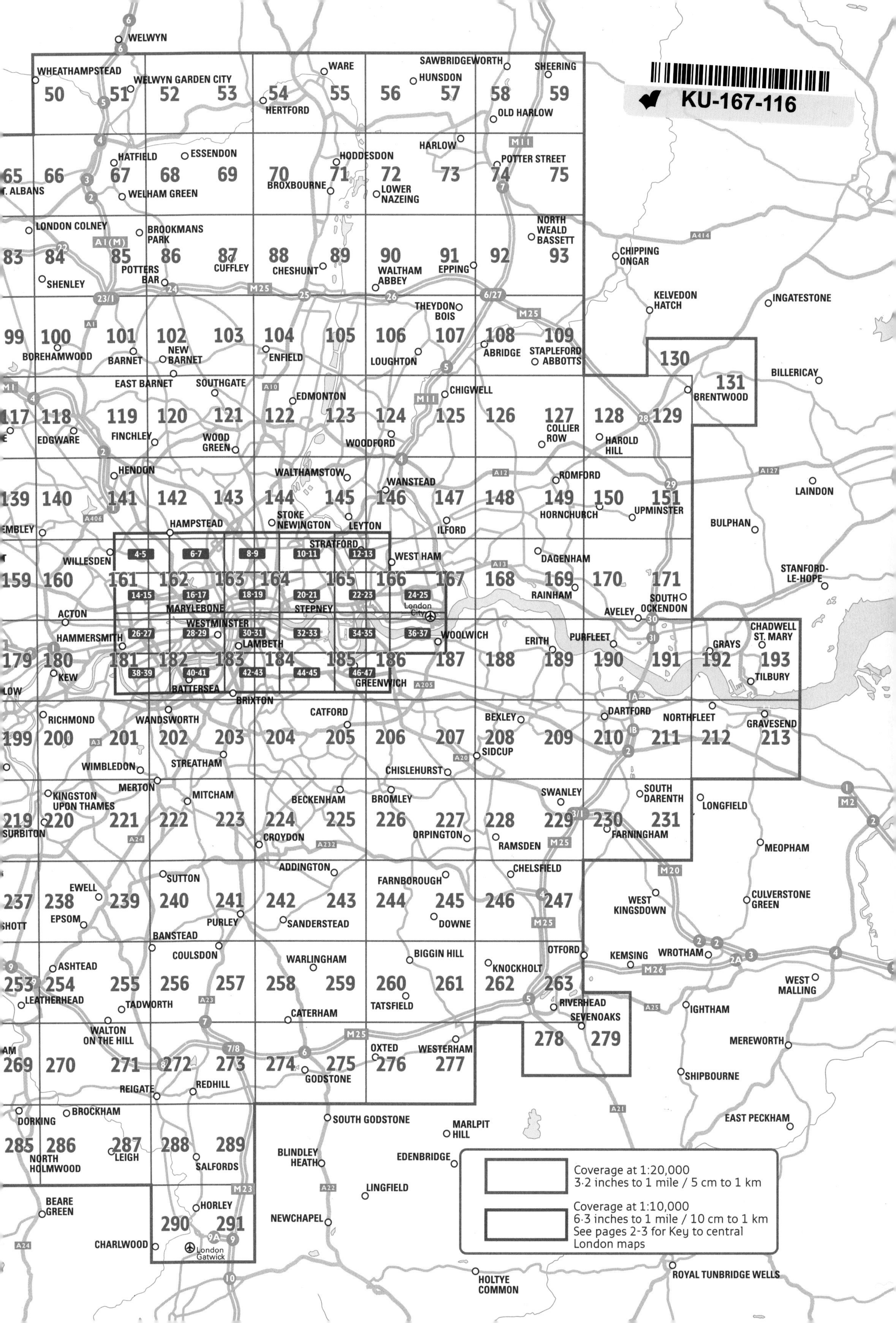

KU-167-116

WELWYN
WHEATHAMPSTEAD 50 51 WELWYN GARDEN CITY 52 53 54 HERTFORD 55 WARE 56 HUNSDON 57 SAWBRIDGEWORTH 58 OLD HARLOW 59 SHEERING

65 ST. ALBANS 66 67 HATFIELD 68 ESSENDON 69 WELHAM GREEN 70 BROXBOURNE 71 HODDESDON 72 LOWER NAZEING 73 HARLOW 74 POTTER STREET 75

83 84 LONDON COLNEY SHENLEY 85 POTTERS BAR 86 BROOKMANS PARK 87 CUFFLEY 88 CHESHUNT 89 90 WALTHAM ABBEY 91 EPPING 92 93 NORTH WEALD BASSETT

CHIPPING ONGAR KELVEDON HATCH INGATESTONE

99 100 BOREHAMWOOD 101 BARNET 102 NEW BARNET 103 104 ENFIELD 105 106 LOUGHTON 107 THEYDON BOIS 108 ABRIDGE 109 STAPLEFORD ABBOTTS 130 131 BRENTWOOD BILLERICAY

117 118 EDGWARE 119 FINCHLEY EAST BARNET 120 121 SOUTHGATE WOOD GREEN 122 EDMONTON 123 124 WOODFORD 125 CHIGWELL 126 127 COLLIER ROW 128 HAROLD HILL 129

139 140 WEMBLEY 141 HENDON 142 HAMPSTEAD 143 144 WALTHAMSTOW STOKE NEWINGTON 145 LEYTON 146 WANSTEAD 147 ILFORD 148 149 ROMFORD HORNCHURCH 150 151 UPMINSTER LAINDON BULPHAN

4-5 6-7 8-9 10-11 12-13 14-15 16-17 18-19 20-21 22-23 24-25

159 160 WILLESDEN 161 162 MARYLEBONE 163 164 STRATFORD 165 STEPNEY 166 WEST HAM London City 167 168 169 DAGENHAM RAINHAM 170 171 SOUTH OCKENDON AVELEY STANFORD-LE-HOPE

26-27 28-29 30-31 32-33 34-35 36-37 38-39 40-41 42-43 44-45 46-47

179 180 ACTON HAMMERSMITH KEW 181 182 WESTMINSTER 183 LAMBETH BATTERSEA 184 BRIXTON 185 186 GREENWICH 187 WOOLWICH 188 189 ERITH 190 PURFLEET 191 192 GRAYS 193 CHADWELL ST. MARY TILBURY

199 RICHMOND 200 201 WANDSWORTH 202 203 STREATHAM WIMBLEDON 204 205 CATFORD 206 207 208 BEXLEY SIDCUP 209 210 DARTFORD 211 NORTHFLEET 212 213 GRAVESEND CHISLEHURST

219 SURBITON 220 KINGSTON UPON THAMES 221 MERTON 222 MITCHAM 223 224 CROYDON BECKENHAM 225 226 BROMLEY 227 ORPINGTON 228 RAMSDEN 229 SWANLEY 230 FARNINGHAM 231 SOUTH DARENTH LONGFIELD MEOPHAM

237 EPSOM 238 EWELL 239 240 SUTTON 241 PURLEY 242 ADDINGTON SANDERSTEAD 243 244 FARNBOROUGH 245 DOWNE 246 CHELSFIELD 247 WEST KINGSDOWN CULVERSTONE GREEN

253 LEATHERHEAD 254 ASHTEAD 255 BANSTEAD TADWORTH 256 COULSDON 257 258 WARLINGHAM 259 CATERHAM 260 TATSFIELD BIGGIN HILL 261 262 KNOCKHOLT 263 OTFORD RIVERHEAD SEVENOAKS KEMSING WROTHAM WEST MALLING IGHTHAM

269 270 WALTON ON THE HILL 271 REIGATE 272 273 REDHILL 274 GODSTONE 275 OXTED 276 WESTERHAM 277 278 279 MEREWORTH SHIPBOURNE

DORKING BROCKHAM SOUTH GODSTONE MARLPIT HILL EAST PECKHAM
285 286 NORTH HOLMWOOD 287 LEIGH 288 289 SALFORDS BLINDLEY HEATH EDENBRIDGE LINGFIELD
BEARE GREEN 290 HORLEY 291 CHARLWOOD London Gatwick NEWCHAPEL
HOLTYE COMMON ROYAL TUNBRIDGE WELLS

Coverage at 1:20,000
3·2 inches to 1 mile / 5 cm to 1 km

Coverage at 1:10,000
6·3 inches to 1 mile / 10 cm to 1 km
See pages 2-3 for Key to central London maps

London Underground map

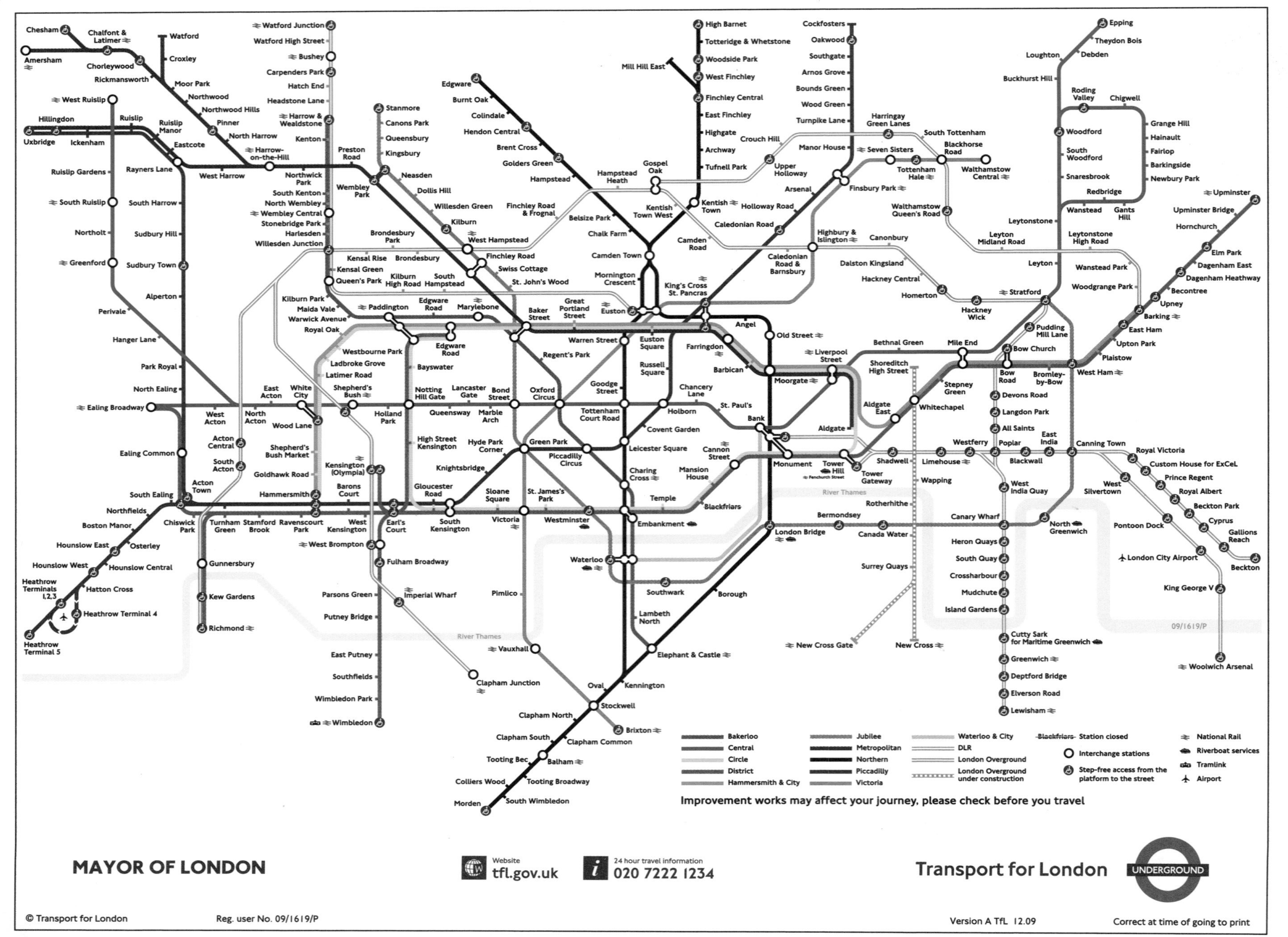

Collins GREATER LONDON STREETFINDER

CONTENTS

CENTRAL AREA MAPS

Key to central London maps 2-3
Key to map symbols 3
Central area maps 4-47

LONDON STREET MAPS

Key to London street maps 48-49
Key to map symbols 49
London street maps 50-291

URBAN AREA MAPS

Key to London urban area maps 292-293
Key to map symbols 293
London urban area maps 294-311

INFORMATION PAGES

M25 London orbital motorway 312-313
Airport plans 314
London Congestion Charging and
Low Emission zones 315
Index to street names, places of interest,
place names, stations, hospitals, schools,
colleges and universities 316-480
Administrative areas 482-483

Key to central London maps

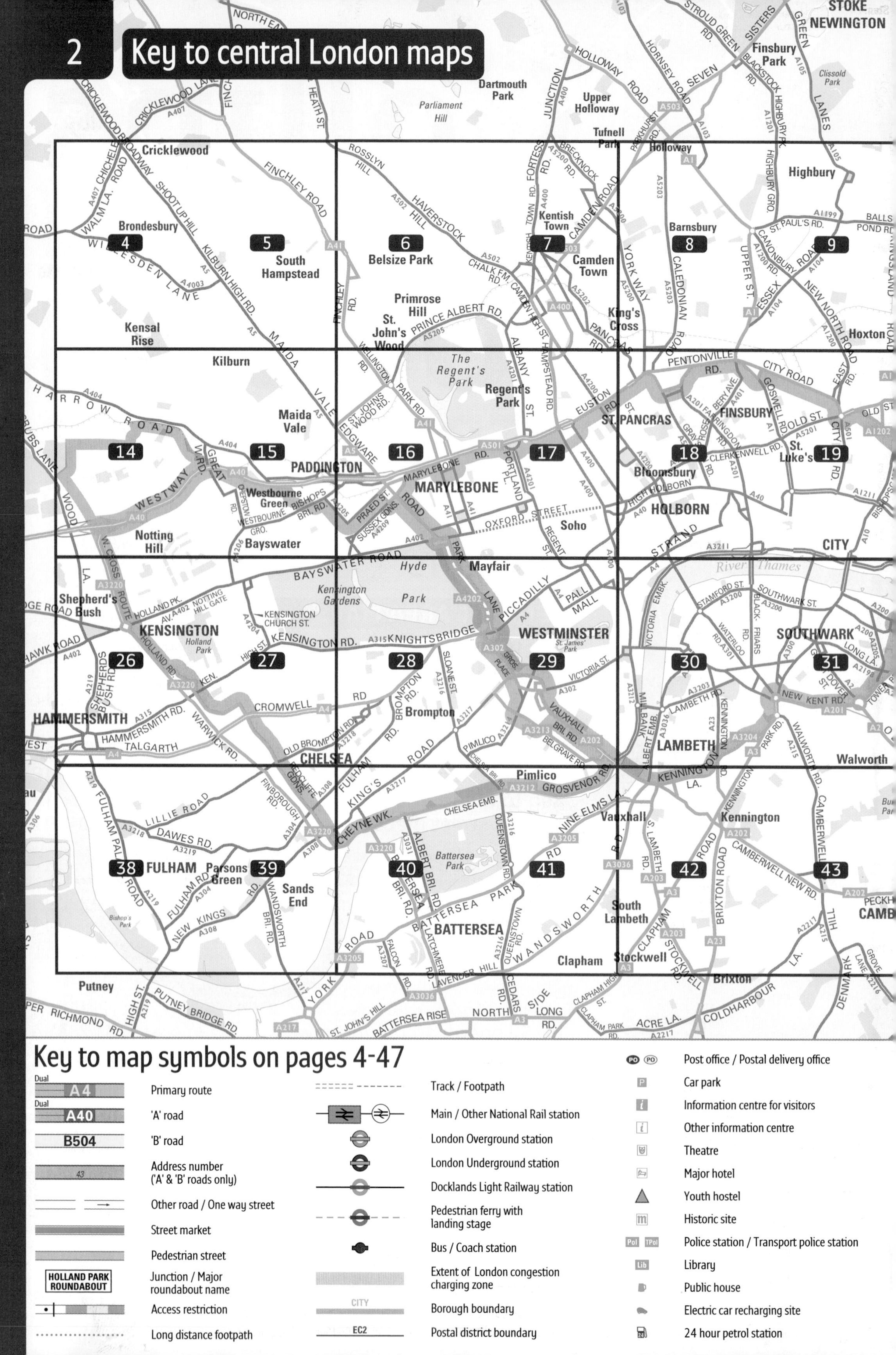

Key to map symbols on pages 4-47

Dual A4	Primary route
Dual A40	'A' road
B504	'B' road
43	Address number ('A' & 'B' roads only)
	Other road / One way street
	Street market
	Pedestrian street
HOLLAND PARK ROUNDABOUT	Junction / Major roundabout name
	Access restriction
	Long distance footpath
	Track / Footpath
	Main / Other National Rail station
	London Overground station
	London Underground station
	Docklands Light Railway station
	Pedestrian ferry with landing stage
	Bus / Coach station
	Extent of London congestion charging zone
CITY	Borough boundary
EC2	Postal district boundary
PO PO	Post office / Postal delivery office
P	Car park
i	Information centre for visitors
i	Other information centre
	Theatre
	Major hotel
	Youth hostel
m	Historic site
Pol TPol	Police station / Transport police station
Lib	Library
	Public house
	Electric car recharging site
24	24 hour petrol station

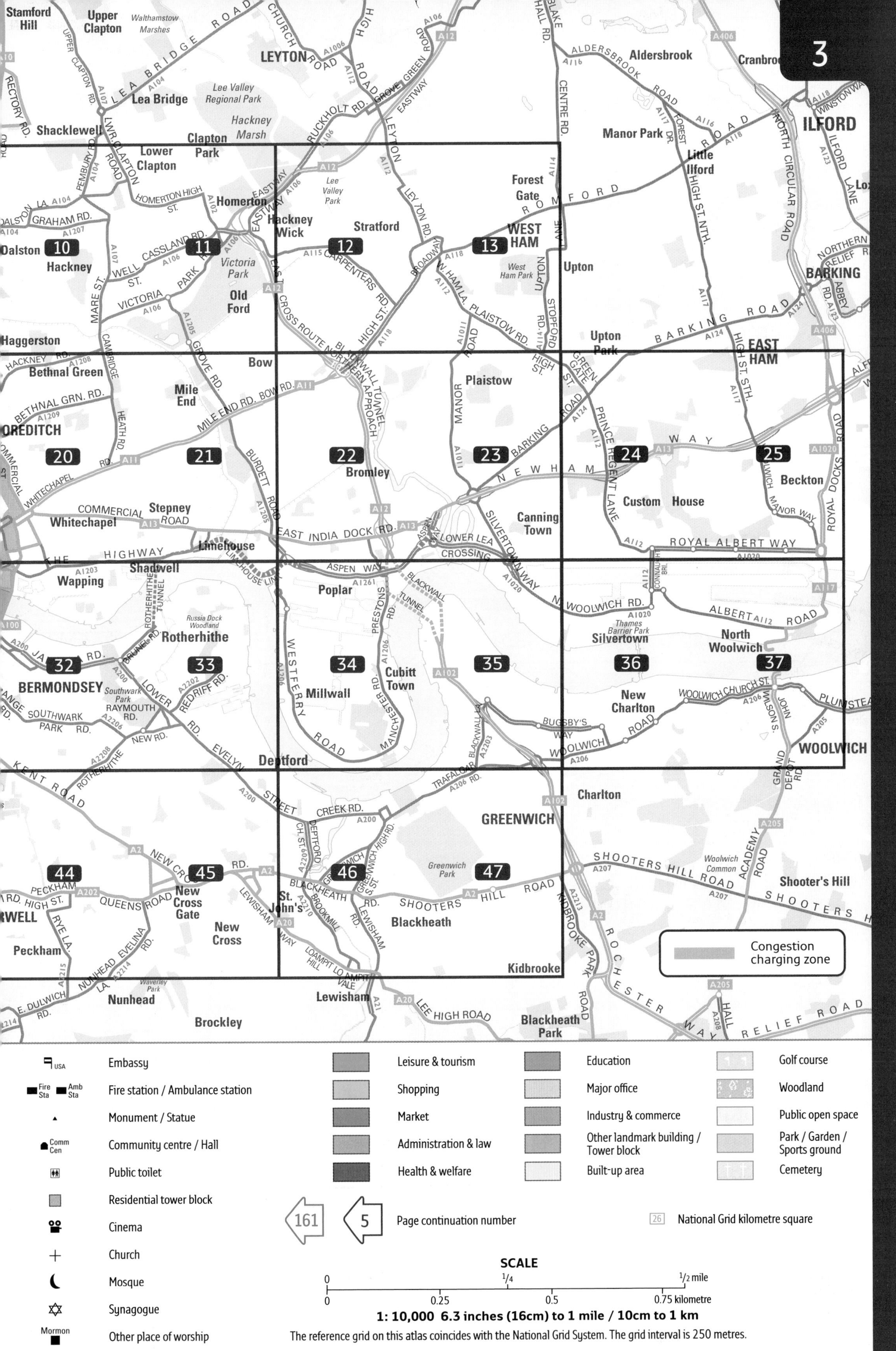
3
Stamford Hill
Upper Clapton
Walthamstow Marshes
LEYTON
Aldersbrook
Cranbrook
ILFORD
Lea Bridge
Lee Valley Regional Park
Hackney Marsh
Shacklewell
Lower Clapton
Clapton Park
Manor Park
Little Ilford
Forest Gate
Homerton
Hackney Wick
Lee Valley Park
Stratford
WEST HAM
West Ham Park
Upton
Dalston
Hackney
Victoria Park
Old Ford
BARKING
Haggerston
Bethnal Green
Bow
Mile End
Plaistow
Upton Park
EAST HAM
SHOREDITCH
Bromley
Custom House
Beckton
Whitechapel
Stepney
Limehouse
Canning Town
Wapping
Shadwell
Poplar
Russia Dock Woodland
Rotherhithe
Thames Barrier Park
Silvertown
North Woolwich
BERMONDSEY
Southwark Park
Millwall
Cubitt Town
New Charlton
WOOLWICH
Deptford
Charlton
GREENWICH
Greenwich Park
Woolwich Common
Shooter's Hill
Peckham
New Cross Gate
New Cross
St. John's
Blackheath
Kidbrooke
Nunhead
Waverley Park
Lewisham
Brockley
Blackheath Park
10
11
12
13
20
21
22
23
24
25
32
33
34
35
36
37
44
45
46
47
Congestion charging zone
Embassy
Fire station / Ambulance station
Monument / Statue
Community centre / Hall
Public toilet
Residential tower block
Cinema
Church
Mosque
Synagogue
Other place of worship
Leisure & tourism
Shopping
Market
Administration & law
Health & welfare
Education
Major office
Industry & commerce
Other landmark building / Tower block
Built-up area
Golf course
Woodland
Public open space
Park / Garden / Sports ground
Cemetery
161
5
Page continuation number
26
National Grid kilometre square
SCALE
0
1/4
1/2 mile
0
0.25
0.5
0.75 kilometre
1: 10,000 6.3 inches (16cm) to 1 mile / 10cm to 1 km
The reference grid on this atlas coincides with the National Grid System. The grid interval is 250 metres.

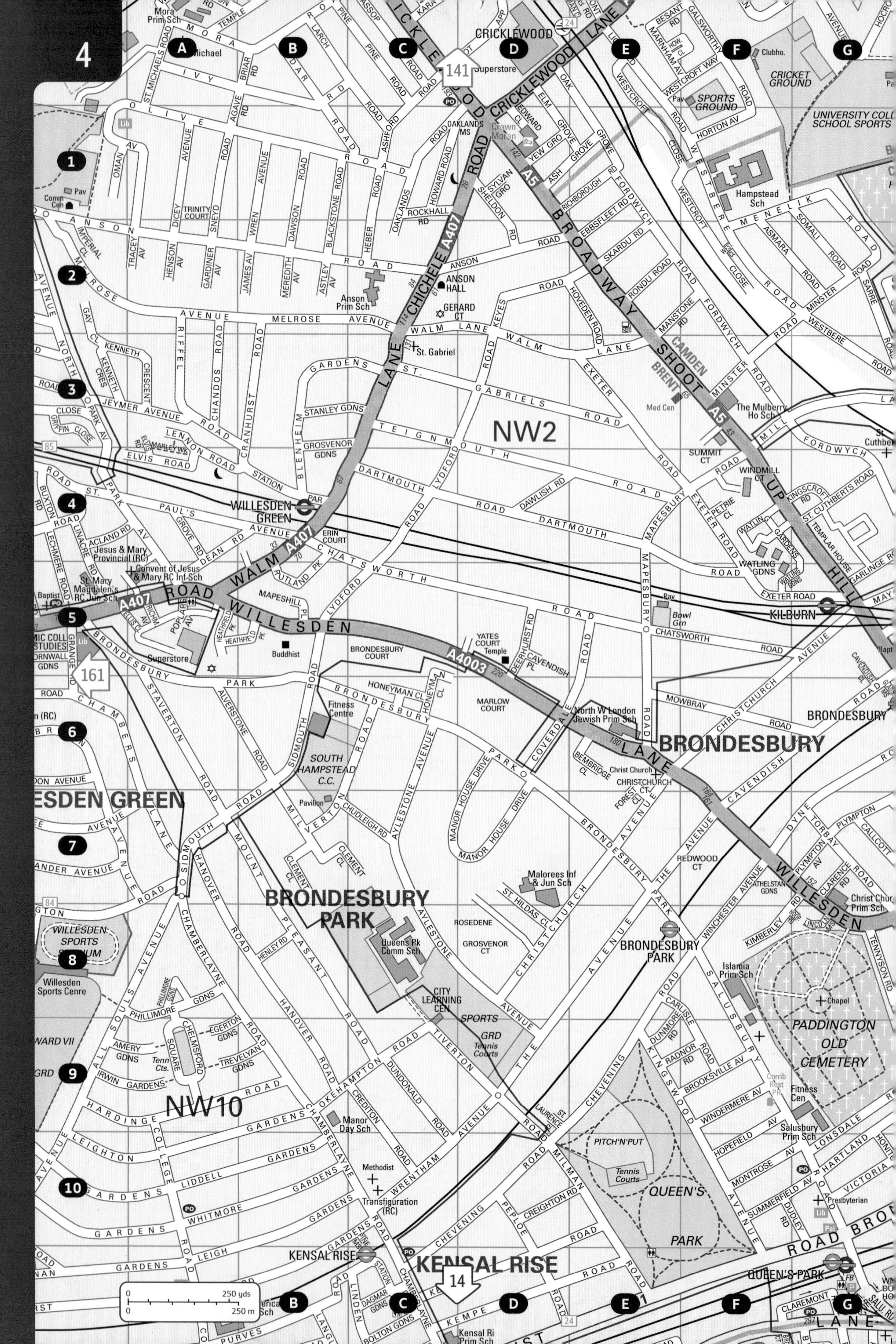

A
B
C
D
E
F
G
1
2
3
4
5
6
7
8
9
10
141
161
14
CRICKLEWOOD
NW2
NW10
BRONDESBURY
BRONDESBURY PARK
KENSAL RISE
ESDEN GREEN
WILLESDEN GREEN
KILBURN
QUEEN'S PARK
CRICKLEWOOD LANE
CRICKLEWOOD BROADWAY
SHOOT UP HILL
CHICHELE ROAD
WALM LANE
WILLESDEN LANE
A5
A407
A4003
MORA ROAD
OLIVE ROAD
ANSON ROAD
MELROSE AVENUE
ST. GABRIELS ROAD
TEIGNMOUTH ROAD
DARTMOUTH ROAD
CHATSWORTH ROAD
BRONDESBURY PARK
CHRISTCHURCH AVENUE
SALUSBURY ROAD
CHAMBERLAYNE ROAD
MOUNT PLEASANT ROAD
OKEHAMPTON ROAD
CHEVENING ROAD
MILMAN ROAD
KEMPE ROAD
Hampstead Sch
CRICKET GROUND
UNIVERSITY COLL SCHOOL SPORTS
SPORTS GROUND
The Mulberry Ho Sch
Anson Prim Sch
ANSON HALL
St. Gabriel
Jesus & Mary Provincial (RC)
Convent of Jesus & Mary RC Inf Sch
St. Mary Magdalen's RC Jun Sch
Superstore
Buddhist
Temple
North W London Jewish Prim Sch
Christ Church
SOUTH HAMPSTEAD C.C.
Fitness Centre
Pavilion
Malorees Inf & Jun Sch
Queens Pk Comm Sch
CITY LEARNING CEN
SPORTS GRD
Tennis Courts
Islamia Prim Sch
PADDINGTON OLD CEMETERY
Chapel
Salusbury Prim Sch
Presbyterian
PITCH'N'PUT
QUEEN'S PARK
Manor Day Sch
Methodist
Transfiguration (RC)
WILLESDEN SPORTS STADIUM
Willesden Sports Centre
Christ Church Prim Sch
Kensal Ri Prim Sch
Med Cen
Bowl Grn
CAMDEN
BRENT
0
250 yds
250 m

5
H
J
K
L
M
N
P
1
2
3
4
5
6
7
8
9
10
142
15
6
NW3
NW6
NW8
WEST HAMPSTEAD
SOUTH HAMPSTEAD
KILBURN
FORTUNE GREEN
HAMPSTEAD
HAMPSTEAD C.C.
FINCHLEY ROAD
FINCHLEY ROAD & FROGNAL
WEST HAMPSTEAD (THAMESLINK)
WEST HAMPSTEAD
SOUTH HAMPSTEAD
KILBURN HIGH ROAD
KILBURN PARK
KILBURN HIGH ROAD
MAIDA ROAD
BELSIZE ROAD
ABBEY ROAD
WEST END LANE
FINCHLEY ROAD
FITZJOHN'S AV
HEATH ST
FROGNAL
PLATT'S LANE
KIDDERPORE AVENUE
REDINGTON ROAD
ARKWRIGHT ROAD
BROADHURST GARDENS
COMPAYNE GARDENS
CLEVE ROAD
CANFIELD GARDENS
GREENCROFT GARDENS
WOODCHURCH ROAD
ABERDARE GARDENS
GOLDHURST TERRACE
ACOL ROAD
QUEX RD
MILL LANE
SUMATRA ROAD
MAYGROVE ROAD
IVERSON ROAD
LYMINGTON RD
FAWLEY ROAD
HILLFIELD ROAD
WEECH RD
INGHAM ROAD
BOUNDARY ROAD
LOUDOUN ROAD
CARLTON HILL
SPRINGFIELD ROAD
ALEXANDRA ROAD
HILGROVE ROAD
GREVILLE ROAD
PRIORY ROAD
MORTIMER CRESCENT
CAMDEN
WESTMINSTER
B510
B511
B520
B509
B507
B413
A41
A4
Emmanuel C of E Prim Sch
Beckford Prim Sch
Camden Arts Cen
Quality Hotel
Holiday Inn Express
O2 Shopping Centre
VUE
Superstore
Freud Museum
Kilburn Grange Park
Maygrove Peace Park
Webheath Estate
Abbey Road Estate
Mortimer Estate
The Jack Taylor Sch
George Eliot Inf & Jun Schs
Quintin Kynaston Sch
The American Sch in London
Abercorn School
St. Mary's RC Prim Sch
St. Augustine's Prim Sch
St. Augustine's HighSch
Salvation Army
Sacred Heart of Jesus (RC)
St. Mary's Kilburn C of E Prim Sch
University Coll Sch
University Coll Jun Sch
European Sch of Management
Sports Ground
Tennis Courts
Central Sch of Speech & Drama
St. Thomas More (RC)
Holy Trinity Prim Sch
S. Hampstead High Sch
North Br Ho Jun Sch
Southbank Int Sch
Charteris Comm Sports Cen
Kingsgate Prim Sch
Everyman
Zoroastrian
Snowman Ho
Casterbridge
Greville Hall
Vivian Ct
St. George's Catholic School, Maida Vale
Barbara Brosnan Court
Hosp of St. John & St. Eliza

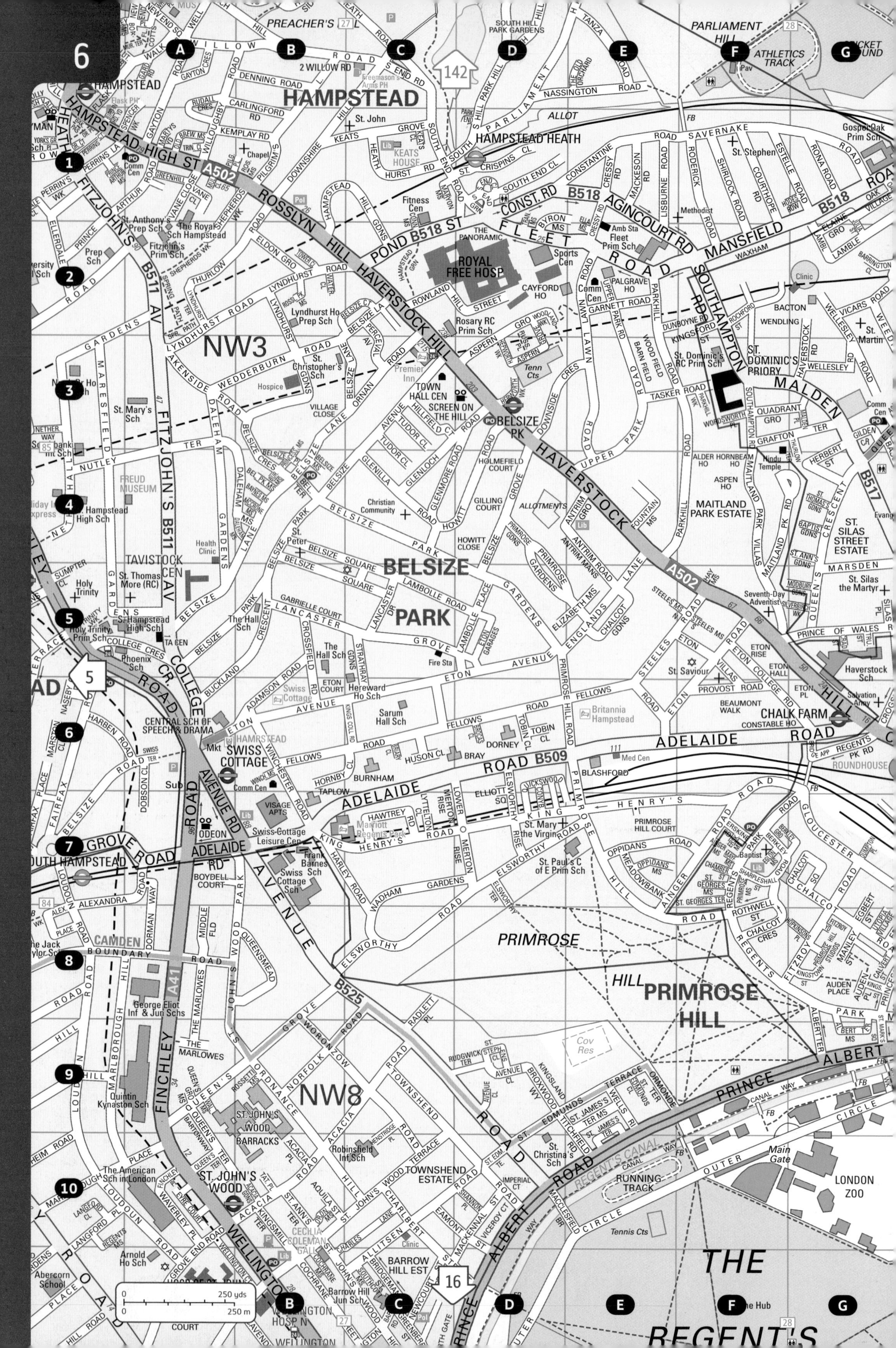
HAMPSTEAD
NW3
BELSIZE
PARK
NW8
PRIMROSE
HILL
PRIMROSE
HILL
THE
REGENT'S
HAMPSTEAD HEATH
ROYAL
FREE HOSP
SWISS
COTTAGE
CHALK FARM
BELSIZE
PK
ST. JOHN'S
WOOD
LONDON
ZOO
ROUNDHOUSE
RUNNING
TRACK
PARLIAMENT
HILL
ATHLETICS
TRACK
HAMPSTEAD HIGH ST
A502
ROSSLYN HILL
HAVERSTOCK HILL
HAVERSTOCK
FITZJOHN'S AV
B511
ADELAIDE ROAD
B509
FINCHLEY ROAD
A41
AVENUE RD
WELLINGTON
PRINCE ALBERT ROAD
B525
AGINCOURT RD
MANSFIELD ROAD
B518
SOUTHAMPTON RD
MALDEN ROAD
FLEET ROAD
POND ST
KEATS HOUSE
FREUD MUSEUM
ODEON
CAMDEN
ST. DOMINIC'S PRIORY
MAITLAND PARK ESTATE
ST. SILAS STREET ESTATE
TOWNSHEND ESTATE
SOUTH HAMPSTEAD
142
5
16
27
28
250 yds
250 m
A
B
C
D
E
F
G
1
2
3
4
5
6
7
8
9
10

H
J
K
L
M
N
P
1
2
3
4
5
6
7
8
9
10
TUFNELL PARK
GOSPEL OAK
NW5
N7
KENTISH TOWN
NW1
N1
CAMDEN TOWN
KING'S CROSS
REGENT'S PARK
TUFNELL PARK
KENTISH TOWN
KENTISH TOWN WEST
CAMDEN ROAD
CAMDEN TOWN
MORNINGTON CRESCENT
Parliament Hill Sch
Lido
Acland Burghley Sch
Youth Cen
Baptist
St. Cosmas
Comm Cen
Eleanor Palmer Prim Sch
St. Benet & All Saints
Fitness Cen
Fire Sta
Apostolic
FORUM CLUB
City Farm
Carlton Prim Sch
Recycle Cen
Royal Mail Delivery Off
Our Lady (RC)
Resource Cen
Luther Tyndale
BRECKNOCK ROAD ESTATE
HILLDROP ESTATE
Tufnell Pk Prim Sch
Bridge Sch
Holloway School
LONDON MET UNI - Halls of Residence
H.M.P. HOLLOWAY
Kentish Town C of E Prim Sch
Kentish Town Mkt (Indoor)
St. Patrick's Cath Prim Sch
WESTMINSTER KINGSWAY COLL
Torriano Jun Sch
Torriano Inf Sch
St. Luke
The Bridge Sch
Brecknock Prim Sch
MAIDEN EST
Rhyl Prim Sch
Sports Cen
Pitches
CANTELOWES GDNS
Health Cen
Hope Chapel
Congregational
CATH
Camden Sch for Girls
St. Paul
CAMDEN SQ GDNS
Irish Comm Cen
Day Hosp
Spiritualist
Holy Trinity C of E Prim Sch
Chalcot Sch
Zen Society
CLARENCE WAY EST
PLAY AREA
DENTON
Stables Mkt
THE OPEN UNI IN LONDON
Hawley Lock
M.T.V. Studios
Superstore
Camden Lock Mkt
Camden Lock
FILM MAKERS CO-OP
Holiday Inn
Youth Cen
Primrose Hill Prim Sch
Camden Mkt
UNI
Inf Sch
St. Michael with All Saints
TRANS. Pol
AGAR GROVE ESTATE
LULWORTH
ST. JAMES GATE
STAR WHARF
St. Michael's Camden Town Prim Sch
Our Lady's RC Prim Sch
GREEK CATH
ST. MARTIN'S GARDENS
The Cavendish Sch
PLAZA
ODEON
Our Lady (RC)
Sports Cen
Cecil Sharp House
Fitness Cen
JEWISH MUS
Jehovah's Witness
CURNOCK EST
Methodist
Richard Cobden Prim Sch
Parcelforce
ROYAL VETERINARY COLL
ST. PANCRAS HOSPITAL
CORONERS CT
ST. PANCRAS GARDENS
St. Pancras
Camley Street Natural Park
Gas Works
DEPOT
THEATRO TECHNIS
THE WORKING MEN'S COLL
GODWIN COURT
LEARNING CEN
South Camden Comm Sch
Sports Cen
Edith Neville Prim Sch
Comm Cen
North Br Ho Snr Sch
Gloucester Gate
Danish St. Ch
TA CEN
REGENT'S PARK BARRACKS
DEPOT
Gtr Lon Ho
Health Cen
OUTER CIRCLE
GORDON HO RD
HIGHGATE RD
FORTESS ROAD
BRECKNOCK ROAD
CAMDEN ROAD
KENTISH TOWN RD
ROYAL COLLEGE ST
ST. PANCRAS WAY
CAMDEN HIGH ST
CAMDEN PARK RD
YORK WAY
AGAR GROVE
CHALK FARM RD
PARKWAY
DELANCEY STREET
ALBANY ST
HAMPSTEAD RD
EVERSHOLT ST
PANCRAS ROAD
MIDLAND RD
LEIGHTON RD
TORRIANO AV
PRINCE OF WALES ROAD
MALDEN CRES
FERDINAND ST
ISLIP STREET
GAISFORD STREET
PATSHULL ROAD
LAWFORD ROAD
BARTHOLOMEW ROAD
ROCHESTER ROAD
GRAFTON ROAD
CASTLE ROAD
HAWLEY RD
CROWNDALE RD
PRATT ST
ARLINGTON ROAD
MORNINGTON CRES
OAKLEY SQ
A400
A5200
A503
A5202
A5205
B518
B512
143
8
17

HOLLOWAY
LOWER HOLLOWAY
BARNSBURY
ISLINGTON
KING'S CROSS
N7
NW1
H.M.P. HOLLOWAY
H.M.P. PENTONVILLE
EMIRATES STADIUM ARSENAL FC
HIGHBURY FIELDS
CALEDONIAN PARK
SPORTS GROUND
PARADISE PARK
LAYCOCK STREET PARK
BARNSBURY SQ GDN
ARUNDEL SQ GDN
THORNHILL SQ
BINGFIELD PARK
BARNARD PARK
GIBSON SQ GDNS
MARKET ROAD GDNS
REGENT'S CANAL
Camley Street Natural Park
Karting Track
DEPOT
Gas Works
KINGS PLACE
BATTLEBRIDGE BASIN
HOLLOWAY ROAD
CALEDONIAN ROAD
HIGHBURY & ISLINGTON
CALEDONIAN ROAD & BARNSBURY
DRAYTON PARK
ANGEL
KING'S CROSS
NAGS HEAD
CAMDEN ROAD
YORK WAY
CALEDONIAN ROAD
HOLLOWAY ROAD
LIVERPOOL ROAD
UPPER STREET
PENTONVILLE ROAD
COPENHAGEN STREET
RICHMOND AVENUE
HORNSEY ROAD
TOLLINGTON ROAD
PARKHURST ROAD
HILLMARTON ROAD
MARKET ROAD
BREWERY ROAD
HEMINGFORD ROAD
WHARFDALE RD
ST. PANCRAS WAY
MIDLAND ROAD
A1
A503
A5203
A5200
A103
B515
A501
143
7
18
0 250 yds
0 250 m

H
J
K
L
M
N
P
1
2
3
4
5
6
7
8
9
10
144
10
19
N16
N5
N1
E8
HIGHBURY
CANONBURY
KINGSLAND
DE BEAUVOIR TOWN
HOXTON
SHOREDITCH
HIGHBURY ESTATE
DALSTON KINGSLAND
DALSTON JUNCTION
HAGGERSTON
CANONBURY
ESSEX ROAD
HIGHBURY GROVE
A1201
A1199
A1200
A104
A105
A10
B104
B102
PAUL'S ROAD
BALLS POND ROAD
ESSEX ROAD
NEW NORTH ROAD
NEWINGTON GRN
NEWINGTON GREEN ROAD
GREEN LANES
ALBION ROAD
MILDMAY PARK
MILDMAY GROVE NORTH
MILDMAY GROVE SOUTH
SOUTHGATE ROAD
HACKNEY
ISLINGTON
KINGSLAND ROAD
KINGSLAND HIGH ST
STOKE NEWINGTON
ST. PAUL'S RD
GROSVENOR AVENUE
CANONBURY PARK NORTH
CANONBURY PARK SOUTH
CANONBURY GROVE
NORTHCHURCH ROAD
ENGLEFIELD ROAD
DOWNHAM ROAD
DE BEAUVOIR ROAD
CULFORD ROAD
MORTIMER ROAD
STAMFORD ROAD
ORSMAN ROAD
EAGLE WHARF ROAD
SHEPHERDESS WALK
WENLOCK STREET
PITFIELD STREET
HOXTON STREET
REGENT'S CANAL
KINGSLAND BASIN
WENLOCK BASIN
CITY ROAD BASIN
ROSEMARY GDNS
SHOREDITCH SPORTS GRD PARK
SHOREDITCH PARK GARDEN
Britannia Leisure Cen
Kingsland Shopping Cen
DE BEAUVOIR ESTATE
COLVILLE ESTATE
HOBBS PLACE ESTATE
WHITMORE ESTATE
KINGSGATE ESTATE
DOVERCOURT EST
SHELLGROVE EST
MAYVILLE ESTATE
MILTON GARDEN ESTATE
PARKVIEW ESTATE
FROGMORE IND EST
LONDON MET UNI (Ladbroke Ho)
Highbury Flds Sch Annexe
Highbury Gro Sch
Highbury Quad Prim Sch
Newington Grn Prim Sch
Grasmere Prim Sch
Horizon Spec Sch
Shacklewell Prim Sch
Princess May Prim Sch
St. Matthias C of E Prim Sch
St. Jude's & St. Paul's C of E Prim Sch
De Beauvoir Prim Sch
Our Lady & St. Joseph RC Prim Sch
The Childrens Ho Upr Sch
Rotherfield Prim Sch
New North Comm Sch
St. Mary's C of E Prim Sch
Islington Green Sch
Thomas Fairchild Prim Sch
Hanover Prim Sch
Whitmore Prim Sch
Burbage Prim Sch
St. Joan of Arc RC Prim Sch
ESTORICK GALL
GEFFRYE MUSEUM
GAINSBOROUGH STUDIOS
ROSEMARY THEATRE & PH
Salvation Army
Harecourt United Reformed Church
JEWISH BURIAL GRD
ST. PAUL'S SHRUBBERY

A
B
C
D
E
F
G
1
2
3
4
5
6
7
8
9
10
N16
SHACKLEWELL
HACKNEY DOWNS
HACKNEY
E8
DALSTON
LONDON FIELDS
HAGGERSTON
HAGGERSTON PARK
E2
N1
SOUTH HACKNEY
144
9
20
DALSTON KINGSLAND (open 2010)
DALSTON JUNCTION (open 2010)
HAGGERSTON (open 2010)
HOXTON (open 2010)
HACKNEY CENTRAL
CAMBRIDGE HEATH
KINGSLAND HIGH ST
STOKE NEWINGTON ROAD
KINGSLAND ROAD
DALSTON LANE
GRAHAM ROAD
QUEENSBRIDGE ROAD
MARE STREET
PEMBURY ROAD
AMHURST ROAD
HACKNEY ROAD
CAMBRIDGE HEATH ROAD
VICTORIA PARK ROAD
LWR CLAPTON RD
CLAPTON ROAD
CRICKETFIELD ROAD
DOWNS PARK ROAD
RICHMOND ROAD
FOREST ROAD
MIDDLETON ROAD
ALBION DRIVE
SHRUBLAND ROAD
WHISTON ROAD
REGENTS ROW
A10
A104
A107
A1207
A102
A106
B108
B127
A1208
Kingsland Shopping Cen
Petchey Academy
Mossbourne Comm. Academy
London Fields Lido
BUS DEPOT
Gas Works
Hackney City Farm
0 250 yds
0 250 m

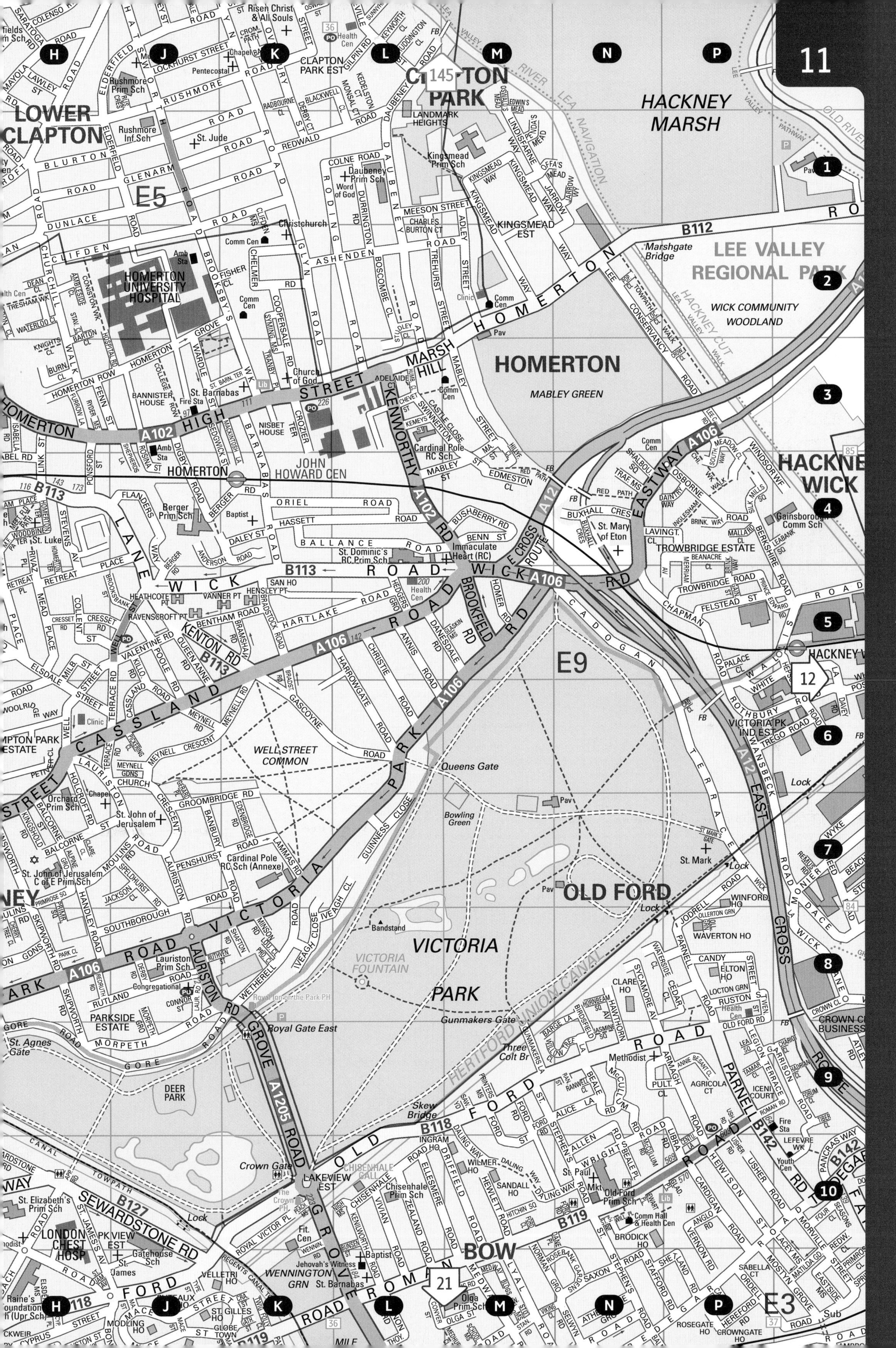
11
LOWER CLAPTON
E5
CLAPTON PARK
145
HACKNEY MARSH
RIVER LEA
LEA NAVIGATION
LEE VALLEY REGIONAL PARK
WICK COMMUNITY WOODLAND
HACKNEY CUT
HOMERTON
MABLEY GREEN
HOMERTON UNIVERSITY HOSPITAL
JOHN HOWARD CEN
KINGSMEAD EST
TROWBRIDGE ESTATE
HACKNEY WICK
12
E9
WELL STREET COMMON
Queens Gate
Bowling Green
OLD FORD
VICTORIA PARK
VICTORIA FOUNTAIN
Bandstand
Royal Gate East
Gunmakers Gate
HERTFORD UNION CANAL
DEER PARK
Crown Gate
LAKEVIEW EST
St. Agnes Gate
PARKSIDE ESTATE
LONDON CHEST HOSP
BOW
21
E3
WENNINGTON GRN
HOMERTON HIGH STREET
CASSLAND ROAD
VICTORIA PARK ROAD
WICK ROAD
EASTWAY
EAST CROSS ROUTE
GROVE ROAD
OLD FORD ROAD
ROMAN ROAD
SEWARDSTONE RD
PARNELL ROAD
A102
A106
A12
A1205
B112
B113
B118
B119
B127
B142

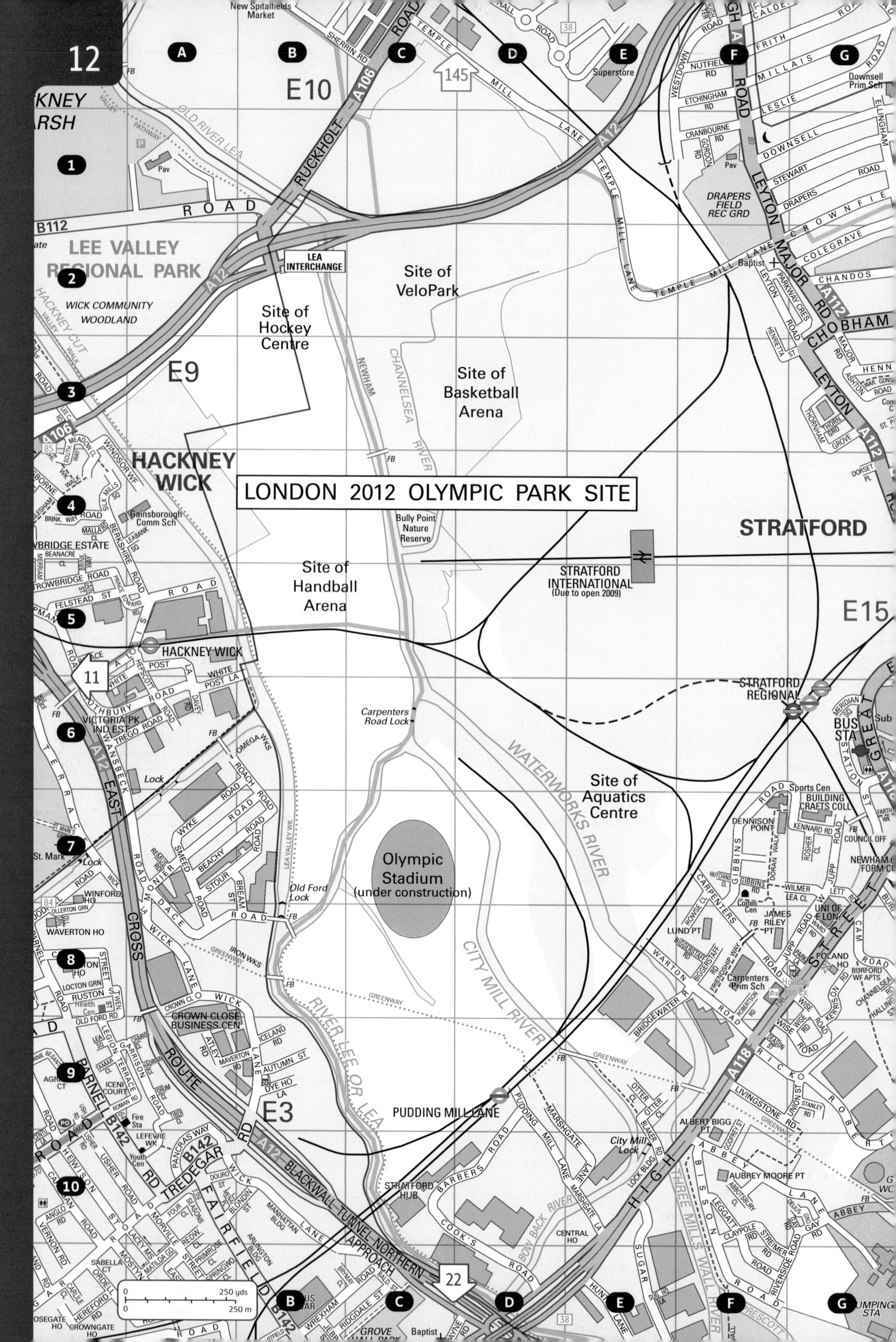
A
B
C
D
E
F
G
1
2
3
4
5
6
7
8
9
10
New Spitalfields Market
SHERRIN RD
TEMPLE MILL LANE
145
E10
RUCKHOLT ROAD
A106
Superstore
38
WESTDOWN ROAD
NUTFIELD RD
ETCHINGHAM RD
CRANBOURNE RD
GORDON RD
HIGH ROAD LEYTON
FRITH ROAD
MILLAIS ROAD
LESLIE ROAD
Downsell Prim Sch
DOWNSELL ROAD
ELLINGHAM ROAD
STEWART ROAD
DRAPERS ROAD
DRAPERS FIELD REC GRD
CROWNFIELD ROAD
COLEGRAVE ROAD
CHANDOS ROAD
Baptist
LEYTON ROAD
PARKWAY CRES
HENRIETTA ST
MAJOR RD
LEYTON MAJOR RD
A112
CHOBHAM ROAD
HACKNEY MARSH
VALLEY PATHWAY
OLD RIVER LEA
Pav
ROAD
B112
LEE VALLEY REGIONAL PARK
A12
LEA INTERCHANGE
Site of VeloPark
Site of Hockey Centre
WICK COMMUNITY WOODLAND
HACKNEY CUT
E9
NEWHAM
CHANNELSEA RIVER
Site of Basketball Arena
HACKNEY WICK
FB
LONDON 2012 OLYMPIC PARK SITE
THORNHAM GRO
THORN GRO
GROVE
DORSET PL
STRATFORD
Gainsborough Comm Sch
BRINK WAY
MALLARD CL
TROWBRIDGE ESTATE
TROWBRIDGE ROAD
BEANACRE CL
MERIAM CL
BERKSHIRE ROAD
PRINCE EDWARD RD
FELSTEAD ST
Bully Point Nature Reserve
Site of Handball Arena
STRATFORD INTERNATIONAL
(Due to open 2009)
E15
HACKNEY WICK
WHITE POST LA
HEPSCOTT RD
DAVEY RD
11
VICTORIA PK IND EST
TREGO ROAD
WANSBECK RD
Carpenters Road Lock
STRATFORD REGIONAL
MERIDIAN SQ
BUS STA
GREAT EASTERN
Sub
OMEGA WKS
ROACH ROAD
Lock
WYKE ROAD
WATERWORKS RIVER
Site of Aquatics Centre
Sports Cen
BUILDING CRAFTS COLL
DENNISON POINT
KENNARD RD
GIBBINS RD
DORAN WALK
ROSHER CL
COUNCIL OFF
NEWHAM 6 FORM COLL
St. Mark
Lock
WINFORD HO
WAVERTON HO
A12 EAST CROSS ROUTE
MONIER ROAD
SMEED ROAD
BEACHY ROAD
STOUR ROAD
BREAM ST
DACE ROAD
LEA VALLEY WK
Old Ford Lock
Olympic Stadium
(under construction)
CARPENTERS ROAD
HUTCHINS CL
WILMER LEA CL
JAMES RILEY PT
UNI OF E LON
LUND PT
ROWSE CL
JUPP ROAD
POLAND HO
BURFORD WF APTS
WICK LANE
GREENWAY
IRON WKS
CITY MILL RIVER
WARTON ROAD
BIGGERSTAFF RD
FRIENDSHIP WAY
Carpenters Prim Sch
Holiday Inn Ex
KERRISON RD
CHANNELSEA
LOCTON GRN
RUSTON ST
OLD FORD RD
Health Cen
CROWN CL
CROWN CLOSE BUSINESS CEN
BRIDGEWATER RD
ROBERTSON RD
WISE ROAD
RIVER LEE OR LEA
ICELAND RD
ATLEY RD
MAVERTON RD
AUTUMN ST
DYE HO LA
GARRISON RD
LEGION TERRACE
ICENI COURT
ROMAN RD
PARNELL RD
B142
Fire Sta
LEFEVRE WK
Youth Cen
E3
PUDDING MILL LANE
MARSHGATE LANE
OTTER CL
City Mill Lock
BLAKER RD
LIVINGSTONE RD
UNION ST
STANLEY RD
ROBERTS RD
ALBERT BIGG PT
GODFREY ST
ABBEY LANE
AUBREY MOORE PT
PANCRAS WAY
TREDEGAR RD
USHER ROAD
HEWISON ST
DOURO ST
FAIRFIELD RD
BLONDIN ST
MANHATTAN BLDG
A12 BLACKWALL TUNNEL NORTHERN APPROACH
STRATFORD HUB
BARBERS ROAD
PUDDING MILL LANE
COOK'S ROAD
BOW BACK RIVER
CENTRAL HO
LOCK BLDG
SUGAR HOUSE LANE
THREE MILLS WALL RIVER
BISSON RD
LEGGATT RD
CLAYPOLE RD
STREIMER RD
RIVERSIDE ROAD
GAY RD
ABBOTSBURY CL
A118 HIGH STREET
ANGLO RD
VERNON RD
SABELLA CT
MOSTYN
ORDELL RD
HEREFORD RD
CROWNGATE HO
ARLINGTON BLDG
WREXHAM RD
RIDGDALE ST
BALDOCK ST
BRYMAY CL
GROVE HALL PARK
Baptist
HUNT'S LANE
22
250 yds
250 m
PUMPING STA

H
J
K
L
M
N
P
146
JEWISH CEMETERY
WEST HAM CEMETERY
Chapel
AVENUE ROAD ESTATE
FOREST GATE
Forest Gate Comm Sch
Odessa Inf Sch
St. James' C of E Jun Sch
FOREST LANE PK
Maryland Prim Sch
Colegrave Prim Sch
St. Francis' RC Prim Sch
MARYLAND
Earlham Prim Sch
Azhar Academy Girls Sch
E7
Leisure Cen
Sarah Bonnell Sch
UNI OF E LONDON (Stratford Campus)
Superstore
PICTURE HO
ARTS CEN
THEATRE ROYAL
The Stratford Centre
STRATFORD OFFICE VILLAGE
CONF & LEISURE CEN
NEWHAM COLL OF FURTHER ED (Stratford Campus)
REC GRD
Sports Halls
Park Prim Sch
CLAPTON FC
WEST HAM PARK
SPORTS GROUND
WEST HAM
Bandstand
Tennis Courts
THE CEDARS
166
Stratford Sch
St. Antony's RC Prim Sch
St. Bonaventure's RC Sch
Rokeby Sch
John F. Kennedy Sch
SPORTS GND
West Ham Ch Prim Sch
Portway Prim Sch
E13
Selwyn Prim Sch
STRATFORD MARKET DEPOT
Sub Sta
Ranelagh Prim Sch
Manor Prim Sch
PLAISTOW
Curwen Prim Sch
Eleanor Smith Sch
23
Channelsea Ho Bus
A112
A11
A118
A114
B164
B165
A1011
ROMFORD ROAD
LEYTONSTONE RD
FOREST LANE
WOODGRANGE ROAD
UPTON LANE
PORTWAY
PLAISTOW ROAD
NEW PLAISTOW RD
MANOR ROAD
BROADWAY
ANGEL LANE
THE GROVE
WEST HAM LANE
VICARAGE LANE
DENSHAM
STOPFORD ROAD
CLEGG ST
HIGH STREET
1
2
3
4
5
6
7
8
9
10

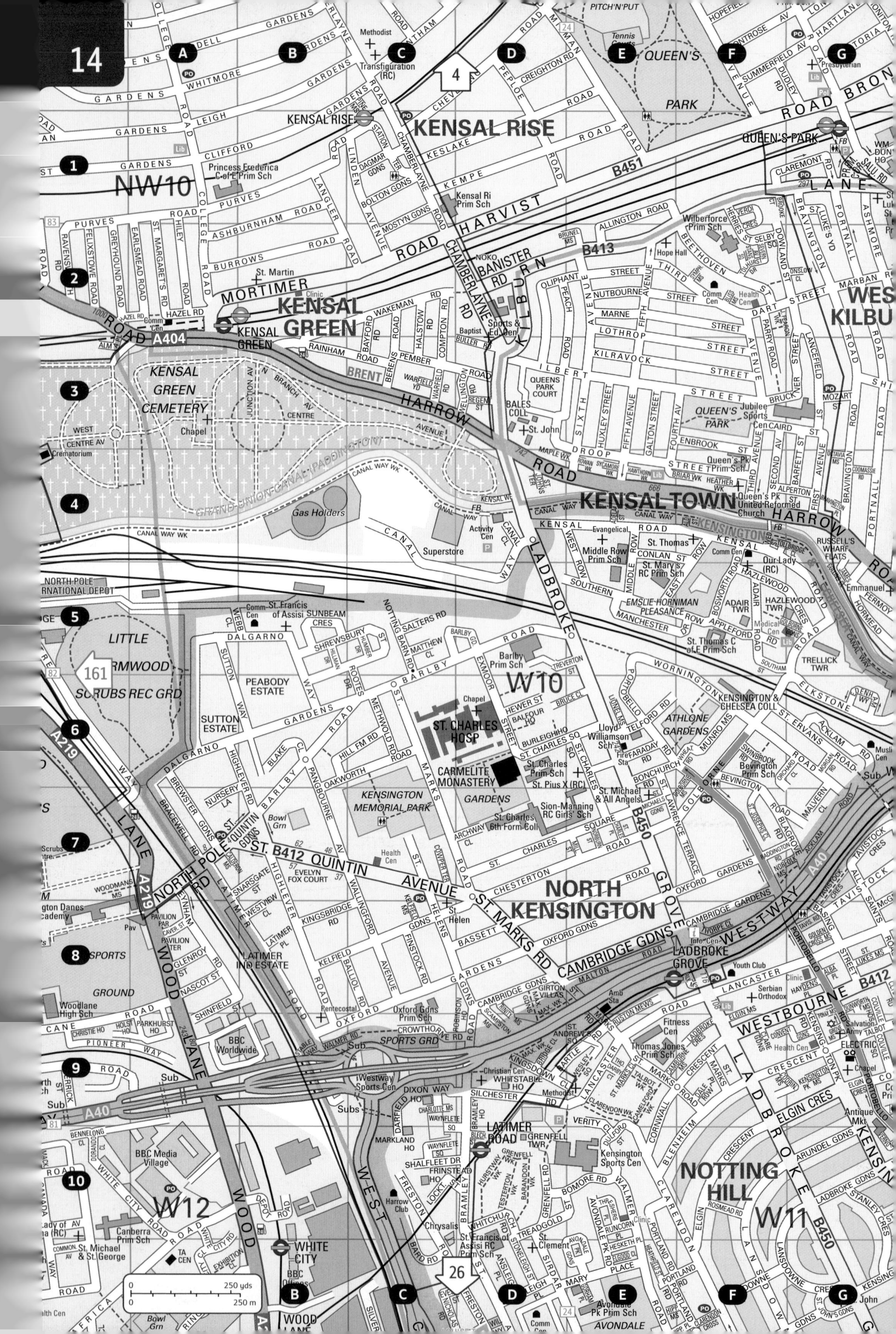
A
B
C
D
E
F
G
1
2
3
4
5
6
7
8
9
10
4
161
26
NW10
W10
W11
W12
KENSAL RISE
KENSAL GREEN
KENSAL TOWN
NORTH KENSINGTON
NOTTING HILL
WEST KILBURN
QUEEN'S PARK
KENSAL GREEN CEMETERY
LITTLE WORMWOOD SCRUBS REC GRD
GRAND UNION CANAL (PADDINGTON)
Gas Holders
Superstore
ST. CHARLES HOSP
CARMELITE MONASTERY
KENSINGTON MEMORIAL PARK
PEABODY ESTATE
SUTTON ESTATE
LATIMER IND ESTATE
BBC Worldwide
BBC Media Village
WHITE CITY
LATIMER ROAD
LADBROKE GROVE
WESTBOURNE PARK
KENSAL RISE
QUEEN'S PARK
HARROW ROAD
LADBROKE GROVE
WESTWAY
WOOD LANE
NORTH POLE RD
ST. QUINTIN AVENUE
ST. MARKS RD
CAMBRIDGE GDNS
KENSINGTON & CHELSEA COLL
TRELLICK TWR
SPORTS GROUND
SPORTS GRD
Westway Sports Cen
Kensington Sports Cen
Thomas Jones Prim Sch
A404
A40
A219
B412
B413
B450
B451
0
250 yds
250 m

KILBURN
KILBURN PARK
NW6
NW8
W9
W2
MAIDA VALE
MAIDA HILL
ST. JOHN'S WOOD
WESTBOURNE GREEN
PADDINGTON
BAYSWATER
ROYAL OAK
WARWICK AVENUE
PADDINGTON RECREATION GROUND
ATHLETICS TRACK
CRICKET GROUND
Little Venice
PADDINGTON GREEN
BRUNEL ESTATE
HALLFIELD EST
BARRIE ESTATE
BBC Studios
Paddington Sports Club
Bowling Greens
Europa House
Colonnade
GOODS SHED
BUS GARAGE
Portobello Junction
WESTBOURNE PARK
WESTBOURNE GREEN SPORTS COMPLEX
WARWICK EST
KINGDOM ST
LONDON STREET
Lancaster Gate
MAIDA VALE
ABBEY ROAD
CARLTON VALE
SHIRLAND ROAD
HARROW ROAD
WESTWAY
ELGIN AVENUE
SUTHERLAND AVENUE
RANDOLPH AVENUE
LAUDERDALE ROAD
CLIFTON GDNS
BLOMFIELD ROAD
WARWICK AVENUE
FORMOSA ST
EDGWARE ROAD
BISHOPS BRIDGE ROAD
WESTBOURNE GROVE
WESTBOURNE PARK VILLAS
PORCHESTER ROAD
QUEENSWAY
CHEPSTOW ROAD
PEMBRIDGE VILLAS
GT WESTERN RD
BAYSWATER ROAD
EASTBOURNE TER
CRAVEN HILL
KILBURN PARK ROAD
GROVE END ROAD
HAMILTON TERRACE
A5
A40
A404
A4206
A4207
A402
B413
B414
B411
B415
B507
5
16
27
H
J
K
L
M
N
P
1
2
3
4
5
6
7
8
9
10

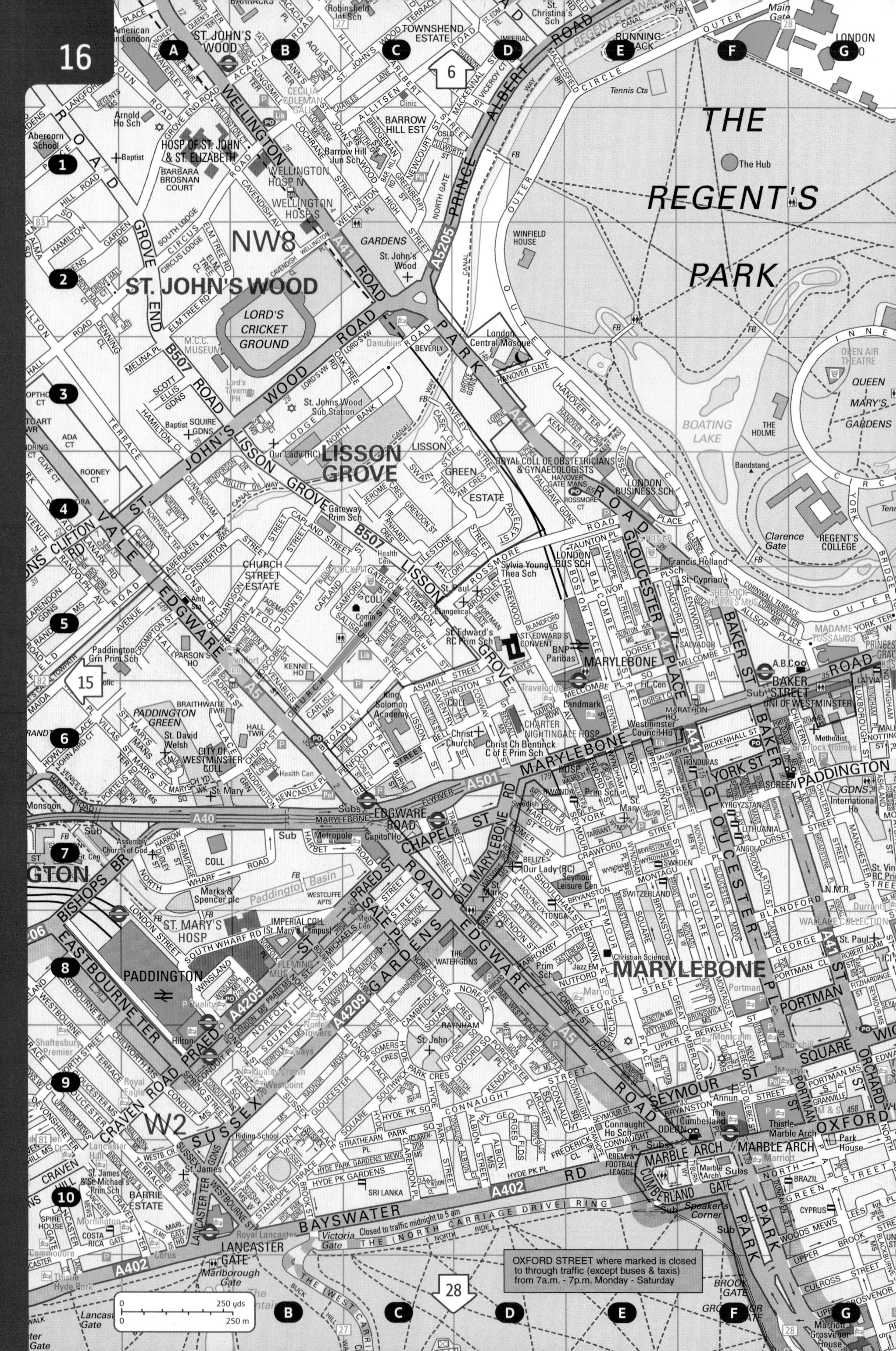
A
B
C
D
E
F
G
1
2
3
4
5
6
7
8
9
10
6
15
28
ST. JOHN'S WOOD
NW8
THE REGENT'S PARK
LORD'S CRICKET GROUND
M.C.C. MUSEUM
LISSON GROVE
MARYLEBONE
PADDINGTON
W2
EDGWARE ROAD
MARBLE ARCH
BAKER STREET
LANCASTER GATE
PADDINGTON GREEN
CHURCH STREET ESTATE
LISSON GREEN ESTATE
BARROW HILL EST
TOWNSHEND ESTATE
HOSP OF ST. JOHN & ST. ELIZABETH
WELLINGTON HOSP N
WELLINGTON HOSP S
London Central Mosque
LONDON BUSINESS SCH
REGENT'S COLLEGE
OPEN AIR THEATRE
QUEEN MARY'S GARDENS
BOATING LAKE
THE HOLME
The Hub
WINFIELD HOUSE
ROYAL COLL OF OBSTETRICIANS & GYNAECOLOGISTS
MADAME TUSSAUDS
SHERLOCK HOLMES MUS
WALLACE COLLECTION
ST. MARY'S HOSP
IMPERIAL COLL (St. Mary's Campus)
Marks & Spencer plc
Paddington Basin
CITY OF WESTMINSTER COLL
UNI OF WESTMINSTER
Westminster Council Ho
CHARTER NIGHTINGALE HOSP
PRINCE ALBERT ROAD
WELLINGTON ROAD
PARK ROAD
ST. JOHN'S WOOD ROAD
EDGWARE ROAD
MARYLEBONE ROAD
BAYSWATER ROAD
OXFORD STREET
GLOUCESTER PLACE
BAKER ST
SUSSEX GARDENS
PRAED ST
A41
A5
A40
A501
A402
A5205
A4205
A4209
B507
THE (NORTH CARRIAGE DRIVE) RING
Closed to traffic midnight to 5 am
OXFORD STREET where marked is closed to through traffic (except buses & taxis) from 7a.m. - 7p.m. Monday - Saturday
250 yds
250 m

H
J
K
L
M
N
P
1
2
3
4
5
6
7
8
9
10
7
18
29
REGENT'S PARK
NW1
Cumberland Gate
Gloucester Gate
Parks Dept
CAPEL MANOR COLLEGE
ALBANY STREET
REGENT'S PARK BARRACKS
ST. GEORGE'S CATHEDRAL
CUMBERLAND MARKET EST
MORNINGTON CRESCENT
CROWNDALE
HAMPSTEAD ROAD
EVERSHOLT
OAKLEY SQ
SOMERS TOWN
BRITISH LIBRARY
ST. PANCRAS INT.
MIDLAND ROAD
EUSTON
BRITISH TRANSPORT POLICE
EUSTON POLICE STATION
BUS STA
EUSTON ROAD
EUSTON SQUARE
WARREN ST
GT. PORTLAND ST
REGENT'S PARK
PARK SQUARE GARDENS
PARK CRES
ROYAL ACADEMY OF MUSIC
LONDON CLINIC
PORTLAND HOSP
WC1
UCL (Main Site)
U.C.L. HOSP
GOWER ST
TOTTENHAM CT RD
WOBURN PL
TAVISTOCK SQ GDNS
RUSSELL SQ GARDENS
UNIVERSITY OF LONDON
Senate Ho.
BLOOMSBURY
THE BRITISH MUSEUM
BEDFORD SQUARE
GOODGE ST
MORTIMER ST
UNI OF WESTMINSTER (Cavendish Campus)
B.B.C. Radio
All Souls
CAVENDISH SQ
OXFORD CIRCUS
OXFORD ST
JOHN LEWIS
DEBENHAMS
SELFRIDGES
BOND ST
REGENT ST
W1
LIBERTY
PALLADIUM
HAMLEYS
CARNABY ST
SOHO
SOHO SQUARE
CHARING CROSS RD
NEW OXFORD ST
TOTTENHAM COURT RD
CENTREPOINT
LEICESTER SQ
Trocadero Cen
PICCADILLY CIRCUS
Eros
SHAFTESBURY AV
GROSVENOR SQUARE
MAYFAIR
NEW BOND ST
CONDUIT ST
ROYAL ACAD. OF ARTS
Immaculate Conception (RC)

A
B
C
D
E
F
G
1
2
3
4
5
6
7
8
9
10
8
17
30
NW1
SOMERS TOWN
BRITISH LIBRARY
ST. PANCRAS INT.
KING'S CROSS
KING'S CROSS & ST. PANCRAS
PENTONVILLE
PENTONVILLE ROAD
A501
CALEDONIAN
WHARFDALE
ANGEL
FINSBURY
ST. PANCRAS
EUSTON RD
GRAY'S INN RD
KING'S CROSS RD
WC1
CORAM'S FIELDS
GUILFORD
HOSP FOR CHILDREN
RUSSELL SQUARE GARDENS
UNIVERSITY OF LONDON
BLOOMSBURY
THE BRITISH MUSEUM
GRAY'S INN GARDENS
CLERKENWELL RD
FARRINGDON
HOLBORN
A40
HOLBORN
LINCOLN'S INN FIELDS
WC2
KINGSWAY
ALDWYCH
STRAND
COVENT GARDEN
LEICESTER SQ
CHANCERY LANE
FLEET STREET
ROYAL COURTS OF JUSTICE
TEMPLE
VICTORIA EMBANKMENT
BLACKFRIARS MILLENNIUM PIER
H.M.S. PRESIDENT
THAMES
0 250 yds
0 250 m

SHOREDITCH
HOXTON
N1
EC1
EC2
EC3
EC4
E1
BARBICAN
BROADGATE
ST. LUKE'S
LIVERPOOL STREET
MANSION HOUSE
MONUMENT
BANK
MOORGATE
OLD STREET
BARBICAN
ST. PAUL'S CATHEDRAL
ST. BARTHOLOMEW'S HOSPITAL
BUNHILL FIELDS BURIAL GRD
FINSBURY SQ
CITY ROAD
OLD STREET
LONDON WALL
CHEAPSIDE
BISHOPSGATE
HOUNDSDITCH
KINGSLAND RD
SHOREDITCH HIGH STREET
GREAT EASTERN STREET
NEW NORTH RD
CITY ROAD BASIN
WENLOCK BASIN
REGENT'S CANAL
KINGS SQUARE GDN
FENCHURCH ST
TOWER HILL
SOUTHWARK
MILLENNIUM BRIDGE
CANNON ST
9
20
31
H
J
K
L
M
N
P
1
2
3
4
5
6
7
8
9
10

HAGGERSTON
Haggerston Park
Sports Ground
Hackney City Farm
Haggerston Sch
Randal Cremer Prim Sch
Hoxton (open 2010)
Geffrye Museum
St. Chad
Gas Works
St. Casimir (RC)
Cambridge Heath
Peterley Bus Cen
Parmiter Ind Cen
Hackney Road
A1208
Hadrian Est
Ion Square Gardens
St. Peter
E2
Mowlem Prim Sch
Bishops Way
St. John's Prim Sch
York Hall Leisure Cen
Our Lady (RC)
Museum of Childhood
Raine's Foundation Sch (Lwr Sch)
Beatrice Tate Sch
George Loveless Ho
Dorset Est
Columbia Prim Sch
Columbia Rd
Elver Gardens
Oaklands Sch
Elizabeth Selby Inf Sch
Lawdale Jun Sch
Old Bethnal Green Road
BETHNAL GREEN
Charles Dickens Ho
Bethnal Green
Bethnal Grn Est
Bethnal Green Gdns
Tower Hamlets Coll (Bethnal Grn Cen)
Bethnal Grn Technology Coll
Gosset B118
Mildmay Mission Hosp
Virginia Prim Sch
Arnold Circus
Calvert Av
Crowne Plaza
Green Street
Weavers Fields
St. Mathew
United Reformed
Hague Prim Sch
Three Colts La B135
Old Nichol
Club Row
Redchurch
St. Matthias Prim Sch
William Davis Prim Sch
Bethnal Green
Cheshire Street
Dunbridge St
SHOREDITCH
Sclater St
Shoreditch High Street (open 2010)
Sports Centre
Stewart Headlam Prim Sch
Spitalfields City Farm
Allen Gdns
Thomas Buxton Inf & Jun Sch
Jewish Burial Ground
Swanlea Sch
Superstore
Cambridge Heath Rd A107
Commercial St A1202
St. Anne's Prim Sch
St. Anne (RC)
Osmani Prim Sch
Keen Students Sch
Sports Cen
E1
Whitechapel
Mile End
Old Spitalfields Market
ABN AMRO
Christ Church
Christ Ch C of E Sch
Bethnal Grn Training Cen
Royal London Hosp
Whitechapel Rd A11
Toynbee Hall
Canon Barnett Prim Sch
Aldgate East
London Met Uni
Kobi Nazrul Prim Sch
Madani Girls Sch
Barts and The London
Sch of Nursing & Midwifery
Commercial Road A13
Houndsditch
Aldgate
Aldgate High St
Bus Sta
Royal Bank of Scotland
Harry Gosling Prim Sch
Mulberry Sch for Girls
Bigland Grn Prim Sch
St. Mary & St. Michael Prim Sch
WHITECHAPEL
EC3
Fenchurch St
Minories
Mansell St
Leman Street
Alie Street
Prescot St
Cable St
Royal Mint St
Tower Gateway
Tower Hill
Shadwell
Blue Gate Flds Inf & Jun Schs
Mulberry Sch For Girls
St. George
The Highway A1203
Shapla Prim Sch
St. Paul's C of E Prim Sch
Tobacco Dock
Under development
Tower of London
Trinity Tower
10
19
32
250 yds
250 m

H
J
K
L
M
N
P
11
BOW
ROMAN ROAD
B119
MILE END PARK
MILE END
MILE END HOSPITAL
QUEEN MARY- UNI OF LONDON
JEWISH BURIAL GROUND
MILE END ROAD
A11
BOW ROAD
E3
ROYAL LON. HOSP (ST. CLEMENTS)
TOWER HAMLETS CEMETERY PARK
BURDETT ROAD
A1205
GLOBE ROAD
SEWARDSTONE RD
B127
B118
LONDON CHEST HOSP
MEATH GARDENS
SPORTS GRD
STEPNEY GREEN
OCEAN ESTATE
SHANDY PARK
RAGGED SCHOOL MUSEUM
Mile End Park Leisure Cen
MILE END STADIUM
LONDON INDEP. HOSP
STEPNEY
STEPNEY GREEN PARK
B121
B140
BEN JONSON ROAD
ST. PAULS WAY
E14
LOCKSLEY ESTATE
COMMERCIAL ROAD
A13
LIMEHOUSE
LIMEHOUSE BASIN
CABLE STREET
B126
ROTHERHITHE TUNNEL
NARROW STREET
ROPEMAKERS FIELD
A1203
WEST INDIA DOCK RD
WESTFERRY
Bow Common Lane
22
THAMES
33
KING EDWARD VII MEMORIAL PK
LIMEHOUSE CUT
1
2
3
4
5
6
7
8
9
10

A
B
C
D
E
F
G
1
2
3
4
5
6
7
8
9
10
12
21
34
E3
E14
E15
BROMLEY
BOW ROAD
BOW CHURCH
DEVONS ROAD
BROMLEY BY BOW
LANGDON PARK
ALL SAINTS
WESTFERRY
POPLAR
BLACKWALL
BLACKWALL TUNNEL NORTHERN APPROACH
BOW RD
BOW ROAD
DEVAS STREET
DEVONS ROAD
ST. PAULS WAY
BOW COMMON LANE
EAST INDIA DOCK ROAD
WEST INDIA DOCK RD
POPLAR HIGH STREET
ASPEN WAY
ABBOTT ROAD
FAIRFIELD ROAD
THREE MILL LANE
TOWER HAMLETS CEMETERY PARK
GROVE HALL PARK
LEE VALLEY PARK
LEE VALLEY PARK-THREE MILLS GREEN
MEMORIAL GARDENS
BARTLETT PARK
JOLLY'S GREEN
GAS WORKS
Gas Works
Three Mills Studios
Superstore
Dudley Stationers
Mail Centre
BARRATT IND PK
BOW TRIANGLE BUS. CEN
THOMAS ROAD IND EST
LANSBURY EST
BOW BRIDGE ESTATE
DEVONS ESTATE
POPLAR BUSINESS PARK
TOWER HAMLETS COLL
LIMEHOUSE CUT
LIMEHOUSE CAUSEWAY
PUMPING STA
TWELVETREES BUS PK
ROYAL LON. HOSP (ST. CLEMENTS)
Global Switch
East India Dock Ho
COUNCIL OFFICES
0
250 yds
250 m

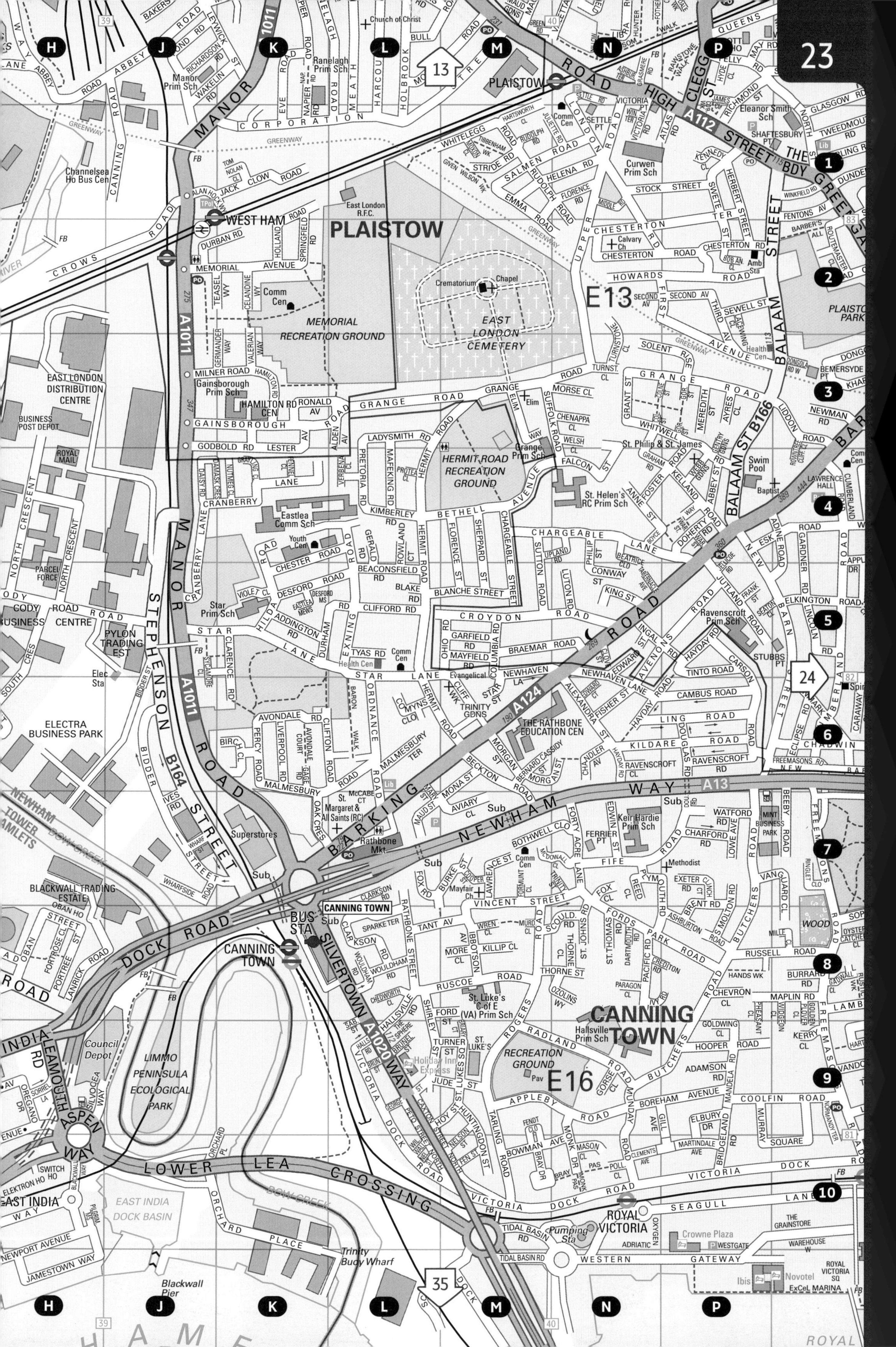
H
J
K
L
M
N
P
13
PLAISTOW
Church of Christ
Ranelagh Prim Sch
Manor Prim Sch
CORPORATION
GREENWAY
MANOR
A1011
FB
Channelsea Ho Bus Cen
JACK CLOW ROAD
WEST HAM
CROWS ROAD
DURBAN RD
MEMORIAL AVENUE
East London R.F.C.
PLAISTOW
Comm Cen
MEMORIAL RECREATION GROUND
Crematorium
Chapel
EAST LONDON CEMETERY
E13
WHITELEGG
STRIDE RD
SALMEN ROAD
HELENA RD
EMMA ROAD
Curwen Prim Sch
STOCK STREET
CHESTERTON RD
Calvary Ch
HOWARDS ROAD
SECOND AV
SEWELL ST
SOLENT RISE
Health Cen
BALAAM STREET
Eleanor Smith Sch
SHAFTESBURY PT
TWEEDMOUTH RD
HIGH STREET
A112
CLEGG ST
QUEENS ROAD
RICHMOND
GLASGOW RD
THE GREENWAY
Lib
1
2
3
4
5
6
7
8
9
10
PLAISTOW PARK
Amb Sta
EAST LONDON DISTRIBUTION CENTRE
BUSINESS POST DEPOT
ROYAL MAIL
MILNER ROAD
Gainsborough Prim Sch
HAMILTON RD CEN
GAINSBOROUGH
GODBOLD RD
LESTER
GRANGE ROAD
Elim
MORSE CL
CHENAPPA CL
SUFFOLK ROAD
GRANGE ROAD
LIDDON ROAD
NEWMAN RD
BALAAM ST B166
LADYSMITH RD
PRETORIA RD
MAFEKING RD
HERMIT ROAD RECREATION GROUND
Grange Prim Sch
FALCON ST
St. Philip & St. James
Swim Pool
Baptist
St. Helen's RC Prim Sch
CRANBERRY
Eastlea Comm Sch
KIMBERLEY RD
BETHELL AVENUE
CHARGEABLE LANE
CHARGEABLE STREET
Youth Cen
CHESTER ROAD
BEACONSFIELD RD
DESFORD ROAD
BLAKE RD
BLANCHE STREET
CROYDON ROAD
CLIFFORD RD
GARFIELD RD
MAYFIELD RD
BRAEMAR ROAD
CONWAY
KING ST
BARKING ROAD
Ravenscroft Prim Sch
HAYDAY RD
TINTO ROAD
CAMBUS ROAD
LING ROAD
KILDARE ROAD
RAVENSCROFT RD
ELKINGTON ROAD
STUBBS PT
24
CODY BUSINESS CENTRE
CODY ROAD
PYLON TRADING EST
Star Prim Sch
STAR LANE
TYAS RD
Comm Cen
Health Cen
Evangelical
NEWHAVEN LANE
A124
THE RATHBONE EDUCATION CEN
Elec Sta
ELECTRA BUSINESS PARK
STEPHENSON STREET
B164
MANOR ROAD
AVONDALE RD
MALMESBURY TER
MALMESBURY
Lib
St. Margaret & All Saints (RC)
Rathbone Mkt
NEWHAM WAY
A13
Sub
Keir Hardie Prim Sch
WATFORD RD
CHARFORD RD
MINT BUSINESS PARK
Superstores
BLACKWALL TRADING ESTATE
DOCK ROAD
CANNING TOWN
BUS STA
CANNING TOWN
Mayfair Ch
VINCENT STREET
Methodist
FIFE
RUSSELL ROAD
WOOD
BURRARD RD
SILVERTOWN WAY
A1020
RUSCOE ROAD
St. Luke's C of E (VA) Prim Sch
CANNING TOWN
Hallsville Prim Sch
RADLAND ROAD
CHEVRON
MAPLIN RD
KERRY CL
HOOPER ROAD
ADAMSON RD
Holiday Inn Express
RECREATION GROUND
Pav
E16
APPLEBY ROAD
BOREHAM AVENUE
COOLFIN ROAD
MURRAY SQUARE
Council Depot
LIMMO PENINSULA ECOLOGICAL PARK
EAST INDIA
LEAMOUTH RD
ASPEN WAY
LOWER LEA CROSSING
VICTORIA DOCK ROAD
BOW CREEK
EAST INDIA DOCK BASIN
ORCHARD PLACE
NEWPORT AVENUE
JAMESTOWN WAY
Trinity Buoy Wharf
Blackwall Pier
35
ROYAL VICTORIA
TIDAL BASIN RD
Pumping Sta
SEAGULL LANE
Crowne Plaza
WESTGATE
WESTERN GATEWAY
THE GRAINSTORE
Ibis
Novotel
ROYAL VICTORIA SQ
ExCeL MARINA
NEWHAM
TOWER HAMLETS
ROYAL

24
A
B
C
D
E
F
G
1
2
3
4
5
6
7
8
9
10
BOLEYN GRD - WEST HAM UTD FC
Lister Comm Sch
Southern Rd Prim Sch
Plaistow Prim Sch
PLAISTOW HOSP
166
Quality Hotel
Our Lady (RC)
EAST HAM
St. Mary the Virgin
Eleanor Smith Sch
SHAFTESBURY PT
PLAYING FLD
Youth Cen
Pav
Christian
St. Martin
Central Pk Prim Sch
Elim Pentecostal
BARKING ROAD
A124
A112
B167
B166
B167 STREET
CENTRAL PARK ROAD
GREENGATE STREET
BALAAM STREET
PLAISTOW PARK
JACOBS HO
Health Cen
Amb Sta
E13
E16
PRINCE REGENT LANE
TUNMARSH LANE
HUMBERSTONE
New City Prim Sch
Brampton Prim Sch
BRAMPTON PARK
GREENWAY
St. Andrew's
ST. ANDREWS ROAD
Comm Cen
Swim Pool
Baptist
Pol
NEWHAM UNIVERSITY HOSPITAL
NEWHAM CENTRE FOR MENTAL HEALTH
Brampton Manor Sch
Roman Rd Prim Sch
PLAYING FIELDS
Sports Hall
Kaizen Prim Sch
NEWHAM 6TH FORM COLL
Fire Sta
Cumberland Sch
Medical Cen
TERENCE MCMILLAN STADIUM
Tollgate Prim Sch
Leisure Cen
EAST HAM INDUSTRIAL ESTATE
BECKTON DISTRICT PARK NORTH
NEWHAM WAY
A13
23
Spiritualist
Ghana Seventh-Day Adventist
John F. Kennedy Post 16 Annex
TOLLGATE ROAD
MINT BUSINESS PARK
Tenn Cts
CANNING TOWN REC GRD
Rosetta Prim Sch
WOOD
Lib
Baptist
Health Cen
Fellowship
Scott Wilkie Prim Sch
KING GEORGE V PARK
CUSTOM HOUSE
Ellen Wilkinson Prim Sch
Newham City Farm
Christian Cen
Comm Cen
St. Joachim's RC Prim Sch
St. Anne (RC)
MARGARET MCMILLAN HO
Ascension
The Royal Docks Comm Sch
Calverton Prim Sch
Hospice
KING GEORGE AVENUE
STANSFELD ROAD
ALLOT
CONNAUGHT ROUNDABOUT
ROYAL ALBERT ROUNDABOUT
VICTORIA DOCK ROAD
CUSTOM HOUSE for ExCeL
PRINCE REGENT
BUS STA
Premier Inn
Crowne Plaza
THE GRAINSTORE
WAREHOUSE W
ExCeL London
Novotel
Ibis
ROYAL VICTORIA SQ
EASTERN GATEWAY
Ramada
DOCKSIDE ROAD
London Regatta Centre
Boathouse
THE ROYALS BUSINE
CONNAUGHT BRIDGE
36
Sunborn Yacht Hotel
ROYAL VICTORIA DOCK
0 250 yds
0 250 m
41
42

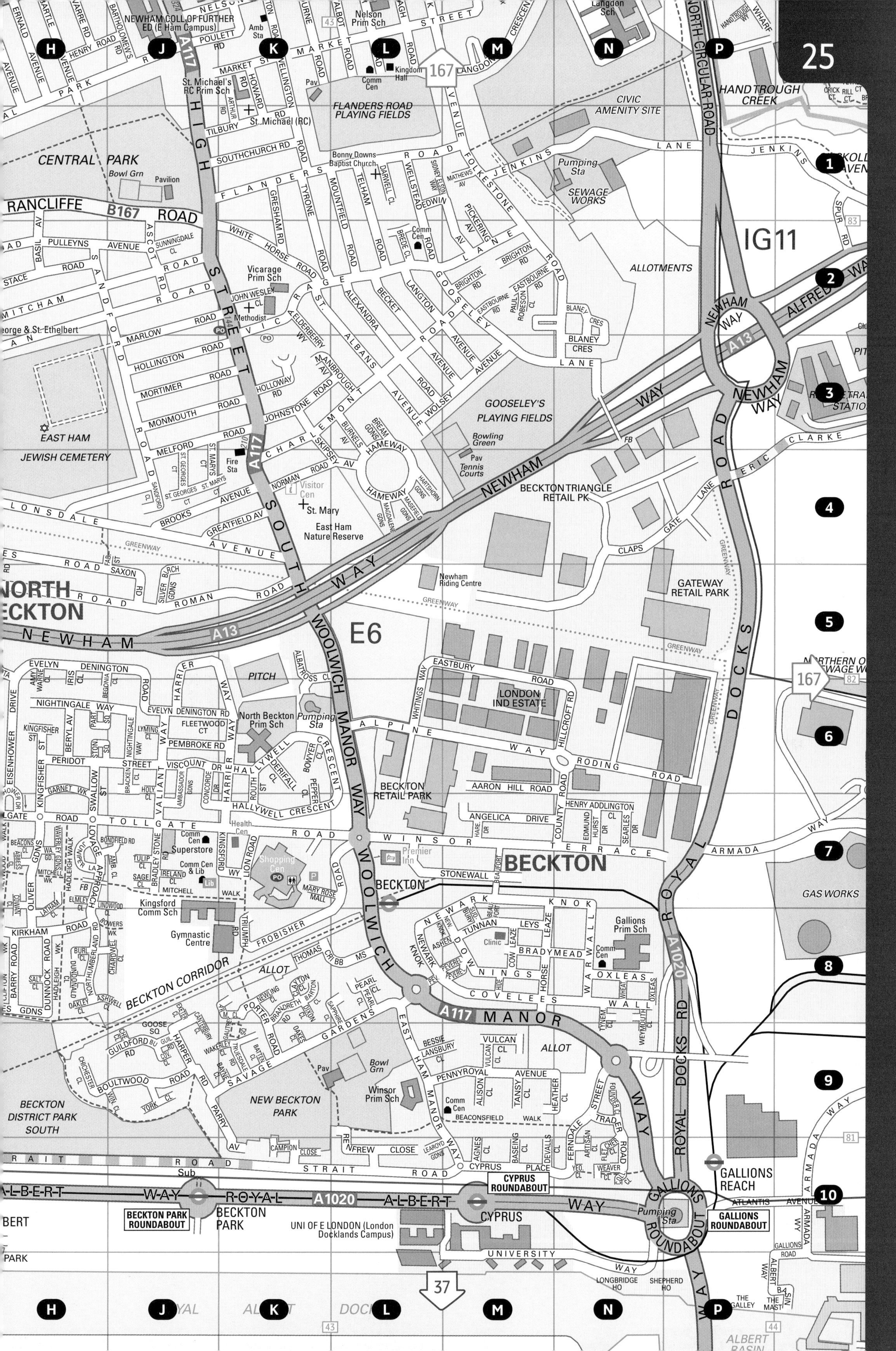

H
J
K
L
M
N
P
167
NEWHAM COLL OF FURTHER ED (E Ham Campus)
Nelson Prim Sch
Kingdom Hall
Comm Cen
St. Michael's RC Prim Sch
St. Michael (RC)
FLANDERS ROAD PLAYING FIELDS
HANDTROUGH CREEK
CIVIC AMENITY SITE
NORTH CIRCULAR ROAD
CENTRAL PARK
Bowl Grn
Pavilion
Bonny Downs Baptist Church
Pumping Sta
SEWAGE WORKS
RANCLIFFE
B167
ROAD
HIGH STREET
A117
IG11
ALLOTMENTS
Vicarage Prim Sch
JOHN WESLEY CL
Methodist
NEWHAM WAY
A13
ALFRED WAY
BLANEY CRES
EAST HAM JEWISH CEMETERY
GOOSELEY'S PLAYING FIELDS
Bowling Green
Pav
Tennis Courts
Fire Sta
Visitor Cen
St. Mary
East Ham Nature Reserve
BECKTON TRIANGLE RETAIL PK
ERIC CLARKE LANE
LONSDALE AVENUE
GREENWAY
Newham Riding Centre
GATEWAY RETAIL PARK
NORTH BECKTON
ROMAN ROAD
SOUTH STREET
E6
ROYAL DOCKS ROAD
PITCH
North Beckton Prim Sch
Pumping Sta
WOOLWICH MANOR WAY
EASTBURY ROAD
LONDON IND ESTATE
ALPINE WAY
RODING ROAD
HILLCROFT RD
NORTHERN OUTFALL SEWAGE WORKS
BECKTON RETAIL PARK
AARON HILL ROAD
HENRY ADDLINGTON CL
TOLLGATE ROAD
WINSOR TERRACE
ARMADA WAY
Health Cen
Comm Cen
Superstore
Shopping Cen
Premier Inn
BECKTON
GAS WORKS
Comm Cen & Lib
MARY ROSE MALL
STONEWALL
Kingsford Comm Sch
Gymnastic Centre
Gallions Prim Sch
Clinic
BECKTON CORRIDOR
ALLOT
A1020
A117 MANOR WAY
Bowl Grn
Winsor Prim Sch
BECKTON DISTRICT PARK SOUTH
NEW BECKTON PARK
STRAIT ROAD
CYPRUS ROUNDABOUT
GALLIONS REACH
ROYAL ALBERT WAY
A1020
BECKTON PARK ROUNDABOUT
BECKTON PARK
CYPRUS
UNI OF E LONDON (London Docklands Campus)
GALLIONS ROUNDABOUT
UNIVERSITY WAY
ATLANTIS AVENUE
LONGBRIDGE HO
SHEPHERD HO
THE GALLEY
THE MAST
37
ALBERT BASIN
43
44
1
2
3
4
5
6
7
8
9
10

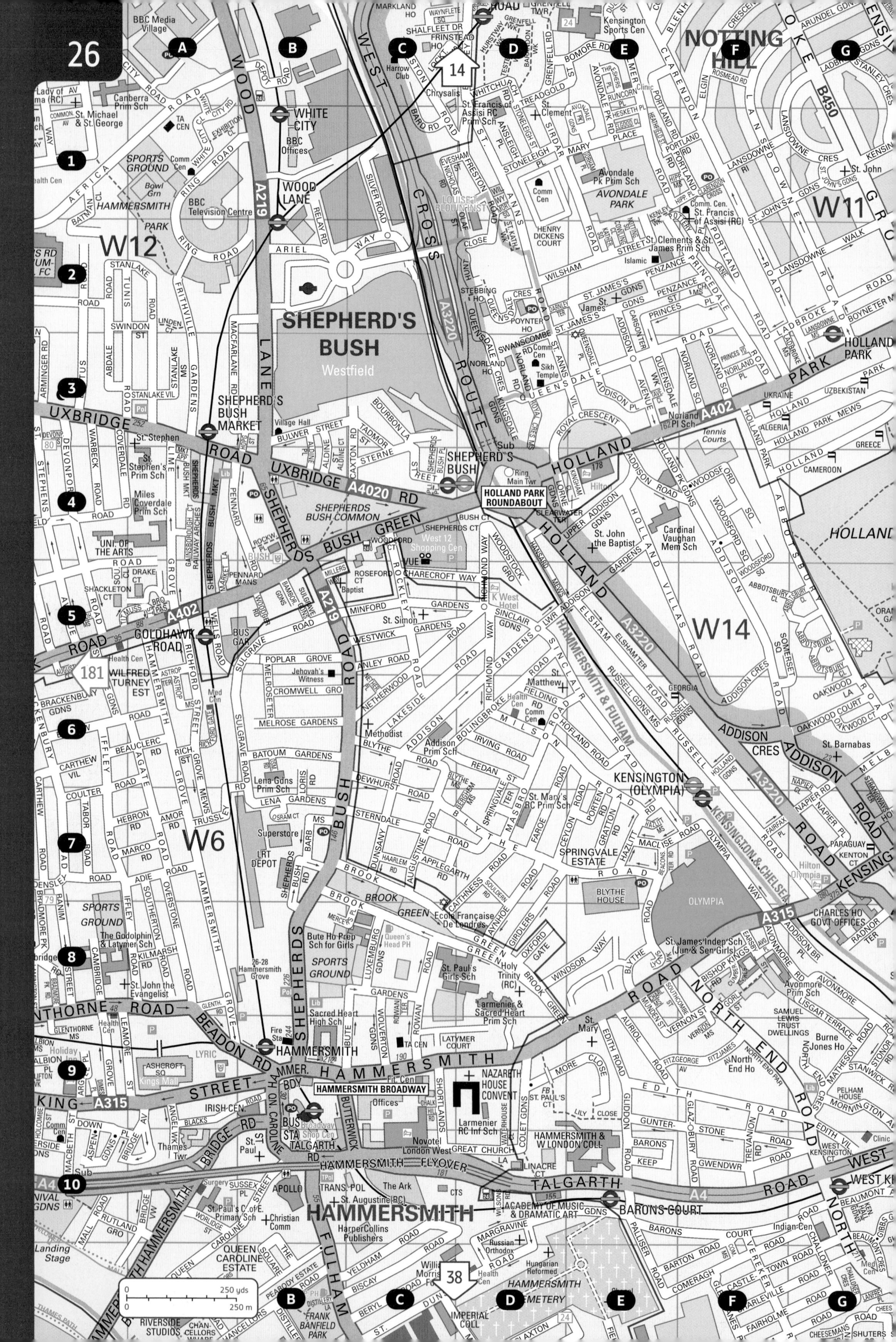
A
B
C
D
E
F
G
1
2
3
4
5
6
7
8
9
10
14
38
181
NOTTING HILL
W11
W12
W14
W6
SHEPHERD'S BUSH
Westfield
HAMMERSMITH
WHITE CITY
WOOD LANE
BBC Media Village
BBC Television Centre
HAMMERSMITH PARK
SHEPHERD'S BUSH MARKET
HOLLAND PARK ROUNDABOUT
HOLLAND PARK
SHEPHERDS BUSH COMMON
KENSINGTON (OLYMPIA)
OLYMPIA
BLYTHE HOUSE
GOLDHAWK ROAD
HAMMERSMITH BROADWAY
HAMMERSMITH FLYOVER
BARONS COURT
WEST KENSINGTON
HAMMERSMITH CEMETERY
AVONDALE PARK
UXBRIDGE ROAD
A4020
A402
A219
A3220
A315
A4
B450
HOLLAND ROAD
TALGARTH ROAD
FULHAM PALACE ROAD
WEST CROSS ROUTE
SHEPHERDS BUSH GREEN
NORTH END ROAD
ADDISON ROAD
BROOK GREEN
LYRIC
APOLLO
RIVERSIDE STUDIOS
FRANK BANFIELD PARK
HarperCollins Publishers
St. Paul's Girls Sch
The Godolphin & Latymer Sch
SPORTS GROUND
ACADEMY OF MUSIC & DRAMATIC ART
0
250 yds
0
250 m

H
J
K
L
M
N
P
1
2
3
4
5
6
7
8
9
10
15
28
39
W2
W8
SW7
SW5
KENSINGTON
KENSINGTON GARDENS
SOUTH KENSINGTON
EARLS COURT
PARK
ROUND POND
BAYSWATER ROAD
NOTTING HILL GATE
QUEENSWAY
HIGH ST. KENSINGTON
GLOUCESTER ROAD
EARLS COURT
KENSINGTON HIGH ST
KENSINGTON CHURCH STREET
PALACE GARDENS TER
CAMPDEN HILL ROAD
HOLLAND STREET
KENSINGTON ROAD
PALACE GATE
QUEEN'S GATE
CROMWELL ROAD
WEST CROMWELL RD
EARLS COURT RD
WARWICK ROAD
OLD BROMPTON ROAD
BROMPTON ROAD
REDCLIFFE GDNS
PEMBROKE RD
LADBROKE SQUARE GARDENS
KENSINGTON PALACE
KENSINGTON TOWN HALL
Holland Park Sch
CRICKET GROUND
LEIGHTON HO MUS
LINLEY SAMBOURNE HOUSE
Victoria Statue
William III Statue
Physical Energy Statue
Speke Monument
Peter Pan
Bandstand
Albert Memorial
Lancaster Gate
North Porchester Terrace Gate
Inverness Terrace Gate
Black Lion Gate
Orme Square Gate
Diana Mem Playground
Palace Gate
Queen's Gate
ROYAL ALBERT HALL
ROYAL COLL OF ART
ROYAL COLL OF MUSIC
IMPERIAL COLLEGE
EARLS COURT EXHIBITION CENTRE
LILLIE BRIDGE DEPOT
LONDON ELECTRONICS COLL
ST. JAMES'S & LUCIE CLAYTON COLL
CROMWELL HOSP
Superstore
A402
A4
A3220
A3218
B325 GLOUCESTER RD
B415

A
B
C
D
E
F
G
1
2
3
4
5
6
7
8
9
10
16
27
40
HYDE PARK
KENSINGTON GARDENS
W2
SW7
SW3
BROMPTON
BAYSWATER RD
A402
MARBLE ARCH
CUMBERLAND GATE
Speakers' Corner
PARK LANE
LANCASTER GATE
Marlborough Gate
The Fountains
Lancaster Gate
Speke Monument
Peter Pan
THE LONG WATER
Bird Sanctuary
Physical Energy Statue
Queens Temple
SERPENTINE ROAD
THE SERPENTINE
Pier
Lido
Diana Princess of Wales Memorial
SERPENTINE GALLERY
Bandstand
War Memorial
Holocaust Memorial
ROTTEN ROW
Albert Gate
HYDE PARK CORNER
Edinburgh Gate
Prince of Wales Gate
Rutland Gate
Coalbrookdale Gate
Albert Memorial
Alexandra Gate
Queen's Gate
SOUTH CARRIAGE DRIVE
Closed to traffic midnight to 5 am
HYDE PARK BARRACKS
KENSINGTON RD
A315
KNIGHTSBRIDGE
KENSINGTON GORE
ROYAL ALBERT HALL
ROYAL COLL OF ART
Royal Geographical Society
IMPERIAL COLL
ROYAL COLL OF MUSIC
PRINCE CONSORT RD
EXHIBITION RD
GOETHE INSTITUT
RUSSIAN ORTH CATH
HARVEY NICHOLS
HARRODS
BROMPTON RD
A4
BEAUCHAMP PL
PONT STREET
B319
SLOANE STREET
A3216
SOUTH KENSINGTON
SCIENCE MUSEUM
NATURAL HISTORY MUSEUM
VICTORIA & ALBERT MUSEUM
Brompton Oratory
Holy Trinity
CROMWELL RD
Lycée Français Charles de Gaulle Sch
THURLOE PL
PELHAM STREET
ONSLOW SQUARE
FULHAM ROAD
A308
A3218
SYDNEY STREET
THE ROYAL MARSDEN
ROYAL BROMPTON HOSP
B304
KING'S ROAD
SAMUEL LEWIS TRUST DWELLINGS
SUTTON EST
CHELSEA CLOISTERS
GUINNESS TRUST BLDGS
CADOGAN SQUARE
CADOGAN PLACE
CADOGAN HALL
SLOANE SQ
PETER JONES
LOWER SLOANE ST
Saatchi Gallery
DUKE OF YORK SQ
BURTON'S COURT
B302
CHELSEA BRIDGE RD
ROYAL HOSPITAL
MUSEUM
Marriott Grosvenor House
A4202
PARK LANE
CHESHAM PL
B310
PIMLICO RD
Chelsea
Sports Cen
250 yds
250 m

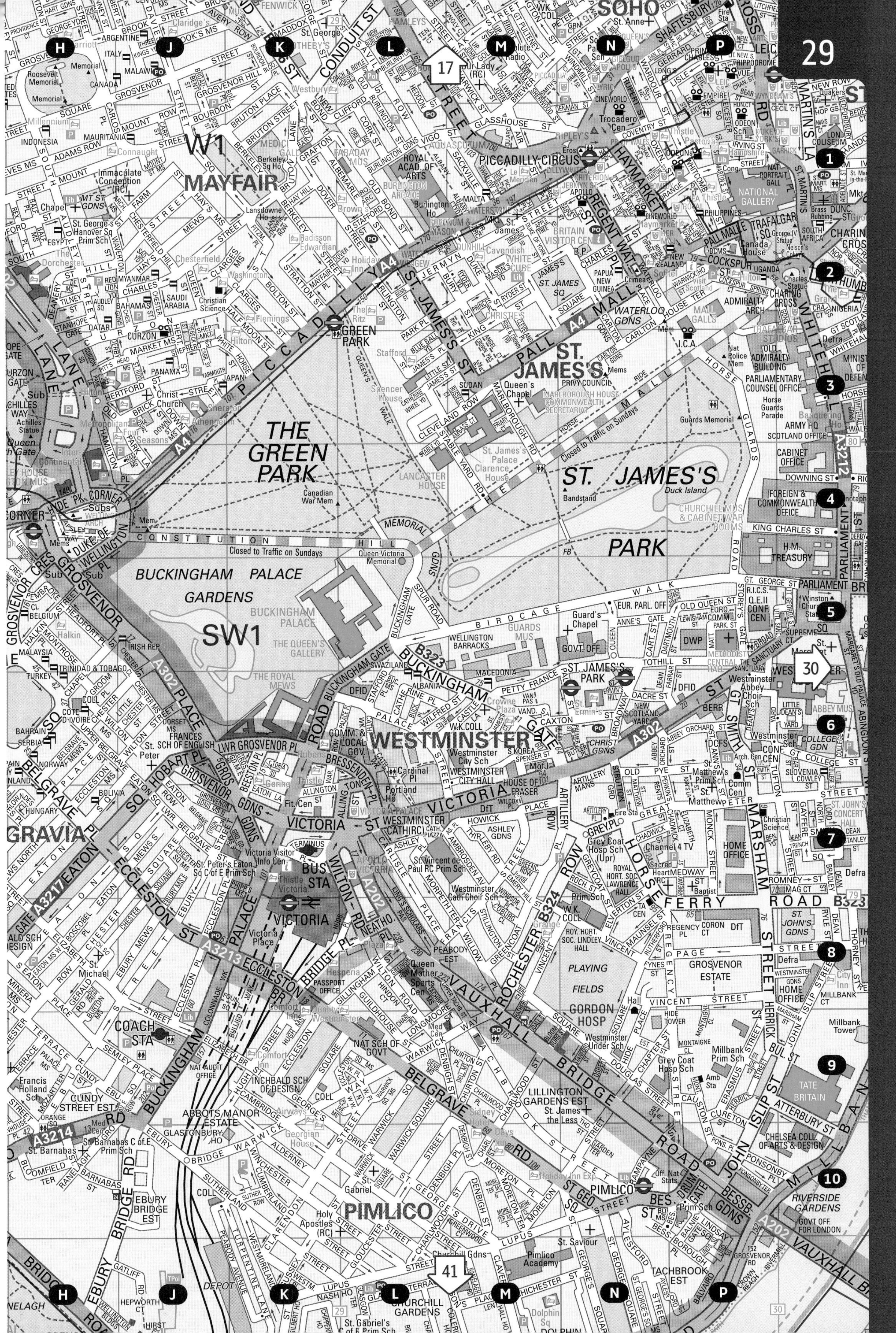
H
J
K
L
M
N
P
1
2
3
4
5
6
7
8
9
10
17
30
41
SOHO
W1
MAYFAIR
THE GREEN PARK
ST. JAMES'S
ST. JAMES'S PARK
BUCKINGHAM PALACE GARDENS
BUCKINGHAM PALACE
SW1
WESTMINSTER
GRAVIA
PIMLICO
PICCADILLY CIRCUS
PICCADILLY
GREEN PARK
HYDE PK. CORNER
CONSTITUTION HILL
Closed to Traffic on Sundays
Closed to Traffic on Sundays
THE MALL
BIRDCAGE WALK
PALL MALL
HAYMARKET
REGENT ST
ST. JAMES'S ST
TRAFALGAR SQ
NATIONAL GALLERY
WHITEHALL
HORSE GUARDS ROAD
H.M. TREASURY
FOREIGN & COMMONWEALTH OFFICE
CABINET OFFICE
DOWNING ST
KING CHARLES ST
PARLIAMENT ST
VICTORIA ST
VICTORIA
BUS STA
COACH STA
BUCKINGHAM PALACE ROAD
VAUXHALL BRIDGE ROAD
BELGRAVE RD
HORSEFERRY ROAD
MARSHAM STREET
JOHN ISLIP ST
MILLBANK
TATE BRITAIN
PLAYING FIELDS
GORDON HOSP
GROSVENOR ESTATE
HOME OFFICE
LILLINGTON GARDENS EST
CHURCHILL GARDENS
TACHBROOK EST
EBURY BRIDGE EST
ECCLESTON ST
GROSVENOR PLACE
GROSVENOR CRES
DUKE OF WELLINGTON PL
ST. JAMES'S PARK
PIMLICO
RIVERSIDE GARDENS
DEPOT

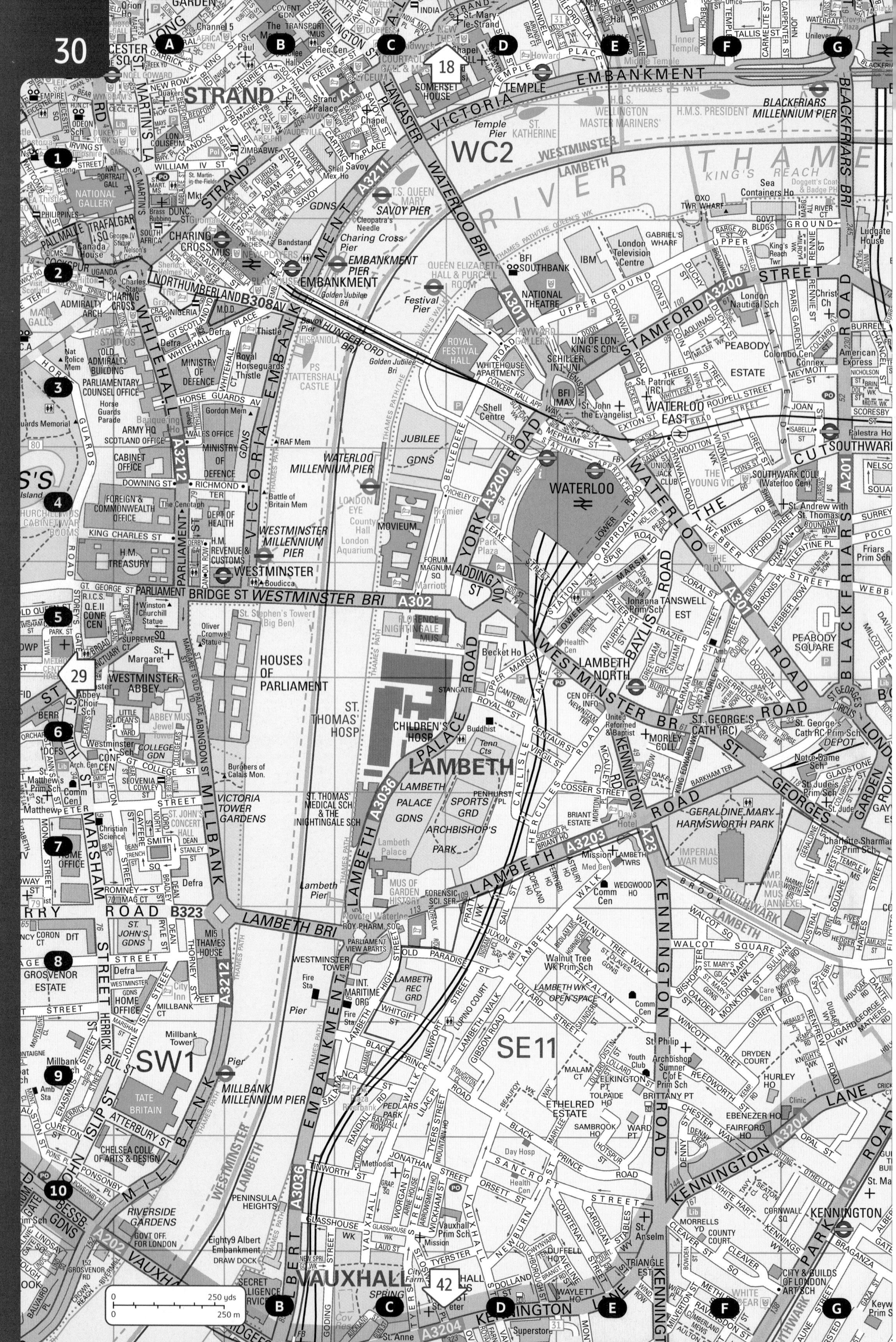
STRAND
WC2
RIVER THAMES
KING'S REACH
VICTORIA EMBANKMENT
WATERLOO BRI
WESTMINSTER BRI
LAMBETH BRI
BLACKFRIARS BRI
STAMFORD STREET
THE CUT
WATERLOO
WESTMINSTER
CHARING CROSS
EMBANKMENT
TEMPLE
LAMBETH NORTH
KENNINGTON
VAUXHALL
LAMBETH
SE11
SW1
HOUSES OF PARLIAMENT
WESTMINSTER ABBEY
NATIONAL GALLERY
ROYAL FESTIVAL HALL
NATIONAL THEATRE
ST. THOMAS' HOSP
LAMBETH PALACE GDNS
ARCHBISHOP'S PARK
VICTORIA TOWER GARDENS
GERALDINE MARY HARMSWORTH PARK
IMPERIAL WAR MUS
TATE BRITAIN
MILLBANK
WHITEHALL
KENNINGTON ROAD
KENNINGTON LANE
LAMBETH ROAD
WESTMINSTER BR ROAD
ALBERT EMBANKMENT
18
29
42
A
B
C
D
E
F
G
1
2
3
4
5
6
7
8
9
10
250 yds
250 m

H
J
K
L
M
N
P
19
BLACKFRIARS
EC4
MILLENNIUM BRIDGE
SOUTHWARK BRIDGE
Southwark Bridge Steps
CANNON ST
Swan Lane Pier
LONDON BRIDGE
MONUMENT
EASTCHEAP
GREAT TOWER ST
LOWER THAMES STREET
H. M. Revenue & Customs
Old Billingsgate Mkt
TOWER HILL
TOWER OF LONDON
1
EC3
Tower Millennium Pier
2
TOWER BRIDGE
TOWER HAMLETS
SOUTHWARK
H.M.S. BELFAST
BANKSIDE PIER
SHAKESPEARE'S GLOBE THEATRE
BANKSIDE GALLERY
TATE MODERN
Financial Times
CLINK PRISON MUS
GOLDEN HINDE
LONDON BRIDGE HOSPITAL
LONDON BRIDGE CITY PIER
Hay's Galleria
SOUTHWARK CATHEDRAL
VINOPOLIS
Borough Mkt
BRAMAH MUS
TOOLEY ST
LONDON DUNGEON
MORE LONDON PLACE
CITY HALL (Greater London Authority)
POTTERS FIELDS PARK
3
SOUTHWARK ST
A3200
SE1
SOUTHWARK
UNION STREET
BOROUGH HIGH STREET
ST. THOMAS STREET
A200
GUY'S HOSP
LONDON BRIDGE
BERMONDSEY STREET
CRUCIFIX LA
DRUID ST
4
BLACKFRIARS ROAD
A300
MARSHALSEA RD
BOROUGH
THE BOROUGH
LONG LANE
LEATHERMARKET GARDENS
TYERS EST
NEWHAM COLL
5
TOWER BRIDGE RD
32
A2198
TABARD GARDENS
TABARD GARDENS ESTATE
ELIM ESTATE
CLUNY EST
ABBEY ST
6
BOROUGH ROAD
LONDON SOUTH BANK UNI
NEWINGTON CAUSEWAY
GREAT DOVER STREET
KING'S COLLEGE (Hall Of Residence)
A2
ROCKINGHAM ESTATE
LAWSON EST
MEAKIN EST
A100
TOWER BRIDGE RD
GRANGE RD
7
A2206
A201
ELEPHANT & CASTLE
NEW KENT ROAD
BRICKLAYER'S ARMS ROUNDABOUT
OLD KENT RD
HAROLD ESTATE
8
NEWINGTON
NEWINGTON BUTTS
WALWORTH ROAD
Bricklayer's Arms Distribution Centre
Royal Mail
MANDELA WAY
9
EAST STREET
WALWORTH
SE17
A215
ALVEY EST
SURREY SQUARE PARK
KINGLAKE EST
OLD KENT ROAD
DUNTON RD
10
43
FARADAY GARDENS
AYLESBURY EST
SURREY GDNS

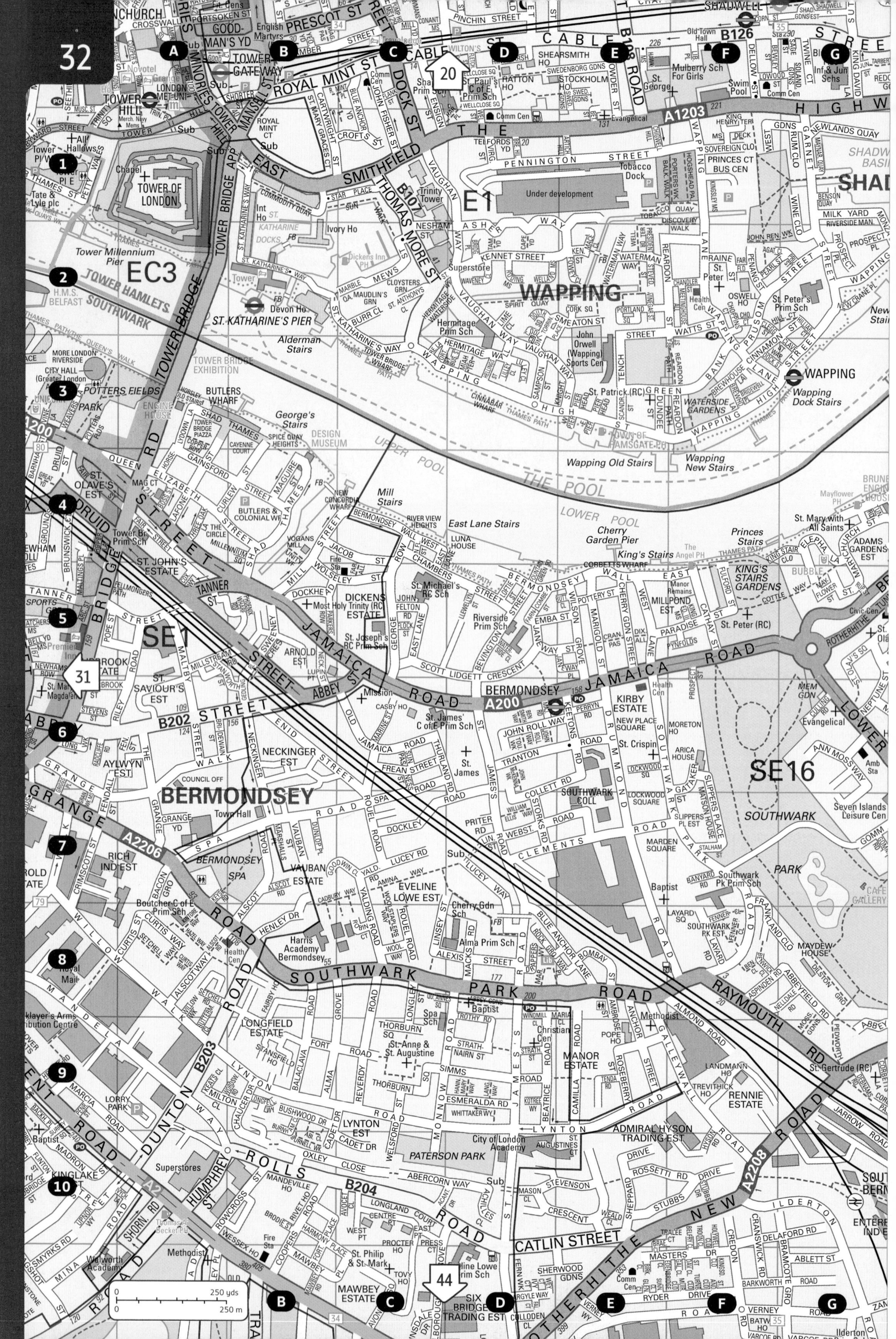
A
B
C
D
E
F
G
1
2
3
4
5
6
7
8
9
10
20
31
44
TOWER HILL
TOWER GATEWAY
SHADWELL
ROYAL MINT ST
PRESCOT ST
CABLE ST
HIGHWAY
THE HIGHWAY
A1203
B126
EAST SMITHFIELD
TOWER OF LONDON
Tower Millennium Pier
EC3
E1
TOWER HAMLETS
SOUTHWARK
H.M.S. BELFAST
TOWER BRIDGE
TOWER BRIDGE APP
ST. KATHARINE'S PIER
ST. KATHARINE DOCKS
Ivory Ho
Tobacco Dock
Under development
PENNINGTON STREET
WAPPING
WAPPING LANE
WAPPING HIGH STREET
Wapping Dock Stairs
Wapping Old Stairs
Wapping New Stairs
St. Peter
Hermitage Prim Sch
John Orwell (Wapping) Sports Cen
Alderman Stairs
MORE LONDON RIVERSIDE
CITY HALL (Greater London Authority)
POTTERS FIELDS PARK
BUTLERS WHARF
George's Stairs
DESIGN MUSEUM
TOWER BRIDGE EXHIBITION
UPPER POOL
THE POOL
LOWER POOL
Mill Stairs
East Lane Stairs
Cherry Garden Pier
King's Stairs
Princes Stairs
KING'S STAIRS GARDENS
St. Mary with All Saints
Mayflower PH
A200
SHAD THAMES
QUEEN ELIZABETH STREET
TOOLEY STREET
JAMAICA ROAD
BERMONDSEY
SE1
SE16
DRUID STREET
TANNER ST
DICKENS ESTATE
Most Holy Trinity (RC)
St. Joseph's RC Prim Sch
St. Michael's RC Sch
Riverside Prim Sch
ST. SAVIOUR'S EST
B202
NECKINGER EST
AYLWYN EST
BERMONDSEY
Town Hall
SPA ROAD
GRANGE ROAD
A2206
RICH IND EST
BERMONDSEY SPA
VAUBAN ESTATE
EVELINE LOWE EST
Cherry Gdn Sch
Alma Prim Sch
Harris Academy Bermondsey
SOUTHWARK PARK ROAD
St. James
KIRBY ESTATE
St. Crispin
SOUTHWARK COLL
SOUTHWARK PARK
Seven Islands Leisure Cen
Southwark Pk Prim Sch
MAYDEW HOUSE
RAYMOUTH RD
LONGFIELD ESTATE
St. Anne & St. Augustine
MANOR ESTATE
RENNIE ESTATE
ADMIRAL HYSON TRADING EST
LYNTON EST
PATERSON PARK
City of London Academy
B204
ROLLS ROAD
DUNTON ROAD
B203
OLD KENT ROAD
A2
Superstores
LORRY PARK
Royal Mail
Walworth Academy
St. Philip & St. Mark
MAWBEY ESTATE
SIX BRIDGES TRADING EST
CATLIN STREET
A2208
NEW ROTHERHITHE ROAD
ILDERTON ROAD
St. Gertrude (RC)
0
250 yds
0
250 m

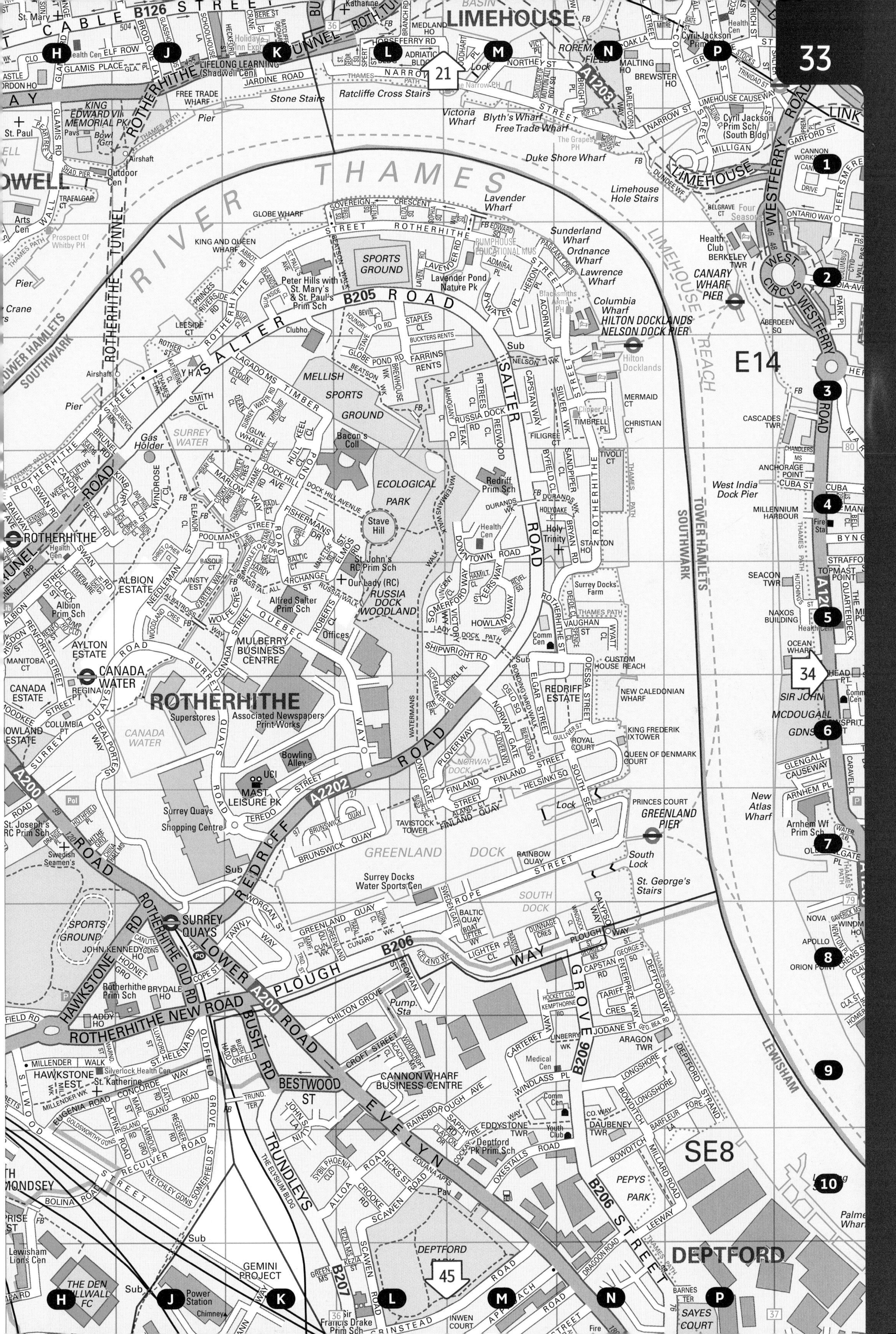
LIMEHOUSE
ROTHERHITHE
DEPTFORD
RIVER THAMES
LIMEHOUSE REACH
E14
SE8
ROTHERHITHE TUNNEL
SALTER ROAD
B205
REDRIFF ROAD
A2202
LOWER ROAD
A200
EVELYN STREET
PLOUGH WAY
B206
GROVE STREET
ROTHERHITHE NEW ROAD
ROTHERHITHE OLD RD
HAWKSTONE RD
BUSH RD
BESTWOOD ST
TRUNDLEYS RD
WESTFERRY ROAD
WESTFERRY CIRCUS
NARROW ST
LIMEHOUSE CAUSEWAY
CABLE STREET
B126
GLAMIS PLACE
JARDINE ROAD
A1203
SPORTS GROUND
MELLISH SPORTS GROUND
ECOLOGICAL PARK
Stave Hill
RUSSIA DOCK WOODLAND
SURREY WATER
CANADA WATER
GREENLAND DOCK
SOUTH DOCK
NORWAY DOCK
Surrey Quays Shopping Centre
Associated Newspapers Print Works
MAST LEISURE PK
Bowling Alley
Surrey Docks Water Sports Cen
Surrey Docks Farm
CANADA WATER
SURREY QUAYS
ROTHERHITHE
HILTON DOCKLANDS NELSON DOCK PIER
CANARY WHARF PIER
GREENLAND PIER
Limehouse Hole Stairs
Lavender Pond Nature Pk
Peter Hills with St. Mary's & St. Paul's Prim Sch
Alfred Salter Prim Sch
Redriff Prim Sch
Albion Prim Sch
Rotherhithe Prim Sch
Deptford Pk Prim Sch
Cyril Jackson Prim Sch
Arnhem Wf Prim Sch
KING EDWARD VII MEMORIAL PK
ALBION ESTATE
AYLTON ESTATE
CANADA ESTATE
MULBERRY BUSINESS CENTRE
CANNON WHARF BUSINESS CENTRE
REDRIFF ESTATE
HAWKSTONE EST.
PEPYS PARK
DEPTFORD PARK
SIR JOHN MCDOUGALL GDNS
West India Dock Pier
New Atlas Wharf
TOWER HAMLETS
SOUTHWARK
LEWISHAM
THE DEN MILLWALL FC
H J K L M N P
1 2 3 4 5 6 7 8 9 10
21
34
45

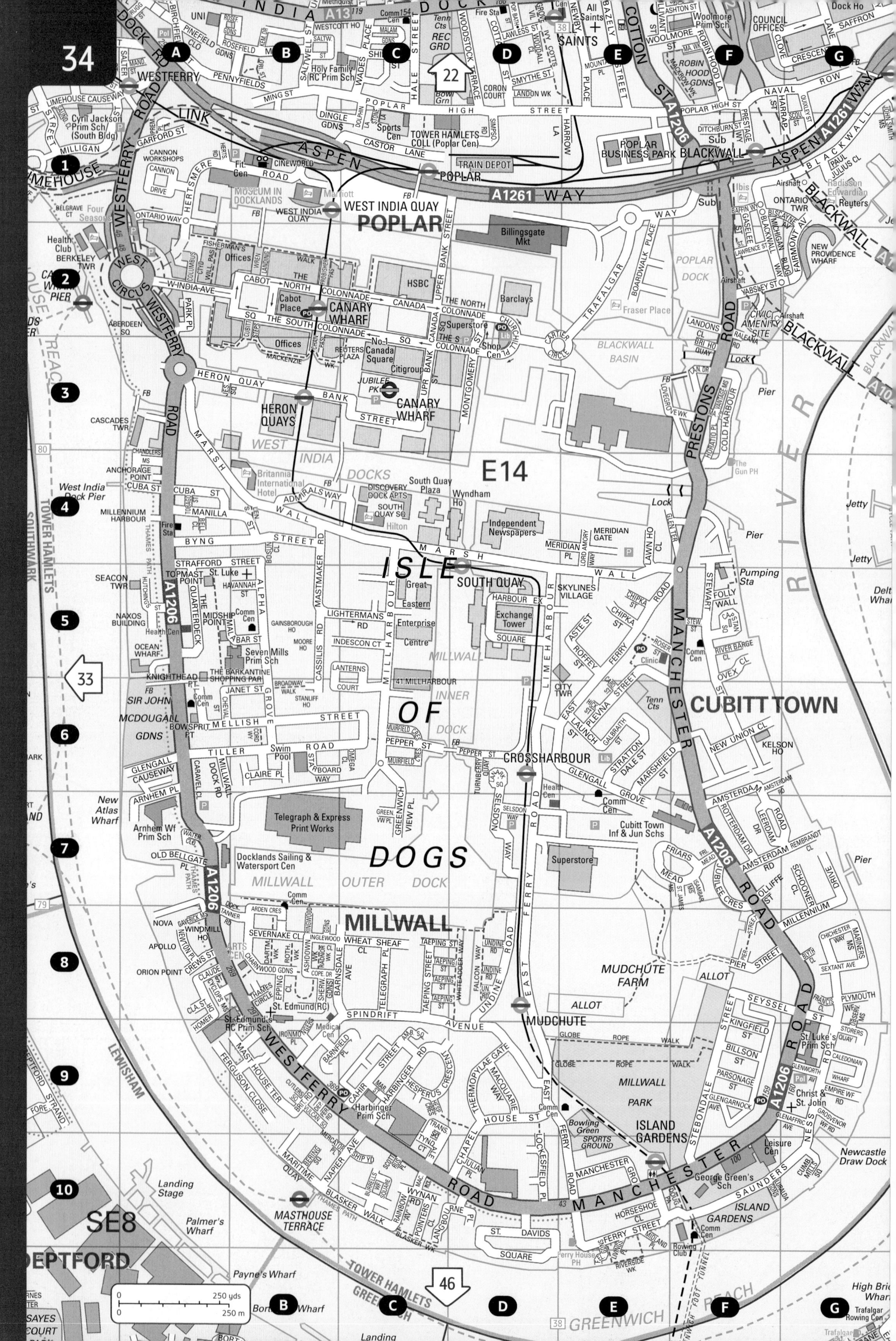
22
33
46
A
B
C
D
E
F
G
1
2
3
4
5
6
7
8
9
10
POPLAR
ISLE OF DOGS
CUBITT TOWN
MILLWALL
E14
SE8
DEPTFORD
LIMEHOUSE
WESTFERRY
WEST INDIA QUAY
POPLAR
CANARY WHARF
HERON QUAYS
SOUTH QUAY
CROSSHARBOUR
MUDCHUTE
ISLAND GARDENS
BLACKWALL
WEST INDIA DOCK RD
A13
A1261
A1206
ASPEN WAY
POPLAR HIGH STREET
WESTFERRY ROAD
MANCHESTER ROAD
PRESTONS ROAD
EAST FERRY ROAD
MARSH WALL
LIMEHARBOUR
HERON QUAY
WEST INDIA AVE
NORTH COLONNADE
SOUTH COLONNADE
CANADA SQ
UPPER BANK STREET
BANK STREET
TRAFALGAR WAY
COTTON ST
SAUNDERS NESS ROAD
SPINDRIFT AVENUE
WEST INDIA DOCKS
MILLWALL INNER DOCK
MILLWALL OUTER DOCK
POPLAR DOCK
BLACKWALL BASIN
Billingsgate Mkt
Museum in Docklands
Cineworld
Marriott
HSBC
Barclays
Citigroup
Cabot Place
No.1 Canada Square
Reuters Plaza
Jubilee Pk
Britannia International Hotel
Hilton
South Quay Plaza
Wyndham Ho
Independent Newspapers
Meridian Gate
Great Eastern Enterprise Centre
41 Millharbour
Exchange Tower
Skylines Village
Telegraph & Express Print Works
Docklands Sailing & Watersport Cen
Mudchute Farm
Millwall Park
Tower Hamlets Coll (Poplar Cen)
Train Depot
Poplar Business Park
Fraser Place
Civic Amenity Site
Sir John McDougall Gdns
Arnhem Wf Prim Sch
Cubitt Town Inf & Jun Schs
George Green's Sch
Harbinger Prim Sch
St. Edmund's RC Prim Sch
Seven Mills Prim Sch
Holy Family RC Prim Sch
Cyril Jackson Prim Sch (South Bldg)
Woolmore Prim Sch
St. Luke's Prim Sch
Masthouse Terrace
Landing Stage
Palmer's Wharf
Payne's Wharf
West India Dock Pier
New Atlas Wharf
Newcastle Draw Dock
Greenwich Foot Tunnel
RIVER THAMES
TOWER HAMLETS
SOUTHWARK
LEWISHAM
GREENWICH
0
250 yds
250 m

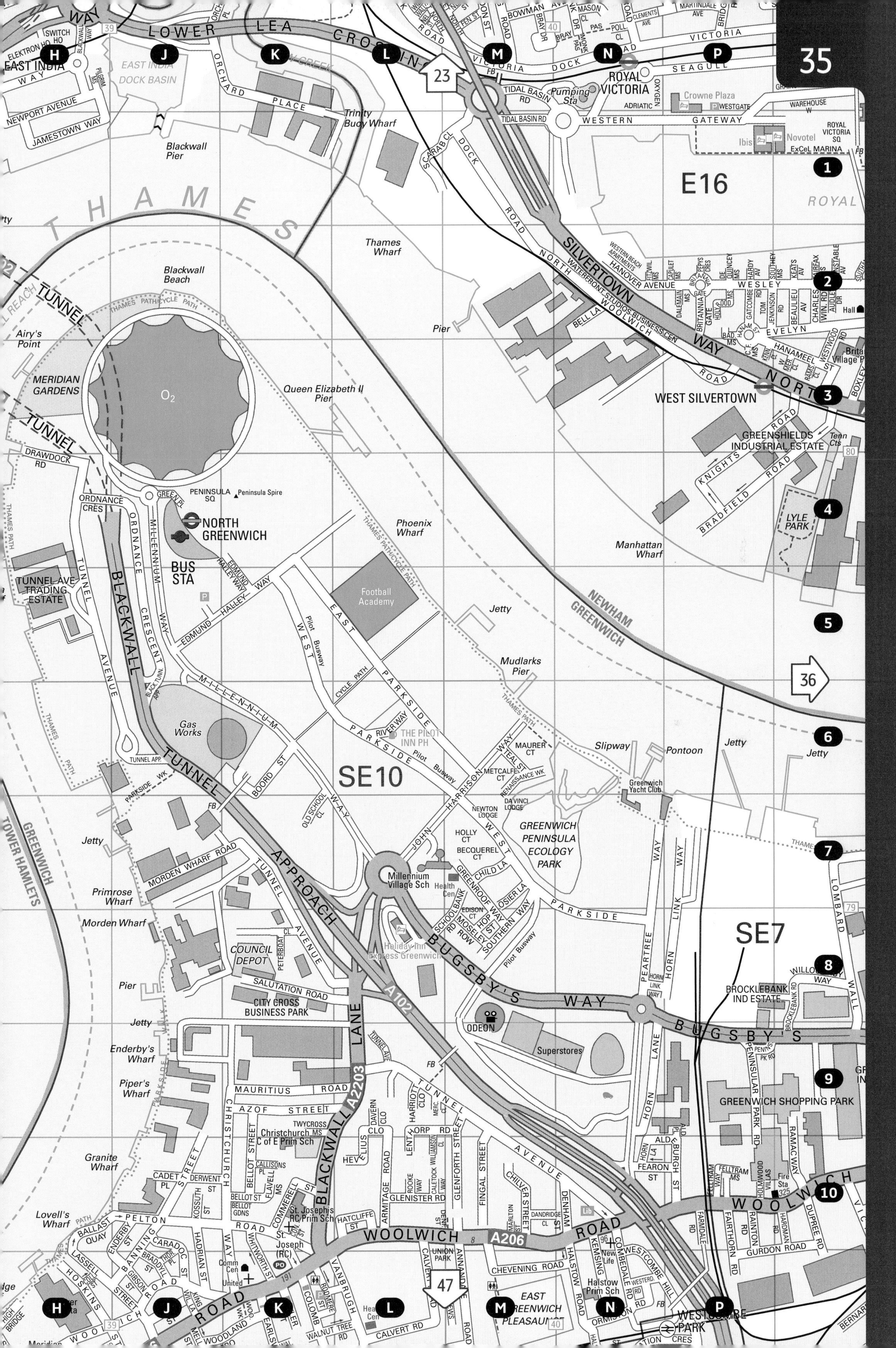

THAMES
E16
SE10
SE7
WEST SILVERTOWN
NORTH GREENWICH
O2
ROYAL VICTORIA
GREENWICH PENINSULA ECOLOGY PARK
GREENWICH SHOPPING PARK
BROCKLEBANK IND ESTATE
GREENSHIELDS INDUSTRIAL ESTATE
TUNNEL AVE TRADING ESTATE
CITY CROSS BUSINESS PARK
MERIDIAN GARDENS
LYLE PARK
EAST INDIA DOCK BASIN
Blackwall Pier
Blackwall Beach
Airy's Point
Thames Wharf
Queen Elizabeth II Pier
Phoenix Wharf
Manhattan Wharf
Mudlarks Pier
Football Academy
Gas Works
Millennium Village Sch
Holiday Inn Express Greenwich
ODEON
Superstores
COUNCIL DEPOT
Primrose Wharf
Morden Wharf
Enderby's Wharf
Piper's Wharf
Granite Wharf
Lovell's Wharf
Greenwich Yacht Club
NEWHAM
GREENWICH
TOWER HAMLETS
SILVERTOWN WAY
BLACKWALL TUNNEL APPROACH
BUGSBY'S WAY
WOOLWICH ROAD
LOWER LEA CROSSING
A102
A206
A2203
23
36
47

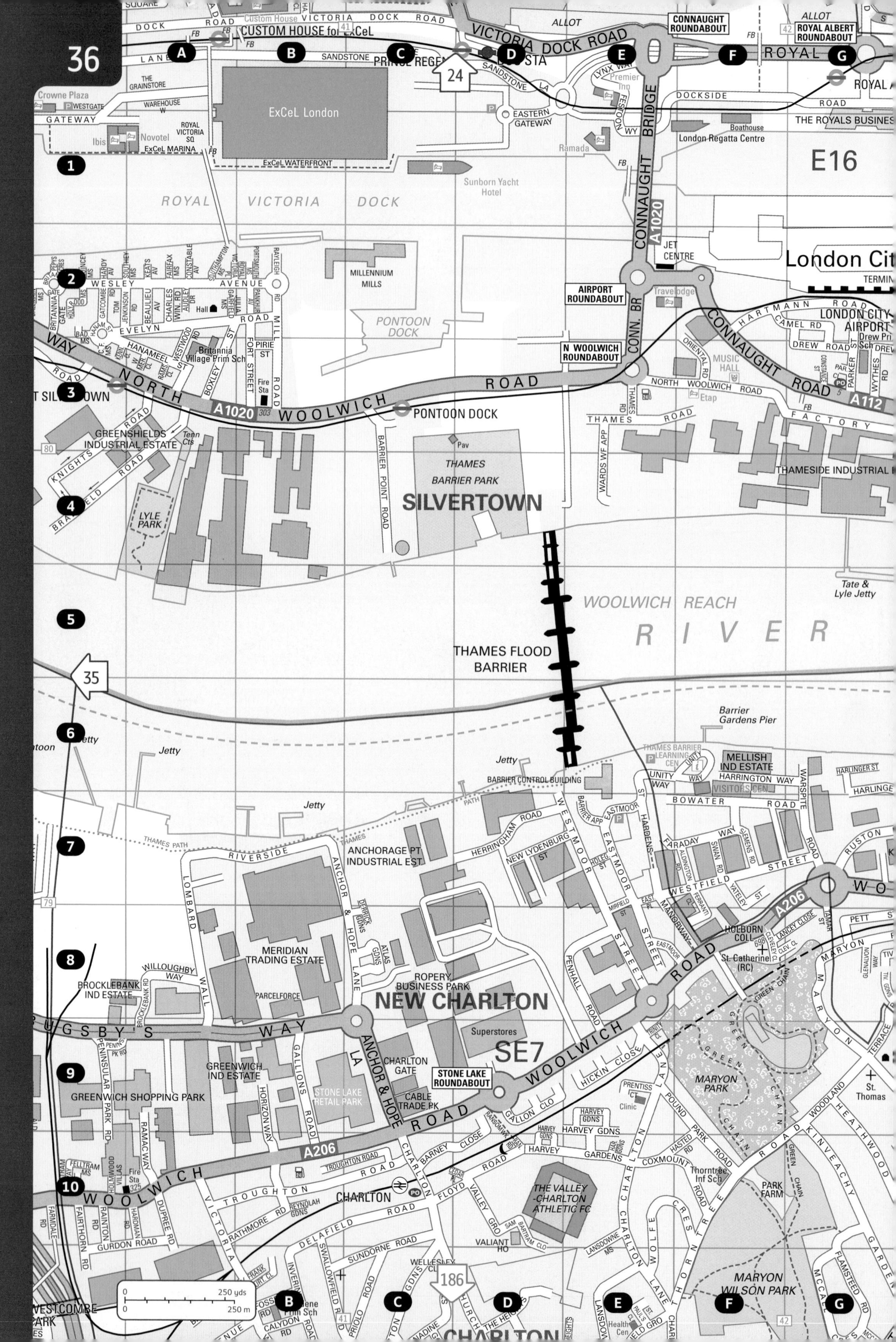
CUSTOM HOUSE for ExCeL
VICTORIA DOCK ROAD
CONNAUGHT ROUNDABOUT
ROYAL ALBERT ROUNDABOUT
24
ExCeL London
ExCeL MARINA
ExCeL WATERFRONT
Crowne Plaza
Ibis
Novotel
Sunborn Yacht Hotel
ROYAL VICTORIA DOCK
E16
London Regatta Centre
THE ROYALS BUSINESS
CONNAUGHT BRIDGE
A1020
JET CENTRE
London City
AIRPORT ROUNDABOUT
N WOOLWICH ROUNDABOUT
MILLENNIUM MILLS
PONTOON DOCK
LONDON CITY AIRPORT
CONNAUGHT ROAD
A112
NORTH WOOLWICH ROAD
WESLEY AVENUE
Britannia Village Prim Sch
GREENSHIELDS INDUSTRIAL ESTATE
THAMES BARRIER PARK
SILVERTOWN
THAMESIDE INDUSTRIAL
LYLE PARK
WOOLWICH REACH
RIVER
Tate & Lyle Jetty
THAMES FLOOD BARRIER
35
Barrier Gardens Pier
THAMES BARRIER LEARNING CEN
MELLISH IND ESTATE
BARRIER CONTROL BUILDING
ANCHORAGE PT INDUSTRIAL EST.
MERIDIAN TRADING ESTATE
BROCKLEBANK IND ESTATE
ROPERY BUSINESS PARK
NEW CHARLTON
Superstores
SE7
STONE LAKE ROUNDABOUT
GREENWICH IND ESTATE
GREENWICH SHOPPING PARK
STONE LAKE RETAIL PARK
CABLE TRADE PK
A206
WOOLWICH ROAD
MARYON PARK
THE VALLEY -CHARLTON ATHLETIC FC
CHARLTON
Thorntree Inf Sch
PARK FARM
MARYON WILSON PARK
186
WESTCOMBE PARK
250 yds
250 m

GALLIONS REACH
BECKTON PARK ROUNDABOUT
BECKTON PARK
CYPRUS ROUNDABOUT
CYPRUS
GALLIONS ROUNDABOUT
A1020
25
UNI OF E LONDON (London Docklands Campus)
UNIVERSITY WAY
ROYAL ALBERT DOCK
ALBERT BASIN
KING GEORGE V DOCK
City Airport
HARTMANN ROAD
NEWLAND STREET
ALBERT ROAD
A112
FACTORY ROAD
NORTH WOOLWICH
STANDARD INDUSTRIAL ESTATE
BT London Teleport
Pump Sta
KING GEORGE V
WOOLWICH MANOR WAY
A117
ALBERT ROAD
ROYAL VICTORIA GDNS
Waldair Wharf
PIER ROAD
North Woolwich Pier
Woolwich Ferry Pier
THAMES
NEWHAM
GREENWICH
WOOLWICH FOOT TUNNEL
WOOLWICH FREE VEHICLE FERRY
SE28
187
WOOLWICH ARSENAL PIER
WOOLWICH
GREENWICH HERITAGE CEN
FIREPOWER
THAMES PATH
South Pontoon
NEW FERRY APP
WOOLWICH HIGH ST
MKT HILL
BERESFORD ST
A206
PLUMSTEAD ROAD
WOOLWICH CHURCH STREET
WOOLWICH DOCKYARD IND EST
WOOLWICH DOCKYARD
SE18
JOHN WILSON ST
A205
WELLINGTON STREET
B210
TOWN HALL
WOOLWICH NEW RD
WOOLWICH ARSENAL
GRAND DEPOT ROAD
A2065
ARTILLERY PLACE
ROYAL ARTILLERY BARRACKS
HILLREACH
BARRACK FIELD
187
Mulgrave Pond
St. Peter's RC Prim Sch
Foxfield Prim Sch
RAGLAN ROAD
FREDERICK PLACE
BURRAGE PLACE
Nightingale Prim Sch
St. Margaret's C of E Prim Sch
H J K L M N P
1 2 3 4 5 6 7 8 9 10

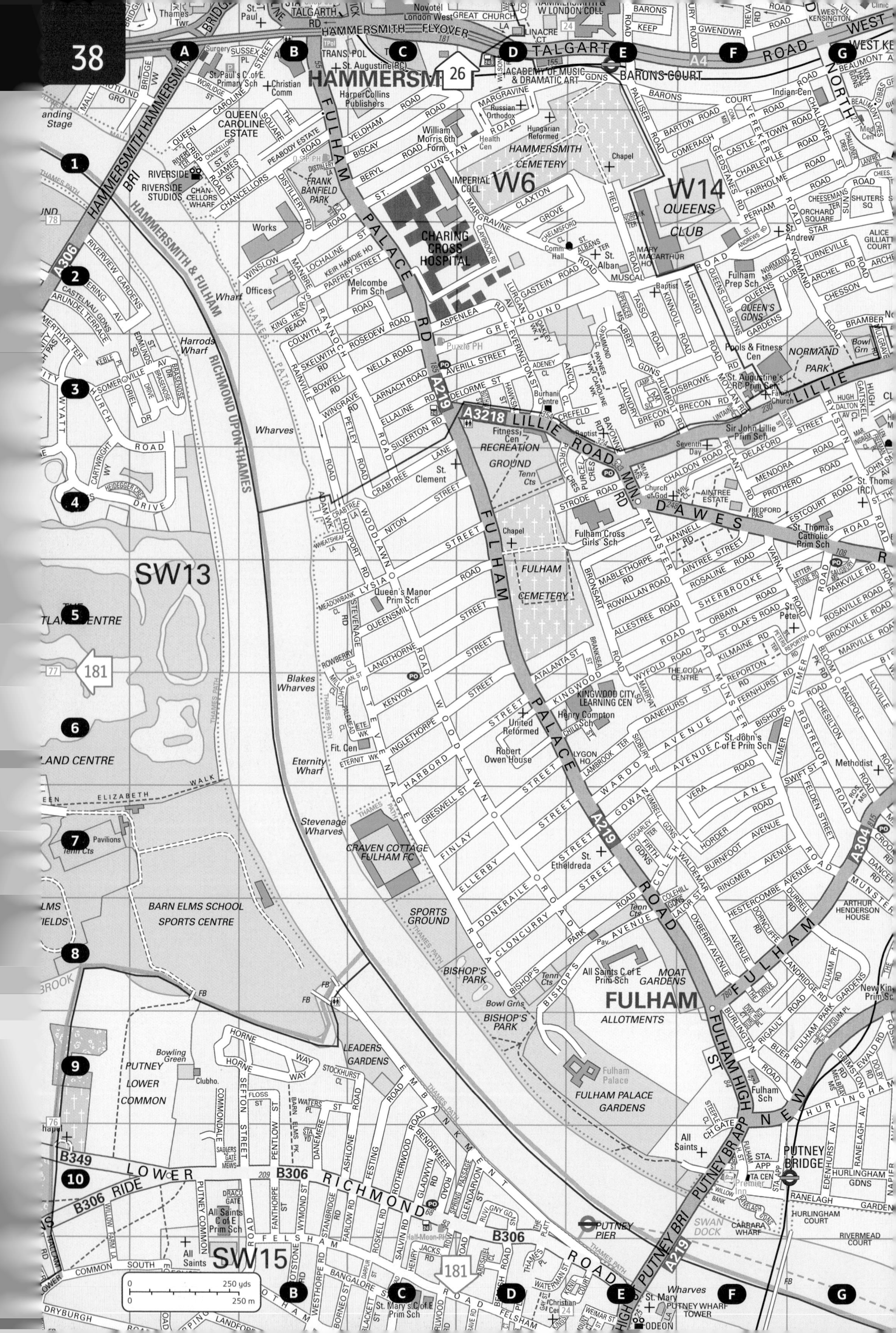
HAMMERSMITH FLYOVER
TALGARTH RD
26
HAMMERSMITH
BARONS COURT
A4 ROAD
WEST
Queen Caroline Estate
Riverside Studios
Frank Banfield Park
Charing Cross Hospital
W6
Hammersmith Cemetery
W14
Queens Club
Margravine
Fulham Palace Rd
A219
A3218 LILLIE ROAD
Recreation Ground
Fulham Cemetery
Hammersmith Bri
A306
Hammersmith & Fulham
Richmond upon Thames
Thames Path
SW13
181
Harrods Wharf
Wharves
Blakes Wharves
Eternity Wharf
Stevenage Wharves
Craven Cottage Fulham FC
Sports Ground
Bishop's Park
Queen's Manor Prim Sch
Fulham Cross Girls' Sch
Kingwood City Learning Cen
Henry Compton Sch
Robert Owen House
St. John's C of E Prim Sch
St. Thomas Catholic Prim Sch
Normand Park
Queen's Gdns
Dawes Rd
Munster Rd
Fulham
Moat Gardens
Allotments
Fulham Palace
Fulham Palace Gardens
All Saints C of E Prim Sch
Fulham High St
Putney Bri
Putney Bridge
Hurlingham Court
Putney Pier
Swan Dock
Carrara Wharf
Putney Wharf Tower
Barn Elms School Sports Centre
Putney Lower Common
Leaders Gardens
Lower Richmond Rd
B306
B349
SW15
Felsham Road
Embankment
Putney Common
A304
Fulham Rd
New Kings Rd
Hurlingham Gdns
Ranelagh Gardens
Rivermead Court
Arthur Henderson House
0 250 yds 250 m

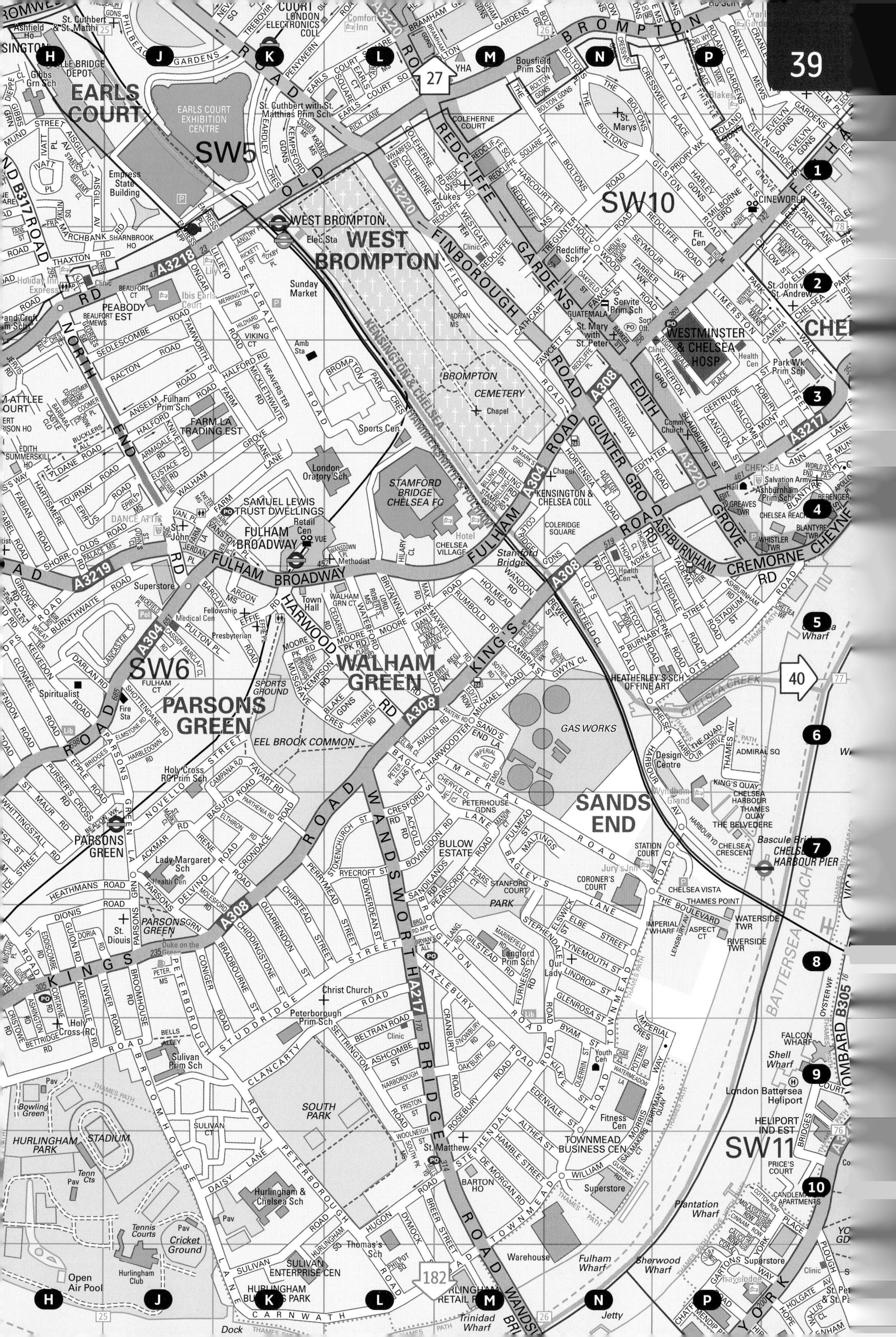
EARLS COURT
EARLS COURT EXHIBITION CENTRE
SW5
Empress State Building
WEST BROMPTON
BROMPTON CEMETERY
Chapel
SW10
STAMFORD BRIDGE CHELSEA FC
CHELSEA VILLAGE
FULHAM BROADWAY
KENSINGTON & CHELSEA COLL
COLERIDGE SQUARE
WESTMINSTER & CHELSEA HOSP
CHELSEA
SW6
PARSONS GREEN
WALHAM GREEN
EEL BROOK COMMON
GAS WORKS
SANDS END
CHELSEA HARBOUR
CHELSEA HARBOUR PIER
HEATHERLEY'S SCH OF FINE ART
BATTERSEA REACH
London Battersea Heliport
SW11
SOUTH PARK
HURLINGHAM PARK
STADIUM
Hurlingham Club
Cricket Ground
Open Air Pool
Fulham Wharf
Sherwood Wharf
Plantation Wharf
Shell Wharf
FALCON WHARF
Chelsea Wharf
Trinidad Wharf
TOWNMEAD BUSINESS CEN
HURLINGHAM BUSINESS PARK
SULIVAN ENTERPRISE CEN
OLD BROMPTON ROAD
FULHAM ROAD
KING'S ROAD
NORTH END ROAD
NEW KING'S ROAD
WANDSWORTH BRIDGE ROAD
FINBOROUGH ROAD
REDCLIFFE GARDENS
EDITH GROVE
GUNTER GRO
CREMORNE RD
CHEYNE
LOTS ROAD
IMPERIAL ROAD
TOWNMEAD ROAD
HARWOOD RD
PARSONS GREEN LA
PETERBOROUGH ROAD
STUDDRIDGE STREET
CARNWATH
A3218
A3220
A304
A308
A3219
A3217
A217
B317
B305
27
40
182
H
J
K
L
M
N
P
1
2
3
4
5
6
7
8
9
10

A
B
C
D
E
F
G
1
2
3
4
5
6
7
8
9
10
28
39
182
THE ROYAL MARSDEN
ROYAL BROMPTON HOSP
St. Luke
SW3
SW10
SW11
SW6
CHELSEA
FULHAM ROAD
KING'S ROAD
CHEYNE WALK
CHELSEA EMBANKMENT
WESTMINSTER & CHELSEA HOSP
CINEWORLD
BURTON'S COURT
ROYAL HOSPITAL CHELSEA
NATIONAL ARMY MUSEUM
MUSEUM
CHELSEA PHYSIC GARDEN
CADOGAN PIER
KENSINGTON & CHELSEA
WANDSWORTH
ALBERT BRIDGE
BATTERSEA BRIDGE
BATTERSEA PARK
CHILDREN'S ZOO
Peace Pagoda
Fountain Lake
Bandstand
REC GRDS
CARRIAGE DRIVE NORTH
PRINCE OF WALES DR
ALBERT BRIDGE ROAD
BATTERSEA PARK ROAD
BATTERSEA BRIDGE ROAD
WESTBRIDGE ROAD
LOMBARD ROAD
FALCON ROAD
LATCHMERE ROAD
FALCON PARK
ROYAL COLL OF ART
Chelsea Wharf
CHELSEA HARBOUR PIER
Bascule Bridge
London Battersea Heliport
Plantation Wharf
Shell Wharf
Christchurch
Superstores
Superstore
Church of the Ascension
250 yds
250 m

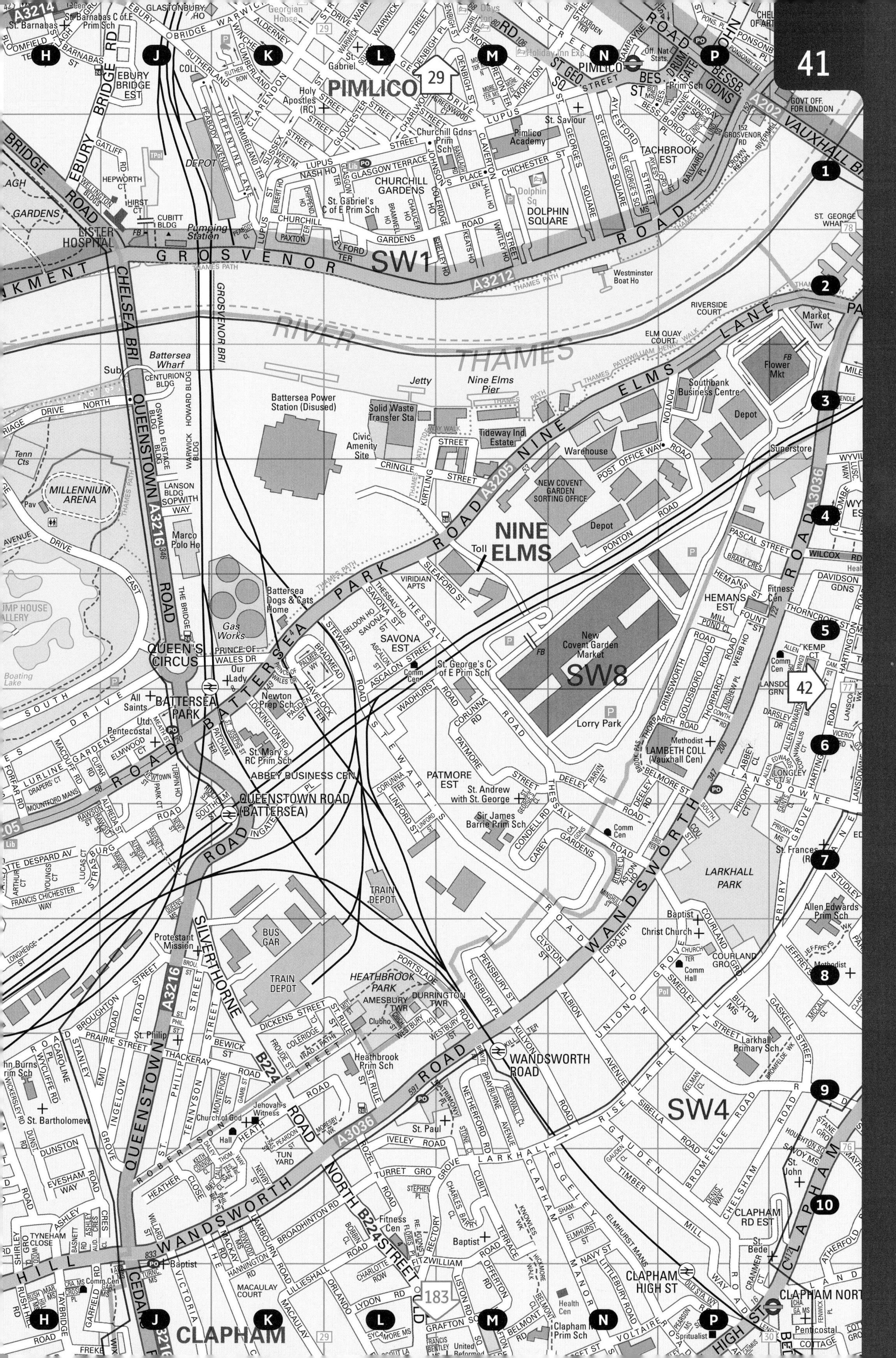
PIMLICO
29
SW1
GROSVENOR ROAD
A3212
RIVER THAMES
NINE ELMS LANE
NINE ELMS
SW8
New Covent Garden Market
Lorry Park
NEW COVENT GARDEN SORTING OFFICE
Battersea Power Station (Disused)
Nine Elms Pier
Jetty
Market Twr
Flower Mkt
Southbank Business Centre
Depot
Warehouse
Superstore
Tideway Ind Estate
Solid Waste Transfer Sta
Civic Amenity Site
BATTERSEA PARK ROAD
A3205
QUEENSTOWN ROAD
A3216
CHELSEA BRI
GROSVENOR BRI
Battersea Wharf
MILLENNIUM ARENA
Gas Works
Battersea Dogs & Cats Home
QUEEN'S CIRCUS
BATTERSEA PARK
QUEENSTOWN ROAD (BATTERSEA)
ABBEY BUSINESS CEN.
PATMORE EST
SAVONA EST
St. Andrew with St. George
Sir James Barrie Prim Sch
LAMBETH COLL (Vauxhall Cen)
HEMANS EST
42
LARKHALL PARK
WANDSWORTH ROAD
A3036
TRAIN DEPOT
BUS GAR
HEATHBROOK PARK
Heathbrook Prim Sch
WANDSWORTH ROAD
SW4
CLAPHAM RD EST
CLAPHAM HIGH ST
CLAPHAM NORTH
CLAPHAM
183
DOLPHIN SQUARE
CHURCHILL GARDENS
Pimlico Academy
TACHBROOK EST
EBURY BRIDGE EST
LISTER HOSPITAL
Westminster Boat Ho
VAUXHALL BRIDGE ROAD
A202
GOVT OFF. FOR LONDON
H
J
K
L
M
N
P
1
2
3
4
5
6
7
8
9
10

A
B
C
D
E
F
G
1
2
3
4
5
6
7
8
9
10
30
41
183
RIVERSIDE GARDENS
GOVT OFF. FOR LONDON
PENINSULA HEIGHTS
Eighty9 Albert Embankment
DRAW DOCK
SECRET INTELLIGENCE SERVICE
VAUXHALL
SPRING GDNS
VAUXHALL GDNS EST
VAUXHALL BRI
BRIDGEFOOT
ALBERT
SW1
SE11
KENNINGTON LANE
KENNINGTON
KENNINGTON PARK
KENNINGTON OVAL
THE OVAL SURREY C.C.C.
GAS WORKS
GASWORKS GALLERY
VAUXHALL PARK
SW8
SW9
SW4
SOUTH LAMBETH
SOUTH LAMBETH ROAD
WANDSWORTH RD
BUS STATION
PARRY ST
Flower Mkt
Southbank Business Centre
Depot
Superstore
WYVIL EST
HEMANS EST
LANSDOWNE GRN
LARKHALL PARK
STUDLEY ESTATE
STOCKWELL
STOCKWELL GARDENS EST
STOCKWELL PARK ESTATE
CLAPHAM RD EST
CLAPHAM ROAD
CLAPHAM NORTH
CLAPHAM HIGH ST
LAMBETH HOSPITAL
MURSELL ESTATE
CALDWELL GARDENS ESTATE
COWLEY ESTATE
ANGELL TOWN ESTATE
LOUGHBOROUGH ESTATE
MAX ROACH PARK
SLADE GDNS
MOSTYN GDNS
BRIXTON ROAD
CAMBERWELL NEW ROAD
HARLEYFORD ROAD
STOCKWELL ROAD
BRIXTON ACADEMY
BUS GAR
OVAL
SPORTS GRD
WYCK GARDENS
250 yds
250 m

WALWORTH
SE17
CAMBERWELL
SE5
SE15
BURGESS PARK
SURREY SQUARE PARK
SURREY GDNS
FARADAY GARDENS
AYLESBURY EST
ELIZABETH EST
WYNDHAM ESTATE
ELMINGTON ESTATE
DOWLAS ESTATE
BURGESS BUSINESS PARK
GREEK CATHEDRAL
CAMBERWELL GREEN
CAMBERWELL CHURCH ST
PECKHAM
DENMARK HILL
CAMBERWELL ROAD
ALBANY ROAD
WELLS WAY
SOUTHAMPTON WAY
CAMBERWELL GROVE
DOG KENNEL HILL
CHAMPION PK
COLDHARBOUR LANE
KING'S COLLEGE HOSPITAL
MAUDSLEY HOSPITAL
WILLIAM BOOTH COLL
RUSKIN PARK
LUCAS GDNS
SCEAUX GDNS
SPORTS GRD
CAMBERWELL COLL OF ARTS
S LONDON GALL
TOWN HALL
VALMAR TRADING ESTATE
CRAWFORD ESTATE
CHAMPION PARK EST
DOG KENNEL HILL EST
CHAMPION HILL ESTATE
LOUGHBOROUGH JUNCTION
PELICAN ESTATE
Kart Track
Tennis Cen
Bowl Grn
Football Pitch
ALLOT
PITCHES
Bandstand
A215
A202
A2216
A2217
B214
31
44
184

SE5
SE1
SE15
SE16
PECKHAM
PATERSON PARK
ROLLS ROAD
ABERCORN WAY
STEVENSON CRESCENT
CATLIN STREET
ROTHERHITHE NEW ROAD
ILDERTON ROAD
VERNEY ROAD
MAWBEY ESTATE
SIX BRIDGES TRADING EST
Eveline Lowe Prim Sch
St. Philip & St. Mark
Walworth Academy
Cobourg Prim Sch
LONCROFT ROAD
SPORTS GRD
NEATE STREET
SURREY LINEAR CANAL PARK
TRAFALGAR AV B215
OSSORY ROAD
GLENGALL ROAD
Superstores
Cantium Retail Park
Mountain of Fire
OLD KENT ROAD A2
KENT PARK IND EST
Gas Works
Christ Church
LEYTON SQ PK
PECKHAM PARK ROAD B216
FRIARY ESTATE
FRANCISCAN FRIARY
LEDBURY EST
Haymerle Sch
Church of Christ
LINDLEY ESTATE
WILLOWBROOK RD
PECKHAM HILL B215 STREET
COMMERCIAL WAY
BELLS GARDEN EST
Gloucester Prim Sch
DANIEL GDNS
St. Luke
Oliver Goldsmith Prim Sch
CAMBERWELL COLL OF ARTS
S LONDON GALL
OLIVER-GOLDSMITH ESTATE
TUSTIN ESTATE
Pilgrims' Way Prim Sch
BRIMMINGTON PARK
St. John with St. Andrew
QUEENS ROAD PECKHAM
PECKHAM HIGH STREET
QUEENS ROAD
A202
PELICAN ESTATE
The Academy at Peckham
Aylesham Centre
HANOVER PK
CLIFTON ESTATE
Tuke Sch
John Donne Prim Sch
COSSALL PARK
St. Thomas the Apostle Coll
Highshore Sch
Rye Lane Mkt
PREMIER
PECKHAM RYE
SPORTS GROUND
WARWICK GDNS
All Saints
St. James (RC)
RYE LANE
A2215
St. Mary Magdalene Prim Sch
Church of God
SOUTHWARK ADULT ED (Thomas Calton Cen)
Bellenden Prim Sch
Gospel Hall
Faith Chapel
Revival Church
St. Saviour
Salvation Army
EVELINA ROAD
NUNHEAD LANE A2214
Rye Oak Prim Sch
DOG KENNEL HILL EST
Dog Kennel Hill Prim Sch
250 yds
250 m
32
43
184

DEPTFORD
SE8
SE14
NEW CROSS GATE
NEW CROSS
SE4
NUNHEAD
NUNHEAD CEMETERY
DEPTFORD PARK
FOLKESTONE GARDENS
FORDHAM PARK
TELEGRAPH HILL PARK
NEW CROSS GATE CUTTING NATURE RESERVE
BRIDGE HOUSE MEADOWS
SAYES COURT PARK
THE DEN MILLWALL FC
NEW CROSS ROAD
LEWISHAM WAY
BROCKLEY
33
46
185

A
B
C
D
E
F
G
1
2
3
4
5
6
7
8
9
10
34
45
185
DEPTFORD
SE8
E14
SE10
SE13
SE14
ST. JOHN'S
LEWISHAM
GREENWICH
Palmer's Wharf
Payne's Wharf
Borthwick Wharf
MASTHOUSE TERRACE
TOWER HAMLETS
GREENWICH REACH
Landing Stage
Sailing Centre
Wood Wharf
GREENWICH PIER
CUTTY SARK
CUTTY SARK GDNS
TRINITY COLL OF MUSIC
UNI OF GREENWICH (Maritime Greenwich Campus)
QUEEN'S HOUSE
NATIONAL MARITIME MUS
ISLAND GARDENS
George Green's
MANCHESTER ROAD
ST. DAVIDS SQUARE
FERRY STREET
HORSESHOE CL
SAYES COURT PARK
Charlotte Turner Prim Sch
Grinling Gibbons Prim Sch
Barnardo's Cen
Methodist
MCMILLAN STUDENT VILLAGE
CREEK ROAD
A200
ROMNEY ROAD
A206
Laban
St. Nicholas with St. Lukes
St. Alfege with St. Peters Prim Sch
St. Alfege
BARDSLEY LANE
ROYAL HILL
CROOMS HILL
Circus Gate
GREENWICH HIGH ROAD
GREENWICH SOUTH STREET
James Wolfe Prim Sch
GREENWICH CEN BUS. PK
BROOKMARSH IND EST
GREENWICH
FAIRCHARM TRADING EST
DEPTFORD
St. Paul
St. Joseph's Prim Sch
Our Lady (RC)
ALBANY EMPIRE
COMMUNITY ED LEWISHAM
Tidemill Prim Sch
DEPTFORD CHURCH STREET
DEPTFORD HIGH STREET
A2209
LEWISHAM COLL (Deptford Campus)
DEPTFORD BRIDGE
Addey & Stanhope Sch
DEPTFORD BDY
FLORENCE B218 RD
BLACKHEATH ROAD
BLACKHEATH HILL
SHOOTERS HILL
A2
BLACKHEATH BUS. EST
EGERTON DRIVE
B208
NORMAN ROAD
GREENWICH SCH OF MANAGEMENT
QUEEN ELIZAB. COLL
Richard I PH
St. Ursula's Convent Sch
B209
Superstores
Water Works
BROOKMILL ROAD
A2210
BROOKMILL PARK
RAVENSBOURNE RIVER
Lucas Vale Prim Sch
FRIENDLY GARDENS
St. Stephen's C of E Prim Sch
Ashmead Jun Sch
LEWISHAM WAY
Welsh Presbyterian
LEWISHAM COLL (Lewisham Way Campus)
Morden Mt Prim Sch
ELVERSON ROAD
LEWISHAM ROAD
A2211
RIVER QUAGGY
GREYLADIES GARDENS
Superstore
GRANVILLE PK ADULT LEARNING CEN
LOAMPIT HILL
A20
LOAMPIT VALE
THURSTON ROAD
THURSTON RD IND EST
Lewisham Br Prim Sch
BUS STA
St. Stephen with St. Mark
LEWISHAM HIGH ST
BELMONT
Clock Twr
RIVERDALE
KAREN COURT
250 yds
250 m

H
J
K
L
M
N
P
35
186
1
2
3
4
5
6
7
8
9
10
WOOLWICH ROAD
A206
TRAFALGAR ROAD
Power Sta
Lovell's Wharf
Granite Wharf
Meridian Prim Sch
Arches Leisure Cen
MAZE HILL
EAST GREENWICH PLEASAUNCE
WESTCOMBE PARK
SE7
A102
ONE TREE HILL
GREENWICH PARK
ROYAL OBSERVATORY GREENWICH (FLAMSTEED HOUSE)
Peter Harrison Planetarium
THE GARDENS
THE WILDERNESS (DEER PARK)
Croom's Hill Gate
Blackheath Gate
Bandstand
RANGER'S HOUSE
John Roan Sec Sch
Blackheath High Sch
Invicta Inf Sch
Kingdom Hall
VANBRUGH PARK
WESTCOMBE PARK ROAD
B210
CHARLTON WAY
SHOOTERS HILL ROAD
A2
BLACKHEATH
SE3
PRINCE OF WALES ROAD
B212
Blackheath Nursery & Prep Sch
The Pointer Sch
Bardon Lodge
KIDBROOKE GROVE
A2213
Morden College
Chapel
St. James
SPORTS GROUNDS
All Saints Cof E Prim Sch
All Saints
Clarendon Hotel
Blackheath High Sch (Jun Dept)
John Ball Sch
BLACKHEATH
BLACKHEATH VILLAGE
Quakers
Our Lady (RC)
St. Michael & All Angels
BLACKHEATH HALLS
Brooklands JMI Sch
BLACKHEATH HOSP
Mormons
LEE TERRACE
B220
LEE HILL
St. Matthew Academy
CEMETERY
Wingfield Prim Sch
KIDB

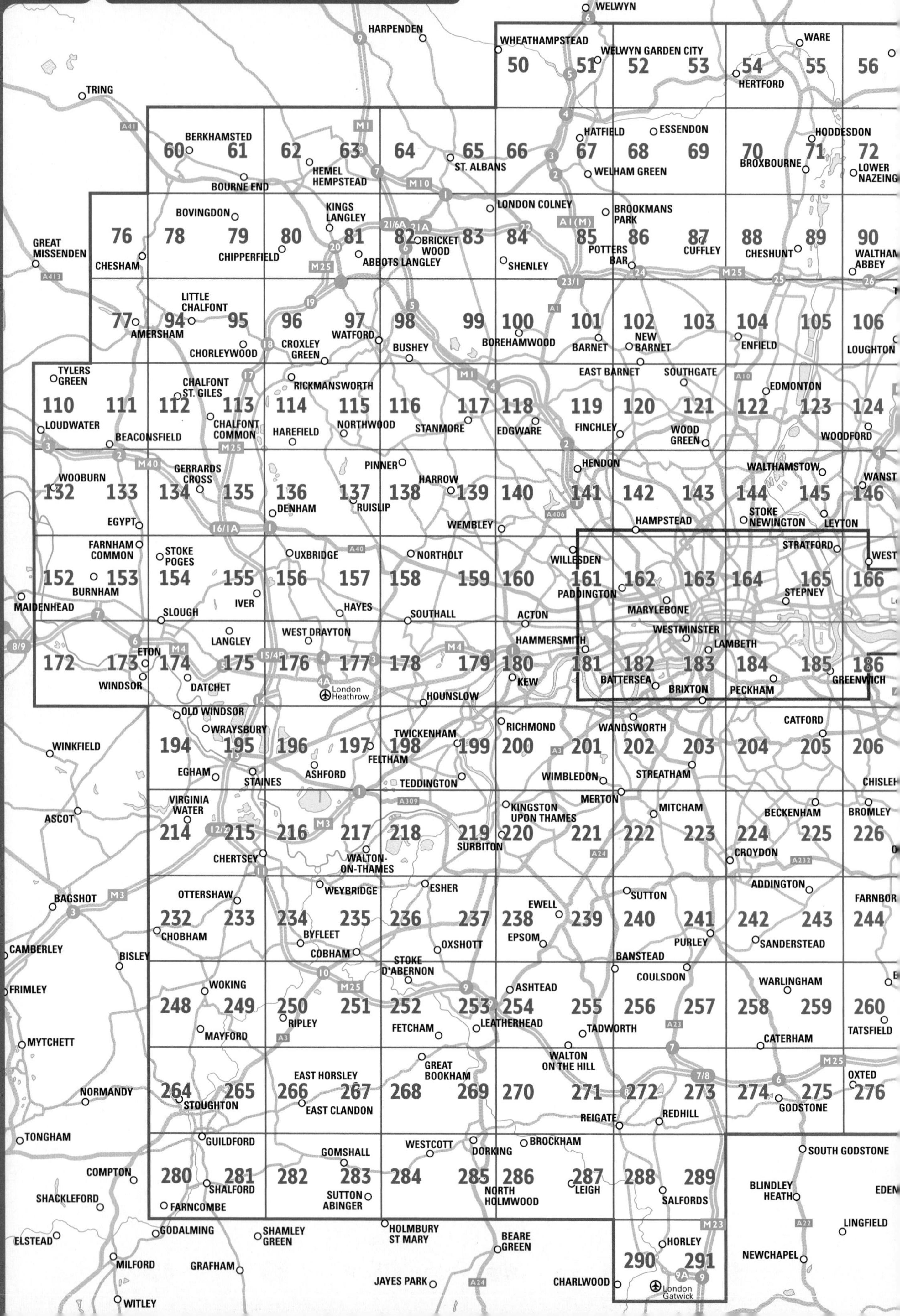

Key to London street maps

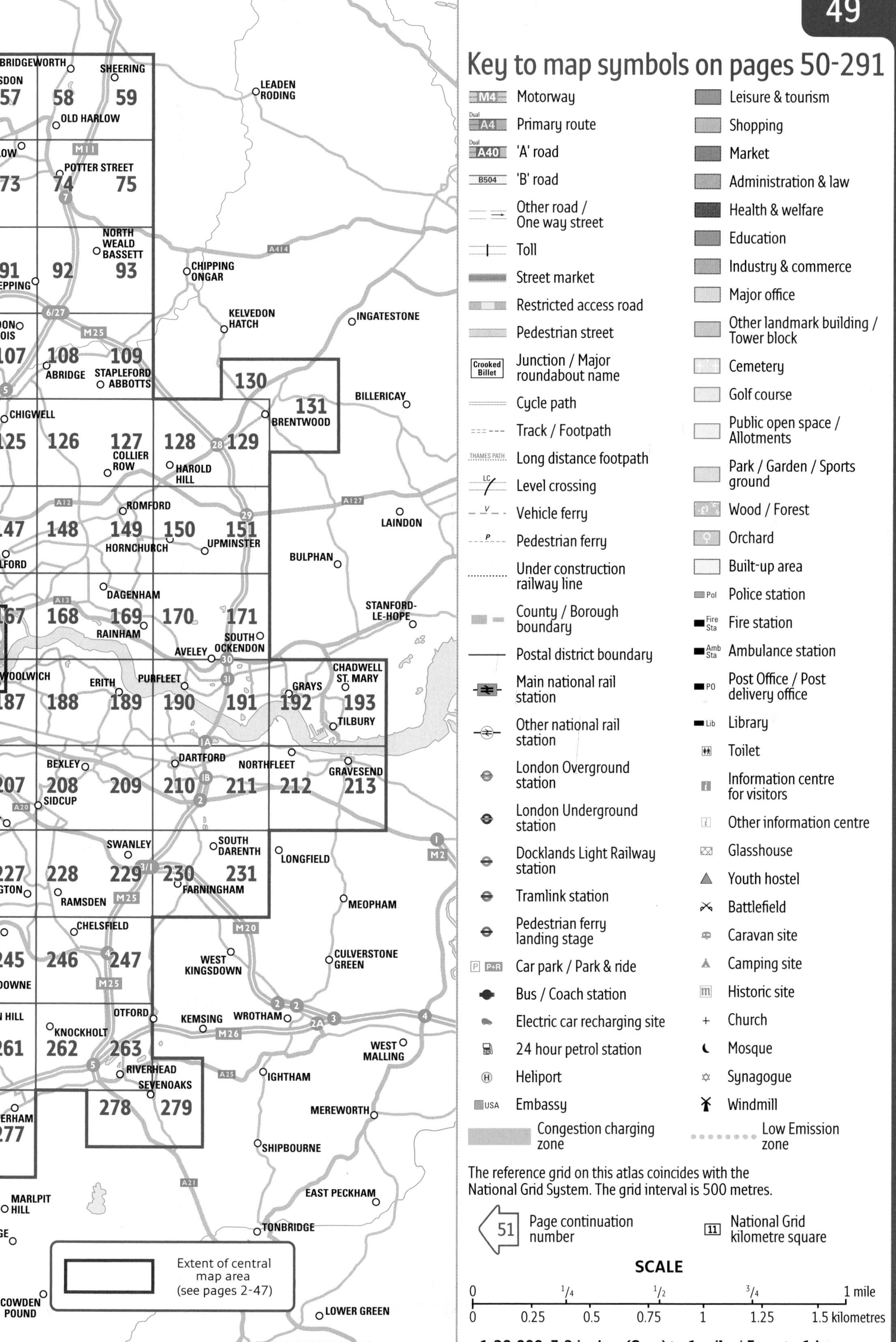
WBRIDGEWORTH
SHEERING
NSDON
57
58
59
OLD HARLOW
LEADEN RODING
RLOW
M11
POTTER STREET
73
74
75
NORTH WEALD BASSETT
91
92
93
EPPING
A414
CHIPPING ONGAR
YDON BOIS
6/27
M25
KELVEDON HATCH
INGATESTONE
107
108
109
ABRIDGE
STAPLEFORD ABBOTTS
130
131
BRENTWOOD
BILLERICAY
CHIGWELL
125
126
127
128
129
COLLIER ROW
HAROLD HILL
A12
ROMFORD
A127
LAINDON
147
148
149
150
151
HORNCHURCH
UPMINSTER
ILFORD
BULPHAN
DAGENHAM
A13
STANFORD-LE-HOPE
167
168
169
170
171
RAINHAM
SOUTH OCKENDON
AVELEY
WOOLWICH
ERITH
PURFLEET
GRAYS
CHADWELL ST. MARY
187
188
189
190
191
192
193
TILBURY
DARTFORD
NORTHFLEET
BEXLEY
GRAVESEND
207
208
209
210
211
212
213
SIDCUP
A20
SWANLEY
SOUTH DARENTH
LONGFIELD
M2
227
228
229
230
231
FARNINGHAM
RAMSDEN
M25
MEOPHAM
CHELSFIELD
M20
245
246
247
WEST KINGSDOWN
CULVERSTONE GREEN
DOWNE
M25
OTFORD
KEMSING
WROTHAM
KNOCKHOLT
M26
WEST MALLING
261
262
263
RIVERHEAD
A25
IGHTHAM
SEVENOAKS
278
279
STERHAM
277
MEREWORTH
SHIPBOURNE
A21
MARLPIT HILL
EAST PECKHAM
TONBRIDGE
Extent of central map area (see pages 2-47)
COWDEN POUND
LOWER GREEN
ROYAL TUNBRIDGE WELLS
Key to map symbols on pages 50-291
M4 Motorway
Dual A4 Primary route
Dual A40 'A' road
B504 'B' road
Other road / One way street
Toll
Street market
Restricted access road
Pedestrian street
Crooked Billet Junction / Major roundabout name
Cycle path
Track / Footpath
THAMES PATH Long distance footpath
LC Level crossing
V Vehicle ferry
P Pedestrian ferry
Under construction railway line
County / Borough boundary
Postal district boundary
Main national rail station
Other national rail station
London Overground station
London Underground station
Docklands Light Railway station
Tramlink station
Pedestrian ferry landing stage
P P+R Car park / Park & ride
Bus / Coach station
Electric car recharging site
24 hour petrol station
Heliport
USA Embassy
Congestion charging zone
Leisure & tourism
Shopping
Market
Administration & law
Health & welfare
Education
Industry & commerce
Major office
Other landmark building / Tower block
Cemetery
Golf course
Public open space / Allotments
Park / Garden / Sports ground
Wood / Forest
Orchard
Built-up area
Pol Police station
Fire Sta Fire station
Amb Sta Ambulance station
PO Post Office / Post delivery office
Lib Library
Toilet
Information centre for visitors
Other information centre
Glasshouse
Youth hostel
Battlefield
Caravan site
Camping site
Historic site
Church
Mosque
Synagogue
Windmill
Low Emission zone
The reference grid on this atlas coincides with the National Grid System. The grid interval is 500 metres.
51 Page continuation number
11 National Grid kilometre square
SCALE
0 1/4 1/2 3/4 1 mile
0 0.25 0.5 0.75 1 1.25 1.5 kilometres
1:20,000 3.2 inches (8cm) to 1 mile / 5 cm to 1 km

LAMERWOOD
COUNTRY CLUB
CODICOTE ROAD
SCRATCHING GROVE
DOWDELL'S WOOD
FISH WOOD
THREEGROVES WOOD
CHERRYTREE SPRING
CONEYDALE SPRING
WARREN WOOD
Ayot Place
AL6
BLADDER WOOD
AYOT GREENWAY
ROBINSON'S WOOD
BOWLE'S WOOD
WATEREND
Sparrowhall Farm
Wheathampstead
SPORTS GRD
ALLOT
Marford Farm
River Lee or Lea
GRAYS WOOD
COWPER'S SPRING
PARK MEAD SPRING
WATEREND LANE
CHARLIES CROFT
DAVID'S DINGLE
B653 MARFORD ROAD
WRIGHT WAY
Chalkdell Farm
Flint Bridge
BLUEBELL HILL WOOD
Devil's Dyke Earthworks
The Slad Earthworks
Samuels Farm
FLINT BRIDGE PLANTATION
Clubhouse
Brocket Hall
THE BROADWATER
Beech Hyde Farm
AL4
GREEN
LAMB'S GROVE
Warren Farm
The John Bunyan PH
PEARMAN'S SPRING
KENT'S DELL
SPRITE FIELD SPRING
Upper Cromer Hyde Farm
BROCKET PARK
Coleman Green
FLETCHER'S WICK
CROMER HYDE LANE
Crooked Chimney PH
Cromer Hyde
FURZEFIELD WOOD
Nomansland Farm
WELWYN HATFIELD
ST. ALBANS
BENSTEAD'S WOOD
WET GROVE
LONG GROVE SPRING
LONG GROVE PLANTATION
Cromerhyde Farm
TOWER HILL LANE
TITNOL'S WOOD
HAMMOND'S LANE
Hammond's Farm
Symondshyde Farm
DOGS HEART SPRING
CHALKDELL WOOD
SYMONDS HYDE
SYMONDSHYDE GREAT WOOD
SYMONDSHYDE PICNIC AREA
AL10
HAMMOND'S WOOD
HARLOWDELL SPRING
HILL WOOD
FURZE FIELD
COOPERS GREEN LANE
PET CEM
HOME OFFICE SCIENTIFIC DEVELOPMENT BRANCH
Fairfold's Farm
Sutton's Farm
WOODCOCK HILL
Astwick Manor
Astwick Manor Farm
Fielder Centre
MANOR ROAD
FROBISHER WAY
HATFIELD BUSINESS PARK
Offices
66
SAND AND GRAVEL PIT
HOOK'S
0 500 yds
0 500 m
CL CM CN CP CQ CR CS
05 06 07 08 09 10 11 12 13 14
19 20 21
11 12 13 14

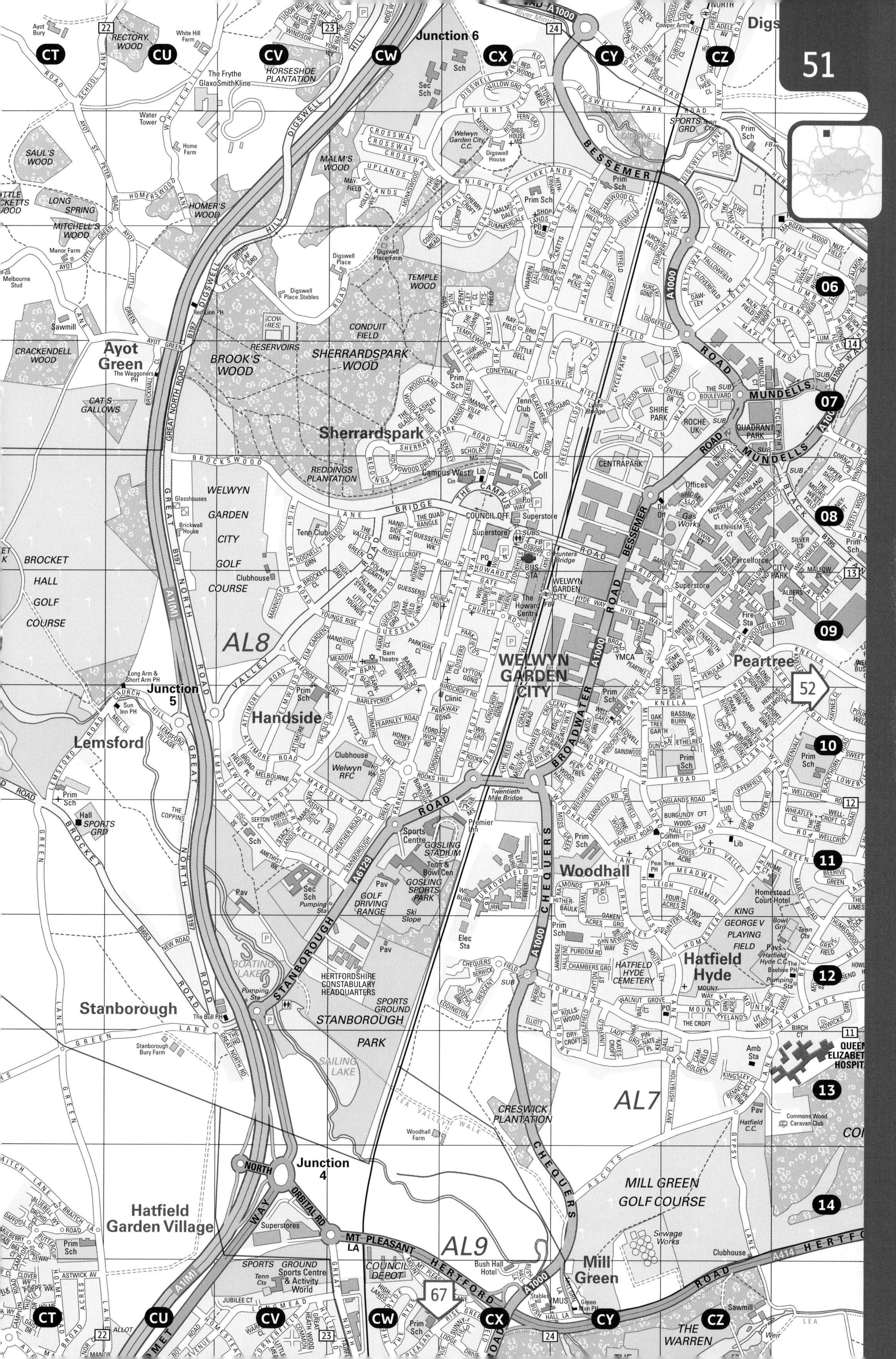

Junction 6
Ayot Green
Sherrardspark
SHERRARDSPARK WOOD
BROOK'S WOOD
WELWYN GARDEN CITY GOLF COURSE
BROCKET HALL GOLF COURSE
AL8
Handside
Lemsford
Junction 5
WELWYN GARDEN CITY
Peartree
Woodhall
Hatfield Hyde
Stanborough
STANBOROUGH PARK
AL7
Junction 4
Hatfield Garden Village
AL9
MILL GREEN GOLF COURSE
Mill Green
QUEEN ELIZABETH HOSPITAL
BESSEMER ROAD
BROADWATER ROAD
CHEQUERS
STANBOROUGH ROAD
GREAT NORTH ROAD
A1(M)
A1000
A6129
A414
HERTFORD ROAD
MOUNDELLS
52
67
CT
CU
CV
CW
CX
CY
CZ
06
07
08
09
10
11
12
13
14

Holdens
Tewin
AL6
Archers Green
PANSHANGER AERODROME
Panshanger
Peartree
AL7
Hall Grove
Cole Green
Hatfield
AL9
QUEEN ELIZABETH II HOSPITAL
THE COMMONS
MILL GREEN GOLF COURSE
PANSHANGER GOLF COURSE
MONEYHOLE LANE PARK
HENRY WOOD
BIRCHALL WOOD
HIGH GROVE
ROLLS WOOD
GREAT CAPTAIN'S WOOD
BROCKET HILL
DAWLEY WOOD
DAWLEY PLANTATION
BRAMFIELD PARK WOOD
HOME WOOD
WESTLEY WOOD
RECTORY WOOD
FLEXLEYS WOOD
LAMB DELL WOOD
RED WOOD
POPLARS GREEN
POPLAR GROVE
HERTFORD ROAD
A414 HERTFORD ROAD
HATFIELD ROAD
COLE GREEN WAY
PANSHANGER LANE
BIRCHALL LANE
HOLWELL LANE
MUNDELLS
BLACK FAN ROAD
EAST HERTS
WELWYN HATFIELD
River Mimram
River Lee or Lea
51
68
500 yds
500 m

DH
DJ
DK
DL
DM
DN
DP
29
30
31
Bramfield
Bramfield Place Farm
PRIEST WOOD
Waterford Hall
BARLEYCROFT GROVE
BULLSMILL LANE
HIGH ROAD
A119
NORTH ROAD
VICARAGE
BRAMFIELD LANE
SACOMBE LANE
Waterford
WATERFORD PLANTATION
WATERFORD COMMON
WATERFORD HEATH COMMUNITY NATURE PARK
WATERFORD MARSH
TIMBER ORCHARD
HOLLY GROVE ROAD
TATTLE HILL
BRAMFIELD
OAKFIELD PLANTATION
GOLDINGS
Goldings Hall
GREAT MOLE WOOD
06
07
08
09
10
11
12
13
14
Prim Sch
GREAT MOLEWOOD
HIGH MOLEWOOD
HOOK'S BUSHES
BARNSLEYS WOOD
CHATTERSFIELD PLANTATION
HANGING GROVE
Broadoak End
ICEHOUSE WOOD
Windyridge Farm
ELEVEN ACRE WOOD
River Beane
Goldings Canal
Bengeo
LITTLE MOLE WOOD
SELEBROOM WOOD
ARCHER'S SPRING
LONG WOOD
Comm Cen
Lafarge Redlands Aggregates
WELWYN ROAD
HERTFORD CEMETERY
ALLOT
EVERGREEN WOOD
GARDEN WOOD
BROADWATER
Weir
BLAKEMORE WOOD
SAND PIT
Golden Griffin PH
B1000
Sec Sch
HERTFORD NORTH
SG14
LADY HUGHES'S WOOD
CHESHER'S PLANTATION
HERTFORD COUNTY HOSP
54
HERTFORD
GASCOYNE
OSIER BEDS
CHELMSFORD WOOD
HERTINGFORDBURY ROAD
A414
BYPASS
CHISEL SHELF
GREEN
Mill Farm
Epcombs
THE COURTYARD
THE MILL
Hertingfordbury
White Horse Hotel
Hall
Prince of Wales PH
MAYFLOWER CL
Tenn Cts
Hertingfordbury C.C.
Sch
TERRACE WOOD
Terrace Wood Nursery
THE OLD COACH ROAD
COACH ROAD
War Memorial
Prim Sch
The Bury Farm
COLE GREEN WAY
LEA VALLEY WALK
Birch Green
Birch Grove Nursery
FOXDELLS
River Lee or Lea
Riverside Garden Centre
PONTERS GROVE
Letty Green Fruit Farm
Eastendgreen Farm
SOUTHFIELD WOOD
Bayfordbury Park Farm
Letty Green
Rochfords Nursery
Pipers End
East End Green
CHALK DELL
SG13
THE PINETUM
B158
GROTTO WOOD
Bayfordbury
Bayfordbury Mansion
Roxford
GRAVEL PIT
Uni of Herts-Field Station & Observatory
Glasshouse
Woolmers Park
GRAVEFIELD GROVE
Home Farm
SPRING WOOD
THE PIGHTLE
LARCH PLANTATION
HOOK'S GROVE
SAILOR'S GROVE
GRAVEL PIT
69
Water Hall Farm
BROADGREEN WOOD

DQ
DR
DS
DT
DU
DV
DW
33
34
35
05
06
07
08
09
10
11
12
13
14
53
70
ST JOHNS WOOD
Pumping Sta
Elec Sta
Depot
OAK WOOD
WARE CEM
WATERFORD HEATH COMMUNITY NATURE PARK
SG14
EIGHT ACRE PLANTATION
COWSHED CORNER
Ware Park Farm
Ware Park Manor
Ware Park
MONASTERY
Nursery
Bardon Farm
GREAT MOLE WOOD
BENGEO MEADOWS
Kennel Corner
Sec Sch
Prim Sch
Swim Pool
SPORTS GRD
Tenn Cts
Lido
Bowl Green
Clubho
Lock
Weir
FB
River Lee or Lea
Manifold Ditch
LEA VALLEY WALK
Black Ditch
KING'S MEADS
New River
Chadwell Spring
Clubhouse
CHADWELL SPRINGS GOLF COURSE
HERTFORD ROAD
Bengeo
Water Tower
SPORTS GRD
THE VINEYARD
LITTLE MOLE WOOD
THE WARREN
River Beane
Hertford Lock
LOCK HOUSE IND EST
MEAD LANE IND EST
MEAD BUSINESS CENTRE
DICKER MILL IND EST
HARTHAM COMMON
Pitch 'n' Putt
Superstore
WARE ROAD
A119
STANSTEAD ROAD
B1502
A10
Fitness Cen
Madford Retail Pk
Fire Sta
Mus
Shop Cen
Lib
Castle
Castle Hall
Royal Mail Delivery Off
MAG CT
HERTFORD
GASCOYNE WAY
LONDON ROAD
A414
COUNTY HALL
FOXHOLES BUSINESS PARK
WATERMARK WAY
BURIAL GRD
Sec Sch
Foxholes Farm
Rush Green Farm
Hertford Town FC
Cricket Ground
Hertford Cricket Club
BALLS PARK
THE CANAL
B1197
Jenningsbury Court
Moat
Amwell Place Farm
Dunkirks Farm
Caravan Club Site
GREAT STOCK WOOD
LITTLE STOCK WOOD
Hertford Heath
Water Tower
Comm Cen
SPORTS GRD
THE ARBORETUM
Swallow Grove Farm
SG13
BALLS WOOD
HERTFORD HEATH NATURE RESERVE
HIGH WOOD
Research Centre
Bayfordbury Mansion
Brickendonbury
Brickendon Brook
HOBBYHORSE WOOD
ERMINE STREET ROMAN ROAD
EAST HERTS
SAILOR'S GROVE
Clements Farm
THE GROVE
Blackfields Farm
East Herts Equestrian Centre
MANGROVE LANE
MORGANS WALK
BOX
0
500 yds
500 m

DX
DY
DZ
EA
EB
EC
ED
36
37
38
06
07
08
09
10
11
12
13
14
SG12
EN11
WARE
Easneye
Great Amwell
St. Margarets
Stanstead Abbotts
Hailey
Woollensbrook
LEE VALLEY REGIONAL PARK
AMWELL QUARRY NATURE RESERVE
RYE MEADS NATURE RESERVE
RSPB RYE MEADS
JACKSON'S GROVE
PRIOR'S WOOD
LADY GROVE
DOGHOUSE WOOD
YOUNG WOOD
WIDBURY WOOD
MEAD WOOD
EASNEYE WOOD
PETER'S WOOD
POST WOOD
LEAFYOAK WOOD
MUCH WOOD
GOLDING'S WOOD
HAILEY WOOD
DELLS WOOD
KING GEORGE'S FLD
PRESDALES RECREATION GROUND
St. Margaretsbury Rec Grd
All Nations Christian Coll
Amwell Roundabout
Van Hage Garden Centre
Great Cozens
Morley Hall
Moat
Swades Farm
Newhole Farm
Ford
Waters Place Farm
The Dairy Farm
Widburyhill Farm
Amwellbury Farm
Brokengall Hill
Hardmead Lock
Stanstead Lock
The Maltings
Rye House Gatehouse
RYE HOUSE SPEEDWAY
Sewage Works
Filter Beds
Sludge Lagoons
Visitor Centre
Showman's Caravan Site
Ryegate Farm
Glasshouses
The Galley Hall PH
HIGH A1170 ST
A1170
A414
B1004
B181
B1502
A10
HODDESDON BYPASS
RIVER LEE NAVIGATION
LEE VALLEY CYCLE ROUTE
HOLLYCROSS ROAD
CAPPELL LA
AMWELL LANE
STATION ROAD
LOWER ROAD
WALNUT TREE WALK
HERTFORD ROAD
HAILEY LANE
ST. MARGARET'S ROAD
WARE ROAD
LONDON ROAD
HIGH STREET
ROYDON ROAD
HUNSDON ROAD
NETHERFIELD LANE
WIDBURY HILL
71
56

Hunsdon
Hunsdonbury
Briggens Park
Stanstead Abbotts
SG12
EN11
CM19
HOGHAM'S WOOD
HOGHAM'S PLANTATION
TOWNLANDS
THISTLY WOOD
HULL WOOD
DOGHOUSE WOOD
LADY GROVE
YOUNG WOOD
BIRCH WOOD
MOAT WOOD
NEWGATE WOOD
BALLARD'S WOOD
THIRSTY SPRING
BLACK BUSHES
THE WILDERNESS
SLOE GROVE
BURY PLANTATION
LORD'S WOOD
SQUARE SPRING
LONG SPRING
POGDEN'S WOOD
COLDHARBOUR WOOD
THE GROVE
BRIGGENS HOUSE HOTEL GOLF COURSE
Briggens House Hotel
HUNSDON MEAD
EASTWICK MEAD
ROYDON MEAD
RYE MEADS NATURE RESERVE
LEE VALLEY REGIONAL PARK
ROYDON PARK
HOME FARM INDUSTRIAL ESTATE
HARLOW BUSINESS PARK
STANSTEAD ROAD
EASTWICK ROAD
HARCAMLOW WAY
HERTFORDSHIRE
ESSEX
EAST HERTS
EPPING FOREST
Sewage Works
Filter Beds
Sludge Lagoons
RYE HOUSE SPEEDWAY
KARTING
A414
B180
B181
B1004
55
72

CM21
CM20
Gilston Park
Pye Corner
Eastwick
Little Parndon
Netteswell
Mark Hall
HARLOW
TOWN PARK
MARSHLAND WOOD
LAWNS WOOD
EASTWICK WOOD
QUEEN'S WOOD
BATTLES WOOD
MAPLECROFT WOOD
BLACK HUT WOOD
MOLE WOOD
GOLDEN GROVE
SAYES COPPICE
NEW PLANTATION
TUCK'S SPRING
GIBSON'S SHAW
ROUNDSELL SHAW
RECTORY PLANTATION
FOX EARTHS
THE CHASE
The Mount
Golden Hill
THE MANOR OF GROVES GOLF COURSE AND COUNTRY CLUB
SAND AND GRAVEL PIT
HOLLINGSON MEADS
HERTFORDSHIRE
PARNDON MEAD
CANONS BROOK GOLF COURSE
HARLOW STADIUM
PRINCESS ALEXANDRA HOSPITAL
Eastwick Lodge Roundabout
Burnt Mill Roundabout
Crown Gate Roundabout
EASTWICK ROAD
EDINBURGH WAY
FIFTH / ALLENDE AVENUE
ELIZABETH WAY
SECOND AVENUE
FOURTH AVENUE
ACTONS LANE
PENNYS LANE
BAKERS LANE
WALLIS LANE
HIGH WYCH ROAD
REDRICKS LANE
GILSTON LANE
EASTWICK HALL LANE
COCKROBIN LANE
A1169
A414
A1019
58
73

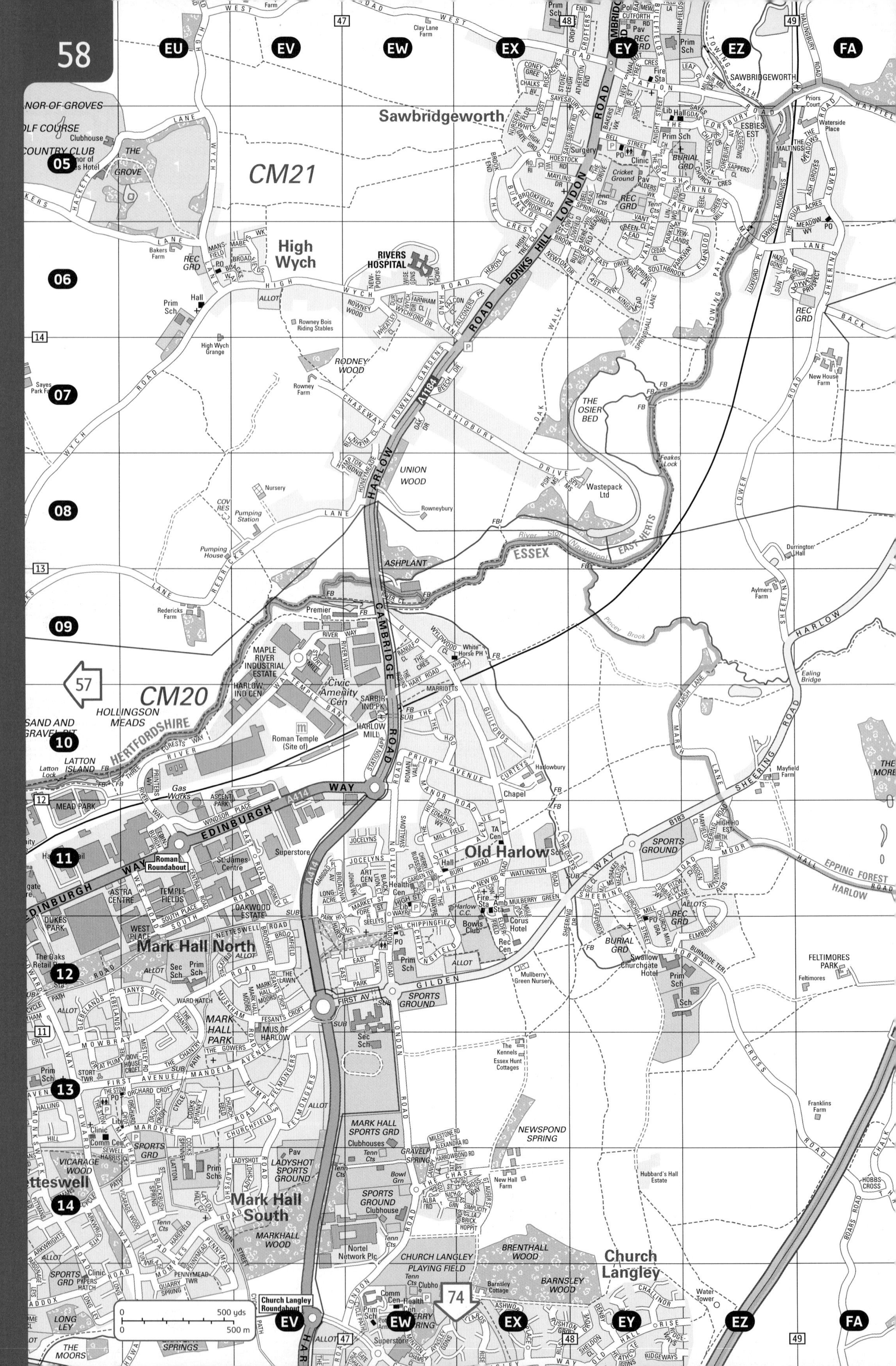
EU
EV
EW
EX
EY
EZ
FA
05
06
07
08
09
10
11
12
13
14
Sawbridgeworth
CM21
High Wych
RIVERS HOSPITAL
Rowney Bois Riding Stables
RODNEY WOOD
Rowney Farm
High Wych Grange
UNION WOOD
Rowneybury
THE OSIER BED
Feakes Lock
Wastepack Ltd
Pumping Station
Pumping House
Redericks Farm
Nursery
ASHPLANT
River Stort (Navigation)
ESSEX
EAST HERTS
HERTFORDSHIRE
Pincey Brook
Premier Inn
MAPLE RIVER INDUSTRIAL ESTATE
HARLOW IND CEN
Civic Amenity Cen
SARBIR IND PK
HARLOW MILL
Roman Temple (Site of)
CM20
HOLLINGSON MEADS
SAND AND GRAVEL PIT
LATTON ISLAND
Latton Lock
57
Gas Works
MEAD PARK
EDINBURGH WAY
Roman Roundabout
St James Centre
Superstore
ASTRA CENTRE
TEMPLE FIELDS
DUKES PARK
OAKWOOD ESTATE
WEST PLACE
Mark Hall North
The Oaks Retail Park
MARK HALL PARK
MUS OF HARLOW
Old Harlow
Hallowbury
Chapel
Bowls Club
Corus Hotel
Mulberry Green Nursery
SPORTS GROUND
MARK HALL SPORTS GRD
LADYSHOT SPORTS GROUND
Mark Hall South
MARKHALL WOOD
Nortel Network Plc
CHURCH LANGLEY PLAYING FIELD
Church Langley Roundabout
BRENTHALL WOOD
BARNSLEY WOOD
Church Langley
NEWSPOND SPRING
The Kennels
Essex Hunt Cottages
New Hall Farm
Hubbard's Hall Estate
Water Tower
HOBBS CROSS
Franklins Farm
FELTIMORES PARK
Feltimores
Swallow Churchgate Hotel
BURIAL GRD
Mayfield Farm
Ealing Bridge
Aylmers Farm
Durrington Hall
New House Farm
Priors Court
Waterside Place
Clay Lane Farm
Bakers Farm
Sayes Park Farm
Clubhouse
THE GROVE
VICARAGE WOOD
Netteswell
LONG LEY
THE MOORS
A1184
A414
B183
74
47
48
49
500 yds
500 m

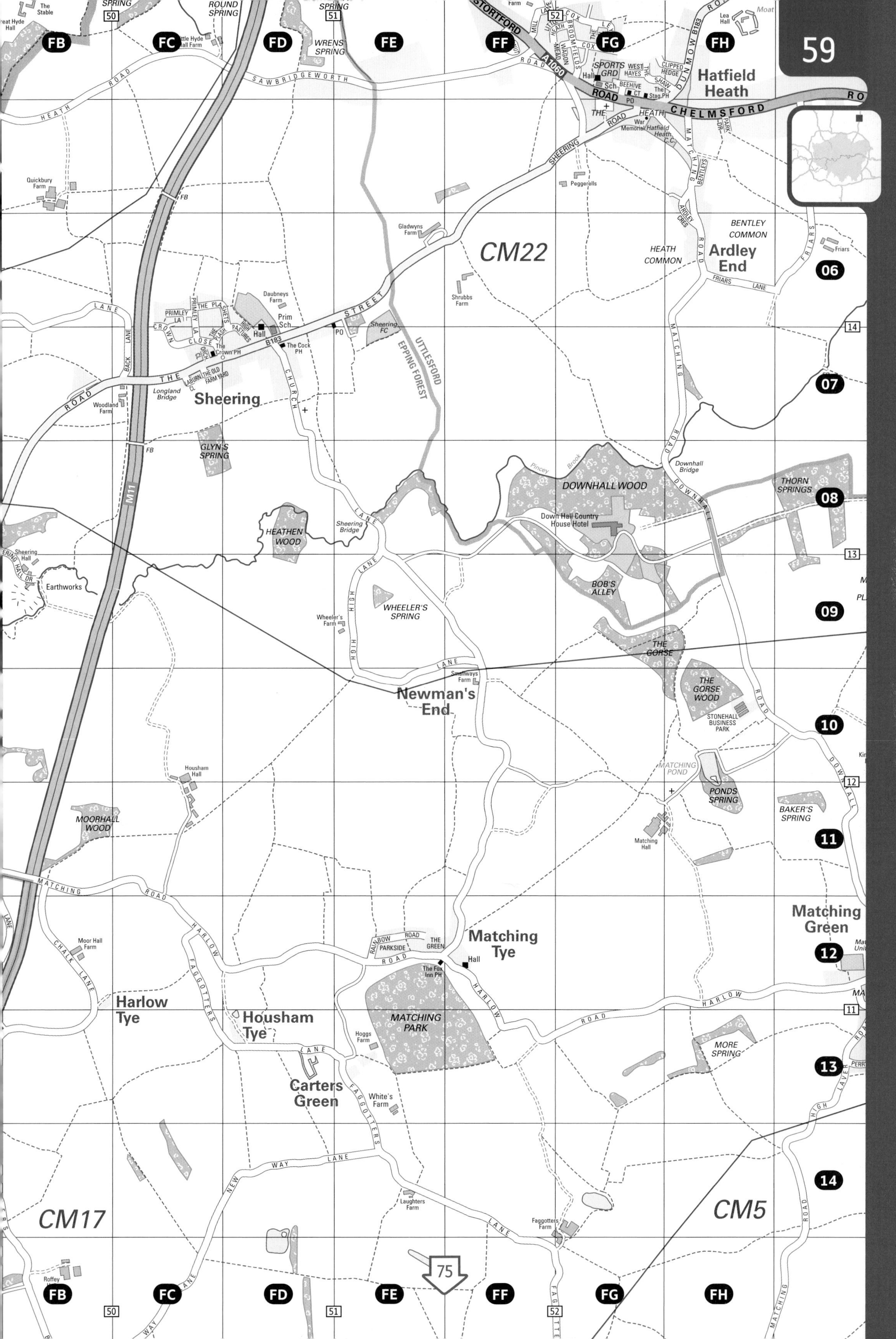
FB
FC
FD
FE
FF
FG
FH
Hatfield Heath
Ardley End
Sheering
Newman's End
Matching Tye
Matching Green
Harlow Tye
Housham Tye
Carters Green
CM22
CM17
CM5
M11
B183
A1060
DOWNHALL WOOD
Down Hall Country House Hotel
HEATHEN WOOD
WHEELER'S SPRING
BOB'S ALLEY
THE GORSE
THE GORSE WOOD
STONEHALL BUSINESS PARK
PONDS SPRING
BAKER'S SPRING
THORN SPRINGS
MOORHALL WOOD
MATCHING PARK
MORE SPRING
GLYN'S SPRING
UTTLESFORD
EPPING FOREST
SAWBRIDGEWORTH ROAD
HEATH ROAD
CHELMSFORD ROAD
SHEERING ROAD
THE STREET
CHURCH LANE
HIGH LANE
MATCHING ROAD
HARLOW ROAD
FAGGOTTERS LANE
NEW WAY LANE
CHALK LANE
DOWN HALL ROAD
FRIARS LANE
BENTLEY COMMON
HEATH COMMON
Housham Hall
Matching Hall
Faggotters Farm
Laughters Farm
White's Farm
Hoggs Farm
Moor Hall Farm
Quickbury Farm
Woodland Farm
Gladwyns Farm
Shrubbs Farm
Daubneys Farm
Peggerells
Wheeler's Farm
Smallways Farm
Downhall Bridge
Sheering Bridge
Longland Bridge
Earthworks
Sheering Hall
Roffey
The Fox Inn PH
The Crown PH
The Cock PH
Prim Sch
Sheering FC
MATCHING POND
75
06
07
08
09
10
11
12
13
14
50
51
52

AS
AT
AU
AV
AW
AX
AY
98
99
00
NORTHCHURCH COMMON NT
FIRTHSDEN BEECHES
NATIONAL TRUST
Hill Farm
Pumping Station
Gorseside Farm
Northchurch Farm
BERKHAMSTED GOLF COURSE
15
16
17
18
19
20
21
22
23
24
09
08
07
06
Dudswell
GRAND UNION CANAL
ALLOT
HP4
BERKHAMSTED
Well Farm
Clubhouse
Tenn Cts
Pav
REC GRD
HIGH STREET
A4251
B4506
CEM
Sec Sch
New Farm
Northchurch
RECYLING CEN
CANAL-SIDE
BERKHAMSTED PLACE
SPORTS GRD
Sch
PO
Social Cen
Hospice
THE ROOKERY
Woodcock Hill
COX DELL
Youth Club
Sports Cen
Health Cen
GOSSOMS END
The Mansion
BERKHAMSTED CASTLE (ruins)
Bowl Grn
Tenn Club
Berkhamsted Town FC
Superstore
THE MOOR
Amb Sta
Fire Sta
Clinic
CIVIC CEN
Lib
Hall
Fit Cen
Pol
THE PLANTATION
Prim Sch
REC GRD
Prep Sch
CEM
BERKHAMSTED BYPASS
A41
A416
KINGS ROAD
KINGSHILL WAY
LONDON ROAD
Tower
PLAYING FIELD
National Film & Television Archive
Ashlyns Farm
Ashlyns Hall
Prim Sch
PANCAKE WOOD
FIRS WOOD
WILLOW WOOD
HOCKERIDGE WOOD
CHESHAM ROAD
SANDPIT GREEN
DROPPING'S WOOD
COKER'S SPRING
Johns Lane Farm
Sch
Haresfoot Farm
William Hill Farm
Hockeridge Farm
HP5
Brickies Farm
Harriotts End Farm
THE LARCHES
Snowhill Farm
Old Oak Farm
HEATHEN GROVE
Sewage Works
DACORUM HERTFORDSHIRE
CHILTERN BUCKINGHAMSHIRE
Ashley Green
Flamstead Farm
Whelpley Hill Farm
Kenmore Farm
SHORT WOOD
GREAT WOOD
78
0 500 yds
0 500 m
Sale's Farm
Spencer's Farm
Hemming's Farm

AZ
BA
BB
BC
BD
BE
BF
GREAT FRITHDEN COPSE
NATIONAL TRUST
LITTLE FRITHSDEN COPSE
Hollybush Farm
FRITHSDEN VINES
Alford Arms PH
Crossways Farm
HERDIN'S WOOD
Strathgade Farm
Bingham's Park Farm
Poultry Farm
BROWN'S SPRING WOOD
HOLLYBUSH WOOD
Rumblers Farm
Woodcroft Farm
CATSTAIL WOOD
BERKHAMSTED GOLF COURSE
Grims Ditch
SPORTS GRD
Potten End
Potten-End Farm
DELL WOOD
Martins Pond PH
Boxted Farm
COV RES
Bowling Green
Little Heath Park
Gutteridge Farm
GUTTERIDGE WOOD
LITTLE HEATH NT
Little Heath Farm
Boxted Pig Farm
Gadebridge
SPORTS GROUND
Little Heath Great Farm
Lower Little Heath Farm
Fields End Farm
WARNERS END
Warners End
BULLBEGGAR'S WOOD
HP1
SHRUB HILL COMMON
NORTHRIDGE PARK
Chaulden
Berkhamsted Sewage Works
GRAND UNION CANAL
River Bulbourne
Broadway Farm
Pix Farm
Pouchen End Farm
The Three Horseshoes PH
Watermill Hotel
Cress Farm
White Horse PH & The Anchor PH
Bourne End Farm
Bourne End
BOURNE END MILLS
CHAULDEN LANE PLAYING FIELD
Rugby Ground
CONVENT
Moorend Farm
HEMEL HEMPSTEAD
Lower Farm
Vale Farm
Premier Inn
GREEN CROFT
HAY WOOD
UPPER ROUGHDOWN
Prep Sch
HANGING WOOD
Clubhouse
LITTLE HAY GOLF COMPLEX
HP3
BOXMOOR GOLF COURSE
SHEETHANGER COMMON
COLESHILL WOOD
GORSEFIELD WOOD
BURY WOOD
Felden Lodge
Howe's Retreat
Tower Farm
Felden Grange
Felden Manor
Longcroft Farm
COVERED RESERVOIR
A4251
A41
A4146
B4505
KINGS LANGLEY BYPASS
BERKHAMSTED BYPASS
LONDON ROAD
16
17
18
19
20
21
22
23
24
62
79

BG
BH
BJ
BK
BL
BM
BN
05
06
07
08
09
15
16
17
18
19
20
21
22
23
24
61
80
VARNEY'S WOOD
Lovetts End Farm
Wood Farm
The Red Lion PH
A4146
THRIFT WOOD
Grist House Farm
Watercress Beds
Strathgade Farm
Noake Mill
Fish Farm
Gaddesden Hall
Piccotts End Garden Centre
Fish Ponds
River Gade
Electricity Station
BUZZARD ROAD
CASTLE WOOD
New Farm House
Piccotts End
DELL WOOD
Piccotts End Farm
Boars Head PH
PICCOTTS END LANE
CYCLE TRACK
GROVEHILL PLAYING FIELDS
Grovehill
MARGARET LLOYD PARK
Cupid Green
Amenity Site
Tenn Cts
REDBOURN ROAD
LINK ROAD
A4147
Superstore
Clubhouse
PENNINE WAY SPORTS GROUND
YEWTREE WOOD
SWALLOWDALE LA
WIDMORE WOOD
HOWE GROVE
Marchmont Farm
WARNERS END WOOD
HOME WOOD
GADEBRIDGE HILL
PARK
SPORTS GROUND
Gadebridge
SPORTS GROUND
GADEBRIDGE PARK
LEIGHTON BUZZARD ROAD
Highfield
RANDALL PARK
Highfield House
PLAYING FLD
HP1
WARNERS END
VALLEY
Bowling Greens
ARTS CEN
QUEENSWAY
KEEN FIELDS
Fire Sta
Amb Sta
West Herts Coll
Hammerfield
William Crook House
NORTHRIDGE PARK
DACORUM CIVIC CENTRE
DACORUM PAVILION
Superstore
BUS STA
Adeyfield
REITH FIELDS
HEATH LANE CEMETERY
HEMEL HEMPSTEAD GENERAL HOSP
HEMEL HEMPSTEAD
The Travelodge
Marlowes Centre
ST. ALBANS ROAD
A414
JARMAN PARK
Leisure World
Cinema
Ice Arena
DACORUM ATHLETICS TRACK
SKI CENTRE
Plough Roundabout
Hotel Riverside
CONVENT
Rugby Ground
Cricket Ground
Boxmoor
Sports Cen
STATION ROAD
Cricket Club
LONDON ROAD
A4251
TWO WATERS RD
TWO WATERS WAY
LIME WALK
Fishery Inn PH
HP3
Bennetts End
BELSWAINS PLAYING FIELDS
Tennis Courts
Swan PH
ROUGHDOWN VILLAS RD
UPPER ROUGHDOWN
LOWER ROUGHDOWN
Gas Holder
Gas Holders
Glasshouses
ORAM PLACE
KINGS LANGLEY BYPASS
A41
Three Fields Farm
Felden
HOME WOOD
APSLEY MILLS RETAIL PARK
Superstore
Holiday Inn Express
APSLEY
Apsley
SHENDISH MANOR GOLF COURSE
HEN'S HEAD WOOD
Howe's Retreat
Felden Lodge
Tower Farm
FEATHERBED LANE
GRAND UNION CANAL
LANGLEY
0
500 yds
500 m

BP
BQ
BR
BS
BT
BU
BV
08
09
10
Dane End Farm
Med Cen
Superstore
Prim Sch
HEMEL HEMPSTEAD ROAD
CYCLE PATH
Bohemia House
Hill Farm
Prim Schs
Comm Cen
Wood End Farm
DACORUM
ST. ALBANS
CHERRY TREE LANE
Cherry Tree Farm
LILLY LANE
PUNCH BOWL LANE
HP2
16
BRICKFIELDS IND EST
PRATTS DELL
Southend Farm
AL3
17
Old Jeromes
Butler's Farm
HEMEL HEMPSTEAD INDUSTRIAL ESTATE
McDONALD BUS. PK
MAYLANDS
Oil Tanks
HOGG END LANE
BOUNDARY WAY
BUNCEFIELD LANE
Buncefield Terminal
Oil Tanks
Kettlewell's Farm
18
GROVELANDS BUS. CEN
SARACEN INDUSTRIAL AREA
KENTISH WOOD
WINDMILLHILL WOOD
THE VISTAS
THE WILDERNESS
CHALK DELL
GORHAMBURY
Dixons Group Plc
WOOD LANE END
WOODWELLS FARM CEMETERY
Depot
BRUCE'S PLANTATION
19
Peoplebuilding
Fitness Cen
A4147 MAYLANDS AVENUE
BREAKSPEAR WAY
Caravan Club
Elec Sta
Holiday Inn
B.P. Plc
MARCHMONT HOUSE POND
Junctions 7 & 8
Gorhambury (Ruins)
64
BRICKKILN WOOD
20
Mayers Farm Stud Cottages
07
M1
Prim Sch
Westwick Farm
Leverstock Green
Leverstock Green FC
Comm Cen
Lib
Westwick Hall
21
SQUARE WOOD
Westwick Row Farm
Cricket Ground
Pav
LEVERSTOCK GREEN ROAD
Hill End Farm
Tenn Club
Sch
WESTWICK ROW
HEMEL HEMPSTEAD ROAD
A4147
Corner Farm
Westwick House
BEECHTREE LANE
22
Prim Sch
Sports Cen
Sec Sch
CATSDELL BOTTOM
THREE RIVERS
BEDMOND ROAD
BLACKWATER LANE
06
LONGFIELD SPRING
A414
APPSPOND LANE
Maiden Crouch Farm
BLACKWATER WOOD
23
Bunkers Farm
Well Farm
Sch
SILVERTHORN DRIVE
BUNKERS LANE
Highwood Hall Farm
POTTERS CROUCH PLANTATION
APPSPOND WOOD
24
WOODHALL LANE
High Herts Farm
The Swan PH
LONG DEANS
81
Bedmond House
Rose Acre
WD5
BEDMOND LANE
HIGH

BW
BX
BY
BZ
CA
CB
CC
12
13
14
15
16
17
18
19
20
21
22
23
24
09
08
07
06
Punch Bowl PH
Pumping Sta
BUSH WOOD
Childwick Bury
KIEMART'S SPRING WOOD
Hill Farm
New Jerome Cottage
THE PLANTATION
PUNCH BOWL LANE
WATLING STREET (ROMAN ROAD)
A5183 REDBOURN ROAD
River Ver
Mill Race
Woodlands Farm
TOULMIN DRIVE SPORTS GROUND
Stafford Farm
Stafford Stud
LADIES GROVE WOOD
BATCH WOOD
HOGG END LANE
WHITEHEDGE SPRING
Bow Bridge
Golf & Tennis Cen
Batchwood Hall
Bowling Green
BATCHWOOD HALL GOLF COURSE
Butler's Farm
AL3
Maynes Farm
WINDMILLHILL WOOD
CHURCHYARD MEADOW
GORHAMBURY DRIVE
ONE ACRE
Gorhambury
THE WILDERNESS
CHALK DELL
GORHAMBURY
GILPINS
HUGO'S SPINNEY
Shepherds Cottage
Course of Roman Wall
A5183 REDBOURN ROAD
VERULAM
FOLLY
ALBANY LODGE
ST. ALBANS CITY HOSP
Hospice
REC GRD
Gorhambury (Ruins)
63
CYPRESS WOOD
The Fosse
KINGSBURY WATERMILL
St. Michael's Bridge
BELL MEADOW
VERULAMIUM MUSEUM
Roman Open Air Theatre
LORD BACON'S MOUNT
TEMPLE WOOD
Site of Roman Verulamium
Mayers Farm Stud Cottages
Prae Wood House
Tennis Courts
PRAE WOOD
HEMEL HEMPSTEAD ROAD
VERULAMIUM PARK
Hypocaust
Pav
Prae Wood Farm
SQUARE WOOD
Verulam Hills
ATHLETICS TRACK
Leisure Centre
Superstore
Prim Sch
ABBEY VIEW GOLF COURSE
Hill End Farm
A4147 HEMEL HEMPSTEAD ROAD
SPORTS GROUND
St. Stephens
WATLING
A414
LONGFIELD SPRING
Maiden Crouch Farm
MADAM'S WOOD
Windridge Farm
BIRCH WOOD
NETHERWAY
OPEN SPACE
Sec Sch
A5183 STREET
APPSPOND WOOD
BEDMOND LANE
Westfields Farm
PARK WOOD
Holly Bush PH
RAGGED HALL LANE
Potters Crouch East Farm
Potters Crouch Farm
SQUARE WOOD
SCRUBBS WOOD
Cuckman's Farm
AL2
REC GRD
ALLOT
ST. JULIAN'S WOOD
M1
WD5
Potters Crouch
0 500 yds
0 500 m
82
WATLING STREET CARAVAN (TRAVELLERS)
A405
Plaistowes Farm
WELLFIELD

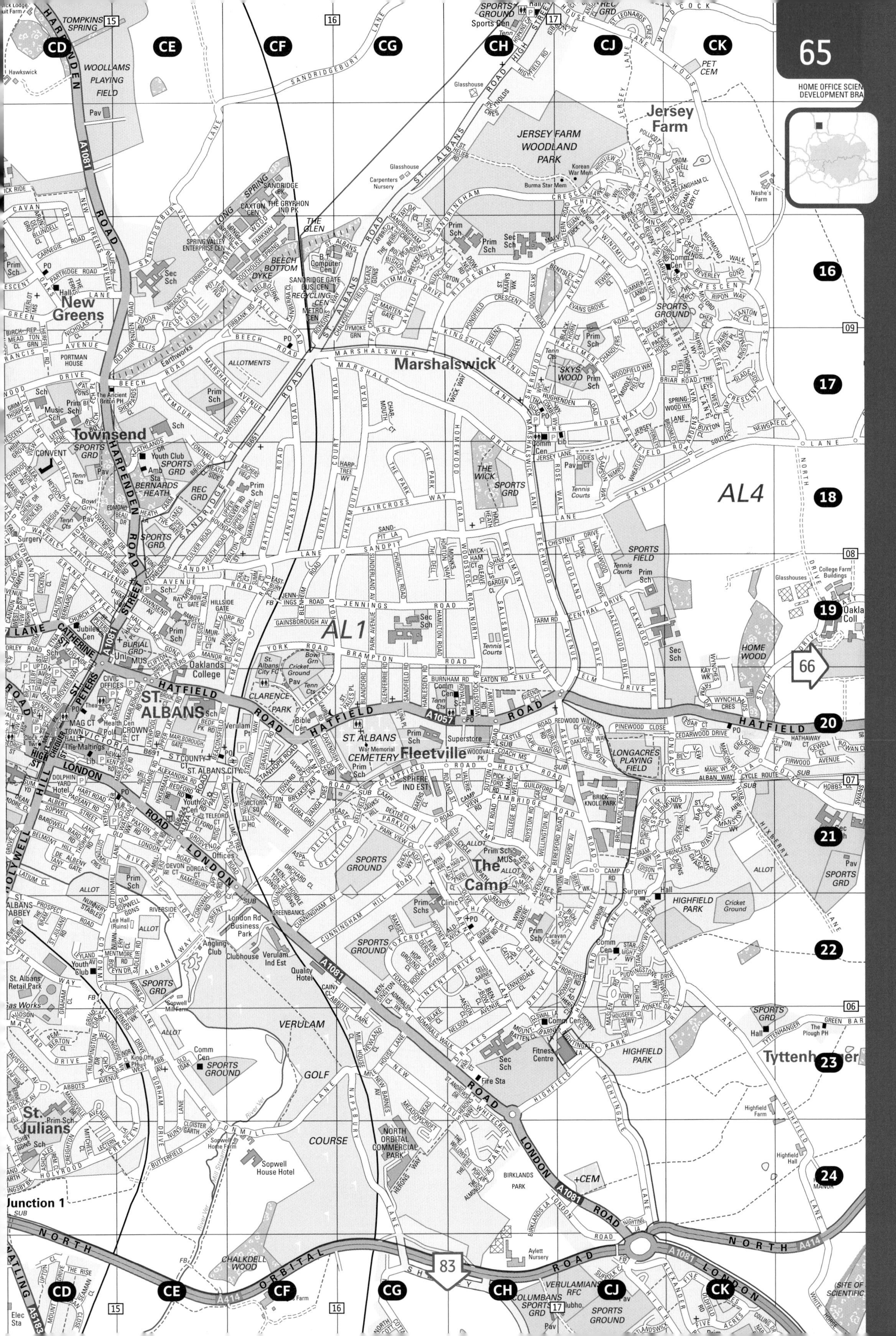
CD
CE
CF
CG
CH
CJ
CK
15
16
17
HOME OFFICE SCIENTIFIC DEVELOPMENT BRANCH
16
17
18
19
20
21
22
23
24
09
08
07
06
66
83
TOMPKINS SPRING
WOOLLAMS PLAYING FIELD
HARPENDEN ROAD
A1081
SANDRIDGEBURY LANE
SPORTS GROUND
Sports Cen
PET CEM
Jersey Farm
JERSEY FARM WOODLAND PARK
Korean War Mem
Burma Star Mem
Glasshouse
Carpenters Nursery
Nashe's Farm
SANDRIDGE PK
THE GRYPHON IND PK
CAXTON CEN
SPRING VALLEY ENTERPRISE CEN
THE GLEN
BEECH BOTTOM DYKE
B.T. Computer Cen
SANDRIDGE GATE BUS CEN
RECYCLING CEN
METRO CEN
New Greens
PORTMAN HOUSE
ALLOTMENTS
Earthworks
Marshalswick
SKYS WOOD
Townsend
The Ancient Briton PH
SPORTS GRD
Youth Club
BERNARDS HEATH
REC GRD
CONVENT
THE WICK
SPORTS GRD
AL4
AL1
Tennis Courts
SPORTS FIELD
Glasshouses
College Farm Buildings
Oaklands Coll
HOME WOOD
Oaklands College
St. Albans City Cricket Ground
CLARENCE PARK
ST. ALBANS
CIVIC OFFICES
HATFIELD ROAD
A1057
ST. ALBANS CEMETERY
War Memorial
Fleetville
Superstore
LONGACRES PLAYING FIELD
BRICK KNOLL PARK
SPHERE IND EST
The Maltings
ST. ALBANS CITY
LONDON ROAD
The Camp
SPORTS GROUND
HIGHFIELD PARK
Cricket Ground
SPORTS GRD
ST. ALBANS ABBEY
Lee Hall (Ruins)
London Rd Business Park
Angling Club
Clubhouse
Verulam Ind Est
Quality Hotel
St. Albans Retail Park
Sopwell Mill Farm
VERULAM GOLF COURSE
Comm Cen
SPORTS GROUND
Sopwell Home Farm
Sopwell House Hotel
NORTH ORBITAL COMMERCIAL PARK
Fire Sta
Fitness Centre
HIGHFIELD PARK
Tyttenhanger
The Plough PH
Highfield Farm
Highfield Hall
BIRKLANDS PARK
CEM
Aylett Nursery
St. Julians
Junction 1
NORTH ORBITAL ROAD
A414
CHALKDELL WOOD
VERULAMIANS RFC
SPORTS GROUND
(SITE OF SCIENTIFIC

CL
CM
CN
CP
CQ
CR
CS
50
65
84
HOME OFFICE SCIENTIFIC DEVELOPMENT BRANCH
Fairfold's Farm
Sutton's Farm
WOODCOCK HILL
Astwick Manor
Astwick Manor Farm
MANOR ROAD
Fielder Centre
HATFIELD BUSINESS PARK
Offices
FROBISHER WAY
SAND AND GRAVEL PIT
SAND & GRAVEL PIT
HOOK'S WOOD
SLEEVE HALL WOOD
BALL'S COVERT
OAK WOOD
Nashe's Farm
Beech Farm
ASH GREEN
Oak Farm
ROUND WOOD
HOME COVERT
WELWYN HATFIELD
ST. ALBANS
AL10
University of Hertfordshire de Havilland Campus
Sports Cen
Fitness Cen
BISHOP SQUARE
Ramada
Prim Sch
COOPERS GREEN LANE
OAKLANDS LANE
NORTH DRIVE
HOUSE LANE
RIPON WAY
NEWGATE CL
ST. ALBANS ROAD WEST
POPLARS
BRAMBLE ROAD
ELLENBROOK
COMET WAY
Radio Nursery
Popefield Farm
Wilkin's Green
Ellenbrook
College Farm Buildings
Glasshouses
Oaklands Coll
Tenn Cts
BAGGYMEAD SPRING
Notcutts Garden Cen.
A1057
HATFIELD ROAD
Smallford
Smallford Nursery
Wilkin's Green Farm
Nast Hyde Farm
ALBAN WAY CYCLE ROUTE
Junction 3
RYDERS AV
ROEHYDE WAY
STATION ROAD
Superstores
Coll
AL4
Sleapshyde
Sleapshyde Farm
SLEAPSHYDE LANE
SMITHS CRES
SLEAPCROSS GARDENS
A414
JOHNSON'S SPRING
Bullen's Green
Sec Sch
Pav
SPORTS GRD
ALLOT
Cricket Ground
HIXBERRY LANE
HEATH ROAD
Smallford Farm
BUTTERWICK LANE
BARLEY MOW CARAVAN PARK
Barley Mow Stables
ORBITAL
HIGH STREET
SPORTS GRD
Prim Sch
Tenn Cts
Clubhouse
BURIAL GRD
Hall
Roundhouse Farm
Colney Heath
Pumping Sta
ROESTOCK PARK
ROESTOCK LANE
Queens Head PH
Colney Heath Farm
FELLOWES LANE
TOLLGATE ROAD
DELLSOME LANE
Roestock
Tollgate Farm
SPORTS GRD
Hall
GREEN BARLEY
The Plough PH
Tyttenhanger
SAND AND GRAVEL PIT
River Colne
PARK CORNER
Highfield Farm
Highfield Hall
HIGHFIELD MANOR
HIGHFIELD LANE
KNIGHT'S WOOD
BLOUNT SPRING
ST. ALBANS HERTSMERE
Warren Farm
THE WARREN
FREDERICK'S WOOD
WELWYN HATFIELD
Tyttenhanger Farm
COURSERS ROAD
NORTH ORBITAL A414
LONDON
COPPICE
GARDEN WOOD
THE NEW PLANTATION
Tyttenhanger House
Coursers Farm
0 500 yds
0 500 m
15
16
17
18
19
20
21
22
23
24
06
07
08
09
19
20
21

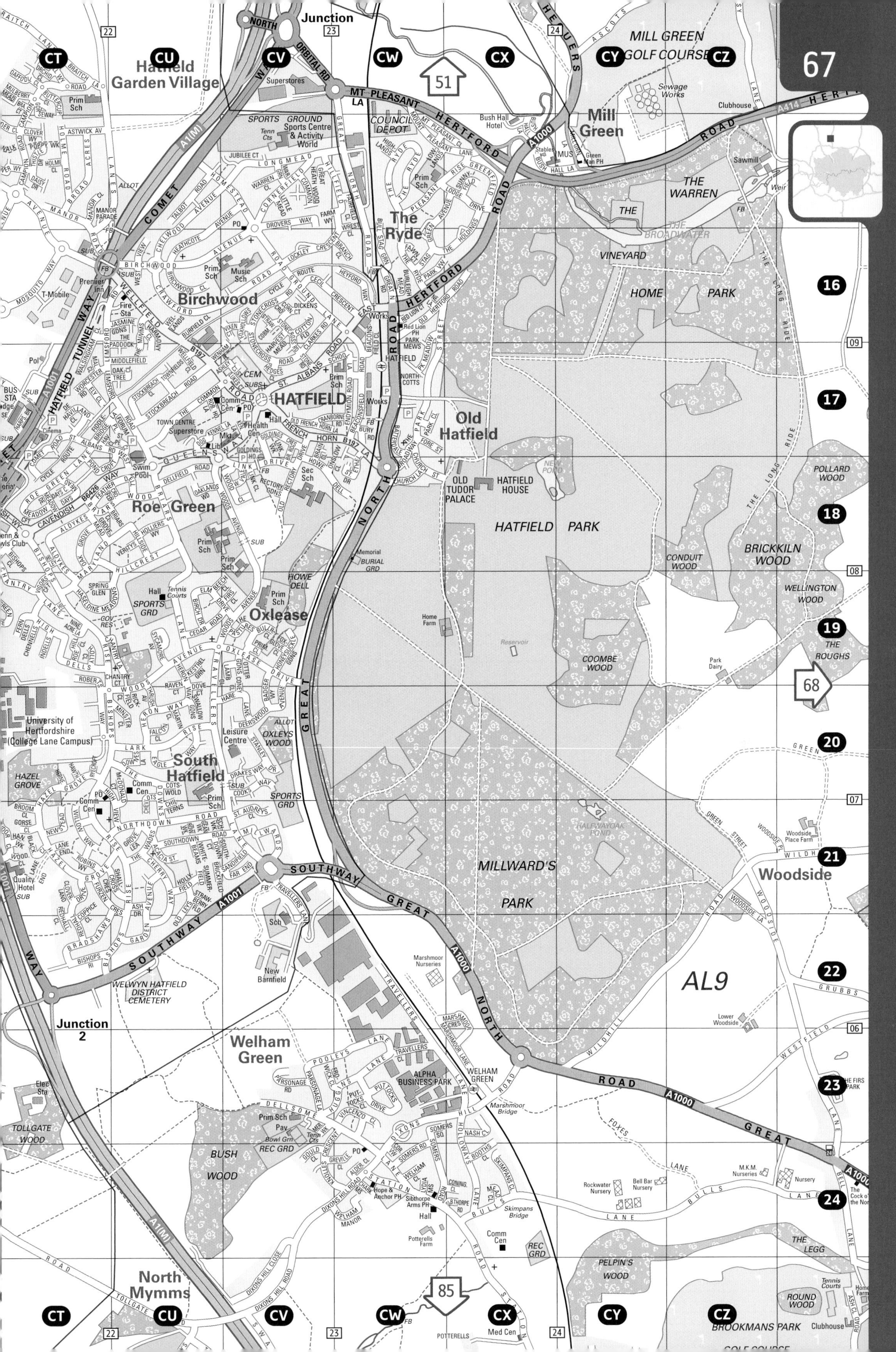
67
Junction 23
Hatfield Garden Village
MILL GREEN GOLF COURSE
Mill Green
51
CT
CU
CV
CW
CX
CY
CZ
MT PLEASANT LA
HERTFORD ROAD
COMET WAY
HATFIELD TUNNEL
Superstores
SPORTS GROUND
Sports Centre & Activity World
COUNCIL DEPOT
Bush Hall Hotel
Sewage Works
Clubhouse
Sawmill
THE WARREN
THE BROADWATER
VINEYARD
HOME PARK
The Ryde
Birchwood
HATFIELD
Old Hatfield
Roe Green
Oxlease
South Hatfield
OLD TUDOR PALACE
HATFIELD HOUSE
HATFIELD PARK
NEW POND
POLLARD WOOD
BRICKKILN WOOD
CONDUIT WOOD
WELLINGTON WOOD
THE ROUGHS
COOMBE WOOD
Home Farm
Reservoir
Park Dairy
68
HALFWAYOAK POND
MILLWARD'S PARK
Woodside
Woodside Place Farm
AL9
University of Hertfordshire (College Lane Campus)
HAZEL GROVE
OXLEYS WOOD
SPORTS GRD
Leisure Centre
SOUTHWAY
GREAT NORTH ROAD
A1000
A1001
A1(M)
WELWYN HATFIELD DISTRICT CEMETERY
Junction 2
Welham Green
New Barnfield
Marshmoor Nurseries
ALPHA BUSINESS PARK
WELHAM GREEN
Marshmoor Bridge
TOLLGATE WOOD
BUSH WOOD
REC GRD
Skimpans Bridge
Rockwater Nursery
Bell Bar Nursery
M.K.M. Nurseries
Nursery
Lower Woodside
THE LEGG
PELPIN'S WOOD
ROUND WOOD
North Mymms
85
Potterells Farm
POTTERELLS
Med Cen
Comm Cen
BROOKMANS PARK
Clubhouse
16
17
18
19
20
21
22
23
24
09
08
07
06
22
23
24

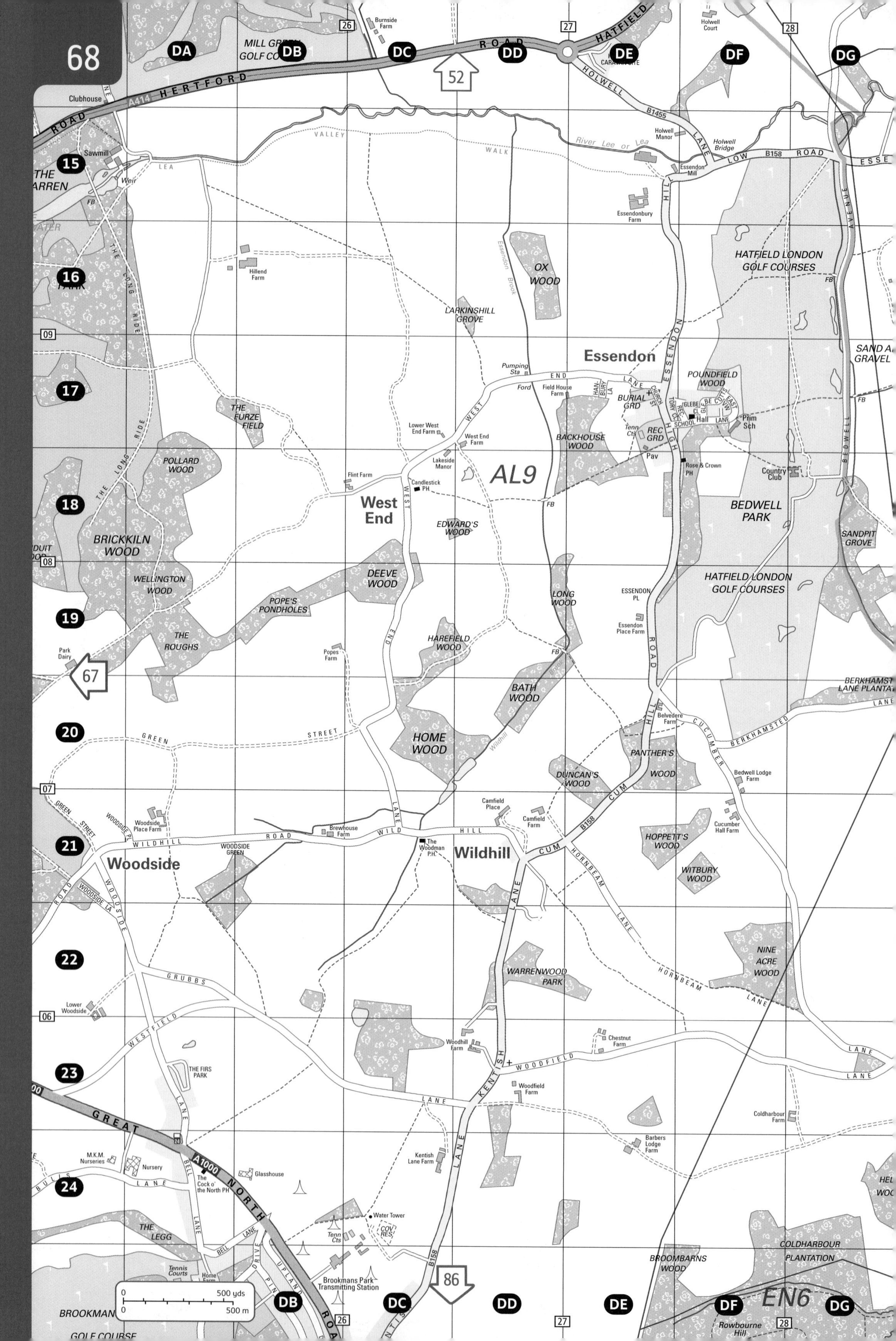

DA
DB
DC
DD
DE
DF
DG
MILL GREEN GOLF COURSE
Burnside Farm
Holwell Court
HERTFORD ROAD
HATFIELD ROAD
A414
52
CARAVAN SITE
HOLWELL
B1455
Clubhouse
VALLEY WALK
River Lee or Lea
Holwell Manor
Holwell Bridge
LANE
LOW B158 ROAD
ESSENDON
Essendon Mill
Sawmill
Weir
LEA
THE WARREN
FB
Essendonbury Farm
HILL
AVENUE
Hillend Farm
Essendon Brook
OX WOOD
HATFIELD LONDON GOLF COURSES
THE LONG RIDE
LARKINSHILL GROVE
Essendon
Pumping Sta
END LANE
Ford
Field House Farm
HANBURY LA
BURIAL GRD
CHURCH ST
POUNDFIELD WOOD
GLEBE CL
GLEBE COTTS
EAST
SCHOOL LANE
Hall
Prim Sch
TORY CL
REC GRD
Tenn Cts
Pav
Rose & Crown PH
BACKHOUSE WOOD
THE FURZE FIELD
WEST END
Lower West End Farm
West End Farm
Lakeside Manor
Candlestick PH
Flint Farm
POLLARD WOOD
AL9
West End
BEDWELL
Country Club
BEDWELL PARK
SAND A GRAVEL
FB
EDWARD'S WOOD
BRICKKILN WOOD
SANDPIT GROVE
WELLINGTON WOOD
DEEVE WOOD
LONG WOOD
POPE'S PONDHOLES
ESSENDON PL
Essendon Place Farm
THE ROUGHS
HAREFIELD WOOD
Park Dairy
67
Popes Farm
BATH WOOD
Brook
BERKHAMSTED LANE PLANTA
Belvedere Farm
CUCUMBER
BERKHAMSTED LANE
GREEN STREET
HOME WOOD
Wildhill
PANTHER'S WOOD
DUNCAN'S WOOD
Bedwell Lodge Farm
GREEN STREET
Camfield Place
Camfield Farm
CUM CUM
Cucumber Hall Farm
WOODSIDE PL
Woodside Place Farm
Brewhouse Farm
WILDHILL ROAD
WILD HILL
The Woodman P.H.
Wildhill
HOPPETT'S WOOD
WOODSIDE GREEN
HORNBEAM LANE
WITBURY WOOD
Woodside
WOODSIDE LA
WOODSIDE
B158
NINE ACRE WOOD
GRUBBS
WARRENWOOD PARK
HORNBEAM LANE
Lower Woodside
WESTFIELD
Chestnut Farm
Woodhill Farm
KENTISH
WOODFIELD
LANE
THE FIRS PARK
Woodfield Farm
GREAT NORTH ROAD
A1000
Coldharbour Farm
Barbers Lodge Farm
Kentish Lane Farm
M.K.M. Nurseries
Nursery
BELL LANE
The Cock o' the North PH
Glasshouse
BULLS LANE
HEL WOO
Water Tower
COV RES
THE LEGG
Tenn Cts
BELL LANE
DRIVE
UPLANDS
COLDHARBOUR PLANTATION
Tennis Courts
Home Farm
Brookmans Park Transmitting Station
B158
86
BROOMBARNS WOOD
EN6
500 yds
500 m
BROOKMANS GOLF COURSE
Rowbourne Hill
15
16
17
18
19
20
21
22
23
24
26
27
28
09
08
07
06

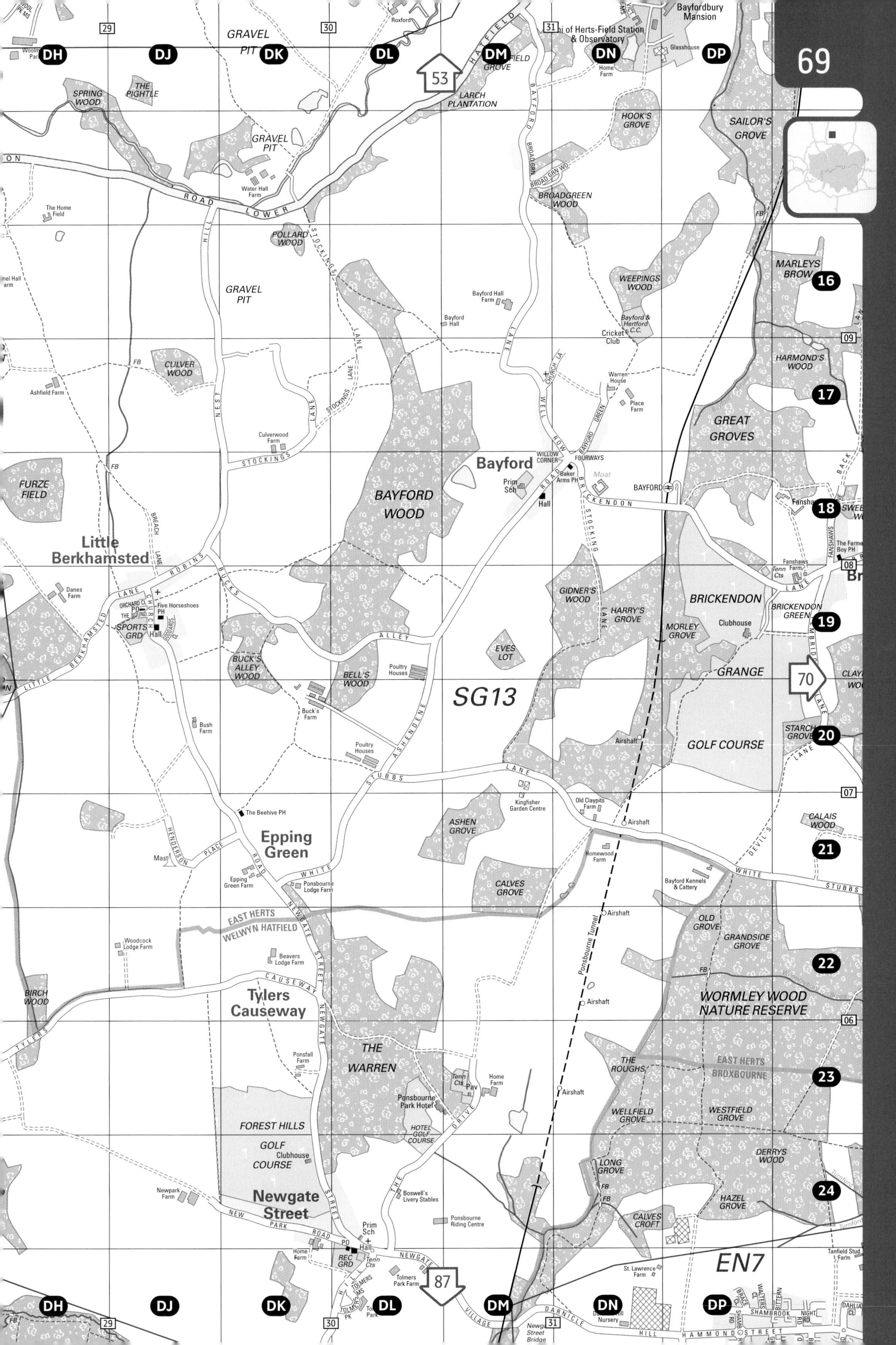

GRAVEL PIT
Roxford
Bayfordbury Mansion
Uni of Herts-Field Station & Observatory
Glasshouse
HATFIELD ROAD
HATFIELD GROVE
53
LARCH PLANTATION
Home Farm
SPRING WOOD
THE PIGHTLE
HOOK'S GROVE
SAILOR'S GROVE
GRAVEL PIT
Water Hall Farm
LOWER ROAD
BROAD GRN WD
BROADGREEN WOOD
The Home Field
POLLARD WOOD
HILL
STOCKINGS LANE
BAYFORD LANE
MARLEYS BROW
WEEPINGS WOOD
GRAVEL PIT
Bayford Hall Farm
Bayford Hall
Bayford & Hertford C.C.
Cricket Club
CULVER WOOD
Ashfield Farm
FB
CHURCH LA
Warren House
Place Farm
HARMOND'S WOOD
GREAT GROVES
NEST
Culverwood Farm
STOCKINGS
WELL ROW
BAYFORD GREEN
WILLOW CORNER
FOURWAYS
FURZE FIELD
Bayford
Prim Sch
Baker Arms PH
Moat
BAYFORD
BAYFORD WOOD
Hall
BRICKENDON
Fanshaws
The Farmers Boy PH
Fanshaws Farm
Tenn Cts
Little Berkhamsted
BREACH LANE
ROBINS
BUCKS
GIDNER'S WOOD
HARRY'S GROVE
BRICKENDON
BRICKENDON GREEN
Danes Farm
ORCHARD CL
THE BOUND
Five Horseshoes PH
SPORTS GRD
GODDARDS CL
LITTLE BERKHAMSTED LANE
MORLEY GROVE
Clubhouse
ALLEY
EVES LOT
BUCK'S ALLEY WOOD
BELL'S WOOD
Poultry Houses
GRANGE
70
SG13
Buck's Farm
ASHENDENE
Bush Farm
Airshaft
GOLF COURSE
STARCH GROVE
Poultry Houses
STUBBS LANE
Kingfisher Garden Centre
Old Claypits Farm
CALAIS WOOD
The Beehive PH
ASHEN GROVE
Epping Green
HENDERSON PLACE
Mast
Homewood Farm
DEVIL'S LANE
WHITE STUBBS
Epping Green Farm
Ponsbourne Lodge Farm
CALVES GROVE
Bayford Kennels & Cattery
EAST HERTS
WELWYN HATFIELD
Airshaft
OLD GROVE
GRANDSIDE GROVE
Woodcock Lodge Farm
Beavers Lodge Farm
NEWGATE STREET
CAUSEWAY
Ponsbourne Tunnel
WORMLEY WOOD NATURE RESERVE
BIRCH WOOD
Tylers Causeway
TYLERS
THE WARREN
THE ROUGHS
EAST HERTS
BROXBOURNE
Ponsfall Farm
Tenn Cts
Pav
Home Farm
Ponsbourne Park Hotel
WELLFIELD GROVE
WESTFIELD GROVE
FOREST HILLS
GOLF
Clubhouse
COURSE
HOTEL GOLF COURSE
THE DRIVE
DERRYS WOOD
LONG GROVE
Newpark Farm
Newgate Street
Boswell's Livery Stables
HAZEL GROVE
NEW PARK ROAD
Ponsbourne Riding Centre
CALVES CROFT
Prim Sch
Hall
PO
Home Farm
REC GRD
Tenn Cts
NEWGATE
EN7
St. Lawrence Farm
Tanfield Stud Farm
Tolmers Park Farm
87
TOLMERS MS
TOLMERS PK
VILLAGE
DARNICLE HILL
Nursery
Newgate Street Bridge
HAMMOND STREET
SHAMBROOK
NIGHTINGALE
DAHLIA CL
DH
DJ
DK
DL
DM
DN
DP
29
30
31
16
17
18
19
20
21
22
23
24
09
08
07
06

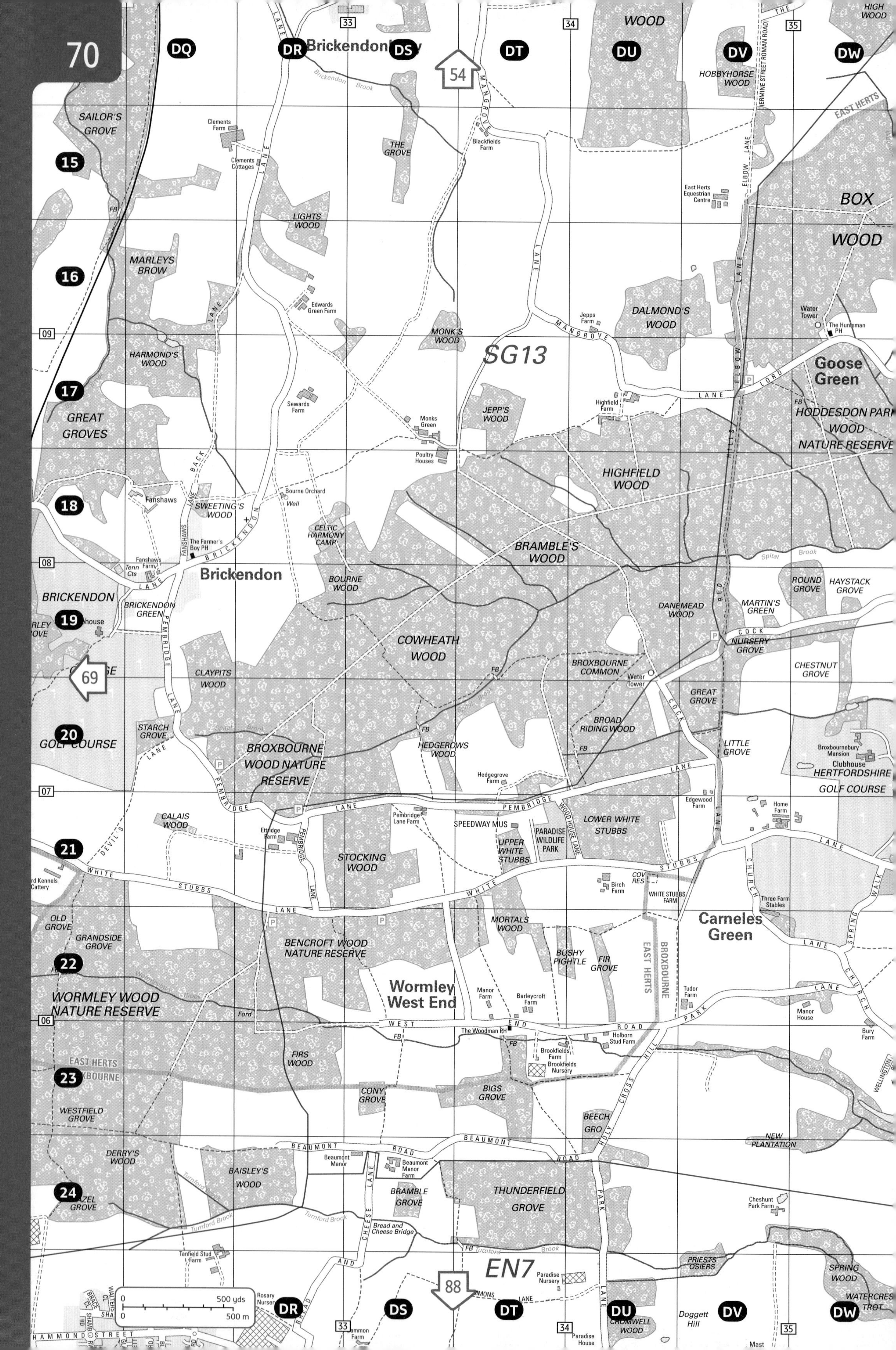

DQ
DR
Brickendonbury
DS
DT
DU
DV
DW
54
WOOD
HIGH WOOD
HOBBYHORSE WOOD
SAILOR'S GROVE
Clements Farm
Clements Cottages
THE GROVE
Blackfields Farm
East Herts Equestrian Centre
LIGHTS WOOD
BOX WOOD
MARLEYS BROW
Edwards Green Farm
Water Tower
The Huntsman PH
DALMOND'S WOOD
Jepps Farm
MONK'S WOOD
HARMOND'S WOOD
SG13
Goose Green
GREAT GROVES
Sewards Farm
Monks Green
JEPP'S WOOD
Highfield Farm
HODDESDON PARK WOOD NATURE RESERVE
Poultry Houses
HIGHFIELD WOOD
Fanshaws
Bourne Orchard
Well
SWEETING'S WOOD
CELTIC HARMONY CAMP
The Farmer's Boy PH
BRAMBLE'S WOOD
Brickendon
BOURNE WOOD
ROUND GROVE
HAYSTACK GROVE
BRICKENDON
BRICKENDON GREEN
DANEMEAD WOOD
MARTIN'S GREEN
NURSERY GROVE
COWHEATH WOOD
69
CLAYPITS WOOD
BROXBOURNE COMMON
Water Tower
CHESTNUT GROVE
GREAT GROVE
STARCH GROVE
GOLF COURSE
BROAD RIDING WOOD
BROXBOURNE WOOD NATURE RESERVE
HEDGEROWS WOOD
LITTLE GROVE
Broxbournebury Mansion
Clubhouse
HERTFORDSHIRE GOLF COURSE
Hedgegrove Farm
CALAIS WOOD
Pembridge Lane Farm
SPEEDWAY MUS
PARADISE WILDLIFE PARK
LOWER WHITE STUBBS
Edgewood Farm
Home Farm
UPPER WHITE STUBBS
STOCKING WOOD
Birch Farm
WHITE STUBBS FARM
OLD GROVE
MORTALS WOOD
Carneles Green
Three Farm Stables
GRANDSIDE GROVE
BENCROFT WOOD NATURE RESERVE
BUSHY PIGHTLE
FIR GROVE
EAST HERTS
BROXBOURNE
Wormley West End
WORMLEY WOOD NATURE RESERVE
Manor Farm
Barleycroft Farm
Tudor Farm
Manor House
Bury Farm
The Woodman PH
Holborn Stud Farm
Brookfields Farm
Brookfields Nursery
FIRS WOOD
CONY GROVE
BIGS GROVE
WESTFIELD GROVE
BEECH GRO
NEW PLANTATION
DERRY'S WOOD
Beaumont Manor
Beaumont Manor Farm
BAISLEY'S WOOD
BRAMBLE GROVE
THUNDERFIELD GROVE
Cheshunt Park Farm
HAZEL GROVE
Bread and Cheese Bridge
Tanfield Stud Farm
PRIESTS OSIERS
EN7
Paradise Nursery
SPRING WOOD
88
Doggett Hill
CROMWELL WOOD
Paradise House
Mast
0 500 yds
0 500 m
15
16
17
18
19
20
21
22
23
24
09
08
07
06
33
34
35

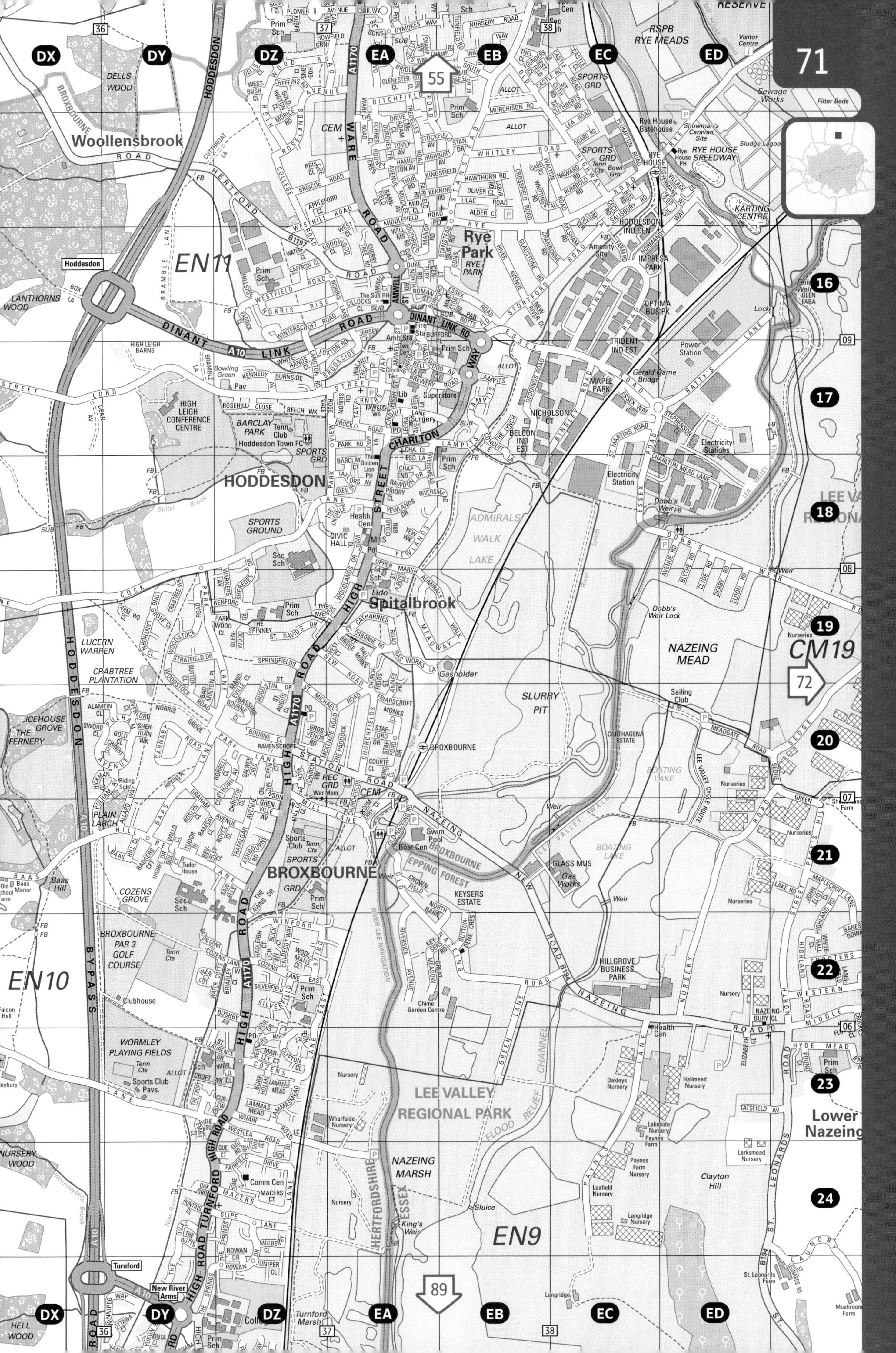
DX
DY
DZ
EA
EB
EC
ED
55
72
89
16
17
18
19
20
21
22
23
24
09
08
07
06
36
37
38
RSPB RYE MEADS
Woollensbrook
DELLS WOOD
HODDESDON
EN11
Rye Park
RYE HOUSE
RYE HOUSE SPEEDWAY
KARTING CENTRE
HODDESDON IND CEN
IMPRESA PARK
OPTIMA BUS PK
TRIDENT IND EST
Power Station
Gerald Game Bridge
NICHOLSON CT
BELCON IND EST
Electricity Stations
Electricity Station
Dobb's Weir
Dobb's Weir Lock
NAZEING MEAD
CM19
DINANT LINK ROAD
HIGH LEIGH CONFERENCE CENTRE
BARCLAY PARK
Hoddesdon Town FC
LANTHORNS WOOD
Hoddesdon
ADMIRALS WALK LAKE
Spitalbrook
SLURRY PIT
LUCERN WARREN
CRABTREE PLANTATION
ICEHOUSE GROVE
THE FERNERY
BROXBOURNE
Gasholder
CARTHAGENA ESTATE
BOATING LAKE
LEE VALLEY CYCLE ROUTE
Sailing Club
GLASS MUS
Gas Works
KEYSERS ESTATE
EPPING FOREST
HILLGROVE BUSINESS PARK
COZENS GROVE
BROXBOURNE PAR 3 GOLF COURSE
EN10
WORMLEY PLAYING FIELDS
LEE VALLEY REGIONAL PARK
NAZEING MARSH
FLOOD RELIEF CHANNEL
RIVER LEE NAVIGATION
HERTFORDSHIRE
ESSEX
King's Weir
Sluice
EN9
Lower Nazeing
Clayton Hill
Turnford
New River Arms
Turnford Marsh
HELL WOOD
NURSERY WOOD
HODDESDON BYPASS
A10
A1170
B194
B1197

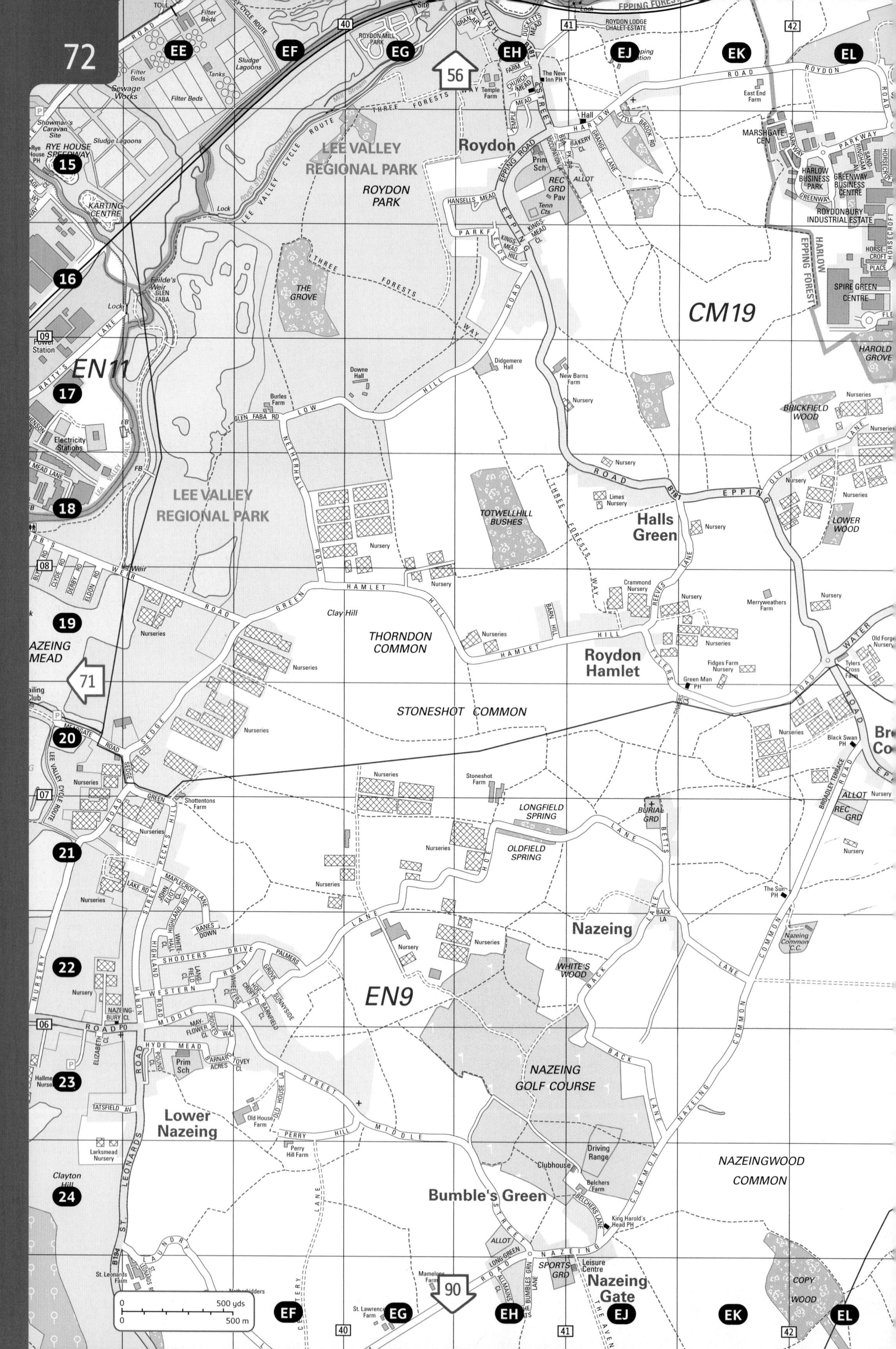

EE
EF
EG
EH
EJ
EK
EL
56
Roydon
LEE VALLEY REGIONAL PARK
ROYDON PARK
THE GROVE
EN11
CM19
HARLOW BUSINESS PARK
GREENWAY BUSINESS CENTRE
ROYDONBURY INDUSTRIAL ESTATE
SPIRE GREEN CENTRE
HAROLD GROVE
BRICKFIELD WOOD
LOWER WOOD
Halls Green
TOTWELLHILL BUSHES
THORNDON COMMON
Clay Hill
Roydon Hamlet
STONESHOT COMMON
NAZEING MEAD
71
LONGFIELD SPRING
OLDFIELD SPRING
Nazeing
WHITE'S WOOD
EN9
NAZEING GOLF COURSE
Lower Nazeing
Bumble's Green
NAZEINGWOOD COMMON
Nazeing Gate
COPY WOOD
90
500 yds
500 m

BROOK GOLF COURSE
HARLOW STADIUM
Harlow Town FC
OAK WOOD
Little Parndon
PRINCESS ALEXANDRA HOSPITAL
57
Netteswell
CM20
Harlow College
HARLOW
Harvey Centre
CIVIC CEN
WATER GARDENS
Crown Gate Roundabout
SECOND AVENUE
A1025
THE MOORS
LONG LEY
NETTLESWELL PLANTATION
Pinnacles
GlaxoSmith Kline
COLDHARBOUR PINNACLES ESTATE
CRAMMOND PARK
HARLOW BUSINESS CENTRE
Whitehall Roundabout
Hare Street
THIRD AVENUE
NEW FRONTIERS SCIENCE PARK
Great Parndon
PARNDON WOOD
ELIZABETH WAY
A1169
CM18
PLAYING FIELD
Passmores House
Passmores
Brays Grove
Tye Green
BUSH FAIR PLAYING FIELDS
Katherines
UPPER WOOD
SOUTHERN WAY
Staple Tye Shop Cen
Stewards
THE LATTON BUSH CENTRE
Latton Bush
Sumners
Leisure Centre
BURNETT'S WOOD
MAUND'S WOOD
74
Kingsmoor
PARNDON WOOD CEM
PARNDON WOOD NATURE RESERVE
RISDEN'S WOOD
HOSPITAL WOOD
Jacks Hatch
Rye Hill
HARLOW EPPING FOREST
Water Tower
Dorrington Farm
Rivetts Farm
Lodge Farm
THREE FORESTS WAY
CM16
Marles Farm
Sumners Farm
Travellers Friend PH
EPPING GREEN
Epping Green
Epping Green House
EPPING LONG GRN
B181
Cobbin's Brook
91
Epping Upland
Pinch Timber Farm
Hayleys Manor Farm
BARN MEADOW
UPLAND ROAD
Rose Farm
EM
EN
EP
EQ
ER
ES
ET
43
44
45
16
17
18
19
20
21
22
23
24
09
08
07
06

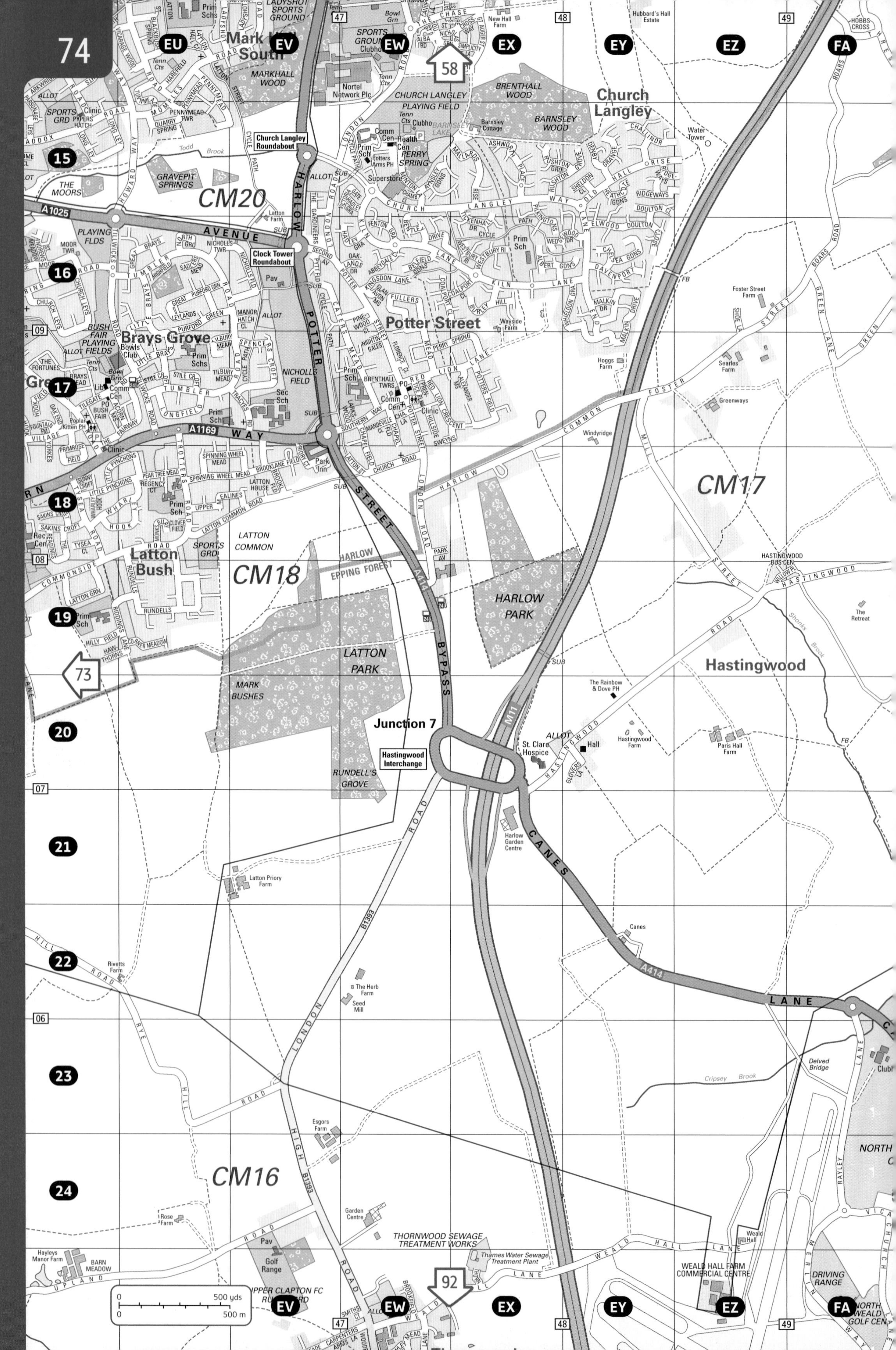
EU
EV
EW
EX
EY
EZ
FA
58
Mark Hall South
MARKHALL WOOD
Nortel Network Plc
CHURCH LANGLEY PLAYING FIELD
BRENTHALL WOOD
Church Langley
BARNSLEY WOOD
Barnsley Cottage
New Hall Farm
Hubbard's Hall Estate
HOBBS CROSS
Water Tower
Church Langley Roundabout
PERRY SPRING
Superstore
Potters Arms PH
GRAVEPIT SPRINGS
THE MOORS
CM20
A1025
AVENUE
HARLOW
Latton Farm
PLAYING FLDS
MOOR TWR
Clock Tower Roundabout
Pav
POTTER
Potter Street
Wayside Farm
Foster Street Farm
BUSH FAIR PLAYING FIELDS
Brays Grove
Bowls Club
Prim Schs
ALLOT
NICHOLLS FIELD
Sec Sch
Hoggs Farm
Searles Farm
Greenways
FOSTER
COMMON
Windyridge
A1169
WAY
Clinic
Park Inn
STREET
CHURCH ROAD
LATTON COMMON
CM18
Latton Bush
SPORTS GRD
HARLOW EPPING FOREST
HARLOW PARK
A414
CM17
HASTINGWOOD BUS CEN
HASTINGWOOD
The Retreat
ROAD
Hastingwood
The Rainbow & Dove PH
LATTON PARK
MARK BUSHES
BYPASS
73
Junction 7
Hastingwood Interchange
RUNDELL'S GROVE
M11
St. Clare Hospice
Hall
Hastingwood Farm
Paris Hall Farm
Harlow Garden Centre
CANES
Latton Priory Farm
B1393
Canes
Rivetts Farm
The Herb Farm
Seed Mill
LANE
Delved Bridge
Club
Cripsey Brook
LONDON
RYE HILL ROAD
HIGH
Esgors Farm
NORTH
CM16
Garden Centre
Rose Farm
THORNWOOD SEWAGE TREATMENT WORKS
Thames Water Sewage Treatment Plant
Pav
Golf Range
Hayleys Manor Farm
BARN MEADOW
UPLAND
WEALD HALL LANE
Weald Hall
WEALD HALL FARM COMMERCIAL CENTRE
DRIVING RANGE
NORTH WEALD GOLF CEN
92
0 500 yds
0 500 m
15
16
17
18
19
20
21
22
23
24
47
48
49
09
08
07
06

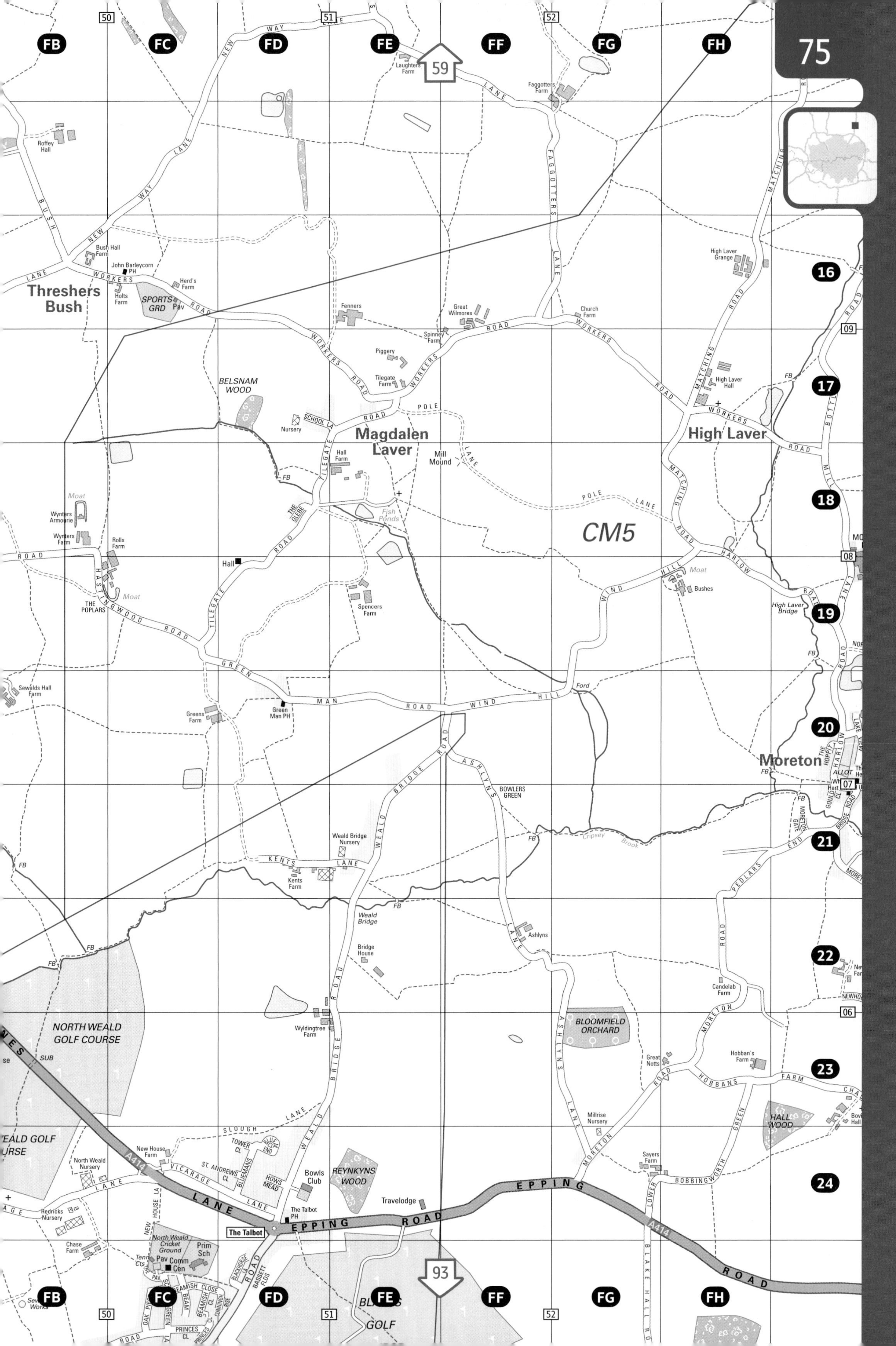

59
93
FB
FC
FD
FE
FF
FG
FH
50
51
52
16
17
18
19
20
21
22
23
24
09
08
07
06
Roffey Hall
Laughters Farm
Faggotters Farm
Threshers Bush
Bush Hall Farm
John Barleycorn PH
Herd's Farm
Holts Farm
SPORTS GRD
Pav
Fenners
Great Wilmores
Church Farm
High Laver Grange
Spinney Farm
Piggery
Tilegate Farm
High Laver Hall
BELSNAM WOOD
Nursery
Magdalen Laver
Hall Farm
Mill Mound
High Laver
Moat
Wynters Armourie
Wynters Farm
Rolls Farm
Fish Ponds
CM5
Hall
Bushes
THE POPLARS
Spencers Farm
High Laver Bridge
Sewalds Hall Farm
Greens Farm
Green Man PH
Ford
Moreton
ALLOT
BOWLERS GREEN
Weald Bridge Nursery
Cripsey Brook
Kents Farm
Weald Bridge
Ashlyns
Bridge House
Candelab Farm
NORTH WEALD GOLF COURSE
Wyldingtree Farm
BLOOMFIELD ORCHARD
Great Notts
Hobban's Farm
HALL WOOD
Millrise Nursery
New House Farm
North Weald Nursery
Bowls Club
REYNKYNS WOOD
Sayers Farm
Travelodge
The Talbot PH
The Talbot
Redricks Nursery
Chase Farm
North Weald Cricket Ground
Prim Sch
Pav
Comm Cen
Tenn Cts
GOLF
WORKERS ROAD
POLE LANE
MATCHING ROAD
HARLOW ROAD
WIND HILL
GREEN MAN ROAD
HASTINGWOOD ROAD
TILEGATE ROAD
THE GLEBE
SCHOOL LA
NEW WAY LANE
BUSH LANE
FAGGOTTERS LANE
WEALD BRIDGE ROAD
ASHLYNS LANE
KENTS LANE
PEDLARS END
MORETON ROAD
HOBBANS FARM
GREEN
BOBBINGWORTH
LOWER
BLAKE HALL RD
MORETON GATE
EPPING ROAD
A414
VICARAGE LANE
SLOUGH LANE
TOWER CL
BLUE MAN END
ST. ANDREWS CL
BLUMANS
HOWS MEAD
LANE
NEW HOUSE LA
BASSETT FLDS
BEAMISH CLOSE
PRINCES CL
OAK PIECE
BEAM
CUNNINGHAM RISE

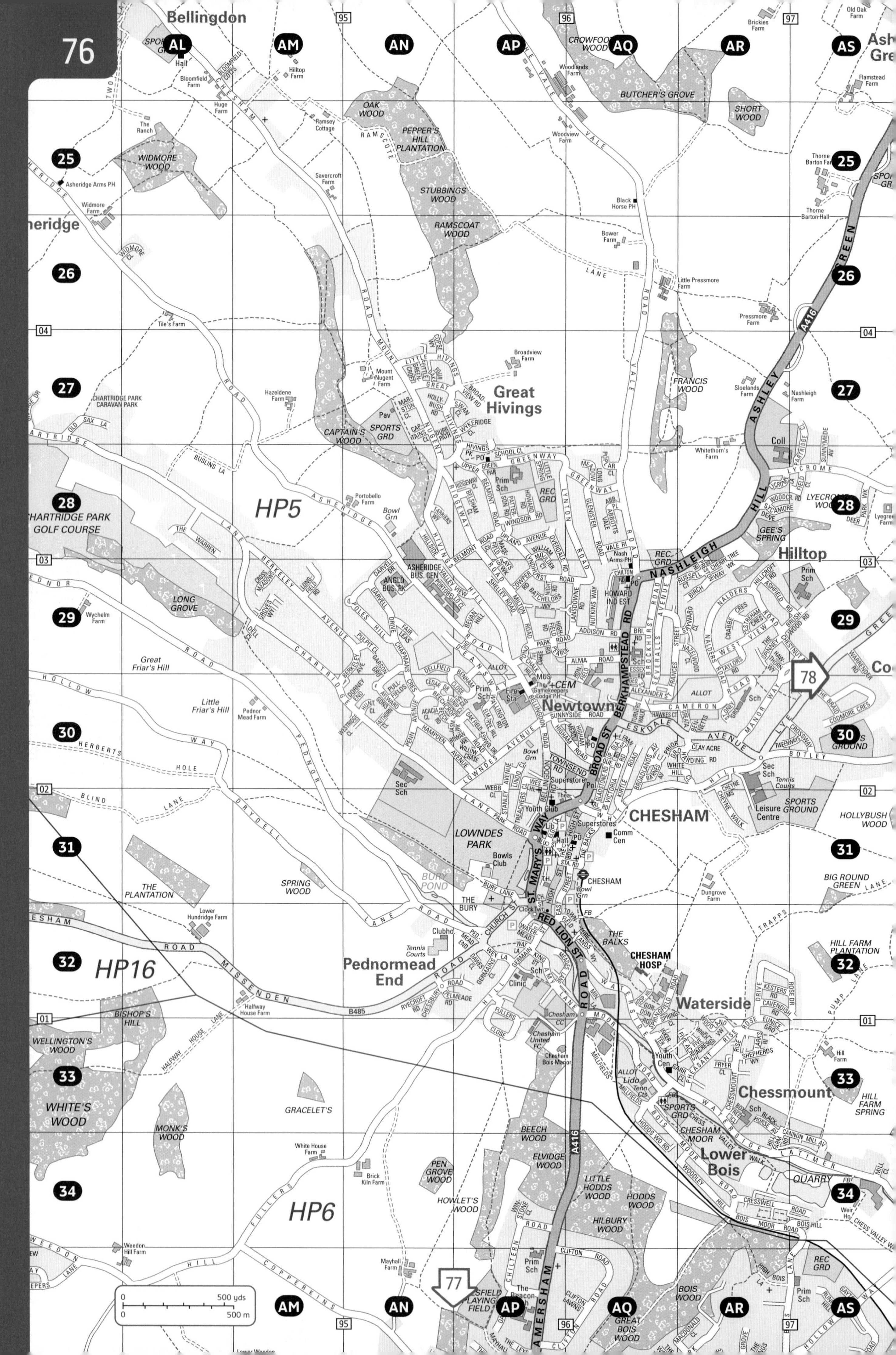
Bellingdon
AL
AM
AN
AP
AQ
AR
AS
95
96
97
Hall
Bloomfield Farm
Hilltop Farm
Huge Farm
The Ranch
Ramsey Cottage
OAK WOOD
PEPPER'S HILL PLANTATION
CROWFOOT WOOD
Woodlands Farm
BUTCHER'S GROVE
SHORT WOOD
Brickies Farm
Old Oak Farm
Flamstead Farm
Woodview Farm
WIDMORE WOOD
Asheridge Arms PH
Widmore Farm
Savercroft Farm
STUBBINGS WOOD
RAMSCOAT WOOD
Black Horse PH
Thorne Barton Farm
Thorne Barton Hall
Bower Farm
Little Pressmore Farm
Pressmore Farm
Tile's Farm
Broadview Farm
Mount Nugent Farm
Hazeldene Farm
CHARTRIDGE PARK CARAVAN PARK
Great Hivings
FRANCIS WOOD
Sloelands Farm
Nashleigh Farm
CAPTAIN'S WOOD
SPORTS GRD
Pav
Whitethorn's Farm
Coll
Portobello Farm
Bowl Grn
HP5
CHARTRIDGE PARK GOLF COURSE
ASHERIDGE BUS. CEN
ANGLO BUS. PK
Nash Arms PH
HOWARD IND EST
Hilltop
GEE'S SPRING
Lyegreen Farm
LONG GROVE
Wychelm Farm
Great Friar's Hill
Little Friar's Hill
Pednor Mead Farm
Newtown
Gamekeepers Lodge PH
CEM
MUS
Fire Sta
Prim Sch
78
Sec Sch
Superstore
Youth Club
CHESHAM
Superstores
Comm Cen
LOWNDES PARK
Bowls Club
BURY POND
THE BURY
SPRING WOOD
THE PLANTATION
Lower Hundridge Farm
Clock Twr
Tennis Courts
Leisure Centre
SPORTS GROUND
HOLLYBUSH WOOD
BIG ROUND GREEN
Dungrove Farm
THE BALKS
CHESHAM HOSP
HILL FARM PLANTATION
Pednormead End
HP16
Clubho.
Halfway House Farm
Clinic
Chesham CC
Chesham United FC
Chesham Bois Manor
Waterside
BISHOP'S HILL
WELLINGTON'S WOOD
B485
Youth Cen
Lido
Chessmount
HILL FARM SPRING
Hill Farm
WHITE'S WOOD
MONK'S WOOD
GRACELET'S
CHESHAM MOOR
BEECH WOOD
ELVIDGE WOOD
A416
Lower Bois
QUARRY
White House Farm
Brick Kiln Farm
PEN GROVE WOOD
HOWLET'S WOOD
LITTLE HODDS WOOD
HODDS WOOD
HILBURY WOOD
HP6
Weedon Hill Farm
Mayhall Farm
77
PLAYING FIELD
The Beacon
GREAT BOIS WOOD
BOIS WOOD
REC GRD
Prim Sch
500 yds
500 m
25
26
27
28
29
30
31
32
33
34
04
03
02
01
NASHLEIGH HILL
ASHLEY GREEN
BROAD ST
BERKHAMSTEAD RD
ST. MARY'S WAY
RED LION ST
AMERSHAM ROAD
MISSENDEN ROAD
ASHERIDGE ROAD
CHARTRIDGE LANE
PEDNOR ROAD
HOLLOW WAY
BOTLEY ROAD
LYCROME ROAD
WATERSIDE
FULLERS HILL
COPPERKINS LANE
CLIFTON ROAD

76
94
111
AMERSHAM
Amersham Old Town
Chesham Bois
Lower Bois
Coleshill
HP5
HP6
HP7
HP8
AMERSHAM HOSPITAL
WEEDONHILL WOOD
OSTLER'S WOOD
HUNDRED ACRES
BRENTFORD WOOD
RODGER'S WOOD
DAVID'S WOOD
PARSONAGE WOOD
HERVINES PARK
SPORTS GROUND
Crematorium
Superstore
AMERSHAM BYPASS
LONDON ROAD EAST
LONDON ROAD WEST
WOODSIDE ROAD
STATION ROAD
CHESHAM ROAD
GORE HILL
WHIELDEN LANE

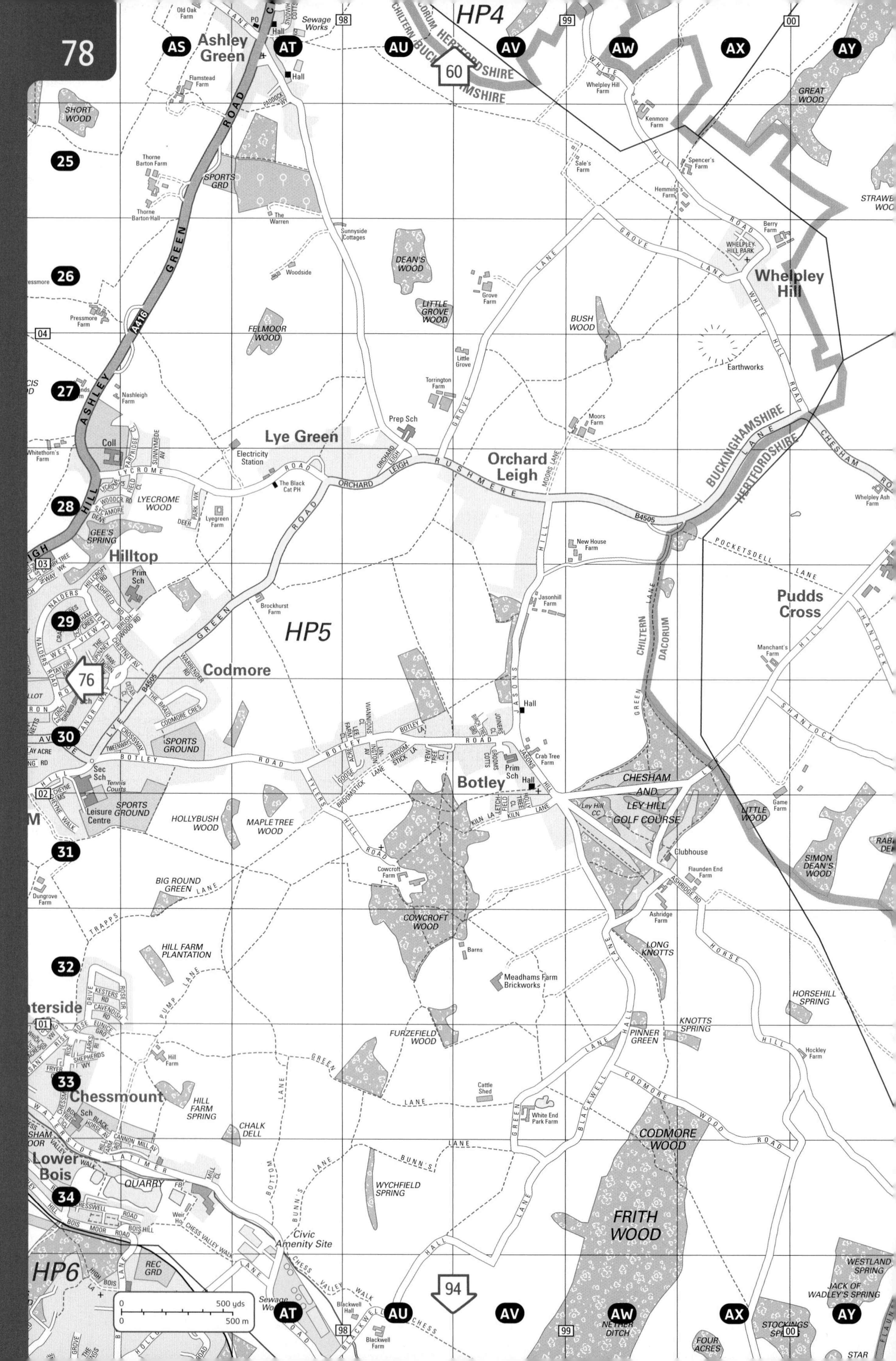

Ashley Green
HP4
HP5
HP6
Whelpley Hill
Lye Green
Orchard Leigh
Hilltop
Codmore
Botley
Pudds Cross
Chessmount
Lower Bois
CHILTERN
DACORUM
BUCKINGHAMSHIRE
HERTFORDSHIRE
SHORT WOOD
GREAT WOOD
DEAN'S WOOD
LITTLE GROVE WOOD
FELMOOR WOOD
BUSH WOOD
LYECROME WOOD
GEE'S SPRING
HOLLYBUSH WOOD
MAPLE TREE WOOD
BIG ROUND GREEN
COWCROFT WOOD
HILL FARM PLANTATION
LONG KNOTTS
HORSEHILL SPRING
FURZEFIELD WOOD
KNOTTS SPRING
PINNER GREEN
HILL FARM SPRING
CHALK DELL
CODMORE WOOD
WYCHFIELD SPRING
FRITH WOOD
WESTLAND SPRING
JACK OF WADLEY'S SPRING
SIMON DEAN'S WOOD
LITTLE WOOD
FOUR ACRES
CHESHAM AND LEY HILL GOLF COURSE
SPORTS GRD
SPORTS GROUND
REC GRD
QUARRY
Civic Amenity Site
Earthworks
Leisure Centre
Meadhams Farm Brickworks
60
76
94
500 yds
500 m

AZ
BA
BB
BC
BD
BE
BF
01
02
03
04
HANGING WOOD
Prep Sch
HAY WOOD
Clubhouse
COLESHILL WOOD
LITTLE HAY GOLF COMPLEX
Clubhouse
61
BOXMOOR GOLF COURSE
SHEETHANGER COMMON
Felden Lodge
Howe's Retreat
HP1
UPPER BOURNE END LANE
COVERED RESERVOIR
RAMACRE WOOD
GORSEFIELD WOOD
BOX LANE
BOX ROAD
B4505
BURY RISE
BURY WOOD
Longcroft Farm
LONGCROFT
SHOTHANGER WAY
BUSHFIELD ROAD
RAINHILL SPRING
RAINHILL DELL
KINGSHILL DELL
Macdonald Bobsleigh Hotel
Disused Airfield
H.M. THE MOUNT PRISON
Duckhall Farm
Honours Farm
HEMPSTEAD ROAD
Random Farm
HOMEFIELD SPRING
SHORTRIDGE WOOD
OLD DEAN
FLAUNDEN LANE
BULSTRODE LANE
26
27
28
29
30
31
32
33
34
STONEY LANE
Bury Farm
Lib
Sch
Hall
PO
CHURCH STREET
Lane Farm
Dormers
Nuffield Farm
RUCKLERS LANE
LONGCROFT LANE
CHIPPERFIELD ROAD
CHESHAM ROAD
Bovingdon
Rent Street Farm
Darley Ash
Street Farm
Greinan Farm
Bulstrode Farm
Bovingdon Grange
Grange Farm
Pav Bovingdon FC
rickworks
Cross Farm
HP3
Pav
BOVINGDON GREEN
Green Farm
Bryants Nurseries
BAKER'S WOOD
Bell Farm
Long Lane Farm
Wyevale Garden Centre
Tenements Farm
80
Stoney Lane Nursery
The Boot PH
Tuffs Farm
Frenches Farm
Chipperfield House
Riding School
Cottingham Farm
Mast
Meadow Way Farm
Shantock Nursery
Shantock Farm
Chiltern Farm
VENUS HILL
Venus Hill Dairy Farm
Crumlin Farm
Garden Centre
WD4
New Maulden Farm
Hogpits Bottom
HOLLY HEDGES LANE
WOODMAN'S WOOD
Prim Sch
Tenn Cts
ALLOT
Rose Farm
FIR WOOD
HOGPITS BOTTOM
Bricklayer's Arms PH
Woodman's Farm
OLLEBERRIE LANE
WINDMILL HILL
CHIPPERFIELD
LOWER PLANTATION
LITTLE WINDMILL HILL
Cherry Tree Farm
Stables
Sharlowe's Farm
Dale Farm
WD3
Olleberrie Farm
PENMAN'S GREEN
The Plough PH
Belsize
FLAUNDEN SPRING
Flaunden
Hall
FLAUNDEN LANE
Whitedell Farm
Hillmeads Farm
Springview Farm
LIMEDELL SPRING
Newhouse Farm
BRAGMANS LANE
Rose Hall Farm
DEBARDINE WOOD
ROSEHALL WOOD
PLOUGH WOOD
HILLMEADS SPRING
HANGING CROFT
Moonshine Farm
Great Sarratt Hall Farm
Great Sarratt Hall
Mast
R.A.F. Chenies
DACORUM
THREE RIVERS
TOP SPRING
OLDCROFT WOOD
LONG WOOD
95
DAFFODIL SPRING
Martin Top Farm
BRAMBLE
HANGINGLANE WOOD
The Boot PH

Felden
HP3
Apsley
SHENDISH MANOR
GOLF COURSE
SHENDISH MANOR
CONFERENCE CENTRE
APSLEY MILLS
RETAIL PARK
Superstore
Holiday Inn
Express
GRAND UNION CANAL
LONDON ROAD
A4251
A41
LANGLEY BYPASS
KINGS LANGLEY BYPASS
HEMPSTEAD ROAD
GREAT WOOD
PHASELS WOOD
Phasels Wood
Activity Centre
OLD
DEAN
RUCKLERS LANE
BARNES LANE
BULSTRODE LANE
FEATHERBED LANE
HIGHCROFT ROAD
Felden
Lodge
Howe's
Retreat
Tower
Farm
Felden
Grange
Felden
Manor
Three Fields
Farm
COCK'S
HEAD
WOOD
HEN'S HEAD
WOOD
THE
COURTYARD
RUCKLERS
WOOD
DARK
WOOD
MERCEYS
WOOD
THE
HANGINGS
THE
NUCKET
Badgerdell
Barnes
Farm
Barnes
Lodge
Eagle Inn
PH
SCATTERDELLS
WOOD
THE
GROVE
THE
WINGS
KING LANGLEY
COMMON
Kings
Langley
C.C.
Sec
Sch
Prim Sch
Premier
Travel Inn
Hill
Farm
Priory
(Remains of)
Rectory Farm
Kings
Langley
CHIPPERFIELD ROAD
Meggacres
Farm
Whippendell
Farm
Whippendell
Bottom
Whippendell
Hill
Ballspond
Farm
Kings Langley
Riding School
Garden
Centre
Chipperfield
Prim
Sch
Two Brewers PH
War
Mem
Chipperfield
CC
Rose
Farm
WD4
ROOKERY
WOOD
Manor House
Berrybush Farm
Sunbury Hill
Farm
LANGLEY LODGE LANE
Burlew Farm
Middle
Farm
Langley
Lodge
Langley Lodge Farm
Wayside Farm
CHIPPERFIELD COMMON
PENMAN'S
GREEN
Belsize
DACORUM
THREE RIVERS
Hillmeads
Farm
Callipers
Hall
Callipers
Hall Farm
Cart &
Horses PH
QUICKMOOR LANE
Baytree Farm
DEBARDINE
WOOD
PLOUGH WOOD
HILLMEADS
SPRING
Commonwood
Dellfield
COMMONWOOD
COMMON
Bucks Hill Farm
Bucks
Hill
BUCKS HILL
BERRYBUSHES
WOOD
BERRYBUSHES
WOOD
DELLSHOT
SPRING
Model Farm
SHEEPCOTE
SPRING
HAWK
SPRING
BEECHEN
BOTTOM
Little
Westwood
Farm
Great
Sarratt Hall
Sarratt
The
Boot PH
M25
62
79
96
BG
BH
BJ
BK
BL
BM
BN
25
26
27
28
29
30
31
32
33
34
04
03
02
01
05
06
07
500 yds
500 m

BP
BQ
BR
BS
BT
BU
BV
63
POTTERS CROUCH PLANTATION
LONG DEANS
HP3
Highwood Hall Farm
High Herts Farm
Bedmond House
Rose Acre
Sports Hall
Radio Station
Hyde Meadow Farm
HYDE LANE SPRING
Hyde Springs
Hyde Farm
Pimlico House
Little Abbots
NEW PLANTATION
Hyde Lane Farm
Hart Hall Farm
Hart Hall
Green End Farm
White House Farm
Woodlands Poultry Farm
Leewood Farm
Verulam Farm
NEWLANDS PARK
WELLFIELD SPRING
DEADMAN WOOD
BEDMOND WOOD
White Hart PH
Whitehouse Farm
PIECORNER WOOD
HANGING WOOD
FURZEFIELD WOOD
JOB'S WOOD
Bedmond
Hilltop Farm
HIGH VIEW CARAVAN PARK
MOOR WOOD
BEDMOND PLAYING FIELDS
Prim Sch
Bell Inn PH
Ninnings Farm
Poultry Farm
Millhouse Farm
Searches Farm
LONG SPRING
Benmore Farm
Glasshouse
GREAT NOTLEY
Tenements Farm
WD5
M25
Junction 21A
STOWES WOOD
Numbers Farm
KINGLEY PK
LONG WOOD
Mansion House Farm
LITTLE NOTLEY
COV RES
ST. ALBANS THREE RIVERS
82
Fishing Club
ROUND WOOD
Wind Turbine & Renewable Energy Systems
KINGS LANGLEY
CEM
Lib
Fortunes Farm
BLOOM WOOD
ABBOTS LANGLEY
MANOR HOUSE GROUNDS
Youth Cen
Pol
ALLOT
LEAVESDEN CT
Clinic
TANNERS WOOD
LEAVESDEN COUNTRY PARK
Junction 20
WATFORD ROAD
GRAND UNION CANAL
Hall
Prim Sch
Health Cen
Comm Cen
WOODSIDE STADIUM
Leisure Cen
HILL FARM IND EST
WD25
ALBAN WOOD
WOODSIDE PLAYING FIELDS
Hunton Bridge
SOUTH WAY PLAYING FLD
Tennis Courts
Bowl Grn
Woodside
Watford Town C.C.
Cinema
Leisure Park
The Waterside PH
Leavesden Studios
Hunton Park
Langleybury
THE ROOKERY
SPORTS GROUND
Langleybury Children's Farm
A41
A405
NORTH ORBITAL ROAD
Medical Cen
Home Farm
Leavesden Green
Kingswood
KINGSWAY
97
Airshafts
REC
Garston
NORTH WATFORD CEMETERY
STANBOROUGH PARK
WESTERN AVENUE
Hunton Bridge
M1

APPSPOND WOOD
PARK WOOD
Westfields Farm
BW
BX
BY
BZ
CA
CB
CC
64
Holly Bush PH
Potters Crouch East Farm
Potters Crouch Farm
SQUARE WOOD
SCRUBBS WOOD
Cuckman's Farm
RAGGED HALL LANE
BEDMOND LANE
ROBERT
WARREN RD
BUTT FIELD VIEW
WATLING STREET
ALLOT
REC GRD
Prim Sch
ST. JULIAN'S WOOD
WATLING STREET CARAVAN SITE (TRAVELLERS)
Potters Crouch
25
WELLFIELD SPRING
CHISWELL GREEN LANE
FURZEBUSHES LANE
Plaistowes Farm
GREENWOOD PARK
Pavs
Tennis Courts
Three Hammers PH
Royal Entemological Society
Bone Hill
RNRS GDNS OF THE ROSE
Chiswellgreen Farm
AL2
26
WHITEHOUSE LANE
Chiswell Green
TIPPENDELL LANE
04
Whitehouse Farm
Noke Farm
Noke Lane Business Centre
Thistle
NOKE LANE
BLUNTS LANE
WATFORD ROAD
NORTH ORBITAL ROAD
A405
MAYFLOWER ROAD
How Wood
Burston Manor Farm
Moat
Garden Cen
Birchwood Farm
Burston Nursery
Prim Sch
27
HOLT WOOD
Holt Farm
Millhouse Farm
Searches Farm
SEARCHES LANE
LYE LANE
BIRCH WOOD
Open air pool
SPIELPLATZ
Tennis Courts
28
Tenements Farm
WD5
M25
M1
Junction 21A
SUNFOLKS
Kettlewell Farm
Lye House
Clubhouse
Cricket Ground
03
Junction 21 M25
Junction 6A M1
WINCH HILL WOOD
Bricket Wood
29
BLACKGREEN WOOD
GRAVEL PIT
ST. ALBANS
THREE RIVERS
81
BLACKGREEN WOOD
SMUG OAK GREEN BUSINESS CENTRE
HORSESHOE BUSINESS PARK
Social Club
30
CHEQUERS LANE
Junction 6
Fortunes Farm
Waterdale
SMUG OAK GREEN
The Gate PH
SMUG OAK LANE
Pav
BLOOM WOOD
Prim Sch
BRICKET WOOD
SPORTS GROUND
THE LAKES
Sports Centre
02
31
Sec Sch
Sports Centre
BENSKINS SPORTS GRD
Household Waste Centre
Depot
Crem
Brookdell Farm
NOTTLERS WOOD
Nottlers House
BRICKET WOOD
Lib
Pumping Sta
ELMS LANE
PENFOLD PARK GOLF COURSE
BUILDING RESEARCH ESTABLISHMENT
SPORTS GRD
JACK WILLIAM'S WOOD
WD25
Sec Sch
32
Sec Sch
Garston Manor Sch
NEW PLANTATION
Site of Roman Villa
BUCKNALLS LANE
01
Prim Sch
COMMON
WOODSIDE STADIUM
Leisure Cen
PITCH
Prim Sch
MUTCHETTS WOOD
WD25
33
WOODSIDE PLAYING FIELDS
Watford Town C.C.
Three Horseshoes PH
Little Munden Farm
River Colne
Premier Inn
Leisure Park
A405
KINGSWAY
ST. ALBANS ROAD
COLDHARBOUR PLANTATION
FOUR ACRE PLANTATION
GARSTON PARK
CRAB WOOD
Munden
PEARTREE WOOD
Ford
34
Medical Cen
GARSTON PARK PARADE
ST. ALBANS
HERTSMERE
Kingswood
A412
MUNDEN SPRING
Munden House
Sch
GARSTON
98
0 500 yds
0 500 m
Sch
BX
BY
BZ
CA
CB
CC
12
13
14
STANBOROUGH PARK
Meriden

AL1
AL4
AL2
WD7
Park Street
Frogmore
Colney Street
LONDON COLNEY
RADLETT
SHENLEY PARK
NORTH ORBITAL ROAD
NORTH ORBITAL COMMERCIAL PARK
LONDON ROAD
CHALKDELL WOOD
Hedges Farm
VERULAMIANS RFC
COLUMBANS SPORTS GRD
SPORTS GROUND
Radlett Aerodrome (Disused)
GRAVEL PIT
BROAD COLNEY LAKES NATURE RESERVE
Broad Colney Bridge
River Colne
Fir Tree Farm
ALL SAINTS PASTORAL CENTRE
QUARRY
COLNEY PARK
VENTURA PARK
PARK IND EST
CARU PARK
FROGMORE HOME PARK
Premier Inn
Colney Street Farm
The George & Dragon PH
Old Parkbury
Harper Lane Rail Depot
HARPERBURY HOSPITAL
RADLETT GOLF CENTRE
HOUND'S WOOD
NINE ACRES
Houndswood Farm
Harper Lodge Farm and Stables
Netherwylde Farm
Hill Farm
Oakridge Lane Sewage Treatment Works
PORTERS PARK GOLF COURSE
SAND PLANTATION
The Shenley Cricket Centre
COW BANKS
RIVERSIDE ESTATE
WATLING STREET
RADLETT ROAD
M25
A5183
B556
B5378
A414
A1081
65
84
99
CD
CE
CF
CG
CH
CJ
CK
26
27
28
29
30
31
32
33
34
15
16
17
04
03
02
01

CT
CU
CV
CW
CX
CY
CZ
67
North Mymms
NORTH MYMMS PARK
North Mymms Park Training Centre
Water End
The Woodman Inn PH
The Old Maypole PH
BRICK KILN WOOD
PELPIN'S WOOD
BROOKMANS PARK GOLF COURSE
BROOKMANS PARK
26
27
28
29
30
31
32
33
34
GOBIONS OPEN SPACE
GOBIONS GARDEN
GOBIONS POND
AL9
Blue Bridge
Deep Bottom
SWALLOW HOLES
CANGSLEY WOOD
Royal Veterinary College (Hawkshead)
HAWKSHEAD WOOD
MYMMSHALL WOOD
WELWYN HATFIELD
HERTSMERE
SPORTS GROUND
PILVAGE WOOD
Royal Veterinary College (Boltons Park Farm)
Site of Motte & Baileys
POTTERS BAR GOLF COURSE
86
THE ENTERPRISE CENTRE
FURZEFIELD WOOD
CRANBORNE INDUSTRIAL ESTATE
KING GEORGE V PLAYING FLDS
Warrengate Farm
Mimms Hall Farm
Windmore Hall
Town Farm
Black Horse PH
The White Hart PH
South Mimms
EN6
POTTERS BAR
Wyllyotts Cen & Mus
Bridgefoot
Bridgefoot House
Dugdale Hill
Rydal Mount
Rydal Mount Stables
Premier Inn South Mimms
Bignell's Corner
South Mimms Services
Days Inn
Cancer Research UK
Nat Inst for Biological Standards & Control
Blanche Farm
Junction 23 (M25) Junction 1 A1(M)
101
M25
A1(M)
Elm Farm
Bentley Heath Farm
Bentley Heath
Garden Centre
22
23
24

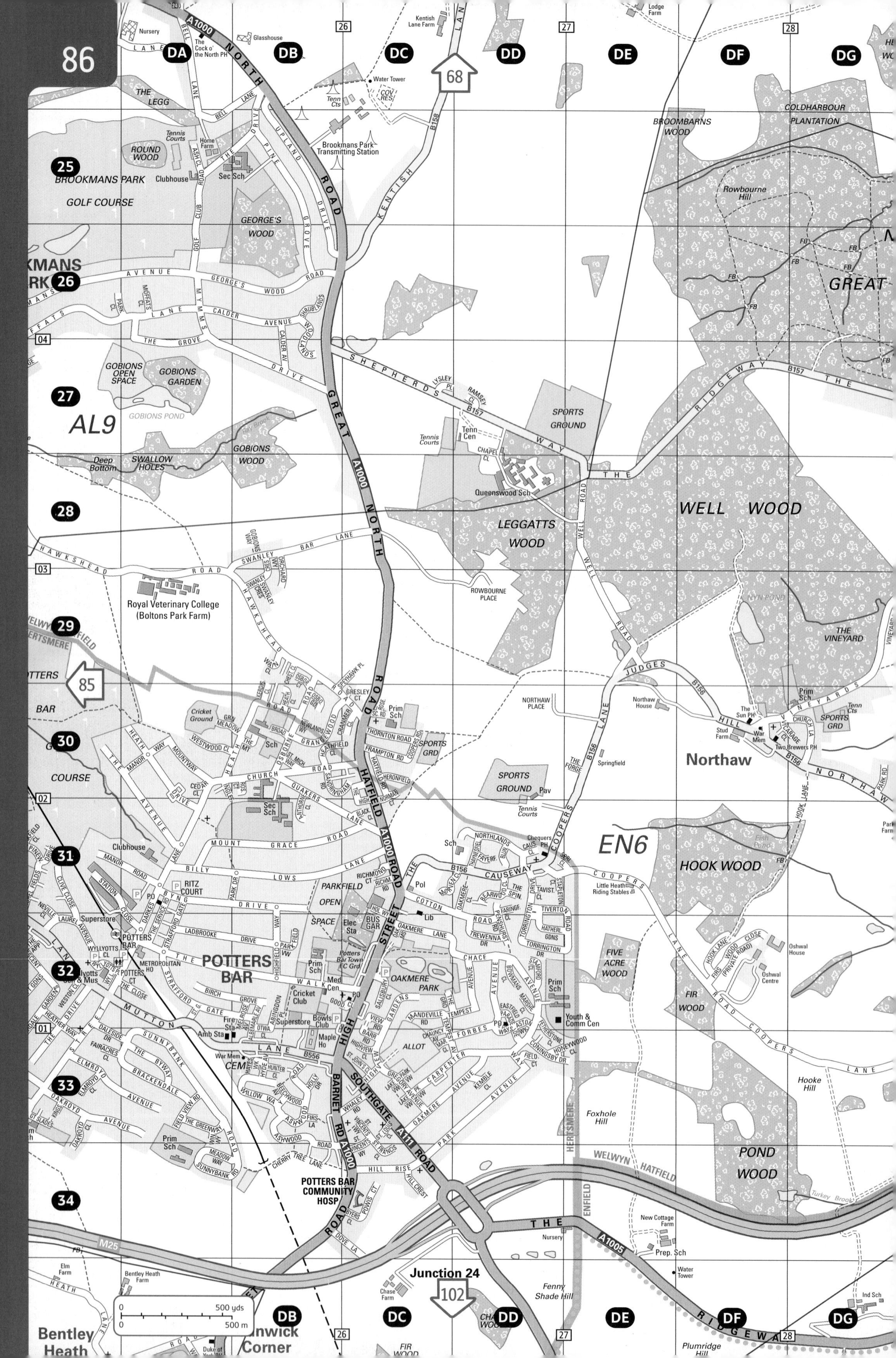

68
85
102
DA
DB
DC
DD
DE
DF
DG
25
26
27
28
29
30
31
32
33
34
BROOKMANS PARK
GOLF COURSE
THE LEGG
ROUND WOOD
GEORGE'S WOOD
Brookmans Park Transmitting Station
Water Tower
Kentish Lane Farm
Lodge Farm
BROOMBARNS WOOD
COLDHARBOUR PLANTATION
Rowbourne Hill
GREAT
AL9
GOBIONS OPEN SPACE
GOBIONS GARDEN
GOBIONS POND
GOBIONS WOOD
Deep Bottom
SWALLOW HOLES
SHEPHERDS WAY
SPORTS GROUND
Queenswood Sch
LEGGATTS WOOD
WELL WOOD
ROWBOURNE PLACE
Royal Veterinary College (Boltons Park Farm)
HAWKSHEAD ROAD
GREAT NORTH ROAD
A1000
THE RIDGEWAY
B157
B156
NORTHAW PLACE
Northaw House
Northaw
THE VINEYARD
NYN POND
SPORTS GROUND
Tennis Courts
EN6
HOOK WOOD
Little Heath Riding Stables
FIVE ACRE WOOD
FIR WOOD
Oshwal House
Oshwal Centre
POTTERS BAR
PARKFIELD OPEN SPACE
OAKMERE PARK
Cricket Club
Superstore
Youth & Comm Cen
COURSE
Foxhole Hill
Hooke Hill
POND WOOD
WELWYN HATFIELD
HERTSMERE
ENFIELD
M25
A1005
Junction 24
POTTERS BAR COMMUNITY HOSP
New Cottage Farm
Prep. Sch
Water Tower
Fenny Shade Hill
Bentley Heath Farm
Elm Farm
Chase Farm
Bentley Heath
Ganwick Corner
Plumridge Hill
500 yds
500 m

DH
DJ
DK
DL
DM
DN
DP
GOLF COURSE
Clubhouse
Newgate Street
69
Boswell's Livery Stabl
LONG GROVE
HAZEL GROVE
CALVES CROFT
NEW PARK ROAD
Prim Sch
Hall
PO
REC GRD
Tenn Cts
Home Farm
SG13
NEWGATE STREET VILLAGE
Tolmers Park Farm
Tolmers Park
St. Lawrence Farm
Tanfield Stud
Darnicle Hill Nursery
DARNICLE HILL
HAMMOND STREET
Newgate Street Bridge
SHAMBROOK
NORTHAW
Justice Hill
Postern Bridge
CARBONE HILL
Burleigh Farm
WOOD
Grimes Bottom
Cuffley Camp
26
Ashfield Nurseries
WORMLEY WOOD
Tolmers Scout Camp
TOLMERS ROAD
HOME WOOD
Nursery
Theobold Nursery
04
BROOKSIDE
HOMEWOOD
TOLMERS
27
Elm Farm
RIDGEWAY
Carbone Bottom
BRADGATE
FARM CL
CHESHUNT COMMON
Springfield Nursery
Weald View Nursery
HANDPOST HILL ROAD
Nyn Manor Farm
THE RIDGEWAY
B157
HANYARDS
HIGHFIELDS
THE DRIVEWAY
FOXES LA
STARLING LA
THE MEADWAY
Prim Sch
WOODLAND WY
ROBINSON AVENUE
28
House Farm
Goff's Oak PH
SPORTS GRD
Surgery
THE DRIVE
03
Thornton's Farm
PLOUGH
Cuffley Hills Farm
Cuffley
Brook Farm
CUFFLEY HILL
B156
PEMBROKE DRIVE
ISABELLE CL
Hempshill Brook
FB
Health Cen
Lib
Hall
CUFFLEY
STATION ROAD
Youth Cen
MOORHURST AV
29
KING JAMES AV
JAMES AVENUE
CHURCH
EAST
Goffs Oak
Prim Sch
Poyndon Farm
88
Temps Hill
KINGSWELL RIDE
BURLEIGH WAY
COLESDALE
THEOBALDS
Prim Sch
SOUTH DR
BROXBOURNE
WELWYN HATFIELD
BROADFIELDS
SILVER
EN7
ORCHID CL
30
Pumping Sta
JONES
Tenn Club
KING GEORGE'S FIELD
Clubho
Bowling Grn
Coles Hill
Wells Farm
NORTHAW ROAD
02
ROAD WEST
B156
Colesdale Farm
NORTHAW BROOK
Soper's Viaduct
BURNT FARM RIDE
Burnt Farm
31
CATTLEGATE HILL
OLD PARK
(PRIVATE ROAD)
NURSERY PLANTATION
Northaw Brook
CATTLEGATE WOOD
Robin Hill
CATTLINS
32
01
WOODGATE AV
OAKWELL DR
COOPERS LANE ROAD
Barvin Hill
Cattlegate Farm
Cattlegate
TILEKILN OSIERS
HERTFORDSHIRE
M25
33
CINDER ASH
Woodhurst Farm
Owls Hall Farm
Turkey Brook
HERTFORDSHIRE
M25
The Paddocks
Glasshouse
South Hill
Oak Hill Farm
Glasgow Stud
EN2
CATTLEGATE ROAD
34
Holly Hill Farm
CREWS HILL
Garden Centre
Culver Garden Centre
Country World
Nursery
Sloeman's Farm
Clubhouse
Woldens Nursery & Garden Centre
Browns of Crews Hill Nurseries
WHITEWEBBS
103
CREWS HILL GOLF COURSE
Woldens Nurseries
ROSEWOOD DR
WROXHAM GDNS
CYPRESS AV
Crews Hill
WHITEWEBBS WOOD
ST. NICHOLAS HO
29
30
31

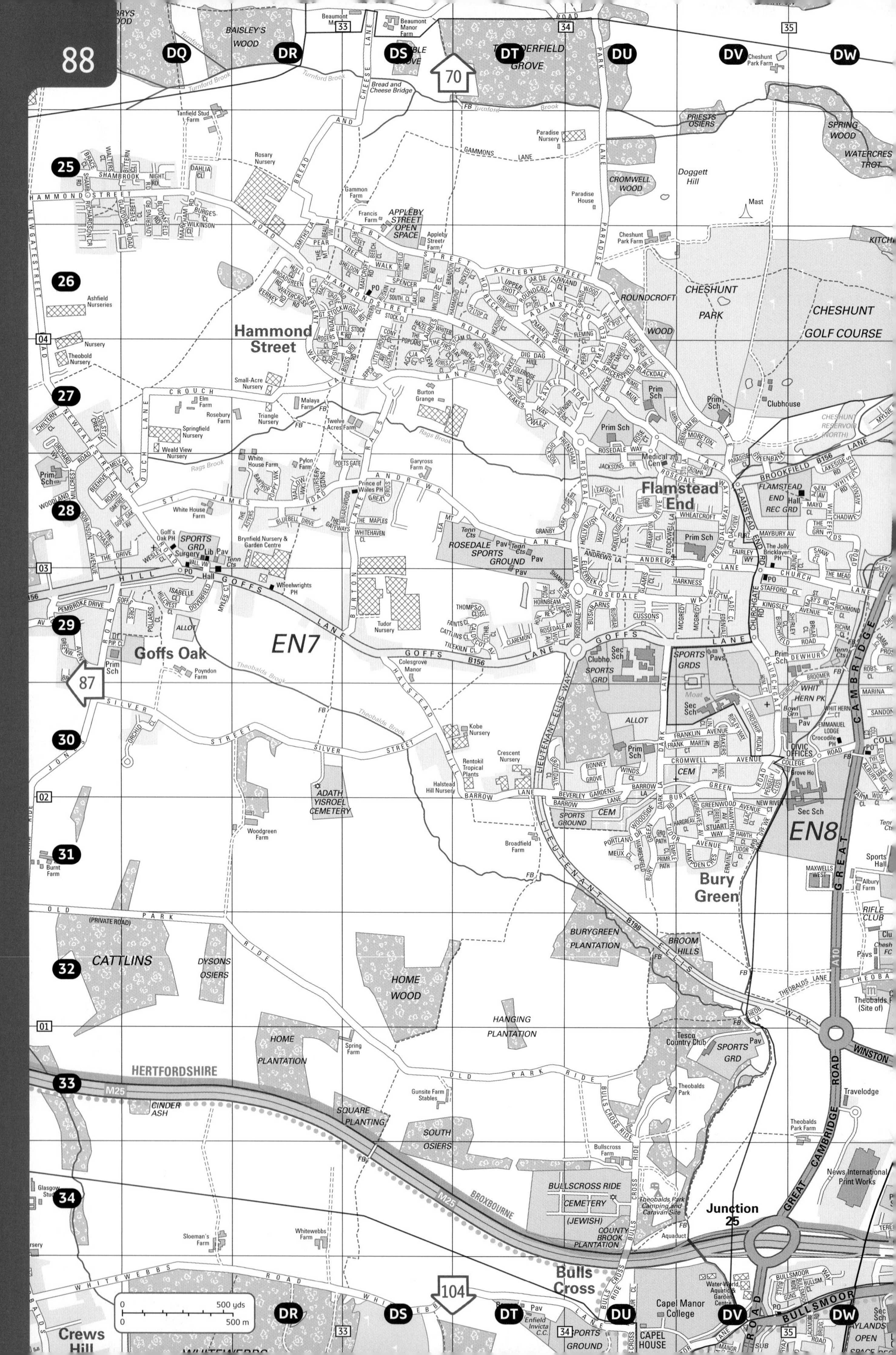

DQ
DR
DS
DT
DU
DV
DW
70
87
104
BAISLEY'S WOOD
Turnford Brook
Beaumont Manor Farm
Bread and Cheese Bridge
PRIESTS OSIERS
SPRING WOOD
WATERCRESS TROT
GAMMONS LANE
Paradise Nursery
Tanfield Stud Farm
Rosary Nursery
Gammon Farm
Doggett Hill
CROMWELL WOOD
Paradise House
Mast
Cheshunt Park Farm
APPLEBY STREET OPEN SPACE
Appleby Street Farm
Francis Farm
HAMMOND STREET
APPLEBY STREET
ROUNDCROFT
CHESHUNT PARK
WOOD
CHESHUNT GOLF COURSE
Hammond Street
Ashfield Nurseries
Nursery
Theobold Nursery
Small-Acre Nursery
CROUCH LANE
Elm Farm
Malaya Farm
Burton Grange
Rosebury Farm
Triangle Nursery
Twelve Acres Farm
Springfield Nursery
Weald View Nursery
Rags Brook
Clubhouse
CHESHUNT RESERVOIR (NORTH)
White House Farm
Pylon Farm
Garyross Farm
Prince of Wales PH
ST JAMES ROAD
ANDREWS LANE
Flamstead End
FLAMSTEAD END REC GRD
White House Farm
Goff's Oak PH
SPORTS GRD
Surgery
Brynfield Nursery & Garden Centre
ROSEDALE SPORTS GROUND
Wheelwrights PH
GOFFS LANE
Tudor Nursery
EN7
Goffs Oak
Poyndon Farm
Colesgrove Manor
Theobalds Brook
B156
SPORTS GRDS
Moat
Sec Sch
ALLOT
Kobe Nursery
SILVER STREET
Crescent Nursery
Rentokil Tropical Plants
Halstead Hill Nursery
ADATH YISROEL CEMETERY
Woodgreen Farm
Broadfield Farm
BARROW LANE
LIEUTENANT ELLIS WAY
CEM
Bury Green
EN8
Sec Sch
CIVIC OFFICES
Burnt Farm
OLD PARK RIDE
(PRIVATE ROAD)
CATTLINS
DYSONS OSIERS
BURYGREEN PLANTATION
BROOM HILLS
HOME WOOD
HANGING PLANTATION
B198
THEOBALDS LANE
Theobalds (Site of)
HOME PLANTATION
Spring Farm
Tesco Country Club
SPORTS GRD
WINSTON
HERTFORDSHIRE
M25
CINDER ASH
SQUARE PLANTING
Gunsite Farm Stables
SOUTH OSIERS
Theobalds Park
Travelodge
Theobalds Park Farm
GREAT CAMBRIDGE ROAD
A10
Bullscross Farm
BULLSCROSS RIDE
CEMETERY (JEWISH)
Theobalds Park Camping and Caravan Site
COUNTY BROOK PLANTATION
BROXBOURNE
Junction 25
News International Print Works
Glasgow Stud
Sloeman's Farm
Whitewebbs Farm
Aquaduct
WHITEWEBBS ROAD
Bulls Cross
Water World, Aquatic & Garden Centre
Capel Manor College
CAPEL HOUSE
BULLSMOOR LANE
Enfield Invicta C.C.
SPORTS GROUND
Crews Hill
0 500 yds
0 500 m
25
26
27
28
29
30
31
32
33
34
33
34
35

Wormley
NAZEING MARSH
HERTFORDSHIRE
ESSEX
EN10
Turnford
College
HOLYFIELD LAKE
LEE VALLEY REGIONAL PARK
Sailing Club
Holyfield Marsh
Holyfield Hall Farm
Elec Station
Lee Valley Park Farm & Information Service
Holyfield
Hayes Hill
THE NIGHTLEYS
NORTH METROPOLITAN PIT
SEVENTY ACRES LAKE
Cheshunt Lock
Grubbs Hill
HOMEFIELD WOOD
EN9
KENNEL WOOD
CHESHUNT
GRUNDY PARK
WALTHAM ABBEY WOODS
Cornmill Meadows
BOWYER'S WATER
ROYAL GUNPOWDER MILLS
WALTHAM CROSS
Waltham Marsh
Cheshunt Marsh
WALTHAM ABBEY (Ruins)
ABBEY GARDENS
LARSENS REC GRD
TOWN MEAD
Holdbrook
Freezywater
RAMMEY MARSH
CEM
SPORTS GROUND
HIGH ROAD TURNFORD
GREAT CAMBRIDGE RD
HODDESDON ROAD
HALFHIDE LANE
STATION ROAD
ELEANOR CROSS RD
MONARCHS WAY
MERIDIAN WAY
MOLLISON AVENUE
HOLYFIELD
CROOKED MILE
SEWARDSTONE RD
RIVER LEE NAVIGATION
LEA VALLEY WALK
A10
A121
A1055
B194
B176
M25
DX
DY
DZ
EA
EB
EC
ED
36
37
38
04
03
02
01
26
27
28
29
30
31
32
33
34
71
90
105

Bumble's Green
72
NAZEINGWOOD COMMON
Nazeing Gate
EN9
Aimes Green
Holyfield
Upshire
Copthall Green
WALTHAM ABBEY
89
106
GALLEYHILL WOOD
DEERPARK WOOD
STOCKING GROVE
WARLIES PARK

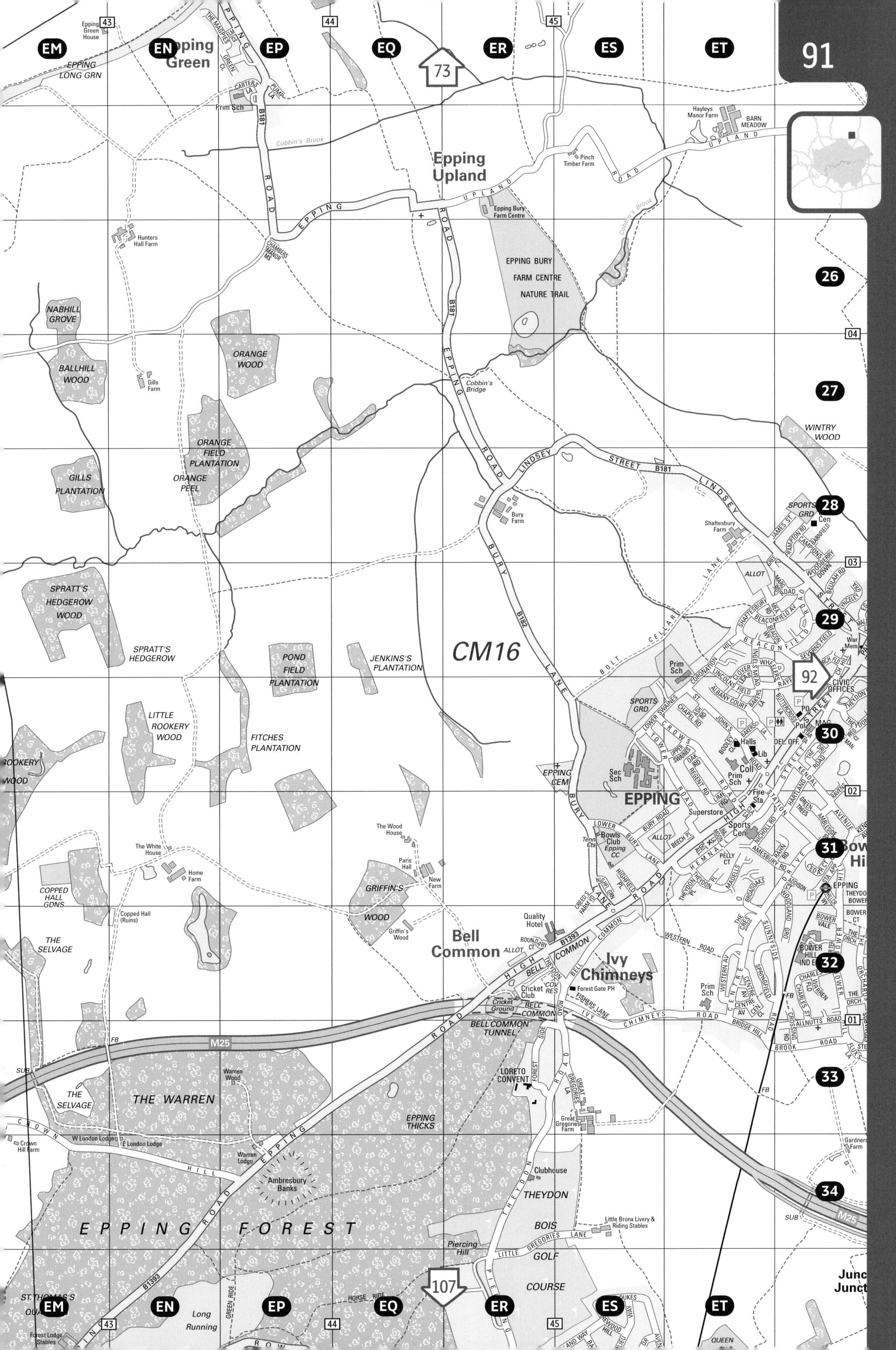
Epping Green
Epping Upland
EPPING BURY FARM CENTRE NATURE TRAIL
NABHILL GROVE
BALLHILL WOOD
ORANGE WOOD
ORANGE FIELD PLANTATION
ORANGE PEEL
GILLS PLANTATION
SPRATT'S HEDGEROW WOOD
SPRATT'S HEDGEROW
POND FIELD PLANTATION
JENKINS'S PLANTATION
CM16
LITTLE ROOKERY WOOD
FITCHES PLANTATION
ROOKERY WOOD
COPPED HALL GDNS
THE SELVAGE
GRIFFIN'S WOOD
Bell Common
Ivy Chimneys
EPPING
WINTRY WOOD
M25
THE WARREN
EPPING THICKS
BELL COMMON TUNNEL
LORETO CONVENT
Ambresbury Banks
EPPING FOREST
THEYDON BOIS GOLF COURSE
Piercing Hill
Long Running
Hunters Hall Farm
Gills Farm
Bury Farm
Shaftesbury Farm
Hayleys Manor Farm
BARN MEADOW
Pinch Timber Farm
Epping Bury Farm Centre
Cobbin's Bridge
Cobbin's Brook
The White House
Home Farm
Copped Hall (Ruins)
The Wood House
Paris Hall
New Farm
Griffin's Wood
Quality Hotel
Forest Gate PH
Great Gregories Farm
Little Bronx Livery & Riding Stables
Gardners Farm
Warren Wood
Warren Lodge
W London Lodge
E London Lodge
Crown Hill Farm
Forest Lodge Stables
73
92
107
EM EN EP EQ ER ES ET
26 27 28 29 30 31 32 33 34
43 44 45
04 03 02 01

EU
EV
EW
EX
EY
EZ
FA
74
THORNWOOD SEWAGE TREATMENT WORKS
Thames Water Sewage Treatment Plant
Garden Centre
Rose Farm
Hayleys Manor Farm
BARN MEADOW
UPLAND ROAD
Pav
Golf Range
UPPER CLAPTON FC RUGBY GRD
WEALD HALL LANE
Weald Hall
WEALD HALL FARM COMMERCIAL CENTRE
DRIVING RANGE
NORTH WEALD GOLF CEN
Thornwood
Moat
NORTH WEALD AIRFIELD
Hangar
Gliding Club
WOODSIDE COMMERCIAL ESTATE
M11
B1393
WINTRY WOOD
STUMP ROAD
WOODSIDE
EPPING ROAD
B181
Superstore
Clubhouse
NORTH WEALD PAR 3 GOLF COURSE
ROUGHTALLEY'S WOOD
Norway House
Piggery
THE LOWER FOREST
EPPING FOREST BURIAL PARK
Carisbrooke Farm
Wintry Park Farm
SPORTS GRD
Comm Cen
Shaftesbury Farm
Elec Sta
EPPING PLAIN
ALLOT
Amb Sta
Health Cen
ST. MARGARET'S HOSPITAL
SPENCER CLOSE HOSPITAL
GERNON BUSHES
Coopersale Cricket Club
Pav
Prim Sch
PO
Coopersale
CM16
91
War Mem
CIVIC OFFICES
SPORTS GRDS
Tenn Cts
POSTERNIANE SPRING
HAWKSHILL WOOD
BIRCHING COPPICE
MOUNT WOOD
FORTY ACRES
REDYN'S WOOD
Coopersale Farm
Coopersale House
Halls
Lib
Coll
Prim Sch
Fire Sta
Superstore
Sports Cen
Epping Ongar Railway
Stonards Farm
STONARDS HILL
HOUBLONS HILL
Gaynes Park House
Gaynes Park
MOUNT QUARTER
ONGAR DOWN
GRAVEL PIT WOOD
Theydon Oak PH
Bower Hill
EPPING
THEYDON BOWER
BOWER CT
BOWER VALE
BOWER HILL IND EST
ESSEX WAY
High Warren
Mount End
Fiddlers Hamlet
COOPERSALE STREET
Home Farm
MOUNT ROAD
Merry Fiddlers PH
Hornes Farm
STEWARDS GREEN ROAD
Masons Bridge Farm
Searles Hall
Prim Sch
BEACHET WOOD
Sawkins Farm
Little Thorn Hall Farm
HOBBS CROSS ROAD
Gardners Farm
Farm
Sch
Hobbs Cross Road Sewage Works
North House
Clubhouse
HOBBS CROSS GOLF CENTRE
Mount Hill Farm
THE ROUGH PATCH
Theydon Mount
M25
Junction 6 (M11)
Junction 27 (M25)
108
LONG PLANTATION
ICEHOUSE PLANTATION
BARBER'S WOOD
Garnish Hall
500 yds
500 m
0
25
26
27
28
29
30
31
32
33
34
04
03
02
01
47
48
49

North Weald Bassett
Blakes Golf Course
Reynkyns Wood
Travelodge
The Talbot
Epping Road
Toot Hill
Toot Hill Golf Course
Greensted Green
Clatterford End
CM5
RM4
Knightsland Wood
Northlands Wood
Ongar Park Wood
High Wood
Pewley Wood
Miller's Grove
Dolman's Spring
Greensted Wood
Icehouse Wood
Twentyacre Wood
Berwick Ham
Long Spring
Hanging Spring
Round Spring
Well Eaves
Essex Way
Blake Hall Road
School Road
Berwick Lane
Tawney Common
Mutton Row
Old Rectory Road
75
109

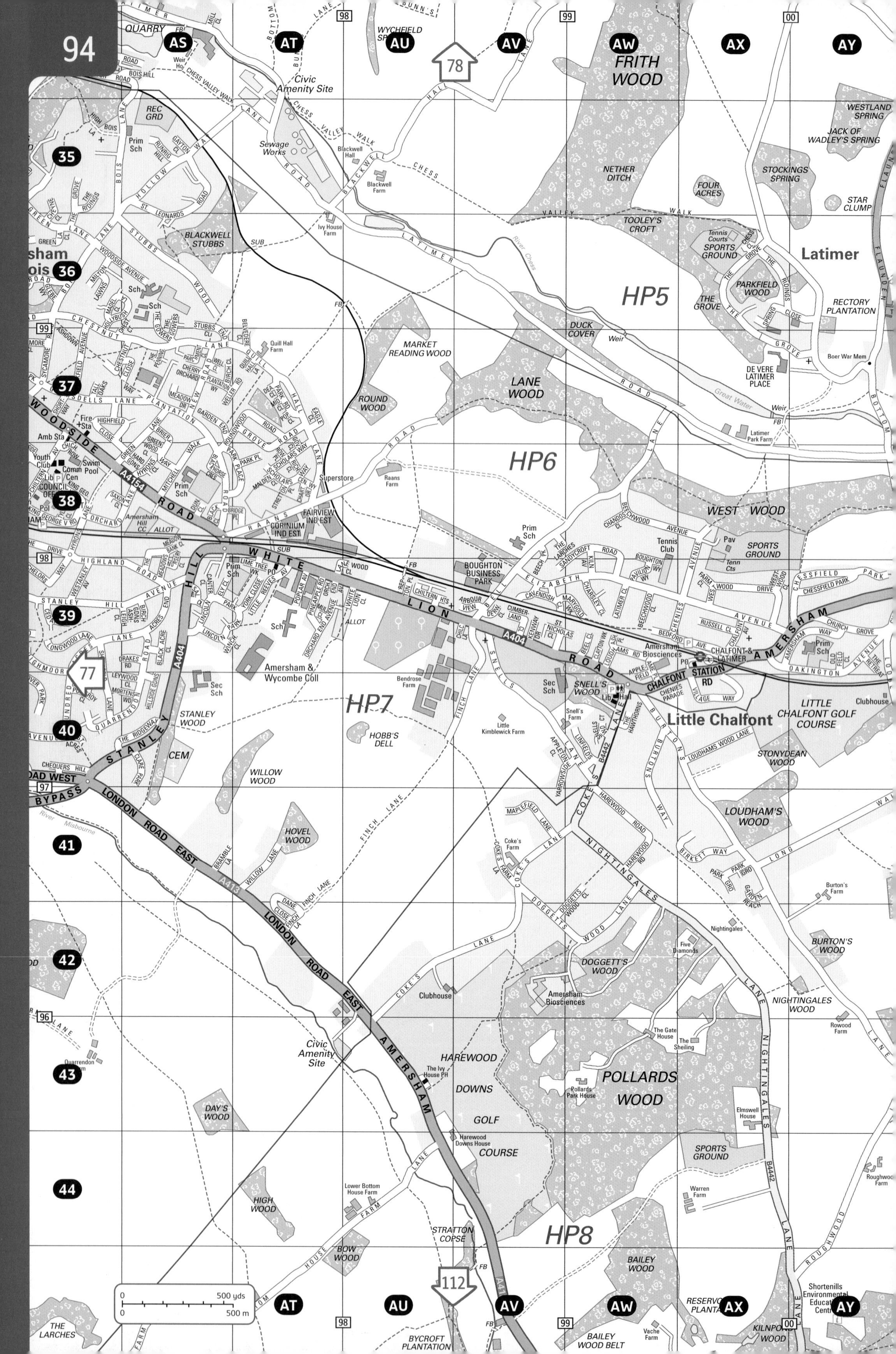

AS
AT
AU
AV
AW
AX
AY
98
99
00
78
112
77
35
36
37
38
39
40
41
42
43
44
97
96
QUARRY
Civic Amenity Site
Sewage Works
Blackwell Hall
Blackwell Farm
Ivy House Farm
WYCHFIELD
FRITH WOOD
WESTLAND SPRING
JACK OF WADLEY'S SPRING
NETHER DITCH
FOUR ACRES
STOCKINGS SPRING
STAR CLUMP
TOOLEY'S CROFT
Tennis Courts
SPORTS GROUND
Latimer
PARKFIELD WOOD
THE GROVE
RECTORY PLANTATION
HP5
DUCK COVER
Weir
Boer War Mem
DE VERE LATIMER PLACE
Great Water
Latimer Park Farm
REC GRD
Prim Sch
BLACKWELL STUBBS
CHESS VALLEY WALK
LATIMER ROAD
River Chess
MARKET READING WOOD
LANE WOOD
ROUND WOOD
Quill Hall Farm
HP6
Raans Farm
Superstore
FAIRVIEW IND EST
CORINIUM IND EST
WEST WOOD
Tennis Club
SPORTS GROUND
Pav
Tenn Cts
BOUGHTON BUSINESS PARK
Amersham Biosciences
CHALFONT & LATIMER
CHALFONT STATION RD
Little Chalfont
LITTLE CHALFONT GOLF COURSE
Clubhouse
STONYDEAN WOOD
LOUDHAM'S WOOD
Burton's Farm
BURTON'S WOOD
NIGHTINGALES WOOD
Rowood Farm
Nightingales
Five Diamonds
DOGGETT'S WOOD
Amersham Biosciences
The Gate House
The Sheiling
POLLARDS WOOD
Pollards Park House
Elmswell House
SPORTS GROUND
Warren Farm
Roughwood Farm
Shortenills Environmental Education Centre
BAILEY WOOD
HP8
BAILEY WOOD BELT
Vache Farm
KILNPOND WOOD
WOODSIDE ROAD
A4154
A404
WHITE LION ROAD
AMERSHAM ROAD
Fire Sta
Amb Sta
Youth Club
Comm Cen
Swim Pool
Lib
COUNCIL OFFS
Pol
Amersham Hill CC
Sch
Amersham & Wycombe Coll
Sec Sch
STANLEY WOOD
CEM
HP7
Bendrose Farm
HOBB'S DELL
Little Kimblewick Farm
Snell's Farm
SNELL'S WOOD
WILLOW WOOD
HOVEL WOOD
Coke's Farm
Clubhouse
HAREWOOD DOWNS GOLF COURSE
The Ivy House PH
Harewood Downs House
Civic Amenity Site
LONDON ROAD EAST
A413
DAY'S WOOD
HIGH WOOD
Lower Bottom House Farm
STRATTON COPSE
BOW WOOD
BYCROFT PLANTATION
THE LARCHES
Quarrendon Farm
NIGHTINGALES LANE
B4442
River Misbourne
0 500 yds
0 500 m

HP3
WD3
Chenies
Chorleywood
Chorleywood Bottom
The Swillet
Heronsgate
FLAUNDEN GROVE
BALDWIN'S WOOD
MOUNT WOOD
CHORLEYWOOD COMMON
CHORLEYWOOD GOLF COURSE
AMERSHAM ROAD
CHENIES ROAD
RICKMANSWORTH ROAD
BUCKINGHAMSHIRE
HERTFORDSHIRE
DACORUM
THREE RIVERS
CHILTERN
79
96
113

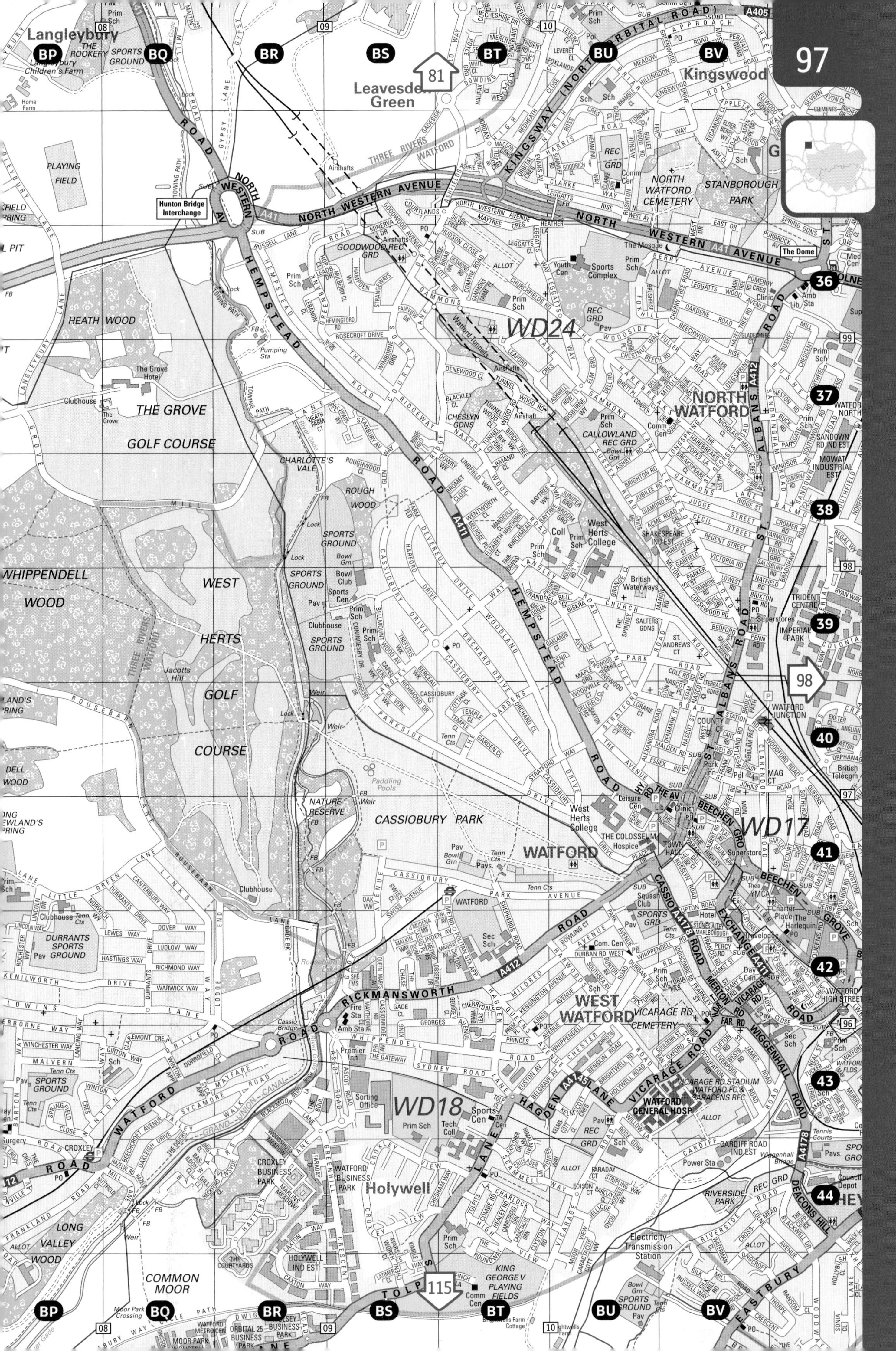
Langleybury
THE ROOKERY
SPORTS GROUND
Langleybury Children's Farm
Leavesden Green
81
Kingswood
NORTH WATFORD CEMETERY
STANBOROUGH PARK
PLAYING FIELD
Hunton Bridge Interchange
NORTH WESTERN AVENUE
GOODWOOD REC GRD
Sports Complex
The Mosque
The Dome
HEATH WOOD
WD24
The Grove Hotel
THE GROVE GOLF COURSE
NORTH WATFORD
CALLOWLAND REC GRD
CHARLOTTE'S VALE
ROUGH WOOD
SPORTS GROUND
West Herts College
WHIPPENDELL WOOD
WEST HERTS GOLF COURSE
Jacotts Hill
British Waterways
TRIDENT CENTRE
IMPERIAL PARK
MOWAT INDUSTRIAL EST
SANDOWN RD IND EST
98
WATFORD JUNCTION
CASSIOBURY PARK
NATURE RESERVE
Paddling Pools
WATFORD
THE COLOSSEUM
TOWN HALL
WD17
DURRANTS SPORTS GROUND
WEST WATFORD
VICARAGE RD CEMETERY
VICARAGE RD STADIUM WATFORD FC & SARACENS RFC
WATFORD GENERAL HOSP
WD18
Holywell
CROXLEY BUSINESS PARK
WATFORD BUSINESS PARK
HOLYWELL IND EST
LONG VALLEY WOOD
COMMON MOOR
KING GEORGE V PLAYING FIELDS
115
RIVERSIDE PARK
GARDIFF ROAD IND EST
Electricity Transmission Station
Power Sta
BP
BQ
BR
BS
BT
BU
BV
36
37
38
39
40
41
42
43
44
08
09
10

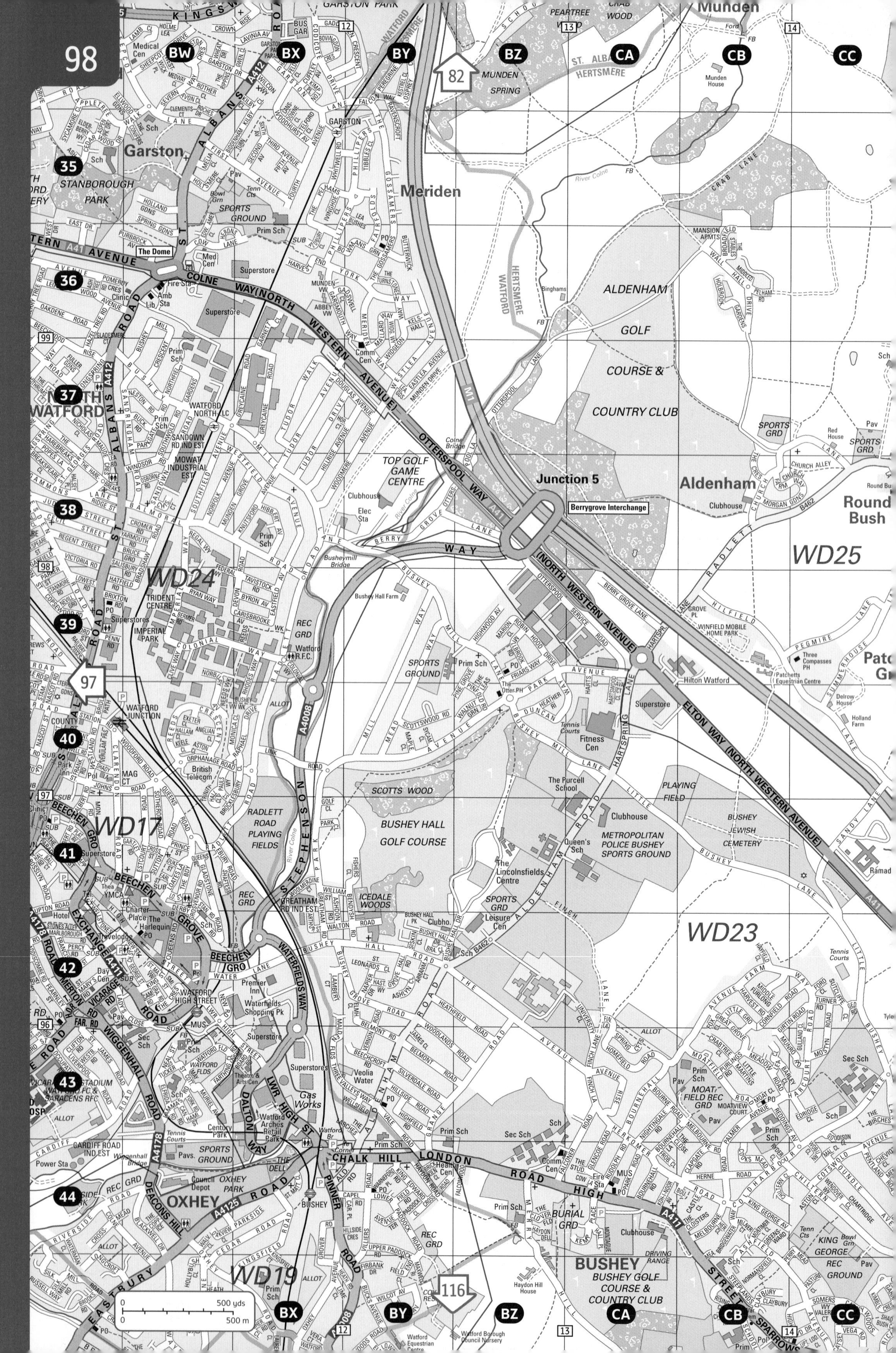
Garston
Meriden
North Watford
Aldenham
Round Bush
Oxhey
Bushey
WD17
WD19
WD23
WD24
WD25
Junction 5
Berrygrove Interchange
The Dome
Stanborough Park
Aldenham Golf Course & Country Club
Top Golf Game Centre
Bushey Hall Golf Course
Radlett Road Playing Fields
Metropolitan Police Bushey Sports Ground
Bushey Jewish Cemetery
Bushey Golf Course & Country Club
Watford Junction
Watford High Street
Watford North
Mowat Industrial Est
Sandown Rd Ind Est
Greatham Rd Ind Est
Cardiff Road Ind Est
Imperial Park
Trident Centre
Scotts Wood
Icedale Woods
Munden Spring
Munden House
Hilton Watford
The Purcell School
Queen's Sch
The Lincolnsfields Centre
Watford Arches Retail Park
Waterfields Shopping Pk
Watford F.C. & Saracens RFC Stadium
Watford R.F.C.
Colne Way (North Western Avenue)
Otterspool Way
Elton Way (North Western Avenue)
St Albans Road
Hartspring Lane
Aldenham Road
London Road
High Road
Chalk Hill
Pinner Road
Wiggenhall Road
Deacons Hill
Eastbury Road
Beechen Grove
Exchange Road
Stephenson Way
Waterfields Way
Dalton Way
Lwr High St
M1
A41
A411
A412
A4008
A4125
A4178
B462
BW
BX
BY
BZ
CA
CB
CC
35
36
37
38
39
40
41
42
43
44
82
97
116
0
500 yds
500 m

Oakridge Lane Sewage Treatment Works
CD
CE
CF
CG
CH
CJ
CK
PARK
GOLF COURSE
SAND PLANTATION
The Shenley Cricket Centre
Clubhouse
83
Starveacres
Blackbirds Farm
THE GORSE
RADLETT
Prim Sch
Blackbirds Country Fare (Garden Centre)
Kemprow Farm
SCRUBBITTS WOOD
SPORTS GRD
FIR SPRING
ALLOT
Tenn & Squash Club
CEM
WD7
36
99
High Cross House
Tabard R.F.C.
Radlett C.C.
Cobden Hill
Cat & Fiddle PH
WELLHOUSE DELL
Cricket Ground
37
Battlers Green
Battlers Green Farm
Home Farm
COBDENHILL DELL
MOSES DELL
KENDAL WOOD
Tenn Cts
Fish Pond
38
Little Kendals Farm
Kendal Hall Farm
Organ Hall Farm
Letchmore Heath
The Fruit Farm
Schs
LITTLE KENDALS WOOD
98
Aldenham Grange
Aldenham Cottage
Hall
Three Horseshoes PH
War Mem
PLAYING FIELD
Pav
39
Bhaktivedanta Manor Hare Krishna Temple
SPORTS GRD
Sports Cen
Aldenham Sch
SPORTS GROUND
Boydens Hill
Medburn Cottages
PLAYING FIELD
100
ELSTREE
North Medburn Farm
North Medburn Stables
40
Electricity Transfer Station
Slades Farm
Letchmore Lodge
DRIVING RANGE
97
Battle Axes PH
ALDENHAM PARK WOODLAND
Waggon & Horses PH
Clubhouse
GOLF
The Haberdasher's Aske's Sch for Boys
Medburn Bridge
South Medburn Farm
41
ELSTREE AERODROME
Hilfield Farm
Flying Club
Hangars
The Haberdasher's Aske's Sch for Girls
COURSE
Boathouse
Hilfield Castle
Pages Farm
WD6
ALDENHAM
42
DAM
HILFIELD PARK RESERVOIR
Sewage Works
Home Farm
ALLOT
Pumping Sta
96
PARK
Elli Dani Farm (Stables)
Lister Institute
DAM
Boathouse
Hertsmere Borough Council Cemetery
43
Hart's Farm Stables
ALDENHAM COUNTRY PARK
Sailing Club
ELSTREE
ALDENHAM RESERVOIR
SPORTS GROUND
Prim Sch
44
Caldecote Farm
Berkeley Cottage
ELSTREE HILL OPEN SPACE
Comm Cen
CONVENT Sch
Gas Pumping Sta
117
CENTENNIAL PARK
The Leys
ELSTREE OPEN SPACE

CL
CM
CN
CP
CQ
CR
CS
84
99
118
35
36
37
38
39
40
41
42
43
44
WD7
WD6
BIG PURSLEY WOOD
LITTLE PURSLEY WOOD
CROSS OAKS WOOD
BIRCH WOOD
Green Street
Well End
BOREHAMWOOD
ELSTREE
GOLF COURSE
DRIVING RANGE
HERTSMERE BOROUGH COUNCIL CEMETERY
ABERFORD PARK
MEADOW PARK
AYCLIFFE ROAD PITCHES
SPORTS GROUND
MAXWELL PK
RIPON PARK
ROWLEY LANE GOLF COURSE
ROWLEY LANE SPORTS GRD
G.E.C. SPORTS GROUND
A1 DRIVING RANGE
DEACONS HILL OPEN SPACE
SCRATCH WOOD
FROGHALL WOOD
BOYS HILL WOOD
THISTLE WOOD
GRAVEL PIT WOOD
ELSTREE OPEN SPACE
Deacons Hill
Furze Hill
High Canons
Crossoaks Farm
Auriol Farm
Wood Hall Farm
Wood Hall
Kitwells Farm
Villa Scalabrini
Lyndhurst
SILVER HILL
High Canons Farm
Bucketsland Farm
Wheatsheaf Farm
Maxwelton Nurseries
Well End Farm
Holly Cottage
Strangeways Farm
Rowley Farm
Mops & Brooms PH
Holmshill House
Ridge Farm
Organ Hall Farm
South Medburn Farm
Elli Dani Farm (Stables)
Woodcock Hill Farm
Airshafts
Elstree Manor
Penniwells Farm
The Leys
Arkley Park
Hyver Hall
Stirling Corner
Stirling Retail Pk
STIRLING IND CEN
Elstree Park
Borehamwood Shopping Park
Metropolis Centre
B.B.C. Elstree Studios
Elstree Film Studios
Oaklands College
Hertswood School (Annex)
DEVONSHIRE BUSINESS PARK
BOREHAMWOOD IND PARK
Millennium Studios
Hertsmere Ind Pk
KENILWORTH PARK
Kinetic Bus Cen
Capital Bus Pk
ELSTREE & BOREHAMWOOD
Gas Works
CIVIC OFFS
War Memorial
Elstree Inn
Superstore
Holiday Inn
Premier Inn
The Venue
New Horizons
The Garden Nursery
Tokonoma Bonsai
The White Horse PH
London Colney C.C.
Pursley Farm
Cowley Hill Farm
ELSTREE TUNNEL
A411
A5135
B5378
A1
BARNET BYPASS
ELSTREE HILL NORTH
ELSTREE HILL SOUTH
BARNET LANE
ELSTREE WAY
SHENLEY ROAD
GREEN STREET
COWLEY HILL
ROWLEY LANE
CROSSOAKS LANE
SUMMERSWOOD LANE
HIGH CANONS
WELL END ROAD
BUCKETTSLAND LANE
WOODHALL LANE
ALLUM LANE
FURZEHILL ROAD
MANOR WAY
AYCLIFFE ROAD
THEOBALD STREET
GATESHEAD ROAD
LONDON LOOP
0
500 yds
500 m

CT
CU
CV
CW
CX
CY
CZ
85
M25
Bignell's Corner
South Mimms Services
Days Inn
Nat Inst for Biological Standards & Control
Blanche Farm
Junction 23 (M25) Junction 1 A1(M)
A1(M)
Summerswood Farm
Dancers Hill
Dancershill House
Laurel Lodge
Laurel House
Norfolk Lodge
Mausoleum
Bentley Heath
Elm Farm
Wrotham Park
WROTHAM PARK
Tennis Courts
Pool
Dyrham Park Farm
Mimmshall Brook
DYRHAM PARK GOLF COURSE
Country Club
Pool
Tennis Courts
DYRHAM PARK
Valentine's Farm
Green Dragon Inn PH
Knightsland Farm
Lower Kitt's End Farm
Wrotham Business Park
Kitt's End
Kitt's End Farm
A1000
Deadman's Bottom
36
37
38
39
40
41
42
43
44
99
98
97
96
THE SHIRE LONDON GOLF COURSE
ALLOTMENTS
Clubhouse
OLD FOLD MANOR GOLF COURSE
MOAT
Old Fold Manor
Monken Hadley
Battle of Barnet 1471
Rectory Farm
102
A1081
Fold Farm
EN5
Electricity Sta
BYNG ROAD PLAYING FIELDS
High Barnet
Barnet Elizabethans R.F.C.
ALLOT
Homestead Farm
POOR CLARE MONASTERY
HERTSMERE
BARNET
SPORTS GROUND
Hadley
KING GEORGE'S FIELD
BARNET
SPORTS GROUND
The Spires Shop Cen
BARNET TRADING EST
Woodlands Farm
Rowley Green Farm
ARKLEY OPEN SPACE
Nursery
Three Elms Farm
A411
WHALEBONE PARK
BARNET HOSP
Rowley Green
ARKLEY GOLF COURSE
ARKLEY RISE ESTATE OPEN SPACE
CEMETERY
CHIPPING BARNET
HIGH BARNET
Barnet Coll
THE BULL THEATRE
Arkley Manor Farm
Clubhouse
War Memorial
Water Tower
Arkley
BELLS HILL ALLOT
Underhill
Clubhouse
SPORTS GROUND
BARNET PLAYING FIELDS
WHITINGS HILL OPEN SPACE
LONDON LOOP / DOLLIS VALLEY GREENWALK
Ducks Island
KING GEORGE V PLAYING FIELDS
Barnet Gate
Whitings Hill Farm
Cottage Farm
SPORTS GROUND
GRANGE PLAYING FIELDS
PLAYING FIELD
Tennis Courts
Dollis Brook
OLD ELIZABETHANS (BARNET) MEMORIAL PLAYING FIELDS
119
Brent Lodge Farm
N20
Sec Sch
SOUTH HERTS GOLF
22
23
24

DA
DB
DC
DD
DE
DF
DG
POTTERS BAR COMMUNITY HOSP
86
M25
Junction 24
THE RIDGEWAY
A1005
WELWYN HATFIELD
POND WOOD
New Cottage Farm
Nursery
Prep. Sch
Water Tower
Fenny Shade Hill
CHASE WOOD
Chase Farm
Elm Farm
Bentley Heath Farm
35
Bentley Heath
Garden Centre
Ganwick Corner
Duke of York PH
Pav
Cricket Ground
FIR WOOD
Plumridge Hill
Ind Sch
PLUMRIDGE WOOD
South Barvin Farm
VAULT HILL WOOD
36
Wrotham Park
Pool
WROTHAM PARK
99
Three Oak Hill
Hornbeam Hills
HERTFORDSHIRE
A111
Cockshot Hill
Plumridge Farm
Salmon's Brook
Deadman's Bottom
Ganwick Farm
SPOILBANK WOOD
HERTSMERE
ENFIELD
Slopers Pond Farm
Roundhedge Hill
37
Wrotham Business Park
A1000
GREAT NORTH ROAD
WAGGON ROAD
ENFIELD
BARTRAMS QUASH
CLAREMONT ROAD
COURTLEIGH AV
KINGWELL ROAD
Monken Mead Brook
Tenn Club
Prim Sch
West Lodge Park Hotel
ASH WOOD
38
HADLEY WOOD
LANCASTER AVENUE
HADLEY WOOD
Great Broadgates Hill
BEECH HILL
FERNY HILL
Ferny Hill Farm
98
Clubhouse
FERNYHILL WOOD
39
Monken Hadley
Battle of Barnet
Rectory Farm
Sch
Prim Sch
War Memorial
101
CAMLET WAY
BEECH HILL PARK
HADLEY WOOD GOLF COURSE
ROUGH LOT
COCKFOSTERS ROAD
Green Brook
Fish Ponds
SEEDFIELD SPINNEY
Bournwell Hill
COVERT WAY OPEN SPACE
Sewit's Hill
40
MONKEN HADLEY COMMON
Priddeon's Hill
Newman's Hill
ENFIELD
BARNET
EN4
BEECH HILL LAKE
Water Tower
OAK WOOD
Hadley
97
TUDOR GOLF COURSE
TUDOR SPORTS GRD
KING GEORGE'S FIELD
EN5
Clubhouse
Tenn Cts
Sec Sch
Prim Sch
41
BARNET
SPORTS GROUND
Tenn Ct
ALLOT
Gas Works
Ludgrove Hall
War Memorial
Monument
CHURCH WAY
SOUTH CL
STREET
BARNET TRADING EST
THE BULL THEATRE
Barnet Coll
Sports Cen
VICTORIA REC GRD
SPORTS GROUND
Pav
Bowl Club
TRENT PARK CEM
COCKFOSTERS
42
Sec Sch
HIGH BARNET
NEW BARNET
COCKFOSTERS
A110
A111
BARNET
96
Med Cen
Prim Sch
Comm Cen
Superstore
NEW BARNET
EAST BARNET ROAD
43
Amb Sta
Fire Sta
A1000
GREAT NORTH ROAD
BARNET HILL
STATION ROAD
Health Cen
Hall
CAT HILL
BARNET FC
Clubhouse
Underhill SPORTS GROUND
Valley Cen
BROOKHILL ROAD
Lib
Prim Sch
Sec Sch
Prim Sch
MUS
Middlesex Uni
Sch
B193
LONGMORE AVENUE
BARNET PLAYING FIELDS
44
Pavs.
Prim Sch
KING GEORGE V PLAYING FIELDS
EAST BARNET
Oak Hill College
N20
WYATTS FARM OPEN SPACE
120
OAKLEIGH PARK
OAK HILL PARK
Bandstand
Miniature Golf Course
Bowl Grn
Prim Sch
Sec Sch
500 yds
500 m
26
27
28
GOLF

103
M25
29
30
31
DH
DJ
DK
DL
DM
DN
DP
87
South Hill
Oak Hill Farm
Glasgow Stud
Sloeman's Farm
Holly Hill Farm
CREWS HILL
Clubhouse
Garden Centre
Culver Garden Centre
Country World
ROAD
BURNT FM RIDE
Nursery
Woldens Nursery & Garden Centre
Browns of Crews Hill Nurseries
Woldens Nurseries
CREWS HILL GOLF COURSE
ST. NICHOLAS HO
Holyhill Brook
LODGE
EAST
WHITEWEBBS
THEOBALDS PARK
BEECH AV
ROSEWOOD DR
WROXHAM GDNS
CYPRESS AV
GOLF RIDE
Kings Oak Riding Stables
Crews Hill
TINGEYS TOP LANE
Wilfwoods Water Garden Centre
WILDWOOD
Botany Bay
Pav
Botany Bay C.C.
Botany Bay Farm
LITTLE BEECHILL WOOD
Kings Oak Plain
Glasshouses
SUB
Hill Side Nursery
Prim Sch
ROSEDALE CL
ST. JOHNS PK HOME EST
STRAYFIELD ROAD
A1005
THE RIDGEWAY
RECTORY FARM ROAD
North Enfield CC
The Fallow Buck PH
FLASH LANE
CLAY HILL
Anglo Aquarium Plant
LONDON LOOP
Queenswood Farm
Rectory Farm
Turkey Brook
LONDON LOOP/RECTORY FARM ROAD
STRAYFIELD ROAD CEMETERY
Rendlesham Viaduct
Kingswood
Clay Hill
36
37
38
39
40
41
42
43
44
99
98
97
96
DUNCAN'S WOOD
CHASE
EN2
HILLY FIELDS PARK
COOK'S HOLE ROAD
LAVENDER HILL CEMETERY
Cuckolds Hill
Park Farms
THE KING'S OAK HOSPITAL
CHASE FARM HOSPITAL
Royal Chace Hotel
CAMLET MOAT
MOAT WOOD
HADLEY ROAD
Parkside Farm
Pumping Station
Amb Sta
FOUR HILLS EST
Camlet Hill
RIDE WOOD
Vicarage Farm
Leeging Beech Gutter
Salmon's Brook
LAVENDER HILL
GORDON HILL
Fish Pond
WILLIAMS WOOD
ICEHOUSE WOOD
Hog Hill
104
Comfort Hotel
Middlesex University
Well
Monument
SHAWS WOOD
NUFFIELD HOSP
Tennis Courts
Pav
SPORTS GROUND
TRENT PARK GOLF COURSE
Merryhills Brook
SLADES HILL
WINDMILL HILL
A110
World's End
ENFIELD GOLF COURSE
Clubhouse
ENFIELD CHASE
FB
TRIANGULAR WOOD
South Lodge Farm
Trent Park Equestrian Centre
Driving Range
Clubhouse
ENFIELD ROAD
CHEYNE WALK
GRANGE PARK
BUSH HILL PARK GOLF COURSE
Sec Sch
Prim Sch
OAKWOOD
BRAMLEY ROAD
PRIORY
Superstore
Health Cen
SPORTS GROUND
N21
GRANGE PARK
OAKWOOD PARK
Pitch 'n' Putt
YACHTING POND
Chaseside Works
SPORTS GRD
121
WINCHMORE HILL
N14
A111
RIDGE LANES
Green Dragon PH
ALLOT
Leisure

DQ
DR
DS
DT
DU
DV
DW
33
34
35
88
M25
BROXBOURNE
BULLSCROSS RIDE
CEMETERY (JEWISH)
COUNTY BROOK PLANTATION
Theobalds Park Camping and Caravan Site
Junction 25
News International Print Works
GREAT CAMBRIDGE ROAD
Sloeman's Farm
Whitewebbs Farm
WHITEWEBBS ROAD
35
Crews Hill
Wilfwoods Water Garden Centre
WHITEWEBBS WOOD
WHITEWEBBS PARK
WHITEWEBBS GOLF COURSE
White Webbs House
Roman Villa
Enfield Invicta C.C.
Bulls Cross
SPORTS GROUND
Capel Manor College
CAPEL HOUSE
Water World, Aquatic & Garden Centre
BULLSMOOR
AYLANDS OPEN SPACE
WILDWOOD
36
Hill Side Nursery
Myddelton Farm
BULLS CROSS FIELD
Orchardside Nurseries
Myddelton House
Gardens
New River (Old Course)
Turkey Brook
LONDON LOOP
ALLOTMENTS
Aylands Sch
Cuffley Brook
99
Prim Sch
ST. JOHNS PK HOME EST
North Enfield CC
The Fallow Buck PH
EN2
Brayside Farm
Clubhouse
37
Queenswood Farm
CLAY HILL
FLASH LANE
BEGGARS HOLLOW
Rose & Crown PH
FORTY HALL COUNTRY PARK
Maiden's Bridge
TURKEY STREET
Bullsmoor
Kingswood
Clay Hill
Clay Hill House
Bandstand
Forty Hill
Forty Hall Farm
FORTY HALL & MUSEUM
THE DELL
War Memorial
CEMETERY
Crematorium
HILLY FIELDS PARK
ALLOTMENTS
Clock House
Clockhouse Nursery
38
LAVENDER HILL CEMETERY
COOK'S HOLE ROAD
PHIPPS HATCH LANE
FOUR HILLS EST
REC GRD
Prim Schs
FORTY HILL
98
HOE LANE
39
GORDON HILL
LAVENDER HILL
Health Cen
ENFIELD CEMETERY (JEWISH)
CARTERHATCH LANE
Tenn Cts
SPORTS GROUND
Pavs
103
Sec Sch
REC GRD
Holtwhites Hotel
Fitness Centre
QUEEN ELIZABETH STADIUM
40
CHASE SIDE
PARSONAGE LANE
EN1
ENFIELD PLAYING FIELDS
SPORTS GROUND
97
ENFIELD TOWN
SPORTS GROUND
CIVIC CENTRE
ENFIELD
BASEBALL GROUND
Superstores
ENFIELD RETAIL PK
Enfield Coll
HERTFORD ROAD
41
WINDMILL HILL
A110
ENFIELD CHASE
CHURCH ST
SOUTHBURY ROAD
Palace Gardens
Palace Exchange
CECIL ROAD
Superstore
Leisure Cen
Cinema
Tenn Cts
TOWN PARK
42
BUSH HILL PARK
Clubhouse
SOUTHBURY
CHEYNE WALK
96
BUSH HILL PARK GOLF COURSE
MARTINBRIDGE TRADING ESTATE
HASLEMERE BUSINESS CENTRE
Middlesex University
GRANGE PARK
43
Clubhouse
Enfield C.C.
BUSH HILL PARK
Bowls & Tenn Club
GREAT CAMBRIDGE IND EST
A1010
HERTFORD RD HIGH STREET
N21
44
A105
VILLAGE ROAD
PARK AVENUE
GREEN DRAGON LANE
ALLOTMENTS
KING GEORGE'S FLD
JUBILEE PARK
122
0 500 yds
0 500 m
DR
DS
DT
DU
DV
DW
33
34
35

EE
EF
EG
EH
EJ
EK
EL
90
WALTHAM ABBEY
Prim Schs
SPORTS GROUND
Waltham Abbey FC
Swim Pool
Marriott Waltham Abbey
HONEY LANE
Junction 26
M25
Skillet Hill Farm
Southend Farm
Upshire Hall
SOUTHEND LANE
CLAY PIGEON RANGE
The Lodge
Sudbury Farm
Woodbine Inn PH
WOODBINE CLOSE
Woodgreen Farm
POTKILN WOOD
BRAMBLY SHAW
Woodredon House
CONYBURY WOOD
Woodredon Farm
Woodredon Riding School
STABLES SHAW
35
36
37
38
39
40
41
42
43
44
LODGE LANE
Quinton Hill Farm
Sewardstone Roundabout
DOWDING WAY
A121
EN9
Inner Lodge
POPLARS SHAW
LORD PADGETS WOOD
Volunteer PH
HONEY LANE PLAIN
WALTHAM ABBEY CEMETERY (JEWISH)
WOODRIDDEN
HONEY LANE QUARTERS
SUNSHINE PLAIN
THREE FORESTS WAY
WAKE ROAD
Tile Hill Farm
Round Hills
Darrens Nursery
Beechview Nursery
Pinetree Nursery
AVEY LANE
Felicia Nursery
Providence Nursery
Normandy Nursery
Beech Hill Park
Hanbury Riding School
BEECH HILL PARK
HIGH BEECH GOLF COURSE
Clubho
Avey Lane Farm
Premier Inn
PYNEST GRN
Pynest Green
High Beech Riding School
Duke of Wellington PH
WELLINGTON
High Beech Nursery
Avey Cottages
Bowl Club
Y.H.A.
Earthworks
King's Oak PH
Epping Forest Field Cen
Sewardstone Nursery
THOMPSON'S WOOD
Mott Street Nursery
GRAVEL HILL
MANOR ROAD
Paul's Nursery
Prim Sch
Manor House
Oak Farm
MOTT STREET
EPPING
Mount Pleasant
LITTLE MONK WOOD
Court Hill
Bellringers
Wake Valley
NEW ROAD
A104
Broom Hill
BLACKWEIR POND
Blackweir Hill
105
ALDERGROVE WOOD
PEPPER ALLEY
High Beech C.C.
High Beech
Wallsgrove House
CHURCH ROAD
LIPPITTS HILL
Barn Hill
BLIND LANE
GREEN LANE
Kate's Cellar
Loughton Camp
Shelley's Hill
Robin Hood PH
IG10
HILL WOOD
CENTENARY WALK
FOREST
Day's Farm
Elms Caravan & Camping Park
Police Training Centre
Pipers Farm
Owl PH
Suntrap Field Study Centre
FERNHILL WOOD
Staples Hill
Strawberry Hill
EARL'S PATH
Springfield Farm
Piggeries
WHITEHOUSE PLAIN
Carrolls Farm
WEST ESSEX GOLF COURSE
Clubhouse
BANCHET FIELD
ROUND THICKET
FAIRMEAD POND
GREEN RIDE
Prim Schs
STAPLES ROAD
Health Cen
The Scout Association
GILWELL LANE
ALMHOUSE PLAIN
Fairmead Bottom
North Long Hills
STRAWBERRY HILL PONDS
E4
Sewardstonebury
Long Hills
Glasshouses
Tenn Cts
Bury Farm
HORNBEAM LA
WOODMAN'S GLADE
BURY WOOD
HORSE RIDE
Obelisk
Cuckoo Pits
Grimston's Oak
Oaklands Sch
Fire Sta
Superstore
Sec Sch
Tenn Club
LOUGHTON
CHINGFORD GOLF COURSE
Magpie Hill
CONNAUGHT WATER
Warren Hill
Warren Hill House
North Farm House
CHINGFORD PLAIN
Holmhurst
124
QUEEN ELIZABETH'S HUNTING LODGE
A1069
Buckhurst Hill
Warren Wood PH
THE WARREN
Tenn & Bowl Club
Oak Hall
CHINGFORD
0 500 yds
0 500 m

EPPING FOREST
THEYDON BOIS GOLF COURSE
Theydon Bois
CM16
RM4
IG7
Debden Green
Debden
LOUGHTON
LOUGHTON GOLF COURSE
Wake Arms
Junction 5
WOOLSTON MANOR GOLF COURSE
Rolls Park Roundabout
Little London
THEYDON MEAD
THEYDON BOIS CEMETERY
QUEEN MARY & WESTFIELD COLLEGE SPORTS GROUND
M11
A121
A1168
A113
A1112
B172
B1393
91
108
125

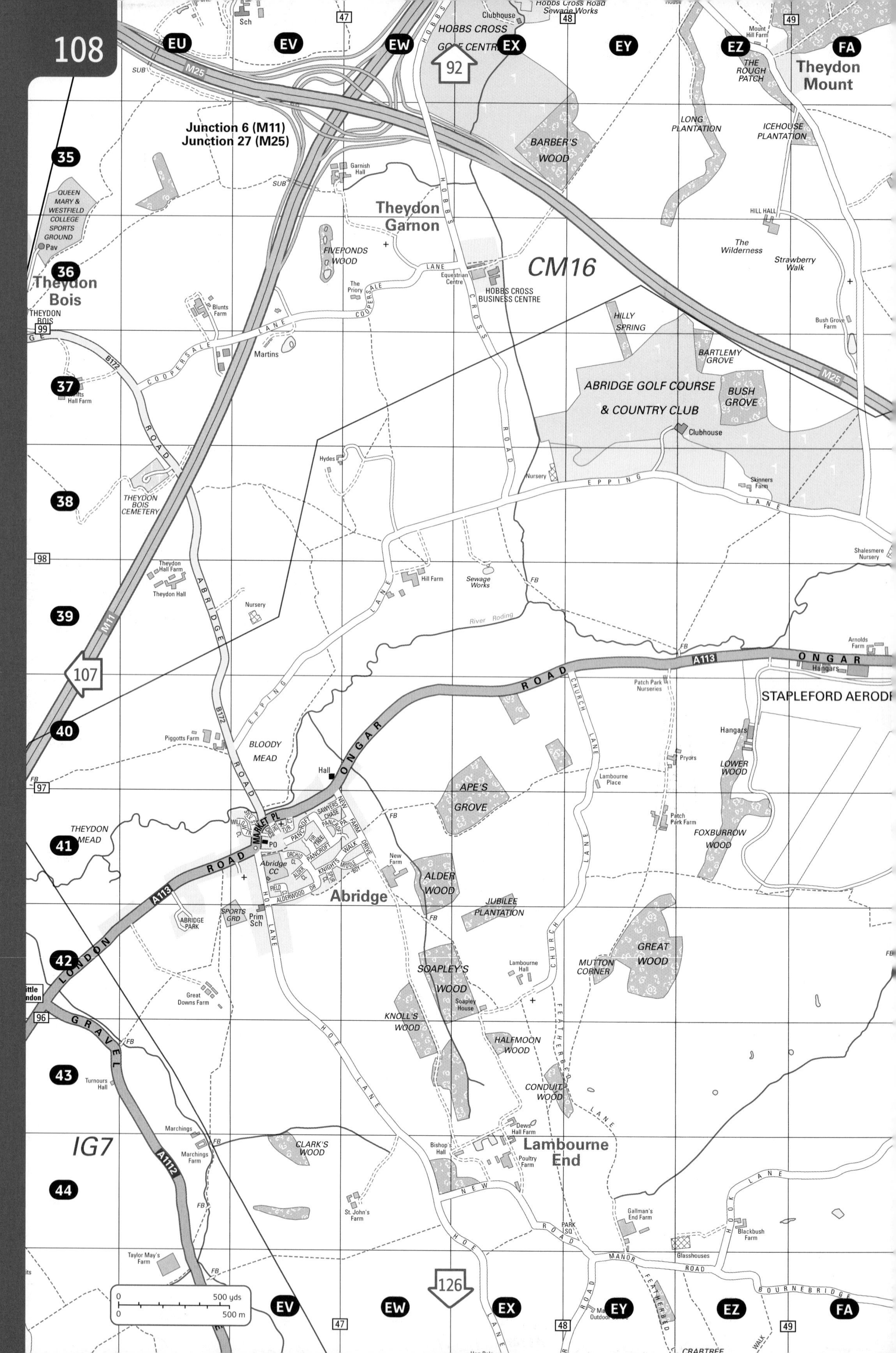
Junction 6 (M11)
Junction 27 (M25)
Theydon Garnon
Theydon Bois
Theydon Mount
CM16
HOBBS CROSS GOLF CENTRE
BARBER'S WOOD
ABRIDGE GOLF COURSE & COUNTRY CLUB
BUSH GROVE
BARTLEMY GROVE
HILLY SPRING
LONG PLANTATION
ICEHOUSE PLANTATION
FIVEPONDS WOOD
HOBBS CROSS BUSINESS CENTRE
QUEEN MARY & WESTFIELD COLLEGE SPORTS GROUND
THEYDON BOIS CEMETERY
Theydon Hall
Hill Farm
Sewage Works
River Roding
BLOODY MEAD
APE'S GROVE
STAPLEFORD AERODROME
LOWER WOOD
FOXBURROW WOOD
Abridge
ALDER WOOD
JUBILEE PLANTATION
SOAPLEY'S WOOD
KNOLL'S WOOD
HALFMOON WOOD
CONDUIT WOOD
GREAT WOOD
MUTTON CORNER
THEYDON MEAD
ABRIDGE PARK
Lambourne End
CLARK'S WOOD
IG7
Great Downs Farm
Marchings Farm
Taylor May's Farm
St. John's Farm
Gallman's End Farm
Blackbush Farm
Glasshouses
ONGAR ROAD
LONDON ROAD
EPPING LANE
HOE LANE
CHURCH LANE
MANOR ROAD
GRAVEL LANE
A113
A1112
B172
M11
M25
92
107
126
0 500 yds
0 500 m

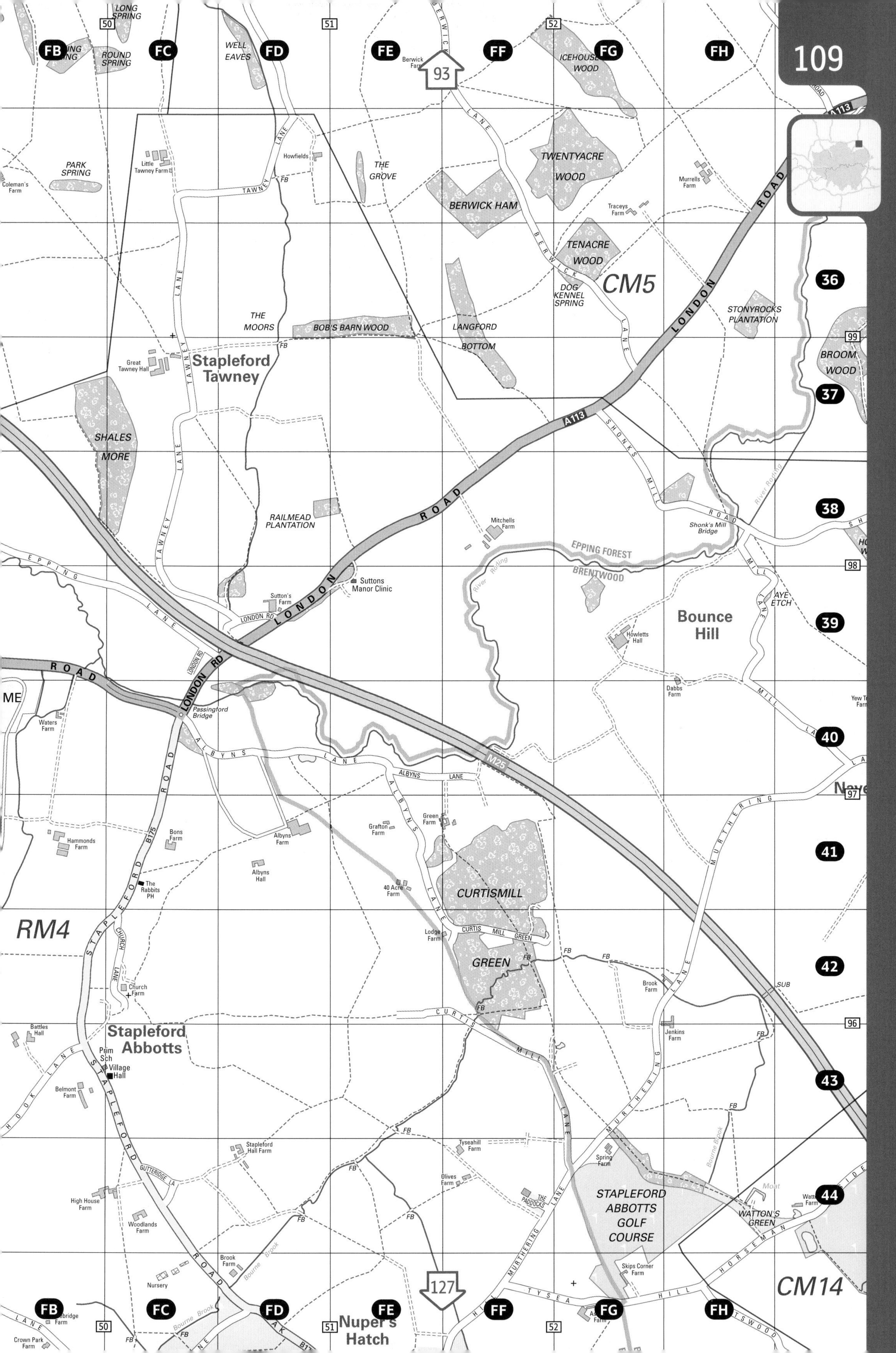
LONG SPRING
ROUND SPRING
WELL EAVES
FB
FC
FD
FE
FF
FG
FH
50
51
52
Berwick Farm
93
ICEHOUSE WOOD
A113
PARK SPRING
Coleman's Farm
Little Tawney Farm
Howfields
TAWNEY LANE
THE GROVE
TWENTYACRE WOOD
BERWICK HAM
Murrells Farm
Traceys Farm
ROAD
TENACRE WOOD
BERWICK LANE
DOG KENNEL SPRING
CM5
LONDON
36
STONYROCKS PLANTATION
THE MOORS
BOB'S BARN WOOD
LANGFORD BOTTOM
99
BROOM WOOD
Great Tawney Hall
Stapleford Tawney
37
SHALES MORE
SHONKS MILL
River Roding
38
RAILMEAD PLANTATION
Mitchells Farm
Shonk's Mill Bridge
ROAD
EPPING FOREST
BRENTWOOD
98
EPPING LANE
Suttons Manor Clinic
Sutton's Farm
LONDON RD
AYE ETCH
Bounce Hill
39
Howletts Hall
ROAD
Dabbs Farm
Yew Tree Farm
Waters Farm
Passingford Bridge
ALBYNS LANE
40
M25
ALBYNS LANE
97
Green Farm
Grafton Farm
Bons Farm
Hammonds Farm
Albyns Farm
B175
MURTHERING
41
Albyns Hall
The Rabbits PH
40 Acre Farm
CURTISMILL
RM4
Lodge Farm
CURTIS MILL GREEN
CHURCH LANE
GREEN
42
Brook Farm
SUB
Church Farm
CURTIS MILL
96
Battles Hall
Stapleford Abbotts
Prim Sch
Village Hall
Jenkins Farm
43
Belmont Farm
HOOK LANE
STAPLEFORD
Tyseahill Farm
Stapleford Hall Farm
Spring Farm
Bourne Brook
GUTTERIDGE LA
Olives Farm
THE PADDOCKS
STAPLEFORD ABBOTTS GOLF COURSE
Moat
44
WATTON'S GREEN
High House Farm
Woodlands Farm
HORSEMAN
Brook Farm
Nursery
Skips Corner Farm
127
TYSEA HILL
CM14
Crown Park Farm
Nuper's Hatch
Bourne Brook

HP15
TYLERS GREEN
COMMON WOOD
THE LARCHES
CHARCOLE GROVE
THE COPSE
PENNHOUSE GROVE
Winchmore Hill
PUGH'S WOOD
BROOK WOOD
ROUND WOOD
BRANCHES WOOD
GLORY BELT
KING'S WOOD
SPORTS GRD
SPORTS GROUND
Penn
VICARAGE WOOD
DOWNHAM GROVE
WESTFIELD PIECES
WITHERIDGE WOOD
PENBURY GROVE
CHURCH PATH WOOD
Knotty Green
POND WOOD
HP10
GATEMOOR WOOD
CORKERS WOOD
STANDERS WOOD
WYCOMBE HEIGHTS GOLF CENTRE
MAGPIE WOOD
DRIVING RANGE
COPPICE WOOD
VINEYARD
LONGFIELD WOOD
Forty Green
THROSHERS WOOD
SNIGGS WOOD
ROUNDHEADS WOOD
HOGBACK WOOD
Loudwater
Holtspur
CUT-THROAT WOOD
Junction 3
FLACKWELL HEATH
FENNELL'S WOOD
LITTLE GOMMS WOOD
B474
A40
132
500 yds
500 m

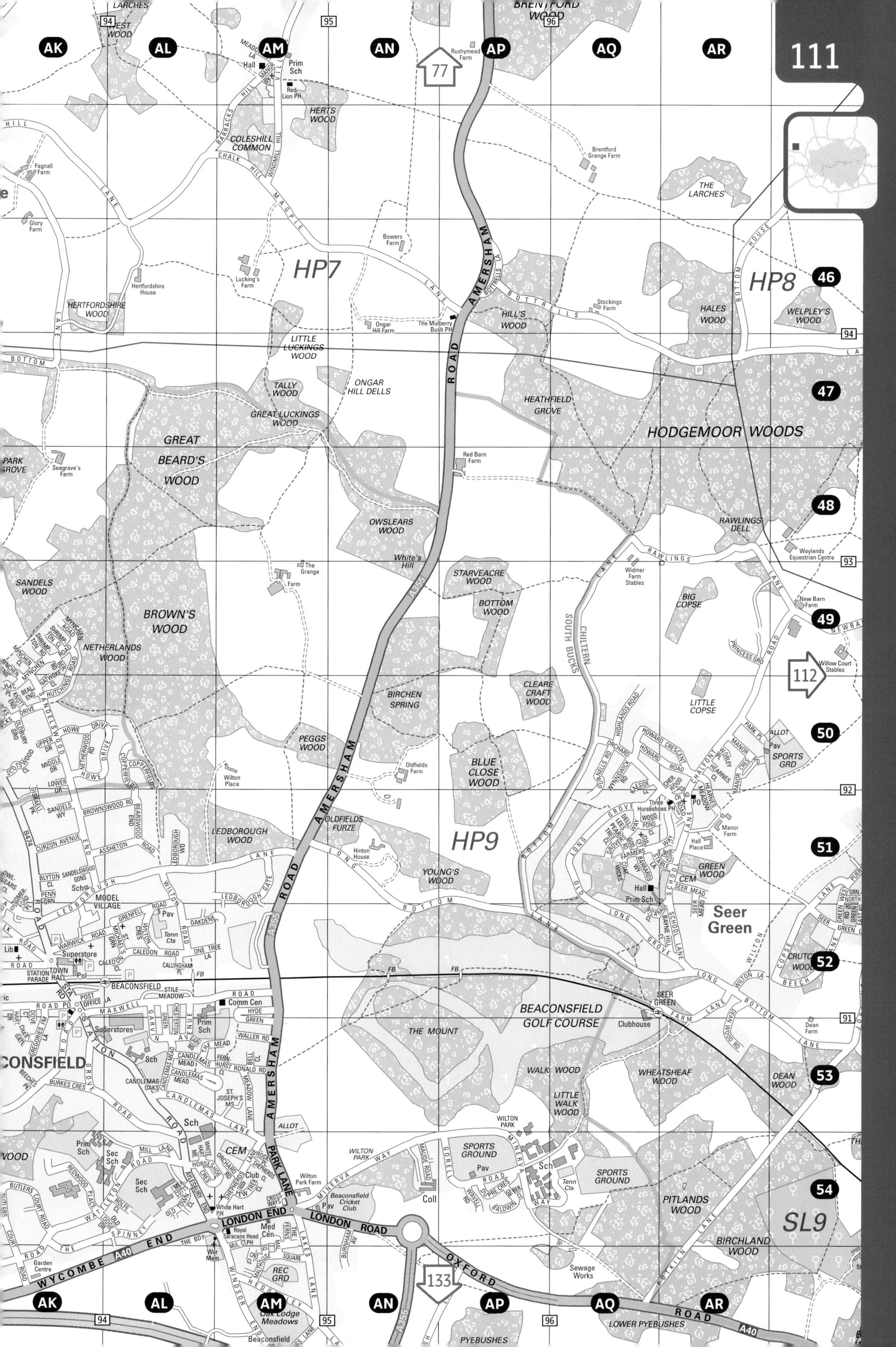

AK AL AM AN AP AQ AR
77
HP7
HP8
HP9
SL9
46 47 48 49 50 51 52 53 54
112
133
94 95 96 93 92 91
COLESHILL COMMON
HERTS WOOD
THE LARCHES
HERTFORDSHIRE WOOD
LITTLE LUCKINGS WOOD
ONGAR HILL DELLS
TALLY WOOD
GREAT LUCKINGS WOOD
GREAT BEARD'S WOOD
HILL'S WOOD
HALES WOOD
WELPLEY'S WOOD
HEATHFIELD GROVE
HODGEMOOR WOODS
OWSLEARS WOOD
RAWLINGS DELL
SANDELS WOOD
BROWN'S WOOD
NETHERLANDS WOOD
STARVEACRE WOOD
BOTTOM WOOD
BIG COPSE
BIRCHEN SPRING
CLEARE CRAFT WOOD
LITTLE COPSE
PEGGS WOOD
BLUE CLOSE WOOD
LEDBOROUGH WOOD
OLDFIELDS FURZE
YOUNG'S WOOD
GREEN WOOD
Seer Green
BEACONSFIELD GOLF COURSE
THE MOUNT
WALK WOOD
LITTLE WALK WOOD
WHEATSHEAF WOOD
DEAN WOOD
PITLANDS WOOD
BIRCHLAND WOOD
SPORTS GROUND
SPORTS GRD
MODEL VILLAGE
CONSFIELD
AMERSHAM ROAD
PARK LANE
LONDON END
LONDON ROAD
OXFORD ROAD
WYCOMBE END
LOWER PYEBUSHES
PYEBUSHES
Oak Lodge Meadows
Beaconsfield

AS
AT
AU
AV
AW
AX
AY
98
99
00
94
111
134
45
46
47
48
49
50
51
52
53
54
HP7
HP8
HP9
Chalfont St. Giles
Butlers Cross
Seer Green
Jordans
Layter's Green
HIGH WOOD
BOW WOOD
STRATTON COPSE
BAILEY WOOD
RESERVOIR PLANTATION
BAILEY WOOD BELT
KILNPOND WOOD
Shortenills Environmental Education Centre
SHORTENILLS WOOD
OAK PLANTATION
DELLGARDEN PLANTATION
THE LARCHES
BYCROFT PLANTATION
PERRYFIELD PLANTATION
RUSHCROFT WOOD
HALES WOOD
WELPLEY'S WOOD
MILLFIELD PLANTATION
GEMOOR WOODS
RAWLINGS DELL
BIG COPSE
LITTLE COPSE
Waylands Equestrian Centre
New Barn Farm
Highclere Farm
Willow Court Stables
Clubhouse
DRIVING RANGE
OAKLAND PARK GOLF COURSE
Youth Club
MILTON'S COTTAGE
SPORTS GRD
Bowling Green
CEM
Dibden Hill
Bramleys Farm
Dibden Hill Farm
Greyhound Track
Bowstridge
TURNER'S WOOD
Turner's Wood Farm
FOXDELL WOOD
PLAYING FIELD
Harmony Nurseries
LONG WOOD
FARM WOOD
Grove Farm
ROUND WOOD
MIDDLE WOOD
OUTFIELD PLANTATION
CHALFONT GROVE
Outfield Farm
Windmill Farm
POND WARREN WOOD
GROVE WOOD
Woodlands Farm
BIRCH PLANTATION
MONTAGUE'S DELL
Tennis Club
SPORTS GROUND
CRUTCHES WOOD
OLD JORDANS & MAYFLOWER BARN
Jordans Farm
Y.H.A.
Dean Farm
SPRING WOOD
Welders House
Stone Dean Farm
WELDERS WOOD
Leisure Centre
HOSP
DEAN WOOD
WEEDONS DELL
MOUNTHILL WOOD
THE ASH BEDS
THIRTY ACRE KNOLL
GREAT LEGS WOOD
MALMS WOOD
GOLDHILL COMMON
Layter's Green Farm
MOBILE HOME PARK
BIRCHLAND WOOD
HIGH WOOD
BEECH WOOD
Parkwood Farm
Stampwell Farm
BIRCH WOOD
AUSTENWOOD COMMON
Bowl Club
GREEN WOOD
Manor Farm
LONDON ROAD
AMERSHAM ROAD
GRAVEL HILL
A413
A40
B4442
0 500 yds
0 500 m

Chorleywood Bottom
The Swillet
Heronsgate
Mill End
Junction 17
GROVESPRING WOOD
PHILIPSHILL WOOD
NEWLAND GORSE
NEWLAND PARK
CHILTERN OPEN AIR MUSEUM
Buckinghamshire Chilterns University College
SPORTS GROUND
BOTTOM WOOD
LADYWALK WOOD
WD3
Maple Cross Roundabout
FIVE PLANTATIONS
POLLARDSHILL WOOD
Maple Cross
BEECHEN WOOD
Chalfont Common
KILN WOOD
ROBERT'S WOOD
SL9
ROUND ROCKET PLANTATION
QUARRY & LANDFILL SITE
MIDDLE WOOD
BLOOM WOOD
CEM
FRANKLINS SPRING
Maple Lodge Sewage Treatment Works
PLAYING FIELDS
LYNSTERS LAKE
UB9
West Hyde
PYNESFIELD LAKE
GRAVEL PIT
CHALFONT ST. PETER
HOGTROUGH WOOD
GERRARDS CROSS GOLF COURSE
Horseshoe Bay
Sailing Club
LITTLE HANGING WOOD
Denham Grove
NOCKHILL WOOD
JUNIPER WOOD
THREE RIVERS
SOUTH BUCKS
BUCKINGHAMSHIRE
HERTFORDSHIRE
M25
A405
A412
DENHAM WAY
95
114
135

RICKMANSWORTH
Moneyhill
Mill End
Batchworth
WD3
MOOR PARK GOLF COURSE
BATCHWORTH PARK GOLF COURSE
STOCKER'S LAKE NATURE RESERVE
Batchworth Heath
Hill End
HAREFIELD
UB9
HAREFIELD HOSPITAL
BISHOP'S WOOD
PARK WOOD
CROXLEY HALL WOOD
WOODCOCK HILL CEMETERY
WOODCOCK HILL INDUSTRIAL ESTATE
HERTFORDSHIRE
HILLINGDON
THREE RIVERS
96
113
136
BG
BH
BJ
BK
BL
BM
BN
05
06
07
45
46
47
48
49
50
51
52
53
54
94
93
92
91
0 500 yds
0 500 m

BP
BQ
BR
BS
BT
BU
BV
97
137
116
46
47
48
49
50
51
52
53
54
WD18
WD19
HA6
HA5
Holywell
Moor Park
MOOR PARK ESTATE
Eastbury
NORTHWOOD
Northwood Hills
OXHEY
SOUTH OXHEY PLAYING FIELDS
COMMON MOOR
LONG VALLEY WOOD
WATFORD BUSINESS PARK
CROXLEY BUSINESS PARK
HOLYWELL IND EST
KING GEORGE V PLAYING FIELDS
SPORTS GROUND
Electricity Transmission Station
WOLSEY BUSINESS PARK
ORBITAL 25 BUSINESS PARK
MOOR PARK INDUSTRIAL CENTRE
VALE INDUSTRIAL ESTATE
TOLPITS LANE
Tolpits Plantation
The Withey Bed Wood
Brightwells Spring
HAMPERMILL LAKE
HAMPERMILL LANE
RUNNING TRACK
Merchant Taylor's Sch
GOLF COURSE
SANDY LODGE GOLF COURSE
SANDY LODGE LANE
HAMPERMILL WOOD
BIG WOOD
Ox Pasture Spring
OLD FURZE FIELD
YOUNG HANGINGS
OLD HANGINGS
THE PLANTATION
BECK MASON'S WOOD
Northwood Headquarters
BATHEND CLUMP
BATCHWORTH LANE
RICKMANSWORTH ROAD
MOUNT VERNON HOSPITAL
THE GRAVEL PITS
WATFORD ROAD
SANDY LANE
WILD WOODS
St. John's Sch
PINNER WOOD
PINNER HILL GOLF COURSE
PINNER PARK
HOGS BACK OPEN SPACE
NORTHWOOD GOLF COURSE
HASTE HILL GOLF COURSE
NORTHWOOD CEMETERY
RUISLIP NATURE RESERVE
COPSE WOOD
DUCKS HILL
HIGH STREET
PINNER ROAD
A404
A4125
A4145
A4180
HILLINGDON
THREE RIVERS
POOR'S FIELD
YOUNGWOOD

BW
BX
BY
BZ
CA
CB
CC
98
115
138
45
46
47
48
49
50
51
52
53
54
94
93
92
91
12
13
14
BUSHEY
BUSHEY GOLF COURSE & COUNTRY CLUB
WATFORD HEATH
SPOILBANKS
SHERWOODS WOOD
MARGEHOLES WOOD
GOLF DRIVING RANGE
OXHEY PARK GOLF COURSE
WD19
WD23
WD23
SOUTH OXHEY PLAYING FIELDS
Ox Pasture Spring
Warren Dell
MERRY HILL
CARPENDERS PARK
HARTSBOURNE GOLF COURSE & COUNTRY CLUB
SOUTH OXHEY
POND WOOD
WOODWALKS
CARPENDERS PARK CEMETERY
MUTTON WOOD
LEVELS WOOD
Grim's Dyke Hotel
WEALD WOOD
GRIM'S DYKE GOLF COURSE
BECK MAN'S WOOD
SANDPIT WOOD
HERTFORDSHIRE
HERTSMERE
HARROW
STONY WOOD
NANSCOT WOOD
WILD WOODS
THREE RIVERS
SADDLERS MEAD REC GROUND
HATCH END
SHAFTESBURY PLAYING FIELDS
PINNER WOOD
PINNER HILL GOLF COURSE
HA5
PINNERWOOD PARK
HATCH END PLAYING FIELD
RAGHUVANSHI CHARITABLE TRUST SPORTS GROUND
PINNER PARK
SPORTS GROUND
BANNISTER STADIUM
MONTESOLE PLAYING FIELDS
PINNER GREEN
LITTLE COMMON
HA2
HEADSTONE MANOR
KING GEORGE REC GROUND
HILL MEAD NATURE PARK
Haydon Hill House
Watford Borough Council Nursery
Watford Equestrian Centre
Carpenders Park Farm
Oxhey Lane Farm
Grimswood House
Highcroft
Pinnerwood Farm
Pinner Park Farm
UXBRIDGE ROAD
OXHEY LANE
EASTBURY LANE
PINNER ROAD
LONDON ROAD
HIGH STREET
SPARROWS HERNE
RICKMANSWORTH RD
ST. THOMAS' DRIVE
A4008
A4125
A411
A410
A404
B4542
0 500 yds
0 500 m

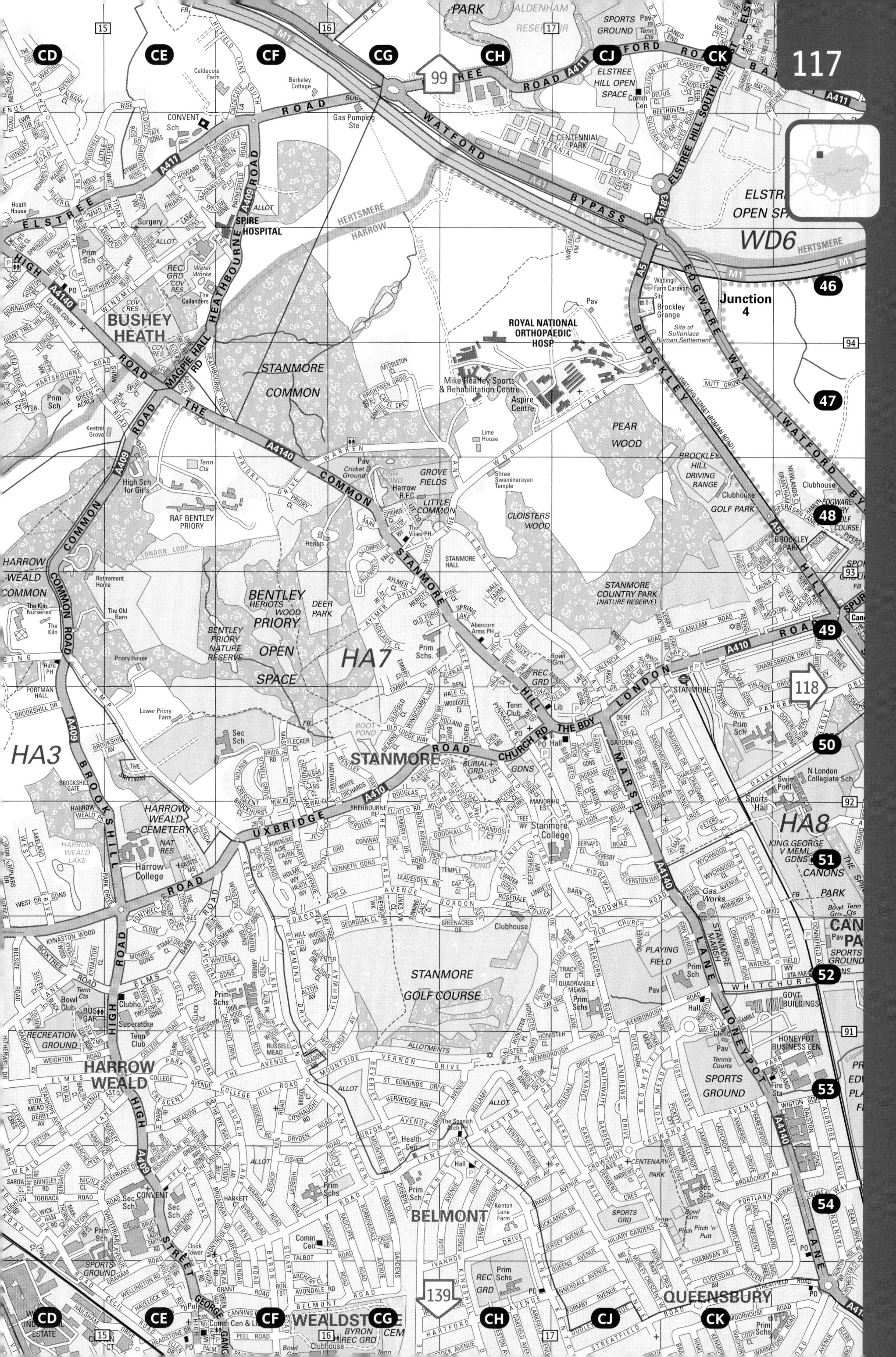
CD
CE
CF
CG
CH
CJ
CK
15
16
17
99
118
139
94
93
92
91
46
47
48
49
50
51
52
53
54
ELSTREE ROAD
WATFORD BY-PASS
A41
A411
M1
A5
A5183
A4140
A409
A410
HERTSMERE
HARROW
WD6
HA7
HA3
HA8
Junction 4
BUSHEY HEATH
SPIRE HOSPITAL
STANMORE COMMON
ROYAL NATIONAL ORTHOPAEDIC HOSP
Mike Heafey Sports & Rehabilitation Centre
Aspire Centre
PEAR WOOD
CLOISTERS WOOD
BROCKLEY HILL DRIVING RANGE
GOLF PARK
STANMORE COUNTRY PARK (NATURE RESERVE)
BENTLEY PRIORY OPEN SPACE
BENTLEY PRIORY NATURE RESERVE
RAF BENTLEY PRIORY
HARROW WEALD COMMON
HARROW WEALD CEMETERY
Harrow College
STANMORE
STANMORE GOLF COURSE
Stanmore College
STANMORE MARSH
HARROW WEALD
BELMONT
QUEENSBURY
WEALDSTONE
CANONS PARK
KING GEORGE V MEML GDNS
N London Collegiate Sch
HONEYPOT BUSINESS CEN
SPORTS GROUND
RECREATION GROUND
ELSTREE HILL OPEN SPACE
CENTENNIAL PARK
BROCKLEY HILL
EDGWARE WAY
WATLING STREET (ROMAN ROAD)
Site of Sulloniace Roman Settlement
UXBRIDGE ROAD
CHURCH RD
LONDON ROAD
MARSH LANE
HONEYPOT LANE
HIGH ROAD
BROOKSHILL
COMMON ROAD
KENTON LANE
HIGH STREET
GEORGE STREET
WHITCHURCH LANE
GORDON AVENUE
VERNON DRIVE
THE BDY

CL
CM
CN
CP
CQ
CR
CS
100
117
140
DEACONS HILL OPEN SPACE
Deacons Hill
SCRATCH WOOD
FROGHALL WOOD
BOYS HILL WOOD
THISTLE WOOD
CLUMP OF TREES WOOD
TARGET WOOD
GRAVEL PIT WOOD
MILL HILL GOLF COURSE
NUT WOOD
HEMMINGS WOOD
STONEY WOOD
Stirling Corner
ELSTREE OPEN SPACE
WD6
HERTSMERE
BARNET
Junction 4
London Gateway Services
EDGWAREBURY CEMETERY
EDGWAREBURY PARK
BROCKLEY HILL DRIVING RANGE
EDGWAREBURY GOLF COURSE
Canons Corner
Apex Corner
CONVENT
STONEGROVE PARK
EDGWARE
HA8
KING GEORGE V MEML GDNS
CANONS PARK
CHANDOS RECREATION GROUND
EDGWARE COMMUNITY HOSPITAL
BURNT OAK
WATLING PARK
LYNDHURST PARK
ADASTRAL ESTATE
HA7
HONEYPOT BUSINESS CEN
PRINCE EDWARD PLAYING FIELD
MONTROSE PLAYING FIELDS
NW LONDON HEALTH PROTECTION UNIT
BLOOD TRANSFUSION CENTRE
COLINDALE BUSINESS PK
COLINDALE
QUEENSBURY
BRITISH LIBRARY NEWSPAPERS
45
46
47
48
49
50
51
52
53
54
19
20
21
91
92
93
94
A411
A41
A5
A410
A5100
A5109
A4140
M1
A1
500 yds
500 m

Barnet Gate
Ducks Island
101
N20
OLD ELIZABETHANS (BARNET) MEMORIAL PLAYING FIELDS
GRANGE PLAYING FIELDS
OLD CHOLMELEIAN SPORTS GROUND
TOTTERIDGE FIELDS NATURE RESERVE
TOTTERIDGE PARK
TOTTERIDGE COMMON
TOTTERIDGE
TOTTERIDGE VILLAGE
TOTTERIDGE GREEN
HENDON PARK WOOD
BEECH WOOD
HIGHWOOD PARK
Highwood Hill
Holcombe Dales
DARLANDS LAKE NATURE RESERVE
Consolata Missionary Coll
Folly Farm
SPORTS GROUND
Clubhouses
Burtonhole Farm
Nat Inst for Medical Research
NW7
N12
120
THE MILL FIELD
CHALET ESTATE
MARSHALL ESTATE
Mill Hill Circus
MILL HILL
ARRANDENE OPEN SPACE
Featherstone Hill
MILL HILL PARK
MILL HILL CEM
Drivers Hill
Watch Tower House
BITTACY HILL PARK
FINCHLEY GOLF COURSE
Nether Court (Clubhouse)
Council Depot
MILL HILL EAST
CHASE LODGE PLAYING FIELD
METRO GOLF RANGE
HENDON GOLF COURSE
Crematorium
HENDON CEMETERY
BARNET COPTHALL STADIUM
COPTHALL PLAYING FIELDS
COPTHALL SPORTS GROUND
Junction 2
Five Ways Corner
HOLDERS HILL
CHURCH END
FINCHLEY CENTRAL
N3
NW4
SUNNY HILL PARK
NW9
RAF MUSEUM
Pentavia Retail Park
Mill Hill Ind Est
WINDSOR OPEN SPACE
Bridgewater Hotel Hendon Hall
141
WATFORD WAY
GREAT NORTH WAY
HENDON LANE
REGENTS PARK ROAD
CT
CU
CV
CW
CX
CY
CZ
22
23
24
46
47
48
49
50
51
52
53
54

DA
DB
DC
DD
DE
DF
DG
102
119
142
45
46
47
48
49
50
51
52
53
54
EAST BARNET
Oak Hill College
OAK HILL PARK
EN4
SOUTH HERTS GOLF COURSE
N20
BROOK FARM OPEN SPACE
WYATTS FARM OPEN SPACE
KING GEORGE V PLAYING FIELDS
BARNET PLAYING FIELDS
DAME ALICE OWEN'S GRD
OAKLEIGH PARK
TOTTERIDGE & WHETSTONE
TOTTERIDGE GREEN
WHETSTONE
Consolata Missionary Coll
SWAN LANE OPEN SPACE
NORTH MIDDLESEX GOLF COURSE
BRUNSWICK PARK
MIDDLESEX UNI
BETHUNE PARK GOLF COURSE
FRIARY PARK
FRIERN BARNET
N12
WOODSIDE PARK
NORTH FINCHLEY
FINCHLEY
COPPETTS WOOD
WEST FINCHLEY
FINCHLEY MEMORIAL HOSP
GLEBELANDS OPEN SPACE
VICTORIA PARK
FINCHLEY CENTRAL
CHURCH END
N3
MUSWELL HILL SPORTS GROUND
COPPETTS WOOD HOSP
ST. PANCRAS & ISLINGTON CEMETERY
Crematorium
COLDFALL WOOD
N2
N10
TOTTERIDGE LANE
A5109
A109
OAKLEIGH ROAD NORTH
A1000
HIGH ROAD
BALLARDS LANE
A598
A1003
WOODHOUSE ROAD
FRIERN BARNET LANE
NORTH CIRCULAR ROAD
A406
EAST END RD
A504
500 yds
500 m

DH
DJ
DK
DL
DM
DN
DP
103
OAKWOOD
OAKWOOD PARK
WINCHMORE HILL
GROVELANDS PARK
N14
N21
OSIDGE
SOUTHGATE
PRIORY HOSPITAL
SOUTHGATE CEMETERY
PALMERS GREEN
ARNOS PARK
NEW SOUTHGATE
BROOMFIELD PARK
N13
N11
BOWES PARK
MUSWELL HILL GOLF COURSE
N22
WOOD GREEN
NOEL PARK
ALEXANDRA PALACE
ALEXANDRA PARK
MUSWELL HILL
HORNSEY
THE PAULIN GROUND
CLOWES SPORTS GROUND
HAZELWOOD SPORTS GRD
TOTTENHALL SPORTS GROUND
NEW RIVER SPORTS CENTRE
FRIERN BRIDGE RETAIL PARK
TRAIN DEPOT
122
143
46
47
48
49
50
51
52
53
54
29
30
31

DQ
DR
DS
DT
DU
DV
DW
104
121
144
45
46
47
48
49
50
51
52
53
54
N21
N13
N22
N17
N18
N9
RIDGE AVENUE
GREAT CAMBRIDGE ROAD
HERTFORD ROAD
JUBILEE PARK
LOWER EDMONTON
EDMONTON
UPPER EDMONTON
TOTTENHAM
TOTTENHAM HALE
TOTTENHAM MARSHES
EDMONTON CEMETERY
FIRS FARM PLAYING FIELDS
CLOWES SPORTS GROUND
THE PAULIN GROUND
CHURCH STREET REC GRD
CHURCHFIELD REC GRD
PYMMES PARK
TATEM PARK REC GRD
HOLLY-WOOD GDNS
Great Cambridge Junction
STERLING WAY
SILVER STREET
ANGEL ROAD
CONDUIT LANE
Kenninghall
NORTH MIDDLESEX UNIVERSITY HOSPITAL
TOTTENHALL SPORTS GROUND
BOUNDARY PLAYING FIELDS
SPORTS GROUND
LANDMARK COMMERCIAL CENTRE
EDMONTON FEDERATION CEMETERY (JEWISH)
WESTERN SYNAGOGUE CEMETERY
TOTTENHAM PARK CEMETERY
MONTAGU RECREATION GROUND
CRAIG PARK
TRIUMPH TRADING EST
HOTSPUR IND EST
MOWLEM TRADING ESTATE
TOTTENHAM CEMETERY
BRUCE CASTLE PARK
TOTTENHAM HOTSPUR FC
WHITE HART LANE
THE ROUNDWAY
LORDSHIP LANE
LORDSHIP RECREATION GROUND
BROADWATER FARM EST
TOWER GDNS
PEABODY EST
BRUCE GROVE
LEE VALLEY TECHNOPARK
DOWN LANE REC GRD
MILMEAD INDUSTRIAL CENTRE
LOCKWOOD RESERVOIR
MERIDIAN WAY
WATERMEAD WAY
LRT DEPOT
DOWNHILLS PARK
500 yds
500 m

DX
DY
DZ
EA
EB
EC
ED
36
37
38
105
124
145
46
47
48
49
50
51
52
53
54
LEE VALLEY
WILLIAM
GIRLING
RESERVOIR
GOLF
COURSE
LEE VALLEY
REGIONAL
PARK
DEEPHAMS
SEWAGE
TREATMENT
WORKS
BANBURY
RESERVOIR
CHINGFORD
E4
FRIDAY
HILL
CHINGFORD
HATCH
SOUTH
CHINGFORD
HIGHAMS
PARK
HALE END
HIGHAM
HILL
E17
WALTHAMSTOW
IG8
CHINGFORD MOUNT
CEMETERY
LARKS
WOOD
THE
HAWK
WOOD
POLE
HILL
MANSFIELD
PARK
RIDGEWAY
PARK
LLOYD
PARK
WALTHAMSTOW
STADIUM
(closed)
EPPING
FOREST
Crooked Billet
Cooks Ferry
Hall La
Wood
Street
The
Bell
LEA VALLEY VIADUCT
SOUTHEND ROAD
NORTH CIRCULAR
KINGS HEAD HILL
NEW ROAD
HALL LANE
OLD CHURCH ROAD
CHINGFORD MOUNT ROAD
CHINGFORD ROAD
LARKSHALL ROAD
WALTHAM WAY
SEWARDSTONE ROAD
MANSFIELD HILL
A110
A112
A1009
A1037
A406
A503
A104
A1055
B160
B169
B179
B179

EE
EF
EG
EH
EJ
EK
EL
40
41
42
106
123
146
45
46
47
48
49
50
51
52
53
54
94
93
92
91
IG10
IG9
IG8
E4
E17
E18
CHINGFORD PLAIN
QUEEN ELIZABETH'S HUNTING LODGE
RANGERS ROAD
A1069
CHINGFORD
THE WARREN
HATCH FOREST
Tenn & Bowl Club
CHINGFORD GREEN
BARN HOPPETT
Buckhurst Hill
Warren Hill House
Holmhurst
Oak Hall
Warren Wood PH
EPPING NEW ROAD
MANOR ROAD
ROEBUCK GRN
ROEBUCK LANE
Cricket Ground
WHITEHALL PLAIN
WHITEHALL ROAD
A110
FRIDAY HILL
PIMP HALL PARK
BLUEHOUSE GROVE
SPORTS GROUND
HATCH FOREST
HATCH GROVE
THE BIRBECK
REED'S FOREST
Hatch Plain
Bancroft's Sch
PALMERSTON ROAD
B170
BUCKHURST HILL
QUEENS ROAD
Holiday Inn Express
HOLLY HOUSE HOSP
Amb Sta
Elec Sta
LORD'S BUSHES
Knighton Wood
MONKHAMS LANE
Woodford Wells
WOODFORD GOLF COURSE
The Lops
NEW ROAD
HATCH LA
CHINGFORD AVENUE
WOODFORD GREEN
A1009
THE HIGHAMS PARK
BOATING LAKE
HIGHAMS PARK
HALE END
WOODFORD R.F.C.
Woodford Wells Club
Cricket Ground
Horse & Well PH
RAY PARK
RODING VALLEY
LUXBOROUGH LANE TREATMENT WORKS
LOUGHTON R.F.C. Clubho.
BANCROFT R.F.C.
LONDON GUILDHALL UNI SPORTS GRD
EPPING FOREST
ASHTON PLAYING FIELD
RUNNING TRACK
Gas Works
SPORTS PITCH
WOODFORD
BROADMEAD
HIGH ROAD
CHIGWELL ROAD
A113
DARTNALLS PLAYING FLD
PLAYING FLDS
ORCHARD EST
ALLOTMENTS
OLD MONOVIANS SPORTS GRD
WANSTEAD Clubhouse RFC
SPORTS GROUND
EPPING FOREST
WALTHAMSTOW FOREST
County Hotel
Royal Oak PH
Churchill Statue
Woodford Green C.C.
St. Margaret's
THE OAKS
FOREST DRIVE
SOUTHEND ROAD
NORTH CIRCULAR ROAD
A406
Waterworks Corner
George Lane Roundabout
Charlie Brown's Roundabout
SOUTH WOODFORD
WOODFORD TRADING ESTATE
UNITY TRADING ESTATE
Cocked Hat PH
Snaresbrook Coll
Junction
ONSLOW GDNS
A1199
A503
Hyland Ho Sch
COV RES
NEW ROAD
0
500 yds
500 m

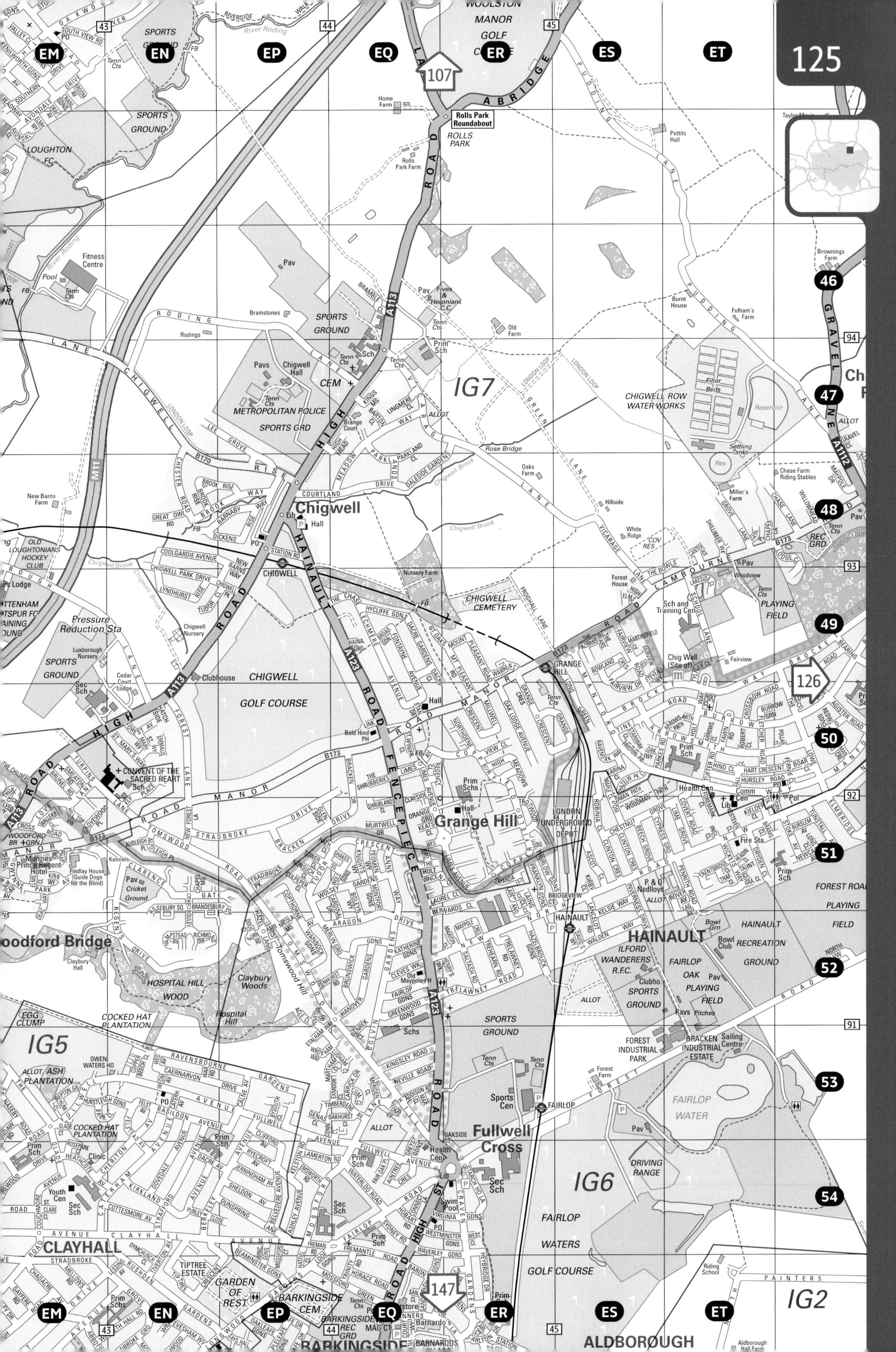
EM
EN
EP
EQ
ER
ES
ET
107
126
147
WOOLSTON MANOR GOLF COURSE
River Roding
SPORTS GROUND
LOUGHTON FC
Rolls Park Roundabout
ROLLS PARK
Home Farm
Rolls Park Farm
Pettits Hall
ABRIDGE ROAD
PUDDING LANE
Fitness Centre
Pool
Pav
Bramstones
Rodings
RODING LANE
CHIGWELL LANE
SPORTS GROUND
Chigwell Hall
CEM
METROPOLITAN POLICE SPORTS GRD
IG7
Oaks Farm
Old Farm
Burnt House
Fulham's Farm
CHIGWELL ROW WATER WORKS
Filter Beds
Reservoir
Settling Tanks
Browning Farm
GRAVEL LANE
ALLOT
Chase Farm Riding Stables
Miller's Farm
Rose Bridge
VICARAGE LANE
GREEN LANE
New Barns Farm
M11
Chigwell
HAINAULT ROAD
HIGH ROAD
A113
A123
A1112
B170
B173
CHIGWELL
Hillside
White Ridge
COV RES
Forest House
LAMBOURNE ROAD
Sch and Training Cen
PLAYING FIELD
OLD LOUGHTONIANS HOCKEY CLUB
Nursery Farm
CHIGWELL CEMETERY
Chig Well (Site of)
Pressure Reduction Sta
Chigwell Nursery
Luxborough Nursery
SPORTS GROUND
GRANGE HILL
Cedar Court Lodge
CHIGWELL GOLF COURSE
Clubhouse
MANOR ROAD
Bald Hind PH
FENCEPIECE ROAD
CONVENT OF THE SACRED HEART
Grange Hill
LONDON UNDERGROUND DEPOT
Health Cen
Fire Sta
FOREST ROAD
PLAYING FIELD
Manzies Prince Regent Hotel
Findlay House (Guide Dogs for the Blind)
Cricket Ground
Woodford Bridge
HAINAULT
P & O Nedlloyd
HAINAULT RECREATION GROUND
ILFORD WANDERERS R.F.C.
FAIRLOP OAK PLAYING FIELD
Claybury Hall
HOSPITAL HILL WOOD
Claybury Woods
Hospital Hill
Tomswood Hill
SPORTS GROUND
FOREST INDUSTRIAL PARK
BRACKEN INDUSTRIAL ESTATE
Sailing Centre
EGG CLUMP
COCKED HAT PLANTATION
IG5
ALLOT ASH PLANTATION
FOREST ROAD
FAIRLOP WATER
Fullwell Cross
FAIRLOP
DRIVING RANGE
IG6
FAIRLOP WATERS GOLF COURSE
CLAYHALL
TIPTREE ESTATE
GARDEN OF REST
BARKINGSIDE CEM
Riding School
PAINTERS
IG2
ALDBOROUGH
BARKINGSIDE

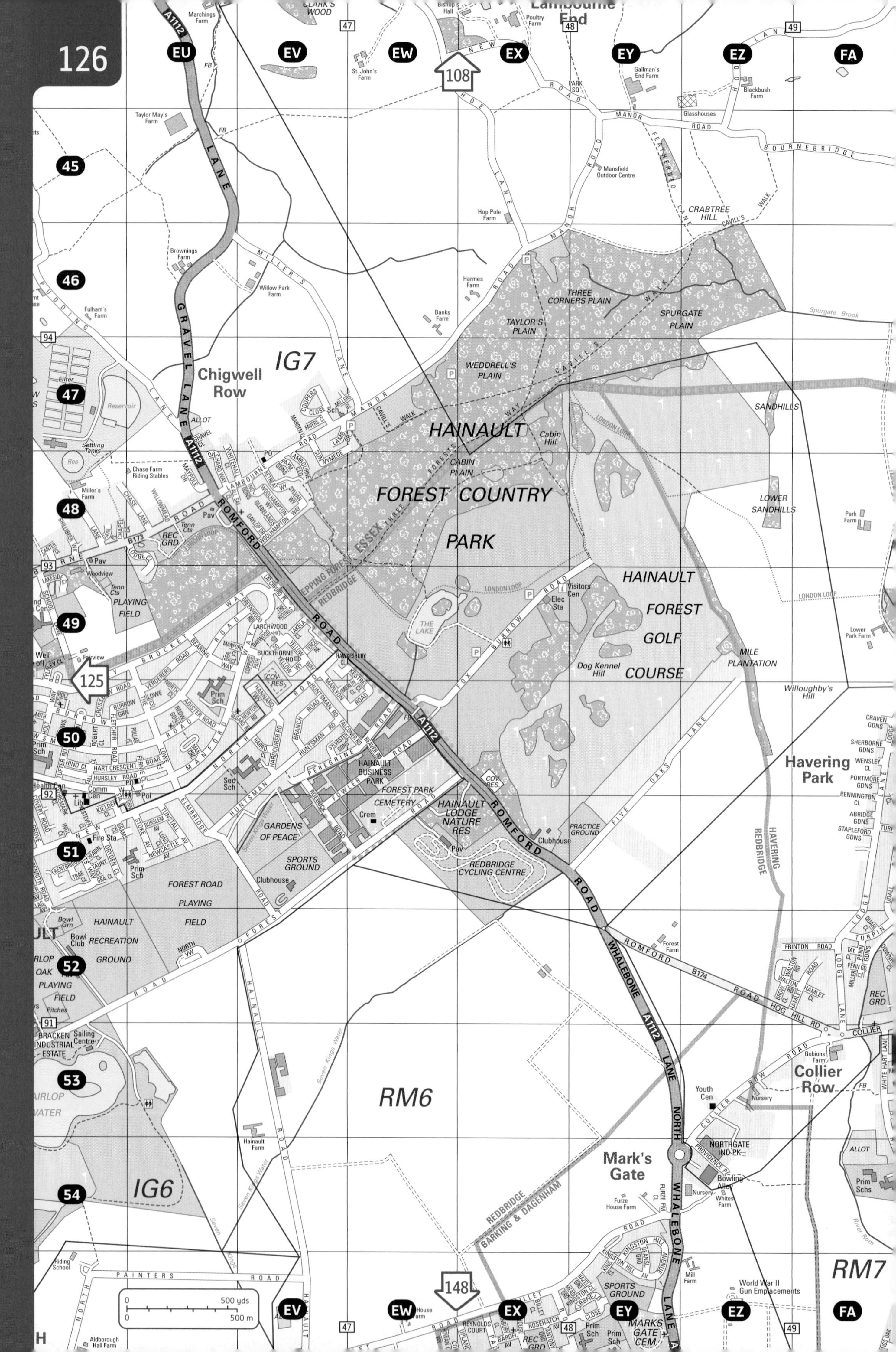

EU
EV
EW
EX
EY
EZ
FA
108
125
148
45
46
47
48
49
50
51
52
53
54
IG7
IG6
RM6
RM7
Chigwell Row
HAINAULT FOREST COUNTRY PARK
HAINAULT FOREST GOLF COURSE
Havering Park
Collier Row
Mark's Gate
THE LAKE
THREE CORNERS PLAIN
TAYLOR'S PLAIN
SPURGATE PLAIN
WEDDRELL'S PLAIN
CABIN PLAIN
Cabin Hill
CRABTREE HILL
SANDHILLS
LOWER SANDHILLS
MILE PLANTATION
Dog Kennel Hill
Willoughby's Hill
HAINAULT BUSINESS PARK
FOREST PARK CEMETERY
GARDENS OF PEACE
SPORTS GROUND
HAINAULT LODGE NATURE RES
REDBRIDGE CYCLING CENTRE
FOREST ROAD PLAYING FIELD
HAINAULT RECREATION GROUND
NORTHGATE IND PK
BRACKEN INDUSTRIAL ESTATE
GRAVEL LANE
ROMFORD ROAD
MANOR ROAD
FOX BURROW ROAD
FIVE OAKS LANE
WHALEBONE LANE NORTH
HAINAULT ROAD
FOREST ROAD
PAINTERS ROAD
COLLIER ROW ROAD
HOG HILL RD
BOURNEBRIDGE LANE
REDBRIDGE
HAVERING
BARKING & DAGENHAM
EPPING FOREST
ESSEX
0 500 yds
0 500 m

FB
FC
FD
FE
FF
FG
FH
109
CM14
Nuper's Hatch
NOAK HILL ROAD
TYSEA HILL
Noak Hill
STRAIGHTS PLANTATION
PALACE PLANTATION
SANDPITS PLANTATION
WITCH HILL PLANTATION
HILLY PARK
EPPING FOREST
ESSEX
HAVERING
BRENTWOOD
EPPING FOREST
46
47
48
49
50
51
52
53
54
94
93
92
91
TRENCH POND PLANTATION
PYRGO PARK
FOXBURROW WOOD
SOUTH PARK PLANTATION
Havering-atte-Bower
ST. FRANCIS HOSPICE
RM4
PHEASANT WOOD
AVENUE WOOD
HAVERING COUNTRY PARK
PINE WOOD
ROUND WOOD
BIG FIELD
BEAN FIELD
KILN WOOD
FURRY FIELD
BEDFORD'S PARK
SPORTS GROUND
BOWER WOOD
SPRING WOODS
LARCH WOOD
NURSERY WOOD
BEDFORD'S PARK
Chase Cross
BEDFORDS LAKE
128
RM5
RM1
RISEBRIDGE GOLF COURSE
RISE PARK
LAWNS REC GRD
RM3
ROMFORD GOLF COURSE
RM2
RAPHAEL PARK
GIDEA PARK SPORTS GRD
Gidea Park
EASTERN AVENUE
EAST
MAIN ROAD
149
50
51
52
KING GEORGE'S PLAYING FIELDS
HUBBINET IND EST

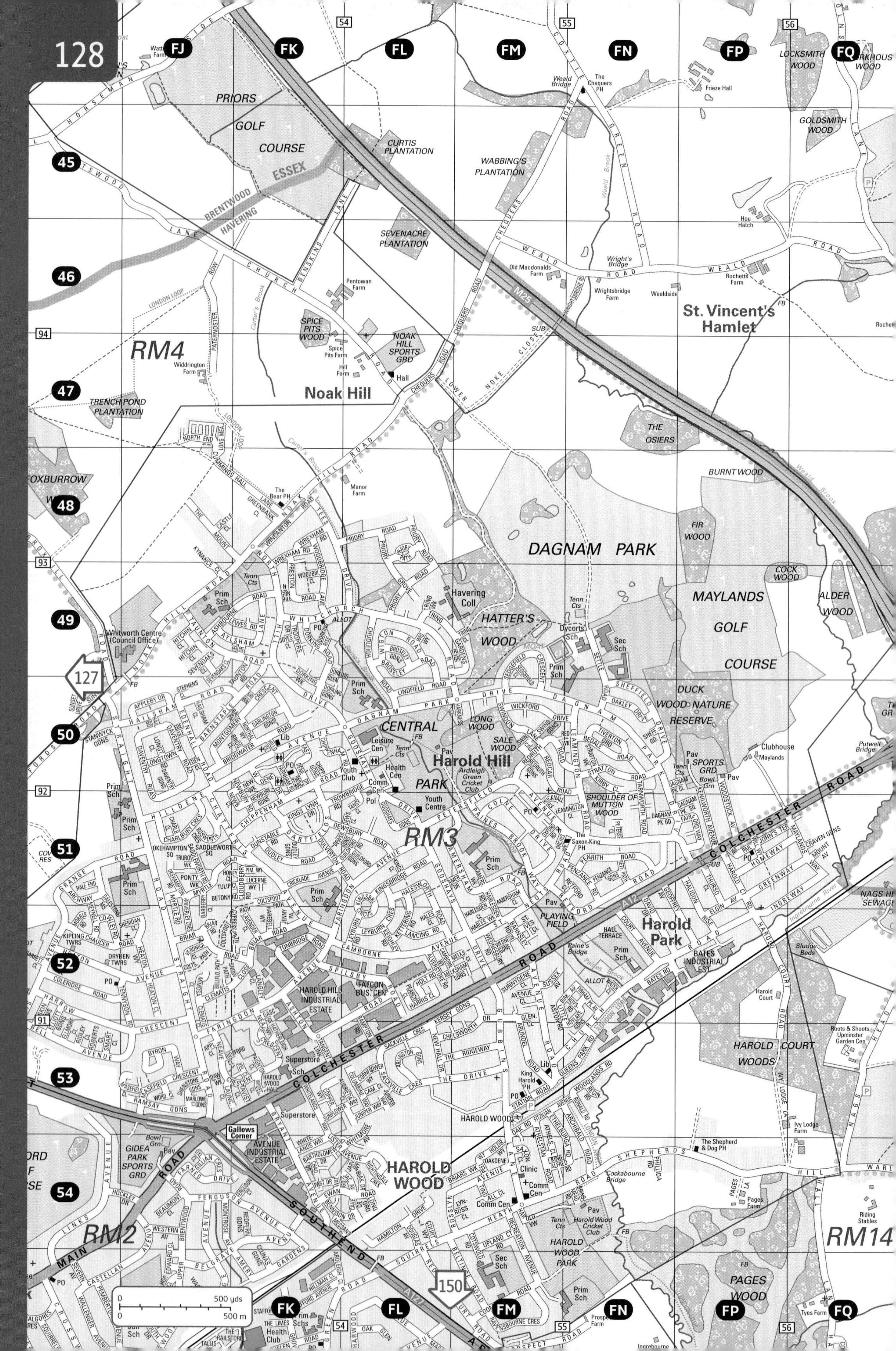
Noak Hill
Harold Hill
Harold Park
Harold Wood
St. Vincent's Hamlet
DAGNAM PARK
MAYLANDS GOLF COURSE
PRIORS GOLF COURSE
RM4
RM3
RM2
RM14
CENTRAL PARK
HAROLD COURT WOODS
HAROLD WOOD PARK
COLCHESTER ROAD
SOUTHEND ROAD
ESSEX
BRENTWOOD
HAVERING
DUCK WOOD NATURE RESERVE
HATTER'S WOOD
PAGES WOOD
500 yds
500 m

127
150

BRENTWOOD
CM14
CM15
CM13
WEALD COUNTRY PARK
South Weald
Brook Street
Warley
Great Warley
WARLEY COUNTRY PARK
Junction 28
BRENTWOOD BYPASS
HIGH STREET
LONDON ROAD
BROOK STREET
SHENFIELD ROAD
INGRAVE ROAD
ONGAR ROAD
WEALD ROAD
HIGHWOOD HOSP
MARILLAC HOSPITAL
SPIRE HARTSWOOD HOSP
ESSEX NUFFIELD HOSP
MASCALLS PARK
THORNDON PARK GOLF COURSE
HOLDEN'S WOOD
BARRACK WOOD
ELLEN'S WOOD
WARLEY PLACE NATURE RESERVE
BRENTWOOD LEISURE PARK
BRENTWOOD
HAVERING
ESSEX
130
131
151

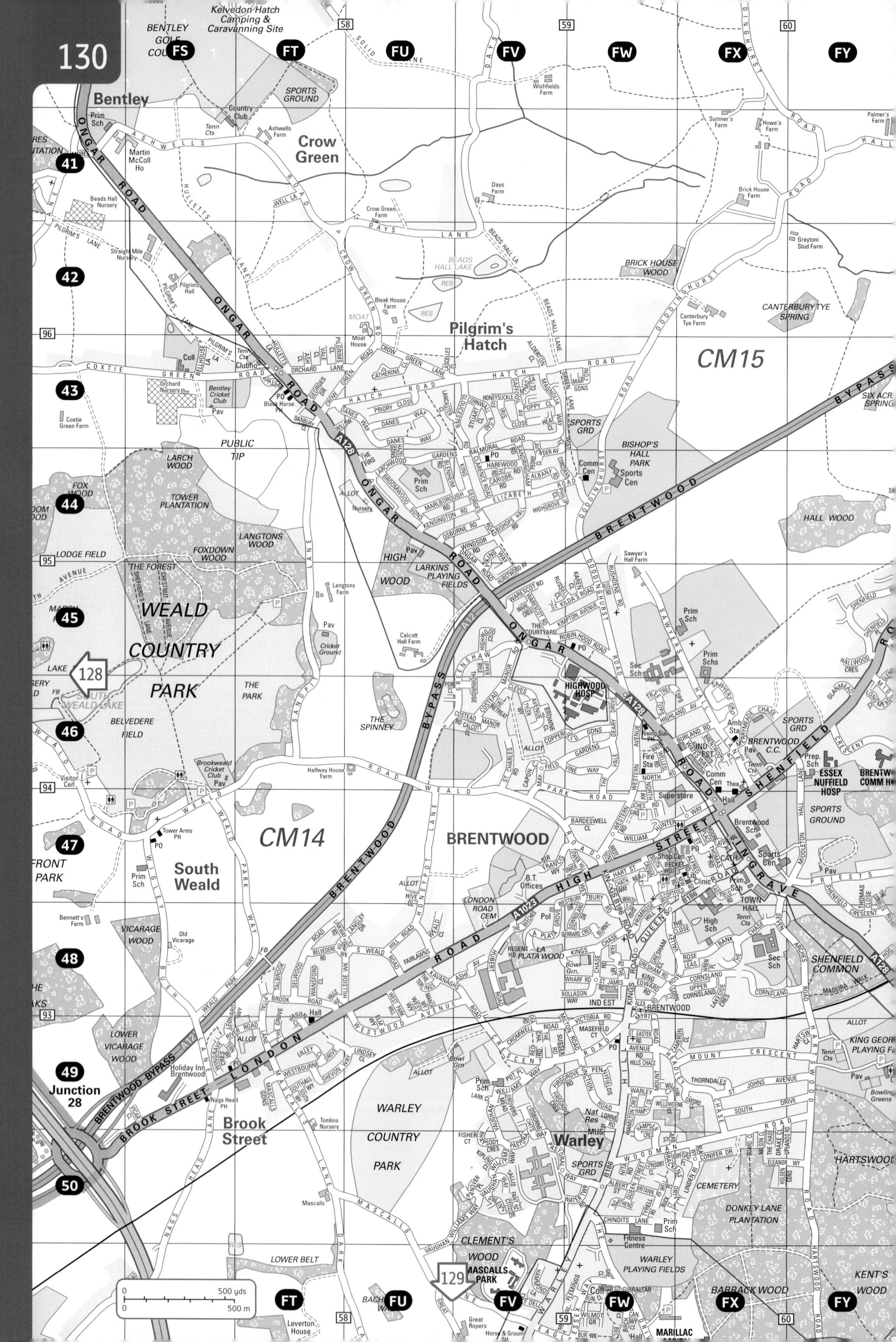
Kelvedon Hatch Camping & Caravanning Site
Bentley Golf Course
Bentley
Prim Sch
Martin McColl Ho
Country Club
Sports Ground
Tenn Cts
Ashwells Farm
Crow Green
Ashwells Road
Days Lane
Wishfields Farm
Sumner's Farm
Howe's Farm
Palmer's Farm
Beads Hall Nursery
Days Farm
Crow Green Farm
Brick House Farm
Graytoni Stud Farm
Pilgrim's Lane
Straight Mile Nursery
Pilgrims Hall
Beads Hall Lake
Res
Brick House Wood
Bleak House Farm
Moat
Moat House
Canterbury Tye Farm
Canterbury Tye Spring
Pilgrim's Hatch
CM15
Ongar Road
Coxtie Green Road
Coll
Tenn Cts
Clubho
Orchard Nursery
Bentley Cricket Club
Pav
Coxtie Green Farm
Black Horse PH
PO
Hatch Road
Doddinghurst Road
Sports Grd
Bishop's Hall Park
Sports Cen
Comm Cen
Six Acre Spring
Public Tip
Larch Wood
Fox Wood
Tower Plantation
Prim Sch
Allot
Nursery
Hall Wood
Brentwood Bypass
A128
A12
Langtons Wood
Foxdown Wood
Lodge Field
The Forest
Weald Country Park
High Wood
Larkins Playing Fields
Sawyer's Hall Farm
Langtons Farm
Pav
Cricket Ground
Calcott Hall Farm
Prim Sch
Prim Schs
Sec Sch
Highwood Hosp
Lake
128
South Weald Lake
The Park
Belvedere Field
The Spinney
Brookweald Cricket Club
Halfway House Farm
Weald Road
Visitor Cen
Rising Sun PH
Fire Sta
Ind Est
Comm Cen
Amb Sta
Brentwood C.C.
Sports Grd
Essex Nuffield Hosp
Brentwood Comm H
Prep. Sch
Sports Ground
Superstore
Thea
Hall
Brentwood Sch
Shenfield Road
CM14
Brentwood
Tower Arms PH
PO
South Weald
Prim Sch
Front Park
High Street
Shop Cen
Lib
Clinic
Prim Sch
Town Hall
High Sch
Tenn Cts
Sports Cen
Pav
Ingrave Road
Priests Lane
B.T. Offices
London Road Cem
Pol
Allot
Bennett's Farm
Vicarage Wood
Old Vicarage
Regent La Plata Wood
Bowl Grn.
Ind Est
Shenfield Common
Sec Sch
Brentwood
Lower Vicarage Wood
A1023
Hall
Allot
Holiday Inn Brentwood
Junction 28
Brentwood Bypass
Brook Street
Nags Head PH
Bowl Grn
Allot
Prim Sch
Warley Country Park
Tomlins Nursery
Nat Res
Mus
Warley
Sports Grd
Cemetery
Donkey Lane Plantation
King George Playing Fields
Tenn Cts
Pav
Bowling Greens
Hartswood
Mascalls
Chindits Lane
Prim Sch
Fitness Centre
Warley Playing Fields
Clement's Wood
Lower Belt
129
Mascalls Park
Barrack Wood
Kent's Wood
Coll
Great Ropers
Horse & Groom
Leverton House
Marillac
0 500 yds
0 500 m
41 42 43 44 45 46 47 48 49 50
93 94 95 96
58 59 60
FS FT FU FV FW FX FY

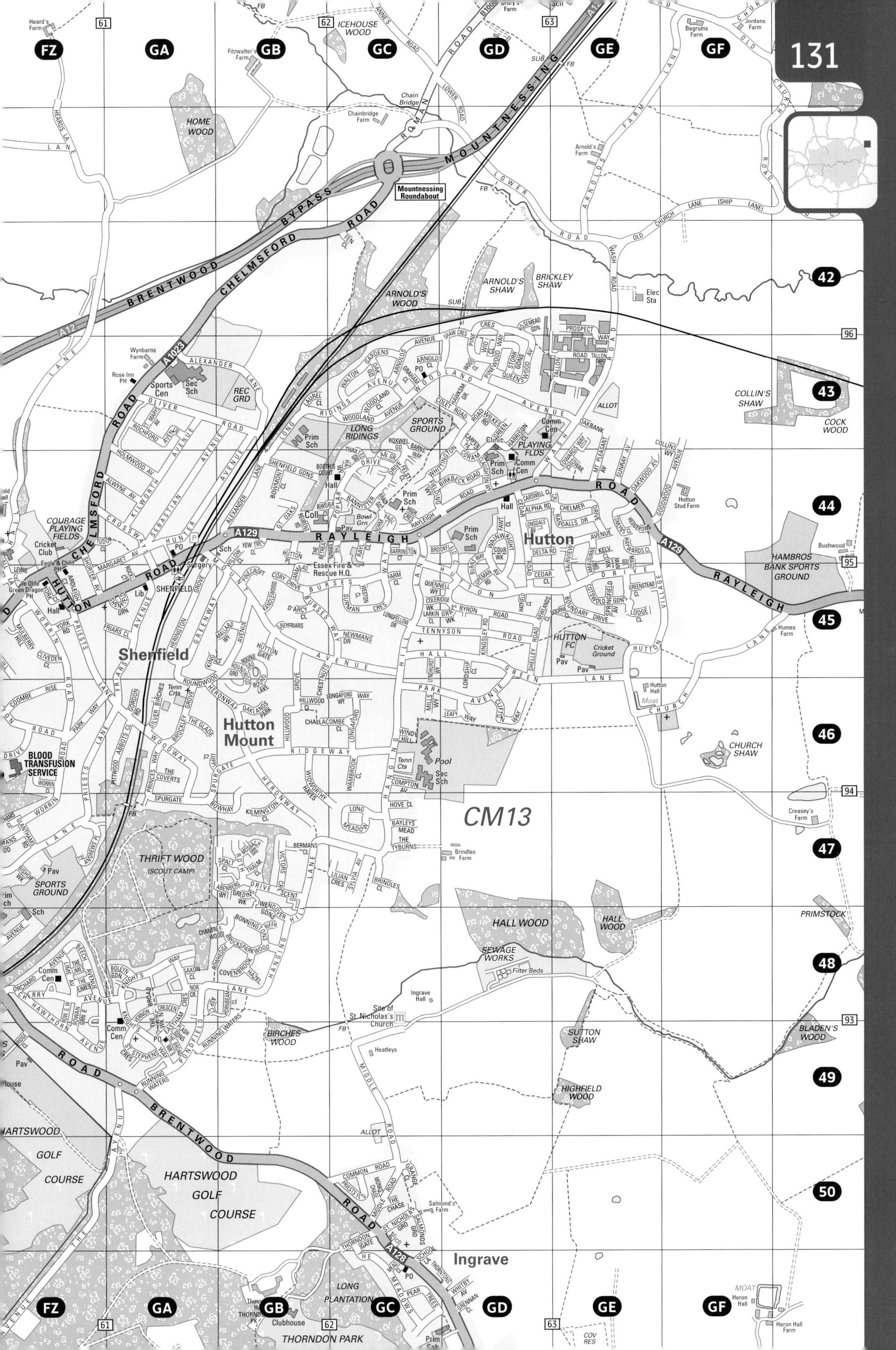
FZ
GA
GB
GC
GD
GE
GF
61
62
63
96
95
94
93
42
43
44
45
46
47
48
49
50
Heard's Farm
ICEHOUSE WOOD
Fitzwalter's Farm
Begrums Farm
Jordans Farm
HOME WOOD
Chain Bridge
Chainbridge Farm
Mountnessing Roundabout
MOUNTNESSING
BRENTWOOD BYPASS
CHELMSFORD ROAD
A12
A1023
Arnold's Farm
ARNOLDS FARM LANE
CHURCH LANE (SHIP LANE)
LOWER ROAD
WASH ROAD
Elec Sta
ARNOLD'S WOOD
ARNOLD'S SHAW
BRICKLEY SHAW
COLLIN'S SHAW
COCK WOOD
Wynbarns Farm
Rose Inn PH
Sports Cen
Sec Sch
REC GRD
LONG RIDINGS
SPORTS GROUND
PLAYING FLDS
Comm Cen
Prim Sch
ALLOT
Hutton Stud Farm
COURAGE PLAYING FIELDS
Cricket Club
A129
RAYLEIGH ROAD
HUTTON ROAD
SHENFIELD
Essex Fire & Rescue H.Q.
Hutton
HAMBROS BANK SPORTS GROUND
Bushwood
Humes Farm
Shenfield
HUTTON FC
Cricket Ground
Hutton Hall
Moat
BLOOD TRANSFUSION SERVICE
Hutton Mount
Pool
CHURCH SHAW
CM13
Creasey's Farm
THRIFT WOOD (SCOUT CAMP)
SPORTS GROUND
Brindles Farm
HALL WOOD
PRIMSTOCK
SEWAGE WORKS
Filter Beds
Ingrave Hall
Site of St. Nicholas's Church
BIRCHES WOOD
SUTTON SHAW
BLADEN'S WOOD
Heatleys
HIGHFIELD WOOD
BRENTWOOD ROAD
HARTSWOOD GOLF COURSE
ALLOT
Salmond's Farm
A128
Ingrave
LONG PLANTATION
Clubhouse
THORNDON PARK
Heron Hall
Heron Hall Farm
MOAT

FLACKWELL HEATH GOLF COURSE
Wooburn Green
Wooburn
HP10
WOOBURN PARK
BOURNE END
SL8
WOOLMAN'S WOOD
HEDSOR GOLF COURSE
BURWOOD ESTATE
HEDSOR PARK
SL6
SL1
LAMBOURNE GOLF COURSE
Cookham
CLIVEDEN NT
Junction 3
110
152

HP9
SL9
SL2
Junction 2
Hedgerley
EGYPT
Farnham Common
BURTLEY WOOD
BOWER WOOD
EGYPT WOODS
BURNHAM BEECHES
Beaconsfield Service Area
WINDSOR ROAD
COLLINSWOOD ROAD
BEACONSFIELD ROAD
OXFORD ROAD
LONDON END
WYCOMBE END
M40
A40
A355

111
134
153

AS
AT
AU
AV
AW
AX
AY
112
BIRCHLAND WOOD
HIGH WOOD
BEECH WOOD
MALMS WOOD
MOBILE HOME PARK
Parkwood Farm
SPORTS GRD
Prim Sch
SPORTS GRD
AUSTENWOOD COMMON
55
OXFORD ROAD
A40
BIRCH WOOD
SIBLET'S WOOD
CHANTRY WOOD
Bellhouse Hotel
56
Mumfords Farm
Raylands Farm
Wapsey's Wood Landfill Site
ROAD
CHILTERN
SOUTH BUCKS
89
SAND AND GRAVEL PIT
FURTHER WARREN WOOD
WEST PLANTATION
SL9
57
Jarretts Hill
GERRARDS CROSS
The Bull Hotel
BULSTRODE
Bulstrode
PARK
58
Slade Farm
MENAGERIE WOOD
GROVE PLANTATION
Bulstrode Camp
Crab Hill
GERRARDS CROSS COMMON
88
HEDGERLEY GREEN
59
SUTTON'S WOOD
133
Ponders
French Horn PH
Clubhouse
Cricket Ground
Hedgerley
LEITH GROVE
RSPB NATURE RESERVE
CHURCH WOOD
The White Horse PH
UPPER MEADOW
High Meadows
60
87
HANGING WOOD
61
HEDGERLEY PARK
MOUNTHILL WOOD
Mount Hill Farm
BLACK GROVE
Park House
DUKE'S ORCHARD
Riding Stables
M40
62
PARKSIDE CEMETERY
PICKERIDGE WOOD
Low Farm
Hedgerley Park Farm
Tara
TIMBER WOOD
HAY WOOD
86
STOKE WOOD
Pickeridge Farm
Kestrel Farm
SL3
Fulmer
Fulmer Hall
63
SL2
Church Farm
Fulmer House Farm
Alder Bourne
STOKE COMMON
64
BROCKHURST WOOD
STOKE COMMON
FRAME WOOD
PENN WOOD
Fernacres Farm
Fernacres House
Fulmer C.C.
Black Firs
154
0 500 yds
0 500 m
AT
AU
AV
AW
AX
AY
Framewood Manor
WEXHAM PLACE
PARSON'S WOOD
FULMER COMMON
98
99
00

GERRARDS CROSS GOLF COURSE
NOCKHILL WOOD
JUNIPER WOOD
GREAT HALINGS WOOD
LITTLE HANGING WOOD
Denham Grove
NORTHMOOR HILL (NATURE RESERVE)
DENHAM MARSH WOOD
DENHAM AERODROME
DENHAM GOLF COURSE
Denham Green
Higher Denham
UB9
TOM WILLIAM'S WOOD
BRADBURY'S ISLAND
CAPS WOOD
Tatling End
BAKER'S WOOD
THE RANCHO
GALLOWS WOOD
MILL WOOD
LITTLE GALLOWS WOOD
NABOTH
GALDWINS WOOD
BROADSPRING WOOD
HAWKS WOOD
FURZENEY WOOD
Junction 16 (M25)
Junction 1a (M40)
GOSSAMS WOOD
BROWN'S WOOD
OLDHOUSE WOOD
PARKSPRING WOOD
MOUNT FIDGET WOOD
LANGLEY COMMON
SL0
LONG COPPICE
Denham Roundabout
M25
M40
A40
A412
A413
NORTH ORBITAL ROAD
DENHAM AVENUE
AMERSHAM ROAD
OXFORD ROAD
113
136
155

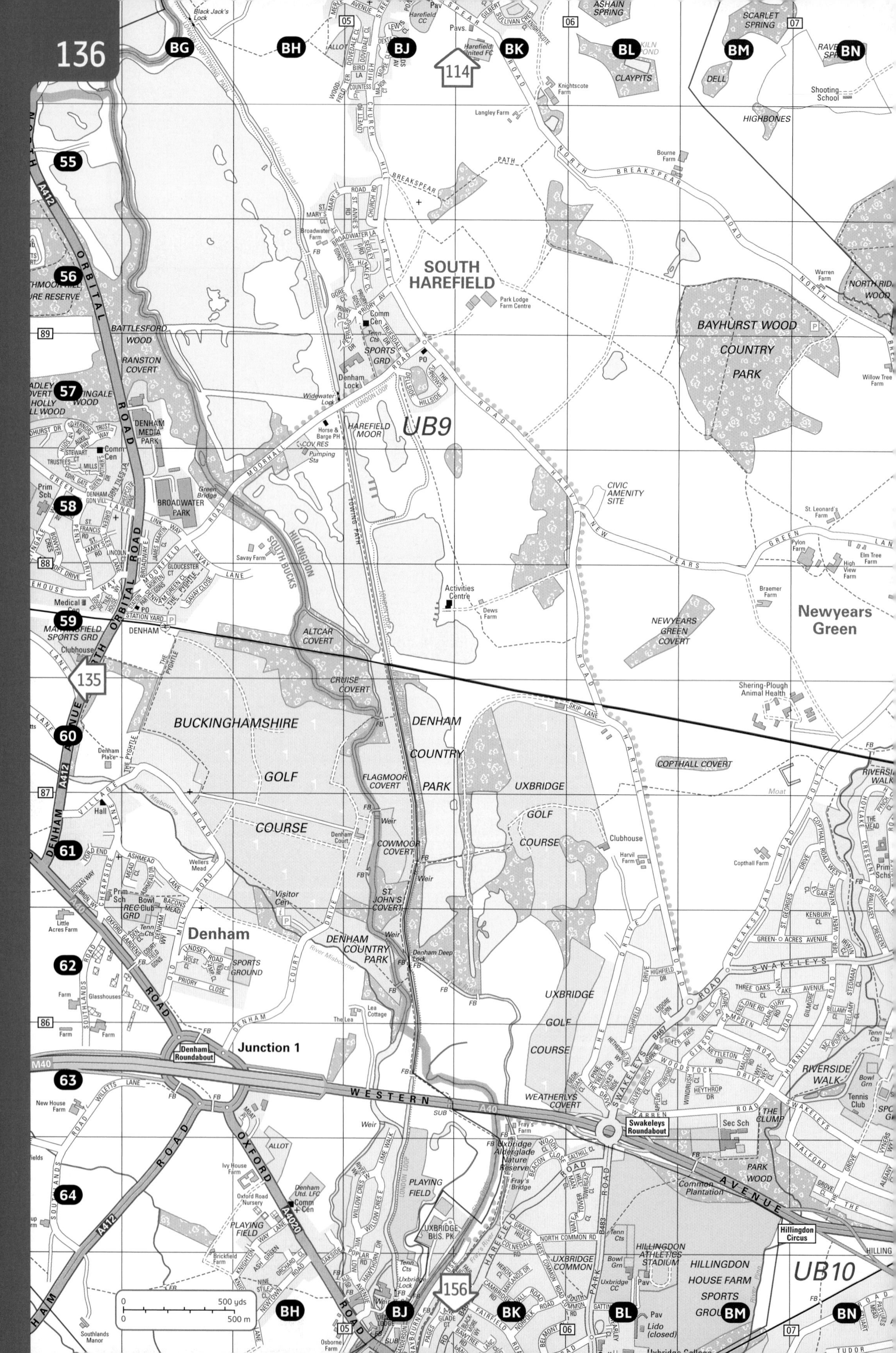
BG
BH
BJ
BK
BL
BM
BN
114
135
156
SOUTH HAREFIELD
UB9
UB10
Denham
Newyears Green
Junction 1
Denham Roundabout
Swakeleys Roundabout
Hillingdon Circus
ORBITAL ROAD
NORTH ORBITAL ROAD
DENHAM AVENUE
A412
A40
A4020
B467
B483
M40
WESTERN AVENUE
OXFORD ROAD
HAREFIELD ROAD
MOORHALL ROAD
NORTH HYDE
BREAKSPEAR ROAD
SOUTH BREAKSPEAR ROAD
BREAKSPEAR PATH
NORTH BREAKSPEAR ROAD
SKIP LANE
NEW YEARS GREEN LANE
SWAKELEYS ROAD
SWAKELEYS DRIVE
VILLAGE ROAD
SAVAY LANE
DENHAM COURT DRIVE
PARK ROAD
Grand Union Canal
River Misbourne
Frays River
London Loop
Towing Path
South Bucks
Hillingdon
Black Jack's Lock
Denham Lock
Widewater Lock
Denham Deep Lock
Uxbridge Lock
Harefield CC
Harefield United FC
ASHAIN SPRING
SCARLET SPRING
KILN POND
CLAYPITS
DELL
HIGHBONES
Shooting School
Knightscote Farm
Langley Farm
Bourne Farm
Warren Farm
NORTH RIDE WOOD
BAYHURST WOOD COUNTRY PARK
Willow Tree Farm
Park Lodge Farm Centre
CIVIC AMENITY SITE
St. Leonard's Farm
Pylon Farm
Elm Tree Farm
High View Farm
Braemer Farm
NEWYEARS GREEN COVERT
Shering-Plough Animal Health
COPTHALL COVERT
Copthall Farm
Activities Centre
Dews Farm
Broadwater Farm
Comm Cen
SPORTS GRD
Horse & Barge PH
COV RES
Pumping Sta
HAREFIELD MOOR
BATTLESFORD WOOD
RANSTON COVERT
DENHAM MEDIA PARK
BROADWATER PARK
Green Bridge
Savay Farm
ALTCAR COVERT
CRUISE COVERT
BUCKINGHAMSHIRE GOLF COURSE
DENHAM COUNTRY PARK
FLAGMOOR COVERT
COWMOOR COVERT
ST. JOHN'S COVERT
UXBRIDGE GOLF COURSE
Clubhouse
Harvil Farm
Denham Court
Visitor Cen
Wellers Mead
Denham Place
Hall
Prim Sch
REC GRD
SPORTS GROUND
Little Acres Farm
Glasshouses
Lea Cottage
The Lea
New House Farm
Ivy House Farm
Oxford Road Nursery
PLAYING FIELD
Denham Utd. LFC
UXBRIDGE BUS. PK
Brickfield Farm
Southlands Manor
Osborne Farm
Fray's Farm
Uxbridge Alderglade Nature Reserve
Fray's Bridge
WEATHERLYS COVERT
UXBRIDGE COMMON
HILLINGDON ATHLETICS STADIUM
Uxbridge CC
Lido (closed)
HILLINGDON HOUSE FARM SPORTS GROUND
Common Plantation
PARK WOOD
THE CLUMP
Sec Sch
RIVERSIDE WALK
Tennis Club
MARTINFIELD SPORTS GRD
Medical Cen
STATION YARD
DENHAM
ALLOT
Pav
Pavs.
Weir
FB
55
56
57
58
59
60
61
62
63
64
05
06
07
86
87
88
89
0
500 yds
500 m

Northwood Hills
HA6
HA5
HA4
COPSE WOOD
YOUNG WOOD
MAD BESS WOOD
POOR'S FIELD
RUISLIP NATURE RESERVE
RUISLIP LIDO
RUISLIP COMMON
PARK WOOD
EASTCOTE VILLAGE
EASTCOTE
RUISLIP
RUISLIP MANOR
RUISLIP GOLF COURSE
ICKENHAM
RUISLIP GARDENS
RAF NORTHOLT
WEST RUISLIP
SOUTH RUISLIP
CAVENDISH REC GRD
BESSINGBY FIELD
KINGS COLLEGE PLAYING FIELDS
NEW POND FARM FIELDS
ODYSSEY BUSINESS PARK
BRAINTREE INDUSTRIAL ESTATE
DUCKS HILL ROAD
BURY STREET
HIGH STREET
WEST END ROAD
RICKMANSWORTH RD
WESTERN AVENUE
115
138
157
BP
BQ
BR
BS
BT
BU
BV
08
09
10
56
57
58
59
60
61
62
63
64
89
88
87
86

BW
BX
BY
BZ
CA
CB
CC
116
137
158
55
56
57
58
59
60
61
62
63
64
12
13
14
89
88
87
86
PINNER GREEN
MONTESOLE PLAYING FIELDS
LITTLE COMMON
PINNER
PINNER MEMORIAL PARK
PINNER NEW CEMETERY
PINNER VILLAGE GARDENS
CUCKOO HILL
HA5
EASTCOTE VILLAGE
EASTCOTE
THE CROFT PLAYING FIELD
NORTH HARROW
HEADSTONE
HEADSTONE MANOR RECREATION GROUND
SPORTS GROUND
WEST HARROW
WEST HARROW REC GRD
RAYNERS LANE
HA2
ROXBOURNE PARK
CAVENDISH REC GRD
PINE GDNS
BESSINGBY FIELD
Streamside Reservation
RECREATION GROUND
NEWTON PARK WEST
NEWTON FM ECOLOGY PK
SOUTH HARROW
ALEXANDRA PARK
ROXETH REC GRD
DEANE PARK
SOUTH RUISLIP
SOUTH RUISLIP PLAYING FIELD
BRAINTREE INDUSTRIAL ESTATE
ODYSSEY BUSINESS PARK
Ruislip Retail Park
Victoria Retail Park
Brook Retail Park
HA4
Civic Amenity Site
NORTHOLT RECREATION GRD
EARLSMEAD STADIUM
Harrow Borough FC
UB5
LORD HALSBURY MEMORIAL GRD
Air Traffic Radio Sta
A404
A4090
A312
B466
GEORGE V AVENUE
PINNER ROAD
STATION RD
IMPERIAL DRIVE
ALEXANDRA AVENUE
NORTHOLT ROAD
PETTS HILL
WEST END ROAD
VICTORIA ROAD
EASTCOTE LANE
CANNON LANE
FIELD END ROAD
UXBRIDGE RD
HIGH ROAD
RAYNERS LANE
WHITTINGTON WAY
WHITTON AV W
0 500 yds
0 500 m

CD
CE
CF
CG
CH
CJ
CK
117
159
140
56
57
58
59
60
61
62
63
64
15
16
17
86
87
88
89
HA7
HA3
HA1
HA9
HA0
UB6
QUEENSBURY
WEALDSTONE
KENTON
NORTH WEMBLEY
HARROW ON THE HILL
SUDBURY
PRESTON
WAVERLEY INDUSTRIAL ESTATE
HARROW & WEALDSTONE
KENTON RECREATION GROUND
University of Westminster
NORTHWICK PARK HOSP
ST. MARK'S HOSP
OLYMPIC MEDICAL INSTITUTE
NORTHWICK PARK
HARROW SCHOOL PLAYING FIELDS
HARROW SCHOOL GOLF COURSE
MINIATURE RIFLE RANGE
BOWDEN HOUSE
CLEMENTINE CHURCHILL HOSPITAL
CHASEWOOD PARK
SPORTS GROUND
VALE FARM SPORTS GROUND
WEMBLEY FC
BARHAM PARK
WEMBLEY COMMERCIAL CENTRE
PRESTON PARK
KING EDWARD VII PARK
WOODCOCK PARK
JOHN BILLAM SPORTS GRD
ST. LUKE'S HOSPICE
THE GROVE OPEN SPACE
HARROW HILL GOLF COURSE
BYRON REC GRD
CIVIC AMENITY SITE
THE HAWTHORN CENTRE
HARROW REC
SUDBURY HILL HARROW
SUDBURY HILL
SUDBURY & HARROW ROAD
SUDBURY TOWN
WEMBLEY CENTRAL
NORTH WEMBLEY
SOUTH KENTON
NORTHWICK PARK
HARROW-ON-THE-HILL
COLLEGE BUS STA
KENTON ROAD
WATFORD ROAD
HARROW ROAD
EAST LANE
KENTON LANE
SHEEPCOTE ROAD
STATION ROAD
GREENFORD ROAD
WHITTON AVENUE WEST
EASTCOTE AVENUE
SUDBURY COURT DRIVE
ROXETH HILL
BESSBOROUGH ROAD
LOWER ROAD
A4006
A404
A409
A4088
A4090
A4005
A312
A4089

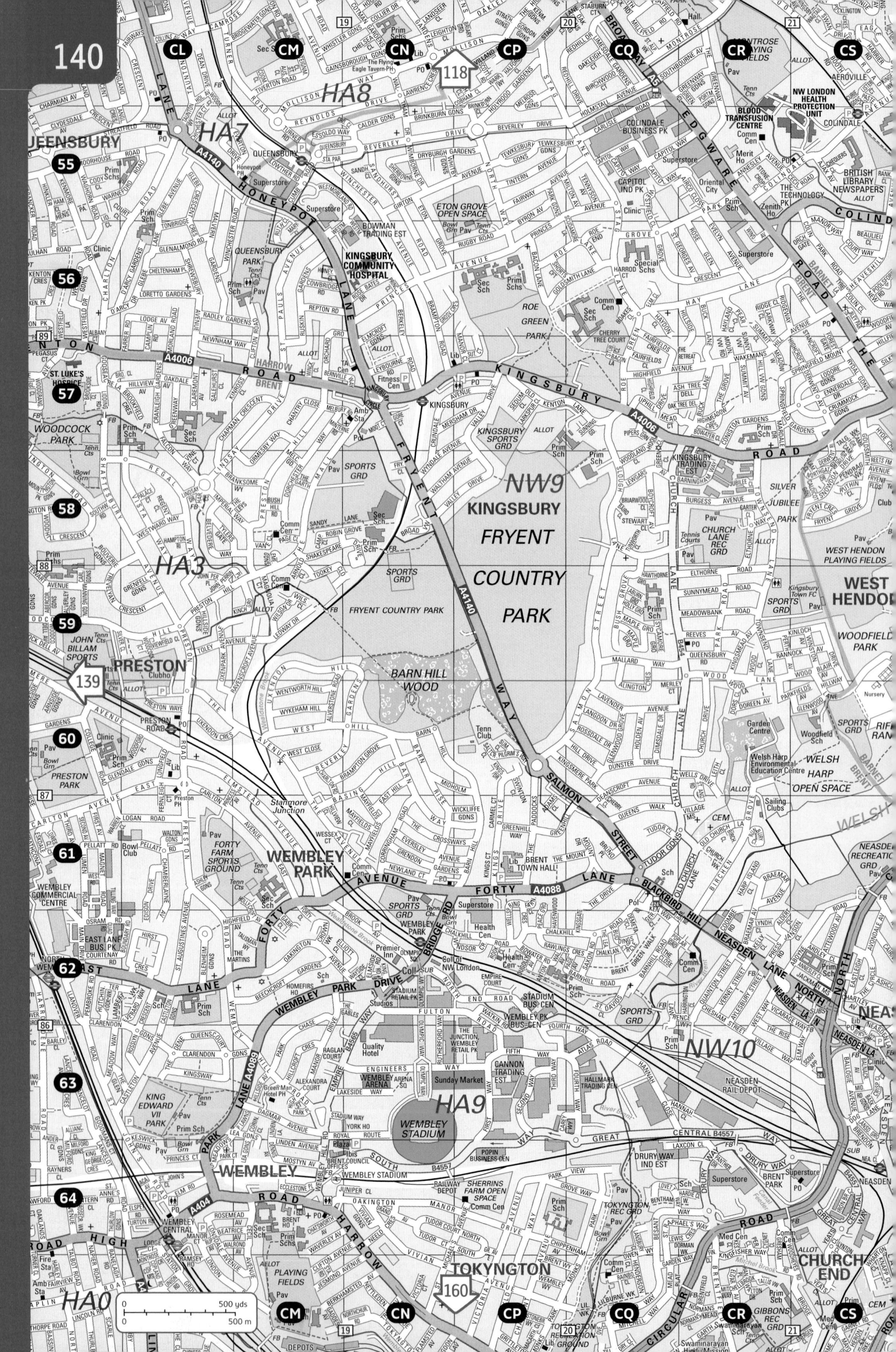
CL
CM
CN
CP
CQ
CR
CS
118
HA8
HA7
QUEENSBURY
55
56
57
58
59
60
61
62
63
64
139
160
19
20
21
COLINDALE
COLINDALE BUSINESS PK
NW LONDON HEALTH PROTECTION UNIT
BLOOD TRANSFUSION CENTRE
BRITISH LIBRARY NEWSPAPERS
MONTROSE PLAYING FIELDS
EDGWARE ROAD
HONEYPOT LANE
KINGSBURY COMMUNITY HOSPITAL
QUEENSBURY PARK
ETON GROVE OPEN SPACE
BOWMAN TRADING EST
CAPITOL IND PK
ROE GREEN PARK
KINGSBURY ROAD
KINGSBURY
KINGSBURY SPORTS GRD
ST. LUKE'S HOSPICE
WOODCOCK PARK
NW9
KINGSBURY
FRYENT
COUNTRY
PARK
FRYENT COUNTRY PARK
FRYENT WAY
A4140
A4006
HA3
KINGSBURY TRADING EST
SILVER JUBILEE PARK
CHURCH LANE REC GRD
WEST HENDON PLAYING FIELDS
WEST HENDON
WOODFIELD PARK
PRESTON
JOHN BILLAM SPORTS
PRESTON PARK
BARN HILL WOOD
WELSH HARP OPEN SPACE
Welsh Harp Environmental Education Centre
NEASDEN RECREATION GRD
WEMBLEY PARK
FORTY FARM SPORTS GROUND
FORTY AVENUE
FORTY LANE
A4088
BRENT TOWN HALL
SALMON STREET
BLACKBIRD HILL
NEASDEN LANE
WEMBLEY COMMERCIAL CENTRE
EAST LANE BUS. PK
WEMBLEY PARK DRIVE
STADIUM RETAIL PK
THE JUNCTION, WEMBLEY RETAIL PK
WEMBLEY ARENA
Sunday Market
CANNON TRADING EST
HALLMARK TRADING CEN
HA9
WEMBLEY STADIUM
NW10
NEASDEN RAIL DEPOT
KING EDWARD VII PARK
WEMBLEY
WEMBLEY CENTRAL
DRURY WAY IND EST
BRENT PARK
SHERRINS FARM OPEN SPACE
TOKYNGTON REC GRD
TOKYNGTON
PLAYING FIELDS
HA0
CHURCH END
GIBBONS REC GRD
NORTH CIRCULAR ROAD
HARROW ROAD
HIGH ROAD
A404
A4089
B4557
500 yds
500 m

CT
CU
CV
CW
CX
CY
CZ
119
HOLDERS HILL
SUNNY HILL PARK
RAF MUSEUM
GARDEN HOSP
Bridgewater Hotel Hendon Hall
N3
Middlesex Uni
CHURCH ROAD
FINCHLEY
NORTH CIRCULAR ROAD
Henlys Corner
THE HYDE
HENDON
Sch of Jewish Studies
CARMELITE MONASTERY
NW4
HENDON PARK
HENDON CENTRAL
PRINCES PARK
HOOP LANE CEMETERY (JEWISH)
GARDEN OF REMEMBRANCE
Welsh Harp
Brent Cross Shopping Centre
Brent Cross Interchange
BRENT CROSS
Junction 1
NW11
GREEK CATH
142
BRENT RESERVOIR
Staples Corner
Brent South Shopping Pk
CLITTERHOUSE PLAYING FIELDS
Hendon FC
AQUARIUS BUSINESS PARK
WELLINGTON PARK EST
BASING HILL PK
CHILDS HILL PK
CHILDS HILL
DOLLIS HILL
GLADSTONE PARK
CRICKLEWOOD
UNIVERSITY COLLEGE SCHOOL SPORTS GRD
HAMPSTEAD CEMETERY
BARNET
CAMDEN
NW8
NW2
161
WILLESDEN
KILBURN
56
57
58
59
60
61
62
63
64

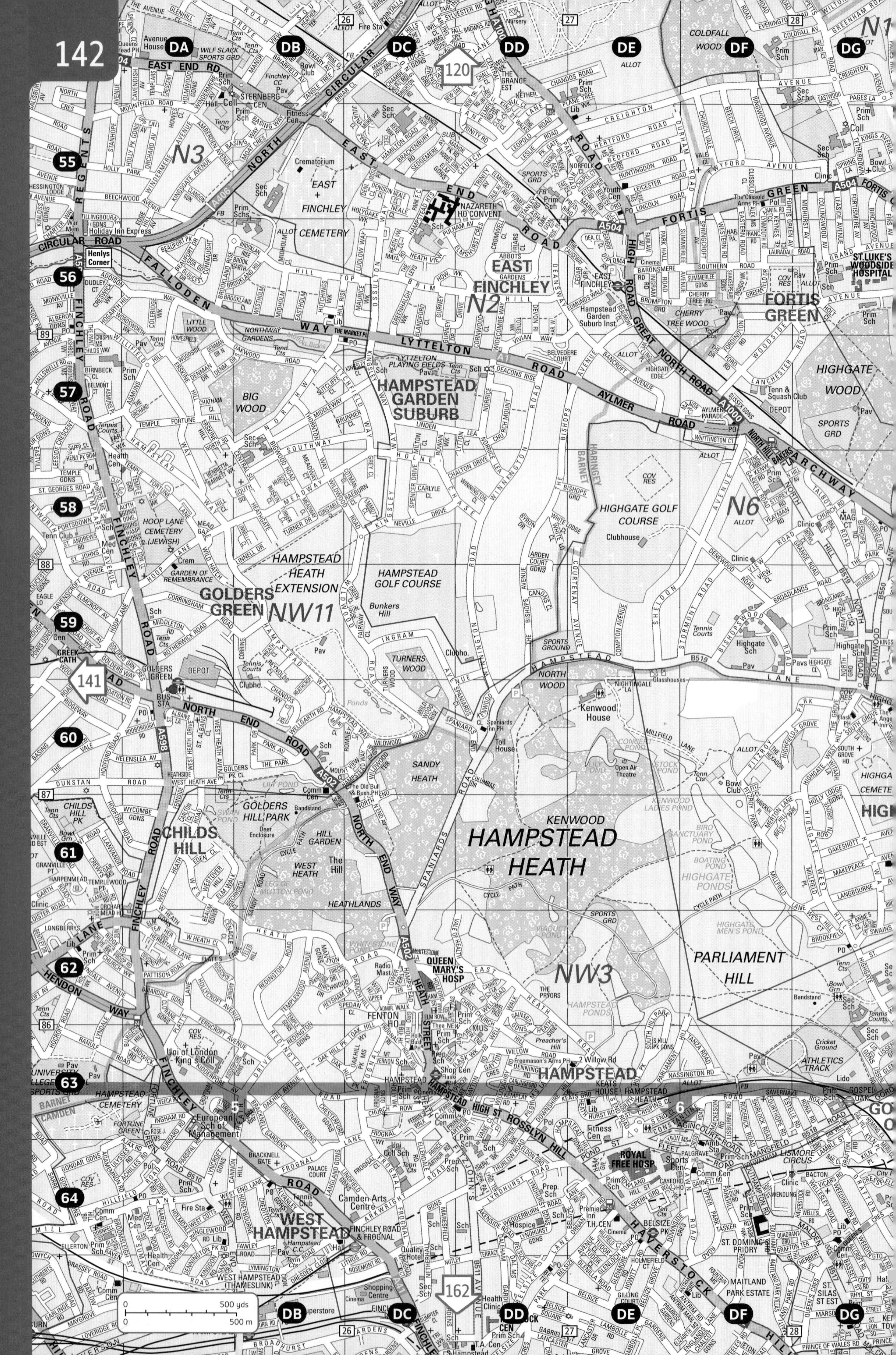

DA
DB
DC
DD
DE
DF
DG
26
27
28
120
55
56
57
58
59
60
61
62
63
64
89
88
87
86
141
162
N3
N2
N6
NW11
NW3
EAST FINCHLEY
FORTIS GREEN
HAMPSTEAD GARDEN SUBURB
GOLDERS GREEN
CHILDS HILL
HAMPSTEAD HEATH
HAMPSTEAD
WEST HAMPSTEAD
PARLIAMENT HILL
HIGHGATE WOOD
HIGHGATE GOLF COURSE
HAMPSTEAD GOLF COURSE
HAMPSTEAD HEATH EXTENSION
EAST FINCHLEY CEMETERY
HOOP LANE CEMETERY (JEWISH)
HAMPSTEAD CEMETERY
GOLDERS HILL PARK
BIG WOOD
LITTLE WOOD
TURNERS WOOD
CHERRY TREE WOOD
COLDFALL WOOD
NORTH WOOD
SANDY HEATH
WEST HEATH
HILL GARDEN
HEATHLANDS
KENWOOD
Kenwood House
HIGHGATE PONDS
ATHLETICS TRACK
ROYAL FREE HOSP
QUEEN MARY'S HOSP
ST.LUKE'S WOODSIDE HOSPITAL
NAZARETH HO CONVENT
Henlys Corner
Holiday Inn Express
GARDEN OF REMEMBRANCE
LYTTELTON PLAYING FIELDS
European Sch of Management
Uni of London King's Coll
Camden Arts Centre
MAITLAND PARK ESTATE
ST. DOMINIC'S PRIORY
LISMORE CIRCUS
NORTH CIRCULAR ROAD
FALLODEN WAY
LYTTELTON ROAD
AYLMER ROAD
GREAT NORTH ROAD
HIGH ROAD
EAST END ROAD
FORTIS GREEN
ARCHWAY ROAD
HAMPSTEAD LANE
SPANIARDS ROAD
NORTH END ROAD
NORTH END WAY
HEATH STREET
FINCHLEY ROAD
HENDON WAY
ROSSLYN HILL
HAVERSTOCK HILL
REGENTS PARK ROAD
A406
A1000
A504
A598
A502
A41
B519
BARNET
CAMDEN
HARINGEY
0 500 yds
0 500 m

DH
DJ
DK
DL
DM
DN
DP
121
NOEL PARK
ALEXANDRA PALACE
ALEXANDRA
PARK
N22
MUSWELL HILL
HORNSEY
N8
CROUCH END
QUEEN'S WOOD
HARRINGAY
STROUD GREEN
FINSBURY
N4
PARK
FINSBURY PARK
N19
WHITTINGTON HOSPITAL
HIGHGATE CEMETERY
UPPER HOLLOWAY
DARTMOUTH PARK
TUFNELL PARK
HOLLOWAY
N7
LOWER HOLLOWAY
KENTISH TOWN
NW5
HIGHBURY
N5
EMIRATES STADIUM
ARSENAL FC
H.M. PRISON HOLLOWAY
144
163
56
57
58
59
60
61
62
63
64
CANONBURY
PENTONVILLE

DQ
DR
DS
DT
DU
DV
DW
122
143
164
55
56
57
58
59
60
61
62
63
64
N22
N17
N15
N4
N16
N5
E5
E8
LORDSHIP RECREATION GROUND
BELMONT REC GRD
WEST GREEN
DOWNHILLS PARK
CHESTNUTS PARK
ST ANN'S HOSPITAL
SEVEN SISTERS
SOUTH TOTTENHAM
TOTTENHAM HALE
TOTTENHAM MARSHES
WALTHAMSTOW RESERVOIR
DOWN LANE REC GRD
LEE VALLEY TECHNOPARK
CHESNUT ESTATE
LOCKWOOD INDUSTRIAL PARK
Tottenham Hale Retail Park
THE HIGH CROSS CENTRE
MARKFIELD REC GRD
WARWICK RESERVOIR EAST
WARWICK RESERVOIR WEST
SPRINGHILL SPORTS GRD
COPPERMILL PLAYING FIELD
LEE VALLEY REGIONAL
Walthamstow Marsh Nature Reserve
SPRINGFIELD PARK
WOODBERRY DOWN ESTATE
MANOR HOUSE
STAMFORD HILL
STAMFORD HILL ESTATE
UPPER CLAPTON
CLAPTON COMMON
ABNEY PARK CEMETERY
STOKE NEWINGTON
CLISSOLD PARK
SPORTS GROUND
NORTH MILLFIELDS RECREATION GROUND
SHACKLEWELL
HACKNEY DOWNS
HIGHBURY
DALSTON
HACKNEY CENTRAL
AMHURST A107
SEVEN SISTERS ROAD
GREEN LANES
STAMFORD HILL
STOKE NEWINGTON HIGH ST
BALLS POND ROAD
DALSTON LANE
LEA BRIDGE ROAD
0 500 yds
0 500 m

DX
DY
DZ
EA
EB
EC
ED
HIGHAM HILL
LLOYD PARK
WALTHAMSTOW
CHESTNUTS SHOWGROUND
UPLANDS BUSINESS PARK
FOREST TRADING EST
Blackhorse Road
Wood Street
THORPE COOMBE HOSP
UPPER WALTHAMSTOW
E17
DOUGLAS EYRE PLAYING FIELDS
WALTHAMSTOW CENTRAL
WALTHAMSTOW QUEENS ROAD
WALTHAMSTOW CEM
Whipps Cross
WHIPPS CROSS UNIVERSITY HOSPITAL
ST. JAMES'S PARK
LOW HALL SPORTS GROUND
LEYTON IND VILLAGE
FOREST BUSINESS PK
ALLOTMENTS
LEYTONSTONE
LEYTON FC
E10
LEYTON
LEYTON MIDLAND RD
SEYMOUR ROAD PLAYING FIELD
MARSH LANE PLAYING FIELD
LEYTON MARSHES
Lee Valley Ice Centre
THE WATERWORKS NATURE RESERVE
LEE VALLEY PITCH & PUTT GOLF COURSE
TEMPLE MILLS DEPOT
LEYTON ORIENT FC
SIDMOUTH PARK
ST. PATRICK'S RC CEMETERY
LEA BRIDGE
HACKNEY MARSH
New Spitalfields Market
CLAPTON PARK
LOWER CLAPTON
LEE VALLEY REGIONAL PARK
Lea Interchange
WICK COMMUNITY WOODLAND
DRAPERS FIELD REC. GRD
HOMERTON
MABLEY GREEN
E9
HACKNEY WICK
LONDON 2012 OLYMPIC PARK SITE
E15
STRATFORD INTERNATIONAL (Due to open 2009)
STRATFORD
123
146
165
56
57
58
59
60
61
62
63
64

SOUTH WOODFORD
E18
EPPING FOREST
SNARESBROOK
SNARESBROOK CROWN COURT
WHIPPS CROSS UNIVERSITY HOSPITAL
LEYTONSTONE
E11
WANSTEAD
WANSTEAD FLATS
WANSTEAD GOLF COURSE
WANSTEAD PARK
ALDERSBROOK
CITY OF LONDON CEMETERY
MANOR PARK
MANOR PARK CEMETERY
WEST HAM CEMETERY
E15
FOREST GATE
E7
WOODGRANGE PARK CEMETERY
IG4
Junction 4
SPIRE RODING HOSP
Redbridge Roundabout
Charlie Brown's Roundabout
Waterworks Corner
Green Man Roundabout
NORTH CIRCULAR ROAD
EASTERN AVENUE
ROMFORD ROAD
WOODFORD NEW ROAD
HOLLYBUSH HILL
HERMON HILL
ALDERSBROOK ROAD
WOODGRANGE ROAD
LEYTONSTONE ROAD
HIGH ROAD
BLAKE HALL ROAD
CENTRE ROAD
BUSH ROAD
CAMBRIDGE PARK
WHIPPS CROSS ROAD
SOUTHEND ROAD
EE
EF
EG
EH
EJ
EK
EL
55
56
57
58
59
60
61
62
63
64
124
145
166
500 yds
500 m

EM
EN
EP
EQ
ER
ES
ET
125
CLAYHALL
FAIRLOP WATERS
GOLF COURSE
IG5
IG6
ALDBOROUGH HATCH
BARKINGSIDE
GARDEN OF REST
BARKINGSIDE CEM
56
57
KING GEORGE HOSPITAL
GANTS HILL
NEWBURY PARK
EASTERN AVENUE
WOODFORD AVENUE
CRANBROOK ROAD
IG2
SEVEN KINGS PARK
REDBRIDGE
VALENTINES PARK
58
59
SEVEN KINGS
148
60
CRANBROOK
MELBOURNE FIELD
IG1
IG3
61
ILFORD
HIGH ROAD
GREEN LANE
SOUTH PARK
62
63
LOXFORD
LITTLE ILFORD PARK
BARKING PARK
LONGBRIDGE ROAD
64
E12
167
ILFORD LANE
A12
A406
A123
A118
A1083
A124
A1400
NORTH CIRCULAR ROAD
SPORTS GROUND
DEPOT

EU
EV
EW
EX
EY
EZ
FA
47
48
49
126
168
147
55
56
57
58
59
60
61
62
63
64
86
87
88
89
Mark's Gate
IG2
RM6
RM8
RM9
IG3
IG11
CHADWELL HEATH
GOODMAYES
BECONTREE
Becontree Heath
KING GEORGE HOSPITAL
GOODMAYES HOSPITAL
Redbridge College
EASTERN AVENUE
A12
HIGH ROAD
A118
GREEN LANE
A1083
WHALEBONE LANE NORTH
WHALEBONE LANE SOUTH
A1112
LONGBRIDGE ROAD
A124
WOOD LANE
HEATHWAY
A1240
PORTERS AVENUE
A1153
LONDON ROAD
BILLET ROAD
PAINTERS ROAD
SPORTS GROUND
WARREN PARK GOLF CENTRE
ST. CHADS PARK
KINGS PARK
GOODMAYES PARK
VALENCE PARK
PARSLOES PARK
MAYESBROOK PARK
WESTLANDS PLAYING FIELDS
WEST HAM UNITED FC TRAINING GROUND
MIRRAVALE TRADING ESTATE
ELDENWALL IND ESTATE
MARKS GATE CEM
BARKING FC Clubhouse
ARENA
World War II Gun Emplacements
Little Heath
Moby Dick
DAGENHAM
DAGENHAM HEATHWAY
0
500 yds
500 m

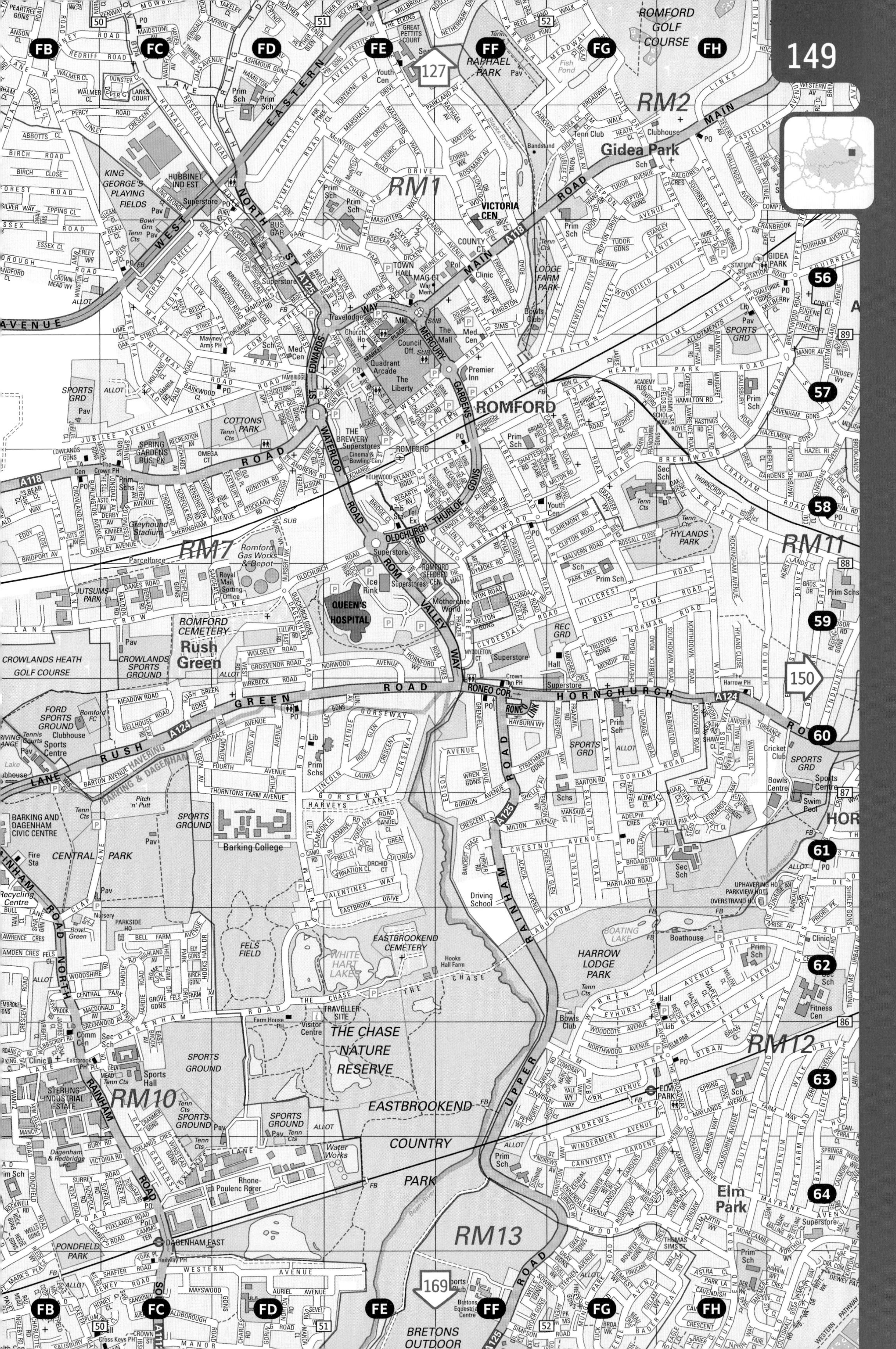
149
FB
FC
FD
FE
FF
FG
FH
ROMFORD GOLF COURSE
RAPHAEL PARK
RM2
Gidea Park
RM1
VICTORIA CEN
KING GEORGE'S PLAYING FIELDS
HUBBINET IND EST
NORTH EASTERN
MAIN ROAD
A118
A125
LODGE FARM PARK
ROMFORD
The Mall
The Liberty
Quadrant Arcade
THE BREWERY
COTTONS PARK
RM7
Romford Gas Works & Depot
Greyhound Stadium
QUEEN'S HOSPITAL
ROMFORD CEMETERY
Rush Green
CROWLANDS HEATH GOLF COURSE
CROWLANDS SPORTS GROUND
RM11
HYLANDS PARK
HORNCHURCH ROAD
A124
RUSH GREEN ROAD
ROM VALLEY WAY
RAINHAM ROAD
BARKING AND DAGENHAM CIVIC CENTRE
CENTRAL PARK
Barking College
FELS FIELD
EASTBROOKEND CEMETERY
WHITE HART LAKES
HARROW LODGE PARK
THE CHASE NATURE RESERVE
EASTBROOKEND COUNTRY PARK
RM10
STERLING INDUSTRIAL ESTATE
Rhone-Poulenc Rorer
DAGENHAM EAST
PONDFIELD PARK
RM12
Elm Park
ELM PARK
RM13
BRETONS OUTDOOR
UPPER RAINHAM ROAD
127
150
169
56
57
58
59
60
61
62
63
64
50
51
52
86
87
88
89

HAROLD WOOD
128
RM3
RM2
PAGES WOOD
HAROLD WOOD PARK
Ardleigh Green
Havering College of Further Educ
Emerson Park
RM11
149
HORNCHURCH
UPMINSTER GOLF COURSE
UPMINSTER
RM12
ST. GEORGES HOSPITAL
Hacton
Elm Park
170
Corbets Tey
PARKLANDS OPEN SPACE
GAYNES PARKWAY
HORNCHURCH STADIUM
UPMINSTER PARK
ST. ANDREW'S PARK
ELLIOT PLAYING FIELDS
FIELDERS SPORTS GRD
LANGTON GDNS
HORNCHURCH CEM
SOUTHEND ARTERIAL ROAD
HIGH STREET
UPMINSTER ROAD
ST. MARY'S LANE
FJ
FK
FL
FM
FN
FP
FQ
55
56
57
58
59
60
61
62
63
64
0 500 yds
0 500 m

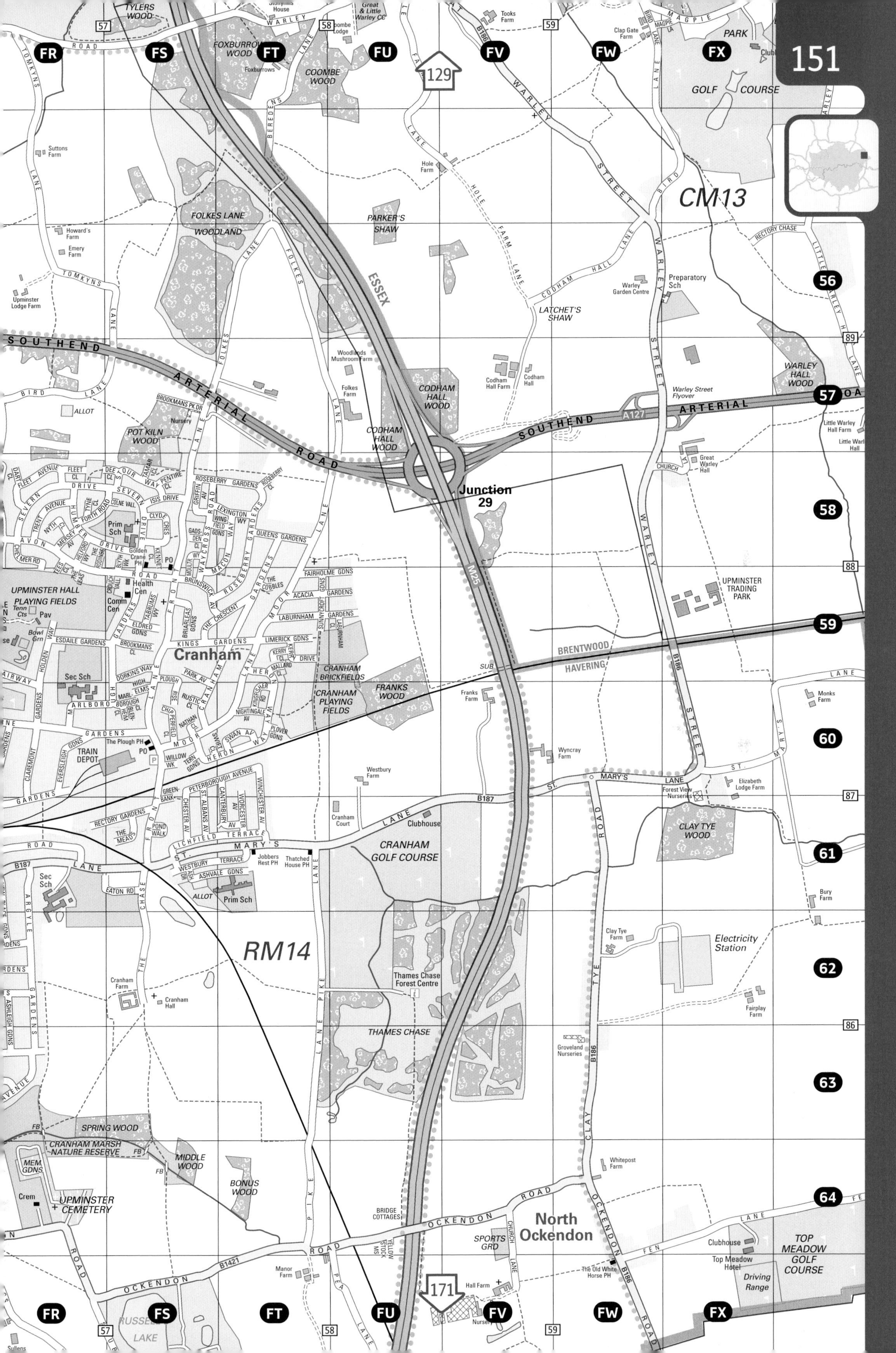
CM13
RM14
Cranham
North Ockendon
Junction 29
SOUTHEND ARTERIAL ROAD
M25
A127
B186
B187
B1421
ESSEX
BRENTWOOD
HAVERING
UPMINSTER TRADING PARK
UPMINSTER HALL PLAYING FIELDS
CRANHAM GOLF COURSE
THAMES CHASE
Thames Chase Forest Centre
CRANHAM MARSH NATURE RESERVE
UPMINSTER CEMETERY
SPRING WOOD
MIDDLE WOOD
BONUS WOOD
CLAY TYE WOOD
FRANKS WOOD
CRANHAM BRICKFIELDS
CRANHAM PLAYING FIELDS
CODHAM HALL WOOD
FOLKES LANE WOODLAND
POT KILN WOOD
PARKER'S SHAW
LATCHET'S SHAW
WARLEY HALL WOOD
FOXBURROW WOOD
COOMBE WOOD
TYLERS WOOD
GOLF COURSE
TOP MEADOW GOLF COURSE
Electricity Station
TRAIN DEPOT
129
171
FR FS FT FU FV FW FX
56 57 58 59 60 61 62 63 64

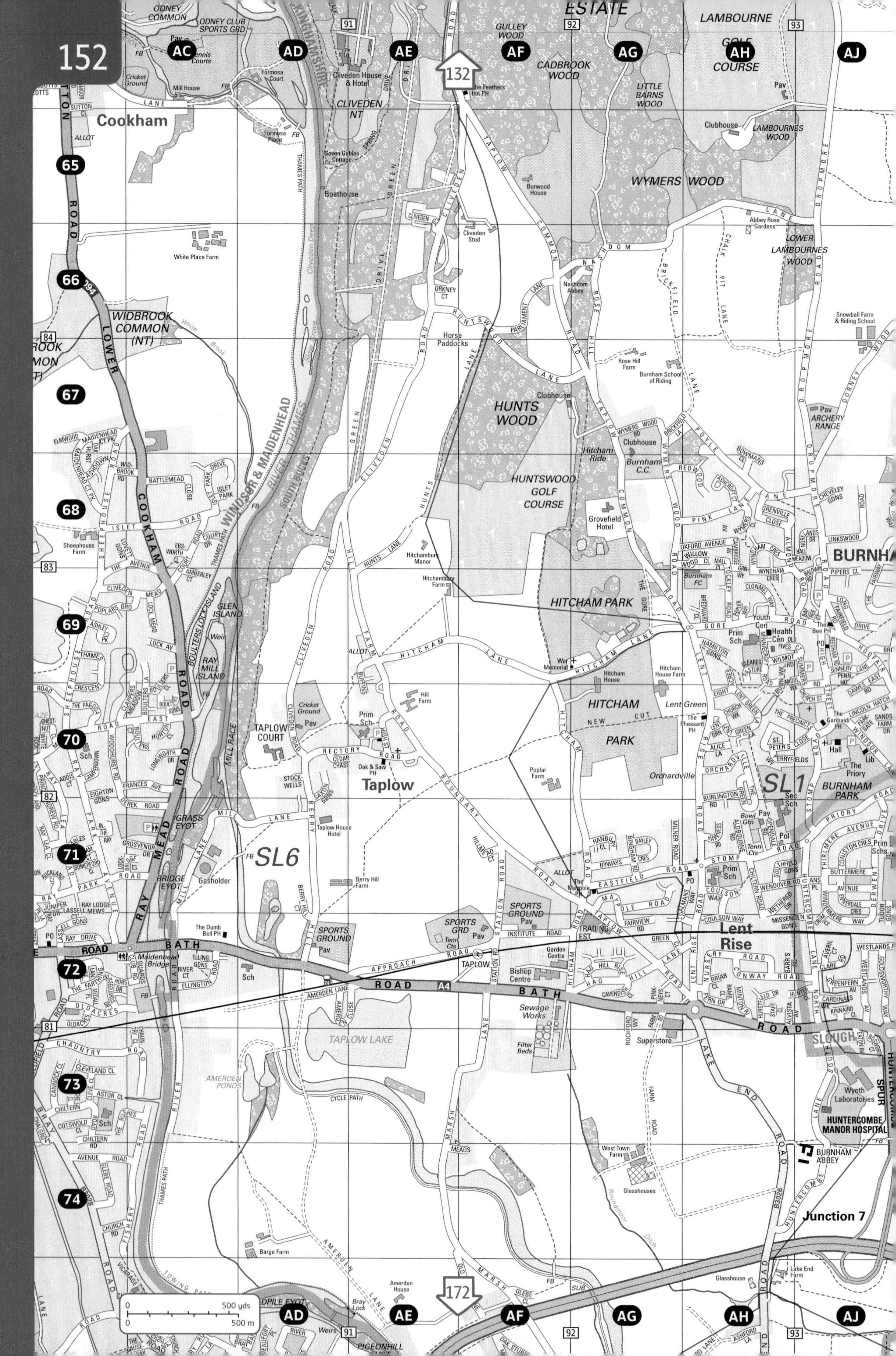

132
172
Cookham
WIDBROOK COMMON (NT)
ODNEY COMMON
ODNEY CLUB SPORTS GRD
Cliveden House & Hotel
CLIVEDEN NT
CADBROOK WOOD
GULLEY WOOD
LITTLE BARNS WOOD
LAMBOURNE GOLF COURSE
LAMBOURNES WOOD
WYMERS WOOD
LOWER LAMBOURNES WOOD
White Place Farm
Cliveden Stud
Burwood House
Nashdom Abbey
Abbey Rose Gardens
Horse Paddocks
HUNTS WOOD
Rose Hill Farm
Burnham School of Riding
Snowball Farm & Riding School
ARCHERY RANGE
HUNTSWOOD GOLF COURSE
Grovefield Hotel
Burnham C.C.
Hitcham Ride
Hitchambury Manor
Hitchambury Farm
HITCHAM PARK
BURNHAM
Burnham FC
Sheephouse Farm
GLEN ISLAND
RAY MILL ISLAND
BOULTERS LOCK ISLAND
WINDSOR & MAIDENHEAD
SOUTH BUCKS
RIVER THAMES
War Memorial
Hitcham House
Hitcham House Farm
Lent Green
The Pheasant PH
TAPLOW COURT
Cricket Ground
Hill Farm
Oak & Saw PH
Taplow
Poplar Farm
Orchardville
SL1
BURNHAM PARK
The Priory
SL6
Taplow House Hotel
Berry Hill Farm
GRASS EYOT
BRIDGE EYOT
Gasholder
The Dumb Bell PH
SPORTS GROUND
SPORTS GRD
TRADING EST
Garden Centre
Bishop Centre
Lent Rise
Maidenhead Bridge
TAPLOW
Sewage Works
Filter Beds
Superstore
TAPLOW LAKE
AMERDEN PONDS
CYCLE PATH
West Town Farm
Glasshouses
Wyeth Laboratories
HUNTERCOMBE MANOR HOSPITAL
BURNHAM ABBEY
Junction 7
Barge Farm
Amerden House
Bray Lock
Weirs
Lake End Farm
Glasshouse
SLOUGH
COOKHAM ROAD
BATH ROAD
A4
A4094
B3026
Junction 7
500 yds
500 m

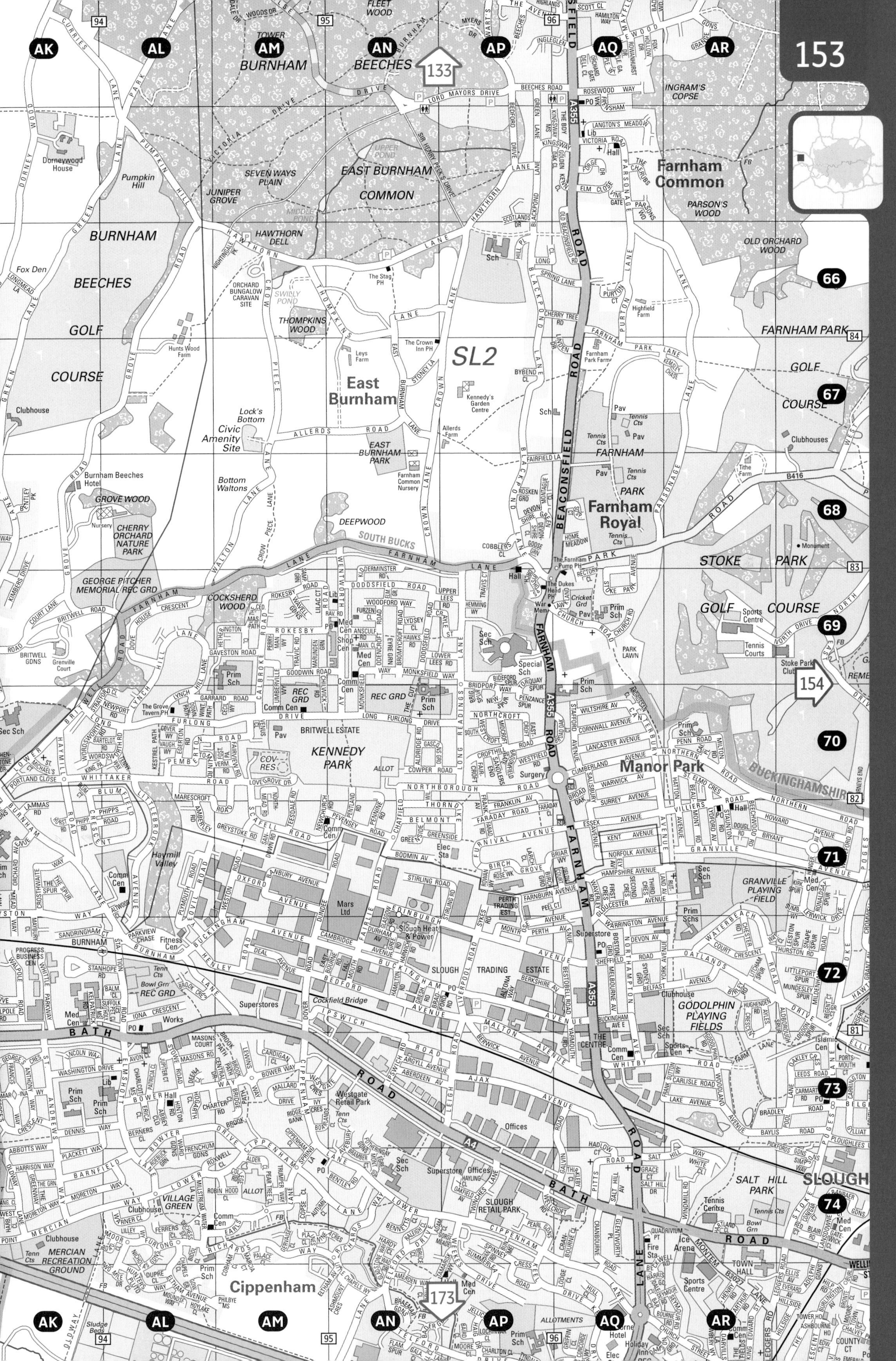

AK
AL
AM
AN
AP
AQ
AR
94
95
96
133
154
173
66
67
68
69
70
71
72
73
74
81
82
83
84
BURNHAM BEECHES
FLEET WOOD
TOWER WOOD
INGRAM'S COPSE
Farnham Common
PARSON'S WOOD
OLD ORCHARD WOOD
FARNHAM PARK
GOLF COURSE
Clubhouses
Tithe Farm
B416
Monument
STOKE PARK GOLF COURSE
Sports Centre
Tennis Courts
Stoke Park Club
Dorneywood House
Pumpkin Hill
SEVEN WAYS PLAIN
EAST BURNHAM COMMON
UPPER POND
MIDDLE POND
JUNIPER GROVE
HAWTHORN DELL
BURNHAM BEECHES GOLF COURSE
Fox Den
Clubhouse
ORCHARD BUNGALOW CARAVAN SITE
SWILLY POND
THOMPKINS WOOD
The Stag PH
Hunts Wood Farm
Leys Farm
The Crown Inn PH
SL2
East Burnham
Kennedy's Garden Centre
Lock's Bottom
Civic Amenity Site
EAST BURNHAM PARK
Farnham Common Nursery
Allerds Farm
Bottom Waltons
Burnham Beeches Hotel
GROVE WOOD
CHERRY ORCHARD NATURE PARK
DEEPWOOD
GEORGE PITCHER MEMORIAL REC GRD
COCKSHERD WOOD
Highfield Farm
Farnham Park Farm
FARNHAM PARK
Farnham Royal
The Farnham Pump PH
The Dukes Head PH
War Mem
Cricket Grd
PARK LAWN
BRITWELL GDNS
Grenville Court
Sec Sch
The Grove Tavern PH
BRITWELL ESTATE
KENNEDY PARK
Manor Park
BUCKINGHAMSHIRE
Haymill Valley
Mars Ltd
Slough Heat & Power
SLOUGH TRADING ESTATE
Superstore
GRANVILLE PLAYING FIELD
GODOLPHIN PLAYING FIELDS
PROGRESS BUSINESS CEN
Fitness Cen
Works
Superstores
Cockfield Bridge
Westgate Retail Park
Offices
SLOUGH RETAIL PARK
VILLAGE GREEN
MERCIAN RECREATION GROUND
Cippenham
Sludge Beds
ALLOTMENTS
SALT HILL PARK
Ice Arena
TOWN HALL
Sports Centre
SLOUGH
A355
A4
B3027
BEACONSFIELD ROAD
FARNHAM ROAD
BATH ROAD
STOKE PARK

AS
AT
AU
AV
AW
AX
AY
134
153
174
STOKE COMMON
BROCKHURST WOOD
FRAME WOOD
PENN WOOD
FULMER COMMON
PARSON'S WOOD
OLD ORCHARD WOOD
STOKE POGES
Offices
FARNHAM PARK
GOLF COURSE
Clubhouses
HOME WOOD
Teikyo Japanese Sch
WEXHAM SPRINGS
UPTON WOOD
DOG KENNEL FIELD
SPRUCE WOOD
Wexham Street
NUFFIELD HOSP
CUCKOO PEN
SL2
ROWLEY WOOD
ROWLEYFIELD LARCHES
ROWLEY SLIP
WALK WOOD
WEXHAM PARK GOLF COURSE
GROTES WOOD
GALLIONS WOOD
SPRING WOOD
HOLLYBUSH WOOD
STOKE PARK GOLF COURSE
GRAY'S FIELD
Monument to Thomas Gray
GARDEN OF REMEMBRANCE
Stoke Park Club Hotel
Stoke Green
WEXHAM PARK HOSPITAL
SL3
ROWLEY LAKE
BUCKINGHAMSHIRE
THE LANES GOLF COURSE
STONE'S WOOD
Pinewood Hotel
GRANVILLE PLAYING FIELD
CEMETERY
Crematorium
ARTS CENTRE
GODOLPHIN PLAYING FIELDS
George Green
SL1
SLOUGH
SALT HILL PARK
Grand Union Canal
Slough Nursery
Middle Green
BLOOM PARK
WELLINGTON ST
Queensmere Shop Centre
UXBRIDGE ROAD
A4
A412
B416
500 yds
500 m

BLACK PARK COUNTRY PARK
LANGLEY PARK COUNTRY PARK
IVER HEATH
IVER
Shreding Green
IVER GOLF COURSE
Pinewood Film Studios
Heatherden Hall
LONG COPPICE
OLDHOUSE WOOD
BROWN'S WOOD
LANGLEY COMMON
STRAWBERRY WOOD
NATURE RESERVE
DIAMOND WOOD
CHESTNUT WOOD
FOXES GUTTER
COLUMN LARCHES
RHODODENDRON GARDENS
LANGLEY PARK WOOD
ROUGHGROUND WOOD
ARBORETUM
BROOM WARREN
CHANDLERS HILL
THE CLUMP
PLAYING FIELD
Five Points
SL0
UB9
M25
A412
A4007
B470
BUCKINGHAMSHIRE
SLOUGH
SOUTH BUCKS
Grand Union Canal (Slough Arm)
Sewage Works
Recycling Centre
135
156
175
AZ
BA
BB
BC
BD
BE
BF
66
67
68
69
70
71
72
73
74

BG
BH
BJ
BK
BL
BM
BN
65
66
67
68
69
70
71
72
73
74
84
83
82
81
05
06
07
136
155
176
UB9
UB10
UB8
UB7
SL0
UXBRIDGE
UXBRIDGE MOOR
COWLEY
HILLINGDON
IVER
YIEWSLEY
WEST DRAYTON
Hillingdon Circus
HILLINGDON HOUSE FARM SPORTS GROUNDS
HILLINGDON ATHLETICS STADIUM
UXBRIDGE COMMON
Uxbridge College (Uxbridge Campus)
Lido (closed)
HILLINGDON COURT PARK
BIG CLUMP
American Community Sch
HILLINGDON GOLF COURSE
HILLINGDON & UXBRIDGE CEMETERY
Brunel University
Halls of Residence
BRUNEL UNIVERSITY SPORTS PARK
UNIVERSITY PLAYING FIELDS
Milton Hulchings Garden Centre
HILLINGDON HOSPITAL
COLHAM GREEN REC GRD
Stockley Academy
Apple Tree Roundabout
Colham Roundabout
PLAYING FIELD
SPORTS GROUND
Uxbridge FC
HORTON IND PARK
RAINBOW INDUSTRIAL ESTATE
West Drayton Coal Depot
Water Treatment Works
Sewage Works
FARLOWS LAKE
LITTLE BRITAIN LAKE
COWLEY LAKE
HUNTSMOOR PARK
Huntsmoor Park Farm
Filter Beds
TOMO INDUSTRIAL EST
ZODIAC BUSINESS PARK
Cowley Retail Park
COWLEY HALL REC GRD
COWLEY BUSINESS PARK
BRIDGE WORKS
CHILTERN BUSINESS VILLAGE
SARUM COMPLEX
MIDAS INDUSTRIAL ESTATE
Royal Mail Sorting Off.
ROCKINGHAM REC GRD
CIVIC OFFICES
The Pavilions
The Chimes
HIGHBRIDGE ESTATE
The Compass Group
Electricity Sub Station
Iver Nature Study Cen
Mansfield Farm
Watergate Farm
Southlands Manor
Brickfield Farm
Ivy House Farm
Oxford Road Nursery
Osborne Farm
Denham Lodge
Alderglade Nature Reserve
Common Plantation
PARK WOOD
Palmer's Moor Farm
Delaford Manor
Coppins Farm
Lower Delaford
Woodlands Park
Delaford Park
Iver Lodge
Thorney Weir House
R.A.F. Uxbridge
RIFLE RANGE
SPORTS GRD
Red Lion Hotel
Tudor Cottage
CONEY GREEN
DEPOT
HILLINGDON HILL
HILLINGDON ROAD
COWLEY ROAD
COWLEY HIGH ROAD
FALLING LANE
OXFORD ROAD
ROCKINGHAM RD
ST. JOHNS ROAD
UXBRIDGE ROAD
PARK ROAD
HARLINGTON ROAD
STOCKLEY RD
DRAYTON PARK VIEW RD
ROYAL LANE
COLHAM AVENUE
PACKET BOAT LANE
TROUT LANE
IVER LANE
A4020
A4007
A408
A437
B470
B483
B467
M25
BUCKINGHAMSHIRE
SOUTH BUCKS
Grand Union Canal
Frays River
River Pinn
Colne Brook
Alder Bourne
GOLF COURSE
500 yds
500 m

RAF NORTHOLT
137
HA4
NORTH HILLINGDON
WESTERN AVENUE
A40
FREEZELAND COVERT
CUTTHROAT WOOD
GUTTERIDGE WOOD
NATURE RESERVE
MEADOWS NATURE RESERVE
Polish War Memorial
C & L GOLF & COUNTRY CLUB
WEST END ROAD
THE GORSE
HILLINGDON
EALING
LANE COVERT
WEST LONDON SHOOTING SCHOOL
UB5
HOME COVERT
POLE HILL OPEN SPACE
HARE PLANTATION
SPORTS GROUND
YEADING BROOK MEADOWS NATURE RESERVE
GROSVENOR PLAYING FIELD
YEADING
158
HAYES SHRUB
HAYES PARK
GRANGE PK
UB4
BELMORE PLAYING FIELDS
HAYES END
RECREATION GROUND
UXBRIDGE ROAD
A4020
ROSEDALE PARK
GRASSY MEADOW
MEMORIAL GDNS
HAYES STADIUM
HAYES
BARRA HALL PARK
BELL HOUSE FLD
WARREN PARK
THE PARKWAY
Lombardy Retail Park
Uxbridge College Hayes Community Campus
Stilwell Roundabout
Ossie Garvin Roundabout
HEXAGON BUSINESS CENTRE
HAYES METRO CENTRE
STOCKLEY PARK GOLF COURSE
STOCKLEY PARK
DAWLEY ROAD
UB3
E.M.I. SPORTS GROUND
UB11
Grand Union Canal
ABENGLEN INDUSTRIAL ESTATE
WARNFORD IND EST
HAYES TOWN
177
PASADENA TRADING EST
PROVIDENT INDUSTRIAL ESTATE
MINET COUNTRY PARK
HAYES BYPASS
A312
A437
BP
BQ
BR
BS
BT
BU
BV
66
67
68
69
70
71
72
73
74

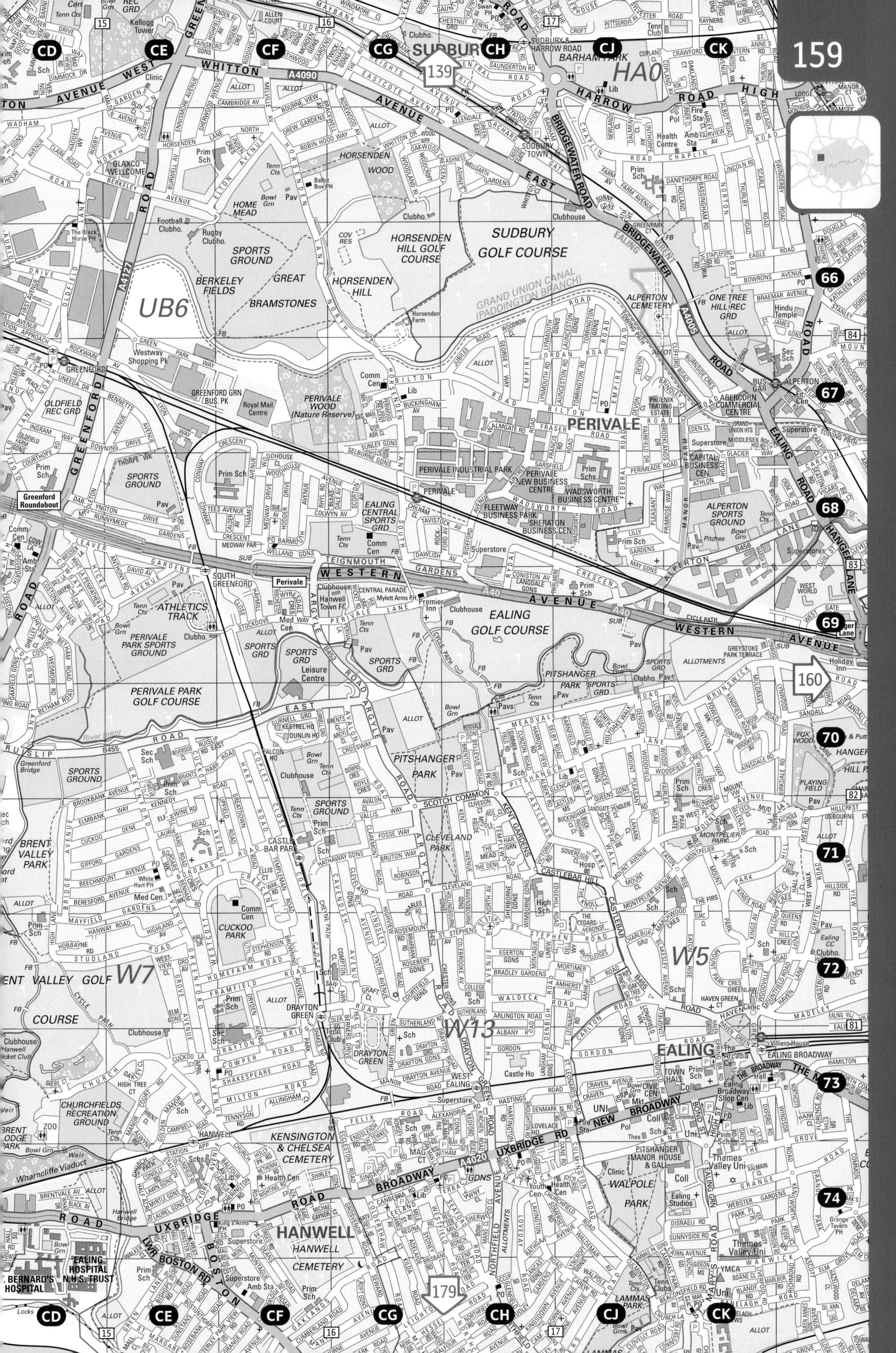
CD
CE
CF
CG
CH
CJ
CK
SUDBURY
HA0
BARHAM PARK
139
WHITTON AVENUE WEST
EASTCOTE AVENUE
HARROW ROAD
HORSENDEN WOOD
SUDBURY GOLF COURSE
HORSENDEN HILL GOLF COURSE
SPORTS GROUND
HOME MEAD
BERKELEY FIELDS
GREAT BRAMSTONES
HORSENDEN HILL
UB6
GRAND UNION CANAL (PADDINGTON BRANCH)
ALPERTON CEMETERY
ONE TREE HILL REC GRD
GREENFORD
OLDFIELD REC GRD
PERIVALE WOOD (Nature Reserve)
PERIVALE
PERIVALE INDUSTRIAL PARK
ALPERTON
ABERCORN COMMERCIAL CENTRE
CAPITAL BUSINESS CEN
ALPERTON SPORTS GROUND
EALING CENTRAL SPORTS GRD
Greenford Roundabout
SOUTH GREENFORD
Perivale
WESTERN AVENUE
ATHLETICS TRACK
PERIVALE PARK SPORTS GROUND
EALING GOLF COURSE
PERIVALE PARK GOLF COURSE
PITSHANGER PARK
160
66
67
68
69
70
71
72
73
74
BRENT VALLEY PARK
CUCKOO PARK
CLEVELAND PARK
W7
W13
W5
BRENT VALLEY GOLF COURSE
DRAYTON GREEN
EALING
EALING BROADWAY
CHURCHFIELDS RECREATION GROUND
KENSINGTON & CHELSEA CEMETERY
PITSHANGER MANOR HOUSE & GALL
WALPOLE PARK
HANWELL
HANWELL CEMETERY
EALING HOSPITAL N.H.S. TRUST
ST. BERNARD'S HOSPITAL
LAMMAS PARK
Thames Valley Uni
179
UXBRIDGE ROAD
NEW BROADWAY

WEMBLEY
TOKYNGTON
CHURCH END
HA0
HA9
ALPERTON
STONEBRIDGE
PARK ROYAL
HARLESDEN
NORTH ACTON
WEST ACTON
ACTON
EAST ACTON
EALING COMMON
W3
W5
NORTH CIRCULAR ROAD
WESTERN AVENUE
HANGER LANE
EALING ROAD
HARROW ROAD
UXBRIDGE ROAD
HIGH STREET
GUNNERSBURY AVENUE
HORN LANE
VICTORIA ROAD
OLD OAK COMMON LANE
TWYFORD ABBEY
CENTRAL MIDDLESEX HOSPITAL
PARK ROYAL CEN
FRIARY PARK INDUSTRIAL ESTATE
ACTON PARK
ACTON CEMETERY
EALING BROADWAY
CL
CM
CN
CP
CQ
CR
CS
65
66
67
68
69
70
71
72
73
74
140
159
180
0
500 yds
500 m

CT
CU
CV
CW
CX
CY
CZ
141
NW2
WILLESDEN
WILLESDEN GREEN
BRONDESBURY
BRONDESBURY PARK
NW10
NW6
KILBURN
KENSAL RISE
QUEEN'S PARK
KENSAL GREEN
WEST KILBURN
KENSAL TOWN
MAIDA HILL
ST. MARY'S RC CEMETERY
KENSAL GREEN CEMETERY
GRAND UNION CANAL (Paddington Branch)
W10
W9
OLD OAK COMMON
WORMWOOD SCRUBS
LINFORD CHRISTIE STADIUM
QUEEN CHARLOTTE & CHELSEA HOSP
HAMMERSMITH HOSPITAL
H.M. PRISON WORMWOOD SCRUBS
ST. CHARLES HOSP
NORTH KENSINGTON
W12
WESTWAY
NOTTING HILL
SHEPHERD'S BUSH
Westfield
LOFTUS ROAD STADIUM QPR FC
HOLLAND PARK
KENSINGTON
W8
162
181
14
66
67
68
69
70
71
72
73
74
22
23
24

DA
DB
DC
DD
DE
DF
DG
142
WEST HAMPSTEAD
ROYAL FREE HOSP
BELSIZE PARK
NW3
NW6
SOUTH HAMPSTEAD
SWISS COTTAGE
FINCHLEY ROAD
HAVERSTOCK HILL
CHALK FARM
PRIMROSE HILL
NW8
ST. JOHN'S WOOD
LORD'S CRICKET GROUND
WELLINGTON HOSP
HOSPITAL OF ST. JOHN & ST. ELIZ.
LONDON ZOO
NW1
THE REGENT'S PARK
QUEEN MARY'S GARDENS
KILBURN
KILBURN HIGH ROAD
MAIDA VALE
MAIDA HILL
W9
LISSON GROVE
MARYLEBONE
161
WESTBOURNE GREEN
PADDINGTON
ST. MARY'S HOSP
W2
BAYSWATER
WESTWAY
EDGWARE ROAD
MARBLE ARCH
OXFORD STREET where marked is closed to through traffic (except buses & taxis) from 7a.m.-7p.m. Monday - Saturday
KENSINGTON GARDENS
HYDE PARK
THE SERPENTINE
THE LONG WATER
ROUND POND
KENSINGTON PALACE
W8
SW7
NOTTING HILL GATE
KENSINGTON
HOLLAND PARK
KNIGHTSBRIDGE
182
65
66
67
68
69
70
71
72
73
74
26
27
28
0 500 yds
0 500 m

DH
DJ
DK
DL
DM
DN
DP
143
HOLLOWAY
LOWER HOLLOWAY
KENTISH TOWN
CAMDEN TOWN
KING'S CROSS
BARNSBURY
ISLINGTON
N1
N7
PENTONVILLE
SOMERS TOWN
ST. PANCRAS
FINSBURY
CLERKENWELL
EC1
WC1
BLOOMSBURY
HOLBORN
WC2
SOHO
W1
STRAND
EC4
MAYFAIR
ST. JAMES'S
SW1
THE GREEN PARK
ST. JAMES'S PARK
SE1
SOUTHWARK
THE BOROUGH
REGENT'S PARK
RIVER
66
67
68
69
70
71
72
73
74
164
183
EUSTON ROAD
PENTONVILLE RD
CALEDONIAN ROAD
YORK WAY
CAMDEN ROAD
GRAY'S INN ROAD
FARRINGDON ROAD
HOLBORN
KINGSWAY
OXFORD STREET
REGENT STREET
PICCADILLY
VICTORIA EMBANKMENT
BLACKFRIARS
WATERLOO
BUCKINGHAM PALACE

DQ
DR
DS
DT
DU
DV
DW
144
163
184
33
34
35
65
66
67
68
69
70
71
72
73
74
CANONBURY
KINGSLAND
HACKNEY
DALSTON
E8
SOUTH HACKNEY
N1
DE BEAUVOIR TOWN
HOXTON
HAGGERSTON
E2
BETHNAL GREEN
ST. LUKE'S
SHOREDITCH
CLERKENWELL
EC1
BROADGATE
BARBICAN
EC2
STEPNEY
E1
WHITECHAPEL
EC4
SHADWELL
WAPPING
SOUTHWARK
SE1
BOROUGH
THAMES
REGENT'S CANAL
LONDON FIELDS
TOWER OF LONDON
LONDON BRIDGE HOSP
GUY'S HOSPITAL
ROYAL LONDON HOSP
MOORFIELDS EYE HOSP
MILDMAY MISS. HOSP
ST. JOSEPH'S HOSPICE
LONDON CHEST HOSP
TATE MODERN
SHAKESPEARE GLOBE THEATRE
500 yds
500 m

DX
DY
DZ
EA
EB
EC
ED
HOMERTON
E9
HACKNEY WICK
145
LONDON 2012 OLYMPIC PARK SITE
STRATFORD INTERNATIONAL (Due to open 2009)
E15
STRATFORD
VICTORIA PARK
OLD FORD
MILE END
BOW
E3
TOWER HAMLETS CEMETERY PARK
BROMLEY
MILE END PARK
MILE END STADIUM
LEE VALLEY PARK
LIMEHOUSE
E14
POPLAR
ISLE
WEST INDIA DOCKS
CANARY WHARF
SE16
SE10
RIVER THAMES
166
185
LIMMO PENINSULA ECOLOGICAL PARK
CANNING TOWN
BLACKWALL
NORTH GREENWICH
QUEEN MARY UNIVERSITY OF LONDON
ROYAL LON. HOSP (ST. CLEMENTS)
THREE MILLS GREEN
LANGDON PARK
BARTLETT PARK
STEPNEY GREEN PARK
66
67
68
69
70
71
72
73
74

166
EE
EF
EG
EH
EJ
EK
EL
146
13
FOREST GATE
E7
WOODGRANGE PARK CEMETERY
PLASHET JEWISH CEMETERY
PLASHET PARK
STRATFORD
Stratford Cen
Uni of East Lon
WEST HAM PARK
WEST HAM
UPTON
UPTON PARK
PRIORY PARK
BOLEYN GRD WEST HAM UTD. FC
E15
PLAISTOW
EAST LONDON CEMETERY
MEMORIAL RECREATION GROUND
PLAISTOW PARK
PLAISTOW HOSP
24
LEE VALLEY REGIONAL PARK
165
E13
NEWHAM UNIVERSITY HOSPITAL
TERENCE McMILLAN STADIUM
BRAMPTON PARK
EAST HAM JEWISH CEMETERY
E6
BECKTON DISTRICT PARK NORTH
CUSTOM HOUSE
BECKTON DISTRICT PARK SOUTH
CANNING TOWN
KING GEORGE V PARK
ELECTRA BUSINESS PARK
BLACKWALL TRADING EST
LIMMO PENINSULA ECOLOGICAL PARK
LOWER LEA CROSSING
ExCeL London
ROYAL VICTORIA DOCK
E16
Millennium Mills
Connaught Roundabout
Royal Albert Roundabout
Airport Roundabout
N Woolwich Roundabout
CONNAUGHT BRIDGE
LONDON
SE10
O2
SILVERTOWN
THAMES BARRIER PARK
THAMESIDE INDUSTRIAL EST
186
RIVER
WOOLWICH REACH
THAMES FLOOD
500 yds
500 m
40
41
42
65
66
67
68
69
70
71
72
73
74
84
83
82
81

EM
EN
EP
EQ
ER
ES
ET
43
44
45
LOXFORD
LITTLE ILFORD PARK
147
BARKING PARK
BARKING PARK REC GRD
Indoor Bowl Club
E12
SPORTS GROUND
LONGBRIDGE ROAD
FANSHAWE AV
NORTHERN RELIEF ROAD
NORTH CIRCULAR ROAD
A406
A124
A123
A13
A117
A1020
A112
A116
BARKING
BARKING HOSPITAL
UPNEY
RIPPLE ROAD
TRIPPLESIDE BURIAL GROUND
BARKING INDUSTRIAL PARK
ALFREDS WAY IND ESTATE
WAYSIDE COMMERCIAL EST
IG11
ALFREDS WAY
BARKING BYPASS
BARKING ROAD REC GRD
TOWN HALL
Movers Lane
GREATFIELDS PARK
LYON BUSINESS PARK
ABBEY WHARF INDUSTRIAL ESTATE
KATELLA TRADING EST
BARKING BUSINESS CENTRE
THAMES ROAD
RIVER ROAD BUSINESS PARK
168
IO CENTRE
TRAFALGAR BUSINESS CENTRE
BUZZARD CREEK INDUSTRIAL ESTATE
CREEKMOUTH
BARKING FLOOD BARRIER
Gravel Works
BECKTON REACH SEWAGE TREATMENT WORKS
Filter Beds
Northern Outfall Sewage Works
Gallions Reach Shopping Park
GEMINI BUSINESS PARK
Gas Works
DLR DEPOT
GOOSELEY'S PLAYING FIELDS
BECKTON TRIANGLE RETAIL PARK
GATEWAY RETAIL PARK
FLANDERS RD PLAYING FLDS
LONDON IND EST
BECKTON RETAIL PARK
BECKTON
NEW BECKTON PARK
25
Cyprus Roundabout
Gallions Roundabout
GALLIONS REACH
Uni of East London
ALBERT DOCK
CITY AIRPORT
KING GEORGE V DOCK
KING GEORGE V
STANDARD INDUSTRIAL ESTATE
ROYAL VICTORIA GDNS
North Woolwich Pier
Woolwich Ferry Pier
37
187
MARGARET NESS OR TRIPCOCK POINT
SE28
GALLIONS HILL
THAMESMEAD
H.M. PRISON
WOOLWICH CROWN CT
66
67
68
69
70
71
72
73
74
81
82
83
84

EU
EV
EW
EX
EY
EZ
FA
148
BARKING FC
ARENA
PARSLOES PARK
RM9
DAGENHAM
DAGENHAM HEATHWAY
A1240
HEATHWAY
A1153
PORTERS AVENUE
LODGE AVENUE
BECONTREE
HEDGEMANS ROAD
IVYHOUSE ROAD
GORESBROOK ROAD
GORESBROOK PARK
CASTLE GREEN
GORESBROOK SPORTS GROUND
BARKING R.F.C.
RIPPLESIDE BURIAL GROUND
Lodge Avenue Junction
BARKING INDUSTRIAL PARK
ALFREDS WAY
ALFREDS WAY IND ESTATE
RENWICK IND ESTATE
RIPPLE ROAD
A13
WAYSIDE COMMERCIAL EST
TRAIN DEPOT
RIPPLESIDE COMMERCIAL ESTATE
MAYBELLS COMM EST
THAMES AVENUE
FORD MOTOR WORKS
Freight Depot
DAGENHAM DOCK
CHOATS ROAD
BARKING BUSINESS CENTRE
RIVERSIDE INDUSTRIAL ESTATE
THAMES ROAD
Thameside Park City Farm
The Ripple Nature Reserve
IG11
THAMES GATEWAY PARK
BREACH LANE
HINDMANS WAY
POWER STATION
Power Station
Horse Shoe Corner
THUNDERER ROAD
Oil Storage Depot
CHEQUERS LANE
167
CREEKMOUTH
TRAFALGAR BUSINESS CENTRE
BUZZARD CREEK INDUSTRIAL ESTATE
Superstore
RIVER ROAD
Gravel Works
BARKING BARRIER
Barking or False Point
Pier
Jetty
BARKING & DAGENHAM
NEWHAM
GREENWICH
BEXLEY
CROSSNESS LIGHTHOUSE
THAMESMEAD NORTH
Ecology Study Area
Driving Range
RIVERSIDE GOLF COURSE
SE2
Crossness Pumping Station
COVERED RESERVOIRS
Crossness Sewage Treatment Works
Sludge Incinerator
SPORTS GROUND
CROSSWAY PARK
Thamesmead Town FC
MANORWAY GREEN
MOORINGS
THAMESMEAD
CENTRAL WAY
CARLYLE ROAD
HARROW MANORWAY
EASTERN WAY
A2016
SOUTHMERE PARK
LAKESIDE CENTRE
SOUTHMERE
ERITH MARSHES
CROSSNESS NATURE RESERVE
BIRCHMERE PARK
SE28
ABBEY WOOD PARK
WOODLAND WAY
DA18
Bexley Business Academy
188
65
66
67
68
69
70
71
72
73
74
47
48
49
81
82
83
84
0
500 yds
500 m

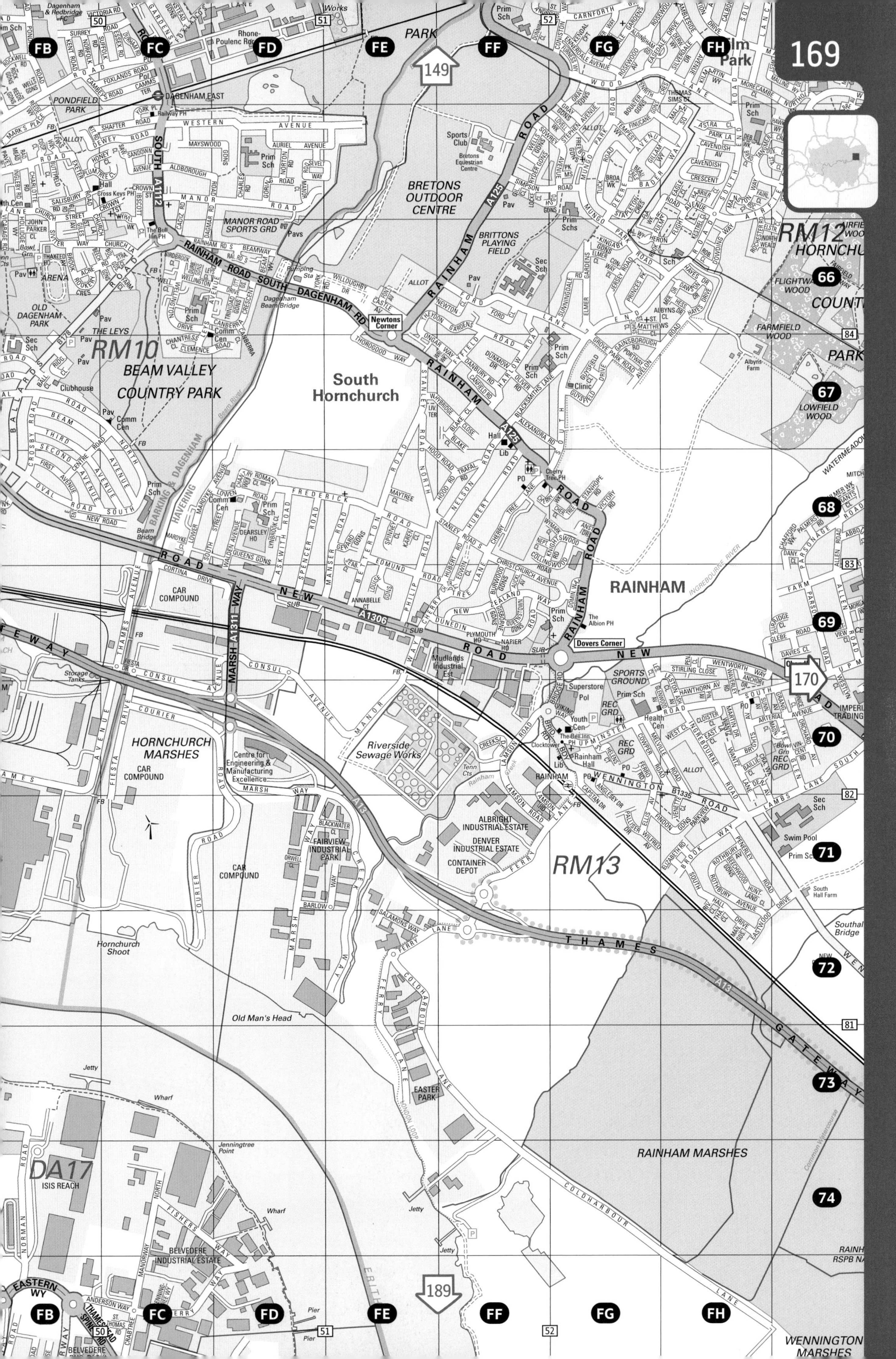
FB
FC
FD
FE
FF
FG
FH
149
170
189
RM10
RM12
RM13
DA17
HORNCHURCH
RAINHAM
South Hornchurch
BRETONS OUTDOOR CENTRE
BRITTONS PLAYING FIELD
BEAM VALLEY COUNTRY PARK
OLD DAGENHAM PARK
PONDFIELD PARK
MANOR ROAD SPORTS GRD
HORNCHURCH MARSHES
RAINHAM MARSHES
WENNINGTON MARSHES
Riverside Sewage Works
ALBRIGHT INDUSTRIAL ESTATE
DENVER INDUSTRIAL ESTATE
CONTAINER DEPOT
FAIRVIEW INDUSTRIAL PARK
BELVEDERE INDUSTRIAL ESTATE
Mudlands Industrial Est
CAR COMPOUND
Centre for Engineering & Manufacturing Excellence
Storage Tanks
SPORTS GROUND
FARMFIELD WOOD
LOWFIELD WOOD
FLIGHTWAY WOOD
Albyns Farm
South Hall Farm
Southall Bridge
Old Man's Head
Jenningtree Point
Hornchurch Shoot
ISIS REACH
EASTER PARK
Newtons Corner
Dovers Corner
DAGENHAM EAST
RAINHAM ROAD SOUTH
DAGENHAM RD
RAINHAM ROAD
NEW ROAD
A1306
A125
A1112
A13
THAMES GATEWAY
MARSH WAY
A1311
FERRY LANE
COLDHARBOUR LANE
THAMES AVENUE
B1335
WENNINGTON ROAD
SOUTH STREET
UPMINSTER ROAD SOUTH
BRIDGE RD
RAINHAM
Clocktower
Rainham Hall
Superstore
INGREBOURNE RIVER
Beam River
Common Watercourse
Jetty
Wharf
Pier
50
51
52
81
82
83
84
66
67
68
69
70
71
72
73
74

FJ
FK
FL
FM
FN
FP
FQ
54
55
56
150
169
190
65
66
67
68
69
70
71
72
73
74
84
83
82
81
RM12
AIRFIELD WOOD
HORNCHURCH
COUNTRY
PARK
PINEWOOD
FLIGHTWAY WOOD
FARMFIELD WOOD
LOWFIELD WOOD
ABBEY WOOD
Albyns Farm
Superstore
Prim Sch
MAYBANK AVENUE
MORECAMBE CL
ASTRA CL
PARK LA
CAVENDISH
CRESCENT
DEWEY PATH
WESTERN PATHWAY
EASTERN PATHWAY
LONDON LOOP / INGREBOURNE VALLEY GREEN WAY
FB
White Hart PH
Park Corner Farm
PARK FARM ROAD
Lodge Farm
Rainham Lodge Farm
POND ROAD
BERWICK
PARKLAND AVENUE
PARKLANDS OPEN SPACE
Corbets Tey Sch
Corbets Tey
Huntsman Hounds PH
Poultry Farm
Harwood Hall
HARWOOD HALL LANE
Stables
Gardners Cor Hall
Central Farm
AVELEY ROAD
BONNETTS WOOD
LANE
SAND & GRAVEL PIT
Civic Amenity Site
BERWICK GLADES
BERWICK WOODS
LITTLE GERPINS LANE
Gerpins Farm
GERPINS LANE
SAND AND GRAVEL PIT
Berwick Ponds Farm
BERWICK POND
WATERMEADOW
INGREBOURNE RIVER
ABBEY WOOD LANE
Berwick Manor
Berwick Manor Farm
White Post Corner
WARWICK LANE
WARWICK WOOD
WHITE POST WOOD
ROMFORD
LAKESIDE
CARDINAL WY
THORN LANE
FAIRVIEW
KING EDWARD AVENUE
STOKE
FARM ROAD
PARSONAGE ROAD
ALLEN ROAD
NORTH ROAD
Prim Sch
CEM
KENWAY
RAINHAM CEMETERY (JEWISH)
LAUNDERS LANE
Saxon Horn PH
UPMINSTER RD
Chandlers Corner
SPRING FARM PARK
Tennis Cts
Pav
IMPERIAL TRADING EST
A1306 NEW ROAD
SOUTH END
ALLOT
REC GRD
SOUTH LANE
LAMBS LANE
Sec Sch
RM13
Swim Pool
Prim Sch
South Hall Farm
Southall Bridge
NEW COTTAGES
WENNINGTON ROAD
East Hall Farm
EAST HALL LANE
CHURCH LANE
Wennington Hall
Premier Travel Inn
Willow Farm
Hall
THE GREEN
Fire Sta
Lennards
Wennington
Moat
Bretts Farm
Sir Henry Gurnett PH
Moor Hall
The Marisco PH
PO
KENNINGTON PARK
New Farm
SANDY LANE
B1335
Sandy Lane Farm
A13
GATEWAY
Common Watercourse
RAINHAM MARSHES
RAINHAM MARSHES RSPB NATURE RESERVE
WENNINGTON MARSHES
LANE
0
500 yds
0
500 m
PURFLEET IND PARK
LONDON ROAD
A1306
PURFLEET ROAD
Nursery
Clubhouse
SPORTS GROUND
TOPLANDS AV
BUCHANAN CL
LOWLANDS
Hall
Lib
ARNHEM AVENUE
MYRTLE GRO
CENTRAL
SHANNON
NETHAN DR
ROWAN GROVE

North Ockendon
SOUTH OCKENDON
Aveley
RM14
RM15
RM16
UPMINSTER CEMETERY
MIDDLE WOOD
BONUS WOOD
SPORTS GRD
TOP MEADOW GOLF
Top Meadow Hotel
Driving Range
Clubhouse
RUSSELL'S LAKE
STUBBERS ADVENTURE CENTRE
COYS LAKE
HAVERING
THURROCK
SAND AND GRAVEL PIT
FREEMAN'S SHAW
THE WILDERNESS
WHITEHALL WOOD
BELHUS WOODS COUNTRY PARK
LITTLE BRICKKILN WOOD
BRICKKILN WOOD
BELHUS CHASE
FORD AVELEY PLANT
SOUTH OCKENDON REC GRD
OAK WOOD
ASH PLANTATION
ROOKERY
BONNYGATE WOOD
SPORTS GROUND
THE SHRUBBERY
BELHUS PARK GOLF COURSE
DILKES PARK
BELHUS PARK
LITTLE PALMER'S SHAW
GREAT PALMER'S SHAW
MARDYKE VALLEY GOLF COURSE
North Stifford
HANGMAN'S WOOD
MILLARD'S GARDEN
BRANNETT'S WOOD
MARDYKE WOODS
DAVY DOWN RIVERSIDE PARK
LOW WELL WOOD
BRICKBARN WOOD
COMBE WOOD
Junction 30
KARTING CEN
LAKESIDE COACH PARK
THURROCK ARTERIAL ROAD
FIELDS OF PEACE
M25
A13
B1421
B186
B1335
151
191
66
67
68
69
70
71
72
73
74
84
83
82
81
57
58
59
FR
FS
FT
FU
FV
FW
FX

AC
AD
AE
AF
AG
AH
AJ
152
91
92
93
ABBEY
Junction 7
Glasshouses
Barge Farm
Amerden House
HEADPILE EYOT
Bray Lock
Weirs
PIGEONHILL EYOT
Waterside PH
Bray
Crown Inn P.H.
Jesus Hospital
Bray Bridge
ALLOT
Cricket Grd
THE CAUSEWAY
The Cut
M4
New Thames Bridge
Weir Bank
Hall
Prim Sch
HARCOURT ROAD
OAK STUBBS LANE
Dorney Reach
Hotel
MONKEY ISLAND
DORNEY REACH ROAD
Glasshouse
Lake End Farm
ASHFORD LANE
CYCLE PATH
Dorney
VILLAGE B3026 ROAD
Dorney Court
Court Farm
Pigeonhouse Farm
Riding School
WINDSOR ROAD
BRAY MARINA
Clubhouse
QUEEN'S EYOT
GRAVEL PIT
CEM
Works
Holyport
A308
LYNGFIELD PARK
SL6
DORNEY LAKE
BUCKINGHAMSHIRE
WINDSOR & MAIDENHEAD
RIVER THAMES
TOWING PATH
SOUTH BUCKS
Bray Studios
Oakley Court Hotel
Pitch 'n' Putt
FERNDALE PARK
The Guild House
Queen's Head PH
Wayside Stables Equestrian Centre
Stroud Farm
Windsor Marina
Bullock's Hatch Bridge
The Retreat Farm
Fifield
Coningsby Farm
GREEN LANE
B3024
The Rising Sun PH
Ledger Farm
The Fifield Inn PH
Fifield House
Braywood C.C. Pav
Prim Sch
Banham Farm
OAKLEY GREEN ROAD
Kimbers Farm
Oakley Place Farm
Oakley Green
Bishops Farmhouse
The Greene Oak PH
Windsor Garden Centre
Ye Olde Red Lion PH
Broom Farm
Gale House Farm
Tarbay Farm
TARBAY LANE
Braywood House
BRAY WOOD
Lakeside Racing Stables
Darkhole Bridge
DARKHOLE RIDE
Nightingale Corner
HOLLIDAY'S PLAIN
NOBBSCROOK
WINDSOR FOREST
Wakers Farm
New Lodge Farm
DRIFT ROAD
WINDSOR & MAIDENHEAD
BRACKNELL FOREST
Foliejon Park Farm
New Lodge
NOBBSCROOK COPSE
FISH POND
Windsor Hill
500 yds
500 m
75
76
77
78
79
80
81
82
83
84

AK
AL
AM
AN
AP
AQ
AR
153
174
Cippenham
SL1
SL4
M4
Junction 6
Chalvey
Eton Wick
DORNEY COMMON
Boveney
ETON
Clewer Village
Dedworth
Clewer Green
Clewer New Town
WINDSOR
WASTE WATER TREATMENT WORKS
ETON WICK COMMON
ETON GREAT COMMON
ETON COLLEGE GOLF COURSE
THE PLAYING FIELDS
ROYAL WINDSOR RACECOURSE
RIVER THAMES
JUBILEE RIVER
MERCIAN RECREATION GROUND
SUTHERLAND GRANGE
WINDSOR RACECOURSE PARK HOMES
CLEWER PARK
DEDWORTH MANOR OPEN SPACE
CLEWER MEMORIAL REC GRD
MAIDENHEAD ROAD
A308
A332
A355
B3026
B3022
B3024
WINDSOR & ETON RELIEF ROAD
TUNS LANE
KINGS ROAD
ALBERT ROAD
ST. LEONARDS ROAD
WINKFIELD ROAD
WINDSOR CEMETERY
QUEEN MARY'S PLANTATION
HOG COMMON
GARRISON SPORTS GROUND
CAVALRY EXERCISE GROUNDS
WINDSOR GREAT PARK
KING EDWARD VII HOSP
PRINCESS MARGARET HOSP
HOUSEHOLD CAVALRY MUS
Combermere Barracks
Victoria Barracks
THE BROCAS
DEADWATER FIREWORK AIT
SPORTS GROUND
ALEXANDRA GDNS
WINDSOR & ETON CENTRAL
WINDSOR & ETON RIVERSIDE
Eton College
ASH PLANTATION
WITHY COVER
DININGROOM CLOSE
SPITAL MEADOW
PADDOCKHILL COPSE
NEW COVER
LEGOLAND
76
77
78
79
80
81
82
83
84

SLOUGH
Upton Park
Upton
SL1
UPTON COURT PARK
AGARS PLOUGH PLAYING FIELDS
THAMES VALLEY ATHLETICS CENTRE
DITTON PARK
KEDERMISTER PARK
THE HOME PARK RECREATION GROUND
DATCHET GOLF COURSE
WINDSOR CASTLE
DATCHET
WINDSOR
SL4
THE HOME PARK
FROGMORE GARDENS
Southlea
HAM ISLAND
ROYAL GARDENS
Sunnymeads
154
173
194

IVER GOLF COURSE
BUCKINGHAMSHIRE
SLOUGH
SOUTH BUCKS
LANGLEY
LANGLEY BUSINESS CENTRE
E. Berkshire Coll
MEMORIAL GROUND
Richings Park
SL0
RICHINGS PARK GOLF COURSE AND COUNTRY CLUB
HOME WOOD
Royal Mail Distribution Centre
HARVEY PARK
AXIS PARK
Junction 15 (M25)
Junction 4B (M4)
M4
OAK PLANTATION
OLD WOOD
Sewage Works
LAKESIDE IND EST
Junction 5
Brands Hill
COLNBROOK BYPASS
Colnbrook
THE QUEEN MOTHER RESERVOIR
SL3
PIPPINS PARK
COLNBROOK GOLF RANGE
Poyle
BRITANNIA INDUSTRIAL EST
MCKAY TRADING ESTATE
POYLE TECH CEN
TRIDENT INDUSTRIAL ESTATE
Horton
Arthur Jacob Nature Reserve
Junction 14
TW19
WINDSOR & MAIDENHEAD
SURREY
WRAYSBURY
155
176
195

YIEWSLEY
WEST DRAYTON
THORNEY
THORNEY PARK GOLF COURSE
SL0
UB7
Junction 15 (M25)
Junction 4B (M4)
M4
M25
HARMONDSWORTH MOOR
PROSPECT PARK
Harmondsworth
Sipson
SL3
Longford
Longford Roundabout
COLNBROOK BYPASS
BATH ROAD
NORTHERN PERIMETER ROAD
TW6
TW19
TERMINAL 5
TERMINAL 3
Control Tower
Junction 14
BEDFONT COURT ESTATE
HARMONDSWORTH MOOR COUNTRY PARK
HARMONDSWORTH IMMIGRATION REMOVAL CEN
SIPSON WAR MEML. REC GRD
HEATHROW COACH CEN
BRITISH AIRWAYS CARGO CENTRE
SPELTHORNE
SURREY
156
175
196
500 yds
500 m

HAYES TOWN
UB11
UB3
HARLINGTON
CRANFORD
CRANFORD COUNTRYSIDE PARK
HEATHROW AIRPORT (LONDON)
HATTON
TW4
TW5
TW14
MINET COUNTRY PARK
Junction 4
Junction 3
Junction 4A
STOCKLEY PARK
BOURNE FARM FIELD
PINKWELL PARK
CHERRY LANE CEMETERY
IMPERIAL COLLEGE SPORTS GROUND
LITTLE HARLINGTON FIELD
SIPSON MEADOW
SAM PHILIP REC GRD
CRANE MEADOW
AVENUE PARK
HOUNSLOW HEATH GOLF COURSE
HOUNSLOW URBAN FARM
Waggoners Roundabout
Hatton Cross
Cherry Lane Roundabout
TERMINAL 1
TERMINAL 2
NORTH HYDE RD
BATH ROAD
GREAT SOUTH-WEST ROAD
THE PARKWAY
HIGH STREET
STATION ROAD
DAWLEY ROAD
M4
A4
A30
A312
A437
A408
157
178
197

SOUTHALL
MINET COUNTRY PARK
UB3
UB1
UB2
NORWOOD GREEN
NORTH HYDE
AIRLINKS GOLF COURSE
BRITISH AIRWAYS SPORTS GROUND
Heston Services
HESTON
OSTERLEY PARK HOUSE
OSTERLEY
LAMPTON
LAMPTON PARK
TW5
TW4
TW3
HOUNSLOW WEST
HOUNSLOW
SUTTON PLAYING FIELD
Waggoners Roundabout
Henlys Roundabout
158
177
198
BW
BX
BY
BZ
CA
CB
CC
75
76
77
78
79
80
81
82
83
84
Junction 3
0 500 yds
0 500 m

CD
CE
CF
CG
CH
CJ
CK
159
HANWELL
HANWELL CEMETERY
EALING HOSPITAL N.H.S. TRUST
ST. BERNARD'S HOSPITAL
UXBRIDGE ROAD
BROADWAY
A4020
Thames Valley Uni
PITSHANGER MANOR HOUSE & GALL
WALPOLE PARK
Ealing Studios
LAMMAS PARK
LAMMAS
W7
W13
W5
SPORTS GROUND
WATERSIDE TRADING CENTRE
BRENT RIVER PARK
ELTHORNE PARK
ELTHORNE PARK EXTENSION
RIVER BRENT BUS PARK
LONG WOOD (Nature Reserve)
M4
OSTERLEY PARK NT
WYKE GREEN GOLF COURSE
BOSTON MANOR
BOSTON MANOR HOUSE
LONDON PLAYING FIELDS
Grand Union Canal
SOUTH EALING
NORTHFIELDS
LITTLE EALING
SOUTH EALING CEMETERY
PHOENIX PARK
Junction 2
DEPOT
MACFARLANE SPORT FIELD
B.A.A. SPORTS GRD
CENTAURS BUSINESS CEN
WEST CROSS CENTRE
BRENTSIDE EXECUTIVE CENTRE
BRENTFORD BUSINESS CENTRE
GlaxoSmithKline
BRENTFORD
BRENTFORD FC
WATERMANS ARTS CEN
180
Gillette Corner
GREAT WEST ROAD
A4
TW7
TW8
TW9
TW1
SPRING GROVE
ISLEWORTH
WOODLANDS
SYON PARK
SYON HOUSE
Battles of Brentford 1016 & 1642
London Butterfly House
WEST MIDDLESEX UNIVERSITY HOSP
BOTANIC GA
ARBORETUM
KEW
QUEEN'S COTTAGE GARDENS
Queen Charlotte's Cottage
RIVER THAMES
ISLEWORTH AIT
Duke of Northumberland Estate
ROYAL MID-SURREY GOLF COURSE (OLD DEER PARK)
Kew Observatory
OBSERVATORY GARDENS
OLD DEER PARK RECREATION GROUND
RICHMOND ATHLETIC GROUND
ROYAL HOSP
Richmond Circus
RICHMOND GREEN
MOGDEN SEWAGE TREATMENT WORKS
WORTON HALL INDUSTRIAL ESTATE
VICTORY BUSINESS CENTRE
REDLEES PARK
THORNBURY PLAYING FIELDS
ST MARGARETS
St. Margarets Roundabout
199
TWICKENHAM ROAD
LONDON ROAD
A315
A310
A3004
A316
76
77
78
79
80
81
82
83
84
15
16
17

CL
CM
CN
CP
CQ
CR
CS
160
EALING COMMON
ACTON
EAST ACTON
W5
W3
W4
TW8
TW9
SW14
SOUTH ACTON
ACTON PARK
BEDFORD PARK
GUNNERSBURY
GUNNERSBURY PARK
SOUTH EALING CEMETERY
POPEFIELD PLAYING FIELDS
SOUTHFIELDS PLAYING FIELDS
KENSINGTON CEMETERY
CLAYPONDS HOSP
Junction 1
Junction 2
Chiswick Rbt
Gunnersbury Park
Kew Bridge
Kew Green
BRENTFORD
CHISWICK
CHISWICK HOUSE GROUNDS
CHISWICK HOUSE
TURNHAM GREEN
GROVE PARK
KEW
KEW PALACE
ROYAL BOTANIC GARDENS
OLIVER'S ISLAND
BRENTFORD AIT
THE NATIONAL ARCHIVES
RIVER THAMES
CHISWICK CEMETERY
DUKE'S MEADOW
DUKE'S MEADOWS GOLF CHISWICK BRIDGE
CIVIL SERVICE SPORTS GROUND
RIVERSIDE RECREATION GROUND
HAMMERSMITH CEMETERY
NORTH SHEEN
NORTH SHEEN CEMETERY
MORTLAKE
EAST SHEEN
Chalkers Corner
Manor Circus
Milestone Green
Richmond Circus
RICHMOND
RICHMOND ATHLETIC GROUND
ROYAL HOSP
QUEEN'S COTTAGE GARDENS
OLD DEER PARK
PESTHOUSE COMMON
EAST SHEEN COMMON (NT)
NATIONAL TENNIS CENTRE
PALEWELL COMMON
BARNES BRIDGE
BARNES HOSP
HOUNSLOW
RICHMOND UPON THAMES
179
200
75
76
77
78
79
80
81
82
83
84
19
20
21
0 500 yds
0 500 m

CT
CU
CV
CW
CX
CY
CZ
SHEPHERD'S BUSH
161
KENSINGTON
HOLLAND PARK
W14
W12
W6
W8
SW5
SW6
SW13
SW15
HAMMERSMITH
EARLS COURT
CASTELNAU
THE WETLANDS CENTRE
BARNES
PARSONS GREEN
FULHAM
PUTNEY
WANDSWORTH
ROEHAMPTON
RIVER THAMES
OLYMPIA
HAMMERSMITH CEMETERY
QUEENS CLUB
CHARING CROSS HOSP
FULHAM CEMETERY
BARNES COMMON
BARN ELMS PLAYING FIELDS
WANDSWORTH PARK
HURLINGHAM PARK
FULHAM PALACE GARDENS
CRAVEN COTTAGE FULHAM FC
LOFTUS ROAD STADIUM QPR FC
EARLS COURT EXHIBITION CENTRE
UXBRIDGE ROAD
GOLDHAWK ROAD
KING STREET
GREAT WEST ROAD
HAMMERSMITH ROAD
TALGARTH ROAD
WEST CROMWELL ROAD
LILLIE ROAD
FULHAM PALACE ROAD
NEW KINGS ROAD
UPPER RICHMOND ROAD
LOWER RICHMOND ROAD
CASTELNAU
ROCKS LANE
PUTNEY BRIDGE
WANDSWORTH BRIDGE
182
201
76
77
78
79
80
81
82
83
84
22
23
24
26
38

DA
DB
DC
DD
DE
DF
DG
KENSINGTON GARDENS
HYDE PARK
ROUND POND
THE SERPENTINE
162
W8
SW7
KENSINGTON
HOLLAND PARK
75
76
77
78
79
80
81
82
83
84
KENSINGTON PALACE
SERPENTINE GALLERY
KENSINGTON ROAD
KENSINGTON GORE
KNIGHTSBRIDGE
HYDE PARK CORNER
ROYAL ALBERT HALL
Royal Coll of Music
Imperial Coll
SCIENCE MUSEUM
NATURAL HISTORY MUSEUM
VICTORIA & ALBERT MUSEUM
SOUTH KENSINGTON
CROMWELL ROAD
BELGRAVIA
BROMPTON
SW5
EARLS COURT
EARLS COURT EXHIBITION CENTRE
SW10
THE ROYAL MARSDEN
ROYAL BROMPTON HOSP
ROYAL HOSPITAL CHELSEA
SW3
WEST BROMPTON
BROMPTON CEMETERY
CHELSEA
CHELSEA & WEST. HOSP
EMBANKMENT
KENSINGTON & CHELSEA
WANDSWORTH
181
STAMFORD BRIDGE CHELSEA FC
BATTERSEA PARK
CHILDREN'S ZOO
Peace Pagoda
WALHAM GREEN
PARSONS GREEN
EEL BROOK COMMON
SANDS END
SW6
SOUTH PARK
HURLINGHAM PARK
LONDON BATTERSEA HELIPORT
SW11
39
40
CLAPHAM JUNCTION
HAMMERSMITH & FULHAM
SW15
SW18
WANDSWORTH
WANDSWORTH TOWN
CLAPHAM COMMON
202
BOLINGBROKE HOSP
500 yds
500 m

DH
DJ
DK
DL
DM
DN
DP
163
184
203
ST. JAMES'S
THE GREEN PARK
ST. JAMES'S PARK
SW1
SE1
WESTMINSTER
VICTORIA
PIMLICO
LAMBETH
SE11
VAUXHALL
KENNINGTON
NINE ELMS
SW8
RIVER THAMES
SOUTH LAMBETH
STOCKWELL
SW9
SE5
BATTERSEA
CLAPHAM
BRIXTON
SW4
SE24
CLAPHAM COMMON
SOUTHWARK
WATERLOO
HOUSES OF PARLIAMENT
BUCKINGHAM PALACE
THE OVAL (SURREY C.C.C.)
New Covent Garden Market
Battersea Power Station (Disused)
LAMBETH HOSPITAL
76
77
78
79
80
81
82
83
84
41
42

DQ
DR
DS
DT
DU
DV
DW
164
WAPPING
SOUTHWARK
SE1
GUY'S HOSPITAL
LONDON BRIDGE
TOWER BRIDGE EXHIBITION
THE BOROUGH
NEWINGTON
BERMONDSEY
ROTHERHITHE
SOUTHWARK PARK
SE17
WALWORTH
BURGESS PARK
CAMBERWELL
PECKHAM
SE5
SE15
KING'S COLLEGE HOSPITAL
MAUDSLEY HOSPITAL
RUSKIN PARK
SE24
SE22
DULWICH COMMUNITY HOSP
PECKHAM RYE COMMON
PECKHAM RYE PARK
NUNHEAD
75
76
77
78
79
80
81
82
83
84
183
43
44
204
0 500 yds
0 500 m
DR
DS
DT
DU
DV
DW

DX
DY
DZ
EA
EB
EC
ED
165
ISLE
OF
DOGS
SE16
ROTHERHITHE
CUBITT
TOWN
MILLWALL
MUDCHUTE
FARM
E14
SE10
DEPTFORD
SE8
SE14
NEW CROSS
GATE
NEW
CROSS
ST
JOHN'S
GREENWICH
GREENWICH
PARK
NATIONAL
MARITIME MUSEUM
ROYAL
OBSERVATORY
GREENWICH
(Flamsteed House)
QUEEN'S
HOUSE
SE3
BLACKHEAT
SE4
HILLY
FIELDS
LEWISHAM
SE13
BROCKLEY
LADYWELL
BROCKLEY
CEMETERY
LADYWELL
CEMETERY
TELEGRAPH
HILL
PARK
DEPTFORD
PARK
PEPYS
PARK
MILLWALL
PARK
ISLAND
GARDENS
WEST INDIA DOCKS
MILLWALL
OUTER DOCK
GREENLAND
DOCK
SURREY
WATER
SOUTHWARK
TOWER HAMLETS
LEWISHAM
GREENWICH
A200
A2
A20
A206
A1206
A2209
A2210
A2211
A21
A2202
A102
A1203
76
77
78
79
80
81
82
83
84
186
205
36
37
38
45
46

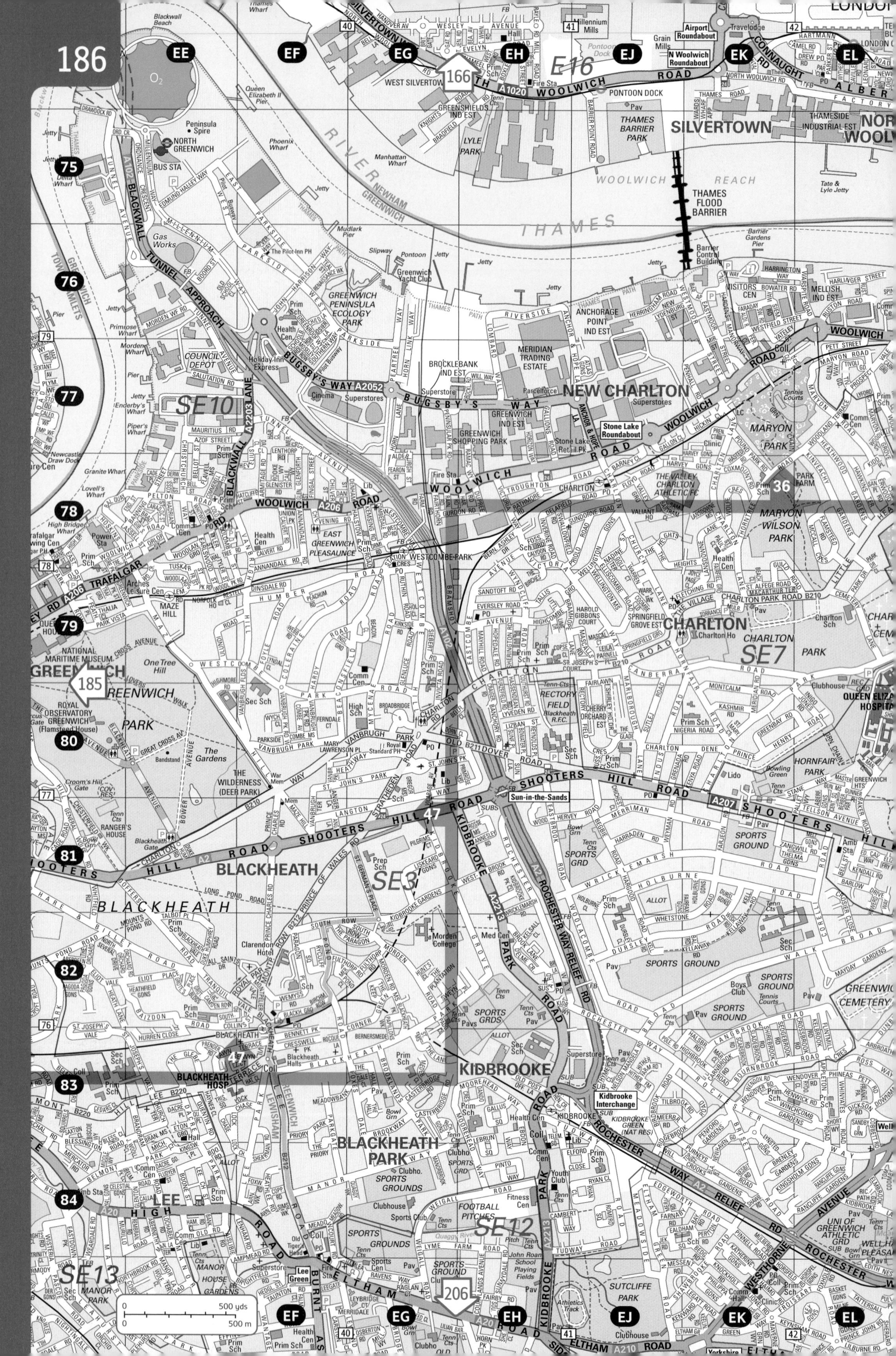

EE
EF
EG
EH
EJ
EK
EL
75
76
77
78
79
80
81
82
83
84
166
185
206
36
47
E16
SE10
SE3
SE7
SE12
SE13
SILVERTOWN
NEW CHARLTON
CHARLTON
CHARLTON PARK
BLACKHEATH
BLACKHEATH PARK
KIDBROOKE
LEE
GREENWICH
GREENWICH PARK
MARYON PARK
MARYON WILSON PARK
HORNFAIR PARK
SUTCLIFFE PARK
RIVER THAMES
WOOLWICH REACH
THAMES FLOOD BARRIER
THAMES BARRIER PARK
NORTH GREENWICH
Peninsula Spire
GREENWICH PENINSULA ECOLOGY PARK
BLACKWALL TUNNEL APPROACH
BUGSBY'S WAY
WOOLWICH ROAD
SHOOTERS HILL ROAD
ROCHESTER WAY RELIEF RD
KIDBROOKE PARK ROAD
ELTHAM ROAD
LEE HIGH ROAD
BURNT ASH
Airport Roundabout
N Woolwich Roundabout
Stone Lake Roundabout
Sun-in-the-Sands
Kidbrooke Interchange
Lee Green
NATIONAL MARITIME MUSEUM
ROYAL OBSERVATORY GREENWICH (Flamsteed House)
THE WILDERNESS (DEER PARK)
THE VALLEY CHARLTON ATHLETIC FC
QUEEN ELIZA HOSPITA
GREENWICH CEMETERY
UNI OF GREENWICH ATHLETIC GRD
BLACKHEATH HOSP
FOOTBALL PITCHES
SPORTS GROUND
0 500 yds
0 500 m

188
EU
EV
EW
EX
EY
EZ
FA
168
187
208
47
48
49
75
76
77
78
79
80
81
82
83
84
SOUTHMERE PARK
ERITH MARSHES
CROSSNESS NATURE RESERVE
LAKESIDE CENTRE
SOUTHMERE
BIRCHMERE PARK
SE28
DA18
WOODLAND WAY
Bexley Business Academy
ABBEY WOOD PARK
THISTLEBROOK INDUSTRIAL EST
HARROW MANORWAY
EASTERN WAY
Birchmere Business Park
Civic Amenity Site
WEST THAMESMEAD BUSINESS PARK
EASTERN IND EST
Gas Works
SE18
ABBEY WOOD
PLUMSTEAD GARDENS
Lesnes Abbey (ruins)
ABBEY WOOD
ABBEY WOOD CARAVAN CLUBS SITE
SE2
BOSTALL HEATH
Hospice
HURST ESTATE
WEST HEATH
ALBERT ROAD ESTATE
BELVEDERE SPORTS GRD
BOSTALL HILL
BOSTALL HEATH
CLAM FIELD RECREATION GROUND
BOSTALL WOODS
GOLDIE LEIGH HOSPITAL
PLUMSTEAD CEMETERY
WOOLWICH CEMETERY
EAST WICKHAM
EAST WICKHAM OPEN SPACE
DA16
WICKHAM LANE
STEVENS PARK
BEXLEYHEATH
DA7
WELLING
WELLING HIGH STREET
Welling United FC & Erith and Belvedere FC
DANSON
PARK
Danson Mansion
Bexley Grammar Sch
BEXLEYHEATH CEMETERY
Broadway Shop Centre
DA6
BEXLEYHEATH
BROADWAY
CROOK LOG
DANSON ROAD
A2016
A206
A207
A209
A2041
A221
B213
0 500 yds
0 500 m

RAINHAM MARSHES
FB
FC
FD
FE
FF
FG
FH
50
51
52
169
190
209
76
77
78
79
80
81
82
83
84
RM13
DA17
DA8
DA1
BELVEDERE
LESSNESS HEATH
ERITH
NORTHUMBERLAND HEATH
BARNEHURST
BARNES CRAY
CRAYFORD MARSHES
RIVER THAMES
ERITH REACH
ERITH RANDS
HAVERING
BEXLEY
Coldharbour Point
FREIGHTMASTER ESTATE
COLDHARBOUR LANE
BELVEDERE INDUSTRIAL ESTATE
CHURCH MANORWAY INDUSTRIAL ESTATE
CRABTREE MANORWAY IND EST
BELVEDERE BUS. PARK
Erith Oil Works
EUROPA TRADING ESTATE
EASTERN WY
BRONZE AGE WAY
A2016
FRASER ROAD
A206
QUEEN'S ROAD
SOUTH RD
NORTHEND ROAD
BEXLEY ROAD
Atlas Trade Park
ERITH CEMETERY
FRANK'S PARK
Bexley Coll
ERITH & DISTRICT HOSP
MONASTERY
ERITH STADIUM
Erith Town F.C.
ERITH REC GRD
Sports Centre
MANFORD IND EST
ANCHOR BAY IND EST
CHURCH TRADING EST
SLADE GREEN
POWER IND EST
SPORTS GROUND
HOWBURY LANE REC GRDS
Howbury Farm
RAIL DEPOT
The Grange
Chemical Works
OPTIMA PARK
THAMES ROAD
Waste Reception Centre
Crayside Industrial Est
BURSTED WOOD
BARNEHURST GOLF COURSE
MARTENS GROVE PARK
SHENSTONE PARK
BAKERS FIELD
Perry Street Farm
Victoria Scott Court
ACORN INDUSTRIAL PARK
WATLING STREET
A207
LONDON ROAD
A220
A2000
PERRY STREET
CRAYFORD
Stanham Farm
The Saltings
Sailing Club
Concrete Works
Superstore
Erith Deep Wharf Jetty
Chalk Fm Wharf
Landing Stage
Sludge Pipeline
Jetty
Pier
Wharf
ISIS REACH
RAINHAM RSPB

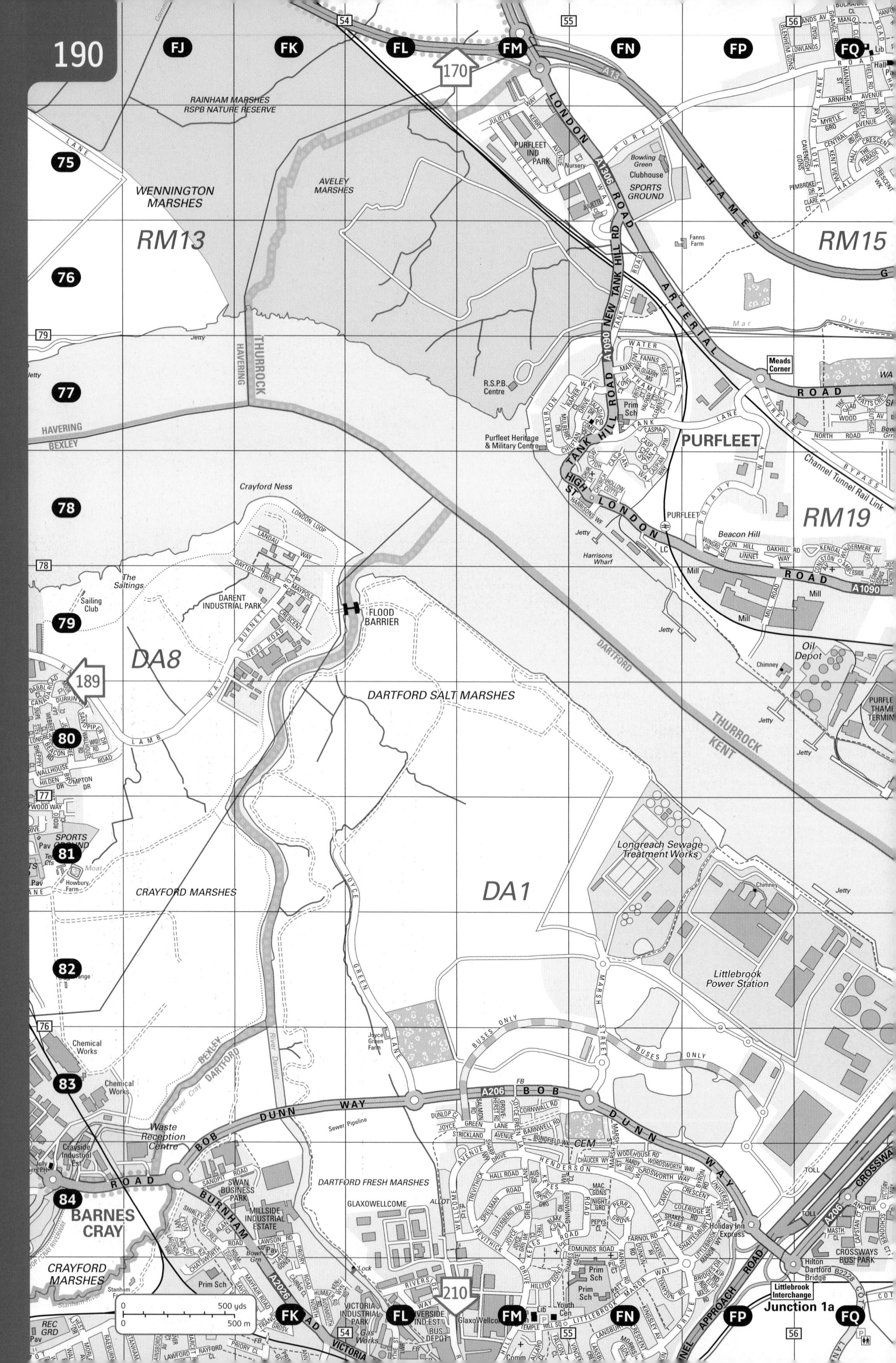

170
189
210
RAINHAM MARSHES
RSPB NATURE RESERVE
WENNINGTON MARSHES
RM13
AVELEY MARSHES
PURFLEET IND PARK
Bowling Green
Clubhouse
SPORTS GROUND
Fanns Farm
RM15
LONDON ROAD
A1306
NEW TANK HILL RD
A1090
TANK HILL ROAD
ARTERIAL ROAD
THAMES
Meads Corner
R.S.P.B. Centre
Purfleet Heritage & Military Centre
PURFLEET
Channel Tunnel Rail Link
RM19
Beacon Hill
Harrisons Wharf
Jetty
Mill
Oil Depot
Chimney
HAVERING
THURROCK
BEXLEY
DARTFORD
KENT
Crayford Ness
The Saltings
Sailing Club
DARENT INDUSTRIAL PARK
FLOOD BARRIER
DA8
DARTFORD SALT MARSHES
CRAYFORD MARSHES
DA1
Longreach Sewage Treatment Works
Littlebrook Power Station
JOYCE GREEN LANE
Joyce Green Farm
MARSH STREET
BUSES ONLY
Chemical Works
Waste Reception Centre
Crayside Industrial Est
BOB DUNN WAY
A206
River Darent
River Cray
Sewer Pipeline
DARTFORD FRESH MARSHES
GLAXOWELLCOME
SWAN BUSINESS PARK
MILLSIDE INDUSTRIAL ESTATE
VICTORIA INDUSTRIAL PARK
BURNHAM ROAD
A2026
BARNES CRAY
CRAYFORD MARSHES
Holiday Inn Express
Hilton Dartford Bridge
CROSSWAYS BUS PARK
Littlebrook Interchange
Junction 1a
APPROACH ROAD
TOLL
CROSSWAYS
FJ
FK
FL
FM
FN
FP
FQ
75
76
77
78
79
80
81
82
83
84
54
55
56
0
500 yds
500 m

Junction 30
Junction 31
West Thurrock
CHAFFORD HUNDRED
RM16
South Stifford
RM20
DA2
DA9
DA10
RIVER THAMES
Lakeside
LAKESIDE RETAIL PK
WATERGLADE INDUSTRIAL PK
FROGMORE ESTATE
WEST THURROCK MARSHES
STONENESS LIGHTHOUSE
Oil Storage Depot
Crossways
Stone
Greenhithe
QUEEN ELIZABETH II BRIDGE
TUNNEL
ARTERIAL ROAD
A1306
A13
M25
A126
A1090
A226
WEST THURROCK WAY
CANTERBURY WAY
OLIVER ROAD
LONDON ROAD
CROSSWAYS BOULEVARD
Stonehouse Corner
Thurrock Services
Thurrock FC
WARREN GORGE
LION GORGE
ST. CLEMENT'S OR FIDDLER'S REACH
171
192
211
FR
FS
FT
FU
FV
FW
FX
76
77
78
79
80
81
82
83
84

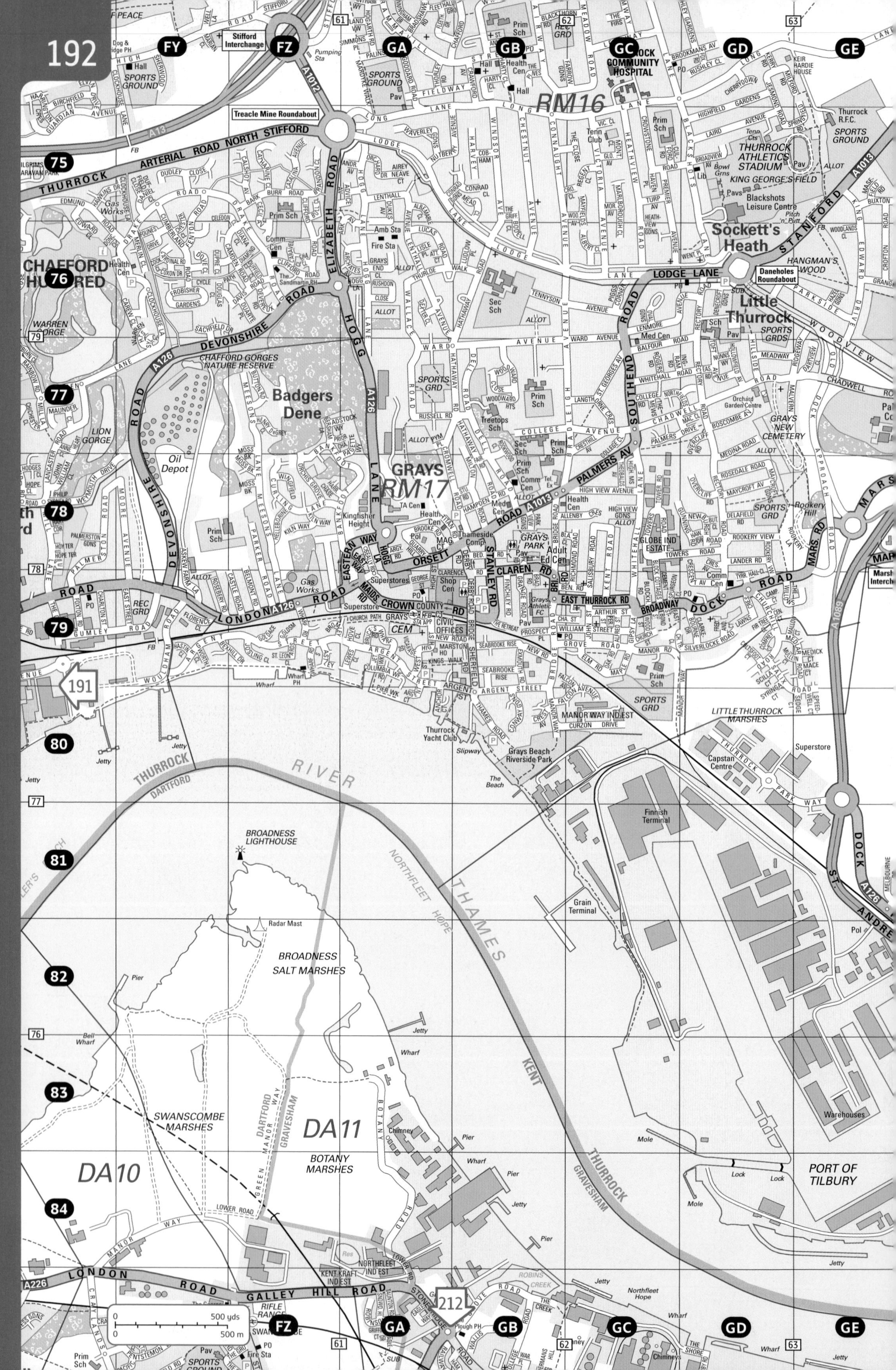

FY
FZ
GA
GB
GC
GD
GE
Stifford Interchange
Treacle Mine Roundabout
Daneholes Roundabout
RM16
RM17
GRAYS
Sockett's Heath
Little Thurrock
CHAFFORD HUNDRED
Badgers Dene
CHAFFORD GORGES NATURE RESERVE
WARREN GORGE
LION GORGE
Oil Depot
THURROCK ATHLETICS STADIUM
KING GEORGE'S FIELD
Blackshots Leisure Centre
Thurrock R.F.C.
HANGMAN'S WOOD
GRAYS NEW CEMETERY
Rookery Hill
GLOBE IND ESTATE
LITTLE THURROCK MARSHES
Capstan Centre
Finnish Terminal
Grain Terminal
Thurrock Yacht Club
Grays Beach Riverside Park
MANOR WAY IND EST
BROADNESS LIGHTHOUSE
Radar Mast
BROADNESS SALT MARSHES
SWANSCOMBE MARSHES
BOTANY MARSHES
DA10
DA11
PORT OF TILBURY
Warehouses
RIVER THAMES
NORTHFLEET HOPE
THURROCK
DARTFORD
KENT
GRAVESHAM
NORTHFLEET IND EST
KENT KRAFT IND EST
ARTERIAL ROAD NORTH STIFFORD
THURROCK
ELIZABETH ROAD
HOGG LANE
DEVONSHIRE ROAD
LONDON ROAD
ORSETT ROAD
PALMERS AV
SOUTHEND ROAD
LODGE LANE
STANFORD ROAD
CHADWELL ROAD
DOCK ROAD
EAST THURROCK RD
BROADWAY
STANLEY RD
CLAREN. RD
GALLEY HILL ROAD
LONDON ROAD
A13
A126
A1012
A1013
A1089
A226
75
76
77
78
79
80
81
82
83
84
61
62
63
76
77
78
79
191
212
0
500 yds
0
500 m

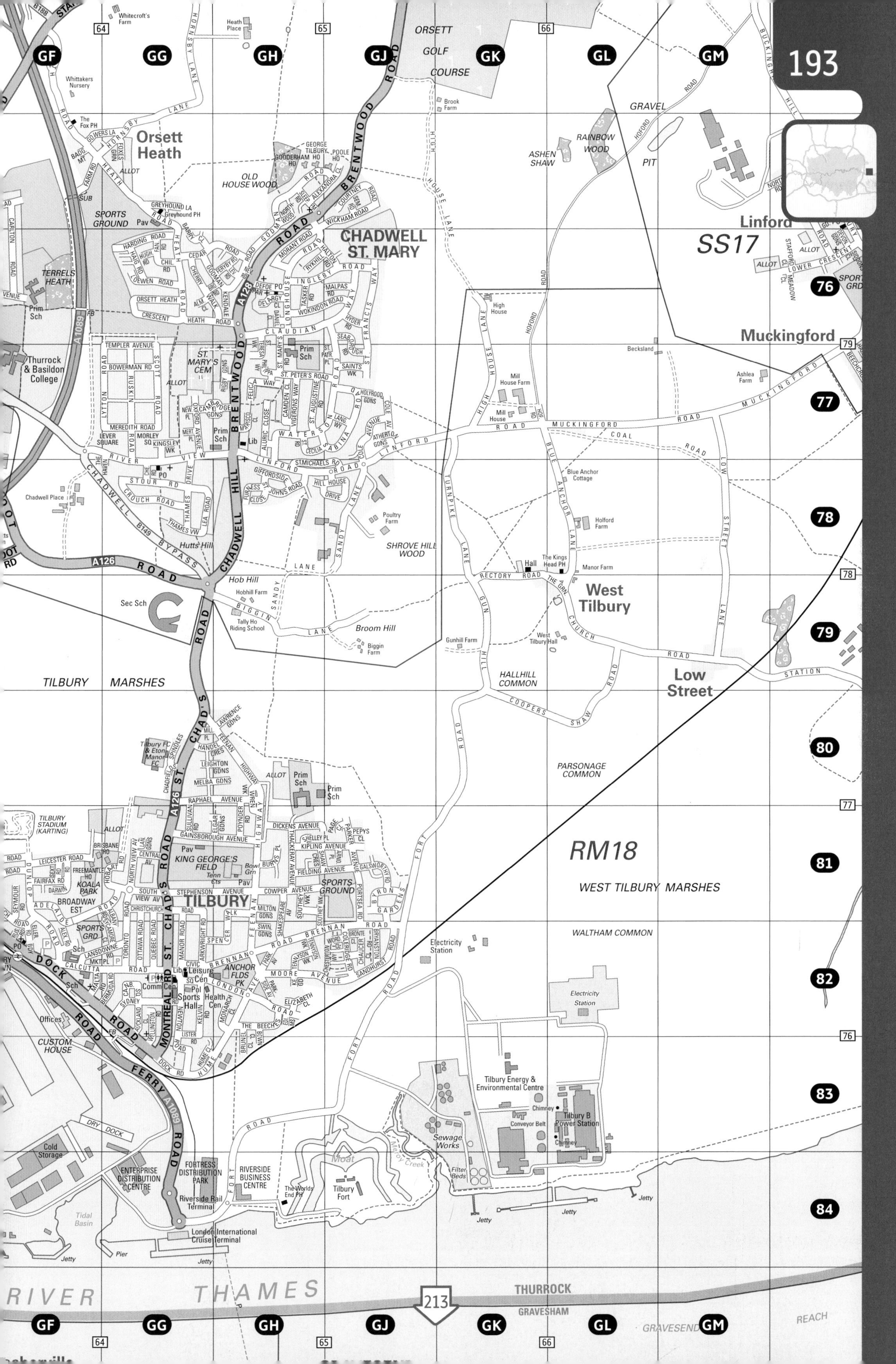

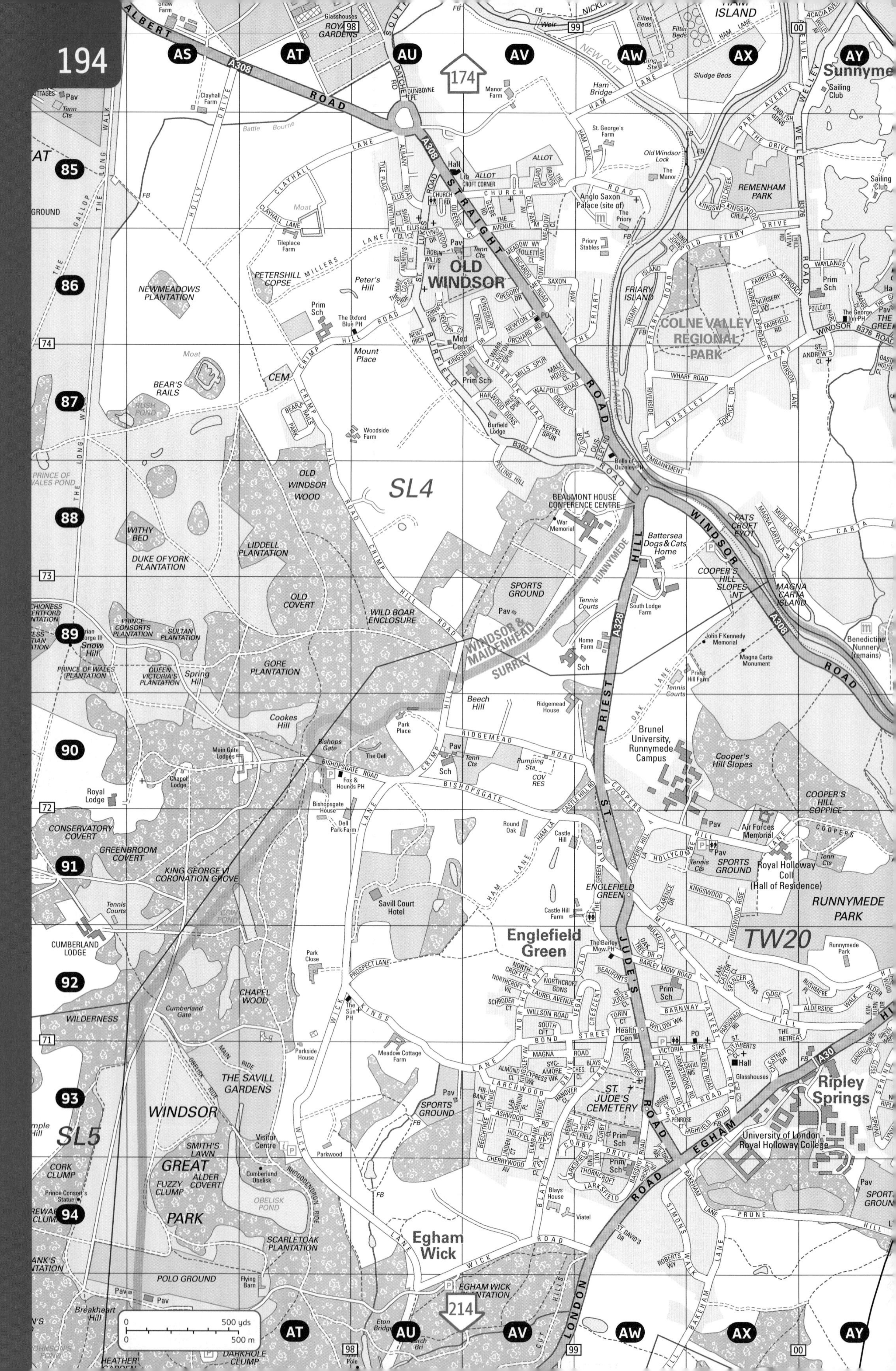
OLD WINDSOR
Englefield Green
Egham Wick
Ripley Springs
SL4
SL5
TW20
WINDSOR GREAT PARK
COLNE VALLEY REGIONAL PARK
RUNNYMEDE PARK
174
214

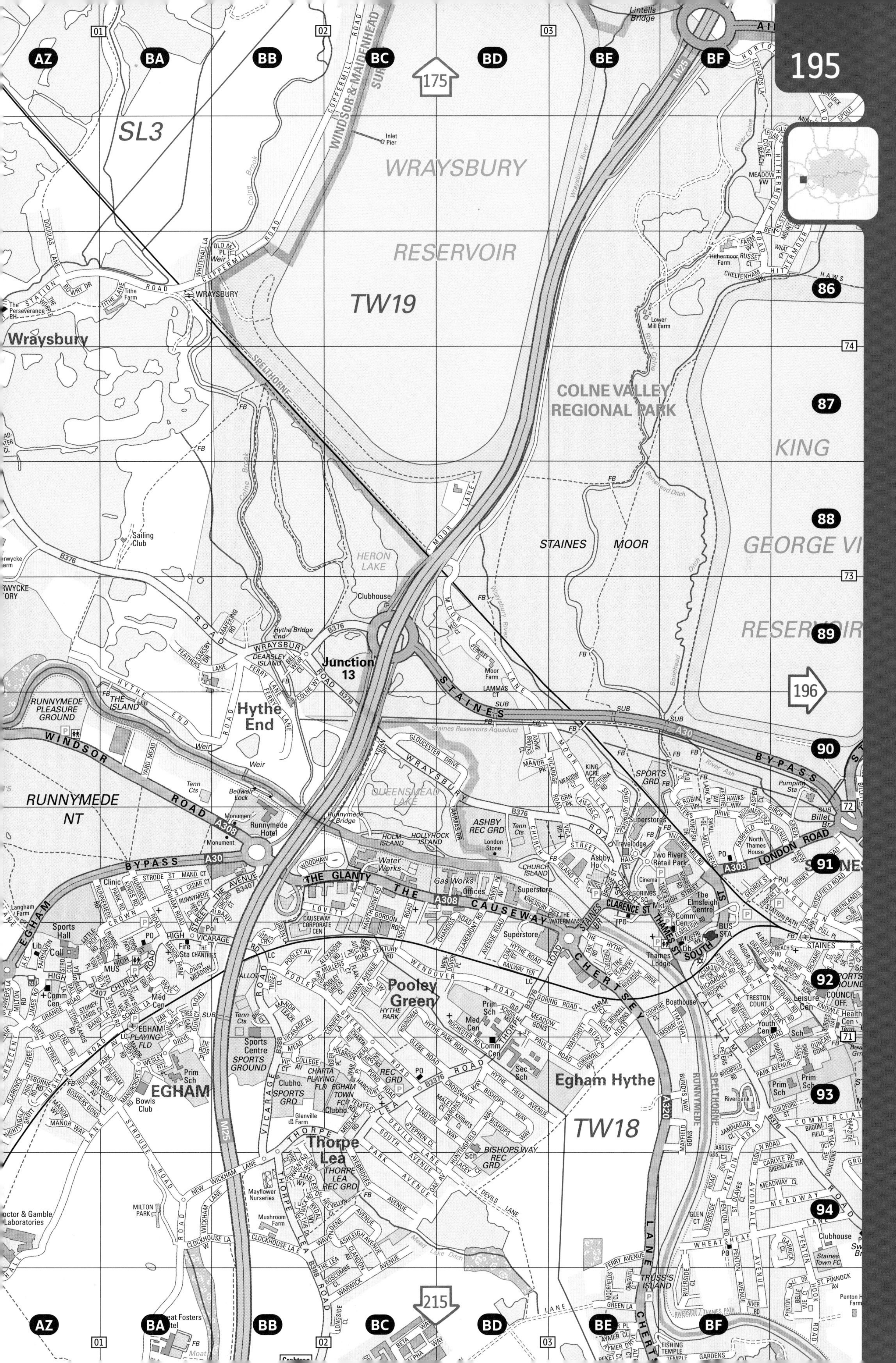

AZ
BA
BB
BC
BD
BE
BF
01
02
03
175
215
196
86
87
88
89
90
91
92
93
94
74
73
72
71
SL3
WRAYSBURY
RESERVOIR
TW19
TW18
Wraysbury
COLNE VALLEY REGIONAL PARK
KING GEORGE VI RESERVOIR
STAINES MOOR
HERON LAKE
Junction 13
Hythe End
RUNNYMEDE PLEASURE GROUND
RUNNYMEDE NT
Runnymede Hotel
THE ISLAND
Bell Weir Lock
QUEENSMEAD LAKE
HOLM ISLAND
HOLLYHOCK ISLAND
ASHBY REC GRD
CHURCH ISLAND
Two Rivers Retail Park
The Elmsleigh Centre
STAINES
EGHAM
Pooley Green
Thorpe Lea
Egham Hythe
TRUSS'S ISLAND
WINDSOR & MAIDENHEAD
SPELTHORNE
RUNNYMEDE
M25
A30
A308
A320
B376
B388
B3376
B3407
WINDSOR ROAD
EGHAM BYPASS
STAINES BYPASS
LONDON ROAD
THE CAUSEWAY
THE GLANTY
CHERTSEY LANE
STAINES ROAD
WRAYSBURY ROAD
COPPERMILL ROAD
HYTHE END ROAD
STROUDE ROAD
Lintells Bridge
Inlet Pier
Lower Mill Farm
Hithermoor Farm
Moor Farm
Sailing Club
Clubhouse
Water Works
Gas Works
Staines Reservoirs Aqueduct
Runnymede Bridge
Mayflower Nurseries
Mushroom Farm
Glenville Farm
Bowls Club
Sports Centre
Staines Town FC
Riverbank

BG
BH
BJ
BK
BL
BM
BN
176
195
216
85
86
87
88
89
90
91
92
93
94
STANWELL MOOR
STANWELL
STAINES
ASHFORD
TW19
TW18
TW17
KING GEORGE VI RESERVOIR
STAINES RESERVOIRS
CARGO TERMINAL
BRITISH AIRWAYS CARGO CENTRE
SPELTHORNE
SURREY
HILLINGDON
SOUTHERN PERIMETER ROAD
STANWELL MOOR ROAD
A3044
LONDON ROAD
A30
STAINES BYPASS
A308
KINGSTON ROAD
BEDFONT ROAD
ASHFORD HOSPITAL
Superstore
The Bull Dog
Crooked Billet Roundabout
Fordbridge Roundabout
H.M. Prison Bronzefield
SHORTWOOD COMMON
FORDBRIDGE PARK
ASHFORD MANOR GOLF COURSE
GRAVEL PIT
Electricity Station
STAINES PARK MINI RAILWAY
RECREATION GROUND
BURIAL GROUND
BLACKBURN TRADING ESTATE
CAMGATE CENTRE
Virgin Atlantic Cargo
SPORTS GROUND
QUEEN MARY
0 500 yds
0 500 m

BP
BQ
BR
BS
BT
BU
BV
08
09
10
177
198
217
86
87
88
89
90
91
92
93
94
74
73
72
71
HATTON
Hatton Cross
HATTON CROSS
TW6
TERMINAL 4
Terminal Four Roundabout
Hilton
Catering Centre
Park & Fly
SOUTH-WEST ROAD
GREAT SOUTH-WEST ROAD
SOUTHERN PERIMETER ROAD
TW14
BEDFONT RECREATION GROUND
Bedfont FC
Clubhouse
HOUNSLOW URBAN FARM
HATTON CEM
Superstore
Asylum & Immigration Tribunal
MERCURY CENTRE
FALCON EST
GRIFFIN CENTRE
Civic Amenity Site
DONKEY WOOD
BALANCING RESERVOIR
DUKE OF NORTHUMBERLAND'S RIVER
HILLINGDON
HOUNSLOW
STAINES ROAD
A315
SPORTS GROUND
SPORTS GRD
FELTHAM ARENAS
GLEBELANDS PLAYING FIELDS
BEDFONT LANE REC GRD
FELTHAM PARK
HOUNSLOW ROAD
HARLINGTON ROAD WEST
HARLINGTON ROAD EAST
A244
A312
THE PARKWAY
FAGGS ROAD
Clockhouse Roundabout
Clockhouse Place
Royal Oak PH
NEW SQUARE
Cisco Systems
CEM
BEDFONT LAKES COUNTRY PARK
Information Centre
B3003
EAST BEDFONT
H.M. Young Offenders Institution & Remand Centre
SPELTHORNE
GROSVENOR PARK
FELTHAM
FELTHAM BUSINESS COMPLEX
ICG & DGC
Travelodge
St. Giles Hotel
LOWER FELTHAM
HIGH STREET
ASHFORD RD
Three Horseshoes PH
TW13
Hanworth Garden Centre
Staines R.F.C.
SNAKEY LANE
ASHFORD IND EST
TW15
LAKESIDE SPORTS GROUND
SURREY
FELTHAMHILL
Running Horse PH
KING GEORGE'S FIELD
B.P. Sunbury Business Park
Pumping Station
Filter Beds
TW16
CHERTSEY ROAD
CADBURY ROAD
A308
STAINES ROAD WEST
Clubhouse
The Shears
Junction 1
Sunbury Cross
Sunbury Cross Cen
SUNBURY
KEMPTON PARK (RACE DAYS ONLY)
Grandstand
ASHFORD COMMON WATER TREATMENT WORKS
TRADING ESTATE
DOLPHIN
M3
Leisure Cen
Fitness Centre
Adult Cen
Staines Reservoirs Aqueduct
PARK
RACECOURSE

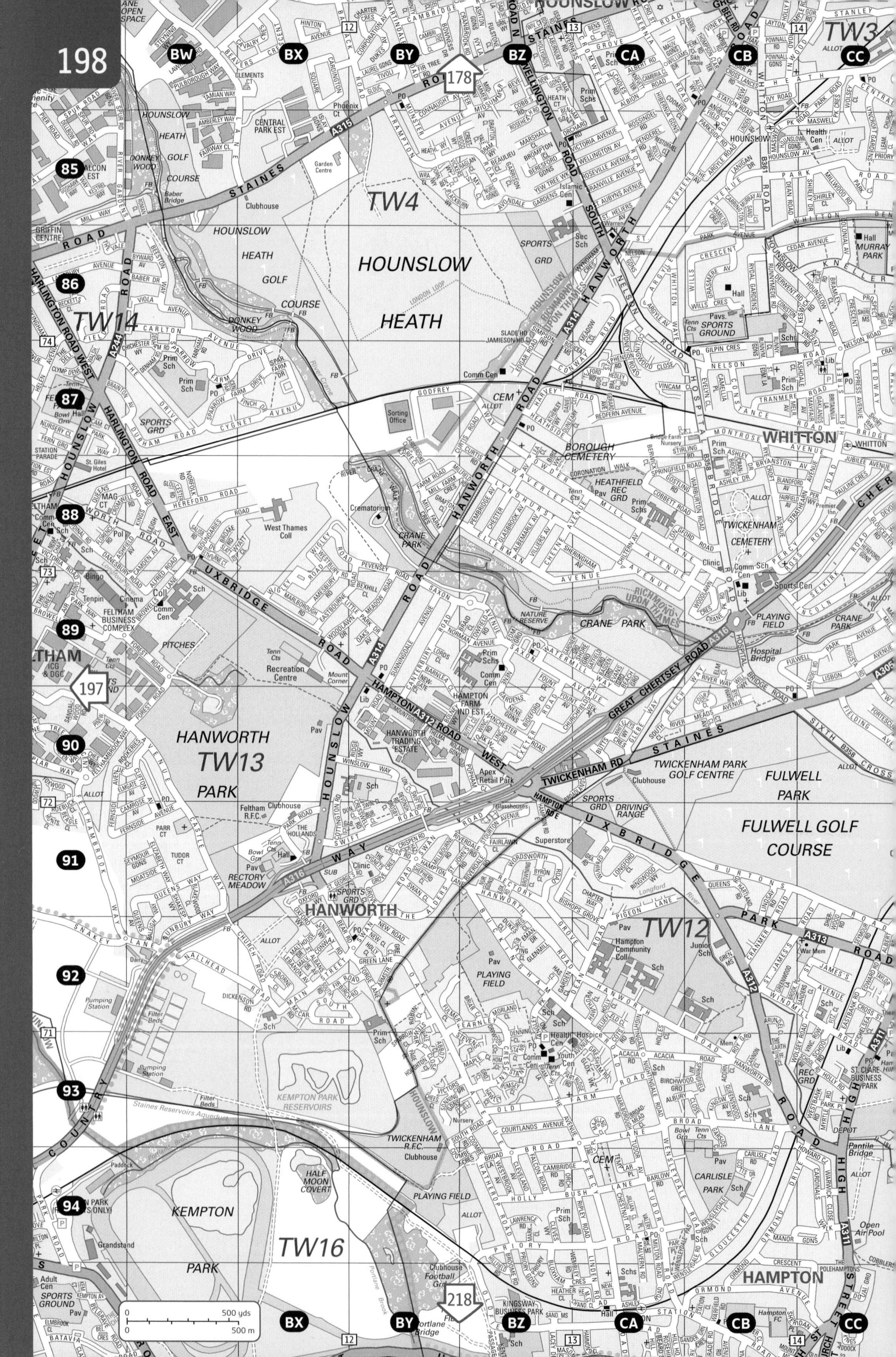
BW
BX
BY
BZ
CA
CB
CC
178
85
86
87
88
89
90
91
92
93
94
197
218
TW3
TW4
TW12
TW13
TW14
TW16
HOUNSLOW HEATH
HOUNSLOW HEATH GOLF COURSE
HANWORTH PARK
HANWORTH
WHITTON
HAMPTON
KEMPTON PARK
KEMPTON PARK RESERVOIRS
FULWELL PARK
FULWELL GOLF COURSE
TWICKENHAM PARK GOLF CENTRE
CRANE PARK
BOROUGH CEMETERY
TWICKENHAM CEMETERY
HEATHFIELD REC GRD
CENTRAL PARK EST
West Thames Coll
Crematorium
Recreation Centre
HAMPTON FARM IND EST
HANWORTH TRADING ESTATE
Apex Retail Park
Feltham R.F.C.
RECTORY MEADOW
HALF MOON COVERT
TWICKENHAM R.F.C.
CARLISLE PARK
KINGSWAY BUSINESS PARK
ST. CLARE BUSINESS PARK
FELTHAM BUSINESS COMPLEX
Hampton Community Coll
STAINES ROAD
UXBRIDGE ROAD
HANWORTH ROAD
GREAT CHERTSEY ROAD
HOUNSLOW ROAD
HARLINGTON ROAD EAST
HARLINGTON ROAD WEST
SWIFT WAY
HAMPTON ROAD WEST
TWICKENHAM RD
HIGH STREET
COUNTRY WAY
Staines Reservoirs Aqueduct
0
500 yds
0
500 m

ROEHAMPTON
SW15
PUTNEY
WANDSWORTH
EAST PUTNEY
PUTNEY HEATH
ROEHAMPTON GOLF COURSE
Roehampton University
Froebel College
Digby Stuart College
Southlands College
QUEEN MARY'S UNI HOSP
ROEHAMPTON PLAYING FIELDS
S. Thames Coll
Downshire Ho
ROYAL HOSPITAL
Tibbet's Corner
Roehampton Lane
Kingsfarm Plantation
RICHMOND PARK GOLF COURSE
PUTNEY VALE CEMETERY
Stag Lane
PUTNEY VALE
WINDMILL MUSEUM
PARKSIDE HOSPITAL
Parkside Oncology Clinic
LONDON SCOTTISH GOLF COURSE
WIMBLEDON
COMMON
BLUEGATE GRAVEL PIT (DISUSED)
ROYAL WIMBLEDON GOLF COURSE
CANNIZARO PARK
Cannizaro House Hotel
Fishponds Wood Nature Reserve
Caesar's Camp
Shadwell Wood
LADY JANE'S WOOD
WOLFSON NEUROREHAB CENTRE
COPSE HILL
SW20
OBERON PLAYING FIELD
SPORTS GROUND
COTTENHAM PARK
SW18
SOUTHFIELDS
WIMBLEDON PARK EST
WIMBLEDON PARK Stadium
WIMBLEDON PARK GOLF COURSE
WIMBLEDON PARK
ALL ENGLAND LAWN TENNIS & CROQUET CLUB
SW19
WIMBLEDON
DUNDONALD REC GRD
MERTON PARK
CT CU CV CW CX CY CZ
181
202
221
86 87 88 89 90 91 92 93 94

DA
DB
DC
DD
DE
DF
DG
182
WANDSWORTH
WEST HILL
WANDSWORTH HIGH ST
EAST HILL
ARMOURY WAY
WANDSWORTH COMMON
BATTERSEA RISE
CLAPHAM COMMON
CLAPHAM COMMON W SIDE
ST. JOHN'S HILL
SPENCER PARK
SW11
BOLINGBROKE HOSP
WANDSWORTH COMMON
TRINITY ROAD
H.M. PRISON WANDSWORTH
WANDSWORTH CEMETERY
EARLSFIELD
SOUTHFIELDS
SW18
MERTON ROAD
BUCKHOLD ROAD
GARRATT LANE
DURNSFORD ROAD
KING GEORGE'S PARK
BURNTWOOD LANE
NIGHTINGALE LANE
BALHAM
BALHAM HIGH ROAD
SW17
CENTRAL LONDON GOLF CENTRE
SPRINGFIELD HOSPITAL
STREATHAM CEMETERY
UPPER TOOTING
TOOTING BEC
Tooting Bec
GARRATT GREEN
SUMMERSTOWN
WIMBLEDON STADIUM
WIMBLEDON PARK
SW19
201
WIMBLEDON CEMETERY
PLOUGH LANE
HAYDONS ROAD
LAMBETH CEMETERY
ST. GEORGE'S HOSPITAL
Tooting Bdy
TOOTING BROADWAY
MITCHAM ROAD
TOOTING HIGH STREET
WANDLE MEADOW NAT. PK
TOOTING GRAVENEY
COLLIER'S WOOD
LONDON ROAD CEMETERY
FIGGE'S MARSH
SOUTH WIMBLEDON
MERTON HIGH STREET
THE BROADWAY
WIMBLEDON
MERANTUN WAY
222
MERTON INDUSTRIAL PARK
ABBEY REC GRD
85
86
87
88
89
90
91
92
93
94
0 500 yds
0 500 m

DH
DJ
DK
DL
DM
DN
DP
183
CLAPHAM COMMON
SW4
BRIXTON
CLAPHAM PARK
SW2
SE24
BROCKWELL PARK
H.M. PRISON BRIXTON
STREATHAM HILL
SE21
TULSE HILL
86
87
88
89
90
91
92
93
94
74
73
72
71
204
TOOTING BEC COMMON
WEST NORWOOD CEMETERY
WEST NORWOOD
SE27
STREATHAM PARK
STREATHAM
TOOTING GRAVENEY COMMON
TOOTING BEC ATHLETICS TRACK
SW16
STREATHAM COMMON
THE ROOKERY
NORWOOD GROVE RECREATION GROUND
PLAYING FIELD
SE19
BIGGIN WOOD
STREATHAM VALE
NORBURY PARK
NORBURY
223
29
30
31
POYNDERS ROAD
CHRISTCHURCH ROAD
BRIXTON HILL
STREATHAM HIGH ROAD
TULSE HILL
NORWOOD ROAD
KNIGHTS HILL
BEC ROAD
MITCHAM LANE
STREATHAM COMMON NORTH
CROWN LANE
BEULAH HILL
CLAPHAM COMMON SOUTH SIDE
CAVENDISH ROAD
ACRE LANE
DULWICH ROAD
THURLOW PARK ROAD
CROXTED ROAD

DQ
DR
DS
DT
DU
DV
DW
184
SE24
SE22
SE21
SE27
SE26
SE19
SE20
85
86
87
88
89
90
91
92
93
94
203
224
33
34
35
74
73
72
71
HERNE HILL
EAST DULWICH
BROCKWELL PARK
DULWICH
PECKHAM RYE COMMON
PECKHAM RYE PARK
CAMBERWELL OLD CEMETERY
TULSE HILL
DULWICH PARK
DULWICH & SYDENHAM HILL GOLF COURSE
SYDENHAM HILL WOOD (NATURE RESERVE)
DULWICH WOOD
HORNIMAN GDNS
WEST DULWICH
WEST NORWOOD CEMETERY
WEST NORWOOD
UPPER SYDENHAM
SYDENHAM WELLS PARK
NORWOOD PARK
NORWOOD
CRYSTAL PALACE PARK
CRYSTAL PALACE NATIONAL SPORTS CENTRE
NORWOOD NEWTOWN
UPPER NORWOOD
SYDENHAM
PENGE
ANERLEY
HERNE HILL VELODROME
SOUTH BANK UNIVERSITY SPORTS GROUND
DULWICH COMMUNITY HOSP
DULWICH PICTURE GALL
HALF MOON LANE
VILLAGE WAY
CROXTED ROAD
THURLOW PARK ROAD
DULWICH COMMON
LORDSHIP LANE
LONDON ROAD
DARTMOUTH ROAD
KIRKDALE
WESTWOOD HILL
CRYSTAL PALACE PARK ROAD
CRYSTAL PALACE PARADE
COLLEGE ROAD
GIPSY HILL
ANERLEY HILL
ANERLEY ROAD
CHURCH ROAD
BEULAH HILL
KNIGHTS HILL
NORWOOD ROAD
CROWN DALE
CENTRAL HILL
WESTOW HILL
DULWICH WOOD PK
SYDENHAM HILL
Tulse Hill
Forest Hill
The Grove
0
500 yds
500 m

DX
DY
DZ
EA
EB
EC
ED
185
BROCKLEY
SE4
LADYWELL
LADYWELL CEMETERY
BROCKLEY CEMETERY
HILLY FIELDS
UNIVERSITY HOSPITAL LEWISHAM
LEWISHAM PARK
SE13
HITHER GREEN
MANOR PARK
CAMBERWELL NEW CEMETERY
HONOR OAK PARK
HONOR OAK SPORTS GRD
BLYTHE HILL FIELDS
BROCKLEY HILL PARK
SE23
MOUNTFIELD PARK PLAYING FIELDS
Catford Gyratory
CATFORD
BROWNHILL ROAD
S CIRCULAR
STANSTEAD ROAD
FOREST HILL
SOUTH CIRCULAR ROAD
CATFORD HILL
SE6
BROMLEY ROAD
PERRY HILL
BELL GREEN
BELLINGHAM
FORSTER MEMORIAL PARK
MAYOW PARK
LOWER SYDENHAM
SOUTHEND
SOUTHEND LANE
BROMLEY HILL
HOME PARK
BECKENHAM PLACE PARK
GOLF COURSE
NEW BECKENHAM
KENT C.C.C.
CRYSTAL PALACE FC TRAINING GROUND
ROYAL BANK OF SCOTLAND SPORTS GOUND
SUMMERHOUSE HILL WOOD
BR3
BR2
CATOR PARK
BECKENHAM
SHORTLANDS GOLF COURSE
BROMLEY PARK
THE SLOANE HOSPITAL
206
225
86
87
88
89
90
91
92
93
94

EE
EF
EG
EH
EJ
EK
EL
186
205
226
85
86
87
88
89
90
91
92
93
94
LEE
HITHER GREEN
SE13
SE12
SE6
MANOR PARK
MANOR HOUSE GARDENS
Lee Green
ELTHAM ROAD
A20 ROAD
SIDCUP ROAD
ELTHAM A210 ROAD
WESTHORNE AV
WESTHORNE AVENUE
Yorkshire Grey
Clifton's Roundabout
KIDBROOKE PARK
SUTCLIFFE PARK
UNI OF GREENWICH ATHLETIC GRD
ROCHESTER WAY
MIDDLE PARK FIELD
QUEENSCROFT REC GRD
ELTHAM
ELTHAM PALACE
KING JOHN PLAYING FIELDS
CIVIL SERVICE SPORTS GROUNDS
OLD COLFEIANS SPORTS GROUND
LEWISHAM
GREENWICH
Colfe's Sch
CHILTONIAN IND ESTATE
S CIRCULAR ROAD
ST. MILDREDS ROAD
BURNT ASH HILL
BARING ROAD
NORTHBROOK PARK
GROVE PARK
HITHER GREEN CEMETERY
Crematorium
MOTTINGHAM
MOTTINGHAM LANE
UNI OF WESTMINSTER SPORTS GROUND
MOTTINGHAM SPORTS GROUND
CHINBROOK ESTATE
CHINBROOK MEADOWS
LOWER MARVELS WOOD
MARVELS WOOD
GROVE PARK CEMETERY
ELMSTEAD WOOD
ELMSTEAD
SUNDRIDGE PARK GOLF COURSE
SUNDRIDGE
Sundridge Park
ROCKPIT WOOD
ELMSTEAD WOODS
BR1
BR2
FORSTER MEM PARK
WHITEFOOT LANE
DOWNHAM
DOWNHAM FIELDS
DOWNHAM PLAYING FIELDS
SHAFTESBURY PARK REC GRD
PLAISTOW
KING'S MEADOW PLAYING FIELDS
BURNT ASH LANE
BROMLEY ROAD
BROMLEY HILL
LONDON ROAD
A21
LEWISHAM BOROUGH SPORTS GROUND
MIDLAND BANK SPORTS GROUND
WARREN AVE PLAYING FIELDS
SHORTLANDS GOLF
THE SLOANE HOSPITAL
BROMLEY PARK
BROMLEY NORTH
SUNDRIDGE PARK
Widmore Green
COLLEGE RD
TWEEDY RD
500 yds
500 m

DA16
EM
EN
EP
EQ
ER
ES
ET
187
ROCHESTER WAY RELIEF ROAD
ELTHAM PARK SOUTH
ELTHAM WARREN GOLF COURSE
Crematorium
EAST ROCHESTER
SPORTS GROUND
Greenwich Environment Curriculum Service
BEXLEY ROAD
A210
BLACKFEN ROAD
ELTHAM HIGH ST
AVERY HILL
AVERY HILL PARK
University of Greenwich Avery Hill Campus
CAMBRIDGE MISSION SPORTS GROUND
CHARLTON ATHLETIC FC TRAINING GRD
FOOTSCRAY PLAYING FIELDS
MILLWALL FC TRAINING GRD
ROYAL BLACKHEATH GOLF COURSE
TARN BIRD SANCTUARY
SE9
FOOTSCRAY ROAD
A211
BLACKFEN
DA15
HOLLY OAK WOOD PK
86
87
88
89
90
91
92
93
94
LAMORBEY
NEW ELTHAM
FAIRY HILL REC GRD
OLD FARM PARK
KING GEORGE'S REC GRD
208
SIDCUP ROAD
A20
LONGLANDS
JACK NICKLAUS GOLF CENTRE
FLAMINGO PK SPORTS GRD
LONGLANDS REC GRD
MAIN ROAD
SIDCUP
DA14
SIDCUP BYPASS
STATION ROAD
A222
BELMONT LANE OPEN SPACE
Kemnal Manor Stables
Beaver's Wood
CHISLEHURST CEMETERY
Hoblands Wood
OLD ELTHAMIANS SPORTS GRD
UNIVERSITY COLLEGE LONDON SPORTS GRD
BR7
CHISLEHURST WEST
WHYTES WOODLAND
Bird Sanctuary
Ravensbourne Coll
WHITE HORSE HILL
A208
HIGH STREET
CHISLEHURST
CAMDEN PARK
CHISLEHURST GOLF COURSE
CHISLEHURST COMMON
PERRY STREET
SCADBURY PARK
NATURE RESERVE
PARK WOOD
Scadbury Moated Manor House Site
QUEEN MARY'S HOSP
Frognal Corner
BROMLEY LANE
227
43
44
45
The Larches

EU
EV
EW
EX
EY
EZ
FA
188
DA16
DANSON
PARK
THE LAKE
The Boathouse
Danson Mansion
Bexley Grammar Sch
DA6
BEXLEYHEATH
BROADWAY
Broadway Shop Centre
BEXLEYHEATH GOLF COURSE
BEXLEY
ROCHESTER WAY
BLACKFEN ROAD
Danson Interchange
EAST ROCHESTER WAY
BLENDON ROAD
BRIDGEN ROAD
PARKHILL ROAD
BEXLEY PARK WOOD
BLACKFEN
HOLLY OAK WOOD PK
PENHILL PARK
PENHILL ROAD
RIVERSIDE WALK
SIDCUP GOLF COURSE
DA15
LAMORBEY PARK
Rose Bruford College
MORBEY
HURST ROAD
ABBEYHILL PARK
RUTLAND CEM SHAW
ALBANY PARK
DA5
Bexley Cricket Club
SIDCUP
KING GEORGE'S REC GRD
207
Sidcup Arts Cen
WARING PARK
GOLDSMITH COLLEGE SPORTS GRD
THE ALDERS
NORTH CRAY
NORTH CRAY WOOD
STABLE MEADOW
DA14
FOOTS CRAY MEADOWS
Foots Cray Place
GATTONS WOOD
GATTONS PLANTATION
SIDCUP HIGH STREET
STATION ROAD
ELM ROAD
THE GREEN
SIDCUP PLACE
SIDCUP TECHNOLOGY CENTRE
QUEEN MARY'S HOSP
Frognal Corner
FOOTS CRAY
FOOTS CRAY HIGH ST
MAIDSTONE RD
NORTH CRAY ROAD
Ruxley Corner
RUXLEY CORNER INDUSTRIAL ESTATE
RUXLEY WOOD
Ruxley Manor Garden Centre
SCADBURY PARK NATURE RESERVE
LITTLE WOOD
Irish Plantation
Scadbury Moated Manor House Site
Crittall's Corner
EDGINGTON WAY
SEVENOAKS
SIDCUP BYPASS
A20
BR5
228
RUXLEY PARK GOLF COURSE
CRAY VALLEY
CRAYFIELDS BUSINESS PARK
85
86
87
88
89
90
91
92
93
94
0 500 yds
0 500 m

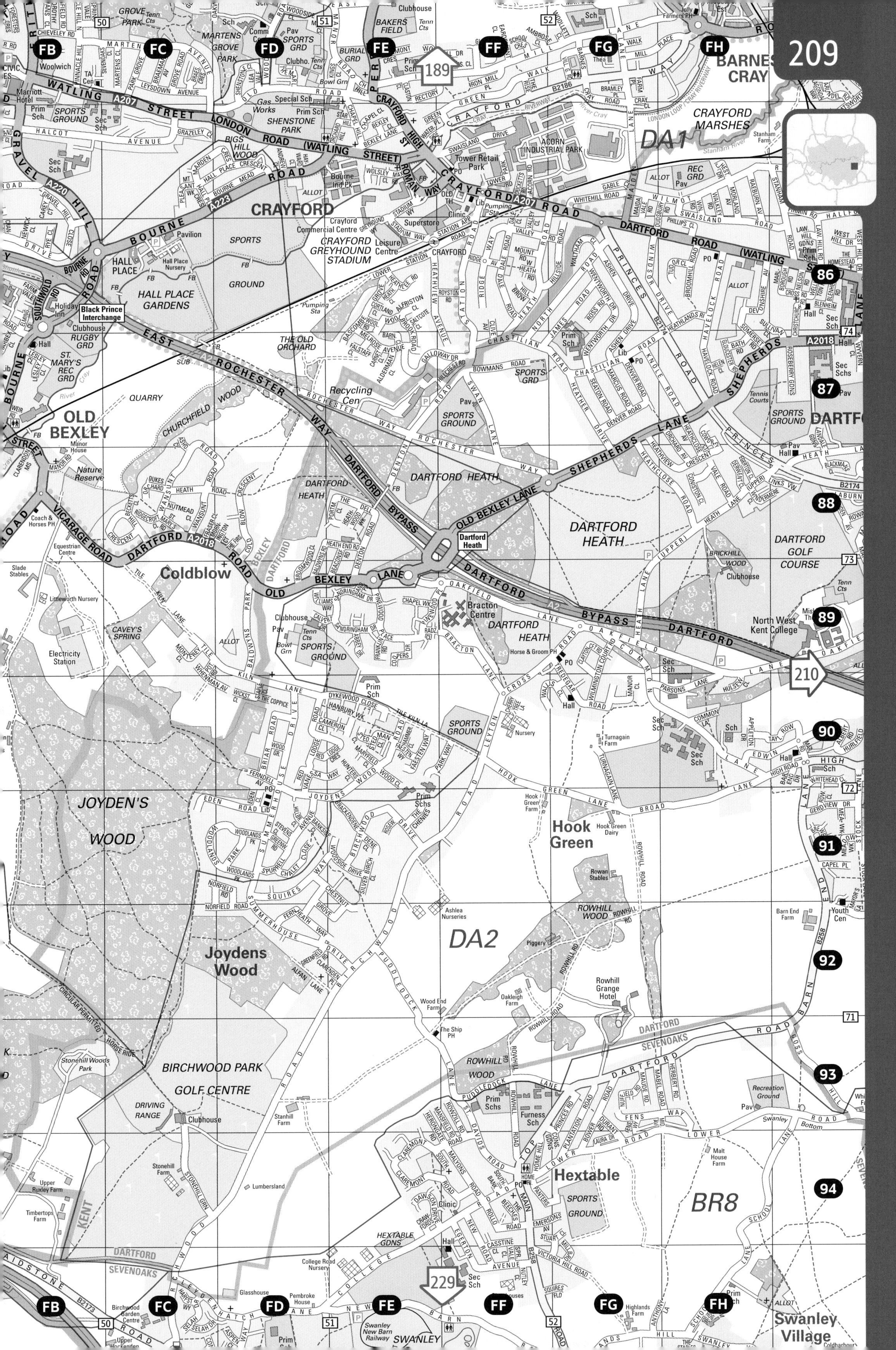

FB
FC
FD
FE
FF
FG
FH
189
BARNES CRAY
CRAYFORD MARSHES
DA1
GROVE PARK
MARTENS GROVE PARK
BAKERS FIELD
BURIAL GRD
SPORTS GRD
Woolwich
Marriott Hotel
SPORTS GROUND
WATLING STREET
A207
LONDON ROAD (WATLING STREET)
SHENSTONE PARK
Special Sch
CRAYFORD HIGH ST
RIVERWAY
ACORN INDUSTRIAL PARK
Tower Retail Park
BIGS HILL WOOD
GRAVEL HILL
A220
A223
BOURNE ROAD
CRAYFORD
Crayford Commercial Centre
CRAYFORD GREYHOUND STADIUM
Leisure Centre
Superstore
CRAYFORD ROAD
DARTFORD ROAD (WATLING STREET)
HALL PLACE
HALL PLACE GARDENS
SPORTS GROUND
Pavilion
Black Prince Interchange
Holiday Inn
RUGBY GRD
ST. MARY'S REC GRD
EAST ROCHESTER WAY
A2
THE OLD ORCHARD
Recycling Cen
QUARRY
CHURCHFIELD WOOD
OLD BEXLEY
Nature Reserve
Manor House
DARTFORD HEATH
DARTFORD BYPASS
ROCHESTER WAY
SHEPHERDS LANE
OLD BEXLEY LANE
Dartford Heath
DARTFORD HEATH
DARTFORD GOLF COURSE
86
87
88
89
90
91
92
93
94
DARTFORD
SPORTS GROUND
Tennis Courts
North West Kent College
210
VICARAGE ROAD
DARTFORD ROAD
A2018
Coldblow
OLD BEXLEY LANE
Equestrian Centre
Slade Stables
Littleworth Nursery
CAVEY'S SPRING
Electricity Station
Bracton Centre
DARTFORD HEATH
Horse & Groom PH
SPORTS GROUND
JOYDEN'S WOOD
Hook Green
Hook Green Farm
Hook Green Dairy
Turnagain Farm
Rowan Stables
ROWHILL WOOD
Ashlea Nurseries
DA2
Piggery
Joydens Wood
Rowhill Grange Hotel
Oakleigh Farm
Wood End Farm
The Ship PH
ROWHILL WOOD
BIRCHWOOD PARK GOLF CENTRE
DRIVING RANGE
Clubhouse
Stonehill Woods Park
Stanhill Farm
Stonehill Farm
Lumbersland
Upper Ruxley Farm
Timbertops Farm
KENT
DARTFORD
SEVENOAKS
DARTFORD ROAD
Furness Sch
Hextable
SPORTS GROUND
BR8
Recreation Ground
Swanley Bottom
Malt House Farm
HEXTABLE GDNS
College Road Nursery
Glasshouse
Pembroke House
Birchwood Garden Centre
229
Highlands Farm
Swanley New Barn Railway
SWANLEY
Swanley Village
Barn End Farm
Youth Cen
B258
B2173
50
51
52
71
72
73
74

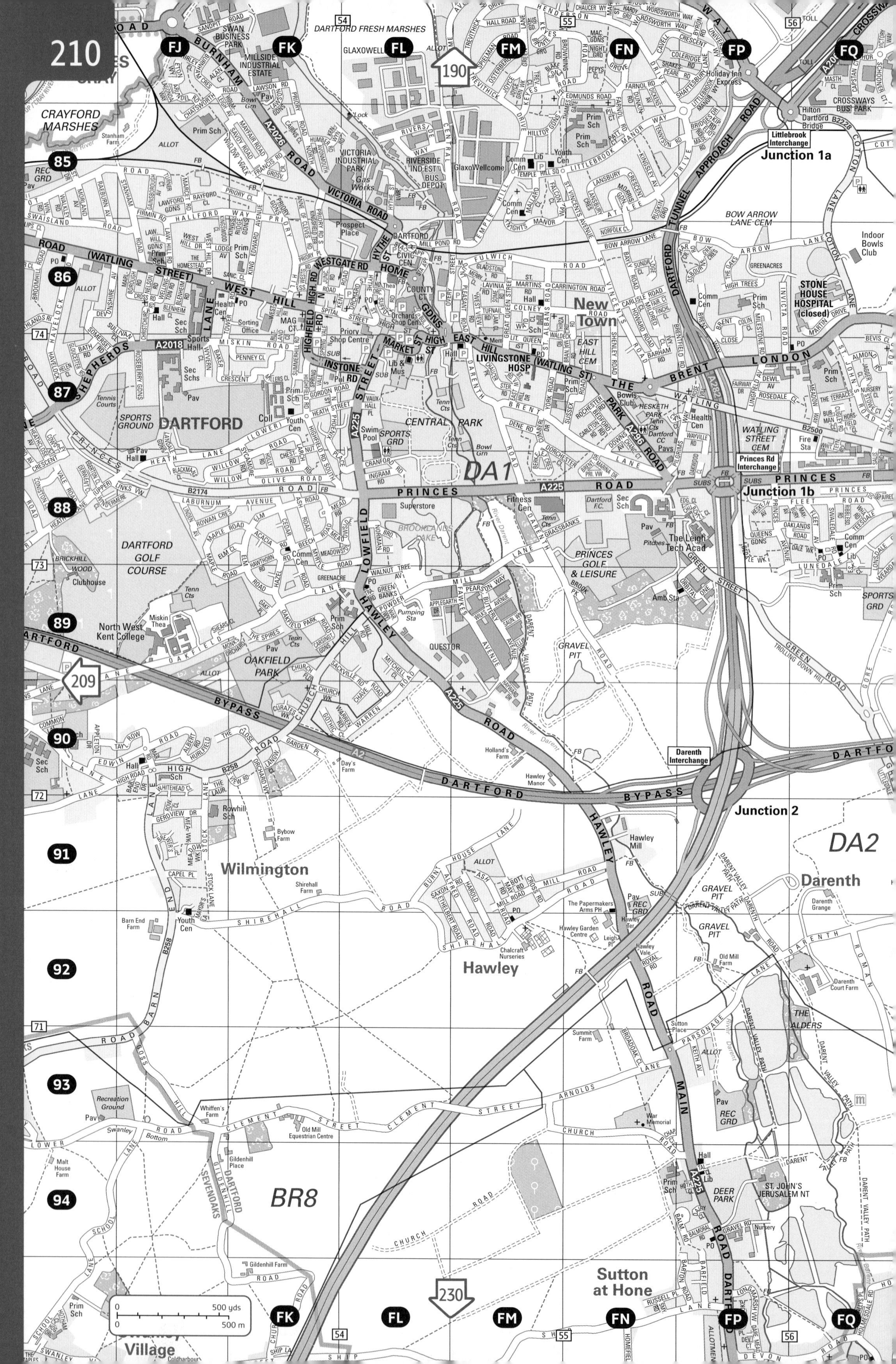

Crossways
Thames Europort
Johnson's Wharf
Jetty
Superstore
Quadrant Court
Newtons Court
Crossways Boulevard
St. Mary's Road
Charles Street
Travelodge
Stone Crossing
Elizabeth Street
Stone
Greenhithe
Knockhall
London Road
A226
Swanscombe Heritage Park
Nat Res
Leisure Centre
DA9
DA10
DA13
DA4
Stone Rec Grd
Stone Cem
Bluewater Parkway
Bluewater Shopping Centre
The Village
Cinema
Water Circus
Darent Valley Hospital
Watling Street
A296
Bean Interchange
A2
Dartford Bypass
Darenth Wood
The Thrift
Chalk Pit
Caravan Site
Bean
Badger's Mount
Ladies Wood
Lords Wood
Beacon Wood Country Park
Waller Park
Lane End
Green Street Green
Betsham
South Darenth
St. Margaret's Farm
Manor Farm Garden Centre
Shellbank
Sandbanks
Highcross
Westwood Farm
Wheatsheaf PH
Walnut Tree Farm
Chalkcroft
Ryecroft Farm
Ryecroft Wood
Gill's Farm
Quarry
FR FS FT FU FV FW FX
86 87 88 89 90 91 92 93 94
57 58 59
191
212
231

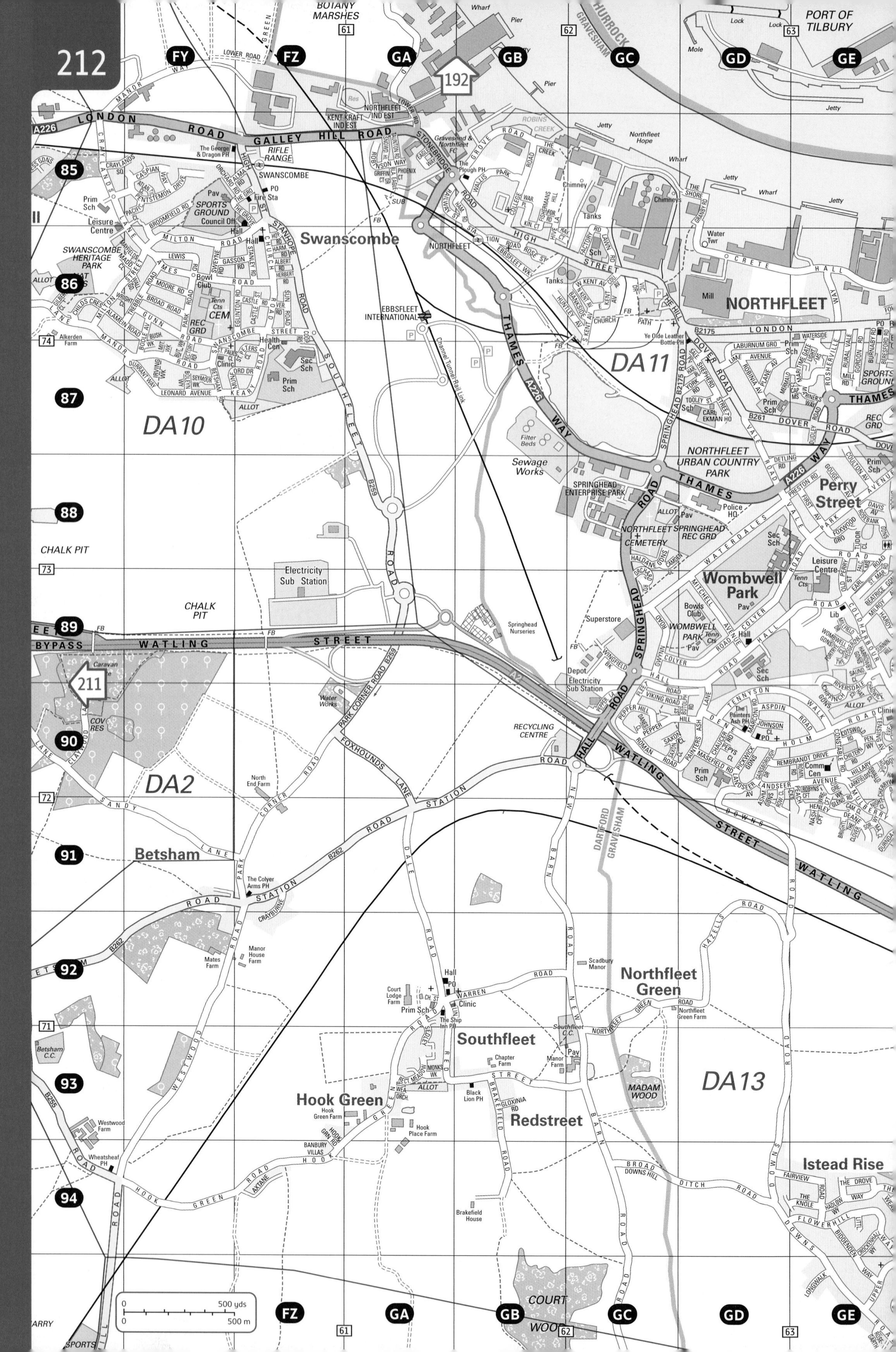
BOTANY MARSHES
PORT OF TILBURY
Swanscombe
NORTHFLEET
DA11
DA10
DA2
DA13
EBBSFLEET INTERNATIONAL
Perry Street
Wombwell Park
NORTHFLEET URBAN COUNTRY PARK
Betsham
Northfleet Green
Southfleet
Hook Green
Redstreet
Istead Rise
WATLING STREET
THAMES WAY
LONDON ROAD
GALLEY HILL ROAD
SPRINGHEAD ROAD
STATION ROAD
SOUTHFLEET ROAD
Sewage Works
Electricity Sub Station
CHALK PIT
MADAM WOOD
COURT WOOD
192
211

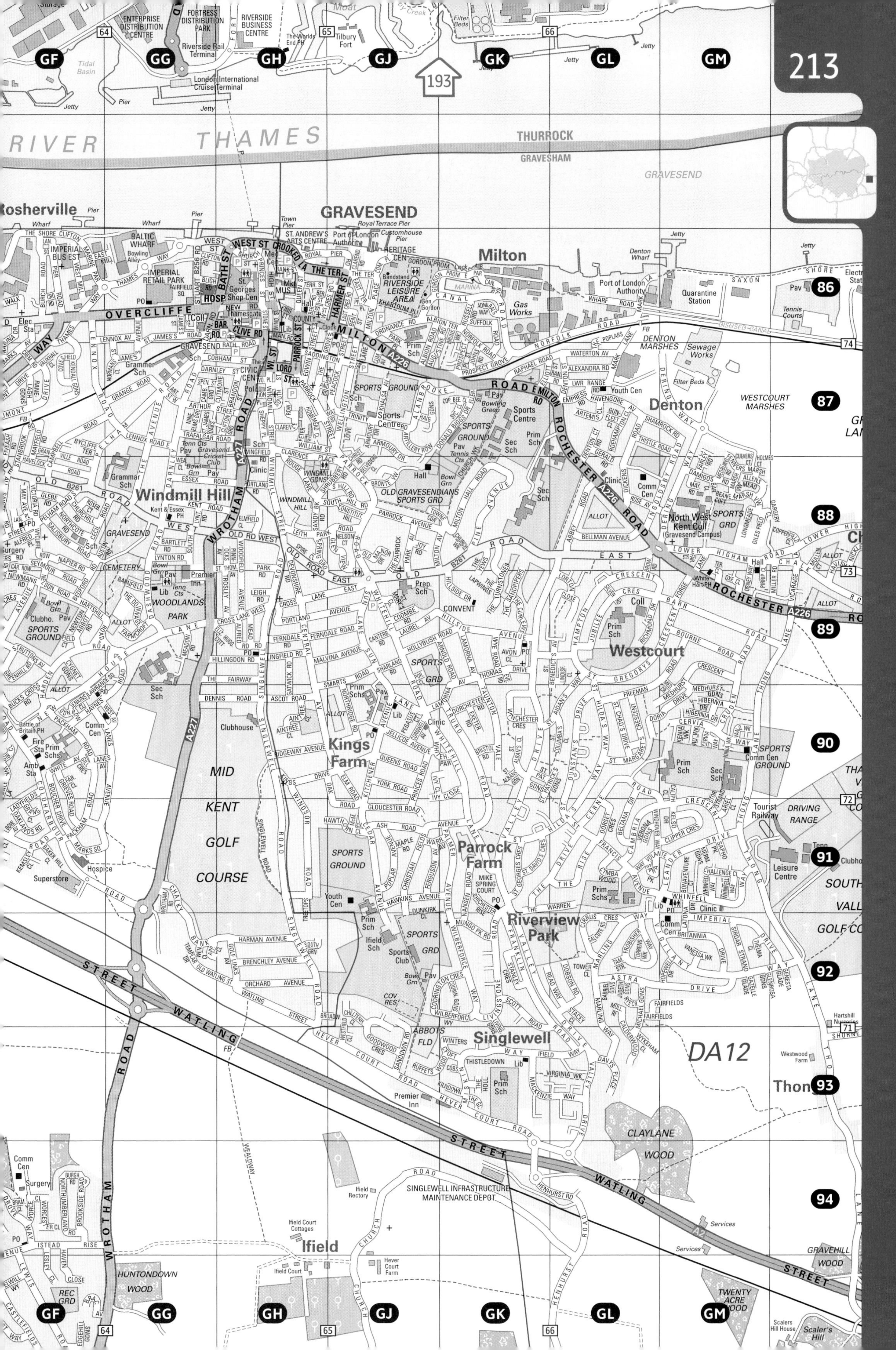

RIVER THAMES
THURROCK
GRAVESHAM
GRAVESEND
Rosherville
Milton
Denton
Windmill Hill
Westcourt
Kings Farm
Parrock Farm
Riverview Park
Singlewell
Ifield
Thong
DA12
MID KENT GOLF COURSE
CLAYLANE WOOD
HUNTONDOWN WOOD
TWENTY ACRE WOOD
GRAVEHILL WOOD
WESTCOURT MARSHES
DENTON MARSHES
ENTERPRISE DISTRIBUTION CENTRE
FORTRESS DISTRIBUTION PARK
RIVERSIDE BUSINESS CENTRE
Tilbury Fort
London International Cruise Terminal
Riverside Rail Terminal
Royal Terrace Pier
IMPERIAL RETAIL PARK
RIVERSIDE LEISURE AREA
OLD GRAVESENDIANS SPORTS GRD
WOODLANDS PARK
SINGLEWELL INFRASTRUCTURE MAINTENANCE DEPOT
North West Kent Coll (Gravesend Campus)
OVERCLIFFE
MILTON ROAD
ROCHESTER ROAD
WROTHAM ROAD
WATLING STREET
A226
A227
A2
B261
GF
GG
GH
GJ
GK
GL
GM
64
65
66
193
74
73
72
71
86
87
88
89
90
91
92
93
94

Egham Wick
Royal Holloway College
The American Comm Sch
VIRGINIA WATER
Virginia Water
WENTWORTH
Wentworth
GOLF COURSE
GU25
GU24
SL5
Longcross
LONGCROSS
CHERTSEY COMMON
BARROW HILLS GOLF COURSE
THE VALLEY GARDENS
VIRGINIA WATER PLANTATION
BELVEDERE WOOD
KING GEORGE V PLAYING FIELD
Clubhouse
CHRISTCHURCH ROAD
LONDON ROAD
BLACKNEST ROAD
CHOBHAM LANE
WELLINGTON AVENUE
500 yds
500 m

AZ
BA
BB
BC
BD
BE
BF
01
02
03
195
216
233
TW20
TW18
KT16
KT15
Stroude
Thorpe
Thorpe Green
THORPE GREEN
Lyne
CHERTSEY
Great Fosters Hotel
Luddington House
Oaktree Nursery
Nursery
Mayflower Nurseries
Crabtree Corner
THORPE INDUSTRIAL EST
EGHAM BUSINESS VILLAGE
TASIS England
Manor Farm
Spring Farm
Woodcock Farm
SPORTS GROUND
THE MOAT
LONGSIDE LAKE
MANOR LAKE
THORPE PARK
Mountbatten Pavilion
Abbey Lake
ST. ANN'S LAKE
WATER GARDENS
Britannia Arena
CEMEX UK
TRUSS'S ISLAND
PENTON HOOK ISLAND
PENTON HOOK MARINA
PENTON PARK (Caravan Park)
Staines Town FC
Yacht Basin
Weir
Hurst Stud Farm
Tennis Courts
Home Farm
Rose & Crown PH
ANCHOR COPSE
Junction 2 (M3), Junction 12 (M25)
St. Anne's Chapel (remains of)
ST. ANN'S HILL PARK
Sludge Lagoons
Lyne Sewage Works
Filter Beds
Recycling Centre
Redlands Farm
Lyne Hill Farm
Ruxbury Farm
Twynersh House PH
Chertsey Cricket Club
Chertsey Town FC
ABBEYFIELDS REC GRD
GOGMORE FM PK
Grange Gardens Nursery
Lynefield Farm
Hillside Farm
Chilsey Green Farm
ELM FARM CARAVAN PARK
Almner Priory
Nursery
The Brooks Riding Centre
THE ROUGH
Merrywood Farm
Lyne Court
Lyne Place Manor
Piggery
LYNE COPSE
RECREATION GROUND
Pantiles Nurseries
HERSHAM COPSE
FAN GROVE
Great Cockcrow Railway
Cockcrow Hill
FANGROVE PARK
Lynwood Farm
Lyne Acres Farm
Trys Hill Farm
Fan Court
Westbrook Farm
Squires Nursery
Hardwick Court Farm
Pannells Farm
Fox Hills Farm
White Lodge Centre
RUNNYMEDE HOSP
ST. PETER'S HOSP
Silverlands Farm
FOXHILLS GOLF COURSE
Clubhouse
Foxhills Country Club
Foxhills
HOME WOOD
HOMEWOOD PARK
Botleys Mansion
Hillswood Business Park
Church Farm
Kitchenride
ALLOTMENTS
SPORTS GROUND
REC GRD
SANDGATES
Sec Sch
Woodside Farm
Junction 11
ADDLESTONE CEMETERY
Health Club
Shop Cen
Comm Hall
M25
M3
A320
A317
B386
B388
B389
B375
THORPE BYPASS
MILL HOUSE LANE
GUILDFORD ROAD
STAINES ROAD
CHERTSEY LANE
LYNE LANE
LYNE CROSSING
HOLLOWAY HILL
STONEHILL ROAD
ST. PETER'S WAY
ALMNERS ROAD
HARDWICK LANE
WATERY LANE
RUXBURY ROAD
ST. ANNS HILL ROAD
PYRCROFT ROAD
CHILSEY GREEN RD
BARKER ROAD
EASTWORTH ROAD
HANWORTH LANE
TRYS HILL
COLDHARBOUR LANE
ROSEMARY LANE
NORLANDS LANE
MONKS WALK
OLD COACH ROAD
96
97
98
99
100
101
102
103
104
66
67
68
69

196
215
234
BG
BH
BJ
BK
BL
BM
BN
05
06
07
69
68
67
66
95
96
97
98
99
100
101
102
103
104
TW18
KT16
KT15
QUEEN
MARY
RESERVOIR
LALEHAM
CHERTSEY
ADDLESTONE MOOR
GRAVEL
Clubhouse
Sweep's Bridge
Staines Town FC
SPORTS GROUND
Penton Hook Farm
Garden Centre
Penton Hook Lock
ARCADIA CARAVANS
Glasshouse
Pumping Sta
Intake Channel
Gas Pipeline Sta
ROUND COPSE
PENTON HOOK ISLAND
PENTON HOOK
PENTON HOOK MARINA
Yacht Basin
Manor Farm
Prim Sch
Hall
Youth Club
Three Horseshoes PH
SPORTS GRD
Pav
War Mem
Nursery
PENTON PARK (Caravan Park)
Mountbatten Pavilion
Abbey Lake
STAINES ROAD
Clubhouse
LALEHAM GOLF COURSE
LALEHAM BURWAY
RESERVOIR
Filter Beds
Water Works
Rowing Club
LALEHAM PARK
Laleham Abbey
LALEHAM PARK SPORTS GROUND
Camp Site
Laleham Nurseries
Shepperton Studios
THE GREEN
Squires Bridge
REC GRD
Staines Rd Farm
Prim Sch
Sailing Club
M3
Earthworks
ABBEYFIELDS REC GRD
Abbey Bridge
Abbey Chase House
Chertsey Cricket Club
Chertsey Town FC
Old TH
Shop Cen
GOGMORE FM PK
Comm Hall
Health Club
SPORTS GRD
Weir
Chertsey Lock
ABBEYFIELDS MOBILE HOME PARK
CHERTSEY BRIDGE ROAD
Dumsey Eyot
RYEPECK MEADOW MOORINGS
Riversleigh Farm
RECREATION GROUND
Prim Sch
SPORTS GROUND
Health Cen
FORDWATER TRADING EST
Fordwater Bridge
Marina
DOCKETT EDDY
Dockett Point
CHERTSEY MEADS
PHARAOH'S ISLAND
Shepperton Lock
LOCK ISLAND
HAMHAUGH ISLAND
Hamhaugh Point
Hamm Court Farm
Coll
Fire Sta
Woburn Park Farm
Hatch Farm
WOBURN PARK
Tennis Cen
St. George's College
The Plantation Nursery
ADDLESTONE CEMETERY
ABBEY MOOR GOLF COURSE
Pannells Farm
Woodside Farm
Junction 11
The George
Bowl Grn
VICTORY PARK
Superstore
Health Cen
Crouch Oak PH
SPORTS GRD
MEADOWLANDS PARK
Thales
BOURNE BUS PK
RHM Culinary Brands
WEYBRIDGE BUSINESS PARK
Black Boy Bridge
Weybridge Lock
The Bull Dogs
HOSP
A317
A320
B375
B376
B377
0 500 yds
0 500 m

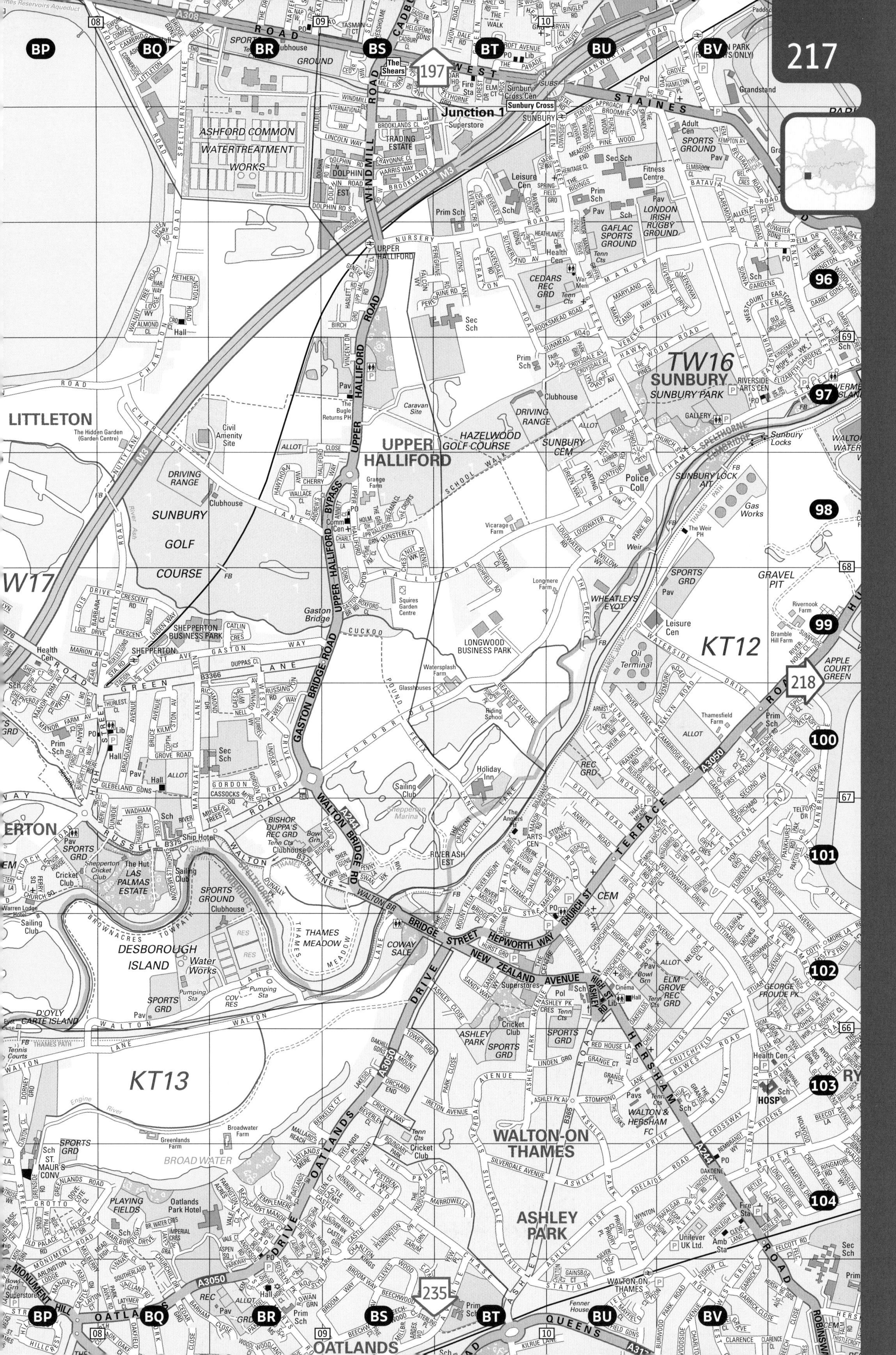

ASHFORD COMMON WATER TREATMENT WORKS
Junction 1
SUNBURY
TW16
UPPER HALLIFORD
HAZELWOOD GOLF COURSE
SUNBURY GOLF COURSE
LITTLETON
TW17
KT12
KT13
WALTON-ON-THAMES
ASHLEY PARK
DESBOROUGH ISLAND
OATLANDS
SHEPPERTON BUSINESS PARK
LONGWOOD BUSINESS PARK
GRAVEL PIT
SUNBURY LOCK AIT
WHEATLEYS EYOT
BROAD WATER

KEMPTON PARK
RACECOURSE
TW16
HAMPTON
TW12
SUNBURY
KT12
KT8
WEST MOLESEY
QUEEN ELIZABETH II RESERVOIR
ISLAND BARN RESERVOIR
KNIGHTS RESERVOIR
BESSBOROUGH RESERVOIR
STAIN HILL RESERVOIRS
KT10
RYDENS
Lower Green
SANDOWN PARK RACECOURSE
HERSHAM VILLAGE GOLF COURSE
HURST PARK
198
217
236
BW
BX
BY
BZ
CA
CB
CC
95
96
97
98
99
100
101
102
103
104

CL
CM
CN
CP
CQ
CR
CS
200
COOMBE
COOMBE WOOD GOLF COURSE
KT2
KINGSTON HOSPITAL
NORBITON
KINGSTON UPON THAMES
KINGSTON CEMETERY
KT1
NEW MALDEN
BERRYLANDS
KT3
SURBITON CEMETERY
HOGSMILL PUBLIC OPEN SPACE
KT5
SURBITON
SURBITON HOSP
KT6
ALEXANDRA REC GRD
HOGSMILL OPEN SPACE
OLD MALDEN
MALDEN MANOR
TOLWORTH
TOLWORTH HOSPITAL
Tolworth Junction
Hook Junction
KING GEORGES FIELD
KT9
238
219
KINGSTON UNIVERSITY SPORTS GRD
MAORI SPORTS GROUND
RIVERHILL SPORTS GRD
WANDGAS ATHLETIC GROUND
KING EDWARD REC GRD
RED LION BUSINESS PARK
KINGSTON BYPASS
KINGSTON ROAD
EWELL ROAD
MALDEN WAY
COOMBE LANE WEST
KINGSTON HILL
CAMBRIDGE ROAD
LONDON ROAD
SURBITON HILL ROAD
BRIGHTON ROAD
HOOK ROAD
PENRHYN ROAD
HIGH STREET
RICHMOND ROAD
95
96
97
98
99
100
101
102
103
104
500 yds
500 m

CT
CU
CV
CW
CX
CY
CZ
201
WOLFSON NEUROREHAB CENTRE
COPSE HILL
OBERON PLAYING FIELD
COTTENHAM PARK
COTTENHAM PK REC GRD
DUNDONALD REC GRD
NELSON HOSP
JOHN INNES REC GRD
WIMBLEDON CHASE
RAYNES PARK
SW20
PRINCE GEORGE'S PLAYING FIELD
MESSINES PLAYING FLD
JOSEPH HOOD RECREATION GROUND
BUSHEY MEAD
CANNON HILL COMMON
RAYNES PARK PLAYING FIELDS
SW19
MERTON PARK
SOUTH MERTON
MOSTYN GARDENS
MORDEN
WEST BARNES
MOTSPUR PARK
FULHAM F.C. TRAINING GROUND
THE SIR JOSEPH HOOD MEMORIAL PLAYING FIELDS
MOTSPUR PARK
SPORTS GROUND
OLD BLUES R.F.C.
MORDEN CEMETERY
MERTON & SUTTON JOINT CEMETERY
MORDEN PARK
MORDEN SPORTS GROUND
SM4
KING GEORGE'S FIELD
The Woodstock
GARTH ROAD IND CEN
MANOR PARK REC GRD
ST. ANTHONY'S HOSP
SM3
SUTTON CEMETERY
WORCESTER PARK
KT4
FAIRLANDS PARK
NORTH CHEAM
239
Queen Victoria
SM1
COLLINGWOOD REC GRD
222
Malden Junction
Shannon Corner
Coombe Lane
A3
A238
A298
A24
A217
A2043
B282
B279
B286
B235
KINGSTON ROAD
COOMBE LANE
WORPLE ROAD
BUSHEY ROAD
GRAND DRIVE
MARTIN WAY
LONDON ROAD
EPSOM ROAD
STONECOT HILL
CENTRAL ROAD
CHEAM COMMON ROAD
MALDEN ROAD
BEVERLEY WAY
KINGSTON BY PASS
ST. DUNSTAN'S HILL
OLDFIELDS ROAD
96
97
98
99
100
101
102
103
104
22
23
24

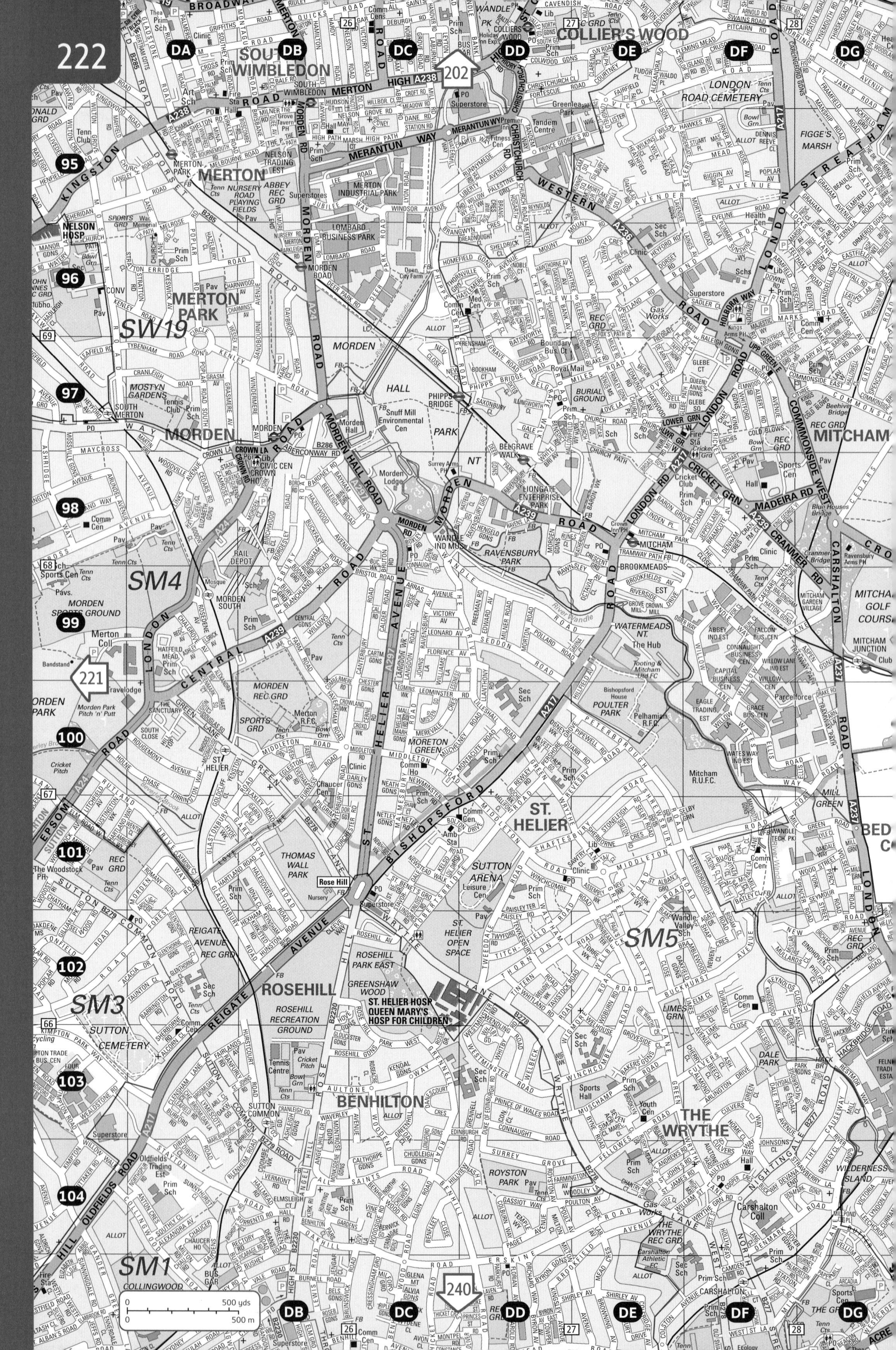
DA
DB
DC
DD
DE
DF
DG
SOUTH WIMBLEDON
COLLIER'S WOOD
202
MERTON HIGH
A238
MERANTUN WAY
LONDON ROAD CEMETERY
FIGGE'S MARSH
MERTON
NELSON TRADING EST
ABBEY REC GRD
MERTON INDUSTRIAL PARK
LOMBARD BUSINESS PARK
MERTON PARK
SW19
MORDEN
HALL
PARK
NT
MOSTYN GARDENS
MORDEN HALL ROAD
Snuff Mill Environmental Cen
Morden Hall
Morden Lodge
PHIPPS BRIDGE
BELGRAVE WALK
LIONGATE ENTERPRISE PARK
BURIAL GROUND
MITCHAM
COMMONSIDE WEST
CRICKET GRN
MADEIRA RD
A239
A217
A236
A24
A297
SM4
MORDEN SOUTH
RAVENSBURY PARK
BROOKMEADS
WATERMEADS NT
The Hub
MORDEN SPORTS GROUND
Merton Coll
221
MORDEN REC GRD
SPORTS GRD
POULTER PARK
Pelhamians R.F.C.
Mitcham R.U.F.C.
ABBEY IND EST
CONNAUGHT BUSINESS CEN
CAPITAL BUSINESS CEN
EAGLE TRADING EST
GRACE BUS CEN
WILLOW LANE IND EST
MITCHAM GOLF COURSE
MITCHAM JUNCTION
MORETON GREEN
ST. HELIER
MILL GREEN
CENTRAL ROAD
LONDON ROAD
BISHOPSFORD ROAD
ST. HELIER AVENUE
THOMAS WALL PARK
Rose Hill
SUTTON ARENA
ST. HELIER OPEN SPACE
SM5
REIGATE AVENUE REC GRD
ROSEHILL PARK EAST
GREENSHAW WOOD
ST. HELIER HOSP
QUEEN MARY'S HOSP FOR CHILDREN
ROSEHILL
ROSEHILL RECREATION GROUND
SM3
SUTTON CEMETERY
BENHILTON
SUTTON COMMON
THE WRYTHE
DALE PARK
ROYSTON PARK
THE WRYTHE REC GRD
Carshalton Coll
WILDERNESS ISLAND
SM1
COLLINGWOOD
REIGATE AVENUE
OLDFIELDS ROAD
EPSOM ROAD
A24
A217
A237
B278
B2230
95
96
97
98
99
100
101
102
103
104
26
27
28
66
67
68
69
240
500 yds
500 m

STREATHAM VALE
STREATHAM COMMON
NORBURY
NORBURY PARK
BIG WOOD
SW16
STREATHAM PARK CEMETERY
PLAYING FIELDS
POLLARDS HILL
GREEN LANE SPORTS GROUND
CR7
THORNTON HEATH
CR4
MITCHAM
COMMON
SHERWOOD PK
WINDMILL TRADING EST
PLAYING FIELD
SPORTS GRD
CROYDON CEMETERY
Croydon Athletic FC
Croydon Boys FC
Thornton Heath Pond
MAYDAY UNIVERSITY HOSPITAL
QUEEN'S ROAD CEMETERY
BROAD GREEN
THORNTON ROAD IND EST
MERTON
SUTTON
Hundred Acre Bridge
Traq Motor Sport Circuits
RIFLE RANGE
TRAMSHEDS IND EST
THERAPIA LANE
Lombard Roundabout
VALLEY POINT IND EST
Beddington Farm
Sorting Office
Sewage Works
Filter Beds
Sludge Beds
RESERVOIR
Mile Road Bridge
PIONEERS INDUSTRIAL PARK
AMPERE WAY
CR0
WADDON MARSH
BEDDINGTON TRADING PARK
Roman Bath House (Site of)
BEDDINGTON
HACKBRIDGE
SM6
BEDDINGTON PARK
THE GRANGE GARDENS
SPORTS GRD
PROGRESS BUSINESS PK
CROYDON SUB STATION
MILL LANE TRADING ESTATE
WADDON
WANDLE PARK
Civic Amenity Site
WEST CROYDON
Whitgift Centre
CHURCH STREET
REEVES CORNER
DUPPAS HILL
Croydon Flyover
Fiveways
LONDON ROAD
MITCHAM ROAD
PURLEY WAY
CROYDON ROAD
DUPPAS HILL RD
A23
A236
A232
A235
B272
B273
B266
203
224
241
96
97
98
99
100
101
102
103
104
DH
DJ
DK
DL
DM
DN
DP
29
30
31

DQ
DR
DS
DT
DU
DV
DW
UPPER NORWOOD
PENGE
204
SE19
SE20
ANERLEY
BETTS PARK
BEAULIEU HEIGHTS
SOUTH NORWOOD GROUNDS
SPORTS GROUND
ORCHARD SCHOOL SPORTS CENTRE
SOUTH NORWOOD LAKE
SOUTH NORWOOD
GRANGEWOOD PARK
BECKENHAM CEMETERY
SOUTH NORWOOD COUNTRY PARK
SE25
SELHURST PARK-CRYSTAL PALACE FC
CR7
THORNTON HEATH
GREEN LANE SPORTS GROUND
NORWOOD JUNCTION
SOUTH NORWOOD REC GRD
CROYDON AND RYLANDS FIELDS
CROYDON SPORTS ARENA
CROYDON DRIVING RANGE
223
QUEEN'S ROAD CEMETERY
MAYDAY UNIVERSITY HOSPITAL
SELHURST
WOODSIDE
ASHBURTON PARK
SHIRLEY OAKS HOSPITAL
CROYDON
ADDISCOMBE
CR0
WHITGIFT PLAYING FIELDS
SHIRLEY PARK GOLF COURSE
HOCKEY PITCH
LLOYD PARK
COOMBE PARK
SPORTS GROUND
PARK HILL
242
95
96
97
98
99
100
101
102
103
104
33
34
35
66
67
68
69
0
500 yds
0
500 m

DX
DY
DZ
EA
EB
EC
ED
205
BECKENHAM
NEW BECKENHAM
LEWISHAM
BROMLEY
RAVENSBOURNE
THE SLOANE HOSPITAL
SHORTLANDS
BECKENHAM HOSPITAL
CROYDON RD REC GROUND
BR3
BR2
ELMERS END
KELSEY PARK
EDEN PARK
PARK LANGLEY
UPPER ELMERS END
CROUCH OAK WOOD
MONKS ORCHARD
BETHLEM ROYAL HOSPITAL
HIGH BROOM WOOD
LANGLEY PARK GOLF COURSE
THE ROOKERY
WEST WICKHAM
BLAKE REC GRD
The Swan Junction
SPRING PARK WOOD
BR4
SHIRLEY
FOXES WOOD
PINEWOODS
KENNEL WOOD
SPRING PARK
SPARROWS DEN PLAYING FIELDS
CONEY HALL REC GRD
243
226
96
97
98
99
100
101
102
103
104
36
37
38
66
67
68
69
A222
A214
A234
A232
A2015
A2022
B230
B251
BECKENHAM ROAD
CROYDON ROAD
BROMLEY ROAD
HIGH STREET
MANOR ROAD
SOUTH EDEN PARK RD
LINKS WAY
WICKHAM ROAD
HAYES LANE
STATION RD
GLEBE WAY
ADDINGTON

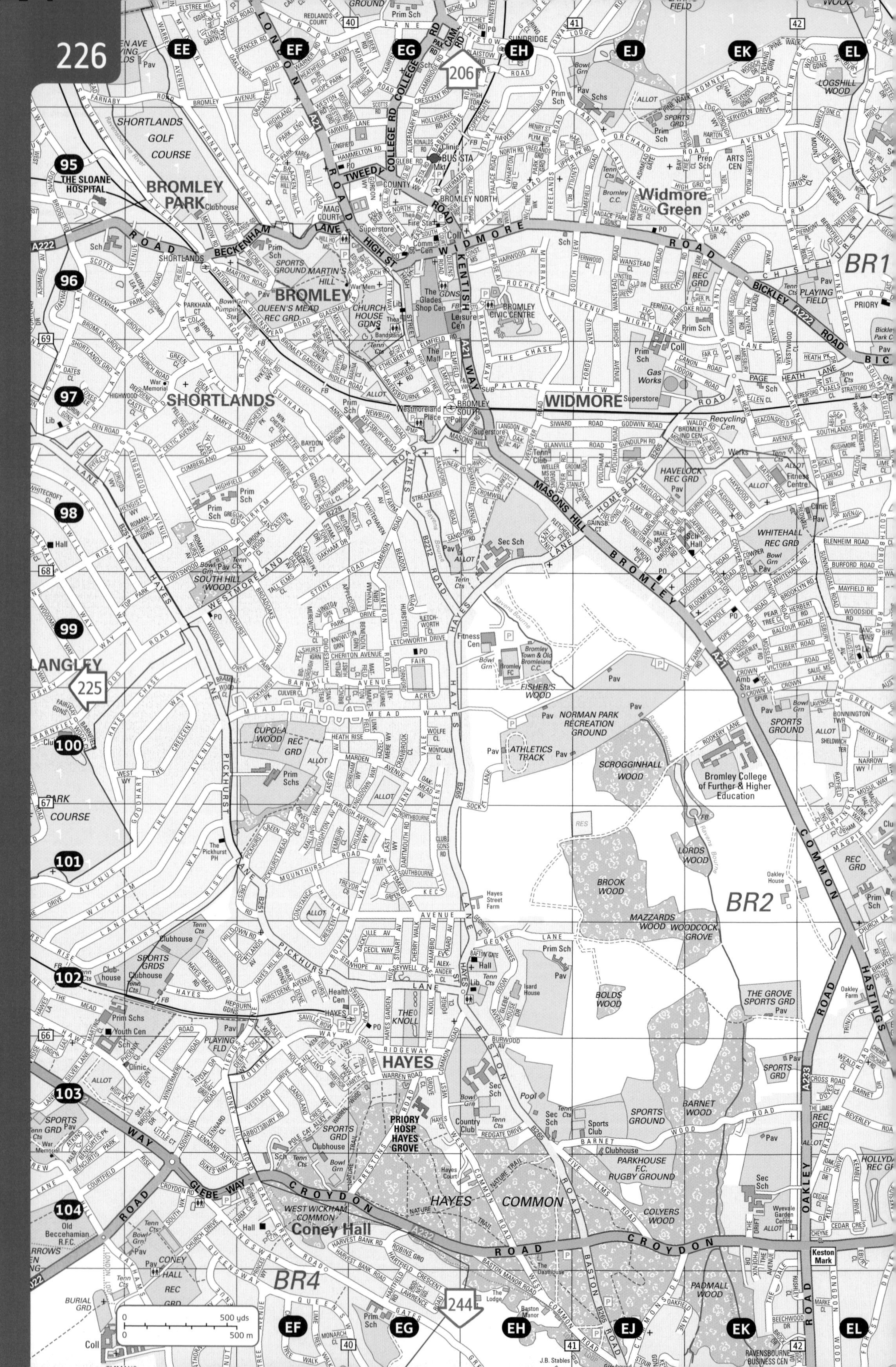
EE
EF
EG
EH
EJ
EK
EL
206
95
96
97
98
99
100
101
102
103
104
225
244
SHORTLANDS GOLF COURSE
THE SLOANE HOSPITAL
BROMLEY PARK
SHORTLANDS
BROMLEY
Widmore Green
WIDMORE
BR1
BR2
BR4
LANGLEY
SOUTH HILL WOOD
CUPOLA WOOD
NORMAN PARK RECREATION GROUND
ATHLETICS TRACK
SCROGGINHALL WOOD
Bromley College of Further & Higher Education
LORDS WOOD
BROOK WOOD
MAZZARDS WOOD
WOODCOCK GROVE
BOLDS WOOD
THE GROVE SPORTS GRD
BARNET WOOD
SPORTS GROUND
PARKHOUSE F.C. RUGBY GROUND
COLYERS WOOD
PADMALL WOOD
HAYES
HAYES COMMON
WEST WICKHAM COMMON
Coney Hall
PRIORY HOSP HAYES GROVE
THE KNOLL
FISHER'S WOOD
HAVELOCK REC GRD
WHITEHALL REC GRD
LOGSHILL WOOD
Keston Mark
BROMLEY CIVIC CENTRE
The Glades Shop Cen
QUEEN'S MEAD REC GRD
MARTIN'S HILL
CHURCH HOUSE GDNS
BROMLEY NORTH
BROMLEY SOUTH
SHORTLANDS
A21
A222
A232
A233
B265
BECKENHAM ROAD
WIDMORE ROAD
BICKLEY ROAD
MASONS HILL
BROMLEY COMMON
HASTINGS ROAD
OAKLEY ROAD
CROYDON ROAD
GLEBE WAY
HAYES LANE
PICKHURST LANE
WESTMORELAND ROAD
KENTISH WAY
HIGH ST
LONDON ROAD
0 500 yds
0 500 m
J.B. Stables

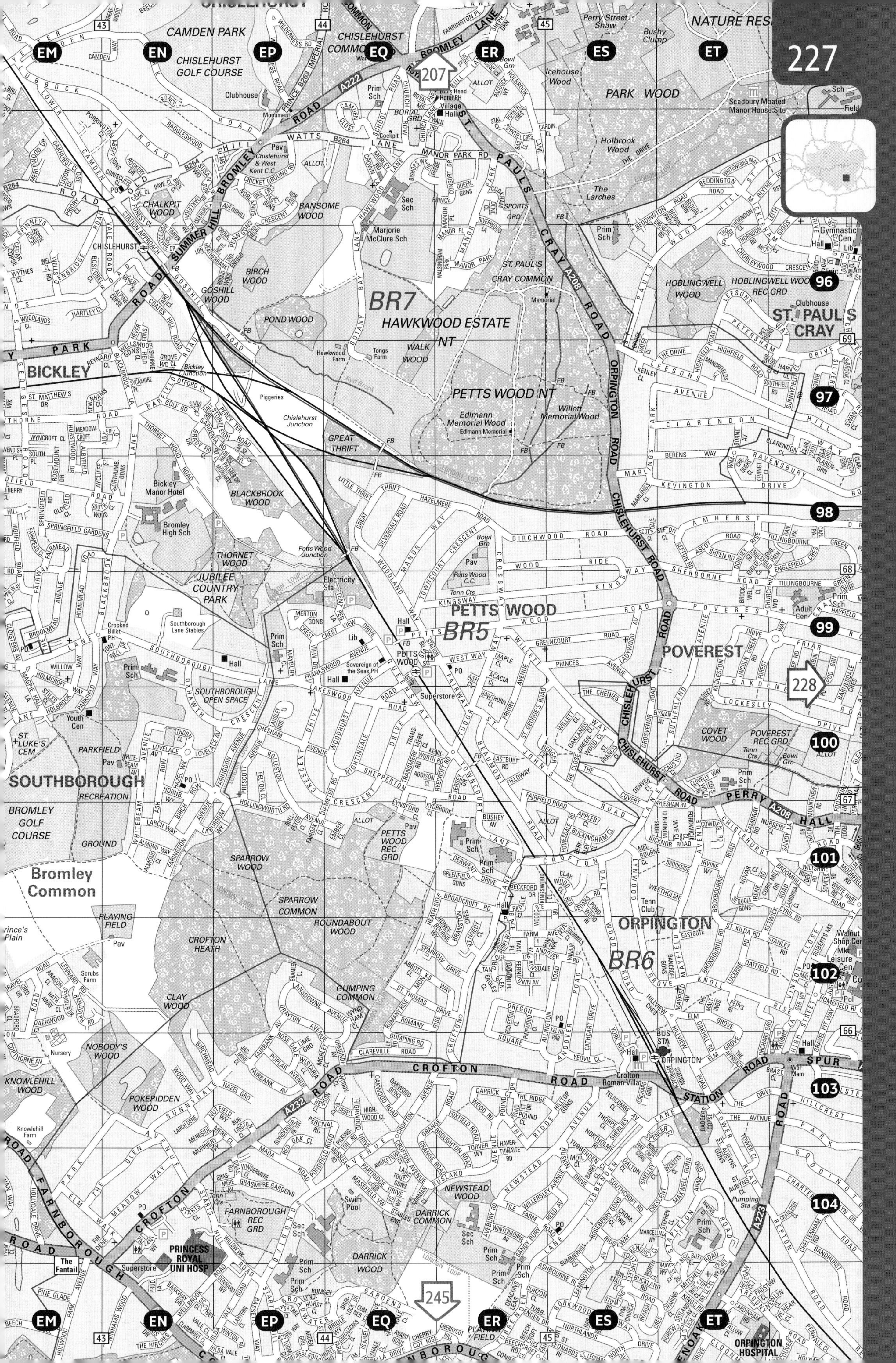
EM
EN
EP
EQ
ER
ES
ET
207
245
228
96
97
98
99
100
101
102
103
104
CAMDEN PARK
CHISLEHURST GOLF COURSE
CHISLEHURST COMMON
Perry Street Shaw
Bushy Clump
NATURE RESERVE
PARK WOOD
Icehouse Wood
Scadbury Moated Manor House Site
Holbrook Wood
The Larches
BROMLEY LANE
ST. PAUL'S CRAY ROAD
A208
A222
B264
PRINCE IMPERIAL ROAD
CHALKPIT WOOD
BANSOME WOOD
Marjorie McClure Sch
CHISLEHURST
SUMMER HILL
BIRCH WOOD
GOSHILL WOOD
POND WOOD
BR7
HAWKWOOD ESTATE NT
WALK WOOD
ST. PAUL'S CRAY COMMON
HOBLINGWELL WOOD
HOBLINGWELL WOOD REC GRD
ST. PAUL'S CRAY
BICKLEY
Bickley Junction
Chislehurst Junction
GREAT THRIFT
PETTS WOOD NT
Edlmann Memorial Wood
Willett Memorial Wood
Kyd Brook
Bickley Manor Hotel
BLACKBROOK WOOD
Bromley High Sch
ORPINGTON ROAD
CHISLEHURST ROAD
THORNET WOOD
JUBILEE COUNTRY PARK
Petts Wood Junction
PETTS WOOD
BR5
POVEREST
COVET WOOD
POVEREST REC GRD
SOUTHBOROUGH OPEN SPACE
SOUTHBOROUGH
ST. LUKE'S CEM
PARKFIELD
BROMLEY GOLF COURSE
RECREATION GROUND
Bromley Common
SPARROW WOOD
SPARROW COMMON
ROUNDABOUT WOOD
PETTS WOOD REC GRD
PLAYING FIELD
CROFTON HEATH
CLAY WOOD
GUMPING COMMON
ORPINGTON
BR6
PERRY HALL ROAD
NOBODY'S WOOD
KNOWLEHILL WOOD
POKERIDDEN WOOD
CROFTON ROAD
A232
Crofton Roman Villa
STATION ROAD
SPUR ROAD
A223
FARNBOROUGH ROAD
FARNBOROUGH REC GRD
NEWSTEAD WOOD
DARRICK COMMON
DARRICK WOOD
PRINCESS ROYAL UNI HOSP
ORPINGTON HOSPITAL
The Fantail
LONDON LOOP

EU
EV
EW
EX
EY
EZ
FA
95
96
97
98
99
100
101
102
103
104
47
48
49
69
68
67
66
208
227
246
DA14
BR7
BR5
BR6
SIDCUP BYPASS
A20
A224
A223
A232
A208
B258
SEVENOAKS WAY
CRAY AVENUE
COURT ROAD (ORPINGTON BYPASS)
EDGINGTON
Crittall's Corner
Scadbury Moated Manor House Site
Irish Plantation
Field Study Centre
Youth Cen
ST. PAUL'S CRAY
HOBLINGWELL WOOD REC GRD
CRAYFIELDS BUSINESS PARK
CRAYFIELDS IND PARK
RUXLEY PARK GOLF COURSE
Ruxley Manor Garden Centre
RUXLEY WOOD
CRAY VALLEY GOLF COURSE
Ski Centre
Fitness Cen
DRIVING RANGE
Clubhouse
Barnfield Bank
Pilgrim Hill
Lower Hockenden Farm
Simon's Field Shaw
The Small House
PAULS CRAY HILL PARK
HIGHLANDS WOOD
HOCKENDEN WOOD
Hogspring Cottages
Milewood
MURRAY BUSINESS CEN
SPRINGVALE RETAIL PARK
Gas Works
Superstores
ST. MARY CRAY
BUS GARAGE
NUGENT SHOPPING PARK
NUGENT IND PARK
ST MARY CRAY
ST. MARY CRAY REC GRD
THE WARREN
Sheepcote Farm
Ringland Farm
CHILD'S WOOD
Blueberry Farm
Kevington Farm
Derry Downs
GRIGG'S CROSS
KYNASTON WOOD
Waldens Farm
Crouch Farm
Walden Manor
Heather's Holdings
Bleak House Farm
POVEREST
POVEREST REC GRD
PERRY HALL ROAD
PRIORY GARDENS
BROMLEY MUS
GRASSMEADE RECREATION GROUND
RAMSDEN
Eastwood Farm
GRIFF'S WOOD
HOLLINGBOURNE TWR
BEKESBOURNE TWR
Piggery
Byways Nurseries
SAGE WENTS
Crownwood Farm
Cookham Hill Farm
Cookham Farm
SPUR ROAD
Goddington House
Goddington
GODDINGTON PARK
ROUNDS SMALLAMS
Bowling Green
LILLY'S WOOD
BLACK BUSH WOOD
ORPINGTON HOSPITAL
Tennis Courts
500 yds
500 m

Hextable
SWANLEY PARK
SWANLEY
BR8
Crockenhill
Hulberry
Junction 3 (M
Junction 1 (M
PEDHAM
209
230
247

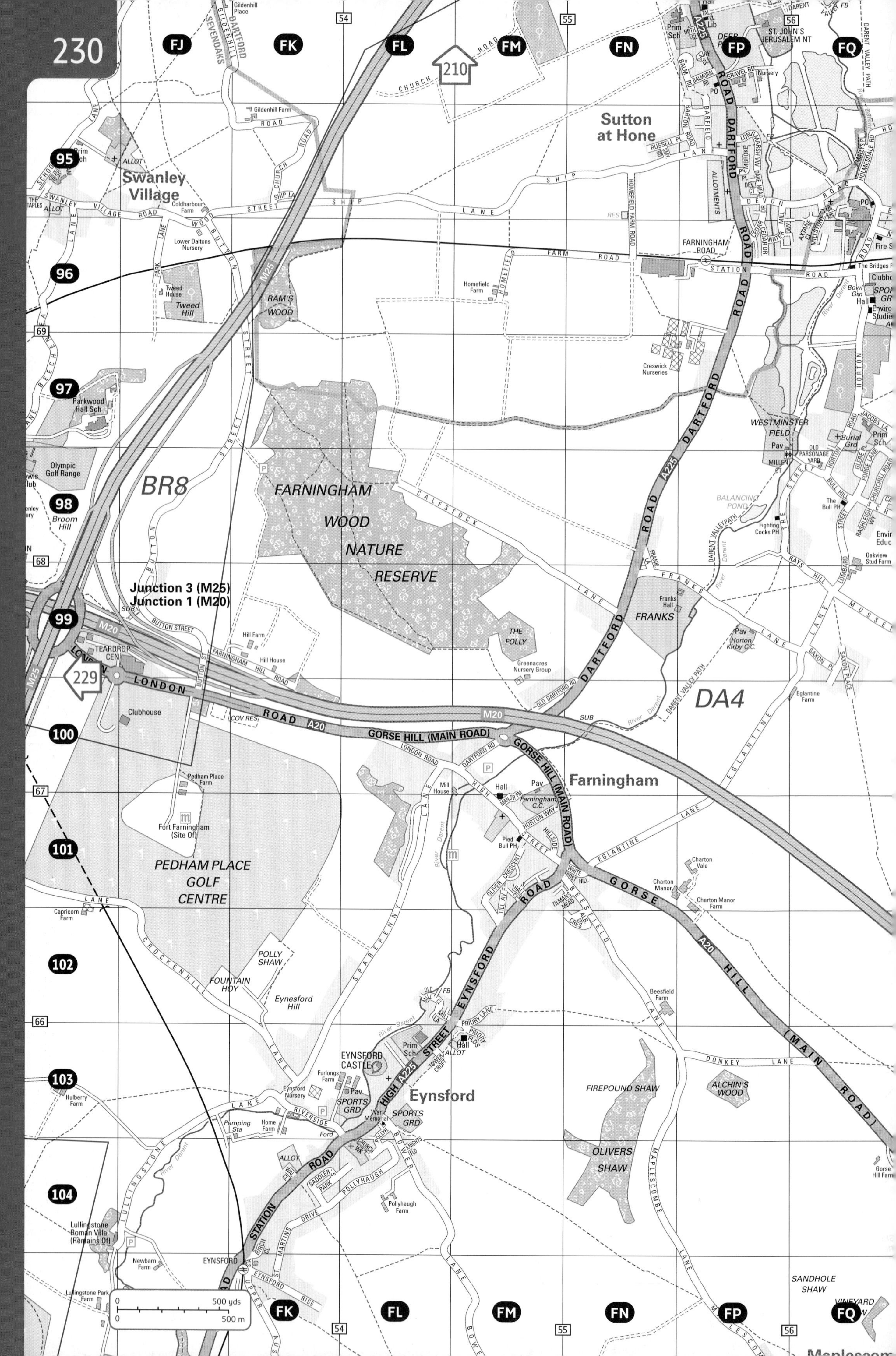
FJ
FK
FL
FM
FN
FP
FQ
210
229
Sutton at Hone
Swanley Village
Farningham
Eynsford
BR8
DA4
FARNINGHAM WOOD NATURE RESERVE
PEDHAM PLACE GOLF CENTRE
Junction 3 (M25)
Junction 1 (M20)
M25
M20
A20
A225
DARTFORD ROAD
LONDON ROAD
GORSE HILL (MAIN ROAD)
GORSE HILL (MAIN ROAD)
SHIP LANE
FARNINGHAM ROAD
STATION ROAD
HIGH STREET
EYNSFORD ROAD
EYNSFORD CASTLE
WESTMINSTER FIELD
FRANKS
THE FOLLY
RAM'S WOOD
Tweed Hill
Broom Hill
Olympic Golf Range
Parkwood Hall Sch
POLLY SHAW
FOUNTAIN HOY
Eynesford Hill
FIREPOUND SHAW
OLIVERS SHAW
ALCHIN'S WOOD
SANDHOLE SHAW
Lullingstone Roman Villa (Remains Of)
Fort Farningham (Site Of)
Creswick Nurseries
Greenacres Nursery Group
Charton Manor
Beesfield Farm
Pollyhaugh Farm
95
96
97
98
99
100
101
102
103
104
54
55
56
66
67
68
69
0 500 yds
0 500 m

South Darenth
Horton Kirby
Dean Bottom
Pinden
Mile End Green
Hartley Green
Fawkham Green
DA2
DA3
TN15
HORTON WOOD
GROVE WOOD
HOPKINS SPRING WOOD
HATCHFIELD WOOD
CHURCHDOWN WOOD
RYECROFTS WOOD
PENNIS WOOD
YEWFIELD SHAW
CHOAKS WOOD
SAXTEN'S WOOD
GABRIEL SPRING WOOD
SHETLEY SHAWS
FAWKHAM MANOR HOSPITAL
FAWKHAM VALLEY GOLF COURSE
REDLIBBETS GOLF COURSE
BRANDS HATCH MOTOR RACING
BRANDS HATCH KARTING
QUARRY
DARTFORD
SEVENOAKS
211
FR
FS
FT
FU
FV
FW
FX
57
58
59
96
97
98
99
100
101
102
103
104

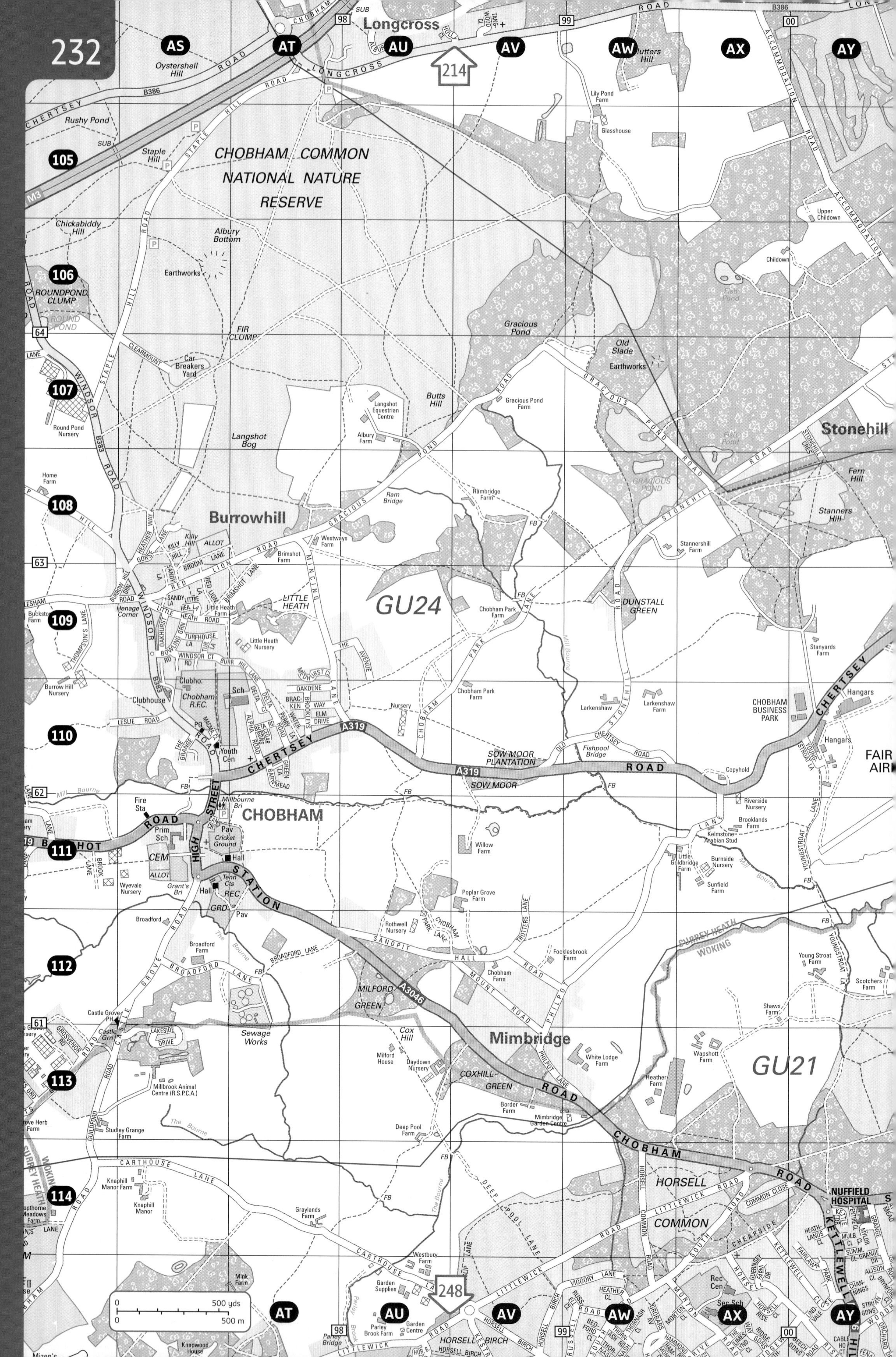
AS
AT
AU
AV
AW
AX
AY
Longcross
214
Oystershell Hill
Rushy Pond
105
Staple Hill
CHOBHAM COMMON NATIONAL NATURE RESERVE
Chickabiddy Hill
Albury Bottom
Earthworks
106
ROUNDPOND CLUMP
64
FIR CLUMP
Car Breakers Yard
107
Round Pond Nursery
Lily Pond Farm
Glasshouse
Upper Childown
Childown
Gracious Pond
Old Slade
Earthworks
Gracious Pond Farm
Butts Hill
Langshot Equestrian Centre
Albury Farm
Langshot Bog
Stonehill
Fern Hill
Stanners Hill
Home Farm
108
Burrowhill
Rambridge Farm
Ram Bridge
Westways Farm
Brimshot Farm
Stannershill Farm
63
LITTLE HEATH
GU24
DUNSTALL GREEN
Henage Corner
109
Buckstone Farm
Little Heath Farm
Chobham Park Farm
Little Heath Nursery
Stanyards Farm
Burrow Hill Nursery
Clubho.
Chobham R.F.C.
Sch
Clubhouse
Chobham Park Farm
Nursery
Larkenshaw
Larkenshaw Farm
CHOBHAM BUSINESS PARK
Hangars
110
Youth Cen
A319
SOW MOOR PLANTATION
Fishpool Bridge
Copyhold
FAIR AIR
62
SOW MOOR
Riverside Nursery
Fire Sta
Millbourne Bri
CHOBHAM
Prim Sch
Pav
Cricket Ground
Willow Farm
Brooklands Farm
Kelmstone Arabian Stud
111
CEM
Hall
Little Goldbridge Farm
Burnside Nursery
Wyevale Nursery
ALLOT
Grant's Bri
Hall
Tenn Cts
REC
GRD
Pav
Poplar Grove Farm
Sunfield Farm
Broadford
Rothwell Nursery
Broadford Farm
Focklesbrook Farm
WOKING
Young Strood Farm
112
Chobham Farm
MILFORD GREEN
A3046
Scotchers Farm
Shaws Farm
61
Castle Grove PH
Castle Grn
Sewage Works
Cox Hill
Mimbridge
White Lodge Farm
Wapshott Farm
GU21
113
Milford House
Daydown Nursery
COXHILL GREEN
Heather Farm
Millbrook Animal Centre (R.S.P.C.A.)
Border Farm
Mimbridge Garden Centre
Grove Herb Farm
Studley Grange Farm
Deep Pool Farm
HORSELL
Knaphill Manor Farm
114
Knaphill Manor
Graylands Farm
HORSELL COMMON
NUFFIELD HOSPITAL
Westbury Farm
Mink Farm
Rec Cen
Sec Sch
0 500 yds
0 500 m
Garden Supplies
248
98
Parley Bridge
Parley Brook Farm
Garden Centre
HORSELL BIRCH
Knepwood House
99
00

OTTERSHAW
KT16
KT15
KT14
GU22
ROW TOWN
WOODHAM
SHEERWATER
WEST BYFLEET
Pyrford
Junction 11
OTTERSHAW PARK
GREAT WOOD
BIRCH WOOD
HOYT WOOD
NEW ZEALAND GOLF COURSE
HORSELL COMMON
QUEENWOOD GOLF COURSE
HOMEWOOD PARK
McLaren Technology Centre
GUILDFORD ROAD
CHERTSEY ROAD
CHOBHAM ROAD
ST. PETER'S WAY
WOODHAM LANE
SHEERWATER ROAD
OLD WOKING ROAD
MURRAY ROAD
SPINNEY HILL
BASINGSTOKE CANAL
215
234
249

BG
BH
BJ
BK
BL
BM
BN
216
233
250
Junction 11
105
106
107
108
109
110
111
112
113
114
ADDLESTONE
ROW TOWN
NEW HAW
KT15
KT14
GU22
GU23
WOODHAM
WEST BYFLEET
DARTNELL PARK
BYFLEET
BROOKLANDS
WEYBRID
St. George's College
The Plantation Nursery
HOSPITALLER CONVENT
SAYES COURT PUBLIC OPEN SPACE
Crockford Bridge
Crockford Bridge Farm
Coxes Lock
Weybridge Lock
Black Boy Bridge
WEYBRIDGE BUSINESS PARK
RIVERSIDE PARK
PLAYING FIELDS
Brooklands College
Crickets Hill
Conduit Hill
Weybridge Junction
Addlestone Junction
Nine Arches Bridge
Water Works
SEVEN ARCHES APPROACH
Seven Arches Bridge
MERCEDES-BENZ WORLD
BROOKLANDS MUSEUM
Procter & Gamble
THE HEIGHTS
Sony UK
CENTRAL VETERINARY LABORATORY
DRIVING RANGE
TOP GOLF ADDLESTONE GOLF COURSE
Coomelands Farm
Hall's Farm
Grange Farm
Charwood Farm
Fallow Farm
Electricity Station
BYFLEET & NEW HAW
Byfleet Junction
BROOKLANDS INDUSTRIAL PARK
TRADE CITY
BYFLEET TECHNICAL CENTRE
BROOKLANDS COMMUNITY PARK
Paddocks Retail Pk
Horizon Business Village
Fitness Club
HEATHERVALE REC GRD
HEATHERVALE CARAVAN PARK
Botton Lock
CAMPHILL INDUSTRIAL ESTATE
Scotland Lock
BASINGSTOKE CANAL
PLAYING FIELD
OLD WOOD
TINS WOOD
Wey Retail Pk
Plough Bridge
Plough Bridge Farm
Bluegates Hole
Byfleet Mill
Mouchel Parkman
Murray's Bridge
Tennis Courts
DODD'S WOOD
Dodd's Bridge
Health Club
TRADITIONS GOLF COURSE
COMMON MEADOWS
River Wey
Sewage Works
Filter Beds
Manor House
THE ISLAND
Park Barn Farm
Wey Manor Farm
Clubhouse
A317
A318
A245
M25
B3121
B385
B374
WEYBRIDGE ROAD
HIGH STREET
BRIGHTON ROAD
NEW HAW ROAD
BYFLEET ROAD
OYSTER LANE
PARVIS ROAD
OLD WOKING ROAD
BARNES WALLIS DR
SOPWITH DR
WOODHAM LANE
CHURCH ROAD
STATION ROAD
500 yds
500 m

BP
BQ
BR
BS
BT
BU
BV
217
ASHLEY PARK
OATLANDS PARK
BURWOOD PARK
WALTON-ON-THAMES
QUEENS ROAD
OATLANDS DRIVE
HERSHAM ROAD
KT12
KT13
KT11
106
107
108
109
110
111
112
113
114
236
63
62
61
64
WALTON COMMON
UPPER COMMON
BURHILL GOLF COURSE (OLD COURSE)
BURHILL GOLF COURSE (NEW COURSE)
WHITELEY VILLAGE
ST. GEORGE'S HILL
ST. GEORGE'S HILL GOLF COURSE
SEVEN HILLS ROAD
BURWOOD ROAD
BYFLEET ROAD
A245
A3
PORTSMOUTH ROAD
PAINSHILL PARK
SILVERMERE GOLF COURSE
FOXHOLM COVERT
ESHER ROAD
OLD COMMON
COBHAM COMMUNITY HOSP
BETWEEN STREETS
HIGH ST
RIVERHILL
MILL RD
STOKE
COBHAM
251
08
09
10

HERSHAM
ESHER
WEST END
KT12
KT11
ESHER COMMON
FAIRMILE COMMON
OXSHOTT HEATH
Claremont Park
Fairmile
HERSHAM RIVERSIDE PARK
WEST END COMMON
CLAREMONT LANDSCAPE GARDEN (NT)
MOORE PLACE GOLF COURSE
CLAREMONT PARK GOLF COURSE
PRINCESS ALICE HOSPICE
COBHAM COMMUNITY HOSP
LITTLE HEATH COMMON
WATERCUT COPSE
KNOWLE HILL PARK
PORTSMOUTH ROAD
ESHER BYPASS
HERSHAM BYPASS
218
235
252

HINCHLEY WOOD
LITTLEWORTH COMMON
KINGSTON BYPASS
A309
D.W.P. OFFICE
219
Hook Junction
KING EDWARD REC GRD
SPORTS GROUND
SURBITON GOLF COURSE
MEMLORIAL GRD
HINCHLEY WOOD
Telegraph Hill
Semaphore House
RUGBY GRD
SPORTS GRD
LOVELACE PLAYING FIELD
Esher Cricket Club
Slough Farm
Manor Farm
Elm Farm
LOWER WOOD
CHESSINGTON NORTH
CLAYGATE
KT10
SPORTS GROUND
THE GRAPSOME
CHURCH FIELDS
CHESSINGTON SOUTH
CLAYGATE COMMON
Vale Farm
Horringdon Farm
Oak Cottages
BARWELL LAKE
Winey Hill
Holiday Inn
KT9
CHESSINGTON WORLD OF ADVENTURES
BARWELL BUSINESS PARK
CHESSINGTON GOLF CENTRE
Driving Range
238
SURREY
KINGSTON UPON THAMES
HOLROYDS PLANTATION
SIXTY ACRE WOOD
BIRCH WOOD
MILBOURNEHOLD PLANTATION
GREAT OAK
Premier Inn
Park Farm
KT22
LIMEKILN WOOD
JUBILEE WOOD
Electricity Station
Garden Centre
CHESSINGTON WOOD
OLD CARPENTERS PLANTATION
EPSOM COTTAGE
Malden Rushett
BRICKYARD PLANTATION
MILBOURNEHOLD WOOD
SILVERGLADE BUSINESS PARK
NEW WOOD
Glanmire Farm
Byhurst Farm
STOKE WOOD
PRINCE'S COVERTS
Bunkers Hill
Woodcock Corner
Rushett Farm
OXSHOTT
Telegraph Hill
COV RES
KT21
D'ABERNON CHASE
Ashtead Roman Villa (Site of)
THE FOREST
ELMBRIDGE
MOLE VALLEY
Horns Hill
253
LEATHERHEAD GOLF COURSE
LEATHERHEAD ROAD
A243
A3
ESHER BYPASS
B280
OAK LANE
FAIROAK LANE
RUSHETT LANE
CD
CE
CF
CG
CH
CJ
CK
15
16
17
61
62
63
64
106
107
108
109
110
111
112
113
114

CL
CM
CN
CP
CQ
CR
CS
220
237
254
19
20
21
61
62
63
64
105
106
107
108
109
110
111
112
113
114
KT9
KT19
KT18
KT21
HOOK
CHESSINGTON
HORTON
EPSOM
WEST EWELL
EPSOM COMMON
HORTON COUNTRY PARK
HORTON PARK COUNTRY CLUB GOLF COURSE
CHESSINGTON GOLF CENTRE
HOGSMILL RIVERSIDE OPEN SPACE
KING GEORGE'S FIELD
KING GEORGE'S TRADING EST
DAVIS ROAD IND PK
CHESSINGTON TRADE PARK
HOOK RISE SOUTH IND PK
KINGSTON BUS. CEN.
CHURCH FIELDS
BUTCHERS GROVE
GREAT WOOD
FOUR ACRE WOOD
POND WOOD
NEWTON WOOD
HOOK ROAD ARENA
ST. EBBA'S HOSPITAL
WEST PARK HOSPITAL
NEW EPSOM & EWELL COTTAGE HOSP
EPSOM GENERAL HOSP
LONG GROVE PARK
HORTON PARK CHILDREN'S FARM
OLD HALEYBURIANS R.F.C.
KING GEORGE V REC GRD
LONGMEAD BUS. PK
LONGMEAD IND EST
NONSUCH INDUSTRIAL ESTATE
KINGSTON UPON THAMES
SURREY
EPSOM & EWELL
KINGSTON BYPASS
CHESSINGTON ROAD
HOOK ROAD
RUXLEY LANE
CHRIST CHURCH ROAD
UPPER HIGH STREET
SOUTH STREET
ASHLEY AV
The Quadrant
Woodcock Corner
Stamford Grn
THE FOREST
500 yds
500 m

CT
CU
CV
CW
CX
CY
CZ
221
NORTH CHEAM
Queen Victoria
KT4
CUDDINGTON REC GRD
STONELEIGH
STONELEIGH Lib
Beggar's Hill
EWELL BYPASS
Organ Crossroads
NONSUCH PARK
OAK PLANTATION
Nonsuch Mansion
THE WOOD
Diana's Dyke
Cuddington Church (Site of)
SM3
CHEAM REC GRD
CHEAM PARK
CHEAM
Cheam Village
SM1
Sutton Water Services
PERRETS FIELD
SEARS PARK
ST. DUNSTAN'S HILL
BELMONT RISE
SM2
240
106
107
108
109
110
111
112
113
114
EWELL
EWELL EAST Clubhouse
EAST EWELL
KT17
Glyn Old Boys FC
Nescot
CUDDINGTON GOLF COURSE
SM7
SURREY
EPSOM & EWELL
SUTTON
REIGATE & BANSTEAD
BANSTEAD DOWNS GOLF COURSE
RIFLE RANGE
NORTH LOOE
Epsom College
EPSOM DOWNS
Drift Bridge Hotel
Drift Br
Banstead Crossroads
NORK
255
BOLT LA
ALEXANDRA REC GRD
PLAYING FIELDS
Hatch Furlong
Bourne Hall Mus & Lib
Superstore
22
23
24

DA
DB
DC
DD
DE
DF
DG
222
SM1
COLLINGWOOD REC GRD
ROYSTON PARK
CARSHALTON
THE WRYTHE REC GRD
Carshalton Coll
WILDERNESS ISLAND
THE GROVE
WEST SUTTON
SUTTON
CARSHALTON ROAD
HIGH ST
POUND ST
CARSHALTON PARK
CARSHALTON WAR MEMORIAL HOSP
CARSHALTON BEECHES
SPORTS GRD
Sutton High Sch
105
106
107
108
109
110
111
112
113
114
SM2
OVERTON PARK REC GRD
239
SM5
WELLFIELD PLANTATION
CARSHALTON BEECHES
SUTTON HOSPITAL
Uni of Lon Institute of Cancer Research
ROYAL MARSDEN HOSP
BELMONT
BANSTEAD DOWNS
BANSTEAD DOWNS GOLF COURSE
BANSTEAD COMMON
H.M. PRISON DOWNVIEW
H.M. PRISON HIGH DOWN
OAKS SPORTS CENTRE GOLF COURSE
Oaks Sports Cen
THE OAKS PARK
LITTLE WOODCOTE
PLAYING FIELD
LITTLE WOODCOTE ESTATE
WOODMANSTERNE LANE
WOODMANSTERNE PARK RECREATION GROUND
SPORTS GROUND
RIFFET WOOD
BIG WOOD
CLOCKHOUSE REC GRD
CROYDON ROAD
WINKWORTH A2022
SM7
256
WOODMANSTERNE
Banstead Crossroads
RIFLE RANGE
500 yds
500 m

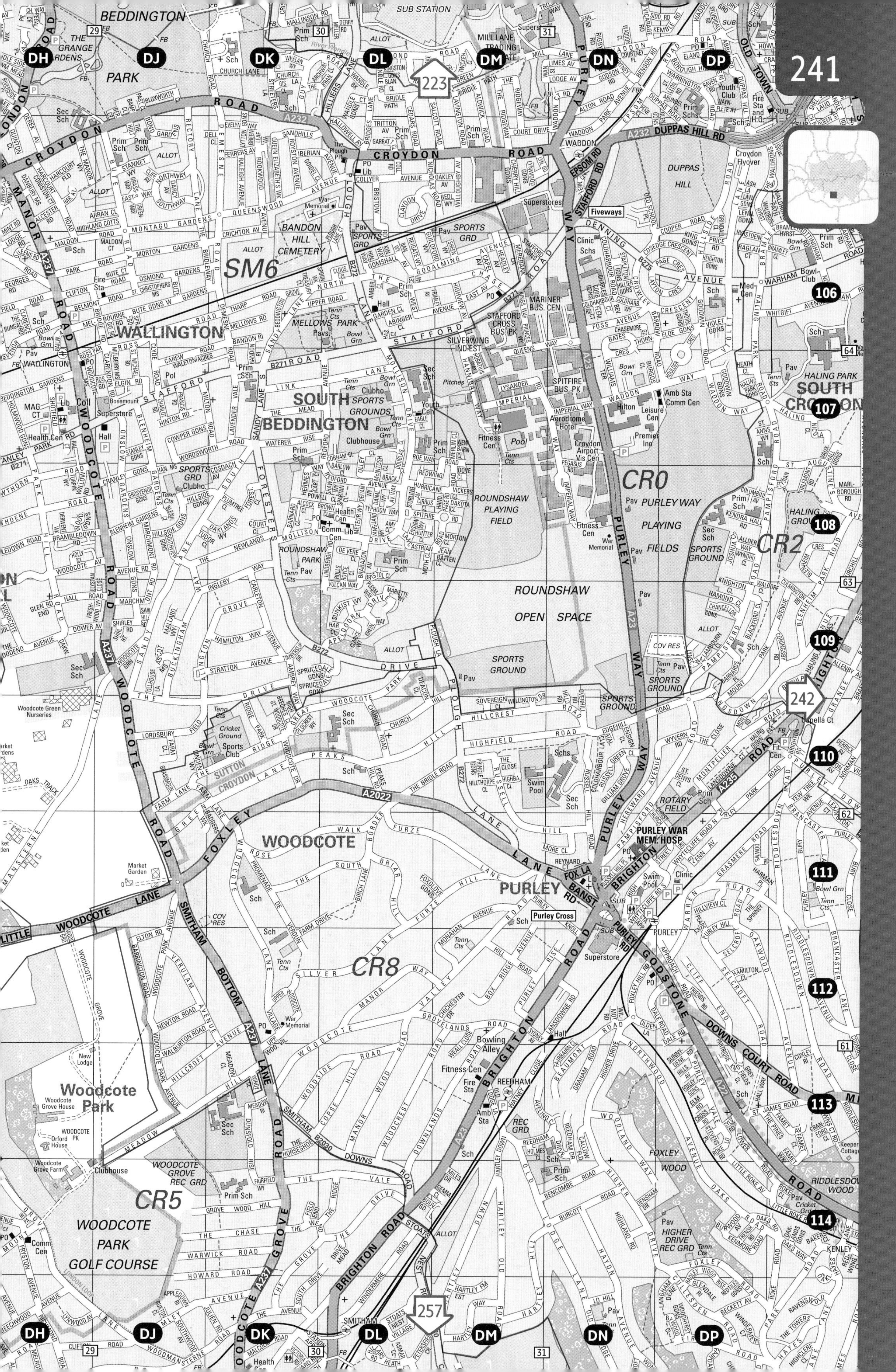
BEDDINGTON
THE GRANGE GARDENS
PARK
DH
DJ
DK
DL
DM
DN
DP
223
SUB STATION
MILL LANE TRADING ESTATE
CROYDON ROAD
A232
DUPPAS HILL RD
DUPPAS HILL
Croydon Flyover
WADDON
Fiveways
BANDON HILL CEMETERY
SM6
WALLINGTON
SOUTH BEDDINGTON
STAFFORD ROAD
B271 ROAD
SILVERWING IND EST
STAFFORD CROSS BUS PK
MARINER BUS. CEN
SPITFIRE BUS. PK
IMPERIAL WAY
Aerodrome Hotel
Croydon Airport Vis Cen
ROUNDSHAW PLAYING FIELD
CR0
PURLEY WAY PLAYING FIELDS
ROUNDSHAW OPEN SPACE
SPORTS GROUND
SOUTH CROYDON
HALING PARK CROSS
CR2
106
107
108
109
110
111
112
113
114
242
A23
PURLEY WAY
A237
WOODCOTE ROAD
A2022
FOXLEY LANE
WOODCOTE
PURLEY
Purley Cross
PURLEY WAR MEM. HOSP
BRIGHTON ROAD
A235
GODSTONE ROAD
A22
DOWNS COURT ROAD
CR8
SMITHAM BOTTOM LANE
Woodcote Park
CR5
WOODCOTE PARK GOLF COURSE
WOODCOTE GROVE REC GRD
FOXLEY WOOD
HIGHER DRIVE REC GRD
RIDDLESDOWN WOOD
KENLEY
REEDHAM
SMITHAM
257
29
30
31
61
62
63
64

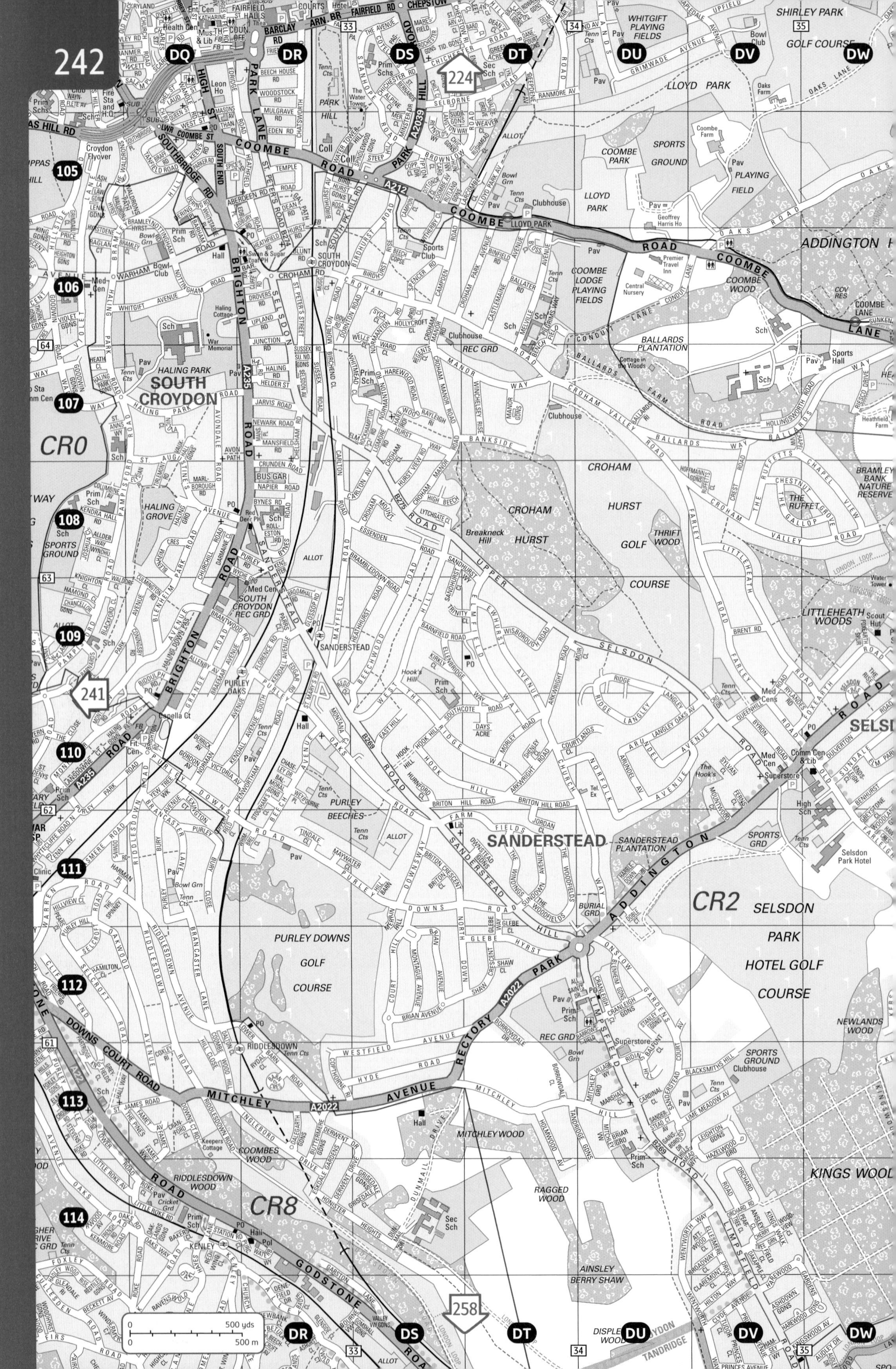
DQ
DR
DS
DT
DU
DV
DW
224
WHITGIFT PLAYING FIELDS
SHIRLEY PARK GOLF COURSE
LLOYD PARK
COOMBE PARK
SPORTS GROUND
PLAYING FIELD
LLOYD PARK
COOMBE ROAD
A212
PARK LANE
HIGH ST
SOUTH END
BRIGHTON ROAD
A235
PARK HILL ROAD
A2039
Croydon Flyover
105
106
107
108
109
110
111
112
113
114
64
63
62
61
33
34
35
SOUTH CROYDON
HALING PARK
CR0
HALING GROVE
SPORTS GROUND
SOUTH CROYDON REC GRD
SANDERSTEAD
PURLEY OAKS
241
ADDINGTON H
COOMBE LODGE PLAYING FIELDS
COOMBE WOOD
BALLARDS PLANTATION
CROHAM HURST GOLF COURSE
CROHAM HURST
Breakneck Hill
THRIFT WOOD
REC GRD
BRAMLEY BANK NATURE RESERVE
THE RUFFETT
LITTLEHEATH WOODS
SELSDON ROAD
SELSD
SANDERSTEAD
SANDERSTEAD PLANTATION
ADDINGTON ROAD
CR2
SELSDON PARK HOTEL GOLF COURSE
Selsdon Park Hotel
NEWLANDS WOOD
SPORTS GROUND
PURLEY DOWNS GOLF COURSE
PURLEY BEECHES
RECTORY PARK
A2022
MITCHLEY AVENUE
MITCHLEY WOOD
RAGGED WOOD
KINGS WOOD
DOWNS COURT ROAD
COOMBES WOOD
RIDDLESDOWN WOOD
CR8
GODSTONE ROAD
KENLEY
AINSLEY BERRY SHAW
LIMPSFIELD ROAD
B269
TANDRIDGE
258
0 500 yds
0 500 m

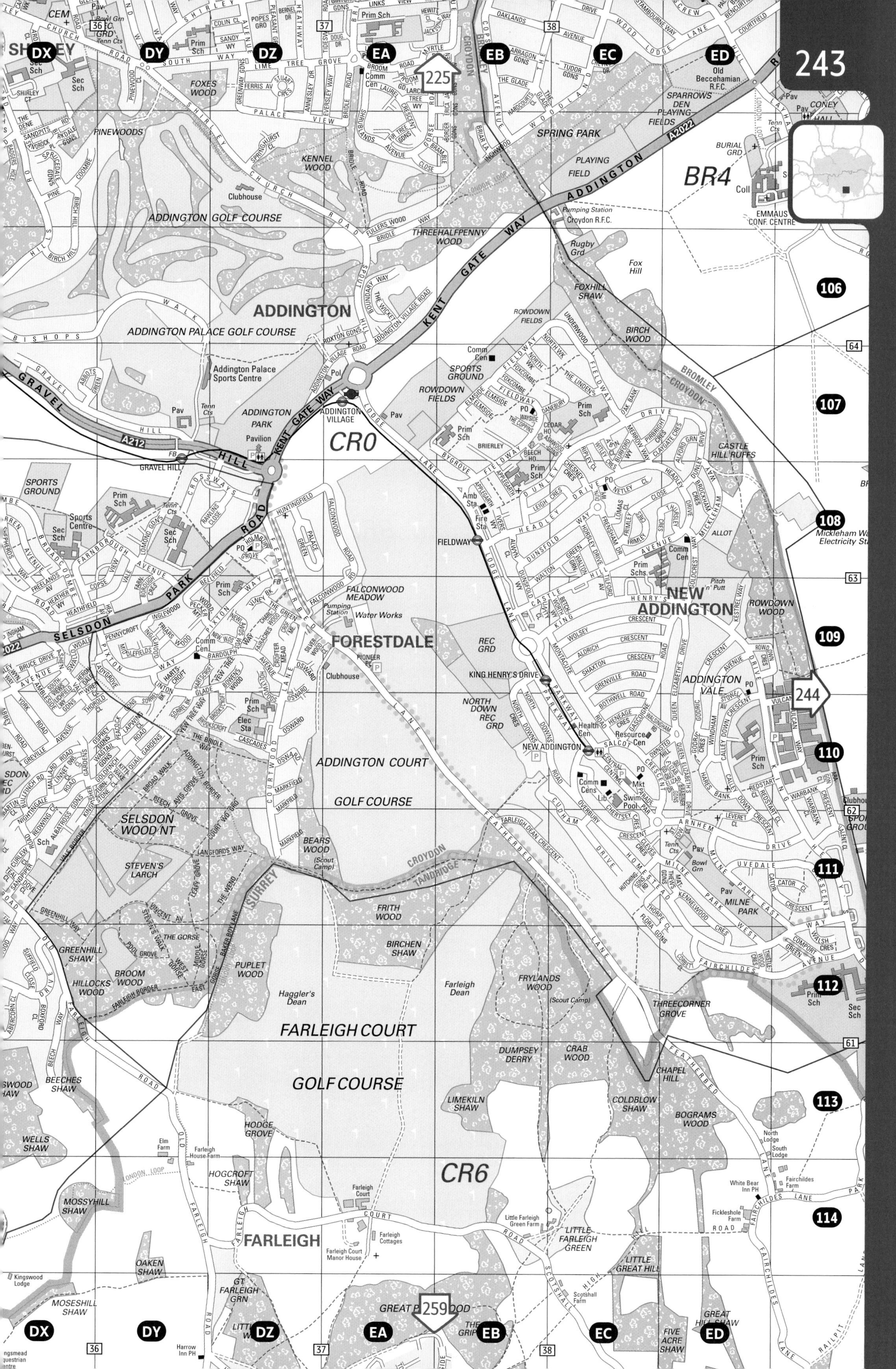
ADDINGTON
ADDINGTON GOLF COURSE
ADDINGTON PALACE GOLF COURSE
Addington Palace Sports Centre
ADDINGTON PARK
ADDINGTON VILLAGE
CR0
BR4
SPRING PARK
KENNEL WOOD
THREEHALFPENNY WOOD
FOXES WOOD
PINEWOODS
FORESTDALE
NEW ADDINGTON
ADDINGTON VALE
FALCONWOOD MEADOW
ADDINGTON COURT GOLF COURSE
SELSDON WOOD NT
FRITH WOOD
BIRCHEN SHAW
FARLEIGH COURT GOLF COURSE
FARLEIGH
CR6
LITTLE FARLEIGH GREEN
KENT GATE WAY
ADDINGTON ROAD
GRAVEL HILL
SELSDON PARK ROAD
FEATHERBED LANE
ROWDOWN FIELDS
FOXHILL SHAW
BIRCH WOOD
CASTLE HILL RUFFS
ROWDOWN WOOD
THREECORNER GROVE
CHAPEL HILL
BOGRAMS WOOD
COLDBLOW SHAW
CRAB WOOD
DUMPSEY DERRY
LIMEKILN SHAW
FRYLANDS WOOD
HODGE GROVE
HOGCROFT SHAW
MOSSYHILL SHAW
WELLS SHAW
BEECHES SHAW
OAKEN SHAW
MOSESHILL SHAW
GREENHILL SHAW
HILLOCKS WOOD
BROOM WOOD
PUPLET WOOD
STEVEN'S LARCH
BEARS WOOD
FIVE ACRE SHAW
LITTLE GREAT HILL
GREAT HILL SHAW
SPARROWS DEN PLAYING FIELDS
Old Beccehamian R.F.C.
Croydon R.F.C.
EMMAUS CONF. CENTRE
DX DY DZ EA EB EC ED
225
244
259
106 107 108 109 110 111 112 113 114
36 37 38
61 62 63 64

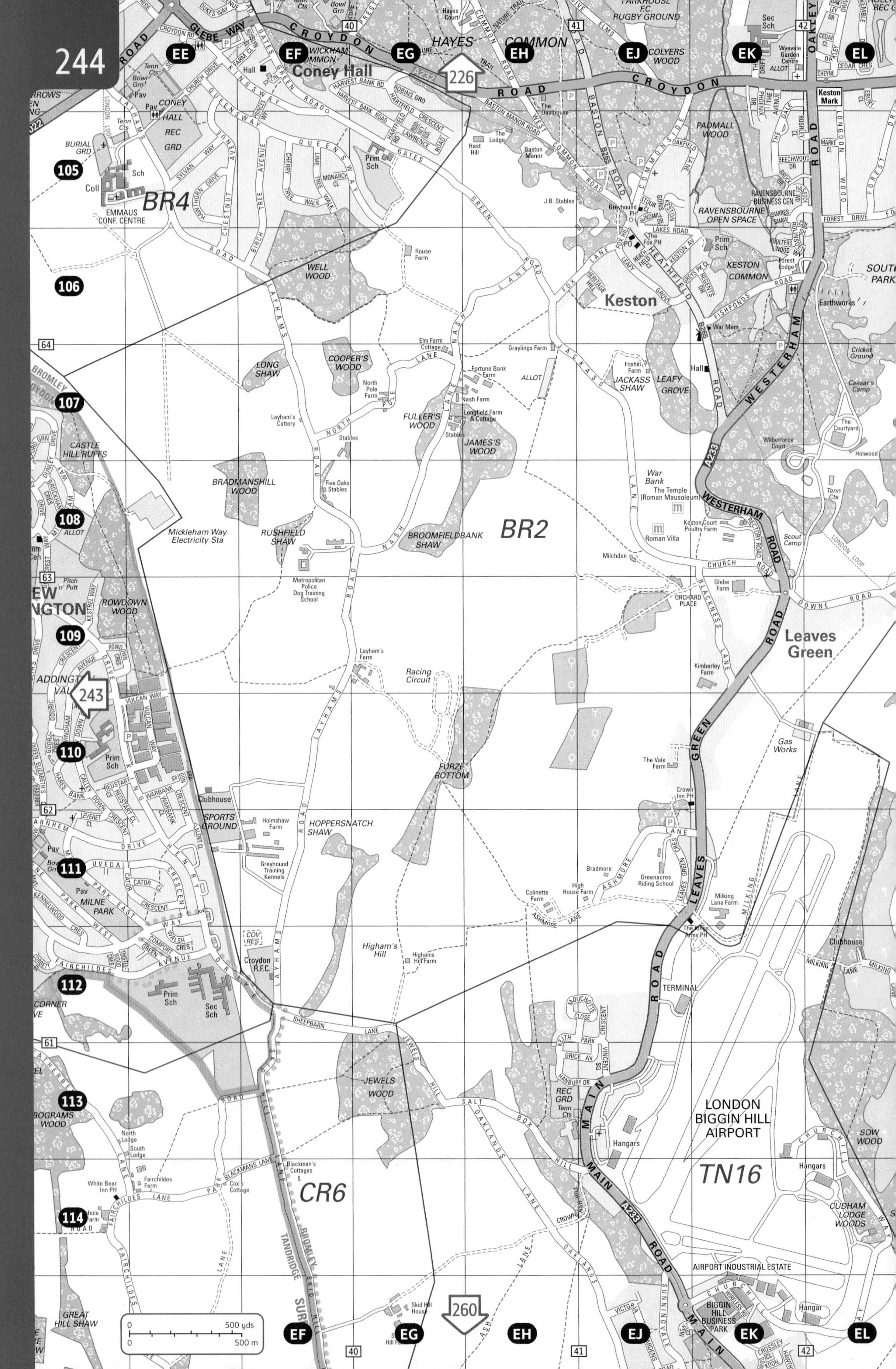
Coney Hall
Keston
Leaves Green
BR4
BR2
CR6
TN16
LONDON BIGGIN HILL AIRPORT
HAYES COMMON
KESTON COMMON
RAVENSBOURNE OPEN SPACE
WESTERHAM ROAD
CROYDON ROAD
LAYHAMS ROAD
MAIN ROAD
LEAVES GREEN ROAD
226
243
260

EM
EN
EP
EQ
ER
ES
ET
43
44
45
227
246
261
FARNBOROUGH
COMMON
FARNBOROUGH
PRINCESS ROYAL UNI HOSP
Superstore
The Fantail
FARNBOROUGH REC GRD
Swim Pool
NEWSTEAD WOOD
DARRICK WOOD
PLAYING FIELD
ORPINGTON HOSPITAL
Sports Club
SPORTS GRD
STRAWBERRY FLDS
HIGH STREET
B2158
FARNBOROUGH HILL
SEVENOAKS ROAD
SEVENOAKS WAY
A21
A223
LAKE WOOD
NINHAMS WOOD
COVERED RESERVOIRS
BROOM BANK
Mill Hill
CHURCH END PLANTATION
BR6
RAMUS WOOD
Green Street Green
COCKSETT PLANTATION
Cocksett Hill
GLENTRAMMON REC GRD
Sevenoaks Lodge
SHIRE LANE
Lower Hook Farm
North End Farm
HIGH ELMS COUNTRY PARK
Nature Centre
Woodpiece
WHITELANDS WOOD
Clubhouse
Clockhouse
BLACKLANDS
THE ROOKERY
LONDON LOOP
North End Farm Cottages
BOGEY LANE
Denbarn Farm
Rose & Crown PH
Chelsfield Hall Farm
ROUNDS WOOD
HIGH ELMS GOLF COURSE
NATURE FIELD
Farthing Street Farm
Farthings
Orange Court
Meadow Cottage
Green Acres
Hazels
Little Crowhill
The Rookery
Cuckoo Lodge
CUCKOO WOOD
Gorringes Farm
GREAT MOLLOMS WOOD
LITTLE MOLLOMS WOOD
BURNT GORSE
Grasslands Farm
Avondale Farm
Long Acre
Prim Sch
SPORTS GRD
Downe
The Queens Head PH
Petleys Farm
Petleys
Downe Hall
Hall
Christmas Tree Farm
The Shack
Endsleigh
White Earth
Snag Farm
Southfields
Hazelwood
Rose Cottage
FOXBERRY WOOD
HOMEFIELD SPRING
Hang Grove Farm
SQUARE SHAW
HAZEL WOOD
The Oaks
Snag Lane Farm
THOMPSON WOOD
Downe Lodge
Downe Court Manor
Downe Court Farm
DOWN HOUSE DARWIN MUSEUM
DOWNE BANK NATURE RESERVE
Norsted Manor Farm
WEST KENT GOLF COURSE
Buxton Browne Research Institute
Downe C.C.
Pav
LORDFIELD SHAW
The Shaws (Girl Guide Camp)
Mace Farm
Mace Farm Cottages
BROOM WOOD
HIGH WOOD
HANG GROVE
Beechwood
The Boundary
Hostye Farm
KANGLES WOOD
MACE LANE
TN14
Church Hill Farm
LADIES WOOD
SPENCERS GROVE
Luxted Farm
FOXBURROW WOOD
NEW YEARS WOOD
NEWLANDS WOOD
TWENTY ACRE SHAW
HOOK WOOD
BIRD HOUSE WOOD
DOWNE ACTIVITY CENTRE
Clock Tower
Angus Home
SPORTS GRD
New Year Cottage
BIRCHES CROFT
LEASONS WOOD
Open Air Pool
BROMLEY CROFT
Single Street
Bottom Farm
Tenn Cts
Cudham
JOCKEY WOOD
OAKES SHAW
106
107
108
109
110
111
112
113
114
61
62
63
64

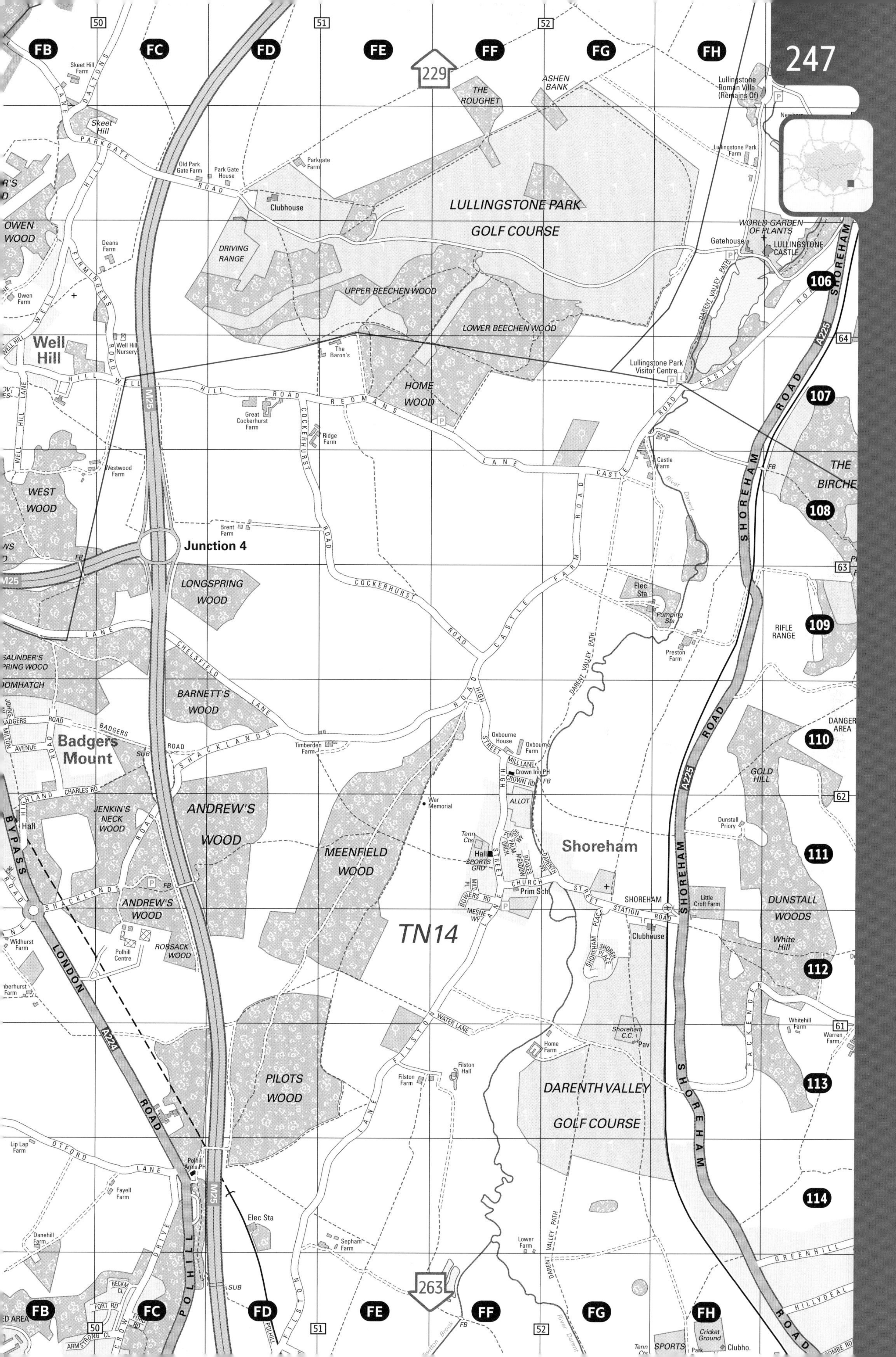

LULLINGSTONE PARK GOLF COURSE
UPPER BEECHEN WOOD
LOWER BEECHEN WOOD
HOME WOOD
THE ROUGHET
ASHEN BANK
Lullingstone Roman Villa (Remains Of)
WORLD GARDEN OF PLANTS
LULLINGSTONE CASTLE
Lullingstone Park Visitor Centre
Well Hill
Junction 4
LONGSPRING WOOD
BARNETT'S WOOD
Badgers Mount
ANDREW'S WOOD
MEENFIELD WOOD
JENKIN'S NECK WOOD
ROBSACK WOOD
Shoreham
TN14
PILOTS WOOD
DARENTH VALLEY GOLF COURSE
DUNSTALL WOODS
GOLD HILL
RIFLE RANGE
WEST WOOD
OWEN WOOD
SHOREHAM ROAD
LONDON ROAD
POLHILL
CASTLE FARM ROAD
COCKERHURST ROAD
REDMANS LANE
HIGH STREET
FILSTON LANE
DARENT VALLEY PATH

AS
AT
AU
AV
AW
AX
AY
232
264
GU21
GU24
GU3
115
116
117
118
119
120
121
122
123
124
98
99
00
59
58
57
56
Horsell Common
Horsell
Horsell Birch
Horsell Moor
Littlewick Common
Goldsworth Park
Goldsworth Park Trading Estate
Goldsworth Park Rec Grd
Traciovs Copse
Knaphill
Knaphill Manor
Lansbury Estate
Waterers Park
Woking Cemetery
Crematorium
St. John's
St. John's Lye
Mount Hermon
Hook Heath
Woking Golf Course
Mayford
Hoe Valley Linear Park
Sutton Green Golf Course
Worplesdon Golf Course
Worplesdon
Smart's Heath
Prey Heath
Fisher's Hill
Martlands Ind Est
Burdenshot Hill
Bridley Copse
Beech Hill
Pye Hill
Whitmoor
Lockfield Drive
A324
A320
A3046
B380
Egley Road
Guildford Road
Hermitage Road
Amstel Way
Littlewick Road
Carthouse Lane
Saunders Lane
Smarts Heath Road
Prey Heath Road
Hook Heath Road
Mile Path
Basingstoke Canal
500 yds
500 m

AZ
BA
BB
BC
BD
BE
BF
01
02
03
233
250
265
116
117
118
119
120
121
122
123
124
59
58
57
56
WEST BYFLEET
GOLF COURSE
Pyrford
Prim Sch
Comm Cen
PYRFORD COMMON
THE ROUGH
Pyrford Court
The Bothy
WOKING
Maybury
GU22
HOEBRIDGE GOLF CENTRE
Driving Range
Clubhouse
Monument Hill
Fox Hill
Hoebridge Farm
Sewage Works
Filter Beds
Pumping Sta
Woking Park Farm
OLDHILL COPSE
Newark Priory (Remains)
Church Farm
Lady Place
Pyrford Village
Wheelers Farm
Abbey Stream Bridge
Newark Mill Bridge
The Seven Stars PH
Papercourt Farm
Papercourt Lock
Old Woking
HIGH STREET
A247
BURIAL GRD
Riverdale Farm
WOKING PARK
Leisure Cen
Swim Pool
Sec Sch
Coll
Westfield
GU4
GU23
SAND PIT
Prews Farm
Mill
Sailing Club
Send
Send Marsh
Christian Centre
Hall
Cart Bridge
Carbridge House
Moorlane Farm
Nursery
Fisher's Farm
Lower Westfield Farm
Runtley Wood Farm
Triggs Lock Bridge
Triggs Lock
Cricketshill Farm
Concorde C.C.
Sendholme
Wareham's Farm
CEM
Sendbarns
Stables
WOKING BUSINESS PARK
KINGSWEY BUSINESS PARK
RIVER COURT
GENESIS BUSINESS PARK
CHERTSEY ROAD
A320
A245
B382
B367
B368
B380
B381
BROADMEAD ROAD
SEND ROAD
SEND BARNS LANE
NEWARK LANE
CHURCH HILL
UPSHOT LANE
OLD WOKING ROAD
RIVER WEY
WOKING GUILDFORD

TRADITIONS GOLF COURSE
PYRFORD GOLF COURSE
THE WISLEY GOLF COURSE
DRIVING RANGE
WISLEY COMMON
ROYAL HORTICULTURAL SOCIETY GARDEN WISLEY
Wisley
KT14
COMMON MEADOWS
River Wey
BUXTON WOOD
M25
WOOLGER'S WOOD
GU22
Pyrford Green
Pyrford Village
PEATMOOR WOOD
LOCK COPSE
Pyrford Marina
WALSHAM PLANTATION
WALSHAM MEADOW
Irish Hole
Newark Priory (Remains)
Abbey Stream
RIPLEY GREEN
SPORTS GRD
Ockham Park
Elm Corner
OCKHAM COMMON
Battleston Hill
PORTSMOUTH ROAD
RIPLEY BYPASS
OCKHAM PARK
PARK WOOD
Ripley
Ockham
GU23
Send Marsh
GARLICK'S ARCH COPSE
LOVELAND'S COPSE
ROBOROW WOOD
BACHELOR'S COPSE
BRAMBLERIDE COPSE
SHEPPARDSGROVE COPSE
GROVE HEATH
HUNGRY HILL
Sewage Works
Sailing Club
Wren's Nest
Pinetum
Bicentenary Glasshouse
Aberconway House
Dodd's Bridge
Murray's Bridge
Wisley Bridge
Stratford Bridge
Newark New Bridge
Newark Lock
Walsham Lock
Pyrford Lock
The Anchor PH
The Seven Stars PH
Jovial Sailor PH
Half Moon PH
249
234
266
0 500 yds
0 500 m

PAINSHILL PARK
KT11
KT24
OCKHAM COMMON
Junction 10
Wisley Interchange
Martyr's Green
May's Green
Downside
COBHAM PARK
THE DRIFT GOLF COURSE
EFFINGHAM COMMON
EFFINGHAM JUNCTION
HOOK WOOD
CHAFFERS COPSE
STUMPS GROVE
BARNSTHORNS WOOD
HATCHFORD PARK
HATCHFORD WOOD
CHATLEY HEATH
CHATLEY WOOD
NORTON WOOD
BRAMBLE WOOD
BRICKFIELD COPSE
LITTLE BRICKFIELD COPSE
OLD OAK COMMON
THE NEW PRESERVE
PEAKED ROUGH
ROUNDABOUT
CLAMP ROUGH
GALLOWS GROVE
BUSHY THICKET
THICKET COPSE
TRULLIBER COPSE
TANNERS COPSE
HUNT'S COPSE
THE BOGS
BREACH HILL WOOD
LODGE COPSE
ELMBRIDGE
GUILDFORD
PORTSMOUTH ROAD
POINTERS ROAD
OCKHAM LANE
OLD LANE
HORSLEY ROAD
DOWNSIDE ROAD
PLOUGH LANE
CHILBROOK ROAD
GOOSE GREEN
BETWEEN STREETS
HIGH ST
RIVERHILL
THE LAKE
River Mole
235
252
267

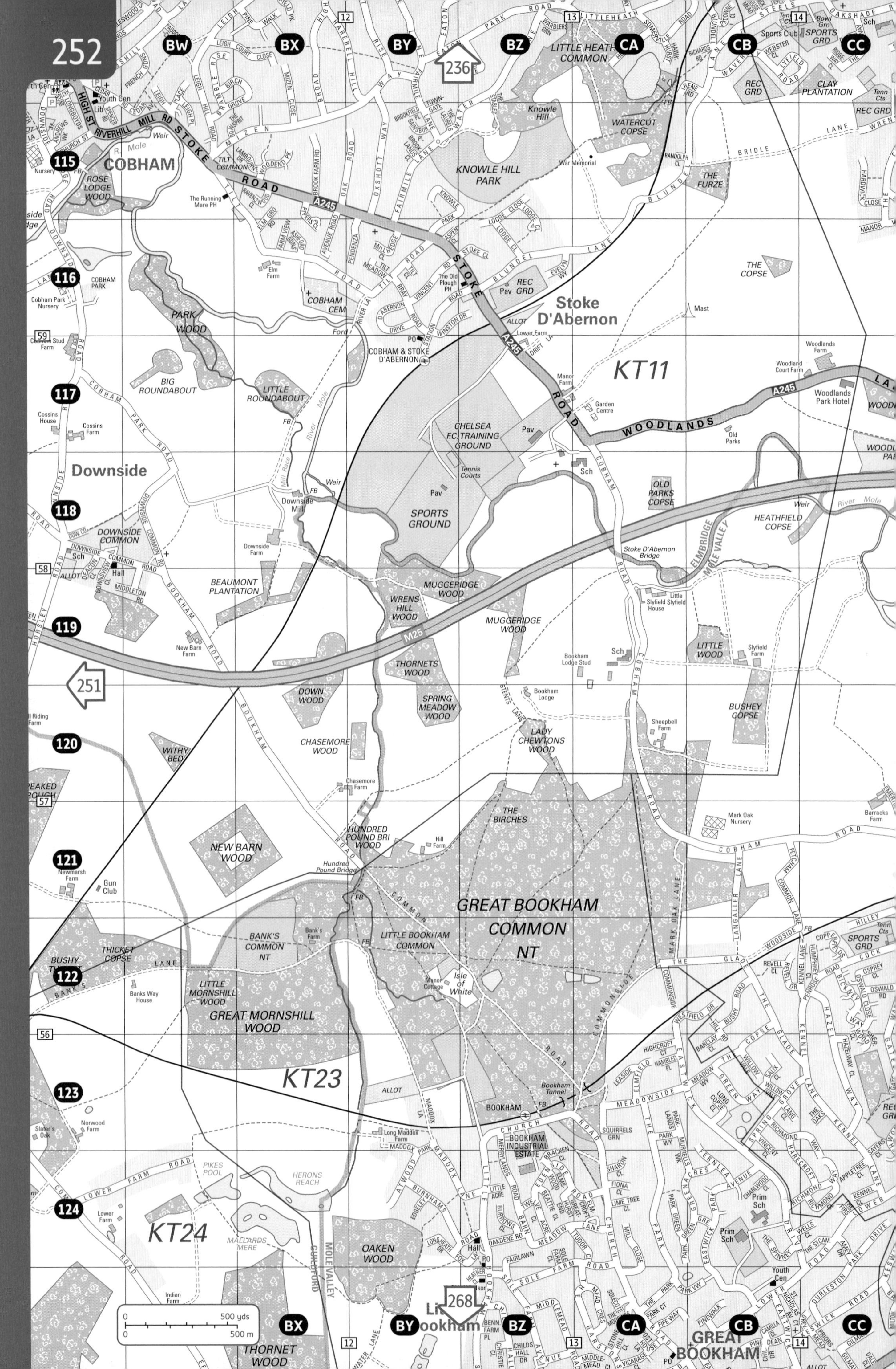

BW
BX
BY
BZ
CA
CB
CC
236
LITTLE HEATH COMMON
SPORTS GRD
REC GRD
CLAY PLANTATION
COBHAM
ROSE LODGE WOOD
KNOWLE HILL PARK
WATERCUT COPSE
THE FURZE
War Memorial
The Running Mare PH
STOKE ROAD
A245
COBHAM PARK
Cobham Park Nursery
COBHAM CEM
The Old Plough PH
THE COPSE
Stoke D'Abernon
COBHAM & STOKE D'ABERNON
PARK WOOD
BIG ROUNDABOUT
LITTLE ROUNDABOUT
KT11
Woodlands Park Hotel
WOODLANDS
Old Parks
CHELSEA F.C. TRAINING GROUND
Downside
SPORTS GROUND
Downside Mill
OLD PARKS COPSE
HEATHFIELD COPSE
DOWNSIDE COMMON
Downside Farm
Stoke D'Abernon Bridge
ELMBRIDGE
MOLE VALLEY
BEAUMONT PLANTATION
MUGGERIDGE WOOD
WRENS HILL WOOD
M25
New Barn Farm
THORNETS WOOD
LITTLE WOOD
Slyfield Farm
Bookham Lodge Stud
Bookham Lodge
251
DOWN WOOD
SPRING MEADOW WOOD
BUSHEY COPSE
WITHY BED
CHASEMORE WOOD
LADY CHEWTONS WOOD
Sheepbell Farm
Chasemore Farm
THE BIRCHES
Mark Oak Nursery
Barracks Farm
NEW BARN WOOD
HUNDRED POUND BRI WOOD
Hundred Pound Bridge
Hill Farm
Newmarsh Farm
Gun Club
GREAT BOOKHAM COMMON NT
BANK'S COMMON NT
LITTLE BOOKHAM COMMON
THICKET COPSE
BUSHY
Banks Way House
LITTLE MORNSHILL WOOD
GREAT MORNSHILL WOOD
Isle of White
KT23
ALLOT
Bookham Tunnel
BOOKHAM
Norwood Farm
Long Maddox Farm
BOOKHAM INDUSTRIAL ESTATE
PIKES POOL
HERONS REACH
Lower Farm
KT24
MALLARDS MERE
OAKEN WOOD
Prim Sch
Youth Cen
Indian Farm
268
GREAT BOOKHAM
THORNET WOOD
GUILDFORD
500 yds
500 m
115
116
117
118
119
120
121
122
123
124

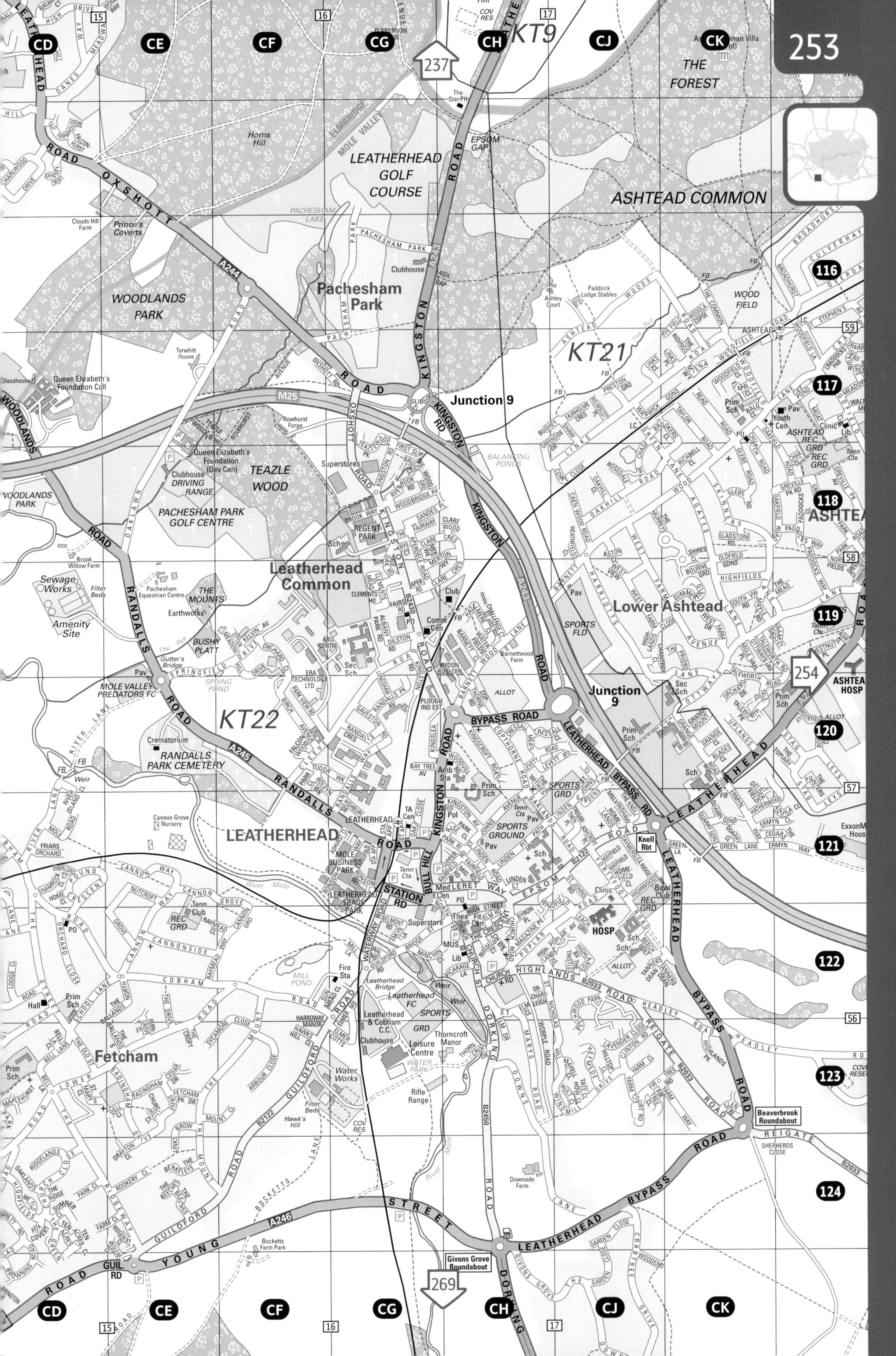
KT9
THE FOREST
ASHTEAD COMMON
LEATHERHEAD GOLF COURSE
EPSOM GAP
Horns Hill
MOLE VALLEY
ELMBRIDGE
The Star PH
Clouds Hill Farm
Prince's Coverts
WOODLANDS PARK
Pachesham Park
Clubhouse
Paddock Lodge Stables
Ashley Court
KT21
WOOD FIELD
Tyrwhitt House
Queen Elizabeth's Foundation Coll
Junction 9
M25
Rowhurst Forge
Queen Elizabeth's Foundation (Dev Cen)
TEAZLE WOOD
Clubhouse DRIVING RANGE
PACHESHAM PARK GOLF CENTRE
BALANCING PONDS
REGENT PARK
Leatherhead Common
Lower Ashtead
ASHTEAD REC GRD
Sewage Works
Filter Beds
Amenity Site
Pachesham Equestrian Centre
THE MOUNTS
Earthworks
BUSHY PLATT
SPRING POND
MOLE VALLEY PREDATORS FC
Gutter's Bridge
ERA TECHNOLOGY LTD
Barnettwood Farm
SPORTS FLD
KT22
Crematorium
RANDALLS PARK CEMETERY
PLOUGH IND EST
ALLOT
Junction 9
Cannon Grove Nursery
LEATHERHEAD
MOLE BUSINESS PARK
LEATHERHEAD TRADE PARK
SPORTS GROUND
Knoll Rbt
ASHTEAD HOSP
River Mole
MILL POND
Fire Sta
Leatherhead Bridge
Leatherhead FC
Leatherhead & Cobham C.C.
Thorncroft Manor
Leisure Centre
Water Works
Rifle Range
HOSP
Fetcham
Hawk's Hill
Downside Farm
Beaverbrook Roundabout
SHEPHERDS CLOSE
Bocketts Farm Park
Givons Grove Roundabout
OXSHOTT ROAD
KINGSTON ROAD
RANDALLS ROAD
LEATHERHEAD BYPASS RD
LEATHERHEAD ROAD
BYPASS ROAD
YOUNG STREET
GUILDFORD ROAD
DORKING ROAD
REIGATE ROAD
HEADLEY ROAD
A244
A243
A245
A246
B2122
B2033
B2450
237
254
269
CD
CE
CF
CG
CH
CJ
CK
15
16
17
56
57
58
59
116
117
118
119
120
121
122
123
124

EPSOM COMMON
NEWTON WOOD
FOREST
COMMON
WOOD FIELD
ASHTEAD
Ashtead Park
City of London Freemen's School
ASHTEAD HOSP
KT21
KT18
KT22
EPSOM
EPSOM GENERAL HOSP
Woodcote
RAC WOODCOTE PARK GOLF COURSE
Woodcote Park Country Club
HALFMOON CLUMP
WORLDS END
THE GROVE
The Durdans
LANGLEY BOTTOM WOOD
Langley Vale
THE WARREN
EPSOM & EWELL
MOLE VALLEY
ADDLESTEAD WOOD
LITTLE HURST WOOD
Tyrrell's Wood
TYRRELL'S WOOD
HAMBLETON WOOD
HEADLEY COURT
HOOK WOOD
GREAT HURST WOOD
PIGNUT WOOD
NOWER WOOD
OYSTER HILL NT
TYRRELL'S WOOD GOLF COURSE
COSTAL WOOD
Headley
Beaverbrook Roundabout
ExxonMobil House
Chase Farm Stud
Clubhouse
M25
A24
B2033
238
253
270
CL
CM
CN
CP
CQ
CR
CS
115
116
117
118
119
120
121
122
123
124
0 500 yds
0 500 m

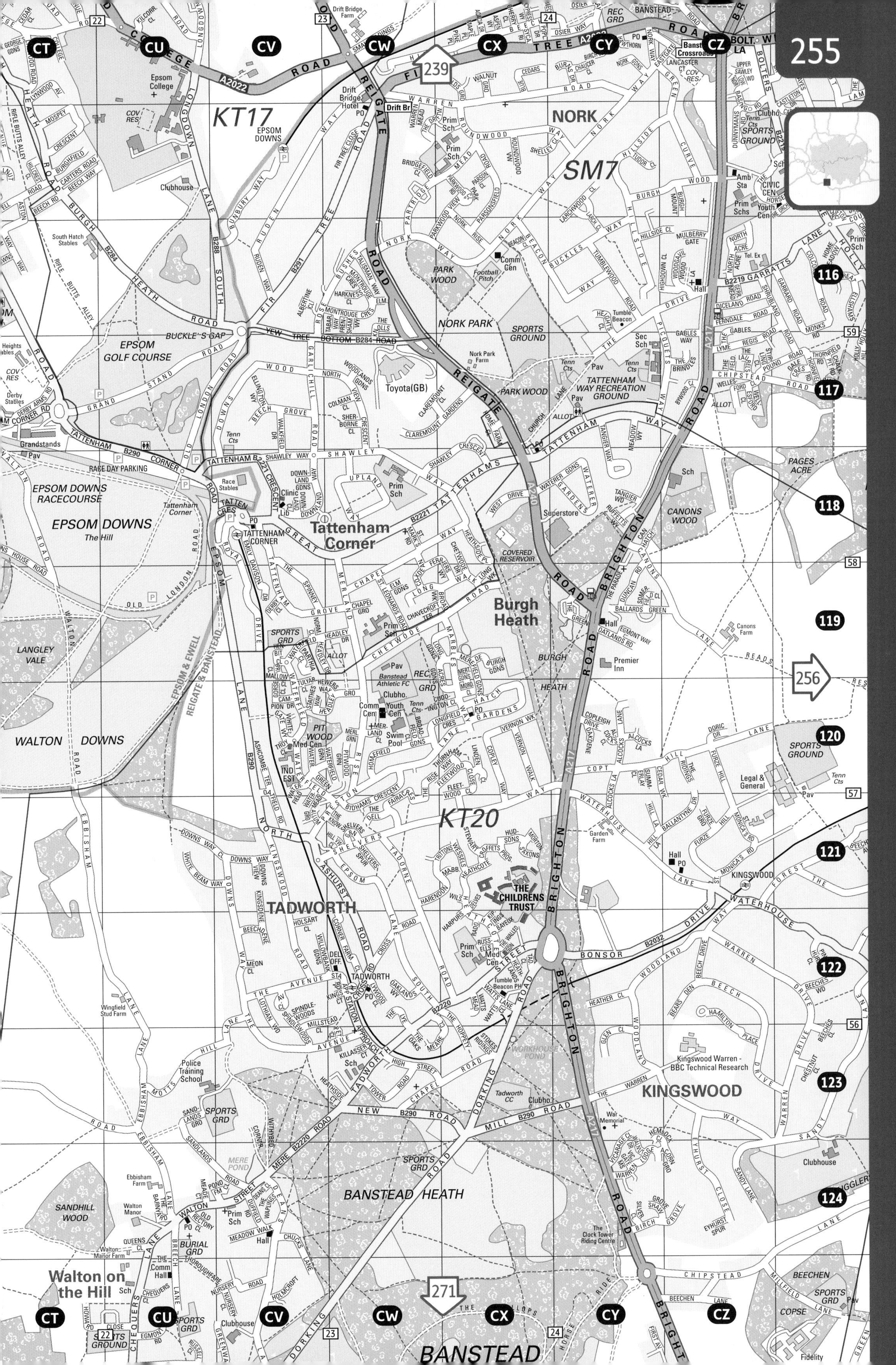
KT17
EPSOM DOWNS
NORK
SM7
Epsom College
EPSOM GOLF COURSE
BUCKLE'S GAP
PARK WOOD
NORK PARK
SPORTS GROUND
Toyota(GB)
Nork Park Farm
TATTENHAM WAY RECREATION GROUND
EPSOM DOWNS RACECOURSE
EPSOM DOWNS
The Hill
Tattenham Corner
Burgh Heath
BURGH HEATH
CANONS WOOD
PAGES ACRE
Canons Farm
Premier Inn
COVERED RESERVOIR
Superstore
LANGLEY VALE
WALTON DOWNS
KT20
THE CHILDRENS TRUST
TADWORTH
KINGSWOOD
Kingswood Warren - BBC Technical Research
Legal & General
Tadworth CC
BANSTEAD HEATH
SANDHILL WOOD
Walton on the Hill
Police Training School
Wingfield Stud Farm
Ebbisham Farm
Walton Manor
The Clock Tower Riding Centre
BEECHEN COPSE
BANSTEAD
Fidelity
239
256
271
116
117
118
119
120
121
122
123
124
CT
CU
CV
CW
CX
CY
CZ
22
23
24
56
57
58
59

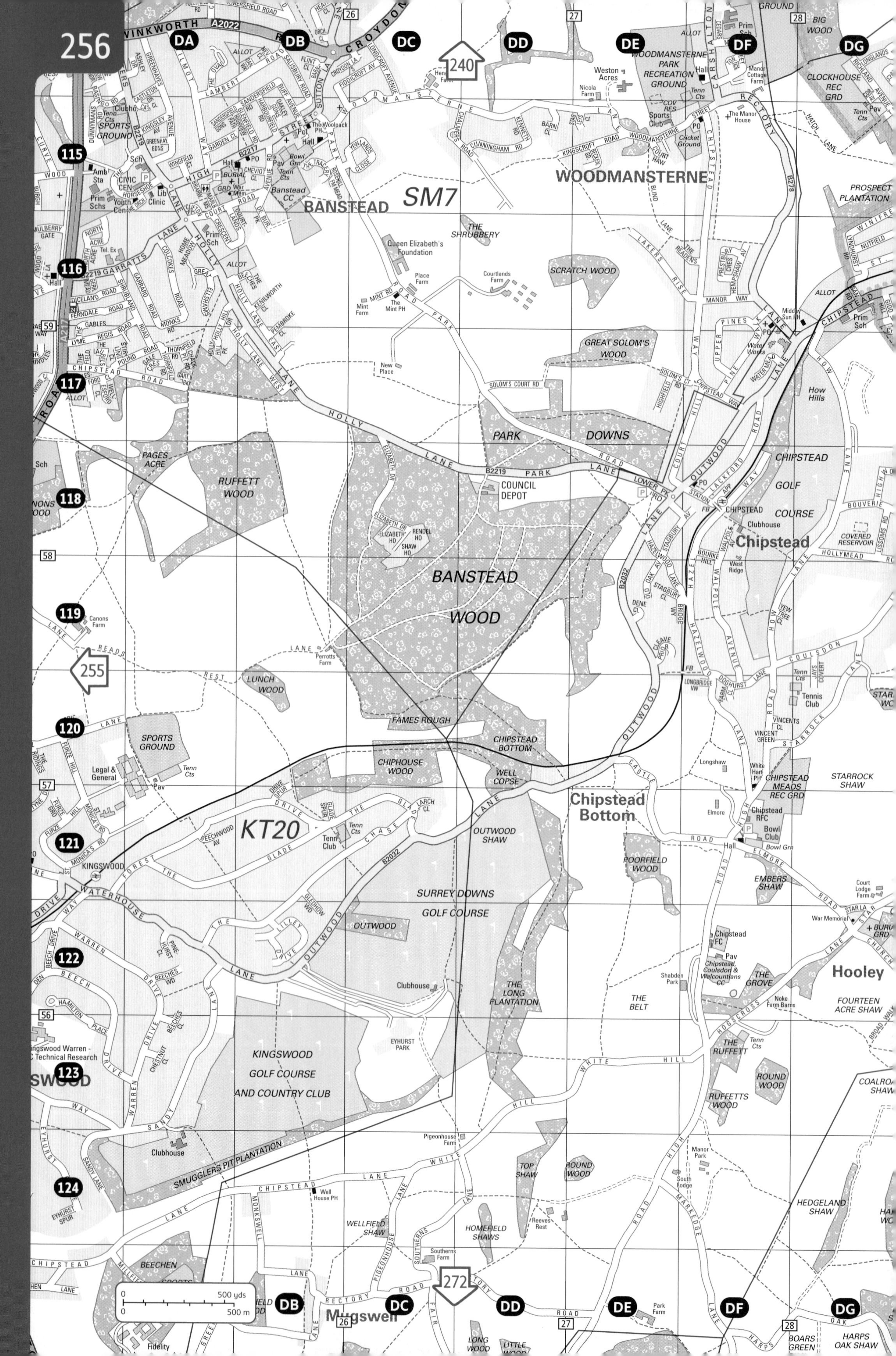

256
DA
DB
DC
DD
DE
DF
DG
240
255
272
26
27
28
59
58
57
56
115
116
117
118
119
120
121
122
123
124
WINKWORTH
A2022
CROYDON
BANSTEAD
SM7
WOODMANSTERNE
WOODMANSTERNE PARK RECREATION GROUND
CLOCKHOUSE REC GRD
BIG WOOD
PROSPECT PLANTATION
SPORTS GROUND
THE SHRUBBERY
Queen Elizabeth's Foundation
SCRATCH WOOD
GREAT SOLOM'S WOOD
PARK
DOWNS
PAGES ACRE
RUFFETT WOOD
COUNCIL DEPOT
BANSTEAD
WOOD
CHIPSTEAD GOLF COURSE
Chipstead
How Hills
COVERED RESERVOIR
LUNCH WOOD
FAMES ROUGH
CHIPSTEAD BOTTOM
CHIPHOUSE WOOD
WELL COPSE
Chipstead Bottom
STARROCK SHAW
CHIPSTEAD MEADS REC GRD
SPORTS GROUND
Legal & General
KT20
KINGSWOOD
OUTWOOD SHAW
SURREY DOWNS
GOLF COURSE
OUTWOOD
POORFIELD WOOD
EMBERS SHAW
Hooley
FOURTEEN ACRE SHAW
THE GROVE
THE BELT
THE LONG PLANTATION
THE RUFFETT
ROUND WOOD
RUFFETTS WOOD
KINGSWOOD GOLF COURSE AND COUNTRY CLUB
EYHURST PARK
SMUGGLERS PIT PLANTATION
TOP SHAW
ROUND WOOD
HEDGELAND SHAW
WELLFIELD SHAW
HOMEFIELD SHAWS
BEECHEN
Mugswell
HARPS OAK SHAW
BOARS GREEN
LONG WOOD
0 500 yds
0 500 m

WOODCOTE PARK GOLF COURSE
COULSDON
Old Coulsdon
KENLEY
CR8
CR5
CR3
RH1
COULSDON MANOR GOLF COURSE
HARTLEY BUSHES
FARTHING OR FAIRDEAN DOWNS
HAPPY VALLEY PARK
SURREY NATIONAL GOLF COURSE
Chaldon
ALDERSTEAD HEATH
THE GULLET
DEVILS DEN WOOD
BOXERS WOOD
NETHERNE WOOD
FIGGS WOOD
FURZEFIELD WOOD
FRYERN BROOM WOOD
WILLEY BROOM WOOD
BROAD WOOD
PILES WOOD
LORD'S WOOD
SPARTICLES WOOD
STONYFIELD SHAW
MARLFIELD SHAW
DUNSTAN'S WOOD
TWINERS WOOD
POSTERN WOOD
STAR SHAW
THREE CORNERED SHAW
PETERSHOLE SHAW
DITCHES SHAW
GRASSCUTS SHAW
CHURCH GREEN
COULSDON COMMON
GRANGE PARK
BETTS MEAD RECREATION GR
HIGHER DRIVE REC GRD
BROTHERS FIELD
Rook Hill
CROYDON
TANDRIDGE
SURREY
BRIGHTON ROAD
A23
A237
B2030
B2031
B276
Junction 7
Mersham Tunnel
241
258
273
DH
DJ
DK
DL
DM
DN
DP
116
117
118
119
120
121
122
123
124
29
30
31
56
57
58
59

DQ
DR
DS
DT
DU
DV
DW
242
257
274
RIDDLESDOWN WOOD
RAGGED WOOD
KINGS WOOD
AINSLEY BERRY SHAW
CR2
DISPLEY'S WOOD
CROYDON
TANDRIDGE
GODSTONE ROAD
KENLEY
CR8
BOURNE PARK
Gas Works
SURREY
PLAYING FIELDS
Hamsey Green
SPORTS GROUND
THE DOBBIN
TITHEPIT SHAW
WHYTELEAFE RECREATION GROUND
KENLEY COMMON
Whyteleafe
WHYTELEAFE
UPPER WARLINGHAM
BETTS MEAD RECREATION GROUND
Wattenden Arms PH
KENLEY AERODROME
Joysons Hill
BURIAL GROUND
COXES WOOD
BLIZE WOOD
Whyteleafe FC
WHYTELEAFE SOUTH
Ofcom (Spectrum Management Office)
RAF Mem
Surrey Hills Gliding Club
Travelodge
Coulsdon
CR5
RYDON'S WOOD
MANOR PARK
WINDMILL SHAW
SUBWAYS
COULSDON COMMON
Burntwood Hill
ROUND SHAW
Birchwood House Farm
Sports Centre
Stony Hill
BIRCH WOOD
Caterham-on-the-Hill
CATERHAM BYPASS
A22
CATERHAM
CR3
SURREY NATIONAL GOLF COURSE
Clubhouse
WESTWAY COMMON
COV RES
PARK SHAW
CATERHAM DENE HOSP
QUEEN'S PARK
SPORTS GRD
Fryern Farm
Tillingdown Farm
RUGBY GROUND
Rook Hill
MARIE CURIE CENTRE
THE NORTH DOWNS HOSP
CARR'S CROFT
0 500 yds
0 500 m
33
34
35
56
57
58
59
115
116
117
118
119
120
121
122
123
124

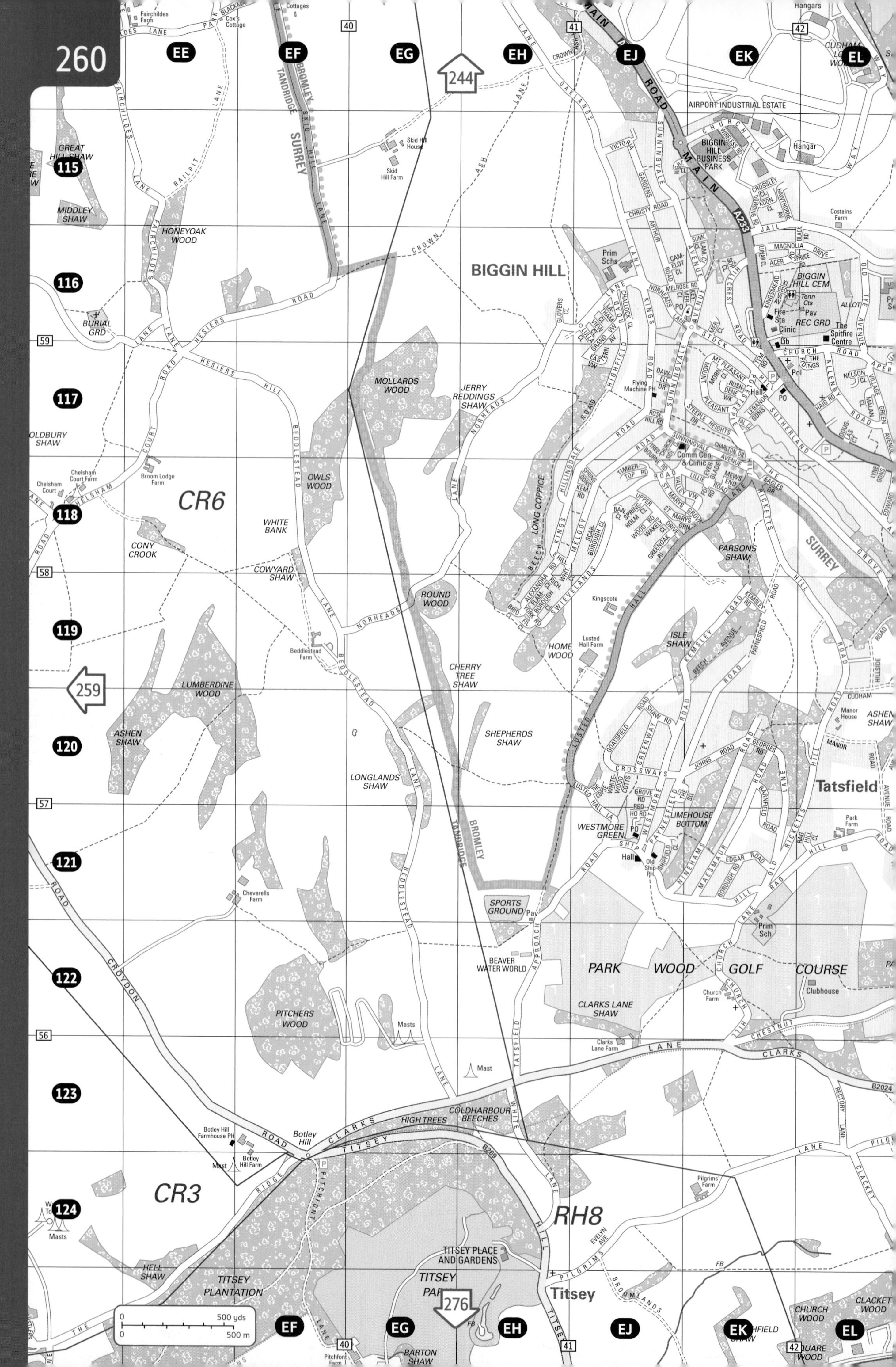
EE
EF
EG
EH
EJ
EK
EL
244
BROMLEY
TANDRIDGE
SURREY
SKID HILL LANE
Skid Hill House
Skid Hill Farm
Fairchildes Farm
Cox's Cottage
Cottages
FAIRCHILDES LANE
RAILPIT LANE
GREAT HILL SHAW
MIDDLEY SHAW
HONEYOAK WOOD
115
116
117
118
119
120
121
122
123
124
BURIAL GRD
HESIERS ROAD
HESIERS HILL
CROWN ROAD
CROWN ASH LANE
OAKLANDS
AIRPORT INDUSTRIAL ESTATE
BIGGIN HILL BUSINESS PARK
Hangars
Hangar
CUDHAM
MAIN ROAD
A233
BIGGIN HILL
Prim Schs
BIGGIN HILL CEM
Tenn Cts
Pav
REC GRD
Fire Sta
Clinic
Lib
Pol
The Spitfire Centre
Costains Farm
MOLLARDS WOOD
JERRY REDDINGS SHAW
NORHEADS LANE
Flying Machine PH
LONG COPPICE
Comm Cen & Clinic
OLDBURY SHAW
Chelsham Court Farm
Chelsham Court
Broom Lodge Farm
CHELSHAM COURT ROAD
CR6
OWLS WOOD
WHITE BANK
BEDDLESTEAD LANE
CONY CROOK
COWYARD SHAW
ROUND WOOD
PARSONS SHAW
Kingscote
Lusted Hall Farm
HOME WOOD
ISLE SHAW
LUSTED HALL LANE
Beddlestead Farm
259
LUMBERDINE WOOD
CHERRY TREE SHAW
CUDHAM
Manor House
ASHEN SHAW
ASHEN SHAW
SHEPHERDS SHAW
LONGLANDS SHAW
Tatsfield
WESTMORE GREEN
LIMEHOUSE BOTTOM
Park Farm
Old Ship PH
Hall
Cheverells Farm
SPORTS GROUND
Pav
BEAVER WATER WORLD
PARK WOOD GOLF COURSE
Prim Sch
Clubhouse
CLARKS LANE SHAW
Church Farm
Clarks Lane Farm
CROYDON ROAD
PITCHERS WOOD
Masts
Mast
CLARKS LANE
B2024
COLDHARBOUR BEECHES
HIGH TREES
Botley Hill
Botley Hill Farmhouse PH
Botley Hill Farm
TITSEY ROAD
B269
PITCHFONT LANE
CR3
RH8
Pilgrims Farm
WHITE LANE
TITSEY PLACE AND GARDENS
TITSEY PARK
276
HELL SHAW
TITSEY PLANTATION
Titsey
PILGRIMS LANE
BROOMLANDS
CHURCH WOOD
CLACKET WOOD
SQUARE WOOD
BARTON SHAW
Pitchfont Farm
500 yds
500 m
40
41
42
56
57
58
59

EM
EN
EP
EQ
ER
ES
ET
245
277
262
LADEN WOOD
SPENCERS GROVE
Luxted Farm
LUXTED ROAD
BR6
TWENTY ACRE SHAW
Church Hill Farm
CUDHAM ROAD
DOWNE ACTIVITY CENTRE
Clock Tower
BIRD HOUSE WOOD
BIRDHOUSE LANE
LEASONS WOOD
Open Air Pool
BROMLEY CROFT
Single Street
SINGLE STREET
STRAKES SHAW
Sports Centre
Chavic Park Farm Riding School
Prim Sch
The Old Jail PH
JAIL LANE
BERRY'S HILL
BERRY'S GREEN ROAD
Berry's Green
Homeleigh Farm
Brickyard Farm
Littlewood Farm
Aperfield
PIMLICO WOOD
Foal Farm
Clubhouse
CHERRY LODGE GOLF COURSE
Warren Farm
RESTAVON PARK
BLACKBUSH SHAW
Bottom Farm
CHURCH HILL
Cudham Court Farm
SPORTS GRD
Tenn Cts
Blacksmiths Arms PH
Angus Home
Cudham
LORD DARBY MS
Cacket's Farm
CACKETS LANE
Cacket's Cottages
Cottage Farm
Cudham Parish Hall
TN14
Parsonage Farm
Underhill Farm
Corkers Farm
Rosehaugh Farm
Maple Farm
SOUTH CUDHAM LANE
NEW BARN LANE
THE GROVE
Horns Green
Cedar Farm
The Manor
Thrift Farm
THRIFT LANE
Little Rosemary Farm
FOXBURROW WOOD
NEWYEARS WOOD
HOOK WOOD
NEW YEARS LANE
COPHALL WOOD
Shelleys
SHELLEYS LANE
Letts Green
BROOM WOOD
BASTON WOOD
LITTLE JOCKEYS WOOD
KNOCKHOLT WOOD
BURLINGS LANE
Beeches Farm
Mountross Farm
The Tally Ho PH
Hazlet Wood Farm
MAIN ROAD
STONEINGS LANE
116
117
118
119
120
121
122
123
124
59
58
57
56
43
44
45
MAIN ROAD
WINIFRED'S ROAD
LOTUS RD
CLARENCE ROAD
BELVEDERE ROAD
WOODBURY ROAD
Fox & Hounds PH
WITHINS WOOD
Stud Farm
A233
South Street
TN16
Great South Street Farm
Park Farm
Silverbeach Farm
Buckhurst Farm
OLD HARROW LANE
GRAY'S WOOD
SHELLEM WOOD
Southwood Farm
CUDHAM FRITH
BOMBERS LANE
Milena Stables
KENT
SOUTH
THE SEVENOAKS
BROMLEY
VIEWLANDS AV
NOWER
Brasted Hill Farm
THE NOWER
HOGTROUGH HILL
JOELAND'S WOOD
Hogtrough Hill
SILVERSTEAD LANE
GRAYS ROAD
Westerham Riding School
BUCKHURST
Hawley's Corner
The Spinning Wheel PH
Gray's Farm
TATSFIELD
PALACE ROAD
WESTERHAM
Westerham Heights Nurseries
BROOMCOCKS WOOD
NORTH DOWNS WAY
CHESTNUT AVENUE
Little Betsom's Farm
ROUND SHAW
Betsom's Hill
WHITELANDS SHAW
Ceme Easter
Pumping Sta
Tatsfield Court Farm
PILGRIMS WAY
HILL
LONDON ROAD
HOLYWELL SHAW
PARK WOOD
Gaysham
ROWTYE WOOD
Force Green
Force Green Farm
FORCE GREEN LANE
HARTLEY WOOD
M25
Charmans Farm
Park Farm
River Darent
WESTERHAM WOOD
BEGGARS LANE
CLACKET GREEN
ASH RD
ELM RD
HARTLEY ROAD
OAK RD
MADAN CL
A25
FB
Prim
CROYDON ROAD

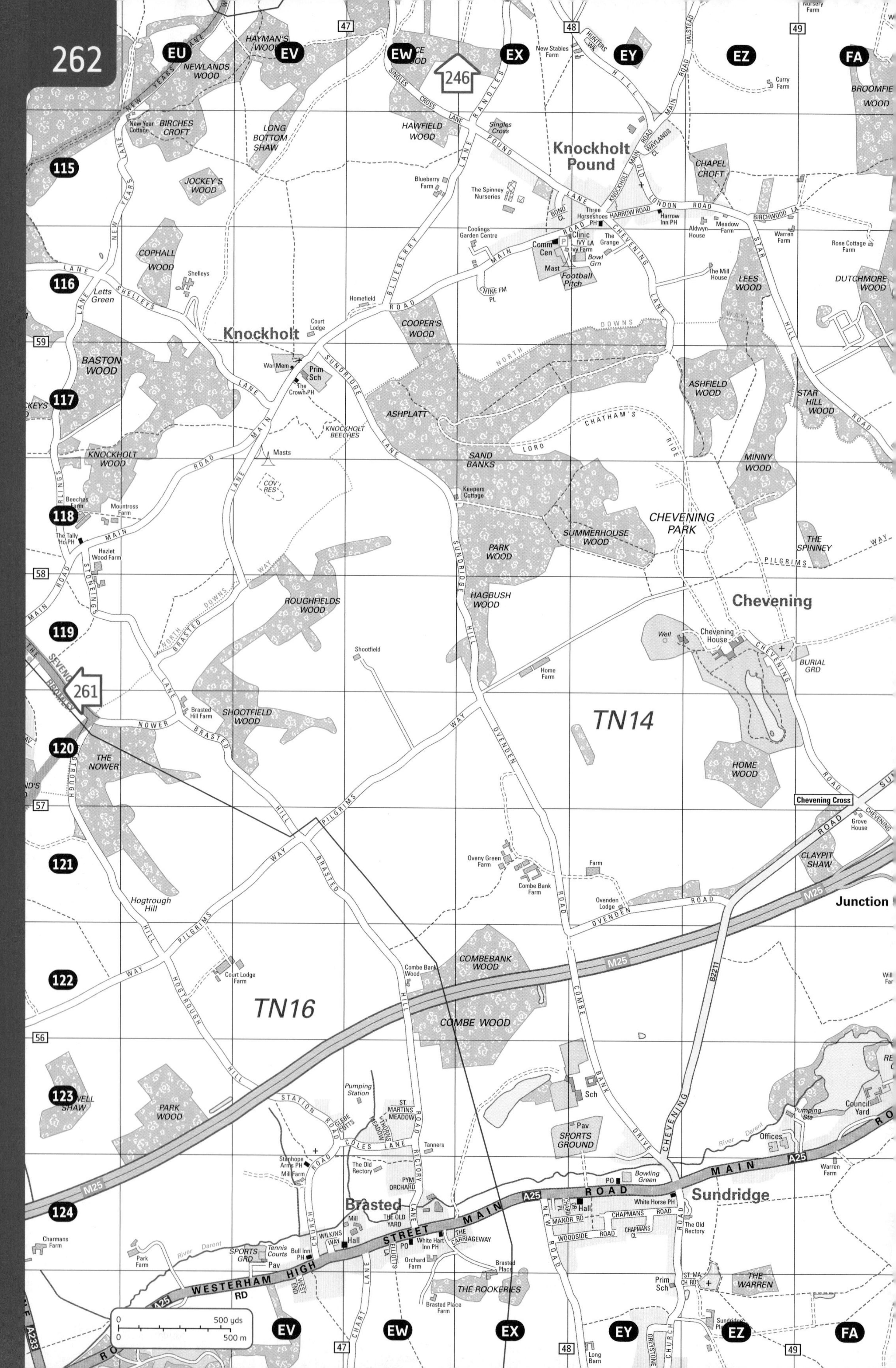

246
261
EU
EV
EW
EX
EY
EZ
FA
115
116
117
118
119
120
121
122
123
124
47
48
49
59
58
57
56
NEWLANDS WOOD
HAYMAN'S WOOD
NEW YEARS LANE
New Year Cottage
BIRCHES CROFT
LONG BOTTOM SHAW
SINGLES CROSS LANE
HAWFIELD WOOD
RANDLES LANE
Singles Cross
POUND LANE
New Stables Farm
HUNTERS WK
HILL
HALSTEAD ROAD
MAIN ROAD
WAYLANDS CL
Curry Farm
BROOMFIELD WOOD
Knockholt Pound
CHAPEL CROFT
JOCKEY'S WOOD
Blueberry Farm
The Spinney Nurseries
OLD
BOND CL
Three Horseshoes PH
HARROW ROAD
Harrow Inn PH
LONDON ROAD
Aldwyn House
Meadow Farm
BIRCHWOOD LA
Warren Farm
Rose Cottage Farm
COPHALL WOOD
Coolings Garden Centre
Clinic
IVY LA
Ivy Farm
Comm Cen
The Grange
Bowl Grn
Mast
Football Pitch
CHEVENING LANE
STAR HILL
LANE
Shelleys
Letts Green
SHELLEYS
BLUEBERRY LANE
MAIN ROAD
CHINE FM PL
The Mill House
LEES WOOD
DUTCHMORE WOOD
Homefield
Court Lodge
COOPER'S WOOD
NORTH DOWNS WAY
Knockholt
BASTON WOOD
War Mem
Prim Sch
The Crown PH
SUNDRIDGE LANE
ASHFIELD WOOD
STAR HILL WOOD
ASHPLATT
KNOCKHOLT BEECHES
CHATHAM'S
LORD
RIDE
KNOCKHOLT WOOD
Masts
SAND BANKS
MINNY WOOD
RILLINGS
COV RES
Keepers Cottage
Beeches Farm
Mountross Farm
CHEVENING PARK
The Tally Ho PH
SUMMERHOUSE WOOD
THE SPINNEY
Hazlet Wood Farm
PARK WOOD
PILGRIMS WAY
STONINGS
ROUGHFIELDS WOOD
HAGBUSH WOOD
SUNDRIDGE HILL
Chevening
BRASTED LANE
Well
Chevening House
Shootfield
BURIAL GRD
SEVENOAKS
Home Farm
Brasted Hill Farm
NOWER
SHOOTFIELD WOOD
TN14
OVENDEN
THE NOWER
HOME WOOD
STROUGH
Chevening Cross
CHEVENING ROAD
Grove House
CLAYPIT SHAW
Oveny Green Farm
Farm
Combe Bank Farm
Ovenden Lodge
OVENDEN ROAD
M25
Junction
Hogtrough Hill
HOGTROUGH HILL
Court Lodge Farm
Combe Bank Wood
COMBEBANK WOOD
B2211
TN16
COMBE WOOD
COMBE BANK DRIVE
PARK WOOD
STATION ROAD
Pumping Station
ST. MARTINS MEADOW
GLEBE COTTS
THORNS MEADOW
Sch
Pav
SPORTS GROUND
Pumping Sta
Council Yard
River Darent
Offices
A25
Tanners
COLES LANE
RECTORY LANE
Stanhope Arms PH
Mill Farm
The Old Rectory
PYM ORCHARD
Bowling Green
PO
Warren Farm
Brasted
Mill
THE OLD YARD
MAIN ROAD
White Horse PH
Sundridge
Hall
CHAPMANS ROAD
MANOR RD
NEW ROAD
The Old Rectory
WOODSIDE ROAD
CHAPMANS CL
Charmans Farm
WILKINS WAY
Hall
HIGH STREET
White Hart Inn PH
THE CARRIAGEWAY
Park Farm
SPORTS GRD
Tennis Courts
Bull Inn PH
Pav
ELLIOTTS LA
Orchard Farm
Brasted Place
WESTERHAM RD
WEST END
CHART LANE
THE ROOKERIES
Prim Sch
ST. MARY'S CH RD
THE WARREN
Brasted Place Farm
Sundridge Place
A233
0 500 yds
0 500 m
GREYSTONE
CHURCH
Long Barn

Otford
Twitton
Dunton Green
Longford
Chipstead
Riverhead
Bessels Green
TN14
TN13
SEVENOAKS WILDLIFE RESERVE
Sevenoaks
247
278
279

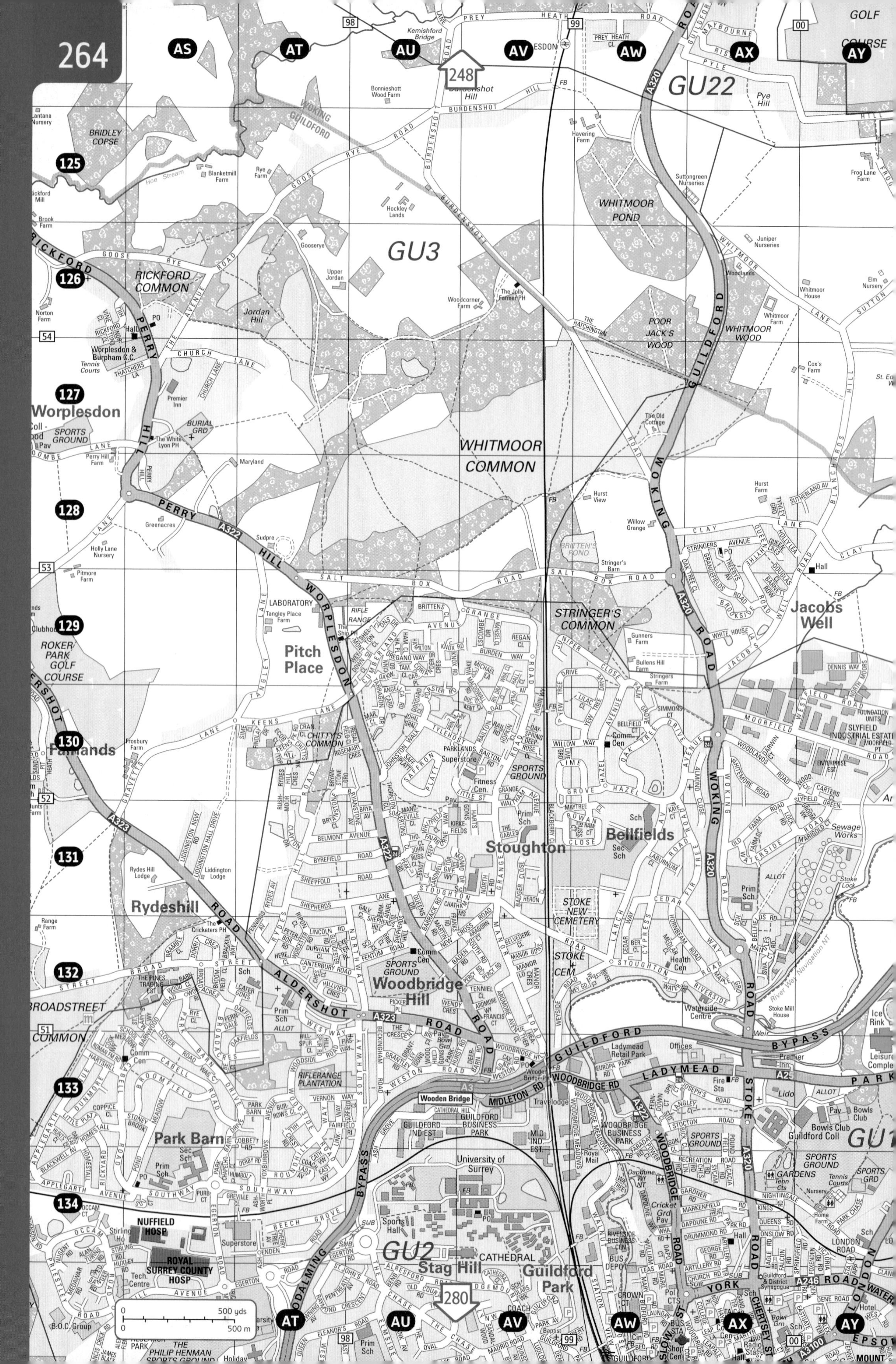
AS
AT
AU
AV
AW
AX
AY
248
280
GU22
GU3
GU2
GU1
125
126
127
128
129
130
131
132
133
134
Kemishford Bridge
Burdenshott Hill
Bonnieshott Wood Farm
BRIDLEY COPSE
Blanketmill Farm
Rye Farm
Hockley Lands
Gooserye
Upper Jordan
RICKFORD COMMON
Jordan Hill
Woodcorner Farm
The Jolly Farmer PH
Havering Farm
Suttongreen Nurseries
WHITMOOR POND
Pye Hill
Frog Lane Farm
Juniper Nurseries
Woodlands
Whitmoor House
Elm Nursery
POOR JACK'S WOOD
Whitmoor Farm
WHITMOOR WOOD
Cox's Farm
Norton Farm
Worplesdon & Burpham C.C.
Tennis Courts
Premier Inn
Worplesdon
SPORTS GROUND
BURIAL GRD
The White Lyon PH
Perry Hill Farm
Maryland
The Old Cottage
WHITMOOR COMMON
Hurst View
Hurst Farm
Willow Grange
Greenacres
Sudpre
Holly Lane Nursery
BRITTEN'S POND
Stringer's Barn
Pitmore Farm
LABORATORY
Tangley Place Farm
RIFLE RANGE
The Ship PH
ROKER PARK GOLF COURSE
Pitch Place
STRINGER'S COMMON
Gunners Farm
Bullens Hill Farm
Stringers Farm
Jacobs Well
SLYFIELD INDUSTRIAL ESTATE
CHITTY'S COMMON
Fairlands
Frosbury Farm
Parklands Superstore
Fitness Cen.
SPORTS GROUND
Prim Sch
Stoughton
Bellfields
Sec Sch
Sewage Works
Rydes Hill Lodge
Liddington Lodge
Rydeshill
The Cricketers PH
STOKE NEW CEMETERY
STOKE CEM
Health Cen
Range Farm
THE PINES TRADING EST
Woodbridge Hill
BROADSTREET COMMON
Comm Cen
Prim Sch
SPORTS GROUND
RIFLERANGE PLANTATION
Waterside Centre
Stoke Mill House
River Wey Navigation NT
Ladymead Retail Park
Offices
Premier Inn
Ice Rink
Leisure Complex
Wooden Bridge
GUILDFORD IND EST
GUILDFORD BUSINESS PARK
MID. IND. EST.
Travelodge
WOODBRIDGE BUSINESS PARK
Royal Mail
Fire Sta
Lido
Bowls Club
Guildford Coll
SPORTS GROUND
GARDENS
Park Barn
University of Surrey
Sports Hall
Cricket Grd
Dapdune Wf NT
RIVERSIDE BUSINESS CEN
BUS DEPOT
NUFFIELD HOSP
ROYAL SURREY COUNTY HOSP
Superstore
Tech. Centre
Stag Hill
CATHEDRAL
Guildford Park
CROWN CTS
BUS STA
Guildford & District Synagogue
B.O.C. Group
PHILIP HENMAN
GUILDFORD BYPASS
WOODBRIDGE ROAD
WOKING ROAD
GUILDFORD ROAD
ALDERSHOT ROAD
PERRY HILL
WORPLESDON ROAD
SALT BOX ROAD
STOKE ROAD
YORK ROAD
LONDON ROAD
LADYMEAD
A320
A322
A323
A3
A25
A246
A3100
500 yds
500 m

Send
Send Marsh
Sutton Green
GU23
Sendgrove
SUTTON PARK
BURPHAM COURT FARM PARK
FRITHYS WOOD
COTTS WOOD
GU4
Burpham
Abbotswood
Bushy Hill
Merrow
GUILDFORD GOLF COURSE
MERROW COMMON
CHALK PIT
SUTHERLAND MEMORIAL PARK
SPORTS GROUND
COPSE EDGE
HIGHCOTTS WOOD
LONDON ROAD
RIPLEY BYPASS
EPSOM ROAD
CLANDON ROAD
SEND BARNS LANE
CLAY LANE
NEW INN LANE
BOXGROVE ROAD
GUILDFORD ROAD
RIVER WEY NAVIGATION NT
249
266
281

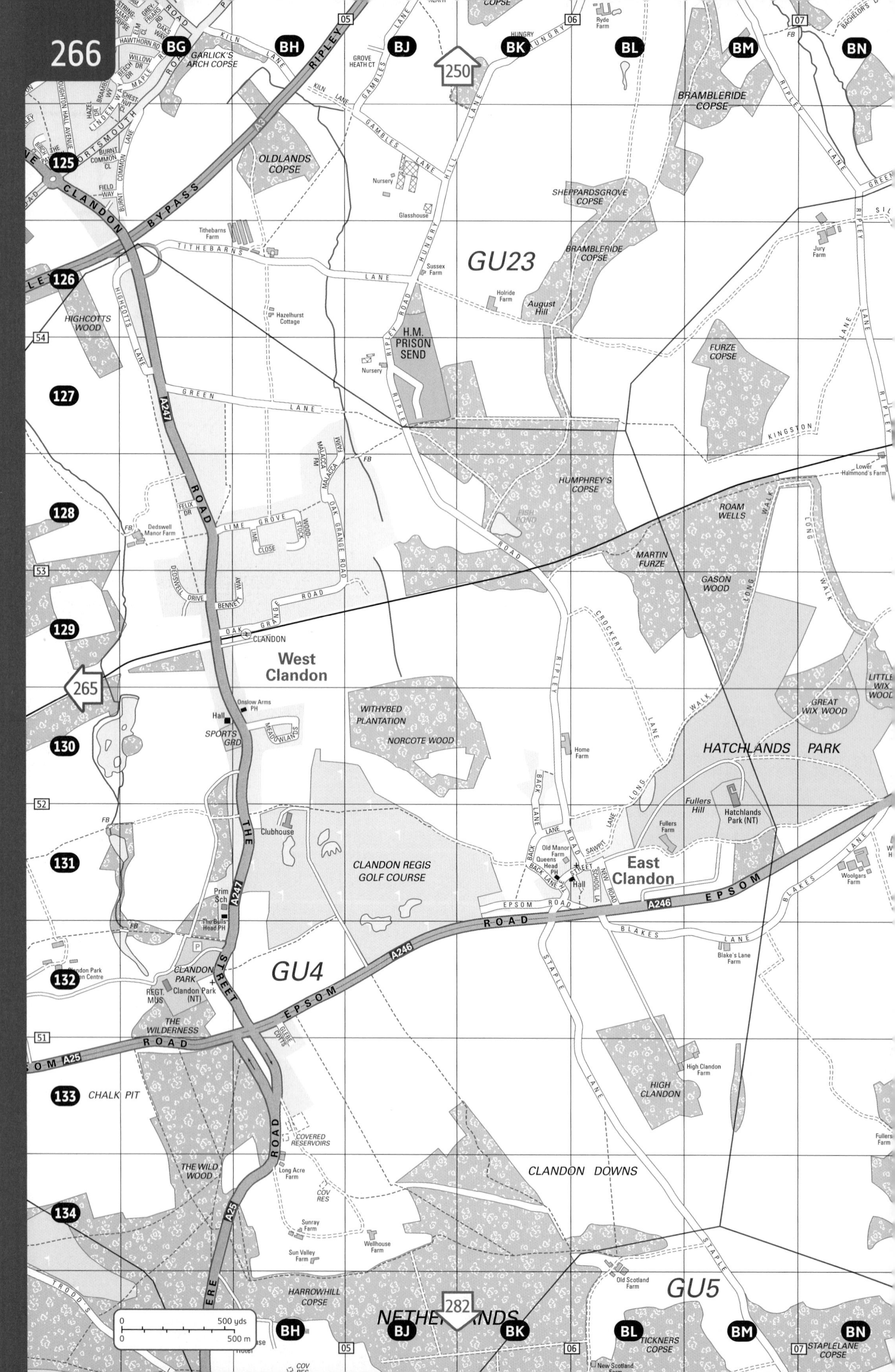
West Clandon
East Clandon
GU23
GU4
GU5
HATCHLANDS PARK
CLANDON REGIS GOLF COURSE
CLANDON DOWNS
H.M. PRISON SEND
OLDLANDS COPSE
BRAMBLERIDE COPSE
SHEPPARDSGROVE COPSE
HUMPHREY'S COPSE
FURZE COPSE
ROAM WELLS
MARTIN FURZE
GASON WOOD
GREAT WIX WOOD
WITHYBED PLANTATION
NORCOTE WOOD
HIGHCOTTS WOOD
HIGH CLANDON
THE WILD WOOD
HARROWHILL COPSE
TICKNERS COPSE
STAPLELANE COPSE
CLANDON PARK
THE WILDERNESS
CHALK PIT
CLANDON BYPASS
EPSOM ROAD
THE STREET
RIPLEY ROAD
HUNGRY HILL LANE
GAMBLES LANE
TITHEBARNS LANE
GREEN LANE
STAPLE LANE
BLAKES LANE
LONG WALK
KINGSTON
CROCKERY LANE
A247
A246
A25
A3
250
265
282
0 500 yds
0 500 m

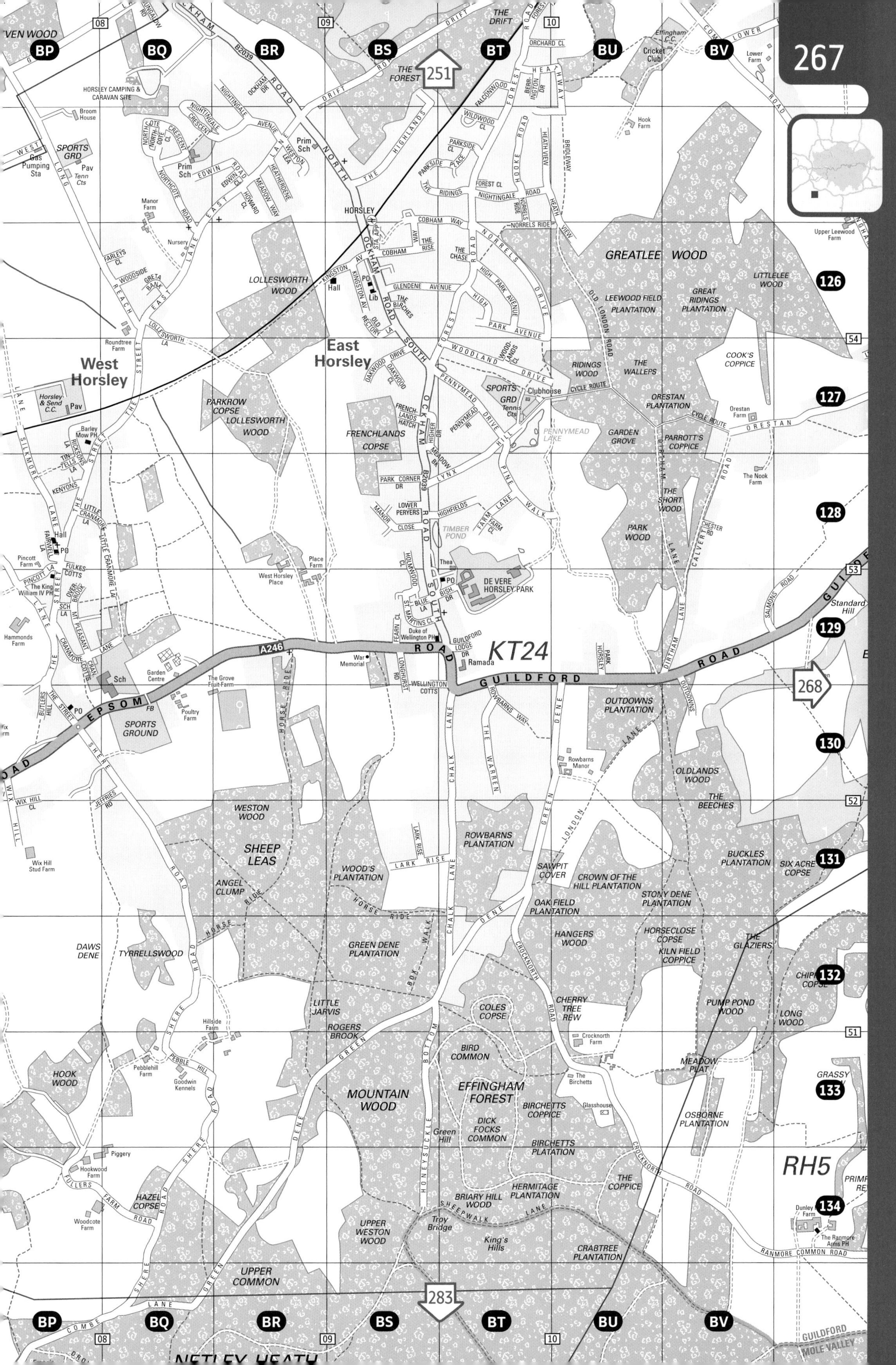

West Horsley
East Horsley
KT24
RH5
HORSLEY
LOLLESWORTH WOOD
PARKROW COPSE
FRENCHLANDS COPSE
GREATLEE WOOD
LITTLELEE WOOD
LEEWOOD FIELD PLANTATION
GREAT RIDINGS PLANTATION
COOK'S COPPICE
RIDINGS WOOD
THE WALLEPS
ORESTAN PLANTATION
GARDEN GROVE
PARROTT'S COPPICE
THE SHORT WOOD
PARK WOOD
DE VERE HORSLEY PARK
PENNYMEAD LAKE
TIMBER POND
OUTDOWNS PLANTATION
OLDLANDS WOOD
THE BEECHES
BUCKLES PLANTATION
SIX ACRE COPSE
WESTON WOOD
SHEEP LEAS
ANGEL CLUMP
WOOD'S PLANTATION
ROWBARNS PLANTATION
SAWPIT COVER
CROWN OF THE HILL PLANTATION
STONY DENE PLANTATION
OAK FIELD PLANTATION
HANGERS WOOD
HORSECLOSE COPSE
KILN FIELD COPPICE
THE GLAZIERS
DAWS DENE
TYRRELLSWOOD
GREEN DENE PLANTATION
LITTLE JARVIS
ROGERS BROOK
COLES COPSE
CHERRY TREE REW
PUMP POND WOOD
LONG WOOD
BIRD COMMON
MEADOW PLAT
HOOK WOOD
MOUNTAIN WOOD
EFFINGHAM FOREST
BIRCHETTS COPPICE
DICK FOCKS COMMON
BIRCHETTS PLATATION
OSBORNE PLANTATION
GRASSY
HAZEL COPSE
BRIARY HILL WOOD
HERMITAGE PLANTATION
THE COPPICE
UPPER WESTON WOOD
King's Hills
CRABTREE PLANTATION
UPPER COMMON
NETLEY HEATH
A246
B2039
EPSOM ROAD
GUILDFORD ROAD
OCKHAM ROAD NORTH
OCKHAM ROAD SOUTH
CHALK LANE
SHERE ROAD
CROCKNORTH ROAD
RANMORE COMMON ROAD
HONEYSUCKLE BOTTOM
GREEN DENE
THE STREET
LONG REACH
EAST LANE
OLD LONDON ROAD
DIRTHAM LANE
SHEEPWALK LANE
COMBE LANE
FULLERS FARM ROAD
ORESTAN LANE
CYCLE ROUTE
GUILDFORD
MOLE VALLEY
Effingham C.C.
Cricket Club
Hook Farm
Upper Leewood Farm
Orestan Farm
The Nook Farm
Standard Hill
Rowbarns Manor
Crocknorth Farm
The Birchetts
Glasshouse
Dunley Farm
The Ranmore Arms PH
Troy Bridge
Green Hill
Hillside Farm
Pebblehill Farm
Goodwin Kennels
Piggery
Hookwood Farm
Woodcote Farm
Wix Hill Stud Farm
Hammonds Farm
Pincott Farm
The King William IV PH
Barley Mow PH
Roundtree Farm
Manor Farm
Nursery
Broom House
HORSLEY CAMPING & CARAVAN SITE
Gas Pumping Sta
SPORTS GRD
Horsley & Send C.C.
West Horsley Place
Place Farm
Garden Centre
The Grove Fruit Farm
Poultry Farm
SPORTS GROUND
War Memorial
Duke of Wellington PH
Ramada
Clubhouse
BP BQ BR BS BT BU BV
08 09 10
54 53 52 51
126 127 128 129 130 131 132 133 134

251
268
283

Little Bookham
GREAT BOOKHAM
Effingham
KT24
KT23
EFFINGHAM GOLF COURSE
MOLE VALLEY
RANMORE COMMON NT
POLESDEN LACEY NT
THORNET WOOD
OAKEN WOOD
KING GEORGE V PLAYING FIELD
LEATHERHEAD ROAD
GUILDFORD ROAD
RANMORE COMMON ROAD
252
267
284
BW
BX
BY
BZ
CA
CB
CC
0 500 yds
0 500 m

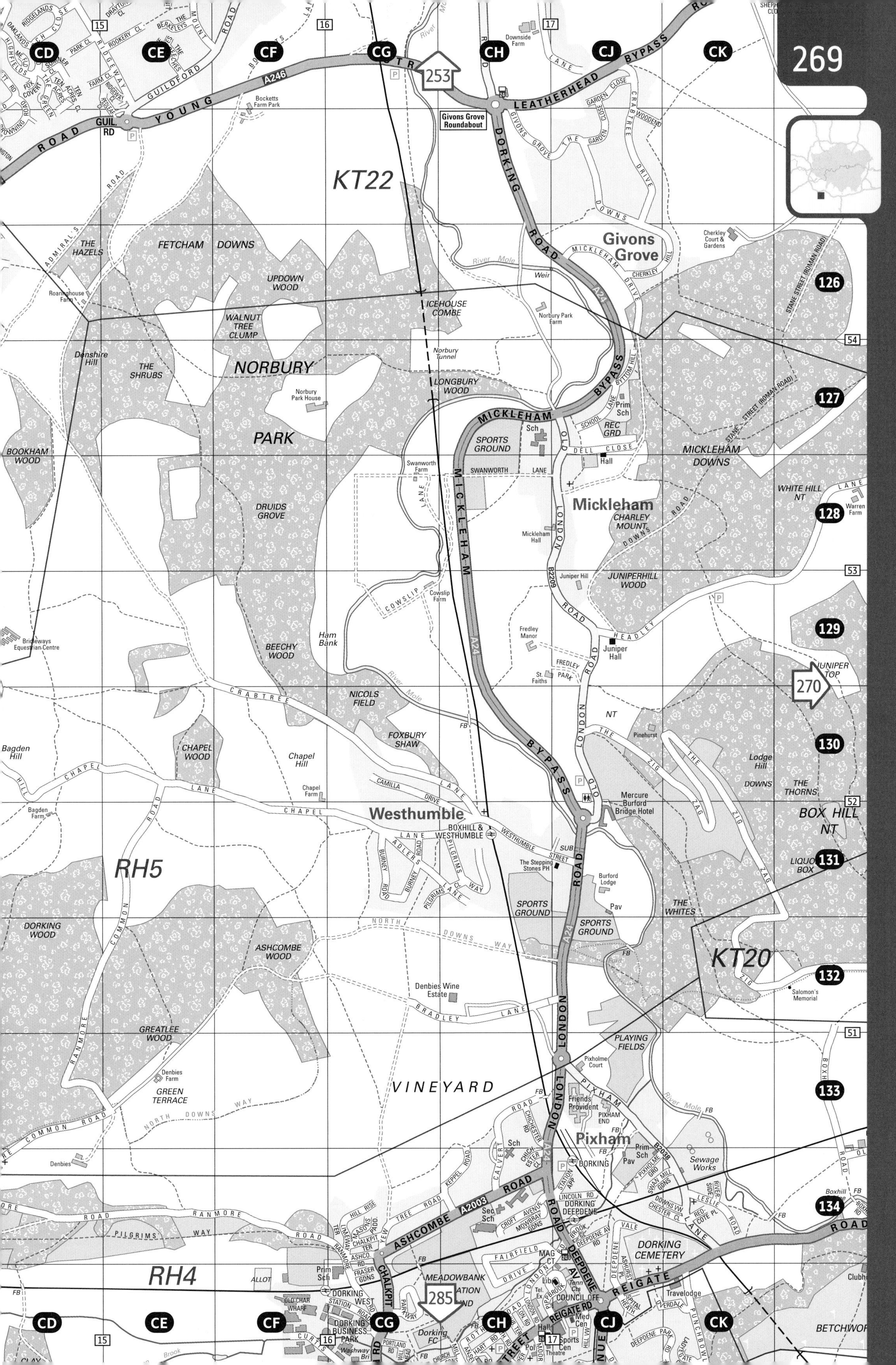
CD
CE
CF
CG
CH
CJ
CK
253
Givons Grove Roundabout
LEATHERHEAD BYPASS
GUILDFORD ROAD
YOUNG
A246
Bocketts Farm Park
Downside Farm
KT22
DORKING ROAD
Givons Grove
Cherkley Court & Gardens
126
FETCHAM DOWNS
THE HAZELS
UPDOWN WOOD
ICEHOUSE COMBE
Norbury Park Farm
Weir
River Mole
WALNUT TREE CLUMP
Denshire Hill
THE SHRUBS
NORBURY
PARK
Norbury Park House
Norbury Tunnel
LONGBURY WOOD
MICKLEHAM BYPASS
127
54
STANE STREET (ROMAN ROAD)
BOOKHAM WOOD
SPORTS GROUND
Swanworth Farm
SWANWORTH LANE
MICKLEHAM DOWNS
Mickleham
CHARLEY MOUNT
WHITE HILL NT
Warren Farm
128
DRUIDS GROVE
Mickleham Hall
Juniper Hill
JUNIPERHILL WOOD
53
COWSLIP
Cowslip Farm
Ham Bank
Fredley Manor
HEADLEY ROAD
Juniper Hall
129
Brideways Equestrian Centre
BEECHY WOOD
St. Faiths
JUNIPER TOP
270
CRABTREE
NICOLS FIELD
FOXBURY SHAW
NT
Pinehurst
130
Bagden Hill
CHAPEL WOOD
Chapel Hill
Lodge Hill
DOWNS
THE THORNS
THE ZIG ZAG
CHAPEL LANE
Chapel Farm
CAMILLA DRIVE
Westhumble
Mercure Burford Bridge Hotel
52
BOX HILL NT
Bagden Farm
BOXHILL & WESTHUMBLE
WESTHUMBLE STREET
RH5
The Stepping Stones PH
Burford Lodge
LIQUOR BOX
131
SPORTS GROUND
Pav
THE WHITES
DORKING WOOD
COMMON
NORTH DOWNS WAY
ASHCOMBE WOOD
KT20
132
Denbies Wine Estate
Salomon's Memorial
BRADLEY LANE
GREATLEE WOOD
PLAYING FIELDS
51
Pixholme Court
Denbies Farm
GREEN TERRACE
VINEYARD
Friends Provident
PIXHAM END
133
RANMORE COMMON ROAD
Pixham
Sewage Works
Denbies
DORKING
DORKING DEEPDENE
134
RANMORE ROAD
PILGRIMS' WAY
ASHCOMBE ROAD
A2003
DORKING CEMETERY
REIGATE ROAD
RH4
ALLOT
CHALKPIT
MEADOWBANK
285
DORKING WEST
DORKING BUSINESS PARK
Dorking FC
COUNCIL OFF
Travelodge
BETCHWORTH
15
16
17

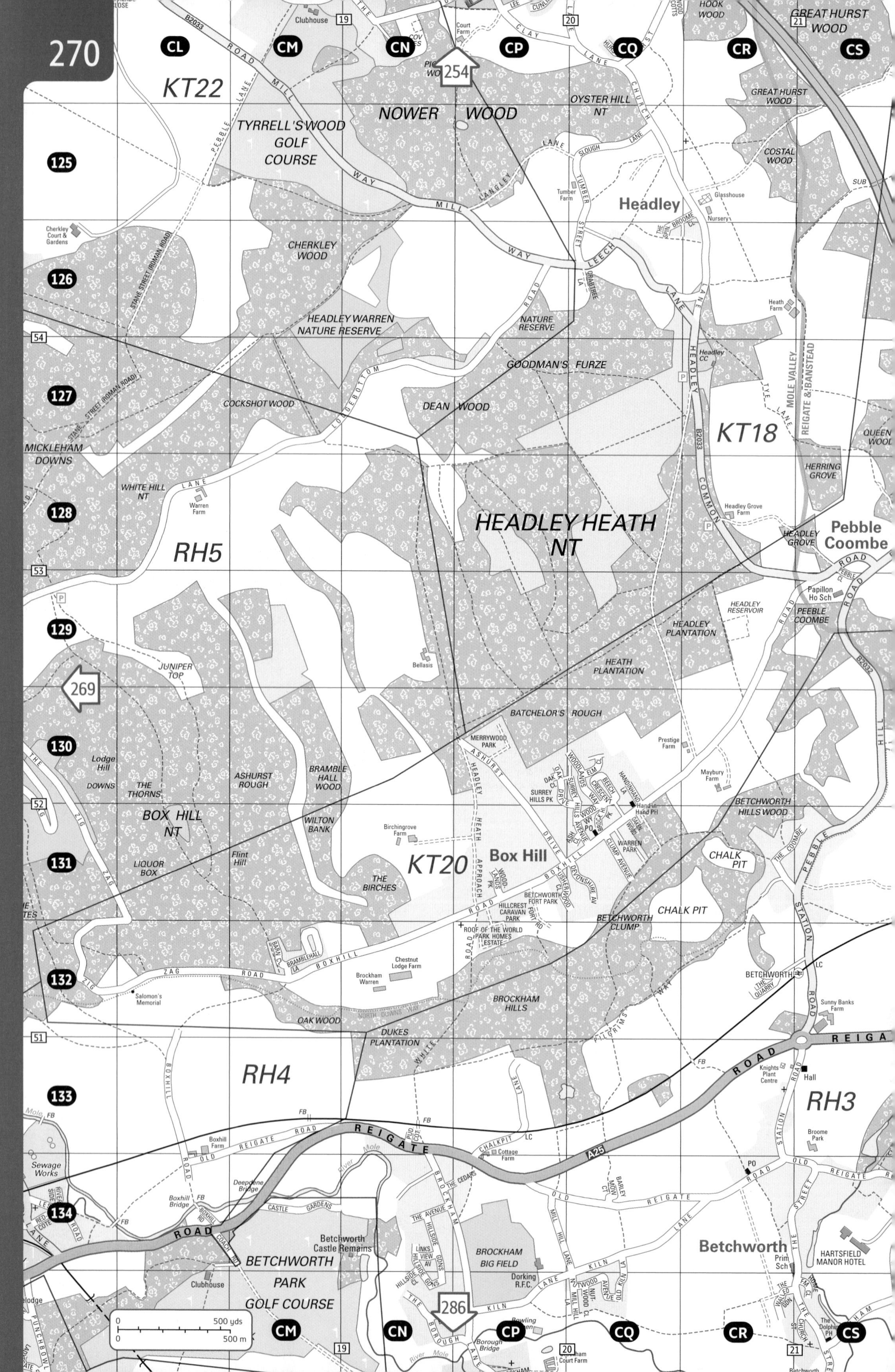

CL
CM
CN
CP
CQ
CR
CS
19
20
21
254
269
286
125
126
127
128
129
130
131
132
133
134
54
53
52
51
KT22
KT18
KT20
RH5
RH4
RH3
Clubhouse
Court Farm
HOOK WOOD
GREAT HURST WOOD
NOWER WOOD
OYSTER HILL NT
TYRRELL'S WOOD GOLF COURSE
Cherkley Court & Gardens
CHERKLEY WOOD
Headley
Glasshouse
Nursery
Tumber Farm
COSTAL WOOD
HEADLEY WARREN NATURE RESERVE
NATURE RESERVE
GOODMAN'S FURZE
Headley CC
Heath Farm
MOLE VALLEY
REIGATE & BANSTEAD
COCKSHOT WOOD
DEAN WOOD
MICKLEHAM DOWNS
WHITE HILL NT
Warren Farm
QUEEN WOOD
HERRING GROVE
HEADLEY HEATH NT
Headley Grove Farm
HEADLEY GROVE
Pebble Coombe
Papillon Ho Sch
HEADLEY RESERVOIR
PEEBLE COOMBE
HEADLEY PLANTATION
HEATH PLANTATION
JUNIPER TOP
Bellasis
BATCHELOR'S ROUGH
MERRYWOOD PARK
Prestige Farm
Maybury Farm
Lodge Hill
DOWNS
THE THORNS
ASHURST ROUGH
BRAMBLE HALL WOOD
BOX HILL NT
WILTON BANK
Birchingrove Farm
SURREY HILLS PK
Hand-in Hand PH
WARREN PARK
BETCHWORTH HILLS WOOD
CHALK PIT
Box Hill
LIQUOR BOX
Flint Hill
THE BIRCHES
HILLCREST CARAVAN PARK
BETCHWORTH FORT PARK
BETCHWORTH CLUMP
ROOF OF THE WORLD PARK HOMES ESTATE
Chestnut Lodge Farm
Brockham Warren
BROCKHAM HILLS
Salomon's Memorial
OAK WOOD
DUKES PLANTATION
NORTH DOWNS WAY
PILGRIMS WAY
BETCHWORTH
Sunny Banks Farm
Knights Plant Centre
Hall
Sewage Works
Boxhill Farm
Cottage Farm
Boxhill Bridge
Deepdene Bridge
River Mole
Broome Park
PO
Betchworth Castle Remains
BETCHWORTH PARK GOLF COURSE
Clubhouse
BROCKHAM BIG FIELD
Dorking R.F.C.
Betchworth
Prim Sch
HARTSFIELD MANOR HOTEL
Borough Bridge
Bowling Green
Brockham Court Farm
The Dolphin PH
B2033
B2032
A25
REIGATE ROAD
OLD REIGATE ROAD
ZIG ZAG ROAD
BOXHILL ROAD
HEADLEY COMMON ROAD
MILL WAY
LEECH LANE
CLAY LANE
CHURCH LANE
TUMBER STREET
LODGEBOTTOM ROAD
STANE STREET (ROMAN ROAD)
PEBBLE LANE
PEBBLE HILL
STATION ROAD
ASHURST DRIVE
HEADLEY HEATH APPROACH
CASTLE GARDENS
COACH RD
BROCKHAM LANE
KILN LANE
MILL HILL LANE
THE STREET
0
500 yds
500 m

Walton on the Hill
BANSTEAD HEATH
BANSTEAD
KT20
HEATH
WALTON HEATH GOLF COURSE
WALTON HEATH
CHUSSEX PLAIN
Lower Kingswood
Mogador
MARGERY WOOD NT
Buckland
RH2
REIGATE
REIGATE HEATH GOLF COURSE
REIGATE HEATH
DORKING ROAD
BRIGHTON ROAD
BUCKLAND ROAD
M25
A217
A25
B2220
B2032
Pfizer
LITTLE HEATH
ROUND WOOD
DEWRIDING PLANTATION
Lady Hill
Thistle Hill
Buckland Hills
Mount Hill
Conybury Hill
Juniper Hill
Colley Hill
THE HORSESHOE
THE SADDLE KNOB
QUEEN'S PARK
NORTHLAND SHAW
BUSHY SHAW
COLLEYLAND SHAW
BUSHFIELD COPPICE
COLLEY COPSE
COLLEY WOOD
SAND AND GRAVEL PIT
THE ALDERS
FOUR ACRE UPPER WOODS
THE BEECHES
NORTH DOWNS WAY
PILGRIMS WAY
255
272
287
126
127
128
129
130
131
132
133
134
22
23
24
51
52
53
54

DA
DB
DC
DD
DE
DF
DG
26
27
28
256
271
288
125
126
127
128
129
130
131
132
133
134
54
53
52
51
Clubhouse
Mugswell
CR5
KT20
RH2
Lower Kingswood
Upper Gatton
Margery
Gatton
Coles Meads
REIGATE
REDHILL
Reigate Hill Interchange
Junction 8
M25
A217
A242
A25
A23
B2034
BRIGHTON ROAD
REIGATE HILL
CROYDON ROAD
GATTON BOTTOM
RECTORY LANE
CHIPSTEAD LANE
MILLFIELD LANE
BABYLON LANE
BLACKHORSE LANE
MERSTHAM RD
LONDON ROAD
LONDON RD
HIGH STREET
CHURCH STREET
REIGATE ROAD
HATCHLANDS RD
STATION RD
PARK ROAD
BELL ST
CASTLEFIELD RD
NUTWOOD NT
REIGATE HILL NT
GATTON PARK
THE LAKE
TEMPLE WOOD
SERPENTINE WOOD
HIGH BEECHES
JUBILEE PLANTATIONS
UPPER GATTON WOOD
UPPER GATTON PARK
DELL WOOD
GATWICK WOOD
GRUB WOOD
MILLFIELD WOOD
COLTS BUSHES
LONG WOOD
LITTLE WOOD
FURZEFIELD COPSE
FURZEFIELD SHAW
HARPS OAK SHAW
BOARS GREEN SHAW
HEDGELAND SHAW
WELLFIELD SHAW
HOMEFIELD SHAWS
TOP SHAW
MAJORITY PLANTATION
THE CROSSWAYS
GROVE SHAW
GLEBE SHAW
GATLANDS SHAW
CATSBRAIN SHAW
CATSBRAIN EAST
GATTON FIELD SHAW
MANSHIPS SHAW
PARK SHAW
TOWER WOOD
GREAT BUCK WOOD
WINGATE HILL
HALFMOON CLUMP
THE BURPIT
GREENCLUMP HILL
TWO ACRE WOOD
BLACKHORSE WOOD
FOUR ACRE UPPER WOODS
THE BEECHES
QUEEN'S PARK
COVERED RESERVOIR
REC GRD
SPORTS GROUND
SPORTS GRD
BEECHEN COPSE
Fidelity Investments Int.
Ashtead Hill
Kingswood Hill
GATTON BOTTOM
REIGATE HILL GOLF COURSE
Driving Range
WRAY COMMON
REIGATE CEMETERY
PRIORY POND
PRIORY PARK
Site of Reigate Castle
Site of Priory
Reigate Coll
East Surrey Coll
East Surrey Hosp
HOP GARDEN POND
ENGINE POND
Highways Livery Stables
Orchard Cottage Riding Stables
Home Field Farm
Southerns Farm
Park Farm
Boars Green Farm
Crossways Farm
Whitehall Farm
Margery Farm
Margery Hall Stud
Kingswood Manor
Kingswood Hall
Reeves Rest
Manor Hotel
Surrey Fire & Rescue Service HQ
Johnston House
Bowls Club
TA Centre
0 500 yds
0 500 m

DH
DJ
DK
DL
DM
DN
DP
257
289
274
SPARTICLES WOOD
Airshafts
ALDERSTEAD HEATH
Chaldon
FRYERN BROOM WOOD
B2031
DEAN LANE
ROOK LANE
Rook Hill
Hall
Prim Sch
WILLEY BROOM WOOD
Clubhouse
SIX BROTHERS FIELD
CR3
BIRCHWOOD LANE
PILGRIMS LANE
Uplands Farm
Tollsworth Manor
Earthworks
Mersham Tunnel
Junction 7
LONDON ROAD
COVERED RESERVOIR
Alderstead Farm
THE SHRUBBERY
ALDERSTEAD HILL
BEECH ROAD
SHEPHERDS HILL
CHURCH HILL
LIME WORKS ROAD
JOLLIFFE RD
RIDGEBUSHES WOOD
Hilltop Farm
HILLTOP LANE
Masts
PILGRIMS LANE
NORTH DOWNS WAY
PILGRIM'S WAY
Willey Park Farm
NORTH DOWNS
Ockley Hill
M23
SUB
PILGRIMS' WAY
Junction 8 (M23), Junction 7 (M25)
OCKLEY WOOD
BEDLAMS BANK
White Hill
ROCKSHAW ROAD
SPRINGBOTTOM ROAD
HERONSWOOD MERE
WITHY SHAW
BOTTOM
A23
NORTH ROAD
FB
Hall
Merstham
MERSTHAM
Pav
Mersham CC
Home Farm
GATTON PARK
FURZEFIELD WOOD
WARWICK WOLD ROAD
PENDELL WOOD
BLACK BUSHES
M25
RADSTOCK ROAD
HUDDLESTON CRESCENT
CHESTERTON DR
Comm Cen
Prim Sch
MANSFIELD DRIVE
PORTLAND HOUSE
PORTLAND DR
NAILSWORTH CRES
DUNDREY CRES
DELABOLE ROAD
RADSTOCK WAY
BOLSOVER GRO
Prim Sch
SOUTH ROAD
HIGH ST
THE GROVE
BUSHETTS GRO
BLETCHINGLEY ROAD
AVENUE
OAKWOOD RD
Warwick Wold
REGENT CL
Health Cen
Lib
Pav
WORSTED GREEN
MANOR RD
ALBERT RD
ENDSLEIGH RD
PO
SUTTON GDNS
Sch
Darby House
Redhill Brook
Pav
Tennis Courts
Sch
MERSTHAM ROAD
THE CROSSWAYS
SOUTHCOTE RD
SPORTS GROUND
ALLOT
NUTFIELD
ALBURY ROAD
DEANS RD
South Merstham
DEVON ROAD
MELTON RD
BOURNE RD
SEWAGE WORKS
REIGATE & BANSTEAD
TANDRIDGE
Pendell Farm
WATER LANE
ROAD
QUARRYSIDE BUSINESS PARK
WYECLIFFE GDNS
CHILBERTON
TILERS CLOSE
MILL LANE
PENDELL CT
Sch
Pendell House
Brewer Street Farm
MERCERS PARK COUNTRY PARK
RH1
NUTFIELD MARSH ROAD
Ford Bridge
HOLMETHORPE IND EST
TROWERS WAY
HOLMETHORPE AVENUE
Lake Farm
NUTFIELD ROAD
Cricket Ground
Pav
CHILMEAD LANE
Inn on the Pond PH
MARSH
COCKLEY PLANTATION
SANDY LANE
Holmethorpe
Chilmead Farm
CORMONGERS LANE
PEYTON'S COTTAGES
Glebe House
Nursery
LITTLE COMMON LANE
Bletchingley
ALLOT
PUBLIC TIP
PARK WOOD
Nutfield Court
CHURCH HILL
LITTLE COMMON
Nutfield
BLETCHINGLEY ROAD
HIGH STREET
CASTLE STREET
Castle Hill
Hall
HUNTERS GATE
Capenor Nursery
Robert Denholm House
COOMBES COPPICE
STANLEY'S WOOD
NUTFIELD CEMETERY
ROAD
A25
FOX HOLE
HOLMESDALE PARK
NORTH PARK
Nutfield Priory Hotel
SPORTS GRD
Furze Hill
Castle Hill Farm
Nutfield Lodge
Stockers Hill
FULLERS WOOD LANE
Priory Farm Plant Centre
Priory Farm
STENERS HILL
NUTFIELD PRIORY LAKE
HOGTROUGH LANE
Bower Hill
SANDY LANE
KENTWYNS RISE
Kentwyns
Prim
REDSTONE CEMETERY
Sandhills Farm
29
30
31
51
52
53
54
126
127
128
129
130
131
132
133
134

CATERHAM
CR3
MARIE CURIE CENTRE
THE NORTH DOWNS HOSP
RUGBY GROUND
Clubhouse
SPORTS GRD
Sports Centre
OLDPARK SHAW
TEN ACRE SHAW
TUPWOOD SCRUBS
FOSTERDOWN WOOD
Fosterdown Fort
Gravelly Hill
Weather Station
EIGHT ACRE WOOD
White Hill
QUARRY HANGERS
SPRING BOTTOM
QUARRY WOOD
ROCKY SHAW
BLACK BUSHES
CONDUIT SHAW
PENDELL WOOD
M25
KITCHEN COPSE
Orpheus Centre
RH1
SAND PIT
ELM PLATT
Godstone
Godstone Interchange
GODSTONE HILL
BLETCHINGLEY ROAD
BLETCHINGLEY GOLF COURSE
Bletchingley
A25
HIGH STREET
CASTLE STREET
Castle Hill
STANLEY'S WOOD
HARLINGS SHAW
TILBURSTOWHILL PLANTATION
GRAVELHILL WOOD
ELEVEN ACRE SHAW
LONG SHAW
Tilburstow Hill
CROOKEDFIELD SHAW
Sandhills Farm
500 yds
500 m

DX
DY
DZ
EA
EB
EC
ED
259
276
RH8
OXTED
Tandridge
Church Town
NORTH DOWNS GOLF COURSE
GODSTONE GOLF COURSE
TANDRIDGE GOLF COURSE
LITTLE CHURCH WOOD
WHISTLERS WOOD
TEMPLEHILL PLANTATION
GREAT CHURCH WOOD NATURE RESERVE
MARDEN PARK
ROOKERY
STUBBS COPSE
SPORTS GROUND
THE RUMPS
WHITFIELD PLANTATION
HAZEL SHAW
HORSE SHAW
HANGING WOOD
SOUTH HAWKE
RYE SHAW
RYE WOOD
ROBINS GROVE WOOD
THE ABBEYS
LODGE WOOD
ARMITAGE WOOD
HAMFIELD SHAW
FIVE ACRE SHAW
CHALKPIT WOOD
CHALK PITS
OXTED QUARRY
CHALK PIT
BEECH PLANTATION NT
OXTED DOWNS NT
FLOWER WOOD
PALMERS WOOD OILFIELD
SAND PIT
THE MOUNT
THE BOGS
MASTER PARK
MOORE'S SHAW
GLEBE WATER
OLDPARK WOOD
CASTLEHILL WOOD
THE ENTERDENT
HOPGARDEN WOOD
DEAN SHAW
STOW COPPICE
MAIZENHALL SHAW
THE BIRCHES
NEW BUSTONS WOOD
BUSTONS WOOD
ROUND WOOD
STONEPIT SHAW
REDDINGS WOOD
SOUTHLANDS SHAWS
SOUTHLANDS WOOD
BUSHEY CROFT REC GRD
BROADHAM GREEN
Airshaft
Oxted Tunnel
M25
A22
A25
B2236
GODSTONE ROAD
OXTED ROAD
WEST HILL
GODSTONE BYPASS
EASTBOURNE ROAD
GANGERS HILL
TANDRIDGE HILL LANE
TANDRIDGE LANE
HOGTROUGH LANE
BARROW GREEN ROAD
SANDY LANE
CHALKPIT LANE
FLOWER LANE
CHURCH LANE
JACKASS LANE
SOUTHLANDS LANE
BROADHAM GREEN RD
GIBBS BROOK LANE
Tandridge Priory
Riding Centre
Barrow Green Court
Barrow Green Farm
Ridgeway Manor
Tandridge Hill Farm
Chaldens Farm
Flint Hall Farm
Rooks Nest
Flower Farm
Knights Garden Centre
Round Lodge
Little Court Farm
Tandridge Court
Tandridge Court Farm
Barley Mow PH
Tandridge Hall
Sewage Works
Filter Beds
Leigh Mill House
Leigh Place
The Glebe House
Southlands
Southlands Lodge
Rose Farm
Perrysfield Farm
Perrysfield
Stockett's Manor
Haycutter PH
Stonehall Farm
Oxted Place
Mill Barn
Newhouse Farm
Clubhouse
Masts
126
127
128
129
130
131
132
133
134
36
37
38
51
52
53
54

EE
EF
EG
EH
EJ
EK
EL
40
41
42
260
TITSEY PLACE AND GARDENS
TITSEY PARK
Titsey
CR3
HELL SHAW
TITSEY PLANTATION
OXTED DOWNS NT
PILGRIMS
ROUGHFIELD SHAW
CHURCH WOOD
CLACKET WOOD
SQUARE WOOD
Premier Inn
TITSEY WOOD
BARTON SHAW
Pitchfont Farm
Limpsfield Lodge Farm
Park Farm
M25
54
CHALKPIT WOOD
ASHEN COPPICE
Broomlands Farm
SAND PIT
SPORTS GROUND
GRUBSTREET SHAW
GRUBSTREET COPSE
Prim Schs
Tennis Courts
Sports Hall
Sec Sch
Limpsfield
RH8
53
MASTER PARK
OXTED
Swim Pool
Gas Holder
Health Cen
COUNCIL OFF
Fire Sta
Superstore
275
WESTERHAM ROAD
A25
EAST HILL
WEST HILL
LIMPSFIELD CHART
Pebble Hill
Court Langley
St. Michael's
ANDREWS WOOD
LIMPSFIELD COMMON
GOLF COURSE
Limpsfield Chart
Wildshaw
Swallowfield
WEST HEATH
Woodhurst Bridge
Limpsfield Tunnel
52
LITTLE HEATH NT
Chartfield House
Tenchley's Park
Mill Barn
Stonehall Farm
Stonehamme
THE ALDERS
TENCHLEY'S WOOD
Boulthurst Farm
HURST GREEN
Health Centre
Haycutter PH
Hurst Green
LOAMPIT WOOD
Whitegates Farm
51
Crabbett Wood
Crabbett Wood Farm
CRABBETT WOOD
Tenchleys Manor
RUNNING TRACK
REC GRD
Doghurst
ITCHINGWOOD COMMON
Perrysfield Farm
Perrysfield
Coltsford Mill
FAIRVIEW IND EST
Red Lane Farm
PARISHCROFT WOOD
Parishcroft Wood Farm
Stockett's Manor
Holland
Depot
Sewage Works
Filter Beds
POWDERDICK SHAW
The Diamond PH
Connerton Stables
Stockenden Farm
Rose Farm
Clubhouse
Oxted R.F.C.
Upper Gincox Farm
HONESLAND WOOD
COLLESTERS WOOD
MOLLSTONES WOOD
0 500 yds
0 500 m
125
126
127
128
129
130
131
132
133
134

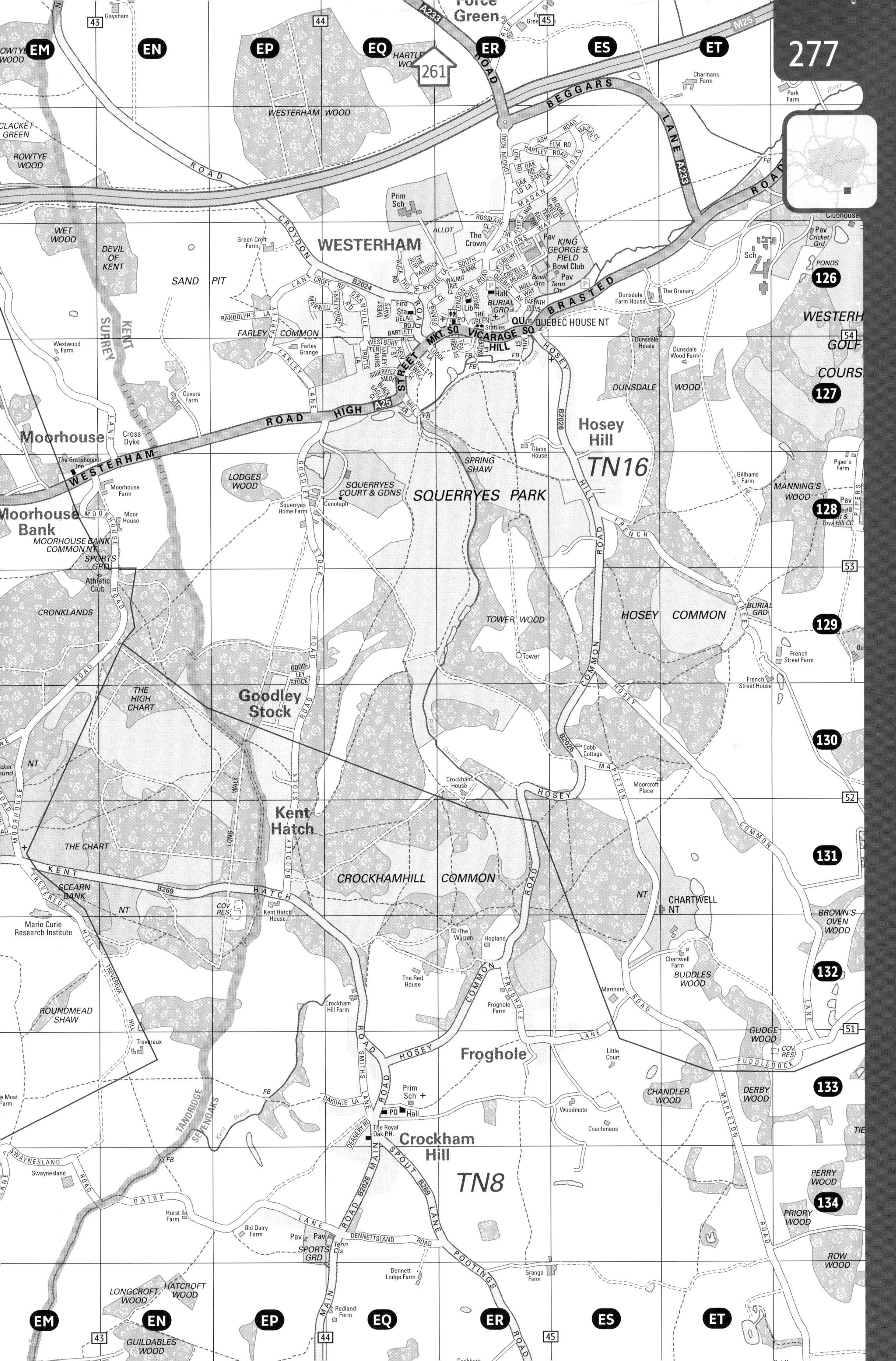

WESTERHAM
Hosey Hill
TN16
SQUERRYES PARK
Goodley Stock
Kent Hatch
CROCKHAMHILL COMMON
Froghole
Crockham Hill
TN8
Moorhouse
Moorhouse Bank
WESTERHAM WOOD
SURREY
KENT
TANDRIDGE
SEVENOAKS
HOSEY COMMON
TOWER WOOD
DUNSDALE WOOD
CHARTWELL NT
Marie Curie Research Institute
THE HIGH CHART
THE CHART
CRONKLANDS
ROUNDMEAD SHAW
BEGGARS LANE
WESTERHAM ROAD
CROYDON ROAD
HIGH STREET
QUEBEC HOUSE NT
SQUERRYES COURT & GDNS
M25
A233
A25
B2024
B2026
B269
261
126
127
128
129
130
131
132
133
134

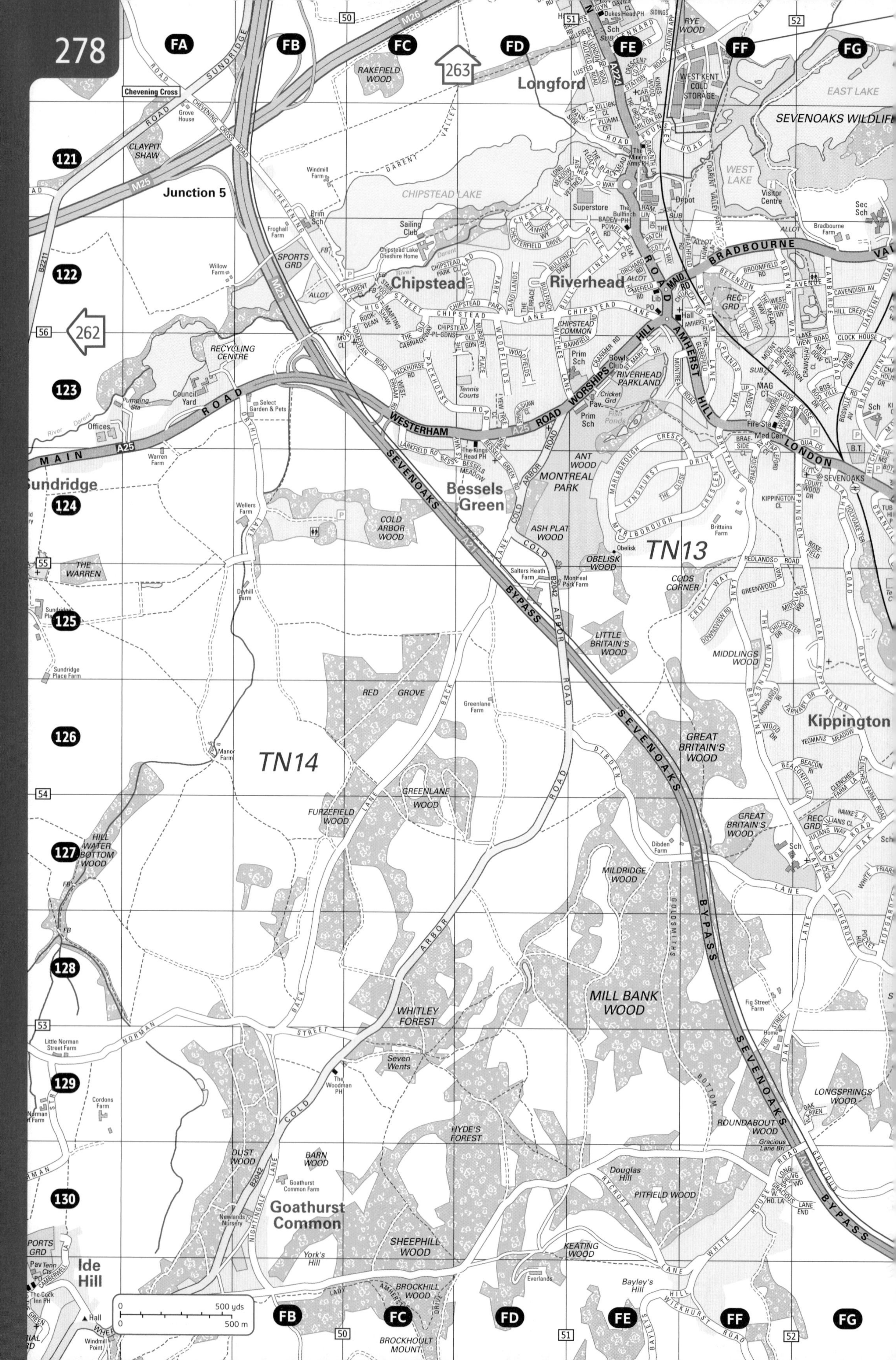
FA
FB
FC
FD
FE
FF
FG
263
262
Chevening Cross
Junction 5
Longford
Chipstead
Riverhead
Bessels Green
Sundridge
TN13
TN14
Kippington
Goathurst Common
Ide Hill
CHIPSTEAD LAKE
SEVENOAKS WILDLIFE
EAST LAKE
WEST LAKE
RAKEFIELD WOOD
CLAYPIT SHAW
RECYCLING CENTRE
COLD ARBOR WOOD
MONTREAL PARK
ASH PLAT WOOD
OBELISK WOOD
THE WARREN
RED GROVE
GREENLANE WOOD
FURZEFIELD WOOD
LITTLE BRITAIN'S WOOD
GREAT BRITAIN'S WOOD
MIDDLINGS WOOD
MILDRIDGE WOOD
MILL BANK WOOD
WHITLEY FOREST
HYDE'S FOREST
DUST WOOD
BARN WOOD
PITFIELD WOOD
SHEEPHILL WOOD
KEATING WOOD
BROCKHILL WOOD
BROCKHOULT MOUNT
LONGSPRINGS WOOD
ROUNDABOUT WOOD
HILL WATER BOTTOM WOOD
SEVENOAKS BYPASS
WESTERHAM ROAD
MAIN ROAD
COLD ARBOR ROAD
BACK LANE
NORMAN STREET
121
122
123
124
125
126
127
128
129
130
50
51
52
53
54
55
56
0 500 yds
0 500 m

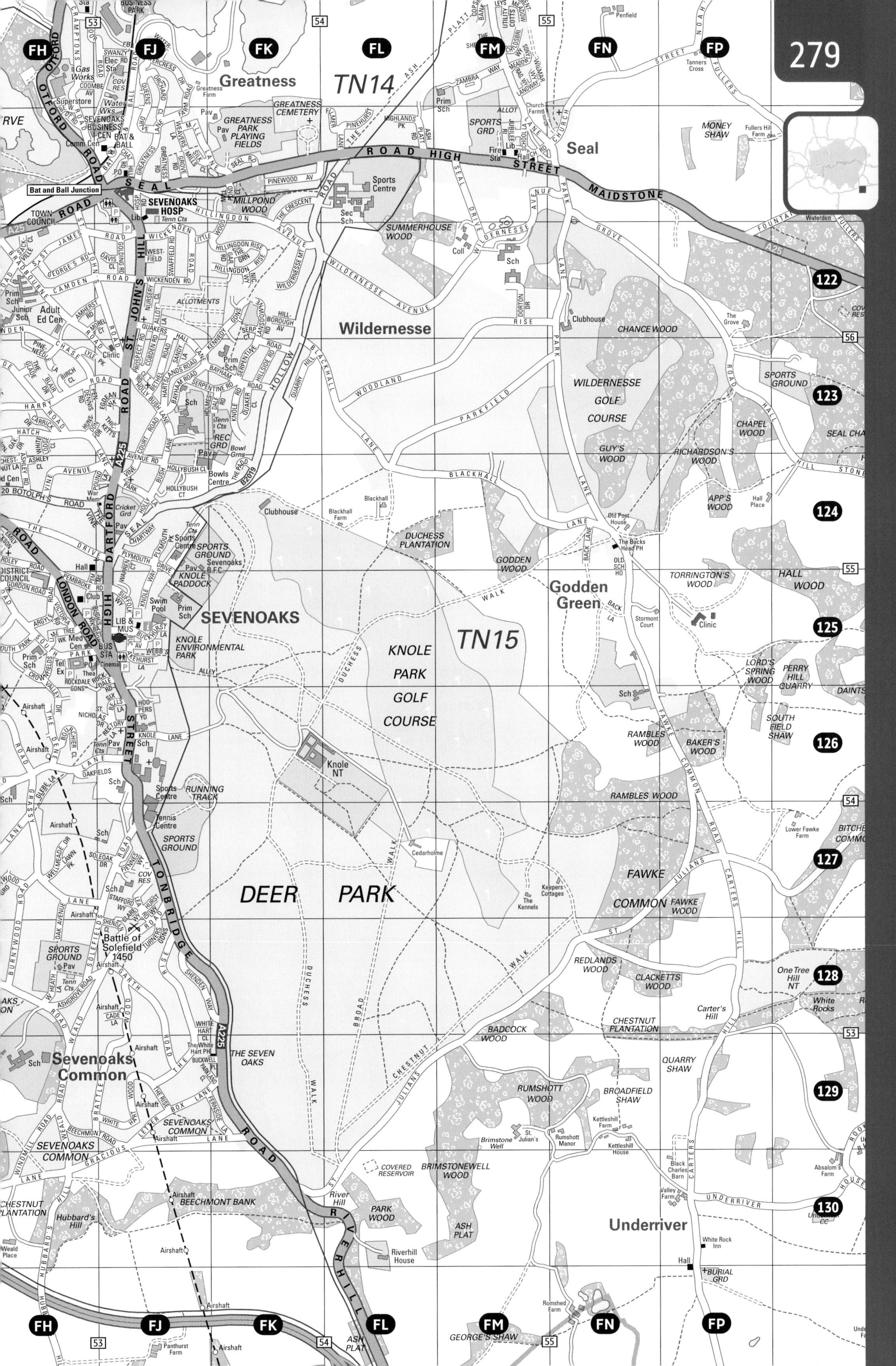

264
GU2
Stag Hill
CATHEDRAL
Guildford Park
NUFFIELD HOSP
ROYAL SURREY COUNTY HOSP
University of Surrey
SURREY RESEARCH PARK
THE PHILIP HENMAN SPORTS GROUND
Onslow Arboretum
Onslow Village
GUILDFORD
GUILDFORD CEMETERY
Charlottevil
MOUNT ALVERNIA HOSP
CASTLE
SUNNYDOWN PLANTATION
MANOR COPSE
PICCARD'S ROUGH
St. Catherine's Chapel
The College of Law
Artington
SURREY POLICE H.Q.
SHALFORD PARK
WEST WARREN
EAST WARREN
Littleton
GU3
LOSELEY PARK
LOSELEY HOUSE
RUSH CROFT
ASHEN COPSE
PIPKIN COPSE
PUDDOCK COPSE
THE GROVE
OLD CLAYPITS WOOD
QUADRUM INDUSTRIAL PARK
SHALFORD
PEAS MARSH
Peasmarsh
TRUNLEY HEATH
GOSDEN COMMON
Binscombe
GU7
BROADWATER PARK GOLF COURSE
FARNCOMBE
BRAMLEY GOLF COURSE
RIFLE RANGE
CENTAUR PLACE TRAINING COURSE
A3
A31
A3100
A281
A248
A246
B3000
PORTSMOUTH ROAD
GUILDFORD ROAD
BROADFORD ROAD
HORSHAM ROAD
THE STREET
HOG'S BACK
NORTH DOWNS WAY
PILGRIMS WAY
AS
AT
AU
AV
AW
AX
AY
98
99
00
49
48
47
46
135
136
137
138
139
140
141
142
143
144
0
500 yds
500 m

AZ
BA
BB
BC
BD
BE
BF
01
02
03
265
282
EPSOM ROAD
GUILDFORD GOLF COURSE
Clubhouse
MERROW DOWNS
WALNUT TREE BOTTOM
HAREWARREN
THE ROUGHS
Newlands Corner
Visitor Centre
136
137
138
139
140
141
142
143
144
49
48
47
46
ALBURY DOWNS
SPORTS GROUND
Pav
DOWNSIDE ROAD
WARREN ROAD
LITTLE WARREN CL
Warren Farm
Burwood Farm
GU1
ALLOT
PEWLEY DOWN
WHITE LANE
LONGDOWN
COV RES
HALFPENNY LANE
White Lane Farm
GU5
Newbarn
PILGRIMS WAY
GUILDFORD LANE
Tyting Farm
Whinney Hill
South Warren Farm
FARTHING COPSE
CHANTRIES
HALFPENNY COPSE
St. Martha's Priory Lodge
St. Martha's Hill
NORTH DOWNS WAY
Great Halfpenny Farm
GU4
Old Great Halfpenny
LIDWELL COPSE
Tilling Bourne
POSTFORD POND
MILL LA
Chilworth Manor
Little Halfpenny Farm
SHALFORD ROAD
Manor Farm
MUD WOOD
BLACKSMITH LANE
Lockner Farm
War Memorial
DORKING ROAD
A248
CUCKOO COPSE
Chilworth
CHILWORTH
Prim Sch
FISH POND
Tangley Mere
SPORTS GROUND
BRADSTONE BROOK SPORTS GROUND
SHALFORD COMMON
LOCKNER HOLT
Glasshouse
Chilworth Hill
Tangley Hill
FRANCISCAN FRIARY
NATIONAL TRUST
ROSEMARY HILL
Hornhatch Farm
RICES CORNER
Great Tangley Manor House
Great Tangley Manor Farm
WONERSH COMMON
Lower Chinthurst Farm
Blackheath
The Villagers PH
Blackheath C.C.
BLACKHEATH LANE
LITTLEFORD LANE
Hall
Derry's Hill
DERRY'S WOOD
HEATHFIELDS
Chinthurst Farm
Southlands Equestrian Centre
Tower
Chinthurst Hill
CEM
GU5
BARNETT HILL CONFERENCE CENTRE
ST. MARY'S DERRYWOOD
NORTHBROOK HILL
Hallam's Farm
St. Catherine's Schs
The Grantley Arms PH
Wonersh
Wonersh Court
Wonersh House
St. John's Seminary
B2128
B2129
Bramley
Northcote Farm
Holmcroft Nursery
GREEN LANE
MILL LANE
A281

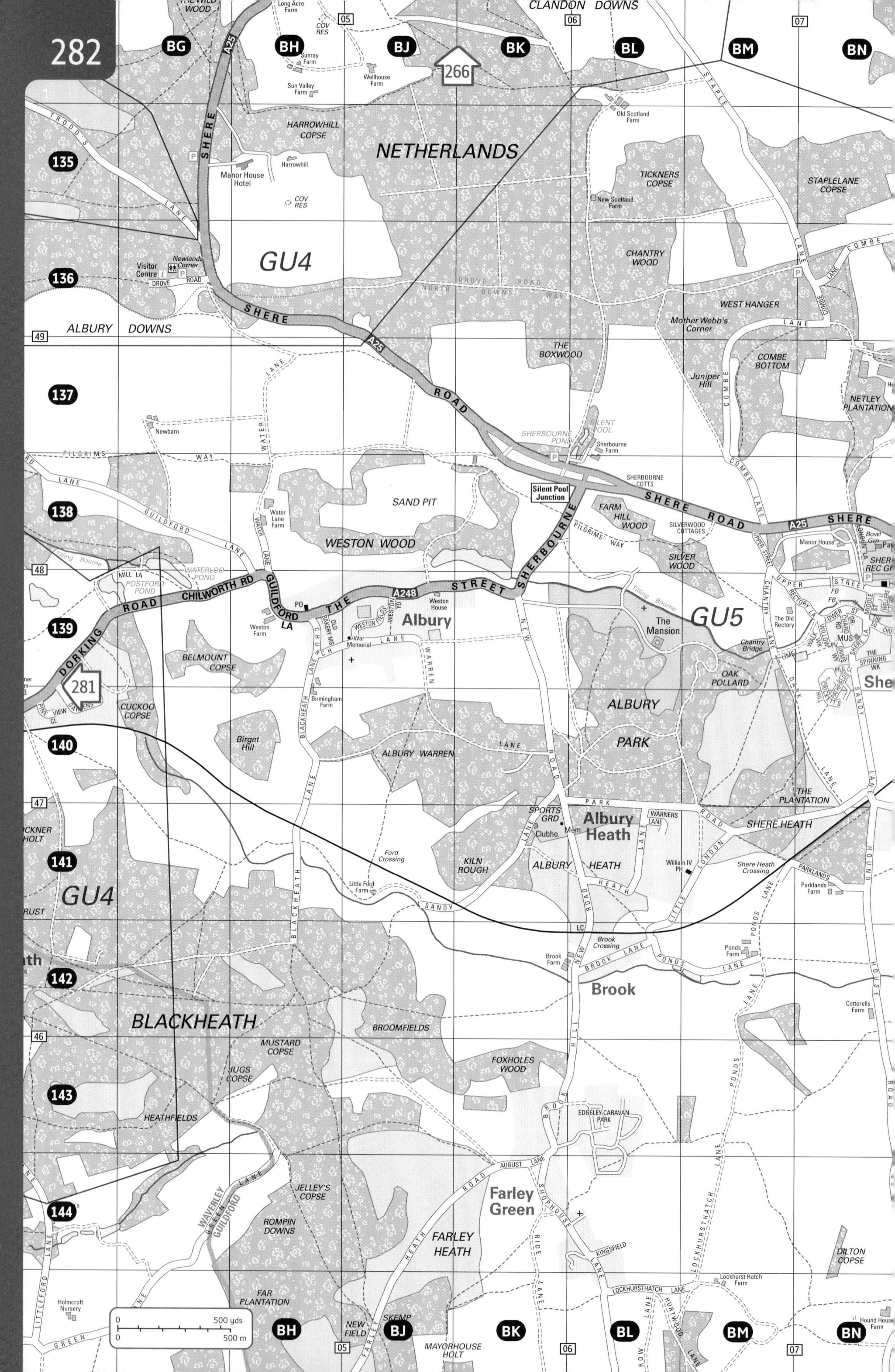
CLANDON DOWNS
NETHERLANDS
GU4
ALBURY DOWNS
Manor House Hotel
Newlands Corner
Visitor Centre
HARROWHILL COPSE
TICKNERS COPSE
STAPLELANE COPSE
CHANTRY WOOD
WEST HANGER
Mother Webb's Corner
COMBE BOTTOM
NETLEY PLANTATION
THE BOXWOOD
Juniper Hill
Sherbourne Farm
SHERBOURNE POND
SILENT POOL
Silent Pool Junction
SAND PIT
WESTON WOOD
FARM HILL WOOD
SILVER WOOD
SILVERWOOD COTTAGES
SHERBOURNE COTTS
Newbarn
Water Lane Farm
Albury
Weston House
Weston Farm
War Memorial
The Mansion
GU5
Chantry Bridge
OAK POLLARD
ALBURY PARK
The Old Rectory
BELMOUNT COPSE
CUCKOO COPSE
Birget Hill
Birmingham Farm
ALBURY WARREN
THE PLANTATION
SHERE HEATH
Albury Heath
ALBURY HEATH
KILN ROUGH
William IV PH
Shere Heath Crossing
Parklands Farm
Ford Crossing
Little Ford Farm
Brook Crossing
Brook Farm
Brook
Ponds Farm
Cotterells Farm
BLACKHEATH
BROOMFIELDS
MUSTARD COPSE
JUGS COPSE
FOXHOLES WOOD
HEATHFIELDS
EDGELEY CARAVAN PARK
JELLEY'S COPSE
ROMPIN DOWNS
Farley Green
FARLEY HEATH
DILTON COPSE
Lockhurst Hatch Farm
FAR PLANTATION
Holmcroft Nursery
NEW FIELD
MAYORHOUSE HOLT
Hound House Farm
GU4
SHERE ROAD
A25
A248
THE STREET
CHILWORTH RD
DORKING ROAD
GUILDFORD LA
NEW ROAD
PARK ROAD
LITTLE LONDON
SANDY LANE
BROOK LANE
PONDS LANE
LOCKHURSTHATCH LANE
AUGUST LANE
SHOPHOUSE LANE
FARLEY HEATH ROAD
BROOK HILL
WAVERLEY LANE
0 500 yds
0 500 m
266
281

BP
BQ
BR
BS
BT
BU
BV
08
09
10
267
284
KT24
RH5
UPPER COMMON
UPPER WESTON WOOD
HERMITAGE PLANTATION
THE COPPICE
King's Hills
CRABTREE PLANTATION
NETLEY HEATH
OAKEN GROVE
GREATLEE WOOD
Francis Corner
Gravelhill Gate
GREAT KINGS WOOD
LITTLE KINGS WOOD NT
Gallows Gate
HACKHURST DOWNS
Colkitchen Hole
OLD SIMM'S COPSE
DUNLEY WOOD
Colekitchen Farm
Kings Holt
NETLEY PARK NT
HACKHURST DOWN NT
Netley House
ROUND DOWN
New Barn Farm
Churchfield Farm
Hackhurst Farm
Nursery
Gomshall
GOMSHALL
PINEY COPSE NT
FIRTREE COPSE
THE ROUGH
ABINGER ROUGHS
NATIONAL TRUST
THE PADDOCKS
BROOMY DOWNS
THE PLANTATION
BIRCHIN COPSE
Netley Farm
Pumping Sta
Fire Sta
SPORTS GRD
GOMSHALL MARSH
Abinger Arms PH
Abinger Hammer
Sch
Abinger Hall Stables
Towerhill Farm
Cricket Ground
Clubhouse
Hall
Crossways Farm
Paddington Farm
Burrows Farm
A25
SHERE ROAD
STATION ROAD
DORKING ROAD
GUILDFORD ROAD
Tilling Bourne
Burrows Lea Farm
Burrows Cross
ENGINE WOOD
ELLIX WOOD
ELLIX PLANTATION
Home Farm
Hazel Brow Farm
Burrows Cross House
Raikes Farm
B2126
HORSHAM ROAD
Sutton Place Farm Nursery
Sutton Abinger
Frolbury Manor
Hoe
CONY COPSE
WOODHOUSE COPSE
Lane End Farm
SPORTS GRD
Smoky Hole
High Lawns
Hazel Hall
Colman's Hill
TENNINGSHOOK WOOD
FELDAY HOUSES
Y.H.A.
Peaslake
The Hurtwood Inn PH
Hurtwood Chase
RIDING COPSE
PASTU
136
137
138
139
140
141
142
143
144
49
48
47
46

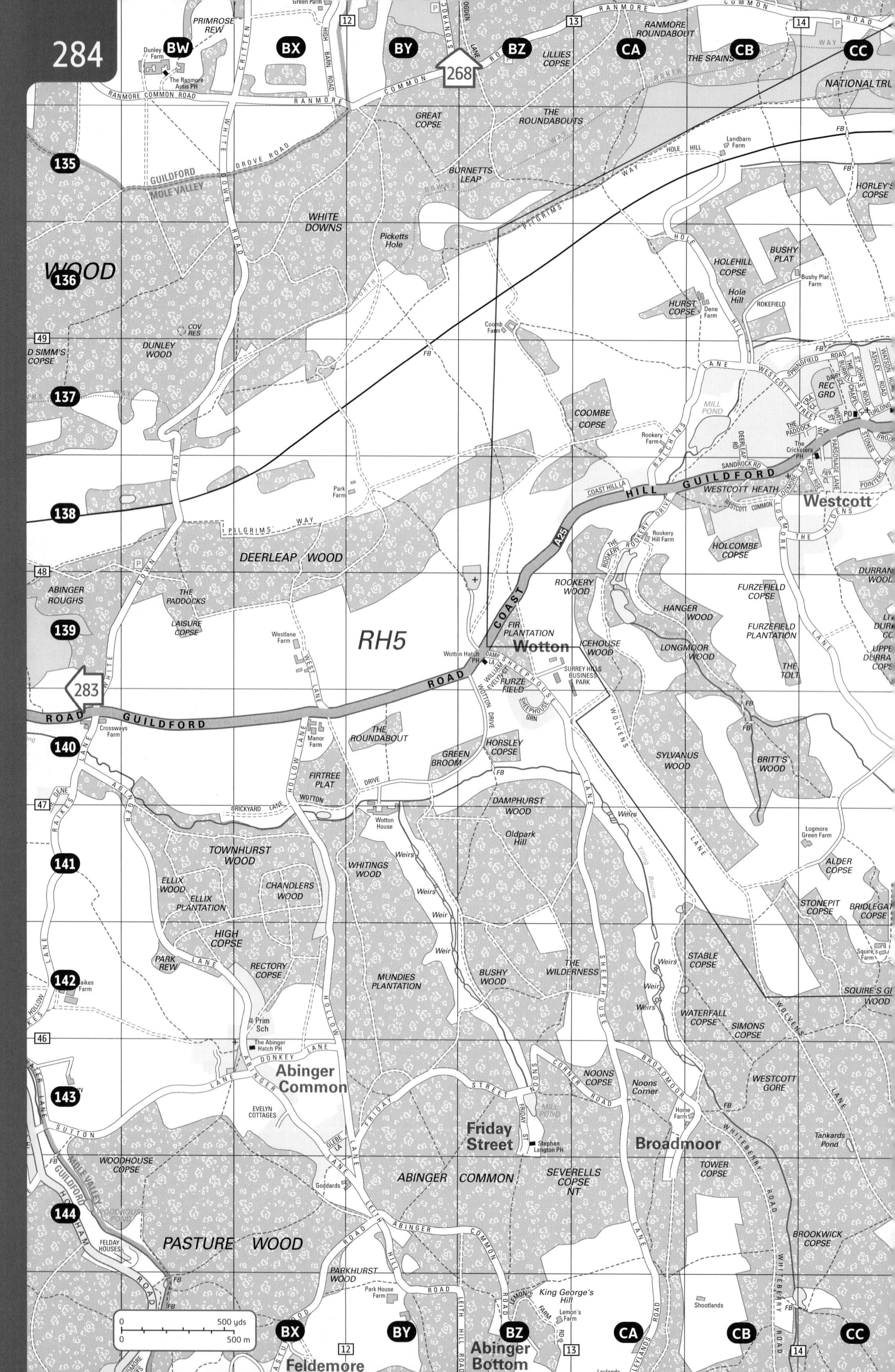

BW
BX
BY
BZ
CA
CB
CC
268
283
135
136
137
138
139
140
141
142
143
144
12
13
14
49
48
47
46
RANMORE COMMON ROAD
Dunley Farm
The Ranmore Arms PH
PRIMROSE REW
CRITTEN
HIGH BARN ROAD
Green Farm
STONYROCK
OGDEN LANE
RANMORE COMMON
RANMORE ROUNDABOUT
LILLIES COPSE
THE SPAINS
NATIONAL TRU
GREAT COPSE
THE ROUNDABOUTS
WHITE DOWN ROAD
DROVE ROAD
GUILDFORD
MOLE VALLEY
BURNETTS LEAP
Landbarn Farm
HOLE HILL
HORLEY'S COPSE
WHITE DOWNS
Picketts Hole
PILGRIMS' WAY
WOOD
COV RES
DUNLEY WOOD
SIMM'S COPSE
BUSHY PLAT
Bushy Plat Farm
HOLEHILL COPSE
Hole Hill
ROKEFIELD
HURST COPSE
Dene Farm
Coomb Farm
FB
WESTCOTT
SPRINGFIELD ROAD
REC GRD
MILL POND
COOMBE COPSE
Rookery Farm
BALCHINS
DEERLEAP RD
SANDROCK RD
The Cricketers PH
Park Farm
COAST HILL LA
GUILDFORD
WESTCOTT HEATH
WESTCOTT COMMON
Westcott
Rookery Hill Farm
HOLCOMBE COPSE
DEERLEAP WOOD
ABINGER ROUGHS
THE PADDOCKS
LAISURE COPSE
ROOKERY WOOD
HANGER WOOD
FURZEFIELD COPSE
FURZEFIELD PLANTATION
DURRAN WOOD
A25
COAST
FIR PLANTATION
Wotton
ICEHOUSE WOOD
LONGMOOR WOOD
Westlane Farm
RH5
Wotton Hatch PH
SURREY HILLS BUSINESS PARK
THE TOLT
ROAD
WEST LANE
FURZE FIELD
SHEEPHOUSE GRN
WOTTON DRIVE
ROAD GUILDFORD
Crossways Farm
Manor Farm
THE ROUNDABOUT
HORSLEY COPSE
GREEN BROOM
SYLVANUS WOOD
BRITT'S WOOD
WOLVENS
FIRTREE PLAT
HOLLOW LANE
BRICKYARD LANE
WOTTON DRIVE
DAMPHURST WOOD
RAIKES LANE
ABINGER
Wotton House
Weirs
Oldpark Hill
Logmore Green Farm
TOWNHURST WOOD
WHITINGS WOOD
ALDER COPSE
ELLIX WOOD
CHANDLERS WOOD
ELLIX PLANTATION
Weir
STONEPIT COPSE
BRIDLEGATE COPSE
HIGH COPSE
PARK REW
RECTORY COPSE
MUNDIES PLANTATION
BUSHY WOOD
THE WILDERNESS
STABLE COPSE
Squire's Farm
Raikes Farm
SQUIRE'S GREEN WOOD
WATERFALL COPSE
SIMONS COPSE
Prim Sch
The Abinger Hatch PH
DONKEY LANE
Abinger Common
NOONS CORNER ROAD
NOONS COPSE
Noons Corner
BROADMOOR
WESTCOTT GORE
EVELYN COTTAGES
FRIDAY STREET
Friday Street
MILL POND
Stephan Langton PH
Broadmoor
Home Farm
Tankards Pond
WOODHOUSE COPSE
GLEBE LA
ABINGER COMMON
SEVERELLS COPSE NT
TOWER COPSE
WHITEBERRY ROAD
Goddards
SUTTON
HORSHAM ROAD
FELDAY HOUSES
PASTURE WOOD
LEITH HILL
ABINGER COMMON
BROOKWICK COPSE
PARKHURST WOOD
Park House Farm
ROAD
King George's Hill
Lemon's Farm
Shootlands
LEITH HILL ROAD
LEMON'S FARM RD
LEYLANDS LANE
500 yds
500 m
Feldemore
Abinger Bottom

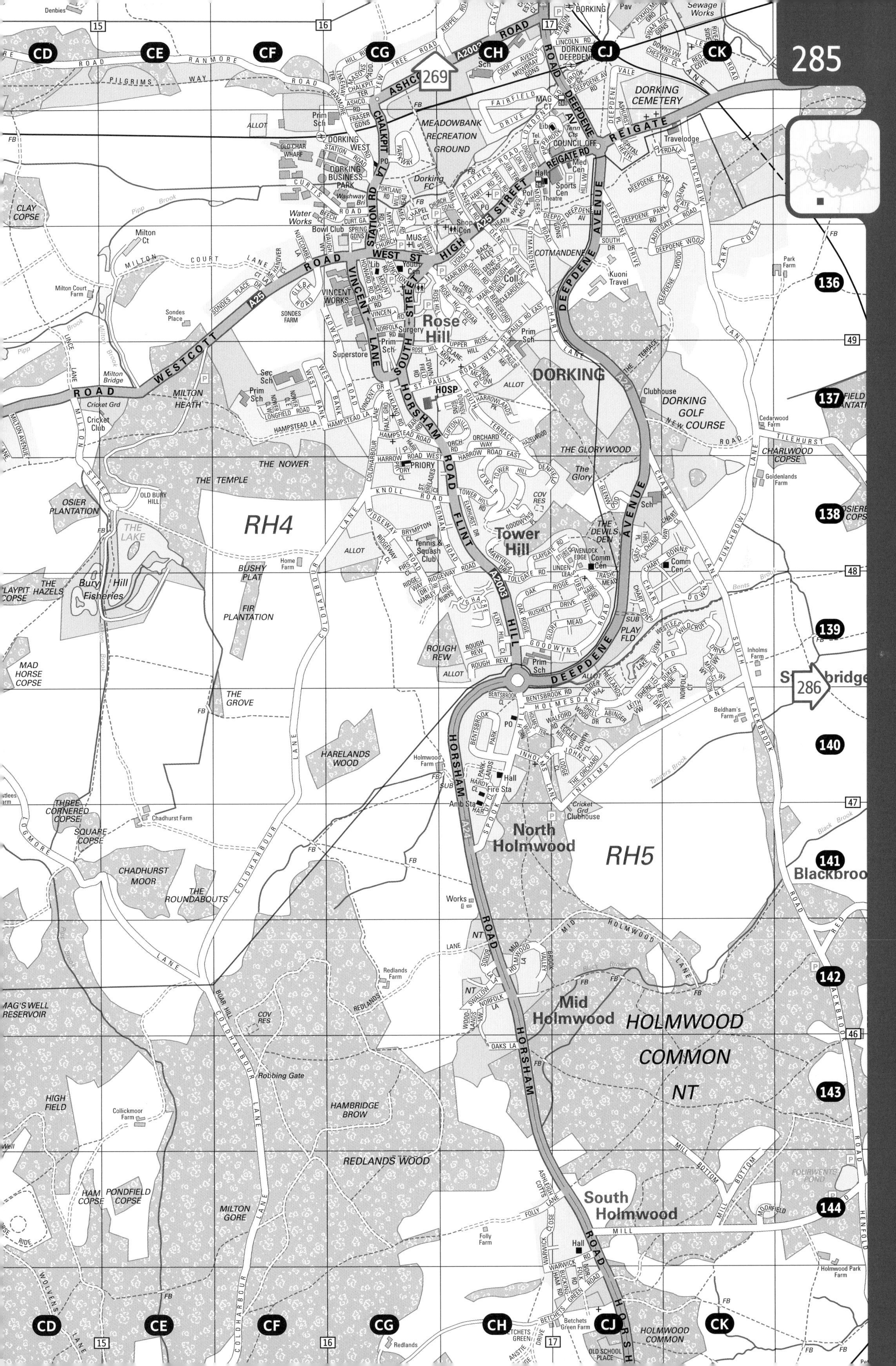
CD
CE
CF
CG
CH
CJ
CK
269
286
136
137
138
139
140
141
142
143
144
49
48
47
46
15
16
17
DORKING
Rose Hill
Tower Hill
North Holmwood
Mid Holmwood
South Holmwood
HOLMWOOD COMMON NT
RH4
RH5
DORKING CEMETERY
MEADOWBANK RECREATION GROUND
DORKING GOLF COURSE
THE GLORY WOOD
THE NOWER
THE TEMPLE
MILTON HEATH
Bury Hill Fisheries
THE LAKE
FIR PLANTATION
BUSHY PLAT
THE GROVE
HARELANDS WOOD
CHADHURST MOOR
THE ROUNDABOUTS
SQUARE COPSE
THREE CORNERED COPSE
MAD HORSE COPSE
CLAY COPSE
OSIER PLANTATION
THE HAZELS
REDLANDS WOOD
HAMBRIDGE BROW
MILTON GORE
HIGH FIELD
HAM COPSE
PONDFIELD COPSE
CHARLWOOD COPSE
HOLMWOOD COMMON
Blackbrook
WESTCOTT ROAD
RANMORE ROAD
PILGRIMS WAY
DEEPDENE AVENUE
REIGATE ROAD
HORSHAM ROAD
FLINT HILL
COLDHARBOUR LANE
CHART LANE
PUNCHBOWL LANE
MILL ROAD
A25
A24
A2003
HOSP
Dorking FC
Sports Cen
Superstore
Travelodge
Kuoni Travel
Robbing Gate
Chadhurst Farm
Redlands Farm
Folly Farm
Holmwood Park Farm
Betchets Green Farm

CL
CM
CN
CP
CQ
CR
CS
270
285
RH4
RH3
RH5
BETCHWORTH PARK GOLF COURSE
BETCHWORTH PARK
Betchworth Castle Remains
Clubhouse
Boxhill
Deepdene Bridge
Betchworth
HARTSFIELD MANOR HOTEL
BROCKHAM BIG FIELD
Dorking R.F.C.
Bowling Green
Borough Bridge
River Mole
Brockham Court Farm
Tanner's Bridge
Hall
Prim Sch
Brockham
SPORTS GRD
ALLOT
OLD PARK WOOD
DENDY'S WOOD
Betchworth House
Betchworth Bridge
The Dolphin PH
Park Farm
Pondtail Farm
GREENSAND WAY
FIELD PLANTATION
Cedarwood Farm
CHARLWOOD COPSE
Goldenlands Farm
OSIERBED COPSE
Feltons Farm
Gadbrook Farm
DUFFLES PLANTATION
Strood Green
Stroodgreen Farm
THE ROUGH
GADBROOK COPSE
Bushbury Farm
Tanners Brook
TWEED WOOD
Gadbrook House
SCAMMELLS COPSE
Inholms Farm
Stonebridge
Beldham Farm
Bents Brook
ROOTHILL WOOD
Root Hill
HIGHRIDGE WOOD
Hall Farm
Ashcroft Farm
Root Hill Farm
ORCHARD COPSE
Hook Farm
Black Brook
Great Brockhamhurst
Great Brockhamhurst Farm
Blunts Place Farm
Oakleigh Grange
HOOK COPSE
Blackbrook
KILN COPSE
Westwood Farm
Bunce Common
TWENTY ACRE SHAW
SCAMMELLS GROVE
Gad Brook
JESSIES ROUGH
Brook Lodge Farm
Waterlands Farm
Shellwood Manor
Shellwood Farm
HITHER HAWESREW
Lodge Farm
Hawesrew Farm
SNELLING PLANTED FIELD
NEW BARN SHAW
FOURWENTS POND
Wymbleton Farm
BROOKFIELD COPSE
BIRCH PLATT'S
Holmwood Park Farm
Filter Beds
SEWAGE WORKS
SIX ACRE COPSE
FURZEFIELD COPSE
BROADLANDS ROUGH
Ewood Farm
Swires Farm
Hammond's Farm
Petersfield
0 500 yds
0 500 m
19
20
21
46
47
48
49
135
136
137
138
139
140
141
142
143
144

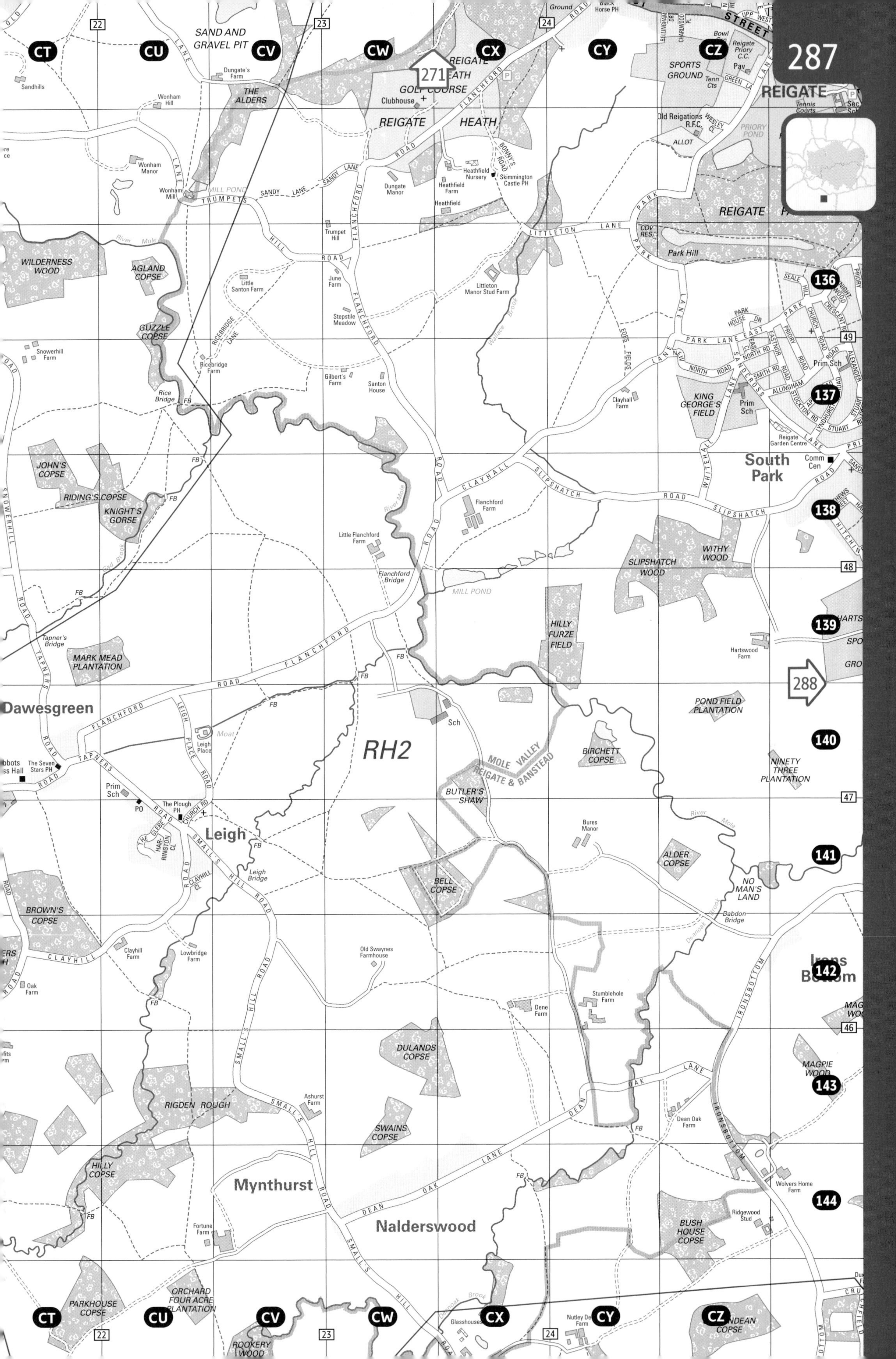

SAND AND GRAVEL PIT
Dungate's Farm
Sandhills
Wonham Hill
THE ALDERS
REIGATE HEATH GOLF COURSE
Clubhouse
REIGATE HEATH
Wonham Manor
Wonham Mill
MILL POND
TRUMPETS HILL ROAD
SANDY LANE
Dungate Manor
Heathfield Nursery
Heathfield Farm
Heathfield
Skimmington Castle PH
FLANCHFORD ROAD
BONNY'S ROAD
SPORTS GROUND
Reigate Priory C.C.
REIGATE
Old Reigations R.F.C.
PRIORY POND
ALLOT
REIGATE
PARK LANE
LITTLETON LANE
COV RES
Park Hill
WILDERNESS WOOD
AGLAND COPSE
Trumpet Hill
June Farm
Little Santon Farm
Littleton Manor Stud Farm
Stepstile Meadow
GUZZLE COPSE
RICEBRIDGE LANE
Ricebridge Farm
Snowerhill Farm
Gilbert's Farm
Santon House
Rice Bridge
Wallace Brook
EDS FIELDS
PARK LANE EAST
NORTH ROAD
KING GEORGE'S FIELD
Prim Sch
Clayhall Farm
Reigate Garden Centre
South Park
Comm Cen
JOHN'S COPSE
RIDING'S COPSE
KNIGHT'S GORSE
River Mole
CLAYHALL ROAD
SLIPSHATCH ROAD
Flanchford Farm
Little Flanchford Farm
Flanchford Bridge
MILL POND
SLIPSHATCH WOOD
WITHY WOOD
Gad Brook
SNOWERHILL ROAD
Tapner's Bridge
MARK MEAD PLANTATION
HILLY FURZE FIELD
Hartswood Farm
Dawesgreen
FLANCHFORD ROAD
LEIGH PLACE ROAD
Moat
Leigh Place
The Seven Stars PH
TAPNERS ROAD
RH2
Sch
MOLE VALLEY
REIGATE & BANSTEAD
POND FIELD PLANTATION
BIRCHETT COPSE
NINETY THREE PLANTATION
BUTLER'S SHAW
Prim Sch
PO
The Plough PH
CHURCH RD
Leigh
THE GLEBE
HARRINGTON CL
Leigh Bridge
CLAYHILL CL
Bures Manor
ALDER COPSE
River Mole
NO MAN'S LAND
BELL COPSE
BROWN'S COPSE
Clayhill Farm
Lowbridge Farm
Old Swaynes Farmhouse
Dabdon Bridge
Deanoak Brook
Irons Bottom
Oak Farm
Dene Farm
Stumblehole Farm
IRONSBOTTOM
SMALL'S HILL ROAD
DULANDS COPSE
MAGPIE WOOD
RIGDEN ROUGH
Ashurst Farm
DEAN OAK LANE
Dean Oak Farm
SWAINS COPSE
HILLY COPSE
Mynthurst
Wolvers Home Farm
Fortune Farm
Nalderswood
Ridgewood Stud
BUSH HOUSE COPSE
PARKHOUSE COPSE
ORCHARD FOUR ACRE PLANTATION
Deanoak Brook
Glasshouses
Nutley Dean Farm
ROOKERY WOOD
NUTLEY DEAN COPSE
CT CU CV CW CX CY CZ
22 23 24
49 48 47 46
136 137 138 139 140 141 142 143 144

271
288

DA
DB
DC
DD
DE
DF
DG
REIGATE
REDHILL
272
REIGATE CEMETERY
PRIORY PARK
REIGATE PARK
REDHILL COMMON
Earlswood
Mead Vale
Woodhatch
South Park
EARLSWOOD COMMON
REDHILL AND REIGATE GOLF COURSE
EARLSWOOD LAKES
EAST SURREY HOSPITAL
EARLSWOOD SEWAGE WORKS
Doversgreen
FELLAND COPSE
HARTSWOOD SPORTS GROUND
RH2
TURNER'S SHAW
287
PETRIDGEWOOD COMMON
HOME GROVE
BENTING WOOD
HOLLOW SHAW
KILN FIELD PLANTATION
TWELVE ACRE PLANTATION
NINETY THREE PLANTATION
POND FIELD PLANTATION
WITHY WOOD
Sidlow
Salfords
Irons Bottom
NO MAN'S LAND
MAGPIE WOOD
FONTIGARRY FARM BUSINESS PARK
SAXLEY HILL
RH6
BUSH HOUSE COPSE
COLLENDEAN COPSE
290
500 yds
500 m
135
136
137
138
139
140
141
142
143
144
49
48
47
46
26
27
28
A25
A23
A2044
A217
B2034
COCKSHOT HILL
WOODHATCH ROAD
DOVERS GREEN ROAD
REIGATE ROAD
BRIGHTON ROAD
HORLEY ROAD
LONESOME LANE
MEATH GREEN LANE
IRONSBOTTOM
KINNERSLEY MANOR
LODGE LANE
BONEHURST ROAD

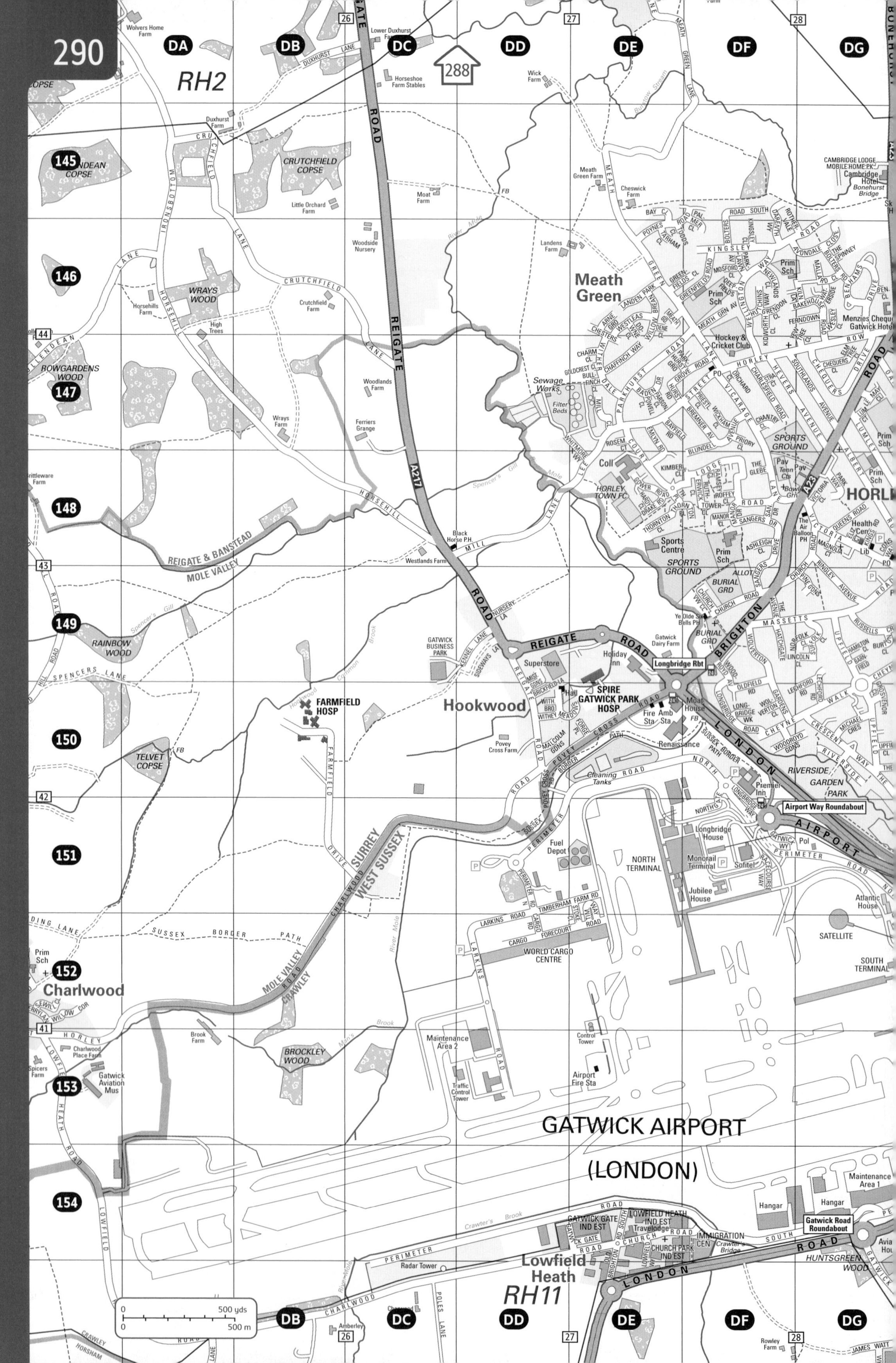

RH2
288
DA
DB
DC
DD
DE
DF
DG
26
27
28
Wolvers Home Farm
Lower Duxhurst Farm
DUXHURST LANE
Horseshoe Farm Stables
Wick Farm
Duxhurst Farm
CRUTCHFIELD
CRUTCHFIELD COPSE
IRONSBOTTOM
Little Orchard Farm
Moat Farm
REIGATE ROAD
A217
Meath Green Farm
Cheswick Farm
CAMBRIDGE LODGE MOBILE HOME PK
Cambridge Hotel
Bonehurst Bridge
145
146
147
148
149
150
151
152
153
154
44
43
42
41
ROWGARDENS WOOD
WRAYS WOOD
Horsehills Farm
High Trees
Crutchfield Farm
Woodside Nursery
Landens Farm
Meath Green
Woodlands Farm
Ferriers Grange
Wrays Farm
Sewage Works
Filter Beds
Hockey & Cricket Club
Prim Sch
Menzies Chequers Gatwick Hotel
SPORTS GROUND
Coll
HORLEY TOWN FC
Sports Centre
BURIAL GRD
HORLEY
Health Cen
Lib
The Air Balloon PH
Black Horse P.H
Westlands Farm
REIGATE & BANSTEAD
MOLE VALLEY
HORSEHILL
MILL LANE
RAINBOW WOOD
SPENCERS LANE
GATWICK BUSINESS PARK
Superstore
Holiday Inn
Gatwick Dairy Farm
Longbridge Rbt
Ye Olde Six Bells PH
BRIGHTON ROAD
REIGATE ROAD
FARMFIELD HOSP
Hookwood
SPIRE GATWICK PARK HOSP
Fire Sta
Amb Sta
Moat House
Renaissance
Povey Cross Farm
TELVET COPSE
FARMFIELD DRIVE
SURREY
WEST SUSSEX
Cleaning Tanks
Premier Inn
Airport Way Roundabout
LONDON ROAD
AIRPORT WAY
Longbridge House
Fuel Depot
NORTH TERMINAL
Monorail Terminal
Sofitel
Jubilee House
Atlantic House
SATELLITE
SOUTH TERMINAL
RIVERSIDE GARDEN PARK
SUSSEX BORDER PATH
WORLD CARGO CENTRE
LARKINS ROAD
CHARLWOOD ROAD
MOLE VALLEY
CRAWLEY
Prim Sch
Charlwood
Brook Farm
Charlwood Place Farm
Gatwick Aviation Mus
Spicers Farm
BROCKLEY WOOD
Maintenance Area 2
Traffic Control Tower
Control Tower
Airport Fire Sta
GATWICK AIRPORT
(LONDON)
Maintenance Area 1
Hangar
Hangar
Gatwick Road Roundabout
GATWICK GATE IND EST
LOWFIELD HEATH IND EST
Travelodge
IMMIGRATION CEN
CHURCH PARK IND EST
Crawter's Bridge
HUNTSGREEN WOOD
Radar Tower
Lowfield Heath
RH11
PERIMETER ROAD
Amberley
Rowley Farm
POLES LANE
0 500 yds
0 500 m

RH1
RH6
RH10
289
Hunters Moon Farm
The Castle PH
MILLERS COPSE
Rookswood Farm
ROOKERY HILL
COLDLAND WOOD
Philips Research Laboratories
CROSSOAK LA
Hathersham Farm
THE ROOKERY
COURTOAK GREEN
Burstow Stream
Greatlake Farm
LONGYARDS SHAW
Burstow Manor
BURSTOW BUSINESS CENTRE
Hollesley Farm
Elec Sta
The Farmhouse PH
Tanyard Farm
BROOK WOOD
Sewage Works
Smallfield Grid Sub Station
ALDER BED
LOST SEVENS
LANGSHOTT WOOD
OAK BED
WEATHERHILL COMMON
GATWICK METRO CENTRE
Gas Holder Sta
BRIDGE IND EST
Prim Sch
Swim Pool
Sec Sch
Harrowsley Green Farm
THE CRAVENS
CAREYS WOOD
HAYES WK
SPORTS GRD
PLAYING FIELDS
The Plough PH
Green Farm
Wilgers Farm
Haroldslea Poultry Farm
Farney Glen Farm
BRIDGEHAM WOOD
Smallfield
Site of Thunderfield Castle
Lower Broadbridge Farm
Broadmead Farm
Hall
LABURNUM CT
HORLEY
THE ROUGHS
THE PLANTATION
REIGATE & BANSTEAD
TANDRIDGE
Flightpath Farm
Broadbridge Stables
BELLHATCH WOOD
COLLINS WOOD
Junction 9a
Junction 9
Airport Way Roundabout East
SUSSEX BORDER PATH
M23
A23
Monorail Terminal
First Point
Hilton
Schlumberger House
GATWICK AIRPORT
BUS/COACH STA
BRIDGES WOOD
WEST SUSSEX
SURREY
Broadfield Farm
Burstow
Redeham Hall
Fern Court Farm
Gatwick House
Mushroom Farm
EASTLANDS SHAW
Keepers Corner
EFFINGHAM
CRAWLEY
TANDRIDGE
Rivington Farm
Teizers Farm
Burstow Hall
Burstow Nurseries
HORLEYLAND WOOD
The Shipley Bridge Inn PH
Shipley Bridge
KILN HEATH
B2037
B2036
New House Farm
Riding School
Filter Beds
Sludge Lagoons
UPPER PICKETT'S
ALLEN'S WOOD
Courtlands
Burstow Park Farm
Burstow Park
Sewage Works
The Parsons Pig PH
Hollybush Farm
KING GEORGE'S FIELD
Pav
Oldlands Farm
The Greyhound PH
BLACKCORNER WOOD
GATWICK INTERNATIONAL DISTRIBUTION
DH DJ DK DL DM DN DP
29 30 31
146 147 148 149 150 151 152 153 154
44 43 42 41

Key to London urban maps

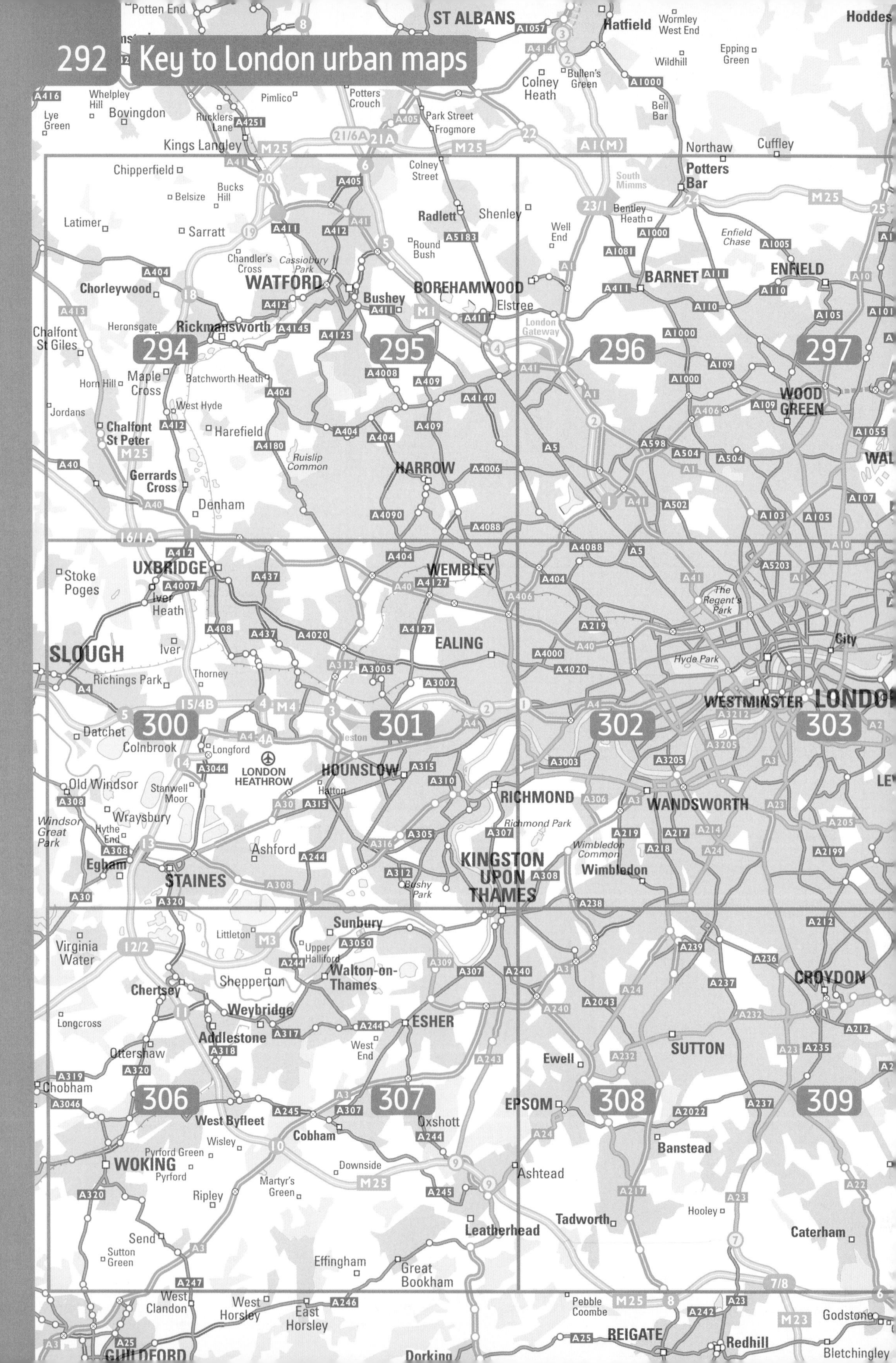

Key to map symbols on pages 294-311

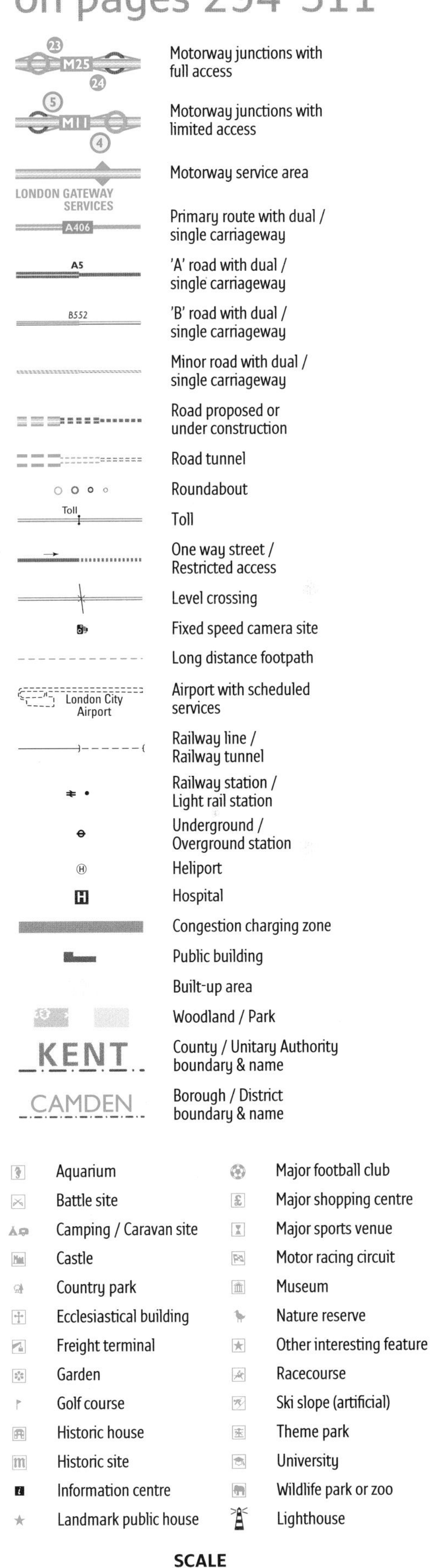

SCALE

0 1/2 1 1 1/2 2 miles

0 1 2 3 4 kilometres

1:63,360 1 inch (2.5cm) to 1 mile / 1.6 cm to 1 km

Orchard Leigh
BOVINGDON
Codmore
Botley
Cowcroft Wood
Hogpits Bottom
Fir Wood
Chipperfield
Chipperfield Common
Belsize
KINGS LANGLEY
Hunton Bridge
Flaunden
Chessmount
Lower Bois
Frith Wood
Long Wood
Latimer
Flaunden Grove
Baldwin's Wood
Hanginglane Wood
Limeshill Wood
Dawes Common
Sarratt
Sandfield Wood
Scatterdells Wood
Berrybushes Wood
Beechen Bottom
Juniper Hill
Templepan Wood
Heath Wood
Lane Wood
West Wood
Mount Wood
Chenies
Chenies Manor House
Turveylane Wood
Great Wood
Whippendell Wood
Harrocks Wood
Welling Grove
LITTLE CHALFONT
CHILTERN
THREE RIVERS
Beechengrove Wood
Loudwater
Pollards Wood
CHORLEYWOOD
CROXLEY GREEN
Chorleywood Bottom
RICKMANSWORTH
Bailey Wood
Philipshill Wood
The Swillet
Grovespring Wood
Heronsgate
Mill End
Moneyhill
CHALFONT ST. GILES
Buckinghamshire Chilterns University College
Chiltern Open Air Museum
Newland Park
Bottom Wood
Batchworth
Moor Park
Butlers Cross
Chalfont Common
Maple Cross
Batchworth Heath
Hill End
NORTHWOOD
CHALFONT ST. PETER
Jordans
Pearson's Wood
Bishop's Wood
Mount Vernon Hospital
Layter's Green
Mounthill Wood
Great Legs Wood
Park Wood
Harefield
Hogtrough Wood
Copse Wood
Siblet's Wood
Nockhill Wood
Juniper Wood
Great Halings Wood
South Harefield
Mad Bess Wood
Ruislip Common
BUCKINGHAMSHIRE
HILLINGDON
Denham Aerodrome
Denham Marsh Wood
Bulstrode Park
GERRARDS CROSS
Denham Green
Higher Denham
RSPB Nature Reserve Church Wood
Hedgerley
Hanging Wood
Mounthill Wood
Tatling End
South Bucks Council Office
DENHAM
Denham Country Park
Ickenham
Galdwins Wood
Hawks Wood
Stoke Common
M25
M40
A404
A412
A413
A40
300
0 1/2 1 mile
0 1 2 km

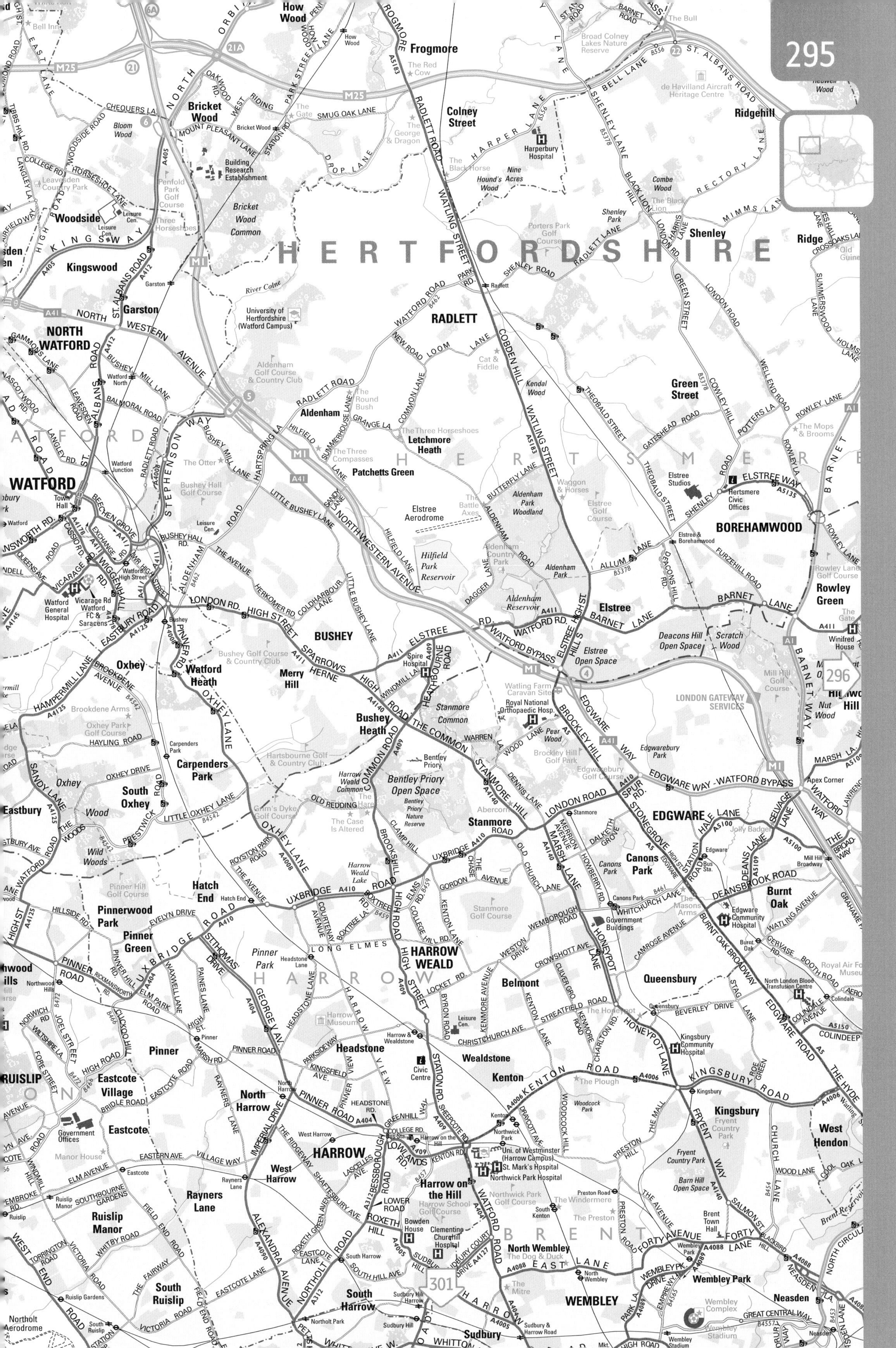
HERTFORDSHIRE
HERTSMERE
WATFORD
HARROW
BRENT
Frogmore
Colney Street
Ridgehill
Bricket Wood
How Wood
Woodside
Kingswood
Garston
NORTH WATFORD
RADLETT
Aldenham
Letchmore Heath
Patchetts Green
Green Street
Shenley
Ridge
BOREHAMWOOD
Elstree
Rowley Green
BUSHEY
Merry Hill
Bushey Heath
Watford Heath
Oxhey
Carpenders Park
South Oxhey
Eastbury
Stanmore
EDGWARE
Canons Park
Burnt Oak
Hatch End
Pinnerwood Park
Pinner Green
Pinner
HARROW WEALD
Belmont
Queensbury
Headstone
Wealdstone
Kenton
Kingsbury
West Hendon
North Harrow
Eastcote Village
Eastcote
RUISLIP
Ruislip Manor
South Ruislip
Rayners Lane
West Harrow
HARROW
Harrow on the Hill
North Wembley
WEMBLEY
Wembley Park
Neasden
South Harrow
Sudbury
Elstree Aerodrome
Hilfield Park Reservoir
Aldenham Reservoir
Bentley Priory Open Space
Stanmore Common
Harrow Weald Common
Fryent Country Park
Barn Hill Open Space
Deacons Hill Open Space
Scratch Wood
LONDON GATEWAY SERVICES
Northolt Aerodrome
M25
M1
A41
A411
A5
A1
296
301

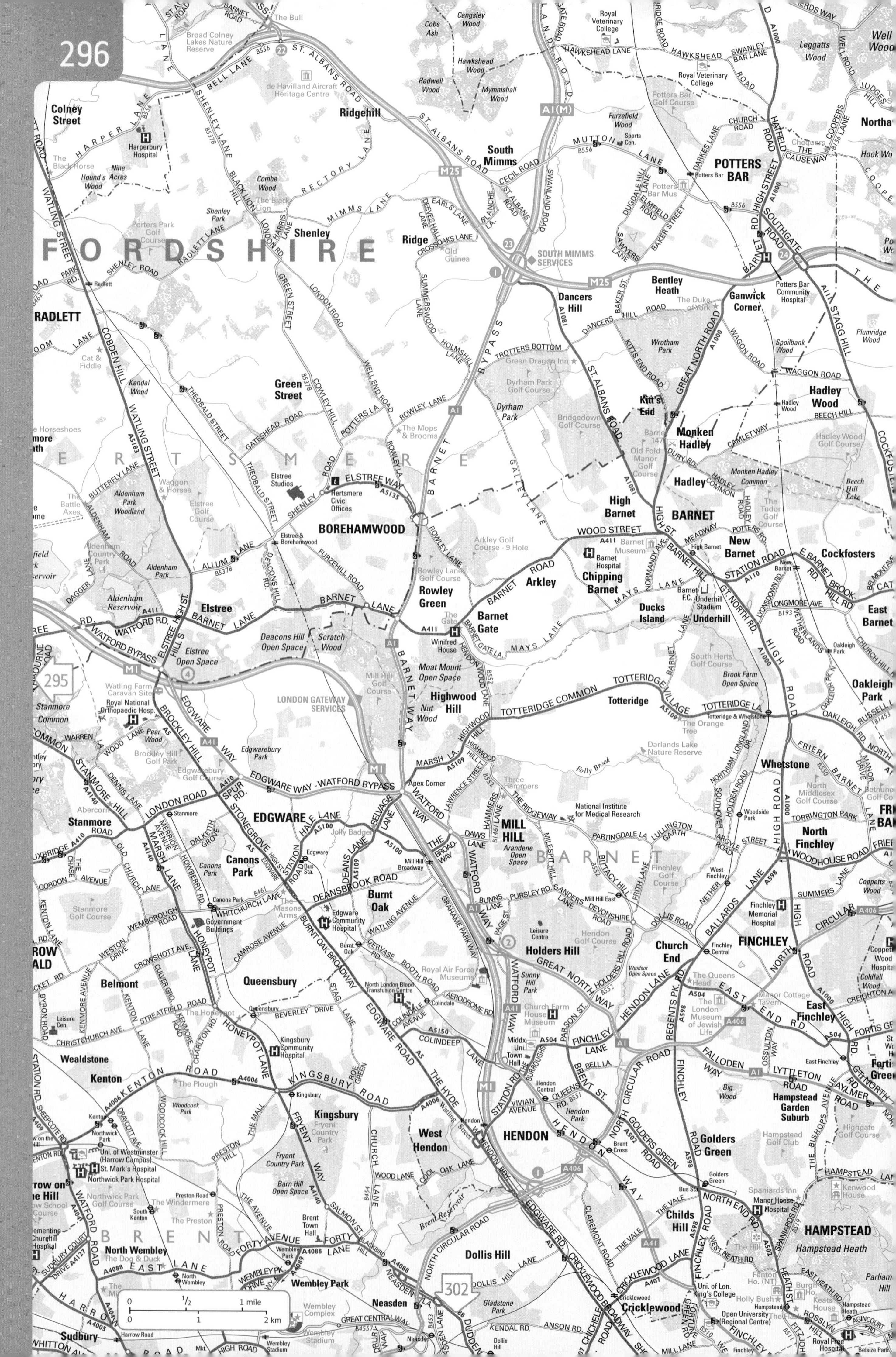

Colney Street
Broad Colney Lakes Nature Reserve
The Bull
de Havilland Aircraft Heritage Centre
Ridgehill
Cangsley Wood
Cobs Ash
Hawkshead Wood
Redwell Wood
Mymmshall Wood
Royal Veterinary College
HAWKSHEAD LANE
SWANLEY BAR LANE
Leggatts Wood
Potters Bar Golf Course
Harperbury Hospital
The Black Horse
Nine Acres
Hound's Wood
Combe Wood
The Black Lion
Shenley Park
Shenley
Porters Park Golf Course
South Mimms
Ridge
Old Guinea
SOUTH MIMMS SERVICES
POTTERS BAR
Potters Bar Mus
Potters Bar Community Hospital
FORDSHIRE
RADLETT
Radlett
Cat & Fiddle
Kendal Wood
Green Street
Bentley Heath
Dancers Hill
Ganwick Corner
The Duke of York
Wrotham Park
Spoilbank Wood
Plumridge Wood
Green Dragon Inn
Dyrham Park Golf Course
Dyrham Park
Bridgedown Golf Course
Kitt's End
Monken Hadley
Hadley Wood
Hadley Wood Golf Course
Old Fold Manor Golf Course
Hadley
Monken Hadley Common
Beech Hill Lake
The Tudor Golf Course
The Mops & Brooms
HERTSMERE
Elstree Studios
Hertsmere Civic Offices
BOREHAMWOOD
Elstree & Borehamwood
Waggon & Horses
Aldenham Park Woodland
Elstree Golf Course
Aldenham Country Park
Aldenham Park
Aldenham Reservoir
High Barnet
BARNET
Arkley Golf Course - 9 Hole
Barnet Museum
Barnet Hospital
Chipping Barnet
Arkley
New Barnet
Cockfosters
Rowley Lane Golf Course
Rowley Green
Barnet Gate
Elstree
Ducks Island
Underhill Stadium
Underhill
East Barnet
Deacons Hill Open Space
Scratch Wood
Winifred House
Elstree Open Space
Watling Farm Caravan Site
Royal National Orthopaedic Hosp.
Moat Mount Open Space
Mill Hill Golf Course
LONDON GATEWAY SERVICES
Highwood Hill
Nut Wood
South Herts Golf Course
Brook Farm Open Space
Totteridge
Oakleigh Park
The Orange Tree
Darlands Lake Nature Reserve
Stanmore Common
Pear Wood
Brockley Hill Golf Park
Edgwarebury Park
Edgwarebury Golf Course
Apex Corner
Three Hammers
National Institute for Medical Research
Whetstone
North Middlesex Golf Course
Stanmore
EDGWARE
Jolly Badger
MILL HILL
Arandene Open Space
BARNET
North Finchley
Canons Park
Mill Hill Broadway
Finchley Golf Course
West Finchley
Coppetts Wood
Stanmore Golf Course
Government Buildings
The Masons Arms
Burnt Oak
Edgware Community Hospital
Mill Hill East
Leisure Centre
Hendon Golf Course
Holders Hill
Church End
FINCHLEY
Finchley Memorial Hospital
Finchley Central
Belmont
Queensbury
Royal Air Force Museum
North London Blood Transfusion Centre
Sunny Hill Park
Windsor Open Space
The Queens Head
Manor Cottage Tavern
East Finchley
The London Museum of Jewish Life
Colindale
The Honeypot
Church Farm House Museum
Middx Uni.
Town Hall
Kingsbury Community Hospital
Leisure Cen.
Wealdstone
Kenton
The Plough
Kingsbury
Hendon Central
Hendon Park
Big Wood
Hampstead Garden Suburb
Woodcock Park
Fryent Country Park
West Hendon
HENDON
Brent Cross
Golders Green
Hampstead Golf Club
Highgate Golf Course
Uni. of Westminster (Harrow Campus)
St. Mark's Hospital
Northwick Park Hospital
Northwick Park Golf Course
Preston Road
The Windermere
Barn Hill Open Space
Brent Reservoir
Spaniards Inn
Manor House Hospital
Kenwood House
South Kenton
The Preston
BRENT
Brent Town Hall
Childs Hill
HAMPSTEAD
Hampstead Heath
North Wembley
The Dog & Duck
Dollis Hill
Wembley Park
Neasden
Gladstone Park
Cricklewood
Uni. of Lon. King's College
Open University (Regional Centre)
Fenton Ho. (NT)
Burgh Ho.
Keats House
Royal Free Hospital
Wembley Complex
Wembley Stadium
Sudbury
Harrow Road
Dollis Hill
295
302
0 1/2 1 mile
0 1 2 km
WATLING STREET
BARNET BYPASS
BARNET WAY
EDGWARE WAY
GREAT NORTH ROAD
GREAT NORTH WAY
WATFORD WAY
NORTH CIRCULAR ROAD
EDGWARE ROAD
KINGSBURY ROAD
KENTON ROAD

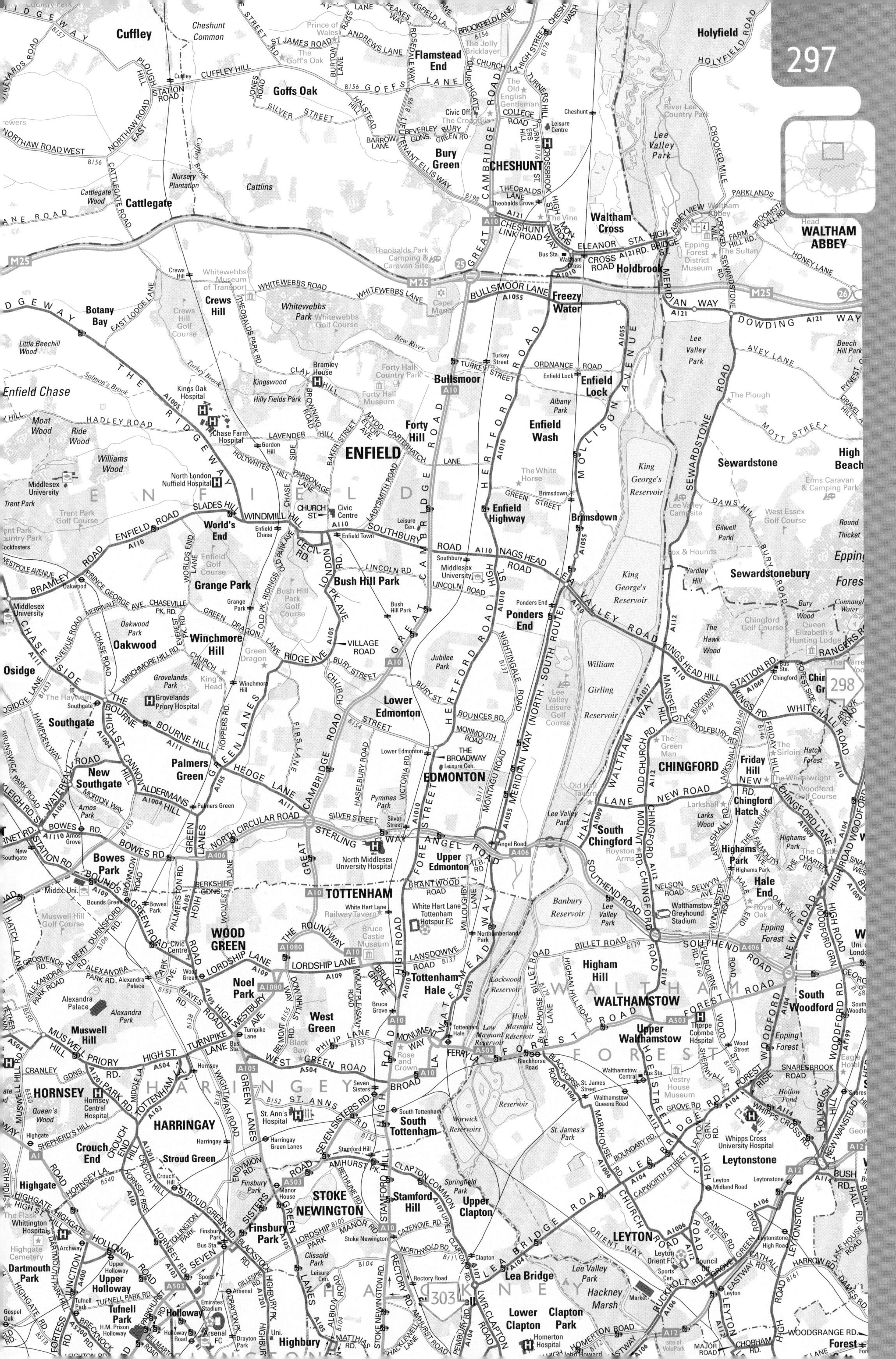

Cuffley
Cheshunt Common
Goffs Oak
Flamstead End
Holyfield
Bury Green
CHESHUNT
Cattlegate
Cattlins
Waltham Cross
WALTHAM ABBEY
Holdbrook
Crews Hill
Botany Bay
Whitewebbs Park
Freezy Water
Bullsmoor
Enfield Lock
Enfield Chase
Forty Hill
ENFIELD
Enfield Wash
Enfield Highway
Brimsdown
Sewardstone
High Beach
World's End
Grange Park
Bush Hill Park
Ponders End
Sewardstonebury
King George's Reservoir
William Girling Reservoir
Oakwood
Winchmore Hill
Osidge
Southgate
Lower Edmonton
CHINGFORD
Palmers Green
New Southgate
EDMONTON
Upper Edmonton
Friday Hill
Chingford Hatch
South Chingford
Bowes Park
TOTTENHAM
Higham Park
Hale End
WOOD GREEN
Banbury Reservoir
Higham Hill
Noel Park
Tottenham Hale
WALTHAMSTOW
South Woodford
Muswell Hill
West Green
Upper Walthamstow
HORNSEY
HARRINGAY
South Tottenham
Crouch End
Stroud Green
Leytonstone
Highgate
STOKE NEWINGTON
Stamford Hill
Upper Clapton
Finsbury Park
LEYTON
Dartmouth Park
Upper Holloway
Lea Bridge
Tufnell Park
Holloway
Highbury
Lower Clapton
Clapton Park
Hackney Marsh
Forest
M25
A10
A406
298
303

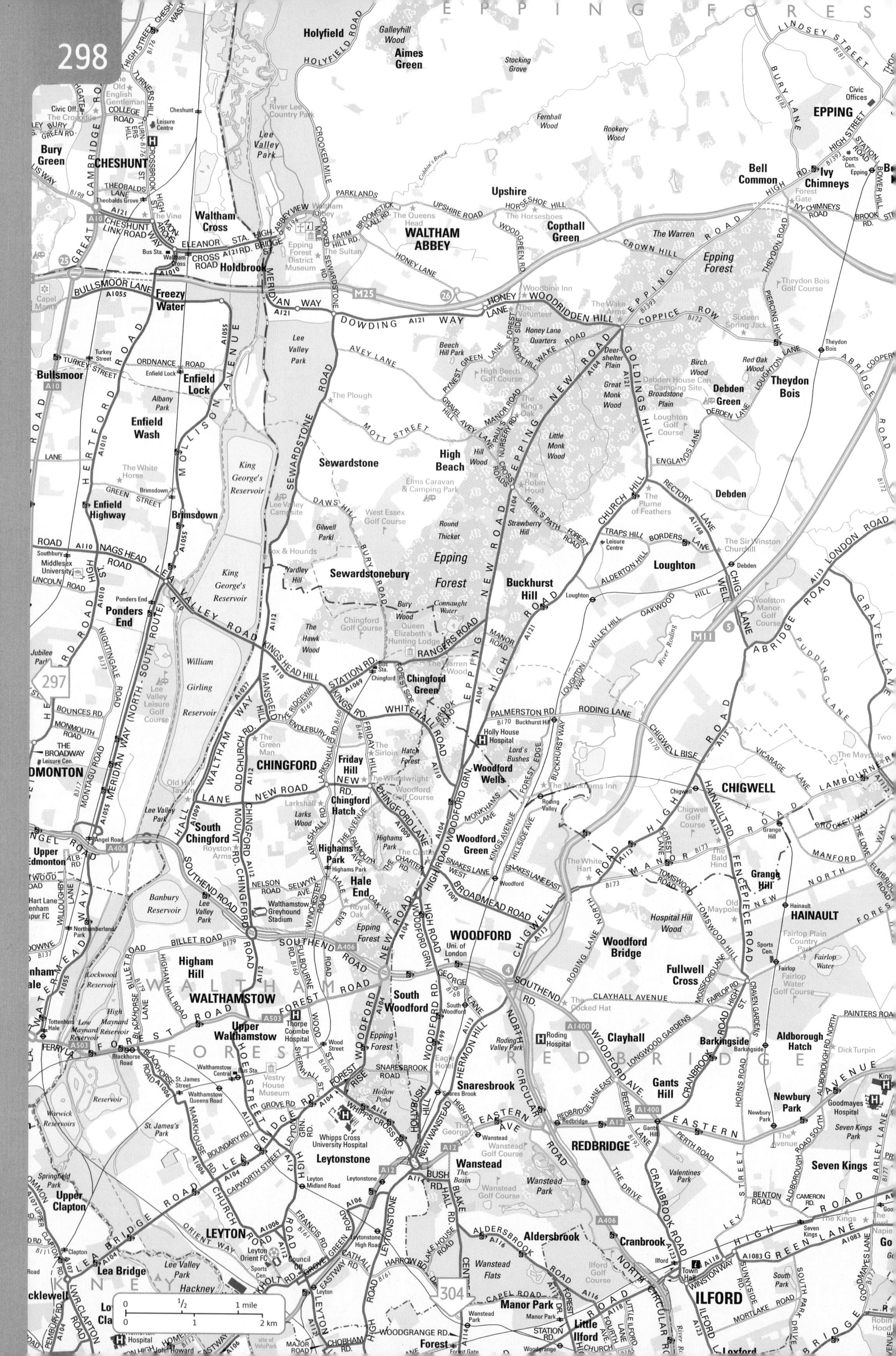
EPPING FOREST
Holyfield
Galleyhill Wood
Aimes Green
Stocking Grove
EPPING
Civic Offices
Bury Green
CHESHUNT
Lee Valley Park
River Lee Country Park
Fernhall Wood
Rookery Wood
Bell Common
Ivy Chimneys
Upshire
Waltham Cross
WALTHAM ABBEY
Copthall Green
The Warren
Epping Forest District Museum
Holdbrook
Epping Forest
Freezy Water
Theydon Bois Golf Course
M25
DOWDING WAY
MERIDIAN WAY
BULLSMOOR LANE
WOODRIDDEN HILL
COPPICE ROW
Honey Lane Quarters
Beech Hill Park
High Beech Golf Course
Deer-shelter Plain
Birch Wood
Red Oak Wood
Theydon Bois
Bullsmoor
Enfield Lock
Debden Green
Great Monk Wood
Broadstone Plain
Albany Park
Enfield Wash
The Plough
Loughton Golf Course
Little Monk Wood
High Beach
Sewardstone
King George's Reservoir
Elms Caravan & Camping Park
Debden
The Robin Hood
The Plume of Feathers
Enfield Highway
Brimsdown
Lee Valley Campsite
West Essex Golf Course
Gilwell Park
Round Thicket
Strawberry Hill
Leisure Centre
The Sir Winston Churchill
Middlesex University
Epping Forest
Loughton
Sewardstonebury
Buckhurst Hill
Yardley Hill
Ponders End
Bury Wood
Connaught Water
Woolston Manor Golf Course
Chingford Golf Course
Queen Elizabeth's Hunting Lodge
The Hawk Wood
M11
William Girling Reservoir
RANGERS ROAD
297
Lee Valley Leisure Golf Course
Chingford Green
The Warren Wood
River Roding
Holly House Hospital
Lord's Bushes
Hatch Forest
Friday Hill
CHINGFORD
The Green Man
The Sirloin
Woodford Wells
EDMONTON
The Maypole
CHIGWELL
Chingford Hatch
The Monkhams Inn
Larkshall
Larks Wood
Chigwell Golf Course
Lee Valley Park
South Chingford
Higham Park
Woodford Green
Upper Edmonton
Royston Arms
The Castle
The White Hart
The Bald Hind
Grange Hill
Hale End
Banbury Reservoir
Walthamstow Greyhound Stadium
Royal Oak
Hospital Hill Wood
HAINAULT
Epping Forest
Old Maypole
Fairlop Plain Country Park
WOODFORD
Woodford Bridge
Uni. of London
Higham Hill
Fairlop Water
Lockwood Reservoir
Fullwell Cross
Fairlop Water Golf Course
WALTHAMSTOW
South Woodford
CLAYHALL AVENUE
The Cocked Hat
PAINTERS ROAD
Upper Walthamstow
Thorpe Coombe Hospital
Clayhall
Roding Hospital
Barkingside
Aldborough Hatch
Dick Turpin
Low Maynard Reservoir
High Maynard Reservoir
Epping Forest
Roding Valley Park
FOREST
REDBRIDGE
Vestry House Museum
Eagle Hotel
Snaresbrook
Gants Hill
Newbury Park
Goodmayes Hospital
Reservoir
Warwick Reservoirs
St. James's Park
Hollow Pond
Whipps Cross University Hospital
The George
Wanstead Golf Course
REDBRIDGE
Seven Kings Park
Leytonstone
Wanstead
The Basin
Wanstead Park
Valentines Park
Seven Kings
Upper Clapton
Springfield Park
LEYTON
Aldersbrook
Cranbrook
Leyton Orient FC
Lee Valley Park
Wanstead Flats
Ilford Golf Course
Lea Bridge
Hackney
304
Manor Park
ILFORD
South Park
Little Ilford
Forest Gate
Hospital
0 ½ 1 mile
0 1 2 km

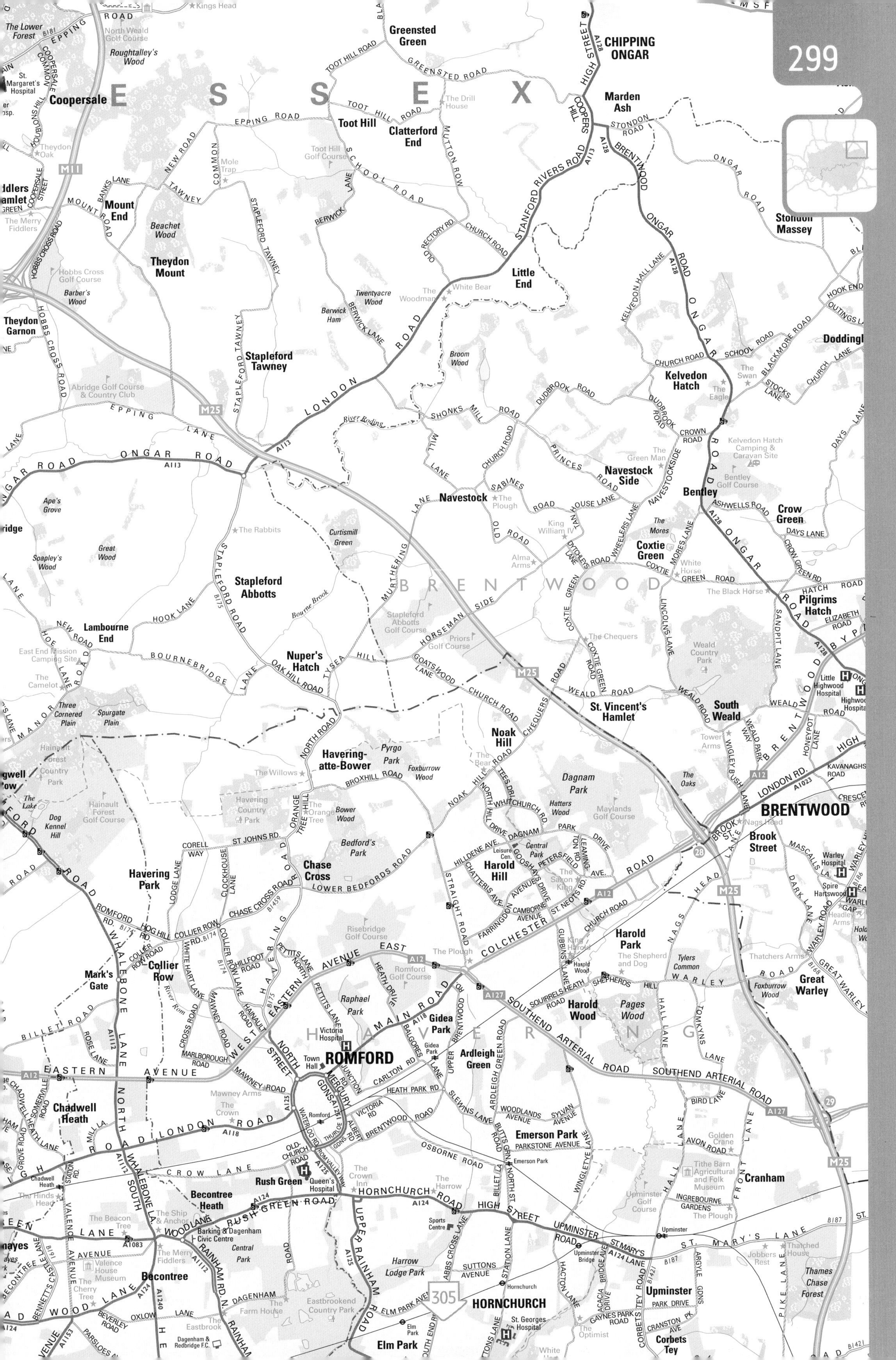
ESSEX
BRENTWOOD
HAVERING
CHIPPING ONGAR
Greensted Green
Marden Ash
Toot Hill
Clatterford End
Coopersale
The Lower Forest
North Weald Golf Course
Roughtalley's Wood
St. Margaret's Hospital
Theydon Oak
Mount End
Beachet Wood
Theydon Mount
Hobbs Cross Golf Course
Barber's Wood
Theydon Garnon
Stapleford Tawney
Toot Hill Golf Course
Mole Trap
The Drill House
Berwick Ham
Twentyacre Wood
The Woodman
The White Bear
Little End
Broom Wood
Stondon Massey
Kelvedon Hatch
The Swan
The Eagle
Kelvedon Hatch Camping & Caravan Site
Doddinghurst
Abridge Golf Course & Country Club
Ape's Grove
Soapley's Wood
Great Wood
Curtismill Green
The Rabbits
Navestock
The Plough
Navestock Side
The Green Man
Bentley
Bentley Golf Course
Crow Green
King William IV
Alma Arms
The Mores
Coxtie Green
White Horse
The Black Horse
Pilgrims Hatch
Stapleford Abbotts
Lambourne End
East End Mission Camping Site
The Camelot
Nuper's Hatch
Stapleford Abbotts Golf Course
Priors Golf Course
The Chequers
Weald Country Park
Little Highwood Hospital
Highwood Hospital
South Weald
St. Vincent's Hamlet
Three Cornered Plain
Spurgate Plain
Hainault Forest Country Park
The Lake
Dog Kennel Hill
Hainault Forest Golf Course
Havering-atte-Bower
Pyrgo Park
Foxburrow Wood
The Willows
Noak Hill
The Bear
Dagnam Park
Hatters Wood
Maylands Golf Course
Tower Arms
The Oaks
BRENTWOOD
Nags Head
Brook Street
Warley Hospital
Spire Hartswood
Havering Country Park
The Orange Tree
Bower Wood
Bedford's Park
Chase Cross
Havering Park
Leisure Cen.
Central Park
Harold Hill
The Saxon King
Risebridge Golf Course
The Plough
Harold Park
The Shepherd and Dog
King Harold
Tylers Common
Thatchers Arms
Headley Arms
Great Warley
Foxburrow Wood
Mark's Gate
Collier Row
Romford Golf Course
Raphael Park
Gidea Park
Harold Wood
Pages Wood
Victoria Hospital
Town Hall
ROMFORD
Ardleigh Green
Chadwell Heath
Mawney Arms
The Crown
Emerson Park
Golden Crane
Tithe Barn Agricultural and Folk Museum
Cranham
Upminster Golf Course
The Plough
Rush Green
Queen's Hospital
The Crown Inn
The Harrow
Becontree Heath
The Ship & Anchor
Barking & Dagenham Civic Centre
Central Park
The Beacon Tree
The Merry Fiddlers
Valence House Museum
The Cherry Tree
Becontree
The Hinds Head
Harrow Lodge Park
Sports Centre
HORNCHURCH
Upminster
Upminster Bridge
Jobbers Rest
Thatched House
Thames Chase Forest
Eastbrookend Country Park
The Farm House
Eastbrook
Dagenham & Redbridge F.C.
Elm Park
St. Georges Hospital
The Optimist
Corbets Tey
305
M25
M11
A12
A127
A113
A128
A118
A124
A125
EPPING ROAD
ONGAR ROAD
LONDON ROAD
STANFORD RIVERS ROAD
SOUTHEND ARTERIAL ROAD
EASTERN AVENUE
COLCHESTER ROAD
MAIN ROAD
HORNCHURCH ROAD
UPPER RAINHAM ROAD
HIGH STREET
WHALEBONE LANE NORTH
WARLEY ROAD

0 1/2 1 mile
0 1 2 km

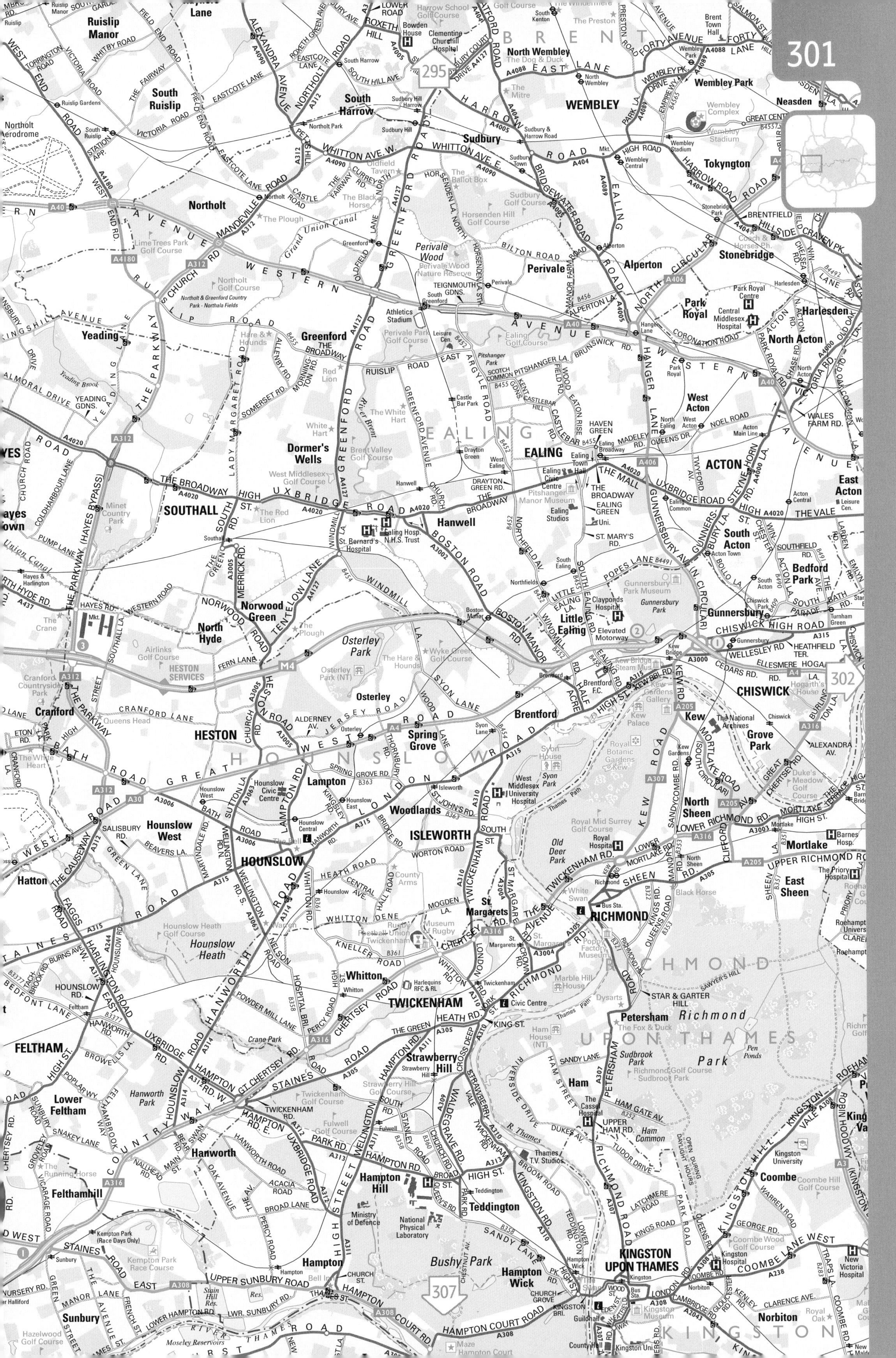
Ruislip Manor
South Ruislip
Northolt Aerodrome
South Harrow
North Wembley
WEMBLEY
Wembley Park
Neasden
Sudbury
Tokyngton
Northolt
Perivale
Alperton
Stonebridge
Harlesden
Park Royal
North Acton
Yeading
Greenford
West Acton
Dormer's Wells
EALING
ACTON
East Acton
SOUTHALL
Hanwell
South Acton
Bedford Park
Norwood Green
North Hyde
Little Ealing
Gunnersbury
Osterley Park
Cranford
HESTON
Osterley
Brentford
CHISWICK
Spring Grove
Kew
Grove Park
HOUNSLOW
Lampton
Woodlands
ISLEWORTH
North Sheen
Mortlake
Hounslow West
Hatton
East Sheen
St. Margarets
RICHMOND
Hounslow Heath
Whitton
TWICKENHAM
FELTHAM
Petersham
Richmond Park
Strawberry Hill
Ham
Lower Feltham
Hanworth
Kingston Vale
Felthamhill
Hampton Hill
Coombe
Teddington
Hampton
Bushy Park
Hampton Wick
KINGSTON UPON THAMES
Sunbury
Norbiton
295
302
307
M4
A4
A40
A316
A205
A308
A3

BRENT
South Wembley
WEMBLEY
Wembley Park
Wembley Complex
Wembley Stadium
Dollis Hill
Neasden
Tokyngton
Sudbury
Brent Town Hall
Swaminarayan Hindi Mission
Gladstone Park
Willesden
Willesden Community Hospital
Childs Hill
Cricklewood
Brondesbury
HAMPSTEAD
Hampstead Heath
Belsize Park
South Hampstead
Primrose Hill
St. John's Wood
Kilburn
Kensal Rise
Maida Vale
PADDINGTON
Stonebridge
Alperton
Perivale
Park Royal
Central Middlesex Hospital
Harlesden
North Acton
West Acton
Wormwood Scrubs
Linford Christie Stadium
H.M. Prison Wormwood Scrubs
Hammersmith Hospital
Queen Charlotte & Chelsea Hosp.
St. Charles Hospital
Princess Louise Hosp.
Westbourne Green
Bayswater
Notting Hill
Hyde Park
Kensington Gardens
Holland Park
KENSINGTON
EALING
Ealing Studios
Pitshanger Manor Museum
ACTON
East Acton
South Acton
Bedford Park
Shepherd's Bush
B.B.C. Television Centre
Loftus Road Queens Park Rangers F.C.
HAMMERSMITH
Olympia
Imp. Coll
Victoria & Albert Museum
Science Mus.
Nat. Hist. Mus.
Brompton
CHELSEA
Hanwell
Little Ealing
Gunnersbury Park
Gunnersbury Park Museum
Gunnersbury
Claypond Hospital
Elevated Motorway
CHISWICK
Hogarth's House
Kew Bridge Steam Museum
Brentford
Brentford F.C.
Kew
Kew Palace
Royal Botanic Gardens Kew
The National Archives
Grove Park
Castelnau
The Wetlands Centre
Charing Cross Hospital
Queens Club
FULHAM
Craven Cottage Fulham FC
Fulham Palace
Parsons Green
Walham Green
Sands End
Stamford Bridge Chelsea FC
Syon House
Syon Park
West Middlesex University Hospital
Royal Mid Surrey Golf Course
Old Deer Park
North Sheen
Mortlake
BARNES
Putney
HAMMERSMITH & FULHAM
East Sheen
RICHMOND
St. Margarets
Roehampton
Queen Mary's Hospital
Putney Heath
WANDSWORTH
Royal Hospital
Southfields
Earlsfield
H.M. Prison Wandsworth
RICHMOND UPON THAMES
Richmond Park
Petersham
Ham House
Ham
Ham Common
Pen Ponds
Richmond Park Golf Course
Wimbledon Windmill Museum
Wimbledon Park
Wimbledon Common
Putney Vale
Kingston Vale
London Scottish Golf Course
All England Lawn Tennis & Croquet Club
Summerstown
Upper Tooting
Tooting Graveney
Twickenham
Teddington
Thames T.V. Studios
Kingston University
Coombe
Coombe Hill Golf Course
Royal Wimbledon Golf Course
WIMBLEDON
Copse Hill
Wolfson Medical Rehabilitation Centre
KINGSTON UPON THAMES
Hampton Wick
Bushy Park
Norbiton
New Malden
Raynes Park
Bushey Mead
MERTON
Nelson Hospital
Collier's Wood
MITCHAM
KINGSTON
0 1/2 1 mile
0 1 2 km
296
301
308

Finsbury Park
LEYTON
Lea Bridge
Lee Valley Park
Hackney Marsh
Dartmouth Park
Upper Holloway
Tufnell Park
Holloway
Highbury
Shacklewell
Lower Clapton
Clapton Park
Homerton
Hackney Wick
Stratford
Kentish Town
Barnsbury
Dalston
Hackney
Victoria Park
Old Ford
Camden Town
King's Cross
Hoxton
Haggerston
Bethnal Green
Bow
Plaistow
Regent's Park
ST. PANCRAS
FINSBURY
St. Luke's
SHOREDITCH
Mile End
Bromley
Bloomsbury
HOLBORN
Soho
Whitechapel
Stepney
Limehouse
Canning Town
Mayfair
Wapping
Shadwell
Poplar
WESTMINSTER
SOUTHWARK
Rotherhithe
BERMONDSEY
Millwall
Cubitt Town
LAMBETH
Walworth
Deptford
Pimlico
Kennington
Vauxhall
CAMBERWELL
Peckham
New Cross Gate
New Cross
St. John's
Blackheath
South Lambeth
Clapham
Stockwell
Brixton
Nunhead
Lewisham
Kidbrooke
Brockley
Herne Hill
Ladywell
Clapham Park
East Dulwich
Honor Oak
Honor Oak Park
Hither Green
DULWICH
Streatham Hill
Tulse Hill
Catford
West Dulwich
Forest Hill
Grove Park
West Norwood
Upper Sydenham
Lower Sydenham
Bell Green
Bellingham
Southend
Downham
STREATHAM
SYDENHAM
Streatham Park
Furzedown
Norwood New Town
New Beckenham
Plaistow
Streatham Vale
Norwood
Penge
BECKENHAM
Norbury
Upper Norwood
South Norwood
Elmers End
Shortlands
304
309
297

298
303
310
Leyton
Aldersbrook
Cranbrook
Ilford
Wanstead Flats
Lee Valley Park
Hackney Marsh
Lower Clapton
Clapton Park
Manor Park
Little Ilford
Forest Gate
Homerton
Hackney Wick
Stratford
West Ham
Upton
Loxford
Barking
Victoria Park
Old Ford
Upton Park
East Ham
Newham
Bow
Tower Hamlets
Mile End
Plaistow
Bromley
Stepney
Canning Town
Custom House
Beckton
Creekmouth
Whitechapel
Limehouse
Shadwell
Wapping
Poplar
Rotherhithe
Silvertown
North Woolwich
Thamesmead
Thamesmead West
London City Airport
Royal Victoria Dock
Royal Albert Dock
Royal George V Dock
The O2
Millwall
Cubitt Town
Bermondsey
Deptford
New Charlton
Woolwich
Plumstead
Charlton
Greenwich
New Cross
New Cross Gate
St. John's
Blackheath
Shooter's Hill
East Wickham
Kidbrooke
Lewisham
Nunhead
Brockley
Blackheath Park
Welling
Falconwood
Ladywell
Lee
Eltham
Avery Hill
Blackfen
Honor Oak
Honor Oak Park
Hither Green
Catford
Forest Hill
Lamorbey
New Eltham
Mottingham
Grove Park
Longlands
Bell Green
Bellingham
Lower Sydenham
Southend
Downham
Elmstead
Sidcup
Sydenham
New Beckenham
Sundridge
Chislehurst West
Plaistow
Chislehurst
Penge
Beckenham
Anerley
Bromley
Widmore
Shortlands
Bickley
River Thames
Thames Barrier
Greenwich
Lewisham
0 ½ 1 mile
0 1 2 km

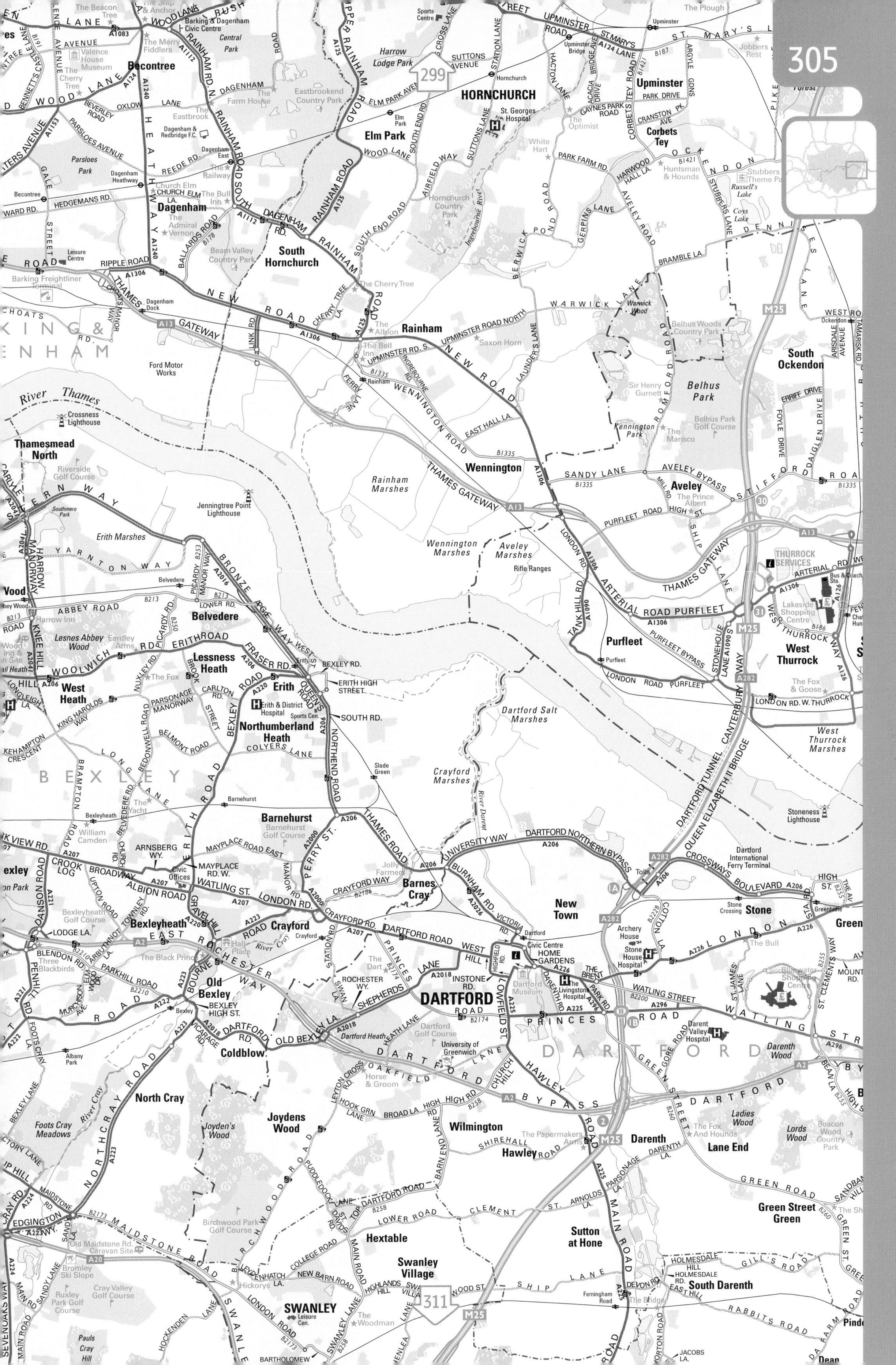
Becontree
Valence House Museum
Barking & Dagenham Civic Centre
Central Park
Harrow Lodge Park
299
HORNCHURCH
St. Georges Hospital
Upminster
Upminster Bridge
Corbets Tey
Elm Park
Eastbrookend Country Park
Dagenham & Redbridge F.C.
Parsloes Park
Dagenham
Hornchurch Country Park
Ingrebourne River
South Hornchurch
Beam Valley Country Park
Barking Freightliner Terminal
Dagenham Dock
Rainham
Saxon Horn
Belhus Woods Country Park
Warwick Wood
South Ockendon
Belhus Park
Sir Henry Gurnett
Belhus Park Golf Course
Kennington Park
Ford Motor Works
River Thames
Crossness Lighthouse
Thamesmead North
Riverside Golf Course
Rainham Marshes
Wennington
Aveley
Jenningtree Point Lighthouse
Erith Marshes
Wennington Marshes
Aveley Marshes
Rifle Ranges
THURROCK SERVICES
Lakeside Shopping Centre
Belvedere
Purfleet
West Thurrock
Lesnes Abbey Wood
Lessness Heath
Erith
West Heath
Erith & District Hospital
Northumberland Heath
Dartford Salt Marshes
West Thurrock Marshes
BEXLEY
Crayford Marshes
River Darent
Stoneness Lighthouse
Barnehurst
Barnehurst Golf Course
DARTFORD TUNNEL
QUEEN ELIZABETH II BRIDGE
Dartford International Ferry Terminal
Bexleyheath
Barnes Cray
New Town
Stone
Bexleyheath Golf Course
Crayford
Archery House
Stone House Hospital
Greenhithe
Old Bexley
DARTFORD
Dartford Museum
Livingstone Hospital
Darent Valley Hospital
Bluewater Shopping Centre
Dartford Heath
Dartford Golf Course
University of Greenwich
Darenth Wood
Coldblow
North Cray
Foots Cray Meadows
Joyden's Wood
Joydens Wood
Wilmington
Hawley
Darenth
Lane End
Ladies Wood
Lords Wood
Beacon Wood Country Park
Birchwood Park Golf Course
Hextable
Sutton at Hone
Green Street Green
Swanley Village
South Darenth
SWANLEY
Cray Valley Golf Course
Ruxley Park Golf Course
Bromley Ski Slope
Pauls Cray Hill
311
M25
A2
A13
A282

Egham Wick
Thorpe Lea
SPELTHORNE
Queen Mary Reservoir
300
Royal Holloway College
Virginia Water
Stroude
Thorpe
Thorpe Green
Laleham
Littleton
VIRGINIA WATER
Laleham Golf Course
Laleham Park Camping Site
Sunbury Golf Course
M3
M25
Chertsey
Shepperton
Wentworth Golf Course
Longcross
Hersham Copse
Lyne
Fan Grove
Bog Wood
Silver Birch Caravan Site
Chertsey Meads
Desborough Island
Addlestone Moor
Abbey Moor Golf Course
Barrow Hills Golf Course
Foxhills Golf Course
St. Peter's Hospital
Runnymede Hospital
Woburn Park
Addlestone
Weybridge
Elmbridge Museum
Chobham Common
RUNNYMEDE
Elmbridge Civic Cen.
Queenswood Golf Course
Row Town
Ottershaw
Stonehill
New Haw
Burrowhill
SURREY HEATH
Ottershaw Park
Brox Copse
Central Veterinary Labs.
Brooklands
Brooklands Museum
Great Wood
Chobham
Fairoaks Airport
Birch Wood
Hoyt Wood
QUEEN MARYS DR.
THE BROADWAY
Byfleet & New Haw
St. George's Hill Golf Course
New Zealand Golf Course
Woodham
Dartnell Park
Mimbridge
Horsell Common
Bleak House
West Byfleet
Byfleet
Broadoaks Government Offices
Silvermere Golf Course
Cobham Bus Museum
Sheerwater
Basingstoke Canal
Nuffield Hospital
West Byfleet Golf Course
Traditions Golf Course
Horsell
WOKING
Pyrford
Wisley
Goldsworth Park
Maybury
The Anchor
The Wisley Golf Course
Wisley Common
Pyrford Green
Mount Hermon
Beechcroft Hospital
St. John's
Knaphill
Hoebridge Golf Centre
Pyrford Village
Pyrford Golf Course
Wisley Gardens (RHS)
Ockham Common
Bolder Mere
Elm Corner
Woking Park
Leisure Cen.
Newark Priory (rems)
Martyr's Green
Hook Heath
Old Woking
Woking Golf Course
River Wey
Ripley Green
Half Moon
Ockham
Chaffers Copse
Westfield
The Cricketers
Mayford
Oakham Park
Ripley
Stumps Grove
New Inn
Westfield Common
Services
Sutton Green Golf Course
Send
Send Marsh
Jovial Sailor
Barnsthorns Wood
Worplesdon
Horsley Camping & Caravan Site
Sutton Green
The Fox & Hounds
Whitmoor Pond
Jolly Farmer
Poor Jack's Wood
Sendgrove
Lollesworth Wood
H.M. Prison Send
GUILDFORD
Jacobs Well
Sutton Park
Sutton Place
Whitmoor Common
Burpham Court Farm Park
Frithy's Wood
West Clandon
West Horsley
King William IV
Stringer's Common
Clandon
Cotts Wood
Onslow Arms Inn
Hatchlands Park
Burpham
Christ College Ski Slope
Clandon Regis Golf Course
Queens Head
East
0 1/2 1 mile
0 1 2 km

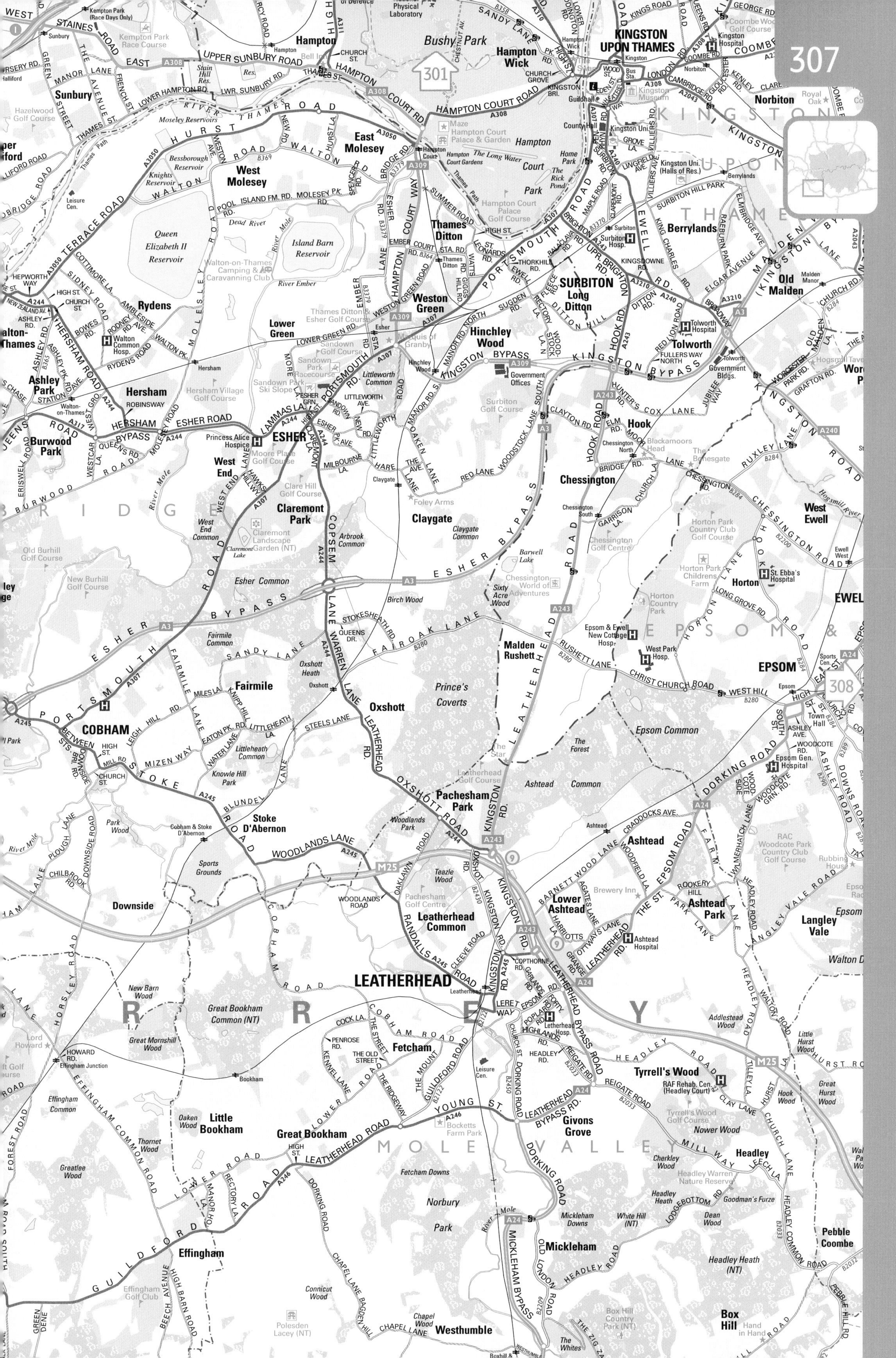
301
308
KINGSTON UPON THAMES
Hampton
Hampton Wick
Bushy Park
Kempton Park Race Course
Sunbury
Hampton Court Palace & Garden
East Molesey
West Molesey
Queen Elizabeth II Reservoir
Island Barn Reservoir
Thames Ditton
Weston Green
Surbiton
SURBITON
Long Ditton
Berrylands
Norbiton
Old Malden
Tolworth
Hinchley Wood
Lower Green
Rydens
Walton-on-Thames
Hersham
Ashley Park
Burwood Park
ESHER
West End
Claremont Park
Claygate
Chessington
Hook
Chessington World of Adventures
Esher Common
Prince's Coverts
Malden Rushett
Oxshott
Fairmile
COBHAM
Stoke D'Abernon
Pachesham Park
Horton
West Ewell
EWELL
EPSOM
Epsom Common
Ashtead Common
Ashtead
Lower Ashtead
Ashtead Park
Langley Vale
Downside
Leatherhead Common
LEATHERHEAD
Fetcham
Tyrrell's Wood
Great Bookham
Little Bookham
Givons Grove
Headley
Effingham
Norbury Park
Mickleham
Westhumble
Box Hill
Pebble Combe
Headley Heath (NT)
Fetcham Downs
Polesden Lacey (NT)
KINGSTON BYPASS
ESHER BYPASS
PORTSMOUTH ROAD
LEATHERHEAD ROAD
KINGSTON RD.
M25
A3
A24
A243
A244
A245
A246
A307
A308
A309
MOLE VALLEY
SURREY
EPSOM & EWELL
KINGSTON UPON THAMES

KINGSTON UPON THAMES
Norbiton
New Malden
Raynes Park
Bushey Mead
MORDEN
MERTON
MITCHAM
Copse Hill
Hampton Court Park
Berrylands
Motspur Park
West Barnes
Morden Park
St. Helier
Rosehill
SURBITON
Long Ditton
Old Malden
Hinchley Wood
Tolworth
Worcester Park
North Cheam
Benhilton
The Wrythe
CARSHALTON
Hook
Chessington
Stoneleigh
CHEAM
SUTTON
West Ewell
Horton
EWELL
East Ewell
Carshalton Beeches
Malden Rushett
EPSOM
Belmont
Banstead Downs
North Looe
BANSTEAD
Woodmansterne
Epsom Common
Pachesham Park
Ashtead
Nork
Tattenham Corner
Lower Ashtead
Ashtead Park
Langley Vale
Epsom Downs
Burgh Heath
Walton Downs
Tadworth
Kingswood
Chipstead Bottom
Tyrrell's Wood
Givons Grove
Walton on the Hill
Banstead Heath
Mugswell
Headley
Mickleham
Pebble Coombe
Walton Heath
Lower Kingswood
Mogador
Margery
Box Hill
Westhumble
KINGSTON
UPON
THAMES
SUTTON
EPSOM & EWELL
REIGATE & BANSTEAD
KINGSTON BYPASS
M25
302
307
0 1/2 1 mile
0 1 2 km

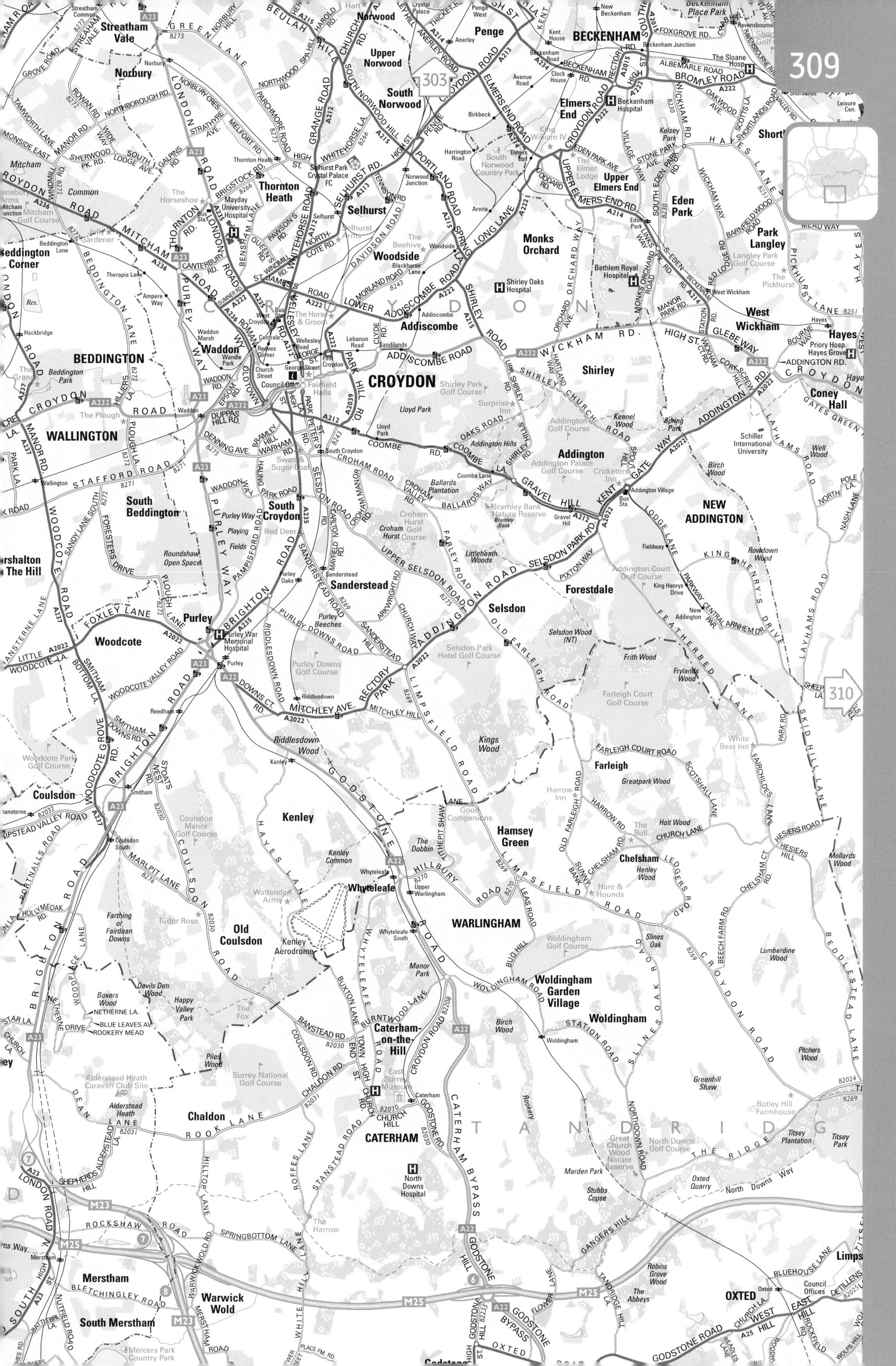

Streatham Vale
Norbury
Mitcham
Common
Thornton Heath
Upper Norwood
South Norwood
Norwood
Penge
BECKENHAM
Beckenham Place Park
Elmers End
Upper Elmers End
Eden Park
Park Langley
Shortlands
Selhurst
Woodside
Addiscombe
Monks Orchard
Shirley Oaks Hospital
Beddington Corner
BEDDINGTON
Waddon
CROYDON
WALLINGTON
South Beddington
South Croydon
Shirley
Addington
Lloyd Park
West Wickham
Hayes
Coney Hall
NEW ADDINGTON
Forestdale
Selsdon
Sanderstead
Purley
Woodcote
Coulsdon
Kenley
Kenley Aerodrome
Whyteleafe
Hamsey Green
Farleigh
Chelsham
WARLINGHAM
Old Coulsdon
Woldingham Garden Village
Woldingham
Caterham-on-the-Hill
CATERHAM
Chaldon
Merstham
South Merstham
Warwick Wold
OXTED
Limpsfield
CROYDON
TANDRIDGE
M23
M25
A23
A22
A232
A212
A2022
303
310

304
309
BECKENHAM
Elmers End
Upper Elmers End
Eden Park
Shortlands
BROMLEY
Widmore
Bickley
Southborough
Petts Wood
Poverest
ORPINGTON
Monks Orchard
Park Langley
West Wickham
Hayes
Shirley
Coney Hall
Keston
Bromley Common
Farnborough
Chelsfield
Green Street Green
Addington
NEW ADDINGTON
Forestdale
Selsdon
Leaves Green
Downe
Hazelwood
Farleigh
Hamsey Green
Chelsham
BIGGIN HILL
Aperfield
Single Street
Cudham
Berry's Green
Horns Green
WARLINGHAM
South Street
Tatsfield
Woldingham Garden Village
Woldingham
Titsey
Westerham
Hosey Hill
Limpsfield
OXTED
Limpsfield Chart
Goodley Stock
Kent Hatch
Godstone
London Biggin Hill Airport
Princess Royal University Hospital
Clacket Lane Services
Down House (Darwin Museum)
Titsey Park
Squerryes Court
TANDRIDGE
BROMLEY
M25
A21
A22
A25
A232
A233
A2022
B269
CROYDON ROAD
WESTERHAM ROAD
PILGRIMS WAY
North Downs Way
0 ½ 1 mile
0 1 2 km

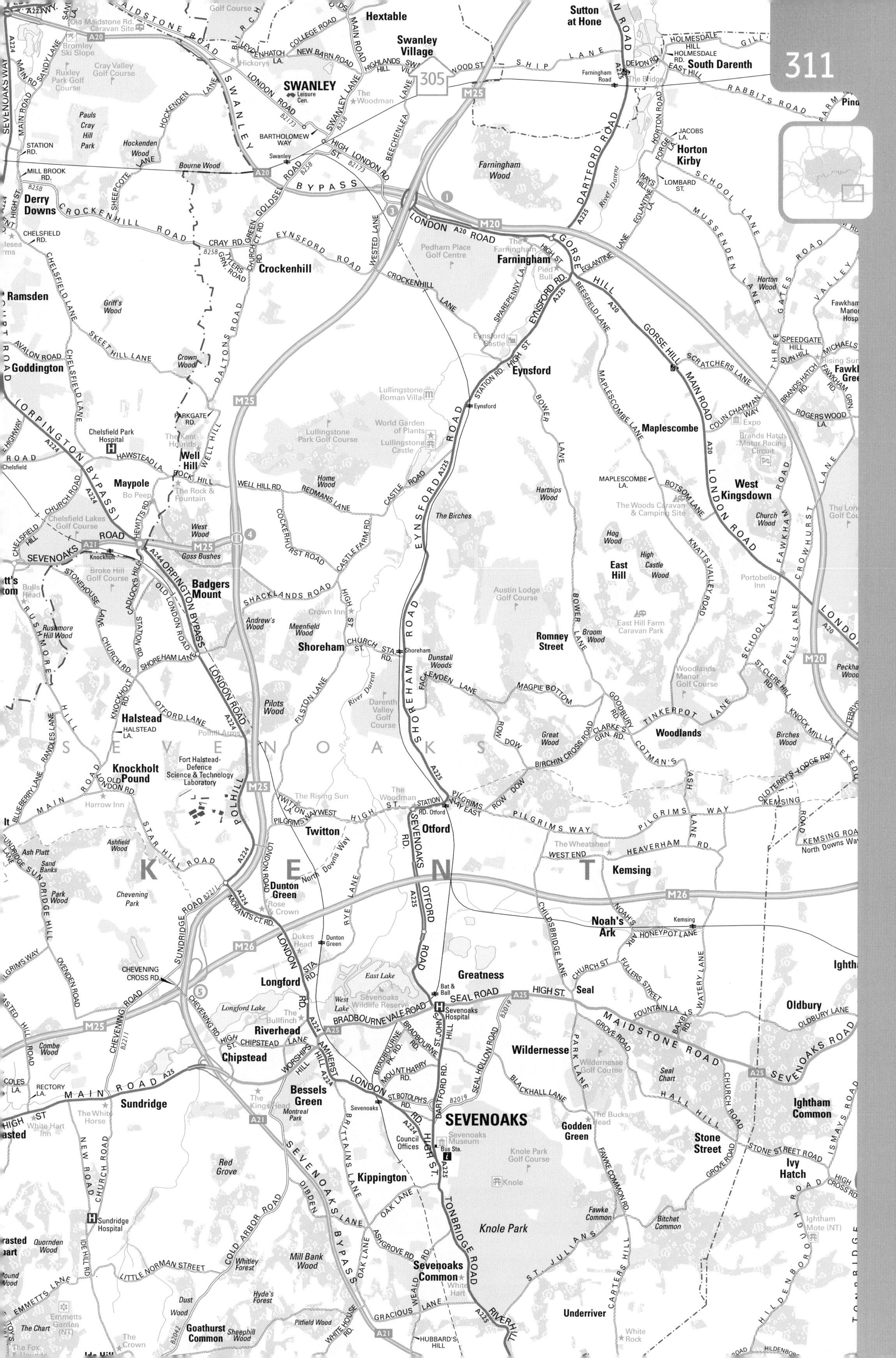

Hextable
Sutton at Hone
Swanley Village
305
SWANLEY
South Darenth
Horton Kirby
Farningham Wood
Derry Downs
Crockenhill
Farningham
Pedham Place Golf Centre
Ramsden
Goddington
Eynsford
Eynsford Castle
Lullingstone Roman Villa
Lullingstone Park Golf Course
World Garden of Plants
Lullingstone Castle
Maplescombe
West Kingsdown
Chelsfield Park Hospital
Well Hill
Maypole
Chelsfield Lakes Golf Course
Badgers Mount
Broke Hill Golf Course
East Hill
Romney Street
Austin Lodge Golf Course
Shoreham
Halstead
Knockholt Pound
Fort Halstead-Defence Science & Technology Laboratory
Woodlands
Darenth Valley Golf Course
Twitton
Otford
Kemsing
Noah's Ark
Dunton Green
Longford
Greatness
Seal
Oldbury
Riverhead
Chipstead
Wilderness
Sundridge
Bessels Green
SEVENOAKS
Sevenoaks Hospital
Sevenoaks Museum
Knole Park Golf Course
Knole
Knole Park
Godden Green
Stone Street
Ightham Common
Ivy Hatch
Kippington
Sevenoaks Common
Underriver
Goathurst Common
Sundridge Hospital
Emmetts Garden (NT)
Ightham Mote (NT)
SEVENOAKS
KENT
M25
M20
M26
A20
A21
A25
A224
A225

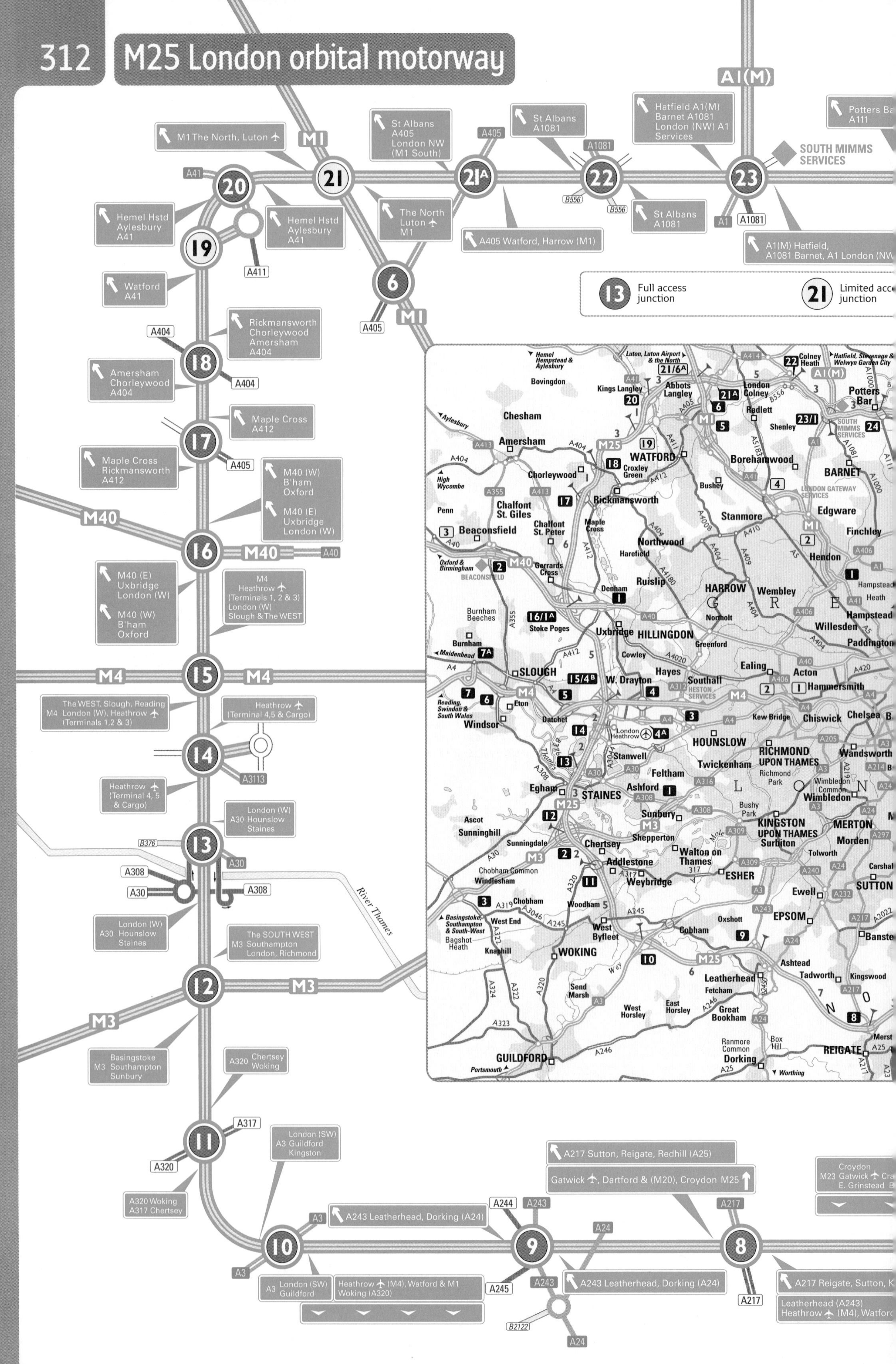
312
M25 London orbital motorway
A1(M)
M1
M1 The North, Luton
St Albans A405 London NW (M1 South)
A405
St Albans A1081
A1081
Hatfield A1(M) Barnet A1081 London (NW) A1 Services
Potters Ba A111
SOUTH MIMMS SERVICES
A41
20
21
21A
22
23
B556
St Albans A1081
A1
A1081
A1(M) Hatfield, A1081 Barnet, A1 London (NW
Hemel Hstd Aylesbury A41
Hemel Hstd Aylesbury A41
The North Luton M1
A405 Watford, Harrow (M1)
19
A411
6
A405
Watford A41
13 Full access junction
21 Limited acc junction
A404
Rickmansworth Chorleywood Amersham A404
18
Amersham Chorleywood A404
A404
Maple Cross A412
17
Maple Cross Rickmansworth A412
A405
M40 (W) B'ham Oxford
M40 (E) Uxbridge London (W)
M40
16
M40
A40
M40 (E) Uxbridge London (W)
M40 (W) B'ham Oxford
M4 Heathrow (Terminals 1, 2 & 3) London (W) Slough & The WEST
M4
15
M4
The WEST, Slough, Reading M4 London (W), Heathrow (Terminals 1,2 & 3)
Heathrow (Terminal 4,5 & Cargo)
14
A3113
Heathrow (Terminal 4, 5 & Cargo)
London (W) A30 Hounslow Staines
B376
13
A308
A30
A30
A308
River Thames
London (W) A30 Hounslow Staines
The SOUTH WEST M3 Southampton London, Richmond
12
M3
M3
Basingstoke M3 Southampton Sunbury
A320 Chertsey Woking
A317
11
A320
London (SW) A3 Guildford Kingston
A320 Woking A317 Chertsey
A217 Sutton, Reigate, Redhill (A25)
Gatwick, Dartford & (M20), Croydon M25
Croydon M23 Gatwick E. Grinstead
A3
A243 Leatherhead, Dorking (A24)
A244
A243
A217
A24
10
9
8
A3
A3 London (SW) Guildford
Heathrow (M4), Watford & M1 Woking (A320)
A245
A243
A243 Leatherhead, Dorking (A24)
A217
A217 Reigate, Sutton, K
Leatherhead (A243) Heathrow (M4), Watford
B2122
A24
WATFORD
Rickmansworth
HARROW
HILLINGDON
SLOUGH
Windsor
HOUNSLOW
RICHMOND UPON THAMES
KINGSTON UPON THAMES
STAINES
WOKING
GUILDFORD
EPSOM
ESHER
SUTTON
MERTON
REIGATE
BARNET
Borehamwood
Potters Bar
Chesham
Amersham
Beaconsfield
Uxbridge
Ealing
Hammersmith
Wembley
Edgware
Leatherhead
Dorking
Weybridge
Chertsey
Addlestone
Egham
Feltham
Twickenham
Wimbledon
Kingswood
Box Hill

Enfield
Hertford
A10

Waltham
Abbey
Loughton
A121

M11 London (N.E.), Stansted, Harlow, Cambridge

Chelmsford
Romford A12
Brentwood
A1023

Potters Bar
A111

A10 London (N & C), Hertford, Enfield

Waltham
Abbey
Loughton
A121

M11 London (N.E.), Stansted, Harlow, Cambridge

Chelmsford
A12
Brentwood
A1023

Basildon
Southend
A127

Primary road junction

Romford
Basildon
Southend
A127

Dagenham
Thurrock A13
(Lakeside)
Tilbury
(A1306, A126)
(A1090)
Thurrock Services

London (E & C)
Barking
Docklands
Tilbury
Basildon
Non motorway traffic

THURROCK SERVICES

Thurrock (Lakeside) Services A1306
Purfleet (A1090)
W. Thurrock (A126)

Tunnel (Northbound)
Bridge (Southbound)
River Thames

Dartford Crossing

Toll

Swanscombe
Erith A206
Bluewater

Swanscombe (A226)
Erith A206

Dartford Toll Tunnel
Dagenham (A13) The North (M11, M1) (M25)

Dartford A225

London, Canterbury (M2)
Non-motorway traffic

London
Canterbury (M2)
Non-motorway traffic

A2 London (SE & C), Bexleyheath
Canterbury (M2), Dartford (A225)

London
(SE & C)
Lewisham
A20
Dover
Channel
Tunnel
Maidstone
M20

London (SE & C)
Lewisham
A20
Channel Tunnel
Maidstone
M20

Bromley
A21
Orpington
A224

London (SE)
Bromley
A21
Orpington
(A224)

M25 Gatwick (M23) Heathrow (M4)
Sevenoaks Hastings A21

Maidstone
Channel Tnl M26 (M20)
Dover
Sevenoaks, Hastings A21

A22 Eastbourne Godstone, Caterham Westerham (A25)

(M20, M11)
Dartford
Maidstone
Sevenoaks (A21)
M25

Westerham (A25)
Dartford & (M11)
Maidstone (M20)
M25

CLACKET LANE SERVICES

E. Grinstead
Eastbourne
Caterham
Godstone
A22
Redhill
(A25)

Brighton
M23(S) Crawley
Gatwick

(M1) & Waford, Reigate (A217)
Heathrow (M4) M25

M23(N) Croydon

(A240)

M25

2 Full junction
2 Restricted junction

0 2 4 miles
0 2 4 6 km

Key to map symbols

- Short stay car park
- Mid stay car park
- Long stay car park
- London underground station
- Railway station
- Monorail station
- Information centre for tourists
- Bus station
- Major hotel

Luton

Tel. 01582 405100
www.london-luton.co.uk

Stansted

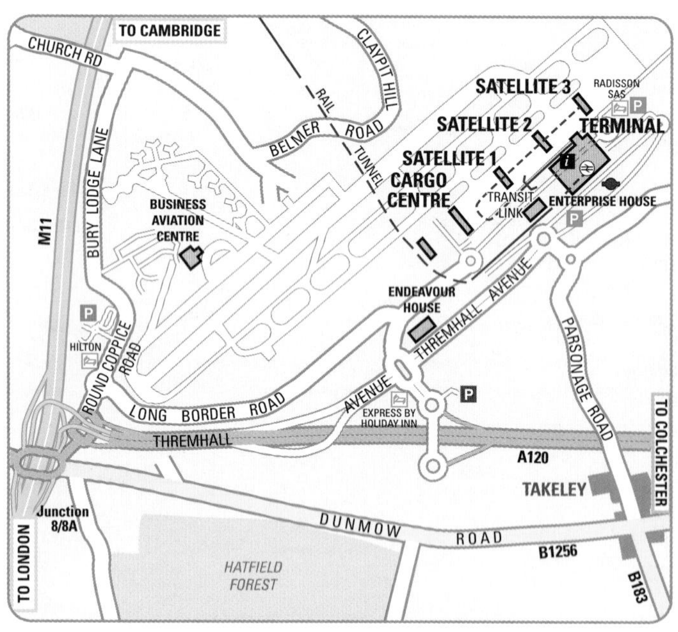

Tel. 0870 000 0303
www.stanstedairport.com

Heathrow

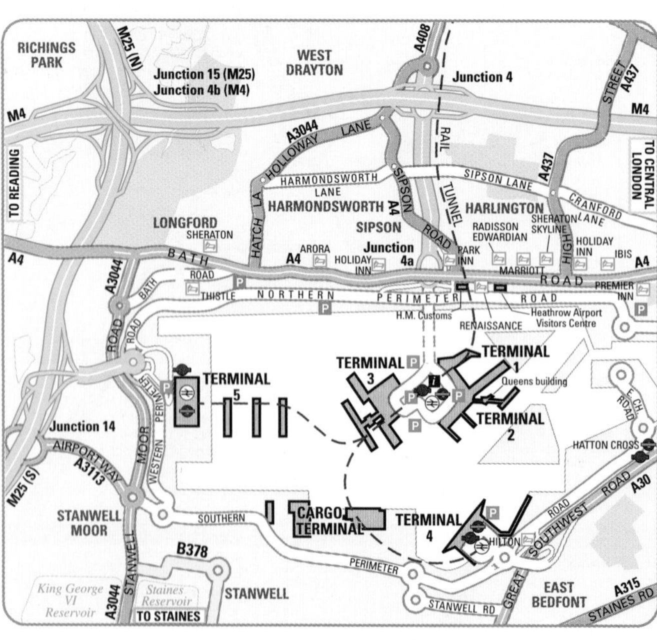

Tel. 0870 000 0123
www.heathrowairport.com

Gatwick

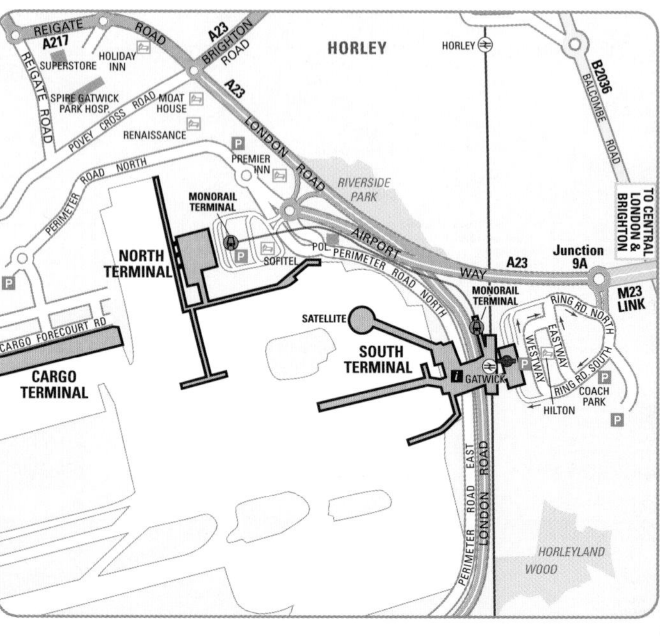

Tel. 0870 000 2468
www.gatwickairport.com

Congestion Charging Zone

The London Congestion Charging Zone was introduced to reduce traffic congestion within Central London.

● The eastern section of the zone operates inside the 'Inner Ring Road' linking Marylebone Road, Euston Road, Pentonville Road, Tower Bridge, Elephant and Castle, Vauxhall Bridge and Park Lane. The western section of the zone is bounded by Harrow Road, the West Cross Route, the inner southbound arm of the Earls Court one way system, Chelsea Embankment, Vauxhall Bridge Road and Park Lane. The route around the zone and between the two sections is exempt from charge (see map below).

● The daily operating time is from 7am to 6pm, Monday to Friday, excluding public holidays and the period between Christmas Day and New Year's Day.

● Payment of the daily £8 Congestion Charge, either in advance or on the day of travel, allows the registered vehicle to enter, drive around and leave the congestion zone as many times as required on that one day.

● Payments can be made in a variety of ways but in all cases the vehicle registration number and the dates to be paid for must be given.
Charges can be paid:

- online at www.cclondon.com
- by phone on 0845 900 1234
- by text message for drivers who have pre-registered on the website or telephone.
- by post by requesting an application form from Congestion Charging, PO Box 2982, Coventry, CV7 8WR, or downloading the form from the website and posting to the same address.
- at self-service machines in major car parks within the congestion zone.
- at newsagents, convenience stores or petrol stations throughout the Greater London area where you see the Congestion Charging sign or the PayPoint logo.

PayPoint

● Further information, including vehicles eligible for exemption or a discount, can be found on the website **www.cclondon.com** or by telephoning 0845 900 1234.

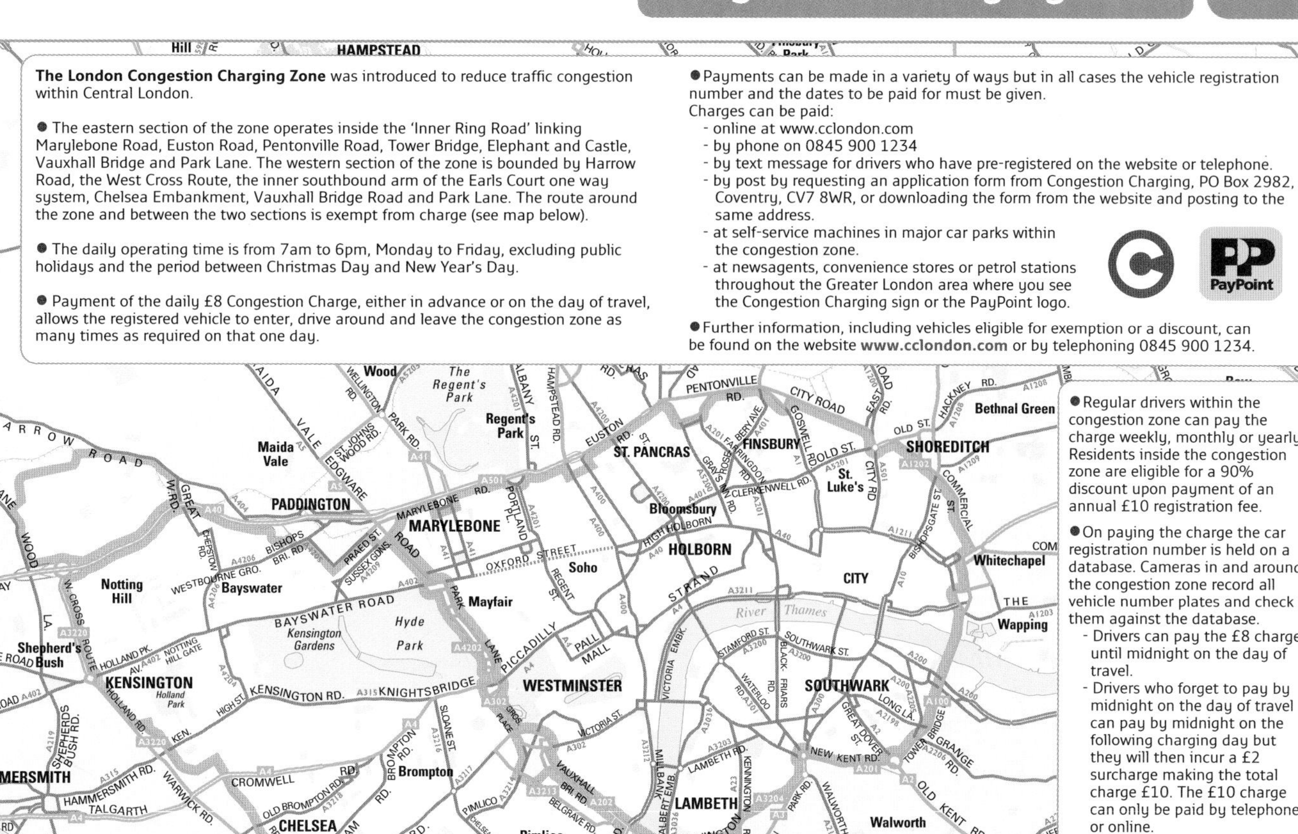

This symbol is shown on traffic signs when approaching, entering and leaving the congestion charging zone.

Congestion charging zone

● Regular drivers within the congestion zone can pay the charge weekly, monthly or yearly. Residents inside the congestion zone are eligible for a 90% discount upon payment of an annual £10 registration fee.

● On paying the charge the car registration number is held on a database. Cameras in and around the congestion zone record all vehicle number plates and check them against the database.

- Drivers can pay the £8 charge until midnight on the day of travel.
- Drivers who forget to pay by midnight on the day of travel can pay by midnight on the following charging day but they will then incur a £2 surcharge making the total charge £10. The £10 charge can only be paid by telephone or online.

Any driver who has not paid before midnight on the following charging day will be sent a £120 Penalty Charge Notice (PCN). Payment within 14 days will reduce this to £60. Failure to pay within 28 days will result in the penalty being increased to £180.

Low Emission Zone

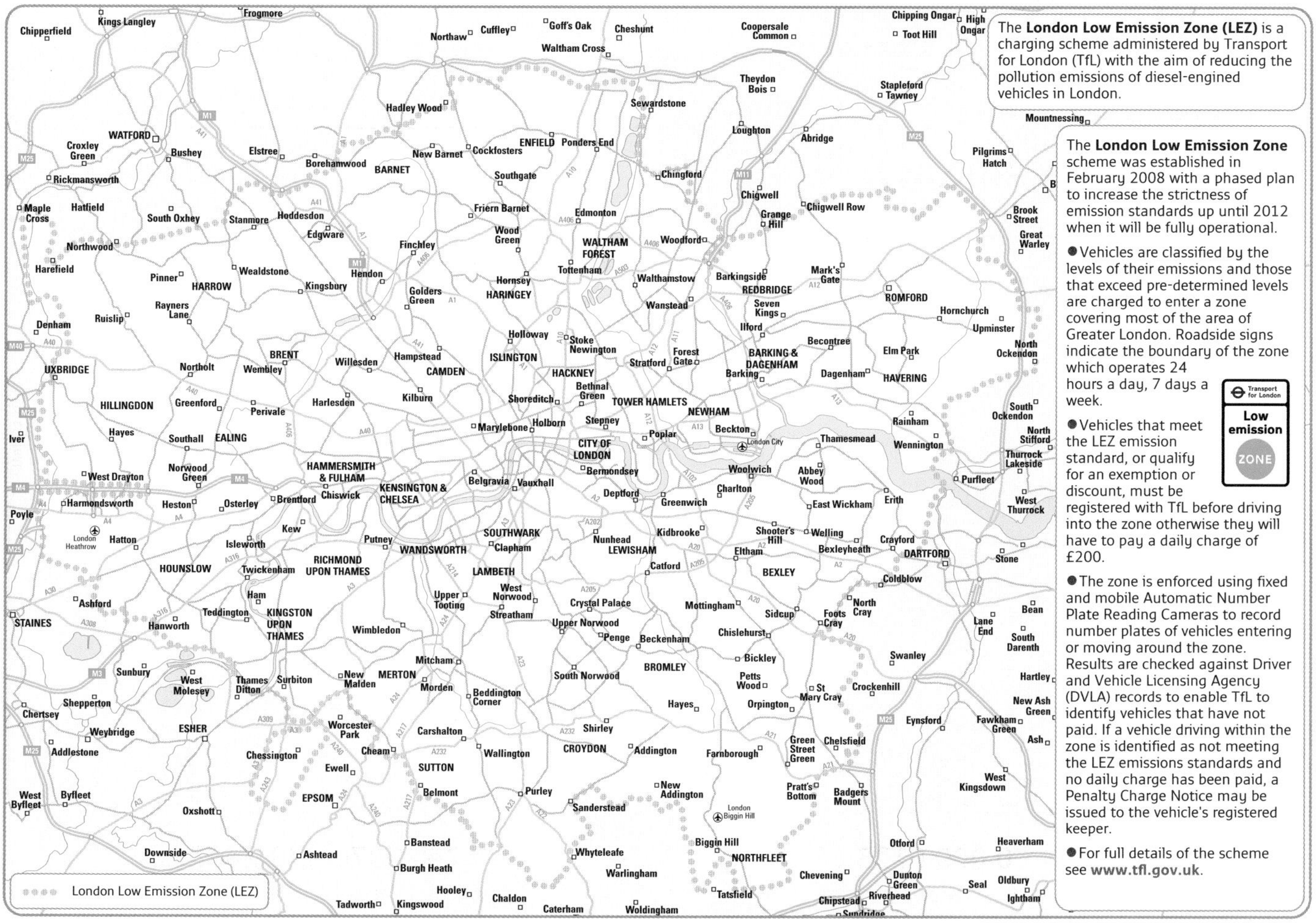

The **London Low Emission Zone (LEZ)** is a charging scheme administered by Transport for London (TfL) with the aim of reducing the pollution emissions of diesel-engined vehicles in London.

The **London Low Emission Zone** scheme was established in February 2008 with a phased plan to increase the strictness of emission standards up until 2012 when it will be fully operational.

● Vehicles are classified by the levels of their emissions and those that exceed pre-determined levels are charged to enter a zone covering most of the area of Greater London. Roadside signs indicate the boundary of the zone which operates 24 hours a day, 7 days a week.

Transport for London
Low emission
ZONE

● Vehicles that meet the LEZ emission standard, or qualify for an exemption or discount, must be registered with TfL before driving into the zone otherwise they will have to pay a daily charge of £200.

● The zone is enforced using fixed and mobile Automatic Number Plate Reading Cameras to record number plates of vehicles entering or moving around the zone. Results are checked against Driver and Vehicle Licensing Agency (DVLA) records to enable TfL to identify vehicles that have not paid. If a vehicle driving within the zone is identified as not meeting the LEZ emissions standards and no daily charge has been paid, a Penalty Charge Notice may be issued to the vehicle's registered keeper.

● For full details of the scheme see **www.tfl.gov.uk**.

London Low Emission Zone (LEZ)

Notes on how to use the index

The index starting on page 318 combines entries for street names, place names, places of interest, stations, hospitals, schools, colleges and universities.

Place names are shown in capital letters,
e.g. **ACTON**, W3 . . . . **160** CN74
These include towns, villages and other localities within the area covered by this atlas.

Places of interest are shown with a star symbol,
e.g. ★ **British Mus, The** WC1 . . **17** P7
These include parks, museums, galleries, other important buildings and tourist attractions.

Other features are shown by symbols as listed :-

Symbol	Feature	Symbol	Feature
⇌	Railway station	H	Hospital
	London Overground station	Sch	School
⊖	London Underground station	Coll	College
DLR	Docklands Light Railway station	Uni	University
Tra	Tramlink station	Jct	Road junction
Riv	Pedestrian ferry landing stage	●	Selected industrial estate / commercial building
	Bus station		Selected major shop / shopping centre / market

All other entries are for street names.

When there is more than one feature with exactly the same name then that name is shown only once in the index.
It is then followed by a list of entries for each postal district that contains a feature with that same name. London postal district references are given first in alpha-numeric order and are followed by either the post town or locality in alphabetical order. For example, there are three streets called **Ardley Close** in this atlas and the index entry shows that one of these is in London postal district NW10, one is in London postal district SE6 and one is in Ruislip HA4.
e.g. **Ardley Cl**, NW10 . . . .**140** CS62
SE6 . . . .**205** DY90
Ruislip HA4 . . . .**137** BQ59

In cases where there are two or more streets of the same name in the same postal area, extra information is given in brackets to aid location.
Some postal areas are abbreviated and a full list of locality and post town abbreviations used in this atlas is given on the following page.

All entries are followed by the page number and grid reference on which the name will be found. So, in the example above, **Ardley Close,** NW10 will be found on page **140** in square CS62.

All entries are indexed to the largest scale map on which they are shown.

The index also contains some features which are not actually named on the maps because there is not enough space. In these cases the adjoining or nearest named thoroughfare to such a street is shown in *italic.* The reference indicates where the unnamed street is located *off* the named thoroughfare.
e.g. **Baird Cl**, E10 *off Marconi Rd*. **145** EA60

A strict letter-by-letter alphabetical order is followed in this index. All non-alphabetic characters such as spaces, hyphens or apostrophes have not been included in the index order. For example **Belle Vue Road** and **Bellevue Road** will be found listed together.

Names beginning with a definite article (i.e. **The**) are indexed from their second word onwards with the definite article being placed at the end of the name.
e.g. **Avenue, The,** E4 . . . . **123** ED51

Standard terms such as **Avenue, Close, Rise** and **Road** are abbreviated in the index but are ordered alphabetically as if given in full. So, for example, **Abbots Ri** comes before **Abbots Rd.** A list of these abbreviations is given below.

General abbreviations

A&E Accident & Emergency
Acad Academy
All Alley
App Approach
Apts Apartments
Arc Arcade
Assoc Association
Av Avenue
Ave Avenue
BUPA British United Provident Association
Bdy Broadway
Bk Bank
Bldg Building
Bldgs Buildings
Boul Boulevard
Bowl Bowling
Br Bridge
C of E Church of England
Cath Cathedral, Catholic
CCC County Cricket Club
Cem Cemetery
Cen Central, Centre
Cft Croft
Cfts Crofts
Ch Church
Chyd Churchyard
Circ Circus
Cl Close
Co County
Coll College
Comb Combined
Comm Community
Comp Comprehensive
Conf Conference
Cont Continuing
Conv Convent
Cor Corner
Cors Corners
Cotts Cottages
Cres Crescent
Ct Court
Ctyd Courtyard
Del Delivery
Dep Depot
Dept Department
Dev Development
Dr Drive
Dws Dwellings
E East
Ed Education, Educational
Embk Embankment
Est Estate
Ex Exchange
Exhib Exhibition
Ext Extension
FC Football Club
Fit Cen Fitness Centre
Fld Field
Flds Fields
Fm Farm
GM Grant Maintained
Gall Gallery
Gar Garage
Gdn Garden
Gdns Gardens
Gen General
Gra Grange
Gram Grammar
Grd Ground
Grds Grounds
Grn Green
Grns Greens
Gro Grove
Gros Groves
Gt Great
HQ Headquarters
Ho House
Hos Houses
Hosp Hospital
HPRU Human Psycho-pharmacology Research Unit
Hts Heights
Ind Industrial
Indep Independent
Inf Infant(s)
Inst Institute
Int International
JM Junior Mixed
JMI Junior Mixed & Infant(s)
Jun Junior
Junct Junction
La Lane
Las Lanes
Lib Library
Lit Literary
Lo Lodge
Lwr Lower
Mans Mansions
Med Medical
Med Medicine
Mem Memorial
Met Metropolitan
Mid Middle
Mkt Market
Ms Mews
Mt Mount
Mus Museum
N North
NHS National Health Service
Nat National
Nurs Nursery
Off Office
PO Post Office
PRU Pupil Referral Unit
Par Parade
Pas Passage
Pk Park
Pl Place
Pol Police
Poly Polytechnic
Prec Precinct
Prep Preparatory
Prim Primary
Prom Promenade
Pt Point
Quad Quadrant
RC Roman Catholic
Rbt Roundabout
Rd Road
Rds Roads
Rehab Rehabilitation
Ri Rise
S South
Sch School
Schs Schools
Sec Secondary
Sen Senior
Shop Shopping
Spec Special
Sq Square
St Street
St. Saint
Sta Station
Sts Streets
Sub Subway
TA Territorial Army
Tech Technical, Technology
Tenn Tennis
Ter Terrace
Thea Theatre
Trd Trading
Twr Tower
Twrs Towers
Uni University
Upr Upper
VA Voluntary Aided
VC Voluntary Controlled
Vet Veterinary
Vil Villas
Vil Villa
Vw View
W West
Wd Wood
Wds Woods
Wf Wharf
Wk Walk
Wks Works
Yd Yard

Locality & post town abbreviations

Note: In the following list of abbreviations post towns are in **bold** type.

Abb.L.	**Abbots Langley**
Abin.Com.	Abinger Common
Abin.Ham.	Abinger Hammer
Add.	**Addlestone**
Alb.Hth	Albury Heath
Ald.	Aldenham
Amer.	**Amersham**
Amer.O.T.	Amersham Old Town
Art.	Artington
Ash.Grn	Ashley Green
Ashf.	**Ashford**
Ashtd.	**Ashtead**
Ayot St.P.	Ayot Saint Peter
B.End	Bourne End
B.Stort.	Bishop's Stortford
Bad.Dene	Badgers Dene
Bad.Mt	Badgers Mount
Bans.	**Banstead**
Bark.	**Barking**
Barn.	**Barnet**
Barne.	Barnehurst
Beac.	**Beaconsfield**
Beck.	**Beckenham**
Bedd.	Beddington
Bedd.Cor.	Beddington Corner
Bell.	Bellingdon
Belv.	**Belvedere**
Berk.	**Berkhamsted**
Berry's Grn	Berry's Green
Bet.	**Betchworth**
Bex.	**Bexley**
Bexh.	**Bexleyheath**
Bigg.H.	Biggin Hill
Birch Grn	Birch Green
Bkhm	Bookham
Bletch.	Bletchingley
Borwd.	**Borehamwood**
Bov.	Bovingdon
Box H.	Box Hill
Bramfld	Bramfield
Brent.	**Brentford**
Brick.Wd	Bricket Wood
Broad.Com.	Broadley Common
Brock.	Brockham
Brom.	Bromley
Brook.Pk	Brookmans Park
Brox.	**Broxbourne**
Brwd.	**Brentwood**
Buck.H.	**Buckhurst Hill**
Burgh Hth	Burgh Heath
Burn.	Burnham
Bushey Hth	Bushey Heath
Carp.Pk	Carpenders Park
Cars.	**Carshalton**
Cat.	**Caterham**
Ch.End	Church End
Ch.Lang.	Church Langley
Ch.St.G.	**Chalfont Saint Giles**
Chad.Hth	Chadwell Heath
Chad.Spr.	Chadwell Springs
Chad.St.M.	Chadwell Saint Mary
Chaff.Hun.	Chafford Hundred
Chal.St.P.	Chalfont Saint Peter
Chan.Cr.	Chandlers Cross
Chap.End	Chapmore End
Charl.	Charlwood
Chel.	Chelsham
Chels.	Chelsfield
Cher.	**Chertsey**
Chesh.	**Chesham**
Chesh.B.	Chesham Bois
Chess.	**Chessington**
Chev.	Chevening
Chig.	**Chigwell**
Chilw.	Chilworth
Chipper.	Chipperfield
Chis.	**Chislehurst**
Chob.Com.	Chobham Common
Chorl.	Chorleywood
Chsht	Cheshunt
Cipp.	Cippenham
Clay.	Claygate
Cob.	**Cobham**
Cockfos.	Cockfosters
Cole Grn	Cole Green
Colesh.	Coleshill
Coll.Row	Collier Row
Coln.Hth	Colney Heath
Coln.St	Colney Street
Colnbr.	Colnbrook
Cooper.	Coopersale
Couls.	**Coulsdon**
Cran.	Cranford
Craw.	Crawley
Cray.	Crayford
Crock.	Crockenhill
Crock.H.	Crockham Hill
Crox.Grn	Croxley Green
Croy.	**Croydon**
Dag.	**Dagenham**
Dance.H.	Dancers Hill
Dart.	**Dartford**
Denh.	Denham
Dor.	**Dorking**
Dorney R.	Dorney Reach
Down.	Downside
Dunt.Grn	Dunton Green
E.Barn.	East Barnet
E.Bed.	East Bedfont
E.Burn.	East Burnham
E.Clan.	East Clandon
E.Ewell	East Ewell
E.Hors.	East Horsley
E.Mol.	**East Molesey**
E.Til.	East Tilbury
Earls.	Earlswood
Eastcote Vill.	Eastcote Village
Eden.	Edenbridge
Edg.	**Edgware**
Eff.	Effingham
Eff.Junct.	Effingham Junction
Egh.	**Egham**
Elm Pk	Elm Park
Elm.Wds	Elmstead Woods
Els.	Elstree
Enf.	**Enfield**
Eng.Grn	Englefield Green
Epp.	**Epping**
Epp.Grn	Epping Green
Epp.Upl.	Epping Upland
Epsom Com.	Epsom Common
Essen.	Essendon
Ewell E.	Ewell East
Ewell W.	Ewell West
Eyns.	Eynsford
Far.Grn	Farley Green
Farn.Com.	Farnham Common
Farn.Royal	Farnham Royal
Farnboro.	Farnborough
Farnc.	Farncombe
Fawk.	Fawkham
Fawk.Grn	Fawkham Green
Felt.	**Feltham**
Fetch.	Fetcham
Flack.Hth	Flackwell Heath
Flam.	Flamstead
Flaun.	Flaunden
Fnghm	Farningham
Forty Grn	Forty Green
Frog.	Frogmore
Gat.	Gatwick
Gdmg.	Godalming
Gdse.	**Godstone**
Geo.Grn	George Green
Ger.Cr.	**Gerrards Cross**
Gidea Pk	Gidea Park
Gilston Pk	Gilston Park
Godden Grn	Godden Green
Goms.	Gomshall
Grav.	**Gravesend**
Green.	**Greenhithe**
Grn St Grn	Green Street Green
Grnf.	**Greenford**
Gt Amwell	Great Amwell
Gt Warley	Great Warley
Guil.	**Guildford**
H.Wyc.	High Wycombe
Hackbr.	Hackbridge
Had.Wd	Hadley Wood
Halst.	Halstead
Han.	Hanworth
Har.	**Harrow**
Har.Hill	Harrow on the Hill
Har.Wld	Harrow Weald
Hare.	Harefield
Harl.	**Harlow**
Harling.	Harlington
Harm.	Harmondsworth
Harold Wd	Harold Wood
Hast.	Hastingwood
Hat.	**Hatfield**
Hat.Hth	Hatfield Heath
Hav.at.Bow.	Havering-atte-Bower
Haz.	Hazlemere
Hedg.	Hedgerley
Hem.H.	**Hemel Hempstead**
Herons.	Heronsgate
Hert.	**Hertford**
Hert.Hth	Hertford Heath
Hext.	Hextable
High Barn.	High Barnet
Hinch.Wd	Hinchley Wood
Hkwd	Hookwood
Hlgdn	Hillingdon
Hmptn H.	Hampton Hill
Hmptn W.	Hampton Wick
Hmptn.	**Hampton**
Hodd.	**Hoddesdon**
Holm.	Holmwood
Holm.St.M.	Holmbury Saint Mary
Holt.	Holtspur
Holy.	Holyport
Horl.	**Horley**
Horn.	**Hornchurch**
Hort.Kir.	Horton Kirby
Houns.	**Hounslow**
Houns.W.	Hounslow West
Hunt.Br.	Hunton Bridge
Hutt.	Hutton
Hyde Hth	Hyde Heath
Ickhm	Ickenham
Ilf.	**Ilford**
Islw.	**Isleworth**
Ken.	**Kenley**
Kes.	**Keston**
Kgfld	Kingfield
Kgswd	Kingswood
Kings L.	**Kings Langley**
Kings.T.	**Kingston upon Thames**
Knap.	Knaphill
Knock.	Knockholt
Knock.P.	Knockholt Pound
Knot.Grn	Knotty Green
Lamb.End	Lambourne End
Let.Hth	Letchmore Heath
Letty Grn	Letty Green
Lmpfld	Limpsfield
Lmpfld Cht	Limpsfield Chart
Lmsfd	Lemsford
Lon.Col.	London Colney
Lon.Gat.Air.	London Gatwick Airport
Lon.Hthrw Air.	London Heathrow Airport
Lon.Hthrw Air.N	London Heathrow Airport N
Long Dit.	Long Ditton
Long.	**Longfield**
Longcr.	Longcross
Loud.	Loudwater
Loug.	**Loughton**
Lt.Berk.	Little Berkhamsted
Lt.Chal.	Little Chalfont
Lt.Hth	Little Heath
Lt.Warley	Little Warley
Lthd.	**Leatherhead**
Lvsdn	Leavesden
Lwfld Hth	Lowfield Heath
Lwr Kgswd	Lower Kingswood
Lwr Naze.	Lower Nazeing
Magd.Lav.	Magdalen Laver
Maid.	Maidenhead
Map.Cr.	Maple Cross
Mark Hall N.	Mark Hall North
Match.Grn	Matching Green
Match.Tye	Matching Tye
Mdgrn	Middlegreen
Merst.	Merstham
Mick.	Mickleham
Mid Holm.	Mid Holmwood
Mimbr.	Mimbridge
Mitch.	**Mitcham**
Mitch.Com.	Mitcham Common
Mord.	**Morden**
Mots.Pk	Motspur Park
Mtnsg	Mountnessing
N.Har.	North Harrow
N.Holm.	North Holmwood
N.Mal.	**New Malden**
N.Mymms	North Mymms
N.Ock.	North Ockendon
N.Stfd	North Stifford
N.Wld Bas.	North Weald Bassett
N.Wld Bas.N.	North Weald Bassett North
Nave.	Navestock
Nave.S.	Navestock Side
Naze.	Nazeing
Naze.Gate	Nazeing Gate
New Adgtn	New Addington
New Barn.	New Barnet
Newgate St	Newgate Street
Northumb.Hth	Northumberland Heath
Nthch	Northchurch
Nthflt	Northfleet
Nthlt.	**Northolt**
Nthwd.	**Northwood**
Nutfld	Nutfield
Oakl.	Oaklands
Oakley Grn	Oakley Green
Ock.	Ockham
Old Harl.	Old Harlow
Old Wind.	Old Windsor
Old Wok.	Old Woking
Ong.	Ongar
Ons.Vill.	Onslow Village
Orch.L.	Orchard Leigh
Orp.	**Orpington**
Ott.	Ottershaw
Oxt.	**Oxted**
Pans.	Panshanger
Park St	Park Street
Peasl.	Peaslake
Peasm.	Peasmarsh
Petts Wd	Petts Wood
Picc.End	Piccotts End
Pilg.Hat.	Pilgrim's Hatch
Pnr.	**Pinner**
Pond.End	Ponders End
Port.Wd	Porters Wood
Pot.B.	**Potters Bar**
Pott.Cr.	Potters Crouch
Pott.End	Potten End
Pott.St	Potter Street
Pr.Bot.	Pratt's Bottom
Pur.	**Purley**
Purf.	**Purfleet**
Putt.	Puttenham
Rad.	**Radlett**
Rain.	**Rainham**
Ran.Com.	Ranmore Common
Rayners La	Rayners Lane
Red.	**Redhill**
Redbn	Redbourn
Reig.	**Reigate**
Rich.	**Richmond**
Rick.	**Rickmansworth**
Rod.Val.	Roding Valley
Roe Grn	Roe Green
Rom.	**Romford**
Rosh.	Rosherville
Ruis.	**Ruislip**
Runny.	Runnymede
Rush Grn	Rush Green
Rvrhd	Riverhead
Rydes.	Rydeshill
S.Croy.	**South Croydon**
S.Darenth	South Darenth
S.Har.	South Harrow
S.Holm.	South Holmwood
S.Merst.	South Merstham
S.Mimms	South Mimms
S.Nutfld	South Nutfield
S.Ock.	**South Ockendon**
S.Oxhey	South Oxhey
S.Park	South Park
S.Ruis.	South Ruislip
S.Stfd	South Stifford
S.Wld	South Weald
S.le H.	Stanford-le-Hope
Salf.	Salfords
Sand.	Sandridge
Saw.	**Sawbridgeworth**
Scad.Pk	Scadbury Park
Seer Grn	Seer Green
Send M.	Send Marsh
Sev.	**Sevenoaks**
Shalf.	Shalford
Sham.Grn	Shamley Green
Sheer.	Sheerwater
Shenf.	Shenfield
Shep.	**Shepperton**
Shipley Br	Shipley Bridge
Shore.	Shoreham
Short.	Shortlands
Sid.	**Sidcup**
Slade Grn	Slade Green
Slou.	**Slough**
St.Alb.	**Saint Albans**
St.Geo.H.	Saint George's Hill
St.John's	Saint John's
St.M.Cray	Saint Mary Cray
St.P.Cray	Saint Paul's Cray
Stai.	**Staines**
Stan.	**Stanmore**
Stanboro.	Stanborough
Stanfd.Riv.	Stanford Rivers
Stans.Abb.	Stanstead Abbotts
Stanw.	Stanwell
Stanw.M.	Stanwell Moor
Stap.Abb.	Stapleford Abbotts
Stap.Taw.	Stapleford Tawney
Sthflt	Southfleet
Sthl Grn	Southall Green
Sthl.	**Southall**
Stoke D'Ab.	Stoke D'Abernon
Stoke P.	Stoke Poges
Strood Grn	Strood Green
Sun.	Sunbury-on-Thames
Sund.	Sundridge
Surb.	**Surbiton**
Sutt.	**Sutton**
Sutt.Grn	Sutton Green
Sutt.H.	Sutton at Hone
Swan.	**Swanley**
Swans.	**Swanscombe**
T.Ditt.	**Thames Ditton**
Tad.	**Tadworth**
Tand.	Tandridge
Tap.	Taplow
Tats.	Tatsfield
Tedd.	**Teddington**
Th.Hth.	**Thornton Heath**
They.B.	Theydon Bois
They.Gar.	Theydon Garnon
They.Mt	Theydon Mount
Thnwd	Thornwood
Thres.B.	Threshers Bush
Til.	**Tilbury**
Tkgtn	Tokyngton
Turnf.	Turnford
Twick.	**Twickenham**
Tyr.Wd	Tyrrell's Wood
Tytten.	Tyttenhanger
Undrvr	Underriver
Upmin.	**Upminster**
Uxb.	**Uxbridge**
Vir.W.	**Virginia Water**
W.Byf.	**West Byfleet**
W.Clan.	West Clandon
W.Ewell	West Ewell
W.Hors.	West Horsley
W.Hyde	West Hyde
W.Mol.	**West Molesey**
W.Thur.	West Thurrock
W.Til.	West Tilbury
W.Wick.	**West Wickham**
Wal.Abb.	**Waltham Abbey**
Wal.Cr.	**Waltham Cross**
Wall.	**Wallington**
Walt.	**Walton-on-Thames**
Walt.Hill	Walton on the Hill
Warl.	**Warlingham**
Wat.	**Watford**
Wat.Oak.	Water Oakley
Waterf.	Waterford
Wdf.Grn.	**Woodford Green**
Wdhm	Woodham
Wealds.	Wealdstone
Well.	**Welling**
Welw.	Welwyn
Welw.G.C.	**Welwyn Garden City**
Wem.	**Wembley**
Wenn.	Wennington
West Dr.	**West Drayton**
West.	**Westerham**
Westc.	Westcott
Westh.	Westhumble
Wey.	**Weybridge**
Wheat.	Wheathampstead
Whel.Hill	Whelpley Hill
Whiteley Vill.	Whiteley Village
Whyt.	Whyteleafe
Wilm.	Wilmington
Winch.Hill	Winchmore Hill
Wind.	**Windsor**
Wink.	Winkfield
Wok.	**Woking**
Wold.	Woldingham
Won.	Wonersh
Woob.Grn	Wooburn Green
Woob.Moor	Wooburn Moor
Wor.Pk.	**Worcester Park**
Worp.	Worplesdon
Wrays.	Wraysbury
Wyc.End	Wycombe End
Yiew.	Yiewsley

1 - Add

● **1 Canada Sq**, E14 34 C3
200 Pentonville Rd, Hall of Res, N1 18 C1
★ **2 Willow Rd**, NW3 142 DE63
● **30 St. Mary Axe**, EC3 *off St. Mary Axe* 19 P8
● **99 Bishopsgate**, EC2 *off Bishopsgate* 19 N8

A

Aaron Hill Rd, E6 25 M6
Abady Ho, SW1 *off Page St* 29 P8
Abberley Ms, SW4 *off Cedars Rd* 183 DH83
Abberton Wk, Rain. RM13 *off Ongar Way* 169 FE66
Abbess Cl, E6 25 H7
SW2 203 DP88
Abbeville Ms, SW4 183 DK84
Abbeville Rd, N8 *off Barrington Rd* 143 DK56
SW4 203 DJ86
Abbey Av, St.Alb. AL3 64 CA23
Wembley HA0 160 CL68
● **Abbey Business Cen**, SW8 41 K6
Abbey Chyd, Wal.Abb. EN9 89 EC33
Abbey Cl, E5 144 DU63
SW8 41 P6
Hayes UB3 157 BV74
Northolt UB5 *off Invicta Gro* 158 BZ69
Pinner HA5 137 BV55
Romford RM1 149 FG58
Slough SL1 153 AL73
Woking GU22 249 BE116
Abbey C of E Prim Sch, The, St.Alb. AL1 *off Grove Rd* 65 CD21
Abbey Ct, Wal.Abb. EN9 89 EB34
Abbey Cres, Belv. DA17 188 FA77
Abbeydale Cl, Harl. CM17 74 EW16
Abbeydale Rd, Wem. HA0 160 CN67
Abbey Dr, SW17 *off Church La* 202 DG92
Abbots Langley WD5 81 BU32
Dartford DA2 209 FE89
Staines TW18 216 BJ98
Abbeyfield Cl, Mitch. CR4 222 DE96
Abbeyfield Rd, SE16 32 G8
Abbeyfields Cl, NW10 160 CN68
Abbeyfields Mobile Home Pk, Cher. KT16 216 BK101
Abbey Gdns, NW8 15 N1
SE16 32 D8
SW1 *off Great Coll St* 30 A6
W6 38 E2
Chertsey KT16 216 BG100
Chislehurst BR7 227 EN95
Waltham Abbey EN9 89 EC33
Abbey Grn, Cher. KT16 216 BG100
Abbey Gro, SE2 188 EV77
Abbeyhill Rd, Sid. DA15 208 EW89
● **Abbey Ind Est**, Mitch. CR4 222 DF99
Wembley HA0 160 CM67
Abbey La, E15 12 F10
Beckenham BR3 205 EA94
Abbey Manor Coll, John Evelyn Ed Cen, SE4 *off Dressington Av* 205 EA86
● **Abbey Mead Ind Pk**, Wal.Abb. EN9 89 EC34
Abbey Meadows, Cher. KT16 216 BJ101
Abbey Ms, E17 *off Leamington Av* 145 EA57
Isleworth TW7 179 CH81
Abbey Mill End, St.Alb. AL3 64 CC21
Abbey Mill La, St.Alb. AL3 64 CC21
Abbey Mills, St.Alb. AL3 64 CC21
Abbey Orchard St, SW1 29 P6
Abbey Par, SW19 *off Merton High St* 202 DC94
W5 *off Hanger La* 160 CM69
Abbey Pk, Beck. BR3 205 EA94
Abbey Pk La, Burn. SL1 133 AL61
Abbey Pl, Dart. DA1 *off Priory Rd N* 210 FK85
Abbey Prim Sch, Mord. SM4 *off Glastonbury Rd* 222 DB101
Abbey Retail Pk, Bark. IG11 167 EP67
Abbey Rd, E15 13 H10
NW6 5 L7
NW8 5 N9
NW10 160 CP68
SE2 188 EX77
SW19 202 DC94
Barking IG11 167 EP66
Belvedere DA17 188 EX77
Bexleyheath DA7 188 EY84
Chertsey KT16 216 BH101
Croydon CR0 223 DP104
Enfield EN1 104 DS43
Gravesend DA12 213 GL88
Greenhithe DA9 211 FW85
Ilford IG2 147 ER57
Shepperton TW17 216 BN102
South Croydon CR2 243 DX110
Virginia Water GU25 214 AX99
Waltham Cross EN8 89 DY34
Woking GU21 248 AW117
Abbey Rd Est, NW8 5 L9
Abbey St, E13 23 P4
SE1 31 P6
Abbey Ter, SE2 188 EW77
● **Abbey Trd Est**, SE26 205 DZ92
Abbey Vw, NW7 119 CT48
Radlett WD7 99 CF35
Waltham Abbey EN9 89 EB33
Watford WD25 98 BX36
Abbey Vw Rd, St.Alb. AL3 64 CC20
Abbey Vw Rbt, Wal.Abb. EN9 89 EB33
Abbey Wk, W.Mol. KT8 218 CB97
Abbey Way, SE2 188 EX76
● **Abbey Wf Ind Est**, Bark. IG11 167 ER68
ABBEY WOOD, SE2 188 EV76
⇌ **Abbey Wood** 188 EW76
Abbey Wd La, Rain. RM13 170 FK68
Abbey Wd Rd, SE2 188 EV77
Abbey Wd Sch, SE2 *off Eynsham Dr* 188 EU76
Abbot Cl, Byfleet KT14 234 BK110
Staines TW18 196 BK94
Abbot Ct, SW8 *off Hartington Rd* 42 A5
Abbot Rd, Guil. GU1 280 AX136
Abbots Av, Epsom KT19 238 CN111
St. Albans AL1 65 CE23
Abbots Av W, St.Alb. AL1 65 CD23
Abbotsbury Cl, E15 12 F10
W14 26 F5
Abbotsbury Gdns, Pnr. HA5 138 BW58
Abbotsbury Ms, SE15 184 DW83
Abbotsbury Prim Sch, Mord. SM4 *off Abbotsbury Rd* 222 DB99
Abbotsbury Rd, W14 26 F4
Bromley BR2 226 EF103
Morden SM4 222 DB99
Abbots Cl, Guil. GU2 280 AS137
Orpington BR5 227 EQ102
Rainham RM13 170 FJ68
Ruislip HA4 138 BX62
Shenfield CM15 131 GA46
Abbots Dr, Har. HA2 138 CA61
Virginia Water GU25 214 AW98
Abbots Fld, Grav. DA12 *off Ruffets Wd* 213 GJ93
Abbotsfield Sch, Hlgdn UB10 *off Clifton Gdns* 157 BP68
Abbotsford Av, N15 144 DQ56
Abbotsford Cl, Wok. GU22 *off Onslow Cres* 249 BA117
Abbotsford Gdns, Wdf.Grn. IG8 124 EG52
Abbotsford Lo, Nthwd. HA6 115 BS50
Abbotsford Rd, Ilf. IG3 148 EU61
Abbots Gdns, N2 142 DD56
W8 27 L7
Abbots Grn, Croy. CR0 243 DX107
Abbotshade Rd, SE16 33 K2
Abbotshall Av, N14 121 DJ48
Abbotshall Rd, SE6 205 ED88
Abbot's Hill Sch, Hem.H. HP3 *off Bunkers La* 81 BP25
Abbots La, SE1 31 P3
Kenley CR8 258 DQ116
ABBOTS LANGLEY, WD5 81 BR31
Abbots Langley Sch, Abb.L. WD5 *off Parsonage Cl* 81 BT30
Abbotsleigh Cl, Sutt. SM2 240 DB108
Abbotsleigh Rd, SW16 203 DJ91
Abbots Manor Est, SW1 29 J9
Abbotsmede Cl, Twick. TW1 199 CF89
Abbots Pk, SW2 203 DN88
St. Albans AL1 65 CF22
Abbot's Pl, NW6 5 L8
Abbots Pl, Borwd. WD6 100 CP37
Abbots Ri, Kings L. WD4 80 BM26
Redhill RH1 272 DG132
Abbot's Rd, E6 166 EK67
Abbots Rd, Abb.L. WD5 81 BS30
Edgware HA8 118 CQ52
Abbots Ter, N8 143 DL58
Abbotstone Rd, SW15 181 CW83
Abbot St, E8 10 A4
Abbots Vw, Kings L. WD4 80 BM27
Abbots Wk, W8 27 L7
Windsor SL4 173 AL82
Abbots Way, Beck. BR3 225 DY99
Chertsey KT16 215 BF101
Guildford GU1 265 BD133
Abbotsweld, Harl. CM18 73 ER18
Abbotsweld Prim Sch, Harl. CM18 *off Partridge Rd* 73 ER17
Abbotswell Rd, SE4 205 DZ85
ABBOTSWOOD, Guil. GU1 265 AZ132
Abbotswood, Guil. GU1 265 AZ131
Abbotswood Cl, Belv. DA17 *off Coptefield Dr* 188 EY76
Guildford GU1 265 AZ131
Abbotswood Dr, Wey. KT13 235 BR110
Abbotswood Gdns, Ilf. IG5 147 EM55
Abbotswood Rd, SE22 184 DS84
SW16 203 DK90
Abbotswood Way, Hayes UB3 157 BV74
Abbots Yd, Guil. GU1 *off Walnut Tree Cl* 280 AW135
Abbott Av, SW20 221 CX96
Abbott Cl, Hmptn. TW12 198 BY93
Northolt UB5 158 BZ65
Abbott Rd, E14 22 E7
Abbotts Cl, N1 9 J5
SE28 168 EW73
Romford RM7 149 FB55
Swanley BR8 229 FG98
Uxbridge UB8 156 BK71
Abbotts Cres, E4 123 ED49
Enfield EN2 103 DP40
Abbotts Dr, Wal.Abb. EN9 90 EG33
Wembley HA0 139 CH61
Abbotts Pk Rd, E10 145 EC59
Abbotts Pl, Chesh. HP5 76 AQ28
Abbotts Ri, Stans.Abb. SG12 55 ED11
Abbotts Rd, Barn. EN5 102 DB42
Mitcham CR4 223 DJ98
Southall UB1 158 BY74
Sutton SM3 221 CZ104
Abbott's Tilt, Hersham KT12 218 BY104
Abbotts Vale, Chesh. HP5 76 AQ28
Abbotts Wk, Bexh. DA7 188 EX80
Caterham CR3 *off Gaist Av* 258 DV122
Abbotts Way, Slou. SL1 153 AK74
Stanstead Abbotts SG12 55 ED11
Abbotts Wf, E14 22 A8
Abbs Cross Gdns, Horn. RM12 150 FJ60
Abbs Cross La, Horn. RM12 150 FJ63
Abbs Cross Sch, Horn. RM12 *off Abbs Cross La* 150 FJ62
Abchurch La, EC4 19 M10
Abchurch Yd, EC4 19 L10
Abdale Rd, W12 161 CV74
Abel Cl, Hem.H. HP2 62 BM20
Abel Smith Sch, Hert. SG13 *off Churchfields* 54 DR09
Abenberg Way, Hutt. CM13 131 GB47
● **Abenglen Ind Est**, Hayes UB3 177 BR75
Aberavon Rd, E3 21 M3
Abercairn Rd, SW16 203 DJ94
Aberconway Rd, Mord. SM4 222 DB97
Abercorn Cl, NW7 119 CY52
NW8 15 N1
South Croydon CR2 243 DX112
● **Abercorn Commercial Cen**, Wem. HA0 159 CK67
Abercorn Cres, Har. HA2 138 CB60
Abercorn Dell, Bushey WD23 116 CC47
Abercorn Gdns, Har. HA3 139 CK59
Romford RM6 148 EV58
Abercorn Gro, Ruis. HA4 137 BR56
Abercorn Ms, Rich. TW10 *off Kings Rd* 180 CM84
Abercorn Pl, NW8 15 N2
Abercorn Rd, NW7 119 CY52
Stanmore HA7 117 CJ52
Abercorn Sch, NW8 15 P1
Abercorn Wk, NW8 15 N2
Abercorn Way, SE1 32 C10
Woking GU21 248 AU118
Abercrombie Dr, Enf. EN1 *off Linwood Cres* 104 DU39
Abercrombie St, SW11 40 D8
Abercrombie Way, Harl. CM18 73 EQ16
Aberdale Ct, SE16 *off Garter Way* 33 J5
Aberdale Gdns, Pot.B. EN6 85 CZ33
Aberdare Cl, W.Wick. BR4 225 EC103
Aberdare Gdns, NW6 5 M7
NW7 119 CX52
Aberdare Rd, Enf. EN3 104 DW42
Aberdeen Av, Slou. SL1 153 AN73
Aberdeen La, N5 9 H2
Aberdeen Par, N18 *off Angel Rd* 122 DV50
Aberdeen Pk, N5 9 H2
Aberdeen Pk Ms, N5 9 K1
Aberdeen Pl, NW8 16 A5
Aberdeen Rd, N5 9 J1
N18 122 DV50
NW10 141 CT64
Croydon CR0 242 DQ105
Harrow HA3 117 CF54
Aberdeen Sq, E14 33 P2
Aberdeen Ter, SE3 46 G8
Aberdour Rd, Ilf. IG3 148 EV62
Aberdour Sch, Burgh Hth KT20 *off Brighton Rd* 255 CZ118
Aberdour St, SE1 31 N8
Aberfeldy St, E14 22 F8
Aberford Gdns, SE18 186 EL81
Aberford Rd, Borwd. WD6 100 CN40
Aberfoyle Rd, SW16 203 DK93
Abergeldie Rd, SE12 206 EH86
Abernethy Rd, SE13 186 EE84
Abersham Rd, E8 10 B2
Abery St, SE18 187 ES77
Abigail Ms, Rom. RM3 *off King Alfred Rd* 128 FM54
Ability Twrs, EC1 19 J2
Abingdon Cl, NW1 7 N5
SE1 32 B10
SW19 202 DC93
Uxbridge UB10 156 BM67
Woking GU21 248 AV118
Abingdon Pl, Pot.B. EN6 86 DB32
Abingdon Rd, N3 120 DC54
SW16 223 DL96
W8 27 J6
Abingdon St, SW1 30 A6
Abingdon Vil, W8 27 J7
Abingdon Way, Orp. BR6 246 EV105
Abinger Av, Sutt. SM2 239 CW109
Abinger Cl, Bark. IG11 148 EU63
Bromley BR1 226 EL97
New Addington CR0 243 EC107
North Holmwood RH5 285 CJ140
Wallington SM6 241 DL106
ABINGER COMMON, Dor. RH5 284 BX143
Abinger Common Rd, Dor. RH5 284 BY144
Abinger Common Sch, Abin.Com. RH5 *off Abinger La* 284 BX142
Abinger Dr, Red. RH1 288 DE136
Abinger Gdns, Islw. TW7 179 CE83
Abinger Gro, SE8 45 N3
ABINGER HAMMER, Dor. RH5 283 BT139
Abinger Hammer Village Sch, Abin.Ham. RH5 *off Hackhurst La* 283 BT139
Abinger Keep, Horl. RH6 *off Langshott La* 291 DJ147
Abinger La, Dor. RH5 283 BV140
Abinger Ms, W9 15 J4
Abinger Rd, W4 180 CS76
Abinger Way, Guil. GU4 265 BB129
Ablett St, SE16 44 G1
Abney Gdns, N16 *off Stoke Newington High St* 144 DT61
Aboyne Dr, SW20 221 CU96
Aboyne Est, SW17 202 DD90
Aboyne Lo Sch, St.Alb. AL3 *off Etna Rd* 65 CD19
Aboyne Rd, NW10 140 CS62
SW17 202 DD90
Abraham Cl, Wat. WD19 115 BV49
ABRIDGE, Rom. RM4 108 EV41
Abridge Cl, Wal.Cr. EN8 105 DX35
Abridge Gdns, Rom. RM5 126 FA51
Abridge Pk, Abridge RM4 108 EU42
Abridge Rd, Abridge RM4 108 EU39
Chigwell IG7 125 ER44
Theydon Bois CM16 107 ES36
Abridge Way, Bark. IG11 168 EV68
Abyssinia Cl, SW11 *off Cairns Rd* 182 DE84
Abyssinia Rd, SW11 *off Auckland Rd* 182 DE84
Acacia Av, N17 122 DR52
Brentford TW8 179 CH80
Hayes UB3 157 BT72
Hornchurch RM12 149 FF61
Mitcham CR4 *off Acacia Rd* 223 DH96
Ruislip HA4 137 BU60
Shepperton TW17 216 BN99
Wembley HA9 140 CL64
West Drayton UB7 156 BM73
Woking GU22 248 AX120
Wraysbury TW19 174 AY84
● **Acacia Business Cen**, E11 *off Howard Rd* 146 EE62
Acacia Cl, SE8 33 L9
SE20 *off Selby Rd* 224 DU96
Chesham HP5 76 AN30
Cheshunt EN7 88 DS27
Petts Wood BR5 227 ER99
Stanmore HA7 117 CE51
Woodham KT15 233 BF110
Acacia Ct, Wal.Abb. EN9 *off Farthingale La* 90 EG34
Acacia Dr, Bans. SM7 239 CX114
Sutton SM3 221 CZ102
Upminster RM14 150 FN63
Woodham KT15 233 BF110
Acacia Gdns, NW8 6 B10
Upminster RM14 151 FT59
West Wickham BR4 225 EC103
Acacia Gro, SE21 204 DR89
Berkhamsted HP4 60 AV20
New Malden KT3 220 CR97
Acacia Ms, Harm. UB7 176 BK79
Acacia Pl, NW8 6 B10
Acacia Rd, E11 146 EE61
E17 145 DY58
N22 121 DN53
NW8 6 B10
SW16 223 DL95
W3 160 CQ73
Beckenham BR3 225 DZ97
Dartford DA1 210 FK88
Enfield EN2 104 DR39
Greenhithe DA9 211 FS86
Guildford GU1 264 AX134
Hampton TW12 198 CA93
Mitcham CR4 223 DH96
Staines TW18 196 BH92
Acacias, The, Barn. EN4 102 DD43
Acacia St, Hat. AL10 67 CU21
Acacia Wk, Swan. BR8 229 FD96
Acacia Way, Sid. DA15 207 ET88
Academia Way, N17 122 DS51
Academy at Peckham, The, SE15 44 B7
Academy Ct, Borwd. WD6 100 CN42
Academy Flds Cl, Rom. RM2 149 FG57
Academy Flds Rd, Rom. RM2 149 FH57
Academy Gdns, W8 27 J4
Croydon CR0 224 DT102
Northolt UB5 158 BX68
Academy Pl, SE18 187 EM81
Academy Rd, SE18 187 EM81
Acanthus Dr, SE1 32 C10
Acanthus Rd, SW11 40 G10
Accommodation La, Harm. UB7 176 BJ79
Accommodation Rd, NW11 141 CZ59
Longcross KT16 214 AX104
A.C. Ct, T.Ditt. KT7 *off Harvest La* 219 CG100
Ace Par, Chess. KT9 *off Hook Rd* 220 CL104
Acer Av, Hayes UB4 158 BY71
Rainham RM13 170 FK69
Acer Ct, Enf. EN3 105 DY41
Acer Rd, Bigg.H. TN16 260 EK116
Acers, Park St AL2 82 CC28
Acfold Rd, SW6 39 L7
Achilles Cl, SE1 32 D10
Hemel Hempstead HP2 62 BM18
Achilles Pl, Wok. GU21 248 AW117
Achilles Rd, NW6 5 H2
Achilles St, SE14 45 N5
Achilles Way, W1 28 G3
Acklam Rd, W10 14 G7
Acklington Dr, NW9 118 CS53
Ackmar Rd, SW6 39 J7
Ackroyd Dr, E3 21 P6
Ackroyd Rd, SE23 205 DX87
Acland Burghley Sch, NW5 *off Burghley Rd* 143 DJ63
Acland Cl, SE18 *off Clothworkers Rd* 187 ER80
Acland Cres, SE5 184 DR83
Acland Rd, NW2 161 CV65
Acle Cl, Ilf. IG6 125 EP52
Acme Rd, Wat. WD24 97 BU38
Acock Gro, Nthlt. UB5 138 CB63
Acol Cres, Ruis. HA4 137 BV64
Acol Rd, NW6 5 K7
Aconbury Rd, Dag. RM9 168 EV67
Acorn Cl, E4 123 EA50
Chislehurst BR7 207 EQ92
Enfield EN2 103 DP39
Hampton TW12 198 CB93
Horley RH6 291 DJ147
Romford RM1 *off Pettits La* 127 FE54
Slough SL3 *off Tamar Way* 175 BB78
Stanmore HA7 117 CH52
Acorn Ct, Ilf. IG2 147 ES58
Acorn Gdns, SE19 224 DT95
W3 160 CR71
Acorn Gro, Hayes UB3 177 BT80
Kingswood KT20 255 CY124
Ruislip HA4 137 BT63
Woking GU22 *off Old Sch Pl* 248 AY121
● **Acorn Ind Pk**, Dart. DA1 209 FF85
Acorn La, Cuffley EN6 87 DL29
Acorn Ms, Harl. CM18 73 ET17
Acorn Par, SE15 44 E5
Acorn Pl, Wat. WD24 97 BU37
Acorn Rd, Dart. DA1 209 FF85
Hemel Hempstead HP3 62 BN21
Acorns, The, Chig. IG7 125 ES49
Smallfield RH6 291 DP148
Acorns Inf Sch, The, Betchworth Site, Bet. RH3 *off The Street* 270 CR134
Leigh Site, Leigh RH2 *off Tapners Rd* 287 CU140
Acorn St, Hunsdon SG12 56 EK08
Acorns Way, Esher KT10 236 CC106
Acorn Wk, SE16 33 M2
Acorn Way, SE23 205 DX90
Beckenham BR3 225 EC99
Orpington BR6 245 EP105
Acre Dr, SE22 184 DU84
Acrefield Rd, Chal.St.P. SL9 134 AX55
Acre La, SW2 183 DL84
Carshalton SM5 240 DG105
Wallington SM6 240 DG105
Acre Pas, Wind. SL4 173 AR81
Acre Path, Nthlt. UB5 *off Arnold Rd* 158 BY65
Acre Rd, SW19 202 DD93
Dagenham RM10 169 FB66
Kingston upon Thames KT2 220 CL95
Acres End, Amer. HP7 77 AS39
Acres Gdns, Tad. KT20 255 CX119
Acre Vw, Horn. RM11 150 FL56
Acre Way, Nthwd. HA6 115 BT53
Acrewood, Hem.H. HP2 62 BL20
Acrewood Way, St.Alb. AL4 66 CM20
Acris St, SW18 202 DC85
ACTON, W3 160 CN74
Acton & W London Coll, W3 *off Gunnersbury La* 160 CP74
⊖ **Acton Central** 160 CR74
Acton Cl, N9 122 DU47
Cheshunt EN8 89 DY31
Acton High Sch, W3 *off Gunnersbury La* 180 CN75
Acton Hill Ms, W3 *off Uxbridge Rd* 160 CP74
Acton Ho, W3 160 CQ72
Acton La, NW10 160 CS68
W3 180 CQ75
W4 180 CR76
⇌ **Acton Main Line** 160 CQ72
Acton Ms, E8 10 A8
● **Acton Pk Est**, W3 180 CR75
Actons La, High Wych CM21 57 EQ05
Acton St, WC1 18 C3
⊖ **Acton Town** 180 CN75
Acuba Rd, SW18 202 DB89
Acworth Cl, N9 122 DW45
Ada Cl, N11 120 DF48
Ada Ct, W9 15 P3
Ada Gdns, E14 22 G8
E15 13 L9
Adair Cl, SE25 224 DV97
Adair Gdns, Cat. CR3 258 DQ121
Adair Rd, W10 14 F5
Adair Twr, W10 14 F5
Adam & Eve Ct, W1 17 M8
Adam & Eve Ms, W8 27 K6
Adam Cl, SE6 205 DZ91
Slough SL1 153 AN74
Adam Ct, SW7 27 P8
Adam Meere Ho, E1 *off Tarling St* 20 G9
Adam Rd, E4 123 DZ51
Adams Cl, N3 120 DA52
NW9 140 CP61
Surbiton KT5 220 CM100
Adams Ct, EC2 19 M8
Adamsfield, Wal.Cr. EN7 88 DU27
Adams Gdns Est, SE16 32 G4
Adams Ho, N16 *off Stamford Hill* 144 DT60
Harlow CM20 *off Post Office Rd* 57 ER14
Adams Ms, N22 121 DM52
SW17 202 DF89
Adamson Rd, E16 23 P9
NW3 6 B6
Adamson Way, Beck. BR3 225 EC99
Adams Pl, N7 8 D3
Adams Quarter, Brent. TW8 *off Tallow Rd* 179 CJ79
Adamsrill Cl, Enf. EN1 104 DR44
Adamsrill Prim Sch, SE26 *off Adamsrill Rd* 205 DY90
Adamsrill Rd, SE26 205 DY91
Adams Rd, N17 122 DR54
Beckenham BR3 225 DY99
Adams Row, W1 29 H1
Adams Sq, Bexh. DA6 *off Regency Way* 188 EY83
Adam St, WC2 30 B1
Adams Wk, Kings.T. KT1 220 CL96
Adams Way, Croy. CR0 224 DT100
Adam Wk, SW6 38 B4
Ada Pl, E2 10 D9
Adare Wk, SW16 203 DM90
Ada Rd, SE5 43 N5
Wembley HA0 139 CJ62
Adastral Est, NW9 118 CS53
Ada St, E8 10 E9
Adcock Wk, Orp. BR6 *off Borkwood Pk* 245 ET105
Adderley Gdns, SE9 207 EN91
Adderley Gro, SW11 *off Culmstock Rd* 202 DG85
Adderley Rd, Har. HA3 117 CF53
Adderley St, E14 22 E9
Addey & Stanhope Sch, SE14 46 A6
ADDINGTON, Croy. CR0 243 DZ106
Addington Border, Croy. CR0 243 DY110
Addington Cl, Wind. SL4 173 AN83
Addington Ct, SW14 180 CR83
Addington Dr, N12 120 DC51
Addington Gro, SE26 205 DY91
Addington High Sch, New Adgtn CR0 *off Fairchildes Av* 244 EE112
Addington Rd, E3 22 A2
E16 23 K5
N4 143 DN59
Croydon CR0 223 DN102
South Croydon CR2 242 DU111
West Wickham BR4 226 EE103
Addington Sq, SE5 43 K4
Addington St, SE1 30 D5
Addington Village 243 EA107
● **Addington Village Interchange** 243 EA107
Addington Village Rd, Croy. CR0 243 EA106
Addis Cl, Enf. EN3 105 DX39
ADDISCOMBE, Croy. CR0 224 DT102
Addiscombe 224 DU102
Addiscombe Av, Croy. CR0 224 DU101
Addiscombe Cl, Har. HA3 139 CJ57
Addiscombe Ct Rd, Croy. CR0 224 DS102
Addiscombe Gro, Croy. CR0 224 DR103
Addiscombe Rd, Croy. CR0 224 DS103
Watford WD18 97 BV42
Addison Av, N14 103 DH44
W11 26 E2
Hounslow TW3 178 CC81
Addison Br Pl, W14 26 G8
Addison Cl, Cat. CR3 258 DR122
Northwood HA6 115 BU53
Petts Wood BR5 227 EQ100
Addison Ct, Epp. CM16 92 EU31
Addison Cres, W14 26 F6
Addison Dr, SE12 *off Eltham Rd* 206 EH85
Addison Gdns, W14 26 C6
Grays RM17 *off Palmers Dr* 192 GC77
Surbiton KT5 220 CM98
Addison Gro, W4 180 CS76
● **Addison Ind Est**, Ruis. HA4 138 BY63
Addison Pl, W11 26 E3
Southall UB1 *off Atherton Pl* 158 CA73
Addison Prim Sch, W14 26 C6
Addison Rd, E11 146 EG58
E17 145 EB57
SE25 224 DU98
W14 26 G6
Bromley BR2 226 EJ99
Caterham CR3 258 DR121
Chesham HP5 76 AQ29
Enfield EN3 104 DW39
Guildford GU1 280 AY135
Ilford IG6 125 EQ53
Teddington TW11 199 CH93

Addison Rd, Wok. GU21
off Chertsey Rd 249 AZ117
Addison's Cl, Croy. CR0 225 DZ103
Addison Way, NW11 141 CZ56
Hayes UB3 157 BU72
Northwood HA6 115 BT53
Addle Hill, EC4 19 H10
ADDLESTONE, KT15 234 BJ106
⇌ Addlestone 234 BK105
ADDLESTONE MOOR, Add. KT15 216 BG103
Addlestone Moor, Add. KT15 216 BJ103
Addlestone Pk, Add. KT15 234 BH106
Addlestone Rd, Add. KT15 234 BL105
Addy Ho, SE16 33 H9
Adecroft Way, W.Mol. KT8 218 CC97
Adela Av, N.Mal. KT3 221 CV99
Adelaide Av, SE4 185 DZ84
Adelaide Cl, SW9
off Broughton Dr 183 DN84
Enfield EN1 104 DS38
Slough SL1
off Amerden Way 173 AN75
Stanmore HA7 117 CG49
Adelaide Cotts, W7 179 CF75
Adelaide Ct, E9 11 L3
Waltham Cross EN8
off Queens Way 89 DZ34
Adelaide Gdns, Rom. RM6 148 EY57
Adelaide Gro, W12 161 CU74
Adelaide Pl, Wey. KT13 235 BR105
Adelaide Rd, E10 145 EB62
NW3 6 B7
SW18 off Putney Br Rd 202 DA85
W13 159 CG74
Ashford TW15 196 BK92
Chislehurst BR7 207 EP92
Hounslow TW5 178 BY81
Ilford IG1 147 EP61
Richmond TW9 180 CM84
Southall UB2 178 BY77
Surbiton KT6 220 CL99
Teddington TW11 199 CF93
Tilbury RM18 193 GF81
Walton-on-Thames KT12 217 BU104
Adelaide Sq, Wind. SL4 173 AR82
Adelaide St, WC2 30 A1
St. Albans AL3 65 CD19
Adelaide Ter, Brent. TW8 179 CK78
Adela St, W10 14 E4
Adelina Gro, E1 20 G6
Adelina Ms, SW12 203 DK88
Adeline Pl, WC1 17 P7
Adeliza Cl, Bark. IG11
off North St 167 EQ66
Adelphi Ct, SE16
off Garter Way 33 J5
Adelphi Cres, Hayes UB4 157 BT69
Hornchurch RM12 149 FG61
Adelphi Gdns, Slou. SL1 174 AS75
Adelphi Rd, Epsom KT17 238 CR113
Adelphi Ter, WC2 30 B1
Adelphi Way, Hayes UB4 157 BT69
Adeney Cl, W6 38 D3
Aden Gro, N16 9 L1
Adenmore Rd, SE6 205 EA87
Aden Rd, Enf. EN3 105 DY42
Ilford IG1 147 EP59
Aden Ter, N16 144 DR63
ADEYFIELD, Hem.H. HP2 62 BN20
Adeyfield Gdns, Hem.H. HP2 62 BM19
Adeyfield Rd, Hem.H. HP2 62 BM20
Sch Adeyfield Sch, Hem.H. HP2
off Longlands 62 BN20
Adhara Rd, Nthwd. HA6
off Vega Cres 115 BU50
Adhern Ct, St.Alb. AL1 65 CJ22
Adie Rd, W6 26 A7
Adine Rd, E13 24 A4
Adisham Ho, E5
off Pembury Rd 10 E2
● Adler Ind Est, Hayes UB3 177 BR75
Adlers La, Westh. RH5 269 CG131
Adler St, E1 20 C8
Adley St, E5 11 M1
Adlington Cl, N18 122 DR50
Admaston Rd, SE18 187 EQ80
Admiral Cl, Orp. BR5 228 EX98
Admiral Ct, NW4
off Barton Cl 141 CU57
Admiral Ho, Tedd. TW11
off Twickenham Rd 199 CG91
● Admiral Hyson Trd Est, SE16 32 E9
Admiral Pl, N8 143 DP56
SE16 33 M2
Admirals Cl, E18 146 EH56
Colney Heath AL4 66 CR23
Admirals Ct, Guil. GU1 265 BB133
Admiral Seymour Rd, SE9 187 EM84
Admirals Gate, SE10 46 D6
Admiral Sq, SW10 39 P6
Admiral's Rd, Lthd. KT22, KT23 269 CD126
Admiral Stirling Ct, Wey. KT13
off Weybridge Rd 234 BM105
Admiral St, SE8 46 B7
Hertford SG13 54 DU09
Admirals Wk, NW3 142 DC62
Coulsdon CR5 257 DM120
Admiral's Wk, Dor. RH5 268 CB130
Admirals Wk, Green. DA9 211 FV85
Hoddesdon EN11 71 EA19
St. Albans AL1 65 CG23
Admirals Way, E14 34 B4
Gravesend DA12 213 GK86
★ Admiralty Arch, SW1 29 P2
Admiralty Cl, SE8 46 A6
West Drayton UB7 176 BL75
Admiralty Way, Tedd. TW11 199 CF93
Admiral Wk, W9 15 K6
Admiral Way, Berk. HP4 60 AT17
Adnams Wk, Rain. RM13
off Lovell Wk 169 FF65
Adolf St, SE6 205 EB91
Adolphus Rd, N4 143 DP61
Adolphus St, SE8 45 P4
Adomar Rd, Dag. RM8 148 EX62
Adpar St, W2 16 A5
Adrian Av, NW2
off North Circular Rd 141 CV60
Adrian Cl, Barn. EN5 101 CX44
Harefield UB9 114 BK53
Adrian Ms, SW10 39 M2
Adrian Rd, Abb.L. WD5 81 BS31
Adrians Wk, Slou. SL2 154 AT74
Adriatic, E16 23 N10
Adriatic Bldg, E14 21 L10
Adrienne Av, Sthl. UB1 158 BZ70
Adstock Ms, Chal.St.P. SL9
off Church La 112 AX53
Adstock Way, Bad.Dene RM17 192 FZ77
Sch ADT Coll, SW15
off West Hill 201 CZ85
Coll Adult Coll of Barking & Dagenham, The, Dag. RM9
off Fanshawe Cres 148 EZ64
Coll Adult Ed Coll Bexley, Brampton Rd Adult Ed Cen, Bexh. DA7
off Brampton Rd 188 EX83
Crayford Manor Ho Adult Ed Cen, Dart. DA1
off Mayplace Rd E 189 FE83
Southlake Cen, SE2
off Seacourt Rd 188 EX75
Advance Rd, SE27 204 DQ91
Advent Ct, Wdf.Grn. IG8
off Wood La 124 EF50
Adventurers Ct, E14
off Newport Av 35 H1
Advent Way, N18 123 DX50
Advice Av, Grays RM16 192 GA75
Adys Rd, SE15 44 B10
Aegean Apts, E16
off Western Gateway 35 P1
Aerodrome Rd, NW4 119 CT54
NW9 119 CT54
Aerodrome Way, Houns. TW5 178 BW79
Aeroville, NW9 118 CS54
Affleck St, N1 18 D1
Afghan Rd, SW11 40 C9
★ Africa Cen, WC2 18 A10
Afton Dr, S.Ock. RM15 171 FV72
Agamemnon Rd, NW6 5 H2
Agar Cl, Surb. KT6 220 CM103
Agar Gro, NW1 7 M7
Agar Gro Est, NW1 7 M7
Agar Pl, NW1 7 M7
Agars Pl, Datchet SL3 174 AU79
Agar St, WC2 30 A1
Agate Cl, E16 24 F9
NW10 160 CN69
Agate Rd, W6 26 A6
Agates La, Ashtd. KT21 253 CK118
Agatha Cl, E1 32 F2
Agaton Rd, SE9 207 EQ89
Agave Rd, NW2 4 A1
Agdon St, EC1 18 G4
Agincourt Rd, NW3 6 E1
Agister Rd, Chig. IG7 126 EU50
Agnes Av, Ilf. IG1 147 EP63
Agnes Cl, E6 25 M10
Agnesfield Cl, N12 120 DE51
Agnes Gdns, Dag. RM8 148 EX63
Agnes Rd, W3 161 CT74
Agnes Scott Ct, Wey. KT13
off Palace Dr 217 BP104
Agnes St, E14 21 P8
Agnew Rd, SE23 205 DX87
Agraria Rd, Guil. GU2 280 AV135
Agricola Ct, E3 11 P9
Agricola Pl, Enf. EN1 104 DT43
Aidan Cl, Dag. RM8 148 EY63
Aileen Wk, E15 13 M6
Ailsa Av, Twick. TW1 199 CG85
Ailsa Rd, Twick. TW1 199 CH85
Ailsa St, E14 22 F6
AIMES GREEN, Wal.Abb. EN9 90 EF28
Ainger Ms, NW3 6 F7
Ainger Rd, NW3 6 E7
Ainsdale Cl, Orp. BR6 227 ER102
Ainsdale Cres, Pnr. HA5 138 CA55
Ainsdale Dr, SE1 44 C1
Ainsdale Rd, W5 159 CK70
Watford WD19 116 BW48
Ainsdale Way, Wok. GU21 248 AU118
Ainsley Av, Rom. RM7 149 FB58
Ainsley Cl, N9 122 DS46
Ainsley St, E2 20 F3
Ainslie Wk, SW12 203 DH87
Ainslie Wd Cres, E4 123 EB50
Ainslie Wd Gdns, E4 123 EB49
Sch Ainslie Wd Prim Sch, E4
off Ainslie Wd Rd 123 EB50
Ainslie Wd Rd, E4 123 EA50
Ainsty Est, SE16 33 J5
Ainsworth Cl, NW2 141 CU62
SE15 43 P8
Ainsworth Rd, E9 10 G7
Croydon CR0 223 DP103
Ainsworth Way, NW8 5 N8
Aintree Av, E6 166 EL67
Aintree Cl, Colnbr. SL3 175 BE81
Gravesend DA12 213 GH90
Uxbridge UB8 157 BP72
Aintree Cres, Ilf. IG6 125 EQ54
Aintree Est, SW6 38 F4
Aintree Gro, Upmin. RM14 150 FM62
Aintree Rd, Perivale UB6 159 CH68
Aintree St, SW6 38 F5
Airco Cl, NW9 140 CR55
Aird Ct, Hmptn. TW12
off Oldfield Rd 218 BZ95
Aird Ho, SE1
off Rockingham St 31 J7
Airdrie Cl, N1 8 C7
Hayes UB4 off Glencoe Rd 158 BY71
Airedale, Hem.H. HP2
off Wharfedale 62 BL17
Airedale Av, W4 181 CT77
Airedale Av S, W4
off Netheravon Rd S 181 CT78
Airedale Cl, Dart. DA2 210 FQ88
Airedale Rd, SW12 202 DF87
W5 179 CJ76
Aire Dr, S.Ock. RM15 171 FV70
Airey Neave Ct, Grays RM17 192 GA75
Airfield Way, Horn. RM12 169 FH65
Watford WD25 81 BT34
★ Air Forces Mem, Egh. TW20 194 AX91
Airlie Gdns, W8 27 J3
Ilford IG1 147 EP60
● Air Links Ind Est, Houns. TW5 178 BW78
Air Pk Way, Felt. TW13 197 BV89
● Airport Ind Est, Bigg.H. TN16 244 EK114
Jct Airport Rbt, E16 36 E2
Airport Way, Gat. RH6 290 DG151
Staines TW19 175 BF84
Jct Airport Way Rbt, Horl. RH6 290 DF151
Jct Airport Way Rbt E, Horl. RH6 291 DH151
Air St, W1 29 M1
Airthrie Rd, Ilf. IG3 148 EV61
Aisgill Av, W14 39 H1
Aisher Rd, SE28 168 EW73
Aisher Way, Rvrhd TN13 278 FE121
Aislibie Rd, SE12 186 EE84
Aiten Pl, W6 off Standish Rd 181 CU77
Aitken Cl, E8 10 C8
Mitcham CR4 222 DF101
Aitken Rd, SE6 205 EB89
Barnet EN5 101 CW43
Aitman Dr, Brent. TW8
off Chiswick High Rd 180 CN78
Ait's Vw, W.Mol. KT8
off Victoria Av 218 CB97
Ajax Av, NW9 140 CS55
Slough SL1 153 AP73
Ajax Rd, NW6 5 H2
● Ajax Wks, Bark. IG11 167 EP66
Akabusi Cl, Croy. CR0 224 DU100
Akehurst La, Sev. TN13 279 FJ125
Akehurst St, SW15 201 CU86
Akeman Cl, St.Alb. AL3
off Meautys 64 BZ22
Akenside Rd, NW3 6 A3
Akerman Rd, SW9 42 G7
Surbiton KT6 219 CJ100
Akers Way, Chorl. WD3 95 BD44
Sch Akiva Prim Sch, N3
off East End Rd 120 DA54
Alabama St, SE18 187 ER80
Alacross Rd, W5 179 CJ75
Alamaro Lo, SE10
off Renaissance Wk 35 M6
Alamein Cl, Brox. EN10 71 DX20
Alamein Gdns, Dart. DA2 211 FR87
Alamein Rd, Swans. DA10 211 FX86
Alanbrooke, Grav. DA12 213 GJ87
Alan Cl, Dart. DA1 190 FJ84
Alandale Dr, Pnr. HA5 115 BV54
Aland Ct, SE16 33 M7
Alander Ms, E17 145 EC56
Alan Dr, Barn. EN5 101 CY44
Alan Gdns, Rom. RM7 148 FA59
Alan Hilton Ct, Ott. KT16
off Cheshire Cl 233 BD107
Alan Hocken Way, E15 23 J1
Alan Rd, SW19 201 CY92
Alanthus Cl, SE12 206 EF86
Alan Way, Geo.Grn SL3 154 AY72
Alaska, E16 off Seagull La 23 N10
Alaska Bldg, SE13
off Deals Gateway 46 C7
Alaska St, SE1 30 E3
Alba Cl, Hayes UB4
off Ramulis Dr 158 BX70
Albacore Cres, SE13 205 EB86
Alba Gdns, NW11 141 CY58
Albain Cres, Ashf. TW15 196 BL89
Alba Ms, SW18 202 DA89
Alban Av, St.Alb. AL3 65 CD18
Alban Cres, Borwd. WD6 100 CP39
Farningham DA4 230 FN102
Alban Highwalk, EC2
off London Wall 19 K7
Alban Pk, St.Alb. AL4 66 CM20
Albans Vw, Wat. WD25 81 BV33
Alban Way Cycle Route, Hat. AL10 66 CQ20
St. Albans AL1, AL4 65 CK20
Sch Alban Wd Prim Sch, Wat. WD25 off The Brow 81 BV32
Albany, W1 29 L1
Albany, The, Wdf.Grn. IG8 124 EF49
Albany Cl, N15 143 DP56
SW14 180 CP84
Bexley DA5 208 EW87
Bushey WD23 99 CD44
Esher KT10 236 CA109
Reigate RH2 272 DA132
Uxbridge UB10 136 BN64
Coll Albany Coll, NW4
off Queens Rd 141 CW57
Hendry Ho, NW4
off Hendon Way 141 CV57
Albany Ct, E4
off Chelwood Cl 105 EB44
E10 145 EA59
Epping CM16 91 ET30
Harrow HA3 139 CK56
Albany Ctyd, W1 29 M1
Albany Cres, Clay. KT10 237 CE107
Edgware HA8 118 CN52
Albany Gate, Chesh. HP5
off Bellingdon Rd 76 AP30
Albany Hts, Grays RM17
off Hogg La 192 GA78
H Albany Lodge Comm Treatment Cen, St.Alb. AL3 64 CC19
Albany Mans, SW11 40 D5
Albany Ms, N1 8 E6
SE5 43 K3
Bromley BR1 206 EG93
Kingston upon Thames KT2 199 CK93
St. Albans AL2
off North Orbital Rd 82 CA27
Sutton SM1 off Camden Rd 240 DB106
Ware SG12 off Albany Quay 55 DY06
⇌ Albany Park 208 EX89
Albany Pk, Colnbr. SL3 175 BD81
Albany Pk Av, Enf. EN3 104 DW39
Albany Pk Rd, Kings.T. KT2 199 CK93
Leatherhead KT22 253 CG119
Albany Pas, Rich. TW10 200 CM85
Albany Pl, Brent. TW8
off Albany Rd 180 CL79
Egham TW20 195 BA91
Albany Quay, Ware SG12 55 DY06
Albany Rd, E10 145 EA59
E12 146 EK63
E17 145 DY58
N4 143 DM58
N18 122 DV50
SE5 43 L3
SE17 43 L3
SW19 202 DB92
W13 159 CH73
Belvedere DA17 188 EZ79
Bexley DA5 208 EW87
Brentford TW8 179 CK79
Chislehurst BR7 207 EP92
Enfield EN3 105 DX37
Hersham KT12 236 BX105
Hornchurch RM12 149 FG60
New Malden KT3 220 CR98
Old Windsor SL4 194 AU85
Pilgrim's Hatch CM15 130 FV44
Richmond TW10
off Albert Rd 200 CL85
Romford RM6 148 EZ58
Tilbury RM18 193 GG81
Windsor SL4 173 AQ82
Albanys, The, Reig. RH2 272 DA131
Sch Albany Sch, Enf. EN3
off Bell La 105 DX38
Sch Albany Sch, The, Horn. RM12
off Broadstone Rd 149 FH61
Albany St, NW1 7 J10
Albany Vw, Buck.H. IG9 124 EG46
Alba Pl, W11 14 G8
Alba Rd, Harl. CM17 58 EW14
Albatross Cl, E6 25 K5
Albatross Ct, Hert. SG13
off Tee Side 54 DV08
Albatross Gdns, S.Croy. CR2 243 DX111
Albatross St, SE18 187 ES80
Albatross Way, SE16 33 J5
Hatfield AL10 66 CR18
Albemarle, SW19 201 CX89
Albemarle App, Ilf. IG2 147 EP58
Albemarle Av, Chsht EN8 88 DW28
Potters Bar EN6 86 DB33
Twickenham TW2 198 BZ88
Albemarle Cl, Grays RM17 192 GA75
Albemarle Gdns, Ilf. IG2 147 EP58
New Malden KT3 220 CR98
Albemarle Pk, Stan. HA7
off Marsh La 117 CJ50
Sch Albemarle Prim Sch, SW19
off Princes Way 201 CY89
Albemarle Rd, Beck. BR3 225 EB95
East Barnet EN4 120 DE45
Albemarle St, W1 29 K1
Albemarle Way, EC1 18 G5
Albeny Gate, St.Alb. AL1 65 CD21
Albermarle Pk, Beck. BR3
off Albemarle Rd 225 EB95
Alberon Gdns, NW11 141 CZ56
Alberta Av, Sutt. SM1 239 CY105
Alberta Dr, Smallfield RH6 291 DN148
Alberta Est, SE17 31 H10
Alberta Rd, Enf. EN1 104 DT44
Erith DA8 189 FC81
Alberta St, SE17 30 G10
Albert Av, E4 123 EA49
SW8 42 C5
Chertsey KT16 216 BG97
Albert Barnes Ho, SE1 31 J7
Albert Basin, E16 37 P1
Albert Basin Way, E16 37 P1
Albert Bigg Pt, E15 12 F9
Albert Br, SW3 40 D3
SW11 40 D3
Albert Br Rd, SW11 40 D4
Albert Carr Gdns, SW16 203 DL92
Albert Cl, E9 10 F9
N22 121 DK53
Grays RM16 192 GC76
Slough SL1
off Hencroft St S 174 AT76
Albert Ct, SW7 28 A5
Waltham Cross EN8
off Queens Way 89 DZ34
Albert Cres, E4 123 EA49
Albert Dr, SW19 201 CY89
Staines TW18 195 BF92
Woking GU21 233 BD114
Albert Embk, SE1 42 B1
Albert Gdns, E1 21 J9
Harlow CM17 74 EX16
Albert Gate, SW1 28 F4
Albert Gro, SW20 221 CX95
Albert Hall Mans, SW7 28 A5
Albert Ho, SE28
off Erebus Dr 187 EQ76
Albertine Cl, Epsom KT17 255 CV116
Albert Mans, SW11 40 E6
★ Albert Mem, SW7 28 A4
Albert Ms, E14 off Narrow St 21 L10
N4 143 DM60
SE4 off Arabin Rd 185 DY84
W8 27 N6
Redhill RH1 off Reed Dr 288 DG137
Albert Murray Cl, Grav. DA12
off Armoury Dr 213 GJ87
Albert Pl, N3 120 DA53
N17 off High Rd 144 DT55
W8 27 M5
Eton Wick SL4
off Common Rd 173 AN78
Albert Rd, E10 145 EC61
E16 37 H3
E17 145 EA57
E18 146 EH55
N4 143 DM60
N15 144 DS58
N22 121 DJ53
NW4 141 CX56
NW6 15 H1
NW7 119 CT50
SE9 206 EL90
SE20 205 DX94
SE25 224 DU98
W5 159 CH70
Addlestone KT15 216 BK104
Ashford TW15 196 BM92
Ashtead KT21 254 CM118
Belvedere DA17 188 EZ78
Bexley DA5 208 FA86
Bromley BR2 226 EK99
Buckhurst Hill IG9 124 EK47
Chelsfield BR6 246 EU106
Chesham HP5 76 AQ31
Dagenham RM8 148 EZ60
Dartford DA2 210 FJ90
East Barnet EN4 102 DC42
Englefield Green TW20 194 AX93
Epsom KT17 239 CT113
Hampton Hill TW12 198 CC92
Harrow HA2 138 CC55
Hayes UB3 177 BS76
Horley RH6 290 DG147
Hounslow TW3 178 CA84
Ilford IG1 147 EP62
Kingston upon Thames KT1 220 CM96
Mitcham CR4 222 DF97
New Malden KT3 221 CT98
Richmond TW10 200 CL85
Romford RM1 149 FF57
St. Mary Cray BR5 228 EV100
South Merstham RH1 273 DJ129
Southall UB2 178 BX76
Sutton SM1 240 DD106
Swanscombe DA10 212 FZ86
Teddington TW11 199 CF93
Twickenham TW1 199 CF88
Warlingham CR6 259 DZ117
West Drayton UB7 156 BL74
Windsor SL4 174 AS84
Albert Rd Est, Belv. DA17 188 EZ78
Albert Rd N, Reig. RH2 271 CZ133
Watford WD17 97 BV41
Albert Rd S, Wat. WD17 97 BV41
Albert Sleet Ct, N9
off Colthurst Dr 122 DV48
Albert Sq, E15 13 K3
SW8 42 C5
Albert St, N12 120 DC50
NW1 7 K9
St. Albans AL1 65 CD21
Slough SL1 174 AT76
Warley CM14 130 FW50
Windsor SL4 173 AP81
Albert Ter, NW1 6 G8
NW10 160 CR67
W6 off Beavor La 181 CU78
Buckhurst Hill IG9 124 EK47
Albert Ter Ms, NW1 6 G9
Albert Way, SE15 44 E4
Albion Av, N10 120 DG53
SW8 41 N8
Albion Cl, W2 16 D10
Hertford SG13 54 DS08
Romford RM7 149 FD58
Slough SL2 154 AU74
Albion Cres, Ch.St.G. HP8 112 AV48
Albion Dr, E8 10 A7
Albion Est, SE16 33 J5
Albion Gro, N16 144 DS63
Albion Hill, Hem.H. HP2
off Wolsey Rd 62 BK21
Loughton IG10 106 EJ43
Albion Ho, E16 off Church St 37 N3
Woking GU21 249 AZ117
Albion Ms, N1 8 E8
NW6 4 G6
W2 16 D9
W6 off Galena Rd 181 CV77
Albion Par, N16
off Albion Rd 144 DR63
Gravesend DA12 213 GK86
Albion Pk, Loug. IG10 106 EK43
Albion Pl, EC1 18 G6
SE25 224 DU97
W6 181 CV77
Windsor SL4 173 AN82
Sch Albion Prim Sch, SE16 33 H5
Albion Riverside Bldg, SW11 40 D4
Albion Rd, E17 145 EC55
N16 9 M2
N17 122 DT54
Bexleyheath DA6 188 EZ84
Chalfont St. Giles HP8 112 AV47
Gravesend DA12 213 GJ87
Hayes UB3 157 BS72
Hounslow TW3 178 CA84
Kingston upon Thames KT2 220 CQ95
Reigate RH2 288 DC135
St. Albans AL1 65 CF20
Sutton SM2 240 DD107
Twickenham TW2 199 CE88
Albion Sq, E8 10 A7
Albion St, SE16 33 H5
W2 16 D9
Croydon CR0 223 DP102
Albion Ter, E8 10 A7
Gravesend DA12 213 GJ86
Albion Vil Rd, SE26 204 DW90
Albion Wk, N1 18 B1
Albion Way, EC1 19 J7
SE13 185 EC84
Wembley HA9
off North End Rd 140 CP62
Albion Yd, N1 18 B1
Albon Ho, SW18
off Neville Gill Cl 202 DB86
● Albright Ind Est, Rain. RM13 169 FF71
Albrighton Rd, SE22 184 DS83
Albuhera Cl, Enf. EN2 103 DN39
ALBURY, Guil. GU5 282 BJ139
Albury Av, Bexh. DA7 188 EY82
Isleworth TW7 179 CF80
Sutton SM2 239 CW109
Albury Cl, Epsom KT19 238 CP109
Hampton TW12 198 CA93
Longcross KT16 214 AU104
Albury Ct, Sutt. SM1
off Ripley Gdns 240 DC105
Albury Dr, Pnr. HA5 116 BX52
Albury Gro Rd, Chsht EN8 89 DX30
ALBURY HEATH, Guil. GU5 282 BL141
Albury Heath, Albury GU5 282 BL141
Albury Keep, Horl. RH6
off Langshott La 291 DH147
Albury Ms, E12 146 EJ60
Albury Pk, Albury GU5 282 BL140
Albury Ride, Chsht EN8 89 DX31
Albury Rd, Chess. KT9 238 CL106
Guildford GU1 281 AZ135
Hersham KT12 235 BS107
South Merstham RH1 273 DJ129
Albury St, SE8 46 A3
Albury Wk, Chsht EN8 88 DW30
Albyfield, Brom. BR1 227 EM97
Albyn Ho, Hem.H. HP2 62 BK19
Albyn Rd, SE8 46 A7
Albyns Cl, Rain. RM13 169 FG66
Albyns La, Rom. RM4 109 FC40
Alcester Cres, E5 144 DV61
Alcester Rd, Wall. SM6 241 DH105
Alcock Cl, Wall. SM6 241 DK108
Alcock Rd, Houns. TW5 178 BX80
Alcocks Cl, Kgswd KT20 255 CY120
Alcocks La, Kgswd KT20 255 CY120
Alconbury, Welw.G.C. AL7 52 DE08
Alconbury Cl, Borwd. WD6 100 CM39
Alconbury Rd, E5 144 DU61
Alcorn Cl, Sutt. SM3 222 DA103
Alcott Cl, W7
off Westcott Cres 159 CF71
Alcuin Ct, Stan. HA7
off Old Ch La 117 CJ52
ALDBOROUGH HATCH, Ilf. IG2 147 ES55
Aldborough Rd, Dag. RM10 169 FC65
Upminster RM14 150 FM61
Aldborough Rd N, Ilf. IG2 147 ET57
Aldborough Rd S, Ilf. IG3 147 ES60
Aldborough Spur, Slou. SL1 154 AS72
Aldbourne Rd, W12 161 CT74
Burnham SL1 152 AH71
Aldbridge St, SE17 31 P10
Aldburgh Ms, W1 17 H8

Aldbury Av, Wem. HA9 160 CP66
Aldbury Cl, St.Alb. AL4
off Larkswood Ri 65 CJ15
Watford WD25 98 BX36
Aldbury Gro, Welw.G.C. AL7 52 DB09
Aldbury Ms, N9 122 DR45
Aldbury Rd, Mill End WD3 113 BF45
Aldebert Ter, SW8 42 B5
Aldeburgh Cl, E5
off Southwold Rd 144 DV61
Aldeburgh Pl, SE10 35 P9
Woodford Green IG8 124 EG49
Aldeburgh St, SE10 35 N10
Alden Av, E15 23 L3
ALDENHAM, Wat. WD25 98 CB38
Aldenham Av, Rad. WD7 99 CG36
★ **Aldenham Country Pk**, Borwd. WD6 99 CG43
Aldenham Dr, Uxb. UB8 157 BP70
Aldenham Gro, Rad. WD7 83 CH34
Aldenham Rd, Bushey WD23 98 BZ42
Elstree WD6 99 CH42
Letchmore Heath WD25 99 CE39
Radlett WD7 99 CG35
Watford WD19 98 BX44
Sch **Aldenham Sch**, Els. WD6
off Aldenham Rd 99 CF40
Aldenham St, NW1 17 M1
Aldenholme, Wey. KT13 235 BS107
Aldensley Rd, W6 181 CV76
Alden Vw, Wind. SL4 173 AK81
Alder Av, Upmin. RM14 150 FM63
Alderbourne La, Fulmer SL3 134 AX63
Iver SL0 135 BA64
Sch **Alderbrook Prim Sch**, SW12
off Oldridge Rd 203 DH87
Alderbrook Rd, SW12 203 DH86
Alderbury Rd, SW13 181 CU79
Slough SL3 175 AZ75
Alderbury Rd W, Slou. SL3 175 AZ75
Alder Cl, SE15 44 B3
Englefield Green TW20 194 AY92
Erith DA18 188 EZ75
Hoddesdon EN11 71 EB15
Park Street AL2 82 CB28
Slough SL1 153 AM74
Aldercombe La, Cat. CR3 274 DS127
Alder Ct, N11 *off Cline Rd* 121 DJ51
Aldercroft, Couls. CR5 257 DM116
Alder Dr, S.Ock. RM15
off Laburnum Gro 171 FW70
Alder Gro, NW2 141 CV61
Aldergrove Gdns, Houns. TW3
off Bath Rd 178 BY82
Aldergrove Wk, Horn. RM12
off Pembrey Way 170 FJ65
Alder Ho, NW3 6 F4
Alderley Ct, Berk. HP4 60 AV20
Alderman Av, Bark. IG11 168 EU69
Aldermanbury, EC2 19 K8
Aldermanbury Sq, EC2 19 K7
Alderman Cl, Dart. DA1 209 FE87
North Mymms AL9 67 CW24
🔒 **Alderman Judge Mall**, Kings.T. KT1 *off Eden St* 220 CL96
Aldermans Hill, N13 121 DL49
Alderman's Wk, EC2 19 N7
Aldermary Rd, Brom. BR1 226 EG95
Alder Ms, N19 *off Bredgar Rd* 143 DJ61
Aldermoor Rd, SE6 205 DZ90
Alderney Av, Houns. TW5 178 CB80
Alderney Gdns, Nthlt. UB5 158 BZ66
Alderney Ho, N1 *off Arran Wk* 9 K5
Alderney Ms, SE1 31 L6
Alderney Rd, E1 21 J4
Erith DA8 189 FG80
Alderney St, SW1 29 K10
Alder Rd, SW14 180 CR83
Denham UB9 156 BJ65
Iver SL0 155 BC68
Sidcup DA14 207 ET90
Alders, The, N21 103 DN44
SW16 203 DJ91
Feltham TW13 198 BY91
Hounslow TW5 178 BZ79
West Byfleet KT14 234 BJ112
West Wickham BR4 225 EB102
Alders Av, Wdf.Grn. IG8 124 EE51
ALDERSBROOK, E12 146 EH61
Aldersbrook Av, Enf. EN1 104 DS40
Aldersbrook Dr, Kings.T. KT2 200 CM93
Aldersbrook La, E12 147 EM62
Sch **Aldersbrook Prim Sch**, E12
off Ingatestone Rd 146 EJ60
Aldersbrook Rd, E11 146 EH61
E12 146 EK62
Alders Cl, E11 146 EH61
W5 179 CK76
Edgware HA8 118 CQ50
● **Alders Ct**, Welw.G.C. AL7 52 DA09
Aldersey Gdns, Bark. IG11 167 ER65
Aldersey Rd, Guil. GU1 265 AZ134
Aldersford Cl, SE4 205 DX85
Aldersgate St, EC1 19 J8
Alders Gro, E.Mol. KT8 219 CD99
Aldersgrove, Wal.Abb. EN9
off Roundhills 90 EE34
Aldersgrove Av, SE9 206 EJ90
Aldershot Rd, NW6 5 H8
Guildford GU2, GU3 264 AT132
Alderside Wk, Eng.Grn TW20 194 AY92
Aldersmead Av, Croy. CR0 225 DX100
Aldersmead Rd, Beck. BR3 205 DY94
Alderson Pl, Sthl. UB2 158 CC74
Alderson St, W10 14 F4
Alders Rd, Edg. HA8 118 CQ50
Reigate RH2 272 DB132
Alderstead La, Merst. RH1 273 DK126
Alders Wk, Saw. CM21 58 EY05
Alderton Cl, NW10 140 CR62
Loughton IG10 107 EN42
Pilgrim's Hatch CM15 130 FV43
Alderton Cres, NW4 141 CV57
Alderton Hall La, Loug. IG10 107 EN42
Alderton Hill, Loug. IG10 106 EL43
Sch **Alderton Inf Sch**, Loug. IG10
off Alderton Hall La 107 EN43
Sch **Alderton Jun Sch**, Loug. IG10
off Alderton Hall La 107 EN43
Alderton Ms, Loug. IG10
off Alderton Hall La 107 EN42
Alderton Ri, Loug. IG10 107 EN42
Alderton Rd, SE24 184 DQ83
Croydon CR0 224 DT101
Alderton Way, NW4 141 CV57
Loughton IG10 107 EM43
Alderville Rd, SW6 39 H8
Alder Wk, Ilf. IG1 147 EQ64
Watford WD25
off Aspen Pk Dr 97 BV35
Alder Way, Swan. BR8 229 FD96
Alderwick Dr, Houns. TW3 179 CD83
Alderwood Cl, Abridge RM4 108 EV41
Caterham CR3 274 DS125
Alderwood Dr, Abridge RM4 108 EV41
Alderwood Ms, Barn. EN4 102 DC38
Sch **Alderwood Prim Sch**, SE9 *off Rainham Cl* 207 ES86
Alderwood Rd, SE9 207 ER86
Aldford St, W1 28 G2
⊖ **Aldgate** 20 A9
⊖ **Aldgate** 20 A9
Aldgate, EC3 20 A9
Aldgate Av, E1 20 A8
🔒 **Aldgate Barrs Shop Cen**, E1 20 B8
⊖ **Aldgate East** 20 B8
Aldgate High St, EC3 20 A9
Aldham Dr, S.Ock. RM15 171 FW71
Aldin Av N, Slou. SL1 174 AU75
Aldin Av S, Slou. SL1 174 AU75
Aldine Ct, W12 26 B4
Aldine Pl, W12 26 B3
Aldine St, W12 26 B4
Aldingham Ct, Horn. RM12
off Easedale Dr 149 FG64
Aldingham Gdns, Horn. RM12 149 FG64
Aldington Cl, Dag. RM8 148 EW59
Aldington Rd, SE18 36 F7
Aldis Ms, SW17 202 DE92
Enfield EN3 105 EA37
Aldis St, SW17 202 DE92
Aldock, Welw.G.C. AL7 52 DA12
Aldred Rd, NW6 5 J2
Aldren Rd, SW17 202 DC90
Aldrich Cres, New Adgtn CR0 243 EC109
Aldriche Way, E4 123 EC51
Aldrich Gdns, Sutt. SM3 221 CZ104
Aldrich Ter, SW18
off Lidiard Rd 202 DC89
Aldridge Av, Edg. HA8 118 CP48
Enfield EN3 105 EA38
Ruislip HA4 138 BX61
Stanmore HA7 118 CL53
Aldridge Ri, N.Mal. KT3 220 CS101
Aldridge Rd, Slou. SL2 153 AN70
Aldridge Rd Vil, W11 15 H7
Aldridge Wk, N14 121 DL45
Aldrien Ct, N9
off Galahad Rd 122 DU48
Aldrington Rd, SW16 203 DJ92
Aldsworth Cl, W9 15 L5
Aldwick, St.Alb. AL1 65 CH22
Aldwick Cl, SE9 207 ER90
Aldwick Rd, Croy. CR0 223 DM104
Aldworth Gro, SE13 205 EC86
Aldworth Rd, E15 13 J7
Aldwych, WC2 18 C10
Aldwych Av, Ilf. IG6 147 EQ56
Aldwych Cl, Horn. RM12 149 FG61
Aldwych Underpass, WC2
off Kingsway 18 C9
Aldwyck Ct, Hem.H. HP1 62 BJ19
Aldykes, Hat. AL10 67 CT18
Alers Rd, Bexh. DA6 208 EX85
Alesia Cl, N22 121 DL52
Alestan Beck Rd, E16 24 F8
Alexa Ct, W8 27 L8
Sutton SM2
off Mulgrave Rd 240 DA107
Alexander Av, NW10 161 CV66
Alexander Cl, Barn. EN4 102 DD42
Bromley BR2 226 EG102
Sidcup DA15 207 ES85
Southall UB2 158 CC74
Twickenham TW2 199 CF89
Alexander Ct, Chsht EN8 89 DX30
Alexander Cres, Cat. CR3 258 DQ121
Alexander Evans Ms, SE23
off Sunderland Rd 205 DX88
Sch **Alexander First Sch**, Oakley Grn SL4 *off Kenneally Row* 172 AJ82
★ **Alexander Fleming Laboratory Mus**, W2 16 B8
Alexander Godley Cl, Ashtd. KT21 254 CM119
Alexander Ho, Kings.T. KT2
off Kingsgate Rd 220 CL95
Alexander La, Brwd. CM13, CM15 131 GB44
Sch **Alexander McLeod Prim Sch**, SE2 *off Fuchsia St* 188 EV78
Alexander Ms, SW16 203 DJ92
W2 15 L8
Harlow CM17 74 EX17
Alexander Pl, SW7 28 C8
Oxted RH8 276 EE128
Alexander Rd, N19 143 DL62
Bexleyheath DA7 188 EX82
Chislehurst BR7 207 EP92
Coulsdon CR5 257 DH115
Egham TW20 195 BB92
Greenhithe DA9 211 FW85
Hertford SG14 53 DN09
London Colney AL2 83 CJ25
Reigate RH2 288 DA137
Alexander Sq, SW3 28 C8
Alexander St, W2 15 K8
Chesham HP5 76 AQ30
Alexanders Wk, Cat. CR3 274 DT126
Alexandra Av, N22 121 DK53
SW11 40 G6
W4 180 CR80
Harrow HA2 138 BZ60
Southall UB1 158 BZ73
Sutton SM1 222 DA104
Warlingham CR6 259 DZ117
Alexandra Cl, SE8 45 N2
Ashford TW15 197 BR94
Grays RM16 193 GH75
Harrow HA2
off Alexandra Av 138 CA62
Staines TW18 196 BK93
Swanley BR8 229 FE96
Walton-on-Thames KT12 217 BU103
Alexandra Cotts, SE14 45 P7
Alexandra Ct, N14 103 DJ43
N16 9 P1
W9 15 P4
Ashford TW15 197 BR93
Alexandra Ct, Wal.Cr. EN8
off Alexandra Way 89 DZ34
Wembley HA9 140 CM63
Alexandra Cres, Brom. BR1 206 EF93
Alexandra Dr, SE19 204 DS92
Surbiton KT5 220 CN101
Alexandra Gdns, N10 143 DH56
W4 180 CS80
Carshalton SM5 240 DG109
Hounslow TW3 178 CB82
Alexandra Gro, N4 143 DP60
N12 120 DB50
Sch **Alexandra Inf Sch**, Beck. BR3 *off Kent Ho Rd* 205 DX94
Kingston upon Thames KT2
off Alexandra Rd 200 CN94
Sch **Alexandra Jun Sch**, SE26
off Cator Rd 205 DX93
Alexandra Ms, N2 142 DF55
SW19 *off Alexandra Rd* 201 CZ93
Sch **Alexandra Nurs & Inf & Jun Schs**, Houns. TW3
off Denbigh Rd 178 CB82
★ **Alexandra Palace**, N22 121 DK54
⇌ **Alexandra Palace** 121 DL54
Alexandra Palace Way, N22 143 DJ55
Alexandra Pk Rd, N10 121 DH54
N22 121 DK54
Sch **Alexandra Pk Sch**, N11
off Bidwell Gdns 121 DJ53
Alexandra Pl, NW8 5 P8
SE25 224 DR99
Croydon CR0
off Alexandra Rd 224 DS102
Guildford GU1 281 AZ136
Sch **Alexandra Prim Sch**, N22
off Western Rd 121 DM54
Alexandra Rd, E6 25 L2
E10 145 EC62
E17 145 DZ58
E18 146 EH55
N8 143 DN55
N9 122 DV45
N10 121 DH51
N15 144 DR57
NW4 141 CX56
NW8 5 P8
SE26 205 DX93
SW14 180 CR83
SW19 201 CZ93
W4 180 CR75
Addlestone KT15 234 BK105
Ashford TW15 197 BR94
Biggin Hill TN16 260 EH119
Borehamwood WD6 100 CR38
Brentford TW8 179 CK79
Brentwood CM14 130 FW48
Chadwell Heath RM6 148 EX58
Chipperfield WD4 80 BG30
Croydon CR0 224 DS102
Enfield EN3 105 DX42
Englefield Green TW20 194 AW93
Epsom KT17 239 CT113
Erith DA8 189 FF79
Gravesend DA12 213 GL87
Harlow CM17 58 EW13
Hemel Hempstead HP2 62 BK20
Hounslow TW3 178 CB82
Kings Langley WD4 80 BN29
Kingston upon Thames KT2 200 CN94
Mitcham CR4 202 DE94
Rainham RM13 169 FF67
Richmond TW9 180 CM82
Romford RM1 149 FF58
St. Albans AL1 65 CE20
Sarratt WD3 96 BG36
Slough SL1 173 AR76
Thames Ditton KT7 219 CF99
Tilbury RM18 193 GF82
Twickenham TW1 199 CJ86
Uxbridge UB8 156 BK68
Warlingham CR6 259 DY117
Watford WD17 97 BU40
Windsor SL4 173 AR82
Sch **Alexandra Sch**, S.Har. HA2
off Alexandra Av 138 CA61
Alexandra Sq, Mord. SM4 222 DA99
Alexandra St, E16 23 N6
SE14 45 M4
Alexandra Ter, Guil. GU1 280 AY135
Alexandra Wk, SE19 204 DS92
South Darenth DA4
off Gorringe Av 231 FS96
Alexandra Way, Epsom KT19 238 CN111
Waltham Cross EN8 89 DZ34
Alexandria Rd, W13 159 CG73
Alex Ct, Hem.H. HP2
off Alexandra Rd 62 BK19
Alexis St, SE16 32 C8
Alfan La, Dart. DA2 209 FD92
Alfearn Rd, E5 144 DW63
Alford Cl, Guil. GU4 265 AZ131
Alford Grn, New Adgtn CR0 243 ED107
Alford Ho, N6 143 DJ58
Alford Pl, N1 19 K1
Alford Rd, Erith DA8 189 FD78
Alfoxton Av, N15 143 DP56
Alfreda St, SW11 41 J6
Alfred Cl, W4 180 CR77
Alfred Ct, Whyt. CR3
off Godstone Rd 258 DU119
Alfred Gdns, Sthl. UB1 158 BY73
Alfred Ms, W1 17 N6
Alfred Pl, WC1 17 N6
Northfleet DA11 213 GF88
Alfred Prior Ho, E12 147 EN63
Alfred Rd, E15 13 L2
SE25 224 DU99
W2 15 K6
W3 160 CQ74
Aveley RM15 170 FQ74
Belvedere DA17 188 EZ78
Brentwood CM14 130 FX47
Buckhurst Hill IG9 124 EK47
Feltham TW13 198 BW89
Gravesend DA11 213 GH89
Hawley DA2 210 FL91
Kingston upon Thames KT1 220 CL97
Sutton SM1 240 DC106
Sch **Alfred Salter Prim Sch**, SE16 33 K5
Alfred's Gdns, Bark. IG11 167 ES68
Alfred St, E3 21 P1
Grays RM17 192 GC79
Alfreds Way, Bark. IG11 167 EQ69
● **Alfreds Way Ind Est**, Bark. IG11 168 EU67
Alfreton Cl, SW19 201 CX90
Alfriston, Surb. KT5 220 CM99
Alfriston Av, Croy. CR0 223 DL101
Harrow HA2 138 CA58
Alfriston Cl, Dart. DA1 209 FE86
Surbiton KT5 220 CM100
Alfriston Rd, SW11 202 DF85
Sch **Alfriston Sch**, Knot.Grn HP9 *off Penn Rd* 110 AJ49
Algar Cl, Islw. TW7
off Algar Rd 179 CG83
Stanmore HA7 117 CF50
Algar Rd, Islw. TW7 179 CG83
Algarve Rd, SW18 202 DB88
Algernon Rd, NW4 141 CU58
NW6 5 J9
SE13 46 C10
Algers Cl, Loug. IG10 106 EK43
Algers Mead, Loug. IG10 106 EK43
Algers Rd, Loug. IG10 106 EK43
Algiers Rd, SE13 185 EA84
Alibon Gdns, Dag. RM10 148 FA64
Alibon Rd, Dag. RM9, RM10 148 EZ64
Alice Cl, New Barn. EN5 102 DC42
Alice Ct, SW15 181 CZ84
Alice Gilliatt Ct, W14 38 G2
Alice La, E3 11 N9
Burnham SL1 152 AH70
Alice Ms, Tedd. TW11
off Luther Rd 199 CF92
Alice Ruston Pl, Wok. GU22 248 AW119
Alice St, SE1 31 N7
Alice Thompson Cl, SE12 206 EJ89
Alice Wk, W5 159 CJ71
Alice Walker Cl, SE24
off Shakespeare Rd 183 DP84
Alice Way, Houns. TW3 178 CB84
Alicia Av, Har. HA3 139 CH56
Alicia Cl, Har. HA3 139 CJ56
Alicia Gdns, Har. HA3 139 CH56
Alie St, E1 20 B9
Alington Cres, NW9 140 CQ60
Alington Gro, Wall. SM6 241 DJ109
Alison Cl, E6 25 M9
Croydon CR0
off Shirley Oaks Rd 225 DX102
Woking GU21 248 AY115
Aliwal Rd, SW11 182 DE84
Alkerden La, Green. DA9 211 FW86
Swanscombe DA10 211 FW86
Alkerden Rd, W4 180 CS78
Alkham Rd, N16 144 DT61
Alkham Twr, Orp. BR5 228 EW98
Allan Barclay Cl, N15 144 DT58
Allan Cl, N.Mal. KT3 220 CR99
Allandale, Hem.H. HP2 62 BK18
St. Albans AL3 64 CB23
Allandale Av, N3 141 CY55
Allandale Cres, Pot.B. EN6 85 CY32
Allandale Pl, Orp. BR6 228 EX104
Allandale Rd, Enf. EN3 105 DX36
Hornchurch RM11 149 FF59
Allan Way, W3 160 CQ71
Allard Cl, Chsht EN7 88 DT27
Orpington BR5 228 EW101
Allard Cres, Bushey Hth WD23 116 CC46
Allard Gdns, SW4 203 DK85
Allard Way, Brox. EN10 71 DY21
Allardyce St, SW4 183 DM84
Allbrook Cl, Tedd. TW11 199 CE92
Allcot Cl, Felt. TW14 197 BT88
Allcroft Rd, NW5 7 H3
Allder Way, S.Croy. CR2 241 DP108
Alldicks Rd, Hem.H. HP3 62 BM22
Allenby Av, S.Croy. CR2 242 DQ109
Allenby Cl, Grnf. UB6 158 CA69
Allenby Cres, Grays RM17 192 GB78
Allenby Dr, Horn. RM11 150 FL60
Sch **Allenby Prim Sch**, Sthl. UB1 *off Allenby Rd* 158 CA72
Allenby Rd, SE23 205 DY90
SE28 187 EQ76
Biggin Hill TN16 260 EL117
Southall UB1 158 CA72
Allen Cl, Mitch. CR4 223 DH95
Shenley WD7 *off Russet Dr* 84 CL32
Sunbury-on-Thames TW16 217 BV95
Allen Ct, Dor. RH4
off High St 285 CH136
Greenford UB6 139 CF64
Hatfield AL10
off Drakes Way 67 CV20
Allendale Av, Sthl. UB1 158 CA72
Allendale Cl, SE5 43 L8
SE26 205 DX92
Dartford DA2
off Princes Rd 211 FR88
Allendale Rd, Grnf. UB6 159 CH65
Allende Av, Harl. CM20 57 ER13
Allen Edwards Dr, SW8 42 A6
Sch **Allen Edwards Prim Sch**, SW4 42 A7
Allenford Ho, SW15
off Tunworth Cres 201 CT86
Allen Ho Pk, Wok. GU22 248 AW120
Allen Pl, Twick. TW1
off Church St 199 CG88
Allen Rd, E3 21 N10
N16 144 DS63
Beckenham BR3 225 DX96
Bookham KT23 268 CB126
Croydon CR0 223 DM101
Rainham RM13 170 FJ69
Sunbury-on-Thames TW16 217 BV95
Allensbury Pl, NW1 7 P7
Allens Mead, Grav. DA12 213 GM88
Allens Rd, Enf. EN3 104 DW43
Allen St, W8 27 K6
Allenswood, SW19
off Albert Dr 201 CY88
Allenswood Rd, SE9 186 EL83
Allen Way, Datchet SL3 174 AW81
Allerds Rd, Farn.Royal SL2 153 AM67
Allerford Ct, Har. HA2 138 CB57
Allerford Rd, SE6 205 EB91
Allerton Cl, Borwd. WD6 100 CM38
Allerton Ct, NW4
off Holders Hill Rd 119 CX54
Allerton Rd, N16 144 DQ61
Borehamwood WD6 100 CL38
Allerton Wk, N7
off Durham Rd 143 DM61
Allestree Rd, SW6 38 E5
Alleyn Cres, SE21 204 DR89
Alleyndale Rd, Dag. RM8 148 EW61
Alleyn Pk, SE21 204 DR89
Southall UB2 178 BZ77
Alleyn Rd, SE21 204 DR90
Sch **Alleyn's Sch**, SE22
off Townley Rd 204 DS85
Allfarthing La, SW18 202 DB86
Sch **Allfarthing Prim Sch**, SW18
off St. Ann's Cres 202 DC86
Allgood Cl, Mord. SM4 221 CX100
Allgood St, E2 20 B1
Allhallows La, EC4 31 L1
★ **All Hallows-on-the-Wall C of E Ch**, EC2 19 M7
Allhallows Rd, E6 24 G7
All Hallows Rd, N17 122 DS53
Allhusen Gdns, Fulmer SL3
off Alderbourne La 134 AY63
Alliance Cl, Houns. TW4
off Vimy Cl 198 BZ85
Wembley HA0 139 CK63
● **Alliance Ct**, W3
off Alliance Rd 160 CP71
Alliance Rd, E13 24 C5
SE18 188 EU79
W3 160 CP70
Allied Ct, N1 9 P7
Allied Way, W3 *off Larden Rd* 180 CS75
Allingham Cl, W7 159 CF73
Allingham Ct, Gdmg. GU7
off Summers Rd 280 AT144
Allingham Ms, N1 9 J10
Allingham Rd, Reig. RH2 288 DA137
Allingham St, N1 9 J10
Allington Av, N17 122 DS51
Allington Cl, SW19
off High St Wimbledon 201 CX92
Gravesend DA12
off Farley Rd 213 GM88
Greenford UB6 158 CC66
Allington Ct, Enf. EN3 105 DX43
Slough SL2 154 AT73
Allington Rd, NW4 141 CV57
W10 14 E2
Harrow HA2 138 CC57
Orpington BR6 227 ER103
Allington St, SW1 29 L7
Allis Ms, Harl. CM17
off Tatton St 58 EW14
Allison Cl, SE10 46 F7
Waltham Abbey EN9 90 EG33
Allison Gro, SE21 204 DS88
Allison Rd, N8 143 DN57
W3 160 CQ72
Allitsen Rd, NW8 16 C1
Allmains Cl, Naze.Gate EN9 90 EH25
Coll **All Nations Christian Coll**, Easneye SG12 55 EC08
Allnutts Rd, Epp. CM16 92 EU33
Allnutt Way, SW4 203 DK85
Alloa Rd, SE8 33 K10
Ilford IG3 148 EU61
Allonby Dr, Ruis. HA4 137 BP59
Allonby Gdns, Wem. HA9 139 CJ60
Allonby Ho, E14 21 L7
Allotment La, Sev. TN13 279 FJ122
Allotment Way, NW2
off Midland Ter 141 CX62
Alloway Cl, Wok. GU21
off Inglewood 248 AV118
Alloway Rd, E3 21 M2
Allport Ms, E1 21 H5
DLR **All Saints** 22 E10
Sch **All Saints Benhilton C of E Prim Sch**, Sutt. SM1
off All Saints Rd 222 DB104
Sch **All Saints Carshalton C of E Prim Sch**, Cars. SM5
off Rotherfield Rd 240 DG106
Sch **All Saints Cath Sch & Tech Coll**, Dag. RM8 *off Terling Rd* 148 FA60
All Saints Cl, N9 122 DT47
SW8 42 A6
Chigwell IG7 126 EU48
Swanscombe DA10
off High St 212 FZ85
Sch **All Saints C of E Jun Sch**, SE19 *off Upper Beulah Hill* 224 DS95
Sch **All Saints' C of E Prim Sch**, N20 *off Oakleigh Rd N* 120 DD47
NW2 *off Cricklewood La* 141 CZ62
Sch **All Saints C of E Prim Sch**, SE3 47 J8
SW6 38 E8
SW15 38 A10
SW19 *off East Rd* 202 DC94
All Saints Cres, Wat. WD25 82 BX33
All Saints Dr, SE3 47 K8
South Croydon CR2 242 DT112
Sch **All Saints Inf Sch**, SE19
off Upper Beulah Hill 224 DS95
All Saints La, Crox.Grn WD3 96 BN44
All Saints Ms, Har. HA3 117 CE51
All Saints Pas, SW18
off Wandsworth High St 202 DA85
All Saints Rd, SW19 202 DC94
W3 180 CQ76
W11 14 G7
Northfleet DA11 213 GF88
Sutton SM1 222 DB104
All Saints St, N1 8 C10
All Saints Twr, E10 145 EB59
Allsop Pl, NW1 16 F5
All Souls Av, NW10 161 CV68
Sch **All Souls C of E Prim Sch**, W1 17 L7
All Souls Pl, W1 17 K7
Allum Cl, Els. WD6 100 CL42
Allum Gro, Tad. KT20 255 CV121
Allum La, Els. WD6 100 CM42
Allum Way, N20 120 DC46
Allwood Cl, SE26 205 DX91
Allwood Rd, Chsht EN7 88 DT27
Allyn Cl, Stai. TW18
off Penton Rd 195 BF93
Alma Av, E4 123 EC52
Hornchurch RM12 150 FL63
Almack Rd, E5 10 G1
Alma Cl, Knap. GU21 248 AS118
Alma Cres, Sutt. SM1 239 CY106
Alma Cut, St.Alb. AL1 65 CE21
Alma Gro, SE1 32 B9
Alma Pl, NW10 *off Harrow Rd* 161 CV69
SE19 204 DT94
Thornton Heath CR7 223 DN99
Sch **Alma Prim Sch**, SE16 32 D8
Enfield EN3 *off Alma Rd* 105 DX43
Alma Rd, N10 120 DG52
SW18 202 DC85
Carshalton SM5 240 DE106
Chesham HP5 76 AQ29
Enfield EN3 105 DY43
Esher KT10 219 CE102
Eton Wick SL4 173 AM77
Northchurch HP4 60 AS17
Orpington BR5 228 EX103

Alma Rd, Reig. RH2 . . . 272 DB133
St. Albans AL1 . . . 65 CE21
Sidcup DA14 . . . 208 EU90
Southall UB1 . . . 158 BY73
Swanscombe DA10 . . . 212 FZ85
Windsor SL4 . . . 173 AQ82
Alma Row, Har. HA3 . . . 117 CD53
Alma Sq, NW8 . . . 15 P2
Alma St, E15 . . . 12 G4
NW5 . . . 7 K4
Alma Ter, SW18 . . . 202 DD87
W8 off Allen St . . . 27 K7
Almeida St, N1 . . . 8 G7
Almeric Rd, SW11 . . . 182 DF84
Almer Rd, SW20 . . . 201 CU94
Almington St, N4 . . . 143 DL60
Almners Rd, Lyne KT16 . . . 215 BC100
Almond Av, W5 . . . 180 CL76
Carshalton SM5 . . . 222 DF103
Uxbridge UB10 . . . 137 BP62
West Drayton UB7 . . . 176 BN76
Woking GU22 . . . 248 AX121
Almond Cl, SE15 . . . 44 D9
Bromley BR2 . . . 227 EN101
Englefield Green TW20 . . . 194 AV93
Feltham TW13
off Highfield Rd . . . 197 BU88
Grays RM16 . . . 193 GG76
Guildford GU1 . . . 264 AX130
Hayes UB3 . . . 157 BS73
Ruislip HA4 off Roundways . . . 137 BT62
Shepperton TW17 . . . 217 BQ96
Windsor SL4 . . . 173 AP82
Almond Dr, Swan. BR8 . . . 229 FD96
Almond Gro, Brent. TW8 . . . 179 CH80
Almond Rd, N17 . . . 122 DU52
SE16 . . . 32 F8
Burnham SL1 . . . 152 AH68
Dartford DA2 . . . 210 FQ87
Epsom KT19 . . . 238 CR111
Almonds, The, St.Alb. AL1 . . . 65 CH24
Almonds Av, Buck.H. IG9 . . . 124 EG47
Almond Wk, Hat. AL10
off Southdown Rd . . . 67 CU21
Almond Way, Borwd. WD6 . . . 100 CP42
Bromley BR2 . . . 227 EN101
Harrow HA2 . . . 116 CB54
Mitcham CR4 . . . 223 DK99
Almons Way, Slou. SL2 . . . 154 AV71
Almorah Rd, N1 . . . 9 L7
Hounslow TW5 . . . 178 BX81
Alms Heath, Ock. GU23 . . . 251 BP121
Almshouse La, Chess. KT9 . . . 237 CJ109
Enfield EN1 . . . 104 DV37
Almshouses, The, Dor. RH4
off Cotmandene . . . 285 CH135
Alnwick Gro, Mord. SM4
off Bordesley Rd . . . 222 DB98
Alnwick Rd, E16 . . . 24 C9
SE12 . . . 206 EH87
ALPERTON, Wem. HA0 . . . 160 CM67
⊖ Alperton . . . 160 CL67
Sch Alperton Comm Sch, Lwr Sch,
Wem. HA0 off Ealing Rd . . . 160 CL67
Upr Sch & 6th Form Cen, Wem.
HA0 off Stanley Av . . . 160 CL66
Alperton La, Perivale UB6 . . . 159 CK69
Wembley HA0 . . . 159 CK69
Alperton St, W10 . . . 14 F4
Alphabet Gdns, Cars. SM5 . . . 222 DD100
Alphabet Sq, E3 . . . 22 B6
● Alpha Business Pk,
N.Mymms AL9 . . . 67 CW23
Alpha Cl, NW1 . . . 16 D4
Alpha Ct, Whyt. CR3 . . . 258 DU118
Alpha Gro, E14 . . . 34 B5
Alpha Pl, NW6 . . . 5 K10
SW3 . . . 40 D2
Sch Alpha Prep Sch, Har. HA1
off Hindes Rd . . . 139 CE57
Alpha Rd, E4 . . . 123 EB48
N18 . . . 122 DU51
SE14 . . . 45 P6
Chobham GU24 . . . 232 AT110
Croydon CR0 . . . 224 DS102
Enfield EN3 . . . 105 DY42
Hutton CM13 . . . 131 GD44
Surbiton KT5 . . . 220 CM100
Teddington TW11 . . . 199 CD92
Uxbridge UB10 . . . 157 BP70
Woking GU22 . . . 249 BB116
Alpha St, SE15 . . . 44 C9
Alpha St N, Slou. SL1 . . . 174 AU75
Alpha St S, Slou. SL1 . . . 174 AT76
Alpha Way, Egh. TW20 . . . 215 BC95
Alphea Cl, SW19 . . . 202 DE94
Alpine Av, Surb. KT5 . . . 220 CQ103
Alpine Cl, Croy. CR0 . . . 224 DS104
Alpine Copse, Brom. BR1 . . . 227 EN96
Alpine Gro, E9 . . . 11 H7
Alpine Rd, E10 . . . 145 EB61
SE16 . . . 33 H9
Redhill RH1 . . . 272 DG131
Walton-on-Thames KT12 . . . 217 BU101
Alpine Vw, Cars. SM5 . . . 240 DE106
Alpine Wk, Stan. HA7 . . . 117 CE47
Alpine Way, E6 . . . 25 L6
Alresford Rd, Guil. GU2 . . . 280 AU135
Alric Av, NW10 . . . 160 CR66
New Malden KT3 . . . 220 CS97
Alroy Rd, N4 . . . 143 DN59
Alsace Rd, SE17 . . . 31 N10
Alscot Rd, SE1 . . . 32 B8
Alscot Way, SE1 . . . 32 A8
Alsford Wf, Berk. HP4 . . . 60 AX19
Alsike Rd, SE2 . . . 188 EX76
Erith DA18 . . . 188 EY76
Alsom Av, Wor.Pk. KT4 . . . 239 CU105
Alsop Cl, Lon.Col. AL2 . . . 84 CL27
Alston Cl, Long Dit. KT6 . . . 219 CH101
Alston Rd, N18 . . . 122 DV50
SW17 . . . 202 DD91
Barnet EN5 . . . 101 CY41
Hemel Hempstead HP1 . . . 62 BG21
● Alston Wks, Barn. EN5 . . . 101 CY41
Altair Cl, N17 . . . 122 DT51
Altair Way, Nthwd. HA6 . . . 115 BT49
Altash Way, SE9 . . . 207 EM89
Altenburg Av, W13 . . . 179 CH76
Altenburg Gdns, SW11 . . . 182 DF84
Alterton Cl, Wok. GU21 . . . 248 AU117
Alt Gro, SW19
off St. George's Rd . . . 201 CZ94
Altham Gdns, Wat. WD19 . . . 116 BX49
Altham Gro, Harl. CM20 . . . 57 ET12
Altham Rd, Pnr. HA5 . . . 116 BY52
Althea St, SW6 . . . 39 M9
Althorne Gdns, E18 . . . 146 EF56
Althorne Rd, Red. RH1 . . . 288 DG136
Althorne Way, Dag. RM10 . . . 148 FA61
Althorp Cl, Barn. EN5 . . . 119 CU45
Althorpe Gro, SW11 . . . 40 B6
Althorpe Ms, SW11 . . . 40 B7
Althorpe Rd, Har. HA1 . . . 138 CC57
Althorp Rd, SW17 . . . 202 DF88
St. Albans AL1 . . . 65 CE19
Altima Ct, SE22
off East Dulwich Rd . . . 184 DU84
Altmore Av, E6 . . . 167 EM66
Sch Altmore Inf Sch, E6
off Altmore Av . . . 167 EM67
Altona Rd, Loud. HP10 . . . 110 AC52
Alton Av, Stan. HA7 . . . 117 CF52
Altona Way, Slou. SL1 . . . 153 AP72
Alton Cl, Bex. DA5 . . . 208 EY88
Isleworth TW7 . . . 179 CF82
Alton Ct, Stai. TW18 . . . 215 BE95
Alton Gdns, Beck. BR3 . . . 205 EA94
Twickenham TW2 . . . 199 CD87
Alton Ho, E3
off Bromley High St . . . 22 D2
Alton Rd, N17 . . . 144 DR55
SW15 . . . 201 CU88
Croydon CR0 . . . 223 DN104
Richmond TW9 . . . 180 CL84
Sch Alton Sch, The, SW15
off Danebury Av . . . 200 CS86
Alton St, E14 . . . 22 C7
Altwood Cl, Slou. SL1 . . . 153 AL71
Altyre Cl, Beck. BR3 . . . 225 DZ99
Altyre Rd, Croy. CR0 . . . 224 DR103
Altyre Way, Beck. BR3 . . . 225 DZ99
Aluric Cl, Grays RM16 . . . 193 GH77
Alvanley Gdns, NW6 . . . 5 L2
Alva Way, Wat. WD19 . . . 116 BX47
Alverstoke Rd, Rom. RM3 . . . 128 FL52
Alverstone Av, SW19 . . . 202 DA89
East Barnet EN4 . . . 120 DE45
Alverstone Gdns, SE9 . . . 207 EQ88
Alverstone Rd, E12 . . . 147 EN63
NW2 . . . 4 A6
New Malden KT3 . . . 221 CT98
Wembley HA9 . . . 140 CM60
Alverston Gdns, SE25 . . . 224 DS99
Alverton, St.Alb. AL3
off Green La . . . 64 CC17
Alverton St, SE8 . . . 45 N1
Alveston Av, Har. HA3 . . . 139 CH55
Alveston Sq, E18 . . . 124 EG54
Alvey Est, SE17 . . . 31 N9
Alvey St, SE17 . . . 31 N10
Alvia Gdns, Sutt. SM1 . . . 240 DC105
Alvington Cres, E8 . . . 10 A2
Alvista Av, Tap. SL6 . . . 152 AH72
Alway Av, Epsom KT19 . . . 238 CQ106
Alwen Gro, S.Ock. RM15 . . . 171 FV71
Alwold Cres, SE12 . . . 206 EH86
Alwyn Av, W4 . . . 180 CR78
Alwyn Cl, Els. WD6 . . . 100 CM44
New Addington CR0 . . . 243 EB108
Alwyne Av, Shenf. CM15 . . . 131 GA44
Alwyne Ct, Wok. GU21 . . . 248 AY116
Alwyne La, N1 . . . 9 H6
Alwyne Pl, N1 . . . 9 J5
Alwyne Rd, N1 . . . 9 H6
SW19 . . . 201 CZ93
W7 . . . 159 CE73
Alwyne Sq, N1 . . . 9 J4
Alwyne Vil, N1 . . . 9 H6
Alwyn Gdns, NW4 . . . 141 CU56
W3 . . . 160 CP72
Alwyns Cl, Cher. KT16
off Alwyns La . . . 216 BG100
Alwyns La, Cher. KT16 . . . 215 BF100
Alyngton, Nthch HP4 . . . 60 AS16
Alyth Gdns, NW11 . . . 142 DA58
Alzette Ho, E2 . . . 21 J2
Amalgamated Dr, Brent. TW8 . . . 179 CG79
Amanda Cl, Chig. IG7 . . . 125 ER51
Amanda Ct, Slou. SL3 . . . 174 AX76
Amanda Ms, Rom. RM7 . . . 149 FC57
Amazon Apts, N8
off New River Av . . . 143 DM56
Amazon St, E1 . . . 20 E9
Ambassador Cl, Houns. TW3 . . . 178 BY82
Ambassador Gdns, E6 . . . 25 J7
Ambassador's Ct, SW1 . . . 29 M3
Ambassador Sq, E14 . . . 34 C9
Amber Av, E17 . . . 123 DY53
Amber Ct, SW17 . . . 202 DG91
Staines TW18
off Laleham Rd . . . 195 BF92
Ambercroft Way, Couls. CR5 . . . 257 DP119
Amberden Av, N3 . . . 142 DA55
Ambergate St, SE17 . . . 31 H10
Amber Gro, NW2 . . . 141 CX60
Amber La, Ilf. IG6 . . . 125 EP52
Amberley Cl, Orp. BR6 . . . 245 ET106
Pinner HA5 . . . 138 BZ55
Send GU23 . . . 265 BF125
Amberley Ct, Maid. SL6 . . . 152 AC69
Sidcup DA14 . . . 208 EW92
Amberley Dr, Wdhm KT15 . . . 233 BF110
Amberley Gdns, Enf. EN1 . . . 122 DS45
Epsom KT19 . . . 239 CT105
Amberley Gro, SE26 . . . 204 DV91
Croydon CR0 . . . 224 DT101
Amberley Pl, Wind. SL4
off Peascod St . . . 173 AR81
Amberley Rd, E10 . . . 145 EA59
N13 . . . 121 DM47
SE2 . . . 188 EX79
W9 . . . 15 K6
Buckhurst Hill IG9 . . . 124 EJ46
Enfield EN1 . . . 122 DT45
Slough SL2 . . . 153 AL71
Amberley Way, Houns. TW4 . . . 198 BW85
Morden SM4 . . . 221 CZ101
Romford RM7 . . . 149 FB56
Uxbridge UB10 . . . 156 BL69
Amber Ms, N22
off Brampton Pk Rd . . . 143 DN55
Amberry Ct, Harl. CM20 . . . 57 ER14
Amberside Cl, Islw. TW7 . . . 199 CD86
Amberside Ct, Hem.H. HP3
off Hardings Cl . . . 62 BH23
Amber St, E15 . . . 13 H5
Amber Wf, E2 . . . 10 A9
Amberwood Cl, Wall. SM6 . . . 241 DL106
Amberwood Ri, N.Mal. KT3 . . . 220 CS100
Ambient Ho, Enf. EN3
off Tysoe Av . . . 105 DZ36
Amblecote, Cob. KT11 . . . 236 BY111
Amblecote Cl, SE12 . . . 206 EH90
Amblecote Meadows, SE12 . . . 206 EH90
Amblecote Rd, SE12 . . . 206 EH90
Sch Ambler Prim Sch, N4
off Blackstock Rd . . . 143 DP61
Ambler Rd, N4 . . . 143 DP62
Ambleside, SW19
off Albert Dr . . . 201 CY88
Bromley BR1 . . . 205 ED93
Epping CM16 . . . 92 EU31
Purfleet RM19 . . . 190 FQ78
Ambleside Av, SW16 . . . 203 DK91
Beckenham BR3 . . . 225 DY99
Hornchurch RM12 . . . 149 FH64
Walton-on-Thames KT12 . . . 218 BW102
Ambleside Cl, E9 . . . 11 H2
E10 . . . 145 EB59
N17 off Drapers Rd . . . 144 DT55
Redhill RH1 . . . 289 DH139
Ambleside Cres, Enf. EN3 . . . 105 DX41
Ambleside Dr, Felt. TW14 . . . 197 BT88
Ambleside Gdns, SW16 . . . 203 DK92
Ilford IG4 . . . 146 EL56
South Croydon CR2 . . . 243 DX109
Sutton SM2 . . . 240 DC107
Wembley HA9 . . . 139 CK60
Ambleside Pt, SE15 . . . 44 G4
Ambleside Rd, NW10 . . . 161 CT66
Bexleyheath DA7 . . . 188 FA82
Ambleside Wk, Uxb. UB8
off High St . . . 156 BK67
Ambleside Way, Egh. TW20 . . . 195 BB94
Ambrey Way, Wall. SM6 . . . 241 DK109
Ambrooke Rd, Belv. DA17 . . . 188 FA76
Ambrosden Av, SW1 . . . 29 M7
Ambrose Av, NW11 . . . 141 CY59
Ambrose Cl, E6 . . . 25 J7
Crayford DA1 . . . 189 FF84
Orpington BR6
off Stapleton Rd . . . 227 ET104
Ambrose Ms, SW11 . . . 40 E9
Ambrose St, SE16 . . . 32 E8
Ambrose Wk, E3 . . . 22 A1
● AMC Business Cen, NW10 . . . 160 CP69
Amelia Cl, W3 . . . 160 CP74
Amelia St, SE17 . . . 31 H10
Amelle Gdns, Rom. RM3
off Greenway . . . 128 FP51
Amen Cor, EC4 . . . 19 H9
SW17 . . . 202 DF93
Amen Ct, EC4 . . . 19 H8
Amenity Way, Mord. SM4 . . . 221 CW101
Amerden Cl, Tap. SL6 . . . 152 AD72
Amerden La, Tap. SL6 . . . 152 AD74
Amerden Way, Slou. SL1 . . . 173 AN75
Sch American Comm Sch, Cobham
Int Sch, Cob. KT11
off Portsmouth Rd . . . 236 BW110
Egham Int Sch, Egh. TW20
off London Rd . . . 214 AW96
Hillingdon Int Sch, Hlgdn
UB10 off Vine La . . . 156 BM67
Sch American Sch in London,
The, NW8 . . . 6 A10
America Sq, EC3 . . . 20 A10
America St, SE1 . . . 31 J3
Amerland Rd, SW18 . . . 201 CZ86
AMERSHAM, HP6 & HP7 . . . 77 AP38
⇌ Amersham . . . 77 AQ38
⊖ Amersham . . . 77 AQ38
Coll Amersham & Wycombe Coll,
Amersham Campus, Amer.
HP7 off Stanley Hill . . . 94 AT39
Chesham Campus, Chesh.
HP5 off Lycrome Rd . . . 76 AR28
Amersham Av, N18 . . . 122 DR51
Amersham Bypass, Amer. HP7 . . . 77 AN41
Amersham Cl, Rom. RM3 . . . 128 FM51
Amersham Dr, Rom. RM3 . . . 128 FL51
Amersham Gro, SE14 . . . 45 N4
H Amersham Hosp,
Amer. HP7 . . . 77 AN41
★ Amersham Mus,
Amer. HP7 . . . 77 AP40
AMERSHAM OLD TOWN,
Amer. HP7 . . . 77 AP39
Amersham Pl, Amer. HP7 . . . 94 AW39
Amersham Rd, SE14 . . . 45 N5
Beaconsfield HP9 . . . 111 AM53
Chalfont St. Giles HP8 . . . 94 AU43
Chalfont St. Peter SL9 . . . 112 AX49
Chesham HP5 . . . 77 AP35
Chesham Bois HP6 . . . 77 AP36
Coleshill HP7 . . . 111 AP46
Croydon CR0 . . . 224 DQ100
Gerrards Cross SL9 . . . 135 BB59
Little Chalfont HP6 . . . 94 AX39
Rickmansworth WD3 . . . 95 BB39
Romford RM3 . . . 128 FM51
Sch Amersham Sch, The, Amer.
HP7 off Stanley Hill . . . 77 AS40
Amersham Vale, SE14 . . . 45 P4
Amersham Wk, Rom. RM3 . . . 128 FM51
Amersham Way, Amer. HP6 . . . 94 AX39
Amery Gdns, NW10 . . . 161 CV67
Romford RM2 . . . 150 FK55
Amery Rd, Har. HA1 . . . 139 CG61
Amesbury, Wal.Abb. EN9 . . . 90 EG32
Amesbury Av, SW2 . . . 203 DL89
Amesbury Cl, Epp. CM16
off Amesbury Rd . . . 91 ET31
Worcester Park KT4 . . . 221 CW102
Amesbury Dr, E4 . . . 105 EB44
Amesbury Rd, Brom. BR1 . . . 226 EK97
Dagenham RM9 . . . 168 EX66
Epping CM16 . . . 91 ET31
Feltham TW13 . . . 198 BX89
Amesbury Twr, SW8 . . . 41 L8
Ames Rd, Swans. DA10 . . . 212 FY86
Amethyst Cl, N11 . . . 121 DK52
Amethyst Ct, Enf. EN3
off Enstone Rd . . . 105 DY41
Amethyst Rd, E15 . . . 13 H1
Amethyst Wk, Welw.G.C. AL8 . . . 51 CV11
Amey Dr, Bkhm KT23 . . . 252 CC124
Amherst Av, W13 . . . 159 CJ72
Amherst Cl, Orp. BR5 . . . 228 EU98
Amherst Dr, Orp. BR5 . . . 227 ET98
Amherst Hill, Sev. TN13 . . . 278 FE122
Amherst Pl, Sev. TN13 . . . 278 FF122
Amherst Rd, W13 . . . 159 CJ72
Sevenoaks TN13 . . . 279 FH122
Sch Amherst Sch, Rvrhd
TN13 off Witches La . . . 278 FE123
Amhurst Gdns, Islw. TW7 . . . 179 CF81
Amhurst Par, N16
off Amhurst Pk . . . 144 DT59
Amhurst Pk, N16 . . . 144 DR59
Amhurst Pas, E8 . . . 10 C1
Amhurst Rd, E8 . . . 10 E3
N16 . . . 144 DT63
Amhurst Ter, E8 . . . 10 C1
Amhurst Wk, SE28
off Roman Sq . . . 168 EU74
Amicia Gdns, Stoke P. SL2 . . . 154 AT67
Amidas Gdns, Dag. RM8 . . . 148 EV63
Amiel St, E1 . . . 21 H4
Amies St, SW11 . . . 40 E10
Amina Way, SE16 . . . 32 C7
Amis Av, Epsom KT19 . . . 238 CP107
New Haw KT15 . . . 234 BG111
Amis Rd, Wok. GU21 . . . 248 AS119
Amity Gro, SW20 . . . 221 CW95
Amity Rd, E15 . . . 13 L8
Ammanford Grn, NW9
off Ruthin Cl . . . 140 CS58
Amner Rd, SW11 . . . 202 DG86
Amor Rd, W6 . . . 26 A7
Amott Rd, SE15 . . . 184 DU83
Amoy Pl, E14 . . . 22 A9
Ampere Way, Croy. CR0 . . . 223 DL101
Ampleforth Cl, Orp. BR6 . . . 246 EW105
Ampleforth Rd, SE2 . . . 188 EV75
Ampthill Sq Est, NW1 . . . 17 M1
Ampton Pl, WC1 . . . 18 C3
Ampton St, WC1 . . . 18 C3
Amroth Cl, SE23 . . . 204 DV88
Amroth Grn, NW9
off Fryent Gro . . . 140 CS58
Amstel Way, Wok. GU21 . . . 248 AT118
Amsterdam Rd, E14 . . . 34 F7
Amundsen Ct, E14
off Napier Av . . . 34 B10
Amwell Cl, Enf. EN2 . . . 104 DR43
Watford WD25
off Phillipers . . . 98 BY35
Amwell Common, Welw.G.C.
AL7 . . . 52 DB10
Amwell Ct, Hodd. EN11 . . . 71 EA16
Waltham Abbey EN9 . . . 90 EF33
Amwell Ct Est, N4 . . . 144 DQ60
Amwell End, Ware SG12 . . . 55 DX06
Amwell Hill, Gt Amwell SG12 . . . 55 DZ08
Amwell La, Ware SG12 . . . 55 EA09
Amwell Pl, Hert.Hth SG13 . . . 54 DW11
Jct Amwell Rbt, Ware SG12 . . . 55 DZ11
Amwell St, EC1 . . . 18 E2
Hoddesdon EN11 . . . 71 EA17
Sch Amwell Vw Sch, Stans.Abb.
SG12 off Station Rd . . . 55 EB11
Amyand Cotts, Twick. TW1
off Amyand Pk Rd . . . 199 CH86
Amyand La, Twick. TW1
off Marble Hill Gdns . . . 199 CH87
Amyand Pk Gdns, Twick. TW1
off Amyand Pk Rd . . . 199 CH87
Amyand Pk Rd, Twick. TW1 . . . 199 CG87
Amy Cl, Wall. SM6 . . . 241 DL108
Sch Amy Johnson Prim Sch, Wall.
SM6 off Mollison Dr . . . 241 DL108
Amy La, Chesh. HP5 . . . 76 AP32
Amy Rd, Oxt. RH8 . . . 276 EE129
Amyruth Rd, SE4 . . . 205 EA85
Amy Warne Cl, E6 . . . 25 H6
Anatola Rd, N19
off Dartmouth Pk Hill . . . 143 DH61
Ancaster Cres, N.Mal. KT3 . . . 221 CU100
Ancaster Ms, Beck. BR3 . . . 225 DX97
Ancaster Rd, Beck. BR3 . . . 225 DX97
Ancaster St, SE18 . . . 187 ES80
Anchorage Cl, SW19 . . . 202 DA92
Anchorage Pt, E14 . . . 33 P4
● Anchorage Pt Ind Est, SE7 . . . 36 C7
Anchor & Hope La, SE7 . . . 36 B7
● Anchor Bay Ind Est, Erith
DA8 . . . 189 FG79
Anchor Boul, Dart. DA2 . . . 190 FQ84
Anchor Cl, Bark. IG11 . . . 168 EV69
Cheshunt EN8 . . . 89 DX28
Anchor Ct, Grays RM17 . . . 192 GA80
Anchor Dr, Rain. RM13 . . . 169 FH69
Anchor Ho, SW18
off Smugglers Way . . . 182 DB84
Anchor La, Hem.H. HP1 . . . 62 BH21
Anchor Ms, N1 . . . 9 P5
SW11 off Westbridge Rd . . . 40 B7
SW12 . . . 203 DH86
🔒 Anchor Retail Pk, E1 . . . 21 H5
Anchor St, SE16 . . . 32 E8
Anchor Ter, E1 . . . 21 H5
Anchor Wf, E3 off Watts Gro . . . 22 C6
Anchor Yd, EC1 . . . 19 K4
Ancill Cl, W6 . . . 38 D3
Ancona Rd, NW10 . . . 161 CU68
SE18 . . . 187 ER78
Andace Pk Gdns, Brom. BR1 . . . 226 EJ95
Andalus Rd, SW9 . . . 183 DL83
Ander Cl, Wem. HA0 . . . 139 CK63
Andermans, Wind. SL4 . . . 173 AK81
Anderson Cl, N21 . . . 103 DM43
W3 . . . 160 CR72
Epsom KT19 . . . 238 CP112
Guildford GU2
off Tylehost . . . 264 AV130
Harefield UB9 . . . 114 BG53
Sutton SM3 . . . 222 DA102
Anderson Ct, Red. RH1 . . . 288 DG137
Anderson Dr, Ashf. TW15 . . . 197 BQ91
Anderson Ho, Bark. IG11
off The Coverdales . . . 167 ER68
Anderson Pl, Houns. TW3 . . . 178 CB84
Anderson Rd, E9 . . . 11 J4
Shenley WD7 . . . 84 CN33
Weybridge KT13 . . . 217 BR104
Woodford Green IG8 . . . 146 EK55
Andersons Sq, N1 . . . 8 G9
Anderson St, SW3 . . . 28 E10
Anderson Way, Belv. DA17 . . . 189 FB75
Anderton Cl, SE5 . . . 184 DR83
Andmark Ct, Sthl. UB1
off Herbert Rd . . . 158 BZ74
Andover Av, E16 . . . 24 E9
Andover Cl, Epsom KT19 . . . 238 CR111
Feltham TW14 . . . 197 BT88
Greenford UB6 . . . 158 CB70
Uxbridge UB8 . . . 156 BH68
Andover Est, N7 . . . 143 DM61
Andover Pl, NW6 . . . 5 L10
Andover Rd, N7 . . . 143 DM61
Orpington BR6 . . . 227 ER102
Twickenham TW2 . . . 199 CD88
Andrea Av, Grays RM16 . . . 192 GA75
Andre St, E8 . . . 10 D2
Andrew Borde St, WC2 . . . 17 P8
Andrew Cl, Dart. DA1 . . . 209 FD85
Ilford IG6 . . . 125 ER51
Shenley WD7 . . . 84 CM33
Andrewes Gdns, E6 . . . 24 G8
Andrewes Ho, EC2 . . . 19 K7
Sch Andrew Ewing Prim Sch,
Heston TW5
off Westbrook Rd . . . 178 BZ80
Andrew Hill La, Hedg. SL2 . . . 133 AQ61
Andrew Pl, SW8 . . . 41 P6
Andrew Reed Ho, SW18
off Linstead Way . . . 201 CY87
Andrews Cl, E6 . . . 24 G8
Buckhurst Hill IG9 . . . 124 EJ47
Epsom KT17 . . . 239 CT114
Harrow HA1
off Bessborough Rd . . . 139 CD59
Hemel Hempstead HP2
off Church St . . . 62 BK18
Orpington BR5 . . . 228 EX97
Worcester Park KT4 . . . 221 CX103
Andrews Crosse, WC2 . . . 18 E9
Andrewsfield, Welw.G.C. AL7 . . . 52 DC09
Andrews La, Chsht EN7 . . . 88 DU28
Sch Andrews La Prim Sch, Chsht
EN7 off Andrews La . . . 88 DV28
Andrews Pl, SE9 . . . 207 EP86
Dartford DA2 . . . 209 FE89
Andrew's Rd, E8 . . . 10 E9
Andrew St, E14 . . . 22 E8
Andrews Wk, SE17 . . . 43 H3
Andwell Cl, SE2 . . . 188 EV75
Anelle Ri, Hem.H. HP3 . . . 62 BM24
Anemone Ct, Enf. EN3
off Enstone Rd . . . 105 DY41
ANERLEY, SE20 . . . 224 DV95
⇌ Anerley . . . 204 DV94
Anerley Gro, SE19 . . . 204 DT94
Anerley Hill, SE19 . . . 204 DT93
Anerley Pk, SE20 . . . 204 DU94
Anerley Pk Rd, SE20 . . . 204 DV94
Anerley Rd, SE19 . . . 204 DU94
SE20 . . . 204 DU94
Anerley Sta Rd, SE20 . . . 224 DV95
Anerley St, SW11 . . . 40 F8
Anerley Vale, SE19 . . . 204 DT94
Anfield Cl, SW12
off Belthorn Cres . . . 203 DJ87
Angas Ct, Wey. KT13 . . . 235 BQ106
⊖ Angel . . . 8 F10
Angel All, E1 . . . 20 B8
Angel Cl, N18 . . . 122 DT49
Hampton Hill TW12
off Windmill Rd . . . 198 CC93
Angel Cor Par, N18
off Fore St . . . 122 DU49
Angel Ct, EC2 . . . 19 M8
SW1 . . . 29 M3
SW17 . . . 202 DF91
Jct Angel Edmonton, N18
off Angel Rd . . . 122 DU50
Angelfield, Houns. TW3 . . . 178 CB84
Angel Gate, EC1 . . . 19 H2
Guildford GU1 off High St . . . 280 AX136
Angel Hill, Sutt. SM1 . . . 222 DB104
Angel Hill Dr, Sutt. SM1 . . . 222 DB104
Angelica Cl, West Dr. UB7
off Lovibonds Av . . . 156 BM72
Angelica Dr, E6 . . . 25 M7
Angelica Gdns, Croy. CR0 . . . 225 DX102
Angelica Rd, Guil. GU2 . . . 264 AU130
Angelis Apts, N1
off Graham St . . . 19 H1
Angel La, E15 . . . 13 H4
Hayes UB3 . . . 157 BR71
Angell Pk Gdns, SW9 . . . 42 F10
Angell Rd, SW9 . . . 42 F10
Angell Town Est, SW9 . . . 42 E8
Angel Ms, E1 . . . 20 F10
N1 . . . 18 F1
SW15 . . . 201 CU87
Angel Pas, EC4 . . . 31 L1
Angel Pl, N18 . . . 122 DU50
SE1 . . . 31 L4
Reigate RH2
off Cockshot Hill . . . 288 DB137
⇌ Angel Road . . . 122 DW50
Angel Rd, N18 . . . 122 DV50
Harrow HA1 . . . 139 CE58
Thames Ditton KT7 . . . 219 CG101
● Angel Rd Wks, N18 . . . 122 DW50
Angel Southside, EC1 . . . 18 F1
Angel Sq, EC1 . . . 18 F1
Angel St, EC1 . . . 19 J8
Angel Wk, W6 . . . 26 A9
Angel Way, Rom. RM1 . . . 149 FE57
Angel Wf, N1 off Eagle Wf Rd . . . 164 DQ68
Angerstein La, SE3 . . . 47 M6
Angle Cl, Uxb. UB10 . . . 156 BN67
Anglefield Rd, Berk. HP4 . . . 60 AU19
Angle Grn, Dag. RM8 . . . 148 EW60
Angle Pl, Berk. HP4 . . . 60 AU19
Angle Rd, Grays RM20 . . . 191 FX79
Anglers Cl, Rich. TW10
off Locksmeade Rd . . . 199 CJ91
Angler's La, NW5 . . . 7 K5
Anglers Reach, Surb. KT6 . . . 219 CK99
Anglesea Av, SE18 . . . 37 N9
Anglesea Ms, SE18 . . . 37 N9
Anglesea Pl, Grav. DA11
off Clive Rd . . . 213 GH86
Anglesea Rd, SE18 . . . 37 N9
Kingston upon Thames KT1 . . . 219 CK98
Orpington BR5 . . . 228 EW100
Anglesea Ter, W6
off Wellesley Av . . . 181 CV76
Anglesey Cl, Ashf. TW15 . . . 196 BN90
Anglesey Ct Rd, Cars. SM5 . . . 240 DG107
Anglesey Dr, Rain. RM13 . . . 169 FG70
Anglesey Gdns, Cars. SM5 . . . 240 DG107
Anglesey Rd, Enf. EN3 . . . 104 DV42
Watford WD19 . . . 116 BW50
Anglesmede Cres, Pnr. HA5 . . . 138 CA55
Anglesmede Way, Pnr. HA5 . . . 138 BZ55
Angles Rd, SW16 . . . 203 DL91
Anglia Cl, N17 off Park La . . . 122 DV52
Anglia Ct, Dag. RM8
off Spring Cl . . . 148 EX60
Anglia Ho, E14 . . . 21 M9
Anglian Cl, Wat. WD24 . . . 98 BW40
Anglian Rd, E11 . . . 145 ED62
Anglia Wk, E6 . . . 167 EM67
● Anglo Business Pk,
Chesh. HP5 . . . 76 AN29
Anglo Rd, E3 . . . 11 P10
Angrave Ct, E8 . . . 10 B8
Angrave Pas, E8 . . . 10 B8
Angus Cl, Chess. KT9 . . . 238 CN106
Angus Dr, Ruis. HA4 . . . 138 BW63
Angus Gdns, NW9 . . . 118 CR53

Angus Home, Cudham TN14 261 ER115
Angus Rd, E13 24 D3
Angus St, SE14 45 M4
Anhalt Rd, SW11 40 D4
Anisdowne Cl, Abin.Ham. RH5 283 BT142
Ankerdine Cres, SE18 187 EP81
Ankerwycke Priory, Wrays. TW19 194 AY89
Anlaby Rd, Tedd. TW11 199 CE92
Anley Rd, W14 26 C5
Anmersh Gro, Stan. HA7 117 CK53
Annabel Cl, E14 22 C9
Annabelle Ct, Rain. RM13 169 FE69
Anna Cl, E8 10 B8
Annalee Gdns, S.Ock. RM15 171 FV71
Annalee Rd, S.Ock. RM15 171 FV71
Annandale Gro, Uxb. UB10 137 BQ62
Annandale Rd, SE10 47 L1
W4 180 CS77
Croydon CR0 224 DU103
Guildford GU2 280 AV136
Sidcup DA15 207 ES87
Anna Neagle Cl, E7
off Dames Rd 146 EG63
Annan Way, Rom. RM1 127 FD53
Anne Boleyn Ct, SE9
off Avery Hill Rd 207 ER86
Anne Boleyn's Wk, Kings.T. KT2 200 CL92
Sutton SM3 239 CX108
Anne Case Ms, N.Mal. KT3
off Sycamore Gro 220 CR97
Anne Compton Ms, SE12 206 EF87
Anne Goodman Ho, E1
off Jubilee St 20 G8
Anne Heart Cl, Chaff.Hun. RM16 191 FX77
Anne of Cleeves Ct, SE9
off Avery Hill Rd 207 ER86
Anne of Cleves Rd, Dart. DA1 210 FK85
Anners Cl, Egh. TW20 215 BC97
Annesley Av, NW9 140 CR55
Annesley Cl, NW10 140 CS62
Annesley Dr, Croy. CR0 225 DZ104
Annesley Rd, SE3 186 EH81
Annesley Wk, N19
off Highgate Hill 143 DJ61
Annesmere Gdns, SE3
off Highbrook Rd 186 EK83
Anne St, E13 23 N4
Anne's Wk, Cat. CR3 258 DS120
Annett Cl, Shep. TW17 217 BS98
Annette Cl, Har. HA3
off Spencer Rd 117 CE54
Annette Cres, N1 9 K7
Annette Rd, N7 143 DM63
Annett Rd, Walt. KT12 217 BU101
Anne Way, Ilf. IG6 125 EQ51
West Molesey KT8 218 CB98
Annie Besant Cl, E3 11 P9
Annie Brooks Cl, Stai. TW18 195 BD90
Annie Taylor Ho, E12
off Walton Rd 147 EN63
Annifer Way, S.Ock. RM15 171 FV71
Anningsley Pk, Ott. KT16 233 BD110
Anning St, EC2 19 P4
Annington Rd, N2 142 DF55
Annis Rd, E9 11 L5
Ann La, SW10 40 A4
Ann Moss Way, SE16 32 G6
Ann's Cl, SW1 28 F5
Ann's Pl, E1 20 A7
Ann St, SE18 187 ER77
Annsworthy Av, Th.Hth. CR7
off Grange Pk Rd 224 DR97
Annsworthy Cres, SE25
off Grange Rd 224 DR96
Annunciation RC Inf Sch, The, Edg. HA8 off Thirleby Rd 118 CR53
Annunciation RC Jun Sch, The, Edg. HA8 off The Meads 118 CR51
Anscuff Rd, Slou. SL2 153 AN69
Ansdell Rd, SE15 44 G8
Ansdell St, W8 27 M6
Ansdell Ter, W8 27 M6
Ansell Gro, Cars. SM5 222 DG102
Ansell Rd, SW17 202 DE90
Dorking RH4 285 CH135
Anselm Cl, Croy. CR0 224 DT104
Anselm Rd, SW6 39 J3
Pinner HA5 116 BZ52
Ansford Rd, Brom. BR1 205 EC92
Ansleigh Pl, W11 26 D1
Ansley Cl, S.Croy. CR2 242 DV114
Anslow Gdns, Iver SL0 155 BD68
Anslow Pl, Slou. SL1 152 AJ71
Anson Cl, Bov. HP3 79 AZ27
Romford RM7 127 FB54
St. Albans AL1 65 CH22
Anson Ho, E1 21 L5
Anson Pl, SE28 187 ER75
Anson Prim Sch, NW2 4 C2
Anson Rd, N7 7 M1
NW2 4 C2
Anson Ter, Nthlt. UB5 158 CB65
Anson Wk, Nthwd. HA6 115 BQ49
Anstead Dr, Rain. RM13 169 FG68
Anstey Rd, SE15 44 C10
Anstey Wk, N15 143 DP56
Anstice Cl, W4 180 CS80
Anston Ct, Guil. GU2
off Southway 264 AS134
Anstridge Path, SE9 207 ER86
Anstridge Rd, SE9 207 ER86
Antelope Av, Grays RM16
off Hogg La 192 GA76
Antelope Rd, SE18 37 J6
Antelope Wk, Surb. KT6
off Maple Rd 219 CK99
Anthony Cl, NW7 118 CS49
Dunton Green TN13 278 FE121
Watford WD19 116 BW46
Anthony La, Swan. BR8 229 FG95
Anthony Rd, SE25 224 DU100
Borehamwood WD6 100 CM40
Greenford UB6 159 CE68
Welling DA16 188 EU81
Anthony Roper Prim Sch, The, Eyns. DA4 off High St 230 FL103
Anthonys, Wok. GU21 233 BB112
Anthony St, E1 20 F8
Anthony Way, N18 123 DX51
Slough SL1 153 AK73
Anthony W Ho, Brock. RH3
off Wheelers La 286 CP136
Anthorne Cl, Pot.B. EN6 86 DB31
Anthus Ms, Nthwd. HA6 115 BS52
Antigua Cl, SE19
off Salters Hill 204 DR92
Antigua Wk, SE19 204 DR92
Antill Rd, E3 21 L2
N15 144 DU56
Antill Ter, E1 21 J8
Antlands La, Shipley Br RH6 291 DK153
Antlands La E, Horl. RH6 291 DL153
Antlands La W, Horl. RH6 291 DL153
Antlers Hill, E4 105 EB43
Antoinette Ct, Abb.L. WD5
off Dairy Way 81 BT29
Anton Cres, Sutt. SM1 222 DA104
Antoneys Cl, Pnr. HA5 116 BX54
Antonine Gate, St.Alb. AL3 64 CA21
Antonine Hts, SE1 31 N5
Anton Pl, Wem. HA9 140 CP62
Anton Rd, S.Ock. RM15 171 FV70
Anton St, E8 10 D2
Antony Ho, E5 off Pembury Pl 10 E3
Antrim Gro, NW3 6 E4
Antrim Mans, NW3 6 D4
Antrim Rd, NW3 6 E4
Antrobus Cl, Sutt. SM1 239 CZ106
Antrobus Rd, W4 180 CQ77
Anvil Cl, SW16 203 DJ94
Bovingdon HP3
off Yew Tree Dr 79 BB28
Anvil Ct, Langley SL3
off Blacksmith Row 175 BA77
Anvil La, Cob. KT11 235 BU114
Anvil Pl, St.Alb. AL2 82 CA26
Anvil Rd, Sun. TW16 217 BU97
Anvil Ter, Dart. DA2
off Pinewood Pl 209 FE89
Anworth Cl, Wdf.Grn. IG8 124 EH51
Anyards Rd, Cob. KT11 235 BV113
Anzio Gdns, Cat. CR3 258 DQ121
Apeldoorn Dr, Wall. SM6 241 DL109
Aperdele Rd, Lthd. KT22 253 CG118
APERFIELD, West. TN16 261 EM117
Aperfield Rd, Bigg.H. TN16 260 EL117
Erith DA8 189 FF79
Apers Av, Wok. GU22 249 AZ121
Apex Cl, Beck. BR3 225 EB95
Apex Cor, NW7 118 CR49
● Apex Ind Est, NW10
off Hythe Rd 161 CT70
Apex Retail Pk, Felt. TW13 198 BZ90
● Apex Twr, N.Mal. KT3 220 CS97
Apley Rd, Reig. RH2 288 DA137
Aplin Way, Islw. TW7 179 CE81
Apollo, E14 34 A8
Apollo Av, Brom. BR1
off Rodway Rd 226 EH95
Northwood HA6 115 BU50
Apollo Cl, Horn. RM12 149 FH61
★ Apollo Hammersmith, W6 26 B10
Apollo Pl, E11 146 EE62
SW10 40 A4
St. John's GU21
off Church Rd 248 AU119
★ Apollo Thea, W1 17 N10
★ Apollo Victoria Thea, SW1 29 L7
Apollo Way, SE28
off Broadwater Rd 187 ER76
Hemel Hempstead HP2 62 BM18
Apostle Way, Th.Hth. CR7 223 DP96
Apothecary St, EC4 18 G9
Appach Rd, SW2 203 DN85
Apperlie Dr, Horl. RH6 291 DJ150
Apple Blossom Ct, SW8
off Pascal St 41 P4
Appleby Cl, E4 123 EC51
N15 144 DR57
Petts Wood BR5 227 ES101
Twickenham TW2 199 CD89
Uxbridge UB8 157 BQ72
Appleby Ct, W3
off Newport Rd 180 CQ75
Appleby Dr, Rom. RM3 128 FJ50
Appleby Gdns, Felt. TW14 197 BT88
Appleby Grn, Rom. RM3
off Appleby Dr 128 FJ50
Appleby Rd, E8 10 D6
E16 23 M9
Appleby St, E2 10 A10
Cheshunt EN7 88 DT26
Apple Cotts, Bov. HP3 79 BA27
Applecroft, Nthch HP4 60 AS17
Park Street AL2 82 CB28
Applecroft Rd, Welw.G.C. AL8 51 CV09
Applecroft Sch, Welw.G.C. AL8 off Applecroft Rd 51 CV10
Appledore Av, Bexh. DA7 189 FC81
Ruislip HA4 137 BV62
Appledore Cl, SW17 202 DF89
Bromley BR2 226 EF99
Edgware HA8 118 CN53
Romford RM3 128 FJ53
Appledore Cres, Sid. DA14 207 ES90
Appledore Way, NW7
off Tavistock Av 119 CX52
Appledown Ri, Couls. CR5 257 DJ115
Applefield, Amer. HP7 94 AW39
Appleford Cl, Hodd. EN11 71 DZ15
Appleford Rd, W10 14 F5
Apple Garth, Brent. TW8 179 CK77
Applegarth, Clay. KT10 237 CF106
New Addington CR0 243 EB108
Applegarth Dr, Dart. DA1 210 FL89
Ilford IG2 147 ET56
Applegarth Ho, Erith DA8 189 FF82
Applegarth Nurs & Inf & Jun Schs, New Adgtn CR0
off Bygrove 243 EB107
Applegarth Rd, SE28 168 EV74
W14 26 C7
Applegate, Brwd. CM14 130 FT43
Apple Gro, Chess. KT9 238 CL105
Enfield EN1 104 DS41
Apple Mkt, Kings.T. KT1
off Eden St 219 CK96
Apple Orchard, Swan. BR8 229 FD98
Apple Orchard, The, Hem.H. HP2 off Highfield La 62 BM18
Apple Rd, E11 146 EE62
Appleshaw Cl, Grav. DA11 213 GG92
Appleton Cl, Amer. HP7 94 AV40
Bexleyheath DA7 189 FB82
Harlow CM19 73 EQ16
Appleton Dr, Dart. DA2 209 FH90
Appleton Gdns, N.Mal. KT3 221 CU100
Appleton Rd, SE9 186 EL83
Loughton IG10 107 EP41
Appleton Sq, Mitch. CR4
off Silbury Av 222 DE95
Appleton Way, Horn. RM12 150 FK60
Apple Tree Av, Uxb. UB8 156 BM71
West Drayton UB7 156 BM71
Appletree Cl, SE20
off Jasmine Gro 224 DV95
Leatherhead KT22 252 CC124
Appletree Ct, Guil. GU4 265 BD131
Appletree Gdns, Barn. EN4 102 DE42
Appletree La, Slou. SL3 174 AW76
Apple Tree Rbt, West Dr. UB7 156 BM73
Appletree Wk, Chesh. HP5
off Cresswell Rd 76 AR34
Watford WD25 81 BV34
Apple Tree Yd, SW1 29 M2
Applewood Cl, N20 120 DE46
NW2 141 CV62
Ickenham UB10 136 BL63
Applewood Dr, E13 24 A4
Appold St, EC2 19 N6
Erith DA8 189 FF79
Apprentice Gdns, Nthlt. UB5 158 BZ69
Apprentice Way, E5
off Clarence Rd 144 DV63
Approach, The, NW4 141 CX57
W3 160 CR72
Enfield EN1 104 DV40
Orpington BR6 227 ET103
Potters Bar EN6 85 CZ32
Upminster RM14 150 FP62
Approach Cl, N16 9 N2
Approach Rd, E2 20 G1
SW20 221 CW96
Ashford TW15 197 BQ93
Barnet EN4 102 DD42
Edgware HA8 118 CP51
Purley CR8 241 DP112
St. Albans AL1 65 CE21
Taplow SL6 152 AE72
West Molesey KT8 218 CA99
Appspond La, Pott.Cr. AL2 63 BV23
Aprey Gdns, NW4 141 CW56
April Cl, W7 159 CE73
Ashtead KT21 254 CM117
Feltham TW13 197 BU90
Orpington BR6 245 ET106
April Glen, SE23 205 DX90
April St, E8 10 B1
Aprilwood Cl, Wdhm KT15 233 BF111
Apsledene, Grav. DA12
off Miskin Way 213 GK93
APSLEY, Hem.H. HP3 80 BK25
⇌ Apsley 80 BL25
Apsley Cl, Har. HA2 138 CC57
Apsley Grn, Hem.H. HP3
off London Rd 80 BL25
★ Apsley Ho (Wellington Mus), W1 28 G4
Apsley Mills Retail Pk, Hem.H. HP3 62 BL24
Apsley Rd, SE25 224 DV98
New Malden KT3 220 CQ97
Apsley Way, NW2 141 CU61
W1 29 H4
● Aquarius Business Pk, NW2 141 CT60
Aquarius Way, Nthwd. HA6 115 BU50
★ Aquatic Experience, Brent. TW8 179 CH81
Aquila Cl, Lthd. KT22 254 CL121
Aquila St, NW8 6 B10
Aquinas St, SE1 30 F2
Aquis Ct, St.Alb. AL3 64 CC20
Arabella Dr, SW15 180 CS84
Arabia Cl, E4 123 ED45
Arabin Rd, SE4 185 DY84
Aragon Av, Epsom KT17 239 CV109
Thames Ditton KT7 219 CF99
Aragon Cl, Brom. BR2 227 EM102
Enfield EN2 103 DM38
Hemel Hempstead HP2 63 BQ15
Loughton IG10 106 EL44
New Addington CR0 244 EE110
Romford RM5 127 FB51
Sunbury-on-Thames TW16 197 BT94
Aragon Dr, Ilf. IG6 125 EQ52
Ruislip HA4 138 BX60
Aragon Pl, Mord. SM4 221 CX101
Aragon Prim Sch, Mord. SM4 off Aragon Rd 221 CY101
Aragon Rd, Kings.T. KT2 200 CL92
Morden SM4 221 CX100
Aragon Twr, SE8 33 N9
Aragon Wk, Byfleet KT14 234 BM113
Aragorn Ct, Guil. GU2 264 AV132
Aran Ct, Wey. KT13
off Mallards Reach 217 BR103
Arandora Cres, Rom. RM6 148 EV59
Aran Dr, Stan. HA7 117 CJ49
Aran Hts, Ch.St.G. HP8 112 AV49
Aran Ms, N7
off Barnsbury Gro 8 E6
Arbery Rd, E3 21 L2
Arbor Cl, Beck. BR3 225 EB96
Arbor Ct, N16 144 DR61
Arboretum Pl, Bark. IG11
off Ripple Rd 167 EQ66
Arborfield Cl, SW2 203 DM88
Slough SL1 174 AS76
Arbor Rd, E4 123 ED48
Arbour, The, Hert. SG13 54 DR11
Arbour Cl, Fetch. KT22 253 CF123
Warley CM14 130 FW50
Arbour Rd, Enf. EN3 105 DX42
Arbour Sq, E1 21 J9
Arbour Vale Sch, Slou. SL2 off Farnham Rd 153 AP69
Arbour Vw, Amer. HP7 94 AV39
Arbour Way, Horn. RM12 149 FH64
Arbroath Grn, Wat. WD19 115 BU48
Arbroath Rd, SE9 186 EL83
Arbrook Chase, Esher KT10 236 CC107
Arbrook Cl, Orp. BR5 228 EU97
Arbrook La, Esher KT10 236 CC107
Arbury Ter, SE26 204 DU90
Arbuthnot La, Bex. DA5 208 EY86
Arbuthnot Rd, SE14 45 J8
Arbutus Cl, Red. RH1 288 DC136
Arbutus Rd, Red. RH1 288 DC136
Arbutus St, E8 10 A8
Arcade, The, EC2 19 N7
Croydon CR0 off High St 224 DQ104
Hatfield AL10
off Wellfield Rd 67 CV17
Arcade, The, Rom. RM3 128 FK50
Arcade Pl, Rom. RM1 149 FE57
Arcadia Av, N3 120 DA53
Arcadia Caravans, Stai. TW18 216 BH95
Arcadia Cen, The, W5 159 CK73
Arcadia Cl, Cars. SM5 240 DG105
Arcadian Av, Bex. DA5 208 EY86
Arcadian Cl, Bex. DA5 208 EY86
Arcadian Gdns, N22 121 DM52
Arcadian Pl, SW18 201 CY87
Arcadian Rd, Bex. DA5 208 EY86
Arcadia St, E14 22 B8
Arcany Rd, S.Ock. RM15 171 FV70
Archangel St, SE16 33 K5
Archates Av, Grays RM16 192 GA76
Archbishop Lanfranc Sch, The, Croy. CR0 off Mitcham Rd 223 DL100
Archbishops Pl, SW2 203 DM86
Archbishop Sumner C of E Prim Sch, SE11 30 F9
Archbishop Tenison's C of E High Sch, Croy. CR0
off Selborne Rd 224 DT104
Archbishop Tenison's Sch, SE11 42 D3
Archdale Pl, N.Mal. KT3 220 CP97
Archdale Rd, SE22 204 DT85
Archdeacon Cambridge's C of E Prim Sch, Twick. TW2
off The Green 199 CE89
Archel Rd, W14 38 G2
Archer Cl, Kings L. WD4 80 BM29
Kingston upon Thames KT2 200 CL94
Archer Ho, N1
off Phillipp St 9 P9
SW11 40 A8
Archer Ms, Hmptn H. TW12
off Windmill Rd 198 CC93
Archer Rd, SE25 224 DV98
Orpington BR5 228 EU99
Archers, Harl. CM19 73 EP20
Archers Cl, Hert. SG14 54 DQ08
Archers Ct, S.Ock. RM15 171 FV71
Archers Dr, Enf. EN3 104 DW40
Archers Fld, St.Alb. AL1 65 CF18
ARCHERS GREEN, Welw. AL6 52 DE08
Archer Sq, SE14 45 L3
Archers Ride, Welw.G.C. AL7 52 DB11
Archer St, W1 17 N10
Archer Ter, West Dr. UB7
off Yew Av 156 BL73
Archer Way, Swan. BR8 229 FF96
Archery Cl, W2 16 D9
Harrow HA3 139 CF55
Archery Pl, Goms. GU5 283 BQ139
Archery Rd, SE9 207 EM85
Archery Steps, W2
off St. Georges Flds 16 D10
Arches, SW9 off Ridgeway Rd 183 DP83
Arches, The, SW6 38 G8
SW8
off New Covent Gdn Mkt 41 P4
WC2 30 B2
Harrow HA2 138 CB61
Windsor SL4 173 AQ81
Archfield, Welw.G.C. AL7 51 CY06
● Archgate Business Cen, N12 off High Rd 120 DC50
Archibald Cl, Enf. EN3 105 DX36
Archibald Ms, W1 29 H1
Archibald Rd, N7 7 N1
Romford RM3 128 FN53
Archibald St, E3 22 A3
Archie Cl, West Dr. UB7 176 BN75
Archie St, SE1 31 P5
Architectural Assoc Sch of Architecture, WC1 17 P7
Arch Rd, Hersham KT12 218 BX104
Arch St, SE1 31 J7
⊖ Archway 143 DJ61
Archway, Rom. RM3 127 FH51
● Archway Business Cen, N19 off Wedmore St 143 DK62
Archway Campus, The, N19 off Highgate Hill 143 DJ61
Archway Cl, N19
off Archway Rd 143 DJ61
SW19 202 DB91
W10 14 C7
Wallington SM6 223 DK104
Archway Mall, N19 143 DJ61
Archway Ms, SW15
off Putney Br Rd 181 CY84
Dorking RH4 off Chapel Ct 285 CG135
Archway Pl, Dor. RH4
off Chapel Ct 285 CG135
Archway Rd, N6 142 DG58
N19 143 DJ60
Archway St, SW13 180 CS83
Arcola St, E8 10 A2
Arcon Dr, Nthlt. UB5 158 BY70
Arctic St, NW5 7 J3
Arcus Rd, Brom. BR1 206 EE93
Ardbeg Rd, SE24 204 DR86
Arden Cl, SE28 168 EX72
Bovingdon HP3 79 BA28
Bushey Heath WD23 117 CF45
Harrow HA1 139 CD62
Reigate RH2 288 DB138
Arden Ct Gdns, N2 142 DD58
Arden Cres, E14 34 B8
Dagenham RM9 168 EW66
Arden Est, N1 19 N1
Arden Gro, Orp. BR6 245 EP105
Arden Ho, SW9 42 B9
Arden Ms, E17 145 EB57
Arden Mhor, Pnr. HA5 137 BV56
Arden Rd, N3 141 CY55
W13 159 CJ73
Ardens Way, St.Alb. AL4 65 CK18
Ardent Cl, SE25 224 DS97
Ardesley Wd, Wey. KT13 235 BS105
Ardfern Av, SW16 223 DN97
Ardfillan Rd, SE6 205 ED88
Ardgowan Rd, SE6 206 EE87
Ardilaun Rd, N5 144 DQ63
Ardingly Cl, Croy. CR0 225 DX104
Ardleigh Cl, Horn. RM11 150 FK55
Ardleigh Ct, Shenf. CM15 131 FZ45
Ardleigh Gdns, Hutt. CM13
off Fairview Av 131 GE44
Sutton SM3 222 DA101
ARDLEIGH GREEN, Horn. RM11 150 FJ56
Ardleigh Grn Inf Sch, Horn. RM11 off Ardleigh Grn Rd 150 FK55
Ardleigh Grn Jun Sch, Horn. RM11 off Ardleigh Grn Rd 150 FK55
Ardleigh Grn Rd, Horn. RM11 150 FK57
Ardleigh Ms, Ilf. IG1
off Bengal Rd 147 EP62
Ardleigh Rd, E17 123 DZ53
N1 9 M5
Ardleigh Ter, E17 123 DZ53
Ardley Cl, NW10 140 CS62
SE6 205 DY90
Ruislip HA4 137 BQ59
Ardley Cres, Hat.Hth CM22 59 FH05
ARDLEY END, B.Stort. CM22 59 FH06
Ardlui Rd, SE27 204 DQ89
Ardmay Gdns, Surb. KT6 220 CL99
Ardmere Rd, SE13 205 ED86
Ardmore Av, Guil. GU2 264 AV132
Ardmore La, Buck.H. IG9 124 EH45
Ardmore Pl, Buck.H. IG9 124 EH45
Ardmore Rd, S.Ock. RM15 171 FV70
Ardmore Way, Guil. GU2 264 AV132
Ardoch Rd, SE6 205 ED89
Ardra Rd, N9 123 DX48
Ardrossan Cl, Slou. SL2 153 AQ70
Ardrossan Gdns, Wor.Pk. KT4 221 CU104
Ardross Av, Nthwd. HA6 115 BS50
Ardshiel Cl, SW15
off Bemish Rd 181 CX83
Ardshiel Dr, Red. RH1 288 DE136
Ardwell Av, Ilf. IG6 147 EQ57
Ardwell Rd, SW2 203 DL89
Ardwick Rd, NW2 142 DA63
Arena 224 DW99
● Arena, The, Enf. EN3 105 DZ38
Arena Shop Pk, N4 143 DP58
Arena Sq, Wem. HA9 140 CN63
Arewater Grn, Loug. IG10 107 EM39
Argali Ho, Erith DA18
off Kale Rd 188 EY76
Argall Av, E10 145 DX59
Argall Way, E10 145 DX60
Argenta Way, NW10 160 CP66
Argent Cl, Egh. TW20 195 BC93
Argent Ct, Barn. EN5 102 DC42
Grays RM17 192 GA80
Argento Twr, SW18 202 DB86
Argent St, Grays RM17 192 FY79
Argent Way, Chsht EN7 88 DR26
Argles Cl, Green. DA9
off Cowley Av 211 FU85
Argon Ms, SW6 39 K5
Argon Rd, N18 122 DW50
Argosy Gdns, Stai. TW18 195 BF93
Argosy La, Stanw. TW19 196 BK87
Argus Cl, Rom. RM7 127 FB53
Argus Way, Nthlt. UB5 158 BY69
Argyle Av, Houns. TW3 198 CA86
Argyle Cl, W13 159 CG70
Argyle Gdns, Upmin. RM14 151 FR61
Argyle Pas, N17 122 DT53
Argyle Pl, W6 181 CV77
Argyle Prim Sch, WC1 18 A2
Argyle Rd, E1 21 J4
E15 13 J1
E16 24 B9
N12 120 DA50
N17 122 DU53
N18 122 DU49
W13 159 CG71
Barnet EN5 101 CW42
Greenford UB6 159 CF69
Harrow HA2 138 CB58
Hounslow TW3 198 CB85
Ilford IG1 147 EN61
Sevenoaks TN13 279 FH125
Teddington TW11 199 CE92
Argyle Sq, WC1 18 B2
Argyle St, WC1 18 A2
Argyle Wk, WC1 18 B3
Argyle Way, SE16 44 D1
Argyll Av, Slou. SL1 153 AN73
Southall UB1 158 CB74
Argyll Cl, SW9 42 C10
Argyll Gdns, Edg. HA8 118 CP54
Argyll Rd, SE18 187 EQ76
W8 27 J5
Grays RM17 192 GA78
Hemel Hempstead HP2 62 BL15
Argyll St, W1 17 L9
Aria Ho, WC2 18 B8
Arica Ho, SE16 32 F6
Arica Rd, SE4 185 DY84
Ariel Cl, Grav. DA12 213 GM91
Ariel Rd, NW6 5 J5
Ariel Way, W12 26 B2
Hounslow TW4 177 BV83
Arisdale Av, S.Ock. RM15 171 FV71
Aristotle Rd, SW4 183 DK83
Arizona Bldg, SE13
off Deals Gateway 46 C7
Ark Acad, Wem. HA9
off Forty Av 140 CN61
Ark Av, Grays RM16 192 GA76
Arkell Gro, SE19 203 DP94
Arkindale Rd, SE6 205 EC90
Arklay Cl, Uxb. UB8 156 BM70
ARKLEY, Barn. EN5 101 CU43
Arkley Ct, Hem.H. HP2
off Arkley Rd 63 BP15
Arkley Cres, E17 145 DZ57
Arkley Dr, Barn. EN5 101 CU42
Arkley La, Barn. EN5 101 CU41
Arkley Pk, Barn. EN5 100 CR44
Arkley Rd, E17 145 DZ57
Hemel Hempstead HP2 63 BP15
Arkley Vw, Barn. EN5 101 CV42
Arklow Ct, Chorl. WD3
off Station App 95 BD42
Arklow Ho, SE17 43 L2
Arklow Ms, Surb. KT6
off Vale Rd S 220 CL103
Arklow Rd, SE14 45 N3
Arkwright Rd, NW3 5 N3
Colnbrook SL3 175 BE82
South Croydon CR2 242 DT110
Tilbury RM18 193 GG82
Arkwrights, Harl. CM20 57 ET14
Arlesey Cl, SW15 201 CY85
Arlesford Rd, SW9 42 B10
Arlingford Rd, SW2 203 DN85
Arlingham Ms, Wal.Abb. EN9 off Sun St 89 EC33
Arlington, N12 120 DA48
Arlington Av, N1 9 K9
Arlington Bldg, E3 12 B10
Arlington Cl, SE13 205 ED85
Sidcup DA15 207 ES87
Sutton SM1 222 DA103
Twickenham TW1 199 CJ86
Arlington Ct, W3
off Mill Hill Rd 160 CP74

Arlington Ct, Hayes UB3
off Shepiston La 177 BR78
Reigate RH2
off Oakfield Dr. 272 DB132
Arlington Cres, Wal.Cr. EN8 . . . . 89 DY34
Arlington Dr, Cars. SM5 . . . . . . 222 DF103
Ruislip HA4 . . . . 137 BR58
Arlington Gdns, W4 . . . . 180 CQ78
Ilford IG1 . . . . 147 EN60
Romford RM3 . . . . 128 FL53
Arlington Grn, NW7 . . . . 119 CX52
Arlington Lo, SW2 . . . . 183 DM84
Weybridge KT13 . . . . 235 BP105
Arlington Ms, Twick. TW1
off Arlington Rd 199 CJ86
Arlington Pl, SE10 . . . . 46 E5
Arlington Rd, N14 . . . . 121 DH47
NW1 . . . . 7 K9
W13 . . . . 159 CH72
Ashford TW15 . . . . 196 BM92
Richmond TW10 . . . . 199 CK89
Surbiton KT6 . . . . 219 CK100
Teddington TW11 . . . . 199 CF91
Twickenham TW1 . . . . 199 CJ86
Woodford Green IG8 . . . . . . 124 EG53
Arlington Sq, N1 . . . . 9 K9
Arlington St, SW1 . . . . 29 L2
Arlington Way, EC1 . . . . 18 F2
Arliss Way, Nthlt. UB5 . . . . 158 BW67
Arlow Rd, N21 . . . . 121 DN46
Armada Ct, SE8 . . . . 46 A3
Grays RM16 off Hogg La . . . 192 GA76
Armadale Cl, N17 . . . . 144 DV56
Armadale Rd, SW6 . . . . 39 J4
Feltham TW14 . . . . 197 BU85
Woking GU21 . . . . 248 AU117
Armada Way, E6 . . . . 167 EQ73
Armagh Rd, E3 . . . . 11 P9
Armand Cl, Wat. WD17 . . . . 97 BT38
Armfield Cl, W.Mol. KT8 . . . . . . 218 BZ99
Armfield Cres, Mitch. CR4 . . . . 222 DF96
Armfield Rd, Enf. EN2 . . . . 104 DR39
Arminger Rd, W12 . . . . 161 CV74
Armistice Gdns, SE25 . . . . 224 DU97
Armitage Cl, Loud. WD3 . . . . 96 BK42
Armitage Rd, NW11 . . . . 141 CZ60
SE10 . . . . 35 L10
Armor Rd, Purf. RM19 . . . . 191 FR77
Armour Cl, N7 . . . . 8 C5
Armoury Dr, Grav. DA12 . . . . . . 213 GJ87
Armoury Rd, SE8 . . . . 46 D9
Armoury Way, SW18 . . . . 202 DA85
Armstead Wk, Dag. RM10 . . . . . 168 FA66
Armstrong Av, Wdf.Grn. IG8 . . 124 EE51
Armstrong Cl, E6 . . . . 25 K8
Borehamwood WD6 . . . . 100 CQ41
Bromley BR1 . . . . 226 EL97
Dagenham RM8 . . . . 148 EX59
Halstead TN14 . . . . 263 FB115
London Colney AL2 . . . . 84 CL27
Pinner HA5 . . . . 137 BU58
Walton-on-Thames KT12 . . . 217 BU100
Armstrong Cres, Cockfos. EN4 . 102 DD41
Armstrong Gdns, Shenley WD7 . 84 CL32
Armstrong Pl, Hem.H. HP1
off High St 62 BK19
Armstrong Rd, NW10 . . . . 160 CS66
SE18 . . . . 187 EQ76
SW7 . . . . 28 A7
W3 . . . . 161 CT74
Englefield Green TW20 . . . . . 194 AW93
Feltham TW13 . . . . 198 BY92
Armstrong Way, Sthl. UB2 . . . . 178 CB75
Armytage Rd, Houns. TW5 . . . . 178 BX80
Arnal Cres, SW18 . . . . 201 CY87
Arncliffe Cl, N11 . . . . 120 DG51
Arncroft Ct, Bark. IG11
off Renwick Rd 168 EV69
Arndale Wk, SW18
off Garratt La 202 DB85
Arndale Way, Egh. TW20
off Church Rd 195 BA92
Arne Gro, Horl. RH6 . . . . 290 DE146
Orpington BR6 . . . . 227 ET104
Arne Ho, SE11 . . . . 30 C10
Arne St, WC2 . . . . 18 B9
Arnett Cl, Rick. WD3 . . . . 96 BG44
Sch Arnett Hills JMI Sch, Rick.
WD3 off Berry La 96 BG44
Arnett Sq, E4 . . . . 123 DZ51
Arnett Way, Rick. WD3 . . . . 96 BG44
Arne Wk, SE3 . . . . 186 EF84
Arneways Av, Rom. RM6 . . . . . . 148 EX55
Arneway St, SW1 . . . . 29 P7
Arnewood Cl, SW15 . . . . 201 CU88
Oxshott KT22 . . . . 236 CB113
Arney's La, Mitch. CR4 . . . . . . 222 DG100
Arngask Rd, SE6 . . . . 205 ED87
Arnhem Av, Aveley RM15 . . . . . 170 FQ74
Arnhem Dr, New Adgtn CR0 . . 243 ED111
Arnhem Pl, E14 . . . . 34 A7
Arnhem Way, SE22
off East Dulwich Gro 204 DS85
Arnhem Wf, E14 off Arnhem Pl . 34 A7
Sch Arnhem Wf Prim Sch, E14 . . 34 A7
Arnison Rd, E.Mol. KT8 . . . . 219 CD98
Arnold Av E, Enf. EN3 . . . . 105 EA38
Arnold Av W, Enf. EN3 . . . . 105 DZ38
Arnold Bennett Way, N8
off Burghley Rd 143 DN55
Arnold Circ, E2 . . . . 20 A3
Arnold Cl, Har. HA3 . . . . 140 CM59
Arnold Cres, Islw. TW7 . . . . 199 CD85
Arnold Dr, Chess. KT9 . . . . 237 CK107
Arnold Est, SE1 . . . . 32 B5
Arnold Gdns, N13 . . . . 121 DP50
Sch Arnold Ho Sch, NW8 . . . . . . 16 A1
Arnold Pl, Til. RM18 . . . . 193 GJ81
Arnold Rd, E3 . . . . 22 A2
N15 . . . . 144 DT55
SW17 . . . . 202 DF94
Dagenham RM9, RM10 . . . . . 168 EZ66
Gravesend DA12 . . . . 213 GJ89
Northolt UB5 . . . . 158 BX65
Staines TW18 . . . . 196 BJ94
Waltham Abbey EN9 . . . . 105 EC36
Woking GU21 . . . . 249 BB116
Arnolds Av, Hutt. CM13 . . . . . . 131 GC43
Arnolds Cl, Hutt. CM13 . . . . . . 131 GC43
Arnolds Fm La, Mtnsg CM13 . . 131 GE41
Arnolds La, Sutt.H. DA4 . . . . . . 210 FM93
⊖ Arnos Grove 121 DJ49
Arnos Gro, N14 . . . . 121 DK49
Arnos Rd, N11 . . . . 121 DJ50
Arnott Cl, SE28
off Applegarth Rd 168 EW73
W4 . . . . 180 CR77
Arnould Av, SE5 . . . . 184 DR84
Arnsberg Way, Bexh. DA7 . . . . 188 FA84
Arnside Gdns, Wem. HA9 . . . . . 139 CK60
Arnside Rd, Bexh. DA7 . . . . 188 FA81
Arnside St, SE17 . . . . 43 K2
Arnulf St, SE6 . . . . 205 EB91
Arnulls Rd, SW16 . . . . 203 DN93
Arodene Rd, SW2 . . . . 203 DM86
Arosa Rd, Twick. TW1 . . . . 199 CK86
Arpley Sq, SE20 off High St . . . 204 DW94
Arragon Gdns, SW16 . . . . 203 DL94
West Wickham BR4 . . . . 225 EB104
Arragon Rd, E6 . . . . 166 EK67
SW18 . . . . 202 DB88
Twickenham TW1 . . . . 199 CG87
Arran Cl, Erith DA8 . . . . 189 FD79
Hemel Hempstead HP3 . . . . . 63 BQ22
Wallington SM6 . . . . 241 DH105
Arran Dr, E12 . . . . 146 EK60
Arran Grn, Wat. WD19
off Prestwick Rd 116 BX49
Arran Ms, W5 . . . . 160 CM74
Arranmore Ct, Bushey WD23 . . . 98 BY42
Arran Rd, SE6 . . . . 205 EB89
Arran Wk, N1 . . . . 9 J6
Arran Way, Esher KT10 . . . . . . 218 CB103
Arras Av, Mord. SM4 . . . . 222 DC99
Arretine Cl, St.Alb. AL3 . . . . 64 BZ22
Arreton Mead, Horsell GU21 . . 232 AY114
Arrol Ho, SE1 . . . . 31 K7
Arrol Rd, Beck. BR3 . . . . 224 DW97
Arrow Rd, E3 . . . . 22 C2
Arrowscout Wk, Nthlt. UB5
off Wayfarer Rd 158 BY69
Arrowsmith Cl, Chig. IG7 . . . . . 125 ET50
Arrowsmith Ho, SE11 . . . . 30 C10
Arrowsmith Path, Chig. IG7 . . . 125 ET50
Arrowsmith Rd, Chig. IG7 . . . . 125 ES50
Loughton IG10 . . . . 106 EL41
⊖ Arsenal 143 DN62
★ Arsenal FC, N5 . . . . 8 E1
Arsenal Rd, SE9 . . . . 187 EM82
Arsenal Way, SE18 . . . . 187 EQ76
Arta Ho, E1 . . . . 21 H9
Artemis Cl, Grav. DA12 . . . . . . 213 GL87
Arterberry Rd, SW20 . . . . 201 CW94
Arterial Av, Rain. RM13 . . . . . . 169 FH70
Arterial Rd N Stifford,
Grays RM17 . . . . 192 FY75
Arterial Rd Purfleet, Purf.
RM19 . . . . 190 FN76
Arterial Rd W Thurrock,
Grays RM16, RM20 . . . . 191 FU76
Artesian Cl, NW10 . . . . 160 CR66
Hornchurch RM11 . . . . 149 FF58
Artesian Gro, Barn. EN5 . . . . . 102 DC41
Artesian Rd, W2 . . . . 15 J9
Artesian Wk, E11 . . . . 146 EE62
Arthingworth St, E15 . . . . 13 J8
Arthur Ct, SW11 . . . . 41 H7
W2 . . . . 15 L8
Arthurdon Rd, SE4 . . . . 205 EA85
Arthur Gro, SE18 . . . . 187 EQ77
Arthur Henderson Ho, SW6 . . . . 38 G8
Arthur Horsley Wk, E7 . . . . 13 M2
★ Arthur Jacob Nature Reserve,
Slou. SL3 . . . . 175 BC83
Arthur Newton Ho, SW11
off Lavender Rd 40 B10
Arthur Rd, E6 . . . . 167 EM68
N7 . . . . 143 DM63
N9 . . . . 122 DT47
SW19 . . . . 202 DA90
Biggin Hill TN16 . . . . 260 EJ115
Kingston upon Thames KT2 . 200 CN94
New Malden KT3 . . . . 221 CV99
Romford RM6 . . . . 148 EW59
St. Albans AL1 . . . . 65 CH20
Slough SL1 . . . . 173 AR75
Windsor SL4 . . . . 173 AP81
Arthur's Br Rd, Wok. GU21 . . . 248 AW117
Arthur St, EC4 . . . . 31 M1
Bushey WD23 . . . . 98 BX42
Erith DA8 . . . . 189 FF80
Gravesend DA11 . . . . 213 GG87
Grays RM17 . . . . 192 GC79
Arthur St W, Grav. DA11 . . . . . . 213 GG87
Arthur Toft Ho, Grays RM17
off New Rd 192 GB79
Arthur Walls Ho, E12
off Grantham Rd 147 EN62
Artichoke Dell, Chorl. WD3 . . . . 95 BE43
Artichoke Hill, E1 . . . . 32 E1
Artichoke Pl, SE5 . . . . 43 L6
Artillery Cl, Ilf. IG2
off Horns Rd 147 EQ58
Artillery La, E1 . . . . 19 P7
W12 . . . . 161 CU72
Artillery Mans, SW1 . . . . 29 N6
Artillery Pas, E1 . . . . 19 P7
Artillery Pl, SE18 . . . . 37 K9
SW1 . . . . 29 N7
Harrow HA3
off Chicheley Rd 116 CC52
Artillery Rd, Guil. GU1 . . . . 280 AX135
Artillery Row, SW1 . . . . 29 N7
Gravesend DA12 . . . . 213 GJ87
Artillery Ter, Guil. GU1 . . . . 264 AX134
ARTINGTON, Guil. GU3 . . . . . . 280 AW139
Artington Cl, Orp. BR6 . . . . 245 EQ105
Artington Wk, Guil. GU2 . . . . . 280 AW137
Artisan Cl, E6 . . . . 25 N10
Artisan Cres, St.Alb. AL3 . . . . . . 64 CC19
Artizan St, E1 . . . . 19 P8
Sch Arts Ed Sch London, The,
W4 off Bath Rd 180 CS77
Arundel Av, Epsom KT17 . . . . . 239 CV110
Morden SM4 . . . . 221 CZ98
South Croydon CR2 . . . . 242 DU110
Arundel Cl, E15 . . . . 13 K1
SW11 . . . . 202 DE85
Bexley DA5 . . . . 208 EZ86
Cheshunt EN8 . . . . 88 DW28
Croydon CR0 . . . . 223 DP104
Hampton Hill TW12 . . . . 198 CB92
Hemel Hempstead HP2 . . . . . . 63 BP19
Arundel Ct, N12 . . . . 120 DE51
Harrow HA2 . . . . 138 CA63
Slough SL3 . . . . 174 AX77
Arundel Dr, Borwd. WD6 . . . . . 100 CQ43
Harrow HA2 . . . . 138 BZ63
Orpington BR6 . . . . 246 EV106
Woodford Green IG8 . . . . 124 EG52
Arundel Gdns, N21 . . . . 121 DN46
W11 . . . . 14 G10
Edgware HA8 . . . . 118 CR52
Ilford IG3 . . . . 148 EU61
Arundel Gt Ct, WC2 . . . . 18 D10
Arundel Gro, N16 . . . . 9 N2
St. Albans AL3 . . . . 65 CD15
Arundel Pl, N1 . . . . 8 E5
Arundel Rd, Abb.L. WD5 . . . . 81 BU32
Cockfosters EN4 . . . . 102 DE41
Croydon CR0 . . . . 224 DR100
Dartford DA1 . . . . 190 FJ84
Dorking RH4 . . . . 285 CG136
Hounslow TW4 . . . . 178 BW83
Kingston upon Thames KT1 . 220 CP96
Romford RM3 . . . . 128 FM53
Sutton SM2 . . . . 239 CZ108
Uxbridge UB8 . . . . 156 BH68
Arundel Sq, N7 . . . . 8 E5
Arundel St, WC2 . . . . 18 D10
Arundel Ter, SW13 . . . . 181 CV79
Arvon Rd, N5 . . . . 8 F2
Asbaston Ter, Ilf. IG1
off Buttsbury Rd 147 EQ64
Ascalon Ho, SW8
off Ascalon St 41 L5
Ascalon St, SW8 . . . . 41 L5
Ascension Rd, Rom. RM5 . . . . . 127 FC51
● Ascent Pk, Harl. CM20 . . . . . . 58 EU10
Ascham Dr, E4
off Rushcroft Rd 123 EB52
Ascham End, E17 . . . . 123 DY53
Ascham St, NW5 . . . . 7 L2
Aschurch Rd, Croy. CR0 . . . . . 224 DT101
Ascot Cl, Els. WD6 . . . . 100 CN43
Ilford IG6 . . . . 125 ES51
Northolt UB5 . . . . 138 CA64
Ascot Gdns, Enf. EN3 . . . . 104 DW37
Hornchurch RM12 . . . . 150 FL63
Southall UB1 . . . . 158 BZ71
Ascot Ms, Wall. SM6 . . . . 241 DJ109
Ascot Rd, E6 . . . . 25 J2
N15 . . . . 144 DR57
N18 . . . . 122 DU49
SW17 . . . . 202 DG93
Feltham TW14 . . . . 196 BN88
Gravesend DA12 . . . . 213 GH90
Orpington BR5 . . . . 227 ET98
Watford WD18 . . . . 97 BS43
Ascots La, Welw.G.C. AL7 . . . . . 51 CY14
Ascott Av, W5 . . . . 180 CL75
Ascot Ter, Gt Amwell SG12
off Yearling Cl 55 DZ08
Ashanti Ms, E8 . . . . 10 F3
Ashbeam Cl, Gt Warley CM13 . 129 FW51
Ashbourne, St.Alb. AL2 . . . . 82 BZ31
Ashbourne Av, E18 . . . . 146 EH56
N20 . . . . 120 DF47
NW11 . . . . 141 CZ57
Bexleyheath DA7 . . . . 188 EY80
Harrow HA2 . . . . 139 CD61
Ashbourne Cl, N12 . . . . 120 DB49
W5 . . . . 160 CN71
Coulsdon CR5 . . . . 257 DJ118
Ashbourne Ct, E5
off Daubeney Rd 145 DY63
Ashbourne Gdns, Hert. SG13 . . 54 DS11
Ashbourne Gro, NW7 . . . . 118 CR50
SE22 . . . . 204 DT85
W4 . . . . 180 CS78
Ashbourne Ho, Slou. SL1 . . . . . 174 AS75
Coll Ashbourne Indep 6th
Form Coll, W8 . . . . 27 L4
Ashbourne Par, W5
off Ashbourne Rd 160 CM70
Ashbourne Ri, Orp. BR6 . . . . . . 245 ER105
Ashbourne Rd, W5 . . . . 160 CM71
Broxbourne EN10 . . . . 71 DZ21
Mitcham CR4 . . . . 202 DG93
Romford RM3 . . . . 128 FJ49
Ashbourne Sq, Nthwd. HA6 . . . 115 BS51
Ashbourne Ter, SW19 . . . . 202 DA94
Ashbourne Way, NW11 . . . . 141 CZ57
Ashbridge Rd, E11 . . . . 146 EE59
Ashbridge St, NW8 . . . . 16 C5
Ashbrook Rd, N19 . . . . 143 DK60
Dagenham RM10 . . . . 149 FB62
Old Windsor SL4 . . . . 194 AV87
Ashburn Gdns, SW7 . . . . 27 N8
Ashburnham Av, Har. HA1 . . . . 139 CF58
Ashburnham Cl, N2 . . . . 142 DD55
Sevenoaks TN13
off Fiennes Way 279 FJ127
Watford WD19 . . . . 115 BU48
Ashburnham Dr, Wat. WD19 . . . 115 BU48
Ashburnham Gdns, Har. HA1 . 139 CF58
Upminster RM14 . . . . 150 FP60
Ashburnham Gro, SE10 . . . . 46 D5
Ashburnham Pk, Esher KT10 . 236 CC105
Ashburnham Pl, SE10 . . . . 46 D5
Sch Ashburnham Prim Sch,
SW10 . . . . 40 A4
Ashburnham Retreat, SE10 . . . . 46 D5
Ashburnham Rd, NW10 . . . . 14 A2
SW10 . . . . 39 P5
Belvedere DA17 . . . . 189 FC77
Richmond TW10 . . . . 199 CH90
Ashburnham Twr, SW10
off Blantyre St 40 A4
Ashburn Pl, SW7 . . . . 27 N8
Ashburton Av, Croy. CR0 . . . . . 224 DV102
Ilford IG3 . . . . 147 ES63
Ashburton Cl, Croy. CR0 . . . . . 224 DU102
Sch Ashburton Comm Sch,
Croy. CR0 off Shirley Rd . . 224 DV101
Ashburton Ct, Pnr. HA5 . . . . . . 138 BX55
Ashburton Gdns, Croy. CR0 . . . 224 DU103
Sch Ashburton Jun & Inf Sch,
Croy. CR0 off Long La 224 DV100
Ashburton Rd, E16 . . . . 23 P8
Croydon CR0 . . . . 224 DU102
Ruislip HA4 . . . . 137 BU61
Ashburton Ter, E13 . . . . 13 N10
Ashburton Triangle, N5
off Drayton Pk 143 DN63
Ashbury Cl, Hat. AL10 . . . . 66 CS18
Ashbury Cres, Guil. GU4 . . . . . 265 BC132
Ashbury Dr, Uxb. UB10 . . . . . . 137 BP61
Ashbury Gdns, Rom. RM6 . . . . 148 EX57
Ashbury Pl, SW19 . . . . 202 DC93
Ashbury Rd, SW11 . . . . 40 G10
Ashby Av, Chess. KT9 . . . . 238 CN107
Ashby Cl, Horn. RM11
off Holme Rd 150 FN60
Ashby Gdns, St.Alb. AL1 . . . . . . 65 CD24
Ashby Gro, N1 . . . . 9 K6
Ashby Ho, N1 . . . . 9 K6
Ashby Ms, SE4 . . . . 45 N9
SW2 off Prague Pl 203 DL85
Ashby Rd, N15 . . . . 144 DU57
SE4 . . . . 45 P9
Watford WD24 . . . . 97 BU38
Ashby St, EC1 . . . . 19 H3
Ashby Wk, Croy. CR0 . . . . 224 DQ100
Ashby Way, Sipson UB7 . . . . . . 176 BN80
Ashchurch Gro, W12 . . . . 181 CU75
Ashchurch Pk Vil, W12 . . . . 181 CU76
Ashchurch Ter, W12 . . . . 181 CU76
Ash Cl, SE20 . . . . 224 DW96
Abbots Langley WD5 . . . . 81 BR32
Brookmans Park AL9 . . . . 86 DA25
Carshalton SM5 . . . . 222 DF103
Edgware HA8 . . . . 118 CQ49
Harefield UB9 . . . . 114 BK53
New Malden KT3 . . . . 220 CR96
Petts Wood BR5 . . . . 227 ER99
Pilgrim's Hatch CM15 . . . . . . 130 FT43
Pyrford GU22 . . . . 250 BG115
Romford RM5 . . . . 127 FB52
Sidcup DA14 . . . . 208 EV90
Slough SL3 . . . . 175 BB76
South Merstham RH1 . . . . . . 273 DJ130
Stanmore HA7 . . . . 117 CG51
Swanley BR8 . . . . 229 FC96
Tadworth KT20 . . . . 270 CQ131
Watford WD25 . . . . 97 BV35
Woking GU22 . . . . 248 AY120
Ashcombe, Welw.G.C. AL8 . . . . . 51 CY05
Ashcombe Av, Surb. KT6 . . . . . 219 CK101
Ashcombe Cl, Ashf. TW15 . . . . 196 BK90
Ashcombe Gdns, Edg. HA8 . . . 118 CN49
Ashcombe Ho, Enf. EN3 . . . . . . 105 DX41
Ashcombe Pk, NW2 . . . . 140 CS62
Ashcombe Rd, SW19 . . . . 202 DA92
Carshalton SM5 . . . . 240 DG107
Dorking RH4 . . . . 269 CG134
Merstham RH1 . . . . 273 DJ127
Sch Ashcombe Sch, The, Dor.
RH4 off Ashcombe Rd 269 CH134
Ashcombe Sq, N.Mal. KT3 . . . . 220 CQ97
Ashcombe St, SW6 . . . . 39 L9
Ashcombe Ter, Tad. KT20 . . . . . 255 CV120
Ash Copse, Brick.Wd AL2 . . . . . . 82 BZ31
Ash Ct, N11 off Cline Rd 121 DJ51
Epsom KT19 . . . . 238 CQ105
Ashcroft, Pnr. HA5 . . . . 116 CA51
Shalford GU4 . . . . 280 AY141
Ashcroft Av, Sid. DA15 . . . . 208 EU86
Ashcroft Ct, N20
off Oakleigh Rd N 120 DD47
Broxbourne EN10
off Winford Dr 71 DZ22
Burnham SL1 . . . . 152 AH68
Ashcroft Cres, Sid. DA15 . . . . . 208 EU86
Ashcroft Dr, Denh. UB9 . . . . . . 135 BF58
Ashcroft Pk, Cob. KT11 . . . . . . 236 BY112
Ashcroft Pl, Lthd. KT22 . . . . . . 253 CJ121
Ashcroft Ri, Couls. CR5 . . . . . . 257 DL116
Ashcroft Rd, E3 . . . . 21 L3
Chessington KT9 . . . . 220 CM104
Ashcroft Sq, W6 . . . . 26 A9
Ashdale, Bkhm KT23 . . . . 268 CC126
Ashdale Cl, Stai. TW19 . . . . 196 BL89
Twickenham TW2 . . . . 198 CC87
Ashdale Gro, Stan. HA7 . . . . . . 117 CF51
Ashdale Rd, SE12 . . . . 206 EH88
Ashdales, St.Alb. AL1 . . . . 65 CD24
Ashdale Way, Twick. TW2
off Ashdale Cl 198 CC87
Ashdene, SE15 . . . . 44 E6
Pinner HA5 . . . . 138 BW55
Ashdene Cl, Ashf. TW15 . . . . . . 197 BQ94
Ashdon Cl, Hutt. CM13
off Poplar Dr 131 GC44
South Ockendon RM15
off Afton Dr 171 FV72
Woodford Green IG8 . . . . 124 EH51
Ashdon Rd, NW10 . . . . 160 CS67
Bushey WD23 . . . . 98 BX41
Ashdown Cl, Beck. BR3 . . . . . . 225 EB96
Bexley DA5 . . . . 209 FC87
Reigate RH2 . . . . 288 DB138
Woking GU22
off Guildford Rd 248 AY118
Ashdown Ct, E17 . . . . 123 EC54
Ashdown Cres, NW5 . . . . 6 G3
Cheshunt EN8 . . . . 89 DY28
Ashdown Dr, Borwd. WD6 . . . . 100 CM40
Ashdown Gdns, S.Croy. CR2 . . 258 DV115
Ashdown Pl, T.Ditt. KT7 . . . . . . 219 CG100
Ashdown Rd, Enf. EN3 . . . . 104 DW41
Epsom KT17 . . . . 239 CT113
Kingston upon Thames KT1 . 220 CL96
Reigate RH2 . . . . 288 DB138
Uxbridge UB10 . . . . 156 BN68
Ashdown Wk, E14 . . . . 34 B8
Romford RM7 . . . . 127 FB54
Ashdown Way, SW17 . . . . 202 DG89
Amersham HP6 . . . . 77 AR37
Ash Dr, Hat. AL10 . . . . 67 CU21
Redhill RH1 . . . . 289 DH136
Ashen, E6 . . . . 25 L8
Sch Ashen Cross, Slou. SL3 . . . . 155 BB71
Ashenden, SE17 . . . . 31 J8
Ashendene Rd, Bayford SG13 . . 69 DL20
Ashenden Rd, E5 . . . . 11 K2
Guildford GU2 . . . . 280 AT135
Ashenden Wk, Farn.Com. SL2 . 133 AR63
Ashen Dr, Dart. DA1 . . . . 209 FG86
Ashen Gro, SW19 . . . . 202 DA90
Ashentree Ct, EC4 . . . . 18 F9
Ashen Vale, S.Croy. CR2 . . . . . . 243 DX109
● Asheridge Business Cen,
Chesh. HP5 . . . . 76 AN29
Asheridge Rd, Chesh. HP5 . . . . . 76 AM28
Asher Loftus Way, N11 . . . . 120 DF51
Asher Way, E1 . . . . 32 D2
Ashfield Av, Bushey WD23 . . . . . 98 CB44
Feltham TW13 . . . . 197 BV88
Ashfield Cl, Ashtd. KT21 . . . . . 254 CL119
Beckenham BR3 . . . . 205 EA94
Richmond TW10 . . . . 200 CL88
Sch Ashfield Jun Sch,
Bushey WD23
off School La 116 CB45
Ashfield La, Chis. BR7 . . . . 207 EQ93
Ashfield Par, N14 . . . . 121 DK46
Ashfield Rd, N4 . . . . 144 DQ58
N14 . . . . 121 DJ48
W3 . . . . 161 CT74
Chesham HP5 . . . . 76 AR29
Ashfields, Loug. IG10 . . . . 107 EM40
Reigate RH2 . . . . 272 DB132
Watford WD25 . . . . 97 BT35
Ashfield St, E1 . . . . 20 E7
Ashfield Yd, E1 . . . . 20 G7
ASHFORD, TW15 . . . . 196 BM92
⇌ Ashford 196 BL91
Ashford Av, N8 . . . . 143 DL56
Ashford TW15 . . . . 197 BP93
Brentwood CM14 . . . . 130 FV48
Hayes UB4 . . . . 158 BX72
Ashford Cl, E17 . . . . 145 DZ58
Ashford TW15 . . . . 196 BL91
Sch Ashford C of E Prim Sch, Ashf.
TW15 off School Rd 197 BP93
Ashford Cres, Ashf. TW15 . . . . . 196 BL90
Enfield EN3 . . . . 104 DW40
Ashford Gdns, Cob. KT11 . . . . . 252 BX116
Ashford Grn, Wat. WD19 . . . . . . 116 BX50
H Ashford Hosp, Ashf. TW15 . 196 BL89
● Ashford Ind Est, Ashf.
TW15 . . . . 197 BQ91
Ashford La, Dorney SL4 . . . . . . 172 AH75
Maidenhead SL6 . . . . 172 AG75
Ashford Ms, N17 . . . . 122 DU53
Sch Ashford Pk Prim Sch,
Ashf. TW15
off Station Cres 196 BK91
Ashford Rd, E6 . . . . 167 EN65
E18 . . . . 124 EH54
NW2 . . . . 4 C1
Ashford TW15 . . . . 197 BQ94
Feltham TW13 . . . . 197 BT90
Iver SL0 . . . . 155 BC66
Staines TW18 . . . . 216 BK95
Ashford St, N1 . . . . 19 N2
Ash Grn, Denh. UB9 . . . . 156 BH65
Ash Gro, E8 . . . . 10 F9
N10 . . . . 143 DH56
N13 . . . . 122 DQ48
NW2 . . . . 4 D1
SE20 . . . . 224 DW96
W5 . . . . 180 CL75
Amersham HP6 . . . . 77 AN36
Enfield EN1 . . . . 122 DS45
Feltham TW14 . . . . 197 BS88
Guildford GU2 . . . . 264 AU134
Harefield UB9 . . . . 114 BK53
Hayes UB3 . . . . 157 BR73
Hemel Hempstead HP3 . . . . . 62 BM24
Hounslow TW5 . . . . 178 BX81
Southall UB1 . . . . 158 CA71
Staines TW18 . . . . 196 BJ93
Stoke Poges SL2 . . . . 154 AT66
Wembley HA0 . . . . 139 CG63
West Drayton UB7 . . . . 156 BM73
West Wickham BR4 . . . . 225 EC103
Ashgrove Rd, Ashf. TW15 . . . . . 197 BQ92
Bromley BR1 . . . . 205 ED93
Ilford IG3 . . . . 147 ET60
Sevenoaks TN13 . . . . 278 FG127
Ash Gros, Saw. CM21 . . . . 58 FA05
Sch Ashgrove Sch, Brom.
BR1 off Widmore Rd 226 EH96
Ash Hill Cl, Bushey WD23 . . . . . 116 CB46
Ash Hill Dr, Pnr. HA5 . . . . 138 BW55
Ash Ho, SE1
off Longfield Est 32 B9
● Ash Ind Est,
Harl. CM19 . . . . 73 EM16
Ashingdon Cl, E4 . . . . 123 EC48
Ashington Ho, E1
off Barnsley St 20 F4
Ashington Rd, SW6 . . . . 39 H8
Ash Island, E.Mol. KT8 . . . . 219 CD97
Ashlake Rd, SW16 . . . . 203 DL91
Ashland Pl, W1 . . . . 16 G6
Ash La, Horn. RM11
off Wiltshire Av 150 FM56
Romford RM1 . . . . 127 FG51
Windsor SL4 . . . . 173 AK82
Ashlar Pl, SE18 . . . . 37 N9
Ashlea Rd, Chal.St.P. SL9 . . . . . 112 AX54
Ashleigh Av, Egh. TW20 . . . . . . 195 BC94
Ashleigh Cl, Amer. HP7 . . . . 77 AS39
Horley RH6 . . . . 290 DF148
Ashleigh Cotts, Dor. RH5 . . . . . 285 CH144
Ashleigh Ct, Wal.Abb. EN9
off Lamplighters Cl 90 EG34
Ashleigh Gdns, Sutt. SM1 . . . . 222 DB103
Upminster RM14 . . . . 151 FR62
Ashleigh Pt, SE23
off Dacres Rd 205 DX90
Ashleigh Rd, SE20 . . . . 224 DV97
SW14 . . . . 180 CS83
Ashley Av, Epsom KT18 . . . . . . 238 CR113
Ilford IG6 . . . . 125 EP54
Morden SM4 . . . . 222 DA99
🔒 Ashley Cen, Epsom KT18 . . 238 CR113
Ashley Cl, NW4 . . . . 119 CW54
Bookham KT23 . . . . 268 BZ125
Hemel Hempstead HP3 . . . . . 62 BM22
Pinner HA5 . . . . 115 BV54
Sevenoaks TN13 . . . . 279 FH124
Walton-on-Thames KT12 . . . 217 BT102
Welwyn Garden City AL8 . . . . . 51 CW07
Sch Ashley C of E Prim Sch, Walt.
KT12 off Ashley Rd 217 BU102
Ashley Ct, Epsom KT18 . . . . 238 CR113
Hatfield AL10 . . . . 67 CU17
Woking GU21 . . . . 248 AT118
Ashley Cres, N22 . . . . 121 DN54
SW11 . . . . 41 H10
Ashley Dr, Bans. SM7 . . . . 240 DA114
Borehamwood WD6 . . . . 100 CQ43
Isleworth TW7 . . . . 179 CE79
Penn HP10 . . . . 110 AC45
Twickenham TW2 . . . . 198 CB87
Walton-on-Thames KT12 . . . 217 BU104
Ashley Gdns, N13 . . . . 122 DQ49
SW1 . . . . 29 M7
Orpington BR6 . . . . 245 ES106
Richmond TW10 . . . . 199 CK90
Shalford GU4 . . . . 281 AZ141
Wembley HA9 . . . . 140 CL61
ASHLEY GREEN, Chesh. HP5 . . 60 AS24
Ashley Grn Rd, Chesh. HP5 . . . . 76 AR27
Ashley Gro, Loug. IG10
off Staples Rd 106 EL41
Ashley La, NW4 . . . . 119 CW54
NW7 . . . . 119 CW54
Croydon CR0 . . . . 241 DP105
ASHLEY PARK, Walt. KT12 . . . 217 BT104
Ashley Pk Av, Walt. KT12 . . . . . 217 BT103
Ashley Pk Cres, Walt. KT12 . . . . 217 BT102
Ashley Pk Rd, Walt. KT12 . . . . . 217 BU103
Ashley Pl, SW1 . . . . 29 L7
Ashley Ri, Walt. KT12 . . . . 235 BU105
Ashley Rd, E4 . . . . 123 EA50
E7 . . . . 166 EJ66
N17 . . . . 144 DU55
N19 . . . . 143 DL60
SW19 . . . . 202 DB93
Enfield EN3 . . . . 104 DW40
Epsom KT18 . . . . 238 CR114
Hampton TW12 . . . . 218 CA95

Ashley Rd, Hert. SG14 53 DN10
Richmond TW9
off Jocelyn Rd 180 CL83
St. Albans AL1 65 CJ20
Sevenoaks TN13 279 FH123
Thames Ditton KT7 219 CF100
Thornton Heath CR7 223 DM98
Uxbridge UB8 156 BH68
Walton-on-Thames KT12 217 BU102
Westcott RH4 284 CC137
Woking GU21 248 AT118
Ashleys, Rick. WD3 113 BF45
Ashley Sq, Epsom KT18 238 CR113
Ashley Wk, NW7 119 CW52
Ashling Rd, Croy. CR0 224 DU102
Ashlin Rd, E15 13 H1
Ashlone Rd, SW15 38 B10
Ashlyn Cl, Bushey WD23 98 BY42
Ashlyn Gro, Horn. RM11 150 FK55
Ashlyns Ct, Berk. HP4 60 AV20
Ashlyns La, Ong. CM5 75 FG23
Ashlyns Pk, Cob. KT11 236 BY113
Ashlyns Rd, Berk. HP4 60 AV20
Epping CM16 91 ET30
Sch Ashlyns Sch, Berk. HP4
off Chesham Rd 60 AW21
Ashlyns Way, Chess. KT9 237 CK107
Ashmead, N14 103 DJ43
Ashmead Dr, Denh. UB9 136 BG61
Ashmead Gate, Brom. BR1 226 EJ95
Ashmead Ho, E9
off Kingsmead Way 11 M2
Ashmead La, Denh. UB9 136 BG61
Ashmead Pl, Amer. HP7 94 AW39
Sch Ashmead Prim Sch, SE8 46 A8
Ashmead Rd, SE8 46 A8
Feltham TW14 197 BU88
Ashmeads Ct, Shenley WD7 83 CK33
Ashmere Av, Beck. BR3 225 ED96
Ashmere Cl, Sutt. SM3 239 CW106
Ashmere Gro, SW2 183 DL84
Ash Ms, Epsom KT18 238 CS113
Ashmill St, NW1 16 C6
Ashmole Pl, SW8 42 D3
Sch Ashmole Prim Sch, SW8 42 D3
Sch Ashmole Sch, N14
off Cecil Rd 121 DJ46
Ashmole St, SW8 42 D3
Ashmore Cl, SE15 44 B5
Ashmore Ct, Houns. TW5
off Wheatlands 178 CA79
Ashmore Gdns, Hem.H. HP3 63 BP21
Northfleet DA11 212 GD91
Ashmore Gro, Well. DA16 187 ER83
Ashmore La, Kes. BR2 244 EH111
Ashmore Rd, W9 15 H4
Ashmount Cres, Slou. SL1 173 AN75
Sch Ashmount Prim Sch, N19
off Ashmount Rd 143 DJ59
Ashmount Rd, N15 144 DT57
N19 143 DJ59
Ashmount Ter, W5 179 CK77
Ashmour Gdns, Rom. RM1 127 FD54
Ashneal Gdns, Har. HA1 139 CD62
Ashness Gdns, Grnf. UB6 159 CH65
Ashness Rd, SW11 202 DF85
Ash Platt, The, Seal TN14,TN15 279 FL121
Ash Platt Rd, Seal TN15 279 FL121
Ash Ride, Enf. EN2 103 DN35
Ashridge Cl, Bov. HP3 79 AZ28
Harrow HA3 139 CJ58
Ashridge Cres, SE18 187 EQ80
Ashridge Dr, Brick.Wd AL2 82 BY30
Watford WD19 116 BW50
Ashridge Gdns, N13 121 DK50
Pinner HA5 138 BY56
Ashridge Ri, Berk. HP4 60 AT18
Ashridge Rd, Chesh. HP5 78 AW31
Ashridge Way, Mord. SM4 221 CZ97
Sunbury-on-Thames TW16 197 BU93
Ash Rd, E15 13 K2
Croydon CR0 225 EA103
Dartford DA1 210 FK88
Gravesend DA12 213 GJ91
Hawley DA2 210 FM91
Orpington BR6 245 ET108
Shepperton TW17 216 BN98
Sutton SM3 221 CY101
Westerham TN16 277 ER125
Woking GU22 248 AX120
Ash Row, Brom. BR2 227 EN101
ASHTEAD, KT21 254 CL118
⇌ Ashtead 253 CK117
Ashtead Common, Ashtd.
KT21 253 CJ115
Ashtead Gap, Lthd. KT22 253 CH116
H Ashtead Hosp, Ashtd.
KT21 254 CL119
ASHTEAD PARK, Ashtd. KT21 254 CN118
Ashtead Rd, E5 144 DU59
Ashtead Wds Rd, Ashtd. KT21 253 CJ117
Ashton Cl, Hersham KT12 235 BV107
Sutton SM1 240 DA105
Ashton Ct, E4
off Connington Cres 124 EE48
Romford RM6 off High Rd 148 EY58
Ashton Gdns, Houns. TW4 178 BZ84
Romford RM6 148 EY58
Sch Ashton Ho Sch, Islw. TW7
off Eversley Cres 179 CD81
Ashton Rd, E15 12 G3
Enfield EN3 105 DY36
Romford RM3 128 FK52
Woking GU21 248 AT117
Ashton St, E14 22 F10
Ashtree Av, Mitch. CR4 222 DD96
Ash Tree Cl, Croy. CR0 225 DY100
Ashtree Cl, Orp. BR6 245 EP105
Ash Tree Cl, Surb. KT6 220 CL102
Ashtree Cl, St.Alb. AL1
off Granville Rd 65 CF20
Waltham Abbey EN9
off Farthingale La 90 EG34
Ash Tree Dell, NW9 140 CQ57
Ash Tree Fld, Harl. CM20 57 EN13
Ash Tree Rd, Wat. WD24 97 BV36
Ash Tree Way, Croy. CR0 225 DY99
Ashtree Way, Hem.H. HP1 62 BG21
Ashurst Cl, SE20 224 DV95
Dartford DA1 189 FF83
Kenley CR8 258 DR115
Ashurst Cl, Lthd. KT22 253 CG121
Northwood HA6 115 BS52
Ashurst Dr, Box H. KT20 270 CP130
Ilford IG2, IG6 147 EP58
Shepperton TW17 216 BL99
Ashurst Pl, Dor. RH4 269 CJ134
Ashurst Rd, N12 120 DE50
Barnet EN4 102 DF43
Tadworth KT20 255 CV121
Ashurst Wk, Croy. CR0 224 DV103
Ash Vale, Map.Cr. WD3 113 BD50
Ashvale Dr, Upmin. RM14 151 FS61
Ashvale Gdns, Rom. RM5 127 FD50
Upminster RM14 151 FS61
Ashvale Rd, SW17 202 DF92
Ashview Cl, Ashf. TW15 196 BL93
Ashview Gdns, Ashf. TW15 196 BL92
Ashville Rd, E11 145 ED61
Ash Wk, SW2 203 DM88
South Ockendon RM15 171 FX69
Wembley HA0 139 CJ63
Ashwater Rd, SE12 206 EG88
Ashway Cen, The, Kings.T.
KT2 off Elm Cres 220 CL95
Ashwell Cl, E6 25 H8
Ashwell Pl, Wat. WD24 97 BU37
Ashwells Manor Dr, Penn
HP10 110 AC47
Ashwells Rd, Pilg.Hat. CM15 130 FS41
Ashwell St, St.Alb. AL3 65 CD19
Ashwells Way, Ch.St.G. HP8 112 AW47
Ashwick Cl, Cat. CR3 274 DU125
Ashwindham Ct, Wok. GU21
off Raglan Rd 248 AT118
Ashwin St, E8 10 A4
Ashwood, Warl. CR6 258 DW120
Ashwood Av, Rain. RM13 169 FH70
Uxbridge UB8 156 BN72
Ashwood Dr, Chesh. HP5 76 AP30
Ashwood Gdns, Hayes UB3
off Cranford Dr 177 BT77
New Addington CR0 243 EB107
Ashwood Ms, St.Alb. AL1
off Prospect Rd 65 CD22
Ashwood Pk, Fetch. KT22 252 CC124
Woking GU22 249 BA118
Ashwood Pl, Bean DA2
off Bean La 211 FV90
Ashwood Rd, E4 123 ED48
Englefield Green TW20 194 AV93
Potters Bar EN6 86 DB33
Woking GU22 249 AZ118
Ashworth Cl, SE5 43 L8
Ashworth Pl, Guil. GU2 264 AT134
Harlow CM17 74 EX15
Ashworth Rd, W9 15 M2
Asker Ho, N7
off Tufnell Pk Rd 143 DL63
Askern Cl, Bexh. DA6 188 EX84
Aske St, N1 19 N2
Askew Cres, W12 181 CT75
Askew Fm La, Grays RM17 192 FY78
Askew Rd, W12 161 CT74
Northwood HA6 115 BR47
Askham Ct, W12 161 CU74
Askham Rd, W12 161 CU74
Askill Dr, SW15 201 CY85
Askwith Rd, Rain. RM13 169 FD69
Asland Rd, E15 13 J9
Aslett St, SW18 202 DB87
Asmara Rd, NW2 4 F2
Asmar Cl, Couls. CR5 257 DL115
Asmuns Hill, NW11 142 DA57
Asmuns Pl, NW11 141 CZ57
Asolando Dr, SE17 31 K9
Aspasia Cl, St.Alb. AL1 65 CF21
Aspdin Rd, Nthflt DA11 212 GD90
Aspect Ct, SW6 39 P8
Aspects, Sutt. SM1 240 DB106
Aspects Ct, Slou. SL1
off Windsor Rd 174 AS75
Aspen Cl, N19
off Hargrave Pk 143 DJ61
W5 180 CM75
Bricket Wood AL2 82 BY30
Guildford GU4 265 BD131
Orpington BR6 246 EU106
Slough SL2 off Birch Gro 153 AP71
Staines TW18 195 BF90
Stoke D'Abernon KT11 252 BY116
Swanley BR8 229 FD95
West Drayton UB7 156 BM74
Aspen Copse, Brom. BR1 227 EM96
Aspen Ct, Brwd. CM13 131 GA48
Hayes UB3 177 BS77
Virginia Water GU25 214 AY98
Aspen Dr, Wem. HA0 139 CG63
Aspen Gdns, W6 181 CV78
Ashford TW15 197 BQ92
Mitcham CR4 222 DG99
Aspen Grn, Erith DA18 188 EZ76
Aspen Gro, Pnr. HA5 137 BT55
Upminster RM14 150 FN63
Aspen Ho, NW3 6 F4
Warlingham CR6
off East Parkside 259 EB115
Aspen La, Nthlt. UB5 158 BY69
Aspenlea Rd, W6 38 C2
Aspen Pk Dr, Wat. WD25 97 BV35
Aspens Pl, Hem.H. HP1 61 BF23
Aspen Sq, Wey. KT13 217 BR104
Aspen Vale, Whyt. CR3
off Whyteleafe Hill 258 DT118
Aspen Way, E14 34 B1
Banstead SM7 239 CX114
Enfield EN3 105 DX35
Feltham TW13 197 BV90
South Ockendon RM15 171 FX69
Welwyn Garden City AL7 52 DC10
Aspern Gro, NW3 6 D3
Aspfield Row, Hem.H. HP1 62 BH18
Aspinall Rd, SE4 45 K10
Aspinden Rd, SE16 32 F8
Aspley Rd, SW18 202 DB85
Asplins Rd, N17 122 DU53
Asprey Ct, Cat. CR3 258 DT123
Asprey Gro, Cat. CR3 258 DU124
Asprey Ms, Beck. BR3 225 DZ99
Asprey Pl, Brom. BR1
off Chislehurst Rd 226 EL96
Asquith Cl, Dag. RM8 148 EW60
Assam St, E1 20 C8
Assata Ms, N1 9 H4
Assembly Pas, E1 21 H6
Assembly Wk, Cars. SM5 222 DE101
Assher Rd, Hersham KT12 218 BY104
Assheton Rd, Beac. HP9 111 AK51
Assurance Cotts, Belv. DA17
off Heron Hill 188 EZ78
Astall Cl, Har. HA3 117 CE53
Astbury Business Pk, SE15
off Station Pas 44 G6
Astbury Ho, SE11 30 E7
Astbury Rd, SE15 44 G6
Astede Pl, Ashtd. KT21 254 CM118
Astell St, SW3 28 D10
Aster Ct, E5 144 DW61
Asters, The, Chsht EN7 88 DR28
Aste St, E14 34 E5
Asteys Row, N1 9 H7
Asthall Gdns, Ilf. IG6 147 EQ56
Astleham Rd, Shep. TW17 216 BL97
Astle St, SW11 40 G8
Astley, Grays RM17 192 FZ79
Astley Av, NW2 4 B2
Sch Astley Cooper Sch, The, Hem.H.
HP2 off St. Agnells La 62 BN15
Astley Ho, SE1
off Rowcross St 32 B10
Astley Rd, Hem.H. HP1 62 BJ20
● Astolat Ind Est, Peasm.
GU3 280 AV142
Aston Av, Har. HA3 139 CJ59
Aston Cl, Ashtd. KT21 253 CJ118
Bushey WD23 98 CC44
Sidcup DA14 208 EU90
Watford WD24 98 BW40
Aston Ct, N4 off Queens Dr 144 DQ61
Aston Gra, Hert. SG14 54 DR07
Aston Grn, Houns. TW4 178 BW82
Aston Ho, SW8 41 N7
Sch Aston Ho Sch, Jun Sch,
W5 off Aston Rd 159 CK72
Sen Sch, W5
off Montpelier Rd 159 CK71
Aston Mead, Wind. SL4 173 AL80
Aston Ms, Rom. RM6 148 EW59
Aston Pl, SW16
off Averil Gro 203 DP93
Aston Rd, SW20 221 CW96
W5 159 CK72
Claygate KT10 237 CE106
Astons Rd, Nthwd. HA6 115 BQ48
Aston St, E14 21 L8
Aston Ter, SW12
off Cathles Rd 203 DH86
Astonville St, SW18 202 DA88
Aston Way, Epsom KT18 255 CT115
Potters Bar EN6 86 DD32
Astor Av, Rom. RM7 149 FC58
Astor Cl, Add. KT15 234 BK105
Kingston upon Thames KT2 200 CP93
Astoria Wk, SW9 183 DN83
● Astra Business Cen,
Red. RH1 288 DG144
● Astra Cen, Harl. CM20 57 ET11
Astra Cl, Horn. RM12 169 FH65
Astra Dr, Grav. DA12 213 GL92
Astrop Ms, W6 26 A6
Astrop Ter, W6 26 A6
Astwick Av, Hat. AL10 67 CT15
Astwood Ms, SW7 27 N8
Asylum Arch Rd, Red. RH1 288 DF137
Asylum Rd, SE15 44 F4
Atalanta Cl, Pur. CR8 241 DN110
Atalanta St, SW6 38 D6
Atbara Ct, Tedd. TW11 199 CH93
Atbara Rd, Tedd. TW11 199 CH93
Atcham Rd, Houns. TW3 178 CC84
Atcost Rd, Bark. IG11 168 EU71
Atheldene Rd, SW18 202 DB88
Sch Athelney Prim Sch, SE6
off Athelney St 205 EA90
Athelney St, SE6 205 EA90
Athelstan Cl, Rom. RM3 128 FM53
Athelstane Gro, E3 21 N1
Athelstane Ms, N4
off Stroud Grn Rd 143 DN60
Athelstan Gdns, NW6 4 F7
Athelstan Ho, E9
off Kingsmead Way 11 N2
Sch Athelstan Ho Sch, Hmptn.
TW12 off Percy Rd 218 CA95
Athelstan Rd, Hem.H. HP3 62 BM23
Kingston upon Thames KT1 220 CM98
Romford RM3 128 FM53
Athelstan Wk N, Welw.G.C. AL7 51 CY10
Athelstan Wk S, Welw.G.C. AL7 51 CX10
Athelstan Way, Orp. BR5 228 EU95
Athelstone Rd, Har. HA3 117 CD54
Athena Cl, Har. HA2
off Byron Hill Rd 139 CE61
Kingston upon Thames KT1 220 CM97
Athena Ct, SE1 off Long La 31 N5
Athenaeum Ct, N5 9 K1
Athenaeum Pl, N10 143 DH55
Athenaeum Rd, N20 120 DC46
Athena Pl, Nthwd. HA6
off The Drive 115 BT53
Athenia Cl, Goffs Oak EN7 87 DN29
Athenlay Rd, SE15 205 DX85
Athens Gdns, W9 15 J5
Atherden Rd, E5 144 DW63
Atherfield Rd, Reig. RH2 288 DC137
Atherfold Rd, SW9 42 A10
Atherley Way, Houns. TW4 198 BZ87
Atherstone Ct, W2 15 M6
Atherstone Ms, SW7 27 P8
Atherton Cl, Shalf. GU4 280 AY140
Stanwell TW19 196 BK86
Atherton Ct, Eton SL4
off Meadow La 173 AR80
Atherton Dr, SW19 201 CX91
Atherton Gdns, Grays RM16 193 GJ77
Atherton Hts, Wem. HA0 159 CJ65
Atherton Ms, E7 13 M4
Atherton Pl, Har. HA2 139 CD55
Southall UB1 158 CA73
Atherton Rd, E7 13 M3
SW13 181 CU80
Ilford IG5 124 EL54
Atherton St, SW11 40 D8
Athlone, Clay. KT10 237 CE107
Athlone Cl, E5 10 F2
Radlett WD7 99 CG36
Athlone Rd, SW2 203 DM87
Athlone Sq, Wind. SL4
off Ward Royal 173 AQ81
Athlone St, NW5 7 H4
Athlon Rd, Wem. HA0 159 CK68
Athol Cl, Pnr. HA5 115 BV53
Athole Gdns, Enf. EN1 104 DS43
Athol Gdns, Pnr. HA5 115 BV53
Atholl Ho, W9 15 N3
Atholl Rd, Ilf. IG3 148 EU59
Athol Rd, Erith DA8 189 FC78
Athol Sq, E14 22 F9
Athol Way, Uxb. UB10 156 BN69
Atkins Cl, Wok. GU21
off Greythorne Rd 248 AU118
Atkins Dr, W.Wick. BR4 225 ED103
Atkinson Cl, Orp. BR6
off Martindale Av 246 EU106
Atkinson Ho, SW11
off Austin Rd 40 G7
Atkinson Rd, E16 24 D7
Atkins Rd, E10 145 EB58
SW12 203 DK87
Atlanta Boul, Rom. RM1 149 FE58
Atlanta Bldg, SE13
off Deals Gateway 46 C7
Atlantic, E16 off Seagull La 23 N10
Atlantic Cl, Swans. DA10 212 FY85
Atlantic Rd, SW9 183 DN84
Atlantis Av, E16 25 P10
Atlantis Cl, Bark. IG11 168 EV69
● Atlas Business Cen, NW2 141 CV61
Atlas Gdns, SE7 36 C8
Atlas Ms, E8 10 B4
N7 8 D5
Atlas Rd, E13 23 P1
N11 121 DH51
NW10 160 CS69
Dartford DA1
off Cornwall Rd 190 FM83
Wembley HA9 140 CQ63
● Atlas Trade Pk, Erith DA8 189 FD78
Atley Rd, E3 12 A9
● Atlip Cen, Wem. HA0
off Atlip Rd 160 CL67
Atlip Rd, Wem. HA0 160 CL67
Atney Rd, SW15 181 CY84
Atria Rd, Nthwd. HA6 115 BU50
● Atrium, The, Uxb. UB8
off Harefield Rd 156 BJ66
Attenborough Cl, Wat. WD19 116 BY48
Atterbury Cl, West. TN16 277 ER126
Atterbury Rd, N4 143 DN58
Atterbury St, SW1 29 P9
Attewood Av, NW10 140 CS62
Attewood Rd, Nthlt. UB5 158 BY65
Attfield Cl, N20 120 DD47
Attimore Cl, Welw.G.C. AL8 51 CV10
Attimore Rd, Welw.G.C. AL8 51 CV10
Attle Cl, Uxb. UB10 156 BN68
Attlee Cl, Hayes UB4 157 BV69
Thornton Heath CR7 224 DQ100
Attlee Ct, Grays RM17 192 GA76
Attlee Dr, Dart. DA1 210 FN85
Attlee Rd, SE28 168 EV73
Hayes UB4 157 BU69
Attlee Ter, E17 145 EB56
Attneave St, WC1 18 E3
Attwood Cl, S.Croy. CR2 242 DV114
Atwater Cl, SW2 203 DN88
Atwell Cl, E10
off Belmont Pk Rd 145 EB58
Atwell Pl, T.Ditt. KT7 219 CF102
Atwell Rd, SE15 44 D9
Atwood, Bkhm KT23 252 BY124
Atwood Av, Rich. TW9 180 CN82
Sch Atwood Prim Sch, S.Croy.
CR2 off Limpsfield Rd 242 DU113
Atwood Rd, W6 181 CV77
Atwoods All, Rich. TW9
off Leyborne Pk 180 CN81
Auber Cl, Hodd. EN11 55 DZ14
Aubert Ct, N5 143 DP63
Aubert Pk, N5 143 DP63
Aubert Rd, N5 143 DP63
Aubrey Av, Lon.Col. AL2 83 CJ26
Aubrey Beardsley Ho, SW1
off Vauxhall Br Rd 29 M9
Aubrey Moore Pt, E15 12 F10
Aubrey Pl, NW8 15 N1
Aubrey Rd, E17 145 EA55
N8 143 DL57
W8 27 H2
Aubreys Rd, Hem.H. HP1 61 BE21
Aubrey Wk, W8 27 H3
Aubrietia Cl, Rom. RM3 128 FL53
Auburn Cl, SE14 45 L5
Aubyn Hill, SE27 204 DQ91
Aubyn Sq, SW15 181 CU84
Auckland Av, Rain. RM13 169 FF69
Auckland Cl, SE19 224 DT95
Enfield EN1 104 DV37
Tilbury RM18 193 GG82
Auckland Gdns, SE19 224 DS95
Auckland Hill, SE27 204 DQ91
Auckland Ri, SE19 224 DS95
Auckland Rd, E10 145 EB62
SE19 224 DT95
SW11 182 DE84
Caterham CR3 258 DS122
Ilford IG1 147 EP60
Kingston upon Thames KT1 220 CM98
Potters Bar EN6 85 CY32
Auckland St, SE11 42 C1
Auden Dr, Borwd. WD6 100 CN43
Auden Pl, NW1 6 G8
Sutton SM3
off Wordsworth Dr 239 CW105
Audleigh Pl, Chig. IG7 125 EN51
Audley Cl, N10 121 DH52
SW11 41 H10
Addlestone KT15 234 BH106
Borehamwood WD6 100 CN41
Audley Ct, E18 146 EF56
Pinner HA5
off Rickmansworth Rd 116 BW54
Audley Dr, E16 36 A2
Warlingham CR6 258 DW115
Audley Firs, Hersham KT12 236 BW105
Audley Gdns, Ilf. IG3 147 ET61
Loughton IG10 107 EQ40
Waltham Abbey EN9 89 EC34
Audley Pl, Sutt. SM2 240 DB108
Sch Audley Prim Sch, Cat. CR3
off Whyteleafe Rd 258 DT121
Audley Rd, NW4 141 CV58
W5 160 CM71
Enfield EN2 103 DP40
Richmond TW10 200 CM85
Audley Sq, W1 29 H2
Audley Wk, Orp. BR5 228 EW100
Audrey Cl, Beck. BR3 225 EB100
Audrey Gdns, Wem. HA0 139 CH61
Audrey Rd, Ilf. IG1 147 EP62
Audrey St, E2 10 C10
Audric Cl, Kings.T. KT2 220 CN95
Audwick Cl, Chsht EN8 89 DX28
Augur Cl, Stai. TW18 195 BF92
Augurs La, E13 24 B2
Augusta Cl, W.Mol. KT8
off Freeman Dr 218 BZ97
Augusta Rd, Twick. TW2 198 CC89
Augusta St, E14 22 C8
August End, Geo.Grn SL3 154 AY72
Augustine Cl, Colnbr. SL3 175 BE83
Augustine Ct, Wal.Abb. EN9
off Beaulieu Dr 89 EB33
Whyteleafe CR3
off Godstone Rd 258 DU119
Augustine Rd, W14 26 C7
Gravesend DA12 213 GJ87
Harrow HA3 116 CB53
Orpington BR5 228 EX97
August La, Albury GU5 282 BK144
Augustus Cl, W12
off Goldhawk Rd 181 CV75
Brentford TW8 179 CJ80
St. Albans AL3 64 CA22
Stanmore HA7 117 CK48
Augustus Ct, SE1 31 N8
Augustus Ho, NW1
off Augustus St 17 L2
Augustus La, Orp. BR6 228 EU103
Augustus Rd, SW19 201 CY88
Augustus St, NW1 17 K1
Aulay Lawrence Ct, N9
off Menon Dr 122 DV48
Aultone Way, Cars. SM5 222 DF104
Sutton SM1 222 DB103
Aultone Yd, Cars. SM5 222 DF104
Aulton Pl, SE11 42 F1
Aurelia Gdns, Croy. CR0 223 DM99
Aurelia Rd, Croy. CR0 223 DL100
Auriel Av, Dag. RM10 169 FD65
Auriga Ms, N1 9 M2
Auriol Cl, Wor.Pk. KT4
off Auriol Pk Rd 220 CS104
Auriol Dr, Grnf. UB6 159 CD66
Uxbridge UB10 156 BN65
Sch Auriol Jun Sch, Ewell
KT19 off Vale Rd 239 CT105
Auriol Pk Rd, Wor.Pk. KT4 220 CS104
Auriol Rd, W14 26 E9
Aurum Cl, Horl. RH6 291 DH149
Austell Gdns, NW7 118 CS48
Austen Apts, SE20
off Croydon Rd 224 DV96
Austen Cl, SE28 168 EV74
Greenhithe DA9 211 FW85
Loughton IG10 107 ER41
Tilbury RM18
off Coleridge Rd 193 GJ82
Austen Gdns, Dart. DA1 190 FM84
Austen Ho, NW6 15 J2
Austen Rd, Erith DA8 189 FB80
Guildford GU1 281 AZ135
Harrow HA2 138 CB61
Austenway, Chal.St.P. SL9 134 AX55
Austen Way, Slou. SL3 175 AZ79
Austenwood Cl, Chal.St.P. SL9 112 AW54
Austenwood La, Chal.St.P. SL9 112 AX54
Austin Av, Brom. BR2 226 EL99
Austin Cl, SE23 205 DZ87
Coulsdon CR5 257 DP118
Twickenham TW1 199 CJ85
Austin Ct, E6 off Kings Rd 166 EJ67
Austin Friars, EC2 19 M8
Austin Friars Pas, EC2 19 M8
Austin Friars Sq, EC2 19 M8
Austin Rd, SW11 40 G7
Hayes UB3 177 BT75
Northfleet DA11 213 GF88
Orpington BR5 228 EU100
Austin's La, Uxb. UB10 137 BQ62
Austins Mead, Bov. HP3 79 BB28
Austins Pl, Hem.H. HP2
off St. Mary's Rd 62 BK19
Austin St, E2 20 A3
Austin Waye, Uxb. UB8 156 BJ67
Austral Cl, Sid. DA15 207 ET90
Austral Dr, Horn. RM11 150 FK59
Australia Rd, W12 161 CV73
Slough SL1 154 AV74
Austral St, SE11 30 G8
Austyn Gdns, Surb. KT5 220 CP102
Austyns Pl, Ewell KT17 239 CU109
Autumn Cl, SW19 202 DC93
Enfield EN1 104 DU39
Slough SL1 153 AM74
Autumn Dr, Sutt. SM2 240 DB109
Autumn Glades, Hem.H. HP3 63 BQ22
Autumn Gro, Brom. BR1 206 EH93
Welwyn Garden City AL7 52 DB11
Autumn St, E3 12 B9
Auxiliaries Way, Uxb. UB9 135 BF57
Avalon Cl, SW20 221 CY96
W13 159 CG71
Enfield EN2 103 DN40
Orpington BR6 228 EX104
Watford WD25 82 BY32
Avalon Ct, Bushey WD23 98 CA40
Avalon Rd, SW6 39 L6
W13 159 CG70
Orpington BR6 228 EW103
Avante Ct, Kings.T. KT1 219 CK97
Avard Gdns, Orp. BR6 245 EQ105
Avarn Rd, SW17 202 DF93
Avebury, Slou. SL1 153 AN74
Avebury Ct, N1
off Avebury St 9 L9
Hemel Hempstead HP2 62 BN17
Avebury Pk, Surb. KT6 219 CK101
Avebury Rd, E11
off Southwest Rd 145 ED60
SW19 221 CZ95
Orpington BR6 227 ER104
Avebury St, N1 9 L9
AVELEY, S.Ock. RM15 171 FR73
Aveley Bypass, S.Ock. RM15 170 FQ73
Aveley Cl, Aveley RM15 171 FR74
Erith DA8 189 FF79
Sch Aveley Prim Sch, Aveley
RM15 off Stifford Rd 171 FS74
Aveley Rd, Rom. RM1 149 FD56
Upminster RM14 170 FP65
Aveline St, SE11 42 E1
Aveling Cl, Pur. CR8 241 DM113
Aveling Pk Rd, E17 123 EA54
Avelon Rd, Rain. RM13 169 FG67
Romford RM5 127 FD51
Ave Maria La, EC4 19 H9
Avenell Rd, N5 143 DP62
Avening Rd, SW18
off Brathway Rd 202 DA87
Avening Ter, SW18 202 DA86
Avenons Rd, E13 23 N5
Avenue, The, E4 123 ED51
E11 (Leytonstone) 146 EF61
E11 (Wanstead) 146 EH58
N3 120 DA54
N8 143 DN55

Avenue, The, N10 121 DJ54
N11 121 DH49
N17 122 DS54
NW6 4 E7
NW10 off Hillside 160 CR67
SE10 46 G4
SW4 202 DG85
SW11 202 DE87
SW18 202 DE87
W4 180 CS76
W13 159 CH73
Amersham HP7 77 AQ38
Barnet EN5 101 CY41
Beckenham BR3 225 EB95
Bexley DA5 208 EX87
Brentwood CM13 129 FW51
Brockham RH3 270 CN134
Bromley BR1 226 EK97
Bushey WD23 98 BZ42
Carshalton SM5 240 DG108
Cheam SM3 239 CW108
Chobham GU24 232 AT109
Claygate KT10 237 CE107
Coulsdon CR5 257 DK115
Cowley UB8 156 BK70
Cranford TW5 177 BU81
Croydon CR0 224 DS104
Datchet SL3 174 AV81
Egham TW20 195 BB91
Epsom KT17 239 CV108
Farnham Common SL2 133 AP64
Gravesend DA11 213 GG88
Greenhithe DA9 191 FV84
Hampton TW12 198 BZ93
Harrow HA3 117 CF53
Hatch End HA5 116 CA52
Hemel Hempstead HP1 61 BE19
Hertford SG14 53 DP07
Hoddesdon EN11 71 DZ19
Horley RH6 290 DF149
Hornchurch RM12 150 FJ61
Hounslow TW3 198 CB85
Ickenham UB10 136 BN63
Isleworth TW7 179 CD79
Keston BR2 226 EK104
Leatherhead KT22 237 CF112
Loughton IG10 106 EK44
Nazeing EN9 90 EJ25
New Haw KT15 234 BG110
Northwood HA6 115 BQ51
Old Windsor SL4 194 AV85
Orpington BR6 227 ET103
Pinner HA5 138 BZ58
Potters Bar EN6 85 CZ30
Radlett WD7 83 CG33
Richmond TW9 180 CM82
Romford RM1 149 FD56
St. Paul's Cray BR5 208 EV94
South Nutfield RH1 289 DL137
Staines TW18 216 BH95
Sunbury-on-Thames TW16 217 BV95
Surbiton KT5 220 CM100
Sutton SM2 239 CZ109
Tadworth KT20 255 CV122
Twickenham TW1 199 CJ85
Watford WD17 97 BU40
Wembley HA9 140 CM61
West Drayton UB7 176 BL76
West Wickham BR4 225 EC101
Westerham TN16 261 EM122
Whyteleafe CR3 258 DU119
Worcester Park KT4 221 CT103
Worplesdon GU3 264 AS127
Wraysbury TW19 174 AX83
Avenue App, Kings L. WD4 80 BN30
Avenue Cl, N14 103 DJ44
NW8 6 D9
Hounslow TW5 177 BU81
Romford RM3 128 FM52
Tadworth KT20 255 CV122
West Drayton UB7 176 BK76
Avenue Ct, Tad. KT20
off The Avenue 255 CV123
Avenue Cres, W3 180 CP75
Hounslow TW5 177 BV80
Avenue Dr, Slou. SL3 155 AZ71
Avenue Elmers, Surb. KT6 220 CL99
Avenue Gdns, SE25 224 DU97
SW14 180 CS83
W3 180 CP75
Horley RH6 291 DJ149
Hounslow TW5 177 BU80
Teddington TW11 199 CF94
Avenue Gate, Loug. IG10 106 EJ44
● Avenue Ind Est, E4 123 DZ51
Romford RM3 128 FK54
Avenue Ms, N10 143 DH55
Avenue Pk Rd, SE27 203 DP89
Sch Avenue Prim Sch, E12
off Meanley Rd 146 EL64
Cheam SM2 off Avenue Rd 240 DA110
Avenue Ri, Bushey WD23 98 CA43
Tram Avenue Road 225 DX96
Avenue Rd, E7 146 EH64
N6 143 DJ59
N12 120 DC49
N14 121 DH45
N15 144 DR57
NW3 6 A6
NW8 6 B7
NW10 161 CT68
SE20 224 DW95
SE25 224 DU96
SW16 223 DK96
SW20 221 CV96
W3 180 CP75
Banstead SM7 256 DB115
Beckenham BR3 224 DW95
Belvedere DA17 189 FC77
Bexleyheath DA7 188 EY83
Brentford TW8 179 CJ78
Caterham CR3 258 DR122
Chadwell Heath RM6 148 EV59
Cobham KT11 252 BX116
Epsom KT18 238 CR114
Erith DA8 189 FC80
Feltham TW13 197 BT90
Hampton TW12 218 CB95
Harold Wood RM3 128 FM52
Hoddesdon EN11 71 ED19
Isleworth TW7 179 CF81
Kingston upon Thames KT1 220 CL97
New Malden KT3 220 CS98
Pinner HA5 138 BY55
St. Albans AL1 65 CE19
Sevenoaks TN13 279 FJ123
Southall UB1 178 BZ75
Staines TW18 195 BD92
Sutton SM2 240 DA110
Avenue Rd, Tats. TN16 260 EL120
Teddington TW11 199 CG94
Theydon Bois CM16 107 ER36
Wallington SM6 241 DJ108
Warley CM14 130 FW49
Woodford Green IG8 124 EJ51
Avenue Rd Est, E11
off High Rd Leytonstone 145 ED63
Avenue S, Surb. KT5 220 CM101
Avenue Ter, N.Mal. KT3
off Kingston Rd 220 CQ97
Watford WD19 98 BY44
Averil Ct, Tap. SL6 152 AJ72
Averil Gro, SW16 203 DP93
Averill St, W6 38 C3
Avern Gdns, W.Mol. KT8 218 CB98
Avern Rd, W.Mol. KT8 218 CB99
Avery Fm Row, SW1 29 J9
Avery Gdns, Ilf. IG2 147 EM57
AVERY HILL, SE9 207 EQ86
★ Avery Hill Pk, SE9 207 EQ86
Avery Hill Rd, SE9 207 ER86
Avery Row, W1 17 J10
Avey La, High Beach IG10 106 EH39
Waltham Abbey EN9 105 ED36
Avia Cl, Hem.H. HP3 62 BK24
Aviary Cl, E16 23 M7
Aviary Rd, Wok. GU22 250 BG116
● Aviator Pk, Add. KT15 216 BK104
Aviemore Cl, Beck. BR3 225 DZ99
Aviemore Way, Beck. BR3 225 DY99
Sch Avigdor Hirsch Torah Temimah Prim Sch,
NW2 off Parkside 141 CV63
Avignon Rd, SE4 45 K10
Avington Cl, Guil. GU1
off London Rd 264 AY134
Avington Ct, SE1
off Old Kent Rd 31 P9
Avington Gro, SE20 204 DW94
Avion Cres, NW9 119 CU53
Avior Dr, Nthwd. HA6 115 BT49
Avis Gro, Croy. CR0 243 DY110
Avis Sq, E1 21 K8
Avoca Rd, SW17 202 DG91
Avocet Cl, SE1 32 C10
St. Albans AL3 64 CC17
Avocet Ms, SE28 187 ER76
Avon Cl, Add. KT15 234 BG107
Gravesend DA12 213 GK89
Hayes UB4 158 BW70
Slough SL1 153 AL73
Sutton SM1 240 DC105
Watford WD25 82 BW34
Worcester Park KT4 221 CU103
Avon Ct, Buck.H. IG9
off Chequers 124 EH46
Greenford UB6
off Braund Av 158 CB70
Avondale Av, N12 120 DB50
NW2 140 CS62
Barnet EN4 120 DF46
Esher KT10 219 CG104
Staines TW18 195 BF94
Worcester Park KT4 221 CT102
Avondale Cl, Hersham KT12
off Pleasant Pl 236 BW106
Horley RH6 290 DF146
Loughton IG10 125 EM45
Avondale Ct, E11 146 EE60
E16 23 K6
E18 124 EH53
Avondale Cres, Enf. EN3 105 DY41
Ilford IG4 146 EK57
Avondale Dr, Hayes UB3 157 BU74
Loughton IG10 125 EM45
Avondale Gdns, Houns. TW4 198 BZ85
Avondale Ho, SE1
off Avondale Sq 44 C1
Avondale Pk Gdns, W11 26 E1
Sch Avondale Pk Prim Sch, W11 26 E1
Avondale Pk Rd, W11 14 E10
Avondale Ri, SE15 44 A10
Avondale Rd, E16 23 K6
E17 145 EA59
N3 120 DC53
N13 121 DN47
N15 143 DP57
SE9 206 EL89
SW14 180 CR83
SW19 202 DB92
Ashford TW15 196 BK90
Bromley BR1 206 EE93
Harrow HA3 139 CF55
South Croydon CR2 242 DQ107
Welling DA16 188 EW82
Avondale Sq, SE1 44 C1
Avon Grn, S.Ock. RM15 171 FV72
Sch Avon Ho Sch, Wdf.Grn. IG8
off High Rd Woodford Grn 124 EG49
Avonley Rd, SE14 45 H5
Avonmead, Wok. GU21
off Silversmiths Way 248 AW118
Avon Ms, Pnr. HA5 116 BZ53
Avonmore Av, Guil. GU1 265 AZ133
Avonmore Gdns, W14
off Avonmore Rd 26 G9
Avonmore Pl, W14 26 F8
Sch Avonmore Prim Sch, W14 26 F8
Avonmore Rd, W14 26 G8
Avonmor Ms, Ripley GU23 250 BH122
Avonmouth Rd, Dart. DA1 210 FK85
Avonmouth St, SE1 31 J6
Avon Path, S.Croy. CR2 242 DQ107
Avon Pl, SE1 31 K5
Avon Rd, E17 145 ED55
SE4 46 A10
Greenford UB6 158 CA70
Sunbury-on-Thames TW16 197 BT94
Upminster RM14 151 FR58
Avon Sq, Hem.H. HP2 62 BM15
Avonstowe Cl, Orp. BR6 227 EQ104
Avontar Rd, S.Ock. RM15 171 FV70
Avon Way, E18 146 EG55
Avonwick Rd, Houns. TW3 178 CB82
Avril Way, E4 123 EC50
Avro Way, Wall. SM6 241 DL108
Weybridge KT13 234 BL110
Awlfield Av, N17 122 DR53
Awliscombe Rd, Well. DA16 187 ET82
Axes La, Red. RH1 289 DJ141
Axe St, Bark. IG11 167 EQ67
Axholme Av, Edg. HA8 118 CN53
Axiom Apts, Rom. RM1
off Mercury Gdns 149 FF56
● Axis Cen, Lthd. KT22 253 CF119
Axis Ct, SE10 47 J2
SE16 off East La 32 D4
● Axis Pk, Langley SL3 175 BB78
Axminster Cres, Well. DA16 188 EW81
Axminster Rd, N7 143 DL62
Axon Pl, Ilf. IG1 147 EQ61
Axtaine Rd, Orp. BR5 228 EX101
Axtane, Sthflt DA13 212 FZ94
Axtane Cl, Sutt.H. DA4 230 FQ96
Axwood, Epsom KT18 254 CQ115
Aybrook St, W1 16 G7
Aycliffe Cl, Brom. BR1 227 EM98
Aycliffe Dr, Hem.H. HP2 62 BL16
Sch Aycliffe Dr Prim Sch, Hem.H.
HP2 off Aycliffe Dr 62 BL16
Aycliffe Rd, W12 161 CT74
Borehamwood WD6 100 CL39
Ayebridges Av, Egh. TW20 195 BC94
Aylands Cl, Wem. HA9
off Preston Rd 140 CL61
Aylands Rd, Enf. EN3 104 DW36
Sch Aylands Sch, Enf. EN3
off Keswick Dr 104 DW36
Aylesbury Cl, E7 13 M4
Aylesbury Ct, Sutt. SM1
off Benhill Wd Rd 222 DC104
Aylesbury Cres, Slou. SL1 153 AR72
Aylesbury End, Beac. HP9 111 AL54
Aylesbury Est, SE17 43 M1
Aylesbury Rd, SE17 43 M1
Bromley BR2 226 EG97
Aylesbury St, EC1 18 G5
NW10 140 CR62
Aylesford Av, Beck. BR3 225 DY99
Aylesford St, SW1 29 N10
🔒 Aylesham Cen, SE15 44 C7
Aylesham Cl, NW7 119 CU52
Aylesham Rd, Orp. BR6 227 ET101
Ayles Rd, Hayes UB4 157 BV69
Aylestone Av, NW6 4 C8
Aylesworth Av, Slou. SL2
off Doddsfield Rd 153 AN69
Aylesworth Spur, Old Wind.
SL4 194 AV87
Aylets Fld, Harl. CM18 73 ES19
Aylett Rd, SE25 224 DV98
Isleworth TW7 179 CE82
Upminster RM14 150 FQ61
Ayley Cft, Enf. EN1 104 DU43
Ayliffe Cl, Kings.T. KT1
off Cambridge Gdns 220 CN96
Aylmer Cl, Stan. HA7 117 CG49
Aylmer Dr, Stan. HA7 117 CG49
Aylmer Par, N2 142 DF57
Aylmer Rd, E11 146 EF60
N2 142 DE57
W12 180 CS75
Dagenham RM8 148 EY62
Ayloffe Rd, Dag. RM9 168 EZ65
Sch Ayloff Prim Sch, Elm Pk
RM12 off South End Rd 149 FH63
Ayloffs Cl, Horn. RM11 150 FL57
Ayloffs Wk, Horn. RM11 150 FK57
Aylsham Dr, Uxb. UB10 137 BR62
Aylsham La, Rom. RM3 128 FJ49
Aylsham Rd, Hodd. EN11 71 EC15
Aylton Est, SE16 33 H5
Sch Aylward First & Mid Sch, Stan.
HA7 off Pangbourne Dr 117 CK50
Aylward Gdns, Chesh. HP5 76 AN30
Aylward Rd, SE23 205 DX89
SW20 221 CZ96
Sch Aylward Sch, N18
off Windmill Rd 122 DR49
Aylwards Ri, Stan. HA7 117 CG49
Aylward St, E1 20 G8
Aylwyn Est, SE1 31 P6
Aymer Cl, Stai. TW18 215 BE95
Aymer Dr, Stai. TW18 215 BE95
Aynhoe Rd, W14 26 D8
Aynho St, Wat. WD18 97 BV43
Aynscombe Angle, Orp. BR6 228 EV101
Aynscombe La, SW14 180 CQ83
Aynscombe Path, SW14
off Thames Bk 180 CQ82
Aynsley Gdns, Harl. CM17 74 EW15
AYOT GREEN, Welw. AL6 51 CU07
Ayot Grn, Welw. AL6 51 CU06
Ayot Greenway, St.Alb. AL4 50 CN06
Ayot Little Grn, Ayot St.P. AL6 51 CT06
Ayot Path, Borwd. WD6 100 CN37
Ayot St. Peter Rd, Welw. AL6 51 CT05
Ayr Ct, W3 160 CN71
Ayres Cl, E13 23 P3
Ayres St, SE1 31 K4
Ayr Grn, Rom. RM1 127 FE52
Ayrsome Rd, N16 144 DS62
Ayrton Gould Ho, E2 21 K2
Ayrton Rd, SW7 28 A6
Ayr Way, Rom. RM1 127 FE52
Aysgarth Ct, Sutt. SM1
off Sutton Common Rd 222 DB104
Aysgarth Rd, SE21 204 DS86
Aytoun Pl, SW9 42 D9
Aytoun Rd, SW9 42 D9
Azalea Cl, W7 159 CF74
Ilford IG1 147 EP64
London Colney AL2 83 CH27
Azalea Ct, Wok. GU22 248 AX119
Woodford Green IG8
off The Bridle Path 124 EE52
Azalea Dr, Swan. BR8 229 FD98
Azalea Ho, Felt. TW13
off Bedfont La 197 BV88
Azalea Wk, Pnr. HA5 137 BV57
Azalea Way, Geo.Grn SL3
off Blinco La 154 AY72
Azania Ms, NW5 7 J4
Azenby Rd, SE15 44 A8
Sch Azhar Acad Girl's Sch, E7 13 N4
Azile Everitt Ho, SE18
off Blendon Ter 187 EQ78
Azof St, SE10 35 K9

B

Baalbec Rd, N5 9 H3
Baas Hill, Brox. EN10 71 DX21
Baas Hill Cl, Brox. EN10 71 DY21
Baas La, Brox. EN10 71 DY21
Babbacombe Cl, Chess. KT9 237 CK106
Babbacombe Gdns, Ilf. IG4 146 EL56
Babbacombe Rd, Brom. BR1 226 EG95
Baber Dr, Felt. TW14 198 BW86
Babington Ct, WC1
off Ormond Cl 18 B6
Sch Babington Ho Sch, Chis.
BR7 off Grange Dr 207 EM93
Babington Ri, Wem. HA9 160 CN65
Babington Rd, NW4 141 CV56
SW16 203 DK92
Dagenham RM8 148 EW64
Hornchurch RM12 149 FH60
Babmaes St, SW1 29 N1
Babylon La, Lwr Kgswd KT20 272 DA127
Bacchus Wk, N1 19 N1
Bachelors Acre, Wind. SL4 173 AR81
Bachelor's La, Wok. GU23 250 BN124
Baches St, N1 19 M3
Back, The, Pott.End HP4 61 BB16
Back All, Dor. RH4 285 CH136
Back Ch La, E1 20 C10
Back Grn, Hersham KT12 236 BW107
Back Hill, EC1 18 E5
Backhouse Pl, SE17 31 P9
Back La, N8 143 DL57
NW3 off Heath St 142 DC63
Bexley DA5 208 FA87
Brentford TW8 179 CK79
Buckhurst Hill IG9 124 EK47
Chalfont St. Giles HP8 112 AU48
Chenies WD3 95 BB38
East Clandon GU4 266 BK130
Edgware HA8 118 CQ53
Godden Green TN15 279 FN124
Hertford SG13 70 DQ18
Ide Hill TN14 278 FC126
Letchmore Heath WD25 99 CE39
Nazeing EN9 72 EJ23
North Stifford RM16 171 FW74
Purfleet RM19 191 FS76
Richmond TW10 199 CJ90
Romford RM6
off St. Chad's Rd 148 EY59
Sheering CM22 58 FA06
Tewin AL6 52 DE05
Backley Gdns, SE25 224 DU100
Back of High St, Chobham
GU24 off High St 232 AS111
Back Path, Red. RH1 274 DQ133
Back Rd, Sid. DA14 208 EU91
Backs, The, Chesh. HP5 76 AQ31
Back St, Harl. CM17
off Broadway Av 58 EW11
Bacon Gro, SE1 32 A7
Bacon La, NW9 140 CP56
Edgware HA8 118 CN53
Bacon Link, Rom. RM5 127 FB51
Sch Bacon's Coll, SE16 33 L4
Bacons Dr, Cuffley EN6 87 DL29
Bacons La, N6 142 DG60
Bacons Mead, Denh. UB9 136 BG61
Bacon St, E1 20 B4
E2 20 B4
Bacon Ter, Dag. RM8
off Fitzstephen Rd 148 EV64
Bacton, NW5 6 F2
Bacton St, E2 21 H2
Badburgham Ct, Wal.Abb. EN9 90 EF33
Baddeley Cl, Enf. EN3 105 EA37
Baddow Cl, Dag. RM10 168 FA67
Woodford Green IG8 124 EK51
Baddow Wk, N1 9 J8
Baden Cl, Stai. TW18 196 BG94
Baden Dr, Horl. RH6 290 DE147
Baden Pl, SE1 31 L4
Baden Powell Cl, Dag. RM9 168 EY67
Surbiton KT6 220 CM103
Sch Baden-Powell Prim Sch,
E5 off Ferron Rd 144 DV62
Baden Powell Rd, Sev. TN13 278 FE121
Baden Rd, N8 143 DK56
Guildford GU2 264 AU132
Ilford IG1 147 EP64
Bader Cl, Ken. CR8 258 DR115
Welwyn Garden City AL7 52 DC09
Bader Gdns, Slou. SL1 173 AN75
Bader Wk, Nthflt DA11 212 GE90
Bader Way, Rain. RM13 169 FG65
Badger Cl, Felt. TW13 197 BV90
Guildford GU2 264 AV131
Hounslow TW4 178 BW83
Ilford IG2 147 EQ59
Badgers Cl, Ashf. TW15 196 BM92
Borehamwood WD6
off Kingsley Av 100 CM40
Enfield EN2 103 DP41
Harrow HA1 139 CD58
Hayes UB3 157 BS73
Hertford SG13 54 DV09
Woking GU21 248 AW118
Badgers Copse, Orp. BR6 227 ET103
Worcester Park KT4 221 CT103
Badgers Cft, N20 119 CY46
SE9 207 EN90
Broxbourne EN10 71 DY21
Hemel Hempstead HP2 63 BR21
BADGERS DENE, Grays RM17 192 FZ77
Badgers Hill, Vir.W. GU25 214 AW99
Badgers Hole, Croy. CR0 243 DX105
Badgers La, Warl. CR6 258 DW120
BADGERS MOUNT, Sev. TN14 247 FB110
Badgers Mt, Orsett RM16 193 GF75
Badgers Ri, Bad.Mt TN14 246 FA110
Badgers Rd, Bad.Mt TN14 247 FB110
Badgers Wk, Chorl. WD3 95 BF42
New Malden KT3 220 CS96
Purley CR8 241 DK111
Whyteleafe CR3 258 DT119
Badgers Wd, Chaldon CR3 274 DQ125
Farnham Common SL2 133 AQ64
Badger Way, Hat. AL10 67 CV20
Badingham Dr, Fetch. KT22 253 CE123
Badlis Rd, E17 123 EA54
Badlow Cl, Erith DA8 189 FE80
Badma Cl, N9 off Hudson Way 122 DW48
Badminton Cl, Borwd. WD6 100 CN40
Harrow HA1 139 CE56
Northolt UB5 158 CA65
Badminton Ms, E16 35 P2
Badminton Pl, Brox. EN10 71 DY20
Badminton Rd, SW12 202 DG86
Badric Ct, SW11 40 B9
Badsworth Rd, SE5 43 J5
Baffin Way, E14 34 F1
Bafton Gate, Brom. BR2 226 EH102
Bagden Hill, Westh. RH5 269 CD130
Bagley Cl, West Dr. UB7 176 BL75
Bagley's La, SW6 39 M7
Bagleys Spring, Rom. RM6 148 EY56
Bagot Cl, Ashtd. KT21 254 CM116
Bagshot Ct, SE18
off Prince Imperial Rd 187 EN81
Bagshot Rd, Enf. EN1 122 DT45
Englefield Green TW20 194 AW94
Bagshot St, SE17 43 P1
Bahram Rd, Epsom KT19 238 CR110
Baildon St, SE8 45 P5
Bailey Cl, E4 123 EC49
N11 121 DK52
SE28 167 ES74
Purfleet RM19
off Gabion Av 191 FR77
Windsor SL4 173 AN82
Bailey Cres, Chess. KT9 237 CK108
Bailey Ho, SE18
off Berber Par 186 EL81
Bailey Ms, SW2 203 DN85
W4 off Herbert Gdns 180 CP79
Bailey Pl, SE26 205 DX93
Bailey Rd, Westc. RH4 284 CC137
Baillie Cl, Rain. RM13 169 FH70
Baillie Rd, Guil. GU1 281 AZ135
Baillies Wk, W5
off Liverpool Rd 179 CK75
Bainbridge Cl, Ham TW10
off Latchmere Cl 200 CL92
Bainbridge Rd, Dag. RM9 148 EZ63
Bainbridge St, WC1 17 P8
Baines Cl, S.Croy. CR2
off Brighton Rd 242 DR106
Baines Wk, Chesh. HP5
off High St 76 AP31
Bainton Mead, Wok. GU21 248 AU117
Baird Av, Sthl. UB1 158 CB73
Baird Cl, E10 off Marconi Rd 145 EA60
NW9 140 CQ58
Bushey WD23
off Ashfield Av 98 CB44
Slough SL1 173 AP75
Baird Gdns, SE19 204 DS91
Baird Rd, Enf. EN1 104 DV42
Baird St, EC1 19 K4
Bairny Wd App, Wdf.Grn. IG8
off Broadway Cl 124 EH51
Bairstow Cl, Borwd. WD6 100 CL39
Baizdon Rd, SE3 47 J9
Bakeham La, Eng.Grn TW20 194 AW94
Bakehouse Ms, Hmptn. TW12 198 CA94
Bakehouse Rd, Horl. RH6 290 DF146
Baker Boy La, Croy. CR0 243 DZ112
Baker Cres, Dart. DA1 210 FJ87
Baker Hill Cl, Nthflt DA11 213 GF91
Baker La, Mitch. CR4 222 DG96
Baker Pas, NW10 off Baker Rd 160 CS67
Baker Pl, Epsom KT19 238 CQ107
Baker Rd, NW10 160 CS67
SE18 186 EL80
Bakers Av, E17 145 EB58
Bakers Cl, Ken. CR8 242 DQ114
St. Albans AL1 65 CG21
Bakers Ct, SE25 224 DS97
Bakerscroft, Chsht EN8 89 DX28
Bakers End, SW20 221 CY96
Bakers Fld, N7 143 DK63
Bakers Gdns, Cars. SM5 222 DE103
Bakers Gro, Welw.G.C. AL7 52 DC08
Bakers Hall Ct, EC3 31 P1
Bakers Hill, E5 144 DW60
New Barnet EN5 102 DB40
Bakers La, N6 142 DF58
Epping CM16 91 ET30
High Wych CM21 57 ET05
Bakers Mead, Gdse. RH9 274 DW130
Baker's Ms, W1 16 G8
Bakers Ms, Orp. BR6 245 ET107
Bakers Orchard, Woob.Grn
HP10 132 AE58
Bakers Pas, NW3 5 P1
Baker's Rents, E2 20 A3
Bakers Rd, Chsht EN7 88 DV30
Uxbridge UB8 156 BK66
Bakers Row, E15 13 J10
Baker's Row, EC1 18 E5
⊖ Baker Street 16 F6
Baker St, NW1 16 F5
W1 16 F6
Enfield EN1 104 DR41
Hertford SG13 54 DS09
Potters Bar EN6 101 CY35
Weybridge KT13 234 BN105
Bakers Wk, Saw. CM21 58 EY05
Bakers Wd, Denh. UB9 135 BD60
Baker's Yd, EC1 18 E5
Uxbridge UB8
off Bakers Rd 156 BK66
Bakery Cl, SW9 42 D6
Roydon CM19 72 EJ15
Bakery Path, Edg. HA8
off Station Rd 118 CP51
Bakery Pl, SW11
off Altenburg Gdns 182 DF84
Bakewell Way, N.Mal. KT3 220 CS96
Balaams La, N14 121 DK47
Balaam St, E13 23 P4
Balaclava Rd, SE1 32 B9
Surbiton KT6 219 CJ101
Bala Grn, NW9
off Snowdon Dr 140 CS58
Balcary Gdns, Berk. HP4 60 AS20
Balcaskie Rd, SE9 207 EM85
Balchen Rd, SE3 186 EK82
Balchier Rd, SE22 204 DV86
Balchins La, Westc. RH4 284 CA138
Balcombe Cl, Bexh. DA6 188 EX84
Balcombe Gdns, Horl. RH6 291 DJ149
Balcombe Rd, Horl. RH6 291 DH147
Balcombe St, NW1 16 E5
Balcon Ct, W5 off Boileau Rd 160 CM72
Balcon Way, Borwd. WD6 100 CQ39
Balcorne St, E9 11 H7
Balder Ri, SE12 206 EH89
Balderton St, W1 17 H9
Baldocks Rd, They.B. CM16 107 ES35
Baldock St, E3 22 C1
Ware SG12 55 DX06
Baldock Way, Borwd. WD6 100 CM39
Baldry Gdns, SW16 203 DL93
Baldwin Cres, SE5 43 J6
Guildford GU4 265 BC132
Baldwin Gdns, Houns. TW3
off Chamberlain Gdns 178 CC81
Baldwin Rd, SW11 202 DG86
Beaconsfield HP9 111 AP54
Burnham SL1 152 AJ69
Baldwins, Welw.G.C. AL7 52 DB09
Baldwin's Gdns, EC1 18 E6
Baldwins Hill, Loug. IG10 107 EM40

Baldwins La, Crox.Grn WD3 96 BN42
Baldwins Shore, Eton SL4 173 AR79
Baldwin St, EC1 19 L3
Baldwin Ter, N1 9 J10
Baldwyn Gdns, W3 160 CQ73
Baldwyns Pk, Bex. DA5 209 FD89
Baldwyns Rd, Bex. DA5 209 FD89
Balearic Apts, E16
off Western Gateway 35 P1
Bale Rd, E1 21 L6
Bales Coll, W10 14 D3
Balfern Gro, W4 180 CS78
Balfern St, SW11 40 D7
Balfe St, N1 18 B1
Balfont Cl, S.Croy. CR2 242 DU113
Balfour Av, W7 159 CF74
Woking GU22 248 AY122
● Balfour Business Cen, Sthl. UB2 178 BX76
Balfour Gro, N20 120 DF48
Balfour Ho, W10 14 D6
Balfour Ms, N9 off Fore St 122 DU48
W1 29 H2
Bovingdon HP3 79 AZ27
Balfour Pl, SW15 181 CV84
W1 29 H1
Balfour Rd, N5 9 J1
SE25 224 DU98
SW19 202 DB94
W3 160 CQ71
W13 179 CG75
Bromley BR2 226 EK99
Carshalton SM5 240 DF108
Grays RM17 192 GC77
Harrow HA1 139 CD57
Hounslow TW3 178 CB83
Ilford IG1 147 EP61
Southall UB2 178 BX76
Weybridge KT13 234 BN105
Balfour St, SE17 31 L8
Hertford SG14 54 DQ08
Balfron Twr, E14 22 E8
Balgonie Rd, E4 123 ED46
Balgores Cres, Rom. RM2 149 FH55
Balgores La, Rom. RM2 149 FH55
Balgores Sq, Rom. RM2 149 FH56
Balgowan Cl, N.Mal. KT3 220 CS99
Balgowan Prim Sch, Beck. BR3 off Balgowan Rd 225 DY96
Balgowan Rd, Beck. BR3 225 DY97
Balgowan St, SE18 187 ET77
BALHAM, SW12 202 DF88
⇌ Balham 203 DH88
⊖ Balham 203 DH88
Balham Continental Mkt, SW12 off Shipka Rd 203 DH88
Balham Gro, SW12 202 DG87
Balham High Rd, SW12 202 DG88
SW17 202 DG89
Balham Hill, SW12 203 DH87
Balham New Rd, SW12 203 DH87
Balham Pk Rd, SW12 202 DF88
Balham Rd, N9 122 DU47
Balham Sta Rd, SW12 203 DH88
Balkan Wk, E1 32 E1
Balladier Wk, E14 22 C7
Ballamore Rd, Brom. BR1 206 EG90
Ballance Rd, E9 11 K4
Ballands N, The, Fetch. KT22 253 CE122
Ballands S, The, Fetch. KT22 253 CE123
Ballantine St, SW18 182 DC84
Ballantyne Cl, SE9 206 EL91
Ballantyne Dr, Kgswd KT20 255 CZ121
Ballard Cl, Kings.T. KT2 200 CR94
Ballard Grn, Wind. SL4 173 AL80
Ballards Cl, Dag. RM10 169 FB67
Ballards Fm Rd, Croy. CR0 242 DU107
South Croydon CR2 242 DU107
Ballards Grn, Tad. KT20 255 CY119
Ballards La, N3 120 DA53
N12 120 DA53
Oxted RH8 276 EJ129
Ballards Ms, Edg. HA8 118 CN51
Ballards Ri, S.Croy. CR2 242 DU107
Ballards Rd, NW2 141 CU61
Dagenham RM10 169 FB67
Ballards Way, Croy. CR0 242 DV107
South Croydon CR2 242 DU107
Ballast Quay, SE10 35 H10
Ballater Cl, Wat. WD19 116 BW49
Ballater Rd, SW2 183 DL84
South Croydon CR2 242 DT106
Ball Ct, EC3 off Castle Ct 19 M9
Ballenger Ct, Wat. WD18 97 BV41
Ballina St, SE23 205 DX87
Ballingdon Rd, SW11 202 DG86
Ballinger Ct, Berk. HP4 60 AV20
Ballinger Pt, E3 22 C2
Ballinger Way, Nthlt. UB5 158 BY70
Balliol Av, E4 123 ED49
Balliol Rd, N17 122 DS53
W10 14 B8
Welling DA16 188 EV82
Balloch Rd, SE6 205 ED88
Ballogie Av, NW10 140 CS63
Ballow Cl, SE5 43 N5
Balls Pk, Hert. SG13 54 DT11
Balls Pond Pl, N1 9 M4
Balls Pond Rd, N1 9 M4
Balmain Cl, W5 159 CK74
Balmer Rd, E3 21 N1
Balmes Rd, N1 9 M8
Balmoral Apts, W2
off Praed St 16 C7
Balmoral Av, N11 120 DG50
Beckenham BR3 225 DY98
Balmoral Cl, SW15 201 CX86
Park Street AL2 82 CC28
Slough SL1 153 AL72
Balmoral Ct, Wor.Pk. KT4 221 CV103
Balmoral Cres, W.Mol. KT8 218 CA97
Balmoral Dr, Borwd. WD6 100 CR43
Hayes UB4 157 BT71
Southall UB1 158 BZ70
Woking GU22 249 BC116
Balmoral Gdns, W13 179 CG76
Bexley DA5 208 EZ87
Ilford IG3 147 ET60
South Croydon CR2 242 DR110
Windsor SL4 173 AR83
Balmoral Gro, N7 8 C5
Balmoral Ms, W12 181 CT76
Balmoral Rd, E7 146 EJ63
E10 145 EB61
NW2 161 CV65
Abbots Langley WD5 81 BU32
Enfield EN3 105 DX36
Harrow HA2 138 CA63
Hornchurch RM12 150 FK62
Kingston upon Thames KT1 220 CM98
Pilgrim's Hatch CM15 130 FV44
Romford RM2 149 FH56
Sutton at Hone DA4 210 FP94
Watford WD24 98 BW38
Worcester Park KT4 221 CV104
Balmoral Way, Sutt. SM2 240 DA110
Balmore Cl, E14 22 F8
Balmore Cres, Barn. EN4 102 DG43
Balmore St, N19 143 DH61
Balmuir Gdns, SW15 181 CW84
Balnacraig Av, NW10 140 CS63
Balniel Gate, SW1 29 P10
Balquhain Cl, Ashtd. KT21 253 CK117
Balsams Cl, Hert. SG13 54 DR11
Baltic Apts, E16
off Western Gateway 35 P1
Baltic Cl, SW19 202 DD94
Baltic Ct, SE16 33 K4
Baltic Pl, N1 9 P9
Baltic Quay, SE16 33 M8
Baltic St E, EC1 19 J5
Baltic St W, EC1 19 J5
Baltic Wf, Grav. DA11 213 GG86
Baltimore Ho, SW18
off Juniper Dr 182 DC84
Baltimore Pl, Well. DA16 187 ET82
Balvaird Pl, SW1 41 P1
Balvernie Gro, SW18 201 CZ87
Bamber Ho, Bark. IG11
off St. Margarets 167 EQ67
Bamber Rd, SE15 44 A6
Bamboo Ct, E5 144 DW61
Bamborough Gdns, W12 26 B5
Bamford Av, Wem. HA0 160 CM67
Bamford Rd, Bark. IG11 167 EQ65
Bromley BR1 205 EC92
Bamford Way, Rom. RM5 127 FB50
Bampfylde Cl, Wall. SM6 223 DJ104
Bampton Dr, NW7 119 CU52
Bampton Rd, SE23 205 DX90
Romford RM3 128 FL52
Bampton Way, Wok. GU21 248 AU118
Banavie Gdns, Beck. BR3 225 EC95
Banbury Av, Slou. SL1 153 AM71
Banbury Cl, Enf. EN2
off Holtwhites Hill 103 DP39
Banbury Ct, WC2 18 A10
Sutton SM2 240 DA108
● Banbury Enterprise Cen, Croy. CR0 off Factory La 223 DP103
Banbury Rd, E9 11 J7
E17 123 DX52
Banbury St, SW11 40 D8
Watford WD18 97 BU43
Banbury Vil, Grav. DA13 212 FZ94
Banbury Wk, Nthlt. UB5
off Brabazon Rd 158 CA68
Banchory Rd, SE3 186 EH80
Bancroft Av, N2 142 DE57
Buckhurst Hill IG9 124 EG47
Bancroft Chase, Horn. RM12 149 FF61
Bancroft Cl, Ashf. TW15
off Feltham Hill Rd 196 BN92
Bancroft Ct, SW8 42 A6
Northolt UB5 158 BW67
Reigate RH2 272 DB134
Bancroft Gdns, Har. HA3 116 CC53
Orpington BR6 227 ET102
Bancroft Rd, E1 21 H3
Harrow HA3 116 CC54
Reigate RH2 272 DA134
Bancroft's Sch, Wdf.Grn. IG8
off High Rd Woodford Grn 124 EG48
Banders Ri, Guil. GU1 265 BC133
Band La, Egh. TW20 195 AZ92
Bandon Cl, Uxb. UB10 156 BM67
Bandon Hill Prim Sch, Wall. SM6 off Sandy La S 241 DK107
Bandon Ri, Wall. SM6 241 DK106
Banes Down, Lwr Naze. EN9 72 EE22
Banfield Rd, SE15 184 DV83
Bangabandhu Prim Sch, E2 21 H3
Bangalore St, SW15 181 CW83
Bangor Cl, Nthlt. UB5 138 CB64
Bangors Cl, Iver SL0 155 BE72
Bangors Rd N, Iver SL0 155 BD67
Bangors Rd S, Iver SL0 155 BE71
Banim St, W6 181 CV76
Banister Ms, NW6 5 L6
Banister Rd, W10 14 D2
⊖ Bank 19 L9
DLR Bank 19 L9
Bank, The, N6
off Cholmeley Pk 143 DH60
Bank Av, Mitch. CR4 222 DD96
Bank Ct, Dart. DA1
off High St 210 FL86
Hemel Hempstead HP1 62 BJ21
Bank End, SE1 31 K2
Bankfoot, Bad.Dene RM17 192 FZ77
Bankfoot Rd, Brom. BR1 206 EE91
Bankhurst Rd, SE6 205 DZ87
Bank La, SW15 200 CS85
Kingston upon Thames KT2 200 CL94
Bank Ms, Sutt. SM1
off Sutton Ct Rd 240 DC107
Bank Mill, Berk. HP4 60 AY19
Bank Mill La, Berk. HP4 60 AY20
★ Bank of England, EC2 19 L9
★ Bank of England Mus, EC2 19 M9
Bank Pl, Brwd. CM14
off High St 130 FW47
Bank Rd, Penn HP10 110 AC47
Banks Ho, SE1 31 J7
Banksian Wk, Islw. TW7 179 CE81
Banksia Rd, N18 122 DW50
Bankside, SE1 31 J1
Dunton Green TN13 278 FE121
Enfield EN2 103 DP39
Northfleet DA11 212 GC86
South Croydon CR2 242 DT107
Southall UB1 158 BX74
Woking GU21
off Wyndham Rd 248 AV118
Bankside Av, SE13 185 EB83
Northolt UB5
off Townson Av 157 BU68
Bankside Cl, N4 144 DQ58
Bexley DA5 209 FD91
Biggin Hill TN16 260 EJ118
Bankside Cl, Cars. SM5 240 DE107
Harefield UB9 114 BG51
Isleworth TW7 179 CF84
Bankside Dr, T.Ditt. KT7 219 CH102
★ Bankside Gall, SE1 31 H1
Bankside Lofts, SE1 31 H2
Bankside Pier 31 J1
Bankside Rd, Ilf. IG1 147 EQ64
Bankside Way, SE19
off Lunham Rd 204 DS93
Banks La, Bexh. DA6 188 EZ84
Bank's La, Eff. KT24 251 BV122
Banks La, Epp. CM16 92 EY32
Banks Rd, Borwd. WD6 100 CQ40
Banks Spur, Slou. SL1
off Cooper Way 173 AP75
Bank St, E14 34 B3
Gravesend DA12 213 GH86
Sevenoaks TN13 279 FH125
Banks Way, E12 147 EN63
Guildford GU4 265 AZ131
Bankton Rd, SW2 183 DN84
Bankwell Rd, SE13 186 EE84
Bann Cl, S.Ock. RM15 171 FV73
Banner Cl, Purf. RM19
off Brimfield Rd 191 FR77
Bannerman Ho, SW8 42 C3
Banner St, EC1 19 K5
Banning St, SE10 47 J1
Bannister Cl, SW2 203 DN88
Greenford UB6 139 CD64
Slough SL3 174 AY75
Bannister Dr, Hutt. CM13 131 GC44
Bannister Gdns, Orp. BR5
off Main Rd 228 EW97
Bannister Ho, E9 11 J3
Harrow HA3
off Headstone Dr 139 CE55
Bannister's Rd, Guil. GU2 280 AT136
Bannockburn Prim Sch, SE18
off Plumstead High St 187 ET77
Bannockburn Rd, SE18 187 ES77
Bannow Cl, Epsom KT19 238 CS105
★ Banqueting Ho, SW1 30 A3
BANSTEAD, SM7 256 DB115
⇌ Banstead 239 CY114
Banstead Comm Jun Sch, Bans. SM7 off The Horseshoe 255 CZ115
Banstead Ct, W12
off Hilary Rd 161 CT73
Banstead Crossroads, Bans. SM7 239 CZ114
Banstead Gdns, N9 122 DS48
Banstead Inf Sch, Bans. SM7
off The Horseshoe 255 CZ115
Banstead Rd, Bans. SM7 239 CX112
Carshalton SM5 240 DE107
Caterham CR3 258 DR121
Epsom KT17 239 CV110
Purley CR8 241 DN111
Banstead Rd S, Sutt. SM2 240 DD110
Banstead St, SE15 44 G10
Banstead Way, Wall. SM6 241 DL106
Banstock Rd, Edg. HA8 118 CP51
Banting Dr, N21 103 DM43
Banton Cl, Enf. EN1
off Central Av 104 DV40
Bantry St, SE5 43 M5
Banwell Rd, Bex. DA5
off Woodside La 208 EX86
Banyard Rd, SE16 32 F7
Banyards, Horn. RM11 150 FL56
Bapchild Pl, Orp. BR5
off Okemore Gdns 228 EW98
Baptist Gdns, NW5 6 G4
Barandon Wk, W11 14 D10
Barataria Pk, Ripley GU23 249 BF121
Barbara Brosnan Ct, NW8 16 A1
Barbara Castle Cl, SW6 39 H3
Barbara Cl, Shep. TW17 217 BP99
Barbara Hucklesby Cl, N22
off The Sandlings 121 DP54
Barbara Speake Stage Sch, W3 off East Acton La 160 CS73
Barbauld Rd, N16 144 DS62
Barbel Cl, Wal.Cr. EN8 89 EA34
Barber Cl, N21 121 DN45
Barberry Cl, Rom. RM3 128 FJ52
Barberry Rd, Hem.H. HP1 62 BG20
Barber's All, E13 24 A2
Barbers Rd, E15 12 C10
BARBICAN, EC2 19 J7
⇌ Barbican 19 H6
⊖ Barbican 19 H6
★ Barbican Arts & Conf Cen, EC2 19 K6
Barbican Rd, Grnf. UB6 158 CB72
Barb Ms, W6 26 B7
Barbon Cl, WC1 18 B6
Barbot Cl, N9 122 DU48
Barchard St, SW18 202 DB85
Barchester Cl, W7 159 CF74
Uxbridge UB8 156 BJ70
Barchester Rd, Har. HA3 117 CD54
Slough SL3 175 AZ75
Barchester St, E14 22 C7
Barclay Cl, SW6 39 J5
Fetcham KT22 252 CB123
Hertford Heath SG13 54 DV11
Watford WD18 97 BU44
Barclay Ct, Hodd. EN11 71 EA18
Slough SL1 173 AQ75
Barclay Oval, Wdf.Grn. IG8 124 EG49
Barclay Path, E17 145 EC57
Barclay Prim Sch, E10
off Canterbury Rd 145 ED58
Barclay Rd, E11 146 EE60
E13 24 C5
E17 145 EC57
N18 122 DR51
SW6 39 J5
Croydon CR0 224 DR104
Barclay Way, W.Thur. RM20 191 FT78
Barcombe Av, SW2 203 DL89
Barcombe Cl, Orp. BR5 227 ET97
Barden Cl, Hare. UB9 114 BJ52
Barden St, SE18 187 ES80
Bardeswell Cl, Brwd. CM14 130 FW47
Bardfield Av, Rom. RM6 148 EX55
Bardney Rd, Mord. SM4 222 DB98
Bardolph Av, Croy. CR0 243 DZ109
Bardolph Rd, N7 143 DL63
Richmond TW9
off St. Georges Rd 180 CM83
Bardon Wk, Wok. GU21
off Bampton Way 248 AV117
Bard Rd, W10 26 C1
Bards Cor, Hem.H. HP1
off Laureate Way 62 BH19
Bardsey Pl, E1 20 G5
Bardsey Wk, N1 9 K5
Bardsley Cl, Croy. CR0 224 DT104
Bardsley La, SE10 46 E3
Bardwell Ct, St.Alb. AL1 65 CD21
Bardwell Rd, St.Alb. AL1 65 CD21
Barfett St, W10 14 G4
Barfield, Sutt.H. DA4 230 FP95
Barfield Av, N20 120 DE47
Barfield Rd, E11 146 EF60
Bromley BR1 227 EN97
Barfields, Bletch. RH1 273 DP133
Loughton IG10 107 EN42
Barfields Gdns, Loug. IG10
off Barfields 107 EN42
Barfields Path, Loug. IG10 107 EN42
Barfleur La, SE8 33 N9
Barfolds, N.Mymms AL9
off Dixons Hill Rd 67 CW23
Barford Cl, NW4 119 CU53
Barford St, N1 8 F9
Barforth Rd, SE15 184 DV83
Barfreston Way, SE20 224 DV95
Bargate Cl, SE18 187 ET78
New Malden KT3 221 CU101
Bargate Ct, Guil. GU2
off Chapelhouse Cl 264 AS134
Barge Ct, Green. DA9 191 FW84
Barge Ho Rd, E16 37 N3
Barge Ho St, SE1 30 F2
Barge La, E3 11 M9
Bargery Rd, SE6 205 EB88
Barge Wk, E.Mol. KT8 219 CD97
Kingston upon Thames KT1, KT2 219 CK95
Walton-on-Thames KT12 218 BX97
Bargrove Av, Hem.H. HP1 62 BG21
Bargrove Cl, SE20 204 DU94
Bargrove Cres, SE6
off Elm La 205 DZ89
Barham Av, Els. WD6 100 CM41
Barham Cl, Brom. BR2 226 EL102
Chislehurst BR7 207 EP92
Gravesend DA12 213 GM88
Romford RM7 127 FB54
Wembley HA0 159 CH65
Weybridge KT13 235 BQ105
Barham Prim Sch, Wem. HA0 off Danethorpe Rd 159 CJ65
Barham Rd, SW20 201 CU94
Chislehurst BR7 207 EP92
Dartford DA1 210 FN87
South Croydon CR2 242 DQ105
Baring Cl, SE12 206 EG89
Baring Cres, Beac. HP9 110 AJ52
Baring Prim Sch, SE12
off Linchmere Rd 206 EG87
Baring Rd, SE12 206 EG87
Beaconsfield HP9 110 AJ52
Cockfosters EN4 102 DD41
Croydon CR0 224 DU102
Baring St, N1 9 L9
Barkantine Shop Par, The, E14 34 A5
Bark Burr Rd, Grays RM16 192 FZ75
Barker Cl, Cher. KT16 215 BE101
New Malden KT3
off England Way 220 CP98
Northwood HA6 115 BT52
Richmond TW9 180 CP82
Barker Dr, NW1 7 M7
Barker Ms, SW4 183 DH84
Barker Rd, Cher. KT16 215 BE101
Barker St, SW10 39 N2
Barker Wk, SW16 203 DK90
Barkham Rd, N17 122 DR52
Barkham Ter, SE1 30 F6
Bark Hart Rd, Orp. BR6 228 EV102
BARKING, IG11 167 EP67
⇌ Barking 167 EQ66
⊖ Barking 167 EQ66
Barking Abbey Sch, Lwr Sch, Bark. IG11
off Longbridge Rd 147 ES64
Upr Sch, Bark. IG11
off Sandringham Rd 167 ET65
Barking & Dagenham Civic Cen, Dag. RM10 149 FB61
● Barking Business Cen, Bark. IG11 168 EU69
Barking Coll, Rush Grn RM7
off Dagenham Rd 149 FD61
Barking Hosp, Bark. IG11 167 ET66
● Barking Ind Pk, Bark. IG11 167 ET67
Barking Rd, E6 24 D1
E13 24 A3
E16 23 L7
BARKINGSIDE, Ilf. IG6 147 EP55
⊖ Barkingside 147 ER56
Bark Pl, W2 15 L10
Barkston Gdns, SW5 27 L10
Barkston Path, Borwd. WD6 100 CN37
Barkway Ct, N4 off Queens Dr 144 DQ61
Barkway Dr, Orp. BR6 245 EN105
Barkwood Cl, Rom. RM7 149 FC57
Barkworth Rd, SE16 44 F1
Barlborough St, SE14 45 H4
Barlby Gdns, W10 14 C5
Barlby Prim Sch, W10 14 D5
Barlby Rd, W10 14 C6
Barlee Cres, Uxb. UB8 156 BJ71
Barle Gdns, S.Ock. RM15 171 FV72
Barley Brow, Wat. WD25 81 BV31
Barley Cl, Bushey WD23 98 CB43
Wembley HA0 139 CK63
Barleycorn Way, E14 21 N10
Hornchurch RM11 150 FM58
Barley Cft, Harl. CM18 73 ER19
Hemel Hempstead HP2 63 BQ20
Hertford SG14 54 DR07
Barleycroft Grn, Welw.G.C. AL8 51 CW09
Barleycroft Rd, Welw.G.C. AL8 51 CW10
Barley Flds, Woob.Grn HP10 132 AE55
Barleyfields Cl, Rom. RM6 148 EV59
Barley La, Ilf. IG3 148 EU60
Romford RM6 148 EV58
Barley La Prim Sch, Chad.Hth RM6 off Huxley Dr 148 EV59
Barleymead, Horl. RH6
off Oatlands 291 DJ147
Barley Mow Caravan Pk, St.Alb. AL4 66 CM22
Barley Mow Ct, Bet. RH3 270 CQ134
Barley Mow La, St.Alb. AL4 66 CL23
Barley Mow Pas, EC1 19 H7
W4 180 CR78
Barley Mow Rd, Eng.Grn TW20 194 AW92
Barley Mow Way, Shep. TW17 216 BN98
Barley Ponds Cl, Ware SG12 55 DZ06
Barley Ponds Rd, Ware SG12 55 DZ06
● Barley Shotts Business Pk, W10 off Acklam Rd 14 G6
Barlow Cl, Hat. AL10 66 CR16
Wallington SM6 241 DL108
Barlow Dr, SE18 186 EL81
Barlow Ho, SE16
off Rennie Est 32 F9
Barlow Pl, W1 29 K1
Barlow Rd, NW6 5 H4
W3 160 CP74
Hampton TW12 198 CA94
Barlow St, SE17 31 M8
Barlow Way, Rain. RM13 169 FD71
Barmeston Rd, SE6 205 EB89
Barmor Cl, Har. HA2 116 CB54
Barmouth Av, Perivale UB6 159 CF68
Barmouth Rd, SW18 202 DC86
Croydon CR0 225 DX103
Barnabas Ct, N21
off Cheyne Wk 103 DN43
Barnabas Rd, E9 11 K3
Barnaby Cl, Har. HA2 138 CC61
Barnaby Pl, SW7 28 A9
Barnaby Way, Chig. IG7 125 EP48
Barnacre Cl, Uxb. UB8 156 BK72
Barnacres Rd, Hem.H. HP3 80 BM25
Barnard Acres, Lwr Naze. EN9 72 EE23
Barnard Cl, SE18 37 M8
Chislehurst BR7 227 ER95
Sunbury-on-Thames TW16
off Oak Gro 197 BV94
Wallington SM6 241 DK108
Barnard Ct, Wok. GU21 248 AS118
Barnard Gdns, Hayes UB4 157 BV70
New Malden KT3 221 CU98
Barnard Grn, Welw.G.C. AL7 51 CZ10
Barnard Gro, E15 13 L7
Barnard Hill, N10 120 DG54
Barnard Ms, SW11 182 DE84
Barnardo Dr, Ilf. IG6 147 EQ56
Barnardo Gdns, E1 21 J10
Barnardo St, E1 21 J9
Barnardos Village, Ilf. IG6 147 EQ55
Barnard Rd, SW11 182 DE84
Enfield EN1 104 DV40
Mitcham CR4 222 DG97
Warlingham CR6 259 EB119
Barnard's Inn, EC1 18 F8
Barnards Pl, S.Croy. CR2 241 DP109
Barnard Way, Hem.H. HP3 62 BL21
Barnato Cl, W.Byf. KT14 234 BL112
Barnby Sq, E15 13 J8
Barnby St, E15 13 J8
NW1 17 M1
Barn Cl, Ashf. TW15 197 BP92
Banstead SM7 256 DD115
Epsom KT18
off Woodcote Side 254 CP115
Farnham Common SL2 133 AP63
Hemel Hempstead HP3 62 BM23
Northolt UB5 158 BW68
Radlett WD7 99 CG35
Tadworth KT20 270 CM132
Welwyn Garden City AL8 51 CW09
Barn Cres, Pur. CR8 242 DR113
Stanmore HA7 117 CJ51
Barncroft Cl, Loug. IG10 107 EN43
Uxbridge UB8 157 BP71
Barncroft Grn, Loug. IG10 107 EN43
Barn Cft Prim Sch, E17
off Brunel Rd 145 DY58
Barncroft Prim Sch, Hem.H. HP2 off Washington Av 62 BK15
Barncroft Rd, Berk. HP4 60 AT20
Loughton IG10 107 EN43
Barncroft Way, St.Alb. AL1 65 CG21
Barndicott, Welw.G.C. AL7 52 DC09
Barneby Cl, Twick. TW2
off Rowntree Rd 199 CE88
BARNEHURST, Bexh. DA7 189 FD83
⇌ Barnehurst 189 FC82
Barnehurst Av, Bexh. DA7 189 FC81
Erith DA8 189 FC81
Barnehurst Cl, Erith DA8 189 FC81
Barnehurst Inf Sch, Northumb.Hth DA8
off Barnehurst Cl 189 FC81
Barnehurst Jun Sch, Northumb.Hth DA8
off Barnehurst Cl 189 FC81
Barnehurst Rd, Bexh. DA7 189 FC82
Barn Elms Pk, SW15 38 B9
Barn End Cen, Wilm. DA2
off High Rd 210 FJ90
Barn End Dr, Dart. DA2 210 FJ90
Barn End La, Dart. DA2 210 FJ92
BARNES, SW13 181 CU82
⇌ Barnes 181 CU83
Barnes Av, SW13 181 CU80
Chesham HP5 76 AQ30
Southall UB2 178 BZ77
⇌ Barnes Bridge 180 CS82
Barnes Br, SW13 180 CS82
W4 180 CS82
Barnesbury Ho, SW4 203 DK85
Barnes Cl, E12 146 EK63
★ Barnes Common, SW13 181 CU83
Barnes Ct, E16 24 D6
Barnet EN5 102 DB42
Woodford Green IG8 124 EK50
BARNES CRAY, Dart. DA1 189 FH84
Barnes Cray Cotts, Dart. DA1
off Maiden La 209 FG85
Barnes Cray Prim Sch, Cray. DA1 off Iron Mill La 189 FG84
Barnes Cray Rd, Dart. DA1 189 FG84
Barnesdale Cres, Orp. BR5 228 EU100
Barnes End, N.Mal. KT3 221 CU99
Barnes High St, SW13 181 CT82
Barnes Hosp, SW14 180 CS83
Barnes Ho, Bark. IG11
off St. Marys 167 ER67
Barnes La, Kings L. WD4 80 BH27
Barnes Pikle, W5 159 CK73
Barnes Prim Sch, SW13
off Cross St 181 CT83
Barnes Ri, Kings L. WD4 80 BM27
Barnes Rd, N18 122 DW49
Godalming GU7 280 AS143
Ilford IG1 147 EQ64
Barnes St, E14 21 L9
Barnes Ter, SE8 45 P1
Barnes Wallis Cl, Eff. KT24 268 BX127
Barnes Wallis Dr, Wey. KT13 234 BL111
Barnes Way, Iver SL0 155 BF73
BARNET, EN4 & EN5 101 CZ41
Barnet Bypass, Barn. EN5 100 CS41
Borehamwood WD6 100 CS41

Coll Barnet Coll, Grahame Pk Cen,
NW9 off Grahame Pk Way . 119 CT53
Montagu Rd Cen, NW4
off Montagu Rd. 141 CU58
N London Business Pk Cen,
N11 off Oakleigh Rd S 120 DG47
Stanhope Rd Cen, N12
off Stanhope Rd 120 DD50
Wood St Cen, Barn. EN5
off Wood St 101 CZ42
Barnet Dr, Brom. BR2. . . . . 226 EL103
BARNET GATE, Barn. EN5 . . . . 101 CT44
Barnet Gate La, Barn. EN5 . . . . 101 CT44
Barnet Gro, E2. . . . . 20 C2
Barnet Hill, Barn. EN5. . . . . 102 DA42
H Barnet Hosp, Barn. EN5 . . . 101 CX42
Barnet La, N20. . . . . 119 CZ46
Barnet EN5. . . . . 101 CZ44
Elstree WD6. . . . . 99 CK44
★ Barnet Mus, Barn. EN5
off Wood St 101 CY42
Barnet Rd, Barn. EN5 . . . . 101 CV43
London Colney AL2 . . . . 84 CL27
Potters Bar EN6. . . . . 102 DA35
Barnett Cl, Erith DA8 . . . . 189 FF82
Leatherhead KT22. . . . . 253 CH119
Wonersh GU5 . . . . 281 BC143
Barnett La, Won. GU5. . . . . 281 BB144
● Barnet Trd Est, High Barn.
EN5. . . . . 101 CZ41
Barnett Row, Jacobs Well
GU4 . . . . 264 AX129
Barnetts Shaw, Oxt. RH8 . . . . . 275 ED127
Barnett St, E1 . . . . 20 E8
Barnetts Way, Oxt. RH8 . . . . . . 275 ED127
Sch Barnett Wd Inf Sch, Ashtd.
KT21 off Barnett Wd La 253 CK117
Barnett Wd La, Ashtd. KT21 . . . 253 CJ119
Leatherhead KT22. . . . . 253 CH120
Barnet Way, NW7 . . . . 118 CR45
Barnet Wd Rd, Brom. BR2 . . . . 226 EJ103
Barney Cl, SE7. . . . . 36 C10
Barn Fld, NW3. . . . . 6 E3
Barnfield, Bans. SM7 . . . . 240 DB114
Epping CM16. . . . . 92 EU28
Gravesend DA11 . . . . 213 GG89
Hemel Hempstead HP3 . . . . . 62 BM23
Horley RH6 . . . . 290 DG149
Iver SL0 . . . . 155 BE72
New Malden KT3 . . . . 220 CS100
Slough SL1 . . . . 153 AK74
Barnfield Av, Croy. CR0 . . . . . . 224 DW103
Kingston upon Thames KT2. 199 CK91
Mitcham CR4. . . . . 223 DH98
Barnfield Cl, N4
off Crouch Hill. 143 DL59
SW17 . . . . 202 DC90
Coulsdon CR5 . . . . 258 DQ119
Greenhithe DA9. . . . . 211 FT86
Hoddesdon EN11 . . . . 71 EA15
Lower Nazeing EN9 . . . . 72 EF22
Swanley BR8. . . . . 229 FC101
Barnfield Gdns, SE18
off Barnfield Rd. 187 EP79
Kingston upon Thames KT2. 178 CL91
Barnfield Pl, E14 . . . . 34 B9
Sch Barnfield Prim Sch, Edg.
HA8 off Silkstream Rd 118 CQ53
Barnfield Rd, SE18 . . . . 187 EP79
W5 . . . . 159 CJ70
Belvedere DA17 . . . . 188 EZ79
Edgware HA8. . . . . 118 CQ53
Orpington BR5 . . . . 228 EX97
St. Albans AL4. . . . . 65 CJ17
Sevenoaks TN13 . . . . 278 FD123
South Croydon CR2 . . . . 242 DS109
Tatsfield TN16 . . . . 260 EK120
Welwyn Garden City AL7. . . . . 51 CY11
Barnfield Way, Oxt. RH8 . . . . . 276 EG133
Barnfield Wd Cl, Beck. BR3. . . . 225 ED100
Barnfield Wd Rd, Beck. BR3 . . . 225 ED100
Barnham Dr, SE28 . . . . 167 ET74
Barnham Rd, Grnf. UB6 . . . . . . 158 CC69
Barnham St, SE1. . . . . 31 P4
Barnhill, Pnr. HA5 . . . . 138 BW57
Barn Hill, Roydon CM19. . . . . . . 72 EH19
Wembley HA9. . . . . 140 CP61
Barnhill Av, Brom. BR2. . . . . . . 226 EF99
Sch Barnhill Comm High Sch,
Hayes UB4
off Yeading La 158 BW69
Barnhill La, Hayes UB4. . . . . . . 157 BV69
Barnhill Rd, Hayes UB4 . . . . . . 157 BV70
Wembley HA9. . . . . 140 CQ62
Barnhurst Path, Wat. WD19 . . . 116 BW50
Barningham Way, NW9 . . . . . . 140 CR58
Barn Lea, Mill End WD3 . . . . . . 114 BG46
Barnlea Cl, Felt. TW13. . . . . 198 BY89
Barnmead, Chobham GU24. . . 232 AT110
Barn Mead, Harl. CM18 . . . . 73 ER17
Theydon Bois CM16 . . . . 107 ES36
Toot Hill CM5. . . . . 93 FE29
Barnmead Gdns, Dag. RM9 . . . 148 EZ64
Barn Meadow, Epp.Upl. CM16
off Upland Rd 91 ET25
Barn Meadow La, Bkhm KT23. 252 BZ124
Barnmead Rd, Beck. BR3 . . . . . 225 DY95
Dagenham RM9 . . . . 148 EZ64
Barnock Cl, Dart. DA1 . . . . 209 FE87
Barn Ri, Wem. HA9 . . . . 140 CN60
BARNSBURY, N1 . . . . 8 D6
Barnsbury Cl, N.Mal. KT3. . . . . 220 CQ98
Barnsbury Cres, Surb. KT5. . . . 220 CQ102
Barnsbury Est, N1 . . . . 8 D9
Barnsbury Gro, N7 . . . . 8 D5
Sch Barnsbury Inf Sch, Wok.
GU22 off Hawthorn Rd. . . . 248 AX121
Sch Barnsbury Jun Sch, Wok.
GU22 off Almond Av 248 AX121
Barnsbury La, Surb. KT5 . . . . . 220 CP103
Barnsbury Pk, N1 . . . . 8 E6
Barnsbury Rd, N1 . . . . 8 E10
Barnsbury Sq, N1 . . . . 8 E7
Barnsbury St, N1 . . . . 8 E7
Barnsbury Ter, N1 . . . . 8 D7
Barns Ct, Harl. CM19 . . . . 73 EN20
Waltham Abbey EN9 . . . . 90 EG32
Barnscroft, SW20. . . . . 221 CV97
Barnsdale Av, E14 . . . . 34 B8
Barnsdale Cl, Borwd. WD6. . . . 100 CM39
Barnsdale Rd, W9 . . . . 15 H4
Barnsfield Pl, Uxb. UB8 . . . . . . 156 BJ66
Barnside Ct, Welw.G.C. AL8. . . . 51 CW09
Barnsley Rd, Rom. RM3 . . . . . . 128 FM52
Barnsley St, E1 . . . . 20 F4
Barnstaple La, SE13
off Lewisham High St. 185 EC84
Barnstaple Path, Rom. RM3. . . 128 FJ50
Barnstaple Rd, Rom. RM3 . . . . 128 FJ50
Barnstaple Rd, Ruis. HA4. . . . . 138 BW62
Barnston Wk, N1 . . . . 9 J8
Barnston Way, Hutt. CM13. . . . 131 GC43
Barn St, N16 . . . . 144 DS61
Barnsway, Kings L. WD4 . . . . . . 80 BL28
Barnway, Eng.Grn TW20. . . . . . 194 AW92
Barn Way, Wem. HA9 . . . . 140 CN60
Barnwell Rd, SW2. . . . . 203 DN85
Dartford DA1 . . . . 190 FM83
Barnwood Cl, N20. . . . . 119 CZ46
W9 . . . . 15 L5
Guildford GU2. . . . . 264 AS132
Ruislip HA4
off Lysander Rd. 137 BR61
Barnwood Rd, Guil. GU2 . . . . . 264 AS133
Barnyard, The, Walt.Hill KT20. . 255 CU124
Baron Cl, N11. . . . . 120 DG50
Sutton SM2 . . . . 240 DB110
Baroness Rd, E2 . . . . 20 B2
Baronet Gro, N17
off St. Paul's Rd. 122 DU53
Baronet Rd, N17 . . . . 122 DU53
Baron Gdns, Ilf. IG6 . . . . 147 EQ55
Baron Gro, Mitch. CR4 . . . . 222 DE98
Baron Ho, SW19
off Chapter Way 222 DD95
Baron Rd, Dag. RM8. . . . . 148 EX60
Barons, The, Twick. TW1 . . . . . 199 CH86
⊖ Barons Court. 26 E10
Barons Ct, Wall. SM6
off Whelan Way. 223 DK104
Barons Ct Rd, W14 . . . . 26 E10
Baronsfield Rd, Twick. TW1. . . . 199 CH86
Barons Gate, Barn. EN4 . . . . . . 102 DE44
Barons Hurst, Epsom KT18 . . . 254 CQ116
Barons Keep, W14. . . . . 26 E10
Barons Mead, Har. HA1 . . . . . . 139 CE56
Baronsmead Rd, SW13 . . . . . . 181 CU81
Baronsmede, W5. . . . . 180 CM75
Baronsmere Rd, N2 . . . . 142 DE56
Barons Pl, SE1. . . . . 30 F5
Baron St, N1 . . . . 8 E10
Barons Wk, Croy. CR0. . . . . 225 DY100
Barons Way, Egh. TW20. . . . . . 195 BD93
Reigate RH2. . . . . 288 DA138
Baron Wk, E16. . . . . 23 L6
Mitcham CR4. . . . . 222 DE98
Baroque Ct, Houns. TW3
off Prince Regent Rd. 178 CC83
Barque Ms, SE8. . . . . 46 A2
Barrack La, Wind. SL4. . . . . 173 AR82
Barrack Path, Wok. GU21 . . . . . 248 AT118
Barrack Rd, Guil. GU2 . . . . 264 AU132
Hounslow TW4 . . . . 178 BX84
Barrack Row, Grav. DA11 . . . . . 213 GH86
Barracks, The, Add. KT15 . . . . . 216 BH104
Barracks Hill, Colesh. HP7. . . . . 111 AM45
Barracks La, Barn. EN5
off High St 101 CY41
Barra Cl, Hem.H. HP3 . . . . 63 BP23
Barra Hall Circ, Hayes UB3. . . . 157 BS72
Barra Hall Rd, Hayes UB3 . . . . 157 BS73
Barrards Way, Seer Grn HP9. . . 111 AQ51
Barrass Cl, Enf. EN3 . . . . 105 EA37
Barratt Av, N22 . . . . 121 DM54
● Barratt Ind Pk, E3 . . . . 22 E5
Southall UB1 . . . . 178 CA75
Barratt Way, Har. HA3
off Tudor Rd. 139 CD55
Barrenger Rd, N10. . . . . 120 DF53
Barrens Brae, Wok. GU22. . . . . 249 BA118
Barrens Cl, Wok. GU22. . . . . . . 249 BA118
Barrens Pk, Wok. GU22. . . . . . . 249 BA118
Barrett Cl, Rom. RM3 . . . . 127 FH52
Barrett Rd, E17 . . . . 145 EC56
Fetcham KT22 . . . . 252 CC124
Barretts Grn Rd, NW10. . . . . . . 160 CQ68
Barretts Gro, N16 . . . . 9 P2
Barretts Rd, Dunt.Grn TN13 . . . 263 FD120
Barrett St, W1 . . . . 17 H9
Barrhill Rd, SW2 . . . . 203 DL89
Barricane, Wok. GU21 . . . . 248 AV119
Barrie Cl, Couls. CR5. . . . . 257 DJ115
Barriedale, SE14 . . . . 45 M8
Barrie Est, W2 . . . . 16 A10
Barrier App, SE7 . . . . 36 E7
Barrier Pt Rd, E16 . . . . 36 C3
Barrier Pt Twr, E16
off Barrier Pt Rd 36 C4
Barringer Sq, SW17 . . . . 202 DG91
Barrington Cl, NW5. . . . . 6 G2
Ilford IG5 . . . . 125 EM53
Loughton IG10
off Barrington Rd 107 EQ42
Barrington Ct, W3
off Cheltenham Pl. 180 CP75
Dorking RH4
off Barrington Rd 285 CG137
Hutton CM13. . . . . 131 GC44
Barrington Dr, Fetch. KT22. . . . 269 CD125
Harefield UB9 . . . . 114 BG52
Barrington Grn, Loug. IG10 . . . 107 EQ42
Barrington Lo, Wey. KT13. . . . . 235 BQ106
Barrington Ms, Welw.G.C. AL7. . 52 DB10
Barrington Pk Gdns, Ch.St.G.
HP8. 112 AX46
Sch Barrington Prim Sch, Bexh.
DA7 off Barrington Rd 188 EX82
Barrington Rd, E12 . . . . 167 EN65
N8. . . . . 143 DK57
SW9 . . . . 183 DP83
Bexleyheath DA7 . . . . 188 EX82
Dorking RH4 . . . . 285 CG137
Loughton IG10. . . . . 107 EQ41
Purley CR8. . . . . 241 DJ112
Sutton SM3 . . . . 222 DA102
Barrington Vil, SE18 . . . . 187 EN81
Barrow Av, Cars. SM5 . . . . 240 DF108
Barrow Cl, N21 . . . . 121 DP48
Barrowdene Cl, Pnr. HA5
off Paines La 116 BY54
Barrowell Grn, N21. . . . . 121 DP47
Barrowfield Cl, N9. . . . . 122 DV48
Barrow Gdns, Red. RH1 . . . . . . 273 DH132
Barrowgate Rd, W4. . . . . 180 CQ78
Barrow Grn Rd, Oxt. RH8. . . . . . 275 EC128
Barrow Hedges Cl, Cars. SM5 . 240 DE108
Sch Barrow Hedges Prim Sch,
Cars. SM5 off Harbury Rd . 240 DE108
Barrow Hedges Way, Cars.
SM5 . . . . 240 DE108
Barrow Hill, Wor.Pk. KT4 . . . . . 220 CS103
Barrow Hill Cl, Wor.Pk. KT4 . . . . 220 CS103
Barrow Hill Est, NW8 . . . . 16 C1
Sch Barrow Hill Jun Sch, NW8. . 16 C1
Barrow Hill Rd, NW8 . . . . 16 C1
Barrow La, Chsht EN7 . . . . 88 DT30
Barrow Pt Av, Pnr. HA5. . . . . . . 116 BY54
Barrow Pt La, Pnr. HA5. . . . . . . 116 BY54
Barrow Rd, SW16 . . . . 203 DK93
Croydon CR0 . . . . 241 DN106
Barrowsfield, S.Croy. CR2 . . . . . 242 DT112
Barrows Rd, Harl. CM19. . . . . . . 73 EM15
Barrow Wk, Brent. TW8. . . . . . . 179 CJ79
Barr Rd, Grav. DA12 . . . . 213 GM89
Potters Bar EN6. . . . . 86 DC33
Barrsbrook Fm Rd, Cher. KT16 . 215 BE102
Barrsbrook Hall, Cher. KT16. . . 215 BE102
Barrs Rd, NW10. . . . . 160 CR66
Barr's Rd, Tap. SL6 . . . . 152 AH72
Barry Av, N15. . . . . 144 DT58
Bexleyheath DA7 . . . . 188 EY80
Windsor SL4 . . . . 173 AQ80
Barry Cl, Grays RM16. . . . . 193 GG75
Orpington BR6 . . . . 227 ES104
St. Albans AL2. . . . . 82 CB25
Barry Ho, SE16
off Rennie Est 32 F10
Barry Rd, E6. . . . . 25 H8
NW10 . . . . 160 CQ66
SE22 . . . . 204 DU86
Bars, The, Guil. GU1 . . . . 280 AX135
Barset Rd, SE15 . . . . 44 G10
Barson Cl, SE20 . . . . 204 DW94
Barston Rd, SE27 . . . . 204 DQ89
Barstow Cres, SW2. . . . . 203 DM88
Bartel Cl, Hem.H. HP3. . . . . 63 BR22
Bartelotts Rd, Slou. SL2. . . . . . . 153 AK70
Barter St, WC1. . . . . 18 B7
Barters Wk, Pnr. HA5
off High St 138 BY55
Barth Ms, SE18 . . . . 187 ES77
Bartholomew Cl, EC1 . . . . 19 J7
SW18 . . . . 182 DC84
Bartholomew Ct, E14
off Newport Av 35 H1
Dorking RH4 off South St. . . . 285 CG137
Bartholomew Dr, Harold Wd
RM3 . . . . 128 FK54
Bartholomew La, EC2. . . . . 19 M9
Bartholomew Pl, EC1 . . . . 19 J7
Bartholomew Rd, NW5 . . . . 7 M5
Bartholomew Sq, E1 . . . . 20 F4
EC1 . . . . 19 K4
Bartholomew St, SE1. . . . . 31 L7
Bartholomew Vil, NW5. . . . . 7 L5
Bartholomew Way, Swan. BR8. 229 FE97
Barth Rd, SE18 . . . . 187 ES77
Bartle Av, E6 . . . . 166 EL68
Bartle Rd, W11. . . . . 14 D9
Bartlett Cl, E14 . . . . 22 B8
Bartlett Ct, EC4. . . . . 18 F8
Bartlett Rd, Grav. DA11 . . . . . . 213 GG88
Westerham TN16. . . . . 277 EQ126
Bartletts, Chal.St.P. SL9 . . . . . . 112 AY52
Bartletts Mead, Hert. SG14 . . . . 54 DR06
Bartletts Pas, EC4 . . . . 18 F8
Bartlett St, S.Croy. CR2 . . . . . . 242 DR106
Bartlow Gdns, Rom. RM5 . . . . . 127 FD53
Barton, The, Cob. KT11. . . . . . . 236 BX112
Barton Av, Rom. RM7. . . . . 149 FB60
Barton Cl, E6 . . . . 25 K8
E9 . . . . 11 H2
NW4. 141 CU57
SE15. . . . . 44 F10
Addlestone KT15. . . . . 234 BG107
Bexleyheath DA6 . . . . 208 EY85
Chigwell IG7 . . . . 125 EQ47
Shepperton TW17 . . . . 217 BP100
Barton Ct, Whyt. CR3 . . . . 258 DU119
Barton Grn, N.Mal. KT3 . . . . . . 220 CR96
Barton Ho, E3 off Bow Rd 22 C2
N1. . . . . 9 H6
SW6 . . . . 39 M10
Barton Meadows, Ilf. IG6. . . . . 147 EQ56
Barton Pl, Guil. GU4
off London Rd. 265 BB131
Barton Rd, W14. . . . . 38 E1
Bramley GU5. . . . . 281 BA144
Hornchurch RM12. . . . . 149 FG60
Sidcup DA14 . . . . 208 EY93
Slough SL3 . . . . 175 AZ75
Sutton at Hone DA4 . . . . 230 FP95
Bartons, The, Els. WD6 . . . . 99 CK44
Barton St, SW1. . . . . 30 A6
Bartonway, NW8. . . . . 6 A9
Barton Way, Borwd. WD6. . . . . 100 CN40
Croxley Green WD3 . . . . 97 BP43
Bartram Cl, Uxb. UB8. . . . . 157 BP70
Bartram Rd, SE4. . . . . 205 DY85
Bartrams La, Barn. EN4 . . . . . . 102 DC38
Bartrop Cl, Goffs Oak EN7 . . . . . 88 DR28
Barts Cl, Beck. BR3 . . . . 225 EA99
Barville Cl, SE4
off St. Norbert Rd 185 DY84
● Barwell Business Pk,
Chess. KT9. . . . . 237 CK108
Barwell La, Chess. KT9. . . . . . . 237 CJ108
Barwick Dr, Uxb. UB8 . . . . 157 BP71
Barwick Ho, W3. . . . . 180 CQ75
Barwick Rd, E7 . . . . 146 EH63
Barwood Av, W.Wick. BR4 . . . . 225 EB102
Bascombe Gro, Dart. DA1 . . . . . 209 FE87
Bascombe St, SW2. . . . . 203 DN86
Basden Gro, Felt. TW13 . . . . . . 198 CA89
Basedale Rd, Dag. RM9 . . . . . . 168 EV66
Baseing Cl, E6. . . . . 25 M10
Basevi Way, SE8 . . . . 46 C2
Basford Way, Wind. SL4. . . . . . . 173 AK83
Bashley Rd, NW10 . . . . 160 CR70
Basil Av, E6 . . . . 25 H2
Basildene Rd, Houns. TW4. . . . 178 BX82
Basildon Av, Ilf. IG5. . . . . 125 EN53
Basildon Cl, Sutt. SM2 . . . . 240 DB109
Watford WD18. . . . . 97 BQ44
Basildon Rd, SE2. . . . . 188 EU78
Basildon Sq, Hem.H. HP2. . . . . . 62 BM16
Basil Gdns, SE27. . . . . 204 DQ92
Croydon CR0
off Primrose La 225 DX102
Basil Ms, Harl. CM17
off Square St. 58 EW14
Basilon Rd, Bexh. DA7 . . . . 188 EY82
Basil St, SW3 . . . . 28 E6
Basin App, E14 . . . . 21 M9
Basing Cl, T.Ditt. KT7 . . . . 219 CF101
Basing Ct, SE15. . . . . 44 B7
Basingdon Way, SE5. . . . . 184 DR84
Basing Dr, Bex. DA5 . . . . 208 EZ86
Basingfield Rd, T.Ditt. KT7 . . . . 219 CF101
Basinghall Av, EC2 . . . . 19 L7
Basinghall Gdns, Sutt. SM2. . . . 240 DB109
Basinghall St, EC2 . . . . 19 L8
Basing Hill, NW11 . . . . 141 CZ60
Wembley HA9. . . . . 140 CM61
Basing Ho, Bark. IG11
off St. Margarets. 167 ER67
Basing Ho Yd, E2. . . . . 19 P2
Basing Pl, E2 . . . . 19 P2
Basing Rd, Bans. SM7 . . . . 239 CZ114
Mill End WD3. . . . . 113 BF46
Basing St, W11 . . . . 14 G8
Basing Way, N3. . . . . 142 DA55
Thames Ditton KT7. . . . . 219 CF101
Basire St, N1 . . . . 9 J8
Baskerville Gdns, NW10. . . . . . . 140 CS63
Baskerville Rd, SW18 . . . . 202 DE87
Basket Gdns, SE9. . . . . 206 EL85
Baslow Cl, Har. HA3 . . . . 117 CD53
Baslow Wk, E5. . . . . 145 DX63
Basnett Rd, SW11 . . . . 40 H10
Basque Ct, SE16 . . . . 33 J4
Bassano St, SE22 . . . . 204 DT85
Bassant Rd, SE18 . . . . 187 ET79
Bassein Pk Rd, W12 . . . . 181 CT75
Basset Cl, New Haw KT15 . . . . . 234 BH110
Bassett Cl, Sutt. SM2 . . . . 240 DB109
Bassett Dr, Reig. RH2. . . . . 272 DA133
Bassett Flds, N.Wld Bas. CM16. 93 FD25
Bassett Gdns, Islw. TW7. . . . . . . 178 CC80
North Weald Bassett CM16 . . . 93 FB26
Bassett Ho, Dag. RM9 . . . . 168 EV67
Bassett Rd, W10 . . . . 14 D8
Uxbridge UB8
off Oxford Rd 156 BJ66
Woking GU22 . . . . 249 BC116
Bassetts Cl, Orp. BR6. . . . . 245 EP105
Bassett St, NW5 . . . . 6 G3
Bassetts Way, Orp. BR6 . . . . . . 245 EP105
Bassett Way, Grnf. UB6 . . . . 158 CB72
Slough SL2
off Pemberton Rd 153 AL70
Bassil Rd, Hem.H. HP2 . . . . 62 BK21
Bassingbourne Cl, Brox. EN10. . 71 DZ20
Bassingburn Wk, Welw.G.C. AL7. 51 CZ10
Bassingham Rd, SW18. . . . . 202 DC87
Wembley HA0. . . . . 159 CK65
Bassishaw Highwalk, EC2
off Aldermanbury Sq 19 K7
Bastable Av, Bark. IG11. . . . . . . 167 ES68
Bastion Highwalk, EC2. . . . . 19 J7
● Bastion Ho, EC2
off London Wall. 19 J7
Bastion Rd, SE2 . . . . 188 EU78
Baston Manor Rd, Brom. BR2 . 226 EH104
Baston Rd, Brom. BR2 . . . . 226 EH102
Sch Baston Sch, Hayes BR2
off Baston Rd 226 EH103
Bastwick St, EC1. . . . . 19 J4
Basuto Rd, SW6 . . . . 39 J7
⇌ Bat & Ball 279 FJ121
Jct Bat & Ball Junct, Sev.
TN14. 279 FH121
Bat & Ball Rd, Sev. TN14 . . . . . 279 FJ121
Batavia Cl, Sun. TW16 . . . . 218 BW95
Batavia Ms, SE14 . . . . 45 M5
Batavia Rd, SE14. . . . . 45 M5
Sunbury-on-Thames TW16. . 217 BV95
Batchelor St, N1 . . . . 8 E10
Batchelors Way, Amer. HP7 . . . . 77 AR39
Chesham HP5 . . . . 76 AP29
Batchwood Dr, St.Alb. AL3 . . . . 64 CC17
Batchwood Gdns, St.Alb. AL3. . 65 CD17
Batchwood Grn, Orp. BR5 . . . . 228 EU97
Batchwood Hall, St.Alb. AL3 . . . 64 CB17
Sch Batchwood Sch, St.Alb.
AL3 off Townsend Dr 65 CD17
Batchwood Vw, St.Alb. AL3. . . . 64 CC18
BATCHWORTH, Rick. WD3 . . . . 114 BM47
BATCHWORTH HEATH, Rick.
WD3 . . . . 114 BN49
Batchworth Heath Hill, Rick.
WD3 . . . . 114 BN49
Batchworth Hill, Rick. WD3 . . . 114 BM48
Batchworth La, Nthwd. HA6 . . . 115 BS50
Jct Batchworth Rbt, Rick. WD3. 114 BK46
Bateman Cl, Bark. IG11
off Glenny Rd 167 EQ65
Bateman Ho, SE17 . . . . 42 G3
Bateman Rd, E4 . . . . 123 EA51
Croxley Green WD3 . . . . 96 BN44
Bateman's Bldgs, W1 . . . . 17 N9
Batemans Ms, Warley CM14
off Vaughan Williams Way . 130 FV49
Bateman's Row, EC2 . . . . 19 P4
Bateman St, W1 . . . . 17 N9
Bates Cl, Geo.Grn SL3 . . . . 154 AY72
Bates Cres, SW16. . . . . 203 DJ94
Croydon CR0. . . . . 241 DN106
● Bates Ind Est, Harold Wd
RM3. 128 FP52
Bateson St, SE18 . . . . 187 ES77
Bateson Way, Wok. GU21. . . . . 233 BC114
Bates Rd, Rom. RM3. . . . . 128 FN52
Bate St, E14. . . . . 21 P10
Bates Wk, Add. KT15 . . . . 234 BJ108
● B.A.T. Export Ho,
Wok. GU21 . . . . 248 AY117
Batford Cl, Welw.G.C. AL7 . . . . . 52 DB10
Bath Cl, SE15. . . . . 44 F5
Bath Ct, EC1 . . . . 18 E5
EC1 (St. Luke's Est)
off St. Luke's Est 19 L3
Bathgate Rd, SW19. . . . . 201 CX90
Bath Ho, SE1 off Bath Ter. 31 K6
Bath Ho Rd, Croy. CR0. . . . . . . 223 DL102
Bath Pas, Kings.T. KT1
off St. James Rd 219 CK96
Bath Pl, EC2. . . . . 19 N3
Barnet EN5. . . . . 101 CZ41
Bath Rd, E7 . . . . 166 EK65
N9. . . . . 122 DV47
W4 . . . . 180 CS77
Colnbrook SL3. . . . . 175 BB79
Dartford DA1 . . . . 209 FH87
Harlington UB3 . . . . 177 BQ81
Hounslow TW3, TW4, TW5,
TW6 . . . . 178 BX82
Romford RM6 . . . . 148 EY58
Slough SL1 . . . . 153 AP74
Taplow SL6 . . . . 152 AF72
West Drayton UB7 . . . . 176 BK81
Baths Rd, Brom. BR2 . . . . 226 EK98
Bath St, EC1 . . . . 19 K3
Gravesend DA11 . . . . 213 GH86
Bath Ter, SE1 . . . . 31 J7
Bathurst Av, SW19
off Brisbane Av 222 DB95
Bathurst Cl, Iver SL0 . . . . 175 BF75
Bathurst Gdns, NW10 . . . . 161 CV68
Bathurst Ms, W2. . . . . 16 A10
Bathurst Rd, Hem.H. HP2. . . . . . . 62 BK17
Ilford IG1 . . . . 147 EP60
Bathurst St, W2. . . . . 16 A10
Bathurst Wk, Iver SL0. . . . . 175 BE75
Bathway, SE18 . . . . 37 M8
Batley Cl, Mitch. CR4 . . . . 222 DF101
Batley Pl, N16 . . . . 144 DT62
Batley Rd, N16
off Stoke Newington High St. 144 DT62
Enfield EN2 . . . . 104 DQ39
Batman Cl, W12 . . . . 161 CV74
Baton Cl, Purf. RM19 . . . . 191 FR77
Batoum Gdns, W6. . . . . 26 B6
Batson Ho, E1
off Fairclough St. 20 D9
Batson St, W12 . . . . 181 CU75
Batsworth Rd, Mitch. CR4 . . . . 222 DD97
Batten Av, Wok. GU21 . . . . 248 AS119
Battenburg Wk, SE19
off Brabourne Cl. 204 DS92
Batten Cl, E6 . . . . 25 K9
Batten St, SW11 . . . . 40 D10
Batterdale, Hat. AL9 . . . . 67 CW17
Battersby Rd, SE6. . . . . 205 ED89
BATTERSEA, SW11 . . . . 40 F6
Battersea Br, SW3 . . . . 40 B4
SW11 . . . . 40 B4
Battersea Br Rd, SW11. . . . . 40 C5
● Battersea Business Cen,
SW11 off Lavender Hill. . . . 182 DG83
Battersea Ch Rd, SW11 . . . . 40 B6
★ Battersea Dogs Home, SW8. 41 K5
Battersea High St, SW11 . . . . . . 40 B7
★ Battersea Park, SW11 . . . . . . 40 F4
⇌ Battersea Park. 41 J6
Battersea Pk Rd, SW8 . . . . 41 J6
SW11 . . . . 40 C9
Battersea Ri, SW11 . . . . 202 DE85
Battersea Sq, SW11
off Battersea High St 40 B7
Coll Battersea Tech Coll, SW11 . . 40 F7
Battery Rd, SE28. . . . . 187 ES75
Battis, The, Rom. RM1
off South St. 149 FE57
Battishill Gdns, N1
off Waterloo Ter. 8 G7
Battishill St, N1. . . . . 8 G7
Battlebridge Ct, N1. . . . . 8 B10
Battle Br La, SE1. . . . . 31 N3
Battlebridge La, Merst. RH1. . . 273 DH130
Battle Br Rd, NW1. . . . . 18 A1
Battle Cl, SW19. . . . . 202 DC93
Battledean Rd, N5. . . . . 8 G2
Battlefield Rd, St.Alb. AL1 . . . . . 65 CF18
Battlemead Cl, Maid. SL6 . . . . . 152 AC68
Battle Rd, Belv. DA17 . . . . 189 FC77
Erith DA8 . . . . 189 FC77
BATTLERS GREEN, Rad. WD7 . . 99 CE37
Battlers Grn Dr, Rad. WD7. . . . . 99 CE37
Batts Hill, Red. RH1 . . . . 272 DE132
Reigate RH2. . . . . 272 DD132
Batty St, E1 . . . . 20 D8
Batwa Ho, SE16 . . . . 44 F1
Baudwin Rd, SE6 . . . . 206 EE89
Baugh Rd, Sid. DA14 . . . . 208 EW92
Baulk, The, SW18 . . . . 202 DA87
Bavant Rd, SW16 . . . . 223 DL96
Bavaria Rd, N19. . . . . 143 DL61
Bavdene Ms, NW4
off The Burroughs. 141 CV56
Bavent Rd, SE5. . . . . 43 K9
Bawdale Rd, SE22. . . . . 204 DT85
Bawdsey Av, Ilf. IG2 . . . . 147 ET56
Bawtree Cl, Sutt. SM2 . . . . 240 DC110
Bawtree Rd, SE14. . . . . 45 L4
Uxbridge UB8 . . . . 156 BK65
Bawtry Rd, N20. . . . . 120 DF48
Baxendale, N20. . . . . 120 DC47
Baxendale St, E2. . . . . 20 C2
Baxter Av, Red. RH1 . . . . 272 DE134
Baxter Cl, Brom. BR1
off Stoneleigh Rd 227 EP97
Slough SL1 . . . . 174 AS76
Southall UB2. . . . . 178 CB75
Uxbridge UB10 . . . . 157 BP69
Baxter Gdns, Noak Hill RM3
off North End. 128 FJ47
Baxter Ho, E3
off Bromley High St 22 C2
Baxter Rd, E16. . . . . 24 D8
N1. . . . . 9 M5
N18. . . . . 122 DV49
NW10 . . . . 160 CS70
Ilford IG1 . . . . 147 EP64
Bayards, Warl. CR6 . . . . 258 DW118
Bay Cl, Horl. RH6 . . . . 290 DE145
Bay Ct, W5. . . . . 180 CL76
Baycroft Cl, Pnr. HA5 . . . . 138 BW55
Baydon Ct, Brom. BR2 . . . . 226 EF97
Bayes Cl, SE26 . . . . 204 DW92
Bayeux, Tad. KT20. . . . . 255 CX122
Bayeux Ho, SE7
off Springfield Gro 186 EJ79
Bayfield Rd, SE9. . . . . 186 EK84
Horley RH6 . . . . 290 DE147
BAYFORD, Hert. SG13 . . . . 69 DM18
⇌ Bayford 69 DN18
BAYFORDBURY, Hert. SG13. . . . 53 DM13
Bayford Cl, Hem.H. HP2 . . . . 63 BQ15
Hertford SG13. . . . . 54 DQ11
Bayford Grn, Bayford SG13 . . . . 69 DN18
Bayford La, Bayford SG13 . . . . . 53 DM14
Bayford Ms, E8 . . . . 10 F7
Sch Bayford Prim Sch, Bayford
SG13 off Ashendene Rd. . . . 69 DM18
Bayford Rd, NW10 . . . . 14 C3
Bayford St, E8 . . . . 10 F7
Baygrove Ms, Hmptn W. KT1. . 219 CJ95
Bayham Pl, NW1. . . . . 7 L10
Bayham Rd, W4. . . . . 180 CR76
W13 . . . . 159 CH73
Morden SM4. . . . . 222 DB98
Sevenoaks TN13 . . . . 279 FJ123
Bayham St, NW1 . . . . 7 L9
Bayhorne La, Horl. RH6 . . . . . . 291 DJ150
Bayhurst Dr, Nthwd. HA6. . . . . 115 BT51
★ Bayhurst Wood Country Pk,
Uxb. UB9 . . . . 136 BM56
Bayleaf Cl, Hmptn H. TW12 . . . 199 CD92
Bayley Cres, Burn. SL1. . . . . . . 152 AG71
Bayleys Mead, Hutt. CM13. . . . 131 GC47
Bayley St, WC1 . . . . 17 N7
Bayley Wk, SE2
off Woolwich Rd 188 EY78
Baylie Ct, Hem.H. HP2
off Baylie La 62 BL18
Baylie La, Hem.H. HP2 . . . . 62 BL18

Sch Baylis Ct Sch, Slou. SL1 off Gloucester Av 153 AR71
Baylis Ms, Twick. TW1 199 CG87
Baylis Par, Slou. SL1 off Oatlands Dr 154 AS72
Baylis Rd, SE1 30 E5
  Slough SL1 153 AR73
Bayliss Av, SE28 168 EX73
Bayliss Cl, N21 103 DL43
  Southall UB1 158 CB72
Bayliss Ct, Guil. GU1 off Mary Rd 280 AW135
Bayly Rd, Dart. DA1 210 FN86
Bay Manor La, Grays RM20 191 FT79
Baymans Wd, Shenf. CM15 130 FY47
Bayne Cl, E6 25 K9
Bayne Hill Cl, Seer Grn HP9 111 AR52
Baynes Cl, Enf. EN1 104 DU40
Baynes Ms, NW3 6 B4
Baynes St, NW1 7 M7
Baynham Cl, Bex. DA5 208 EZ86
Baynton Rd, Wok. GU22 249 BB120
Bayonne Rd, W6 38 E3
Bays Fm Ct, West Dr. UB7 176 BJ80
Bayshill Ri, Nthlt. UB5 158 CB65
Bayston Rd, N16 144 DT62
BAYSWATER, W2 15 M9
⊖ Bayswater 15 L10
Bayswater Rd, W2 16 B10
Baythorne St, E3 21 P6
Bay Tree Av, Lthd. KT22 253 CG120
🔒 Baytree Cen, Brwd. CM14 off High St 130 FW47
Bay Tree Cl, Brom. BR1 226 EJ95
Baytree Cl, Chsht EN7 88 DT27
Bay Tree Cl, Ilf. IG6 off Hazel La 125 EP52
Baytree Cl, Park St AL2 82 CB27
  Sidcup DA15 207 ET88
Bay Tree Ct, Burn. SL1 152 AJ69
Baytree Ho, E4 off Dells Cl. 123 EB45
Baytree Ms, SE17 31 L8
Baytree Rd, SW2 183 DM84
Bay Trees, Oxt. RH8 276 EH133
Baytree Wk, Wat. WD17 97 BT38
Baywood Sq, Chig. IG7 126 EV49
Bazalgette Cl, N.Mal. KT3 220 CR99
Bazalgette Ct, W6 off Great W Rd 181 CU78
Bazalgette Gdns, N.Mal. KT3 220 CR99
Bazely St, E14 22 E10
Bazile Rd, N21 103 DN44
Beacham Cl, SE7 186 EK78
Beachborough Rd, Brom. BR1 205 EC91
Beachcroft Av, Sthl. UB1 158 BZ74
Beachcroft Rd, E11 146 EE62
Beachcroft Way, N19 143 DK60
Beach Gro, Felt. TW13 198 CA89
Beach's Ho, Stai. TW18 196 BG92
Beachy Rd, E3 12 A7
Beacon Cl, Bans. SM7 255 CX116
  Beaconsfield HP9 110 AG54
  Chalfont St. Peter SL9 112 AY52
  Uxbridge UB8 136 BK64
Beacon Dr, Bean DA2 211 FV90
Beaconfield Av, Epp. CM16 91 ET29
Beaconfield Rd, Epp. CM16 91 ET29
Beaconfields, Sev. TN13 278 FF126
Beaconfield Way, Epp. CM16 91 ET29
Beacon Gate, SE14 45 J9
Beacon Gro, Cars. SM5 240 DG105
Beacon Hill, N7 8 A2
  Penn HP10 110 AD48
  Purfleet RM19 190 FP78
  Woking GU21 248 AW118
Sch Beacon Hill Sch, S.Ock. RM15 off Erriff Dr 171 FU71
  Post 16 Provision, S.Ock. RM15 off Fortin Cl. 171 FU73
Beacon Ri, Sev. TN13 278 FG126
Beacon Rd, SE13 205 ED86
  Erith DA8 189 FH80
  London Heathrow Airport TW6 196 BN86
  Ware SG12 55 EA05
Jct Beacon Rd Rbt, Lon.Hthrw Air. TW6 197 BP86
Beacons, The, Hat. AL10 off Beaconsfield Cl 67 CW17
  Loughton IG10 107 EN38
Sch Beacon Sch, The, Bans. SM7 off Picquets Way 255 CY117
  Chesham Bois HP6 off Amersham Rd 77 AP35
Beacons Cl, E6 25 H7
BEACONSFIELD, HP9 110 AJ53
⇌ Beaconsfield 111 AL52
Beaconsfield Cl, N11 120 DG49
  SE3 47 N2
  W4 180 CQ78
  Hatfield AL10 67 CW17
Beaconsfield Common La, Slou. SL2 133 AQ57
Beaconsfield Gdns, Clay. KT10 237 CE108
Sch Beaconsfield High Sch, Beac. HP9 off Wattleton Rd 111 AL54
Beaconsfield Par, SE9 off Beaconsfield Rd 206 EL91
Beaconsfield Pl, Epsom KT17 238 CS112
Sch Beaconsfield Prim Sch, Sthl. UB1 off Beaconsfield Rd 178 BY75
Beaconsfield Rd, E10 145 EC61
  E16 23 L5
  E17 145 DZ58
  N9 122 DU49
  N11 120 DG48
  N15 144 DS56
  NW10 161 CT65
  SE3 47 M3
  SE9 206 EL89
  SE17 43 M1
  W4 180 CR76
  W5 179 CJ75
  Bexley DA5 209 FE88
  Bromley BR1 226 EK97
  Claygate KT10 237 CE108
  Croydon CR0 224 DR100
  Enfield EN3 105 DX37
  Epsom KT18 254 CR119
  Hatfield AL10 67 CW17
  Hayes UB4 158 BW74
Beaconsfield Rd, N.Mal. KT3 220 CR96
  St. Albans AL1 65 CE20
  Slough SL2 153 AQ68
  Southall UB1 158 BX74
  Surbiton KT5 220 CM101
  Twickenham TW1 199 CH86
  Woking GU22 249 AZ120
Sch Beaconsfield Sch, The, Beac. HP9 off Wattleton Rd 111 AL54
Beaconsfield Ter, Rom. RM6 148 EX58
Beaconsfield Ter Rd, W14 26 E7
Beaconsfield Wk, E6 25 M9
  SW6 39 H7
Beacontree Av, E17 123 ED53
Beacontree Rd, E11 146 EF59
Beacon Way, Bans. SM7 255 CX116
  Rickmansworth WD3 114 BG45
★ Beacon Wd Country Pk, Dart. DA2 211 FV91
Beadles La, Oxt. RH8 275 ED130
Beadlow Cl, Cars. SM5 off Olveston Wk 222 DD100
Beadman Pl, SE27 off Norwood High St 203 DP91
Beadman St, SE27 203 DP91
Beadnell Rd, SE23 205 DX88
Beadon Rd, W6 26 A9
  Bromley BR2 226 EG98
Beads Hall La, Pilg.Hat. CM15 130 FV42
Beaford Gro, SW20 221 CY97
Beagle Cl, Felt. TW13 197 BV91
  Radlett WD7 99 CF37
Beagles Cl, Orp. BR5 228 EX103
Beak St, W1 17 M10
Beal Cl, Well. DA16 188 EU81
Beale Cl, N13 121 DP50
Beale Pl, E3 11 N10
Beale Rd, E3 11 N9
Beales La, Wey. KT13 216 BN104
Beales Rd, Bkhm KT23 268 CB127
Sch Beal High Sch, Ilf. IG4 off Woodford Br Rd 146 EL56
Bealings End, Beac. HP9 111 AK50
Beal Rd, Ilf. IG1 147 EN61
Beam Av, Dag. RM10 169 FB67
Beames Rd, NW10 160 CR67
Beaminster Gdns, Ilf. IG6 125 EP54
Beaminster Ho, SW8 off Dorset Rd 42 C4
Beamish Cl, N.Wld Bas. CM16 93 FC25
Beamish Dr, Bushey Hth WD23 116 CC46
Beamish Ho, SE16 off Rennie Est 32 G9
Beamish Rd, N9 122 DU46
  Orpington BR5 228 EW101
Sch Beam Prim Sch, Dag. RM10 off Oval Rd N 169 FC68
Beamway, Dag. RM10 169 FD66
BEAN, Dart. DA2 211 FV90
Beanacre Cl, E9 11 P4
Beane Cft, Grav. DA12 213 GM88
Beane River Vw, Hert. SG14 54 DQ09
Beane Rd, Hert. SG14 53 DP09
Jct Bean Interchange, Dart. DA2 211 FU89
Bean La, Bean DA2 211 FV89
Sch Bean Prim Sch, Bean DA2 off School La 211 FW91
Bean Rd, Bexh. DA6 188 EX84
  Greenhithe DA9 211 FV85
Beanshaw, SE9 207 EN91
Beansland Gro, Rom. RM6 126 EY54
Bear All, EC4 18 G8
Bear Cl, Rom. RM7 149 FB58
Beardell St, SE19 204 DT93
Beardow Gro, N14 103 DJ44
Beard Rd, Kings.T. KT2 200 CM92
Beardsfield, E13 13 N9
Beard's Hill, Hmptn. TW12 218 CA95
Beard's Hill Cl, Hmptn. TW12 off Beard's Hill 218 CA95
Beardsley Ter, Dag. RM8 off Fitzstephen Rd 148 EV64
Beardsley Way, W3 180 CR75
Beards Rd, Ashf. TW15 197 BS93
Bearfield Rd, Kings.T. KT2 200 CL94
Bear Gdns, SE1 31 J2
Bearing Cl, Chig. IG7 126 EU49
Bearing Way, Chig. IG7 126 EU49
Bear La, SE1 31 H2
Bear Rd, Felt. TW13 198 BX92
Bears Den, Kgswd KT20 255 CZ122
Bears Rails Pk, Old Wind. SL4 194 AT87
Bearstead Ri, SE4 205 DZ85
Bearsted Ter, Beck. BR3 225 EA95
Bear St, WC2 17 P10
Bearswood End, Beac. HP9 111 AL51
Bearwood Cl, Add. KT15 off Ongar Pl 234 BG107
  Potters Bar EN6 86 DD31
Beasleys Ait La, Sun. TW16 217 BT100
Beasleys Yd, Uxb. UB8 off Warwick Pl 156 BJ66
Beaton Cl, SE15 44 B6
  Greenhithe DA9 191 FV84
Beatrice Av, SW16 223 DM97
  Wembley HA9 140 CL64
Beatrice Cl, E13 23 N4
  Pinner HA5 off Reid Cl 137 BU56
Beatrice Ct, Buck.H. IG9 124 EK47
Beatrice Gdns, Nthflt DA11 212 GE89
Beatrice Pl, W8 27 L7
Beatrice Rd, E17 145 EA57
  N4 143 DN59
  N9 122 DW45
  SE1 32 D9
  Oxted RH8 276 EE129
  Richmond TW10 off Albert Rd 200 CM85
  Southall UB1 158 BZ74
Sch Beatrice Tate Sch, E2 20 F2
Beatrice Wilson Flats, Sev. TN13 off Rockdale Rd 279 FH125
Sch Beatrix Potter Prim Sch, SW18 off Magdalen Rd 202 DC88
Beatson Wk, SE16 33 L2
Beattie Cl, Bkhm KT23 252 BZ124
  Feltham TW14 197 BT88
Beattock Ri, N10 143 DH56
Beatty Av, Guil. GU1 265 BA133
Beatty Rd, N16 144 DS63
  Stanmore HA7 117 CJ51
  Waltham Cross EN8 89 DZ34
Beatty St, NW1 7 L10
Beattyville Gdns, Ilf. IG6 147 EN55
Beauchamp Cl, W4 off Beaumont Rd 180 CQ76
Beauchamp Ct, Stan. HA7 off Hardwick Cl 117 CJ50
Beauchamp Gdns, Mill End WD3 114 BG46
Beauchamp Pl, SW3 28 D6
Beauchamp Rd, E7 166 EH66
  SE19 224 DR95
  SW11 182 DE84
  East Molesey KT8 218 CB99
  Sutton SM1 240 DA106
  Twickenham TW1 199 CG87
  West Molesey KT8 218 CB99
Beauchamps, Welw.G.C. AL7 52 DB10
Beauchamp St, EC1 18 E7
Beauchamp Ter, SW15 off Dryburgh Rd 181 CV83
Beauclare Cl, Lthd. KT22 off Delderfield 253 CK121
Sch Beauclerc Inf Sch, Sun. TW16 off French St. 218 BW97
Beauclerc Rd, W6 181 CV76
Beauclerk Cl, Felt. TW13 off Florence Rd 197 BV88
Beaudesert Ms, West Dr. UB7 176 BL75
Beaufort, E6 25 M8
Beaufort Av, Har. HA3 139 CG56
Beaufort Cl, E4 off Higham Sta Av 123 EB51
  SW15 201 CV87
  W5 160 CM71
  Chafford Hundred RM16 off Clifford Rd 192 FZ76
  North Weald Bassett CM16 92 FA27
  Reigate RH2 271 CZ133
  Romford RM7 149 FC56
  Woking GU22 249 BC116
Sch Beaufort Comm Prim Sch, Wok. GU21 off Kirkland Av 248 AT116
Beaufort Ct, SW6 39 J2
  Richmond TW10 199 CJ91
Beaufort Dr, NW11 142 DA56
Beaufort Gdns, NW4 141 CW58
  SW3 28 D6
  SW16 203 DM94
  Hounslow TW5 178 BY81
  Ilford IG1 147 EN60
Beaufort Ms, SW6 39 H2
Beaufort Pk, NW11 142 DA56
Beaufort Pl, Bray SL6 172 AD75
Beaufort Rd, W5 160 CM71
  Kingston upon Thames KT1 220 CL98
  Reigate RH2 271 CZ133
  Richmond TW10 199 CJ91
  Ruislip HA4 off Lysander Rd 137 BR61
  Twickenham TW1 199 CJ87
  Woking GU22 249 BC116
Beauforts, Eng.Grn TW20 194 AW92
Beaufort St, SW3 40 B3
Beaufort Way, Epsom KT17 239 CU108
Beaufoy Rd, N17 122 DS52
Beaufoy Wk, SE11 30 D9
Beaulieu Av, E16 36 A2
  SE26 204 DV91
Beaulieu Cl, NW9 140 CS56
  SE5 43 M10
  Datchet SL3 174 AV81
  Hounslow TW4 198 BZ85
  Mitcham CR4 222 DG95
  Twickenham TW1 199 CK87
  Watford WD19 116 BW46
Beaulieu Dr, Pnr. HA5 138 BX58
  Waltham Abbey EN9 89 EB32
Beaulieu Gdns, N21 122 DQ45
Beaulieu Pl, W4 180 CQ76
Beauly Way, Rom. RM1 127 FE53
Beaumanor Gdns, SE9 207 EN91
Beaumaris Dr, Wdf.Grn. IG8 124 EK52
Beaumaris Grn, NW9 off Goldsmith Av 140 CS58
Beaumaris Twr, W3 180 CP75
Beaumayes Cl, Hem.H. HP1 62 BH21
Beaumont Av, W14 26 G10
  Harrow HA2 138 CB58
  Richmond TW9 180 CM83
  St. Albans AL1 65 CH18
  Wembley HA0 139 CJ64
Beaumont Cl, N2 142 DE56
  Kingston upon Thames KT2 200 CN94
  Romford RM2 128 FJ54
Beaumont Cres, W14 26 G10
  Rainham RM13 169 FG65
Beaumont Dr, Ashf. TW15 197 BR92
  Northfleet DA11 212 GE87
  Worcester Park KT4 221 CV102
Beaumont Gdns, NW3 142 DA62
  Hutton CM13 off Bannister Dr 131 GC44
Beaumont Gate, Rad. WD7 99 CG35
Beaumont Gro, E1 21 J5
Beaumont Ms, W1 17 H6
  Pinner HA5 138 BY55
Beaumont Pk Dr, Roydon CM19 72 EH15
Beaumont Pl, W1 17 M4
  Barnet EN5 101 CZ39
  Isleworth TW7 199 CF85
  Watford WD18 off Brightwell Rd 97 BU43
Sch Beaumont Prim Sch, E10 off Burchell Rd 145 EB60
  Purley CR8 off Old Lo La 241 DN114
Beaumont Ri, N19 143 DK60
Beaumont Rd, E10 145 EB59
  E13 24 B3
  SE19 204 DQ93
  SW19 201 CY87
  W4 180 CQ76
  Broxbourne EN10 70 DR24
  Petts Wood BR5 227 ER100
  Purley CR8 241 DN113
  Slough SL2 153 AR70
  Windsor SL4 173 AQ82
Beaumonts, Red. RH1 288 DF143
Sch Beaumont Sch, St.Alb. AL4 off Oakwood Dr 65 CJ19
Beaumont Sq, E1 21 J6
Beaumont St, W1 17 H6
Beaumont Vw, Chsht EN7 88 DR26
Beaumont Wk, NW3 6 F6
● Beaumont Wks, St.Alb. AL1 off Hedley Rd 65 CH20
Beauvais Ter, Nthlt. UB5 158 BX69
Beauval Rd, SE22 204 DT86
Beaverbank Rd, SE9 207 ER88
Jct Beaverbrook Rbt, Lthd. KT22 253 CK123
Beaver Cl, SE20 off Lullington Rd 204 DU94
  Hampton TW12 218 CB95
  Morden SM4 221 CW101
Beaver Gro, Nthlt. UB5 off Jetstar Way 158 BY69
Beaver Rd, Ilf. IG6 126 EW50
Beavers Cl, Guil. GU3 264 AS133
Sch Beavers Comm Prim Sch, Houns. TW4 off Arundel Rd 178 BW83
Beavers Cres, Houns. TW4 178 BW84
Beavers La, Houns. TW4 178 BW83
Beaverwood Rd, Chis. BR7 207 ES93
Sch Beaverwood Sch for Girls, Chis. BR7 off Beaverwood Rd 207 ES93
Beavor Gro, W6 off Beavor La 181 CU78
Beavor La, W6 181 CU77
Beazley Cl, Ware SG12 55 DY05
Bebbington Rd, SE18 187 ES77
Beblets Cl, Orp. BR6 245 ET106
Beccles Dr, Bark. IG11 167 ES65
Beccles St, E14 21 P10
Bec Cl, Ruis. HA4 138 BX62
Beck Cl, SE13 46 C7
Beck Ct, Beck. BR3 225 DX97
BECKENHAM, BR3 225 EA95
● Beckenham Business Cen, Beck. BR3 205 DY93
Beckenham Gdns, N9 122 DS48
Beckenham Gro, Brom. BR2 225 ED96
⇌ Beckenham Hill 205 EC92
Beckenham Hill Rd, SE6 205 EB92
  Beckenham BR3 205 EB92
H Beckenham Hosp, Beck. BR3 225 DZ96
⇌ Beckenham Junction 225 EA95
Trm Beckenham Junction 225 EA95
Beckenham La, Brom. BR2 226 EE96
Beckenham Pl Pk, Beck. BR3 205 EB94
Trm Beckenham Road 225 DY95
Beckenham Rd, Beck. BR3 225 DX95
  West Wickham BR4 225 EB101
Beckenshaw Gdns, Bans. SM7 256 DE115
Beckers, The, N16 144 DU63
Becket Av, E6 25 L2
Becket Cl, SE25 224 DU100
  Great Warley CM13 129 FW51
Becket Fold, Har. HA1 off Courtfield Cres 139 CF57
Becket Ho, Brwd. CM14 130 FW47
Becket Rd, N18 122 DW49
Beckets Sq, Berk. HP4 off Bridle Way 60 AU17
Becket St, SE1 31 L6
Beckett Av, Ken. CR8 257 DP115
Beckett Chase, Slou. SL3 off Olivia Dr 175 AZ78
Beckett Cl, NW10 160 CR65
  SW16 203 DK89
  Belvedere DA17 off Tunstock Way 188 EY76
Beckett Ho, SW9 42 B9
Beckett Rd, Couls. CR5 257 DK122
Becketts, Hert. SG14 53 DN10
Beckett's Av, St.Alb. AL3 64 CC17
Becketts Cl, Bex. DA5 209 FC88
  Feltham TW14 197 BV86
  Orpington BR6 227 ET104
Becketts Pl, Hmptn W. KT1 219 CK95
Beckett Wk, Beck. BR3 205 DY93
Beckford Cl, W14 27 H9
Beckford Dr, Orp. BR5 227 ER101
Beckford Pl, SE17 43 K1
Sch Beckford Prim Sch, NW6 5 H3
Beckford Rd, Croy. CR0 224 DT100
Beckham Ho, SE11 off Marylee Way 30 D9
Beckingham Rd, Guil. GU2 264 AU132
Beckings Way, Flack.Hth HP10 132 AC56
Beck La, Beck. BR3 225 DX97
Becklow Gdns, W12 off Becklow Rd 181 CU75
Becklow Ms, W12 off Becklow Rd 181 CT75
Becklow Rd, W12 181 CU75
Beckman Cl, Halst. TN14 263 FC115
Sch Beckmead Sch, Beck. BR3 off Monks Orchard Rd 225 EA102
Beck River Pk, Beck. BR3 225 DZ95
Beck Rd, E8 10 E8
Becks Rd, Sid. DA14 208 EU90
BECKTON, E6 25 M7
DLR Beckton 25 L7
DLR Beckton Park 25 K10
Jct Beckton Pk Rbt, E16 25 J10
● Beckton Retail Pk, E6 25 L6
Beckton Rd, E16 23 M6
🔒 Beckton Triangle Retail Pk, E6 25 M4
Beck Way, Beck. BR3 225 DZ97
Beckway Rd, SW16 223 DK96
Beckway St, SE17 31 M9
Beckwell Rd, Slou. SL1 173 AQ75
Beckwith Rd, SE24 204 DR86
Beclands Rd, SW17 202 DG93
Becmead Av, SW16 203 DK91
  Harrow HA3 139 CH57
Becondale Rd, SE19 204 DS92
BECONTREE, Dag. RM8 148 EY62
⊖ Becontree 168 EW66
Becontree Av, Dag. RM8 148 EV63
BECONTREE HEATH, Dag. RM8 148 FA60
Sch Becontree Prim Sch, Dag. RM8 off Stevens Rd 148 EV62
Becquerel Ct, SE10 35 M7
Bective Pl, SW15 off Bective Rd 181 CZ84
Bective Rd, E7 146 EG63
  SW15 181 CZ84
Becton Pl, Erith DA8 189 FB80
Bedale Rd, Enf. EN2 104 DQ38
  Romford RM3 128 FN50
Bedale St, SE1 31 L3
Bedale Wk, Dart. DA2 210 FP88
BEDDINGTON, Croy. CR0 223 DK103
BEDDINGTON CORNER, Mitch. CR4 222 DG101
Beddington Cross, Croy. CR0 223 DK102
Beddington Fm Rd, Croy. CR0 223 DL102
Beddington Gdns, Cars. SM5 240 DG107
  Wallington SM6 241 DH107
Beddington Grn, Orp. BR5 227 ET95
Beddington Gro, Wall. SM6 241 DK106
Sch Beddington Inf Sch, Wall. SM6 off Croydon Rd 241 DJ105
Trm Beddington Lane 223 DJ100
Beddington La, Croy. CR0 223 DJ99
● Beddington La Ind Est, Croy. CR0 223 DJ100
Sch Beddington Pk Prim Sch, Bedd. CR0 off Derry Rd 223 DK104
Beddington Path, Orp. BR5 227 ET95
Beddington Rd, Ilf. IG3 147 ET59
  Orpington BR5 227 ES96
● Beddington Trd Pk, Croy. CR0 223 DL102
Beddlestead La, Warl. CR6 260 EF117
Bede Cl, Pnr. HA5 116 BX53
Sch Bedelsford Sch, Kings.T. KT1 off Grange Rd 220 CL97
Bedens Rd, Sid. DA14 208 EY93
Bede Rd, Rom. RM6 148 EW58
Bedevere Rd, N9 122 DU48
Bedfont Cl, Felt. TW14 197 BQ86
  Mitcham CR4 222 DG96
Bedfont Ct, Stai. TW19 176 BH84
Bedfont Ct Est, Stai. TW19 176 BG83
Bedfont Grn Cl, Felt. TW14 197 BQ88
Sch Bedfont Inf & Nurs & Jun Schs, E.Bed. TW14 off Hatton Rd 197 BS86
Bedfont La, Felt. TW13, TW14 197 BT87
Bedfont Rd, Felt. TW13, TW14 197 BS89
  Stanwell TW19 196 BL86
Bedford Av, WC1 17 P7
  Amersham HP6 94 AW39
  Barnet EN5 101 CZ43
  Hayes UB4 157 BV72
  Slough SL1 153 AM72
Bedfordbury, WC2 18 A10
Bedford Cl, N10 120 DG52
  W4 180 CS79
  Chenies WD3 95 BB38
  Woking GU21 248 AW115
Bedford Cor, W4 180 CS77
Bedford Ct, WC2 30 A1
Bedford Cres, Enf. EN3 105 DY35
Bedford Dr, Farn.Com. SL2 133 AP64
Bedford Gdns, W8 27 J3
  Hornchurch RM12 150 FJ61
Bedford Hill, SW12 203 DH88
  SW16 203 DH88
Bedford Ho, SW4 183 DL84
  Guildford GU1 off Bedford Rd 280 AW135
Bedford Ms, N2 142 DE55
  SE6 off Aitken Rd 205 EB89
BEDFORD PARK, W4 180 CR76
Bedford Pk, Croy. CR0 224 DQ102
Bedford Pk Cor, W4 off Bath Rd 180 CS77
Bedford Pk Rd, St.Alb. AL1 65 CE20
Bedford Pas, SW6 38 F4
Bedford Pl, WC1 18 A6
  Croydon CR0 224 DR102
Bedford Rd, E6 167 EN67
  E17 123 EA54
  E18 124 EG54
  N2 142 DE55
  N8 143 DK58
  N9 122 DV45
  N15 144 DS56
  N22 121 DL53
  NW7 118 CS47
  SW4 183 DL83
  W4 180 CR76
  W13 159 CH73
  Dartford DA1 210 FN87
  Grays RM17 192 GB78
  Guildford GU1 280 AW135
  Harrow HA1 138 CC58
  Ilford IG1 147 EP62
  Northfleet DA11 213 GF89
  Northwood HA6 115 BQ48
  Orpington BR6 228 EV103
  Ruislip HA4 137 BT63
  St. Albans AL1 65 CE21
  Sidcup DA15 207 ES90
  Twickenham TW2 199 CD90
  Worcester Park KT4 221 CW103
Bedford Row, WC1 18 D6
Bedford Sq, WC1 17 P7
Bedford St, WC2 18 A10
  Berkhamsted HP4 60 AX19
  Watford WD24 97 BV39
Bedford Ter, SW2 off Lyham Rd 203 DL85
Bedford Way, WC1 17 P5
Bedgebury Gdns, SW19 201 CY89
Bedgebury Rd, SE9 186 EK84
Bedivere Rd, Brom. BR1 206 EG90
Bedlam Ms, SE11 30 E8
Bedlow Way, Croy. CR0 241 DM105
BEDMOND, Abb.L. WD5 81 BS27
Bedmond Hill, Pimlico HP3 81 BS25
Bedmond La, Abb.L. WD5 81 BV25
  St. Albans AL2, AL3 64 BX24
Bedmond Rd, Abb.L. WD5 81 BT29
  Hemel Hempstead HP3 63 BS23
Sch Bedmond Village Prim & Nurs Sch, Bedmond WD5 off Meadow Way 81 BT28
Sch Bedonwell Inf Sch, Belv. DA17 off Bedonwell Rd 188 EY79
Sch Bedonwell Jun Sch, Belv. DA17 off Bedonwell Rd 188 EY79
Bedonwell Rd, SE2 188 EY79
  Belvedere DA17 188 FA79
  Bexleyheath DA7 188 FA79
Bedser Cl, SE11 42 D2
  Thornton Heath CR7 224 DQ97
  Woking GU21 249 BA116
Bedser Dr, Grnf. UB6 139 CD64
Bedster Gdns, W.Mol. KT8 218 CB96
Bedwardine Rd, SE19 204 DS94
Bedwell Av, Essen. AL9 68 DG18
Bedwell Cl, Welw.G.C. AL7 51 CY10
Bedwell Gdns, Hayes UB3 177 BS78
Bedwell Pk, Essen. AL9 68 DF18
Bedwell Rd, N17 122 DS53
  Belvedere DA17 188 FA78
Beeby Rd, E16 24 A7
Beech Av, N20 120 DE46
  W3 160 CS74
  Brentford TW8 179 CH80
  Brentwood CM13 131 FZ48
  Buckhurst Hill IG9 124 EH47
  Effingham KT24 268 BX129
  Enfield EN2 103 DN35
  Radlett WD7 83 CG33
  Ruislip HA4 137 BV60
  Sidcup DA15 208 EU87
  South Croydon CR2 242 DR111
  Swanley BR8 229 FF98
  Tatsfield TN16 260 EK119
  Upminster RM14 150 FP62
Beech Bottom, St.Alb. AL3 65 CD17
Beech Cl, N9 104 DU44
  SE8 45 P3
  SW15 201 CU87
  SW19 201 CW93
  Ashford TW15 197 BR92

Beech Cl, Byfleet KT14 . . . . **234** BL112
Carshalton SM5 . . . . **222** DF103
Cobham KT11 . . . . **236** CA112
Dorking RH4 . . . . **285** CF135
Effingham KT24 . . . . **268** BX128
Hatfield AL10. . . . . **67** CU19
Hersham KT12 . . . . **236** BW105
Hornchurch RM12. . . . . **149** FH62
Loughton IG10. . . . . **107** EP41
Stanwell TW19
off St. Mary's Cres **196** BK87
Sunbury-on-Thames TW16
off Harfield Rd. **218** BX96
Ware SG12. . . . . **55** DX08
West Drayton UB7 . . . . **176** BN76
Beech Cl Ct, Cob. KT11. . . . . . **236** BZ111
Beech Copse, Brom. BR1 . . . . . **227** EM96
South Croydon CR2 . . . . **242** DS106
Beech Ct, E17 . . . . **145** ED55
SE9. . . . . **206** EL86
Ilford IG1 . . . . **147** EN62
Beech Cres, Box H. KT20 . . . . . **270** CQ130
Beechcroft, Ashtd. KT21. . . . . . **254** CM119
Chislehurst BR7 . . . . **207** EN94
Beechcroft Av, NW11 . . . . **141** CZ59
Bexleyheath DA7 . . . . **189** FD81
Croxley Green WD3 . . . . **97** BQ44
Harrow HA2. . . . . **138** CA59
Kenley CR8 . . . . **258** DR115
New Malden KT3 . . . . **220** CQ95
Beechcroft Cl, Houns. TW5. . . . **178** BY80
Orpington BR6 . . . . **245** ER105
Beechcroft Gdns, Wem. HA9 . . **140** CM62
Beechcroft Lo, Sutt. SM2
off Devonshire Rd. **240** DC108
Beechcroft Manor, Wey. KT13 . **217** BR104
Beechcroft Rd, E18 . . . . **124** EH54
SW14 . . . . **180** CQ83
SW17 . . . . **202** DE89
Bushey WD23 . . . . **98** BY43
Chesham HP5 . . . . **76** AN30
Chessington KT9. . . . . **238** CM105
Orpington BR6 . . . . **245** ER105
Beechdale, N21. . . . . **121** DM47
Beechdale Rd, SW2 . . . . **203** DM86
Beech Dell, Kes. BR2. . . . . **245** EM105
Beechdene, Tad. KT20. . . . . **255** CV122
Beech Dr, N2. . . . . **142** DF55
Berkhamsted HP4 . . . . **60** AW20
Borehamwood WD6 . . . . **100** CM40
Kingswood KT20. . . . . **255** CZ122
Reigate RH2. . . . . **272** DD134
Ripley GU23 . . . . **250** BG124
Sawbridgeworth CM21 . . . . . **58** EW07
Beechen Cliff Way, Islw. TW7
off Henley Cl **179** CF81
Beechen Gro, Pnr. HA5. . . . . . . **138** BZ55
Watford WD17. . . . . **98** BW42
Beechen La, Lwr Kgswd KT20. **271** CZ125
Beechenlea La, Swan. BR8. . . . . **229** FH97
Beechen Wd, Map.Cr. WD3. . . . . **113** BD49
Beeches, The, Amer. HP6 . . . . . . **77** AN36
Banstead SM7. . . . . **256** DB116
Beaconsfield HP9 . . . . **110** AH54
Bramley GU5. . . . . **281** AZ144
Brentwood CM14 . . . . **130** FV48
Chorleywood WD3 . . . . **95** BF43
Fetcham KT22 . . . . **253** CE124
Hounslow TW3 . . . . **178** CB81
Park Street AL2 . . . . **83** CE27
Swanley BR8. . . . . **209** FF94
Tilbury RM18. . . . . **193** GH82
Beeches Av, Cars. SM5. . . . . . . **240** DE108
Beeches Cl, SE20
off Genoa Rd. **224** DW95
Kingswood KT20. . . . . **256** DA123
Beeches Dr, Farn.Com. SL2 . . . **133** AP64
Beeches Pk, Beac. HP9 . . . . **111** AK53
Beeches Rd, SW17 . . . . **202** DE90
Farnham Common SL2 . . . . . . **133** AP64
Sutton SM3. . . . . **221** CY102
Beeches Wk, Cars. SM5 . . . . . . **240** DD109
Beeches Way, B.End SL8 . . . . . . **132** AD61
Beeches Wd, Kgswd KT20 . . . . . **256** DA122
Beech Fm Rd, Warl. CR6. . . . . . . **259** EC120
Beechfield, Bans. SM7 . . . . **240** DB113
Hoddesdon EN11 . . . . **55** EA13
Kings Langley WD4. . . . . **80** BM30
Sawbridgeworth CM21 . . . . . . **58** EZ05
Beechfield Cl, Borwd. WD6 . . . **100** CL40
Beechfield Cotts, Brom. BR1
off Widmore Rd. **226** EJ96
Beechfield Gdns, Rom. RM7 . . **149** FC59
Beechfield Rd, N4. . . . . **144** DQ58
SE6. . . . . **205** DZ88
Bromley BR1 . . . . **226** EJ96
Erith DA8 . . . . **189** FE80
Hemel Hempstead HP1 . . . . . **62** BH21
Ware SG12. . . . . **55** DZ05
Welwyn Garden City AL7 . . . . **51** CY11
Beechfield Sch, Wat. WD24
off Gammons La. **97** BU37
Beechfield Wk, Wal.Abb. EN9. . **105** ED35
Beech Gdns, EC2
off White Lyon Ct **19** J6
W5 . . . . **180** CL75
Dagenham RM10 . . . . **169** FB66
Woking GU21 . . . . **248** AY115
Beech Gro, Add. KT15 . . . . **234** BH105
Amersham HP7. . . . . **77** AQ39
Aveley RM15. . . . . **170** FQ74
Bookham KT23 . . . . **268** CA127
Caterham CR3 . . . . **274** DS126
Croydon CR0. . . . . **243** DY110
Epsom KT18 . . . . **255** CV117
Guildford GU2. . . . . **264** AT134
Ilford IG6 . . . . **125** ES51
Mayford GU22 . . . . **248** AX123
Mitcham CR4. . . . . **223** DK98
New Malden KT3 . . . . **220** CR97
Beech Hall, Ott. KT16 . . . . **233** BC108
Beech Hall Cres, E4. . . . . **123** ED52
Beech Hall Rd, E4 . . . . **123** EC52
Beech Hill, Barn. EN4. . . . . **102** DD38
Woking GU22 . . . . **248** AX123
Beech Hill Av, Barn. EN4 . . . . . . **102** DC39
Beech Hill Ct, Berk. HP4. . . . . . . **60** AX18
Beech Hill Gdns, Wal.Abb. EN9. **106** EH37
Beechhill Rd, SE9 . . . . **207** EN85
Beech Holt, Lthd. KT22. . . . . **253** CJ122
Beech Ho, NW3
off Maitland Pk Vil. **6** F4
Croydon CR0. . . . . **243** EB107
Beech Ho Rd, Croy. CR0. . . . . . **224** DR104
Beech Hyde La, Wheat. AL4 . . . . **50** CM07
Beech La, Buck.H. IG9. . . . . **124** EH47
Guildford GU2. . . . . **280** AW137
Jordans HP9 . . . . **112** AS52
Beech Lawn, Guil. GU1 . . . . . . **281** AZ135
Beech Lawns, N12 . . . . **120** DD50
Beech Lo, Stai. TW18
off Farm Cl. **195** BE92
Beechmeads, Cob. KT11. . . . . . . **236** BX113
Beechmont Av, Vir.W. GU25. . . **214** AX99
Beechmont Cl, Brom. BR1 . . . . . **206** EE92
Beechmont Rd, Sev. TN13 . . . . . **279** FH129
Beechmore Gdns, Sutt. SM3 . . **221** CX103
Beechmore Rd, SW11. . . . . **40** F7
Beechmount Av, W7 . . . . **159** CD71
Beecholme, Bans. SM7 . . . . **239** CY114
Beecholme Av, Mitch. CR4. . . . **223** DH95
Beecholme Est, E5 . . . . **144** DV62
Beecholme Prim Sch, Mitch.
CR4 *off Edgehill Rd*. **223** DH95
Beecholm Ms, Chsht EN8 . . . . . . **89** DX28
Beech Pk, Amer. HP6 . . . . **94** AV39
Beechpark Way, Wat. WD17. . . . **97** BS37
Beech Pl, Epp. CM16 . . . . **91** ET31
St. Albans AL3. . . . . **65** CD17
Beech Rd, N11 . . . . **121** DL51
SW16 . . . . **223** DL96
Biggin Hill TN16 . . . . **260** EH118
Dartford DA1 . . . . **210** FK88
Epsom KT17 . . . . **255** CT115
Feltham TW14 . . . . **197** BS87
Merstham RH1 . . . . **273** DJ126
Orpington BR6 . . . . **246** EU108
Reigate RH2. . . . . **272** DA131
St. Albans AL3. . . . . **65** CE17
Sevenoaks TN13
off Victoria Rd **279** FH125
Slough SL3 . . . . **174** AY75
Watford WD24. . . . . **97** BU37
Weybridge KT13
off St. Marys Rd **235** BR105
Beechrow, Ham TW10 . . . . **200** CL91
Beech St, EC2 . . . . **19** J6
Romford RM7 . . . . **149** FC56
Beechtree Av, Eng.Grn TW20. . **194** AV93
Beech Tree Cl, N1 . . . . **8** E6
Stanmore HA7. . . . . **117** CJ50
Beech Tree Glade, E4 . . . . **124** EF46
Beechtree La, St.Alb. AL3. . . . . . **63** BV22
Beech Tree La, Stai. TW18
off Staines Rd. **216** BH96
Beech Tree Pl, Sutt. SM1
off St. Nicholas Way **240** DB106
Beech Vale, Wok. GU22
off Hill Vw Rd. **249** AZ118
Beechvale Cl, N12. . . . . **120** DE50
Beech Wk, NW7. . . . . **118** CS51
Dartford DA1 . . . . **189** FG84
Epsom KT17 . . . . **239** CU111
Hoddesdon EN11 . . . . **71** DZ17
Beech Way, NW10. . . . . **160** CR66
Beechway, Bex. DA5. . . . . **208** EX86
Beech Way, Epsom KT17 . . . . . . **255** CT115
Beechway, Guil. GU1 . . . . **265** BB133
Beech Way, S.Croy. CR2. . . . . . . **243** DX113
Twickenham TW2 . . . . **198** CA90
Beech Waye, Ger.Cr. SL9 . . . . . **135** AZ59
Beechwood Av, N3 . . . . **141** CZ55
Amersham HP6. . . . . **94** AW38
Chorleywood WD3 . . . . **95** BB42
Coulsdon CR5 . . . . **257** DH115
Greenford UB6 . . . . **158** CB69
Harrow HA2. . . . . **138** CB62
Hayes UB3. . . . . **157** BR73
Kingswood KT20. . . . . **256** DA121
Orpington BR6 . . . . **245** ES106
Potters Bar EN6. . . . . **86** DB33
Richmond TW9 . . . . **180** CN81
Ruislip HA4 . . . . **137** BT61
St. Albans AL1. . . . . **65** CH18
Staines TW18. . . . . **196** BH93
Sunbury-on-Thames TW16. . **197** BU93
Thornton Heath CR7. . . . . **223** DP98
Uxbridge UB8 . . . . **156** BN72
Weybridge KT13 . . . . **235** BS105
Beechwood Circle, Har. HA2
off Beechwood Gdns **138** CB62
Beechwood Cl, NW7. . . . . **118** CR50
Amersham HP6. . . . . **94** AW39
Cheshunt EN7 . . . . **88** DS26
Hertford SG13. . . . . **54** DT09
Knaphill GU21. . . . . **248** AS117
Long Ditton KT6 . . . . **219** CJ101
Weybridge KT13 . . . . **235** BS105
Beechwood Ct, Cars. SM5. . . . . **240** DF105
Sunbury-on-Thames TW16. . **197** BU93
Beechwood Cres, Bexh. DA7 . . **188** EX83
Beechwood Dr, Cob. KT11 . . . . . **236** CA111
Keston BR2 . . . . **244** EK105
Woodford Green IG8 . . . . **124** EF50
Beechwood Gdns, NW10
off St. Annes Gdns **160** CM69
Caterham CR3. . . . . **258** DU122
Harrow HA2. . . . . **138** CB62
Ilford IG5 . . . . **147** EM57
Rainham RM13 . . . . **169** FH71
Slough SL1 . . . . **174** AS75
Beechwood Gro, W3. . . . . **160** CS73
Long Ditton KT6 . . . . **219** CJ101
Beechwood La, Warl. CR6 . . . . . **259** DX119
Beechwood Manor, Wey. KT13. **235** BS105
Beechwood Ms, N9 . . . . **122** DU47
Beechwood Pk, E18 . . . . **146** EG55
Chorleywood WD3 . . . . **95** BF42
Hemel Hempstead HP3 . . . . . . **61** BF24
Leatherhead KT22. . . . . **253** CJ123
Beechwood Ri, Chis. BR7. . . . . . **207** EP91
Watford WD24. . . . . **97** BV36
Beechwood Rd, E8 . . . . **10** A4
N8. . . . . **143** DK56
Beaconsfield HP9 . . . . **110** AJ53
Caterham CR3. . . . . **258** DU122
Knaphill GU21. . . . . **248** AS117
Slough SL2 . . . . **153** AR71
South Croydon CR2 . . . . **242** DS109
Virginia Water GU25. . . . . **214** AU101
Beechwood Sch, SW16
off Leigham Ct Rd. **203** DL90
Slough SL2
off Long Readings La **153** AP69
Beechwoods Ct, SE19
off Crystal Palace Par **204** DT92
Beechwood Vil, Red. RH1. . . . . . **288** DG144
Beechworth Cl, NW3 . . . . **142** DA61
Beecot La, Walt. KT12. . . . . **218** BW103
Beecroft La, SE4
off Beecroft Rd **205** DY85
Beecroft Ms, SE4
off Beecroft Rd **205** DY85
Beecroft Rd, SE4. . . . . **205** DY85
Beehive Cl, E8 . . . . **10** A6
Elstree WD6. . . . . **99** CK44
Uxbridge UB10
off Honey Hill **156** BM66
Beehive Ct, Rom. RM3
off Arundel Rd. **128** FM52
Beehive Grn, Welw.G.C. AL7 . . . **52** DA11
Beehive La, Ilf. IG1, IG4 . . . . . . **147** EM58
Welwyn Garden City AL7. . . . **52** DA12
Beehive Pas, EC3. . . . . **19** N9
Beehive Pl, SW9 . . . . **183** DN83
Beehive Rd, Goffs Oak EN7 . . . . **87** DP28
Staines TW18. . . . . **195** BF92
Beehive Way, Reig. RH2 . . . . . . **288** DB138
Beeken Dene, Orp. BR6
off Isabella Dr **245** EQ105
Beel Cl, Amer. HP7 . . . . **94** AW39
Beeleigh Rd, Mord. SM4 . . . . . . **222** DB98
Beesfield La, Fnghm DA4. . . . . . **230** FN101
Beeston Cl, E8. . . . . **10** C2
Watford WD19 . . . . **116** BX49
Beeston Dr, Chsht EN8. . . . . **89** DX27
Beeston Pl, SW1 . . . . **29** K7
Beeston Rd, Barn. EN4. . . . . . . **102** DD44
Beeston Way, Felt. TW14 . . . . . **198** BW86
Beethoven Rd, Els. WD6. . . . . . . **99** CJ44
Beethoven St, W10 . . . . **14** F2
Beeton Cl, Pnr. HA5 . . . . **116** CA52
Begbie Rd, SE3 . . . . **186** EJ81
Beggars Bush La, Wat. WD18. . . **97** BR43
Beggar's Hill, Epsom KT17. **239** CT107
Beggars Hill, Epsom KT17 . . . **239** CT108
Beggars Hollow, Enf. EN2 . . . . **104** DR37
Beggars La, Abin.Ham. RH5. . . **283** BT137
Westerham TN16. . . . . **277** ER125
Beggars Roost La, Sutt. SM1. . **240** DA107
Begonia Cl, E6. . . . . **25** H6
Begonia Pl, Hmptn. TW12
off Gresham Rd. **198** CA93
Begonia Wk, W12
off Du Cane Rd **161** CT72
Beira St, SW12 . . . . **203** DH87
Beis Chinuch Lebonos Girls Sch,
N4 *off Woodberry Gro* **144** DQ59
Beis Malka Girls' Sch, N16
off Alkham Rd **144** DT60
Beis Rochel D'Satmar Girls' Sch,
N16 *off Amhurst Pk* **144** DS59
Beis Yaakov Prim Sch, NW9
off Edgware Rd. **140** CR55
Bejun Ct, New Barn. EN5
off Station App **102** DC42
Beken Ct, Wat. WD25
off First Av. **98** BW35
Bekesbourne St, E14 . . . . **21** L9
Bekesbourne Twr, Orp. BR5 . . **228** EX102
★ **Bekonscot Model Village**,
Beac. HP9. . . . . **111** AK51
Belcanto London Acad,
SE9 *off Passey Pl* **207** EM86
Belcher Rd, Hodd. EN11
off Amwell St **71** EA16
Belchers La, Naze.Gate EN9. . . . **72** EJ24
● **Belcon Ind Est**, Hodd. EN11 . **71** EB17
Belcroft Cl, Brom. BR1 . . . . **206** EF94
Beldam Haw, Halst. TN14. . . . . . **246** FA112
Beldham Gdns, W.Mol. KT8. . . . **218** CB97
Belfairs Dr, Rom. RM6 . . . . **148** EW59
Belfairs Grn, Wat. WD19 . . . . . **116** BX50
Belfast Av, Slou. SL1 . . . . **153** AQ72
Belfast Rd, N16 . . . . **144** DT61
SE25. **224** DV98
Belfield Gdns, Harl. CM17 . . . . . **74** EW16
Belfield Rd, Epsom KT19 . . . . . **238** CR109
Belfont Wk, N7 . . . . **8** B1
Belford Gro, SE18. . . . . **37** L9
Belford Rd, Borwd. WD6. . . . . . **100** CM38
Belfort Rd, SE15 . . . . **45** H8
Belfour Ter, N3
off Squires La **120** DB54
Belfry Av, Hare. UB9 . . . . **114** BG53
Belfry Cl, SE16. . . . . **32** F10
Bromley BR1 . . . . **227** EP98
Belfry La, Rick. WD3 . . . . **114** BJ46
Belfry Shop Cen, Red. RH1 . **272** DF133
Belgrade Rd, N16 . . . . **9** P1
Hampton TW12 . . . . **218** CB95
Belgrave Av, Rom. RM2 . . . . . . **150** FJ55
Watford WD18. . . . . **97** BT43
Belgrave Cl, N14
off Prince George Av. **103** DJ43
NW7 . . . . **118** CR50
W3 *off Avenue Rd*. **180** CP75
Hersham KT12 . . . . **235** BV105
Orpington BR5 . . . . **228** EW98
St. Albans AL4. . . . . **65** CJ16
Belgrave Ct, E14 . . . . **33** P1
Belgrave Cres, Sun. TW16 . . . . **217** BV95
Belgrave Dr, Kings L. WD4. . . . . **81** BQ28
Belgrave Gdns, N14 . . . . **103** DK43
NW8. . . . . **5** M9
Stanmore HA7
off Copley Rd. **117** CJ50
Belgrave Hts, E11 . . . . **146** EG60
Belgrave Manor, Wok. GU22 . . **248** AY119
Belgrave Ms, Uxb. UB8 . . . . **156** BK70
Belgrave Ms N, SW1. . . . . **28** G5
Belgrave Ms S, SW1. . . . . **29** H6
Belgrave Ms W, SW1 . . . . **28** G6
Belgrave Pl, SW1 . . . . **29** H6
Belgrave Rd, E10. . . . . **145** EC60
E11 . . . . **146** EG61
E13 . . . . **24** B4
E17 . . . . **145** EA57
SE25. . . . . **224** DT98
SW1 . . . . **29** L9
SW13 . . . . **181** CT80
Hounslow TW4 . . . . **178** BZ83
Ilford IG1 . . . . **147** EM60
Mitcham CR4. . . . . **222** DD97
Slough SL1 . . . . **154** AS73
Sunbury-on-Thames TW16. . **217** BV95
Belgrave Sq, SW1. . . . . **28** G6
Belgrave St, E1 . . . . **21** K9
Belgrave Ter, Wdf.Grn. IG8 . . . . **124** EG48
Belgrave Walk **222** DD97
Belgrave Wk, Mitch. CR4 . . . . . . **222** DD97
Belgrave Yd, SW1 . . . . **29** J7
BELGRAVIA, SW1 . . . . **28** G7
Belgravia Cl, Barn. EN5. . . . . . . **101** CZ41
Belgravia Gdns, Brom. BR1 . . . . **206** EE93
Belgravia Ho, SW4 . . . . **203** DK86
Belgravia Ms, Kings.T. KT1. . . . **219** CK98
Belgrove St, WC1 . . . . **18** A2
Belham Rd, Kings L. WD4 . . . . . . **80** BM28
Belham Wk, SE5 . . . . **43** M6
Belhaven Ct, Borwd. WD6 . . . . . **100** CM39
Belhus Chase, Aveley RM15 . . . **171** FR71
Belhus Chase Sch, Aveley
RM15 *off Nethan Dr* **171** FR73
Belhus Pk, Aveley RM15. . . . . . **171** FS73
Belinda Rd, SW9. . . . . **183** DP83
Belitha Vil, N1 . . . . **8** D6
Bell, The, E17. . . . . **145** EA55
Bellamy Cl, E14. . . . . **34** A4
W14 . . . . **39** H1
Edgware HA8. . . . . **118** CQ48
Uxbridge UB10 . . . . **136** BN62
Watford WD17. . . . . **97** BU39
Bellamy Dr, Stan. HA7 . . . . **117** CH53
Bellamy Ho, SW17
off Garratt La. **202** DD91
Hounslow TW5 . . . . **178** CA79
Bellamy Rd, E4 . . . . **123** EB51
Cheshunt EN8 . . . . **89** DY29
Enfield EN2 . . . . **104** DR40
Bellamy St, SW12. . . . . **203** DH87
Bel La, Felt. TW13
off Butts Cotts. **198** BZ90
Bellarmine Cl, SE28 . . . . **187** ET75
Bellasis Av, SW2. . . . . **203** DL89
Bell Av, Rom. RM3 . . . . **127** FH53
West Drayton UB7 . . . . **176** BM77
Bell Br Rd, Cher. KT16 . . . . **215** BF102
Bellchambers Cl,
Lon.Col. AL2 . . . . **83** CJ26
Bell Cl, Beac. HP9 . . . . **111** AM53
Bedmond WD5 . . . . **81** BT27
Greenhithe DA9. . . . . **211** FT85
Pinner HA5. . . . . **116** BW54
Ruislip HA4 . . . . **137** BT62
Slough SL2 . . . . **154** AV71
Bellclose Rd, West Dr. UB7. . . . **176** BL75
BELL COMMON, Epp. CM16 . . . . **91** ER32
Bell Common, Epp. CM16 . . . . . **91** ES32
Bell Common Tunnel, Epp.
CM16 . . . . **91** ER33
Bell Ct, Surb. KT5
off Barnsbury La. **220** CP103
Bell Cres, Couls. CR5
off Maple Way. **257** DH121
Bell Dr, SW18 . . . . **201** CY87
Bellefield Rd, Orp. BR5. . . . . . . **228** EV99
Bellefields Rd, SW9 . . . . **183** DM83
Bellegrove Cl, Well. DA16. . . . . **187** ET82
Bellegrove Par, Well. DA16
off Bellegrove Rd **187** ET83
Bellegrove Rd, Well. DA16 . . . . **187** ER82
Bellenden Prim Sch, SE15 . . **44** C10
Bellenden Rd, SE15 . . . . **44** B8
Bellerbys Coll, SE8 . . . . **46** B3
Bellestaines Pleasaunce, E4 . . **123** EA47
Belleville Prim Sch, SW11
off Webbs Rd. **202** DF85
Belleville Rd, SW11. . . . . **202** DF85
Belle Vue, Grnf. UB6 . . . . **159** CD67
Belle Vue Cl, Stai. TW18 . . . . . . **216** BG95
Belle Vue Est, NW4
off Bell La **141** CW56
Belle Vue La, Bushey Hth
WD23. . . . . **117** CD46
Bellevue Ms, N11 . . . . **120** DG50
Bellevue Par, SW17
off Bellevue Rd **202** DE88
Belle Vue Pk, Th.Hth. CR7. . . . . **224** DQ97
Bellevue Pl, E1 . . . . **20** G5
Slough SL1 . . . . **174** AT76
Belle Vue Rd, E17 . . . . **123** ED54
Bellevue Rd, N11. . . . . **120** DG49
Belle Vue Rd, NW4 . . . . **141** CW56
Bellevue Rd, SW13. . . . . **181** CU82
SW17 . . . . **202** DE88
W13 . . . . **159** CH70
Bexleyheath DA6 . . . . **208** EZ85
Belle Vue Rd, Downe BR6
off Standard Rd. **245** EN110
Bellevue Rd, Horn. RM11 . . . . . **150** FM60
Kingston upon Thames KT1. **220** CL97
Romford RM5 . . . . **127** FC51
Belle Vue Rd, Ware SG12 . . . . . . **55** DZ06
Bellevue Ter, Hare. UB9 . . . . . . **114** BG52
Bellew St, SW17. . . . . **202** DC90
Bell Fm Av, Dag. RM10. . . . . . . **149** FC62
Bell Fm Jun Sch, Hersham
KT12 *off Hersham Rd*. **236** BW105
Bellfield, Croy. CR0. . . . . **243** DY109
Bellfield Av, Har. HA3 . . . . **116** CC51
Bellfield Cl, SE3. . . . . **47** P4
Bellfield Ct, Guil. GU1 . . . . **264** AW130
BELLFIELDS, Guil. GU1 . . . . . . **264** AW131
Bellfields Rd, Guil. GU1 . . . . . . **264** AX132
Bellflower Cl, E6 . . . . **24** G6
Bellflower Path, Rom. RM3 . . . **128** FJ52
Bell Gdns, E17
off Markhouse Rd. **145** DZ57
Orpington BR5 . . . . **228** EW99
Bellgate, Hem.H. HP2. . . . . **62** BL17
Bellgate Ms, NW5 *off York Ri*. . **143** DH62
Bellgate Prim Sch, Hem.H.
HP2 *off Fletcher Way* **62** BL18
BELL GREEN, SE6. . . . . **205** DZ90
Bell Grn, SE26. . . . . **205** DZ90
Bovingdon HP3. . . . . **79** BB27
Bell Grn La, SE26 . . . . **205** DY92
Bellhaven, E15. . . . . **13** H4
Bell Hill, Croy. CR0
off Surrey St **224** DQ103
Bellhouse La, Pilg.Hat. CM14. . **130** FS43
Bellhouse Rd, Rom. RM7. . . . . . **149** FC60
Bellina Ms, NW5. . . . . **7** K1
● **Bell Ind Est**, W4
off Cunnington St. **180** CQ77
Bellingdon Rd, Chesh. HP5 . . . . **76** AP31
BELLINGHAM, SE6. . . . . **205** EB90
⇌ **Bellingham** **205** EB90
Bellingham Ct, Bark. IG11
off Renwick Rd **168** EV69
Bellingham Dr, Reig. RH2 . . . . . **271** CZ134
Bellingham Grn, SE6 . . . . **205** EA90
Bellingham Rd, SE6 . . . . **205** EB90
● **Bellingham Trd Est**, SE6
off Franthorne Way. **205** EB90
Bell Inn Yd, EC3. . . . . **19** M9
Bell La, E1 . . . . **20** A7
E16 . . . . **35** N2
NW4. . . . . **141** CX56
Amersham HP6, HP7 . . . . **94** AV39
Bedmond WD5 . . . . **81** BT27
Berkhamsted HP4 . . . . **60** AS18
Brookmans Park AL9 . . . . **86** DA25
Broxbourne EN10. . . . . **71** DY21
Enfield EN3 . . . . **105** DX38
Eton Wick SL4 . . . . **173** AM77
Fetcham KT22 . . . . **253** CD123
Hertford SG14. . . . . **54** DR09
Hoddesdon EN11 . . . . **71** EA17
London Colney AL2 . . . . **84** CL29
Twickenham TW1
off The Embankment. **199** CG88
Wembley HA9
off Magnet Rd. **139** CK61
Bell La Cl, Fetch. KT22 . . . . **253** CD123
Bell La Comb Sch, Lt.Chal.
HP6 *off Bell La*. **94** AV38
Bell La Prim Sch, NW4
off Bell La **141** CX56
Bellmaker Ct, E3 . . . . **22** A6
Bellman Av, Grav. DA12 . . . . . . **213** GL88
Bellmarsh Rd, Add. KT15 . . . . . . **234** BH105
Bell Mead, Saw. CM21 . . . . **58** EY05
Bell Meadow, SE19
off Dulwich Wd Av **204** DS91
Godstone RH9. . . . . **274** DV132
Bellmount Wd Av, Wat. WD17 . . **97** BS39
Bello Cl, SE24 . . . . **203** DP87
Bellot Gdns, SE10. . . . . **35** K10
Bellot St, SE10 . . . . **35** K10
Bell Par, Wind. SL4
off St. Andrews Av **173** AM82
Bellridge Pl, Knot.Grn HP9 . . . . **110** AH49
Bellring Cl, Belv. DA17 . . . . **188** FA79
Bell Rd, E.Mol. KT8. . . . . **219** CD99
Enfield EN1 . . . . **104** DR39
Hounslow TW3 . . . . **178** CB84
Bells All, SW6 . . . . **39** J9
Bells Gdn Est, SE15 . . . . **44** C5
Bells Hill, Barn. EN5 . . . . **101** CX43
Bell's Hill, Stoke P. SL2. . . . . . . **154** AU67
Bells Hill Grn, Stoke P. SL2. . . . **154** AU66
Bells La, Horton SL3. . . . . **175** BB83
Bell St, NW1 . . . . **16** C6
SE18. . . . . **186** EL81
Reigate RH2. . . . . **272** DA134
Sawbridgeworth CM21 . . . . . . **58** EY05
Bellswood La, Iver SL0. . . . . **155** BB71
Belltrees Gro, SW16 . . . . **203** DM92
Bell Vw, St.Alb. AL4 . . . . **65** CK20
Windsor SL4 . . . . **173** AM83
Bell Vw Cl, Wind. SL4. . . . . **173** AM82
Bell Water Gate, SE18. . . . . **37** M6
Bell Weir Cl, Stai. TW19. . . . . . . **195** BB89
Bellwether La, Outwood RH1 . **289** DP143
Bell Wf La, EC4 . . . . **31** K1
Bellwood Rd, SE15. . . . . **185** DX84
Bell Yd, WC2 . . . . **18** E8
Bell Yd Ms, SE1. . . . . **31** P5
Belmarsh Rd, SE28
off Western Way **187** ES75
BELMONT, Har. HA3. . . . . **117** CG54
BELMONT, Sutt. SM2. . . . . **240** DB111
⇌ **Belmont**. **240** DA110
Belmont, Mill Hill Prep Sch,
NW7 *off The Ridgeway* **119** CU48
Belmont, Slou. SL2. . . . . **153** AN71
Weybridge KT13
off Egerton Rd. **235** BQ107
Belmont Av, N9. . . . . **122** DU46
N13. . . . . **121** DL50
N17. . . . . **144** DQ55
Barnet EN4. . . . . **102** DF43
Guildford GU2. . . . . **264** AT131
New Malden KT3 . . . . **221** CU99
Southall UB2 . . . . **178** BY76
Upminster RM14. . . . . **150** FM61
Welling DA16. . . . . **187** ES83
Wembley HA0. . . . . **160** CM67
Belmont Circle, Har. HA3 . . . . . **117** CH53
Belmont Cl, E4 . . . . **123** ED50
N20. . . . . **120** DB46
SW4 . . . . **183** DJ83
Cockfosters EN4 . . . . **102** DF42
Uxbridge UB8 . . . . **156** BK65
Woodford Green IG8 . . . . **124** EH49
Belmont Cotts, Colnbr. SL3
off High St **175** BC80
Belmont Ct, NW11 . . . . **141** CZ57
Belmont First & Mid Schs,
Har.Wld HA3
off Hibbert Rd **117** CF54
Belmont Gro, SE13. . . . . **46** G10
W4 *off Belmont Ter*. **180** CR77
Belmont Hall Ct, SE13
off Belmont Gro **185** ED83
Belmont Hill, SE13 . . . . **185** ED83
St. Albans AL1. . . . . **65** CD21
Belmont Inf Sch, N22
off Rusper Rd **144** DQ55
Belmont Jun Sch, N22
off Rusper Rd **144** DQ55
Belmont La, Chis. BR7 . . . . **207** EQ92
Stanmore HA7. . . . . **117** CJ52
Belmont Ms, SW19
off Chapman Sq **201** CX89
Belmont Pk, SE13. . . . . **185** ED84
Belmont Pk Cl, SE13. . . . . **185** ED84
Belmont Pk Rd, E10 . . . . **145** EB58
Belmont Pk Sch, E10
off Leyton Grn Rd. **145** EC58
Belmont Prim Sch, W4
off Belmont Rd **180** CR77
Erith DA8 *off Belmont Rd*. . . **188** FA80
Belmont Ri, Sutt. SM2 . . . . **239** CZ107
Belmont Rd, N15. . . . . **144** DQ56
N17. . . . . **144** DQ56
SE25. . . . . **224** DV99
SW4 . . . . **183** DJ83
W4 *off Chiswick High Rd* . . . **180** CR77
Beckenham BR3 . . . . **225** DZ96
Bushey WD23 . . . . **98** BY43
Chesham HP5 . . . . **76** AP29
Chislehurst BR7 . . . . **207** EP92
Erith DA8. . . . . **188** FA80
Grays RM17. . . . . **192** FZ78
Harrow HA3. . . . . **139** CF55
Hemel Hempstead HP3 . . . . . . **62** BL24
Hornchurch RM12. . . . . **150** FK62
Ilford IG1 . . . . **147** EQ62
Leatherhead KT22. . . . . **253** CG122
Reigate RH2. . . . . **288** DC135
Sutton SM2 . . . . **240** DA110
Twickenham TW2 . . . . **199** CD89
Uxbridge UB8 . . . . **156** BK66
Wallington SM6 . . . . **241** DH106
Belmont St, NW1. . . . . **7** H6
Belmont Ter, W4 . . . . **180** CR77
Belmor, Els. WD6 . . . . **100** CN43
Belmore Av, Hayes UB4 . . . . **157** BU72
Woking GU22 . . . . **249** BD116
Belmore La, N7. . . . . **7** P3
Belmore Prim Sch, Hayes
UB4 *off Owen Rd* **157** BV69
Belmore St, SW8 . . . . **41** N6
Beloe Cl, SW15 . . . . **181** CU83

Belper Ct, E5 off Pedro St 145 DX63
Belsham Cl, Chesh. HP5 76 AP28
Belsham St, E9 10 G4
BELSIZE, Rick. WD3 79 BF33
Belsize Av, N13 121 DM51
NW3 6 B4
W13 179 CH76
Belsize Cl, Hem.H. HP3 62 BN21
St. Albans AL4 65 CJ15
Belsize Ct, NW3 6 B2
Belsize Cres, NW3 6 B3
Belsize Gdns, Sutt. SM1 240 DB105
Belsize Gro, NW3 6 D4
Belsize La, NW3 6 A5
Belsize Ms, NW3 6 B4
BELSIZE PARK, NW3 6 C5
⊖ Belsize Park 6 D3
Belsize Pk, NW3 6 A5
Belsize Pk Gdns, NW3 6 B4
Belsize Pk Ms, NW3 6 B4
Belsize Pl, NW3 6 B4
Belsize Rd, NW6 5 P7
Harrow HA3 117 CD52
Hemel Hempstead HP3 62 BN21
Belsize Sq, NW3 6 B4
Belsize Ter, NW3 6 B4
Belson Rd, SE18 37 J8
Belswains Grn, Hem.H. HP3 off Belswains La 62 BL23
Belswains La, Hem.H. HP3 80 BM25
Sch Belswains Prim Sch, Hem.H. HP3 off Barnfield 62 BM24
Beltana Dr, Grav. DA12 213 GL91
Beltane Dr, SW19 201 CX90
Belthorn Cres, SW12 203 DJ87
Beltinge Rd, Rom. RM3 150 FM55
Beltona Gdns, Chsht EN8 89 DX27
Belton Rd, E7 166 EH66
E11 146 EE63
N17 144 DS55
NW2 161 CU65
Berkhamsted HP4 60 AU18
Sidcup DA14 208 EU91
Belton Way, E3 22 A6
Beltran Rd, SW6 39 L9
Beltwood Rd, Belv. DA17 189 FC77
BELVEDERE, DA17 189 FB77
⇌ Belvedere 188 FA76
Belvedere, The, SW10 39 P7
Belvedere Av, SW19 201 CY92
Ilford IG5 125 EP54
Belvedere Bldgs, SE1 31 H5
● Belvedere Business Pk, Belv. DA17 189 FB75
Belvedere Cl, Amer. HP6 94 AT36
Esher KT10 236 CB106
Gravesend DA12 213 GJ88
Guildford GU2 264 AV132
Teddington TW11 199 CE92
Weybridge KT13 234 BN106
Belvedere Ct, N1 9 N8
N2 142 DD57
Belvedere Dr, SW19 201 CY92
Belvedere Gdns, St.Alb. AL2 82 CA27
West Molesey KT8 218 BZ99
Belvedere Gro, SW19 201 CY92
Belvedere Ho, Felt. TW13 197 BU88
Belvedere Ind Est, Belv. DA17 189 FC76
Sch Belvedere Inf Sch, Belv. DA17 off Mitchell Cl 189 FB76
Sch Belvedere Jun Sch, Belv. DA17 off Mitchell Cl 189 FB76
Belvedere Ms, SE3 47 P5
SE15 184 DW83
Belvedere Pl, SE1 31 H5
SW2 183 DM84
Belvedere Rd, E10 145 DY60
SE1 30 D4
SE2 168 EX74
SE19 204 DT94
W7 179 CF76
Bexleyheath DA7 188 EZ83
Biggin Hill TN16 261 EM118
Brentwood CM14 130 FT48
Belvederes, The, Reig. RH2 288 DB137
Belvedere Sq, SW19 201 CY92
Belvedere Strand, NW9 119 CT54
Belvedere Way, Har. HA3 140 CL58
Belvoir Cl, SE9 206 EL90
Belvoir Ho, SW1 off Vauxhall Br Rd 29 M8
Belvoir Rd, SE22 204 DU87
Belvue Cl, Nthlt. UB5 158 CA66
Belvue Rd, Nthlt. UB5 158 CA66
Sch Belvue Sch, Nthlt. UB5 off Rowdell Rd 158 CA67
Bembridge Cl, NW6 4 E6
Bembridge Ct, Slou. SL1 off Park St 174 AT75
Bembridge Gdns, Ruis. HA4 137 BR61
Bemersyde Pt, E13 24 A3
Bemerton Est, N1 8 B7
Bemerton St, N1 8 C8
Bemish Rd, SW15 181 CX83
Bempton Dr, Ruis. HA4 137 BV61
Bemsted Rd, E17 145 DZ55
Benares Rd, SE18 187 ET77
Benbow Cl, St.Alb. AL1 65 CH22
Benbow Rd, W6 181 CV76
Benbow St, SE8 46 B2
Benbow Waye, Uxb. UB8 156 BJ71
Benbrick Rd, Guil. GU2 280 AU135
Benbury Cl, Brom. BR1 205 EC92
Bence, The, Egh. TW20 215 BB97
Bench Fld, S.Croy. CR2 242 DT107
Benchleys Rd, Hem.H. HP1 61 BF21
Bench Manor Cres, Chal.St.P. SL9 112 AW54
Bencombe Rd, Pur. CR8 241 DN114
Bencroft, Chsht EN7 88 DU26
Bencroft Rd, SW16 203 DJ94
Hemel Hempstead HP2 62 BL20
Bencurtis Pk, W.Wick. BR4 225 ED104
Bendall Ms, NW1 16 D6
Bendemeer Rd, SW15 38 C10
Bendish Pt, SE28 187 EQ75
Bendish Rd, E6 166 EL66
Bendmore Av, SE2 188 EU78
Bendon Valley, SW18 202 DB87
Bendysh Rd, Bushey WD23 98 BY41
Benedict Cl, Belv. DA17 off Tunstock Way 188 EY76
Orpington BR6 227 ES104
Benedict Dr, Felt. TW14 197 BR87
Benedictine Gate, Wal.Cr. EN8 89 DY27
Sch Benedict Prim Sch, Mitch. CR4 off Church Rd 222 DD97
Benedict Rd, SW9 42 D10
Mitcham CR4 222 DD97
Benedicts Wf, Bark. IG11 off Town Quay 167 EP67
Benedict Way, N2 142 DC55
Benenden Grn, Brom. BR2 226 EG99
Benen-Stock Rd, Stai. TW19 195 BF85
Benets Rd, Horn. RM11 150 FN60
Benett Gdns, SW16 223 DL96
Benfleet Cl, Cob. KT11 236 BY112
Sutton SM1 222 DC104
Benfleet Way, N11 120 DG47
Benford Rd, Hodd. EN11 71 DZ19
Bengal Ct, EC3 off Birchin La 19 M9
Bengal Rd, Ilf. IG1 147 EP63
Bengarth Dr, Har. HA3 117 CD54
Bengarth Rd, Nthlt. UB5 158 BX67
BENGEO, Hert. SG14 54 DQ07
Bengeo Gdns, Rom. RM6 148 EW58
Bengeo Meadows, Hert. SG14 54 DR06
Bengeo Ms, Hert. SG14 54 DQ06
Sch Bengeo Prim Sch, Hert. SG14 off The Avenue 54 DQ06
Bengeo St, Hert. SG14 54 DQ08
Bengeworth Rd, SE5 43 J10
Harrow HA1 139 CG61
Ben Hale Cl, Stan. HA7 117 CH49
Benham Cl, SW11 182 DD83
Chesham HP5 76 AP29
Chessington KT9 237 CJ107
Coulsdon CR5 257 DP118
Benham Gdns, Houns. TW4 198 BZ85
Benham Rd, W7 159 CE71
Benhams Cl, Horl. RH6 290 DG146
Benhams Dr, Horl. RH6 290 DG146
Benhams Pl, NW3 off Holly Wk 142 DC63
Benhill Av, Sutt. SM1 240 DB105
Benhill Rd, SE5 43 M5
Sutton SM1 222 DC104
Benhill Wd Rd, Sutt. SM1 222 DC104
BENHILTON, Sutt. SM1 222 DB103
Benhilton Gdns, Sutt. SM1 222 DB104
Benhurst Av, Horn. RM12 149 FH62
Benhurst Cl, S.Croy. CR2 243 DX110
Benhurst Ct, SW16 203 DN92
Benhurst Gdns, S.Croy. CR2 242 DW110
Benhurst La, SW16 203 DN92
Sch Benhurst Prim Sch, Elm Pk RM12 off Benhurst Av 149 FH62
Beningfield Dr, Lon.Col. AL2 83 CH27
Benington Ct, N4 off Brownswood Rd 144 DQ61
Benin St, SE13 205 ED87
Benison Ct, Slou. SL1 off Hencroft St S 174 AT76
Benjafield Cl, N18 off Brettenham Rd 122 DV49
Benjamin Cl, E8 10 D9
Hornchurch RM11 149 FG58
Benjamin La, Wexham SL3 154 AV70
Benjamin Ms, SW12 203 DJ87
Benjamin St, EC1 18 G6
Ben Jonson Ho, EC2 off The Barbican 19 K6
Sch Ben Jonson Prim Sch, E1 21 M5
Ben Jonson Rd, E1 21 K7
Benledi Rd, E14 22 G8
Benn Cl, Oxt. RH8 276 EG134
Bennelong Cl, W12 161 CV73
Bennerley Rd, SW11 202 DE85
Bennets Ctyd, SW19 off Watermill Way 222 DC95
Bennetsfield Rd, Uxb. UB11 157 BP74
Bennet's Hill, EC4 19 H10
Bennet St, SW1 29 L2
Bennett Cl, Cob. KT11 235 BU113
Hampton Wick KT1 219 CJ95
Hounslow TW4 198 BY85
Northwood HA6 115 BT52
Welling DA16 188 EU82
Welwyn Garden City AL7 51 CZ13
Bennett Gro, SE13 46 D7
Bennett Ho, SW1 off Page St 29 P8
Bennett Pk, SE3 47 L10
Bennett Rd, E13 24 C5
N16 9 N1
SW9 42 F9
Romford RM6 148 EY58
Bennetts, Chesh. HP5 76 AR30
Bennetts Av, Croy. CR0 225 DY103
Greenford UB6 159 CE67
Bennetts Castle La, Dag. RM8 148 EW63
Bennetts Cl, N17 122 DT51
Colney Heath AL4 66 CR23
Mitcham CR4 223 DH95
Slough SL1 153 AN74
Bennetts Copse, Chis. BR7 206 EL93
BENNETTS END, Hem.H. HP3 62 BM23
Bennetts End Cl, Hem.H. HP3 62 BM21
Bennetts End Rd, Hem.H. HP3 62 BM21
Bennetts Fm Pl, Bkhm KT23 268 BZ125
Bennetts Gate, Hem.H. HP3 off Kimps Way 62 BN23
Bennett St, W4 180 CS79
Bennetts Way, Croy. CR0 225 DY103
Bennetts Yd, SW1 29 P7
Uxbridge UB8 off High St 156 BJ66
Bennett Way, Lane End DA2 211 FR91
West Clandon GU4 266 BG129
Benning Cl, Wind. SL4 173 AK83
Benningfield Gdns, Berk. HP4 60 AY17
Benningholme Rd, Edg. HA8 118 CS51
Bennington Dr, Borwd. WD6 100 CM39
Bennington Rd, N17 122 DS53
Woodford Green IG8 124 EE52
Bennions Cl, Horn. RM12 off Franklin Rd 170 FK65
Bennison Dr, Harold Wd RM3 128 FK54
Benn St, E9 11 M4
Benn's Wk, Rich. TW9 off Rosedale Rd 180 CL84
Benrek Cl, Ilf. IG6 125 EQ53
Bensbury Cl, SW15 201 CV87
Bensham Cl, Th.Hth. CR7 224 DQ98
Bensham Gro, Th.Hth. CR7 224 DQ96
Bensham La, Croy. CR0 223 DP101
Thornton Heath CR7 223 DP98
Bensham Manor Rd, Th.Hth. CR7 224 DQ98
Sch Bensham Manor Sch, Th.Hth. CR7 off Ecclesbourne Rd 224 DQ99
Bensington Ct, Felt. TW14 197 BR86
Benskin Rd, Wat. WD18 97 BU43
Benskins La, Noak Hill RM4 128 FK46
Bensley Cl, N11 120 DF50
Ben Smith Way, SE16 32 D6
Benson Av, E6 24 D1
Benson Cl, Houns. TW3 178 CA84
Slough SL2 154 AU74
Uxbridge UB8 156 BL71
Benson Ct, SW8 off Hartington Rd 42 A6
Enfield EN3 off Harston Dr 105 EA38
Sch Benson Prim Sch, Croy. CR0 off West Way 225 DY104
Benson Quay, E1 32 G1
Benson Rd, SE23 204 DW88
Croydon CR0 223 DN104
Grays RM17 192 GB79
🔒 Bentall Cen, The, Kings.T. KT1 219 CK96
Bentfield Gdns, SE9 off Aldersgrove Av 206 EJ90
Benthall Gdns, Ken. CR8 258 DQ117
Sch Benthal Prim Sch, N16 off Benthal Rd 144 DU62
Benthal Rd, N16 144 DU61
Bentham Av, Wok. GU21 249 BC115
Bentham Ct, N1 9 J7
Bentham Ho, SE1 off Falmouth Rd 31 L6
Bentham Rd, E9 11 J5
SE28 168 EV73
Bentham Wk, NW10 140 CQ64
Ben Tillet Cl, Bark. IG11 168 EU66
Ben Tillett Cl, E16 37 J3
Bentinck Cl, NW8 off Prince Albert Rd 16 D1
Gerrards Cross SL9 134 AX57
Bentinck Ms, W1 17 H8
Bentinck Rd, West Dr. UB7 156 BK74
Bentinck St, W1 17 H8
Bentley Ct, SE13 off Whitburn Rd 185 EC84
Bentley Dr, NW2 141 CZ62
Harlow CM17 74 EW16
Ilford IG2 147 EQ58
Weybridge KT13 234 BN109
BENTLEY HEATH, Barn. EN5 101 CZ35
Bentley Heath La, Barn. EN5 85 CY34
Bentley Ms, Enf. EN1 104 DR44
Bentley Pk, Burn. SL1 153 AK68
★ Bentley Priory Open Space, Stan. HA7 117 CF49
Bentley Rd, N1 9 P5
Hertford SG14 53 DL08
Slough SL1 153 AN74
Bentleys, Hat.Hth CM22 59 FH05
Bentley St, Grav. DA12 213 GJ86
Bentley Way, Stan. HA7 117 CG50
Woodford Green IG8 124 EG48
Sch Bentley Wd High Sch for Girls, Stan. HA7 off Bridges Rd 117 CF50
Benton Rd, Ilf. IG1 147 ER60
Watford WD19 116 BX50
Bentons La, SE27 204 DQ91
Bentons Ri, SE27 204 DR92
Bentry Cl, Dag. RM8 148 EY61
Bentry Rd, Dag. RM8 148 EY61
Bentsbrook Cl, N.Holm. RH5 285 CH140
Bentsbrook Pk, N.Holm. RH5 285 CH140
Bentsbrook Rd, N.Holm. RH5 285 CH140
Bentsley Cl, St.Alb. AL4 65 CJ16
Sch Bentworth Prim Sch, W12 off Bentworth Rd 161 CV72
Bentworth Rd, W12 161 CV72
Benville Ho, SW8 42 D5
Benwell Ct, Sun. TW16 217 BU95
Benwell Rd, N7 8 E1
Benwick Cl, SE16 32 F8
Benworth St, E3 21 P2
Benyon Path, S.Ock. RM15 off Tyssen Pl 171 FW69
Sch Benyon Prim Sch, S.Ock. RM15 off Tyssen Pl 171 FW68
Benyon Rd, N1 9 M8
Benyon Wf, E8 9 P8
Beomonds Row, Cher. KT16 off Heriot Rd 216 BG101
Sch Beormund Sch, SE1 31 M5
Berberis Cl, Guil. GU1 264 AW132
Berberis Ho, Felt. TW13 off Highfield Rd 197 BU89
Berberis Wk, West Dr. UB7 176 BL77
Berber Par, SE18 186 EL81
Berber Pl, E14 22 A10
Berber Rd, SW11 202 DF85
Berberry Cl, Edg. HA8 off Larkspur Gro 118 CQ49
Berceau Wk, Wat. WD17 97 BS39
Bercta Rd, SE9 207 EQ89
Berdan Ct, Enf. EN3 off George Lovell Dr 105 EA37
Bere Cl, Green. DA9 off Ingress Pk Av 211 FW85
Berecroft, Harl. CM18 73 ER20
Beredens La, Gt Warley CM13 151 FT55
Berefeld, Hem.H. HP2 62 BK18
Berengers Pl, Dag. RM9 168 EV65
Berenger Twr, SW10 40 A4
Berenger Wk, SW10 off Blantyre St 40 A4
Berens Rd, NW10 14 C3
Orpington BR5 228 EX99
Berens Way, Chis. BR7 227 ET98
Beresford Av, N20 120 DF47
W7 159 CD71
Slough SL2 154 AW74
Surbiton KT5 220 CP102
Twickenham TW1 199 CJ86
Wembley HA0 160 CM67
Beresford Dr, Brom. BR1 226 EL97
Woodford Green IG8 124 EJ49
Beresford Gdns, Enf. EN1 104 DS42
Hounslow TW4 198 BZ85
Romford RM6 148 EY57
Beresford Rd, E4 124 EE46
E17 123 EB53
N2 142 DE55
N5 9 L3
N8 143 DN57
Dorking RH4 285 CH136
Harrow HA1 139 CD57
Kingston upon Thames KT2 220 CM95
Mill End WD3 113 BF46
New Malden KT3 220 CQ98
Northfleet DA11 212 GE87
St. Albans AL1 65 CH21
Southall UB1 158 BX74
Beresford Rd, Sutt. SM2 239 CZ108
Beresford Sq, SE18 37 N8
Beresford St, SE18 37 N7
Beresford Ter, N5 9 K3
Berestede Rd, W6 181 CT78
Bere St, E1 21 K10
Bergenia Ho, Felt. TW13 off Bedfont La 197 BV88
Bergen Sq, SE16 33 M6
Berger Cl, Petts Wd BR5 227 ER100
Sch Berger Prim Sch, E9 11 J4
Berger Rd, E9 11 J4
Berghem Ms, W14 26 D7
Berghers Hill, Woob.Grn HP10 132 AF59
Bergholt Av, Ilf. IG4 146 EL57
Bergholt Cres, N16 144 DS59
Bergholt Ms, NW1 7 M7
Berglen Ct, E14 21 L9
Bericot Way, Welw.G.C. AL7 52 DC09
Bering Sq, E14 34 B10
Bering Wk, E16 24 E9
Berisford Ms, SW18 202 DB86
Berkeley Av, Bexh. DA7 188 EX81
Chesham HP5 76 AN30
Greenford UB6 159 CE65
Hounslow TW4 177 BU82
Ilford IG5 125 EN54
Romford RM5 127 FC52
Berkeley Cl, Abb.L. WD5 81 BT32
Chesham HP5 off Berkeley Av 76 AN30
Elstree WD6 100 CN43
Hornchurch RM11 150 FP61
Kingston upon Thames KT2 200 CL94
Petts Wood BR5 227 ES101
Potters Bar EN6 85 CY32
Ruislip HA4 137 BU62
Staines TW19 195 BD89
Ware SG12 54 DW05
Berkeley Ct, N14 103 DJ44
Croxley Green WD3 off Mayfare 97 BR43
Guildford GU1 off London Rd 264 AY134
Wallington SM6 223 DJ104
Weybridge KT13 217 BR103
Berkeley Cres, Barn. EN4 102 DD43
Dartford DA1 210 FM88
Berkeley Dr, Horn. RM11 150 FN60
West Molesey KT8 218 BZ97
Berkeley Gdns, N21 122 DR45
W8 27 K3
Claygate KT10 237 CG107
Walton-on-Thames KT12 217 BT101
West Byfleet KT14 233 BF114
Berkeley Ho, E3 21 P3
Berkeley Ms, W1 16 F8
Berkeley Pl, SW19 201 CX93
Epsom KT18 254 CR115
Sch Berkeley Prim Sch, Heston TW5 off Cranford La 178 BX80
Berkeley Rd, E12 146 EL64
N8 143 DK57
N15 144 DR58
NW9 140 CN56
SW13 181 CU81
Loudwater HP10 110 AC53
Uxbridge UB10 157 BQ66
Berkeleys, The, Fetch. KT22 253 CE124
Berkeley Sq, W1 29 K1
Berkeley St, W1 29 K1
Berkeley Twr, E14 33 P2
Berkeley Wk, N7 off Durham Rd 143 DM61
Berkeley Waye, Houns. TW5 178 BX80
Berkerley Ms, Sun. TW16 218 BW97
Berkhampstead Rd, Belv. DA17 188 FA78
Chesham HP5 76 AQ30
BERKHAMSTED, HP4 60 AW17
⇌ Berkhamsted 60 AW18
Berkhamsted Av, Wem. HA9 160 CM65
Berkhamsted Bypass, Berk. HP4 60 AV21
Hemel Hempstead HP1 61 BB23
★ Berkhamsted Castle, Berk. HP4 60 AX18
Sch Berkhamsted Collegiate Sch, Castle Campus, Berk. HP4 off Castle St 60 AW19
Kings Campus, Berk. HP4 off Kings Rd 60 AV19
Prep Sch, Berk. HP4 off Kings Rd 60 AV19
Berkhamsted Hill, Berk. HP4 60 AY17
Berkhamsted La, Essen. AL9 68 DF20
Berkhamsted Pl, Berk. HP4 60 AW17
Berkhamsted Rd, Hem.H. HP1 61 BD17
Berkley Av, Wal.Cr. EN8 89 DX34
Berkley Cl, St.Alb. AL4 65 CJ16
Berkley Ct, Berk. HP4 off Mill St 60 AW19
Berkley Cres, Grav. DA12 off Milton Rd 213 GJ86
Berkley Gro, NW1 6 F7
Berkley Rd, NW1 6 F7
Beaconsfield HP9 111 AK49
Gravesend DA12 213 GH86
Berks Hill, Chorl. WD3 95 BC43
Berkshire Av, Slou. SL1 153 AP72
Berkshire Cl, Cat. CR3 258 DR122
Berkshire Gdns, N13 121 DN51
N18 122 DV50
Berkshire Rd, E9 11 P4
Berkshire Sq, Mitch. CR4 off Berkshire Way 223 DL98
Berkshire Way, Horn. RM11 150 FN57
Mitcham CR4 223 DL98
Bermans Cl, Hutt. CM13 131 GB47
Bermans Way, NW10 140 CS63
Bermer Rd, Wat. WD24 98 BW39
BERMONDSEY, SE1 32 A7
⊖ Bermondsey 32 D6
Bermondsey Sq, SE1 31 P6
Bermondsey St, SE1 31 N3
● Bermondsey Trd Est, SE16 off Rotherhithe New Rd 32 G10
Bermondsey Wall E, SE16 32 D5
Bermondsey Wall W, SE16 32 C4
Bermuda Rd, Til. RM18 193 GG82
Bernal Cl, SE28 off Haldane Rd 168 EX73
Bernard Ashley Dr, SE7 186 EH78
Bernard Av, W13 179 CH76
Bernard Cassidy St, E16 23 M6
Bernard Gdns, SW19 201 CZ92
Bernard Gro, Wal.Abb. EN9 off Beaulieu Dr 89 EB33
Bernard Rd, N15 144 DT57
Bernard Rd, Rom. RM7 149 FC59
Wallington SM6 241 DH105
Bernards Cl, Ilf. IG6 125 EQ51
Bernard Shaw Ho, NW10 off Knatchbull Rd 160 CR67
Sch Bernards Heath Inf Sch, St.Alb. AL1 off Sandridge Rd 65 CF18
Sch Bernards Heath Jun Sch, St.Alb. AL3 off Watson Av 65 CE17
Bernard St, WC1 18 A5
Gravesend DA12 213 GH86
St. Albans AL3 65 CD19
Bernays Cl, Stan. HA7 117 CJ51
Bernays Gro, SW9 183 DM84
Bernel Dr, Croy. CR0 225 DZ104
Berne Rd, Th.Hth. CR7 224 DQ99
Berners Cl, Slou. SL1 153 AL73
Berners Dr, W13 159 CG72
Broxbourne EN10 off Berners Way 71 DZ23
St. Albans AL1 65 CD23
Bernersmede, SE3 47 N10
Berners Ms, W1 17 M7
Berners Pl, W1 17 M8
Berners Rd, N1 8 F10
N22 121 DN53
Berners St, W1 17 M7
Berners Way, Brox. EN10 71 DZ23
Berney Rd, Croy. CR0 224 DR101
Bernhardt Cres, NW8 16 C4
Bernhart Cl, Edg. HA8 118 CQ52
Bernice Cl, Rain. RM13 170 FJ70
Bernville Way, Har. HA3 140 CM57
Bernwell Rd, E4 124 EE48
Berricot Grn, Tewin AL6 52 DE08
Berridge Grn, Edg. HA8 118 CN52
Berridge Ms, NW6 5 J2
Berridge Rd, SE19 204 DS92
Berries, The, Sand. AL4 65 CG16
Berriman Rd, N7 143 DM62
Berrington Dr, E.Hors. KT24 251 BT124
Berriton Rd, Har. HA2 138 BZ60
Berry Av, Wat. WD24 97 BU36
Berrybank Cl, E4 off Greenbank Cl 123 EC47
Berry Cl, N21 121 DP46
Dagenham RM10 148 FA64
Hornchurch RM12 off Airfield Way 150 FJ64
Rickmansworth WD3 114 BH45
Berry Ct, Houns. TW4 off Raglan Cl 198 BZ85
Berrydale Rd, Hayes UB4 158 BY70
Berryfield, Slou. SL2 154 AW72
Berryfield Cl, E17 145 EB56
Bromley BR1 226 EL95
Berry Fld Pk, Amer. HP6 77 AP37
Berryfield Rd, SE17 31 H10
Jct Berrygrove Interchange, Wat. WD25 98 CA38
Berry Gro La, Wat. WD25 98 CA39
Sch Berrygrove Prim Sch, Wat. WD25 off Fourth Av 98 BX35
Berryhill, SE9 187 EP84
Berry Hill, Stan. HA7 117 CK49
Taplow SL6 152 AD71
Berry Hill Ct, Tap. SL6 152 AD71
Berryhill Gdns, SE9 187 EP84
BERRYLANDS, Surb. KT5 220 CM99
⇌ Berrylands 220 CN98
Berrylands, SW20 221 CW97
Orpington BR6 228 EW104
Surbiton KT5 220 CN99
Berrylands Rd, Surb. KT5 220 CM100
Berry La, SE21 204 DR91
Hersham KT12 off Burwood Rd 236 BX106
Rickmansworth WD3 114 BH46
Berryman Cl, Dag. RM8 off Bennetts Castle La 148 EW62
Berrymans La, SE26 205 DX91
Berrymead, Hem.H. HP2 62 BM19
Berry Meade, Ashtd. KT21 254 CM117
Berry Meade Cl, Ashtd. KT21 off Berry Meade 254 CM117
Berrymead Gdns, W3 160 CQ74
Sch Berrymede Inf Sch, W3 off Park Rd N 180 CP75
Sch Berrymede Jun Sch, W3 off Osborne Rd 180 CP75
Berrymede Rd, W4 180 CR76
Berry Pl, EC1 19 H3
Berryscroft Ct, Stai. TW18 196 BJ94
Berryscroft Rd, Stai. TW18 196 BJ94
BERRY'S GREEN, West. TN16 261 EP116
Berry's Grn Rd, Berry's Grn TN16 261 EP116
Berry's Hill, Berry's Grn TN16 261 EP115
Berrys La, Byfleet KT14 234 BK111
Berry St, EC1 19 H4
Berry Wk, Ashtd. KT21 254 CM119
Berry Way, W5 180 CL76
Rickmansworth WD3 114 BH45
Bersham La, Bad.Dene RM17 192 FZ77
Bertal Rd, SW17 202 DD91
Berther Rd, Horn. RM11 150 FK59
Berthold Ms, Wal.Abb. EN9 89 EB33
Berthon St, SE8 46 B4
Bertie Rd, NW10 161 CU65
SE26 205 DX93
Bertram Cotts, SW19 202 DA94
Bertram Rd, NW4 141 CU58
Enfield EN1 104 DU42
Kingston upon Thames KT2 200 CN94
Bertram St, N19 143 DH61
Bertram Way, Enf. EN1 104 DT42
Bertrand St, SE13 46 C10
Bertrand Way, SE28 168 EV73
Bert Rd, Th.Hth. CR7 224 DQ99
Berwick Av, Hayes UB4 158 BX72
Slough SL1 153 AP73
Berwick Cl, Beac. HP9 111 AP54
Stanmore HA7 off Gordon Av 117 CF51
Twickenham TW2 198 CA87
Waltham Cross EN8 89 EA34
Berwick Cres, Sid. DA15 207 ES86
Berwick Gdns, Sutt. SM1 222 DC104
Berwick La, Stanfd.Riv. CM5 109 FF36
Berwick Pl, Welw.G.C. AL7 51 CX12
Berwick Pond Cl, Rain. RM13 170 FK68
Berwick Pond Rd, Rain. RM13 170 FL68
Upminster RM14 170 FM66
Berwick Rd, E16 24 C9
N22 121 DP53
Borehamwood WD6 100 CM38
Rainham RM13 170 FK68
Welling DA16 188 EV81
Berwick St, W1 17 N9

Berwick Way, Orp. BR6 228 EU102
Sevenoaks TN14 279 FH121
Berwyn Av, Houns. TW3 178 CB81
Berwyn Rd, SE24 203 DP88
Richmond TW10 180 CP84
Beryl Av, E6 25 H6
Beryl Ho, SE18 off Spinel Cl 187 ET78
Beryl Rd, W6 38 C1
Berystede, Kings.T. KT2 200 CP94
Besant Ct, N1 9 M3
Besant Pl, SE22
off Hayes Gro 184 DT84
Besant Rd, NW2 141 CY63
Besant Wk, N7
off Newington Barrow Way 143 DM61
Besant Way, NW10 140 CQ64
Besley St, SW16 203 DJ93
Bessant Dr, Rich. TW9 180 CP81
Bessborough Gdns, SW1 29 P10
Bessborough Pl, SW1 29 N10
Bessborough Rd, SW15 201 CU88
Harrow HA1 139 CD60
Bessborough St, SW1 29 N10
BESSELS GREEN, Sev. TN13 278 FC124
Bessels Grn Rd, Sev. TN13 278 FD123
Bessels Meadow, Sev. TN13 278 FD124
Bessels Way, Sev. TN13 278 FC124
Bessemer Cl, Slou. SL3 175 AZ78
Sch Bessemer Gra Prim Sch,
SE5 off Dylways 184 DR84
Bessemer Rd, SE5 43 K9
Welwyn Garden City AL7,
AL8 51 CY05
Bessie Lansbury Cl, E6 25 L9
Bessingby Rd, Ruis. HA4 137 BU61
Bessingham Wk, SE4
off Aldersford Cl 205 DX85
Besson St, SE14 45 H6
Bessy St, E2 21 H2
Bestobell Rd, Slou. SL1 153 AQ72
Bestwood St, SE8 33 K9
Beswick Ms, NW6 5 M3
Betam Rd, Hayes UB3 177 BR75
Beta Pl, SW4 off Santley St 183 DM84
Beta Rd, Chobham GU24 232 AT110
Woking GU22 249 BB116
Beta Way, Egh. TW20 215 BC95
BETCHWORTH, RH3 270 CR134
⇌ Betchworth 270 CR132
Betchworth Cl, Sutt. SM1
off St. Barnabas Rd 240 DD106
Betchworth Fort Pk, Tad. KT20 270 CP131
Betchworth Rd, Ilf. IG3 147 ES61
Betchworth Way, New Adgtn
CR0 243 EC109
Betenson Av, Sev. TN13 278 FF122
Betham Rd, Grnf. UB6 159 CD69
Bethany Cl, Horn. RM12 150 FJ61
Bethany Pl, Wok. GU21 248 AX118
Bethany Waye, Felt. TW14 197 BS87
Bethecar Rd, Har. HA1 139 CE57
Bethell Av, E16 23 L4
Ilford IG1 147 EN59
Bethel Rd, Sev. TN13 279 FJ123
Welling DA16 188 EW83
Bethersden Cl, Beck. BR3 205 DZ94
Sch Beth Jacob Gram Sch for Girls,
NW4 off Stratford Rd 141 CX56
H Bethlem Royal Hosp, Beck.
BR3 225 EA101
BETHNAL GREEN, E2 20 E2
⇌ Bethnal Green 20 E4
⊖ Bethnal Green 20 G3
Bethnal Grn Est, E2 20 G3
Bethnal Grn Rd, E1 20 A4
E2 20 A4
Sch Bethnal Grn Tech Coll, E2 20 B3
Coll Bethnal Grn Training Cen,
E1 20 C6
Sch Beths Gram Sch, Bex.
DA5 off Hartford Rd 209 FB86
Bethune Av, N11 120 DF49
Bethune Rd, N16 144 DR59
NW10 160 CR70
Bethwin Rd, SE5 43 H4
Betjeman Cl, Chsht EN7
off Rosedale Way 88 DU28
Coulsdon CR5 257 DM117
Pinner HA5 138 CA56
Betjeman Gdns, Chorl. WD3 95 BD42
Betjeman Way, Hem.H. HP1 62 BH18
Betley Ct, Walt. KT12 217 BV104
Betony Cl, Croy. CR0
off Primrose La 225 DX102
Betony Rd, Rom. RM3 128 FJ51
Betoyne Av, E4 124 EE49
BETSHAM, Grav. DA13 212 FY91
Betsham Rd, Erith DA8 189 FF80
Southfleet DA13 211 FX92
Swanscombe DA10 212 FY87
Betstyle Rd, N11 121 DH49
Betterton Dr, Sid. DA14 208 EY89
Betterton Rd, Rain. RM13 169 FE69
Betterton St, WC2 18 A9
Bettles Cl, Uxb. UB8 156 BJ68
Bettoney Vere, Bray SL6 172 AC75
Bettons Pk, E15 13 K9
Bettridge Rd, SW6 39 H9
Betts Cl, Beck. BR3 225 DY96
Betts La, Naze. EN9 72 EJ21
Betts Ms, E17 145 DZ58
Betts St, E1 32 E1
Betts Way, SE20 224 DV95
Long Ditton KT6 219 CH102
Sch Betty Layward Prim Sch,
N16 off Clissold Rd 144 DR62
Betula Cl, Ken. CR8 258 DR115
Betula Wk, Rain. RM13 170 FK69
Between Sts, Cob. KT11 235 BU114
Beulah Av, Th.Hth. CR7
off Beulah Rd 224 DQ96
Beulah Cl, Edg. HA8 118 CP48
Beulah Cres, Th.Hth. CR7 224 DQ96
Beulah Gro, Croy. CR0 224 DQ100
Beulah Hill, SE19 203 DP93
Sch Beulah Inf & Nurs Sch, Th.Hth.
CR7 off Furze Rd 224 DQ97
Sch Beulah Jun Sch, Th.Hth.
CR7 off Beulah Rd 224 DQ97
Beulah Path, E17
off Addison Rd 145 EB57
Beulah Rd, E17 145 EB57
SW19 201 CZ94
Epping CM16 92 EU29
Hornchurch RM12 150 FJ62
Sutton SM1 240 DA105
Thornton Heath CR7 224 DQ97
Beulah Wk, Wold. CR3 259 DY120
Beult Rd, Dart. DA1 189 FG83
Bevan Av, Bark. IG11 168 EU66
Bevan Cl, Hem.H. HP3 62 BK22
Bevan Ct, Croy. CR0 241 DN106
Bevan Hill, Chesh. HP5 76 AP29
Bevan Ho, Grays RM16
off Laird Av 192 GD75
Bevan Pk, Epsom KT17 239 CT111
Bevan Pl, Swan. BR8 229 FF98
Bevan Rd, SE2 188 EV78
Barnet EN4 102 DF42
Bevans Cl, Green. DA9
off Johnsons Way 211 FW86
Bevan St, N1 9 K9
Bevan Way, Horn. RM12 150 FM63
Bev Callender Cl, SW8 41 J10
Bevenden St, N1 19 M2
Bevercote Wk, Belv. DA17
off Osborne Rd 188 EZ79
Beveridge Rd, NW10 160 CS66
Beverley Av, SW20 221 CT95
Hounslow TW4 178 BZ84
Sidcup DA15 207 ET87
Beverley Cl, N21 122 DQ46
SW11 off Maysoule Rd 182 DD84
SW13 181 CT82
Addlestone KT15 234 BK106
Broxbourne EN10 71 DY21
Chessington KT9 237 CJ105
Enfield EN1 104 DS42
Epsom KT17 239 CW111
Hornchurch RM11 150 FM59
Weybridge KT13 217 BS103
Beverley Cotts, SW15
off Kingston Vale 200 CS90
Beverley Ct, N14 121 DJ45
N20 off Farnham Cl 120 DC45
SE4 45 P10
Beverley Cres, Wdf.Grn. IG8 124 EH53
Beverley Dr, Edg. HA8 140 CP55
Beverley Gdns, NW11 141 CY59
SW13 181 CT83
Cheshunt EN7 88 DT30
Hornchurch RM11 150 FM59
St. Albans AL4 65 CK16
Stanmore HA7 117 CG53
Welwyn Garden City AL7 52 DC09
Wembley HA9 140 CM60
Worcester Park KT4
off Green La 221 CU102
Beverley Hts, Reig. RH2 272 DB132
Beverley Hyrst, Croy. CR0
off Addiscombe Rd 224 DT103
Beverley La, SW15 201 CT90
Kingston upon Thames KT2 200 CS94
Beverley Ms, E4
off Beverley Rd 123 ED51
Beverley Path, SW13 181 CT82
Beverley Rd, E4 123 ED51
E6 24 F2
SE20 off Wadhurst Cl 224 DV96
SW13 181 CT83
W4 181 CT78
Bexleyheath DA7 189 FC82
Bromley BR2 226 EL103
Dagenham RM9 148 EY63
Kingston upon Thames KT1 219 CJ95
Mitcham CR4 223 DK98
New Malden KT3 221 CU98
Ruislip HA4 137 BU61
Southall UB2 178 BY77
Sunbury-on-Thames TW16 217 BT95
Whyteleafe CR3 258 DS116
Worcester Park KT4 221 CW103
● Beverley Trd Est, Mord.
SM4 off Garth Rd 221 CX101
Beverley Way, SW20 221 CT95
New Malden KT3 221 CT95
Beverly, NW8 16 C3
Beversbrook Rd, N19 143 DK62
Beverstone Rd, SW2 203 DM85
Thornton Heath CR7 223 DN98
Beverston Ms, W1 16 E7
Bevil Ct, Hodd. EN11
off Molesworth 55 EA14
Bevill Allen Cl, SW17 202 DF92
Bevill Cl, SE25 224 DU97
Bevin Cl, SE16 33 L2
Bevin Ct, WC1 18 D2
Bevington Path, SE1
off Tanner St 32 A5
Sch Bevington Prim Sch, W10 14 F6
Bevington Rd, W10 14 F6
Beckenham BR3 225 EB96
Bevington St, SE16 32 D5
Bevin Rd, Hayes UB4 157 BU69
Bevin Sq, SW17 202 DF90
Bevin Way, WC1 18 E2
Bevis Cl, Dart. DA2 210 FQ87
Bevis Marks, EC3 19 P8
Bewcastle Gdns, Enf. EN2 103 DL42
Bew Ct, SE22 off Lordship La 204 DU87
Bewdley St, N1 8 E6
Bewick Ms, SE15 44 E5
Bewick St, SW8 41 K9
Bewley Cl, Chsht EN8 89 DX31
Bewley St, E1 20 F10
SW19 202 DC93
Bewlys Rd, SE27 203 DP92
Bexhill Cl, Felt. TW13 198 BY89
Bexhill Dr, Grays RM17 192 FY79
Bexhill Rd, N11 121 DK50
SE4 205 DZ87
SW14 180 CQ83
Bexhill Wk, E15 13 K9
BEXLEY, DA5 208 FA86
⇌ Bexley 208 FA88
Coll Bexley Cen for Music & Dance,
Sid. DA15 off Station Rd 208 EU90
Bexley Cl, Dart. DA1 209 FE85
Coll Bexley Coll, Holly Hill Campus,
Belv. DA17 off Holly Hill Rd 189 FB78
Sidcup Campus, Sid.
DA14 off Main Rd 207 ET91
Tower Rd Campus, Belv.
DA17 off Tower Rd 189 FC77
Bexley Gdns, N9 122 DR48
Chadwell Heath RM6 148 EV57
Sch Bexley Gram Sch, Well. DA16
off Danson La 188 EV84
BEXLEYHEATH, DA6 & DA7 208 EZ85
⇌ Bexleyheath 188 EY82
Sch Bexleyheath Sch, Bexh.
DA6 off Graham Rd 188 FA83
Bexley High St, Bex. DA5 208 FA87
Bexley La, Dart. DA1 209 FE85
Sidcup DA14 208 EW90
Bexley Rd, SE9 207 EP85
Erith DA8 189 FC80
Bexley St, Wind. SL4 173 AQ81
Beyers Gdns, Hodd. EN11 55 EA14
Beyers Prospect, Hodd. EN11 55 EA13
Beyers Ride, Hodd. EN11 55 EA13
Beynon Rd, Cars. SM5 240 DF106
Bianca Rd, SE15 44 C3
Bibsworth Rd, N3 119 CZ54
Bibury Cl, SE15 43 P3
Bicester Rd, Rich. TW9 180 CN83
Bickenhall St, W1 16 F6
Bickersteth Rd, SW17 202 DF93
Bickerton Rd, N19 143 DJ61
BICKLEY, Brom. BR1 227 EM97
⇌ Bickley 226 EL97
Bickley Cres, Brom. BR1 226 EL98
Bickley Pk Rd, Brom. BR1 226 EL97
Sch Bickley Pk Sch, Nurs &
Pre-Prep, Brom. BR1
off Page Heath La 226 EK97
Sch Bickley Prim Sch, Brom.
BR1 off Nightingale La 226 EJ96
Bickley Rd, E10 145 EB59
Bromley BR1 226 EK96
Bickley St, SW17 202 DE92
Bicknell Cl, Guil. GU1 264 AW133
Bicknell Rd, SE5 184 DQ83
Bickney Way, Fetch. KT22 252 CC122
Bicknoller Cl, Sutt. SM2 240 DB110
Bicknoller Rd, Enf. EN1 104 DT39
Bicknor Rd, Orp. BR6 227 ES101
Bidborough Cl, Brom. BR2 226 EF99
Bidborough St, WC1 18 A3
Biddenden Way, SE9 207 EN91
Istead Rise DA13 212 GE94
Biddenham Turn, Wat. WD25 98 BW35
Bidder St, E16 23 J6
Biddestone Rd, N7 8 C1
Biddles Cl, Slou. SL1 153 AL74
Biddulph Rd, W9 15 L3
South Croydon CR2 242 DQ109
Bideford Av, Perivale UB6 159 CH68
Bideford Cl, Edg. HA8 118 CN53
Feltham TW13 198 BZ90
Romford RM3 128 FJ53
Bideford Gdns, Enf. EN1 122 DS45
Bideford Rd, Brom. BR1 206 EF90
Enfield EN3 105 DZ38
Ruislip HA4 137 BV62
Welling DA16 188 EV80
Bideford Spur, Slou. SL2 153 AP69
Bidhams Cres, Tad. KT20 255 CW121
Bidwell Gdns, N11 121 DJ52
Bidwell St, SE15 44 F7
★ Big Ben (St. Stephens Twr),
SW1 30 B5
Bigbury Cl, N17 122 DS52
Big Common La, Bletch. RH1 273 DP133
Biggerstaff Rd, E15 12 E8
Biggerstaff St, N4 143 DN61
Biggin Av, Mitch. CR4 222 DF95
BIGGIN HILL, West. TN16 260 EH116
Biggin Hill, SE19 203 DP94
● Biggin Hill Business Pk,
West. TN16 260 EK115
Biggin Hill Cl, Kings.T. KT2 199 CJ92
Sch Biggin Hill Prim Sch, Bigg.H.
TN16 off Old Tye Av 260 EL116
Biggin La, Grays RM16 193 GH79
Biggin Way, SE19 203 DP94
Bigginwood Rd, SW16 203 DP94
Biggs Gro Rd, Chsht EN7 88 DR27
Biggs Row, SW15
off Felsham Rd 181 CX83
Big Hill, E5 144 DV60
Sch Bigland Grn Prim Sch, E1 20 E9
Bigland St, E1 20 E9
Bignell Rd, SE18 187 EP78
Jet Bignell's Cor, S.Mimms EN6 85 CU34
Bignold Rd, E7 13 P1
Bigwood Rd, NW11 142 DB57
Biko Cl, Uxb. UB8
off Sefton Way 156 BJ72
Billet Cl, Rom. RM6 148 EX55
Billet La, Berk. HP4 60 AU18
Hornchurch RM11 150 FK60
Iver SL0 155 BB69
Slough SL3 155 BB73
Billet Rd, E17 123 DX54
Romford RM6 148 EV55
Staines TW18 196 BG90
Billets Hart Cl, W7 179 CE75
● Billet Wks, E17 123 DZ53
Bill Faust Ho, E1
off Tarling St 20 G9
Bill Hamling Cl, SE9 207 EM89
Billingford Cl, SE4 185 DX84
Billing Pl, SW10 39 M4
Billing Rd, SW10 39 M4
Billings Cl, Dag. RM9
off Ellerton Rd 168 EW66
🔒 Billingsgate Mkt, E14 34 D2
Billing St, SW10 39 M4
Billington Ms, W3
off High St 160 CP74
Billington Rd, SE14 45 J5
Billinton Hill, Croy. CR0 224 DR103
Billiter Sq, EC3 19 P10
Billiter St, EC3 19 P9
Bill Nicholson Way, N17
off High Rd 122 DT52
Billockby Cl, Chess. KT9 238 CM107
Billson St, E14 34 F9
Billy Lows La, Pot.B. EN6 86 DA31
Bilsby Gro, SE9 206 EK91
Bilton Cl, Poyle SL3 175 BE82
Bilton Rd, Erith DA8 189 FG80
Perivale UB6 159 CH67
Bilton Twrs, W1
off Great Cumberland Pl 16 F9
Bilton Way, Enf. EN3 105 DY39
Hayes UB3 177 BV75
Bina Gdns, SW5 27 N9
Bincote Rd, Enf. EN2 103 DM41
Binden Rd, W12 181 CT76
Bindon Grn, Mord. SM4 222 DB98
Binfield Rd, SW4 42 B7
Byfleet KT14 234 BL112
South Croydon CR2 242 DT106
Bingfield St, N1 8 B8
Bingham Cl, Hem.H. HP1 61 BF18
South Ockendon RM15 171 FV72
Bingham Ct, N1 9 H6
Bingham Dr, Stai. TW18 196 BK94
Woking GU21 248 AT118
Bingham Pl, W1 16 G6
Bingham Pt, SE18 37 P9
Bingham Rd, Burn. SL1 152 AG71
Croydon CR0 224 DU102
Bingham St, N1 9 L4
Bingley Rd, E16 24 C8
Bingley Rd, Grnf. UB6 158 CC71
Hoddesdon EN11 71 EC17
Sunbury-on-Thames TW16 197 BU94
Binley Ho, SW15
off Highcliffe Dr 201 CU86
Binne Ho, SE1 off Bath Ter 31 J7
Binney St, W1 17 H10
Binns Rd, W4 180 CS78
Binns Ter, W4 off Binns Rd 180 CS78
Binscombe Cres, Gdmg. GU7 280 AS144
Binsey Wk, SE2 168 EW74
Binstead Cl, Hayes UB4 158 BY71
Binyon Cres, Stan. HA7 117 CF50
Birbetts Rd, SE9 207 EM89
Birchall La, Cole Grn SG14 52 DF12
Birchall Wd, Welw.G.C. AL7 52 DC10
Bircham Path, SE4
off Aldersford Cl 205 DX85
Birchanger Rd, SE25 224 DU99
Birch Av, N13 122 DQ48
Caterham CR3 258 DR124
Leatherhead KT22 253 CF120
West Drayton UB7 156 BM72
Birch Circle, Gdmg. GU7 280 AT143
Birch Cl, E16 23 K6
N19 143 DJ61
SE15 44 D9
Amersham HP6 77 AS37
Banstead SM7 239 CY114
Brentford TW8 179 CH80
Buckhurst Hill IG9 124 EK48
Eynsford DA4 230 FK104
Hounslow TW3 179 CD83
Iver SL0 155 BD68
New Haw KT15 234 BK109
Romford RM7 149 FB55
Send GU23 265 BF125
Sevenoaks TN13 279 FH123
South Ockendon RM15 171 FX69
Teddington TW11 199 CG92
Woking GU21 248 AW119
Birch Copse, Brick.Wd AL2 82 BY30
Birch Ct, Nthwd. HA6
off Rickmansworth Rd 115 BQ51
Welwyn Garden City AL7 52 DA12
Birch Cres, Horn. RM11 150 FL56
South Ockendon RM15 171 FX69
Uxbridge UB10 156 BM67
Birchcroft Cl, Chaldon CR3 274 DQ125
Birchdale, Ger.Cr. SL9 134 AX60
Birchdale Cl, W.Byf. KT14 234 BJ111
Birchdale Gdns, Rom. RM6 148 EX59
Birchdale Rd, E7 146 EJ64
Birchdene Dr, SE28 188 EU75
Birchdown Ho, E3 22 C3
Birch Dr, Hat. AL10 67 CU19
Maple Cross WD3 113 BD50
Birchen Cl, NW9 140 CR61
Birchend Cl, S.Croy. CR2 242 DR107
Birchen Gro, NW9 140 CR61
Bircherley Ct, Hert. SG14
off Priory St 54 DR09
🔒 Bircherley Grn Shop Cen, Hert.
SG14 off Green St 54 DR09
Bircherley St, Hert. SG14 54 DR09
Birches, The, E12
off Station Rd 146 EL63
N21 103 DM44
SE7 186 EH79
Beaconsfield HP9 110 AH53
Brentwood CM13 130 FY48
Bushey WD23 98 CC43
East Horsley KT24 267 BS126
Hemel Hempstead HP3 61 BF23
North Weald Bassett CM16 93 FB26
Orpington BR6 245 EN105
Swanley BR8 229 FE96
Waltham Abbey EN9
off Honey La 90 EF34
Woking GU22
off Heathside Rd 249 AZ118
Birches Cl, Epsom KT18 254 CS115
Mitcham CR4 222 DF97
Pinner HA5 138 BY57
Birches La, Goms. GU5 283 BQ141
Birchfield, N.Stfd RM16 171 FX74
Birchfield Cl, Add. KT15 234 BH105
Coulsdon CR5 257 DM116
Birchfield Gro, Epsom KT17 239 CW110
Birchfield Rd, Chsht EN8 88 DV29
Birchfield St, E14 22 A10
Birch Gdns, Amer. HP7 77 AS39
Dagenham RM10 149 FC62
Birchgate Ms, Tad. KT20
off Bidhams Cres 255 CW121
BIRCH GREEN, Hert. SG14 53 DJ11
Birch Grn, NW9
off Clayton Fld 118 CS52
Hemel Hempstead HP1 61 BF19
Hertford SG14 53 DJ12
Staines TW18 196 BG91
Birch Gro, E11 146 EE62
SE12 206 EF87
W3 160 CN74
Cobham KT11 236 BW114
Kingswood KT20 255 CY124
Potters Bar EN6 86 DA32
Shepperton TW17 217 BS96
Slough SL2 153 AP71
Welling DA16 188 EU84
Windsor SL4 173 AK81
Woking GU22 249 BD115
Birchgrove Ho, Rich. TW9
off Strand Dr 180 CP80
Birch Hill, Croy. CR0 243 DX106
Birchington Cl, Bexh. DA7 189 FB81
Orpington BR5
off Hart Dyke Rd 228 EW102
Birchington Ho, E5 10 E2
Birchington Rd, N8 143 DK58
NW6 5 K8
Surbiton KT5 220 CM101
Windsor SL4 173 AN82
Birchin La, EC3 19 M9
Birchlands Av, SW12 202 DF87
Birch La, Flaun. HP3 79 BB33
Purley CR8 241 DL111
Birch Leys, Hem.H. HP2
off Hunters Oak 63 BQ15
Birchmead, Orp. BR6 227 EN103
Watford WD17 97 BT38
Birchmead Av, Pnr. HA5 138 BW56
Birchmead Cl, St.Alb. AL3 65 CD17
● Birchmere Business Pk,
SE28 188 EU75
Birchmere Row, SE3 47 M9
Birchmore Wk, N5 144 DQ62
Birch Pk, Har. HA3 116 CC52
Birch Pl, Green. DA9 211 FS86
Birch Rd, Felt. TW13 198 BX92
Godalming GU7 280 AT143
Romford RM7 149 FB55
Birch Row, Brom. BR2 227 EN101
Birch Tree Av, W.Wick. BR4 244 EF106
Birch Tree Gro, Ley Hill HP5 78 AV30
Birch Tree Wk, Wat. WD17 97 BT37
Birch Tree Way, Croy. CR0 224 DV103
Birch Vale, Cob. KT11 236 CA112
Birch Vw, Epp. CM16 92 EV29
Birchville Ct, Bushey Hth WD23
off Heathbourne Rd 117 CE46
Birch Wk, Borwd. WD6 100 CN39
Erith DA8 189 FC79
Mitcham CR4 223 DH95
West Byfleet KT14 234 BG112
Birch Way, Chesh. HP5 76 AR29
Hatfield AL10
off Crawford Rd 67 CV16
Birchway, Hayes UB3 157 BU74
Birch Way, Lon.Col. AL2 83 CK27
Redhill RH1 289 DH136
Warlingham CR6 259 DY118
BIRCHWOOD, Hat. AL10 67 CU16
Birchwood, Shenley WD7 84 CN34
Waltham Abbey EN9
off Roundhills 90 EE34
Birchwood Av, N10 142 DG55
Beckenham BR3 225 DZ98
Hatfield AL10 67 CU16
Sidcup DA14 208 EV89
Wallington SM6 222 DG104
Sch Birchwood Av Prim Sch, Hat.
AL10 off Birchwood Av 67 CV16
Birchwood Cl, Gt Warley CM13 129 FW51
Hatfield AL10 67 CU16
Horley RH6 291 DH147
Morden SM4 222 DB98
Birchwood Ct, N13 121 DP50
Edgware HA8 118 CQ54
Birchwood Dr, NW3 142 DB62
Dartford DA2 209 FE91
West Byfleet KT14 234 BG112
Birchwood Gro, Hmptn. TW12 198 CA93
Birchwood La, Chaldon CR3 273 DP125
Esher KT10 237 CD110
Knockholt Pound TN14 262 EZ115
Leatherhead KT22 237 CD110
Birchwood Pk Av, Swan. BR8 229 FE97
Sch Birchwood Prim Sch, Swan.
BR8 off Russett Way 229 FD95
Birchwood Rd, SW17 203 DH92
Dartford DA2 209 FE92
Petts Wood BR5 227 ER98
Swanley BR8 229 FC95
West Byfleet KT14 234 BG112
Birchwood Ter, Swan. BR8
off Birchwood Rd 229 FC95
Birchwood Way, Park St AL2 82 CB28
Birdbrook Cl, Dag. RM10 169 FC66
Hutton CM13 131 GB44
Birdbrook Rd, SE3 186 EJ83
Birdcage Wk, SW1 29 M5
Harlow CM20 57 EQ14
Coll Bird Coll, Sid. DA14
off Birkbeck Rd 208 EU90
Birdcroft Rd, Welw.G.C. AL8 51 CW09
Birdham Cl, Brom. BR1 226 EL99
Birdhouse La, Downe BR6 261 EN115
Birdhurst Av, S.Croy. CR2 242 DR105
Birdhurst Gdns, S.Croy. CR2 242 DR105
Birdhurst Ri, S.Croy. CR2 242 DS106
Birdhurst Rd, SW18 182 DC84
SW19 202 DE93
South Croydon CR2 242 DS106
Birdie Way, Hert. SG13 54 DV08
Bird in Bush Rd, SE15 44 D4
Bird-in-Hand La, Brom. BR1 226 EK96
Bird-in-Hand Ms, SE23
off Dartmouth Rd 204 DW89
Bird-in-Hand Pas, SE23
off Dartmouth Rd 204 DW89
Bird in Hand Yd, NW3 5 P1
Bird La, Gt Warley CM13 151 FX55
Harefield UB9 114 BJ54
Upminster RM14 151 FR57
Birds Cl, Welw.G.C. AL7 52 DB11
Birds Fm Av, Rom. RM5 127 FB53
Birdsfield La, E3 11 N8
Birds Hill Dr, Oxshott KT22 237 CD113
Birds Hill Ri, Oxshott KT22 237 CD113
Birds Hill Rd, Oxshott KT22 237 CD112
Bird St, W1 17 H9
Birdswood Dr, Wok. GU21 248 AS119
Bird Wk, Twick. TW2 198 BZ88
Birdwood Av, SE13 205 ED86
Birdwood Cl, S.Croy. CR2 243 DX111
Teddington TW11 199 CE91
Birfield Rd, Loud. HP10 110 AC53
⇌ Birkbeck 224 DW97
Tra Birkbeck 224 DW97
Birkbeck Av, W3 160 CQ73
Greenford UB6 158 CC67
Uni Birkbeck Coll, Main Bldg,
WC1 17 P5
Clore Management Cen, WC1 17 P5
Gordon Ho & Ingold Laboratories,
WC1 17 N4
Gordon Sq, WC1 17 P4
Russell Sq, WC1 17 P6
Birkbeck Gdns, Wdf.Grn. IG8 124 EF47
Birkbeck Gro, W3 180 CR75
Birkbeck Hill, SE21 203 DP89
Birkbeck Ms, E8 10 A3
W3 160 CR74
Birkbeck Pl, SE21 204 DQ88
Sch Birkbeck Prim Sch, Sid.
DA14 off Alma Rd 208 EV90
Birkbeck Rd, E8 10 A3
N8 143 DL56
N12 120 DC50
N17 122 DT53
NW7 119 CT50
SW19 202 DB92
W3 160 CR74
W5 179 CJ77
Beckenham BR3 224 DW96
Enfield EN2 104 DR39
Hutton CM13 131 GD44
Ilford IG2 147 ER57
Romford RM7 149 FD60

Birkbeck Rd, Sid. DA14 208 EU90
Birkbeck St, E2 20 F3
Birkbeck Way, Grnf. UB6 158 CC67
Birkdale Av, Pnr. HA5 138 CA55
Romford RM3 128 FM52
Birkdale Cl, SE16 44 E1
SE28 168 EX72
Orpington BR6 227 ER101
Birkdale Gdns, Croy. CR0 243 DX105
Watford WD19 116 BX48
Birkdale Rd, SE2 188 EU77
W5 160 CL70
Birkenhead Av, Kings.T. KT2 220 CM96
Birkenhead St, WC1 18 B2
Birken Ms, Nthwd. HA6 115 BP50
Birkett Way, Ch.St.G. HP8 94 AX41
Birkhall Rd, SE6 205 ED88
Birkheads Rd, Reig. RH2 272 DA133
Birklands La, St.Alb. AL1 83 CH25
Birklands Pk, St.Alb. AL1 65 CH24
Birkwood Cl, SW12 203 DK87
Birley Rd, N20 120 DC47
Slough SL1 153 AR72
Birley St, SW11 40 G9
Birling Rd, Erith DA8 189 FD80
Birnam Cl, Send M. GU23 250 BG124
Birnam Rd, N4 143 DM61
Birnbeck Cl, NW11 141 CZ57
Birnbeck Ct, NW11
off Finchley Rd 141 CZ57
Birrell Ho, SW9 42 C9
Birse Cres, NW10 140 CS63
Birstall Grn, Wat. WD19 116 BX49
Birstall Rd, N15 144 DS57
Birtley Path, Borwd. WD6 100 CL39
Biscayne Av, E14 34 F1
Biscay Rd, W6 38 C1
Biscoe Cl, Houns. TW5 178 CA79
Biscoe Way, SE13 185 ED83
Bisenden Rd, Croy. CR0 224 DS103
Bisham Cl, Cars. SM5 222 DF102
Bisham Gdns, N6 142 DG60
Bishop Butt Cl, Orp. BR6 227 ET104
Bishop Cen, Tap. SL6 152 AF72
Bishop Challoner Cath Collegiate Sch, E1 21 H9
Bishop Challoner Sch, Short. BR2 *off Bromley Rd* 225 ED96
Bishop David Brown Sch, The, Sheer. GU21
off Albert Dr 233 BD113
Bishop Douglass Sch, N2
off Hamilton Rd 142 DC55
Bishop Duppa's Pk, Shep. TW17 217 BR101
Bishop Fox Way, W.Mol. KT8 218 BZ98
Bishop Gilpin C of E Prim Sch, SW19 *off Lake Rd* 201 CZ92
Bishop John Robinson Prim Sch, SE28 *off Hoveton Rd* 168 EW73
Bishop Justus C of E Sch, Brom. BR2
off Magpie Hall La 226 EL101
Bishop Ken Rd, Har. HA3 117 CF54
Bishop Kings Rd, W14 26 F8
Bishop Perrin C of E Prim Sch, Whitton TW2
off Hospital Br Rd 198 CB88
Bishop Ramsey C of E Sch, Ruis. HA4
off Hume Way 137 BU59
Bishop Ridley C of E Prim Sch, Well. DA16
off Northumberland Av 187 ES84
Bishop Rd, N14 121 DH45
Bishop's Av, E13 166 EH67
SW6 38 D8
Bishops Av, Brom. BR1 226 EJ96
Elstree WD6 100 CM43
Northwood HA6 115 BS49
Romford RM6 148 EW58
Bishops Av, The, N2 142 DD59
Bishops Br, W2 15 P8
Bishops Br Rd, W2 15 M9
Bishops Cl, E17 145 EB56
Bishop's Cl, N19 143 DJ62
Bishops Cl, SE9 207 EQ89
W4 180 CQ78
Barnet EN5 101 CX44
Bishop's Cl, Couls. CR5 257 DN118
Bishops Cl, Enf. EN1
off Central Av 104 DV40
Hatfield AL10 67 CT18
Richmond TW10 199 CK90
St. Albans AL4 65 CG16
Bishop's Cl, Sutt. SM1 222 DA104
Bishops Cl, Uxb. UB10 156 BN68
Bishop's Ct, EC4 18 G8
WC2 18 E8
Bishops Ct, Abb.L. WD5 81 BT31
Cheshunt EN8
off Churchgate 88 DV30
Greenhithe DA9 211 FS85
Bishops Dr, Felt. TW14 197 BR86
Northolt UB5 158 BY67
Bishops Fm Cl, Oakley Grn SL4 172 AH82
Bishopsfield, Harl. CM18 73 ES18
Bishopsford Comm Sch, Mord. SM4 *off Lilleshall Rd* 222 DD100
Bishopsford Rd, Mord. SM4 222 DC101
Bishops Garth, St.Alb. AL4
off Bishops Cl 65 CG16
Bishopsgate, EC2 19 N9
Bishopsgate Arc, EC2 19 P7
Bishopsgate Chyd, EC2 19 N7
Bishopsgate Inst, EC2 19 P7
Bishopsgate Rd, Eng.Grn TW20 194 AT90
Bishopsgate Sch, Egh. TW20
off Bishopsgate Rd 194 AU90
Bishops Gro, N2 142 DD58
Hampton TW12 198 BZ91
Bishop's Hall, Kings.T. KT1 219 CK96
Bishops Hall Rd, Pilg.Hat. CM15 130 FV44
Bishopshalt Sch, Hlgdn UB8 *off Royal La* 156 BM69
Bishop's Hatfield Girls' Sch, Hat. AL10 *off Woods Av* 67 CU18
Bishops Hill, Walt. KT12 217 BU101
Bishops Ho, SW8
off South Lambeth Rd 42 B5
Bishopsmead, SE5
off Camberwell Rd 43 K5
Bishops Mead, Hem.H. HP1 62 BH22
Bishopsmead Cl, E.Hors. KT24
off Ockham Rd S 267 BS128
Epsom KT19 238 CR110
Bishopsmead Dr, E.Hors. KT24 267 BT129
Bishopsmead Par, E.Hors. KT24
off Ockham Rd S 267 BS129
Bishops Orchard, Farn.Royal SL2 153 AP69
Bishop's Pk, SW6 38 C8
Bishop's Pk Rd, SW6 38 D8
Bishops Pk Rd, SW16 223 DL95
Bishops Pl, Sutt. SM1
off Lind Rd 240 DC106
Bishop Sq, Hat. AL10 66 CS17
Bishops Ri, Hat. AL10 67 CT22
Bishops Rd, N6 142 DG58
SW6 38 G5
Bishop's Rd, SW11 40 D4
Bishops Rd, W7 179 CE75
Croydon CR0 223 DP101
Hayes UB3 157 BQ71
Slough SL1 174 AU75
Bishops Sq, E1 19 P6
Bishops Ter, SE11 30 F8
Bishopsthorpe Rd, SE26 205 DX91
Bishop Stopford's Sch, Enf. EN1 *off Brick La* 104 DV40
Bishop St, N1 9 J8
Bishops Wk, Chis. BR7 227 EQ95
Croydon CR0 243 DX106
Bishop's Wk, Pnr. HA5
off High St 138 BY55
Bishops Wk, Woob.Grn HP10 132 AE58
Bishops Way, E2 10 F10
Egham TW20 195 BD93
Bishops Wd, Wok. GU21 248 AT117
Bishops Wood Hosp, Nthwd. HA6 115 BP51
Bishopswood Rd, N6 142 DF59
Bishop Thomas Grant Catholic Sch, SW16
off Belltrees Gro 203 DM92
Bishop Wk, Shenf. CM15 131 FZ47
Bishop Wand C of E Sch, The, Sun. TW16 *off Laytons La* 217 BT96
Bishop Wilfred Wd Cl, SE15 44 D8
Bishop Winnington-Ingram C of E Prim Sch, Ruis. HA4
off Southcote Ri 137 BR59
Biskra, Wat. WD17 97 BU39
Bisley Cl, Wal.Cr. EN8 89 DX33
Worcester Park KT4 221 CW102
Bisley Ho, SW19 201 CX89
Bispham Rd, NW10 160 CM69
Bisson Rd, E15 12 F10
Bisterne Av, E17 145 ED55
Bittacy Busines Cen, NW7 119 CY52
Bittacy Cl, NW7 119 CX51
Bittacy Ct, NW7
off Bittacy Hill 119 CY52
Bittacy Hill, NW7 119 CX51
Bittacy Pk Av, NW7 119 CX51
Bittacy Ri, NW7 119 CW51
Bittacy Rd, NW7 119 CX51
Bittams La, Cher. KT16 233 BE105
Bittern Cl, Chsht EN7 88 DQ25
Hayes UB4 158 BX71
Hemel Hempstead HP3 80 BM25
Bitterne Dr, Wok. GU21 248 AT117
Bittern Pl, N22 121 DM54
Bittern St, SE1 31 J5
Bittoms, The, Kings.T. KT1 219 CK97
Bixley Cl, Sthl. UB2 178 BZ77
Black Acre Cl, Amer. HP7 77 AS39
Blackacre Rd, They.B. CM16 107 ES37
Blackall St, EC2 19 N4
Blackberry Cl, Guil. GU1 264 AV131
Shepperton TW17
off Cherry Way 217 BS98
Blackberry Fm Cl, Houns. TW5 178 BY80
Blackberry Fld, Orp. BR5 228 EU95
Blackbird Hill, NW9 140 CQ61
Blackbirds La, Ald. WD25 99 CD35
Blackbird Yd, E2 20 B2
Blackborne Rd, Dag. RM10 168 FA65
Blackborough Cl, Reig. RH2 272 DC134
Blackborough Rd, Reig. RH2 288 DC135
Black Boy La, N15 144 DQ57
Black Boy Wd, Brick.Wd AL2 82 CA30
Blackbridge Rd, Wok. GU22 248 AX119
BLACKBROOK, Dor. RH5 286 CL141
Blackbrook La, Brom. BR1, BR2 227 EN97
Blackbrook Rd, Dor. RH5 285 CK140
Black Bull Yd, EC1
off Hatton Wall 18 E6
Blackburn, The, Bkhm KT23
off Little Bookham St 252 BZ124
Blackburne's Ms, W1 16 G10
Blackburn Rd, NW6 5 L5
Blackburn Trd Est, Stanw. TW19 196 BM86
Blackburn Way, Houns. TW4 198 BY85
Blackbury Cl, Pot.B. EN6 86 DC31
Blackbush Av, Rom. RM6 148 EX57
Blackbush Cl, Sutt. SM2 240 DB108
Blackbush Spring, Harl. CM20 58 EU14
Black Cut, St.Alb. AL1 65 CE21
Blackdale, Chsht EN7 88 DU27
Blackdown Av, Wok. GU22 249 BE115
Blackdown Cl, N2 120 DC54
Woking GU22 249 BC116
Blackdown Ter, SE18
off Prince Imperial Rd 187 EM80
Black Eagle Cl, West. TN16 277 EQ127
Black Eagle Dr, Nthflt DA11 212 GA85
Black Eagle Sq, West. TN16
off High St 277 EQ127
Blackett Cl, Stai. TW18 215 BE96
Blackett St, SW15 181 CX83
Blacketts Wd Dr, Chorl. WD3 95 BB43
Black Fan Cl, Enf. EN2 104 DQ39
Black Fan Rd, Welw.G.C. AL7 52 DB09
BLACKFEN, Sid. DA15 207 ET87
Blackfen Par, Sid. DA15
off Blackfen Rd 208 EU86
Blackfen Rd, Sid. DA15 207 ES85
Blackfen Sch for Girls, Sid. DA15 *off Blackfen Rd* 208 EV86
Blackford Cl, S.Croy. CR2 241 DP109
Blackford Rd, Wat. WD19 116 BX50
Blackford's Path, SW15
off Roehampton High St 201 CU87
Blackfriars 19 H10
Blackfriars Br, EC4 18 G10
SE1 18 G10
Blackfriars Ct, EC4 18 G10
Black Friars La, EC4 18 G10
Blackfriars Millennium Pier 18 F10
Blackfriars Pas, EC4 18 G10
Blackfriars Rd, SE1 30 G5
Black Gates, Pnr. HA5
off Moss La 138 BZ55
Black Grn Wd Cl, Park St AL2 82 CB29
Blackhall La, Sev. TN15 279 FK123
BLACKHEATH, SE3 47 K7
BLACKHEATH, Guil. GU4 281 BE142
Blackheath, SE3 47 M7
Blackheath 47 K10
Blackheath Av, SE10 47 H5
Blackheath Bluecoat C of E Sch, SE3
off Old Dover Rd 186 EH80
Blackheath Business Est, SE10 46 E7
Blackheath Conservatoire of Music & The Arts, SE3 47 L10
Blackheath Gro, SE3 47 L9
Wonersh GU5 281 BB143
Blackheath High Sch, Jun Dept, SE3 47 M9
Sen Dept, SE3 47 N4
Blackheath Hill, SE10 46 D7
Blackheath Hosp, The, SE3 186 EE83
Blackheath La, Albury GU5 282 BH140
Guildford GU4, GU5 281 BD143
Blackheath Nurs & Prep Sch, SE3 47 N6
BLACKHEATH PARK, SE3 186 EF84
Blackheath Pk, SE3 47 M10
Blackheath Ri, SE13 46 E9
Blackheath Rd, SE10 46 C6
Blackheath Vale, SE3 47 K8
Blackheath Village, SE3 47 L9
Blackhills, Esher KT10 236 CA109
Blackhorse Av, Chesh. HP5 76 AR33
Blackhorse Cl, Amer. HP6 77 AS38
Black Horse Cl, Wind. SL4 173 AK82
Black Horse Ct, SE1 31 M6
Blackhorse Cres, Amer. HP6 77 AS38
Blackhorse Lane 224 DU101
Blackhorse La, E17 145 DX55
Croydon CR0 224 DU101
North Weald Bassett CM16 93 FD25
Reigate RH2 272 DB129
South Mimms EN6 84 CS30
Blackhorse Ms, E17
off Blackhorse La 145 DX55
Black Horse Pl, Uxb. UB8
off Waterloo Rd 156 BJ67
Blackhorse Road 145 DX56
Blackhorse Road 145 DX56
Blackhorse Rd, E17 145 DX56
Blackhorse Rd, E17 145 DX56
SE8 45 M2
Sidcup DA14 208 EU91
Woking GU22 248 AS122
Blackhouse Fm, Egh. TW20
off Coldharbour La 215 BC97
Black Lake Cl, Egh. TW20 215 BA95
Blacklands Dr, Hayes UB4 157 BQ70
Blacklands Meadow, Nutfld RH1 273 DL133
Blacklands Rd, SE6 205 EC91
Blacklands Ter, SW3 28 E9
Blackley Cl, Wat. WD17 97 BT37
Black Lion Ct, Harl. CM17 58 EW11
Black Lion Hill, Shenley WD7 84 CL32
Black Lion La, W6 181 CU77
Black Lion Ms, W6
off Black Lion La 181 CU77
Blackmans Cl, Dart. DA1 210 FJ88
Blackmans La, Warl. CR6 244 EE114
Blackmead, Rvrhd TN13 278 FE121
Blackmoor La, Wat. WD18 97 BR43
Blackmore Av, Sthl. UB1 159 CD74
Blackmore Cl, Grays RM17 192 GB78
Blackmore Ct, Wal.Abb. EN9 90 EG33
Blackmore Cres, Wok. GU21 249 BB115
Blackmore Dr, NW10 160 CP66
Blackmore Rd, Buck.H. IG9 124 EL45
Blackmores, Harl. CM19 73 EP15
Blackmores Gro, Tedd. TW11 199 CG93
Blackmore Twr, W3
off Stanley Rd 180 CQ76
Blackmore Way, Uxb. UB8 156 BK65
Blackness La, Kes. BR2 244 EK109
Woking GU22 248 AY119
Black Park Country Pk, Slou. SL3 155 AZ67
Black Pk Rd, Slou. SL3 155 AZ68
Black Path, E10 145 DX59
Blackpond La, Slou. SL2 153 AP66
Blackpool Gdns, Hayes UB4 157 BS70
Blackpool Rd, SE15 44 E9
Black Prince Cl, Byfleet KT14 234 BM114
Black Prince Interchange, Bex. DA5 209 FB86
Black Prince Rd, SE1 30 C9
SE11 30 D9
Black Rod Cl, Hayes UB3 177 BT76
Blackshaw Rd, SW17 202 DC91
Blackshots La, Grays RM16 192 GD75
Blacksmith Cl, Ashtd. KT21 254 CM119
Blacksmith La, Chilw. GU4 281 BC139
Blacksmith Row, Slou. SL3 175 BA77
Blacksmiths Cl, Gt Amwell SG12 55 EA08
Romford RM6 148 EW58
Blacksmiths Hill, S.Croy. CR2 242 DU113
Blacksmiths La, Cher. KT16 216 BG101
Denham UB9 135 BC61
Orpington BR5 228 EW99
Rainham RM13 169 FF67
St. Albans AL3 64 CB20
Staines TW18 216 BH97
Blacksmiths Way, High Wych CM21 58 EU06
Blacks Rd, W6 26 A9
Blackstock Ms, N4
off Blackstock Rd 143 DP61
Blackstock Rd, N4 143 DP61
N5 143 DP61
Blackstone Cl, Red. RH1 288 DE135
Blackstone Est, E8 10 D7
Blackstone Hill, Red. RH1 288 DE135
Blackstone Ho, SW1
off Churchill Gdns 41 L1
Blackstone Rd, NW2 4 B2
Black Swan Ct, Ware SG12
off Baldock St 55 DX06
Black Swan Yd, SE1 31 N4
Black's Yd, Sev. TN13
off Bank St 279 FJ125
Blackthorn Av, West Dr. UB7 176 BN77
Blackthorn Cl, Reig. RH2 288 DC136
St. Albans AL4 65 CJ17
Watford WD25 81 BV32
Blackthorn Ct, Houns. TW5 178 BY80
Blackthorn Dell, Slou. SL3 174 AW76
Blackthorne Av, Croy. CR0 224 DW101
Blackthorne Cl, Hat. AL10 67 CT21
Blackthorne Cres, Colnbr. SL3 175 BE83
Blackthorne Dr, E4 123 ED49
Blackthorne Rd, Bigg.H. TN16 260 EK116
Bookham KT23 268 CC126
Colnbrook SL3 175 BE83
Blackthorn Gro, Bexh. DA7 188 EX83
Blackthorn Rd, Ilf. IG1 147 ER64
Reigate RH2 288 DC136
Welwyn Garden City AL7 52 DA10
Blackthorn St, E3 22 B5
Blackthorn Way, Warley CM14 130 FX50
Blacktree Ms, SW9 183 DN83
Blackwall 34 F1
Blackwall La, SE10 35 K10
Blackwall Pier, E14 35 J1
Blackwall Trd Est, E14 23 H7
Blackwall Tunnel, E14 34 G1
Blackwall Tunnel App, SE10 35 J5
Blackwall Tunnel Northern App, E3 12 B10
E14 22 E2
Blackwall Way, E14 34 F1
Blackwater Cl, E7 13 M1
Rainham RM13 169 FD71
Blackwater La, Hem.H. HP3 63 BS23
Blackwater Rd, Sutt. SM1
off High St 240 DB105
Blackwater St, SE22 204 DT85
Blackwell Cl, E5 145 DX63
Harrow HA3 117 CD52
Blackwell Dr, Wat. WD19 98 BW44
Blackwell Gdns, Edg. HA8 118 CN48
Blackwell Hall La, Chesh. HP5 78 AW33
Blackwell Rd, Kings L. WD4 80 BN29
Blackwood Av, N18
off Harbet Rd 123 DX50
Blackwood Cl, W.Byf. KT14 234 BJ112
Blackwood Ct, Brox. EN10
off Groom Rd 89 DZ26
Blackwood St, SE17 31 L10
Blade Ct, Rom. RM7
off Oldchurch Rd 149 FE58
Blade Ms, SW15 181 CZ84
Bladen Cl, Wey. KT13 235 BR107
Blades Cl, Lthd. KT22 253 CK120
Blades Ct, SW15 181 CZ84
Bladindon Dr, Bex. DA5 208 EW87
Bladon Cl, Guil. GU1 265 BA133
Bladon Gdns, Har. HA2 138 CB58
Blagdens Cl, N14 121 DJ47
Blagdens La, N14 121 DK47
Blagdon Rd, SE13 205 EB86
New Malden KT3 221 CT98
Blagdon Wk, Tedd. TW11 199 CJ93
Blagrove Rd, W10 14 F7
Blair Av, NW9 140 CS59
Esher KT10 218 CC103
Blair Cl, N1 9 K4
Hayes UB3 177 BU77
Sidcup DA15 207 ES85
Blairderry Rd, SW2 203 DL89
Blair Dr, Sev. TN13 279 FH123
Blairhead Dr, Wat. WD19 115 BV48
Blair Ho, SW9 42 C8
Blair Peach Prim Sch, Sthl. UB1 *off Beaconsfield Rd* 158 BX74
Blair Rd, Slou. SL1 154 AS74
Blair St, E14 22 F9
Blake Apts, N8
off New River Av 143 DM55
Blake Av, Bark. IG11 167 ES67
Blakeborough Dr, Harold Wd RM3 128 FL54
Blake Cl, W10 14 B6
Carshalton SM5 222 DE101
Hayes UB4 157 BR68
Rainham RM13 169 FF67
St. Albans AL1 65 CG23
Welling DA16 187 ES81
Blakeden Dr, Clay. KT10 237 CF107
Blakefield Gdns, Couls. CR5 257 DM118
Blake Gdns, SW6 39 L6
Dartford DA1 190 FM84
Blake Hall Cres, E11 146 EG60
Blake Hall Rd, E11 146 EG59
Blakehall Rd, Cars. SM5 240 DF107
Blake Hall Rd, Ong. CM5 93 FG25
Blake Ho, Beck. BR3 205 EA93
Blakemere Rd, Welw.G.C. AL8 51 CX07
Blake Ms, Rich. TW9
off High Pk Rd 180 CN81
Blakemore Gdns, SW13
off Lonsdale Rd 181 CV79
Blakemore Rd, SW16 203 DL90
Thornton Heath CR7 223 DM99
Blakemore Way, Belv. DA17 188 EY76
Blakeney Av, Beck. BR3 225 DZ95
Blakeney Cl, E8 10 C2
N20 120 DC46
NW1 7 N7
Epsom KT19 238 CR111
Blakeney Rd, Beck. BR3 205 DZ94
Blakenham Rd, SW17 202 DF91
Blaker Ct, SE7 *off Fairlawn* 186 EJ80
Blake Rd, E16 23 L5
N11 121 DJ52
Croydon CR0 224 DS103
Mitcham CR4 222 DE97
Blaker Rd, E15 12 E9
Blakes Av, N.Mal. KT3 221 CT99
Blakes Ct, Saw. CM21
off Church St 58 EY05
Blake's Grn, W.Wick. BR4 225 EC102
Blakes La, E.Clan. GU4 266 BL132
New Malden KT3 221 CT99
West Horsley KT24 266 BM131
Blakesley Av, W5 159 CJ72
Blakesley Ho, E12
off Grantham Rd 147 EN62
Blakesley Wk, SW20
off Kingston Rd 221 CZ96
Blakes Rd, SE15 43 P4
Blakes Ter, N.Mal. KT3 221 CU99
Blake St, SE8 46 A2
Blakesware Gdns, N9 122 DR45
Blakes Way, Til. RM18
off Coleridge Rd 193 GJ82
Blakewood Cl, Felt. TW13 198 BW91
Blanchard Cl, SE9 206 EL90
Blanchard Dr, Wat. WD18
off Cassio Pl 97 BS42
Blanchard Gro, Enf. EN3 105 EB38
Blanchard Ms, Harold Wd RM3 *off Avenue Rd* 128 FM52
Blanchards Hill, Guil. GU4 264 AY128
Blanchard Way, E8 10 D5
Blanch Cl, SE15 44 G5
Blanchedowne, SE5 184 DR84
Blanche La, S.Mimms EN6 85 CT34
Blanche Nevile Sch, N10
off Burlington Rd 142 DG55
Blanche St, E16 23 L5
Blanchland Rd, Mord. SM4 222 DB99
Blanchmans Rd, Warl. CR6 259 DY118
Blandfield Rd, SW12 202 DG86
Blandford Av, Beck. BR3 225 DY96
Twickenham TW2 198 CB88
Blandford Cl, N2 142 DC56
Croydon CR0 223 DL104
Romford RM7 149 FB56
Slough SL3 174 AX76
Woking GU22 249 BB117
Blandford Ct, Slou. SL3
off Blandford Rd S 174 AX76
Blandford Cres, E4 123 EC45
Blandford Rd, W4 180 CS76
W5 179 CK75
Beckenham BR3 224 DW96
St. Albans AL1 65 CG20
Southall UB2 178 CA77
Teddington TW11 199 CD92
Blandford Rd N, Slou. SL3 174 AX76
Blandford Rd S, Slou. SL3 174 AX76
Blandford Sq, NW1 16 D5
Blandford St, W1 16 F8
Blandford Waye, Hayes UB4 158 BW72
Bland St, SE9 186 EK84
Blaney Cres, E6 25 N3
Blanford Ms, Reig. RH2 272 DD134
Blanford Rd, Reig. RH2 288 DC135
Blanmerle Rd, SE9 207 EP88
Blann Cl, SE9 206 EK86
Blantyre St, SW10 40 A4
Blantyre Twr, SW10 40 A4
Blantyre Wk, SW10
off Blantyre St 40 A4
Blashford, NW3 6 E6
Blashford St, SE13 205 ED87
Blasker Wk, E14 34 B10
Blattner Cl, Els. WD6 100 CL42
Blawith Rd, Har. HA1 139 CE56
Blaxland Ter, Chsht EN8
off Davison Dr 89 DX28
Blaydon Cl, N17 122 DV52
Ruislip HA4 137 BS59
Blaydon Wk, N17 122 DV52
Blays Cl, Eng.Grn TW20 194 AW93
Blays La, Eng.Grn TW20 194 AV94
Bleak Hill La, SE18 187 ET79
Blean Gro, SE20 204 DW94
Bleasdale Av, Perivale UB6 159 CG68
Blechynden St, W10 14 D10
Bleddyn Cl, Sid. DA15 208 EW86
Bledlow Cl, NW8 16 B5
SE28 168 EW73
Bledlow Ri, Grnf. UB6 158 CC68
Bleeding Heart Yd, EC1 18 F7
Blegberry Gdns, Berk. HP4 60 AS19
Blegborough Rd, SW16 203 DJ93
Blemundsbury, WC1
off Dombey St 18 C6
Blencarn Cl, Wok. GU21 248 AT116
Blendon Dr, Bex. DA5 208 EX86
Blendon Path, Brom. BR1
off Hope Pk 206 EF94
Blendon Rd, Bex. DA5 208 EX86
Blendon Ter, SE18 187 EQ78
Blendworth Pt, SW15
off Wanborough Dr 201 CV88
Blenheim Av, Ilf. IG2 147 EN58
Blenheim Cen, The, Houns. TW3 178 CB82
Blenheim Cl, N21
off Elm Pk Rd 122 DQ46
SE12 206 EH88
SW20 221 CW97
Dartford DA1 210 FJ86
Greenford UB6
off Leaver Gdns 159 CD68
Romford RM7 149 FC56
Sawbridgeworth CM21 58 EW07
Slough SL3 155 AZ74
Upminster RM14 151 FS60
Wallington SM6 241 DJ108
Watford WD19 116 BX45
West Byfleet KT14
off Madeira Rd 233 BF113
Blenheim Ct, N19 143 DL61
Bromley BR2 *off Durham Av* 226 EF98
Sidcup DA14 207 ER90
Sutton SM2
off Wellesley Rd 240 DC107
Waltham Cross EN8
off Eleanor Cross Rd 89 DZ34
Woodford Green IG8
off Navestock Cres 124 EJ53
Blenheim Cres, W11 14 E10
Ruislip HA4 137 BR61
South Croydon CR2 242 DQ108
Blenheim Dr, Well. DA16 187 ET81
Blenheim Gdns, NW2 4 B4
SW2 203 DM86
Aveley RM15 170 FP74
Kingston upon Thames KT2 200 CP94
South Croydon CR2 242 DU112
Wallington SM6 241 DJ107
Wembley HA9 140 CL62
Woking GU22 248 AV119
Blenheim Gro, SE15 44 B9
Blenheim High Sch, Epsom KT19 *off Longmead Rd* 238 CR110
Blenheim Ms, Shenley WD7 84 CL33
Blenheim Pk Rd, S.Croy. CR2 242 DQ109
Blenheim Pas, NW8 5 N10
Blenheim Pl, Tedd. TW11 199 CF92
Blenheim Prim Sch, Orp. BR6 *off Blenheim Rd* 228 EW103
Blenheim Ri, N15 144 DT56
Blenheim Rd, E6 24 E2
E15 146 EE63
E17 145 DX55
NW8 5 N10
SE20 *off Maple Rd* 204 DW94
SW20 221 CW97
W4 180 CS76
Abbots Langley WD5 81 BU33
Barnet EN5 101 CX41
Bromley BR1 226 EL98

Blenheim Rd, Dart. DA1 210 FJ86
Epsom KT19 238 CR111
Harrow HA2 138 CB58
Northolt UB5 158 CB65
Orpington BR6 228 EW103
Pilgrim's Hatch CM15 130 FU44
St. Albans AL1 65 CF19
Sidcup DA15 208 EW88
Slough SL3 174 AX77
Sutton SM1 222 DA104
Blenheim Shop Cen, SE20 204 DW94
Blenheim St, W1 17 J9
Blenheim Ter, NW8 5 N10
Blenheim Way, Islw. TW7 179 CG81
North Weald Bassett CM16 92 FA27
Blenhiem Ct, Welw.G.C. AL7 51 CZ08
Blenkarne Rd, SW11 202 DF86
Blenkin Cl, St.Alb. AL3 64 CC16
Bleriot Rd, Houns. TW5 178 BW80
Blessbury Rd, Edg. HA8 118 CQ53
Blessed Dominic RC Prim Sch, NW9 off Lanacre Av 119 CT54
Blessed Sacrament RC Prim Sch, N1 8 C9
Blessington Cl, SE13 185 ED83
Blessington Rd, SE13 185 ED83
Blessing Way, Bark. IG11 168 EW68
BLETCHINGLEY, Red. RH1 274 DQ132
Bletchingley Adult Ed Cen, Bletch. RH1
off Stychens La 274 DQ133
Bletchingley Cl, Merst. RH1 273 DJ129
Thornton Heath CR7 223 DP98
Bletchingley Rd, Gdse. RH9 274 DU131
Merstham RH1 273 DJ129
Nutfield RH1 273 DN133
Bletchley Ct, N1 19 L1
Bletchley St, N1 19 K1
Bletchmore Cl, Harling. UB3 177 BR78
Bletsoe Wk, N1 9 K10
Blewbury Ho, SE2
off Yarnton Way 188 EX75
Bligh Rd, Grav. DA11 213 GG86
Bligh's Ct, Sev. TN13
off Bligh's Wk 279 FH125
Bligh's Rd, Sev. TN13
off High St 279 FJ125
Bligh's Wk, Sev. TN13 279 FH125
Blincoe Cl, SW19 201 CX89
Blinco La, Geo.Grn SL3 154 AY72
Blind La, Bans. SM7 256 DE115
Betchworth RH3 286 CQ137
High Beach IG10 106 EE40
Waltham Abbey EN9 90 EJ33
Blindman's La, Chsht EN8 89 DX30
Bliss Cres, SE13 46 D8
Blissett St, SE10 46 E6
Bliss Ho, Enf. EN1 104 DT38
Bliss Ms, W10 14 F2
Blisworth Cl, Hayes UB4 158 BY70
Blithbury Rd, Dag. RM9 168 EV65
Blithdale Rd, SE2 188 EU77
Blithfield St, W8 27 L7
Blockhouse Rd, Grays RM17 192 GC79
Blockley Rd, Wem. HA0 139 CH61
Bloemfontein Av, W12 161 CV74
Bloemfontein Rd, W12 161 CV73
Bloemfontein Way, W12
off Bloemfontein Rd 161 CV74
Blomfield Ct, SW11 40 B7
Blomfield Ms, W2 15 N7
Blomfield Rd, W9 15 N6
Blomfield St, EC2 19 M7
Blomfield Vil, W2 15 M7
Blomville Rd, Dag. RM8 148 EY62
Blondell Cl, Harm. UB7 176 BK79
Blondel St, SW11 40 G8
Blondin Av, W5 179 CJ77
Blondin St, E3 12 A10
Bloomburg St, SW1 29 M9
Bloomfield Cl, Knap. GU21 248 AS118
Bloomfield Ct, E10
off Brisbane Rd 145 EB62
Bloomfield Cres, Ilf. IG2 147 EP58
Bloomfield Pl, W1 17 K10
Bloomfield Rd, N6 142 DG58
SE18 187 EP78
Bromley BR2 226 EK99
Cheshunt EN7 88 DQ25
Kingston upon Thames KT1 220 CL98
Bloomfield Ter, SW1 29 H10
Westerham TN16 277 ES125
Bloom Gro, SE27 203 DP90
Bloomhall Rd, SE19 204 DR92
Bloom Pk Rd, SW6 38 G5
BLOOMSBURY, WC1 17 P7
Bloomsbury Cl, NW7 119 CU52
W5 160 CM73
Epsom KT19 238 CR110
Bloomsbury Ct, WC1 18 B7
Guildford GU1
off St. Lukes Sq 281 AZ135
Pinner HA5 138 BZ55
Bloomsbury Ho, SW4 203 DK86
Bloomsbury Ms, Wdf.Grn. IG8 off Waltham Rd 124 EL51
Bloomsbury Pl, SW18 202 DC85
WC1 18 B6
Bloomsbury Sq, WC1 18 B7
Bloomsbury St, WC1 17 P7
Bloomsbury Way, WC1 18 A8
Blore Cl, SW8 41 N7
Blore Ct, W1 17 N9
Blossom Cl, W5 180 CL75
Dagenham RM9 168 EZ67
South Croydon CR2 242 DT106
Blossom Ho Sch, SW20
off The Drive 201 CW94
Blossom La, Enf. EN2 104 DQ39
Blossom St, E1 19 P6
Blossom Way, Uxb. UB10 156 BM66
West Drayton UB7 176 BN77
Blossom Waye, Houns. TW5 178 BY80
Blount St, E14 21 M8
Bloxam Gdns, SE9 206 EL85
Bloxhall Rd, E10 145 DZ60
Bloxham Cres, Hmptn. TW12 198 BZ94
Bloxworth Cl, Wall. SM6 223 DJ104
Blucher Rd, SE5 43 K5
Blucher St, Chesh. HP5 76 AP31
Blue Anchor All, Rich. TW9
off Kew Rd 180 CL84
Blue Anchor La, SE16 32 D8
West Tilbury RM18 193 GL77
Blue Anchor Yd, E1 20 C10
Blue Ball La, Egh. TW20 195 AZ92
Blue Ball Yd, SW1 29 L3
Blue Barn La, Wey. KT13 234 BN111
Bluebell Av, E12 146 EK64
Bluebell Cl, E9 10 G8
SE26 204 DT91
Hemel Hempstead HP1
off Sundew Rd 61 BE21
Hertford SG13 54 DU09
Northolt UB5 158 BZ65
Orpington BR6 227 EQ103
Rush Green RM7 149 FE61
Wallington SM6 223 DH102
Bluebell Ct, Wok. GU22 248 AX119
Bluebell Dr, Bedmond WD5 81 BT27
Cheshunt EN7 88 DR28
Bluebell La, E.Hors. KT24 267 BS129
Bluebell Way, Hat. AL10 51 CT14
Ilford IG1 167 EP65
Blueberry Cl, St.Alb. AL3 65 CD16
Woodford Green IG8 124 EG51
Blueberry Gdns, Couls. CR5 257 DM116
Blueberry La, Knock. TN14 262 EW116
Bluebird La, Dag. RM10 168 FA66
Bluebird Way, SE28 187 ER75
Bricket Wood AL2 82 BY30
Bluebridge Av, Brook.Pk AL9 85 CY27
Bluebridge Rd, Brook.Pk AL9 85 CY26
Blue Cedars, Bans. SM7 239 CX114
Blue Cedars Pl, Cob. KT11 236 BX112
Bluecoat Cl, Hert. SG14
off Railway St 54 DR09
Bluecoats Av, Hert. SG14 54 DR09
Bluecoat Yd, Ware SG12 55 DX06
Bluefield Cl, Hmptn. TW12 198 CA92
Blue Gate Flds Inf & Jun Schs, E1 20 G10
Bluegates, Ewell KT17 239 CU108
Bluehouse Gdns, Oxt. RH8 276 EG128
Blue Ho Hill, St.Alb. AL3 64 CA20
Bluehouse La, Oxt. RH8 276 EG127
Bluehouse Rd, E4 124 EE48
Blue Leaves Av, Couls. CR5 257 DK121
Bluelion Pl, SE1 31 N6
Bluemans, N.Wld Bas. CM16 75 FD24
Bluemans End, N.Wld Bas. CM16 75 FD24
Blueprint Apts, SW12
off Balham Gro 203 DH87
Blue Sch, The, Islw. TW7
off North St 179 CG83
Bluett Rd, Lon.Col. AL2 83 CK27
Bluewater Ho, SW18
off Smugglers Way 182 DB84
Bluewater Parkway, Bluewater DA9 211 FS87
Bluewater Shop Cen, Green. DA9 211 FT87
Blumfield Ct, Slou. SL1 153 AK70
Blumfield Cres, Slou. SL1 153 AK70
Blundel La, Stoke D'Ab. KT11 236 CB114
Blundell Av, Horl. RH6 290 DF148
Blundell Cl, E8 10 C2
St. Albans AL3 65 CD16
Blundell Rd, Edg. HA8 118 CR53
Blundell St, N7 8 B6
Blunden Cl, Dag. RM8 148 EW60
Blunden Dr, Slou. SL3 175 BB77
Blunesfield, Pot.B. EN6 86 DD31
Blunt Rd, S.Croy. CR2 242 DR106
Blunts Av, Sipson UB7 176 BN80
Blunts La, St.Alb. AL2 82 BW27
Blunts Rd, SE9 207 EN85
Blurton Rd, E5 11 H1
Blyth Cl, E14 34 G8
Borehamwood WD6 100 CM39
Twickenham TW1
off Grimwood Rd 199 CF86
Blythe Cl, SE6 205 DZ87
Iver SL0 155 BF72
Blythe Hill, SE6 205 DZ87
Orpington BR5 227 ET95
Blythe Hill La, SE6 205 DZ87
Blythe Hill Pl, SE23
off Brockley Pk 205 DY87
Blythe Ms, W14 26 C6
Blythe Rd, W14 26 E8
Hoddesdon EN11 71 ED19
Blythe St, E2 20 E2
Blytheswood Pl, SW16
off Curtis Fld Rd 203 DM91
Blythe Vale, SE6 205 DZ88
Blyth Rd, E17 145 DZ59
SE28 168 EW73
Bromley BR1 226 EF95
Hayes UB3 177 BS75
Blyth's Wf, E14 33 M1
Blythswood Rd, Ilf. IG3 148 EU60
Blyth Wk, Upmin. RM14 151 FS58
Blythway, Welw.G.C. AL7 51 CZ06
Blyth Wd Pk, Brom. BR1
off Blyth Rd 226 EF95
Blythwood Rd, N4 143 DL59
Pinner HA5 116 BX53
Blyton Cl, Beac. HP9 111 AK51
Bnois Jerusalem Sch, N16 off Amhurst Pk 144 DS59
Boades Ms, NW3 off New End 142 DD63
Boadicea Cl, Slou. SL1 153 AK74
Boadicea St, N1 8 C9
Boakes Cl, NW9 140 CQ56
Boakes Meadow, Shore. TN14 247 FF111
Boar Cl, Chig. IG7 126 EU50
Boardman Av, E4 105 EB43
Boardman Cl, Barn. EN5 101 CY43
Board Sch Rd, Wok. GU21 249 AZ116
Boardwalk Pl, E14 34 E2
Boar Hill, Dor. RH5 285 CF142
Boarlands Cl, Slou. SL1 153 AM73
Boarlands Path, Slou. SL1
off Brook Path 153 AM73
Boar's Head Yd, Brent. TW8
off Brent Way 179 CK80
Boars Rd, Harl. CM17 58 FA14
Boatemah Wk, SW9
off Peckford Pl 42 E9
Boathouse Wk, SE15 44 B4
Richmond TW9 180 CL81
Boat Lifter Way, SE16 33 M8
Bob Anker Cl, E13 23 P2
Bobbin Cl, SW4 41 L10
Bobby Moore Way, N10 120 DF52
Bob Dunn Way, Dart. DA1 190 FJ84
Bob Marley Way, SE24
off Mayall Rd 183 DN84
Bobs La, Rom. RM1 127 FG52
Bocketts La, Lthd. KT22 253 CF124
Bockhampton Rd, Kings.T. KT2 200 CM94
Bocking St, E8 10 E8
Boddicott Cl, SW19 201 CY89
Boddington Gdns, W3 180 CN75
Bodell Cl, Grays RM16 192 GB76
Bodiam Cl, Enf. EN1 104 DR40
Bodiam Rd, SW16 203 DK94
Bodiam Way, NW10 160 CM69
Bodicea Ms, Houns. TW4 198 BZ87
Bodle Av, Swans. DA10 212 FY87
Bodley Cl, Epp. CM16 91 ET30
New Malden KT3 220 CS99
Bodley Manor Way, SW2
off Hambridge Way 203 DN87
Bodley Rd, N.Mal. KT3 220 CR100
Bodmin Av, Slou. SL2 153 AN71
Bodmin Cl, Har. HA2 138 BZ62
Orpington BR5 228 EW102
Bodmin Gro, Mord. SM4 222 DB99
Bodmin St, SW18 202 DA88
Bodnant Gdns, SW20 221 CU97
Bodney Rd, E8 10 E3
Bodwell Cl, Hem.H. HP1 61 BF19
Boeing Way, Sthl. UB2 177 BV76
Boevey Path, Belv. DA17 188 EZ79
Bogey La, Orp. BR6 245 EN108
Bognor Gdns, Wat. WD19 116 BW50
Bognor Rd, Well. DA16 188 EX81
Bohemia, Hem.H. HP2 62 BL19
Bohemia Pl, E8 10 F4
Bohn Rd, E1 21 L6
Bohun Gro, Barn. EN4 102 DE44
Boileau Par, W5
off Boileau Rd 160 CM72
Boileau Rd, SW13 181 CU80
W5 160 CM72
Bois Av, Amer. HP6 77 AP36
Bois Hall Rd, Add. KT15 234 BK105
Bois Hill, Chesh. HP5 76 AS34
Bois La, Amer. HP6 77 AR35
Bois Moor Rd, Chesh. HP5 76 AQ33
Boissy Cl, St.Alb. AL4 66 CL21
Bolberry Rd, Coll.Row RM5 127 FD50
Bolden St, SE8 46 C8
Bolderwood Way, W.Wick. BR4 225 EB103
Boldmere Rd, Pnr. HA5 138 BW59
Boleyn Av, Enf. EN1 104 DV39
Epsom KT17 239 CV110
Boleyn Cl, E17 145 EA56
Chafford Hundred RM16
off Clifford Rd 192 FZ76
Hemel Hempstead HP2
off Parr Cres 63 BQ15
Loughton IG10
off Roding Gdns 106 EL44
Staines TW18
off Chertsey La 195 BE92
Boleyn Ct, Brox. EN10 71 DY21
Buckhurst Hill IG9 124 EG46
Boleyn Dr, Ruis. HA4 138 BX61
St. Albans AL1 65 CD22
West Molesey KT8 218 BZ97
Boleyn Gdns, Brwd. CM13 131 GA48
Dagenham RM10 169 FC66
West Wickham BR4 225 EB103
Boleyn Gro, W.Wick. BR4 225 EC103
Boleyn Rd, E6 166 EK68
E7 13 P7
N16 9 P3
Boleyn Wk, Lthd. KT22 253 CF120
Boleyn Way, Barn. EN5 102 DC41
Ilford IG6 125 EQ51
Swanscombe DA10 212 FY87
Bolina Rd, SE16 33 H10
Bolingbroke Gro, SW11 182 DE84
Bolingbroke Hosp, SW11 202 DE85
Bolingbroke Rd, W14 26 D6
Bolingbroke Wk, SW11 40 B5
Bolingbroke Way, Hayes UB3 157 BR74
Bolingbrook, St.Alb. AL4 65 CG16
Bolliger Ct, NW10
off Park Royal Rd 160 CQ70
Bollo Br Rd, W3 180 CP76
Bollo La, W3 180 CP75
W4 180 CQ77
Bolney Gate, SW7 28 C5
Bolney St, SW8 42 C5
Bolney Way, Felt. TW13 198 BY90
Bolsover Dr, Merst. RH1 273 DL129
Bolsover St, W1 17 K5
Bolstead Rd, Mitch. CR4 223 DH95
Bolster Gro, N22 121 DK52
Bolt Cellar La, Epp. CM16 91 ES29
Bolt Ct, EC4 18 F9
Bolters La, Bans. SM7 239 CZ114
Bolters Rd, Horl. RH6 290 DG146
Bolters Rd S, Horl. RH6 290 DF146
Boltmore Cl, NW4 141 CX55
Bolton Av, Wind. SL4 173 AQ83
Bolton Cl, SE20 off Selby Rd 224 DU96
Chessington KT9 237 CK107
Bolton Cres, SE5 42 F3
Windsor SL4 173 AQ83
Bolton Dr, Mord. SM4 222 DC101
Bolton Gdns, NW10 14 C1
SW5 27 L10
Bromley BR1 206 EF93
Teddington TW11 199 CG93
Bolton Gdns Ms, SW10 27 N10
Bolton Rd, E15 13 M5
N18 122 DT50
NW8 5 M9
NW10 160 CS67
W4 180 CQ80
Chessington KT9 237 CK107
Harrow HA1 138 CC56
Windsor SL4 173 AQ83
Boltons, The, SW10 27 N10
Wembley HA0 139 CF63
Woodford Green IG8 124 EG49
Boltons Cl, Wok. GU22 250 BG116
Boltons La, Harling. UB3 177 BQ80
Woking GU22 250 BG116
Boltons Pl, SW5 27 N10
Bolton St, W1 29 K2
Bolton Wk, N7 off Durham Rd 143 DM61
Bombay St, SE16 32 E8
Bombers La, West. TN16 261 ER119
Bomer Cl, Sipson UB7 176 BN80
Bomore Rd, W11 14 D10
Bonar Pl, Chis. BR7 206 EL94
Bonar Rd, SE15 44 C5
Bonaventure Ct, Grav. DA12 213 GM91
Bonchester Cl, Chis. BR7 207 EN94
Bonchurch Cl, Sutt. SM2 240 DB108
Bonchurch Rd, W10 14 E6
W13 159 CH74
Bond Cl, Iver SL0 155 BB66
Knockholt Pound TN14 262 EX115
West Drayton UB7 156 BM72
Bond Ct, EC4 19 L9
Bondfield Av, Hayes UB4 157 BU69
Bondfield Rd, E6 25 H7
Bondfield Wk, Dart. DA1 190 FM84
Bond Gdns, Wall. SM6 241 DJ105
Bonding Yd Wk, SE16 33 M5
Bond Prim Sch, Mitch. CR4 off Bond Rd 222 DF96
Bond Rd, Mitch. CR4 222 DE96
Surbiton KT6 220 CM103
Warlingham CR6 259 DX118
Bonds La, Mid Holm. RH5 285 CH142
Bond Street 17 H9
Bond St, E15 13 J2
W4 180 CS77
W5 159 CK73
Englefield Green TW20 194 AV92
Grays RM17 192 GC79
Bondway 42 B2
Bondway, SW8 42 B3
Bonehurst Rd, Horl. RH6 288 DG144
Salfords RH1 288 DG142
Bone Mill La, Gdse. RH9
off Eastbourne Rd 275 DY134
Boneta Rd, SE18 37 J7
Bonfield Rd, SE13 185 EC84
Bonham Cl, Belv. DA17 188 EZ78
Bonham Gdns, Dag. RM8 148 EX61
Bonham Rd, SW2 203 DM85
Dagenham RM8 148 EX61
Bonheur Rd, W4 180 CR75
Bonhill St, EC2 19 M5
Boniface Gdns, Har. HA3 116 CB52
Boniface Rd, Uxb. UB10 137 BP62
Boniface Wk, Har. HA3 116 CB52
Bonington Ho, Enf. EN1
off Ayley Cft 104 DU43
Bonington Rd, Horn. RM12 150 FK64
Bonita Ms, SE4 45 J10
Bonks Hill, Saw. CM21 58 EX06
Bon Marche Ter Ms, SE27
off Gipsy Rd 204 DS91
Bonner Ct, Chsht EN8
off Coopers Wk 89 DX28
Bonner Hill Rd, Kings.T. KT1 220 CM97
Bonner Prim Sch, E2 21 H1
Bonner Rd, E2 10 G10
Bonners Cl, Wok. GU22 248 AY122
Bonnersfield Cl, Har. HA1 139 CF58
Bonnersfield La, Har. HA1 139 CG58
Bonner St, E2 21 H1
Bonner Wk, Grays RM16
off Clifford Rd 192 FZ76
Bonnett Ms, Horn. RM11 150 FL60
Bonneville Gdns, SW4 203 DJ86
Bonneville Prim Sch, SW4
off Bonneville Gdns 203 DJ86
Bonney Gro, Chsht EN7 88 DU30
Bonneygrove Prim Sch, Chsht EN7 off Dark La 88 DU30
Bonney Way, Swan. BR8 229 FE96
Bonnington Ho, N1
off Killick St 18 C1
Bonningtons, Brwd. CM13 131 GB48
Bonnington Sq, SW8 42 C2
Bonnington Twr, Brom. BR2 226 EL100
Bonnygate Prim Sch, S.Ock. RM15 off Arisdale Av 171 FV71
Bonny's Rd, Reig. RH2 287 CX135
Bonny St, NW1 7 L7
Bonser Rd, Twick. TW1 199 CF89
Bonsey Cl, Wok. GU22 248 AY121
Bonsey La, Wok. GU22 248 AY121
Bonseys La, Chobham GU24 233 AZ110
Bonsor Dr, Kgswd KT20 255 CY122
Bonsor St, SE5 43 N5
Bonus Pastor Cath Coll, Lwr Sch, Brom. BR1
off Churchdown 206 EE91
Upr Sch, Brom. BR1
off Winlaton Rd 206 EE91
Bonville Gdns, NW4
off Handowe Cl 141 CU56
Bonville Rd, Brom. BR1 206 EF92
Bookbinders' Cotts, N20
off Manor Dr 120 DF48
Booker Cl, E14 21 P7
Booker Rd, N18 122 DU50
Bookham 252 BZ123
Bookham Ct, Lthd. KT23
off Church Rd 252 BZ123
Mitcham CR4 222 DD97
Bookham Gro, Bkhm KT23 268 CB126
Bookham Ind Est, Bkhm KT23 252 BZ123
Bookham Rd, Down. KT11 252 BW119
Book Ms, WC2 17 P9
Boone Ct, N9 122 DW48
Boones Rd, SE13 186 EE84
Boone St, SE13 186 EE84
Boord St, SE10 35 K6
Boot All, St.Alb. AL1
off Market Pl 65 CD20
Boothby Rd, N19 143 DK61
Booth Cl, E9 10 F9
SE28 168 EV73
Booth Dr, Stai. TW18 196 BK93
Booth Ho, Brent. TW8
off London Rd 179 CJ80
Booth La, EC4 19 J10
Booth Rd, NW9 118 CS54
Croydon CR0
off Waddon New Rd 223 DP103
Booths Cl, N.Mymms AL9 67 CX24
Booth's Ct, Hutt. CM13 131 GB44
Booth's Pl, W1 17 M7
Boot St, N1 19 N3
Bordars Rd, W7 159 CE71
Bordars Wk, W7 159 CE71
Borden Av, Enf. EN1 104 DR44
Border Cres, SE26 204 DV92
Border Gdns, Croy. CR0 243 EB105
Bordergate, Mitch. CR4 222 DE95
Border Rd, SE26 204 DV92
Borderside, Slou. SL2 154 AU72
Borders La, Loug. IG10 107 EN42
Bordesley Rd, Mord. SM4 222 DB98
Bordon Wk, SW15 201 CU87
Boreas Wk, N1 19 H1
Boreham Av, E16 23 N9
Boreham Cl, E11
off Hainault Rd 145 EC60
Boreham Holt, Els. WD6 100 CM42
Boreham Rd, N22 122 DQ54
BOREHAMWOOD, WD6 100 CP41
Borehamwood Ind Pk, Borwd. WD6 100 CR40
Borehamwood Shop Pk, Borwd. WD6 100 CN41
Borgard Rd, SE18 37 J8
Borham Ms, Hodd. EN11 55 EA13
Borkwood Pk, Orp. BR6 245 ET105
Borkwood Way, Orp. BR6 245 ES105
Borland Cl, Green. DA9
off Steele Av 211 FU85
Borland Rd, SE15 184 DW84
Teddington TW11 199 CH93
Bornedene, Pot.B. EN6 85 CY31
Borneo St, SW15 181 CW83
Borough 31 K5
BOROUGH, THE, SE1 31 J5
Borough, The, Brock. RH3 286 CN135
Borough High St, SE1 31 J5
Borough Hill, Croy. CR0 223 DP104
Borough Mkt, SE1 31 L3
Borough Rd, SE1 30 G6
Isleworth TW7 179 CE81
Kingston upon Thames KT2 220 CN95
Mitcham CR4 222 DE96
Tatsfield TN16 260 EK121
Borough Sq, SE1 31 J5
Borough Way, Pot.B. EN6 85 CY32
Borrell Cl, Brox. EN10 71 DZ20
Borrett Cl, SE17 43 J1
Borrodaile Rd, SW18 202 DB86
Borrowdale Av, Har. HA3 117 CG54
Borrowdale Cl, N2 120 DC54
Egham TW20
off Derwent Rd 195 BB94
Ilford IG4 146 EL56
South Croydon CR2 242 DT113
Borrowdale Ct, Enf. EN2 104 DQ39
Hemel Hempstead HP2 62 BL17
Borrowdale Dr, S.Croy. CR2 242 DT112
Borthwick Ms, E15 13 J1
Borthwick Rd, E15 13 J1
NW9 off West Hendon Bdy 141 CT58
Borthwick St, SE8 46 A1
Borwick Av, E17 145 DZ55
Bosanquet Cl, Uxb. UB8 156 BK70
Bosanquet Rd, Hodd. EN11 71 EC15
Bosbury Rd, SE6 205 EC90
Boscastle Rd, NW5 143 DH62
Boscobel Cl, Brom. BR1 227 EM96
Boscobel Pl, SW1 29 H8
Boscobel St, NW8 16 B5
Bosco Cl, Orp. BR6 245 ET105
Boscombe Av, E10 145 ED59
Grays RM17 192 GD77
Hornchurch RM11 150 FK60
Boscombe Circ, NW9
off Warmwell Av 118 CR54
Boscombe Cl, E5 11 L2
Egham TW20 215 BC95
Boscombe Gdns, SW16 203 DL93
Boscombe Rd, SW17 202 DG93
SW19 222 DB95
W12 161 CU74
Worcester Park KT4 221 CW102
Bose Cl, N3 off Claremont Pk 119 CY53
Bosgrove, E4 123 EC46
Boshers Gdns, Egh. TW20 195 AZ93
Boss Ho, SE1 32 A4
Boss St, SE1 32 A4
Bostall Heath, SE2 188 EW78
Bostall Hill, SE2 188 EU78
Bostall La, SE2 188 EV78
Bostall Manorway, SE2 188 EV77
Bostall Pk Av, Bexh. DA7 188 EY80
Bostall Rd, Orp. BR5 208 EV94
Bostal Row, Bexh. DA7
off Harlington Rd 188 EZ83
Bostock Ho, Houns. TW5 178 CA79
Boston Gdns, W4 180 CS79
W7 179 CG77
Brentford TW8 179 CG77
Boston Gro, Ruis. HA4 137 BQ58
Slough SL1 153 AQ72
Boston Manor 179 CG77
Boston Manor Ho, Brent. TW8 179 CH78
Boston Manor Rd, Brent. TW8 179 CH77
Boston Pk Rd, Brent. TW8 179 CJ78
Boston Pl, NW1 16 E5
Boston Rd, E6 24 G2
E17 145 EA58
W7 159 CE74
Croydon CR0 223 DM100
Edgware HA8 118 CQ52
Bostonthorpe Rd, W7 179 CE75
Boston Vale, W7 179 CG77
Bosun Cl, E14 34 B4
Bosville Av, Sev. TN13 278 FG123
Bosville Dr, Sev. TN13 278 FG123
Bosville Rd, Sev. TN13 278 FG123
Boswell Cl, Orp. BR5
off Killewarren Way 228 EW100
Shenley WD7 84 CL32
Boswell Ct, WC1 18 B6
Boswell Path, Hayes UB3
off Croyde Av 177 BT77
Boswell Rd, Th.Hth. CR7 224 DQ98
Boswell Row, Cat. CR3
off Croydon Rd 258 DU122
Boswell St, WC1 18 B6
Bosworth Cl, E17 123 DZ53
Bosworth Ct, Slou. SL1 152 AJ73
Bosworth Cres, Rom. RM3 128 FJ51
Bosworth Ho, Erith DA8
off Saltford Cl 189 FE78
Bosworth Rd, N11 121 DK51
W10 14 F5
Barnet EN5 102 DA41
Dagenham RM10 148 FA63
BOTANY BAY, Enf. EN2 103 DK36
Botany Bay La, Chis. BR7 227 EQ97
Botany Cl, Barn. EN4 102 DE42
Botany Rd, Nthflt DA11 192 GA83
Botany Way, Purf. RM19 190 FP78
Boteley Cl, E4 123 ED47
Botery's Cross, Red. RH1 273 DP133
Botham Cl, Edg. HA8 118 CQ52
Botham Dr, Slou. SL1 174 AS76
Botha Rd, E13 24 B6
Bothwell Cl, E16 23 M7
Bothwell Rd, New Adgtn CR0 243 EC110
Bothwell St, W6 38 D3
BOTLEY, Chesh. HP5 78 AV30
Botley La, Chesh. HP5 78 AU30
Botley Rd, Chesh. HP5 78 AT30
Hemel Hempstead HP2 62 BN15
Botolph All, EC3 19 N10
Botolph La, EC3 31 M1

Botsford Rd, SW20 221 CY96
Bottom Ho Fm La, Ch.St.G. HP8 112 AT45
Bottom La, Chesh. HP5 78 AT34
Kings Langley WD4 96 BH35
Seer Green HP9 111 AP51
Bottrells Cl, Ch.St.G. HP8 112 AT47
Bottrells La, Ch.St.G. HP8 112 AT47
Coleshill HP7 111 AP46
Bott Rd, Hawley DA2 210 FM91
Botts Ms, W2 15 K9
Botts Pas, W2 15 K9
Botwell Common Rd, Hayes UB3 157 BR73
Botwell Cres, Hayes UB3 157 BS72
Sch Botwell Ho RC Prim Sch, Hayes UB3 off Botwell La 177 BT75
Botwell La, Hayes UB3 157 BS74
Boucher Cl, Tedd. TW11 199 CF92
Boucher Dr, Nthflt DA11 213 GF90
Boucher Wk, Rain. RM13 off Deere Av 169 FG65
Boughton Av, Brom. BR2 226 EF101
● Boughton Business Pk, Amer. HP6 94 AV39
Boughton Hall Av, Send GU23 249 BF124
Boughton Rd, SE28 187 ES76
Boughton Way, Amer. HP6 94 AW38
Boulcott St, E1 21 K9
Boulevard, The, SW6 39 P7
SW17 off Balham High Rd 202 DG89
SW18 off Smugglers Way 182 DB84
Greenhithe DA9 off Ingress Pk Av 191 FW84
Watford WD18 97 BR43
Welwyn Garden City AL7 51 CZ07
Wembley HA9 off Engineers Way 140 CN63
Woodford Green IG8 125 EN51
Boulevard Dr, NW9 119 CT54
Boulmer Rd, Uxb. UB8 156 BJ69
Boulogne Rd, Croy. CR0 224 DQ100
Boulter Cl, Brom. BR1 227 EP97
Boulter Gdns, Rain. RM13 169 FG65
Boulters Cl, Maid. SL6 152 AC70
Slough SL1 off Amerden Way 173 AN75
Boulters Ct, Maid. SL6 152 AC70
Boulters Gdns, Maid. SL6 152 AC70
Boulters La, Maid. SL6 152 AC70
Boulters Lock Island, Maid. SL6 152 AC69
Boulthurst Way, Oxt. RH8 276 EH132
Boulton Ho, Brent. TW8 off Green Dragon La 180 CL78
Boulton Rd, Dag. RM8 148 EY62
Boultwood Rd, E6 25 H9
Bounce, The, Hem.H. HP2 62 BK18
BOUNCE HILL, Rom. RM4 109 FH39
Bounces La, N9 122 DV47
Bounces Rd, N9 122 DV46
Boundaries Rd, SW12 202 DF89
Feltham TW13 198 BW88
Boundary, The, Lt.Berk. SG13 69 DJ19
Boundary Av, E17 145 DZ59
● Boundary Business Cen, Wok. GU21 249 BA115
● Boundary Business Ct, Mitch. CR4 222 DD97
Boundary Cl, SE20 off Haysleigh Gdns 224 DU96
Barnet EN5 101 CZ39
Ilford IG3 off Loxford La 147 ES63
Kingston upon Thames KT1 220 CP97
Southall UB2 178 CA78
Boundary Ct, Epp. CM16 91 ER32
Welwyn Garden City AL7 off Boundary La 51 CZ13
Boundary Dr, Hert. SG14 54 DR07
Hutton CM13 131 GE45
Boundary La, E13 24 E3
SE17 43 K3
Welwyn Garden City AL7 51 CY12
Boundary Pk, Wey. KT13 217 BS103
Boundary Pas, E2 20 A4
Boundary Pl, Woob.Grn HP10 132 AD55
Boundary Rd, E13 24 D1
E17 145 DZ59
N9 104 DW44
N22 143 DP55
NW8 5 M9
SW19 202 DD93
Ashford TW15 196 BJ92
Barking IG11 167 EQ68
Carshalton SM5 241 DH107
Chalfont St. Peter SL9 112 AX52
High Wycombe HP10 110 AC54
Pinner HA5 138 BX58
Romford RM1 149 FG58
St. Albans AL1 65 CE18
Sidcup DA15 207 ES85
Taplow SL6 152 AE70
Upminster RM14 150 FN62
Wallington SM6 241 DH107
Wembley HA9 140 CL62
Woking GU21 249 BA116
Boundary Row, SE1 30 G4
Boundary St, E2 20 A3
Erith DA8 189 FF80
Boundary Way, Croy. CR0 243 EA106
Hemel Hempstead HP2 63 BQ18
Watford WD25 81 BV32
Woking GU21 249 BA115
Boundary Yd, Wok. GU21 off Boundary Rd 249 BA116
Boundfield Rd, SE6 206 EE91
⊖ Bounds Green 121 DK51
● Bounds Grn Ind Est, N11 121 DH51
Sch Bounds Grn Inf Sch, N11 off Bounds Grn Rd 121 DK52
Sch Bounds Grn Jun Sch, N11 off Bounds Grn Rd 121 DL52
Bounds Grn Rd, N11 121 DJ51
N22 121 DJ51
Bourbon La, W12 26 C3
Bourchier Cl, Sev. TN13 279 FH126
Bourchier St, W1 17 N10
Bourdon Pl, W1 17 K10
Bourdon Rd, SE20 224 DW96
Bourdon St, W1 17 K10
Bourke Cl, NW10 160 CS65
SW4 203 DL86
Bourke Hill, Chipstead CR5 256 DF118
Bourlet Cl, W1 17 L7
Bourn Av, N15 144 DR56
Barnet EN4 102 DD43
Uxbridge UB8 156 BN70
Bournbrook Rd, SE3 186 EK83
Bourne, The, N14 121 DK46
Bovingdon HP3 79 BA27
Ware SG12 55 DX05
Bourne Av, N14 121 DL47
Chertsey KT16 216 BG97
Hayes UB3 177 BQ76
Ruislip HA4 138 BW64
Windsor SL4 173 AQ84
Bournebridge Cl, Hutt. CM13 131 GE45
Bournebridge La, Stap.Abb. RM4 126 EZ45
● Bourne Business Pk, Add. KT15 234 BK105
Bourne Cl, Brox. EN10 71 DZ20
Chilworth GU4 281 BB140
Isleworth TW7 179 CE83
Thames Ditton KT7 219 CF103
Ware SG12 55 DX05
West Byfleet KT14 234 BH113
Bourne Ct, Ruis. HA4 137 BV64
Bourne Dr, Mitch. CR4 222 DD96
BOURNE END, Hem.H. HP1 61 BC22
Bourne End, Horn. RM11 150 FN59
Bourne End La, Hem.H. HP1 61 BC22
● Bourne End Mills, Hem.H. HP1 61 BB22
Bourne End Rd, Maid. SL6 132 AD62
Northwood HA6 115 BS49
Bourne Est, EC1 18 E6
Bournefield Rd, Whyt. CR3 off Godstone Rd 258 DT118
Bourne Gdns, E4 123 EB49
Bourne Gro, Ashtd. KT21 253 CK119
Bournehall Av, Bushey WD23 98 CA43
Bournehall La, Bushey WD23 98 CA44
★ Bourne Hall Mus, Epsom KT17 239 CT109
Sch Bournehall Prim Sch, Bushey WD23 off Bournehall Av 98 CB43
Bournehall Rd, Bushey WD23 98 CA44
Bourne Hill, N13 121 DL46
Bourne Hill Cl, N13 off Bourne Hill 121 DM47
● Bourne Ind Pk, Dart. DA1 209 FE85
Bourne La, Cat. CR3 258 DR121
Bourne Mead, Bex. DA5 209 FD85
Bournemead, Bushey WD23 98 CB44
Bournemead Av, Nthlt. UB5 157 BU68
Bournemead Cl, Nthlt. UB5 157 BU68
Bourne Meadow, Egh. TW20 215 BB98
Bournemead Way, Nthlt. UB5 157 BV68
Bourne Ms, Gdse. RH9 274 DW130
Bournemouth Cl, SE15 44 D9
Bournemouth Rd, SE15 44 D9
SW19 222 DA95
Bourne Pk Cl, Ken. CR8 258 DS115
Bourne Pl, W4 180 CR78
Chertsey KT16 216 BH102
Sch Bourne Prim Sch, Ruis. HA4 off Cedar Av 158 BW65
Bourne Rd, E7 146 EF62
N8 143 DL58
Berkhamsted HP4 60 AT18
Bexley DA5 209 FB86
Bromley BR2 226 EK98
Bushey WD23 98 CA43
Dartford DA1 209 FC86
Godalming GU7 280 AT143
Gravesend DA12 213 GM89
Slough SL1 173 AQ75
South Merstham RH1 273 DJ130
Virginia Water GU25 214 AX99
Bourneside, Vir.W. GU25 214 AU101
Bourneside Cres, N14 121 DK46
Bourneside Gdns, SE6 205 EC92
Bourneside Rd, Add. KT15 234 BK105
Bourne St, SW1 28 G9
Croydon CR0 off Waddon New Rd 223 DP103
Bourne Ter, W2 15 L6
Bourne Vale, Brom. BR2 226 EG101
Bournevale Rd, SW16 203 DL91
Bourne Vw, Grnf. UB6 159 CF65
Kenley CR8 258 DR115
Bourne Way, Add. KT15 234 BJ106
Bromley BR2 226 EF103
Epsom KT19 238 CQ105
Sutton SM1 239 CZ106
Swanley BR8 229 FC97
Woking GU22 248 AX122
Bournewood Rd, SE18 188 EU80
Orpington BR5 228 EV101
Bournville Rd, SE6 205 EA87
Bournwell Cl, Barn. EN4 102 DF41
Bourton Cl, Hayes UB3 157 BU74
Sch Bousfield Prim Sch, SW5 27 N10
Bousfield Rd, SE14 45 J8
Bousley Ri, Ott. KT16 233 BD108
Sch Boutcher C of E Prim Sch, SE1 32 A8
Boutflower Rd, SW11 182 DE84
Boutique Hall, SE13 off Lewisham Cen 185 EC84
Bouton Pl, N1 off Waterloo Ter 8 G7
Bouverie Gdns, Har. HA3 139 CK58
Purley CR8 241 DL114
Bouverie Ms, N16 144 DS61
Bouverie Pl, W2 16 B8
Bouverie Rd, N16 144 DS61
Chipstead CR5 256 DG118
Harrow HA1 138 CC59
Bouverie St, EC4 18 F9
Bouverie Way, Slou. SL3 174 AY78
Bouvier Rd, Enf. EN3 104 DW38
BOVENEY, Wind. SL4 173 AK79
Boveney Cl, Slou. SL1 off Amerden Way 173 AN75
Boveney New Rd, Eton Wick SL4 173 AL77
Boveney Rd, SE23 205 DX87
Dorney SL4 172 AJ77
Boveney Wd La, Burn. SL1 132 AJ62
Bovey Way, S.Ock. RM15 171 FV71
Bovill Rd, SE23 205 DX87
BOVINGDON, Hem.H. HP3 79 BA28
Bovingdon Av, Wem. HA9 160 CN65
Bovingdon Cl, N19 off Brookside Rd 143 DJ61
Bovingdon Cres, Wat. WD25 82 BX34
Bovingdon La, NW9 118 CS53
Sch Bovingdon Prim Sch, Bov. HP3 off High St 79 BB27
Bovingdon Rd, SW6 39 L7
Bovingdon Sq, Mitch. CR4 off Leicester Av 223 DL98
BOW, E3 21 M1
Bow Arrow La, Dart. DA1, DA2 210 FN86
Bowater Cl, NW9 140 CR57
SW2 203 DL86
Bowater Gdns, Sun. TW16 217 BV96
Bowater Pl, SE3 186 EH80
Bowater Ridge, St.Geo.H. KT13 235 BR110
Bowater Rd, SE18 36 F7
Wembley HA9 140 CP62
Bow Br Est, E3 22 C2
DLR Bow Church 22 B3
Bow Chyd, EC4 19 K9
Bow Common La, E3 21 N5
Bowden Cl, Felt. TW14 197 BS88
Bowden Dr, Horn. RM11 150 FL60
H Bowden Ho, Har.Hill HA1 139 CE61
Bowden St, SE11 42 F1
Bowditch, SE8 33 N10
Bowdon Rd, E17 145 EA59
Bowen Dr, SE21 204 DS90
Bowen Rd, Har. HA1 138 CC59
Bowen St, E14 22 D8
Bowens Wd, Croy. CR0 243 DZ109
Bowen Way, Couls. CR5 257 DK122
Bower Av, SE10 47 K5
Bower Cl, Nthlt. UB5 158 BW68
Romford RM5 127 FD52
Bower Ct, Epp. CM16 92 EU32
Woking GU22 off Princess Rd 249 BB116
Bowerdean St, SW6 39 L7
Bower Fm Rd, Hav.at.Bow. RM4 127 FC48
BOWER HILL, Epp. CM16 92 EU31
Bower Hill, Epp. CM16 92 EU32
Bower Hill Cl, S.Nutfld RH1 289 DL137
● Bower Hill Ind Est, Epp. CM16 92 EU32
Bower Hill La, S.Nutfld RH1 289 DK135
Bower La, Eyns. DA4 230 FL103
Bowerman Av, SE14 45 M3
Bowerman Rd, Grays RM16 193 GG77
Sch Bower Pk Sch, Rom. RM1 off Havering Rd 127 FE51
Bower Rd, Swan. BR8 209 FG94
Bowers Av, Nthflt DA11 213 GF91
Bowers Cl, Guil. GU4 off Cotts Wd Dr 265 BA129
Bowers Fm Dr, Guil. GU4 265 BA130
Bowers La, Guil. GU4 265 BA129
Bowers Rd, Shore. TN14 247 FF111
Bower St, E1 21 J9
Bowers Wk, E6 25 H8
Bower Ter, Epp. CM16 92 EU32
Bower Vale, Epp. CM16 92 EU32
Bower Way, Slou. SL1 153 AM73
Bowery Ct, Dag. RM10 off St. Mark's Pl 169 FB65
Bowes Cl, Sid. DA15 208 EV86
Bowes-Lyon Cl, Wind. SL4 off Ward Royal 173 AQ81
Bowes-Lyon Ms, St.Alb. AL3 65 CD20
BOWES PARK, N22 121 DL51
⇌ Bowes Park 121 DL51
Sch Bowes Prim Sch, N11 off Bowes Rd 121 DK50
Bowes Rd, N11 121 DH50
N13 121 DL50
W3 160 CS73
Dagenham RM8 148 EW63
Staines TW18 195 BE92
Walton-on-Thames KT12 217 BV103
Bowfell Rd, W6 38 B3
Bowford Av, Bexh. DA7 188 EY81
Bowgate, St.Alb. AL1 65 CE19
Bowhay, Hutt. CM13 131 GA47
Bowhill Cl, SW9 42 F4
Bowie Cl, SW4 203 DK87
Bowland Rd, SW4 183 DK84
Woodford Green IG8 124 EJ51
Bowland Yd, SW1 28 F5
Bow La, EC4 19 K9
N12 120 DC53
Morden SM4 221 CY100
Bowl Ct, EC2 19 P5
Bowlers Grn, Magd.Lav. CM5 75 FF21
Bowlers Orchard, Ch.St.G. HP8 112 AU48
Bowles Grn, Enf. EN1 104 DV36
Bowley Cl, SE19 204 DT93
Bowley La, SE19 204 DT92
Bowling Cl, Uxb. UB10 off Birch Cres 156 BM67
Bowling Ct, Wat. WD18 97 BU42
Bowling Grn Cl, SW15 201 CV87
Bowling Grn La, EC1 18 F4
Bowling Grn Pl, SE1 31 L4
Bowling Grn Rd, Chobham GU24 232 AS109
Bowling Grn Row, SE18 37 J7
Bowling Grn St, SE11 42 E2
Bowling Grn Wk, N1 19 N2
Bowling Rd, Ware SG12 55 DY06
Bowls, The, Chig. IG7 125 ES49
Bowls Cl, Stan. HA7 117 CH50
Bowman Av, E16 23 M10
Bowman Ms, SW18 201 CZ88
Bowmans Cl, W13 159 CH74
Burnham SL1 152 AH67
Potters Bar EN6 86 DD32
Bowmans Ct, Hem.H. HP2 62 BK18
Bowmans Grn, Wat. WD25 98 BX36
Sch Bowmansgreen Prim Sch, Lon.Col. AL2 off Telford Rd 83 CJ27
Bowmans Lea, SE23 204 DW87
Bowmans Meadow, Wall. SM6 223 DH104
Bowmans Ms, E1 20 C10
Bowman's Ms, N7 off Seven Sisters Rd 143 DL62
Bowmans Pl, N7 off Holloway Rd 143 DL62
Bowmans Rd, Dart. DA1 209 FF87
● Bowman Trd Est, NW9 140 CN56
Bowmead, SE9 207 EM89
Bowmont Cl, Hutt. CM13 131 GB44
Bowmore Wk, NW1 7 P6
Bown Cl, Til. RM18 193 GH82
Bowness Cl, E8 10 A5
Bowness Cres, SW15 200 CS92
Bowness Dr, Houns. TW4 178 BY84
Bowness Rd, SE6 205 EB87
Bexleyheath DA7 189 FB82
Bowness Way, Horn. RM12 149 FG64
Bowood Rd, SW11 182 DG84
Enfield EN3 105 DX40
Bowring Grn, Wat. WD19 116 BW50
⊖ Bow Road 22 A2
Bow Rd, E3 21 P3
Bowrons Av, Wem. HA0 159 CK66
Bowry Dr, Wrays. TW19 195 AZ86
Sch Bow Sch, E3 22 B1
Bowsher Ct, Ware SG12 55 DY06
Bowsley Ct, Felt. TW13 off Highfield Rd 197 BU89
Bowsprit, The, Cob. KT11 252 BW115
Bowsprit Pt, E14 34 A6
Bow St, E15 13 J3
WC2 18 B9
Bowstridge La, Ch.St.G. HP8 112 AW51
● Bow Triangle Business Cen, E3 22 B3
Bowyer Cl, E6 25 K6
Bowyer Ct, E4 off The Ridgeway 123 EC46
Bowyer Cres, Denh. UB9 135 BF58
Bowyer Dr, Slou. SL1 153 AL74
Bowyer Pl, SE5 43 K4
Bowyers, Hem.H. HP2 62 BK18
Bowyers Cl, Ashtd. KT21 254 CM118
Bowyer St, SE5 43 J4
Boxall Rd, SE21 204 DS86
Box Elder Cl, Edg. HA8 118 CQ50
Boxfield, Welw.G.C. AL7 52 DB12
Boxford Cl, S.Croy. CR2 243 DX112
Boxgrove Av, Guil. GU1 265 BA132
Boxgrove La, Guil. GU1 265 BA133
Sch Boxgrove Prim Sch, SE2 off Boxgrove Rd 188 EW76
Guildford GU1 off Boxgrove La 265 BB133
Boxgrove Rd, SE2 188 EW76
Guildford GU1 265 BA133
BOX HILL, Tad. KT20 270 CP131
Boxhill, Hem.H. HP2 62 BK18
⇌ Boxhill & Westhumble 269 CH131
Boxhill Rd, Box H. KT20 270 CP131
Dorking RH4 270 CL133
Sch Box Hill Sch, Mick. RH5 off Old London Rd 269 CH127
Boxhill Way, Strood Grn RH3 286 CP138
Box La, Bark. IG11 168 EV68
Hemel Hempstead HP3 61 BE24
Hoddesdon EN11 71 DX16
Boxley Rd, Mord. SM4 222 DC98
Boxley St, E16 36 A3
BOXMOOR, Hem.H. HP1 62 BH22
Sch Boxmoor Ho Sch, Hem.H. HP3 off Box La 61 BF23
Sch Boxmoor Prim Sch, Hem.H. HP1 off Cowper Rd 62 BG21
Boxmoor Rd, Har. HA3 139 CH56
Romford RM5 127 FC50
Boxoll Rd, Dag. RM9 148 EZ63
Box Ridge Av, Pur. CR8 241 DM112
Boxted Cl, Buck.H. IG9 124 EL46
Boxted Rd, Hem.H. HP1 61 BF18
Box Tree Cl, Chesh. HP5 76 AR33
Boxtree La, Har. HA3 116 CC53
Boxtree Rd, Har. HA3 117 CD52
Boxtree Wk, Orp. BR5 228 EX102
Box Tree Wk, Red. RH1 288 DC136
Box Wk, Lthd. KT24 267 BS132
Boxwell Rd, Berk. HP4 60 AV19
Boxwood Cl, West Dr. UB7 off Hawthorne Cres 176 BM75
Boxwood Way, Warl. CR6 259 DX117
Boxworth Cl, N12 120 DD50
Boxworth Gro, N1 8 D8
Boyard Rd, SE18 37 N10
Boyce Cl, Borwd. WD6 100 CL39
Boyce St, SE1 30 D3
Boyce Way, E13 23 N4
Boycroft Av, NW9 140 CQ58
Boyd Av, Sthl. UB1 158 BZ74
Boyd Cl, Kings.T. KT2 200 CN94
Boydell Ct, NW8 6 A7
Boyd Rd, SW19 202 DD93
Boyd St, E1 20 C9
Boyes Cres, Lon.Col. AL2 83 CH26
Boyfield St, SE1 31 H5
Boyland Rd, Brom. BR1 206 EF92
Boyle Av, Stan. HA7 117 CG51
Boyle Cl, Uxb. UB10 156 BM68
Boyle Fm Island, T.Ditt. KT7 219 CG100
Boyle Fm Rd, T.Ditt. KT7 219 CG100
Boyle St, W1 17 L10
Boyne Av, NW4 141 CX56
Boyne Rd, SE13 46 F10
Dagenham RM10 148 FA62
Boyne Ter Ms, W11 26 G2
Boyseland Ct, Edg. HA8 118 CQ47
Boyson Rd, SE17 43 L2
Boyton Cl, E1 21 H4
N8 143 DL55
Boyton Rd, N8 143 DL55
Brabant Ct, EC3 19 N10
Brabant Rd, N22 121 DM54
Brabazon Av, Wall. SM6 241 DL108
Brabazon Rd, Houns. TW5 178 BW80
Northolt UB5 158 CA68
Brabazon St, E14 22 C8
Brabiner Gdns, Croy. CR0 243 ED110
Brabourne Cl, SE19 204 DS92
Brabourne Cres, Bexh. DA7 188 EZ79
Brabourne Hts, NW7 118 CS48
Brabourne Ri, Beck. BR3 225 EC99
Brabourn Gro, SE15 44 G9
Brace Cl, Chsht EN7 87 DP25
Bracer Ho, N1 off Nuttall St 9 P10
Bracewell Av, Grnf. UB6 139 CF64
Bracewell Rd, W10 14 A7
Bracewood Gdns, Croy. CR0 224 DT104
Bracey Ms, N4 off Bracey St 143 DL61
Bracey St, N4 143 DL61
Bracken, The, E4 off Hortus Rd 123 EC47
Bracken Av, SW12 202 DG86
Croydon CR0 225 EB104
Brackenbridge Dr, Ruis. HA4 138 BX62
Brackenbury Gdns, W6 181 CV76
Sch Brackenbury Prim Sch, W6 off Dalling Rd 181 CV76
Brackenbury Rd, N2 142 DC55
W6 181 CV76
Bracken Cl, E6 25 J7
Bookham KT23 252 BZ124
Borehamwood WD6 100 CP39
Farnham Common SL2 133 AR63
Sunbury-on-Thames TW16 197 BT93
Twickenham TW2 198 CA87
Woking GU22 249 AZ118
Bracken Ct, Hat. AL10 51 CT14
Brackendale, N21 121 DM47
Potters Bar EN6 86 DA33
Brackendale Cl, Houns. TW3 178 CB81
Brackendale Gdns, Upmin. RM14 150 FQ63
Brackendene, Brick.Wd AL2 82 BZ30
Dartford DA2 209 FE91
Brackendene Cl, Wok. GU21 249 BA115
Bracken Dr, Chig. IG7 125 EP51
Bracken End, Islw. TW7 199 CD85
Brackenfield Cl, E5 144 DV62
Brackenforde, Slou. SL3 174 AW75
Bracken Gdns, SW13 181 CU82
Brackenhill, Berk. HP4 60 AY18
Cobham KT11 236 CA111
Bracken Hill Cl, Brom. BR1 226 EF95
Bracken Hill La, Brom. BR1 226 EF95
● Bracken Ind Est, Ilf. IG6 125 ET53
Bracken Ms, E4 off Hortus Rd 123 EC46
Romford RM7 148 FA58
Bracken Path, Epsom KT18 238 CP113
Brackens, The, Enf. EN1 122 DS45
Hemel Hempstead HP2 off Heather Way 62 BK19
Orpington BR6 246 EU106
Brackens Dr, Warley CM14 130 FW50
Brackenside, Horl. RH6 off Stockfield 291 DH147
Bracken Way, Chobham GU24 232 AT110
Guildford GU3 264 AS132
Brackenwood, Sun. TW16 217 BU95
Brackley, Wey. KT13 235 BR106
Brackley Av, SE15 184 DV83
Brackley Cl, Wall. SM6 241 DL108
Brackley Rd, W4 180 CS78
Beckenham BR3 205 DZ94
Brackley Sq, Wdf.Grn. IG8 124 EK52
Brackley St, EC1 19 J6
Brackley Ter, W4 180 CS78
Bracklyn Cl, N1 9 L10
Bracklyn Ct, N1 9 L10
Bracklyn St, N1 9 L10
Bracknell Cl, N22 121 DN53
Bracknell Gdns, NW3 5 L1
Bracknell Gate, NW3 5 L2
Bracknell Pl, Hem.H. HP2 62 BM16
Bracknell Way, NW3 5 L1
Bracondale, Esher KT10 236 CC107
Bracondale Rd, SE2 188 EU77
H Bracton Cen, The, Dart. DA2 209 FF89
Bracton La, Dart. DA2 209 FF89
Bradbery, Map.Cr. WD3 113 BD50
Bradbourne Pk Rd, Sev. TN13 278 FG123
Bradbourne Rd, Bex. DA5 208 FA87
Grays RM17 192 GB79
Sevenoaks TN13 279 FH122
Sch Bradbourne Sch, The, Sev. TN13 off Bradbourne Vale Rd 278 FG121
Bradbourne St, SW6 39 K8
Bradbourne Vale Rd, Sev. TN13 278 FF122
Bradbury Cl, Borwd. WD6 100 CP39
Southall UB2 178 BZ77
Bradbury Ct, SW20 off Clifton Pk Av 221 CW96
Bradbury Gdns, Fulmer SL3 134 AX63
Bradbury Ms, N16 9 P3
Bradbury St, N16 9 P3
Bradd Cl, S.Ock. RM15 171 FW69
Braddock Cl, Coll.Row RM5 127 FC51
Isleworth TW7 179 CF83
Braddon Rd, Rich. TW9 180 CM83
Braddyll St, SE10 47 J1
Bradenham Av, Well. DA16 188 EU84
Bradenham Cl, SE17 43 L2
Bradenham Rd, Har. HA3 139 CH56
Hayes UB4 157 BS69
Bradenhurst Cl, Cat. CR3 274 DT126
Braden St, W9 15 L5
Bradfield Cl, Guil. GU4 265 BA131
Woking GU22 248 AY118
Bradfield Dr, Bark. IG11 148 EU64
Bradfield Ho, SW8 off Wandsworth Rd 41 N8
Bradfield Rd, E16 35 P4
Ruislip HA4 138 BY64
Bradford Cl, N17 122 DT51
SE26 off Coombe Rd 204 DV91
Bromley BR2 227 EM102
Bradford Dr, Epsom KT19 239 CT107
Bradford Rd, W3 off Warple Way 180 CS75
Heronsgate WD3 113 BC45
Ilford IG1 147 ER60
Slough SL1 153 AN72
Bradgate, Cuffley EN6 87 DK27
Bradgate Cl, Cuffley EN6 87 DK28
Bradgate Rd, SE6 205 EA86
Brading Cres, E11 146 EH61
Brading Rd, SW2 203 DM87
Croydon CR0 223 DM100
Brading Ter, W12 181 CV76
Bradiston Rd, W9 15 H2
Bradleigh Av, Grays RM17 192 GC77
Bradley Cl, N1 8 F10
N7 8 B5
Belmont SM2 off Station Rd 240 DA110
Bradley Gdns, W13 159 CH72
Bradley Ho, E3 off Bromley High St 22 D1
Bradley La, Dor. RH5 269 CG132
Bradley Lynch Ct, E2 off Morpeth St 21 J2
Bradley Ms, SW17 202 DF88
Bradley Rd, N22 121 DM54
SE19 204 DQ93
Enfield EN3 105 DY38
Slough SL1 153 AR73
Waltham Abbey EN9 105 EC36
Bradley Stone Rd, E6 25 J7
Bradman Row, Edg. HA8 off Pavilion Way 118 CQ52
Bradmead, SW8 41 K5
Bradmore Ct, Enf. EN3 off Enstone Rd 105 DY41
Bradmore Grn, Brook.Pk AL9 85 CY26
Coulsdon CR5 off Coulsdon Rd 257 DM118
Bradmore La, Brook.Pk AL9 85 CW27
Bradmore Pk Rd, W6 181 CV76
Bradmore Way, Brook.Pk AL9 85 CY26
Coulsdon CR5 257 DL117
Bradshaw Cl, SW19 202 DA93
Windsor SL4 173 AL81
Bradshaw Dr, NW7 119 CX52
Bradshawe Waye, Uxb. UB8 156 BL71

Bradshaw Rd, Wat. WD24 . . . . . 98 BW39
Bradshaws, Hat. AL10 . . . . 67 CT22
Bradshaws Cl, SE25 . . . . 224 DU97
Bradstock Rd, E9 . . . . 11 K5
Epsom KT17 . . . . 239 CU106
Bradstone Brook, Shalf. GU4 . 281 BA141
Brad St, SE1 . . . . 30 F3
Bradwell Av, Dag. RM10 . . . . . 148 FA61
Bradwell Cl, E18 . . . . 146 EF56
Hornchurch RM12 . . . . 169 FH65
Bradwell Ct, Whyt. CR3
off Godstone Rd 258 DU119
Bradwell Grn, Hutt. CM13 . . . . 131 GC44
Bradwell Ms, N18
off Lyndhurst Rd 122 DU49
Bradwell Rd, Buck.H. IG9 . . . . 124 EL46
Bradwell St, E1 . . . . 21 K3
Brady Av, Loug. IG10 . . . . 107 EQ40
Brady Dr, Brom. BR1 . . . . 227 EN97
Bradymead, E6 . . . . 25 M8
Sch Brady Prim Sch, Rain. RM13
off Wennington Rd 170 FJ71
Brady St, E1 . . . . 20 E5
Braemar Av, N22 . . . . 121 DL53
NW10 . . . . 140 CR62
SW19 . . . . 202 DA89
Bexleyheath DA7 . . . . 189 FC84
South Croydon CR2 . . . . . . 242 DQ109
Thornton Heath CR7 . . . . . . 223 DN97
Wembley HA0 . . . . 159 CK66
Braemar Cl, SE16 . . . . 32 E10
Braemar Gdns, NW9 . . . . 118 CR53
Hornchurch RM11 . . . . 150 FN58
Sidcup DA15 . . . . 207 ER90
Slough SL1 . . . . 173 AN75
West Wickham BR4 . . . . 225 EC102
Braemar Rd, E13 . . . . 23 M5
N15 . . . . 144 DS57
Brentford TW8 . . . . 179 CK79
Worcester Park KT4 . . . . . . 221 CV104
Braemer Ho, W9 . . . . 15 N3
Braeside, Beck. BR3 . . . . 205 EA92
New Haw KT15 . . . . 234 BH111
Braeside Av, SW19 . . . . 221 CY95
Sevenoaks TN13 . . . . 278 FF124
Braeside Cl, Pnr. HA5
off The Avenue 116 CA52
Sevenoaks TN13 . . . . 278 FF123
Braeside Cres, Bexh. DA7 . . . . 189 FC84
Braeside Rd, SW16 . . . . 203 DJ94
Sch Braeside Sch, Jun Sch, Buck.H.
IG9 off Palmerston Rd 124 EJ47
Sen Sch, Buck.H. IG9
off High Rd 124 EH46
Braes Mead, S.Nutfld RH1 . . . . 289 DL135
Braes St, N1 . . . . 9 H6
Braesyde Cl, Belv. DA17 . . . . . 188 EZ77
Brafferton Rd, Croy. CR0 . . . . 242 DQ105
Braganza St, SE17 . . . . 30 G10
Bragg Cl, Dag. RM8
off Porters Av 168 EV65
Bragmans La, Flaun. HP3 . . . . . 79 BB34
Sarratt WD3 . . . . 79 BE33
Braham St, E1 . . . . 20 B9
Braid, The, Chesh. HP5 . . . . . . 76 AS30
Braid Av, W3 . . . . 160 CS72
Braid Cl, Felt. TW13 . . . . 198 BZ89
Braid Ct, W4 off Lawford Rd . . 180 CQ80
Braidwood Pas, EC1
off Cloth St 19 J6
Braidwood Rd, SE6 . . . . 205 ED88
Braidwood St, SE1 . . . . 31 N3
Brailsford Cl, Mitch. CR4 . . . . 202 DE94
Brailsford Rd, SW2 . . . . 203 DN85
Brain Cl, Hat. AL10 . . . . 67 CV18
Sch Braintcroft Prim Sch, NW2
off Warren Rd 141 CT61
Brainton Av, Felt. TW14 . . . . . . 197 BV87
Braintree Av, Ilf. IG4 . . . . 146 EL56
● Braintree Ind Est, Ruis.
HA4 . . . . 137 BV63
Braintree Rd, Dag. RM10 . . . . . 148 FA62
Ruislip HA4 . . . . 137 BV63
Braintree St, E2 . . . . 20 G4
Braithwaite Av, Rom. RM7 . . . . 148 FA59
Braithwaite Gdns, Stan. HA7 . . 117 CJ53
Braithwaite Ho, EC1 . . . . 19 K4
Braithwaite Rd, Enf. EN3 . . . . . 105 DZ41
Braithwaite Twr, W2 . . . . 16 A6
Brakefield Rd, Sthflt DA13 . . . 212 GB93
Brakey Hill, Bletch. RH1 . . . . . 274 DS134
Brakynbery, Nthch HP4 . . . . . . 60 AS16
Bramah Grn, SW9 . . . . 42 F6
★ Bramah Mus, SE1 . . . . 31 K3
Bramalea Cl, N6 . . . . 142 DG58
Bramall Cl, E15 . . . . 13 L2
Bramall Ct, N7 . . . . 8 C4
Bramber Ct, Brent. TW8
off Sterling Pl 180 CL77
Slough SL1 . . . . 153 AN74
Bramber Ho, Kings.T. KT2
off Kingsgate Rd 220 CL95
Bramber Rd, N12 . . . . 120 DE50
W14 . . . . 38 G2
Bramber Way, Warl. CR6 . . . . . 259 DZ116
Brambleacres Cl, Sutt. SM2 . . 240 DA108
Bramble Av, Bean DA2 . . . . . . 211 FW90
Bramble Banks, Cars. SM5 . . . 240 DG109
Bramblebury Rd, SE18 . . . . . . 187 EQ78
Bramble Cl, N15 . . . . 144 DU56
Beckenham BR3 . . . . 225 EC99
Chalfont St. Peter SL9
off Garners Rd 112 AY51
Chigwell IG7 . . . . 125 EQ46
Croydon CR0 . . . . 243 EA105
Guildford GU3 . . . . 264 AS132
Oxted RH8 . . . . 276 EH133
Redhill RH1 . . . . 288 DG136
Shepperton TW17
off Halliford Cl 217 BR97
Stanmore HA7 . . . . 117 CK52
Uxbridge UB8 . . . . 156 BM71
Watford WD25 . . . . 81 BU34
Bramble Cft, Erith DA8 . . . . . . 189 FC77
Brambledene Cl, Wok. GU21 . . 248 AW118
Brambledown, Stai. TW18 . . . . 216 BG95
Brambledown Cl, W.Wick. BR4 . 226 EE99
Brambledown Rd, Cars. SM5 . . 240 DG108
South Croydon CR2 . . . . 242 DS108
Wallington SM6 . . . . 241 DH108
Bramblefield Cl, Long. DA3 . . . 231 FX97
Bramble Gdns, W12 . . . . 161 CT73
Bramblehall La, Tad. KT20 . . . . 270 CM132
Bramble La, Amer. HP7 . . . . 77 AS41
Hampton TW12 . . . . 198 BZ93
Hoddesdon EN11 . . . . 71 DY17
Sevenoaks TN13 . . . . 279 FH128
Upminster RM14 . . . . 170 FQ67
Bramble Mead, Ch.St.G. HP8 . . 112 AU48
Bramble Ri, Cob. KT11 . . . . 252 BW115
Harlow CM20 . . . . 57 EQ14
Bramble Rd, Hat. AL10 . . . . 66 CR18
Brambles, The, Chsht EN8 . . . . . 89 DX31
Chigwell IG7 off Clayside . . . 125 EQ51
St. Albans AL1 . . . . 65 CD22
West Drayton UB7 . . . . 176 BL77
Brambles Cl, Cat. CR3 . . . . 258 DS122
Isleworth TW7 . . . . 179 CG80
Brambles Fm Dr, Uxb. UB10 . . 156 BN69
Sch Brambletye Jun Sch, Red. RH1
off Brambletye Pk Rd 288 DG136
Brambletye Pk Rd, Red. RH1 . . 288 DG135
Bramble Wk, Epsom KT18 . . . . 238 CP114
Bramble Way, Ripley GU23 . . . 249 BF124
Bramblewood, Merst. RH1 . . . . 273 DH129
Bramblewood Cl, Cars. SM5 . . . 222 DE102
Brambling Cl, Bushey WD23 . . . 98 BY42
Brambling Ri, Hem.H. HP2 . . . . . 62 BL17
Bramblings, The, E4 . . . . 123 ED49
Bramcote Av, Mitch. CR4 . . . . . 222 DF98
Bramcote Ct, Mitch. CR4
off Bramcote Av 222 DF98
Bramcote Gro, SE16 . . . . 32 G10
Bramcote Rd, SW15 . . . . 181 CV84
Bramdean Cres, SE12 . . . . 206 EG88
Bramdean Gdns, SE12 . . . . 206 EG88
Bramerton Rd, Beck. BR3 . . . . 225 DZ97
Bramerton St, SW3 . . . . 40 C2
Bramfield, Wat. WD25
off Garston La 82 BY34
Bramfield Ct, N4
off Queens Dr 144 DQ61
Bramfield La, Waterf. SG14 . . . . 53 DL05
Bramfield Rd, SW11 . . . . 202 DE86
Hertford SG14 . . . . 53 DL06
Bramford Ct, N14 . . . . 121 DK47
Bramford Rd, SW18 . . . . 182 DC84
Bramham Gdns, SW5 . . . . 27 L10
Chessington KT9 . . . . 237 CK105
Bramhope La, SE7 . . . . 186 EH79
Bramlands Cl, SW11 . . . . 182 DE83
Bramleas, Wat. WD18 . . . . 97 BT42
Bramley Av, Couls. CR5 . . . . . . 257 DJ115
● Bramley Business Cen,
Bramley GU5
off Station Rd 281 AZ144
Bramley Cl, E17 . . . . 123 DY54
N14 . . . . 103 DH43
Chertsey KT16 . . . . 216 BH102
Eastcote HA5 . . . . 137 BT55
Hayes UB3 . . . . 157 BU73
Istead Rise DA13 . . . . 213 GF94
Orpington BR6 . . . . 227 EP102
Redhill RH1
off Abinger Dr 288 DE136
South Croydon CR2 . . . . 241 DP106
Staines TW18 . . . . 196 BJ93
Swanley BR8 . . . . 229 FE98
Twickenham TW2 . . . . 198 CC86
Woodford Green IG8
off Orsett Ter 124 EJ52
Bramley Ct, Wat. WD25
off Orchard Av 81 BV31
Welling DA16 . . . . 188 EV81
Bramley Cres, SW8 . . . . 41 P4
Ilford IG2 . . . . 147 EN58
Bramley Gdns, Wat. WD19 . . . . 116 BW50
Bramley Gro, Ashtd. KT21 . . . . 254 CL119
Bramley Hill, S.Croy. CR2 . . . . 241 DP106
Bramley Ho, SW15
off Tunworth Cres 201 CT86
W10 . . . . 14 D9
Bramley Ho Ct, Enf. EN2 . . . . . 104 DR37
Bramley Hyrst, S.Croy. CR2 . . . 242 DQ105
Bramley Par, N14 . . . . 103 DJ42
Bramley Pl, Dart. DA1 . . . . 189 FG84
Bramley Rd, N14 . . . . 103 DH43
W5 . . . . 179 CJ76
W10 . . . . 14 D10
Cheam SM2 . . . . 239 CX109
Sutton SM1 . . . . 240 DD106
Sch Bramley Sch, Walt.Hill
KT20 off Chequers La 271 CU125
Bramley Shaw, Wal.Abb. EN9 . . . 90 EF33
Bramley Wk, Horl. RH6 . . . . 291 DJ148
Bramley Way, Ashtd. KT21 . . . . 254 CM117
Hounslow TW4 . . . . 198 BZ85
St. Albans AL4 . . . . 65 CJ21
West Wickham BR4 . . . . 225 EB103
Brammas Cl, Slou. SL1 . . . . 173 AQ76
Brampton Cl, E5 . . . . 144 DV61
Cheshunt EN7 . . . . 88 DU28
Brampton Gdns, N15 . . . . 144 DQ57
Hersham KT12 . . . . 236 BW106
Brampton Gro, NW4 . . . . 141 CV56
Harrow HA3 . . . . 139 CG56
Wembley HA9 . . . . 140 CN60
Brampton La, NW4 . . . . 141 CW56
Sch Brampton Manor Sch, E6 . . 24 E4
Brampton Pk Rd, N22 . . . . 143 DN55
Sch Brampton Prim Sch, E6 . . . 24 G3
Bexleyheath DA7
off Brampton Rd 188 EX82
Brampton Rd, E6 . . . . 24 F4
N15 . . . . 144 DQ57
NW9 . . . . 140 CN56
SE2 . . . . 188 EW79
Bexleyheath DA7 . . . . 188 EX80
Croydon CR0 . . . . 224 DT101
Hillingdon UB10 . . . . 157 BP68
St. Albans AL1 . . . . 65 CG19
Watford WD19 . . . . 115 BU48
Brampton Ter, Borwd. WD6 . . . 100 CN38
Bramshaw Gdns, Wat. WD19 . . 116 BX50
Bramshaw Ri, N.Mal. KT3 . . . . 220 CS100
Bramshaw Rd, E9 . . . . 11 K5
Bramshill Cl, Chig. IG7
off Tine Rd 125 ES50
Bramshill Gdns, NW5 . . . . 143 DH62
Bramshill Rd, NW10 . . . . 161 CT68
Bramshot Av, SE7 . . . . 47 P1
Bramshot Way, Wat. WD19 . . . . 115 BU47
Bramston Cl, Ilf. IG6 . . . . 125 ET51
Bramston Rd, NW10 . . . . 161 CU68
SW17 . . . . 202 DC90
Bramwell Cl, Sun. TW16 . . . . . . 218 BX96
Bramwell Ho, SE1
off Harper Rd 31 K7
SW1 . . . . 41 L1
Bramwell Ms, N1 . . . . 8 D8
Brancaster Dr, NW7 . . . . 119 CT52
Brancaster La, Pur. CR8 . . . . . 242 DQ112
Brancaster Pl, Loug. IG10 . . . . 107 EM41
Brancaster Rd, E12 . . . . 147 EM63
SW16 . . . . 203 DL90
Ilford IG2 . . . . 147 ER58
Brancepeth Gdns, Buck.H. IG9 . 124 EG47
Branch Cl, Hat. AL10 . . . . 67 CW16
Branch Hill, NW3 . . . . 142 DC62
Branch Pl, N1 . . . . 9 M8
Branch Rd, E14 . . . . 21 L10
Ilford IG6 . . . . 126 EV50
Park Street AL2 . . . . 83 CD27
St. Albans AL3 . . . . 64 CB19
Branch St, SE15 . . . . 43 P5
Brancker Rd, Har. HA3 . . . . 139 CK55
Brancroft Way, Enf. EN3 . . . . . . 105 DY39
Brand Cl, N4 . . . . 143 DP60
Brandesbury Sq, Wdf.Grn. IG8 . 125 EN51
Sch Brandlehow Prim Sch, SW15
off Brandlehow Rd 181 CZ84
Brandlehow Rd, SW15 . . . . 181 CZ84
Brandon Cl, Chaff.Hun. RM16 . . 192 FZ75
Cheshunt EN7 . . . . 88 DS26
Brandon Est, SE17 . . . . 43 H3
Brandon Gros Av, S.Ock. RM15 . 171 FW69
Brandon Ms, EC2
off The Barbican 19 L7
Brandon Rd, E17 . . . . 145 EC55
N7 . . . . 8 A6
Dartford DA1 . . . . 210 FN87
Southall UB2 . . . . 178 BZ78
Sutton SM1 . . . . 240 DB105
Brandon St, SE17 . . . . 31 J9
Gravesend DA11 . . . . 213 GH87
Brandram Ms, SE13 . . . . 186 EE83
Brandram Rd, SE13 . . . . 186 EE83
Brandreth Rd, E6 . . . . 25 K8
SW17 . . . . 203 DH89
Brandries, The, Wall. SM6 . . . . 223 DK104
BRANDS HILL, Slou. SL3 . . . . . 175 BB79
Brandsland, Reig. RH2 . . . . 288 DB138
Brands Rd, Slou. SL3 . . . . 175 BB79
Brand St, SE10 . . . . 46 E5
Brandville Gdns, Ilf. IG6 . . . . . 147 EP56
Brandville Rd, West Dr. UB7 . . . 176 BL75
Brandy Way, Sutt. SM2 . . . . . . 240 DA108
Sch Branfil Inf Sch, Upmin.
RM14 off Cedar Av 150 FN63
Sch Branfil Jun Sch, Upmin.
RM14 off Cedar Av 150 FN63
Branfill Rd, Upmin. RM14 . . . . . 150 FP61
Brangbourne Rd, Brom. BR1 . . . 205 EC92
Brangton Rd, SE11 . . . . 42 D1
Brangwyn Cres, SW19 . . . . 222 DD95
Branksea St, SW6 . . . . 38 E5
Branksome Av, N18 . . . . 122 DT51
Branksome Cl, Hem.H. HP2 . . . . 62 BN19
Teddington TW11 . . . . 199 CD91
Walton-on-Thames KT12 . . . 218 BX103
Branksome Rd, SW2 . . . . 203 DL85
SW19 . . . . 222 DA95
Branksome Way, Har. HA3 . . . . 140 CL58
New Malden KT3 . . . . 220 CQ95
Bransby Rd, Chess. KT9 . . . . . 238 CL107
Branscombe Gdns, N21 . . . . . . 121 DN45
Branscombe St, SE13 . . . . 46 D10
Bransdale Cl, NW6 . . . . 5 K8
Bransell Cl, Swan. BR8 . . . . . . 229 FC100
Bransgrove Rd, Edg. HA8 . . . . . 118 CM53
Branston Cres, Petts Wd BR5 . . 227 ER102
Branstone Rd, Rich. TW9 . . . . . 180 CM81
Branton Rd, Green. DA9 . . . . . . 211 FT86
Brants Wk, W7 . . . . 159 CE70
Brantwood Av, Erith DA8 . . . . . 189 FC80
Isleworth TW7 . . . . 179 CG84
Brantwood Cl, E17 . . . . 145 EB55
West Byfleet KT14
off Brantwood Gdns 234 BG113
Brantwood Ct, W.Byf. KT14
off Brantwood Dr 233 BF113
Brantwood Dr, W.Byf. KT14 . . . 233 BF113
Brantwood Gdns, Enf. EN2 . . . . 103 DL42
Ilford IG4 . . . . 146 EL56
West Byfleet KT14 . . . . 233 BF113
Brantwood Rd, N17 . . . . 122 DT51
SE24 . . . . 204 DQ85
Bexleyheath DA7 . . . . 189 FB82
South Croydon CR2 . . . . 242 DQ109
Brantwood Way, Orp. BR5 . . . . 228 EW97
Brasenose Dr, SW13 . . . . 38 A3
Brasher Cl, Grnf. UB6 . . . . 139 CD64
Brassett Pt, E15 . . . . 13 K9
Brassey Cl, Felt. TW14 . . . . 197 BU88
Oxted RH8 . . . . 276 EG129
Brassey Hill, Oxt. RH8 . . . . 276 EG130
Brassey Rd, NW6 . . . . 5 H4
Oxted RH8 . . . . 276 EF130
Brassey Sq, SW11 . . . . 40 G10
Brassie Av, W3 . . . . 160 CS72
Brass Tally All, SE16 . . . . 33 K5
BRASTED, West. TN16 . . . . 262 EW124
Brasted Cl, SE26 . . . . 204 DW91
Bexleyheath DA6 . . . . 208 EX85
Orpington BR6 . . . . 227 ET103
Sutton SM2 . . . . 240 DA110
Brasted Hill, Knock. TN14 . . . . . 262 EU120
Brasted Hill Rd, Brasted TN16 . 262 EV121
Brasted La, Knock. TN14 . . . . . 262 EU119
Brasted Rd, Erith DA8 . . . . 189 FE80
Westerham TN16 . . . . 277 ES126
Brathway Rd, SW18 . . . . 202 DA87
Bratley St, E1 . . . . 20 C5
Brattle Wd, Sev. TN13 . . . . 279 FH129
Braund Av, Grnf. UB6 . . . . 158 CB70
Braundton Av, Sid. DA15 . . . . . 207 ET88
Braunston Dr, Hayes UB4 . . . . . 158 BY70
Bravington Cl, Shep. TW17 . . . . 216 BM99
Bravington Pl, W9 . . . . 14 G4
Bravington Rd, W9 . . . . 14 G4
Bravingtons Wk, N1 . . . . 18 B1
Brawlings La, Chal.St.P. SL9 . . . 113 BA49
Brawne Ho, SE17 . . . . 43 H3
Braxfield Rd, SE4 . . . . 185 DY84
Braxted Pk, SW16 . . . . 203 DM93
BRAY, Maid. SL6 . . . . 172 AC76
Bray, NW3 . . . . 6 D6
Brayards Rd, SE15 . . . . 44 E9
Braybank, Bray SL6 . . . . 172 AC75
Braybourne Cl, Uxb. UB8 . . . . . 156 BJ65
Braybourne Dr, Islw. TW7 . . . . . 179 CF80
Braybrooke Gdns, SE19
off Fox Hill 204 DS94
Braybrook St, W12 . . . . 161 CT71
Brayburne Av, SW4 . . . . 41 M9
Bray Cl, Borwd. WD6 . . . . 100 CQ39
Bray SL6 . . . . 172 AC76
Bray Ct, Maid. SL6 . . . . 172 AC77
Braycourt Av, Walt. KT12 . . . . . 217 BV101
Bray Cres, SE16 . . . . 33 J4
Braydon Rd, N16 . . . . 144 DT60
Bray Dr, E16 . . . . 23 M10
Brayfield Rd, Bray SL6 . . . . 172 AC75
Brayfield Ter, N1 . . . . 8 E7
Brayford Sq, E1 . . . . 21 H8
Bray Gdns, Wok. GU22 . . . . 249 BE116
Bray Pas, E16 . . . . 23 N10
Bray Pl, SW3 . . . . 28 E9
Bray Rd, NW7 . . . . 119 CX51
Guildford GU2 . . . . 280 AV135
Stoke D'Abernon KT11 . . . . . . 252 BY116
BRAYS GROVE, Harl. CM18 . . . . 74 EU17
Sch Brays Gro Comm Coll, Harl.
CM18 off Tracyes Rd 74 EV17
Brays Mead, Harl. CM18 . . . . 73 ET17
Bray Springs, Wal.Abb. EN9
off Roundhills 90 EE34
Brayton Gdns, Enf. EN2 . . . . . . 103 DK42
Braywood Av, Egh. TW20 . . . . . 195 AZ93
Sch Braywood C of E First Sch,
Oakley Grn SL4
off Oakley Grn Rd 172 AE82
Braywood Rd, SE9 . . . . 187 ER84
Brazier Cres, Nthlt. UB5 . . . . . . 158 BZ70
Braziers Fld, Hert. SG13 . . . . 54 DT09
Brazil Cl, Bedd. CR0 . . . . 223 DL101
Breach Barn Mobile Home Pk,
Wal.Abb. EN9 . . . . 90 EH29
Breach Barns La, Wal.Abb.
EN9 . . . . 90 EF30
Breach La, Dag. RM9 . . . . 168 FA69
Little Berkhamsted SG13 . . . . 69 DJ18
Breach Rd, Grays RM20 . . . . . . 191 FT79
Bread & Cheese La, Chsht EN7 . 88 DR25
Bread St, EC4 . . . . 19 K9
Breakfield, Couls. CR5 . . . . 257 DL116
Breakmead, Welw.G.C. AL7 . . . . 52 DB10
Breakneck Hill, Green. DA9 . . . 211 FV85
Breakspear Av, St.Alb. AL1 . . . . 65 CF21
Breakspear Ct, Abb.L. WD5 . . . . 81 BT30
Breakspeare Cl, Wat. WD24 . . . . 97 BV38
Breakspeare Rd, Abb.L. WD5 . . . 81 BS31
Sch Breakspeare Sch, Abb.L. WD5
off Gallows Hill La 81 BS31
Sch Breakspear Inf & Jun Schs,
Ickhm UB10
off Bushey Rd 136 BN61
Breakspear Path, Hare. UB9 . . . 136 BJ55
Breakspear Pl, Abb.L. WD5
off Hanover Gdns 81 BT30
Breakspear Rd, Ruis. HA4 . . . . . 137 BP59
Breakspear Rd N, Hare. UB9 . . . 136 BN57
Breakspear Rd S, Ickhm UB9,
UB10 . . . . 136 BM62
Breakspears Dr, Orp. BR5 . . . . 228 EU95
Breakspears Ms, SE4 . . . . 46 A9
Breakspears Rd, SE4 . . . . 46 A10
Breakspear Way, Hem.H. HP2 . . . 63 BQ20
Breaks Rd, Hat. AL10 . . . . 67 CV18
Bream Cl, N17 . . . . 144 DV56
Bream Gdns, E6 . . . . 25 L3
Breamore Cl, SW15 . . . . 201 CU88
Breamore Rd, Ilf. IG3 . . . . 147 ET61
Bream's Bldgs, EC4 . . . . 18 E8
Bream St, E3 . . . . 12 B7
Breamwater Gdns, Rich. TW10 . 199 CH90
Brearley Cl, Edg. HA8 . . . . 118 CQ52
Uxbridge UB8 . . . . 156 BL65
Sch Breaside Prep Sch, Brom.
BR1 off Orchard Rd 226 EK95
Breasley Cl, SW15 . . . . 181 CV84
Brechin Pl, SW7 . . . . 27 P9
Brecken Cl, St.Alb. AL4 . . . . 65 CG16
Sch Brecknock Prim Sch, NW1 . . 7 P4
Brecknock Rd, N7 . . . . 7 N2
N19 . . . . 143 DJ63
Brecknock Rd Est, N19 . . . . 7 M1
Breckonmead, Brom. BR1
off Wanstead Rd 226 EJ96
Brecon Cl, Mitch. CR4 . . . . 223 DL98
Worcester Park KT4 . . . . 221 CW103
Brecon Grn, NW9
off Goldsmith Av 140 CS58
Brecon Ms, N7 . . . . 7 N3
Brecon Rd, W6 . . . . 38 F3
Enfield EN3 . . . . 104 DW42
Brede Cl, E6 . . . . 25 L2
Bredgar, SE13 . . . . 205 EC85
Bredgar Rd, N19 . . . . 143 DJ61
Bredhurst Cl, SE20 . . . . 204 DW93
Bredinghurst, SE22 . . . . 204 DU87
Sch Bredinghurst Sch, SE15
off Stuart Rd 185 DX84
Bredon Rd, Croy. CR0 . . . . 224 DT101
Bredune, Ken. CR8 . . . . 258 DR115
Bredward Cl, Burn. SL1 . . . . . . 152 AH69
Breech La, Walt.Hill KT20 . . . . 255 CU124
Breer St, SW6 . . . . 39 L10
Breezers Hill, E1 . . . . 32 D1
Breeze Ter, Chsht EN8
off Collet Cl 89 DX28
Brember Rd, Har. HA2 . . . . 138 CC61
Bremer Ms, E17 . . . . 145 EB56
Bremer Rd, Stai. TW18 . . . . 196 BG90
Bremner Av, Horl. RH6 . . . . 290 DF147
Bremner Cl, Swan. BR8 . . . . . . 229 FG98
Bremner Rd, SW7 . . . . 27 P5
Brenchley Av, Grav. DA11 . . . . 213 GH92
Brenchley Cl, Brom. BR2 . . . . . 226 EF100
Chislehurst BR7 . . . . 227 EN95
Brenchley Gdns, SE23 . . . . 204 DW86
Brenchley Rd, Orp. BR5 . . . . . . 227 ET95
Bren Ct, Enf. EN3
off Colgate Pl 105 EA37
Brendans Cl, Horn. RM11 . . . . . 150 FL60
Brenda Rd, SW17 . . . . 202 DF89
Brenda Ter, Swans. DA10
off Manor Rd 212 FY87
Brende Gdns, W.Mol. KT8 . . . . . 218 CB98
Brendon Av, NW10 . . . . 140 CS63
Brendon Cl, Erith DA8 . . . . 189 FE81
Esher KT10 . . . . 236 CC107
Harlington UB3 . . . . 177 BQ80
Brendon Ct, Rad. WD7
off The Avenue 83 CH34
Brendon Dr, Esher KT10 . . . . . . 236 CC107
Brendon Gdns, Har. HA2 . . . . . 138 CB63
Ilford IG2 . . . . 147 ES57
Brendon Gro, N2 . . . . 120 DC54
Brendon Rd, SE9 . . . . 207 ER89
Dagenham RM8 . . . . 148 EZ60
Brendon St, W1 . . . . 16 D8
Brendon Way, Enf. EN1 . . . . . . 122 DS45
Brenley Cl, Mitch. CR4 . . . . 222 DG97
Brenley Gdns, SE9 . . . . 186 EK84
Brennan Rd, Til. RM18 . . . . 193 GH82
Brent, The, Dart. DA1, DA2 . . . . 210 FN87
Coll Brent Adult Coll, NW10
off Morland Gdns 160 CR67
Brent Cl, Bex. DA5 . . . . 208 EY88
Dartford DA2 . . . . 210 FP86
Brentcot Cl, W13 . . . . 159 CH70
Brent Cres, NW10 . . . . 160 CM68
⊖ Brent Cross 141 CX59
Brent Cross Gdns, NW4
off Cooper Rd 141 CX58
Jct Brent Cross Interchange,
The, NW2 . . . . 141 CX59
🛍 Brent Cross Shop Cen,
NW4 . . . . 141 CW59
Brentfield, NW10 . . . . 160 CP66
Brentfield Cl, NW10 . . . . 160 CR65
Brentfield Gdns, NW2
off Hendon Way 141 CX59
Brentfield Ho, NW10
off Stonebridge Pk 160 CR66
Sch Brentfield Prim Sch, NW10
off Meadow Garth 160 CR65
Brentfield Rd, NW10 . . . . 160 CR65
Dartford DA1 . . . . 210 FN86
BRENTFORD, TW8 . . . . 179 CK79
⇌ Brentford 179 CJ79
● Brentford Business Cen,
Brent. TW8 . . . . 179 CH80
Brentford Cl, Hayes UB4 . . . . . 158 BX70
★ Brentford FC, Brent. TW8 . . 179 CK79
Sch Brentford Sch for Girls,
Brent. TW8
off Boston Manor Rd 179 CK79
Brent Grn, NW4 . . . . 141 CW57
Brent Grn Wk, Wem. HA9 . . . . . 140 CQ62
Brenthall Twrs, Harl. CM17 . . . . 74 EW17
Brentham Way, W5 . . . . 159 CK70
Brenthouse Rd, E9 . . . . 10 G6
Brenthurst Rd, NW10 . . . . 141 CT64
Sch Brent Knoll Sch, SE23
off Mayow Rd 205 DX90
Brentlands Dr, Dart. DA1 . . . . . 210 FN88
Brent La, Dart. DA1 . . . . 210 FM87
Brent Lea, Brent. TW8 . . . . 179 CJ80
Brentmead Cl, W7 . . . . 159 CE73
Brentmead Gdns, NW10 . . . . . . 160 CM68
Brentmead Pl, NW11
off North Circular Rd 141 CX58
● Brent New Enterprise Cen,
NW10 off Cobbold Rd 161 CT65
Brenton St, E14 . . . . 21 M8
🛍 Brent Pk, NW10 . . . . 140 CR64
Brent Pk Rd, NW4 . . . . 141 CV59
NW9 . . . . 141 CU60
Brent Pl, Barn. EN5 . . . . 102 DA43
Sch Brent Prim Sch, The, Dart.
DA2 off London Rd 210 FQ87
Brent Rd, E16 . . . . 23 P8
SE18 . . . . 187 EP80
Brentford TW8 . . . . 179 CJ79
South Croydon CR2 . . . . 242 DV109
Southall UB2 . . . . 178 BW76
Brent Side, Brent. TW8 . . . . . . 179 CJ79
Brentside Cl, W13 . . . . 159 CG70
● Brentside Executive Cen,
Brent. TW8 . . . . 179 CH79
Sch Brentside High Sch, W7
off Greenford Av 159 CE70
Sch Brentside Prim Sch, W7
off Kennedy Rd 159 CE70
🛍 Brent S Shop Pk, NW2 . . . . 141 CW60
Brent St, NW4 . . . . 141 CW56
Brent Ter, NW2 . . . . 141 CW61
Brentvale Av, Sthl. UB1 . . . . . . 159 CD74
Wembley HA0 . . . . 160 CM67
Brent Vw Rd, NW9 . . . . 141 CU59
Brent Way, N3 . . . . 120 DA51
Brentford TW8 . . . . 179 CK80
Dartford DA2 . . . . 210 FP86
Wembley HA9 . . . . 160 CP65
Brentwick Gdns, Brent. TW8 . . 180 CL77
BRENTWOOD, CM13 - CM15 . . 130 FU47
⇌ Brentwood 130 FW48
Brentwood Bypass, Brwd.
CM14, CM15 . . . . 129 FR49
Brentwood Cl, SE9 . . . . 207 EQ88
H Brentwood Comm Hosp
& Minor Injuries Unit,
Brwd. CM15 . . . . 130 FY46
Sch Brentwood Co High Sch,
Brwd. CM14
off Seven Arches Rd 130 FX48
Brentwood Ct, Add. KT15 . . . . . 234 BH105
Brentwood Ho, SE18
off Shooters Hill Rd 186 EK80
★ Brentwood Mus,
Brwd. CM14 . . . . 130 FW49
Brentwood Pl, Brwd. CM15 . . . 130 FX46
Sch Brentwood Prep Sch,
Brwd. CM15
off Middleton Hall La 130 FY46
Brentwood Rd, Brwd. CM13 . . . 131 GA49
Grays RM16 . . . . 193 GH77
Romford RM1, RM2 . . . . 149 FF58
Sch Brentwood Sch, Brwd.
CM15 off Ingrave Rd 130 FX47
Sch Brentwood Ursuline Conv
High Sch, Brwd. CM14
off Queens Rd 130 FX47
Brereton Ct, Hem.H. HP3 . . . . . . 62 BL22
Brereton Rd, N17 . . . . 122 DT52
Bressay Dr, NW7 . . . . 119 CU52
Bressenden Pl, SW1 . . . . 29 K6
Bressey Av, Enf. EN1 . . . . 104 DU39
Bressey Gro, E18 . . . . 124 EF54
Bretlands Rd, Cher. KT16 . . . . . 215 BE103
Breton Ho, EC2
off The Barbican 19 K6
Brett Cl, N16 . . . . 144 DS61
Northolt UB5
off Broomcroft Av 158 BX69
Brett Ct, N9 . . . . 122 DW47
Cheshunt EN8
off Coopers Wk 89 DX28
Brett Cres, NW10 . . . . 160 CR66
Brettell St, SE17 . . . . 43 M1
Brettenham Av, E17 . . . . 123 EA53
Sch Brettenham Prim Sch, N18
off Brettenham Rd 122 DU49
Brettenham Rd, E17 . . . . 123 EA54
N18 . . . . 122 DU49
Brett Gdns, Dag. RM9 . . . . 168 EY66
Brettgrave, Epsom KT19 . . . . . . 238 CQ110
Brett Ho Cl, SW15
off Putney Heath La 201 CX86
Brett Pas, E8 . . . . 10 F3
Brett Pl, Wat. WD24 . . . . 97 BU37
Brett Rd, E8 . . . . 10 F3
Barnet EN5 . . . . 101 CW43
Brevet Cl, Purf. RM19 . . . . 191 FR77
Brewer's Fld, Dart. DA2 . . . . . . 210 FJ91

Brewer's Grn, SW1 29 N6
Brewers Hall Gdns, EC2 19 K7
Brewers La, Rich. TW9 199 CK85
Brewer St, W1 17 M10
Bletchingley RH1 274 DQ131
★ Brewery, The, EC1 19 K6
Brewery, The, Rom. RM1 149 FE57
Brewery Cl, Wem. HA0 139 CG64
Brewery La, Byfleet KT14 234 BL113
Hoddesdon EN11 71 EA17
Sevenoaks TN13
off High St 279 FJ125
Twickenham TW1 199 CF87
Brewery Rd, N7 8 A6
SE18 187 ER78
Bromley BR2 226 EL102
Hoddesdon EN11 71 EA17
Woking GU21 248 AX117
Brewery Sq, EC1 18 G4
SE1 32 A3
Brewery Wk, Rom. RM1 149 FE57
Brewhouse La, E1 32 F3
SW15 181 CY83
Hertford SG14 54 DQ09
Brewhouse Rd, SE18 37 K8
Brew Ho Rd, Strood Grn RH3
off Tanners Meadow 286 CP138
Brewhouse Wk, SE16 33 L3
Brewhouse Yd, EC1 19 H4
Gravesend DA12
off Queen St 213 GH86
Brewood Rd, Dag. RM8 168 EV65
Brewster Gdns, W10 14 A6
Brewster Ho, E14 21 N10
Brewster Rd, E10 145 EB60
Brian Av, S.Croy. CR2 242 DS112
Brian Cl, Horn. RM12 149 FH63
Briane Rd, Epsom KT19 238 CQ110
Brian Rd, Rom. RM6 148 EW57
Briant Est, SE1 30 E7
Briant Ho, SE1 30 D7
Briants Cl, Pnr. HA5 116 BZ54
Briant St, SE14 45 J6
Briar Av, SW16 203 DM94
Briarbank Rd, W13 159 CG72
Briar Banks, Cars. SM5 240 DG109
Briarcliff, Hem.H. HP1 61 BE19
Briar Cl, N2 142 DB55
N13 122 DQ48
Buckhurst Hill IG9 124 EK47
Cheshunt EN8 88 DW29
Hampton TW12 198 BZ92
Isleworth TW7 199 CF85
Potten End HP4 61 BA16
Taplow SL6 152 AH72
Warlingham CR6 259 EA116
West Byfleet KT14 234 BH111
Briar Ct, Sutt. SM3 239 CW105
Briar Cres, Nthlt. UB5 158 CB65
Briardale Gdns, NW3 142 DA62
Briarfield Av, N3 120 DB54
Briarfield Cl, Bexh. DA7 188 FA82
Briar Gdns, Brom. BR2 226 EF102
Briar Gro, S.Croy. CR2 242 DU113
Briar Hill, Pur. CR8 241 DL111
Briaris Cl, N17 122 DV52
Briar La, Cars. SM5 240 DG109
Croydon CR0 243 EB105
Briarleas Gdns, Upmin. RM14 151 FS59
Briarley Cl, Brox. EN10 71 DZ22
Briar Pas, SW16 223 DL97
Briar Pl, SW16 223 DM97
Briar Rd, NW2 141 CW63
SW16 223 DL97
Bexley DA5 209 FD90
Harrow HA3 139 CJ57
Romford RM3 128 FJ52
St. Albans AL4 65 CJ17
Send GU23 249 BB123
Shepperton TW17 216 BN99
Twickenham TW2 199 CE88
Watford WD25 81 BU34
Briars, The, Bushey Hth WD23 117 CE45
Cheshunt EN8 89 DY31
Harlow CM18 73 ES18
Hertford SG13 54 DU09
Sarratt WD3 96 BH36
Slough SL3 175 AZ78
Briars Cl, Hat. AL10 67 CU18
Briars Ct, Oxshott KT22 237 CD114
Briars La, Hat. AL10 67 CU18
Briars Wk, Rom. RM3 128 FL54
Briarswood, Goffs Oak EN7 88 DS28
Briars Wd, Hat. AL10 67 CT18
Horley RH6 291 DJ147
Briarswood Way, Orp. BR6 245 ET106
Briar Wk, SW15 181 CV84
W10 14 E4
Edgware HA8 118 CQ52
West Byfleet KT14 234 BG112
Briarway, Berk. HP4 60 AW20
Briar Way, Guil. GU4 265 BB130
Slough SL2 153 AQ71
West Drayton UB7 176 BN75
Briarwood, Bans. SM7 256 DA115
Briarwood Cl, NW9 140 CQ58
Feltham TW13 197 BS90
Briarwood Ct, Wor.Pk. KT4
off The Avenue 221 CU102
Briarwood Dr, Nthwd. HA6 115 BU54
Briarwood Rd, SW4 203 DK85
Epsom KT17 239 CU107
Briary Cl, NW3 6 C6
Briary Ct, E16 23 M9
Sidcup DA14 208 EV92
Briary Gdns, Brom. BR1 206 EH92
Briary Gro, Edg. HA8 118 CP54
Briary La, N9 122 DT48
Brick Ct, EC4 18 E9
Grays RM17
off Columbia Wf Rd 192 GA79
Brickcroft, Brox. EN10 89 DY26
Brickcroft Hoppit, Harl. CM17 58 EX14
Brickenden Ct, Wal.Abb. EN9 90 EF33
BRICKENDON, Hert. SG13 70 DQ19
BRICKENDONBURY, Hert. SG13 54 DR14
Brickendon Grn, Brickendon
SG13 70 DQ19
Brickendon La, Hert. SG13 70 DQ18
Brickett Rd, St.Alb. AL1 65 CD20
Brickett Cl, Ruis. HA4 137 BQ57
BRICKET WOOD, St.Alb. AL2 82 BZ29
⇌ Bricket Wood 82 CA30
Brick Fm Cl, Rich. TW9 180 CP81
Brickfield, Hat. AL10 67 CU21
Brickfield Av, Hem.H. HP3 63 BP21
Brickfield Cl, E9 10 F5
Brentford TW8 179 CJ80
Brickfield Cotts, SE18 187 ET79
Brickfield Fm Gdns, Orp. BR6 245 EQ105
Brickfield La, Barn. EN5 101 CT44
Burnham SL1 152 AG67
Harlington UB3 177 BR79
Hookwood RH6 290 DD150
Brickfield Rd, SW19 202 DB91
Coopersale CM16 92 EX29
Outwood RH1 289 DN142
Thornton Heath CR7 223 DP95
Brickfields, Har. HA2 139 CD61
Brickfields, The, Ware SG12 54 DV05
● Brickfields Ind Est,
Hem.H. HP2 63 BP16
Brickfields La, Cooper. CM16
off Brickfield Rd 92 EX29
Brickfields Way, West Dr. UB7 176 BM76
Brick Kiln Cl, Wat. WD19 98 BY44
Brick Kiln La, Oxt. RH8 276 EJ131
Brick Knoll Pk, St.Alb. AL1 65 CJ21
Brickland Ct, N9
off The Broadway 122 DU47
Brick La, E1 20 B4
E2 20 B3
Enfield EN1, EN3 104 DV40
Stanmore HA7 117 CK52
● Bricklayer's Arms Distribution
Cen, SE1 31 P9
Jct Bricklayer's Arms Rbt, SE1 31 L8
Brickmakers La, Hem.H. HP3 63 BP21
Brick St, W1 29 J3
Brickwall Cl, Ayot St.P. AL6 51 CU07
Brickwall La, Ruis. HA4 137 BS60
Brickwood Cl, SE26 204 DV90
Brickwood Rd, Croy. CR0 224 DS103
Brickyard La, Wotton RH5 284 BW141
Brideale Cl, SE15 44 B3
Bride Ct, EC4 18 G9
Bride La, EC4 18 G9
Bridel Ms, N1 8 G9
Brides Pl, N1 9 N7
Bride St, N7 8 D5
Bridewain St, SE1 32 A6
Bridewell Pl, E1 32 F3
EC4 18 G9
Bridford Ms, W1 17 K6
Bridge, The, SW8 41 J5
Harrow HA3 139 CE55
Kings Langley WD4 81 BP29
Sch Bridge Acad, E2 10 B9
Bridge App, NW1 6 G6
Bridge Av, W6 181 CW78
W7 159 CD71
Upminster RM14 150 FN61
Bridge Barn La, Wok. GU21 248 AW117
Bridge Cl, W10 14 D9
Brentwood CM13 131 FZ49
Byfleet KT14 234 BM112
Dartford DA2 191 FR83
Enfield EN1 104 DV40
Romford RM7 149 FE58
Slough SL1 153 AM73
Staines TW18 195 BE91
Teddington TW11 199 CF91
Walton-on-Thames KT12 217 BT101
Woking GU21 248 AW117
Bridge Cotts, Upmin. RM14 151 FU64
Bridge Ct, E14
off Newport Av 23 H10
Welwyn Garden City AL7 51 CZ09
Woking GU21 248 AX117
Bridge Dr, N13 121 DM49
Bridge End, E17 123 EC53
Bridge End Cl, Kings.T. KT2
off Clifton Rd 220 CN95
Bridgefield Cl, Bans. SM7 255 CW115
Bridgefield Rd, Sutt. SM1 240 DA107
Bridgefields, Welw.G.C. AL7 51 CZ08
Bridgefoot, SE1 42 A1
Ware SG12 off High St 55 DX06
Bridgefoot La, Pot.B. EN6 85 CX33
Bridge Gdns, N16 9 L1
Ashford TW15 197 BQ94
East Molesey KT8 219 CD98
Bridge Gate, N21
off Ridge Av 122 DQ45
● Bridgegate Cen, Welw.G.C.
AL7 off Martinfield 51 CZ08
Bridgeham Cl, Wey. KT13
off Mayfield Rd 234 BN106
Bridgeham Way, Smallfield
RH6 291 DP148
Bridge Hill, Epp. CM16 91 ET33
Bridgehill Cl, Guil. GU2 264 AU133
Wembley HA0 159 CK67
Bridge Ho, NW3
off Adelaide Rd 6 G6
SW8 off St. George Wf 42 A1
Bridge Ho Quay, E14 34 F3
● Bridge Ind Est, Horl. RH6 291 DH148
Bridgeland Rd, E16 23 P10
Bridgelands Cl, Beck. BR3 205 DZ94
Bridge La, NW11 141 CY57
SW11 40 D7
Virginia Water GU25 214 AY99
Bridgeman Dr, Wind. SL4 173 AN82
Bridgeman Rd, N1 8 C7
Teddington TW11 199 CG93
Bridgeman St, NW8 16 C1
Bridge Meadows, SE14 45 J2
Bridge Ms, Wok. GU21
off Bridge Barn La 248 AX117
Bridgend Rd, SW18 182 DC84
Enfield EN1 104 DW35
Bridgenhall Rd, Enf. EN1 104 DT39
Bridgen Rd, Bex. DA5 208 EY86
Bridge Pk, SW18 202 DA85
Guildford GU4 265 BC131
Bridge Pl, SW1 29 K8
Amersham HP6 77 AS38
Croydon CR0 224 DR101
Watford WD17
off Lower High St 98 BX43
Bridgepoint Pl, N6
off Hornsey La 143 DJ60
Bridgeport Pl, E1 32 D2
Bridger Cl, Wat. WD25 82 BX33
Bridge Rd, E6 167 EM66
E15 13 H7
E17 145 DZ59
N9 off Fore St 122 DU48
N22 121 DL53
Bridge Rd, NW10 160 CS65
Beckenham BR3 205 DZ94
Bexleyheath DA7 188 EY82
Chertsey KT16 216 BH101
Chessington KT9 238 CL106
East Molesey KT8 219 CE98
Epsom KT17 239 CT112
Erith DA8 189 FF81
Grays RM17 192 GB78
Hounslow TW3 179 CD82
Hunton Bridge WD4 81 BQ33
Isleworth TW7 179 CD83
Orpington BR5 228 EV100
Rainham RM13 169 FF70
Southall UB2 178 BZ75
Sutton SM2 240 DB107
Twickenham TW1 199 CH86
Uxbridge UB8 156 BJ68
Wallington SM6 241 DJ106
Welwyn Garden City AL7, AL8 51 CW08
Wembley HA9 140 CN62
Weybridge KT13 234 BM105
Bridge Rd E, Welw.G.C. AL7 51 CY08
Bridge Row, Croy. CR0
off Cross Rd 224 DR102
Sch Bridge Sch, The,
Prim Dept, N7 7 P4
Sec Dept, N7 7 P1
Bridges Cl, Horl. RH6 291 DK148
Bridges Ct, SW11 40 A10
Bridges Dr, Dart. DA1 210 FP85
Bridges La, Croy. CR0 241 DL105
Bridges Pl, SW6 39 H6
Bridges Rd, SW19 202 DB93
Stanmore HA7 117 CF50
Bridges Rd Ms, SW19
off Bridges Rd 202 DB93
Bridge St, SW1 30 A5
W4 180 CR77
Berkhamsted HP4 60 AX19
Colnbrook SL3 175 BD80
Guildford GU1 280 AW135
Hemel Hempstead HP1 62 BJ21
Leatherhead KT22 253 CG122
Pinner HA5 138 BX55
Richmond TW9 199 CK85
Staines TW18 195 BE91
Walton-on-Thames KT12 217 BT102
Bridge Ter, E15 13 H7
SE13 off Mercator Rd 185 ED84
Bridgetown Cl, SE19
off St. Kitts Ter 204 DS92
Bridge Vw, W6 26 A10
Greenhithe DA9 191 FV84
Bridgeview Ct, Ilf. IG6 125 ER51
Bridgewater Cl, Chis. BR7 227 ES97
Bridgewater Ct, Slou. SL3 175 BA78
Bridgewater Gdns, Edg. HA8 118 CM54
Bridgewater Hill, Nthch HP4 60 AT16
Bridgewater Rd, E15 12 E9
Berkhamsted HP4 60 AU17
Wembley HA0 159 CJ66
Weybridge KT13 235 BR107
Sch Bridgewater Sch, Berk.
HP4 off Bridle Way 60 AU17
Bridgewater Sq, EC2 19 J6
Bridgewater St, EC2 19 J6
Bridgewater Ter, Wind. SL4 173 AR81
Bridgewater Way, Bushey WD23 98 CB44
Windsor SL4
off Bridgewater Ter 173 AR81
Bridge Way, N11
off Pymmes Grn Rd 121 DJ48
NW11 141 CZ57
Bridgeway, Bark. IG11 167 ET66
Bridge Way, Chipstead CR5 256 DE119
Cobham KT11 235 BT113
Twickenham TW2 198 CC87
Uxbridge UB10 137 BP64
Bridgeway, Wem. HA0 160 CL66
Bridgeway St, NW1 17 M1
Bridge Wf, Cher. KT16 216 BJ101
Bridge Wf Rd, Islw. TW7
off Church St 179 CH83
Bridgewood Cl, SE20 204 DV94
Bridgewood Rd, SW16 203 DK94
Worcester Park KT4 239 CU105
● Bridge Wks, Uxb. UB8 156 BJ70
Bridge Yd, SE1 31 M2
Bridgford St, SW18 202 DC90
Bridgman Rd, W4 180 CQ76
Bridgwater Cl, Rom. RM3 128 FK50
Bridgwater Rd, Rom. RM3 128 FJ50
Ruislip HA4 137 BU63
Bridgwater Wk, Rom. RM3 128 FK50
Bridle Cl, Enf. EN3 105 DZ37
Epsom KT19 238 CR106
Hoddesdon EN11 55 EA13
Kingston upon Thames KT1 219 CK98
St. Albans AL3 65 CE18
Sunbury-on-Thames TW16
off Forge La 217 BU97
Bridle End, Epsom KT17 239 CT114
Bridle La, W1 17 M10
Cobham KT11 252 CB115
Leatherhead KT22 252 CB115
Loudwater WD3 96 BK41
Twickenham TW1 199 CH86
Bridle Ms, Barn. EN5
off High St 101 CZ42
Bridle Path, Bedd. CR0 223 DM104
Watford WD17 97 BV40
Bridle Path, The, Epsom KT17 239 CV110
Woodford Green IG8 124 EE52
Bridlepath Way, Felt. TW14 197 BS88
Bridle Rd, Clay. KT10 237 CH107
Croydon CR0 225 EA104
Epsom KT17 239 CT113
Pinner HA5 138 BW58
Bridle Rd, The, Pur. CR8 241 DL110
Bridle Way, Berk. HP4 60 AU17
Croydon CR0 243 EA106
Great Amwell SG12 55 EA09
Hoddesdon EN11 55 EA14
Orpington BR6 245 EQ105
Bridle Way, The, Croy. CR0 243 DY110
Bridleway, The, Wall. SM6 241 DJ105
Bridleway Cl, Epsom KT17 239 CW110
Bridle Way N, Hodd. EN11 55 EA13
Bridle Way S, Hodd. EN11 55 EA14
Bridlington Cl, Bigg.H. TN16 260 EH119
Bridlington Rd, N9 122 DV45
Watford WD19 116 BX48
Bridlington Spur, Slou. SL1 173 AP76
Bridport Av, Rom. RM7 149 FB58
Bridport Pl, N1 9 M10
Bridport Rd, N18 122 DS50
Greenford UB6 158 CB67
Thornton Heath CR7 223 DN97
Bridport Ter, SW8 41 N7
Bridport Way, Slou. SL2 153 AP70
Bridstow Pl, W2 15 K8
Brief St, SE5 42 G8
Brier Lea, Lwr Kgswd KT20 271 CZ126
Brierley, New Adgtn CR0 243 EB107
Brierley Av, N9 122 DW46
Brierley Cl, SE25 224 DU98
Hornchurch RM11 150 FJ58
Brierley Rd, E11 145 ED63
SW12 203 DJ89
Brierly Cl, Guil. GU2 264 AU132
Brierly Gdns, E2 21 H1
Brier Rd, Tad. KT20 255 CV119
Briery Ct, Chorl. WD3 96 BG42
Hemel Hempstead HP2 62 BN19
Briery Fld, Chorl. WD3 96 BG42
Briery Way, Amer. HP6 77 AS37
Hemel Hempstead HP2 62 BN18
Brigade Cl, Har. HA2 139 CD61
Brigade Pl, Cat. CR3 258 DQ122
Brigade St, SE3 47 L9
Brigadier Av, Enf. EN2 104 DQ39
Brigadier Hill, Enf. EN2 104 DQ38
Brigeford Cl, E5 144 DU61
BRIGGENS PARK, Ware SG12 56 EJ11
Briggs Cl, Mitch. CR4 223 DH95
Bright Cl, Belv. DA17 188 EX77
Brightfield Rd, SE12 206 EF85
Bright Hill, Guil. GU1 280 AX136
Brightlands, Nthflt DA11 212 GE91
Brightlands Rd, Reig. RH2 272 DC132
Brightling Rd, SE4 205 DZ86
Brightlingsea Pl, E14 21 N10
Brightman Rd, SW18 202 DD88
Brighton Av, E17 145 DZ57
Brighton Cl, Add. KT15 234 BJ106
Uxbridge UB10 157 BP66
Brighton Dr, Nthlt. UB5 158 CA65
Brighton Gro, SE14 45 L6
Brighton Rd, E6 25 M2
N2 120 DC54
N16 144 DS63
Addlestone KT15 234 BJ105
Banstead SM7 239 CZ114
Coulsdon CR5 257 DJ119
Horley RH6 290 DF149
Purley CR8 242 DQ110
Redhill RH1 288 DF135
South Croydon CR2 242 DQ106
Surbiton KT6 219 CJ100
Sutton SM2 240 DB109
Tadworth KT20 255 CY119
Watford WD24 97 BU38
Brighton Spur, Slou. SL2 153 AP70
Brighton Ter, SW9 183 DM84
Redhill RH1 off Hooley La 288 DF135
Brights Av, Rain. RM13 169 FH70
Brightside, The, Enf. EN3 105 DX39
Brightside Av, Stai. TW18 196 BJ94
Brightside Rd, SE13 205 ED86
Bright St, E14 22 D8
Brightview Cl, Brick.Wd AL2 82 BY29
Brightwell Cl, Croy. CR0
off Sumner Rd 223 DN102
Brightwell Cres, SW17 202 DF92
Brightwell Rd, Wat. WD18 97 BU43
Brightwen Gro, Stan. HA7 117 CG47
Sch Brigidine Sch Windsor,
Wind. SL4 off King's Rd 173 AR83
Brig Ms, SE8 46 A3
Brigstock Rd, Belv. DA17 189 FB77
Coulsdon CR5 257 DH115
Thornton Heath CR7 223 DN99
Brill Pl, NW1 17 P1
Brimfield Rd, Purf. RM19 191 FR77
Brim Hill, N2 142 DC56
Brimpsfield Cl, SE2 188 EV76
BRIMSDOWN, Enf. EN3 105 DY41
⇌ Brimsdown 105 DY41
Brimsdown Av, Enf. EN3 105 DY40
● Brimsdown Ind Est,
Enf. EN3 105 DY39
Sch Brimsdown Inf & Jun Schs,
Enf. EN3 off Green St 105 DX41
Brimshot La, Chobham GU24 232 AS109
Brimstone Cl, Orp. BR6 246 EW108
Brimstone Ho, E15
off Victoria St 13 J6
Brimstone La, Dor. RH5 286 CM143
Brimstone Wk, Berk. HP4 60 AT17
Sch Brindishe Prim Sch, SE12
off Wantage Rd 206 EF85
Brindle Gate, Sid. DA15 207 ES88
Brindle La, Forty Grn HP9 110 AG51
Brindles, Horn. RM11 150 FL56
Brindles, The, Bans. SM7 255 CZ117
Brindles Cl, Hutt. CM13 131 GC47
Brindley Cl, Bexh. DA7 189 FB83
Wembley HA0 159 CJ67
Brindley Ho, SW2
off New Pk Rd 203 DL87
Brindley St, SE14 45 N7
Brindley Way, Brom. BR1 206 EG92
Hemel Hempstead HP3
off London Rd 80 BM25
Southall UB1 158 CB73
Brindwood Rd, E4 123 DZ48
Brinkburn Cl, SE2 188 EU77
Edgware HA8 118 CP54
Brinkburn Gdns, Edg. HA8 140 CN55
Brinkley, Kings.T. KT1
off Burritt Rd 220 CN96
Brinkley Rd, Wor.Pk. KT4 221 CV103
Brinklow Ct, St.Alb. AL3 64 CB23
Brinklow Cres, SE18 187 EP80
Brinklow Ho, W2 15 K6
Brinkworth Rd, Ilf. IG5 146 EL55
Brinkworth Way, E9 11 P4
Brinley Cl, Chsht EN8 88 DW31
Brinsdale Rd, NW4 141 CX56
Brinsley Ho, E1
off Tarling St 20 G9
Brinsley Rd, Har. HA3 117 CD54
Brinsmead, Frog. AL2 83 CD27
Brinsmead Rd, Rom. RM3 128 FN54
Brinsworth Cl, Twick. TW2 199 CD89
Brinton Wk, SE1 30 G3
Brion Pl, E14 22 E7
Brisbane Av, SW19 222 DB95
Brisbane Ho, Til. RM18 193 GF81
Brisbane Rd, E10 145 EB61
W13 179 CG75
Ilford IG1 147 EP59
Brisbane St, SE5 43 L5
Briscoe Cl, E11 146 EF61
Hoddesdon EN11 71 DZ15
Briscoe Rd, SW19 202 DD93
Hoddesdon EN11 71 DZ15
Briscoe Rd, Rain. RM13 170 FJ68
Briset Rd, SE9 186 EK83
Briset St, EC1 18 G6
Briset Way, N7 143 DM61
Brisson Cl, Esher KT10 236 BZ107
Bristol Cl, Houns. TW4
off Harvey Rd 198 CA87
Stanwell TW19 196 BL86
Wallington SM6 241 DL108
Bristol Gdns, SW15
off Portsmouth Rd 201 CW87
W9 15 M5
Bristol Ho, SE11
off Lambeth Wk 30 E7
Bristol Ms, W9 15 M5
Bristol Pk Rd, E17 145 DY56
Bristol Rd, E7 166 EJ65
Gravesend DA12 213 GK90
Greenford UB6 158 CB67
Morden SM4 222 DC99
Bristol Way, Slou. SL1 154 AS74
Briston Gro, N8 143 DL58
Briston Ms, NW7 119 CU52
Bristowe Cl, SW2 203 DN86
Bristow Rd, SE19 204 DS92
Bexleyheath DA7 188 EY81
Croydon CR0 241 DL105
Hounslow TW3 178 CC83
★ Britain at War Experience,
SE1 31 N3
Britannia Bldg, N1
off Ebenezer St 19 L2
● Britannia Business Pk,
Wal.Cr. EN8 89 DZ34
Britannia Cl, SW4
off Bowland Rd 183 DK84
Erith DA8 189 FF79
Northolt UB5 158 BX69
Britannia Ct, Kings.T. KT2
off Skerne Wk 219 CK95
Britannia Dr, Grav. DA12 213 GM92
Britannia Gate, E16 35 P2
● Britannia Ind Est,
Colnbr. SL3 175 BD82
Britannia La, Twick. TW2 198 CC87
Britannia Rd, E14 34 B9
N12 120 DC48
SW6 39 L5
Chesham HP5 76 AQ29
Ilford IG1 147 EP62
Surbiton KT5 220 CM101
Waltham Cross EN8 89 DZ34
Warley CM14 130 FW50
Britannia Row, N1 9 H8
Britannia St, WC1 18 C2
Sch Britannia Village Prim Sch,
E16 36 A3
Britannia Wk, N1 19 L2
Britannia Way, NW10 160 CP70
SW6 39 M5
Stanwell TW19 196 BK87
★ British Dental Assoc Mus,
W1 17 J7
British Gro, W4 181 CT78
British Gro N, W4
off Middlesex Ct 181 CT78
British Gro Pas, W4 181 CT78
British Gro S, W4
off British Gro Pas 181 CT78
British Legion Rd, E4 124 EF47
★ British Lib, NW1 17 P2
★ British Lib Newspapers,
NW9 140 CS55
★ British Med Assoc, WC1 17 P4
★ British Mus, The, WC1 17 P7
★ British Red Cross Mus &
Archives, SW1 19 L6
Coll British Sch of Osteopathy,
SE1 31 K5
British St, E3 21 P3
Coll British Transport Pol Training
Sch, Walt.Hill KT20
off Sandlands Gro 255 CU123
Briton Cl, S.Croy. CR2 242 DS111
Briton Cres, S.Croy. CR2 242 DS111
Briton Hill Rd, S.Croy. CR2 242 DS110
Coll BRIT Sch for Performing Arts
& Tech, The, Croy. CR0
off The Crescent 224 DR100
Brittain Rd, Dag. RM8 148 EY62
Hersham KT12 236 BX106
Brittains La, Sev. TN13 278 FF123
Brittany Ho, Enf. EN2
off Chantry Cl 104 DQ38
Brittany Pt, SE11 30 E9
Britten Cl, NW11 142 DB60
Elstree WD6
off Rodgers Cl 99 CK44
Brittenden Cl, Orp. BR6 245 ES107
Brittenden Par, Grn St Grn BR6
off Glentrammon Rd 245 ET107
Britten Dr, Sthl. UB1 158 CA72
Brittens Cl, Guil. GU2 264 AU129
Britten St, SW3 40 C1
Brittidge Rd, NW10
off Paulet Way 160 CS66
Britton Av, St.Alb. AL3 65 CD20
Britton Cl, SE6
off Brownhill Rd 205 ED87
Sch Brittons Sch, Rain. RM13
off Ford La 169 FF66
Britton St, EC1 18 G5
Britwell Dr, Berk. HP4 60 AY17
Britwell Est, Slou. SL2 153 AM70
Britwell Gdns, Burn. SL1 153 AK69
Britwell Rd, Burn. SL1 153 AK69
Brixham Cres, Ruis. HA4 137 BU60
Brixham Gdns, Ilf. IG3 147 ES64
Brixham Rd, Well. DA16 188 EX81
Brixham St, E16 37 K3
BRIXTON, SW2 183 DL84
⇌ Brixton 183 DN84
⊖ Brixton 183 DN84
★ Brixton Acad, The, SW9 42 E10
Brixton Hill, SW2 203 DL87
Brixton Hill Pl, SW2 203 DL87
Brixton Oval, SW2 183 DN84
Brixton Rd, SW9 42 E5
Watford WD24 97 BV39
Brixton Sta Rd, SW9 183 DN84
Brixton Village Mkt, SW9
off Coldharbour La 183 DN84
Brixton Water La, SW2 203 DM85
Broad Acre, Brick.Wd AL2 82 BY30
Broadacre, Stai. TW18 196 BG92
Broadacre Cl, Uxb. UB10 137 BP62
Broad Acres, Gdmg. GU7 280 AS143
Broadacres, Guil. GU3 264 AS132
Broad Acres, Hat. AL10 67 CT15

Broadbent Cl, N6 . . . 143 DH60
Broadbent St, W1 . . . 17 J10
Broadberry Ct, N18 . . . 122 DV50
Broadbridge Cl, SE3 . . . 47 N4
Broadbridge La, Smallfield RH6 . . . 291 DN148
Broad Cl, Hersham KT12 . . . 218 BX104
Broad Common Est, N16 *off Osbaldeston Rd* . . . 144 DU60
Broadcoombe, S.Croy. CR2 . . . 242 DW108
Broad Ct, WC2 . . . 18 B9
Welwyn Garden City AL7 . . . 51 CY09
Broadcroft, Hem.H. HP2 . . . 62 BK18
Broadcroft Av, Stan. HA7 . . . 117 CK54
Broadcroft Rd, Petts Wd BR5 . . . 227 ER101
Broad Ditch Rd, Sthflt DA13 . . . 212 GC94
Broadeaves Cl, S.Croy. CR2 . . . 242 DS106
Broadfield, Ald.WD25 . . . 98 CB36
Harlow CM20 . . . 57 ES14
● **Broadfield Cl**, Croy. CR0 *off Progress Way* . . . 223 DM103
Broadfield Cl, NW2 . . . 141 CW62
Romford RM1 . . . 149 FF57
Tadworth KT20 . . . 255 CW120
Broadfield Ct, Bushey Hth WD23 . . . 117 CE47
Sch **Broadfield Inf Sch**, Hem.H. HP2 *off Broadfield Rd* . . . 62 BM20
Sch **Broadfield Jun Sch**, Hem.H. HP2 *off Windmill Rd* . . . 62 BM20
Broadfield La, NW1 . . . 8 A6
Broadfield Pl, Welw.G.C. AL8 . . . 51 CV10
Broadfield Rd, SE6 . . . 206 EE87
Hemel Hempstead HP2 . . . 62 BM20
Peaslake GU5 . . . 283 BR142
Broadfields, E.Mol. KT8 . . . 219 CD100
Goffs Oak EN7 . . . 87 DP29
Harrow HA2 . . . 116 CB54
High Wych CM21 . . . 58 EV06
Broadfields Av, N21 . . . 121 DN45
Edgware HA8 . . . 118 CP49
Sch **Broadfields Co Prim Sch**, Harl. CM20 *off Freshwaters* . . . 57 ES14
Broadfields Hts, Edg. HA8 . . . 118 CP49
Broadfields La, Wat. WD19 . . . 115 BV46
Sch **Broadfields Prim Sch**, Edg. HA8 *off Broadfields Av* . . . 118 CN47
Broadfield Sq, Enf. EN1 . . . 104 DV40
Broadfields Way, NW10 . . . 141 CT64
Broadfield Way, Buck.H. IG9 . . . 124 EJ48
Broadford, Shalf. GU4 . . . 280 AX141
Broadford La, Chobham GU24 . . . 232 AT112
● **Broadford Pk**, Shalf. GU4 . . . 280 AX141
Sch **Broadford Prim Sch**, Harold Hill RM3 *off Faringdon Av* . . . 128 FK51
Broadford Rd, Peasm. GU3 . . . 280 AW142
BROADGATE, EC2 . . . 19 M6
Broadgate, E13 . . . 166 EJ68
Waltham Abbey EN9 . . . 90 EF33
Broadgate Circle, EC2 . . . 19 N6
Broadgate Rd, E16 . . . 24 E8
Broadgates Av, Barn. EN4 . . . 102 DB39
Broadgates Rd, SW18 *off Ellerton Rd* . . . 202 DD88
BROAD GREEN, Croy. CR0 . . . 223 DN100
Broad Grn, Bayford SG13 . . . 69 DM15
Broad Grn Av, Croy. CR0 . . . 223 DP101
Broadgreen Rd, Chsht EN7 . . . 88 DR26
Broad Grn Wd, Bayford SG13 . . . 69 DM15
Broadham Grn Rd, Oxt. RH8 . . . 275 ED132
Broadham Pl, Oxt. RH8 . . . 275 ED131
Broadhead Strand, NW9 . . . 119 CT53
Broadheath Dr, Chis. BR7 . . . 207 EM92
Broad Highway, Cob. KT11 . . . 236 BX114
Broadhinton Rd, SW4 . . . 41 K10
Broadhurst, Ashtd. KT21 . . . 254 CL116
Broadhurst Av, Edg. HA8 . . . 118 CP49
Ilford IG3 . . . 147 ET63
Broadhurst Cl, NW6 . . . 5 N5
Richmond TW10 *off Lower Gro Rd* . . . 200 CM85
Broadhurst Gdns, NW6 . . . 5 L5
Chigwell IG7 . . . 125 EQ49
Reigate RH2 . . . 288 DB137
Ruislip HA4 . . . 138 BW61
Broadhurst Wk, Rain. RM13 . . . 169 FG65
Broadlake Cl, Lon.Col. AL2 . . . 83 CK27
Broadlands, Bad.Dene RM17 *off Bankfoot* . . . 192 FZ78
Hanworth TW13 . . . 198 BZ90
Horley RH6 . . . 291 DJ147
Broadlands Av, SW16 . . . 203 DL89
Chesham HP5 . . . 76 AQ31
Enfield EN3 . . . 104 DV41
Shepperton TW17 . . . 217 BQ100
Broadlands Cl, N6 . . . 142 DG59
SW16 . . . 203 DL89
Enfield EN3 . . . 104 DV41
Waltham Cross EN8 . . . 89 DX34
Broadlands Dr, Warl. CR6 . . . 258 DW119
Broadlands Rd, N6 . . . 142 DF59
Bromley BR1 . . . 206 EH91
Broadlands Way, N.Mal. KT3 . . . 221 CT100
Broad La, EC2 . . . 19 N6
N8 *off Tottenham La* . . . 143 DM57
N15 . . . 144 DT56
Beaconsfield HP9 . . . 132 AH55
Dartford DA2 . . . 209 FG91
Hampton TW12 . . . 198 CA93
Wooburn Green HP10 . . . 132 AG58
Broad Lawn, SE9 . . . 207 EN89
Broadlawns Ct, Har. HA3 . . . 117 CF53
Broadleaf Gro, Welw.G.C. AL8 . . . 51 CV06
BROADLEY COMMON, Wal.Abb. EN9 . . . 72 EL20
Broadley Gdns, Shenley WD7 *off Queens Way* . . . 84 CL32
Broadley Rd, Harl. CM19 . . . 73 EM19
Broadley St, NW8 . . . 16 B6
Broadley Ter, NW1 . . . 16 D5
Waltham Abbey EN9 . . . 72 EL21
Broadmark Rd, Slou. SL2 . . . 154 AV73
Broadmayne, SE17 . . . 31 K10
Broadmead, SE6 . . . 205 EA90
Ashtead KT21 . . . 254 CM117
Horley RH6 . . . 291 DJ147
Broadmead Av, Wor.Pk. KT4 . . . 221 CU101
Broadmead Cl, Hmptn. TW12 . . . 198 CA93
Pinner HA5 . . . 116 BY52
Sch **Broadmead Junior, Inf & Nurs Sch**, Croy. CR0 *off Sydenham Rd* . . . 224 DR101
Broadmead Rd, Hayes UB4 . . . 158 BY70
Northolt UB5 . . . 158 BY70
Woking GU22, GU23 . . . 249 BB122
Woodford Green IG8 . . . 124 EG51
Broadmeads, Send GU23 *off Broadmead Rd* . . . 249 BB122
Ware SG12 . . . 55 DX06
Sch **Broadmere Comm Prim Sch**, Sheer. GU21 *off Devonshire Av* . . . 233 BD113
BROADMOOR, Dor. RH5 . . . 284 CA143
Broadmoor, Dor. RH5 . . . 284 CA143
Broad Oak, Slou. SL2 . . . 153 AQ70
Sunbury-on-Thames TW16 . . . 197 BT93
Woodford Green IG8 . . . 124 EH50
Broadoak Av, Enf. EN3 . . . 105 DX35
Broad Oak Cl, E4 . . . 123 EA50
Orpington BR5 . . . 228 EU96
Broadoak Cl, Sutt.H. DA4 . . . 210 FN93
Broadoak Ct, SW9 *off Gresham Rd* . . . 183 DN83
Broad Oak Ct, Slou. SL2 . . . 153 AQ70
BROADOAK END, Hert. SG14 . . . 53 DM07
Broad Oak La, Hert. SG14 . . . 53 DM07
Broad Oak Manor, Hert. SG14 . . . 53 DM07
Broadoak Rd, Erith DA8 . . . 189 FD80
Broadoaks, Epp. CM16 . . . 91 ET31
Broadoaks Cres, W.Byf. KT14 . . . 234 BH114
Broadoaks Way, Brom. BR2 . . . 226 EF99
Broad Platts, Slou. SL3 . . . 174 AX76
Broad Ride, Egh. TW20 . . . 214 AU96
Broad Rd, Swans. DA10 . . . 212 FY86
Broad Sanctuary, SW1 . . . 29 P5
Broadstone Pl, W1 . . . 16 G7
Broadstone Rd, Horn. RM12 . . . 149 FG61
Broad St, Chesh. HP5 . . . 76 AQ30
Dagenham RM10 . . . 168 FA66
Hemel Hempstead HP2 . . . 62 BK19
Rydeshill GU3 . . . 264 AS132
Teddington TW11 . . . 199 CF93
Broad St Av, EC2 . . . 19 N7
Broad St Pl, EC2 . . . 19 M7
Broadstrood, Loug. IG10 . . . 107 EN38
Broad Vw, NW9 . . . 140 CN58
Broadview Av, Grays RM16 . . . 192 GD75
Broadview Ho, Enf. EN3 *off Tysoe Av* . . . 105 DZ36
Broadview Rd, SW16 . . . 203 DJ94
Chesham HP5 . . . 76 AP27
Broadwalk, E18 . . . 146 EF55
Broad Wk, N21 . . . 121 DM47
NW1 . . . 17 J3
SE3 . . . 186 EJ83
W1 . . . 28 G2
Caterham CR3 . . . 258 DT122
Coulsdon CR5 . . . 256 DG123
Croydon CR0 . . . 243 DY110
Epsom KT18 . . . 255 CX119
Harlow CM20 . . . 57 ER14
Broadwalk, Har. HA2 . . . 138 CA57
Broad Wk, Houns. TW5 . . . 178 BX81
Orpington BR6 . . . 228 EX104
Richmond TW9 . . . 180 CM80
Sevenoaks TN15 . . . 279 FL128
Broad Wk, The, W8 . . . 27 M1
East Molesey KT8 . . . 219 CF97
Broadwalk, The, Nthwd. HA6 . . . 115 BQ54
Broadwalk Ct, W8 . . . 27 K2
Broad Wk La, NW11 . . . 141 CZ59
Broad Wk N, The, Brwd. CM13 . . . 131 GA49
🔒 **Broadwalk Shop Cen**, Edg. HA8 . . . 118 CN51
Broad Wk S, The, Brwd. CM13 . . . 131 GA49
Broadwall, SE1 . . . 30 F2
Broadwater, Berk. HP4 . . . 60 AW18
Potters Bar EN6 . . . 86 DB30
Broadwater Cl, Hersham KT12 . . . 235 BU106
Woking GU21 . . . 233 BD112
Wraysbury TW19 . . . 195 AZ87
Broadwater Cres, Welw.G.C. AL7 . . . 51 CX10
Broad Water Cres, Wey. KT13 . . . 217 BQ104
Broadwater Fm Est, N17 . . . 122 DR54
Sch **Broadwater Fm Prim Sch**, N17 *off Moira Cl* . . . 122 DR54
Broadwater Gdns, Hare. UB9 . . . 136 BH56
Orpington BR6 . . . 245 EP105
Broadwater La, Hare. UB9 . . . 136 BH56
● **Broadwater Pk**, Denh. UB9 . . . 136 BG58
Broadwater Pk, Maid. SL6 . . . 172 AE78
Broadwater Pl, Wey. KT13 *off Oatlands Dr* . . . 217 BS103
Sch **Broadwater Prim Sch**, SW17 *off Broadwater Rd* . . . 202 DE91
Broadwater Ri, Guil. GU1 . . . 265 BA134
Broadwater Rd, N17 . . . 122 DS53
SE28 . . . 187 ER76
SW17 . . . 202 DE91
Welwyn Garden City AL7 . . . 51 CY10
Broadwater Rd N, Hersham KT12 . . . 235 BT106
Broadwater Rd S, Hersham KT12 . . . 235 BT106
Sch **Broadwater Sch**, Farnc. GU7 *off Summers Rd* . . . 280 AU143
Broadway, E15 . . . 13 H7
SW1 . . . 29 N6
W7 . . . 159 CG74
W13 . . . 159 CG74
Barking IG11 . . . 167 EQ67
Bexleyheath DA6, DA7 . . . 188 EY84
Grays RM17 . . . 192 GC79
Potters Bar EN6 *off Darkes La* . . . 85 CZ32
Rainham RM13 . . . 169 FG70
Romford RM2 . . . 149 FG55
Staines TW18 *off Kingston Rd* . . . 196 BH93
Swanley BR8 . . . 229 FC100
Tilbury RM18 . . . 193 GF82
Broadway, The, E4 . . . 123 EC51
E13 . . . 24 A1
N8 . . . 143 DL58
N9 . . . 122 DU47
N14 *off Winchmore Hill Rd* . . . 121 DK46
N22 . . . 121 DN54
NW7 . . . 118 CS50
SW13 *off The Terrace* . . . 180 CS82
SW19 . . . 201 CZ93
W5 . . . 159 CK73
W7 *off Cherington Rd* . . . 159 CE74
Amersham HP7 . . . 77 AP40
Beaconsfield HP9 *off Penn Rd* . . . 111 AK52
Cheam SM3 . . . 239 CY107
Chesham HP5 . . . 76 AP31
Croydon CR0 *off Croydon Rd* . . . 241 DL105
Dagenham RM8 . . . 148 EZ61
Farnham Common SL2 . . . 153 AQ65
Greenford UB6 . . . 158 CC70
Hatfield AL9 . . . 67 CW17
Hornchurch RM12 . . . 149 FH63
Laleham TW18 . . . 216 BJ97
Loughton IG10 . . . 107 EQ42
New Haw KT15 . . . 234 BG110
Broadway, The, Pnr. HA5 . . . 116 BZ52
Southall UB1 . . . 158 BX73
Stanmore HA7 . . . 117 CJ50
Sutton SM1 *off Manor La* . . . 240 DC106
Thames Ditton KT7 *off Hampton Ct Way* . . . 219 CE102
Watford WD17 . . . 98 BW41
Wealdstone HA3 . . . 117 CE54
Wembley HA9 *off East La* . . . 140 CL62
Woking GU21 . . . 249 AZ117
Woodford Green IG8 . . . 124 EH51
Wycombe End HP9 . . . 111 AL54
Broadway Av, Croy. CR0 . . . 224 DR99
Harlow CM17 . . . 58 EV11
Twickenham TW1 . . . 199 CH86
Broadway Cl, Amer. HP7 . . . 77 AP40
South Croydon CR2 . . . 242 DV114
Woodford Green IG8 . . . 124 EH51
Broadway Ct, SW19 . . . 201 CZ93
Amersham HP7 . . . 77 AP40
Broadway E, Denh. UB9 . . . 136 BG59
Broadway Est, Til. RM18 . . . 193 GF81
Broadway Gdns, Mitch. CR4 . . . 222 DE98
🔒 **Broadway Mkt**, SW17 . . . 202 DF91
Broadway Mkt, E8 . . . 10 D9
Broadway Mkt Ms, E8 . . . 10 D9
Broadway Ms, E5 . . . 144 DT59
N13 *off Elmdale Rd* . . . 121 DM50
N21 *off Compton Rd* . . . 121 DP46
Broadway Par, N8 . . . 143 DL58
Hayes UB3 *off Coldharbour La* . . . 157 BU74
Hornchurch RM12 *off The Broadway* . . . 149 FH63
Broadway Pl, SW19 *off Hartfield Rd* . . . 201 CZ93
🔒 **Broadway Shop Cen**, W6 . . . 26 B9
Bexleyheath DA6 . . . 188 FA84
Broadway Wk, E14 . . . 34 B6
Broadwick St, W1 . . . 17 M10
Broadwood, Grav. DA11 . . . 213 GH92
Broadwood Av, Ruis. HA4 . . . 137 BS58
Broadwood Rd, Couls. CR5 . . . 257 DK121
Broadwood Ter, W8 *off Pembroke Rd* . . . 27 H8
Broad Yd, EC1 . . . 18 G5
Brocas Cl, NW3 . . . 6 D6
Brocas St, Eton SL4 . . . 173 AR80
Brocas Ter, Eton SL4 . . . 173 AQ80
Brockbridge Ho, SW15 *off Tangley Gro* . . . 201 CT86
Brockdene Dr, Kes. BR2 . . . 244 EK105
Brockdish Av, Bark. IG11 . . . 147 ET64
Brockenhurst, W.Mol. KT8 . . . 218 BZ100
Brockenhurst Av, Wor.Pk. KT4 . . . 220 CS102
Brockenhurst Cl, Wok. GU21 . . . 233 AZ114
Brockenhurst Gdns, NW7 . . . 118 CS50
Ilford IG1 . . . 147 EQ64
Brockenhurst Ms, N18 *off Lyndhurst Rd* . . . 122 DU49
Brockenhurst Rd, Croy. CR0 . . . 224 DV101
Brockenhurst Way, SW16 . . . 223 DK96
Brocket Cl, Chig. IG7 *off Brocket Way* . . . 125 ET50
Brocket Pk, Lmsfd AL8 . . . 50 CS10
Brocket Rd, Grays RM16 . . . 193 GG76
Hoddesdon EN11 . . . 71 EA17
Welwyn Garden City AL8 . . . 51 CT11
Brockett Cl, Welw.G.C. AL8 . . . 51 CV09
Brocket Way, Chig. IG7 . . . 125 ES50
Brock Grn, S.Ock. RM15 *off Cam Grn* . . . 171 FV72
BROCKHAM, Bet. RH3 . . . 286 CP136
Brockham Cl, SW19 . . . 201 CZ92
Brockham Cres, New Adgtn CR0 . . . 243 ED108
Brockham Dr, SW2 *off Fairview Pl* . . . 203 DM87
Ilford IG2 . . . 147 EP58
Brockham Grn, Brock. RH3 . . . 286 CP135
Brockham Hill Pk, Box H. KT20 . . . 270 CQ131
Brockhamhurst Rd, Bet. RH3 . . . 286 CN141
Brockham Keep, Horl. RH6 *off Langshott La* . . . 291 DJ147
Brockham La, Brock. RH3 . . . 270 CN134
Sch **Brockham Sch**, Brock. RH3 *off Wheelers La* . . . 286 CP136
Brockham St, SE1 . . . 31 K6
Brockhill, Wok. GU21 . . . 248 AU117
Brockhurst Cl, Stan. HA7 . . . 117 CF51
Brockhurst Rd, Chesh. HP5 . . . 76 AQ29
Brockill Cres, SE4 . . . 185 DY84
Brocklebank Ct, Whyt. CR3 . . . 258 DU118
Brocklebank Ho, E16 *off Glenister St* . . . 37 M3
● **Brocklebank Ind Est**, SE7 . . . 35 P8
Brocklebank Rd, SE7 . . . 36 A9
SW18 . . . 202 DC87
Brocklehurst St, SE14 . . . 45 K4
Brocklesbury Cl, Wat. WD24 . . . 98 BW41
Brocklesby Rd, SE25 . . . 224 DV98
Brockles Mead, Harl. CM19 . . . 73 EQ19
BROCKLEY, SE4 . . . 205 DY85
⇌ **Brockley** . . . 45 M10
Brockley Av, Stan. HA7 . . . 118 CL48
Brockley Cl, Stan. HA7 . . . 118 CL49
Brockley Combe, Wey. KT13 . . . 235 BR105
Brockley Cres, Rom. RM5 . . . 127 FC52
Brockley Cross, SE4 . . . 45 N10
Brockley Footpath, SE15 . . . 184 DW84
Brockley Gdns, SE4 . . . 45 N8
Brockley Gro, SE4 . . . 205 DZ85
Hutton CM13 . . . 131 GA46
Brockley Hall Rd, SE4 . . . 205 DY86
Brockley Hill, Stan. HA7 . . . 117 CJ46
Brockley Ms, SE4 . . . 205 DY85
Brockley Pk, SE23 . . . 205 DY87
Stanmore HA7 . . . 118 CL48
Sch **Brockley Prim Sch**, SE4 *off Brockley Rd* . . . 205 DZ85
Brockley Ri, SE23 . . . 205 DY86
Brockley Rd, SE4 . . . 45 M10
Brockleyside, Stan. HA7 . . . 117 CK49
Brockley Vw, SE23 . . . 205 DY87
Brockley Way, SE4 . . . 205 DX85
Brockman Ri, Brom. BR1 . . . 205 ED91
Brock Pl, E3 . . . 22 C5
Brock Rd, E13 . . . 24 B6
Brocks Dr, Sutt. SM3 . . . 221 CY104
Brockshot Cl, Brent. TW8 . . . 179 CK79
Brocksparkwood, Brwd. CM13 . . . 131 GB48
Brock St, SE15 . . . 44 G10
Brockswood La, Welw.G.C. AL8 . . . 51 CU08
Brockton Cl, Rom. RM1 . . . 149 FF56
Brock Way, Vir.W. GU25 . . . 214 AW99
Brockway Cl, E11 . . . 146 EE60
Guildford GU1 . . . 265 BB132
Brockweir, E2 . . . 20 G1
Brockwell Av, Beck. BR3 . . . 225 EB99
Brockwell Cl, Orp. BR5 . . . 227 ET99
★ **Brockwell Park**, SE24 . . . 203 DP86
Brockwell Pk Gdns, SE24 . . . 203 DN87
Brockwell Pk Row, SW2 . . . 203 DN86
Broderick Gro, Bkhm KT23 *off Lower Shott* . . . 268 CA126
Brodewater Rd, Borwd. WD6 . . . 100 CP40
Brodia Rd, N16 . . . 144 DS62
Brodick Ho, E3 . . . 11 N10
Brodie Ho, SE1 *off Coopers Rd* . . . 32 B10
Brodie Rd, E4 . . . 123 EC46
Enfield EN2 . . . 104 DQ38
Guildford GU1 . . . 280 AY135
Brodie St, SE1 . . . 32 B10
Brodlove La, E1 . . . 21 J10
Brodrick Gro, SE2 . . . 188 EV77
Brodrick Rd, SW17 . . . 202 DE89
Brograve Gdns, Beck. BR3 . . . 225 EB96
Broke Ct, Guil. GU4 *off Speedwell Cl* . . . 265 BC131
Broke Fm Dr, Orp. BR6 . . . 246 EW109
Broken Furlong, Eton SL4 . . . 173 AP78
Brokengate La, Denh. UB9 . . . 135 BC60
Broken Wf, EC4 . . . 19 J10
Brokes Cres, Reig. RH2 . . . 272 DA132
Brokesley St, E3 . . . 21 N3
Brokes Rd, Reig. RH2 . . . 272 DA132
Broke Wk, E8 . . . 10 B8
Bromar Rd, SE5 . . . 43 P10
Bromborough Grn, Wat. WD19 . . . 116 BW50
Bromefield, Stan. HA7 . . . 117 CJ53
Bromefield Ct, Wal.Abb. EN9 . . . 90 EG33
Bromehead Rd, E1 . . . 20 G8
Bromehead St, E1 . . . 20 G8
Bromell's Rd, SW4 . . . 183 DJ84
Brome Rd, SE9 . . . 187 EM83
Bromet Cl, Wat. WD17 . . . 97 BT38
Sch **Bromet Prim Sch**, Wat. WD19 *off Oxhey Rd* . . . 116 BX45
Bromfelde Rd, SW4 . . . 41 P10
Bromfelde Wk, SW4 . . . 41 P9
Bromfield St, N1 . . . 8 F10
Bromford Cl, Oxt. RH8 . . . 276 EG133
Bromhall Rd, Dag. RM8, RM9 . . . 168 EV65
Bromhedge, SE9 . . . 207 EM90
Bromholm Rd, SE2 . . . 188 EV76
Bromleigh Cl, Chsht EN8 . . . 89 DY28
Bromleigh Ct, SE23 *off Lapse Wd Wk* . . . 204 DV89
BROMLEY, BR1 & BR2 . . . 226 EF96
BROMLEY, E3 . . . 22 D5
Bromley, Grays RM17 . . . 192 FZ79
Coll **Bromley Adult Ed Coll**, Kentwood Cen, SE20 *off Kingsdale Rd* . . . 205 DX94
Poverest Cen, Orp. BR5 *off Poverest Rd* . . . 228 EU99
Widmore Cen, Brom. BR1 *off Nightingale La* . . . 226 EJ97
Bromley Av, Brom. BR1 . . . 206 EE94
⊖ **Bromley-by-Bow** . . . 22 D4
Bromley Cl, Harl. CM20 . . . 58 EV11
Coll **Bromley Coll of Further & Higher Ed**, Anerley, SE20 *off Hawthorn Gro* . . . 224 DW95
Beckenham Learning Cen, Beck. BR3 *off Beckenham Rd* . . . 225 DZ95
Old Town Hall, Brom. BR1 *off Tweedy Rd* . . . 226 EG96
Rookery La Campus, Brom. BR2 *off Rookery La* . . . 226 EK100
BROMLEY COMMON, Brom. BR2 . . . 227 EM101
Bromley Common, Brom. BR2 . . . 226 EJ98
Bromley Cres, Brom. BR2 . . . 226 EF97
Ruislip HA4 . . . 137 BT63
Bromley Gdns, Brom. BR2 . . . 226 EF97
Bromley Gro, Brom. BR2 . . . 225 ED96
Bromley Hall Rd, E14 . . . 22 E6
Sch **Bromley High Sch GDST**, Brom. BR1 *off Blackbrook La* . . . 227 EN98
Bromley High St, E3 . . . 22 C2
Bromley Hill, Brom. BR1 . . . 206 EE92
● **Bromley Ind Cen**, Brom. BR1 . . . 226 EJ97
Bromley La, Chis. BR7 . . . 207 EQ94
★ **Bromley Mus**, Orp. BR6 . . . 228 EV101
⇌ **Bromley North** . . . 226 EG95
⊖ **Bromley North** . . . 226 EG95
BROMLEY PARK, Brom. BR1 . . . 226 EE95
Bromley Pk, Brom. BR1 *off London Rd* . . . 226 EF95
Bromley Pl, W1 . . . 17 L6
Bromley Rd, E10 . . . 145 EB58
E17 . . . 123 EA54
N17 . . . 122 DT53
N18 . . . 122 DR48
SE6 . . . 205 EB88
Beckenham BR3 . . . 225 EB95
Chislehurst BR7 . . . 227 EP95
Downham BR1 . . . 205 EC91
Shortlands BR2 . . . 225 EC96
Sch **Bromley Rd Inf Sch**, Beck. BR3 *off Bromley Rd* . . . 225 EB95
⇌ **Bromley South** . . . 226 EG97
Bromley St, E1 . . . 21 K7
BROMPTON, SW3 . . . 28 C7
Brompton Arc, SW3 . . . 28 E5
Brompton Cl, SE20 *off Selby Rd* . . . 224 DU96
Hounslow TW4 . . . 198 BZ85
Brompton Dr, Erith DA8 . . . 189 FH80
Brompton Gro, N2 . . . 142 DE56
★ **Brompton Oratory**, SW7 . . . 28 C7
Brompton Pk Cres, SW6 . . . 39 L3
Brompton Pl, SW3 . . . 28 D6
Brompton Rd, SW1 . . . 28 D6
SW3 . . . 28 C8
SW7 . . . 28 D6
Brompton Sq, SW3 . . . 28 C6
Brompton Ter, SE18 *off Prince Imperial Rd* . . . 187 EN81
Bromwich Av, N6 . . . 142 DG61
Bromyard Av, W3 . . . 160 CS74
Bromyard Ho, SE15 . . . 44 E4
W3 . . . 160 CS74
Bromycroft Rd, Slou. SL2 . . . 153 AN69
BRONDESBURY, NW2 . . . 4 E6
⊖ **Brondesbury** . . . 4 G6
Brondesbury Ct, NW2 . . . 4 C5
Brondesbury Ms, NW6 . . . 5 J7
BRONDESBURY PARK, NW6 . . . 4 B7
⊖ **Brondesbury Park** . . . 4 E8
Brondesbury Pk, NW2 . . . 161 CV65
NW6 . . . 4 E7
Brondesbury Rd, NW6 . . . 4 G10
Brondesbury Vil, NW6 . . . 5 H10
Bronsart Rd, SW6 . . . 38 E5
Bronsdon Way, Denh. UB9 . . . 135 BF61
Bronson Rd, SW20 . . . 221 CX96
Bronte Cl, E7 *off Bective Rd* . . . 146 EG63
Erith DA8 . . . 189 FB80
Ilford IG2 . . . 147 EN57
Slough SL1 . . . 174 AS75
Tilbury RM18 . . . 193 GJ82
Bronte Gro, Dart. DA1 . . . 190 FM84
Bronte Ho, NW6 . . . 15 K2
Sch **Bronte Sch**, Grav. DA11 *off Pelham Rd* . . . 213 GG87
Bronte Vw, Grav. DA12 . . . 213 GJ88
Bronti Cl, SE17 . . . 43 K1
Bronze Age Way, Belv. DA17 . . . 189 FC76
Erith DA8 . . . 189 FC76
Bronze St, SE8 . . . 46 B4
BROOK, Guil. GU5 . . . 282 BL142
Brook Av, Dag. RM10 . . . 169 FB66
Edgware HA8 . . . 118 CP51
Wembley HA9 . . . 140 CN62
Brookbank, Enf. EN1 . . . 104 DV37
Wooburn Green HP10 . . . 132 AC60
Brookbank Av, W7 . . . 159 CD71
Brookbank Rd, SE13 . . . 185 EA83
Brook Cl, NW7 . . . 119 CY52
SW17 . . . 202 DG89
SW20 . . . 221 CV97
W3 . . . 160 CN74
Borehamwood WD6 . . . 100 CP41
Dorking RH4 . . . 269 CJ134
Epsom KT19 . . . 238 CS109
Romford RM2 . . . 127 FF53
Ruislip HA4 . . . 137 BS59
Stanwell TW19 . . . 196 BM87
Sch **Brook Comm Prim Sch**, E8 . . . 10 D3
Brook Ct, Bark. IG11 *off Spring Pl* . . . 167 EQ68
Buckhurst Hill IG9 . . . 124 EH46
Brook Cres, E4 . . . 123 EA49
N9 . . . 122 DV49
Slough SL1 . . . 153 AL72
Brookdale, N11 . . . 121 DJ49
Brookdale Av, Upmin. RM14 . . . 150 FN62
Brookdale Cl, Upmin. RM14 . . . 150 FP62
Brookdale Rd, E17 . . . 145 EA55
SE6 . . . 205 EB86
Bexley DA5 . . . 208 EY86
Brookdene Av, Wat. WD19 . . . 115 BV45
Brookdene Dr, Nthwd. HA6 . . . 115 BT52
Brookdene Rd, SE18 . . . 187 ET77
Brook Dr, SE11 . . . 30 F7
Harrow HA1 . . . 138 CC56
Radlett WD7 . . . 83 CF33
Ruislip HA4 . . . 137 BS58
Brooke Av, Har. HA2 . . . 138 CC62
Brooke Cl, Bushey WD23 . . . 116 CC45
Brooke Ct, W10 . . . 14 F1
Brookehowse Rd, SE6 . . . 205 EB90
Brook End, Saw. CM21 . . . 58 EX05
Brookend Rd, Sid. DA15 . . . 207 ES88
Brooke Rd, E5 . . . 144 DU62
E17 . . . 145 EC56
N16 . . . 144 DT62
Grays RM17 . . . 192 GA78
Brooker Rd, Wal.Abb. EN9 . . . 89 EC34
Brookers Cl, Ashtd. KT21 . . . 253 CJ117
Brooke's Ct, EC1 . . . 18 E6
Brookes Mkt, EC1 . . . 18 F6
Brooke St, EC1 . . . 18 E7
Brooke Way, Bushey WD23 . . . 116 CC45
Brook Fm Rd, Cob. KT11 . . . 252 BX115
Brookfield, N6 . . . 142 DG62
Godalming GU7 . . . 280 AU143
Thornwood CM16 . . . 92 EW25
Woking GU21 . . . 248 AV116
Coll **Brookfield Adult Learning Cen**, Uxb. UB8 *off Park Rd* . . . 156 BL65
Brookfield Av, E17 . . . 145 EC56
NW7 . . . 119 CV51
W5 . . . 159 CK70
Sutton SM1 . . . 240 DD105
🔒 **Brookfield Cen**, Chsht EN8 . . . 89 DX27
Brookfield Cl, NW7 . . . 119 CV51
Ashtead KT21 . . . 254 CL120
Hutton CM13 . . . 131 GC44
Ottershaw KT16 . . . 233 BD107
Redhill RH1 . . . 288 DG140
Brookfield Ct, Grnf. UB6 . . . 158 CC69
Harrow HA3 . . . 139 CK57
Brookfield Cres, NW7 . . . 119 CV51
Harrow HA3 . . . 140 CL57
Brookfield Gdns, Chsht EN8 . . . 89 DX27
Claygate KT10 . . . 237 CF107
Sch **Brookfield Ho Sch**, Wdf.Grn. IG8 *off Alders Av* . . . 124 EE51
Brookfield La E, Chsht EN8 . . . 89 DX27
Brookfield La W, Chsht EN8 . . . 88 DV28
Brookfield Pk, NW5 . . . 143 DH62
Brookfield Path, Wdf.Grn. IG8 . . . 124 EE51
Brookfield Pl, Cob. KT11 . . . 252 BY115
Sch **Brookfield Prim Sch**, N19 *off Chester Rd* . . . 143 DH61
Sutton SM3 *off Ridge Rd* . . . 221 CY102
🔒 **Brookfield Retail Pk**, Chsht EN8 . . . 89 DX26
Brookfield Rd, E9 . . . 11 M5
N9 . . . 122 DU48
W4 . . . 180 CR75
Wooburn Green HP10 . . . 132 AD60
Brookfields, Enf. EN3 . . . 105 DX42
Sawbridgeworth CM21 . . . 58 EX05
Brookfields Av, Mitch. CR4 . . . 222 DE99
Brook Gdns, E4 . . . 123 EB49
SW13 . . . 181 CT83
Kingston upon Thames KT2 . . . 220 CQ95
Brook Gate, W1 . . . 28 F1
Brook Grn, W6 . . . 26 D8
Chobham GU24 *off Brookleys* . . . 232 AT110
Brook Hill, Far.Grn GU5 . . . 282 BK143
Oxted RH8 . . . 275 EC130
Brookhill Cl, SE18 . . . 187 EP78
East Barnet EN4 . . . 102 DE43
Brookhill Rd, SE18 . . . 187 EP78
Barnet EN4 . . . 102 DE43
Brookhouse Dr, Woob.Grn HP10 . . . 132 AC60
Brookhouse Gdns, E4 . . . 124 EE49
Brookhurst Rd, Add. KT15 . . . 234 BH107
● **Brook Ind Est**, Hayes UB4 . . . 158 BX74
Brooking Cl, Dag. RM8 . . . 148 EW62

Brooking Rd, E7 13 P2
Brookland Cl, NW11 142 DA56
Brookland Garth, NW11 142 DB56
Brookland Hill, NW11 142 DA56
Brookland Inf & Jun Schs, NW11 off Hill Top 142 DB56
Brookland Inf Sch, Chsht EN8 off Elm Dr 89 DY28
Brookland Jun Sch, Chsht EN8 off Elm Dr 89 DY28
Brookland Ri, NW11 142 DA56
BROOKLANDS, Wey. KT13 234 BM109
Brooklands, Dart. DA1 210 FL88
Brooklands App, Rom. RM1 149 FD56
Brooklands Av, SW19 202 DB89
Sidcup DA15 207 ER89
Brooklands Cl, Cob. KT11 252 BY115
Romford RM7 off Marshalls Rd 149 FD56
Sunbury-on-Thames TW16 217 BS95
Brooklands Coll, Ashford Campus, Ashf. TW15 off Church Rd 196 BM91
Weybridge Campus, Wey. KT13 off Heath Rd 234 BM107
Brooklands Ct, New Haw KT15 234 BK110
St. Albans AL1 65 CE20
Weybridge KT13 235 BP108
Brooklands Dr, Perivale UB6 159 CJ67
Weybridge KT13 234 BM110
Brooklands Gdns, Horn. RM11 150 FJ57
Potters Bar EN6 85 CY32
● Brooklands Ind Pk, Wey. KT13 234 BL110
Brooklands La, Rom. RM7 149 FD56
Weybridge KT13 234 BM107
★ Brooklands Mus, Wey. KT13 234 BN109
Brooklands Pk, SE3 47 N10
Brooklands Pas, SW8 41 N6
Brooklands Pl, Hmptn. TW12 198 CB92
Brooklands Prim Sch, SE3 47 P10
Brooklands Rd, Rom. RM7 149 FD56
Thames Ditton KT7 219 CF102
Weybridge KT13 235 BP107
Brooklands Sch, Reig. RH2 off Wray Pk Rd 272 DB132
Brooklands Way, Red. RH1 272 DE132
Brook La, SE3 186 EH82
Albury GU5 282 BL142
Berkhamsted HP4 60 AV18
Bexley DA5 208 EX86
Bromley BR1 206 EG93
Sawbridgeworth CM21 58 EX05
Send GU23 249 BE122
● Brook La Business Cen, Brent. TW8 off Brook La N 179 CK78
Brooklane Fld, Harl. CM18 74 EV18
Brook La N, Brent. TW8 179 CK78
Brooklea Cl, NW9 118 CS53
Brookleys, Chobham GU24 232 AT110
Brooklyn Av, SE25 224 DV98
Loughton IG10 106 EL42
Brooklyn Cl, Cars. SM5 222 DE103
Woking GU22 248 AY119
Brooklyn Ct, Wok. GU22 off Brooklyn Rd 248 AY119
Brooklyn Gro, SE25 224 DV98
Brooklyn Pas, W12 26 A5
Brooklyn Rd, SE25 224 DV98
Bromley BR2 226 EK99
Woking GU22 248 AY118
Brooklyn Way, West Dr. UB7 176 BK76
Brookmans Av, Brook.Pk AL9 85 CY26
Brookmans Cl, Upmin. RM14 151 FS59
BROOKMANS PARK, Hat. AL9 85 CY26
⇌ Brookmans Park 85 CX27
Brookmans Pk Dr, Upmin. RM14 151 FS57
Brookmans Pk Prim Sch, Brook.Pk AL9 off Bradmore Way 85 CY26
● Brookmarsh Ind Est, SE10 46 C4
Brook Mead, Epsom KT19 238 CS107
Brookmead Av, Brom. BR1 227 EM99
Brookmead Cl, Orp. BR5 228 EV101
● Brookmead Ind Est, Croy. CR0 223 DJ100
Brook Meadow, N12 120 DB49
Brook Meadow Cl, Wdf.Grn. IG8 124 EE51
Brookmeadow Way, Wal.Abb. EN9 off Breach Barn Mobile Home Pk 90 EH30
Brookmead Rd, Croy. CR0 223 DJ100
Brookmeads Est, Mitch. CR4 222 DE99
Brookmead Way, Orp. BR5 228 EV100
Brook Ms, Chig. IG7 off High Rd 125 EP48
Brook Ms N, W2 15 P10
Brookmill Cl, Wat. WD19 off Brookside Rd 115 BV45
Brookmill Rd, SE8 46 B6
Brook Par, Chig. IG7 off High Rd 125 EP48
Brook Pk, Dart. DA1 210 FN89
Brook Pk Cl, N21 103 DP44
Brook Path, Loug. IG10 106 EL42
Slough SL1 153 AM73
Brook Pl, Barn. EN5 102 DA43
Brook Retail Pk, Ruis. HA4 138 BX64
Brook Ri, Chig. IG7 125 EN48
Brook Rd, N8 143 DL56
N22 143 DM55
NW2 141 CU61
Borehamwood WD6 100 CN40
Brentwood CM14 130 FT48
Buckhurst Hill IG9 124 EG47
Chilworth GU4 281 BC140
Epping CM16 92 EU33
Ilford IG2 147 ES58
Loughton IG10 106 EL43
Merstham RH1 273 DJ129
Northfleet DA11 212 GE88
Redhill RH1 288 DF135
Romford RM2 127 FF53
Sawbridgeworth CM21 58 EX06
Surbiton KT6 220 CL103
Swanley BR8 229 FD97
Thornton Heath CR7 224 DQ98
Brook Rd, Twick. TW1 199 CG86
Waltham Cross EN8 89 DZ34
Brook Rd S, Brent. TW8 179 CK79
Brooks Av, E6 25 J4
Brooksbank St, E9 11 J5
Brooksby Ms, N1 8 F6
Brooksby St, N1 8 F7
Brooksby's Wk, E9 11 J2
Brooks Cl, SE9 207 EN89
Weybridge KT13 234 BN110
Brooks Ct, Hert. SG14 53 DM08
Brookscroft, Croy. CR0 243 DY110
Brookscroft Rd, E17 123 EB53
Brooksfield, Welw.G.C. AL7 52 DB08
Brookshill, Har. HA3 117 CD50
Brookshill Av, Har. HA3 117 CD50
Brookshill Dr, Har. HA3 117 CD50
Brookshill Gate, Har.Wld HA3 117 CD50
Brookside, Ilf. IG3 off Barley La 148 EU58
Brookside, N21 103 DM44
Carshalton SM5 240 DG106
Chertsey KT16 215 BE101
Colnbrook SL3 175 BC80
East Barnet EN4 102 DE44
Harlow CM19 73 EM17
Hatfield AL10 66 CR18
Hertford SG13 54 DS09
Hoddesdon EN11 71 DZ17
Hornchurch RM11 150 FL57
Ilford IG6 125 EQ51
Jacobs Well GU4 264 AX129
Orpington BR6 227 ET101
South Mimms EN6 85 CU32
Uxbridge UB10 156 BM66
Waltham Abbey EN9 off Broomstick Hall Rd 90 EE32
Brookside Av, Ashf. TW15 196 BJ92
Wraysbury TW19 174 AY83
Brookside Cl, Barn. EN5 101 CY44
Feltham TW13 197 BU90
Kenton HA3 139 CK57
South Harrow HA2 138 BY63
Brookside Cres, Cuffley EN6 87 DL27
Worcester Park KT4 off Green La 221 CU102
Brookside Gdns, Enf. EN1 104 DV37
Brookside Inf & Jun Schs, Harold Hill RM3 off Dagnam Pk Dr 128 FL50
Brookside Prim Sch, Hayes UB4 off Perth Av 158 BW69
Brookside Rd, N9 122 DV49
N19 143 DJ61
NW11 141 CY58
Hayes UB4 158 BW73
Istead Rise DA13 213 GF94
Watford WD19 115 BV45
Brookside S, E.Barn. EN4 120 DG45
Brookside Wk, N3 119 CY54
N12 120 DA51
NW4 141 CY56
NW11 141 CY56
Brookside Way, Croy. CR0 225 DX100
Brooks La, W4 180 CN79
Brook's Ms, W1 17 J10
Brook Sq, SE18 off Barlow Dr 186 EL81
Brooks Rd, E13 13 N9
W4 180 CN78
BROOK STREET, Brwd. CM14 130 FS49
Brook St, N17 off High Rd 122 DT54
W1 17 H10
W2 16 B10
Belvedere DA17 189 FB78
Brentwood CM14 130 FS50
Erith DA8 189 FB79
Kingston upon Thames KT1 220 CL96
Windsor SL4 173 AR82
Brooksville Av, NW6 4 F9
Brooks Way, Orp. BR5 228 EW96
Brook Vale, Erith DA8 189 FB81
Brook Valley, Mid Holm. RH5 285 CH142
Brookview Rd, SW16 203 DJ92
Brookville Rd, SW6 38 G5
Brook Wk, N2 120 DD53
Edgware HA8 118 CR51
Brookway, SE3 186 EG83
Brook Way, Chig. IG7 125 EN48
Leatherhead KT22 253 CG118
Rainham RM13 169 FH71
Brookwood, Horl. RH6 off Stockfield 291 DH147
Brookwood Av, SW13 181 CT83
Brookwood Cl, Brom. BR2 226 EF98
Brookwood Rd, SW18 201 CZ88
Hounslow TW3 178 CB81
Broom Av, Orp. BR5 228 EV96
Broom Cl, Brom. BR2 226 EL100
Cheshunt EN7 88 DU27
Esher KT10 236 CB106
Hatfield AL10 67 CT21
Teddington TW11 199 CK94
Broomcroft Av, Nthlt. UB5 158 BW69
Broomcroft Cl, Wok. GU22 249 BD116
Broomcroft Dr, Wok. GU22 249 BD115
Broome Cl, Headley KT18 270 CQ126
Broome Ho, E5 10 E2
Broome Pl, Aveley RM15 171 FR74
Broome Rd, Hmptn. TW12 198 BZ94
Broomer Pl, Chsht EN8 88 DW29
Broome Way, SE5 43 L5
Broom Fm Est, Wind. SL4 172 AJ82
Broomfield, E17 145 DZ59
Guildford GU2 264 AS133
Harlow CM20 58 EV12
Park Street AL2 82 CC27
Staines TW18 196 BG93
Sunbury-on-Thames TW16 217 BU95
Broomfield Av, N13 121 DM50
Broxbourne EN10 89 DY26
Loughton IG10 107 EM44
Broomfield Cl, Guil. GU3 264 AS132
Romford RM5 127 FD52
Broomfield Ct, Wey. KT13 235 BP107
Broomfield Gate, Slou. SL2 153 AP70
Broomfield Ho Sch, Kew TW9 off Broomfield Rd 180 CM81
Broomfield La, N13 121 DM49
Broomfield Pk, Westc. RH4 284 CC137
Broomfield Pl, W13 159 CH74
Broomfield Ride, Oxshott KT22 237 CD112
Broomfield Ri, Abb.L. WD5 81 BR32
Broomfield Rd, N13 121 DL50
W13 159 CH74
Beckenham BR3 225 DY97
Bexleyheath DA6 208 FA85
New Haw KT15 234 BH111
Richmond TW9 180 CM81
Broomfield Rd, Rom. RM6 148 EX59
Sevenoaks TN13 278 FF122
Surbiton KT5 220 CM102
Swanscombe DA10 212 FY86
Teddington TW11 off Melbourne Rd 199 CJ93
Broomfields, Esher KT10 236 CC106
Broomfield Sch, N14 off Wilmer Way 121 DK50
Broomfield St, E14 22 B7
Broom Gdns, Croy. CR0 225 EA104
Broom Gro, Wat. WD17 97 BU38
Broomgrove Gdns, Edg. HA8 118 CN53
Broomgrove Rd, SW9 42 D9
Broom Hall, Oxshott KT22 237 CD114
Broomhall End, Wok. GU21 off Broomhall La 248 AY116
Broomhall La, Wok. GU21 248 AY116
Broomhall Rd, S.Croy. CR2 242 DR109
Woking GU21 248 AY116
Broom Hill, Hem.H. HP1 61 BE21
Stoke Poges SL2 154 AU66
Broomhill Ct, Wdf.Grn. IG8 off Broomhill Rd 124 EG51
Broomhill Ri, Bexh. DA6 208 FA85
Broomhill Rd, SW18 202 DA85
Dartford DA1 209 FH86
Ilford IG3 148 EU61
Orpington BR6 228 EU101
Woodford Green IG8 124 EG51
Broomhills, Sthflt DA13 off Betsham Rd 212 FY91
Welwyn Garden City AL7 52 DA08
Broomhill Wk, Wdf.Grn. IG8 124 EF52
Broom Ho, Slou. SL3 175 AZ77
Broomhouse La, SW6 39 J9
Broomhouse Rd, SW6 39 J8
Broomlands La, Oxt. RH8 276 EJ125
Broom La, Chobham GU24 232 AS109
Broomleys, St.Alb. AL4 65 CK17
Broomloan La, Sutt. SM1 222 DA103
Broom Lock, Tedd. TW11 199 CJ93
Broom Mead, Bexh. DA6 208 FA85
Broom Pk, Tedd. TW11 199 CK94
Broom Rd, Croy. CR0 225 EA104
Teddington TW11 199 CJ93
Brooms Cl, Welw.G.C. AL8 51 CX06
● Broomsleigh Business Pk, SE26 off Worsley Br Rd 205 DZ92
Broomsleigh St, NW6 5 H3
Broomstick Hall Rd, Wal.Abb. EN9 90 EE33
Broomstick La, Chesh. HP5 78 AU30
Broom Water, Tedd. TW11 199 CJ93
Broom Water W, Tedd. TW11 199 CJ92
Broom Way, Wey. KT13 235 BS105
Broomwood Cl, Bex. DA5 209 FD89
Croydon CR0 225 DX99
Broomwood Gdns, Pilg.Hat. CM15 130 FU44
Broomwood Hall Sch, SW12 off Nightingale La 202 DG87
Broomwood Rd, SW11 202 DF86
Orpington BR5 228 EV96
Broseley Gdns, Rom. RM3 128 FL49
Broseley Gro, SE26 205 DY92
Broseley Rd, Rom. RM3 128 FL49
Broster Gdns, SE25 224 DT97
Brougham Rd, E8 10 C8
W3 160 CQ72
Brougham St, SW11 40 F8
Brough Cl, SW8 42 B5
Kingston upon Thames KT2 199 CK92
Broughinge Rd, Borwd. WD6 100 CP40
Broughton Av, N3 141 CY55
Richmond TW10 199 CH90
Broughton Dr, SW9 183 DN84
Broughton Gdns, N6 143 DJ58
Broughton Rd, SW6 39 L7
W13 159 CH73
Orpington BR6 227 ER103
Otford TN14 263 FG116
Thornton Heath CR7 223 DN100
Broughton Rd App, SW6 39 L8
Broughton St, SW8 41 J8
Broughton Way, Rick. WD3 114 BG45
Brouncker Rd, W3 180 CQ75
Brow, The, Ch.St.G. HP8 112 AX48
Redhill RH1 off Spencer Way 288 DG139
Watford WD25 81 BV33
Brow Cl, Orp. BR5 off Brow Cres 228 EX101
Brow Cres, Orp. BR5 228 EW102
Browells La, Felt. TW13 197 BV89
Brownacres Towpath, Wey. KT13 217 BP102
Brown Cl, Wall. SM6 241 DK108
Browne Cl, Brwd. CM14 130 FV46
Romford RM5 127 FB50
Woking GU22 249 BB120
Brownfields, Welw.G.C. AL7 51 CZ08
Brownfields Ct, Welw.G.C. AL7 off Brownfields 52 DA08
Brownfield St, E14 22 D9
Browngraves Rd, Harling. UB3 177 BQ80
Brown Hart Gdns, W1 17 H10
Brownhill Rd, SE6 205 EB87
Browning Av, W7 159 CF72
Sutton SM1 240 DE105
Worcester Park KT4 221 CV102
Browning Cl, E17 145 EC56
W9 15 P5
Collier Row RM5 126 EZ52
Hampton TW12 198 BZ91
Welling DA16 187 ES81
Browning Ms, W1 17 J7
Browning Rd, E11 146 EF59
E12 167 EM65
Dartford DA1 190 FM84
Enfield EN2 104 DR38
Fetcham KT22 269 CD125
Browning St, SE17 31 K10
Browning Wk, Til. RM18 off Coleridge Rd 193 GJ82
Browning Way, Houns. TW5 178 BX81
Brownlea Gdns, Ilf. IG3 148 EU61
Brownlow Cl, Barn. EN4 102 DD43
Brownlow Ms, WC1 18 D5
Brownlow Rd, E7 off Woodford Rd 146 EG63
E8 10 B8
N3 120 DB52
N11 121 DL51
NW10 160 CS66
W13 159 CG74
Berkhamsted HP4 60 AW18
Borehamwood WD6 100 CN42
Croydon CR0 242 DS105
Brownlow Rd, Red. RH1 272 DE134
Brownlow St, WC1 18 D7
Brownrigg Rd, Ashf. TW15 196 BN91
Brown Rd, Grav. DA12 213 GL88
Brown's Bldgs, EC3 19 P9
Brownsea Wk, NW7 off Sanders La 119 CX51
Browns La, NW5 7 J3
Effingham KT24 268 BX127
Brownspring Dr, SE9 207 EP91
Browns Rd, E17 145 EA55
Surbiton KT5 220 CM101
Brown's Sch, Orp. BR6 off Hawstead La 246 EZ106
Browns Spring, Pott.End HP4 61 BC16
Brown St, W1 16 E8
Brownswell Rd, N2 120 DD54
Brownswood Rd, N4 143 DP62
Beaconsfield HP9 111 AK51
Broxash Rd, SW11 202 DG86
BROXBOURNE, EN10 71 DZ21
⇌ Broxbourne 71 EA20
Broxbourne Av, E18 146 EH56
Broxbournebury Ms, Brox. EN10 off White Stubbs La 70 DW21
● Broxbourne Business Cen, Chsht EN8 off Fairways 89 DX26
Broxbourne C of E Prim Sch, Brox. EN10 off Mill La 71 DZ21
Broxbourne Common, Brox. EN10 70 DU19
Broxbourne Rd, E7 146 EG62
Orpington BR6 227 ET101
Broxbourne Sch, The, Brox. EN10 off High Rd 71 DZ21
Broxburn Dr, S.Ock. RM15 171 FV73
Broxburn Par, S.Ock. RM15 off Broxburn Dr 171 FV73
Broxhill Rd, Hav.at.Bow. RM4 127 FH48
Broxholme Cl, SE25 off Whitehorse La 224 DR98
Broxholm Rd, SE27 203 DN90
Brox La, Ott. KT16 233 BD109
Brox Ms, Ott. KT16 off Brox Rd 233 BC107
Brox Rd, Ott. KT16 233 BC107
Broxted Ms, Hutt. CM13 off Bannister Dr 131 GC44
Broxted Rd, SE6 205 DZ89
Broxwood Way, NW8 6 D9
Bruce Av, Horn. RM12 150 FK61
Shepperton TW17 217 BQ100
★ Bruce Castle Mus, N17 122 DS53
Bruce Castle Rd, N17 122 DT53
Bruce Cl, W10 14 D6
Byfleet KT14 234 BK113
Slough SL1 153 AN74
Welling DA16 188 EV81
Bruce Dr, S.Croy. CR2 243 DX109
Bruce Gdns, N20 off Balfour Gro 120 DF48
⇌ Bruce Grove 122 DT54
Bruce Gro, N17 off High Rd 122 DT54
Bruce Gro, N17 122 DS53
Orpington BR6 228 EU102
Watford WD24 98 BW38
Bruce Gro Prim Sch, N17 off Sperling Rd 122 DT54
Bruce Hall Ms, SW17 202 DG91
Bruce Rd, E3 22 C3
NW10 160 CR66
SE25 224 DR98
Barnet EN5 off St. Albans Rd 101 CY41
Harrow HA3 117 CE54
Mitcham CR4 202 DG94
Bruce's Wf Rd, Grays RM17 192 GA79
Bruce Wk, Wind. SL4 173 AK82
Bruce Way, Wal.Cr. EN8 89 DX33
Bruckner St, W10 14 F3
Brudenell, Wind. SL4 173 AM83
Brudenell Rd, SW17 202 DF90
Bruffs Meadow, Nthlt. UB5 158 BY65
Bruford Ct, SE8 46 B3
Bruges Pl, NW1 7 M7
Brumana Cl, Wey. KT13 235 BP107
Brumfield Rd, Epsom KT19 238 CQ106
Brummel Cl, Bexh. DA7 189 FC83
★ Brunei Gall, WC1 17 P6
Brunel 154 AT74
Brunel Cl, SE19 204 DT93
Hounslow TW5 177 BV80
Northolt UB5 158 BZ69
Romford RM1 149 FE56
Tilbury RM18 193 GH83
★ Brunel Engine Ho, SE16 32 G4
Brunel Est, W2 15 J7
Brunel Ho, N16 off Stamford Hill 144 DT60
Brunel Ms, W10 14 D2
Brunel Pl, Sthl. UB1 158 CB72
Brunel Rd, E17 145 DY58
SE16 32 G5
W3 160 CS71
Woodford Green IG8 125 EM50
Brunel St, E16 23 L9
Brunel Uni, Runnymede Campus, Eng.Grn TW20 off Coopers Hill La 194 AW90
Uxbridge Campus, Uxb. UB8 off Kingston La 156 BK69
Brunel Wk, N15 144 DS56
Twickenham TW2 off Stephenson Rd 198 CA87
Brunel Way, Slou. SL1 154 AT74
Brune St, E1 20 A7
Brunlees Ho, SE1 off Bath Ter 31 J7
Brunner Cl, NW11 142 DB57
Brunner Ct, Ott. KT16 233 BC106
Brunner Rd, E17 145 DY57
W5 159 CK70
Bruno Pl, NW9 140 CQ61
Brunswick Av, N11 120 DG48
Upminster RM14 151 FS59
Brunswick Cl, Bexh. DA6 188 EX84
Pinner HA5 138 BY58
Thames Ditton KT7 219 CF102
Twickenham TW2 199 CD90
Walton-on-Thames KT12 218 BW103
Brunswick Ct, EC1 off Tompion St 18 G3
SE1 31 P5
SW1 off Regency St 29 P9
Barnet EN4 102 DD43
Upminster RM14 off Waycross Rd 151 FS59
Brunswick Cres, N11 120 DG48
Brunswick Gdns, W5 160 CL69
W8 27 K3
Ilford IG6 125 EQ52
Brunswick Gro, N11 120 DG48
Cobham KT11 236 BW113
● Brunswick Ind Pk, N11 121 DH49
Brunswick Ms, SW16 off Potters La 203 DK93
W1 16 F8
BRUNSWICK PARK, N11 120 DF48
Brunswick Pk, SE5 43 M6
Brunswick Pk Gdns, N11 120 DG47
Brunswick Pk Prim Sch, N14 off Osidge La 120 DG47
SE5 43 M5
Brunswick Pk Rd, N11 120 DG47
Brunswick Pl, N1 19 M3
NW1 17 H4
SE19 204 DU94
Brunswick Quay, SE16 33 K7
Brunswick Rd, E10 145 EC60
E14 off Blackwall Tunnel Northern App 22 F9
N15 144 DS57
W5 159 CK70
Bexleyheath DA6 188 EX84
Enfield EN3 105 EA38
Kingston upon Thames KT2 220 CN95
Sutton SM1 240 DB105
Brunswick Shop Cen, WC1 18 A4
Brunswick Sq, N17 122 DT51
WC1 18 B5
Brunswick St, E17 145 EC57
Brunswick Vil, SE5 43 N6
Brunswick Wk, Grav. DA12 213 GK87
Brunswick Way, N11 121 DH49
Brunton Pl, E14 21 M9
Brushfield St, E1 19 P6
Brushmakers Ct, Chesh. HP5 off Higham Rd 76 AP30
Brushrise, Wat. WD24 97 BU36
Brushwood Cl, E14 22 D6
Brushwood Dr, Chorl. WD3 95 BC42
Brushwood Jun Sch, Chesh. HP5 off Brushwood Rd 76 AS29
Brushwood Rd, Chesh. HP5 76 AR29
Brussels Rd, SW11 182 DD84
Bruton Cl, Chis. BR7 207 EM94
Bruton La, W1 29 K1
Bruton Pl, W1 29 K1
Bruton Rd, Mord. SM4 222 DC99
Bruton St, W1 29 K1
Bruton Way, W13 159 CG71
Bryan Av, NW10 161 CV66
Bryan Cl, Sun. TW16 197 BU94
Bryan Rd, SE16 33 N4
Bryan's All, SW6 39 L8
Bryanston Av, Twick. TW2 198 CB88
Bryanston Cl, Sthl. UB2 178 BZ77
Bryanstone Av, Guil. GU2 264 AU131
Bryanstone Cl, Guil. GU2 264 AT131
Bryanstone Ct, Sutt. SM1 off Oakhill Rd 240 DC105
Bryanstone Gro, Guil. GU2 264 AT130
Bryanstone Rd, N8 143 DK57
Waltham Cross EN8 89 DZ34
Bryanston Ms E, W1 16 E7
Bryanston Ms W, W1 16 E7
Bryanston Pl, W1 16 E7
Bryanston Rd, Til. RM18 193 GJ82
Bryanston Sq, W1 16 E7
Bryanston St, W1 16 E9
Bryant Av, Rom. RM3 128 FK53
Slough SL2 153 AR71
Bryant Cl, Barn. EN5 101 CZ43
Bryant Ct, E2 10 A10
W3 160 CR74
Bryant Rd, Nthlt. UB5 158 BW69
Bryant Row, Noak Hill RM3 off Long Meadow 128 FJ47
Bryant St, E15 13 H7
Bryantwood Rd, N7 8 E2
Brycedale Cres, N14 121 DK49
Bryce Rd, Dag. RM8 148 EW63
Brydale Ho, SE16 33 J8
Bryden Cl, SE26 205 DY92
Brydges Pl, WC2 30 A1
Brydges Rd, E15 13 H2
Brydon Wk, N1 8 B8
Bryer Ct, EC2 off Bridgewater St 19 J6
Bryer Pl, Wind. SL4 173 AK83
Bryett Rd, N7 143 DL62
Brymay Cl, E3 22 B1
Brympton Cl, Dor. RH4 285 CG138
Brynford Cl, Wok. GU21 248 AY115
Brynmaer Rd, SW11 40 E7
Bryn-y-Mawr Rd, Enf. EN1 104 DT42
Bryony Cl, Loug. IG10 107 EP42
Uxbridge UB8 156 BM71
Bryony Rd, W12 161 CU73
Guildford GU1 265 BB131
Bryony Way, Sun. TW16 197 BT93
BSix, Brooke Ho 6th Form Coll, E5 off Kenninghall Rd 144 DV62
Bubblestone Rd, Otford TN14 263 FH116
Buccleuch Rd, Datchet SL3 174 AU80
Buchanan Cl, N21 103 DM43
Aveley RM15 170 FQ74
Buchanan Ct, Borwd. WD6 100 CQ40
Buchanan Gdns, NW10 161 CV68
Buchan Cl, Uxb. UB8 156 BJ69
Buchan Rd, SE15 45 H10
Bucharest Rd, SW18 202 DC87
Buckbean Path, Rom. RM3 off Clematis Cl 128 FJ52
Buckden Cl, N2 off Southern Rd 142 DF56
SE12 206 EF86
Buckettsland La, Borwd. WD6 100 CR38
Buckfast Ct, W13 off Romsey Rd 159 CG73
Buckfast Rd, Mord. SM4 222 DB98
Buckfast St, E2 20 D3
Buckham Thorns Rd, West. TN16 277 EQ126
Buck Hill Wk, W2 28 B1
Buckhold Rd, SW18 202 DA86
Buckhurst Av, Cars. SM5 222 DE102
Sevenoaks TN13 279 FJ125
Buckhurst Cl, Red. RH1 272 DE132
BUCKHURST HILL, IG9 124 EH45
⊖ Buckhurst Hill 124 EK47
Buckhurst Hill Comm Prim Sch, Buck.H. IG9 off Lower Queens Rd 124 EL47
Buckhurst La, Sev. TN13 279 FJ125
Buckhurst Rd, West. TN16 261 EN121

Buckhurst St, E1 20 F5
Buckhurst Way, Buck.H. IG9 124 EK49
Buckingham Arc, WC2 30 B1
Buckingham Av, N20 120 DC45
Feltham TW14 197 BV86
Perivale UB6 159 CG67
Slough SL1 153 AN72
Thornton Heath CR7 223 DN95
Welling DA16 187 ES84
West Molesey KT8 218 CB97
Buckingham Av E, Slou. SL1 153 AQ72
Buckingham Chambers, SW1
off Greencoat Pl 29 M8
Buckingham Cl, W5 159 CJ71
Enfield EN1 104 DS40
Guildford GU1 265 AZ133
Hampton TW12 198 BZ92
Hornchurch RM11 150 FK58
Petts Wood BR5 227 ES101
Buckingham Coll Prep Sch,
Pnr. HA5 *off Rayners La* 138 BZ59
Buckingham Coll Sch, Har.
HA1 *off Hindes Rd* 139 CE57
Buckingham Ct, NW4 141 CU55
Loughton IG10
off Rectory La 107 EN40
Buckingham Dr, Chis. BR7 207 EP92
Buckingham Gdns, Edg. HA8 118 CM52
Slough SL1 174 AT75
Thornton Heath CR7 223 DN96
West Molesey KT8 218 CB96
Buckingham Gate, SW1 29 L5
London Gatwick Airport RH6 291 DJ152
Buckingham Gro, Uxb. UB10 156 BN68
Buckingham La, SE23 205 DY87
Buckingham Lo, N10 143 DJ56
Hoddesdon EN11
off Taverners Way 71 EA17
Buckingham Ms, N1 9 P5
NW10 161 CT68
SW1 29 L6
★ **Buckingham Palace**, SW1 29 K5
Buckingham Palace Rd, SW1 29 J9
Buckingham Pl, SW1 29 L6
Buckingham Prim Sch, Hmptn.
TW12 *off Buckingham Rd* 198 BZ92
Buckingham Rd, E10 145 EB62
E11 146 EJ57
E15 13 L2
E18 124 EF53
N1 9 N5
N22 121 DL53
NW10 161 CT68
Borehamwood WD6 100 CR42
Edgware HA8 118 CM52
Gravesend DA11
off Dover Rd 212 GD87
Hampton TW12 198 BZ91
Harrow HA1 139 CD57
Ilford IG1 147 ER61
Kingston upon Thames KT1 220 CM98
Mitcham CR4 223 DL99
Richmond TW10 199 CK89
Watford WD24 98 BW37
Buckinghamshire Chilterns Uni Coll, Chalfont Campus,
Ch.St.G. HP8
off Gorelands La 113 BA47
Buckingham St, WC2 30 B1
Buckingham Way, Wall. SM6 241 DJ109
BUCKLAND, Bet. RH3 271 CU133
Buckland Av, Slou. SL3 174 AV77
Buckland Cl, NW7 119 CU49
Buckland Ct Gdns, Bet. RH3 271 CU133
Buckland Cres, NW3 6 A6
Windsor SL4 173 AM81
Buckland Gate, Wexham SL3 154 AV68
Buckland La, Bet. RH3 271 CU130
Tadworth KT20 271 CT129
Buckland Prim Sch, Laleham
TW18 *off Berryscroft Rd* 196 BJ94
Buckland Ri, Pnr. HA5 116 BW53
Buckland Rd, E10 145 EC61
Chessington KT9 238 CM106
Lower Kingswood KT20 271 CZ128
Orpington BR6 245 ES105
Reigate RH2 271 CX133
Sutton SM2 239 CW110
Bucklands, The, Rick. WD3 114 BG45
Bucklands Rd, Tedd. TW11 199 CJ93
Buckland St, N1 19 M1
Buckland Wk, W3 160 CQ74
Morden SM4 222 DC98
Buckland Way, Wor.Pk. KT4 221 CW102
Buck La, NW9 140 CR57
Bucklebury, NW1 17 L4
Bucklebury Cl, Holy. SL6 172 AC78
Buckleigh Av, SW20 221 CY97
Buckleigh Rd, SW16 203 DK93
Buckleigh Way, SE19 224 DT95
Buckler Ct, N7 *off Eden Gro* 8 D3
Buckler Gdns, SE9
off Southold Ri 207 EM90
Bucklers All, SW6 39 H3
Bucklersbury, EC4 19 L9
Bucklersbury Pas, EC4 19 L9
Bucklers Cl, Brox. EN10 71 DZ22
Bucklers Ct, Warley CM14 130 FW50
Bucklers Way, Cars. SM5 222 DF104
Buckles Ct, Belv. DA17
off Fendyke Rd 188 EX76
Buckles La, S.Ock. RM15 171 FW71
Buckle St, E1 20 B8
Buckles Way, Bans. SM7 255 CY116
Buckley Cl, SE23 204 DV87
Dartford DA1 189 FF82
Buckley Rd, NW6 5 H7
Buckley St, SE1 30 E3
Buckmaster Cl, SW9 42 E10
Buckmaster Rd, SW11 182 DE84
Bucknalls Cl, Wat. WD25 82 BY32
Bucknalls Dr, Brick.Wd AL2 82 BZ31
Bucknalls La, Wat. WD25 82 BX32
Bucknall St, WC2 17 P8
Bucknall Way, Beck. BR3 225 EB98
Bucknell Cl, SW2 183 DM84
Buckner Rd, SW2 183 DM84
Bucknills Cl, Epsom KT18 238 CP114
Buckrell Rd, E4 123 ED47
Bucks All, Hert. SG13 69 DK19
Bucks Av, Wat. WD19 116 BY45
Bucks Cl, W.Byf. KT14 234 BH114
Bucks Cross Rd, Nthflt DA11 213 GF90
Orpington BR6 246 EY106
BUCKS HILL, Kings L. WD4 80 BK34
Bucks Hill, Kings L. WD4 80 BK34
Buckstone Cl, SE23 204 DW86
Buckstone Rd, N18 122 DU51
Buck St, NW1 7 K7
Buckters Rents, SE16 33 L3
Buckthorne Ho, Chig. IG7 126 EV49
Buckthorne Rd, SE4 205 DY86
Buckton Rd, Borwd. WD6 100 CM38
Buck Wk, E17 *off Wood St* 145 ED56
Buckwell Pl, Sev. TN13 279 FJ129
Budd Cl, N12 120 DB49
Buddcroft, Welw.G.C. AL7 52 DB08
Buddings Circle, Wem. HA9 140 CQ62
Budd's All, Twick. TW1 199 CJ85
Budebury Rd, Stai. TW18 196 BG92
Bude Cl, E17 145 DZ57
Budge La, Mitch. CR4 222 DF101
Budgen Dr, Red. RH1 272 DG131
Budge Row, EC4 19 L10
Budge's Wk, W2 27 N2
Budgin's Hill, Orp. BR6 246 EW112
Budleigh Cres, Well. DA16 188 EW81
Budoch Ct, Ilf. IG3 148 EU61
Budoch Dr, Ilf. IG3 148 EU61
Buer Rd, SW6 38 F9
Buff Av, Bans. SM7 240 DB114
Buffers La, Lthd. KT22
off Kingston Rd 253 CG119
Buffins, Tap. SL6 152 AE69
Bug Hill, Wold. CR3 259 DX120
Bugsby's Way, SE7 35 P9
SE10 35 L8
Buick Ho, Kings.T. KT2 220 CN96
Building 22, SE18
off Carriage St 37 P7
Building 36, SE18
off Marlborough Rd 187 EQ76
Building 45, SE18
off Hopton Rd 37 P6
Building 47, SE18
off Marlborough Rd 187 EQ76
Building 48, SE18
off Marlborough Rd 187 EQ76
Building 49, SE18
off Argyll Rd 187 EQ76
Building 50, SE18
off Argyll Rd 187 EQ76
Building Crafts Coll, E15 12 G7
Bulbourne Cl, Berk. HP4 60 AT17
Hemel Hempstead HP1 62 BG21
Bulganak Rd, Th.Hth. CR7 224 DQ98
Bulinga St, SW1 29 P9
Bulkeley Av, Wind. SL4 173 AP82
Bulkeley Cl, Eng.Grn TW20 194 AW91
Bullace Cl, Hem.H. HP1 62 BG19
Bullace La, Dart. DA1 210 FL86
Bullace Row, SE5 43 K6
Bull All, Well. DA16
off Welling High St 188 EV83
Bullards Pl, E2 21 J2
Bullbanks Rd, Belv. DA17 189 FC77
Bullbeggars La, Berk. HP4 61 AZ20
Godstone RH9 274 DW132
Woking GU21 248 AV116
Bull Cl, Grays RM16 192 FZ75
Bull Dog, The, Ashf. TW15 196 BL89
Bullen Ho, E1 20 F5
BULLEN'S GREEN, St.Alb. AL4 66 CS22
Bullens Grn La, Coln.Hth AL4 66 CS23
Bullen St, SW11 40 C8
Buller Cl, SE15 44 C5
Buller Rd, N17 122 DU54
N22 121 DN54
NW10 14 D3
Barking IG11 167 ES66
Thornton Heath CR7 224 DR96
Bullers Cl, Sid. DA14 208 EY92
Bullers Wd Dr, Chis. BR7 206 EL94
Bullers Wd Sch, Chis. BR7
off St. Nicolas La 226 EL95
Bullescroft Rd, Edg. HA8 118 CN48
Bullfinch Cl, Horl. RH6 290 DE147
Sevenoaks TN13 278 FD122
Bullfinch Dene, Sev. TN13 278 FD122
Bullfinch La, Sev. TN13 278 FD122
Bullfinch Rd, S.Croy. CR2 243 DX110
Bullhead Rd, Borwd. WD6 100 CQ41
Bull Hill, Hort.Kir. DA4 230 FQ98
Leatherhead KT22 253 CG121
Bullied Way, SW1 29 K9
Bull Inn Ct, WC2 30 B1
Bullivant Cl, Green. DA9 211 FU85
Bullivant St, E14 22 E9
Bull La, N18 122 DS50
Chislehurst BR7 207 ER94
Dagenham RM10 149 FB62
Gerrards Cross SL9 134 AX55
Sutton Green GU4 265 AZ126
Bullocks La, Hert. SG13 54 DQ11
Bull Plain, Hert. SG14 54 DR09
Bull Rd, E15 13 L10
Bullrush Cl, Cars. SM5 222 DE103
Croydon CR0 224 DS100
Hatfield AL10 67 CV19
Bullrush Gro, Uxb. UB8 156 BJ70
Bull's All, SW14 180 CR82
● **Bullsbridge Ind Est**,
Sthl. UB2 177 BV77
Bulls Br Rd, Sthl. UB2 177 BV76
Bullsbrook Rd, Hayes UB4 158 BW74
BULLS CROSS, Wal.Cr. EN7 104 DT35
Bulls Cross, Enf. EN2 104 DU37
Bulls Cross Ride, Wal.Cr. EN7 104 DU35
Bulls Gdns, SW3 28 D8
Bull's Head Pas, EC3 19 N9
Bullsland Gdns, Chorl. WD3 95 BB44
Bullsland La, Chorl. WD3 95 BB44
Gerrards Cross SL9 113 BB45
Bulls La, Hat. AL9 67 CZ24
BULLSMOOR, Enf. EN1 104 DV37
Bullsmoor Cl, Wal.Cr. EN8 104 DW35
Bullsmoor Gdns, Wal.Cr. EN8 104 DV35
Bullsmoor La, Enf. EN1, EN3 104 DW35
Waltham Cross EN7 104 DU35
Bullsmoor Ride, Wal.Cr. EN8 104 DW35
Bullsmoor Way, Wal.Cr. EN8 104 DV35
Bull Stag Grn, Hat. AL9 67 CW15
Bullwell Cres, Chsht EN8 89 DY29
Bull Yd, SE15 44 D7
Gravesend DA12
off High St 213 GH86
Bulmer Gdns, Har. HA3 139 CK59
Bulmer Ms, W11 27 J2
Bulmer Pl, W11 27 J2
Bulmer Wk, Rain. RM13 170 FJ68
Bulow Est, SW6 39 M7
Bulstrode Av, Houns. TW3 178 BZ82
Bulstrode Cl, Chipper. WD4 79 BE29
Bulstrode Ct, Ger.Cr. SL9 134 AX58
Bulstrode Gdns, Houns. TW3 178 BZ83
Bulstrode La, Chipper. WD4 78 BE29
Felden HP3 80 BG27
Bulstrode Pl, W1 17 H7
Bulstrode Pl, Slou. SL1 174 AT76
Bulstrode Rd, Houns. TW3 178 CA83
Bulstrode St, W1 17 H8
Bulstrode Way, Ger.Cr. SL9 134 AX57
Bulwer Ct Rd, E11 145 ED60
Bulwer Gdns, Barn. EN5 102 DC42
Bulwer Rd, E11 145 ED59
N18 122 DS49
Barnet EN5 102 DB42
Bulwer St, W12 26 B3
BUMBLE'S GREEN, Wal.Abb.
EN9 72 EG24
Bumbles Grn La, Naze.Gate
EN9 90 EH25
Bunbury Way, Epsom KT17 255 CV116
Bunby Rd, Stoke P. SL2 154 AT66
BUNCE COMMON, Reig. RH2 286 CR141
Bunce Common Rd, Leigh
RH2 286 CR141
Bunce Dr, Cat. CR3 258 DR123
Buncefield La, Hem.H. HP2 63 BR20
● **Buncefield Terminal**,
Hem.H. HP2 63 BR18
Bunces Cl, Eton Wick SL4 173 AP78
Bunces La, Wdf.Grn. IG8 124 EF52
Bundys Way, Stai. TW18 195 BF93
Bungalow Rd, SE25 224 DS98
Woking GU23 251 BQ124
Bungalows, The, SW16 203 DH94
Wallington SM6 241 DH106
Bunhill Row, EC1 19 L4
Bunhouse Pl, SW1 28 G10
Bunkers Hill, NW11 142 DC59
Belvedere DA17 188 FA77
Sidcup DA14 208 EZ90
Bunkers La, Hem.H. HP3 80 BN25
Bunning Way, N7 8 B6
Bunnsfield, Welw.G.C. AL7 52 DC08
Bunns La, NW7 119 CT51
Bunn's La, Chesh. HP5 78 AU34
Bunsen St, E3 11 L10
Bunten Meade, Slou. SL1 153 AP74
Buntingbridge Rd, Ilf. IG2 147 ER57
Bunting Cl, N9
off Dunnock Cl 123 DX46
Mitcham CR4 222 DF99
Bunton St, SE18 37 M7
Bunyan Ct, EC2
off The Barbican 19 J6
Bunyan Rd, E17 145 DY55
Bunyard Dr, Wok. GU21 233 BC114
Bunyons Cl, Gt Warley CM13 129 FW51
Buonaparte Ms, SW1 29 N10
Burbage Cl, SE1 31 L7
Cheshunt EN8 89 DY31
Hayes UB3 157 BR72
Burbage Prim Sch, N1 9 N10
Burbage Rd, SE21 204 DR86
SE24 204 DQ86
Burberry Cl, N.Mal. KT3 220 CS96
Burbidge Rd, Shep. TW17 216 BN98
Burbridge Way, N17 122 DT54
Burcham St, E14 22 D8
Burcharbro Rd, SE2 188 EX79
Burchell Ct, Bushey WD23
off Catsey La 116 CC45
Burchell Rd, E10 145 EB60
SE15 44 F7
Burcher Gale Gro, SE15 43 P4
Burchets Hollow, Peasl. GU5 283 BR144
Burchetts Way, Shep. TW17 217 BP100
Burchett Way, Rom. RM6 148 EZ58
Burch Rd, Nthflt DA11 213 GF86
Burchwall Cl, Rom. RM5 127 FC52
Burcote, Wey. KT13 235 BR107
Burcote Rd, SW18 202 DD88
Burcott Gdns, Add. KT15 234 BJ107
Burcott Rd, Pur. CR8 241 DN114
Burden Cl, Brent. TW8 179 CJ78
Burdenshot Hill, Worp. GU3 264 AU125
Burdenshott Av, Rich. TW10 180 CP84
Burdenshott Rd, Wok. GU22 264 AU125
Worplesdon GU3 264 AU125
Burden Way, E11 146 EH61
Guildford GU2 264 AV129
Burder Cl, N1 9 P4
Burder Rd, N1 9 P4
Burdett Av, SW20 221 CU95
Burdett Cl, W7
off Cherington Rd 159 CF74
Sidcup DA14 208 EY92
Burdett Coutts C of E Prim Sch, SW1 29 N7
Burdett Ms, NW3 6 B4
W2 15 L8
Burdett Rd, E3 21 M4
E14 21 M4
Croydon CR0 224 DR100
Richmond TW9 180 CM82
Burdetts Rd, Dag. RM9 168 EZ67
Burdett St, SE1 30 E6
Burdock Cl, Croy. CR0 225 DX102
Burdock Rd, N17 144 DU55
Burdon La, Sutt. SM2 239 CY108
Burdon Pk, Sutt. SM2 239 CZ109
Burfield Cl, SW17 202 DD91
Hatfield AL10 67 CU16
Burfield Dr, Warl. CR6 258 DW119
Burfield Rd, Chorl. WD3 95 BB43
Old Windsor SL4 194 AU86
Burford Cl, Dag. RM8 148 EW62
Ilford IG6 147 EQ56
Uxbridge UB10 136 BL63
Burford Gdns, N13 121 DM48
Hoddesdon EN11 71 EB16
Slough SL1
off Buttermere Av 152 AJ71
Burford La, Epsom KT17 239 CW111
Burford Ms, Hodd. EN11
off Burford St 71 EA16
Burford Pl, Hodd. EN11 71 EA16
Burford Rd, E6 24 G2
E15 12 G7
SE6 205 DZ89
Brentford TW8 180 CL78
Bromley BR1 226 EL98
Sutton SM1 222 DA103
Worcester Park KT4 221 CT101
Burford St, Hodd. EN11 71 EA17
Burford Wk, SW6 39 M5
Burford Way, New Adgtn CR0 243 EC107
Burford Wf Apts, E15 12 G8
Burgage La, Ware SG12 55 DX06
Burgate Cl, Dart. DA1 189 FF83
Burges Cl, Horn. RM11 150 FM58
Burges Ct, E6 167 EN66
Burges Gro, SW13 181 CV80
Burges Rd, E6 166 EL66
Burgess Av, NW9 140 CR58
● **Burgess Business Pk**, SE5 43 M4
Burgess Cl, Chsht EN7 88 DQ25
Feltham TW13 198 BY91
Burgess Ct, Borwd. WD6
off Belford Rd 100 CM38
Burgess Hill, NW2 142 DA63
Burgess Ms, SW19 202 DB93
Burgess Rd, E15 13 J1
Sutton SM1 240 DB105
Burgess St, E14 22 A7
Burgess Wd Gro, Beac. HP9 110 AH53
Burgess Wd Rd, Beac. HP9 110 AH53
Burgess Wd Rd S, Beac. HP9 132 AH55
Burge St, SE1 31 M7
Burges Way, Stai. TW18 196 BG92
Burgett Rd, Slou. SL1 173 AP76
Burghfield, Epsom KT17 255 CT115
Burghfield Rd, Istead Rise
DA13 213 GF94
BURGH HEATH, Tad. KT20 255 CX119
Burgh Heath Rd, Epsom KT17 238 CS114
★ **Burgh Ho** (Hampstead Mus),
NW3 *off New End Sq* 142 DD63
Burghill Rd, SE26 205 DY91
Burghley Av, Borwd. WD6 100 CQ43
New Malden KT3 220 CR95
Burghley Hall Cl, SW19 201 CY87
Burghley Ho, SW19 201 CY90
Burghley Pl, Mitch. CR4 222 DF99
Burghley Rd, E11 146 EE60
N8 143 DN55
NW5 7 K2
SW19 201 CX91
Chafford Hundred RM16 191 FW76
Burghley Twr, W3 161 CT73
Burgh Mt, Bans. SM7 255 CZ115
Burgh St, N1 9 H10
Burgh Wd, Bans. SM7 255 CY115
Burgon St, EC4 19 H9
Burgos Cl, Croy. CR0 241 DN107
Burgos Gro, SE10 46 C6
Burgoyne Hatch, Harl. CM20
off Momples Rd 58 EU14
Burgoyne Rd, N4 143 DP58
SE25 224 DT98
SW9 42 C10
Sunbury-on-Thames TW16 197 BT93
Burgundy Cft, Welw.G.C. AL7 51 CZ11
Burgundy Ho, Enf. EN2
off Bedale Rd 104 DQ38
Burham Cl, SE20 *off Maple Rd* 204 DW94
Burhill, Hersham KT12 235 BU109
Burhill Comm Inf Sch, Hersham
KT12 *off Pleasant Pl* 236 BX107
Burhill Gro, Pnr. HA5 116 BY54
Burhill Rd, Hersham KT12 236 BW107
Burke Cl, SW15 180 CS84
Burke Ho, SW11
off Maysoule Rd 182 DD84
Burkes Cl, Beac. HP9 132 AH55
Burkes Cres, Beac. HP9 111 AK53
Burkes Par, Beac. HP9
off Station Rd 111 AK52
Burkes Rd, Beac. HP9 110 AJ54
Burke St, E16 23 M7
Burket Cl, Sthl. UB2
off Kingsbridge Rd 178 BZ77
Burland Rd, SW11 202 DF85
Brentwood CM15 130 FX46
Romford RM5 127 FC51
Burlea Cl, Hersham KT12 235 BV106
Burleigh Av, Sid. DA15 207 ET85
Wallington SM6 222 DG104
Burleigh Cl, Add. KT15 234 BH106
Romford RM7 149 FB56
Burleigh Gdns, N14 121 DJ46
Ashford TW15 197 BQ92
Woking GU21 249 AZ116
Burleigh Ho, W10 14 D6
Burleigh Mead, Hat. AL9 67 CW16
Burleigh Pk, Cob. KT11 236 BY112
Burleigh Pl, SW15 201 CX85
Burleigh Prim Sch, Chsht
EN8 *off Blindman's La* 89 DX29
Burleigh Rd, Add. KT15 234 BH105
Cheshunt EN8 89 DY32
Enfield EN1 104 DS42
Hemel Hempstead HP2 63 BQ21
Hertford SG13 54 DU08
St. Albans AL1 65 CH20
Sutton SM3 221 CY102
Uxbridge UB10 157 BP67
Burleigh St, WC2 18 C10
Burleigh Wk, SE6 205 EC88
Burleigh Way, Cuffley EN6 87 DL30
Enfield EN2 *off Church St* 104 DR41
Burley Cl, E4 123 EA50
SW16 223 DK96
Burley Hill, Harl. CM17 74 EX16
Burley Orchard, Cher. KT16 216 BG100
Burley Rd, E16 24 C7
Burlingham Cl, Guil. GU4
off Gilliat Dr 265 BD132
Burlings La, Knock. TN14 261 ET118
Burlington Arc, W1 29 L1
Burlington Av, Rich. TW9 180 CN81
Romford RM7 149 FB58
Slough SL1 174 AS75
Burlington Cl, E6 25 H8
W9 15 H5
Feltham TW14 197 BR87
Orpington BR6 227 EP103
Pinner HA5 137 BV55
Burlington Danes Acad,
W12 *off Wood La* 161 CV72
Burlington Gdns, W1 29 L1
W3 160 CQ74
W4 180 CQ78
Romford RM6 148 EY59
Burlington Inf & Nurs Sch,
N.Mal. KT3
off Burlington Rd 221 CT98
Burlington Jun Sch, N.Mal.
KT3 *off Burlington Rd* 221 CT98
Burlington La, W4 180 CS80
Burlington Ms, SW15 201 CZ85
W3 160 CQ74
Burlington Pl, SW6 38 F9
Reigate RH2 272 DA134
Woodford Green IG8 124 EG48
Burlington Ri, E.Barn. EN4 120 DE46
Burlington Rd, N10
off Tetherdown 142 DG55
N17 122 DU53
SW6 38 F8
W4 180 CQ78
Burnham SL1 152 AH70
Enfield EN2 104 DR39
Isleworth TW7 179 CD81
Burlington Rd, N.Mal. KT3 221 CU98
Slough SL1 174 AS75
Thornton Heath CR7 224 DQ96
Burman Cl, Dart. DA2 210 FQ87
Burma Rd, N16 144 DR63
Longcross KT16 214 AT104
Burmester Rd, SW17 202 DC90
Burnaby Cres, W4 180 CP79
Burnaby Gdns, W4 180 CQ79
Burnaby Rd, Nthflt DA11 212 GE87
Burnaby St, SW10 39 N5
Burnbrae Cl, N12 120 DB51
Burnbury Rd, SW12 203 DJ88
Burn Cl, Add. KT15 234 BK105
Oxshott KT22 252 CC115
Burncroft Av, Enf. EN3 104 DW40
Burndell Way, Hayes UB4 158 BX71
Burne Jones Ho, W14 26 G9
Burnell Av, Rich. TW10 199 CJ92
Welling DA16 188 EU82
Burnell Gdns, Stan. HA7 117 CK53
Burnell Rd, Sutt. SM1 240 DB105
Burnell Wk, SE1 32 B10
Great Warley CM13 129 FW51
Burnels Av, E6 25 L3
Burness Cl, N7 8 C4
Uxbridge UB8 156 BK68
Burne St, NW1 16 C6
Burnet Av, Guil. GU1 265 BB131
Burnet Cl, Hem.H. HP3 62 BL21
Burnet Gro, Epsom KT19 238 CQ113
Burnett Cl, E9 11 H3
Burnett Ho, SE13 46 F9
Burnett Pk, Harl. CM19 73 EP20
Burnett Rd, Erith DA8 190 FK79
Ilford IG6 125 EP52
Burnett Sq, Hert. SG14 53 DM08
Burnetts Rd, Wind. SL4 173 AL81
Burney Av, Surb. KT5 220 CM99
Burney Cl, Fetch. KT22 268 CC125
Burney Dr, Loug. IG10 107 EP40
Burney Ho, Lthd. KT22
off Highbury Dr 253 CG121
Burney Rd, Westh. RH5 269 CG131
Burney St, SE10 46 F4
Burnfoot Av, SW6 38 F7
Burnfoot Ct, SE22 204 DV88
BURNHAM, Slou. SL1 152 AJ68
⇌ **Burnham** 153 AK72
Burnham, NW3 6 C6
Burnham Av, Beac. HP9 133 AN55
Uxbridge UB10 137 BQ63
Burnham Cl, NW7 119 CU52
SE1 32 B9
Enfield EN1 104 DS38
Wealdstone HA3 139 CG56
Windsor SL4 173 AK82
Burnham Ct, NW4 141 CW56
Burnham Cres, E11 146 EJ56
Dartford DA1 190 FJ84
Burnham Dr, Reig. RH2 272 DA133
Worcester Park KT4 221 CX103
Burnham Gdns, Croy. CR0 224 DT101
Hayes UB3 177 BR76
Hounslow TW4 177 BV81
Burnham Gram Sch, Burn.
SL1 *off Hogfair La* 153 AK70
Burnham Hts, Slou. SL1
off Goldsworthy Way 152 AJ72
Burnham La, Slou. SL1 153 AL72
Burnham Rd, E4 123 DZ50
Beaconsfield HP9 133 AL58
Dagenham RM9 168 EV66
Dartford DA1 190 FJ84
Morden SM4 222 DB99
Romford RM7 149 FD55
St. Albans AL1 65 CG20
Sidcup DA14 208 EY89
Burnhams Gro, Epsom KT19 238 CP111
Burnhams Rd, Bkhm KT23 252 BY124
Burnham St, E2 20 G2
Kingston upon Thames KT2 220 CN95
Burnham Upr Sch, Burn.
SL1 *off Opendale Rd* 152 AH71
Burnham Wk, Slou. SL2 133 AN64
Burnham Way, SE26 205 DZ92
W13 179 CH77
Burnhill Cl, SE15 44 F4
Burnhill Rd, Beck. BR3 225 EA96
Burnley Cl, Wat. WD19 116 BW50
Burnley Rd, NW10 141 CU64
SW9 42 C8
Grays RM20 191 FT81
Burnsall St, SW3 28 D10
Burns Av, Chad.Hth RM6 148 EW59
Feltham TW14 197 BU86
Sidcup DA15 208 EV86
Southall UB1 158 CA73
Burns Cl, E17 145 EC56
SW19 202 DD93
Carshalton SM5 240 DG109
Erith DA8 189 FF81
Hayes UB4 157 BT71
Welling DA16 187 ET81
Burns Dr, Bans. SM7 239 CY114
Burnside, Ashtd. KT21 254 CM118
Hertford SG14 53 DN10
Hoddesdon EN11 71 DZ17
St. Albans AL1 65 CH22
Sawbridgeworth CM21 58 EX05
Burnside Av, E4 123 DZ51
Burnside Cl, SE16 33 K2
Barnet EN5 102 DA41
Hatfield AL10
off Homestead Rd 67 CU15
Twickenham TW1 199 CG86
Burnside Cres, Wem. HA0 159 CK67
Burnside Rd, Dag. RM8 148 EW61
Burnside Ter, Harl. CM17 58 EZ12
Burns Pl, Til. RM18 193 GH81
Burns Rd, NW10 161 CT67
SW11 40 E8
W13 179 CH75
Wembley HA0 159 CK68
Burns Ter, Esher KT10
off Farm Rd 218 CB103
Burns Way, Houns. TW5 178 BX82
Hutton CM13 131 GD45
Burnt Ash Hts, Brom. BR1 206 EH92
Burnt Ash Hill, SE12 206 EF86
Burnt Ash La, Brom. BR1 206 EG93

Burnt Ash Prim Sch, Brom. BR1 off Rangefield Rd 206 EG92
Burnt Ash Rd, SE12 206 EF85
Burnt Common Cl, Ripley GU23 265 BF125
Burnt Common La, Ripley GU23 266 BG125
Burnt Fm Ride, Enf. EN2 87 DP34
  Waltham Cross EN7 87 DP31
Burnt Ho La, Hawley DA2 210 FL91
Burnthwaite Rd, SW6 39 H5
Burnt Mill, Harl. CM20 57 EQ13
Burnt Mill Cl, Harl. CM20 off Burnt Mill La 57 EQ12
● Burnt Mill Ind Est, Harl. CM20 57 EQ12
Burnt Mill La, Harl. CM20 57 EQ12
Burnt Mill Rbt, Harl. CM20 57 ER12
Burnt Mill Sch, Harl. CM20 off First Av 57 ES13
BURNT OAK, Edg. HA8 118 CQ52
⊖ Burnt Oak 118 CQ53
Burnt Oak Bdy, Edg. HA8 118 CN52
Burnt Oak Flds, Edg. HA8 118 CQ53
Burnt Oak Jun Sch, Sid. DA15 off Burnt Oak La 208 EU88
Burnt Oak La, Sid. DA15 208 EU86
Burntwood, Brwd. CM14 130 FW48
Burntwood Av, Horn. RM11 150 FK58
Burntwood Cl, SW18 202 DD88
  Caterham CR3 258 DU121
Burntwood Gra Rd, SW18 202 DD88
Burntwood Gro, Sev. TN13 279 FH127
Burntwood La, SW17 202 DE89
  Caterham CR3 258 DU121
Burntwood Rd, Sev. TN13 279 FH128
Burntwood Sch, SW17 off Burntwood La 202 DD89
Burntwood Vw, SE19 off Bowley La 204 DT92
Burn Wk, Burn. SL1 152 AH70
Burnway, Horn. RM11 150 FL59
Buross St, E1 20 F9
BURPHAM, Guil. GU1 265 BB130
Burpham, Guil. GU4 265 BC129
Burpham Cl, Hayes UB4 158 BX71
★ Burpham Court Fm Pk, Guil. GU4 265 AZ128
Burpham La, Guil. GU4 265 BA129
Burpham Prim Sch, Burpham GU4 off Burpham La 265 BA130
Burrage Gro, SE18 187 EQ77
Burrage Pl, SE18 187 EP78
Burrage Rd, SE18 187 EQ79
  Redhill RH1 272 DG132
Burrard Rd, E16 24 A8
  NW6 5 J2
Burr Cl, E1 32 C2
  Bexleyheath DA7 188 EZ83
  London Colney AL2 off Waterside 84 CL27
Burrell, The, Westc. RH4 284 CC137
Burrell Cl, Croy. CR0 225 DY100
  Edgware HA8 118 CP47
Burrell Row, Beck. BR3 off High St 225 EA96
Burrell St, SE1 30 G2
Burrells Wf Sq, E14 34 C10
Burrell Twrs, E10 145 EA59
Burrfield Dr, Orp. BR5 228 EX99
Burr Hill La, Chobham GU24 232 AS109
Burritt Rd, Kings.T. KT1 220 CN96
Burroughs, The, NW4 141 CV57
Burroughs Gdns, NW4 141 CV56
Burroughs Par, NW4 off The Burroughs 141 CV56
Burroway Rd, Slou. SL3 175 BB76
Burrow Cl, Chig. IG7 off Burrow Rd 125 ET50
Burrowfield, Welw.G.C. AL7 51 CX11
Burrow Grn, Chig. IG7 125 ET50
BURROWHILL, Wok. GU24 232 AS108
Burrow Rd, SE22 184 DS84
  Chigwell IG7 125 ET50
Burrows Chase, Wal.Abb. EN9 105 ED36
Burrows Cl, Bkhm KT23 252 BZ124
  Guildford GU2 264 AT133
  Penn HP10 110 AC45
Burrows Cross, Shere GU5 283 BQ141
Burrows La, Goms. GU5 283 BQ140
Burrows Ms, SE1 30 G4
Burrows Rd, NW10 14 A2
Burrow Wk, SE21 204 DQ87
Burr Rd, SW18 202 DA87
Bursdon Cl, Sid. DA15 207 ET89
Burses Way, Hutt. CM13 131 GB45
Bursland Rd, Enf. EN3 105 DX42
Burslem Av, Ilf. IG6 126 EU51
Burslem St, E1 20 D9
Burstead Cl, Cob. KT11 236 BX113
Bursted Wd Prim Sch, Bexh. DA7 off Swanbridge Rd 189 FB82
Burstock Rd, SW15 181 CY84
Burston Dr, Park St AL2 82 CC28
Burston Rd, SW15 201 CX85
Burston Vil, SW15 off St. John's Av 201 CX85
BURSTOW, Horl. RH6 291 DN152
● Burstow Business Cen, Horl. RH6 291 DP146
Burstow Prim Sch, Smallfield RH6 off Wheelers La 291 DP148
Burstow Rd, SW20 221 CY95
Burtenshaw Rd, T.Ditt. KT7 219 CG101
Burtley Cl, N4 144 DQ60
Burton Av, Wat. WD18 97 BU42
Burton Cl, Chess. KT9 237 CK108
  Horley RH6 290 DG149
  Thornton Heath CR7 224 DR97
Burton Ct, SW3 off Franklin's Row 28 F10
Burton Dr, Enf. EN3 105 EA37
Burton Gdns, Houns. TW5 178 BZ81
Burton Gro, SE17 43 L1
Burtonhole Cl, NW7 119 CX49
Burtonhole La, NW7 119 CY49
Burton La, SW9 42 F8
  Goffs Oak EN7 88 DS29
Burton Ms, SW1 29 H9
Burton Pl, WC1 17 P3
Burton Rd, E18 146 EH55
Burton Rd, NW6 5 H7
  SW9 42 G8
  Kingston upon Thames KT2 200 CL94
  Loughton IG10 107 EQ42
Burtons La, Ch.St.G. HP8 95 AZ43
  Rickmansworth WD3 95 AZ43
Burtons Rd, Hmptn H. TW12 198 CB91
Burton St, WC1 17 P3
Burtons Way, Ch.St.G. HP8 94 AW40
Burton Way, Wind. SL4 173 AL83
Burtwell La, SE27 204 DR91
Burwash Ct, Orp. BR5 off Rookery Gdns 228 EW99
Burwash Ho, SE1 31 M5
Burwash Rd, SE18 187 ER78
Burway Cres, Cher. KT16 216 BG97
Burwell Av, Grnf. UB6 159 CE65
Burwell Cl, E1 20 F9
Burwell Rd, E10 145 DY60
Burwell Wk, E3 22 B4
Burwood Av, Brom. BR2 226 EH103
  Kenley CR8 241 DP114
  Pinner HA5 138 BW57
Burwood Cl, Guil. GU1 265 BD133
  Hersham KT12 236 BW107
  Reigate RH2 272 DD134
  Surbiton KT6 220 CN102
Burwood Gdns, Rain. RM13 169 FF69
BURWOOD PARK, Walt. KT12 235 BT106
Burwood Pk, Cob. KT11 235 BS112
Burwood Pk Rd, Hersham KT12 235 BV105
Burwood Pl, W2 16 D8
  Barnet EN4 102 DC39
Burwood Rd, Hersham KT12 235 BV107
Burwood Sch, Orp. BR6 off Avalon Rd 228 EX103
Bury, The, Chesh. HP5 76 AP31
  Hemel Hempstead HP1 62 BJ19
Bury Av, Hayes UB4 157 BS68
  Ruislip HA4 137 BQ58
Bury Cl, SE16 33 K2
  Woking GU21 248 AX116
Bury Ct, EC3 19 P8
Burycroft, Welw.G.C. AL8 51 CY06
Burydell La, Park St AL2 83 CD27
Bury Fm, Amer. HP7 off Gore Hill 77 AQ40
Bury Flds, Guil. GU2 280 AW136
Buryfield Ter, Ware SG12 off Priory St 54 DW06
Buryfield Way, Ware SG12 54 DW05
BURY GREEN, Wal.Cr. EN7 88 DV31
Bury Grn, Hem.H. HP1 62 BJ19
Bury Grn Rd, Chsht EN7 88 DU31
Bury Gro, Mord. SM4 222 DB99
Bury Hill, Hem.H. HP1 62 BH19
Bury Hill Cl, Hem.H. HP1 62 BJ19
Buryholme, Brox. EN10 71 DZ23
Bury La, Chesh. HP5 76 AP31
  Epping CM16 91 ES31
  Rickmansworth WD3 114 BK46
  Woking GU21 248 AW116
Bury Meadows, Rick. WD3 114 BK46
Bury Pl, WC1 18 A7
Bury Ri, Hem.H. HP3 79 BD25
Bury Rd, E4 106 EE43
  N22 143 DN55
  Dagenham RM10 149 FB64
  Epping CM16 91 ES31
  Harlow CM17 58 EW11
  Hatfield AL10 67 CW17
  Hemel Hempstead HP1 62 BJ19
Burys Ct Sch, Leigh RH2 off Flanchford Rd 287 CX140
Buryside Cl, Ilf. IG2 147 ET56
Bury St, EC3 19 P9
  N9 122 DU46
  SW1 29 M2
  Guildford GU2 280 AW136
  Ruislip HA4 137 BQ57
Bury St W, N9 122 DR45
Bury Wk, SW3 28 C9
Busbridge Ho, E14 22 B7
Busby Ms, NW5 off Busby Pl 7 N4
Busby Pl, NW5 7 N4
Busby St, E2 20 B4
Busch Cl, Islw. TW7 179 CH81
Bushbaby Cl, SE1 31 N7
Bushbarns, Chsht EN7 88 DU29
Bushberry Rd, E9 11 M4
Bushbury La, Bet. RH3 286 CN139
Bushby Av, Brox. EN10 71 DZ22
Bush Cl, Add. KT15 234 BJ106
  Ilford IG2 147 ER57
Bush Cotts, SW18 off Putney Br Rd 202 DA85
Bush Ct, W12 26 D4
Bushell Cl, SW2 203 DM89
Bushell Grn, Bushey Hth WD23 117 CD47
Bushell St, E1 32 D3
Bushell Way, Chis. BR7 207 EN92
Bush Elms Rd, Horn. RM11 149 FG59
Bushetts Gro, Merst. RH1 273 DH129
BUSHEY, WD23 116 CA45
⊖ Bushey 98 BX44
Bushey & Oxhey Inf Sch, Bushey WD23 off Aldenham Rd 98 BY43
Bushey Av, E18 146 EF55
  Petts Wood BR5 227 ER101
Bushey Cl, E4 123 EC48
  Kenley CR8 258 DS116
  Uxbridge UB10 137 BP61
  Welwyn Garden City AL7 52 DB10
Bushey Ct, SW20 221 CV96
Bushey Cft, Harl. CM18 73 ES17
  Oxted RH8 275 EC130
Bushey Down, SW12 off Bedford Hill 203 DH89
Bushey Grn, Welw.G.C. AL7 52 DB10
Bushey Gro Rd, Bushey WD23 98 BX42
Bushey Hall Dr, Bushey WD23 98 BY42
Bushey Hall Pk, Bushey WD23 98 BY42
Bushey Hall Rd, Bushey WD23 98 BX42
Bushey Hall Sch, Bushey WD23 off London Rd 98 BZ44
BUSHEY HEATH, Bushey WD23 117 CE46
Bushey Heath Prim Sch, Bushey WD23 off The Rutts 117 CD46
Bushey Hill Rd, SE5 43 P7
Bushey La, Sutt. SM1 240 DA105
Bushey Lees, Sid. DA15 off Fen Gro 207 ET86
Bushey Ley, Welw.G.C. AL7 52 DB10
Bushey Manor Jun Sch, Bushey WD23 off Grange Rd 98 BY44
BUSHEY MEAD, SW20 221 CX97
Bushey Meads Sch, Bushey WD23 off Coldharbour La 98 CC43
Bushey Mill Cres, Wat. WD24 98 BW37
Bushey Mill La, Bushey WD23 98 BZ40
  Watford WD24 98 BW37
Bushey Rd, E13 24 C1
  N15 144 DS58
  SW20 221 CV97
  Croydon CR0 225 EA103
  Hayes UB3 177 BS77
  Sutton SM1 240 DB105
  Uxbridge UB10 136 BN61
Bushey Shaw, Ashtd. KT21 253 CH117
Bushey Vw Wk, Wat. WD24 98 BX40
Bushey Way, Beck. BR3 225 ED100
Bush Fair, Harl. CM18 73 ET17
Bushfield Cl, Edg. HA8 118 CP47
Bushfield Cres, Edg. HA8 118 CP47
Bushfield Dr, Red. RH1 288 DG139
Bushfield Rd, Bov. HP3 79 BC25
Bushfields, Loug. IG10 107 EN43
Bushfield Wk, Swans. DA10 212 FY86
Bush Gro, NW9 140 CQ59
  Stanmore HA7 117 CK53
Bushgrove Rd, Dag. RM8 148 EX63
Bush Hall La, Hat. AL9 67 CX15
Bush Hill, N21 122 DQ45
BUSH HILL PARK, Enf. EN1 104 DS43
⇌ Bush Hill Park 104 DT44
Bush Hill Pk Prim Sch, Enf. EN1 off Main Av 104 DU43
Bush Hill Rd, N21 104 DR44
  Harrow HA3 140 CM58
Bush Ho, SE18 off Berber Par 186 EL80
  Harlow CM18 off Bush Fair 73 ET17
● Bush Ind Est, N19 143 DJ62
  NW10 160 CR70
Bush La, EC4 19 L10
  Send GU23 249 BD124
Bushmead Cl, N15 off Duffield Dr 144 DT56
Bushmoor Cres, SE18 187 EQ80
Bushnell Rd, SW17 203 DH89
Bush Rd, E8 10 E9
  E11 146 EF59
  SE8 33 K8
  Buckhurst Hill IG9 124 EK49
  Richmond TW9 180 CM79
  Shepperton TW17 216 BM99
Bushway, Dag. RM8 148 EX63
Bushwood, E11 146 EF60
Bushwood Cl, N.Mymms AL9 off Dellsome La 67 CV23
Bushwood Dr, SE1 32 B9
Bushwood Rd, Rich. TW9 180 CN79
Bushy Cl, Rom. RM1 127 FD51
BUSHY HILL, Guil. GU1 265 BC132
Bushy Hill Dr, Guil. GU1 265 BB132
Bushy Hill Jun Sch, Guil. GU1 off Sheeplands Av 265 BD133
★ Bushy Park, Tedd. TW11 219 CF95
Bushy Pk, Hmptn H. TW12 219 CF95
  Teddington TW11 219 CF95
Bushy Pk Gdns, Tedd. TW11 199 CD92
Bushy Pk Rd, Tedd. TW11 199 CH94
Bushy Rd, Fetch. KT22 252 CB122
  Teddington TW11 199 CF93
Business Acad Bexley, The, Prim Sch, Erith DA18 off Yarnton Way 188 EY75
  Sec Sch, Erith DA18 off Yarnton Way 188 EY75
★ Business Design Cen, N1 8 F9
● Business Pk 8, Lthd. KT22 off Barnett Wd La 253 CH119
● Business Village, The, Slou. SL2 154 AV74
Buslins La, Chesh. HP5 76 AL28
Butcher Row, E1 21 K10
  E14 21 K10
Butchers La, Sev. TN15 231 FX103
Butchers Ms, Hayes UB3 off Hemmen La 157 BT73
Butchers Rd, E16 23 P8
Butcher Wk, Swans. DA10 212 FY87
Bute Av, Rich. TW10 200 CL89
Bute Ct, Wall. SM6 241 DJ106
Bute Gdns, W6 26 C9
  Wallington SM6 241 DJ106
Bute Gdns W, Wall. SM6 241 DJ106
Bute Ho Prep Sch for Girls, W6 26 C8
Bute Ms, NW11 off Northway 142 DB57
Bute Rd, Croy. CR0 223 DN102
  Ilford IG6 147 EP57
  Wallington SM6 241 DJ105
Bute St, SW7 28 A8
Bute Wk, N1 9 L5
Butler Av, Har. HA1 139 CD59
Butler Cl, Edg. HA8 off Scott Rd 118 CP54
Butler Ct, Wem. HA0 off Harrow Rd 139 CG63
Butler Ho, Grays RM17 off Argent St 192 GB79
Butler Pl, SW1 29 N6
Butler Rd, NW10 161 CT66
  Dagenham RM8 148 EV63
  Harrow HA1 138 CC59
Butlers & Colonial Wf, SE1 32 B4
Butlers Cl, Amer. HP6 77 AN37
  Hounslow TW4 178 BZ83
  Windsor SL4 173 AK82
Butlers Ct, Wal.Cr. EN8 off Trinity La 89 DY32
Butlers Ct Rd, Beac. HP9 111 AK54
Butlers Ct Sch, Beac. HP9 off Wattleton Rd 111 AK54
BUTLERS CROSS, Beac. HP9 112 AT49
Butlers Dene Rd, Wold. CR3 259 DZ120
Butlers Dr, E4 105 EC38
Butlers Hill, W.Hors. KT24 267 BP130
Butler St, E2 21 H2
  Uxbridge UB10 157 BP70
Butlers Wf, SE1 32 A3
Butler Wk, Grays RM17 off Palmers Dr 192 GD77
Buttell Cl, Grays RM17 192 GD78
Buttercross La, Epp. CM16 92 EU30
Buttercup Cl, Hat. AL10 51 CT14
  Northolt UB5 158 BY65
  Romford RM3 off Copperfields Way 128 FK53
Buttercup Sq, Stanw. TW19 off Diamedes Av 196 BK88
Butterfield, Woob.Grn HP10 132 AD59
Butterfield Cl, N17 off Devonshire Rd 122 DQ51
  SE16 32 E5
Butterfield Cl, Twick. TW1 199 CF86
Butterfield Ho, SE18 off Berber Par 186 EL80
Butterfield La, St.Alb. AL1 65 CE24
Butterfields, E17 145 EC57
Butterfield Sq, E6 25 J9
Butterfly La, SE9 207 EP86
  Elstree WD6 99 CG41
Butterfly Wk, Warl. CR6 258 DW120
Butterfly Wk Shop Cen, SE5 43 K7
Butter Hill, Cars. SM5 222 DG104
  Dorking RH4 off South St 285 CG136
  Wallington SM6 222 DG104
Butteridges Cl, Dag. RM9 168 EZ67
Butterly Av, Dart. DA1 210 FM89
Buttermere Av, Slou. SL1 152 AJ71
Buttermere Cl, E15 13 H1
  SE1 32 A9
  Feltham TW14 197 BT88
  Morden SM4 221 CX100
  St. Albans AL1 65 CH21
Buttermere Dr, SW15 201 CY85
Buttermere Gdns, Pur. CR8 242 DR113
Buttermere Rd, Orp. BR5 228 EX98
Buttermere Wk, E8 10 B5
Buttermere Way, Egh. TW20 off Keswick Rd 195 BB94
Buttersweet Ri, Saw. CM21 58 EY06
Butterwick, W6 26 B9
  Watford WD25 98 BY36
Butterwick La, St.Alb. AL4 66 CN22
Butterworth Gdns, Wdf.Grn. IG8 124 EG51
Buttesland St, N1 19 M2
Buttfield Cl, Dag. RM10 169 FB65
Butt Fld Vw, St.Alb. AL1 64 CC24
Buttlehide, Map.Cr. WD3 113 BD50
Buttmarsh Cl, SE18 37 P10
Buttondene Cres, Brox. EN10 71 EB22
Button Rd, Grays RM17 192 FZ77
Button St, Swan. BR8 230 FJ96
Butts, The, Brent. TW8 179 CK79
  Broxbourne EN10 71 DY24
  Otford TN14 263 FH116
  Sunbury-on-Thames TW16 off Elizabeth Gdns 218 BW97
Buttsbury Rd, Ilf. IG1 147 EQ64
Butts Cotts, Felt. TW13 198 BZ90
Butts Cres, Han. TW13 198 CA90
Butts End, Hem.H. HP1 62 BG18
Butts Grn Rd, Horn. RM11 150 FK58
Buttsmead, Nthwd. HA6 115 BQ52
Butts Piece, Nthlt. UB5 off Longhook Gdns 157 BV68
Butts Rd, Brom. BR1 206 EE92
  Woking GU21 248 AY117
Buxhall Cres, E9 11 N4
Buxlow Prep Sch, Wem. HA9 off Castleton Gdns 140 CL62
Buxted Rd, E8 10 A6
  N12 120 DE50
  SE22 184 DS84
Buxton Av, Cat. CR3 258 DS121
Buxton Cl, N9 122 DW47
  Epsom KT19 238 CP111
  St. Albans AL4 65 CK17
  Woodford Green IG8 124 EK51
Buxton Ct, N1 19 K2
Buxton Cres, Sutt. SM3 239 CY105
Buxton Dr, E11 146 EE56
  New Malden KT3 220 CR96
Buxton Gdns, W3 160 CP73
Buxton Ho, SW11 off Maysoule Rd 182 DD84
Buxton La, Cat. CR3 258 DR120
Buxton Ms, SW4 41 P8
Buxton Path, Wat. WD19 116 BW48
Buxton Pl, Cat. CR3 258 DR120
Buxton Rd, E4 123 ED45
  E6 24 G2
  E15 13 J3
  E17 145 DY56
  N19 143 DK60
  NW2 161 CV65
  SW14 180 CS83
  Ashford TW15 196 BK92
  Erith DA8 189 FD80
  Grays RM16 192 GE75
  Ilford IG2 147 ES58
  Theydon Bois CM16 107 ES36
  Thornton Heath CR7 223 DP99
  Waltham Abbey EN9 90 EG32
Buxton St, E1 20 B5
● Buzzard Creek Ind Est, Bark. IG11 167 ET71
Byam St, SW6 39 N9
Byards Cft, SW16 223 DK95
Byatt Wk, Hmptn. TW12 off Victors Dr 198 BY93
Bybend Cl, Farn.Royal SL2 153 AP67
Bychurch End, Tedd. TW11 199 CF92
Bycliffe Ter, Grav. DA11 213 GF87
Bycroft Rd, Sthl. UB1 158 CA70
Bycroft St, SE20 off Penge La 205 DX94
Bycullah Av, Enf. EN2 103 DP41
Bycullah Rd, Enf. EN2 103 DP41
Byde St, Hert. SG14 54 DQ08
Bye, The, W3 160 CS72
Byegrove Ct, SW19 off Byegrove Rd 202 DD94
Byegrove Rd, SW19 202 DD93
Byers Cl, Pot.B. EN6 86 DC34
Byewaters, Wat. WD18 97 BQ44
Byeway, The, SW14 180 CQ83
Bye Way, The, Har. HA3 117 CE53
Byeway, The, Rick. WD3 114 BL47
Byeways, Twick. TW2 198 CB90
Byeways, The, Surb. KT5 220 CN99
Byfeld Gdns, SW13 181 CU81
Byfield, Welw.G.C. AL8 51 CY06
Byfield Cl, SE16 33 M4
Byfield Pas, Islw. TW7 179 CG83
Byfield Rd, Islw. TW7 179 CG83
BYFLEET, W.Byf. KT14 234 BM113
⇌ Byfleet & New Haw 234 BK110
Byfleet Prim Sch, Byfleet KT14 off Kings Head La 234 BK111
Byfleet Rd, Byfleet KT14 234 BN112
  Cobham KT11 235 BS113
  New Haw KT15 234 BK108
● Byfleet Tech Cen, Byfleet KT14 234 BK111
Byford Cl, E15 13 K7
Bygrove, New Adgtn CR0 243 EB107
Bygrove Prim Sch, E14 22 C9
Bygrove St, E14 22 C9
Byland Cl, N21 121 DM45
Byland Cl, Mord. SM4 off Bolton Dr 222 DD101
Bylands, Wok. GU22 249 BA119
Bylands Cl, SE2 188 EV76
  SE16 33 K2
Byne Rd, SE26 204 DW93
  Carshalton SM5 222 DE103
Bynes Rd, S.Croy. CR2 242 DR108
Byng Dr, Pot.B. EN6 86 DA31
Bynghams, Harl. CM19 73 EM17
Byng Pl, WC1 17 N5
Byng Rd, Barn. EN5 101 CX41
Byng St, E14 34 A4
Bynon Av, Bexh. DA7 188 EY83
Bypass Rd, Lthd. KT22 253 CH120
Byre, The, N14 103 DH44
Byrefield Rd, Guil. GU2 264 AT131
Byre Rd, N14 102 DG44
Byrne Rd, SW12 203 DH88
Byron Av, E12 166 EL65
  E18 146 EF55
  NW9 140 CP56
  Borehamwood WD6 100 CN43
  Coulsdon CR5 257 DL115
  Hounslow TW4 177 BU82
  New Malden KT3 221 CU99
  Sutton SM1 240 DD105
  Watford WD24 98 BX39
Byron Av E, Sutt. SM1 240 DD105
Byron Cl, E8 10 C8
  SE26 205 DY91
  SE28 168 EW74
  SW16 203 DL93
  Hampton TW12 198 BZ91
  Knaphill GU21 248 AS117
  Waltham Cross EN7 off Allard Cl 88 DT27
  Walton-on-Thames KT12 218 BY102
Byron Ct, W9 15 K4
  Enfield EN2 103 DP40
  Harrow HA1 139 CE58
  Windsor SL4 173 AN83
Byron Ct Prim Sch, Wem. HA0 off Spencer Rd 139 CJ61
Byron Dr, N2 142 DD58
  Erith DA8 189 FB80
Byron Gdns, Sutt. SM1 240 DD105
  Tilbury RM18 193 GJ81
Byron Hill Rd, Har. HA2 139 CD60
Byron Ho, Beck. BR3 205 EA93
  Slough SL3 175 BB78
Byron Ms, NW3 6 D2
  W9 15 K4
Byron Pl, Lthd. KT22 253 CH122
Byron Prim Sch, Couls. CR5 off St. Davids 257 DM117
Byron Rd, E10 145 EB60
  E17 145 EA55
  NW2 141 CV61
  NW7 119 CU50
  W5 160 CM74
  Addlestone KT15 234 BL105
  Dartford DA1 190 FP84
  Harrow HA1 139 CE58
  Hutton CM13 131 GD45
  South Croydon CR2 242 DV110
  Wealdstone HA3 117 CF54
  Wembley HA0 139 CJ62
Byron St, E14 22 E8
Byron Ter, N9 104 DW44
Byron Way, Hayes UB4 157 BS70
  Northolt UB5 158 BY69
  Romford RM3 128 FJ53
  West Drayton UB7 176 BM77
Bysouth Cl, N15 144 DR56
  Ilford IG5 125 EP53
By the Mt, Welw.G.C. AL7 51 CX10
By the Wd, Wat. WD19 116 BX47
Bythorn St, SW9 183 DM83
Byton Rd, SW17 202 DF93
Byttom Hill, Mick. RH5 269 CJ127
Byward Av, Felt. TW14 198 BW86
Byward St, EC3 31 P1
Bywater Pl, SE16 33 M2
Bywater St, SW3 28 E10
Byway, The, Epsom KT19 239 CT105
  Potters Bar EN6 86 DA33
  Sutton SM2 240 DD109
Byways, Berk. HP4 60 AY18
  Burnham SL1 152 AG71
Byways, The, Ashtd. KT21 off Skinners La 253 CK118
Bywell Pl, W1 17 L7
Bywood Av, Croy. CR0 224 DW100
Bywood Cl, Bans. SM7 255 CZ117
  Kenley CR8 257 DP115
By-Wood End, Chal.St.P. SL9 113 AZ50
Byworth Wk, N19 off Courtauld Rd 143 DL60

C

Cabbell Pl, Add. KT15 234 BJ105
Cabbell St, NW1 16 C7
Cabell Rd, Guil. GU2 264 AS133
Caberfeigh Cl, Red. RH1 272 DD134
Cabinet Way, E4 123 DZ51
Cable Ho Ct, Wok. GU21 248 AY115
Cable Pl, SE10 46 F6
Cable St, E1 20 C10
● Cable Trade Pk, SE7 36 C9
Cabot Pl, E14 34 B2
Cabot Sq, E14 34 B2
Cabot Way, E6 off Parr Rd 166 EK67
Cabrera Av, Vir.W. GU25 214 AW100
Cabrera Cl, Vir.W. GU25 214 AX100
Cabul Rd, SW11 40 C9
Cacket's Cotts, Cudham TN14 261 ES115
Cackets La, Cudham TN14 261 ER115
Cactus Cl, SE15 43 P8
Cactus Wk, W12 off Du Cane Rd 161 CT72
Cadbury Cl, Islw. TW7 179 CG81
  Sunbury-on-Thames TW16 197 BS94
Cadbury Rd, Sun. TW16 197 BS94
Cadbury Way, SE16 32 B7
Caddington Cl, Barn. EN4 102 DE43
Caddington Rd, NW2 141 CY62
Caddis Cl, Stan. HA7 117 CF52
Caddy Cl, Egh. TW20 195 BA92
Cade La, Sev. TN13 279 FJ128
Cadell Cl, E2 20 B1
Cade Rd, SE10 46 G6
Cader Rd, SW18 202 DC86
Cadet Dr, SE1 32 B10
Cadet Pl, SE10 35 J10

Cadiz Ct, Dag. RM10
off Rainham Rd S 169 FD66
Cadiz Rd, Dag. RM10 169 FC66
Cadiz St, SE17 43 K1
Cadley Ter, SE23 204 DW89
Cadlocks Hill, Halst.TN14 246 EZ110
Cadman Cl, SW9
off Langton Rd 42 G5
Cadmer Cl, N.Mal. KT3 220 CS98
Cadmore Cl, Hert. SG14
off The Ridgeway 53 DM07
Cadmore La, Chsht EN8 89 DX28
Cadmus Cl, SW4
off Aristotle Rd 183 DK83
Cadnam Pt, SW15
off Dilton Gdns 201 CV88
Cadogan Av, Dart. DA2 211 FR87
Cadogan Cl, E9 11 P6
Beckenham BR3
off Albemarle Rd 225 ED95
Harrow HA2 138 CB63
Teddington TW11 199 CE92
Cadogan Ct, Sutt. SM2 240 DB107
Cadogan Gdns, E18 146 EH55
N3 120 DB53
N21 103 DN43
SW3 28 F8
Cadogan Gate, SW1 28 F8
Cadogan La, SW1 28 G7
Cadogan Pier 40 D3
Cadogan Pl, SW1 28 F6
Kenley CR8 258 DQ117
Cadogan Rd, SE18 37 P6
Surbiton KT6 219 CK99
Cadogan Sq, SW1 28 F7
Cadogan St, SW3 28 E9
Cadogan Ter, E9 11 N5
Cadoxton Av, N15 144 DT58
Cadwallon Rd, SE9 207 EP89
Caedmon Rd, N7 143 DM63
Caenshill Pl, Wey. KT13 234 BN108
Caenshill Rd, Wey. KT13 234 BN108
Caenwood Cl, Wey. KT13 234 BN107
Caen Wd Rd, Ashtd. KT21 253 CJ118
Caerleon Cl, Clay. KT10 237 CH108
Sidcup DA14 208 EW92
Caerleon Ter, SE2
off Blithdale Rd 188 EV77
Caernarvon Cl, Hem.H. HP2 62 BK20
Hornchurch RM11 150 FN60
Mitcham CR4 223 DL97
Caernarvon Dr, Ilf. IG5 125 EN53
Caesars Wk, Mitch. CR4 222 DF99
Caesars Way, Shep. TW17 217 BR100
Cage Pond Rd, Shenley WD7 84 CM33
Cages Wd Dr, Farn.Com. SL2 133 AP63
Cage Yd, Reig. RH2
off High St 272 DA134
Cahill St, EC1 19 K5
Cahir St, E14 34 C9
Caillard Rd, Byfleet KT14 234 BL111
Cain Cl, St.Alb. AL1 65 CF22
Cains La, Felt. TW14 197 BS85
Caird St, W10 14 F3
Cairn Av, W5 159 CK74
Cairncross Ms, N8
off Felix Av 143 DL58
Cairndale Cl, Brom. BR1 206 EF94
Cairnfield Av, NW2 140 CS62
Cairngorm Cl, Tedd. TW11
off Vicarage Rd 199 CG92
Cairngorm Pl, Slou. SL2 153 AR70
Cairns Av, Wdf.Grn. IG8 124 EL51
Cairns Cl, Dart. DA1 210 FK85
St. Albans AL4 65 CK21
Cairns Ms, SE18 *off Bell St* 186 EL81
Cairns Rd, SW11 202 DE85
Cairn Way, Stan. HA7 117 CF51
Cairo New Rd, Croy. CR0 223 DP103
Cairo Rd, E17 145 EA56
Caishowe Rd, Borwd. WD6 100 CP39
Caister Cl, Hem.H. HP2 62 BL21
Caistor Ms, SW12
off Caistor Rd 203 DH87
Caistor Pk Rd, E15 13 M9
Caistor Rd, SW12 203 DH87
Caithness Dr, Epsom KT18 238 CR114
Caithness Gdns, Sid. DA15 207 ET86
Caithness Rd, W14 26 C8
Mitcham CR4 203 DH94
Calabria Rd, N5 8 G4
Calais Cl, Chsht EN7 88 DR26
Calais Gate, SE5 42 G6
Calais St, SE5 43 H6
Calbourne Av, Horn. RM12 149 FH64
Calbourne Rd, SW12 202 DF87
Calbroke Ct, Slou. SL2
off Calbroke Rd 153 AM69
Calbroke Rd, Slou. SL2 153 AM70
Calcott Cl, Brwd. CM14 130 FV46
Calcott Wk, SE9 206 EK91
Calcroft Av, Green. DA9 211 FW85
Calcutta Rd, Til. RM18 193 GF82
Caldbeck, Wal.Abb. EN9 89 ED34
Caldbeck Av, Wor.Pk. KT4 221 CU103
Caldecot Av, Chsht EN7 88 DT29
Caldecote Gdns, Bushey WD23 99 CE44
Caldecote La, Bushey WD23 117 CF45
Caldecot Rd, SE5 43 K8
Caldecott Way, E5 145 DX62
Caldecot Way, Brox. EN10 71 DZ22
Calder Av, Brook.Pk AL9 86 DB26
Perivale UB6 159 CF68
Calder Cl, Enf. EN1 104 DS41
Calder Ct, Rom. RM1 149 FD56
Slough SL3 175 AZ78
Calder Gdns, Edg. HA8 140 CN55
Calderon Pl, W10 14 A7
Calderon Rd, E11 145 EC63
Calder Rd, Mord. SM4 222 DC99
Caldervale Rd, SW4 203 DK85
Calder Way, Colnbr. SL3 175 BF83
Calderwood, Grav. DA12 213 GL92
Calderwood Pl, Barn. EN4 102 DB39
Calderwood St, SE18 37 M8
Caldicot Grn, NW9 140 CS58
Caldicott Sch, Farn.Royal
SL2 *off Crown La* 153 AP66
Caldwell Gdns Est, SW9 42 E6
Caldwell Rd, Wat. WD19 116 BX49
Caldwell St, SW9 42 D5
Caldy Rd, Belv. DA17 189 FB76
Caldy Wk, N1 9 J6
Caleb St, SE1 31 J4
Caledon Cl, Beac. HP9 111 AK52
Caledonian Cl, Ilf. IG3 148 EV60
⊖ **Caledonian Road** 8 B4
Caledonian Rd, N1 18 B1
N7 8 C4
Caledonian Road & Barnsbury 8 D6
Caledonian Sq, NW1 7 N4
Caledonian Way, Gat. RH6
off Queen's Gate 291 DH151
Caledonian Wf, E14 34 G9
Caledonia Rd, Stai. TW19 196 BL88
Caledonia St, N1 18 B1
Caledon Pl, Guil. GU4
off Darfield Rd 265 BA131
Caledon Rd, E6 166 EL67
Beaconsfield HP9 111 AL52
London Colney AL2 83 CK26
Wallington SM6 240 DG105
Cale St, SW3 28 C10
Caletock Way, SE10 35 L10
Calfstock La, Fnghm DA4 230 FL98
Calico Row, SW11 39 P10
Calidore Cl, SW2 203 DM86
California Bldg, SE13
off Deals Gateway 46 C6
California Cl, Sutt. SM2 240 DA110
California La, Bushey Hth
WD23 117 CD46
California Rd, N.Mal. KT3 220 CP98
Caliph Cl, Grav. DA12 213 GM90
Callaby Ter, N1 9 M5
Callaghan Cl, SE13 186 EE84
Callander Rd, SE6 205 EB89
Callan Gro, S.Ock. RM15 171 FV73
Callard Av, N13 121 DP50
Callcott Rd, NW6 4 G7
Callcott St, W8 27 J2
Callendar Rd, SW7 28 A6
Calley Down Cres, New Adgtn
CR0 243 ED110
Callingham Cl, E14 21 P7
Callingham Pl, Beac. HP9 111 AL52
Callis Fm Cl, Stanw. TW19
off Bedfont Rd 196 BL86
Callisons Pl, SE10 35 K10
Callis Rd, E17 145 DZ58
Callisto Ct, Hem.H. HP2
off Jupiter Dr 62 BM17
Callow Fld, Pur. CR8 241 DN113
Callow Hill, Vir.W. GU25 214 AW97
Callowland Cl, Wat. WD24 97 BV38
Callow St, SW3 39 P2
Calluna Ct, Wok. GU22
off Heathside Rd 249 AZ118
Calmington Rd, SE5 43 P1
Calmont Rd, Brom. BR1 205 ED93
Calmore Cl, Horn. RM12 150 FJ64
Calne Av, Ilf. IG5 125 EP53
Calonne Rd, SW19 201 CX91
Calshot Av, Chaff.Hun. RM16 192 FZ75
Calshot Rd, Lon.Hthrw Air.
TW6 176 BN82
Calshot St, N1 8 C10
Calshot Way, Enf. EN2 103 DP41
London Heathrow Airport
TW6 *off Calshot Rd* 177 BP82
Calthorpe Gdns, Edg. HA8
off Jesmond Way 118 CL50
Sutton SM1 222 DC104
Calthorpe St, WC1 18 D4
Calton Av, SE21 204 DS85
Hertford SG14 53 DM08
Calton Ct, Hert. SG14
off Calton Av 53 DM09
Calton Rd, New Barn. EN5 102 DC44
Calverley Cl, Beck. BR3 205 EB93
Calverley Ct, Epsom KT19
off Kingston Rd 238 CR105
Calverley Cres, Dag. RM10 148 FA61
Calverley Gdns, Har. HA3 139 CK59
Calverley Gro, N19 143 DK60
Calverley Rd, Epsom KT17 239 CU107
Calvert Av, E2 19 P3
Calvert Cl, Belv. DA17 188 FA77
Epsom KT19 238 CP110
Sidcup DA14 208 EY93
Calvert Cres, Dor. RH4
off Calvert Rd 269 CH134
Calvert Dr, Dart. DA2 209 FD89
Calverton, SE5 43 M2
Calverton Prim Sch, E16 24 F9
Calverton Rd, E6 167 EN67
Calvert Rd, SE10 47 L1
Barnet EN5 101 CX40
Dorking RH4 269 CH134
Effingham KT24 267 BV128
Calvert's Bldgs, SE1 31 L3
Calvert St, NW1 6 G8
Calvin Cl, Orp. BR5 228 EX97
Calvin St, E1 20 A5
Calydon Rd, SE7 186 EH78
Calypso Cres, SE15 44 A4
Calypso Way, SE16 33 N7
Camac Rd, Twick. TW2 199 CD88
Camarthen Grn, NW9 140 CS57
Cambalt Rd, SW15 201 CX85
Cambell Inf Sch, Dag. RM9
off Langley Cres 168 EX66
Cambell Jun Sch, Dag. RM9
off Langley Cres 168 EX66
Camberley Av, SW20 221 CV96
Enfield EN1 104 DS42
Camberley Cl, Sutt. SM3 221 CX104
Camberley Rd, Lon.Hthrw Air.
TW6 176 BN83
Cambert Way, SE3 186 EH84
CAMBERWELL, SE5 43 K5
● **Camberwell Business Cen**,
SE5 43 L5
Camberwell Ch St, SE5 43 L7
Camberwell Coll of Arts,
Peckham Rd, SE5 43 P6
Wilson Rd, SE5 43 N7
Camberwell Glebe, SE5 43 N7
Camberwell Grn, SE5 43 K6
Camberwell Grn, SE5 43 L6
Camberwell Gro, SE5 43 M7
Camberwell New Rd, SE5 42 E3
Camberwell Pas, SE5 43 K6
Camberwell Rd, SE5 43 K3
Camberwell Sta Rd, SE5 43 J7
Cambeys Rd, Dag. RM10 149 FB64
Camborne Av, W13 179 CH75
Romford RM3 128 FL52
Camborne Cl, Lon.Hthrw Air.
TW6 *off Camborne Rd* 176 BN83
Camborne Dr, Hem.H. HP2 62 BL16
Camborne Ms, SW18
off Camborne Rd 202 DA87
W11 14 E9
Camborne Rd, SW18 202 DA87
Croydon CR0 224 DU101
London Heathrow Airport
TW6 176 BN83
Camborne Rd, Mord. SM4 221 CX99
Sidcup DA14 208 EW90
Sutton SM2 240 DA108
Welling DA16 187 ET82
Camborne Way, Houns. TW5 178 CA81
London Heathrow Airport
TW6 *off Camborne Rd* 176 BN83
Romford RM3 128 FL52
Cambourne Av, N9 123 DX45
Cambray Rd, SW12 203 DJ88
Orpington BR6 227 ET101
Cambria Cl, Houns. TW3 178 CA84
Sidcup DA15 207 ER88
Cambria Ct, Felt. TW14 197 BV87
Cambria Cres, Grav. DA12 213 GL91
Cambria Gdns, Stai. TW19 196 BL87
Cambria Ho, SE26
off High Level Dr 204 DU91
Erith DA8 *off Larner Rd* 189 FE80
Cambrian Av, Ilf. IG2 147 ES57
Cambrian Cl, SE27 203 DP90
Cambrian Grn, NW9 140 CS57
Cambrian Gro, Grav. DA11 213 GG87
Cambrian Rd, E10 145 EA59
Richmond TW10 200 CM86
Cambrian Way, Hem.H. HP2 62 BL17
Cambria Rd, SE5 43 J10
Cambria St, SW6 39 M5
Cambridge Av, NW6 5 K10
Burnham SL1 152 AH68
Greenford UB6 139 CF64
New Malden KT3 221 CT96
Romford RM2 150 FJ55
Slough SL1 153 AM72
Welling DA16 187 ET84
Cambridge Barracks Rd, SE18 37 K9
Cambridge Circ, WC2 17 P9
Cambridge Cl, E17 145 DZ58
N22 *off Pellatt Gro* 121 DN53
NW10 *off Lawrence Way* 140 CQ62
SW20 221 CV95
Cheshunt EN8 88 DW29
East Barnet EN4 120 DG46
Harmondsworth UB7 176 BK79
Hounslow TW4 178 BY84
Woking GU21 248 AT118
Cambridge Cotts, Rich. TW9 180 CN79
Cambridge Cres, E2 20 E1
Teddington TW11 199 CG92
Cambridge Dr, SE12 206 EG85
Potters Bar EN6 85 CX31
Ruislip HA4 138 BW61
Cambridge Gdns, N10 120 DG53
N13 121 DN50
N17
off Great Cambridge Rd 122 DR52
N21 122 DR45
NW6 5 K10
W10 14 F8
Enfield EN1 104 DU40
Grays RM16 193 GG77
Kingston upon Thames KT1 220 CN96
Cambridge Gate, NW1 17 K3
Cambridge Gate Ms, NW1 17 K3
Cambridge Grn, SE9 207 EP88
Cambridge Gro, SE20 224 DV95
W6 181 CV77
Cambridge Gro Rd, Kings.T.
KT1 220 CN96
⇌ **Cambridge Heath** 10 E10
Cambridge Heath Rd, E1 20 F6
E2 20 F6
Cambridge Ho, Wind. SL4
off Ward Royal 173 AQ81
Cambridge Lo Mobile Home Pk,
Horl. RH6 290 DG145
Cambridge Mans, SW11 40 E7
Cambridge Par, Enf. EN1
off Great Cambridge Rd 104 DU39
Cambridge Pk, E11 146 EG59
Twickenham TW1 199 CK87
Cambridge Pk Rd, E11
off Cambridge Pk 146 EG59
Cambridge Pl, W8 27 M5
Cambridge Rd, E4 123 ED46
E11 146 EF58
NW6 15 J2
SE20 224 DV97
SW11 40 E7
SW13 181 CT82
SW20 221 CU95
W7 179 CF75
Ashford TW15 197 BQ94
Barking IG11 167 EQ66
Beaconsfield HP9 110 AJ53
Bromley BR1 206 EG94
Carshalton SM5 240 DE107
Hampton TW12 198 BZ94
Harlow CM20 58 EW09
Harrow HA2 138 CA57
Hounslow TW4 178 BY84
Ilford IG3 147 ES60
Kingston upon Thames KT1,
KT2 220 CM96
Mitcham CR4 223 DJ97
New Malden KT3 220 CS98
Richmond TW9 180 CN80
St. Albans AL1 65 CH21
Sidcup DA14 207 ES91
Southall UB1 158 BZ74
Teddington TW11 199 CF91
Twickenham TW1 199 CK86
Uxbridge UB8 156 BK65
Walton-on-Thames KT12 217 BV100
Watford WD18 98 BW42
West Molesey KT8 218 BZ98
Cambridge Rd N, W4 180 CP78
Cambridge Rd S, W4 180 CP78
Cambridge Row, SE18 187 EP78
Cambridge Sch, W6
off Cambridge Gro 181 CV77
Cambridge Sch of English,
The, WC2 18 B8
Cambridge Sq, W2 16 C8
Redhill RH1 288 DG137
Cambridge St, SW1 29 K9
Cambridge Ter, N13 121 DN50
NW1 17 K3
Berkhamsted HP4 60 AX19
Cambridge Ter Ms, NW1 17 K3
Cambridge Tutors Coll, Croy.
CR0 *off Water Twr Hill* 242 DS105
Cambstone Cl, N11 120 DG47
Cambus Cl, Hayes UB4 158 BY71
Cambus Rd, E16 23 P6
Camdale Rd, SE18 187 ET80
★ **Camden Arts Cen**, NW3 5 N3
Camden Av, Felt. TW13 198 BW89
Hayes UB4 158 BW73
Camden Cl, Chad.St.M. RM16 193 GH77
Chislehurst BR7 207 EQ94
Gravesend DA11 212 GC88
Camden Gdns, NW1 7 K7
Sutton SM1 240 DB106
Thornton Heath CR7 223 DP97
Camden Gro, Chis. BR7 207 EP93
Camden High St, NW1 7 K8
Camden Hill Rd, SE19 204 DS93
Camdenhurst St, E14 21 M8
Camden Jun Sch, Cars.
SM5 *off Camden Rd* 240 DF105
Camden La, N7 7 P3
★ **Camden Lock Mkt &**
Waterbuses, NW1 7 J7
Camden Lock Pl, NW1 7 J7
Camden Ms, NW1 7 M6
Camden Pk Rd, NW1 7 N4
Chislehurst BR7 207 EM94
Camden Pas, N1 8 G10
Camden Road 7 L7
Camden Rd, E11 146 EH58
E17 145 DZ58
N7 7 L7
NW1 7 N4
Bexley DA5 208 EZ88
Carshalton SM5 240 DF105
Grays RM16 192 FY76
Sevenoaks TN13 279 FH122
Sutton SM1 240 DA106
Camden Row, SE3 47 K9
Camden Sch for Girls, NW5 7 M5
Camden Sq, NW1 7 N6
SE15 44 A6
Camden St, NW1 7 L8
Camden Ter, NW1 7 N5
CAMDEN TOWN, NW1 7 L9
⊖ **Camden Town** 7 K8
Camden Wk, N1 8 G9
Camden Way, Chis. BR7 207 EM94
Thornton Heath CR7 223 DP97
Camelford Wk, W11 14 E9
Camel Gro, Kings.T. KT2 199 CK92
Camellia Cl, Rom. RM3 128 FL53
Camellia Ct, Wdf.Grn. IG8
off The Bridle Path 124 EE52
Camellia Ho, Felt. TW13
off Tilley Rd 197 BV88
Camellia Pl, Twick. TW2 198 CB87
Camellia St, SW8 42 A5
Camelot Cl, SE28 187 ER75
SW19 202 DA91
Biggin Hill TN16 260 EJ116
Camelot Ho, NW1 7 P4
Camelot Prim Sch, SE15 44 E3
Camelot St, SE15 44 E3
Camel Rd, E16 36 F2
Camera Pl, SW10 40 A3
Cameron Cl, N18 122 DV49
N20 *off Myddelton Pk* 120 DE47
Bexley DA5 209 FD90
Warley CM14 130 FW49
Cameron Ct, Ware SG12 55 DX05
Cameron Dr, Wal.Cr. EN8 89 DX34
Cameron Ho, SE5
off Comber Gro 43 J5
Cameron Ho Sch, SW3 40 B2
Cameron Pl, E1 20 F8
SW16 203 DN89
Cameron Rd, SE6 205 DZ89
Bromley BR2 226 EG98
Chesham HP5 76 AQ30
Croydon CR0 223 DP100
Ilford IG3 147 ES60
Cameron Sq, Mitch. CR4 222 DE95
Camerton Cl, E8 10 B5
Camfield, Welw.G.C. AL7 51 CZ13
Camfield Pl, Essen. AL9 68 DD21
● **Camgate Cen**, Stanw.
TW19 196 BM86
Cam Grn, S.Ock. RM15 171 FV72
Camilla Cl, Bkhm KT23 268 CB125
Sunbury-on-Thames TW16 197 BT93
Camilla Dr, Westh. RH5 269 CG130
Camilla Rd, SE16 32 E9
Camille Cl, SE25 224 DU97
Camlan Rd, Brom. BR1 206 EF91
Camlet St, E2 20 A4
Camlet Way, Barn. EN4 102 DA40
St. Albans AL3 64 CB19
Camley St, NW1 7 P10
★ **Camley St Natural Pk**, NW1 7 P10
Camm Av, Wind. SL4 173 AL83
Camm Gdns, Kings.T. KT1
off Church Rd 220 CM96
Thames Ditton KT7 219 CE101
Camms Ter, Dag. RM10 149 FC64
Camomile Av, Mitch. CR4 222 DF95
Camomile Rd, Rush Grn RM7 149 FD61
Camomile St, EC3 19 N8
Camomile Way, West Dr. UB7 156 BL72
CAMP, THE, St.Alb. AL1 65 CH21
Campana Rd, SW6 39 J6
Campbell Av, Ilf. IG6 147 EQ56
Woking GU22 249 AZ121
Campbell Cl, SE18
off Moordown 187 EN81
SW16 203 DK91
Byfleet KT14 234 BK112
Harlow CM17
off Carters Mead 74 EV16
Romford RM1 127 FE51
Ruislip HA4 137 BU58
Twickenham TW2 199 CD89
Campbell Ct, N17 122 DT53
SE22 *off Lordship La* 204 DU87
Campbell Cft, Edg. HA8 118 CN50
Campbell Dr, Beac. HP9 110 AJ51
Campbell Gordon Way, NW2 141 CV63
Campbell Rd, E3 22 B2
E6 166 EL67
E15 13 L1
E17 145 DZ56
N17 122 DU53
W7 159 CE73
Caterham CR3 258 DR121
Croydon CR0 223 DP101
East Molesey KT8
off Hampton Ct Rd 219 CF97
Gravesend DA11 213 GF88
Twickenham TW2 199 CD89
Weybridge KT13 234 BN108
Campbell Wk, N1 8 B8
Campdale Rd, N7 143 DK62
Campden Cres, Dag. RM8 148 EV63
Wembley HA0 139 CH61
Campden Gro, W8 27 K4
Campden Hill, W8 27 J4
Campden Hill Ct, W8 27 K4
Campden Hill Gdns, W8 27 H2
Campden Hill Gate, W8 27 J4
Campden Hill Pl, W11 27 H2
Campden Hill Rd, W8 27 K5
Campden Hill Sq, W8 27 H2
Campden Hill Twrs, W11 27 J2
Campden Ho Cl, W8 27 J4
Campden Rd, S.Croy. CR2 242 DS106
Uxbridge UB10 136 BM62
Campden St, W8 27 J3
Campden Way, Dag. RM8 148 EV63
Campen Cl, SW19 201 CY89
Camp End Rd, Wey. KT13 235 BR110
Camperdown St, E1 20 B9
Campfield Rd, SE9 206 EK87
Hertford SG14 53 DP09
St. Albans AL1 65 CG21
Camphill Ct, W.Byf. KT14 234 BG112
● **Camphill Ind Est**, W.Byf.
KT14 234 BH111
Camphill Rd, W.Byf. KT14 234 BG112
Campine Cl, Chsht EN8
off Welsummer Way 89 DX28
Campion Cl, E6 25 K10
Croydon CR0 242 DS105
Denham UB9 136 BG62
Harrow HA3 140 CM58
Hillingdon UB8 156 BM71
Northfleet DA11 212 GE91
Rush Green RM7 149 FD61
Watford WD25 81 BU33
Campion Ct, Grays RM17 192 GD79
Wembley HA0 *off Elmore Cl* 160 CL68
Campion Dr, Tad. KT20 255 CV120
Campion Gdns, Wdf.Grn. IG8 124 EG50
Campion Pl, SE28 168 EV74
Campion Rd, SW15 181 CW84
Hatfield AL10 67 CT15
Hemel Hempstead HP1 61 BE21
Isleworth TW7 179 CF81
Campions, Epp. CM16 92 EU28
Loughton IG10 107 EN38
Campions, The, Borwd. WD6 100 CN38
Campion Sch, The, Horn.
RM11 *off Wingletye La* 150 FM56
Campions Cl, Borwd. WD6 100 CP37
Campions Ct, Berk. HP4 60 AU20
Campion Ter, NW2 141 CX62
Campion Way, Edg. HA8 118 CQ49
Cample La, S.Ock. RM15 171 FU73
Camplin Rd, Har. HA3 140 CL57
Camplin St, SE14 45 K4
Camp Prim & Nurs Sch,
St.Alb. AL1 *off Camp Rd* 65 CH21
Camp Rd, SW19 201 CV92
Gerrards Cross SL9 134 AX59
St. Albans AL1 65 CJ21
Woldingham CR3 259 DY120
Campsbourne, The, N8
off High St 143 DL56
Campsbourne Rd, N8 143 DL55
Campsbourne Sch &
Children's Cen, N8
off Nightingale La 143 DL55
Campsey Gdns, Dag. RM9 168 EV66
Campsey Rd, Dag. RM9 168 EV66
Campsfield Rd, N8 143 DL55
Campshill Pl, SE13
off Campshill Rd 205 EC85
Campshill Rd, SE13 205 EC85
Campus, The, Welw.G.C. AL8 51 CX08
Campus Rd, E17 145 DZ58
Campus Way, NW4 141 CV56
Camp Vw, SW19 201 CV92
Camp Vw Rd, St.Alb. AL1 65 CH21
Cam Rd, E15 12 G8
Camrose Av, Edg. HA8 118 CM53
Erith DA8 189 FB79
Feltham TW13 197 BV91
Camrose Cl, Croy. CR0 225 DY101
Morden SM4 222 DA98
Camrose St, SE2 188 EU78
Canada Av, N18 122 DQ51
Redhill RH1 288 DG138
Canada Cres, W3 160 CQ71
Canada Dr, Red. RH1 288 DG138
Canada Est, SE16 33 H6
Canada Fm Rd, Long. DA3 231 FU99
South Darenth DA4 231 FU98
Canada Gdns, SE13 205 EC85
Canada La, Brox. EN10 89 DY25
Canada Rd, W3 160 CQ70
Byfleet KT14 234 BK111
Cobham KT11 236 BW113
Erith DA8 189 FH80
Slough SL1 174 AV75
Canadas, The, Brox. EN10 89 DY25
Canada Sq, E14 34 C2
Canada St, SE16 33 J5
⊖ **Canada Water** 33 H5
Canada Way, W12 161 CV73
Canadian Av, SE6 205 EB88
Canadian Mem Av, Egh. TW20 214 AT96
Canal App, SE8 45 L1
Canal Bk Ms, Wok. GU21
off Vale Fm Rd 248 AY117
Canal Basin, Grav. DA12 213 GK86
Canal Boul, NW1 7 N4
Canal Bldg, N1
off Shepherdess Wk 9 K10
Canal Cl, E1 21 L4
W10 14 D4
Canal Ct, Berk. HP4 60 AY20
● **Canal Est**, Langley SL3 175 BA75
Canal Gro, SE15 44 D2
Canal Path, E2 10 A9
Canal Rd, Grav. DA12 213 GJ86
● **Canalside**, Berk. HP4 60 AT17
Canal Side, Hare. UB9 114 BG52
Canalside, Red. RH1 273 DH131
Canal St, SE5 43 L3
Canal Wk, N1 9 M8
NW10 *off West End Cl* 160 CQ66
SE26 204 DW92
Croydon CR0 224 DS100
Canal Way, N1 9 K10
NW1 16 D2
NW8 16 C3
NW10 161 CT70
W2 15 M6
W9 15 H6

Canal Way, W10 . . . 15 H6
Harefield UB9 . . . 114 BG51
Canal Way Wk, W10 . . . 14 C4
Canal Wf, Slou. SL3 . . . 175 BA75
⊖ Canary Wharf . . . 34 C3
DLR Canary Wharf . . . 34 B2
RB Canary Wharf Pier . . . 33 P2
Canberra Cl, NW4 . . . 141 CU55
Dagenham RM10 . . . 169 FD66
Hornchurch RM12 . . . 150 FJ63
St. Albans AL3 . . . 65 CF16
Canberra Cres, Dag. RM10 . . . 169 FD66
Canberra Dr, Hayes UB4 . . . 158 BW69
Northolt UB5 . . . 158 BW69
Canberra Pl, Rich. TW9
off Marksbury Av . . . 180 CN83
Sch Canberra Prim Sch, W12
off Australia Rd . . . 161 CV73
Canberra Rd, E6
off Barking Rd . . . 167 EM67
SE7 . . . 186 EJ79
W13 . . . 159 CG74
Bexleyheath DA7 . . . 188 EX79
London Heathrow Airport
TW6 . . . 176 BN83
Canberra Sq, Til. RM18 . . . 193 GG82
Canbury Av, Kings.T. KT2 . . . 220 CM95
● Canbury Business Pk,
Kings.T. KT2 off Elm Cres . . 220 CL95
Canbury Ms, SE26
off Wells Pk Rd . . . 204 DU90
Canbury Pk Rd, Kings.T. KT2 . . 220 CL95
Canbury Pas, Kings.T. KT2 . . . 219 CK95
Canbury Path, Orp. BR5 . . . 228 EU98
Sch Canbury Sch, Kings.T. KT2
off Kingston Hill . . . 200 CP93
Cancell Rd, SW9 . . . 42 F6
Candahar Rd, SW11 . . . 40 C9
Cander Way, S.Ock. RM15 . . . 171 FV73
Candlefield Cl, Hem.H. HP3
off Candlefield Rd . . . 62 BN23
Candlefield Rd, Hem.H. HP3 . . . 62 BN23
Candlefield Wk, Hem.H. HP3
off Candlefield Rd . . . 62 BN23
Candle Gro, SE15 . . . 184 DV83
Candlemakers Apts, SW11 . . . 40 A10
Candlemas La, Beac. HP9 . . . 111 AL53
Candlemas Mead, Beac. HP9 . . 111 AL53
Candlemas Oaks, Beac. HP9 . . . 111 AL53
Candler Ms, Twick. TW1 . . . 199 CG87
Candler St, N15 . . . 144 DR58
Candlerush Cl, Wok. GU22 . . . 249 BB117
Candlestick La, Wal.Cr. EN7
off Park La . . . 88 DV27
Candle St, E1 . . . 21 L6
Candover Cl, Harm. UB7 . . . 176 BK80
Candover Rd, Horn. RM12 . . . 149 FH60
Candover St, W1 . . . 17 L7
Candy Cft, Bkhm KT23 . . . 268 CB125
Candy St, E3 . . . 11 P8
Cane Hill, Harold Wd RM3
off Bennison Dr . . . 128 FK54
Caneland Ct, Wal.Abb. EN9 . . . 90 EF34
Canes La, Hast. CM17 . . . 74 EX21
North Weald Bassett CM16 . . 74 FA23
Canewdon Cl, Wok. GU22 . . . 248 AY119
Caney Ms, NW2 . . . 141 CX61
Canfield Dr, Ruis. HA4 . . . 137 BV64
Canfield Gdns, NW6 . . . 5 N5
Canfield Pl, NW6 . . . 5 N5
Canfield Rd, Rain. RM13 . . . 169 FF67
Woodford Green IG8 . . . 124 EL52
Canford Av, Nthlt. UB5 . . . 158 BY67
Canford Cl, Enf. EN2 . . . 103 DN40
Canford Dr, Add. KT15 . . . 216 BH103
Canford Gdns, N.Mal. KT3 . . . 220 CR100
Canford Pl, Tedd. TW11 . . . 199 CH93
Canford Rd, SW11 . . . 202 DG85
Cangels Cl, Hem.H. HP1 . . . 61 BF22
Canham Rd, SE25 . . . 224 DS97
W3 . . . 180 CS75
Can Hatch, Tad. KT20 . . . 255 CY118
Canmore Gdns, SW16 . . . 203 DJ94
Sch Cann Hall Prim Sch, E11
off Cann Hall Rd . . . 146 EF62
Cann Hall Rd, E11 . . . 13 J1
Canning Cres, N22 . . . 121 DM53
Canning Cross, SE5 . . . 43 N9
Canning Pas, W8 . . . 27 N6
Canning Pl, W8 . . . 27 N6
Canning Pl Ms, W8 . . . 27 N5
Canning Rd, E15 . . . 23 J1
E17 . . . 145 DY56
N5 . . . 143 DP62
Croydon CR0 . . . 224 DT103
Harrow HA3 . . . 139 CF55
Cannington Rd, Dag. RM9 . . . 168 EW65
CANNING TOWN, E16 . . . 23 N8
⊖ Canning Town . . . 23 K8
⊖ Canning Town . . . 23 K8
⊖ Canning Town . . . 23 K8
DLR Canning Town, E16 . . . 23 K8
Cannizaro Rd, SW19 . . . 201 CW93
Cannonbury Av, Pnr. HA5 . . . 138 BX58
Cannon Cl, SW20 . . . 221 CW97
Hampton TW12 . . . 198 CB93
Cannon Ct, EC1
off Brewhouse Yd . . . 19 H4
Cannon Cres, Chobham GU24 . 232 AS111
Cannon Dr, E14 . . . 34 A1
Cannon Gate, Slou. SL2
off Uxbridge Rd . . . 154 AW73
Cannon Gro, Fetch. KT22 . . . 253 CE121
Cannon Hill, N14 . . . 121 DK48
NW6 . . . 5 K2
Cannon Hill Cl, Bray SL6 . . . 172 AC77
Cannon Hill La, SW20 . . . 221 CY97
Cannon La, NW3 . . . 142 DD62
Pinner HA5 . . . 138 BY60
Sch Cannon La First & Mid Schs,
Pnr. HA5
off Cannonbury Av . . . 138 BX58
Cannon Ms, Wal.Abb. EN9 . . . 89 EB33
Cannon Mill Av, Chesh. HP5 . . . 76 AR33
Cannon Pl, NW3 . . . 142 DD62
SE7 . . . 37 H10
Cannon Rd, N14 . . . 121 DL48
Bexleyheath DA7 . . . 188 EY81
Watford WD18 . . . 98 BW43
Cannonside, Fetch. KT22 . . . 253 CE122
Cannons Meadow, Tewin AL6 . . 52 DE06
⇌ Cannon Street . . . 31 L1
⊖ Cannon Street . . . 31 L1
Cannon St, EC4 . . . 19 J9
St. Albans AL3 . . . 65 CD19
Cannon St Rd, E1 . . . 20 E8
● Cannon Trd Est, Wem. HA9 . 140 CP63
Cannon Way, Fetch. KT22 . . . 253 CE121
West Molesey KT8 . . . 218 CA98
● Cannon Wf Business Cen,
SE8 . . . 33 L9
● Cannon Workshops, E14 . . 34 A1
Canon All, EC4
off St. Paul's Chyd . . . 19 H9
Canon Av, Rom. RM6 . . . 148 EW57
Sch Canon Barnett Prim Sch, E1 . 20 B8
Canon Beck Rd, SE16 . . . 33 H4
Canonbie Rd, SE23 . . . 204 DW87
CANONBURY, N1 . . . 9 H5
Canonbury . . . 9 J3
Canonbury Cres, N1 . . . 9 J6
Canonbury Gro, N1 . . . 9 J6
Canonbury La, N1 . . . 8 G6
Canonbury Pk N, N1 . . . 9 J5
Canonbury Pk S, N1 . . . 9 J5
Canonbury Pl, N1 . . . 9 H5
Sch Canonbury Prim Sch, N1 . . . 9 H5
Canonbury Rd, N1 . . . 8 G5
Enfield EN1 . . . 104 DS39
Canonbury Sq, N1 . . . 9 H6
Canonbury St, N1 . . . 9 J6
Canonbury Vil, N1 . . . 9 H6
Canonbury Yd, N1 . . . 9 K8
Canonbury Yd W, N1 . . . 9 H5
Canon Mohan Cl, N14
off Farm La . . . 103 DH44
Sch Canon Palmer Cath
High Sch, Ilf. IG3
off Aldborough Rd S . . . 147 ES60
Canon Rd, Brom. BR1 . . . 226 EJ97
Canon Row, SW1 . . . 30 A5
Canons Brook, Harl. CM19 . . . 73 EN15
Canons Cl, N2 . . . 142 DD59
Edgware HA8 . . . 118 CM51
Radlett WD7 . . . 99 CH35
Reigate RH2 . . . 271 CZ133
Jct Canons Cor, Edg. HA8 . . . 118 CL49
Canons Ct, Edg. HA8 . . . 118 CM51
Canons Dr, Edg. HA8 . . . 118 CL51
Canons Gate, Chsht EN8 . . . 89 DZ26
Harlow CM20 . . . 57 EN14
Sch Canons High Sch, Edg.
HA8 off Shaldon Rd . . . 118 CM54
Canon's Hill, Couls. CR5 . . . 257 DN117
Canons La, Tad. KT20 . . . 255 CY118
Canonsleigh Rd, Dag. RM9 . . . 168 EV66
CANONS PARK, Edg. HA8 . . . 118 CL52
⊖ Canons Park . . . 118 CL52
Canons Pk Cl, Edg. HA8
off Donnefield Av . . . 118 CL52
Canons Rd, Ware SG12 . . . 54 DW05
Canon St, N1 . . . 9 J9
Canons Wk, Croy. CR0 . . . 225 DX104
Canopus Way, Nthwd. HA6 . . . 115 BU49
Staines TW19 . . . 196 BL87
Canopy La, Harl. CM17 . . . 58 EW14
Canrobert St, E2 . . . 20 E2
Cantelowes Rd, NW1 . . . 7 P5
Canterbury Av, Ilf. IG1 . . . 146 EL59
Sidcup DA15 . . . 208 EW89
Slough SL2 . . . 153 AQ70
Upminster RM14 . . . 151 FT60
Canterbury Cl, E6 . . . 25 J8
Amersham HP7 . . . 77 AS39
Beckenham BR3 . . . 225 EB95
Chigwell IG7 . . . 125 ET48
Dartford DA1 . . . 210 FN87
Greenford UB6 . . . 158 CB72
Northwood HA6 . . . 115 BT51
Worcester Park KT4 . . . 221 CX103
Canterbury Ct, Dor. RH4
off Station Rd . . . 285 CG135
Canterbury Cres, SW9 . . . 183 DN83
Canterbury Gro, SE27 . . . 203 DP90
Canterbury Ho, E3 off Bow Rd . 22 C2
SE1 . . . 30 D6
Borehamwood WD6 . . . 100 CN40
Erith DA8 off Arthur St . . . 189 FF80
Canterbury Ms, Oxshott KT22 . 236 CC113
Windsor SL4 . . . 173 AN82
Canterbury Par, S.Ock. RM15 . . 171 FW69
Canterbury Pl, SE17 . . . 31 H9
Canterbury Rd, E10 . . . 145 EC59
NW6 . . . 15 J1
Borehamwood WD6 . . . 100 CN40
Croydon CR0 . . . 223 DM101
Feltham TW13 . . . 198 BY90
Gravesend DA12 . . . 213 GJ89
Guildford GU2 . . . 264 AT132
Harrow HA1, HA2 . . . 138 CB57
Morden SM4 . . . 222 DC99
Watford WD17 . . . 97 BV40
Canterbury Ter, NW6 . . . 5 J10
Canterbury Way, Crox.Grn WD3 . 97 BQ41
Great Warley CM13 . . . 129 FW51
Purfleet RM19 . . . 191 FS80
Cantium Retail Pk, SE1 . . . 44 C2
Cantley Gdns, SE19 . . . 224 DT95
Ilford IG2 . . . 147 EQ58
Cantley Rd, W7 . . . 179 CG76
Canton St, E14 . . . 22 A9
Cantrell Rd, E3 . . . 21 P5
Cantwell Rd, SE18 . . . 187 EP80
Canute Gdns, SE16 . . . 33 J8
Canvey St, SE1 . . . 31 H2
Capability Way, Green. DA9 . . . 191 FW84
Cape Cl, Bark. IG11 . . . 167 EP65
Capel Av, Wall. SM6 . . . 241 DM106
Capel Cl, N20 . . . 120 DC48
Bromley BR2 . . . 226 EL102
Capel Ct, EC2 . . . 19 M9
SE20 . . . 224 DW95
Capel Cres, Stan. HA7 . . . 117 CG47
Capel Gdns, Ilf. IG3 . . . 147 ET63
Pinner HA5 . . . 138 BZ56
Capella Rd, Nthwd. HA6 . . . 115 BT50
Capell Av, Chorl. WD3 . . . 95 BC43
Capell Rd, Chorl. WD3 . . . 95 BC43
Capell Way, Chorl. WD3 . . . 95 BD43
Coll Capel Manor Coll,
Regent's Pk, NW1 . . . 17 H3
Sch Capel Manor Coll & Gdns, Enf.
EN1 off Bullsmoor La . . . 104 DU35
Sch Capel Manor Prim Sch, Enf.
EN1 off Bullsmoor La . . . 104 DV35
Capel Pl, Dart. DA2 . . . 210 FJ91
Capel Pt, E7 . . . 146 EH63
Capel Rd, E7 . . . 146 EH63
E12 . . . 146 EK63
Barnet EN4 . . . 102 DE44
Capel Rd, Enf. EN1 . . . 104 DV36
Watford WD19 . . . 98 BY44
Capel Vere Wk, Wat. WD17 . . . 97 BS39
Capener's Cl, SW1 . . . 28 G5
Capern Rd, SW18
off Cargill Rd . . . 202 DC88
Cape Rd, N17
off High Cross Rd . . . 144 DU55
St. Albans AL1 . . . 65 CH20
Cape Yd, E1 . . . 32 D2
H Capio Nightingale Hosp,
NW1 . . . 16 D6
● Capital Business Cen,
Mitch. CR4 . . . 222 DF99
Wembley HA0 . . . 159 CK68
● Capital Business Pk,
Borwd. WD6 . . . 100 CQ41
Sch Capital City Acad, NW10
off Doyle Gdns . . . 161 CV67
Coll Capital Coll, SE15 . . . 44 F4
Coll Capital Coll (CIFE) London
Sch of Insurance, WC1 . . . 18 C6
Capital E Apts, E16
off Western Gateway . . . 35 P1
Capital Interchange Way,
Brent. TW8 . . . 180 CN78
● Capital Pk, Old Wok. GU22 . 249 BB121
● Capital Pl, Harl. CM19
off Lovet Rd . . . 73 EN16
● Capitol Ind Pk, NW9 . . . 140 CQ55
Capitol Way, NW9 . . . 140 CQ55
Capland St, NW8 . . . 16 B4
Caple Par, NW10
off Harley Rd . . . 160 CS68
Caple Rd, NW10 . . . 161 CT68
Capon Cl, Brwd. CM14 . . . 130 FV46
Caponfield, Welw.G.C. AL7 . . . 52 DB11
Cappell La, Stans.Abb. SG12 . . . 55 ED10
Capper St, WC1 . . . 17 M5
Caprea Cl, Hayes UB4
off Triandra Way . . . 158 BX71
Capri Rd, Croy. CR0 . . . 224 DT102
● Capstan Cen, Til. RM18 . . . 192 GD80
Capstan Cl, Rom. RM6 . . . 148 EV58
Capstan Ct, Dart. DA2 . . . 190 FQ84
Capstan Dr, Rain. RM13 . . . 169 FG70
Capstan Ms, Grav. DA11 . . . 212 GE87
Capstan Ride, Enf. EN2 . . . 103 DN40
Capstan Rd, SE8 . . . 33 N8
Capstan Sq, E14 . . . 34 F5
Capstan's Wf, Wok. GU21 . . . 248 AT118
Capstan Way, SE16 . . . 33 M3
Capstone Rd, Brom. BR1 . . . 206 EF91
● Capswood Business Cen,
Denh. UB9 . . . 135 BB60
Captain Cook Cl, Ch.St.G. HP8 . 112 AU49
Captains Cl, Chesh. HP5 . . . 76 AN27
Captains Wk, Berk. HP4 . . . 60 AX20
Capthorne Av, Har. HA2 . . . 138 BY60
Capuchin Cl, Stan. HA7 . . . 117 CH51
Capulet Ms, E16 . . . 35 P2
Capulet Sq, E3 . . . 22 D3
Capworth St, E10 . . . 145 EA60
Caractacus Cottage Vw,
Wat. WD18 . . . 115 BU45
Caractacus Grn, Wat. WD18 . . . 97 BT44
Caradoc Cl, W2 . . . 15 J8
Caradoc St, SE10 . . . 35 J10
Caradon Cl, E11 . . . 146 EE60
Woking GU21 . . . 248 AV118
Caradon Way, N15 . . . 144 DR56
Caravan La, Rick. WD3 . . . 114 BL45
Caravel Cl, E14 . . . 34 A6
Grays RM16 . . . 192 FZ76
Caravelle Gdns, Nthlt. UB5
off Javelin Way . . . 158 BX69
Caravel Ms, SE8 . . . 46 A2
Caraway Cl, E13 . . . 24 A6
Caraway Pl, Guil. GU2 . . . 264 AU129
Wallington SM6 . . . 223 DH104
Carberry Rd, SE19 . . . 204 DS93
Carbery Av, W3 . . . 180 CM75
Carbis Cl, E4 . . . 123 ED46
Carbis Rd, E14 . . . 21 N8
Carbone Hill, Newgate St SG13 . 87 DK26
Northaw EN6 . . . 87 DJ27
Carbuncle Pas Way, N17 . . . 122 DU54
Carburton St, W1 . . . 17 K6
Carbury Cl, Horn. RM12 . . . 170 FJ65
Cardale St, E14 . . . 34 E5
Cardamom Cl, Guil. GU2 . . . 264 AU130
Carde Cl, Hert. SG14 . . . 53 DM08
Carden Rd, SE15 . . . 184 DV83
Cardiff Cl, Rom. RM5 . . . 127 FD52
Cardiff Rd, W7 . . . 179 CG76
Enfield EN3 . . . 104 DV42
Watford WD18 . . . 97 BV44
● Cardiff Rd Ind Est,
Wat. WD18 . . . 97 BV44
Cardiff St, SE18 . . . 187 ES80
Cardiff Way, Abb.L. WD5 . . . 81 BU32
Cardigan Cl, Slou. SL1 . . . 153 AM73
Woking GU21 . . . 248 AS118
Cardigan Gdns, Ilf. IG3 . . . 148 EU61
Cardigan Pl, SE3 . . . 47 J8
Cardigan Rd, E3 . . . 11 P10
SW13 . . . 181 CU82
SW19 off Haydons Rd . . . 202 DC93
Richmond TW10 . . . 200 CL86
Cardigan St, SE11 . . . 30 E10
Cardigan Wk, N1
off Ashby Gro . . . 9 K6
Cardinal Av, Borwd. WD6 . . . 100 CP41
Kingston upon Thames KT2 . 200 CL92
Morden SM4 . . . 221 CY100
Cardinal Bourne St, SE1 . . . 31 M7
Cardinal Cap All, SE1
off New Globe Wk . . . 31 J1
Cardinal Cl, Chsht EN7 . . . 88 DT26
Chislehurst BR7 . . . 227 ER95
Edgware HA8 off Abbots Rd . 118 CR52
Morden SM4 . . . 221 CY101
South Croydon CR2 . . . 242 DU113
Worcester Park KT4 . . . 239 CU105
Cardinal Ct, Borwd. WD6
off Cardinal Av . . . 100 CP41
Cardinal Cres, N.Mal. KT3 . . . 220 CQ96
Cardinal Dr, Ilf. IG6 . . . 125 EQ51
Walton-on-Thames KT12 . . 218 BX102
Cardinal Gro, St.Alb. AL3 . . . 64 CB22
Cardinal Hinsley Cl, NW10 . . . 161 CU68
Sch Cardinal Hinsley Mathematics
& Computing Coll, NW10
off Harlesden Rd . . . 161 CU67
Sch Cardinal Newman Catholic
Prim Sch, Hersham KT12
off Arch Rd . . . 218 BX104
Cardinal Pl, SW15 . . . 181 CX84
Sch Cardinal Pole RC Sch, E9 . . . 11 L3
Annexe, E9 . . . 11 K7
Cardinal Rd, Chaff.Hun. RM16 . 192 FY76
Feltham TW13 . . . 197 BV88
Ruislip HA4 . . . 138 BX60
Sch Cardinal Rd Inf & Nurs Sch,
Felt. TW13 off Cardinal Rd . 197 BV88
Cardinals Wk, Hmptn. TW12 . . . 198 CC94
Sunbury-on-Thames TW16 . 197 BS93
Taplow SL6 . . . 152 AJ72
Cardinals Way, N19 . . . 143 DK60
Sch Cardinal Vaughan Mem Sch,
W14 . . . 26 E4
Cardinal Wk, SW1
off Palace St . . . 29 L6
Cardinal Way, Har. HA3 . . . 139 CE55
Rainham RM13 . . . 170 FK68
Sch Cardinal Wiseman Sch, The,
Grnf. UB6
off Greenford Rd . . . 158 CC71
Cardine Ms, SE15 . . . 44 E4
Cardingham, Wok. GU21 . . . 248 AU117
Cardington Sq, Houns. TW4 . . 178 BX84
Cardington St, NW1 . . . 17 L2
Cardinham Rd, Orp. BR6 . . . 245 ET105
Cardozo Rd, N7 . . . 8 B2
Cardrew Av, N12 . . . 120 DD50
Cardrew Cl, N12 . . . 120 DD50
Cardross St, W6 . . . 181 CV76
Sch Cardwell Prim Sch, SE18 . . . 37 J8
Cardwell Rd, N7 . . . 143 DL63
Cardwells Keep, Guil. GU2 . . . 264 AU131
Cardy Rd, Hem.H. HP1 . . . 62 BH21
Carew Cl, N7 . . . 143 DM61
Chafford Hundred RM16 . . 192 FY76
Coulsdon CR5 . . . 257 DP119
Carew Ct, Sutt. SM2 . . . 240 DB109
Sch Carew Manor Sch, Wall.
SM6 off Church Rd . . . 223 DK104
Carew Rd, N17 . . . 122 DU54
W13 . . . 179 CJ75
Ashford TW15 . . . 197 BQ93
Mitcham CR4 . . . 222 DG96
Northwood HA6 . . . 115 BS51
Thornton Heath CR7 . . . 223 DP97
Wallington SM6 . . . 241 DJ107
Carew St, SE5 . . . 43 H8
Carew Way, Orp. BR5 . . . 228 EW102
Watford WD19 . . . 116 BZ48
Carey Cl, Wind. SL4 . . . 173 AP83
Carey Ct, Bexh. DA6 . . . 209 FB85
Carey Gdns, SW8 . . . 41 N7
Carey La, EC2 . . . 19 J8
Carey Pl, SW1 . . . 29 N9
Carey Rd, Dag. RM9 . . . 148 EY63
Careys Cft, Berk. HP4 . . . 60 AU16
Carey's Fld, Dunt.Grn TN13 . . 263 FE120
Carey St, WC2 . . . 18 D9
Careys Wd, Smallfield RH6 . . . 291 DP148
Carey Way, Wem. HA9 . . . 140 CP63
Carfax Pl, SW4
off Holwood Pl . . . 183 DK84
Carfax Rd, Hayes UB3 . . . 177 BT78
Hornchurch RM12 . . . 149 FF63
Carfree Cl, N1 . . . 8 F6
Cargill Rd, SW18 . . . 202 DB88
Cargo Forecourt Rd, Gat. RH6 . 290 DD152
Cargo Rd, Gat. RH6 . . . 290 DD152
Cargreen Pl, SE25
off Cargreen Rd . . . 224 DT98
Cargreen Rd, SE25 . . . 224 DT98
Carholme Rd, SE23 . . . 205 DZ88
Carisbrook Cl, Enf. EN1 . . . 104 DT39
Carisbrooke Av, Bex. DA5 . . . 208 EX88
Watford WD24 . . . 98 BX39
Carisbrooke Cl, Horn. RM11 . . 150 FN60
Hounslow TW4 . . . 198 BY87
Stanmore HA7 . . . 117 CK54
Carisbrooke Ct, Slou. SL1 . . . 154 AT73
Carisbrooke Gdns, SE15 . . . 44 B4
Carisbrooke Ho, Kings.T. KT2
off Kingsgate Rd . . . 220 CL95
Carisbrooke Rd, E17 . . . 145 DY56
Bromley BR2 . . . 226 EJ98
Mitcham CR4 . . . 223 DK98
St. Albans AL2 . . . 82 CB26
Carisbrook Rd, Pilg.Hat. CM15 . 130 FV44
Carker's La, NW5 . . . 7 J2
Carlbury Cl, St.Alb. AL1 . . . 65 CH21
Carl Ekman Ho, Grav. DA11 . . 212 GD87
Carleton Av, Wall. SM6 . . . 241 DK109
Carleton Cl, Esher KT10 . . . 219 CD102
Carleton Pl, Hort.Kir. DA4 . . . 230 FQ98
Carleton Rd, N7 . . . 7 N2
Cheshunt EN8 . . . 89 DX28
Dartford DA1 . . . 210 FN87
Carlile Cl, E3 . . . 21 P1
Carlina Gdns, Wdf.Grn. IG8 . . . 124 EH50
Carlingford Gdns, Mitch. CR4 . 202 DF94
Carlingford Rd, N15 . . . 143 DP55
NW3 . . . 142 DD63
Morden SM4 . . . 221 CX100
Carlisle Av, EC3 . . . 19 P9
W3 . . . 160 CS72
St. Albans AL1, AL3 . . . 65 CD18
Carlisle Cl, Kings.T. KT2 . . . 220 CN95
Pinner HA5 . . . 138 BY59
Carlisle Gdns, Har. HA3 . . . 139 CK59
Ilford IG1 . . . 146 EL58
Sch Carlisle Inf Sch, Hmptn.
TW12 off Broad La . . . 198 CB93
Carlisle La, SE1 . . . 30 D7
Carlisle Ms, NW8 . . . 16 B6
Carlisle Pl, N11 . . . 121 DH49
SW1 . . . 29 L7
Carlisle Rd, E10 . . . 145 EA61
N4 . . . 143 DN59
NW6 . . . 4 E8
NW9 . . . 140 CQ55
Dartford DA1 . . . 210 FN86
Hampton TW12 . . . 198 CB94
Romford RM1 . . . 149 FF57
Slough SL1 . . . 153 AR73
Sutton SM1 . . . 239 CZ106
Carlisle St, W1 . . . 17 N9
Carlisle Wk, E8 . . . 10 A5
Carlisle Way, SW17 . . . 202 DG92
Carlos Pl, W1 . . . 29 H1
Carlow St, NW1 . . . 7 L10
Carlton Av, N14 . . . 103 DK43
Feltham TW14 . . . 198 BW86
Greenhithe DA9 . . . 211 FS86
Harrow HA3 . . . 139 CH57
Hayes UB3 . . . 177 BS77
South Croydon CR2 . . . 242 DS108
Carlton Av E, Wem. HA9 . . . 140 CL60
Carlton Av W, Wem. HA0 . . . 139 CH61
Carlton Cl, NW3 . . . 142 DA61
Borehamwood WD6 . . . 100 CR42
Chessington KT9 . . . 237 CK107
Edgware HA8 . . . 118 CN50
Carlton Cl, Nthlt. UB5
off Whitton Av W . . . 138 CC64
Upminster RM14 . . . 150 FP61
Woking GU21 . . . 233 AZ114
Carlton Ct, SW9 . . . 42 G6
Ilford IG6 . . . 147 ER55
Uxbridge UB8 . . . 156 BK71
Carlton Cres, Sutt. SM3 . . . 239 CY105
Carlton Dr, SW15 . . . 201 CY85
Ilford IG6 . . . 147 ER55
Carlton Gdns, SW1 . . . 29 N3
W5 . . . 159 CJ72
Carlton Grn, Red. RH1 . . . 272 DE131
Carlton Gro, SE15 . . . 44 E6
Carlton Hill, NW8 . . . 5 N9
Carlton Ho, Felt. TW14 . . . 197 BT87
Carlton Ho Ter, SW1 . . . 29 N3
Carlton Par, Orp. BR6 . . . 228 EV101
Sevenoaks TN13
off St. John's Hill . . . 279 FJ122
Carlton Pk Av, SW20 . . . 221 CW96
Carlton Pl, Nthwd. HA6 . . . 115 BP50
Weybridge KT13
off Castle Vw Rd . . . 235 BP105
Sch Carlton Prim Sch, NW5 . . . 7 H3
Carlton Rd, E11 . . . 146 EF60
E12 . . . 146 EK63
E17 . . . 123 DY53
N4 . . . 143 DN59
N11 . . . 120 DG50
SW14 . . . 180 CQ83
W4 . . . 180 CR75
W5 . . . 159 CJ73
Erith DA8 . . . 189 FB79
Grays RM16 . . . 193 GF75
New Malden KT3 . . . 220 CS96
Redhill RH1 . . . 272 DF131
Reigate RH2 . . . 272 DD132
Romford RM2 . . . 149 FG57
Sidcup DA14 . . . 207 ET92
Slough SL2 . . . 154 AV73
South Croydon CR2 . . . 242 DR107
Sunbury-on-Thames TW16 . . 197 BT94
Walton-on-Thames KT12 . . 217 BV101
Welling DA16 . . . 188 EV83
Woking GU21 . . . 233 BA114
Carlton Sq, E1 . . . 21 J4
Carlton St, SW1 . . . 29 N1
Carlton Ter, E11 . . . 146 EH57
N18 . . . 122 DR48
SE26 . . . 204 DW90
Carlton Twr Pl, SW1 . . . 28 F6
Carlton Tye, Horl. RH6 . . . 291 DJ148
Carlton Vale, NW6 . . . 15 K1
Sch Carlton Vale Inf Sch, NW6 . . 15 H2
Carlton Vil, SW15
off St. John's Av . . . 201 CX85
Carlwell St, SW17 . . . 202 DE92
Carlyle Av, Brom. BR1 . . . 226 EK97
Southall UB1 . . . 158 BZ73
Carlyle Cl, N2 . . . 142 DC58
West Molesey KT8 . . . 218 CB96
Carlyle Ct, SW10
off Chelsea Harbour . . . 39 P6
Carlyle Gdns, Sthl. UB1 . . . 158 BZ73
Carlyle Lo, New Barn. EN5
off Richmond Rd . . . 102 DC43
Carlyle Ms, E1 . . . 21 K4
Carlyle Pl, SW15 . . . 181 CX84
Carlyle Rd, E12 . . . 146 EL63
NW10 . . . 160 CR67
SE28 . . . 168 EV73
W5 . . . 179 CJ78
Croydon CR0 . . . 224 DU103
Staines TW18 . . . 195 BF94
★ Carlyle's Ho, SW3 . . . 40 C3
Carlyle Sq, SW3 . . . 40 B1
Carly Ms, E2 . . . 20 C3
Carlyon Av, Har. HA2 . . . 138 BZ63
Carlyon Cl, Wem. HA0 . . . 160 CL67
Carlyon Rd, Hayes UB4 . . . 158 BW72
Wembley HA0 . . . 160 CL68
Carlys Cl, Beck. BR3 . . . 225 DX96
Carmalt Gdns, SW15 . . . 181 CW84
Hersham KT12 . . . 236 BW106
Carmarthen Pl, SE1 . . . 31 N4
Carmarthen Rd, Slou. SL1 . . . 154 AS73
Carmel Cl, Wok. GU22 . . . 248 AY118
Carmel Ct, W8 . . . 27 L4
Wembley HA9 . . . 140 CP61
Carmelite Cl, Har. HA3 . . . 116 CC53
Carmelite Rd, Har. HA3 . . . 116 CC53
Carmelite St, EC4 . . . 18 F10
Carmelite Wk, Har. HA3 . . . 116 CC53
Carmelite Way, Har. HA3 . . . 116 CC54
Carmel Way, Rich. TW9 . . . 180 CP82
Carmen Ct, Borwd. WD6
off Belford Rd . . . 100 CM38
Carmen St, E14 . . . 22 C8
Carmichael Av, Green. DA9
off Lightermans Way . . . 191 FW84
Carmichael Cl, SW11
off Darien Rd . . . 182 DD83
Ruislip HA4 . . . 137 BU63
Carmichael Ms, SW18 . . . 202 DD87
Carmichael Rd, SE25 . . . 224 DU99
Carminia Rd, SW17 . . . 203 DH89
Carnaby Rd, Brox. EN10 . . . 71 DY20
Carnaby St, W1 . . . 17 L9
Carnach Grn, S.Ock. RM15 . . . 171 FV73
Carnac St, SE27 . . . 204 DR91
Carnanton Rd, E17 . . . 123 ED53
Carnarvon Av, Enf. EN1 . . . 104 DT41
Carnarvon Dr, Hayes UB3 . . . 177 BQ76
Carnarvon Rd, E10 . . . 145 EC58
E15 . . . 13 L4
E18 . . . 124 EF53
Barnet EN5 . . . 101 CY41
Carnation Cl, Rush Grn RM7 . . 149 FE61
Carnation St, SE2 . . . 188 EV78
Carnbrook Ms, SE3
off Carnbrook Rd . . . 186 EK83
Carnbrook Rd, SE3 . . . 186 EK83
Carnecke Gdns, SE9 . . . 206 EL85
Carnegie Cl, Enf. EN3 . . . 105 EB38
Surbiton KT6
off Fullers Av . . . 220 CM103
Carnegie Pl, SW19 . . . 201 CX90
Carnegie Rd, St.Alb. AL3 . . . 65 CD16
Carnegie St, N1 . . . 8 C9
CARNELES GREEN, Brox. EN10 . 70 DV22
Carnet Cl, Dart. DA1 . . . 209 FE87
Carnforth Cl, Epsom KT19 . . . 238 CP107
Carnforth Gdns, Horn. RM12 . . 149 FG64
Carnforth Rd, SW16 . . . 203 DK94
Carnie Lo, SW17
off Manville Rd . . . 203 DH90
Carnoustie Cl, SE28 . . . 168 EX72
Carnoustie Dr, N1 . . . 8 C7

Camwath Rd, SW6 182 DA83
Caro La, Hem.H. HP3 62 BN22
Carol Cl, NW4 141 CX56
Carolina Cl, E15 13 J3
Carolina Rd, Th.Hth. CR7 223 DP96
Caroline Cl, N10 121 DH54
SW16 203 DM90
W2 27 M1
Croydon CR0 242 DS105
Isleworth TW7 179 CD80
West Drayton UB7 176 BK75
Caroline Ct, Ashf. TW15 197 BP93
Stanmore HA7
off The Chase 117 CG51
Caroline Gdns, SE15 44 E4
Caroline Pl, SW11 41 H9
W2 15 M10
Harlington UB3 177 BS80
Watford WD19 98 BY44
Caroline Pl Ms, W2 27 M1
Caroline Rd, SW19 201 CZ94
Caroline St, E1 21 K9
Caroline Ter, SW1 28 G9
Caroline Wk, W6 38 E3
Carol St, NW1 7 L8
Carolyn Cl, Wok. GU21 248 AT119
Carolyn Dr, Orp. BR6 228 EU104
● **Carolyn Ho**, Croy. CR0
off Dingwall Rd 224 DR103
Caroon Dr, Sarratt WD3 96 BH36
Carpenders Av, Wat. WD19 116 BY48
CARPENDERS PARK,
Wat. WD19 116 BZ47
⊖ **Carpenders Park** 116 BX48
Carpenter Cl, Epsom KT17 239 CT109
Carpenter Gdns, N21 121 DP47
Carpenter Path, Hutt. CM13 131 GD43
Carpenters Arms La, Thnwd
CM16 92 EV25
Carpenters Arms Path, SE9
off Eltham High St 207 EM86
Carpenters Cl, Barn. EN5 102 DB44
Carpenters Ct, Twick. TW2 199 CE89
Carpenters Ms, N7 8 B3
Carpenters Pl, SW4 183 DK84
Carpenters Prim Sch, E15 12 F8
Carpenters Rd, E15 12 F7
Enfield EN1 104 DW36
Carpenter St, W1 29 J1
Carpenters Wd Dr, Chorl. WD3 95 BB42
Carpenter Way, Pot.B. EN6 86 DC33
Carrack Ho, Erith DA8
off Saltford Cl 189 FE78
Carrara Cl, SW9 183 DP84
Carrara Ms, E8 10 C3
Carrara Wf, SW6 38 F10
Carr Cl, Stan. HA7 117 CG51
Carre Ms, SE5 43 H7
Carr Gro, SE18 37 H8
Carriage Dr E, SW11 40 G4
Carriage Dr N, SW11 41 H3
Carriage Dr S, SW11 40 E6
Carriage Dr W, SW11 40 E5
Carriage Ms, Ilf. IG1 147 EQ61
Carriage Pl, N16 144 DR62
SW16 203 DJ92
Carriages, The, Ware SG12
off Station Rd 55 DY07
Carriage St, SE18 37 P7
Carriageway, The, Brasted
TN16 262 EX124
Carrick Cl, Islw. TW7 179 CG83
Carrick Dr, Ilf. IG6 125 EQ53
Sevenoaks TN13 279 FH123
Carrick Gdns, N17
off Flexmere Rd 122 DS52
Carrick Gate, Esher KT10 218 CC104
Carrick Ms, SE8 46 A2
Carriden Ct, Hert. SG14
off The Ridgeway 53 DM07
Carrill Way, Belv. DA17 188 EX77
Carrington Av, Borwd. WD6 100 CP43
Hounslow TW3 198 CB85
Carrington Cl, Arkley EN5 101 CU43
Borehamwood WD6 100 CQ43
Croydon CR0 225 DY101
Kingston upon Thames KT2 200 CQ92
Redhill RH1 272 DF133
Carrington Gdns, E7
off Woodford Rd 146 EG63
Carrington Pl, Esher KT10 236 CB105
Carrington Rd, Dart. DA1 210 FM86
Richmond TW10 180 CN84
Slough SL1 154 AS73
Carrington Sq, Har. HA3 116 CC52
Carrington St, W1 29 J3
Carrol Cl, NW5 7 J1
Carroll Av, Guil. GU1 265 BB134
Carroll Cl, E15 13 K3
Carroll Hill, Loug. IG10 107 EM41
Carronade Ct, N7
off Eden Gro 8 D3
Carronade Pl, SE28 187 EQ76
Carron Cl, E14 22 D8
Carroun Rd, SW8 42 C4
Carroway La, Grnf. UB6 159 CD69
Carrow Rd, Dag. RM9 168 EV66
Walton-on-Thames KT12 218 BX104
Carr Rd, E17 123 DZ54
Northolt UB5 158 CA65
Carrs La, N21 104 DQ43
Carr St, E14 21 M7
CARSHALTON, SM5 240 DD105
⇌ **Carshalton** 240 DF105
CARSHALTON BEECHES,
Cars. SM5 240 DD109
⇌ **Carshalton Beeches** 240 DF107
Carshalton Boys Sports Coll,
Cars. SM5
off Winchcombe Rd 222 DE103
Carshalton Coll, Cars. SM5
off Nightingale Rd 222 DF104
Carshalton Gro, Sutt. SM1 240 DD105
Carshalton High Sch for Girls,
Cars. SM5 *off West St* 222 DF104
CARSHALTON ON THE HILL,
Cars. SM5 240 DG109
Carshalton Pk Rd, Cars. SM5 240 DF106
Carshalton Pl, Cars. SM5 240 DG105
Carshalton Rd, Bans. SM7 240 DF114
Carshalton SM5 240 DC106
Mitcham CR4 222 DG98
Sutton SM1 240 DC106
Carshalton War Mem Hosp,
Cars. SM5 240 DF107
Carsington Gdns, Dart. DA1 210 FK89
Carslake Rd, SW15 201 CW86
Carson Rd, E16 23 P5
SE21 204 DQ89
Carson Rd, Cockfos. EN4 102 DF42
Carson Ter, W11 26 E2
Carstairs Rd, SE6 205 EC90
Carston Cl, SE12 206 EF85
Carswell Cl, Hutt. CM13 131 GD44
Ilford IG4 146 EK56
Carswell Rd, SE6 205 EC87
Cartbridge Cl, Send GU23
off Send Rd 249 BB123
Cartel Cl, Purf. RM19 191 FR77
Carter Cl, NW9 140 CR58
Romford RM5 127 FB52
Wallington SM6 241 DK108
Windsor SL4 173 AN82
Carter Dr, Rom. RM5 127 FB52
Carteret St, SW1 29 N5
Carteret Way, SE8 33 M9
Carterhatch Inf Sch, Enf.
EN1 *off Carterhatch La* 104 DV39
Carterhatch Jun Sch, Enf.
EN1 *off Carterhatch La* 104 DV39
Carterhatch La, Enf. EN1 104 DU40
Carterhatch Rd, Enf. EN3 104 DW40
Carter Ho, SW11
off Petergate 182 DC84
Carter La, EC4 19 H9
Carter Pl, SE17 43 K1
Carter Rd, E13 166 EH67
SW19 202 DD93
Carters Cl, Guil. GU1 264 AY130
Worcester Park KT4 221 CX103
Carters Cotts, Red. RH1 288 DE136
Cartersfield Rd, Wal.Abb. EN9 89 EC34
CARTERS GREEN, Harl. CM17 59 FD13
Carters Hill, Undrvr TN15 279 FP127
Carters Hill Cl, SE9 206 EJ88
Carters La, SE23 205 DY89
Epping Green CM16 73 EP24
Woking GU22 249 BC120
Carters Mead, Harl. CM17 74 EV16
Cartersmead Cl, Horl. RH6 291 DH147
Carters Rd, Epsom KT17 255 CT115
Carters Row, Nthflt DA11 213 GF88
Carter St, SE17 43 J2
Carters Yd, SW18 202 DA85
Carter Wk, Penn HP10 110 AC47
Carthagena Est, Brox. EN10 71 EC20
Carthew Rd, W6 181 CV76
Carthew Vil, W6 181 CV76
Carthouse La, Wok. GU21 232 AS114
Carthusian St, EC1 19 J6
Cartier Circle, E14 34 D3
Carting La, WC2 30 B1
Cart La, E4 123 ED45
Cartmel, NW1 17 L2
Cartmel Cl, N17
off Heybourne Rd 122 DV52
Reigate RH2 272 DE133
Cartmel Gdns, Mord. SM4 222 DC99
Cartmel Rd, Bexh. DA7 188 FA81
Carton St, W1 16 F8
Cart Path, Wat. WD25 82 BW33
Cartridge Pl, SE18 37 P7
Cartwright Gdns, WC1 18 A3
Cartwright Rd, Dag. RM9 168 EZ66
Cartwright St, E1 20 B10
Cartwright Way, SW13 181 CV80
Carve Ley, Welw.G.C. AL7 52 DB10
Carver Cl, W4 180 CQ76
Carver Rd, SE24 204 DQ86
Carville Cres, Brent. TW8 180 CL77
Cary Rd, E11 146 EE63
Carysfort Rd, N8 143 DK57
N16 144 DR62
Cary Wk, Rad. WD7 83 CH34
Casby Ho, SE16 32 C6
Cascade Av, N10 143 DJ56
Cascade Cl, Buck.H. IG9
off Cascade Rd 124 EK47
Orpington BR5 228 EW97
Cascade Rd, Buck.H. IG9 124 EK47
Cascades, Croy. CR0 243 DZ110
Cascades Twr, E14 34 P3
Caselden Cl, Add. KT15 234 BJ106
Casella Rd, SE14 45 J5
Casewick Rd, SE27 203 DP91
Casey Cl, NW8 16 C3
Casimir Rd, E5 144 DV62
Casino Av, SE24 204 DQ85
Caspian Cl, Purf. RM19 190 FN77
Caspian St, SE5 43 L4
Caspian Wk, E16 24 E9
Caspian Way, Purf. RM19 190 FN78
Swanscombe DA10 212 FY85
Caspian Wf, E3 *off Violet Rd* 22 C6
Cassandra Cl, Nthlt. UB5 139 CD63
Cassandra Gate, Chsht EN8 89 DZ27
Casselden Rd, NW10 160 CR66
Cassel Hosp, The, Ham
TW10 199 CK91
Cassidy Rd, SW6 39 J5
Cassilda Rd, SE2 188 EU77
Cassilis Rd, E14 34 B5
Twickenham TW1 199 CH85
Cassiobridge, Wat. WD18 97 BR42
Cassiobridge Rd, Wat. WD18 97 BS42
Cassiobury Av, Felt. TW14 197 BT86
Cassiobury Ct, Wat. WD17 97 BS40
Cassiobury Dr, Wat. WD17 97 BT40
Cassiobury Inf & Nurs Sch,
Wat. WD17
off Bellmount Wd Av 97 BS39
Cassiobury Jun Sch,
Wat. WD17 *off*
Bellmount Wd Av 97 BS39
★ **Cassiobury Park**, Wat. WD18 97 BS41
Cassiobury Pk, Wat. WD18 97 BS41
Cassiobury Pk Av, Wat. WD18 97 BS41
Cassiobury Rd, E17 145 DX57
Cassio Pl, Wat. WD18 97 BS42
Cassio Rd, Wat. WD18 97 BV41
Cassis Ct, Loug. IG10 107 EQ42
Cassland Rd, E9 11 H6
Thornton Heath CR7 224 DR98
Casslee Rd, SE6 205 DZ87
Cassocks Sq, Shep. TW17 217 BR100
Casson St, E1 20 C7
Casstine Cl, Swan. BR8 209 FF94
Castalia Sq, E14
off Roserton St 34 E5
Castano Ct, Abb.L. WD5 81 BS31
Castellain Rd, W9 15 N5
Castellan Av, Rom. RM2 149 FH55
Castellane Cl, Stan. HA7
off Daventer Dr 117 CF52
Castello Av, SW15 201 CW85
Castell Rd, Loug. IG10 107 EQ39
CASTELNAU, SW13 181 CU79
Castelnau, SW13 181 CV79
Castelnau Gdns, SW13
off Arundel Ter 181 CV79
Castelnau Pl, SW13
off Castelnau 181 CV79
Castelnau Row, SW13
off Lonsdale Rd 181 CV79
Casterbridge, NW6 5 M8
Casterbridge Rd, SE3 186 EG83
Casterton St, E8 10 F5
Castile Gdns, Kings L. WD4 80 BM29
Castile Rd, SE18 37 M8
Castilion Prim Sch, SE28
off Copperfield Rd 168 EW72
Castille Ct, Wal.Cr. EN8 89 DZ34
Castillon Rd, SE6 206 EE89
Castlands Rd, SE6 205 DZ89
Castle Av, E4 123 ED50
Datchet SL3 174 AU79
Epsom KT17 239 CU109
Rainham RM13 169 FE66
West Drayton UB7 156 BL73
Castlebar Hill, W5 159 CH71
Castlebar Ms, W5 159 CJ71
⇌ **Castle Bar Park** 159 CF71
Castlebar Pk, W5 159 CH70
Castlebar Rd, W5 159 CJ71
Castlebar Sch, W13
off Hathaway Gdns 159 CF71
Castle Baynard St, EC4 19 H10
Castlebrook Cl, SE11 30 G8
Castle Cl, E9 11 L3
SW19 201 CX90
W3 180 CP75
Bletchingley RH1 274 DQ133
Bromley BR2 226 EE97
Bushey WD23 98 CB44
Hoddesdon EN11 55 EC14
Reigate RH2 288 DB138
Romford RM3 128 FJ48
Sunbury-on-Thames TW16
off Percy Bryant Rd 197 BS94
Castlecombe Dr, SW19 201 CX87
Castlecombe Prim Sch, SE9
off Castlecombe Rd 206 EL92
Castlecombe Rd, SE9 206 EL91
Castle Cor, Bletch. RH1
off Overdale 274 DQ133
Castle Ct, EC3 19 M9
SE26 *off Champion Rd* 205 DY91
SW15 181 CY83
Castledine Rd, SE20 204 DV94
Castle Dr, Horl. RH6 291 DJ150
Ilford IG4 146 EL58
Reigate RH2 288 DA138
Castle Fm, Wind. SL4 173 AK82
Castle Fm Rd, Shore. TN14 247 FF109
Castlefield Rd, Reig. RH2 272 DA133
Castleford Av, SE9 207 EP88
Castleford Cl, N17 122 DT51
Borehamwood WD6 100 CM38
Castle Gdns, Dor. RH4 270 CM134
Castlegate, Rich. TW9 180 CM83
Castle Gateway, Berk. HP4 60 AW17
Castle Grn, Wey. KT13 217 BS104
Castle Gro Rd, Chobham
GU24 232 AS113
Castlehaven Rd, NW1 7 J7
Castle Hill, Berk. HP4 60 AW17
Guildford GU1 280 AX136
Longfield DA3 231 FX99
Windsor SL4 173 AR81
Castle Hill Av, Berk. HP4 60 AW18
New Addington CR0 243 EB109
Castle Hill Cl, Berk. HP4 60 AV18
Castle Hill Prim Sch, Chess.
KT9 *off Buckland Rd* 238 CM105
Chessington KT9
off Moor La 238 CM106
New Addington CR0
off Dunley Dr 243 EC107
Castle Hill Rd, Egh. TW20 194 AV91
Castle La, SW1 29 M6
Castleleigh Ct, Enf. EN2 104 DR43
Castlemaine Av, Epsom KT17 239 CV109
South Croydon CR2 242 DT106
Castlemaine Twr, SW11 40 F8
Castlemain St, E1 20 E6
Castlemead, SE5 43 K5
Castle Mead, Hem.H. HP1 62 BH22
Castle Ms, N12 *off Castle Rd* 120 DC50
NW1 7 J5
SW17 202 DE91
Hampton TW12
off Station Rd 218 CB95
Weybridge KT13 217 BS104
Castle Par, Epsom KT17
off Ewell Bypass 239 CU108
Castle Pl, NW1 7 K5
W4 *off Windmill Rd* 180 CS77
Castle Pt, E13 24 D1
Castlereagh St, W1 16 D8
Castle Rd, N12 120 DC50
NW1 7 J5
Chipstead CR5 256 DE120
Dagenham RM9 168 EV67
Enfield EN3 105 DY39
Epsom KT18 254 CP115
Eynsford DA4 247 FH107
Grays RM17 192 FZ79
Hoddesdon EN11 55 EB14
Isleworth TW7 179 CF82
Northolt UB5 158 CB65
St. Albans AL1 65 CH20
Shoreham TN14 247 FG108
Southall UB2 178 BZ76
Swanscombe DA10 212 FZ86
Weybridge KT13 217 BS104
Woking GU21 233 AZ114
Castle Sq, Bletch. RH1 274 DQ133
Guildford GU1 280 AX136
Castle St, E6 166 EJ68
Berkhamsted HP4 60 AW19
Bletchingley RH1 273 DP133
Greenhithe DA9 211 FU85
Guildford GU1 280 AX136
Hertford SG14 54 DQ10
Kingston upon Thames KT1 220 CL96
Slough SL1 174 AT76
Swanscombe DA10 212 FZ86
Castleton Av, Bexh. DA7 189 FD81
Wembley HA9 140 CL63
Castleton Cl, Bans. SM7 256 DA115
Croydon CR0 225 DY100
Castleton Dr, Bans. SM7 256 DA115
Castleton Gdns, Wem. HA9 140 CL62
Castleton Rd, E17 123 ED54
SE9 206 EK91
Ilford IG3 148 EU60
Mitcham CR4 223 DK98
Castleton Rd, Ruis. HA4 138 BX60
Castletown Rd, W14 38 F1
Castle Vw, Epsom KT18 238 CP114
Castleview Cl, N4 144 DQ60
Castleview Gdns, Ilf. IG1 146 EL58
Castleview Rd, Slou. SL3 174 AW77
Castle Vw Rd, Wey. KT13 235 BP105
Castleview Sch, Slou. SL3
off Woodstock Av 174 AX77
Castle Wk, Reig. RH2
off London Rd 272 DA134
Sunbury-on-Thames TW16
off Elizabeth Gdns 218 BW97
Castle Way, SW19 201 CX90
Epsom KT17 *off Castle Av* 239 CU109
Feltham TW13 198 BW91
Castlewood Dr, SE9 187 EM82
Castlewood Rd, N15 144 DU58
N16 144 DU59
Cockfosters EN4 102 DD41
Castle Yd, N6 *off North Rd* 142 DG59
SE1 31 H2
Richmond TW10 *off Hill St* 199 CK85
Castor La, E14 34 C1
Catalina Av, Chaff.Hun. RM16 192 FZ75
Catalina Rd, Lon.Hthrw Air.
TW6 *off Cromer Rd* 176 BN82
Catalin Ct, Wal.Abb. EN9
off Howard Cl 89 ED33
Catalonia Apts, Wat. WD18
off Linden Av 97 BT42
Catalpa Cl, Guil. GU1
off Cedar Way 264 AW132
Catalpa Ct, SE13
off Hither Grn La 205 ED86
Cater Gdns, Guil. GU3 264 AT132
CATERHAM, CR3 258 DU123
⇌ **Caterham** 258 DU124
Caterham Av, Ilf. IG5 125 EM54
Caterham Bypass, Cat. CR3 258 DV120
Caterham Cl, Cat. CR3 258 DS120
Caterham Ct, Wal.Abb. EN9 90 EF34
Caterham Dene Hosp,
Cat. CR3 258 DT123
Caterham Dr, Couls. CR5 257 DP118
Caterham High Sch, Ilf.
IG5 *off Caterham Av* 125 EM54
CATERHAM-ON-THE-HILL,
Cat. CR3 258 DT122
Caterham Rd, SE13 185 EC83
Caterham Sch, Cat. CR3
off Harestone Valley Rd 274 DT126
Caterham Valley Comm
Learning Cen, Cat. CR3
off Beechwood Rd 258 DU122
Catesby St, SE17 31 M9
CATFORD, SE6 205 EB88
⇌ **Catford** 205 EA87
⇌ **Catford Bridge** 205 EA87
Catford Bdy, SE6 205 EB87
Catford Gyratory, SE6 205 EB87
Catford High Sch, SE6
off Bellingham Rd 205 EC90
Catford Hill, SE6 205 DZ89
Catford Ms, SE6
off Holbeach Rd 205 EB87
Catford Rd, SE6 205 EA88
Cathall Rd, E11 145 ED62
Catham Cl, St.Alb. AL1 65 CH22
Catharine Cl, Chaff.Hun. RM16 192 FZ75
Cathay St, SE16 32 F5
Cathay Wk, Nthlt. UB5
off Brabazon Rd 158 CA68
Cathcart Dr, Orp. BR6 227 ES103
Cathcart Hill, N19 143 DJ62
Cathcart Rd, SW10 39 M2
Cathcart St, NW5 7 J4
Cathedral Cl, Guil. GU2 280 AV135
Cathedral Ct, St.Alb. AL3 64 CB22
Cathedral Hill, Guil. GU2 264 AU133
● **Cathedral Hill Ind Est**, Guil.
GU2 *off Cathedral Hill* 264 AU133
★ **Cathedral of the Holy Spirit**
Guildford, Guil. GU2 264 AV134
Cathedral Piazza, SW1 29 L7
Cathedral Pl, Brwd. CM14 130 FX47
Cathedral Sch of St. Saviour &
St. Mary Overie, The, SE1 31 K4
Cathedral St, SE1 31 L2
Cathedral Vw, Guil. GU2 264 AT134
Cathedral Wk, SW1 29 L6
Catherall Rd, N5 144 DQ62
Catherine Cl, Byfleet KT14 234 BL114
Hemel Hempstead HP2
off Parr Cres 63 BQ15
Loughton IG10
off Roding Gdns 107 EM44
Pilgrim's Hatch CM15 130 FU43
Catherine Ct, N14
off Conisbee Ct 103 DJ43
Catherine Dr, Rich. TW9 180 CL84
Sunbury-on-Thames TW16 197 BT93
Catherine Gdns, Houns. TW3 179 CD84
Catherine Griffiths Ct, EC1 18 F4
Catherine Gro, SE10 46 C6
Catherine Ho, N1
off Phillipp St 9 P9
Catherine Howard Ct, SE9
off Avery Hill Rd 207 ER86
Weybridge KT13
off Old Palace Rd 217 BP104
Catherine of Aragon Ct, SE9
off Avery Hill Rd 207 EQ86
Catherine Parr Ct, SE9
off Avery Hill Rd 207 ER86
Catherine Pl, SW1 29 L6
Harrow HA1 139 CF57
Catherine Rd, Enf. EN3 105 DY36
Romford RM2 149 FH57
Surbiton KT6 219 CK99
Catherine's Cl, West Dr. UB7
off Money La 176 BK76
Catherine St, WC2 18 C10
St. Albans AL3 65 CD19
Catherine Wheel All, E1 19 P7
Catherine Wheel Rd, Brent.
TW8 179 CK80
Catherine Wheel Yd, SW1 29 L3
Catherwood Ct, N1
off Murray Gro 19 L1
Cat Hill, Barn. EN4 102 DE44
Cathles Rd, SW12 203 DH86
Cathnor Rd, W12 181 CV75
Cathrow Ms, Hodd. EN11 55 EA14
Catisfield Rd, Enf. EN3 105 DY37
Catkin Cl, Hem.H. HP1 62 BH19
Catlin Cres, Shep. TW17 217 BR99
Catlin Gdns, Gdse. RH9 274 DV130
Catling Cl, SE23 204 DW90
Catlins La, Pnr. HA5 137 BV55
Catlin St, SE16 44 D1
Hemel Hempstead HP3 62 BH23
Cator Cl, New Adgtn CR0 244 EE111
Cator Cres, New Adgtn CR0 243 ED111
Cator La, Beck. BR3 225 DZ96
Cato Rd, SW4 183 DK83
Cator Pk Sch, Beck. BR3
off Lennard Rd 205 DY94
Cator Rd, SE26 205 DX93
Carshalton SM5 240 DF106
Cator St, SE15 44 A3
Cato St, W1 16 D7
Catsey La, Bushey WD23 116 CC45
Catsey Wds, Bushey WD23 116 CC45
Catterick Cl, N11 120 DG51
Catterick Way, Borwd. WD6 100 CM39
Cattistock Rd, SE9 206 EL92
CATTLEGATE, Enf. EN2 87 DL33
Cattlegate Hill, Northaw EN6 87 DK31
Cattlegate Rd, Enf. EN2 87 DL34
Northaw EN6 87 DK31
Cattley Cl, Barn. EN5 101 CY42
Cattlins Cl, Chsht EN7 88 DS29
Catton St, WC1 18 C7
Cattsdell, Hem.H. HP2 62 BL18
Caughley Ho, SE11
off Lambeth Wk 30 E7
Caulfield Rd, E6 167 EM66
SE15 44 F8
Causeway, The, N2 142 DE56
SW18 182 DB84
SW19 201 CX92
Bray SL6 172 AC75
Carshalton SM5 222 DG104
Chessington KT9 238 CL105
Claygate KT10 237 CF108
Feltham TW14 177 BU84
Hounslow TW4 177 BU84
Potters Bar EN6 86 DC31
Staines TW18 195 BC91
Sutton SM2 240 DC109
Teddington TW11
off Broad St 199 CF93
Causeway Cl, Pot.B. EN6 86 DD31
● **Causeway Corporate Cen**,
Stai. TW18 195 BB91
Causeway Ct, Wok. GU21
off Bingham Dr 248 AT118
Causeyware Rd, N9 122 DV45
Causton Rd, N6 143 DH59
Causton Sq, Dag. RM10 168 FA66
Causton St, SW1 29 P9
Cautherly La, Gt Amwell SG12 55 DZ10
Cautley Av, SW4 203 DJ85
Cavalier Cl, Rom. RM6 148 EX56
Cavalier Gdns, Hayes UB3 157 BR72
Cavalier Ho, W5
off Uxbridge Rd 159 CJ73
Cavalry Barracks, Houns. TW4 178 BX83
Cavalry Cres, Houns. TW4 178 BX84
Windsor SL4 173 AQ83
Cavalry Gdns, SW15 201 CY85
Cavalry Sq, SW3 28 F10
Cavan Dr, St.Alb. AL3 65 CD15
Cavan Pl, Pnr. HA5 116 BZ53
Cavaye Pl, SW10 39 P1
Cavell Cres, Dart. DA1 190 FN84
Harold Wood RM3 128 FL54
Cavell Dr, Enf. EN2 103 DN40
Cavell Rd, N17 122 DR52
Cheshunt EN7 88 DT27
Cavell St, E1 20 F6
Cavell Way, Epsom KT19 238 CN111
Cavendish Av, N3 120 DA54
NW8 16 B1
W13 159 CG71
Erith DA8 189 FC79
Harrow HA1 139 CD63
Hornchurch RM12 169 FH65
New Malden KT3 221 CV99
Ruislip HA4 137 BV64
Sevenoaks TN13 278 FG122
Sidcup DA15 208 EU87
Welling DA16 187 ET83
Woodford Green IG8 124 EH53
Cavendish Cl, N18 122 DV50
NW6 4 G5
NW8 16 B2
Amersham HP6 94 AV39
Hayes UB4 157 BS71
Sunbury-on-Thames TW16 197 BT93
Taplow SL6 152 AG72
Cavendish Coll, WC1 17 N6
Cavendish Ct, EC3 19 P8
Croxley Green WD3
off Mayfare 97 BR43
Sunbury-on-Thames TW16 197 BT93
Cavendish Cres, Els. WD6 100 CN42
Hornchurch RM12 169 FH65
Cavendish Dr, E11 145 ED60
Claygate KT10 237 CE106
Edgware HA8 118 CM51
Cavendish Gdns, SW4 203 DJ86
Aveley RM15 190 FQ75
Barking IG11 147 ES64
Ilford IG1 147 EN60
Redhill RH1 272 DG133
Romford RM6 148 EY57
Cavendish Ms N, W1 17 K6
Cavendish Ms S, W1 17 K7
Cavendish Par, SW4 *off*
Clapham Common S Side 203 DH86
Hounslow TW4 *off Bath Rd* 178 BY82
Cavendish Pl, NW2 4 D5
W1 17 K8
Bromley BR1 227 EM97
Cavendish Prim Sch, W4
off Edensor Rd 180 CS80
Cavendish Rd, E4 123 EC51
N4 143 DN58
N18 122 DV50
NW6 4 F7
SW12 203 DH86
SW19 202 DD94
W4 180 CQ81
Barnet EN5 101 CW41
Chesham HP5 76 AR32
Croydon CR0 223 DP102
New Malden KT3 221 CT99
Redhill RH1 272 DG134

Cavendish Rd, St.Alb. AL1 65 CF20
Sunbury-on-Thames TW16 197 BT93
Sutton SM2 240 DC108
Weybridge KT13 235 BQ108
Woking GU22 248 AX119
Cavendish Sch, The, NW1 7 K8
Hemel Hempstead HP1
off Warners End Rd 62 BH19
Cavendish Sq, W1 17 K8
Longfield DA3 231 FX97
Cavendish St, N1 19 L1
Cavendish Ter, Felt. TW13 197 BU89
Cavendish Wk, Epsom KT19 238 CP111
Cavendish Way, Hat. AL10 67 CT18
West Wickham BR4 225 EB102
Cavenham Cl, Wok. GU22 248 AY119
Cavenham Gdns, Horn. RM11 150 FJ57
Ilford IG1 147 ER62
Caverleigh Way, Wor.Pk. KT4 221 CU102
Cave Rd, E13 24 B1
Richmond TW10 199 CJ91
Caversham Av, N13 121 DN48
Sutton SM3 221 CY103
Caversham Ct, N11 120 DG48
Caversham Flats, SW3 40 E2
Caversham Rd, N15 144 DQ56
NW5 7 L4
Kingston upon Thames KT1 220 CM96
Caversham St, SW3 40 E2
Caverswall St, W12 14 A8
Caveside Cl, Chis. BR7 227 EN95
Cavill's Wk, Chig. IG7 126 EW47
Romford RM4 126 EX47
Cawcott Dr, Wind. SL4 173 AL81
Cawdor Av, S.Ock. RM15 171 FU73
Cawdor Cres, W7 179 CG77
Cawley Hatch, Harl. CM19 73 EM15
Cawnpore St, SE19 204 DS92
Cawsey Way, Wok. GU21 248 AY117
Caxton Av, Add. KT15 234 BG107
● Caxton Cen, St.Alb. AL3 65 CF15
Caxton Dr, Uxb. UB8 156 BK68
Caxton Gdns, Guil. GU2 264 AV133
Caxton Gro, E3 22 A2
Caxton Hill, Hert. SG13 54 DT09
Caxton Hill Ext Rd, Hert. SG13 54 DT09
Caxton La, Oxt. RH8 276 EL131
Caxton Ms, Brent. TW8
off The Butts 179 CK79
Caxton Ri, Red. RH1 272 DG133
Caxton Rd, N22 121 DM54
SW19 202 DC92
W12 26 C4
Hoddesdon EN11 55 EB13
Southall UB2 178 BX76
Caxtons Ct, Guil. GU1 265 BA132
Caxton St, SW1 29 M6
Caxton St N, E16 23 L9
Caxton Way, Rom. RM1 149 FE56
Watford WD18 97 BR44
Cayenne Ct, SE1 32 B3
Cayford Ho, NW3 6 D2
Caygill Cl, Brom. BR2 226 EF98
Cayley Prim Sch, E14 21 L8
Cayley Rd, Sthl. UB2
off McNair Rd 178 CB76
Cayton Pl, EC1 19 L3
Cayton Rd, Couls. CR5 257 DJ122
Greenford UB6 159 CE68
Cayton St, EC1 19 L3
Cazenove Rd, E17 123 EA53
N16 144 DT61
Cearns Ho, E6 166 EK67
Cearn Way, Couls. CR5 257 DM115
Cecil Av, Bark. IG11 167 ER66
Enfield EN1 104 DT42
Grays RM16 192 FZ75
Hornchurch RM11 150 FL55
Wembley HA9 140 CM64
Cecil Cl, W5 159 CK71
Ashford TW15 197 BQ93
Chessington KT9 237 CK105
Cecil Ct, WC2 29 P1
Barnet EN5 101 CX41
Cecil Cres, Hat. AL10 67 CV16
Cecile Pk, N8 143 DL58
Cecilia Cl, N2 142 DC55
★ Cecilia Coleman Gall, NW8 6 B10
Cecilia Rd, E8 10 C2
Cecil Manning Cl, Perivale
UB6 159 CG67
Cecil Pk, Pnr. HA5 138 BY56
Cecil Pl, Mitch. CR4 222 DF99
Cecil Rd, E11 146 EE62
E13 13 P8
E17 123 EA53
N10 121 DH54
N14 121 DJ46
NW9 140 CS55
NW10 160 CS67
SW19 202 DB94
W3 160 CQ71
Ashford TW15 197 BQ94
Cheshunt EN8 89 DX32
Croydon CR0 223 DM100
Enfield EN2 104 DR42
Gravesend DA11 213 GF88
Harrow HA3 139 CE55
Hertford SG13 54 DQ12
Hoddesdon EN11 71 EC15
Hounslow TW3 178 CC82
Ilford IG1 147 EP63
Iver SL0 155 BE72
Potters Bar EN6 85 CU32
Romford RM6 148 EX59
St. Albans AL1 65 CF20
Sutton SM1 239 CZ107
Cecil Rd Prim & Nurs Sch,
Grav. DA11 off Cecil Rd 213 GF88
★ Cecil Sharp Ho, NW1 7 H8
Cecil St, Wat. WD24 97 BV38
Cecil Way, Brom. BR2 226 EG102
Slough SL2 153 AM70
Cedar Av, Barn. EN4 120 DE45
Cobham KT11 252 BW115
Enfield EN3 104 DW40
Gravesend DA12 213 GJ91
Hayes UB3 157 BU72
Romford RM6 148 EY57
Ruislip HA4 158 BW65
Sidcup DA15 208 EU87
Cedar Av, Twick. TW2 198 CB86
Upminster RM14 150 FN63
Waltham Cross EN8 89 DX33
West Drayton UB7 156 BM74
Cedar Chase, Tap. SL6 152 AD70
Cedar Cl, E3 11 P8
SE21 204 DQ88
SW15 200 CR91
Borehamwood WD6 100 CP42
Bromley BR2 226 EL104
Buckhurst Hill IG9 124 EK47
Carshalton SM5 240 DF107
Chesham HP5 76 AS30
Dorking RH4 285 CH136
East Molesey KT8
off Cedar Rd 219 CE98
Epsom KT17 239 CT114
Esher KT10 236 BZ108
Hertford SG14 53 DP09
Hutton CM13 131 GD45
Ilford IG1 147 ER64
Iver SL0
off Thornbridge Rd 155 BC66
Potters Bar EN6 86 DA30
Reigate RH2 288 DC136
Romford RM7 149 FC56
Sawbridgeworth CM21 58 EY06
Staines TW18 216 BJ97
Swanley BR8 229 FC96
Ware SG12 55 DX07
Warlingham CR6 259 DY119
Cedar Copse, Brom. BR1 227 EM96
Cedar Ct, E11
off Grosvenor Rd 146 EH57
N1 9 K6
SE7 off Fairlawn 186 EJ79
SE9 206 EL86
SW19 201 CX90
Egham TW20 195 BA91
Epping CM16 92 EU31
St. Albans AL4 65 CK20
Cedar Cres, Brom. BR2 226 EL104
Cedarcroft Rd, Chess. KT9 238 CM105
Cedar Dr, N2 142 DE56
Chesham HP5 76 AN30
Fetcham KT22 253 CE123
Loughton IG10 107 EP40
Pinner HA5 116 CA51
Sutton at Hone DA4 230 FP96
Cedar Gdns, Chobham GU24 232 AT110
Sutton SM2 240 DC107
Upminster RM14 150 FQ62
Woking GU21
off St. John's Rd 248 AV118
Cedar Grn, Hodd. EN11 71 EA18
Cedar Gro, W5 180 CL76
Amersham HP7 77 AR39
Bexley DA5 208 EW86
Southall UB1 158 CA71
Weybridge KT13 235 BQ105
Cedar Hts, Rich. TW10 200 CL88
Cedar Hill, Epsom KT18 254 CQ116
Cedar Ho, Croy. CR0 243 EB107
Sunbury-on-Thames TW16 197 BT94
Cedarhurst, Brom. BR1 206 EE94
Cedarhurst Dr, SE9 206 EJ85
Cedar Lawn Av, Barn. EN5 101 CY43
Cedar Lo, Chsht EN8
off High St 89 DX28
Cedar Ms, SW15
off Cambalt Rd 201 CX85
Cedar Mt, SE9 206 EK88
Cedarne Rd, SW6 39 L5
Cedar Pk, Cat. CR3 258 DS121
Chigwell IG7 off High Rd 125 EP49
Cedar Pk Gdns, Rom. RM6 148 EX59
Cedar Pk Rd, Enf. EN2 104 DQ38
Cedar Pl, SE7 36 C10
Northwood HA6 115 BQ51
Cedar Ri, N14 120 DG45
South Ockendon RM15
off Sycamore Way 171 FX70
Cedar Rd, N17 122 DT53
NW2 141 CW63
Berkhamsted HP4 60 AX20
Bromley BR1 226 EJ96
Cobham KT11 235 BV114
Croydon CR0 224 DS103
Dartford DA1 210 FK88
East Molesey KT8 219 CE98
Enfield EN2 103 DP38
Erith DA8 189 FG81
Feltham TW14 197 BR88
Grays RM16 193 GG76
Hatfield AL10 67 CU19
Hornchurch RM12 150 FJ62
Hounslow TW4 178 BW82
Hutton CM13 131 GD44
Romford RM7 149 FC56
Sutton SM2 240 DC107
Teddington TW11 199 CG92
Watford WD19 98 BW44
Weybridge KT13 234 BN105
Woking GU22 248 AV120
Cedars, Bans. SM7 240 DF114
Cedars, The, E15 13 M8
W13 159 CJ72
Bookham KT23 268 CC126
Brockham RH3 270 CN134
Buckhurst Hill IG9 124 EG46
Byfleet KT14 234 BM112
Guildford GU1 265 BA131
Leatherhead KT22 254 CL121
Reigate RH2 272 DD134
Slough SL2 153 AM69
Teddington TW11
off Adelaide Rd 199 CF93
Cedars Av, E17 145 EA57
Mitcham CR4 222 DG98
Rickmansworth WD3 114 BJ46
Cedars Cl, NW4 141 CX55
SE13 185 ED83
Chalfont St. Peter SL9 112 AY50
Cedars Ct, N9 off Church St 122 DT47
Cedars Dr, Uxb. UB10 156 BM68
Cedars Manor Sch, Har.
HA3 off Whittlesea Rd 116 CC53
Cedars Ms, SW4 183 DH84
Cedars Prim Sch, The,
Cran. TW5 off High St 177 BV80
Cedars Rd, E15 13 K4
N21 121 DP47
SW4 183 DH83
SW13 181 CT82
W4 180 CQ78
Beckenham BR3 225 DY96
Croydon CR0 223 DL104
Hampton Wick KT1 219 CJ95
Morden SM4 222 DA98
Cedars Wk, Chorl. WD3 95 BF42
Cedar Ter, Rich. TW9 180 CL84
Cedar Ter Rd, Sev. TN13 279 FJ123
Cedar Tree Gro, SE27 203 DP92
Cedarville Gdns, SW16 203 DM93
Cedar Vista, Kew TW9 180 CL82
Cedar Wk, Clay. KT10 237 CF107
Hemel Hempstead HP3 62 BK22
Kenley CR8 258 DQ116
Kingswood KT20 255 CY120
Waltham Abbey EN9 89 ED34
Welwyn Garden City AL7 52 DB10
Cedar Way, NW1 7 N7
Berkhamsted HP4 60 AX20
Guildford GU1 264 AW132
Slough SL3 174 AY78
Sunbury-on-Thames TW16 197 BS94
Cedarwood Dr, St.Alb. AL4 65 CK20
Cedar Wd Dr, Wat. WD25 97 BV35
Cedra Ct, N16 144 DU60
Cedric Av, Rom. RM1 149 FE55
Cedric Rd, SE9 207 EQ90
Celadon Cl, Enf. EN3 105 DY41
Celandine Cl, E14 22 A7
South Ockendon RM15 171 FW70
Celandine Dr, E8 10 B6
SE28 168 EV74
Celandine Gro, N14 103 DJ43
Celandine Rd, Hersham KT12 236 BY105
Celandine Way, E15 23 K2
Celbridge Ms, W2 15 M8
Celedon Cl, Grays RM16 192 FY75
Celestial Gdns, SE13 185 ED84
Celia Cres, Ashf. TW15 196 BK93
Celia Rd, N19 7 M1
Cell Barnes Cl, St.Alb. AL1 65 CH22
Cell Barnes La, St.Alb. AL1 65 CH23
Cell Fm Av, Old Wind. SL4 194 AV85
Celtic Av, Brom. BR2 226 EE97
Celtic Rd, Byfleet KT14 234 BL114
Celtic St, E14 22 D6
Cement Block Cotts,
Grays RM17 192 GC79
Cemetery Hill, Hem.H. HP1 62 BJ21
Cemetery La, SE7 186 EL79
Lower Nazeing EN9 90 EF25
Shepperton TW17 217 BP101
Cemetery Rd, E7 13 L2
N17 122 DS52
SE2 188 EV80
Cemmaes Ct Rd, Hem.H. HP1 62 BJ20
Cemmaes Meadow, Hem.H.
HP1 62 BJ20
Cenacle Cl, NW3 142 DA62
★ Cenotaph, The, SW1 30 A4
● Centaurs Business Cen,
Islw. TW7 179 CG79
Centaur St, SE1 30 D6
Centaury Ct, Grays RM17 192 GD79
● Centenary Ind Est, Enf.
EN3 105 DZ42
Centenary Rd, Enf. EN3 105 DZ42
Centenary Wk, Loug. IG10 106 EH41
Centenary Way, Amer. HP6 94 AT38
Centennial Av, Els. WD6 117 CH45
Centennial Ct, Els. WD6 117 CJ45
● Centennial Pk, Els. WD6 117 CJ45
Central Av, E11 145 ED61
N2 120 DD54
N9 122 DS48
SW11 40 E5
Aveley RM15 190 FQ75
Enfield EN1 104 DV40
Gravesend DA12 213 GH89
Grays RM20 191 FT77
Harlow CM20 57 ER14
Hayes UB3 157 BU73
Hounslow TW3 178 CC84
Pinner HA5 138 BZ58
Tilbury RM18 193 GG81
Wallington SM6 241 DL106
Waltham Cross EN8 89 DY33
Welling DA16 187 ET82
West Molesey KT8 218 BZ98
● Central Business Cen, NW10
off Great Cen Way 140 CS64
Central Circ, NW4
off Hendon Way 141 CV57
★ Central Criminal Ct
(Old Bailey), EC4 19 H8
Central Dr, Horn. RM12 150 FL62
St. Albans AL4 65 CJ19
Slough SL1 153 AM73
Welwyn Garden City AL7 51 CZ07
Centrale 224 DQ103
Centrale Shop Cen,
Croy. CR0 224 DQ103
Central Foundation Boys' Sch,
EC2 19 M4
Central Foundation Girls' Sch,
Lwr Sch, E3 21 M2
Upr Sch, E3 21 P3
Central Gdns, Mord. SM4 222 DB99
Central Hill, SE19 204 DR92
Central Ho, E15 12 D10
Barking IG11
off Cambridge Rd 167 EQ66
Central Middlesex Hosp,
NW10 160 CQ69
Central Par, E17 off Hoe St 145 EA56
Feltham TW14 198 BW87
Hounslow TW5
off Heston Rd 178 CA80
New Addington CR0 243 EC110
Perivale UB6 159 CG69
Surbiton KT6 220 CL100
Central Pk Av, Dag. RM10 149 FB62
● Central Pk Est, Houns.
TW4 198 BX85
Central Pk Prim Sch, E6 24 F1
Central Pk Rd, E6 24 D1
Central Pl, SE25
off Portland Rd 224 DV98
Central Prim Sch, Wat.
WD17 off Derby Rd 98 BW42
Central Rd, Dart. DA1 210 FL85
Harlow CM20 58 EU11
Morden SM4 222 DA100
Wembley HA0 139 CH64
Worcester Park KT4 221 CU103
Central St. Martins Coll of
Art & Design, WC1 18 C7
Back Hill Site, EC1 18 F5
Byam Shaw Sch of Art, N19
off Elthorne Rd 143 DK61
Catton St Site, WC1 18 C7
Charing Cross Rd Site, WC2 17 P9
Central Sch Footpath, SW14 180 CQ83
Central Sch of Ballet, EC1 18 F5
Central Sch of Speech &
Drama, NW3 6 A6
Central Sq, NW11 142 DB58
Wembley HA9
off Station Gro 140 CL64
West Molesey KT8 218 BZ98
Central St, EC1 19 J3
Central Wk, Epsom KT19
off Station App 238 CR113
Central Way, NW10 160 CQ69
SE28 168 EU74
Carshalton SM5 240 DE108
Feltham TW14 197 BU85
Oxted RH8 275 ED127
● Centrapark, Welw.G.C. AL7 51 CY08
Centre, The, Walt. KT12 217 BT102
Centre Av, W3 160 CR74
W10 14 B3
Epping CM16 91 ET32
Centre Cl, Epp. CM16 91 ET32
Centre Common Rd, Chis.
BR7 207 EQ93
Centre Ct Shop Cen,
SW19 201 CZ93
Centre Dr, Epp. CM16 91 ET32
Centre Grn, Epp. CM16
off Centre Av 91 ET32
● Centrepoint, WC1 17 P8
Centre Pt, SE1 32 C10
Centre Rd, E7 146 EG61
E11 146 EG61
Dagenham RM10 169 FB68
Windsor SL4 172 AJ80
Centre St, E2 20 E1
Centre Way, E17 123 EC52
N9 122 DW47
Centreway Apts, Ilf. IG1
off High Rd 147 EQ61
Centric Cl, NW1 7 J8
Centrillion Pt, Croy. CR0
off Masons Av 242 DQ105
Centrium, Wok. GU22 248 AY117
Centurion Bldg, SW8 41 J3
Centurion Cl, N7 8 C6
Centurion Ct, SE18 37 K9
Hackbridge SM6
off Wandle Rd 223 DH104
Romford RM1 149 FD55
St. Albans AL1
off Camp Rd 65 CG21
Centurion La, E3 11 P10
Centurion Sq, SE18 186 EL81
Centurion Way, Erith DA18 188 FA76
Purfleet RM19 190 FM77
Century Cl, NW4 141 CX57
St. Albans AL3 64 CC19
Century Ct, Wok. GU21 249 AZ116
Century Ms, E5 10 G1
Century Pk, Wat. WD17 98 BW43
Century Rd, E17 145 DY55
Hoddesdon EN11 71 EA16
Staines TW18 195 BC92
Ware SG12 55 DX05
Century Yd, SE23 204 DW89
Cephas Av, E1 21 H4
Cephas St, E1 20 G5
Ceres Rd, SE18 187 ET77
Cerise Rd, SE15 44 D7
Cerne Cl, Hayes UB4 158 BW73
Cerne Rd, Grav. DA12 213 GL91
Morden SM4 222 DC100
Cerney Ms, W2 16 A10
Cerotus Pl, Cher. KT16 215 BF101
Cervantes Ct, W2 15 M9
Northwood HA6
off Green La 115 BT52
Cervia Way, Grav. DA12 213 GM90
Cester St, E2 10 C9
Cestreham Cres, Chesh. HP5 76 AR29
Ceylon Rd, W14 26 D7
Chabot Dr, SE15 184 DV83
Chace Av, Pot.B. EN6 86 DD32
Chace Comm Sch, Enf.
EN1 off Churchbury La 104 DS39
Chacombe Pl, Beac. HP9 111 AK50
Chadacre Av, Ilf. IG5 147 EM55
Chadacre Rd, Epsom KT17 239 CV107
Chadbourn St, E14 22 D7
Chad Cres, N9 122 DW48
Chadd Dr, Brom. BR1 226 EL97
Chadd Grn, E13 13 N9
Chadfields, Til. RM18 193 GG80
Chadhurst Cl, N.Holm. RH5
off Wildcroft Dr 285 CK139
Chadview Ct, Chad.Hth RM6 148 EX59
Chadville Gdns, Rom. RM6 148 EX57
Chadway, Dag. RM8 148 EW60
Chadwell, Ware SG12 54 DW07
Chadwell Av, Chsht EN8 88 DW28
Romford RM6 148 EV59
Chadwell Bypass, Grays RM16 193 GF78
CHADWELL HEATH, Rom.
RM6 148 EX58
⇌ Chadwell Heath 148 EX59
Chadwell Heath Foundation
Sch, The, Chad.Hth RM6
off Christie Gdns 148 EV58
Chadwell Heath La, Rom.
RM6 148 EV57
Chadwell Hill, Grays RM16 193 GH78
Chadwell La, N8 143 DM55
Chadwell Prim Sch, Chad.Hth
RM6 off High Rd 148 EW59
Chadwell Ri, Ware SG12 54 DW07
Chadwell Rd, Grays RM17 192 GC77
CHADWELL ST. MARY,
Grays RM16 193 GJ76
Chadwell St. Mary Prim Sch,
Chad.St.M. RM16
off River Vw 193 GH77
Chadwell St, EC1 18 F2
Chadwick Av, E4 123 ED49
N21 103 DM42
SW19 202 DA93
Chadwick Cl, SW15 201 CT87
W7 off Westcott Cres 159 CF71
Northfleet DA11 212 GE89
Teddington TW11 199 CG93
Chadwick Dr, Harold Wd RM3 128 FK54
Chadwick Ms, W4
off Thames Rd 180 CP79
Chadwick Pl, Long Dit. KT6 219 CJ101
Chadwick Rd, E11 146 EE59
NW10 161 CT67
SE15 44 A9
Ilford IG1 147 EP62
Chadwick St, SW1 29 P7
Chadwick Way, SE28 168 EX73
Chadwin Rd, E13 24 A6
Chadworth Way, Clay. KT10 237 CD106
Chaffers Mead, Ashtd. KT21 254 CM116
Chaffinch Av, Croy. CR0 225 DX100
● Chaffinch Business Pk,
Beck. BR3 225 DX98
Chaffinch Cl, N9 123 DX46
Croydon CR0 225 DX99
Surbiton KT6 220 CN104
Chaffinches Grn, Hem.H. HP3 62 BN24
Chaffinch La, Wat. WD18 115 BT45
Chaffinch Rd, Beck. BR3 225 DY95
Chaffinch Way, Horl. RH6 290 DE147
CHAFFORD HUNDRED,
Grays RM16 191 FX76
⇌ Chafford Hundred 191 FV77
Chafford Hundred Business &
Enterprise Coll, Chaff.Hun.
RM16 off Mayflower Rd 191 FW78
Chafford Hundred Prim Sch,
Grays RM16
off Mayflower Rd 191 FW78
Chafford Sch, The, Rain.
RM13 off Lambs La S 170 FJ71
Chafford Wk, Rain. RM13 170 FJ68
Chafford Way, Rom. RM6 148 EW56
Chagford St, NW1 16 E5
Chailey Av, Enf. EN1 104 DT40
Chailey Cl, Houns. TW5
off Springwell Rd 178 BX81
Chailey Pl, Hersham KT12 236 BY105
Chailey St, E5 144 DW62
Chalbury Wk, N1 8 D10
Chalcombe Rd, SE2 188 EV76
Chalcot Cl, Sutt. SM2 240 DA108
Chalcot Cres, NW1 6 F8
Chalcot Gdns, NW3 6 E5
Chalcot Ms, SW16 203 DL90
Chalcot Rd, NW1 6 G7
Chalcot Sch, NW1 7 J6
Chalcot Sq, NW1 6 G7
Chalcott Gdns, Long Dit. KT6 219 CJ102
Chalcroft Rd, SE13 206 EE85
CHALDON, Cat. CR3 257 DN124
Chaldon Cl, Red. RH1 288 DE136
Chaldon Common Rd, Chaldon
CR3 258 DQ124
Chaldon Path, Th.Hth. CR7 223 DP98
Chaldon Rd, SW6 38 E4
Caterham CR3 258 DR124
Chaldon Way, Couls. CR5 257 DL117
Chale Rd, SW2 203 DL86
Chalet Cl, Berk. HP4 60 AT19
Bexley DA5 209 FD91
Chalet Est, NW7 119 CU49
Chale Wk, Sutt. SM2
off Hulverston Cl 240 DB109
⇌ Chalfont & Latimer 94 AW39
⊖ Chalfont & Latimer 94 AW39
Chalfont Av, Amer. HP6 94 AX39
Wembley HA9 160 CP65
Chalfont Cen for Epilepsy,
Chal.St.P. SL9 112 AY49
Chalfont Cl, Hem.H. HP2 63 BP15
CHALFONT COMMON,
Ger.Cr. SL9 113 AZ49
Chalfont Ct, NW9 141 CT55
Chalfont Grn, N9 122 DS48
● Chalfont Gro, Chal.St.P. SL9 112 AV51
Chalfont La, Chorl. WD3 95 BB43
Gerrards Cross SL9 113 BC51
West Hyde WD3 113 BC51
Chalfont Ms, SW19
off Augustus Rd 201 CZ88
● Chalfont Pk, Chal.St.P. SL9 135 AZ55
Chalfont Rd, N9 122 DS48
SE25 224 DT97
Chalfont St. Giles HP8 113 BB48
Gerrards Cross SL9 113 BB48
Hayes UB3 177 BU75
Maple Cross WD3 113 BD49
Seer Green HP9 111 AR50
CHALFONT ST. GILES, HP8 112 AV47
Chalfont St. Giles Inf Sch
& Nurs, Ch.St.G. HP8
off School La 112 AV48
Chalfont St. Giles Jun Sch,
Ch.St.G. HP8
off Parsonage Rd 112 AV48
CHALFONT ST. PETER,
Ger.Cr. SL9 113 AZ53
Chalfont St. Peter C of E Sch,
Chal.St.P. SL9
off Penn Rd 112 AX53
Chalfont St. Peter Inf Sch,
Chal.St.P. SL9
off Lovel End 112 AW52
Chalfonts & Gerrards Cross
Hosp, Chal.St.P. SL9 112 AX53
Chalfonts Comm Coll,
Chal.St.P. SL9 off Narcot La 112 AW52
Chalfont Sta Rd, Amer. HP7 94 AW40
Chalfont Wk, Pnr. HA5
off Willows Cl 116 BW54
Chalfont Way, W13 179 CH76
Chalford Cl, W.Mol. KT8 218 CA98
Chalforde Gdns, Rom. RM2 149 FH56
Chalford Flats, Woob.Grn HP10 132 AE57
Chalford Rd, SE21 204 DR91
Chalford Wk, Wdf.Grn. IG8 124 EK53
Chalgrove, Welw.G.C. AL7 52 DD08
Chalgrove Av, Mord. SM4 222 DA99
Chalgrove Cres, Ilf. IG5 124 EL54
Chalgrove Gdns, N3 141 CY55
Chalgrove Prim Sch, N3
off Chalgrove Gdns 141 CY55
Chalgrove Rd, N17 122 DV53
Sutton SM2 240 DD108
Chalice Cl, Wall. SM6
off Lavender Vale 241 DK107
Chalice Way, Green. DA9 211 FS85
Chalk Dale, Welw.G.C. AL7 52 DB08
Chalkdell Flds, St.Alb. AL4 65 CG16
Chalkdell Hill, Hem.H. HP2 62 BL20
Chalkenden Cl, SE20 204 DV94
Chalkers Cor, SW14 180 CP83
⊖ Chalk Farm 6 F6
Chalk Fm Rd, NW1 6 G6
Chalk Hill, Chesh. HP5 76 AP29
Coleshill HP7 111 AM45
Watford WD19 98 BX44
Chalkhill Prim Sch, Wem.
HA9 off Barnhill Rd 140 CP62
Chalk Hill Rd, W6 26 C9
Chalkhill Rd, Wem. HA9 140 CP62
Chalklands, Wem. HA9 140 CQ62
Chalk La, Ashtd. KT21 254 CM119
Barnet EN4 102 DF42
East Horsley KT24 267 BT130
Epsom KT18 254 CR115

Chalk La, Harl. CM17 .... 58 FA14
Chalkley Cl, Mitch. CR4 .... 222 DF96
Chalkmill Dr, Enf. EN1 .... 104 DV41
Chalk Paddock, Epsom KT18 .. 254 CR115
Chalk Pit Av, Orp. BR5 .... 228 EW97
Chalkpit La, Bet. RH3 .... 270 CP133
Bookham KT23 .... 268 BZ128
Chalk Pit La, Burn. SL1 .... 152 AH66
Chalkpit La, Dor. RH4 .... 285 CG135
Oxted RH8 .... 275 EC125
Woldingham CR3 .... 275 EC125
Chalk Pit Rd, Bans. SM7 .... 256 DA117
Epsom KT18 .... 254 CQ119
Chalkpit Ter, Dor. RH4 .... 269 CG134
Chalk Pit Way, Sutt. SM1 .... 240 DC106
Chalkpit Wd, Oxt. RH8 .... 275 ED127
Chalk Rd, E13 .... 24 B6
Chalkstone Cl, Well. DA16 .... 188 EU81
Chalkstream Way, Woob.Grn
HP10 off Glory Mill La 132 AE56
Chalkwell Pk Av, Enf. EN1 .... 104 DS42
Chalky Bk, Grav. DA11 .... 213 GG91
Chalky La, Chess. KT9 .... 237 CK109
Challacombe Cl, Hutt. CM13 .. 131 GB46
Challenge Cl, Grav. DA12 .... 213 GM91
Challenge Ct, Lthd. KT22 .... 253 CH119
Twickenham TW2
off Langhorn Dr. 199 CE87
Challenge Rd, Ashf. TW15 .... 197 BQ90
Challice Way, SW2 .... 203 DM88
Challinor, Harl. CM17 .... 74 EY15
Challin St, SE20 .... 224 DW95
Challis Rd, Brent. TW8 .... 179 CK78
Challock Cl, Bigg.H. TN16 .... 260 EJ116
Challoner Cl, N2 .... 120 DD54
Challoner Cres, W14 .... 38 G1
Challoners Cl, E.Mol. KT8 .... 219 CD98
Challoner St, W14 .... 26 G10
Chalmers Ct, Crox.Grn WD3 ... 96 BM44
Chalmers Ho, SW11
off York Rd 182 DC83
Chalmers Rd, Ashf. TW15 .... 197 BP91
Banstead SM7 .... 256 DD115
Chalmers Rd E, Ashf. TW15 .... 197 BP91
Chalmers Wk, SE17 .... 43 H3
Chalmers Way, Felt. TW14 .... 197 BV85
Chaloner Ct, SE1 .... 31 L4
Chalsey Rd, SE4 .... 185 DZ84
Chalton Dr, N2 .... 142 DC58
Chalton St, NW1 .... 17 P2
CHALVEY, Slou. SL1 .... 173 AQ76
Chalvey Gdns, Slou. SL1 .... 174 AS75
Chalvey Gro, Slou. SL1 .... 173 AP75
Chalvey Pk, Slou. SL1 .... 174 AS75
Chalvey Rd E, Slou. SL1 .... 174 AS75
Chalvey Rd W, Slou. SL1 .... 173 AR75
Chamberlain Cl, SE28
off Broadwater Rd. 187 ER76
Harlow CM17 .... 74 EW15
Ilford IG1
off Richmond Rd. 147 EQ62
Chamberlain Cotts, SE5 .... 43 M7
Chamberlain Cres, W.Wick.
BR4 .... 225 EB102
Chamberlain Gdns, Houns.
TW3 .... 178 CC81
Chamberlain La, Pnr. HA5 .... 137 BU56
Chamberlain Pl, E17 .... 145 DY55
Chamberlain Rd, N2 .... 120 DC54
W13 off Midhurst Rd 179 CG75
Chamberlain St, NW1 .... 6 F7
Chamberlain Wk, Felt. TW13
off Burgess Cl 198 BY91
Chamberlain Way, Pnr. HA5 ... 137 BV55
Surbiton KT6 .... 220 CL101
Chamberlayne Av, Wem. HA9 .. 140 CL61
Chamberlayne Rd, NW10 .... 14 C2
Chambers Av, Sid. DA14 .... 208 EY93
Chambersbury La, Hem.H. HP3. 80 BN25
Sch Chambersbury Prim Sch, Hem.H.
HP3 off Hill Common 62 BN23
Chambers Cl, Green. DA9 .... 211 FU85
Chambers Gdns, N2 .... 120 DD53
Chambers Gro, Welw.G.C. AL7 . 51 CY12
Chambers Ho, SW16
off Pringle Gdns 203 DJ91
Chambers La, NW10 .... 161 CV66
Chambers Manor Ms, Epp.Upl.
CM16 .... 91 EP26
Chambers Pl, S.Croy. CR2
off Rolleston Rd 242 DR108
Chambers Rd, N7 .... 143 DL63
Chambers St, SE16 .... 32 C4
Hertford SG14 .... 54 DQ09
Chamber St, E1 .... 20 B10
Chambers Wk, Stan. HA7 .... 117 CH50
Chambon Pl, W6 off Beavor La . 181 CU77
Chambord St, E2 .... 20 B3
Chamers Ct, W12
off Heathstan Rd 161 CU72
Champa Cl, N17 .... 122 DT54
Champion Cres, SE26 .... 205 DY91
Champion Down, Eff. KT24
off Norwood Cl 268 BY128
Champion Gro, SE5 .... 43 M10
Champion Hill, SE5 .... 43 M10
Champion Hill Est, SE5 .... 184 DS83
Champion Pk, SE5 .... 43 L9
Champion Pk Est, SE5 .... 43 M10
Champion Rd, SE26 .... 205 DY91
Upminster RM14 .... 150 FP61
Champions Grn, Hodd. EN11 ... 55 EA14
Champions Way, NW4 .... 119 CV53
NW7 .... 119 CV53
Hoddesdon EN11 .... 55 EA14
Champness Cl, SE27 .... 204 DR91
Champness Rd, Bark. IG11 .... 167 ET65
Champney Cl, Horton SL3 .... 175 BA83
Champneys Cl, Sutt. SM2 .... 239 CZ108
Chance Cl, Grays RM16 .... 192 FZ76
Chancellor Gdns, S.Croy. CR2 . 241 DP109
Chancellor Gro, SE21 .... 204 DQ89
Chancellor Pas, E14 .... 34 B3
Chancellor Pl, NW9 .... 119 CT54
Chancellors Ct, WC1
off Orde Hall St 18 C6
Chancellors Rd, W6 .... 38 A1
Sch Chancellor's Sch,
Brook.Pk AL9
off Pine Gro 86 DB25
Chancellors St, W6 .... 38 A1
Chancellors Wf, W6 .... 38 A1
Chancellor Way, Sev. TN13 .... 278 FG122
Chancelot Rd, SE2 .... 188 EV77
Chancel St, SE1 .... 30 G2
Chancery Cl, St.Alb. AL4 .... 65 CK15
Chancery Ct, Dart. DA1 .... 210 FN87
Egham TW20
off The Chantries 195 BA92
● Chancerygate Business Cen,
Slou. SL3 .... 174 AY75
Chancerygate Cl, Ruis. HA4 ... 138 BY64
Chancerygate Way, Ruis. HA4 . 138 BY63
⊖ Chancery Lane 18 E7
Chancery La, WC2 .... 18 E8
Beckenham BR3 .... 225 EB96
Chancery Ms, SW17 .... 202 DE89
Chance St, E1 .... 20 A4
E2 .... 20 A4
Chanctonbury Chase, Red.
RH1 .... 273 DH134
Chanctonbury Cl, SE9 .... 207 EP90
Chanctonbury Gdns, Sutt.
SM2 .... 240 DB108
Chanctonbury Way, N12 .... 119 CZ49
Chandler Av, E16 .... 23 N6
Chandler Cl, Hmptn. TW12 .... 218 CA95
Chandler Ct, Th.Hth. CR7
off Bensham La 223 DP99
Chandler Rd, Loug. IG10 .... 107 EP39
Chandlers Cl, Felt. TW14 .... 197 BT87
Jct Chandlers Cor, Rain. RM13 . 170 FJ69
CHANDLERS CROSS,
Rick. WD3 .... 96 BM38
Chandlers Dr, Erith DA8 .... 189 FD77
Sch Chandlers Fld Prim Sch,
W.Mol. KT8 off High St 218 CA99
Chandler's La, Chan.Cr. WD3 ... 96 BL37
Chandlers Ms, E14 .... 34 A4
Greenhithe DA9 .... 191 FW84
Chandlers Rd, St.Alb. AL4 .... 65 CJ17
Chandler St, E1 .... 32 F2
Chandlers Way, SW2 .... 203 DN87
Hertford SG14 .... 53 DN09
Romford RM1 .... 149 FE57
Chandler Way, SE15 .... 43 P3
Dorking RH5 .... 285 CJ138
Chandon Lo, Sutt. SM2
off Devonshire Rd 240 DC108
Chandos Av, E17 .... 123 EA54
N14 .... 121 DJ48
N20 .... 120 DC46
W5 .... 179 CJ77
Chandos Cl, Amer. HP6 .... 94 AW38
Buckhurst Hill IG9 .... 124 EH47
Chandos Ct, Stan. HA7 .... 117 CH51
Chandos Cres, Edg. HA8 .... 118 CM52
Chandos Gdns, Couls. CR5 .... 257 DP119
Chandos Par, Edg. HA8
off Chandos Cres 118 CM52
Chandos Pl, WC2 .... 30 A1
Chandos Rd, E15 .... 12 G2
N2 .... 120 DD54
N17 .... 122 DS54
NW2 .... 4 A3
NW10 .... 160 CS70
Borehamwood WD6 .... 100 CM40
Harrow HA1 .... 138 CC57
Pinner HA5 .... 138 BW59
Staines TW18 .... 195 BD92
Chandos St, W1 .... 17 K7
Chandos Way, NW11 .... 142 DB60
Change All, EC3 .... 19 M9
Chanlock Path, S.Ock. RM15
off Carnach Grn 171 FV73
Channel Cl, Houns. TW5 .... 178 CA81
Channel Gate Rd, NW10
off Old Oak La 161 CT69
Channel Ho, E14 .... 21 L7
SE16 off Canada St 33 J5
Channel Islands Est, N1 .... 9 K5
● Channelsea Ho Business Cen,
E15 .... 23 H1
Channelsea Rd, E15 .... 12 G8
Channing Cl, Horn. RM11 .... 150 FM59
Channings, Horsell GU21 .... 248 AY115
Sch Channing Sch for Girls, Jun Sch,
N6 off Highgate High St 143 DH60
Sen Sch, N6
off Highgate High St 143 DH60
Chantilly Way, Epsom KT19 .... 238 CP110
Chanton Dr, Epsom KT17 .... 239 CW110
Sutton SM2 .... 239 CW110
Chantress Cl, Dag. RM10 .... 169 FC67
Chantrey Cl, Ashtd. KT21 .... 253 CJ119
Chantrey Rd, SW9 .... 183 DM83
Chantreywood, Brwd. CM13 .... 131 GA48
Chantries, The, Egh. TW20 .... 195 BA92
Chantry, The, E4
off The Ridgeway 123 EC46
Harlow CM20 .... 58 EU13
Uxbridge UB8 .... 156 BM69
Chantry Cl, NW7
off Hendon Wd La 101 CT44
SE2 off Felixstowe Rd 188 EW76
W9 .... 15 H5
Enfield EN2 .... 104 DQ38
Harrow HA3 .... 140 CM57
Horley RH6 .... 290 DF147
Kings Langley WD4 .... 80 BN29
Sidcup DA14
off Ellenborough Rd 208 EY92
Sunbury-on-Thames TW16 .... 197 BU94
Windsor SL4 .... 173 AN81
Chantry Cotts, Chilw. GU4 .... 281 BB140
Chantry Ct, Cars. SM5 .... 222 DE104
Hatfield AL10 .... 67 CT19
Chantry Cres, NW10 .... 161 CT65
Chantry Ho, Rain. RM13
off Chantry Way 169 FD68
Chantry Hurst, Epsom KT18 .... 254 CR115
Chantry La, Brom. BR2
off Bromley Common 226 EK99
Hatfield AL10 .... 67 CT19
London Colney AL2 .... 83 CK26
Shere GU5 .... 282 BM139
Chantry Pl, Har. HA3 .... 116 CB53
Sch Chantry Prim Sch, Grav.
DA12 off Ordnance Rd 213 GJ86
Chantry Rd, Cher. KT16 .... 216 BJ101
Chessington KT9 .... 238 CM106
Chilworth GU4 .... 281 BB140
Harrow HA3 .... 116 CB53
Sch Chantry Sch, The, Yiew.
UB7 off Falling La 156 BL73
Chantry Sq, W8
off St. Mary's Pl 27 L7
Chantry St, N1 .... 9 H9
Chantry Vw Rd, Guil. GU1 .... 280 AX137
Chantry Way, Mitch. CR4
off Church Rd 222 DD97
Rainham RM13 .... 169 FD68
Chant Sq, E15 .... 13 H7
Chant St, E15 .... 13 H7
Chapel Av, Add. KT15 .... 234 BH105
Chapel Cl, NW10 .... 141 CT64
Brookmans Park AL9 .... 86 DD27
Dartford DA1 .... 209 FE85
Chapel Cl, Grays RM20 .... 191 FV79
Watford WD25 .... 81 BT34
Chapel Cotts, Hem.H. HP2 .... 62 BK18
Chapel Ct, N2 .... 142 DE55
SE1 .... 31 L4
SE18 .... 187 ET79
Dorking RH4 .... 285 CG135
Chapel Cft, Chipper. WD4 .... 80 BG31
Chapel Cfts, Nthch HP4 .... 60 AS17
Chapel End, Chal.St.P. SL9 .... 112 AX54
Hoddesdon EN11 .... 71 EA18
Sch Chapel End Inf & Jun Schs,
E17 off Beresford Rd 123 EB53
Chapel Fm Rd, SE9 .... 207 EM90
Chapel Fld, Harl. CM17 .... 74 EW17
Chapelfields, Stans.Abb. SG12 . 55 ED10
Chapel Gate Ms, SW4
off Bedford Rd 183 DL83
Chapel Gro, Add. KT15 .... 234 BH105
Epsom KT18 .... 255 CW119
Chapel Hill, Dart. DA1 .... 209 FE85
Effingham KT24
off The Street 268 BX127
Chapelhouse Cl, Guil. GU2 .... 264 AS134
Chapel Ho St, E14 .... 34 D10
Chapelier Ho, SW18
off Eastfields Av 182 DA84
Chapel La, Bkhm KT23 .... 268 CC128
Chigwell IG7 .... 125 ET48
Harlow CM17 .... 74 EW17
Letty Green SG14 .... 53 DH13
Pinner HA5 .... 138 BX55
Romford RM6 .... 148 EX59
Stoke Poges SL2 .... 154 AV66
Uxbridge UB8 .... 156 BN72
Westcott RH4 .... 284 CC137
Westhumble RH5 .... 269 CD130
Chapel Mkt, N1 .... 8 E10
Chapel Ms, Wdf.Grn. IG8 .... 125 EN51
Chapel Mill Rd, Kings.T. KT1 .... 220 CM97
Chapelmount Rd, Wdf.Grn.
IG8 .... 125 EM51
Chapel Pk Rd, Add. KT15 .... 234 BH105
Chapel Path, E11 .... 146 EG58
Chapel Pl, EC2 .... 19 N3
N1 .... 8 F10
N17 off White Hart La 122 DT52
W1 .... 17 J9
St. Albans AL1 .... 65 CD23
Chapel Rd, SE27 .... 203 DP91
W13 .... 159 CH74
Bexleyheath DA7 .... 188 FA84
Epping CM16 .... 91 ET30
Hounslow TW3 .... 178 CB83
Ilford IG1 .... 147 EN62
Oxted RH8 .... 276 EJ130
Redhill RH1 .... 272 DF134
Smallfield RH6 .... 291 DP148
Tadworth KT20 .... 255 CW123
Twickenham TW1 .... 199 CH87
Warlingham CR6 .... 259 DX118
Chapel Row, Hare. UB9 .... 114 BJ53
Chapels Cl, Slou. SL1 .... 153 AL74
Chapel Side, W2 .... 15 L10
Chapel Sq, Vir.W. GU25 .... 214 AY98
Chapel Stones, N17 .... 122 DT53
Chapel St, NW1 .... 16 C7
SW1 .... 29 H6
Berkhamsted HP4 .... 60 AW19
Enfield EN2 .... 104 DQ41
Guildford GU1
off Castle St 280 AX136
Hemel Hempstead HP2 .... 62 BK19
Slough SL1 .... 174 AT75
Uxbridge UB8
off Trumper Way 156 BJ67
Woking GU21 .... 249 AZ117
Chapel Ter, Loug. IG10
off Forest Rd 106 EL42
Chapel Vw, S.Croy. CR2 .... 242 DV107
🔒 Chapel Wk, Croy. CR0
off Whitgift Cen 224 DQ103
Chapel Wk, NW4 .... 141 CV56
Bexley DA5 .... 209 FE89
Coulsdon CR5 .... 257 DK122
Dartford DA2 .... 209 FE89
Chapel Way, N7
off Sussex Way 143 DM62
Bedmond WD5 .... 81 BT27
Epsom KT18 .... 255 CW119
Chapel Yd, SW18
off Wandsworth High St 202 DA85
Chaplaincy Gdns,
Horn. RM11 .... 150 FL60
Chaplin Cl, SE1 .... 30 F4
Chaplin Ct, Sutt.H. DA4 .... 210 FN93
Chaplin Cres, Sun. TW16 .... 197 BS93
Chaplin Ms, Slou. SL3 .... 175 AZ78
Chaplin Rd, E15 .... 13 K10
N17 .... 144 DT55
NW2 .... 161 CU65
Dagenham RM9 .... 168 EY66
Wembley HA0 .... 159 CJ65
Chaplin Sq, N12 .... 120 DD52
Chapman Cl, West Dr. UB7 .... 176 BM76
Chapman Ctyd, Chsht EN8 .... 89 DX30
Chapman Cres, Har. HA3 .... 140 CL57
● Chapman Pk Ind Est,
NW10 .... 161 CT65
Chapman Pl, N4 .... 143 DP61
Chapman Rd, E9 .... 11 P5
Belvedere DA17 .... 188 FA78
Croydon CR0 .... 223 DN102
Chapmans Cl, Sund. TN14 .... 262 EY124
Chapmans Cres, Chesh. HP5 .... 76 AN29
Chapman's La, SE2 .... 188 EW77
Belvedere DA17 .... 188 EX77
Chapmans La, Orp. BR5 .... 228 EX96
Chapman Sq, SW19 .... 201 CX89
Chapmans Rd, Sund. TN14 .... 262 EY124
Chapman St, E1 .... 20 E10
Chapone Pl, W1 .... 17 N9
Chapter Chambers, SW1
off Chapter St 29 N9
Chapter Cl, W4 .... 180 CQ76
Uxbridge UB10 .... 156 BM66
Chapter Ct, Egh. TW20
off The Chantries 195 BA92
Chapter Ho Ct, EC4 .... 19 J9
Chapter Ms, Wind. SL4 .... 173 AR80
Chapter Rd, NW2 .... 141 CU64
SE17 .... 43 H1
Chapter St, SW1 .... 29 N9
Chapter Way, SW19 .... 222 DC95
Hampton TW12 .... 198 CA91
Chara Pl, W4 .... 180 CR79
Charcot Ho, SW15
off Highcliffe Dr 201 CT86
Charcroft Gdns, Enf. EN3 .... 105 DX42
Chardin Rd, W4
off Elliott Rd 180 CS77
Chardins Cl, Hem.H. HP1 .... 61 BF19
Chardmore Rd, N16 .... 144 DU60
Chard Rd, Lon.Hthrw Air. TW6
off Heathrow Tunnel App 177 BP82
Chardwell Cl, E6 .... 25 J8
Charecroft Way, W12 .... 26 C5
W14 .... 26 C5
Charfield Ct, W9 .... 15 L5
Charford Rd, E16 .... 23 P7
Chargate Cl, Hersham KT12 .... 235 BT107
Chargeable La, E13 .... 23 M4
Chargeable St, E16 .... 23 M4
Chargrove Cl, SE16 .... 33 K4
Charing Cl, Orp. BR6 .... 245 ET105
⇌ Charing Cross 30 A2
⊖ Charing Cross 30 A2
Charing Cross, SW1 .... 29 P2
H Charing Cross Hosp, W6 .... 38 C2
Charing Cross Rd, WC2 .... 17 P8
Chariot Cl, E3 .... 12 A9
Chariotts Pl, Wind. SL4
off Victoria St 173 AR81
Charkham Ms, N.Mymms AL9 .. 67 CW24
Charlbert St, NW8 .... 6 C10
Charlbury Av, Stan. HA7 .... 117 CK50
Charlbury Cl, Rom. RM3 .... 128 FJ51
Charlbury Cres, Rom. RM3 .... 128 FJ51
Charlbury Gdns, Ilf. IG3 .... 147 ET61
Charlbury Gro, W5 .... 159 CJ72
Charlbury Ho, E12
off Grantham Rd 147 EN62
Charlbury Rd, Uxb. UB10 .... 136 BM62
Charlcot Ms, Slou. SL1 .... 153 AL73
Charldane Rd, SE9 .... 207 EP90
Charlecote Gro, SE26 .... 204 DV90
Charlecote Rd, Dag. RM8 .... 148 EY62
Charlemont Rd, E6 .... 25 K4
Charles Babbage Cl, Chess.
KT9 .... 237 CJ108
Charles Barry Cl, SW4 .... 41 M10
Charles Burton Ct, E5 .... 11 L1
Charles Ch Wk, Ilf. IG1 .... 147 EM58
Charles Cl, Sid. DA14 .... 208 EV91
Charles Cobb Gdns, Croy. CR0 . 241 DN106
Charles Coveney Rd, SE15 .... 44 A6
Charles Cres, Har. HA1 .... 139 CD59
Sch Charles Darwin Sch, Bigg.H.
TN16 off Jail La 261 EM116
Charles Dickens Ho, E2 .... 20 E3
★ Charles Dickens Mus, WC1 . 18 D4
Sch Charles Dickens Prim Sch,
SE1 .... 31 J5
Charles Dickens Ter, SE20
off Maple Rd 204 DW94
Sch Charles Edward Brooke C of E
Girls' Sch, Lwr Sch, SE5 .... 42 G7
Upr Sch, SW9 .... 43 H6
Charlesfield, SE9 .... 206 EJ90
Charlesfield Rd, Horl. RH6 .... 290 DF147
Charles Flemwell Ms, E16 .... 35 P3
Charles Gdns, Slou. SL2 .... 154 AV72
Charles Gardner Ct, N1 .... 19 M2
Charles Grinling Wk, SE18 .... 37 L8
Charles Gro, N14 .... 121 DJ46
Charles Haller St, SW2
off Tulse Hill 203 DN87
Charles Hocking Ho, W3
off Bollo Br Rd 180 CQ75
Charles Ho, N17 off Love La .. 122 DT52
Chertsey KT16
off Guildford St 215 BF102
Windsor SL4
off Ward Royal 173 AQ81
Charles La, NW8 .... 16 B1
Charles Mackenzie Ho, SE16
off Linsey St 32 C8
Charlesmere Gdns, SE28
off Battery Rd 187 ES75
Charles Nex Ms, SE21 .... 204 DQ89
Charles Pl, NW1 .... 17 M3
Charles Rd, E7 off Lens Rd 166 EJ66
SW19 .... 222 DA95
W13 .... 159 CG72
Badgers Mount TN14 .... 247 FB110
Dagenham RM10 .... 169 FD65
Romford RM6 .... 148 EX59
Staines TW18 .... 196 BK93
Charles Rowan Ho, WC1 .... 18 E3
Charles II Pl, SW3
off King's Rd 40 E1
Charles II St, SW1 .... 29 N2
Charles Sevright Dr, NW7 .... 119 CX50
Charles Sq, N1 .... 19 M3
Charles Sq Est, N1 .... 19 M3
Charles St, SW13 .... 180 CS82
W1 .... 29 J2
Berkhamsted HP4 .... 60 AV19
Chertsey KT16 .... 215 BF102
Croydon CR0 .... 224 DQ104
Enfield EN1 .... 104 DT43
Epping CM16 .... 92 EU32
Grays RM17 .... 192 GB79
Greenhithe DA9 .... 211 FT85
Hemel Hempstead HP1 .... 62 BJ21
Hounslow TW3 .... 178 BZ82
Uxbridge UB10 .... 157 BP70
Windsor SL4 .... 173 AQ81
Charleston Cl, Felt. TW13 .... 197 BU90
Charleston St, SE17 .... 31 K9
Charles Townsend Ho, EC1 .... 18 F4
Charles Whincup Rd, E16 .... 36 A2
Charlesworth Cl, Hem.H. HP3 .. 62 BK22
Charlesworth Pl, SW13
off Eleanor Gro 181 CT83
Charleville Circ, SE26 .... 204 DU92
Charleville Ms, Islw. TW7
off Railshead Rd 179 CH84
Charleville Rd, W14 .... 38 F1
Jct Charlie Brown's Rbt, E18 .. 124 EJ54
Charlie Chaplin Wk, SE1 .... 30 D3
off Waterloo Br
Charlieville Rd, Erith DA8
off Northumberland Pk 189 FC80
Charlmont Rd, SW17 .... 202 DF93
Charlock Way, Guil. GU1 .... 265 BB131
Watford WD18 .... 97 BT44
Charlotte Av, Slou. SL2 .... 154 AT73
Charlotte Cl, Ashtd. KT21 .... 254 CL118
Bexleyheath DA6 .... 208 EY85
Ilford IG6 off Connor Cl 125 EQ53
St. Albans AL4 .... 66 CL20
Charlotte Ct, N8 .... 143 DK58
W6 off Invermead Cl 181 CU77
Esher KT10 .... 236 CC106
Charlotte Despard Av, SW11 ... 41 H7
Charlotte Gdns, Rom. RM5 .... 127 FB51
Charlotte Gro, Smallfield RH6 . 291 DN147
Charlotte Ms, W1 .... 17 M6
W10 .... 14 C9
W14 .... 26 E8
Charlotte Pk Av, Brom. BR1 .... 226 EL97
Charlotte Pl, NW9
off Uphill Dr 140 CQ57
SW1 .... 29 L9
W1 .... 17 M7
Grays RM20 .... 191 FV79
Charlotte Rd, EC2 .... 19 N4
SW13 .... 181 CT81
Dagenham RM10 .... 169 FB65
Wallington SM6 .... 241 DJ107
Charlotte Row, SW4 .... 183 DJ83
Sch Charlotte Sharman Prim Sch,
SE11 .... 30 G7
Charlotte Sq, Rich. TW10
off Greville Rd 200 CM86
Charlotte St, W1 .... 17 M6
Charlotte Ter, N1 .... 8 D9
Sch Charlotte Turner Prim Sch,
SE8 .... 46 B2
CHARLOTTEVILLE, Guil. GU1 . 280 AY137
Charlow Cl, SW6 .... 39 N9
CHARLTON, SE7 .... 186 EJ79
⇌ Charlton 36 B10
Charlton, Wind. SL4 .... 172 AJ82
★ Charlton Athletic FC, SE7 .... 36 D10
Charlton Av, Hersham KT12 ... 235 BV105
Charlton Ch La, SE7 .... 36 C10
Charlton Cl, Hodd. EN11 .... 71 EA17
Slough SL1 .... 173 AP75
Uxbridge UB10 .... 137 BP61
Charlton Cres, Bark. IG11 .... 167 ET68
Charlton Dene, SE7 .... 186 EJ80
Charlton Dr, Bigg.H. TN16 .... 260 EK117
Charlton Gdns, Couls. CR5 .... 257 DJ118
● Charlton Gate, SE7 .... 36 C9
Charlton Kings, Wey. KT13 .... 217 BS104
Charlton Kings Rd, NW5 .... 7 N2
Charlton La, SE7 .... 36 E10
Shepperton TW17 .... 217 BS98
Sch Charlton Manor Prim Sch,
SE7 off Indus Rd 186 EK80
Charlton Mead La, Hodd. EN11 . 71 EC18
Charlton Mead La S, Hodd. EN11
off Charlton Mead La 71 ED18
Charlton Pk La, SE7 .... 186 EK80
Charlton Pk Rd, SE7 .... 186 EK79
Charlton Pl, N1 .... 8 G10
Windsor SL4 off Charlton 172 AJ82
Charlton Rd, N9 .... 123 DX46
NW10 .... 160 CS67
SE3 .... 186 EG80
SE7 .... 186 EH80
Harrow HA3 .... 139 CK56
Shepperton TW17 .... 217 BQ97
Wembley HA9 .... 140 CM60
Charlton Row, Wind. SL4
off Charlton 172 AJ82
Sch Charlton Sch, SE7
off Charlton Pk Rd 186 EL79
Charlton Sq, Wind. SL4
off Charlton 172 AJ82
Charlton St, Grays RM20 .... 191 FX79
Charlton Wk, Wind. SL4
off Charlton 172 AJ82
Charlton Way, SE3 .... 47 J7
Hoddesdon EN11 .... 71 EA17
Windsor SL4 .... 172 AJ82
Charlwood, Croy. CR0 .... 243 DZ109
Charlwood Cl, Bkhm KT23 .... 252 CB124
Harrow HA3
off Kelvin Cres 117 CE51
Charlwood Dr, Oxshott KT22 .. 253 CD115
Charlwood Ho, SW1
off Vauxhall Br Rd 29 N9
Richmond TW9
off Strand Dr 180 CP80
Charlwood Pl, SW1 .... 29 M9
Reigate RH2 .... 271 CZ134
Charlwood Rd, SW15 .... 181 CX83
Horley RH6 .... 290 DB152
Charlwood St, SW1 .... 29 M9
Charlwood Ter, SW15 .... 181 CX84
Charman Ho, SW8
off Hemans St 42 A4
Charman Rd, Red. RH1 .... 272 DE134
Charm Cl, Horl. RH6 .... 290 DE147
Charmian Av, Stan. HA7 .... 139 CK55
Charminster Av, SW19 .... 222 DA96
Charminster Ct, Surb. KT6
off Lovelace Gdns 219 CK101
Charminster Rd, SE9 .... 206 EK91
Worcester Park KT4 .... 221 CX102
Charmouth Ct, St.Alb. AL1 .... 65 CG17
Charmouth Ho, SW8
off Dorset Rd 42 C4
Charmouth Rd, St.Alb. AL1 .... 65 CG18
Welling DA16 .... 188 EW81
Charmwood La, Orp. BR6 .... 246 EV109
Charne, The, Otford TN14 .... 263 FG117
Charnock, Swan. BR8 .... 229 FE98
Charnock Rd, E5 .... 144 DV62
Charnwood Av, SW19 .... 222 DA96
Charnwood Cl, N.Mal. KT3 .... 220 CS98
Charnwood Dr, E18 .... 146 EH55
Charnwood Gdns, E14 .... 34 B8
Charnwood Pl, N20 .... 120 DC48
Charnwood Rd, SE25 .... 224 DR99
Enfield EN1 .... 104 DV36
Uxbridge UB10 .... 156 BN68
Charnwood St, E5 .... 144 DU61
Charrington Pl, St.Alb. AL1 .... 65 CF21
Charrington Rd, Croy. CR0
off Drayton Rd 223 DP103
Charrington St, NW1 .... 7 N10
Charsley Cl, Amer. HP6 .... 94 AW39
Charsley Rd, SE6 .... 205 EB89
Charta Rd, Egh. TW20 .... 195 BC92
Chart Cl, Brom. BR2 .... 226 EE95
Croydon CR0 .... 224 DW100
Dorking RH5 .... 285 CK138
Mitcham CR4 .... 222 DF98
Chart Downs, Dor. RH5 .... 285 CJ138
Charter Av, Ilf. IG2 .... 147 ER60
Charter Cl, St.Alb. AL1
off Bricket Rd 65 CE20
Slough SL1 .... 174 AT76
Charter Ct, N.Mal. KT3 .... 220 CS97
Charter Cres, Houns. TW4 .... 178 BY84

Charter Dr, Amer. HP6 94 AT38
Bexley DA5 208 EY87
★ Charterhouse, EC1 19 H6
Charterhouse Av, Wem. HA0 139 CJ63
Charterhouse Bldgs, EC1 19 H5
Charterhouse Dr, Sev. TN13 278 FG123
Charterhouse Ms, EC1 19 H6
Charterhouse Rd, E8 10 C1
Orpington BR6 228 EU104
Charterhouse Sq, EC1 19 H6
Charterhouse Sq Sch, EC1 19 J6
Charterhouse St, EC1 18 F7
Charteris Rd, N4 143 DN60
NW6 5 H9
Woodford Green IG8 124 EH52
● Charter Pl, Uxb. UB8 156 BK66
Charter Pl, Wat. WD17 98 BW42
Charter Pl, Stai. TW18 196 BG93
Charter Rd, Kings.T. KT1 220 CP97
Slough SL1 153 AL73
Charter Rd, The, Wdf.Grn. IG8 124 EE51
Charter Sch, The, SE24
off Red Post Hill 204 DR85
Charters Cl, SE19 204 DS92
Charters Cross, Harl. CM18 73 ER18
Charter Sq, Kings.T. KT1 220 CP96
Charter Way, N3 141 CZ56
N14 103 DJ44
Chartfield Av, SW15 201 CV85
Chartfield Pl, Wey. KT13 235 BP106
Chartfield Rd, Reig. RH2 288 DC135
Chartfield Sq, SW15 201 CX85
Chart Gdns, Dor. RH5 285 CJ139
Chartham Ct, SW9 183 DN83
Chartham Gro, SE27
off Royal Circ. 203 DP90
Chartham Rd, SE25 224 DV97
Chart Hills Cl, SE28
off Fairway Dr 168 EY72
Chart La, Dor. RH4 285 CH136
Reigate RH2 272 DB134
Chart La S, Dor. RH5 285 CJ138
Chartley Av, NW2 140 CS62
Stanmore HA7 117 CF51
Charton Cl, Belv. DA17 188 EZ79
Chartridge Cl, Barn. EN5 101 CU43
Bushey WD23 98 CC44
Chartridge La, Chesh. HP5 76 AM29
Chartridge Way, Hem.H. HP2 63 BQ20
Chart St, N1 19 M2
Chartway, Reig. RH2 272 DB133
Sevenoaks TN13 279 FJ124
★ Chartwell, West. TN16 277 ET131
Chartwell Cl, SE9 207 EQ89
Croydon CR0 224 DR102
Greenford UB6 158 CB67
Waltham Abbey EN9 90 EE33
Chartwell Dr, Orp. BR6 245 ER106
Chartwell Gdns, Sutt. SM3 239 CY105
Chartwell Gate, Beac. HP9 111 AK53
Chartwell Pl, Epsom KT18 238 CS114
Harrow HA2 139 CD61
Sutton SM3 239 CZ105
Chartwell Rd, Nthwd. HA6 115 BT51
Chartwell Way, SE20 224 DV95
Chartwood Pl, Dor. RH4
off South St 285 CG136
Charville La, Hayes UB4 157 BS68
Charville La W, Uxb. UB10 157 BP69
Charville Prim Sch, Hayes
UB4 off Bury Av 157 BS68
Charwood, SW16 203 DN91
Charwood Cl, Shenley WD7 84 CL33
Chasden Rd, Hem.H. HP1 61 BF17
Chase, The, E12 146 EK63
SW4 41 J10
SW16 203 DM94
SW20 221 CY95
Ashtead KT21 253 CJ118
Bexleyheath DA7 189 FB83
Brentwood (Cromwell Rd)
CM14 130 FV49
Brentwood (Seven Arches Rd)
CM14 130 FX48
Brentwood (Woodman Rd)
CM14 130 FX50
Bromley BR1 226 EH97
Chadwell Heath RM6 148 EY58
Chesham HP5 76 AP29
Chigwell IG7 125 EQ49
Coulsdon CR5 241 DJ114
East Horsley KT24 267 BT126
Eastcote HA5 138 BW58
Edgware HA8 118 CP53
Goffs Oak EN7 87 DP28
Grays RM20 191 FX79
Great Amwell SG12 55 EA09
Guildford GU2 280 AU135
Harlow CM17 58 EW14
Hemel Hempstead HP2
off Turners Hill 62 BL21
Hornchurch RM12 149 FE62
Ingrave CM13 131 GC50
Kingswood KT20 256 DA122
Loughton IG10 124 EJ45
Oxshott KT22 252 CC115
Penn HP10 110 AC46
Pinner HA5 138 BZ56
Radlett WD7 99 CF35
Reigate RH2 288 DD135
Romford RM1 149 FE55
Rush Green RM7 149 FD62
Stanmore HA7 117 CG50
Sunbury-on-Thames TW16 217 BV95
Upminster RM14 151 FS62
Uxbridge UB10 136 BN64
Wallington SM6 241 DL106
Watford WD18 97 BS42
Wooburn Green HP10 132 AF59
Chase Br Prim Sch, Twick.
TW2 off Kneller Rd 199 CE86
Chase Cl, Colesh. HP7 77 AN43
Penn HP10 110 AC46
Chase Ct Gdns, Enf. EN2 104 DQ41
CHASE CROSS, Rom. RM1 127 FE51
Chase Cross Rd, Rom. RM5 127 FC52
Chase End, Epsom KT19 238 CR112
Chase Fm Hosp, Enf. EN2 103 DN38
Chasefield Cl, Guil. GU4 265 BA131
Chasefield Rd, SW17 202 DF91
Chase Gdns, E4 123 EA49
Chase Gdns, Twick. TW2 199 CD86
Chase Grn, Enf. EN2 104 DQ41
Chase Grn Av, Enf. EN2 103 DP40
Chase Hill, Enf. EN2 104 DQ41
Chase Ho Gdns, Horn. RM11
off Great Nelmes Chase 150 FM57
Chase La, Chig. IG7 126 EU48
Ilford IG6 147 ER57
Chase La Prim Sch, E4
off York Rd 123 DZ50
Chaseley Dr, W4 180 CP78
South Croydon CR2 242 DR110
Chaseley St, E14 21 L9
Chasemore Cl, Mitch. CR4 222 DF101
Chasemore Gdns, Croy. CR0 241 DN106
Chase Ridings, Enf. EN2 103 DN40
Chase Rd, N14 103 DJ44
NW10 160 CR70
W3 160 CR70
Brentwood CM14 130 FW48
Epsom KT19 238 CR112
Chase Side, N14 102 DG44
Enfield EN2 104 DQ41
Chase Side Av, SW20 221 CY95
Enfield EN2 104 DQ40
Chaseside Cl, Rom. RM1 127 FE51
Chase Side Cres, Enf. EN2 104 DQ39
Chaseside Gdns, Cher. KT16 216 BH101
Chase Side Pl, Enf. EN2
off Chase Side 104 DQ40
Chase Side Prim Sch, Enf.
EN2 off Trinity St 104 DQ40
Chase Sq, Grav. DA11
off High St 213 GH86
Chaseville Par, N21 103 DM43
Chaseville Pk Rd, N21 103 DL43
Chase Way, N14 121 DH47
Chaseways, Saw. CM21 58 EW07
Chasewood Av, Enf. EN2 103 DP40
Chasewood Pk, Har. HA1 139 CE62
Chastilian Rd, Dart. DA1 209 FF87
Chaston Pl, NW5
off Grafton Ter 6 G3
Chatelet Cl, Horl. RH6 291 DH147
Chater Ho, E2 off Roman Rd 21 J2
Chater Infants' Sch, Wat.
WD18 off Southsea Av 97 BU42
Chater Jun Sch, Wat. WD18
off Addiscombe Rd 97 BV42
Chatfield, Slou. SL2 153 AN71
Chatfield Ct, Cat. CR3 258 DR122
Chatfield Dr, Guil. GU4 265 BC132
Chatfield Rd, SW11 182 DC83
Croydon CR0 223 DP102
Chatham Av, Brom. BR2 226 EF101
Chatham Cl, NW11 142 DA57
SE18 37 P6
Sutton SM3 221 CZ101
Chatham Hill Rd, Sev. TN14 279 FJ121
Chatham Ms, Guil. GU2 264 AU131
Chatham Pl, E9 10 G4
Chatham Rd, E17 145 DY55
E18 off Grove Hill 124 EF54
SW11 202 DF86
Kingston upon Thames KT1 220 CN96
Orpington BR6
off Gladstone Rd 245 EQ106
Chatham St, SE17 31 L8
Chatham Way, Brwd. CM14 130 FW47
Chatsfield, Epsom KT17 239 CU110
Chatsfield Pl, W5 160 CL72
Chatsworth Av, NW4 119 CW54
SW20 221 CY95
Bromley BR1 206 EH91
Sidcup DA15 208 EU88
Wembley HA9 140 CM64
Chatsworth Cl, NW4 119 CW54
Borehamwood WD6 100 CN41
West Wickham BR4 226 EF103
Chatsworth Ct, W8 27 J8
Stanmore HA7 off Marsh La 117 CJ50
Chatsworth Cres, Houns. TW3 179 CD84
Chatsworth Dr, Enf. EN1 122 DU45
Chatsworth Est, E5
off Elderfield Rd 145 DX63
Chatsworth Gdns, W3 160 CP73
Harrow HA2 138 CB60
New Malden KT3 221 CT99
Chatsworth Inf & Nurs Sch,
Houns. TW3 off Heath Rd 178 CC84
Chatsworth Inf Sch, Sid.
DA15 off Burnt Oak La 208 EU88
Chatsworth Jun Sch, Houns.
TW3 off Heath Rd 178 CC84
Chatsworth Ms, Wat. WD24 97 BU38
Chatsworth Par, Petts Wd BR5
off Queensway 227 EQ99
Chatsworth Pl, Mitch. CR4 222 DF97
Oxshott KT22 237 CD112
Teddington TW11 199 CG91
Chatsworth Ri, W5 160 CM70
Chatsworth Rd, E5 144 DW62
E15 13 L3
NW2 4 E5
W4 180 CQ79
W5 160 CM70
Croydon CR0 242 DR105
Dartford DA1 210 FJ85
Hayes UB4 157 BV70
Sutton SM3 239 CX106
Chatsworth Way, SE27 203 DP90
Chatteris Av, Rom. RM3 128 FJ51
Chattern Hill, Ashf. TW15 197 BP91
Chattern Rd, Ashf. TW15 197 BQ91
Chatterton Ms, N4
off Chatterton Rd 143 DP62
Chatterton Rd, N4 143 DP62
Bromley BR2 226 EK98
Chatto Rd, SW11 202 DF85
Chaucer Av, Hayes UB4 157 BU71
Hounslow TW4 177 BV82
Richmond TW9 180 CN82
Weybridge KT13 234 BN108
Chaucer Cl, N11 121 DJ50
Banstead SM7 239 CY114
Berkhamsted HP4 60 AT18
Tilbury RM18 193 GJ82
Windsor SL4 173 AR83
Chaucer Ct, N16 9 N1
Guildford GU2 off Lawn Rd 280 AW137
Chaucer Dr, SE1 32 B9
Chaucer Gdns, Sutt. SM1 222 DA104
Chaucer Grn, Croy. CR0 224 DV101
Chaucer Ho, SW1 41 L1
Sutton SM1 222 DA104
Chaucer Pk, Dart. DA1 210 FM87
Chaucer Rd, E7 13 P5
E11 146 EG58
E17 123 EC54
Chaucer Rd, SE24 203 DN85
W3 160 CQ74
Ashford TW15 196 BL91
Northfleet DA11 212 GD90
Romford RM3 127 FH52
Sidcup DA15 208 EW88
Sutton SM1 240 DA105
Welling DA16 187 ES81
Chaucer Way, SW19 202 DD93
Addlestone KT15 234 BG107
Dartford DA1 190 FN84
Hoddesdon EN11 55 EA13
Slough SL1 154 AT74
CHAULDEN, Hem.H. HP1 61 BE21
Chaulden Ho Gdns, Hem.H.
HP1 61 BF21
Chaulden Inf & Nurs Sch,
Hem.H. HP1 off School Row 61 BF21
Chaulden Jun Sch, Hem.H.
HP1 off School Row 61 BF21
Chaulden La, Hem.H. HP1 61 BD22
Chaulden Ter, Hem.H. HP1 61 BF21
Chauncey Cl, N9 122 DU48
Chauncy Av, Pot.B. EN6 86 DC33
Chauncy Ct, Hert. SG14
off Bluecoats Av 54 DR09
Chauncy Sch, The, Ware
SG12 off Park Rd 54 DV05
Chaundrye Cl, SE9 207 EM86
Chauntler Cl, E16 24 B10
Chauntry Cl, Maid. SL6 152 AC73
Chavecroft Ter, Epsom KT18 255 CW119
Chave Rd, Dart. DA2 210 FL90
Chaworth Cl, Ott. KT16 233 BC107
Chaworth Rd, Ott. KT16 233 BC107
CHEAM, Sutt. SM3 239 CX107
⇌ Cheam 239 CY108
Cheam Cl, Tad. KT20
off Waterfield 255 CW121
Cheam Common Infants' Sch,
Wor.Pk. KT4
off Balmoral Rd 221 CV103
Cheam Common Jun Sch,
Wor.Pk. KT4
off Kingsmead Av 221 CV103
Cheam Common Rd,
Wor.Pk. KT4 221 CV103
Cheam Flds Prim Sch, Cheam
SM3 off Stoughton Av 239 CY106
Cheam High Sch, Cheam
SM3 off Chatsworth Rd 239 CY105
Cheam Mans, Sutt. SM3 239 CY108
Cheam Pk Fm Infants' Sch,
Sutt. SM3 off Molesey Dr 221 CY104
Cheam Pk Fm Jun Sch, Sutt.
SM3 off Kingston Av 221 CY104
Cheam Pk Way, Sutt. SM3 239 CY107
Cheam Rd, E.Ewell SM2 239 CX110
Epsom KT17 239 CU109
Sutton SM1 239 CZ107
Cheam St, SE15 44 F10
Cheam Village, Sutt. SM3 239 CY107
Cheapside, EC2 19 K9
N13 off Taplow Rd 122 DQ49
Woking GU21 232 AX114
Cheapside La, Denh. UB9 135 BF61
Chearsley, SE17
off Deacon Way 31 K8
Chedburgh, Welw.G.C. AL7 52 DD08
Cheddar Cl, N11 120 DF51
Cheddar Rd, Lon.Hthrw Air.
TW6 off Cromer Rd 176 BN82
Cheddar Waye, Hayes UB4 157 BV72
Cheddington Rd, N18 122 DS48
Chedworth Cl, E16 23 L8
Cheelson Rd, S.Ock. RM15 171 FW68
Cheeseman Cl, Hmptn. TW12 198 BY93
Cheesemans Ter, W14 38 G1
Cheffins Rd, Hodd. EN11 55 DZ14
Cheldon Av, NW7 119 CX52
Chelford Rd, Brom. BR1 205 ED92
Chelmer Cres, Bark. IG11 168 EV68
Chelmer Dr, Hutt. CM13 131 GE44
South Ockendon RM15 171 FW73
Chelmer Rd, E9 11 K2
Grays RM16 193 GG78
Upminster RM14 151 FR58
Chelmsford Av, Rom. RM5 127 FD52
Chelmsford Cl, E6 25 J9
W6 38 D2
Sutton SM2 240 DA109
Chelmsford Dr, Upmin. RM14 150 FM62
Chelmsford Gdns, Ilf. IG1 146 EL59
Chelmsford Rd, E11 145 ED60
E17 145 EA58
E18 124 EF53
N14 121 DJ45
Hatfield Heath CM22 59 FH05
Hertford SG14 53 DN10
Shenfield CM15 131 FZ44
Chelmsford Sq, NW10 4 A9
CHELSEA, SW3 40 A2
Chelsea & Westminster Hosp,
SW10 39 P3
★ Chelsea Antique Mkt, SW3 40 B2
Chelsea Br, SW1 41 J2
SW8 41 J2
Chelsea Br Rd, SW1 28 G10
Chelsea Cloisters, SW3 28 D9
Chelsea Cl, NW10
off Winchelsea Rd 160 CR67
Edgware HA8 118 CN54
Hampton Hill TW12 198 CC93
Worcester Park KT4 221 CU101
Chelsea Coll of Art & Design,
SW1 30 A10
Chelsea Cres, SW10 39 P7
Chelsea Embk, SW3 40 D3
Chelsea Flds, Hodd. EN11 55 EB13
★ Chelsea FC, SW6 39 L4
Chelsea Gdns, SW1
off Chelsea Br Rd 41 H1
W13 off Hathaway Gdns 159 CF71
Harlow CM17 74 EY16
Sutton SM3 239 CY105
Chelsea Harbour, SW10 39 P7
● Chelsea Harbour Design Cen,
SW10 off Harbour Av 39 P6
Chelsea Harbour Dr, SW10 39 P6
Chelsea Harbour Pier 40 A7
Chelsea Manor Ct, SW3 40 D2
Chelsea Manor Gdns, SW3 40 D2
Chelsea Manor St, SW3 40 C1
Chelsea Ms, Horn. RM11
off St. Leonards Way 149 FH60
Chelsea Pk Gdns, SW3 40 A2
★ Chelsea Physic Gdn, SW3 40 E2
Chelsea Reach Twr, SW10 40 A4
Chelsea Sq, SW3 28 B10
Chelsea Twrs, SW3 40 D1
Chelsea Village, SW6 39 M4
Chelsea Vista, SW6 39 P7
Chelsea Wf, SW10 40 A5
CHELSFIELD, Orp. BR6 246 EW106
⇌ Chelsfield 246 EV106
Chelsfield Av, N9 123 DX45
Chelsfield Gdns, SE26 204 DW90
Chelsfield Grn, N9
off Chelsfield Av 123 DX45
Chelsfield Hill, Orp. BR6 246 EW109
Chelsfield La, Maypole BR6 246 FA108
Orpington BR5, BR6 228 EX101
Sevenoaks TN14 247 FC109
Chelsfield Pk Hosp,
Chels. BR6 246 EZ106
Chelsfield Prim Sch, Chels.
BR6 off Warren Rd 246 EY106
Chelsfield Rd, Orp. BR5 228 EW100
CHELSHAM, Warl. CR6 259 EA117
Chelsham Cl, Warl. CR6 259 DY118
Chelsham Common,
Warl. CR6 259 EA116
Chelsham Common Rd,
Warl. CR6 259 EA117
Chelsham Ct Rd, Warl. CR6 259 ED118
Chelsham Rd, SW4 41 P10
South Croydon CR2 242 DR107
Warlingham CR6 259 EA117
Chelsing Ri, Hem.H. HP2 63 BQ21
Chelston App, Ruis. HA4 137 BU61
Chelston Rd, Ruis. HA4 137 BU60
Chelsworth Cl, Rom. RM3
off Chelsworth Dr 128 FM53
Chelsworth Dr, SE18 187 ER79
Romford RM3 128 FL53
Cheltenham Av, Twick. TW1 199 CG87
Cheltenham Cl, Grav. DA12 213 GJ92
New Malden KT3
off Northcote Rd 220 CQ97
Northolt UB5 158 CB65
Cheltenham Gdns, E6 24 G1
Loughton IG10 106 EL44
Cheltenham Pl, W3 160 CP74
Harrow HA3 140 CL56
Cheltenham Rd, E10 145 EC58
SE15 184 DW84
Orpington BR6 228 EU104
Cheltenham Ter, SW3 28 F10
Cheltenham Vil, Stai. TW19 195 BF86
Chelverton Rd, SW15 181 CX84
Chelveston, Welw.G.C. AL7 52 DD08
Chelwood, N20
off Oakleigh Rd N 120 DD47
Chelwood Av, Hat. AL10 67 CU16
Chelwood Cl, E4 105 EB44
Coulsdon CR5 257 DJ119
Epsom KT17 239 CT112
Northwood HA6 115 BQ52
Chelwood Gdns, Rich. TW9 180 CN82
Chelwood Gdns Pas, Rich. TW9
off Chelwood Gdns 180 CN82
Chelwood Wk, SE4 185 DY84
Chenappa Cl, E13 23 M3
Chenduit Way, Stan. HA7 117 CF50
Chene Dr, St.Alb. AL3 65 CD18
Chene Ms, St.Alb. AL3 65 CD18
Cheney Row, E17 123 DZ53
Cheneys Rd, E11 146 EE62
Cheney St, Pnr. HA5 138 BW57
CHENIES, Rick. WD3 95 BB38
Chenies, The, Dart. DA2 209 FE91
Petts Wood BR6 227 ES100
Chenies Av, Amer. HP6 94 AW39
Chenies Bottom, Chenies WD3 95 BA37
Chenies Ct, Hem.H. HP2
off Datchet Cl 63 BP15
Chenies Hill, Flaun. HP3 79 BB34
★ Chenies Manor, Rick. WD3 95 BA38
Chenies Ms, WC1 17 N5
Chenies Par, Amer. HP7 94 AW40
Chenies Pl, NW1 7 N10
Chenies Rd, Chorl. WD3 95 BD40
Chenies Sch, Chenies WD3
off Latimer Rd 95 BB38
Chenies St, WC1 17 N6
Chenies Way, Wat. WD18 115 BS45
Cheniston Cl, W.Byf. KT14 234 BG113
Cheniston Gdns, W8 27 L6
Chennells, Hat. AL10 67 CT19
Chennestone Prim Sch, Sun.
TW16 off Manor La 217 BV96
Chepstow Av, Horn. RM12 150 FL62
Chepstow Cl, SW15 201 CY86
Chepstow Cres, W11 15 J10
Ilford IG3 147 ES58
Chepstow Gdns, Sthl. UB1 158 BZ72
Chepstow Pl, W2 15 K10
Chepstow Ri, Croy. CR0 224 DS104
Chepstow Rd, W2 15 K8
W7 179 CG76
Croydon CR0 224 DS104
Chepstow Vil, W11 15 H10
Chequers, Buck.H. IG9 124 EH46
Hatfield AL9 51 CX13
Welwyn Garden City AL7 51 CX11
Chequers Cl, NW9 140 CS55
Horley RH6 290 DG147
Orpington BR5 227 ET98
Walton on the Hill KT20 271 CU125
Chequers Dr, Horl. RH6 290 DG147
Chequers Fld, Welw.G.C. AL7 51 CX12
Chequers Gdns, N13 121 DP50
Chequers Hill, Amer. HP7 77 AR40
Chequers La, Dag. RM9 168 EZ70
Walton on the Hill KT20 271 CU125
Watford WD25 82 BW30
Chequers Orchard, Iver SL0 155 BF72
Chequers Par, SE9
off Eltham High St 207 EM86
Chequers Pl, Dor. RH4 285 CH136
Chequers Rd, Brwd. CM14 128 FM46
Loughton IG10 107 EN43
Romford RM3 128 FL47
Chequers Sq, Uxb. UB8
off The Pavilions 156 BJ66
Chequer St, EC1 19 K5
St. Albans AL1 65 CD20
Chequers Wk, Wal.Abb. EN9 90 EF33
Chequers Way, N13 122 DQ50
Chequers Yd, Dor. RH4
off Chequers Pl 285 CH136
Chequer Tree Cl, Knap. GU21 248 AS116
Cherbury Cl, SE28 168 EX72
Cherbury Ct, N1 19 M1
Cherbury St, N1 19 M1
Cherchefelle Ms, Stan. HA7 117 CH50
Cherimoya Gdns, W.Mol.
KT8 off Kelvinbrook 218 CB97
Cherington Rd, W7 159 CF74
Cheriton Av, Brom. BR2 226 EF99
Ilford IG5 125 EM54
Cheriton Cl, W5 159 CJ71
Barnet EN4 102 DF41
St. Albans AL4 65 CK16
Cheriton Ct, Walt. KT12 218 BW102
Cheriton Dr, SE18 187 ER80
Cheriton Ho, E5
off Pembury Rd 10 E2
Cheriton Sq, SW17 202 DG89
Cherkley Hill, Lthd. KT22 269 CJ126
Cherries, The, Slou. SL2 154 AV72
Cherry Acre, Chal.St.P. SL9 112 AX49
Cherry Av, Brwd. CM13 131 FZ48
Slough SL3 174 AX75
Southall UB1 158 BX74
Swanley BR8 229 FD97
Cherry Blossom Cl, N13 121 DP50
Harlow CM17 58 EW11
Cherry Bounce, Hem.H. HP1 62 BK18
Cherry Cl, E17 145 EB57
NW9 119 CT54
SW2 203 DN87
W5 179 CK76
Banstead SM7 239 CX114
Carshalton SM5 222 DF103
Morden SM4 221 CY98
Ruislip HA4 off Roundways 137 BT62
Cherrycot Hill, Orp. BR6 245 ER105
Cherrycot Ri, Orp. BR6 245 EQ105
Cherry Cres, Brent. TW8 179 CH80
Cherry Cft, Crox.Grn WD3 96 BN44
Welwyn Garden City AL8 51 CX05
Cherrycroft Gdns, Pnr. HA5
off Westfield Pk 116 BZ52
Cherrydale, Wat. WD18 97 BT42
Cherrydown Av, E4 123 DZ48
Cherrydown Cl, E4 123 DZ48
Cherrydown Rd, Sid. DA14 208 EX89
Cherrydown Wk, Rom. RM7 127 FB54
Cherry Dr, Forty Grn HP9 110 AH51
Cherry Gdns, Dag. RM9 148 EZ64
Northolt UB5 158 CB66
Cherry Gdn Sch, SE16 32 D8
Cherry Gdn St, SE16 32 E5
Cherry Garth, Brent. TW8 179 CK77
Cherry Grn Cl, Red. RH1 289 DH136
Cherry Gro, Hayes UB3 157 BV74
Uxbridge UB8 157 BP71
Cherry Hill, Har. HA3 117 CE51
Loudwater WD3 96 BH41
New Barnet EN5 102 DB44
St. Albans AL2 82 CA25
Cherry Hill Gdns, Croy. CR0 241 DM105
Cherry Hills, Wat. WD19 116 BY50
Cherry Hollow, Abb.L. WD5 81 BT31
Cherrylands Cl, NW9 140 CQ61
Cherry La, Amer. HP7 77 AN40
West Drayton UB7 176 BM77
Cherry La Prim Sch, West Dr.
UB7 off Sipson Rd 176 BM77
Cherry La Rbt, West Dr.
UB7 177 BP77
Cherry Laurel Wk, SW2
off Beechdale Rd 203 DM86
Cherry Orchard, Amer. HP6 77 AS37
Ashtead KT21 254 CP118
Hemel Hempstead HP1 62 BG18
Staines TW18 196 BG92
Stoke Poges SL2 154 AV66
West Drayton UB7 176 BL75
Cherry Orchard Cl, Orp. BR5 228 EW99
Cherry Orchard Est, SE7 186 EJ80
Cherry Orchard Gdns, Croy.
CR0 off Oval Rd 224 DR103
West Molesey KT8 218 BZ97
Cherry Orchard Prim Sch,
SE7 off Rectory Fld Cres 186 EJ80
Cherry Orchard Rd, Brom.
BR2 226 EL103
Croydon CR0 224 DR103
West Molesey KT8 218 CA97
Cherry Ri, Ch.St.G. HP8 112 AX47
Cherry Rd, Enf. EN3 104 DW38
Cherry St, Rom. RM7 149 FD57
Woking GU21 248 AY118
Cherry Tree Av, Guil. GU2 264 AT134
London Colney AL2 83 CK26
Staines TW18 196 BH93
West Drayton UB7 156 BM72
Cherry Tree Cl, E9 11 H8
Grays RM17 192 GC79
Rainham RM13 169 FG68
Wembley HA0 139 CG63
Cherry Tree Ct, NW9
off Boakes Cl 140 CQ56
SE7 off Fairlawn 186 EJ79
Coulsdon CR5 257 DM118
Cherry Tree Dr, SW16 203 DL90
South Ockendon RM15 171 FX70
Cherry Tree Grn, Hert. SG14 53 DM07
South Croydon CR2 242 DV114
Cherrytree La, Chal.St.P. SL9 112 AX54
Cherry Tree La, Dart. DA2 209 FF90
Epsom KT19
off Christ Ch Rd 238 CN112
Fulmer SL3 155 AZ65
Harlow CM20 57 EP14
Hemel Hempstead HP2 63 BQ17
Heronsgate WD3 113 BC46
Iver SL0 156 BG67
Potters Bar EN6 86 DB34
Rainham RM13 169 FE69
Cherry Tree Ms, Hodd. EN11
off Cherry Tree Rd 71 EA16
Cherry Tree Prim Sch, Wat.
WD24 off Berry Av 97 BU36
Cherry Tree Ri, Buck.H. IG9 124 EJ49
Cherry Tree Rd, E15 13 J2
N2 142 DF56
Beaconsfield HP9 110 AH54
Farnham Royal SL2 153 AQ66
Hoddesdon EN11 71 EA16
Watford WD24 97 BV36
Cherrytrees, Couls. CR5 257 DK121
Cherry Trees Sch, The, E3 22 B3
Cherry Tree Wk, EC1 19 K5
Beckenham BR3 225 DZ98
Chesham HP5 76 AR29
West Wickham BR4 244 EF105
Cherry Tree Way, E13 24 E4
Penn HP10 110 AC46
Stanmore HA7 117 CH51
Cherry Wk, Brom. BR2 226 EG102
Grays RM16 193 GG76
Loudwater WD3 96 BJ40
Rainham RM13 169 FF68
Cherry Way, Epsom KT19 238 CR107

Cherry Way, Hat. AL10 67 CU21
Horton SL3 175 BC83
Shepperton TW17 217 BR98
Cherrywood Av, Eng.Grn TW20 194 AV93
Cherrywood Cl, E3 21 M2
Kingston upon Thames KT2 200 CN94
Cherry Wd Cl, Seer Grn HP9 111 AR50
Cherrywood Dr, SW15 201 CX85
Northfleet DA11 212 GE90
Cherrywood La, Mord. SM4 221 CY98
Cherrywood Lo, SE13
off Oakwood Cl 205 ED86
Cherry Wd Way, W5
off Hanger Vale La 160 CN71
Cherston Gdns, Loug. IG10 107 EN42
Cherston Rd, Loug. IG10 107 EN42
CHERTSEY, KT16 216 BG102
⇌ **Chertsey** 215 BF102
Chertsey Br Rd, Cher. KT16 216 BK101
Chertsey Cl, Ken. CR8 257 DP115
Chertsey Cres, New Adgtn CR0 243 EC110
Chertsey Dr, Sutt. SM3 221 CY103
Chertsey La, Cher. KT16 215 BE95
Epsom KT19 238 CN112
Staines TW18 195 BE92
Chertsey Meads, Cher. KT16 216 BK102
★ **Chertsey Mus**, Cher. KT16
off Windsor St 216 BG100
Chertsey Rd, E11 145 ED61
Addlestone KT15 216 BH103
Ashford TW15 197 BR94
Byfleet KT14 234 BK111
Chobham GU24 232 AY110
Feltham TW13 197 BS92
Ilford IG1 147 ER63
Shepperton TW17 216 BN101
Sunbury-on-Thames TW16 197 BR94
Twickenham TW1, TW2 199 CF86
Woking GU21 233 BA113
Chertsey St, SW17 202 DG92
Guildford GU1 280 AX135
Cherubs, The, Farn.Com. SL2 153 AQ65
Chervil Cl, Felt. TW13 197 BU90
Chervil Ms, SE28 168 EV74
Cherwell Cl, Crox.Grn WD3 96 BN43
Slough SL3 *off Tweed Rd* 175 BB79
Cherwell Ct, Epsom KT19 238 CQ105
Teddington TW11
off Broom Pk 199 CK94
Cherwell Gro, S.Ock. RM15 171 FV73
Cherwell Ho, NW8
off Church St Est 16 B5
Cherwell Way, Ruis. HA4 137 BQ58
Cheryls Cl, SW6 39 M6
Cheselden Rd, Guil. GU1 280 AY135
Cheseman St, SE26 204 DV90
Chesfield Rd, Kings.T. KT2 200 CL94
CHESHAM, HP5 76 AQ31
⊖ **Chesham** 76 AQ31
Chesham Av, Petts Wd BR5 227 EP100
CHESHAM BOIS, Amer. HP6 77 AQ36
Sch **Chesham Bois C of E Comb Sch**,
Amer. HP6 *off Bois La* 77 AS35
Chesham Cl, SW1 28 G7
Romford RM7 149 FD56
Sutton SM2 239 CY110
Chesham Ct, Nthwd. HA6
off Frithwood Av 115 BT51
Chesham Cres, SE20 224 DW96
Sch **Chesham High Sch**, Chesh.
HP5 *off White Hill* 76 AR30
H **Chesham Hosp**, Chesh. HP5 76 AQ32
Chesham La, Ch.St.G. HP8 112 AY48
Chalfont St. Peter SL9 112 AY49
Chesham Ms, SW1 28 G6
Guildford GU1
off Chesham Rd 281 AZ135
Sch **Chesham Pk Comm Coll**, Chesh.
HP5 *off Chartridge La* 76 AN30
Chesham Pl, SW1 28 G7
Sch **Chesham Prep Sch**, Chesh.
HP5 *off Orchard Leigh* 78 AU27
Chesham Rd, SE20 224 DW96
SW19 202 DD92
Amersham HP6 77 AQ38
Ashley Green HP5 60 AT24
Berkhamsted HP4 60 AV21
Bovingdon HP3 78 AY27
Guildford GU1 280 AY135
Kingston upon Thames KT1 220 CN95
Chesham St, NW10 140 CR62
SW1 28 G7
Chesham Ter, W13 179 CH75
Chesham Way, Wat. WD18 97 BS44
Cheshire Cl, E17 123 EB53
SE4 45 N8
Hornchurch RM11 150 FN57
Mitcham CR4 223 DL97
Ottershaw KT16 233 BC107
Cheshire Ct, EC4 18 F9
Slough SL1 *off Sussex Pl* 174 AV75
Cheshire Dr, Lvsdn WD25 81 BT34
Cheshire Gdns, Chess. KT9 237 CK107
Cheshire Ho, N18 122 DV49
Cheshire Rd, N22 121 DM52
Cheshire St, E2 20 B4
Chesholm Rd, N16 144 DS62
CHESHUNT, Wal.Cr. EN8 89 DX31
⇌ **Cheshunt** 89 DZ30
H **Cheshunt Comm Hosp**,
Chsht EN8 89 DY31
Cheshunt Pk, Chsht EN7 88 DV26
Cheshunt Rd, E7 166 EH65
Belvedere DA17 188 FA78
Sch **Cheshunt Sch**, Chsht
EN8 *off College Rd* 88 DW30
Cheshunt Wash, Chsht EN8 89 DY27
Chesil Ct, E2 10 G10
Chesilton Rd, SW6 38 G6
Chesil Way, Hayes UB4 157 BT69
Chesley Gdns, E6 24 F1
Chesney Cres, New Adgtn CR0 243 EC108
Chesney St, SW11 40 G7
Chesnut Est, N17 144 DT55
Chesnut Gro, N17 144 DT55
Chesnut Rd, N17 144 DT55
Chessbury Cl, Chesh. HP5
off Missenden Rd 76 AP32
Chessbury Rd, Chesh. HP5 76 AN32
Chess Cl, Latimer HP5 94 AX36
Loudwater WD3 96 BK42
Chessell Cl, Th.Hth. CR7 223 DP98
Chessfield Pk, Amer. HP6 94 AY39
Chess Hill, Loud. WD3 96 BK42
Chessholme Ct, Sun. TW16 197 BS94
Chessholme Rd, Ashf. TW15 197 BQ93
CHESSINGTON, KT9 238 CL107
Chessington Av, N3 141 CY55
Bexleyheath DA7 188 EY80
Chessington Cl, Epsom KT19 238 CQ107
Sch **Chessington Comm Coll**,
Chess. KT9 *off Garrison La* 237 CK108
Chessington Ct, N3
off Charter Way 141 CZ55
Pinner HA5 138 BZ56
Chessington Hall Gdns, Chess.
KT9 237 CK108
Chessington Hill Pk, Chess.
KT9 238 CN106
Chessington Lo, N3 141 CZ55
Chessington Mans, E10
off Albany Rd 145 EA59
⇌ **Chessington North** 238 CL106
Chessington Rd, Epsom KT17,
KT19 239 CT109
⇌ **Chessington South** 237 CK108
● **Chessington Trade Pk**,
Chess. KT9 238 CN105
Chessington Way, W.Wick. BR4 225 EB103
★ **Chessington World of Adventures**,
Chess. KT9 237 CJ110
Chess La, Loud. WD3 96 BK42
CHESSMOUNT, Chesh. HP5 76 AR33
Chessmount Ri, Chesh. HP5 76 AR33
Chesson Rd, W14 38 G2
Chess Vale Ri, Crox.Grn WD3 96 BM44
Chess Valley Wk, Chesh. HP5 94 AU35
Rickmansworth WD3 96 BL44
Chess Way, Chorl. WD3 96 BG41
Chesswood Way, Pnr. HA5 116 BX54
Chester Av, Rich. TW10 200 CM86
Twickenham TW2 198 BZ88
Upminster RM14 151 FS61
Chester Cl, SW1 29 H5
SW13 181 CV83
Ashford TW15 197 BR92
Chafford Hundred RM16 192 FY76
Dorking RH4 269 CJ134
Guildford GU2 264 AT132
Loughton IG10 107 EQ39
Potters Bar EN6 86 DB29
Richmond TW10 200 CM86
Sutton SM1 222 DA103
Uxbridge UB8 157 BP72
Chester Cl N, NW1 17 K2
Chester Cl S, NW1 17 K3
Chester Cotts, SW1 28 G9
Chester Ct, NW1
off Albany St 17 K3
SE5 43 L5
Chester Cres, E8 10 B3
Chester Dr, Har. HA2 138 BZ58
Chesterfield Cl, Orp. BR5 228 EX98
Chesterfield Dr, Dart. DA1 209 FH85
Esher KT10 219 CG103
Sevenoaks TN13 278 FD122
Chesterfield Gdns, N4 143 DP57
SE10 46 G5
W1 29 J2
Chesterfield Gro, SE22 204 DT85
Chesterfield Hill, W1 29 J1
Chesterfield Ms, N4 143 DP57
Ashford TW15 196 BL91
Chesterfield Rd, E10 145 EC58
N3 120 DA51
W4 180 CQ79
Ashford TW15 196 BL91
Barnet EN5 101 CX43
Enfield EN3 105 DY37
Epsom KT19 238 CR108
Sch **Chesterfield Sch**, Enf. EN3
off Chesterfield Rd 105 DY37
Chesterfield St, W1 29 J2
Chesterfield Wk, SE10 47 H6
Chesterfield Way, SE15 44 G5
Hayes UB3 177 BU75
Chesterford Gdns, NW3 5 M1
Chesterford Ho, SE18
off Shooters Hill Rd 186 EK81
Chesterford Rd, E12 147 EM64
Chester Gdns, W13 159 CH72
Enfield EN3 104 DV44
Morden SM4 222 DC100
Chester Gate, NW1 17 J3
Chester Gibbons Grn, Lon.Col.
AL2 83 CK26
Chester Grn, Loug. IG10 107 EQ39
Chester Ms, E17
off Chingford Rd 123 EA54
SW1 29 J6
Chester Path, Loug. IG10 107 EQ39
Chester Pl, NW1 17 J2
Chester Rd, E7 166 EK66
E11 146 EH58
E16 23 K5
E17 145 DX57
N9 122 DV46
N17 144 DR55
N19 143 DH61
NW1 17 H3
SW19 201 CW93
Borehamwood WD6 100 CQ41
Chigwell IG7 125 EN48
Effingham KT24 267 BV128
Hounslow TW4 177 BV83
Ilford IG3 147 ET60
London Heathrow Airport
TW6 176 BN83
Loughton IG10 107 EP40
Northwood HA6 115 BS52
Sidcup DA15 207 ES85
Slough SL1 153 AR72
Watford WD18 97 BU43
Chester Row, SW1 28 G9
Chesters, Horl. RH6 290 DE146
Chesters, The, N.Mal. KT3 220 CS95
Chester Sq, SW1 29 J8
Chester Sq Ms, SW1 29 J7
Chester St, E2 20 D4
SW1 29 H6
Chester Ter, NW1 17 J2
Chesterton Cl, SW18 202 DA85
Chesham HP5 *off Milton Rd* 76 AP29
Greenford UB6 158 CB68
Chesterton Dr, Merst. RH1 273 DL128
Staines TW19 196 BM88
Chesterton Grn, Beac. HP9 111 AL52
Chesterton Ho, SW11
off Ingrave St 40 B10
Sch **Chesterton Prim Sch**, SW11 40 G7
Chesterton Rd, E13 23 P2
W10 14 D7
Chesterton Sq, W8 27 H8
Chesterton Ter, E13 23 N2
Kingston upon Thames KT1 220 CN96
Chesterton Way, Til. RM18 193 GJ82
Chester Way, SE11 30 F9
Chesthunte Rd, N17 122 DQ53
Chestnut All, SW6 39 H3
Chestnut Av, E7 146 EH63
N8 143 DL57
SW14 *off Thornton Rd* 180 CR83
SW17 203 DJ90
Bluewater DA9 211 FT87
Brentford TW8 179 CK77
Brentwood CM14 130 FS45
Buckhurst Hill IG9 124 EK48
Chesham HP5 76 AR29
East Molesey KT8 219 CF97
Edgware HA8 118 CL51
Epsom KT19 238 CS105
Esher KT10 219 CD101
Grays RM16 192 GB75
Guildford GU2 280 AW138
Hampton TW12 198 CA94
Hornchurch RM12 149 FF61
Northwood HA6 115 BT54
Rickmansworth WD3 96 BG43
Slough SL3 174 AY75
Teddington TW11 219 CF96
Virginia Water GU25 214 AT98
Wembley HA0 139 CH64
West Drayton UB7 156 BM73
West Wickham BR4 244 EE106
Westerham TN16 260 EK122
Weybridge KT13 235 BQ108
Whiteley Village KT12 235 BS109
Chestnut Av N, E17 145 EC56
Chestnut Av S, E17 145 EC56
Chestnut Cl, N14 103 DJ43
N16 144 DR61
SE6 205 EC92
SE14 45 N6
SW16 203 DN91
Addlestone KT15 234 BK106
Amersham HP6 77 AR37
Ashford TW15 197 BP91
Buckhurst Hill IG9 124 EK48
Carshalton SM5 222 DF102
Chalfont St. Peter SL9 113 AZ52
Englefield Green TW20 194 AW93
Hayes UB3 157 BS73
Hornchurch RM12
off Lancaster Dr 150 FJ63
Hunsdon SG12 56 EK06
Kingswood KT20 256 DA123
Northfleet DA11
off Burch Rd 213 GF86
Orpington BR6 246 EU106
Potten End HP4 61 BB17
Redhill RH1
off Haigh Cres 289 DH136
Ripley GU23 250 BG124
Sidcup DA15 208 EU88
Sunbury-on-Thames TW16 197 BT93
West Drayton UB7 177 BP80
Chestnut Copse, Oxt. RH8 276 EG132
Chestnut Ct, SW6 39 H3
Amersham HP6 77 AS37
Surbiton KT6
off Penners Gdns 220 CL101
Chestnut Cres, Whiteley Vill.
KT12 *off Chestnut Av* 235 BS109
Chestnut Dr, E11 146 EG58
Berkhamsted HP4 60 AX20
Bexleyheath DA7 188 EX83
Englefield Green TW20 194 AX93
Harrow HA3 117 CF52
Pinner HA5 138 BX58
St. Albans AL4 65 CH18
Windsor SL4 173 AL84
Chestnut Glen, Horn. RM12 149 FF61
Chestnut Gro, SE20 204 DV94
SW12 202 DG87
W5 179 CK76
Barnet EN4 102 DF43
Brentwood CM14 130 FW47
Dartford DA2 209 FD91
Hoddesdon EN11 55 EB13
Ilford IG6 125 ES51
Isleworth TW7 179 CG84
Mitcham CR4 223 DK98
New Malden KT3 220 CR97
South Croydon CR2 242 DV108
Staines TW18 195 BJ93
Wembley HA0 139 CH64
Woking GU22 248 AY120
Sch **Chestnut Gro Sch**, SW12
off Chestnut Gro 202 DG88
Chestnut Ho, NW3
off Maitland Pk Vil 6 F4
Chestnut La, N20 119 CY46
Amersham HP6 77 AR36
Harlow CM20 57 EP14
Sevenoaks TN13 279 FH124
Weybridge KT13 235 BP106
Sch **Chestnut La Sch**, Amer.
HP6 *off Chestnut La* 77 AS36
Chestnut Manor Cl, Stai.
TW18 196 BH92
Chestnut Mead, Red. RH1
off Oxford Rd 272 DE133
Chestnut Ms, Chal.St.P.
SL9 *off Gold Hill E* 112 AX54
Chestnut Pk, Bray SL6 172 AE77
Chestnut Pl, SE26 204 DT91
Ashtead KT21 254 CL119
Epsom KT17 239 CU111
Weybridge KT13 235 BP106
Chestnut Ri, SE18 187 ER79
Bushey WD23 116 CB45
Chestnut Rd, SE27 203 DP90
SW20 221 CX96
Ashford TW15 197 BP91
Beaconsfield HP9 110 AH54
Dartford DA1 210 FK88
Enfield EN3 105 DY36
Guildford GU1 264 AX134
Horley RH6 290 DG146
Kingston upon Thames KT2 200 CL94
Twickenham TW2 199 CE89
Chestnut Row, N3
off Nether St 120 DA52
Chestnuts, Hutt. CM13 131 GB46
Chestnuts, The, Abridge RM4 108 EV41
Hemel Hempstead HP3 61 BF24
Hertford SG13 54 DR10
Horley RH6 291 DH146
Walton-on-Thames KT12 217 BU103
Sch **Chestnuts Prim Sch**, N15
off Black Boy La 144 DQ57
Chestnut Wk, Byfleet KT14
off Royston Rd 234 BL112
Chalfont St. Peter SL9 112 AY52
Epping Green CM16
off Epping Rd 73 EP24
Sevenoaks TN15 279 FL129
Chestnut Wk, Shep. TW17 217 BS99
Watford WD24 97 BU37
Whiteley Village KT12
off Octagon Rd 235 BS109
Woodford Green IG8 124 EG50
Chestnut Way, Felt. TW13 197 BV90
Cheston Av, Croy. CR0 225 DY103
Chestwood Gro, Uxb. UB10 156 BM66
Cheswick Cl, Dart. DA1 189 FF84
Chesworth Cl, Erith DA8 189 FE81
Chettle Cl, SE1 31 L6
Chettle Ct, N8 143 DN58
Chetwode Dr, Epsom KT18 255 CX118
Chetwode Rd, SW17 202 DF90
Tadworth KT20 255 CW119
Chetwood Wk, E6 25 H7
Chetwynd Av, E.Barn. EN4 120 DF46
Chetwynd Dr, Uxb. UB10 156 BM68
Chetwynd Rd, NW5 143 DH63
Chevalier Cl, Stan. HA7 118 CL49
Cheval Pl, SW7 28 D6
Cheval St, E14 34 A6
Cheveley Cl, Rom. RM3
off Chelsworth Dr 128 FM53
Cheveley Gdns, Burn. SL1 152 AJ68
Chevely Cl, Cooper. CM16 92 EX29
Cheveney Wk, Brom. BR2
off Marina Cl 226 EG97
CHEVENING, Sev. TN14 262 EZ119
Jct **Chevening Cross**, Chev.
TN14 262 FA120
Chevening Cross Rd, Chev.
TN14 262 FA120
Chevening La, Knock.P. TN14 262 EY115
Chevening Rd, NW6 4 E9
SE10 47 M1
SE19 204 DR93
Chevening TN14 262 EZ119
Chipstead TN13 278 FB121
Sundridge TN14 262 EY123
Chevenings, The, Sid. DA14 208 EW90
Sch **Chevening St. Botolph's C of E
Prim Sch**, Sev. TN13
off Chevening Rd 278 FB122
Cheverton Rd, N19 143 DK60
Chevet St, E9 11 L3
Chevington Pl, Horn. RM12
off Chevington Way 150 FK64
Chevington Way, Horn. RM12 150 FK63
Cheviot Cl, Bans. SM7 256 DB115
Bexleyheath DA7 189 FE82
Bushey WD23 98 CC44
Enfield EN1 104 DR40
Harlington UB3 177 BR80
Sutton SM2 240 DD109
Cheviot Gdns, NW2 141 CX61
SE27 203 DP91
Cheviot Gate, NW2 141 CY61
Cheviot Rd, SE27 203 DN92
Hornchurch RM11 149 FG60
Slough SL3 175 BA78
Cheviots, Hat. AL10 67 CU21
Hemel Hempstead HP2 62 BM17
Cheviot Way, Ilf. IG2 147 ES56
Chevron Cl, E16 23 P8
Chevy Rd, Sthl. UB2 178 CC75
Chewton Rd, E17 145 DY56
Cheyham Gdns, Sutt. SM2 239 CX110
Cheyham Way, Sutt. SM2 239 CY110
Cheyne Av, E18 146 EF55
Twickenham TW2 198 BZ88
Cheyne Cl, NW4 141 CW57
Amersham HP6 77 AR36
Bromley BR2 226 EL104
Gerrards Cross SL9 134 AY60
Ware SG12 55 DX05
Cheyne Ct, SW3 40 E2
Banstead SM7 *off Park Rd* 256 DB115
Cheyne Gdns, SW3 40 D2
Cheyne Hill, Surb. KT5 220 CM98
Cheyne Ms, SW3 40 D2
Chesham HP5 76 AR30
Cheyne Pk Dr, W.Wick. BR4 225 EC104
Cheyne Path, W7 159 CF71
Cheyne Pl, SW3 40 E2
Cheyne Rd, Ashf. TW15 197 BR93
Cheyne Row, SW3 40 C3
Cheyne Wk, N21 103 DP43
NW4 141 CW58
SW3 40 D3
SW10 40 A4
Chesham HP5 76 AR31
Croydon CR0 224 DU103
Horley RH6 290 DG149
Longfield DA3
off Cavendish Sq 231 FX97
Cheyneys Av, Edg. HA8 117 CK51
Chichele Gdns, Croy. CR0 242 DS105
Chichele Rd, NW2 4 C2
Oxted RH8 276 EE128
Chicheley Gdns, Har. HA3 116 CC52
Chicheley Rd, Har. HA3 116 CC52
Chicheley St, SE1 30 D4
Chichester Av, Ruis. HA4 137 BR61
Chichester Cl, E6 25 H9
SE3 186 EJ80
Aveley RM15 170 FQ74
Chafford Hundred RM16 191 FX77
Dorking RH4 269 CH134
Hampton TW12 *off Maple Cl* 198 BZ93
Chichester Ct, NW1 7 L6
Epsom KT17 239 CT109
Slough SL1 174 AV75
Stanmore HA7 140 CL55
Chichester Dr, Pur. CR8 241 DM112
Sevenoaks TN13 278 FF125
Chichester Gdns, Ilf. IG1 146 EL59
Chichester Ms, SE27 203 DN91
Chichester Rents, WC2 18 E8
Chichester Ri, Grav. DA12 213 GK91
Chichester Rd, E11 146 EE62
N9 122 DU46
NW6 15 J1
W2 15 M6
Croydon CR0 224 DS104
Dorking RH4 269 CH133
Greenhithe DA9 211 FT85
Chichester Row, Amer. HP6 77 AR38
Chichester St, SW1 41 M1
Chichester Way, E14 34 G8
Feltham TW14 197 BV87
Watford WD25 82 BY33
Chichester Wf, Erith DA8 189 FE78
Chicksand St, E1 20 B7
Chiddingfold, N12 120 DA48
Chiddingstone Av, Bexh. DA7 188 EZ80
Chiddingstone Cl, Sutt. SM2 240 DA110
Chiddingstone St, SW6 39 K8
Chieftan Dr, Purf. RM19 190 FM77
Chieveley Rd, Bexh. DA7 189 FB84
Chiffinch Gdns, Nthflt DA11 212 GE90
Chignell Pl, W13
off Broadway 159 CG74
CHIGWELL, IG7 125 EP48
⊖ **Chigwell** 125 EP49
Chigwell Hill, E1 32 E1
Chigwell Hurst Ct, Pnr. HA5 138 BX55
Chigwell La, Loug. IG10 107 EQ43
Chigwell Pk, Chig. IG7 125 EP49
Chigwell Pk Dr, Chig. IG7 125 EN48
Sch **Chigwell Prim Sch**, Chig.
IG7 *off High Rd* 125 EQ47
Chigwell Ri, Chig. IG7 125 EN47
Chigwell Rd, E18 146 EH55
Woodford Green IG8 124 EJ54
CHIGWELL ROW, Chig. IG7 126 EU47
Sch **Chigwell Row Inf Sch**, Chig.
IG7 *off Lambourne Rd* 126 EV47
Sch **Chigwell Sch**, Chig. IG7
off High Rd 125 EQ47
Chigwell Vw, Rom. RM5
off Lodge La 126 FA51
Chilberton Dr, S.Merst. RH1 273 DJ130
Chilbrook Rd, Down. KT11 251 BU118
Chilcombe Ho, SW15
off Fontley Way 201 CU87
Chilcot Cl, E14 22 D9
Chilcote La, Lt.Chal. HP7 94 AV39
Chilcott Cl, Wem. HA0 139 CJ63
Chilcott Rd, Wat. WD24 97 BS36
Childebert Rd, SW17 203 DH89
Sch **Childeric Prim Sch**, SE14 45 M5
Childeric Rd, SE14 45 M5
Childerley, Kings.T. KT1
off Burritt Rd 220 CN97
Childerley St, SW6 38 E6
Childers, The, Wdf.Grn. IG8 125 EM50
Childers St, SE8 45 M2
Child La, SE10 35 M7
Sch **Children's Ho Upr Sch**,
The, N1 9 N3
H **Children's Trust, The**,
Tad. KT20 255 CX121
Childs Av, Hare. UB9 114 BJ54
Childs Cl, Horn. RM11 150 FJ58
Childs Cres, Swans. DA10 211 FX86
Childs Hall Cl, Bkhm KT23
off Childs Hall Rd 268 BZ125
Childs Hall Dr, Bkhm KT23 268 BZ125
Childs Hall Rd, Bkhm KT23 268 BZ125
CHILDS HILL, NW2 142 DA61
Sch **Childs Hill Prim Sch**, NW2
off Dersingham Rd 141 CY62
Childs Hill Wk, NW2 141 CZ62
Childs La, SE19
off Westow St 204 DS93
Child's Ms, SW5
off Child's Pl 27 L9
Child's Pl, SW5 27 K9
Child's St, SW5 27 K9
Child's Wk, SW5 27 K9
Childs Way, NW11 141 CZ57
Childwick Ct, Hem.H. HP3
off Rumballs Rd 62 BN23
Chilham Cl, Bex. DA5 208 EZ87
Hemel Hempstead HP2 62 BL21
Perivale UB6 159 CG68
Chilham Rd, SE9 206 EL91
Chilham Way, Brom. BR2 226 EG101
Chillerton Rd, SW17 202 DG92
Chillingford Ho, SW17
off Blackshaw Rd 202 DC91
Chillington Dr, SW11 182 DC84
Chillingworth Gdns, Twick.
TW1 *off Tower Rd* 199 CF90
Chillingworth Rd, N7 8 E3
Chilmans Dr, Bkhm KT23 268 CB125
Chilmark Gdns, Merst. RH1 273 DL129
New Malden KT3 221 CT101
Chilmark Rd, SW16 223 DK96
Chilmead La, Nutfld RH1 273 DK132
Chilsey Grn Rd, Cher. KT16 215 BE100
Chiltern Av, Amer. HP6 77 AR38
Bushey WD23 98 CC44
Twickenham TW2 198 CA88
● **Chiltern Business Village**,
Uxb. UB8 156 BH68
Chiltern Cl, Berk. HP4 60 AT18
Bexleyheath DA7 189 FE81
Borehamwood WD6 100 CM40
Bushey WD23 98 CB44
Croydon CR0 224 DS104
Goffs Oak EN7 87 DP27
Ickenham UB10 137 BP61
Staines TW18 196 BG92
Watford WD18 97 BT42
Woking GU22 248 AW122
Worcester Park KT4
off Cotswold Way 221 CW103
● **Chiltern Commerce Cen**,
Chesh. HP5
off Asheridge Rd 76 AN29
Chiltern Cor, Berk. HP4
off Durrants Rd 60 AU18
● **Chiltern Ct**, Chesh. HP5
off Asheridge Rd 76 AN29
Chiltern Dene, Enf. EN2 103 DM42
Chiltern Dr, Mill End WD3 113 BF45
Surbiton KT5 220 CP99
Chiltern Gdns, NW2 141 CX62
Bromley BR2 226 EF98
Hornchurch RM12 150 FJ62
Chiltern Hts, Amer. HP7 94 AU39
Chiltern Hill, Chal.St.P. SL9 112 AY53
Chiltern Hills Rd, Beac. HP9 110 AJ53
★ **Chiltern Open Air Mus**,
Ch.St.G. HP8 113 AZ47
Chiltern Par, Amer. HP6 77 AQ37
Chiltern Pk Av, Berk. HP4 60 AU17
Chiltern Pl, E5 144 DV61
Chiltern Rd, E3 22 B5
Amersham HP6 77 AP35
Burnham SL1 152 AH71
Ilford IG2 147 ES56
Northfleet DA11 212 GE90
Pinner HA5 138 BW57
St. Albans AL4 65 CJ16
Sutton SM2 240 DB109
Chilterns, Hat. AL10 67 CU21
Hemel Hempstead HP2 62 BL18

Chilterns, The, Nthch HP4
off Stoney Cl 60 AT17
Sutton SM2 off Gatton Cl. . . 240 DB109
Chiltern St, W1 . . . . 16 G6
Chiltern Vw Rd, Uxb. UB8 . . . . 156 BJ68
Chiltern Way, Wdf.Grn. IG8 . . . 124 EG48
Chilthorne Cl, SE6
off Ravensbourne Pk Cres . 205 DZ87
Chilton Av, W5. . . . . 179 CK77
Chilton Ct, Penn HP10. . . . . . . 110 AC45
Chilton Ct, Hert. SG14
off The Ridgeway 53 DM07
Walton-on-Thames KT12 . . . 235 BU105
Chilton Grn, Welw.G.C. AL7. . . . 52 DC09
Chilton Gro, SE8. . . . . 33 K9
● Chiltonian Ind Est, SE12 . . 206 EF86
Chilton Rd, Chesh. HP5 . . . . . . 76 AQ29
Edgware HA8. . . . . 118 CN51
Grays RM16. . . . . 193 GG76
Richmond TW9 . . . . 180 CN83
Chiltons, The, E18
off Grove Hill. 124 EG54
Chiltons Cl, Bans. SM7
off High St 256 DB115
Chilton St, E2 . . . . 20 B4
Chilvers Cl, Twick. TW2 . . . . . . 199 CE89
Chilver St, SE10 . . . . 35 M10
Chilwell Gdns, Wat. WD19 . . . . 116 BW49
Chilwick Rd, Slou. SL2. . . . . . . 153 AM69
CHILWORTH, Guil. GU4 . . . . . . 281 BC140
⇌ Chilworth. 281 BE140
Sch Chilworth C of E Inf Sch, Chilw. GU4 off Dorking Rd 281 BD140
Chilworth Ct, SW19 . . . . 201 CX88
Chilworth Gdns, Sutt. SM1 . . . 222 DC104
Chilworth Gate, Brox. EN10
off Silverfield. 71 DZ22
Cheshunt EN8
off Davison Dr. 89 DX28
Chilworth Ms, W2. . . . . 15 P9
Chilworth Rd, Albury GU5 . . . . 282 BG139
Chilworth St, W2. . . . . 15 P9
Chimes Av, N13. . . . . 121 DN50
Chime Sq, St.Alb. AL3 . . . . 65 CE19
🛍 Chimes Shop Cen, The, Uxb. UB8 . . . . 156 BK66
Chimney La, Woob.Grn HP10
off Glory Mill La 132 AE56
China Hall Ms, SE16. . . . . 33 H7
China Ms, SW2 . . . . 203 DM87
★ Chinatown, W1
off Gerrard St 17 P10
Chinbrook Cres, SE12. . . . . 206 EH90
Chinbrook Est, SE9. . . . . 206 EK90
Chinbrook Rd, SE12 . . . . 206 EH90
Chinchilla Dr, Houns. TW4 . . . . 178 BW82
Chindit Cl, Brox. EN10 . . . . 71 DY20
Chindits La, Warley CM14 . . . . 130 FW50
Chine, The, N10. . . . . 143 DJ56
N21. 103 DP44
Dorking RH4 off High St. 285 CH135
Wembley HA0. . . . . 139 CH64
Chine Fm Pl, Knock.P. TN14 . . . 262 EX116
Ching Ct, WC2. . . . . 18 A9
Chingdale Rd, E4 . . . . 124 EE48
CHINGFORD, E4 . . . . 123 EB46
⇌ Chingford. 124 EE45
⊖ Chingford. 124 EE45
Chingford Av, E4 . . . . 123 EB48
Sch Chingford C of E Inf Sch, E4 off Kings Rd 123 ED46
Sch Chingford C of E (VC) Jun Sch, E4 off Cambridge Rd 123 ED46
Sch Chingford Foundation Sch, E4 off Nevin Dr 123 EC46
CHINGFORD GREEN, E4 . . . . . . 124 EF46
Sch Chingford Hall Comm Prim Sch, E4 off Burnside Av . . . 123 DZ51
CHINGFORD HATCH, E4. . . . . . 123 EC49
● Chingford Ind Cen, E4 . . . . . 123 DY50
Chingford La, Wdf.Grn. IG8 . . . 124 EE49
Chingford Mt Rd, E4. . . . . 123 EA49
Chingford Rd, E4. . . . . 123 EA51
E17 . . . . 123 EB53
Chingley Cl, Brom. BR1 . . . . . . 206 EE93
Ching Way, E4 . . . . 123 DZ51
Chinnery Cl, Enf. EN1 . . . . 104 DT39
Chinnor Cres, Grnf. UB6. . . . . . 158 CB68
Chinthurst La, Guil. GU4, GU5 . 280 AY141
Chinthurst Ms, Couls. CR5. . . . 256 DG116
Chinthurst Pk, Shalf. GU4 . . . . 280 AY142
Sch Chinthurst Sch, Tad. KT20
off Tadworth St 255 CW123
Chipka St, E14. . . . . 34 E5
Chipley St, SE14. . . . . 45 L3
Chipmunk Chase, Hat. AL10 . . . 66 CR16
Chipmunk Gro, Nthlt. UB5
off Argus Way 158 BY69
Chippendale All, Uxb. UB8
off Chippendale Waye 156 BK66
Chippendale Ho, SW1 . . . . 41 K1
Chippendale St, E5. . . . . 145 DX62
Chippendale Waye, Uxb. UB8 . 156 BK66
Chippenham Av, Wem. HA9. . . 140 CP64
Chippenham Cl, Pnr. HA5 . . . . 137 BT56
Romford RM3
off Chippenham Rd 128 FK50
Chippenham Gdns, NW6. . . . . . 15 J3
Romford RM3 . . . . 128 FK50
Chippenham Ms, W9 . . . . 15 J5
Chippenham Rd, W9. . . . . 15 J5
Romford RM3 . . . . 128 FK51
Chippenham Wk, Rom. RM3
off Chippenham Rd 128 FK51
CHIPPERFIELD, Kings L. WD4 . . 80 BG31
Chipperfield Cl, Upmin. RM14. 151 FS60
Chipperfield Rd, Bov. HP3 . . . . . 79 BB27
Hemel Hempstead HP3 . . . . . 62 BJ24
Kings Langley WD4. . . . . 80 BK30
Orpington BR5 . . . . 228 EU95
CHIPPING BARNET, Barn. EN5 . 101 CY42
Chipping Cl, Barn. EN5
off St. Albans Rd 101 CY41
Chippingfield, Harl. CM17 . . . . . 58 EW12
CHIPSTEAD, Couls. CR5. . . . . . 256 DF118
CHIPSTEAD, Sev. TN13. . . . . . . 278 FC122
⇌ Chipstead 256 DF118
Chipstead, Chal.St.P. SL9 . . . . . 112 AW53
Chipstead Av, Th.Hth. CR7 . . . 223 DP98
CHIPSTEAD BOTTOM, Couls. CR5. . . . . 256 DE121
Chipstead Cl, SE19 . . . . 204 DT94
Coulsdon CR5 . . . . 256 DG116
Redhill RH1 . . . . 288 DF136
Sutton SM2 . . . . 240 DB109
Chipstead Ct, Knap. GU21
off Creston Av. 248 AS117
Chipstead Gdns, NW2 . . . . 141 CV61
Chipstead La, Chipstead CR5 . 256 DB124
Lower Kingswood KT20. . . . . 271 CZ125
Sevenoaks TN13 . . . . 278 FC122
Chipstead Pk, Sev. TN13. . . . . . 278 FD122
Chipstead Pk Cl, Sev. TN13 . . . 278 FC122
Chipstead Pl Gdns, Sev. TN13 . 278 FC122
Chipstead Rd, Bans. SM7 . . . . 255 CZ117
Erith DA8 . . . . 189 FE80
Chipstead Sta Par, Chipstead CR5 off Station App 256 DF118
Chipstead St, SW6 . . . . 39 K7
Sch Chipstead Valley Prim Sch, Couls. CR5
off Chipstead Valley Rd . . . 256 DG116
Chipstead Valley Rd, Couls. CR5. . . . . 257 DH116
Chipstead Way, Bans. SM7 . . . 256 DF115
Chip St, SW4. . . . . 183 DK83
Chirk Cl, Hayes UB4 . . . . 158 BY70
Chirton Wk, Wok. GU21 . . . . . . 248 AU118
Sch Chisenhale Prim Sch, E3 . . . 11 L10
Chisenhale Rd, E3. . . . . 11 L10
Chisholm Rd, Croy. CR0. . . . . . 224 DS103
Richmond TW10 . . . . 200 CM86
Chisledon Wk, E9 . . . . 11 P4
CHISLEHURST, BR7 . . . . 207 EN94
⇌ Chislehurst 227 EN96
Sch Chislehurst & Sidcup Gram Sch, Sid. DA15
off Hurst Rd. 208 EV89
Chislehurst Av, N12 . . . . 120 DC52
★ Chislehurst Caves, Chis. BR7 off Caveside Cl 227 EN95
Sch Chislehurst C of E Prim Sch, Chis. BR7 off School Rd . . . 207 EQ94
Chislehurst Rd, Brom. BR1 . . . . 226 EK96
Chislehurst BR7 . . . . 226 EK96
Orpington BR5, BR6 . . . . 227 ES98
Richmond TW10 . . . . 200 CL86
Sidcup DA14 . . . . 208 EU92
CHISLEHURST WEST, Chis. BR7. 207 EM92
Chislet Cl, Beck. BR3. . . . . 205 EA94
Chisley Rd, N15. . . . . 144 DS58
Chiswell Ct, Wat. WD24 . . . . 98 BW38
CHISWELL GREEN, St.Alb. AL2. 82 CA26
Chiswell Grn La, St.Alb. AL2 . . 82 BX25
Chiswell Sq, SE3
off Brook La. 186 EH82
Chiswell St, EC1 . . . . 19 K6
SE5. . . . . 43 M4
CHISWICK, W4. . . . . 180 CR79
⇌ Chiswick 180 CQ80
Sch Chiswick & Bedford Pk Prep Sch, W4 off Priory Av 180 CS77
Chiswick Br, SW14 . . . . 180 CQ82
W4 . . . . 180 CQ82
Chiswick Cl, Croy. CR0. . . . . . . 223 DM104
Chiswick Common Rd, W4 . . . . 180 CR77
Sch Chiswick Comm Sch, W4
off Burlington La. 180 CR80
Chiswick Ct, Pnr. HA5 . . . . 138 BZ55
Chiswick Grn Studios, W4
off Evershed Wk 180 CQ77
Chiswick High Rd, W4 . . . . 180 CR77
Brentford TW8. . . . . 180 CM78
★ Chiswick Ho, W4. . . . . 180 CS79
Chiswick Ho Grds, W4 . . . . 180 CR79
Chiswick La, W4 . . . . 180 CS78
Chiswick La S, W4 . . . . 181 CT78
Chiswick Mall, W4. . . . . 181 CT79
W6 . . . . 181 CT79
⊖ Chiswick Park 180 CQ77
Chiswick Pk, W4 . . . . 180 CP77
Chiswick Pier, W4. . . . . 181 CT80
Chiswick Quay, W4. . . . . 180 CQ81
Chiswick Rd, N9 . . . . 122 DU47
W4 . . . . 180 CQ77
Jct Chiswick Rbt, W4 . . . . 180 CN78
Chiswick Sq, W4
off Hogarth Rbt 180 CS79
Chiswick Staithe, W4. . . . . 180 CQ81
Chiswick Ter, W4
off Acton La. 180 CQ77
Chiswick Village, W4. . . . . 180 CP78
Chiswick Wf, W4 . . . . 181 CT79
Chittenden Cl, Hodd. EN11
off Founders Rd 55 EB14
Chittenden Cotts, Wisley GU23 . . . . 250 BL116
Chitterfield Gate, Sipson UB7 . 176 BN80
Chitty's Common, Guil. GU2 . . 264 AT130
Chitty's La, Dag. RM8. . . . . 148 EX61
Chitty St, W1 . . . . 17 M6
Chittys Wk, Guil. GU3. . . . . 264 AT130
Chivalry Rd, SW11 . . . . 202 DE85
Chivenor Gro, Kings.T. KT2 . . . 199 CK92
Chivenor Pl, St.Alb. AL4. . . . . . . 65 CJ22
Chivers Rd, E4. . . . . 123 EB48
Choats Manor Way, Dag. RM9. 168 EZ69
Choats Rd, Bark. IG11. . . . . 168 EW68
Dagenham RM9 . . . . 168 EW68
CHOBHAM, Wok. GU24 . . . . . . 232 AT111
● Chobham Business Pk, Chobham GU24 . . . . 232 AX110
Chobham Cl, Ott. KT16. . . . . . . 233 BB107
★ Chobham Common National Nature Reserve, Wok. GU24 . . . . 232 AS105
Chobham Gdns, SW19. . . . . . . 201 CX89
Chobham La, Longcr. KT16 . . . 214 AV102
Chobham Pk La, Chobham GU24 . . . . 232 AU110
Chobham Rd, E15. . . . . 12 G3
Horsell GU21. . . . . 232 AW113
Ottershaw KT16 . . . . 233 BA108
Woking GU21 . . . . 248 AY116
Sch Chobham St. Lawrence C of E Prim Sch, Chobham GU24
off Bagshot Rd 232 AS111
Choice Vw, Ilf. IG1
off Axon Pl. 147 EQ61
Choir Grn, Knap. GU21. . . . . . . 248 AS117
Cholmeley Cres, N6 . . . . 143 DH59
Cholmeley Pk, N6 . . . . 143 DH60
Cholmley Gdns, NW6. . . . . 5 J2
Cholmley Rd, T.Ditt. KT7 . . . . . 219 CH100
Cholmondeley Av, NW10 . . . . . 161 CU68
Cholmondeley Wk, Rich. TW9 . 199 CJ85
Choppins Ct, E1 . . . . 32 F2
Chopwell Cl, E15. . . . . 13 H7
CHORLEYWOOD, Rick. WD3 . . . 95 BE43
⇌ Chorleywood. 95 BD42
⊖ Chorleywood. 95 BD42
CHORLEYWOOD BOTTOM, Rick. WD3. . . . . 95 BD44
Chorleywood Bottom, Chorl. WD3 . . . . 95 BD43
Chorleywood Cl, Rick. WD3 . . . 114 BK45
Chorleywood Common, Chorl. WD3 . . . . 95 BE42
Chorleywood Cres, Orp. BR5. . 227 ET96
Chorleywood Ho Dr, Chorl. WD3. 95 BE41
Chorleywood Lo La, Chorl. WD3
off Rickmansworth Rd 95 BF41
Sch Chorleywood Prim Sch, Chorl. WD3 off Stag La. 95 BC44
Chorleywood Rd, Rick. WD3 . . . 96 BG42
Choumert Gro, SE15 . . . . 44 C9
Choumert Ms, SE15 . . . . 44 C9
Choumert Rd, SE15 . . . . 44 A10
Choumert Sq, SE15 . . . . 44 C9
Chow Sq, E8 . . . . 10 A2
Chrislaine Cl, Stanw. TW19. . . . 196 BK86
Chrisp St, E14 . . . . 22 C7
Christabel Cl, Islw. TW7 . . . . . . 179 CE83
Christchurch Av, N12 . . . . 120 DC51
NW6. . . . . 4 F6
Erith DA8 . . . . 189 FD79
Harrow HA3. . . . . 139 CH56
Rainham RM13 . . . . 169 FF68
Teddington TW11. . . . . 199 CG92
Wembley HA0. . . . . 160 CL65
Sch Christ Ch Bentinck C of E Prim Sch, NW1 . . . . 16 D6
Sch Christchurch (Brixton) C of E Prim Sch, SW9 . . . . 42 F6
Christchurch Cl, N12
off Summers La 120 DD52
SW19 . . . . 202 DD94
Enfield EN2 . . . . 104 DQ40
St. Albans AL3. . . . . 64 CC19
Sch Christ Ch C of E Inf Sch, Vir.W. GU25 off Christchurch Rd . 214 AV97
Sch Christ Ch C of E Jun Sch, W5 off New Bdy 159 CK73
Ottershaw KT16
off Fletcher Rd. 233 BD107
Sch Christ Ch C of E Prim Sch, Regent's Pk, NW1 . . . . 17 K2
Hampstead, NW3
off Christchurch Hill 142 DD62
SE23 off Perry Vale 205 DX89
SW3. . . . . 40 E2
Sch Christchurch C of E Prim Sch, SW11 . . . . 40 D10
Sch Christ Ch C of E Prim Sch, Barn. EN5 off Byng Rd 101 CX40
Surbiton KT5
off Pine Gdns 220 CN100
Sch Christ Ch C of E Prim Sch & Nurs, Ware SG12
off New Rd 55 DY06
Sch Christ Ch C of E Prim Sch, Purley, Pur. CR8
off Montpelier Rd 241 DP110
Sch Christ Ch C of E Sch, E1. . . . 20 B6
Chorleywood WD3
off Rickmansworth Rd 95 BF41
Christchurch Ct, NW6. . . . . 4 E6
Christchurch Cres, Grav. DA12
off Christchurch Rd. 213 GJ87
Radlett WD7. . . . . 99 CG36
Sch Christ Ch Erith C of E Prim Sch, Erith DA8
off Lesney Pk Rd 189 FD79
Christchurch Gdns, Epsom KT19. . . . . 238 CP111
Harrow HA3. . . . . 139 CG56
Christchurch Grn, Wem. HA0. . 160 CL65
Christchurch Hill, NW3. . . . . . . 142 DD62
Christchurch La, Barn. EN5 . . . 101 CY40
Christ Ch Mt, Epsom KT19. . . . 238 CP112
Sch Christ Ch New Malden Prim Sch, N.Mal. KT3
off Elm Rd 220 CR97
New Malden KT3
off Lime Gro 220 CS97
Christchurch Pk, Sutt. SM2 . . . 240 DC108
Christ Ch Pas, EC1 . . . . 19 H8
Christchurch Pas, NW3. . . . . . . 142 DC62
Barnet EN5. . . . . 101 CY41
Christ Ch Path, Hayes UB3 . . . 177 BQ76
Christchurch Pl, Epsom KT19. . 238 CP111
Hertford SG14
off Port Vale. 54 DQ09
Sch Christ Ch Prim Sch, NW6. . . . 4 G7
SE10. . . . . 35 K10
SE18 off Shooters Hill 187 EN81
Sch Christchurch Prim Sch, Ilf. IG1 off Wellesley Rd 147 EQ60
Christchurch Rd, N8 . . . . 143 DL58
SW2 . . . . 203 DM88
SW14 . . . . 200 CP85
SW19 . . . . 222 DD95
Christ Ch Rd, Beck. BR3
off Fairfield Rd. 225 EA96
Christchurch Rd, Dart. DA1 . . . 210 FJ87
Christ Ch Rd, Epsom KT19. . . . . 238 CL112
Christchurch Rd, Grav. DA12 . . 213 GJ88
Hemel Hempstead HP2 . . . . . . 62 BK19
Ilford IG1 . . . . 147 EP60
Purley CR8. . . . . 241 DP110
Sidcup DA15 . . . . 207 ET91
Christ Ch Rd, Surb. KT5 . . . . . 220 CM100
Christchurch Rd, Til. RM18. . . . 193 GG81
Virginia Water GU25. . . . . 214 AU97
Christchurch Sq, E9 . . . . 10 G9
Sch Christ Ch (Streatham) C of E Prim Sch, SW2
off Cotherstone Rd 203 DM88
Christchurch St, SW3. . . . . 40 E2
Christchurch Ter, SW3. . . . . 40 E2
Christchurch Way, SE10 . . . . . . 35 K9
Woking GU21
off Church St E 249 AZ117
Christian Cl, Hodd. EN11 . . . . . . 55 DZ13
Christian Ct, SE16. . . . . 33 N3
Christian Flds, SW16 . . . . 203 DN94
Christian Flds Av, Grav. DA12 . 213 GJ91
Christian Sq, Wind. SL4
off Ward Royal. 173 AQ81
Christian St, E1 . . . . 20 D8
Christie Cl, Bkhm KT23. . . . . . . 268 BZ125
Broxbourne EN10 . . . . 71 DZ21
Guildford GU1
off Waterside Rd 264 AX131
Christie Ct, N19
off Hornsey Rd 143 DL61
Watford WD18. . . . . 97 BU43
Christie Dr, Croy. CR0. . . . . 224 DU99
Christie Gdns, Rom. RM6. . . . . 148 EV58
Christie Ho, W12
off Du Cane Rd 161 CV72
Christie Rd, E9. . . . . 11 L5
Waltham Abbey EN9
off Deer Pk Way. 105 EB35
Christies Av, Bad.Mt TN14 . . . . 246 FA110
Coll Christie's Ed, W1 . . . . 17 K6
Christie Wk, Cat. CR3 . . . . 258 DR122
Christina Sq, N4 . . . . 143 DP60
Christina St, EC2. . . . . 19 N4
Christine Worsley Cl, N21
off Highfield Rd. 121 DP47
Christmas Hill, Guil. GU4, GU5. 281 AZ141
Christmas La, Farn.Com. SL2 . 133 AQ62
Christopher Av, W7. . . . . 179 CG76
Christopher Cl, SE16. . . . . 33 J4
Hornchurch RM12
off Chevington Way 150 FK63
Sidcup DA15 . . . . 207 ET85
Christopher Ct, Hem.H. HP3
off Seaton Rd 62 BK23
Tadworth KT20 off High St. . . 255 CW123
Christopher Gdns, Dag. RM9 off Wren Rd. 148 EX64
Sch Christopher Hatton Prim Sch, EC1. 18 E5
Christopher Pl, NW1. . . . . 17 P3
🛍 Christopher Pl Shop Cen, St.Alb. AL3 off Market Pl . . . 65 CD20
Christopher Rd, Sthl. UB2 . . . . 177 BV77
Christopher's Ms, W11 . . . . 26 F2
Christopher St, EC2 . . . . 19 M5
Sch Christ's Coll Finchley, N2
off East End Rd 142 DB55
Sch Christ's Coll, Guildford, Guil. GU1 off Larch Av. 264 AW131
Sch Christ's Sch, Rich. TW10
off Queens Rd 200 CN85
Sch Christ the King RC Prim Sch, N4 off Tollington Pk. 143 DM61
Coll Christ the King 6th Form Coll, SE13. 47 H10
Christy Rd, Bigg.H. TN16 . . . . . 260 EJ115
Chryssell Rd, SW9 . . . . 42 F5
Chrystie La, Bkhm KT23. . . . . . 268 CB126
Chubworthy St, SE14. . . . . 45 L3
Chucks La, Walt.Hill KT20. . . . . 255 CV124
Chudleigh Cres, Ilf. IG3. . . . . . . 147 ES63
Chudleigh Gdns, Sutt. SM1 . . . 222 DC104
Chudleigh Rd, NW6 . . . . 4 B7
SE4. . . . . 205 DZ85
Romford RM3 . . . . 128 FL49
Twickenham TW2 . . . . 199 CF87
Chudleigh St, E1. . . . . 21 J8
Chudleigh Way, Ruis. HA4 . . . . 137 BU60
Chulsa Rd, SE26 . . . . 204 DV92
Chumleigh Gdns, SE5
off Chumleigh St. 184 DS79
Chumleigh St, SE5 . . . . 43 N2
Chumleigh Wk, Surb. KT5 . . . . 220 CM98
Church All, Ald. WD25. . . . . 98 CC38
Croydon CR0. . . . . 223 DN102
Gravesend DA11
off High St. 213 GH86
Church App, SE21 . . . . 204 DR90
Cudham TN14
off Cudham La S. 261 EQ115
Egham TW20. . . . . 215 BC97
Stanwell TW19. . . . . 196 BK86
Church Av, E4 . . . . 123 ED51
NW1. . . . . 7 K5
SW14 . . . . 180 CR83
Beckenham BR3 . . . . 225 EA95
Northolt UB5. . . . . 158 BZ66
Pinner HA5 . . . . 138 BY58
Ruislip HA4 . . . . 137 BR60
Sidcup DA14 . . . . 208 EU92
Southall UB2 . . . . 178 BY76
Churchbury Cl, Enf. EN1. . . . . . 104 DS40
Churchbury La, Enf. EN1 . . . . . 104 DR41
Churchbury Rd, SE9. . . . . 206 EK87
Enfield EN1 . . . . 104 DR40
Church Cl, N20 . . . . 120 DE48
W8 . . . . 27 L4
Addlestone KT15. . . . . 234 BH105
Cuffley EN6 . . . . 87 DL29
Edgware HA8. . . . . 118 CQ50
Eton SL4 . . . . 173 AR79
Fetcham KT22 . . . . 253 CD124
Hayes UB4. . . . . 157 BR71
Horsell GU21. . . . . 248 AX116
Hounslow TW3 off Bath Rd . . 178 BZ83
Little Berkhamsted SG13
off Church Rd 69 DJ19
Loughton IG10. . . . . 107 EM40
Lower Kingswood KT20
off Buckland Rd. 271 CZ127
Northwood HA6 . . . . 115 BT52
Radlett WD7. . . . . 99 CG36
Staines TW18
off The Broadway 216 BJ97
Uxbridge UB8 . . . . 156 BH68
West Drayton UB7 . . . . 176 BL76
Church Cor, SW17
off Mitcham Rd. 202 DF92
Church Ct, Reig. RH2 . . . . 272 DB134
Richmond TW9
off George St. 199 CK85
Church Cres, E9. . . . . 11 J6
N3 . . . . 119 CZ53
N10. . . . . 143 DH56
N20. . . . . 120 DE48
St. Albans AL3. . . . . 64 CC19
Sawbridgeworth CM21 . . . . . . 58 EZ05
South Ockendon RM15. . . . . . 171 FW69
Church Cft, St.Alb. AL4. . . . . 65 CJ22
Churchcroft Cl, SW12. . . . . 202 DG87
Churchdown, Brom. BR1 . . . . . 206 EE91
Church Dr, NW9 . . . . 140 CR60
Bray SL6 . . . . 172 AC75
Harrow HA2. . . . . 138 BZ58
West Wickham BR4. . . . . 226 EE104
Church Elm La, Dag. RM10 . . . . 168 FA65
CHURCH END, N3 . . . . 119 CZ53
CHURCH END, NW10 . . . . 160 CS65
Church End, E17 . . . . 145 EB56
NW4. . . . . 141 CV55
Harlow CM19. . . . . 73 EN17
Church Entry, EC4. . . . . 19 H9
Church Est Almshouses, Rich. TW9 off St. Mary's Gro. . . . 180 CM84
Church Fm Cl, Swan. BR8 . . . . . 229 FC100
★ Church Farm Ho Mus, NW4. . . . . 141 CV55
Church Fm La, Sutt. SM3. . . . . 239 CY107
Church Fm Way, Ald. WD25 . . . . 98 CB38
Church Fld, Dart. DA2. . . . . 210 FK89
Church Fld, Epp. CM16. . . . . 92 EU29
Churchfield, Harl. CM20. . . . . . . 58 EU13
Church Fld, Rad. WD7. . . . . 99 CG36
Sevenoaks TN13 . . . . 278 FE122
Churchfield Av, N12 . . . . 120 DC51
Churchfield Cl, Har. HA2. . . . . . 138 CC56
Hayes UB3. . . . . 157 BT73
Churchfield Ms, Slou. SL2 . . . . 154 AU72
Churchfield Path, Chsht EN8 . . . 88 DW29
Churchfield Pl, Shep. TW17
off Chertsey Rd 217 BP101
Weybridge KT13 . . . . 234 BN105
Sch Churchfield Prim Sch, N9 off Latymer Rd 122 DT46
Churchfield Rd, W3. . . . . 160 CQ74
W7 . . . . 179 CE75
W13 . . . . 159 CH74
Chalfont St. Peter SL9. . . . . . 112 AX53
Reigate RH2. . . . . 271 CZ133
Tewin AL6 . . . . 52 DC06
Walton-on-Thames KT12 . . . . 217 BU102
Welling DA16. . . . . 188 EU83
Weybridge KT13 . . . . 234 BN105
Churchfields, E18 . . . . 124 EG53
SE10. . . . . 46 E4
Broxbourne EN10 . . . . 71 EA21
Guildford GU4
off Burpham La. 265 BA129
Hertford SG13 . . . . 54 DR10
Horsell GU21. . . . . 248 AY116
Loughton IG10. . . . . 106 EL42
West Molesey KT8 . . . . 218 CA97
Churchfields Av, Felt. TW13 . . . 198 BZ90
Weybridge KT13 . . . . 235 BP105
Sch Churchfields Infants' Sch, E18 off Churchfields 124 EG53
Sch Churchfields Jun Sch, E18
off Churchfields. 124 EG53
Churchfields La, Brox. EN10
off Station Rd 71 EA20
Sch Churchfields Prim Sch, Beck. BR3 off Churchfields Rd. 225 DX96
Churchfields Rd, Beck. BR3 . . . 225 DX96
Watford WD24. . . . . 97 BT36
Church Gdns, W5 . . . . 179 CK75
Dorking RH4 . . . . 285 CG135
Wembley HA0 . . . . 139 CG63
Church Garth, N19
off Pemberton Gdns 143 DK61
Church Gate, SW6 . . . . 38 F10
Churchgate, Chsht EN8 . . . . 88 DV30
Sch Churchgate C of E Prim Sch, Harl. CM17
off Hobbs Cross Rd. 58 EZ12
Churchgate Gdns, Harl. CM17
off Sheering Rd. 58 EZ11
Churchgate Rd, Chsht EN8 . . . . 88 DV29
Churchgate St, Harl. CM17 . . . . 58 EY11
Church Grn, SW9 . . . . 42 F8
Hayes UB3. . . . . 157 BT72
Hersham KT12 . . . . 236 BW107
St. Albans AL1
off Hatfield Rd. 65 CD19
Church Gro, SE13 . . . . 185 EB84
Amersham HP6. . . . . 94 AY39
Kingston upon Thames KT1. 219 CJ95
Rickmansworth WD3. . . . . 114 BG46
Wexham SL3. . . . . 154 AW71
Church Hill, E17. . . . . 145 EA56
N21. . . . . 121 DM45
SE18. . . . . 37 K7
SW19 . . . . 201 CZ92
Bedmond WD5 . . . . 81 BT26
Carshalton SM5 . . . . 240 DF106
Caterham CR3. . . . . 258 DT124
Crayford DA2. . . . . 189 FE84
Cudham TN14 . . . . 261 EQ115
Dartford DA2 . . . . 210 FK90
Epping CM16. . . . . 92 EU29
Greenhithe DA9. . . . . 211 FS85
Harefield UB9 . . . . 136 BJ55
Harrow HA1. . . . . 139 CE60
Hertford Heath SG13 . . . . 54 DV11
Horsell GU21. . . . . 248 AX116
Lemsford AL8 . . . . 51 CU10
Loughton IG10. . . . . 106 EL41
Merstham RH1 . . . . 273 DH126
Nutfield RH1 . . . . 273 DM133
Orpington BR6 . . . . 228 EU101
Purley CR8. . . . . 241 DL110
Pyrford GU22 . . . . 249 BF117
Shere GU5. . . . . 282 BN139
Tatsfield TN16 . . . . 260 EK122
Sch Church Hill Prim Sch, Barn. EN4 off Burlington Ri. 120 DF45
Church Hill Rd, E17. . . . . 145 EB56
Barnet EN4 . . . . 120 DF45
Surbiton KT6. . . . . 220 CL99
Sutton SM3 . . . . 239 CX105
Church Hill Wd, Orp. BR5. . . . . 227 ET99
Church Hollow, Purf. RM19 . . . 190 FN78
Church Hyde, SE18
off Old Mill Rd. 187 ES79
Churchill Av, Har. HA3 . . . . 139 CH58
Uxbridge UB10 . . . . 157 BP69
Churchill Cl, Dart. DA1 . . . . 210 FP88
Feltham TW14 . . . . 197 BT88
Fetcham KT22 . . . . 253 CE123
Uxbridge UB10 . . . . 157 BP69
Warlingham CR6. . . . . 258 DW117
Sch Churchill C of E Prim Sch, West. TN16 off Rysted La . . 277 EQ125
Churchill Ct, SE18
off Rushgrove St. 37 K9
W5 . . . . 160 CM70
Northolt UB5. . . . . 138 CA64
Staines TW18
off Chestnut Gro 196 BH93
Churchill Cres, N.Mymms AL9
off Dixons Hill Rd 67 CW23
Churchill Dr, Knot.Grn HP9. . . . 110 AJ50
Weybridge KT13 . . . . 217 BQ104
Churchill Gdns, SW1 . . . . 41 L1
W3 . . . . 160 CN72
Sch Churchill Gdns Prim Sch, SW1 . . . . 41 M1
Churchill Gdns Rd, SW1. . . . . . . 41 K1
Churchill Ms, Wdf.Grn. IG8
off High Rd Woodford Grn. 124 EF51
★ Churchill Mus & Cabinet War Rooms, SW1 . . . . 29 P4
Churchill Pl, E14 . . . . 34 D2
Harrow HA1
off Sandridge Cl 139 CE56
Churchill Rd, E16. . . . . 24 C9
NW2. . . . . 161 CV65
NW5. . . . . 143 DH63
Edgware HA8. . . . . 118 CM51
Epsom KT19 . . . . 238 CN111

Churchill Rd, Grav. DA11 213 GF88
Grays RM17 192 GD79
Guildford GU1 280 AY135
Horton Kirby DA4 230 FQ98
St. Albans AL1 65 CG18
Slough SL3 175 AZ77
Smallfield RH6 291 DP148
South Croydon CR2 242 DQ109
Churchill Ter, E4 123 EA49
Churchill Wk, E9 11 H2
Churchill Way, Bigg.H. TN16 244 EK113
Bromley BR1
off Ethelbert Rd 226 EG97
Sunbury-on-Thames TW16 197 BU92
Church Island, Stai. TW18 195 BD91
Church La, E11 146 EE60
E17 145 EB56
N2 142 DD55
N8 143 DM56
N9 122 DU47
N17 122 DS53
NW9 140 CQ61
SW17 203 DH91
SW19 221 CZ95
W5 179 CJ75
Abridge RM4 108 EY40
Albury GU5 282 BH139
Aldenham WD25 98 CB38
Bayford SG13 69 DM17
Berkhamsted HP4 60 AW19
Bletchingley RH1 274 DR133
Bovingdon HP3 79 BB27
Bray SL6 172 AC75
Bromley BR2 226 EL102
Broxbourne EN10 70 DW22
Burstow RH6 291 DL153
Chaldon CR3 257 DN123
Chalfont St. Peter SL9 112 AX53
Chelsham CR6 259 EC116
Cheshunt EN8 88 DV29
Chessington KT9 238 CM107
Chislehurst BR7 227 EQ95
Colney Heath AL4 66 CP22
Coulsdon CR5 256 DG122
Dagenham RM10 169 FB65
Enfield EN1 104 DR41
Godstone RH9 275 DX132
Great Warley CM13 151 FW58
Harrow HA3 117 CF53
Hatfield AL9 67 CW18
Headley KT18 254 CQ124
Hutton CM13 131 GE46
Kings Langley WD4 80 BN29
Loughton IG10 107 EM41
Mill End WD3 114 BG46
Nork SM7 255 CX117
North Ockendon RM14 151 FV64
North Weald Bassett CM16 93 FB26
Northaw EN6 86 DG30
Oxted RH8 276 EE129
Pinner HA5 138 BY55
Purfleet RM19 190 FN78
Richmond TW10 200 CL88
Romford RM1 149 FE56
Sarratt WD3 95 BF38
Send GU23 265 BB126
Sheering CM22 59 FD07
Shere GU5 282 BN139
Stapleford Abbotts RM4 109 FC42
Stoke Poges SL2 154 AT69
Teddington TW11 199 CF92
Thames Ditton KT7 219 CF100
Twickenham TW1 199 CG88
Uxbridge UB8 156 BH68
Wallington SM6 223 DK104
Warlingham CR6 259 DX117
Wennington RM13 170 FK72
Westerham TN16 260 EK122
Wexham SL3 154 AW71
Weybridge KT13 234 BN105
Windsor SL4 173 AR81
Worplesdon GU3 264 AS127
Church La Av, Couls. CR5 257 DH122
Church La Dr, Couls. CR5 257 DH122
CHURCH LANGLEY, Harl. CM17 58 EY14
Sch Church Langley Comm Prim Sch, Ch.Lang. CM17
off Church Langley Way 74 EW15
Jct Church Langley Rbt, Harl. CM17 74 EV15
Church Langley Way, Harl. CM17 74 EW15
Churchley Rd, SE26 204 DV91
Church Leys, Harl. CM18 73 ET16
Church Manor Est, SW9 42 F5
Church Manorway, SE2 187 ET77
Erith DA8 189 FD76
Church Manorway Ind Est, Erith DA8 189 FC76
Churchmead, SE5
off Camberwell Rd 43 K5
Church Mead, Roydon CM19 56 EH14
Churchmead Cl, E.Barn. EN4 102 DE44
Sch Churchmead C of E Sch, Datchet SL3 off Priory Way 174 AV80
Church Meadow, Long Dit. KT6 219 CJ103
Churchmead Rd, NW10 161 CU65
Church Ms, Add. KT15 234 BJ105
Church Mill Gra, Harl. CM17 58 EY12
Churchmore Rd, SW16 223 DJ95
Church Mt, N2 142 DD57
Church Paddock Ct, Wall. SM6 223 DK104
● Church Pk Ind Est, Craw. RH11 290 DE154
Church Pas, EC2
off Gresham St 19 K8
Barnet EN5 off Wood St 101 CZ42
Surbiton KT6 220 CL99
Church Path, E11 146 EG57
E17 off St. Mary Rd 145 EB56
N5 9 H2
N12 120 DC50
N17 off White Hart La 122 DS52
N20 120 DC49
NW10 160 CS66
SW14 180 CR83
SW19 222 DA96
W4 180 CQ76
W7 159 CE74
Bray SL6 172 AC75
Cobham KT11 235 BV114
Coulsdon CR5 257 DN118
Grays RM17 192 GA79
Great Amwell SG12 55 DZ09
Greenhithe DA9 211 FT85
Mitcham CR4 222 DE97
Northfleet DA11 212 GC86
Southall UB1 158 CA74
Church Path, Sthl Grn UB2 178 BZ76
Swanley BR8 off School La 229 FH95
Woking GU21 off High St 249 AZ117
Church Pl, SW1 29 M1
W5 off Church Gdns 179 CK75
Ickenham UB10 137 BQ62
Mitcham CR4 222 DE97
Twickenham TW1
off Church St 199 CG88
Church Ri, SE23 205 DX88
Chessington KT9 238 CM107
Church Rd, E10 145 EB61
E12 146 EL64
E17 123 DY54
N1 9 K5
N6 142 DG58
N17 122 DS53
NW4 141 CV56
NW10 160 CS65
SE19 224 DS95
SW13 181 CT82
SW19 (Wimbledon) 201 CY90
W3 180 CQ75
W7 159 CF74
Addlestone KT15 234 BG106
Ashford TW15 196 BM90
Ashtead KT21 253 CK117
Barking IG11 167 EQ65
Bexleyheath DA7 188 EZ82
Biggin Hill TN16 260 EK117
Bookham KT23 252 BZ123
Bourne End SL8 132 AD62
Brasted TN16 262 EV124
Bromley BR2 226 EG96
Buckhurst Hill IG9 124 EH46
Burstow RH6 291 DN151
Byfleet KT14 234 BM113
Caterham CR3 258 DT123
Chelsfield BR6 246 EY106
Claygate KT10 237 CF107
Cowley UB8 156 BK70
Cranford TW5 177 BV78
Crockenhill BR8 229 FD101
Croydon CR0 223 DP104
East Molesey KT8 219 CD98
Egham TW20 195 BA92
Enfield EN3 104 DW44
Epsom KT17 238 CS112
Erith DA8 189 FC78
Farnborough BR6 245 EQ106
Farnham Royal SL2 153 AQ69
Feltham TW13 198 BX92
Gravesend DA12, DA13 213 GJ94
Greenhithe DA9 211 FS85
Guildford GU1 280 AX135
Halstead TN14 246 EY111
Ham TW10 200 CM92
Harefield UB9 136 BJ55
Harlow CM17 74 EW18
Harold Wood RM3 128 FN53
Hayes UB3 157 BT72
Hemel Hempstead HP3 63 BQ21
Hertford SG14 53 DP08
Heston TW5 178 CA80
High Beach IG10 106 EH40
High Wycombe HP10 110 AD47
Horley RH6 290 DF149
Horsell GU21 248 AY116
Ilford IG2 147 ER58
Isleworth TW7 179 CD81
Iver SL0 155 BC69
Kenley CR8 258 DR115
Keston BR2 244 EK108
Kingston upon Thames KT1 220 CM96
Leatherhead KT22 253 CH122
Leigh RH2 287 CU141
Little Berkhamsted SG13 69 DJ19
Long Ditton KT6 219 CJ103
Lowfield Heath RH11 290 DE154
Mitcham CR4 222 DD96
Noak Hill RM4 128 FK46
Northolt UB5 158 BZ66
Northwood HA6 115 BT52
Old Windsor SL4 194 AV85
Penn HP10 110 AC47
Potten End HP4 61 BB16
Potters Bar EN6 86 DB30
Purley CR8 241 DL110
Redhill RH1 288 DE136
Reigate RH2 288 DA136
Richmond TW9, TW10 200 CL85
St. John's GU21 248 AU119
Seal TN15 279 FM121
Seer Green HP9 111 AR51
Shepperton TW17 217 BP101
Shortlands BR2 226 EE97
Sidcup DA14 208 EU91
Southall UB2 178 BZ76
Stanmore HA7 117 CH50
Sutton SM3 239 CY107
Sutton at Hone DA4 210 FL94
Swanley BR8 230 FK95
Swanscombe DA10 212 FZ86
Teddington TW11 199 CE91
Tilbury RM18 193 GF81
Wallington SM6 223 DJ104
Warlingham CR6 258 DW117
Watford WD17 97 BU39
Welling DA16 188 EV82
Welwyn Garden City AL8 51 CX09
West Drayton UB7 176 BK76
West Ewell KT19 238 CR108
West Tilbury RM18 193 GL79
Whyteleafe CR3 258 DT118
Woldingham CR3 259 DX122
Worcester Park KT4 220 CS102
Church Rd Merton, SW19 222 DD95
Church Rd Twr Block, Stan. HA7 off Church Rd 117 CJ50
Church Row, NW3 5 N1
Chislehurst BR7 207 EQ94
Church Row Ms, Ware SG12
off Church St 55 DX06
Church Side, Epsom KT18 238 CP113
Churchside Cl, Bigg.H. TN16 260 EJ117
Church Sq, Shep. TW17 217 BP101
Tra Church Street 223 DP103
Church St, E15 13 K8
E16 37 N3
N9 122 DS47
NW8 16 B6
W2 16 B6
W4 180 CS79
Amersham HP7 77 AP40
Betchworth RH3 286 CS135
Bovingdon HP3 79 BB27
Burnham SL1 152 AJ70
Chalvey SL1 173 AQ75
Chesham HP5 76 AP31
Church St, Cob. KT11 251 BV115
Croydon CR0 224 DQ103
Dagenham RM10 169 FB65
Dorking RH4 285 CG136
Effingham KT24 268 BX127
Enfield EN2 104 DR41
Epsom KT17 238 CS113
Esher KT10 236 CB105
Essendon AL9 68 DE17
Ewell KT17 239 CU109
Gravesend DA11 213 GH86
Grays RM17 192 GC79
Hampton TW12 218 CC95
Hatfield AL9 67 CW17
Hemel Hempstead HP2 62 BK18
Hertford SG14 54 DR09
Isleworth TW7 179 CH83
Kingston upon Thames KT1 219 CK96
Leatherhead KT22 253 CH122
Old Woking GU22 249 BC121
Reigate RH2 272 DA134
Rickmansworth WD3 114 BL46
St. Albans AL3 65 CD19
Sawbridgeworth CM21 58 EY05
Seal TN15 279 FN121
Shoreham TN14 247 FF111
Slough SL1 174 AT76
Southfleet DA13 212 GA92
Staines TW18 195 BE91
Sunbury-on-Thames TW16 217 BV97
Sutton SM1 off High St 240 DB106
Twickenham TW1 199 CG88
Waltham Abbey EN9 89 EC33
Walton-on-Thames KT12 217 BU102
Ware SG12 55 DX06
Watford WD18 98 BW42
Weybridge KT13 234 BN105
Windsor SL4
off Castle Hill 173 AR81
Church St E, Wok. GU21 249 AZ117
Church St Est, NW8 16 B5
Church St Pas, E15 13 K8
Church St W, Wok. GU21 248 AY117
Church Stretton Rd, Houns. TW3 198 CC85
Church Ter, NW4 141 CV55
SE13 186 EE83
SW8 41 P8
Richmond TW10 199 CK85
Windsor SL4 173 AL82
CHURCH TOWN, Gdse. RH9 275 DX131
● Church Trd Est, Erith DA8 189 FG80
Church Vale, N2 142 DF55
SE23 204 DW89
Church Vw, Aveley RM15 190 FQ75
Broxbourne EN10 71 DZ20
Swanley BR8 off Lime Rd 229 FD97
Upminster RM14 150 FN61
Church Vw Cl, Horl. RH6 290 DF149
Churchview Rd, Twick. TW2 199 CD88
Church Vil, Sev. TN13
off Maidstone Rd 278 FE122
Church Wk, N6 142 DG62
N16 9 M2
NW2 141 CZ62
NW4 141 CW55
NW9 140 CR61
SW13 181 CU81
SW15 201 CV85
SW16 223 DJ96
SW20 221 CW97
Bletchingley RH1 274 DR133
Brentford TW8 179 CJ79
Burnham SL1 152 AH70
Bushey WD23 off High St 98 CA44
Caterham CR3 258 DU124
Chertsey KT16 216 BG101
Dartford DA2 210 FK90
Enfield EN2 104 DR41
Eynsford DA4 230 FL104
Gravesend DA12 213 GK88
Hayes UB3 157 BT72
Horley RH6
off Woodroyd Av 290 DF149
Leatherhead KT22 253 CH122
Outwood RH1 289 DP142
Reigate RH2
off Reigate Rd 272 DC134
Richmond TW9
off Red Lion St 199 CK85
Sawbridgeworth CM21 58 EZ05
Thames Ditton KT7 219 CF100
Walton-on-Thames KT12 217 BU102
Weybridge KT13
off Beales La 216 BN104
Church Wk Shop Cen, Cat. CR3 off Church Wk 258 DU124
Churchward Ho, W14
off Ivatt Pl 39 H1
Church Way, N20 120 DD48
Churchway, NW1 17 P2
Church Way, Barn. EN4 102 DF42
Edgware HA8 118 CN51
Oxted RH8 276 EF132
South Croydon CR2 242 DT110
Churchwell Path, E9 10 G4
Churchwood Gdns, Wdf.Grn. IG8 124 EG49
Churchyard, The, Bray SL6
off Church Dr 172 AC75
Churchyard Row, SE11 31 H8
Church Yd Wk, W2 16 A6
Churston Av, E13 166 EH67
Churston Cl, SW2
off Tulse Hill 203 DP88
Churston Dr, Mord. SM4 221 CX99
Churston Gdns, N11 121 DJ51
Churton Pl, SW1 29 M9
Churton St, SW1 29 M9
Chusan Pl, E14 21 P9
Chuters Cl, Byfleet KT14 234 BL112
Chuters Gro, Epsom KT17 239 CT112
Chyne, The, Ger.Cr. SL9 135 AZ57
Chyngton Cl, Sid. DA15 207 ET90
Cibber Rd, SE23 205 DX89
Cicada Rd, SW18 202 DC85
Cicely Rd, SE15 44 D7
Cillocks Cl, Hodd. EN11 71 EA16
Cimba Wd, Grav. DA12 213 GL91
Cinderella Path, NW11
off North End Rd 142 DB60
Cinderford Way, Brom. BR1 206 EE91
Cinder Path, Wok. GU22 248 AW119
Cinnabar Wf, E1 32 D3
Cinnamon Cl, SE15 44 A4
Croydon CR0 223 DL101
Windsor SL4 173 AM81
Cinnamon Gdns, Guil. GU2 264 AU129
Cinnamon Row, SW11 39 P10
Cinnamon St, E1 32 F3
Cintra Pk, SE19 204 DT94
CIPPENHAM, Slou. SL1 173 AM75
Cippenham Cl, Slou. SL1 153 AM73
Sch Cippenham Inf Sch, Slou. SL1 off Dennis Way 153 AK73
Sch Cippenham Jun Sch, Cipp. SL1 off Elmshott La 153 AL73
Cippenham La, Slou. SL1 153 AM73
Circle, The, NW2 140 CS62
NW7 118 CR50
SE1 32 A4
Tilbury RM18
off Toronto Rd 193 GG81
Circle Gdns, SW19 222 DA96
Byfleet KT14 234 BM113
Circle Rd, Whiteley Vill. KT12 235 BS110
Circuits, The, Pnr. HA5 138 BW56
Circular Rd, N17 144 DT55
Circular Way, SE18 187 EM79
Circus Lo, NW8 16 A2
Circus Ms, W1 16 E6
Circus Pl, EC2 19 M7
Circus Rd, NW8 16 A2
Coll Circus Space, N1 19 N3
Circus St, SE10 46 E5
Cirencester St, W2 15 L6
Cirrus Cl, Wall. SM6 241 DL108
Cirrus Cres, Grav. DA12 213 GL92
Cissbury Ring N, N12 119 CZ50
Cissbury Ring S, N12 119 CZ50
Cissbury Rd, N15 144 DR57
Citadel Pl, SE11 30 C10
Citizen Ho, N7
off Harvist Est 143 DN63
Citizen Rd, N7 143 DN63
● C.I. Twr, N.Mal. KT3 220 CS97
Citron Ter, SE15
off Nunhead La 184 DV83
Coll City & Guilds of London Art Sch, SE11 42 F1
Coll City & Islington Coll, Adult Learning Cen, N19
off Junction Rd 143 DJ61
Cen for Applied Sciences, EC1 18 G2
Cen for Business, Arts & Tech, N7 8 B1
Cen for Health, Social & Child Care, N7 off Holloway Rd 143 DL63
Cen for Lifelong Learning, N4 off Blackstock Rd 143 DP61
Dalby Ho, EC4 18 G1
Coll City & Islington 6th Form Coll, EC1 18 G2
● City Business Cen, SE16
off Lower Rd 32 G5
Coll City Business Coll, EC1 19 H3
Coll City Coll, The, N1 19 L2
● City Cross Business Pk, SE10 35 K8
● City Forum, EC1 19 J2
City Gdn Row, N1 19 H1
City Gate Ho, Ilf. IG2 147 EN58
Coll City Learning Cen, NW10 4 C9
Coll City Lit, Keeley Ho, WC2 18 C9
Stukeley St, WC2 18 B8
City Mill River Towpath, E15
off Blaker Rd 12 E9
Sch City of London Acad (Islington), N1 9 J9
Sch City of London Acad (Southwark), SE1 32 D10
Sch City of London Freemen's Sch, Ashtd. KT21
off Park La 254 CN119
Sch City of London Sch, EC4 19 J10
Sch City of London Sch for Girls, EC2 19 K6
★ City of Westminster Archives Cen, SW1 29 P6
Coll City of Westminster Coll, Cockpit Thea, NW8 16 C5
Cosway St Cen, NW1 16 D6
Maida Vale Cen, W9 15 L3
Paddington Grn Cen, W2 16 A6
Queens Pk Cen, W9 15 J3
● City Pk, Welw.G.C. AL7 52 DA08
● City Pt, EC2 19 L6
City Rd, EC1 18 G1
⇌ City Thameslink 18 G9
City Twr, E14 34 D6
Uni City Uni, Cass Business Sch, EC1 19 L5
Halls of Res & Saddlers Sports Cen, EC1 19 J4
Northampton Sq Campus, EC1 18 G3
Walmsley Bldg, EC1 18 G4
Walter Sickert Hall, N1 19 J2
Uni City Uni - Inns of Ct Sch of Law, Atkin Bldg, WC1 18 D6
Gray's Inn Pl, WC1 18 D7
Princeton St, WC1 18 D6
Uni City Uni - St. Bartholomew Sch of Nursing & Midwifery, E1 20 F7
City Vw, Ilf. IG1
off Axon Pl 147 EQ61
City Vw Apts, N1 9 J7
Cityview Ct, SE22 204 DU87
City Wk, SE1 31 N5
Civic Cl, St.Alb. AL1 65 CD20
Civic Offices, St.Alb. AL1 65 CD20
Civic Sq, Harl. CM20
off South Gate 73 ER15
Tilbury RM18 193 GG82
Civic Way, Ilf. IG6 147 EQ56
Ruislip HA4 138 BX64
Clabon Ms, SW1 28 E7
Clacket La, West. TN16 260 EL124
Clack La, Ruis. HA4 137 BQ60
Clack St, SE16 33 H5
Clacton Rd, E6 24 E2
E17 145 DY58
N17 off Sperling Rd 122 DT54
Claigmar Gdns, N3 120 DB53
Claire Causeway, Dart. DA2 191 FS84
Claire Ct, N12 120 DC48
Bushey Heath WD23 117 CD46
Pinner HA5
off Westfield Pk 116 BZ52
Claire Gdns, Stan. HA7 117 CJ50
Claire Pl, E14 34 B6
Clairvale, Horn. RM11 150 FL59
Clairvale Rd, Houns. TW5 178 BX81
Clairview Rd, SW16 203 DH92
Clairville Ct, Reig. RH2 272 DD134
Clairville Gdns, W7 159 CE74
Clairville Pt, SE23 205 DX90
Clammas Way, Uxb. UB8 156 BJ71
Clamp Hill, Stan. HA7 117 CD49
Clancarty Rd, SW6 39 K9
⇌ Clandon 266 BH129
Clandon Av, Egh. TW20 195 BC94
Clandon Cl, W3 180 CP75
Epsom KT17 239 CT107
Sch Clandon C of E Inf Sch, W.Clan. GU4 off The Street 266 BG131
Clandon Gdns, N3 142 DA55
★ Clandon Park, Guil. GU4 266 BG132
Clandon Pk, W.Clan. GU4 266 BG132
Clandon Rd, Guil. GU1 280 AY135
Ilford IG3 147 ES61
Send GU23 265 BF125
West Clandon GU4 265 BF125
Clandon St, SE8 46 B8
Clanricarde Gdns, W2 27 K1
Clapgate Rd, Bushey WD23 98 CB44
CLAPHAM, SW4 183 DH83
★ Clapham Common, SW4 182 DG84
⊖ Clapham Common 183 DJ84
Jct Clapham Common, SW4 183 DJ84
Clapham Common N Side, SW4 183 DH84
Clapham Common S Side, SW4 203 DH85
Clapham Common W Side, SW4 182 DG84
Clapham Cres, SW4 183 DK84
Clapham Est, SW11 182 DE84
⇌ Clapham High Street 183 DK83
Clapham High St, SW4 183 DK84
⇌ Clapham Junction 182 DD84
⊖ Clapham Junction 182 DD84
Sch Clapham Manor Prim Sch, SW4 off Belmont Rd 183 DJ83
Clapham Manor St, SW4 41 M10
⊖ Clapham North 183 DL83
CLAPHAM PARK, SW4 203 DK86
Clapham Pk Est, SW4 203 DK86
Clapham Pk Rd, SW4 183 DK84
Clapham Rd, SW9 42 D6
Clapham Rd Est, SW4 41 P10
⊖ Clapham South 203 DH86
Clap La, Dag. RM10 149 FB62
Claps Gate La, E6 25 N4
⇌ Clapton 144 DV61
Clapton App, Woob.Grn HP10 132 AD55
Clapton Common, E5 144 DT59
Sch Clapton Girls' Tech Coll, E5 10 G1
CLAPTON PARK, E5 145 DY63
Clapton Pk Est, E5
off Blackwell Cl 145 DX63
Clapton Pas, E5 10 G2
Clapton Sq, E5 10 F2
Clapton Ter, E5
off Clapton Common 144 DU60
Clapton Way, E5 144 DU63
Sch Clara Grant Sch, E3 22 B5
Clara Pl, SE18 37 M8
Clare Cl, N2
off Thomas More Way 142 DC55
Elstree WD6 100 CM44
West Byfleet KT14 234 BG113
Clare Cor, SE9 207 EP87
Clare Cotts, Bletch. RH1 273 DP133
Clare Ct, Aveley RM15 190 FQ75
Northwood HA6 115 BS50
Woldingham CR3 259 EA123
Clare Cres, Lthd. KT22 253 CG118
Claredale, Wok. GU22 248 AY119
Claredale St, E2 20 D1
Clare Dr, Farn.Com. SL2 133 AP63
Clare Gdns, E7 13 N1
W11 14 F9
Barking IG11 167 ET65
Egham TW20
off Mowbray Cres 195 BA92
Clare Hill, Esher KT10 236 CB107
Clare Ho, E3 11 N8
Sch Clare Ho Prim Sch, Beck. BR3 off Oakwood Av 225 EC96
Clare La, N1 9 K7
Clare Lawn Av, SW14 200 CR85
Clare Mkt, WC2 18 C9
Clare Ms, SW6 39 L5
Claremont, Brick.Wd AL2 82 CA31
Cheshunt EN7 88 DT29
Claremont Av, Esher KT10 236 BZ107
Harrow HA3 140 CL57
Hersham KT12 236 BX105
New Malden KT3 221 CU99
Sunbury-on-Thames TW16 217 BV95
Woking GU22 248 AY119
Claremont Cl, E16 37 M3
N1 18 F1
SW2 off Christchurch Rd 203 DM88
Grays RM16 off Premier Av 192 GC76
Hersham KT12 236 BW106
Orpington BR6 245 EN105
South Croydon CR2 258 DV115
Claremont Ct, Dor. RH4 285 CH137
Surbiton KT6
off St. James Rd 219 CK100
Claremont Cres, Crox.Grn WD3 97 BQ43
Dartford DA1 189 FE84
Claremont Dr, Esher KT10 236 CB108
Shepperton TW17 217 BP100
Woking GU22 248 AY119
Claremont End, Esher KT10 236 CB107
Sch Claremont Fan Ct Sch, Esher KT10 off Claremont Dr 236 CB108
Claremont Gdns, Ilf. IG3 147 ES61
Surbiton KT6 220 CL99
Upminster RM14 151 FR60
Claremont Gro, W4
off Edensor Gdns 180 CS80
Woodford Green IG8 124 EJ51
Sch Claremont High Sch, Kenton HA3 off Claremont Av 140 CL57
★ Claremont Landscape Gdn, Esher KT10 236 BZ108
Claremont La, Esher KT10 236 CB105
CLAREMONT PARK, Esher KT10 236 CB108
Claremont Pk, N3 119 CY53
Claremont Pk Rd, Esher KT10 236 CB107
Claremont Pl, Grav. DA11
off Cutmore St 213 GH87

Claremont Prim Sch, NW2 off Claremont Rd 141 CX61
Claremont Rd, E7 146 EH64
E11 off Grove Grn Rd 145 ED62
E17 123 DY54
N6 143 DJ59
NW2 141 CX62
W9 14 F1
W13 159 CG71
Barnet EN4 102 DD37
Bromley BR1 226 EL98
Claygate KT10 237 CE108
Croydon CR0 224 DU102
Harrow HA3 117 CE54
Hornchurch RM11 149 FG58
Redhill RH1 272 DG131
Staines TW18 195 BD92
Surbiton KT6 220 CL100
Swanley BR8 209 FE94
Teddington TW11 199 CF92
Twickenham TW1 199 CH86
West Byfleet KT14 234 BG112
Windsor SL4 173 AQ82
Claremont Sq, N1 18 E1
Claremont St, E16 37 M3
N18 122 DU51
SE10 46 D4
Claremont Way, NW2 141 CW60
● Claremont Way Ind Est, NW2 141 CW60
Claremount Cl, Epsom KT18 255 CW117
Claremount Gdns, Epsom KT18 255 CW117
Clarence Av, SW4 203 DK86
Bromley BR1 226 EL98
Ilford IG2 147 EN58
New Malden KT3 220 CQ96
Upminster RM14 150 FN61
Clarence Cl, Barn. EN4 102 DD43
Bushey Heath WD23 117 CF45
Hersham KT12 236 BW105
Clarence Ct, Egh. TW20 off Clarence St 195 AZ93
Horley RH6 291 DK147
Clarence Cres, SW4 203 DK86
Sidcup DA14 208 EV90
Windsor SL4 173 AQ81
Clarence Dr, Eng.Grn TW20 194 AW91
Clarence Gdns, NW1 17 K3
Clarence Gate, Wdf.Grn. IG8 125 EN51
Clarence Gate Gdns, NW1 off Glentworth St 16 F5
★ Clarence Ho, SW1 29 M4
Clarence La, SW15 200 CS86
Clarence Lo, Hodd. EN11 off Taverners Way 71 EA17
Clarence Ms, E5 10 F2
SE16 33 J3
SW12 203 DH87
Clarence Pl, E5 10 F2
Gravesend DA12 213 GH87
Clarence Rd, E5 144 DV63
E12 146 EK64
E16 23 K5
E17 123 DX54
N15 144 DQ57
N22 121 DL52
NW6 4 G7
SE8 46 C3
SE9 206 EL89
SW19 202 DB93
W4 180 CN78
Berkhamsted HP4 60 AW19
Bexleyheath DA6 188 EY84
Biggin Hill TN16 261 EM118
Bromley BR1 226 EK97
Croydon CR0 224 DR101
Enfield EN3 104 DV43
Grays RM17 192 GA79
Hersham KT12 235 BV105
Pilgrim's Hatch CM15 130 FV44
Redhill RH1 288 DD137
Richmond TW9 180 CM81
St. Albans AL1 65 CF20
Sidcup DA14 208 EV90
Sutton SM1 240 DB105
Teddington TW11 199 CF93
Wallington SM6 241 DH106
Windsor SL4 173 AP81
Clarence Row, Grav. DA12 213 GH87
Clarence St, Egh. TW20 195 AZ93
Kingston upon Thames KT1 220 CL96
Richmond TW9 180 CL84
Southall UB2 178 BX76
Staines TW18 195 BE91
Clarence Ter, NW1 16 F4
Hounslow TW3 178 CB84
Clarence Wk, SW4 42 A8
Redhill RH1 288 DD137
Clarence Way, NW1 7 J6
Horley RH6 291 DK147
South Ockendon RM15 171 FX72
Clarence Way Est, NW1 7 K6
Clarenden Pl, Dart. DA2 209 FD92
Clarendon Cl, E9 11 H7
W2 16 C10
Hemel Hempstead HP2 62 BK19
Orpington BR5 228 EU97
Clarendon Ct, Slou. SL2 154 AV73
Clarendon Cres, Twick. TW2 199 CD90
Clarendon Cross, W11 26 F1
Clarendon Dr, SW15 181 CW84
Clarendon Flds, Chan.Cr. WD3 96 BM38
Clarendon Gdns, NW4 141 CU55
W9 15 P5
Dartford DA2 211 FR87
Ilford IG1 147 EM60
Wembley HA9 140 CL63
Clarendon Gate, Ott. KT16 233 BD107
Clarendon Grn, Orp. BR5 228 EU98
Clarendon Gro, NW1 17 N2
Mitcham CR4 222 DF97
Orpington BR5 228 EU97
Clarendon Ms, W2 16 C9
Ashtead KT21 254 CL119
Bexley DA5 209 FB88
Borehamwood WD6 off Clarendon Rd 100 CN41
Clarendon Path, Orp. BR5 228 EU97
Clarendon Pl, W2 16 C10
Sevenoaks TN13 off Clarendon Rd 278 FG125
Clarendon Prim Sch, Ashf. TW15 off Knapp Rd 196 BM91
Clarendon Ri, SE13 185 EC83
Clarendon Rd, E11 145 ED60
E17 145 EB58
E18 146 EG55
N8 143 DM55
N15 143 DP56
N18 122 DU51
N22 121 DM54
SW19 202 DE94
W5 160 CL69
W11 14 E10
Ashford TW15 196 BM91
Borehamwood WD6 100 CN41
Cheshunt EN8 89 DX29
Croydon CR0 223 DP103
Gravesend DA12 213 GJ86
Harrow HA1 139 CE58
Hayes UB3 177 BT75
Redhill RH1 272 DF133
Sevenoaks TN13 278 FG124
Wallington SM6 241 DJ107
Watford WD17 97 BV40
Clarendon Sch, Hmptn. TW12 off Hanworth Rd 198 CB93
Clarendon St, SW1 41 K1
Clarendon Ter, W9 15 P4
Clarendon Wk, W11 14 E9
Clarendon Way, N21 104 DQ44
Chislehurst BR7 227 ET97
Orpington BR5 227 ET97
Clarens St, SE6 205 DZ89
Clare Pk, Amer. HP7 77 AS40
Clare Pl, SW15 off Minstead Gdns 201 CT87
Clare Pt, NW2 off Claremont Rd 141 CX60
Clare Rd, E11 145 ED58
NW10 161 CU66
SE14 45 N7
Greenford UB6 159 CD65
Hounslow TW4 178 BZ83
Stanwell TW19 196 BL87
Taplow SL6 152 AJ72
Clares, The, Cat. CR3 258 DU124
Clare St, E2 20 F1
Claret Gdns, SE25 224 DS98
Clareville Gro, SW7 27 P9
Clareville Rd, Cat. CR3 258 DU124
Orpington BR5 227 EQ103
Clareville St, SW7 27 P9
Clare Way, Bexh. DA7 188 EY81
Sevenoaks TN13 279 FJ127
Clare Wd, Lthd. KT22 253 CH118
Clarewood Wk, SW9 183 DP84
Clarges Ms, W1 29 J2
Clarges St, W1 29 K2
Claribel Rd, SW9 42 G8
Clarice Way, Wall. SM6 241 DL109
Claridge Rd, Dag. RM8 148 EX60
Clarissa Rd, Rom. RM6 148 EX59
Clarissa St, E8 10 A9
Clark Cl, Erith DA8 189 FG81
Clarkebourne Dr, Grays RM17 192 GD79
Clarke Ct, W6 off Great W Rd 181 CU78
Clarke Grn, Wat. WD25 97 BU35
Clarke Ms, N9 off Plevna Rd 122 DV48
Clarke Path, N16 144 DU60
Clarkes Av, Wor.Pk. KT4 221 CX102
Clarkes Dr, Uxb. UB8 156 BL71
Clarke's Ms, W1 17 H6
Clarkes Rd, Hat. AL10 67 CV17
Clarke Way, Wat. WD25 97 BU35
Clarkfield, Mill End WD3 114 BH46
Clark Lawrence Ct, SW11 off Winstanley Rd 182 DD83
Clarks La, Epp. CM16 91 ET31
Halstead TN14 246 EZ112
Warlingham CR6 260 EF123
Westerham TN16 260 EK123
Clarks Mead, Bushey WD23 116 CC45
Clarkson Ct, Hat. AL10 66 CS17
Clarkson Rd, E16 23 L8
Clarkson Row, NW1 17 L1
Clarksons, The, Bark. IG11 167 EQ68
Clarkson St, E2 20 E2
Clarks Pl, EC2 19 N8
Clarks Rd, Ilf. IG1 147 ER61
Clark St, E1 20 F7
Clark Way, Houns. TW5 178 BX80
Classon Cl, West Dr. UB7 176 BL75
Claston Cl, Dart. DA1 189 FE84
CLATTERFORD END, Ong. CM5 93 FG30
Claude Rd, E10 145 EC61
E13 166 EH67
SE15 44 E9
Claude St, E14 34 A8
Claudia Jones Way, SW2 203 DL86
Claudian Pl, St.Alb. AL3 64 CA22
Claudian Way, Grays RM16 193 GH76
Claudia Pl, SW19 201 CY88
Claudius Cl, Stan. HA7 117 CK48
Claughton Rd, E13 24 D1
Claughton Way, Hutt. CM13 131 GD44
Clauson Av, Nthlt. UB5 138 CB64
Clavell St, SE10 46 E2
Claverdale Rd, SW2 203 DM87
Claverhambury Rd, Wal.Abb. EN9 90 EF29
Clavering Av, SW13 181 CV79
Clavering Cl, Twick. TW1 199 CG91
Clavering Rd, E12 146 EK60
● Claverings Ind Est, N9 123 DX47
Clavering Way, Hutt. CM13 off Poplar Dr 131 GC44
Claverley Gro, N3 120 DA52
Claverley Vil, N3 120 DB52
Claverton Cl, Bov. HP3 79 BA28
Claverton St, SW1 41 M1
Clave St, E1 32 G3
Claxton Gro, W6 38 D1
Claxton Path, SE4 off Hainford Cl 185 DX84
Clay Acre, Chesh. HP5 76 AR30
Clay Av, Mitch. CR4 223 DH96
Claybank Gro, SE13 46 C10
Claybourne Ms, SE19 off Church Rd 204 DS94
Claybridge Rd, SE12 206 EJ91
Claybrook Cl, N2 142 DD55
Claybrook Rd, W6 38 D2
Clayburn Gdns, S.Ock. RM15 171 FV73
Claybury, Bushey WD23 116 CB45
Claybury Bdy, Ilf. IG5 146 EL55
Claybury Hall, Wdf.Grn. IG8 125 EM52
Claybury Rd, Wdf.Grn. IG8 124 EL52
Clay Cor, Cher. KT16 off Eastworth Rd 216 BH102
Claycots Prim Sch, Slou. SL2 off Monksfield Way 153 AN70
Claycroft, Welw.G.C. AL7 52 DB08
Claydon, SE17 off Deacon Way 31 J8
Claydon Dr, Croy. CR0 241 DL105
Claydon End, Chal.St.P. SL9 134 AY55
Claydon La, Chal.St.P. SL9 134 AY55
Claydon Rd, Wok. GU21 248 AU116
Claydown Ms, SE18 37 M10
Clayfarm Rd, SE9 207 EQ89
Clayfields, Penn HP10 110 AC45
CLAYGATE, Esher KT10 237 CE108
⇌ Claygate 237 CD107
Claygate Cl, Horn. RM12 149 FG63
Claygate Cres, New Adgtn CR0 243 EC107
Claygate La, Esher KT10 219 CG103
Thames Ditton KT7 219 CG102
Waltham Abbey EN9 89 ED30
Claygate Lo Cl, Clay. KT10 237 CE108
Claygate Prim Sch, Clay. KT10 off Foley Rd 237 CE108
Claygate Rd, W13 179 CH76
Dorking RH4 285 CH138
CLAYHALL, Ilf. IG5 125 EM54
Clayhall Av, Ilf. IG5 146 EL55
Clayhall La, Old Wind. SL4 194 AT85
Reigate RH2 287 CX138
Clayhanger, Guil. GU4 265 BC132
CLAY HILL, Enf. EN2 104 DQ37
Clay Hill, Enf. EN2 104 DQ37
Clayhill, Surb. KT5 220 CN99
Clayhill Cl, Leigh RH2 287 CU141
Clayhill Cres, SE9 206 EK91
Clayhill Rd, Leigh RH2 287 CT142
Claylands Pl, SW8 42 E4
Claylands Rd, SW8 42 D3
Clay La, Bushey Hth WD23 117 CE45
Edgware HA8 118 CN46
Guildford GU4 264 AY128
Headley KT18 254 CP124
South Nutfield RH1 289 DJ135
Stanwell TW19 196 BM87
Claymill Ho, SE18 187 EQ78
Claymills Ms, Hem.H. HP3 62 BN23
Claymore, Hem.H. HP2 62 BL16
Claymore Cl, Mord. SM4 222 DA101
Claymore Ct, E17 off Billet Rd 123 DY53
Claypit Hill, Wal.Abb. EN9 106 EJ36
Claypole Dr, Houns. TW5 178 BY81
Claypole Rd, E15 12 F10
Clayponds Av, Brent. TW8 180 CL77
Clayponds Gdns, W5 179 CK77
Clayponds Hosp, W5 180 CL77
Clayponds La, Brent. TW8 180 CL78
Clay Rd, The, Loug. IG10 106 EL39
Clayside, Chig. IG7 125 EQ51
Clay's La, Loug. IG10 107 EN39
Clay St, W1 16 F7
Beaconsfield HP9 110 AJ48
Clayton Av, Upmin. RM14 150 FP64
Wembley HA0 160 CL66
Clayton Cl, E6 25 K8
Clayton Cres, N1 8 B9
Brentford TW8 179 CK78
Clayton Cft Rd, Dart. DA2 209 FG89
Clayton Dr, SE8 33 L10
Guildford GU2 264 AT131
Hemel Hempstead HP3 63 BR22
Clayton Fld, NW9 118 CS52
Clayton Mead, Gdse. RH9 274 DV130
Clayton Ms, SE10 46 G6
Clayton Rd, SE15 44 D7
Chessington KT9 237 CJ105
Epsom KT17 238 CS113
Hayes UB3 177 BS75
Isleworth TW7 179 CE83
Romford RM7 149 FC60
Clayton St, SE11 42 E2
Clayton Ter, Hayes UB4 off Jollys La 158 BX71
Clayton Wk, Amer. HP7 94 AW39
Clayton Way, Uxb. UB8 156 BK70
Clay Tye Rd, Upmin. RM14 151 FW63
Claywood Cl, Orp. BR6 227 ES101
Claywood La, Bean DA2 211 FX90
Clayworth Cl, Sid. DA15 208 EV86
Cleall Av, Wal.Abb. EN9 off Quaker La 89 EC34
Cleanthus Cl, SE18 187 EP81
Cleanthus Rd, SE18 187 EP81
Clearbrook Way, E1 21 H8
Cleardene, Dor. RH4 285 CH136
Cleardown, Wok. GU22 249 BB118
Cleares Pasture, Burn. SL1 152 AH69
Clearmount, Chobham GU24 232 AS107
Clears, The, Reig. RH2 271 CY132
Clearwater Pl, Long Dit. KT6 219 CJ100
Clearwater Ter, W11 26 D4
Clearwell Dr, W9 15 L5
Cleave Av, Hayes UB3 177 BS77
Orpington BR6 245 ES107
Cleaveland Rd, Surb. KT6 219 CK99
Cleave Prior, Chipstead CR5 256 DE119
Cleaverholme Cl, SE25 224 DV100
Cleaver Sq, SE11 30 F10
Cleaver St, SE11 30 F10
Cleeve, The, Guil. GU1 265 BA134
Cleeve Ct, Felt. TW14 off Kilross Rd 197 BS88
Cleeve Hill, SE23 204 DV88
Cleeve Pk Gdns, Sid. DA14 208 EV89
Cleeve Pk Sch, Sid. DA14 off Bexley La 208 EW90
Cleeve Rd, Lthd. KT22 253 CF120
● Cleeve Studios, E2 off Boundary St 20 A3
Cleeve Way, SW15 off Danebury Av 201 CT86
Sutton SM1 222 DB102
Clegg St, E1 32 F2
E13 13 P10
Cleland Path, Loug. IG10 107 EP39
Cleland Rd, Chal.St.P. SL9 112 AX54
Clematis Cl, Rom. RM3 128 FJ52
Clematis Gdns, Wdf.Grn. IG8 124 EG50
Clematis St, W12 161 CT73
Clem Attlee Ct, SW6 38 G3
Clem Attlee Par, SW6 off North End Rd 39 H3
Clemence Rd, Dag. RM10 169 FC67
Clemence St, E14 21 N7
Clement Av, SW4 183 DK84
Clement Cl, NW6 4 B7
W4 180 CR76
Clement Cl, Pur. CR8 off Croftleigh Av 257 DP116
Clement Gdns, Hayes UB3 177 BS77
Clementhorpe Rd, Dag. RM9 168 EW65
Clementina Rd, E10 145 DZ60
Clementine Churchill Hosp, Har. HA1 139 CF62
Clementine Cl, W13 off Balfour Rd 179 CH75
Clementine Wk, Wdf.Grn. IG8 off Salway Cl 124 EG52
Clementine Way, Hem.H. HP1 62 BH22
Clement Rd, SW19 201 CY92
Beckenham BR3 225 DX96
Cheshunt EN8 89 DY27
Clements Av, E16 23 N10
Clements Cl, N12 120 DB49
Slough SL1 174 AV75
Clements Ct, Houns. TW4 178 BX84
Ilford IG1 off Clements La 147 EP62
Watford WD25 98 BW35
Clements Ho, Lthd. KT22 253 CG119
Clement's Inn, WC2 18 D9
Clement's Inn Pas, WC2 18 D9
Clements La, EC4 19 M10
Ilford IG1 147 EP62
Clements Mead, Lthd. KT22 253 CG119
Clements Pl, Brent. TW8 179 CK78
Clements Rd, E6 167 EM66
SE16 32 D7
Chorleywood WD3 95 BD43
Ilford IG1 147 EP62
Walton-on-Thames KT12 217 BV103
Clements St, Ware SG12 55 DY06
Clement St, Swan. BR8 210 FK93
Clement Way, Upmin. RM14 150 FM62
Clenches Fm La, Sev. TN13 278 FG126
Clenches Fm Rd, Sev. TN13 278 FG126
Clendon Way, SE18 off Polthorne Gro 187 ER77
Clennam St, SE1 31 K4
Clensham Ct, Sutt. SM1 off Sutton Common Rd 222 DA103
Clensham La, Sutt. SM1 222 DA103
Clenston Ms, W1 16 E8
Cleopatra Cl, Stan. HA7 117 CK48
★ Cleopatra's Needle, WC2 30 C2
Clephane Rd, N1 9 L5
Clere St, EC2 19 M4
Clerics Wk, Shep. TW17 off Gordon Rd 217 BR100
CLERKENWELL, EC1 18 G5
Clerkenwell Cl, EC1 18 F4
Clerkenwell Grn, EC1 18 F5
Clerkenwell Parochial C of E Prim Sch, EC1 18 E2
Clerkenwell Rd, EC1 18 E5
Clerks Cft, Bletch. RH1 274 DR133
Clerks Piece, Loug. IG10 107 EM41
Clermont Rd, E9 10 G8
Clevedon, Wey. KT13 235 BQ106
Clevedon Cl, N16 off Smalley Cl 144 DT62
Clevedon Gdns, Hayes UB3 177 BR76
Hounslow TW5 177 BV81
Clevedon Rd, SE20 225 DX95
Kingston upon Thames KT1 220 CN96
Twickenham TW1 199 CK86
Clevehurst Cl, Stoke P. SL2 154 AT65
Cleveland Av, SW20 221 CZ96
W4 181 CT77
Hampton TW12 198 BZ94
Cleveland Cl, Walt. KT12 217 BV104
Wooburn Green HP10 132 AE55
Cleveland Cres, Borwd. WD6 100 CQ43
Cleveland Dr, Stai. TW18 216 BH96
Cleveland Gdns, N4 144 DQ57
NW2 141 CX61
SW13 181 CT82
W2 15 N9
Worcester Park KT4 220 CS103
Cleveland Gro, E1 20 G5
Cleveland Inf & Jun Schs, Ilf. IG1 off Cleveland Rd 147 EP63
Cleveland Ms, W1 17 L6
Cleveland Pk, Stai. TW19 196 BL86
Cleveland Pk Av, E17 145 EA56
Cleveland Pk Cres, E17 145 EA56
Cleveland Pl, SW1 29 M2
Cleveland Ri, Mord. SM4 221 CX101
Cleveland Rd, E18 146 EG55
N1 9 M7
N9 122 DV45
SW13 181 CT82
W4 off Antrobus Rd 180 CQ76
W13 159 CH71
Hemel Hempstead HP2 63 BP18
Ilford IG1 147 EP62
Isleworth TW7 179 CG84
New Malden KT3 220 CS98
Uxbridge UB8 156 BK68
Welling DA16 187 ET82
Worcester Park KT4 220 CS103
Cleveland Row, SW1 29 L3
Cleveland Sq, W2 15 N9
Cleveland St, W1 17 L5
Cleveland Ter, W2 15 P8
Cleveland Way, E1 20 G5
Hemel Hempstead HP2 63 BP18
Cleveley Cl, SE7 36 F8
Cleveley Cres, W5 160 CL68
Cleveleys Rd, E5 144 DV62
Cleverly Est, W12 161 CU74
Cleve Rd, NW6 5 K6
Sidcup DA14 208 EX90
Cleves Av, Brwd. CM14 130 FV46
Epsom KT17 239 CV109
Cleves Cl, Cob. KT11 235 BV114
Loughton IG10 106 EL44
Cleves Ct, Wind. SL4 173 AM83
Cleves Cres, New Adgtn CR0 243 EC111
Cleves Prim Sch, E6 off Arragon Rd 166 EK67
Cleves Rd, E6 166 EK67
Hemel Hempstead HP2 63 BP15
Richmond TW10 199 CJ90
Cleves Sch, Wey. KT13 off Oatlands Av 235 BT105
Cleves Wk, Ilf. IG6 125 EQ52
Cleves Way, Hmptn. TW12 198 BZ94
Ruislip HA4 138 BX60
Sunbury-on-Thames TW16 197 BT93
Cleves Wd, Wey. KT13 235 BS105
Clewer Av, Wind. SL4 173 AN82
Clewer Ct Rd, Wind. SL4 173 AP80
Clewer Cres, Har. HA3 117 CD53
Clewer Flds, Wind. SL4 173 AQ81
CLEWER GREEN, Wind. SL4 173 AM82
Clewer Grn C of E First Sch, Wind. SL4 off Hatch La 173 AN83
Clewer Hill Rd, Wind. SL4 173 AL82
Clewer Ho, SE2 off Wolvercote Rd 188 EX75
CLEWER NEW TOWN, Wind. SL4 173 AN82
Clewer New Town, Wind. SL4 173 AN82
Clewer Pk, Wind. SL4 173 AN80
CLEWER VILLAGE, Wind. SL4 173 AM80
Clichy Est, E1 21 H7
Clifden Ms, E5 11 K1
Clifden Rd, E5 11 H2
Brentford TW8 179 CK79
Twickenham TW1 199 CF88
Cliff End, Pur. CR8 241 DP112
Cliffe Rd, S.Croy. CR2 242 DR106
Cliffe Wk, Sutt. SM1 off Turnpike La 240 DC106
Clifford Av, SW14 180 CP83
Chislehurst BR7 207 EM93
Ilford IG5 125 EP53
Wallington SM6 241 DJ105
Clifford Cl, Nthlt. UB5 158 BY67
Clifford Dr, SW9 183 DP84
Clifford Gdns, NW10 14 A1
Hayes UB3 177 BR77
Clifford Gro, Ashf. TW15 196 BN91
Clifford Haigh Ho, SW6 off Fulham Palace Rd 181 CX80
Clifford Manor Rd, Guil. GU4 280 AY138
Clifford Rd, E16 23 L5
E17 123 EC54
N9 104 DW44
SE25 224 DU98
Barnet EN5 102 DB41
Chafford Hundred RM16 192 FZ75
Hounslow TW4 178 BX83
Richmond TW10 199 CK89
Wembley HA0 159 CK67
Clifford's Inn Pas, EC4 18 E9
Clifford St, W1 29 L1
Clifford Way, NW10 141 CT63
Cliff Pl, S.Ock. RM15 171 FX69
Cliff Reach, Bluewater DA9 211 FS87
Cliff Richard Ct, Chsht EN8 off High St 89 DX28
Cliff Rd, NW1 7 P4
Cliff Ter, SE8 46 B8
Cliffview Rd, SE13 185 EA83
Cliff Vil, NW1 7 P4
Cliff Wk, E16 23 M6
Clifton Av, E17 145 DX55
N3 119 CZ53
W12 161 CT74
Feltham TW13 198 BW90
Stanmore HA7 117 CH54
Sutton SM2 240 DB111
Wembley HA9 160 CM65
Clifton Cl, Add. KT15 216 BH103
Caterham CR3 258 DR123
Cheshunt EN8 89 DY29
Horley RH6 291 DK148
Orpington BR6 245 EQ106
Clifton Ct, N4 off Biggerstaff St 143 DN61
NW8 16 A4
Woodford Green IG8 off Snakes La W 124 EG51
Clifton Cres, SE15 44 F5
Clifton Est, SE15 44 D7
Clifton Gdns, N15 144 DT58
NW11 141 CZ58
W4 off Dolman Rd 180 CR77
W9 15 N5
Enfield EN2 103 DL42
Uxbridge UB10 157 BP68
Clifton Gro, E8 10 C4
Gravesend DA11 213 GH87
Clifton Hatch, Harl. CM18 off Trotters Rd 74 EU18
Clifton Hill, NW8 5 N9
Clifton Hill Sch, Cat. CR3 off Chaldon Rd 258 DR123
Clifton Lawns, Amer. HP6 77 AQ35
Clifton Lo Boys' Prep Sch, W5 off Mattock La 159 CK73
Clifton Marine Par, Grav. DA11 213 GF86
Clifton Pk Av, SW20 221 CW96
Clifton Pl, SE16 33 H4
W2 16 B10
Banstead SM7 256 DA115
Clifton Prim Sch, Sthl. UB2 off Clifton Rd 178 BY77
Clifton Ri, SE14 45 M5
Windsor SL4 173 AK81
Clifton Rd, E7 166 EK65
E16 23 K6
N1 9 K5
N3 120 DC53
N8 143 DK58
N22 121 DJ53
NW10 161 CU68
SE25 224 DS98
SW19 201 CX93
W9 15 P4
Amersham HP6 77 AP35
Coulsdon CR5 257 DH115
Gravesend DA11 213 GG86
Greenford UB6 158 CC70
Harrow HA3 140 CM57
Hornchurch RM11 149 FG58
Ilford IG2 147 ER58
Isleworth TW7 179 CD82
Kingston upon Thames KT2 200 CM94
London Heathrow Airport TW6 off Inner Ring E 177 BP83
Loughton IG10 106 EL42
Sidcup DA14 207 ES91
Slough SL1 174 AV75
Southall UB2 178 BY77
Teddington TW11 199 CE91
Wallington SM6 241 DH106
Watford WD18 97 BV43
Welling DA16 188 EW83
Cliftons La, Reig. RH2 271 CX131
Clifton's Rbt, SE12 206 EH86
Clifton St, EC2 19 N6
St. Albans AL1 65 CE19
Clifton Ter, N4 143 DN61
Clifton Vil, W9 15 M6
Cliftonville, Dor. RH4 285 CH137
Clifton Wk, E6 25 H8
W6 off Galena Rd 181 CV77
Dartford DA2 off Osbourne Rd 210 FP86
Clifton Way, SE15 44 F5
Borehamwood WD6 100 CN39
Hutton CM13 131 GD46

Clifton Way, Wem. HA0 . . . . . . 160 CL67
Woking GU21 . . . . 248 AT117
Climb, The, Rick. WD3 . . . . 96 BH44
Clinch Ct, E16 . . . . 23 P7
Cline Rd, N11 . . . . 121 DJ51
Guildford GU1 . . . . 281 AZ136
Clinger Ct, N1 . . . . 9 N9
★ Clink Prison Mus, SE1 . . . . . 31 L2
Clink St, SE1 . . . . 31 K2
Clinton Av, E.Mol. KT8 . . . . . . 218 CC98
Welling DA16 . . . . 187 ET84
Clinton Cl, Wey. KT13 . . . . 217 BP104
Clinton Cres, Ilf. IG6 . . . . 125 ES51
Clinton End, Hem.H. HP2 . . . . . 63 BQ20
Clinton Rd, E3 . . . . 21 L3
E7 . . . . 13 P1
N15 . . . . 144 DR56
Leatherhead KT22 . . . . 253 CJ123
Clinton Ter, Sutt. SM1
off Manor La 240 DC105
Clipper Boul, Dart. DA2 . . . . . 191 FS83
Clipper Boul W, Dart. DA2 . . . . 191 FR83
Clipper Cl, SE16 . . . . 33 J4
Clipper Cres, Grav. DA12 . . . . 213 GM91
Clipper Way, SE13 . . . . 185 EC84
Clippesby Cl, Chess. KT9 . . . . . 238 CM108
Clipstone Ms, W1 . . . . 17 L5
Clipstone Rd, Houns. TW3 . . . . 178 CA83
Clipstone St, W1 . . . . 17 K6
Clissold Cl, N2 . . . . 142 DF55
Clissold Ct, N4 . . . . 144 DQ61
Clissold Cres, N16 . . . . 144 DR62
Clissold Rd, N16 . . . . 144 DR62
Clitheroe Av, Har. HA2 . . . . . . 138 CA60
Clitheroe Gdns, Wat. WD19 . . . 116 BX48
Clitheroe Rd, SW9 . . . . 42 B9
Romford RM5 . . . . 127 FC50
Clitherow Av, W7 . . . . 179 CG76
Clitherow Pas, Brent. TW8 . . . . 179 CJ78
Clitherow Rd, Brent. TW8 . . . . . 179 CH78
Clitterhouse Cres, NW2 . . . . . . 141 CW60
Clitterhouse Rd, NW2 . . . . 141 CW60
Clive Av, N18
off Claremont St 122 DU51
Dartford DA1 . . . . 209 FF86
Clive Cl, Pot.B. EN6 . . . . 85 CZ31
Clive Ct, W9 . . . . 15 P4
Slough SL1 . . . . 173 AR75
★ Cliveden, Maid. SL6 . . . . . . 132 AD64
Cliveden Cl, N12
off Woodside Av 120 DC49
Shenfield CM15 . . . . 131 FZ45
Cliveden Gages, Tap. SL6 . . . . . 152 AE65
Cliveden Pl, SW1 . . . . 28 G8
Shepperton TW17 . . . . 217 BP100
Cliveden Rd, SW19 . . . . 221 CZ95
Burnham SL1 . . . . 152 AE65
Taplow SL6 . . . . 152 AE65
Clivedon Ct, W13 . . . . 159 CH71
Clivedon Rd, E4 . . . . 124 EE50
Clive Par, Nthwd. HA6
off Maxwell Rd 115 BS52
Clive Pas, SE21 off Clive Rd 204 DR90
Clive Rd, SE21 . . . . 204 DR90
SW19 . . . . 202 DE93
Belvedere DA17 . . . . 188 FA77
Enfield EN1 . . . . 104 DU42
Esher KT10 . . . . 236 CB105
Feltham TW14 . . . . 197 BU86
Gravesend DA11 . . . . 213 GH86
Great Warley CM13 . . . . 129 FW52
Romford RM2 . . . . 149 FH57
Twickenham TW1 . . . . 199 CF91
Clivesdale Dr, Hayes UB3 . . . . 157 BV74
Clive Way, Enf. EN1 . . . . 104 DU42
Watford WD24 . . . . 98 BW39
Cloak La, EC4 . . . . 19 K10
⇌ Clock House 225 DY96
Clockhouse Av, Bark. IG11 . . . . 167 EQ67
Clockhouse Cl, SW19 . . . . 201 CW90
Clock Ho Cl, Byfleet KT14 . . . . 234 BM112
Clockhouse Cl, Guil. GU1
off Palm Gro 264 AW130
Clockhouse La, Ashf. TW15 . . . 196 BN91
Feltham TW14 . . . . 197 BP89
Grays RM16 . . . . 171 FX74
Romford RM5 . . . . 127 FB52
Clock Ho La, Sev. TN13 . . . . . . 278 FG123
Clockhouse La E, Egh. TW20 . . 195 BB94
Clockhouse La W, Egh. TW20 . . 195 BA94
Clock Ho Mead, Oxshott KT22 . 236 CB114
Clockhouse Ms, Chorl. WD3
off Chorleywood Ho Dr 95 BE41
● Clockhouse Pl, Felt. TW14 . 197 BQ88
Clockhouse Pl, SW15 . . . . 201 CY85
Sch Clockhouse Prim Sch,
Coll.Row RM5
off Clockhouse La 127 FB51
Clock Ho Rd, Beck. BR3 . . . . . . 225 DY97
Jct Clockhouse Rbt,
Felt. TW14 . . . . 197 BP88
★ Clockmakers Company
Collection, The (Guildhall Lib),
EC2 . . . . 19 K8
Clock Twr Ms, N1 . . . . 9 K9
SE28 . . . . 168 EV73
W7 off Uxbridge Rd 159 CE74
Clock Twr Rd, Islw. TW7 . . . . . . 179 CF83
Jct Clock Twr Rbt, Harl. CM17 . . 74 EV16
Clock Vw Cres, N7 . . . . 8 A4
Cloister Cl, Rain. RM13 . . . . . . 169 FH70
Teddington TW11 . . . . 199 CH92
Cloister Gdns, SE25 . . . . 224 DV100
Edgware HA8 . . . . 118 CQ50
Cloister Garth, Berk. HP4 . . . . . 60 AW19
St. Albans AL1 . . . . 65 CE24
Cloister Rd, NW2 . . . . 141 CZ62
W3 . . . . 160 CQ71
Cloisters, The, Bushey WD23 . . . 98 CB44
Guildford GU1
off London Rd 265 BA131
Rickmansworth WD3 . . . . 114 BL45
Welwyn Garden City AL8 . . . . 51 CX09
Windsor SL4 . . . . 173 AN82
Woking GU22 . . . . 249 BB121
Cloisters Av, Brom. BR2 . . . . . . 227 EM99
● Cloisters Business Cen,
SW8 off Battersea Pk Rd 41 K5
Cloisters Ct, Rick. WD3
off The Cloisters 114 BL45
Cloisters Mall, Kings.T. KT1
off Union St 219 CK96
Cloister Wk, Hem.H. HP2
off Townsend 62 BK18
Clonard Way, Pnr. HA5 . . . . 116 CA51
Clonbrock Rd, N16 . . . . 144 DS63
Cloncurry St, SW6 . . . . 38 D8
Clonmel Cl, Har. HA2 . . . . 139 CD61
Clonmell Rd, N17 . . . . 144 DR55
Clonmel Rd, SW6 . . . . 39 H5
Teddington TW11 . . . . 199 CD91
Clonmel Way, Burn. SL1 . . . . . . 152 AH69
Clonmore St, SW18 . . . . 201 CZ88
Cloonmore Av, Orp. BR6 . . . . . . 245 ET105
Clorane Gdns, NW3 . . . . 142 DA62
Sch Clore Shalom Sch, Shenley
WD7 off Hugo Gryn Way . . . 84 CL30
Sch Clore Tikva Sch, Ilf. IG6
off Fullwell Av 125 EQ54
Close, The, E4
off Beech Hall Rd 123 EC52
N14 . . . . 121 DK47
N20 . . . . 119 CZ47
SE3 . . . . 47 H9
Beckenham BR3 . . . . 225 DY98
Berry's Green TN16 . . . . 261 EP116
Bexley DA5 . . . . 208 FA86
Brentwood CM14 . . . . 130 FW48
Brookmans Park AL9 . . . . 85 CY26
Bushey WD23 . . . . 98 CB43
Carshalton SM5 . . . . 240 DE109
Dartford DA2 . . . . 210 FJ90
East Barnet EN4 . . . . 102 DF44
Eastcote HA5 . . . . 138 BW59
Grays RM16 . . . . 192 GC75
Harrow HA2 . . . . 116 CC54
Hillingdon UB10 . . . . 156 BN67
Horley RH6 . . . . 291 DJ150
Isleworth TW7 . . . . 179 CD82
Iver SL0 . . . . 155 BC69
Mitcham CR4 . . . . 222 DF98
New Malden KT3 . . . . 220 CQ96
Petts Wood BR5 . . . . 227 ES100
Potters Bar EN6 . . . . 86 DA32
Purley (Pampisford Rd) CR8 . . 241 DP110
Purley (Russ.Hill) CR8 . . . . . . 241 DM110
Radlett WD7 . . . . 83 CF33
Rayners Lane HA5 . . . . 138 BZ59
Reigate RH2 . . . . 288 DB135
Richmond TW9 . . . . 180 CP83
Rickmansworth WD3 . . . . 114 BJ46
Romford RM6 . . . . 148 EY58
Sevenoaks TN13 . . . . 278 FE124
Sidcup DA14 . . . . 208 EV91
Slough SL1
off St. George's Cres 153 AK73
Strood Green RH3 . . . . 286 CP138
Sutton SM3 . . . . 221 CZ101
Uxbridge UB10 . . . . 156 BL66
Virginia Water GU25 . . . . 214 AW99
Ware SG12 . . . . 55 DY06
Wembley (Barnhill Rd) HA9 . 140 CQ62
Wembley (Lyon Pk Av) HA0 . 160 CL65
West Byfleet KT14 . . . . 234 BG113
Wonersh GU5 . . . . 281 BB144
Closemead Cl, Nthwd. HA6 . . . 115 BQ51
Cloth Ct, EC1 . . . . 19 H7
Cloth Fair, EC1 . . . . 19 H7
Clothier St, E1 . . . . 19 P8
Cloth St, EC1 . . . . 19 J6
Clothworkers Rd, SE18 . . . . . . 187 ER80
Cloudberry Rd, Rom. RM3 . . . . 128 FK51
Cloudesdale Rd, SW17 . . . . 203 DH89
Cloudesley Pl, N1 . . . . 8 E9
Cloudesley Rd, N1 . . . . 8 E8
Bexleyheath DA7 . . . . 188 EZ81
Erith DA8 . . . . 189 FF81
Cloudesley Sq, N1 . . . . 8 E9
Cloudesley St, N1 . . . . 8 F9
Clouston Cl, Wall. SM6 . . . . . . 241 DL106
Clova Rd, E7 . . . . 13 M4
Clove Cres, E14 . . . . 22 F10
Clove Hitch Quay, SW11 . . . . . . 39 P10
Clovelly Av, NW9 . . . . 141 CT56
Uxbridge UB10 . . . . 137 BQ63
Warlingham CR6 . . . . 258 DV118
Clovelly Cl, Pnr. HA5 . . . . 137 BV55
Uxbridge UB10 . . . . 137 BQ63
Clovelly Ct, Horn. RM11 . . . . . 150 FM61
Clovelly Gdns, SE19 . . . . 224 DT95
Enfield EN1 . . . . 122 DS45
Romford RM7 . . . . 127 FB53
Clovelly Rd, N8 . . . . 143 DK56
W4 . . . . 180 CQ75
W5 . . . . 179 CJ75
Bexleyheath DA7 . . . . 188 EY79
Hounslow TW3 . . . . 178 CA82
Clovelly Way, E1 . . . . 21 H8
Harrow HA2 . . . . 138 BZ61
Orpington BR6 . . . . 227 ET100
Clover Cl, E11 off Norman Rd . 145 ED61
Clover Ct, Grays RM17
off Churchill Rd 192 GD79
Woking GU22 . . . . 248 AX118
Cloverdale Gdns, Sid. DA15 . . . 207 ET86
Clover Fld, Harl. CM18 . . . . 74 EU18
Cloverfield, Welw.G.C. AL7 . . . . . 51 CZ06
Clover Fld, The, Bushey WD23 . . 98 BZ44
Cloverfields, Horl. RH6 . . . . . . 291 DH147
Clover Hill, Couls. CR5 . . . . 257 DH121
Cloverland, Hat. AL10 . . . . 67 CT21
Clover Lea, Gdmg. GU7 . . . . . . 280 AS143
Clover Leas, Epp. CM16 . . . . 91 ET30
Cloverleys, Loug. IG10 . . . . 106 EK43
Clover Ms, SW3 . . . . 40 E2
Clover Rd, Guil. GU2 . . . . 264 AS132
Clovers, The, Nthflt DA11 . . . . . 212 GE91
Clover Way, Hat. AL10 . . . . 67 CT15
Hemel Hempstead HP1 . . . . . . 62 BH19
Wallington SM6 . . . . 222 DG102
Clove St, E13 . . . . 23 N5
Clowders Rd, SE6 . . . . 205 DZ90
Clowser Cl, Sutt. SM1
off Turnpike La 240 DC106
Cloysters Grn, E1 . . . . 32 C2
Cloyster Wd, Edg. HA8 . . . . 117 CK52
Club Gdns Rd, Brom. BR2 . . . . 226 EG101
Club Row, E1 . . . . 20 A4
E2 . . . . 20 A4
Clump, The, Rick. WD3 . . . . 96 BG43
Clump Av, Box H. KT20 . . . . . . 270 CQ131
Clumps, The, Ashf. TW15 . . . . . 197 BR91
Clunas Gdns, Rom. RM2 . . . . . . 128 FK54
Clunbury Av, Sthl. UB2 . . . . 178 BZ78
Clunbury Ct, Berk. HP4
off Manor St 60 AX19
Clunbury St, N1 . . . . 19 M1
Cluny Est, SE1 . . . . 31 N6
Cluny Ms, SW5 . . . . 27 J9
Cluny Pl, SE1 . . . . 31 N6
Cluse Ct, N1 . . . . 9 J10
Clutterbucks, Sarratt WD3 . . . . 96 BG36
Clutton St, E14 . . . . 22 D7
Clydach Rd, Enf. EN1 . . . . 104 DT42
Clyde Av, S.Croy. CR2 . . . . 258 DV115
Clyde Circ, N15 . . . . 144 DS56
Clyde Cl, Red. RH1 . . . . 272 DG133
Clyde Cres, Upmin. RM14 . . . . 151 FS58
Clyde Pl, E10 . . . . 145 EB59
Clyde Rd, N15 . . . . 144 DS56
N22 . . . . 121 DK53
Croydon CR0 . . . . 224 DT102
Hoddesdon EN11 . . . . 71 ED19
Stanwell TW19 . . . . 196 BK88
Sutton SM1 . . . . 240 DA106
Wallington SM6 . . . . 241 DJ106
Clydesdale, Enf. EN3 . . . . 105 DX42
Clydesdale Av, Stan. HA7 . . . . . 139 CK55
Clydesdale Cl, Borwd. WD6 . . . 100 CR43
Isleworth TW7 . . . . 179 CF83
Clydesdale Gdns, Rich. TW10 . . 180 CP84
Clydesdale Ho, Erith DA18
off Kale Rd 188 EY75
Clydesdale Rd, W11 . . . . 14 G8
Hornchurch RM11 . . . . 149 FF59
Clydesdale Wk, Brox. EN10
off Tarpan Way 89 DZ25
Clyde Sq, Hem.H. HP2 . . . . 62 BM15
Clyde St, SE8 . . . . 45 P3
Clyde Ter, SE23 . . . . 204 DW89
Hertford SG13 . . . . 54 DU09
Clyde Vale, SE23 . . . . 204 DW89
Clyde Way, Rom. RM1 . . . . 127 FE53
Clydon Cl, Erith DA8 . . . . 189 FE79
Clyfford Rd, Ruis. HA4 . . . . 137 BT63
Clyfton Cl, Brox. EN10 . . . . 71 DZ23
Clymping Dene, Felt. TW14 . . . 197 BV87
Clyston Rd, Wat. WD18 . . . . 97 BT44
Clyston St, SW8 . . . . 41 N8
Clyve Way, Stai. TW18 . . . . 215 BE95
Coach All, Woob.Grn HP10 . . . 132 AF60
Coach & Horses Yd, W1 . . . . 17 K10
Coach Ho La, N5 . . . . 8 G1
SW19 . . . . 201 CX91
Coach Ho Ms, SE14 . . . . 45 J8
Coachhouse Ms, SE20 . . . . 204 DV94
Coach Ho Ms, SE23 . . . . 205 DX86
Redhill RH1 off Mill St 288 DF135
Coach Ho Yd, SW18
off Ebner St 182 DB84
Coachlads Av, Guil. GU2 . . . . . 264 AT134
Coachmaker Ms, SW4
off Fenwick Pl 183 DL83
W4 off Berrymede Rd 180 CR76
Coach Ms, St.Alb. AL1 . . . . 65 CH20
Coach Rd, Brock. RH3 . . . . 270 CL134
Ottershaw KT16 . . . . 233 BC107
Coach Yd Ms, N19 . . . . 143 DL60
Coal Ct, Grays RM17
off Columbia Wf Rd 192 GA79
Coaldale Wk, SE21
off Lairdale Cl 204 DQ87
Coalecroft Rd, SW15 . . . . 181 CW84
Coalmans Way, Burn. SL1 . . . . 152 AH72
Coalport Cl, Harl. CM17 . . . . . . 74 EW16
Coalport Ho, SE11
off Walnut Tree Wk 30 E8
Coal Post Cl, Grn St Grn
BR6 off Lynne Cl 245 ET107
Coal Rd, Til. RM18 . . . . 193 GL77
Coast Hill, Westc. RH4 . . . . . . 284 BZ139
Coast Hill La, Westc. RH4 . . . . 284 CA138
Coaters La, Woob.Grn HP10 . . 132 AE56
Coates Av, SW18 . . . . 202 DE86
Coates Cl, Th.Hth. CR7 . . . . . . 224 DQ97
Coates Dell, Wat. WD25 . . . . 82 BY33
Coates Hill Rd, Brom. BR1 . . . . 227 EN96
Coates Rd, Els. WD6 . . . . 117 CK45
Coate St, E2 . . . . 20 D1
Coates Wk, Brent. TW8 . . . . 180 CL78
Coates Way, Wat. WD25 . . . . 82 BX33
Sch Coates Way JMI & Nurs Sch,
Wat. WD25 off Coates Way . . 82 BY33
Coat Wicks, Seer Grn HP9 . . . . 111 AQ51
Cobalt Cl, Beck. BR3 . . . . 225 DX98
Cobb Cl, Borwd. WD6 . . . . 100 CQ43
Datchet SL3 . . . . 174 AX81
Cobbett Cl, Enf. EN3 . . . . 104 DW36
Cobbett Rd, SE9 . . . . 186 EL83
Guildford GU2 . . . . 264 AS133
Twickenham TW2 . . . . 198 CA88
Cobbetts Av, Ilf. IG4 . . . . 146 EK57
Cobbetts Cl, Wok. GU21 . . . . . . 248 AV117
Cobbetts Hill, Wey. KT13 . . . . . 235 BP107
Cobbett St, SW8 . . . . 42 D5
Cobb Grn, Wat. WD25 . . . . 81 BV32
Cobbins, The, Wal.Abb. EN9 . . . 90 EE33
Cobbinsbank, Wal.Abb. EN9
off Farm Hill Rd 89 ED33
Cobbinsend Rd, Wal.Abb. EN9 . 90 EK29
Cobbins Way, Harl. CM17 . . . . . . 58 EY11
Cobble La, N1 . . . . 8 G6
Cobble Ms, N5 . . . . 144 DQ62
N6 off Highgate W Hill 142 DG60
Cobblers Cl, Farn.Royal SL2 . . 153 AP68
Cobblers Wk, E.Mol. KT8 . . . . . 219 CG95
Hampton TW12 . . . . 198 CC94
Kingston upon Thames KT2 . 219 CG95
Teddington TW11 . . . . 219 CG95
Cobbles, The, Brwd. CM15 . . . . 130 FY47
Upminster RM14 . . . . 151 FT59
Cobblestone Pl, Croy. CR0
off Oakfield Rd 224 DQ102
● Cobbold Est, NW10 . . . . . . 161 CT65
Cobbold Ms, W12
off Cobbold Rd 181 CT75
Cobbold Rd, E11 . . . . 146 EF62
NW10 . . . . 161 CT65
W12 . . . . 180 CS75
Cobb Rd, Berk. HP4 . . . . 60 AT19
Cobb's Ct, EC4
off Pilgrim St 19 H9
Cobb's Rd, Houns. TW4 . . . . . . 178 BZ84
Cobb St, E1 . . . . 20 A7
Cobden Cl, Uxb. UB8 . . . . 156 BJ67
Cobden Hill, Rad. WD7 . . . . 99 CH36
Cobden Rd, E11 . . . . 146 EE62
SE25 . . . . 224 DU99
Orpington BR6 . . . . 245 ER105
Sevenoaks TN13 . . . . 279 FJ123
COBHAM, KT11 . . . . 251 BV115
Cobham, Grays RM16 . . . . 192 GB75
⇌ Cobham & Stoke
D'Abernon 252 BY117
Cobham Av, N.Mal. KT3 . . . . . . 221 CU99
★ Cobham Bus Mus,
Cob. KT11 . . . . 235 BQ112
Cobham Cl, SW11 . . . . 202 DE86
Bromley BR2 . . . . 226 EL101
Edgware HA8 . . . . 118 CP54
Enfield EN1 . . . . 104 DU41
Greenhithe DA9 . . . . 211 FV86
Sidcup DA15 off Park Mead . 208 EV86
Slough SL1 . . . . 173 AM75
Wallington SM6 . . . . 241 DL107
H Cobham Comm Hosp,
Cob. KT11 . . . . 235 BV113
Cobham Gate, Cob. KT11 . . . . . 235 BV114
Cobham Gra, Cob. KT11
off Between Sts 235 BV114
Cobham Ho, Bark. IG11
off St. Margarets 167 EQ67
Erith DA8 off Boundary St . . 189 FF80
Cobham Ms, NW1 . . . . 7 N6
Cobham Pk, Cob. KT11 . . . . 251 BV116
Cobham Pk Rd, Cob. KT11 . . . . 251 BV117
Cobham Pl, Bexh. DA6 . . . . 208 EX85
Cobham Rd, E17 . . . . 123 EC53
N22 . . . . 143 DP55
Fetcham KT22 . . . . 253 CE122
Hounslow TW5 . . . . 178 BW80
Ilford IG3 . . . . 147 ES61
Kingston upon Thames KT1 . 220 CN95
Stoke D'Abernon KT11 . . . . . 252 CA118
Ware SG12 . . . . 55 DZ05
Cobham St, Grav. DA11 . . . . . . 213 GG87
Cobham Ter, Green. DA9
off Bean Rd 211 FV85
Cobham Way, E.Hors. KT24 . . . 267 BS126
Cobill Cl, Horn. RM11 . . . . 150 FJ56
Cobland Rd, SE12 . . . . 206 EJ91
Cobmead, Hat. AL10 . . . . 67 CV16
Coborn Rd, E3 . . . . 21 N1
Coborn St, E3 . . . . 21 P2
Sch Cobourg Prim Sch, SE5 . . . 44 A2
Cobourg Rd, SE5 . . . . 44 A2
Cobourg St, NW1 . . . . 17 M3
Cobsdene, Grav. DA12 . . . . 213 GK93
Cobs Way, New Haw KT15 . . . . 234 BJ110
Coburg Cl, SW1 . . . . 29 M8
Coburg Cres, SW2 . . . . 203 DM88
Coburg Gdns, Ilf. IG5 . . . . 124 EK54
Coburg Rd, N22 . . . . 143 DM55
Cochrane Ms, NW8 . . . . 16 B1
Cochrane Rd, SW19 . . . . 201 CZ94
Cochrane St, NW8 . . . . 16 B1
Cockayne Way, SE8 . . . . 33 M10
Cockbush Av, Hert. SG13 . . . . . . 54 DU08
Cockerell Rd, E17 . . . . 145 DY59
Cockerhurst Rd, Shore. TN14 . . 247 FD107
Cocker Rd, Enf. EN1 . . . . 104 DV36
Cockett Rd, Slou. SL3 . . . . 174 AY76
COCKFOSTERS, Barn. EN4 . . . . 102 DE42
⊖ Cockfosters 102 DG42
Cockfosters Par, Barn. EN4
off Cockfosters Rd 102 DG42
Cockfosters Rd, Barn. EN4 . . . . 102 DF40
Cock Grn, Harl. CM19 . . . . 73 EP17
Cock Hill, E1 . . . . 19 P7
Cock La, EC1 . . . . 18 G7
Broxbourne EN10 . . . . 70 DU20
Fetcham KT22 . . . . 252 CC122
Hoddesdon EN11 . . . . 71 DY19
Cockle Way, Shenley WD7 . . . . . 84 CL33
Cockmannings La, Orp. BR5 . . 228 EX102
Cockmannings Rd, Orp. BR5 . . 228 EX101
Cockpit Steps, SW1 . . . . 29 P5
Cockpit Yd, WC1 . . . . 18 D6
Cockrobin La, Harl. CM20 . . . . . 57 EN08
Ware SG12 . . . . 57 EN05
Cocks Cres, N.Mal. KT3 . . . . . . 221 CT98
Cocksett Av, Orp. BR6 . . . . 245 ES107
Cockshot Hill, Reig. RH2 . . . . . 288 DB136
Cockshot Rd, Reig. RH2 . . . . . . 288 DB135
Cockspur Ct, SW1 . . . . 29 P2
Cockspur St, SW1 . . . . 29 P2
Cocksure La, Sid. DA14 . . . . . . 208 FA90
Cock's Yd, Uxb. UB8
off Bakers Rd 156 BK66
● Coda Cen, The, SW6 . . . . 38 E5
Code St, E1 . . . . 20 B5
Codham Hall La, Gt Warley
CM13 . . . . 151 FV56
Codicote Dr, Wat. WD25 . . . . 82 BX34
Codicote Rd, Welw. AL6 . . . . 50 CL05
Wheathampstead AL4 . . . . . . 50 CL05
Codling Cl, E1 . . . . 32 D2
Codling Way, Wem. HA0 . . . . . . 139 CK63
CODMORE, Chesh. HP5 . . . . 76 AS29
Codmore Cres, Chesh. HP5 . . . . 76 AS30
Codmore Wd Rd, Chesh. HP5 . . 78 AW33
Codrington Ct, Wok. GU21
off Raglan Rd 248 AT118
Codrington Cres, Grav. DA12 . . 213 GJ92
Codrington Gdns, Grav. DA12 . 213 GK92
Codrington Hill, SE23 . . . . 205 DY87
Codrington Ms, W11 . . . . 14 F9
Cody Cl, Har. HA3 . . . . 139 CK55
Wallington SM6
off Alcock Cl 241 DK108
Cody Rd, E16 . . . . 23 H5
● Cody Rd Business Cen, E16 . 23 H5
Coe Av, SE25 . . . . 224 DU100
Coe's All, Barn. EN5
off Wood St 101 CY42
Coe Spur, Slou. SL1 . . . . 173 AP75
Coffey St, SE8 . . . . 46 B4
Coftards, Slou. SL2 . . . . 154 AW72
Cogan Av, E17 . . . . 123 DY53
Cohen Cl, Chsht EN8 . . . . 89 DY31
Coin St, SE1 . . . . 30 E2
Coity Rd, NW5 . . . . 7 H4
Cokers La, SE21
off Perifield 204 DQ88
Coke's Fm La, Ch.St.G. HP8 . . . . 94 AV41
Coke's La, Amer. HP7 . . . . 94 AW41
Chalfont St. Giles HP8 . . . . . . 94 AU42
Coke St, E1 . . . . 20 C8
Colas Ms, NW6 . . . . 5 K8
Colbeck Ms, SW7 . . . . 27 M9
Colbeck Rd, Har. HA1 . . . . 138 CC59
Colberg Pl, N16 . . . . 144 DS59
Colborne Way, Wor.Pk. KT4 . . . 221 CW104
Colbrook Av, Hayes UB3 . . . . . . 177 BR76
Colbrook Cl, Hayes UB3 . . . . . . 177 BR76
Colburn Av, Cat. CR3 . . . . 258 DT124
Pinner HA5 . . . . 116 BY51
Colburn Cres, Guil. GU4
off Sutherland Dr 265 BA131
Colburn Way, Sutt. SM1 . . . . . . 222 DD104
Colby Ms, SE19
off Gipsy Hill 204 DS92
Colby Rd, SE19 . . . . 204 DS92
Walton-on-Thames KT12
off Winchester Rd 217 BU102
Colchester Av, E12 . . . . 147 EM62
Colchester Dr, Pnr. HA5 . . . . . . 138 BX57
Colchester Rd, E10 . . . . 145 EC59
E17 . . . . 145 EA58
Edgware HA8 . . . . 118 CQ52
Northwood HA6 . . . . 115 BU54
Romford RM3 . . . . 128 FK53
Colchester St, E1 . . . . 20 B8
Colcokes Rd, Bans. SM7 . . . . . . 256 DA116
Cold Arbor Rd, Sev. TN13 . . . . . 278 FD124
Coldbath Sq, EC1 . . . . 18 E4
Coldbath St, SE13 . . . . 46 D7
COLDBLOW, Bex. DA5 . . . . 209 FC89
Cold Blow Cres, Bex. DA5 . . . . . 209 FD88
Cold Blow La, SE14 . . . . 45 K3
Cold Blows, Mitch. CR4 . . . . . . 222 DF97
Coldershaw Rd, W13 . . . . 159 CG74
Coldfall Av, N10 . . . . 120 DF54
Sch Coldfall Prim Sch, N10
off Coldfall Av 120 DF54
Coldham Gro, Enf. EN3 . . . . 105 DY37
Cold Harbour, E14 . . . . 34 F3
Coldharbour Cl, Egh. TW20 . . . 215 BC97
Coldharbour Crest, SE9
off Great Harry Dr 207 EN90
Coldharbour La, SE5 . . . . 183 DN84
SW9 . . . . 183 DN84
Bletchingley RH1 . . . . 274 DT134
Bushey WD23 . . . . 98 CB44
Dorking RH4, RH5 . . . . 285 CG138
Egham TW20 . . . . 215 BC97
Hayes UB3 . . . . 157 BU73
Purley CR8 . . . . 241 DN110
Rainham RM13 . . . . 169 FE72
Woking GU22 . . . . 249 BF115
● Coldharbour La Ind Est,
SE5 off Coldharbour La 43 K9
● Coldharbour Pinnacles Est,
Harl. CM19 . . . . 73 EM16
Coldharbour Pl, SE5 . . . . 43 L8
Coldharbour Rd, Croy. CR0 . . . . 241 DN106
Harlow CM19 . . . . 73 EM16
Northfleet DA11 . . . . 212 GE89
West Byfleet KT14 . . . . 233 BF114
Woking GU22 . . . . 249 BF115
Coldharbour Way, Croy. CR0 . . 241 DN106
Coldmoreham Yd, Amer. HP7 . . 77 AM39
Coldshott, Oxt. RH8 . . . . 276 EG133
Coldstream Gdns, SW18 . . . . . . 201 CZ86
Coldstream Rd, Cat. CR3 . . . . . 258 DQ121
Cole Av, Chad.St.M. RM16 . . . . . 193 GJ77
Colebeck Ms, N1 . . . . 9 H5
Colebert Av, E1 . . . . 20 G4
Colebrook, Ott. KT16 . . . . 233 BD107
Colebrook Cl, NW7 . . . . 119 CX52
SW15 . . . . 201 CX87
Colebrooke Av, W13 . . . . 159 CH72
Colebrooke Dr, E11 . . . . 146 EH59
Colebrooke Pl, N1 . . . . 9 H9
Colebrooke Ri, Brom. BR2 . . . . 226 EE96
Colebrooke Rd, Red. RH1 . . . . . 272 DE132
Colebrooke Row, N1 . . . . 18 G1
Colebrook Gdns, Loug. IG10 . . . 107 EP40
Colebrook Ho, E14 . . . . 22 B8
Colebrook La, Loug. IG10 . . . . . 107 EP40
Colebrook Path, Loug. IG10 . . . 107 EP40
Colebrook Pl, Ott. KT16 . . . . . . 233 BB108
Colebrook Rd, SW16 . . . . 223 DL95
Colebrook St, Erith DA8 . . . . . . 189 FF78
Colebrook Way, N11 . . . . 121 DH50
Coleby Path, SE5 . . . . 43 M5
Colechurch Ho, SE1
off Avondale Sq 44 C1
Cole Cl, SE28 . . . . 168 EV74
Coledale Dr, Stan. HA7 . . . . 117 CJ53
Coleford Rd, SW18 . . . . 202 DC85
Cole Gdns, Houns. TW5 . . . . 177 BU80
Sch Colegrave Prim Sch, E15 . . . 13 H3
Colegrave Rd, E15 . . . . 12 G2
COLE GREEN, Hert. SG14 . . . . . . 52 DG12
Cole Grn Bypass, Hert. SG14 . . . 52 DF12
Cole Grn La, Welw.G.C. AL7 . . . . 52 DB11
Cole Grn Way, Hert. SG14 . . . . . . 53 DK12
Colegrove Rd, SE15 . . . . 44 B3
Coleherne Ct, SW5 . . . . 39 M1
Coleherne Ms, SW10 . . . . 39 L1
Coleherne Rd, SW10 . . . . 39 L1
Colehill Gdns, SW6 . . . . 38 E7
Colehill La, SW6 . . . . 38 E7
Colekitchen La, Goms. GU5 . . . 283 BR136
Coleman Cl, SE25 . . . . 224 DU96
Coleman Flds, N1 . . . . 9 K8
COLEMAN GREEN, St.Alb. AL4 . 50 CM10
Coleman Grn La, Wheat. AL4 . . . 50 CM10
Coleman Rd, SE5 . . . . 43 N4
Belvedere DA17 . . . . 188 FA77
Dagenham RM9 . . . . 168 EY65
Colemans Heath, SE9 . . . . 207 EP90
Coleman's La, Lwr Naze. EN9 . . 89 ED26
Colemans La, Ong. CM5 . . . . 93 FH30
Coleman St, EC2 . . . . 19 L8
Colenorton Cres, Eton Wick
SL4 . . . . 173 AL77
Colenso Dr, NW7 . . . . 119 CU52
Colenso Rd, E5 . . . . 144 DW63
Ilford IG2 . . . . 147 ES60
Cole Pk Gdns, Twick. TW1 . . . . . 199 CG86
Cole Pk Rd, Twick. TW1 . . . . 199 CG86
Cole Pk Vw, Twick. TW1
off Hill Vw Rd 199 CG86
Colepits Wd Rd, SE9 . . . . 207 EQ85
Sch Coleraine Pk Prim Sch,
N17 off Glendish Rd 122 DV53
Coleraine Rd, N8 . . . . 143 DN55
SE3 . . . . 47 L3
Coleridge Av, E12 . . . . 166 EL65
Sutton SM1 . . . . 240 DE105
Coleridge Cl, SW8 . . . . 41 K9
Cheshunt EN7 . . . . 88 DT27
Coleridge Cres, Colnbr. SL3 . . . 175 BE81
Coleridge Gdns, NW6 . . . . 5 N7
SW10 . . . . 39 M4
Coleridge Ho, SW1 . . . . 41 L1
Coleridge La, N8 . . . . 143 DL58
Sch Coleridge Prim Sch, N8
off Crouch End Hill 143 DK59
Coleridge Rd, E17 . . . . 145 DZ56
N4 . . . . 143 DN61
N8 . . . . 143 DK58
N12 . . . . 120 DC50
Ashford TW15 . . . . 196 BL91
Croydon CR0 . . . . 224 DW101
Dartford DA1 . . . . 190 FN84
Romford RM3 . . . . 127 FH52
Tilbury RM18 . . . . 193 GJ82
Coleridge Sq, SW10 . . . . 39 N4
W13 . . . . 159 CG72
Coleridge Wk, NW11 . . . . 142 DA56
Hutton CM13 . . . . 131 GC45
Coleridge Way, Borwd. WD6 . . . 100 CN42
Hayes UB4 . . . . 157 BU72
Orpington BR6 . . . . 228 EU100

Coleridge Way, West Dr. UB7 176 BM77
Cole Rd, Twick. TW1 199 CG86
Watford WD17 97 BV39
Colesburg Rd, Beck. BR3 225 DZ97
Coles Cres, Har. HA2 138 CB61
Colescroft Hill, Pur. CR8 257 DN115
Colesdale, Cuffley EN6 87 DL30
Coles Grn, Bushey Hth WD23 116 CC46
Loughton IG10 107 EN39
Coles Grn Ct, NW2 141 CU61
Coles Grn Rd, NW2 141 CU60
COLESHILL, Amer. HP7 77 AM43
Coles Hill, Hem.H. HP1 62 BG18
Coleshill C of E Inf Sch, Colesh. HP7
off Village Rd 77 AM44
Coleshill Flats, SW1
off Pimlico Rd 29 H9
Coleshill La, Winch.Hill HP7 110 AJ45
Coleshill Rd, Tedd. TW11 199 CE93
Coles La, Brasted TN16 262 EW123
Colesmead Rd, Red. RH1 272 DF131
COLES MEADS, Red. RH1 272 DF131
Colestown St, SW11 40 D8
Cole St, SE1 31 K5
Colet Cl, N13 121 DP51
Colet Gdns, W14 26 D10
Colet Rd, Hutt. CM13 131 GC43
Colets Orchard, Otford TN14 263 FH116
Coley Av, Wok. GU22 249 BA118
Coley St, WC1 18 D5
Colfe Rd, SE23 205 DY88
Colfe's Sch, SE12
off Horn Pk La 206 EH86
Colgate Pl, Enf. EN3 105 EA37
Colgrove, Welw.G.C. AL8 51 CW10
Colham Av, West Dr. UB7 156 BL74
Colham Grn Rd, Uxb. UB8 156 BN71
Colham Manor Prim Sch, Hlgdn UB8 off Violet Av 156 BN72
Colham Mill Rd, West Dr. UB7 176 BK75
Colham Rd, Uxb. UB8 156 BM70
Colham Rbt, Uxb. UB8 156 BN73
Colina Ms, N15 143 DP56
Colina Rd, N15 143 DP57
Colin Cl, NW9 140 CS56
Croydon CR0 225 DZ104
Dartford DA2 210 FP86
West Wickham BR4 226 EF104
Colin Cres, NW9 141 CT56
Colindale 140 CS55
Colindale Av, NW9 140 CR55
St. Albans AL1 65 CF22
Colindale Business Pk, NW9 140 CQ55
Colindale Prim Sch, NW9
off Poolsford Rd 141 CT56
Colindeep Gdns, NW4 141 CU57
Colindeep La, NW4 140 CS55
NW9 140 CS55
Colin Dr, NW9 141 CT57
Colinette Rd, SW15 181 CW84
Colin Gdns, NW9 141 CT57
Colin Par, NW9
off Edgware Rd 140 CS56
Colin Pk Rd, NW9 140 CS56
Colin Rd, NW10 161 CU65
Caterham CR3 258 DU123
Colinsdale, N1 8 G9
Colinton Rd, Ilf. IG3 148 EV61
Colin Way, Slou. SL1 173 AP76
Coliston Pas, SW18
off Coliston Rd 202 DA87
Coliston Rd, SW18 202 DA87
Collamore Av, SW18 202 DE88
Collapit Cl, Har. HA1 138 CB57
Collard Av, Loug. IG10 107 EQ40
Collard Cl, Ken. CR8 258 DS120
Collard Grn, Loug. IG10 107 EQ40
Collard Pl, NW1 7 J6
College App, SE10 46 F3
College Av, Egh. TW20 195 BB93
Epsom KT17 239 CT114
Grays RM17 192 GB77
Harrow HA3 117 CE53
Slough SL1 174 AS76
College Cl, E9 10 G2
N18 122 DT50
Grays RM17 192 GC78
Harrow HA3 117 CE52
North Mymms AL9 85 CX28
Twickenham TW2 199 CD88
Ware SG12 55 DX07
College Ct, Chsht EN8 88 DW30
College Cres, NW3 6 A5
Redhill RH1 272 DG131
Windsor SL4 173 AP82
College Cross, N1 8 F7
College Dr, Ruis. HA4 137 BU59
Thames Ditton KT7 219 CE101
College Gdns, E4 123 EB45
N18 122 DT50
SE21 204 DS88
SW17 202 DE89
Enfield EN2 104 DR39
Ilford IG4 146 EL57
New Malden KT3 221 CT99
College Gate, Harl. CM20 73 EQ15
College Grn, SE19 204 DS94
College Gro, NW1 7 N9
College Hill, EC4 19 K10
College Hill Rd, Har. HA3 117 CF53
College La, NW5 143 DH63
Hatfield AL10 66 CS20
Woking GU22 248 AW119
College Ms, SW1 30 A6
SW18 off St. Ann's Hill 202 DB85
★ College of Arms, EC4 19 H10
College of Law, The, Bloomsbury Cen, WC1 17 N6
Bream's Bldgs, EC4 18 E8
Moorgate Cen, EC1 19 L5
Guildford GU3
off Portsmouth Rd 280 AW138
College of N E London, The, Tottenham Cen, N15
off High Rd 144 DT56
Tottenham Grn Cen, N15
off Town Hall App Rd 144 DT56
College of N W London, Kilburn Cen, NW6 5 J8
College of N W London, Wembley Pk Cen, Wem. HA9 off North End Rd 140 CN62
Willesden Cen, NW10
off Dudden Hill La 141 CT64
College Pk Cl, SE13 185 ED84
College Pk Rd, N17
off College Rd 122 DT51
College Pk Sch, W2 15 L9
College Pl, E17 146 EE56
NW1 7 M9
SW10 39 N4
Greenhithe DA9 191 FW84
St. Albans AL3 64 CC20
College Pt, E15 13 L4
College Rd, E17 145 EC57
N17 122 DT51
N21 121 DN47
NW10 14 A1
SE19 204 DT92
SE21 204 DS87
SW19 202 DD93
W13 159 CH72
Abbots Langley WD5 81 BT31
Bromley BR1 206 EG94
Cheshunt EN8 88 DV30
Croydon CR0 224 DR103
Enfield EN2 104 DR40
Epsom KT17 239 CU114
Grays RM17 192 GC77
Guildford GU1 280 AX135
Harrow on the Hill HA1 139 CE58
Harrow Weald HA3 117 CE53
Hertford Heath SG13 54 DW13
Hoddesdon EN11 71 DZ15
Isleworth TW7 179 CF81
Northfleet DA11 212 GB85
St. Albans AL1 65 CH21
Slough SL1 153 AM74
Swanley BR8 229 FE95
Wembley HA9 139 CK60
Woking GU22 249 BB116
College Row, E9 11 J3
College Slip, Brom. BR1 226 EG95
College Sq, Harl. CM20
off College Gate 73 ER15
College St, EC4 19 K10
St. Albans AL3 65 CD20
College Ter, E3 21 N2
N3 off Hendon La 119 CZ54
College Vw, SE9 206 EK88
College Wk, Kings.T. KT1
off Grange Rd 220 CL97
College Way, Ashf. TW15 196 BM91
Hayes UB3 157 BU73
Northwood HA6 115 BR51
Welwyn Garden City AL8 51 CX08
College Yd, NW5 7 K1
Watford WD24
off Gammons La 97 BV38
Collent St, E9 11 H5
Coller Cres, Lane End DA2 211 FS91
Colless Rd, N15 144 DT57
Collet Cl, Chsht EN8 89 DX28
Collet Gdns, Chsht EN8
off Collet Cl 89 DX28
Collett Ho, N16
off Stamford Hill 144 DT60
Collett Rd, SE16 32 D7
Hemel Hempstead HP1 62 BJ20
Ware SG12 55 DX05
Collett Sch, The, Hem.H. HP1 off Lockers Pk La 62 BH19
Collett Way, Sthl. UB2 158 CB74
Colley Hill La, Hedg. SL2 134 AT62
Colleyland, Chorl. WD3 95 BD42
Colley La, Reig. RH2 271 CY132
Colley Manor Dr, Reig. RH2 271 CX133
Colley Way, Reig. RH2 271 CY131
Collier Cl, E6 25 N10
Epsom KT19 238 CN107
Collier Dr, Edg. HA8 118 CN54
COLLIER ROW, Rom. RM5 126 FA53
Collier Row La, Rom. RM5 127 FB52
Collier Row Rd, Rom. RM5 126 EZ53
Colliers, Cat. CR3 274 DU125
Colliers Cl, Wok. GU21 248 AV117
Colliers Shaw, Kes. BR2 244 EK105
Collier St, N1 18 C1
Colliers Water La, Th.Hth. CR7 223 DN99
COLLIER'S WOOD, SW19 202 DD94
Colliers Wood 202 DD94
Collier Way, Guil. GU4 265 BD132
Collindale Av, Erith DA8 189 FB79
Sidcup DA15 208 EU88
Collingbourne Rd, W12 161 CV74
Collingham Gdns, SW5 27 M9
Collingham Pl, SW5 27 L9
Collingham Rd, SW5 27 M8
Collingham Sch, SW5 27 M9
Collings Cl, N22
off Whittington Rd 121 DM51
Collington Cl, Nthflt DA11
off Beresford Rd 212 GE87
Collington St, SE10 47 H1
Collingtree Rd, SE26 204 DW91
Collingwood Av, N10 142 DG55
Surbiton KT5 220 CQ102
Collingwood Cl, SE20 224 DV95
Horley RH6 291 DH147
Twickenham TW2 198 CA86
Collingwood Cres, Guil. GU1 265 BA133
Collingwood Dr, Lon.Col. AL2 83 CK25
Collingwood Pl, Walt. KT12 217 BU104
Collingwood Rd, E17 145 EA58
N15 144 DS56
Mitcham CR4 222 DE96
Rainham RM13 169 FF68
Sutton SM1 222 DA104
Uxbridge UB8 157 BP70
Collingwood Sch, Jun Dept, Wall. SM6 off Maldon Rd 241 DH106
Sen Dept, Wall. SM6
off Springfield Rd 241 DH106
Collingwood St, E1 20 F4
Collins Av, Stan. HA7 118 CL54
Collins Dr, Ruis. HA4 138 BW61
Collins Meadow, Harl. CM19 73 EP15
Collinson Ct, Enf. EN3
off The Generals Wk 105 DY37
Collinson St, SE1 31 J5
Collinson Wk, SE1 31 J5
Collins Rd, N5 144 DQ63
Collins Sq, SE3 47 L9
Collins St, SE3 47 K9
Collins Way, Hutt. CM13 131 GE43
Collinswood Rd, Farn.Com. SL2 133 AN60
Collin's Yd, N1 8 G9
Collinwood Av, Enf. EN3 104 DW41
Collinwood Gdns, Ilf. IG5 147 EM57
Collis All, Twick. TW2
off The Green 199 CE88
Collison Pl, N16 144 DS61
Collis Prim Sch, Tedd. TW11 off Fairfax Rd 199 CH93
Colls Rd, SE15 44 G6
Collum Grn Rd, Slou. SL2 133 AR62
Collyer Av, Croy. CR0 241 DL105
Collyer Pl, SE15 44 C7
Collyer Rd, Croy. CR0 241 DL105
London Colney AL2 83 CJ27
Colman Cl, Epsom KT18 255 CW117
Colman Rd, E16 24 C7
Colmans Hill, Peasl. GU5 283 BS144
Colman Way, Red. RH1 272 DE132
Colmar Cl, E1 21 J4
Colmer Pl, Har. HA3 117 CD52
Colmer Rd, SW16 223 DL95
Colmore Ms, SE15 44 F7
Colmore Rd, Enf. EN3 104 DW42
COLNBROOK, Slou. SL3 175 BD80
Colnbrook Bypass, Slou. SL3 175 BF80
West Drayton UB7 175 BF80
Colnbrook Cl, Lon.Col. AL2 84 CL27
Colnbrook C of E Prim Sch, Colnbr. SL3 off High St 175 BD80
Colnbrook Ct, Slou. SL3 175 BF81
Colnbrook Sch, S.Oxhey WD19 off Hayling Rd 116 BW48
Colnbrook St, SE1 30 G7
Colndale Rd, Colnbr. SL3 175 BE82
Colne Av, Mill End WD3 114 BG47
Watford WD19 97 BV44
West Drayton UB7 176 BJ75
Colne Bk, Horton SL3 175 BC83
Colnebridge Cl, Stai. TW18
off Clarence St 195 BE91
Colne Br Retail Pk, Wat. WD17 off Lower High St 98 BX43
Colne Cl, S.Ock. RM15 171 FW73
Colne Ct, Epsom KT19 238 CQ105
Colnedale Rd, Uxb. UB8 136 BK64
Colne Dr, Rom. RM3 128 FM51
Walton-on-Thames KT12 218 BX104
Colne Gdns, Lon.Col. AL2 84 CL27
Colne Ho, Bark. IG11 167 EP65
Colne Mead, Mill End WD3
off Uxbridge Rd 114 BG47
Colne Orchard, Iver SL0 155 BF72
Colne Pk Caravan Site, West Dr. UB7 176 BJ77
Colne Reach, Stai. TW19 195 BF85
Colne Rd, E5 11 L1
N21 122 DR45
Twickenham TW1, TW2 199 CE88
Colne St, E13 23 N3
Colne Valley, Upmin. RM14 151 FS58
Colne Way, Hem.H. HP2 62 BM15
Staines TW19 195 BB90
Watford WD24, WD25 98 BW36
Colney Flds Shop Pk, Lon.Col. AL2 84 CM28
Colney Hatch La, N10 120 DG52
N11 120 DF51
COLNEY HEATH, St.Alb. AL4 66 CR22
Colney Heath La, St.Alb. AL4 66 CL20
Colney Heath Sch, Coln.Hth AL4 off High St 66 CQ22
Colney Rd, Dart. DA1 210 FM86
COLNEY STREET, St.Alb. AL2 83 CE31
Cologne Rd, SW11 182 DD84
Coloma Conv Girls' Sch, Croy. CR0 off Upper Shirley Rd 225 DX104
Colombo Rd, Ilf. IG1 147 EQ60
Colombo St, SE1 30 G3
Colomb St, SE10 47 K1
Colonels La, Cher. KT16 216 BG100
Colonels Wk, Enf. EN2 103 DP40
Colonial Av, Twick. TW2 198 CC85
Colonial Dr, W4 180 CQ77
Colonial Rd, Felt. TW14 197 BS87
Slough SL1 174 AU75
Colonial Way, Wat. WD24 98 BX39
Colonnade, WC1 18 A5
Colonnade Wk, SW1 29 J9
Colonsay, Hem.H. HP3 63 BQ22
Colony Ms, N1
off Mildmay Gro N 9 M3
Colorado Apts, N8
off Great Amwell La 143 DM55
Colorado Bldg, SE13
off Deals Gateway 46 C7
Colosseum Ter, NW1
off Albany St 17 K4
Colson Gdns, Loug. IG10 107 EN42
Colson Grn, Loug. IG10
off Colson Rd 107 EP42
Colson Path, Loug. IG10 107 EN42
Colson Rd, Croy. CR0 224 DS103
Loughton IG10 107 EP42
Colson Way, SW16 203 DJ91
Colsterworth Rd, N15 144 DT56
Colston Av, Cars. SM5 240 DE105
Colston Cl, Cars. SM5
off West St 240 DF105
Colston Cres, Goffs Oak EN7 87 DP27
Colston Rd, E7 166 EK65
SW14 180 CQ84
Colt Hatch, Harl. CM20 57 EP13
Colthurst Cres, N4 144 DQ61
Colthurst Dr, N9 122 DV48
Colthurst Gdns, Hodd. EN11 71 ED15
Coltishall Rd, Horn. RM12 170 FJ65
Coltman St, E14 21 M7
Colt Ms, Enf. EN3 105 EA37
Coltness Cres, SE2 188 EV78
Colton Gdns, N17 144 DQ55
Colton Rd, Har. HA1 139 CE57
Coltsfoot, Welw.G.C. AL7 52 DB11
Coltsfoot, The, Hem.H. HP1 61 BE21
Coltsfoot Ct, Grays RM17 192 GD79
Coltsfoot Dr, Guil. GU1 265 BA131
West Drayton UB7 156 BL72
Coltsfoot La, Oxt. RH8 276 EF133
Coltsfoot Path, Rom. RM3 128 FJ52
Columbas Dr, NW3 142 DD60
Columbia Av, Edg. HA8 118 CP53
Ruislip HA4 137 BV60
Worcester Park KT4 221 CT101
Columbia Pt, SE16 33 H6
Columbia Prim Sch, E2 20 B2
Columbia Rd, E2 20 A2
E13 23 M6
Broxbourne EN10 89 DY26
Columbia Sq, SW14
off Upper Richmond Rd W 180 CQ84
Columbia Wf Rd, Grays RM17 192 GA79
Columbine Av, E6 24 G7
South Croydon CR2 241 DP108
Columbine Way, SE13 46 E9
Romford RM3 128 FL53
Columbus Ct, SE16
off Rotherhithe St 33 H3
Columbus Ctyd, E14 34 A2
Columbus Gdns, Nthwd. HA6 115 BU53
Columbus Sq, Erith DA8 189 FF79
Colva Wk, N19 off Chester Rd 143 DH61
Colvestone Cres, E8 10 A3
Colvestone Prim Sch, E8 10 A3
Colview Ct, SE9
off Mottingham La 206 EK88
Colville Est, N1 9 N9
Colville Gdns, W11 15 H9
Colville Hos, W11 14 G8
Colville Ms, W11 15 H9
Colville Pl, W1 17 M7
Colville Prim Sch, W11 15 H9
Colville Rd, E11 145 EC62
E17 123 DY54
N9 122 DV46
W3 180 CP76
W11 15 H9
Colville Sq, W11 14 G9
Colville Ter, W11 14 G9
Colvin Cl, SE26 204 DW92
Colvin Gdns, E4 123 EC48
E11 146 EH56
Ilford IG6 125 EQ53
Waltham Cross EN8 105 DX35
Colvin Rd, E6 166 EL66
Thornton Heath CR7 223 DN99
Colwall Gdns, Wdf.Grn. IG8 124 EG50
Colwell Rd, SE22 204 DT85
Colwick Cl, N6 143 DK59
Colwith Rd, W6 38 B3
Colwood Gdns, SW19 202 DD94
Colworth Gro, SE17 31 K9
Colworth Rd, E11 146 EE58
Croydon CR0 224 DU102
Colwyn Av, Perivale UB6 159 CF68
Colwyn Cl, SW16 203 DJ92
Colwyn Cres, Houns. TW3 178 CC81
Colwyn Grn, NW9
off Snowdon Dr 140 CS58
Colwyn Ho, SE1
off Briant Est 30 E7
Colwyn Rd, NW2 141 CV62
Colyer Cl, N1 8 D10
SE9 207 EP89
Colyer Rd, Nthflt DA11 212 GC89
Colyers Cl, Erith DA8 189 FD81
Colyers La, Erith DA8 189 FC81
Colyers Prim Sch, Erith DA8 off Colyers La 189 FD81
Colyers Wk, Erith DA8
off Colyers La 189 FE81
Colyton Cl, Well. DA16 188 EX81
Wembley HA0
off Bridgewater Rd 159 CJ65
Woking GU21 248 AW118
Colyton La, SW16 203 DN92
Colyton Rd, SE22 204 DV85
Colyton Way, N18 122 DU50
Combe, The, NW1 17 K3
Combe Av, SE3 47 M4
Combe Bk Dr, Sund. TN14 262 EY122
Combe Bk Sch, Sund. TN14
off Combe Bk Dr 262 EY123
Combe Bottom, Guil. GU5 282 BM137
Combedale Rd, SE10 35 N10
Combe La, Guil. GU5 283 BP135
Combemartin Rd, SW18 201 CY87
Combe Ms, SE3 47 L4
Comber Cl, NW2 141 CV62
Comber Gro, SE5 43 J6
Comber Gro Prim Sch, SE5 43 J5
Comber Ho, SE5
off Comber Gro 43 K5
Combermere Cl, Wind. SL4 173 AP82
Combermere Rd, SW9 42 C10
Morden SM4 222 DB100
Combe Rd, Gdmg. GU7 280 AS143
Watford WD18 97 BT44
Comberton Rd, E5 144 DV61
Combeside, SE18 187 ET80
Combe St, Hem.H. HP1 62 BJ20
Combwell Cres, SE2 188 EU76
Comely Bk Rd, E17 145 EC57
Comeragh Cl, Wok. GU22 248 AU119
Comeragh Ms, W14 26 F10
Comeragh Rd, W14 38 E1
Comer Cres, Sthl. UB2
off Windmill Av 178 CC75
Comerford Rd, SE4 185 DY84
Comer Ho, Barn. EN5
off Station Rd 102 DC42
Comet Cl, E12 146 EK63
Purfleet RM19 190 FN77
Watford WD25 81 BT34
Comet Pl, SE8 46 A5
Comet Rd, Hat. AL10 67 CT18
Stanwell TW19 196 BK87
Comet St, SE8 46 A5
Comet Way, Hat. AL9, AL10 66 CS19
Comforts Fm Av, Oxt. RH8 276 EF133
Comfort St, SE15 43 N3
Comfrey Ct, Grays RM17 192 GD79
Commerce Rd, N22 121 DM53
Brentford TW8 179 CJ80
Commerce Way, Croy. CR0 223 DM103
Commercial Pl, Grav. DA12 213 GJ86
Commercial Rd, E1 20 C8
E14 21 M9
N17 122 DS51
N18 122 DS50
Guildford GU1 280 AX135
Staines TW18 196 BG93
Commercial St, E1 20 A5
Commercial Way, NW10 160 CP68
SE15 44 A5
Woking GU21 249 AZ117
Commerell St, SE10 35 K10
Commodity Quay, E1 32 B1
Commodore Ho, SW18
off Juniper Dr 182 DC84
Commodore St, E1 21 L5
Common, The, E15 13 L4
W5 160 CL73
Ashtead KT21 253 CK116
Berkhamsted HP4 61 AZ17
Chipperfield WD4 80 BG32
Hatfield AL10 67 CU17
Kings Langley WD4 80 BN28
Penn HP10 110 AC46
Richmond TW10 199 CK90
Shalford GU4 280 AY141
Common, The, Sthl. UB2 178 BW77
Stanmore HA7 117 CE47
West Drayton UB7 176 BJ77
Wonersh GU5 281 BB143
Common Cl, Wok. GU21 232 AX114
Commondale, SW15 38 A9
Commonfield Rd, Bans. SM7 240 DA114
Commonfields, Harl. CM20 57 ES13
Common Gdns, Pott.End HP4 61 BB17
Common Gate Rd, Chorl. WD3 95 BD43
Common La, Burn. SL1 133 AK62
Claygate KT10 237 CG108
Dartford DA2 209 FG89
Eton SL4 173 AQ78
Kings Langley WD4 80 BM28
Letchmore Heath WD25 99 CE39
New Haw KT15 234 BJ109
Radlett WD7 99 CE39
Commonmeadow La, Ald. WD25 82 CB33
Common Mile Cl, SW4 203 DK85
Common Rd, SW13 181 CU83
Chorleywood WD3 95 BD42
Claygate KT10 237 CG107
Dorney SL4 172 AJ77
Eton Wick SL4 173 AM78
Ingrave CM13 131 GC50
Langley SL3 175 BA77
Leatherhead KT23 252 BY121
Redhill RH1 288 DF136
Stanmore HA7 117 CD49
Waltham Abbey EN9 72 EK22
Commons, The, Welw.G.C. AL7 52 DA12
Commonside, Bkhm KT23 252 CA122
Epsom KT18 254 CN115
Keston BR2 244 EJ105
Commonside Cl, Couls. CR5 257 DP120
Sutton SM2 240 DB111
Commonside E, Mitch. CR4 222 DF97
Commonside Rd, Harl. CM18 73 ES19
Commonside W, Mitch. CR4 222 DF97
Commons La, Hem.H. HP2 62 BL19
Commons Wd Caravan Club, Welw.G.C. AL7 52 DA13
Commonswood Sch, Welw.G.C. AL7 off The Commons 52 DB12
Commonwealth Av, W12 161 CV73
Hayes UB3 157 BR72
Commonwealth Rd, N17 122 DU52
Caterham CR3 258 DU123
Commonwealth Way, SE2 188 EV78
COMMONWOOD, Kings L. WD4 80 BH34
Common Wd, Farn.Com. SL2 133 AQ63
Commonwood La, Kings L. WD4 96 BH35
Common Wd La, Penn HP10 110 AD46
Community Cl, Uxb. UB10 137 BQ62
Community Coll Hackney, London Flds, E8 10 F7
Shoreditch Campus, N1 19 P2
Community Ed Lewisham, Brockley Cen, SE23
off Brockley Ri 205 DY88
Granville Pk Adult Learning Cen, SE13 46 F10
Grove Pk Cen, SE12
off Pragnell Rd 206 EH89
Holbeach Cen, SE6
off Doggett Rd 205 EA87
Mornington Cen, SE8 45 P5
Community La, N7 7 N2
Community Learning & Skills Service Friday Hill Cen, E4
off Simmons La 124 EE47
Community Rd, E15 13 H3
Greenford UB6 158 CC67
Community Wk, Esher KT10
off High St 236 CC105
Community Way, Crox.Grn WD3 off Barton Way 97 BP43
Como Rd, SE23 205 DY89
Como St, Rom. RM7 149 FD57
Compass Cl, Ashf. TW15 197 BQ94
Edgware HA8
off Glendale Av 118 CM49
Compass Hill, Rich. TW10 199 CK86
Compass Ho, SW18
off Smugglers Way 182 DB84
Compass La, Brom. BR1
off North St 226 EG95
Compass Pt, Nthch HP4
off Chapel Crfts 60 AS17
Compayne Gdns, NW6 5 L6
Comport Grn, New Adgtn CR0 244 EE112
Compton Av, E6 166 EK68
N1 8 G5
N6 142 DE59
Hutton CM13 131 GC46
Romford RM2 149 FH55
Wembley HA0 139 CJ63
Compton Cl, E3 22 B6
NW1 17 K3
NW11 141 CX62
SE15 44 C5
W13 159 CG72
Edgware HA8 118 CQ52
Esher KT10 236 CC106
Compton Ct, SE19
off Victoria Cres 204 DS92
Slough SL1
off Brook Cres 153 AL72
Compton Cres, N17 122 DQ52
W4 180 CQ79
Chessington KT9 238 CL107
Northolt UB5 158 BX67
Compton Gdns, Add. KT15
off Monks Cres 234 BH106
St. Albans AL2 82 CB26
Compton Ho, SW11
off Parkham St 40 C6
Compton Pas, EC1 19 H4
Compton Pl, WC1 18 A4
Erith DA8 189 FF79
Watford WD19 116 BY48
Compton Ri, Pnr. HA5 138 BY57
Compton Rd, N1 9 H5
N21 121 DN46
NW10 14 C3
SW19 201 CZ93
Croydon CR0 224 DV102
Hayes UB3 157 BS73
Compton Sch, The, N12
off Summers La 120 DE51
Compton St, EC1 18 G4
Compton Ter, N1 8 G5
Comreddy Cl, Enf. EN2 103 DP39
Comus Pl, SE17 31 N9
Comyne Rd, Wat. WD24 97 BT36
Comyn Rd, SW11 182 DE84

Comyns, The, Bushey Hth WD23 116 CC46
Comyns Cl, E16 23 L6
Comyns Rd, Dag. RM9 168 FA66
Conant Ms, E1 20 C10
Conaways Cl, Epsom KT17 239 CU110
Concanon Rd, SW2 183 DM84
Concert Hall App, SE1 30 D3
● Concord Business Cen, W3 off Concord Rd 160 CP71
Concord Cl, Nthlt. UB5 158 BY69
Concorde Cl, Houns. TW3 178 CB82
Uxbridge UB10 156 BL68
Concorde Ct, Wind. SL4 off Green La 173 AN82
Concorde Dr, E6 25 J7
Hemel Hempstead HP2 62 BK20
Concorde Way, SE16 33 J9
Slough SL1 173 AQ75
Concord Rd, W3 160 CP70
Enfield EN3 104 DW43
Concord Ter, Har. HA2 off Coles Cres 138 CB61
Concourse, The, N9 off Edmonton Grn Shop Cen 122 DU47
NW9 119 CT53
Concrete Cotts, Wisley GU23 off Wisley La 250 BL116
Condell Rd, SW8 41 M7
Conder St, E14 21 L8
Condor Ct, Guil. GU2 off Millmead Ter 280 AW136
Condor Path, Nthlt. UB5 off Brabazon Rd 158 CA68
Condor Rd, Stai. TW18 216 BH97
Condor Wk, Horn. RM12 off Heron Flight Av 169 FH66
Condover Cres, SE18 187 EP80
Condray Pl, SW11 40 C5
Sch Conductive Ed Cen, N10 off Muswell Hill 143 DH55
Conduit, The, Bletch. RH1 274 DS129
Conduit Av, SE10 47 H6
Conduit Ct, WC2 18 A10
Conduit La, N18 122 DW50
Croydon CR0 242 DU106
Enfield EN3 off Morson Rd 105 DY44
Hoddesdon EN11 71 EA17
South Croydon CR2 242 DU106
Conduit La E, Hodd. EN11 71 EB17
Conduit Ms, SE18 37 P10
W2 16 A9
Conduit Pas, W2 16 A9
Conduit Pl, W2 16 A9
Conduit Rd, SE18 37 P10
Conduit St, W1 17 K10
Conduit Way, NW10 160 CQ66
Conegar Ct, Slou. SL1 154 AS74
Conewood St, N5 143 DP62
Coney Acre, SE21 204 DQ88
Coneyberry, Reig. RH2 288 DC138
Coney Burrows, E4 124 EE47
Coneybury, Bletch. RH1 274 DS134
Coneybury Cl, Warl. CR6 258 DV119
Coney Cl, Hat. AL10 67 CV19
Coneydale, Welw.G.C. AL8 51 CX07
Coney Gro, Uxb. UB8 156 BN69
Coneygrove Path, Nthlt. UB5 off Arnold Rd 158 BY65
CONEY HALL, W.Wick. BR4 226 EF104
Coney Hill Rd, W.Wick. BR4 226 EE103
Coney Way, SW8 42 D3
Conference Cl, E4 off Greenbank Cl 123 EC47
Conference Rd, SE2 188 EW77
Conford Dr, Shalf. GU4 280 AY141
Congleton Gro, SE18 187 EQ78
Congo Dr, N9 122 DW48
Congo Rd, SE18 187 ER78
Congress Rd, SE2 188 EW77
Congreve Rd, SE9 187 EM83
Waltham Abbey EN9 90 EE33
Congreve St, SE17 31 N8
Congreve Wk, E16 24 E7
Conical Cor, Enf. EN2 104 DQ40
Coniers Way, Guil. GU4 265 BB131
Conifer Av, Rom. RM5 127 FB50
Conifer Cl, Orp. BR6 245 ER105
Reigate RH2 272 DA132
Waltham Cross EN7 88 DT29
Conifer Dr, Warley CM14 130 FX50
Conifer Gdns, SW16 203 DL90
Enfield EN1 104 DS44
Sutton SM1 222 DB103
Conifer La, Egh. TW20 195 BC92
Conifer Pk, Epsom KT17 238 CS111
Conifers, Wey. KT13 235 BS105
Conifers, The, Hem.H. HP3 61 BF23
Watford WD25 98 BW35
Conifers Cl, Tedd. TW11 199 CH94
Conifer Way, Hayes UB3 157 BU73
Swanley BR8 229 FC95
Wembley HA0 139 CJ62
Coniger Rd, SW6 39 J8
Coningesby Dr, Wat. WD17 97 BS39
Coningham Ms, W12 161 CU74
Coningham Rd, W12 181 CV75
Coningsby Av, NW9 118 CS54
Coningsby Bk, St.Alb. AL1 65 CC24
Coningsby Cl, N.Mymms AL9 67 CX24
Coningsby Cotts, W5 off Coningsby Rd 179 CK75
Coningsby Dr, Pot.B. EN6 86 DD33
Coningsby Gdns, E4 123 EB51
Coningsby La, Fifield SL6 172 AC81
Coningsby Rd, N4 143 DP59
W5 179 CJ75
South Croydon CR2 242 DQ109
Conington Rd, SE13 46 D8
Conisbee Ct, N14 103 DJ43
Conisborough Cres, SE6 205 EC90
Coniscliffe Cl, Chis. BR7 227 EN95
Coniscliffe Rd, N13 122 DQ48
Conista Ct, Wok. GU21 off Roundthorn Way 248 AT116
Coniston Av, Bark. IG11 167 ES66
Perivale UB6 159 CH69
Purfleet RM19 190 FQ79
Upminster RM14 150 FQ63
Welling DA16 187 ES83
Coniston Cl, N20 120 DC48
SW13 off Lonsdale Rd 181 CT80
SW20 221 CX100
W4 180 CQ81
Barking IG11 off Coniston Av 167 ES66
Bexleyheath DA7 189 FC81
Dartford DA1 209 FH88
Erith DA8 189 FE80
Coniston Cl, Hem.H. HP3 63 BQ21
Coniston Ct, NW7 off Langstone Way 119 CY52
Wallington SM6 241 DH105
Weybridge KT13 235 BP107
Coniston Cres, Slou. SL1 152 AJ71
Conistone Way, N7 8 B6
Coniston Gdns, N9 122 DW46
NW9 140 CR57
Ilford IG4 146 EL56
Pinner HA5 137 BU56
Sutton SM2 240 DD107
Wembley HA9 139 CJ60
Coniston Ho, SE5 43 J4
Coniston Rd, N10 121 DH54
N17 122 DU51
Bexleyheath DA7 189 FC81
Bromley BR1 206 EE93
Coulsdon CR5 257 DJ116
Croydon CR0 224 DU101
Kings Langley WD4 80 BM28
Twickenham TW2 198 CB86
Woking GU22 249 BB120
Coniston Wk, E9 11 H2
Coniston Way, Chess. KT9 220 CL104
Egham TW20 195 BB94
Hornchurch RM12 149 FG64
Reigate RH2 272 DE133
Conlan St, W10 14 E4
Conley Rd, NW10 160 CS65
Conley St, SE10 35 K10
Connaught Av, E4 123 ED45
SW14 180 CQ83
Ashford TW15 196 BL91
East Barnet EN4 120 DF46
Enfield EN1 104 DS40
Grays RM16 192 GB75
Hounslow TW4 198 BY85
Loughton IG10 106 EK42
Connaught Br, E16 36 E3
● Connaught Business Cen, NW9 off Hyde Est Rd 141 CT57
Mitcham CR4 222 DF99
Connaught Cl, E10 145 DY61
W2 16 C9
Enfield EN1 104 DS40
Hemel Hempstead HP2 62 BN18
Sutton SM1 222 DD103
Uxbridge UB8 157 BQ70
Connaught Ct, E17 off Orford Rd 145 EB56
Buckhurst Hill IG9 off Chequers 124 EH46
Connaught Dr, NW11 142 DA56
Weybridge KT13 234 BN111
Connaught Gdns, N10 143 DH57
N13 121 DP49
Berkhamsted HP4 60 AT16
Morden SM4 222 DC98
Connaught Hts, Uxb. UB10 off Uxbridge Rd 157 BQ70
Connaught Hill, Loug. IG10 106 EK42
Sch Connaught Ho Sch, W2 16 E9
Connaught La, Ilf. IG1 147 EQ61
Connaught Ms, NW3 6 C1
SE18 37 M10
Ilford IG1 off Connaught Rd 147 ER61
Connaught Pl, W2 16 E10
Connaught Rd, E4 124 EE45
E11 145 ED60
E16 36 F2
E17 145 EA57
N4 143 DN59
NW10 160 CS67
SE18 37 M10
W13 159 CH73
Barnet EN5 101 CX44
Harrow HA3 117 CF53
Hornchurch RM12 150 FK62
Ilford IG1 147 ER61
New Malden KT3 220 CS98
Richmond TW10 off Albert Rd 200 CM85
St. Albans AL3 64 CC18
Slough SL1 174 AV75
Sutton SM1 222 DD103
Teddington TW11 199 CD92
Jct Connaught Rbt, E16 24 E10
Sch Connaught Sch for Girls, E11 off Connaught Rd 146 EE60
Annexe, E11 off Madeira Rd 146 EE61
Connaught Sq, W2 16 E9
Connaught St, W2 16 C9
Connaught Way, N13 121 DP49
Connect La, Barkingside IG6 125 EQ54
Connell Cres, W5 160 CM70
Connemara Cl, Borwd. WD6 100 CQ44
Connicut La, Lthd. KT23 268 CB128
Connington Cres, E4 123 ED48
Connop Rd, Enf. EN3 105 DX38
Connor Cl, E11 146 EE60
Ilford IG6 125 EP53
Connor Ct, SW11 off Alfreda St 41 J7
Connor Rd, Dag. RM9 148 EZ63
Connor St, E9 11 J8
Conolly Rd, W7 159 CE74
Conquerors Hill, Wheat. AL4 50 CL07
Conquest Rd, Add. KT15 234 BG106
Conrad Cl, Grays RM16 192 GB75
Conrad Dr, Wor.Pk. KT4 221 CW102
Conrad Gdns, Grays RM16 192 GA75
Conrad Ho, N16 9 N2
Consfield Av, N.Mal. KT3 221 CU98
Consort Cl, Warley CM14 130 FW50
Consort Ms, Islw. TW7 199 CD85
Consort Rd, SE15 44 E8
Consort Way, Horl. RH6 290 DG148
Consort Way E, Horl. RH6 291 DH149
Cons St, SE1 30 F4
Constable Av, E16 36 A2
Constable Cl, N11 off Friern Barnet La 120 DF50
NW11 142 DB58
Hayes UB4 157 BQ68
Constable Cres, N15 144 DU57
Constable Gdns, Edg. HA8 118 CN53
Isleworth TW7 199 CD85
Constable Ho, E14 off Cassilis Rd 34 B5
NW3 6 F6
Constable Ms, Brom. BR1 226 EH96
Dagenham RM8 off Stonard Rd 148 EV63
Constable Rd, Nthflt DA11 212 GE90
Constable Wk, SE21 204 DS90
Constance Cl, SW15 200 CR91
Constance Cres, Brom. BR2 226 EF101
Constance Rd, Croy. CR0 223 DP101
Enfield EN1 104 DS44
Sutton SM1 240 DC105
Twickenham TW2 198 CB87
Constance St, E16 36 G3
Constantine Pl, Hlgdn UB10 156 BM67
Constantine Rd, NW3 6 D1
Constitution Cres, Grav. DA12 off South Hill Rd 213 GJ88
Constitution Hill, SW1 29 J4
Gravesend DA12 213 GJ88
Woking GU22 248 AY119
Constitution Ri, SE18 187 EN81
Consul Av, Dag. RM9 169 FC69
Consul Gdns, Swan. BR8 209 FG94
Content St, SE17 31 K9
Contessa Cl, Orp. BR6 245 ES106
Control Twr Rd, Lon.Hthrw Air. TW6 176 BN83
Convair Wk, Nthlt. UB5 off Kittiwake Rd 158 BX69
Convent Cl, Beck. BR3 205 EC94
Convent Ct, Wind. SL4 173 AN82
Convent Gdns, W5 179 CJ77
W11 14 F9
Convent Hill, SE19 204 DQ93
Convent La, Cob. KT11 235 BS111
Sch Convent of Jesus & Mary Language Coll, NW10 off Crownhill Rd 161 CT67
Sch Convent of Jesus & Mary RC Inf Sch, NW2 4 A5
Convent Rd, Ashf. TW15 196 BN92
Windsor SL4 173 AN82
Convent Way, Sthl. UB2 178 BW77
Conway Cl, Loud. HP10 110 AC53
Rainham RM13 169 FG66
Stanmore HA7 117 CG51
Conway Cres, Perivale UB6 159 CE68
Romford RM6 148 EW59
Conway Dr, Ashf. TW15 197 BQ93
Hayes UB3 177 BQ76
Sutton SM2 240 DB107
Conway Gdns, Enf. EN2 104 DS38
Grays RM17 192 GB80
Mitcham CR4 223 DK98
Wembley HA9 139 CJ59
Conway Gro, W3 160 CR71
Conway Ms, W1 17 L6
Sch Conway Prim Sch, SE18 off Gallosson Rd 187 ES77
Conway Rd, N14 121 DL48
N15 143 DP57
NW2 141 CW61
SE18 187 ER77
SW20 221 CW95
Feltham TW13 198 BX92
Hounslow TW4 198 BZ87
London Heathrow Airport TW6 off Inner Ring E 177 BP83
Taplow SL6 152 AH72
Conway St, E13 23 N5
W1 17 L5
Conway Wk, Hmptn. TW12 off Fearnley Cres 198 BZ93
Conybeare, NW3 6 D6
Conybury Cl, Wal.Abb. EN9 90 EG32
Cony Cl, Chsht EN7 88 DS26
Conyers, Harl. CM20 57 EQ13
Conyers Cl, Hersham KT12 236 BX106
Woodford Green IG8 124 EE51
Conyers Rd, SW16 203 DK92
Conyer St, E3 21 L1
Conyers Way, Loug. IG10 107 EP41
Cooden Cl, Brom. BR1 206 EH94
Cook Ct, SE16 off Rotherhithe St 33 H3
Cooke Cl, Chaff.Hun. RM16 192 FY76
Cookes Cl, E11 146 EF61
Cookes La, Sutt. SM3 239 CY107
Cooke St, Bark. IG11 167 EQ67
Cookham Cl, Sthl. UB2 178 CB75
Cookham Cres, SE16 33 J4
Cookham Dene Cl, Chis. BR7 227 ER95
Cookham Hill, Orp. BR6 228 FA104
Cookham Rd, Sid. DA14 208 FA94
Swanley BR8 228 FA95
Cookhill Rd, SE2 188 EV75
Cook Rd, Dag. RM9 168 EX67
Cooks Cl, E14 off Cabot Sq 34 B2
Chalfont St. Peter SL9 112 AY51
Romford RM5 127 FC53
Jct Cooks Ferry, N18 123 DY50
Cooks Ferry Rbt, N18 off Advent Way 123 DX50
Cook's Hole Rd, Enf. EN2 103 DP38
Cooks Mead, Bushey WD23 98 CB44
Cookson Gro, Erith DA8 189 FB80
Cook Sq, Erith DA8 189 FF80
Cook's Rd, E15 12 C10
Cooks Rd, SE17 42 G2
Cooks Spinney, Harl. CM20 58 EU13
Cooks Vennel, Hem.H. HP1 62 BG18
Cooks Way, Hat. AL10 67 CV20
Coolfin Rd, E16 23 P9
Coolgardie Av, E4 123 EC50
Chigwell IG7 125 EN48
Coolgardie Rd, Ashf. TW15 197 BQ92
Coolhurst Rd, N8 143 DK58
Cool Oak La, NW9 140 CS59
Coomassie Rd, W9 14 G4
COOMBE, Kings.T. KT2 200 CQ94
Coombe, The, Bet. RH3 270 CR131
Coombe Av, Croy. CR0 242 DS105
Sevenoaks TN14 263 FH120
Coombe Bk, Kings.T. KT2 220 CS95
Sch Coombe Boys' Sch, N.Mal. KT3 off College Gdns 221 CU99
Coll Coombe Cliff CETS Cen, Croy. CR0 off Coombe Rd 242 DR105
Coombe Cl, Edg. HA8 118 CM54
Hounslow TW3 178 CA84
Coombe Cor, N21 121 DP46
Coombe Cres, Hmptn. TW12 198 BY94
Coombe Dr, Add. KT15 233 BF107
Kingston upon Thames KT2 200 CR94
Ruislip HA4 137 BV60
Coombe End, Kings.T. KT2 200 CR94
Coombefield Cl, N.Mal. KT3 220 CS99
Coombe Gdns, SW20 221 CU96
Berkhamsted HP4 60 AT18
New Malden KT3 221 CT98
Sch Coombe Girls' Sch, N.Mal. KT3 off Clarence Av 220 CR96
Coombe Hts, Kings.T. KT2 200 CS94
Coombe Hill Ct, Wind. SL4 173 AK84
Coombe Hill Glade, Kings.T. KT2 200 CS94
Sch Coombe Hill Inf & Jun Schs, Kings.T. KT2 off Coombe La W 220 CR95
Coombe Hill Rd, Kings.T. KT2 200 CS94
Mill End WD3 114 BG45
Coombe Ho Chase, N.Mal. KT3 220 CR95
Coombehurst Cl, Barn. EN4 102 DF40
Coombelands La, Add. KT15 234 BG107
Tra Coombe Lane 242 DW106
Jct Coombe La, SW20 221 CT95
Coombe La, SW20 221 CU95
Croydon CR0 242 DV106
Whiteley Village KT12 235 BT109
Coombe La W, Kings.T. KT2 200 CS94
Coombe Lea, Brom. BR1 226 EL97
Coombe Lo, SE7 186 EJ79
Coombe Neville, Kings.T. KT2 200 CR94
Coombe Pk, Kings.T. KT2 200 CR92
Coombe Ridings, Kings.T. KT2 200 CQ92
Coombe Ri, Kings.T. KT2 220 CQ95
Shenfield CM15 131 FZ46
Coombe Rd, N22 121 DN53
NW10 140 CR62
SE26 204 DV91
W4 180 CS78
W13 off Northcroft Rd 179 CH76
Bushey WD23 116 CC45
Croydon CR0 242 DR105
Gravesend DA12 213 GJ89
Hampton TW12 198 BZ93
Kingston upon Thames KT2 220 CN95
New Malden KT3 220 CS96
Romford RM3 150 FM55
Coomber Way, Croy. CR0 223 DK101
Coombes Rd, Dag. RM9 168 EZ67
London Colney AL2 83 CH26
Coombe Vale, Ger.Cr. SL9 134 AY60
Coombe Wk, Sutt. SM1 222 DB104
Coombe Way, Byfleet KT14 234 BM112
Coombewood Dr, Rom. RM6 148 EZ58
Coombe Wd Hill, Pur. CR8 242 DQ112
Coombe Wd Rd, Kings.T. KT2 200 CQ92
Coombfield Dr, Lane End DA2 211 FR91
Coombs St, N1 19 H1
Coomer Ms, SW6 39 H3
Coomer Pl, SW6 39 H3
Coomer Rd, SW6 39 H3
Cooms Wk, Edg. HA8 off East Rd 118 CQ53
Cooperage Cl, N17 off Brantwood Rd 122 DT51
Co-operative Ho, SE15 44 D10
Cooper Av, E17 123 DX53
Cooper Cl, SE1 30 F5
Greenhithe DA9 211 FS85
Smallfield RH6 291 DN148
Cooper Cres, Cars. SM5 222 DF104
Cooper Rd, NW4 141 CX58
NW10 141 CT64
Croydon CR0 241 DN105
Guildford GU1 280 AY136
COOPERSALE, Epp. CM16 92 EX29
Sch Coopersale & Theydon Garnon C of E Prim Sch, Epp. CM16 off Brickfield Rd 92 EX29
Coopersale Cl, Wdf.Grn. IG8 off Navestock Cres 124 EJ52
Coopersale Common, Cooper. CM16 92 EX28
Sch Coopersale Hall Sch, Epp. CM16 off Flux's La 92 EV34
Coopersale La, Epp. CM16 108 EU37
Coopersale Rd, E9 11 K2
Coopersale St, Epp. CM16 92 EW32
Coopers Cl, E1 20 G5
Chigwell IG7 126 EV47
Dagenham RM10 169 FB65
South Darenth DA4 231 FR95
Staines TW18 195 BE92
Sch Coopers' Company & Coborn Sch, Upmin. RM14 off St. Mary's La 151 FR61
Coopers Ct, Gidea Pk RM2 off Kidman Cl 150 FJ55
Hertford SG14 off The Folly 54 DR09
Cooper's Ct, Ware SG12 55 DY06
Coopers Cres, Borwd. WD6 100 CQ39
Coopers Dr, Dart. DA2 209 FE89
Coopers Gate, Coln.Hth AL4 66 CP22
Coopers Grn La, Hat. AL10 50 CS13
St. Albans AL4 66 CL17
Welwyn Garden City AL8 50 CQ14
Coopers Hill La, Egh. TW20 194 AY91
Coopers Hill Rd, Red. RH1 273 DM133
Coopers La, E10 145 EB60
NW1 7 P10
Cooper's La, SE12 206 EH89
Coopers La, Pot.B. EN6 86 DD31
Staines TW18 195 BF91
Sch Cooper's La Prim Sch, SE12 off Pragnell Rd 206 EH89
Coopers La Rd, Pot.B. EN6 86 DE31
Coopers Ms, Beck. BR3 225 EA96
Watford WD25 off High Elms La 82 BW31
Coopers Rd, SE1 44 B1
Northfleet DA11 212 GE88
Potters Bar EN6 86 DC30
Swanscombe DA10 212 FZ86
Cooper's Row, EC3 20 A10
Coopers Row, Iver SL0 155 BC70
Coopers Shaw Rd, Til. RM18 193 GK80
Sch Coopers Tech Coll, Chis. BR7 off Hawkwood La 227 EQ95
Cooper St, E16 23 M7
Coopers Wk, E15 13 J3
Cheshunt EN8 89 DX28
Coopers Yd, N1 8 G6
Cooper's Yd, SE19 204 DS93
Cooper Way, Berk. HP4 off Robertson Rd 60 AX19
Slough SL1 173 AP76
Coote Gdns, Dag. RM8 148 EZ62
Coote Rd, Bexh. DA7 188 EZ81
Dagenham RM8 148 EZ62
Copeland Dr, E14 34 B8
Copeland Ho, SE11 30 D7
Copeland Rd, E17 145 EB57
SE15 44 D9
Copeman Cl, SE26 204 DW92
Copeman Rd, Hutt. CM13 131 GD45
Copenhagen Gdns, W4 180 CQ75
Copenhagen Pl, E14 21 N9
Sch Copenhagen Prim Sch, N1 8 C9
Copenhagen St, N1 8 B9
Copenhagen Way, Walt. KT12 217 BV104
Cope Pl, W8 27 J7
Copers Cope Rd, Beck. BR3 205 DZ93
Cope St, SE16 33 J8
Copford Cl, Wdf.Grn. IG8 124 EL51
Copford Wk, N1 9 J8
Copgate Path, SW16 203 DM93
Copinger Wk, Edg. HA8 off North Rd 118 CP53
Copland Av, Wem. HA0 139 CK64
Copland Cl, Wem. HA0 139 CJ64
Sch Copland Comm Sch & Tech Cen, Wem. HA9 off Cecil Av 140 CM64
Copland Ms, Wem. HA0 160 CL65
Copland Rd, Wem. HA0 160 CL65
Copleigh Dr, Kgswd KT20 255 CY120
Copleston Ms, SE15 44 A10
Copleston Pas, SE15 44 A10
Copleston Rd, SE15 184 DT83
Copley Cl, SE17 43 H3
W7 159 CF71
Redhill RH1 272 DE132
Woking GU21 248 AS119
Copley Dene, Brom. BR1 226 EK95
Copley Pk, SW16 203 DM93
Copley Rd, Stan. HA7 117 CJ50
Copley St, E1 21 J7
Copley Way, Tad. KT20 255 CX120
Copmans Wick, Chorl. WD3 95 BD43
Coppard Gdns, Chess. KT9 237 CJ107
Copped Hall, SE21 off Glazebrook Cl 204 DR89
Epping CM16 91 EN32
Coppelia Rd, SE3 186 EF84
Coppen Rd, Dag. RM8 148 EZ59
Copperas St, SE8 46 C3
Copper Beech Cl, Grav. DA12 213 GK87
Hemel Hempstead HP3 61 BF23
Ilford IG5 125 EN53
Orpington BR5 228 EW99
Windsor SL4 173 AK81
Woking GU22 248 AV121
Copper Beech Ct, Loug. IG10 107 EN39
Copper Beeches, Islw. TW7 179 CD81
Copper Beech Rd, S.Ock. RM15 171 FW69
Copper Cl, N17 122 DV52
SE19 off Auckland Rd 204 DT94
Copperdale Rd, Hayes UB3 177 BU75
Copperfield, Chig. IG7 125 ER51
Copperfield Av, Uxb. UB8 156 BN71
Copperfield Cl, S.Croy. CR2 242 DQ111
Copperfield Ct, Lthd. KT22 off Kingston Rd 253 CG121
Pinner HA5 off Copperfield Way 138 BZ56
Copperfield Dr, N15 144 DT56
Copperfield Gdns, Brwd. CM14 130 FV46
Copperfield Ms, N18 122 DS50
Copperfield Ri, Add. KT15 233 BF106
Copperfield Rd, E3 21 M5
SE28 168 EW72
Copperfields, Beac. HP9 111 AL50
Dartford DA1 off Spital St 210 FL86
Fetcham KT22 252 CC122
Welwyn Garden City AL7 off Forresters Dr 52 DC10
Copperfield St, SE1 31 H4
Copperfields Way, Rom. RM3 128 FK53
Copperfield Ter, Slou. SL2 off Mirador Cres 154 AV73
Copperfield Way, Chis. BR7 207 EQ93
Pinner HA5 138 BZ56
Coppergate Cl, Brom. BR1 226 EH95
Coppergate Ct, Wal.Abb. EN9 off Farthingale La 90 EG34
Copperkins Gro, Amer. HP6 77 AP36
Copperkins La, Amer. HP6 77 AM35
Copper Mead Cl, NW2 141 CW62
Copper Ms, W4 180 CQ76
Copper Mill Dr, Islw. TW7 179 CF82
Coppermill La, E17 144 DW58
Copper Mill La, SW17 202 DC91
Coppermill La, Hare. UB9 113 BE52
Rickmansworth WD3 113 BE52
Sch Coppermill Prim Sch, E17 off Edward Rd 145 DX57
Coppermill Rd, Wrays. TW19 175 BC84
Copper Ridge, Chal.St.P. SL9 113 AZ50
Copper Row, SE1 32 A3
Copperwood, Hert. SG13 54 DT09
Coppetts Cl, N12 120 DE52
Coppetts Rd, N10 120 DG54
H Coppetts Wd Hosp, N10 120 DF53
Sch Coppetts Wd Prim Sch, N10 off Coppetts Rd 120 DG53
Coppice, The, Ashf. TW15 off School Rd 197 BP93
Bexley DA5 209 FD90
Enfield EN2 103 DP42
Hemel Hempstead HP2 63 BP19
Seer Green HP9 111 AR51
Watford WD19 98 BW44
West Drayton UB7 156 BL72
Coppice Cl, SW20 221 CW97
Beckenham BR3 225 EB98
Hatfield AL10 67 CT22
Ruislip HA4 137 BR58
Stanmore HA7 117 CF51
Coppice Dr, SW15 201 CV86
Wraysbury TW19 194 AX87
Coppice End, Wok. GU22 249 BE116
Coppice Fm Rd, Penn HP10 110 AC45
Coppice Hatch, Harl. CM18 73 ER17
Coppice La, Reig. RH2 271 CZ132
Coppice Path, Chig. IG7 126 EV49
Sch Coppice Prim Sch, Chig. IG7 off Manford Way 126 EU50
Coppice Row, They.B. CM16 107 EM36
Coppice Wk, N20 120 DA48
Coppice Way, E18 146 EF56
Hedgerley SL2 133 AR61
Coppies Gro, N11 120 DG49
Copping Cl, Croy. CR0 242 DS105
Coppings, The, Hodd. EN11 off Danemead 55 EA14
Coppins, The, Har. HA3 117 CE51
New Addington CR0 243 EB107
Welwyn Garden City AL8 51 CU11
Coppins Cl, Berk. HP4 60 AS19
Coppins La, Iver SL0 155 BF71

Coppock Cl, SW11 40 C9
Coppsfield, W.Mol. KT8
off Hurst Rd 218 CA97
Copse, The, E4 124 EF46
Amersham HP7 77 AQ38
Beaconsfield HP9 110 AJ51
Caterham CR3 274 DU126
Fetcham KT22 252 CB123
Hemel Hempstead HP1 61 BE18
Hertford SG13 54 DU09
South Nutfield RH1 289 DL136
Tatsfield TN16 260 EJ120
Warlingham CR6 259 DY117
Copse Av, W.Wick. BR4 225 EB104
Copse Cl, SE7 186 EH79
Chilworth GU4 281 BC140
Northwood HA6 115 BQ54
Slough SL1 153 AM74
West Drayton UB7 176 BK76
Copse Edge Av, Epsom KT17 239 CT113
Copse Glade, Surb. KT6 219 CK102
COPSE HILL, SW20 201 CV94
Copse Hill, SW20 201 CV94
Harlow CM19 73 EP18
Purley CR8 241 DL113
Sutton SM2 240 DB108
Copse La, Horl. RH6 291 DJ147
Jordans HP9 112 AS52
Copsem Dr, Esher KT10 236 CB107
Copsem La, Esher KT10 236 CB107
Oxshott KT22 236 CC111
Copsem Way, Esher KT10 236 CC107
Copsen Wd, Oxshott KT22 236 CC111
Copse Rd, Cob. KT11 235 BV113
Redhill RH1 288 DC136
Woking GU21 248 AT118
Copse Vw, S.Croy. CR2 243 DX109
Copse Way, Chesh. HP5 76 AN27
Copse Wd, Iver SL0 155 BD67
Copsewood Cl, Sid. DA15 207 ES86
Copse Wd Ct, Reig. RH2
off Green La 272 DE132
Copsewood Rd, Wat. WD24 97 BV39
Copse Wd Way, Nthwd. HA6 115 BQ52
Copshall Cl, Harl. CM18 73 ES19
Copsleigh Av, Red. RH1 288 DG141
Copsleigh Cl, Salf. RH1 288 DG140
Copsleigh Way, Red. RH1 288 DG140
Coptain Ho, SW18
off Eastfields Av 182 DA84
Coptefield Dr, Belv. DA17 188 EX76
Coptfold Rd, Brwd. CM14 130 FW47
Copthall Av, EC2 19 M8
Copthall Bldgs, EC2 19 L8
Copthall Cl, EC2 19 L8
Chalfont St. Peter SL9 113 AZ52
Copthall Cor, Chal.St.P. SL9 112 AY52
Copthall Ct, EC2 19 L8
Copthall Dr, NW7 119 CU52
Copthall Gdns, NW7 119 CU52
Twickenham TW1 199 CF88
COPTHALL GREEN,
Wal.Abb. EN9 90 EK33
Copthall La, Chal.St.P. SL9 112 AY52
Copthall Rd E, Uxb. UB10 136 BN61
Copthall Rd W, Uxb. UB10 136 BN61
Sch Copthall Sch, NW7
off Pursley Rd 119 CV52
Copthall Way, New Haw KT15 233 BF110
Copt Hill La, Kgswd KT20 255 CY120
Copthorn Av, Brox. EN10 71 DZ21
Copthorne Av, SW12 203 DK87
Bromley BR2 227 EM103
Ilford IG6 125 EP51
Copthorne Chase, Ashf. TW15 196 BM91
Copthorne Cl, Crox.Grn WD3 96 BM43
Shepperton TW17 217 BQ100
Copthorne Gdns, Horn. RM11 150 FN57
Copthorne Ms, Hayes UB3 177 BS77
Copthorne Pl, Eff.Junct. KT24 251 BU122
Copthorne Ri, S.Croy. CR2 242 DR113
Copthorne Rd, Crox.Grn WD3 96 BM44
Leatherhead KT22 253 CH120
Coptic St, WC1 18 A7
Copwood Cl, N12 120 DD49
Coral Apts, E16
off Western Gateway 35 P1
Coral Cl, Rom. RM6 148 EW56
Coral Gdns, Hem.H. HP2 62 BM19
Coraline Cl, Sthl. UB1 158 BZ69
Coralline Wk, SE2 188 EW75
Coral Row, SW11 39 P10
Corals Mead, Welw.G.C. AL7 51 CX10
Coral St, SE1 30 F5
Coram Cl, Berk. HP4 60 AW20
Coram Grn, Hutt. CM13 131 GD44
★ Coram's Flds, WC1 18 B5
Coram St, WC1 18 A5
Coran Cl, N9 123 DX45
Corban Rd, Houns. TW3 178 CA83
Corbar Cl, Barn. EN4 102 DD38
Corbden Cl, SE15 44 B6
Corbet Cl, Wall. SM6 222 DG102
Corbet Ct, EC3 19 M9
Corbet Pl, E1 20 A6
Corbet Rd, Epsom KT17 238 CS110
Corbets Av, Upmin. RM14 150 FP64
CORBETS TEY, Upmin. RM14 170 FQ65
Corbets Tey Rd, Upmin. RM14 150 FP63
Sch Corbets Tey Sch, Upmin.
RM14 off Harwood Hall La 150 FQ64
Corbett Cl, Croy. CR0 243 ED112
Corbett Gro, N22 121 DL52
Corbett Rd, E11 146 EJ58
E17 145 EC55
Corbetts La, SE16 32 G9
Corbetts Pas, SE16 32 G9
Corbicum, E11 146 EE59
Corbidge Ct, SE8 46 C2
Corbiere Ct, SW19
off Thornton Rd 201 CX93
Corbiere Ho, N1 9 N8
Corbin Ho, E3 22 D2
Corbins La, Har. HA2 138 CB62
Corbridge Cres, E2 10 E10
Corbridge Ms, Rom. RM1 149 FF57
Corby Cl, Eng.Grn TW20 194 AW93
St. Albans AL2 82 CA25
Corby Cres, Enf. EN2 103 DL42
Corby Dr, Eng.Grn TW20 194 AV93
Corbylands Rd, Sid. DA15 207 ES87
Corbyn St, N4 143 DL60
Corby Rd, NW10 160 CR68
Corby Way, E3 22 A5
Corcorans, Pilg.Hat. CM15 130 FV44
Cordelia Cl, SE24 183 DP84
Cordelia Gdns, Stai. TW19 196 BL87
Cordelia Rd, Stai. TW19 196 BL87
Cordelia St, E14 22 C8
Cordell Cl, Chsht EN8 89 DY28
Cordell Ho, N15 144 DU57
Corder Cl, St.Alb. AL3 64 CA23
Corderoy Pl, Cher. KT16 215 BE100
Cordingley Rd, Ruis. HA4 137 BR61
Cording St, E14 22 D7
Cordons Cl, Chal.St.P. SL9 112 AX53
Cordrey Gdns, Couls. CR5 257 DL115
Uni Cordwainers at London Coll
of Fashion, EC1 19 J5
Cordwainers Wk, E13 13 P10
Cord Way, E14 34 B6
Cordwell Rd, SE13 206 EE85
Corefield Cl, N11
off Benfleet Way 120 DG47
Corelli Rd, SE3 186 EL82
Corfe Av, Har. HA2 138 CA63
Corfe Cl, Ashtd. KT21 253 CJ118
Borehamwood WD6 100 CR41
Hayes UB4 158 BW72
Hemel Hempstead HP2 62 BL21
Hounslow TW4 198 BY87
Corfe Gdns, Slou. SL1
off Avebury 153 AN74
Corfe Ho, SW8
off Dorset Rd 42 C4
Corfe Twr, W3 180 CP75
Corfield Rd, N21 103 DM43
Corfield St, E2 20 F3
Corfton Rd, W5 160 CL72
Coriander Av, E14 22 G9
Coriander Cres, Guil. GU2 264 AU129
Cories Cl, Dag. RM8 148 EX61
Corinium Cl, Wem. HA9 140 CM63
Corinium Gate, St.Alb. AL3 64 CA22
● Corinium Ind Est, Amer.
HP6 94 AT38
Corinne Rd, N19 7 M1
Corinthian Manorway,
Erith DA8 189 FD77
Corinthian Rd, Erith DA8 189 FD77
Corinthian Way, Stanw. TW19
off Clare Rd 196 BK87
Corker Wk, N7 143 DM61
Corkran Rd, Surb. KT6 219 CK101
Corkscrew Hill, W.Wick. BR4 225 ED103
Cork Sq, E1 32 E2
Cork St, W1 29 L1
Cork St Ms, W1 29 L1
🔒 Cork Tree Retail Pk, E4 123 DY50
Cork Tree Way, E4 123 DY50
Corlett St, NW1 16 C6
Cormongers La, Nutfld RH1 273 DK131
Cormont Rd, SE5 42 G7
Cormorant Cl, E17 123 DX53
Cormorant Ho, Enf. EN3
off Alma Rd 105 DX43
Cormorant Pl, Sutt. SM1
off Sandpiper Rd 239 CZ106
Cormorant Rd, E7 13 M2
Cormorant Wk, Horn. RM12
off Heron Flight Av 169 FH65
Cornbury Rd, Edg. HA8 117 CK52
Corncroft, Hat. AL10 67 CV16
Cornelia Dr, Hayes UB4 158 BW70
Cornelia Pl, Erith DA8
off Queen St 189 FE79
Cornelia St, N7 8 D5
Cornell Cl, Sid. DA14 208 EY93
Cornell Ct, Enf. EN3 105 DY41
Cornell Way, Rom. RM5 126 FA50
Corner, The, W.Byf. KT14 234 BG113
Corner Fm Cl, Tad. KT20 255 CW122
Cornerfield, Hat. AL10 67 CV15
Corner Fielde, SW2
off Streatham Hill 203 DL88
Corner Grn, SE3 47 N9
Corner Hall, Hem.H. HP3 62 BJ22
Corner Hall Av, Hem.H. HP3 62 BK22
Corner Ho St, WC2 30 A2
Corner Mead, NW9 119 CT52
Corner Meadow, Harl. CM18 74 EU19
Corners, Welw.G.C. AL7 52 DA07
Cornerside, Ashf. TW15 197 BQ94
Corner Vw, N.Mymms AL9 67 CW24
Corney Reach Way, W4 180 CS80
Corney Rd, W4 180 CS79
Cornfield Cl, Uxb. UB8 156 BK68
Cornfield Rd, Bushey WD23 98 CB42
Reigate RH2 288 DC135
Cornfields, Gdmg. GU7 280 AT143
Cornfields, The, Hem.H. HP1 62 BH21
Cornflower La, Croy. CR0 225 DX102
Cornflower Ter, SE22 204 DV86
Cornflower Way, Hat. AL10 66 CS15
Romford RM3 128 FL53
Cornford Cl, Brom. BR2 226 EG99
Cornford Gro, SW12 203 DH89
Cornhill, EC3 19 M9
Cornhill Cl, Add. KT15 216 BH103
Cornhill Dr, Enf. EN3 105 DY37
Cornish Ct, N9 122 DV45
Cornish Gro, SE20 204 DV94
Cornish Ho, SE17 42 G3
Brentford TW8
off Green Dragon La 180 CM78
Corn Mead, Welw.G.C. AL8 51 CW06
Cornmill, Wal.Abb. EN9 89 EB33
Corn Mill Dr, Orp. BR6 227 ET101
Cornmill Ms, Wal.Abb. EN9
off Highbridge St 89 EB33
Cornmow Dr, NW10 141 CT64
Cornshaw Rd, Dag. RM8 148 EX60
Cornsland, Brwd. CM14 150 FX48
Cornsland Cl, Upmin. RM14 150 FQ55
Cornsland Ct, Brwd. CM14 130 FW48
Cornthwaite Rd, E5 144 DW62
Cornwall Av, E2 20 G3
N3 120 DA52
N22 121 DL53
Byfleet KT14 234 BM114
Claygate KT10 237 CF108
Slough SL2 153 AQ70
Southall UB1 158 BZ71
Welling DA16 187 ES83
Cornwall Cl, Bark. IG11 167 ET65
Eton Wick SL4 173 AL78
Hornchurch RM11 150 FN56
Waltham Cross EN8 89 DY33
Cornwall Cres, W11 14 E10
Cornwall Dr, Orp. BR5 208 EW94
Cornwall Gdns, NW10 161 CV65
SW7 27 M7
Cornwall Gdns Wk, SW7 27 M7
Cornwall Gate, Purf. RM19
off Fanns Ri 190 FN77
Cornwall Gro, W4 180 CS78
Cornwallis Av, N9 122 DV47
SE9 207 ER89
Cornwallis Cl, Cat. CR3 258 DQ122
Erith DA8 189 FF79
Cornwallis Ct, SW8 42 A6
Cornwallis Gro, N9 122 DV47
Cornwallis Rd, E17 145 DX56
N9 122 DV47
N19 143 DL61
SE18 187 EQ77
Dagenham RM9 148 EX63
Cornwallis Sq, N19 143 DL61
Cornwallis Wk, SE9 187 EM83
Cornwall Ms S, SW7 27 N7
Cornwall Ms W, SW7 27 M7
Cornwall Rd, N4 143 DN59
N15 144 DR57
N18 off Fairfield Rd 122 DU50
SE1 30 E2
Croydon CR0 223 DP103
Dartford DA1 190 FM83
Harrow HA1 138 CC58
Pilgrim's Hatch CM15 130 FV43
Pinner HA5 116 BZ52
Ruislip HA4 137 BT62
St. Albans AL1 65 CE22
Sutton SM2 239 CZ108
Twickenham TW1 199 CG87
Uxbridge UB8 156 BK65
Cornwall Sq, SE11 30 F10
Cornwall St, E1 20 F10
Cornwall Ter, NW1 16 F5
Cornwall Ter Ms, NW1 16 F5
Cornwall Way, Stai. TW18 195 BE93
Corn Way, E11 145 ED62
Cornwell Av, Grav. DA12 213 GJ90
Cornwell Rd, Old Wind. SL4 194 AU86
Cornwood Cl, N2 142 DD57
Cornwood Dr, E1 20 G8
Cornworthy Rd, Dag. RM8 148 EW64
Corona Rd, SE12 206 EG87
Coronation Av, N16
off Victorian Rd 144 DT62
George Green SL3 154 AY72
Windsor SL4 174 AT81
Coronation Cl, Bex. DA5 208 EX86
Ilford IG6 147 EQ56
Coronation Dr, Horn. RM12 149 FH63
Coronation Hill, Epp. CM16 91 ET30
Coronation Rd, E13 24 D3
NW10 160 CN70
Hayes UB3 177 BT77
Ware SG12 55 DX05
Coronation Wk, Twick. TW2 198 CA88
★ Coronet, The, SE1 31 H7
Coronet, The, Horl. RH6 291 DJ150
Coronet St, N1 19 N3
Corporation Av, Houns. TW4 178 BY84
Corporation Row, EC1 18 F4
Corporation St, E15 23 K1
N7 8 A3
Sch Corpus Christi Prim Sch,
N.Mal. KT3
off Chestnut Gro 220 CQ97
Sch Corpus Christi RC Prim Sch,
SW2 off Trent Rd 203 DM85
Annexe, SW2 off Trent Rd 203 DM85
Corrance Rd, SW2 183 DL84
Corran Way, S.Ock. RM15 171 FV73
Corri Av, N14 121 DK49
Corrib Dr, Sutt. SM1 240 DE106
Corrie Gdns, Vir.W. GU25 214 AW101
Corrie Rd, Add. KT15 234 BK105
Woking GU22 249 BC120
Corrigan Av, Couls. CR5 240 DG114
Corrigan Cl, NW4 141 CW55
Corringham Ct, NW11
off Corringham Rd 142 DA59
St. Albans AL1
off Lemsford Rd 65 CF19
Corringham Rd, NW11 142 DA59
Wembley HA9 140 CN61
Corringway, NW11 142 DB59
W5 160 CN70
Corris Grn, NW9 140 CS58
Corry Dr, SW9 183 DP84
Corsair Cl, Stai. TW19 196 BK87
Corsair Rd, Stai. TW19 196 BL87
Corscombe Cl, Kings.T. KT2 200 CQ92
Corsehill St, SW16 203 DJ93
Corsham St, N1 19 M3
Corsica St, N5 8 G4
Cortayne Rd, SW6 39 H8
Cortina Dr, Dag. RM9 169 FC69
Cortis Rd, SW15 201 CV86
Cortis Ter, SW15 201 CV86
Cortland Cl, Dart. DA1 209 FE86
Woodford Green IG8 124 EJ53
Corunna Rd, SW8 41 M6
Corunna Ter, SW8 41 L6
Corve La, S.Ock. RM15 171 FV73
Corvette Sq, SE10 47 H2
Corwell Gdns, Uxb. UB8 157 BQ72
Corwell La, Uxb. UB8 157 BQ72
Cory Dr, Hutt. CM13 131 GB45
Coryton Path, W9 15 H4
Cory Wright Way, Wheat. AL4 50 CL06
Cosbycote Av, SE24 204 DQ85
Cosdach Av, Wall. SM6 241 DK108
Cosedge Cres, Croy. CR0 241 DN106
Cosgrove Cl, N21 122 DQ47
Hayes UB4 off Kingsash Dr 158 BY70
Cosmo Pl, WC1 18 B6
Cosmur Cl, W12 181 CT76
Cossall Wk, SE15 44 E8
Cossar Ms, SW2 203 DN86
Cosser St, SE1 30 E6
Costa St, SE15 44 C9
Costead Manor Rd, Brwd.
CM14 130 FV46
Costell's Meadow, West. TN16 277 ER126
Costins Wk, Berk. HP4
off Robertson Rd 60 AX19
Sch Coston Prim Sch, Grnf.
UB6 off Oldfield La S 158 CC69
Costons Av, Grnf. UB6 159 CD69
Costons La, Grnf. UB6 159 CD69
Coston Wk, SE4
off Hainford Cl 185 DX84
Cosway St, NW1 16 D6
Cotall St, E14 22 B8
Coteford Cl, Loug. IG10 107 EP40
Pinner HA5 137 BU57
Sch Coteford Inf Sch, Eastcote
HA5 off Fore St 137 BU58
Sch Coteford Jun Sch, Eastcote
HA5 off Fore St 137 BT57
Coteford St, SW17 202 DF91
Cotelands, Croy. CR0 224 DS104
Cotesbach Rd, E5 144 DW62
Cotesmore Gdns, Dag. RM8 148 EW63
Cotesmore Rd, Hem.H. HP1 61 BE21
Cotford Rd, Th.Hth. CR7 224 DQ98
Cotham St, SE17 31 K9
Cotherstone, Epsom KT19 238 CR110
Cotherstone Rd, SW2 203 DM88
Cotland Acres, Red. RH1 288 DD136
Cotlandswick, Lon.Col. AL2 83 CJ26
Cotleigh Av, Bex. DA5 208 EX89
Cotleigh Rd, NW6 5 J6
Romford RM7 149 FD58
Cotman Cl, NW11 142 DC58
SW15 201 CX86
Cotmandene, Dor. RH4 285 CH136
Cotmandene Cres, Orp. BR5 228 EU96
Cotman Gdns, Edg. HA8 118 CN54
Cotman Ms, Dag. RM8 148 EW64
Cotmans Cl, Hayes UB3 157 BU74
Coton Rd, Well. DA16 188 EU83
Cotsford Av, N.Mal. KT3 220 CQ99
Cotsmoor, St.Alb. AL1
off Granville Rd 65 CF20
Cotswold, Hem.H. HP2
off Mendip Way 62 BL17
Cotswold Av, Bushey WD23 98 CC44
Cotswold Cl, Bexh. DA7 189 FE82
Hinchley Wood KT10 219 CF104
Kingston upon Thames KT2 200 CP93
St. Albans AL4
off Chiltern Rd 65 CJ15
Slough SL1 173 AP76
Staines TW18 196 BG92
Uxbridge UB8 156 BJ67
Cotswold Ct, EC1 19 J4
N11 120 DG49
Cotswold Gdns, E6 24 F2
NW2 141 CX61
Hutton CM13 131 GE45
Ilford IG2 147 ER59
Cotswold Gate, NW2 141 CY60
Cotswold Grn, Enf. EN2
off Cotswold Way 103 DM42
Cotswold Ms, SW11 40 B7
Cotswold Ri, Orp. BR6 227 ET100
Cotswold Rd, Hmptn. TW12 198 CA93
Northfleet DA11 212 GE90
Romford RM3 128 FM54
Sutton SM2 240 DB110
Cotswolds, Hat. AL10 67 CU20
Cotswold St, SE27
off Norwood High St 203 DP91
Cotswold Way, Enf. EN2 103 DM42
Worcester Park KT4 221 CW103
Cottage Av, Brom. BR2 226 EL102
Cottage Cl, Crox.Grn WD3 96 BM44
Harrow HA2 139 CE61
Ottershaw KT16 233 BC107
Ruislip HA4 137 BR60
Watford WD17 97 BT40
Cottage Fm Way, Egh. TW20
off Green Rd 215 BC97
Cottage Fld Cl, Sid. DA14 208 EW88
Cottage Gdns, Chsht EN8 88 DW29
Cottage Grn, SE5 43 M4
Cottage Gro, SW9 183 DL83
Surbiton KT6 219 CK100
Cottage Pk Rd, Hedg. SL2 133 AR61
Cottage Pl, SW3 28 C6
Cottage Rd, N7 8 C3
Epsom KT19 238 CR108
Cottage St, E14 22 D10
Cottage Wk, N16
off Brooke Rd 144 DT62
Cottenham Dr, NW9 141 CT55
SW20 201 CV94
Cottenham Par, SW20
off Durham Rd 221 CV96
COTTENHAM PARK, SW20 221 CV95
Cottenham Pk Rd, SW20 201 CV94
Cottenham Pl, SW20 201 CV94
Cottenham Rd, E17 145 DZ56
Cotterells, Hem.H. HP1 62 BJ21
Cotterells Hill, Hem.H. HP1 62 BJ20
Cotterill Rd, Surb. KT6 220 CL103
Cottesbrooke Cl, Colnbr. SL3 175 BD81
Cottesbrook St, SE14 45 L4
Cottesloe Ms, SE1 30 F6
Cottesmore Av, Ilf. IG5 125 EN54
Cottesmore Gdns, W8 27 M6
Cottimore Av, Walt. KT12 217 BV102
Cottimore Cres, Walt. KT12 217 BV101
Cottimore La, Walt. KT12 218 BW102
Cottimore Ter, Walt. KT12 217 BV101
Cottingham Chase, Ruis. HA4 137 BU62
Cottingham Rd, SE20 205 DX94
SW8 42 D3
Cottington Rd, Felt. TW13 198 BX91
Cottington St, SE11 30 F10
Cottle Way, SE16 32 F5
Cotton Av, W3 160 CR72
Cotton Cl, E11 146 EE61
Dagenham RM9
off Flamstead Rd 168 EW66
Cotton Dr, Hert. SG13 54 DV08
Cotton Fld, Hat. AL10 67 CV16
Cottongrass Cl, Croy. CR0
off Cornflower La 225 DX102
Cotton Hill, Brom. BR1 205 ED91
Cotton La, Dart. DA2 210 FQ86
Greenhithe DA9 210 FQ85
Cottonmill Cres, St.Alb. AL1 65 CD21
Cottonmill La, St.Alb. AL1 65 CE23
Cotton Rd, Pot.B. EN6 86 DC31
Cotton Row, SW11 39 P10
Cottons App, Rom. RM7 149 FD57
Cottons Ct, Rom. RM7 149 FD57
Cottons Gdns, E2 19 P2
Cottons La, SE1 31 M2
Cotton St, E14 22 E10
Cottrell Ct, SE10
off Greenroof Way 35 M8
Cottrill Gdns, E8 10 E4
Cotts Cl, W7
off Westcott Cres 159 CF72
Cotts Wd Dr, Guil. GU4 265 BA129
Couchmore Av, Esher KT10 219 CE103
Ilford IG5 125 EM54
Coulgate St, SE4 185 DY83
COULSDON, CR5 257 DJ116
Sch Coulsdon C of E Prim Sch,
Couls. CR5
off Bradmore Grn 257 DM118
Coll Coulsdon Coll, Couls. CR5
off Placehouse La 257 DN119
Coulsdon Common, Cat. CR3 258 DQ121
Coulsdon Ct Rd, Couls. CR5 257 DM116
Sch Coulsdon High Sch, Couls.
CR5 off Homefield Rd 257 DP120
Coulsdon La, Chipstead CR5 256 DF119
● Coulsdon N Ind Est, Couls.
CR5 257 DK116
Coulsdon Pl, Cat. CR3 258 DR122
Coulsdon Ri, Couls. CR5 257 DL117
Coulsdon Rd, Cat. CR3 258 DQ121
Coulsdon CR5 257 DM115
⇌ Coulsdon South 257 DK116
Coulser Cl, Hem.H. HP1 62 BG17
Coulson Cl, Dag. RM8 148 EW59
Coulson Ct, Lon.Col. AL2 83 CK27
Coulson St, SW3 28 E10
Coulson Way, Burn. SL1 152 AH71
Coulter Cl, Cuffley EN6 87 DK27
Hayes UB4
off Berrydale Rd 158 BY70
Coulter Rd, W6 181 CV76
Coulton Av, Nthflt DA11 212 GE87
Council Av, Nthflt DA11 212 GC86
Council Cotts, Wisley GU23
off Wisley La 250 BK115
Councillor St, SE5 43 J5
Counter Ct, SE1
off Borough High St 31 L3
Counters Cl, Hem.H. HP1 62 BG20
Counter St, SE1 31 N2
Sch Countess Anne C of E Prim Sch,
Hat. AL10 off School La 67 CW17
Countess Cl, Hare. UB9 114 BJ54
Countess Rd, NW5 7 L2
Countisbury Av, Enf. EN1 122 DT45
Countisbury Gdns, Add. KT15 234 BH106
Country Way, Han. TW13 197 BV94
Sunbury-on-Thames TW16 197 BV94
County Gate, SE9 207 EQ90
New Barnet EN5 102 DB44
County Gro, SE5 43 J6
★ County Hall, SE1 30 C4
County Rd, E6 25 N7
Thornton Heath CR7 223 DP96
County St, SE1 31 K7
Coupland Pl, SE18 187 EQ78
Courage Cl, Horn. RM11 150 FJ58
Courage Wk, Hutt. CM13 131 GD44
Courcy Rd, N8 143 DN55
Courier Rd, Dag. RM9 169 FC70
Courland Gro, SW8 41 P7
Courland Gro Hall, SW8 41 P8
Courland Rd, Add. KT15 216 BH104
Courland St, SW8 41 P7
Course, The, SE9 207 EN90
Coursers Rd, Coln.Hth AL4 84 CN27
Court, The, Ruis. HA4 138 BY63
Warlingham CR6 259 DY118
Courtauld Cl, SE28 168 EU74
★ Courtauld Inst of Art, WC2 18 C10
Courtauld Rd, N19 143 DK60
Courtaulds, Chipper. WD4 80 BH30
Court Av, Belv. DA17 188 EZ78
Coulsdon CR5 257 DN118
Romford RM3 128 FN52
Court Bushes Rd, Whyt. CR3 258 DU120
Court Cl, Har. HA3 139 CK55
Maidenhead SL6 172 AC77
Twickenham TW2 198 CB90
Wallington SM6 241 DK108
Court Cl Av, Twick. TW2 198 CB90
Court Cres, Chess. KT9 237 CK106
Slough SL1 153 AR72
Swanley BR8 229 FE98
Court Downs Rd, Beck. BR3 225 EB96
Court Dr, Croy. CR0 241 DM105
Maidenhead SL6 152 AC68
Stanmore HA7 118 CL49
Sutton SM1 240 DE105
Uxbridge UB10 156 BM67
Courtenay Av, N6 142 DE58
Harrow HA3 116 CC53
Sutton SM2 240 DA109
Courtenay Dr, Beck. BR3 225 ED96
Chafford Hundred RM16
off Clifford Rd 192 FZ76
Courtenay Gdns, Har. HA3 116 CC54
Upminster RM14 150 FQ60
Courtenay Ms, E17
off Cranbrook Ms 145 DY57
Courtenay Pl, E17 145 DY57
Courtenay Rd, E11 146 EF62
E17 145 DX56
SE20 205 DX94
Wembley HA9 139 CK62
Woking GU21 249 BA116
Worcester Park KT4 221 CW104
Courtenay Sq, SE11 42 E1
Courtenay St, SE11 30 E10
Courtens Ms, Stan. HA7 117 CJ52
Court Fm Av, Epsom KT19 238 CR106
Court Fm Cl, Slou. SL1
off Weekes Dr 153 AP74
Court Fm Pk, Warl. CR6 258 DU116
Court Fm Rd, SE9 206 EK89
Northolt UB5 158 CA66
Warlingham CR6 258 DU118
Courtfield, W5
off Castlebar Hill 159 CJ71
Courtfield Av, Har. HA1 139 CF57
Courtfield Cl, Brox. EN10 71 EA20
Courtfield Cres, Har. HA1 139 CF57
Courtfield Gdns, SW5 27 M8
W13 159 CG72
Denham UB9 136 BG62
Ruislip HA4 137 BT61
Courtfield Ms, SW5 27 N9
Courtfield Ri, W.Wick. BR4 225 ED104
Courtfield Rd, SW7 27 M9
Ashford TW15 197 BP93
Court Gdns, N7 8 F5
Courtgate Cl, NW7 119 CT51
Court Grn Hts, Wok. GU22 248 AW120
Court Haw, Bans. SM7 256 DE115
Court Hill, Chipstead CR5 256 DE118
South Croydon CR2 242 DS112
Courthill Rd, SE13 185 EC84
Courthope Rd, NW3 6 F1
SW19 201 CY92
Greenford UB6 159 CD68
Courthope Vil, SW19 201 CY94
Court Ho Gdns, N3 120 DA51
Courthouse Rd, N12 120 DB51
Courtland Av, E4 124 EF47
NW7 118 CR48
SW16 203 DM94
Ilford IG1 147 EM61

Courtland Dr, Chig. IG7 125 EP48
Courtland Gro, SE28 168 EX73
Sch Courtland Prim Sch, NW7
off Courtland Av 118 CS47
Courtland Rd, E6
off Harrow Rd 166 EL67
Courtlands, Rich. TW10 180 CN84
Courtlands Av, SE12 206 EH85
Bromley BR2 226 EF102
Esher KT10 236 BZ107
Hampton TW12 198 BZ93
Richmond TW9 180 CP82
Slough SL3 174 AX77
Courtlands Cl, Ruis. HA4 137 BT59
South Croydon CR2 242 DT110
Watford WD24 97 BS35
Courtlands Cres, Bans. SM7 256 DA115
Courtlands Dr, Epsom KT19 238 CS107
Watford WD17, WD24 97 BS37
Courtlands Rd, Surb. KT5 220 CN101
Court La, SE21 204 DS86
Burnham SL1 153 AK69
Dorney SL4 172 AG76
Epsom KT19 238 CQ113
Iver SL0 156 BG74
Court La Gdns, SE21 204 DS87
Court Lawns, Penn HP10 110 AC46
Courtleas, Cob. KT11 236 CA113
Courtleet Dr, Erith DA8 189 FB81
Courtleigh Av, Barn. EN4 102 DD38
Courtleigh Gdns, NW11 141 CY56
Court Lo Rd, Horl. RH6 290 DE147
Courtman Rd, N17 122 DQ52
Court Mead, Nthlt. UB5 158 BZ69
Courtmead Cl, SE24 204 DQ86
Courtnell St, W2 15 J8
Courtney Cl, SE19 204 DS93
Courtney Cres, Cars. SM5 240 DF108
Courtney Pl, Cob. KT11 236 BZ112
Croydon CR0 223 DN104
Courtney Rd, N7 8 E2
SW19 202 DE94
Croydon CR0 223 DN104
Grays RM16 193 GJ75
London Heathrow Airport
TW6 176 BN83
Courtney Way, Lon.Hthrw Air.
TW6 176 BN83
Court Par, Wem. HA0 139 CH62
Courtrai Rd, SE23 205 DY86
Court Rd, SE9 206 EL89
SE25 224 DT96
Banstead SM7 256 DA116
Caterham CR3 258 DR123
Godstone RH9 274 DW131
Lane End DA2 211 FS92
Maidenhead SL6 152 AC69
Orpington BR6 228 EV101
Southall UB2 178 BZ77
Uxbridge UB10 137 BP64
Courtside, N8 143 DK58
Court St, E1 20 E6
Bromley BR1 226 EG96
Court Way, NW9 140 CS56
W3 160 CQ71
Ilford IG6 147 EQ55
Romford RM3 128 FL54
Twickenham TW2 199 CF87
Courtway, Wdf.Grn. IG8 124 EJ50
Courtway, The, Wat. WD19 116 BY47
Courtwood Dr, Sev. TN13 278 FG124
Court Wd Gro, Croy. CR0 243 DZ111
Courtwood La, Croy. CR0 243 DZ110
Sch Courtwood Prim Sch, Croy.
CR0 off Courtwood La 243 DZ110
Court Yd, SE9 206 EL86
Courtyard, The, N1 8 D6
Brentwood CM15 130 FV45
Hertingfordbury SG14 53 DM10
Keston BR2 244 EL107
Shendish HP3 80 BK26
Courtyard Ho, SW6
off Lensbury Av 39 P8
Courtyard Ms, Orp. BR5
off Dorchester Cl 208 EU94
● Courtyards, The, Wat.
WD18 115 BR45
Courtyards, The, Slou. SL3
off Waterside Dr 175 BA75
Cousin La, EC4 31 L1
Cousins Cl, West Dr. UB7 156 BL73
Couthurst Rd, SE3 186 EH79
Coutts Av, Chess. KT9 238 CL106
Coutts Cres, NW5 142 DG62
Coval Gdns, SW14 180 CP84
Coval La, SW14 180 CP84
Coval Pas, SW14 off Coval Rd 180 CQ84
Coval Rd, SW14 180 CP84
Coveham Cres, Cob. KT11 235 BU113
Covelees Wall, E6 25 M8
Covell Ct, SE8
off Reginald Sq 46 B5
Covenbrook, Brwd. CM13 131 GB48
★ Covent Garden, WC2 18 B10
⊖ Covent Garden 18 A10
Covent Gdn Mkt, WC2 18 B10
Coventry Cl, E6 25 J9
NW6 5 K9
Coventry Rd, E1 20 F4
E2 20 F4
SE25 224 DU98
Ilford IG1 147 EP60
Coventry St, W1 29 N1
Coverack Cl, N14 103 DJ44
Croydon CR0 225 DY101
Coverdale, Hem.H. HP2
off Wharfedale 62 BL17
Coverdale Cl, Stan. HA7 117 CH50
Coverdale Ct, Enf. EN3
off Raynton Rd 105 DY37
Coverdale Gdns, Croy. CR0
off Park Hill Ri 224 DT104
Coverdale Rd, N11 120 DG51
NW2 4 D6
W12 161 CV74
Coverdales, The, Bark. IG11 167 EQ68
Coverdale Way, Slou. SL2 153 AL70
Coverley Cl, E1 20 D6
Great Warley CM13
off Wilmot Grn 129 FW51
Covert, The, Nthwd. HA6 115 BQ53
Petts Wood BR6 227 ES100
Coverton Rd, SW17 202 DE92
Covert Rd, Ilf. IG6 125 ET51
Coverts, The, Hutt. CM13 131 GA46
Coverts Rd, Clay. KT10 237 CF109
Covert Way, Barn. EN4 102 DC40
Covesfield, Grav. DA11 213 GF87
Covet Wd Cl, Orp. BR5 227 ET100
Covey Cl, SW19 222 DB96
Covington Gdns, SW16 203 DP94
Covington Way, SW16 203 DM93
Cowan Cl, E6 25 H7
Cowbridge, Hert. SG14 54 DQ09
Cowbridge La, Bark. IG11 167 EP66
Cowbridge Rd, Har. HA3 140 CM56
Cowcross St, EC1 18 G6
Cowdenbeath Path, N1 8 C8
Cowden Rd, Orp. BR6 227 ET101
Cowden St, SE6 205 EA91
Cowdray Rd, Uxb. UB10 157 BQ67
Cowdray Way, Horn. RM12 149 FF63
Cowdrey Cl, Enf. EN1 104 DS40
Cowdrey Ct, Dart. DA1 209 FH87
Cowdrey Rd, SW19 202 DB92
Cowdry Rd, E9
off East Cross Route 11 N5
Cowen Av, Har. HA2 138 CC61
Cowgate Rd, Grnf. UB6 159 CD68
Cowick Rd, SW17 202 DF91
Cowings Mead, Nthlt. UB5 158 BY66
Cowland Av, Enf. EN3 104 DW42
Cow La, Bushey WD23 98 CA44
Greenford UB6 159 CD68
Watford WD25 98 BW36
Cow Leaze, E6 25 M8
Cowleaze Rd, Kings.T. KT2 220 CL95
Cowles, Chsht EN7 88 DT27
COWLEY, Uxb. UB8 156 BJ70
Cowley Av, Cher. KT16 215 BF101
Greenhithe DA9 211 FT85
● Cowley Business Pk,
Cowley UB8 156 BJ69
Cowley Cl, S.Croy. CR2 242 DW109
Cowley Cres, Hersham KT12 236 BW105
Uxbridge UB8 156 BJ71
Cowley Est, SW9 42 E6
Cowley Hill, Borwd. WD6 100 CP37
Sch Cowley Hill Prim Sch, Borwd.
WD6 off Winstre Rd 100 CP39
Cowley La, Cher. KT16 215 BF101
Cowley Mill Rd, Uxb. UB8 156 BH68
Cowley Pl, NW4 141 CW57
Cowley Retail Pk,
Cowley UB8 156 BK73
Cowley Rd, E11 146 EH57
SW9 42 F7
SW14 180 CS83
W3 161 CT74
Ilford IG1 147 EM59
Romford RM3 127 FH52
Uxbridge UB8 156 BJ68
Sch Cowley St. Laurence C of E
Prim Sch, Cowley UB8
off Worcester Rd 156 BK71
Cowley St, SW1 30 A6
Cowling Cl, W11 26 E2
Cowlins, Harl. CM17 58 EX11
Cowper Av, E6 166 EL66
Sutton SM1 240 DD105
Tilbury RM18 193 GH81
Cowper Cl, Brom. BR2 226 EK98
Chertsey KT16 215 BF100
Welling DA16 208 EU85
Cowper Ct, Wat. WD24 97 BU37
Cowper Cres, Hert. SG14 53 DP07
Cowper Gdns, N14 103 DJ44
Wallington SM6 241 DJ107
Cowper Rd, N14 121 DH46
N16 9 N2
N18 122 DU50
SW19 202 DC93
W3 160 CR74
W7 159 CF73
Belvedere DA17 188 FA77
Berkhamsted HP4 60 AV19
Bromley BR2 226 EK98
Chesham HP5 76 AP29
Hemel Hempstead HP1 62 BH21
Kingston upon Thames KT2 200 CM92
Rainham RM13 169 FG70
Slough SL2 153 AN70
Welwyn Garden City AL7 51 CZ11
Cowpers Ct, EC3
off Birchin La 19 M9
Cowper St, EC2 19 M4
Cowper Ter, W10 14 C7
Cowslip Cl, Uxb. UB10 156 BL66
Cowslip La, Mick. RH5 269 CG129
Woking GU21 248 AV115
Cowslip Rd, E18 124 EH54
Cowslips, Welw.G.C. AL7 52 DC10
Cowthorpe Rd, SW8 41 P6
Cox Cl, Shenley WD7 84 CM32
Coxdean, Epsom KT18 255 CW119
Coxe Pl, Wealds. HA3 139 CG56
Coxfield Cl, Hem.H. HP2 62 BL21
Cox La, Chess. KT9 238 CM105
Epsom KT19 238 CP106
Coxley Ri, Pur. CR8 242 DQ113
Coxmount Rd, SE7 36 E10
Coxon Dr, Chaff.Hun. RM16 192 FY76
Coxson Way, SE1 32 A5
Cox's Wk, SE21 204 DU88
Coxwell Rd, SE18 187 ER78
SE19 204 DS94
Coxwold Path, Chess. KT9
off Garrison La 238 CL108
Cozens La E, Brox. EN10 71 DZ23
Cozens La W, Brox. EN10 71 DY22
Cozens Rd, Ware SG12 55 DZ06
Crabbe Cres, Chesh. HP5 76 AR29
Crabbs Cft Cl, Orp. BR6
off Ladycroft Way 245 EQ106
Crab Hill, Beck. BR3 205 ED94
Crab Hill La, S.Nutfld RH1 289 DM138
Crab La, Ald. WD25 98 CB35
Crabtree Av, Rom. RM6 148 EX56
Wembley HA0 160 CL68
Crabtree Cl, E2 20 A1
Beaconsfield HP9 110 AH54
Bookham KT23 268 CC126
Bushey WD23 98 CB43
Hemel Hempstead HP3 62 BK22
Jct Crabtree Cor, Egh. TW20 215 BB95
Crabtree Ct, Hem.H. HP3
off Crabtree La 62 BL22
Crabtree Dr, Lthd. KT22 253 CJ124
Crabtree Hill, Lamb.End RM4 126 EZ45
Crabtree La, SW6 38 C4
Bookham KT23 268 CC126
Headley KT18 270 CQ126
Hemel Hempstead HP3 62 BK22
Westhumble RH5 269 CF130
● Crabtree Manorway Ind Est,
Belv. DA17 189 FB76
Crabtree Manorway N, Belv.
DA17 189 FC75
Crabtree Manorway S, Belv.
DA17 189 FC76
● Crabtree Office Village, Egh.
TW20 off Eversley Way 215 BC96
Crabtree Rd, Egh. TW20 215 BC96
Crabtree Wk, Brox. EN10 71 DY19
Crackley Meadow, Hem.H. HP2 63 BP15
Cracknell Cl, Enf. EN1 104 DV37
Craddock Rd, Enf. EN1 104 DT41
Craddocks Av, Ashtd. KT21 254 CL117
Craddocks Cl, Ashtd. KT21 254 CN116
Craddocks Par, Ashtd. KT21 254 CL117
Craddock St, NW5 6 G5
Cradhurst Cl, Westc. RH4 284 CC137
Cradley Rd, SE9 207 ER88
Cragg Av, Rad. WD7 99 CF36
Craigavon Rd, Hem.H. HP2 62 BM16
Craigdale Rd, Horn. RM11 149 FF58
Craig Dr, Uxb. UB8 157 BP72
Craigen Av, Croy. CR0 224 DV102
Craigerne Rd, SE3 186 EH80
Craig Gdns, E18 124 EF54
Craigholm, SE18 187 EN82
Craiglands, St.Alb. AL4 65 CK16
Craigmore Twr, Wok. GU22
off Guildford Rd 248 AY119
Craig Mt, Rad. WD7 99 CH35
Craigmuir Pk, Wem. HA0 160 CM67
Craignair Rd, SW2 203 DN87
Craignish Av, SW16 223 DM96
Craig Pk Rd, N18 122 DV50
Craig Rd, Rich. TW10 199 CJ91
Craigs Ct, SW1 30 A2
Craigs Wk, Chsht EN8
off Davison Dr 89 DX28
Craigton Rd, SE9 187 EM84
Craigweil Av, Rad. WD7 99 CH35
Craigweil Cl, Stan. HA7 117 CK50
Craigweil Dr, Stan. HA7 117 CK50
Craigwell Av, Felt. TW13 197 BU90
Craigwell Cl, Stai. TW18 215 BE95
Craik Ct, NW6 15 H1
Crail Row, SE17 31 M9
Crakell Rd, Reig. RH2 288 DC135
Cramer Ct, N.Mal. KT3
off Warwick Rd 220 CQ97
Cramer St, W1 17 H7
Crammerville Wk, Rain. RM13 169 FH70
Crammond Cl, W6 38 E2
● Crammond Pk, Harl. CM19 73 EN16
Cramond Ct, Felt. TW14 197 BS88
Crampshaw La, Ashtd. KT21 254 CM119
Sch Crampton Prim Sch, SE17 31 H10
Crampton Rd, SE20 204 DW93
Cramptons Rd, Sev. TN14 263 FH120
Crampton St, SE17 31 J9
Cranberry Cl, Nthlt. UB5
off Parkfield Av 158 BX68
Cranberry La, E16 23 J5
Cranborne Av, Sthl. UB2 178 CA77
Surbiton KT6 220 CN104
Cranborne Cl, Hert. SG13 54 DQ12
Potters Bar EN6 85 CY31
Cranborne Cres, Pot.B. EN6 85 CY31
Cranborne Gdns, Upmin.
RM14 150 FP61
Welwyn Garden City AL7 51 CZ10
● Cranborne Ind Est, Pot.B.
EN6 85 CY30
Sch Cranborne Prim Sch, Pot.B.
EN6 off Laurel Flds 85 CZ31
Cranborne Rd, Bark. IG11 167 ER67
Cheshunt EN8 89 DX32
Hatfield AL10 67 CV17
Hoddesdon EN11 71 EB16
Potters Bar EN6 85 CY31
Cranborne Waye, Hayes UB4 158 BW73
Cranbourn All, WC2
off Cranbourn St 17 P10
Cranbourne Av, E11 146 EH56
Windsor SL4 173 AM82
Cranbourne Cl, SW16 223 DL97
Hersham KT12 236 BW107
Horley RH6 291 DH146
Slough SL1 153 AQ74
Cranbourne Dr, Hodd. EN11 55 EB13
Pinner HA5 138 BX57
Cranbourne Gdns, NW11 141 CY57
Ilford IG6 147 EQ55
Cranbourne Pas, SE16 32 E5
Sch Cranbourne Prim Sch, Hodd.
EN11 off Bridle Way N 55 EB13
Cranbourne Rd, E12
off High St N 146 EL64
E15 12 F1
N10 121 DH54
Northwood HA6 137 BT55
Slough SL1 153 AQ74
Cranbourn St, WC2 17 P10
CRANBROOK, Ilf. IG1 147 EM60
Cranbrook Cl, Brom. BR2 226 EG100
Sch Cranbrook Coll, Ilf. IG1
off Mansfield Rd 147 EN61
Cranbrook Dr, Esher KT10 218 CC102
Romford RM2 149 FH56
St. Albans AL4 66 CL20
Twickenham TW2 198 CB88
Cranbrook Ho, E5
off Pembury Rd 10 E2
Erith DA8 off Boundary St 189 FF80
Cranbrook La, N11 121 DH49
Cranbrook Ms, E17 145 DY57
Cranbrook Pk, N22 121 DM53
Sch Cranbrook Prim Sch, Ilf.
IG1 off The Drive 147 EM59
Cranbrook Ri, Ilf. IG1 147 EM59
Cranbrook Rd, SE8 46 B7
SW19 201 CY94
W4 180 CS78
Barnet EN4 102 DD44
Bexleyheath DA7 188 EZ81
Hounslow TW4 178 BZ84
Ilford IG1, IG2, IG6 147 EN59
Thornton Heath CR7 224 DQ96
Cranbrook St, E2 21 K1
Cranbury Rd, SW6 39 M8
Crandale Ho, E5
off Pembury Rd 10 E2
Crandon Wk, S.Darenth DA4
off Gorringe Av 231 FS96
Crane Av, W3 160 CQ73
Isleworth TW7 199 CG85
Cranebank Ms, Twick. TW1 179 CG84
Cranebrook, Twick. TW2
off Manor Rd 198 CC89
Crane Cl, Dag. RM10 168 FA65
Harrow HA2 138 CC62
Crane Ct, EC4 18 F9
Epsom KT19 238 CQ105
Cranefield Dr, Wat. WD25 82 BY32
Craneford Cl, Twick. TW2 199 CF87
Craneford Way, Twick. TW2 199 CE87
Crane Gdns, Hayes UB3 177 BT77
Crane Gro, N7 8 F4
Crane Ho, SE15 44 A7
Cranell Grn, S.Ock. RM15 171 FV74
Crane Lo Rd, Houns. TW5 104 BV79
Crane Mead, Ware SG12 55 DY07
● Crane Mead Business Pk,
Ware SG12 55 DY07
Sch Crane Pk Prim Sch, Han.
TW13 off Norman Av 198 BZ89
Crane Pk Rd, Twick. TW2 198 CB89
Crane Rd, Twick. TW2 199 CE88
Cranesbill Cl, NW9
off Annesley Av 140 CR55
Cranes Dr, Surb. KT5 220 CL98
Cranes Pk, Surb. KT5 220 CL98
Cranes Pk Av, Surb. KT5 220 CL98
Cranes Pk Cres, Surb. KT5 220 CM98
Crane St, SE10 46 G1
SE15 44 A6
Craneswater, Hayes UB3 177 BT80
Craneswater Pk, Sthl. UB2 178 BZ78
Cranes Way, Borwd. WD6 100 CQ43
Crane Way, Twick. TW2 198 CC87
Cranfield Cl, SE27
off Norwood High St 204 DQ90
Cranfield Ct, Wok. GU21
off Martindale Rd 248 AU118
Cranfield Cres, Cuffley EN6 87 DL29
Cranfield Dr, NW9 118 CS52
Cranfield Rd, SE4 45 N10
Cranfield Rd E, Cars. SM5 240 DG109
Cranfield Rd W, Cars. SM5 240 DF109
Cranfield Row, SE1 30 F6
CRANFORD, Houns. TW5 177 BU80
Cranford Av, N13 121 DL50
Staines TW19 196 BL87
Cranford Cl, SW20 221 CV95
Purley CR8 242 DQ113
Staines TW19 196 BL87
Sch Cranford Comm Coll, Cran.
TW5 off High St 177 BV79
Cranford Cotts, E1
off Cranford St 21 K10
Cranford Ct, Hert. SG14
off The Ridgeway 53 DM08
Cranford Dr, Hayes UB3 177 BT77
Sch Cranford Inf & Nurs Sch, Cran.
TW4 off Berkeley Av 177 BV82
Sch Cranford Jun Sch, Cran.
TW4 off Woodfield Rd 177 BV82
Cranford La, Hayes UB3 177 BR79
Heston TW5 178 BX80
London Heathrow Airport
TW6 177 BT83
London Heathrow Airport
N TW6 177 BT81
Sch Cranford Pk Prim Sch, Harling.
UB3 off Phelps Way 177 BT77
Cranford Pk Rd, Hayes UB3 177 BT77
Cranford Ri, Esher KT10 236 CC106
Cranford Rd, Dart. DA1 210 FL88
Cranford St, E1 21 K10
Cranford Way, N8 143 DM57
CRANHAM, Upmin. RM14 151 FS59
Cranham Gdns, Upmin. RM14 151 FS60
Cranham Rd, Horn. RM11 149 FH58
Cranhurst Rd, NW2 4 B4
Cranleigh Cl, SE20 224 DV96
Bexley DA5 209 FB86
Cheshunt EN7 88 DU28
Orpington BR6 228 EU104
South Croydon CR2 242 DU112
Cranleigh Ct, Mitch. CR4
off Phipps Br Rd 222 DD97
Cranleigh Dr, Swan. BR8 229 FE98
Cranleigh Gdns, N21 103 DN43
SE25 224 DS97
Barking IG11 167 ER66
Harrow HA3 140 CL57
Kingston upon Thames KT2 200 CM93
Loughton IG10 107 EM44
South Croydon CR2 242 DU112
Southall UB1 158 BZ72
Sutton SM1 222 DB103
● Cranleigh Gdns Ind Est, Sthl.
UB1 off Cranleigh Gdns 158 BZ71
Cranleigh Ms, SW11 40 D9
Cranleigh Rd, N15 144 DQ57
SW19 222 DA97
Esher KT10 218 CC102
Feltham TW13 197 BT91
Wonersh GU5 281 BB144
Cranleigh St, NW1 17 M1
Cranley Cl, Guil. GU1 265 BA134
Cranley Dene, Guil. GU1 265 BA134
Cranley Dene Ct, N10 142 DG56
Cranley Dr, Ilf. IG2 147 EQ59
Ruislip HA4 137 BT61
Cranley Gdns, N10 143 DJ56
N13 121 DM48
SW7 27 P10
Wallington SM6 241 DJ108
Cranley Ms, SW7 27 P10
Cranley Par, SE9
off Beaconsfield Rd 206 EL91
Cranley Pl, SW7 28 A9
Cranley Rd, E13 24 A6
Guildford GU1 265 AZ134
Hersham KT12 235 BS106
Ilford IG2 147 EQ58
Cranmer Av, W13 179 CH76
Cranmer Cl, Mord. SM4 221 CX100
Potters Bar EN6 86 DB30
Ruislip HA4 138 BX60
Stanmore HA7 117 CJ52
Warlingham CR6 259 DY117
Weybridge KT13 234 BN108
Cranmer Ct, SW3 28 D9
SW4 183 DK83
Hampton Hill TW12
off Cranmer Rd 198 CB92
Sch Cranmere Prim Sch, Esher
KT10 off The Drive 218 CC102
Cranmer Fm Cl, Mitch. CR4 222 DF98
Cranmer Gdns, Dag. RM10 149 FC63
Warlingham CR6 259 DY117
Cranmer Ho, SW11
off Surrey La 40 C6
Sch Cranmer Prim Sch, Mitch.
CR4 off Cranmer Rd 222 DF98
Cranmer Rd, E7 146 EH63
SW9 42 F4
Croydon CR0 223 DP104
Edgware HA8 118 CP48
Hampton Hill TW12 198 CB92
Cranmer Rd, Hayes UB3 157 BR72
Kingston upon Thames KT2 200 CL92
Mitcham CR4 222 DF98
Sevenoaks TN13 278 FE123
Cranmer Ter, SW17 202 DD92
Cranmore Av, Islw. TW7 178 CC80
Cranmore Cotts, Lthd. KT24 267 BP129
Cranmore Ct, St.Alb. AL1 65 CF19
Cranmore La, W.Hors. KT24 267 BP129
Cranmore Rd, Brom. BR1 206 EE90
Chislehurst BR7 207 EM92
Sch Cranmore Sch, W.Hors.
KT24 off Epsom Rd 267 BQ130
Cranmore Way, N10 143 DJ56
Cranston Cl, Houns. TW3 178 BY82
Reigate RH2 288 DB135
Uxbridge UB10 137 BR61
Cranston Est, N1 19 M1
Cranston Gdns, E4 123 EB50
Cranston Pk Av, Upmin. RM14 150 FP63
Cranston Rd, SE23 205 DY88
Cranstoun Cl, Guil. GU3 264 AT130
Cranswick Rd, SE16 32 F10
Crantock Rd, SE6 205 EB89
Cranwell Cl, E3 22 C5
St. Albans AL4 65 CJ22
Cranwell Gro, Shep. TW17 216 BM98
Cranwells La, Farn.Com. SL2 133 AQ62
Cranwich Av, N21 122 DR45
Cranwich Rd, N16 144 DR59
Cranwood St, EC1 19 L3
Cranworth Cres, E4 123 ED46
Cranworth Gdns, SW9 42 E7
Craster Rd, SW2 203 DM87
Crathie Rd, SE12 206 EH86
Cravan Av, Felt. TW13 197 BU89
Craven Av, W5 159 CJ73
Southall UB1 158 BZ71
Craven Cl, N16 144 DU59
Hayes UB4 157 BU72
Craven Gdns, SW19 202 DA92
Barking IG11 167 ES68
Collier Row RM5 126 FA50
Harold Wood RM3 128 FQ51
Ilford IG6 125 ER54
Craven Hill, W2 15 P10
Craven Hill Gdns, W2 15 N10
Craven Hill Ms, W2 15 P10
Craven Ms, SW11
off Taybridge Rd 182 DG83
Craven Pk, NW10 160 CS67
Craven Pk Ms, NW10 160 CS66
Craven Pk Rd, N15 144 DT58
NW10 160 CS67
Craven Pas, WC2 30 A2
Craven Rd, NW10 160 CR67
W2 15 P10
W5 159 CJ73
Croydon CR0 224 DV102
Kingston upon Thames KT2 220 CM95
Orpington BR6 228 EX104
Cravens, The, Smallfield RH6 291 DN148
Craven St, WC2 30 A2
Craven Ter, W2 15 P10
Craven Wk, N16 144 DU59
Crawford Av, Wem. HA0 139 CK64
Crawford Cl, Islw. TW7 179 CE82
Crawford Compton Cl, Horn.
RM12 170 FJ65
Crawford Est, SE5 43 K8
Crawford Gdns, N13 121 DP48
Northolt UB5 158 BZ69
Crawford Ms, W1 16 E7
Crawford Pas, EC1 18 E5
Crawford Pl, W1 16 D8
Sch Crawford Prim Sch, SE5 43 K7
Crawford Rd, SE5 43 K7
Hatfield AL10 67 CU16
Crawfords, Swan. BR8 209 FE94
Crawford St, NW10
off Fawood Av 160 CR66
W1 16 E7
Crawley Dr, Hem.H. HP2 62 BM16
Crawley Rd, E10 145 EB60
N22 122 DQ54
Enfield EN1 122 DS45
Crawshaw Rd, Ott. KT16 233 BD107
Crawshay Cl, Sev. TN13 278 FG123
Crawshay Ct, SW9 42 F6
Crawthew Gro, SE22 184 DT84
Cray Av, Ashtd. KT21 254 CL116
Orpington BR5 228 EV99
Craybrooke Rd, Sid. DA14 208 EV91
Crayburne, Sthflt DA13 212 FZ92
Craybury End, SE9 207 EQ89
Cray Cl, Dart. DA1 189 FG84
Craydene Rd, Erith DA8 189 FF81
● Crayfields Business Pk,
Orp. BR5 228 EW95
● Crayfields Ind Pk,
Orp. BR5 228 EW96
CRAYFORD, Dart. DA1 209 FD85
⇌ Crayford 209 FE86
Crayford Cl, E6 24 G8
● Crayford Creek, Dart.
DA1 off Thames Rd 189 FH83
Crayford High St, Dart. DA1 189 FE84
Crayford Rd, N7 143 DK63
Dartford DA1 209 FF85
Crayford Way, Dart. DA1 209 FF85
Crayke Hill, Chess. KT9 238 CL108
Craylands, Orp. BR5 228 EW97
Craylands La, Swans. DA10 211 FX85
Sch Craylands Sch, The, Swans.
DA10 off Craylands La 211 FX85
Craylands Sq, Swans. DA10 211 FX85
Crayle St, Slou. SL2 153 AN69
Craymill Sq, Dart. DA1 189 FF82
Crayonne Cl, Sun. TW16 217 BS95
Cray Riverway, Dart. DA1 209 FF85
Cray Rd, Belv. DA17 188 FA79
Sidcup DA14 208 EW94
Swanley BR8 229 FB100
● Crayside Ind Est,
Cray. DA1 189 FH84
Cray Valley Rd, Orp. BR5 228 EU99
Cray Vw Cl, Orp. BR5
off Mill Brook Rd 228 EW98
Crealock Gro, Wdf.Grn. IG8 124 EF50
Crealock St, SW18 202 DB86
Creasey Cl, Horn. RM11 149 FH61

Creasy Cl, Abb.L. WD5 81 BT31
Creasy Est, SE1 31 N7
Crebor St, SE22 204 DU86
Credenhall Dr, Brom. BR2 227 EM102
Credenhill St, SW16 203 DJ93
Crediton Hill, NW6 5 L2
Crediton Rd, E16 23 N8
NW10 4 C9
Crediton Way, Clay. KT10 237 CG106
Credon Rd, E13 166 EJ68
SE16 32 F10
Credo Way, Grays RM20 191 FV79
Creechurch La, EC3 19 P9
Creechurch Pl, EC3 19 P9
Creed Ct, EC4 off Ludgate Sq 19 H9
Creed La, EC4 19 H9
Creed's Fm Yd, Epp. CM16 91 ES32
Creek, The, Grav. DA11 212 GB85
Sunbury-on-Thames TW16 217 BU99
CREEKMOUTH, Bark. IG11 168 EU70
Creek Rd, SE8 46 A3
SE10 46 A3
Barking IG11 167 ET69
East Molesey KT8 219 CE98
Creekside, SE8 46 C5
Rainham RM13 169 FF70
Creek Way, Rain. RM13 169 FE71
Creeland Gro, SE6 205 DZ88
Cree Way, Rom. RM1 127 FE52
Crefeld Cl, W6 38 D3
Creffield Rd, W3 160 CM73
W5 160 CM73
Creighton Av, E6 166 EK68
N2 142 DE55
N10 120 DG54
St. Albans AL1 65 CD24
Creighton Cl, W12 161 CU73
Creighton Rd, N17 122 DS52
NW6 4 D10
W5 179 CK76
Cremer St, E2 20 A1
Cremorne Est, SW10 40 A4
Cremorne Gdns, Epsom KT19 238 CR109
Cremorne Rd, SW10 39 P5
Northfleet DA11 213 GF87
Crescent, EC3 20 A10
Crescent, The, E17 145 DY57
N11 120 DF49
NW2 141 CV62
SW13 181 CT82
SW19 202 DA90
W3 160 CS72
Abbots Langley WD5 81 BT30
Aldenham WD25 98 CB37
Ashford TW15 196 BM92
Barnet EN5 102 DB41
Beckenham BR3 225 EA95
Belmont SM2 240 DA111
Bexley DA5 208 EW87
Bricket Wood AL2 82 CA30
Caterham CR3 259 EA123
Chertsey KT16
off Western Av 216 BG97
Croxley Green WD3 97 BP44
Croydon CR0 224 DR99
Egham TW20 194 AY93
Epping CM16 91 ET32
Epsom KT18 238 CN114
Greenhithe DA9 211 FW85
Guildford GU2 264 AU132
Harlington UB3 177 BQ80
Harlow CM17 58 EW09
Harrow HA2 139 CD60
Horley RH6 291 DH150
Ilford IG2 147 EN58
Leatherhead KT22 253 CH122
Loughton IG10 106 EK43
New Malden KT3 220 CQ96
Northfleet DA11 213 GF89
Reigate RH2 off Chartway 272 DB134
Sevenoaks TN13 279 FK121
Shepperton TW17 217 BT101
Sidcup DA14 207 ET91
Slough SL1 174 AS75
Southall UB1 178 BZ75
Surbiton KT6 220 CL99
Sutton SM1 240 DD105
Upminster RM14 151 FS59
Watford WD18 98 BW42
Wembley HA0 139 CH61
West Molesey KT8 218 CA98
West Wickham BR4 226 EE100
Weybridge KT13 216 BN104
Crescent Arc, SE10 46 E3
Crescent Av, Grays RM17 192 GD78
Hornchurch RM12 149 FF61
Crescent Cotts, Sev. TN13 263 FE120
Crescent Ct, Surb. KT6 219 CK99
Crescent Dr, Petts Wd BR5 227 EP100
Shenfield CM15 130 FY46
Crescent E, Barn. EN4 102 DC38
Crescent Gdns, SW19 202 DA90
Ruislip HA4 137 BV58
Swanley BR8 229 FC96
Crescent Gro, SW4 183 DJ84
Mitcham CR4 222 DE98
Crescent Ho, SE13
off Ravensbourne Pl 46 C8
Crescent La, SW4 203 DK85
Crescent Ms, N22 121 DL53
Crescent Pl, SW3 28 C8
Crescent Ri, N22 121 DK53
Barnet EN4 102 DE43
Crescent Rd, E4 124 EE45
E6 166 EJ67
E10 145 EB61
E13 13 P8
E18 124 EJ54
N3 119 CZ53
N8 143 DK59
N9 122 DU46
N11 120 DF49
N15 off Carlingford Rd 143 DP55
N22 121 DK53
SE18 37 N10
SW20 221 CX95
Aveley RM15 190 FQ75
Barnet EN4 102 DE43
Beckenham BR3 225 EB96
Bletchingley RH1 274 DQ133
Bromley BR1 206 EG94
Crescent Rd, Cat. CR3 258 DU124
Dagenham RM10 149 FB63
Enfield EN2 103 DP41
Erith DA8 189 FF79
Hemel Hempstead HP2 62 BK20
Kingston upon Thames KT2 200 CN94
Reigate RH2 288 DA136
Shepperton TW17 217 BQ99
Sidcup DA15 207 ET90
Warley CM14 130 FV49
Crescent Row, EC1 19 J5
Crescent Stables, SW15 201 CY85
Crescent St, N1 8 D6
Crescent Vw, Loug. IG10 106 EK44
Crescent Wk, Aveley RM15 190 FQ75
Crescent Way, N12 120 DE51
SE4 185 EA83
SW16 203 DM94
Aveley RM15 171 FR74
Horley RH6 290 DG150
Orpington BR6 245 ES106
Crescent W, Barn. EN4 102 DC38
Crescent Wd Rd, SE26 204 DU90
Cresford Rd, SW6 39 L7
Crespigny Rd, NW4 141 CV58
Cressage Cl, Sthl. UB1 158 CA70
Cressall Cl, Lthd. KT22 253 CH120
Cressall Mead, Lthd. KT22 253 CH120
Cress End, Rick. WD3 114 BG47
Cresset Cl, Stans.Abb. SG12 55 EC12
Cresset Rd, E9 11 H5
Cresset St, SW4 183 DK83
Cressfield Cl, NW5 7 H2
Cressida Rd, N19 143 DJ60
Cressingham Gro, Sutt. SM1 240 DC105
Cressingham Rd, SE13 46 F10
Edgware HA8 118 CR51
Cressinghams, The, Epsom
KT18 238 CR113
Cressington Cl, N16 9 P2
Cress Ms, Brom. BR1 205 ED92
Cress Rd, Slou. SL1 173 AP75
Cresswell Gdns, SW5 27 N10
Cresswell Pk, SE3 47 L10
Cresswell Pl, SW10 27 N10
Cresswell Rd, SE25 224 DU98
Chesham HP5 76 AR34
Feltham TW13 198 BY91
Twickenham TW1 199 CK86
Cresswell Way, N21 121 DN45
Cressy Ct, E1 21 H6
W6 181 CV76
Cressy Ho, E1
off Hannibal Rd 21 H6
Cressy Pl, E1 21 H6
Cressy Rd, NW3 6 E2
Crest, The, N13 121 DN49
NW4 141 CW57
Beaconsfield HP9 110 AG54
Goffs Oak EN7
off Orchard Way 87 DP27
Sawbridgeworth CM21 58 EX05
Surbiton KT5 220 CN99
Cresta Dr, Wdhm KT15 233 BF110
Crest Av, Grays RM17 192 GB80
Crestbrook Av, N13 121 DP48
Crestbrook Pl, N13 121 DP48
Crest Cl, Bad.Mt TN14 247 FB111
Crest Dr, Enf. EN3 104 DW38
Crestfield St, WC1 18 B2
Crest Gdns, Ruis. HA4 138 BW62
Crest Hill, Peasl. GU5 283 BR142
Cresthill Av, Grays RM17 192 GC77
Creston Av, Knap. GU21 248 AS116
Creston Way, Wor.Pk. KT4 221 CX102
Crest Pk, Hem.H. HP2 63 BQ19
Crest Rd, NW2 141 CT61
Bromley BR2 226 EF101
South Croydon CR2 242 DV108
Crest Vw, Green. DA9
off Woodland Way 191 FU84
Pinner HA5 138 BX56
Crest Vw Dr, Petts Wd BR5 227 EP99
Crestway, SW15 201 CV86
Crestwood Way, Houns. TW4 198 BZ85
Creswell Dr, Beck. BR3 225 EB99
Creswick Ct, Welw.G.C. AL7 51 CX10
Sch Creswick Prim & Nurs Sch,
Welw.G.C. AL7
off Chequers 51 CY12
Creswick Rd, W3 160 CP73
Creswick Wk, E3 22 A2
NW11 141 CZ56
Crete Hall Rd, Grav. DA11 212 GD86
Creton St, SE18 37 M7
Creukhorne Rd, NW10 160 CS66
Crewdson Rd, SW9 42 E5
Horley RH6 291 DH148
Crewe Curve, Berk. HP4 60 AT16
Crewe Pl, NW10 161 CT69
Crewe's Av, Warl. CR6 258 DW116
Crewe's Cl, Warl. CR6 258 DW116
Crewe's Fm La, Warl. CR6 259 DX116
Crewe's La, Warl. CR6 259 DX116
CREWS HILL, Enf. EN2 103 DP35
⇌ Crews Hill 87 DM34
Crews St, E14 34 A8
Crewys Rd, NW2 141 CZ61
SE15 44 F9
Crib St, Ware SG12 55 DX05
Crichton Av, Wall. SM6 241 DK106
Crichton Rd, Cars. SM5 240 DF107
Crichton St, SW8 41 L8
Crick Ct, Bark. IG11
off Spring Pl 167 EQ68
Cricketers Arms Rd, Enf. EN2 104 DQ40
Cricketers Cl, N14 121 DJ45
Chessington KT9 237 CK105
Erith DA8 189 FE78
St. Albans AL3
off Stonecross 65 CE19
Cricketers Ct, SE11 30 G9
Cricketers Ms, SW18
off East Hill 202 DB85
Cricketers Ter, Cars. SM5
off Wrythe La 222 DE104
Cricketers Wk, SE26
off Doctors Cl 204 DW92
Cricketfield Rd, E5 10 F1
Cricket Fld Rd, Uxb. UB8 156 BK67
Cricketfield Rd, West Dr. UB7 176 BJ77
Cricket Grn, Mitch. CR4 222 DF97
Sch Cricket Grn Sch, Mitch.
CR4 off Lower Grn W 222 DE97
Cricket Grd Rd, Chis. BR7 227 EP95
Cricket Hill, S.Nutfld RH1 289 DM136
Cricket La, Beck. BR3 205 DY93
Crickett's Hill, Shere GU5 282 BN139
Cricket Way, Wey. KT13 217 BS103
Cricklade Av, SW2 203 DL89
Romford RM3 128 FK51
CRICKLEWOOD, NW2 141 CX62
⇌ Cricklewood 141 CX63
Cricklewood Bdy, NW2 141 CW62
Cricklewood La, NW2 4 D1
Cridland St, E15 13 L9
Crieff Ct, Tedd. TW11 199 CJ94
Crieff Rd, SW18 202 DC86
Criffel Av, SW2 203 DK89
Crimp Hill, Eng.Grn TW20 194 AU90
Crimp Hill Rd, Old Wind. SL4 194 AU88
Crimscott St, SE1 31 P7
Crimsworth Rd, SW8 41 P6
Crinan St, N1 8 B10
Cringle St, SW8 41 L4
Cripplegate St, EC2 19 J6
Cripps Grn, Hayes UB4
off Stratford Rd 157 BV70
Crispe Ho, Bark. IG11
off Dovehouse Mead 167 ER68
Crispen Rd, Felt. TW13 198 BY91
Crispian Cl, NW10 140 CS63
Crispin Cl, Ashtd. KT21 254 CM118
Beaconsfield HP9 110 AJ51
Croydon CR0
off Harrington Cl 223 DL103
Crispin Cres, Croy. CR0 223 DK104
Crispin Ms, NW11 141 CZ57
Crispin Pl, E1 20 A6
Crispin Rd, Edg. HA8 118 CQ51
Crispin St, E1 20 A7
Crispin Way, Farn.Com. SL2 133 AR63
Uxbridge UB8 156 BM70
Crisp Rd, W6 38 A1
Criss Cres, Chal.St.P. SL9 112 AW54
Criss Gro, Chal.St.P. SL9 112 AW54
Cristowe Rd, SW6 39 H8
Criterion Ms, N19 143 DK61
SE24 off Shakespeare Rd 203 DP85
Jct Crittall's Cor, Sid. DA14 208 EV94
Critten La, Dor. RH5 268 BX132
Crockenhall Way, Istead Rise
DA13 212 GE94
CROCKENHILL, Swan. BR8 229 FD101
Crockenhill La, Eyns. DA4 229 FG101
Sch Crockenhill Prim Sch, Crock.
BR8 off Stones Cross Rd 229 FC100
Crockenhill Rd, Orp. BR5 228 EX99
Swanley BR8 228 EZ100
Crockerton Rd, SW17 202 DF89
Crockery La, E.Clan. GU4 266 BL129
Crockford Cl, Add. KT15 234 BJ105
Crockford Pk Rd, Add. KT15 234 BJ106
CROCKHAM HILL, Eden. TN8 277 EQ133
Sch Crockham Hill C of E Prim Sch,
Crock.H. TN8
off Main Rd 277 EQ133
Crockham Way, SE9 207 EN91
Crocknorth Rd, Dor. RH5 267 BU133
East Horsley KT24 267 BT132
Crocus Cl, Croy. CR0
off Cornflower La 225 DX102
Crocus Fld, Barn. EN5 101 CZ44
Croffets, Tad. KT20 255 CX121
Croft, The, E4 124 EE47
NW10 161 CT68
W5 160 CL71
Barnet EN5 101 CX42
Broxbourne EN10 71 DY23
Fetcham KT22 253 CE123
Hounslow TW5 178 BY79
Loughton IG10 107 EN40
Pinner HA5 138 BZ59
Ruislip HA4 138 BW63
St. Albans AL2 82 CA25
Swanley BR8 229 FC97
Welwyn Garden City AL7 51 CZ12
Wembley HA0 139 CJ64
Croft Av, Dor. RH4 269 CH134
West Wickham BR4 225 EC102
Croft Cl, NW7 118 CS48
Belvedere DA17 188 EZ78
Chalfont St. Peter SL9 112 AX54
Chipperfield WD4 80 BG30
Chislehurst BR7 207 EM91
Harlington UB3 177 BQ80
Uxbridge UB10 156 BN66
Croft Cor, Old Wind. SL4 194 AV85
Croft Ct, Borwd. WD6 100 CR41
Croftdown Rd, NW5 142 DG62
Croft End Cl, Chess. KT9
off Ashcroft Rd 220 CM104
Croft End Rd, Chipper. WD4 80 BG30
Crofters, The, Wind. SL4 194 AU86
Crofters Cl, Islw. TW7
off Ploughmans End 199 CD85
Redhill RH1 289 DH136
Stanwell TW19 off Park Rd 196 BK86
Crofters Ct, SE8
off Croft St 33 L9
Crofters Mead, Croy. CR0 243 DZ109
Crofters Rd, Nthwd. HA6 115 BS49
Crofters Way, NW1 7 N8
Croft Fld, Chipper. WD4 80 BG30
Hatfield AL10 67 CU18
Croft Gdns, W7 179 CG75
Ruislip HA4 137 BS60
Crofthill Rd, Slou. SL2 153 AP70
Croft La, Chipper. WD4 80 BG30
Croftleigh Av, Pur. CR8 257 DN116
Croft Lo Cl, Wdf.Grn. IG8 124 EH51
Croft Meadow, Chipper. WD4 80 BG30
Croft Ms, N12 120 DC48
Crofton, Ashtd. KT21 254 CL118
Crofton Av, W4 180 CR80
Bexley DA5 208 EX87
Orpington BR6 227 EQ103
Walton-on-Thames KT12 218 BW104
Crofton Cl, Ott. KT16 233 BC108
Croftongate Way, SE4 205 DY85
Crofton Gro, E4 123 ED49
Sch Crofton Inf Sch, Orp. BR5
off Towncourt La 227 ER101
Sch Crofton Jun Sch, Orp.
BR5 off Towncourt La 227 ER101
Crofton La, Orp. BR5, BR6 227 ER101
⇌ Crofton Park 205 DZ85
Crofton Pk Rd, SE4 205 DZ86
Crofton Rd, E13 24 A4
SE5 43 P7
Grays RM16 192 GE76
Orpington BR6 227 EN104
Crofton Ter, E5
off Studley Cl 11 L2
Richmond TW9 180 CM84
Crofton Way, Barn. EN5
off Wycherley Cres 102 DB44
Enfield EN2 103 DN40
Croft Rd, SW16 223 DN95
SW19 202 DC94
Bromley BR1 206 EG93
Chalfont St. Peter SL9 112 AY54
Enfield EN3 105 DY39
Sutton SM1 240 DE106
Ware SG12 54 DW05
Westerham TN16 277 EP126
Woldingham CR3 259 DZ122
Crofts, The, Hem.H. HP3 63 BP21
Shepperton TW17 217 BS98
Croftside, SE25 off Sunny Bk. 224 DU97
Crofts La, N22 121 DN52
Crofts Path, Hem.H. HP3 63 BP22
Crofts Rd, Har. HA1 139 CG58
Crofts St, E1 32 C1
Croft St, SE8 33 L9
Croft Wk, Brox. EN10 71 DY23
Croftway, NW3 5 K1
Richmond TW10 199 CH90
Croft Way, Sev. TN13 278 FF125
Sidcup DA15 207 ES90
Crogsland Rd, NW1 6 G6
Croham Cl, S.Croy. CR2 242 DS108
Croham Manor Rd, S.Croy.
CR2 242 DS106
Croham Mt, S.Croy. CR2 242 DS108
Croham Pk Av, S.Croy. CR2 242 DT106
Croham Rd, S.Croy. CR2 242 DR106
Croham Valley Rd, S.Croy. CR2 242 DT107
Croindene Rd, SW16 223 DL95
Cromartie Rd, N19 143 DK59
Cromarty Rd, Edg. HA8 118 CP47
Crombie Cl, Ilf. IG4 147 EM57
Crombie Rd, Sid. DA15 207 ER88
Cromer Cl, Uxb. UB8 157 BQ72
CROMER HYDE, Welw.G.C. AL8 50 CS10
Cromer Hyde La, Lmsfd AL8 50 CR10
Crome Rd, NW10 160 CS65
Cromer Pl, Orp. BR6
off Andover Rd 227 ER102
Cromer Rd, E10 145 ED59
N17 122 DU54
SE25 224 DV97
SW17 202 DG93
Chadwell Heath RM6 148 EY58
Hornchurch RM11 150 FK59
London Heathrow Airport
TW6 176 BN83
New Barnet EN5 102 DC42
Romford RM7 149 FC58
Watford WD24 98 BW38
Woodford Green IG8 124 EG49
Sch Cromer Rd Prim Sch, New Barn.
EN5 off Cromer Rd 102 DC41
Cromer St, WC1 18 B3
Cromer Ter, E8 10 C2
Cromer Vil Rd, SW18 201 CZ86
Cromford Cl, Orp. BR6 227 ES104
Cromford Path, E5
off Overbury St 145 DX63
Cromford Rd, SW18 202 DA85
Cromford Way, N.Mal. KT3 220 CR95
Cromlix Cl, Chis. BR7 227 EP96
Crompton Pl, Enf. EN3
off Brunswick Rd 105 EA38
Crompton St, W2 16 A5
Cromwell Av, N6 143 DH60
W6 181 CV78
Bromley BR2 226 EH98
Cheshunt EN7 88 DU30
New Malden KT3 221 CT99
Cromwell Cl, N2 142 DD56
W3 off High St 160 CQ74
Bromley BR2 226 EH98
Chalfont St. Giles HP8 112 AW48
St. Albans AL4 65 CK15
Walton-on-Thames KT12 217 BV102
Cromwell Cres, SW5 27 J8
Cromwell Dr, Slou. SL1 154 AS72
Cromwell Gdns, SW7 28 B7
Cromwell Gro, W6 26 B6
Caterham CR3 258 DQ121
Cromwell Highwalk, EC2
off Silk St 19 K6
H Cromwell Hosp, The, SW5 27 L8
● Cromwell Ind Est, E10 145 DY60
Cromwell Ms, SW7 28 B8
Cromwell Pl, N6 143 DH60
SW7 28 B8
SW14 180 CQ83
W3 off Grove Pl 160 CQ74
◆ Cromwell Road 220 CL95
Cromwell Rd, E7 166 EJ66
E17 145 EC57
N3 120 DC54
N10 120 DG52
SW5 27 K8
SW7 28 A8
SW9 42 G6
SW19 202 DA92
Beckenham BR3 225 DY96
Borehamwood WD6 100 CL39
Caterham CR3 258 DQ121
Cheshunt EN7 88 DV28
Croydon CR0 224 DR101
Feltham TW13 197 BV88
Grays RM17 192 GA77
Hayes UB3 157 BR72
Hertford SG13 54 DT08
Hounslow TW3 178 CA84
Kingston upon Thames KT2 220 CL95
Redhill RH1 272 DF133
Teddington TW11 199 CG93
Walton-on-Thames KT12 217 BV102
Ware SG12 55 DZ06
Warley CM14 130 FV49
Wembley HA0 160 CL68
Worcester Park KT4 220 CR104
Cromwells Ct, Slou. SL3 155 AZ74
Cromwells Mere, Rom. RM1
off Havering Rd 127 FD51
Cromwell St, Houns. TW3 178 CA84
Cromwell Twr, EC2 19 K6
Cromwell Wk, Red. RH1 272 DF134
Crondace Rd, SW6 39 K7
Crondall Ct, N1 19 N1
Crondall Ho, SW15
off Fontley Way 201 CU88
Crondall St, N1 19 M1
Cronin St, SE15 44 A5
Cronks Hill, Red. RH1 288 DC135
Reigate RH2 288 DC135
Cronks Hill Cl, Red. RH1 288 DD136
Cronks Hill Rd, Red. RH1 288 DD136
Jct Crooked Billet, E17 123 EB52
Crooked Billet, SW19 201 CW93
Jct Crooked Billet Rbt,
Stai. TW18 196 BG91
Crooked Billet Yd, E2 19 P2
Crooked La, Grav. DA12 213 GH86
Crooked Mile, Wal.Abb. EN9 89 EC33
Jct Crooked Mile Rbt,
Wal.Abb. EN9 89 EC33
Crooked Usage, N3 141 CY55
Crooked Way, Lwr Naze. EN9 72 EE22
Crooke Rd, SE8 33 L10
Crookham Rd, SW6 38 G7
Crookhams, Welw.G.C. AL7 52 DA07
Crook Log, Bexh. DA6 188 EX83
Sch Crook Log Prim Sch, Bexh.
DA6 off Crook Log 188 EX84
Crookston Rd, SE9 187 EN83
Croombs Rd, E16 24 C7
Crooms Hill, SE10 46 F4
Crooms Hill Gro, SE10 46 F4
Crop Common, Hat. AL10
off Stonecross Rd 67 CV16
Cropley Ct, N1 9 L10
Cropley St, N1 9 L10
Croppath Rd, Dag. RM10 148 FA63
Cropthorne Ct, W9 15 P3
Crosby Cl, Beac. HP9 133 AM55
Feltham TW13 198 BY91
St. Albans AL4 65 CJ23
Crosby Ct, SE1 31 L4
Crosby Rd, E7 13 N4
Dagenham RM10 169 FB68
Crosby Row, SE1 31 L5
Crosby Sq, EC3 19 N9
Crosby Wk, E8 10 A5
SW2 203 DN87
Crosier Cl, SE3 186 EL81
Crosier Rd, Ickhm UB10 137 BQ63
Crosier Way, Ruis. HA4 137 BS62
Crosland Pl, SW11
off Taybridge Rd 182 DG83
Crossacres, Wok. GU22 249 BE115
Cross Av, SE10 47 H3
Crossbow Rd, Chig. IG7 125 ET50
Crossbrook, Hat. AL10 66 CS19
Crossbrook Rd, SE3 186 EL82
Crossbrook St, Chsht EN8 89 DX31
Cross Cl, SE15 44 E8
Cross Deep, Twick. TW1 199 CF89
Cross Deep Gdns, Twick. TW1 199 CF89
Crossett Grn, Hem.H. HP3 63 BQ22
Crossfell Rd, Hem.H. HP3 63 BQ22
Crossfield Cl, Berk. HP4 60 AT19
Crossfield Pl, Wey. KT13 235 BP108
Crossfield Rd, N17 144 DQ55
NW3 6 B5
Hoddesdon EN11 71 EB15
Crossfields, Loug. IG10 107 EP43
St. Albans AL3 64 CB23
Crossfield St, SE8 46 A4
Crossford St, SW9 42 B9
Crossgate, Edg. HA8 118 CN48
Greenford UB6 159 CH65
DLR Crossharbour 34 D6
Crossing Rd, Epp. CM16 92 EU32
Cross Keys Cl, N9
off Balham Rd 122 DU47
W1 17 H7
Sevenoaks TN13 278 FG127
Cross Keys Sq, EC1 19 J7
Cross Lances Rd, Houns. TW3 178 CB84
Crossland Rd, Red. RH1 272 DG134
Thornton Heath CR7 223 DP100
Crosslands, Cher. KT16 215 BE104
Crosslands Av, W5 160 CM74
Southall UB2 178 BZ78
Crosslands Rd, Epsom KT19 238 CR107
Cross La, EC3 31 N1
N8 143 DM56
Beaconsfield HP9 133 AM55
Bexley DA5 208 EZ87
Hertford SG14 53 DP09
Ottershaw KT16 233 BB107
Cross La E, Grav. DA12 213 GH89
Cross Las, Chal.St.P. SL9 112 AY50
Guildford GU1 281 AZ135
Cross Las Cl, Chal.St.P. SL9
off Cross Las 113 AZ50
Cross La W, Grav. DA11 213 GH89
Crosslet St, SE17 31 M8
Crosslet Vale, SE10 46 C7
Crossley Cl, Bigg.H. TN16 260 EK115
Crossleys, Ch.St.G. HP8 112 AW49
Crossley St, N7 8 E4
Crossmead, SE9 207 EM88
Watford WD19 97 BV44
Crossmead Av, Grnf. UB6 158 CA69
Cross Meadow, Chesh. HP5 76 AM29
Crossmount Ho, SE5 43 J4
Crossness La, SE28 168 EX73
★ Crossness Pumping Sta,
SE2 168 EY72
Crossness Rd, Bark. IG11 167 ET69
Cross Oak, Wind. SL4 173 AN82
Crossoak La, Red. RH1 289 DH144
Cross Oak Rd, Berk. HP4 60 AU20
Crossoaks La, Borwd. WD6 100 CR35
South Mimms EN6 84 CS34
Crosspath, The, Rad. WD7 99 CG35
Cross Rd, E4 123 ED46
N11 121 DH50
N22 121 DN52
SE5 43 P8
SW19 202 DA94
Belmont SM2 240 DA110
Bromley BR2 226 EL103
Chadwell Heath RM6 148 EW59
Croydon CR0 224 DR102
Dartford DA1 210 FJ86
Enfield EN1 104 DS42
Feltham TW13 198 BY91
Harrow HA1 139 CD56
Hawley DA2 210 FM91
Hertford SG14 54 DQ08
Kingston upon Thames KT2 200 CM94
Northfleet DA11 213 GF86
Orpington BR5 228 EV99
Purley CR8 241 DP113
Romford RM7 148 FA55
Sidcup DA14
off Sidcup Hill 208 EV91
South Harrow HA2 138 CB62
Sutton SM2 240 DD106
Tadworth KT20 255 CW122
Uxbridge UB8 156 BJ66
Waltham Cross EN8 89 DY33
Watford WD19 98 BY44
Wealdstone HA3 117 CG54
Weybridge KT13 217 BR104
Woodford Green IG8 125 EM51
Cross Rds, High Beach IG10 106 EH40
Crossroads, The, Eff. KT24 268 BX128

Cross St, N1 8 G8
SW13 180 CS82
Erith DA8 off Bexley Rd 189 FE78
Hampton Hill TW12 198 CC92
Harlow CM20 73 ER15
St. Albans AL3
off Spencer St 65 CD20
Uxbridge UB8 156 BJ66
Ware SG12 55 DY06
Watford WD17 98 BW41
Cross Ter, Wal.Abb. EN9
off Stonyshotts 90 EE34
Crossthwaite Av, SE5 184 DR84
Crosstrees Ho, E14
off Cassilis Rd 34 B6
Crosswall, EC3 20 A10
Crossway, N12 120 DD51
N16 9 P3
NW9 141 CT56
Cross Way, NW10 161 CU66
Crossway, SE28 168 EW72
SW20 221 CW98
W13 159 CG70
Chesham HP5 76 AS30
Dagenham RM8 148 EW62
Enfield EN1 122 DS45
Harlow CM17 58 EX14
Hayes UB3 157 BU74
Petts Wood BR5 227 ER98
Pinner HA5 115 BV54
Ruislip HA4 138 BW63
Walton-on-Thames KT12 217 BV103
Welwyn Garden City AL8 51 CW05
Woodford Green IG8 124 EJ49
Crossway, The, N22 121 DP52
SE9 206 EK89
Cross Way, The, Har. HA3 117 CE54
Crossway, The, Uxb. UB10 156 BM68
CROSSWAYS, Dart. DA2 191 FR84
Crossways, N21 104 DQ44
Beaconsfield HP9 111 AM54
Berkhamsted HP4 60 AT20
Effingham KT24 268 BX127
Egham TW20 195 BD93
Hemel Hempstead HP3 63 BP20
Romford RM2 149 FH55
Shenfield CM15 131 GA44
South Croydon CR2 243 DY108
Sunbury-on-Thames TW16 197 BT94
Sutton SM2 240 DD109
Tatsfield TN16 260 EJ120
Crossways, The, Couls. CR5 257 DM119
Guildford GU2 280 AU135
Hounslow TW5 178 BZ80
South Merstham RH1 273 DJ130
Wembley HA9 140 CN61
Crossways Acad, SE4 45 L9
Crossways Boul, Dart. DA2 190 FQ84
Greenhithe DA9 191 FT84
● Crossways Business Pk,
Dart. DA2 190 FQ84
Crossways La, Reig. RH2 272 DC128
Crossways Rd, Beck. BR3 225 EA98
Mitcham CR4 223 DH97
Crosswell Cl, Shep. TW17 217 BQ96
Crosthwaite Way, Slou. SL1 153 AK71
Croston St, E8 10 D8
Crothall Cl, N13 121 DM48
Crouch Av, Bark. IG11 168 EV68
Crouch Cl, Beck. BR3 205 EA93
Crouch Ct, Harl. CM20 57 EQ13
Crouch Cft, SE9 207 EN90
CROUCH END, N8 143 DJ58
Crouch End Hill, N8 143 DK59
Crouchfield, Hem.H. HP1 62 BH21
Hertford SG14 54 DQ06
Crouch Hall Rd, N8 143 DK58
Crouch Hill 143 DM59
Crouch Hill, N4 143 DL58
N8 143 DL58
Crouch La, Goffs Oak EN7 88 DQ28
Crouchman Cl, Grays RM16 192 GB75
Crouchman's Cl, SE26 204 DT90
Crouch Oak La, Add. KT15 234 BJ105
Crouch Rd, NW10 160 CR66
Grays RM16 193 GG78
Crouch Valley, Upmin. RM14 151 FS59
Crowborough Cl, Warl. CR6 259 DY117
Crowborough Dr, Warl. CR6 259 DY118
Crowborough Path, Wat.
WD19 116 BX49
Crowborough Rd, SW17 202 DG93
Crowcroft Cl, Guil. GU2
off Henderson Av 264 AV130
Crowden Way, SE28 168 EW73
Crowder Cl, N12 120 DC53
Crowder St, E1 20 F10
Crow Dr, Halst. TN14 263 FC115
Crowfoot Cl, E9 11 P3
SE28 167 ES74
CROW GREEN, Brwd. CM15 130 FT41
Crow Grn La, Pilg.Hat. CM15 130 FU43
Crow Grn Rd, Pilg.Hat. CM15 130 FT43
Crowhurst Cl, SW9 42 F8
Crowhurst Mead, Gdse. RH9 274 DW130
Crowhurst Way, Orp. BR5 228 EW99
Crowland Av, Hayes UB3 177 BS77
Crowland Gdns, N14 121 DL45
Crowland Prim Sch, N15
off Crowland Rd 144 DU57
Crowland Rd, N15 144 DT57
Thornton Heath CR7 224 DR98
Crowlands Av, Rom. RM7 149 FB58
Crowlands Inf & Jun Schs,
Rom. RM7 off London Rd 149 FC58
Crowland Ter, N1 9 L6
Crowland Wk, Mord. SM4 222 DB100
Crow La, Rom. RM7 148 EZ59
Crowley Cres, Croy. CR0 241 DN106
Crowline Wk, N1
off Clephane Rd 9 K4
Crowmarsh Gdns, SE23
off Tyson Rd 204 DW87
Crown Arc, Kings.T. KT1
off Union St 219 CK96
Crown Ash Hill, West. TN16 244 EH114
Crown Ash La, Warl. CR6 260 EG116
Westerham TN16 260 EG116
Crownbourne Ct, Sutt. SM1
off St. Nicholas Way 240 DB105
● Crown Business Est,
Chesh. HP5
off Berkhampstead Rd 76 AQ30
Crown Cl, E3 12 A8
N22 off Winkfield Rd 121 DN53
NW6 5 L4
NW7 119 CT47
Colnbrook SL3 175 BC80
Hayes UB3 177 BT75
Crown Cl, Orp. BR6 246 EU105
Sheering CM22 59 FC07
Walton-on-Thames KT12 218 BW101
● Crown Cl Business Cen, E3 12 A9
Crown Ct, EC2 19 K9
SE12 206 EH86
WC2 18 B9
Crown Dale, SE19 203 DP93
Crowndale Rd, NW1 7 L10
Crownfield, Brox. EN10 71 EA21
Crownfield Av, Ilf. IG2 147 ES57
Crownfield Inf Sch, Coll.Row
RM7 off White Hart La 126 FA54
Crownfield Jun Sch, Coll.Row
RM7 off White Hart La 126 FA54
Crownfield Rd, E15 12 G2
Crownfields, Sev. TN13 279 FH125
Crown Gate, Harl. CM20 73 ER15
Crowngate Ho, E3 21 P1
Crown Gate Rbt, Harl.
CM18 73 ER15
Crown Hts, Guil. GU1 280 AY137
Crown Hill, Croy. CR0
off Church St 224 DQ103
Epping CM16 91 EM33
Waltham Abbey EN9 91 EM33
Crownhill Rd, NW10 161 CT67
Woodford Green IG8 124 EL52
Crown La, N14 121 DJ46
SW16 203 DN92
Bromley BR2 226 EK99
Chislehurst BR7 227 EQ95
Farnham Royal SL2 153 AN68
High Wycombe HP11 110 AF48
Morden SM4 222 DB97
Virginia Water GU25 214 AX100
Crown La Gdns, SW16 203 DN92
Crown La Prim Sch,
SW16 off Crown La 203 DP92
Crown La Spur, Brom. BR2 226 EK100
Crown Meadow, Colnbr. SL3 175 BB80
Crownmead Way, Rom. RM7 149 FB56
Crown Ms, E13
off Waghorn Rd 166 EJ67
W6 181 CU77
Crown Mill, Mitch. CR4 222 DE99
Crown Office Row, EC4 18 E10
Crown Pas, SW1 29 M3
Kingston upon Thames
KT1 off Church St 219 CK96
Watford WD18
off The Crescent 98 BW42
Crown Pl, EC2 19 N6
NW5 7 K4
SE16 44 F1
Crown Pt Par, SE19
off Beulah Hill 203 DP93
Crown Reach, SW1 41 P1
Crown Ri, Cher. KT16 215 BF102
Watford WD25 82 BW34
Crown Rd, N10 120 DG52
Borehamwood WD6 100 CN39
Enfield EN1 104 DV42
Grays RM17 192 GA79
Ilford IG6 147 ER56
Morden SM4 222 DB98
New Malden KT3 220 CQ95
Orpington BR6 246 EU106
Ruislip HA4 138 BX64
Shoreham TN14 247 FF110
Sutton SM1 240 DB105
Twickenham TW1 199 CH86
Virginia Water GU25 214 AW100
Crown Sq, Wok. GU21
off Commercial Way 249 AZ117
Crownstone Rd, SW2 203 DN85
Crown St, SE5 43 K4
W3 160 CP74
Brentwood CM14 130 FW47
Dagenham RM10 169 FC65
Egham TW20 195 BA92
Harrow HA2 139 CD60
Crown Ter, Rich. TW9 180 CM84
Crowntree Cl, Islw. TW7 179 CF79
Crown Wk, Uxb. UB8
off The Pavilions 156 BJ66
Crown Wk, Hem.H. HP3 62 BL24
Wembley HA9 140 CM62
Crown Way, West Dr. UB7 156 BM74
Crown Wds La, SE9 187 EP82
SE18 187 EP82
Crown Wds Sch, SE9
off Riefield Rd 207 EQ85
Crown Wds Way, SE9 207 ER85
Crown Wks, E2 20 E1
Crown Yd, Houns. TW3
off High St 178 CC83
Crow Piece La, Farn.Royal SL2 153 AM66
Crowshott Av, Stan. HA7 117 CJ53
Crows Rd, E15 23 H2
Barking IG11 167 EP65
Epping CM16 91 ET30
Crowstone Rd, Grays RM16 192 GC75
Crowther Av, Brent. TW8 180 CL77
Crowther Cl, SW6 39 H3
Crowther Rd, SE25 224 DU98
Crowthorne Cl, SW18 201 CZ88
Crowthorne Rd, W10 14 C9
Croxdale Rd, Borwd. WD6 100 CM40
Croxden Cl, Edg. HA8 140 CM55
Croxden Wk, Mord. SM4 222 DC100
Croxford Gdns, N22 121 DP52
Croxford Way, Rom. RM7
off Horace Av 149 FD60
Croxley 97 BP44
● Croxley Business Pk,
Wat. WD18 97 BR44
Croxley Cl, Orp. BR5 228 EV96
CROXLEY GREEN, Rick. WD3 96 BN43
Croxley Grn, Orp. BR5 228 EV95
Croxley Hall Wds, Crox.Grn
WD3 114 BM45
Croxley Rd, W9 15 H3
Croxley Vw, Wat. WD18 97 BS44
Croxted Cl, SE21 204 DQ87
Croxted Ms, SE24 204 DQ86
Croxted Rd, SE21 204 DQ87
SE24 204 DQ87
Croxteth Ho, SW8 41 N8
Croyde Av, Grnf. UB6 158 CC69
Hayes UB3 177 BS77
Croyde Cl, Sid. DA15 207 ER87
CROYDON, CR0 224 DR102
Croydon Coll, Croy. CR0
off College Rd 224 DR103
Croydon Flyover, Croy. CR0 241 DP105
Croydon Gro, Croy. CR0 223 DP102
Croydon High Sch, S.Croy.
CR2 off Old Farleigh Rd 242 DW110
Croydon La, Bans. SM7 240 DB114
Croydon La S, Bans. SM7 240 DB114
Croydon Rd, E13 23 M5
SE20 224 DV96
Beckenham BR3 225 DY98
Beddington CR0 241 DL105
Bromley BR2 226 EF104
Caterham CR3 258 DU122
Keston BR2 226 EJ104
London Heathrow Airport
TW6 177 BP82
Mitcham CR4 222 DG98
Mitcham Common CR0 222 DG98
Reigate RH2 272 DB134
Wallington SM6 241 DH105
Warlingham CR6 259 ED122
West Wickham BR4 226 EE104
Westerham TN16 261 EM123
● Croydon Rd Ind Est, Beck.
BR3 225 DX98
● Croydon Valley Trade Pk, Croy.
CR0 off Beddington Fm Rd 223 DL101
Croyland Rd, N9 122 DU46
Croylands Dr, Surb. KT6 220 CL101
Croysdale Av, Sun. TW16 217 BU97
Crozier Dr, S.Croy. CR2 242 DV110
Crozier Ho, SE3
off Ebdon Way 186 EH83
Crozier Ter, E9 11 K3
Crucible Cl, Rom. RM6 148 EV58
Crucifix La, SE1 31 N4
Cruden Ho, SE17 42 G3
Cruden Rd, Grav. DA12 213 GM90
Cruden St, N1 9 H9
Cruick Av, S.Ock. RM15 171 FW73
Cruikshank Rd, E15 13 K1
Cruikshank St, WC1 18 E2
Crummock Cl, Slou. SL1 152 AJ72
Crummock Gdns, NW9 140 CS57
Crumpsall St, SE2 188 EW77
Crundale Av, NW9 140 CN57
Crundal Twr, Orp. BR5 228 EW102
Crunden Rd, S.Croy. CR2 242 DR108
Crusader Cl, Purf. RM19
off Centurion Way 190 FN77
Crusader Gdns, Croy. CR0
off Cotelands 224 DS104
● Crusader Industrial Est,
N4 off Hermitage Rd 144 DQ58
Crusader Way, Wat. WD18 97 BT44
Crushes Cl, Hutt. CM13 131 GE44
Crusoe Ms, N16 144 DR61
Crusoe Rd, Erith DA8 189 FD78
Mitcham CR4 202 DF94
Crutched Friars, EC3 19 P10
Crutches La, Jordans HP9 112 AS51
Crutchfield La, Hkwd RH6 290 DA145
Walton-on-Thames KT12 217 BV103
Crutchley Rd, SE6 206 EE89
Crystal Av, Horn. RM12 150 FL63
Crystal Ct, SE19
off College Rd 204 DT92
Crystal Ho, SE18
off Spinel Cl 187 ET78
Crystal Palace 204 DU93
★ Crystal Palace FC, SE25 224 DS98
★ Crystal Palace Nat Sports Cen,
SE19 204 DU93
Crystal Palace Par, SE19 204 DT93
★ Crystal Palace Pk, SE19 204 DT92
Crystal Palace Pk Rd, SE26 204 DU92
Crystal Palace Rd, SE22 184 DU84
Crystal Palace Sta Rd, SE19 204 DU93
Crystal Ter, SE19 204 DR93
Crystal Vw Ct, Brom. BR1 205 ED91
Crystal Way, Dag. RM8 148 EW60
Harrow HA1 139 CF57
Crystal Wf, N1 19 H1
Cuba Dr, Enf. EN3 104 DW40
Cuba St, E14 34 A4
Cubitt Bldg, SW1 41 J1
Cubitt Sq, Sthl. UB2
off Windmill Av 158 CC74
Cubitt Steps, E14 34 B2
Cubitt St, WC1 18 D3
Cubitts Yd, WC2 18 B10
Cubitt Ter, SW4 41 M10
CUBITT TOWN, E14 34 F6
Cubitt Town Inf & Jun Schs,
E14 34 F7
Cublands, Hert. SG13 54 DV09
Cuckmans Dr, St.Alb. AL2 82 CA25
Cuckmere Way, Orp. BR5 228 EX102
Cuckoo Av, W7 159 CE70
Cuckoo Dene, W7 159 CD71
Cuckoo Hall La, N9 122 DW45
Cuckoo Hall Prim Sch, N9
off Cuckoo Hall La 123 DX45
Cuckoo Hill, Pnr. HA5 138 BW55
Cuckoo Hill Dr, Pnr. HA5 138 BW55
Cuckoo Hill Rd, Pnr. HA5 138 BW56
Cuckoo La, W7 159 CE73
Cuckoo Pound, Shep. TW17 217 BS99
Cucumber La, Essen. AL9 68 DF20
Hertford SG13 68 DF20
Cudas Cl, Epsom KT19 239 CT105
Cuddington, SE17 31 J8
Cuddington Av, Wor.Pk. KT4 221 CT104
Cuddington Cl, Tad. KT20 255 CW120
Cuddington Comm Prim Sch,
Wor.Pk. KT4
off Salisbury Rd 221 CT104
Cuddington Cft Prim Sch,
Cheam SM2 off West Dr 239 CX109
Cuddington Glade, Epsom
KT19 238 CN112
Cuddington Pk Cl, Bans. SM7 239 CZ113
Cuddington Way, Sutt. SM2 239 CX112
CUDHAM, Sev. TN14 261 ER115
Cudham Cl, Belmont SM2 240 DA110
Cudham C of E Prim Sch,
Bigg.H. TN16 off Jail La 261 EN116
Cudham Dr, New Adgtn CR0 243 EC110
Cudham La N, Cudham TN14 245 ER112
Orpington BR6 245 ES110
Cudham La S, Sev. TN14 261 EQ115
Cudham Pk Rd, Cudham TN14 245 ES110
Cudham Rd, Downe BR6 245 EN111
Tatsfield TN16 260 EL120
Cudham St, SE6 205 EC87
Cudworth St, E1 20 F4
Cuff Cres, SE9 206 EK86
CUFFLEY, Pot.B. EN6 87 DM29
Cuffley 87 DM29
Cuffley Av, Wat. WD25 82 BX34
Cuffley Ct, Hem.H. HP2 63 BQ15
Cuffley Hill, Goffs Oak EN7 87 DN29
Cuffley Sch, Cuffley EN6
off Theobalds Rd 87 DM30
Cuff Pt, E2 20 A2
Cugley Rd, Dart. DA2 210 FQ87
Culford Gdns, SW3 28 F9
Culford Gro, N1 9 N5
Culford Ms, N1 9 N4
Culford Rd, N1 9 N6
Grays RM16 192 GC75
Culgaith Gdns, Enf. EN2 103 DL42
Cullen Sq, S.Ock. RM15 171 FW73
Cullen Way, NW10 160 CQ70
Cullera Cl, Nthwd. HA6 115 BT51
Cullerne Cl, Ewell KT17 239 CT110
Cullesden Rd, Ken. CR8 257 DP115
Culling Rd, SE16 32 G6
Cullings Ct, Wal.Abb. EN9 90 EF33
Cullington Cl, Har. HA3 139 CG56
Cullingworth Rd, NW10 141 CU64
Culloden Cl, SE16 44 D1
Culloden Prim Sch, E14 22 F9
Culloden Rd, Enf. EN2 103 DP40
Culloden St, E14 22 F8
Cullum St, EC3 19 N10
Culmington Rd, W13 179 CJ75
South Croydon CR2 242 DQ109
Culmore Rd, SE15 44 F5
Culmstock Rd, SW11 202 DG85
Culpeper Cl, Ilf. IG6 125 EP51
Culpepper Cl, N18 122 DV50
Culross Cl, N15 144 DQ56
Culross St, W1 28 G1
Culsac Rd, Surb. KT6 220 CL103
Culverden Rd, SW12 203 DJ89
Watford WD19 115 BV48
Culver Dr, Oxt. RH8 276 EE130
Culver Gro, Stan. HA7 117 CJ54
Culverhay, Ashtd. KT21 254 CL116
Culverhouse Gdns, SW16 203 DM90
Culverlands Cl, Stan. HA7 117 CH49
Culverley Rd, SE6 205 EB88
Culver Rd, St.Alb. AL1 65 CE19
Culvers Av, Cars. SM5 222 DF103
Culvers Ct, Grav. DA12 213 GM88
Culvers Cft, Seer Grn HP9 111 AQ51
Culvers Ho Prim Sch, Mitch.
CR4 off Orchard Av 222 DG102
Culvers Retreat, Cars. SM5 222 DF102
Culverstone Cl, Brom. BR2 226 EF100
Culvers Way, Cars. SM5 222 DF103
Culvert La, Uxb. UB8 156 BH68
Culvert Pl, SW11 40 G9
Culvert Rd, N15 144 DS57
SW11 40 F7
Culworth St, NW8 16 C1
Culzean Cl, SE27
off Chatsworth Way 203 DP90
Cumberland Av, NW10 160 CP69
Gravesend DA12 213 GJ87
Guildford GU2 264 AU129
Hornchurch RM12 150 FL62
Slough SL2 153 AQ70
Welling DA16 187 ES83
● Cumberland Business Pk,
NW10 160 CN69
Cumberland Cl, E8 10 A5
SW20 off Lansdowne Rd 201 CX94
Amersham HP7 94 AV39
Epsom KT19 238 CS110
Hemel Hempstead HP3 63 BS24
Hertford SG14 53 DP06
Hornchurch RM12 150 FL62
Ilford IG6 125 EQ53
Twickenham TW1
off Westmorland Cl 199 CH86
Cumberland Ct, Hodd. EN11 71 EA16
Welling DA16
off Bellegrove Rd 187 ES82
Cumberland Cres, W14 26 F8
Cumberland Dr, Bexh. DA7 188 EY80
Chessington KT9 220 CM104
Dartford DA1 210 FM87
Esher KT10 219 CG103
Cumberland Gdns, NW4 119 CX54
WC1 18 D2
Cumberland Gate, W1 28 E10
Cumberland Ho, SE28 187 EQ75
Cumberland Mkt, NW1 17 K2
Cumberland Mkt Est, NW1 17 K2
Cumberland Ms, SE11 42 F1
Cumberland Mills Sq, E14 34 G10
● Cumberland Pk, NW10 161 CU69
Cumberland Pk, W3 160 CQ73
Cumberland Pl, NW1 17 J2
SE6 206 EF88
Sunbury-on-Thames TW16 217 BU98
Cumberland Rd, E12 146 EK63
E13 24 A6
E17 123 DY54
N9 122 DW46
N22 121 DM54
SE25 224 DV100
SW13 181 CT81
W3 160 CQ73
W7 179 CF75
Ashford TW15 196 BK90
Bromley BR2 226 EE98
Chafford Hundred RM16 192 FY75
Harrow HA1 138 CB57
Richmond TW9 180 CN80
Stanmore HA7 140 CM55
Cumberlands, Ken. CR8 258 DR115
Cumberland Sch, E13 24 C4
Cumberland St, SW1 29 K10
Staines TW18 195 BD92
Cumberland Ter, NW1 17 J1
Cumberland Ter Ms, NW1 17 J1
Cumberland Vil, W3
off Cumberland Rd 160 CQ73
Cumberlow Av, SE25 224 DU97
Cumberlow Pl, Hem.H. HP2 63 BQ21
Cumbernauld Gdns, Sun.
TW16 197 BT92
Cumberton Rd, N17 122 DR53
Cumbrae Cl, Slou. SL2
off St. Pauls Av 154 AU74
Cumbrae Gdns, Long Dit. KT6 219 CK103
Cumbrian Av, Bexh. DA7 189 FE81
Cumbrian Gdns, NW2 141 CX61
Cumbrian Way, Uxb. UB8 156 BK67
Cum Cum Hill, Hat. AL9 68 DD21
★ Cuming Mus, SE17
off Walworth Rd 31 J9
Cumley Rd, Toot Hill CM5 93 FE30
Cummings Hall La, Noak Hill
RM3 128 FJ48
Cumming St, N1 18 C1
Cumnor Gdns, Epsom KT17 239 CU107
Cumnor Ho Sch, S.Croy.
CR2 off Pampisford Rd 241 DP109
Cumnor Ri, Ken. CR8 258 DQ117
Cumnor Rd, Sutt. SM2 240 DC107
Cunard Cres, N21 104 DR44
Cunard Pl, EC3 19 P9
Cunard Rd, NW10 160 CR69
Cunard Wk, SE16 33 K8
Cundalls Rd, Ware SG12 55 DY05
Cundy Rd, E16 24 C9
Cundy St, SW1 29 H9
Cundy St Est, SW1 29 H9
Cunliffe Cl, Headley KT18 254 CP124
Cunliffe Rd, Epsom KT19 239 CT105
Cunliffe St, SW16 203 DJ93
Cunningham Av, Enf. EN3 105 DY36
Guildford GU1 265 BA133
Hatfield AL10 66 CR17
St. Albans AL1 65 CF22
Cunningham Cl, Rom. RM6 148 EW57
West Wickham BR4 225 EB103
Cunningham Ct, E10
off Oliver Rd 145 EB62
Cunningham Hill Inf Sch,
St.Alb. AL1
off Cell Barnes La 65 CG21
Cunningham Hill Jun Sch,
St.Alb. AL1
off Cell Barnes La 65 CG22
Cunningham Hill Rd, St.Alb.
AL1 65 CF22
Cunningham Pk, Har. HA1 138 CC57
Cunningham Pl, NW8 16 A4
Cunningham Ri, N.Wld Bas.
CM16 93 FC25
Cunningham Rd, N15 144 DU56
Banstead SM7 256 DD115
Cheshunt EN8 89 DY27
Cunnington St, W4 180 CQ76
Cupar Rd, SW11 41 H6
CUPID GREEN, Hem.H. HP2 62 BN16
Cupid Grn La, Hem.H. HP2 62 BN15
Cupola Cl, Brom. BR1 206 EH92
Curates Wk, Dart. DA2 210 FK90
Cureton St, SW1 29 P9
Curfew Bell Rd, Cher. KT16 215 BF101
Curfew Yd, Wind. SL4
off Thames St 173 AR81
Curie Gdns, NW9 118 CS54
Curlew Cl, SE28 168 EX73
Berkhamsted HP4 60 AW20
South Croydon CR2 243 DX111
Curlew Ct, Brox. EN10 71 DZ23
Surbiton KT6 220 CM104
Curlew Gdns, Guil. GU4 265 BD132
Curlew Ho, Enf. EN3
off Allington Ct 105 DX43
Curlews, The, Grav. DA12 213 GK89
Curlew St, SE1 32 A4
Curlew Ter, Ilf. IG5
off Tiptree Cres 147 EN55
Curlew Way, Hayes UB4 158 BX71
Curling Cl, Couls. CR5 257 DM120
Curling La, Bad.Dene RM17 192 FZ78
Curling Vale, Guil. GU2 280 AU136
Curness St, SE13 185 EC84
Curnick's La, SE27
off Chapel Rd 204 DQ91
Curnock Est, NW1 7 L9
● Curo Pk, Frog. AL2 83 CE27
Curran Av, Sid. DA15 207 ET85
Wallington SM6 222 DG104
Curran Cl, Uxb. UB8 156 BJ70
Currey Rd, Grnf. UB6 159 CD65
Curricle St, W3 160 CS74
Currie Hill Cl, SW19 201 CZ91
Curries La, Slou. SL1 133 AK64
Currie St, Hert. SG13 54 DS09
Curry Ri, NW7 119 CX51
Cursitor St, EC4 18 E8
Curtain Pl, EC2 19 P4
Curtain Rd, EC2 19 N5
Curteys, Harl. CM17 58 EX10
Curthwaite Gdns, Enf. EN2 103 DK42
Curtis Cl, Mill End WD3 114 BG46
Curtis Dr, W3 160 CR72
Curtis Fld Rd, SW16 203 DM91
Curtis Gdns, Dor. RH4 285 CG135
Curtis Ho, N11 121 DH50
Curtis La, Wem. HA0
off Station Gro 140 CL64
Curtismill Cl, Orp. BR5 228 EV97
Curtis Mill Grn, Nave. RM4 109 FF42
Curtis Mill La, Nave. RM4 109 FF42
Curtismill Way, Orp. BR5 228 EV97
Curtis Rd, Dor. RH4 285 CF135
Epsom KT19 238 CQ105
Hemel Hempstead HP3 63 BQ21
Hornchurch RM11 150 FM60
Hounslow TW4 198 BZ87
Curtiss Dr, Lvsdn WD25 81 BT34
Curtis St, SE1 32 A8
Curtis Way, SE1 32 A8
SE28 off Tawney Rd 168 EV73
Berkhamsted HP4 60 AX20
Curvan Cl, Epsom KT17 239 CT110
Curve, The, W12 161 CU73
Curwen Av, E7
off Woodford Rd 146 EH63
Curwen Prim Sch, E13 23 N1
Curwen Rd, W12 181 CU75
Curzon Av, Beac. HP9 111 AK51
Enfield EN3 105 DX43
Hazlemere HP15 110 AC45
Stanmore HA7 117 CG53
Curzon Cl, Haz. HP15 110 AC45
Orpington BR6 245 ER105
Weybridge KT13
off Curzon Rd 234 BN105
Curzon Cres, NW10 161 CT66
Barking IG11 167 ET68
Curzon Dr, Grays RM17 192 GC80
Curzon Gate, W1 28 G3
Curzon Pl, Pnr. HA5 138 BW57
Curzon Rd, N10 121 DH54
W5 159 CH70
Thornton Heath CR7 223 DN100
Weybridge KT13 234 BN105
Curzon Sq, W1 29 H3
Curzon St, W1 29 H3
Cusack Cl, Twick. TW1
off Waldegrave Rd 199 CF91
Cussons Cl, Chsht EN7 88 DU29
CUSTOM HOUSE, E16 24 F8

Custom House for ExCeL 24 B10
Custom Ho Reach, SE16 33 N5
Custom Ho Wk, EC3 31 N1
Cut, The, SE1 30 F4
Slough SL2 153 AN70
Cutcombe Rd, SE5 43 K9
Cuthberga Cl, Bark. IG11
off George St 167 EQ66
Cuthbert Ct, Whyt. CR3
off Godstone Rd 258 DU119
Cuthbert Gdns, SE25 224 DS97
Cuthbert Rd, E17 145 EC55
N18 off Fairfield Rd 122 DU50
Croydon CR0 223 DP103
Cuthberts Cl, Chsht EN7 88 DT29
Cuthbert St, W2 16 A6
Cut Hills, Egh. TW20 214 AV95
Virginia Water GU25 214 AU96
Cuthill Wk, SE5 43 L7
Cutlers Gdns, E1 19 P8
Cutlers Gdns Arc, EC2
off Devonshire Sq 19 P8
Cutlers Sq, E14 34 B9
Cutlers Ter, N1 9 N4
Cutler St, E1 19 P8
Cutmore, Bark. IG11
off Ripple Rd 167 EQ66
Cutmore Dr, Coln.Hth AL4 66 CP22
Cutmore St, Grav. DA11 213 GH87
Cutthroat All, Rich. TW10
off Ham St 199 CJ89
Cutthroat La, Hodd. EN11 71 DZ15
Cutting, The, Red. RH1 288 DF136
Cuttsfield Ter, Hem.H. HP1 61 BF21
★ Cutty Sark, SE10 46 E2
Cutty Sark Ct, Green. DA9
off Low Cl 211 FU85
Cutty Sark for Maritime Greenwich 46 E3
Cutty Sark Gdns, SE10 46 F2
Cuxton Cl, Bexh. DA6 208 EY85
Cwmbran Ct, Hem.H. HP2 62 BM16
Cyclamen Cl, Hmptn. TW12
off Gresham Rd 198 CA93
Cyclamen Rd, Swan. BR8 229 FD98
Cyclamen Way, Epsom KT19 238 CP106
Cyclops Ms, E14 34 A8
Cygnet Av, Felt. TW14 198 BW87
Cygnet Cl, NW10 140 CR64
Borehamwood WD6 100 CQ39
Northwood HA6 115 BQ52
Woking GU21 248 AV116
Cygnet Gdns, Nthflt DA11 213 GF89
Cygnets, The, Felt. TW13 198 BY91
Staines TW18
off Edgell Rd 195 BF92
Cygnets Cl, Red. RH1 272 DG132
Cygnet St, E1 20 B4
Cygnet Vw, Grays RM20 191 FT77
Cygnet Way, Hayes UB4 158 BX71
● Cygnus Business Cen, NW10 161 CT65
Cymbeline Ct, Har. HA1 139 CF58
Cynthia St, N1 18 D1
Cyntra Pl, E8 10 F7
Cypress Av, Enf. EN2 103 DN35
Twickenham TW2 198 CC87
Welwyn Garden City AL7 52 DC10
Cypress Cl, E5 144 DU61
Waltham Abbey EN9 89 ED34
Cypress Ct, Vir.W. GU25 214 AY98
Cypress Gdns, SE4 205 DY85
Cypress Gro, Ilf. IG6 125 ES51
Cypress Inf Sch, SE25
off Cypress Rd 224 DS96
Cypress Jun Sch, SE25
off Cypress Rd 224 DS96
Cypress Path, Rom. RM3 128 FK52
Cypress Pl, W1 17 M5
Cypress Rd, SE25 224 DS96
Guildford GU1 264 AW132
Harrow HA3 117 CD54
Cypress Tree Cl, Sid. DA15 207 ET88
Cypress Wk, Eng.Grn TW20 194 AV93
Watford WD25
off Cedar Wd Dr 97 BV35
Cypress Way, Bans. SM7 239 CX114
Cyprus 25 M10
Cyprus Av, N3 119 CY54
Cyprus Cl, N4
off Atterbury Rd 143 DP58
Cyprus Gdns, N3 119 CY54
Cyprus Pl, E2 21 H1
E6 25 M10
Cyprus Rd, N3 119 CZ54
N9 122 DT47
Cyprus Rbt, E16 25 M10
Cyprus St, E2 20 G1
Cyrena Rd, SE22 204 DT86
Cyril Jackson Prim Sch, N Bldg, E14 21 P10
S Bldg, E14 33 P1
Cyril Mans, SW11 40 F7
Cyril Rd, Bexh. DA7 188 EY82
Orpington BR6 228 EU101
Cyrils Way, St.Alb. AL1
off Maynard Dr 65 CD23
Cyrus St, EC1 19 H4
Czar St, SE8 46 A2

D

Dabbling Cl, Erith DA8 189 FH80
Dabbs Hill La, Nthlt. UB5 138 CB64
D'Abernon Chase, Lthd. KT22 237 CG114
D'Abernon Cl, Esher KT10 236 CA105
D'Abernon Dr, Stoke D'Ab. KT11 252 BY116
Dabin Cres, SE10 46 E6
Dacca St, SE8 45 P2
Dace Rd, E3 12 A8
Dacorum Way, Hem.H. HP1 62 BJ20
Dacre Av, Aveley RM15 171 FR74
Ilford IG5 125 EN54
Dacre Cl, Chig. IG7 125 EQ49
Greenford UB6 158 CB68
Dacre Cres, Aveley RM15 171 FR74
Dacre Gdns, SE13 186 EE84
Borehamwood WD6 100 CR43
Chigwell IG7 125 EQ49
● Dacre Ind Est, Chsht EN8
off Fieldings Rd 89 DZ29
Dacre Pk, SE13 186 EE83
Dacre Pl, SE13 186 EE83
Dacre Rd, E11 146 EF60
E13 166 EH67
Croydon CR0 223 DL101
Dacres Est, SE23 205 DX90
Dacres Rd, SE23 205 DX90
Dacre St, SW1 29 N6
Dade Way, Sthl. UB2 178 BZ78
Dads Wd, Harl. CM20 73 EQ15
Daerwood Cl, Brom. BR2 227 EM102
Daffodil Av, Pilg.Hat. CM15 130 FV43
Daffodil Cl, Croy. CR0 225 DX102
Hatfield AL10 51 CT14
Daffodil Gdns, Ilf. IG1 147 EP64
Daffodil Pl, Hmptn. TW12
off Gresham Rd 198 CA93
Daffodil St, W12 161 CT73
Dafforne Rd, SW17 202 DG90
Dagden Rd, Shalf. GU4 280 AY140
DAGENHAM, RM8 - RM10 168 FA65
Dagenham Av, Dag. RM9 168 EY67
⇌ Dagenham Dock 168 EZ68
⊖ Dagenham East 149 FC64
⊖ Dagenham Heathway 168 EZ65
Dagenham Leisure Pk, Dag. RM9 168 EY67
Dagenham Pk Comm Sch, Dag. RM10 off School Rd 169 FB67
Dagenham Rd, E10 145 DZ60
Dagenham RM10 149 FC63
Rainham RM13 169 FD66
Romford RM7 149 FD62
Dagger La, Els. WD6 99 CG44
Daggs Dell Rd, Hem.H. HP1 61 BE18
Dagley Fm Pk Homes, Shalf. GU4 280 AX140
Dagley La, Shalf. GU4 280 AY140
Dagmar Av, Wem. HA9 140 CM63
Dagmar Gdns, NW10 14 C1
Dagmar Ms, Sthl. UB2
off Dagmar Rd 178 BY76
Dagmar Pas, N1 9 H8
Dagmar Rd, N4 143 DN59
N15 off Cornwall Rd 144 DR56
N22 121 DK53
SE5 43 N7
SE25 224 DS99
Dagenham RM10 169 FC66
Kingston upon Thames KT2 220 CM95
Southall UB2 178 BY76
Windsor SL4 173 AR82
Dagmar Ter, N1 9 H8
Dagnall Cres, Uxb. UB8 156 BJ71
Dagnall Pk, SE25 224 DS100
Dagnall Rd, SE25 224 DS99
Dagnall St, SW11 40 F8
Dagnam Pk Cl, Rom. RM3 128 FN50
Dagnam Pk Dr, Rom. RM3 128 FL50
Dagnam Pk Gdns, Rom. RM3 128 FN51
Dagnam Pk Sq, Rom. RM3 128 FP51
Dagnan Rd, SW12 203 DH87
Dagonet Gdns, Brom. BR1 206 EG90
Dagonet Rd, Brom. BR1 206 EG90
Dahlia Cl, Chsht EN7 88 DQ25
Dahlia Dr, Swan. BR8 229 FF96
Dahlia Gdns, Ilf. IG1 167 EP65
Mitcham CR4 223 DK98
Dahlia Rd, SE2 188 EV77
Dahomey Rd, SW16 203 DJ93
Daiglen Dr, S.Ock. RM15 171 FU73
Daiglen Sch, The, Buck.H. IG9 off Palmerston Rd 124 EJ47
Daimler Way, Wall. SM6 241 DL108
Daines Cl, E12 147 EM62
South Ockendon RM15 171 FU70
Dainford Cl, Brom. BR1 205 ED92
Dainton Cl, Brom. BR1 226 EH95
Daintry Cl, Har. HA3 139 CG56
Daintry Lo, Nthwd. HA6 115 BT52
Daintry Way, E9 11 N4
Dair Ho Sch, Farn.Royal SL2
off Beaconsfield Rd 153 AQ67
Dairsie Rd, SE9 187 EN83
Dairy Cl, NW10 161 CU67
Bromley BR1
off Plaistow La 206 EH94
Sutton at Hone DA4 210 FP94
Thornton Heath CR7 224 DQ96
Westcott RH4 284 CC137
Dairy Fm Pl, SE15 44 G7
Dairyglen Av, Chsht EN8 89 DY31
Dairy La, SE18 37 J9
Crockham Hill TN8 277 EN134
Dairyman Cl, NW2
off Claremont Rd 141 CY62
Dairyman's Wk, Guil. GU4 265 BB129
Dairy Meadow Prim Sch, Sthl. UB2 off Swift Rd 178 BZ76
Dairy Ms, N2 off East End Rd 142 DE56
SW9 183 DL83
Dairy Wk, SW19 201 CY91
Dairy Way, Abb.L. WD5 81 BT29
Daisy Cl, Croy. CR0 225 DX102
Daisy Dobbins Wk, N19
off Hillrise Rd 143 DL59
Daisy Dr, Hat. AL10 67 CT15
Daisy La, SW6 39 J10
Daisy Meadow, Egh. TW20 195 BA92
Daisy Rd, E16 23 J4
E18 124 EH54
Dakin Pl, E1 21 L7
Dakota Bldg, SE13
off Deals Gateway 46 B7
Dakota Cl, Wall. SM6 241 DM108
Dakota Gdns, E6 25 H5
Northolt UB5
off Argus Way 158 BY69
Dalberg Rd, SW2 183 DN84
Dalberg Way, SE2
off Lanridge Rd 188 EX76
Dalby Rd, SW18 182 DC84
Dalbys Cres, N17 122 DS51
Dalby St, NW5 7 J5
Dalcross Rd, Houns. TW4 178 BY82
Dale, The, Kes. BR2 244 EK105
Waltham Abbey EN9 90 EE34
Dale Av, Edg. HA8 118 CM53
Hounslow TW4 178 BY83
Dalebury Rd, SW17 202 DE89
Dale Cl, SE3 47 N10
Addlestone KT15 234 BH106
Bookham KT23 268 CC125
Dartford DA1 209 FF86
Dale Cl, New Barn. EN5 102 DB44
Pinner HA5 115 BV53
South Ockendon RM15 171 FU72
Dale Ct, Saw. CM21
off The Crest 58 EX06
Slough SL1 173 AQ75
Dale Dr, Hayes UB4 157 BT70
Dale End, Dart. DA1
off Dale Rd 209 FF86
Dale Gdns, Wdf.Grn. IG8 124 EH49
Dalegarth Gdns, Pur. CR8 242 DR113
Dale Grn Rd, N11 121 DH48
Dale Gro, N12 120 DC50
Daleham Av, Egh. TW20 195 BA93
Daleham Dr, Uxb. UB8 157 BP72
Daleham Gdns, NW3 6 A3
Daleham Ms, NW3 6 B4
Dalehead, NW1 17 L1
Dalemain Ms, E16 35 P2
Dale Pk Av, Cars. SM5 222 DF103
Dale Pk Rd, SE19 224 DQ95
Dale Rd, NW5 7 H2
SE17 43 H3
Dartford DA1 209 FF86
Greenford UB6 158 CB71
Purley CR8 241 DN112
Southfleet DA13 212 GA91
Sunbury-on-Thames TW16 197 BT94
Sutton SM1 239 CZ105
Swanley BR8 229 FC96
Walton-on-Thames KT12 217 BT101
Dale Row, W11 14 F9
Daleside, Ger.Cr. SL9 134 AY60
Orpington BR6 246 EU106
Daleside Cl, Orp. BR6 246 EU107
Daleside Dr, Pot.B. EN6 85 CZ32
Daleside Gdns, Chig. IG7 125 EQ48
Daleside Rd, SW16 203 DH92
Epsom KT19 238 CR107
Dales Path, Borwd. WD6
off Farriers Way 100 CR43
Dales Rd, Borwd. WD6 100 CR43
Dalestone Ms, Rom. RM3 127 FH51
Dale St, W4 180 CS78
Dale Vw, Erith DA8 189 FF82
Headley KT18 254 CP123
Woking GU21 248 AU118
Dale Vw Av, E4 123 EC47
Dale Vw Cres, E4 123 EC47
Dale Vw Gdns, E4 123 ED48
Daleview Rd, N15 144 DS58
Dale Wk, Dart. DA2 210 FQ88
Dalewood, Welw.G.C. AL7 52 DD10
Dalewood Cl, Horn. RM11 150 FM59
Dalewood Gdns, Wor.Pk. KT4 221 CV103
Dale Wd Rd, Orp. BR6 227 ES101
Daley St, E9 11 K4
Daley Thompson Way, SW8 41 J9
Dalgarno Gdns, W10 14 A6
Dalgarno Way, W10 14 A5
Dalgleish St, E14 21 M9
Daling Way, E3 11 M9
Dalkeith Gro, Stan. HA7 117 CK50
Dalkeith Rd, SE21 204 DQ88
Ilford IG1 147 EQ62
Dallas Rd, NW4 141 CU59
SE26 204 DV90
W5 160 CM71
Sutton SM3 239 CY107
Dallas Ter, Hayes UB3 177 BT76
Dallega Cl, Hayes UB3
off Dawley Rd 157 BR73
Dallinger Rd, SE12 206 EF86
Dalling Rd, W6 181 CV76
Dallington Cl, Hersham KT12 236 BW107
Dallington Sch, EC1 19 H4
Dallington Sq, EC1
off Dallington St 19 H4
Dallington St, EC1 19 H4
Dallin Rd, SE18 187 EP80
Bexleyheath DA6 188 EX84
Dalmain Prim Sch, SE23
off Grove Cl 205 DY88
Dalmain Rd, SE23 205 DX88
Dalmally Rd, Croy. CR0 224 DT101
Dalmeny Av, N7 8 A2
SW16 223 DN96
Dalmeny Cl, Wem. HA0 159 CJ65
Dalmeny Cres, Houns. TW3 179 CD84
Dalmeny Rd, N7 7 P1
Carshalton SM5 240 DG108
Erith DA8 189 FB81
New Barnet EN5 102 DC44
Worcester Park KT4 221 CV104
Dalmeyer Rd, NW10 161 CT65
Dalmore Av, Clay. KT10 237 CF107
Dalmore Rd, SE21 204 DQ89
Dalroy Cl, S.Ock. RM15 171 FU72
Dalrymple Cl, N14 121 DK45
Dalrymple Rd, SE4 185 DY84
DALSTON, E8 10 C6
Dalston Gdns, Stan. HA7 118 CL53
⊖ Dalston Junction 10 A5
⊖ Dalston Kingsland 9 P4
Dalston La, E8 10 A4
Dalton Av, Mitch. CR4 222 DE96
Dalton Cl, Hayes UB4 157 BR70
Orpington BR6 227 ES104
Purley CR8 242 DQ112
Dalton Grn, Slou. SL3 175 AZ79
Dalton Rd, Har.Wld HA3 117 CD54
Daltons Rd, Chels. BR6 229 FB104
Swanley BR8 229 FC102
Dalton St, SE27 203 DP89
St. Albans AL3 65 CD19
Dalton Way, Wat. WD17 98 BX43
Dalwood St, SE5 43 N6
Daly Dr, Brom. BR1 227 EN97
Dalyell Rd, SW9 42 C10
Damascene Wk, SE21
off Lovelace Rd 204 DQ88
Damask Ct, Sutt. SM1
off Cleeve Way 222 DB102
Damask Cres, E16 23 J4
Damask Grn, Hem.H. HP1 61 BE21
Dame Alice Owen's Sch, Pot.B. EN6 off Dugdale Hill La 85 CY33
Damer Ter, SW10 39 P5
Dames Rd, E7 146 EG62
Dame St, N1 9 J10
Dameswick Vw, St.Alb. AL2 82 CA27
Dame Tipping C of E Prim Sch, Hav.at.Bow. RM4
off North Rd 127 FE48
Damien St, E1 20 F8
Damigos Rd, Grav. DA12 213 GM88
Damon Cl, Sid. DA14 208 EV90
Damphurst La, Dor. RH5 284 BZ139
Damson Ct, Swan. BR8 229 FD98
Damson Dr, Hayes UB3 157 BU73
Damson Gro, Slou. SL1 173 AQ75
Damson Way, Cars. SM5 240 DF110
St. Albans AL4 65 CJ18
Damsonwood Rd, Sthl. UB2 178 CA76
Danbrook Rd, SW16 223 DL95
Danbury Cl, Pilg.Hat. CM15 130 FT43
Romford RM6 148 EX55
Danbury Cres, S.Ock. RM15 171 FV72
Danbury Ms, Wall. SM6 241 DH105
Danbury Rd, Loug. IG10 124 EL45
Rainham RM13 169 FF67
Danbury St, N1 9 H10
Danbury Way, Wdf.Grn. IG8 124 EJ51
Danby St, SE15 44 A10
Dancer Rd, SW6 38 G7
Richmond TW9 180 CN83
DANCERS HILL, Barn. EN5 101 CW35
Dancers Hill Rd, Barn. EN5 101 CY36
Dancers La, Barn. EN5 101 CW35
Dandelion Cl, Rush Grn RM7 149 FE61
Dando Cres, SE3 186 EH83
Dandridge Cl, SE10 35 M10
Slough SL3 174 AX77
Dandridge Dr, B.End SL8
off Millside 132 AC60
Danebury, New Adgtn CR0 243 EB107
Danebury Av, SW15 200 CS86
Daneby Rd, SE6 205 EB90
Dane Cl, Amer. HP7 94 AT41
Bexley DA5 208 FA87
Orpington BR6 245 ER106
Dane Ct, Wok. GU22 249 BF115
Danecourt Gdns, Croy. CR0 224 DT104
Danecroft Rd, SE24 204 DQ85
Danegrove Prim Sch, Years 2-6, Barn. EN4
off Windsor Dr 102 DE44
Reception & Year 1, E.Barn. EN4 off Ridgeway Av 102 DF44
Danehill Wk, Sid. DA14
off Hatherley Rd 208 EU90
Daneholes Rbt, Grays RM16 192 GD76
Danehurst Cl, Egh. TW20 194 AY93
Danehurst Gdns, Ilf. IG4 146 EL57
Danehurst St, SW6 38 E6
Daneland, Barn. EN4 102 DF44
Danemead, Hodd. EN11 55 EA14
Danemead Gro, Nthlt. UB5 138 CB64
Danemere St, SW15 38 B10
Dane Pl, E3 11 N10
Dane Rd, N18 122 DW49
SW19 222 DC95
W13 159 CJ74
Ashford TW15 197 BQ93
Ilford IG1 147 EQ64
Otford TN14 263 FE117
Southall UB1 158 BY73
Warlingham CR6 259 DX117
Danes, The, Park St AL2 82 CC28
Danesbury Pk, Hert. SG14 54 DR08
Danesbury Rd, Felt. TW13 197 BV88
Danes Cl, Nthflt DA11 212 GC90
Oxshott KT22 236 CC114
Danescombe, SE12 206 EG88
Danes Ct, Wem. HA9
off North End Rd 140 CP62
Danescourt Cres, Sutt. SM1 222 DC103
Danescroft, NW4 141 CX57
Danescroft Av, NW4 141 CX57
Danescroft Gdns, NW4 141 CX57
Danesdale Rd, E9 11 L5
Danesfield, SE5 43 N2
Ripley GU23 249 BF123
Danesfield Cl, Walt. KT12 217 BV104
Danesfield Manor Sch, Walt. KT12 off Rydens Av 218 BW103
Danes Gate, Har. HA1 139 CE55
Daneshill, Red. RH1 272 DE133
Danes Hill, Wok. GU22 249 BA118
Daneshill Cl, Red. RH1 272 DE133
Danes Hill Sch, Main Sch, Oxshott KT22
off Leatherhead Rd 237 CD114
Pre-Prep Dept, Oxshott KT22 off Steels La 236 CC113
Danes Rd, Rom. RM7 149 FC59
Danesrood, Guil. GU1
off Lower Edgeborough Rd 281 AZ135
Dane St, WC1 18 C7
Danes Way, Oxshott KT22 237 CD114
Pilgrim's Hatch CM15 130 FU43
Daneswood Av, SE6 205 EC90
Daneswood Cl, Wey. KT13 235 BP106
Danethorpe Rd, Wem. HA0 159 CK65
Danetree Cl, Epsom KT19 238 CQ108
Danetree Jun Sch, W.Ewell KT19 off Danetree Rd 238 CQ108
Danetree Rd, Epsom KT19 238 CQ108
Danette Gdns, Dag. RM10 148 EZ61
Daneville Rd, SE5 43 L7
Dangan Rd, E11 146 EG58
Daniel Bolt Cl, E14 22 D6
Daniel Cl, N18 122 DW49
SW17 202 DE93
Chafford Hundred RM16 192 FY75
Grays RM16 193 GH76
Hounslow TW4 198 BZ87
Daniel Gdns, SE15 44 A4
Daniells, Welw.G.C. AL7 52 DA08
Daniell Way, Croy. CR0 223 DL102
Daniel Pl, NW4 141 CV58
Daniel Rd, W5 160 CM73
Daniels La, Warl. CR6 259 DZ116
Daniels Rd, SE15 184 DW83
Daniel Way, Bans. SM7 240 DB114
Dan Leno Wk, SW6 39 L5
Dan Mason Dr, W4 180 CR82
Danses Cl, Guil. GU4 265 BD132
Dansey Pl, W1 17 N10
Dansington Rd, Well. DA16 188 EU84
Danson Cres, Well. DA16 188 EV83
Danson Interchange, Sid. DA15 208 EW86
Danson La, Well. DA16 188 EU84
Danson Mead, Well. DA16 188 EW83
★ Danson Park, Well. DA16 188 EW84
Danson Pk, Bexh. DA6 188 EW84
Danson Prim Sch, Well. DA16 off Danson La 188 EU84
Danson Rd, Bex. DA5 208 EX85
Bexleyheath DA6 208 EX85
Danson Underpass, Sid. DA15 off Danson Rd 208 EW85
Dante Pl, SE11 31 H8
Dante Rd, SE11 30 G8
Danube Apts, N8
off Great Amwell La 143 DM55
Danube St, SW3 28 D10
Danvers Rd, N8 143 DK56
Danvers St, SW3 40 B3
Danvers Way, Cat. CR3 258 DQ123
Danyon Cl, Rain. RM13 170 FJ68
Danziger Way, Borwd. WD6 100 CQ39
Dapdune Ct, Guil. GU1 264 AW134
Dapdune Rd, Guil. GU1 264 AX134
Dapdune Wf, Guil. GU1 264 AW134
Daphne Gdns, E4
off Gunners Gro 123 EC48
Daphne Jackson Rd, Guil. GU2 280 AS135
Daphne St, SW18 202 DC86
Daplyn St, E1 20 C6
Darblay Cl, Sand. AL4 50 CM10
D'Arblay St, W1 17 M9
Darby Cl, Cat. CR3 258 DQ122
Darby Cres, Sun. TW16 218 BW96
Darby Dr, Wal.Abb. EN9 89 EC33
Darby Gdns, Sun. TW16 218 BW96
Darcy Av, Wall. SM6 241 DJ105
Darcy Cl, N20 120 DD47
Cheshunt EN8 89 DY31
Coulsdon CR5 257 DP119
D'Arcy Cl, Hutt. CM13 131 GB45
D'Arcy Dr, Har. HA3 139 CK56
Darcy Gdns, Dag. RM9 168 EZ67
D'Arcy Gdns, Har. HA3 140 CL56
Darcy Ho, E8 10 E8
D'Arcy Pl, Ashtd. KT21 254 CM117
Bromley BR2 226 EG98
Darcy Rd, SW16 223 DL96
D'Arcy Rd, Ashtd. KT21 254 CM117
Darcy Rd, Islw. TW7
off London Rd 179 CG81
D'Arcy Rd, Sutt. SM3 239 CX105
Dare Gdns, Dag. RM8 148 EY62
Darell Prim Sch, Rich. TW9 off Darell Rd 180 CN83
Darell Rd, Rich. TW9 180 CN83
Darent Cl, Chipstead TN13 278 FC122
DARENTH, Dart. DA2 210 FQ91
Darenth Comm Prim Sch, Dart. DA2 off Green St Grn Rd 211 FT93
Darenth Gdns, West. TN16 277 ER126
Darenth Hill, Dart. DA2 210 FQ92
Darenth Interchange, Dart. DA2 210 FP90
Darenth La, Dunt.Grn TN13 278 FE121
South Ockendon RM15 171 FU72
Darenth Pk Av, Dart. DA2 211 FR89
Darenth Rd, N16 144 DT59
Darenth DA2 210 FP91
Dartford DA1 210 FM87
Welling DA16 188 EU81
Darenth Way, Horl. RH6 290 DF145
Shoreham TN14 247 FG111
Darenth Wd Rd, Dart. DA2 211 FS89
● Darent Ind Pk, Erith DA8 190 FJ79
Darent Mead, Sutt.H. DA4 230 FP95
Darent Valley Hosp, Dart. DA2 211 FS88
Darent Valley Path, Dart. DA1, DA2, DA4 210 FM89
Sevenoaks TN13, TN14 263 FG115
Darfield Rd, SE4 205 DZ85
Guildford GU4 265 BA131
Darfield Way, W10 14 C10
Darfur St, SW15 181 CX83
Dargate Cl, SE19
off Chipstead Cl 204 DT94
Darien Rd, SW11 182 DD83
Darkes La, Pot.B. EN6 86 DA32
Darkhole Ride, Wind. SL4 172 AH84
Dark Ho Wk, EC3
off Grant's Quay Wf 31 M1
Dark La, Chsht EN7 88 DU31
Great Warley CM14 129 FU52
Puttenham GU3 282 BM139
Ware (Musley La) SG12 55 DY05
Darlands Dr, Barn. EN5 101 CX43
Darlan Rd, SW6 39 H5
Darlaston Rd, SW19 201 CX94
Darley Cl, Add. KT15 234 BJ106
Croydon CR0 225 DY100
Darley Cft, Park St AL2 82 CB28
Darley Dene Inf Sch, Add. KT15 off Garfield Rd 234 BJ106
Darley Dr, N.Mal. KT3 220 CR96
Darley Gdns, Mord. SM4 222 DB100
Darley Rd, N9 122 DT46
SW11 202 DF86
Darling Rd, SE4 46 A10
Darling Row, E1 20 F5
Darlington Cl, Amer. HP6
off King George V Rd 77 AR38
Darlington Gdns, Rom. RM3 128 FK50
Darlington Path, Rom. RM3
off Darlington Gdns 128 FK50
Darlington Rd, SE27 203 DP92
Darlton Cl, Dart. DA1 189 FF83
Darmaine Cl, S.Croy. CR2 242 DQ108
Darnaway Pl, E14 22 F7
Darndale Cl, E17 123 DZ54
Darnets Fld, Otford TN14 263 FF117
Darnhills, Rad. WD7 99 CG35
Darnicle Hill, Chsht EN7 87 DM25
Darnley Ho, E14 21 M8
Darnley Pk, Wey. KT13 217 BP104
Darnley Rd, E9 10 F5
Gravesend DA11 213 GG88
Grays RM17 off Stanley Rd 192 GB79
Woodford Green IG8 124 EG53
Darnley St, Grav. DA11 213 GG87
Darnley Ter, W11 26 D2
Darns Hill, Swan. BR8 229 FC101
Darrell Cl, Slou. SL3 175 AZ77
Darrell Rd, SE22 204 DU85
Darren Cl, N4 143 DM59
Darrick Wd Inf Sch, Orp. BR6 off Lovibonds Av 245 EP105
Darrick Wd Jun Sch, Orp. BR6 off Lovibonds Av 245 EP105
Darrick Wd Rd, Orp. BR6 227 ER103
Darrick Wd Sch, Orp. BR6
off Lovibonds Av 227 EP104
Darrington Rd, Borwd. WD6 100 CL39
Darris Cl, Hayes UB4 158 BY70
Darsley Dr, SW8 41 P6
Dart, The, Hem.H. HP2 62 BN15
Dart Cl, Slou. SL3 175 BB79
Upminster RM14 151 FR58
Dartfields, Rom. RM3 128 FK51
DARTFORD, DA1 & DA2; DA4 210 FJ87
⇌ Dartford 210 FL86
Dartford Adult Ed Cen, Dart. DA1 off Highfield Rd 210 FK87
Dartford Av, N9 104 DW44

Dartford Bypass, Bex. DA5 209 FE88
Dartford DA2 209 FH89
Dartford Gdns, Chad.Hth RM6
off Heathfield Pk Dr 148 EV57
Sch Dartford Gram Sch, Dart.
DA1 off West Hill 210 FJ86
Sch Dartford Gram Sch for Girls,
Dart. DA1
off Shepherds La 210 FJ87
★ Dartford Heath, Dart. DA1 209 FG88
Dartford Heath, Bex. DA5 209 FF88
Dartford Ho, SE1
off Longfield Est 32 B9
★ Dartford Mus, Dart. DA1 210 FL87
Dartford Rd, Bex. DA5 209 FC88
Dartford DA1 209 FG86
Farningham DA4 230 FP95
Sevenoaks TN13 279 FJ124
Dartford St, SE17 43 K2
Sch Dartford Tech Coll, Dart.
DA1 off Heath La 210 FJ87
Dartford Tunnel, Dart. DA1 191 FR83
Purfleet RM19 191 FR83
Dartford Tunnel App Rd,
Dart. DA1 210 FN86
Dart Grn, S.Ock. RM15 171 FV72
Dartmoor Wk, E14 34 B8
Dartmouth Av, Wok. GU21 233 BC114
Dartmouth Cl, W11 15 H8
Dartmouth Grn, Wok. GU21 233 BD114
Dartmouth Gro, SE10 46 F7
Dartmouth Hill, SE10 46 F7
Dartmouth Ho, Kings.T. KT2
off Kingsgate Rd 220 CL95
DARTMOUTH PARK, NW5 143 DH62
Dartmouth Pk Av, NW5 143 DH62
Dartmouth Pk Hill, N19 143 DH60
NW5 143 DH60
Dartmouth Pk Rd, NW5 143 DH63
Dartmouth Path, Wok. GU21 233 BD114
Dartmouth Pl, SE23
off Dartmouth Rd 204 DW89
W4 180 CS79
Dartmouth Rd, E16 23 N8
NW2 4 C4
NW4 141 CU58
SE23 204 DW90
SE26 204 DW90
Bromley BR2 226 EG101
Ruislip HA4 137 BU62
Dartmouth Row, SE10 46 F8
Dartmouth St, SW1 29 N5
Dartmouth Ter, SE10 46 G7
Dartnell Av, W.Byf. KT14 234 BH112
Dartnell Cl, W.Byf. KT14 234 BH112
Dartnell Ct, W.Byf. KT14 234 BJ112
Dartnell Cres, W.Byf. KT14 234 BH112
DARTNELL PARK, W.Byf. KT14 234 BJ113
Dartnell Pk Rd, W.Byf. KT14 234 BJ111
Dartnell Pl, W.Byf. KT14 234 BH112
Dartnell Rd, Croy. CR0 224 DT101
Dartrey Twr, SW10
off Blantyre St 40 A4
Dartrey Wk, SW10
off Blantyre St 40 A4
Dart St, W10 14 F2
Dartview Cl, Grays RM17 192 GE77
Darvel Cl, Wok. GU21 248 AU116
Darvell Dr, Chesh. HP5 76 AN29
Darvells Yd, Chorl. WD3 95 BD41
Darville Rd, N16 144 DT62
Darvills La, Slou. SL1 173 AR75
Darwell Cl, E6 25 L1
Darwen Pl, E2 10 E9
Darwin Cl, N11 121 DH48
Orpington BR6 245 ER106
St. Albans AL3 65 CE16
Darwin Ct, SE17 31 M9
Guildford GU1 264 AX130
Darwin Dr, Sthl. UB1 158 CB72
Darwin Gdns, Wat. WD19 116 BW50
Darwin Rd, N22 121 DP53
W5 179 CJ78
Slough SL3 175 AZ75
Tilbury RM18 193 GF81
Welling DA16 187 ET83
Darwin St, SE17 31 M8
Daryngton Dr, Grnf. UB6 159 CD68
Guildford GU1 265 BB134
Dashes, The, Harl. CM20 57 ES14
Dashwood Cl, Bexh. DA6 208 FA85
Slough SL3 174 AW77
West Byfleet KT14 234 BJ112
Dashwood Lang Rd, Add.
KT15 234 BK105
Dashwood Rd, N8 143 DM58
Gravesend DA11 213 GG89
Dassett Rd, SE27 203 DP92
Datchelor Pl, SE5 43 M7
DATCHET, Slou. SL3 174 AW81
⇌ Datchet 174 AV81
Datchet Cl, Hem.H. HP2 63 BP15
Datchet Pl, Datchet SL3 174 AV81
Datchet Rd, SE6 205 DZ90
Horton SL3 175 AZ83
Old Windsor SL4 174 AU84
Slough SL3 174 AT77
Windsor SL4 173 AR80
Sch Datchet St. Mary's C of E
Prim Sch, Datchet SL3
off The Green 174 AV81
Datchworth Ct, N4
off Queens Dr 144 DQ62
Datchworth Turn, Hem.H. HP2 63 BQ20
Date St, SE17 43 L1
Daubeney Gdns, N17 122 DQ52
Daubeney Pl, Hmptn. TW12
off High St 218 CC95
Sch Daubeney Prim Sch, E5 11 L1
Daubeney Rd, E5 11 L1
N17 122 DQ52
Daubeney Twr, SE8 33 N9
Dault Rd, SW18 202 DC86
Davall Ho, Grays RM17
off Argent St 192 GB79
Davema Cl, Chis. BR7 227 EN95
Sch Davenant Foundation Sch,
Loug. IG10 off Chester Rd 107 EQ38
Davenant Rd, N19 143 DK61
Croydon CR0
off Duppas Hill Rd 241 DP105
Davenant St, E1 20 D7
Davenham Av, Nthwd. HA6 115 BT49
Sch Davenies Sch, Beac. HP9
off Station Rd 111 AL53
Davenport, Ch.Lang. CM17 74 EY16
Davenport Cl, Tedd. TW11 199 CG93
Davenport Ho, SE11
off Walnut Tree Wk 30 E8
Davenport Rd, SE6 205 EB86
Sidcup DA14 208 EX89
Daventer Dr, Stan. HA7 117 CF52
Daventry Av, E17 145 EA58
Daventry Cl, Colnbr. SL3 175 BF81
Daventry Gdns, Rom. RM3 128 FJ50
Daventry Grn, Rom. RM3
off Hailsham Rd 128 FJ50
Daventry Rd, Rom. RM3 128 FJ50
Daventry St, NW1 16 C6
Davern Cl, SE10 35 L9
Davey Cl, N7 8 D5
N13 121 DM50
Davey Rd, E9 12 A6
Davey St, SE15 44 B3
David Av, Grnf. UB6 159 CE69
David Cl, Harling. UB3 177 BR80
David Dr, Rom. RM3 128 FN51
Davidge Pl, Knot.Grn HP9 110 AJ50
Davidge St, SE1 30 G5
David Lee Pt, E15 13 K9
Sch David Livingstone Prim Sch,
Th.Hth. CR7
off Northwood Rd 224 DQ95
David Ms, W1 16 F6
David Rd, Colnbr. SL3 175 BF82
Dagenham RM8 148 EY61
Davidson Gdns, SW8 42 A5
Davidson La, Har. HA1
off Grove Hill 139 CF59
Sch Davidson Prim Sch, Croy.
CR0 off Dartnell Rd 224 DT101
Davidson Rd, Croy. CR0 224 DT100
Davidson Terraces, E7
off Windsor Rd 146 EH64
Davidson Way, Rom. RM7 149 FE58
Davids Rd, SE23 204 DW88
David St, E15 13 H4
David's Way, Ilf. IG6 125 ES52
David Twigg Cl, Kings.T. KT2 220 CL95
Davies Cl, Croy. CR0 224 DU100
Rainham RM13 170 FJ69
Coll Davies Laing & Dick
Indep Coll, W1 17 H8
Davies La, E11 146 EE61
Sch Davies La Prim Sch, E11
off Davies La 146 EF61
Davies Ms, W1 17 J10
Davies St, W1 17 J10
Hertford SG13 54 DS09
Davies Wk, Islw. TW7 179 CD81
Davies Way, Loud. HP10 110 AC54
Da Vinci Lo, SE10 35 M7
Davington Gdns, Dag. RM8 148 EV64
Davington Rd, Dag. RM8 168 EV65
Davinia Cl, Wdf.Grn. IG8
off Deacon Way 125 EM51
Davis Av, Nthflt DA11 212 GE88
Davis Cl, Sev. TN13 279 FJ122
Davis Ct, St.Alb. AL1 65 CE20
Davison Cl, Chsht EN8 89 DX28
Epsom KT19 238 CP111
Davison Dr, Chsht EN8 89 DX28
Davison Rd, Slou. SL3 175 AZ78
Davis Rd, W3 161 CT74
Aveley RM15 171 FR74
Chafford Hundred RM16 192 FZ76
Chessington KT9 238 CN105
Weybridge KT13 234 BM110
● Davis Rd Ind Pk, Chess.
KT9 238 CN105
Davis St, E13 24 B1
Davisville Rd, W12 181 CU75
Davis Way, Sid. DA14 208 EY93
Davos Cl, Wok. GU22 248 AY119
Davys Cl, Wheat. AL4 50 CL08
Davys Pl, Grav. DA12 213 GL93
Dawell Dr, Bigg.H. TN16 260 EJ117
Dawes Av, Horn. RM12 150 FK62
Isleworth TW7 199 CG85
Dawes Cl, Chesh. HP5 76 AP32
Greenhithe DA9 211 FT85
Dawes Ct, Esher KT10 236 CB105
Dawes E Rd, Burn. SL1 152 AJ70
DAWESGREEN, Reig. RH2 287 CT140
Dawes Ho, SE17 31 L9
Dawes La, Sarratt WD3 95 BE37
Dawes Moor Cl, Slou. SL2 154 AW72
Dawes Rd, SW6 38 E4
Uxbridge UB10 156 BL68
Dawes St, SE17 31 M10
Dawley, Welw.G.C. AL7 51 CZ06
Dawley Av, Uxb. UB8 157 BQ71
Dawley Ct, Hem.H. HP2 62 BM16
Dawley Grn, S.Ock. RM15 171 FU72
Dawley Par, Hayes UB3
off Dawley Rd 157 BQ73
Dawley Ride, Colnbr. SL3 175 BE81
Dawley Rd, Hayes UB3 157 BR73
Uxbridge UB8 157 BQ73
Dawlish Av, N13 121 DL49
SW18 202 DB89
Perivale UB6 159 CG68
Dawlish Dr, Ilf. IG3 147 ES63
Pinner HA5 138 BY57
Ruislip HA4 137 BU61
Sch Dawlish Prim Sch, E10
off Jesse Rd 145 EC60
Dawlish Rd, E10 145 EC61
N17 144 DU55
NW2 4 D4
Dawlish Wk, Rom. RM3 128 FJ53
Dawnay Gdns, SW18 202 DD89
Dawnay Rd, SW18 202 DC89
Bookham KT23 268 CB126
Sch Dawnay Sch, The, Bkhm
KT23 off Griffin Way 268 CA126
Dawn Cl, Houns. TW4 178 BY83
Dawn Cres, E15 13 H8
Dawn Redwood Cl, Horton
SL3 175 BA83
Dawpool Rd, NW2 141 CT61
Daws Hill, E4 105 EC41
Daws La, NW7 119 CT50
Dawson Av, Bark. IG11 167 ES66
Orpington BR5 228 EV96
Dawson Cl, SE18 187 EQ77
Hayes UB3 157 BR71
Windsor SL4 173 AN82
Dawson Dr, Rain. RM13 169 FH66
Swanley BR8 209 FE94
Dawson Gdns, Bark. IG11
off Dawson Av 167 ET66
Dawson Hts Est, SE22 204 DU87
Dawson Pl, W2 15 J10
Dawson Rd, NW2 4 B2
Byfleet KT14 234 BK111
Kingston upon Thames KT1 220 CM97
Dawson St, E2 20 B1
Dawson Ter, N9 122 DW45
Daws Pl, Red. RH1 273 DJ131
Dax Ct, Sun. TW16
off Thames St 218 BW97
Daybrook Rd, SW19 222 DB96
Daye Mead, Welw.G.C. AL7 52 DB12
Daylesford Av, SW15 181 CU84
Daylop Dr, Chig. IG7 126 EV48
Daymer Gdns, Pnr. HA5 137 BV56
Daymerslea Ridge, Lthd. KT22 253 CJ121
Days Acre, S.Croy. CR2 242 DT110
Daysbrook Rd, SW2 203 DM89
Days Cl, Hat. AL10 67 CT18
Dayseys Hill, Outwood RH1 289 DN143
Days La, Pilg.Hat. CM15 130 FU42
Sidcup DA15 207 ES87
Sch Days La Prim Sch, Sid.
DA15 off Days La 207 ET86
Days Mead, Hat. AL10 67 CT18
Dayspring, Guil. GU2 264 AV130
Dayton Dr, Erith DA8 190 FK78
Dayton Gro, SE15 44 G6
Deacon Cl, Down. KT11 251 BV119
Purley CR8 241 DL109
St. Albans AL1
off Creighton Av 65 CD24
Deacon Fld, Guil. GU2
off Cathedral Hill 264 AU133
Deacon Ms, N1 9 M7
Deacon Pl, Cat. CR3 258 DQ123
Deacon Rd, NW2 141 CU64
Kingston upon Thames KT2 220 CM95
Deacons Cl, Els. WD6 100 CN42
Pinner HA5 115 BV54
Deaconsfield Rd, Hem.H. HP3 62 BK23
Deacons Hill, Wat. WD19 98 BW44
Deacons Hill Rd, Els. WD6 100 CM42
Deacons Leas, Orp. BR6 245 ER105
Deacons Ri, N2 142 DD57
Deacons Wk, Hmptn. TW12
off Bishops Gro 198 BZ91
● Deacon Trd Est, E4
off Cabinet Way 123 DZ51
Deacon Way, SE17 31 J8
Woodford Green IG8 125 EM52
Deadfield La, Hert. SG14 52 DF13
Deadhearn La, Ch.St.G. HP8 112 AY46
Deadman's Ash La, Sarratt WD3 96 BH36
Deakin Cl, Wat. WD18
off Chenies Way 115 BS45
Deal Av, Slou. SL1 153 AM72
Deal Ms, W5 179 CK77
Deal Porters Way, SE16 33 H6
Deal Rd, SW17 202 DG93
Deals Gateway, SE13 46 B6
Deal St, E1 20 C6
Dealtry Rd, SW15 181 CW84
Deal Wk, SW9 42 E5
Deanacre Cl, Chal.St.P. SL9 112 AY51
Dean Av, Hodd. EN11 71 DX17
DEAN BOTTOM, Dart. DA4 231 FV97
Dean Bradley St, SW1 30 A7
Dean Cl, E9 11 H2
SE16 33 K3
Uxbridge UB10 156 BM66
Windsor SL4 173 AK83
Woking GU22 249 BE115
Dean Ct, SW8
off Thorncroft St 42 A5
Wembley HA0 139 CH62
Deancroft Rd, Chal.St.P. SL9 112 AY51
Deancross St, E1 20 G9
Dean Dr, Stan. HA7 118 CL54
Deane Av, Ruis. HA4 138 BW64
Deane Cft Rd, Pnr. HA5 137 BV58
Deanery Cl, N2 142 DE56
Deanery Ms, W1 29 H2
Deanery Rd, E15 13 J5
Crockham Hill TN8 277 EQ134
Deanery St, W1 29 H2
Sch Deanesfield Prim Sch, Ruis.
HA4 off Queens Wk 138 BX63
Deane Way, Ruis. HA4 137 BV58
Dean Farrar St, SW1 29 N6
Dean Fld, Bov. HP3 79 BA27
Dean Gdns, E17 145 ED56
W13 off Northfield Av 159 CH74
Deanhill Ct, SW14 180 CP84
Deanhill Rd, SW14 180 CP84
Dean Ho, E1 off Tarling St 20 G9
N16 off Stamford Hill 144 DT60
Dean La, EC4
off New Fetter La 18 F8
Redhill RH1 257 DH123
Dean Moore Cl, St.Alb. AL1 65 CD21
Dean Oak La, Leigh RH2 287 CW144
Dean Rd, NW2 4 A5
SE28 168 EU73
Croydon CR0 242 DR105
Hampton TW12 198 CA92
Hounslow TW3 198 CB85
Dean Ryle St, SW1 30 A8
Deansbrook Cl, Edg. HA8 118 CQ51
Sch Deansbrook Inf Sch, NW7
off Hale Dr 118 CQ51
Sch Deansbrook Jun Sch,
NW7 off Hale Dr 118 CQ51
Deansbrook Rd, Edg. HA8 118 CQ52
Deans Bldgs, SE17 31 L9
Deans Cl, W4 180 CP79
Abbots Langley WD5 81 BR32
Amersham HP6 94 AT37
Dean's Cl, Croy. CR0 224 DT104
Deans Cl, Edg. HA8 118 CQ51
Stoke Poges SL2 154 AV67
Walton on the Hill KT20 255 CV124
Deans Ct, EC4 19 H9
Deanscroft Av, NW9 140 CQ61
Deans Dr, N13 121 DP51
Edgware HA8 118 CR50
● Deans Factory Est, Rain.
RM13 off Lambs La N 170 FK70
Deansfield, Cat. CR3 274 DT125
Sch Deansfield Prim Sch, SE9
off Dairsie Rd 187 EN83
Deans Gdns, St.Alb. AL4 65 CG16
Dean's Gate Cl, SE23 205 DX90
Deans La, W4 off Deans Cl 180 CP79
Edgware HA8 118 CQ51
Nutfield RH1 273 DN133
Walton on the Hill KT20 255 CV124
Deans Ms, W1 17 K8
Deans Rd, W7 159 CF74
South Merstham RH1 273 DJ130
Sutton SM1 222 DB104
Warley CM14 130 FW49
Dean Stanley St, SW1 30 A7
Dean St, E7 13 N2
W1 17 N8
Deans Wk, Couls. CR5 257 DN118
Deansway, N2 142 DD56
N9 122 DS48
Chesham HP5 76 AP29
Deans Way, Edg. HA8 118 CQ50
Deansway, Hem.H. HP3 62 BM23
Dean's Yd, SW1 29 P6
Dean Trench St, SW1 30 A7
Dean Wk, Bkhm KT23 268 CB126
Edgware HA8
off Deansbrook Rd 118 CQ51
Deanway, Ch.St.G. HP8 112 AU48
Dean Way, Sthl. UB2 178 CB75
Dean Wd Rd, Jordans HP9 111 AR52
Dearne Cl, Stan. HA7 117 CG50
De'Arn Gdns, Mitch. CR4 222 DE97
Dearsley Ho, Rain. RM13 169 FD68
Dearsley Rd, Enf. EN1 104 DU41
Deason St, E15 12 F9
De Barowe Ms, N5 9 H1
DEBDEN, Loug. IG10 107 ER41
⊖ Debden 107 EQ42
Debden Cl, NW9 off Kenley Av 118 CS54
Kingston upon Thames
KT2 199 CK92
Woodford Green IG8 124 EJ52
DEBDEN GREEN, Loug. IG10 107 EQ38
Debden Grn, Loug. IG10 107 EP38
Debden La, Loug. IG10 107 EP38
Sch Debden Pk High Sch, Loug.
IG10 off Willingale Rd 107 ER40
Debden Rd, Loug. IG10 107 EP38
Debden Wk, Horn. RM12 169 FH65
De Beauvoir, N1
off Tottenham Rd 9 P5
De Beauvoir Cres, N1 9 N8
De Beauvoir Est, N1 9 M8
Sch De Beauvoir Prim Sch, N1 9 P5
De Beauvoir Rd, N1 9 N6
De Beauvoir Sq, N1 9 P7
DE BEAUVOIR TOWN, N1 9 M8
Debenham Rd, Chsht EN7 88 DV27
Debnams Rd, SE16 32 G9
De Bohun Av, N14 103 DH44
Sch De Bohun Prim Sch, N14
off Green Rd 103 DH43
Deborah Cl, Islw. TW7 179 CE81
Deborah Cres, Ruis. HA4 137 BR59
Debrabant Cl, Erith DA8 189 FD79
De Brome Rd, Felt. TW13 198 BW88
De Burgh Gdns, Tad. KT20 255 CX119
De Burgh Pk, Bans. SM7 256 DB115
Deburgh Rd, SW19 202 DC94
Decies Way, Stoke P. SL2 154 AU67
Decima St, SE1 31 N6
Deck Cl, SE16 33 K4
Decoy Av, NW11 141 CY57
De Crespigny Pk, SE5 43 L8
Dedswell Dr, W.Clan. GU4 266 BG128
DEDWORTH, Wind. SL4 173 AL81
Dedworth Dr, Wind. SL4 173 AL81
Sch Dedworth Grn First Sch,
Wind. SL4 off Smiths La 173 AL82
Sch Dedworth Mid Sch, Wind.
SL4 off Smiths La 173 AL82
Dedworth Rd, Wind. SL4 173 AK83
Dee, The, Hem.H. HP2 62 BM15
Dee Cl, Upmin. RM14 151 FS58
Deeley Rd, SW8 41 N6
Deena Cl, W3 160 CM72
Slough SL1 153 AL73
Deep Acres, Amer. HP6 77 AN36
Deepdale, SW19 201 CX91
Deepdale Av, Brom. BR2 226 EF98
Deepdale Cl, N11 120 DG51
Deepdene, W5 160 CM70
Potters Bar EN6 85 CX31
Deepdene Av, Croy. CR0 224 DT104
Dorking RH4, RH5 269 CJ134
Deepdene Av Rd, Dor. RH4 269 CJ134
Deepdene Cl, E11 146 EG56
Deepdene Ct, N21 103 DP44
Bromley BR2 226 EE97
Deepdene Dr, Dor. RH5 285 CJ135
Deepdene Gdns, SW2 203 DM87
Dorking RH4 285 CH135
Deepdene Pk Rd, Dor. RH5 285 CJ135
Deepdene Path, Loug. IG10 107 EN42
Deepdene Pt, SE23
off Dacres Rd 205 DX90
Deepdene Rd, SE5 184 DR84
Loughton IG10 107 EN42
Welling DA16 188 EU83
Deepdene Vale, Dor. RH4 285 CJ135
Deepdene Wd, Dor. RH5 285 CJ136
Deep Fld, Datchet SL3 174 AV80
Deepfields, Horl. RH6 290 DF146
Deepfield Way, Couls. CR5 257 DL116
Deep Pool La, Chobham GU24 232 AV114
Deeprose Cl, Guil. GU2 264 AV130
Deepwell Cl, Islw. TW7 179 CG81
Deepwood La, Grnf. UB6 159 CD69
Deerbarn Rd, Guil. GU2 264 AV133
Deerbrook Rd, SE24 203 DP88
Deer Cl, Hert. SG13 54 DT09
Deercote Ct, Chsht EN8
off Glen Luce 89 DX31
Deerdale Rd, SE24 184 DQ84
Deere Av, Rain. RM13 169 FG65
Deerfield Cl, NW9 141 CT57
Ware SG12 55 DX05
Deerhurst Cl, Felt. TW13 197 BU91
Deerhurst Cres, Hmptn H.
TW12 198 CC92
Deerhurst Rd, NW2 4 D5
SW16 203 DM92
Deerings Dr, Pnr. HA5 137 BU57
Deerings Rd, Reig. RH2 272 DB134
Deerleap Gro, E4 105 EB43
Deerleap La, Sev. TN14 246 EX113
Deerleap Rd, Westc. RH4 284 CB137
Dee Rd, Rich. TW9 180 CM84
Windsor SL4 172 AJ80
Deer Pk, Harl. CM19 73 EN18
Deer Pk Cl, Kings.T. KT2 200 CP94
Deer Pk Gdns, Mitch. CR4 222 DD97
Deer Pk Rd, SW19 222 DB96
Deer Pk Wk, Chesh. HP5 76 AS28
Deer Pk Way, Wal.Abb. EN9 105 EB36
West Wickham BR4 226 EF103
Deers Fm Cl, Wisley GU23 250 BL116
Deerswood Av, Hat. AL10 67 CV20
Deerswood Cl, Cat. CR3 258 DU124
Deeside Rd, SW17 202 DD90
Dee St, E14 22 F8
Deeves Hall La, Pot.B. EN6 84 CS33
Dee Way, Epsom KT19 238 CS110
Romford RM1 127 FE53
Defence Cl, SE28 167 ES74
H Defence Medical Rehab Cen
Headley Ct, Epsom KT18 254 CP123
Coll Defence Sch of Languages,
Seer Grn HP9 off Wilton Pk 111 AP54
Defiance Wk, SE18 37 J7
Defiant Way, Wall. SM6 241 DL108
Defoe Av, Rich. TW9 180 CN80
Defoe Cl, SE16 33 N5
SW17 202 DE93
Erith DA8 off Selkirk Dr 189 FF81
Defoe Ho, EC2
off The Barbican 19 J6
Defoe Par, Grays RM16 193 GH76
Defoe Pl, EC2
off The Barbican 19 K6
SW17 off Lessingham Av 202 DF91
Defoe Rd, N16 144 DS61
Defoe Way, Rom. RM5 126 FA51
De Frene Rd, SE26 205 DX91
De Gama Pl, E14
off Maritime Quay 34 B10
Degema Rd, Chis. BR7 207 EP92
Dehar Cres, NW9 141 CU59
★ De Havilland Aircraft Heritage
Cen, St.Alb. AL2 84 CP29
De Havilland Cl, Hat. AL10 67 CT17
Dehavilland Cl, Nthlt. UB5 158 BX69
De Havilland Ct, Ilf. IG1
off Piper Way 147 ER60
Shenley WD7
off Armstrong Gdns 84 CL32
De Havilland Dr, SE18 187 EP79
Weybridge KT13 234 BL111
Sch De Havilland Prim Sch, Hat.
AL10 off Travellers La 67 CU20
De Havilland Rd, Edg. HA8 118 CP54
Hounslow TW5 178 BW80
De Havilland Way, Abb.L. WD5 81 BT32
Stanwell TW19 196 BK86
Deimos Dr, Hem.H. HP2 62 BN17
Dekker Rd, SE21 204 DS86
Delabole Rd, Merst. RH1 273 DL129
Delacourt Rd, SE3
off Old Dover Rd 186 EH80
Delafield Ho, E1 20 D9
Delafield Rd, SE7 36 B10
Grays RM17 192 GD78
Delaford Cl, Iver SL0 155 BF72
Delaford Rd, SE16 32 F10
Delaford St, SW6 38 F4
Delagarde Rd, West. TN16 277 EQ126
Delahay Ri, Berk. HP4 60 AV17
Delamare Cres, Croy. CR0 224 DW100
Delamare Rd, Chsht EN8 89 DZ30
Delamere Ct, E17
off Hawker Pl 123 EC54
Delamere Gdns, NW7 118 CR51
Delamere Rd, SW20 221 CX95
W5 160 CL74
Borehamwood WD6 100 CP39
Hayes UB4 158 BX73
Reigate RH2 288 DB138
Delamere St, W2 15 N6
Delamere Ter, W2 15 M6
Delancey Pas, NW1 7 K9
Delancey St, NW1 7 J9
Delaporte Cl, Epsom KT17 238 CS112
De Lapre Cl, Orp. BR5 228 EX101
De Lara Way, Wok. GU21 248 AX118
Delargy Cl, Grays RM16 193 GH76
De Laune St, SE17 42 G1
Delaware Rd, W9 15 L4
Delawyk Cres, SE24 204 DQ86
Delcombe Av, Wor.Pk. KT4 221 CW102
Delderfield, Lthd. KT22 253 CK120
Delft Way, SE22
off East Dulwich Gro 204 DS85
Delhi Rd, Enf. EN1 122 DT45
Delhi St, N1 8 B9
Delia St, SW18 202 DB87
Delisle Rd, SE28 167 ES74
Delius Cl, Els. WD6 99 CJ44
Delius Gro, E15 12 G10
Dell, The, SE2 188 EU78
SE19 224 DT95
Bexley DA5 209 FE88
Brentford TW8 179 CJ79
Chalfont St. Peter SL9 112 AY51
Feltham TW14 197 BV87
Great Warley CM13 129 FV51
Greenhithe DA9 211 FV85
Hertford SG13 54 DQ12
Horley RH6 291 DH147
Northwood HA6 115 BS47
Penn HP10 110 AC46
Pinner HA5 116 BX54
Radlett WD7 99 CG36
Reigate RH2 272 DA133
St. Albans AL1 65 CG18
Tadworth KT20 255 CW121
Waltham Abbey EN9
off Greenwich Way 105 EC36
Wembley HA0 139 CH64
Woking GU21 248 AW118
Woodford Green IG8 124 EH48
Della Path, E5 144 DV62
Dellbow Rd, Felt. TW14 197 BV85
Dell Cl, E15 13 H8
Chesham HP5 76 AM29
Farnham Common SL2 133 AQ64
Fetcham KT22 253 CE123
Mickleham RH5 269 CJ127
Wallington SM6 241 DJ105
Woodford Green IG8 124 EH48
Dellcott Cl, Welw.G.C. AL8 51 CV08
Dellcut Rd, Hem.H. HP2 62 BN18
Dell Fm Rd, Ruis. HA4 137 BR57
Dellfield, Chesh. HP5 76 AN29
St. Albans AL1 65 CF21
Dellfield Av, Berk. HP4 60 AV17
Dellfield Cl, Beck. BR3 225 EC95
Berkhamsted HP4 60 AU17
Radlett WD7 99 CE35
Watford WD17 97 BU40
Dellfield Cres, Uxb. UB8 156 BJ70
Dellfield Par, Cowley UB8
off High St 156 BJ70
Dellfield Rd, Hat. AL10 67 CU18
Dell La, Epsom KT17 239 CU106
Dell Leas, Seer Grn HP9 111 AQ51
Dellmeadow, Abb.L. WD5 81 BS30

Dell Meadow, Hem.H. HP3 . . . . 62 BL24
Dell Orchard, Winch.Hill HP7
off Fagnall La 110 AJ45
Dellors Cl, Barn. EN5 . . . . 101 CX43
Dellow Cl, Ilf. IG2 . . . . 147 ER59
Dellow St, E1 . . . . 20 F10
Dell Ri, Park St AL2 . . . . 82 CB26
Dell Rd, Enf. EN3 . . . . 104 DW38
Epsom KT17 . . . . 239 CU107
Grays RM17 . . . . 192 GB77
Watford WD24 . . . . 97 BU37
West Drayton UB7 . . . . 176 BM76
Dells, The, Hem.H. HP3 . . . . 63 BP21
Dells Cl, E4 . . . . 123 EB45
Teddington TW11
off Middle La 199 CF93
Dellside, Hare. UB9 . . . . 136 BJ57
Dell Side, Wat. WD24 . . . . 97 BU37
Dell's Ms, SW1 . . . . 29 M9
Dellsome La, Coln.Hth AL4 . . . . . 66 CS23
North Mymms AL9 . . . . 67 CV23
Dellswood Cl, Hert. SG13 . . . . . . 54 DS10
Dells Wd Cl, Hodd. EN11 . . . . . . 55 DZ14
Dell Wk, N.Mal. KT3 . . . . 220 CS96
Dell Way, W13 . . . . 159 CJ72
Dellwood, Rick. WD3 . . . . 114 BH46
Dellwood Gdns, Ilf. IG5 . . . . 147 EN55
Delmar Av, Hem.H. HP2 . . . . 63 BR21
Delmare Cl, SW9 . . . . 183 DM84
Delmeade Rd, Chesh. HP5 . . . . . 76 AN32
Delme Cres, SE3 . . . . 186 EH82
Delmey Cl, Croy. CR0 . . . . 224 DT104
Deloraine St, SE8 . . . . 46 A7
Delorme St, W6 . . . . 38 C3
Delta Bungalows, Horl. RH6
off Michael Cres 290 DG150
● Delta Cen, Wem. HA0
off Mount Pleasant 160 CM67
Delta Cl, Chobham GU24 . . . . . 232 AT110
Worcester Park KT4 . . . . 220 CS104
Delta Ct, NW2 . . . . 141 CU61
Delta Dr, Horl. RH6
off Cheyne Wk 290 DG150
Delta Gain, Wat. WD19 . . . . 116 BX47
Delta Gro, Nthlt. UB5 . . . . 158 BX69
Delta Ho, N1 off Nile St 19 L2
● Delta Pk Ind Est, Enf. EN3 . 105 DZ40
Delta Rd, Chobham GU24 . . . . 232 AT110
Hutton CM13 . . . . 131 GD44
Woking GU21 . . . . 249 BA116
Worcester Park KT4 . . . . 220 CS104
Delta St, E2 . . . . 20 C2
Delta Way, Egh. TW20 . . . . 215 BC95
De Luci Rd, Erith DA8 . . . . 189 FC78
Sch De Lucy Prim Sch, SE2
off Cookhill Rd 188 EV75
De Lucy St, SE2 . . . . 188 EV77
Delvan Cl, SE18
off Ordnance Rd 187 EN80
Delvers Mead, Dag. RM10 . . . . 149 FC63
Delverton Rd, SE17 . . . . 43 H1
Delves, Tad. KT20 . . . . 255 CX121
Delvino Rd, SW6 . . . . 39 J7
De Mandeville Gate, Enf. EN1
off Southbury Rd 104 DU42
De Mel Cl, Epsom KT19 . . . . . . 238 CP112
Demesne Rd, Wall. SM6 . . . . . . 241 DK106
Demeta Cl, Wem. HA9 . . . . 140 CQ62
De Montfort Par, SW16
off Streatham High Rd 203 DL90
De Montfort Rd, SW16 . . . . 203 DL90
De Morgan Rd, SW6 . . . . 39 M10
Dempster Cl, Long Dit. KT6 . . . 219 CJ102
Dempster Rd, SW18 . . . . 202 DC85
Denbar Par, Rom. RM7
off Mawney Rd 149 FC56
Denberry Dr, Sid. DA14 . . . . . . 208 EV90
Denbigh Cl, W11 . . . . 15 H10
Chislehurst BR7 . . . . 207 EM93
Hemel Hempstead HP2 . . . . . . 62 BL21
Hornchurch RM11 . . . . 150 FN56
Ruislip HA4 . . . . 137 BT61
Southall UB1 . . . . 158 BZ72
Sutton SM1 . . . . 239 CZ106
Denbigh Dr, Hayes UB3 . . . . . . 177 BQ75
Denbigh Gdns, Rich. TW10 . . . . 200 CM85
Denbigh Ms, SW1 . . . . 29 L9
Denbigh Pl, SW1 . . . . 29 L10
Denbigh Rd, E6 . . . . 24 E3
W11 . . . . 15 H10
W13 . . . . 159 CH73
Hounslow TW3 . . . . 178 CB82
Southall UB1 . . . . 158 BZ72
Denbigh St, SW1 . . . . 29 L9
Denbigh Ter, W11 . . . . 15 H10
Denbridge Rd, Brom. BR1 . . . . . 227 EM96
Denby Gra, Harl. CM17 . . . . 74 EY15
Denby Rd, Cob. KT11 . . . . 236 BW113
Den Cl, Beck. BR3 . . . . 225 ED97
Dendridge Cl, Enf. EN1 . . . . 104 DV37
Dene, The, W13 . . . . 159 CH71
Abinger Hammer RH5 . . . . . . 283 BV141
Croydon CR0 . . . . 243 DX105
Sevenoaks TN13 . . . . 279 FH126
Sutton SM2 . . . . 239 CZ111
Wembley HA9 . . . . 140 CL63
West Molesey KT8 . . . . 218 BZ99
Dene Av, Houns. TW3 . . . . 178 BZ83
Sidcup DA15 . . . . 208 EV87
Dene Cl, SE4 . . . . 185 DY83
Bromley BR2 . . . . 226 EF102
Coulsdon CR5 . . . . 256 DE119
Dartford DA2 . . . . 209 FE91
Guildford GU1 . . . . 265 BB132
Horley RH6 . . . . 290 DE146
Worcester Park KT4 . . . . 221 CT103
Dene Ct, Stan. HA7 . . . . 117 CJ50
Denecroft Cres, Uxb. UB10 . . . . 157 BP67
Denecroft Gdns, Grays RM17 . 192 GD76
Dene Dr, Orp. BR6 . . . . 228 EV104
Denefield Dr, Ken. CR8 . . . . 258 DR115
Dene Gdns, Stan. HA7 . . . . 117 CJ50
Thames Ditton KT7 . . . . 219 CG103
Sch Deneholm Prim Sch, Grays
RM16 off Culford Rd 192 GC75
Dene Holm Rd, Nthflt DA11 . . . 212 GD90
Denehurst Gdns, NW4 . . . . 141 CW58
W3 . . . . 160 CP74
Richmond TW10 . . . . 180 CN84
Twickenham TW2 . . . . 199 CD87
Woodford Green IG8 . . . . 124 EH49
Dene Path, S.Ock. RM15 . . . . . . 171 FU72
Dene Pl, Wok. GU21 . . . . 248 AV118
Dene Rd, N11 . . . . 120 DF46
Ashtead KT21 . . . . 254 CM119
Buckhurst Hill IG9 . . . . 124 EK46
Dartford DA1 . . . . 210 FM87
Guildford GU1 . . . . 280 AY135
Northwood HA6 . . . . 115 BS51
Denes, The, Hem.H. HP3
off Barnacres Rd 62 BM24
Dene St, Dor. RH4 . . . . 285 CH136
Dene St Gdns, Dor. RH4 . . . . . . 285 CH136
Denewood, New Barn. EN5 . . . 102 DC43
Denewood Cl, Wat. WD17 . . . . . 97 BT37
Denewood Rd, N6 . . . . 142 DF58
Denfield, Dor. RH4 . . . . 285 CH138
Denford St, SE10 . . . . 35 L10
Dengie Wk, N1 . . . . 9 J8
DENHAM, Uxb. UB9 . . . . 136 BG62
⇌ Denham 136 BG59
★ Denham Aerodrome,
Uxb. UB9 . . . . 135 BD57
Denham Av, Denh. UB9 . . . . 135 BF61
Denham Cl, Denh. UB9 . . . . 136 BG62
Hemel Hempstead HP2 . . . . . . 62 BN15
Welling DA16
off Park Vw Rd 188 EW83
Denham Ct Dr, Denh. UB9 . . . . 136 BH63
Denham Cres, Mitch. CR4 . . . . . 222 DF98
Denham Dr, Ilf. IG2 . . . . 147 EQ58
Denham Gdn Village,
Denh. UB9 . . . . 135 BF58
⇌ Denham Golf Club 135 BD59
DENHAM GREEN, Uxb. UB9 . . 135 BE58
Denham Grn Cl, Denh. UB9 . . . 136 BG59
Denham Grn La, Denh. UB9 . . 135 BE57
Denham La, Chal.St.P. SL9 . . . . 113 BA53
Denham Lo, Denh. UB9 . . . . . . 156 BJ65
● Denham Media Pk,
Denh. UB9 . . . . 136 BG57
Denham Rd, N20 . . . . 120 DF48
Denham UB9 . . . . 155 BE65
Egham TW20 . . . . 195 BA91
Epsom KT17 . . . . 239 CT112
Feltham TW14 . . . . 198 BW86
Iver SL0 . . . . 155 BD67
Denham Rbt, Uxb. UB9 . . . . . 136 BG63
Denham St, SE10 . . . . 35 N10
Sch Denham Village Inf Sch, Denh.
UB9 off Cheapside La 135 BF61
Denham Wk, Chal.St.P. SL9 . . . 113 AZ51
Denham Way, Bark. IG11 . . . . . . 167 ES67
Borehamwood WD6 . . . . 100 CR39
Denham UB9 . . . . 136 BG62
Maple Cross WD3 . . . . 113 BE50
Denholme Rd, W9 . . . . 15 H2
Denholme Wk, Rain. RM13
off Ryder Gdns 169 FF65
Denholm Gdns, Guil. GU4 . . . . 265 BA131
Denison Cl, N2 . . . . 142 DC55
Denison Rd, SW19 . . . . 202 DD93
W5 . . . . 159 CJ70
Feltham TW13 . . . . 197 BT91
Deniston Av, Bex. DA5 . . . . 208 EY88
Denis Way, SW4 . . . . 41 P10
Denleigh Gdns, N21 . . . . 121 DN46
Thames Ditton KT7 . . . . 219 CE100
Denman Dr, NW11 . . . . 142 DA57
Ashford TW15 . . . . 197 BP93
Claygate KT10 . . . . 237 CG106
Denman Dr N, NW11 . . . . 142 DA57
Denman Dr S, NW11 . . . . 142 DA57
Denman Pl, W1
off Great Windmill St 29 N1
Denman Rd, SE15 . . . . 44 A7
Denman St, W1 . . . . 29 N1
Denmark Av, SW19 . . . . 201 CY94
Denmark Cl, Mord. SM4 . . . . . . 222 DA99
Denmark Gdns, Cars. SM5 . . . . 222 DF104
Denmark Gro, N1 . . . . 8 E10
⇌ Denmark Hill 43 L9
Denmark Hill, SE5 . . . . 43 L7
Denmark Hill Dr, NW9 . . . . 141 CT56
Denmark Hill Est, SE5 . . . . 184 DR84
Denmark Pl, E3 . . . . 22 B2
WC2 . . . . 17 P8
Denmark Rd, N8 . . . . 143 DN56
NW6 . . . . 15 H1
SE5 . . . . 43 J7
SE25 . . . . 224 DU99
SW19 . . . . 201 CX93
W13 . . . . 159 CH73
Bromley BR1 . . . . 226 EH95
Carshalton SM5 . . . . 222 DF104
Guildford GU1 . . . . 280 AY135
Kingston upon Thames KT1 . 220 CL97
Twickenham TW2 . . . . 199 CD90
Denmark St, E11
off High Rd Leytonstone . . 146 EE62
E13 . . . . 24 A6
N17 . . . . 122 DV53
WC2 . . . . 17 P9
Watford WD17 . . . . 97 BV40
Denmark Ter, N2
off Fortis Grn 142 DF55
Denmark Wk, SE27 . . . . 204 DQ91
Denmead Cl, Ger.Cr. SL9 . . . . . 134 AY59
Denmead Ho, SW15
off Highcliffe Dr 201 CT86
Denmead Rd, Croy. CR0 . . . . . . 223 DP102
Sch Denmead Sch, Hmptn. TW12
off Wensleydale Rd 198 CB94
Dennan Rd, Surb. KT6 . . . . 220 CM102
Dennard Way, Farnboro. BR6 . . 245 EP105
Denner Rd, E4 . . . . 123 EA47
Denne Ter, E8 . . . . 10 B9
Dennett Rd, Croy. CR0 . . . . 223 DN102
Dennetts Gro, SE14 . . . . 45 J8
Dennettsland Rd, Crock.H. TN8 . 277 EQ134
Dennetts Rd, SE14 . . . . 45 H7
Denning Av, Croy. CR0 . . . . 241 DN105
Denning Cl, NW8 . . . . 15 P2
Hampton TW12 . . . . 198 BZ93
Denning Ms, SW12 . . . . 202 DG86
Denning Pt, E1 . . . . 20 A8
Denning Rd, NW3 . . . . 142 DD63
Dennington Cl, E5
off Detmold Rd 144 DV61
Dennington Pk Rd, NW6 . . . . 5 K4
Denningtons, The, Wor.Pk. KT4 . 220 CS103
Dennis Av, Wem. HA9 . . . . 140 CM64
Dennis Cl, Ashf. TW15 . . . . 197 BR94
Redhill RH1 . . . . 272 DE132
Dennises La, S.Ock. RM15 . . . . 171 FU66
Upminster RM14 . . . . 171 FS67
Dennis Gdns, Stan. HA7 . . . . . . 117 CJ50
Dennis La, Stan. HA7 . . . . 117 CH48
Dennison Pt, E15 . . . . 12 F7
Dennis Pk Cres, SW20 . . . . 221 CY95
Dennis Reeve Cl, Mitch. CR4 . . 222 DF95
Dennis Rd, E.Mol. KT8 . . . . 218 CC98
Gravesend DA11 . . . . 213 GG90
Dennis Way, Guil. GU1 . . . . 264 AY129
Slough SL1 . . . . 153 AK73
Denny Av, Wal.Abb. EN9 . . . . . . 89 ED34
Denny Cl, E6 . . . . 24 G7
Denny Cres, SE11 . . . . 30 F9
Denny Gdns, Dag. RM9
off Canonsleigh Rd 168 EV66
Denny Gate, Chsht EN8 . . . . 89 DZ27
Denny Rd, N9 . . . . 122 DV46
Slough SL3 . . . . 175 AZ77
Dennys La, Berk. HP4 . . . . 60 AT21
Denny St, SE11 . . . . 30 F10
De Novo Pl, St.Alb. AL1
off Granville Rd 65 CF20
Den Rd, Brom. BR2 . . . . 225 ED97
Densham Dr, Pur. CR8 . . . . 241 DN114
Densham Rd, E15 . . . . 13 K8
Densley Cl, Welw.G.C. AL8 . . . . . 51 CX07
Densole Cl, Beck. BR3
off Kings Hall Rd 225 DY95
Densworth Gro, N9 . . . . 122 DW47
Dent Cl, S.Ock. RM15 . . . . 171 FU72
DENTON, Grav. DA12 . . . . 213 GL87
Denton, NW1 . . . . 7 H5
Denton Cl, Barn. EN5 . . . . 101 CW43
Redhill RH1 . . . . 288 DG139
Denton Ct Rd, Grav. DA12 . . . . 213 GL87
Denton Gro, Walt. KT12 . . . . . . 218 BX103
Denton Rd, N8 . . . . 143 DM57
N18 . . . . 122 DS49
Bexley DA5 . . . . 209 FE89
Dartford DA1 . . . . 209 FE88
Twickenham TW1 . . . . 199 CK86
Welling DA16 . . . . 188 EW80
Denton St, SW18 . . . . 202 DB86
Gravesend DA12 . . . . 213 GL87
Denton Ter, Bex. DA5
off Denton Rd 209 FE89
Denton Way, E5 . . . . 145 DX62
Woking GU21 . . . . 248 AT118
Dents Gro, Lwr Kgswd KT20 . . 271 CZ128
Dents Rd, SW11 . . . . 202 DF86
Denvale Wk, Wok. GU21 . . . . . . 248 AU118
Denver Cl, Petts Wd BR6 . . . . . 227 ES100
● Denver Ind Est, Rain.
RM13 . . . . 169 FF71
Denver Rd, N16 . . . . 144 DS59
Dartford DA1 . . . . 209 FG87
Denyer St, SW3 . . . . 28 D9
Denziloe Av, Uxb. UB10 . . . . . . 157 BP69
Denzil Rd, NW10 . . . . 141 CT64
Guildford GU2 . . . . 280 AV135
Deodar Rd, SW15 . . . . 181 CY84
Deodora Cl, N20 . . . . 120 DE48
★ Department for Environment,
Food & Rural Affairs (Defra),
SW1 . . . . 30 A3
★ Department for Transport
(DfT), SW1 . . . . 29 P8
★ Department of Health,
SW1 . . . . 30 A4
Depot App, NW2 . . . . 141 CX63
Depot Rd, W12 . . . . 14 B10
Epsom KT17 . . . . 238 CS113
Hounslow TW3 . . . . 179 CD83
DEPTFORD, SE8 . . . . 45 P1
⇌ Deptford 46 A4
DLR Deptford Bridge 46 B6
Deptford Br, SE8 . . . . 46 B6
Deptford Bdy, SE8 . . . . 46 A6
Deptford Ch St, SE8 . . . . 46 B3
Deptford Ferry Rd, E14 . . . . 34 B9
Deptford Grn, SE8 . . . . 46 B3
Sch Deptford Grn Sch,
Lwr Sch, SE14 . . . . 45 M4
Upr Sch, SE14 . . . . 45 N4
Deptford High St, SE8 . . . . 46 A3
Sch Deptford Pk Prim Sch, SE8 . 33 M10
Deptford Strand, SE8 . . . . 33 P9
● Deptford Trd Est, SE8 . . . . . . 45 L2
Deptford Wf, SE8 . . . . 33 N8
De Quincey Ho, SW1
off Lupus St 41 L1
De Quincey Ms, E16 . . . . 35 P2
De Quincey Rd, N17 . . . . 122 DR53
Derby Arms Rd, Epsom KT18 . 255 CT117
Derby Av, N12 . . . . 120 DC50
Harrow HA3 . . . . 117 CD53
Romford RM7 . . . . 149 FC58
Upminster RM14 . . . . 150 FM62
Derby Cl, Epsom KT18 . . . . 255 CV119
Derby Ct, E5 off Overbury St . . 145 DX63
Derby Gate, SW1 . . . . 30 A4
Derby Hill, SE23 . . . . 204 DW89
Derby Hill Cres, SE23 . . . . 204 DW89
Derby Ho, SE11
off Walnut Tree Wk 30 E8
Derby Rd, E7 . . . . 166 EJ66
E9 . . . . 11 J8
E18 . . . . 124 EF53
N18 . . . . 122 DW50
SW14 . . . . 180 CP84
SW19 off Russell Rd 202 DA94
Croydon CR0 . . . . 223 DP103
Enfield EN3 . . . . 104 DV43
Grays RM17 . . . . 192 GB78
Greenford UB6 . . . . 158 CB67
Guildford GU2 . . . . 264 AT134
Hoddesdon EN11 . . . . 71 ED19
Hounslow TW3 . . . . 178 CB84
Surbiton KT5 . . . . 220 CN102
Sutton SM1 . . . . 239 CZ107
Uxbridge UB8 . . . . 156 BJ68
Watford WD17 . . . . 98 BW41
Derby Rd Br, Grays RM17 . . . . 192 GB79
● Derby Rd Ind Est, Houns.
TW3 off Derby Rd 178 CB84
Derbyshire St, E2 . . . . 20 D3
Derby Sq, The, Epsom KT19
off High St 238 CR113
Derby Stables Rd, Epsom
KT18 . . . . 254 CS117
Derby St, W1 . . . . 29 H3
Dereham Pl, EC2 . . . . 19 P3
Romford RM5 . . . . 127 FB51
Dereham Rd, Bark. IG11 . . . . . . 167 ET65
Derehams Av, Loud. HP10 . . . . 110 AC52
Derehams La, Loud. HP10 . . . . 110 AC53
Derek Av, Epsom KT19 . . . . 238 CN106
Wallington SM6 . . . . 241 DH105
Wembley HA9 . . . . 160 CP66
Derek Cl, Ewell KT19 . . . . 238 CP106
Derek Walcott Cl, SE24
off Shakespeare Rd 183 DP84
Derham Gdns, Upmin. RM14 . . 150 FQ62
Deri Av, Rain. RM13 . . . . 169 FH70
Dericote St, E8 . . . . 10 D8
Deridene Cl, Stanw. TW19 . . . . 196 BL86
Derifall Cl, E6 . . . . 25 K6
Dering Pl, Croy. CR0 . . . . 242 DQ105
Dering Rd, Croy. CR0 . . . . 242 DQ105
Dering St, W1 . . . . 17 J9
Dering Way, Grav. DA12 . . . . . . 213 GM87
Derinton Rd, SW17 . . . . 202 DF91
Derley Rd, Sthl. UB2 . . . . 178 BW76
Dermody Gdns, SE13 . . . . 205 ED85
Dermody Rd, SE13 . . . . 205 ED85
Deronda Rd, SE24 . . . . 203 DP88
De Ros Pl, Egh. TW20 . . . . 195 BA93
Deroy Cl, Cars. SM5 . . . . 240 DF107
Derrick Av, S.Croy. CR2 . . . . . . 242 DQ110
Derrick Gdns, SE7 . . . . 36 C7
Derrick Rd, Beck. BR3 . . . . 225 DZ97
Derry Av, S.Ock. RM15 . . . . 171 FU72
Derrydown, Wok. GU22 . . . . . . 248 AW121
DERRY DOWNS, Orp. BR5 . . . . 228 EX100
Derry Downs, Orp. BR5 . . . . . . 228 EW100
Derry Leys, Hat. AL10 . . . . 66 CS16
Derry Rd, Croy. CR0 . . . . 223 DL104
Derry St, W8 . . . . 27 L5
Dersingham Av, E12 . . . . 147 EN64
Sch Dersingham Inf Sch, E12
off Dersingham Av 147 EN64
Dersingham Rd, NW2 . . . . 141 CY62
Derwent Av, N18 . . . . 122 DR50
NW7 . . . . 118 CR50
NW9 . . . . 140 CS57
SW15 . . . . 200 CS91
Barnet EN4 . . . . 120 DF46
Pinner HA5 . . . . 116 BY51
Uxbridge UB10 . . . . 136 BN62
Derwent Cl, Add. KT15 . . . . 234 BK106
Amersham HP7 . . . . 94 AV39
Claygate KT10 . . . . 237 CE107
Dartford DA1 . . . . 209 FH88
Feltham TW14 . . . . 197 BT88
Watford WD25 . . . . 82 BW34
Derwent Cres, N20 . . . . 120 DC48
Bexleyheath DA7 . . . . 188 FA82
Stanmore HA7 . . . . 117 CJ54
Derwent Dr, Hayes UB4 . . . . . . 157 BS71
Petts Wood BR5 . . . . 227 ER101
Purley CR8 . . . . 242 DR113
Slough SL1 . . . . 152 AJ71
Derwent Gdns, Ilf. IG4 . . . . 146 EL56
Wembley HA9 . . . . 139 CJ59
Derwent Gro, SE22 . . . . 184 DT84
Derwent Par, S.Ock. RM15 . . . . 171 FU72
Derwent Ri, NW9 . . . . 140 CS58
Derwent Rd, N13 . . . . 121 DM49
SE20 . . . . 224 DU96
SW20 . . . . 221 CX100
W5 . . . . 179 CJ76
Egham TW20 . . . . 195 BB94
Hemel Hempstead HP3 . . . . . . 63 BQ21
Southall UB1 . . . . 158 BZ72
Twickenham TW2 . . . . 198 CB86
Derwent St, SE10 . . . . 35 J10
Derwent Wk, Wall. SM6 . . . . . . 241 DH108
Sch Derwentwater Prim Sch,
W3 off Shakespeare Rd 160 CQ74
Derwentwater Rd, W3 . . . . 160 CQ74
Derwent Way, Horn. RM12 . . . . 149 FH64
Derwent Yd, W5
off Northfield Av 179 CJ76
De Salis Rd, Uxb. UB10 . . . . . . 157 BQ70
Desborough Cl, W2 . . . . 15 M6
Hertford SG14 . . . . 53 DP06
Shepperton TW17 . . . . 216 BN101
Welwyn Garden City AL7 . . . . . 52 DB12
Desborough Ho, W14
off North End Rd 39 H2
Desborough St, W2 . . . . 15 L6
Desenfans Rd, SE21 . . . . 204 DS86
● Deseronto Trd Est,
Slou. SL3 . . . . 174 AY75
Desford Ct, Ashf. TW15
off Desford Way 196 BM89
Desford Ms, E16 . . . . 23 K5
Desford Rd, E16 . . . . 23 K5
Desford Way, Ashf. TW15 . . . . . 196 BM89
★ Design Mus, SE1 . . . . 32 B3
Desmond Rd, Wat. WD24 . . . . . . 97 BT36
Desmond St, SE14 . . . . 45 M3
Desmond Tutu Dr, SE23
off St. Germans Rd 205 DY88
De Soissons Cl, Welw.G.C.
AL8 . . . . 51 CV11
Despard Rd, N19 . . . . 143 DJ60
Sch De Stafford Sch, Cat. CR3
off Burntwood La 258 DT121
Desvignes Dr, SE13 . . . . 205 ED86
De Tany Ct, St.Alb. AL1 . . . . 65 CD21
Detillens La, Oxt. RH8 . . . . 276 EG129
Detling Cl, Horn. RM12 . . . . 150 FJ64
Detling Rd, Brom. BR1 . . . . 206 EG92
Erith DA8 . . . . 189 FD80
Northfleet DA11 . . . . 212 GD88
Detmold Rd, E5 . . . . 144 DW61
Deva Cl, St.Alb. AL3 . . . . 64 CA22
Devalls Cl, E6 . . . . 25 M10
Devana End, Cars. SM5 . . . . . . 222 DF104
Devas Rd, SW20 . . . . 221 CW95
Devas St, E3 . . . . 22 D4
Devenay Rd, E15 . . . . 13 L7
Devenish Rd, SE2 . . . . 188 EU75
Deventer Cres, SE22 . . . . 204 DS85
Deveraux Cl, Beck. BR3 . . . . . . 225 EC99
De Vere Cl, Wall. SM6 . . . . 241 DL108
De Vere Gdns, W8 . . . . 27 N5
Ilford IG1 . . . . 147 EM61
Deverell St, SE1 . . . . 31 L7
De Vere Ms, W8 . . . . 27 N6
Devereux Ct, WC2 . . . . 18 E9
Devereux Dr, Wat. WD17 . . . . . . 97 BS38
Devereux La, SW13 . . . . 181 CV80
Devereux Rd, SW11 . . . . 202 DF86
Grays RM16 . . . . 192 FZ76
Windsor SL4 . . . . 173 AR82
De Vere Wk, Wat. WD17 . . . . 97 BS40
Deverill Ct, SE20 . . . . 224 DW95
Deverills Way, Slou. SL3 . . . . . 175 BC77
Deveron Gdns, S.Ock. RM15 . . 171 FU71
Deveron Way, Rom. RM1 . . . . . 127 FE53
Devey Cl, Kings.T. KT2 . . . . 200 CS94
Devils La, Egh. TW20 . . . . 195 BD94
Devil's La, Hert. SG13 . . . . 69 DP21
Devitt Cl, Ashtd. KT21 . . . . 254 CN116
Devizes St, N1 . . . . 9 M9
Devoil Cl, Guil. GU4 . . . . 265 BB130
Devoke Way, Walt. KT12 . . . . . 218 BX103
Devon Av, Slou. SL1 . . . . 153 AQ72
Twickenham TW2 . . . . 198 CC88
Devon Bk, Guil. GU2
off Portsmouth Rd 280 AW137
Devon Cl, N17 . . . . 144 DT55
Buckhurst Hill IG9 . . . . 124 EH47
Kenley CR8 . . . . 258 DT116
Perivale UB6 . . . . 159 CJ67
Devon Ct, Buck.H. IG9
off Chequers 124 EH46
St. Albans AL1 . . . . 65 CE21
Sutton at Hone DA4 . . . . 230 FP95
Devon Cres, Red. RH1 . . . . 272 DD134
Devoncroft Gdns, Twick. TW1 . . 199 CG87
Devon Gdns, N4 . . . . 143 DP58
Devonhurst Pl, W4
off Heathfield Ter 180 CR78
Devonia Gdns, N18 . . . . 122 DQ51
Devonia Rd, N1 . . . . 9 H10
Devon Mans, SE1
off Tooley St 32 A4
Devon Mead, Hat. AL10
off Chipmunk Chase 66 CR16
Devonport Gdns, Ilf. IG1 . . . . . 147 EM58
Devonport Ms, W12
off Devonport Rd 161 CV74
Devonport Rd, W12 . . . . 181 CV75
Devonport St, E1 . . . . 21 J9
Devon Ri, N2 . . . . 142 DD56
Devon Rd, Bark. IG11 . . . . 167 ES67
Hersham KT12 . . . . 236 BW105
South Merstham RH1 . . . . 273 DJ130
Sutton SM2 . . . . 239 CY109
Sutton at Hone DA4 . . . . 230 FP95
Watford WD24 . . . . 98 BX39
Devons Est, E3 . . . . 22 D3
Devonshire Av, Amer. HP6 . . . . . 77 AP37
Box Hill KT20 . . . . 270 CQ131
Dartford DA1 . . . . 209 FH86
Sutton SM2 . . . . 240 DC108
Woking GU21 . . . . 233 BC114
● Devonshire Business Pk,
Borwd. WD6 . . . . 100 CR41
Devonshire Cl, E15 . . . . 13 K1
N13 . . . . 121 DN49
W1 . . . . 17 J6
Amersham HP6 . . . . 77 AQ37
Farnham Royal SL2 . . . . 153 AP68
Devonshire Cres, NW7 . . . . 119 CX52
Devonshire Dr, SE10 . . . . 46 C5
Long Ditton KT6 . . . . 219 CK102
Devonshire Gdns, N17 . . . . 122 DQ51
N21 . . . . 122 DQ45
W4 . . . . 180 CQ80
Devonshire Grn, Farn.Royal
SL2 . . . . 153 AP68
Devonshire Gro, SE15 . . . . 44 F3
Devonshire Hill La, N17 . . . . . . 122 DQ51
Sch Devonshire Hill Prim Sch,
N17 off Weir Hall Rd 122 DR51
Devonshire Ho, SE1
off Bath Ter 31 J6
Sutton SM2
off Devonshire Av 240 DC108
Sch Devonshire Ho Prep Sch,
NW3 . . . . 5 P2
Devonshire Ms, SW10
off Park Wk 40 A2
W4 . . . . 180 CS78
Devonshire Ms N, W1 . . . . 17 J6
Devonshire Ms S, W1 . . . . 17 J6
Devonshire Ms W, W1 . . . . 17 J5
Devonshire Pas, W4 . . . . 180 CS78
Devonshire Pl, NW2 . . . . 142 DA62
W1 . . . . 17 H5
W8 . . . . 27 L7
Devonshire Pl Ms, W1 . . . . 17 H5
Sch Devonshire Prim Sch, Sutt.
SM2 off Devonshire Av . . . 240 DC108
Devonshire Rd, E16 . . . . 24 B8
E17 . . . . 145 EA58
N9 . . . . 122 DW46
N13 . . . . 121 DM49
N17 . . . . 122 DQ51
NW7 . . . . 119 CX52
SE9 . . . . 206 EL89
SE23 . . . . 204 DW88
SW19 . . . . 202 DE94
W4 . . . . 180 CS78
W5 . . . . 179 CJ76
Bexleyheath DA6 . . . . 188 EY84
Carshalton SM5 . . . . 240 DG105
Croydon CR0 . . . . 224 DR101
Eastcote HA5 . . . . 138 BW58
Feltham TW13 . . . . 198 BY90
Gravesend DA12 . . . . 213 GH88
Grays RM16 . . . . 192 FY77
Harrow HA1 . . . . 139 CD58
Hatch End HA5 . . . . 116 BZ53
Hornchurch RM12 . . . . 150 FJ61
Ilford IG2 . . . . 147 ER59
Orpington BR6 . . . . 228 EU101
Southall UB1 . . . . 158 CA71
Sutton SM2 . . . . 240 DC108
Weybridge KT13 . . . . 234 BN105
Devonshire Row, EC2 . . . . 19 P7
Devonshire Row Ms, W1 . . . . . . 17 K5
Devonshire Sq, EC2 . . . . 19 P8
Bromley BR2 . . . . 226 EH98
Devonshire St, W1 . . . . 17 H6
W4 . . . . 180 CS78
Devonshire Ter, W2 . . . . 15 P9
Devonshire Way, Croy. CR0 . . . 225 DY103
Hayes UB4 . . . . 157 BV72
DLR Devons Road 22 C4
Devons Rd, E3 . . . . 22 B6
Devon St, SE15 . . . . 44 F3
Devon Way, Chess. KT9 . . . . . . 237 CJ106
Epsom KT19 . . . . 238 CP106
Uxbridge UB10 . . . . 156 BM68
Devon Waye, Houns. TW5 . . . . . 178 BZ80
De Walden St, W1 . . . . 17 H7
Dewar Spur, Slou. SL3 . . . . 175 AZ79
Dewar St, SE15 . . . . 184 DU83
Dewberry Gdns, E6 . . . . 24 G6
Dewberry St, E14 . . . . 22 E7
Dewey La, SW2 off Tulse Hill . . 203 DN86
Dewey Path, Horn. RM12 . . . . . 170 FJ65
Dewey Rd, N1 . . . . 8 E10
Dagenham RM10 . . . . 169 FB65
Dewey St, SW17 . . . . 202 DF92
Dewgrass Gro, Wal.Cr. EN8 . . . 105 DX35
Dewhurst Rd, W14 . . . . 26 C6
Cheshunt EN8 . . . . 88 DW29
Sch Dewhurst St. Mary C of E
Prim Sch, Chsht EN8
off Churchgate 88 DW29
Dewlands, Gdse. RH9 . . . . 274 DW131
Dewlands Av, Dart. DA2 . . . . . . 210 FP87
Dewlands Ct, NW4
off Holders Hill Rd 119 CX54
Dewsbury Cl, Pnr. HA5 . . . . 138 BY58
Romford RM3 . . . . 128 FL51

Dewsbury Ct, W4 off Chiswick Rd 180 CQ77
Dewsbury Gdns, Rom. RM3 128 FK51
Worcester Park KT4 221 CU104
Dewsbury Rd, NW10 141 CU64
Romford RM3 128 FK51
Dewsbury Ter, NW1 7 K8
Dexter Cl, Grays RM17 192 GA76
St. Albans AL1 65 CG21
Dexter Ho, Erith DA18 off Kale Rd 188 EY76
Dexter Rd, Barn. EN5 101 CX44
Harefield UB9 114 BJ54
Deyncourt Gdns, Upmin. RM14 150 FQ61
Deyncourt Rd, N17 122 DQ53
Deynecourt Gdns, E11 146 EJ56
D'Eynsford Rd, SE5 43 L6
Dhonan Ho, SE1 off Longfield Est 32 B8
Diadem Ct, W1 17 N9
Dial Cl, Green. DA9 211 FW85
Dialmead, Ridge EN6 off Crossoaks La 85 CT34
Dial Wk, The, W8 27 M4
Diamedes Av, Stanw. TW19 196 BK87
Diameter Rd, Petts Wd BR5 227 EP101
Diamond Cl, Dag. RM8 148 EW60
Grays RM16 192 FZ76
Diamond Rd, Ruis. HA4 138 BX63
Slough SL1 174 AU75
Watford WD24 97 BU38
Diamond St, NW10 160 CR66
SE15 43 P5
Diamond Ter, SE10 46 F6
Diamond Way, SE8 46 B4
Diana Cl, E18 124 EH53
SE8 45 P2
Chafford Hundred RM16 192 FZ76
George Green SL3 154 AY72
Sidcup DA14 208 EY89
Diana Gdns, Surb. KT6 220 CM103
Diana Ho, SW13 181 CT81
★ Diana Princess of Wales Mem, W2 28 C4
Diana Rd, E17 145 DZ55
Diana Wk, Horl. RH6 off High St 291 DH148
Dianne Way, Barn. EN4 102 DE43
Dianthus Cl, SE2 off Carnation St 188 EV78
Chertsey KT16 215 BE101
Dianthus Ct, Wok. GU22 248 AX118
Diban Av, Horn. RM12 149 FH63
Dibden Hill, Ch.St.G. HP8 112 AW49
Dibden La, Ide Hill TN14 278 FE126
Dibden St, N1 9 H8
Dibdin Cl, Sutt. SM1 222 DA104
Dibdin Ho, W9 5 L10
Dibdin Rd, Sutt. SM1 222 DA104
Diceland Rd, Bans. SM7 255 CZ116
Dicey Av, NW2 4 A2
Dickens Av, N3 120 DC53
Dartford DA1 190 FN84
Tilbury RM18 193 GH81
Uxbridge UB8 157 BP72
Dickens Cl, Chsht EN7 88 DU26
Erith DA8 189 FB80
Hayes UB3 off Croyde Av 177 BS77
Richmond TW10 200 CL89
St. Albans AL3 65 CD19
Dickens Ct, Hat. AL10 67 CV16
Dickens Dr, Add. KT15 233 BF107
Chislehurst BR7 207 EQ93
Dickens Est, SE1 32 C5
SE16 32 C5
Dickens Ho, NW6 15 J2
Dickens La, N18 122 DS50
Dickens Ms, EC1 18 G6
Dickenson Cl, N9 off Croyland Rd 122 DU46
Dickenson Rd, N8 143 DL59
Feltham TW13 198 BW92
Dickensons La, SE25 224 DU99
Dickensons Pl, SE25 224 DU100
Dickenson Way, Ware SG12 55 DX05
Dickens Pl, Colnbr. SL3 175 BE81
Dickens Ri, Chig. IG7 125 EN48
Dickens Rd, E6 166 EK68
Gravesend DA12 213 GL88
Dickens Sq, SE1 31 K6
Dickens St, SW8 41 K8
Dickens Way, Rom. RM1 149 FE56
Dickenswood Cl, SE19 203 DP94
Dickerage La, N.Mal. KT3 220 CQ97
Dickerage Rd, Kings.T. KT1 220 CQ95
New Malden KT3 220 CQ95
● Dicker Mill Est, Hert. SG13 54 DR08
Dickinson Av, Crox.Grn WD3 96 BN44
Dickinson Ct, EC1 off Brewhouse Yd 19 H5
Dickinson Quay, Hem.H. HP3 80 BL25
Dickinson Sq, Crox.Grn WD3 96 BN44
Dickson, Chsht EN7 87 DT27
Dickson Fold, Pnr. HA5 138 BX56
Dickson Rd, SE9 186 EL83
Dick Turpin Way, Felt. TW14 177 BT84
Didsbury Cl, E6 off Barking Rd 167 EM67
Dieppe Cl, W14 27 H10
Digby Cres, N4 144 DQ61
Digby Gdns, Dag. RM10 168 FA67
Digby Pl, Croy. CR0 224 DT104
Digby Rd, E9 11 J3
Barking IG11 167 ET66
Digby St, E2 21 H3
Digby Wk, Horn. RM12 off Pembrey Way 170 FJ65
Digby Way, Byfleet KT14 off High Rd 234 BM112
Dig Dag Hill, Chsht EN7 88 DT27
Digdens Ri, Epsom KT18 254 CQ115
Digon St, E1 21 J7
Dighton Ct, SE5 43 J3
Dighton Rd, SW18 202 DC85
Dignum St, N1 8 E10
Digswell Cl, Borwd. WD6 100 CN38
Digswell Hill, Welw. AL6 51 CU06
Digswell Ho, Welw.G.C. AL8 51 CX05
Digswell Ho Ms, Welw.G.C. AL8 51 CX05
Digswell La, Welw. AL6 51 CX06
Digswell Pl, Welw.G.C. AL8 51 CW06
Digswell Ri, Welw.G.C. AL8 51 CX07
Digswell Rd, Welw.G.C. AL8 51 CY06
Digswell St, N7 8 F4
Dilhorne Cl, SE12 206 EH90
Sch Dilkes Prim Sch, S.Ock. RM15 off Garron La 171 FT72
Dilke St, SW3 40 F2
● Dilloway Yd, Sthl. UB2 off The Green 178 BY75
Dillwyn Cl, SE26 205 DY91
Dilston Cl, Nthlt. UB5 off Yeading La 158 BW69
Dilston Gro, SE16 32 G8
Dilston Rd, Lthd. KT22 253 CG119
Dilton Gdns, SW15 201 CU88
Dilwyn Ct, E17 off Hillyfield 123 DY54
Dimes Pl, W6 off King St 181 CV77
Dimmock Dr, Grnf. UB6 139 CD64
Dimmocks La, Sarratt WD3 96 BH36
Dimond Cl, E7 13 P1
Dimsdale Dr, NW9 140 CQ60
Enfield EN1 104 DU44
Slough SL2 133 AM63
Dimsdale St, Hert. SG14 54 DQ09
Dimsdale Wk, E13 13 P9
Dimson Cres, E3 22 A4
Dinant Link Rd, Hodd. EN11 71 DY16
Dingle, The, Uxb. UB10 157 BP68
Dingle Cl, Barn. EN5 101 CT44
Dingle Gdns, E14 34 B1
Dingle Rd, Ashf. TW15 197 BP92
Dingley La, SW16 203 DK89
Dingley Pl, EC1 19 K3
Dingley Rd, EC1 19 J3
Dingwall Av, Croy. CR0 224 DQ103
Dingwall Gdns, NW11 142 DA58
Dingwall Rd, SW18 202 DC87
Carshalton SM5 240 DF109
Croydon CR0 224 DR103
Dinmont St, E2 10 E10
Dinmore, Bov. HP3 79 AZ28
Dinsdale Cl, Wok. GU22 249 AZ118
Dinsdale Gdns, SE25 224 DS98
New Barnet EN5 102 DB43
Dinsdale Rd, SE3 47 L2
Dinsmore Rd, SW12 203 DH87
Dinton Rd, SW19 202 DD93
Kingston upon Thames KT2 200 CM94
Dione Rd, Hem.H. HP2 off Saturn Way 62 BM17
Diploma Av, N2 142 DE56
Diploma Ct, N2 off Diploma Av 142 DE56
Dirdene Cl, Epsom KT17 239 CT112
Dirdene Gdns, Epsom KT17 239 CT112
Dirdene Gro, Epsom KT17 238 CS112
Dirleton Rd, E15 13 L8
Dirtham La, Eff. KT24 267 BU127
Disbrowe Rd, W6 38 E3
● Discovery Business Pk, SE16 off St. James's Rd 32 D7
Discovery Dock Apts E, E14 34 C4
Discovery Dock Apts W, E14 34 C4
Sch Discovery Prim Sch & Children's Cen, SE28 off Battery Rd 167 ET74
Discovery Wk, E1 32 E1
Dishforth La, NW9 118 CS53
Disney Ms, N4 143 DP57
Disney Pl, SE1 31 K4
Disney St, SE1 31 K4
Dison Cl, Enf. EN3 105 DX39
Disraeli Cl, SE28 168 EW74
W4 off Acton La 180 CR76
Disraeli Ct, Slou. SL3 off Sutton Pl 175 BB79
Disraeli Gdns, SW15 off Fawe Pk Rd 181 CZ84
Disraeli Pk, Beac. HP9 111 AK50
Disraeli Rd, E7 13 P4
NW10 160 CQ68
SW15 181 CY84
W5 159 CK74
Diss St, E2 20 A2
Distaff La, EC4 19 J10
Distillery La, W6 38 B1
Distillery Rd, W6 38 B1
Distillery Wk, Brent. TW8 180 CL79
Distin St, SE11 30 E9
District Rd, Wem. HA0 139 CH64
Ditch All, SE10 46 D7
Ditchburn St, E14 34 F1
Ditches La, Cat. CR3 257 DM122
Coulsdon CR5 257 DL120
Ditches Ride, The, Loug. IG10 107 EN37
Ditchfield Rd, Hayes UB4 158 BY70
Hoddesdon EN11 55 EA14
Dittisham Rd, SE9 206 EL91
Ditton Cl, T.Ditt. KT7 219 CG101
Dittoncroft Cl, Croy. CR0 242 DS105
Ditton Gra Cl, Long Dit. KT6 219 CK102
Ditton Gra Dr, Long Dit. KT6 219 CK102
Ditton Hill, Long Dit. KT6 219 CJ102
Ditton Hill Rd, Long Dit. KT6 219 CJ102
Ditton Lawn, T.Ditt. KT7 219 CG102
Ditton Pk, Slou. SL3 174 AX78
Ditton Pk Rd, Slou. SL3 174 AY79
Ditton Pl, SE20 224 DV95
Ditton Reach, T.Ditt. KT7 219 CH100
Ditton Rd, Bexh. DA6 208 EX85
Datchet SL3 174 AX81
Slough SL3 175 AZ79
Southall UB2 178 BZ78
Surbiton KT6 220 CL102
Sch Divine Saviour RC Prim Sch, The, Abb.L. WD5 off Broomfield Ri 81 BR32
Divis Way, SW15 off Dover Pk Dr 201 CV86
Divot Pl, Hert. SG13 54 DV08
Dixon Clark Ct, N1 8 G5
Dixon Cl, E6 25 K8
Dixon Dr, Wey. KT13 234 BM110
Dixon Ho, W10 14 C9
Dixon Pl, W.Wick. BR4 225 EB102
Dixon Rd, SE14 45 M6
SE25 224 DS97
Dixon's All, SE16 32 E5
Dixon's Ct, Ware SG12 off Crane Mead 55 DY06
Dixons Hill Cl, N.Mymms AL9 85 CV25
Dixons Hill Rd, N.Mymms AL9 85 CU25
Dixon Way, NW10 off Church Rd 160 CS66
Dobbin Cl, Har. HA3 117 CG54
Dobb's Weir, Hodd. EN11 71 EC18
Dobb's Weir Rd, Hodd. EN11 71 EE18
Roydon CM19 71 ED18
Dobell Path, SE9 off Dobell Rd 207 EM85
Dobell Rd, SE9 207 EM85
Doble Ct, S.Croy. CR2 242 DU111
Dobree Av, NW10 161 CV66
Dobson Cl, NW6 6 A7
Dobson Rd, Grav. DA12 213 GL92
Doby Ct, EC4 19 K10
Dockers Tanner Rd, E14 34 A7
Dockett Eddy, Cher. KT16 216 BL102
Dockett Eddy La, Shep. TW17 216 BM102
Dockhead, SE1 32 B5
Dock Hill Av, SE16 33 K4
Dockland St, E16 37 L3
Dockley Rd, SE16 32 C7
● Dockley Rd Ind Est, SE16 off Rouel Rd 32 C7
Dock Rd, E16 35 M1
Barking IG11 167 EQ68
Brentford TW8 179 CK80
Grays RM17 192 GD79
Tilbury RM18 193 GF82
Dockside Rd, E16 24 F10
Dock St, E1 20 C10
Dockwell Cl, Felt. TW14 177 BU84
Sch Doctor Challoner's Gram Sch, Amer. HP6 off Chesham Rd 77 AQ38
Sch Doctor Challoner's High Sch, Lt.Chal. HP7 off Coke's La 94 AV40
Doctor Johnson Av, SW17 203 DH90
★ Doctor Johnson's Ho, EC4 18 F9
Doctors Cl, SE26 204 DW92
Doctors Commons Rd, Berk. HP4 60 AV20
Doctors La, Chaldon CR3 257 DN123
Sch Doctor Triplett's C of E Prim Sch, Hayes UB3 off Hemmen La 157 BT72
Docwra's Bldgs, N1 9 N4
Dodbrooke Rd, SE27 203 DN90
Dodd Ho, SE16 off Rennie Est 32 F9
Doddinghurst Rd, Brwd. CM15 130 FW44
Doddington Gro, SE17 42 G2
Doddington Pl, SE17 42 G2
Dodd's Cres, W.Byf. KT14 234 BH114
Doddsfield Rd, Slou. SL2 153 AN69
Dodds La, Ch.St.G. HP8 112 AU47
Piccotts End HP2 62 BJ16
Dodd's La, Wok. GU22 234 BG114
Dodds Pk, Brock. RH3 286 CP136
Dodsley Pl, N9 122 DW48
Dodson St, SE1 30 F5
Dod St, E14 21 P8
Dodwood, Welw.G.C. AL7 52 DB10
Doebury Wk, SE18 off Prestwood Cl 188 EU79
Doel Cl, SW19 202 DC94
Doggett Rd, SE6 205 EA87
Doggetts Ct, E.Barn. EN4 102 DE43
Doggetts Fm Rd, Denh. UB9 135 BC59
Doggetts Way, St.Alb. AL1 64 CC22
Doggetts Wd Cl, Ch.St.G. HP8 94 AV42
Doggetts Wd La, Ch.St.G. HP8 94 AV41
Doghurst Av, Harling. UB3 177 BP80
Doghurst Dr, West Dr. UB7 177 BP80
Doghurst La, Chipstead CR5 256 DF120
Dog Kennel Grn, Ran.Com. RH5 268 BX133
Dog Kennel Hill, SE22 184 DS83
Dog Kennel Hill Est, SE22 184 DS83
Sch Dog Kennel Hill Prim Sch, SE22 43 P10
Dog Kennel La, Chorl. WD3 95 BF42
Hatfield AL10 67 CU17
Dog La, NW10 140 CS63
Dognell Grn, Welw.G.C. AL8 51 CV08
Dogwood Cl, Nthflt DA11 212 GE91
Doherty Rd, E13 23 P4
● Dokal Ind Est, Sthl. UB2 off Hartington Rd 178 BY76
Dolben St, SE1 30 G3
Dolby Rd, SW6 38 G9
Dolland St, SE11 42 D1
Dollis Av, N3 119 CZ53
Dollis Brook Wk, Barn. EN5 101 CY44
Dollis Cres, Ruis. HA4 138 BW60
DOLLIS HILL, NW2 141 CV62
⊖ Dollis Hill 141 CU64
Dollis Hill Av, NW2 141 CV62
Dollis Hill La, NW2 141 CV62
Sch Dollis Inf Sch, NW7 off Pursley Rd 119 CW52
Sch Dollis Jun Sch, NW7 off Pursley Rd 119 CW52
● Dollis Ms, N3 120 DA53
Dollis Pk, N3 119 CZ53
Dollis Rd, N3 119 CY52
NW7 119 CY52
Dollis Valley Dr, Barn. EN5 101 CZ44
Dollis Valley Grn Wk, N20 off Totteridge La 120 DC47
Barnet EN5 101 CY44
Dollis Valley Way, Barn. EN5 101 CZ44
Dolman Cl, N3 off Avondale Rd 120 DC54
Dolman Rd, W4 180 CR77
Dolman St, SW4 183 DM84
Dolphin App, Rom. RM1 149 FF56
Dolphin Cl, SE16 33 J4
SE28 168 EX72
Surbiton KT6 219 CK100
Dolphin Ct, NW11 141 CY58
Slough SL1 174 AV75
Staines TW18 196 BG90
Dolphin Ct N, Stai. TW18 196 BG90
● Dolphin Est, Sun. TW16 217 BS95
Dolphin Ho, SW18 off Smugglers Way 182 DB84
Dolphin La, E14 34 C1
Dolphin Pt, Purf. RM19 191 FS78
Dolphin Rd, Nthlt. UB5 158 BZ68
Slough SL1 174 AV75
Sunbury-on-Thames TW16 217 BS95
Dolphin Rd N, Sun. TW16 217 BR95
Dolphin Rd S, Sun. TW16 217 BR95
Dolphin Rd W, Sun. TW16 217 BR95
Dolphin Sq, SW1 41 M1
W4 180 CS80
Dolphin St, Kings.T. KT1 220 CL95
Dolphin Twr, SE8 45 P3
Dolphin Way, Purf. RM19 191 FS78
Dolphin Yd, St.Alb. AL1 65 CD20
Ware SG12 off East St 55 DX06
Dombey St, WC1 18 C6
Coll Dome, The, Wat. WD25 98 BW36
Dome Hill, Cat. CR3 274 DS127
Dome Hill Pk, SE26 204 DT91
Dome Hill Peak, Cat. CR3 274 DS126
Domett Cl, SE5 184 DR84
Dome Way, Red. RH1 272 DF133
Domfe Pl, E5 off Rushmore Rd 144 DW63
Domingo St, EC1 19 J4
Dominica Cl, E13 24 D1
Dominic Ct, Wal.Abb. EN9 89 EB33
● Dominion Business Pk, N9 off Goodwin Rd 123 DX47
Dominion Cl, Houns. TW3 179 CD82
Dominion Dr, Rom. RM5 127 FB51
Dominion Rd, Croy. CR0 224 DT101
Southall UB2 178 BY76
Dominion St, EC2 19 M6
★ Dominion Thea, W1 17 P8
Dominion Way, Rain. RM13 169 FG69
Domonic Dr, SE9 207 EP91
Domville Cl, N20 120 DD47
Donald Biggs Dr, Grav. DA12 213 GK87
Donald Dr, Rom. RM6 148 EW57
Donald Rd, E13 166 EH67
Croydon CR0 223 DM100
Donaldson Rd, NW6 5 H9
SE18 187 EN81
Donald Wds Gdns, Surb. KT5 220 CP103
Donato Dr, SE15 43 N3
Doncaster Dr, Nthlt. UB5 138 BZ64
Doncaster Gdns, N4 144 DQ58
Northolt UB5 138 BZ64
Doncaster Grn, Wat. WD19 116 BW50
Doncaster Rd, N9 122 DV45
Doncaster Way, Upmin. RM14 150 FM62
Doncel Ct, E4 123 ED45
Doncella Cl, Chaff.Hun. RM16 191 FX76
Donegal St, N1 18 D1
Doneraile St, SW6 38 D8
Dongola Rd, E1 21 L6
E13 24 A3
N17 144 DS55
Dongola Rd W, E13 24 A3
Sch Donhead Wimbledon Coll Prep Sch, SW19 off Edge Hill 201 CX94
Donington Av, Ilf. IG6 147 EQ57
Donkey All, SE22 204 DU87
Donkey La, Abin.Com. RH5 284 BX143
Enfield EN1 104 DU40
Farningham DA4 230 FP103
Horley RH6 291 DK152
West Drayton UB7 176 BJ77
Donkin Ho, SE16 off Rennie Est 32 F9
Donnay Cl, Ger.Cr. SL9 134 AX58
Donne Ct, SE24 204 DQ86
Donnefield Av, Edg. HA8 118 CL52
Donne Gdns, Wok. GU22 249 BE115
Donne Pl, SW3 28 D8
Mitcham CR4 223 DH98
Donne Rd, Dag. RM8 148 EW61
Donnington Ct, NW10 161 CV66
Sch Donnington Prim Sch, NW10 off Uffington Rd 161 CV66
Donnington Rd, NW10 161 CV66
Dunton Green TN13 263 FD120
Harrow HA3 139 CK57
Worcester Park KT4 221 CU103
Donnybrook Rd, SW16 203 DJ94
Donovan Av, N10 121 DH54
Donovan Cl, Epsom KT19 238 CR110
Donovan Ct, SW10 off Drayton Gdns 40 A1
Donovan Pl, N21 103 DM43
Don Phelan Cl, SE5 43 M6
Don Way, Rom. RM1 127 FE52
Doods Pk Rd, Reig. RH2 272 DC133
Doods Pl, Reig. RH2 272 DC133
Doods Rd, Reig. RH2 272 DC133
Doods Way, Reig. RH2 272 DD133
Doone Cl, Tedd. TW11 199 CG93
Doon St, SE1 30 E3
Dorado Gdns, Orp. BR6 228 EX104
Doral Way, Cars. SM5 240 DF106
Dorando Cl, W12 161 CV73
Doran Dr, Red. RH1 272 DD134
Doran Gdns, Red. RH1 272 DD134
Doran Gro, SE18 187 ES80
Doran Wk, E15 12 F7
Dora Rd, SW19 202 DA92
Dora St, E14 21 N8
Dora Way, SW9 42 F9
Dorcas Ct, St.Alb. AL1 65 CE21
Dorchester Av, N13 122 DQ49
Bexley DA5 208 EX88
Harrow HA2 138 CC58
Hoddesdon EN11 71 EA15
Dorchester Cl, Dart. DA1 210 FM87
Northolt UB5 138 CB64
Orpington BR5 208 EU94
Dorchester Ct, N14 121 DH45
SE24 204 DQ85
Croxley Green WD3 off Mayfare 97 BQ43
Woking GU22 249 BA116
Dorchester Dr, SE24 204 DQ85
Feltham TW14 197 BS86
Dorchester Gdns, E4 123 EA49
NW11 142 DA56
Dorchester Gro, W4 180 CS78
Dorchester Ho, Rich. TW9 off Strand Dr 180 CP80
Dorchester Ms, N.Mal. KT3 off Elm Rd 220 CR98
Twickenham TW1 199 CJ87
Sch Dorchester Prim Sch, Wor.Pk. KT4 off Dorchester Rd 221 CW102
Dorchester Rd, Grav. DA12 213 GK90
Morden SM4 222 DB101
Northolt UB5 138 CB64
Weybridge KT13 217 BP104
Worcester Park KT4 221 CW102
Dorchester Way, Har. HA3 140 CM58
Dorchester Waye, Hayes UB4 158 BW72
Dorcis Av, Bexh. DA7 188 EY82
Dordrecht Rd, W3 160 CS74
Dore Av, E12 147 EN64
Doreen Av, NW9 140 CR60
Dore Gdns, Mord. SM4 222 DB101
Dorell Cl, Sthl. UB1 158 BZ71
Dorey Ho, Brent. TW8 off London Rd 179 CJ80
Doria Dr, Grav. DA12 213 GL90
Dorian Rd, Horn. RM12 149 FG60
Doria Rd, SW6 39 H8
Doric Dr, Kgswd KT20 255 CZ120
Doric Way, NW1 17 N2
Dorie Ms, N12 120 DB49
Dorien Rd, SW20 221 CX96
Dorin Ct, Warl. CR6 258 DV119
Dorincourt, Wok. GU22 249 BE115
Doris Ashby Cl, Perivale UB6 159 CG67
Doris Av, Erith DA8 189 FC81
Doris Rd, E7 13 P6
Ashford TW15 197 BR93
DORKING, RH4 & RH5 285 CH137
⇌ Dorking 269 CJ134
Coll Dorking Adult Learning Cen, Dor. RH4 off Dene St 285 CH136
★ Dorking & District Mus, Dor. RH4 285 CG136
● Dorking Business Pk, Dor. RH4 285 CG135
Dorking Cl, SE8 45 N2
Worcester Park KT4 221 CX103
⇌ Dorking Deepdene 269 CJ134
Dorking Gdns, Rom. RM3 128 FK50
H Dorking Gen Hosp, Dor. RH4 285 CG137
Dorking Glen, Rom. RM3 128 FK49
Dorking Ri, Rom. RM3 128 FK49
Dorking Rd, Abin.Ham. RH5 283 BS139
Bookham KT23 268 CB126
Chilworth GU4, GU5 281 BF139
Epsom KT18 254 CN116
Gomshall GU5 283 BR139
Leatherhead KT22 253 CH122
Romford RM3 128 FK49
Tadworth KT20 255 CX123
Dorking Wk, Rom. RM3 128 FK49
⇌ Dorking West 285 CG135
Dorkins Way, Upmin. RM14 151 FS59
Dorlcote Rd, SW18 202 DD87
Dorling Dr, Epsom KT17 239 CT112
Dorly Cl, Shep. TW17 217 BS99
Dorman Pl, N9 off Newdales Cl 122 DU47
Dormans Cl, Nthwd. HA6 115 BR52
Dorman Wk, NW10 140 CQ64
Dorman Way, NW8 6 A8
● Dorma Trd Pk, E10 145 DX60
Dormay St, SW18 202 DB85
Dormer Cl, E15 13 L4
Barnet EN5 101 CX43
Dormers Av, Sthl. UB1 158 CA72
Dormers Ri, Sthl. UB1 158 CB72
DORMER'S WELLS, Sthl. UB1 158 CB73
Sch Dormers Wells High Sch, Sthl. UB1 off Dormers Wells La 158 CA72
Sch Dormers Wells Inf & Jun Schs, Sthl. UB1 off Dormers Wells La 158 CB73
Dormers Wells La, Sthl. UB1 158 CA72
Dormie Cl, St.Alb. AL3 64 CC18
Dormywood, Ruis. HA4 137 BT57
Dornberg Cl, SE3 47 P4
Dornberg Rd, SE3 off Banchory Rd 186 EH80
Dorncliffe Rd, SW6 38 F8
Dornels, Slou. SL2 154 AW72
DORNEY, Wind. SL4 172 AH76
Dorney, NW3 6 D6
★ Dorney Ct, Wind. SL4 172 AG77
Dorney End, Chesh. HP5 76 AN30
Dorney Gro, Wey. KT13 217 BP103
DORNEY REACH, Maid. SL6 172 AF76
Dorney Reach Rd, Dorney R. SL6 172 AF76
Dorney Ri, Orp. BR5 227 ET98
Sch Dorney Sch, Dorney R. SL6 off Harcourt Cl 172 AF76
Dorney Way, Houns. TW4 198 BY85
Dorney Wd Rd, Burn. SL1 133 AK63
Dornfell St, NW6 5 H3
Dornford Gdns, Couls. CR5 258 DQ119
Dornton Rd, SW12 203 DH89
South Croydon CR2 242 DR106
Dorothy Av, Wem. HA0 160 CL66
Sch Dorothy Barley Inf Sch, Dag. RM8 off Davington Rd 148 EV64
Sch Dorothy Barley Jun Sch, Dag. RM8 off Ivinghoe Rd 148 EV64
Dorothy Evans Cl, Bexh. DA7 189 FB84
Dorothy Gdns, Dag. RM8 148 EV63
Dorothy Rd, SW11 182 DF83
Dorrell Pl, SW9 off Brixton Rd 183 DN84
Dorriens Cft, Berk. HP4 60 AT16
Dorrien Wk, SW16 203 DK89
Dorrington Ct, SE25 224 DS96
Dorrington Gdns, Horn. RM12 150 FK60
Dorrington Pt, E3 22 C2
Dorrington St, EC1 18 E6
Dorrington Way, Beck. BR3 225 EC99
Dorrit Cres, Guil. GU3 264 AS132
Dorrit Ms, N18 122 DS49
Dorrit St, SE1 31 K4
Dorrit Way, Chis. BR7 207 EQ93
Dorrofield Cl, Crox.Grn WD3 97 BQ43
Dors Cl, NW9 140 CR60
Dorset Av, Hayes UB4 157 BS69
Romford RM1 149 FD55
Southall UB2 178 CA77
Welling DA16 187 ET84
Dorset Bldgs, EC4 18 G9
Dorset Cl, NW1 16 E6
Berkhamsted HP4 60 AT18
Hayes UB4 157 BS69
Dorset Cres, Grav. DA12 213 GL91
Dorset Dr, Edg. HA8 118 CM51
Woking GU22 249 BB117
Dorset Est, E2 20 B2
Dorset Gdns, Mitch. CR4 223 DM98
Dorset Ho, Enf. EN3 105 DX37
Dorset Ms, N3 120 DA53
SW1 29 J6
Dorset Pl, E15 12 G4
Dorset Ri, EC4 18 G9
Dorset Rd, E7 166 EJ66
N15 144 DR56
N22 121 DL53
SE9 206 EL89
SW8 42 B4
SW19 222 DA95
W5 179 CJ76
Ashford TW15 196 BK90
Beckenham BR3 225 DX97
Harrow HA1 138 CC58
Mitcham CR4 222 DE96
Sutton SM2 240 DA110
Windsor SL4 173 AQ82
Sch Dorset Rd Inf Sch, SE9 off Dorset Rd 206 EL89
Dorset Sq, NW1 16 E5
Epsom KT19 238 CR110
Dorset St, W1 16 F7
Sevenoaks TN13 off High St 279 FJ125

Dorset Way, Byfleet KT14 234 BK110
Twickenham TW2 199 CD88
Uxbridge UB10 156 BM68
Dorset Waye, Houns. TW5 178 BZ80
Dorton Cl, SE15 43 P5
Coll **Dorton Coll of Further Ed**, Seal TN15 *off Seal Dr* 279 FM122
Dorton Dr, Sev. TN15 279 FM122
Sch **Dorton Ho Sch**, Seal TN15 *off Wildernesse Av* 279 FM122
Dorton Way, Ripley GU23 250 BH121
Dorville Cres, W6 181 CV76
Dorville Rd, SE12 206 EF85
Dothill Rd, SE18 187 ER80
Douai Gro, Hmptn. TW12 218 CC95
Sch **Douay Martyrs Sch, The**, Ickhm UB10 *off Edinburgh Dr* 137 BP63
Doubleday Rd, Loug. IG10 107 EQ41
Doughty Ms, WC1 18 C5
Doughty St, WC1 18 C4
Douglas Av, E17 123 EA53
New Malden KT3 221 CV98
Romford RM3 128 FL54
Watford WD24 98 BX37
Wembley HA0 160 CL66
Douglas Cl, Chaff.Hun. RM16 192 FY76
Ilford IG6 125 EP52
Jacobs Well GU4 264 AX128
Stanmore HA7 117 CG50
Wallington SM6 241 DL108
Douglas Ct, Cat. CR3 258 DQ122
Westerham TN16 260 EL117
Douglas Cres, Hayes UB4 158 BW70
Douglas Dr, Croy. CR0 225 EA104
Douglas Gdns, Berk. HP4 60 AT18
Douglas Ho, Chsht EN8 *off Coopers Wk* 89 DX28
Douglas La, Wrays. TW19 195 AZ85
Douglas Ms, NW2 141 CY62
Banstead SM7 *off North Acre* 255 CZ116
Douglas Path, E14 34 F10
Douglas Rd, E4 124 EE45
E16 23 P7
N1 9 J6
N22 121 DN53
NW6 4 G8
Addlestone KT15 216 BH104
Esher KT10 218 CB103
Hornchurch RM11 149 FF58
Hounslow TW3 178 CB83
Ilford IG3 148 EU58
Kingston upon Thames KT1 220 CP96
Reigate RH2 272 DA133
Slough SL2 153 AR71
Stanwell TW19 196 BK86
Surbiton KT6 220 CM103
Welling DA16 188 EV81
Douglas Sq, Mord. SM4 222 DA100
Douglas St, SW1 29 N9
Douglas Ter, E17 *off Penrhyn Av* 123 DZ53
Douglas Way, SE8 45 P5
Welwyn Garden City AL7 52 DC09
Doug Siddons Ct, Grays RM17 *off Elm Rd* 192 GC79
Doulton Cl, Harl. CM17 74 EY16
Doulton Ho, SE11 *off Lambeth Wk* 30 D7
Doulton Ms, NW6 5 M4
Doultons, The, Stai. TW18 196 BG94
Dounesforth Gdns, SW18 202 DB88
Dounsell Ct, Pilg.Hat. CM15 *off Ongar Rd* 130 FU44
Douro Pl, W8 27 M6
Douro St, E3 12 A10
Douthwaite Sq, E1 32 D2
Dove App, E6 24 G7
Dove Cl, NW7 119 CT52
Chafford Hundred RM16 192 FY76
Northolt UB5 *off Wayfarer Rd* 158 BX70
South Croydon CR2 243 DX111
Wallington SM6 241 DM108
Dovecot Cl, Pnr. HA5 137 BV57
Dovecote Av, N22 143 DN55
Dovecote Cl, Wey. KT13 217 BP104
Dovecote Gdns, SW14 *off Avondale Rd* 180 CR83
Dovecote Ho, SE16 *off Canada St* 33 J5
Dove Ct, EC2 19 L9
Beaconsfield HP9 111 AK52
Hatfield AL10 67 CU20
Dovedale Av, Har. HA3 139 CJ58
Ilford IG5 125 EN54
Dovedale Cl, Guil. GU4 *off Weylea Av* 265 BA131
Harefield UB9 114 BJ54
Welling DA16 188 EU81
Dovedale Ri, Mitch. CR4 202 DF94
Dovedale Rd, SE22 204 DV85
Dartford DA2 210 FQ88
Dovedon Cl, N14 121 DL47
Dove Ho Cres, Slou. SL2 153 AL69
Dovehouse Cft, Harl. CM20 58 EU13
Dove Ho Gdns, E4 123 EA47
Dovehouse Grn, Wey. KT13 *off Rosslyn Pk* 235 BR105
Dovehouse Mead, Bark. IG11 167 ER68
Dovehouse St, SW3 28 C10
Dove La, Pot.B. EN6 86 DB34
Dove Ms, SW5 27 N9
Doveney Cl, Orp. BR5 228 EW97
Dove Pk, Chorl. WD3 95 BB44
Pinner HA5 116 CA52
Dover Cl, NW2 *off Brent Ter* 141 CX61
Romford RM5 127 FC54
Dovercourt Av, Th.Hth. CR7 223 DN98
Dovercourt Est, N1 9 M5
Dovercourt Gdns, Stan. HA7 118 CL50
Dovercourt La, Sutt. SM1 222 DC104
Dovercourt Rd, SE22 204 DS86
Doverfield, Goffs Oak EN7 88 DQ29
Doverfield Rd, SW2 203 DL86
Guildford GU4 265 BA131
Dover Flats, SE1 31 P9
Dover Gdns, Cars. SM5 222 DF104
Dover Ho Rd, SW15 181 CU84
Doveridge Gdns, N13 121 DP49
Dove Rd, N1 9 L4
Dove Row, E2 10 C9
Dover Pk Dr, SW15 201 CV86
Dover Patrol, SE3 *off Kidbrooke Way* 186 EH82
Dover Rd, E12 146 EJ61
N9 122 DW47
SE19 204 DR93
Northfleet DA11 212 GD87
Romford RM6 148 EY58
Slough SL1 153 AM72
Sch **Dover Rd Comm Prim Sch**, Nthflt DA11 *off Dover Rd E* 212 GE88
Dover Rd E, Grav. DA11 212 GE87
Jct **Dovers Cor**, Rain. RM13 169 FG69
DOVERSGREEN, Reig. RH2 288 DB139
Dovers Grn Rd, Reig. RH2 288 DB139
Sch **Dovers Grn Sch**, Reig. RH2 *off Rushetts Rd* 288 DC138
Doversmead, Knap. GU21 248 AS116
Dover St, W1 29 K1
Dover Way, Crox.Grn WD3 97 BQ42
Dover Yd, W1 29 K2
Doves Cl, Brom. BR2 226 EL103
Doves Yd, N1 8 F9
Dovet Ct, SW8 42 C6
Doveton Rd, S.Croy. CR2 242 DR106
Doveton St, E1 20 G4
Dove Wk, SW1 28 G10
Hornchurch RM12 *off Heron Flight Av* 169 FH65
Dowanhill Rd, SE6 205 ED88
Dowd Cl, N11 *off Nurserymans Rd* 120 DG47
Dowdeswell Cl, SW15 180 CS84
Dowding Pl, Stan. HA7 117 CG51
Dowding Rd, Bigg.H. TN16 260 EK115
Uxbridge UB10 156 BM66
Dowding Wk, Nthflt DA11 212 GE90
Dowding Way, Horn. RM12 169 FH66
Leavesden WD25 81 BT34
Waltham Abbey EN9 105 ED36
Dowdney Cl, NW5 7 M3
Dower Av, Wall. SM6 241 DH109
Dower Cl, Knot.Grn HP9 110 AJ50
Dower Pk, Wind. SL4 173 AL84
Dowgate Hill, EC4 19 L10
Dowland St, W10 14 F2
Dowlans Cl, Bkhm KT23 268 CA127
Dowlans Rd, Bkhm KT23 268 CB127
Dowlas Est, SE5 43 N4
Dowlas St, SE5 43 N4
Dowlerville Rd, Orp. BR6 245 ET107
Dowley Wd, Welw.G.C. AL7 52 DB10
Dowling Ct, Hem.H. HP3 62 BK23
Dowman Cl, SW19 *off Nelson Gro Rd* 222 DB95
Downage, NW4 141 CW55
Downage, The, Grav. DA11 213 GG89
Downalong, Bushey Hth WD23 117 CD46
Downbank Av, Bexh. DA7 189 FD81
Downbarns Rd, Ruis. HA4 138 BX62
Downbury Ms, SW18 *off Merton Rd* 202 DA86
Down Cl, Nthlt. UB5 157 BV68
Sch **Downderry Prim Sch**, Brom. BR1 *off Downderry Rd* 206 EE91
Downderry Rd, Brom. BR1 205 ED90
DOWNE, Orp. BR6 245 EM111
Downe Av, Cudham TN14 245 EQ112
Downe Cl, Horl. RH6 290 DE146
Welling DA16 188 EW80
Downedge, St.Alb. AL3 64 CB19
Downe Ho, SE7 *off Springfield Gro* 186 EJ79
Sch **Downe Manor Prim Sch**, Nthlt. UB5 *off Down Way* 157 BV69
Downend, SE18 *off Moordown* 187 EP80
Sch **Downe Prim Sch**, Downe BR6 *off High Elms Rd* 245 EN111
Downer Dr, Sarratt WD3 96 BG36
Downer Meadow, Gdmg. GU7 280 AS143
Downe Rd, Cudham TN14 245 EQ114
Keston BR2 244 EK109
Mitcham CR4 222 DF96
Downers Cotts, SW4 *off Old Town* 183 DJ84
Downes Cl, Twick. TW1 *off St. Margarets Rd* 199 CH86
Downes Ct, N21 121 DN46
Downes Rd, St.Alb. AL4 65 CH16
Downfield, Wor.Pk. KT4 221 CT102
Downfield Cl, W9 15 L5
Hertford Heath SG13 54 DW11
Sch **Downfield JMI Sch**, Chsht EN8 *off Downfield Rd* 89 DY31
Downfield Rd, Chsht EN8 89 DY31
Hertford Heath SG13 54 DW09
Downfields, Welw.G.C. AL8 51 CV11
Downhall Rd, Hat.Hth CM22 59 FH08
Down Hall Rd, Kings.T. KT2 219 CK95
Downhall Rd, Match.Grn CM17 59 FH08
DOWNHAM, Brom. BR1 206 EF92
Downham Cl, Rom. RM5 126 FA52
Downham La, Brom. BR1 205 ED92
Downham Rd, N1 9 L7
Downham Way, Brom. BR1 205 ED92
Downhills Av, N17 144 DR55
Downhills Pk Rd, N17 144 DQ55
Sch **Downhills Prim Sch**, N15 *off Philip La* 144 DR56
Downhills Way, N17 144 DQ55
★ **Down Ho - Darwin Mus**, Orp. BR6 245 EN112
Downhurst Av, NW7 118 CR50
Downing Av, Guil. GU2 280 AT135
Downing Cl, Har. HA2 138 CC55
Downing Ct, Borwd. WD6 *off Bennington Dr* 100 CM39
Downing Dr, Grnf. UB6 159 CD67
Downing Path, Slou. SL2 153 AL70
Downing Rd, Dag. RM9 168 EZ67
Downings, E6 25 M8
Downing St, SW1 30 A4
Downings Wd, Map.Cr. WD3 113 BD50
Downland Cl, N20 120 DC46
Coulsdon CR5 241 DH114
Epsom KT18 255 CV118
Downland Gdns, Epsom KT18 255 CV118
Downlands, Wal.Abb. EN9 90 EE34
Downlands Rd, Pur. CR8 241 DL113
Downland Way, Epsom KT18 255 CV118
Downleys Cl, SE9 206 EL89
Downman Rd, SE9 186 EL83
Down Pl, W6 181 CV77
Water Oakley SL4 172 AG79
Down Rd, Guil. GU1 265 BB134
Teddington TW11 199 CH93
Downs, The, SW20 201 CX94
Harlow CM20 73 ES15
Hatfield AL10 67 CU20
Leatherhead KT22 269 CJ125
Downs Av, Chis. BR7 207 EM92
Dartford DA1 210 FN87
Epsom KT18 238 CS114
Pinner HA5 138 BZ58
Downs Br Rd, Beck. BR3 225 ED95
Downsbury Ms, SW18 *off Merton Rd* 202 DA85
Downs Ct, Sutt. SM2 240 DB111
Downs Ct Rd, Pur. CR8 241 DP112
Sch **Downsell Prim Sch**, E15 *off Downsell Rd* 145 ED63
Downsell Rd, E15 12 F1
Sch **Downsend Sch**, Lthd. KT22 *off Leatherhead Rd* 253 CK120
Downsfield, Hat. AL10 *off Sandifield* 67 CV21
Downsfield Rd, E17 145 DY58
Downshall Av, Ilf. IG3 147 ES58
Sch **Downshall Prim Sch**, Seven Kings IG3 *off Meads La* 147 ES59
Downs Hill, Beck. BR3 205 ED94
Southfleet DA13 212 GC94
Downs Hill Rd, Epsom KT18 238 CS114
Downshire Hill, NW3 6 B1
Downs Ho Rd, Epsom KT18 255 CT118
DOWNSIDE, Cob. KT11 251 BV118
Downside, Cher. KT16 215 BF102
Epsom KT18 238 CS114
Hemel Hempstead HP2 62 BL19
Sunbury-on-Thames TW16 217 BU95
Twickenham TW1 199 CF90
Downside Br Rd, Cob. KT11 251 BV115
Downside Cl, SW19 202 DC93
Downside Common, Down. KT11 251 BV118
Downside Common Rd, Down. KT11 251 BV118
Downside Cres, NW3 6 D3
W13 159 CG70
Downside Orchard, Wok. GU22 *off Park Rd* 249 BA117
Downside Rd, Down. KT11 251 BV116
Guildford GU4 281 BB135
Sutton SM2 240 DD107
Downside Wk, Brent. TW8 *off Sidney Gdns* 179 CJ79
Northolt UB5 158 BZ69
Downsland Dr, Brwd. CM14 130 FW48
Downs La, E5 *off Downs Rd* 144 DV63
Hatfield AL10 67 CU20
Leatherhead KT22 253 CH123
Downs Pk Rd, E5 10 D2
E8 10 B2
Sch **Downs Prim Sch & Nurs, The**, Harl. CM20 *off The Hides* 73 ES15
Downs Rd, E5 144 DU63
Beckenham BR3 225 EB96
Coulsdon CR5 257 DK118
Dorking RH5 269 CJ128
Enfield EN1 104 DS42
Epsom KT18 254 CS115
Istead Rise DA13 212 GD91
Purley CR8 241 DP111
Slough SL3 174 AX75
Sutton SM2 240 DB110
Thornton Heath CR7 224 DQ95
Downs Side, Sutt. SM2 239 CZ111
Down St, W1 29 J3
West Molesey KT8 218 CA99
Down St Ms, W1 29 J3
Downs Vw, Dor. RH4 269 CJ134
Isleworth TW7 179 CF81
Tadworth KT20 255 CV121
Downsview Av, Wok. GU22 249 AZ121
Downsview Cl, Down. KT11 251 BV119
Downs Vw Cl, Orp. BR6 246 EW110
Downsview Cl, Swan. BR8 229 FF97
Downsview Ct, Guil. GU1 *off Hazel Av* 264 AW130
Downsview Gdns, SE19 203 DP94
Dorking RH4 285 CH137
Sch **Downsview Prim Sch**, SE19 *off Biggin Way* 204 DQ94
Swanley BR8 *off Beech Av* 229 FG97
Downsview Rd, SE19 204 DQ94
Downs Vw Rd, Bkhm KT23 268 CC126
Downsview Rd, Sev. TN13 278 FF125
Sch **Downsview Sch**, E5 *off Downs Rd* 144 DV63
Downs Way, Bkhm KT23 268 CC126
Epsom KT18 255 CT116
Downsway, Guil. GU1 265 BD134
Orpington BR6 245 ES106
Downs Way, Oxt. RH8 276 EE127
Downsway, S.Croy. CR2 242 DS111
Downs Way, Tad. KT20 255 CV121
Downsway, Whyt. CR3 258 DT116
Downsway, The, Sutt. SM2 240 DC109
Downs Way Cl, Tad. KT20 255 CU121
Sch **Downs Way Sch**, Oxt. RH8 *off Downs Way* 276 EE128
Downs Wd, Epsom KT18 255 CV117
Downswood, Reig. RH2 272 DE131
Downton Av, SW2 203 DL89
Downtown Rd, SE16 33 M4
Down Way, Nthlt. UB5 157 BV69
Dowrey St, N1 8 E8
Dowry Wk, Wat. WD17 97 BT38
Dowsett Rd, N17 122 DT54
Dowson Cl, SE5 184 DR84
Doyce St, SE1 31 J4
Doyle Cl, Erith DA8 189 FE81
Doyle Gdns, NW10 161 CU67
Doyle Rd, SE25 224 DU98
Doyle Way, Til. RM18 *off Coleridge Rd* 193 GJ82
D'Oyley St, SW1 28 G8
D'Oyly Carte Island, Wey. KT13 217 BP102
Doynton St, N19 143 DH61
Draco Gate, SW15 38 A10
Draco St, SE17 43 J2
Dragonfly Cl, E13 24 B2
Dragon La, Wey. KT13 234 BN110
Dragon Rd, SE15 43 N3
Hatfield AL10 66 CS17
Dragoon Rd, SE8 45 N1
Dragor Rd, NW10 160 CQ70
Drake Av, Cat. CR3 258 DQ122
Slough SL3 174 AX77
Staines TW18 195 BF92
Drake Cl, SE16 33 K4
Drake Cl, Warley CM14 130 FX50
Drake Ct, SE19 204 DT92
W12 26 A5
Harrow HA2 138 BZ60
Drake Cres, SE28 168 EW72
Drakefell Rd, SE4 45 J9
SE14 45 J9
Drakefield Rd, SW17 202 DG90
Drake Ho, SW8 *off St. George Wf* 42 A1
Drakeley Ct, N5 143 DP63
Drake Ms, Brom. BR2 226 EJ98
Hornchurch RM12 *off Fulmar Rd* 169 FG66
Drake Rd, SE4 46 A10
Chafford Hundred RM16 192 FY76
Chessington KT9 238 CN106
Croydon CR0 223 DM101
Harrow HA2 138 BZ61
Horley RH6 290 DE148
Mitcham CR4 222 DG100
Drakes Cl, Chsht EN8 89 DX28
Esher KT10 236 CA106
Drakes Ctyd, NW6 5 H6
Drakes Dr, Nthwd. HA6 115 BP53
St. Albans AL1 65 CH23
Drakes Dr Mobile Home Pk, St.Alb. AL1 *off Drakes Dr* 65 CH22
Drakes Meadow, Harl. CM17 58 EY11
Drakes Rd, Amer. HP7 77 AR39
Drake St, WC1 18 C7
Enfield EN2 104 DR39
Drakes Wk, E6 167 EM67
Drakes Way, Hat. AL10 67 CV20
Woking GU22 248 AX122
Drakewood Rd, SW16 203 DK94
Draper Cl, Belv. DA17 188 EZ77
Isleworth TW7 179 CD82
Draper Ct, Horn. RM12 150 FL61
Draper Ho, SE1 31 H8
Draper Pl, N1 *off Dagmar Ter* 9 H8
Drapers' Ct, SW11 41 H6
Drapers' Cres, Whiteley Vill. KT12 *off Octagon Rd* 235 BT110
Drapers Rd, E15 12 F1
N17 144 DT55
Enfield EN2 103 DP40
Drappers Way, SE16 32 D8
Draven Cl, Brom. BR2 226 EF101
Drawdock Rd, SE10 35 H3
Drawell Cl, SE18 187 ES78
Drax Av, SW20 201 CV94
Draxmont, SW19 201 CY93
Draycot Rd, E11 146 EH58
Surbiton KT6 220 CN102
Draycott Av, SW3 28 D8
Harrow HA3 139 CH58
Draycott Cl, NW2 141 CX62
SE5 43 L5
Harrow HA3 139 CH58
Draycott Ms, SW6 39 H8
Draycott Pl, SW3 28 E9
Draycott Ter, SW3 28 F8
Dray Ct, Guil. GU2 *off The Chase* 280 AV135
Drayford Cl, W9 15 H4
Dray Gdns, SW2 203 DM85
Draymans Ms, SE15 44 A9
Draymans Way, Islw. TW7 179 CF83
Drayside Ms, Sthl. UB2 *off Kingston Rd* 178 BZ75
Drayson Cl, Wal.Abb. EN9 90 EE32
Drayson Ms, W8 27 K5
Drayton Av, W13 159 CG73
Loughton IG10 107 EM44
Orpington BR6 227 EP102
Potters Bar EN6 85 CY32
Drayton Br Rd, W7 159 CF73
W13 159 CF73
Drayton Cl, Fetch. KT22 253 CE124
Hounslow TW4 198 BZ85
Ilford IG1 147 ER60
Drayton Ford, Rick. WD3 114 BG48
Drayton Gdns, N21 121 DP45
SW10 27 P10
W13 159 CG73
West Drayton UB7 176 BL75
⇌ **Drayton Green** 159 CF72
Drayton Grn, W13 159 CG73
Sch **Drayton Grn Prim Sch**, W13 *off Drayton Gro* 159 CG73
Drayton Grn Rd, W13 159 CH73
Drayton Gro, W13 159 CG73
Sch **Drayton Ho Sch**, Guil. GU1 *off Austen Rd* 281 AZ135
Sch **Drayton Manor High Sch**, W7 *off Drayton Br Rd* 159 CF73
⇌ **Drayton Park** 8 F2
Drayton Pk, N5 8 E3
Drayton Pk Ms, N5 8 E2
Sch **Drayton Pk Prim Sch**, N5 8 F2
Drayton Rd, E11 145 ED60
N17 122 DS54
NW10 161 CT67
W13 159 CG73
Borehamwood WD6 100 CN42
Croydon CR0 223 DP103
Drayton Waye, Har. HA3 139 CH58
Dreadnought Cl, SW19 222 DD96
Drenon Sq, Hayes UB3 157 BT73
Dresden Cl, NW6 5 M4
Dresden Ho, SE11 *off Lambeth Wk* 30 D8
Dresden Rd, N19 143 DJ60
Dresden Way, Wey. KT13 235 BQ106
Dressington Av, SE4 205 EA86
Drew Av, NW7 119 CY51
Drew Gdns, Grnf. UB6 159 CF65
Drew Meadow, Farn.Com. SL2 133 AQ63
Drew Pl, Cat. CR3 258 DR123
Sch **Drew Prim Sch**, E16 36 G3
Drew Rd, E16 36 G3
Drews Pk, Knot.Grn HP9 110 AH49
Drewstead Rd, SW16 203 DK89
Drey, The, Chal.St.P. SL9 112 AY50
Driffield Rd, E3 11 M10
Drift, The, Brom. BR2 226 EK104
Jct **Drift Br**, Epsom KT17 255 CW115
Drift La, Cob. KT11 252 BZ117
Drift Rd, Lthd. KT24 251 BT124
Winkfield SL4 172 AD84
Drift Way, Colnbr. SL3 175 BC81
Richmond TW10 200 CM88
Driftway, The, Bans. SM7 255 CW115
Hemel Hempstead HP2 62 BM20
Leatherhead KT22 *off Downs La* 253 CH123
Mitcham CR4 222 DG95
Driftwood Av, St.Alb. AL2 82 CA26
Driftwood Dr, Ken. CR8 257 DP117
Drill Hall Rd, Cher. KT16 216 BG101
Dorking RH4 *off Westcott Rd* 285 CG136
Drinkwater Rd, Har. HA2 138 CB61
Drive, The, E4 123 ED45
E17 145 EB56
E18 146 EG56
N3 120 DA52
N6 142 DF57
N11 121 DJ51
NW10 *off Longstone Av* 161 CT67
NW11 141 CY59
SW6 38 F8
SW16 223 DM97
SW20 201 CW94
W3 160 CQ72
Amersham HP7 77 AR38
Artington GU3 280 AV138
Ashford TW15 197 BR94
Banstead SM7 255 CY117
Barking IG11 167 ET66
Beckenham BR3 225 EA96
Bexley DA5 208 EW86
Brookmans Park AL9 86 DA25
Buckhurst Hill IG9 124 EJ45
Chalfont St. Peter SL9 112 AY52
Chislehurst BR7 227 ET97
Cobham KT11 236 BY114
Collier Row RM5 127 FC53
Coulsdon CR5 241 DL114
Datchet SL3 174 AV81
Edgware HA8 118 CN50
Enfield EN2 104 DR39
Epsom KT19 239 CT107
Erith DA8 189 FB80
Esher KT10 218 CC102
Feltham TW14 198 BW87
Fetcham KT22 253 CE122
Goffs Oak EN7 87 DP28
Gravesend DA12 213 GK91
Great Warley CM13 130 FW50
Guildford GU2 *off Beech Gro* 264 AT134
Harlow CM20 57 ES14
Harold Wood RM3 128 FL53
Harrow HA2 138 CA59
Headley KT18 254 CN124
Hertford SG14 54 DQ07
High Barnet EN5 101 CY41
Hoddesdon EN11 71 EA15
Horley RH6 291 DH149
Hounslow TW3 179 CD82
Ilford IG1 147 EM60
Isleworth TW7 179 CD82
Kingston upon Thames KT2 200 CQ94
Loughton IG10 106 EL41
Morden SM4 222 DD99
New Barnet EN5 102 DC44
Newgate Street SG13 69 DL24
Northwood HA6 115 BS54
Onslow Village GU2 280 AT136
Orpington BR6 227 ET103
Potters Bar EN6 85 CZ33
Radlett WD7 83 CG34
Rickmansworth WD3 96 BJ44
Sawbridgeworth CM21 58 EY05
Scadbury Park BR7 227 ES95
Sevenoaks TN13 279 FH124
Sidcup DA14 208 EV90
Slough SL3 174 AY75
Surbiton KT6 220 CL101
Sutton SM2 239 CZ112
Thornton Heath CR7 224 DR98
Tyrrell's Wood KT22 254 CN124
Uxbridge UB10 136 BL63
Virginia Water GU25 215 AZ99
Wallington SM6 241 DJ110
Watford WD17 97 BR37
Wembley HA9 140 CQ61
West Wickham BR4 225 ED101
Woking GU22 248 AV120
Wraysbury TW19 194 AX85
Drive Mead, Couls. CR5 241 DL114
Drive Rd, Couls. CR5 257 DM119
Drive Spur, Kgswd KT20 256 DB121
Driveway, The, E17 145 EA58
Cuffley EN6 87 DL28
Drodges Cl, Bramley GU5 281 AZ143
Droitwich Cl, SE26 204 DU90
Dromey Gdns, Har. HA3 117 CF52
Dromore Rd, SW15 201 CY86
Dronfield Gdns, Dag. RM8 148 EW64
Droop St, W10 14 E4
Drop La, Brick.Wd AL2 82 CB30
Sch **Dropmore Inf Sch**, Burn. SL1 *off Littleworth Rd* 132 AJ62
Dropmore Pk, Burn. SL1 132 AH62
Dropmore Rd, Burn. SL1 152 AJ67
Drove Rd, Dor. RH5 284 BW135
Guildford GU4 282 BG136
Drovers Mead, Warley CM14 130 FV49
Drovers Pl, SE15 44 F4
Drovers Rd, S.Croy. CR2 242 DR106
Drovers Way, N7 8 A4
Hatfield AL10 67 CV15
St. Albans AL3 65 CD20
Seer Green HP9 111 AQ51
Droveway, Loug. IG10 107 EP40
Drove Way, The, Istead Rise DA13 212 GE94
Druce Rd, SE21 204 DS86
Drudgeon Way, Bean DA2 211 FV90
Druids Cl, Ashtd. KT21 254 CM120
Druid St, SE1 31 P4
Druids Way, Brom. BR2 225 ED98
Drumaline Ridge, Wor.Pk. KT4 220 CS103
Drummond Av, Rom. RM7 149 FD56
Drummond Cl, Erith DA8 189 FE81
Drummond Cres, NW1 17 N2
Drummond Dr, Stan. HA7 117 CF52
Drummond Gdns, Epsom KT19 238 CP111
Drummond Gate, SW1 29 P10
Drummond Ho, Wind. SL4 *off Balmoral Gdns* 173 AR83
Drummond Pl, Twick. TW1 199 CH86
Drummond Rd, E11 146 EH58
SE16 32 E6
Croydon CR0 224 DQ103
Guildford GU1 264 AX134
Romford RM7 149 FD56
Drummonds, The, Buck.H. IG9 124 EH47
Epping CM16 92 EU30
Drummonds Pl, Rich. TW9 180 CL84
Drummond St, NW1 17 L4
Drum St, E1 20 B8
Drury Cres, Croy. CR0 223 DN103
Drury La, WC2 18 B9

Drury La, Hunsdon SG12 . . . . . . **56** EK06
Drury Rd, Har. HA1 . . . . **138** CC59
Drury Way, NW10 . . . . **140** CR64
● **Drury Way Ind Est**, NW10 . . **140** CQ64
Dryad St, SW15 . . . . **181** CX83
Dryburgh Gdns, NW9 . . . . **140** CN55
Dryburgh Rd, SW15 . . . . **181** CV83
Drycroft, Welw.G.C. AL7 . . . . **51** CY13
Drydell La, Chesh. HP5 . . . . **76** AM31
Dryden Av, W7 . . . . **159** CF72
Dryden Cl, SW4 . . . . **203** DK85
Ilford IG6 . . . . **125** ET51
Dryden Ct, SE11 . . . . **30** F9
Dryden Pl, Til. RM18
off Fielding Av **193** GH81
Dryden Rd, SW19 . . . . **202** DC93
Enfield EN1 . . . . **104** DS44
Harrow HA3 . . . . **117** CF53
Welling DA16 . . . . **187** ES81
Dryden St, WC2 . . . . **18** B9
Dryden Twrs, Rom. RM3 . . . . . . **127** FH52
Dryden Way, Orp. BR6 . . . . **228** EU102
Dryfield Cl, NW10 . . . . **160** CQ65
Dryfield Rd, Edg. HA8 . . . . **118** CQ51
Dryfield Wk, SE8 . . . . **46** A2
Dryhill La, Sund.TN14 . . . . **278** FB123
Dryhill Rd, Belv. DA17 . . . . **188** EZ79
Dryland Av, Orp. BR6 . . . . **245** ET105
Drylands Rd, N8 . . . . **143** DL58
Drynham Pk, Wey. KT13 . . . . . . **217** BS104
Drysdale Av, E4 . . . . **123** EB45
Drysdale Cl, Nthwd. HA6
off Northbrook Dr **115** BS52
Drysdale Pl, N1 . . . . **19** P2
Drysdale St, N1 . . . . **19** P3
Duarte Pl, Grays RM16 . . . . **192** FZ76
Dublin Av, E8 . . . . **10** D8
Dubrae Cl, St.Alb. AL3 . . . . **64** CA22
Du Burstow Ter, W7 . . . . **179** CE75
Ducal St, E2 . . . . **20** B3
Du Cane Ct, SW17 . . . . **202** DG88
Du Cane Rd, W12 . . . . **161** CT72
Duchess Cl, N11 . . . . **121** DH50
Sutton SM1 . . . . **240** DC105
Duchess Ct, Wey. KT13 . . . . **217** BR104
Duchess Gro, Buck.H. IG9 . . . . . **124** EH47
Duchess Ms, W1 . . . . **17** K7
Duchess of Bedford's Wk, W8 . . **27** J5
Duchess of Kent Cl, Guil.
GU2 . . . . **264** AV130
Duchess St, W1 . . . . **17** K7
Slough SL1 . . . . **153** AL74
Duchess Wk, Sev.TN15 . . . . **279** FL125
Duchy Pl, SE1 . . . . **30** F2
Duchy Rd, Barn. EN4 . . . . **102** DD38
Duchy St, SE1 . . . . **30** F2
Ducie Ho, SE7
off Springfield Gro **186** EJ79
Ducie St, SW4 . . . . **183** DM84
Duckett Ms, N4 . . . . **143** DP58
Duckett Rd, N4 . . . . **143** DP58
Ducketts Mead, Roydon
CM19 . . . . **56** EH14
Ducketts Rd, Dart. DA1 . . . . **209** FF85
Duckett St, E1 . . . . **21** L6
Ducking Stool Ct, Rom. RM1 . . **149** FE56
Duck La, W1 . . . . **17** N9
Thornwood CM16 . . . . **92** EW26
Duck Lees La, Enf. EN3 . . . . **105** DY42
Duckling La, Saw. CM21
off Vantorts Rd **58** EY05
Ducks Hill, Nthwd. HA6 . . . . . . **114** BN54
Ducks Hill Rd, Nthwd. HA6 . . . . **115** BP54
Ruislip HA4 . . . . **115** BP54
DUCKS ISLAND, Barn. EN5 . . . **101** CX44
Ducks Wk, Twick.TW1 . . . . **199** CJ85
Du Cros Dr, Stan. HA7 . . . . **117** CK51
Du Cros Rd, W3 *off The Vale* . . . **160** CS74
Dudden Hill La, NW10 . . . . **141** CT63
Duddington Cl, SE9 . . . . **206** EK91
Dudley Av, Har. HA3 . . . . **139** CJ55
Waltham Cross EN8 . . . . **89** DX32
Dudley Cl, Add. KT15 . . . . **216** BJ104
Bovingdon HP3 . . . . **79** BA27
Chafford Hundred RM16 . . . . . **192** FY75
Dudley Ct, NW11 . . . . **141** CZ56
Slough SL1 *off Upton Rd* **174** AU76
Dudley Dr, Mord. SM4 . . . . **221** CY101
Ruislip HA4 . . . . **137** BV64
Dudley Gdns, W13 . . . . **179** CH75
Harrow HA2 . . . . **139** CD60
Romford RM3 . . . . **128** FK51
Dudley Gro, Epsom KT18 . . . . . **238** CQ114
Dudley Ho, W2
off North Wf Rd **16** A7
Dudley Ms, SW2
off Bascombe St **203** DN86
Dudley Pl, Hayes UB3 . . . . **177** BR77
Dudley Rd, E17 . . . . **123** EA54
N3 . . . . **120** DB54
NW6 . . . . **4** F10
SW19 . . . . **202** DA93
Ashford TW15 . . . . **196** BM92
Feltham TW14 . . . . **197** BQ88
Harrow HA2 . . . . **138** CC61
Ilford IG1 . . . . **147** EP63
Kingston upon Thames KT1 . **220** CM97
Northfleet DA11 . . . . **212** GE87
Richmond TW9 . . . . **180** CM82
Romford RM3 . . . . **128** FK51
Southall UB2 . . . . **178** BX75
Walton-on-Thames KT12 . . . **217** BU100
Dudley St, W2 . . . . **16** A7
Dudlington Rd, E5 . . . . **144** DW61
Dudmaston Ms, SW3 . . . . **28** B10
Dudrich Cl, N11 . . . . **120** DF51
Dudrich Ms, SE22 . . . . **204** DT85
Dudsbury Rd, Dart. DA1 . . . . . . **209** FG86
Sidcup DA14 . . . . **208** EV93
Dudset La, Houns.TW5 . . . . **177** BU81
Duffell Ho, SE11 . . . . **30** D10
Dufferin Av, EC1 . . . . **19** L5
Dufferin St, EC1 . . . . **19** K5
Duffield Cl, Grays (Daniel Cl)
RM16 . . . . **192** FY75
Grays (Davis Rd) RM16 . . . . . **192** FZ76
Harrow HA1 . . . . **139** CF57
Duffield Dr, N15 . . . . **144** DT56
Duffield La, Stoke P. SL2 . . . . . **154** AT65
Duffield Pk, Stoke P. SL2 . . . . . **154** AU69
Duffield Rd, Walt.Hill KT20 . . . **255** CV124
Duffins Orchard, Ott. KT16 . . . . **233** BC108
Duff St, E14 . . . . **22** C9
Dufour's Pl, W1 . . . . **17** M9
Dugard Way, SE11 . . . . **30** G8
Dugdale Hill La, Pot.B. EN6 . . . . **85** CY33
Dugdales, Crox.Grn WD3 . . . . . . **96** BN42
Duggan Dr, Chis. BR7 . . . . **206** EL92
Dugolly Av, Wem. HA9 . . . . **140** CP62
Duke Gdns, Ilf. IG6
off Duke Rd **147** ER56
Duke Humphrey Rd, SE3 . . . . . . **47** K6
Duke of Cambridge Cl, Twick.
TW2 . . . . **199** CD86
Duke of Edinburgh Rd, Sutt.
SM1 . . . . **222** DD103
Duke of Wellington Av, SE18 . . . **37** P7
Duke of Wellington Pl, SW1 . . . . **29** H4
Duke of York Sq, SW3 . . . . **28** F9
Duke of York St, SW1 . . . . **29** M2
Duke Pl, Slou. SL1
off Montague Rd **154** AT73
Duke Rd, W4 . . . . **180** CR78
Ilford IG6 . . . . **147** ER56
Dukes Av, N3 . . . . **120** DB53
N10 . . . . **143** DJ55
W4 . . . . **180** CR78
Edgware HA8 . . . . **118** CM51
Grays RM17 . . . . **192** GA75
Harrow HA1 . . . . **139** CE56
Hounslow TW4 . . . . **178** BY84
Kingston upon Thames KT2 . **199** CJ91
New Malden KT3 . . . . **221** CT97
North Harrow HA2 . . . . **138** BZ58
Northolt UB5 . . . . **158** BY66
Richmond TW10 . . . . **199** CJ91
Theydon Bois CM16 . . . . **107** ES35
Dukes Cl, Ashf.TW15 . . . . **197** BQ91
Gerrards Cross SL9 . . . . **134** AX60
Hampton TW12 . . . . **198** BZ92
North Weald Bassett CM16 . . **93** FB27
● **Dukes Ct**, Wok. GU21 . . . . **249** AZ117
Dukes Ct, E6 . . . . **167** EN67
Dukes Dr, Slou. SL2 . . . . **133** AM64
Dukes Gate, W4 *off Acton La* . . **180** CQ77
Dukes Grn Av, Felt.TW14 . . . . . . **197** BU85
Dukes Head Yd, N6
off Highgate High St **143** DH60
Dukes Hill, Wold. CR3 . . . . **259** DY120
Duke Shore Pl, E14 . . . . **33** N1
Duke Shore Wf, E14 . . . . **33** M1
Dukes Kiln Dr, Ger.Cr. SL9 . . . . **134** AW60
Dukes La, W8 . . . . **27** K4
Gerrards Cross SL9 . . . . **134** AY59
Dukes Lo, Nthwd. HA6
off Eastbury Av **115** BS50
Duke's Meadows, W4 . . . . **180** CR81
Dukes Ms, N10 . . . . **143** DH55
Duke's Ms, W1 . . . . **17** H8
Dukes Orchard, Bex. DA5 . . . . . . **209** FC88
● **Dukes Pk**, Harl. CM20 . . . . **57** ET12
Duke's Pas, E17 . . . . **145** EC56
Dukes Pl, EC3 . . . . **19** P9
Dukes Ride, Ger.Cr. SL9 . . . . . . **134** AY60
North Holmwood RH5 . . . . . . **285** CK139
Uxbridge UB10 . . . . **136** BL63
Dukes Rd, E6 . . . . **167** EN67
W3 . . . . **160** CN71
Duke's Rd, WC1 . . . . **17** P3
Dukes Rd, Hersham KT12 . . . . . **236** BX106
Dukesthorpe Rd, SE26 . . . . **205** DX91
Duke St, SW1 . . . . **29** M2
W1 . . . . **17** H8
Hoddesdon EN11 . . . . **71** EA16
Richmond TW9 . . . . **179** CK84
Sutton SM1 . . . . **240** DD105
Watford WD17 . . . . **98** BW41
Windsor SL4 . . . . **173** AP80
Woking GU21 . . . . **249** AZ117
Duke St Hill, SE1 . . . . **31** M2
Dukes Valley, Ger.Cr. SL9 . . . . . **134** AV61
Dukes Way, Berk. HP4 . . . . **60** AU17
Uxbridge UB8
off Waterloo Rd **156** BJ67
West Wickham BR4 . . . . **226** EE104
Dukes Wd Av, Ger.Cr. SL9 . . . . **134** AY60
Dukes Wd Dr, Ger.Cr. SL9 . . . . **134** AW60
Duke's Yd, W1 . . . . **17** H10
Dulas St, N4 . . . . **143** DM60
Dulford St, W11 . . . . **14** E10
Dulka Rd, SW11 . . . . **202** DF85
Sch **Dulverton Prim Sch**, SE9
off Dulverton Rd **207** ER89
Dulverton Rd, SE9 . . . . **207** EQ89
Romford RM3 . . . . **128** FK51
Ruislip HA4 . . . . **137** BU60
South Croydon CR2 . . . . **242** DW110
DULWICH, SE21 . . . . **204** DS87
Sch **Dulwich Coll**, SE21
off College Rd **204** DS89
★ **Dulwich Coll Picture Gall**,
SE21 . . . . **204** DS87
Sch **Dulwich Coll Prep Sch**,
SE21 *off Alleyn Pk* **204** DS90
Dulwich Common, SE21 . . . . . . **204** DS88
SE22 . . . . **204** DS88
H **Dulwich Comm Hosp**,
SE22 . . . . **184** DS84
Sch **Dulwich Hamlet Jun Sch**,
SE21 *off Dulwich Village* . . . **204** DS86
Dulwich Lawn Cl, SE22
off Colwell Rd **204** DT85
Dulwich Oaks, The, SE21 . . . . . **204** DS90
Dulwich Ri Gdns, SE22
off Lordship La **204** DT85
Dulwich Rd, SE24 . . . . **203** DN85
Dulwich Village, SE21 . . . . **204** DS86
Sch **Dulwich Village C of E Inf Sch**, SE21
off Dulwich Village **204** DS86
Dulwich Way, Crox.Grn WD3 . . . **96** BN43
Dulwich Wd Av, SE19 . . . . **204** DS91
Dulwich Wd Pk, SE19 . . . . **204** DS91
Dumas Way, Wat. WD18 . . . . **97** BS42
Dumbarton Av, Wal.Cr. EN8 . . . . **89** DX34
Dumbarton Rd, SW2 . . . . **203** DL86
Dumbleton Cl, Kings.T. KT1
off Gloucester Rd **220** CP95
Dumbletons, The, Map.Cr.
WD3 . . . . **113** BE49
Dumbreck Rd, SE9 . . . . **187** EM84
Dumfries Cl, Wat. WD19 . . . . . . **115** BT48
Dumont Rd, N16 . . . . **144** DS62
Dumpton Pl, NW1 . . . . **6** G7
Dumsey Eyot, Cher. KT16 . . . . . **216** BK101
Dumville Dr, Gdse. RH9 . . . . . . **274** DV131
Dunally Pk, Shep.TW17 . . . . . . **217** BR101
Dunbar Av, SW16 . . . . **223** DN96
Beckenham BR3 . . . . **225** DY98
Dagenham RM10 . . . . **148** FA62
Dunbar Cl, Hayes UB4 . . . . **157** BU71
Slough SL2 . . . . **154** AU72
Dunbar Ct, Sutt. SM1 . . . . **240** DD106
Walton-on-Thames KT12 . . . **218** BW103
Dunbar Gdns, Dag. RM10 . . . . . **148** FA64
Dunbar Rd, E7 . . . . **13** P5
N22 . . . . **121** DN53
New Malden KT3 . . . . **220** CQ98
Dunbar St, SE27 . . . . **204** DQ90
Dunblane Cl, Edg. HA8
off Tayside Dr **118** CP47
Dunblane Rd, SE9 . . . . **186** EL83
Dunboe Pl, Shep.TW17 . . . . . . **217** BQ101
Dunboyne Pl, Old Wind. SL4 . . **174** AU84
Dunboyne Rd, NW3 . . . . **6** E2
Dunbridge Ho, SW15
off Highcliffe Dr **201** CT86
Dunbridge St, E2 . . . . **20** D4
Duncan Cl, Barn. EN5 . . . . **102** DC42
Welwyn Garden City AL7 . . . . **51** CY10
Duncan Dr, Guil. GU1 . . . . **265** BA133
Duncan Gdns, Stai.TW18 . . . . . **196** BG93
Duncan Gro, W3 . . . . **160** CS72
Duncannon Cres, Wind. SL4 . . **173** AK83
Duncannon Pl, Green. DA9 . . . **191** FW84
Duncannon St, WC2 . . . . **30** A1
Duncan Rd, E8 . . . . **10** E8
Richmond TW9 . . . . **180** CL84
Tadworth KT20 . . . . **255** CY119
Duncan St, N1 . . . . **8** G10
Duncans Yd, West.TN16
off Market Sq **277** ER126
Duncan Ter, N1 . . . . **18** G1
Duncan Way, Bushey WD23 . . . . **98** BZ40
Dunch St, E1 . . . . **20** F9
Duncombe Cl, Amer. HP6 . . . . . . **77** AS38
Hertford SG14 . . . . **54** DQ07
Duncombe Ct, Stai.TW18 . . . . . **195** BF94
Duncombe Hill, SE23 . . . . **205** DY87
Sch **Duncombe Prim Sch**,
N19 *off Sussex Way* **143** DL60
Duncombe Rd, N19 . . . . **143** DK60
Hertford SG14 . . . . **54** DQ08
Northchurch HP4 . . . . **60** AS17
Sch **Duncombe Sch**,
Hert. SG14
off Warren Pk Rd **54** DQ08
Duncrievie Rd, SE13 . . . . **205** ED86
Duncroft, SE18 . . . . **187** ES80
Windsor SL4 . . . . **173** AM83
Duncroft Cl, Reig. RH2 . . . . **271** CZ133
Dundalk Rd, SE4 . . . . **185** DY83
Dundas Gdns, W.Mol. KT8 . . . . **218** CB97
Dundas Ms, Enf. EN3 . . . . **105** EA37
Dundas Rd, SE15 . . . . **44** G8
Dundee Ho, W9 . . . . **15** N2
Dundee Rd, E13 . . . . **24** A1
SE25 . . . . **224** DV99
Slough SL1 . . . . **153** AM72
Dundee St, E1 . . . . **32** E3
Dundee Way, Enf. EN3 . . . . **105** DY41
Dundee Wf, E14 . . . . **33** N1
Dundela Gdns, Wor.Pk. KT4 . . . **239** CV105
Dundonald Cl, E6 . . . . **25** H8
Sch **Dundonald Prim Sch**, SW19
off Dundonald Rd **201** CZ94
Tra **Dundonald Road** **201** CZ94
Dundonald Rd, NW10 . . . . **4** C9
SW19 . . . . **201** CY94
Dundrey Cres, Merst. RH1 . . . . . **273** DL129
Dunedin Dr, Cat. CR3 . . . . **274** DS125
Dunedin Ho, E16
off Manwood St **37** K3
Dunedin Rd, E10 . . . . **145** EB62
Ilford IG1 . . . . **147** EQ60
Rainham RM13 . . . . **169** FF69
Dunedin Way, Hayes UB4 . . . . . **158** BW70
Dunelm Gro, SE27 . . . . **204** DQ91
Dunelm St, E1 . . . . **21** J8
Dunfee Way, W.Byf. KT14 . . . . . . **234** BL112
Dunfield Gdns, SE6 . . . . **205** EB91
Dunfield Rd, SE6 . . . . **205** EB92
Dunford Rd, N7 . . . . **8** D1
Dungarvan Av, SW15 . . . . **181** CU84
Dungates La, Buckland RH3 . . . **271** CU133
Dunheved Cl, Th.Hth. CR7 . . . . **223** DN100
Dunheved Rd N, Th.Hth. CR7 . . **223** DN100
Dunheved Rd S, Th.Hth. CR7 . . **223** DN100
Dunheved Rd W, Th.Hth. CR7 . . **223** DN100
Dunhill Pt, SW15
off Dilton Gdns **201** CV88
Dunholme Grn, N9 . . . . **122** DT48
Dunholme La, N9
off Dunholme Rd **122** DT48
Dunholme Rd, N9 . . . . **122** DT48
Dunkeld Rd, SE25 . . . . **224** DR98
Dagenham RM8 . . . . **148** EV61
Dunkellin Gro, S.Ock. RM15 . . . **171** FU71
Dunkellin Way, S.Ock. RM15 . . . **171** FU72
Dunkery Rd, SE9 . . . . **206** EK91
Dunkin Rd, Dart. DA1 . . . . **190** FN84
Dunkirk Cl, Grav. DA12 . . . . **213** GJ92
Dunkirks Ms, Hert. SG13
off Queens Rd **54** DR11
Dunkirk St, SE27 . . . . **204** DQ91
Dunlace Rd, E5 . . . . **11** H2
Dunleary Cl, Houns.TW4 . . . . . . **198** BZ87
Dunley Dr, New Adgtn CR0 . . . **243** EB108
Dunlin Cl, Red. RH1 . . . . **288** DE139
Dunlin Ct, Enf. EN3
off Teal Cl **104** DW36
Dunlin Ho, W13 . . . . **159** CF70
Dunlin Ri, Guil. GU4 . . . . **265** BD132
Dunlin Rd, Hem.H. HP2 . . . . **62** BL15
Dunloe Av, N17 . . . . **144** DR55
Dunloe St, E2 . . . . **20** A1
Dunlop Cl, Dart. DA1 . . . . **190** FL83
Tilbury RM18
off Dunlop Rd **193** GF82
Dunlop Pl, SE16 . . . . **32** B7
Dunlop Rd, Til. RM18 . . . . **193** GF81
Dunmail Dr, Pur. CR8 . . . . **242** DS114
Dunmore Pt, E2 . . . . **20** A3
Dunmore Rd, NW6 . . . . **4** E9
SW20 . . . . **221** CW95
Dunmow Cl, Felt.TW13 . . . . **198** BX91
Loughton IG10 . . . . **106** EL44
Romford RM6 . . . . **148** EW57
Dunmow Dr, Rain. RM13 . . . . . . **169** FF67
Dunmow Ho, Dag. RM9 . . . . **168** EV67
Dunmow Rd, E15 . . . . **13** H1
Dunmow Wk, N1 . . . . **9** J8
Dunnage Cres, SE16 . . . . **33** M8
Dunnets, Knap. GU21 . . . . **248** AS117
Dunning Cl, S.Ock. RM15 . . . . . **171** FU72
Dunningford Cl, Horn. RM12 . . **149** FF64
Sch **Dunningford Prim Sch**,
Elm Pk RM12
off Upper Rainham Rd **149** FF64
Dunn Mead, NW9
off Field Mead **119** CT52
Dunnock Cl, N9 . . . . **123** DX46
Borehamwood WD6 . . . . **100** CN42
Dunnock Rd, E6 . . . . **25** H8
Dunns Pas, WC1 . . . . **18** B8
Dunn St, E8 . . . . **10** A2
Dunny La, Chipper. WD4 . . . . **79** BE32
Dunnymans Rd, Bans. SM7 . . . **255** CZ115
Dunollie Pl, NW5 . . . . **7** M2
Dunollie Rd, NW5 . . . . **7** L2
Dunoon Rd, SE23 . . . . **204** DW87
Dunottar Cl, Red. RH1 . . . . **288** DD136
Sch **Dunottar Sch**, Reig. RH2
off High Trees Rd **288** DD135
Dunraven Av, Red. RH1 . . . . . . **289** DH141
Dunraven Dr, Enf. EN2 . . . . **103** DN40
Dunraven Rd, W12 . . . . **161** CU74
Sch **Dunraven Sch**, Lwr Sch, SW16
off Mount Nod Rd **203** DM90
Upr Sch, SW16
off Leigham Ct Rd **203** DM90
Dunraven St, W1 . . . . **16** F10
Dunsany Rd, W14 . . . . **26** C7
Dunsborough Pk, Ripley GU23 . **250** BJ120
Dunsbury Cl, Sutt. SM2
off Nettlecombe Cl **240** DB109
Dunsdon Av, Guil. GU2 . . . . **280** AV135
Dunsfold Ri, Couls. CR5 . . . . . . **241** DK113
Dunsfold Way, New Adgtn CR0 . **243** EB108
Dunsford Way, SW15 . . . . **201** CV86
Dunsmore Cl, Bushey WD23 . . . . **99** CD44
Hayes UB4 . . . . **158** BX70
Dunsmore Rd, Walt. KT12 . . . . **217** BV100
Dunsmore Way, Bushey
WD23 . . . . **99** CD44
Dunsmure Rd, N16 . . . . **144** DS60
Dunspring La, Ilf. IG5 . . . . **125** EP54
Dunstable Cl, Rom. RM3
off Dunstable Rd **128** FK51
Dunstable Ms, W1 . . . . **17** H6
Dunstable Rd, Rich.TW9 . . . . . . **180** CL84
Romford RM3 . . . . **128** FK51
West Molesey KT8 . . . . **218** BZ98
Dunstall Grn, Chobham GU24 . **232** AW109
Dunstall Rd, SW20 . . . . **201** CV93
Dunstalls, Harl. CM19 . . . . **73** EN19
Dunstall Way, W.Mol. KT8 . . . . **218** CB97
● **Dunstall Welling Est**, Well.
DA16 *off Leigh Pl* **188** EV82
Dunstan Cl, N2
off Thomas More Way **142** DC55
Dunstan Ct, Whyt. CR3
off Godstone Rd **258** DU119
Dunstan Ho, E1
off Stepney Grn **21** H6
Dunstan Rd, NW11 . . . . **141** CZ60
Coulsdon CR5 . . . . **257** DK117
Dunstans Gro, SE22 . . . . **204** DV86
Dunstans Rd, SE22 . . . . **204** DU87
Dunster Av, Mord. SM4 . . . . **221** CX102
Dunster Cl, Barn. EN5 . . . . **101** CX42
Harefield UB9 . . . . **114** BH53
Romford RM5 . . . . **127** FC54
Dunster Ct, EC3 . . . . **19** N10
Borehamwood WD6
off Kensington Way **100** CR41
Dunster Cres, Horn. RM11 . . . . . **150** FN61
Dunster Dr, NW9 . . . . **140** CQ60
Dunster Gdns, NW6 . . . . **5** H6
Slough SL1 *off Avebury* **153** AN73
Dunsters Mead, Welw.G.C. AL7 . **52** DA11
Dunsterville Way, SE1 . . . . **31** M5
Dunster Way, Har. HA2 . . . . **138** BY62
Wallington SM6
off Helios Rd **222** DG102
Dunston Rd, E8 . . . . **10** A9
SW11 . . . . **41** H9
Dunston St, E8 . . . . **10** A8
Dunton Cl, Surb. KT6 . . . . **220** CL102
DUNTON GREEN, Sev.TN13 . . . **263** FC119
⇌ **Dunton Green** **263** FF119
Sch **Dunton Grn Prim Sch**,
Dunt.Grn TN13
off London Rd **263** FE120
Dunton Rd, E10 . . . . **145** EB59
SE1 . . . . **32** A10
Romford RM1 . . . . **149** FE56
Duntshill Rd, SW18 . . . . **202** DB88
Dunvegan Cl, W.Mol. KT8 . . . . . **218** CB98
Dunvegan Rd, SE9 . . . . **187** EM84
Dunwich Rd, Bexh. DA7 . . . . **188** EZ81
Dunworth Ms, W11 . . . . **14** G8
Duplex Ride, SW1 . . . . **28** F5
Dupont Rd, SW20 . . . . **221** CX96
Duppas Av, Croy. CR0
off Violet La **241** DP105
Duppas Cl, Shep.TW17 . . . . **217** BR99
Duppas Hill La, Croy. CR0
off Duppas Hill Rd **241** DP105
Duppas Hill Rd, Croy. CR0 . . . . **241** DP105
Duppas Hill Ter, Croy. CR0 . . . . **223** DP104
Sch **Duppas Jun Sch**, Croy.
CR0 *off Goodwin Rd* **241** DP106
Duppas Rd, Croy. CR0 . . . . **223** DN104
Dupre Cl, Chaff.Hun. RM16 . . . **192** FY76
Slough SL1 . . . . **173** AL75
Dupre Cres, Beac. HP9 . . . . **111** AP54
Dupree Rd, SE7 . . . . **36** A10
Du Pre Wk, Woob.Grn HP10
off Stratford Dr **132** AD59
Dura Den Cl, Beck. BR3 . . . . **205** EB94
Durand Cl, Cars. SM5 . . . . **222** DF102
Durand Gdns, SW9 . . . . **42** D6
Sch **Durand Prim Sch**, SW9 . . . . **42** D6
Cowley Rd Annexe, SW9 . . . **42** F7
Durands Wk, SE16 . . . . **33** M4
Durand Way, NW10 . . . . **160** CQ66
Durant Rd, Swan. BR8 . . . . **209** FG93
Durants Pk Av, Enf. EN3 . . . . . . **105** DX42
Durants Rd, Enf. EN3 . . . . **104** DW42
Sch **Durants Sch**, Enf. EN3
off Pitfield Way **104** DW39
Durant St, E2 . . . . **20** C2
Durban Gdns, Dag. RM10 . . . . . **169** FC66
Durban Rd, E15 . . . . **23** J2
E17 . . . . **123** DZ53
N17 . . . . **122** DS51
SE27 . . . . **204** DQ91
Beckenham BR3 . . . . **225** DZ96
Ilford IG2 . . . . **147** ES60
Durban Rd E, Wat. WD18 . . . . . . **97** BU42
Durban Rd W, Wat. WD18 . . . . . . **97** BU42
Durbin Rd, Chess. KT9 . . . . **238** CL105
Sch **Durdans Pk Prim Sch**, Sthl.
UB1 *off King Georges Dr* . . . **158** BZ71
Durdans Rd, Sthl. UB1 . . . . **158** BZ72
Durell Gdns, Dag. RM9 . . . . **148** EX64
Durell Rd, Dag. RM9 . . . . **148** EX64
Durfey Pl, SE5 . . . . **43** M4
Durfold Dr, Reig. RH2 . . . . **272** DC134
Durford Cres, SW15 . . . . **201** CU88
Durham Av, Brom. BR2 . . . . **226** EF98
Hounslow TW5 . . . . **178** BZ78
Romford RM2 . . . . **150** FJ56
Slough SL1 . . . . **153** AN72
Woodford Green IG8 . . . . **124** EK50
Durham Cl, SW20
off Durham Rd **221** CV96
Guildford GU2 . . . . **264** AT132
Sawbridgeworth CM21 . . . . . . **58** EW06
Stanstead Abbotts SG12 . . . . **55** EB10
Durham Hill, Brom. BR1 . . . . **206** EF91
Durham Ho St, WC2 . . . . **30** B1
Durham Pl, SW3 . . . . **40** E1
Ilford IG1 *off Eton Rd* **147** EQ63
Durham Ri, SE18 . . . . **187** EQ78
Durham Rd, E12 . . . . **146** EK63
E16 . . . . **23** K5
N2 . . . . **142** DE55
N7 . . . . **143** DM61
N9 . . . . **122** DU47
SW20 . . . . **221** CV95
W5 . . . . **179** CK76
Borehamwood WD6 . . . . **100** CQ41
Bromley BR2 . . . . **226** EF97
Dagenham RM10 . . . . **149** FC64
Feltham TW14 . . . . **198** BW87
Harrow HA1 . . . . **138** CB57
Sidcup DA14 . . . . **208** EV92
Durham Row, E1 . . . . **21** K7
Durham St, SE11 . . . . **42** C1
Durham Ter, W2 . . . . **15** L8
Durham Wf Dr, Brent.TW8 . . . . **179** CJ80
Durham Yd, E2 . . . . **20** E2
Duriun Way, Erith DA8 . . . . **189** FH80
Durleston Pk Dr, Bkhm KT23 . . **268** CC125
Durley Av, Pnr. HA5 . . . . **138** BY59
Durley Gdns, Orp. BR6 . . . . **246** EV105
Durley Rd, N16 . . . . **144** DS59
Durlston Rd, E5 . . . . **144** DU61
Kingston upon Thames KT2 . **200** CL93
Durndale La, Nthflt DA11 . . . . . **213** GF91
Durnell Way, Loug. IG10 . . . . . . **107** EN41
Durnford St, N15 . . . . **144** DS57
SE10 . . . . **46** F3
Durning Rd, SE19 . . . . **204** DR92
Durnsford Av, SW19 . . . . **202** DA89
Durnsford Ct, Enf. EN3
off Enstone Rd **105** DY41
Durnsford Rd, N11 . . . . **121** DK53
SW19 . . . . **202** DA89
Durrants Cl, Rain. RM13 . . . . . . **170** FJ68
Durrants Dr, Crox.Grn WD3 . . . . **97** BQ42
Durrants Hill Rd, Hem.H. HP3 . . **62** BK23
Durrants La, Berk. HP4 . . . . **60** AT18
Durrants Path, Chesh. HP5 . . . . . **76** AN27
Durrants Rd, Berk. HP4 . . . . **60** AT18
Durrant Way, Orp. BR6 . . . . **245** ER106
Swanscombe DA10 . . . . **212** FY87
Durrell Rd, SW6 . . . . **38** G7
Durrell Way, Shep.TW17 . . . . . **217** BR100
Durrington Av, SW20 . . . . **221** CW95
Durrington Pk Rd, SW20 . . . . . **221** CW94
Durrington Rd, E5 . . . . **11** L1
Durrington Twr, SW8 . . . . **41** M8
Dursley Cl, SE3 . . . . **186** EJ82
Dursley Gdns, SE3 . . . . **186** EK81
Dursley Rd, SE3 . . . . **186** EJ82
Sch **Durston Ho Sch**, W5
off Castlebar Rd **159** CK72
Durward St, E1 . . . . **20** E6
Durweston Ms, W1 . . . . **16** F6
Durweston St, W1 . . . . **16** F6
Dury Falls Cl, Horn. RM11 . . . . . **150** FM60
Dury Rd, Barn. EN5 . . . . **101** CZ39
Dutch Barn Cl, Stanw.TW19 . . . **196** BK86
Dutch Elm Av, Wind. SL4 . . . . . . **174** AT80
Dutch Gdns, Kings.T. KT2 . . . . . **200** CP93
Dutch Yd, SW18
off Wandsworth High St **202** DA85
Dutton St, SE10 . . . . **46** E6
Dutton Way, Iver SL0 . . . . **155** BE72
Duxberry Cl, Brom. BR2
off Southborough La **226** EL99
Duxford Cl, Horn. RM12 . . . . . . **169** FH65
Duxford Ho, SE2
off Wolvercote Rd **188** EX75
Duxhurst La, Reig. RH2 . . . . **288** DB144
Duxons Turn, Hem.H. HP2
off Maylands Av **63** BP19
Dwight Ct, SW6 . . . . **38** F8
Dwight Rd, Wat. WD18 . . . . **115** BR45
Sch **Dycorts Sch**, Harold Hill
RM3 *off Settle Rd* **128** FN49
Dye Ho La, E3 . . . . **12** B9
Dyer Ct, Enf. EN3
off Manton Rd **105** EA37
Dyer's Bldgs, EC1 . . . . **18** E7
Dyers Fld, Smallfield RH6 . . . . . **291** DP148
Dyers Hall Rd, E11 . . . . **146** EE60
Dyers La, SW15 . . . . **181** CV84
Dyers Way, Rom. RM3 . . . . **127** FH52
Dyke Dr, Orp. BR5 . . . . **228** EW102
Dykes Path, Wok. GU21
off Bentham Av **249** BC115
Dykes Way, Brom. BR2 . . . . **226** EF97
Dykewood Cl, Bex. DA5 . . . . **209** FE90
Dylan Cl, Els. WD6 . . . . **117** CK45
Dylan Rd, SE24 . . . . **183** DP84
Belvedere DA17 . . . . **188** FA76
Dylways, SE5 . . . . **184** DR84
Dymchurch Cl, Ilf. IG5 . . . . **125** EN54
Orpington BR6 . . . . **245** ES105
Dymes Path, SW19
off Queensmere Rd **201** CX89
Dymock St, SW6 . . . . **39** L10
Dymoke Grn, St.Alb. AL4 . . . . **65** CG16
Dymoke Rd, Horn. RM11 . . . . . . **149** FF59
Dymokes Way, Hodd. EN11 . . . . . **55** EA14
Dymond Est, SW17
off Glenburnie Rd **202** DE90
Dyneley Rd, SE12 . . . . **206** EJ91
Dyne Rd, NW6 . . . . **4** F7
Dynevor Rd, N16 . . . . **144** DS62
Richmond TW10 . . . . **200** CL85
Dynham Rd, NW6 . . . . **5** J6
Dyott St, WC1 . . . . **18** A8
Dyrham La, Barn. EN5 . . . . **101** CU36
Dysart Av, Kings.T. KT2 . . . . **199** CJ92
Sch **Dysart Sch**, Surb. KT6
off Ewell Rd **220** CM101
Dysart St, EC2 . . . . **19** M5
Dyson Cl, Wind. SL4 . . . . **173** AP83
Dyson Rd, E11 . . . . **146** EE58
E15 . . . . **13** M5
Dysons Cl, Wal.Cr. EN8 . . . . **89** DX33
Dysons Rd, N18 . . . . **122** DV50

E

Eade Rd, N4 ... 144 DQ59
Eagans Cl, N2 ... 142 DD55
Eagle Av, Rom. RM6 ... 148 EY58
Eagle Cl, SE16 ... 44 G1
Amersham HP6 ... 94 AT37
Enfield EN3 ... 104 DW42
Hornchurch RM12 ... 169 FH65
Wallington SM6 ... 241 DL107
Waltham Abbey EN9 ... 90 EG34
Eagle Ct, EC1 ... 18 G6
Hertford SG13 ... 54 DV08
Eagle Dr, NW9 ... 118 CS54
Eagle Hts, SW11
off Bramlands Cl ... 40 C10
Eagle Hill, SE19 ... 204 DR93
Eagle Ho Ms, SW4
off Narbonne Av ... 203 DJ85
Sch Eagle Ho Sch, Mitch.
CR4 off London Rd ... 222 DF96
Eagle La, E11 ... 146 EG56
Eagle Lo, NW11 ... 141 CZ59
Eagle Ms, N1 ... 9 N5
Eagle Pl, SW1 ... 29 M1
SW7 ... 27 P10
Eagle Rd, Guil. GU1 ... 280 AX135
London Heathrow Airport
TW6 ... 177 BT83
Wembley HA0 ... 159 CK66
Eagles Dr, Tats. TN16 ... 260 EK118
Eaglesfield Rd, SE18 ... 187 EP80
Eagles Rd, Green. DA9 ... 191 FV84
Eagle St, WC1 ... 18 C7
Eagle Ter, Wdf.Grn. IG8 ... 124 EH52
● Eagle Trd Est, Mitch. CR4 ... 222 DF100
Eagle Way, Gt Warley CM13 ... 129 FV51
Hatfield AL10 ... 67 CU20
Northfleet DA11 ... 212 GA85
Eagle Wf Rd, N1 ... 9 K10
Eagling Cl, E3 ... 22 B3
Sch Ealdham Prim Sch, SE9
off Eltham Sq ... 186 EJ84
Ealdham Sq, SE9 ... 186 EJ84
EALING, W5 ... 159 CJ73
Coll Ealing & W London Coll,
W5 off Ealing Grn ... 159 CK74
⇌ Ealing Broadway ... 159 CK73
⊖ Ealing Broadway ... 159 CK73
Ealing Bdy Shop Cen, W5 ... 159 CK73
Coll Ealing City Learning Cen,
W3 off Gunnersbury La ... 180 CN75
Ealing Cl, Borwd. WD6 ... 100 CR39
Sch Ealing Coll Upr Sch, W13
off The Avenue ... 159 CH72
★ Ealing Common, W5 ... 160 CL74
⊖ Ealing Common ... 160 CM74
Jct Ealing Common, W5 ... 160 CM73
Ealing Grn, W5 ... 159 CK74
H Ealing Hosp NHS Trust,
Sthl. UB1 ... 179 CD75
Coll Ealing Indep Coll, W5
off New Bdy ... 159 CJ73
Ealing Pk Gdns, W5 ... 179 CJ77
Ealing Rd, Brent. TW8 ... 179 CK78
Northolt UB5 ... 158 CA66
Wembley HA0 ... 159 CK67
Ealing Village, W5 ... 160 CL72
Eamont Cl, Ruis. HA4 ... 137 BP59
Eamont St, NW8 ... 6 C10
Eardemont Cl, Dart. DA1 ... 189 FF84
Eardley Cres, SW5 ... 39 K1
Eardley Pt, SE18 ... 37 P9
Sch Eardley Prim Sch, SW16
off Cunliffe St ... 203 DJ93
Eardley Rd, SW16 ... 203 DJ92
Belvedere DA17 ... 188 FA78
Sevenoaks TN13 ... 279 FH124
Earhart Way, Houns. TW4 ... 177 BU83
Earl Cl, N11 ... 121 DH50
Earldom Rd, SW15 ... 181 CW84
Earle Gdns, Kings.T. KT2 ... 200 CL93
Earleswood, Cob. KT11 ... 236 BX112
Earlham Gro, E7 ... 13 L3
N22 ... 121 DM52
Sch Earlham Prim Sch, E7 ... 13 M3
N22 off Earlham Gro ... 121 DN52
Earlham St, WC2 ... 17 P9
Earl Ri, SE18 ... 187 ER77
Earl Rd, SW14 ... 180 CQ84
Northfleet DA11 ... 212 GE89
Earlsbrook Rd, Red. RH1 ... 288 DF136
EARLS COURT, SW5 ... 27 H10
⊖ Earls Court ... 27 K9
★ Earls Court Exhib Cen,
SW5 ... 27 J10
Earls Ct Gdns, SW5 ... 27 L9
Earls Ct Rd, SW5 ... 27 K8
W8 ... 27 K8
Earls Ct Sq, SW5 ... 27 L10
Earls Cres, Har. HA1 ... 139 CE56
Earlsdown Ho, Bark. IG11
off Wheelers Cross ... 167 ER68
Earlsferry Way, N1 ... 8 B7
EARLSFIELD, SW18 ... 202 DC88
⇌ Earlsfield ... 202 DC88
Earlsfield, Holy. SL6 ... 172 AC77
Earlsfield Ho, Kings.T. KT2
off Kingsgate Rd ... 219 CK95
Sch Earlsfield Prim Sch, SW18
off Tranmere Rd ... 202 DC89
Earlsfield Rd, SW18 ... 202 DC88
Earlshall Rd, SE9 ... 187 EM84
Earls Ho, Rich. TW9
off Strand Dr ... 180 CP80
Earls La, Slou. SL1 ... 153 AM74
South Mimms EN6 ... 84 CS32
Earlsmead, Har. HA2 ... 138 BZ63
Sch Earlsmead First & Mid Sch,
S.Har. HA2 off Arundel Dr ... 138 BZ63
Sch Earlsmead Prim Sch, N15
off Broad La ... 144 DT57
Earlsmead Rd, N15 ... 144 DT57
NW10 ... 14 A2
Earl's Path, Loug. IG10 ... 106 EJ40
Earls Ter, W8 ... 27 H7
Earlsthorpe Ms, SW12 ... 202 DG86
Earlsthorpe Rd, SE26 ... 205 DX91
Earlstoke St, EC1 ... 18 G2
Earlston Gro, E9 ... 10 F9
Earl St, EC2 ... 19 N6
Watford WD17 ... 98 BW41
Earls Wk, W8 ... 27 J7
Dagenham RM8 ... 148 EV63
Earls Way, Orp. BR6
off Station Rd ... 227 ET103
EARLSWOOD, Red. RH1 ... 288 DF136
⇌ Earlswood ... 288 DF136
Earlswood Av, Th.Hth. CR7 ... 223 DN99
Earlswood Gdns, Ilf. IG5 ... 147 EN55
Sch Earlswood Inf & Nurs Sch,
Red. RH1
off St. John's Rd ... 288 DG135
Earlswood Rd, Red. RH1 ... 288 DF135
Earlswood St, SE10 ... 47 K1
Early Ms, NW1 ... 7 K8
Earnshaw St, WC2 ... 17 P8
Earsby St, W14 ... 26 F8
Easby Cres, Mord. SM4 ... 222 DB100
Easebourne Rd, Dag. RM8 ... 148 EW64
Easedale Dr, Horn. RM12 ... 149 FG64
Easedale Ho, Islw. TW7
off Summerwood Rd ... 199 CF85
Eashing Pt, SW15
off Wanborough Dr ... 201 CV88
Easington Pl, Guil. GU1
off Maori Rd ... 281 AZ135
Easington Way, S.Ock. RM15 ... 171 FU71
Easley's Ms, W1 ... 17 H8
EASNEYE, Ware SG12 ... 55 EC06
● East 10 Enterprise Pk, E10
off Argall Way ... 145 DY60
Coll East 15 Acting Sch, Loug.
IG10 off Rectory La ... 107 EP41
EAST ACTON, W3 ... 160 CR74
⊖ East Acton ... 161 CT72
East Acton La, W3 ... 160 CS73
Sch East Acton Prim Sch, W3
off East Acton La ... 160 CS73
East Arbour St, E1 ... 21 J8
East Av, E12 ... 166 EL66
E17 ... 145 EB56
Hayes UB3 ... 177 BT75
Southall UB1 ... 158 BZ73
Wallington SM6 ... 241 DM106
Whiteley Village KT12
off Octagon Rd ... 235 BT110
East Bk, N16 ... 144 DS59
Eastbank Rd, Hmptn H. TW12 ... 198 CC92
EAST BARNET, Barn. EN4 ... 102 DE44
East Barnet Rd, Barn. EN4 ... 102 DE44
Sch East Barnet Sch, Barn.
EN4 off Chestnut Gro ... 102 DF44
EAST BEDFONT, Felt. TW14 ... 197 BS88
Coll East Berkshire Coll, Langley
Campus, Langley SL3
off Station Rd ... 175 BA76
Windsor Campus, Wind. SL4
off St. Leonards Rd ... 173 AQ82
Eastbourne Av, W3 ... 160 CR72
Eastbourne Gdns, SW14 ... 180 CQ83
Eastbourne Ms, W2 ... 15 P8
Eastbourne Rd, E6 ... 25 M2
E15 ... 13 K9
N15 ... 144 DS58
SW17 ... 202 DG93
W4 ... 180 CQ79
Brentford TW8 ... 179 CJ78
Feltham TW13 ... 198 BX89
Godstone RH9 ... 274 DW132
Slough SL1 ... 153 AM72
Eastbourne Ter, W2 ... 15 P8
Eastbournia Av, N9 ... 122 DV48
Eastbridge, Slou. SL2 ... 174 AV75
Eastbrook Av, N9 ... 122 DW45
Dagenham RM10 ... 149 FC63
Eastbrook Cl, Wok. GU21 ... 249 BA116
Sch Eastbrook Comp Sch, Dag.
RM10 off Dagenham Rd ... 149 FC63
Eastbrook Dr, Rom. RM7 ... 149 FE62
Sch Eastbrook Prim Sch, Hem.H.
HP2 off St. Agnells La ... 62 BN15
Eastbrook Rd, SE3 ... 186 EH80
Waltham Abbey EN9 ... 90 EE33
Eastbrook Way, Hem.H. HP2 ... 62 BL20
EAST BURNHAM, Slou. SL2 ... 153 AN67
East Burnham La, Farn.Royal
SL2 ... 153 AN67
East Burrowfield, Welw.G.C.
AL7 ... 51 CX11
EASTBURY, Nthwd. HA6 ... 115 BS49
Eastbury Av, Bark. IG11 ... 167 ES67
Enfield EN1 ... 104 DS39
Northwood HA6 ... 115 BS50
Sch Eastbury Comp Sch, Bark.
IG11 off Rosslyn Rd ... 167 ES65
Eastbury Ct, Bark. IG11 ... 167 ES67
St. Albans AL1 ... 65 CF19
Sch Eastbury Fm JMI Sch & Nurs,
Nthwd. HA6 off Bishops Av ... 115 BT49
Eastbury Gro, W4 ... 180 CS78
★ Eastbury Manor Ho, Bark.
IG11 ... 167 ET67
Eastbury Pl, Nthwd. HA6
off Eastbury Av ... 115 BT50
Sch Eastbury Prim Sch, Bark.
IG11 off Dawson Av ... 167 ET66
Eastbury Rd, E6 ... 25 L5
Kingston upon Thames KT2 ... 200 CL94
Northwood HA6 ... 115 BS51
Petts Wood BR5 ... 227 ER100
Romford RM7 ... 149 FD58
Watford WD19 ... 115 BV45
Eastbury Sq, Bark. IG11 ... 167 ET67
Eastbury Ter, E1 ... 21 J5
Eastcastle St, W1 ... 17 L8
Eastcheap, EC3 ... 19 M10
East Churchfield Rd, W3 ... 160 CR74
East Ch Rd, Lon.Hthrw Air.
TW6 ... 177 BS82
EAST CLANDON, Guil. GU4 ... 266 BL131
East Cl, W5 ... 160 CN70
Barnet EN4 ... 102 DG42
Greenford UB6 ... 158 CC68
Rainham RM13 ... 169 FH70
St. Albans AL2 ... 82 CB25
Eastcombe Av, SE7 ... 186 EH79
East Common, Ger.Cr. SL9 ... 134 AY58
EASTCOTE, Pnr. HA5 ... 138 BW58
⊖ Eastcote ... 138 BW59
Eastcote, Orp. BR6 ... 227 ET102
Eastcote Av, Grnf. UB6 ... 139 CG64
Harrow HA2 ... 138 CB61
West Molesey KT8 ... 218 BZ99
Eastcote La, Har. HA2 ... 138 CA62
Northolt UB5 ... 158 CA66
Eastcote La N, Nthlt. UB5 ... 158 BZ65
Eastcote Pl, Pnr. HA5 ... 137 BV58
Sch Eastcote Prim Sch, Well.
DA16 off Eastcote Rd ... 187 ER83
Eastcote Rd, Eastcote Vill. HA5 ... 137 BU58
Harrow HA2 ... 138 CC62
Pinner HA5 ... 138 BX57
Ruislip HA4 ... 137 BS59
Welling DA16 ... 187 ER82
Eastcote St, SW9 ... 42 C9
Eastcote Vw, Pnr. HA5 ... 138 BW56
EASTCOTE VILLAGE, Pnr. HA5 ... 137 BV57
Eastcourt, Sun. TW16 ... 218 BW96
East Ct, Wem. HA0 ... 139 CJ61
Sch Eastcourt Sch, Ilf. IG3
off Eastwood Rd ... 148 EU60
East Cres, N11 ... 120 DF49
Enfield EN1 ... 104 DT43
Windsor SL4 ... 173 AM81
East Cres Rd, Grav. DA12 ... 213 GJ86
Eastcroft, Slou. SL2 ... 153 AP70
Eastcroft Rd, Epsom KT19 ... 238 CS108
East Cross Route, E3 ... 11 P6
E9 ... 11 M5
⇌ East Croydon ... 224 DR103
Tra East Croydon ... 224 DR103
Eastdean Av, Epsom KT18 ... 238 CP113
East Dene Dr, Harold Hill RM3 ... 128 FK50
Eastdown Pk, SE13 ... 185 ED84
East Dr, Cars. SM5 ... 240 DE109
Oaklands AL4 ... 66 CL19
Orpington BR5 ... 228 EV100
Sawbridgeworth CM21 ... 58 EY06
Stoke Poges SL2 ... 154 AS69
Virginia Water GU25 ... 214 AU101
Watford WD25 ... 97 BV35
East Duck Lees La, Enf. EN3 ... 105 DY42
EAST DULWICH, SE22 ... 204 DU86
⇌ East Dulwich ... 184 DS84
East Dulwich Gro, SE22 ... 204 DS86
East Dulwich Rd, SE15 ... 184 DT84
SE22 ... 184 DT84
EAST END GREEN, Hert. SG14 ... 53 DK13
East End Rd, N2 ... 142 DC55
N3 ... 120 DA54
East End Way, Pnr. HA5 ... 138 BY55
East Entrance, Dag. RM10 ... 169 FB68
Eastergate, Beac. HP9 ... 110 AJ51
Eastern Av, E11 ... 146 EJ58
Aveley RM15 ... 170 FQ74
Chertsey KT16 ... 216 BG97
Ilford IG2, IG4 ... 146 EL58
Pinner HA5 ... 138 BX59
Romford RM6 ... 148 EW56
Waltham Cross EN8 ... 89 DY33
West Thurrock RM20 ... 191 FT79
Eastern Av E, Rom. RM1,
RM2, RM3 ... 149 FD55
Eastern Av W, Rom. RM1,
RM5, RM6, RM7 ... 148 EY56
Eastern Dr, B.End SL8 ... 132 AC59
Eastern Gateway, E16 ... 36 D1
● Eastern Ind Est,
Erith DA18 ... 188 FA75
Eastern Pathway, Horn. RM12 ... 170 FJ67
Eastern Perimeter Rd,
Lon.Hthrw Air. TW6 ... 177 BT83
Eastern Quay Apts, E16
off Rayleigh Rd ... 36 B2
Eastern Rd, E13 ... 166 EH68
E17 ... 145 EC57
N2 ... 142 DF55
N22 ... 121 DL53
SE4 ... 185 EA84
Grays RM17 ... 192 GD77
Romford RM1 ... 149 FE57
Jct Eastern Rbt, Ilf. IG1 ... 147 EQ61
Eastern Vw, Bigg.H. TN16 ... 260 EJ117
Easternville Gdns, Ilf. IG2 ... 147 EQ58
Eastern Way, SE2 ... 168 EX74
SE28 ... 188 EU75
Belvedere DA17 ... 189 FB75
Erith DA18 ... 168 EX74
Grays RM17 ... 192 GA79
● Easter Pk, Rain. RM13 ... 169 FE73
EAST EWELL, Sutt. SM2 ... 239 CX110
East Ferry Rd, E14 ... 34 D8
Eastfield Av, Wat. WD24 ... 98 BX39
Eastfield Cl, Slou. SL1
off St. Laurence Way ... 174 AU76
Eastfield Cotts, Hayes UB3 ... 177 BR78
Eastfield Ct, St.Alb. AL4
off Southfield Way ... 65 CK17
Eastfield Gdns, Dag. RM10 ... 148 FA63
Eastfield Par, Pot.B. EN6 ... 86 DD32
Sch Eastfield Prim Sch, Enf.
EN3 off Eastfield Rd ... 105 DX38
Eastfield Rd, E17 ... 145 EA56
N8 ... 143 DL55
Brentwood CM14 ... 130 FX47
Burnham SL1 ... 152 AG71
Dagenham RM9, RM10 ... 148 FA63
Enfield EN3 ... 105 DX38
Redhill RH1 ... 289 DJ135
Waltham Cross EN8 ... 89 DY32
Eastfields, Pnr. HA5 ... 138 BW57
Eastfields Av, SW18 ... 182 DA84
Eastfields Rd, W3 ... 160 CQ71
Mitcham CR4 ... 222 DG96
Eastfield St, E14 ... 21 M7
EAST FINCHLEY, N2 ... 142 DD56
⊖ East Finchley ... 142 DE56
East Flint, Hem.H. HP1 ... 61 BF19
East Gdns, SW17 ... 202 DE93
Woking GU22 ... 249 BC117
Eastgate, Bans. SM7 ... 239 CY114
East Gate, Harl. CM20 ... 57 EQ14
● Eastgate Business Pk, E10 ... 145 DY60
Eastgate Cl, SE28 ... 168 EX72
Eastgate Gdns, Guil. GU1 ... 280 AY135
Eastglade, Nthwd. HA6 ... 115 BS50
Pinner HA5 ... 138 BY55
East Gorse, Croy. CR0 ... 243 DY112
East Grn, Hem.H. HP3 ... 80 BM25
East Hall La, Wenn. RM13 ... 170 FK72
East Hall Rd, Orp. BR5 ... 228 EY101
EAST HAM, E6 ... 24 F1
⊖ East Ham ... 166 EL66
Eastham Cl, Barn. EN5 ... 101 CY43
Eastham Cres, Brwd. CM13 ... 131 GA49
● East Ham Ind Est, E6 ... 24 G5
East Ham Manor Way, E6 ... 25 L8
East Ham Mkt Hall, E6
off Myrtle Rd ... 166 EL67
★ East Ham Nature Reserve
& Visitor Cen, E6 ... 25 K4
East Harding St, EC4 ... 18 F8
East Heath Rd, NW3 ... 142 DD62
East Hill, SW18 ... 202 DB85
Biggin Hill TN16 ... 260 EH118
Dartford DA1 ... 210 FM87
East Hill, Oxt. RH8 ... 276 EE129
South Croydon CR2 ... 242 DS110
South Darenth DA4 ... 230 FQ95
Wembley HA9 ... 140 CN61
Woking GU22 ... 249 BC116
East Hill Dr, Dart. DA1 ... 210 FM87
East Hill Rd, Oxt. RH8 ... 276 EE129
Eastholm, NW11 ... 142 DB56
East Holme, Erith DA8 ... 189 FD81
Eastholme, Hayes UB3 ... 157 BU74
EAST HORSLEY, Lthd. KT24 ... 267 BS127
DLR East India ... 23 H10
East India Dock Rd, E14 ... 21 P9
East India Way, Croy. CR0 ... 224 DT102
East Kent Av, Nthflt DA11 ... 212 GC86
Eastlake Ho, NW8
off Frampton St ... 16 B5
Eastlake Rd, SE5 ... 43 H9
Eastlands Cl, Oxt. RH8 ... 275 ED127
Eastlands Cres, SE21 ... 204 DT86
Eastlands Way, Oxt. RH8 ... 275 ED127
East La, SE16 ... 32 C5
Abbots Langley WD5 ... 81 BU29
Kingston upon Thames KT1
off High St ... 219 CK97
South Darenth DA4 ... 231 FR96
Watford WD25 ... 81 BU29
Wembley HA0, HA9 ... 139 CK62
West Horsley KT24 ... 267 BQ125
● East La Business Pk,
Wem. HA9 ... 139 CK62
Eastlea Av, Wat. WD25 ... 98 BY37
Sch Eastlea Comm Sch, E16 ... 23 K4
Eastlea Ms, E16 ... 23 K5
Eastleigh Av, Har. HA2 ... 138 CB61
Eastleigh Cl, NW2 ... 140 CS62
Sutton SM2 ... 240 DB108
Eastleigh Rd, E17 ... 123 DZ54
Bexleyheath DA7 ... 189 FC82
Eastleigh Wk, SW15 ... 201 CU87
Eastleigh Way, Felt. TW14 ... 197 BU88
East Lo La, Enf. EN2 ... 103 DK36
East Mall, Rom. RM1
off Mercury Gdns ... 149 FE57
H Eastman Dental Hosp, WC1 ... 18 C3
Eastman Rd, W3 ... 160 CR74
Eastman Way, Epsom KT19 ... 238 CP110
Hemel Hempstead HP2 ... 62 BN17
East Mascalls, SE7
off Mascalls Rd ... 186 EJ79
East Mead, Ruis. HA4 ... 138 BX62
Welwyn Garden City AL7 ... 52 DB12
Eastmead, Wok. GU21 ... 248 AV117
Eastmead Av, Grnf. UB6 ... 158 CB69
Eastmead Cl, Brom. BR1 ... 226 EL96
East Meads, Guil. GU2 ... 280 AT135
Eastmearn Rd, SE21 ... 204 DQ89
East Mill, Grav. DA11 ... 213 GF86
East Milton Rd, Grav. DA12 ... 213 GK87
East Mimms, Hem.H. HP2 ... 62 BL19
EAST MOLESEY, KT8 ... 219 CD98
Eastmont Rd, Esher KT10 ... 219 CE103
Eastmoor Pl, SE7 ... 36 E7
Eastmoor St, SE7 ... 36 E7
East Mt St, E1 ... 20 F7
Eastney Rd, Croy. CR0 ... 223 DP102
Eastney St, SE10 ... 46 G1
Eastnor, Bov. HP3 ... 79 BA28
Eastnor Cl, Reig. RH2 ... 287 CZ137
Eastnor Rd, SE9 ... 207 EQ88
Reigate RH2 ... 288 DA136
Easton Gdns, Borwd. WD6 ... 100 CR42
Easton St, WC1 ... 18 E3
Eastor, Welw.G.C. AL7 ... 52 DA06
East Pk, Harl. CM17 ... 58 EV12
Sawbridgeworth CM21 ... 58 EY06
East Pk Cl, Rom. RM6 ... 148 EX57
East Parkside, SE10 ... 35 L5
Warlingham CR6 ... 259 EA116
East Pas, EC1 ... 19 H6
East Pier, E1 ... 32 E3
East Pl, SE27
off Pilgrim Hill ... 204 DQ91
East Pt, SE1 ... 32 C10
East Poultry Av, EC1 ... 18 G7
⊖ East Putney ... 201 CY85
East Ramp, Lon.Hthrw Air.
TW6 ... 177 BP81
East Ridgeway, Cuffley EN6 ... 87 DK29
East Rd, E15 ... 13 N9
N1 ... 19 L3
SW3 ... 40 G1
SW19 ... 202 DC93
Barnet EN4 ... 120 DG46
Chadwell Heath RM6 ... 148 EY57
Edgware HA8 ... 118 CP53
Enfield EN3 ... 104 DW38
Feltham TW14 ... 197 BR87
Harlow CM20 ... 58 EV11
Kingston upon Thames KT2 ... 220 CL95
Reigate RH2 ... 271 CZ133
Rush Green RM7 ... 149 FD59
Welling DA16 ... 188 EV82
West Drayton UB7 ... 176 BM77
Weybridge KT13 ... 235 BR108
East Rochester Way, SE9 ... 187 ES84
Bexley DA5 ... 208 EX86
Sidcup DA15 ... 187 ES84
East Row, E11 ... 146 EG58
W10 ... 14 E5
Eastry Av, Brom. BR2 ... 226 EF100
Eastry Rd, Erith DA8 ... 188 FA80
East Shalford La, Guil. GU4 ... 280 AY139
EAST SHEEN, SW14 ... 180 CR84
East Sheen Av, SW14 ... 180 CR84
Sch East Sheen Prim Sch, SW14
off Upper Richmond Rd W ... 180 CS84
Eastside Ms, E3 ... 22 A1
Eastside Rd, NW11 ... 141 CZ56
East Smithfield, E1 ... 32 B1
East St, SE17 ... 31 K10
Barking IG11 ... 167 EQ66
Bexleyheath DA7 ... 188 FA84
Bookham KT23 ... 268 CB125
Brentford TW8 ... 179 CJ80
Bromley BR1 ... 226 EG96
Chertsey KT16 ... 216 BG101
Chesham HP5 ... 76 AP32
Epsom KT17 ... 238 CS113
Grays RM17 ... 192 GC79
Hemel Hempstead HP2 ... 62 BK20
South Stifford RM20 ... 192 FY79
Ware SG12 ... 55 DX06
Coll East Surrey College,
Gatton Pt N, Red. RH1
off Claremont Rd ... 272 DG130
Gatton Pt S, Red. RH1
off College Cres ... 272 DG131
East Surrey Gro, SE15 ... 44 A5
H East Surrey Hosp,
Red. RH1 ... 288 DG138
★ East Surrey Mus,
Cat. CR3 ... 258 DU124
East Tenter St, E1 ... 20 B9
East Ter, Grav. DA12 ... 213 GJ86
East Thurrock Rd, Grays RM17 ... 192 GB79
East Twrs, Pnr. HA5 ... 138 BX57
East Vale, W3 off The Vale ... 161 CT74
East Vw, E4 ... 123 EC50
Barnet EN5 ... 101 CZ41
Essendon AL9 ... 68 DF17
Eastview Av, SE18 ... 187 ES80
Eastville Av, NW11 ... 141 CZ58
East Wk, E.Barn. EN4 ... 120 DG45
Harlow CM20 ... 57 ER14
Hayes UB3 ... 157 BU74
Reigate RH2 ... 272 DB134
Eastway, E9 ... 11 N4
East Way, E11 ... 146 EH57
Eastway, Beac. HP9 ... 110 AG54
East Way, Brom. BR2 ... 226 EG101
Croydon CR0 ... 225 DY103
Eastway, Epsom KT19 ... 238 CQ112
Gatwick RH6 ... 291 DH152
East Way, Guil. GU2 ... 264 AT134
Hayes UB3 ... 157 BU75
Eastway, Mord. SM4 ... 221 CX99
East Way, Ruis. HA4 ... 137 BU60
Eastway, Wall. SM6 ... 241 DJ105
Eastway Cres, Har. HA2
off Eliot Dr ... 138 CB61
Eastwell Cl, Beck. BR3 ... 225 DY95
EASTWICK, Harl. CM20 ... 57 EP11
Eastwick Ct, SW19
off Victoria Dr ... 201 CX88
Eastwick Cres, Mill End WD3 ... 113 BF47
Eastwick Dr, Bkhm KT23 ... 252 CA123
Eastwick Hall La, Harl. CM20 ... 57 EN09
EAST WICKHAM, Well. DA16 ... 188 EU80
Sch East Wickham Inf Sch, Well.
DA16 off Wickham St ... 187 ET81
Sch East Wickham Jun Sch, Well.
DA16 off Wickham St ... 188 EU81
Sch Eastwick Inf Sch, Bkhm
KT23 off Eastwick Dr ... 252 CB124
Sch Eastwick Jun Sch, Bkhm
KT23 off Eastwick Dr ... 252 CB124
Jct Eastwick Lo Rbt,
Harl. CM20 ... 57 EQ11
Eastwick Pk Av, Bkhm KT23 ... 252 CB124
Eastwick Rd, Bkhm KT23 ... 268 CB125
Harlow CM20 ... 57 EM11
Hersham KT12 ... 235 BV106
Hunsdon SG12 ... 56 EK08
Stanstead Abbotts SG12 ... 56 EF12
Eastwick Row, Hem.H. HP2 ... 62 BN21
Eastwood Cl, E18
off George La ... 124 EG54
N7 ... 8 D2
N17
off Northumberland Gro ... 122 DV52
Eastwood Ct, Hem.H. HP2 ... 62 BN19
Eastwood Dr, Rain. RM13 ... 169 FH72
Eastwood Rd, E18 ... 124 EG54
N10 ... 120 DG54
Bramley GU5 ... 281 AZ144
Ilford IG3 ... 148 EU59
West Drayton UB7 ... 176 BN75
East Woodside, Bex. DA5 ... 208 EY88
Eastwood St, SW16 ... 203 DJ93
Eastworth Rd, Cher. KT16 ... 216 BG102
Eatington Rd, E10 ... 145 ED57
Eaton Av, Slou. SL1 ... 152 AJ73
Eaton Cl, SW1 ... 28 G9
Stanmore HA7 ... 117 CH49
Eaton Ct, Guil. GU1 ... 265 BA132
Eaton Dr, SW9 ... 183 DP84
Kingston upon Thames KT2 ... 200 CN94
Romford RM5 ... 127 FB52
Eaton Gdns, Brox. EN10 ... 71 DY22
Dagenham RM9 ... 168 EY66
Eaton Gate, SW1 ... 28 G8
Northwood HA6 ... 115 BQ51
Eaton Ho, E14
off Westferry Circ ... 33 P1
Eaton La, SW1 ... 29 K7
Eaton Ms N, SW1 ... 28 G8
Eaton Ms S, SW1 ... 29 H8
Eaton Ms W, SW1 ... 29 H8
Eaton Pk, Cob. KT11 ... 236 BY114
Eaton Pk Rd, N13 ... 121 DN47
Cobham KT11 ... 236 BY114
Eaton Pl, SW1 ... 28 G7
Eaton Ri, E11 ... 146 EJ57
W5 ... 159 CK72
Eaton Rd, NW4 ... 141 CW57
Enfield EN1 ... 104 DS41
Hemel Hempstead HP2 ... 63 BP17
Hounslow TW3 ... 179 CD84
St. Albans AL1 ... 65 CH20
Sidcup DA14 ... 208 EX89
Sutton SM2 ... 240 DD107
Upminster RM14 ... 151 FS61
Eaton Row, SW1 ... 29 J6
Eatons Mead, E4 ... 123 EA47
Eaton Sq, SW1 ... 29 J6
Longfield DA3
off Bramblefield Cl ... 231 FX97
Eaton Ter, SW1 ... 28 G8
Eaton Ter Ms, SW1 ... 28 G8
Eatonville Rd, SW17 ... 202 DF89
Eatonville Vil, SW17
off Eatonville Rd ... 202 DF89
Eaton Way, Borwd. WD6 ... 100 CM39
Eaves Cl, Add. KT15 ... 234 BJ107
Ebbas Way, Epsom KT18 ... 254 CP115
Ebb Ct, E16
off Albert Basin Way ... 167 EQ73
Ebbens Rd, Hem.H. HP3 ... 62 BK23
Ebbett Ct, W3
off Victoria Rd ... 160 CR71
Ebbisham Cl, Dor. RH4
off Nower Rd ... 285 CG136
Ebbisham Dr, SW8 ... 42 C2
Ebbisham La, Walt.Hill KT20 ... 255 CT121
Ebbisham Rd, Epsom KT18 ... 238 CP114
Worcester Park KT4 ... 221 CW103
⇌ Ebbsfleet International ... 212 GA86
Ebbsfleet Rd, NW2 ... 4 E2
Ebbsfleet Wk, Nthflt DA11 ... 212 GB86
Ebdon Way, SE3 ... 186 EH83
Ebenezer Ho, SE11 ... 30 F9
Ebenezer St, N1 ... 19 L2
Ebenezer Wk, SW16 ... 223 DJ95
Ebley Cl, SE15 ... 44 A3
Ebner St, SW18 ... 202 DB85
Ebor Cotts, SW15 ... 200 CS90
Ebor St, E1 ... 20 A4

Ebrington Rd, Har. HA3 139 CK58
Ebsworth Cl, Maid. SL6 152 AC68
Ebsworth St, SE23 205 DX87
Eburne Rd, N7 143 DL62
Ebury App, Rick. WD3
off Ebury Rd 114 BK46
Ebury Br, SW1 29 J10
Ebury Br Est, SW1 29 J10
Ebury Br Rd, SW1 41 H1
Ebury Cl, Kes. BR2 226 EL104
Northwood HA6 115 BQ50
Ebury Ms, SE27 203 DP90
SW1 29 H8
Ebury Ms E, SW1 29 J8
Ebury Rd, Rick. WD3 114 BK46
Watford WD17 98 BW41
Ebury Sq, SW1 29 H9
Ebury St, SW1 29 J8
Ebury Way Cycle Path, The,
Rick. WD3 115 BP45
Watford WD18 115 BP45
Ecclesbourne Cl, N13 121 DN50
Ecclesbourne Gdns, N13 121 DN50
Sch Ecclesbourne Inf Sch, Th.Hth.
CR7 off Bensham La 224 DQ99
Sch Ecclesbourne Jun Sch, Th.Hth.
CR7 off Bensham La 224 DQ99
Ecclesbourne Rd, N1 9 K7
Thornton Heath CR7 224 DQ99
Eccles Hill, N.Holm. RH5 285 CJ140
Eccles Rd, SW11 182 DF84
Eccleston Br, SW1 29 K8
Eccleston Cl, Cockfos. EN4 102 DF42
Orpington BR6 227 ER102
Eccleston Cres, Rom. RM6 148 EU59
Ecclestone Ct, Wem. HA9
off St. John's Rd 140 CL64
Ecclestone Pl, Wem. HA9 140 CM64
Eccleston Ms, SW1 29 H7
Eccleston Pl, SW1 29 J8
Eccleston Rd, W13 159 CG73
Eccleston Sq, SW1 29 K9
Eccleston Sq Ms, SW1 29 L9
Eccleston St, SW1 29 J7
Echelforde Dr, Ashf. TW15 196 BN91
Sch Echelford Prim Sch, The,
Ashf. TW15 off Park Rd 197 BP92
Echo Hts, E4 123 EB46
Echo Pit Rd, Guil. GU1 280 AY138
Echo Sq, Grav. DA12
off Old Rd E 213 GJ89
Eckford St, N1 8 E10
Eckington Ho, N15 144 DR58
Eckstein Rd, SW11 182 DE84
Eclipse Ho, N22
off Station Rd 121 DM54
Eclipse Rd, E13 24 A6
Ecob Cl, Guil. GU3 264 AT130
Sch Ecole Française de Londres,
W6 26 D8
Ecton Rd, Add. KT15 234 BH105
Ector Rd, SE6 206 EE89
Edbrooke Rd, W9 15 J4
Eddington Cres, Welw.G.C. AL7 51 CX12
Eddiscombe Rd, SW6 39 H8
Eddy Cl, Rom. RM7 149 FB58
Eddystone Rd, SE4 205 DY85
Eddystone Twr, SE8 33 M9
Eddystone Wk, Stai. TW19 196 BL87
Eddy St, Berk. HP4 60 AU18
Ede Cl, Houns. TW3 178 BZ83
Edenbridge Cl, SE16 44 F1
Orpington BR5 228 EX98
Edenbridge Rd, E9 11 K7
Enfield EN1 104 DS44
Eden Cl, NW3 142 DA61
W8 27 K6
Bexley DA5 209 FD91
Enfield EN3 105 EA38
New Haw KT15 234 BH110
Slough SL3 175 BA78
Wembley HA0 159 CK67
Edencourt Rd, SW16 203 DH93
Edencroft, Bramley GU5 281 AZ144
Edendale Rd, Bexh. DA7 189 FD81
Edenfield Gdns, Wor.Pk. KT4 221 CT104
Eden Grn, S.Ock. RM15 171 FV71
Eden Gro, E17 145 EB57
N7 8 D3
NW10 off St. Andrews Rd 161 CV65
Eden Gro Rd, Byfleet KT14 234 BL113
Edenhall Cl, Hem.H. HP2 63 BR21
Romford RM3 128 FJ50
Edenhall Glen, Rom. RM3 128 FJ50
Edenhall Rd, Rom. RM3 128 FJ50
Sch Edenham High Sch, Croy.
CR0 off Orchard Way 225 DZ101
Edenham Way, W10 14 G6
Eden Ho, SE16 off Canada St 33 J5
Edenhurst Av, SW6 38 G10
Eden Ms, SW17
off Huntspill St 202 DC90
EDEN PARK, Beck. BR3 225 EA99
⇌ Eden Park 225 EA99
Eden Pk Av, Beck. BR3 225 DY98
Eden Pl, Grav. DA12
off Lord St 213 GH87
Eden Rd, E17 145 EB57
SE27 203 DP92
Beckenham BR3 225 DY98
Bexley DA5 209 FC91
Croydon CR0 242 DR105
Edenside Rd, Bkhm KT23 252 BZ124
Edensor Gdns, W4 180 CS80
Edensor Rd, W4 180 CS80
Eden St, Kings.T. KT1 219 CK96
Edenvale, Goffs Oak EN7 88 DV29
Edenvale Cl, Mitch. CR4
off Edenvale Rd 202 DG94
Edenvale Rd, Mitch. CR4 202 DG94
Edenvale St, SW6 39 M9
Eden Wk, Kings.T. KT1
off Eden Wk Shop Cen 220 CL96
Eden Wk Shop Cen,
Kings.T. KT1 220 CL96
Eden Way, E3 off Old Ford Rd 11 P9
Beckenham BR3 225 DZ99
Warlingham CR6 259 DY118
Ederline Av, SW16 223 DM97
Edes Flds, Reig. RH2 287 CY136
Edgar Cl, Swan. BR8 229 FF97
Edgar Ho, E11 146 EG59
Edgar Kail Way, SE22 184 DS84
Edgarley Ter, SW6 38 E7
Edgar Rd, E3 22 D2
Hounslow TW4 198 BZ87
Romford RM6 148 EX59
South Croydon CR2 242 DR109
Tatsfield TN16 260 EK121
Edgar Rd, West Dr. UB7 156 BL73
Edgars Ct, Welw.G.C. AL7 51 CY10
Edgar Wallace Cl, SE15 43 P4
Edgbaston Dr, Shenley WD7 84 CL32
Edgbaston Rd, Wat. WD19 115 BV48
Edgeborough Way, Brom. BR1 206 EK94
Edgebury, Chis. BR7 207 EP91
Sch Edgebury Prim Sch, Chis.
BR7 off Belmont La 207 EQ91
Edgebury Wk, Chis. BR7 207 EQ91
● Edge Business Cen, NW2 141 CV61
Edge Cl, Wey. KT13 234 BN108
Edgecombe Ho, SW19 201 CY88
Edgecoombe, S.Croy. CR2 242 DW108
Edgecoombe Cl, Kings.T. KT2 200 CR94
Edgecote Cl, W3
off Cheltenham Pl 160 CQ74
Edgecot Gro, N15 144 DS57
Edgefield Av, Bark. IG11 167 ET66
Edgefield Cl, Dart. DA1 210 FP88
Redhill RH1 288 DG139
Sch Edge Gro Sch, Ald. WD25
off High Cross 98 CC37
Edge Hill, SE18 187 EP79
SW19 201 CX94
Edge Hill Av, N3 142 DA56
Edge Hill Ct, SW19 201 CX94
Edgehill Ct, Walt. KT12
off St. Johns Dr 218 BW102
Edgehill Gdns, Dag. RM10 148 FA63
Edgehill Rd, W13 159 CJ71
Chislehurst BR7 207 EQ90
Mitcham CR4 223 DH95
Purley CR8 241 DN110
Edgeley, Bkhm KT23 252 BY124
Edgeley Caravan Pk,
Far.Grn GU5 282 BL143
Edgeley La, SW4
off Edgeley Rd 183 DK83
Edgeley Rd, SW4 41 N10
Edgell Cl, Vir.W. GU25 215 AZ97
Edgell Rd, Stai. TW18 195 BF92
Edgel St, SW18
off Ferrier St 182 DB84
Edge Pt Cl, SE27 203 DP92
Edge St, W8 27 K2
Edgewood Dr, Orp. BR6 245 ET106
Edgewood Grn, Croy. CR0 225 DX102
Edgeworth Av, NW4 141 CU57
Edgeworth Cl, NW4 141 CU57
Whyteleafe CR3 258 DU118
Edgeworth Cres, NW4 141 CU57
Edgeworth Rd, SE9 186 EJ84
Cockfosters EN4 102 DE42
Edgington Rd, SW16 203 DK93
Edgington Way, Sid. DA14 208 EW94
Edgson Ho, SW1
off Ebury Br Rd 29 J10
EDGWARE, HA8 118 CP50
⊖ Edgware 118 CP51
⊖ Edgware 118 CN51
Edgwarebury Gdns, Edg. HA8 118 CN50
Edgwarebury La, Edg. HA8 118 CN49
Elstree WD6 118 CL45
H Edgware Comm Hosp,
Edg. HA8 118 CP52
Edgware Ct, Edg. HA8
off High St 118 CN51
Sch Edgware Inf Sch, Edg. HA8
off High St 118 CN51
Sch Edgware Jun Sch, Edg.
HA8 off Heming Rd 118 CN51
⊖ Edgware Road 16 C7
Edgware Rd, NW2 141 CV60
NW9 140 CR55
W2 16 D8
Edgware Rd Sub, W2
off Edgware Rd 16 C7
Edgware Way, Edg. HA8 118 CM49
Edinburgh Av, Mill End WD3 96 BG44
Slough SL1 153 AN71
Edinburgh Cl, E2 20 G1
Pinner HA5 138 BX59
Uxbridge UB10 137 BP63
Edinburgh Ct, SW20 221 CX99
Kingston upon Thames KT1
off Watersplash Cl 220 CL97
Edinburgh Cres, Wal.Cr. EN8 89 DY33
Edinburgh Dr, Abb.L. WD5 81 BU32
Ickenham UB10 137 BP63
Romford RM7
off Eastern Av W 149 FC56
Staines TW18 196 BK93
Edinburgh Gdns, Wind. SL4 173 AR83
Edinburgh Gate, SW1 28 E4
Denham UB9 135 BF58
Harlow CM20 57 ER12
Edinburgh Ho, W9 15 M2
Edinburgh Ms, Til. RM18 193 GH82
Edinburgh Pl, Harl. CM20 58 EU11
Sch Edinburgh Prim Sch, E17
off Edinburgh Rd 145 DZ57
Edinburgh Rd, E13 166 EH68
E17 145 EA57
N18 122 DU50
W7 179 CF75
Sutton SM1 222 DC103
Edinburgh Way, Harl. CM20 57 ER12
Edington Rd, SE2 188 EV76
Enfield EN3 104 DW40
Edison Av, Horn. RM12 149 FF61
Edison Cl, E17 off Exeter Rd 145 EA57
Hornchurch RM12
off Edison Av 149 FF60
St. Albans AL4 65 CJ21
West Drayton UB7 176 BM75
Edison Ct, SE10 35 M8
Watford WD18 97 BU44
Edison Dr, Sthl. UB1 158 CB72
Wembley HA9 140 CL62
Edison Gro, SE18 187 ET80
Edison Rd, N8 143 DK58
Bromley BR2 226 EG96
Enfield EN3 105 DZ40
Welling DA16 187 ET81
Edis St, NW1 6 G8
Edith Cavell Cl, N19
off Hillrise Rd 143 DL59
Edith Cavell Way, SE18 186 EL81
Edith Gdns, Surb. KT5 220 CP101
Edith Gro, SW10 39 N3
Edithna St, SW9 42 B10
Edith Nesbit Wk, SE9 206 EL85
Sch Edith Neville Prim Sch,
NW1 17 N1
Edith Rd, E6 166 EK66
E15 13 H2
N11 121 DK52
SE25 224 DR99
Edith Rd, SW19 202 DB93
W14 26 E9
Orpington BR6 246 EU106
Romford RM6 148 EX58
Edith Row, SW6 39 M6
Edith St, E2 10 C10
Edith Summerskill Ho, SW6 39 H3
Edith Ter, SW10 39 N4
Edith Vil, SW15
off Bective Rd 181 CY84
W14 26 G9
Edith Yd, SW10 39 P4
Edlyn Cl, Berk. HP4 60 AT18
Edmansons Cl, N17
off Bruce Gro 122 DS53
Edmeston Cl, E9 11 M4
Edmond Beaufort Dr, St.Alb.
AL3 65 CD18
Edmonds Ct, W.Mol. KT8
off Avern Rd 218 CB99
EDMONTON, N9 122 DU49
Sch Edmonton Co Sch, Lwr Sch,
N9 off Little Bury St 122 DS46
Upr Sch, Enf. EN1
off Great Cambridge Rd 122 DT45
⇌ Edmonton Green 122 DU47
⊖ Edmonton Green 122 DU47
Edmonton Grn, N9
off The Green 122 DU47
Edmonton Grn Mkt, N9
off Edmonton Grn Shop Cen 122 DV47
Edmonton Grn Shop Cen,
N9 122 DV47
● Edmonton Trade Pk, N18
off Eley Rd 122 DW50
Edmund Ct, Beac. HP9
off North Dr 132 AG55
Edmund Gro, Felt. TW13 198 BZ89
Edmund Halley Way, SE10 35 J5
Edmund Hurst Dr, E6 25 N7
Edmund Rd, Chaff.Hun. RM16 191 FX75
Mitcham CR4 222 DE97
Orpington BR5 228 EW100
Rainham RM13 169 FE68
Welling DA16 188 EU83
Edmunds Av, Orp. BR5 228 EX97
Edmunds Cl, Hayes UB4 158 BW71
Edmunds Ms, Kings L. WD4 80 BN29
Edmunds Rd, Hert. SG14 53 DM08
Edmunds Twr, Harl. CM19 73 EQ15
Edmund St, SE5 43 L4
Edmunds Wk, N2 142 DE56
Edmunds Way, Slou. SL2 154 AV71
Sch Edmund Waller Prim Sch,
SE14 45 J8
Edna Rd, SW20 221 CX96
Edna St, SW11 40 C7
Edrich Ho, SW4 42 A7
Edric Ho, SW1 off Page St 29 P8
Edrick Rd, Edg. HA8 118 CQ51
Edrick Wk, Edg. HA8 118 CQ51
Edric Rd, SE14 45 J4
Edridge Cl, Bushey WD23 98 CC43
Hornchurch RM12 150 FK64
Edridge Rd, Croy. CR0 224 DQ104
Edson Cl, Wat. WD25 81 BT33
Edulf Rd, Borwd. WD6 100 CP39
Edward Amey Cl, Wat. WD25 98 BW36
Edward Av, E4 123 EB51
Morden SM4 222 DD99
Sch Edward Betham C of E
Prim Sch, Grnf. UB6
off Oldfield La S 158 CC68
Edward Cl, N9 122 DT45
NW2 4 D1
Abbots Langley WD5 81 BT32
Chafford Hundred RM16 191 FX76
Hampton Hill TW12
off Edward Rd 198 CC92
Romford RM2 150 FJ55
St. Albans AL1 65 CF21
Edward Ct, E16 23 N6
Hemel Hempstead HP3 62 BK24
Staines TW18 196 BJ93
Waltham Abbey EN9 90 EF33
Edwardes Pl, W8 27 H7
Edwardes Sq, W8 27 J6
Edward Gro, Barn. EN4 102 DD43
Edward Ho, Red. RH1
off Royal Earlswood Pk 288 DG137
Edward Ms, NW1 17 K1
Edward Pauling Ho, Felt. TW14
off Westmacott Dr 197 BT87
Sch Edward Pauling Prim Sch, Felt.
TW13 off Redford Cl 197 BS89
Edward Pl, SE8 45 P3
Edward Rd, E17 145 DX56
SE20 205 DX94
Barnet EN4 102 DD43
Biggin Hill TN16 260 EL118
Bromley BR1 206 EH94
Chislehurst BR7 207 EP92
Coulsdon CR5 257 DK115
Croydon CR0 224 DS101
Feltham TW14 197 BR85
Hampton Hill TW12 198 CC92
Harrow HA2 138 CC55
Northolt UB5 158 BW68
Romford RM6 148 EY58
Edward's Av, Ruis. HA4 157 BV65
Edwards Cl, Hutt. CM13 131 GE44
Worcester Park KT4 221 CX103
Edwards Cotts, N1 8 G5
Edwards Ct, Slou. SL1 174 AS75
Waltham Cross EN8
off Turners Hill 89 DX31
Edwards Dr, N11
off Gordon Rd 121 DK52
Edward II Av, Byfleet KT14 234 BM114
Edwards Gdns, Swan. BR8 229 FD98
Edwards La, N16 144 DR61
Edwards Ms, N1 8 F6
W1 16 G9
Edward Sq, N1 8 C9
SE16 33 M2
Edwards Rd, Belv. DA17 188 FA77
Edward St, E16 23 N5
SE8 45 N4
SE14 45 M4
Edward's Way, SE4
off Adelaide Av 205 EA85
Edwards Way, Hutt. CM13 131 GE44
Edwards Yd, Wem. HA0
off Mount Pleasant 160 CL67
Edward Temme Av, E15 13 L7
Edward Tyler Rd, SE12 206 EH89
Edward Way, Ashf. TW15 196 BM89
Sch Edward Wilson Prim Sch,
W2 15 L6
Edwina Gdns, Ilf. IG4 146 EL57
Edwin Av, E6 25 L1
Edwin Cl, Bexh. DA7 188 EZ79
Rainham RM13 169 FF69
West Horsley KT24 267 BR125
Edwin Hall Pl, SE13
off Hither Grn La 205 ED86
Sch Edwin Lambert Sch, Horn.
RM11 off Malvern Rd 149 FG59
Edwin Pl, Croy. CR0
off Cross Rd 224 DR102
Edwin Rd, Dart. DA2 209 FH90
Edgware HA8 118 CR51
Twickenham TW1, TW2 199 CF88
West Horsley KT24 267 BQ125
Edwin's Mead, E9
off Lindisfarne Way 145 DY63
Edwin St, E1 21 H4
E16 23 N7
Gravesend DA12 213 GH87
Edwyn Cl, Barn. EN5 101 CW44
Edwyn Ho, SW18
off Neville Gill Cl 202 DB86
Eel Brook Cl, SW6 39 L6
Eel Brook Studios, SW6 39 K5
Eel Pie Island, Twick. TW1 199 CG88
Effie Pl, SW6 39 K5
Effie Rd, SW6 39 K5
EFFINGHAM, Lthd. KT24 268 BY127
Effingham Cl, Sutt. SM2 240 DB108
Effingham Common, Eff.
KT24 251 BU123
Effingham Common Rd, Eff.
KT24 251 BU123
Effingham Ct, Wok. GU22
off Constitution Hill 248 AY119
Effingham Hill, Dor. RH5 268 BX132
⇌ Effingham Junction 251 BU123
Effingham Pl, Eff. KT24 268 BX127
Effingham Rd, N8 143 DN57
SE12 206 EE85
Croydon CR0 223 DM101
Long Ditton KT6 219 CH101
Reigate RH2 288 DB135
Effort St, SW17 202 DE92
Effra Par, SW2 203 DN85
Effra Rd, SW2 183 DN84
SW19 202 DB93
Egan Cl, Ken. CR8 258 DR120
Egan Way, Hayes UB3 157 BS73
Egbert St, NW1 6 G8
Egbury Ho, SW15
off Tangley Gro 201 CT86
Egdean Wk, Sev. TN13 279 FJ123
Egeremont Rd, SE13 46 D8
Egerton Av, Swan. BR8 209 FF94
Egerton Cl, Dart. DA1 209 FH88
Pinner HA5 137 BU56
Egerton Ct, Guil. GU2
off Egerton Rd 264 AS134
Egerton Cres, SW3 28 D8
Egerton Dr, SE10 46 C6
Egerton Gdns, NW4 141 CV56
NW10 4 A9
SW3 28 C7
W13 159 CH72
Ilford IG3 147 ET62
Egerton Gdns Ms, SW3 28 D7
Egerton Pl, SW3 28 D7
Weybridge KT13 235 BQ107
Egerton Rd, N16 144 DT59
SE25 224 DS97
Berkhamsted HP4 60 AU17
Guildford GU2 264 AS134
New Malden KT3 221 CT98
Slough SL2 153 AL70
Twickenham TW2 199 CE87
Wembley HA0 160 CM66
Weybridge KT13 235 BQ107
Sch Egerton-Rothesay Nurs &
Pre-Prep Sch, Berk. HP4
off Charles St 60 AV19
Sch Egerton-Rothesay Sch, Berk.
HP4 off Durrants La 60 AT19
Egerton Ter, SW3 28 D7
Egerton Way, Hayes UB3 177 BP80
Eggardon Ct, Nthlt. UB5
off Lancaster Rd 158 CC65
Egg Fm La, Kings L. WD4 81 BP30
Egg Hall, Epp. CM16 92 EU29
Egglesfield Cl, Berk. HP4 60 AS17
EGHAM, TW20 195 BA93
⇌ Egham 195 BA92
● Egham Business Village,
Egh. TW20 215 BC96
Egham Bypass, Egh. TW20 195 AZ92
Egham Cl, SW19 201 CY89
Sutton SM3 221 CY103
Egham Cres, Sutt. SM3 221 CX104
Egham Hill, Egh. TW20 194 AX93
EGHAM HYTHE, Stai. TW18 195 BE93
★ Egham Mus, Egh. TW20 195 BA92
Egham Rd, E13 24 B6
Eghams Cl, Knot.Grn HP9 110 AJ51
Eghams Wd Rd, Beac. HP9 110 AH51
EGHAM WICK, Egh. TW20 194 AU94
Eglantine La, Dart. DA4 230 FN101
Eglantine Rd, SW18 202 DC85
Egleston Rd, Mord. SM4 222 DB100
Egley Dr, Wok. GU22 248 AX122
Egley Rd, Wok. GU22 248 AX122
Eglington Ct, SE17 43 J2
Eglington Rd, E4 123 ED45
Eglinton Hill, SE18 187 EP79
Sch Eglinton Prim Sch & Early
Years Cen, SE18
off Paget Ri 187 EN80
Eglinton Rd, SE18 187 EN79
Swanscombe DA10 212 FZ86
Eglise Rd, Warl. CR6 259 DY117
Egliston Ms, SW15 181 CW83
Egliston Rd, SW15 181 CW83
Eglon Ms, NW1 6 F7
Egmont Av, Surb. KT6 220 CM102
Egmont Pk Rd, Walt.Hill KT20 271 CU125
Egmont Rd, N.Mal. KT3 221 CT98
Surbiton KT6 220 CM102
Sutton SM2 240 DC108
Walton-on-Thames KT12 217 BV101
Egmont St, SE14 45 K5
Egmont Way, Tad. KT20 255 CY119
Egremont Gdns, Slou. SL1 153 AN74
Egremont Ho, SE13 46 D8
Egremont Rd, SE27 203 DN90
Egret Ct, Enf. EN3
off Teal Cl 104 DW36
Egret Way, Hayes UB4 158 BX71
EGYPT, Slou. SL2 133 AQ63
Egypt La, Farn.Com. SL2 133 AP61
Eider Cl, E7 13 L2
Hayes UB4 off Cygnet Way 158 BX71
Eight Acres, Burn. SL1 152 AH70
Eighteenth Rd, Mitch. CR4 223 DL98
Eighth Av, E12 147 EM63
Hayes UB3 157 BU74
Eileen Rd, SE25 224 DR99
Eindhoven Cl, Cars. SM5 222 DG102
Eisenhower Dr, E6 25 H7
Elaine Gro, NW5 6 G2
Elam Cl, SE5 43 H9
Elam St, SE5 43 H8
Eland Pl, Croy. CR0
off Eland Rd 223 DP104
Eland Rd, SW11 40 F10
Croydon CR0 223 DP104
Sch Elangeni Sch, Amer. HP6
off Woodside Av 77 AS36
Elan Rd, S.Ock. RM15 171 FU71
Elba Pl, SE17 31 K8
Elberon Av, Croy. CR0 223 DJ100
Elbe St, SW6 39 N8
Elborough Rd, SE25 224 DU99
Elborough St, SW18 202 DA88
Elbow La, Hert.Hth SG13 70 DV17
Elbow Meadow, Colnbr. SL3 175 BF81
Elbury Dr, E16 23 P9
Elcho St, SW11 40 C5
Elcot Av, SE15 44 E4
● Eldenwall Ind Est,
Dag. RM8 148 EZ60
Elder Av, N8 143 DL57
Elderbek Cl, Chsht EN7 88 DU28
Elderberry Cl, Ilf. IG6
off Hazel La 125 EP52
Elderberry Gro, SE27
off Linton Gro 204 DQ91
Elderberry Rd, W5 180 CL75
Elderberry Way, E6 25 K2
Watford WD25 97 BV35
Elder Cl, N20 120 DB47
Guildford GU4 265 BA131
Sidcup DA15 207 ET88
West Drayton UB7 156 BL73
Elder Ct, Bushey Hth WD23 117 CE47
Elderfield, Harl. CM17 58 EX11
Welwyn Garden City AL7 52 DB10
Elderfield Pl, SW17 203 DH91
Elderfield Rd, E5 11 H1
Stoke Poges SL2 154 AT65
Elderfield Wk, E11 146 EH57
Elderflower Way, E15 13 J6
Elder Gdns, SE27 204 DQ91
Elder Oak Cl, SE20 224 DV95
Elder Rd, SE27 204 DQ92
Eldersley Cl, Red. RH1 272 DF132
Elderslie Cl, Beck. BR3 225 EB99
Elderslie Rd, SE9 207 EN85
Elder St, E1 20 A6
Elderton Rd, SE26 205 DY91
Eldertree Pl, Mitch. CR4
off Eldertree Way 223 DJ95
Eldertree Way, Mitch. CR4 223 DH95
Elder Wk, N1 9 H8
SE13 off Bankside Av 185 EC83
Elder Way, Langley SL3 175 AZ75
North Holmwood RH5 285 CJ140
Rainham RM13 170 FK69
Elderwood Pl, SE27 204 DQ92
Eldon Av, Borwd. WD6 100 CN40
Croydon CR0 224 DW103
Hounslow TW5 178 CA80
Eldon Gro, NW3 6 B2
Sch Eldon Inf Sch, N9
off Eldon Rd 122 DW46
Sch Eldon Jun Sch, N9
off Eldon Rd 122 DW46
Eldon Pk, SE25 224 DV98
Eldon Rd, E17 145 DZ56
N9 122 DW47
N22 121 DP53
W8 27 M7
Caterham CR3 258 DR121
Hoddesdon EN11 71 ED19
Eldon St, EC2 19 M7
Eldon Way, NW10 160 CP68
Eldred Dr, Orp. BR5 228 EW103
Eldred Gdns, Upmin. RM14 151 FS59
Eldred Rd, Bark. IG11 167 ES67
Eldrick Ct, Felt. TW14 197 BR88
Eldridge Cl, Felt. TW14 197 BU88
Eldridge Ct, Dag. RM10
off St. Mark's Pl 169 FB65
Eleanor Av, Epsom KT19 238 CR110
St. Albans AL3 65 CD18
Eleanor Cl, N15 144 DT55
SE16 33 J4
Eleanor Cres, NW7 119 CX49
Eleanor Cross Rd, Wal.Cr. EN8 89 DY34
Eleanor Gdns, Barn. EN5 101 CX43
Dagenham RM8 148 EZ62
Eleanor Gro, SW13 180 CS83
Ickenham UB10 137 BP62
Sch Eleanor Palmer Prim Sch,
NW5 7 L1
Eleanor Rd, E8 10 E5
E15 13 M5
N11 121 DL51
Chalfont St. Peter SL9 112 AW53
Hertford SG14 54 DQ08
Waltham Cross EN8 89 DY33
Sch Eleanor Smith Sch, E13 24 A1
Eleanor St, E3 22 A3
Eleanor Wk, SE18 37 J9
Greenhithe DA9 191 FW84
Eleanor Way, Wal.Cr. EN8 89 DZ34
Warley CM14 130 FX50
Electra Av, Lon.Hthrw Air.
TW6 177 BT83
● Electra Business Pk, E16 23 H6
Electric Av, SW9 183 DN84
Enfield EN3 105 DZ36
Electric La, SW9 183 DN84
Electric Par, E18
off George La 124 EG54
Surbiton KT6 219 CK100
Elektron Ho, E14 23 H10
Element Ho, Enf. EN3
off Tysoe Av 105 DZ36
⇌ Elephant & Castle 31 J8
⊖ Elephant & Castle 31 J8

Elephant & Castle, SE1 31 H7
Elephant & Castle Shop Cen, SE1 off Elephant & Castle 31 J8
Elephant La, SE16 32 G4
Elephant Rd, SE17 31 J8
Elers Rd, W13 179 CJ75
Hayes UB3 177 BR77
Eleven Acre Ri, Loug. IG10 107 EM41
● Eley Est, N18 122 DW50
Eley Rd, N18 123 DX50
Eley Rd Retail Pk, N18 123 DX50
Elfindale Rd, SE24 204 DQ85
Elfin Gro, Tedd. TW11 off Broad St 199 CF92
Elford Cl, SE3 186 EH84
Elfort Rd, N5 143 DN63
Elfrida Cres, SE6 205 EA91
Sch Elfrida Prim Sch, SE6 off Elfrida Cres 205 EB91
Elfrida Rd, Wat. WD18 98 BW43
Elf Row, E1 21 H10
Elfwine Rd, W7 159 CE71
Elgal Cl, Orp. BR6 245 EP106
Elgar Av, NW10 160 CR65
SW16 223 DL97
W5 180 CL75
Surbiton KT5 220 CP101
Elgar Cl, E13 off Bushey Rd 166 EJ68
SE8 46 A5
Buckhurst Hill IG9 124 EK47
Elstree WD6 117 CJ45
Uxbridge UB10 136 BN61
Elgar Gdns, Til. RM18 193 GH81
Elgar St, SE16 33 M6
Elgin Av, W9 15 L3
W12 181 CU75
Ashford TW15 197 BQ93
Harrow HA3 117 CH54
Romford RM3 128 FP52
Elgin Cl, W12 181 CV75
Elgin Cres, W11 14 G9
Caterham CR3 258 DU122
London Heathrow Airport TW6 off Eastern Perimeter Rd 177 BS82
Elgin Dr, Nthwd. HA6 115 BS52
Elgin Gdns, Guil. GU1 265 BA133
Elgin Ms, W11 14 F9
Elgin Ms N, W9 15 M2
Elgin Ms S, W9 15 M2
Elgin Pl, Wey. KT13 235 BQ107
Elgin Rd, N22 121 DJ54
Broxbourne EN10 71 DZ24
Cheshunt EN8 88 DW30
Croydon CR0 224 DT102
Ilford IG3 147 ES60
Sutton SM1 222 DC104
Wallington SM6 241 DJ107
Weybridge KT13 234 BN106
Elgiva La, Chesh. HP5 76 AP31
Elgood Av, Nthwd. HA6 115 BU51
Elgood Cl, W11 26 E1
Elham Cl, Brom. BR1 206 EK94
Elham Ho, E5 off Pembury Rd 18 E3
Elia Ms, N1 18 G1
Elias Pl, SW8 42 E3
Elia St, N1 18 G1
Elibank Rd, SE9 187 EN84
Elim Est, SE1 31 N6
Elim St, SE1 31 M6
Elim Way, E13 23 M3
Eliot Bk, SE23 204 DV89
Sch Eliot Bk Prim Sch, SE26 off Thorpewood Av 204 DV89
Eliot Cotts, SE3 47 K9
Eliot Ct, N15 off Tynemouth Rd 144 DT56
Eliot Dr, Har. HA2 138 CB61
Eliot Gdns, SW15 181 CU84
Eliot Hill, SE13 46 F9
Eliot Ms, NW8 15 P1
Eliot Pk, SE13 46 F9
Eliot Pl, SE3 47 J9
Eliot Rd, Dag. RM9 148 EX63
Dartford DA1 210 FP85
Eliot Vale, SE3 47 H9
Elizabethan Cl, Stanw. TW19 196 BK87
Elizabethan Way, Stanw. TW19 196 BK87
Elizabeth Av, N1 9 K8
Amersham HP6 94 AV39
Enfield EN2 103 DP41
Ilford IG1 147 ER61
Staines TW18 196 BJ93
Elizabeth Blackwell Ho, N22 off Progress Way 121 DN53
Elizabeth Br, SW1 29 J9
Elizabeth Cl, E14 22 C9
W9 15 P4
Barnet EN5 101 CX41
Hertford SG14 off Welwyn Rd 53 DM09
Lower Nazeing EN9 71 ED23
Romford RM7 127 FB53
Sutton SM1 239 CZ105
Tilbury RM18 193 GH82
Welwyn Garden City AL7 52 DC09
Elizabeth Clyde Cl, N15 144 DS56
Elizabeth Cotts, Kew TW9 180 CM81
Elizabeth Ct, SW1 29 P7
Godalming GU7 280 AS144
Gravesend DA11 off St. James's Rd 213 GG86
Horley RH6 290 DG148
Kingston upon Thames KT2 off Lower Kings Rd 220 CL95
St. Albans AL4 off Villiers Cres 65 CK17
Watford WD17 97 BT38
Woodford Green IG8 off Navestock Cres 124 EJ52
Elizabeth Dr, Bans. SM7 256 DC118
Theydon Bois CM16 107 ES36
Elizabeth Est, SE17 43 L2
Elizabeth Fry Pl, SE18 186 EL81
Elizabeth Fry Rd, E8 10 F7
Elizabeth Gdns, W3 161 CT74
Isleworth TW7 179 CG84
Stanmore HA7 117 CJ51
Sunbury-on-Thames TW16 218 BW97
Sch Elizabeth Garrett Anderson Language Coll, N1 8 D10
Elizabeth Ho, Bans. SM7 256 DC118
Elizabeth Huggins Cotts, Grav. DA11 213 GG89
Elizabeth Ms, NW3 6 D5
Elizabeth Pl, N15 144 DR56
Elizabeth Ride, N9 122 DV45
Elizabeth Rd, E6 166 EK67
N15 144 DS57
Godalming GU7 280 AS144
Grays RM16 192 FZ76
Pilgrim's Hatch CM15 130 FV44
Rainham RM13 169 FH71
Sch Elizabeth Selby Inf Sch, E2 20 D2
Elizabeth Sq, SE16 33 L1
Elizabeth St, SW1 29 H8
Greenhithe DA9 211 FS85
Elizabeth Ter, SE9 207 EM86
Elizabeth Way, SE19 204 DR94
Feltham TW13 198 BW91
Harlow CM19, CM20 73 EM16
Orpington BR5 228 EW99
Stoke Poges SL2 154 AT67
Elizabeth Wheeler Ho, Brom. BR1 off The Mall 226 EG97
Eliza Cook Cl, Green. DA9 off Watermans Way 191 FV84
Elkanette Ms, N20 off Ridgeview Rd 120 DC47
Elkington Pt, SE11 30 E9
Elkington Rd, E13 24 A5
Elkins, The, Rom. RM1 127 FE54
Elkins Gdns, Guil. GU4 265 BA131
Elkins Rd, Hedg. SL2 134 AS61
Elkstone Rd, W10 14 G6
Ella Cl, Beck. BR3 225 EA96
Ellacott Ms, SW16 203 DK89
Ellaline Rd, W6 38 C3
Ella Ms, NW3 6 E1
Ellanby Cres, N18 122 DV49
Elland Cl, Barn. EN5 102 DD43
Elland Rd, SE15 184 DW84
Walton-on-Thames KT12 218 BX103
Ella Rd, N8 143 DL59
Ellement Cl, Pnr. HA5 138 BX57
Ellenborough Pl, SW15 181 CU84
Ellenborough Rd, N22 122 DQ53
Sidcup DA14 208 EX92
Ellenbridge Way, S.Croy. CR2 242 DS109
ELLENBROOK, Hat. AL10 66 CR19
Ellenbrook Cl, Wat. WD24 off Hatfield Rd 97 BV39
Ellenbrook Cres, Hat. AL10 off Ellenbrook La 66 CR18
Ellenbrook La, Hat. AL10 66 CS19
Ellen Cl, Brom. BR1 226 EK97
Hemel Hempstead HP2 62 BM19
Ellen Ct, N9 off Densworth Gro 122 DW47
Ellen St, E1 20 D9
Ellen Webb Dr, Wealds. HA3 139 CE55
Ellen Wilkinson Ho, E2 off Usk St 21 J2
Sch Ellen Wilkinson Prim Sch, E6 24 G7
Sch Ellen Wilkinson Sch for Girls, The, W3 off Queens Dr 160 CM72
Elleray Rd, Tedd. TW11 199 CF93
Ellerby St, SW6 38 D7
Ellerdale Cl, NW3 5 N1
Ellerdale Rd, NW3 5 P1
Ellerdale St, SE13 185 EB84
Ellerdine Rd, Houns. TW3 178 CC84
Ellerker Gdns, Rich. TW10 200 CL86
Ellerman Av, Twick. TW2 198 BZ88
Ellerman Rd, Til. RM18 193 GF82
Ellerslie, Grav. DA12 213 GK87
Ellerslie Gdns, NW10 161 CU67
Ellerslie Rd, W12 161 CV74
● Ellerslie Sq Ind Est, SW2 203 DL85
Ellerton, NW6 5 H3
Ellerton Gdns, Dag. RM9 168 EW66
Ellerton Rd, SW13 181 CU81
SW18 202 DD88
SW20 201 CU94
Dagenham RM9 168 EW66
Surbiton KT6 220 CM103
Ellery Rd, SE19 204 DR94
Ellery St, SE15 44 E9
Elles Av, Guil. GU1 265 BB134
Ellesborough Cl, Wat. WD19 116 BW50
Ellesmere Av, NW7 118 CR48
Beckenham BR3 225 EB96
Ellesmere Cl, E11 146 EF57
Datchet SL3 174 AU79
Ruislip HA4 137 BQ59
Ellesmere Dr, S.Croy. CR2 242 DV114
Ellesmere Gdns, Ilf. IG4 146 EL57
Ellesmere Gro, Barn. EN5 101 CZ43
Ellesmere Pl, Walt. KT12 235 BS106
Ellesmere Rd, E3 11 L10
NW10 141 CU64
W4 180 CR79
Berkhamsted HP4 60 AX19
Greenford UB6 158 CC70
Twickenham TW1 199 CJ86
Weybridge KT13 235 BR107
Ellesmere St, E14 22 C8
Ellice Rd, Oxt. RH8 276 EF129
Ellies Ms, Ashf. TW15 196 BL89
Elliman Av, Slou. SL2 154 AS73
Ellingfort Rd, E8 10 F6
Ellingham Cl, Hem.H. HP2 62 BN18
Sch Ellingham Prim Sch, Chess. KT9 off Ellingham Rd 237 CK108
Ellingham Rd, E15 145 ED63
W12 181 CU75
Chessington KT9 237 CK107
Hemel Hempstead HP2 62 BM19
Ellington Ct, Tap. SL6 off Ellington Rd 152 AC72
Ellington Gdns, Tap. SL6 152 AC72
Ellington Ho, SE1 31 K6
Ellington Rd, N10 143 DH56
Feltham TW13 197 BT91
Hounslow TW3 178 CB82
Taplow SL6 152 AC72
Ellington St, N7 8 E5
Ellington Way, Epsom KT18 255 CV117
Elliot Cl, E15 13 J7
Elliot Rd, NW4 141 CV58
Stanmore HA7 117 CG51
Elliott Av, Ruis. HA4 137 BV61
Elliott Cl, Welw.G.C. AL7 51 CX12
Wembley HA9 140 CM62
Elliott Gdns, Rom. RM3 127 FH53
Shepperton TW17 216 BN98
Elliott Rd, SW9 42 G5
W4 180 CS77
Bromley BR2 226 EK98
Thornton Heath CR7 223 DP98
Sch Elliott Sch, SW15 off Pullman Gdns 201 CW86
Elliotts Cl, Cowley UB8 156 BJ71
Elliotts La, Brasted TN16 262 EW124
Elliott's Pl, N1 9 H9
Elliott Sq, NW3 6 D6
Elliotts Row, SE11 30 G8
Elliott St, Grav. DA12 213 GK87
Ellis Av, Chal.St.P. SL9 113 AZ53
Onslow Village GU2 280 AT136
Rainham RM13 169 FG71
Slough SL1 174 AS75
Ellis Cl, NW10 off High Rd 161 CV65
SE9 207 EQ89
Coulsdon CR5 257 DM120
Edgware HA8 118 CS51
Hoddesdon EN11 55 DZ13
Swanley BR8 229 FD98
Elliscombe Rd, SE7 186 EJ78
Ellis Ct, W7 159 CF71
Ellis Fm Cl, Wok. GU22 248 AX122
Ellisfield Dr, SW15 201 CT87
Ellis Flds, St.Alb. AL3 65 CE17
Ellis Ho, St.Alb. AL1 65 CF21
Ellison Cl, Wind. SL4 173 AM83
Ellison Gdns, Sthl. UB2 178 BZ77
Ellison Ho, SE13 46 E8
Ellison Rd, SW13 181 CT82
SW16 203 DK94
Sidcup DA15 207 ER88
Ellis Rd, Couls. CR5 257 DM120
Mitcham CR4 222 DF100
Southall UB2 158 CC74
Ellis St, SW1 28 F8
Elliston Ho, SE18 37 L9
Ellis Way, Dart. DA1 210 FM89
Ellmore Cl, Rom. RM3 127 FH53
Ellora Rd, SW16 203 DK92
Ellsworth St, E2 20 E2
Ellwood Ct, W9 15 L5
Ellwood Gdns, Wat. WD25 81 BV34
Ellwood Ri, Ch.St.G. HP8 112 AW47
Ellwood Rd, Beac. HP9 110 AH54
Elmar Grn, Slou. SL2 153 AN69
Elmar Rd, N15 144 DR56
Elm Av, W5 160 CL74
Carshalton SM5 240 DF110
Ruislip HA4 137 BU60
Upminster RM14 150 FP62
Watford WD19 116 BY45
Elmbank, N14 121 DL45
Elmbank Av, Barn. EN5 101 CW42
Englefield Green TW20 194 AV93
Guildford GU2 280 AU135
Elm Bk Dr, Brom. BR1 226 EK96
Elm Bk Gdns, SW13 180 CS82
Elmbank Way, W7 159 CD71
Elmbourne Dr, Belv. DA17 189 FB77
Elmbourne Rd, SW17 203 DG90
Elmbridge, Harl. CM17 58 EZ12
Elmbridge Av, Surb. KT5 220 CP99
Elmbridge Cl, Ruis. HA4 137 BU58
Elmbridge Dr, Ruis. HA4 137 BT57
Elmbridge La, Wok. GU22 249 AZ119
★ Elmbridge Mus, Wey. KT13 234 BN105
Elmbridge Rd, Ilf. IG6 126 EU51
Elmbridge Wk, E8 10 D6
Elmbrook Cl, Sun. TW16 217 BV95
Elmbrook Gdns, SE9 186 EL84
Elmbrook Rd, Sutt. SM1 239 CZ105
Elm Cl, E11 146 EH58
N19 143 DJ61
NW4 141 CX57
SW20 off Grand Dr 221 CW98
Amersham HP6 77 AQ38
Box Hill KT20 270 CQ130
Buckhurst Hill IG9 124 EK47
Carshalton SM5 222 DF102
Dartford DA1 210 FJ88
Epping Green CM16 73 EP24
Farnham Common SL2 153 AQ65
Harrow HA2 138 CB58
Hayes UB3 157 BU72
Leatherhead KT22 253 CH122
Ripley GU23 250 BG124
Romford RM7 127 FB54
South Croydon CR2 242 DS107
Stanwell TW19 196 BK88
Surbiton KT5 220 CQ101
Twickenham TW2 198 CB89
Waltham Abbey EN9 89 ED34
Warlingham CR6 259 DX117
Woking GU21 248 AX115
ELM CORNER, Wok. GU23 250 BN119
Elmcote Way, Crox.Grn WD3 96 BM44
Elm Ct, EC4 18 E10
Mitcham CR4 off Armfield Cres 222 DF96
Sunbury-on-Thames TW16 197 BT94
Elmcourt Rd, SE27 203 DP89
Sch Elm Ct Sch, SE27 off Elmcourt Rd 204 DQ89
Elm Cres, W5 160 CL74
Kingston upon Thames KT2 220 CL95
Elmcroft, N8 143 DM57
Elm Cft, Datchet SL3 174 AW81
Elmcroft, Lthd. KT23 252 CA124
Elmcroft Av, E11 146 EH57
N9 104 DV44
NW11 141 CZ59
Sidcup DA15 207 ET86
Elmcroft Cl, E11 146 EH56
W5 159 CK72
Chessington KT9 220 CL104
Feltham TW14 197 BT86
Elmcroft Cres, NW11 141 CY59
Harrow HA2 138 CA55
Elmcroft Dr, Ashf. TW15 196 BN92
Chessington KT9 220 CL104
Elmcroft Gdns, NW9 140 CN57
Elmcroft Rd, Orp. BR6 228 EU101
Elmcroft St, E5 144 DW63
Elmdale Rd, N13 121 DM50
Elmdene, Surb. KT5 220 CQ102
Elmdene Av, Horn. RM11 150 FM57
Elmdene Cl, Beck. BR3 225 DZ99
Elmdene Ct, Wok. GU22 off Constitution Hill 248 AY118
Elmdene Rd, SE18 187 EP78
Elmdon Pl, Guil. GU1 off Buckingham Cl 265 AZ133
Elmdon Rd, Houns. TW4 178 BX82
London Heathrow Airport TW6 177 BT83
South Ockendon RM15 171 FU71
Elm Dr, Chsht EN8 89 DY28
Chobham GU24 232 AT110
Harrow HA2 138 CB58
Hatfield AL10 67 CU19
Elm Dr, Lthd. KT22 253 CH122
St. Albans AL4 65 CJ20
Sunbury-on-Thames TW16 218 BW96
Swanley BR8 229 FD96
Elmer Av, Hav.at.Bow. RM4 127 FE48
Elmer Cl, Enf. EN2 103 DM41
Rainham RM13 169 FG66
Elmer Cotts, Fetch. KT22 253 CG123
Elmer Gdns, Edg. HA8 118 CP52
Isleworth TW7 179 CD83
Rainham RM13 169 FG66
Elmer Ms, Fetch. KT22 253 CG123
Elmer Rd, SE6 205 EC87
Elmers Ct, Beac. HP9 off Post Office La 111 AK52
Elmers Dr, Tedd. TW11 off Kingston Rd 199 CH93
ELMERS END, Beck. BR3 225 DY97
⇌ Elmers End 225 DX98
Tram Elmers End 225 DX98
Elmers End Rd, SE20 224 DW96
Beckenham BR3 224 DW96
Elmerside Rd, Beck. BR3 225 DY98
Elmers Rd, SE25 224 DU101
Elm Fm Caravan Pk, Lyne KT16 215 BC101
Elmfield, Bkhm KT23 252 CA123
Elmfield Av, N8 143 DL57
Mitcham CR4 222 DG95
Teddington TW11 199 CF92
Elmfield Cl, Grav. DA11 213 GH88
Harrow HA1 139 CE61
Potters Bar EN6 85 CY33
Elmfield Pk, Brom. BR1 226 EG97
Elmfield Rd, E4 123 EC47
E17 145 DX58
N2 142 DD55
SW17 202 DG89
Bromley BR1 226 EG97
Potters Bar EN6 85 CY33
Southall UB2 178 BY76
Elmfield Way, W9 15 J6
South Croydon CR2 242 DT109
Elm Friars Wk, NW1 7 P7
Elm Gdns, N2 142 DC55
Claygate KT10 237 CF107
Enfield EN2 104 DR38
Epsom KT18 255 CW119
Mitcham CR4 223 DK98
North Weald Bassett CM16 93 FB26
Welwyn Garden City AL8 51 CV09
Elmgate Av, Felt. TW13 197 BV90
Elmgate Gdns, Edg. HA8 118 CR50
Elm Grn, W3 160 CS72
Hemel Hempstead HP1 61 BE18
Elmgreen Cl, E15 13 K8
Sch Elmgreen Sch, The, SE27 off Gipsy Rd 204 DQ91
Elm Gro, N8 143 DL58
NW2 141 CX63
SE15 44 B8
SW19 201 CY94
Berkhamsted HP4 60 AV19
Caterham CR3 258 DS122
Epsom KT18 238 CQ114
Erith DA8 189 FD80
Harrow HA2 138 CA59
Hornchurch RM11 150 FL58
Kingston upon Thames KT2 220 CL95
Orpington BR6 227 ET102
Sutton SM1 240 DB105
Watford WD24 97 BU37
West Drayton UB7 off Willow Av 156 BM73
Woodford Green IG8 124 EF50
Elmgrove Cres, Har. HA1 139 CF57
Sch Elmgrove First Sch, Kenton HA3 off Kenmore Av 139 CG56
Elmgrove Gdns, Har. HA1 139 CG57
Sch Elmgrove Mid Sch, Kenton HA3 off Kenmore Av 139 CG56
Elm Gro Par, Wall. SM6 off Butter Hill 222 DG104
Elm Gro Rd, SW13 181 CU82
W5 180 CL75
Cobham KT11 252 BX116
Elmgrove Rd, Croy. CR0 224 DV101
Harrow HA1 139 CF57
Weybridge KT13 234 BN105
Elm Hall Gdns, E11 146 EH58
Elm Hatch, Harl. CM18 off St. Andrews Meadow 73 ET16
Elmhurst, Belv. DA17 188 EY79
Elmhurst Av, N2 142 DD55
Mitcham CR4 203 DH94
Elmhurst Ct, Bushey WD23 98 BY42
Elmhurst Ct, Guil. GU1 off Lower Edgeborough Rd 281 AZ135
Elmhurst Dr, E18 124 EG54
Dorking RH4 285 CH138
Hornchurch RM11 150 FJ60
Elmhurst Mans, SW4 41 N10
Sch Elmhurst Prim Sch, E7 off Upton Pk Rd 166 EH66
Elmhurst Rd, E7 166 EH66
N17 122 DS54
SE9 206 EL89
Enfield EN3 104 DW37
Slough SL3 175 BA76
Sch Elmhurst Sch, S.Croy. CR2 off South Pk Hill Rd 242 DR106
Elmhurst St, SW4 41 N10
Elmhurst Vil, SE15 off Cheltenham Rd 184 DW84
Elmhurst Way, Loug. IG10 125 EM45
Elmington Cl, Bex. DA5 209 FB86
Elmington Est, SE5 43 M4
Elmington Rd, SE5 43 L6
Elmira St, SE13 185 EB83
Elm La, SE6 205 DZ89
Woking GU23 251 BP118
Elm Lawn Cl, Uxb. UB8 156 BL66
Elm Lawns Cl, St.Alb. AL1 off Avenue Rd 65 CE19
Elmlea Dr, Hayes UB3 157 BS72
Elmlee Cl, Chis. BR7 207 EM93
Elmley Cl, E6 25 H7
Elmley St, SE18 187 ER77
Elm Ms, Rich. TW10 200 CM86
Elmore Cl, Wem. HA0 160 CL68
Elmore Rd, E11 145 EC62
Chipstead CR5 256 DF121
Enfield EN3 105 DX39
Elmores, Loug. IG10 107 EN41
Elmore St, N1 9 K6
Elm Par, Horn. RM12 149 FH63
Sidcup DA14 off Main Rd 208 EU91
ELM PARK, Horn. RM12 149 FH64
⊖ Elm Park 149 FH63
Elm Pk, SW2 203 DM86
Stanmore HA7 117 CH50
Elm Pk Av, N15 144 DT57
Hornchurch RM12 149 FG63
Elm Pk Ct, Pnr. HA5 138 BW55
Elm Pk Gdns, NW4 141 CX57
SW10 40 A1
South Croydon CR2 242 DW110
Elm Pk La, SW3 40 A1
Elm Pk Mans, SW10 39 P2
Elm Pk Rd, E10 145 DY60
N3 119 CZ52
N21 122 DQ45
SE25 224 DT97
SW3 40 A2
Pinner HA5 116 BW54
Elm Pl, SW7 28 A10
Ashford TW15 off Limes Cl 196 BN92
Elm Quay Ct, SW8 41 N2
Elm Rd, E7 13 M4
E11 145 ED61
E17 145 EC57
N22 off Granville Rd 121 DP53
SW14 180 CQ83
Aveley RM15 170 FQ74
Barnet EN5 101 CZ42
Beckenham BR3 225 DZ96
Chessington KT9 238 CL105
Claygate KT10 237 CF107
Dartford DA1 210 FK88
Epsom KT17 239 CT107
Erith DA8 189 FG81
Feltham TW14 197 BR88
Godalming GU7 280 AT143
Gravesend DA12 213 GJ90
Grays RM17 192 GC79
Greenhithe DA9 211 FS86
Horsell GU21 249 AZ115
Kingston upon Thames KT2 220 CM95
Leatherhead KT22 253 CH122
New Malden KT3 220 CR98
Orpington BR6 246 EU108
Penn HP10 110 AD46
Purley CR8 241 DP113
Redhill RH1 272 DE134
Romford RM7 127 FB54
Sidcup DA14 208 EU91
Thornton Heath CR7 224 DR98
Wallington SM6 222 DG102
Warlingham CR6 259 DX117
Wembley HA9 140 CL64
Westerham TN16 277 ES125
Windsor SL4 173 AP83
Woking GU21 248 AX118
Elm Rd W, Sutt. SM3 221 CZ101
Elm Row, NW3 142 DC62
Elmroyd Av, Pot.B. EN6 85 CZ33
Elmroyd Cl, Pot.B. EN6 85 CZ33
Elms, The, SW13 181 CT83
Hertford SG13 54 DU09
Loughton IG10 106 EF40
Warlingham CR6 258 DW115
Elms Av, N10 143 DH55
NW4 141 CX57
Elmscott Gdns, N21 104 DQ44
Elmscott Rd, Brom. BR1 206 EE92
Elms Ct, Wem. HA0 139 CF63
Elms Cres, SW4 203 DJ86
Elmscroft Gdns, Pot.B. EN6 85 CZ32
Elmsdale Rd, E17 145 DZ56
Elms Fm Rd, Horn. RM12 150 FJ64
Elms Gdns, Dag. RM9 148 EZ63
Wembley HA0 139 CG63
Elmshaw Rd, SW15 201 CU85
Elmshorn, Epsom KT17 255 CW116
Elmshott La, Slou. SL1 153 AL73
Elmshurst Cres, N2 142 DD56
Elmside, Guil. GU2 280 AU135
New Addington CR0 243 EB107
Elmside Rd, Wem. HA9 140 CN62
Elms La, Wem. HA0 139 CG63
Elmsleigh Av, Har. HA3 139 CH56
Elmsleigh Cen, The, Stai. TW18 195 BF91
Elmsleigh Ct, Sutt. SM1 222 DB104
Elmsleigh Rd, Stai. TW18 195 BF92
Twickenham TW2 199 CD89
Elmslie Cl, Epsom KT18 238 CQ114
Woodford Green IG8 125 EM51
Elmslie Pt, E3 21 P7
Elms Ms, W2 16 A10
Elms Pk Av, Wem. HA0 139 CG63
Elms Rd, SW4 203 DJ85
Chalfont St. Peter SL9 112 AY52
Harrow HA3 117 CE52
Ware SG12 55 EA05
ELMSTEAD, Chis. BR7 206 EK92
Elmstead Av, Chis. BR7 207 EM92
Wembley HA9 140 CL60
Elmstead Cl, N20 120 DA47
Epsom KT19 238 CS106
Sevenoaks TN13 278 FE122
Elmstead Cres, Well. DA16 188 EW79
Elmstead Gdns, Wor.Pk. KT4 221 CU104
Elmstead Glade, Chis. BR7 207 EM93
Elmstead La, Chis. BR7 207 EM92
Elmstead Rd, Erith DA8 189 FE81
Ilford IG3 147 ES61
West Byfleet KT14 234 BG113
⇌ Elmstead Woods 206 EL93
Elmstone Rd, SW6 39 J6
Elm St, WC1 18 D5
Elmsway, Ashf. TW15 196 BM92
Elmswell Ct, Hert. SG14 off The Ridgeway 53 DM08
Elmswood, Bkhm KT23 252 BZ124
Chigwell IG7 off Copperfield 125 ER51
Elmsworth Av, Houns. TW3 178 CB82
Elm Ter, NW2 142 DA62
SE9 207 EN86
Grays RM20 191 FV79
Harrow HA3 117 CD52
Elm Tree Av, Esher KT10 219 CD101
Elm Tree Cl, NW8 16 A2
Ashford TW15 off Convent Rd 197 BP92
Elmtree Cl, Byfleet KT14 234 BL113
Elm Tree Cl, Cher. KT16 215 BE103
Horley RH6 290 DG147
Northolt UB5 158 BZ68
Elm Tree Ct, SE7 off Fairlawn 186 EJ79
Elmtree Hill, Chesh. HP5 76 AP30
Elm Tree Rd, NW8 16 A2
Elmtree Rd, Tedd. TW11 199 CE91
Sch Elmtree Sch, Chesh. HP5 off Elmtree Hill 76 AP30

Elm Tree Wk, Chorl. WD3 95 BF42
Elm Wk, NW3 142 DA61
SW20 221 CW98
Orpington BR6 227 EM104
Radlett WD7 99 CF36
Romford RM2 149 FG55
Elm Way, N11 120 DG51
NW10 140 CS63
Brentwood CM14 130 FU48
Epsom KT19 238 CR106
Rickmansworth WD3 114 BH46
Worcester Park KT4 221 CW104
Elmwood, Saw. CM21 58 EZ06
Welwyn Garden City AL8 51 CV10
Elmwood Av, N13 121 DL50
Borehamwood WD6 100 CP42
Feltham TW13 197 BU89
Harrow HA3 139 CG57
Elmwood Cl, Ashtd. KT21 253 CK117
Epsom KT17 239 CU108
Wallington SM6 222 DG103
Elmwood Ct, SW11 41 J6
Ashtead KT21
off Elmwood Cl 253 CK117
Wembley HA0 139 CG62
Elmwood Cres, NW9 140 CQ56
Elmwood Dr, Bex. DA5 208 EY87
Epsom KT17 239 CU107
Elmwood Gdns, W7 159 CE72
Elmwood Gro, Hem.H. HP3 62 BM23
Sch Elmwood Inf Sch, Croy.
CR0 off Lodge Rd 223 DP100
Sch Elmwood Jun Sch, Croy.
CR0 off Lodge Rd 223 DP101
Elmwood Pk, Ger.Cr. SL9 134 AY60
Sch Elm Wd Prim Sch, SE27
off Carnac St 204 DR90
Elmwood Rd, SE24 204 DR85
W4 180 CQ79
Croydon CR0 223 DP101
Mitcham CR4 222 DF97
Redhill RH1 272 DG130
Slough SL2 154 AV73
Elmworth Gro, SE21 204 DR89
Elnathan Ms, W9 15 M5
Elphinstone Rd, E17 123 DZ54
Elphinstone St, N5 143 DP63
Elppin Ct, Brox. EN10 71 DZ20
Elrick Cl, Erith DA8
off Queen St 189 FE79
Elrington Rd, E8 10 C5
Woodford Green IG8 124 EG50
Elruge Cl, West Dr. UB7 176 BK76
Elsa Rd, Well. DA16 188 EV82
Elsa St, E1 21 L7
Elsdale St, E9 11 H5
Elsden Ms, E2 21 H1
Elsden Rd, N17 122 DT53
Elsdon Rd, Wok. GU21 248 AU117
Elsenham Rd, E12 147 EM64
Elsenham St, SW18 201 CZ88
Elsham Rd, E11 146 EE62
W14 26 E5
Elsham Ter, W14 26 E5
Elsiedene Rd, N21 122 DQ45
Elsiemaud Rd, SE4 205 DZ85
Elsie Rd, SE22 184 DT84
Elsinge Rd, Enf. EN1 104 DV36
Elsinore Av, Stai. TW19 196 BL87
Elsinore Gdns, NW2 141 CY62
Elsinore Rd, SE23 205 DY88
Elsinore Way, Rich. TW9
off Lower Richmond Rd 180 CP83
Sch Elsley Prim Sch, Wem. HA9
off Tokyngton Av 160 CM65
Elsley Rd, SW11 40 F10
Sch Elsley Sch, SW11 40 G10
Elsons Ms, Welw.G.C. AL7 52 DB09
Elspeth Rd, SW11 182 DF84
Wembley HA0 140 CL64
Elsrick Av, Mord. SM4 222 DA99
Elstan Way, Croy. CR0 225 DY101
Elstead Cl, Sutt. SM3
off Stonecot Hill 221 CY102
Elsted St, SE17 31 M9
Elstow Cl, SE9 207 EN85
Ruislip HA4 138 BX59
Elstow Gdns, Dag. RM9 168 EY67
Elstow Rd, Dag. RM9 168 EY66
ELSTREE, Borwd. WD6 99 CK43
★ Elstree Aerodrome, Borwd.
WD6 99 CF41
⇌ Elstree & Borehamwood 100 CM42
Elstree Cl, Horn. RM12 169 FH66
Elstree Gdns, N9 122 DV46
Belvedere DA17 188 EY77
Ilford IG1 147 EQ64
Elstree Hill, Brom. BR1 206 EE94
Elstree Hill N, Els. WD6 99 CK44
Elstree Hill S, Els. WD6 117 CJ45
Elstree Pk, Borwd. WD6 100 CR44
Elstree Rd, Bushey Hth WD23 117 CD45
Elstree WD6 99 CG44
Elstree Way, Borwd. WD6 100 CP41
Elswick Rd, SE13 46 C10
Elswick St, SW6 39 N8
Elsworth Cl, Felt. TW14 197 BS88
Elsworthy, T.Ditt. KT7 219 CE100
Elsworthy Ri, NW3 6 D6
Elsworthy Rd, NW3 6 D7
Elsworthy Ter, NW3 6 D7
Elsynge Rd, SW18 202 DD85
ELTHAM, SE9 206 EK86
⇌ Eltham 207 EM85
Bus Eltham 207 EM85
Eltham Av, Slou. SL1 173 AL75
Slough (east section) SL1 173 AM75
Sch Eltham C of E Prim Sch,
SE9 off Roper St 207 EM85
Sch Eltham Coll Jun Sch, SE9
off Mottingham La 206 EK88
Sch Eltham Coll Sen Sch, SE9
off Grove Pk Rd 206 EK89
Eltham Grn, SE9 206 EJ85
Eltham Grn Rd, SE9 186 EJ84
Sch Eltham Grn Sch, SE9
off Queenscroft Rd 206 EK86
Eltham High St, SE9 207 EM86
Eltham Hill, SE9 206 EK85
Sch Eltham Hill Tech Coll for Girls,
SE9 off Eltham Hill 206 EL86
★ Eltham Palace, SE9 206 EL87
Eltham Palace Rd, SE9 206 EJ86
Eltham Pk Gdns, SE9 187 EN84
Eltham Rd, SE9 206 EJ85
SE12 206 EF85
Elthiron Rd, SW6 39 K7
Elthorne Av, W7 179 CF75
Elthorne Ct, Felt. TW13 198 BW88
Sch Elthorne Pk High Sch,
W7 off Westlea Rd 179 CF76
Elthorne Pk Rd, W7 179 CF75
Elthorne Rd, N19 143 DK61
NW9 140 CR59
Uxbridge UB8 156 BK68
Elthorne Way, NW9 140 CR58
Elthruda Rd, SE13 205 ED86
Eltisley Rd, Ilf. IG1 147 EP63
Elton Av, Barn. EN5 101 CZ43
Greenford UB6 159 CF65
Wembley HA0 139 CH64
Elton Cl, Kings.T. KT1 199 CJ94
Elton Ho, E3 11 P8
Elton Pk, Wat. WD17 97 BV40
Elton Pl, N16 9 N2
Elton Rd, Hert. SG14 54 DQ08
Kingston upon Thames KT2 220 CM95
Purley CR8 241 DJ112
Elton Way, Wat. WD25 98 CB40
Eltringham St, SW18 182 DC84
Eluna Apts, E1
off Wapping La 32 F1
Elvaston Ms, SW7 27 P6
Elvaston Pl, SW7 27 N7
Elveden Cl, Wok. GU22 250 BH117
Elveden Pl, NW10 160 CN68
Elveden Rd, NW10 160 CN68
Elvedon Rd, Cob. KT11 235 BV111
Feltham TW13 197 BT90
Elvendon Rd, N13 121 DL51
Elver Gdns, E2 20 D2
Elverson Ms, SE8 46 C9
DLR Elverson Road 46 D9
Elverson Rd, SE8 46 D8
Elverton St, SW1 29 N8
Elvet Av, Rom. RM2 150 FJ56
Elvin Dr, N.Stfd RM16 171 FX74
Elvington Grn, Brom. BR2 226 EF99
Elvington La, NW9 118 CS53
Elvino Rd, SE26 205 DY92
Elvis Rd, NW2 4 A4
Elwell Cl, Egh. TW20
off Mowbray Cres 195 BA92
Elwick Rd, S.Ock. RM15 171 FW72
Elwill Way, Beck. BR3 225 EC98
Elwin St, E2 20 C2
Elwood, Harl. CM17 74 EY16
Elwood Cl, Barn. EN5 102 DC42
Elwood St, N5 143 DP62
Elwyn Gdns, SE12 206 EG87
Ely Av, Slou. SL1 153 AQ71
Ely Cl, Amer. HP7 77 AS39
Erith DA8 189 FF82
Hatfield AL10 67 CT17
New Malden KT3 221 CT96
Ely Ct, EC1 18 F7
Ely Gdns, Borwd. WD6 100 CR43
Dagenham RM10 149 FC62
Ilford IG1 146 EL59
Elyne Rd, N4 143 DN58
Ely Pl, EC1 18 F7
Guildford GU2
off Canterbury Rd 264 AT132
Woodford Green IG8 125 EN51
Ely Rd, E10 145 EC58
Croydon CR0 224 DR99
Hounslow West TW4 178 BW83
London Heathrow Airport TW6
off Eastern Perimeter Rd 177 BT82
St. Albans AL1 65 CH21
Elysian Av, Orp. BR5 227 ES100
Elysian Pl, S.Croy. CR2 242 DQ108
Elysium Bldg, The, SE8 33 K10
Elysium Pl, SW6 38 G9
Elysium St, SW6 38 G9
Elystan Cl, Wall. SM6 241 DH109
Elystan Pl, SW3 28 D10
Elystan St, SW3 28 C9
Elystan Wk, N1 8 E9
Emanuel Av, W3 160 CQ72
Emanuel Dr, Hmptn. TW12 198 BZ92
Sch Emanuel Sch, SW11
off Battersea Ri 202 DE85
⊖ Embankment 30 B2
Embankment, SW15 38 C9
Embankment, The, Twick. TW1 199 CG88
Wraysbury TW19 194 AW87
Embankment Gdns, SW3 40 F2
Riv Embankment Pier 30 C2
Embankment Pl, WC2 30 B2
Embassy Ct, Sid. DA14 208 EV90
Welling DA16
off Welling High St 188 EV83
Embassy Gdns, Beck. BR3
off Blakeney Rd 225 DZ95
Emba St, SE16 32 D5
● Ember Cen, Walt. KT12 218 BY103
Ember Cl, Add. KT15 234 BK106
Petts Wood BR5 227 EQ101
Embercourt Rd, T.Ditt. KT7 219 CE100
Ember Fm Av, E.Mol. KT8 219 CD100
Ember Fm Way, E.Mol. KT8 219 CD100
Ember Gdns, T.Ditt. KT7 219 CE101
Ember La, E.Mol. KT8 219 CD101
Esher KT10 219 CD101
Ember Rd, Slou. SL3 175 BB76
Emberson Way, N.Wld Bas.
CM16 93 FC26
Emberton, SE5 43 N2
Emberton Ct, EC1
off Tompion St 18 G3
Embleton Rd, SE13 185 EB83
Watford WD19 115 BU48
Embleton Wk, Hmptn. TW12
off Fearnley Cres 198 BZ93
Embry Cl, Stan. HA7 117 CG49
Embry Dr, Stan. HA7 117 CG51
Embry Way, Stan. HA7 117 CG50
Emden Cl, West Dr. UB7 176 BN75
Emden St, SW6 39 M6
Emerald Cl, E16 24 G9
Emerald Ct, Slou. SL1 174 AS75
Emerald Gdns, Dag. RM8 148 FA60
Emerald Rd, NW10 160 CR67
Emerald Sq, Sthl. UB2 178 BX76
Emerald St, WC1 18 C6
Emerson Apts, N8
off Chadwell La 143 DM55
Emerson Ct, Woob.Grn HP10 132 AE57
Emerson Dr, Horn. RM11 150 FK59
Emerson Gdns, Har. HA3 140 CM58
EMERSON PARK, Horn. RM11 150 FL58
⇌ Emerson Park 150 FL59
Sch Emerson Pk Sch, Horn.
RM11 off Wych Elm Rd 150 FP59
Emerson Rd, Ilf. IG1 147 EN59
Emersons Av, Swan. BR8 209 FF94
Emerson St, SE1 31 J2
Emerton Cl, Bexh. DA6 188 EY84
Emerton Ct, Nthch HP4
off Emerton Garth 60 AS16
Emerton Garth, Nthch HP4 60 AS16
Emerton Rd, Lthd. KT22 252 CC120
Emery Hill St, SW1 29 M7
Emery St, SE1 30 F6
Emes Rd, Erith DA8 189 FC80
Emilia Cl, Enf. EN3 104 DV43
Emily Davison Dr, Epsom
KT18 255 CV118
Emily Jackson Cl, Sev. TN13 279 FH124
Emley Rd, Add. KT15 216 BG104
Emlyn Gdns, W12 180 CS75
Emlyn La, Lthd. KT22 253 CG122
Emlyn Rd, W12 180 CS75
Horley RH6 290 DE147
Redhill RH1 288 DG136
Emma Ho, Rom. RM1
off Market Link 149 FE56
Emmanuel Cl, Guil. GU2 264 AU131
Sch Emmanuel C of E Prim Sch,
NW6 5 K2
Emmanuel Lo, Chsht EN8 88 DW30
Emmanuel Rd, SW12 203 DJ88
Northwood HA6 115 BT52
Emma Rd, E13 23 M1
Emma's Cres, Stans.Abb.
SG12 55 EB11
Emma St, E2 10 E10
Emmaus Way, Chig. IG7 125 EN50
Emmett Cl, Shenley WD7 84 CL33
Emmetts Cl, Wok. GU21 248 AW117
Emmott Av, Ilf. IG6 147 EQ57
Emmott Cl, E1 21 M5
NW11 142 DC58
Emms Pas, Kings.T. KT1 219 CK96
Emperor Cl, Berk. HP4 60 AT16
Emperor's Gate, SW7 27 M7
Empire Av, N18 122 DQ50
Empire Ct, Wem. HA9 140 CP62
Empire Par, N18
off Empire Av 122 DR51
Empire Rd, Perivale UB6 159 CJ67
Empire Sq, N7 143 DL62
SE1 31 L5
SE20 off High St 205 DX94
Empire Sq E, SE1
off Empire Sq 31 L5
Empire Sq S, SE1
off Empire Sq 31 L5
Empire Sq W, SE1
off Empire Sq 31 L5
Empire Vil, Red. RH1 288 DG144
Empire Wk, Green. DA9 191 FW84
Empire Way, Wem. HA9 140 CM63
Empire Wf Rd, E14 34 G9
Empress App, SW6 39 J1
Bus Empress Approach Bus
Terminus 39 J2
Empress Av, E4 123 EB52
E12 146 EJ61
Ilford IG1 147 EM61
Woodford Green IG8 124 EF52
Empress Dr, Chis. BR7 207 EP93
Empress Ms, SE5 43 J8
Empress Pl, SW6 39 J1
Empress Rd, Grav. DA12 213 GL87
Empress St, SE17 43 K2
Empson St, E3 22 D4
Emsworth Cl, N9 122 DW46
Emsworth Rd, Ilf. IG6 125 EP54
Emsworth St, SW2 203 DM89
Emu Rd, SW8 41 H9
Ena Rd, SW16 223 DL97
Enborne Grn, S.Ock. RM15 171 FU71
Enbrook St, W10 14 F3
Endale Cl, Cars. SM5 222 DF103
Endeavour Rd, Chsht EN8 89 DY27
Sch Endeavour Sch, The, Brwd.
CM15 off Hogarth Av 131 FZ48
Endeavour Way, SW19 202 DB91
Barking IG11 168 EU68
Croydon CR0 223 DK101
Endell St, WC2 18 A8
Enderby St, SE10 47 H1
Enderley Cl, Har. HA3
off Enderley Rd 117 CE53
Enderley Rd, Har. HA3 117 CE53
Endersby Rd, Barn. EN5 101 CW43
Endersleigh Gdns, NW4 141 CU56
Endlebury Rd, E4 123 EB47
Endlesham Rd, SW12 202 DG87
Endsleigh Cl, S.Croy. CR2 242 DW110
Endsleigh Gdns, WC1 17 N4
Hersham KT12 236 BW106
Ilford IG1 147 EM61
Surbiton KT6 219 CJ100
● Endsleigh Ind Est, Sthl.
UB2 178 BZ77
Endsleigh Pl, WC1 17 P4
Endsleigh Rd, W13 159 CG73
South Merstham RH1 273 DJ129
Southall UB2 178 BY77
Endsleigh St, WC1 17 N4
Endway, Surb. KT5 220 CN101
Endwell Rd, SE4 45 M9
Endymion Ct, Hat. AL10
off Endymion Rd 67 CW17
Endymion Ms, Hat. AL10
off Endymion Rd 67 CW17
Endymion Rd, N4 143 DN59
SW2 203 DM86
Hatfield AL10 67 CW17
Energen Cl, NW10 160 CS65
ENFIELD, EN1 - EN3 104 DT41
⇌ Enfield Chase 104 DQ41
Enfield Cl, Uxb. UB8 156 BK68
Coll Enfield Coll, Enf. EN3
off Hertford Rd 104 DW41
Sch Enfield Co Sch, Lwr Sch, Enf.
EN2 off Rosemary Av 104 DS39
Upr Sch, Enf. EN2
off Holly Wk 104 DR41
● Enfield Enterprise Cen, Enf.
EN3 off Queensway 104 DW43
Sch Enfield Gram Sch, Lwr Sch,
Enf. EN1 off Baker St 104 DR40
Upr Sch, Enf. EN2
off Market Pl 104 DR41
ENFIELD HIGHWAY, Enf. EN3 104 DW41
ENFIELD LOCK, Enf. EN3 105 DZ37
⇌ Enfield Lock 105 DY37
Enfield Lock, Enf. EN3 105 EA38
Enfield Retail Pk, Enf. EN1 104 DV41
Enfield Rd, N1 9 P7
W3 180 CP75
Brentford TW8 179 CK78
Enfield EN2 103 DK42
Enfield Rd, Lon.Hthrw Air. TW6
off Eastern Perimeter Rd 177 BS82
Jct Enfield Rd Rbt, Lon.Hthrw Air.
TW6 177 BS82
ENFIELD TOWN, Enf. EN2 104 DR40
⇌ Enfield Town 104 DS42
Enfield Wk, Brent. TW8 179 CK78
ENFIELD WASH, Enf. EN3 105 DX38
Enford St, W1 16 E6
Engadine Cl, Croy. CR0 224 DT104
Engadine St, SW18 201 CZ88
Engate St, SE13 185 EC84
Engayne Gdns, Upmin. RM14 150 FP60
Sch Engayne Prim Sch, Upmin.
RM14 off Severn Dr 151 FS58
Engel Pk, NW7 119 CW51
Engineer Cl, SE18 187 EN79
Engineers Way, Wem. HA9 140 CN63
Engineer's Wf, Nthlt. UB5 158 BZ70
Englands La, NW3 6 E5
Loughton IG10 107 EN40
England Way, N.Mal. KT3 220 CP98
Englefield Cl, Croy. CR0
off Queen's Rd 224 DQ100
Enfield EN2 103 DN40
Englefield Green TW20
off Alexandra Rd 194 AW93
Orpington BR5 227 ET99
Englefield Cres, Orp. BR5 227 ET98
ENGLEFIELD GREEN, Egh.
TW20 194 AV92
Englefield Grn, Eng.Grn TW20 194 AW91
Sch Englefield Grn Inf Sch, Eng.Grn
TW20 off Barley Mow Rd 194 AW92
Englefield Path, Orp. BR5 227 ET98
Englefield Rd, N1 9 L5
Orpington BR5 228 EU98
Engleheart Dr, Felt. TW14 197 BT86
Engleheart Rd, SE6 205 EB87
Englehurst, Eng.Grn TW20 194 AW93
Englemere Pk, Oxshott KT22 236 CB114
Englewood Rd, SW12 203 DH86
Engliff La, Wok. GU22 249 BF116
English Gdns, Wrays. TW19 174 AX84
English Grds, SE1 31 N3
Sch English Martyrs' Cath
Prim Sch, SE17 31 M9
Sch English Martyrs RC Prim Sch,
E1 20 B9
English St, E3 21 N4
Enid Cl, Brick.Wd AL2 82 BZ31
Enid St, SE16 32 B6
Enmore Av, SE25 224 DU99
Enmore Gdns, SW14 200 CR85
Enmore Rd, SE25 224 DU99
SW15 181 CW84
Southall UB1 158 CA70
Ennerdale Av, Horn. RM12 149 FG64
Stanmore HA7 139 CJ55
Ennerdale Cl, Felt. TW14 197 BT88
St. Albans AL1 65 CH22
Sutton SM1 239 CZ105
Ennerdale Cres, Slou. SL1 152 AJ71
Ennerdale Dr, NW9 140 CS57
Watford WD25 82 BW33
Ennerdale Gdns, Wem. HA9 139 CJ60
Ennerdale Ho, E3 21 N4
Ennerdale Rd, Bexh. DA7 188 FA81
Richmond TW9 180 CM82
Ennersdale Rd, SE13 205 ED85
Ennismore Av, W4 181 CT77
Greenford UB6 159 CE65
Guildford GU1 265 AZ134
Ennismore Gdns, SW7 28 C5
Thames Ditton KT7 219 CE100
Ennismore Gdns Ms, SW7 28 C6
Ennismore Ms, SW7 28 C6
Ennismore St, SW7 28 C6
Ennis Rd, N4 143 DN60
SE18 187 EQ79
Ensign Cl, Lon.Hthrw Air. TW6 177 BS83
Purley CR8 241 DN110
Stanwell TW19 196 BK88
Ensign Dr, N13 122 DQ48
Ensign Ho, SW8
off St. George Wf 42 A2
Ensign St, E1 20 C10
Ensign Way, Stanw. TW19 196 BK88
Wallington SM6 241 DL108
Enslin Rd, SE9 207 EN86
Ensor Ms, SW7 28 A10
Enstone Rd, Enf. EN3 105 DY41
Uxbridge UB10 136 BM62
Enterdent, The, Gdse. RH9 275 DX133
Enterdent Rd, Gdse. RH9 274 DW134
● Enterprise Cen, The,
Pot.B. EN6 85 CY30
Enterprise Cl, Croy. CR0 223 DN102
● Enterprise Distribution Cen,
Til. RM18 193 GG84
● Enterprise Est, Guil. GU1 264 AY130
Enterprise Ho, E9 10 G7
● Enterprise Ind Est, SE16 32 G10
Enterprise Way, NW10 161 CU69
SW18 182 DA84
Hemel Hempstead HP2 63 BQ18
Teddington TW11 199 CF92
Enterprize Way, SE8 33 N8
Entertainment Av, SE10
off Millennium Way 35 J3
Envoy Av, Lon.Hthrw Air. TW6 177 BT83
Jct Envoy Av Rbt, Lon.Hthrw Air.
TW6 177 BT83
Eothen Cl, Cat. CR3 258 DU124
Epirus Ms, SW6 39 J4
Epirus Rd, SW6 39 H4
EPPING, CM16 91 ES31
⊖ Epping 92 EU31
Epping Cl, E14 34 B8
Romford RM7 149 FB55
★ Epping Forest, Epp. CM16
& Loug. IG10 106 EJ39
Coll Epping Forest Coll, Loug.
IG10 off Borders La 107 EP42
★ Epping Forest District Mus,
Wal.Abb. EN9 off Sun St 89 EC33
Coll Epping Forest Fld Cen,
High Beach IG10
off Wake Rd 106 EJ38
Epping Glade, E4 105 EC44
EPPING GREEN, Epp. CM16 73 EN24
EPPING GREEN, Hert. SG13 69 DK21
Epping Grn, Hem.H. HP2 62 BN15
Epping Grn Rd, Epp.Grn CM16 73 EN21
Epping La, Stap.Taw. RM4 108 EV40
Epping Long Grn, Epp.Grn
CM16 73 EM24
Epping New Rd, Buck.H. IG9 124 EH47
Loughton IG10 106 EH43
Epping Pl, N1 8 F5
Sch Epping Prim Sch, Epp.
CM16 off St. John's Rd 91 ET30
Epping Rd, Epp. CM16 107 EM36
Epping Green CM16 91 ER27
North Weald Bassett CM16 92 EW28
North Weald Bassett North
CM16 75 FD24
Ongar CM5 75 FF24
Roydon CM19 72 EK18
Toot Hill CM5 93 FC30
Waltham Abbey EN9 72 EK18
EPPING UPLAND, Epp. CM16 91 EQ25
Sch Epping Upland C of E Prim Sch,
Epp.Grn CM16
off Carters La 73 EP24
Epping Way, E4 105 EB44
Epple Rd, SW6 39 H6
EPSOM, KT17 - KT19 238 CQ114
⇌ Epsom 238 CR113
Coll Epsom Adult Ed Cen, Epsom
KT17 off Church St 238 CS113
Sch Epsom & Ewell High Sch,
W.Ewell KT19
off Ruxley La 238 CQ106
● Epsom Business Pk, Epsom
KT17 238 CS111
Epsom Cl, Bexh. DA7 189 FB83
Northolt UB5 138 BZ64
Sch Epsom Coll, Epsom KT17
off College Rd 239 CU114
⇌ Epsom Downs 255 CV115
Epsom Downs, Epsom KT18 255 CT118
● Epsom Downs Metro Cen,
Tad. KT20 off Waterfield 255 CV120
★ Epsom Downs Racecourse,
Epsom KT18 255 CT118
Epsom Gap, Lthd. KT22 253 CH115
H Epsom Gen Hosp, Epsom
KT18 254 CQ115
Epsom La N, Epsom KT18 255 CV118
Tadworth KT20 255 CV118
Epsom La S, Tad. KT20 255 CW121
Sch Epsom Prim Sch, Epsom
KT19 off Pound La 238 CR111
Epsom Rd, E10 145 EC58
Ashtead KT21 254 CM118
Croydon CR0 241 DN105
Epsom KT17 239 CT110
Guildford GU1, GU4 265 BE133
Ilford IG3 147 ET58
Leatherhead KT22 253 CH121
Morden SM4 221 CZ101
Sutton SM3 221 CZ101
West Horsley KT24 267 BP130
Epsom Sq, Lon.Hthrw Air. TW6
off Eastern Perimeter Rd 177 BT82
Epsom Way, Horn. RM12 150 FM63
Epstein Rd, SE28 168 EU74
Epworth Rd, Islw. TW7 179 CH80
Epworth St, EC2 19 M5
Equana Apts, SE8 33 L10
Equinox Ho, Bark. IG11 167 EQ65
Equity Ms, W5 159 CK74
Equity Sq, E2 20 B3
Erasmus St, SW1 29 P9
Erbin Ct, N9 off Galahad Rd 122 DU47
Erconwald St, W12 161 CT72
Erebus Dr, SE28 187 EQ76
Eresby Dr, Beck. BR3 225 EA102
Eresby Pl, NW6 5 J7
Erica Cl, Slou. SL1 153 AL73
Erica Ct, Swan. BR8
off Azalea Dr 229 FE98
Woking GU22 248 AX118
Erica Gdns, Croy. CR0 243 EB105
Erica St, W12 161 CU73
Eric Clarke La, Bark. IG11 25 P4
Eric Cl, E7 13 N1
Ericcson Cl, SW18 202 DA85
Eric Fletcher Ct, N1
off Essex Rd 9 K6
Eric Rd, E7 13 N1
NW10 161 CT65
Romford RM6 148 EX59
Ericson Ho, N16
off Stamford Hill 144 DS60
Eric Steele Ho, St.Alb. AL2 82 CB27
Eric St, E3 21 N4
Eridge Grn Cl, Orp. BR5 228 EW102
Eridge Rd, W4 180 CR76
Erin Cl, Brom. BR1 206 EE94
Ilford IG3 148 EU58
Erin Ct, NW2 4 B4
Erindale, SE18 187 ER79
Erindale Ter, SE18 187 ER79
Eriswell Cres, Hersham KT12 235 BS107
Eriswell Rd, Hersham KT12 235 BT105
ERITH, DA8; DA18 189 FD79
⇌ Erith 189 FE78
H Erith & District Hosp,
Erith DA8 189 FD79
Erith Ct, Purf. RM19 190 FN77
Erith Cres, Rom. RM5 127 FC53
Erith High St, Erith DA8 189 FE78
★ Erith Lib & Mus,
Erith DA8
off Walnut Tree Rd 189 FE78
● Erith Riverside, Erith DA8 189 FE79
Erith Rd, Belv. DA17 188 FA78
Bexleyheath DA7 189 FB84
Erith DA8 189 FB84
Sch Erith Sch, Erith DA8
off Avenue Rd 189 FD80
Erkenwald Cl, Cher. KT16 215 BE101
Erlanger Rd, SE14 45 K8
Erlesmere Gdns, W13 179 CG76
Ermine Cl, Chsht EN7 88 DV31
Hounslow TW4 178 BW82
St. Albans AL3 64 CA21
Ermine Ho, N17
off Moselle St 122 DT52
Ermine Ms, E2 10 A9
Ermine Rd, N15 144 DT58
SE13 185 EB83
Ermine Side, Enf. EN1 104 DU43
Ermington Rd, SE9 207 EQ89
Ermyn Cl, Lthd. KT22 253 CK121
Ermyn Way, Lthd. KT22 253 CK121
Ernald Av, E6 166 EL68
Ernan Cl, S.Ock. RM15 171 FU71

Ernan Rd, S.Ock. RM15 . . . . 171 FU71
Erncroft Way, Twick. TW1 . . . . . 199 CF86
Ernest Av, SE27 . . . . 203 DP91
Sch Ernest Bevin Coll, SW17
off Beechcroft Rd 202 DE89
Ernest Cl, Beck. BR3 . . . . 225 EA99
Ernest Gdns, W4 . . . . 180 CP79
Ernest Gro, Beck. BR3 . . . . 225 DZ99
Ernest Rd, Horn. RM11 . . . . 150 FL58
Kingston upon Thames KT1 . 220 CP96
Ernest Sq, Kings.T. KT1 . . . . . . 220 CP96
Ernest St, E1 . . . . 21 K5
Ernle Rd, SW20 . . . . 201 CV94
Ernshaw Pl, SW15
off Carlton Dr. 201 CY85
★ Eros, W1 . . . . 29 N1
Eros Ho, SE6
off Brownhill Rd 205 EB87
Erpingham Rd, SW15 . . . . 181 CW83
Erridge Rd, SW19 . . . . 222 DA96
Erriff Dr, S.Ock. RM15 . . . . 171 FT71
Errington Cl, Grays RM16
off Cedar Rd 193 GH76
Hatfield AL10 . . . . 66 CS17
Errington Dr, Wind. SL4 . . . . . . 173 AN81
Errington Rd, W9 . . . . 15 H4
Errol Gdns, Hayes UB4 . . . . 157 BV70
New Malden KT3 . . . . 221 CU98
Erroll Rd, Rom. RM1 . . . . 149 FF56
Errol St, EC1 . . . . 19 K5
Erskine Cl, Sutt. SM1 . . . . 222 DE104
Erskine Cres, N17 . . . . 144 DV56
Erskine Hill, NW11 . . . . 142 DA57
Erskine Ho, SE7
off Springfield Gro 186 EJ79
Erskine Ms, NW3 . . . . 6 F7
Erskine Rd, E17 . . . . 145 DZ56
NW3 . . . . 6 F7
Sutton SM1 . . . . 240 DD105
Watford WD19 . . . . 116 BW48
Erwood Rd, SE7 . . . . 37 H10
Esam Way, SW16 . . . . 203 DN92
Esbies Est, Saw. CM21 . . . . 58 EZ05
Escomb Ct, Whyt. CR3
off Godstone Rd 258 DU119
Escombe Dr, Guil. GU2 . . . . 264 AV129
Escott Gdns, SE9 . . . . 206 EL91
Escott Pl, Ott. KT16 . . . . 233 BC107
Escot Way, Barn. EN5 . . . . 101 CW43
Coll ESCP-EAP European Sch of
Management, NW3 . . . . 5 K1
Escreet Gro, SE18 . . . . 37 L8
Esdaile Gdns, Upmin. RM14 . . 151 FR59
Esdaile La, Hodd. EN11 . . . . 71 EA18
ESHER, KT10 . . . . 236 CB105
⇌ Esher 219 CD103
Esher Av, Rom. RM7 . . . . 149 FC58
Sutton SM3 . . . . 221 CX104
Walton-on-Thames KT12 . . 217 BU101
Esher Bypass, Chess. KT9 . . . . . 237 CH108
Cobham KT11 . . . . 235 BU112
Esher KT10 . . . . 237 CH108
Sch Esher Ch Sch, Esher KT10
off Milbourne La 236 CC106
Esher Cl, Bex. DA5 . . . . 208 EY88
Esher KT10 . . . . 236 CB106
Sch Esher C of E High Sch,
Esher KT10 off More La . . . 218 CA104
Coll Esher Coll, T.Ditt. KT7
off Weston Grn Rd 219 CE101
Jct Esher Common, Esher
KT10 . . . . 236 CC110
Esher Cres, Lon.Hthrw Air. TW6
off Eastern Perimeter Rd . . 177 BS82
Esher Gdns, SW19 . . . . 201 CX89
Esher Grn, Esher KT10 . . . . 236 CB105
Sch Esher Grn Adult Learning Cen,
Esher KT10 off Esher Grn. . 236 CB105
Esher Grn Dr, Esher KT10 . . . . 218 CB104
Esher Ms, Mitch. CR4 . . . . 222 DF97
Esher Pk Av, Esher KT10 . . . . . 236 CC105
Esher Pl Av, Esher KT10 . . . . . 236 CB105
Esher Rd, E.Mol. KT8 . . . . 219 CD100
Hersham KT12 . . . . 236 BX106
Ilford IG3 . . . . 147 ES62
Eskdale, NW1 . . . . 17 L1
London Colney AL2 . . . . 84 CM27
Eskdale Av, Chesh. HP5 . . . . . . 76 AQ30
Northolt UB5 . . . . 158 BZ67
Eskdale Cl, Dart. DA2 . . . . 210 FQ89
Wembley HA9 . . . . 139 CK61
Eskdale Ct, Hem.H. HP2
off Lonsdale 62 BL17
Eskdale Gdns, Pur. CR8 . . . . . . 242 DR114
Eskdale Rd, Bexh. DA7 . . . . 188 FA82
Uxbridge UB8 . . . . 156 BH68
Eskley Gdns, S.Ock. RM15 . . . . 171 FV70
Eskmont Ridge, SE19 . . . . 204 DS94
Esk Rd, E13 . . . . 23 P4
Esk Way, Rom. RM1 . . . . 127 FD52
Esmar Cres, NW9 . . . . 141 CU59
Esme Ho, SW15 . . . . 181 CT84
Esmeralda Rd, SE1 . . . . 32 D9
Esmond Cl, Rain. RM13
off Dawson Dr. 169 FH66
Esmond Gdns, W4
off South Par 180 CR77
Esmond Rd, NW6 . . . . 5 H9
W4 . . . . 180 CR77
Esmond St, SW15 . . . . 181 CY84
Esparto St, SW18 . . . . 202 DB87
Essendene Cl, Cat. CR3 . . . . . . 258 DS123
Sch Essendene Lo Sch, Cat.
CR3 off Essendene Rd 258 DS123
Essendene Rd, Cat. CR3 . . . . . 258 DS123
Essenden Rd, Belv. DA17 . . . . . 188 FA78
South Croydon CR2 . . . . 242 DS108
Sch Essendine Prim Sch, W9 . . . 15 K3
Essendine Rd, W9 . . . . 15 K4
ESSENDON, Hat. AL9 . . . . 68 DE17
Sch Essendon C of E Prim Sch,
Essen. AL9 off School La . . . 68 DF17
Essendon Gdns, Welw.G.C. AL7 . 51 CZ09
Essendon Hill, Essen. AL9 . . . . . 68 DE17
Essendon Pl, Essen. AL9 . . . . . . 68 DE19
Essendon Rd, Hert. SG13 . . . . . . 68 DG15
Essex Av, Islw. TW7 . . . . 179 CE83
Slough SL2 . . . . 153 AQ71
Essex Cl, E17 . . . . 145 DY56
Addlestone KT15 . . . . 234 BJ105
Morden SM4 . . . . 221 CX101
Essex Cl, Rom. RM7 . . . . 149 FB56
Ruislip HA4 . . . . 138 BX60
Essex Ct, EC4 . . . . 18 E9
SW13 . . . . 181 CT82
Essex Gdns, N4 . . . . 143 DP58
Hornchurch RM11 . . . . 150 FM57
Essex Gro, SE19 . . . . 204 DR93
Essex Ho, E14 . . . . 22 C8
Essex La, Kings L. WD4 . . . . 81 BS33
Essex Pk, N3 . . . . 120 DB51
Essex Pk Ms, W3 . . . . 160 CS74
Essex Pl, W4 . . . . 180 CQ77
Essex Pl Sq, W4
off Chiswick High Rd 180 CR77
Sch Essex Prim Sch, E12
off Sheridan Rd. 147 EM64
⇌ Essex Road 9 J7
Essex Rd, E4 . . . . 124 EE46
E10 . . . . 145 EC58
E12 . . . . 146 EL64
E17 . . . . 145 DY58
E18 . . . . 124 EH54
N1 . . . . 9 J7
NW10 . . . . 160 CS66
W3 . . . . 160 CQ73
W4 off Belmont Ter 180 CR77
Barking IG11 . . . . 167 ER66
Borehamwood WD6 . . . . 100 CN41
Chadwell Heath RM6 . . . . . . 148 EW59
Chesham HP5 . . . . 76 AQ29
Dagenham RM10 . . . . 149 FC64
Dartford DA1 . . . . 210 FK86
Enfield EN2 . . . . 104 DR42
Gravesend DA11 . . . . 213 GG88
Grays RM20 . . . . 191 FU79
Hoddesdon EN11 . . . . 71 EC18
Longfield DA3 . . . . 231 FX96
Romford RM7 . . . . 149 FB56
Watford WD17 . . . . 97 BU40
Essex Rd S, E11 . . . . 145 ED59
Essex St, E7 . . . . 13 N2
WC2 . . . . 18 E10
St. Albans AL1 . . . . 65 CE19
Essex Twr, SE20 . . . . 224 DV95
Essex Vil, W8 . . . . 27 J5
Essex Way, Epp. CM16 . . . . 92 EV32
Great Warley CM13 . . . . 129 FW51
Hoddesdon EN11 . . . . 71 EC17
Ongar CM5 . . . . 93 FF29
Essex Wf, E5 . . . . 144 DW61
Essian St, E1 . . . . 21 L6
Essoldo Way, Edg. HA8 . . . . . . 140 CM55
Estate Way, E10 . . . . 145 DZ60
Estcourt Rd, SE25 . . . . 224 DV100
SW6 . . . . 38 G4
Watford WD17 . . . . 98 BW41
Estella Av, N.Mal. KT3 . . . . 221 CV98
Estelle Rd, NW3 . . . . 6 F1
Esterbrooke St, SW1 . . . . 29 N9
Este Rd, SW11 . . . . 40 C10
Estfeld Cl, Hodd. EN11 . . . . 55 EB14
Esther Cl, N21 . . . . 121 DN45
Esther Rd, E11 . . . . 146 EE59
Estoria Cl, SW2 . . . . 203 DN87
★ Estorick Collection of Modern
Italian Art, N1 . . . . 9 H5
Estreham Rd, SW16 . . . . 203 DK93
Estridge Cl, Houns. TW3 . . . . . . 178 CA84
Estuary Cl, Bark. IG11 . . . . 168 EV69
Eswyn Rd, SW17 . . . . 202 DF91
Etchingham Pk Rd, N3 . . . . 120 DB52
Etchingham Rd, E15 . . . . 145 EC63
Eternit Wk, SW6 . . . . 38 B6
Etfield Gro, Sid. DA14 . . . . 208 EV92
Ethel Bailey Cl, Epsom KT19 . . 238 CN112
Ethelbert Cl, Brom. BR1 . . . . . . 226 EG97
Ethelbert Gdns, Ilf. IG2 . . . . 147 EM57
Ethelbert Rd, SW20 . . . . 221 CX95
Bromley BR1 . . . . 226 EG97
Erith DA8 . . . . 189 FC80
Hawley DA2 . . . . 210 FL91
Orpington BR5 . . . . 228 EX97
Ethelbert St, SW12 . . . . 203 DH88
Ethelburga Rd, Rom. RM3 . . . . 128 FM53
Ethelburga St, SW11 . . . . 40 D6
Ethelburga Twr, SW11 . . . . 40 D6
Ethelden Av, N10 . . . . 143 DJ56
Ethelden Rd, W12 . . . . 161 CV74
Ethelred Cl, Welw.G.C. AL7 . . . . 51 CZ10
Ethelred Ct, Whyt. CR3
off Godstone Rd 258 DU119
Ethelred Est, SE11 . . . . 30 D9
Ethel Rd, E16 . . . . 24 A9
Ashford TW15 . . . . 196 BL92
Ethel St, SE17 . . . . 31 J9
Ethel Ter, Orp. BR6 . . . . 246 EW109
Ethelwine Pl, Abb.L. WD5
off The Crescent 81 BT30
Etheridge Grn, Loug. IG10 . . . . 107 EQ41
Etheridge Rd, NW4 . . . . 141 CW59
Loughton IG10 . . . . 107 EP40
Etherley Rd, N15 . . . . 144 DQ57
Etherow St, SE22 . . . . 204 DU86
Etherstone Grn, SW16 . . . . 203 DN91
Etherstone Rd, SW16 . . . . 203 DN91
Ethnard Rd, SE15 . . . . 44 E3
Ethorpe Cl, Ger.Cr. SL9 . . . . 134 AY57
Ethorpe Cres, Ger.Cr. SL9 . . . . 134 AY57
Ethronvi Rd, Bexh. DA7 . . . . . . 188 EY83
Etloe Rd, E10 . . . . 145 EA61
Etna Rd, St.Alb. AL3 . . . . 65 CD19
ETON, Wind. SL4 . . . . 173 AQ80
Eton Av, N12 . . . . 120 DC52
NW3 . . . . 6 C6
Barnet EN4 . . . . 102 DE44
Hounslow TW5 . . . . 178 BZ79
New Malden KT3 . . . . 220 CR99
Wembley HA0 . . . . 139 CH63
Eton Cl, SW18 . . . . 202 DB87
Datchet SL3 . . . . 174 AU79
Sch Eton Coll, Eton SL4
off High St 173 AR79
Eton Coll Rd, NW3 . . . . 6 F5
Eton Ct, NW3 . . . . 6 B6
Eton SL4 . . . . 173 AR80
Staines TW18 . . . . 195 BF92
Wembley HA0 . . . . 139 CJ63
Sch Eton End PNEU Sch, Datchet
SL3 off Eton Rd 174 AU79
Eton Garages, NW3 . . . . 6 D5
Eton Gro, NW9 . . . . 140 CN55
SE13 . . . . 186 EE83
Eton Hall, NW3 . . . . 6 F5
Sch Eton Ho The Manor Sch, SW4
off Clapham Common
N Side 183 DH84
Eton Pl, NW3 . . . . 6 G6
Sch Eton Porny C of E First Sch,
Eton SL4 off High St 173 AR79
Eton Ri, NW3 . . . . 6 F5
Eton Rd, NW3 . . . . 6 E6
Datchet SL3 . . . . 174 AT78
Hayes UB3 . . . . 177 BT80
Ilford IG1 . . . . 147 EQ64
Orpington BR6 . . . . 246 EV105
Eton Sq, Eton SL4 . . . . 173 AR80
Eton St, Rich. TW9 . . . . 200 CL85
Eton Vil, NW3 . . . . 6 F5
Eton Way, Dart. DA1 . . . . 190 FJ84
ETON WICK, Wind. SL4 . . . . 173 AM77
Sch Eton Wick C of E First Sch,
Eton Wick SL4
off Sheepcote Rd 173 AN78
Eton Wick Rd, Wind. SL4 . . . . . 173 AL77
Etta St, SE8 . . . . 45 M2
Etton Cl, Horn. RM12 . . . . 150 FL61
Ettrick St, E14 . . . . 22 F8
Etwell Pl, Surb. KT5 . . . . 220 CM100
Euclid Way, Grays RM20 . . . . . . 191 FT78
Euesden Cl, N9 . . . . 122 DV48
Eugene Cl, Rom. RM2 . . . . 150 FJ56
Eugenia Rd, SE16 . . . . 33 H9
Eugenie Ms, Chis. BR7 . . . . 227 EP95
Eunice Gro, Chesh. HP5 . . . . 76 AR32
Eureka Gdns, Epp.Grn CM16 . . . 73 EN21
Eureka Rd, Kings.T. KT1
off Washington Rd 220 CN96
Coll Eurocentres, Lee Grn, SE3
off Meadowcourt Rd. 186 EF84
London Cen, SW1 . . . . 29 K9
Euro Cl, NW10 . . . . 161 CU65
Coll Europa Cen for Modern
Languages, Horn. RM11
off The Walk 150 FM61
Europa Pk Rd, Guil. GU1 . . . . . 264 AW133
Europa Pl, EC1 . . . . 19 J3
Europa Rd, Hem.H. HP2
off Jupiter Dr 62 BM17
● Europa Trd Est, Erith DA8 . . 189 FD78
Europe Rd, SE18 . . . . 37 K7
Eustace Bldg, SW8 . . . . 41 J3
Eustace Pl, SE18 . . . . 37 J8
Eustace Rd, E6 . . . . 24 G2
SW6 . . . . 39 J4
Guildford GU4 . . . . 265 BD132
Romford RM6 . . . . 148 EX59
⇌ Euston 17 M2
⇔ Euston 17 M2
⊖ Euston 17 M2
⊖ Euston 17 N3
Euston Av, Wat. WD18 . . . . 97 BT43
Euston Cen, NW1
off Triton Sq 17 L4
Euston Gro, NW1 . . . . 17 N3
Euston Rd, N1 . . . . 18 A2
NW1 . . . . 17 K5
Croydon CR0 . . . . 223 DN102
⊖ Euston Square 17 M4
Euston Sq, NW1 . . . . 17 N3
Euston Sta Colonnade, NW1 . . . 17 N3
Euston St, NW1 . . . . 17 M4
● Euston Twr, NW1 . . . . 17 L4
Evan Cook Cl, SE15 . . . . 44 G7
Evandale Rd, SW9 . . . . 42 F8
Evangelist Rd, NW5 . . . . 7 K1
Evans Av, Wat. WD25 . . . . 97 BT35
● Evans Business Cen, NW2 . 141 CU62
Evans Cl, E8 . . . . 10 B5
Croxley Green WD3 . . . . 96 BN43
Greenhithe DA9 . . . . 211 FU85
Evansdale, Rain. RM13
off New Zealand Way 169 FF69
Evans Gro, Felt. TW13 . . . . 198 CA89
St. Albans AL4 . . . . 65 CJ16
Evans Rd, SE6 . . . . 206 EE89
Evanston Av, E4 . . . . 123 EC52
Evanston Gdns, Ilf. IG4 . . . . 146 EL58
Evans Wf, Hem.H. HP3 . . . . 62 BL24
Eva Rd, Rom. RM6 . . . . 148 EW59
H Evelina Children's Hosp,
SE1 . . . . 30 C6
Evelina Rd, SE15 . . . . 44 G10
SE20 . . . . 205 DX94
Eveline Lowe Est, SE16 . . . . 32 C7
Sch Eveline Lowe Prim Sch,
SE1 . . . . 44 D1
Eveline Rd, Mitch. CR4 . . . . 222 DF95
Evelyn Av, NW9 . . . . 140 CR56
Ruislip HA4 . . . . 137 BT58
Titsey RH8 . . . . 260 EJ124
Evelyn Cl, Twick. TW2 . . . . 198 CB87
Woking GU22 . . . . 248 AX120
Evelyn Cotts, Dor. RH5 . . . . . . 284 BX143
Evelyn Ct, N1 . . . . 19 L1
Evelyn Cres, Sun. TW16 . . . . . . 217 BT95
Evelyn Denington Rd, E6 . . . . . . 25 H5
Evelyn Dr, Pnr. HA5 . . . . 116 BX52
Evelyn Fox Ct, W10 . . . . 14 B7
Evelyn Gdns, SW7 . . . . 40 A1
Godstone RH9 . . . . 274 DW130
Richmond TW9 . . . . 180 CL84
Evelyn Gro, W5 . . . . 160 CM74
Southall UB1 . . . . 158 BZ72
Evelyn Rd, E16 . . . . 35 P2
E17 . . . . 145 EC56
SW19 . . . . 202 DB92
W4 . . . . 180 CR76
Cockfosters EN4 . . . . 102 DF42
Ham TW10 . . . . 199 CJ90
Richmond TW9 . . . . 180 CL83
Evelyns Cl, Uxb. UB8 . . . . 156 BN72
Evelyn Sharp Cl, Rom. RM2
off Amery Gdns. 150 FK55
Evelyn St, SE8 . . . . 33 L9
Evelyn Ter, Rich. TW9 . . . . 180 CL83
Evelyn Wk, N1 . . . . 19 L1
Great Warley CM13
off Essex Way 129 FW51
Evelyn Way, Epsom KT19 . . . . . 238 CN111
Stoke D'Abernon KT11 . . . . . 252 BZ116
Sunbury-on-Thames TW16 . . 217 BT95
Wallington SM6 . . . . 241 DK105
Evelyn Yd, W1 . . . . 17 N8
Evening Hill, Beck. BR3 . . . . . . 205 EC94
Evensyde, Wat. WD18 . . . . 97 BR44
Evenwood Cl, SW15 . . . . 201 CY85
Everard Av, Brom. BR2 . . . . 226 EG102
Slough SL1 . . . . 174 AS75
Everard Cl, St.Alb. AL1 . . . . 65 CD22
Everard La, Cat. CR3
off Tillingdown Hill 258 DU122
Everard Way, Wem. HA9 . . . . . 140 CL62
Everatt Cl, SW18
off Amerland Rd 201 CZ86
Everdon Rd, SW13 . . . . 181 CU79
Everest Cl, Nthflt DA11 . . . . . . 212 GE90
Everest Ct, Wok. GU21
off Langmans Way 248 AS116
Everest Pl, E14 . . . . 22 E6
Swanley BR8 . . . . 229 FD98
Everest Rd, SE9 . . . . 206 EL85
Stanwell TW19 . . . . 196 BK87
Everest Way, Hem.H. HP2 . . . . . 62 BN19
Everett Cl, Bushey Hth WD23 . . 117 CE46
Cheshunt EN7 . . . . 88 DQ25
Pinner HA5 . . . . 137 BT55
Everett Wk, Belv. DA17
off Osborne Rd 188 EZ78
Everglade, Bigg.H. TN16 . . . . . 260 EK118
Everglade Strand, NW9 . . . . . . 119 CT53
Evergreen Cl, SE20 . . . . 204 DW94
Evergreen Ct, Stanw. TW19
off Evergreen Way 196 BK87
Evergreen Oak Av, Wind. SL4 . . 174 AU83
Evergreen Sq, E8 . . . . 10 A6
Evergreen Wk, Hem.H. HP3 . . . . 62 BL22
Evergreen Way, Hayes UB3 . . . 157 BT73
Stanwell TW19 . . . . 196 BK87
Everilda St, N1 . . . . 8 D9
Evering Rd, E5 . . . . 144 DT62
N16 . . . . 144 DT62
Everington Rd, N10 . . . . 120 DF54
Everington St, W6 . . . . 38 D2
Everitt Rd, NW10 . . . . 160 CR69
Everlands Cl, Wok. GU22 . . . . . 248 AY118
Everlasting La, St.Alb. AL3 . . . . . 64 CC19
Everleigh St, N4 . . . . 143 DM60
Eve Rd, E11 . . . . 13 J1
E15 . . . . 23 K1
N17 . . . . 144 DS55
Isleworth TW7 . . . . 179 CG84
Woking GU21 . . . . 249 BB115
Eversfield Gdns, NW7 . . . . 118 CS51
Eversfield Rd, Reig. RH2 . . . . . 272 DB134
Richmond TW9 . . . . 180 CM82
Evershed Wk, W4 . . . . 180 CQ76
Eversholt Ct, Barn. EN5
off Lyonsdown Rd 102 DC43
Eversholt St, NW1 . . . . 7 M10
Evershot Rd, N4 . . . . 143 DM60
Eversleigh Gdns, Upmin.
RM14 . . . . 151 FR60
Eversleigh Rd, E6 . . . . 166 EK67
N3 . . . . 119 CZ52
SW11 . . . . 40 G9
Barnet EN5 . . . . 102 DC43
Eversley Av, Bexh. DA7 . . . . 189 FD82
Wembley HA9 . . . . 140 CN61
Eversley Cl, N21 . . . . 103 DM44
Loughton IG10 . . . . 107 EQ41
Eversley Cres, N21 . . . . 103 DM44
Isleworth TW7 . . . . 179 CD81
Ruislip HA4 . . . . 137 BS61
Eversley Cross, Bexh. DA7 . . . . 189 FE82
Eversley Mt, N21 . . . . 103 DM44
Eversley Pk, SW19 . . . . 201 CV92
Eversley Pk Rd, N21 . . . . 103 DM44
Sch Eversley Prim Sch, N21
off Chaseville Pk Rd 103 DM43
Eversley Rd, SE7 . . . . 186 EH79
SE19 . . . . 204 DR94
Surbiton KT5 . . . . 220 CM98
Eversley Way, Croy. CR0 . . . . . . 243 EA105
Egham TW20 . . . . 215 BC96
Everthorpe Rd, SE15 . . . . 184 DT83
Everton Bldgs, NW1 . . . . 17 L3
Everton Dr, Stan. HA7 . . . . 140 CM55
Everton Rd, Croy. CR0 . . . . 224 DU102
Evesham Av, E17 . . . . 123 EA54
Evesham Cl, Grnf. UB6 . . . . 158 CB68
Reigate RH2 . . . . 271 CZ133
Sutton SM2 . . . . 240 DA108
Evesham Ct, W13
off Tewkesbury Rd. 159 CG74
Evesham Grn, Mord. SM4 . . . . 222 DB100
Evesham Rd, E15 . . . . 13 L8
N11 . . . . 121 DJ50
Gravesend DA12 . . . . 213 GK89
Morden SM4 . . . . 222 DB100
Reigate RH2 . . . . 271 CZ134
Evesham Rd N, Reig. RH2 . . . . 271 CZ133
Evesham St, W11 . . . . 26 C1
Evesham Wk, SE5 . . . . 43 L8
SW9 . . . . 42 E7
Evesham Way, SW11 . . . . 41 H10
Ilford IG5 . . . . 147 EN55
Evreham Rd, Iver SL0 . . . . 155 BE72
Evron Pl, Hert. SG14
off Fore St 54 DR09
Evry Rd, Sid. DA14 . . . . 208 EW93
Ewald Rd, SW6 . . . . 38 G9
Ewanrigg Ter, Wdf.Grn. IG8 . . . 124 EJ50
Ewan Rd, Harold Wd RM3 . . . . 128 FK54
Ewart Gro, N22 . . . . 121 DN53
Ewart Pl, E3 . . . . 11 N10
Ewart Rd, SE23 . . . . 205 DX87
Ewe Cl, N7 . . . . 8 B4
Ewelands, Horl. RH6 . . . . 291 DJ147
EWELL, Epsom KT17 . . . . 239 CU110
Ewell Bypass, Epsom KT17 . . . 239 CU108
Sch Ewell Castle Sch, Ewell
KT17 off Church St 239 CU109
Ewell Ct Av, Epsom KT19 . . . . . 238 CS106
Ewell Downs Rd, Epsom KT17 . 239 CU111
⇌ Ewell East 239 CV110
Sch Ewell Gro Inf & Nurs Sch,
Ewell KT17 off West St 239 CT109
Ewell Ho Gro, Epsom KT17 . . . 239 CT110
Ewellhurst Rd, Ilf. IG5 . . . . 124 EL54
Ewell Pk Gdns, Epsom KT17 . . 239 CU108
Ewell Pk Way, Ewell KT17 . . . . 239 CU107
Ewell Rd, Long Dit. KT6 . . . . . . 219 CH101
Surbiton KT6 . . . . 220 CL100
Sutton SM3 . . . . 239 CY107
⇌ Ewell West 238 CS109
Ewelme Rd, SE23 . . . . 204 DW88
Ewen Cres, SW2 . . . . 203 DN87
Ewer St, SE1 . . . . 31 J3
Ewhurst Av, S.Croy. CR2 . . . . . . 242 DT109
Ewhurst Cl, E1 . . . . 21 H7
Sutton SM2 . . . . 239 CW109
Ewhurst Ct, Mitch. CR4
off Phipps Br Rd 222 DD97
Ewhurst Rd, SE4 . . . . 205 DZ86
Exbury Rd, SE6 . . . . 205 EA89
Excalibur Ct, N9
off Galahad Rd 122 DU48
Excel Ct, WC2 . . . . 29 P1
★ ExCeL London, E16 . . . . 36 B1
ExCeL Marina, E16 . . . . 36 A1
Excelsior Cl, Kings.T. KT1
off Washington Rd 220 CN96
Excelsior Gdns, SE13 . . . . 46 E9
ExCeL Waterfront, E16 . . . . 36 B1
Exchange, The, E1
off Commercial St 20 A5
Exchange Arc, EC2 . . . . 19 P6
Exchange Cl, N11
off Benfleet Way 120 DG47
Exchange Ct, WC2 . . . . 30 B1
Exchange Ho, N8 . . . . 143 DL58
Exchange Pl, EC2 . . . . 19 N6
Exchange Rd, Wat. WD18 . . . . . 97 BV42
Exchange Sq, EC2 . . . . 19 N6
Exchange St, Rom. RM1 . . . . . . 149 FE57
Exchange Wk, Pnr. HA5 . . . . . . 138 BY59
Exeforde Av, Ashf. TW15 . . . . . . 196 BN91
Exeter Cl, E6 . . . . 25 J8
Watford WD24 . . . . 98 BW40
Exeter Ct, Surb. KT6
off Maple Rd 220 CL99
Exeter Gdns, Ilf. IG1 . . . . 146 EL60
Exeter Ho, SW15
off Putney Heath 201 CW86
Exeter Ms, NW6 . . . . 5 L5
SW6 . . . . 39 J4
Exeter Pl, Guil. GU2 . . . . 264 AT132
Exeter Rd, E16 . . . . 23 P7
E17 . . . . 145 EA57
N9 . . . . 122 DW47
N14 . . . . 121 DH46
NW2 . . . . 4 F5
Croydon CR0 . . . . 224 DS101
Dagenham RM10 . . . . 169 FB65
Enfield EN3 . . . . 105 DX41
Feltham TW13 . . . . 198 BZ90
Gravesend DA12 . . . . 213 GK90
Harrow HA2 . . . . 138 BY61
London Heathrow Airport
TW6 . . . . 177 BS83
Welling DA16 . . . . 187 ET82
Exeter St, WC2 . . . . 18 B10
Exeter Way, SE14 . . . . 45 N5
London Heathrow Airport
TW6 . . . . 177 BS82
Exford Gdns, SE12 . . . . 206 EH88
Exford Rd, SE12 . . . . 206 EH89
Exhibition Cl, W12 . . . . 26 A1
Exhibition Rd, SW7 . . . . 28 B5
Exmoor Cl, Ilf. IG6 . . . . 125 EQ53
Exmoor St, W10 . . . . 14 D5
Exmouth Mkt, EC1 . . . . 18 E4
Exmouth Ms, NW1 . . . . 17 M3
Exmouth Pl, E8 . . . . 10 E7
Exmouth Rd, E17 . . . . 145 DZ57
Grays RM17 . . . . 192 GB79
Hayes UB4 . . . . 157 BS69
Ruislip HA4 . . . . 138 BW62
Welling DA16 . . . . 188 EW81
Exmouth St, E1 . . . . 21 H8
Exning Rd, E16 . . . . 23 L5
Exon Apts, Rom. RM1
off Mercury Gdns 149 FE56
Exon St, SE17 . . . . 31 N9
Explorer Av, Stai. TW19 . . . . . . 196 BL88
Explorer Dr, Wat. WD18 . . . . 97 BT44
Express Dr, Ilf. IG3 . . . . 148 EV60
Exton Gdns, Dag. RM8 . . . . 148 EW64
Exton Rd, NW10 . . . . 160 CQ66
Exton St, SE1 . . . . 30 E3
Eyebright Cl, Croy. CR0
off Primrose La 225 DX102
Eyhurst Av, Horn. RM12 . . . . . . 149 FG62
Eyhurst Cl, NW2 . . . . 141 CU61
Kingswood KT20 . . . . 255 CZ123
Eyhurst Pk, Tad. KT20 . . . . 256 DC123
Eyhurst Spur, Kgswd KT20 . . . 255 CZ124
Eylewood Rd, SE27 . . . . 204 DQ92
Eynella Rd, SE22 . . . . 204 DT87
Eynham Rd, W12 . . . . 14 A7
EYNSFORD, Dart. DA4 . . . . 230 FL103
★ Eynsford Castle, Dart. DA4 . 230 FL103
Eynsford Cl, Petts Wd BR5 . . . . 227 EQ101
Eynsford Cres, Bex. DA5 . . . . . 208 EW88
Eynsford Rd, Fnghm DA4 . . . . . 230 FM102
Greenhithe DA9 . . . . 211 FW85
Ilford IG3 . . . . 147 ES61
Swanley BR8 . . . . 229 FD100
Eynsham Dr, SE2 . . . . 188 EU77
Eynswood Dr, Sid. DA14 . . . . . 208 EV92
Eyot Gdns, W6 . . . . 181 CT78
Eyot Grn, W4 . . . . 181 CT78
Eyre Cl, Rom. RM2 . . . . 149 FH56
Eyre Ct, NW8 . . . . 6 A10
Eyre Grn, Slou. SL2 . . . . 153 AN69
Eyre St Hill, EC1 . . . . 18 E5
Eyston Dr, Wey. KT13 . . . . 234 BN110
Eythorne Ct, Epsom KT17
off Windmill La 239 CT112
Eythorne Rd, SW9 . . . . 42 F6
Eywood Rd, St.Alb. AL1 . . . . 64 CC22
Ezra St, E2 . . . . 20 B2

F

Faber Gdns, NW4 . . . . 141 CU57
Fabian Rd, SW6 . . . . 39 H4
Fabian St, E6 . . . . 25 H5
Fackenden La, Shore. TN14 . . . 247 FH113
Factory La, N17 . . . . 122 DT54
Croydon CR0 . . . . 223 DN102
Factory Rd, E16 . . . . 36 G3
Northfleet DA11 . . . . 212 GC86
Factory Sq, SW16 . . . . 203 DL93
Factory Yd, W7 . . . . 159 CE74
Faesten Way, Bex. DA5 . . . . 209 FE90
Faggotters La, High Laver CM5 . 75 FF15
Matching Tye CM17 . . . . 59 FE13
Faggotts Cl, Rad. WD7 . . . . 99 CJ35
Faggs Rd, Felt. TW14 . . . . 197 BU85
Fagnall La, Winch.Hill HP7 . . . . 110 AJ45
Fagus Av, Rain. RM13 . . . . 170 FK69
Faints Cl, Chsht EN7 . . . . 88 DS29
Fairacre, Hem.H. HP3 . . . . 62 BM24
New Malden KT3 . . . . 220 CS97
Fairacres, SW15 . . . . 181 CU84
Fair Acres, Brom. BR2 . . . . 226 EG99
Fairacres, Cob. KT11 . . . . 236 BX112
Croydon CR0 . . . . 243 DZ109
Redhill RH1 . . . . 289 DJ142
Ruislip HA4 . . . . 137 BT59
Tadworth KT20 . . . . 255 CW121
Windsor SL4 . . . . 173 AK82
Fairacres Cl, Pot.B. EN6 . . . . 85 CZ33
● Fairacres Ind Est,
Wind. SL4 . . . . 172 AJ82
Fairbairn Cl, Pur. CR8 . . . . 241 DN113
Fairbairn Grn, SW9 . . . . 42 F6
Fairbank Av, Orp. BR6 . . . . 227 EP103
Fairbank Est, N1 . . . . 19 M1
Fairbanks Rd, N17 . . . . 144 DT55
Fairborne Way, Guil. GU2 . . . . . 264 AU131
Fairbourne, Cob. KT11 . . . . 236 BX113

Fairbourne Cl, Wok. GU21 248 AU118
Fairbourne La, Cat. CR3 258 DQ122
Fairbourne Rd, N17 144 DS55
Fairbridge Rd, N19 143 DK61
Fairbrook Cl, N13 121 DN50
Fairbrook Rd, N13 121 DN51
Fairburn Cl, Borwd. WD6 100 CN39
Fairburn Ct, SW15 201 CY85
Fairburn Ho, N16
off Stamford Hill 144 DS60
W14 off Ivatt Pl 39 H1
Fairby Ho, SE1 32 B8
Fairby Rd, SE12 206 EH85
● Faircharm Trd Est, SE8 46 C4
Fairchild Cl, SW11 40 B9
Fairchildes Av, New Adgtn CR0 243 ED112
Fairchildes La, Warl. CR6 243 ED114
Sch Fairchildes Prim Sch,
New Adgtn CR0
off Fairchildes Av 244 EE112
Fairchild Pl, EC2 19 P5
Fairchild St, EC2 19 P5
Fair Cl, Bushey WD23
off Claybury 116 CB45
Fairclough Cl, Nthlt. UB5 158 BZ70
Fairclough St, E1 20 D9
Faircroft, Slou. SL2 153 AP70
Faircross Av, Bark. IG11 167 EQ65
Romford RM5 127 FD52
Faircross Par, Bark. IG11 167 ES65
Faircross Way, St.Alb. AL1 65 CG18
Fairdale Gdns, SW15 181 CV84
Hayes UB3 157 BU74
Fairdene Rd, Couls. CR5 257 DK117
Fairey Av, Hayes UB3 177 BT77
Fairfax Av, Epsom KT17 239 CV109
Redhill RH1 272 DE133
Fairfax Cl, Oxt. RH8 275 ED130
Walton-on-Thames KT12 217 BV102
Fairfax Ct, Dart. DA1 210 FN86
Fairfax Gdns, SE3 186 EK81
Fairfax Ms, E16 36 A2
SW15 181 CW84
Amersham HP7 77 AN40
Fairfax Pl, NW6 5 P7
W14 26 F7
Fairfax Rd, N8 143 DN56
NW6 5 P7
W4 180 CS76
Grays RM17 192 GB78
Hertford SG13 54 DT08
Teddington TW11 199 CG93
Tilbury RM18 193 GF81
Woking GU22 249 BB120
Fairfax Way, N10 120 DG52
(rail symbol) Fairfield 220 CL96
Fairfield App, Wrays. TW19 194 AX86
Fairfield Av, NW4 141 CV58
Datchet SL3 174 AW80
Edgware HA8 118 CP51
Horley RH6 290 DG149
Ruislip HA4 137 BQ59
Staines TW18 195 BF91
Twickenham TW2 198 CB88
Upminster RM14 150 FQ62
Watford WD19 116 BW48
Fairfield Cl, N12 120 DC49
Datchet SL3 174 AX80
Dorking RH4
off Fairfield Dr 269 CH134
Enfield EN3
off Scotland Grn Rd N 105 DY42
Ewell KT19 238 CS106
Guildford GU2 264 AU133
Hatfield AL10 67 CW15
Hornchurch RM12 149 FG60
Mitcham CR4 202 DE94
Northwood HA6
off Thirlmere Gdns 115 BP50
Radlett WD7 99 CE37
Sidcup DA15 207 ET86
Fairfield Cotts, Lthd. KT23 268 CB125
Fairfield Ct, NW10 161 CU67
Northwood HA6
off Windsor Cl 115 BU54
Fairfield Cres, Edg. HA8 118 CP51
Fairfield Dr, SW18 202 DB85
Broxbourne EN10 71 DZ24
Dorking RH4 269 CH134
Harrow HA2 138 CC55
Perivale UB6 159 CJ67
Fairfield E, Kings.T. KT1 220 CL96
Fairfield Gdns, N8 143 DL57
Fairfield Gro, SE7 186 EK78
★ Fairfield Halls, Croy. CR0 224 DR104
Sch Fair Fld Jun Sch, Rad.
WD7 off Watford Rd 99 CE36
Fairfield La, Farn.Royal SL2 153 AP68
Fairfield N, Kings.T. KT1 220 CL96
Fairfield Pk, Cob. KT11 236 BX114
Fairfield Path, Croy. CR0 224 DR104
Fairfield Pathway,
Horn. RM12 170 FJ66
Fairfield Pl, Kings.T. KT1 220 CL97
Fairfield Ri, Guil. GU2 264 AT133
Fairfield Rd, E3 12 A10
E17 123 DY54
N8 143 DL57
N18 122 DU49
W7 179 CG76
Beckenham BR3 225 EA96
Bexleyheath DA7 188 EZ82
Brentwood CM14 130 FW48
Bromley BR1 206 EG94
Burnham SL1 152 AJ69
Croydon CR0 224 DS104
Epping CM16 92 EV29
Hoddesdon EN11 71 EA15
Ilford IG1 167 EP65
Kingston upon Thames KT1 220 CL96
Leatherhead KT22 253 CH121
Petts Wood BR5 227 ER100
Southall UB1 158 BZ72
Uxbridge UB8 156 BK65
West Drayton UB7 156 BL74
Woodford Green IG8 124 EG51
Wraysbury TW19 194 AX86
Fairfields, Cher. KT16 216 BG102
Gravesend DA12 213 GL92
Fairfields Cl, NW9 140 CQ57
Fairfields Cres, NW9 140 CQ56
Fairfield S, Kings.T. KT1 220 CL97
Sch Fairfields Prim Sch, Chsht
EN7 off Rosedale Way 88 DU27
Fairfield Sq, Grav. DA11 213 GG86
Fairfields Rd, Houns. TW3 178 CC83
Fairfield St, SW18 202 DB85
● Fairfield Trade Pk, Kings.T.
KT1 220 CM97
Fairfield Wk, Chsht EN8 89 DY28
Leatherhead KT22
off Fairfield Rd 253 CH121
Fairfield Way, Barn. EN5 102 DA43
Coulsdon CR5 241 DK114
Epsom KT19 238 CS106
Fairfield W, Kings.T. KT1 220 CL96
Fairfolds, Wat. WD25 98 BY36
Fairfoot Rd, E3 22 A5
Fairford Av, Bexh. DA7 189 FD81
Croydon CR0 225 DX99
Fairford Cl, Croy. CR0 225 DY99
Reigate RH2 272 DC132
Romford RM3
off Fairford Way 128 FP51
West Byfleet KT14 233 BF114
Fairford Ct, Sutt. SM2
off Grange Rd 240 DB108
Fairford Gdns, Wor.Pk. KT4 221 CT104
Fairford Ho, SE11 30 F9
Fairford Way, Rom. RM3 128 FP51
Fairgreen, Barn. EN4 102 DF41
Fair Grn, Saw. CM21
off The Square 58 EY05
Fairgreen E, Barn. EN4 102 DF41
Fairgreen Par, Mitch. CR4
off London Rd 222 DF97
Fairgreen Rd, Th.Hth. CR7 223 DP99
Fairham Av, S.Ock. RM15 171 FU73
Fairhaven, Egh. TW20 195 AZ92
Fairhaven Av, Croy. CR0 225 DX100
Fairhaven Cres, Wat. WD19 115 BU48
Fairhaven Rd, Red. RH1 272 DG130
Fairhazel Gdns, NW6 5 M5
Fairhill, Hem.H. HP3 62 BM24
Fairholme, Felt. TW14 197 BR87
Fairholme Av, Rom. RM2 149 FG57
Fairholme Cl, N3 141 CY56
Fairholme Cres, Ashtd. KT21 253 CJ117
Hayes UB4 157 BT70
Fairholme Gdns, N3 141 CY55
Upminster RM14 151 FT59
Sch Fairholme Prim Sch, Felt.
TW14 off Peacock Av 197 BR88
Fairholme Rd, W14 38 F1
Ashford TW15 196 BL92
Croydon CR0 223 DN101
Harrow HA1 139 CF57
Ilford IG1 147 EM59
Sutton SM1 239 CZ107
Fairholt Cl, N16 144 DS60
Fairholt Rd, N16 144 DR60
Fairholt St, SW7 28 D6
Fairkytes Av, Horn. RM11 150 FK60
Fairland Rd, E15 13 L5
Fairlands Av, Buck.H. IG9 124 EG47
Sutton SM1 222 DA103
Thornton Heath CR7 223 DM98
Fairlands Ct, SE9
off North Pk 207 EN86
Fair La, Chipstead CR5 272 DC125
Fairlawn, SE7 186 EJ79
Bookham KT23 252 BZ124
Weybridge KT13 235 BS106
Fairlawn Av, N2 142 DE56
W4 180 CQ77
Bexleyheath DA7 188 EX82
Fairlawn Cl, N14 103 DJ44
Claygate KT10 237 CF107
Feltham TW13 198 BZ91
Kingston upon Thames KT2 200 CQ93
Fairlawn Ct, SE7
off Fairlawn 186 EJ80
Fairlawn Dr, Red. RH1 288 DE136
Woodford Green IG8 124 EG52
● Fairlawn Enterprise Pk,
Salf. RH1 288 DG143
Fairlawnes, Wall. SM6
off Maldon Rd 241 DH106
Fairlawn Gdns, Sthl. UB1 158 BZ73
Fairlawn Gro, W4 180 CQ77
Banstead SM7 240 DD113
Fairlawn Pk, SE26 205 DY92
Windsor SL4 173 AL84
Woking GU21 232 AY114
Sch Fairlawn Prim Sch, SE23
off Honor Oak Rd 204 DW87
Fairlawn Rd, SW19 201 CZ94
Banstead SM7 240 DD112
Carshalton SM5 240 DC111
Fairlawns, Brwd. CM14 130 FU48
Horley RH6 291 DH149
Pinner HA5 116 BW54
Sunbury-on-Thames TW16 217 BU97
Twickenham TW1 199 CJ86
Watford WD17 97 BT38
Woodham KT15 233 BF111
Fairlawns Cl, Horn. RM11 150 FM59
Staines TW18 196 BH93
Fairlead Ho, E14
off Cassilis Rd 34 B6
Fairlea Pl, W5 159 CK70
Fair Leas, Chesh. HP5 76 AN29
Fairley Way, Chsht EN7 88 DV28
Fairlie Ct, E3
off Stroudley Wk 22 C2
Fairlie Gdns, SE23 204 DW87
Fairlie Rd, Slou. SL1 153 AN72
Fairlight Av, E4 123 ED47
NW10 160 CS68
Windsor SL4 173 AR82
Woodford Green IG8 124 EG51
Fairlight Cl, E4 123 ED47
Worcester Park KT4 239 CW105
Fairlight Dr, Uxb. UB8 156 BK65
Fairlight Rd, SW17 202 DD91
(Underground symbol) Fairlop 125 ER53
Fairlop Cl, Horn. RM12 169 FH65
Fairlop Gdns, Ilf. IG6 125 EQ52
Sch Fairlop Prim Sch, Ilf. IG6
off Colvin Gdns 125 EQ53
Fairlop Rd, E11 145 ED59
Ilford IG6 125 EQ54
Fairmark Dr, Uxb. UB10 156 BN65
Fairmead, Brom. BR1 227 EM98
Surbiton KT5 220 CP102
Woking GU21 248 AW118
Fairmead Cl, Brom. BR1 227 EM98
Hounslow TW5 178 BX80
New Malden KT3 220 CR97
Fairmead Cres, Edg. HA8 118 CQ48
Fairmead Gdns, Ilf. IG4 146 EL57
Fairmead Ho, E9
off Kingsmead Way 11 M1
Fairmead Rd, N19 143 DK62
Croydon CR0 223 DM102
Loughton IG10 106 EH42
Fairmeads, Cob. KT11 236 BZ113
Loughton IG10 107 EP40
Fairmeadside, Loug. IG10 106 EJ43
FAIRMILE, Cob. KT11 236 BZ112
Fairmile Av, SW16 203 DK92
Cobham KT11 236 BY114
Fairmile Ct, Cob. KT11 236 BY112
Fairmile Ho, Tedd. TW11
off Twickenham Rd 199 CG91
Fairmile La, Cob. KT11 236 BX112
Fairmile Pk Copse, Cob. KT11 236 BZ112
Fairmile Pk Rd, Cob. KT11 236 BZ113
Fairmont Av, E14 34 G2
Fairmont Cl, Belv. DA17 188 EZ78
Fairmount Rd, SW2 203 DM86
Fairoak Cl, Ken. CR8 257 DP115
Oxshott KT22 237 CD112
Petts Wood BR5 227 EP101
Fairoak Dr, SE9 207 ER85
Fairoak Gdns, Rom. RM1 127 FE54
Fairoak Gro, Enf. EN3 105 DX37
Fair Oak La, Chess. KT9 237 CF111
Oxshott KT22 237 CF111
Fair Oak Pl, Ilf. IG6 125 EQ54
Fairseat Cl, Bushey Hth WD23
off Hive Rd 117 CE47
Fairs Rd, Lthd. KT22 253 CG119
Fairstead Wk, N1 9 J8
Fairstone Ct, Horl. RH6
off Tanyard Way 291 DH147
Fair St, SE1 31 P4
Hounslow TW3 off High St 178 CC83
Fairthorn Rd, SE7 35 P10
Fairtrough Rd, Orp. BR6 246 EV112
Fairview, Epsom KT17 239 CW111
Erith DA8 off Guild Rd 189 FF80
Potters Bar EN6
off Hawkshead Rd 86 DB29
Ruislip HA4
off The Fairway 138 BW63
Fairview Av, Hutt. CM13 131 GE45
Rainham RM13 170 FK68
Wembley HA0 159 CK65
Woking GU22 248 AY118
Fairview Cl, E17 123 DY53
Chigwell IG7 125 ES49
Woking GU22
off Fairview Av 249 AZ118
Fairview Ct, NW4 119 CX54
Ashford TW15 196 BN92
Fairview Cres, Har. HA2 138 CA60
Fairview Dr, Chig. IG7 125 ES49
Orpington BR6 245 ER105
Shepperton TW17 216 BM99
Watford WD17 97 BS36
Fairview Gdns, Wdf.Grn. IG8 124 EH53
● Fairview Ind Est, Amer. HP6 94 AT38
Oxted RH8 276 EG133
● Fairview Ind Pk,
Rain. RM13 169 FD71
Fairview Pl, SW2 203 DM87
Fairview Rd, N15 144 DT57
SW16 223 DM95
Chigwell IG7 125 ES49
Enfield EN2 103 DN39
Epsom KT17 239 CT111
Istead Rise DA13 212 GD94
Slough SL2 153 AM70
Sutton SM1 240 DD106
Taplow SL6 152 AG72
Fairview Way, Edg. HA8 118 CN49
Fairwater Av, Well. DA16 188 EU84
Fairwater Dr, New Haw KT15 234 BK109
Fairway, SW20 221 CW97
Bexleyheath DA6 208 EY85
Carshalton SM5 240 DC111
Chertsey KT16 216 BH102
Guildford GU1 265 BD133
Hemel Hempstead HP3 62 BM24
Petts Wood BR5 227 ER99
Sawbridgeworth CM21 58 EY05
Virginia Water GU25 214 AV100
Ware SG12 54 DW07
Woodford Green IG8 124 EJ50
Fairway, The, N13 122 DQ48
N14 103 DH44
NW7 118 CR48
W3 160 CS72
Abbots Langley WD5 81 BR32
Bromley BR1 227 EM99
Burnham SL1 152 AJ68
Flackwell Heath HP10 132 AC56
Gravesend DA11 213 GG89
Harlow CM18 73 ET17
Leatherhead KT22 253 CG118
New Barnet EN5 102 DB44
New Malden KT3 220 CR95
Northolt UB5 158 CC65
Northwood HA6 115 BS49
Ruislip HA4 138 BX62
Upminster RM14 150 FQ59
Uxbridge UB10 156 BM68
Wembley HA0 139 CH62
West Molesey KT8 218 CB97
Weybridge KT13 234 BN111
Fairway Av, NW9 140 CP55
Borehamwood WD6 100 CP40
West Drayton UB7 156 BJ74
Fairway Cl, NW11 142 DC59
Croydon CR0 225 DY99
Epsom KT19 238 CQ105
Hounslow TW4 198 BW85
Park Street AL2 82 CC27
West Drayton UB7
off Fairway Av 156 BK74
Woking GU22 248 AU119
Fairway Ct, NW7
off The Fairway 118 CR48
Hemel Hempstead HP3
off Fairway 62 BM24
Fairway Dr, SE28 168 EX72
Dartford DA2 210 FP87
Greenford UB6 158 CB66
Fairway Gdns, Beck. BR3 225 ED100
Ilford IG1 147 EQ64
Sch Fairway Prim Sch, The,
NW7 off The Fairway 118 CR47
Fairways, Ashf. TW15 197 BP93
Cheshunt EN8 89 DX26
Kenley CR8 258 DQ117
Stanmore HA7 118 CL54
Teddington TW11 199 CK94
Waltham Abbey EN9 90 EE34
Fairways, The, Red. RH1 288 DD137
● Fairways Business Pk,
E10 off Lammas Rd 145 DY61
Fairweather Cl, N15 144 DS56
Fairweather Rd, N16 144 DU58
Fairwell La, W.Hors. KT24 267 BP128
Fairwyn Rd, SE26 205 DY91
Faithorn Cl, Chesh. HP5 76 AN30
Fakenham Cl, NW7 119 CU52
Northolt UB5
off Goodwood Dr 158 CA65
Fakruddin St, E1 20 D5
Falaise, Egh. TW20 194 AY92
Falcon Av, Brom. BR1 226 EL98
Grays RM17 192 GB79
Falconberg Ct, W1 17 P8
Falconberg Ms, W1 17 N8
Sch Falconbrook Prim Sch,
SW11 40 B10
● Falcon Business Cen,
Mitch. CR4 222 DF99
Romford RM3 128 FL52
Falcon Cl, W4
off Sutton La S 180 CQ79
Dartford DA1 210 FM85
Hatfield AL10 67 CU20
Northwood HA6 115 BS52
Sawbridgeworth CM21 58 EW06
Waltham Abbey EN9
off Kestrel Rd 90 EG34
Falcon Ct, EC4 18 E9
Woking GU21 233 BC113
Falcon Cres, Enf. EN3 105 DX43
Falcon Dr, Stanw. TW19 196 BK86
Falconer Ct, N17
off Compton Cres 122 DQ52
Falconer Rd, Bushey WD23 98 BZ44
Ilford IG6 126 EV50
Sch Falconer Sch, Bushey
WD23 off Falconer Rd 98 BZ43
Falconers Pk, Saw. CM21 58 EX06
Falconer Wk, N7
off Newington Barrow Way 143 DM61
● Falcon Est, Felt. TW14 197 BV85
Falcon Gro, SW11 40 C10
Falcon Ho, W13 159 CF70
Falconhurst, Oxshott KT22 253 CD115
Falcon La, SW11 182 DE83
Falcon Ms, Grav. DA11 212 GE88
● Falcon Pk Ind Est, NW10 140 CS64
Falcon Ridge, Berk. HP4 60 AW20
Falcon Rd, SW11 40 C9
Enfield EN3 105 DX43
Guildford GU1 280 AX135
Hampton TW12 198 BZ94
Falcons Cl, Bigg.H. TN16 260 EK117
Falcons Cft, Woob.Moor HP10 132 AE55
Sch Falcons Sch for Boys, The,
W4 off Burnaby Gdns 180 CQ79
Sch Falcons Sch for Girls, The,
W5 off Gunnersbury Av 160 CM74
Falcon St, E13 23 N4
Falcon Ter, SW11 182 DE83
Falcon Way, E11 146 EG56
E14 34 D8
NW9 118 CS54
Feltham TW14 197 BV85
Harrow HA3 140 CL57
Hornchurch RM12 169 FG66
Sunbury-on-Thames TW16 217 BS96
Watford WD25 82 BY34
Welwyn Garden City AL7 51 CY07
Falcon Wf, SW11 40 A9
FALCONWOOD, Well. DA16 187 ER83
(rail symbol) Falconwood 187 EQ84
Jct Falconwood, SE9 187 EQ84
Falconwood, Bushey WD23 98 BZ44
East Horsley KT24 251 BT124
Egham TW20 194 AY92
Falcon Wd, Lthd. KT22 253 CF120
Falconwood Av, Well. DA16 187 ER82
Falconwood Par, Well. DA16 187 ES84
Falconwood Rd, Croy. CR0 243 EA108
Falcourt Cl, Sutt. SM1 240 DB106
Falkirk Cl, Horn. RM11 150 FN60
Falkirk Gdns, Wat. WD19 116 BX50
Falkirk Ho, W9 15 M2
Falkirk St, N1 19 P1
Falkland Av, N3 120 DA52
N11 120 DG49
Falkland Gdns, Dor. RH4
off Harrow Rd W 285 CG137
Falkland Gro, Dor. RH4 285 CG137
Falkland Pk Av, SE25 224 DS97
Falkland Pl, NW5 7 L2
Falkland Rd, N8 143 DN56
NW5 7 L2
Barnet EN5 101 CY40
Dorking RH4 285 CG137
Sch Falkner Ho Sch, SW7 27 P9
Fallaize Av, Ilf. IG1
off Riverdene Rd 147 EP63
Falling La, West Dr. UB7 156 BL73
Falloden Way, NW11 142 DA56
Fallow Cl, Chig. IG7 125 ET50
Fallow Ct, SE16 44 D1
Fallow Ct Av, N12 120 DC52
Fallowfield, N4
off Six Acres Est 143 DM61
Bean DA2 211 FV90
Stanmore HA7 117 CG48
Welwyn Garden City AL7 51 CZ06
Fallowfield Cl, Hare. UB9 114 BJ53
Fallowfield Ct, Stan. HA7 117 CG48
Fallow Flds, Loug. IG10 124 EJ45
Fallowfields Dr, N12 120 DE51
Fallowfield Wk, Hem.H. HP1
off Tollpit End 62 BG17
Fallowfield Way, Horl. RH6 291 DH147
Fallow Ri, Hert. SG13 54 DS09
Fallows Cl, N2 120 DC54
Fallsbrook Rd, SW16 203 DJ94
Falman Cl, N9
off Croyland Rd 122 DU46
Falmer Rd, E17 145 EB55
N15 144 DQ57
Enfield EN1 104 DS42
Falmouth Av, E4 123 ED50
Falmouth Cl, N22 121 DM52
SE12 206 EF85
Falmouth Ct, St.Alb. AL3 65 CD18
Falmouth Gdns, Ilf. IG4 146 EL57
Falmouth Ho, SE11
off Seaton Cl 30 F10
Kingston upon Thames KT2
off Kingsgate Rd 219 CK95
Falmouth Rd, SE1 31 K6
Hersham KT12 236 BW105
Slough SL1 153 AN72
Falmouth St, E15 13 H3
Falmouth Way, E17
off Gosport Rd 145 DZ57
Falstaff Cl, Cray. DA1 209 FE87
Falstaff Gdns, St.Alb. AL1 64 CB23
Falstaff Ms, Hmptn H. TW12
off Hampton Rd 199 CD92
Falstone, Wok. GU21 248 AV118
Fambridge Cl, SE26 205 DZ91
Fambridge Ct, Rom. RM7 149 FD57
Fambridge Rd, Dag. RM8 148 FA60
Famet Av, Pur. CR8 242 DQ113
Famet Cl, Pur. CR8 242 DQ113
Famet Gdns, Ken. CR8
off Godstone Rd 242 DQ113
Famet Wk, Pur. CR8 242 DQ113
Fane St, W14 39 H2
Fangrove Pk, Lyne KT16 215 BB102
Fanhams Rd, Ware SG12 55 DY05
★ Fan Mus, SE10 46 F4
Fanns Ri, Purf. RM19 190 FN77
Fann St, EC1 19 J5
EC2 19 J5
Fanshawe, The, Dag. RM9
off Gale St 168 EX66
Fanshawe Av, Bark. IG11 167 EQ65
Fanshawe Ct, Hert. SG14
off Byde St 54 DQ08
Fanshawe Cres, Dag. RM9 148 EY64
Hornchurch RM11 150 FK58
Ware SG12 54 DW05
Fanshawe Rd, Grays RM16 193 GG76
Richmond TW10 199 CJ91
Fanshawe St, Hert. SG14 53 DP08
Fanshaws La, Brickendon SG13 70 DQ18
Fanshaw St, N1 19 N2
Jct Fantail, The, Orp. BR6 245 EM105
Fantail Cl, SE28
off Greenhaven Dr 168 EW72
Fantasia Ct, Warley CM14 130 FV50
Fanthorpe St, SW15 38 B10
Faraday Av, Sid. DA14 208 EU89
Faraday Cl, N7 8 D5
Slough SL2 153 AP71
Watford WD18 97 BR44
Faraday Ct, Wat. WD18 97 BU44
Faraday Lo, SE10
off Renaissance Wk 35 M6
★ Faraday Mus, W1 29 L1
Faraday Pl, W.Mol. KT8 218 CA98
Faraday Rd, E15 13 L5
SW19 202 DA93
W3 160 CQ73
W10 14 E6
Guildford GU1 264 AW133
Slough SL2 153 AP71
Southall UB1 158 CB73
Welling DA16 188 EU83
West Molesey KT8 218 CA98
Faraday Way, SE18 36 E7
Croydon CR0
off Ampere Way 223 DM102
Orpington BR5 228 EV98
Fareham Rd, Felt. TW14 198 BW87
Fareham St, W1 17 N8
Far End, Hat. AL10 67 CV21
Farewell Pl, Mitch. CR4 222 DE95
Faringdon Av, Brom. BR2 227 EP100
Romford RM3 128 FJ53
Faringford Cl, Pot.B. EN6 86 DD31
Faringford Rd, E15 13 J7
Farington Acres, Wey. KT13 217 BR104
Faris Barn Dr, Wdhm KT15 233 BF112
Faris La, Wdhm KT15 233 BF111
Farjeon Rd, SE3 186 EK81
Farland Rd, Hem.H. HP2 62 BN21
FARLEIGH, Warl. CR6 243 DZ114
Farleigh Av, Brom. BR2 226 EF100
Farleigh Border, Croy. CR0 243 DY112
Farleigh Ct, Guil. GU2
off Chapelhouse Cl 264 AS134
Farleigh Ct Rd, Warl. CR6 243 DZ114
Farleigh Dean Cres, Croy. CR0 243 EB111
Farleigh Pl, N16 144 DT63
Sch Farleigh Prim Sch, Warl.
CR6 off Farleigh Rd 259 DY117
Farleigh Rd, N16 144 DT63
New Haw KT15 234 BG111
Warlingham CR6 259 DX118
Farleton Cl, Wey. KT13 235 BR107
Farley Common, West. TN16 277 EP126
Farleycroft, West. TN16 277 EQ126
Farley Dr, Ilf. IG3 147 ES60
FARLEY GREEN, Guil. GU5 282 BK144
Farley Heath, Albury GU5 282 BJ144
Farley La, West. TN16 277 EP127
Farley Ms, SE6 205 EC87
Farley Nurs, West. TN16 277 EQ127
Farley Pk, Oxt. RH8 275 ED130
Farley Pl, SE25 224 DU98
Farley Rd, SE6 205 EB87
Gravesend DA12 213 GM88
South Croydon CR2 242 DV108
Farleys Cl, W.Hors. KT24 267 BQ126
Farlington Pl, SW15
off Roehampton La 201 CV87
Farlow Cl, Nthflt DA11 213 GF90
Farlow Rd, SW15 181 CX83
Farlton Rd, SW18 202 DB87
Farman Gro, Nthlt. UB5
off Wayfarer Rd 158 BX69
Farm Av, NW2 141 CY62
SW16 203 DL91
Harrow HA2 138 BZ59
Swanley BR8 229 FC97
Wembley HA0 159 CJ65
Farmborough Cl, Har. HA1
off Pool Rd 139 CD59
Farm Cl, SW6 39 K4
Amersham HP6 94 AX39
Barnet EN5 101 CW43
Borehamwood WD6 99 CK38
Buckhurst Hill IG9 124 EJ48
Byfleet KT14 234 BM112
Cheshunt EN8 88 DW30
Chipstead CR5 256 DF120
Cuffley EN6 87 DK27
Dagenham RM10 169 FC66
East Horsley KT24 267 BT128
Fetcham KT22 253 CD124
Guildford GU1 264 AX131
Hertford SG14 53 DN09
Holyport SL6 172 AC78
Hutton CM13 131 GC45
Lyne KT16 215 BA100
Roydon CM19 56 EH14
Shenley WD7 84 CL30
Shepperton TW17 216 BN101
Southall UB1 158 CB73

Farm Cl, Stai. TW18 195 BE92
Sutton SM2 240 DD108
Uxbridge UB10 137 BP61
Wallington SM6 241 DJ110
Welwyn Garden City AL8 51 CW09
West Wickham BR4 226 EE104
Farmcote Rd, SE12 206 EG88
Farm Ct, NW4 141 CU55
Farm Cres, Lon.Col. AL2 83 CG26
Slough SL2 154 AV71
Farmcroft, Grav. DA11 213 GG89
Farmdale Rd, SE10 35 P10
Carshalton SM5 240 DE108
Farm Dr, Croy. CR0 225 DZ103
Purley CR8 241 DK112
Farm End, E4 106 EE43
Northwood HA6
off Drakes Dr 115 BP53
Farmer Rd, E10 145 EB60
Farmers Cl, Wat. WD25 81 BV33
Farmers Ct, Wal.Abb. EN9
off Winters Way 90 EG33
Farmers Pl, Chal.St.P. SL9 112 AW54
Farmers Rd, SE5 43 H4
Staines TW18 195 BE92
Farmer St, W8 27 J2
Farmers Way, Seer Grn HP9 111 AQ51
Farmery Ct, Berk. HP4 60 AY17
Farm Fld, Wat. WD17 97 BS38
Farmfield Dr, Charl. RH6 290 DB150
[H] Farmfield Hosp, Horl. RH6 290 DB150
Farmfield Rd, Brom. BR1 206 EE92
Farm Flds, S.Croy. CR2 242 DS111
Farm Gro, Knot.Grn HP9 110 AJ50
Farm Hill Rd, Wal.Abb. EN9 89 ED33
Farm Ho Cl, Brox. EN10 89 DZ25
Farmhouse Cl, Wok. GU22 249 BD115
Farmhouse La, Hem.H. HP2 62 BN18
Farmhouse Rd, SW16 203 DJ94
Farmilo Rd, E17 145 DZ59
Farmington Av, Sutt. SM1 222 DD104
Farmlands, Enf. EN2 103 DN39
Pinner HA5 137 BU56
Farmlands, The, Nthlt. UB5 158 BZ65
Farmland Wk, Chis. BR7 207 EP92
Farm La, N14 102 DG44
SW6 39 K3
Addlestone KT15 234 BG107
Ashtead KT21 254 CN116
Carshalton SM5 240 DF110
Croydon CR0 225 DZ103
East Horsley KT24 267 BT128
Epsom KT18 254 CP119
Hoddesdon EN11 71 EC15
Jordans HP9 111 AR52
Loudwater WD3 96 BH41
Purley CR8 241 DJ110
Send GU23 249 BC123
Slough SL1 153 AR73
● Farm La Trd Cen, SW6 39 J3
Farm Lea, Woob.Grn HP10 132 AF56
Farmleigh, N14 121 DJ45
Farmleigh Gro, Hersham KT12 235 BT106
Farm Pl, W8 27 J2
Berkhamsted HP4 60 AT18
Dartford DA1 189 FG84
Farm Rd, N21 121 DP46
NW10 160 CR67
Chorleywood WD3 95 BA42
Edgware HA8 118 CP51
Esher KT10 218 CB102
Hoddesdon EN11 71 EC16
Hounslow TW4 198 BY88
Morden SM4 222 DB99
Northwood HA6 115 BQ50
Orsett RM16 193 GF75
Rainham RM13 170 FJ69
St. Albans AL1 65 CH19
Sevenoaks TN14 279 FJ121
Staines TW18 196 BH93
Sutton SM2 240 DD108
Taplow SL6 152 AG72
Warlingham CR6 259 DY119
Woking GU22 249 BB120
Farmstead Rd, SE6 205 EB91
Harrow HA3 117 CD53
Farm St, W1 29 J1
Farm Vale, Bex. DA5 209 FB86
Farm Vw, Cob. KT11 252 BX116
Lower Kingswood KT20 271 CZ127
Farm Wk, NW11 141 CZ57
Guildford GU2
off Wilderness Rd 280 AT136
Horley RH6
off Court Lo Rd 290 DF148
Farm Way, Buck.H. IG9 124 EJ49
Bushey WD23 98 CB42
Farmway, Dag. RM8 148 EW63
Farm Way, Hat. AL10 67 CV15
Hornchurch RM12 149 FH63
Northwood HA6 115 BS49
Staines TW19 195 BF86
Worcester Park KT4 221 CW104
Farm Yd, Wind. SL4 173 AR80
Farnaby Dr, Sev. TN13 278 FF126
Farnaby Rd, SE9 186 EJ84
Bromley BR1, BR2 205 ED94
Farnan Av, E17 123 EA54
Farnan Rd, SW16 203 DL92
FARNBOROUGH, Orp. BR6 245 EP106
Farnborough Av, E17 145 DY55
South Croydon CR2 243 DX108
Farnborough Cl, Wem. HA9 140 CP61
Farnborough Common, Orp.
BR6 227 EM104
Farnborough Cres, Brom.
BR2 off Saville Row 226 EF102
South Croydon CR2 243 DY109
Farnborough Hill, Orp. BR6 245 ER106
Farnborough Ho, SW15
off Fontley Way 201 CU88
[Sch] Farnborough Prim Sch,
Farnboro. BR6
off Farnborough Hill 245 EQ106
Farnborough Way, Orp. BR6 245 EQ105
Farnburn Av, Slou. SL1 153 AP71
⇌ Farncombe 280 AT144
[Sch] Farncombe C of E Inf Sch,
Farnc. GU7 off Grays Rd 280 AS144
Farncombe St, SE16 32 D5
Godalming GU7 280 AS144
Farndale Av, N13 121 DP48
Farndale Cres, Grnf. UB6 158 CC69
Farnell Ms, SW5 27 L10
Weybridge KT13
off Thames St 217 BP104
Farnell Pl, W3 160 CP73
Farnell Rd, Islw. TW7 179 CD83
Staines TW18 196 BG90
Farnes Dr, Rom. RM2 128 FJ54
Farney Fld, Peasl. GU5 283 BR142
Farnham Cl, N20 120 DC45
Bovingdon HP3 79 BA28
Sawbridgeworth CM21 58 EW06
FARNHAM COMMON, Slou.
SL2 153 AQ65
[Sch] Farnham Common Inf Sch,
Farn.Com. SL2
off Beaconsfield Rd 133 AQ63
[Sch] Farnham Common Jun Sch,
Farn.Com. SL2
off Sherbourne Wk 133 AQ63
Farnham Gdns, SW20 221 CV96
[Sch] Farnham Grn Prim Sch,
Seven Kings IG3
off Royal Cl 148 EU58
Farnham La, Slou. SL2 153 AN68
Farnham Pk La, Farn.Royal
SL2 153 AQ66
Farnham Pl, SE1 31 H3
Farnham Rd, Guil. GU1, GU2 280 AT137
Ilford IG3 147 ET59
Romford RM3 128 FK50
Slough SL1, SL2 153 AQ71
Welling DA16 188 EW82
[H] Farnham Rd Hosp,
Guil. GU2 280 AV136
FARNHAM ROYAL, Slou. SL2 153 AQ68
Farnham Royal, SE11 42 D1
FARNINGHAM, Dart. DA4 230 FN100
Farningham Cres, Cat. CR3
off Commonwealth Rd 258 DU123
Farningham Hill Rd, Fnghm
DA4 230 FJ99
⇌ Farningham Road 230 FP96
Farningham Rd, N17 122 DU52
Caterham CR3 258 DU123
Farnley, Wok. GU21 248 AT117
Farnley Rd, E4 124 EE45
SE25 224 DR98
Farnol Rd, Dart. DA1 190 FN84
Farnsworth Ct, SE10
off West Parkside 35 M7
Faro Cl, Brom. BR1 227 EN96
Faroe Rd, W14 26 D7
Faroma Wk, Enf. EN2 103 DN39
Farquhar Rd, SE19 204 DT92
SW19 202 DA90
Farquharson Rd, Croy. CR0 224 DQ102
Farquhar St, Hert. SG14 54 DQ08
Farraline Rd, Wat. WD18 97 BV42
Farrance Rd, Rom. RM6 148 EY58
Farrance St, E14 21 P9
Farrans Ct, Har. HA3 139 CH59
Farrant Av, N22 121 DN54
Farrant Cl, Orp. BR6 246 EU108
Farrant Way, Borwd. WD6 100 CL39
Farr Av, Bark. IG11 168 EU68
Farrell Ho, E1 21 H9
Farren Rd, SE23 205 DY89
Farrer Ms, N8 off Farrer Rd 143 DJ56
Farrer Rd, N8 143 DJ56
Harrow HA3 140 CL57
Farrer's Pl, Croy. CR0 243 DX105
Farriday Cl, St.Alb. AL3 65 CE16
Farrier Cl, Brom. BR1 226 EK97
Sunbury-on-Thames TW16 217 BU98
Uxbridge UB8
off Horseshoe Dr 156 BN72
Farrier Pl, Sutt. SM1 222 DA104
Farrier Rd, Nthlt. UB5 158 CA68
Farriers, Gt Amwell SG12 55 EA09
Farriers Cl, Bov. HP3 79 BB28
Epsom KT17 238 CS111
Gravesend DA12 213 GM88
Farriers Ct, Sutt. SM3
off Forge La 239 CY108
Watford WD25 81 BV32
Farriers End, Brox. EN10 89 DZ26
Farriers Ms, SE15 44 G10
Farriers Rd, Epsom KT17 238 CS112
Farrier St, NW1 7 K6
Farriers Way, Borwd. WD6 100 CQ44
Chesham HP5 76 AN28
Farrier Wk, SW10 39 N2
⇌ Farringdon 18 F6
⊖ Farringdon 18 F6
Farringdon Ho, Rich. TW9
off Strand Dr 180 CP80
Farringdon La, EC1 18 F5
Farringdon Rd, EC1 18 E4
Farringdon St, EC4 18 G8
Farringford Cl, St.Alb. AL2 82 CA26
Farrington Av, Orp. BR5 228 EV97
Farrington Pl, Chis. BR7 207 ER94
Northwood HA6 115 BT49
[Sch] Farringtons Sch, Chis.
BR7 off Perry St 207 ER94
Farrins Rents, SE16 33 L3
Farrow La, SE14 45 H4
Farrow Pl, SE16 33 L6
Farr Rd, Enf. EN2 104 DR39
Farthingale Ct, Wal.Abb. EN9 90 EG34
Farthingale La, Wal.Abb. EN9 90 EG34
Farthingale Wk, E15 12 G7
Farthing All, SE1 32 C5
Farthing Cl, Dart. DA1 190 FM84
Watford WD18 98 BW43
Farthing Ct, NW7 119 CY52
Farthing Flds, E1 32 F2
Farthing Grn La, Stoke P. SL2 154 AU68
Farthings, Knap. GU21 248 AS116
Farthings, The, Amer. HP6
off Milton Lawns 77 AR36
Hemel Hempstead HP1 62 BH20
Kingston upon Thames KT2 220 CN95
Farthings Cl, E4 124 EE48
Pinner HA5 137 BV58
Farthing St, Downe BR6 245 EM108
Farthing Way, Couls. CR5 257 DK117
Farwell Rd, Sid. DA14 208 EV90
Farwig La, Brom. BR1 226 EF95
Fashion St, E1 20 A7
Fashoda Rd, Brom. BR2 226 EK98
Fassett Rd, E8 10 D4
Kingston upon Thames KT1 220 CL98
Fassett Sq, E8 10 C4
Fassnidge Way, Uxb. UB8
off Oxford Rd 156 BJ66
Fauconberg Rd, W4 180 CQ79
Faulkner Cl, Dag. RM8 148 EX59
Faulkner's All, EC1 18 G6
Faulkners Rd, Hersham KT12 236 BW106
Faulkner St, SE14 45 H6
Fauna Cl, Rom. RM6 148 EW59
Stanmore HA7 117 CK49
Faunce St, SE17 42 G2
Favart Rd, SW6 39 K6
Faverolle Grn, Chsht EN8 89 DX28
Faversham Av, E4 124 EE46
Enfield EN1 104 DR44
Faversham Cl, Chig. IG7 126 EV47
Faversham Rd, SE6 205 DZ87
Beckenham BR3 225 DZ96
Morden SM4 222 DB100
[Sch] Fawbert & Barnard Infants' Sch,
Saw. CM21 off Knight St 58 EY05
[Sch] Fawbert & Barnard's
Prim Sch, Harl. CM17
off London Rd 58 EW12
Fawcett Cl, SW11 40 B9
SW16 203 DN91
Fawcett Est, E5 144 DU60
Fawcett Rd, NW10 161 CT67
Croydon CR0 224 DQ104
Windsor SL4 173 AP81
Fawcett St, SW10 39 N2
Fawcus Cl, Clay. KT10 237 CE107
Fawe Pk Rd, SW15 181 CZ84
Fawe St, E14 22 D7
Fawke Common, Undrvr TN15 279 FP127
Fawke Common Rd, Sev.
TN15 279 FP126
Fawkes Av, Dart. DA1 210 FM89
[Sch] Fawkham C of E Prim Sch,
Long. DA3 off Valley Rd 231 FV102
FAWKHAM GREEN, Long.
DA3 231 FV104
Fawkham Grn Rd, Fawk.Grn
DA3 231 FV104
Fawkham Ho, SE1
off Longfield Est 32 B9
[H] Fawkham Manor Hosp,
Fawk. DA3 231 FW102
Fawkham Rd, Long. DA3 231 FX97
Fawkon Wk, Hodd. EN11 71 EA17
Fawley Rd, NW6 5 L3
Fawnbrake Av, SE24 203 DP85
Fawn Ct, Hat. AL9 67 CW16
Fawn Rd, E13 166 EJ68
Chigwell IG7 125 ET50
Fawns Manor Cl, Felt. TW14 197 BQ88
Fawns Manor Rd, Felt. TW14 197 BR88
Fawood Av, NW10 160 CR66
Fawsley Cl, Colnbr. SL3 175 BE80
Fawters Cl, Hutt. CM13 131 GD44
Fayerfield, Pot.B. EN6 86 DD31
Faygate Cres, Bexh. DA6 208 FA85
Faygate Rd, SW2 203 DM89
Fay Grn, Abb.L. WD5 81 BR33
Fayland Av, SW16 203 DJ92
Faymore Gdns, S.Ock. RM15 171 FU72
Feacey Down, Hem.H. HP1 62 BG18
Fearn Cl, E.Hors. KT24 267 BS129
Fearney Mead, Mill End WD3 114 BG46
Fearnley Cres, Hmptn. TW12 198 BY92
Fearnley Rd, Welw.G.C. AL8 51 CW10
Fearnley St, Wat. WD18 97 BV42
Fearns Mead, Warley CM14
off Bucklers Ct 130 FW50
Fearon St, SE10 35 N10
Featherbed La, Croy. CR0 243 DZ108
Hemel Hempstead HP3 62 BJ24
Romford RM4 126 EY45
Warlingham CR6 243 ED113
Feather Dell, Hat. AL10 67 CT18
Feathers La, Wrays. TW19 195 BA89
Feathers Pl, SE10 47 H2
Featherstone Av, SE23 204 DV89
Featherstone Gdns, Borwd.
WD6 100 CQ42
[Sch] Featherstone High Sch, Sthl.
UB2 off Montague Waye 178 BY76
● Featherstone Ind Est,
Sthl. UB2 178 BY75
[Sch] Featherstone Prim Sch, Sthl.
UB2 off Western Rd 178 BW77
Featherstone Rd, NW7 119 CV51
Southall UB2 178 BY76
Featherstone St, EC1 19 L4
Featherstone Ter, Sthl. UB2 178 BY76
Featley Rd, SW9 42 G10
Federal Rd, Perivale UB6 159 CJ68
Federal Way, Wat. WD24 98 BW38
Federation Rd, SE2 188 EV77
Fee Fm Rd, Clay. KT10 237 CF108
Feenan Highway, Til. RM18 193 GH80
Feeny Cl, NW10 141 CT63
Felbridge Av, Stan. HA7 117 CG53
Felbridge Cl, SW16 203 DN91
Sutton SM2 240 DB109
Felbridge Ho, SE22
off Pytchley Rd 184 DS83
Felbrigge Rd, Ilf. IG3 147 ET61
Felcott Cl, Hersham KT12 218 BW104
Felcott Rd, Hersham KT12 218 BW104
Felday Hos, Holm.St.M. RH5 283 BV144
Felday Rd, SE13 205 EB86
Abinger Hammer RH5 283 BT140
FELDEN, Hem.H. HP3 62 BG24
Felden Cl, Pnr. HA5 116 BY52
Watford WD25 82 BX34
Felden Dr, Felden HP3 62 BG24
Felden La, Felden HP3 62 BG24
Felden St, SW6 38 G6
Feldman Cl, N16 144 DU60
Feldspar Ct, Enf. EN3
off Enstone Rd 105 DY41
Felgate Ms, W6 181 CV77
Felhampton Rd, SE9 207 EP89
Felhurst Cres, Dag. RM10 149 FB63
Felicia Way, Grays RM16 193 GH77
Felipe Rd, Chaff.Hun. RM16 191 FW76
Felix Av, N8 143 DL58
Felix Dr, W.Clan. GU4 266 BG128
Felix La, Shep. TW17 217 BS100
Felix Pl, SW2 off Talma Rd 203 DN85
Felix Rd, W13 159 CG73
Walton-on-Thames KT12 217 BU100
Felixstowe Ct, E16 37 P3
Felixstowe Rd, N9 122 DU49
N17 144 DT55
NW10 161 CV69
SE2 188 EV76
Felland Way, Reig. RH2 288 DC138
Fellbrigg Rd, SE22 204 DT85
Fellbrigg St, E1 20 F5
Fellbrook, Rich. TW10 199 CH90
Fellmongers Path, SE1 31 P5
Fellmongers Yd, Croy. CR0
off Surrey St 224 DQ104
Fellowes Cl, Hayes UB4
off Paddington Cl 158 BX70
Fellowes La, Coln.Hth AL4 66 CS23
Fellowes Rd, Cars. SM5 222 DE104
Fellows Ct, E2 20 A1
Fellows Rd, NW3 6 B6
Fell Rd, Croy. CR0 224 DQ104
Felltram Ms, SE7 35 P10
Felltram Way, SE7 35 P10
Fell Wk, Edg. HA8
off East Rd 118 CQ53
Felmersham Cl, SW4 183 DK84
Felmingham Rd, SE20 224 DW96
Felmongers, Harl. CM20 58 EV13
● Felnex Trd Est, Wall. SM6 222 DG103
Felsberg Rd, SW2 203 DL86
Fels Cl, Dag. RM10 149 FB62
Fels Fm Av, Dag. RM10 149 FC62
Felsham Rd, SW15 181 CX83
Felspar Cl, SE18 187 ET78
Felstead Av, Ilf. IG5 125 EN53
Felstead Cl, N13 121 DN50
Hutton CM13 131 GC44
Felstead Gdns, E14 46 E1
Felstead Rd, E11 146 EG59
Epsom KT19 238 CR111
Loughton IG10 124 EL45
Orpington BR6 228 EU103
Romford RM5 127 FC51
Waltham Cross EN8 89 DY32
Felstead St, E9 11 P5
Felsted Rd, E16 24 E9
FELTHAM, TW13 & TW14 197 BV89
⇌ Feltham 197 BV88
Feltham Av, E.Mol. KT8 219 CE98
Felthambrook Way, Felt. TW13 197 BV90
● Feltham Business Complex,
Felt. TW13 197 BV89
[Coll] Feltham City Learning Cen,
Felt. TW13
off Browells La 198 BW89
[Sch] Feltham Comm Coll, Felt.
TW13 off Browells La 198 BW89
FELTHAMHILL, Felt. TW13 197 BU92
[Sch] Feltham Hill Inf & Nurs Sch,
Felt. TW13
off Bedfont Rd 197 BT90
[Sch] Feltham Hill Jun Sch,
Felt. TW13
off Ashford Rd 197 BT90
Feltham Hill Rd, Ashf. TW15 197 BP92
Feltham Rd, Ashf. TW15 197 BP91
Mitcham CR4 222 DF96
Redhill RH1 288 DF139
Feltham Wk, Red. RH1 288 DF139
● Feltimores Pk, Harl. CM17 58 FA12
Felton Cl, Borwd. WD6 100 CL38
Broxbourne EN10 89 DZ25
Petts Wood BR5 227 EP100
[Sch] Feltonfleet Sch, Cob.
KT11 off Byfleet Rd 235 BS113
Felton Gdns, Bark. IG11
off Sutton Rd 167 ES67
Felton Lea, Sid. DA14 207 ET92
Felton Rd, W13
off Camborne Av 179 CJ75
Barking IG11
off Sutton Rd 167 ES68
Felton St, N1 9 M9
Fencepiece Rd, Chig. IG7 125 EQ50
Ilford IG6 125 EQ50
Fenchurch Av, EC3 19 N9
Fenchurch Bldgs, EC3 19 P9
Fenchurch Pl, EC3 19 P10
⇌ Fenchurch Street 19 P10
Fenchurch St, EC3 19 N10
Fen Cl, Shenf. CM15 131 GC42
Fen Ct, EC3 19 N9
Fendall Rd, Epsom KT19 238 CQ106
Fendall St, SE1 31 P7
Fendt Cl, E16 23 M9
Fendyke Rd, Belv. DA17 188 EX76
Fenelon Pl, W14 27 H9
Fenemore Rd, Ken. CR8 258 DR119
Fengates Rd, Red. RH1 272 DE134
Fen Gro, Sid. DA15 207 ET86
Fenham Rd, SE15 44 D5
Fen La, SW13 181 CV81
North Ockendon RM14 151 FW64
Fenman Ct, N17
off Shelbourne Rd 122 DV53
Fenman Gdns, Ilf. IG3 148 EV60
Fenn Cl, Brom. BR1 206 EG93
Fennel Cl, E16 23 K4
Croydon CR0
off Primrose La 225 DX102
Guildford GU1 265 BB131
Fennells, Harl. CM19 73 EQ20
Fennells Mead, Epsom KT17 239 CT109
Fennel St, SE18 187 EN79
Fenner Cl, SE16 32 F8
Fenner Ho, Walt. KT12 235 BU105
Fenner Rd, Grays RM16 191 FW77
Fenners Marsh, Grav. DA12 213 GM88
Fenner Sq, SW11
off Thomas Baines Rd 182 DD83
Fennings, The, Amer. HP6 77 AR36
Fenning St, SE1 31 N4
Fenn St, E9 11 H3
Fenns Way, Wok. GU21 248 AY115
Fennycroft Rd, Hem.H. HP1 62 BG17
Fensomes All, Hem.H. HP2
off Queensway 62 BK19
Fensomes Cl, Hem.H. HP2
off Broad St 62 BK19
Fenstanton Av, N12 120 DD50
[Sch] Fenstanton Prim Sch,
SW2 off Abbots Pk 203 DN88
Fen St, E16 23 M10
Fens Way, Swan. BR8 209 FG93
Fenswood Cl, Bex. DA5 208 FA85
Fentiman Rd, SW8 42 B3
Fentiman Way, Har. HA2 138 CB61
Hornchurch RM11 150 FL60
Fenton Av, Stai. TW18 196 BJ93
Fenton Cl, E8 10 B4
SW9 42 C8
Chislehurst BR7 207 EM92
Redhill RH1 272 DG134
Fenton Gra, Harl. CM17 74 EW16
★ Fenton Ho, NW3 142 DC62
Fenton Ho, Houns. TW5 178 CA79
Fenton Rd, N17 122 DQ52
Chafford Hundred RM16 192 FY76
Redhill RH1 272 DG134
Fentons Av, E13 24 A1
Fentum Rd, Guil. GU2 264 AU132
Fenwick Cl, SE18 187 EN79
Woking GU21 248 AV118
Fenwick Gro, SE15 184 DU83
Fenwick Path, Borwd. WD6 100 CM38
Fenwick Pl, SW9 183 DL83
South Croydon CR2
off Columbine Av 241 DP108
Fenwick Rd, SE15 184 DU83
Ferdinand Pl, NW1 7 H6
Ferdinand St, NW1 7 H5
Ferguson Av, Grav. DA12 213 GJ91
Romford RM2 128 FJ54
Surbiton KT5 220 CM99
Ferguson Cl, E14 34 A9
Bromley BR2 225 ED97
Ferguson Ct, Rom. RM2 128 FK54
Ferguson Dr, W3 160 CR72
Fergus Rd, N5 9 H3
Ferme Pk Rd, N4 143 DL57
N8 143 DL57
Fermor Rd, SE23 205 DY88
Fermoy Rd, W9 14 G5
Greenford UB6 158 CB70
Fern Av, Mitch. CR4 223 DK98
Fernbank, Buck.H. IG9 124 EH46
Fernbank Av, Horn. RM12 150 FJ63
Walton-on-Thames KT12 218 BY101
Wembley HA0 139 CF63
Fernbank Ms, SW12 203 DH86
Fernbank Rd, Add. KT15 234 BG106
Fernbrook Av, Sid. DA15
off Blackfen Rd 207 ES85
Fernbrook Cres, SE13 206 EE86
Fernbrook Dr, Har. HA2 138 CB59
Fernbrook Rd, SE13 206 EE86
Ferncliff Rd, E8 10 C2
Fern Cl, N1 9 N10
Broxbourne EN10 71 DZ23
Erith DA8
off Hollywood Way 189 FH81
Warlingham CR6 259 DY118
Ferncroft Av, N12 120 DE51
NW3 142 DA62
Ruislip HA4 138 BW61
Ferndale, Brom. BR1 226 EJ96
Guildford GU3 264 AS132
Ferndale Av, E17 145 ED57
Chertsey KT16 215 BE104
Hounslow TW4 178 BY83
Ferndale Cl, Bexh. DA7 188 EY81
Ferndale Ct, SE3 47 M4
Ferndale Cres, Uxb. UB8 156 BJ69
Ferndale Pk, Bray SL6 172 AE79
Ferndale Rd, E7 166 EH66
E11 146 EE61
N15 144 DT58
SE25 224 DV99
SW4 183 DL84
SW9 183 DM83
Ashford TW15 196 BK92
Banstead SM7 255 CZ116
Enfield EN3 105 DY37
Gravesend DA12 213 GH89
Romford RM5 127 FC54
Woking GU21 249 AZ116
Ferndale St, E6 25 N10
Ferndale Ter, Har. HA1 139 CF56
Ferndale Way, Orp. BR6 245 ER106
Ferndell Av, Bex. DA5 209 FD90
Fern Dells, Hat. AL10 67 CT19
Fern Dene, W13
off Templewood 159 CH71
Ferndene, Brick.Wd AL2 82 BZ31
Ferndene Rd, SE24 184 DQ84
Fernden Ri, Gdmg. GU7 280 AS144
Fernden Way, Rom. RM7 149 FB58
Ferndown, Horl. RH6 290 DF146
Hornchurch RM11 150 FM58
Northwood HA6 115 BU54
Ferndown Av, Orp. BR6 227 ER102
Ferndown Cl, Guil. GU1 281 BA135
Pinner HA5 116 BY52
Sutton SM2 240 DD107
Ferndown Ct, Guil. GU1 264 AW133
Ferndown Gdns, Cob. KT11 236 BW113
Ferndown Rd, SE9 206 EK87
Watford WD19 116 BW48
Fern Dr, Hem.H. HP3 62 BL21
Taplow SL6 152 AH72
Fernecroft, St.Alb. AL1 65 CD23
Fernery, The, Stai. TW18 195 BE92
Fernes Cl, Uxb. UB8 156 BJ72
Ferney Ct, Byfleet KT14
off Ferney Rd 234 BK112
Ferney Meade Way, Islw. TW7 179 CG82
Ferney Rd, Byfleet KT14 234 BK112
Cheshunt EN7 88 DR26
East Barnet EN4 120 DG45
Fern Gro, Felt. TW14 197 BV87
Welwyn Garden City AL8 51 CX05
Ferngrove Cl, Fetch. KT22 253 CE122
Fernhall Dr, Ilf. IG4 146 EK57
Fernhall La, Wal.Abb. EN9 90 EK31
Fernham Rd, Th.Hth. CR7 224 DQ97
Fernhead Rd, W9 15 H2
Fernheath Way, Dart. DA2 209 FD92
Fernhill, Oxshott KT22 237 CD114
Fernhill Cl, Wok. GU22 248 AW120
Fernhill Ct, E17 123 ED54
Fernhill Gdns, Kings.T. KT2 199 CK92
Fern Hill La, Harl. CM18 73 ES19
Fernhill La, Wok. GU22 248 AW120
Fernhill Pk, Wok. GU22 248 AW120
[Sch] Fern Hill Prim Sch,
Kings.T. KT2
off Richmond Rd 200 CL93
Fernhill Rd, Horl. RH6 291 DK152
Fernhills, Hunt.Br. WD4 81 BR33
Fernhill St, E16 37 K3
Fernholme Rd, SE15 205 DX85
Fernhurst Cl, Beac. HP9 111 AM53
Fernhurst Gdns, Edg. HA8 118 CN51
Fernhurst Rd, SW6 38 F6
Ashford TW15 197 BQ91
Croydon CR0 224 DU101
Fernie Cl, Chig. IG7 126 EU50
Fernihough Cl, Wey. KT13 234 BN111
Fernlands Cl, Cher. KT16 215 BE104
Fern La, Houns. TW5 178 BZ78
Fernlea, Bkhm KT23 252 CB124
Fernlea Pl, Cob. KT11 236 BX112
Fernlea Rd, SW12 203 DH88
Mitcham CR4 222 DG96
Fernleigh Cl, W9 15 H2
Croydon CR0 241 DN105
Walton-on-Thames KT12 217 BV104
Fernleigh Ct, Har. HA2 116 CB54
Wembley HA9 140 CL61
Fernleigh Rd, N21 121 DN47

Fernley Cl, Eastcote HA5 . . . . . **137** BU56
Fernleys, St.Alb. AL4. . . . . **65** CJ17
Ferns, The, Beac. HP9 . . . . **111** AM54
Hatfield AL10
off Campion Rd. **67** CT15
St. Albans AL3. . . . . **65** CD16
Fernsbury St, WC1 . . . . **18** E3
Ferns Cl, Enf. EN3 . . . . **105** DY36
South Croydon CR2 . . . . **242** DV110
Fernshaw Rd, SW10. . . . . **39** N3
Fernside, NW11 . . . . **142** DA61
Buckhurst Hill IG9. . . . . **124** EH46
Fernside Av, NW7 . . . . **118** CR48
Feltham TW13 . . . . **197** BV91
Fernside La, Sev.TN13 . . . . **279** FJ129
Fernside Rd, SW12. . . . . **202** DF88
Fernsleigh Cl, Chal.St.P. SL9. . . **112** AY51
Ferns Rd, E15. . . . . **13** L5
Fern St, E3. . . . . **22** B5
Fernthorpe Rd, SW16. . . . . **203** DJ93
Ferntower Rd, N5 . . . . **9** L2
Fern Twrs, Cat. CR3. . . . . **274** DU125
Fernville La, Hem.H. HP2 . . . . . . **62** BK20
Fern Wk, SE16 . . . . **44** D1
Ashford TW15
off Ferndale Rd. **196** BK92
Fern Way, Wat. WD25 . . . . **97** BU35
Fernways, Ilf. IG1
off Cecil Rd **147** EP63
Fernwood, SW19
off Albert Dr. **201** CZ88
Fernwood Av, SW16 . . . . **203** DK91
Wembley HA0
off Bridgewater Rd **139** CJ64
Fernwood Cl, Brom. BR1 . . . . . **226** EJ96
Fernwood Cres, N20 . . . . **120** DF48
Ferny Hill, Barn. EN4. . . . . **102** DF38
Ferranti Cl, SE18 . . . . **36** F7
Ferraro Cl, Houns. TW5. . . . . . . **178** CA79
Ferrers Av, Wall. SM6 . . . . **241** DK105
West Drayton UB7 . . . . **176** BK75
Ferrers Cl, Slou. SL1 . . . . **153** AL74
Ferrers Rd, SW16 . . . . **203** DK92
Ferrestone Rd, N8. . . . . **143** DM56
Ferrey Ms, SW9. . . . . **42** F9
Ferriby Cl, N1. . . . . **8** E6
● **Ferrier Ind Est**, SW18 . . . . . **182** DB84
Ferrier Pt, E16 . . . . **23** N7
Ferrier St, SW18 . . . . **182** DB84
Ferriers Way, Epsom KT18 . . . . **255** CW119
Ferring Cl, Har. HA2 . . . . **138** CC60
Ferrings, SE21 . . . . **204** DS89
Ferris Av, Croy. CR0 . . . . **225** DZ104
Ferris Rd, SE22 . . . . **184** DU84
Ferron Rd, E5. . . . . **144** DV62
Ferro Rd, Rain. RM13 . . . . **169** FG70
Ferrour Ct, N2 . . . . **142** DD55
Ferry Av, Stai. TW18 . . . . **195** BE94
Ferrybridge Ho, SE11 . . . . **30** D7
Ferryhills Cl, Wat. WD19 . . . . . **116** BW48
Ferry Ho, E5
off Harrington Hill. **144** DW60
Ferry La, N17. . . . . **144** DU56
SW13 . . . . **181** CT79
Brentford TW8. . . . . **180** CL79
Chertsey KT16. . . . . **216** BH98
Guildford GU2
off Portsmouth Rd **280** AW138
Laleham TW18. . . . . **216** BJ97
Rainham RM13 . . . . **169** FE72
Richmond TW9 . . . . **180** CM79
Shepperton TW17 . . . . **216** BN102
Wraysbury TW19. . . . . **195** BB89
● **Ferry La Ind Est**, E17. . . . . . **145** DX55
Ferry La Prim Sch, N17
off Jarrow Rd **144** DV56
Ferryman's Quay, SW6. . . . . **39** N9
Ferrymead Av, Grnf. UB6 . . . . . **158** CA69
Ferrymead Dr, Grnf. UB6 . . . . . **158** CA68
Ferrymead Gdns, Grnf. UB6 . . **158** CC68
Ferrymoor, Rich. TW10 . . . . **199** CH90
Ferry Pl, SE18 . . . . **37** M7
Ferry Rd, SW13 . . . . **181** CU80
Bray SL6 . . . . **172** AC75
Teddington TW11. . . . . **199** CH92
Thames Ditton KT7. . . . . **219** CH100
Tilbury RM18. . . . . **193** GG83
Twickenham TW1 . . . . **199** CH88
West Molesey KT8 . . . . **218** CA97
Ferry Sq, Brent. TW8. . . . . **179** CK79
Shepperton TW17 . . . . **217** BP101
Ferry St, E14 . . . . **34** E10
Feryby Rd, Grays RM16 . . . . . **193** GH76
Feryngs Cl, Harl. CM17
off Watlington Rd **58** EX11
Fesants Cft, Harl. CM20 . . . . . **58** EV12
Festing Rd, SW15. . . . . **38** C10
Festival Cl, Bex. DA5 . . . . **208** EX88
Erith DA8 *off Betsham Rd* . . **189** FF80
Uxbridge UB10 . . . . **157** BP67
Festival Ct, Sutt. SM1
off Cleeve Way **222** DB101
Festival Path, Wok. GU21 . . . . . **248** AT119
Festival Pier. **30** C2
Festival Wk, Cars. SM5. . . . . . . **240** DF106
Festoon Way, E16 . . . . **24** E10
FETCHAM, Lthd. KT22 . . . . **253** CD123
Fetcham Common La, Fetch.
KT22. . . . . **252** CB121
Fetcham Downs, Fetch. KT22 . **269** CE126
Fetcham Pk Dr, Fetch. KT22. . . **253** CE123
Fetcham Village Inf Sch, Fetch.
KT22 *off School La* **253** CD122
Fetherstone Cl, Pot.B. EN6. . . . **86** DD32
Fetherton Ct, Bark. IG11
off Spring Pl **167** EQ68
Fetter La, EC4 . . . . **18** F9
Ffinch St, SE8 . . . . **46** A4
Fiddicroft Av, Bans. SM7 . . . . **240** DB114
● **Fiddlebridge Ind Cen**, Hat.
AL10 *off Lemsford Rd*. **67** CT17
Fiddlebridge La, Hat. AL10. . . . . **67** CT17
Fiddlers Cl, Green. DA9 . . . . . . **191** FV84
FIDDLERS HAMLET, Epp. CM16. **92** EW32
Fidgeon Cl, Brom. BR1 . . . . **227** EN97
Fidler Pl, Bushey WD23
off Ashfield Av. **98** CB44
Field Cl, E4. . . . . **123** EB51
NW2. **141** CU61
Abridge RM4 . . . . **108** EV41
Bromley BR1 . . . . **226** EJ96
Buckhurst Hill IG9. . . . . **124** EJ48
Chesham HP5 . . . . **76** AS28
Chessington KT9. . . . . **237** CJ106
Guildford GU4. . . . . **265** BD132
Harlington UB3 . . . . **177** BQ80
Hounslow TW4 . . . . **177** BV81
Ruislip HA4 *off Field Way*. . . **137** BQ60
Sandridge AL4. . . . . **65** CG16
Field Cl, S.Croy. CR2. . . . . **242** DV114
West Molesey KT8 . . . . **218** CB99
Fieldcommon La, Walt. KT12 . . **218** BZ101
Field Ct, WC1. . . . . **18** D7
Gravesend DA11 . . . . **213** GF89
Oxted RH8 . . . . **276** EE127
Field End, Barn. EN5. . . . . **101** CV42
Coulsdon CR5 . . . . **241** DK114
Northolt UB5 . . . . **158** BX65
Ruislip HA4 . . . . **158** BW65
Fieldend, Twick. TW1 . . . . **199** CF91
Field End Cl, Wat. WD19 . . . . . **116** BY45
Field End Inf & Jun Schs, Ruis.
HA4 *off Field End Rd* **138** BX61
Field End Ms, Wat. WD19
off Field End Cl **116** BY45
Fieldend Rd, SW16 . . . . **223** DJ95
Field End Rd, Pnr. HA5. . . . . . . **137** BV58
Ruislip HA4 . . . . **138** BY63
Fielders Cl, Enf. EN1
off Woodfield Cl. **104** DS42
Harrow HA2. . . . . **138** CC60
Fielders Grn, Guil. GU1 . . . . . . **265** AZ134
Fielders Way, Shenley WD7 . . . . **84** CL33
Fieldfare Rd, SE28. . . . . **168** EW73
Fieldgate La, Mitch. CR4 . . . . . **222** DE97
Fieldgate St, E1. . . . . **20** D7
Fieldhouse Cl, E18 . . . . **124** EG53
Fieldhouse Rd, SW12. . . . . **203** DJ88
Fieldhurst, Slou. SL3 . . . . **175** AZ78
Fieldhurst Cl, Add. KT15 . . . . . **234** BH106
Field Inf Sch, Wat. WD18
off Neal St. **98** BW43
Fielding Av, Til. RM18. . . . . . . **193** GH81
Twickenham TW2 . . . . **198** CC90
Fielding Co Prim Sch, W13
off Wyndham Rd. **179** CH76
Fielding Gdns, Slou. SL3 . . . . . **174** AW75
Fielding Ho, NW6 . . . . **15** K2
Fielding La, Brom. BR2. . . . . . . **226** EJ98
Fielding Ms, SW13
off Castelnau. **181** CV79
Fielding Rd, W4. . . . . **180** CR76
W14 . . . . **26** D6
Fieldings, The, SE23 . . . . **204** DW88
Banstead SM7. . . . . **255** CZ117
Horley RH6 . . . . **291** DJ147
Woking GU21 . . . . **248** AT116
Fieldings Rd, Chsht EN8. . . . . . . **89** DZ29
Fielding St, SE17. . . . . **43** J2
Fielding Wk, W13. . . . . **179** CH76
Fielding Way, Hutt. CM13. . . . . **131** GC44
Field Jun Sch, Wat. WD18
off Watford Fld Rd. **98** BW43
Field La, Brent. TW8 . . . . **179** CJ80
Godalming GU7
off The Oval **280** AT144
Teddington TW11. . . . . **199** CG92
Field Mead, NW7. . . . . **118** CS52
NW9 . . . . **118** CS52
Fieldpark Gdns, Croy. CR0. . . . **225** DY102
Field Pl, Gdmg. GU7. . . . . **280** AS144
New Malden KT3 . . . . **221** CT100
Field Pt, E7 *off Station Rd* **146** EG63
Field Rd, E7 . . . . **146** EF63
N17. . . . . **144** DR55
W6 . . . . **38** E1
Aveley RM15 . . . . **170** FQ74
Denham UB9 . . . . **135** BE63
Feltham TW14 . . . . **197** BV86
Hemel Hempstead HP2 . . . . . . **62** BN21
Watford WD19 . . . . **98** BY44
Fields, The, Slou. SL1 . . . . **173** AR75
Fields Ct, Pot.B. EN6. . . . . **86** DD33
Fields End La, Hem.H. HP1 . . . . . **61** BE18
Fieldsend Rd, Sutt. SM3. . . . . . **239** CY106
Fields Est, E8. . . . . **10** D7
Fieldside Cl, Orp. BR6
off State Fm Av. **245** EQ105
Fieldside Rd, Brom. BR1 . . . . . **205** ED92
Fields Pk Cres, Rom. RM6 . . . . **148** EX57
Field St, WC1. . . . . **18** C2
Fieldview, SW18. . . . . **202** DD88
Field Vw, Egh. TW20. . . . . **195** BC92
Feltham TW13 . . . . **197** BR91
Fieldview, Horl. RH6
off Stockfield. **291** DH147
Field Vw Cl, Rom. RM7. . . . . . . **148** FA55
Fieldview Ct, Slou. SL1 . . . . . . **153** AQ71
Staines TW18
off Burges Way **196** BG93
Field Vw Ri, Brick.Wd AL2 . . . . . **82** BY29
Field Vw Rd, Pot.B. EN6. . . . . . . **86** DA33
Fieldway **243** EB108
Fieldway, NW10. . . . . **160** CQ66
Fieldway, Amer. HP7 . . . . **77** AP41
Berkhamsted HP4. . . . . **60** AY21
Field Way, Bov. HP3 . . . . **79** BA27
Chalfont St. Peter SL9. . . . . . . **112** AX52
Fieldway, Dag. RM8 . . . . **148** EV63
Field Way, Grnf. UB6. . . . . **158** CB67
Hoddesdon EN11 . . . . **55** EC13
Fieldway, New Adgtn CR0 . . . . **243** EB107
Petts Wood BR5. . . . . **227** ER100
Field Way, Rick. WD3. . . . . **114** BH46
Ripley GU23 . . . . **265** BF125
Ruislip HA4 . . . . **137** BQ60
Fieldway, Stans.Abb. SG12 . . . . **55** EB11
Field Way, Uxb. UB8. . . . . **156** BK70
Fieldway Cres, N5. . . . . **8** F3
Fiennes Cl, Dag. RM8. . . . . **148** EW60
Fiennes Way, Sev. TN13 . . . . . . **279** FJ127
Fiesta Dr, Dag. RM9 . . . . **169** FC70
Fifehead Cl, Ashf. TW15 . . . . . **196** BL93
Fife Rd, E16 . . . . **23** N7
N22. . . . . **121** DP52
SW14 . . . . **200** CQ85
Kingston upon Thames KT1. **220** CL96
Fife Ter, N1 . . . . **8** D10
Fife Way, Lthd. KT23. . . . . **268** CA125
FIFIELD, Maid. SL6 . . . . **172** AD81
Fifield La, Wink. SL4 . . . . **172** AD84
Fifield Path, SE23
off Bampton Rd. **205** DX90
Fifield Rd, Maid. SL6 . . . . **172** AD80
Fifth Av, E12. . . . . **147** EM63
W10 . . . . **14** E3
Grays RM20. . . . . **191** FU79
Harlow CM20 . . . . **57** ER13
Hayes UB3. . . . . **157** BT74
Watford WD25. . . . . **98** BX35
Fifth Cross Rd, Twick. TW2 . . . . **199** CD89
Fifth Way, Wem. HA9 . . . . **140** CP63
Figges Rd, Mitch. CR4 . . . . **202** DG94
Figgswood, Couls. CR5 . . . . **257** DJ122
Fig St, Sev. TN14. . . . . **278** FF129
Fig Tree Cl, NW10
off Craven Pk. **160** CS67
Figtree Hill, Hem.H. HP2 . . . . . . **62** BK19
Filby Rd, Chess. KT9. . . . . **238** CM107
Filey Av, N16 . . . . **144** DU60
Filey Cl, Bigg.H. TN16 . . . . **260** EH119
Sutton SM2 . . . . **240** DC108
Filey Spur, Slou. SL1 . . . . **173** AP75
Filey Waye, Ruis. HA4. . . . . **137** BU61
Filigree Ct, SE16 . . . . **33** M3
Fillebrook Av, Enf. EN1 . . . . **104** DS40
Fillebrook Rd, E11 . . . . **145** ED60
Fillingham Way, Hat. AL10 . . . . . **66** CS16
Filmer La, Sev. TN14. . . . . **279** FL121
Filmer Rd, SW6. . . . . **38** G6
Windsor SL4 . . . . **173** AK82
Filston La, Sev. TN14 . . . . **247** FE113
Filston Rd, Erith DA8
off Riverdale Rd **189** FC78
Filton Cl, NW9 . . . . **118** CS54
Finborough Rd, SW10 . . . . **39** L2
SW17 . . . . **202** DF93
Finchale Rd, SE2 . . . . **188** EU76
Fincham Cl, Uxb. UB10 . . . . **137** BQ62
Finch Av, SE27. . . . . **204** DR91
Finch Cl, NW10 . . . . **140** CR64
Barnet EN5. . . . . **102** DA43
Hatfield AL10
off Eagle Way **67** CU20
Finchdale, Hem.H. HP1. . . . . **62** BG20
Finchdean Ho, SW15
off Tangley Gro **201** CT87
Finch Dr, Felt. TW14 . . . . **198** BX87
Finch End, Penn HP10. . . . . **110** AC47
Finches, The, Hert. SG13 . . . . . . **54** DV09
Finches Av, Crox.Grn WD3 . . . . . **96** BM41
Finches Ri, Guil. GU1 . . . . **265** BC132
Finch Gdns, E4 . . . . **123** EA50
Finch Grn, Chorl. WD3 . . . . **95** BF42
Finchingfield Av, Wdf.Grn. IG8. **124** EJ52
Finch La, EC3. . . . . **19** M9
Amersham HP7. . . . . **94** AV40
Bushey WD23 . . . . **98** CA43
Knotty Green HP9 . . . . **110** AJ50
FINCHLEY, N3. . . . . **120** DB53
Finchley Catholic High Sch,
N12 *off Woodside La* **120** DB48
Finchley Central **120** DA53
Finchley Cl, Dart. DA1 . . . . **210** FN86
Finchley Ct, N3 . . . . **120** DB51
Finchley La, NW4 . . . . **141** CW56
Finchley Mem Hosp, N12. . **120** DC52
Finchley Pk, N12 . . . . **120** DC49
Finchley Pl, NW8. . . . . **6** A10
Finchley Road **5** N4
Finchley Rd, NW2 . . . . **142** DA62
NW3 . . . . **5** N4
NW8. . . . . **6** A9
NW11 . . . . **141** CZ58
Grays RM17. . . . . **192** GB79
Finchley Road & Frognal **5** N3
Finchley Way, N3. . . . . **120** DA52
Finch Ms, SE15 . . . . **44** A6
Finchmoor, Harl. CM18 . . . . **73** ER18
Finch Rd, Berk. HP4 . . . . **60** AU19
Guildford GU1. . . . . **264** AX134
Finden Rd, E7 . . . . **146** EH64
Findhorn Av, Hayes UB4 . . . . . . **157** BV71
Findhorn St, E14 . . . . **22** F8
Findlay Dr, Guil. GU3 . . . . **264** AT130
Findon Cl, SW18 . . . . **202** DA86
Harrow HA2. . . . . **138** CB62
Findon Ct, Add. KT15 . . . . **233** BF106
Findon Gdns, Rain. RM13 . . . . **169** FG71
Findon Rd, N9 . . . . **122** DV46
W12 . . . . **181** CU75
Fine Bush La, Hare. UB9 . . . . . **137** BP58
Fingal St, SE10 . . . . **35** M10
Finglesham Cl, Orp. BR5
off Westwell Cl **228** EX102
Finians Cl, Uxb. UB10. . . . . **156** BM66
Finland Quay, SE16 . . . . **33** L7
Finland Rd, SE4. . . . . **185** DY83
Finland St, SE16 . . . . **33** M6
Finlay Gdns, Add. KT15 . . . . . . **234** BJ105
Finlays Cl, Chess. KT9 . . . . **238** CN106
Finlay St, SW6. . . . . **38** C7
Finnart Cl, Wey. KT13 . . . . **235** BQ105
Finnart Ho Dr, Wey. KT13
off Vaillant Rd **235** BQ105
Finney La, Islw. TW7. . . . . **179** CG81
Finnis St, E2 . . . . **20** F3
Finnymore Rd, Dag. RM9. . . . . . **168** EY66
FINSBURY, EC1. . . . . **18** F2
Finsbury Av, EC2 . . . . **19** M7
Finsbury Av Sq, EC2 . . . . **19** M7
Finsbury Circ, EC2. . . . . **19** M7
Finsbury Cotts, N22 . . . . **121** DL52
Finsbury Ct, Wal.Cr. EN8
off Parkside **89** DY34
Finsbury Est, EC1 . . . . **18** F3
Finsbury Ho, N22 . . . . **121** DL53
Finsbury Mkt, EC2 . . . . **19** N5
FINSBURY PARK, N4 . . . . **143** DN60
★ **Finsbury Park**, N4 . . . . **143** DP59
Finsbury Park **143** DN61
Finsbury Park **143** DN61
Finsbury Park **143** DN61
Finsbury Pk Av, N4. . . . . **144** DQ58
Finsbury Pk Rd, N4. . . . . **143** DP61
Finsbury Pavement, EC2 . . . . . . **19** M6
Finsbury Rd, N22 . . . . **121** DM53
Finsbury Sq, EC2. . . . . **19** M6
Finsbury St, EC2 . . . . **19** L6
● **Finsbury Twr**, EC1 . . . . **19** L5
Finsbury Way, Bex. DA5. . . . . . . **208** EZ86
Finsen Rd, SE5 . . . . **184** DQ83
Finstock Rd, W10. . . . . **14** C8
Finton Ho Sch, SW17
off Trinity Rd **202** DF89
Finucane Dr, Orp. BR5 . . . . **228** EW101
Finucane Gdns, Rain. RM13 . . . **169** FG65
Finucane Ri, Bushey Hth WD23. **116** CC47
Finway Ct, Wat. WD18
off Whippendell Rd. **97** BT43
Finway Rd, Hem.H. HP2. . . . . . . **63** BP16
Fiona Cl, Bkhm KT23 . . . . **252** CA124
Firbank Cl, E16 . . . . **24** E6
Enfield EN2
off Gladbeck Way **104** DQ42
Firbank Dr, Wat. WD19 . . . . **116** BY45
Woking GU21 . . . . **248** AV119
Firbank La, Wok. GU21. . . . . . . **248** AV119
Firbank Pl, Eng.Grn TW20 . . . . **194** AV93
Firbank Rd, SE15. . . . . **44** F8
Romford RM5 . . . . **127** FB50
St. Albans AL3. . . . . **65** CF16
Fir Cl, Walt. KT12. . . . . **217** BU101
Fircroft Cl, Stoke P. SL2 . . . . . . **154** AU65
Woking GU22 . . . . **249** AZ118
Fircroft Ct, Wok. GU22
off Fircroft Cl **249** AZ118
Fircroft Gdns, Har. HA1 . . . . . . **139** CE62
Fircroft Prim Sch, SW17
off Fircroft Rd **202** DF90
Fircroft Rd, SW17 . . . . **202** DF89
Chessington KT9. . . . . **238** CM105
Englefield Green TW20. . . . . **194** AW94
Fir Dene, Orp. BR6 . . . . **227** EM104
Firdene, Surb. KT5 . . . . **220** CQ102
Fire Bell All, Surb. KT6 . . . . . . **220** CL100
Firecrest Dr, NW3 . . . . **142** DB62
Firefly Gdns, E6. . . . . **24** G5
Firemans Run, S.Darenth
DA4 *off East Hill* **230** FQ95
★ **Firepower**, SE18 . . . . **37** P6
Fire Sta All, Barn. EN5
off Christchurch La **101** CY40
Firethorn Cl, Edg. HA8
off Larkspur Gro **118** CQ49
Firfield Rd, Add. KT15. . . . . . . **234** BG105
Firfields, Wey. KT13 . . . . **235** BP107
Fir Gra Av, Wey. KT13 . . . . **235** BP106
Fir Gro, N.Mal. KT3. . . . . **221** CT100
Firgrove, St.John's GU21 . . . . . **248** AU119
Fir Gro Rd, SW9 . . . . **42** F8
Firham Pk Av, Rom. RM3 . . . . . **128** FN52
Firhill Rd, SE6 . . . . **205** EA91
Firlands, Horl. RH6
off Stockfield **291** DH147
Weybridge KT13 . . . . **235** BS107
Firle Ct, Epsom KT17
off Dirdene Gdns **239** CT112
Firmans Ct, E17. . . . . **145** ED56
Firmingers Rd, Orp. BR6 . . . . . **247** FB106
Firmin Rd, Dart. DA1 . . . . **210** FJ85
Fir Pk, Harl. CM19. . . . . **73** EP18
Fir Rd, Felt. TW13 . . . . **198** BX92
Sutton SM3 . . . . **221** CZ102
Firs, The, E6. . . . . **166** EL66
E17 *off Leucha Rd*. **145** DY57
N20. **120** DD46
W5 . . . . **159** CK71
Artington GU3. . . . . **280** AV138
Bexley DA5 . . . . **209** FD88
Bookham KT23 . . . . **252** CC124
Caterham CR3
off Chatfield Ct **258** DR122
Cheshunt EN7 . . . . **88** DS27
Pilgrim's Hatch CM15 . . . . . . **130** FU44
St. Albans AL1. . . . . **65** CH24
Tadworth KT20 . . . . **271** CZ126
Welwyn Garden City AL8. . . . **51** CW05
Firs Av, N10 . . . . **142** DG55
N11 . . . . **120** DG51
SW14 . . . . **180** CQ84
Windsor SL4 . . . . **173** AM83
Firsby Av, Croy. CR0. . . . . **225** DX102
Firsby Rd, N16. . . . . **144** DT60
Firs Cl, N10 . . . . **142** DG55
SE23 . . . . **205** DX87
Claygate KT10 . . . . **237** CE107
Dorking RH4 . . . . **285** CG138
Hatfield AL10. . . . . **67** CV19
Iver SL0
off Thornbridge Rd **155** BC67
Mitcham CR4. . . . . **223** DH96
Firscroft, N13. . . . . **122** DQ48
Firsdene Cl, Ott. KT16
off Slade Rd. **233** BD107
Firs Dr, Houns. TW5 . . . . **177** BV80
Loughton IG10. . . . . **107** EN39
Slough SL3 . . . . **155** AZ74
Firs End, Chal.St.P. SL9. . . . . . **134** AY55
Firs Fm Prim Sch, N13
off Rayleigh Rd **122** DR48
Firsgrove Cres, Warley CM14. . **130** FV49
Firsgrove Rd, Warley CM14 . . . **130** FV49
Firside Gro, Sid. DA15 . . . . **207** ET88
Firs La, N13 . . . . **122** DQ48
N21. . . . . **122** DQ47
Potters Bar EN6. . . . . **86** DB33
Firs Pk, The, Hat. AL9 . . . . **68** DA23
Firs Pk Av, N21 . . . . **122** DR46
Firs Pk Gdns, N21. . . . . **122** DQ46
Firs Rd, Ken. CR8 . . . . **257** DP115
First Av, E12. . . . . **146** EL63
E13 . . . . **23** N2
E17 . . . . **145** EA57
N18. **122** DW49
NW4 . . . . **141** CW56
SW14 . . . . **180** CS83
W3 . . . . **161** CT74
W10 . . . . **14** G4
Amersham HP7. . . . . **77** AQ40
Bexleyheath DA7 . . . . **188** EW80
Dagenham RM10 . . . . **169** FB68
Enfield EN1 . . . . **104** DT44
Epsom KT19 . . . . **238** CS109
Grays RM20. . . . . **191** FU79
Greenford UB6 . . . . **159** CD66
Harlow CM17, CM20 . . . . **57** ER14
Hayes UB3. . . . . **157** BT74
Lower Kingswood KT20. . . . . **271** CY125
Northfleet DA11. . . . . **212** GE88
Romford RM6 . . . . **148** EW57
Waltham Abbey EN9 *off Breach Barn Mobile Home Pk* **90** EH30
Walton-on-Thames KT12 . . . . **217** BV100
Watford WD25. . . . . **98** BW35
Wembley HA9 . . . . **139** CK61
West Molesey KT8 . . . . **218** BZ98
First Cl, W.Mol. KT8 . . . . **218** CC97
First Cres, Slou. SL1 . . . . **153** AQ71
First Cross Rd, Twick. TW2 . . . . **199** CE89
First Dr, NW10. . . . . **160** CQ66
● **First Quarter**, Epsom KT19 . **238** CS110
First Slip, Lthd. KT22 . . . . **253** CG118
First St, SW3. . . . . **28** D8
Firstway, SW20. . . . . **221** CW96
First Way, Wem. HA9 . . . . **140** CP63
Firs Wk, Nthwd. HA6. . . . . **115** BR51
Woodford Green IG8 . . . . **124** EG50
Firsway, Guil. GU2 . . . . **264** AT133
Firswood Av, Epsom KT19. . . . . **239** CT106
Firs Wd Cl, Pot.B. EN6. . . . . **86** DF32
Firth Gdns, SW6. . . . . **38** E7
Fir Tree Av, Mitch. CR4 . . . . **222** DG96
Stoke Poges SL2. . . . . **154** AT70
West Drayton UB7 . . . . **176** BN76
Fir Tree Cl, SW16. . . . . **203** DJ92
W5 . . . . **160** CL72
Epsom KT17 . . . . **255** CW115
Esher KT10 . . . . **236** CC106
Ewell KT19. . . . . **239** CT105
Grays RM17. . . . . **192** GD79
Hemel Hempstead HP3 . . . . . . **62** BN21
Leatherhead KT22. . . . . **253** CJ123
Orpington BR6 . . . . **245** ET106
Romford RM1 . . . . **149** FD55
Firtree Ct, Els. WD6. . . . . **100** CM42
Fir Tree Gdns, Croy. CR0. . . . . . **243** EA105
Fir Tree Gro, Cars. SM5. . . . . . . **240** DF108
Fir Tree Hill, Chan.Cr. WD3 . . . . . **96** BM38
Fir Tree Pl, Ashf. TW15
off Percy Av. **196** BN92
Fir Tree Rd, Bans. SM7 . . . . **239** CW114
Epsom KT17 . . . . **255** CV116
Guildford GU1. . . . . **264** AX131
Hounslow TW4 . . . . **178** BY84
Leatherhead KT22. . . . . **253** CJ123
Fir Trees, Abridge RM4 . . . . **108** EV41
Fir Trees Cl, SE16. . . . . **33** M3
Fir Tree Wk, Dag. RM10
off Wheel Fm Dr **149** FC62
Enfield EN1 . . . . **104** DR41
Reigate RH2. . . . . **272** DD134
Firwood Av, St.Alb. AL4 . . . . **66** CL20
Firwood Cl, Wok. GU21 . . . . **248** AS119
Firwood Rd, Vir.W. GU25 . . . . . **214** AS100
Fisgard Ct, Grav. DA12
off Admirals Way. **213** GK86
Fisher Cl, E9. . . . . **11** K2
Croydon CR0. . . . . **224** DT102
Enfield EN3 . . . . **105** EB37
Greenford UB6 . . . . **158** CA69
Hersham KT12 . . . . **235** BV105
Kings Langley WD4. . . . . **80** BN29
Fisher Ct, Warley CM14 . . . . . . **130** FV50
Fisher Ho, N1 . . . . **8** E9
Fisherman Cl, Rich. TW10. . . . . **199** CJ91
Fishermans Dr, SE16 . . . . **33** K4
Fishermans Hill, Nthflt DA11 . . **212** GB85
Fisherman's Wk, E14. . . . . **34** A2
Fishermans Wk, SE28
off Tugboat St **187** ES75
Fishermans Way, Hodd. EN11 . . **71** ED15
Fisher Rd, Har. HA3. . . . . **117** CF54
Fishers, Horl. RH6
off Ewelands **291** DJ147
Fishers Cl, SW16. . . . . **203** DK90
Bushey WD23 . . . . **98** BY41
Waltham Cross EN8 . . . . **89** EA34
Fishers Ct, SE14 . . . . **45** J6
Fishersdene, Clay. KT10. . . . . . **237** CG108
Fishers Grn La, Wal.Abb. EN9 . . **89** EB29
Fishers Hatch, Harl. CM20 . . . . **57** ES14
Fishers La, W4 . . . . **180** CR77
Epping CM16. . . . . **91** ES32
Fisher St, E16 . . . . **23** N6
WC1. **18** B7
Fishers Way, Belv. DA17. . . . . . **169** FC74
Fisherton St, NW8 . . . . **16** A5
Fishery Pas, Hem.H. HP1
off Fishery Rd **62** BG22
Fishery Rd, Hem.H. HP1. . . . . . . **62** BG22
Maidenhead SL6. . . . . **152** AC74
Fishguard Spur, Slou. SL1 . . . . **174** AV75
Fishguard Way, E16. . . . . **37** P4
Fishing Temple, Stai. TW18. . . . **215** BF95
Fishponds Rd, SW17 . . . . **202** DE91
Keston BR2 . . . . **244** EK106
Fishpool St, St.Alb. AL3. . . . . . . **64** CB20
Fish St Hill, EC3 . . . . **19** M10
Fisk Cl, Sun. TW16 . . . . **197** BT93
Fitzalan Rd, N3 . . . . **141** CY55
Claygate KT10 . . . . **237** CE108
Fitzalan St, SE11 . . . . **30** E8
Fitzgeorge Av, W14. . . . . **26** E9
New Malden KT3 . . . . **220** CR95
Fitzgerald Av, SW14 . . . . **180** CS83
Fitzgerald Cl, E11
off Fitzgerald Rd **146** EG57
Fitzgerald Ho, E14. . . . . **22** D9
SW9 . . . . **42** E9
Hayes UB3. . . . . **157** BV74
Fitzgerald Rd, E11 . . . . **146** EG57
SW14 . . . . **180** CR83
Thames Ditton KT7. . . . . **219** CG100
Fitzhardinge St, W1 . . . . **16** G8
Fitzherbert Ho, Rich. TW10
off Kingsmead. **200** CM86
Fitzhugh Gro, SW18 . . . . **202** DD86
Fitzilian Av, Rom. RM3. . . . . . . **128** FM53
Fitzjames Av, W14. . . . . **26** F9
Croydon CR0. . . . . **224** DU103
Fitzjohn Av, Barn. EN5 . . . . . . **101** CY43
Fitzjohn Cl, Guil. GU4. . . . . **265** BC131
Fitzjohn's Av, NW3 . . . . **6** A3
Fitzjohn's Prim Sch, NW3 . . . **6** A2
Fitzmaurice Ho, SE16
off Rennie Est **32** F9
Fitzmaurice Pl, W1 . . . . **29** K2
Fitzneal St, W12 . . . . **161** CT72
Fitzrobert Pl, Egh. TW20. . . . . . **195** BA93
Fitzroy Cl, N6. . . . . **142** DF60
Fitzroy Ct, W1 . . . . **17** M5
Fitzroy Cres, W4 . . . . **180** CR80
Fitzroy Gdns, SE19. . . . . **204** DS94
Fitzroy Ms, W1. . . . . **17** L5
Fitzroy Pk, N6 . . . . **142** DF60
Fitzroy Pl, Reig. RH2. . . . . **272** DD134
Fitzroy Rd, NW1 . . . . **6** F8
Fitzroy Sq, W1 . . . . **17** L5
Fitzroy St, W1 . . . . **17** L5
Fitzroy Yd, NW1 . . . . **6** G8
Fitzsimmons Ct, NW10
off Knatchbull Rd **160** CR67
Fitzstephen Rd, Dag. RM8. . . . . **148** EV64
Fitzwarren Gdns, N19. . . . . **143** DJ60
Fitzwilliam Av, Rich. TW9. . . . . **180** CM82
Fitzwilliam Cl, N20. . . . . **120** DG46
Fitzwilliam Ct, Harl. CM17. . . . **58** EY11
Fitzwilliam Ms, E16 . . . . **35** N2
Fitzwilliam Rd, SW4. . . . . **41** L10
Fitzwygram Cl, Hmptn H.
TW12 . . . . **198** CC92
Five Acre, NW9 . . . . **119** CT53
Fiveacre Cl, Th.Hth. CR7. . . . . . **223** DN100
Five Acres, Chesh. HP5. . . . . . . **76** AR33
Harlow CM18. . . . . **73** ES18
Kings Langley WD4. . . . . **80** BM29
London Colney AL2 . . . . **83** CK25
Wooburn Green HP10. . . . . . . **132** AF56
Five Acres Av, Brick.Wd AL2. . . . **82** BZ29
Five Ash Rd, Grav. DA11. . . . . . **213** GF87
Five Bell All, E14 . . . . **21** P9
Five Elms Prim Sch, Dag.
RM9 *off Wood La* **148** EZ62
Five Elms Rd, Brom. BR2. . . . . . **226** EH104
Dagenham RM9 . . . . **148** EZ62
Five Flds Cl, Wat. WD19 . . . . . **116** BZ48

Five Oaks, Add. KT15 233 BF107
Five Oaks La, Chig. IG7 126 EY51
Five Oaks Ms, Brom. BR1 206 EG90
Jct Five Points, Iver SL0 155 BB69
Fives Ct, SE11 30 G8
Jct Fiveways, Croy. CR0 241 DN105
Jct Five Ways Cor, NW4 119 CV53
Fiveways Rd, SW9 42 F8
Five Wents, Swan. BR8 229 FG96
Fladbury Rd, N15 144 DR58
Fladgate Rd, E11 146 EE58
Flag Cl, Croy. CR0 225 DX102
Flagon Ct, Croy. CR0
off Lower Coombe St 242 DQ105
Flags, The, Hem.H. HP2 63 BP20
Flagstaff Cl, Wal.Abb. EN9 89 EB33
Flagstaff Ho, SW8
off St. George Wf 42 A2
Flagstaff Rd, Wal.Abb. EN9 89 EB33
Flag Wk, Pnr. HA5 137 BU58
Flambard Rd, Har. HA1 139 CG58
Flamborough Cl, Bigg.H. TN16 260 EH119
Flamborough Rd, Ruis. HA4 137 BU62
Flamborough Spur, Slou. SL1 173 AN75
Flamborough St, E14 21 L8
Flamborough Wk, E14 21 L9
Flamingo Cl, Hat. AL10 66 CR17
Flamingo Gdns, Nthlt. UB5
off Jetstar Way 158 BY69
Flamingo Wk, Horn. RM12 169 FG65
FLAMSTEAD END, Wal.Cr. EN7 88 DU28
Sch Flamstead End Prim Sch, Chsht EN7
off Longfield La 88 DU27
Flamstead End Rd, Chsht EN8 88 DV28
Flamstead Gdns, Dag. RM9
off Flamstead Rd 168 EW66
Flamstead Rd, Dag. RM9 168 EW66
Flamsted Av, Wem. HA9 160 CN65
Flamsteed Rd, SE7 186 EL78
Flanchford Rd, W12 181 CT76
Reigate RH2 271 CX134
Flanders Ct, Egh. TW20 195 BC92
Flanders Cres, SW17 202 DF94
Flanders Rd, E6 25 K1
W4 180 CS77
Flanders Way, E9 11 J4
Flandrian Cl, Enf. EN3 105 EA38
Flank St, E1 20 C10
Flannery Ct, SE16
off Drummond Rd 32 E6
Flash La, Enf. EN2 103 DP37
Flask Cotts, NW3
off New End Sq 142 DD63
Flask Wk, NW3 5 P1
Flatfield Rd, Hem.H. HP3 62 BN22
Flather Cl, SW16
off Blegborough Rd 203 DJ92
Flat Iron Sq, SE1
off Union St 31 K3
FLAUNDEN, Hem.H. HP3 79 BB33
Flaunden Bottom, Chesh. HP5 94 AY36
Flaunden HP3 94 AY35
Flaunden Hill, Flaun. HP3 79 AZ33
Flaunden La, Hem.H. HP3 79 BB32
Rickmansworth WD3 79 BD33
Flaunden Pk, Flaun. HP3 79 BA32
Flavell Ms, SE10 35 K10
Flavian Cl, St.Alb. AL3 64 BZ22
Flaxen Cl, E4 off Flaxen Rd 123 EB48
Flaxen Rd, E4 123 EB48
Flaxley Rd, Mord. SM4 222 DB100
Flaxman Ct, W1 17 N9
Flaxman Rd, SE5 43 H9
Flaxman Ter, WC1 17 P3
Flaxton Rd, SE18 187 ER81
Flecker Cl, Stan. HA7 117 CF50
Fleece Dr, N9 122 DU49
Sch Fleecefield Prim Sch, N18
off Brettenham Rd 122 DU49
Fleece Rd, Long Dit. KT6 219 CJ102
Fleece Wk, N7 8 B4
Fleeming Cl, E17
off Pennant Ter 123 DZ54
Fleeming Rd, E17 123 DZ54
Fleet Av, Dart. DA2 210 FQ88
Upminster RM14 151 FR58
Fleet Cl, Ruis. HA4 137 BQ58
Upminster RM14 151 FR58
West Molesey KT8 218 BZ99
Fleetdale Par, Dart. DA2
off Fleet Av 210 FQ88
Sch Fleetdown Inf Sch, Dart. DA2 off Lunedale Rd 210 FQ89
Sch Fleetdown Jun Sch, Darenth DA2 off Lunedale Rd 210 FQ89
Fleet La, W.Mol. KT8 218 BZ100
Fleet Pl, EC4
off Limeburner La 18 G8
Sch Fleet Prim Sch, NW3 6 E2
Fleet Rd, NW3 6 D2
Dartford DA2 210 FQ88
Northfleet DA11 212 GC90
Fleetside, W.Mol. KT8 218 BZ100
Fleet Sq, WC1 18 D3
Fleet St, EC4 18 E9
Fleet St Hill, E1 20 C5
FLEETVILLE, St.Alb. AL1 65 CG20
Sch Fleetville Inf & Nurs Sch, St.Alb. AL1 off Woodstock Rd S 65 CH20
Sch Fleetville Jun Sch, St.Alb. AL1 off Hatfield Rd 65 CG20
Fleetway, Egh. TW20 215 BC97
● Fleetway Business Pk, Perivale UB6 159 CH68
Fleetwood Cl, E16 24 E6
Chalfont St. Giles HP8 112 AU49
Chessington KT9 237 CK108
Croydon CR0 224 DT104
Tadworth KT20 255 CW120
Fleetwood Ct, E6 25 J6
West Byfleet KT14 234 BG113
Fleetwood Gro, W3
off East Acton La 160 CS73
Fleetwood Rd, NW10 141 CU64
Kingston upon Thames KT1 220 CP97
Slough SL2 154 AT74
Fleetwood Sq, Kings.T. KT1 220 CP97
Fleetwood St, N16
off Stoke Newington Ch St 144 DS61
Fleetwood Way, Wat. WD19 116 BW49
Fleming Cl, W9 15 J5
Cheshunt EN7 88 DU26
Fleming Ct, W2 16 A6
Croydon CR0 241 DN106
Fleming Cres, Hert. SG14
off Tudor Way 53 DN09
Fleming Dr, N21 103 DM43
Fleming Gdns, Harold Wd RM3
off Bartholomew Dr 128 FK54
Tilbury RM18
off Fielding Av 193 GJ81
Fleming Mead, Mitch. CR4 202 DE94
Fleming Rd, SE17 43 H2
Chafford Hundred RM16 191 FW77
Southall UB1 158 CB72
Waltham Abbey EN9 105 EB35
Flemings, Gt Warley CM13 129 FW51
Fleming Wk, NW9
off Pasteur Cl 118 CS54
Fleming Way, SE28 168 EX73
Isleworth TW7 179 CF83
Flemish Flds, Cher. KT16 216 BG101
Flemming Av, Ruis. HA4 137 BV60
Flempton Rd, E10 145 DY59
Fletcher Cl, E6 25 N10
Ottershaw KT16 233 BE107
St. John's GU21 248 AT118
Fletcher La, E10 145 EC59
Fletcher Path, SE8 46 B5
Fletcher Rd, W4 180 CQ76
Chigwell IG7 125 ET50
Ottershaw KT16 233 BD107
Fletchers Cl, Brom. BR2 226 EH98
Fletcher St, E1 20 D10
Fletcher Way, Hem.H. HP2 62 BJ18
Fletching Rd, E5 144 DW62
SE7 186 EJ79
Fletton Rd, N11 121 DL52
Fleur de Lis St, E1 19 P5
Fleur Gates, SW19 201 CX87
Flexley Wd, Welw.G.C. AL7 51 CZ06
Flex Meadow, Harl. CM19 72 EL16
Flexmere Gdns, N17
off Flexmere Rd 122 DR53
Flexmere Rd, N17 122 DR53
Flight App, NW9 119 CT54
Flimwell Cl, Brom. BR1 206 EE92
Flinders Cl, St.Alb. AL1 65 CG22
Flint Cl, E15 13 L6
Banstead SM7 240 DB114
Bookham KT23 268 CC126
Green Street Green BR6
off Lynne Cl 245 ET107
Redhill RH1 272 DF133
Flint Down Cl, Orp. BR5 228 EU95
Flint Hill, Dor. RH4 285 CH138
Flint Hill Cl, Dor. RH4 285 CH139
Flintlock Cl, Stai. TW19 176 BG84
Flintmill Cres, SE3 186 EL82
Flinton St, SE17 31 P10
Flint St, SE17 31 M9
Grays RM20 191 FV79
Flint Way, St.Alb. AL3 64 CC15
Flitcroft St, WC2 17 P8
Floathaven Cl, SE28 168 EU74
Floats, The, Rvrhd TN13 278 FE121
Flock Mill Pl, SW18 202 DB88
Flockton St, SE16 32 C5
Flodden Rd, SE5 43 J7
Flood La, Twick. TW1
off Church La 199 CG88
Flood Pas, SE18 37 J7
Flood St, SW3 40 D1
Flood Wk, SW3 40 D2
Flora Cl, E14 22 C9
Stanmore HA7 118 CL48
Flora Gdns, W6 181 CV77
Croydon CR0 243 EC111
Romford RM6 148 EW58
Sch Flora Gdns Prim Sch, W6
off Dalling Rd 181 CV77
Flora Gro, St.Alb. AL1 65 CF21
Flora Ho, E3 off Garrison Rd 12 A9
Floral Ct, Ashtd. KT21
off Rosedale 253 CJ118
Floral Dr, Lon.Col. AL2 83 CK26
Floral Pl, N1
off Northampton Gro 9 L3
Floral St, WC2 18 A10
Flora St, Belv. DA17 188 EZ78
Florence Av, Enf. EN2 104 DQ41
Morden SM4 222 DC99
New Haw KT15 234 BG111
Florence Cantwell Wk, N19
off Hillrise Rd 143 DL59
Florence Cl, Grays RM20 192 FY79
Harlow CM17 74 EW17
Hornchurch RM12 150 FL61
Walton-on-Thames KT12
off Florence Rd 217 BV101
Watford WD25 97 BU35
Florence Ct, W9
off Maida Vale 15 P3
Florence Dr, Enf. EN2 103 DQ41
Florence Elson Cl, E12 147 EN63
Florence Gdns, W4 180 CQ79
Romford RM6 off Roxy Av 148 EW59
Staines TW18 196 BH94
Florence Nightingale Ho, N1
off Nightingale Rd 9 K5
★ Florence Nightingale Mus, SE1 30 C5
Florence Rd, E6 166 EJ67
E13 23 N1
N4 143 DN60
SE2 188 EW76
SE14 45 P7
SW19 202 DB93
W4 180 CR76
W5 160 CL73
Beckenham BR3 225 DX96
Bromley BR1 226 EG95
Feltham TW13 197 BV88
Kingston upon Thames KT2 200 CM94
South Croydon CR2 242 DR109
Southall UB2 178 BX77
Walton-on-Thames KT12 217 BV101
Florence St, E16 23 M4
N1 8 G7
NW4 141 CW56
Florence Ter, SE14 45 P6
SW15 off Roehampton Vale 200 CS90
Florence Way, SW12 202 DF88
Uxbridge UB8 156 BJ66
Florence White Ct, N9
off Colthurst Dr 122 DV48
Florey Sq, N21
off Highlands Av 103 DM43
Florfield Pas, E8 10 F5
Florfield Rd, E8 10 F5
Florian Av, Sutt. SM1 240 DD105
Florian Rd, SW15 181 CY84
Florida Cl, Bushey Hth WD23 117 CD47
Florida Ct, Brom. BR2
off Westmoreland Rd 226 EF98
Florida Rd, Shalf. GU4 280 AY140
Thornton Heath CR7 223 DP95
Florida St, E2 20 C3
Florin Ct, EC1 19 J6
SE1 off Tanner St 32 A5
Floris Pl, SW4 41 L10
Floriston Av, Uxb. UB10 157 BQ66
Floriston Cl, Stan. HA7 117 CH53
Floriston Ct, Nthlt. UB5 138 CB64
Floriston Gdns, Stan. HA7 117 CH53
Floss St, SW15 38 B9
Flower & Dean Wk, E1 20 B7
Flower Cres, Ott. KT16 233 BB107
Flowerfield, Otford TN14 263 FF117
Flowerhill Way, Istead Rise DA13 212 GE94
Flower La, NW7 119 CT50
Godstone RH9 275 DY128
Flower Ms, NW11 141 CY58
Flower Pot Cl, N15
off St. Ann's Rd 144 DT58
Flowers Cl, NW2 141 CU62
Flowersmead, SW17 202 DG89
Flowers Ms, N19
off Archway Rd 143 DJ61
Flower Wk, Guil. GU2 280 AW137
Flower Wk, The, SW7 27 N5
Floyd Rd, SE7 36 C10
Floyds La, Wok. GU22 250 BG116
Floyer Cl, Rich. TW10 200 CM85
Fludyer St, SE13 186 EE84
Flux's La, Epp. CM16 92 EU33
Flyer's Way, The, West. TN16 277 ER126
● Flyers Way Ind Est, West. TN16 off The Flyer's Way 277 ER126
Fogerty Cl, Enf. EN3 105 EB37
Fold Cft, Harl. CM20 57 EN14
Foley Cl, Beac. HP9 110 AJ51
Foley Ho, E1 off Tarling St 20 G9
Foley Ms, Clay. KT10 237 CE108
Foley Rd, Bigg.H. TN16 260 EK118
Claygate KT10 237 CE108
Foley St, W1 17 L7
Foley Wd, Clay. KT10 237 CF108
Folgate St, E1 19 P6
Foliot Ho, N1
off Priory Grn Est 8 C10
Foliot St, W12 161 CT72
Folkes La, Upmin. RM14 151 FT57
Folkestone Ct, Slou. SL3 175 BA78
Folkestone Rd, E6 25 M1
E17 145 EB56
N18 122 DU49
Folkingham La, NW9 118 CR53
Folkington Cor, N12 119 CZ50
Follet Dr, Abb.L. WD5 81 BT31
Follett Cl, Old Wind. SL4 194 AV86
Follett St, E14 22 E9
Folly, The, Hert. SG14 54 DR09
Folly Av, St.Alb. AL3 64 CC19
Folly Cl, Rad. WD7 99 CF36
Follyfield Rd, Bans. SM7 240 DA114
Folly La, E4 123 DZ52
E17 123 DY53
St. Albans AL3 64 CC19
South Holmwood RH5 285 CH144
Folly Ms, W11 14 G9
Folly Pathway, Rad. WD7 99 CF35
Folly Vw, Stans.Abb. SG12 55 EB10
Folly Wall, E14 34 F5
Fontaine Rd, SW16 203 DM94
Fontarabia Rd, SW11 182 DG84
Fontayne Av, Chig. IG7 125 EQ49
Rainham RM13 169 FE66
Romford RM1 127 FE54
Fontenelle, SE5 43 N6
Fontenoy Rd, SW12 203 DH89
Fonteyne Gdns, Wdf.Grn. IG8 124 EJ54
Fonthill Cl, SE20
off Selby Rd 224 DU96
Fonthill Ms, N4 143 DM61
Fonthill Rd, N4 143 DM60
Font Hills, N2 120 DC54
● Fontigarry Fm Business Pk, Reig. RH2 288 DC143
Fontley Way, SW15 201 CU87
Fontmell Cl, Ashf. TW15 196 BN92
St. Albans AL3 65 CE18
Fontmell Pk, Ashf. TW15 196 BM92
Fontwell Cl, Har. HA3 117 CE52
Northolt UB5 158 CA65
Fontwell Dr, Brom. BR2 227 EN99
Fontwell Pk Gdns, Horn. RM12 150 FL63
Foord Cl, Dart. DA2 211 FS89
Football La, Har. HA1 139 CE60
Footbury Hill Rd, Orp. BR6 228 EU101
Footpath, The, SW15 201 CU85
FOOTS CRAY, Sid. DA14 208 EV93
Foots Cray High St, Sid. DA14 208 EW93
Foots Cray La, Sid. DA14 208 EW88
Footscray Rd, SE9 207 EN86
Forbench Cl, Ripley GU23 250 BH122
Forbes Av, Pot.B. EN6 86 DD33
Forbes Cl, NW2 141 CU62
Hornchurch RM11
off St. Leonards Way 149 FH60
Forbes Ct, SE19 204 DS92
Forbe's Ride, Wind. SL4 172 AG84
Forbes St, E1 20 D9
Forbes Way, Ruis. HA4 137 BV61
Forburg Rd, N16 144 DU60
FORCE GREEN, West. TN16 261 ER124
Force Grn La, West. TN16 261 ER124
Fordbridge Cl, Cher. KT16 216 BH102
Fordbridge Pk, Sun. TW16 217 BT100
Fordbridge Rd, Ashf. TW15 196 BM92
Shepperton TW17 217 BS100
Sunbury-on-Thames TW16 217 BS100
Jct Fordbridge Rbt, Ashf. TW15 196 BL93
Ford Cl, E3 11 M10
Ashford TW15 196 BL93
Bushey WD23 98 CC42
Harrow HA1 139 CD59
Rainham RM13 169 FF66
Shepperton TW17 216 BN98
Thornton Heath CR7 223 DP100
Fordcroft Rd, Orp. BR5 228 EV99
Forde Av, Brom. BR1 226 EJ97
Fordel Rd, SE6 205 ED88
Ford End, Denh. UB9 135 BF61
Woodford Green IG8 124 EH51
Fordham Cl, Barn. EN4 102 DE41
Hornchurch RM11 150 FN59
Worcester Park KT4 221 CV102
Fordham Rd, Barn. EN4 102 DD41
Fordham St, E1 20 D8
Fordhook Av, W5 160 CM73
Fordingley Rd, W9 15 H3
Fordington Ho, SE26
off Sydenham Hill Est 204 DV90
Fordington Rd, N6 142 DF57
Ford La, Iver SL0 156 BG72
Rainham RM13 169 FF66
Fordmill Rd, SE6 205 EA89
Ford Rd, E3 11 N10
Ashford TW15 196 BM91
Chertsey KT16 216 BH102
Dagenham RM9, RM10 168 EZ66
Northfleet DA11 212 GB85
Old Woking GU22 249 BB120
Fords Gro, N21 122 DQ46
Fords Pk Rd, E16 23 N8
Ford Sq, E1 20 F7
Ford St, E3 11 M9
E16 23 L8
Fordwater Rd, Cher. KT16 216 BH102
● Fordwater Trd Est, Cher. KT16 216 BJ102
Fordwich Cl, Hert. SG14 53 DN09
Orpington BR6 227 ET101
Fordwich Hill, Hert. SG14 53 DN09
Fordwich Ri, Hert. SG14 53 DN09
Fordwich Rd, Welw.G.C. AL8 51 CW10
Fordwych Rd, NW2 4 G3
Fordyce Cl, Horn. RM11 150 FM59
Fordyce Ho, SW16
off Colson Way 203 DJ91
Fordyce Rd, SE13 205 EC86
Fordyke Rd, Dag. RM8 148 EZ61
Forebury, The, Saw. CM21 58 EY05
Forebury Av, Saw. CM21 58 EZ05
Forebury Cres, Saw. CM21 58 EZ05
Forefield, St.Alb. AL2 82 CA27
★ Foreign & Commonwealth Office, SW1 29 P4
Foreign St, SE5 43 H8
Foreland Ct, NW4 119 CY53
Forelands Pl, Saw. CM21
off Bell St 58 EY05
Foreland St, SE18
off Plumstead Rd 187 ER77
Forelands Way, Chesh. HP5 76 AQ32
Foremark Cl, Ilf. IG6 125 ET50
Foreshore, SE8 33 P9
Forest, The, E11 146 EE56
Forest App, E4 124 EE45
Woodford Green IG8 124 EF52
Forest Av, E4 124 EE45
Chigwell IG7 125 EN50
Hemel Hempstead HP3 62 BK22
● Forest Business Pk, E10 145 DX59
Forest Cl, E11 146 EF57
NW6 4 E7
Chislehurst BR7 227 EN95
East Horsley KT24 267 BT125
Waltham Abbey EN9 106 EE37
Woking GU22 249 BD115
Woodford Green IG8 124 EH48
Forest Ct, E4 124 EF46
E11 146 EE56
Forest Cres, Ashtd. KT21 254 CN116
Forest Cft, SE23 204 DV89
FORESTDALE, Croy. CR0 243 EA109
Forestdale, N14 121 DK49
Forestdale Cen, The, Croy. CR0 off Holmbury Gro 243 DZ108
Sch Forestdale Prim Sch, Croy. CR0 off Pixton Way 243 DZ109
Forest Dr, E12 146 EK62
Keston BR2 244 EL105
Kingswood KT20 255 CZ121
Sunbury-on-Thames TW16 197 BT94
Theydon Bois CM16 107 ES36
Woodford Green IG8 123 ED52
Forest Dr E, E11 145 ED59
Forest Dr W, E11 145 EC59
Forest Edge, Buck.H. IG9 124 EJ49
Forester Rd, SE15 184 DV84
Foresters Cl, Chsht EN7 88 DS27
Wallington SM6 241 DK108
Woking GU21 248 AT118
Foresters Cres, Bexh. DA7 189 FB84
Foresters Dr, E17 145 ED56
Wallington SM6 241 DK108
Sch Foresters Prim Sch, Wall. SM6 off Redford Av 241 DK107
Forest Gdns, N17 122 DT54
FOREST GATE, E7 13 N3
⇌ Forest Gate 13 P2
Forest Gate, NW9 140 CS56
Sch Forest Gate Comm Sch, E7 13 P2
Forest Glade, E4 124 EE49
E11 146 EE58
North Weald Bassett CM16 92 EY27
Forest Gro, E8 10 A5
Forest Hts, Buck.H. IG9 124 EG47
FOREST HILL, SE23 205 DX88
⇌ Forest Hill 204 DW89
Jct Forest Hill, SE23 204 DW89
● Forest Hill Business Cen, SE23 off Clyde Vale 204 DW89
● Forest Hill Ind Est, SE23
off Perry Vale 204 DW89
Forest Hill Rd, SE22 204 DV85
SE23 204 DV85
Sch Forest Hill Sch, SE23
off Dacres Rd 205 DX90
Forestholme Cl, SE23 204 DW89
● Forest Ind Pk, Ilf. IG6 125 ES53
Forest La, E7 13 N3
E15 13 K4
Chigwell IG7 125 EN50
Leatherhead KT24 251 BT124
Forest Mt Rd, Wdf.Grn. IG8 123 ED52
Forest Pt, E7 off Windsor Rd 146 EH64
Fore St, EC2 19 K7
N9 122 DU50
N18 122 DT51
Harlow CM17 58 EW11
Hatfield AL9 67 CW17
Hertford SG14 54 DR09
Pinner HA5 137 BU57
Fore St Av, EC2 19 L7
Forest Ridge, Beck. BR3 225 EA97
Keston BR2 244 EL105
Forest Ri, E17 145 ED57
Forest Rd, E7 146 EG63
E8 10 A5
E11 145 ED59
E17 144 DW56
Forest Rd, N9 122 DV46
N17 144 DW56
Cheshunt EN8 89 DX29
Enfield EN3 105 DY36
Erith DA8 189 FG81
Feltham TW13 198 BW89
Ilford IG6 125 ES53
Leatherhead KT24 251 BU123
Loughton IG10 106 EK41
Richmond TW9 180 CN80
Romford RM7 149 FB55
Sutton SM3 222 DA102
Watford WD25 81 BV33
Windsor SL4 173 AK82
Woking GU22 249 BD115
Woodford Green IG8 124 EG48
Sch Forest Sch, E17
off College Pl 146 EE56
Forest Side, E4 124 EF45
E7 146 EH63
Buckhurst Hill IG9 124 EJ46
Epping CM16 91 ER33
Waltham Abbey EN9 106 EJ36
Worcester Park KT4 221 CT102
Forest St, E7 13 N2
● Forest Trd Est, E17 145 DX55
Forest Vw, E4 123 ED45
E11 146 EF59
Forest Vw Av, E10 145 ED57
Forest Vw Rd, E12 146 EL63
E17 123 EC53
Loughton IG10 106 EK42
Forest Wk, N10 121 DH53
Bushey WD23
off Millbrook Rd 98 BZ39
Forest Way, N19
off Hargrave Pk 143 DJ61
Ashtead KT21 254 CM117
Loughton IG10 106 EL41
Orpington BR5 227 ET99
Sidcup DA15 207 ER87
Waltham Abbey EN9 106 EK35
Woodford Green IG8 124 EH49
● Forest Wks, E17
off Forest Rd 145 DX55
Forfar Rd, N22 121 DP53
SW11 41 H6
Forge, The, Northaw EN6 86 DE30
Forge Av, Couls. CR5 257 DN120
Forge Br La, Couls. CR5 257 DH121
Forge Cl, Brom. BR2 226 EG102
Chipperfield WD4 80 BG31
Harlington UB3
off High St 177 BR79
Forge Dr, Clay. KT10 237 CG108
Farnham Common SL2 153 AQ65
Forge End, Amer. HP7 77 AP40
St. Albans AL2 82 CA26
Woking GU21 248 AY117
Forgefield, Bigg.H. TN16
off Main Rd 260 EK116
Forge La, Felt. TW13 198 BY92
Gravesend DA12 213 GM89
Horton Kirby DA4 230 FQ98
Northwood HA6 115 BS52
Richmond TW10
off Petersham Rd 200 CL88
Sunbury-on-Thames TW16 217 BU97
Sutton SM3 239 CY108
Sch Forge La Prim Sch, Han. TW13 off Forge La 198 BY92
Forge Ms, Croy. CR0
off Addington Village Rd 243 EA106
Forge Pl, NW1 7 H5
Horley RH6 290 DE150
Forge Steading, Bans. SM7
off Salisbury Rd 256 DB115
Forge Way, Shore. TN14 247 FF111
Forlong Path, Nthlt. UB5
off Cowings Mead 158 BY65
Forman Pl, N16
off Farleigh Rd 144 DT63
Formation, The, E16 37 N4
Formby Av, Stan. HA7 139 CJ55
Formby Cl, Slou. SL3 175 BC77
Formosa St, W9 15 N5
Formunt Cl, E16 23 M7
Forres Cl, Hodd. EN11 71 EA15
Forres Gdns, NW11 142 DA58
Sch Forres Prim Sch, Hodd. EN11 off Stanstead Rd 55 EB14
Forrester Path, SE26 204 DW91
Forresters Dr, Welw.G.C. AL7 52 DC10
Forrest Gdns, SW16 223 DM97
Forrest Pl, Shere GU5
off Wellers Ct 282 BN139
Forris Av, Hayes UB3 157 BT74
Forset St, W1 16 D8
Forstal Cl, Brom. BR2
off Ridley Rd 226 EG97
Forster Cl, Wdf.Grn. IG8 123 ED52
Sch Forster Pk Prim Sch, SE6
off Boundfield Rd 206 EE90
Forster Rd, E17 145 DY58
N17 144 DT55
SW2 203 DL87
Beckenham BR3 225 DY97
Croydon CR0
off Windmill Rd 224 DQ101
Guildford GU2 264 AU130
Forsters Cl, Rom. RM6 148 EZ58
Forster's Way, SW18 202 DB88
Forsters Way, Hayes UB4 157 BV72
Forston St, N1 9 L10
Forsyte Cres, SE19 224 DS95
Forsyth Ct, Dag. RM10
off St. Mark's Pl 169 FB65
Forsyth Gdns, SE17 43 H2
Forsyth Ho, SW1
off Tachbrook St 29 M10
Forsythia Cl, Ilf. IG1 147 EP64
Forsythia Gdns, Slou. SL3 174 AY76
Forsythia Pl, Guil. GU1
off Larch Av 264 AW132
Forsyth Path, Wok. GU21 233 BD113
Forsyth Pl, Enf. EN1 104 DS43
Forsyth Rd, Wok. GU21 233 BC114
Forterie Gdns, Ilf. IG3 148 EU62
Fortescue Av, E8 10 F7
Twickenham TW2 198 CC90
Fortescue Rd, SW19 202 DD94
Edgware HA8 118 CR53
Weybridge KT13 234 BM105
Fortess Gro, NW5 7 L2
Fortess Rd, NW5 7 K2
Fortess Wk, NW5 7 K2
Fortess Yd, NW5 7 K1
Forthbridge Rd, SW11 182 DG84
Forth Rd, Upmin. RM14 151 FR58

Fortin Cl, S.Ock. RM15 171 FU73
Fortin Path, S.Ock. RM15 171 FU73
Fortin Way, S.Ock. RM15 171 FU73
Fortis Cl, E16 24 C9
FORTIS GREEN, N2 142 DF56
Fortis Grn, N2 142 DE56
N10 142 DE56
Fortis Grn Av, N2 142 DF55
Fortis Grn Rd, N10 142 DG55
Fortismere Av, N10 142 DG55
Sch Fortismere Sch, N10
off Tetherdown 142 DG55
Coll Fortismere Sch 6th Form Cen, N10 *off Tetherdown* 142 DG55
Fort La, Reig. RH2 272 DB130
Fortnam Rd, N19 143 DK61
★ Fortnum & Mason, W1 29 L2
Fortnums Acre, Stan. HA7 117 CF51
● Fortress Distribution Pk, Til. RM18 193 GG84
Fort Rd, SE1 32 B9
Box Hill KT20 270 CP131
Guildford GU1 280 AY137
Halstead TN14 263 FC115
Northolt UB5 158 CA66
Tilbury RM18 193 GH84
Fortrose Cl, E14 23 H8
Fortrose Gdns, SW2 203 DL88
Fortrye Cl, Nthflt DA11 212 GE89
Fort St, E1 19 P7
E16 36 B3
Fortuna Cl, N7 8 D4
Fortune Gate Rd, NW10 160 CS67
Fortune Grn Rd, NW6 5 J1
Fortune La, Els. WD6 99 CK44
Fortune Pl, SE1 44 B1
Fortunes, The, Harl. CM18 73 ET17
Fortunes Mead, Nthlt. UB5 158 BY65
Fortune St, EC1 19 K5
Fortune Wk, SE28
off Broadwater Rd 187 ER76
Fortune Way, NW10 161 CU69
Forty Acre La, E16 23 N7
Forty Av, Wem. HA9 140 CM62
Forty Cl, Wem. HA9 140 CM61
Forty Footpath, SW14 180 CQ83
Fortyfoot Rd, Lthd. KT22 253 CJ121
FORTY GREEN, Beac. HP9 110 AH50
Forty Grn Rd, Knot.Grn HP9 110 AH51
★ Forty Hall & Mus, Enf. EN2 104 DT38
FORTY HILL, Enf. EN2 104 DS37
Forty Hill, Enf. EN2 104 DT38
Sch Forty Hill C of E Prim Sch, Enf. EN2 *off Forty Hill* 104 DU37
Forty La, Wem. HA9 140 CP61
Forum, The, W.Mol. KT8 218 CB98
Forum Cl, E3 12 A9
★ Forum Club, NW5 7 K2
Forum Magnum Sq, SE1 30 C4
Forum Pl, Hat. AL10 67 CU17
Forumside, Edg. HA8
off Station Rd 118 CN51
Forum Way, Edg. HA8
off High St 118 CN51
Forval Cl, Mitch. CR4 222 DF99
Forward Dr, Har. HA3 139 CF56
Fosbery Ct, Enf. EN3
off Sten Cl 105 EA37
Fosbury Ms, W2 27 M1
Foscote Ms, W9 15 K5
Foscote Rd, NW4 141 CV58
Foskett Rd, SW6 38 G9
Foss Av, Croy. CR0 241 DN106
Sch Fossdene Prim Sch, SE7
off Victoria Way 186 EH78
Fossdene Rd, SE7 186 EH78
Fossdyke Cl, Hayes UB4 158 BY71
Fosse Way, W13 159 CG71
West Byfleet KT14
off Brantwood Dr 233 BF113
Fossil Rd, SE13 185 EA83
Fossington Rd, Belv. DA17 188 EX77
Foss Rd, SW17 202 DD91
Fossway, Dag. RM8 148 EW61
Foster Av, Wind. SL4 173 AL83
Foster Cl, Chsht EN8 89 DX30
Fosterdown, Gdse. RH9 274 DV129
Foster La, EC2 19 J8
Foster Rd, E13 23 N4
W3 160 CS73
W4 180 CR78
Hemel Hempstead HP1 62 BG22
Fosters Cl, E18 124 EH53
Chislehurst BR7 207 EM92
Fosters Path, Slou. SL2 153 AM70
Sch Foster's Prim Sch, Well. DA16 *off Westbrooke Rd* 188 EW83
Foster St, NW4 141 CW56
Harlow CM17 74 EY17
Foster Wk, NW4 *off Foster St* 141 CW56
Fothergill Cl, E13 13 N10
Fothergill Dr, N21 103 DL43
Fotheringay Gdns, Slou. SL1 153 AN73
Fotheringham Rd, Enf. EN1 104 DT42
Fotherley Rd, Mill End WD3 113 BF47
Foubert's Pl, W1 17 L9
Foulden Rd, N16 144 DT63
Foulden Ter, N16
off Foulden Rd 144 DT63
Sch Foulds Prim Sch, Barn. EN5 *off Byng Rd* 101 CX41
Foulis Ter, SW7 28 B10
Foulser Rd, SW17 202 DF90
Foulsham Rd, Th.Hth. CR7 224 DQ97
● Foundation Units, Guil. GU1 264 AY130
Founder Cl, E6 25 N9
Founders Cl, Nthlt. UB5 158 BZ69
Founders Ct, EC2 19 L8
Founders Gdns, SE19 204 DQ94
Founders Rd, Hodd. EN11 55 EB14
★ Foundling Mus, WC1 18 B4
Foundry Cl, SE16 33 L2
Foundry Ct, Slou. SL2 154 AT74
Foundry Gate, Wal.Cr. EN8
off York Rd 89 DY33
Foundry La, Horton SL3 175 BB83
Foundry Ms, NW1 17 M4
Hounslow TW3
off New Rd 178 CB84
Foundry Pl, E1 20 G6
Founes Dr, Chaff.Hun. RM16 192 FY76
Fountain Cl, E5
off Lower Clapton Rd 144 DV62
SE18 37 N10
Uxbridge UB8 157 BQ71
Fountain Ct, EC4 18 E10
Eynsford DA4
off Pollyhaugh 230 FL103
Fountain Dr, SE19 204 DT91
Carshalton SM5 240 DF109
Hertford SG13 54 DT8
Fountain Fm, Harl. CM18 73 ET17
Fountain Gdns, Wind. SL4 173 AR83
Fountain Grn Sq, SE16 32 D5
Fountain Ho, SW6
off The Boulevard 39 P8
SW8 *off St. George Wf* 42 B1
Fountain La, Sev. TN15 279 FP122
Fountain Ms, N5
off Highbury Gra 9 J1
NW3 6 E4
Fountain Pl, SW9 42 F7
Waltham Abbey EN9 89 EC34
Fountain Rd, SW17 202 DD92
Redhill RH1 288 DE136
Thornton Heath CR7 224 DQ96
Fountains, The, Loug. IG10
off Fallow Flds 124 EK45
Fountains Av, Felt. TW13 198 BZ90
Fountains Cl, Felt. TW13 198 BZ89
Fountains Cres, N14 121 DL45
Fountain Sq, SW1 29 J8
Fountain Wk, Nthflt DA11 212 GE86
Fountayne Rd, N15 144 DU56
N16 144 DU61
Fount St, SW8 41 P5
Fouracres, SW12
off Little Dimocks 203 DH89
Four Acres, Cob. KT11 236 BY113
Fouracres, Enf. EN3 105 DY39
Four Acres, Guil. GU1 265 BC132
Welwyn Garden City AL7 51 CZ11
Four Acres, The, Saw. CM21 58 EZ06
Fouracres Dr, Hem.H. HP3 62 BM22
Fouracres Wk, Hem.H. HP3 62 BM22
Fourdinier Way, Hem.H. HP3 62 BK23
Four Hills Est, Enf. EN2 104 DQ38
Fourland Wk, Edg. HA8 118 CQ51
Fournier St, E1 20 A6
Four Oaks, Chesh. HP5 76 AN27
Four Seasons Cl, E3 12 A10
● Four Seasons Cres, Sutt. SM3 221 CZ103
Sch Four Swannes Prim Sch, Wal.Cr. EN8 *off King Edward Rd* 89 DY33
Fourth Av, E12 147 EM63
W10 14 E3
Grays RM20 191 FU79
Harlow CM19, CM20 73 EM15
Hayes UB3 157 BT74
Romford RM7 149 FD60
Watford WD25 98 BX35
Fourth Cross Rd, Twick. TW2 199 CD89
Fourth Dr, Couls. CR5 257 DK116
Fourth Way, Wem. HA9 140 CQ63
Four Trees, St.Alb. AL2 64 CB24
Four Tubs, The, Bushey WD23 117 CD45
Fourways, Bayford SG13 69 DN18
St. Albans AL4
off Hatfield Rd 66 CM20
Fourways Mkt, N.Mymms AL9 *off Dixons Hill Rd* 67 CW24
Four Wents, Cob. KT11 235 BV113
Four Wents, The, E4
off Kings Rd 123 ED47
Fowey Av, Ilf. IG4 146 EK57
Fowey Cl, E1 32 E2
Fowler Cl, SW11 182 DD83
Fowler Rd, E7 146 EG63
N1 9 H7
Ilford IG6 126 EV51
Mitcham CR4 222 DG96
Fowlers Cl, Sid. DA14
off Thursland Rd 208 EY92
Fowlers Mead, Chobham GU24 *off Windsor Rd* 232 AS110
Fowlers Wk, W5 159 CK70
Fowley Cl, Wal.Cr. EN8 89 DZ34
Fowley Mead Pk, Wal.Cr. EN8 89 EA34
Fownes St, SW11 40 D10
Foxacre, Cat. CR3
off Town End Cl 258 DS122
Fox All, Wat. WD18
off Lower High St 98 BW43
Fox & Knot St, EC1 19 H6
Foxberry Rd, SE4 185 DY83
Foxberry Wk, Nthflt DA11
off Rowmarsh Cl 212 GD91
Foxboro Rd, Red. RH1 272 DG132
Foxborough Cl, Slou. SL3 175 BA78
Foxborough Gdns, SE4 205 EA86
Sch Foxborough Sch, Langley SL3 *off Common Rd* 175 BA78
Foxbourne Rd, SW17 202 DG89
Fox Burrow Rd, Chig. IG7 126 EX50
Foxburrows Av, Guil. GU2 264 AT134
Foxbury Av, Chis. BR7 207 ER93
Foxbury Cl, Brom. BR1 206 EH93
Orpington BR6 246 EU106
Foxbury Dr, Orp. BR6 246 EU107
Foxbury Rd, Brom. BR1 206 EG93
Fox Cl, E1 21 H4
E16 23 N7
Bushey WD23 98 CB42
Elstree WD6 99 CK44
Orpington BR6 246 EU106
Romford RM5 127 FB50
Weybridge KT13 235 BR106
Woking GU22 249 BD115
Foxcombe, New Adgtn CR0 243 EB107
Foxcombe Cl, E6
off Boleyn Rd 166 EK68
Foxcombe Rd, SW15
off Alton Rd 201 CU88
Foxcote, SE5 43 P1
Fox Covert, Fetch. KT22 253 CD124
Foxcroft, St.Alb. AL1 65 CG22
Foxcroft Rd, SE18 187 EP81
Foxdell, Nthwd. HA6 115 BR51
Foxdells, Birch Grn SG14 53 DJ12
Foxdell Way, Chal.St.P. SL9 112 AY50
Foxearth Cl, Bigg.H. TN16 260 EL118
Foxearth Rd, S.Croy. CR2 242 DW110
Foxearth Spur, S.Croy. CR2 242 DW109
Foxenden Rd, Guil. GU1 280 AY135
Foxes Cl, Hert. SG13 54 DV09
Foxes Dale, SE3 47 N10
Bromley BR2 225 ED97
Foxes Dr, Wal.Cr. EN7 88 DU29
Foxes Grn, Orsett RM16 193 GG75
Foxes La, Cuffley EN6 87 DL28
North Mymms AL9 67 CY23
Foxes Path, Sutt.Grn GU4 265 AZ126
Foxfield Cl, Nthwd. HA6 115 BT51
Sch Foxfield Prim Sch, SE18
off Sandbach Pl 187 EQ78
Foxfield Rd, Orp. BR6 227 ER103
Foxglove Cl, N9 122 DW46
Hatfield AL10 67 CV19
Hoddesdon EN11
off Castle Cl 55 EC14
Sidcup DA15 208 EU86
Southall UB1 158 BY73
Stanwell TW19 196 BK88
Foxglove Gdns, E11 146 EJ56
Guildford GU4 265 BC132
Purley CR8 241 DL111
Foxglove La, Chess. KT9 238 CN105
Foxglove Path, SE28
off Crowfoot Cl 167 ES74
Foxglove Rd, Rush Grn RM7 149 FE61
South Ockendon RM15 171 FW71
Foxgloves, The, Hem.H. HP1 61 BE21
Foxglove St, W12 161 CT73
Foxglove Way, Wall. SM6 223 DH102
Foxgrove, N14 121 DL48
Fox Gro, Walt. KT12 217 BV101
Foxgrove Av, Beck. BR3 205 EB94
Foxgrove Dr, Wok. GU21 249 BA115
Foxgrove Path, Wat. WD19 116 BX50
Foxgrove Rd, Beck. BR3 205 EB94
Foxhall Rd, Upmin. RM14 150 FQ64
Foxham Rd, N19 143 DK62
Foxhanger Gdns, Wok. GU22
off Oriental Rd 249 BA116
Foxherne, Slou. SL3 174 AW75
Fox Hill, SE19 204 DT94
Keston BR2 244 EJ106
Foxhill, Wat. WD24 97 BU36
Fox Hill Gdns, SE19 204 DT94
Foxhills, Wok. GU21 248 AW117
Foxhills Cl, Ott. KT16 233 BB107
Foxhills Ms, Cher. KT16 215 BB104
Foxhills Rd, Ott. KT16 233 BA105
Foxhole Rd, SE9 206 EL85
Foxholes, Wey. KT13 235 BR106
Foxholes Av, Hert. SG13 54 DT09
● Foxholes Business Pk, Hert. SG13 54 DT09
Fox Hollow Cl, SE18 187 ES78
Fox Hollow Dr, Bexh. DA7 188 EX83
Foxhollow Dr, Farn.Com. SL2 133 AQ64
Foxhollows, Hat. AL10 67 CV16
London Colney AL2 83 CJ26
Foxholt Gdns, NW10 160 CQ66
Foxhome Cl, Chis. BR7 207 EN93
Foxhounds La, Grav. DA13 212 GA90
Fox Ho, SW11 *off Maysoule Rd* 182 DD84
Chertsey KT16
off Fox La N 215 BF102
Fox Ho Rd, Belv. DA17 189 FB77
Foxlake Rd, Byfleet KT14 234 BM112
Foxlands Cl, Wat. WD25 81 BU34
Foxlands Cres, Dag. RM10 149 FC64
Foxlands La, Dag. RM10 149 FC64
Foxlands Rd, Dag. RM10 149 FC64
Fox La, N13 121 DM48
W5 160 CL70
Bookham KT23 252 BY124
Caterham CR3 257 DP121
Keston BR2 244 EH106
Reigate RH2 272 DB131
Fox La N, Cher. KT16 215 BF102
Fox La S, Cher. KT16
off Guildford St 215 BF102
Foxlees, Wem. HA0 139 CG63
Foxley Cl, E8 10 C2
Loughton IG10 107 EP40
Redhill RH1 288 DG139
Foxley Ct, Sutt. SM2 240 DC108
Foxley Gdns, Pur. CR8 241 DP113
Foxley Hill Rd, Pur. CR8 241 DN112
Foxley Ho, E3
off Bromley High St 22 D2
Foxley La, Pur. CR8 241 DK111
Foxley Rd, SW9 42 F4
Kenley CR8 241 DP114
Thornton Heath CR7 223 DP98
Foxleys, Wat. WD19 116 BY48
Foxley Sq, SW9 42 G6
Foxmead Cl, Enf. EN2 103 DM41
Foxmoor Ct, Denh. UB9
off Broadway E 136 BG58
Foxmore St, SW11 40 E7
Foxon Cl, Cat. CR3 258 DS121
Foxon La, Cat. CR3 258 DR121
Foxon La Gdns, Cat. CR3 258 DS121
Sch Fox Prim Sch, W8 27 J2
Fox Rd, E16 23 L7
Slough SL3 174 AX77
Fox's Path, Mitch. CR4 222 DE96
Foxton Gro, Mitch. CR4 222 DD96
Foxton Rd, Grays RM20 191 FX79
Hoddesdon EN11 71 DZ17
Foxwarren, Clay. KT10 237 CF109
Foxwell Ms, SE4 45 M10
Foxwell St, SE4 45 M10
Fox Wd, Walt. KT12 235 BT108
Foxwood Chase, Wal.Abb. EN9 105 EC35
Foxwood Cl, NW7 118 CS49
Feltham TW13 197 BV90
Foxwood Grn Cl, Enf. EN1 104 DS44
Foxwood Gro, Nthflt DA11 212 GE88
Pratt's Bottom BR6 246 EW110
Foxwood Rd, SE3 186 EF84
Bean DA2 211 FV90
Foyle Dr, S.Ock. RM15 171 FU71
Foyle Rd, N17 122 DU53
SE3 47 L3
Frailey Cl, Wok. GU22 249 BB116
Frailey Hill, Wok. GU22 249 BB116
Framewood Rd, Slou. SL2, SL3 154 AW66
Framfield Cl, N12 120 DA48
Framfield Ct, Enf. EN1 104 DS44
Framfield Rd, N5 8 G2
W7 159 CE72
Mitcham CR4 202 DG94
Framlingham Cres, SE9 206 EL91
Framlingham Cl, E5
off Detmold Rd 144 DW61
Frampton Cl, Sutt. SM2 240 DA108
Frampton Ct, Denh. UB9
off Denham Grn La 135 BF58
Frampton Pk Est, E9 10 G6
Frampton Pk Rd, E9 10 G5
Frampton Rd, Epp. CM16 92 EU28
Hounslow TW4 198 BY85
Potters Bar EN6 86 DC30
Frampton St, NW8 16 A5
Hertford SG14 54 DR09
Francemary Rd, SE4 205 EA85
Frances & Dick James Ct, NW7
off Langstone Way 119 CY52
Frances Av, Chaff.Hun. RM16 191 FW77
Maidenhead SL6 152 AC70
Sch Frances Bardsley Sch for Girls, Rom. RM1
off Brentwood Rd 149 FH58
Frances Gdns, S.Ock. RM15 171 FT72
Coll Frances King Sch of English, South Kensington, SW7 27 P8
Victoria, SW1 29 K6
Frances Rd, E4 123 EA51
Windsor SL4 173 AR82
Frances St, SE18 37 J8
Chesham HP5 76 AQ30
Franche Ct Rd, SW17 202 DC90
Franchise St, Chesh. HP5 76 AQ30
Francis Av, Bexh. DA7 188 FA82
Feltham TW13 197 BU90
Ilford IG1 147 ER61
St. Albans AL3 64 CC17
Sch Francis Bacon Maths & Computing Coll, St.Alb. AL1 *off Drakes Dr* 65 CH23
Francis Barber Cl, SW16
off Well Cl 203 DM91
Francis Bentley Ms, SW4
off Old Town 183 DJ83
Sch Franciscan Prim Sch, SW17
off Franciscan Rd 202 DG92
Franciscan Rd, SW17 202 DF92
Francis Chichester Way, SW11 41 H7
Francis Cl, E14 34 G8
Epsom KT19 238 CR105
Shepperton TW17 216 BN98
Francisco Cl, Chaff.Hun. RM16 191 FW77
Sch Francis Combe Sch & Comm Coll, Wat. WD25
off Horseshoe La 82 BW32
Francis Ct, Guil. GU2 264 AV132
Francis Gro, SW19 201 CZ93
Sch Francis Holland Sch, Marylebone, NW1 16 E4
Belgravia, SW1 29 H9
Francis Pl, N6
off Holmesdale Rd 143 DH59
Francis Rd, E10 145 EC60
N2 142 DF56
Caterham CR3 258 DR122
Croydon CR0 223 DP101
Dartford DA1 210 FK85
Harrow HA1 139 CG57
Hounslow TW4 178 BX82
Ilford IG1 147 ER61
Orpington BR5 228 EX97
Perivale UB6 159 CH68
Pinner HA5 138 BW57
Wallington SM6 241 DJ107
Ware SG12 55 DX05
Watford WD18 97 BV42
Francis St, E15 13 J3
SW1 29 L8
Ilford IG1 147 ER61
Francis Ter, N19 143 DJ62
Francis Ter Ms, N19
off Francis Ter 143 DJ62
Francis Wk, N1 8 C8
Francis Way, Slou. SL1 153 AK73
Francklyn Gdns, Edg. HA8 118 CN48
Francombe Gdns, Rom. RM1 149 FG58
Franconia Rd, SW4 203 DJ85
Frank Bailey Wk, E12
off Gainsborough Av 147 EN64
Sch Frank Barnes Sch for Deaf Children, NW3 6 B7
Frank Burton Cl, SE7
off Victoria Way 186 EH78
Frank Dixon Cl, SE21 204 DS88
Frank Dixon Way, SE21 204 DS88
Frankfurt Rd, SE24 204 DQ85
Frankham St, SE8 46 A5
Frankland Cl, SE16 32 F7
Croxley Green WD3 114 BN45
Woodford Green IG8 124 EJ50
Frankland Rd, E4 123 EA50
SW7 28 A7
Croxley Green WD3 97 BP44
Franklands Dr, Add. KT15 233 BF108
Franklin Av, Chsht EN7 88 DV30
Slough SL2 153 AP70
Franklin Cl, N20 120 DC45
SE13 46 C7
SE27 203 DP90
Colney Heath AL4 66 CS22
Hemel Hempstead HP3 62 BL23
Kingston upon Thames KT1 220 CN97
Franklin Ct, Guil. GU2
off Humbolt Cl 264 AT134
Franklin Cres, Mitch. CR4 223 DJ98
Franklin Ho, NW9 141 CT59
Franklin Pas, SE9 186 EL83
Franklin Pl, SE13 46 C7
Franklin Rd, SE20 204 DW94
Bexleyheath DA7 188 EY81
Dartford DA2 209 FE89
Gravesend DA12 213 GK92
Hornchurch RM12 170 FJ65
Watford WD17 97 BV40
Franklins, Map.Cr. WD3 113 BE49
Franklins Ms, Har. HA2 138 CC61
Franklin Sq, W14 39 H1
Franklin's Row, SW3 28 F10
Franklin St, E3 22 D2
N15 144 DS58
Franklin Way, Croy. CR0 223 DL101
Frank Lunnon Cl, B.End SL8 132 AC60
Franklyn Cres, Wind. SL4 173 AK83
Franklyn Gdns, Ilf. IG6 125 ER51
Franklyn Rd, NW10 161 CT66
Walton-on-Thames KT12 217 BU100
Frank Martin Ct, Wal.Cr. EN7 88 DU30
Franks Av, N.Mal. KT3 220 CQ98
Franksfield, Peasl. GU5 283 BS144
Franks La, Hort.Kir. DA4 230 FN98
Franks Rd, Guil. GU2 264 AU131
Frank St, E13 23 P5
Frank Sutton Way, Slou. SL1 153 AR73
Frankswood Av, Petts Wd BR5 227 EP99
West Drayton UB7 156 BM72
Frank Towell Ct, Felt. TW14 197 BU87
Franlaw Cres, N13 122 DQ49
Franmil Rd, Horn. RM12 149 FG60
Fransfield Gro, SE26 204 DV90
Frant Cl, SE20 204 DW94
Franthorne Way, SE6 205 EB89
Frant Rd, Th.Hth. CR7 223 DP99
Fraser Cl, E6 24 G8
Bexley DA5 209 FC88
Fraser Ct, W12
off Heathstan Rd 161 CU72
Fraser Gdns, Dor. RH4 285 CG135
Fraser Ho, Brent. TW8
off Green Dragon La 180 CM78
Fraser Rd, E17 145 EB57
N9 122 DV48
Cheshunt EN8 89 DY28
Erith DA8 189 FC78
Perivale UB6 159 CH67
Fraser St, W4 180 CS78
Frating Cres, Wdf.Grn. IG8 124 EG51
Frays Av, West Dr. UB7 176 BK75
Frays Cl, West Dr. UB7 176 BK76
Frays Lea, Uxb. UB8 156 BJ68
Frays Waye, Uxb. UB8 156 BJ67
Frazer Av, Ruis. HA4 138 BW64
Frazer Cl, Rom. RM1 149 FF59
Frazier St, SE1 30 E5
Frean St, SE16 32 C6
Freda Corbett Cl, SE15 44 C4
Frederica Rd, E4 123 ED45
Frederica St, N7 8 C6
Frederick Andrews Ct, Grays RM17 192 GD79
Sch Frederick Bremer Sch, E17 *off Fulbourne Rd* 123 EC54
Frederick Cl, W2 16 D10
Sutton SM1 239 CZ105
Frederick Ct, NW2 141 CY62
Frederick Cres, SW9 42 G5
Enfield EN3 104 DW40
Frederick Gdns, Croy. CR0 223 DP100
Sutton SM1 239 CZ106
Frederick Pl, SE18 37 N10
Frederick Rd, SE17 43 H2
Rainham RM13 169 FD68
Sutton SM1 239 CZ106
Frederick's Pl, EC2 19 L9
Fredericks Pl, N12 120 DC49
Frederick Sq, SE16 33 L1
Frederick's Row, EC1 18 G2
Frederick St, WC1 18 C3
Frederick Ter, E8 10 A7
Frederick Vil, W7
off Lower Boston Rd 159 CE74
Frederic Ms, SW1 28 F5
Frederic St, E17 145 DY57
Fredley Pk, Mick. RH5 269 CJ129
Fredora Av, Hayes UB4 157 BT70
Fred White Wk, N7 8 B4
Fred Wigg Twr, E11 146 EF61
Freeborne Gdns, Rain. RM13 169 FG65
Freedom Cl, E17 145 DY56
Freedom Rd, N17 122 DR54
Freedom St, SW11 40 F8
Freedown La, Sutt. SM2 240 DC113
Freegrove Rd, N7 8 B3
Freeland Pk, NW4 119 CY54
Freeland Rd, W5 160 CM73
Freelands Av, S.Croy. CR2 243 DX109
Freelands Gro, Brom. BR1 226 EH95
Freelands Rd, Brom. BR1 226 EH95
Cobham KT11 235 BV114
Freeland Way, Erith DA8
off Slade Grn Rd 189 FG81
Freeling St, N1 8 C7
Freeman Cl, Nthlt. UB5 158 BY66
Shepperton TW17 217 BS98
Freeman Ct, N7
off Tollington Way 143 DL62
Chesham HP5 *off Barnes Av* 76 AQ30
Freeman Dr, W.Mol. KT8 218 BZ97
Freeman Rd, Grav. DA12 213 GL90
Morden SM4 222 DD99
Freemans Acre, Hat. AL10
off Cunningham Av 66 CR17
Freemans Cl, Stoke P. SL2 154 AT65
Freemans La, Hayes UB3 157 BS73
Freemantle Av, Enf. EN3 105 DX43
Sch Freemantles Sch, Wok. GU22
off Smarts Heath Rd 248 AW122
Freemantle St, SE17 31 N10
Freeman Way, Horn. RM11 150 FL58
★ Freemason's Hall (United Grand Lo of England), WC2 18 B8
Freemasons Pl, Croy. CR0
off Freemasons Rd 224 DS102
Freemasons Rd, E16 24 A7
Croydon CR0 224 DS102
Free Prae Rd, Cher. KT16 216 BG102
Freesia Cl, Orp. BR6 245 ET106
Freethorpe Cl, SE19 224 DR95
Free Trade Wf, E1 21 J10
Freezeland Way, Hlgdn UB10
off Long La 157 BP65
FREEZYWATER, Wal.Cr. EN8 105 DY35
Sch Freezywater St. George's Prim Sch, Enf. EN3
off Hertford Rd 105 DX36
★ Freightliners Fm, N7 8 D4
● Freightmaster Est, Rain. RM13 189 FG76
Freke Rd, SW11 182 DG83
Fremantle Ho, Til. RM18 193 GF81
Fremantle Rd, Belv. DA17 188 FA77
Ilford IG6 125 EQ54
Fremont St, E9 10 G8
French Apts, The, Pur. CR8
off Lansdowne Rd 241 DN112
Frenchaye, Add. KT15 234 BJ106
Frenches, The, Red. RH1 272 DG132
Frenches Ct, Red. RH1
off Frenches Rd 272 DG132
Frenches Rd, Red. RH1 272 DG132
French Gdns, Cob. KT11 236 BW114
French Horn La, Hat. AL10 67 CV17
Frenchlands Hatch, E.Hors. KT24 267 BS127
French Ordinary Ct, EC3 19 P10
French Pl, E1 19 P4
French Row, St.Alb. AL3
off Market Pl 65 CD20
French's Cl, Stans.Abb. SG12 55 EB11
French St, Sun. TW16 218 BW96
Westerham TN16 277 ES128
French's Wells, Wok. GU21 248 AV117
Frenchum Gdns, Slou. SL1 153 AL74
Frendsbury Rd, SE4 185 DY84
Frensham, Chsht EN7 88 DT27
Frensham Cl, Sthl. UB1 158 BZ70
Frensham Ct, Mitch. CR4 222 DD97
Frensham Dr, SW15 201 CU89
New Addington CR0 243 EC108
Frensham Rd, SE9 207 ER89
Kenley CR8 241 DP114

Frensham St, SE15 44 D3
Frensham Wk, Farn.Com. SL2 133 AQ64
Frensham Way, Epsom KT17 255 CW116
Frere St, SW11 40 D8
Freshborough Ct, Guil. GU1
off Lower Edgeborough Rd 281 AZ135
Freshfield Av, E8 10 A7
Freshfield Cl, SE13
off Mercator Rd 185 ED84
Freshfield Dr, N14 121 DH45
Freshfields, Croy. CR0 225 DZ101
Freshfields Av, Upmin. RM14 150 FP64
Freshford St, SW18 202 DC90
Freshmount Gdns, Epsom
KT19 238 CP111
Freshwater Cl, SW17 202 DG93
Freshwater Rd, SW17 202 DG93
Dagenham RM8 148 EX60
Freshwaters, Harl. CM20
off School La 57 ES14
Freshwell Av, Rom. RM6 148 EW56
Fresh Wf, Bark. IG11 167 EP67
● Fresh Wf Est, Bark. IG11
off Fresh Wf 167 EP67
Freshwood Cl, Beck. BR3 225 EB95
Freshwood Way, Wall. SM6 241 DH109
Freston Gdns, Barn. EN4 102 DG43
Freston Pk, N3 119 CZ54
Freston Rd, W10 14 C10
W11 26 D1
Freta Rd, Bexh. DA6 208 EZ85
Fretherne Rd, Welw.G.C. AL8 51 CX09
★ Freud Mus, NW3 6 A4
Frewin Rd, SW18 202 DD88
Friar Ms, SE27 203 DP90
Friar Rd, Hayes UB4 158 BX70
Orpington BR5 228 EU99
Friars, The, Chig. IG7 125 ES49
Harlow CM19 73 EN17
Friars Av, N20 120 DE48
SW15 201 CT90
Shenfield CM15 131 GA46
Friars Cl, E4 123 EC48
N2 142 DD56
SE1 30 G3
Ilford IG1 147 ER60
Northolt UB5
off Broomcroft Av 158 BX69
Shenfield CM15 131 FZ45
Friarscroft, Brox. EN10 71 EA20
Friars Fld, Nthch HP4
off Herons Elm 60 AS16
Friars Gdns, W3
off St. Dunstans Av 160 CR72
Friars Gate, Guil. GU2 280 AU136
Friars Gate Cl, Wdf.Grn. IG8 124 EG49
Friars La, Hat.Hth CM22 59 FH06
Richmond TW9 199 CK85
Friars Mead, E14 34 E7
Friars Ms, SE9 207 EN85
Friars Orchard, Fetch. KT22 253 CD121
Friars Pl La, W3 160 CR73
Friars Prim Sch, SE1 31 H4
Friars Ri, Wok. GU22 249 BA118
Friars Rd, E6 166 EK67
Virginia Water GU25 214 AX98
Friars Stile Pl, Rich. TW10
off Friars Stile Rd 200 CL86
Friars Stile Rd, Rich. TW10 200 CL86
Friar St, EC4 19 H9
Friars Wk, N14 121 DH46
SE2 188 EX78
Friars Way, W3 160 CR72
Bushey WD23 98 BZ39
Chertsey KT16 216 BG100
Kings Langley WD4 80 BN30
Friars Wd, Croy. CR0 243 DY109
Friary, The, Old Wind. SL4 194 AW86
Waltham Cross EN8 89 DZ33
Friary Br, Guil. GU1 280 AW135
Friary Cl, N12 120 DE50
Friary Ct, SW1 29 M3
Woking GU21 248 AT118
Friary Est, SE15 44 D3
Friary Island, Wrays. TW19 194 AW86
Friary La, Wdf.Grn. IG8 124 EG49
Friary Pk Est, W3
off Friary Rd 160 CR72
Friary Pas, Guil. GU1
off Friary St 280 AW136
Friary Rd, N12 120 DD49
SE15 44 D3
W3 160 CR72
Wraysbury TW19 194 AW86
Friary Shop Cen, The, Guil.
GU1 off Onslow St 280 AW135
Friary St, Guil. GU1 280 AW136
Friary Way, N12 120 DE49
FRIDAY HILL, E4 123 ED47
Friday Hill, E4 124 EE47
Friday Hill E, E4 124 EE48
Friday Hill W, E4 124 EE47
Friday Rd, Erith DA8 189 FD78
Mitcham CR4 202 DF94
FRIDAY STREET, Dor. RH5 284 BZ143
Friday St, EC4 19 J9
Abinger Common RH5 284 BZ143
Frideswide Pl, NW5 7 L3
Friendly Pl, SE13 46 D7
Friendly St, SE8 46 A8
Friendly St Ms, SE8
off Friendly St 46 A8
Friends Av, Chsht EN8 89 DX31
Friendship Wk, Nthlt. UB5
off Wayfarer Rd 158 BX69
Friendship Way, E15 12 F8
Friends Rd, Croy. CR0 224 DR104
Purley CR8 241 DP112
Friend St, EC1 18 G2
Friends Wk, Stai. TW18 195 BF92
Uxbridge UB8
off Bakers Rd 156 BK66
FRIERN BARNET, N11 120 DE49
Friern Barnet La, N11 120 DE49
N20 120 DE49
Friern Barnet Rd, N11 120 DF50
Friern Barnet Sch, N11
off Hemington Av 120 DF50
Friern Br Retail Pk, N11 121 DH51
Friern Cl, Chsht EN7 88 DS26
Friern Ct, N20 120 DD48
Friern Mt Dr, N20 120 DC45
Friern Pk, N12 120 DC50
Friern Rd, SE22 204 DU86
Friern Watch Av, N12 120 DC49
Frigate Ms, SE8 46 A2
Frimley Av, Horn. RM11 150 FN60
Wallington SM6 241 DL106
Frimley Cl, SW19 201 CY89
New Addington CR0 243 EC108
Frimley Ct, Sid. DA14 208 EV92
Frimley Cres, New Adgtn CR0 243 EC108
Frimley Gdns, Mitch. CR4 222 DE97
Frimley Rd, Chess. KT9 238 CL106
Hemel Hempstead HP1 61 BE19
Ilford IG3 147 ES62
Frimley Way, E1 21 J4
Fringewood Cl, Nthwd. HA6 115 BP53
Frinstead Gro, Orp. BR5 228 EX98
Frinstead Ho, W10 14 C10
Frinsted Rd, Erith DA8 189 FD80
Frinton Cl, Wat. WD19 115 BV47
Frinton Dr, Wdf.Grn. IG8 123 ED52
Frinton Ms, Ilf. IG2 147 EN58
Frinton Rd, E6 24 E3
N15 144 DS58
SW17 202 DG93
Romford RM5 126 EZ52
Sidcup DA14 208 EY89
Friston Path, Chig. IG7 125 ES50
Friston St, SW6 39 L9
Friswell Pl, Bexh. DA6 188 FA84
Fritham Cl, N.Mal. KT3 220 CS100
Frith Ct, NW7 119 CY52
Frithe, The, Slou. SL2 154 AV72
Frith Knowle, Hersham KT12 235 BV106
Frith La, NW7 119 CY52
Frith Manor Prim Sch, N12
off Lullington Garth 119 CZ50
Frith Rd, E11 145 EC63
Croydon CR0 224 DQ103
Frithsden Copse, Pott.End HP4 61 AZ15
Frithsden Rd, Berk. HP4 60 AY17
Friths Dr, Reig. RH2 272 DB131
Frith St, W1 17 N9
Frithville Gdns, W12 26 A2
Frithwald Rd, Cher. KT16 215 BF101
Frithwood Av, Nthwd. HA6 115 BS51
Frithwood Prim Sch, Nthwd.
HA6 off Carew Rd 115 BT51
Frizlands La, Dag. RM10 149 FB63
Frobisher Cl, Bushey WD23 98 CA44
Kenley CR8 off Hayes La 258 DQ117
Pinner HA5 138 BX59
Frobisher Cres, EC2
off The Barbican 19 K6
Staines TW19 196 BL87
Frobisher Gdns, Chaff.Hun.
RM16 192 FY76
Guildford GU1 265 BA133
Staines TW19 196 BL87
Frobisher Ms, Enf. EN2 104 DR42
Frobisher Pas, E14 34 B2
Frobisher Pl, SE15 44 G7
Frobisher Rd, E6 25 K8
N8 143 DN56
Erith DA8 189 FF80
St. Albans AL1 65 CJ22
Frobisher St, SE10 47 K2
Frobisher Way, Grav. DA12 213 GL92
Greenhithe DA9 191 FV84
Hatfield AL10 66 CR15
Froggy La, Denh. UB9 135 BD62
Froghall La, Chig. IG7 125 ER49
FROGHOLE, Eden. TN8 277 ER133
Froghole La, Eden. TN8 277 ER132
Frog La, Sutt.Grn GU4 264 AY125
Frogley Rd, SE22 184 DT84
Frogmoor La, Rick. WD3 114 BK47
FROGMORE, St.Alb. AL2 83 CE28
Frogmore, SW18 202 DA85
St. Albans AL2 83 CD27
Frogmore Av, Hayes UB4 157 BS69
Frogmore Cl, Slou. SL1 173 AN75
Sutton SM3 221 CX104
Frogmore Dr, Wind. SL4 174 AS81
● Frogmore Est, Grays
RM20 191 FU78
Frogmore Gdns, Hayes UB4 157 BS70
Sutton SM3 239 CY105
Frogmore Home Pk,
St.Alb. AL2 83 CD27
● Frogmore Ind Est, N5 9 J1
NW10 160 CQ69
Frogmore Rd, Hem.H. HP3 62 BK23
Frognal, NW3 5 N4
Frognal Av, Har. HA1 139 CF56
Sidcup DA14 208 EU92
Frognal Cl, NW3 5 N2
Frognal Cor, Sid. DA14 207 ET93
Frognal Ct, NW3 5 P4
Frognal Gdns, NW3 5 N1
Frognal La, NW3 5 L2
Frognal Par, NW3
off Frognal Ct 5 P4
Frognal Pl, Sid. DA14 208 EU93
Frognal Ri, NW3 142 DC63
Frognal Way, NW3 5 N1
Froissart Rd, SE9 206 EK85
Frome Rd, N22 143 DP55
Fromer Rd, Woob.Grn HP10 132 AD59
Frome Sq, Hem.H. HP2
off Waveney 62 BM15
Frome St, N1 9 J10
Fromondes Rd, Sutt. SM3 239 CY106
Front, The, Pott.End HP4 61 BB16
Front La, Upmin. RM14 151 FS59
Frostic Wk, E1 20 B7
Froude St, SW8 41 K9
Frowick Cl, N.Mymms AL9 67 CW23
Frowyke Cres, S.Mimms EN6 85 CU32
Fruen Rd, Felt. TW14 197 BT87
Fruiterers Pas, EC4
off Southwark Br 31 K1
Fryatt Rd, N17 122 DR52
Fry Cl, Rom. RM5 126 FA50
Fryday Gro Ms, SW12 203 DJ87
Fryent Cl, NW9 140 CN58
Fryent Cres, NW9 140 CS58
Fryent Flds, NW9 140 CS58
Fryent Gro, NW9 140 CS58
Fryent Prim Sch, NW9
off Church La 140 CQ59
Fryent Way, NW9 140 CN57
Fryer Cl, Chesh. HP5 76 AR33
Fryern Wd, Chaldon CR3 258 DQ124
Frying Pan All, E1 20 A7
Frymley Vw, Wind. SL4 173 AK81
Fry Rd, E6 166 EK66
NW10 161 CT67
Fryston Av, Couls. CR5 241 DH114
Croydon CR0 224 DU103
Fryth Mead, St.Alb. AL3 64 CB19
Fuchsia Cl, Rush Grn RM7 149 FE61
Fuchsia St, SE2 188 EV78
Fulbeck Dr, NW9 118 CS53
Fulbeck Wk, Edg. HA8
off Burrell Cl 118 CP47
Fulbeck Way, Har. HA2 116 CC54
Fulbourne Cl, Red. RH1
off Dennis Cl 272 DE132
Fulbourne Rd, E17 123 EC53
Fulbourne St, E1 20 E6
Fulbrook Av, New Haw KT15 234 BG111
Fulbrook La, S.Ock. RM15 171 FT73
Fulbrook Ms, N19
off Junction Rd 143 DJ63
Fulbrook Rd, N19
off Junction Rd 143 DJ63
Fulford Gro, Wat. WD19 115 BV47
Fulford Rd, Cat. CR3 258 DR121
Epsom KT19 238 CR108
Fulford St, SE16 32 F5
FULHAM, SW6 38 E8
⊖ Fulham Broadway 39 K4
Fulham Bdy, SW6 39 K4
Fulham Bdy Retail Cen,
SW6 off Fulham Bdy 39 K4
Fulham Cl, Uxb. UB10 157 BQ71
Fulham Ct, SW6 39 J6
Fulham Cross Girls' Sch,
SW6 38 E4
★ Fulham FC, SW6 38 C7
Fulham High St, SW6 38 F9
★ Fulham Palace, SW6 38 E9
Fulham Palace Rd, SW6 38 D4
W6 26 B10
Fulham Pk Gdns, SW6 38 G9
Fulham Pk Rd, SW6 38 G8
Fulham Prep Sch,
Pre-Prep, SW6 38 F9
Prep, W14 38 F2
Fulham Prim Sch, SW6 39 J3
Fulham Rd, SW3 40 A1
SW6 39 M4
SW10 40 A1
Fulkes Cotts, Lthd. KT24 267 BP128
Fullarton Cres, S.Ock. RM15 171 FT72
Fullbrooks Av, Wor.Pk. KT4 221 CT102
Fullbrook Sch, New Haw
KT15 off Selsdon Rd 234 BG111
Fuller Cl, E2 20 C4
Bushey WD23 117 CD45
Orpington BR6 245 ET106
Fuller Gdns, Wat. WD24 97 BV37
Fuller Rd, Dag. RM8 148 EV62
Watford WD24 97 BV37
Fullers Av, Surb. KT6 220 CM103
Woodford Green IG8 124 EF52
Fullers Cl, Chesh. HP5 76 AP32
Romford RM5 127 FC52
Waltham Abbey EN9 90 EG33
Fullers Fm Rd, W.Hors. KT24 267 BP134
★ Fuller's Griffin Brewery,
W4 181 CT79
Fullers Hill, Chesh. HP5 76 AM34
Hyde Heath HP6 76 AM34
Westerham TN16
off Market Sq 277 ER126
Fullers La, Rom. RM5 127 FC52
Fullers Mead, Harl. CM17 74 EW16
Fullers Rd, E18 124 EF53
Fuller St, NW4 141 CW56
Fullers Way N, Surb. KT6 220 CM104
Fullers Way S, Chess. KT9 238 CL105
Fullers Wd, Croy. CR0 243 EA106
Fullers Wd La, S.Nutfld RH1 273 DJ134
Fuller Ter, Ilf. IG1
off Oaktree Gro 147 ER64
Fullerton Cl, Byfleet KT14 234 BM114
Fullerton Dr, Byfleet KT14 234 BL114
Fullerton Rd, SW18 202 DC85
Byfleet KT14 234 BM114
Carshalton SM5 240 DE109
Croydon CR0 224 DT101
Fullerton Way, Byfleet KT14 234 BL114
Fuller Way, Crox.Grn WD3 96 BN43
Hayes UB3 177 BT78
Fullmer Way, Wdhm KT15 233 BF110
Fullwell Av, Ilf. IG5, IG6 125 EM53
FULLWELL CROSS, Ilf. IG6 125 ER53
Fullwell Cross Rbt, Ilf. IG6
off High St 125 ER54
Fullwood Prim Sch, Barkingside
IG6 off Burford Cl 147 EQ56
Fullwoods Ms, N1 19 M2
Fulmar Cl, Surb. KT5 220 CM100
Fulmar Cres, Hem.H. HP1 62 BG21
Fulmar Rd, Horn. RM12 169 FG66
Fulmead St, SW6 39 M7
FULMER, Slou. SL3 134 AX63
Fulmer Cl, Hmptn. TW12 198 BY92
Fulmer Common Rd, Fulmer
SL3 155 AZ65
Iver SL0 155 AZ65
Fulmer Dr, Ger.Cr. SL9 134 AY61
Fulmer Inf Sch, Fulmer
SL3 off Alderbourne La 134 AY63
Fulmer La, Fulmer SL3 134 AY62
Gerrards Cross SL9 135 BB60
Fulmer Ri, Fulmer SL3 155 AZ65
Fulmer Rd, E16 24 E7
Fulmer SL3 134 AY63
Gerrards Cross SL9 134 AY59
Fulmer Way, W13 179 CH76
Gerrards Cross SL9 134 AY58
Fulready Rd, E10 145 ED57
Fulstone Cl, Houns. TW4 178 BZ84
Fulthorp Rd, SE3 47 M8
Fulton Ct, Borwd. WD6
off Aycliffe Rd 100 CM38
Enfield EN3
off Harston Dr 105 EA38
Fulton Ms, W2 15 N10
Fulton Rd, Wem. HA9 140 CN62
Fulvens, Peasl. GU5 283 BS143
Fulvens Cotts, Peasl. GU5 283 BS142
⇌ Fulwell 199 CD91
Fulwell Pk Av, Twick. TW2 198 CB89
Fulwell Rd, Tedd. TW11 199 CD91
Fulwich Rd, Dart. DA1 210 FM86
Fulwood Av, Wem. HA0 160 CM67
Fulwood Cl, Hayes UB3 157 BT72
Fulwood Gdns, Twick. TW1 199 CF86
Fulwood Pl, WC1 18 D7
Fulwood Wk, SW19 201 CY88
Furber St, W6 181 CV76
Furham Feild, Pnr. HA5 116 CA52
Furley Rd, SE15 44 D5
Furlong Cl, Wall. SM6 223 DH102
Furlong Rd, N7 8 F4
Westcott RH4 284 CC137
Furlongs, Hem.H. HP1 62 BG19
Furlongs, The, Esher KT10 218 CB104
Furlong Way, Gat. RH6
off Racecourse Way 290 DF151
Great Amwell SG12 55 DZ09
Furlough, The, Wok. GU22
off Pembroke Rd 249 BA117
Furmage St, SW18 202 DB87
Furneaux Av, SE27 203 DP92
Furner Cl, Dart. DA1 189 FF83
Furness, Wind. SL4 172 AJ82
Furness Cl, Grays RM16 193 GH78
Furness Pl, Wind. SL4
off Furness 172 AJ82
Furness Prim Sch, NW10
off Palermo Rd 161 CU68
Furness Rd, NW10 161 CU68
SW6 39 M8
Harrow HA2 138 CB59
Morden SM4 222 DB101
Furness Row, Wind. SL4
off Furness 172 AJ82
Furness Sch, Hext. BR8
off Rowhill Rd 209 FF93
Furness Sq, Wind. SL4
off Furness 172 AJ82
Furness Wk, Wind. SL4
off Furness 172 AJ82
Furness Way, Horn. RM12 149 FG64
Windsor SL4 172 AJ82
Furnival Av, Slou. SL2 153 AP71
Furnival Cl, Vir.W. GU25 214 AX100
Furnival St, EC4 18 E8
Furrowfield, Hat. AL10
off Stonecross Rd 67 CV16
Furrow La, E9 11 H3
Furrows, The, Hare. UB9 136 BJ57
Walton-on-Thames KT12 218 BW103
Furrows Pl, Cat. CR3 258 DT123
Fursby Av, N3 120 DA51
Furse Av, St.Alb. AL4 65 CG17
Further Acre, NW9 119 CT54
Furtherfield, Abb.L. WD5 81 BS32
Furtherfield Cl, Croy. CR0 223 DN100
Further Grn Rd, SE6 206 EE87
Furtherground, Hem.H. HP2 62 BL21
Furzebushes La, St.Alb. AL2 82 BY25
Furze Cl, Horl. RH6 291 DK148
Redhill RH1 272 DF133
Watford WD19 116 BW50
FURZEDOWN, SW17 202 DG92
Furzedown Cl, Egh. TW20 194 AY93
Furzedown Dr, SW17 203 DH92
Furzedown Hall, SW17
off Spalding Rd 203 DH92
Furzedown Prim Sch, SW17
off Beclands Rd 202 DG93
Furzedown Rd, SW17 203 DH92
Sutton SM2 240 DC111
Furze Fm Cl, Rom. RM6 126 EY54
Furzefield, Chsht EN8 88 DV28
Furze Fld, Oxshott KT22 237 CD113
Furzefield Cl, Chis. BR7 207 EP93
Furzefield Ct, Pot.B. EN6 85 CY31
Furzefield Cres, Reig. RH2 288 DC136
Furzefield Prim Comm Sch,
Merst. RH1
off Delabole Rd 273 DK128
Furzefield Rd, SE3 186 EH79
Beaconsfield HP9 110 AJ53
Reigate RH2 288 DC136
Welwyn Garden City AL7 51 CY10
Furzeground Way, Uxb. UB11 157 BQ74
Furze Gro, Kgswd KT20 255 CZ121
Furzeham Rd, West Dr. UB7 176 BL75
Furze Hill, Kgswd KT20 255 CZ120
Purley CR8 241 DL111
Redhill RH1
off Linkfield La 272 DE133
Furzehill Par, Borwd. WD6
off Shenley Rd 100 CN41
Furzehill Rd, Borwd. WD6 100 CN42
Furzehill Sq, St.M.Cray BR5 228 EV98
Furze Inf Sch, Chad.Hth
RM6 off Bennett Rd 148 EY58
Furze La, Gdmg. GU7 280 AT143
Purley CR8 241 DL111
Furzen Cl, Slou. SL2 153 AN69
Furzen Cres, Hat. AL10 67 CT21
Furze Rd, Add. KT15 233 BF107
Hemel Hempstead HP1 61 BE21
Thornton Heath CR7 224 DQ97
Furze St, E3 22 B6
Furze Vw, Chorl. WD3 95 BC44
Furzewood, Sun. TW16 217 BU95
Fuschia Ct, Wdf.Grn. IG8
off The Bridle Path 124 EE52
Fusedale Way, S.Ock. RM15 171 FT73
Fuzzens Wk, Wind. SL4 173 AL82
Fyefoot La, EC4
off Queen Victoria St 19 J10
Fyfe Apts, N8
off Chadwell La 143 DM55
Fyfe Way, Brom. BR1
off Widmore Rd 226 EG96
Fyfield, N4
off Six Acres Est 143 DN61
Fyfield Cl, Brom. BR2 225 ED98
Fyfield Ct, E7 13 N4
Fyfield Dr, S.Ock. RM15 171 FT73
Fyfield Rd, E17 145 ED55
SW9 42 F10
Enfield EN1 104 DS41
Rainham RM13 169 FF67
Woodford Green IG8 124 EJ52
Fynes St, SW1 29 N8

G

Gabion Av, Purf. RM19 191 FR77
Gable Cl, Abb.L. WD5 81 BS32
Dartford DA1 209 FG85
Pinner HA5 116 CA52
Gable Ct, SE26
off Lawrie Pk Av 204 DV91
Gables, The, Bans. SM7 255 CZ117
Guildford GU2 264 AV131
Hemel Hempstead HP2
off Chapel St 62 BK19
Oxshott KT22 236 CC112
Wembley HA9 140 CN62
Gables Av, Ashf. TW15 196 BM92
Borehamwood WD6 100 CM41
Gables Cl, SE5 43 N6
SE12 206 EG88
Chalfont St. Peter SL9 112 AY49
Datchet SL3 174 AU79
Kingfield GU22
off Kingfield Rd 249 AZ120
Gables Ct, Kgfld GU22
off Kingfield Rd 249 AZ120
Gables Way, Bans. SM7 255 CZ117
Gabriel Cl, Chaff.Hun. RM16 191 FW76
Feltham TW13 198 BX91
Romford RM5 127 FC52
Gabriel Gdns, Grav. DA12 213 GL92
Gabrielle Cl, Wem. HA9 140 CM62
Gabrielle Ct, NW3 6 B5
Gabriel Ms, NW2 141 CZ61
Gabriel Spring Rd, Fawk.Grn
DA3 231 FR103
Gabriel Spring Rd (East),
Fawk.Grn DA3 231 FS103
Gabriel St, SE23 205 DX87
Gabriel's Wf, SE1 30 E2
Gadbrook Rd, Bet. RH3 286 CS139
Gad Cl, E13 24 A2
Gaddesden Av, Wem. HA9 160 CM65
Gaddesden Cres, Wat. WD25 82 BX34
Gaddesden Gro, Welw.G.C.
AL7 off Widford Rd 52 DC09
Gade Av, Wat. WD18 97 BS42
Gade Bk, Crox.Grn WD3 97 BR42
GADEBRIDGE, Hem.H. HP1 61 BF18
Gadebridge La, Hem.H. HP1 62 BJ18
Gadebridge Rd, Hem.H. HP1 62 BG18
Gadebury Hts, Hem.H. HP1 62 BJ20
Gade Cl, Hayes UB3 157 BV74
Hemel Hempstead HP1 62 BH17
Watford WD18 97 BS42
Gadesden Rd, Epsom KT19 238 CQ107
Gadeside, Wat. WD25 97 BS35
Gade Twr, Hem.H. HP3 80 BN25
Gade Valley Cl, Kings L. WD4 80 BN28
Gade Valley JMI Sch,
Hem.H. HP1
off Gadebridge Rd 62 BH19
Gade Vw Gdns, Kings L. WD4 81 BQ32
Gadeview Rd, Hem.H. HP3 62 BK24
Gadsbury Cl, NW9 141 CT58
Gadsden Cl, Upmin. RM14 151 FS58
Gadswell Cl, Wat. WD25 98 BX36
Gadwall Cl, E16 24 A8
Gadwall Way, SE28 187 ER75
Gage Rd, E16 23 K6
Gage St, WC1 18 B6
Gainford St, N1 8 E8
Gainsboro Gdns, Grnf. UB6 139 CE64
Gainsborough Av, E12 147 EN64
Dartford DA1 210 FJ85
St. Albans AL1 65 CF19
Tilbury RM18 193 GG81
Gainsborough Cl, Beck. BR3 205 EA94
Esher KT10 219 CE102
Gainsborough Comm Sch,
E9 12 A4
Gainsborough Ct, N12 120 DB50
W12 26 A5
Bromley BR2 226 EJ98
Walton-on-Thames KT12 235 BU105
Gainsborough Dr, Nthflt DA11 212 GD90
South Croydon CR2 242 DU113
Gainsborough Gdns, NW3 6 A1
NW11 141 CZ59
Edgware HA8 118 CM54
Isleworth TW7 199 CD85
Gainsborough Ho, E14 34 B5
Enfield EN1 off Ayley Cft 104 DU43
Gainsborough Ms, SE26
off Panmure Rd 204 DV90
Gainsborough Pl, Chig. IG7 125 ET48
Cobham KT11 252 BY115
Gainsborough Prim Sch,
E15 23 K3
Gainsborough Rd, E11 146 EE59
E15 23 J3
N12 120 DB50
W4 181 CT77
Dagenham RM8 148 EV63
Epsom KT19 238 CQ110
Hayes UB4 157 BQ68
New Malden KT3 220 CR101
Rainham RM13 169 FG67
Richmond TW9 180 CM83
Woodford Green IG8 124 EL51
Gainsborough Sq, Bexh. DA6
off Regency Way 188 EX83
Gainsborough St, E9 11 P5
Gainsborough Studios, N1 9 L9
Gainsford Rd, E17 145 DZ56
Gainsford St, SE1 32 A4
Gainswood, Welw.G.C. AL7 51 CY10
Gairloch Rd, SE5 43 P8
Gaisford St, NW5 7 L4
Gaist Av, Cat. CR3 258 DU122
Gaitskell Ct, SW11 40 B8
Gaitskell Rd, SE9 207 EQ88
Gaitskell Way, SE1
off Weller St 31 J4
Galahad Cl, Slou. SL1 173 AN75
Galahad Rd, N9 122 DU48
Bromley BR1 206 EG90
Galata Rd, SW13 181 CU80
Galatea Sq, SE15 44 E10
Galaxy, E14 off Crews St 34 A8
Galba Ct, Brent. TW8
off Augustus Cl 179 CK80
Galbraith St, E14 34 E6
Galdana Av, Barn. EN5 102 DC41
Galeborough Av, Wdf.Grn. IG8 123 ED52
Gale Cl, Hmptn. TW12 198 BY93
Mitcham CR4 222 DD97
Gale Cres, Bans. SM7 256 DA117
Galena Ho, SE18
off Grosmont Rd 187 ET78
Galena Rd, W6 181 CV77
Galen Cl, Epsom KT19 238 CN111
Galen Pl, WC1 18 B7
Galesbury Rd, SW18 202 DC86
Gales Cl, Guil. GU4
off Gilliat Dr 265 BD132
Gales Gdns, E2 20 F3
Gale St, E3 22 B6
Dagenham RM9 168 EX67
Gales Way, Wdf.Grn. IG8 124 EL52
Galey Grn, S.Ock. RM15
off Bovey Way 171 FV71
Galgate Cl, SW19 201 CY88
Gallants Fm Rd, E.Barn. EN4 120 DE45
Galleon Boul, Dart. DA2 191 FR84
Galleon Cl, SE16 33 H4
Erith DA8 189 FD77

Galleon Ho, SW8
off St. George Wf 42 A2
Galleon Ms, Grav. DA11
off Maritime Gate 212 GE87
Galleon Rd, Chaff.Hun. RM16 191 FW77
Galleons Dr, Bark. IG11 168 EU69
Galleons La, Geo.Grn SL3 154 AX71
Galleria, The, Hat. AL10 66 CS18
Gallery Ct, Egh. TW20
off The Chantries 195 BA92
Gallery Gdns, Nthlt. UB5 158 BX68
Gallery Rd, SE21 204 DR88
Galley, The, E16 37 P1
Galley Grn, Hailey SG13 55 EA13
Galley Hill, Hem.H. HP1 61 BF18
Waltham Abbey EN9 90 EF30
Galley Hill Rd, Nthflt DA11 212 FZ85
Swanscombe DA10 212 FZ85
Galley La, Barn. EN5 101 CV41
Galleymead Rd, Colnbr. SL3 175 BF81
Galleywall Rd, SE16 32 E9
Galleywood Cres, Rom. RM5 127 FD51
Galliard Cl, N9 104 DW44
Galliard Prim Sch, N9
off Galliard Rd 104 DU44
Galliard Rd, N9 122 DU46
Gallia Rd, N5 9 H3
Gallica Ct, Sutt. SM1
off Cleeve Way 222 DB102
Gallions Cl, Bark. IG11 168 EU69
Gallions Mt Prim Sch,
SE18 *off Purrett Rd* 187 ET78
Gallions Prim Sch, E6 25 N8
Gallions Reach 25 P10
Gallions Reach Shop Pk,
E6 167 EQ71
Gallions Rd, E16
off Armada Way 167 EQ73
SE7 36 B9
Gallions Rbt, E16 25 N10
Gallions Vw Rd, SE28
off Goldfinch Rd 187 ES75
Gallon Cl, SE7 36 D9
Gallop, The, S.Croy. CR2 242 DV108
Sutton SM2 240 DC108
Gallops, The, Esher KT10 218 CB104
Tadworth KT20 271 CV126
Gallosson Rd, SE18 187 ES77
Galloway Chase, Slou. SL2 154 AU73
Galloway Cl, Brox. EN10 89 DZ26
Galloway Dr, Dart. DA1 209 FE87
Galloway Path, Croy. CR0 242 DR105
Galloway Rd, W12 161 CU74
Gallows Cor, Harold Wd
RM3 128 FK53
Gallows Hill, Kings L. WD4 81 BQ31
Gallows Hill La, Abb.L. WD5 81 BQ32
Gallus Cl, N21 103 DM44
Gallus Sq, SE3 186 EH83
Gallys Rd, Wind. SL4 173 AK82
Galpins Rd, Th.Hth. CR7 223 DM98
Galsworthy Av, E14 21 M7
Romford RM6 148 EV59
Galsworthy Cl, SE28 168 EV74
Galsworthy Cres, SE3
off Merriman Rd 186 EJ81
Galsworthy Rd, NW2 141 CY63
Chertsey KT16 216 BG101
Kingston upon Thames KT2 200 CP94
Tilbury RM18 193 GJ81
Galsworthy Ter, N16 144 DS62
Galton St, W10 14 E4
Galva Cl, Barn. EN4 102 DG42
Galvani Way, Croy. CR0
off Ampere Way 223 DM102
Galveston Rd, SW15 201 CZ85
Galvin Rd, Slou. SL1 153 AQ74
Galvins Cl, Guil. GU2 264 AU131
Galway Cl, SE16 44 F1
Galway Ho, EC1 19 K3
Galway St, EC1 19 K3
Gambetta St, SW8 41 K9
Gambia St, SE1 31 H3
Gambier Ho, EC1 19 K2
Gambles La, Ripley GU23 250 BJ124
Gambole Rd, SW17 202 DE91
Games Ho, SE7
off Springfield Gro 186 EJ79
Games Rd, Barn. EN4 102 DF41
Gamlen Rd, SW15 181 CX84
Gammon Cl, Hem.H. HP3 62 BN21
Gammons Fm Cl, Wat. WD24 97 BT36
Gammons La, Brox. EN10 88 DT25
Watford WD24 97 BV38
Gamuel Cl, E17 145 EA58
Gander Grn Cres, Hmptn.
TW12 218 CA95
Gander Grn La, Sutt.
SM1, SM3 221 CY103
Ganders Ash, Wat. WD25 81 BU33
Gandhi Cl, E17 145 EA58
Gandolfi St, SE15 43 N3
Gangers Hill, Gdse. RH9 275 EA127
Woldingham CR3 275 EA127
Ganghill, Guil. GU1 265 BA132
Ganley Ct, SW11
off Newcomen Rd 182 DD83
Ganley Rd, SW11 40 B10
Gant Ct, Wal.Abb. EN9 90 EF34
Ganton St, W1 17 L10
Ganton Wk, Wat. WD19 116 BX49
GANTS HILL, Ilf. IG2 147 EN57
Gants Hill 147 EN58
Gants Hill, Ilf. IG2
off Eastern Av 147 EN58
Gantshill Cres, Ilf. IG2 147 EN57
Ganwick, Barn. EN5 102 DA36
GANWICK CORNER,
Barn. EN5 102 DB35
Ganymede Pl, Hem.H. HP2
off Jupiter Dr 62 BM18
Gap Rd, SW19 202 DA92
Garage Rd, W3 160 CN72
Garand Ct, N7 8 D2
Garbrand Wk, Epsom KT17 239 CT109
Garbutt Pl, W1 17 H6
Garbutt Rd, Upmin. RM14 150 FQ61
Garden Av, Bexh. DA7 188 FA83
Hatfield AL10 67 CU22
Mitcham CR4 203 DH94
Garden City, Edg. HA8 118 CN51
Garden Cl, E4 123 EA50
SE12 206 EH90
SW15 201 CV87
Addlestone KT15 234 BK105
Arkley EN5 101 CW42
Ashford TW15 197 BQ93
Banstead SM7 256 DA115
Hampton TW12 198 BZ92
Garden Cl, Lthd. KT22 253 CJ124
New Malden KT3 220 CS98
Northolt UB5 158 BY67
Ruislip HA4 137 BS61
St. Albans AL1 65 CH19
Wallington SM6 241 DL106
Watford WD17 97 BT40
Garden Cotts, Orp. BR5
off Main Rd 228 EW96
Garden Ct, EC4 18 E10
N12 *off Holden Rd* 120 DB50
Richmond TW9 180 CM81
Stanmore HA7 117 CJ50
Welwyn Garden City AL7 51 CY08
West Molesey KT8
off Avern Rd 218 CB98
Garden Ct Business Cen,
Welw.G.C. AL7
off Garden Ct 51 CZ08
Garden End, Amer. HP6 77 AS37
Gardeners Cl, N11 120 DG47
SE9 206 EL90
Gardeners Rd, Croy. CR0 223 DP102
Gardeners Wk, Bkhm KT23 268 CB126
Garden Fld La, Berk. HP4 61 AZ21
Garden Flds JMI Sch, St.Alb.
AL3 *off Townsend Dr* 65 CD17
Garden Hosp, The, NW4 141 CW55
Garden Ho Sch, SW3 28 F10
Gardenia Rd, Brom. BR1 227 EN97
Enfield EN1 104 DS44
Gardenia Way, Wdf.Grn. IG8 124 EG50
Garden La, SW2
off Christchurch Rd 203 DM88
Bromley BR1 206 EH93
Garden Ms, W2 27 K1
Slough SL1
off Littledown Rd 154 AT74
Garden Pl, E8 10 B8
Dartford DA2 210 FK90
Garden Prim Sch, Mitch.
CR4 *off Abbotts Rd* 223 DK97
Garden Reach, Ch.St.G. HP8 94 AX41
Garden Rd, NW8 15 P2
SE20 224 DW95
Abbots Langley WD5 81 BS31
Bromley BR1 206 EH94
Richmond TW9 180 CN83
Sevenoaks TN13 279 FK122
Walton-on-Thames KT12 217 BV100
Garden Row, SE1 30 G7
Northfleet DA11 213 GF90
Gardens, The, E5 144 DT59
SE22 184 DU84
Beckenham BR3 225 EC96
Brookmans Park AL9 85 CY27
Esher KT10 236 CA105
Feltham TW14 197 BR85
Harrow HA1 138 CC58
Pinner HA5 138 BZ58
Watford WD17 97 BT40
Garden St, E1 21 K7
Garden Suburb Inf Sch,
NW11 *off Childs Way* 141 CZ57
Garden Suburb Jun Sch,
NW11 *off Childs Way* 141 CZ57
Garden Ter, SW1 29 N10
Garden Ter Rd, Harl. CM17 58 EW11
Garden Wk, EC2 19 N3
Beckenham BR3
off Hayne Rd 225 DZ95
Coulsdon CR5 257 DH123
Garden Way, NW10 160 CQ65
Loughton IG10 107 EN38
Gardiner Av, NW2 4 A2
Gardiner Cl, Dag. RM8 148 EX63
Enfield EN3 105 DX44
Orpington BR5 228 EW96
Gardiners, The, Harl. CM17 74 EV15
Gardner Cl, E11 146 EH58
Gardner Ct, EC1
off Brewery Sq 18 G4
N5 9 J1
Gardner Gro, Felt. TW13 198 BZ89
Gardner Ind Est, Beck. BR3 205 DY92
Gardner Pl, Felt. TW14 197 BV86
Gardner Rd, E13 24 A4
Guildford GU1 264 AW134
Gardners La, EC4 19 J10
Gardnor Rd, NW3 *off Flask Wk* 142 DD63
Gard St, EC1 19 H2
Garendon Gdns, Mord. SM4 222 DB101
Garendon Rd, Mord. SM4 222 DB101
Gareth Cl, Wor.Pk. KT4
off Burnham Dr 221 CX103
Gareth Dr, N9 122 DU47
Gareth Gro, Brom. BR1 206 EG91
Garfield Ms, SW11
off Garfield Rd 183 DH83
Garfield Pl, Wind. SL4
off Russell St 173 AR81
Garfield Prim Sch, N11
off Springfield Rd 121 DJ50
SW19 *off Garfield Rd* 202 DC93
Garfield Rd, E4 123 ED46
E13 23 M5
SW11 182 DG83
SW19 202 DC92
Addlestone KT15 234 BJ106
Enfield EN3 104 DW42
Twickenham TW1 199 CG88
Garfield St, Wat. WD24 97 BV38
Garford St, E14 34 A1
Garganey Wk, SE28 168 EX73
Garibaldi Rd, Red. RH1 288 DF135
Garibaldi St, SE18 187 ES77
Garland Cl, Chsht EN8 89 DY31
Hemel Hempstead HP2 62 BK19
Garland Ct, SE17
off Wansey St 31 K9
Garland Dr, Houns. TW3 178 CC82
Garland Ho, N16 144 DR62
Kingston upon Thames KT2
off Kingsgate Rd 220 CL95
Garland Rd, SE18 187 ER80
Bromley BR1 227 EP97
Stanmore HA7 118 CL53
Ware SG12 55 DY06
Garlands Ct, Croy. CR0
off Chatsworth Rd 242 DR105
Garlands Rd, Lthd. KT22 253 CH121
Redhill RH1 288 DF135
Garland Way, Cat. CR3 258 DR122
Hornchurch RM11 150 FL56
Garlichill Rd, Epsom KT18 255 CV117
Garlick Hill, EC4 19 K10
Garlic St, Dor. RH5 268 BZ133
Garlies Rd, SE23 205 DY90
Garlinge Rd, NW2 4 G5
Garman Cl, N18 122 DR50
Garman Rd, N17 122 DW52
Garnault Ms, EC1 18 F3
Garnault Pl, EC1 18 F3
Garnault Rd, Enf. EN1 104 DT38
Garner Cl, Dag. RM8 148 EX60
Garner Dr, Brox. EN10 89 DY26
Garner Rd, E17 123 EC53
Garners Cl, Chal.St.P. SL9 112 AY51
Garners End, Chal.St.P. SL9 112 AY51
Garners Rd, Chal.St.P. SL9 112 AY51
Garner St, E2 20 D1
Garnet Cl, Slou. SL1 173 AN75
Garnet Rd, NW10 160 CS65
Thornton Heath CR7 224 DR98
Garnet St, E1 32 G1
Garnett Cl, SE9 187 EM83
Watford WD24 98 BX37
Garnett Dr, Brick.Wd AL2 82 BZ29
Garnett Rd, NW3 6 E2
Garnett Way, E17
off McEntee Av 123 DY53
Garnet Wk, E6 25 H6
Garnham Cl, N16
off Garnham St 144 DT61
Garnham St, N16 144 DT61
Garnies Cl, SE15 44 A4
Garnon Mead, Cooper. CM16 92 EX28
Garrad's Rd, SW16 203 DK90
Garrard Cl, Bexh. DA7 188 FA83
Chislehurst BR7 207 EP92
Garrard Rd, Bans. SM7 256 DA116
Slough SL2 153 AL70
Garrard Wk, NW10
off Garnet Rd 160 CS65
Garratt Cl, Croy. CR0 241 DL105
Garratt Ho, N16
off Stamford Hill 144 DS60
Garratt La, SW17 202 DD91
SW18 202 DB85
Garratt Pk Sch, SW18
off Waldron Rd 202 DC90
Garratt Rd, Edg. HA8 118 CN52
Garratts Cl, Hert. SG14 54 DQ09
Garratts La, Bans. SM7 255 CZ116
Garratts Rd, Bushey WD23 116 CC45
Garratt Ter, SW17 202 DE91
Garrett Cl, W3 *off Jenner Av* 160 CR71
Chesham HP5 76 AQ33
Garrett St, EC1 19 K4
Garrick Av, NW11 141 CY58
Garrick Cl, SW18 182 DC84
W5 160 CL70
Hersham KT12 235 BV105
Richmond TW9
off Old Palace La 199 CK85
Staines TW18 196 BG94
Garrick Ct, Edg. HA8 118 CM49
Garrick Cres, Croy. CR0 224 DS103
Garrick Dr, NW4 119 CW54
SE28 187 ER76
Garrick Gdns, W.Mol. KT8 218 CA97
Garrick Pk, NW4 119 CX54
Garrick Rd, NW9 141 CT58
Greenford UB6 158 CB70
Richmond TW9 180 CN82
Garrick Rd Ind Est, NW9 141 CT57
Garricks Ho, Kings.T. KT1 219 CK96
Garrick St, WC2 18 A10
Gravesend DA11
off Barrack Row 213 GH86
Garrick Way, NW4 141 CX56
Garrison Cl, SE18
off Red Lion La 187 EN80
Hounslow TW4 198 BZ85
Garrison La, Chess. KT9 237 CK108
Garrison Par, Purf. RM19
off Comet Cl 190 FN77
Garrison Rd, E3 11 P9
Garrolds Cl, Swan. BR8 229 FD96
Garron La, S.Ock. RM15 171 FT72
Garry Cl, Rom. RM1 127 FE52
Garry Way, Rom. RM1 127 FE52
Garsdale Cl, N11 120 DG51
Garside Cl, SE28 187 ER76
Hampton TW12 198 CB93
Garsington Ms, SE4 185 DZ83
Garsmouth Way, Wat. WD25 82 BX36
Garson Cl, Esher KT10
off Garson Rd 236 BZ107
Garson Gro, Chesh. HP5 76 AN29
Garson La, Wrays. TW19 194 AX87
Garson Mead, Esher KT10 236 BZ106
Garson Rd, Esher KT10 236 BZ107
GARSTON, Wat. WD25 98 BW35
Garston 98 BX35
Garston Cres, Wat. WD25 82 BW34
Garston Dr, Wat. WD25 82 BW34
Garston Gdns, Ken. CR8
off Godstone Rd 258 DR115
Garston La, Ken. CR8 242 DR114
Watford WD25 82 BX34
Garston Manor Sch, Wat.
WD25 *off Horseshoe La* 82 BW32
Garston Pk Par, Wat. WD25 82 BX34
Garstons, The, Bkhm KT23 268 CA125
Garter Way, SE16 33 J5
Garth, The, N12
off Holden Rd 120 DB50
Abbots Langley WD5 81 BR33
Cobham KT11 236 BY113
Hampton Hill TW12 198 CB93
Harrow HA3 140 CM58
Garth Cl, W4 180 CR78
Kingston upon Thames KT2 200 CM92
Morden SM4 221 CX101
Ruislip HA4 138 BX60
Garth Ct, W4 180 CR78
Garth Ho, NW2
off Granville Rd 141 CZ61
Garthland Dr, Barn. EN5 101 CV43
Garth Ms, W5
off Greystoke Gdns 160 CL70
Garthorne Rd, SE23 205 DX87
Garth Rd, NW2 141 CZ61
W4 180 CR79
Kingston upon Thames KT2 200 CM92
Morden SM4 221 CW100
Sevenoaks TN13 279 FJ128
South Ockendon RM15 171 FW70
Garth Rd Ind Cen,
Mord. SM4 221 CX101
Garthside, Ham TW10 200 CL92
Garthway, N12 120 DE51
Gartlet Rd, Wat. WD17 98 BW41
Gartmoor Gdns, SW19 201 CZ88
Gartmore Rd, Ilf. IG3 147 ET60
Garton Bk, Bans. SM7 256 DA117
Garton Pl, SW18 202 DC86
Gartons Cl, Enf. EN3 104 DW43
Gartons Way, SW11 182 DC83
Garvary Rd, E16 24 B9
Garvin Av, Beac. HP9 111 AL52
Garvin Ms, Beac. HP9 111 AL53
Garvock Dr, Sev. TN13 278 FG126
Garway Rd, W2 15 L9
Garwood Cl, N17 122 DV53
Gascoigne Gdns, Wdf.Grn.
IG8 124 EE52
Gascoigne Pl, E2 20 A3
Gascoigne Prim Sch, Bark.
IG11 *off Gascoigne Rd* 167 EQ67
Gascoigne Rd, Bark. IG11 167 EQ67
New Addington CR0 243 EC110
Weybridge KT13 217 BP104
Gascons Gro, Slou. SL2 153 AN70
Gascony Av, NW6 5 J7
Gascoyne Cl, Rom. RM3 128 FK52
South Mimms EN6 85 CU32
Gascoyne Dr, Dart. DA1 189 FF82
Gascoyne Rd, E9 11 K6
Gascoyne Way, Hert.
SG13, SG14 54 DQ09
Gaselee St, E14 34 F1
Gaskarth Rd, SW12 203 DH86
Edgware HA8 118 CQ53
Gaskell Rd, N6 142 DF58
Gaskell St, SW4 42 A8
Gaskin St, N1 8 G8
Gaspar Cl, SW5 27 M8
Gaspar Ms, SW5 27 M8
Gassiot Rd, SW17 202 DF91
Gassiot Way, Sutt. SM1 222 DD104
Gasson Rd, Swans. DA10 212 FY86
Gastein Rd, W6 38 D2
Gaston Bell Cl, Rich. TW9 180 CM83
Gaston Br Rd, Shep. TW17 217 BS99
Gaston Rd, Mitch. CR4 222 DG97
Gaston Way, Shep. TW17 217 BR99
Gasworks Gall, SE11 42 D2
Gas Wks La, Brox. EN10 71 EA19
Gataker St, SE16 32 F6
Gatcombe Ho, SE22
off Pytchley Rd 184 DS83
Gatcombe Ms, W5 160 CM73
Gatcombe Rd, E16 35 P2
N19 143 DK62
Gatcombe Way, Barn. EN4 102 DF41
Gate Cl, Borwd. WD6 100 CQ39
Gatecroft, Hem.H. HP3 62 BM22
Gate End, Nthwd. HA6 115 BU52
Gateforth St, NW8 16 C5
Gatehill Rd, Nthwd. HA6 115 BT52
Gatehope Dr, S.Ock. RM15 171 FT72
Gatehouse Cl, Kings.T. KT2 200 CQ94
Windsor SL4
off St. Leonards Rd 173 AP83
Gatehouse Sch, E2 11 J10
Gate Ho Sq, SE1 31 K2
Gateley Rd, SW9 183 DM83
Gate Ms, SW7 28 D5
Gater Dr, Enf. EN2 104 DR39
Gatesborough St, EC2 19 N4
Gatesden Cl, Fetch. KT22 252 CC123
Gatesden Rd, Fetch. KT22 252 CC123
Gates Grn Rd, Kes. BR2 244 EG105
West Wickham BR4 226 EF104
Gateshead Rd, Borwd. WD6 100 CM39
Gateside Rd, SW17 202 DF90
Gatestone Rd, SE19 204 DS93
Gate St, WC2 18 C8
Gate Studios, Borwd. WD6 100 CN42
Gateway, SE17 43 K2
Gate Way, Wey. KT13
off Palace Dr 217 BP104
Gateway, The, Wat. WD18 97 BS43
Woking GU21 233 BB114
Gateway Acad, The, Grays
RM16 *off Marshfoot Rd* 193 GG79
Gateway Business Cen,
SE26 205 DY93
SE28 *off Tom Cribb Rd* 187 ER76
Gateway Cl, Nthwd. HA6 115 BQ51
Gateway Ct, Ilf. IG2 147 EN58
Gateway Ind Est, NW10 161 CT69
Gateway Ms, E8 10 A2
Gateway Prim Sch, NW8 16 B4
Gateway Prim Sch, The,
Dart. DA2
off Milestone Rd 210 FP86
Gateway Retail Pk, E6 25 P5
Gateway Rd, E10 145 EB62
Gateways, Guil. GU1 265 BA134
Gateways, The, SW3 28 D9
Goffs Oak EN7 88 DR28
Gatewick Cl, Slou. SL1 154 AS74
Gatfield Gro, Felt. TW13 198 CA89
Gathorne Rd, N22 121 DN54
Gathorne St, E2 21 K1
Gatley Av, Epsom KT19 238 CP106
Gatley Dr, Guil. GU4 265 AZ131
Gatliff Cl, SW1
off Ebury Br Rd 41 J1
Gatliff Rd, SW1 41 H1
Gatling Rd, SE2 188 EU78
Gatonby St, SE15 44 B6
Gatting Cl, Edg. HA8 118 CQ52
Gatting Way, Uxb. UB8 156 BL65
GATTON, Reig. RH2 272 DF128
Gatton Bottom, Merst. RH1 273 DH127
Reigate RH2 272 DE127
Gatton Cl, Reig. RH2 272 DC131
Sutton SM2 240 DB109
Gatton Pk, Reig. RH2 272 DF129
Gatton Pk Rd, Red. RH1 272 DD132
Reigate RH2 272 DD132
Gatton Prim Sch, SW17
off Gatton Rd 202 DE91
Gatton Rd, SW17 202 DE91
Reigate RH2 272 DC131
Gattons Way, Sid. DA14 208 EZ91
Gatward Cl, N21 103 DP44
Gatward Grn, N9 122 DT47
Gatwick Airport (London),
Gat. RH6 290 DD153
Gatwick Airport 291 DH152
Gatwick Business Pk,
Hkwd RH6 290 DC149
Gatwick Gate, Craw. RH11 290 DD154
Gatwick Gate Ind Est,
Lwfld Hth RH11 290 DE154
Gatwick Metro Cen,
Horl. RH6 291 DH147
Gatwick Rd, SW18 201 CZ87
Gatwick RH6 290 DG154
Gravesend DA12 213 GH90
Gatwick Rd Rbt,
Horl. RH6 290 DG154
Gatwick Way, Gat. RH6 290 DF151
Hornchurch RM12
off Haydock Cl 150 FM63
Gauden Cl, SW4 41 N10
Gauden Rd, SW4 41 N9
Gaumont App, Wat. WD17 97 BV41
Gaumont Ter, W12
off Lime Gro 26 A4
Gauntlet Cl, Nthlt. UB5 158 BY66
Gauntlett Ct, Wem. HA0 139 CH64
Gauntlett Rd, Sutt. SM1 240 DD106
Gaunt St, SE1 31 H6
Gautrey Rd, SE15 45 H8
Gautrey Sq, E6 25 K9
Gavel Cen, The, St.Alb.
AL3 *off Porters Wd* 65 CF16
Gavell Rd, Cob. KT11 235 BU113
Gavel St, SE17 31 M8
Gavenny Path, S.Ock. RM15 171 FT72
Gaverick Ms, E14 34 A8
Gaveston Cl, Byfleet KT14 234 BM113
Gaveston Dr, Berk. HP4 60 AV17
Gavestone Cres, SE12 206 EH87
Gavestone Rd, SE12 206 EH87
Gaveston Rd, Lthd. KT22 253 CG120
Slough SL2 153 AL69
Gaviller Pl, E5
off Clarence Rd 144 DV63
Gavina Cl, Mord. SM4 222 DE99
Gavin St, SE18 187 ES77
Gaviots Cl, Ger.Cr. SL9 135 AZ60
Gaviots Grn, Ger.Cr. SL9 134 AY60
Gaviots Way, Ger.Cr. SL9 134 AY59
Gawain Wk, N9 *off Galahad Rd* 122 DU48
Gawber St, E2 21 H2
Gawdrey Cl, Chesh. HP5
off Five Acres 76 AR33
Gawsworth Cl, E15 13 K2
Gawthorne Ct, E3
off Mostyn Gro 22 A1
Gawton Cres, Couls. CR5 257 DJ121
Gay Cl, NW2 141 CV64
Gaydon Ho, W2 15 M6
Gaydon La, NW9 118 CS53
Gayfere Rd, Epsom KT17 239 CU106
Ilford IG5 147 EM55
Gayfere St, SW1 30 A7
Gayford Rd, W12 181 CT75
Gay Gdns, Dag. RM10 149 FC63
Gayhurst, SE17 43 M2
Gayhurst Comm Sch, E8 10 D6
Gayhurst Rd, E8 10 C6
Gayhurst Sch, Sen Sch,
Chal.St.P. SL9
off Bull La 134 AW56
Jun Sch, Ger.Cr. SL9
off Maltmans La 134 AW56
Gayler Cl, Bletch. RH1 274 DT133
Gaylor Rd, Nthlt. UB5 138 BZ64
Tilbury RM18 192 GE81
Gaynes Ct, Upmin. RM14 150 FP63
Gaynesford Rd, SE23 205 DX89
Carshalton SM5 240 DF108
Gaynes Hill Rd, Wdf.Grn. IG8 124 EL51
Gaynes Pk, Cooper. CM16 92 EY31
Gaynes Pk Rd, Upmin. RM14 150 FN63
Gaynes Rd, Upmin. RM14 150 FP61
Gaynes Sch, Upmin. RM14
off Brackendale Gdns 150 FQ64
Gay Rd, E15 12 G10
Gaysham Av, Ilf. IG2 147 EN57
Gaysham Hall, Ilf. IG5 147 EP55
Gay St, SW15 181 CX83
Gayton Cl, Amer. HP6 77 AS35
Ashtead KT21 254 CL118
Gayton Ct, Har. HA1 139 CF58
Gayton Cres, NW3 142 DD63
Gayton Ho, E3 22 B5
Gayton Rd, NW3 6 A1
SE2 *off Florence Rd* 188 EW76
Harrow HA1 139 CF58
Gayville Rd, SW11 202 DF86
Gaywood Av, Chsht EN8 89 DX30
Gaywood Cl, SW2 203 DM88
Gaywood Est, SE1 30 G7
Gaywood Rd, E17 145 EA55
Ashtead KT21 254 CM118
Gaywood St, SE1 31 H7
Gaza St, SE17 42 G1
Gazelle Glade, Grav. DA12 213 GM92
Gazelle Ho, E15 13 J4
Gean Ct, N11 *off Cline Rd* 121 DJ51
Gean Wk, Hat. AL10 67 CU21
Gearies Infants' Sch, Ilf.
IG2 *off Waremead Rd* 147 EP57
Gearies Jun Sch, Ilf. IG2
off Gantshill Cres 147 EP57
Geariesville Gdns, Ilf. IG6 147 EP56
Gearing Cl, SW17 202 DG91
Geary Cl, Smallfield RH6 291 DP150
Geary Ct, N9
off The Broadway 122 DU47
Geary Dr, Brwd. CM14, CM15 130 FW46
Geary Rd, NW10 141 CU64
Geary St, N7 8 D3
Geddes Pl, Bexh. DA6
off Market Pl 188 FA84
Geddes Rd, Bushey WD23 98 CC42
Geddings Rd, Hodd. EN11 71 EB17
Geddington Ct, Wal.Cr. EN8
off Eleanor Way 89 EA34
Gedeney Rd, N17 122 DQ53
Gedling Ho, SE22
off Quorn Rd 184 DT83
Gedling Pl, SE1 32 B6
Geere Rd, E15 13 M9
Gees Ct, W1 17 H9
Gee St, EC1 19 J4
Geffrye Ct, N1 19 P1
Geffrye Est, N1 19 P1
Geffrye Mus, E2 19 P1
Geffrye St, E2 10 A10
Geisthorp Ct, Wal.Abb. EN9 90 EG33
Geldart Rd, SE15 44 E5
Geldeston Rd, E5 144 DU61
Gellatly Rd, SE14 45 H8
Gell Cl, Uxb. UB10 136 BM62
Gelsthorpe Rd, Rom. RM5 127 FB52
Gemini Business Pk, E6 167 ER71
Gemini Gro, Nthlt. UB5
off Javelin Way 158 BY69

Gemini Ho, E3
off Garrison Rd 12 A9
● Gemini Project, SE14 45 K1
Gemmell Cl, Pur. CR8 241 DM114
Genas Cl, Ilf. IG6 125 EP53
General Gordon Pl, SE18 37 N8
Generals Wk, The, Enf. EN3 105 DY37
General Wolfe Rd, SE10 47 H6
● Genesis Business Pk,
Wok. GU21 249 BC115
Genesis Cl, Stanw. TW19 196 BM88
Genesta Rd, SE18 187 EP79
Geneva Cl, Shep. TW17 217 BS96
Geneva Dr, SW9 183 DN84
Geneva Gdns, Rom. RM6 148 EY57
Geneva Rd, Kings.T. KT1 220 CL98
Thornton Heath CR7 224 DQ99
Genever Cl, E4 123 EA50
Genista Rd, N18 122 DV50
Genoa Av, SW15 201 CW85
Genoa Rd, SE20 224 DW95
Genotin Ms, Horn. RM12 150 FJ64
Genotin Rd, Enf. EN1 104 DR41
Genotin Ter, Enf. EN1
off Genotin Rd 104 DR41
Gentian Row, SE13 46 E7
Gentlemans Row, Enf. EN2 104 DQ41
Gentry Gdns, E13 23 P4
Genyn Rd, Guil. GU2 280 AV136
Geoffrey Av, Rom. RM3 128 FN51
Geoffrey Cl, SE5 43 J9
Geoffrey Gdns, E6 24 G1
Geoffrey Rd, SE4 45 N10
Sch George Abbot Sch, Guil.
GU1 off Woodruff Av 265 BB132
George Avey Cft, N.Wld Bas.
CM16 93 FB26
George Beard Rd, SE8 33 N9
George Belt Ho, E2 21 J2
George Comberton Wk, E12
off Gainsborough Av 147 EN64
George Ct, WC2 30 B1
George Cres, N10 120 DG52
George Crook's Ho, Grays
RM17 off New Rd 192 GB79
George Downing Est, N16 144 DT61
George Eliot Ho, SW1
off Vauxhall Br Rd 29 M9
Sch George Eliot Inf Sch, NW8 6 A8
Sch George Eliot Jun Sch, NW8 6 A8
George Elliston Ho, SE1
off Old Kent Rd 44 C1
George V Av, Pnr. HA5 138 CA55
George V Cl, Pnr. HA5 138 CA55
Watford WD18 97 BT42
George V Way, Perivale UB6 159 CH67
Sarratt WD3 96 BG36
George Gange Way, Wealds.
HA3 139 CE55
GEORGE GREEN, Slou. SL3 154 AX72
George Grn Dr, Geo.Grn SL3 155 AZ71
George Grn Rd, Geo.Grn SL3 154 AX72
Sch George Green's Sch, E14 34 F10
George Gros Rd, SE20 224 DU95
★ George Inn, SE1 31 L3
George Inn Yd, SE1 31 L3
Georgelands, Ripley GU23 250 BH121
George La, E18 124 EG54
SE13 205 EC86
Bromley BR2 226 EH102
Jct George La Rbt, E18 124 EG54
George Lansbury Ho, N22
off Progress Way 121 DN53
George Loveless Ho, E2 20 B2
George Lovell Dr, Enf. EN3 105 EA37
George Lowe Ct, W2 15 L6
George Mathers Rd, SE11 30 G8
George Ms, NW1 17 L3
SW9 42 E9
Enfield EN2 off Church St 104 DR41
Sch George Mitchell Sch, E10
off Farmer Rd 145 EB60
George Rd, E4 123 EA51
Godalming GU7 280 AS144
Guildford GU1 264 AX134
Kingston upon Thames KT2 200 CP94
New Malden KT3 221 CT98
George Row, SE16 32 C5
Georges Cl, Orp. BR5 228 EW97
Georges Dr, Flack.Hth HP10 132 AC56
Pilgrim's Hatch CM15 130 FT43
Georges Mead, Els. WD6 99 CK44
Sch George Spicer Prim Sch, Enf.
EN1 off Southbury Rd 104 DT41
George Sq, SW19
off Mostyn Rd 221 CZ97
George's Rd, N7 8 D3
Georges Rd, Tats. TN16 260 EK120
Georges Sq, SW6 39 H2
Georges Ter, Cat. CR3
off Coulsdon Rd 258 DR122
Tfl George Street 224 DQ103
George St, E16 23 L9
W1 16 F8
W7 off Uxbridge Rd 159 CE74
Barking IG11 167 EQ66
Berkhamsted HP4 60 AY19
Chesham HP5 76 AQ30
Croydon CR0 224 DR103
Grays RM17 192 GA79
Hemel Hempstead HP2 62 BK19
Hertford SG14 54 DQ09
Hounslow TW3 178 BZ82
Richmond TW9 199 CK85
Romford RM1 149 FF58
St. Albans AL3 64 CC20
Southall UB2 178 BY77
Staines TW18 195 BF91
Uxbridge UB8 156 BK66
Watford WD18 98 BW42
Sch George St Prim Sch, Hem.H.
HP2 off George St 62 BK19
George's Wd Rd, Brook.Pk AL9 86 DA26
George Taylor Ct, N9
off Colthurst Dr 122 DV48
George Tilbury Ho, Grays
RM16 193 GH75
Sch George Tomlinson Prim Sch,
E11 off Vernon Rd 146 EE60
Georgetown Cl, SE19
off St. Kitts Ter 204 DS92
Georgette Pl, SE10 46 F5
Georgeville Gdns, Ilf. IG6 147 EP56
Georgewood Rd, Hem.H. HP3 80 BM25
George Wyver Cl, SW19
off Beaumont Rd 201 CY87
George Yd, EC3 19 M9
W1 17 H10
Georgiana St, NW1 7 L8
Georgian Cl, Brom. BR2 226 EH101
Staines TW18 196 BH91
Stanmore HA7 117 CG52
Uxbridge UB10 136 BL63
Georgian Ct, SW16
off Gleneldon Rd 203 DL91
Wembley HA9 160 CN65
Georgian Way, Har. HA1 139 CD61
Georgia Rd, N.Mal. KT3 220 CQ98
Thornton Heath CR7 223 DP95
Georgina Gdns, E2 20 B2
Coll GEOS English Acad, W5
off New Bdy 159 CK73
Geraint Rd, Brom. BR1 206 EG91
Gerald Game Br, Hodd. EN11 71 EC17
Geraldine Rd, SW18 202 DC85
W4 180 CN79
Geraldine St, SE11 30 G7
Gerald Ms, SW1 29 H8
Gerald Rd, E16 23 L4
SW1 29 H8
Dagenham RM8 148 EZ61
Gravesend DA12 213 GL87
Geralds Gro, Bans. SM7 239 CX114
Gerard Av, Houns. TW4 198 CA87
Gerard Ct, NW2 4 C2
Gerard Gdns, Rain. RM13 169 FE68
Gerard Pl, E9 11 J6
Gerard Rd, SW13 181 CT81
Harrow HA1 139 CG58
Gerards Cl, SE16 44 G1
Gerda Rd, SE9 207 EQ89
Gerdview Dr, Dart. DA2 210 FJ91
Germains Cl, Chesh. HP5 76 AP32
Germain St, Chesh. HP5 76 AP32
Germander Way, E15 23 K3
Sch German Sch, The, Rich.
TW10 off Petersham Rd 199 CK88
Gernigan Ho, SW18 202 DD86
Gernon Cl, Rain. RM13
off Jordans Way 170 FK68
Gernon Rd, E3 21 L1
Geron Way, NW2 141 CV60
Gerpins La, Upmin. RM14 170 FM68
Gerrard Cres, Brwd. CM14 130 FV48
Gerrard Gdns, Pnr. HA5 137 BU57
Gerrard Ho, SE14 45 H5
Gerrard Pl, W1 17 P10
Gerrard Rd, N1 9 H10
Gerrards Cl, N14 103 DJ43
GERRARDS CROSS, SL9 134 AX58
⇌ Gerrards Cross 134 AY57
Sch Gerrards Cross C of E Sch,
The, Ger.Cr. SL9
off Moreland Dr 135 AZ59
Gerrards Cross Rd, Stoke P.
SL2 154 AU66
Gerrards Mead, Bans. SM7 255 CZ116
Gerrard St, W1 17 N10
Gerridge St, SE1 30 F5
Gerry Raffles Sq, E15 13 H5
Gertrude Rd, Belv. DA17 188 FA77
Gertrude St, SW10 39 P3
Gervaise Cl, Slou. SL1 153 AM74
Gervase Cl, Wem. HA9 140 CQ62
Gervase Rd, Edg. HA8 118 CQ53
Gervase St, SE15 44 F4
Gews Cor, Chsht EN8 89 DX29
Ghent St, SE6 205 EA89
Ghent Way, E8 10 B4
Giant Arches Rd, SE24 204 DQ87
Giant Tree Hill, Bushey Hth
WD23 117 CD46
Gibbard Ms, SW19 201 CX92
Gibb Cft, Harl. CM18 73 ES19
Gibbfield Cl, Rom. RM6 148 EY55
Gibbins Rd, E15 12 F7
Gibbon Rd, SE15 45 H9
W3 160 CS73
Kingston upon Thames KT2 220 CL95
Gibbons Cl, Borwd. WD6 100 CL39
Gibbons Ms, NW11 141 CZ57
Gibbons Rents, SE1
off Magdalen St 31 N3
Gibbons Rd, NW10 160 CR65
Gibbon Wk, SW15 181 CU84
Gibbs Av, SE19 204 DR92
Gibbs Brook La, Oxt. RH8 275 ED133
Gibbs Cl, SE19 204 DR92
Cheshunt EN8 89 DX29
Gibbs Couch, Wat. WD19 116 BX48
Gibbs Grn, W14 27 H10
Edgware HA8 118 CQ50
Sch Gibbs Grn Sch, W14 27 H10
Gibbs Rd, N18 122 DW49
Gibbs Sq, SE19 204 DR92
Gibney Ter, Brom. BR1
off Durham Hill 206 EF91
Gibraltar Cl, Gt Warley CM13 129 FW51
Gibraltar Cres, Epsom KT19 238 CS110
Gibraltar Ho, Brwd. CM13 129 FW51
Gibraltar Wk, E2 20 B3
● Gibson Business Cen,
N17 off High Rd 122 DT52
Gibson Cl, E1 21 H4
N21 103 DN44
Chessington KT9 237 CJ107
Isleworth TW7 179 CD83
North Weald Bassett CM16
off Beamish Cl 93 FC25
Northfleet DA11 213 GF90
Gibson Ct, Rom. RM1
off Regarth Av 149 FE58
Slough SL3 175 AZ78
Gibson Gdns, N16 144 DT61
Gibson Ms, Twick. TW1
off Richmond Rd 199 CJ87
Gibson Pl, Stanw. TW19 196 BJ86
Gibson Rd, SE11 30 D9
Dagenham RM8 148 EW60
Sutton SM1 240 DB106
Uxbridge UB10 136 BM63
Gibson's Hill, SW16 203 DN93
Gibson Sq, N1 8 F8
Gibson St, SE10 47 J1
Gidd Hill, Couls. CR5 256 DG116
Gidea Av, Rom. RM2 149 FG55
Gidea Cl, Rom. RM2 149 FG55
South Ockendon RM15
off Tyssen Pl 171 FW69
GIDEA PARK, Rom. RM2 149 FG55
⇌ Gidea Park 150 FJ56
Sch Gidea Pk Coll, Gidea Pk
RM2 off Balgores La 149 FG55
Sch Gidea Pk Prim Sch, Gidea Pk
RM2 off Lodge Av 149 FG55
Gideon Cl, Belv. DA17 189 FB77
Gideon Ms, W5 179 CK75
Gideon Rd, SW11 40 G10
Gidian Ct, Park St AL2 83 CD27
Giesbach Rd, N19 143 DJ61
Giffard Rd, N18 122 DS50
Giffard Way, Guil. GU2 264 AU131
Giffin St, SE8 46 A4
Gifford Gdns, W7 159 CD71
Gifford Pl, Warley CM14 130 FX50
Sch Gifford Prim Sch, Nthlt.
UB5 off Greenhill Gdns 158 BZ68
Gifford Rd, NW10 160 CS66
Giffordside, Grays RM16 193 GH78
Gifford St, N1 8 B7
Gift La, E15 13 L8
Giggs Hill, Orp. BR5 228 EU96
Giggs Hill Gdns, T.Ditt. KT7 219 CG102
Giggs Hill Rd, T.Ditt. KT7 219 CG101
Gilbert Cl, SE18 187 EM81
Swanscombe DA10 211 FX86
Sch Gilbert Colvin Prim Sch,
Ilf. IG5 off Strafford Av 125 EN54
Gilbert Gro, Edg. HA8 118 CR53
Gilbert Ho, EC2
off The Barbican 19 K6
SE8 46 B3
SW1 41 K1
Gilbert Pl, WC1 18 A7
Gilbert Rd, SE11 30 F9
SW19 202 DC94
Belvedere DA17 188 FA76
Bromley BR1 206 EG94
Chafford Hundred RM16 191 FW76
Harefield UB9 114 BK54
Pinner HA5 138 BX56
Romford RM1 149 FF56
Gilbert Scott Ct, Amer. HP7 77 AP40
Sch Gilbert Scott Jun & Inf
Comm Schs, S.Croy. CR2
off Farnborough Av 243 DY108
Gilbert St, E15 13 J1
W1 17 H9
Enfield EN3 104 DW37
Hounslow TW3 off High St 178 CC83
Gilbert Way, Berk. HP4 60 AU19
Croydon CR0
off Beddington Fm Rd 223 DL102
Slough SL3 175 AZ78
Gilbert White Cl, Perivale
UB6 159 CG67
Gilbey Cl, Uxb. UB10 137 BP63
Gilbey Rd, SW17 202 DE91
Gilbeys Yd, NW1 7 H7
Gilbey Wk, Woob.Grn HP10
off Stratford Dr 132 AD59
Gilbourne Rd, SE18 187 ET79
Gilda Av, Enf. EN3 105 DY43
Gilda Cres, N16 144 DU60
Gildea Cl, Pnr. HA5 116 CA52
Gildea St, W1 17 K7
Gilden Cl, Harl. CM17 58 EY11
Gilden Cres, NW5 6 G3
Gildenhill Rd, Swan. BR8 210 FJ94
Gilden Way, Harl. CM17 58 EW12
Gilders, Saw. CM21 58 EX05
Gildersome St, SE18
off Nightingale Vale 187 EN79
Gilders Rd, Chess. KT9 238 CM107
Giles Cl, Rain. RM13 170 FK68
Giles Coppice, SE19 204 DT91
Giles Fld, Grav. DA12 213 GM88
Giles Travers Cl, Egh. TW20 215 BC97
Gilfrid Cl, Uxb. UB8 157 BP72
Gilhams Av, Bans. SM7 239 CX112
Gilkes Cres, SE21 204 DS86
Gilkes Pl, SE21 204 DS86
Gillam Way, Rain. RM13 169 FG65
Gillan Grn, Bushey Hth WD23 116 CC47
Gillards Ms, E17
off Gillards Way 145 EA56
Gillards Way, E17 145 EA56
Gill Av, E16 23 P9
Guildford GU2 280 AS135
Gill Cl, Wat. WD18 97 BQ44
Gill Cres, Nthflt DA11 213 GF90
Gillender St, E3 22 E4
E14 22 E4
Sch Gillespie Prim Sch, N5
off Gillespie Rd 143 DP62
Gillespie Rd, N5 143 DN62
Gillett Av, E6 166 EL68
Jct Gillette Cor, Islw. TW7 179 CG80
Gillett Pl, N16 9 P3
Gillett Rd, Th.Hth. CR7 224 DR98
Gillett Sq, N16 9 P3
Gillett St, N16 9 P3
Gillfoot, NW1 17 L1
Gillham Ter, N17 122 DU51
Gilliam Gro, Pur. CR8 241 DN110
Gillian Av, St.Alb. AL1 64 CC24
Gillian Cres, Rom. RM2 128 FJ54
Gillian Pk Rd, Sutt. SM3 221 CZ102
Gillian St, SE13 205 EB85
Gilliat Cl, Iver SL0
off Grange Way 155 BF72
Gilliat Dr, Guil. GU4 265 BD132
Gilliat Rd, Slou. SL1 154 AS73
Gilliat's Grn, Chorl. WD3 95 BD42
Gillies St, NW5 7 H3
Gilling Ct, NW3 6 D4
Gillingham Rd, NW2 141 CY62
Gillingham Row, SW1 29 L8
Gillingham St, SW1 29 K8
Gillison Wk, SE16
off Tranton Rd 32 D6
Gillman Dr, E15 13 L9
Gillmans Rd, Orp. BR5 228 EV102
Gills Hill, Rad. WD7 99 CF35
Gills Hill La, Rad. WD7 99 CF36
Gills Hollow, Rad. WD7 99 CF36
Gill's Rd, S.Darenth DA2, DA4 231 FS95
Gillsted Ct, St.Alb. AL3
off Repton Grn 65 CD17
Gill St, E14 21 P10
Gillum Cl, E.Barn. EN4 120 DF46
Gilmais, Bkhm KT23 268 CC125
Gilman Cres, Wind. SL4 173 AK83
Gilmore Cl, Slou. SL3 174 AW75
Uxbridge UB10 136 BN62
Gilmore Cres, Ashf. TW15 196 BN92
Gilmore Rd, SE13 185 ED84
Gilmour Cl, Wal.Cr. EN7 104 DU35
Gilpin Av, SW14 180 CR84
Gilpin Cl, W2 16 A6
Mitcham CR4 222 DE96
Gilpin Cres, N18 122 DT50
Twickenham TW2 198 CB87
Gilpin Rd, E5 145 DY63
Ware SG12 55 DY07
Gilpin's Gallop, Stans.Abb.
SG12 55 EB11
Gilpins Ride, Berk. HP4 60 AX18
Gilpin Way, Harling. UB3 177 BR80
Gilroy Cl, Rain. RM13 169 FF65
Gilroy Rd, Hem.H. HP2 62 BK19
Gilroy Way, Orp. BR5 228 EV101
Gilsland, Wal.Abb. EN9 106 EE35
Gilsland Pl, Th.Hth. CR7
off Gilsland Rd 224 DR98
Gilsland Rd, Th.Hth. CR7 224 DR98
Gilstead Rd, SW6 39 M8
Gilston La, Gilston Pk CM20 57 EQ09
GILSTON PARK, Harl. CM20 57 EP08
Gilston Rd, SW10 39 P1
Gilton Rd, SE6 206 EE90
Giltspur St, EC1 19 H8
Gilwell Cl, E4
off Antlers Hill 105 EB42
Gilwell La, E4 105 EC42
Gilwell Pk, E4 105 EC41
Gimcrack Hill, Lthd. KT22
off Dorking Rd 253 CH123
Ginsburg Yd, NW3
off Heath St 142 DC63
Gippeswyck Cl, Pnr. HA5
off Uxbridge Rd 116 BX53
⇌ Gipsy Hill 204 DS92
Gipsy Hill, SE19 204 DS91
Gipsy La, SW15 181 CU83
Grays RM17 192 GC79
Gipsy Rd, SE27 204 DQ91
Welling DA16 188 EX81
Gipsy Rd Gdns, SE27 204 DQ91
Giralda Cl, E16 24 E7
Giraud St, E14 22 C8
Girdlers Rd, W14 26 D8
Girdlestone Wk, N19 143 DJ61
Girdwood Rd, SW18 201 CY87
Girling Way, Felt. TW14 177 BU83
Girona Cl, Chaff.Hun. RM16 191 FW76
Gironde Rd, SW6 39 H5
Girtin Rd, Bushey WD23 98 CB43
Girton Av, NW9 140 CN55
Girton Cl, Nthlt. UB5 158 CC65
Girton Ct, Chsht EN8 89 DY30
Girton Gdns, Croy. CR0 225 EA104
Girton Rd, SE26 205 DX92
Northolt UB5 158 CC65
Girton Vil, W10 14 D8
Girton Way, Crox.Grn WD3 97 BQ43
Gisborne Gdns, Rain. RM13 169 FF69
Gisbourne Cl, Wall. SM6 223 DK104
Gisburne Way, Wat. WD24 97 BU37
Gisburn Rd, N8 143 DM56
Gissing Wk, N1 8 F7
Gittens Cl, Brom. BR1 206 EF91
Given Wilson Wk, E13 23 M1
Giverny Ho, SE16
off Canada St 33 J5
GIVONS GROVE, Lthd. KT22 269 CJ126
Givons Gro, Lthd. KT22 269 CH125
Jct Givons Gro Rbt, Lthd.
KT22 269 CH125
Glacier Way, Wem. HA0 159 CK68
Gladbeck Way, Enf. EN2 103 DP42
Gladding Rd, E12 146 EK63
Cheshunt EN7 87 DP25
Glade, The, N21 103 DM44
SE7 186 EJ80
Bromley BR1 226 EK96
Coulsdon CR5 257 DN119
Croydon CR0 225 DX99
Enfield EN2 103 DN41
Epsom KT17 239 CU106
Fetcham KT22 252 CA122
Gerrards Cross SL9 134 AX60
Hutton CM13 131 GA46
Ilford IG5 125 EM53
Kingswood KT20 256 DA121
Penn HP10 110 AC46
Sevenoaks TN13 279 FH123
Staines TW18 196 BH94
Sutton SM2 239 CY109
Upminster RM14 150 FQ64
Welwyn Garden City AL8 51 CW07
West Byfleet KT14 233 BE113
West Wickham BR4 225 EB104
Woodford Green IG8 124 EH48
Glade Cl, Long Dit. KT6 219 CK103
Glade Ct, Ilf. IG5 125 EM53
Uxbridge UB8 156 BJ65
Glade Gdns, Croy. CR0 225 DY101
Glade La, Sthl. UB2 178 CB75
Glade Ms, Guil. GU1 281 AZ135
Sch Glade Prim Sch, Ilf. IG5
off Atherton Rd 125 EM54
Glades, The, Grav. DA12 213 GK93
Hemel Hempstead HP1 61 BE19
Gladeside, N21 103 DM44
Croydon CR0 225 DX100
St. Albans AL4 65 CK17
Gladeside Cl, Chess. KT9 237 CK108
Gladeside Ct, Warl. CR6 258 DV120
Gladesmere Ct, Wat. WD24 97 BV36
Sch Gladesmore Comm Sch,
N15 off Crowland Rd 144 DU57
Gladesmore Rd, N15 144 DT58
Glade Spur, Kgswd KT20 256 DB121
Glades Shop Cen, The,
Brom. BR1 226 EG96
Gladeswood Rd, Belv. DA17 189 FB77
Gladeway, The, Wal.Abb. EN9 89 ED33
Gladiator St, SE23 205 DY86
Glading Ter, N16 144 DT62
Gladioli Cl, Hmptn. TW12
off Gresham Rd 198 CA93
Gladsdale Dr, Pnr. HA5 137 BU56
Gladsmuir Cl, Walt. KT12 218 BW103
Gladsmuir Rd, N19 143 DJ60
Barnet EN5 101 CY40
Gladstone Av, E12 166 EL66
N22 121 DN54
Feltham TW14 197 BU86
Twickenham TW2 199 CD87
Gladstone Ct, SW1
off Regency St 29 P9
SW8 off Havelock Ter 41 K6
SW19 off Gladstone Rd 202 DA94
Gladstone Gdns, Houns. TW3
off Palmerston Rd 178 CC81
Gladstone Ms, N22
off Pelham Rd 121 DN54
Gladstone Ms, NW6 4 G6
SE20 204 DW94
Gladstone Par, NW2
off Edgware Rd 141 CV60
Gladstone Pk Gdns, NW2 141 CV62
Sch Gladstone Pk Prim Sch, NW10
off Sherrick Grn Rd 141 CV64
Gladstone Pl, E3 11 P10
Barnet EN5 101 CX42
Gladstone Rd, SW19 202 DA94
W4 off Acton La 180 CR76
Ashtead KT21 253 CK118
Buckhurst Hill IG9 124 EH46
Chesham HP5 76 AQ31
Croydon CR0 224 DR101
Dartford DA1 210 FM86
Hoddesdon EN11 71 EB16
Kingston upon Thames KT1 220 CN97
Orpington BR6 245 EQ106
Southall UB2 178 BY75
Surbiton KT6 219 CK103
Ware SG12 54 DW05
Watford WD17 98 BW41
Gladstone St, SE1 30 G6
Gladstone Ter, SE27
off Bentons La 204 DQ91
Gladstone Way, Slou. SL1 173 AN75
Wealdstone HA3 139 CE55
Gladwell Rd, N8 143 DM58
Bromley BR1 206 EG93
Gladwin Way, Harl. CM20 57 ER13
Gladwyn Rd, SW15 38 C10
Gladys Rd, NW6 5 K6
Glaisher St, SE8 46 B2
Glaisyer Way, Iver SL0 155 BC68
Glamis Cl, Chsht EN7 88 DU29
Glamis Cres, Hayes UB3 177 BQ76
Glamis Dr, Horn. RM11 150 FL60
Glamis Pl, E1 21 H10
Hemel Hempstead HP2 62 BL19
Glamis Rd, E1 21 H10
Glamis Way, Nthlt. UB5 158 CC65
Glamorgan Cl, Mitch. CR4 223 DL97
Glamorgan Rd, Kings.T. KT1 199 CJ94
Glan Avon Ms, Harl. CM17 74 EW16
Glandford Way, Chad.Hth RM6 148 EV57
Glanfield, Hem.H. HP2
off Bathurst Rd 62 BL17
Glanfield Rd, Beck. BR3 225 DZ98
Glanleam Rd, Stan. HA7 117 CK49
Glanmead, Shenf. CM15 130 FY46
Glanmor Rd, Slou. SL2 154 AV73
Glanthams Cl, Shenf. CM15 130 FY47
Glanthams Rd, Shenf. CM15 131 FZ47
Glanty, The, Egh. TW20 195 BB91
Glanville Dr, Horn. RM11 150 FM60
Glanville Ms, Stan. HA7 117 CG50
Glanville Rd, SW2 203 DL85
Bromley BR2 226 EH97
Glasbrook Av, Twick. TW2 198 BZ88
Glasbrook Rd, SE9 206 EK87
Glaserton Rd, N16 144 DS59
Glasford St, SW17 202 DF93
Glasgow Ho, W9 15 M1
Glasgow Rd, E13 24 A1
N18 off Aberdeen Rd 122 DV50
Slough SL1 153 AN72
Glasgow Ter, SW1 41 L1
Glasier Ct, E15 13 K6
Glaskin Ms, E9 11 M5
Glasse Cl, W13 159 CG73
Glasshill St, SE1 31 H4
Glasshouse Cl, Uxb. UB8 157 BP71
Glasshouse Flds, E1 21 J10
Glasshouse St, W1 29 M1
Glasshouse Wk, SE11 30 B10
Glasshouse Yd, EC1 19 J5
Glasslyn Rd, N8 143 DK57
Glassmill La, Brom. BR2 226 EF96
Glass St, E2 20 F4
Glass Yd, SE18 37 M6
Glastonbury Av, Wdf.Grn. IG8 124 EK52
Glastonbury Cl, Orp. BR5 228 EW102
Glastonbury Ho, SW1 29 J10
Glastonbury Pl, E1 20 G9
Glastonbury Rd, N9 122 DU46
Morden SM4 222 DA101
Glastonbury St, NW6 5 H3
Glaucus St, E3 22 C6
Glazbury Rd, W14 26 F9
Glazebrook Cl, SE21 204 DR89
Glazebrook Rd, Tedd. TW11 199 CF94
Gleave Cl, St.Alb. AL1 65 CH19
Glebe, The, SE3 47 J10
SW16 203 DK91
Chislehurst BR7 227 EQ95
Harlow CM20 off School La 57 ES14
Horley RH6 290 DF148
Kings Langley WD4 80 BN29
Leigh RH2 287 CU141
Magdalen Laver CM5 75 FD18
Watford WD25 82 BW33
West Drayton UB7 176 BM77
Worcester Park KT4 221 CT102
Glebe Av, Enf. EN2 103 DP41
Harrow HA3 140 CL55
Mitcham CR4 222 DE96
Ruislip HA4 157 BV65
Uxbridge UB10 137 BQ63
Woodford Green IG8 124 EG51
Glebe Cl, W4 180 CS78
Bookham KT23 268 CA126
Chalfont St. Peter SL9 112 AX52
Essendon AL9 68 DF17
Hemel Hempstead HP3 62 BL24
Hertford SG14 54 DR07
South Croydon CR2 242 DT111
Taplow SL6 172 AF75
Uxbridge UB10 137 BQ63
Glebe Cotts, Brasted TN16 262 EV123
Essendon AL9 68 DF17
Sutton SM1 off Vale Rd 240 DB105
West Clandon GU4 266 BH132
Glebe Ct, W7 159 CD73
Coulsdon CR5 257 DH115
Guildford GU1 265 AZ134
Mitcham CR4 222 DF97
Sevenoaks TN13 off Oak La 279 FH126
Stanmore HA7 117 CJ50
Glebe Cres, NW4 141 CW56
Harrow HA3 140 CL55
Glebefield, The, Sev. TN13 278 FF123
Sch Glebe First & Mid Sch, Kenton
HA3 off D'Arcy Gdns 140 CL56
Glebe Gdns, Byfleet KT14 234 BK114
New Malden KT3 220 CS101
Glebe Ho Dr, Brom. BR2 226 EH102
Glebe Hyrst, SE19 204 DS91
South Croydon CR2 242 DT112

Glebeland, Hat. AL10
off St. Etheldredas Dr. 67 CW18
Glebeland Gdns, Shep. TW17 217 BQ100
Glebelands, Chig. IG7 126 EV48
Claygate KT10 237 CF109
Dartford DA1 189 FF84
Harlow CM20 57 ET12
Penn HP10 110 AC47
West Molesey KT8 218 CB99
Glebelands Av, E18 124 EG54
Ilford IG2 147 ER59
Glebelands Cl, N12 120 DD53
Glebelands Rd, Felt. TW14 197 BU87
Glebe La, Abin.Com. RH5 284 BX143
Barnet EN5 101 CU43
Harrow HA3 140 CL56
Sevenoaks TN13 279 FH126
Glebe Ms, Sid. DA15 207 ET85
Glebe Path, Mitch. CR4 222 DE97
Glebe Pl, SW3 40 C2
Horton Kirby DA4 230 FQ98
Sch Glebe Prim Sch, Ickhm
UB10 off Sussex Rd 137 BQ63
Glebe Rd, E8 10 A7
N3 120 DC53
N8 143 DM56
NW10 161 CT65
SW13 181 CU82
Ashtead KT21 253 CK118
Bromley BR1 226 EG95
Carshalton SM5 240 DF107
Chalfont St. Peter SL9 112 AW53
Dagenham RM10 169 FB65
Dorking RH4 285 CF136
Egham TW20 195 BC93
Gravesend DA11 213 GF88
Hayes UB3 157 BT74
Hertford SG14 54 DR07
Merstham RH1 257 DH124
Old Windsor SL4 194 AV85
Rainham RM13 170 FJ69
Staines TW18 196 BH93
Stanmore HA7 117 CJ50
Sutton SM2 239 CY109
Uxbridge UB8 156 BJ68
Warlingham CR6 259 DX117
Sch Glebe Sch, W.Wick. BR4
off Hawes La 225 ED103
Glebe Side, Twick. TW1 199 CF86
Glebe Sq, Mitch. CR4 222 DF97
Glebe St, W4 180 CS78
Glebe Ter, W4 off Glebe St 180 CS78
Glebe Way, Amer. HP6 77 AR36
Erith DA8 189 FE79
Hanworth TW13 198 CA90
Hornchurch RM11 150 FL59
South Croydon CR2 242 DT112
West Wickham BR4 225 EC103
Glebeway, Wdf.Grn. IG8 124 EJ50
Gledhow Gdns, SW5 27 N9
Gledhow Wd, Kgswd KT20 256 DB121
Gledstanes Rd, W14 38 F1
Gledwood Av, Hayes UB4 157 BT71
Gledwood Cres, Hayes UB4 157 BT71
Gledwood Dr, Hayes UB4 157 BT71
Gledwood Gdns, Hayes UB4 157 BT71
Gleed Av, Bushey Hth WD23 117 CD47
Gleeson Dr, Orp. BR6 245 ET106
Gleeson Ms, Add. KT15 234 BJ105
Glegg Pl, SW15 181 CX84
Glen, The, Add. KT15 233 BF106
Bromley BR2 226 EE96
Croydon CR0 225 DX104
Eastcote HA5 137 BV57
Enfield EN2 103 DP42
Hemel Hempstead HP2 62 BM15
Northwood HA6 115 BR52
Orpington BR6 227 EM104
Pinner HA5 138 BY59
Rainham RM13 170 FJ70
Slough SL3 174 AW77
Southall UB2 178 BZ78
Wembley HA9 139 CK63
Glenaffric Av, E14 34 F9
Glen Albyn Rd, SW19 201 CX89
Glenalla Rd, Ruis. HA4 137 BT59
Glenalmond Rd, Har. HA3 140 CL56
Glenalvon Way, SE18 36 G8
Glena Mt, Sutt. SM1 240 DC105
Sch Glenarm Coll, Ilf. IG1
off Coventry Rd 147 EP61
Glenarm Rd, E5 10 G2
Glen Av, Ashf. TW15 196 BN91
Glenavon Cl, Clay. KT10 237 CG108
Glenavon Gdns, Slou. SL3 174 AW77
Glenavon Rd, E15 13 K6
Glenbarr Cl, SE9 187 EP83
Glenbow Rd, Brom. BR1 206 EE93
Glenbrook N, Enf. EN2 103 DM42
Sch Glenbrook Prim Sch, SW4
off Clarence Av 203 DK86
Glenbrook Rd, NW6 5 J3
Glenbrook S, Enf. EN2 103 DM42
Glenbuck Ct, Surb. KT6
off Glenbuck Rd 220 CL100
Glenbuck Rd, Surb. KT6 219 CK100
Glenburnie Rd, SW17 202 DF90
Glencairn Dr, W5 159 CH70
Glencairne Cl, E16 24 E6
Glencairn Rd, SW16 223 DL95
Glen Cl, Kgswd KT20 255 CY123
Shepperton TW17 216 BN98
Glencoe Av, Ilf. IG2 147 ER59
Glencoe Dr, Dag. RM10 148 FA63
Glencoe Rd, Bushey WD23 98 CA44
Hayes UB4 158 BY71
Weybridge KT13 216 BN104
Glencorse Grn, Wat. WD19 116 BX49
Glen Ct, Stai. TW18 195 BF94
Glen Cres, Wdf.Grn. IG8 124 EH51
Glendale, Hem.H. HP1 62 BH20
Swanley BR8 229 FF99
Glendale Av, N22 121 DN52
Edgware HA8 118 CM49
Romford RM6 148 EW59
Glendale Cl, SE9 187 EN83
Shenfield CM15 130 FY45
Woking GU21 248 AW118
Glendale Dr, SW19 201 CZ92
Guildford GU4 265 BB130
Glendale Gdns, Wem. HA9 139 CK60
Glendale Ms, Beck. BR3 225 EB95
Glendale Ri, Ken. CR8 257 DP115
Glendale Rd, Erith DA8 189 FC77
Northfleet DA11 212 GE91
Glendale Wk, Chsht EN8 89 DY30
Glendale Way, SE28 168 EW73
Glendall St, SW9 183 DM84
Glendarvon St, SW15 38 D10
Glendean Ct, Enf. EN3
off Tysoe Av 105 DZ36
Glendene Av, E.Hors. KT24 267 BS126
Glendevon Cl, Edg. HA8
off Tayside Dr 118 CP48
Glendish Rd, N17 122 DU53
Glendor Gdns, NW7 118 CR49
Glendower Cres, Orp. BR6 228 EU100
Glendower Gdns, SW14
off Glendower Rd 180 CR83
Glendower Pl, SW7 28 A8
Sch Glendower Prep Sch, SW7 28 A8
Glendower Rd, E4 123 ED46
SW14 180 CR83
Glendown Rd, SE2 188 EU78
Glendun Rd, W3 160 CS73
Gleneagle Ms, SW16
off Ambleside Av 203 DK92
Gleneagle Rd, SW16 203 DK92
Gleneagles, Stan. HA7 117 CH51
Gleneagles Cl, SE16 44 E1
Orpington BR6 227 ER102
Romford RM3 128 FM52
Stanwell TW19 196 BK86
Watford WD19 116 BX49
Gleneagles Grn, Orp. BR6
off Tandridge Dr 227 ER102
Gleneagles Twr, Sthl. UB1 158 CC72
Gleneldon Ms, SW16 203 DL91
Gleneldon Rd, SW16 203 DL91
Glenelg Rd, SW2 203 DL85
Glenesk Rd, SE9 187 EN83
Sch Glenesk Sch, E.Hors. KT24
off Ockham Rd N 267 BR125
Glenester Cl, Hodd. EN11 55 EA14
Glen Faba, Roydon CM19 72 EE16
Glen Faba Rd, Roydon CM19 72 EF17
Glenfarg Rd, SE6 205 ED88
Glenferrie Rd, St.Alb. AL1 65 CG20
Glenfield Cl, Brock. RH3 286 CP138
Glenfield Cres, Ruis. HA4 137 BR59
Glenfield Rd, SW12 203 DJ88
W13 179 CH75
Ashford TW15 197 BP93
Banstead SM7 256 DB115
Brockham RH3 286 CP138
Glenfields, Stoke P. SL2 154 AT67
Glenfield Ter, W13 179 CH75
Glenfinlas Way, SE5 43 H4
Glenforth St, SE10 35 M10
Glengall Causeway, E14 34 A6
Glengall Gro, E14 34 E6
Glengall Rd, NW6 5 H9
SE15 44 B2
Bexleyheath DA7 188 EY83
Edgware HA8 118 CP48
Woodford Green IG8 124 EG51
Glengall Ter, SE15 44 B2
Glen Gdns, Croy. CR0 223 DP104
Glengarnock Av, E14 34 F9
Glengarry Rd, SE22 204 DS85
Glenham Dr, Ilf. IG2 147 EP57
Glenhaven Av, Borwd. WD6 100 CN41
Glenhead Cl, SE9 187 EP83
Glenheadon Cl, Lthd. KT22
off Glenheadon Ri 253 CK123
Glenheadon Ri, Lthd. KT22 253 CK123
Glenhill Cl, N3 120 DA54
Glen Ho, E16 off Storey St 37 M3
Glenhouse Rd, SE9 207 EN85
Glenhurst Av, NW5 142 DG63
Bexley DA5 208 EZ88
Ruislip HA4 137 BQ59
Glenhurst Ct, SE19 204 DT92
Glenhurst Ri, SE19 204 DQ94
Glenhurst Rd, N12 120 DD50
Brentford TW8 179 CJ79
Glenilla Rd, NW3 6 C4
Glenister Ho, Hayes UB3 157 BV74
Glenister Pk Rd, SW16 203 DK94
Glenister Rd, SE10 35 L10
Chesham HP5 76 AQ28
Glenister St, E16 37 M3
Glenkerry Ho, E14 22 E8
Glenlea Path, SE9
off Well Hall Rd 207 EM85
Glenlea Rd, SE9 207 EM85
Glenlion Ct, Wey. KT13 217 BR104
Glenloch Rd, NW3 6 C4
Enfield EN3 104 DW40
Glen Luce, Chsht EN8 89 DX31
Glenluce Rd, SE3 47 N3
Glenlyn Av, St.Alb. AL1 65 CH21
Glenlyon Rd, SE9 207 EN85
Glenmere Av, NW7 119 CU52
Glenmere Row, SE12 206 EG86
Glen Ms, E17 off Glen Rd 145 DZ57
Glenmill, Hmptn. TW12 198 BZ92
Glenmire Ter, Stans.Abb. SG12 55 ED11
Glenmore Cl, Add. KT15 216 BH104
Glenmore Gdns, Abb.L. WD5
off Stewart Cl 81 BU32
Glenmore Rd, NW3 6 C4
Welling DA16 187 ET81
Glenmore Way, Bark. IG11 168 EU69
Glenmount Path, SE18
off Raglan Rd 187 EQ78
Glenn Av, Pur. CR8 241 DP111
Glennie Rd, SE27 203 DN90
Glenny Rd, Bark. IG11 167 EQ65
Glenorchy Cl, Hayes UB4 158 BY71
Glenparke Rd, E7 166 EH65
Glen Ri, Wdf.Grn. IG8 124 EH51
Glen Rd, E13 24 C4
E17 145 DZ57
Chessington KT9 220 CL104
Glen Rd End, Wall. SM6 241 DH109
Glenrosa Gdns, Grav. DA12 213 GM92
Glenrosa St, SW6 39 N8
Glenrose Ct, Sid. DA14 208 EV92
Glenroy St, W12 14 A8
Glensdale Rd, SE4 185 DZ83
Glenshee Cl, Nthwd. HA6
off Rickmansworth Rd 115 BQ51
Glenshiel Rd, SE9 207 EN85
Glenside, Chig. IG7 125 EP51
Glenside Cl, Ken. CR8 258 DR115
Glenside Cotts, Slou. SL1 174 AT76
Glentanner Way, SW17 202 DD90
Glen Ter, E14 34 E4
Glentham Gdns, SW13 181 CV79
Glentham Rd, SW13 181 CU79
Glenthorne Av, Croy. CR0 224 DV102
Glenthorne Cl, Sutt. SM3 222 DA102
Uxbridge UB10 156 BN69
Glenthorne Gdns, Ilf. IG6 147 EN55
Sutton SM3 222 DA102
Sch Glenthorne High Sch, Sutt. SM3
off Sutton Common Rd 222 DA102
Glenthorne Ms, W6
off Glenthorne Rd 181 CV77
Glenthorne Rd, E17 145 DY57
N11 120 DF50
W6 26 A8
Kingston upon Thames KT1 220 CM98
Glenthorpe Rd, Mord. SM4 221 CX99
Glenton Cl, Rom. RM1 127 FE51
Glenton Rd, SE13 186 EE84
Glenton Way, Rom. RM1 127 FE52
Glentrammon Av, Orp. BR6 245 ET107
Glentrammon Cl, Orp. BR6 245 ET107
Glentrammon Gdns, Orp. BR6 245 ET107
Glentrammon Rd, Orp. BR6 245 ET107
Glentworth Pl, Slou. SL1 153 AQ74
Glentworth St, NW1 16 F5
Glenure Rd, SE9 207 EN85
Glenview, SE2 188 EX79
Glen Vw, Grav. DA12 213 GJ88
Glenview Gdns, Hem.H. HP1
off Glenview Rd 62 BH20
Glenview Rd, Brom. BR1 226 EK96
Hemel Hempstead HP1 62 BH20
Glenville Av, Enf. EN2 104 DQ38
Glenville Gro, SE8 45 P5
Glenville Ms, SW18 202 DB87
Glenville Rd, Kings.T. KT2 220 CN95
Glen Wk, Islw. TW7 199 CD85
Glen Way, Wat. WD17 97 BS38
Glenwood, Brox. EN10 71 DZ19
Dorking RH5 285 CJ138
Welwyn Garden City AL7 52 DD10
Glenwood Av, NW9 140 CS60
Rainham RM13 169 FG70
Glenwood Cl, Har. HA1 139 CF57
Glenwood Ct, E18
off Clarendon Rd 146 EG55
Glenwood Dr, Rom. RM2 149 FG56
Glenwood Gdns, Ilf. IG2 147 EN57
Glenwood Gro, NW9 140 CQ60
Glenwood Rd, N15 143 DP57
NW7 118 CS48
SE6 205 DZ88
Epsom KT17 239 CU107
Hounslow TW3 179 CD83
Glenwood Way, Croy. CR0 225 DX100
Glenworth Av, E14 34 G9
Glevum Cl, St.Alb. AL3 64 BZ22
Gliddon Dr, E5 144 DU63
Gliddon Rd, W14 26 E9
Glimpsing Grn, Erith DA18 188 EY76
Glisson Rd, Uxb. UB10 156 BN68
Gload Cres, Orp. BR5 228 EX103
Global App, E3 22 D1
Sch Globe Acad, SE1 31 L7
Globe Ct, Hert. SG14
off Bengeo St 54 DQ07
● Globe Ind Est, Grays RM17 192 GC78
Globe Pond Rd, SE16 33 L3
Sch Globe Prim Sch, E2 21 H2
Globe Rd, E1 21 H2
E2 20 G1
E15 13 L3
Hornchurch RM11 149 FG58
Woodford Green IG8 124 EJ51
Globe Rope Wk, E14 34 E9
Globe St, SE1 31 K6
Globe Ter, E2 20 G2
Globe Town, E2 21 J1
Globe Wf, SE16 33 K1
Globe Yd, W1 17 J9
Glory Cl, Woob.Grn HP10 132 AF56
Glory Hill La, Beac. HP9 132 AF55
Glory Mead, Dor. RH4 285 CH139
Glory Mill La, Woob.Grn HP10 132 AE56
Glossop Rd, S.Croy. CR2 242 DR109
Gloster Rd, N.Mal. KT3 220 CS98
Woking GU22 249 BA120
Gloucester Arc, SW7 27 N8
Gloucester Av, NW1 7 H8
Grays RM16 192 GC75
Hornchurch RM11 150 FN56
Sidcup DA15 207 ES89
Slough SL1 153 AQ71
Waltham Cross EN8 89 DY33
Welling DA16 187 ET84
Gloucester Circ, SE10 46 F4
Gloucester Cl, NW10 160 CR66
Thames Ditton KT7 219 CG102
Gloucester Ct, Denh. UB9 136 BG59
Hatfield AL10
off De Havilland Cl 67 CT17
Richmond TW9 180 CN80
Tilbury RM18 off Dock Rd 193 GF82
Gloucester Cres, NW1 7 J8
Staines TW18 196 BK93
Gloucester Dr, N4 143 DP61
NW11 142 DA56
Staines TW18 195 BC90
Gloucester Gdns, NW11 141 CZ59
W2 15 M8
Cockfosters EN4 102 DG42
Ilford IG1 146 EL59
Sutton SM1 222 DB103
Gloucester Gate, NW1 7 J10
Gloucester Gate Ms, NW1 7 J10
Gloucester Gro, Edg. HA8 118 CR53
Gloucester Ho, NW6 15 K1
Gloucester Ms, E10
off Gloucester Rd 145 EA59
W2 15 P9
Gloucester Ms W, W2 15 N9
Gloucester Par, Sid. DA15 208 EU85
Gloucester Pk, SW7 27 N8
Gloucester Pl, NW1 16 E4
W1 16 F6
Windsor SL4 173 AR82
Gloucester Pl Ms, W1 16 F7
Sch Gloucester Prim Sch, SE15 44 A4
⊖ Gloucester Road 27 P8
Gloucester Rd, E10 145 EA59
E11 146 EH57
E12 147 EM62
E17 123 DX54
N17 122 DR54
N18 122 DT50
SW7 27 N6
W3 180 CQ75
W5 179 CJ75
Barnet EN5 102 DC43
Belvedere DA17 188 EZ78
Croydon CR0 224 DR100
Dartford DA1 209 FH87
Enfield EN2 104 DQ38
Feltham TW13 198 BW88
Gravesend DA12 213 GJ91
Guildford GU2 264 AT132
Hampton TW12 198 CB94
Harrow HA1 138 CB57
Gloucester Rd, Houns. TW4 178 BY84
Kingston upon Thames KT1 220 CP96
Pilgrim's Hatch CM15 130 FV43
Redhill RH1 272 DF133
Richmond TW9 180 CN80
Romford RM1 149 FE58
Teddington TW11 199 CE92
Twickenham TW2 198 CC88
Gloucester Sq, E2 10 C9
W2 16 B9
Woking GU21, GU22
off Church St E 249 AZ117
Gloucester St, SW1 41 L1
Gloucester Ter, W2 15 N8
Gloucester Wk, W8 27 K4
Woking GU21 249 AZ117
Gloucester Way, EC1 18 F3
Glover Cl, SE2 188 EW77
Cheshunt EN7
off Allwood Rd 88 DT27
Glover Dr, N18 122 DW51
Glover Rd, Pnr. HA5 138 BX58
Glovers Cl, Bigg.H. TN16 260 EH116
Hertford SG13 54 DQ11
Glovers Gro, Ruis. HA4 137 BP59
Glovers La, Hast. CM17 74 EY20
Glovers Rd, Reig. RH2 288 DB135
Gloxinia Rd, Sthflt DA13 212 GB93
Gloxinia Wk, Hmptn. TW12 198 CA93
Glycena Rd, SW11 40 F10
Glyn Av, Barn. EN4 102 DD42
Glyn Cl, SE25 224 DS96
Epsom KT17 239 CU109
Glyn Ct, SW16 203 DN90
Stanmore HA7 117 CH51
Glyn Davies Cl, Dunt.Grn TN13 263 FE120
Glyndebourne Pk, Orp. BR6 227 EP103
Glynde Ms, SW3 28 D7
Glynde Rd, Bexh. DA7 188 EX83
Glynde St, SE4 205 DZ86
Glyndon Rd, SE18 187 EQ77
Glyn Dr, Sid. DA14 208 EV91
Glynfield Rd, NW10 160 CS66
Glynne Rd, N22 121 DN54
Glyn Rd, E5 11 K2
Enfield EN3 104 DW42
Worcester Park KT4 221 CX103
Glyn St, SE11 42 C1
Glynswood, Chal.St.P. SL9 113 AZ52
Glynswood Pl, Nthwd. HA6 115 BP52
Sch Glyn Tech Sch, Ewell KT17
off The Kingsway 239 CT111
Glynwood Ct, SE23 204 DW89
Goaters All, SW6 38 G5
GOATHURST COMMON,
Sev. TN14 278 FB130
Goat La, Enf. EN1 104 DT38
Surbiton KT6 219 CJ103
Goat Rd, Mitch. CR4 222 DG101
Goatsfield Rd, Tats. TN16 260 EJ120
Goatswood La, Nave. RM4 127 FH45
Goat Wf, Brent. TW8 180 CL79
Gobions Av, Rom. RM5 127 FD52
Gobions Way, Pot.B. EN6
off Swanley Bar La 86 DB28
Goblins Grn, Welw.G.C. AL7 51 CX10
Godalming Av, Wall. SM6 241 DL106
Godalming Rd, E14 22 C7
Godbold Rd, E15 23 J3
Goddard Cl, Guil. GU2 264 AU130
Shepperton TW17
off Magdalene Rd 216 BM97
Goddard Pl, N19 143 DJ62
Goddard Rd, Beck. BR3 225 DX98
Goddards Cl, Lt.Berk. SG13 69 DJ19
Goddards Way, Ilf. IG1 147 ER60
GODDEN GREEN, Sev. TN15 279 FN125
H Godden Grn Clinic,
Godden Grn TN15 279 FP125
GODDINGTON, Orp. BR6 228 EW104
Goddington Chase, Orp. BR6 246 EV105
Goddington La, Orp. BR6 228 EU104
Godfrey Av, Nthlt. UB5 158 BY67
Twickenham TW2 199 CD87
Godfrey Hill, SE18 37 H9
Godfrey Ho, EC1 19 L3
Godfrey Rd, SE18 37 J9
Godfrey St, E15 12 F10
SW3 28 D10
Godfrey Way, Houns. TW4 198 BY87
Goding St, SE11 42 B1
Godley Cl, SE14 45 H7
Godley Rd, SW18 202 DD88
Byfleet KT14 234 BM113
Godliman St, EC4 19 J9
Godman Rd, SE15 44 E9
Grays RM16 193 GG76
Sch Godolphin & Latymer Sch,
The, W6 off Iffley Rd 181 CV77
Godolphin Cl, N13 121 DP51
Sutton SM2 239 CZ111
Sch Godolphin Inf Sch, Slou.
SL1 off Warrington Av 153 AQ72
Sch Godolphin Jun Sch, Slou.
SL1 off Oatlands Dr 153 AR72
Godolphin Pl, W3 160 CR73
Godolphin Rd, W12 181 CV75
Seer Green HP9 111 AQ51
Slough SL1 153 AR73
Weybridge KT13 235 BR107
Godric Cres, New Adgtn CR0 243 ED110
Godson Rd, Croy. CR0 223 DN104
Godson St, N1 8 E10
Godson Yd, NW6
off Kilburn Pk Rd 15 J3
GODSTONE, RH9 274 DV131
Godstone Bypass, Gdse. RH9 274 DW129
Godstone Grn, Gdse. RH9 274 DV131
Godstone Grn Rd, Gdse. RH9 274 DV131
Godstone Hill, Gdse. RH9 274 DV127
Jct Godstone Interchange,
Gdse. RH9 274 DW128
Godstone Rd, Bletch. RH1 274 DR133
Caterham CR3 258 DU124
Kenley CR8 242 DR114
Oxted RH8 275 EA131
Purley CR8 241 DN112
Sutton SM1 240 DC105
Twickenham TW1 199 CG86
Whyteleafe CR3 258 DT116
Sch Godstone Village Sch, Gdse.
RH9 off Ivy Mill La 274 DV132
Godstow Rd, SE2 188 EW75
Godwin Cl, E4 105 EC38
N1 9 K10
Epsom KT19 238 CQ107
Godwin Ct, NW1 7 M10
Godwin Ho, NW6
off Tollgate Gdns 5 L10
Sch Godwin Jun Sch, E7
off Cranmer Rd 146 EH63
Sch Godwin Prim Sch, Dag.
RM9 off Finnymore Rd 168 EY66
Godwin Rd, E7 146 EH63
Bromley BR2 226 EJ97
Coll Goethe Institut, SW7 28 B6
Goffers Rd, SE3 47 J7
Goffs Cres, Goffs Oak EN7 87 DP29
Goffs La, Goffs Oak EN7 88 DU29
GOFFS OAK, Wal.Cr. EN7 88 DQ29
Goffs Oak Av, Goffs Oak EN7 87 DP28
Sch Goffs Oak Prim Sch, Goffs Oak
EN7 off Millcrest Rd 87 DP28
Goffs Rd, Ashf. TW15 197 BR93
Sch Goffs Sch, Chsht EN7
off Goffs La 88 DU29
Gogmore Fm Cl, Cher. KT16 215 BF101
Gogmore La, Cher. KT16 216 BG101
Goidel Cl, Wall. SM6 241 DK105
Golborne Gdns, W10 14 F5
Golborne Ms, W10 14 E7
Golborne Rd, W10 14 F7
Goldace, Grays RM17 192 FZ79
Golda Cl, Barn. EN5 101 CX44
Goldbeaters Gro, Edg. HA8 118 CS51
Sch Goldbeaters Prim Sch, Edg.
HA8 off Thirleby Rd 118 CR53
Goldcliff Cl, Mord. SM4 222 DA101
Gold Cl, Brox. EN10 71 DY20
Goldcrest Cl, E16 24 E6
SE28 168 EW73
Horley RH6 290 DD147
Goldcrest Ms, W5 159 CK71
Goldcrest Way, Bushey WD23 116 CC46
New Addington CR0 243 ED109
Purley CR8 241 DK110
Goldcroft, Hem.H. HP3 62 BN22
Golden Ct, Islw. TW7 179 CD82
Richmond TW9
off George St 199 CK85
Golden Cres, Hayes UB3 157 BT74
Golden Cross Ms, W11 14 G8
Golden Dell, Welw.G.C. AL7 51 CZ13
★ Golden Hinde, SE1 31 L2
Golden Jubilee Br, SE1 30 C3
WC2 30 B2
Golden La, EC1 19 J5
Golden La Est, EC1 19 J5
Golden Manor, W7 159 CE73
Golden Oak Cl, Farn.Com. SL2 153 AQ65
Golden Plover Cl, E16 24 A8
Golden Sq, W1 17 M10
Golden Yd, NW3
off Heath St 142 DC63
Golders Cl, Edg. HA8 118 CP50
Golders Gdns, NW11 141 CY59
GOLDERS GREEN, NW11 142 DA59
⊖ Golders Green 142 DA59
Golders Green 142 DA60
Golders Grn Cres, NW11 141 CZ59
Golders Grn Rd, NW11 141 CY58
Sch Golders Hill Sch, NW11
off Finchley Rd 142 DA59
Golders Manor Dr, NW11 141 CX58
Golders Pk Cl, NW11 142 DA60
Golders Ri, NW4 141 CX57
Golders Way, NW11 141 CZ59
Goldfinch Cl, Orp. BR6 246 EU106
Goldfinch Gdns, Guil. GU4 265 BD133
Goldfinch Rd, SE28 187 ER76
South Croydon CR2 243 DY110
Goldfinch Way, Borwd. WD6 100 CN42
Goldfort Wk, Wok. GU21
off Langmans Way 248 AS116
Goldhawk Ms, W12
off Devonport Rd 181 CV75
⊖ Goldhawk Road 26 A5
Goldhawk Rd, W6 181 CT77
W12 181 CU76
Goldhaze Cl, Wdf.Grn. IG8 124 EK52
Gold Hill, Edg. HA8 118 CR51
Gold Hill E, Chal.St.P. SL9 112 AX54
Gold Hill N, Chal.St.P. SL9 112 AW53
Gold Hill W, Chal.St.P. SL9 112 AW53
Goldhurst Ter, NW6 5 N7
H Goldie Leigh Hosp, SE2 188 EW79
Golding Cl, Chess. KT9
off Coppard Gdns 237 CJ107
Golding Ct, Ilf. IG1 147 EN62
Goldingham Av, Loug. IG10 107 EQ40
Golding Rd, Sev. TN13 279 FJ122
Goldings, Hert. SG14 53 DN06
Goldings, The, Wok. GU21 248 AT116
Goldings Cres, Hat. AL10 67 CV17
Goldings Hill, Loug. IG10 107 EN39
Goldings Ho, Hat. AL10 67 CV17
Goldings La, Waterf. SG14 53 DN06
Goldings Ri, Loug. IG10 107 EN39
Goldings Rd, Loug. IG10 107 EN39
Golding St, E1 20 D9
Golding Ter, SW11
off Longhedge St 41 H8
Goldington Cl, Hodd. EN11 55 DZ14
Goldington Cres, NW1 7 N10
Goldington St, NW1 7 N10
Gold La, Edg. HA8 118 CR51
Goldman Cl, E2 20 C4
Goldmark Ho, SE3
off Lebrun Sq 186 EH83
Goldney Rd, W9 15 J5
Goldrill Dr, N11 120 DG47
Goldrings Rd, Oxshott KT22 236 CC113
Goldring Way, Lon.Col. AL2 83 CH27
Goldsboro Rd, SW8 41 P6
Goldsborough Cres, E4 123 EC47
H Goldsborough Indep Hosp,
Red. RH1 288 DG138
Goldsdown Cl, Enf. EN3 105 DY40
Goldsdown Rd, Enf. EN3 105 DX40
Goldsel Rd, Swan. BR8 229 FD99
Goldsmid St, SE18 187 ES78
Goldsmith, Grays RM17 192 FZ79
Goldsmith Av, E12 166 EL65
NW9 141 CT58
W3 160 CR73
Romford RM7 148 FA59
Goldsmith Cl, W3 160 CR74
Harrow HA2 138 CB60
Goldsmith Ct, Edg. HA8 118 CM49
Goldsmith La, NW9 140 CP56

Goldsmith Rd, E10 145 EA60
E17 123 DX54
N11 120 DF50
SE15 44 C6
W3 160 CR74
Goldsmiths Bottom, Sev.
TN14 278 FE127
Goldsmiths Cl, Wok. GU21 248 AW118
Goldsmiths Coll, SE14 45 M6
★ Goldsmiths' Hall, EC2 19 J8
Goldsmith's Pl, NW6 5 L9
Goldsmith's Row, E2 20 C1
Goldsmith's Sq, E2 10 D10
Goldsmith St, EC2 19 K8
Goldsmith Way, St.Alb. AL3 64 CC19
Goldstone Cl, Ware SG12
off High Oak Rd 55 DX05
Goldstone Fm Vw, Lthd. KT23 268 CA127
Goldsworth Orchard, Wok.
GU21 off St. John's Rd 248 AU118
GOLDSWORTH PARK, Wok.
GU21 248 AU117
Goldsworth Pk, Wok. GU21 248 AU117
● Goldsworth Pk Trd Est,
Wok. GU21 248 AU116
Goldsworth Prim Sch, Wok.
GU21 off Bridge Barn La 248 AW118
Goldsworth Rd, Wok. GU21 248 AW118
● Goldsworth Rd Ind Est, Wok.
GU21 off Goldsworth Rd 248 AX117
Goldsworthy Gdns, SE16 33 H9
Goldsworthy Way, Slou. SL1 152 AJ72
Goldwell Ho, SE22
off Quorn Rd 184 DS83
Goldwell Rd, Th.Hth. CR7 223 DM98
Goldwin Cl, SE14 45 H6
Goldwing Cl, E16 23 P9
Golf Cl, Bushey WD23 98 BX41
Stanmore HA7 117 CJ52
Thornton Heath CR7
off Kensington Av 223 DN95
Woking GU22 233 BE114
Golf Club Dr, Kings.T. KT2 200 CR94
Golf Club Rd, Brook.Pk AL9 86 DA26
Weybridge KT13 235 BP109
Woking GU22 248 AU120
Golfe Rd, Ilf. IG1 147 ER62
Golf Ho Rd, Oxt. RH8 276 EJ129
Golf Links Av, Grav. DA11 213 GH92
Golf Ride, Enf. EN2 103 DN35
Golf Rd, W5 160 CM72
Bromley BR1 227 EN97
Kenley CR8 258 DR118
Golf Side, Sutt. SM2 239 CY111
Twickenham TW2 199 CD90
Golfside Cl, N20 120 DE48
New Malden KT3 220 CS96
Gollogly Ter, SE7 186 EJ78
Gombards, St.Alb. AL3 65 CD19
Gombards All, St.Alb. AL3
off Worley Rd 65 CD19
Gomer Gdns, Tedd. TW11 199 CG93
Gomer Pl, Tedd. TW11 199 CG93
Gomm Rd, SE16 32 G7
Gomms Wd Cl, Forty Grn HP9 110 AH51
GOMSHALL, Guil. GU5 283 BR139
⇌ Gomshall 283 BR139
Gomshall Av, Wall. SM6 241 DL106
Gomshall Gdns, Ken. CR8 258 DS115
Gomshall La, Shere GU5 282 BN139
Gomshall Rd, Sutt. SM2 239 CW110
Gondar Gdns, NW6 4 G2
Gonnerston, St.Alb. AL3 64 CB19
Gonson St, SE8 46 C3
Gonston Cl, SW19 201 CY89
Gonville Av, Crox.Grn WD3 97 BP44
Gonville Cres, Nthlt. UB5 158 CB65
Gonville Prim Sch, Th.Hth.
CR7 off Gonville Rd 223 DM99
Gonville Rd, Th.Hth. CR7 223 DM99
Gonville St, SW6 38 F10
Gooch Ho, E5 144 DV62
Goodacre Cl, Pot.B. EN6 86 DB32
Goodall Rd, E11 145 EC62
Gooden Ct, Har. HA1 139 CE62
Goodenough Cl, Couls. CR5 257 DN120
Goodenough Rd, SW19 201 CZ94
Goodenough Way, Couls.
CR5 257 DM120
Gooderham Ho, Grays RM16 193 GH75
Goodey Rd, Bark. IG11 167 ET66
Goodge Pl, W1 17 M7
⊖ Goodge Street 17 M6
Goodge St, W1 17 M7
Goodhall Cl, Stan. HA7 117 CG51
Goodhall St, NW10 160 CS69
Goodhart Pl, E14 21 M10
Goodhart Way, W.Wick. BR4 226 EE101
Goodhew Rd, Croy. CR0 224 DU100
Gooding Cl, N.Mal. KT3 220 CQ98
Goodinge Cl, N7 8 A4
Goodison Cl, Bushey WD23 98 CC43
Goodlake Ct, Denh. UB9 135 BF59
GOODLEY STOCK, West. TN16 277 EP130
Goodley Stock, West. TN16 277 EP129
Goodley Stock Rd, Crock.H.
TN8 277 EP131
Westerham TN16 277 EP128
Goodman Cres, SW2 203 DK89
Goodman Pk, Slou. SL2 154 AW74
Goodman Pl, Stai. TW18 195 BF91
Goodman Rd, E10 145 EC59
Goodmans Ct, E1 20 A10
Wembley HA0 139 CK63
Goodman's Stile, E1 20 C8
Goodman's Yd, E1 20 A10
GOODMAYES, Ilf. IG3 148 EV61
⇌ Goodmayes 148 EU60
Goodmayes Av, Ilf. IG3 148 EU60
Goodmayes Hosp, Ilf. IG3 148 EU57
Goodmayes La, Ilf. IG3 148 EU63
Goodmayes Prim Sch, Ilf.
IG3 off Airthrie Rd 148 EV60
Goodmayes Retail Pk,
Rom. RM6 148 EV60
Goodmayes Rd, Ilf. IG3 148 EU60
Goodmead Rd, Orp. BR6 228 EU101
Goodrich Cl, Wat. WD25 97 BU35
Goodrich Prim Sch, SE22
off Dunstans Rd 204 DU86
Goodrich Rd, SE22 204 DT86
Good Shepherd Prim Sch,
Downham BR1
off Moorside Rd 206 EF91
Good Shepherd RC Prim Sch,
New Adgtn CR0
off Dunley Dr. 243 EB108
Good Shepherd RC Prim Sch,
The, W12 off Gayford Rd 181 CT75
Goodson Rd, NW10 160 CS66
Goods Way, NW1 8 A10
Goodway Gdns, E14 22 G8
Goodwill Dr, Har. HA2 138 CA60
Goodwin Cl, SE16 32 B7
Mitcham CR4 222 DD97
Goodwin Ct, Barn. EN4 102 DE44
Waltham Cross EN8 89 DY28
Goodwin Dr, Sid. DA14 208 EX90
Goodwin Gdns, Croy. CR0 241 DP107
Goodwin Meadows, Woob.Grn
HP10 132 AE57
Goodwin Rd, N9 122 DW46
W12 181 CU75
Croydon CR0 241 DP106
Slough SL2 153 AM69
Goodwins Ct, WC2 18 A10
Goodwin St, N4
off Fonthill Rd 143 DN61
Goodwood Av, Enf. EN3 104 DW37
Hornchurch RM12 150 FL63
Hutton CM13 131 GE44
Watford WD24 97 BS35
Goodwood Cl, Hodd. EN11 71 DZ16
Morden SM4 222 DA98
Stanmore HA7 117 CJ50
Goodwood Cres, Grav. DA12 213 GJ93
Goodwood Dr, Nthlt. UB5 158 CA65
Goodwood Path, Borwd.
WD6 off Stratfield Rd 100 CN40
Goodwood Rd, SE14 45 L5
Redhill RH1 272 DF132
Goodworth Rd, Red. RH1 273 DH132
Goodwyn Av, NW7 118 CS50
Goodwyn Sch, NW7
off Hammers La. 119 CU50
Goodwyns Pl, Dor. RH4 285 CH138
Goodwyns Rd, Dor. RH4 285 CH139
Goodwyns Vale, N10 120 DG53
Goodyers Av, Rad. WD7 83 CF33
Goodyers Gdns, NW4 141 CX57
Goosander Way, SE28 187 ER76
Goose Acre, Chesh. HP5 78 AT30
Gooseacre, Welw.G.C. AL7 51 CZ11
Gooseacre La, Har. HA3 139 CK57
Goosecroft, Hem.H. HP1 61 BF19
Goosefields, Rick. WD3 96 BJ44
GOOSE GREEN, Hodd. EN11 70 DW17
Goose Grn, Cob. KT11 251 BU119
Farnham Royal SL2 153 AP68
Gomshall GU5 283 BQ139
Goose Grn Cl, Orp. BR5 228 EU96
Goose Grn Prim Sch, SE22
off Tintagel Cres 184 DT84
Goose La, Wok. GU22 248 AV122
Gooseley La, E6 25 L2
Goosens Cl, Sutt. SM1
off Turnpike La. 240 DC106
Goose Rye Rd, Worp. GU3 264 AT125
Goose Sq, E6 25 J9
Gooshays Dr, Rom. RM3 128 FL50
Gooshays Gdns, Rom. RM3 128 FL51
Gophir La, EC4 19 L10
Gopsall St, N1 9 M9
Goral Mead, Rick. WD3 114 BK46
Goran Ct, N9 off Bedevere Rd 122 DU48
Gordon Av, E4 124 EE51
SW14 180 CS84
Hornchurch RM12 149 FF61
South Croydon CR2 242 DQ110
Stanmore HA7 117 CH51
Twickenham TW1 199 CG85
Gordonbrock Prim Sch, SE4
off Gordonbrock Rd 205 EA85
Gordonbrock Rd, SE4 205 EA85
Gordon Cl, E17 145 EA58
N19 143 DJ61
Chertsey KT16 215 BE104
St. Albans AL1
off Kitchener Cl 65 CH21
Staines TW18 196 BH93
Gordon Cres, Croy. CR0 224 DS102
Hayes UB3 177 BU76
Gordondale Rd, SW19 202 DA89
Gordon Dr, Cher. KT16 215 BE104
Shepperton TW17 217 BR100
Gordon Gdns, Edg. HA8 118 CP54
Gordon Gro, SE5 43 H9
⇌ Gordon Hill 103 DP39
Gordon Hill, Enf. EN2 104 DQ39
Gordon Hosp, SW1 29 N9
Gordon Ho, E1 20 G10
Gordon Ho Rd, NW5 7 H1
Gordon Infants' Sch, Ilf.
IG1 off Golfe Rd 147 ER62
Gordon Pl, W8 27 K4
Gravesend DA12
off East Ter. 213 GJ86
Gordon Prim Sch, SE9
off Craigton Rd 187 EM84
Gordon Prom, Grav. DA12 213 GJ86
Gordon Prom E, Grav. DA12 213 GJ86
Gordon Rd, E4 124 EE45
E11 146 EG58
E15 12 F1
E18 124 EH53
N3 119 CZ52
N9 122 DV47
N11 121 DK52
SE15 44 E7
W4 180 CP79
W5 159 CJ73
W13 159 CH73
Ashford TW15 196 BL90
Barking IG11 167 ES67
Beckenham BR3 225 DZ97
Belvedere DA17 189 FC77
Carshalton SM5 240 DF107
Caterham CR3 258 DR121
Chesham HP5 76 AQ32
Claygate KT10 237 CE107
Dartford DA1 210 FK87
Enfield EN2 104 DQ39
Grays RM16 193 GF75
Harrow HA3 139 CE55
Hounslow TW3 178 CC84
Ilford IG1 147 ER62
Kingston upon Thames KT2 220 CM95
Northfleet DA11 212 GE87
Redhill RH1 272 DG131
Richmond TW9 180 CM82
Gordon Rd, Rom. RM6 148 EZ58
Sevenoaks TN13 279 FH125
Shenfield CM15 131 GA46
Shepperton TW17 217 BR100
Sidcup DA15 207 ES85
Southall UB2 178 BY77
Staines TW18 195 BC91
Surbiton KT5 220 CM101
Waltham Abbey EN9 89 EA34
West Drayton UB7 156 BL73
Windsor SL4 173 AM82
Gordon Sq, WC1 17 P5
Gordon St, E13 23 P3
WC1 17 N4
Gordons Way, Oxt. RH8 275 ED128
Gordon Way, Barn. EN5 101 CZ42
Bromley BR1 226 EG95
Chalfont St. Giles HP8 112 AV48
Gore, The, Burn. SL1 152 AG69
Gore Cl, Hare. UB9 136 BH56
Gore Ct, NW9 140 CN57
Gorefield Pl, NW6 5 J10
Gore Hill, Amer. HP7 77 AP43
Gorelands La, Ch.St.G. HP8 113 AZ47
Gorell Rd, Beac. HP9 111 AP54
Gore Rd, E9 11 H9
SW20 221 CW96
Burnham SL1 152 AH69
Dartford DA2 210 FQ90
Goresbrook Rd, Dag. RM9 168 EV67
Goresbrook Village, Dag. RM9
off Goresbrook Rd 168 EV67
Gore St, SW7 27 P6
GORHAMBURY, St.Alb. AL3 64 BY18
★ Gorhambury, St.Alb. AL3 64 BW19
Gorhambury Dr, St.Alb. AL3 64 BW19
Gorham Dr, St.Alb. AL1 65 CE23
Gorham Pl, W11 26 E1
Goring Cl, Rom. RM5 127 FC53
Goring Gdns, Dag. RM8 148 EW63
Goring Rd, N11 121 DL51
Dagenham RM10 169 FD65
Staines TW18 195 BD92
Gorings Sq, Stai. TW18 195 BE91
Goring St, EC3 19 P8
Goring Way, Grnf. UB6 158 CC68
Gorle Cl, Wat. WD25 81 BU34
Gorleston Rd, N15 144 DR57
Gorleston St, W14 26 F8
Gorman Rd, SE18 37 K8
Gorringe Av, S.Darenth DA4 231 FR96
Gorringe Pk Av, Mitch. CR4 202 DF94
Gorringe Pk Prim Sch, Mitch.
CR4 off Sandy La 222 DG95
Gorse Cl, E16 23 N9
Hatfield AL10 67 CT21
Tadworth KT20 255 CV120
Gorse Ct, Guil. GU4 265 BC132
Gorse Hill, Fnghm DA4 230 FL100
Gorse Hill La, Vir.W. GU25 214 AX98
Gorse Hill Rd, Vir.W. GU25 214 AX98
Gorselands Cl, W.Byf. KT14 234 BJ111
Gorse La, Chobham GU24 232 AS108
Gorse Meade, Slou. SL1 153 AN74
Gorse Ri, SW17 202 DG92
Gorse Rd, Croy. CR0 243 EA105
Orpington BR5 228 FA103
Gorse Wk, West Dr. UB7 156 BL72
Gorseway, Hat. AL10 51 CT14
Romford RM7 149 FD61
Gorst Rd, NW10 160 CQ70
SW11 202 DF86
Gorsuch Pl, E2 20 A2
Gorsuch St, E2 20 A2
Gosberton Rd, SW12 202 DG88
Gosbury Hill, Chess. KT9 238 CL105
Gosden Cl, Bramley GU5 280 AY143
Gosden Common, Bramley
GU5 280 AY143
Gosden Hill Rd, Guil. GU4 265 BC130
Gosden Ho Sch, Bramley
GU5 off Gosden Common 280 AY143
Gosfield Rd, Dag. RM8 148 FA61
Epsom KT19 238 CR112
Gosfield St, W1 17 L6
Gosford Gdns, Ilf. IG4 147 EM57
Gosforth La, Wat. WD19 116 BW48
Gosforth Path, Wat. WD19 115 BU48
Goshawk Gdns, Hayes UB4 157 BS69
Goshawk Way, Felt. TW14 197 BV85
Goslar Way, Wind. SL4 173 AP82
Goslett Ct, Bushey WD23
off Bournehall Av 98 CA43
Goslett Yd, WC2 17 P9
Gosling Cl, Grnf. UB6 158 CA69
Gosling Grn, Slou. SL3 174 AY76
Gosling Rd, Slou. SL3 174 AY76
Gosling Way, SW9 42 F7
Gospatrick Rd, N17 122 DQ52
GOSPEL OAK, NW5 7 H1
Gospel Oak 7 H1
Gospel Oak Prim Sch, NW3 6 G1
Gosport Dr, Horn. RM12 170 FJ65
Gosport Rd, E17 145 DZ57
Gosport Wk, N17
off Yarmouth Cres 144 DV57
Gossage Rd, SE18 187 ER78
Uxbridge UB10 156 BM66
Gossamers, The, Wat. WD25 98 BY36
Gosse Cl, Hodd. EN11 55 DZ14
Gosselin Rd, Hert. SG14 54 DQ07
Gosset St, E2 20 B2
Goss Hill, Dart. DA2 210 FJ93
Swanley BR8 210 FJ93
Gosshill Rd, Chis. BR7 227 EN96
Gossington Cl, Chis. BR7
off Beechwood Ri 207 EP91
Gossoms End, Berk. HP4 60 AU18
Gossoms Ryde, Berk. HP4 60 AU18
Gosterwood St, SE8 45 M2
Gostling Rd, Twick. TW2 198 CA88
Goston Gdns, Th.Hth. CR7 223 DN97
Goswell Arches, Wind. SL4
off Goswell Rd 173 AR81
Goswell Hill, Wind. SL4
off Peascod St 173 AR81
Goswell Rd, EC1 19 J5
Windsor SL4 173 AR81
Gothic Cl, Dart. DA1 210 FK90
Gothic Ct, Hayes UB3
off Sipson La 177 BR79
Gothic Rd, Twick. TW2 199 CD89
Gottfried Ms, NW5
off Fortess Rd 143 DJ63
Goudhurst Rd, Brom. BR1 206 EE92
Gouge Av, Nthflt DA11 212 GE88
Gough Rd, E15 13 L1
Enfield EN1 104 DV40
Gough Sq, EC4 18 F8
Gough St, WC1 18 D4
Gough Wk, E14 22 A9
Gould Cl, N.Mymms AL9 67 CV24
Gould Ct, SE19 204 DS92
Guildford GU4 265 BD132
Goulden Ho App, SW11 40 C8
Goulding Gdns, Th.Hth. CR7 223 DP96
Gould Rd, Felt. TW14 197 BS87
Twickenham TW2 199 CE88
Goulds Grn, Uxb. UB8 157 BP72
Gould Ter, E8 10 F3
Goulston St, E1 20 A8
Goulton Rd, E5 10 F2
Gourley Pl, N15 144 DS57
Gourley St, N15 144 DS57
Gourock Rd, SE9 207 EN85
Govan St, E2 10 D9
Government Row, Enf. EN3 105 EA38
Governors Av, Denh. UB9 135 BF57
Governors Cl, Amer. HP6 94 AT37
Govett Av, Shep. TW17 217 BQ99
Govier Cl, E15 13 K7
Gowan Av, SW6 38 E7
Gowan Rd, NW10 161 CV65
Gowar Fld, S.Mimms EN6 85 CU32
Gower, The, Egh. TW20 215 BB97
Gower Cl, SW4 203 DJ86
Gower Ct, WC1 17 N4
Gower Ho Sch, NW9
off Blackbird Hill 140 CQ61
Gower Ms, WC1 17 N7
Gower Pl, WC1 17 M4
Gower Rd, E7 13 P5
Horley RH6 290 DE148
Isleworth TW7 179 CF79
Weybridge KT13 235 BR107
Gowers, The, Amer. HP6 77 AS36
Harlow CM20 58 EU13
Gowers La, Orsett RM16 193 GF75
Gower St, WC1 17 M4
Gower's Wk, E1 20 C8
Gowings Grn, Slou. SL1 173 AL75
Gowland Pl, Beck. BR3 225 DZ96
Gowlett Rd, SE15 184 DU83
Gowlland Cl, Croy. CR0 224 DU101
Gowrie Pl, Cat. CR3 258 DQ122
Gowrie Rd, SW11 182 DG83
Graburn Way, E.Mol. KT8 219 CD97
Grace Av, Bexh. DA7 188 EZ82
Shenley WD7 83 CK33
● Grace Business Cen,
Mitch. CR4 222 DF100
Gracechurch St, EC3 19 M10
Grace Cl, SE9 206 EK90
Borehamwood WD6 100 CR39
Edgware HA8
off Pavilion Way 118 CQ52
Ilford IG6 125 ET51
Grace Ct, Slou. SL1 153 AQ74
Gracedale Rd, SW16 203 DH92
Gracefield Gdns, SW16 203 DL90
Grace Jones Cl, E8 10 C5
Grace Path, SE26 204 DW91
Grace Pl, E3 22 D3
Grace Rd, Croy. CR0 224 DQ100
Grace's All, E1 20 C10
Graces Ms, SE5 43 M8
Graces Rd, SE5 43 N8
Grace St, E3 22 D3
Gracious La, Sev. TN13 278 FG130
Gracious La End, Sev. TN14 278 FF130
Gracious Pond Rd, Chobham
GU24 232 AT108
Gradient, The, SE26 204 DU91
Graduate Pl, SE1 off Long La 31 N6
Graeme Rd, Enf. EN1 104 DR40
Graemesdyke Av, SW14 180 CP83
Graemesdyke Rd, Berk. HP4 60 AU20
Grafton Cl, W13 159 CG72
George Green SL3 154 AY72
Hounslow TW4 198 BY88
St. Albans AL4
off Princess Diana Dr 65 CK21
West Byfleet KT14
off Madeira Rd 233 BF113
Worcester Park KT4 220 CS104
Grafton Ct, Felt. TW14 197 BR88
Grafton Cres, NW1 7 J5
Grafton Gdns, N4 144 DQ58
Dagenham RM8 148 EY61
Grafton Ho, E3 22 A3
Grafton Inf & Jun Schs,
Dag. RM8
off Grafton Rd 148 EZ61
Grafton Ms, W1 17 L5
Grafton Pk Rd, Wor.Pk. KT4 220 CS103
Grafton Pl, NW1 17 N3
Grafton Prim Sch, N7
off Eburne Rd 143 DL62
Grafton Rd, NW5 7 J4
W3 160 CQ73
Croydon CR0 223 DN102
Dagenham RM8 148 EY61
Enfield EN2 103 DM41
Harrow HA1 138 CC57
New Malden KT3 220 CS97
Worcester Park KT4 220 CR104
Graftons, The, NW2
off Hermitage La 142 DA62
Grafton Sq, SW4 183 DJ83
Grafton St, W1 29 K1
Grafton Ter, NW5 6 F3
Grafton Way, W1 17 L5
WC1 17 L5
West Molesey KT8 218 BZ98
Grafton Yd, NW5 7 K5
Graham Av, W13 179 CH75
Broxbourne EN10 71 DY20
Mitcham CR4 222 DG95
Graham Cl, Croy. CR0 225 EA103
Hutton CM13 131 GC43
St. Albans AL1 65 CD23
Grahame Pk Est, NW9 118 CS53
Grahame Pk Way, NW7 119 CT52
NW9 119 CT54
Graham Gdns, Surb. KT6 220 CL102
Graham Rd, E8 10 C4
E13 23 N4
N15 143 DP55
NW4 141 CV58
SW19 201 CZ94
W4 180 CR76
Bexleyheath DA6 188 FA84
Hampton TW12 198 CA91
Harrow HA3 139 CE55
Mitcham CR4 222 DG95
Purley CR8 241 DN113
Graham St, N1 19 H1
Graham Ter, SW1 28 G9
Grainger Cl, Nthlt. UB5
off Lancaster Rd 138 CC64
Grainger Rd, N22 122 DQ53
Isleworth TW7 179 CF82
Grainge's Yd, Uxb. UB8
off Cross St 156 BJ66
Grainstore, The, E16 24 A10
Gramer Cl, E11 off Norman Rd 145 ED61
Grammar Sch for Girls
Wilmington, The, Dart.
DA2 off Parsons La 209 FH90
Grampian Cl, Harling. UB3 177 BR80
Orpington BR6
off Clovelly Way 227 ET100
Sutton SM2 240 DC108
Grampian Gdns, NW2 141 CY60
Grampian Ho, N9
off Edmonton Grn Shop Cen. 122 DV47
Grampian Way, Slou. SL3 175 BA78
Gramsci Way, SE6 205 EB90
Granard Av, SW15 201 CV85
● Granard Business Cen,
NW7 off Bunns La 118 CS51
Granard Prim Sch, SW15
off Cortis Rd 201 CV86
Granard Rd, SW12 202 DF87
Granaries, The, Wal.Abb. EN9 90 EE34
Granary, The, Roydon CM19 56 EH14
Stanstead Abbotts SG12 55 EC12
Granary Cl, N9 122 DW45
Horley RH6 off Waterside 290 DG146
Granary Ct, E15 13 H4
Granary Mans, SE28 187 EQ75
Granary Rd, E1 20 E5
Granary Sq, N1 8 F5
Granary St, NW1 7 N9
Granby Pk Rd, Chsht EN7 88 DT28
Granby Pl, SE1 30 E5
Granby Rd, SE9 187 EM82
Gravesend DA11 212 GD85
Granby St, E2 20 B4
Granby Ter, NW1 17 L1
Grand Arc, N12
off Ballards La 120 DC50
Grand Av, EC1 19 H6
N10 142 DG56
Surbiton KT5 220 CP99
Wembley HA9 140 CN64
Grand Av E, Wem. HA9 140 CP64
Grand Av Prim & Nurs Sch,
Surb. KT5 off Grand Av 220 CQ100
Grand Dep Rd, SE18 187 EN78
Grand Dr, SW20 221 CW96
Southall UB2 178 CC75
Granden Rd, SW16 223 DL96
Grandfield Av, Wat. WD17 97 BT39
Grandis Cotts, Ripley GU23 250 BH122
Grandison Rd, SW11 202 DF85
Worcester Park KT4 221 CW103
Grand Junct Isle, Sun. TW16
off Lower Hampton Rd 218 BY96
Grand Junct Wf, N1 19 J1
Grand Par, N4 off Green Las 143 DP58
Wembley HA9 off Forty Av. 140 CN61
Grand Par Ms, SW15 201 CY85
Grand Stand Rd, Epsom KT18 255 CT117
Grand Union Canal Wk, W7 179 CE76
Grand Union Cl, W9 15 H6
Grand Union Cres, E8 10 D7
Grand Union Hts, Wem. HA0 159 CK67
● Grand Union Ind Est,
NW10 160 CP68
Grand Union Wk, NW1 7 K7
Wembley HA0 off Water Rd 160 CM67
Grand Union Way, Kings L.
WD4 81 BP29
Southall UB2 178 CA75
Grand Vw Av, Bigg.H. TN16 260 EJ117
Grand Wk, E1 21 M4
Granfield St, SW11 40 B7
Grange, The, N20 120 DC46
SE1 32 A6
SW19 201 CX93
W14 off Lisgar Ter 26 G9
Chobham GU24 232 AS110
Croydon CR0 225 DZ103
Old Windsor SL4 194 AV85
South Darenth DA4 231 FR95
Walton-on-Thames KT12 217 BV103
Wembley HA0 160 CN66
Worcester Park KT4 220 CR104
Grange Av, N12 120 DC50
N20 119 CY45
SE25 224 DS96
East Barnet EN4 120 DE46
Stanmore HA7 117 CH54
Twickenham TW2 199 CE89
Woodford Green IG8 124 EG51
Grangecliffe Gdns, SE25 224 DS96
Grange Cl, Bletch. RH1 274 DR133
Chalfont St. Peter SL9 112 AY53
Edgware HA8 118 CQ50
Guildford GU2 264 AV130
Hayes UB3 157 BS71
Hemel Hempstead HP2 62 BN21
Hertford SG14 53 DP09
Hounslow TW5 178 BZ79
Ingrave CM13 131 GC50
Leatherhead KT22 253 CK120
Merstham RH1 273 DH128
Sidcup DA15 208 EU90
Watford WD17 97 BU39
West Molesey KT8 218 CB98
Westerham TN16 277 EQ126
Woodford Green IG8 124 EG52
Wraysbury TW19 194 AY86
Grange Comm Inf Sch, The,
New Haw KT15
off The Avenue 234 BG110
Grange Ct, WC2 18 D9
Chigwell IG7 125 EQ47
Loughton IG10 106 EK43
Northolt UB5 158 BW68
Staines TW18
off Gresham Rd 196 BG92
Waltham Abbey EN9 89 EC34
Walton-on-Thames KT12 217 BU103
Grangecourt Rd, N16 144 DS60
Grange Cres, SE28 168 EW72
Chigwell IG7 125 ER50
Dartford DA2 210 FP86
Grangedale Cl, Nthwd. HA6 115 BS53
Grange Dr, Chis. BR7 206 EL93
Merstham RH1 273 DH128
Orpington BR6
off Rushmore Hill 246 EW109
Woking GU21 232 AY114
Wooburn Green HP10 132 AD60
Grange End, Smallfield RH6 291 DN148

Grange Est, The, N2 120 DD54
Grange Fm Cl, Har. HA2 138 CC61
Grange Flds, Chal.St.P. SL9 112 AY53
Grangefields Rd, Jacobs Well
GU4 264 AX128
Grange First Sch, S.Har.
HA2 off Welbeck Rd 138 CB60
Grange Gdns, N14 121 DK46
NW3 142 DB62
SE25 224 DS96
Banstead SM7 240 DB113
Farnham Common SL2 133 AR64
Pinner HA5 138 BZ56
Ware SG12 55 DY07
Grange Gro, N1 9 H4
GRANGE HILL, Chig. IG7 125 ER51
⊖ Grange Hill 125 ER49
Grange Hill, SE25 224 DS96
Edgware HA8 118 CQ50
Grangehill Pl, SE9
off Westmount Rd 187 EM83
Grangehill Rd, SE9 187 EM84
Grange Ho, Bark. IG11
off St. Margarets 167 ER67
Erith DA8 189 FG82
Grange La, SE21 204 DT89
Letchmore Heath WD25 99 CD39
Roydon CM19 72 EJ15
Grange Mans, Epsom KT17 239 CT108
Grange Meadow, Bans. SM7 240 DB113
Grange Mid Sch, S.Har.
HA2 off Welbeck Rd 138 CB60
Grangemill Rd, SE6 205 EA90
Grangemill Way, SE6 205 EA89
Grangemount, Lthd. KT22 253 CK120
GRANGE PARK, N21 103 DP43
⇌ Grange Park 103 DP43
Grange Pk, W5 160 CL74
Woking GU21 248 AY115
Grange Pk Av, N21 103 DP44
Grange Pk Inf & Jun Schs,
Hayes UB4
off Lansbury Dr 157 BT70
Grange Pk Pl, SW20 201 CV94
Grange Pk Prep Sch, N21
off The Chine 103 DP44
Grange Pk Prim Sch, N21
off Worlds End La 103 DN42
Grange Pk Rd, E10 145 EB60
Thornton Heath CR7 224 DR98
Grange Pl, NW6 5 J7
Staines TW18 216 BJ96
Walton-on-Thames KT12 217 BU103
Grange Prim Sch, E13 23 M3
SE1 31 N7
W5 off Church Pl 179 CK75
Grange Rd, E10 145 EA60
E13 23 L3
E17 145 DY57
N6 142 DG58
N17 122 DU51
N18 122 DU51
NW10 161 CV65
SE1 31 P6
SE19 224 DR98
SE25 224 DR98
SW13 181 CU81
W4 180 CP78
W5 159 CK74
Aveley RM15 170 FQ74
Bushey WD23 98 BY43
Caterham CR3 274 DU125
Chalfont St. Peter SL9 112 AY53
Chessington KT9 238 CL105
Edgware HA8 118 CR51
Egham TW20 195 AZ92
Elstree WD6 100 CM43
Gravesend DA11 213 GG87
Grays RM17 192 GB79
Guildford GU2 264 AV129
Harrow HA1 139 CG58
Hayes UB3 157 BS72
Hersham KT12 236 BY105
Ilford IG1 147 EP63
Kingston upon Thames KT1 220 CL97
Leatherhead KT22 253 CK120
New Haw KT15 234 BG110
Orpington BR6 227 EQ103
Romford RM3 127 FH51
Sevenoaks TN13 278 FG127
South Croydon CR2 242 DQ110
South Harrow HA2 139 CD61
Southall UB1 178 BY75
Sutton SM2 240 DA108
Thornton Heath CR7 224 DR98
West Molesey KT8 218 CB98
Woking GU21 232 AY114
Granger Way, Rom. RM1 149 FG58
Grange St, N1 9 M9
St. Albans AL3 65 CD19
Grange Vale, Sutt. SM2 240 DB108
Grange Vw Rd, N20 120 DC46
Grange Wk, SE1 31 P6
Grange Wk Ms, SE1 31 P7
Grangeway, N12 120 DB49
NW6 5 J7
Grange Way, Erith DA8 189 FH80
Iver SL0 155 BF72
Grangeway, Smallfield RH6 291 DN148
Woodford Green IG8 124 EJ49
Grangeway, The, N21 103 DP44
Grangeway Gdns, Ilf. IG4 146 EL57
Grangeways Cl, Nthflt DA11 213 GF91
Grangewood, Bex. DA5 208 EZ88
Potters Bar EN6 86 DB30
Wexham SL3 154 AW71
Grangewood Av, Grays RM16 192 GE76
Rainham RM13 170 FJ70
Grangewood Cl, Brwd. CM13
off Knight's Way 131 GA48
Pinner HA5 137 BU57
Grangewood Dr, Sun. TW16
off Spelthorne Gro 197 BT94
Grangewood Indep Sch,
E7 off Chester Rd 166 EK66
Grangewood La, Beck. BR3 205 DZ93
Grangewood Sch, Eastcote
HA5 off Fore St 137 BT57
Grangewood St, E6 166 EJ67
Grangewood Ter, SE25
off Grange Rd 224 DR96
Grange Yd, SE1 32 A7
Granham Gdns, N9 122 DT47
Granite Apts, E15 13 H4
Granite St, SE18 187 ET78
Granleigh Rd, E11 146 EE61
Gransden Av, E8 10 F7
Gransden Rd, W12
off Wendell Rd 181 CT75
Grant Av, Slou. SL1 154 AS72
Grantbridge St, N1 9 H10
Grantchester Cl, Har. HA1 139 CF62
Grant Cl, N14 121 DJ45
N17 122 DS54
Shepperton TW17 217 BP100
Grant Ct, E4
off The Ridgeway 123 EC46
Grantham Cl, Edg. HA8 118 CL48
Grantham Gdns, Rom. RM6 148 EZ58
Ware SG12 55 DY05
Grantham Grn, Borwd. WD6 100 CQ43
Grantham Ms, Berk. HP4 60 AX19
Grantham Pl, W1 29 J3
Grantham Rd, E12 147 EN63
SW9 42 B9
W4 180 CS80
Grantley Cl, Shalf. GU4 280 AY141
Grantley Gdns, Guil. GU2 264 AU133
Grantley Pl, Esher KT10 236 CB106
Grantley Rd, Guil. GU2 264 AU133
Hounslow TW4 178 BW82
Grantley St, E1 21 J3
Grantock Rd, E17 123 ED53
Granton Av, Upmin. RM14 150 FM61
Granton Prim Sch, SW16
off Granton Rd 203 DJ94
Granton Rd, SW16 223 DJ95
Ilford IG3 148 EU60
Sidcup DA14 208 EW93
Grant Pl, Croy. CR0 224 DT102
Grant Rd, SW11 182 DD84
Croydon CR0 224 DT102
Harrow HA3 139 CF55
Grants Cl, NW7 119 CW52
Grants La, Oxt. RH8 276 EJ132
Grant's Quay Wf, EC3 31 M1
Grant St, E13 23 N3
N1 8 E10
Grantully Rd, W9 15 L3
Grant Way, Islw. TW7 179 CG79
Grantwood Cl, Red. RH1
off Bushfield Dr 289 DH139
Granville Av, N9 122 DW48
Feltham TW13 197 BU89
Hounslow TW3 198 CA85
Slough SL2 153 AR71
Granville Cl, Byfleet KT14
off Church Rd 234 BM113
Croydon CR0 224 DS103
Weybridge KT13 235 BQ107
Granville Ct, N1 9 M8
Granville Dene, Bov. HP3 79 BA27
Granville Gdns, SW16 223 DM95
W5 160 CM74
Hoddesdon EN11 55 EA13
Granville Gro, SE13 185 EC83
● Granville Ind Est, NW2 141 CZ61
Granville Ms, Sid. DA14 208 EU91
Granville Pk, SE13 46 F10
Granville Pl, N12 (N.Finchley)
off High Rd 120 DC52
SW6 39 L5
W1 16 G9
Pinner HA5 138 BX55
Granville Pt, NW2 141 CZ61
Granville Rd, E17 145 EB58
E18 124 EH54
N4 143 DM58
N12 120 DB52
N13 off Russell Rd 121 DM51
N22 121 DP53
NW2 141 CZ61
NW6 15 J1
SW18 202 DA87
SW19 off Russell Rd 202 DA94
Barnet EN5 101 CW42
Epping CM16 92 EV29
Gravesend DA11 213 GF87
Hayes UB3 177 BT77
Ilford IG1 147 EP60
Northchurch HP4 60 AS17
Oxted RH8 276 EF129
St. Albans AL1 65 CF20
Sevenoaks TN13 278 FG124
Sidcup DA14 208 EU91
Uxbridge UB10 157 BP65
Watford WD18 98 BW42
Welling DA16 188 EW83
Westerham TN16 277 EQ126
Weybridge KT13 235 BQ107
Woking GU22 249 AZ120
Granville Sch, The, Sev. TN13
off Bradbourne Pk Rd 278 FG123
Granville Sq, SE15 43 P4
WC1 18 D3
Granville St, WC1 18 D3
Grape St, WC2 18 A8
Graphite Sq, SE11 30 C10
Grapsome Cl, Chess. KT9
off Nigel Fisher Way 237 CJ108
Grasdene Rd, SE18 188 EU80
Grasgarth Cl, W3 160 CQ73
Grasholm Way, Slou. SL3 175 BC77
Grasmere Av, SW15 200 CR91
SW19 222 DA97
W3 160 CQ73
Hounslow TW3 198 CB86
Orpington BR6 227 EP104
Ruislip HA4 137 BQ59
Slough SL2 154 AU73
Wembley HA9 139 CK59
Grasmere Cl, Egh. TW20
off Keswick Rd 195 BB94
Feltham TW14 197 BT88
Guildford GU1 265 BB133
Hemel Hempstead HP3 63 BP22
Loughton IG10 107 EM40
Watford WD25 81 BV32
Grasmere Ct, N22
off Palmerston Rd 121 DM51
Grasmere Gdns, Har. HA3 117 CG54
Ilford IG4 147 EM57
Orpington BR6 227 EP104
Grasmere Pt, SE15 44 G4
Grasmere Prim Sch, N16 9 M1
Grasmere Rd, E13 13 N10
N10 121 DH53
N17 122 DU51
SE25 224 DV100
SW16 203 DM92
Bexleyheath DA7 189 FC81
Bromley BR1 226 EF95
Orpington BR6 227 EP104
Purley CR8 241 DP111
St. Albans AL1 65 CH22
Grasmere Way, Byfleet KT14 234 BM112
Grassbanks, Dart. DA1 210 FM88
Grassfield Cl, Couls. CR5 257 DH119
Grasshaven Way, SE28 167 ET74
Grassingham End, Chal.St.P.
SL9 112 AY52
Grassingham Rd, Chal.St.P.
SL9 112 AY52
Grassington Cl, N11 120 DG50
Bricket Wood AL2 82 CA30
Grassington Rd, Sid. DA14 208 EU91
Grasslands, Smallfield RH6 291 DN148
Grassmere, Horl. RH6 291 DH147
Grassmere Rd, Horn. RM11 150 FM56
Grassmount, SE23 204 DV89
Purley CR8 241 DJ110
Grass Pk, N3 119 CZ53
Grass Warren, Tewin AL6 52 DE06
Grassway, Wall. SM6 241 DJ105
Grassy Cl, Hem.H. HP1 62 BG19
Grassy La, Sev. TN13 279 FH126
Grasvenor Av, Barn. EN5 102 DA44
Grasvenor Av Inf Sch, Barn.
EN5 off Grasvenor Av 102 DA44
Gratton Dr, Wind. SL4 173 AL84
Gratton Rd, W14 26 E7
Gratton Ter, NW2 141 CX62
Gravel Cl, Chig. IG7 126 EU47
Graveley, Kings.T. KT1
off Willingham Way 220 CN96
Graveley Av, Borwd. WD6 100 CQ42
Graveley Ct, Hem.H. HP2 63 BQ21
Graveley Dell, Welw.G.C. AL7 52 DB10
Gravel Hill 243 DY108
Gravel Hill, N3 119 CZ54
Bexleyheath DA6 209 FB85
Chalfont St. Peter SL9 112 AY55
Croydon CR0 243 DX107
Hemel Hempstead HP1 62 BH20
High Beach IG10 106 EG38
Leatherhead KT22
off North St 253 CH121
Uxbridge UB8 136 BK64
Gravel Hill Cl, Bexh. DA6 209 FB85
Gravel Hill Prim Sch,
Bexh. DA6
off Watling St 189 FB84
Gravel Hill Ter, Hem.H. HP1 62 BG21
Gravel La, E1 20 A8
Chigwell IG7 126 EU46
Hemel Hempstead HP1 62 BG21
Gravelly Hill, Cat. CR3 274 DS128
Gravelly Ride, SW19 201 CV91
Gravel Path, Berk. HP4 60 AX19
Hemel Hempstead HP1 62 BG20
Gravel Pit La, SE9 207 EQ85
Gravelpits La, Goms. GU5 283 BQ139
Gravel Pit Way, Orp. BR6 228 EU103
Gravel Rd, Brom. BR2 226 EL103
Sutton at Hone DA4 210 FP94
Twickenham TW2 199 CE88
Gravelwood Cl, Chis. BR7 207 EQ90
Gravely Way, Penn HP10 110 AF45
Gravenel Gdns, SW17
off Nutwell St 202 DE92
Graveney Gro, SE20 204 DW94
Graveney Rd, SW17 202 DE91
Graveney Sch, SW17
off Welham Rd 203 DH92
GRAVESEND, DA11 - DA13 213 GJ85
⇌ Gravesend 213 GG87
Gravesend Adult Ed Cen, Grav.
DA11 off Darnley Rd 213 GG86
Gravesend Gram Sch, Grav.
DA12 off Church Wk 213 GK87
Gravesend Gram Sch for Girls,
Grav. DA11 off Pelham Rd 213 GG88
Gravesend Rd, W12 161 CU73
Gravesham Comm Hosp,
The, Grav. DA11 213 GG86
Gravesham Ct, Grav. DA12
off Clarence Row 213 GH87
★ Gravesham Mus, Grav.
DA11 213 GH86
● Graves Yd Ind Est, Well. DA16
off Upper Wickham La 188 EV82
Gravetts La, Guil. GU3 264 AS131
Gray Av, Dag. RM8 148 EZ60
Grayburn Cl, Ch.St.G. HP8 112 AU47
Gray Cl, Add. KT15
off Monks Cres 234 BH106
Gray Gdns, Rain. RM13 169 FG65
Grayham Cres, N.Mal. KT3 220 CR98
Grayham Rd, N.Mal. KT3 220 CR98
Grayland Cl, Brom. BR1 226 EK95
Graylands, They.B. CM16 107 ER37
Woking GU21 248 AY116
Graylands Cl, Wok. GU21 248 AY116
Grayling Cl, E16 23 K4
Grayling Ct, Berk. HP4
off Admiral Way 60 AT17
Grayling Rd, N16 144 DR61
Graylings, The, Abb.L. WD5 81 BR33
Grayling Sq, E2 20 D2
Gray Pl, Ott. KT16
off Clarendon Gate 233 BD107
GRAYS, RM16 & RM17; RM20 192 GA78
⇌ Grays 192 GA79
Grays Conv High Sch, Grays
RM17 off College Av 192 GB77
Grayscroft Rd, SW16 203 DK94
Grays End Cl, Grays RM17 192 GA76
Gray's Fm Prim Sch, Orp.
BR5 off Grays Fm Rd 228 EV95
Grays Fm Rd, Orp. BR5 228 EV95
Graysfield, Welw.G.C. AL7 52 DA12
Grayshott Rd, SW11 40 G9
★ Gray's Inn, WC1 18 D6
Gray's Inn Pl, WC1 18 D7
Gray's Inn Rd, WC1 18 C3
Gray's Inn Sq, WC1 18 E6
Grays La, Ashf. TW15 197 BP91
Gray's La, Ashtd. KT21 254 CM119
Epsom KT18 254 CN120
Grayson Ho, EC1 19 K3
Grays Pk Rd, Stoke P. SL2 154 AU68
Grays Pl, Slou. SL2 154 AT74
Grays Rd, Gdmg. GU7 280 AT144
Slough SL1 154 AT74
Uxbridge UB10 156 BL67
Westerham TN16 261 EP121
Grays Sch Media Arts Coll,
The, Grays RM17
off Hathaway Rd 192 GB76
Grays Shop Cen, Grays
RM17 off High St 192 GA79
Gray St, SE1 30 F5
Grays Wk, Chesh. HP5 76 AP29
Hutton CM13 131 GD45
Grays Wd, Horl. RH6 291 DJ148
Grayswood Gdns, SW20
off Farnham Gdns 221 CV96
Grayswood Pt, SW15
off Norley Vale 201 CU88
Gray's Yd, W1 17 H9
Graywood Ct, N12 120 DC52
Grazebrook Prim Sch,
N16 off Lordship Rd 144 DR61
Grazebrook Rd, N16 144 DR61
Grazeley Cl, Bexh. DA6 209 FC85
Grazeley Ct, SE19
off Gipsy Hill 204 DS92
Grazings, The, Hem.H. HP2 62 BM18
Greatacre, Chesh. HP5 76 AR30
Great Acre Ct, SW4
off Clapham Pk Rd 183 DK84
GREAT AMWELL, Ware SG12 55 DZ10
Great Amwell La, N8 143 DM55
Great Arthur Ho, EC1 19 J5
Great Auger St, Harl. CM17 58 EX14
Great Bell All, EC2 19 L8
Great Benty, West Dr. UB7 176 BL77
Great Bois Wd, Amer. HP6
off Manor Dr 77 AQ36
GREAT BOOKHAM, Lthd.
KT23 268 CB125
★ Great Bookham Common,
Lthd. KT23 252 BZ121
Great Braitch La, Hat. AL10 51 CT14
Great Brays, Harl. CM18 74 EU16
Great Break, Welw.G.C. AL7 52 DB10
Great Brownings, SE21 204 DT91
Great Bushey Dr, N20 120 DB46
Great Cambridge Ind Est,
Enf. EN1 104 DU43
Great Cambridge Junct,
N18 122 DR49
Great Cambridge Rd, N9 122 DS46
N17 122 DR50
N18 122 DR50
Cheshunt EN8 88 DW34
Enfield EN1 104 DU42
Turnford EN10 89 DY26
Great Castle St, W1 17 K8
Great Cen Av, Ruis. HA4 138 BW64
Great Cen St, NW1 16 E6
Great Cen Way, NW10 140 CS64
Wembley HA9 140 CQ63
Great Chapel St, W1 17 N8
Great Chart St, SW11 182 DD84
Great Chertsey Rd, W4 180 CQ82
Feltham TW13 198 CA90
Great Ch La, W6 26 D10
Great Coll St, SW1 30 A6
Great Conduit, Welw.G.C. AL7 52 DC08
Great Cross Av, SE10 47 J5
Great Cullings, Rom. RM7 149 FE61
Great Cumberland Ms, W1 16 E9
Great Cumberland Pl, W1 16 E8
Great Dell, Welw.G.C. AL8 51 CX07
Great Dover St, SE1 31 K5
Greatdown Rd, W7 159 CF70
● Great Eastern Enterprise Cen,
E14 34 C5
Great Eastern Rd, E15 12 G6
Warley CM14 130 FW49
Great Eastern St, EC2 19 N3
Great Eastern Wk, EC2 19 P7
Great Ellshams, Bans. SM7 256 DA116
Great Elms Rd, Brom. BR2 226 EJ98
Hemel Hempstead HP3 62 BM24
Great Fld, NW9 118 CS53
Greatfield Av, E6 25 J4
Greatfield Cl, N19
off Warrender Rd 143 DJ63
SE4 185 EA84
Greatfields Dr, Uxb. UB8 156 BN71
Greatfields Rd, Bark. IG11 167 ER67
Great Fleete Way, Bark. IG11
off Choats Rd 168 EW68
Greatford Dr, Guil. GU1 265 BD134
Great Galley Cl, Bark. IG11 168 EV69
Great Ganett, Welw.G.C. AL7 52 DB11
Great Gdns Rd, Horn. RM11 149 FH58
Great Gatton Cl, Croy. CR0 225 DY101
Great George St, SW1 29 P5
Great Goodwin Dr, Guil. GU1 265 BB132
Great Gregories La, Epp. CM16 91 ES33
Great Gro, Bushey WD23 98 CB42
Great Gros, Goffs Oak EN7 88 DS28
Great Guildford St, SE1 31 J2
Great Hall, SW11
off Battersea Pk Rd 41 H6
Greatham Rd, Bushey WD23 98 BX41
● Greatham Rd Ind Est,
Bushey WD23 98 BX41
Greatham Wk, SW15 201 CU88
Great Harry Dr, SE9 207 EN90
Great Heart, Hem.H. HP2 62 BL18
Great Heath, Hat. AL10 67 CV15
GREAT HIVINGS, Chesh. HP5 76 AP27
Great Hivings, Chesh. HP5 76 AN27
Greathurst End, Bkhm KT23 252 BZ124
Great James St, WC1 18 C5
Great Julians, Rick. WD3 96 BN42
Great Lake Ct, Horl. RH6
off Tanyard Way 291 DH147
Great Ley, Welw.G.C. AL7 51 CY11
Great Leylands, Harl. CM18 74 EU16
Great Marlborough St, W1 17 L9
Great Maze Pond, SE1 31 M4
Great Meadow, Brox. EN10 71 EA22
Great Molewood, Hert. SG14 53 DP06
Great Nelmes Chase, Horn.
RM11 150 FM57
Greatness La, Sev. TN14 279 FJ121
Greatness Rd, Sev. TN14 279 FJ121
Great Newport St, WC2
off Charing Cross Rd 17 P10
Great New St, EC4 18 F8
● Great N Leisure Pk, N12 120 DD52
Great N Rd, N2 142 DE56
N6 142 DE56
Barnet EN5 101 CZ38
Hatfield AL9, AL10 67 CZ23
New Barnet EN5 102 DA43
Potters Bar EN6 86 DB27
Welwyn Garden City AL8 51 CU10
Great N Way, NW4 119 CW54
Great Oak Ct, Hunsdon SG12 56 EK08
Great Oaks, Chig. IG7 125 EQ49
Hutton CM13 131 GB44
Great Oaks Pk, Guil. GU4 265 BB129
Greatorex St, E1 20 C6
Great Ormond St, WC1 18 B6
Great Ormond St Hosp for
Children, The, WC1 18 B5
Great Owl Rd, Chig. IG7 125 EN48
Great Palmers, Hem.H. HP2 62 BM15
Great Pk, Kings L. WD4 80 BM30
GREAT PARNDON, Harl. CM19 73 EP17
Great Percy St, WC1 18 D2
Great Peter St, SW1 29 N7
Great Pettits Ct, Rom. RM1 127 FE54
Great Plumtree, Harl. CM20 57 ET13
⊖ Great Portland Street 17 K5
Great Portland St, W1 17 K6
Great Pulteney St, W1 17 M10
Great Quarry, Guil. GU1 280 AX137
Great Queen St, WC2 18 B9
Dartford DA1 210 FM87
Great Rd, Hem.H. HP2 62 BM19
Great Ropers La, Gt Warley
CM13 129 FU51
Great Russell St, WC1 17 P8
Great St. Helens, EC3 19 N8
Great St. Thomas Apostle, EC4 19 K10
Great Scotland Yd, SW1 30 A3
Great Slades, Pot.B. EN6 85 CZ33
Great Smith St, SW1 29 P6
Great South-West Rd, Felt.
TW14 197 BQ87
Hounslow TW4 177 BT84
Great Spilmans, SE22 204 DS85
Great Stockwood Rd, Chsht
EN7 88 DR26
Great Strand, NW9 119 CT53
Great Sturgess Rd, Hem.H. HP1 61 BF20
Great Suffolk St, SE1 31 H3
Great Sutton St, EC1 19 H5
Great Swan All, EC2 19 L8
Great Tattenhams, Epsom
KT18 255 CV118
Great Thrift, Petts Wd BR5 227 EQ98
Great Till Cl, Otford TN14 263 FE116
Great Titchfield St, W1 17 L8
Great Twr St, EC3 19 N10
Great Trade Cen, NW10
off Hythe Rd 161 CU70
Great Trinity La, EC4 19 K10
Great Turnstile, WC1 18 D7
GREAT WARLEY, Brwd. CM14 129 FV53
Great Warley St, Gt Warley
CM13 129 FU53
Great Western Rd, W2 15 J7
W9 15 H5
W11 15 J7
● Great W Ho, Brent. TW8 179 CJ79
Great W Rd, W4 180 CP78
W6 181 CT78
Brentford TW8 180 CP78
Hounslow TW5 178 BX82
Isleworth TW7 179 CF80
Great Whites Rd, Hem.H. HP3 62 BM22
Great Winchester St, EC2 19 M8
Great Windmill St, W1 17 N10
Greatwood, Chis. BR7 207 EN94
Greatwood Cl, Ott. KT16 233 BC109
Great Woodcote Dr, Pur. CR8 241 DK110
Great Woodcote Pk, Pur. CR8 241 DK110
Great Yd, SE1 31 P4
Greaves Cl, Bark. IG11 167 ER66
Greaves Pl, SW17 202 DE91
Greaves Twr, SW10 39 P4
Grebe Av, Hayes UB4
off Cygnet Way 158 BX72
Grebe Cl, E7 13 M2
E17 123 DY52
Barking IG11 168 EU70
Grebe Ct, Sutt. SM1 239 CZ106
Grebe Crest, Grays RM20 191 FU77
Grecian Cres, SE19 203 DP93
Greding Wk, Hutt. CM13 131 GB47
Greek Ct, W1 17 P9
★ Greek Orthodox Cath of the
Divine Wisdom (St. Sophia),
W2 15 K10
Greek St, W1 17 P9
Greek Yd, WC2 18 A10
Green, The, E4 123 EC46
E11 146 EH58
E15 13 K5
N9 122 DU47
N14 121 DK48
N21 121 DN45
SW14 180 CQ83
SW19 201 CX92
W3 160 CS72
W5 off High St 159 CK73
Amersham HP7 77 AR38
Bexleyheath DA7 188 FA81
Bovingdon HP3 79 BA29
Bromley BR1
off Downham Way 206 EG90
Burgh Heath KT20 255 CY119
Burnham SL1 152 AH70
Carshalton SM5
off High St 240 DG105
Chalfont St. Giles HP8
off High St 112 AW47
Chalvey SL1 173 AR75
Cheshunt EN8 88 DW28
Claygate KT10 237 CF107
Croxley Green WD3 96 BN44
Croydon CR0 243 DZ109
Dartford DA2 211 FR89
Datchet SL3 174 AV80
Englefield Green TW20 194 AW91
Epsom KT17 239 CU111
Feltham TW13 197 BV89
Fetcham KT22 253 CD124
Harefield UB9 114 BJ53
Havering-atte-Bower RM4 127 FE48
Hayes UB3 off Wood End 157 BS72
Hayes BR2 226 EG101
Hounslow TW5
off Heston Rd 178 CA79
Ickenham UB10 137 BQ61
Letchmore Heath WD25 99 CE39
London Colney AL2 83 CK27
Matching Tye CM17 59 FE12
Morden SM4 221 CY98
New Malden KT3 220 CQ97
Otford TN14 263 FH116
Potten End HP4 61 BB17
Pratt's Bottom BR6
off Rushmore Hill 246 EW110
Richmond TW9 199 CK85
Ripley GU23 250 BH121
St. Paul's Cray BR5
off The Avenue 208 EV94
Sarratt WD3 96 BG35

Green, The, Seal TN15
off Church Rd … 279 FM121
Sevenoaks TN13 … 279 FK122
Shepperton TW17 … 217 BS98
Sidcup DA14 … 208 EU91
South Ockendon RM15 … 171 FW69
Southall UB2 … 178 BY76
Sutton SM1 … 222 DB104
Theydon Bois CM16 … 107 ES37
Twickenham TW2 … 199 CE88
Waltham Abbey EN9
off Sewardstone Rd … 89 EC34
Warlingham CR6 … 259 DX117
Welling DA16 … 187 ES84
Welwyn Garden City AL7 … 52 DA11
Wembley HA0 … 139 CG61
Wennington RM13 … 170 FL73
West Drayton UB7 … 176 BK76
West Tilbury RM18 … 193 GL79
Westerham TN16 … 277 ER126
Whiteley Village KT12
off Octagon Rd … 235 BS110
Woldingham CR3 … 259 EA123
Wooburn Green HP10 … 132 AE58
Woodford Green IG8 … 124 EG50
Wraysbury TW19 … 194 AY86
Greenacre, Dart. DA1 … 210 FK89
Knaphill GU21
off Mead Ct … 248 AS116
Windsor SL4 … 173 AL82
Greenacre Cl, Barn. EN5 … 101 CZ38
Northolt UB5 … 138 BZ64
Swanley BR8 … 229 FE96
Greenacre Ct, Eng.Grn TW20 … 194 AW93
Greenacre Gdns, E17 … 145 EC56
Greenacre Pl, Hackbr. SM6
off Park Rd … 223 DH103
Greenacres, N3 … 119 CY54
SE9 … 207 EN86
Barnet EN4 … 102 DD42
Bookham KT23 … 252 CB124
Bushey Heath WD23 … 117 CD47
Green Acres, Croy. CR0 … 224 DT104
Greenacres, Dart. DA2 … 210 FP86
Epping CM16 … 91 ET29
Green Acres, Hem.H. HP2 … 63 BR21
Greenacres, Lwr Kgswd KT20 … 271 CZ128
Oxted RH8 … 276 EE127
Green Acres, Welw.G.C. AL7 … 51 CZ12
Greenacres Av, Uxb. UB10 … 136 BM62
Sch Greenacre Sch, Bans.
SM7 off Sutton La … 240 DB113
Greenacres Cl, Orp. BR6 … 245 EQ105
Rainham RM13 … 170 FL69
Greenacres Dr, Stan. HA7 … 117 CH52
Sch Greenacres Prim Sch, SE9
off Witherston Way … 207 EN89
Greenacre Sq, SE16 … 33 K4
Greenacre Wk, N14 … 121 DK48
Greenall Cl, Chsht EN8 … 89 DY30
Green Arbour Ct, EC1 … 18 G8
Green Av, NW7 … 118 CR49
W13 … 179 CH76
Greenaway Av, N18 … 123 DX51
Greenaway Gdns, NW3 … 5 L1
Green Bk, E1 … 32 E3
N12 … 120 DB49
Greenbank, Chsht EN8 … 88 DV28
Greenbank Av, Wem. HA0 … 139 CG64
Greenbank Cl, E4 … 123 EC47
Romford RM3 … 128 FK48
Greenbank Cres, NW4 … 141 CY56
Greenbank Rd, Wat. WD17 … 97 BR36
Greenbanks, Dart. DA1 … 210 FL89
St. Albans AL1 … 65 CF22
Upminster RM14 … 151 FS60
Greenbay Rd, SE7 … 186 EK80
Greenberry St, NW8 … 16 C1
Greenbrook Av, Barn. EN4 … 102 DC39
Greenbury Cl, Chorl. WD3 … 95 BC41
● Green Business Cen,
Stai. TW18
off The Glanty … 195 BC91
Green Cl, NW9 … 140 CQ58
NW11 … 142 DC59
Bromley BR2 … 226 EE97
Brookmans Park AL9 … 85 CY26
Carshalton SM5 … 222 DF103
Cheshunt EN8 … 89 DY32
Epping Green CM16 … 73 EP24
Feltham TW13 … 198 BY92
Taplow SL6 … 152 AG72
Greencoates, Hert. SG13 … 54 DS10
Greencoat Pl, SW1 … 29 M8
Greencoat Row, SW1 … 29 M7
Sch Green C of E Prim Sch, The,
N17 off Somerset Rd … 144 DT55
Green Common La, Woob.Grn
HP10 … 132 AG59
Greencourt Av, Croy. CR0 … 224 DV103
Edgware HA8 … 118 CP53
Greencourt Gdns, Croy. CR0 … 224 DV102
Greencourt Rd, Petts Wd BR5 … 227 ER99
Green Ct Rd, Swan. BR8 … 229 FD99
Green Cres, Flack.Hth HP10 … 132 AC56
Greencrest Pl, NW2
off Dollis Hill La … 141 CU62
Greencroft, Edg. HA8 … 118 CQ50
Guildford GU1 … 265 BB134
Green Cft, Hat. AL10
off Talbot Rd … 67 CU15
Greencroft Av, Ruis. HA4 … 138 BW61
Greencroft Cl, E6 … 24 G7
Greencroft Gdns, NW6 … 5 L7
Enfield EN1 … 104 DS41
Greencroft Rd, Houns. TW5 … 178 BZ81
Green Curve, Bans. SM7 … 239 CZ114
Green Dale, SE5 … 184 DR84
SE22 … 204 DS85
Green Dale Cl, SE22
off Green Dale … 204 DS85
Greendale Ms, Slou. SL2 … 154 AU73
Greendale Wk, Nthflt DA11 … 212 GE90
Green Dell Way, Hem.H. HP3 … 63 BP20
Green Dene, E.Hors. KT24 … 267 BT131
Green Dragon Ct, SE1 … 31 L2
Green Dragon La, N21 … 103 DP44
Brentford TW8 … 180 CL78
Sch Green Dragon Prim Sch,
Brent. TW8 off North Rd … 180 CL79
Green Dragon Yd, E1 … 20 C7
Green Dr, Maid. SL6 … 152 AE65
Ripley GU23 … 249 BF123
Slough SL3 … 174 AY77
Southall UB1 … 158 CA74
Green E Rd, Jordans HP9 … 112 AS52
Green Edge, Wat. WD25
off Clarke Grn … 97 BU35
Greene Fielde End, Stai. TW18 … 196 BK94
Green Fld Rd, Berk. HP4 … 60 AW19
Green End, N21 … 121 DP47
Chessington KT9 … 238 CL105
● Green End Business Cen,
Sarratt WD3 … 96 BG37
Green End Gdns, Hem.H. HP1 … 62 BG21
Green End La, Hem.H. HP1 … 61 BF20
Greenend Rd, W4 … 180 CS75
Green End Rd, Hem.H. HP1 … 62 BG21
Greener Ct, Enf. EN3
off Martini Dr … 105 EA37
Greenes Ct, Berk. HP4
off Lower Kings Rd … 60 AW18
Greene Wk, Berk. HP4 … 60 AX20
Green Fm Cl, Orp. BR6 … 245 ET106
Greenfell Mans, SE8 … 46 C2
Greenfern Av, Slou. SL1 … 152 AJ72
Greenfield, Hat. AL9 … 67 CX15
Welwyn Garden City AL8 … 51 CX06
Greenfield Av, Surb. KT5 … 220 CP101
Watford WD19 … 116 BX47
Greenfield Dr, N2 … 142 DF56
Bromley BR1 … 226 EJ96
Greenfield End, Chal.St.P. SL9 … 112 AY51
Greenfield Gdns, NW2 … 141 CY61
Dagenham RM9 … 168 EX67
Petts Wood BR5 … 227 ER101
Greenfield Link, Couls. CR5 … 257 DL115
Greenfield Rd, E1 … 20 D7
N15 … 144 DS57
Dagenham RM9 … 168 EW67
Dartford DA2 … 209 FD92
Greenfields, Cuffley EN6
off South Dr … 87 DL30
Loughton IG10 … 107 EN42
Sch Greenfield Sch, Wok. GU22
off Brooklyn Rd … 248 AY119
Greenfields Cl, Gt Warley
CM13 … 129 FW51
Horley RH6 … 290 DE146
Loughton IG10 … 107 EN42
Sch Greenfields Prim Sch, S.Oxhey
WD19 off Ellesborough Cl … 116 BW50
Greenfields Rd, Horl. RH6 … 290 DE146
Greenfield St, Wal.Abb. EN9 … 89 EC34
Greenfield Way, Har. HA2 … 138 CB55
GREENFORD, UB6 … 158 CB69
⇌ Greenford … 159 CD67
⊖ Greenford … 159 CD67
Greenford Av, W7 … 159 CE70
Southall UB1 … 158 BZ73
Greenford Gdns, Grnf. UB6 … 158 CB69
● Greenford Grn Business Pk,
Grnf. UB6 … 159 CE67
Sch Greenford High Sch, Sthl. UB1
off Lady Margaret Rd … 158 CA69
Greenford Rd, Grnf. UB6 … 158 CC71
Harrow HA1 … 139 CE64
Southall UB1 … 158 CC74
Sutton SM1 … 240 DB105
Jct Greenford Rbt, Grnf. UB6 … 159 CD68
Green Gdns, Orp. BR6 … 245 EQ106
Greengate, Grnf. UB6 … 159 CH65
Greengate St, E13 … 24 A1
Green Glade, They.B. CM16 … 107 ES37
Green Glades, Horn. RM11 … 150 FM58
Greenhalgh Wk, N2 … 142 DC56
Greenham Cl, SE1 … 30 E5
Greenham Cres, E4 … 123 DZ51
Greenham Rd, N10 … 120 DG54
Greenham Wk, Wok. GU21 … 248 AW118
Greenhaven Dr, SE28 … 168 EV72
Greenhayes Av, Bans. SM7 … 240 DA114
Greenhayes Cl, Reig. RH2 … 272 DC134
Greenhayes Gdns, Bans. SM7 … 256 DA115
● Greenheath Business Cen,
E2 off Three Colts La … 20 F4
Greenheys Cl, Nthwd. HA6 … 115 BS53
Greenheys Dr, E18 … 146 EF55
Greenheys Pl, Wok. GU22
off White Rose La … 249 AZ118
Greenhill, NW3 … 6 A1
Green Hill, SE18 … 187 EM78
Buckhurst Hill IG9 … 124 EJ46
Downe BR6 … 244 EL112
Greenhill, Sutt. SM1 … 222 DC103
Wembley HA9 … 140 CP61
Greenhill Av, Cat. CR3 … 258 DV121
Greenhill Cres, Wat. WD18 … 97 BS44
Greenhill Gdns, Guil. GU4 … 265 BC131
Northolt UB5 … 158 BZ68
Greenhill Gro, E12 … 146 EL63
Green Hill La, Warl. CR6 … 259 DY117
Greenhill Par, New Barn.
EN5 off Great N Rd … 102 DB43
Greenhill Pk, NW10 … 160 CS67
New Barnet EN5 … 102 DB43
Greenhill Rd, NW10 … 160 CS67
Harrow HA1 … 139 CE58
Northfleet DA11 … 213 GF89
Greenhills, Harl. CM20 … 73 ES15
Greenhills Cl, Rick. WD3 … 96 BH43
Greenhill's Rents, EC1 … 18 G6
Greenhills Ter, N1 … 9 M5
Greenhill Ter, SE18 … 37 K10
Northolt UB5 … 158 BZ68
Greenhill Way, Croy. CR0 … 243 DX111
Harrow HA1 … 139 CE58
Wembley HA9 … 140 CP61
GREENHITHE, DA9 … 211 FV85
⇌ Greenhithe … 211 FU85
Greenhithe Cl, Sid. DA15 … 207 ES87
Greenholm Rd, SE9 … 207 EP85
Green Hundred Rd, SE15 … 44 D3
Greenhurst La, Oxt. RH8 … 276 EG132
Greenhurst Rd, SE27 … 203 DN92
Greening St, SE2 … 188 EW77
Green Knight Ct, N9
off Galahad Rd … 122 DU48
Greenlake Ter, Stai. TW18 … 195 BF94
Greenland Cres, Sthl. UB2 … 178 BW76
Greenland Ms, SE8 … 45 K1
Riv Greenland Pier … 33 N7
Greenland Pl, NW1 … 7 K8
Greenland Quay, SE16 … 33 K8
Greenland Rd, NW1 … 7 K8
Barnet EN5 … 101 CW44
Greenlands, Ott. KT16 … 215 BC104
Greenlands La, NW4 … 119 CV53
Greenlands Rd, Stai. TW18 … 196 BG91
Weybridge KT13 … 217 BP104
Greenland St, NW1 … 7 K8
Greenland Way, Croy. CR0 … 223 DK101
Green La, E4 … 106 EE41
NW4 … 141 CX57
SE9 … 207 EN89
SE20 … 205 DX94
SW16 … 203 DM94
W7 … 179 CE75
Addlestone KT15 … 216 BG104
Amersham HP6 … 77 AS38
Ashtead KT21 … 253 CJ117
Bletchingley RH1 … 274 DS131
Bovingdon HP3 … 79 AZ28
Broxbourne EN10 … 71 EB23
Burnham SL1 … 153 AK66
Byfleet KT14 … 234 BM112
Caterham CR3 … 258 DQ122
Chertsey KT16 … 215 BE103
Chesham HP5 … 78 AV33
Chesham Bois HP6 … 77 AR35
Chessington KT9 … 238 CL109
Chigwell IG7 … 125 ER47
Chipstead CR5 … 272 DA125
Chislehurst BR7 … 207 EP91
Chobham GU24 … 232 AT110
Cobham KT11 … 236 BY112
Croxley Green WD3 … 96 BM43
Dagenham RM8 … 148 EU60
Datchet SL3 … 174 AV81
Edgware HA8 … 118 CN50
Egham TW20 … 195 BB91
Farnham Common SL2 … 133 AP64
Feltham TW13 … 198 BY92
Fifield SL6 … 172 AC81
Godalming GU7 … 280 AS142
Guildford GU1 … 265 BB134
Harrow HA1 … 139 CE62
Hemel Hempstead HP2 … 63 BQ21
Hersham KT12 … 235 BV107
Hounslow TW4 … 177 BV83
Ilford IG1, IG3 … 147 EQ61
Leatherhead KT22 … 253 CK121
Lower Kingswood KT20 … 271 CZ126
Mayford GU24
off Copper Beech Cl … 248 AV121
Morden SM4 … 222 DB100
New Malden KT3 … 220 CQ99
Northwood HA6 … 115 BT52
Ockham GU23 … 251 BP124
Outwood RH1 … 289 DL141
Panshanger AL7 … 52 DD10
Pilgrim's Hatch CM15 … 130 FV43
Purley CR8 … 241 DJ111
Redhill RH1 … 272 DE132
Reigate RH2 … 271 CZ134
St. Albans AL3 … 65 CD16
Shamley Green GU5 … 282 BG144
Shepperton TW17 … 217 BQ100
Shipley Bridge RH6 … 291 DM152
South Ockendon RM15 … 171 FR69
Staines TW18 … 215 BE95
Stanmore HA7 … 117 CH49
Sunbury-on-Thames TW16 … 197 BT94
Thornton Heath CR7 … 223 DN95
Thorpe TW20 … 215 BD95
Threshers Bush CM17 … 74 FA16
Upminster RM14 … 171 FR68
Uxbridge UB8 … 157 BQ71
Waltham Abbey EN9 … 90 EJ34
Warley CM14 … 129 FU52
Warlingham CR6 … 259 DY116
Watford WD19 … 116 BW46
West Clandon GU4 … 266 BG127
West Molesey KT8 … 218 CB99
White Bushes RH1 … 288 DG139
Windsor SL4 … 173 AP82
Worcester Park KT4 … 221 CU102
Green La Av, Hersham KT12 … 236 BW106
Green La Cl, Amer. HP6 … 77 AR36
Byfleet KT14 … 234 BM112
Chertsey KT16 … 215 BE103
Green La Gdns, Th.Hth. CR7 … 224 DQ96
Sch Green La Prim & Nurs Sch,
Wor.Pk. KT4 off Green La … 221 CV101
Green Las, N4 … 144 DQ60
N8 … 143 DP55
N13 … 121 DM51
N15 … 143 DP55
N16 … 144 DQ62
N21 … 121 DP46
Epsom KT19 … 238 CS109
Hatfield AL10 … 51 CT13
Lemsford AL8 … 51 CT11
Sch Green Las Prim Sch, Hat.
AL10 off Green Las … 51 CT14
Green La W, Wok. GU23 … 266 BN125
Greenlaw Ct, W5 … 159 CK72
Greenlaw Gdns, N.Mal. KT3 … 221 CT101
Greenlawn La, Brent. TW8 … 179 CK77
Green Lawns, Ruis. HA4 … 138 BW60
Greenlaw St, SE18 … 37 L7
Green Leaf Av, Wall. SM6 … 241 DK105
Greenleaf Cl, SW2 … 203 DN87
Greenleafe Dr, Ilf. IG6 … 147 EP55
Sch Greenleaf Prim Sch, E17
off Greenleaf Rd … 145 DZ55
Greenleaf Rd, E6
off Redclyffe Rd … 166 EJ67
E17 … 145 DZ55
Greenleaf Way, Har. HA3 … 139 CF55
● Greenlea Pk, SW19 … 202 DD94
Green Leas, Sun. TW16 … 197 BT93
Greenleas, Wal.Abb. EN9 … 105 ED35
Green Leas Cl, Sun. TW16 … 197 BT94
Greenleaves Ct, Ashf. TW15
off Redleaves Av … 197 BP93
Greenleigh Av, St.P.Cray BR5 … 228 EV98
Greenlink Wk, Rich. TW9 … 180 CP81
Green Man Ct, Eastwick CM20
off Eastwick Hall La … 57 EN11
Green Man Gdns, W13 … 159 CG73
Green Man La, W13 … 159 CG74
Feltham TW14 … 177 BU84
Green Manor Way, Grav. DA11 … 192 FZ84
Green Man Pas, W13 … 159 CH73
Green Man Rd, Ong. CM5 … 75 FD19
Jct Green Man Rbt, E11 … 146 EF59
Greenman St, N1 … 9 J7
Green Mead, Esher KT10
off Winterdown Gdns … 236 BZ107
Greenmead Cl, SE25 … 224 DU99
Green Meadow, Pot.B. EN6 … 86 DA30
Greenmeads, Wok. GU22 … 248 AY122
Sch Greenmead Sch, SW15
off St. Margaret's Cres … 201 CV85
Green Moor Link, N21 … 121 DP45
Greenmoor Rd, Enf. EN3 … 104 DW40
Green N Rd, Jordans HP9 … 112 AS51
Greenoak Pl, Cockfos. EN4 … 102 DF40
Greenoak Ri, Bigg.H. TN16 … 260 EJ118
Greenoak Way, SW19 … 201 CX91
Greenock Rd, SW16 … 223 DK95
W3 … 180 CP76
Slough SL1 … 153 AN72
Greenock Way, Rom. RM1 … 127 FE52
Greeno Cres, Shep. TW17 … 216 BN99
⊖ Green Park … 29 L3
Green Pk, Harl. CM20 … 73 ES15
Staines TW18 … 195 BE90
★ Green Park, The, SW1 … 29 K3
Greenpark Ct, Wem. HA0 … 159 CJ66
Green Pk Way, Grnf. UB6 … 159 CE67
Green Pl, SE10 … 35 J4
Dartford DA1 … 209 FE85
Green Pt, E15 … 13 K5
Green Pond Cl, E17 … 145 DZ55
Green Pond Rd, E17 … 145 DY55
Green Ride, Epp. CM16 … 107 EP35
Loughton IG10 … 106 EG43
Green Rd, N14 … 103 DH44
N20 … 120 DC48
Thorpe TW20 … 215 BB98
Greenroof Way, SE10 … 35 M7
Greensand Cl, S.Merst. RH1 … 273 DK128
Green Sand Rd, Red. RH1 … 272 DG133
Greensand Way, Bet. RH3 … 286 CM136
Dorking RH5 … 286 CM136
Godstone RH9 … 274 DV134
South Nutfield RH1 … 289 DP135
Sch Green Sch, The, Islw. TW7
off London Rd … 179 CG81
Greens Cl, The, Loug. IG10 … 107 EN40
Green's Ct, W1 … 17 N10
Green's End, SE18 … 37 N8
Greenshank Cl, E17
off Banbury Rd … 123 DY52
Greenshaw, Brwd. CM14 … 130 FV46
Sch Greenshaw High Sch, Sutt.
SM1 off Grennell Rd … 222 DD103
● Greenshields Ind Est, E16 … 35 P3
Greenside, Bex. DA5 … 208 EY88
Borehamwood WD6 … 100 CN38
Dagenham RM8 … 148 EW60
Slough SL2 … 153 AN71
Swanley BR8 … 229 FD96
Greenside Cl, N20 … 120 DD47
SE6 … 205 ED89
Guildford GU4 … 265 BC131
Greenside Dr, Ashtd. KT21 … 253 CH118
Sch Greenside Prim Sch, W12
off Westville Rd … 181 CU75
Greenside Rd, W12 … 181 CU76
Croydon CR0 … 223 DN101
Greenside Wk, Bigg.H. TN16
off Kings Rd … 260 EH118
Greenslade Av, Ashtd. KT21 … 254 CP119
Sch Greenslade Prim Sch,
SE18 off Erindale … 187 ER79
Greenslade Rd, Bark. IG11 … 167 ER66
Greensleeves Cl, St.Alb. AL4 … 65 CJ21
Greensleeves Dr, Warley CM14 … 130 FV50
Greenstead, Saw. CM21 … 58 EY06
Greenstead Av, Wdf.Grn. IG8 … 124 EJ52
Greenstead Cl, Hutt. CM13 … 131 GE45
Woodford Green IG8
off Greenstead Gdns … 124 EJ51
Greenstead Gdns, SW15 … 201 CU85
Woodford Green IG8 … 124 EJ51
Greensted Ct, Whyt. CR3
off Godstone Rd … 258 DU119
GREENSTED GREEN, Ong.
CM5 … 93 FH28
Greensted Rd, Loug. IG10 … 124 EL45
Ongar CM5 … 93 FG28
Greenstone Ms, E11 … 146 EG58
GREEN STREET, Borwd. WD6 … 100 CP37
Green St, E7 … 166 EH65
E13 … 166 EJ67
W1 … 16 F10
Borehamwood WD6 … 100 CN36
Enfield EN3 … 104 DW40
Harlow CM17 … 58 EX14
Hatfield AL9 … 67 CZ21
Hertford SG14 … 54 DR09
Rickmansworth WD3 … 95 BC40
Shenley WD7 … 100 CN36
Sunbury-on-Thames TW16 … 217 BU95
GREEN STREET GREEN,
Dart. DA2 … 211 FU93
GREEN STREET GREEN,
Orp. BR6 … 245 ES107
Sch Green St Grn Prim Sch,
Grn St Grn BR6
off Vine Rd … 245 ET107
Green St Grn Rd, Dart.
DA1, DA2 … 210 FP88
Greensward, Bushey WD23 … 98 CB44
Green Ter, EC1 … 18 F3
Green Tiles La, Denh. UB9 … 135 BF58
Green Trees, Epp. CM16 … 92 EU31
Green Vale, W5 … 160 CM72
Bexleyheath DA6 … 208 EX85
Greenvale, Welw.G.C. AL7 … 52 DA10
Sch Greenvale Prim Sch, S.Croy.
CR2 off Sandpiper Rd … 243 DX111
Greenvale Rd, SE9 … 187 EM84
Sch Greenvale Sch, SE6
off Waters Rd … 206 EE90
Green Valley, Woob.Grn HP10 … 110 AE54
Green Verges, Stan. HA7 … 117 CK52
Green Vw, Chess. KT9 … 238 CM108
Greenview Av, Beck. BR3 … 225 DY100
Croydon CR0 … 225 DY100
Greenview Cl, W3 … 160 CS74
Green Vw Cl, Bov. HP3 … 79 BA29
Greenview Ct, Ashf. TW15
off Church Rd … 196 BM91
Green Wk, NW4 … 141 CX57
SE1 … 31 N7
Buckhurst Hill IG9 … 124 EL45
Dartford DA1 … 189 FF84
Hampton TW12
off Orpwood Cl … 198 BZ93
Ruislip HA4 … 137 BT60
Southall UB2 … 178 CA78
Woodford Green IG8 … 124 EL51
Green Wk, The, E4 … 123 EC46
Greenway, N14 … 121 DL47
N20 … 120 DA47
Green Way, SE9 … 206 EK85
Greenway, SW20 … 221 CW98
Berkhamsted HP4 … 60 AU19
Green Way, Bkhm KT23 … 252 CB123
Bromley BR2 … 226 EL100
Burnham SL1 … 152 AH69
Greenway, Chesh. HP5 … 76 AP28
Chislehurst BR7 … 207 EN92
Dagenham RM8 … 148 EW61
Greenway, Harl. CM19 … 72 EL15
Hayes UB4 … 157 BV70
Hemel Hempstead HP2 … 63 BP20
Hutton CM13 … 131 GA45
Kenton HA3 … 140 CL57
Pinner HA5 … 115 BV54
Green Way, Red. RH1 … 272 DE132
Greenway, Rom. RM3 … 128 FP51
Green Way, Sun. TW16 … 217 BU98
Greenway, Tats. TN16 … 260 EJ120
Wallington SM6 … 241 DJ105
Woodford Green IG8 … 124 EJ50
Greenway, The, NW9 … 118 CR54
Chalfont St. Peter SL9 … 134 AX55
Enfield EN3 … 105 DX35
Epsom KT18 … 254 CN115
Harrow Weald HA3 … 117 CE53
Hounslow TW4 … 178 BZ84
Ickenham UB10 … 137 BQ61
Mill End WD3 … 114 BG45
Orpington BR5 … 228 EV100
Oxted RH8 … 276 EH133
Pinner HA5 … 138 BZ58
Potters Bar EN6 … 86 DA33
Slough SL1 … 153 AK74
Uxbridge UB8 … 156 BJ68
Greenway Av, E17 … 145 ED56
● Greenway Business Cen,
Harl. CM19 … 72 EL15
Greenway Cl, N4 … 144 DQ61
N11 … 120 DG51
N15 off Copperfield Dr … 144 DT56
N20 … 120 DA47
NW9 … 118 CR54
West Byfleet KT14 … 234 BG113
Greenway Dr, Stai. TW18 … 216 BK95
Sch Greenway First & Nurs Sch,
Berk. HP4 off Crossways … 60 AU19
Greenway Gdns, NW9 … 118 CR54
Croydon CR0 … 225 DZ104
Greenford UB6 … 158 CA69
Harrow HA3 … 117 CE54
Greenway Par, Chesh. HP5 … 76 AP28
Greenways, Abb.L. WD5 … 81 BS32
Beckenham BR3 … 225 EA96
Egham TW20 … 194 AY92
Esher KT10 … 237 CE105
Goffs Oak EN7 … 87 DP29
Hertford SG14 … 53 DN09
Walton on the Hill KT20 … 271 CV125
Woking GU22
off Pembroke Rd … 249 BA117
Greenways, The, Twick. TW1
off South Western Rd … 199 CG86
Greenways Ct, Horn. RM11 … 150 FK58
Greenwell Cl, Gdse. RH9 … 274 DV130
Greenwell St, W1 … 17 K5
Green W Rd, Jordans HP9 … 112 AS52
GREENWICH, SE10 … 46 G4
⇌ Greenwich … 46 D4
DLR Greenwich … 46 D4
● Greenwich Cen Business Pk,
SE10 … 46 D4
Greenwich Ch St, SE10 … 46 F3
Coll Greenwich Comm Coll,
Burrage Cen, SE18
off Burrage Gro … 187 EQ77
Haimo Cen, SE9
off Haimo Rd … 206 EK85
London Leisure Coll, SE7 … 36 E10
New Horizon Cen, SE3
off Telemann Sq … 186 EH83
Plumstead Cen, SE18
off Plumstead Rd … 187 EQ77
Greenwich Ct, Wal.Cr. EN8
off Parkside … 89 DY34
Greenwich Cres, E6 … 24 G7
Greenwich Foot Tunnel, E14 … 46 F1
SE10 … 46 F1
Greenwich Hts, SE18 … 186 EL80
★ Greenwich Heritage Cen,
SE18 … 37 N6
Greenwich High Rd, SE10 … 46 C6
Greenwich Ho, SE13
off Hither Grn La … 205 ED86
● Greenwich Ind Est, SE7 … 36 A9
Shop Greenwich Mkt, SE10 … 46 F3
★ Greenwich Pk, SE10 … 47 J4
Greenwich Pk St, SE10 … 47 H1
Riv Greenwich Pier … 46 E2
Greenwich Quay, SE8 … 46 C3
Coll Greenwich Sch of Management,
SE10 … 46 E4
Shop Greenwich Shop Pk, SE7 … 35 P9
Greenwich S St, SE10 … 46 D6
Greenwich Vw Pl, E14 … 34 C7
Greenwich Way, Wal.Abb. EN9 … 105 EC36
Greenwood, The, Guil. GU1 … 265 BA134
Greenwood Av, Chsht EN7 … 88 DV31
Dagenham RM10 … 149 FB63
Enfield EN3 … 105 DY40
Greenwood Cl, Amer. HP6 … 77 AS37
Bushey Heath WD23
off Langmead Dr … 117 CE45
Cheshunt EN7 … 88 DV31
Morden SM4 … 221 CY98
Petts Wood BR5 … 227 ES100
Seer Green HP9
off Farmers Way … 111 AR51
Sidcup DA15 … 208 EU89
Thames Ditton KT7 … 219 CG102
Woodham KT15 … 233 BF111
Greenwood Ct, SW1 … 29 L10
Greenwood Dr, E4
off Avril Way … 123 EC50
Redhill RH1 … 288 DG139
Watford WD25 … 81 BV34
Greenwood Gdns, N13 … 121 DP48
Caterham CR3 … 274 DU125
Ilford IG6 … 125 EQ52
Oxted RH8 … 276 EG134
Shenley WD7 … 84 CL33
Greenwood Ho, Grays RM17
off Argent St … 192 GB79
Greenwood La, Hmptn H.
TW12 … 198 CB92
Greenwood Pk, Kings.T. KT2 … 200 CS94
Greenwood Pl, NW5 … 7 K2
Sch Greenwood Prim Sch, Nthlt.
UB5 off Wood End Way … 139 CD64
Greenwood Rd, E8 … 10 D5
E13 … 13 M10
Bexley DA5 … 209 FD91
Chigwell IG7 … 126 EV49
Croydon CR0 … 223 DP101
Isleworth TW7 … 179 CE83
Mitcham CR4 … 223 DK97
Thames Ditton KT7 … 219 CG102
Woking GU21 … 248 AS120

Greenwoods, The, S.Har. HA2 138 CC62
Greenwood Ter, NW10 160 CR67
Greenwood Way, Sev. TN13 278 FF125
Green Wrythe Cres, Cars. SM5 222 DE102
Green Wrythe La, Cars. SM5 222 DD100
Sch Green Wrythe Prim Sch, Cars.
SM5 off Green Wrythe La 222 DD100
Greenyard, Wal.Abb. EN9 89 EC33
Greer Rd, Har. HA3 116 CC53
Greet St, SE1 30 F3
Greg Cl, E10 145 EC58
Gregories Fm La, Beac. HP9 111 AK53
Gregories Rd, Beac. HP9 110 AH53
Gregor Ms, SE3 47 P5
Gregory Av, Pot.B. EN6 86 DC33
Gregory Cl, Brom. BR2 226 EE98
Woking GU21 248 AW117
Gregory Cres, SE9 206 EK87
Gregory Dr, Old Wind. SL4 194 AV86
Gregory Ms, Wal.Abb. EN9
off Beaulieu Dr 89 EB32
Gregory Pl, W8 27 L4
Gregory Rd, Hedg. SL2 133 AR61
Romford RM6 148 EX56
Southall UB2 178 CA76
Gregson Cl, Borwd. WD6 100 CQ39
Gregson's Ride, Loug. IG10 107 EN38
Sch Greig City Acad, N8
off High St 143 DL56
Greig Cl, N8 143 DL57
Greig Ter, SE17 43 H2
Grenaby Av, Croy. CR0 224 DR101
Grenaby Rd, Croy. CR0 224 DR101
Grenada Rd, SE7 186 EJ80
Grenade St, E14 21 P10
Grenadier Cl, St.Alb. AL4 65 CJ21
Grenadier Pl, Cat. CR3 258 DQ122
Grenadier St, E16 37 L3
Grenadine Cl, Chsht EN7 88 DT27
Grena Gdns, Rich. TW9 180 CM84
Grenard Cl, SE15 44 C5
Grena Rd, Rich. TW9 180 CM84
Grendon Cl, Horl. RH6 290 DF146
Grendon Gdns, Wem. HA9 140 CN61
Grendon Ho, N1
off Priory Grn Est 18 C1
Grendon St, NW8 16 C4
Grenfell Av, Horn. RM12 149 FF60
Grenfell Cl, Borwd. WD6 100 CQ39
Grenfell Gdns, Har. HA3 140 CL59
Grenfell Ho, SE5
off Comber Gro 43 J5
Grenfell Rd, W11 14 D10
Beaconsfield HP9 111 AL52
Mitcham CR4 202 DF93
Grenfell Twr, W11 14 D10
Grenfell Wk, W11 14 D10
Grennell Cl, Sutt. SM1 222 DD103
Grennell Rd, Sutt. SM1 222 DC103
Grenoble Gdns, N13 121 DN51
Grenside Rd, Wey. KT13 217 BP104
Grenville Av, Brox. EN10 71 DZ21
Grenville Cl, N3 119 CZ53
Burnham SL1 152 AH68
Cobham KT11 236 BX113
Surbiton KT5 220 CQ102
Waltham Cross EN8 89 DX32
Grenville Ct, SE19
off Lymer Av 204 DT92
Grenville Gdns, Wdf.Grn. IG8 124 EJ53
Grenville Ms, N19 143 DL60
Hampton TW12 198 CB92
Grenville Pl, NW7 118 CR50
SW7 27 N7
Grenville Rd, N19 143 DL60
Chafford Hundred RM16 191 FV78
New Addington CR0 243 EC109
Grenville St, WC1 18 B5
Gresford Cl, St.Alb. AL4 65 CK20
Gresham Av, N20 120 DF49
Warlingham CR6 259 DY118
Gresham Cl, Bex. DA5 208 EY86
Brentwood CM14 130 FW48
Enfield EN2 104 DQ41
Oxted RH8 276 EF128
Gresham Ct, Berk. HP4 60 AV20
Gresham Dr, Rom. RM6 148 EV57
Gresham Gdns, NW11 141 CY60
Gresham Pl, N19 143 DK61
Sch Gresham Prim Sch, S.Croy.
CR2 off Limpsfield Rd 242 DU112
Gresham Rd, E6 25 K1
E16 24 B9
NW10 140 CR64
SE25 224 DU98
SW9 183 DN83
Beckenham BR3 225 DY96
Brentwood CM14 130 FW48
Edgware HA8 118 CM51
Hampton TW12 198 CA93
Hounslow TW3 178 CC81
Oxted RH8 276 EF128
Slough SL1 153 AN72
Staines TW18 195 BF92
Uxbridge UB10 156 BN68
Gresham St, EC2 19 J8
Gresham Way, SW19 202 DA90
Gresley Cl, E17 145 DY58
N15 144 DR56
Welwyn Garden City AL8 51 CY08
Gresley Ct, Pot.B. EN6 86 DC30
Gresley Rd, N19 143 DJ60
Gressenhall Rd, SW18 201 CZ86
Gresse St, W1 17 N7
Gresswell Cl, Sid. DA14 208 EU90
Greswell St, SW6 38 C7
Greta Bk, W.Hors. KT24 267 BQ126
Gretton Rd, N17 122 DS52
Greville Av, S.Croy. CR2 243 DX110
Greville Cl, Ashtd. KT21 254 CL119
Guildford GU2 264 AS134
North Mymms AL9 67 CV24
Twickenham TW1 199 CH87
Greville Ct, E5
off Napoleon Rd 144 DV62
Bookham KT23 268 CC125
Greville Hall, NW6 5 L10
Greville Ms, NW6 5 L9
Greville Pk Av, Ashtd. KT21 254 CL118
Greville Pk Rd, Ashtd. KT21 254 CL118
Greville Pl, NW6 5 M10
Sch Greville Prim Sch, The, Ashtd.
KT21 off Stonny Cft 254 CM117
Greville Rd, E17 145 EC56
NW6 5 L10
Richmond TW10 200 CM86
Greville St, EC1 18 F7
Grey Alders, Bans. SM7
off High Beeches 239 CW114
Greycaine Rd, Wat. WD24 98 BX37
Grey Cl, NW11 142 DC58
Greycoat Gdns, SW1
off Greycoat St 29 N7
Sch Grey Coat Hosp Sch,
Lwr Sch, SW1 29 N7
Upr Sch, SW1 29 N9
Greycoat Pl, SW1 29 N7
Greycoat St, SW1 29 N7
Greycot Rd, Beck. BR3 205 EA92
Sch Grey Ct Sch, Rich. TW10
off Ham St 199 CJ90
Grey Eagle St, E1 20 A6
Greyfell Cl, Stan. HA7
off Coverdale Cl 117 CH50
Greyfields Cl, Pur. CR8 241 DP113
Greyfriars, Hutt. CM13 131 GB45
Greyfriars Pas, EC1 19 H8
Greyfriars Rd, Ripley GU23 250 BG124
Greygoose Pk, Harl. CM19 73 EN18
Greyhound Hill, NW4 141 CU55
Greyhound La, SW16 203 DK93
Orsett RM16 193 GG75
South Mimms EN6 85 CU33
Greyhound Rd, N17 144 DS55
NW10 161 CV69
W6 38 D2
W14 38 D2
Sutton SM1 240 DC106
Greyhound Ter, SW16 223 DJ95
Greyhound Way, Dart. DA1 209 FE86
Greyladies Gdns, SE10 46 F7
Greys Pk Cl, Kes. BR2 244 EJ106
Greystead Rd, SE23 204 DW87
Greystoke Av, Pnr. HA5 138 CA55
Greystoke Cl, Berk. HP4 60 AU20
Greystoke Dr, Ruis. HA4 137 BP58
Greystoke Gdns, W5 160 CL70
Enfield EN2 103 DK42
Greystoke Pk Ter, W5 159 CK69
Greystoke Pl, EC4 18 E8
Greystoke Rd, Slou. SL2 153 AM71
Greystone Cl, S.Croy. CR2 242 DW111
Greystone Gdns, Har. HA3 139 CJ58
Ilford IG6 125 EQ54
Greystone Path, E11
off Grove Rd 146 EF59
Greystones Cl, Red. RH1 288 DD136
Greystones Dr, Reig. RH2 272 DC132
Greyswood Av, N18 123 DX51
Greyswood St, SW16 203 DH93
Greythorne Rd, Wok. GU21 248 AU118
Grey Twrs Av, Horn. RM11 150 FK60
Grey Twrs Gdns, Horn. RM11
off Grey Twrs Av 150 FK60
Grice Av, Bigg.H. TN16 244 EH113
Gridiron Pl, Upmin. RM14 150 FP62
Grierson Rd, SE23 205 DX87
Grieves Rd, Nthflt DA11 213 GF90
Griffetts Yd, Chesh. HP5
off Bellingdon Rd 76 AP30
Griffin Av, Upmin. RM14 151 FS58
● Griffin Cen, Felt. TW14 197 BV86
Griffin Cl, NW10 141 CV64
Slough SL1 173 AQ75
Griffin Ct, Ashtd. KT21
off The Warren 254 CL119
Bookham KT23
off Griffin Way 268 CB126
Northfleet DA11 212 GA85
Griffin Manor Way, SE28 187 ER76
Griffin Rd, N17 122 DS54
SE18 187 ER78
Griffins, The, Grays RM16 192 GB75
Griffins Cl, N21 122 DR45
Griffin Wk, Green. DA9
off Church Rd 211 FT85
Griffin Way, Bkhm KT23 268 CA126
Sunbury-on-Thames TW16 217 BU96
Griffith Cl, Dag. RM8
off Gibson Rd 148 EW60
Griffiths Cl, Wor.Pk. KT4 221 CV103
Griffiths Rd, SW19 202 DA94
Griffiths Way, St.Alb. AL1 64 CC22
Griffon Way, Lvsdn WD25 81 BT34
Grifon Rd, Chaff.Hun. RM16 191 FW76
Griggs App, Ilf. IG1 147 EQ61
Griggs Gdns, Horn. RM12
off Tylers Cres 150 FJ64
Griggs Pl, SE1 31 P7
Griggs Rd, E10 145 EC58
Grilse Cl, N9 122 DV49
Grimsby Gro, E16 37 P4
Grimsby St, E2 20 B5
Grimsdells La, Amer. HP6 77 AR37
Grimsdyke Cres, Barn. EN5 101 CW41
Sch Grimsdyke First & Mid Sch,
Hatch End HA5
off Sylvia Av 116 BZ51
Grimsdyke Rd, Pnr. HA5 116 BY52
Grimsel Path, SE5 43 H4
Grimshaw Cl, N6 142 DG59
Grimshaw Way, Rom. RM1 149 FF57
Grimstone Cl, Rom. RM5 127 FB51
Grimston Rd, SW6 38 G9
St. Albans AL1 65 CF21
Grimthorpe Cl, St.Alb. AL3 65 CD17
Grimthorpe Ho, EC1 18 G4
Grimwade Av, Croy. CR0 224 DU104
Grimwade Cl, SE15 44 G10
Grimwood Rd, Twick. TW1 199 CF87
Grindall Cl, Croy. CR0 241 DP105
Grindal St, SE1 30 E5
Grindcobbe, St.Alb. AL1 65 CD23
Grindleford Av, N11 120 DG47
Grindley Gdns, Croy. CR0 224 DT100
Sch Grinling Gibbons Prim Sch,
SE8 45 P3
Grinling Pl, SE8 46 A3
Grinstead Rd, SE8 45 L1
Grisedale Cl, Pur. CR8 242 DS114
Grisedale Gdns, Pur. CR8 242 DS114
Grittleton Av, Wem. HA9 160 CP65
Grittleton Rd, W9 15 J4
Grizedale Ter, SE23 204 DV89
Grobars Av, Wok. GU21 248 AW115
Grocer's Hall Ct, EC2 19 L9
Grogan Cl, Hmptn. TW12 198 BZ93
Groombridge Cl, Hersham
KT12 235 BV106
Welling DA16 208 EU85
Groombridge Rd, E9 11 J7
Groom Cl, Brom. BR2 226 EH98
Groom Cres, SW18 202 DD87
Groomfield Cl, SW17 202 DG91
Groom Pl, SW1 29 H6
Groom Rd, Brox. EN10 89 DZ26
Grooms Cotts, Chesh. HP5 78 AV30
Grooms Dr, Pnr. HA5 137 BU57
Groom Wk, Guil. GU1 264 AY131
Grosmont Rd, SE18 187 ET78
Grosse Way, SW15 201 CV86
Grosvenor Av, N5 9 J3
SW14 180 CS83
Carshalton SM5 240 DF107
Harrow HA2 138 CB58
Hayes UB4 157 BS68
Kings Langley WD4 81 BQ28
Richmond TW10 200 CL85
Grosvenor Cl, Horl. RH6 290 DG150
Iver SL0 155 BD69
Loughton IG10 107 EP39
Grosvenor Cotts, SW1 28 G8
Grosvenor Ct, N14 121 DJ45
NW6 4 D8
Croxley Green WD3
off Mayfare 97 BR43
Guildford GU4 265 BB130
Slough SL1 154 AS72
Sutton SM2
off Brighton Rd 240 DC107
Grosvenor Cres, NW9 140 CN56
SW1 29 H5
Dartford DA1 210 FK85
Uxbridge UB10 157 BP66
Grosvenor Cres Ms, SW1 28 G5
Grosvenor Dr, Horn. RM11 150 FJ60
Loughton IG10 107 EP39
Maidenhead SL6 152 AC71
Grosvenor Est, SW1 29 P8
Grosvenor Gdns, E6 24 E2
N10 143 DJ55
N14 103 DK43
NW2 4 B3
NW11 141 CZ58
SW1 29 J6
SW14 180 CS83
Kingston upon Thames KT2 199 CK93
Upminster RM14 151 FR60
Wallington SM6 241 DJ108
Woodford Green IG8 124 EG51
Grosvenor Gdns Ms E, SW1 29 K6
Grosvenor Gdns Ms N, SW1 29 J7
Grosvenor Gdns Ms S, SW1 29 K7
Grosvenor Gate, W1 28 F1
Grosvenor Hill, SW19 201 CY93
W1 17 J10
Grosvenor Ms, Epsom KT18 254 CR119
Reigate RH2 288 DB137
Grosvenor Pk, SE5 43 J3
Grosvenor Pk Rd, E17 145 EA57
Grosvenor Path, Loug. IG10 107 EP39
Grosvenor Pl, SW1 29 H5
Weybridge KT13
off Vale Rd 217 BR104
Woking GU21
off Burleigh Gdns 249 AZ116
Grosvenor Ri E, E17 145 EB57
Grosvenor Rd, E6 166 EK67
E7 166 EH65
E10 145 EC60
E11 146 EG57
N3 119 CZ52
N9 122 DV46
N10 121 DH53
SE25 224 DU98
SW1 41 J2
W4 180 CP78
W7 159 CG74
Belvedere DA17 188 FA79
Bexleyheath DA6 208 EX85
Borehamwood WD6 100 CN41
Brentford TW8 179 CK79
Broxbourne EN10 71 DZ20
Dagenham RM8 148 EZ60
Epsom KT18 254 CR119
Hounslow TW3 178 BZ83
Ilford IG1 147 EQ62
Northwood HA6 115 BT50
Petts Wood BR5 227 ES100
Richmond TW10 200 CL85
Romford RM7 149 FD59
St. Albans AL1 65 CE21
Southall UB2 178 BZ76
Staines TW18 196 BG94
Twickenham TW1 199 CG87
Wallington SM6 241 DH107
Watford WD17 98 BW42
West Wickham BR4 225 EB102
Grosvenor Sq, W1 17 H10
Kings Langley WD4
off Grosvenor Av 81 BQ28
Grosvenor St, W1 17 J10
Grosvenor Ter, SE5 43 H4
Hemel Hempstead HP1 62 BG21
Grosvenor Vale, Ruis. HA4 137 BT61
Grosvenor Way, E5 144 DW61
Grosvenor Wf Rd, E14 34 G9
Grote's Bldgs, SE3 47 K9
Grote's Pl, SE3 47 J9
Groton Rd, SW18 202 DB89
Grotto, The, Ware SG12 55 DX07
Grotto Pas, W1 17 H6
Grotto Rd, Twick. TW1 199 CF89
Weybridge KT13 217 BP104
Ground La, Hat. AL10 67 CV16
Jct Grove, The, SE22 204 DU88
Grove, The, E15 13 J4
N3 120 DA53
N4 143 DM59
N6 142 DG60
N8 143 DK57
N13 121 DN50
N14 103 DJ43
NW9 140 CR57
NW11 141 CY59
W5 159 CK74
Addlestone KT15 234 BH106
Amersham HP6 77 AR36
Bexleyheath DA6 188 EX84
Biggin Hill TN16 260 EK118
Brentwood CM14 130 FT49
Brookmans Park AL9 86 DA27
Caterham CR3 257 DP121
Chipperfield WD4 80 BJ30
Coulsdon CR5 257 DK115
Edgware HA8 118 CP49
Egham TW20 195 BA92
Enfield EN2 103 DN40
Epsom KT17 238 CS113
Esher KT10 218 CB102
Ewell KT17 239 CT110
Gravesend DA12 213 GH87
Greenford UB6 158 CC72
Horley RH6 291 DH149
Isleworth TW7 179 CE81
Latimer HP5 94 AX36
Potters Bar EN6 86 DC32
Grove, The, Rad. WD7 83 CG34
Sidcup DA14 208 EY91
Slough SL1 174 AU75
Swanley BR8 229 FF97
Swanscombe DA10 212 FZ85
Teddington TW11 199 CG91
Twickenham TW1
off Bridge Rd 199 CH86
Upminster RM14 150 FP63
Uxbridge UB10 136 BN64
Walton-on-Thames KT12 217 BV101
Watford WD17 97 BQ37
West Wickham BR4 225 EB104
Woking GU21 249 AZ116
Grove Av, N3 120 DA52
N10 121 DJ54
W7 159 CE72
Epsom KT17 238 CS113
Pinner HA5 138 BY56
Sutton SM1 240 DA107
Twickenham TW1 199 CF88
Grove Bk, Wat. WD19 116 BX46
Grovebarns, Stai. TW18 196 BG93
Grovebury Cl, Erith DA8 189 FD79
Grovebury Gdns, Park St AL2 82 CC27
Grovebury Rd, SE2 188 EV75
Grove Cl, N14 121 DJ45
SE23 205 DX88
Bromley BR2 226 EG103
Chalfont St. Peter SL9
off Grove La 112 AW53
Epsom KT19 238 CP110
Feltham TW13 198 BY91
Kingston upon Thames KT1 220 CM98
Old Windsor SL4 194 AV87
Slough SL1 off Alpha St S 174 AU76
Uxbridge UB10 136 BN64
Grove Cor, Bkhm KT23
off Lower Shott 268 CA126
Grove Cotts, SW3 40 D2
Grove Ct, Barn. EN5
off High St 101 CZ41
Beaconsfield HP9
off Station Rd 111 AK53
East Molesey KT8
off Walton Rd 219 CD99
Egham TW20 195 BA92
Send GU23 off Send Rd 249 BD123
Waltham Abbey EN9 89 EB33
Grove Cres, E18 124 EF54
NW9 140 CQ56
Croxley Green WD3 96 BN42
Feltham TW13 198 BY91
Kingston upon Thames KT1 220 CL97
Walton-on-Thames KT12 217 BV101
Grove Cres Rd, E15 13 H5
Grovedale Cl, Chsht EN7 88 DT30
Grovedale Rd, N19 143 DK61
Grove Dws, E1 20 G6
Grove End, E18
off Grove Hill 124 EF54
NW5 off Chetwynd Rd 143 DH63
Chalfont St. Peter SL9 112 AW53
Grove End Gdns, NW8
off Grove End Rd 16 A1
Grove End La, Esher KT10 219 CD102
Grove End Rd, NW8 16 A1
Grove Fm Ct, Mitch. CR4
off Brookfields Av 222 DF98
Grove Fm Pk, Nthwd. HA6 115 BR50
Grove Fm Retail Pk,
Chad.Hth RM6 148 EW59
Grove Footpath, Surb. KT5 220 CL98
Grove Gdns, NW4 141 CU56
NW8 16 D3
Dagenham RM10 149 FC62
Enfield EN3 105 DX39
Teddington TW11 199 CG91
Grove Grn Rd, E11 145 EC62
Grove Hall Ct, NW8 15 P2
Grove Hall Rd, Bushey WD23 98 BY42
Grove Heath, Ripley GU23 250 BJ124
Grove Heath Ct, Ripley GU23 250 BJ124
Grove Heath N, Ripley GU23 250 BH122
Grove Heath Rd, Ripley GU23 250 BJ123
Groveherst Rd, Dart. DA1 190 FM83
GROVEHILL, Hem.H. HP2 62 BL16
Grove Hill, E18 124 EF54
Chalfont St. Peter SL9 112 AW52
Harrow HA1 139 CE59
Grove Hill Rd, SE5 43 N10
Harrow HA1 139 CE59
Grovehill Rd, Red. RH1 272 DE134
Grove Ho, Chsht EN8 88 DW30
Grove Ho Rd, N8 143 DL56
Groveland Av, SW16 203 DM94
Groveland Ct, EC4 19 K9
Groveland Rd, Beck. BR3 225 DZ97
Grovelands, Horl. RH6
off The Grove 291 DH149
Park Street AL2 82 CB27
West Molesey KT8 218 CA98
● Grovelands Business Cen,
Hem.H. HP2 63 BQ18
Grovelands Cl, SE5 43 N9
Harrow HA2 138 CB62
Grovelands Ct, N14 121 DK45
Grovelands Rd, N13 121 DM49
N15 144 DU58
Orpington BR5 208 EU94
Purley CR8 241 DL112
Sch Grovelands Sch, Walt.
KT12 off Terrace Rd 217 BV100
Grovelands Way, Grays RM17 192 FZ78
Groveland Way, N.Mal. KT3 220 CQ99
Grove La, SE5 43 L7
Chalfont St. Peter SL9 112 AW53
Chesham HP5 78 AV27
Chigwell IG7 125 ET48
Coulsdon CR5 240 DG113
Epping CM16 off High St 92 EU30
Kingston upon Thames KT1 220 CL98
Uxbridge UB8 156 BM70
Grove La Ter, SE5
off Grove La 43 N10
Grove Lea, Hat. AL10 67 CU21
Groveley Rd, Sun. TW16 197 BT92
Grove Mkt Pl, SE9 207 EM86
Grove Mead, Hat. AL10 67 CT18
Grove Meadow, Welw.G.C. AL7 52 DC09
Grove Ms, W6 26 A6
W11 14 G9
Grove Mill, Mitch. CR4 222 DE99
Grove Mill La, Wat. WD17 97 BP37
Grove Mill Pl, Cars. SM5 222 DG104
GROVE PARK, SE12 206 EG89
GROVE PARK, W4 180 CP80
⇌ Grove Park 206 EG90
◆ Grove Park 206 EH90
Grove Pk, E11 146 EH58
NW9 140 CQ56
SE5 43 N9
Grove Pk Av, E4 123 EB52
Grove Pk Br, W4 180 CQ80
Grove Pk Gdns, W4 180 CP79
Grove Pk Ms, W4 180 CQ80
Sch Grove Pk Prim Sch, W4
off Nightingale Cl 180 CQ79
Grove Pk Rd, N15 144 DS56
SE9 206 EJ90
W4 180 CP80
Rainham RM13 169 FG67
Sch Grove Pk Sch, NW9
off Grove Pk 140 CQ56
Grove Pk Ter, W4 180 CP79
Grove Pas, E2 10 E10
Teddington TW11 199 CG92
Grove Path, Chsht EN7 88 DU31
Grove Pl, NW3
off Christchurch Hill 142 DD62
SW12 203 DH86
W3 160 CQ74
Banstead SM7 240 DF112
Barking IG11
off Clockhouse Av 167 EQ67
North Mymms AL9
off Dixons Hill Rd 67 CW24
Watford WD25 98 CB39
Weybridge KT13 235 BQ106
Sch Grove Prim Sch, Chad.Hth
RM6 off Chadwell Heath La 148 EW57
Grover Cl, Hem.H. HP2 62 BK19
Grove Rd, E3 11 K10
E4 123 EB49
E11 146 EF59
E17 145 EB58
E18 124 EF54
N11 121 DH50
N12 120 DD50
N15 144 DS57
NW2 4 A4
SW13 181 CT82
SW19 202 DC94
W3 160 CQ74
W5 159 CK73
Amersham HP6 94 AT37
Ashtead KT21 254 CM118
Beaconsfield HP9 111 AK53
Belvedere DA17 188 EZ79
Bexleyheath DA7 189 FC84
Borehamwood WD6 100 CN39
Brentford TW8 179 CJ78
Burnham SL1 153 AL67
Chertsey KT16 215 BF100
Cockfosters EN4 102 DE41
East Molesey KT8 219 CD98
Edgware HA8 118 CN51
Epsom KT17 238 CS113
Grays RM17 192 GC79
Guildford GU1 265 BC134
Hemel Hempstead HP1 62 BG22
Horley RH6 290 DE147
Hounslow TW3 178 CB84
Isleworth TW7 179 CE81
Mill End WD3 114 BG47
Mitcham CR4 223 DH96
Northfleet DA11 212 GB85
Northwood HA6 115 BR50
Oxted RH8
off Southlands La 275 EC134
Pinner HA5 138 BZ57
Redhill RH1
off Lower Br Rd 272 DF134
Richmond TW10 200 CM86
Romford RM6 148 EV59
St. Albans AL1 65 CD21
Seal TN15 279 FN122
Sevenoaks TN14 279 FJ121
Shepperton TW17 217 BQ100
Surbiton KT6 219 CK99
Sutton SM1 240 DB107
Tatsfield TN16 260 EJ120
Thornton Heath CR7 223 DN98
Twickenham TW2 199 CD90
Uxbridge UB8 156 BK66
Ware SG12 55 DZ05
Windsor SL4 173 AQ82
Woking GU21 249 AZ116
Sch Grove Rd Prim Sch,
Houns. TW3
off Cromwell Rd 178 CA84
Grove Rd W, Enf. EN3 104 DW37
Grover Rd, Wat. WD19 116 BX45
Groves Cl, B.End SL8 132 AC60
South Ockendon RM15 171 FT73
Grove Shaw, Kgswd KT20 255 CY124
Groveside, Bkhm KT23 268 CA127
Groveside Cl, W3 160 CN72
Bookham KT23 268 CA127
Carshalton SM5 222 DE103
Groveside Rd, E4 124 EE47
Grovestile Waye, Felt. TW14 197 BR87
Grove St, N18 122 DT51
SE8 33 N8
Groves Way, Chesh. HP5 76 AM29
Grove Ter, NW5 143 DH62
Teddington TW11 199 CG91
Grove Ter Ms, NW5
off Grove Ter 143 DH62
Grove Vale, SE22 184 DS84
Chislehurst BR7 207 EN93
Grove Vil, E14 22 D10
Grove Wk, Hert. SG14 54 DQ07
Groveway, SW9 42 D7
Grove Way, Chorl. WD3 95 BB42
Groveway, Dag. RM8 148 EX63
Grove Way, Esher KT10 218 CC101
Uxbridge UB8 156 BK66
Wembley HA9 140 CP64
Grovewood, Rich. TW9
off Sandycombe Rd 180 CN81
Grove Wd Cl, Brom. BR1 227 EN97
Grovewood Cl, Chorl. WD3 95 BB43
Grove Wd Hill, Couls. CR5 241 DK114
Grovewood Pl, Wdf.Grn. IG8 125 EM51
Grubbs La, Hat. AL9 68 DA22
Grub St, Oxt. RH8 276 EJ128
Grummant Rd, SE15 44 A6
Grundy St, E14 22 C9
Gruneisen Rd, N3 120 DB52

● Gryphon Ind Pk, The, Port.Wd AL3 65 CF15
Coll GSA Conservatoire, Guil. GU2 off Millmead Ter 280 AW136
Sch Guardian Angels RC Prim Sch, E3 21 M4
Guardian Av, N.Stfd RM16 191 FX75
Guardian Cl, Horn. RM11 149 FH60
Guards Av, Cat. CR3 258 DQ122
Guards Club Rd, Maid. SL6 152 AC72
Guardsman Cl, Warley CM14 130 FX50
★ Guards Mus, SW1 29 M5
Guards Rd, Wind. SL4 172 AJ82
Guards Wk, Wind. SL4 off Guards Rd 172 AJ82
Gubbins La, Rom. RM3 128 FM52
Gubyon Av, SE24 203 DP85
Guerin Sq, E3 21 N2
Guernsey Cl, Guil. GU4 off Cotts Wd Dr 265 BA129
Hounslow TW5 178 CA81
Guernsey Fm Dr, Wok. GU21 248 AX115
Guernsey Gro, SE24 204 DQ87
Guernsey Ho, N1 9 K5
Enfield EN3 off Eastfield Rd 105 DX38
Guernsey Rd, E11 145 ED60
Guessens Ct, Welw.G.C. AL8 51 CW09
Guessens Gro, Welw.G.C. AL8 51 CW09
Guessens Rd, Welw.G.C. AL8 51 CW09
Guessens Wk, Welw.G.C. AL8 51 CW08
Guibal Rd, SE12 206 EH87
Guildcroft, Guil. GU1 265 BA134
Guildersfield Rd, SW16 203 DL94
GUILDFORD, GU1 - GU5 280 AU137
⇌ Guildford 280 AW135
Guildford 280 AX135
Coll Guildford Adult Learning Cen, Guil. GU1 off Sydenham Rd 280 AY135
Guildford & Godalming Bypass, Guil. GU2, GU3 280 AS136
Guildford Av, Felt. TW13 197 BT89
● Guildford Business Pk, Guil. GU2 264 AV133
Guildford Bypass, Guil. GU1, GU2, GU4 265 AZ131
★ Guildford Castle, Guil. GU1 280 AX136
Coll Guildford Coll, Stoke Pk Campus, Guil. GU1 off Stoke Rd 264 AX133
Sch Guildford Co Sch, Guil. GU2 off Farnham Rd 280 AV136
Guildford Gdns, Rom. RM3 128 FL51
Guildford Gro, SE10 46 D6
Sch Guildford Gro Prim Sch, Guil. GU2 off Southway 264 AS134
Sch Guildford High Sch, Guil. GU1 off London Rd 264 AY134
★ Guildford House Gall, Guil. GU1 off High St 280 AX135
● Guildford Ind Est, Guil. GU2 264 AU133
Guildford La, Albury GU5 282 BH139
Woking GU22 248 AX120
Guildford Lo Dr, E.Hors. KT24 267 BT129
★ Guildford Mus, Guil. GU1 280 AX136
H Guildford Nuffield Hosp, Guil. GU2 264 AS134
GUILDFORD PARK, Guil. GU2 280 AV135
Guildford Pk Av, Guil. GU2 280 AV135
Guildford Pk Rd, Guil. GU2 280 AV135
Guildford Rd, E6 25 J9
E17 123 EC53
SW8 42 B6
Bookham KT23 268 BZ127
Chertsey KT16 215 BE102
Croydon CR0 224 DR100
Dorking RH5 284 BW140
Fetcham KT22 253 CG122
Godalming GU7 280 AU144
Guildford GU3, GU4 264 AX127
Ilford IG3 147 ES61
Leatherhead KT24 268 BW129
Mayford GU22 248 AX122
Romford RM3 128 FL51
St. Albans AL1 65 CH21
Westcott RH4 284 CA138
Woking GU22 248 AY119
Guildford St, Cher. KT16 216 BG101
Staines TW18 196 BG93
Guildford Way, Wall. SM6 241 DL106
★ Guildhall, The, EC2 19 L8
★ Guildhall Art Gall (Guildhall Lib), EC2 19 K8
Guildhall Bldgs, EC2 19 L8
Coll Guildhall Sch of Music & Drama, EC2 19 K6
Hall of Res, EC1 19 L6
Guildhall Yd, EC2 19 K8
Guildhouse St, SW1 29 L8
Guildown Av, N12 120 DB49
Guildford GU2 280 AV137
Guildown Rd, Guil. GU2 280 AV137
Guild Rd, SE7 186 EK78
Erith DA8 189 FF80
Guildsway, E17 123 DZ53
● Guildway, The, Guil. GU3 280 AW140
Guileshill La, Ock. GU23 250 BL123
Guilford Av, Surb. KT5 220 CM99
Guilford Pl, WC1 18 C5
Guilfords, Harl. CM17 58 EX10
Guilford St, WC1 18 B5
Guinery Gro, Hem.H. HP3 62 BM24
Guinevere Gdns, Wal.Cr. EN8 89 DY31
Guinness Cl, E9 11 L7
Hayes UB3 177 BR76
Guinness Ct, E1 20 B9
Woking GU21 off Iveagh Rd 248 AT118
Guinness Sq, SE1 31 N8
Guinness Trust Bldgs, SE1 off Snowsfields 31 N4
SE11 30 G10
SW3 28 E9
SW9 183 DP84
W6 off Fulham Palace Rd 26 B10
Guinness Trust Est, N16 144 DS60
Guion Rd, SW6 39 H8
Gulland Cl, Bushey WD23 98 CC43
Gulland Wk, N1 off Nightingale Rd 9 K5
Gullbrook, Hem.H. HP1 62 BG20
Gullet Wd Rd, Wat. WD25 97 BU35
Gulliver Cl, Nthlt. UB5 158 BZ67
Gulliver Rd, Sid. DA15 207 ES89
Gulliver St, SE16 33 N6
Gull Wk, Horn. RM12 off Heron Flight Av 169 FH66
Gulphs, The, Hert. SG13 54 DR10
Gulston Wk, SW3 28 F9
Gumbrell Ms, Red. RH1 273 DH132
Gumleigh Rd, W5 179 CJ77
Gumley Gdns, Islw. TW7 179 CG83
Sch Gumley Ho RC Conv Sch, Islw. TW7 off St. John's Rd 179 CG83
Gumley Rd, Grays RM20 191 FX79
Gumping Rd, Orp. BR5 227 EQ103
Gundulph Rd, Brom. BR2 226 EJ97
Gunfleet Cl, Grav. DA12 213 GL87
Gun Hill, W.Til. RM18 193 GK79
Gunmakers La, E3 11 M9
Gunnell Cl, SE26 204 DU92
Croydon CR0 224 DU100
Gunner Dr, Enf. EN3 105 EA37
Gunner La, SE18 187 EN78
GUNNERSBURY, W4 180 CP77
⊖ Gunnersbury 180 CP78
⊖ Gunnersbury 180 CP78
Gunnersbury Av, W3 180 CN76
W4 180 CN76
W5 160 CM74
Sch Gunnersbury Catholic Sch for Boys, Brent. TW8 off The Ride 179 CJ78
Gunnersbury Cl, W4 off Grange Rd 180 CP78
Gunnersbury Ct, W3 180 CP75
Gunnersbury Cres, W3 180 CN75
Gunnersbury Dr, W5 180 CM75
Gunnersbury Gdns, W3 180 CN75
Gunnersbury La, W3 180 CN76
Gunnersbury Ms, W4 off Chiswick High Rd 180 CP78
★ Gunnersbury Park, W3 180 CM77
Jct Gunnersbury Pk, W3 180 CM76
Gunnersbury Pk, W3 180 CM77
W5 180 CM77
★ Gunnersbury Park Mus, W3 180 CN76
Gunners Gro, E4 123 EC48
Gunners Rd, SW18 202 DD89
● Gunnery Ter, SE18 187 EQ77
Gunning Rd, Grays RM17 192 GD78
Gunning St, SE18 187 ES77
Gunn Rd, Swans. DA10 212 FY86
Gunpowder Sq, EC4 18 F8
Gunstor Rd, N16 144 DS63
Gun St, E1 20 A7
Gunter Gro, SW10 39 N3
Edgware HA8 118 CR53
Gunters Mead, Esher KT10 236 CC110
Gunterstone Rd, W14 26 E9
Gunthorpe St, E1 20 B7
Gunton Rd, E5 144 DV62
SW17 202 DG93
Gunwhale Cl, SE16 33 K3
Gunyard Ms, SE18 186 EL80
Gurdon Rd, SE7 47 P1
Gurnard Cl, West Dr. UB7 156 BK73
Gurnell Gro, W13 159 CF70
Gurnells Rd, Seer Grn HP9 111 AQ50
Gurney Cl, E15 13 K2
E17 123 DX53
Barking IG11 167 EP65
Beaconsfield HP9 110 AJ53
Gurney Ct Rd, St.Alb. AL1 65 CF18
Gurney Cres, Croy. CR0 223 DM102
Gurney Dr, N2 142 DC57
Gurney Rd, E15 13 J2
SW6 39 N10
Carshalton SM5 240 DG105
Northolt UB5 157 BV69
Gurney's Cl, Red. RH1 288 DF135
Sch Guru Gobind Singh Khalsa Coll, Chig. IG7 off Roding La 125 EM46
Sch Guru Nanak Prim Sch, Hayes UB4 off Springfield Rd 158 BW74
Sch Guru Nanak Sec Sch, Hayes UB4 off Springfield Rd 158 BW74
Guthrie St, SW3 28 C10
Gutteridge La, Stap.Abb. RM4 109 FC44
Gutter La, EC2 19 K8
Guyatt Gdns, Mitch. CR4 off Ormerod Gdns 222 DG96
Guy Barnett Gro, SE3 off Casterbridge Rd 186 EG83
Guy Rd, Wall. SM6 223 DK104
Guyscliff Rd, SE13 205 EC85
Guysfield Cl, Rain. RM13 169 FG67
Guysfield Dr, Rain. RM13 169 FG67
H Guy's Hosp, SE1 31 M4
Guy St, SE1 31 M4
Gwalior Rd, SW15 off Felsham Rd 181 CX83
Gwendolen Av, SW15 201 CX85
Gwendolen Cl, SW15 201 CW85
Gwendolen Ho, Stai. TW19 off Yeoman Dr 196 BL88
Gwendoline Av, E13 166 EH67
Gwendoline Ct, Wal.Cr. EN8 89 DZ34
Gwendwr Rd, W14 26 F10
Gwen Morris Ho, SE5 43 K5
Gwent Cl, Wat. WD25 82 BX34
Gwillim Cl, Sid. DA15 208 EU85
Gwydor Rd, Beck. BR3 225 DX98
Gwydyr Rd, Brom. BR2 226 EF97
Gwyn Cl, SW6 39 N5
Sch Gwyn Jones Prim Sch, E11 off Hainault Rd 145 ED59
Gwynne Av, Croy. CR0 225 DX101
Gwynne Cl, W4 off Pumping Sta Rd 181 CT79
Windsor SL4 173 AL81
Gwynne Ct, Guil. GU2 off Railton Rd 264 AV130
Gwynne Pk Av, Wdf.Grn. IG8 125 EM51
Gwynne Pl, WC1 18 D3
Gwynne Rd, SW11 40 A8
Caterham CR3 258 DR123
Gwynn Rd, Nthflt DA11 212 GC89
Gwynns Wk, Hert. SG13 54 DS09
Gyfford Wk, Chsht EN7 88 DV31
Gylcote Cl, SE5 184 DR84
Gyles Pk, Stan. HA7 117 CJ53
Gyllyngdune Gdns, Ilf. IG3 147 ET61
Gypsy Cl, Gt Amwell SG12 55 DZ11
Jct Gypsy Cor, W3 160 CQ71
Gypsy La, Gt Amwell SG12 55 DZ11
Hunton Bridge WD4 97 BR35
Stoke Poges SL2 134 AS63
Welwyn Garden City AL7 51 CZ13
Gypsy Moth Av, Hat. AL10 66 CS16

H

Haarlem Rd, W14 26 C7
Haberdasher Est, N1 off Haberdasher St 19 M2
Haberdasher Pl, N1 19 M2
Sch Haberdashers' Aske's Boys' Sch, Els. WD6 off Butterfly La 99 CH41
Sch Haberdashers' Aske's Hatcham Coll, SE14 45 L6
Pepys Rd, SE14 45 L9
Sch Haberdashers' Aske's Knights Acad, Brom. BR1 off Launcelot Rd 206 EG91
Sch Haberdashers' Aske's Sch for Girls, Els. WD6 off Aldenham Rd 99 CH42
Haberdasher St, N1 19 M2
Habgood Rd, Loug. IG10 106 EL41
Habitat Cl, SE15 44 F9
Haccombe Rd, SW19 off Haydons Rd 202 DC93
HACKBRIDGE, Wall. SM6 223 DH103
⇌ Hackbridge 223 DH103
Hackbridge Grn, Wall. SM6 222 DG103
Hackbridge Pk Gdns, Cars. SM5 222 DG103
Sch Hackbridge Prim Sch, Wall. SM6 off Hackbridge Rd 222 DG103
Hackbridge Rd, Wall. SM6 222 DG103
Hackett La, Saw. CM21 57 ET05
Hacketts La, Wok. GU22 233 BF114
Hackford Rd, SW9 42 E5
Hackford Wk, SW9 42 D7
Hackforth Cl, Barn. EN5 101 CV43
Hackhurst La, Abin.Ham. RH5 283 BT138
Hackington Cres, Beck. BR3 205 EA93
HACKNEY, E8 10 E5
⊖ Hackney Central 10 E4
★ Hackney City Fm, E2 20 C1
Hackney Cl, Borwd. WD6 100 CR43
⇌ Hackney Downs 10 E4
Sch Hackney Free & Parochial C of E Sch, E9 10 G5
Hackney Gro, E8 off Reading La 10 F5
★ Hackney Marsh, E9 145 DY62
★ Hackney Mus, E8 10 F5
Hackney Rd, E2 20 A3
HACKNEY WICK, E9 12 A4
⊖ Hackney Wick 12 A5
Hackworth Ho, N16 off Stamford Hill 144 DS60
Hackworth Pt, E3 22 B3
Hacon Sq, E8 10 F6
HACTON, Rain. RM13 150 FM64
Hacton Dr, Horn. RM12 150 FK63
Hacton La, Horn. RM12 150 FM62
Upminster RM14 150 FM64
Sch Hacton Prim Sch, Horn. RM12 off Chepstow Av 150 FL63
Hadar Cl, N20 120 DA46
Hadden Rd, SE28 187 ES76
Hadden Way, Grnf. UB6 159 CD65
Haddestoke Gate, Chsht EN8 89 DZ26
Haddington Rd, Brom. BR1 205 ED90
Haddo Ho, SE10 off Haddo St 46 D3
Haddon Cl, Borwd. WD6 100 CN40
Enfield EN1 104 DU44
Hemel Hempstead HP3 62 BN21
New Malden KT3 221 CT99
Weybridge KT13 217 BR104
Haddonfield, SE8 33 K9
Haddon Gro, Sid. DA15 208 EU87
Haddon Rd, Chorl. WD3 95 BC43
Orpington BR5 228 EW99
Sutton SM1 240 DB105
Haddo St, SE10 46 E3
Haden Ct, N4 off Lennox Rd 143 DN61
Haden La, N11 121 DJ49
Hadfield Cl, Sthl. UB1 off Adrienne Av 158 BZ69
Hadfield Rd, Stanw. TW19 196 BK86
Hadlands Cl, Bov. HP3 79 AZ26
Hadleigh Cl, E1 20 G4
SW20 221 CZ96
Shenley WD7 83 CK30
Hadleigh Ct, Brox. EN10 71 DZ22
Hadleigh Dr, Sutt. SM2 240 DA109
Hadleigh Rd, N9 122 DV45
Hadleigh St, E2 21 H3
Hadleigh Wk, E6 25 H8
HADLEY, Barn. EN5 101 CZ40
Hadley Cl, N21 103 DN44
Elstree WD6 100 CM43
Hadley Common, Barn. EN5 102 DA40
Hadley Gdns, W4 180 CR78
Southall UB2 178 BZ78
Hadley Gra, Harl. CM17 74 EW16
Hadley Grn, Barn. EN5 101 CZ40
Hadley Grn Rd, Barn. EN5 101 CZ40
Hadley Grn W, Barn. EN5 101 CZ40
Hadley Gro, Barn. EN5 101 CY40
Hadley Hts, Barn. EN5 off Hadley Rd 102 DB40
Hadley Highstone, Barn. EN5 101 CZ39
Hadley Pl, Wey. KT13 234 BN108
Hadley Ridge, Barn. EN5 101 CZ41
Hadley Rd, Belv. DA17 188 EZ77
Enfield EN2 103 DL38
Hadley Wood EN4 103 DH38
Mitcham CR4 223 DK98
New Barnet EN5 102 DB42
Hadley St, NW1 7 J5
Hadley Way, N21 103 DN44
HADLEY WOOD, Barn. EN4 102 DE38
⇌ Hadley Wood 102 DC38
Sch Hadley Wd Prim Sch, Had.Wd EN4 off Courtleigh Av 102 DC38
Hadley Wd Ri, Ken. CR8 257 DP115
Coll Hadlow Coll Mottingham Cen, SE12 off Mottingham La 206 EJ88
Hadlow Ct, Slou. SL1 153 AQ73
Hadlow Pl, SE19 204 DU94
Hadlow Rd, Sid. DA14 208 EU91
Welling DA16 188 EW80
Hadlow Way, Istead Rise DA13 212 GE94
Hadrian Cl, E3 12 A9
St. Albans AL3 64 BZ22
Staines TW19 196 BL87
Hadrian Ct, Sutt. SM2 off Stanley Rd 240 DB108
Hadrian Est, E2 20 D1
Hadrian Ms, N7 8 D6
Hadrians Ride, Enf. EN1 104 DT43
Hadrian St, SE10 35 J10
Hadrian Way, Stanw. TW19 196 BL87
Hadyn Pk Rd, W12 181 CU75
Hafer Rd, SW11 182 DF84
Hafton Rd, SE6 206 EE88
Hagden La, Wat. WD18 97 BT43
Haggard Rd, Twick. TW1 199 CH87
HAGGERSTON, E2 10 B10
⊖ Haggerston 10 A8
Haggerston Rd, E8 10 A7
Borehamwood WD6 100 CL38
Sch Haggerston Sch, E2 10 B10
Haggerston Studios, E8 off Kingsland Rd 10 A8
Hag Hill La, Tap. SL6 152 AG72
Hag Hill Ri, Tap. SL6 152 AG72
Hagsdell La, Hert. SG13 54 DR10
Hagsdell Rd, Hert. SG13 54 DR10
Sch Hague Prim Sch, E2 20 F4
Hague St, E2 20 D3
Ha-Ha Rd, SE18 187 EM79
Haig Cl, St.Alb. AL1 65 CH21
Haig Dr, Slou. SL1 173 AP75
Haig Gdns, Grav. DA12 213 GJ87
Haigh Cres, Red. RH1 289 DH136
Haig Pl, Mord. SM4 off Green La 222 DA100
Haig Rd, Bigg.H. TN16 260 EL117
Grays RM16 193 GG76
Stanmore HA7 117 CJ50
Uxbridge UB8 157 BP71
Haig Rd E, E13 24 C2
Haig Rd W, E13 24 C2
Haigville Gdns, Ilf. IG6 147 EP56
Hailes Cl, SW19 202 DC93
HAILEY, Hert. SG13 55 DZ13
Hailey Av, Hodd. EN11 55 EA13
Sch Haileybury, Hert. SG13 off College Rd 55 DX13
Haileybury Av, Enf. EN1 104 DT44
Haileybury Rd, Orp. BR6 246 EU105
Hailey Cl, Hailey SG13 55 DY13
Sch Hailey Hall Sch, Hert. SG13 off Hailey La 55 DZ13
Hailey La, Hailey SG13 55 DX14
Hailey Rd, Erith DA18 188 FA75
Hailsham Av, SW2 203 DM89
Hailsham Cl, Rom. RM3 128 FJ50
Surbiton KT6 219 CK101
Hailsham Dr, Har. HA1 139 CD55
Hailsham Gdns, Rom. RM3 128 FJ50
Hailsham Rd, SW17 202 DG93
Romford RM3 128 FJ50
Hailsham Ter, N18 122 DQ50
Sch Haimo Prim Sch, SE9 off Haimo Rd 206 EK85
Haimo Rd, SE9 206 EK85
HAINAULT, Ilf. IG6 125 ES52
⊖ Hainault 125 ES52
● Hainault Business Pk, Ilf. IG6 126 EW50
Hainault Ct, E17 145 ED56
★ Hainault Forest Country Pk, Chig. IG7 126 EW47
Sch Hainault Forest High Sch, Ilf. IG6 off Harbourer Rd 126 EV50
Hainault Gore, Rom. RM6 148 EY57
Hainault Gro, Chig. IG7 125 EQ49
Hainault Rd, E11 145 EC60
Chadwell Heath RM6 148 EZ58
Chigwell IG7 125 EP48
Little Heath RM6 148 EV55
Romford RM5 127 FC54
Hainault St, SE9 207 EP88
Ilford IG1 147 EP61
Haines Cl, N1 9 N7
Haines Ct, Wey. KT13 235 BR106
Haines Wk, Mord. SM4 off Dorchester Rd 222 DB101
Haines Way, Wat. WD25 81 BU34
Hainford Cl, SE4 185 DX84
Haining Cl, W4 off Wellesley Rd 180 CN78
Hainthorpe Rd, SE27 203 DP90
Hainton Cl, E1 20 F9
Halberd Ms, E5 144 DV61
Halbutt Gdns, Dag. RM9 148 EZ62
Halbutt St, Dag. RM9 148 EZ63
Halcomb St, N1 9 N9
Halcot Av, Bexh. DA6 209 FB85
Halcrow St, E1 20 F7
Halcyon Way, Horn. RM11 150 FM60
Haldane Cl, N10 121 DH52
Enfield EN3 105 EB38
Haldane Gdns, Grav. DA11 212 GC88
Haldane Pl, SW18 202 DB88
Haldane Rd, E6 24 G2
SE28 168 EX73
SW6 39 H4
Southall UB1 158 CC73
Haldan Rd, E4 123 EC51
Haldens, Welw.G.C. AL7 51 CZ06
Haldon Cl, Chig. IG7 off Arrowsmith Rd 125 ES50
Haldon Rd, SW18 201 CZ85
Hale, The, E4 123 ED52
N17 144 DU55
Hale Cl, E4 123 EC48
Edgware HA8 118 CQ50
Orpington BR6 245 EQ105
Hale Dr, NW7 118 CQ51
HALE END, E4 123 ED51
Hale End, Rom. RM3 127 FH51
Woking GU22 248 AV121
Hale End Cl, Ruis. HA4 137 BU58
Hale End Rd, E4 123 ED51
E17 123 ED53
Woodford Green IG8 123 ED52
Halefield Rd, N17 122 DU53
Hale Gdns, N17 144 DU55
W3 160 CN74
Hale Gro Gdns, NW7 118 CR50
Hale La, NW7 118 CR50
Edgware HA8 118 CP50
Otford TN14 263 FE117
Hale Path, SE27 203 DP91
Hale Pit Rd, Bkhm KT23 268 CC126
Hale Rd, E6 25 H5
N17 144 DU55
Hertford SG13 54 DR10
Hales Oak, Bkhm KT23 268 CC126
Halesowen Rd, Mord. SM4 222 DB101
Hales Pk, Hem.H. HP2 63 BQ19
Hales Pk Cl, Hem.H. HP2 63 BQ19
Hales Prior, N1 off Calshot St 18 C1
Hales St, SE8 46 A5
Hale St, E14 22 C10
Staines TW18 195 BE91
Haleswood, Cob. KT11 235 BV114
Haleswood Rd, Hem.H. HP2 62 BN19
Halesworth Cl, E5 off Theydon Rd 144 DW61
Romford RM3 128 FL52
Halesworth Rd, SE13 46 C10
Romford RM3 128 FL51
Hale Wk, W7 159 CE71
Haley Rd, NW4 141 CW58
Half Acre, Brent. TW8 179 CK79
Halfacre Hill, Chal.St.P. SL9 112 AY53
Half Acre Rd, W7 159 CE74
Halfhide La, Chsht EN8 89 DX27
Turnford EN10 89 DY26
Halfhides, Wal.Abb. EN9 89 ED33
Half Moon Ct, EC1 19 J7
Half Moon Cres, N1 8 D10
Half Moon La, SE24 204 DQ86
Epping CM16 91 ET31
Half Moon Meadow, Hem.H. HP2 63 BQ15
Half Moon Ms, St.Alb. AL1 off London Rd 65 CD20
Half Moon Pas, E1 20 B9
Half Moon St, W1 29 K2
Half Moon Yd, St.Alb. AL1 off London Rd 65 CD20
Halford Cl, Edg. HA8 118 CP54
Halford Ct, Hat. AL10 66 CS17
Halford Rd, E10 145 ED57
SW6 39 K3
Richmond TW10 200 CL85
Uxbridge UB10 136 BN64
Halfpenny Cl, Chilw. GU4 281 BD140
Halfpenny La, Chilw. GU4 281 BC136
Halfway Ct, Purf. RM19 190 FN77
Halfway Grn, Walt. KT12 217 BV104
Halfway Ho La, Amer. HP6 76 AL33
Halfway St, Sid. DA15 207 ER87
Haliburton Rd, Twick. TW1 199 CG85
Haliday Wk, N1 9 M4
Halidon Cl, E9 10 G2
Halidon Ri, Rom. RM3 128 FP51
Halifax Cl, Brick.Wd AL2 82 BZ30
Leavesden WD25 81 BT34
Teddington TW11 199 CE93
Halifax Rd, Enf. EN2 104 DQ40
Greenford UB6 158 CB67
Heronsgate WD3 113 BC45
Halifax St, SE26 204 DV91
Halifax Way, Welw.G.C. AL7 52 DE09
Halifield Dr, Belv. DA17 188 EY76
Haling Down Pas, S.Croy. CR2 242 DQ109
Haling Gro, S.Croy. CR2 242 DQ108
Sch Haling Manor High Sch, S.Croy. CR2 off Kendra Hall Rd 241 DP108
Haling Pk, S.Croy. CR2 242 DQ107
Haling Pk Gdns, S.Croy. CR2 241 DP107
Haling Pk Rd, S.Croy. CR2 241 DP106
Haling Rd, S.Croy. CR2 242 DR107
Halings La, Denh. UB9 135 BE56
Halkin Arc, SW1 28 G6
Halkingcroft, Slou. SL3 174 AW75
Halkin Ms, SW1 28 G6
Halkin Pl, SW1 28 G6
Halkin St, SW1 29 H5
Hall, The, SE3 47 N10
Hallam Cl, Chis. BR7 207 EM92
Watford WD24 98 BW40
Hallam Gdns, Pnr. HA5 116 BY52
Hallam Ms, W1 17 K6
Hallam Rd, N15 143 DP56
SW13 181 CV83
Hallam St, W1 17 K5
Halland Way, Nthwd. HA6 115 BR51
Hallane Ho, SE27 off Elder Rd 204 DQ92
Hall Av, N18 off Weir Hall Av 122 DR51
Aveley RM15 170 FQ74
Hall Cl, W5 160 CL71
Godalming GU7 280 AS144
Mill End WD3 114 BG46
Hall Ct, Datchet SL3 174 AV80
Teddington TW11 199 CF92
Hall Cres, Aveley RM15 190 FQ75
Hall Dene Cl, Guil. GU1 265 BC133
Hall Dr, SE26 204 DW92
W7 159 CE72
Harefield UB9 114 BJ53
Halley Gdns, SE13 185 ED84
Sch Halley Prim Sch, E14 21 M7
Halley Rd, E7 166 EJ65
E12 166 EK65
Waltham Abbey EN9 105 EB36
Halleys App, Wok. GU21 248 AU118
Halleys Ct, Wok. GU21 off Halleys App 248 AU118
Halleys Ridge, Hert. SG14 53 DN10
Halley St, E14 21 L7
Halleys Wk, Add. KT15 234 BJ108
Hall Fm Cl, Stan. HA7 117 CH49
Hall Fm Dr, Twick. TW2 199 CD87
Hallfield Est, W2 15 N8
Sch Hallfield Inf & Jun Schs, W2 15 M9
Hallford Way, Dart. DA1 210 FJ85
Hall Gdns, E4 123 DZ49
Colney Heath AL4 66 CR23
Hall Gate, NW8 15 P2
Hall Grn La, Hutt. CM13 131 GC45
HALL GROVE, Welw.G.C. AL7 52 DB11
Hall Gro, Welw.G.C. AL7 52 DB11
Hall Heath Cl, St.Alb. AL1 65 CH18
Hall Hill, Oxt. RH8 275 ED131
Seal TN15 279 FP123
Halliards, The, Walt. KT12 off Felix Rd 217 BU100
Halliday Cl, Shenley WD7 84 CL32
Halliday Ho, E1 off Christian St 20 D9
Halliday Sq, Sthl. UB2 159 CD74
Halliford Cl, Shep. TW17 217 BR98
Halliford Rd, Shep. TW17 217 BS99
Sunbury-on-Thames TW16 217 BS99
Sch Halliford Sch, Shep. TW17 off Russell Rd 217 BQ101
Halliford St, N1 9 K6
Halliloo Valley Rd, Wold. CR3 259 DZ119
Hallingbury Ct, E17 145 EB55
Halling Hill, Harl. CM20 57 ET13

Hallings Wf Studios, E15 12 G8
Hallington Cl, Wok. GU21 248 AV117
Halliwell Rd, SW2 203 DM86
Halliwick Rd, N10 120 DG53
Jct **Hall La**, E4 123 DY50
Hall La, E4 123 DY50
NW4 119 CU53
Harlington UB3 177 BR80
Shenfield CM15 131 FZ44
South Ockendon RM15 171 FX68
Upminster RM14 150 FQ60
● **Hallmark Trd Cen**,
Wem. HA9 140 CQ63
Hall Meadow, Burn. SL1 152 AJ68
Hallmead Rd, Sutt. SM1 222 DB104
Sch **Hall Mead Sch**, Upmin. RM14
off Marlborough Gdns 151 FR60
Hallmores, Brox. EN10 71 EA19
Hall Oak Wk, NW6 5 H4
Hallowell Av, Croy. CR0 241 DL105
Hallowell Cl, Mitch. CR4 222 DG97
Hallowell Rd, Nthwd. HA6 115 BS52
Hallowes Cl, Guil. GU2 264 AV129
Hallowes Cres, Wat. WD19 115 BU48
Hallowfield Way, Mitch. CR4 222 DD97
Hallows Gro, Sun. TW16 197 BT92
Hall Pk, Berk. HP4 60 AY20
Hall Pk Gate, Berk. HP4 60 AY21
Hall Pk Hill, Berk. HP4 60 AY21
Hall Pk Rd, Upmin. RM14 150 FQ64
★ **Hall Pl**, Bex. DA5 209 FC86
Hall Pl, W2 16 A5
Woking GU21 249 BA116
Hall Pl Cl, St.Alb. AL1 65 CE19
Hall Pl Cres, Bex. DA5 209 FC85
Hall Pl Dr, Wey. KT13 235 BS106
Hall Pl Gdns, St.Alb. AL1 65 CE19
Hall Rd, E6 167 EM67
E15 145 ED63
NW8 15 P3
Aveley RM15 190 FQ75
Chadwell Heath RM6 148 EW58
Dartford DA1 190 FM84
Gidea Park RM2 149 FH55
Hemel Hempstead HP2 63 BP18
Isleworth TW7 199 CD85
Northfleet DA11 212 GC90
Wallington SM6 241 DH109
Sch **Hall Sch, The**, Jun Sch, NW3 6 B5
Sen Sch, NW3 6 B5
Sch **Hall Sch Wimbledon**, Jun Sch,
SW15 *off Stroud Cres* 201 CU90
Sen Sch, SW20
off The Downs 221 CX95
HALLS GREEN, Harl. CM19 72 EJ18
Hallside Rd, Enf. EN1 104 DT38
Hallsland Way, Oxt. RH8 276 EF133
Hall St, EC1 19 H2
N12 120 DC50
Sch **Hallsville Prim Sch**, E16 23 N9
Hallsville Rd, E16 23 L9
Hallswelle Par, NW11
off Finchley Rd 141 CZ57
Hallswelle Rd, NW11 141 CZ57
Hall Ter, Aveley RM15 191 FR75
Romford RM3 128 FN52
Hall Twr, W2 16 B6
Hall Vw, SE9 206 EK89
Hall Way, Pur. CR8 241 DP113
Hallwood Cres, Shenf. CM15 130 FY45
Hallywell Cres, E6 25 K7
Halons Rd, SE9 207 EN87
Halpin Pl, SE17 31 M9
Halsbrook Rd, SE3 186 EK83
Halsbury Cl, Stan. HA7 117 CH49
Halsbury Rd, W12 161 CV74
Halsbury Rd E, Nthlt. UB5 138 CC63
Halsbury Rd W, Nthlt. UB5 138 CB64
Halse Dr, Slou. SL2 133 AM64
Halsend, Hayes UB3 157 BV74
Halsey Dr, Hem.H. HP1 61 BF18
Halsey Ms, SW3 28 E8
Halsey Pk, Lon.Col. AL2 84 CM27
Halsey Pl, Wat. WD24 97 BV38
Halsey Rd, Wat. WD18 97 BV41
Halsey St, SW3 28 E8
Halsham Cres, Bark. IG11 167 ET65
Halsmere Rd, SE5 43 H6
HALSTEAD, Sev. TN14 246 EZ113
Halstead Cl, Croy. CR0
off Charles St 224 DQ104
Sch **Halstead Comm Prim Sch**,
Halst. TN14 *off Otford La* 246 EZ112
Halstead Ct, N1 19 L1
Halstead Gdns, N21 122 DR46
Halstead Hill, Goffs Oak EN7 88 DS29
Halstead La, Knock.P. TN14 246 EZ114
Sch **Halstead Prep Sch**, Wok.
GU21 *off Woodham Ri* 233 BA114
Halstead Rd, E11 146 EG57
N21 122 DQ46
Enfield EN1 104 DS42
Erith DA8 189 FE81
Halstead Way, Hutt. CM13 131 GC44
Halston Cl, SW11 202 DF86
Sch **Halstow Prim Sch**, SE10 47 N1
Halstow Rd, NW10 14 C3
SE10 35 N10
Halsway, Hayes UB3 157 BU74
Halter Cl, Borwd. WD6 100 CR43
Halton Cl, N11 120 DF51
Park Street AL2 82 CC28
Halton Cross St, N1 9 H8
Halton Pl, N1 9 J8
Halton Rd, N1 9 H6
Grays RM16 193 GH76
Kenley CR8 258 DS120
Halt Robin La, Belv. DA17
off Halt Robin Rd 189 FB77
Halt Robin Rd, Belv. DA17 188 FA77
Haltside, Hat. AL10 66 CS19
Halwick Cl, Hem.H. HP1 62 BH21
HAM, Rich. TW10 199 CK90
Ham, The, Brent. TW8 179 CJ80
Hamara Ghar, E13 166 EJ67
Hambalt Rd, SW4 203 DJ85
Hamble Cl, Ruis. HA4 137 BS61
Woking GU21 248 AU117
Hamble Ct, Tedd. TW11 199 CK94
Hambledon Cl, Uxb. UB8
off Aldenham Dr 157 BP70
Hambledon Gdns, SE25 224 DT97
Hambledon Hill, Epsom KT18 254 CQ116
Hambledon Pl, SE21 204 DS88
Bookham KT23 252 CA123
Hambledon Rd, SW18 201 CZ87
Caterham CR3 258 DR123
Hambledon Vale, Epsom KT18 254 CQ116
Hambledown Rd, Sid. DA15 207 ER87
Hamble La, S.Ock. RM15 171 FT71
Hamble St, SW6 39 M10
Hambleton Cl, Wor.Pk. KT4 221 CW103
Hamble Wk, Nthlt. UB5
off Brabazon Rd 158 CA68
Woking GU21 248 AU118
Hambley Ho, SE16
off Manor Est 32 E9
Hamblings Cl, Shenley WD7 83 CK33
Hambridge Way, SW2 203 DN87
Hambro Av, Brom. BR2 226 EG102
Hambrook Rd, SE25 224 DV97
Hambro Rd, SW16 203 DK93
Sch **Hambrough Prim Sch**,
Sthl. UB1 *off South Rd* 158 BZ74
Hambrough Rd, Sthl. UB1 158 BY74
Hamburgh Ct, Chsht EN8 89 DX28
Ham Cl, Rich. TW10 199 CJ90
Ham Common, Rich. TW10 200 CL91
Ham Cft Cl, Felt. TW13 197 BU90
Hamden Cres, Dag. RM10 149 FB62
Hamel Cl, Har. HA3 139 CK55
Hamelin St, E14 22 E9
Hamels Dr, Hert. SG13 54 DV08
Hamer Cl, Bov. HP3 79 BA28
Hamerton Rd, Nthflt DA11 212 GB85
Hameway, E6 25 L4
Ham Fm Rd, Rich. TW10 199 CK91
Hamfield Cl, Oxt. RH8 275 EC127
Ham Flds, Rich. TW10 199 CG90
Hamfrith Rd, E15 13 L4
Ham Gate Av, Rich. TW10 199 CK90
Hamhaugh Island, Shep.
TW17 216 BN103
★ **Ham Ho**, Rich. TW10 199 CJ88
Hamilton Av, N9 122 DU45
Cobham KT11 235 BU113
Hoddesdon EN11 71 EA15
Ilford IG6 147 EP56
Romford RM1 127 FD54
Surbiton KT6 220 CP102
Sutton SM3 221 CY103
Woking GU22 249 BE115
Hamilton Cl, N17 144 DT55
NW8 16 A3
SE16 33 M5
Bricket Wood AL2 82 CA30
Chertsey KT16 215 BF102
Cockfosters EN4 102 DE42
Epsom KT19 238 CQ112
Feltham TW13 197 BT92
Guildford GU2 264 AU129
Horley RH6 290 DG149
Purley CR8 241 DP112
South Mimms EN6 85 CU33
Teddington TW11 199 CH93
Hamilton Ct, W5 160 CM73
W9 15 N2
Bookham KT23
off Eastwick Pk Av 268 CB125
Hatfield AL10
off Cooks Way 67 CV20
Hamilton Cres, N13 121 DN49
Harrow HA2 138 BZ62
Hounslow TW3 198 CB85
Warley CM14 130 FW49
Hamilton Dr, Guil. GU2 264 AU129
Romford RM3 128 FL54
Hamilton Gdns, NW8 15 P2
Burnham SL1 152 AH69
Hamilton Gordon Ct, Guil.
GU1 *off Langley Cl* 264 AW133
Hamilton Ho, SW8
off St. George Wf 42 A2
Hamilton La, N5 9 H1
Hamilton Mead, Bov. HP3 79 BA27
Hamilton Ms, SW18
off Merton Rd 202 DA88
W1 29 J4
Hamilton Pk, N5 9 H1
Hamilton Pk W, N5 8 G1
Hamilton Pl, N19 143 DK62
W1 29 H3
Guildford GU2 264 AU129
Kingswood KT20 255 CZ122
Sunbury-on-Thames TW16 197 BV94
Hamilton Rd, E15 23 K3
E17 123 DY54
N2 142 DC55
N9 122 DU45
NW10 141 CU64
NW11 141 CX59
SE27 204 DR91
SW19 202 DB94
W4 180 CS75
W5 160 CL73
Berkhamsted HP4 60 AV19
Bexleyheath DA7 188 EY82
Brentford TW8 179 CK79
Cockfosters EN4 102 DE42
Feltham TW13 197 BT91
Harrow HA1 139 CE57
Hayes UB3 157 BV73
Hunton Bridge WD4 81 BQ33
Ilford IG1 147 EP63
Romford RM2 149 FH57
St. Albans AL1 65 CG19
Sidcup DA15 208 EU91
Slough SL1 153 AN72
Southall UB1 158 BZ74
Thornton Heath CR7 224 DR97
Twickenham TW2 199 CE88
Uxbridge UB8 156 BK71
Watford WD19 115 BV48
Coll **Hamilton Rd Cen**, E15 23 K3
● **Hamilton Rd Ind Est**,
SE27 204 DR91
Hamilton Rd Ms, SW19
off Hamilton Rd 202 DB94
Hamilton Sq, N12
off Sandringham Gdns 120 DD51
SE1 31 M4
Hamilton St, SE8 46 A4
Watford WD18 98 BW43
Hamilton Ter, NW8 15 P2
Hamilton Wk, Erith DA8 189 FF80
Hamilton Way, N3 120 DA51
N13 121 DP49
Farnham Common SL2 133 AQ64
Wallington SM6 241 DK109
Ham Island, Old Wind. SL4 174 AX84
Ham La, Eng.Grn TW20 194 AV91
Old Windsor SL4 174 AX84
Hamlea Cl, SE12 206 EG85
Hamlet, The, SE5 184 DR83
Potten End HP4 61 BA16
Hamlet Cl, SE13 186 EE84
Bricket Wood AL2 82 BZ30
Romford RM5 126 FA52
Hamlet Gdns, W6 181 CU77
Hamlet Hill, Roydon CM19 72 EG19
Hamlet Ho, Erith DA8
off Waterhead Cl 189 FE80
Hamlet Ms, SE21
off Thurlow Pk Rd 204 DR88
Hamleton Ter, Dag. RM9
off Flamstead Rd 168 EW66
Hamlet Rd, SE19 204 DT94
Romford RM5 126 FA52
Hamlet Sq, NW2 141 CY62
Hamlets Way, E3 21 N4
Hamlet Way, SE1 31 M4
★ **Hamleys**, W1 17 L10
Hamlin Cres, Pnr. HA5 138 BW57
Hamlin Rd, Sev. TN13 278 FE121
Hamlyn Cl, Edg. HA8 118 CL48
Hamlyn Gdns, SE19 204 DS94
Hamlyn Ho, Felt. TW13
off High St 197 BV88
Hammarskjold Rd, Harl.
CM20 57 EQ14
Hamm Ct, Wey. KT13 216 BL103
Hammelton Grn, SW9 42 G6
Hammelton Rd, Brom. BR1 226 EF95
HAMMERFIELD, Hem.H. HP1 62 BG20
Hammerfield Dr, Abin.Ham.
RH5 283 BT140
Hammer La, Hem.H. HP2 62 BM19
Hammer Par, Wat. WD25 81 BU33
Hammers Gate, St.Alb. AL2 82 CA25
Hammers La, NW7 119 CU50
Hammersley La, Penn HP10,
HP13 110 AC49
HAMMERSMITH, W6 26 B10
⊖ **Hammersmith** 26 B9
⊖ **Hammersmith** 26 B9
Coll **Hammersmith & W London**
Coll, W14 26 E10
Hammersmith Br, SW13 181 CV79
W6 181 CV79
Hammersmith Br Rd, W6 38 A1
Jct **Hammersmith Bdy**, W6 26 B9
Hammersmith Bdy, W6 26 B9
Hammersmith Flyover, W6 26 B10
Hammersmith Gro, W6 26 A7
H **Hammersmith Hosp**, W12 161 CV72
Hammersmith Rd, W6 26 C9
W14 26 C9
Hammersmith Ter, W6 181 CU78
Hammerton Cl, Bex. DA5 209 FE90
Hammet Cl, Hayes UB4 158 BX71
Hammett St, EC3 20 A10
Hamm Moor La, Add. KT15 234 BL106
Hammond Av, Mitch. CR4 223 DH96
Hammond Cl, Barn. EN5 101 CY43
Cheshunt EN7 88 DS26
Greenford UB6
off Lilian Board Way 139 CD64
Hampton TW12 218 CA95
Woking GU21 248 AW115
Hammond Ct, Chsht EN7
off Stocksbridge Cl 88 DS26
Hammond End, Farn.Com.
SL2 133 AP63
Hammond Ho, SE14
off Lubbock St 45 H5
Sch **Hammond JMI & Nurs Sch**,
Hem.H. HP2
off Cambrian Way 62 BM17
Hammond Rd, Enf. EN1 104 DV40
Southall UB2 178 BY76
Woking GU21 248 AW115
Hammonds Cl, Dag. RM8 148 EW62
Hammonds La, Gt Warley
CM13 129 FV51
Hammond's La, Hat. AL10 50 CQ13
Sandridge AL4 50 CN12
HAMMOND STREET,
Wal.Cr. EN7 88 DR26
Hammond St, NW5 7 L4
Hammondstreet Rd, Chsht EN7 88 DR26
Hammond Way, SE28
off Oriole Way 168 EV73
Hamond Cl, S.Croy. CR2 241 DP109
Hamonde Cl, Edg. HA8 118 CP47
Hamond Sq, N1 9 N10
Ham Pk Rd, E7 13 L6
E15 13 L6
Hampden Av, Beck. BR3 225 DY96
Chesham HP5 76 AN30
Hampden Cl, NW1 17 P1
North Weald Bassett CM16 92 FA27
Stoke Poges SL2 154 AU69
Hampden Cres, Chsht EN7 89 DV31
Warley CM14 130 FW49
Sch **Hampden Gurney C of E**
Prim Sch, W1 16 D8
Hampden Gurney St, W1 16 E9
Hampden Hill, Beac. HP9 111 AH53
Ware SG12 55 DZ06
Hampden Hill Cl, Ware SG12 55 DZ05
Hampden La, N17 122 DT53
Hampden Pl, Frog. AL2 83 CE29
Hampden Rd, N8 143 DN56
N10 120 DG52
N17 122 DU53
N19 *off Holloway Rd* 143 DK61
Beckenham BR3 225 DY96
Chalfont St. Peter SL9 112 AX53
Grays RM17 192 GB78
Harrow HA3 116 CC53
Kingston upon Thames KT1 220 CN97
Romford RM5 127 FB52
Slough SL3 175 AZ76
Hampden Sq, N14
off Osidge La 121 DH46
Hampden Way, N14 121 DH47
Watford WD17 97 BS36
Hampermill La, Wat. WD19 115 BT47
Hampshire Av, Slou. SL1 153 AQ71
Hampshire Cl, N18
off Berkshire Gdns 122 DV50
Hampshire Ct, Add. KT15
off Garfield Rd 234 BJ106
Hampshire Hog La, W6
off King St 181 CV77
Hampshire Rd, N22 121 DM52
Hornchurch RM11 150 FN56
Sch **Hampshire Sch, The**,
Pre-Prep, SW7 28 C5
Prep, W2 15 N10
Hampshire St, NW5 7 N4
Hampson Way, SW8 42 C6
⊖ **Hampstead** 142 DC63
Hampstead Av, Wdf.Grn. IG8 125 EN52
Hampstead Cl, SE28 168 EV74
Bricket Wood AL2 82 BZ31
Hampstead Gdns, NW11 142 DA58
Chadwell Heath RM6 148 EV57
HAMPSTEAD GARDEN SUBURB,
N2 142 DC57
Sch **Hampstead Garden Suburb Inst**,
The, N2 *off Beaumont Cl* 142 DE56
Hampstead Grn, NW3 6 C2
Hampstead Gro, NW3 142 DC62
★ **Hampstead Heath**, NW3 142 DD61
⇌ **Hampstead Heath** 6 D1
Hampstead Hts, N2 142 DC56
Hampstead High St, NW3 142 DC63
Hampstead Hill Gdns, NW3 6 B1
Hampstead La, N6 142 DD59
NW3 142 DD59
Dorking RH4 285 CG137
Sch **Hampstead Parochial C of E**
Prim Sch, NW3 5 P1
Hampstead Rd, NW1 7 L10
Dorking RH4 285 CG137
Sch **Hampstead Sch**, NW2 4 F1
Hampstead Sq, NW3 142 DC62
Hampstead Wk, E3
off Waterside Cl 11 P8
Hampstead Way, NW11 142 DC60
HAMPTON, TW12 218 CB95
⇌ **Hampton** 218 CA95
Hampton Cl, N11 121 DH50
NW6 15 J3
SW20 201 CW94
Borehamwood WD6 100 CQ43
Chafford Hundred RM16 191 FW76
Sch **Hampton Comm Coll**, Hmptn.
TW12 *off Hanworth Rd* 198 CA92
⇌ **Hampton Court** 219 CE98
Hampton Ct, N1 8 G5
Hampton Ct Av, E.Mol. KT8 219 CD99
Hampton Ct Cres, E.Mol. KT8 219 CD97
★ **Hampton Court Palace & Pk**,
E.Mol. KT8 219 CE97
Hampton Ct Par, E.Mol. KT8
off Creek Rd 219 CE98
Hampton Ct Pk, E.Mol.
(Home Pk) KT8 219 CG98
Kingston upon Thames
(Home Pk) KT1 219 CG98
Hampton Ct Rd, E.Mol. KT8 219 CF97
Hampton TW12 218 CC96
Kingston upon Thames KT1 219 CF97
Hampton Ct Way, E.Mol. KT8 219 CE100
Esher KT10 219 CE103
Thames Ditton KT7 219 CE103
Hampton Cres, Grav. DA12 213 GL89
● **Hampton Fm Ind Est**,
Felt. TW13 198 BY90
Hampton Gdns, Saw. CM21 58 EW06
Hampton Gro, Epsom KT17 239 CT111
HAMPTON HILL, Hmptn. TW12 198 CC93
● **Hampton Hill Business Pk**,
Hmptn. TW12
off Wellington Rd 198 CC92
Sch **Hampton Hill Jun Sch**,
Hmptn H. TW12
off St. James's Av 198 CC92
Hampton Ho, SW8
off Ascalon St 41 L5
Sch **Hampton Inf Sch**, Hmptn.
TW12 *off Ripley Rd* 198 CA94
Sch **Hampton Jun Sch**, Hmptn.
TW12 *off Percy Rd* 218 CA95
Hampton La, Felt. TW13 198 BY91
Hampton Mead, Loug. IG10 107 EP41
Hampton Ms, NW10
off Minerva Rd 160 CR69
Hampton Ri, Har. HA3 140 CL58
Hampton Rd, E4 123 DZ50
E7 146 EH64
E11 145 ED60
Croydon CR0 224 DQ100
Hampton Hill TW12 199 CD92
Ilford IG1 147 EP63
Redhill RH1 288 DF139
Teddington TW11 199 CD92
Twickenham TW2 199 CD90
Worcester Park KT4 221 CU103
Hampton Rd E, Han. TW13 198 BZ90
Hampton Rd W, Felt. TW13 198 BY89
Sch **Hampton Sch**, Hmptn.
TW12 *off Hanworth Rd* 198 CA92
Hampton St, SE1 31 H9
SE17 31 H9
HAMPTON WICK, Kings.T. KT1 219 CH95
⇌ **Hampton Wick** 219 CJ95
Sch **Hampton Wick Inf & Nurs Sch**,
Hmptn W. TW11
off Normansfield Av 199 CK94
Ham Ridings, Rich. TW10 200 CM92
HAMSEY GREEN, Warl. CR6 258 DW116
Hamsey Grn Gdns, Warl. CR6 258 DV116
Sch **Hamsey Grn Inf Sch**, Warl.
CR6 *off Tithepit Shaw La* 258 DV116
Sch **Hamsey Grn Jun Sch**, Warl.
CR6 *off Tithepit Shaw La* 258 DV116
Hamsey Way, S.Croy. CR2 258 DV115
Hamshades Cl, Sid. DA15 207 ET90
Hamstel Rd, Harl. CM20 57 EP14
Ham St, Rich. TW10 199 CJ89
Ham Vw, Croy. CR0 225 DY100
Ham Yd, W1 17 N10
Hanah Ct, SW19 201 CX94
Hanameel St, E16 35 P2
Hana Ms, E5 10 F1
Hanbury Cl, NW4 141 CW55
Burnham SL1 152 AG71
Cheshunt EN8 89 DX29
Ware SG12 55 DY06
Hanbury Dr, E11
off High Rd Leytonstone 146 EF59
N21 103 DM43
Biggin Hill TN16 244 EH113
Hanbury La, Essen. AL9 68 DE17
Hanbury Ms, N1 9 K9
Hanbury Path, Wok. GU21 233 BD114
Hanbury Rd, N17 122 DV54
W3 180 CP75
Hanbury St, E1 20 A6
Hanbury Wk, Bex. DA5 209 FE90
Hancock Ct, Borwd. WD6 100 CQ39
Hancock Rd, E3 22 E3
SE19 204 DR93
Hancroft Rd, Hem.H. HP3 62 BM22
Hancross Cl, Brick.Wd AL2 82 BY30
Handa Cl, Hem.H. HP3 63 BP23
Handa Wk, N1 9 K4
Hand Ct, WC1 18 D7
Handcroft Rd, Croy. CR0 223 DP101
Handel Cl, Edg. HA8 118 CM51
Handel Cres, Til. RM18 193 GG80
Handel Pl, NW10 160 CR65
Handel St, WC1 18 A4
Handel Way, Edg. HA8 118 CN52
Handen Rd, SE12 206 EE85
Handford Ct, Wat. WD25 82 BX34
Handforth Rd, SW9 42 E4
Ilford IG1
off Winston Way 147 EP62
Handinhand La, Tad. KT20 270 CQ130
Hand La, Saw. CM21 58 EW06
Handley Gate, Brick.Wd AL2 82 BZ29
Handley Gro, NW2 141 CX62
Handley Page Rd, Wall. SM6 241 DM108
Handley Page Way, Coln.St AL2 83 CF30
Handley Rd, E9 11 H8
Handleys Ct, Hem.H. HP2
off Selden Hill 62 BK22
Handowe Cl, NW4 141 CU56
Handpost Hill, Northaw EN6 87 DH28
Handpost Lo Gdns, Hem.H.
HP2 63 BR21
HANDSIDE, Welw.G.C. AL8 51 CV10
Handside Cl, Welw.G.C. AL8 51 CW09
Worcester Park KT4 221 CX102
Handside Grn, Welw.G.C. AL8 51 CW08
Handside La, Welw.G.C. AL8 51 CV11
Hands Wk, E16 23 P8
Handsworth Av, E4 123 ED51
Sch **Handsworth Prim Sch**, E4
off Handsworth Av 123 ED51
Handsworth Rd, N17 144 DR55
Handsworth Way, Wat. WD19 115 BU48
Handtrough Way, Bark. IG11
off Fresh Wf 167 EP68
Hanford Cl, SW18 202 DA88
Hanford Rd, Aveley RM15 170 FQ74
Hanford Row, SW19 201 CW93
Hangar Ruding, Wat. WD19 116 BZ48
Hanger Cl, Hem.H. HP1 62 BH21
Hanger Ct, Knap. GU21 248 AS117
Hanger Grn, W5 160 CN70
Hanger Hill, Wey. KT13 235 BP107
⊖ **Hanger Lane** 160 CM69
Jct **Hanger La**, W5 160 CL69
Hanger La, W5 160 CM70
Hanger Vale La, W5 160 CM72
Hanger Vw Way, W3 160 CN72
Hanging Hill La, Hutt. CM13 131 GB48
Hanging Sword All, EC4 18 F9
Hangrove Hill, Downe BR6 245 EP113
Hankey Pl, SE1 31 M5
Hankins La, NW7 118 CS48
Hanley Cl, Wind. SL4 173 AK81
Hanley Gdns, N4 143 DL60
Hanley Pl, Beck. BR3 205 EA94
Hanley Rd, N4 143 DL60
Hanmer Wk, N7
off Newington Barrow Way 143 DM62
Hannah Cl, NW10 140 CQ63
Beckenham BR3 225 EC97
Hannah Ct, N13 121 DM47
Hannah Mary Way, SE1 32 D9
Hannah Ms, Wall. SM6 241 DJ108
Hannards Way, Ilf. IG6 126 EV50
Hannay La, N8 143 DK59
Hannay Wk, SW16 203 DK89
Hannell Rd, SW6 38 E4
Hannen Rd, SE27
off Norwood High St 203 DP90
Hannibal Rd, E1 21 H6
Stanwell TW19 196 BK87
Hannibal Way, Croy. CR0 241 DM107
Hannington Rd, SW4 183 DH83
Hanover Av, E16 35 N2
Feltham TW13 197 BU88
Hanover Circle, Hayes UB3 157 BQ72
Hanover Cl, Eng.Grn TW20 194 AV93
Merstham RH1 273 DJ128
Richmond TW9 180 CN80
Slough SL1 174 AU76
Sutton SM3 239 CZ105
Windsor SL4
off Hanover Way 173 AM81
Hanover Ct, SE19
off Anerley Rd 204 DT94
W12 *off Uxbridge Rd* 161 CU74
Dorking RH4 285 CF136
Guildford GU1
off Riverside 264 AX132
Hoddesdon EN11
off Jersey Cl 71 EA16
Waltham Abbey EN9
off Quaker La 89 EC34
Woking GU22
off Midhope Rd 248 AY119
Hanover Dr, Chis. BR7 207 EQ91
Hanover Gdns, SE11 42 E3
Abbots Langley WD5 81 BT30
Ilford IG6 125 EQ52
Hanover Gate, NW1 16 D3
Slough SL1
off Cippenham La 153 AN74
Hanover Gate Mans, NW1 16 D4
Hanover Grn, Hem.H. HP1 62 BG22
Hanover Ho, Surb. KT6
off Lenelby Rd 220 CN102
Hanover Mead, Bray SL6 172 AC76
Hanover Pk, SE15 44 C7
Hanover Pl, E3 21 N3
WC2 18 B9
Warley CM14 130 FV50
Sch **Hanover Prim Sch**, N1 9 H10
Hanover Rd, N15 144 DT56
NW10 4 B8
SW19 202 DC94
Hanover Sq, W1 17 K9
Hanover Steps, W2
off St. Georges Flds 16 D9
Hanover St, W1 17 K9
Croydon CR0
off Abbey Rd 223 DP104
Hanover Ter, NW1 16 D3
Hanover Ter Ms, NW1 16 D3
Hanover Wk, Hat. AL10 67 CT21
Weybridge KT13 217 BS104
Hanover Way, Bexh. DA6 188 EX83
Windsor SL4 173 AM82
● **Hanover W Ind Est**, NW10 160 CR68
Hanover Yd, N1 9 H10
Hansard Ms, W14 26 D4
Hansart Way, Enf. EN2
off The Ridgeway 103 DN39

Hanscomb Ms, SW4
off Bromell's Rd ... **183** DJ84
Hans Cres, SW1 ... **28** E6
Hanselin Cl, Stan. HA7 ... **117** CF50
Hansells Mead, Roydon CM19 .. **72** EG15
Hansen Dr, N21 ... **103** DM43
Hanshaw Dr, Edg. HA8 ... **118** CR53
Hansler Gro, E.Mol. KT8 ... **219** CD98
Hansler Rd, SE22 ... **204** DT85
Hansol Rd, Bexh. DA6 ... **208** EY85
Hanson Cl, SW12 ... **203** DH87
SW14 ... **180** CQ83
Beckenham BR3 ... **205** EB93
Guildford GU4 ... **265** AZ131
Loughton IG10 ... **107** EQ40
West Drayton UB7 ... **176** BM76
Hanson Dr, Loug. IG10 ... **107** EQ40
Hanson Gdns, Sthl. UB1 ... **178** BY75
Hanson Grn, Loug. IG10 ... **107** EQ40
Hanson St, W1 ... **17** L6
Hans Pl, SW1 ... **28** F6
Hans Rd, SW3 ... **28** E6
Hans St, SW1 ... **28** F7
Hanway Pl, W1 ... **17** N8
Hanway Rd, W7 ... **159** CD72
Hanway St, W1 ... **17** N8
HANWELL, W7 ... **159** CF74
⇌ **Hanwell** ... **159** CE73
HANWORTH, Felt. TW13 ... **198** BX91
Hanworth La, Cher. KT16 ... **215** BF102
Hanworth Rd, Felt. TW13 ... **197** BV88
Hampton TW12 ... **198** CB93
Hounslow TW3, TW4 ... **178** CB83
Redhill RH1 ... **288** DF139
Sunbury-on-Thames TW16 .. **197** BU94
Hanworth Ter, Houns. TW3 ... **178** CB84
● **Hanworth Trd Est**, Felt.
TW13 ... **198** BY90
Hanyards End, Cuffley EN6 ... **87** DL28
Hanyards La, Cuffley EN6 ... **87** DK28
Hapgood Cl, Grnf. UB6 ... **139** CD64
Harads Pl, E1 ... **32** D1
Harbans Ct, Colnbr. SL3
off Old Bath Rd ... **175** BE81
Harben Rd, NW6 ... **5** P6
Harberson Rd, E15 ... **13** L8
SW12 ... **203** DH88
Harberton Rd, N19 ... **143** DJ60
Harberts Rd, Harl. CM19 ... **73** EP16
Harbet Rd, E4 ... **123** DX50
N18 ... **123** DX50
W2 ... **16** B7
Harbex Cl, Bex. DA5 ... **209** FB87
Sch **Harbinger Prim Sch**, E14 ... **34** C9
Harbinger Rd, E14 ... **34** C9
Harbledown Pl, Orp. BR5
off Okemore Gdns ... **228** EW98
Harbledown Rd, SW6 ... **39** J6
South Croydon CR2 ... **242** DU111
Harbord Cl, SE5 ... **43** L8
Harbord St, SW6 ... **38** C6
Harborne Cl, Wat. WD19 ... **116** BW50
Harborough Av, Sid. DA15 ... **207** ES87
Harborough Cl, Slou. SL1 ... **153** AK74
Harborough Rd, SW16 ... **203** DM91
Harbour Av, SW10 ... **39** P6
Harbourer Cl, Ilf. IG6 ... **126** EV50
Harbourer Rd, Ilf. IG6 ... **126** EV50
Harbour Ex Sq, E14 ... **34** D5
Harbourfield Rd, Bans. SM7 .. **256** DB115
Harbour Reach, SW6
off The Boulevard ... **39** P7
Harbour Rd, SE5 ... **43** J10
Harbour Yd, SW10 ... **39** P7
Harbridge Av, SW15 ... **201** CT87
Harbury Rd, Cars. SM5 ... **240** DE109
Harbut Rd, SW11 ... **182** DD84
Harcamlow Way, Ware SG12 ... **56** EH10
Harcombe Rd, N16 ... **144** DS62
Harcourt, Wrays. TW19 ... **194** AY86
Harcourt Av, E12 ... **147** EM63
Edgware HA8 ... **118** CQ48
Sidcup DA15 ... **208** EW86
Wallington SM6 ... **241** DH105
Harcourt Cl, Dorney R. SL6 ... **172** AF76
Egham TW20 ... **195** BC93
Isleworth TW7 ... **179** CG83
Harcourt Fld, Wall. SM6 ... **241** DH105
Harcourt Lo, Wall. SM6
off Croydon Rd ... **241** DH105
Harcourt Ms, Rom. RM2 ... **149** FF57
Harcourt Rd, E15 ... **23** L1
N22 ... **121** DK53
SE4 ... **185** DY84
SW19 *off Russell Rd* ... **202** DA94
Bexleyheath DA6 ... **188** EY84
Bushey WD23 ... **98** CC43
Dorney Reach SL6 ... **172** AF76
Thornton Heath CR7 ... **223** DM100
Wallington SM6 ... **241** DH105
Windsor SL4 ... **173** AL81
Harcourt St, W1 ... **16** D7
Harcourt Ter, SW10 ... **39** M1
Hardcastle Cl, Croy. CR0 ... **224** DU100
Hardcourts Cl, W.Wick. BR4 ... **225** EB104
Hardell Cl, Egh. TW20 ... **195** BA92
Hardel Ri, SW2 ... **203** DP89
Hardel Wk, SW2
off Papworth Way ... **203** DN87
Harden Fm Cl, Couls. CR5 ... **257** DJ121
Harden Rd, Nthflt DA11 ... **213** GF90
Hardens Manorway, SE7 ... **36** E7
Harders Rd, SE15 ... **44** E8
Hardess St, SE24
off Herne Hill Rd ... **184** DQ83
Hardie Cl, NW10 ... **140** CR64
Hardie Rd, Dag. RM10 ... **149** FC62
Harding Cl, SE17 ... **43** J2
Croydon CR0 ... **224** DT104
Watford WD25 ... **82** BW33
Hardinge Cl, Uxb. UB8 ... **157** BP72
Hardinge Cres, SE18 ... **187** EQ76
Hardinge Rd, N18 ... **122** DS50
NW10 ... **161** CV67
Hardinge St, E1 ... **21** H9
Harding Ho, Hayes UB3 ... **157** BU72
Harding Rd, Bexh. DA7 ... **188** EZ82
Chesham HP5 ... **76** AR30
Epsom KT18 ... **254** CS119
Grays RM16 ... **193** GG76
Hardings, Welw.G.C. AL7 ... **52** DC08
Hardings Cl, Hem.H. HP3 ... **62** BH23
Iver SL0 ... **155** BD69
Harding's Cl, Kings.T. KT2 ... **220** CM95
Hardings La, SE20 ... **205** DX93
Harding Spur, Slou. SL3
off Shaw Gdns ... **175** AZ78
Hardings Row, Iver SL0 ... **155** BC69
Hardingstone Ct, Wal.Cr. EN8
off Eleanor Way ... **89** DZ34
Hardley Cres, Horn. RM11 ... **150** FK56
Hardman Rd, SE7 ... **36** A10
Kingston upon Thames KT2 .. **220** CL96
Hardwick Cl, Oxshott KT22 ... **252** CC115
Stanmore HA7 ... **117** CJ50
Hardwick Cres, Dart. DA2 ... **210** FP86
Hardwicke Av, Houns. TW5 ... **178** CA81
Hardwicke Gdns, Amer. HP6 ... **77** AS38
Hardwicke Ho, E3
off Bromley High St ... **22** C2
Hardwicke Ms, WC1 ... **18** D3
Hardwicke Pl, Lon.Col. AL2 ... **83** CK27
Hardwicke Rd, N13 ... **121** DL51
W4 ... **180** CQ77
Reigate RH2 ... **272** DA133
Richmond TW10 ... **199** CJ91
Hardwicke St, Bark. IG11 ... **167** EQ67
Hardwick Grn, W13 ... **159** CH71
Hardwick La, Lyne KT16 ... **215** BC101
Hardwick Rd, Red. RH1 ... **288** DD136
Hardwick St, EC1 ... **18** F3
Hardwicks Way, SW18 ... **202** DA85
Hardwidge St, SE1 ... **31** N4
Hardy Av, E16 ... **35** P2
Northfleet DA11 ... **212** GE89
Ruislip HA4 ... **137** BV64
Hardy Cl, SE16 ... **33** K5
Barnet EN5 ... **101** CY44
Horley RH6 ... **290** DE148
North Holmwood RH5 ... **285** CH141
Pinner HA5 ... **138** BX59
Slough SL1 ... **153** AN74
Hardy Ct, SW18
off Furmage St ... **202** DB87
Hardy Gro, Dart. DA1 ... **190** FN84
Hardy Pas, N22
off Berners Rd ... **121** DN54
Hardy Rd, E4 ... **123** DZ51
SE3 ... **47** M3
SW19 ... **202** DB94
Hemel Hempstead HP2 ... **62** BM19
Hardy's Ms, E.Mol. KT8 ... **219** CE98
Hardy Way, Enf. EN2 ... **103** DN39
Hare & Billet Rd, SE3 ... **46** G7
Harebell, Welw.G.C. AL7 ... **51** CY13
Harebell Cl, Hert. SG13 ... **54** DV09
Harebell Dr, E6 ... **25** M7
Harebell Hill, Cob. KT11 ... **236** BX114
Harebell Way, Rom. RM3 ... **128** FK52
Harebreaks, The, Wat. WD24 ... **97** BV38
Harecastle Cl, Hayes UB4 ... **158** BY70
Hare Ct, EC4 ... **18** E9
Harecourt Rd, N1 ... **9** J4
Hare Cres, Wat. WD25 ... **81** BU32
Harecroft, Dor. RH4 ... **285** CJ139
Fetcham KT22 ... **252** CB123
Haredale Rd, SE24 ... **184** DQ84
Haredon Cl, SE23 ... **204** DW87
HAREFIELD, Uxb. UB9 ... **114** BL53
Harefield, Esher KT10 ... **237** CE105
Harlow CM20 ... **58** EU14
Sch **Harefield Acad, The**, Hare.
UB9 *off Northwood Way* ... **114** BK53
Harefield Av, Sutt. SM2 ... **239** CY109
Harefield Cl, Enf. EN2 ... **103** DN39
H **Harefield Hosp**, Hare. UB9 .. **114** BJ53
Sch **Harefield Inf Sch**, Hare.
UB9 *off High St* ... **114** BJ53
Sch **Harefield Jun Sch**, Hare.
UB9 *off Park La* ... **114** BJ53
Harefield Ms, SE4 ... **45** N10
Harefield Pl, St.Alb. AL4 ... **65** CK17
Harefield Rd, N8 ... **143** DK57
SE4 ... **185** DZ83
SW16 ... **203** DM94
Rickmansworth WD3 ... **114** BK50
Sidcup DA14 ... **208** EX89
Uxbridge UB8 ... **156** BK65
Hare Hall La, Rom. RM2 ... **149** FH56
Harehatch La, Slou. SL2 ... **133** AL60
Hare Hill, Add. KT15 ... **233** BF107
Hare Hill Cl, Pyrford GU22 ... **250** BG115
Harelands Cl, Wok. GU21 ... **248** AW117
Harelands La, Wok. GU21 ... **248** AW117
Hare La, Clay. KT10 ... **237** CE107
Hatfield AL10 ... **67** CU20
Hare Marsh, E2 ... **20** C4
Sch **Harenc Sch**, Sid. DA14
off Rectory La ... **208** EW92
Harendon, Tad. KT20 ... **255** CW121
Harepark Cl, Hem.H. HP1 ... **61** BF19
Hare Pl, EC4 ... **18** F9
Hare Row, E2 ... **10** F10
Hares Bk, New Adgtn CR0 ... **243** ED110
Haresfield Rd, Dag. RM10 ... **168** FA65
Sch **Haresfoot Sch**, Berk. HP4
off Chesham Rd ... **60** AV22
Harestone Dr, Cat. CR3 ... **258** DT124
Harestone Hill, Cat. CR3 ... **274** DT126
Harestone La, Cat. CR3 ... **274** DS125
H **Harestone Marie Curie Cen**,
Cat. CR3 ... **274** DT125
Harestone Valley Rd, Cat. CR3 .. **274** DT126
HARE STREET, Harl. CM19 ... **73** EP16
Hare St, SE18 ... **37** M7
Harlow CM19 ... **73** EP15
Sch **Hare St Comm Prim Sch & Nurs**,
Harl. CM19 *off Little Gro Fld* .. **73** EQ15
Hare St Springs, Harl. CM19 .. **73** EP15
Hare Ter, Grays RM20
off Mill La ... **191** FX78
Hare Wk, N1 ... **19** P1
Hareward Rd, Guil. GU4 ... **265** BC132
Harewood, Rick. WD3 ... **96** BH43
Harewood Av, NW1 ... **16** D5
Northolt UB5 ... **158** BY66
Harewood Cl, Nthlt. UB5 ... **158** BZ66
Reigate RH2 ... **272** DC132
Harewood Ct, Warl. CR6 ... **259** DY118
Harewood Dr, Ilf. IG5 ... **125** EM54
Harewood Gdns, S.Croy. CR2 .. **258** DV115
Harewood Hill, They.B. CM16 .. **107** ES35
Harewood Pl, W1 ... **17** K9
Slough SL1 ... **174** AU76
Harewood Rd, SW19 ... **202** DE93
Chalfont St. Giles HP8 ... **94** AW41
Isleworth TW7 ... **179** CF80
Pilgrim's Hatch CM15 ... **130** FV44
South Croydon CR2 ... **242** DS107
Watford WD19 ... **115** BV48
Harewood Row, NW1 ... **16** D6
Harewood Ter, Sthl. UB2 ... **178** BZ77
Harfield Gdns, SE5 ... **43** N10
Harfield Rd, Sun. TW16 ... **218** BX96
Harford Cl, E4 ... **123** EB45
Harford Dr, Wat. WD17 ... **97** BS38
Harford Ms, N19 ... **143** DK62
Harford Rd, E4 ... **123** EB45
Harford St, E1 ... **21** L5
Harford Wk, N2 ... **142** DD57
Harfst Way, Swan. BR8 ... **229** FC95
Hargood Cl, Har. HA3 ... **140** CL58
Hargood Rd, SE3 ... **186** EJ81
Hargrave Pk, N19 ... **143** DJ61
Sch **Hargrave Pk Prim Sch**,
N19 *off Hargrave Pk* ... **143** DJ61
Hargrave Pl, N7 ... **7** N3
Hargrave Rd, N19 ... **143** DJ61
Hargreaves Av, Chsht EN7 ... **88** DV30
Hargreaves Cl, Chsht EN7 ... **88** DV31
Hargwyne St, SW9 ... **183** DM83
Haringey Pk, N8 ... **143** DL58
Haringey Pas, N4 ... **143** DP58
N8 ... **143** DN56
Haringey Rd, N8 ... **143** DL56
Coll **Haringey 6th Form Cen**,
N17 *off College Rd* ... **122** DT51
Harington Ter, N9 ... **122** DR48
N18 ... **122** DR48
Harkett Cl, Har. HA3
off Byron Rd ... **117** CF54
Harkett Ct, Har. HA3 ... **117** CF54
Harkness, Chsht EN7 ... **88** DU29
Harkness Cl, Epsom KT17 ... **255** CW116
Romford RM3 ... **128** FM50
Harkness Ct, Sutt. SM1
off Cleeve Way ... **222** DC102
Harkness Ho, E1
off Christian St ... **20** D9
Harkness Rd, Burn. SL1 ... **152** AH71
Hemel Hempstead HP2 ... **62** BK19
Harland Av, Croy. CR0 ... **224** DT104
Sidcup DA15 ... **207** ER90
Harland Cl, SW19 ... **222** DB97
Harland Rd, SE12 ... **206** EG88
Harlands Gro, Orp. BR6 ... **245** EP105
Harlech Gdns, Houns. TW5 ... **178** BW79
Pinner HA5 ... **138** BX59
Harlech Rd, N14 ... **121** DL48
Abbots Langley WD5 ... **81** BU31
Harlech Twr, W3 ... **180** CP75
🔒 **Harlequin, The**, Wat. WD17 .. **98** BW42
Harlequin Av, Brent. TW8 ... **179** CG79
Harlequin Cl, Hayes UB4
off Cygnet Way ... **158** BX71
Isleworth TW7 ... **199** CE85
Harlequin Ho, Erith DA18
off Kale Rd ... **188** EY76
Harlequin Rd, Tedd. TW11 ... **199** CH94
★ **Harlequins RL**, Twick. TW2 .. **199** CE87
Harlescott Rd, SE15 ... **185** DX84
HARLESDEN, NW10 ... **160** CS68
⊖ **Harlesden** ... **160** CR68
⇌ **Harlesden** ... **160** CR68
Harlesden Cl, Rom. RM3 ... **128** FM52
Harlesden Gdns, NW10 ... **161** CT67
Harlesden La, NW10 ... **161** CU67
Sch **Harlesden Prim Sch**,
NW10 *off Acton La* ... **160** CS68
Harlesden Rd, NW10 ... **161** CU67
Romford RM3 ... **128** FM51
St. Albans AL1 ... **65** CG20
Harlesden Wk, Rom. RM3 ... **128** FM52
Harleston Cl, E5
off Theydon Rd ... **144** DW61
Harley Cl, Wem. HA0 ... **159** CK65
Harley Ct, E11
off Blake Hall Rd ... **146** EG59
St. Albans AL4
off Villiers Cres ... **65** CK16
Harley Cres, Har. HA1 ... **139** CD56
Harleyford, Brom. BR1 ... **226** EH95
Harleyford Rd, SE11 ... **42** C2
Harleyford St, SE11 ... **42** E3
Harley Gdns, SW10 ... **39** P1
Orpington BR6 ... **245** ES105
Harley Gro, E3 ... **21** P2
Harley Pl, W1 ... **17** J7
Harley Rd, NW3 ... **6** B7
NW10 ... **160** CS68
Harrow HA1 ... **139** CD56
Harley St, W1 ... **17** J7
H **Harley St Clinic, The**, W1 ... **17** J6
Harling Ct, SW11 ... **40** E8
Harlinger St, SE18 ... **36** G6
Harlings, Hert.Hth SG13 ... **54** DW13
HARLINGTON, Hayes UB3 ... **177** BQ79
Harlington Cl, Harling. UB3
off New Rd ... **177** BQ80
Sch **Harlington Comm Sch**,
Harling. UB3
off Pinkwell La ... **177** BR77
Jun **Harlington Cor**, Hayes
UB3 *off Bath Rd* ... **177** BR81
Harlington Rd, Bexh. DA7 ... **188** EY83
Uxbridge UB8 ... **157** BP71
Harlington Rd E, Felt.
TW13, TW14 ... **197** BV87
Harlington Rd W, Felt. TW14 .. **197** BV86
HARLOW, CM17 - CM20 ... **73** ER15
⇌ **Harlow** ... **57** ER14
Sch **Harlowbury Prim Sch**, Old Harl.
CM17 *off Watlington Rd* ... **58** EX11
● **Harlow Business Cen**,
Harl. CM19 ... **73** EN16
● **Harlow Business Pk**,
Harl. CM19 ... **72** EL15
Coll **Harlow Coll**, Harl. CM20
off Velizy Av ... **57** ES14
Harlow Common, Harl. CM17 .. **74** EW18
Harlow Ct, Hem.H. HP2 ... **62** BN16
Sch **Harlow Flds Sch**, Harl.
CM18 *off Tendring Rd* ... **73** ES17
Harlow Gdns, Rom. RM5 ... **127** FC51
● **Harlow Ind Cen**, Harl. CM20 .. **58** EV10
🔒 **Harlow Mkt**, Harl. CM20
off East Gate ... **57** ER14
⇌ **Harlow Mill** ... **58** EW10
Harlow Potter St Bypass,
Harl. CM17, CM20 ... **74** EV15
Sch **Harlow PRU**, Harl. CM20
off Mowbray Rd ... **58** EU12
🔒 **Harlow Retail Pk**,
Harl. CM20 ... **57** ET11
Harlow Rd, N13 ... **122** DR48
Harlow CM20 ... **58** EW08
Matching Tye CM17 ... **59** FC12
Old Harlow CM17 ... **58** FA09
Rainham RM13 ... **169** FF67
Harlow Rd, Roydon CM19 ... **72** EJ15
Sawbridgeworth CM21 ... **58** EW08
Sheering CM22 ... **58** FA09
⇌ **Harlow Town** ... **57** ER12
HARLOW TYE, Harl. CM17 ... **59** FC12
Harlton Ct, Wal.Abb. EN9 ... **90** EF34
Harlyn Dr, Pnr. HA5 ... **137** BV55
Sch **Harlyn Prim Sch**, Pnr.
HA5 *off Tolcarne Dr* ... **137** BV55
Harman Av, Grav. DA11 ... **213** GH92
Woodford Green IG8 ... **124** EF52
Harman Cl, E4 ... **123** ED49
NW2 ... **141** CY62
SE1 *off Avondale Sq* ... **44** C1
Harman Dr, NW2 ... **141** CY62
Sidcup DA15 ... **207** ET86
Harman Pl, Pur. CR8 ... **241** DP111
Harman Rd, Enf. EN1 ... **104** DT43
Harmer Rd, Swans. DA10 ... **212** FZ86
Harmer St, Grav. DA12 ... **213** GJ86
Harmonds Wd Cl, Brox. EN10 .. **71** DY19
HARMONDSWORTH, West Dr.
UB7 ... **176** BK79
Harmondsworth La, West Dr.
UB7 ... **176** BL79
Sch **Harmondsworth Prim Sch**,
Harm. UB7 *off School Rd* .. **176** BK79
Harmondsworth Rd, West Dr.
UB7 ... **176** BL78
Harmony Cl, NW11 ... **141** CY57
Hatfield AL10 ... **67** CU16
Wallington SM6 ... **241** DL109
Harmony Pl, SE1 ... **32** B10
Harmony Ter, Har. HA2
off Goldsmith Cl ... **138** CB60
Harmony Way, NW4 ... **141** CW56
Harmood Gro, NW1 ... **7** J6
Harmood Pl, NW1 ... **7** J6
Harmood St, NW1 ... **7** J5
Harms Gro, Guil. GU4 ... **265** BC131
Harmsworth Ms, SE11 ... **30** G7
Harmsworth St, SE17 ... **42** G1
Harmsworth Way, N20 ... **119** CZ46
Harness Way, St.Alb. AL4 ... **65** CK17
Harnetts Cl, Swan. BR8 ... **229** FD100
Harold Av, Belv. DA17 ... **188** EZ78
Hayes UB3 ... **177** BT76
Harold Cl, Harl. CM19 ... **73** EM16
Harold Ct, Wal.Cr. EN8
off Alexandra Way ... **89** DZ34
Sch **Harold Ct Prim Sch**, Harold Wd
RM3 *off Church Rd* ... **128** FN52
Harold Ct Rd, Rom. RM3 ... **128** FP51
Harold Cres, Wal.Abb. EN9 ... **89** EC32
Harold Est, SE1 ... **31** P7
Harold Gibbons Ct, SE7 ... **186** EJ79
HAROLD HILL, Rom. RM3 ... **128** FL50
● **Harold Hill Ind Est**,
Rom. RM3 ... **128** FK52
Harold Laski Ho, EC1 ... **18** G3
HAROLD PARK, Rom. RM3 ... **128** FN52
Harold Pl, SE11
off Kennington La ... **42** E1
Harold Rd, E4 ... **123** EC49
E11 ... **146** EE60
E13 ... **166** EH67
N8 ... **143** DM57
N15 ... **144** DT57
NW10 ... **160** CR69
SE19 ... **204** DS93
Hawley DA2 ... **210** FM91
Sutton SM1 ... **240** DD105
Woodford Green IG8 ... **124** EG53
Haroldslea, Horl. RH6 ... **291** DK150
Haroldslea Cl, Horl. RH6 ... **291** DJ150
Haroldslea Dr, Horl. RH6 ... **291** DJ150
Harolds Rd, Harl. CM19 ... **72** EL16
Haroldstone Rd, E17 ... **145** DX57
Harold Vw, Rom. RM3 ... **128** FM54
HAROLD WOOD, Rom. RM3 ... **128** FL54
⇌ **Harold Wood** ... **128** FM53
Harold Wd Hall, Rom. RM3 ... **128** FK53
Sch **Harold Wd Prim Sch**,
Harold Wd RM3
off Recreation Av ... **150** FN55
Harp All, EC4 ... **18** G8
● **Harp Business Cen**, NW2 .. **141** CT61
Harpenden Rd, E12 ... **146** EJ61
SE27 ... **203** DP90
St. Albans AL3 ... **65** CD17
Harpenmead Pt, NW2 ... **141** CZ61
H **Harperbury Hosp**,
Shenley WD7 ... **83** CJ31
Harper Cl, N14
off Alexandra Ct ... **103** DJ43
Chafford Hundred RM16 ... **191** FW78
Harper La, Rad. WD7 ... **83** CG32
Harper Ms, SW17 ... **202** DC90
Harper Rd, E6 ... **25** J9
SE1 ... **31** J6
Harpers Yd, N17
off Ruskin Rd ... **122** DT53
Harpesford Av, Vir.W. GU25 ... **214** AV99
Harp Island Cl, NW10 ... **140** CR61
Harp La, EC3 ... **31** N1
Sch **Harpley Sch**, E1 ... **21** J4
Harpley Sq, E1 ... **21** H3
Harpour Rd, Bark. IG11 ... **167** EQ65
Harp Rd, W7 ... **159** CF70
Harpsden St, SW11 ... **40** G7
Harpsfield Bdy, Hat. AL10 ... **67** CT17
Harps Oak La, Merst. RH1 ... **272** DF125
Harpswood Cl, Couls. CR5 ... **257** DJ122
Harptree Way, St.Alb. AL1 ... **65** CG18
Harpur Ms, WC1 ... **18** C6
Harpurs, Tad. KT20 ... **255** CX122
Harpur St, WC1 ... **18** C6
Harraden Rd, SE3 ... **186** EJ81
Harrap Chase, Bad.Dene RM17 .. **192** FZ78
Harrap St, E14 ... **22** F10
Harrier Av, E11
off Eastern Av ... **146** EH58
Harrier Cl, Horn. RM12 ... **169** FH65
Harrier Ms, SE28 ... **187** ER76
Harrier Rd, NW9 ... **118** CS54
Harriers Cl, W5 ... **160** CL73
Harrier Way, E6 ... **25** K7
Waltham Abbey EN9 ... **90** EG34
Harries Cl, Chesh. HP5
off Deansway ... **76** AP30
Harriescourt, Wal.Abb. EN9 ... **90** EG32
Harries Rd, Hayes UB4 ... **158** BW70
Harriet Cl, E8 ... **10** C8
Harriet Gdns, Croy. CR0 ... **224** DU103
Harriet St, SW1 ... **28** F5
Harriet Tubman Cl, SW2 ... **203** DN87
Harriet Wk, SW1 ... **28** F5
Harriet Walker Way, Rick. WD3 .. **113** BF45
Harriet Way, Bushey WD23 ... **117** CD45
HARRINGAY, N8 ... **143** DN57
⇌ **Harringay** ... **143** DN58
Harringay Gdns, N8 ... **143** DP56
⇌ **Harringay Green Lanes** ... **143** DP58
Harringay Rd, N15 ... **143** DP57
Harrington Cl, NW10 ... **140** CR62
Croydon CR0 ... **223** DL103
Leigh RH2 ... **287** CU141
Windsor SL4 ... **173** AM84
Harrington Ct, W10
off Dart St ... **14** G2
Croydon CR0 *off Altyre Rd* .. **224** DR103
Hertford Heath SG13
off Trinity Rd ... **54** DW12
Harrington Cres, N.Stfd RM16 .. **171** FX74
Harrington Gdns, SW7 ... **27** M9
Harrington Hill, E5 ... **144** DV60
Sch **Harrington Hill Prim Sch**,
E5 *off Harrington Hill* ... **144** DV60
Harrington Ho, NW1 ... **17** L2
Tra **Harrington Road** ... **224** DW97
Harrington Rd, E11 ... **146** EE60
SE25 ... **224** DU98
SW7 ... **28** A8
Harrington Sq, NW1 ... **17** L1
Harrington St, NW1 ... **17** L1
Harrington Way, SE18 ... **36** F6
Harriott Cl, SE10 ... **35** L9
Harriotts Cl, Ashtd. KT21
off Harriotts La ... **253** CJ120
Harriotts La, Ashtd. KT21 ... **253** CJ119
Sch **Harris Acad Bermondsey**,
SE16 ... **32** B8
Sch **Harris Acad Crystal Palace**,
SE19 *off Maberley Rd* ... **224** DT95
Sch **Harris Acad Merton**, Mitch.
CR4 *off Wide Way* ... **223** DK97
Sch **Harris Acad S Norwood**, SE25
off South Norwood Hill ... **224** DT97
Sch **Harris Boys' Acad E Dulwich**,
SE22 *off Peckham Rye* ... **204** DV85
Harris Cl, Enf. EN2 ... **103** DP39
Hounslow TW3 ... **178** CA81
Northfleet DA11 ... **212** GE90
Romford RM3 ... **128** FL52
Harris Gdns, Slou. SL1 ... **173** AQ75
Sch **Harris Girls' Acad E Dulwich**,
SE22 *off Homestall Rd* ... **204** DW85
Harris La, Shenley WD7 ... **84** CN34
Harrison Cl, N20 ... **120** DE46
Hutton CM13 ... **131** GD43
Northwood HA6 ... **115** BQ51
Reigate RH2 ... **288** DB135
Harrison Dr, Brom. BR1 ... **227** EP98
North Weald Bassett CM16 .. **93** FB26
Harrison Rd, Dag. RM10 ... **169** FB65
Waltham Abbey EN9 ... **105** EC35
Harrisons Ri, Croy. CR0 ... **223** DP104
Harrison St, WC1 ... **18** B3
Harrisons Wf, Purf. RM19 ... **190** FN78
Harrison Wk, Chsht EN8 ... **89** DX30
Harrison Way, Sev. TN13 ... **278** FG122
Shepperton TW17 ... **217** BP99
Slough SL1 ... **153** AK74
Harris Rd, Bexh. DA7 ... **188** EY81
Dagenham RM9 ... **148** EZ64
Watford WD25 ... **97** BU35
Harris's La, Ware SG12 ... **54** DW05
Harris St, E17 ... **145** DZ59
SE5 ... **43** M5
Harris Way, Sun. TW16 ... **217** BS95
Harrod Ct, NW9 ... **140** CQ56
Sch **Harrodian Sch, The**, SW13
off Lonsdale Rd ... **181** CT80
★ **Harrods**, SW1 ... **28** E6
Harrogate Ct, Slou. SL3 ... **175** BA78
Harrogate Rd, Wat. WD19 ... **116** BW48
Harrold Rd, Dag. RM8 ... **148** EV64
HARROW, HA1 - HA3 ... **139** CD59
⊖ **Harrow** ... **139** CE58
⇌ **Harrow & Wealdstone** ... **139** CE56
⊖ **Harrow & Wealdstone** ... **139** CE56
★ **Harrow Arts Cen**, Pnr. HA5 .. **116** CB52
Harrow Av, Enf. EN1 ... **104** DT44
Harroway Manor, Fetch. KT22 .. **253** CF122
Harroway Rd, SW11 ... **40** B9
Harrowbond Rd, Harl. CM17 ... **58** EW14
Harrow Bottom Rd, Vir.W.
GU25 ... **215** AZ100
Harrowby Gdns, Nthflt DA11 .. **212** GE89
Harrowby St, W1 ... **16** D8
Harrow Cl, Add. KT15 ... **216** BH103
Chessington KT9 ... **237** CK108
Dorking RH4 ... **285** CG137
Hornchurch RM11 ... **149** FH60
Coll **Harrow Coll**, Harrow-on-the-Hill
Campus, Har. HA1
off Lowlands Rd ... **139** CE59
Harrow Weald Campus, Har.Wld
HA3 *off Brookshill* ... **117** CE51
Harrow Cres, Rom. RM3 ... **127** FH52
Harrowdene Cl, Wem. HA0 ... **139** CK63
Harrowdene Gdns, Tedd. TW11 .. **199** CG93
Harrowdene Rd, Wem. HA0 ... **139** CK62
Harrow Dr, N9 ... **122** DT46
Hornchurch RM11 ... **149** FH60
Harrowes Meade, Edg. HA8 ... **118** CN48
Harrow Flds Gdns, Har. HA1 ... **139** CE62
Coll **Harrow Fire Training Cen**,
Pnr. HA5 *off Pinner Rd* ... **138** CA56
Harrow Gdns, Orp. BR6 ... **246** EV105
Warlingham CR6 ... **259** DZ115
Harrow Gate Gdns, Dor. RH4
off Horsham Rd ... **285** CH138
Harrowgate Rd, E9 ... **11** L5
Harrow Grn, E11 ... **146** EE62
Sch **Harrow High Sch**, Har.
HA1 *off Gayton Rd* ... **139** CG58
Harrowlands Pk, Dor. RH4 ... **285** CH137
Harrow La, E14 ... **34** E1
Godalming GU7 ... **280** AS144
Harrow Manorway, SE2 ... **168** EW74
🔒 **Harrow Mkt**, Slou. SL3 ... **175** BA76
★ **Harrow Mus**, Har. HA2 ... **138** CB55
HARROW ON THE HILL,
Har. HA1 ... **139** CE61
⇌ **Harrow on the Hill** ... **139** CE58
⊖ **Harrow on the Hill** ... **139** CE58
Harrow Pk, Har. HA1 ... **139** CE61
Harrow Pas, Kings.T. KT1
off Market Pl ... **219** CK96
Harrow Pl, E1 ... **19** P8
Harrow Rd, E6 ... **166** EL67
E11 ... **146** EE62
NW10 ... **14** C3
W2 ... **15** L7
W9 ... **15** J5
W10 ... **14** F4
Barking IG11 ... **167** ES67

Harrow Rd, Cars. SM5 240 DE106
Feltham TW14 196 BN88
Ilford IG1 147 EQ63
Knockholt Pound TN14 262 EY115
Slough SL3 175 AZ76
Tokyngton HA9 140 CM64
Warlingham CR6 259 DZ115
Wembley HA0 139 CJ64
Harrow Rd E, Dor. RH4 285 CH138
Harrow Rd W, Dor. RH4 285 CG138
Sch Harrow Sch, Har.Hill HA1
off High St 139 CE60
Harrowsley Ct, Horl. RH6
off Tanyard Way 291 DH147
Harrowsley Grn La, Horl. RH6 291 DJ149
Harrow Vw, Har. HA1, HA2 139 CD56
Hayes UB3 157 BU72
Uxbridge UB10 157 BQ69
Harrow Vw Rd, W5 159 CH70
Harrow Way, Shep. TW17 217 BQ96
Watford WD19 116 BY48
HARROW WEALD, Har. HA3 117 CD53
Harrow Weald Pk, Har. HA3 117 CD51
Sch Harry Gosling Prim Sch, E1 20 D9
Harry's Pl, S.Ock. RM15 171 FX71
Harston Dr, Enf. EN3 105 EA38
Hart Cl, Bletch. RH1 274 DT134
Hart Cor, Grays RM20 191 FX78
Hart Cres, Chig. IG7 125 ET50
Hartcroft Cl, Hem.H. HP3 63 BP21
Hart Dyke Cres, Swan. BR8
off Hart Dyke Rd 229 FD97
Hart Dyke Rd, Orp. BR5 228 EW102
Swanley BR8 229 FD97
Harte Rd, Houns. TW3 178 BZ82
Hartfield Av, Els. WD6 100 CN43
Northolt UB5 157 BV68
Hartfield Cl, Els. WD6 100 CN43
Hartfield Ct, Ware SG12 55 DX05
Hartfield Cres, SW19 201 CZ94
West Wickham BR4 226 EG104
Hartfield Gro, SE20 224 DV95
Hartfield Pl, Nthflt DA11 212 GD87
Hartfield Rd, SW19 201 CZ94
Chessington KT9 237 CK106
West Wickham BR4 244 EG105
Hartfield Ter, E3 22 B1
Hartford Av, Har. HA3 139 CG55
Hartforde Rd, Borwd. WD6 100 CN40
Hartford Rd, Bex. DA5 208 FA86
Epsom KT19 238 CN107
Hart Gdns, Dor. RH4
off Hart Rd 285 CH135
Hart Gro, W5 160 CN74
Southall UB1 158 CA71
Harthall La, Hem.H. HP3 81 BS26
Kings Langley WD4 81 BP28
Hartham Cl, N7 8 B3
Isleworth TW7 179 CG81
Hartham La, Hert. SG14 54 DQ09
Hartham Rd, N7 8 A2
N17 122 DT54
Isleworth TW7 179 CF81
Harting Rd, SE9 206 EL91
Hartington Cl, Farnboro. BR6 245 EQ106
Harrow HA1 139 CE63
Reigate RH2 272 DA132
Hartington Ct, W4 180 CP80
Hartington Rd, E16 24 A9
E17 145 DY58
SW8 42 A5
W4 180 CP80
W13 159 CH73
Southall UB2 178 BY76
Twickenham TW1 199 CH87
Hartismere Rd, SW6 39 H4
Hartlake Rd, E9 11 K5
Hartland Cl, N21
off Elmscott Gdns 104 DQ44
Edgware HA8 118 CN47
New Haw KT15 234 BJ110
Slough SL1 153 AR74
Hartland Dr, Edg. HA8 118 CN47
Ruislip HA4 137 BV62
Hartland Rd, E15 13 L7
N11 120 DF50
NW1 7 J6
NW6 4 G10
Addlestone KT15 234 BG108
Cheshunt EN8 89 DX30
Epping CM16 92 EU31
Hampton Hill TW12 198 CB91
Hornchurch RM12 149 FG61
Isleworth TW7 179 CG83
Morden SM4 222 DA101
Hartlands Cl, Bex. DA5 208 EZ86
Hartland Way, Croy. CR0 225 DY103
Morden SM4 221 CZ101
Hartlepool Ct, E16 37 P3
Hartley Av, E6 166 EL67
NW7 119 CT50
Hartley Cl, NW7 119 CT50
Bromley BR1 227 EM96
Stoke Poges SL3 154 AW67
Hartley Copse, Old Wind. SL4 194 AU86
Hartley Down, Pur. CR8 241 DM114
Hartley Fm Est, Pur. CR8 257 DM115
HARTLEY GREEN, Long. DA3 231 FX99
Hartley Hill, Pur. CR8 257 DM115
Hartley Ho, SE1
off Longfield Est 32 B8
Hartley Old Rd, Pur. CR8 241 DM114
Sch Hartley Prim Sch, E6
off Hartley Av 166 EL67
Hartley Rd, E11 146 EF60
Croydon CR0 223 DP101
Welling DA16 188 EW80
Westerham TN16 277 ER125
Hartley St, E2 21 H2
Hartley Way, Pur. CR8 257 DM115
Hartmann Rd, E16 36 F2
Hartmoor Ms, Enf. EN3 105 DX37
Hartnoll St, N7 8 D2
Harton Cl, Brom. BR1 226 EK95
Harton Rd, N9 122 DV47
Harton St, SE8 46 A6
Hartopp Pt, SW6
off Pellant Rd 38 F4
Hart Rd, Byfleet KT14 234 BL113
Dorking RH4 285 CH135
Harlow CM17 58 EW10
St. Albans AL1 65 CD21
Hartsbourne Av, Bushey Hth
WD23 116 CC47
Hartsbourne Cl, Bushey Hth
WD23 117 CD47
Sch Hartsbourne Prim Sch,
Bushey WD23
off Hartsbourne Rd 117 CD47
Hartsbourne Rd, Bushey Hth
WD23 117 CD47
Hartsbourne Way, Hem.H. HP2 63 BQ21
Harts Cl, Bushey WD23 98 CA40
Hartscroft, Croy. CR0 243 DY109
Harts Gdns, Guil. GU2 264 AV131
Harts Gro, Wdf.Grn. IG8 124 EG50
Hartshill Cl, Uxb. UB10 156 BN65
Hartshill Rd, Nthflt DA11 213 GF89
Hartshill Wk, Wok. GU21 248 AV116
Hartshorn All, EC3 19 P9
Hartshorn Gdns, E6 25 L4
Hartslands Rd, Sev. TN13 279 FJ123
Harts La, SE14 45 L5
Barking IG11 167 EP65
Hartslock Dr, SE2 188 EX75
Hartsmead Rd, SE9 207 EM89
Hartspiece Rd, Red. RH1 288 DG136
Hartspring La, Bushey WD23 98 CA40
Watford WD25 98 CA39
Hart Sq, Mord. SM4 222 DA100
Hart St, EC3 19 P10
Brentwood CM14 130 FW47
Hartsway, Enf. EN3 104 DW42
Hartswood, N.Holm. RH5
off Wildcroft Dr 285 CK139
Hartswood Av, Reig. RH2 288 DA138
Hartswood Cl, Bushey WD23 98 CA40
Warley CM14 130 FY49
Hartswood Gdns, W12 181 CT76
Hartswood Grn, Bushey Hth
WD23 117 CD47
Hartswood Rd, W12 181 CT75
Warley CM14 130 FY49
Hartsworth Cl, E13 23 M1
Hartville Rd, SE18 187 ES77
Hartwell Cl, SW2
off Challice Way 203 DM88
Penn HP10 110 AC45
Hartwell Dr, E4 123 EC51
Beaconsfield HP9 111 AK52
Hartwell St, E8 10 A4
Harvard Hill, W4 180 CP79
Harvard La, W4 180 CQ78
Harvard Rd, SE13 205 EC85
W4 180 CP78
Isleworth TW7 179 CE81
Harvard Wk, Horn. RM12 149 FG63
Harvel Cl, Orp. BR5 228 EU97
Harvel Cres, SE2 188 EX78
Harvest Bk Rd, W.Wick. BR4 226 EF104
Harvest Ct, St.Alb. AL4
off Harvesters 65 CJ16
Shepperton TW17 216 BN98
Harvest End, Wat. WD25 98 BX36
Harvester Rd, Epsom KT19 238 CR110
Harvesters, St.Alb. AL4 65 CK16
Harvesters Cl, Islw. TW7 199 CD85
Harvest Hill, B.End SL8 132 AD61
Harvest La, Loug. IG10 124 EK45
Thames Ditton KT7 219 CG100
Harvest Mead, Hat. AL10 67 CV17
Harvest Rd, Bushey WD23 98 CB42
Englefield Green TW20 194 AX92
Feltham TW13 197 BU91
Harvestside, Horl. RH6 291 DJ147
Harvest Way, Swan. BR8 229 FD101
Harvey, Grays RM16 192 GB75
Harvey Cen, Harl. CM20 73 EQ15
Harvey Cen App, Harl. CM20 73 ER15
Harvey Dr, Hmptn. TW12 218 CB95
Harveyfields, Wal.Abb. EN9 89 EC34
Harvey Gdns, E11 146 EF60
SE7 36 D10
Loughton IG10 107 EP41
Harvey Ho, Brent. TW8
off Green Dragon La 180 CL78
Harvey Orchard, Beac. HP9 110 AJ52
Harvey Rd, E11 146 EF60
N8 143 DM57
SE5 43 L6
Croxley Green WD3 96 BN44
Guildford GU1 280 AY136
Hounslow TW4 198 BZ87
Ilford IG1 147 EP64
London Colney AL2 83 CJ26
Northolt UB5 158 BW66
Slough SL3 175 BB76
Uxbridge UB10 156 BN68
Walton-on-Thames KT12 217 BT101
Sch Harvey Rd Prim Sch, Crox.Grn
WD3 off Harvey Rd 96 BN44
Harveys La, Rom. RM7 149 FD61
Harvey St, N1 9 M9
Harvill Rd, Sid. DA14 208 EX92
Harvil Rd, Hare. UB9 136 BK58
Ickenham UB10 136 BL60
Sch Harvington Sch, W5
off Castlebar Rd 159 CK72
Harvington Wk, E8 10 D6
Harvist Est, N7 143 DM63
Harvist Rd, NW6 14 D2
Harwater Dr, Loug. IG10 107 EM40
Harwell Cl, Ruis. HA4 137 BR60
Harwell Pas, N2 142 DF56
Harwich Rd, Slou. SL1 153 AN72
Harwood Av, Brom. BR1 226 EH96
Hornchurch RM11 150 FL55
Mitcham CR4 222 DE97
Harwood Cl, N12 120 DE51
Tewin AL6 52 DE05
Welwyn Garden City AL8 51 CY05
Wembley HA0 139 CK62
Harwood Dr, Uxb. UB10 156 BM67
Harwood Gdns, Old Wind. SL4 194 AV87
Harwood Hall La, Upmin.
RM14 170 FP65
Harwood Hill, Welw.G.C. AL8 51 CY06
Sch Harwood Hill JMI & Nurs Sch,
Welw.G.C. AL8
off Harwood Hill 51 CY05
Harwood Pk, Red. RH1 288 DG143
Harwood Rd, SW6 39 K5
Harwoods, The, Ware SG12 54 DV05
Harwoods Rd, Wat. WD18 97 BU42
Harwoods Yd, N21
off Wades Hill 121 DN45
Harwood Ter, SW6 39 L6
Hascombe Ter, SE5 43 L8
Hasedines Rd, Hem.H. HP1 62 BG19
Haselbury Rd, N9 122 DS49
N18 122 DS49
Haseldine Meadows, Hat. AL10 67 CT19
Haseldine Rd, Lon.Col. AL2 83 CK26
Haseley End, SE23
off Tyson Rd 204 DW87
Haselrigge Rd, SW4 183 DK84
Sch Haseltine Prim Sch, SE26
off Haseltine Rd 205 DZ91
Haseltine Rd, SE26 205 DZ91
Haselwood Dr, Enf. EN2 103 DP42
Haskard Rd, Dag. RM9 148 EX63
Hasker St, SW3 28 D8
Haslam Av, Sutt. SM3 221 CY102
Haslam Cl, N1 8 F6
Uxbridge UB10 137 BQ61
Haslam Ct, N11
off Waterfall Rd 121 DH49
Haslam St, SE15 44 B5
Haslemere Av, NW4 141 CX58
SW18 202 DB89
W7 179 CG76
W13 179 CG76
Barnet EN4 120 DF46
Hounslow TW5 178 BW82
Mitcham CR4 222 DD96
Haslemere Business Cen,
Enf. EN1 104 DV43
Haslemere Cl, Hmptn. TW12 198 BZ92
Wallington SM6 241 DL106
Haslemere Gdns, N3 141 CZ55
Haslemere Heathrow Est,
Houns. TW4 177 BU82
Haslemere Ind Est, SW18 202 DB89
Sch Haslemere Prim Sch, Mitch.
CR4 off Haslemere Av 222 DD96
Haslemere Rd, N8 143 DK59
N21 121 DP47
Bexleyheath DA7 188 EZ82
Ilford IG3 147 ET61
Thornton Heath CR7 223 DP99
Windsor SL4 173 AN81
Hasler Cl, SE28 168 EV73
Haslett Rd, Shep. TW17 217 BS96
Haslewood Av, Hodd. EN11 71 EA17
Hasluck Gdns, New Barn. EN5 102 DC44
Sch Hasmonean High Sch, Boys,
NW4 off Holders Hill Rd 119 CX54
Girls, NW7 off Page St 119 CU53
Sch Hasmonean Prim Sch,
NW4 off Shirehall La 141 CX57
Hassard St, E2 20 B1
Hassendean Rd, SE3 186 EH79
Hassett Rd, E9 11 K4
Hassocks Cl, SE26 204 DV90
Hassocks Rd, SW16 223 DK95
Hassock Wd, Kes. BR2 244 EK105
Hassop Rd, NW2 141 CX63
Hassop Wk, SE9 206 EL91
Hasted Cl, Green. DA9 211 FW86
Hasted Rd, SE7 36 E10
Hastings Av, Ilf. IG6 147 EQ56
Hastings Cl, SE15 44 C5
Barnet EN5 102 DC42
Grays RM17 192 FY79
Wembley HA0 139 CJ63
Hastings Dr, Surb. KT6 219 CJ100
Hastings Ho, SE18 37 K9
Hastings Pl, Croy. CR0
off Hastings Rd 224 DT102
Hastings Rd, N11 121 DJ50
N17 144 DR55
W13 159 CH73
Bromley BR2 226 EL102
Croydon CR0 224 DT102
Romford RM2 149 FH57
Hastings St, SE18 187 EQ76
WC1 18 A3
Hastings Way, Bushey WD23 98 BY42
Croxley Green WD3 97 BP42
HASTINGWOOD, Harl. CM17 74 EZ19
Hastingwood Business Cen,
Hast. CM17 74 EZ18
Jct Hastingwood Interchange,
Harl. CM17 74 EW20
Hastingwood Rd, Hast. CM17 74 EX20
Magdalen Laver CM5 75 FB19
Hastingwood Trd Est, N18 123 DX51
Hastoe Cl, Hayes UB4 158 BY70
Hasty Cl, Mitch. CR4
off Slade Way 222 DG95
Hat & Mitre Ct, EC1 19 H5
Hatch, The, Enf. EN3 105 DX39
Windsor SL4 172 AJ80
Hatcham Ms Business Cen,
SE14 45 K6
Hatcham Pk Ms, SE14 45 K6
Hatcham Pk Rd, SE14 45 K6
Hatcham Rd, SE15 44 G3
Hatchard Rd, N19 143 DK61
Hatch Cl, Add. KT15 216 BH104
Hatchcroft, NW4 141 CV55
HATCH END, Pnr. HA5 116 BY52
Hatch End 116 BZ52
Sch Hatch End High Sch, Har.
HA3 off Headstone La 116 CB53
Hatchers Ms, SE1 31 P5
Hatchett Rd, Felt. TW14 197 BQ88
Hatch Fm Ms, Add. KT15 216 BJ103
Hatch Gdns, Tad. KT20 255 CX120
Hatchgate, Horl. RH6 290 DF149
Hatchgate Gdns, Burn. SL1 153 AK69
Hatch Gro, Rom. RM6 148 EY56
Hatchingtan, The, Worp. GU3 264 AW126
Hatchlands Ho & Pk,
Guil. GU4 266 BM131
Hatchlands Rd, Red. RH1 272 DE134
Hatch La, E4 123 ED49
Cobham KT11 251 BP119
Coulsdon CR5 256 DG115
Harmondsworth UB7 176 BK80
Ockham GU23 251 BP120
Redhill RH1 289 DM142
Windsor SL4 173 AN83
Hatch Pl, Kings.T. KT2 200 CM92
Hatch Rd, SW16 223 DL96
Pilgrim's Hatch CM15 130 FU43
Hatch Side, Chig. IG7 125 EN50
Hatchwood Cl, Wdf.Grn. IG8
off Sunset Av 124 EF49
Hatcliffe Cl, SE3 47 L10
Hatcliffe St, SE10 35 L10
Hatfeild Cl, Mitch. CR4 222 DD98
Hatfeild Mead, Mord. SM4 222 DA99
Sch Hatfeild Prim Sch, Mord. SM4
off Lower Morden La 221 CY100
HATFIELD, AL9 & AL10 67 CV17
Hatfield 67 CW17
Hatfield Av, Hat. AL10 66 CS15
Hatfield Business Pk,
Hat. AL10 66 CR15
Hatfield Cl, SE14 45 J5
Hornchurch RM12 150 FK64
Hutton CM13 131 GD45
Ilford IG6 147 EP55
Sutton SM2 240 DA109
West Byfleet KT14 234 BH112
Hatfield Cres, Hem.H. HP2 62 BM16
HATFIELD GARDEN VILLAGE,
Hat. AL10 51 CU14
★ Hatfield Ho & Pk, Hat. AL9 67 CX18
HATFIELD HYDE, Welw.G.C. AL7 51 CZ12
Hatfield Ms, Dag. RM9 168 EY66
Hatfield Pk, Hat. AL9 67 CX18
Hatfield Rd, E15 13 K2
W4 180 CR75
W13 159 CG74
Ashtead KT21 254 CM119
Chafford Hundred RM16 191 FX77
Dagenham RM9 168 EY65
Hatfield AL9 52 DE14
Potters Bar EN6 86 DC30
St. Albans AL1, AL4 65 CF20
Slough SL1 174 AU75
Watford WD24 97 BV39
Hatfields, SE1 30 F2
Loughton IG10 107 EP41
Hatfield Tunnel, Hat. AL10 67 CT17
Hathaway Cl, Brom. BR2 227 EM102
Ilford IG6 125 EP51
Ruislip HA4
off Stafford Rd 137 BT63
Stanmore HA7 117 CG50
Hathaway Ct, St.Alb. AL4 66 CL20
Hathaway Cres, E12 167 EM65
Hathaway Gdns, W13 159 CF71
Grays RM17
off Hathaway Rd 192 GA76
Romford RM6 148 EX57
Sch Hathaway Prim Sch, W13
off Hathaway Gdns 159 CF71
Hathaway Rd, Croy. CR0 223 DP101
Grays RM17 192 GB77
Hatherleigh Cl, NW7 119 CX52
Chessington KT9 237 CK106
Morden SM4 222 DA98
Hatherleigh Gdns, Pot.B. EN6 86 DD32
Hatherleigh Rd, Ruis. HA4 137 BU61
Hatherleigh Way, Rom. RM3 128 FK53
Hatherley Cres, Sid. DA14 208 EU89
Hatherley Gdns, E6 24 F4
N8 143 DL58
Hatherley Gro, W2 15 L8
Hatherley Ms, E17 145 EA56
Hatherley Rd, E17 145 DZ56
Richmond TW9 180 CM81
Sidcup DA14 208 EU91
Hatherley St, SW1 29 M9
Hathern Gdns, SE9 207 EN91
Hatherop Rd, Hmptn. TW12 198 BZ94
Hathersage Ct, N1 9 M2
Hathersham Cl, Smallfield
RH6 291 DN147
Hathersham La, Smallfield
RH6 289 DK144
Hatherwood, Lthd. KT22 253 CK121
Hathorne Cl, SE15 44 F8
Hathway St, SE15 45 H9
Hathway Ter, SE14
off Hathway St 45 J9
Hatley Av, Ilf. IG6 147 EQ56
Hatley Cl, N11 120 DF50
Hatley Rd, N4 143 DM61
Hatteraick St, SE16 33 H4
Hattersfield Cl, Belv. DA17 188 EZ77
Hatters La, Wat. WD18 97 BR44
HATTON, Felt. TW14 177 BT84
Hatton Av, Slou. SL2 153 AR70
Hatton Cl, SE18 187 ER80
Chafford Hundred RM16 191 FX76
Northfleet DA11 212 GE90
Hatton Cross 177 BT84
Hatton Cross 177 BT84
Jct Hatton Cross, Felt. TW14 177 BT84
Jct Hatton Cross Rbt,
Lon.Hthrw Air. TW6 177 BS83
Hatton Gdn, EC1 18 F6
Hatton Gdns, Mitch. CR4 222 DF99
Hatton Grn, Felt. TW14 177 BU84
Hatton Gro, West Dr. UB7 176 BK75
Hatton Ho, E1 20 D10
Hatton Ms, Green. DA9 191 FW84
Hatton Pl, EC1 18 F5
Hatton Rd, Chsht EN8 89 DX29
Croydon CR0 223 DN102
Feltham TW14 197 BS85
London Heathrow Airport
TW6 177 BT84
Hatton Row, NW8 16 B5
Sch Hatton Sch, Wdf.Grn.
IG8 off Roding La S 146 EK55
Hatton St, NW8 16 B5
Hatton Wk, Enf. EN2
off London Rd 104 DR42
Hatton Wall, EC1 18 E6
Haul Rd, NW1 8 A10
Haunch of Venison Yd, W1 17 J9
Hauteville Ct Gdns, W6
off Stamford Brook Av 181 CT76
Havana Cl, Rom. RM1
off Exchange St 149 FE57
Havana Rd, SW19 202 DA89
Havannah St, E14 34 B5
Havant Rd, E17 145 EC55
Havelock Cl, W12
off India Way 161 CV73
Havelock Pl, Har. HA1 139 CE58
Sch Havelock Prim Sch, Sthl.
UB2 off Havelock Rd 178 BZ76
Havelock Rd, N17 122 DU54
SW19 202 DC92
Belvedere DA17 188 EZ77
Bromley BR2 226 EJ98
Croydon CR0 224 DT102
Dartford DA1 209 FH87
Gravesend DA11 213 GF88
Harrow HA3 139 CE55
Kings Langley WD4 80 BN28
Southall UB2 178 BZ76
Havelock St, N1 8 B8
Ilford IG1 147 EP61
Havelock Ter, SW8 41 K5
Havelock Wk, SE23 204 DW88
Haven, The, SE26 204 DV92
Grays RM16 193 GF78
Richmond TW9 180 CN83
Sunbury-on-Thames TW16 197 BU94
Havenbury Ind Est, Dor.
RH4 off Station Rd 285 CG135
Haven Cl, SE9 207 EM90
SW19 201 CX90
Esher KT10 219 CE103
Hatfield AL10 67 CT17
Hayes UB4 157 BS71
Istead Rise DA13 213 GF94
Sidcup DA14 208 EW93
Swanley BR8 229 FF96
Haven Ct, Esher KT10
off Portsmouth Rd 219 CE103
Haven Dr, Epsom KT19 238 CP110
Havengore Av, Grav. DA12 213 GL87
Haven Grn, W5 159 CK72
Haven Grn Ct, W5 159 CK72
Havenhurst Ri, Enf. EN2 103 DN40
Haven La, W5 160 CL72
Haven Ms, N1 8 F7
Haven Pl, W5 159 CK73
Esher KT10 219 CE103
Grays RM16 192 GC75
Haven Rd, Ashf. TW15 197 BP91
Havensfield, Chipper. WD4 80 BH31
Haven St, NW1 7 J7
Haven Way, Epsom KT19 238 CP111
Havenwood, Wem. HA9 140 CP62
Havenwood Cl, Gt Warley
CM13 off Wilmot Grn 129 FW51
Havercroft Cl, St.Alb. AL3 64 CB22
Haverfield Gdns, Rich. TW9 180 CN80
Haverfield Rd, E3 21 L2
Haverford Way, Edg. HA8 118 CM53
Haverhill Rd, E4 123 EC46
SW12 203 DJ88
HAVERING-ATTE-BOWER,
Rom. RM4 127 FE48
Coll Havering Coll of Further &
Higher Ed, Ardleigh Grn
Campus, Horn. RM11
off Ardleigh Grn Rd 150 FL56
Quarles Campus, Harold Hill
RM3 off Tring Gdns 128 FL49
Havering Dr, Rom. RM1 149 FE56
Havering Gdns, Rom. RM6 148 EW57
Sch Havering Music Sch, Horn.
RM11 off The Walk 150 FM61
HAVERING PARK, Rom. RM5 126 FA50
Havering Rd, Rom. RM1 149 FD55
Coll Havering 6th Form Coll, Horn.
RM11 off Wingletye La 150 FM60
Havering St, E1 21 J9
Havering Way, Bark. IG11 168 EV69
Havers Av, Hersham KT12 236 BX106
Haversfield Est, Brent. TW8 180 CL78
Haversham Cl, Twick. TW1 199 CK86
Haversham Pl, N6 142 DF61
Haverstock Ct, Orp. BR5 228 EU96
Haverstock Hill, NW3 6 D3
Haverstock Pl, N1
off Haverstock St 19 H2
Haverstock Rd, NW5 6 G3
Sch Haverstock Sch, NW3 6 G5
Haverstock St, N1 19 H1
Haverthwaite Rd, Orp. BR6 227 ER103
Havil St, SE5 43 N5
Havisham Pl, SE19 203 DP93
Hawarden Gro, SE24 204 DQ87
Hawarden Hill, NW2 141 CU62
Hawarden Rd, E17 145 DX56
Caterham CR3 258 DQ121
Haward Rd, Hodd. EN11 71 EC15
Hawbridge Rd, E11 145 ED60
Hawes Cl, Nthwd. HA6 115 BT52
Sch Hawes Down Inf Sch, W.Wick.
BR4 off The Mead 225 ED102
Sch Hawes Down Jun Sch, W.Wick.
BR4 off The Mead 225 ED102
Hawes La, E4 105 EC38
West Wickham BR4 225 EC102
Hawes Rd, N18 122 DV51
Bromley BR1 226 EH95
Tadworth KT20
off Hatch Gdns 255 CX120
Hawes St, N1 9 H7
Haweswater Dr, Wat. WD25 82 BW33
Haweswater Ho, Islw. TW7
off Summerwood Rd 199 CF85
Hawfield Bk, Orp. BR6 228 EX104
Hawfield Gdns, Park St AL2 83 CD26
Hawgood St, E3 22 B7
Hawk Cl, Wal.Abb. EN9 90 EG34
Hawkdene, E4 105 EB44
Sch Hawkedale Inf - A Foundation
Sch, Sun. TW16
off Stratton Rd 217 BT97
Hawkenbury, Harl. CM19 73 EN17
Hawke Pk Rd, N22 143 DP55
Hawke Pl, SE16 33 K4
Hawke Rd, SE19 204 DS93
Hawker Pl, E17 123 EC54
Hawkesbury Cl, Ilf. IG6 126 EV49
Hawkesbury Rd, SW15 201 CV85
Hawkes Cl, Grays RM17
off New Rd 192 GB79
Langley SL3 175 BB76
Hawkes Ct, Chesh. HP5 76 AQ30
Hawkesfield Rd, SE23 205 DY89
Hawkesley Cl, Twick. TW1 199 CG91
Hawke's Pl, Sev. TN13 278 FG127
Hawkes Rd, Felt. TW14 197 BU87
Mitcham CR4 222 DE95
Hawkesworth Cl, Nthwd. HA6 115 BS52
Hawke Twr, SE14 45 L3
Hawkewood Rd, Sun. TW16 217 BU97
Hawkhirst Rd, Ken. CR8 258 DR115
Hawkhurst, Cob. KT11 236 CA114
Hawkhurst Gdns, Chess. KT9 238 CL105
Romford RM5 127 FD51
Hawkhurst Rd, SW16 223 DK95
Hawkhurst Way, N.Mal. KT3 220 CR99
West Wickham BR4 225 EB103
Hawkinge Wk, Orp. BR5 228 EV97
Hawkinge Way, Horn. RM12 170 FJ65
Hawkins Av, Grav. DA12 213 GJ91
Hawkins Cl, NW7
off Hale La 118 CR50
Borehamwood WD6
off Banks Rd 100 CQ40
Harrow HA1 139 CD59
Hawkins Dr, Chaff.Hun. RM16 191 FX75
Hawkins Rd, NW10 160 CS66
Teddington TW11 199 CH93
Hawkins Ter, SE7 37 H10
Hawkins Way, SE6 205 EA92
Bovingdon HP3 79 BA26
Hawkley Gdns, SE27 203 DP89
Hawkridge, NW5 7 H4
Hawkridge Cl, Rom. RM6 148 EW59
Hawkridge Dr, Grays RM17 192 GD78
Hawksbrook La, Beck. BR3 225 EB100

Hawkshaw Cl, SW2
off Tierney Rd 203 DL87
Hawkshead, NW1 17 L2
Hawkshead Cl, Brom. BR1 206 EE94
Hawkshead La, N.Mymms AL9 85 CW28
Hawkshead Rd, NW10 161 CT66
W4 180 CS75
Potters Bar EN6 86 DB29
Hawks Hill, B.End SL8 132 AC61
Hawk's Hill, Lthd. KT22 253 CF123
Hawks Hill, N.Wld Bas. CM16 92 FA27
Hawkshill, St.Alb. AL1 65 CG21
Hawkshill Cl, Esher KT10 236 CA107
Hawks Hill Cl, Fetch. KT22 253 CF123
Hawkshill Dr, Felden HP3 61 BE23
Hawkshill Rd, Slou. SL2 153 AN69
Hawkshill Way, Esher KT10 236 BZ107
Hawkslade Rd, SE15 205 DX85
Hawksley Rd, N16 144 DS62
Hawksmead Cl, Enf. EN3 105 DX35
Hawks Ms, SE10 46 F5
Hawksmoor, Shenley WD7 84 CN33
Hawksmoor Cl, E6 24 G8
SE18 187 ES78
Hawksmoor Grn, Hutt. CM13 131 GD43
Hawksmoor Ms, E1 20 E10
Sch Hawksmoor Prim Sch,
SE28 off Bentham Rd 168 EV74
Hawksmoor St, W6 38 D3
Hawksmouth, E4 123 EB45
Hawks Rd, Kings.T. KT1 220 CM96
Hawkstone Est, SE16 33 H9
Hawkstone Rd, SE16 33 H9
Hawksview, Cob. KT11 236 BZ113
Hawksway, Stai. TW18 195 BF90
Hawkswell Cl, Wok. GU21 248 AT117
Hawkswell Wk, Wok. GU21
off Lockfield Dr 248 AS117
Hawkswood Gro, Fulmer SL3 155 AZ65
Hawkswood La, Ger.Cr. SL9 135 AZ64
Hawk Ter, Ilf. IG5
off Tiptree Cres 147 EN55
Hawkwell Ct, E4
off Colvin Gdns 123 EC48
Hawkwell Ho, Dag. RM8 148 FA60
Hawkwell Wk, N1 9 K8
Hawkwood Cres, E4 105 EB44
Hawkwood Dell, Bkhm KT23 268 CA126
Hawkwood La, Chis. BR7 227 EQ95
Hawkwood Mt, E5 144 DV60
Hawkwood Ri, Bkhm KT23 268 CA126
Hawlands Dr, Pnr. HA5 138 BY59
HAWLEY, Dart. DA2 210 FM92
Hawley Cl, Hmptn. TW12 198 BZ93
Hawley Cres, NW1 7 K7
Sch Hawley Inf Sch, NW1 7 K7
Hawley Ms, NW1 7 J6
Hawley Mill, Dart. DA2 210 FN91
Hawley Rd, N18 123 DX50
NW1 7 K6
Dartford DA1, DA2 210 FL89
HAWLEY'S CORNER,
West. TN16 261 EN121
Hawley St, NW1 7 J7
Hawley Ter, Dart. DA2 210 FN92
Hawley Vale, Dart. DA2 210 FN92
Hawley Way, Ashf. TW15 196 BN92
Haws La, Stai. TW19 196 BG86
Hawstead La, Orp. BR6 246 EZ106
Hawstead Rd, SE6 205 EB86
Hawsted, Buck.H. IG9 124 EH45
Hawthorn Av, E3 11 N8
N13 121 DL50
Brentwood CM13 131 FZ48
Kew TW9 180 CL82
Rainham RM13 169 FH70
Thornton Heath CR7 223 DP95
● Hawthorn Cen, The,
Har. HA1 139 CF56
Hawthorn Cl, Abb.L. WD5 81 BU32
Banstead SM7 239 CY114
Gravesend DA12 213 GH91
Hampton TW12 198 CA92
Hertford SG14 53 DN08
Hounslow TW5 177 BV80
Iver SL0 155 BD68
Petts Wood BR5 227 ER100
Redhill RH1
off Bushfield Dr 288 DG139
Watford WD17 97 BT38
Woking GU22 248 AY120
Hawthorn Cres, SW17 202 DG92
South Croydon CR2 242 DW111
Hawthornden Cl, N12
off Fallowfields Dr 120 DE51
Hawthorndene Cl, Brom.
BR2 226 EF103
Hawthorndene Rd, Brom.
BR2 226 EF103
Hawthorn Dr, Denh. UB9 156 BJ65
Harrow HA2 138 BZ58
West Wickham BR4 244 EE105
Hawthorne Av, Bigg.H. TN16 260 EK115
Carshalton SM5 240 DG108
Cheshunt EN7 88 DV31
Harrow HA3 139 CG58
Mitcham CR4 222 DD96
Ruislip HA4 137 BV58
Hawthorne Cl, N1 9 N4
Bromley BR1 227 EM97
Cheshunt EN7 88 DV31
Sutton SM1
off Aultone Way 222 DC103
Hawthorne Ct, Nthwd. HA6
off Ryefield Cres 115 BU54
Walton-on-Thames KT12
off Ambleside Av 218 BX103
Hawthorne Cres, Slou. SL1 154 AS71
West Drayton UB7 176 BM75
Hawthorne Fm Av, Nthlt. UB5 158 BY67
Hawthorne Gro, NW9 140 CQ59
Hawthorne La, Hem.H. HP1 61 BF19
Hawthorne Ms, Grnf. UB6
off Greenford Rd 158 CC72
Hawthorne Pl, Epsom KT17 238 CS112
Hayes UB3 157 BT73
Hawthorne Rd, E17 145 EA55
Bromley BR1 226 EL97
Radlett WD7 83 CG34
Staines TW18 195 BC92
Hawthornes, Hat. AL10 67 CT20
Hawthorne Way, N9 122 DS47
Guildford GU4 265 BB130
Stanwell TW19 196 BK87
Hawthorn Gdns, W5 179 CK76
Hawthorn Gro, SE20 204 DV94
Barnet EN5 101 CT44
Enfield EN2 104 DR38
Hawthorn Hatch, Brent. TW8 179 CH80
Hawthorn La, Farn.Com. SL2 153 AP65
Sevenoaks TN13 278 FF122
Hawthorn Ms, NW7
off Holders Hill Rd 119 CY53
Hawthorn Pl, Erith DA8 189 FC78
Guildford GU4
off Merrow St 265 BD132
Penn HP10 110 AC47
Hawthorn Rd, N8 143 DK55
N18 122 DT51
NW10 161 CU66
Bexleyheath DA6 188 EZ84
Brentford TW8 179 CH80
Buckhurst Hill IG9 124 EK49
Dartford DA1 210 FK88
Feltham TW13 197 BU88
Hoddesdon EN11 71 EB15
Ripley GU23 250 BG124
Sutton SM1 240 DE107
Wallington SM6 241 DH108
Woking GU22 248 AX120
Hawthorns, Harl. CM18 73 ET19
Welwyn Garden City AL8 51 CX07
Woodford Green IG8 124 EG48
Hawthorns, The, Berk. HP4 60 AU18
Chalfont St. Giles HP8 94 AW40
Colnbrook SL3 175 BF81
Epsom KT17
off Kingston Rd 239 CT107
Hemel Hempstead HP3 61 BF24
Loughton IG10 107 EN42
Maple Cross WD3 113 BD50
Oxted RH8 276 EG133
Ridge EN6 84 CS33
Sch Hawthorns Sch, The, Bletch.
RH1 off Pendell Rd 273 DP131
Hawthorn Wk, W10 14 E4
Hawthorn Way, Chesh. HP5 76 AR29
New Haw KT15 234 BJ110
Redhill RH1 289 DH136
St. Albans AL2 64 CA24
Shepperton TW17 217 BR98
Hawtrees, Rad. WD7 99 CF35
Hawtrey Av, Nthlt. UB5 158 BX68
Hawtrey Cl, Slou. SL1 174 AV75
Hawtrey Dr, Ruis. HA4 137 BU59
Hawtrey Rd, NW3 6 C7
Windsor SL4 173 AQ82
Haxted Rd, Brom. BR1
off North Rd 226 EH95
Haybourn Mead, Hem.H. HP1 62 BH21
Hayburn Way, Horn. RM12 149 FF60
Hay Cl, E15 13 K6
Borehamwood WD6 100 CQ40
Haycroft Cl, Couls. CR5
off Caterham Dr 257 DP118
Haycroft Gdns, NW10 161 CU67
Haycroft Rd, SW2 203 DL85
Surbiton KT6 220 CL104
Hay Currie St, E14 22 D8
Hayday Rd, E16 23 N6
Hayden Ct, Felt. TW13 197 BS91
New Haw KT15 234 BH111
Hayden Rd, Wal.Abb. EN9 105 EC35
Haydens Cl, Orp. BR5 228 EV100
Haydens Pl, W11 14 G8
Haydens Rd, Harl. CM20 73 EQ15
Hayden Way, Rom. RM5 127 FC54
Haydn Av, Pur. CR8 241 DN114
Haydns Ms, W3 160 CQ72
Haydock Av, Nthlt. UB5 158 CA65
Haydock Cl, Horn. RM12 150 FM63
Haydock Grn, Nthlt. UB5
off Haydock Av 158 CA65
Haydon Cl, NW9 140 CQ56
Enfield EN1
off Mortimer Dr 104 DS44
Romford RM3 127 FH52
Haydon Dell, Bushey WD23 98 BZ44
Haydon Dr, Pnr. HA5 137 BU56
Haydon Pk Rd, SW19 202 DB92
Haydon Pl, Guil. GU1 280 AX135
Haydon Rd, Dag. RM8 148 EW61
Watford WD19 98 BY44
Sch Haydon Sch, Eastcote
HA5 off Wiltshire La 137 BT55
⇌ Haydons Road 202 DC92
Haydons Rd, SW19 202 DB92
Haydon St, EC3 20 A10
Haydon Wk, E1 20 B9
Haydon Way, SW11 182 DD84
HAYES, UB3 & UB4 157 BS72
HAYES, Brom. BR2 226 EG103
⇌ Hayes 226 EF102
Hayes, The, Epsom KT18 254 CR119
⇌ Hayes & Harlington 177 BT76
Hayes Barton, Wok. GU22 249 BD116
Hayes Bypass, Hayes
UB3, UB4 158 BX70
Hayes Chase, W.Wick. BR4 226 EE99
Hayes Cl, Brom. BR2 226 EG103
Grays RM20 191 FW79
Hayes Ct, SW2 203 DL88
Hayes Cres, NW11 141 CZ57
Sutton SM3 239 CX105
Hayes Dr, Rain. RM13 169 FH66
HAYES END, Hayes UB3 157 BQ71
Hayes End Cl, Hayes UB4 157 BR70
Hayes End Dr, Hayes UB4 157 BR70
Hayesend Ho, SW17
off Blackshaw Rd 202 DC91
Hayes End Rd, Hayes UB4 157 BR70
Hayesford Pk Dr, Brom. BR2 226 EF99
Hayes Gdn, Brom. BR2 226 EG103
Hayes Gro, SE22 184 DT84
Hayes Hill, Brom. BR2 226 EE102
Hayes Hill Rd, Brom. BR2 226 EF102
Hayes La, Beck. BR3 225 EC97
Bromley BR2 226 EG99
Kenley CR8 242 DQ114
Hayes Mead Rd, Brom. BR2 226 EE102
● Hayes Metro Cen,
Hayes UB4 158 BW73
Hayes Pk, Hayes UB4 157 BS70
Sch Hayes Pk Sch, Hayes
UB4 off Raynton Dr 157 BT70
Hayes Pl, NW1 16 D5
Sch Hayes Prim Sch, Hayes
BR2 off George La 226 EH102
Sch Hayes Prim Sch, The,
Ken. CR8 off Hayes La 257 DP116
Hayes Rd, Brom. BR2 226 EG98
Greenhithe DA9 211 FS87
Southall UB2 177 BV77
Sch Hayes Sch, Hayes BR2
off West Common Rd 226 EH103
Hayes St, Brom. BR2 226 EH102
HAYES TOWN, Hayes UB3 177 BS75
Hayes Wk, Brox. EN10
off Landau Way 89 DZ25
Potters Bar EN6 86 DB33
Smallfield RH6 291 DN147
Hayes Way, Beck. BR3 225 EC98
Hayes Wd Av, Brom. BR2 226 EH102
Hayfield Cl, Bushey WD23 98 CB42
Hayfield Pas, E1 21 H5
Hayfield Rd, Orp. BR5 228 EU99
Hayfields, Horl. RH6
off Ryelands 291 DJ147
Hayfield Yd, E1 21 H5
Haygarth Pl, SW19 201 CX92
Hay Grn, Horn. RM11 150 FN58
Haygreen Cl, Kings.T. KT2 200 CP93
Hay Hill, W1 29 K1
Hayland Cl, NW9 140 CR56
Hay La, NW9 140 CR56
Fulmer SL3 134 AX63
Sch Hay La Sch, NW9
off Grove Pk 140 CQ56
Hayles St, SE11 30 G8
Haylett Gdns, Kings.T. KT1
off Anglesea Rd 219 CK98
Hayley Cl, Chaff.Hun. RM16 191 FW76
Hayling Av, Felt. TW13 197 BU90
Hayling Cl, N16 9 P2
Slough SL1 153 AP74
Hayling Rd, Wat. WD19 115 BV47
Haymaker Cl, Uxb. UB10
off Honey Hill 156 BM66
Hayman Cres, Hayes UB4 157 BR68
Hayman St, N1 9 H7
Haymarket, SW1 29 N1
Haymarket Arc, SW1 29 N1
Haymeads, Welw.G.C. AL8 51 CY06
Haymeads Dr, Esher KT10 236 CC107
Haymer Gdns, Wor.Pk. KT4 221 CU104
Haymerle Rd, SE15 44 C3
Sch Haymerle Sch, SE15 44 C3
Hay Ms, NW3 6 F5
Haymill Cl, Perivale UB6 159 CF69
Haymill Rd, Slou. SL1, SL2 153 AK70
Hayne Rd, Beck. BR3 225 DZ96
Haynes Cl, N11 120 DG48
N17 122 DV52
SE3 186 EE83
Ripley GU23 250 BH122
Slough SL3 175 AZ78
Welwyn Garden City AL7 52 DA10
Haynes Dr, N9 122 DV48
Haynes La, SE19 204 DS93
Haynes Mead, Berk. HP4 60 AU17
Haynes Pk Ct, Horn. RM11
off Slewins Cl 150 FJ57
Haynes Rd, Horn. RM11 150 FK57
Northfleet DA11 213 GF90
Wembley HA0 160 CL66
Hayne St, EC1 19 H6
Haynt Wk, SW20 221 CY97
Hayse Hill, Wind. SL4 173 AK81
Hay's Galleria, SE1 31 N2
Hay's La, SE1 31 N3
Haysleigh Gdns, SE20 224 DU96
Hay's Ms, W1 29 J1
Haysoms Cl, Rom. RM1 149 FE56
Haystall Cl, Hayes UB4 157 BS68
Hay St, E2 10 D9
Hays Wk, Sutt. SM2 239 CX110
Hayter Ct, E11 146 EH61
Hayter Rd, SW2 203 DL85
Hayton Cl, E8 10 B5
Haywain, Oxt. RH8 275 ED130
Hayward Cl, SW19 222 DB95
Dartford DA1 209 FD85
Hayward Copse, Loud. WD3 96 BK42
Hayward Dr, Dart. DA1 210 FM89
★ Hayward Gall, SE1 30 D2
Hayward Gdns, SW15 201 CW86
Hayward Rd, N20 120 DC47
Thames Ditton KT7 219 CG102
Haywards Cl, Chad.Hth RM6 148 EV57
Hutton CM13 131 GE44
Haywards Mead, Eton Wick
SL4 173 AM78
Hayward's Pl, EC1 18 G5
Haywood Cl, Pnr. HA5 116 BX54
Haywood Ct, Wal.Abb. EN9 90 EF34
Haywood Dr, Chorl. WD3 95 BF43
Hemel Hempstead HP3 61 BF23
Haywood Pk, Chorl. WD3 95 BF43
Haywood Ri, Orp. BR6 245 ES105
Haywood Rd, Brom. BR2 226 EK98
Hazel Av, Guil. GU1 264 AW130
West Drayton UB7 176 BN76
Hazelbank, Crox.Grn WD3 97 BQ44
Surbiton KT5 220 CQ102
Hazelbank Ct, Cher. KT16 216 BJ102
Hazelbank Rd, SE6 205 ED89
Chertsey KT16 216 BJ102
Hazelbourne Rd, SW12 203 DH86
Hazelbrouck Gdns, Ilf. IG6 125 ER52
Hazelbury Av, Abb.L. WD5 81 BQ32
Hazelbury Cl, SW19 222 DA96
Hazelbury Grn, N9 122 DS48
Sch Hazelbury Inf Sch, N9
off Haselbury Rd 122 DS48
Sch Hazelbury Jun Sch, N9
off Haselbury Rd 122 DS48
Hazelbury La, N9 122 DS48
Hazel Cl, N13 122 DR48
N19 143 DJ61
NW9 118 CS54
SE15 44 D9
Brentford TW8 179 CH80
Croydon CR0 225 DX101
Englefield Green TW20 194 AV93
Hornchurch RM12 149 FH62
Mitcham CR4 223 DK98
Reigate RH2 288 DC136
Twickenham TW2 198 CC87
Waltham Cross EN7 88 DS26
Hazel Ct, Shenley WD7 84 CM33
Hazelcroft, Pnr. HA5 116 CA51
Hazelcroft Cl, Uxb. UB10 156 BM66
Hazeldean Rd, NW10 160 CR66
Hazeldell Link, Hem.H. HP1 61 BF21
Hazeldell Rd, Hem.H. HP1 61 BE21
Hazeldene, Add. KT15 234 BJ106
Waltham Cross EN8 89 DY32
Hazeldene Ct, Ken. CR8 258 DR115
Hazeldene Dr, Pnr. HA5 138 BW55
Hazeldene Gdns, Uxb. UB10 157 BQ67
Hazeldene Rd, Ilf. IG3 148 EV61
Welling DA16 188 EW82
Hazeldon Rd, SE4 205 DY85
Hazel Dr, Erith DA8 189 FH81
Ripley GU23 265 BF125
South Ockendon RM15 171 FW69
Hazeleigh, Brwd. CM13 131 GB48
Hazeleigh Gdns, Wdf.Grn. IG8 124 EL50
Hazel End, Swan. BR8 229 FE99
Hazel Gdns, Edg. HA8 118 CP49
Grays RM16 192 GE76
Sawbridgeworth CM21 58 EZ06
Hazelgreen Cl, N21 121 DP46
Hazel Gro, SE26 205 DX91
Enfield EN1
off Dimsdale Dr 104 DU44
Feltham TW13 197 BU88
Hatfield AL10 67 CT21
Orpington BR6 227 EP103
Romford RM6 148 EY55
Staines TW18 196 BH93
Watford WD25
off Cedar Wd Dr 97 BV35
Welwyn Garden City AL7 52 DB08
Wembley HA0
off Carlyon Rd 160 CL67
Hazel Gro Est, SE26 205 DX91
Hazel Ho, NW3
off Maitland Pk Rd 6 F4
Hazelhurst, Beck. BR3 225 ED95
Horley RH6 291 DJ147
Hazelhurst Cl, Guil. GU4
off Weybrook Dr 265 BB129
Hazelhurst Rd, SW17 202 DC91
Burnham SL1 152 AJ68
Hazel La, Ilf. IG6 125 EP52
Richmond TW10 200 CL89
Hazell Cres, Rom. RM5 127 FB53
Hazell Pk, Amer. HP7 77 AR39
Hazells Rd, Grav. DA13 212 GD92
Hazellville Rd, N19 143 DK59
Hazell Way, Stoke P. SL2 154 AT65
Hazel Mead, Barn. EN5 101 CV43
Epsom KT17 239 CU110
Hazelmere Cl, Felt. TW14 197 BR86
Leatherhead KT22 253 CH119
Northolt UB5 158 BZ68
Hazelmere Dr, Nthlt. UB5 158 BZ68
Hazelmere Gdns, Horn. RM11 149 FH57
Hazelmere Rd, NW6 5 H8
Northolt UB5 158 BZ68
Petts Wood BR5 227 EQ98
St. Albans AL4 65 CJ17
Hazelmere Wk, Nthlt. UB5 158 BZ68
Hazelmere Way, Brom. BR2 226 EG100
Hazel Ms, N8 143 DN55
Hazel Ri, Horn. RM11 150 FJ58
Hazel Rd, E15 13 J2
NW10 14 A2
Berkhamsted HP4 60 AX20
Dartford DA1 210 FK89
Erith DA8 189 FG81
Park Street AL2 82 CB28
Reigate RH2 288 DC136
West Byfleet KT14 234 BG114
Hazels, The, Welw. AL6 52 DE05
Hazeltree La, Nthlt. UB5 158 BY69
Hazel Tree Rd, Wat. WD24 97 BV37
Hazel Wk, Brom. BR2 227 EN100
North Holmwood RH5
off Lake Vw 285 CJ139
Hazel Way, E4 123 DZ51
SE1 32 A8
Chipstead CR5 256 DF119
Fetcham KT22 252 CC122
Hazelway Cl, Fetch. KT22 252 CC123
HAZELWOOD, Sev. TN14 245 ER111
Hazelwood, Dor. RH4 285 CH137
Loughton IG10 106 EK43
Hazelwood Av, Mord. SM4 222 DB98
Hazelwood Cl, W5 180 CL75
Chesham HP5 76 AR29
Harrow HA2 138 CB56
Hazelwood Ct, NW10
off Neasden La N 140 CS62
Hazelwood Cres, N13 121 DN49
Hazelwood Cft, Surb. KT6 220 CL100
Hazelwood Dr, Pnr. HA5 115 BV54
St. Albans AL4 65 CJ19
Hazelwood Gdns, Pilg.Hat.
CM15 130 FU44
Hazelwood Gro, S.Croy. CR2 242 DV113
Hazelwood Hts, Oxt. RH8 276 EG131
Sch Hazelwood Inf Sch, N13
off Hazelwood La 121 DN49
Sch Hazelwood Jun Sch, N13
off Hazelwood La 121 DN49
Hazelwood La, N13 121 DN49
Abbots Langley WD5 81 BQ32
Chipstead CR5 256 DF119
Hazelwood Pk Cl, Chig. IG7 125 ES50
Hazelwood Rd, E17 145 DY57
Croxley Green WD3 97 BQ44
Cudham TN14 245 ER112
Enfield EN1 104 DT44
Knaphill GU21 248 AS118
Oxted RH8 276 EH132
Sch Hazelwood Sch, Lmpfld
RH8 off Wolfs Hill 276 EG131
Hazlebury Rd, SW6 39 L8
Hazledean Rd, Croy. CR0 224 DR103
Hazledene Rd, W4 180 CQ79
Hazlemere Gdns, Wor.Pk. KT4 221 CV102
Hazlemere Rd, Penn HP10 110 AC45
Slough SL2 154 AW74
Hazlewell Rd, SW15 201 CV85
Hazlewood Cl, E5 145 DY62
Hazlewood Cres, W10 14 F5
Hazlewood Twr, W10 14 F5
Hazlitt Cl, Felt. TW13 198 BY91
Hazlitt Ms, W14 26 E7
Hazlitt Rd, W14 26 E7
Hazon Way, Epsom KT19 238 CQ112
Heacham Av, Uxb. UB10 137 BQ62
Headcorn Pl, Th.Hth. CR7
off Headcorn Rd 223 DM98
Headcorn Rd, N17 122 DT52
Bromley BR1 206 EF92
Thornton Heath CR7 223 DM98
Headfort Pl, SW1 29 H5
Headingley Cl, Chsht EN7 88 DT26
Ilford IG6 125 ET51
Shenley WD7 84 CL32
Headington Pl, Slou. SL2 154 AT74
Headington Rd, SW18 202 DC88
Headlam Rd, SW4 203 DK86
Headlam St, E1 20 F5
Headlands Dr, Berk. HP4 60 AX18
HEADLEY, Epsom KT18 270 CQ125
Headley App, Ilf. IG2 147 EN57
Headley Av, Wall. SM6 241 DM106
Headley Chase, Warley CM14 130 FW49
Headley Cl, Epsom KT19 238 CN107
Headley Common, Gt Warley
CM13 off Warley Gap 129 FV52
Headley Common Rd, Headley
KT18 270 CR127
Tadworth KT20 270 CR127
Headley Ct, SE26 204 DW92
Headley Dr, Epsom KT18 255 CV119
Ilford IG2 147 EP58
New Addington CR0 243 EB108
Headley Gro, Tad. KT20 255 CV120
★ Headley Heath, Epsom
KT18 270 CP128
Headley Heath App, Box H.
KT20 270 CP130
Mickleham RH5 270 CP130
Headley La, Mick. RH5 269 CJ129
Headley Rd, Lthd. KT22 253 CK123
Tyrrell's Wood KT18 254 CN123
Woodcote KT18 254 CP118
Head's Ms, W11 15 J9
HEADSTONE, Har. HA2 138 CC56
Headstone Dr, Har. HA1, HA3 139 CE55
Headstone Gdns, Har. HA2 138 CC56
⊖ Headstone Lane 116 CB53
Headstone La, Har. HA2, HA3 138 CB56
Headstone Rd, Har. HA1 139 CE57
Head St, E1 21 J9
Headway, The, Epsom KT17 239 CT109
Headway Cl, Rich. TW10
off Locksmeade Rd 199 CJ91
Heald St, SE14 46 A6
Healey Rd, Wat. WD18 97 BT44
Healey St, NW1 7 J5
Healy Dr, Orp. BR6 245 ET105
Heanor Ct, E5 off Pedro St 145 DX63
Heards La, Shenf. CM15 131 FZ41
Hearle Way, Hat. AL10 66 CS16
Hearne Ct, Ch.St.G. HP8
off Gordon Way 112 AV48
Hearne Rd, W4 180 CN79
Hearnes Cl, Seer Grn HP9 111 AR50
Hearnes Meadow, Seer Grn
HP9 111 AR50
Hearn Ri, Nthlt. UB5 158 BX67
Hearn Rd, Rom. RM1 149 FF58
Hearn's Bldgs, SE17 31 M9
Hearnshaw St, E14 21 M7
Hearn's Rd, Orp. BR5 228 EW98
Hearn St, EC2 19 P5
Hearnville Rd, SW12 202 DG88
Heart, The, Walt. KT12
off New Zealand Av 217 BU102
H Heart Hosp, The, W1 17 H7
Heath, The, W7
off Lower Boston Rd 159 CE74
Chaldon CR3 258 DQ124
Hatfield Heath CM22 59 FG05
Radlett WD7 83 CG33
Heathacre, Colnbr. SL3
off Park St 175 BE81
Heatham Pk, Twick. TW2 199 CF87
Heath Av, Bexh. DA7 188 EX79
St. Albans AL3 65 CD18
Heathbourne Rd, Bushey Hth
WD23 117 CE47
Stanmore HA7 117 CE47
Heathbridge, Wey. KT13 234 BN108
Sch Heathbrook Prim Sch, SW8 41 L9
Heath Brow, NW3
off North End Way 142 DC62
Hemel Hempstead HP1 62 BJ22
● Heath Business Cen, The,
Salf. RH1 288 DG143
Heath Cl, NW11 142 DB59
W5 160 CM70
Banstead SM7 240 DB114
Harlington UB3 177 BR80
Hemel Hempstead HP1 62 BJ21
Orpington BR5
off Sussex Rd 228 EW100
Potters Bar EN6 86 DB30
Romford RM2 149 FG55
South Croydon CR2 241 DP107
Stanwell TW19 196 BJ86
Heathclose, Swan. BR8
off Moreton Cl 229 FE96
Heath Cl, Vir.W. GU25 214 AX98
Heathclose Av, Dart. DA1 209 FH87
Heathclose Rd, Dart. DA1 209 FG88
Heathcock Ct, WC2
off Exchange Ct 30 B1
Heathcote, Tad. KT20 255 CX121
Heathcote Av, Hat. AL10 67 CU16
Ilford IG5 125 EM54
Heathcote Ct, Ilf. IG5
off Heathcote Av 125 EM54
Heathcote Gdns, Harl. CM17 74 EY15
Heathcote Gro, E4 123 EC48
Heathcote Pt, E9 11 J5
Heathcote Rd, Epsom KT18 238 CR114
Twickenham TW1 199 CH86
Sch Heathcote Sch, E4
off Normanton Pk 124 EE47
Heathcote St, WC1 18 C4
Heathcote Way, West Dr.
UB7 off Tavistock Rd 156 BK74
Heath Cotts, Pot.B. EN6
off Heath Rd 86 DB30
Heath Ct, SE9 207 EQ88
Hertford SG14 53 DM08
Hounslow TW4 178 BZ84
Uxbridge UB8 156 BL66
Heathcroft, NW11 142 DB60
W5 160 CM70
Welwyn Garden City AL7 52 DC09
Heathcroft Av, Sun. TW16 197 BT94
Heathcroft Gdns, E17 123 ED53
Heathdale Av, Houns. TW4 178 BY83
Heathdene, Tad. KT20
off Brighton Rd 255 CY119
Heathdene Dr, Belv. DA17 189 FB77
Heathdene Rd, SW16 203 DM94
Wallington SM6 241 DH108
Heathdown Rd, Wok. GU22 249 BD115
Heath Dr, NW3 5 L1
SW20 221 CW98
Potters Bar EN6 86 DA30
Romford RM2 127 FG53
Send GU23 249 BB123
Sutton SM2 240 DC109
Theydon Bois CM16 107 ES35
Walton on the Hill KT20 271 CU125
Heathedge, SE26 204 DV89
Heath End Rd, Bex. DA5 209 FE88

Heather Av, Rom. RM1 127 FD54
Heatherbank, SE9 187 EM82
Chislehurst BR7 227 EN96
Heatherbank Cl, Cob. KT11 236 BX111
Dartford DA1 209 FE86
Heather Cl, E6 25 N9
N7 143 DM62
SE13 205 ED86
SW8 41 J10
Abbots Langley WD5 81 BU32
Guildford GU2 264 AV132
Hampton TW12 218 BZ95
Isleworth TW7
off Harvesters Cl 199 CD85
Kingswood KT20 255 CY122
New Haw KT15 234 BH110
Pilgrim's Hatch CM15 130 FV43
Redhill RH1 273 DH130
Romford RM1 127 FD53
Uxbridge UB8
off Violet Av 156 BM71
Woking GU21 248 AW115
Heatherdale Cl, Kings.T. KT2 200 CN93
Heatherdene, W.Hors. KT24 267 BR125
Heatherdene Cl, N12
off Bow La 120 DC53
Mitcham CR4 222 DE98
Heatherden Grn, Iver SL0 155 BC67
Heather Dr, Dart. DA1 209 FG87
Enfield EN2 103 DP40
Romford RM1 127 FD54
Heather End, Swan. BR8 229 FD98
Heatherfield La, Wey. KT13 235 BS106
Heatherfields, New Haw KT15 234 BH110
Heatherfold Way, Pnr. HA5 137 BT55
Heather Gdns, NW11 141 CY58
Romford RM1 127 FD54
Sutton SM2 240 DA107
Waltham Abbey EN9 105 EC36
Heather Glen, Rom. RM1 127 FD54
Heatherlands, Horl. RH6
off Stockfield 291 DH147
Sunbury-on-Thames TW16 197 BU93
Heather La, Wat. WD24 97 BT35
West Drayton UB7 156 BL72
Heatherley Dr, Ilf. IG5 146 EL55
Heatherley's Sch of Fine Art,
SW10 39 P5
Heathermount, Guil. GU3
off Broad St 264 AS132
Heather Pk Dr, Wem. HA0 160 CN66
Heather Pl, Esher KT10
off Park Rd 236 CB105
Heather Ri, Bushey WD23 98 BZ40
Heather Rd, E4 123 DZ51
NW2 141 CT61
SE12 206 EG89
Welwyn Garden City AL8 51 CW11
Heathers, The, Stai. TW19 196 BM87
Heatherset Cl, Esher KT10 236 CC106
Heatherset Gdns, SW16 203 DM94
Heatherside Cl, Bkhm KT23 268 BZ125
Heatherside Dr, Vir.W. GU25 214 AU100
Heatherside Gdns, Farn.Com.
SL2 133 AR62
Heatherside Rd, Epsom KT19 238 CR108
Sidcup DA14 off Wren Rd 208 EW90
Heathersland, Dor. RH4
off Goodwyns Rd 285 CJ139
Heatherton Ho Sch, Amer.
HP6 off Copperkins La 77 AQ36
Heatherton Pk, Amer. HP6 77 AP36
Heatherton Ter, N3 120 DB54
Heathervale Caravan Pk,
New Haw KT15 234 BJ110
Heathervale Rd, New Haw
KT15 234 BH110
Heathervale Way, New Haw
KT15 234 BJ110
Heather Wk, W10 14 F4
Edgware HA8 118 CP50
Twickenham TW2
off Hedley Rd 198 CA87
Whiteley Village KT12
off Octagon Rd 235 BT110
Heather Way, Chobham GU24 232 AS108
Hemel Hempstead HP2 62 BK19
Potters Bar EN6 85 CZ32
Romford RM1 127 FD54
South Croydon CR2 243 DX109
Stanmore HA7 117 CF51
Heatherwood Cl, E12 146 EJ61
Heatherwood Dr, Hayes UB4 157 BR68
Heath Fm Ct, Wat. WD17 97 BR37
Heath Fm La, St.Alb. AL3 65 CE18
Heathfield, E4 123 EC48
Chislehurst BR7 207 EQ93
Cobham KT11 236 CA114
Heathfield Av, SW18
off Heathfield Rd 202 DD87
South Croydon CR2 243 DY109
Heathfield Cl, E16 24 E6
Keston BR2 244 EJ106
Potters Bar EN6 86 DB30
Watford WD19 116 BW45
Woking GU22 249 BA118
Heathfield Ct, SE14 45 H4
St. Albans AL1
off Avenue Rd 65 CE19
Heathfield Dr, Mitch. CR4 222 DE95
Redhill RH1 288 DE139
Heathfield Gdns, NW11 141 CX58
SE3 47 J9
SW18 202 DD86
W4 180 CQ78
Croydon CR0
off Coombe Rd 242 DQ105
Heathfield La, Chis. BR7 207 EP93
Heathfield N, Twick. TW2 199 CF87
Heathfield Nurs & Inf &
Jun Schs, Twick. TW2
off Cobbett Rd 198 CA88
Heathfield Pk, NW2 4 A5
Heathfield Pk Dr, Chad.Hth
RM6 148 EV57
Heathfield Ri, Ruis. HA4 137 BQ59
Heathfield Rd, SW18 202 DC86
W3 180 CP75
Bexleyheath DA6 188 EZ84
Bromley BR1 206 EF94
Burnham SL1 132 AG62
Bushey WD23 98 BY42
Croydon CR0 242 DR105
Hersham KT12 236 BY105
Keston BR2 244 EJ106
Sevenoaks TN13 278 FF122
Woking GU22 249 BA118
Heathfield Sch, Pnr. HA5
off Beaulieu Dr 138 BX59
Heathfields Cl, Ashtd. KT21 253 CJ118
Heathfields Ct, Houns. TW4
off Heathlands Way 198 BY85
Heathfield S, Twick. TW2 199 CF87
Heathfield Sq, SW18 202 DD87
Heathfield St, W11 26 E1
Heathfield Ter, SE18 187 ET79
W4 180 CQ78
Heathfield Vale, S.Croy. CR2 243 DX109
Heath Gdns, Twick. TW1 199 CF88
Heathgate, NW11 142 DB58
Hertford Heath SG13 54 DV13
Heathgate Pl, NW3
off Agincourt Rd 6 F2
Heath Gro, SE20 off Maple Rd 204 DW94
Sunbury-on-Thames TW16 197 BT94
Heath Hill, Dor. RH4 285 CH136
Heath Hurst Rd, NW3 6 C1
Heathhurst Rd, S.Croy. CR2 242 DS109
Heathland Rd, N16 144 DS60
Heathlands, Tad. KT20 255 CX122
Heathland Sch, The, Houns.
TW4 off Wellington Rd S 198 BZ86
Heathlands Cl, Sun. TW16 217 BT96
Twickenham TW1 199 CF89
Woking GU21 232 AY114
Heathlands Dr, St.Alb. AL3 65 CE18
Heathlands Ri, Dart. DA1 209 FH86
Heathlands Sch, St.Alb.
AL3 off Heathlands Dr 65 CE17
Heathlands Way, Houns. TW4 198 BY85
Heath La, SE3 47 H9
Albury GU5 282 BL141
Dartford (Lower) DA1 210 FJ88
Dartford (Upper) DA1 209 FG89
Hemel Hempstead HP1 62 BJ22
Hertford Heath SG13 54 DW13
Heathlee Rd, SE3 186 EF84
Dartford DA1 209 FE86
Heathley End, Chis. BR7 207 EQ93
Heathmans Rd, SW6 39 H7
Heath Mead, SW19 201 CX90
Heathmere Prim Sch,
SW15 off Alton Rd 201 CU88
Heath Ms, Ripley GU23 250 BH123
Heath Pk Ct, Rom. RM2
off Heath Pk Rd 149 FG57
Heath Pk Dr, Brom. BR1 226 EL97
Heath Pk Rd, Rom. RM2 149 FG57
Heath Pas, NW3 142 DB61
Heath Ridge Grn, Cob. KT11 236 CA113
Heath Ri, SW15 201 CX86
Bromley BR2 226 EF100
Ripley GU23 250 BH123
Virginia Water GU25 214 AX98
Westcott RH4 284 CC138
Heath Rd, SW8 41 K9
Beaconsfield HP9 132 AG55
Bexley DA5 209 FC88
Caterham CR3 258 DR123
Dartford DA1 209 FF86
Grays RM16 193 GG75
Harrow HA1 138 CC59
Hounslow TW3 178 CB84
Oxshott KT22 236 CC112
Potters Bar EN6 86 DA30
Romford RM6 148 EX59
St. Albans AL1 65 CE19
Thornton Heath CR7 224 DQ97
Twickenham TW1, TW2 199 CF88
Uxbridge UB10 157 BQ70
Watford WD19 116 BX45
Weybridge KT13 234 BN106
Woking GU21 249 AZ115
Heathrow, Goms. GU5 283 BQ139
★ Heathrow Airport (London),
Houns. TW6 177 BP81
Heathrow Cl, West Dr. UB7 176 BH81
⇌ Heathrow Express Terminal
4 197 BP85
⇌ Heathrow Express Terminal
5 176 BJ83
⇌ Heathrow Express Terminals
1,2,3 177 BP83
● Heathrow Int Trd Est,
Houns. TW4 177 BV83
Heathrow Prim Sch, Sipson
UB7 off Harmondsworth La 176 BM79
⊖ Heathrow Terminal 5 176 BJ83
⊖ Heathrow Terminal 4 197 BP85
⊖ Heathrow Terminals 1,2,3 177 BP83
Heathrow Tunnel App,
Lon.Hthrw Air. TW6 177 BP83
Heathrow Vehicle Tunnel,
Lon.Hthrw Air. TW6 177 BP81
Heaths Cl, Enf. EN1 104 DS40
Heath Side, NW3 142 DD63
Heathside, NW11 142 DA60
Colney Heath AL4 66 CP23
Esher KT10 219 CE104
Hounslow TW4 198 BZ87
Heath Side, Petts Wd BR5 227 EQ102
Heathside, St.Alb. AL1 65 CE18
Weybridge KT13 235 BP106
Heathside Av, Bexh. DA7 188 EY81
Heathside Cl, Esher KT10 219 CE104
Ilford IG2 147 ER57
Northwood HA6 115 BR50
Heathside Ct, Tad. KT20 255 CV123
Heathside Cres, Wok. GU22 249 AZ117
Heathside Gdns, Wok. GU22 249 BA117
Heathside Pk Rd, Wok. GU22 249 AZ118
Heathside Pl, Epsom KT18 255 CX118
Heathside Prep Sch,
Lwr Sch, NW3
off Heath St 142 DC63
Upr Sch, NW3 off New End 142 DD63
Heathside Rd, Nthwd. HA6 115 BR49
Woking GU22 249 AZ118
Heathside Sch, Wey. KT13
off Brooklands La 234 BM106
Heathstan Rd, W12 161 CU72
Heath St, NW3 142 DC62
Dartford DA1 210 FK87
Heath Vw, N2 142 DC56
East Horsley KT24 267 BT125
Heathview Av, Dart. DA1 209 FE86
Heath Vw Cl, N2 142 DC56
Heathview Ct, SW19 201 CX89
Heathview Cres, Dart. DA1 209 FG88
Heathview Dr, SE2 188 EX79
Heathview Gdns, SW15 201 CW87
Grays RM16 192 GC75
Heathview Rd, Grays RM16 192 GC75
Thornton Heath CR7 223 DN98
Heath Vil, SE18 187 ET78
SW18 off Cargill Rd 202 DC88
Heathville Rd, N19 143 DL59
Heathwall St, SW11 40 F10
Heathway, SE3 47 N5
Chaldon CR3 274 DQ125
Croydon CR0 225 DZ104
Dagenham RM9, RM10 168 FA66
East Horsley KT24 251 BT124
Heath Way, Erith DA8 189 FC81
Heathway, Iver SL0 155 BD68
Woodford Green IG8 124 EJ49
● Heathway Ind Est, Dag.
RM10 off Manchester Way 149 FB63
Heathwood Gdns, SE7 36 G9
Swanley BR8 229 FC96
Heathwood Pt, SE23
off Dacres Rd 205 DX90
Heathwood Wk, Bex. DA5 209 FE88
Heaton Av, Rom. RM3 127 FH52
Heaton Cl, E4 123 EC48
Romford RM3 128 FJ52
Heaton Ct, Chsht EN8 89 DX29
Heaton Gra Rd, Rom. RM2 127 FF54
Heaton Rd, SE15 44 D10
Mitcham CR4 202 DG94
Heaton Way, Rom. RM3 128 FJ52
Heavens Lea, B.End SL8 132 AC61
Heaven Tree Cl, N1 9 K3
Heaver Rd, SW11 40 B10
Heavers Fm Prim Sch,
SE25 off Dinsdale Gdns 224 DT99
Heavitree Cl, SE18 187 ER78
Heavitree Rd, SE18 187 ER78
Heayfield, Welw.G.C. AL7 52 DC08
Hebden Ct, E2 10 A9
Hebden Ter, N17 off Queen St 122 DS51
Hebdon Rd, SW17 202 DE90
Heber Prim Sch, SE22
off Heber Rd 204 DT86
Heber Rd, NW2 4 C2
SE22 204 DT86
Hebron Rd, W6 181 CV76
Hecham Cl, E17 123 DY54
Heckets Ct, Esher KT10 236 CC111
Heckfield Pl, SW6 39 J5
Heckford Cl, Wat. WD18 97 BQ44
Heckford St, E1 21 K10
Hector Cl, N9 122 DU47
Hector St, SE18 187 ES77
Heddington Gro, N7 8 C2
Heddon Cl, Islw. TW7 179 CG84
Heddon Ct Av, Barn. EN4 102 DF43
Heddon Ct Par, Barn. EN4
off Cockfosters Rd 102 DG43
Heddon Rd, Cockfos. EN4 102 DF43
Heddon St, W1 17 L10
Hedgebrooms, Welw.G.C. AL7 52 DC08
Hedge Hill, Enf. EN2 103 DP39
Hedge La, N13 121 DP48
Hedge Lea, Woob.Grn HP10 132 AD55
Hedgeley, Ilf. IG4 147 EM56
Hedgemans Rd, Dag. RM9 168 EX66
Hedgemans Way, Dag. RM9 168 EY65
Hedge Pl Rd, Green. DA9 211 FT86
HEDGERLEY, Slou. SL2 133 AR60
Hedgerley Ct, Wok. GU21 248 AW117
Hedgerley Gdns, Grnf. UB6 158 CC68
Hedgerley Grn, Hedg. SL2 134 AT58
Hedgerley Hill, Hedg. SL2 133 AR62
Hedgerley La, Beac. HP9 133 AN56
Gerrards Cross SL9 134 AV59
Hedgerley SL2 134 AS58
Hedgerow, Chal.St.P. SL9 112 AY51
Hedge Row, Hem.H. HP1 62 BG18
Hedgerow La, Arkley EN5 101 CV43
Hedgerows, Hutt. CM13 131 GE44
Sawbridgeworth CM21 58 EZ05
Hedgerows, The, Nthflt DA11 212 GE89
Hedgerow Wk, Chsht EN8 89 DX30
Hedgers Cl, Loug. IG10
off Newmans La 107 EN42
Hedgers Gro, E9 11 L5
Hedger St, SE11 30 G8
Hedges, The, St.Alb. AL3 64 CC16
Hedges Cl, Hat. AL10 67 CV17
Hedgeside, Pott.End HP4 61 BA16
Hedgeside Rd, Nthwd. HA6 115 BQ50
Hedge Wk, SE6 205 EB92
Hedgeway, Guil. GU2 280 AU136
Hedgewood Gdns, Ilf. IG5 147 EN56
Hedgewood Sch, Hayes
UB4 off Weymouth Rd 157 BS69
Hedgley Ms, SE12
off Hedgley St 206 EF85
Hedgley St, SE12 206 EF85
Hedingham Cl, N1 9 J7
Horley RH6 291 DJ147
Hedingham Ho, Kings.T. KT2
off Kingsgate Rd 220 CL95
Hedingham Rd, Chaff.Hun.
RM16 191 FW78
Dagenham RM8 148 EV64
Hornchurch RM11 150 FN60
Hedley Av, Grays RM20 191 FW80
Hedley Cl, Rom. RM1
off High St 149 FE57
Hedley Rd, St.Alb. AL1 65 CH20
Twickenham TW2 198 CA87
Hedley Row, N5 9 M2
Hedley Vw, Loud. HP10 110 AD54
Hedsor Hill, B.End SL8 132 AC62
Hedsor La, Burn. SL1 132 AG61
Wooburn Green HP10 132 AG61
Hedsor Pk, Tap. SL6 132 AD63
Hedsor Wf, B.End SL8 132 AC62
Hedworth Av, Wal.Cr. EN8 89 DX33
Heenan Cl, Bark. IG11
off Glenny Rd 167 EQ65
Heene Rd, Enf. EN2 104 DR39
Heideck Gdns, Hutt. CM13
off Victors Cres 131 GB47
Heidegger Cres, SW13
off Wyatt Dr 181 CV80
Heigham Rd, E6 166 EK66
Heighams, Harl. CM19 73 EM18
Heighton Gdns, Croy. CR0 241 DP106
Heights, The, SE7 186 EJ78
Beckenham BR3 205 EC94
Hemel Hempstead HP2
off Saturn Way 62 BM18
Loughton IG10 107 EM40
Nazeing EN9 90 EH25
Northolt UB5 138 BZ64
Weybridge KT13 234 BN110
Heights Cl, SW20 201 CV94
Banstead SM7 255 CY116
Heiron St, SE17 43 H3
Helby Rd, SW4 203 DK86
Helder Gro, SE12 206 EF87
Helder St, S.Croy. CR2 242 DR107
Heldmann Cl, Houns. TW3 179 CD84
Helegan Cl, Orp. BR6 245 ET105
Helena Cl, Barn. EN4 102 DD38
Helena Ho, Red. RH1 288 DG137
Helena Pl, E9 10 F9
Helena Rd, E13 23 M1
E17 145 EA57
NW10 141 CV64
W5 159 CK71
Windsor SL4 173 AR82
Helena Sq, SE16 33 L1
Helen Av, Felt. TW14 197 BV87
Helen Cl, N2
off Thomas More Way 142 DC55
Dartford DA1 209 FH87
West Molesey KT8 218 CB98
Helen Rd, Horn. RM11 150 FK55
Helens Gate, Chsht EN8 89 DZ26
Helenslea Av, NW11 141 CZ60
Helen's Pl, E2 20 G2
Helen St, SE18 37 P8
Helford Cl, Ruis. HA4 137 BS61
Helford Wk, Wok. GU21 248 AU118
Helford Way, Upmin. RM14 151 FR58
Helgiford Gdns, Sun. TW16 197 BS94
Heligan Ho, SE16
off Canada St 33 J5
Helions Rd, Harl. CM19 73 EP15
Helios Rd, Wall. SM6 222 DG102
● Heliport Ind Est, SW11 39 P9
Helix Gdns, SW2 203 DM86
Helix Rd, SW2 203 DM86
Helleborine, Bad.Dene RM17 192 FZ78
Hellen Way, Wat. WD19 116 BW49
Hellings St, E1 32 D3
Hellyer Way, B.End SL8 132 AC60
Helm, The, E16
off Albert Basin Way 37 P1
Helm Cl, Epsom KT19 238 CN112
Helme Cl, SW19 201 CZ92
Helmet Row, EC1 19 K4
Helmore Rd, Bark. IG11 167 ET66
Helmsdale, Wok. GU21
off Winnington Way 248 AV118
Helmsdale Cl, Hayes UB4 158 BY70
Romford RM1 127 FE52
Helmsdale Rd, SW16 223 DJ95
Romford RM1 127 FE52
Helmsley Pl, E8 10 E7
Helperby Rd, NW10 160 CS66
Helsinki Sq, SE16 33 M6
Helston Cl, Pnr. HA5 116 BZ52
Helston Gro, Hem.H. HP2 62 BK16
Helston La, Wind. SL4 173 AN81
Helston Pl, Abb.L. WD5
off Shirley Rd 81 BT32
Helvellyn Cl, Egh. TW20 195 BB94
Helvetia St, SE6 205 DZ89
Hemans Est, SW8 41 P5
Hemans St, SW8 41 P4
Hemberton Rd, SW9 42 A10
HEMEL HEMPSTEAD,
HP1 - HP3 62 BK21
⇌ Hemel Hempstead 62 BG23
Hemel Hempstead 62 BJ20
Hemel Hempstead Gen Hosp,
Hem.H. HP2 62 BK21
● Hemel Hempstead Ind Est,
Hem.H. HP2 63 BP17
Hemel Hempstead Rd, Hem.H.
HP3 63 BR22
Redbourn AL3 63 BQ15
St. Albans AL3 64 CA21
Hemel Hempstead Sch, The,
Hem.H. HP1
off Heath La 62 BJ21
Hemery Rd, Grnf. UB6 139 CD64
Hemingford Cl, N12 120 DD50
Hemingford Rd, N1 8 D9
Sutton SM3 239 CW105
Watford WD17 97 BS36
Heming Rd, Edg. HA8 118 CP52
Hemington Av, N11 120 DF50
Hemingway Cl, NW5 7 H1
Hemlock Cl, Kgswd KT20 255 CY123
Hemlock Rd, W12 161 CT73
Hemmen La, Hayes UB3 157 BT72
Hemming Cl, Hmptn. TW12 218 CA95
Hemmings, The, Berk. HP4 60 AT20
Hemmings Cl, Sid. DA14 208 EV89
Hemmings Mead, Epsom
KT19 238 CP107
Hemming St, E1 20 D5
Hemming Way, Slou. SL2 153 AP69
Watford WD25 97 BU35
Hemnall Ms, Epp. CM16
off Hemnall St 92 EU30
Hemnall St, Epp. CM16 91 ET31
Hempshaw Av, Bans. SM7 256 DF116
Hempson Av, Slou. SL3 174 AW76
Hempstall, Welw.G.C. AL7 52 DB11
Hempstead Cl, Buck.H. IG9 124 EG47
Hempstead La, Pott.End HP4 61 BC17
Hempstead Rd, E17 123 ED54
Bovingdon HP3 79 BA27
Kings Langley WD4 80 BM26
Watford WD17 97 BT39
Hemp Wk, SE17 31 M8
Hemsby Rd, Chess. KT9 238 CM107
Hemsley Rd, Kings L. WD4 81 BP29
Hemstal Rd, NW6 5 J6
Hemsted Rd, Erith DA8 189 FE80
Hemswell Dr, NW9 118 CS53
Hemsworth Ct, N1 9 N9
Hemsworth St, N1 9 N10
Hemus Pl, SW3 40 D1
Hemwood Rd, Wind. SL4 173 AK83
Henage La, Wok. GU22 249 BC120
Hen & Chicken Ct, EC4 18 E9
Henbane Path, Rom. RM3
off Clematis Cl 128 FK52
Henbit Cl, Tad. KT20 255 CV119
Henbury Way, Wat. WD19 116 BX48
Henchley Dene, Guil. GU4 265 BD131
Henchman St, W12 161 CT72
Hencroft St N, Slou. SL1 174 AT75
Hencroft St S, Slou. SL1 174 AT76
Hendale Av, NW4 141 CU55
Henderson Av, Guil. GU2 264 AV130
Henderson Cl, NW10 160 CQ65
Hornchurch RM11 149 FH61
St. Albans AL3 64 CC16
Henderson Dr, NW8 16 A4
Dartford DA1 190 FM84
Henderson Hosp, Sutt.
SM2 240 DB109
Henderson Pl, Bedmond WD5 81 BT27
Epping Green SG13 69 DJ21
Henderson Rd, E7 166 EJ65
N9 122 DV46
SW18 202 DE87
Henderson Rd, Croy. CR0 224 DR100
Hayes UB4 157 BU69
Hendham Rd, SW17 202 DE89
HENDON, NW4 141 CV56
⇌ Hendon 141 CU58
Hendon Av, N3 119 CY53
⊖ Hendon Central 141 CW57
Hendon Gdns, Rom. RM5 127 FC51
Hendon Gro, Epsom KT19 238 CN109
Hendon Hall Ct, NW4
off Parson St 141 CX55
Hendon La, N3 141 CY55
Hendon Pk Row, NW11 141 CZ58
Hendon Prep Sch, NW4
off Tenterden Gro 141 CX55
Hendon Rd, N9 122 DU47
Hendon Sch, NW4
off Golders Ri 141 CX57
Hendon Way, NW2 141 CZ62
NW4 141 CV58
Stanwell TW19 196 BK86
Hendon Wd La, NW7 101 CT44
Hendren Cl, Grnf. UB6
off Dimmock Dr 139 CD64
Hendre Rd, SE1 31 P9
Hendrick Av, SW12 202 DF86
Heneage Cres, New Adgtn
CR0 243 EC110
Heneage La, EC3 19 P9
Heneage St, E1 20 B6
Henfield Cl, N19 143 DJ60
Bexley DA5 208 FA86
Henfield Rd, SW19 221 CZ95
Henfold La, Dor. RH5 286 CL144
Hengelo Gdns, Mitch. CR4 222 DD98
Hengist Rd, SE12 206 EH87
Erith DA8 189 FB80
Hengist Way, Brom. BR2 226 EE98
Hengrave Rd, SE23 205 DX87
Hengrove Ct, Bex. DA5 208 EY88
Hengrove Cres, Ashf. TW15 196 BK90
Henhurst Rd, Cobham DA12 213 GK94
Henley Av, Sutt. SM3 221 CY104
Henley Bk, Guil. GU2 280 AU136
Henley Cl, SE16
off St. Marychurch St 32 G4
Greenford UB6 158 CC68
Isleworth TW7 179 CF81
Henley Ct, N14 121 DJ45
Woking GU22 249 BA120
Henley Cross, SE3 186 EH83
Henley Deane, Nthflt DA11 212 GE91
Henley Dr, SE1 32 B8
Kingston upon Thames KT2 201 CT94
Henley Gdns, Pnr. HA5 137 BV55
Romford RM6 148 EY57
Henley Prior, N1
off Collier St 18 C1
Henley Rd, E16 37 K4
N18 122 DS49
NW10 4 B8
Ilford IG1 147 EQ63
Slough SL1 153 AL72
Henley St, SW11 41 H8
Henley Way, Felt. TW13 198 BX92
Henlow Pl, Rich. TW10 199 CK89
Henlys Cor, N3 141 CZ56
Henlys Rbt, Houns. TW5 178 BW81
Henneker Cl, Rom. RM5 127 FC51
Hennel Cl, SE23 204 DW90
Hennessy Ct, Wok. GU21 233 BC113
Hennessy Rd, N9 122 DW47
Henniker Gdns, E6 24 F2
Henniker Ms, SW3 40 A2
Henniker Pt, E15 13 J3
Henniker Rd, E15 12 G3
Henningham Rd, N17 122 DR53
Henning St, SW11 40 C7
Henrietta Barnett Sch, The,
NW11 off Central Sq 142 DB57
Henrietta Barnett Wk, NW11 142 DA58
Henrietta Cl, SE8 46 B2
Henrietta Ms, WC1 18 B4
Henrietta Pl, W1 17 J9
Henrietta St, E15 12 F2
WC2 18 B10
Henriques St, E1 20 D8
Henry Addlington Cl, E6 25 N7
Henry Cavendish Prim Sch,
SW12 off Hydethorpe Rd 203 DJ88
Henry Cl, Enf. EN2 104 DS38
Henry Compton Sch, SW6 38 E6
Henry Cooper Way, SE9 206 EK90
Henry Darlot Dr, NW7 119 CX50
Henry DeGrey Cl, Grays RM17 192 FZ77
Henry Dent Cl, SE5 184 DR83
Henry Dickens Ct, W11 26 D2
Henry Doulton Dr, SW17 203 DH91
Henry Fawcett Prim Sch,
SE11 42 E2
Henry Grn Prim Sch, Dag.
RM8 off Green La 148 EX61
Henry Jackson Rd, SW15 181 CX83
Henry Macaulay Av, Kings.T.
KT2 219 CK95
Henry Maynard Infants' Sch,
E17 off Maynard Rd 145 EC57
Henry Maynard Jun Sch,
E17 off Addison Rd 145 EC57
Henry Moore Prim Sch,
Harl. CM17 off Kiln La 74 EX17
Henry Peters Dr, Tedd. TW11
off Somerset Gdns 199 CE92
Henry Rd, E6 166 EL68
N4 144 DQ60
Barnet EN4 102 DD43
Slough SL1 173 AR75
Henry's Av, Wdf.Grn. IG8 124 EF50
Henryson Rd, SE4 205 EA85
Henry St, Brom. BR1 226 EH95
Grays RM17
off East Thurrock Rd 192 GC79
Hemel Hempstead HP3 62 BK24
Henry's Wk, Ilf. IG6 125 ER52
Henry Tate Ms, SW16 203 DN92
Henry Wells Sq, Hem.H. HP2
off Aycliffe Dr 62 BL16
Henry Wise Ho, SW1
off Vauxhall Br Rd 29 M9
Hensford Gdns, SE26
off Wells Pk Rd 204 DV91

Henshall Pt, E3 22 C2
Henshall St, N1 9 M5
Henshawe Rd, Dag. RM8 148 EX62
Henshaw St, SE17 31 L8
Hensley Pt, E9 11 K5
Henslowe Rd, SE22 204 DU85
Henslow Way, Wok. GU21 233 BD114
Henson Av, NW2 4 A2
Henson Cl, Orp. BR6 227 EP103
Henson Path, Har. HA3 139 CK55
Henson Pl, Nthlt. UB5 158 BW67
Henstridge Pl, NW8 6 C10
Hensworth Rd, Ashf. TW15 196 BK92
Henty Cl, SW11 40 D5
Henty Wk, SW15 201 CV85
Henville Rd, Brom. BR1 226 EH95
Sch Henwick Prim Sch, SE9
off Henwick Rd 186 EK83
Henwick Rd, SE9 186 EK83
Henwood Side, Wdf.Grn. IG8
off Love La 125 EM51
Hepburn Cl, Chaff.Hun. RM16 191 FX77
Hepburn Ct, S.Mimms EN6 85 CU32
Hepburn Gdns, Brom. BR2 226 EE102
Hepburn Ms, SW11
off Webbs Rd 202 DF85
Hepple Cl, Islw. TW7 179 CH82
Hepplestone Cl, SW15 201 CV86
Hepscott Rd, E9 12 A5
Hepworth Ct, SW1 41 H1
Barking IG11 148 EU64
Hepworth Gdns, Bark. IG11 148 EU64
Hepworth Rd, SW16 203 DL94
Hepworth Wk, NW3 6 D3
Hepworth Way, Walt. KT12 217 BT102
Heracles Cl, Park St AL2 82 CC28
Herald Gdns, Wall. SM6 223 DH104
Herald's Pl, SE11 30 G8
Herald St, E2 20 F4
Herald Wk, Dart. DA1
off Temple Hill Sq 210 FM85
Herbal Hill, EC1 18 F5
Herbert Cres, SW1 28 F6
Knaphill GU21 248 AS118
Herbert Gdns, NW10 161 CV68
W4 180 CP79
Romford RM6 148 EX59
St. Albans AL2 82 CB29
Herbert Ms, SW2
off Bascombe St 203 DN86
Herbert Morrison Ho, SW6 38 G3
Sch Herbert Morrison Prim Sch,
SW8 42 A5
Herbert Pl, SE18
off Plumstead Common Rd 187 EP79
Isleworth TW7 179 CD81
Herbert Rd, E12 146 EL63
E17 145 DZ59
N11 121 DL52
N15 144 DT57
NW9 141 CU58
SE18 187 EN80
SW19 201 CZ94
Bexleyheath DA7 188 EY82
Bromley BR2 226 EK99
Hornchurch RM11 150 FL59
Ilford IG3 147 ES61
Kingston upon Thames KT1 220 CM97
Southall UB1 158 BZ74
Swanley BR8 209 FH93
Swanscombe DA10 212 FZ86
Herbert St, E13 23 P1
NW5 6 G4
Hemel Hempstead HP2
off St. Mary's Rd 62 BK19
Herbert Ter, SE18 187 EP80
Herbrand St, WC1 18 A4
Hercies Rd, Uxb. UB10 156 BM66
Hercules Pl, N7 143 DL62
Hercules Rd, SE1 30 D7
Hercules St, N7 143 DL62
Hercules Way, Lvsdn WD25 81 BT34
Hereford Av, Barn. EN4 120 DF46
Hereford Cl, Epsom KT18 238 CR113
Guildford GU2 264 AT132
Staines TW18 216 BH95
Hereford Copse, Wok. GU22 248 AV119
Hereford Ct, Sutt. SM2
off Worcester Rd 240 DA108
Hereford Gdns, SE13
off Longhurst Rd 206 EE85
Ilford IG1 146 EL59
Pinner HA5 138 BY57
Twickenham TW2 198 CC88
Hereford Ho, NW6 15 K1
Hereford Ms, W2 15 K9
Hereford Pl, SE14 45 N4
Hereford Retreat, SE15 44 C3
Hereford Rd, E3 21 P1
E11 146 EH57
W2 15 K8
W3 160 CP73
W5 179 CJ76
Feltham TW13 198 BW88
Hereford Sq, SW7 27 P9
Hereford St, E2 20 C4
Hereford Way, Chess. KT9 237 CJ106
Herent Dr, Ilf. IG5 146 EL56
Hereward Av, Pur. CR8 241 DN111
Hereward Cl, Wal.Abb. EN9 89 ED32
Hereward Gdns, N13 121 DN50
Hereward Grn, Loug. IG10 107 EQ39
Sch Hereward Ho Sch, NW3 6 C6
Sch Hereward Prim Sch, Loug.
IG10 off Colebrook La 107 EQ39
Hereward Rd, SW17 202 DF91
Herga Ct, Har. HA1 139 CE62
Watford WD17 97 BU40
Herga Rd, Har. HA3 139 CF56
Herington Gro, Hutt. CM13 131 GA45
Sch Herington Ho Sch, Hutt.
CM13 off Mount Av 131 GB44
Heriot Av, E4 123 EA47
Heriot Rd, NW4 141 CW57
Chertsey KT16 216 BG101
Heriots Cl, Stan. HA7 117 CG49
Heritage Av, NW9 119 CT54
Heritage Cl, SW9 183 DP83
Sunbury-on-Thames TW16 217 BU95
Uxbridge UB8 156 BJ70
Heritage Hill, Kes. BR2 244 EJ106
Sch Heritage Ho Sch, Chesh.
HP5 off Cameron Rd 76 AR30
Heritage Lawn, Horl. RH6 291 DJ147
Heritage Pl, SW18
off Earlsfield Rd 202 DC88
Heritage Vw, Har. HA1 139 CF62
Heritage Wk, Chorl. WD3
off Chenies Rd 95 BE41
Herkomer Cl, Bushey WD23 98 CB44
Herkomer Rd, Bushey WD23 98 CA43
Herlwyn Av, Ruis. HA4 137 BS62
Herlwyn Gdns, SW17 202 DF91
Herm Cl, Islw. TW7 178 CC80
Hermes Cl, W9 15 J5
Hermes St, N1 18 E1
Hermes Wk, Nthlt. UB5
off Hotspur Rd 158 CA68
Hermes Way, Wall. SM6 241 DK108
Herm Ho, Enf. EN3
off Eastfield Rd 105 DX38
Hermiston Av, N8 143 DL57
Hermitage, The, SE13 46 F8
SE23 204 DW88
SW13 181 CT81
Feltham TW13 197 BT90
Richmond TW10 199 CK85
Uxbridge UB8 156 BL65
Hermitage Cl, E18 146 EF56
SE2 off Felixstowe Rd 188 EW76
Claygate KT10 237 CG107
Enfield EN2 103 DP40
Shepperton TW17 216 BN98
Slough SL3 174 AW76
Hermitage Ct, E18 146 EG56
NW2 off Hermitage La 142 DA62
Potters Bar EN6
off Southgate Rd 86 DC33
Hermitage Gdns, NW2 142 DA62
SE19 204 DQ93
Hermitage La, N18 122 DR50
NW2 142 DA62
SE25 224 DU100
SW16 203 DM94
Croydon CR0 224 DU100
Windsor SL4 173 AN83
Hermitage Path, SW16 223 DL95
Sch Hermitage Prim Sch, E1 32 D3
Uxbridge UB8
off Belmont Rd 156 BK66
Hermitage Rd, N4 143 DP59
N15 143 DP59
SE19 204 DQ94
Kenley CR8 258 DQ116
Woking GU21 248 AT119
Hermitage Row, E8 10 D3
Sch Hermitage Sch, The, St.John's
GU21 off Oakwood Rd 248 AS119
Hermitage St, W2 16 A7
Hermitage Wk, E18 146 EF56
Hermitage Wall, E1 32 D3
Hermitage Waterside, E1 32 C2
Hermitage Way, Stan. HA7 117 CG53
Hermitage Wds Cres, Wok.
GU21 248 AS119
Hermit Pl, NW6 5 L9
Hermit Rd, E16 23 L6
Hermit St, EC1 18 G2
Hermon Gro, Hayes UB3 157 BU74
Hermon Hill, E11 146 EG57
E18 146 EG57
Herndon Cl, Egh. TW20 195 BA91
Herndon Rd, SW18 202 DC85
Herne Cl, NW10
off North Circular Rd 140 CR64
Hayes UB3 157 BT72
HERNE HILL, SE24 204 DQ85
≠ Herne Hill 203 DP86
Herne Hill, SE24 204 DQ86
Herne Hill Ho, SE24
off Railton Rd 203 DP86
Herne Hill Rd, SE24 43 H10
Sch Herne Hill Sch, SE24
off Herne Hill Rd 204 DQ85
Herne Ms, N18
off Lyndhurst Rd 122 DU49
Herne Pl, SE24 203 DP85
Herne Rd, Bushey WD23 98 CB44
Surbiton KT6 219 CK103
Hernes Cl, Stai. TW18
off Staines Rd 216 BH95
Herneshaw, Hat. AL10 67 CT20
Herns La, Welw.G.C. AL7 52 DB08
Herns Way, Welw.G.C. AL7 52 DA07
Heron Cl, E17 123 DZ54
NW10 160 CS65
Buckhurst Hill IG9 124 EG46
Guildford GU2 264 AV131
Hemel Hempstead HP3 80 BM25
Rickmansworth WD3 114 BK47
Sawbridgeworth CM21 58 EX06
Sutton SM1
off Sandpiper Rd 239 CZ106
Uxbridge UB8 156 BK65
Heron Ct, E5 off Big Hill 144 DV60
Bromley BR2 226 EJ98
Heron Cres, Sid. DA14 207 ES90
Heron Dale, Add. KT15 234 BK106
Herondale, S.Croy. CR2 243 DX109
Herondale Av, SW18 202 DD88
Heron Dr, N4 144 DQ61
Slough SL3 175 BB77
Stanstead Abbotts SG12 55 EC12
Heronfield, Eng.Grn TW20 194 AV93
Potters Bar EN6 86 DC30
Heron Flight Av, Horn. RM12 169 FG66
Herongate Rd, E12 146 EJ61
Cheshunt EN8 89 DY27
Swanley BR8 209 FE93
Heron Hill, Belv. DA17 188 EZ77
Heron Mead, Enf. EN3 105 EA38
Heron Ms, Ilf. IG1
off Balfour Rd 147 EP61
Heron Pl, SE16 33 M2
Harefield UB9 114 BG51
Heron Quay, E14 34 A3
DLR Heron Quays 34 B3
Heron Rd, SE24 184 DQ84
Croydon CR0
off Tunstall Rd 224 DS103
Twickenham TW1 179 CG84
Heronry, The, Hersham KT12 235 BU107
Herons, The, E11 146 EF58
Herons Cft, Wey. KT13 235 BQ107
Herons Elm, Nthch HP4 60 AS16
Heronsforde, W13 159 CJ72
HERONSGATE, Rick. WD3 113 BD45
Heronsgate, Edg. HA8 118 CN50
Sch Heronsgate Prim Sch,
SE28 off Whinchat Rd 187 ER76
Heronsgate Rd, Chorl. WD3 95 BB44
Heronslea, Wat. WD25 83 BW36
Heronslea Dr, Stan. HA7 118 CL50
Heron's Pl, Islw. TW7 179 CH83
Heron Sq, Rich. TW9
off Bridge St 199 CK85
Herons Ri, New Barn. EN4 102 DE42
Herons Way, St.Alb. AL1 65 CH23
Herons Wd, Harl. CM20 57 EP13
Heronswood, Wal.Abb. EN9 90 EE34
Heronswood Ct, Horl. RH6
off Tanyard Way 291 DH147
Heronswood Pl, Welw.G.C. AL7 51 CZ10
Heronswood Rd, Welw.G.C. AL7 52 DA09
● Heron Trd Est, W3
off Alliance Rd 160 CP70
Heron Wk, Nthwd. HA6 115 BS49
Woking GU21
off Blackmore Cres 233 BC114
Heron Way, Felt. TW14 177 BU84
Grays RM20 191 FV78
Hatfield AL10 67 CU19
Heronway, Hutt. CM13 131 GA46
Heron Way, Upmin. RM14 151 FS60
Heronway, Wdf.Grn. IG8 124 EJ49
Herrick Rd, N5 144 DQ62
Herrick St, SW1 29 P8
Herries St, W10 14 F1
Sch Herringham Prim Sch,
Chad.St.M. RM16
off St. Mary's Rd 193 GH77
Herringham Rd, SE7 36 D7
Herrings La, Cher. KT16 216 BG100
Herrongate Cl, Enf. EN1 104 DT40
H Her Royal Highness Princess
Christian's Hosp,
Wind. SL4 173 AQ81
Hersant Cl, NW10 161 CU67
Sch Herschel Gram Sch, Slou.
SL1 off Northampton Av 153 AQ73
Herschell Ms, SE5
off Bicknell Rd 184 DQ83
Herschell Rd, SE23 205 DX87
Herschel Pk Dr, Slou. SL1 174 AT75
Herschel St, Slou. SL1 174 AT75
HERSHAM, Walt. KT12 236 BX107
≠ Hersham 218 BY104
Hersham Bypass, Walt. KT12 235 BV106
Hersham Cen, The,
Walt. KT12 236 BX106
Hersham Cl, SW15 201 CU87
Hersham Gdns, Hersham
KT12 236 BW105
Hersham Rd, Walt. KT12 236 BW105
HERTFORD, SG13 & SG14 53 DP10
Hertford Av, SW14 200 CR85
Hertford Cl, Barn. EN4 102 DD41
H Hertford Co Hosp,
Hert. SG14 53 DP09
Hertford Ct, N13
off Green Las 121 DN48
≠ Hertford East 54 DS09
HERTFORD HEATH, Hert. SG13 54 DV12
Sch Hertford Heath Prim Sch,
Hert.Hth SG13
off Woodland Rd 54 DW12
★ Hertford Mus, Hert. SG14 54 DR09
≠ Hertford North 53 DP09
Hertford Pl, Rick. WD3 113 BF48
Coll Hertford Regional Coll,
Broxbourne Cen, Turnf.
EN10 off High Rd 89 DZ25
Ware Cen, Ware SG12
off Scotts Rd 55 DX07
Hertford Rd, N1 9 P8
N2 142 DE55
N9 122 DV47
Barking IG11 167 EP66
Barnet EN4 102 DC41
Enfield EN3 104 DW41
Great Amwell SG12 55 DZ11
Hatfield AL9 67 CW16
Hertford SG14 52 DB06
Hertford Heath SG13 54 DW13
Hoddesdon EN11 71 DY15
Ilford IG2 147 ES58
Marden Hill SG14 52 DG06
Tewin AL6 52 DE05
Waltham Cross EN8 105 DX37
Ware SG12 54 DW07
Welwyn AL6 52 DB06
Sch Hertford St. Andrew's C of E
Prim Sch, Hert. SG14
off Calton Av 53 DM08
Hertfordshire Co Hall,
Hert. SG13 54 DQ10
Hertford Sq, Mitch. CR4
off Hertford Way 223 DL98
Hertford St, W1 29 J2
Hertford Wk, Belv. DA17
off Hoddesdon Rd 188 FA78
Hertford Way, Mitch. CR4 223 DL98
HERTINGFORDBURY,
Hert. SG14 53 DL10
Sch Hertingfordbury Cowper
Prim Sch, Hert. SG14
off Birch Grn 53 DJ11
Hertingfordbury Rd, Hert. SG14 53 DL11
Hertslet Rd, N7 143 DM62
● Hertsmere Ind Pk,
Borwd. WD6 100 CR41
Sch Hertsmere Jewish Prim Sch,
Rad. WD7 off Watling St 99 CJ38
Hertsmere Rd, E14 34 A1
Hertswood Ct, Barn. EN5
off Hillside Gdns 101 CY42
Sch Hertswood Sch, Lwr Sch,
Borwd. WD6
off Cowley Hill 100 CQ39
Upr Sch, Borwd. WD6
off Thrift Fm La 100 CQ40
Hervey Cl, N3 120 DA53
Hervey Pk Rd, E17 145 DY56
Hervey Rd, SE3 186 EH81
Hervines Ct, Amer. HP6 77 AQ37
Hervines Rd, Amer. HP6 77 AP37
Hesa Rd, Hayes UB3 157 BU72
Hesewall Cl, SW4 41 M9
Hesiers Hill, Warl. CR6 260 EE117
Hesiers Rd, Warl. CR6 260 EE117
Hesketh Av, Dart. DA2 210 FP88
Hesketh Pl, W11 26 E1
Hesketh Rd, E7 146 EG62
Heslop Rd, SW12 202 DF88
Hesper Ms, SW5 27 L10
Hesperus Cres, E14 34 C9
Hessel Rd, W13 179 CG75
Hessel St, E1 20 E9
Hesselyn Dr, Rain. RM13 169 FH66
Hessle Gro, Epsom KT17 239 CT111
Hestercombe Av, SW6 38 F8
Hester Ct, Dag. RM10
off St. Mark's Pl 168 FA65
Hesterman Way, Croy. CR0 223 DL102
Hester Rd, N18 122 DU50
SW11 40 C5
Hester Ter, Rich. TW9
off Chilton Rd 180 CN83
Hestia Ho, SE1
off Royal Oak Yd 31 N5
HESTON, Houns. TW5 178 BZ80
Heston Av, Houns. TW5 178 BY80
Sch Heston Comm Sch, Heston
TW5 off Heston Rd 178 CA80
Heston Gra, Houns. TW5 178 BZ79
Heston Gra La, Houns. TW5 178 BZ79
● Heston Ind Mall, Houns.
TW5 178 BZ80
Sch Heston Inf & Nurs Sch, Heston
TW5 off Heston Rd 178 CA80
Sch Heston Jun Sch, Heston
TW5 off Heston Rd 178 CA80
Heston Rd, Houns. TW5 178 CA80
Redhill RH1 288 DF138
Heston St, SE14 46 A6
Heston Wk, Red. RH1 288 DF138
Heswell Grn, Wat. WD19
off Fairhaven Cres 115 BU48
Hetchleys, Hem.H. HP1 62 BG17
Hetherington Cl, Slou. SL2 153 AM69
Hetherington Rd, SW4 183 DL84
Shepperton TW17 217 BQ96
Hetherington Way, Uxb. UB10 136 BL63
Hethersett Cl, Reig. RH2 272 DC131
Hetley Gdns, SE19 204 DT94
Hetley Rd, W12 161 CV74
Heton Gdns, NW4 141 CU56
Heusden Way, Ger.Cr. SL9 135 AZ60
Hevelius Cl, SE10 35 L10
Hever Ct Rd, Grav. DA12 213 GH93
Hever Cft, SE9 207 EN91
Hever Gdns, Brom. BR1 227 EN96
Heverham Rd, SE18 187 ES77
Hevers Av, Horl. RH6 290 DF147
Hevers Cor, Horl. RH6
off Horley Row 290 DF147
Heversham Rd, Bexh. DA7 188 FA82
Hevingham Dr, Chad.Hth RM6 148 EW57
Hewens Rd, Hayes UB4 157 BQ70
Uxbridge UB10 157 BQ70
Hewer St, W10 14 D6
Hewers Way, Tad. KT20 255 CV120
Hewett Cl, Stan. HA7 117 CH49
Hewett Pl, Swan. BR8 229 FD98
Hewett Rd, Dag. RM8 148 EX64
Hewetts Quay, Bark. IG11 167 EP67
Hewett St, EC2 19 P5
Hewins Cl, Wal.Abb. EN9
off Broomstick Hall Rd 90 EE32
Hewish Rd, N18 122 DS49
Hewison St, E3 11 P10
Hewitt Av, N22 121 DP54
Hewitt Cl, Croy. CR0 225 EA104
Hewitt Rd, N8 143 DN57
Hewitts Rd, Orp. BR6 246 EZ108
Hewlett Rd, E3 11 M10
Hexagon, The, N6 142 DF60
● Hexagon Business Cen,
Hayes UB4 158 BW73
Hexal Rd, SE6 206 EE90
Hexham Gdns, Islw. TW7 179 CG80
Hexham Rd, SE27 204 DQ89
Barnet EN5 102 DB42
Morden SM4 222 DB102
HEXTABLE, Swan. BR8 209 FG94
Sch Hextable Inf Sch, Hext.
BR8 off St. Davids Rd 209 FF93
Sch Hextable Jun Sch, Hext.
BR8 off Rowhill Rd 209 FF93
Sch Hextable Sch, Hext. BR8
off Egerton Av 229 FF95
Hextalls La, Bletch. RH1 274 DR128
Hexton Ct, N4
off Brownswood Rd 144 DQ61
Heybourne Rd, N17 122 DV52
Heybridge Av, SW16 203 DL94
Heybridge Ct, Hert. SG14
off The Ridgeway 53 DM08
Heybridge Dr, Ilf. IG6 125 ER54
Heybridge Way, E10 145 DY59
Heydons Cl, St.Alb. AL3 65 CD18
Heyford Av, SW8 42 B4
SW20 221 CZ97
Heyford Rd, Mitch. CR4 222 DE96
Radlett WD7 99 CF37
Heyford Ter, SW8
off Heyford Av 42 B4
Heyford Way, Hat. AL10 67 CW16
Heygate St, SE17 31 J9
Heylyn Sq, E3 21 P2
Heymede, Lthd. KT22 253 CJ123
Heynes Rd, Dag. RM8 148 EW63
Heysham Dr, Wat. WD19 116 BW50
Heysham La, NW3 142 DB62
Heysham Rd, N15 144 DR58
Heythorp Cl, Wok. GU21 248 AT117
Heythorp St, SW18 201 CZ88
Uni Heythrop Coll, W8 27 L6
Heythrop Dr, Ickhm UB10 136 BM63
Heywood Av, NW9 118 CS53
Heyworth Rd, E5 144 DV63
E15 13 L2
Hibbert Av, Wat. WD24 98 BX38
Hibbert Lo, Chal.St.P. SL9
off Gold Hill E 112 AX54
Hibbert Rd, E17 145 DZ59
Harrow HA3 117 CF54
Hibberts All, Wind. SL4
off Bachelors Acre 173 AR81
Hibbert St, SW11 182 DC83
Hibberts Way, Ger.Cr. SL9 134 AY55
Hibbs Cl, Swan. BR8 229 FD96
Hibernia Dr, Grav. DA12 213 GM90
Hibernia Gdns, Houns. TW3 178 CA84
Hibernia Pt, SE2
off Wolvercote Rd 188 EX75
Hibernia Rd, Houns. TW3 178 CA84
Hibiscus Cl, Edg. HA8
off Campion Way 118 CQ49
Hibiscus Ho, Felt. TW13
off High St 197 BV88
Hichisson Rd, SE15 204 DW85
Hicken Rd, SW2 203 DM85
Hickeys Almshouses, Rich.
TW9 off St. Mary's Gro 180 CM84
Hickin Cl, SE7 36 E9
Hickin St, E14 34 E6
Hickling Rd, Ilf. IG1 147 EP64
Hickman Av, E4 123 EC51
Hickman Cl, E16 24 E7
Broxbourne EN10 71 DX20
Hickman Rd, Rom. RM6 148 EW59
Hickmans Cl, Gdse. RH9 274 DW132
Hickmore Wk, SW4 41 M10
Hickory Cl, N9 122 DU45
Hicks Av, Grnf. UB6 159 CD68
Hicks Cl, SW11 40 C10
Hicks St, SE8 33 L10
Hidalgo Ct, Hem.H. HP2 62 BM18
Hidcote Cl, Wok. GU22 249 BB116
Hidcote Gdns, SW20 221 CV97
Hide, E6 25 M8
Hideaway, The, Abb.L. WD5 81 BU31
Hide Pl, SW1 29 N9
Hide Rd, Har. HA1 139 CD56
Hides, The, Harl. CM20 57 ER14
Hides St, N7 8 D4
Hide Twr, SW1 29 N9
Higgins Rd, Chsht EN7 88 DR27
Higgins Wk, Hmptn. TW12
off Abbott Cl 198 BY93
High, The, Harl. CM20 73 ER15
Highacre, Dor. RH4 285 CH139
High Acres, Abb.L. WD5 81 BR32
Enfield EN2 off Old Pk Vw 103 DN41
HIGHAM HILL, E17 123 DY54
Higham Hill Rd, E17 123 DY54
Higham Mead, Chesh. HP5 76 AQ30
Higham Ms, Nthlt. UB5 158 BZ70
Higham Pl, E17 145 DY55
Higham Rd, N17 144 DR55
Chesham HP5 76 AP30
Woodford Green IG8 124 EG51
Highams Ct, E4 off Friars Cl 123 ED48
● Highams Lo Business Cen,
E17 145 DX55
HIGHAMS PARK, E4 123 ED50
≠ Highams Park 123 ED51
● Highams Pk Ind Est, E4 123 EC51
Sch Highams Pk Sch, E4
off Handsworth Av 123 ED51
Higham Sta Av, E4 123 EB51
Higham St, E17 145 DY55
Higham Vw, N.Wld Bas. CM16 93 FB26
Highbanks Cl, Well. DA16 188 EV80
Highbanks Rd, Pnr. HA5 116 CB50
Highbank Way, N8 143 DN58
HIGH BARNET, Barn. EN5 101 CX40
⊖ High Barnet 102 DA42
High Barn Rd, Dor. RH5 268 BX134
Effingham KT24 268 BX129
Highbarns, Hem.H. HP3 80 BN25
Highbarrow Cl, Pur. CR8 241 DM110
Highbarrow Rd, Croy. CR0 224 DU101
HIGH BEACH, Loug. IG10 106 EG39
High Beech, S.Croy. CR2 242 DS108
Sch High Beech C of E Prim Sch,
Loug. IG10 off Mott St 106 EG39
High Beeches, Bans. SM7 239 CW114
Gerrards Cross SL9 134 AX60
Orpington BR6 246 EU107
Sidcup DA14 208 EY92
Weybridge KT13 235 BS107
High Beeches Cl, Pur. CR8 241 DK110
High Beech Rd, Loug. IG10 106 EL42
High Bois La, Amer. HP6 77 AR35
High Br, SE10 47 H1
Highbridge Cl, Rad. WD7 83 CF33
● Highbridge Est, Uxb. UB8 156 BJ66
Highbridge Rd, Bark. IG11 167 EP67
Highbridge St, Wal.Abb. EN9 89 EA33
High Br Wf, SE10 46 G1
Highbrook Rd, SE3 186 EK83
High Broom Cres, W.Wick.
BR4 225 EB101
HIGHBURY, N5 9 J3
⊖ Highbury & Islington 8 F5
⊖ Highbury & Islington 8 F5
Highbury Av, Hodd. EN11 71 EA15
Thornton Heath CR7 223 DN96
Highbury Cl, N.Mal. KT3 220 CQ98
West Wickham BR4 225 EB103
Highbury Cor, N5 8 G4
Highbury Cres, N5 8 F3
Highbury Dr, Lthd. KT22 253 CG121
Highbury Est, N5 9 K3
Sch Highbury Flds Sch, N5 8 G2
Annexe, N5 9 J2
Highbury Gdns, Ilf. IG3 147 ES61
Highbury Gra, N5 9 H1
Highbury Gro, N5 9 H4
Sch Highbury Gro Sch, N5 9 J3
Highbury Hill, N5 9 H2
Highbury New Pk, N5 9 H4
Highbury Pk, N5 9 H1
Highbury Pl, N5 8 G4
Highbury Quad, N5 143 DP62
Sch Highbury Quad Prim Sch,
N5 9 K1
Highbury Rd, SW19 201 CY92
Highbury Sq, N14
off Burleigh Gdns 121 DJ46
Highbury Sta Rd, N1 8 F5
Highbury Ter, N5 8 G3
Highbury Ter Ms, N5 8 G3
High Canons, Borwd. WD6 100 CQ37
High Cedar Dr, SW20 201 CV94
High Clandon, E.Clan. GU4 266 BL133
Highclere, Guil. GU1 265 BA132
Highclere Cl, Ken. CR8 258 DQ115
Highclere Ct, St.Alb. AL1
off Avenue Rd 65 CE19
Highclere Dr, Hem.H. HP3 62 BN24
Highclere Rd, N.Mal. KT3 220 CR97
Highclere St, SE26 205 DY91
Highcliffe Dr, SW15 201 CT86
Highcliffe Gdns, Ilf. IG4 146 EL57
High Cl, Rick. WD3 96 BJ43
Highcombe, SE7 186 EH79
Highcombe Cl, SE9 206 EK88
High Coombe Pl, Kings.T. KT2 200 CR94
High Coppice, Amer. HP7 77 AQ39
Highcotts La, Guil. GU4 265 BF126
Highcroft, NW9 140 CS57
Highcroft Av, Wem. HA0 160 CN66
Highcroft Ct, Bkhm KT23 252 CA123
Highcroft Gdns, NW11 141 CZ58
Highcroft Rd, N19 143 DL59
Felden HP3 80 BG25
High Cross, Ald. WD25 99 CD37
● High Cross Cen, The, N15 144 DU56
High Cross Rd, N17 144 DU55
Highcross Rd, Sthflt DA13 211 FX92
Highcross Way, SW15 201 CU88
Highdaun Dr, SW16 223 DM98
High Dells, Hat. AL10 67 CT19
Highdown, Wor.Pk. KT4 220 CS103

Highdown Cl, Bans. SM7 255 CZ116
Highdown La, Sutt. SM2 240 DB111
Highdown Rd, SW15 201 CV86
High Dr, N.Mal. KT3 220 CQ95
Oxshott KT22 237 CD114
Woldingham CR3 259 DZ122
High Elms, Chig. IG7 125 ES49
Upminster RM14 151 FS60
Woodford Green IG8 124 EG50
High Elms Cl, Nthwd. HA6 115 BR51
High Elms La, Wat. WD25 81 BV31
High Elms Rd, Downe BR6 245 EP110
HIGHER DENHAM, Uxb. UB9 135 BB59
Higher Dr, Bans. SM7 239 CX112
Leatherhead KT24 267 BS127
Purley CR8 241 DN113
Higher Grn, Epsom KT17 239 CU113
HIGHFIELD, Hem.H. HP2 62 BL18
Highfield, Bans. SM7 256 DE117
Bushey Heath WD23 117 CE47
Chalfont St. Giles HP8 112 AX47
Harlow CM18 74 EU16
Kings Langley WD4 80 BL28
Shalford GU4 280 AY142
Watford WD19 116 BZ48
Highfield Av, NW9 140 CQ57
NW11 141 CX59
Erith DA8 189 FB79
Greenford UB6 139 CE64
Orpington BR6 245 ET106
Pinner HA5 138 BZ57
Wembley HA9 140 CL62
Highfield Cl, N22 121 DN53
NW9 140 CQ57
SE13 205 ED86
Amersham HP6 77 AR37
Englefield Green TW20
off Highfield Rd 194 AW93
Long Ditton KT6 219 CJ102
Northwood HA6 115 BS53
Oxshott KT22 237 CD111
Romford RM5 127 FC51
West Byfleet KT14 234 BG113
Highfield Ct, N14 103 DJ44
Highfield Cres, Horn. RM12 150 FM61
Northwood HA6 115 BS53
Highfield Dr, Brom. BR2 226 EE98
Broxbourne EN10 71 DY21
Caterham CR3 258 DU122
Epsom KT19 239 CT108
Ickenham UB10 136 BL63
West Wickham BR4 225 EB103
Highfield Gdns, NW11 141 CY58
Grays RM16 192 GD75
Highfield Grn, Epp. CM16 91 ES31
Highfield Hill, SE19 204 DR94
Highfield Inf Sch, Short.
BR2 *off Highfield Dr* 226 EE98
Highfield Jun Sch, Short.
BR2 *off South Hill Rd* 226 EE98
Highfield La, Hem.H. HP2 62 BM18
Tyttenhanger AL4 66 CL23
Highfield Link, Rom. RM5 127 FC51
Highfield Manor, St.Alb. AL4 66 CL24
Highfield Ms, NW6 5 L6
Highfield Pk Dr, St.Alb.
AL1, AL4 65 CH23
Highfield Pl, Epp. CM16 91 ES31
Highfield Prim Sch, N21
off Highfield Rd 122 DQ46
Hillingdon UB10
off Charville La W 157 BP69
Highfield Rd, N21 121 DP47
NW11 141 CY58
W3 160 CP71
Berkhamsted HP4 60 AX20
Bexleyheath DA6 208 EZ85
Biggin Hill TN16 260 EJ117
Bromley BR1 227 EM98
Bushey WD23 98 BY43
Caterham CR3 258 DU122
Chertsey KT16 216 BG102
Chesham HP5 76 AP29
Cheshunt EN7 88 DS26
Chislehurst BR7 227 ET97
Dartford DA1 210 FK87
Englefield Green TW20 194 AX93
Feltham TW13 197 BU89
Hertford SG13 54 DR11
Hornchurch RM12 150 FM61
Isleworth TW7 179 CF81
Northwood HA6 115 BS53
Purley CR8 241 DM110
Romford RM5 127 FC52
Sunbury-on-Thames TW16 217 BT98
Surbiton KT5 220 CQ101
Sutton SM1 240 DE106
Walton-on-Thames KT12 217 BU102
West Byfleet KT14 234 BG113
Windsor SL4 173 AM83
Woodford Green IG8 124 EL52
Highfield Rd N, Dart. DA1 210 FK86
Highfields, Ashtd. KT21 253 CK119
Cuffley EN6 87 DL28
East Horsley KT24 267 BS128
Fetcham KT22 253 CD124
Radlett WD7 99 CF35
Highfields Gro, N6 142 DF60
Highfield Twr, Rom. RM5 127 FD50
Highfield Way, Horn. RM12 150 FM61
Potters Bar EN6 86 DB32
Rickmansworth WD3 96 BH44
High Firs, Rad. WD7 99 CF35
Swanley BR8 229 FE98
High Firs Prim Sch,
Swan. BR8
off Court Cres 229 FF98
High Foleys, Clay. KT10 237 CH108
High Gables, Loug. IG10 106 EK43
High Garth, Esher KT10 236 CC107
HIGHGATE, N6 142 DG61
⊖ **Highgate** 143 DH58
**Highgate Acute Mental
Health Cen**, N19 143 DH61
Highgate Av, N6 143 DH58
★ **Highgate Cem**, N6 142 DG60
Highgate Cl, N6 142 DG59
Highgate Edge, N2 142 DE57
Highgate Gro, Saw. CM21 58 EX05
Highgate High St, N6 142 DG60
Highgate Hill, N6 143 DH60
N19 143 DH60
Highgate Ho, SE26
off Sydenham Hill Est 204 DU90
Highgate Jun Sch, N6
off Bishopswood Rd 142 DF59
Highgate Prim Sch, N6
off North Hill 142 DF58
Highgate Rd, NW5 143 DH63
Highgate Sch, N6
off North Rd 142 DG59
Highgate Spinney, N8
off Crescent Rd 143 DK58
Highgate Wk, SE23 204 DW89
Highgate W Hill, N6 142 DG61
Highgate Wd Sch, N8
off Montenotte Rd 143 DJ57
High Gro, SE18 187 ER80
Bromley BR1 226 EJ95
Highgrove, Pilg.Hat. CM15 130 FV44
High Gro, St.Alb. AL3 65 CD18
Welwyn Garden City AL8 51 CW08
Highgrove Cl, N11
off Balmoral Av 120 DG50
Chislehurst BR7 226 EL95
Highgrove Ms, Cars. SM5 222 DF104
Grays RM17 192 GC78
Highgrove Rd, Dag. RM8 148 EW64
Highgrove Way, Ruis. HA4 137 BU58
High Hill, E5
off Mount Pleasant La 144 DV60
High Hill Ferry, E5
off Big Hill 144 DV60
High Hill Rd, Warl. CR6 259 EC115
High Holborn, WC1 18 B8
High Ho Est, Harl. CM17 58 EZ11
High Ho La, Orsett RM16 193 GJ75
West Tilbury RM18 193 GK77
Highland Av, W7 159 CE72
Brentwood CM15 130 FW46
Dagenham RM10 149 FC62
Loughton IG10 106 EL44
Highland Cotts, Wall. SM6 241 DH105
Highland Ct, E18 124 EH53
Highland Cft, Beck. BR3 205 EB92
Highland Dr, Bushey WD23 116 CC45
Hemel Hempstead HP3 63 BP20
Highland Pk, Felt. TW13 197 BT91
Highland Rd, SE19 204 DS93
Amersham HP7 77 AR39
Badgers Mount TN14 247 FB111
Bexleyheath DA6 208 FA85
Bromley BR1, BR2 226 EF95
Lower Nazeing EN9 72 EE22
Northwood HA6 115 BT54
Purley CR8 241 DN114
Highlands, Ashtd. KT21 253 CJ119
Farnham Common SL2 133 AP64
Hatfield AL9 67 CW15
Watford WD19 116 BW46
Highlands, The, Barn. EN5 102 DB43
East Horsley KT24 267 BS125
Edgware HA8 118 CP54
Potters Bar EN6 86 DC30
Rickmansworth WD3 114 BH45
Highlands Av, N21 103 DM43
W3 160 CQ73
Leatherhead KT22 253 CJ122
Highlands Cl, N4
off Mount Vw Rd 143 DL59
Chalfont St. Peter SL9 113 AZ52
Hounslow TW3 178 CB81
Leatherhead KT22 253 CH122
Highlands End, Chal.St.P. SL9 113 AZ52
Highlands Gdns, Ilf. IG1 147 EM60
Highlands Heath, SW15 201 CW87
Highlands Hill, Swan. BR8 229 FG96
Highlands La, Chal.St.P. SL9 113 AZ51
Woking GU22 248 AY122
Highlands Pk, Lthd. KT22 253 CK123
Seal TN15 279 FL121
Highlands Prim Sch, Ilf.
IG1 *off Lennox Gdns* 147 EM60
Highlands Rd, Barn. EN5 102 DA43
Leatherhead KT22 253 CH122
Orpington BR5 228 EV101
Reigate RH2 272 DD133
Seer Green HP9 111 AQ50
Highlands Sch, N21
off Worlds End La 103 DN42
High La, W7 159 CD72
Caterham CR3 259 DZ119
Sheering CM22 59 FE09
Warlingham CR6 259 DZ118
HIGH LAVER, Ong. CM5 75 FH17
High Lawns, Har. HA1 139 CE62
Highlea Cl, NW9 118 CS53
High Leigh Barns, Hodd. EN11 71 DY17
High Level Dr, SE26 204 DU91
Highlever Rd, W10 14 B7
High March Sch, Beac.
HP9 *off Ledborough La* 111 AK51
Highmead, SE18 187 ET80
High Mead, Chig. IG7 125 EQ47
Harrow HA1 139 CE57
West Wickham BR4 225 ED103
Highmead Cres, Wem. HA0 160 CM66
High Meadow Cl, Dor. RH4 285 CH137
Pinner HA5 138 BW56
Highmeadow Cres, NW9 140 CR57
High Meadow Pl, Cher. KT16 215 BF100
High Meadows, Chig. IG7 125 ER50
High Meads Rd, E16 24 E8
High Molewood, Hert. SG14 53 DP07
Highmoor, Amer. HP7 77 AR39
Highmore Rd, SE3 47 K4
High Mt, NW4 141 CU58
High Oak Rd, Ware SG12 55 DX05
High Oaks, Enf. EN2 103 DM38
St. Albans AL3 64 CC15
High Oaks Rd, Welw.G.C. AL8 51 CV08
Highover Pk, Amer. HP7 77 AR40
High Pk Av, E.Hors. KT24 267 BT126
Richmond TW9 180 CN81
High Pk Rd, Rich. TW9 180 CN81
High Pastures, Sheering CM22 59 FD06
High Path, SW19 222 DB95
High Path Rd, Guil. GU1 265 BC134
High Pewley, Guil. GU1 280 AY136
High Pine Cl, Wey. KT13 235 BQ106
High Pines, Warl. CR6 258 DW119
High Pt, N6 142 DG59
SE9 207 EP90
Weybridge KT13 234 BN106
High Ridge, Cuffley EN6 87 DL27
Highridge Cl, Epsom KT18 255 CS115
High Ridge Cl, Hem.H. HP3 80 BK25
Highridge La, Bet. RH3 286 CP140
High Ridge Rd, Hem.H. HP3 80 BK25
High Rd, N2 142 DE56
N11 121 DH50
N12 120 DC51
N15 144 DT58
N17 122 DT53
N20 120 DC45
N22 143 DN55
NW10 (Willesden) 161 CV65
Broxbourne EN10 71 DZ20
High Rd, Buck.H. IG9 124 EH47
Bushey Heath WD23 117 CD46
Byfleet KT14 234 BM112
Chadwell Heath RM6 148 EV60
Chigwell IG7 125 EM50
Chipstead CR5 256 DF121
Cowley UB8 156 BJ71
Eastcote HA5 137 BV56
Epping CM16 91 ER32
Essendon AL9 68 DE17
Harrow Weald HA3 117 CE52
Ilford IG1 147 EP62
Leavesden WD25 97 BT35
Loughton IG10 124 EJ45
North Weald Bassett CM16 93 FB27
Reigate RH2 272 DD126
Seven Kings IG3 147 ET60
Thornwood CM16 92 EV28
Wembley HA0, HA9 139 CK64
Wilmington DA2 210 FJ90
High Rd Ickenham, Uxb. UB10 137 BP62
High Rd Leyton, E10 145 EB60
E15 145 EC62
High Rd Leytonstone, E11 13 J1
E15 146 EE63
High Rd Turnford, Brox. EN10 89 DY25
High Rd Woodford Grn, E18 124 EF52
Woodford Green IG8 124 EF52
High Rd Wormley, Turnf. EN10 71 DY24
Highshore Rd, SE15 44 B8
Highshore Sch, SE15 44 B7
High Silver, Loug. IG10 106 EK42
High Standing, Chaldon CR3 274 DQ125
Highstead Cres, Erith DA8 189 FE81
Highstone Av, E11 146 EG58
High St, E11 146 EG57
E13 13 N10
E15 12 E10
E17 145 DZ57
N8 143 DL56
N14 121 DK46
NW7 119 CV49
NW10 (Harlesden) 161 CT68
SE20 204 DV93
SE25 (S.Norwood) 224 DT98
W3 160 CP74
W5 159 CK73
Abbots Langley WD5 81 BS31
Addlestone KT15 234 BH105
Amersham HP7 77 AM38
Aveley RM15 171 FR74
Banstead SM7 256 DA115
Barkingside IG6 125 EQ54
Barnet EN5 101 CY41
Bean DA2 211 FV90
Beckenham BR3 225 EA96
Bedmond WD5 81 BT27
Berkhamsted HP4 60 AW19
Bletchingley RH1 274 DQ133
Bookham KT23 268 CB125
Bovingdon HP3 79 BA27
Brasted TN16 262 EV124
Bray SL6 172 AC75
Brentford TW8 179 CK79
Brentwood CM14 130 FV47
Bromley BR1 226 EG96
Burnham SL1 152 AJ69
Bushey WD23 98 CA44
Carshalton SM5 240 DG105
Caterham CR3 258 DS123
Chalfont St. Giles HP8 112 AW48
Chalfont St. Peter SL9 112 AY53
Chalvey SL1 173 AQ76
Cheam SM3 239 CY107
Chesham HP5 76 AQ31
Cheshunt EN8 89 DX29
Chipstead TN13 278 FC122
Chislehurst BR7 207 EP93
Chobham GU24 232 AS111
Claygate KT10 237 CF107
Cobham KT11 235 BV114
Colnbrook SL3 175 BC80
Colney Heath AL4 66 CP22
Cowley UB8 156 BJ70
Cranford TW5 177 BV80
Croydon CR0 224 DQ103
Dartford DA1 210 FL86
Datchet SL3 174 AV81
Dorking RH4 285 CH136
Downe BR6 245 EN111
Edgware HA8 118 CN51
Egham TW20 195 BA92
Elstree WD6 99 CK44
Epping CM16 91 ET31
Epsom KT19 238 CR113
Esher KT10 236 CB105
Eton SL4 173 AR79
Ewell KT17 239 CT109
Eynsford DA4 230 FL103
Farnborough BR6 245 EP106
Farningham DA4 230 FM100
Feltham TW13 197 BT90
Godstone RH9 274 DV131
Gravesend DA11 213 GH86
Grays RM17 192 GA79
Green Street Green BR6 245 ET108
Greenhithe DA9 191 FV84
Guildford GU1, GU2 280 AX135
Hampton TW12 198 CC93
Hampton Wick KT1 219 CJ95
Harefield UB9 114 BJ54
Harlington UB3 177 BS78
Harlow CM17 58 EW11
Harmondsworth UB7 176 BK79
Harrow HA1, HA2 139 CE60
Hemel Hempstead HP1 62 BJ18
Hoddesdon EN11 71 EA19
Horley RH6 291 DH148
Hornchurch RM11, RM12 150 FK60
Horsell GU21 248 AV115
Hounslow TW3 178 CC83
Hunsdon SG12 56 EK06
Iver SL0 155 BE72
Kings Langley WD4 80 BN29
Kingston upon Thames KT1 219 CK96
Langley SL3 175 AZ78
Leatherhead KT22 253 CH122
Limpsfield RH8 276 EG128
London Colney AL2 83 CJ25
Merstham RH1 273 DH128
New Malden KT3 220 CS97
Northchurch HP4 60 AS17
Northfleet DA11 212 GB86
Northwood HA6 115 BT53
Nutfield RH1 273 DM133
Old Woking GU22 249 BB121
Orpington BR6 228 EU102
Otford TN14 263 FF116
Oxshott KT22 237 CD113
High St, Oxt. RH8 275 ED130
Pinner HA5 138 BY55
Ponders End EN3 104 DW43
Potters Bar EN6 86 DC33
Purfleet RM19 190 FN78
Purley CR8 241 DN111
Redhill RH1 272 DF134
Reigate RH2 272 DA134
Rickmansworth WD3 114 BK46
Ripley GU23 250 BJ121
Romford RM1 149 FE57
Roydon CM19 56 EH14
Ruislip HA4 137 BS59
St. Albans AL3 65 CD20
St. Mary Cray BR5 228 EW98
Seal TN15 279 FL121
Sevenoaks TN13 279 FJ125
Shepperton TW17 217 BP100
Shoreham TN14 247 FF110
Slough SL1 174 AU75
Southall UB1 158 BZ74
Staines TW18 195 BF91
Stanstead Abbotts SG12 55 EC11
Stanwell TW19 196 BK86
Sutton SM1 240 DB105
Swanley BR8 229 FF98
Swanscombe DA10 212 FZ85
Tadworth KT20 255 CW123
Taplow SL6 152 AE70
Teddington TW11 199 CG92
Thames Ditton KT7 219 CG101
Thornton Heath CR7 224 DQ98
Uxbridge UB8 156 BK67
Waltham Cross EN8 89 DY34
Walton-on-Thames KT12 217 BU102
Ware SG12 55 DX06
Watford WD17 97 BV41
Wealdstone HA3 139 CE55
Wembley HA9 140 CM63
West Molesey KT8 218 CA98
West Wickham BR4 225 EB102
Westerham TN16 277 EQ127
Weybridge KT13 234 BN105
Whitton TW2 198 CC87
Windsor SL4 173 AR81
Woking GU21 248 AY117
Wraysbury TW19 194 AY86
Yiewsley UB7 156 BK74
High St Colliers Wd, SW19 202 DD94
High St Grn, Hem.H. HP2 62 BN18
⊖ **High Street Kensington** 27 L5
High St Ms, SW19 201 CY92
High St N, E6 166 EL67
E12 146 EL64
High St S, E6 167 EM68
High St Wimbledon, SW19 201 CX92
High Timber St, EC4 19 J10
High Tor Cl, Brom. BR1 206 EH94
High Tor Vw, SE28 167 ES74
High Tree Cl, Add. KT15 233 BF106
Sawbridgeworth CM21 58 EX06
High Tree Ct, W7 159 CE73
High Trees, SW2 203 DN88
Barnet EN4 102 DE43
Croydon CR0 225 DY102
Dartford DA2 210 FP86
High Trees Cl, Cat. CR3 258 DT123
High Trees Ct, Brwd. CM14
off Warley Mt 130 FW49
High Trees Rd, Reig. RH2 288 DD135
Highview, Cat. CR3 258 DS124
High Vw, Ch.St.G. HP8 112 AX47
Chorleywood WD3 96 BG42
Gomshall GU5 283 BQ139
Hatfield AL10 67 CT20
Highview, Knap. GU21
off Mulgrave Way 248 AS117
Northolt UB5 158 BY69
High Vw, Pnr. HA5 138 BW56
Sutton SM2 239 CZ111
Watford WD18 97 BT44
Highview Av, Edg. HA8 118 CQ49
High Vw Av, Grays RM17 192 GC78
Highview Av, Wall. SM6 241 DM106
High Vw Caravan Pk, Kings L.
WD4 81 BR28
High Vw Cl, SE19 224 DT96
Loughton IG10 106 EJ43
Highview Cl, Pot.B. EN6 86 DC33
Highview Cres, Hutt. CM13 131 GC44
Highview Gdns, N3 141 CY56
N11 121 DJ50
Edgware HA8 118 CQ49
High Vw Gdns, Grays RM17 192 GC78
Highview Gdns, Pot.B. EN6 86 DC33
St. Albans AL4 65 CJ15
Upminster RM14 150 FP61
Highview Ho, Rom. RM6 148 EY56
Highview Path, Bans. SM7 256 DA115
High Vw Prim Sch, SW11
off Plough Rd 182 DD84
Wallington SM6
off The Chase 241 DL106
High Vw Rd, E18 146 EF55
SE19 204 DR93
Highview Rd, W13 159 CG71
High Vw Rd, Guil. GU2 280 AS137
Highview Rd, Sid. DA14 208 EV91
Highway, The, E1 32 D1
E14 32 D1
Beaconsfield HP9
off Station Rd 111 AK52
Orpington BR6 246 EW106
Stanmore HA7 117 CF53
Sutton SM2 240 DC109
Highway Ct, Beac. HP9
off Station Rd 111 AK52
Highway Prim Sch, The, Orp.
BR6 *off The Highway* 246 EW106
High Wickfield, Welw.G.C. AL7 52 DC10
Highwold, Chipstead CR5 256 DG118
Highwood, Brom. BR2 225 ED97
Highwood Av, N12 120 DC49
Bushey WD23 98 BZ39
Highwood Cl, SE22 204 DU88
Brentwood CM14 130 FV45
Kenley CR8 258 DQ117
Orpington BR6 227 EQ103
Highwood Dr, Orp. BR6 227 EQ103
Highwood Gdns, Ilf. IG5 147 EM57
Highwood Gro, NW7 118 CR50
High Woodhall La, Hem.H. HP3 80 BN25
HIGHWOOD HILL, NW7 119 CU47
Highwood Hill, NW7 119 CT47
Highwood Hosp,
Brwd. CM15 130 FW46
Highwood La, Loug. IG10 107 EN43
Highwood Prim Sch, Bushey
WD23 *off Bushey Mill La* 98 BY39
Highwood Rd, N19 143 DL62
High Wd Rd, Hodd. EN11 71 DZ15
Highwoods, Cat. CR3 274 DS125
Leatherhead KT22 253 CJ121
High Worple, Har. HA2 138 BZ59
Highworth Rd, N11 121 DK51
HIGH WYCH, Saw. CM21 58 EV06
High Wych C of E Prim Sch,
High Wych CM21
off High Wych Rd 58 EU06
High Wych Rd, Saw. CM21 58 EV06
Hilary Av, Mitch. CR4 222 DG97
Hilary Cl, SW6 39 L4
Erith DA8 189 FC81
Hornchurch RM12 150 FK64
Hilary Rd, W12 161 CT72
Hilbert Rd, Sutt. SM3 221 CX104
Hilborough Way, Orp. BR6 245 ER106
Hilbury, Hat. AL10 67 CT19
Hilbury Cl, Amer. HP6 77 AQ35
Hilda Lockert Wk, SW9
off Fiveways Rd 42 G9
Hilda May Av, Swan. BR8 229 FE97
Hilda Rd, E6 166 EK66
E16 23 K5
Hilda Ter, SW9 42 F8
Hilda Vale Cl, Orp. BR6 245 EN105
Hilda Vale Rd, Orp. BR6 245 EN105
Hildenborough Gdns, Brom.
BR1 206 EE93
Hilden Dr, Erith DA8 189 FH80
Hildenlea Pl, Brom. BR2 226 EE96
Hildenley Cl, Merst. RH1
off Malmstone Av 273 DK128
Hildens, The, Westc. RH4 284 CB138
Hilders, The, Ashtd. KT21 254 CP117
Hildreth St, SW12 203 DH88
Hildreth St Ms, SW12
off Hildreth St 203 DH88
Hildyard Rd, SW6 39 K2
Hiley Rd, NW10 14 A1
Hilfield La, Ald. WD25 99 CD41
Hilfield La S, Bushey WD23 99 CF44
Hilgay, Guil. GU1 265 AZ134
Hilgay Cl, Guil. GU1 265 AZ134
Hilgrove Rd, NW6 5 P7
Hiliary Gdns, Stan. HA7 117 CJ54
Hiljon Cres, Chal.St.P. SL9 112 AY53
Hill, The, Cat. CR3 258 DT124
Harlow CM17 58 EW11
Northfleet DA11 212 GC86
Hillars Heath Rd, Couls. CR5 257 DL115
Hillary Av, Nthflt DA11 212 GE90
Hillary Cres, Walt. KT12 218 BW102
Hillary Dr, Islw. TW7 179 CF84
Hillary Ri, Barn. EN5 102 DA42
Hillary Rd, Hem.H. HP2 62 BN19
Slough SL3 174 AY75
Southall UB2 178 CA76
Hill Av, Amer. HP6 77 AQ38
Hill Barn, S.Croy. CR2 242 DS111
Hillbeck Cl, SE15 44 G4
Hillbeck Way, Grnf. UB6 159 CD67
Hillborne Cl, Hayes UB3 177 BU78
Hillborough Av, Sev. TN13 279 FK122
Hillborough Cl, SW19 202 DC94
Hillbrook Gdns, Wey. KT13 234 BN108
Hillbrook Prim Sch, SW17
off Hillbrook Rd 202 DG91
Hillbrook Rd, SW17 202 DF90
Hill Brow, Brom. BR1 226 EK95
Dartford DA1 209 FF86
Hillbrow, N.Mal. KT3 221 CT97
Hillbrow Cl, Bex. DA5 209 FD91
Hillbrow Cotts, Gdse. RH9 274 DW132
Hillbrow Ct, Gdse. RH9 274 DW132
Hillbrow Rd, Brom. BR1 206 EE94
Esher KT10 236 CC105
Hillbury Av, Har. HA3 139 CH57
Hillbury Cl, Warl. CR6 258 DV118
Hillbury Cres, Warl. CR6 258 DW118
Hillbury Gdns, Warl. CR6 258 DW118
Hillbury Rd, SW17 203 DH90
Warlingham CR6 258 DU117
Whyteleafe CR3 258 DU117
Hill Cl, NW2 141 CV62
NW11 142 DA58
Barnet EN5 101 CW43
Chislehurst BR7 207 EP92
Cobham KT11 236 CA112
Harrow HA1 139 CE62
Istead Rise DA13 212 GE94
Purley CR8 242 DQ113
Stanmore HA7 117 CH49
Woking GU21 248 AX116
Wooburn Green HP10 132 AF56
Hill Common, Hem.H. HP3 62 BN24
Hillcote Av, SW16 203 DN94
Hill Ct, Gdmg. GU7 280 AS144
Northolt UB5 138 CA64
Hillcourt Av, N12 120 DB51
Hillcourt Est, N16 144 DR60
Hillcourt Rd, SE22 204 DV86
Hill Cres, N20 120 DB47
Bexley DA5 209 FC88
Harrow HA1 139 CG57
Hornchurch RM11 150 FJ58
Surbiton KT5 220 CM99
Worcester Park KT4 221 CW103
Hillcrest, N6 142 DG59
N21 121 DP45
SE24 184 DR84
Hatfield AL10 67 CU18
Hill Crest, Pot.B. EN6 86 DC34
Hillcrest, St.Alb. AL3 64 CB22
Hill Crest, Sev. TN13 278 FG122
Sidcup DA15 208 EU87
Hillcrest, Wey. KT13 235 BP105
Hillcrest Av, NW11 141 CY57
Chertsey KT16 233 BE105
Edgware HA8 118 CP49
Grays RM20 191 FU79
Pinner HA5 138 BX56
Hillcrest Caravan Pk,
Box H. KT20 270 CP131
Hillcrest Cl, SE26 204 DU91
Beckenham BR3 225 DZ99
Epsom KT18 255 CT115
Goffs Oak EN7 88 DQ29
Hillcrest Ct, Sutt. SM2
off Eaton Rd 240 DD107

Hillcrest Dr, Green. DA9
off Riverview Rd 211 FU85
Hillcrest Gdns, N3 141 CY56
NW2 141 CU62
Esher KT10 219 CF104
Hillcrest Par, Couls. CR5 241 DH114
Hillcrest Rd, E17 123 ED54
E18 124 EF54
W3 160 CN74
W5 160 CL71
Biggin Hill TN16 260 EK116
Bromley BR1 206 EG92
Dartford DA1 209 FF87
Guildford GU2 264 AT133
Hornchurch RM11 149 FG59
Loughton IG10 106 EK44
Orpington BR6 228 EU103
Purley CR8 241 DM110
Shenley WD7 84 CN33
Toot Hill CM5 93 FE30
Whyteleafe CR3 258 DT117
Hillcrest Vw, Beck. BR3 225 DZ100
Hillcrest Way, Epp. CM16 92 EU31
Hillcrest Waye, Ger.Cr. SL9 135 AZ59
Hillcroft, Loug. IG10 107 EN40
Hill Cft, Rad. WD7 83 CG33
Hillcroft Av, Pnr. HA5 138 BZ58
Purley CR8 241 DJ113
Hillcroft Coll, Surb. KT6
off South Bk 220 CL100
Hillcroft Cres, W5 160 CL72
Ruislip HA4 138 BX62
Watford WD19 115 BV46
Wembley HA9 140 CM63
Hillcroft Prim Sch, Cat.
CR3 *off Chaldon Rd* 258 DS123
Hillcroft Rd, E6 25 N6
Chesham HP5 76 AR29
Penn HP10 110 AC46
Hillcroome Rd, Sutt. SM2 240 DD107
Hillcross Av, Mord. SM4 221 CZ99
Hillcross Prim Sch, Mord.
SM4 *off Ashridge Way* 221 CZ98
Hilldale Rd, Sutt. SM1 239 CZ105
Hilldeane Rd, Pur. CR8 241 DN109
Hilldene Av, Rom. RM3 128 FJ51
Hilldene Cl, Rom. RM3 128 FK50
Hilldene Prim Sch, Rom.
RM3 *off Grange Rd* 128 FJ51
Hilldown Rd, SW16 203 DL94
Bromley BR2 226 EE102
Hemel Hempstead HP1 62 BG18
Hill Dr, NW9 140 CQ60
SW16 223 DM97
Leatherhead KT22 253 CF119
Hilldrop Cres, N7 7 P3
Hilldrop Est, N7 7 N2
Hilldrop La, N7 7 P3
Hilldrop Rd, N7 7 N2
Bromley BR1 206 EG93
HILL END, Uxb. UB9 114 BH51
Hillend, SE18 187 EN81
Hill End, Orp. BR6
off The Approach 227 ET103
Hill End La, St.Alb. AL4 65 CJ23
Hill End Rd, Hare. UB9 114 BH51
Hillersdon, Slou. SL2 154 AV71
Hillersdon Av, SW13 181 CU82
Edgware HA8 118 CM50
Hillery Cl, SE17 31 M9
Hilley Fld La, Fetch. KT22 252 CC122
Hill Fm App, Woob.Grn HP10 132 AE55
Hill Fm Av, Wat. WD25 81 BU33
Hill Fm Cl, Wat. WD25 81 BU33
● **Hill Fm Ind Est**, Wat. WD25 81 BT33
Hill Fm La, Ch.St.G. HP8 112 AT46
Hill Fm Rd, W10 14 B6
Chalfont St. Peter SL9 112 AY52
Chesham HP5 76 AR34
Taplow SL6 152 AE68
Uxbridge UB10
off Austin's La 137 BR63
Hillfield, Hat. AL10 67 CV15
Hillfield Av, N8 143 DL57
NW9 140 CS57
Morden SM4 222 DE100
Wembley HA0 160 CL66
Hillfield Cl, Guil. GU1 265 BC132
Harrow HA2 138 CC56
Redhill RH1 272 DG134
Hillfield Ct, NW3 6 C3
Hemel Hempstead HP2 62 BL20
Hillfield Ms, N8 143 DM56
Hillfield Pk, N10 143 DH56
N21 121 DN47
Hillfield Pk Ms, N10 143 DH56
Hillfield Pl, Dunt.Grn TN13 263 FE120
Hillfield Rd, NW6 5 H3
Chalfont St. Peter SL9 112 AY52
Dunton Green TN13 263 FE120
Hampton TW12 198 BZ94
Hemel Hempstead HP2 62 BK20
Redhill RH1 272 DG134
Hillfield Sq, Chal.St.P. SL9 112 AY52
Hillfoot Av, Rom. RM5 127 FC53
Hillfoot Rd, Rom. RM5 127 FC53
Hillford Pl, Red. RH1 288 DG140
Hillgate Pl, SW12 203 DH87
W8 27 J2
Hillgate St, W8 27 J2
Hill Gate Wk, N6 143 DJ58
Hillgrove, Chal.St.P. SL9 113 AZ53
Hill Gro, Felt. TW13
off Watermill Way 198 BZ89
Romford RM1 149 FE55
● **Hillgrove Business Pk**,
Lwr Naze. EN9 71 EC22
Hill Hall, They.Mt CM16 108 EZ35
Hill Ho, E5 144 DV60
Hillhouse, Wal.Abb. EN9 90 EF33
Hill Ho Av, Stan. HA7 117 CF52
Hill Ho Cl, N21 121 DN45
Chalfont St. Peter SL9
off Rickmansworth La 112 AY52
Hillhouse C of E Prim Sch,
Wal.Abb. EN9
off Ninefields 90 EF33
Hill Ho Dr, Chad.St.M. RM16 193 GH78
Hampton TW12 218 CA95
Hillhouse Dr, Reig. RH2 288 DB136
Hill Ho Dr, Wey. KT13 234 BN111
Hill Ho Int Jun Sch, SW1 28 F7
Hill Ho Ms, Brom. BR2 226 EF96
Hill Ho Rd, SW16 203 DM92
Hillhouse Rd, Dart. DA2 210 FQ87
Hillhurst Gdns, Cat. CR3 258 DS120
Hilliard Rd, Nthwd. HA6 115 BT53
Hilliards Ct, E1 32 F2
Hilliards Rd, Uxb. UB8 156 BK72
Hillier Cl, New Barn. EN5 102 DB44
Hillier Gdns, Croy. CR0 241 DN106
Hillier Pl, Chess. KT9 237 CK107
Hillier Rd, SW11 202 DF86
Guildford GU1 265 BA134
Hilliers Av, Uxb. UB8 156 BN69
Hilliers La, Croy. CR0 223 DL104
Hillingdale, Bigg.H. TN16 260 EH118
HILLINGDON, Uxb. UB8 156 BN69
⊖ **Hillingdon** 136 BN64
Hillingdon Av, Sev. TN13 279 FJ121
Staines TW19 196 BL88
Hillingdon Circ, Uxb. UB10 136 BM64
Hillingdon Hill, Uxb. UB10 156 BL69
Hillingdon Hosp, Uxb.
UB8 156 BM71
Hillingdon Manor Sch,
Lwr & Mid Schs, Hayes End
UB8 *off Harlington Rd* 157 BP71
Hillingdon Prim Sch, Hlgdn
UB10 *off Uxbridge Rd* 157 BP69
Hillingdon Ri, Sev. TN13 279 FK122
Hillingdon Rd, Bexh. DA7 189 FC82
Gravesend DA11 213 GG89
Uxbridge UB10 156 BL67
Watford WD25 81 BU34
Hillingdon St, SE17 43 H3
Hillington Gdns, Wdf.Grn. IG8 124 EK54
Hill La, Kgswd KT20 255 CY121
Ruislip HA4 137 BQ60
Hill Ley, Hat. AL10 67 CT18
Hill Leys, Cuffley EN6 87 DL28
Hillman Cl, Horn. RM11 150 FK55
Uxbridge UB8 136 BL64
Hillman Dr, W10 14 B5
Hillman St, E8 10 F5
Hillmarton Rd, N7 8 A2
Hillmead, Berk. HP4 60 AU20
Hillmead Ct, Tap. SL6 152 AF71
Hillmead Dr, SW9 183 DP84
Hill Meadow, Colesh. HP7 77 AM43
Hill Mead Prim Sch, SW9
off Hillmead Dr 183 DP84
Hillmont Rd, Esher KT10 219 CE104
Hillmore Gro, SE26 205 DX92
Hillmount, Wok. GU22
off Constitution Hill 248 AY119
Hill Path, SW16
off Valley Rd 203 DM92
Hill Pl, Farn.Com. SL2 153 AP66
Hillpoint, Loud. WD3 96 BJ43
Hillreach, SE18 37 J10
Hill Ri, N9 104 DV44
NW11 142 DB56
SE23 204 DV88
Chalfont St. Peter SL9 112 AX54
Cuffley EN6 87 DK27
Dorking RH4 269 CG134
Esher KT10 219 CH103
Greenford UB6 158 CC66
Lane End DA2 211 FR92
Potters Bar EN6 86 DC34
Richmond TW10 199 CK85
Rickmansworth WD3 96 BH44
Ruislip HA4 137 BQ60
Slough SL3 175 BA79
Upminster RM14 150 FN61
Hillrise, Walt. KT12 217 BT101
Hillrise Av, Wat. WD24 98 BX38
Hill Ri Cres, Chal.St.P. SL9 112 AY54
Hillrise Rd, N19 143 DL59
Romford RM5 127 FC51
Hill Rd, N10 120 DF53
NW8 15 P1
Brentwood CM14 130 FU48
Carshalton SM5 240 DE107
Dartford DA2 210 FL89
Fetcham KT22 252 CB122
Harrow HA1 139 CG57
Mitcham CR4 223 DH95
Northwood HA6 115 BR51
Pinner HA5 138 BY57
Purley CR8 241 DM112
Sutton SM1 240 DB106
Theydon Bois CM16 107 ES37
Wembley HA0 139 CH62
Hillsboro Rd, SE22 204 DS85
Hillsborough Grn, Wat. WD19 115 BU48
Hills Chace, Warley CM14 130 FW49
Hillsgrove Cl, Well. DA16 188 EW80
Hillsgrove Prim Sch,
Well. DA16
off Sidmouth Rd 188 EW80
Hillside, NW9 140 CR56
NW10 160 CQ67
SW19 201 CX93
Banstead SM7 255 CY115
Chesham HP5 76 AN28
Erith DA8 189 FD77
Farningham DA4 230 FM101
Grays RM17 192 GD77
Harefield UB9 136 BJ57
Harlow CM17 74 EW17
Hatfield AL10 67 CU18
Hoddesdon EN11 71 DZ16
Lane End DA2 211 FS92
New Barnet EN5 102 DC43
Slough SL1 174 AS75
Virginia Water GU25 214 AW100
Ware SG12 54 DW07
Welwyn Garden City AL7 52 DB12
Woking GU22 248 AX120
Hillside, The, Orp. BR6 246 EV109
Hillside Av, N11 120 DF51
Borehamwood WD6 100 CP42
Cheshunt EN8 89 DX31
Gravesend DA12 213 GK89
Purley CR8 241 DP113
Wembley HA9 140 CM63
Woodford Green IG8 124 EJ50
Hillside Cl, NW8 5 M10
Abbots Langley WD5 81 BS32
Banstead SM7 255 CY116
Brockham RH3 286 CN135
Chalfont St. Giles HP8 112 AW48
Chalfont St. Peter SL9 112 AY51
Morden SM4 221 CY98
Woodford Green IG8 124 EJ50
Hillside Ct, St.Alb. AL1
off Hillside Rd 65 CE19
Swanley BR8 229 FG98
Hillside Cres, Chsht EN8 89 DX31
Enfield EN2 104 DR38
Harrow HA2 138 CC60
Northwood HA6 115 BU53
Stanstead Abbotts SG12 55 EB11
Watford WD19 98 BY44
Hillside Dr, Edg. HA8 118 CN51
Gravesend DA12 213 GK89
Hillside Gdns, E17 145 ED55
N6 142 DG58
SW2 203 DN89
Addlestone KT15 233 BF106
Amersham HP7 77 AS40
Barnet EN5 101 CY42
Berkhamsted HP4 60 AX20
Brockham RH3 270 CN134
Edgware HA8 118 CM49
Harrow HA3 140 CL59
Northwood HA6 115 BU52
Wallington SM6 241 DJ108
Hillside Gate, St.Alb. AL1 65 CE19
Hillside Gro, N14 121 DK45
NW7 119 CU52
Hillside Inf & Jun Schs, Nthwd.
HA6 *off Northwood Way* 115 BU52
Hillside La, Brom. BR2 226 EG103
Great Amwell SG12 55 EA10
Hillside Pas, SW2 203 DM89
Hillside Prim Sch, Orp.
BR5 *off Dyke Dr* 228 EW101
Hillside Ri, Nthwd. HA6 115 BU52
Hillside Rd, N15 144 DS59
SW2 203 DN89
W5 160 CL71
Ashtead KT21 254 CM117
Bromley BR2 226 EF97
Bushey WD23 98 BY43
Chorleywood WD3 95 BC43
Coulsdon CR5 257 DM118
Croydon CR0 241 DP106
Dartford DA1 209 FG86
Epsom KT17 239 CV110
Northwood HA6 115 BU52
Pinner HA5 115 BV52
Radlett WD7 99 CH35
St. Albans AL1 65 CE19
Sevenoaks TN13 279 FK123
Southall UB1 158 CA70
Surbiton KT5 220 CM99
Sutton SM2 239 CZ108
Tatsfield TN16 260 EL119
Whyteleafe CR3 258 DU118
Hillside Ter, Hert. SG13 54 DQ11
Hillside Wk, Brwd. CM14 130 FU48
Hills La, Nthwd. HA6 115 BS53
Hillsleigh Rd, W8 27 H2
Hillsmead Way, S.Croy. CR2 242 DU113
Hills Ms, W5 160 CL73
Hills Pl, W1 17 L9
Hillspur Cl, Guil. GU2 264 AT133
Hillspur Rd, Guil. GU2 264 AT133
Hills Rd, Buck.H. IG9 124 EH46
Hillstowe St, E5 144 DW61
Hill St, W1 29 H2
Richmond TW9 199 CK85
St. Albans AL3 64 CC20
● **Hillswood Business Pk**,
Cher. KT16 233 BC105
Hillswood Dr, Cher. KT16 233 BC105
Hillthorpe Cl, Pur. CR8 241 DM110
HILLTOP, Chesh. HP5 76 AR28
Hill Top, NW11 142 DB56
Hilltop, Loug. IG10 107 EN40
Hill Top, Mord. SM4 222 DA100
Sutton SM3 221 CZ101
Hilltop Av, NW10 160 CQ66
Hilltop Cl, Chsht EN7 88 DT26
Guildford GU3 264 AT130
Leatherhead KT22 253 CJ123
Hill Top Cl, Loug. IG10 107 EN41
Hilltop First Sch, Wind.
SL4 *off Clewer Hill Rd* 173 AL83
Hilltop Gdns, NW4 119 CV54
Dartford DA1 210 FM85
Orpington BR6 227 ES103
Hilltop La, Chaldon CR3 273 DN126
Redhill RH1 273 DN126
Hill Top Pl, Loug. IG10 107 EN41
Hilltop Ri, Bkhm KT23 268 CC126
Hilltop Rd, NW6 5 K6
Berkhamsted HP4 60 AW20
Grays RM20 191 FV79
Kings Langley WD4 81 BR27
Reigate RH2 288 DB136
Whyteleafe CR3 258 DS117
Hill Top Vw, Wdf.Grn. IG8 125 EM51
Hilltop Wk, Wold. CR3 259 DY120
Hilltop Way, Stan. HA7 117 CG48
Hillview, SW20 201 CV94
Hill Vw, Berk. HP4 60 AU17
Dorking RH4 285 CJ135
Hillview, Mitch. CR4 223 DL98
Whyteleafe CR3 258 DT117
Hillview Av, Har. HA3 140 CL57
Hornchurch RM11 150 FJ58
Hillview Cl, Pnr. HA5 116 BZ51
Purley CR8 241 DP111
Hill Vw Cl, Tad. KT20 255 CW121
Hillview Cl, Wem. HA9 140 CM61
Hillview Ct, Wok. GU22 249 AZ118
Hillview Cres, Guil. GU2 264 AT132
Ilford IG1 147 EM58
Orpington BR6 227 ES102
Hill Vw Dr, SE28 167 ES74
Hillview Dr, Red. RH1 288 DG135
Hill Vw Dr, Well. DA16 187 ES82
Hillview Gdns, NW4 141 CX56
Hill Vw Gdns, NW9 140 CR57
Hillview Gdns, Chsht EN8 89 DX27
Harrow HA2 138 CA55
Hillview Rd, NW7 119 CX49
Chislehurst BR7 207 EN92
Hill Vw Rd, Clay. KT10 237 CG108
Hillview Rd, Orp. BR6 227 ET102
Pinner HA5 116 BZ52
Sutton SM1 222 DC104
Hill Vw Rd, Twick. TW1 199 CG86
Woking GU22 249 AZ118
Wraysbury TW19 194 AX86
Hillway, N6 142 DG61
NW9 140 CS60
Amersham HP7 77 AP41
Hill Waye, Ger.Cr. SL9 135 AZ58
Hillwood Cl, Hutt. CM13 131 GB46
Hillwood Gro, Hutt. CM13 131 GB46
Hillworth Rd, SW2 203 DN87
Hillyard Rd, W7 159 CE71
Hillyard St, SW9 42 D7
Hillyfield, E17 123 DY54
Hilly Fld, Harl. CM18 73 ET19
Hillyfield Cl, E9 11 M3
Hillyfield Prim Sch, E17
off Higham Hill Rd 145 DY55
Hillyfields, Loug. IG10 107 EN40
Hilly Flds, Welw.G.C. AL7 52 DC08
Hilly Flds Cres, SE4 185 EA83
Hilmay Dr, Hem.H. HP1 62 BH21
Hilperton Rd, Slou. SL1 174 AS75
Hilsea Pt, SW15
off Wanborough Dr 201 CV88
Hilsea St, E5 144 DW63
Hilton Av, N12 120 DD50
Hilton Cl, Uxb. UB8 156 BH68
Hilton Ct, Horl. RH6
off Clarence Way 291 DK147
**Hilton Docklands Nelson
Dock Pier** 33 N2
Hilton Way, S.Croy. CR2 258 DV115
Hilversum Cres, SE22
off East Dulwich Gro 204 DS85
Himalayan Way, Wat. WD18 97 BT43
Himley Rd, SW17 202 DE92
Hinchley Cl, Esher KT10 219 CF104
Hinchley Dr, Esher KT10 219 CF104
Hinchley Manor, Esher KT10 219 CF104
Hinchley Way, Esher KT10 219 CG104
HINCHLEY WOOD, Esher KT10 219 CF104
⇌ **Hinchley Wood** 219 CF104
Hinchley Wd Prim Sch,
Hinch.Wd KT10
off Claygate La 219 CG103
**Hinchley Wd Sch & 6th Form
Cen**, Hinch.Wd KT10
off Claygate La 219 CG103
Hinckley Rd, SE15 184 DU84
Hind Cl, Chig. IG7 125 ET50
Hind Ct, EC4 18 F9
Hind Cres, Erith DA8 189 FD79
Hinde Ms, W1
off Marylebone La 17 H8
Hindes Rd, Har. HA1 139 CD57
Hinde St, W1 17 H8
Hind Gro, E14 22 A9
Hindhead Cl, N16 144 DS60
Uxbridge UB8
off Aldenham Dr 157 BP71
Hindhead Gdns, Nthlt. UB5 158 BY67
Hindhead Grn, Wat. WD19 116 BW50
Hindhead Pt, SW15
off Wanborough Dr 201 CV88
Hindhead Way, Wall. SM6 241 DL106
Hind Ho, N7 *off Harvist Est* 143 DN63
Hindle Ho, E8 10 A1
Hindmans Rd, SE22 204 DU85
Hindmans Way, Dag. RM9 168 EZ70
Hindmarsh Cl, E1 20 D10
Hindon Ct, SW1 29 L8
Hindrey Rd, E5 10 E2
Hindsley's Pl, SE23 204 DW89
Hind Ter, Grays RM20
off Mill La 191 FX78
Hine Cl, Couls. CR5 257 DJ122
Epsom KT19 238 CP111
Hinkler Rd, Har. HA3 139 CK55
Hinkley Cl, Hare. UB9 136 BJ56
Hinksey Cl, Slou. SL3 175 BB76
Hinksey Path, SE2 188 EX76
Hinstock Rd, SE18 187 EQ79
Hinton Av, Houns. TW4 178 BX84
Hinton Cl, SE9 206 EL88
Hinton Rd, N18 122 DS49
SE24 183 DP83
Slough SL1 153 AL73
Uxbridge UB8 156 BJ67
Wallington SM6 241 DJ107
Hintons, Harl. CM19 73 EM19
Hipkins Pl, Brox. EN10 71 DY20
Hipley Ct, Guil. GU1 281 BA135
Hipley St, Wok. GU22 249 BB121
Hippodrome Ms, W11 26 E1
Hippodrome Pl, W11 26 F1
Hirst Ct, SW1 41 J1
Hirst Cres, Wem. HA9 140 CL62
Hispano Ms, Enf. EN3 105 EA37
Hitcham La, Burn. SL1 152 AG69
Taplow SL6 152 AG69
Hitcham Rd, E17 145 DZ59
Burnham SL1 152 AF70
Taplow SL6 152 AF72
Hitchcock Cl, Shep. TW17 216 BM97
Hitchen Hatch La, Sev. TN13 278 FG124
Hitchens Cl, Hem.H. HP1 61 BF19
Hitchin Cl, Rom. RM3 128 FJ49
Hitchings Way, Reig. RH2 288 DA138
Hitchin Sq, E3 11 M10
Hithe Gro, SE16 33 H7
Hitherbaulk, Welw.G.C. AL7 51 CY11
Hitherbroom Rd, Hayes UB3 157 BU74
Hitherbury Cl, Guil. GU2 280 AW137
Hither Fm Rd, SE3 186 EJ83
Hitherfield Prim Sch, SW16
off Hitherfield Rd 203 DN90
Hitherfield Rd, SW16 203 DM89
Dagenham RM8 148 EY61
HITHER GREEN, SE13 206 EE86
⇌ **Hither Green** 206 EE86
Hither Grn La, SE13 205 EC85
Hither Grn Prim Sch,
SE13 *off Beacon Rd* 205 ED86
Hitherlands, SW12 203 DH89
Hither Meadow, Chal.St.P.
SL9 *off Lower Rd* 112 AY54
Hithermoor Rd, Stai. TW19 196 BG85
Hitherway, Welw.G.C. AL8 51 CY05
Hitherwell Dr, Har. HA3 117 CD53
Hitherwood Cl, Horn. RM12
off Swanbourne Dr 150 FK63
Reigate RH2 272 DD132
Hitherwood Dr, SE19 204 DT91
Hive, The, Nthflt DA11
off Fishermans Hill 212 GB85
Hive Cl, Brwd. CM14 130 FU47
Bushey Heath WD23 117 CD47
Hive La, Nthflt DA11 212 GB86
Hive Rd, Bushey Hth WD23 117 CD47
Hivings Hill, Chesh. HP5 76 AN28
Hivings Pk, Chesh. HP5 76 AP28
Hixberry La, St.Alb. AL4 65 CK21
★ **H.M.S. Belfast**, SE1 31 P2
★ **H.M.S. President**, EC4 30 F1
★ **H.M. Treasury**, SW1 30 A4
Hoadly Rd, SW16 203 DK90
Hobart Cl, N20
off Oakleigh Rd N 120 DE47
Hayes UB4 158 BX70
Hobart Dr, Hayes UB4 158 BX70
Hobart Gdns, Th.Hth. CR7 224 DR97
Hobart La, Hayes UB4 158 BX70
Hobart Pl, SW1 29 J6
Richmond TW10
off Chisholm Rd 200 CM86
Hobart Rd, Dag. RM9 148 EX63
Hayes UB4 158 BX70
Ilford IG6 125 EQ54
Tilbury RM18 193 GG81
Worcester Park KT4 221 CV104
Hobart Wk, St.Alb. AL3
off Valley Rd 65 CF16
Hobbans Fm Chase, Ong. CM5 75 FH23
Hobbayne Prim Sch, W7
off Greenford Av 159 CF72
Hobbayne Rd, W7 159 CD72
Hobbes Wk, SW15 201 CV85
Hobbs Cl, Chsht EN8 89 DX29
St. Albans AL4 66 CL21
West Byfleet KT14 234 BH113
Hobbs Cross, Harl. CM17 58 FA14
● **Hobbs Cross Business Cen**,
They.Gar. CM16 108 EX36
Hobbs Cross Rd, Harl. CM17 58 EY12
Theydon Garnon CM16 108 EW35
Hobbs Grn, N2 142 DC55
Hobbs Hill Rd, Hem.H. HP3 62 BL24
Hobbs Hill Wd Prim Sch, Hem.H.
HP3 *off Peascroft Rd* 63 BP22
Hobbs Ms, Ilf. IG3
off Ripley Rd 147 ET61
Hobbs Pl Est, N1 9 N9
Hobbs Rd, SE27 204 DQ91
Hobbs Way, Welw.G.C. AL8 51 CW10
Hobby Horse Cl, Chsht EN7
off Great Stockwood Rd 88 DR26
Hobby St, Enf. EN3 105 DX43
Hobday St, E14 22 C8
Hobill Wk, Surb. KT5 220 CM100
Hoblands End, Chis. BR7 207 ES93
Hobletts Manor Inf & Nurs Sch,
Hem.H. HP2
off Adeyfield Rd 62 BN19
Hobletts Manor Jun Sch,
Hem.H. HP2
off Adeyfield Rd 62 BN19
Hobletts Rd, Hem.H. HP2 62 BM19
Hobsons Cl, Hodd. EN11 55 DZ14
Hobsons Pl, E1 20 C6
Hobtoe Rd, Harl. CM20 57 EN14
Hobury St, SW10 39 P3
Hockenden La, Swan. BR8 229 FB96
Hockeridge Bottom, Berk. HP4 60 AT21
Hockering Gdns, Wok. GU22 249 BA117
Hockering Rd, Wok. GU22 249 BA118
Hocker St, E2 20 A3
Hockett Cl, SE8 33 M8
Hocklands, Welw.G.C. AL7 52 DC08
Hockley Av, E6 166 EL68
Hockley Ct, E18
off Churchfields 124 EG53
Hockley Dr, Rom. RM2 127 FH54
Hockley La, Stoke P. SL2 154 AV67
Hockley Ms, Bark. IG11 167 ES68
Hocroft Av, NW2 141 CZ62
Hocroft Rd, NW2 141 CZ63
Hocroft Wk, NW2 141 CZ62
Hodder Dr, Perivale UB6 159 CF68
HODDESDON, EN11 71 DZ18
Hoddesdon, Hodd. EN11 71 DX16
Hoddesdon Bypass, Brox. EN10 71 DX19
Hertford SG13 55 DY14
Hoddesdon EN11 55 DY14
● **Hoddesdon Ind Cen**,
Hodd. EN11 71 EC15
Hoddesdon Rd, Belv. DA17 188 FA78
Broxbourne EN10 89 DX27
Stanstead Abbotts SG12 55 EC11
Hodds Wd Rd, Chesh. HP5 76 AQ33
Hodes Row, NW3 6 F1
Hodford Rd, NW11 141 CZ61
Hodgemoor Vw, Ch.St.G. HP8 112 AT48
Hodges Cl, Chaff.Hun. RM16 191 FX78
Hodges Way, Wat. WD18 97 BU44
Hodgkin Cl, SE28
off Fleming Way 168 EX73
Hodgkins Ms, Stan. HA7 117 CH50
Hodgson Gdns, Guil. GU4
off Sutherland Dr 265 BA131
Hodings Rd, Harl. CM20 57 EP14
Hodister Cl, SE5 43 K5
Hodnet Gro, SE16 33 J8
Hodsoll Ct, Orp. BR5 228 EX100
Hodson Cl, Har. HA2 138 BZ62
Hodson Cres, Orp. BR5 228 EX100
Hodson Pl, Enf. EN3 105 EA38
HOE, Guil. GU5 283 BS143
Hoe, The, Wat. WD19 116 BX47
Hoe Br Sch, Old Wok. GU22
off Old Woking Rd 249 BC119
Hoebrook Cl, Wok. GU22 248 AX121
Hoechst, Houns. TW4 178 BW83
Hoecroft, Lwr Naze. EN9 72 EF22
Hoe La, Abin.Ham. RH5 283 BT143
Abridge RM4 108 EV43
Enfield EN1, EN3 104 DU38
Nazeing EN9 72 EF22
Peaslake GU5 283 BR144
Ware SG12 55 DX09
Hoe Meadow, Beac. HP9 110 AJ51
Hoestock Rd, Saw. CM21 58 EX05
Hoe St, E17 145 EA56
Hoffmann Gdns, S.Croy. CR2 242 DU108
Hoffman Sq, N1 *off Chart St* 19 M2
Hofland Rd, W14 26 D6
Hoford Rd, Grays RM16 193 GK76
Linford SS17 193 GL75
West Tilbury RM18 193 GK77
Hogan Ms, W2 16 A6
Hogan Way, E5 144 DU61
Hogarth Av, Ashf. TW15 197 BQ93
Brentwood CM15 130 FY48
● **Hogarth Business Pk**, W4 180 CS79
Hogarth Cl, E16 24 E6
W5 160 CL71
Slough SL1 153 AL73
Uxbridge UB8 156 BJ69
Hogarth Ct, EC3 19 P10
SE19 *off Fountain Dr* 204 DT91
Bushey WD23
off Steeplands 116 CB45
Hogarth Cres, SW19 222 DD95
Croydon CR0 224 DQ101
Hogarth Gdns, Houns. TW5 178 CA80
Hogarth Hill, NW11 141 CZ56
Hogarth La, W4 180 CS79
Hogarth Pl, SW5 27 L9
Hogarth Prim Sch,
Brwd. CM15
off Riseway 131 FZ48
Hogarth Reach, Loug. IG10 107 EM43

Hogarth Rd, SW5 27 L9
Dagenham RM8 148 EV64
Edgware HA8 118 CN54
Jct Hogarth Rbt, W4 181 CT79
Hogarth Rbt Flyover, W4
off Burlington La 180 CS79
★ Hogarth's Ho, W4
off Hogarth La 180 CS79
Hogarth Way, Hmptn. TW12 218 CC95
Hogback Wd Rd, Beac. HP9 110 AH51
Hogden La, Lthd. KT23 268 CA129
Ranmore Common RH5 268 BZ132
Hogfair La, Burn. SL1 152 AJ69
Hogg End La, Hem.H. HP2 63 BR17
St. Albans AL3 63 BT17
Hogges Cl, Hodd. EN11
off Conduit La 71 EA17
Hogg La, Els. WD6 99 CG42
Grays RM16, RM17 192 GA76
Hog Hill Rd, Rom. RM5 126 EZ52
Hog Pits, Flaun. HP3 79 BB32
HOGPITS BOTTOM,
Hem.H. HP3 79 BA31
Hogpits Bottom, Flaun. HP3 79 BA32
Hogs Back, Guil. GU3 280 AS137
Hogscross La, Chipstead CR5 256 DF123
Hogsdell La, Hert.Hth SG13 54 DV11
Hogshead Pas, E1 32 F1
Hogshill La, Cob. KT11 235 BV114
Hogs La, Grav. DA11 212 GD90
Hogsmill La, Kings.T. KT1 220 CM97
Hogsmill Way, Epsom KT19 238 CQ106
Hogs Orchard, Swan. BR8 229 FH95
Hogtrough Hill, Brasted TN16 261 ET120
Hogtrough La, Gdse. RH9 275 EA128
Oxted RH8 275 EB128
Redhill RH1 289 DJ135
Holbeach Cl, NW9 118 CS53
Holbeach Gdns, Sid. DA15 207 ES86
Holbeach Ms, SW12 203 DH88
Sch Holbeach Prim Sch, SE6
off Doggett Rd 205 EA87
Holbeach Rd, SE6 205 EA87
Holbeck La, Chsht EN7 88 DT26
Holbeck Row, SE15 44 D5
Holbein Gate, Nthwd. HA6 115 BS50
Holbein Ms, SW1 28 G10
Holbein Pl, SW1 28 G9
Holbein Ter, Dag. RM8
off Marlborough Rd 148 EW63
Holberton Gdns, NW10 161 CV69
HOLBORN, WC2 18 C8
⊖ Holborn 18 B8
Holborn, EC1 18 E7
Holborn Circ, EC1 18 F7
Holborn Cl, St.Alb. AL4 65 CK15
Coll Holborn Coll, SE7 36 F8
Holborn Pl, WC1 18 C7
Holborn Rd, E13 24 A5
Holborn Viaduct, EC1 18 F7
Holborn Way, Mitch. CR4 222 DF96
Holbreck Pl, Wok. GU22
off Heathside Rd 249 AZ118
Holbrook Cl, N19
off Dartmouth Pk Hill 143 DH60
Enfield EN1 104 DT39
Shalford GU4 280 AY142
Holbrooke Ct, N7 143 DL63
Holbrooke Pl, Rich. TW10 199 CK85
Holbrook Gdns, Ald. WD25 98 CB36
Holbrook La, Chis. BR7 207 ER94
Holbrook Meadow, Egh. TW20 195 BC93
Holbrook Rd, E15 23 L1
Holbrook Way, Brom. BR2 227 EM100
Holburne Cl, SE3 186 EJ81
Holburne Gdns, SE3 186 EK81
Holburne Rd, SE3 186 EJ81
Holcombe Cl, West. TN16 277 ER126
Holcombe Hill, NW7 119 CU48
Holcombe Rd, N17 144 DT55
Ilford IG1 147 EN59
Holcombe St, W6 181 CV78
Holcon Ct, Red. RH1 272 DG131
Holcote Cl, Belv. DA17
off Blakemore Way 188 EY76
Holcroft Rd, E9 11 H6
HOLDBROOK, Wal.Cr. EN8 89 EA34
Holdbrook Ct, Wal.Cr. EN8
off Queens Way 89 DZ34
Holdbrook N, Wal.Cr. EN8 89 DZ33
Sch Holdbrook Prim Sch,
Wal.Cr. EN8
off Longcroft Dr 89 DZ34
Holdbrook S, Wal.Cr. EN8
off Queens Way 89 DZ34
Holdbrook Way, Rom. RM3 128 FM54
Holden Av, N12 120 DB50
NW9 140 CQ60
Holdenby Rd, SE4 205 DY85
Holden Cl, Dag. RM8 148 EV62
Hertford SG13 54 DS09
Holden Gdns, Warley CM14 130 FX50
Holdenhurst Av, N12 120 DB52
Holden Pl, Cob. KT11 235 BV114
Holden Pt, E15 13 H4
Holden Rd, N12 120 DB50
HOLDENS, Welw.G.C. AL7 52 DA06
Holden St, SW11 40 G9
Holden Way, Upmin. RM14 151 FR59
Holder Cl, N3 120 DB52
Holdernesse Cl, Islw. TW7 179 CG81
Holdernesse Rd, SW17 202 DF90
Holderness Way, SE27 203 DP92
HOLDERS HILL, NW4 119 CX54
Holders Hill Av, NW4 119 CX54
Holders Hill Circ, NW7
off Dollis Rd 119 CY52
Holders Hill Cres, NW4 119 CX54
Holders Hill Dr, NW4 141 CX55
Holders Hill Gdns, NW4 119 CY54
Holders Hill Rd, NW4 119 CX54
NW7 119 CX54
Holdings, The, Hat. AL9 67 CW16
Holecroft, Wal.Abb. EN9 90 EE34
Hole Fm La, Gt Warley CM13 151 FV55
Holegate St, SE7 36 E7
Hole Hill, Westc. RH4 284 CA136
Holford Ho, SE16
off Manor Est 32 E9
Holford Ms, WC1 18 E1
Holford Pl, WC1 18 D2
Holford Rd, NW3 142 DC62
Guildford GU1 265 BC134
Holford St, WC1 18 E2
Holford Yd, WC1 18 D1
Holgate Av, SW11 182 DD83
Holgate Gdns, Dag. RM10 148 FA64
Holgate Rd, Dag. RM10 148 FA64
HOLLAND, Oxt. RH8 276 EG134
Holland Av, SW20 221 CT95
Sutton SM2 240 DA109
Holland Cl, Brom. BR2 226 EF103
Epsom KT19 238 CQ111
New Barnet EN5 120 DD45
Redhill RH1 272 DF134
Romford RM7 149 FC57
Stanmore HA7 117 CH50
Holland Ct, E17
off Evelyn Rd 145 EC56
NW7 119 CU51
Holland Cres, Oxt. RH8 276 EG133
Holland Dr, SE23 205 DY90
Holland Gdns, W14 26 F6
Brentford TW8 180 CL79
Egham TW20 215 BF96
Watford WD25 98 BW35
Holland Gro, SW9 42 F5
Sch Holland Ho Sch, Edg.
HA8 off Broadhurst Av 118 CP49
Sch Holland Jun Sch, Oxt.
RH8 off Holland Rd 276 EG134
Holland La, Oxt. RH8 276 EG133
★ Holland Pk, W8 26 G4
⊖ Holland Park 26 G3
Holland Pk, W11 26 F3
Holland Pk Av, W11 26 D4
Ilford IG3 147 ES58
Holland Pk Gdns, W14 26 E3
Holland Pk Ms, W11 26 F3
Holland Pk Rd, W14 26 G7
Jct Holland Pk Rbt, W11 26 D4
Sch Holland Pk Sch, W8 27 H4
Holland Pas, N1 9 J8
Holland Pl, W8 27 L4
Holland Ri Ho, SW9 42 D5
Holland Rd, E6 167 EM67
E15 23 K2
NW10 161 CU67
SE25 224 DU99
W14 26 D4
Oxted RH8 276 EG133
Wembley HA0 159 CK65
Hollands, The, Felt. TW13 198 BX91
Woking GU22
off Montgomery Rd 248 AY118
Worcester Park KT4 221 CT102
Hollands Cl, Hunsdon SG12 56 EK06
Holland St, SE1 31 H2
W8 27 K5
Holland Town Est, SW9
off Mandela St 42 F5
Holland Vil Rd, W14 26 E4
Holland Wk, N19
off Duncombe Rd 143 DK60
W8 27 H3
Stanmore HA7 117 CG50
Holland Way, Brom. BR2 226 EF103
Harlow CM17 off Tatton St 58 EW14
Hollar Rd, N16
off Stoke Newington High St 144 DT62
Hollen St, W1 17 N8
Holles Cl, Hmptn. TW12 198 CA93
Holles St, W1 17 K8
Holley Rd, W3 180 CS75
Hollickwood Av, N12 120 DF51
Sch Hollickwood Prim Sch,
N10 off Sydney Rd 121 DH52
Holliday Sq, SW11
off Fowler Cl 182 DD83
Holliday St, Berk. HP4 60 AX19
Hollidge Way, Dag. RM10 169 FB65
Hollie Cl, Smallfield RH6 291 DP149
Hollier Ct, Hat. AL10
off Cranborne Rd 67 CV17
Holliers Way, Hat. AL10 67 CU18
Hollies, The, E11 146 EG57
N20 off Oakleigh Pk N 120 DD46
Bovingdon HP3 79 BA29
Gravesend DA12 213 GK93
Harrow HA3 139 CG56
Oxted RH8 276 EH133
Welwyn Garden City AL8 51 CV13
Hollies Av, Sid. DA15 207 ET89
West Byfleet KT14 233 BF113
Hollies Cl, SW16 203 DN93
Twickenham TW1 199 CF89
Hollies Ct, Add. KT15 234 BJ106
Hollies End, NW7 119 CV50
Hollies Rd, W5 179 CJ77
Hollies Way, SW12
off Bracken Av 202 DG87
Potters Bar EN6 86 DC31
Holligrave Rd, Brom. BR1 226 EG95
Hollingbourne Av, Bexh. DA7 188 EZ80
Hollingbourne Gdns, W13 159 CH71
Hollingbourne Rd, SE24 204 DQ85
Hollingbourne Twr, Orp. BR5 228 EX102
Hollingsworth Rd, Croy. CR0 242 DV107
Hollington Cres, N.Mal. KT3 221 CT100
Hollington Rd, E6 25 J3
N17 122 DU54
Hollingworth Cl, W.Mol. KT8 218 BZ98
Hollingworth Rd, Petts Wd
BR5 227 EP100
Hollingworth Way, West. TN16 277 ER126
Hollins Ho, N7
off Tufnell Pk Rd 143 DL63
Hollis Pl, Grays RM17
off Ward Av 192 GA77
Hollman Gdns, SW16 203 DP93
Hollow, The, Wdf.Grn. IG8 124 EF49
HOLLOWAY, N7 8 B2
Holloway Cl, West Dr. UB7 176 BL78
Holloway Dr, Vir.W. GU25 214 AY98
Holloway Hill, Cher. KT16 235 BC104
Holloway La, Chenies WD3 95 BD36
West Drayton UB7 176 BL79
⊖ Holloway Road 8 D2
Holloway Rd, E6 25 K3
E11 146 EE62
N7 8 F4
N19 143 DK61
Sch Holloway Sch, N7 7 P2
Holloways La, N.Mymms AL9 67 CX23
Holloway St, Houns. TW3 178 CB83
Hollow Cl, Guil. GU2
off Lynwood 280 AV135
Hollow Cotts, Purf. RM19 190 FN78
Hollowfield Av, Grays RM17 192 GD77
Hollowfield Wk, Nthlt. UB5 158 BY65
Hollow Hill La, Iver SL0 155 BB73
Hollow La, Vir.W. GU25 214 AY97
Wotton RH5 284 BX140
Hollows, The, Brent. TW8 180 CM79
Hollow Wk, Kew TW9
off Royal Botanic Gdns 180 CL80
Hollow Way La, Amer. HP6 77 AS35
Chesham HP5 77 AS35
Holly Av, New Haw KT15 234 BG110
Stanmore HA7 118 CL54
Walton-on-Thames KT12 218 BX102
Hollybank Cl, Hmptn. TW12 198 CA92
Hollybank Rd, W.Byf. KT14 234 BG114
Holly Bk Rd, Wok. GU22 248 AV121
Hollyberry La, NW3
off Holly Wk 142 DC63
Hollybrake Cl, Chis. BR7 207 ER94
Hollybush Av, St.Alb. AL2 64 CA24
Hollybush Cl, E11 146 EG57
Harrow HA3 117 CE53
Potten End HP4 61 BD16
Sevenoaks TN13 279 FJ124
Watford WD19 116 BW45
Hollybush Ct, Sev. TN13 279 FJ124
Hollybush Gdns, E2 20 F2
Hollybush Hill, E11 146 EF58
Holly Bush Hill, NW3 142 DC63
Hollybush Hill, Stoke P. SL2 154 AU66
Hollybush La, Amer. HP6 77 AR37
Denham UB9 135 BE63
Holly Bush La, Hmptn. TW12 198 BZ94
Hollybush La, Hem.H. HP1 61 BF19
Iver SL0 155 BB73
Orpington BR6 246 FA107
Ripley GU23 250 BK119
Holly Bush La, Sev. TN13 279 FJ123
Hollybush La, Welw.G.C. AL7 51 CZ13
Hollybush Pl, E2 20 F2
Sch Hollybush Prim Sch, Hert.
SG14 off Fordwich Ri 53 DN09
Hollybush Rd, Chesh. HP5 76 AN27
Gravesend DA12 213 GJ89
Kingston upon Thames KT2 200 CL92
Holly Bush Steps, NW3
off Heath St 142 DC63
Hollybush St, E13 24 B2
Holly Bush Vale, NW3
off Heath St 142 DC63
Hollybush Way, Chsht EN7 88 DU28
Holly Cl, Beck. BR3 225 EC98
Buckhurst Hill IG9 124 EK48
Englefield Green TW20 194 AV93
Farnham Common SL2 133 AQ63
Feltham TW13 198 BY92
Hatfield AL10 67 CT19
Longcross KT16 214 AU104
Wallington SM6 241 DH108
Woking GU21 248 AV119
Hollycombe, Eng.Grn TW20 194 AW91
Holly Cottage Ms, Uxb. UB8
off Pield Heath Rd 156 BN71
Holly Ct, SE10 35 M7
Romford RM1
off Dolphin App 149 FF56
Sutton SM2
off Worcester Rd 240 DA108
Holly Cres, Beck. BR3 225 DZ99
Windsor SL4 173 AK82
Woodford Green IG8 123 ED52
Holly Cft, Hert. SG14 53 DN08
Hollycroft Av, NW3 142 DA62
Wembley HA9 140 CM61
Hollycroft Cl, Sipson UB7 176 BN79
South Croydon CR2 242 DS106
Hollycroft Gdns, Sipson UB7 176 BN79
Hollycross Rd, Ware SG12 55 DZ07
Hollydale Cl, Nthlt. UB5
off Dorchester Rd 138 CB63
Hollydale Dr, Brom. BR2 227 EM104
Sch Hollydale Prim Sch, SE15 45 H9
Hollydale Rd, SE15 44 G7
Hollydell, Hert. SG13 54 DQ11
Hollydene, SE15 44 E6
Hollydown Way, E11 145 ED62
Holly Dr, E4 123 EB45
Berkhamsted HP4 60 AX20
Brentford TW8 179 CG79
Potters Bar EN6 86 DB33
South Ockendon RM15 171 FX70
Windsor SL4 194 AS85
Holly Fm Rd, Sthl. UB2 178 BY78
Holly Fld, Harl. CM19 73 EQ18
Hollyfield, Hat. AL10 67 CU21
Hollyfield Av, N11 120 DF50
Hollyfield Rd, Surb. KT5 220 CM101
Hollyfields, Brox. EN10 89 DY26
Sch Hollyfield Sch & 6th Form
Cen, The, Surb. KT6
off Surbiton Hill Rd 220 CL99
Holly Gdns, Bexh. DA7 189 FC84
West Drayton UB7 176 BM75
Holly Gate, Add. KT15 234 BH105
Holly Grn, Wey. KT13 217 BR104
Holly Gro, NW9 140 CQ59
SE15 44 B8
Bushey WD23 117 CD45
Pinner HA5 116 BY53
Hollygrove Cl, Houns. TW3 178 BZ84
Holly Gro Rd, Bramfld SG14 53 DH07
Hollyhedge Rd, Cob. KT11 235 BV114
Holly Hedges La, Bov. HP3 79 BC30
Rickmansworth WD3 79 BC30
Holly Hedge Ter, SE13 205 ED85
Holly Hill, N21 103 DM44
NW3 142 DC63
Holly Hill Dr, Bans. SM7 256 DA117
Holly Hill Pk, Bans. SM7 256 DA117
Holly Hill Rd, Belv. DA17 189 FB78
Erith DA8 189 FB78
Hollyhock Cl, Hem.H. HP1 61 BE18
Holly Ho, Brwd. CM15
off Sawyers Hall La 130 FX46
H Holly Ho Hosp, Buck.H. IG9 124 EH47
Holly La, Bans. SM7 256 DA116
Holly La E, Bans. SM7 256 DA116
Holly La W, Bans. SM7 256 DA117
Holly Lea, Jacobs Well GU4 264 AX128
Holly Lo, Lwr Kgswd KT20 271 CY126
Holly Lo Gdns, N6 142 DG61
Hollymead, Cars. SM5 222 DF104
Hollymead Rd, Chipstead
CR5 256 DG118
Hollymeoak Rd, Couls. CR5 257 DH119
Holly Ms, SW10 39 P1
Hollymoor La, Epsom KT19 238 CR110
Holly Mt, NW3
off Holly Bush Hill 142 DC63
Hollymount Cl, SE10 46 E6
Sch Hollymount Prim Sch, SW20
off Cambridge Rd 221 CW95
Holly Pk, N3 141 CZ55
N4 143 DM59
Holly Pk Est, N4
off Blythwood Rd 143 DL59
Holly Pk Gdns, N3 142 DA55
Sch Holly Pk Prim Sch, N11
off Bellevue Rd 120 DG50
Holly Pk Rd, N11 120 DG50
W7 159 CF74
Holly Pl, NW3 off Holly Wk 142 DC63
Holly Rd, E11
off Green Man Rbt 146 EF59
W4 off Dolman Rd 180 CR77
Dartford DA1 210 FK88
Enfield EN3 105 DX36
Hampton Hill TW12 198 CC93
Hounslow TW3 178 CB84
Orpington BR6 246 EU108
Reigate RH2 288 DB136
Twickenham TW1 199 CG88
Holly St, E8 10 B6
Holly Ter, N6
off Highgate W Hill 142 DG60
N20 off Swan La 120 DC47
Hollytree Av, Swan. BR8 229 FE96
Hollytree Cl, SW19 201 CX88
Chalfont St. Peter SL9 112 AY50
Holly Tree Cl, Ley Hill HP5 78 AV31
Holly Tree Rd, Cat. CR3
off Elm Gro 258 DS122
Sch Holly Trees Prim Sch,
Warley CM14
off Vaughan Williams Way 130 FV49
Hollyview Cl, NW4 141 CU58
Holly Village, N6
off Swains La 143 DH61
Holly Wk, NW3 5 N1
Enfield EN2 104 DQ41
Richmond TW9 180 CL82
Welwyn Garden City AL8 51 CW05
Holly Way, Mitch. CR4 223 DK98
Hollywood Ct, Els. WD6
off Deacons Hill Rd 100 CM42
Hollywood Gdns, Hayes UB4 157 BV72
Hollywood Hts, Rom. RM1 149 FE58
Hollywood Ms, SW10 39 N2
Hollywood Rd, E4 123 DY50
SW10 39 N1
Hollywoods, Croy. CR0 243 DZ109
Hollywood Way, Erith DA8 189 FH81
Woodford Green IG8 123 ED52
Holman Ho, E2 off Roman Rd 21 J2
Holman Rd, SW11 40 A9
Epsom KT19 238 CQ106
Holmbank Dr, Shep. TW17 217 BS98
Holmbridge Gdns, Enf. EN3 105 DX42
Holmbrook Dr, NW4 141 CX57
Holmbury Ct, SW17 202 DF90
SW19 202 DE94
Holmbury Dr, N.Holm. RH5 285 CJ139
Holmbury Gdns, Hayes UB3 157 BT74
Holmbury Gro, Croy. CR0 243 DZ108
Holmbury Keep, Horl. RH6
off Langshott La 291 DJ147
Holmbury Pk, Brom. BR1 206 EL94
Holmbury Vw, E5 144 DV60
Holmbush Rd, SW15 201 CY86
Holm Cl, Wdhm KT15 233 BE112
Holmcote Gdns, N5 9 J3
Holmcroft, Walt.Hill KT20 271 CV125
Holmcroft Way, Brom. BR2 227 EM99
Holmdale Cl, Borwd. WD6 100 CM40
Holmdale Gdns, NW4 141 CX57
Holmdale Rd, NW6 5 J3
Chislehurst BR7 207 EQ92
Holmdale Ter, N15 144 DS59
Holmdene Av, NW7 119 CU51
SE24 204 DQ85
Harrow HA2 138 CB55
Holmdene Cl, Beck. BR3 225 EC96
Holmead Rd, SW6 39 M5
Holmebury Cl, Bushey Hth
WD23 117 CE47
Holme Chase, Wey. KT13 235 BQ107
Holme Cl, Chsht EN8 89 DY31
Hatfield AL10 67 CT15
Holme Ct, Islw. TW7
off Twickenham Rd 179 CG83
Holmedale, Slou. SL2 154 AW73
Holmefield Ct, NW3 6 D4
Holme Lacey Rd, SE12 206 EF86
Holme Lea, Wat. WD25 82 BW34
Holme Pk, Borwd. WD6 100 CM40
Holme Pl, Hem.H. HP2
off Crest Pk 63 BQ19
Holme Rd, E6 166 EL67
Hatfield AL10 67 CT15
Hornchurch RM11 150 FN60
Holmes Av, E17 145 DZ55
NW7 119 CY50
Holmes Cl, SE22 184 DU84
Purley CR8 241 DM113
Woking GU22 249 AZ121
Holmes Ct, Grav. DA12 213 GM88
Holmesdale, Wal.Cr. EN8 105 DX35
Holmesdale Av, SW14 180 CP83
Redhill RH1 273 DJ131
Holmesdale Cl, SE25 224 DT97
Guildford GU1 265 BB133
Sch Holmesdale Comm Inf Sch,
Reig. RH2 off Alma Rd 272 DB132
Holmesdale Hill, S.Darenth
DA4 230 FQ95
Holmesdale Manor, Red. RH1 272 DG132
Holmesdale Pk, Nutfld RH1 273 DM134
Holmesdale Rd, N6 143 DH59
SE25 224 DR99
Bexleyheath DA7 188 EX82
Croydon CR0 224 DR99
North Holmwood RH5 285 CH140
Reigate RH2 272 DA133
Richmond TW9 180 CM81
Sevenoaks TN13 279 FJ123
South Darenth DA4 230 FQ95
South Nutfield RH1 289 DM136
Teddington TW11 199 CJ94
Holmesdale Ter, N.Holm. RH5 285 CH140
Holmesley Rd, SE23 205 DY86
Holmes Meadow, Harl. CM19 73 EP21
Holmes Pl, SW10 39 P2
Holmes Rd, NW5 7 J4
SW19 202 DC94
Twickenham TW1 199 CF89
Holmes Ter, SE1 30 E4
HOLMETHORPE, Red. RH1 273 DH132
Holmethorpe Av, Red. RH1 273 DH131
● Holmethorpe Ind Est,
Red. RH1 273 DH131
Holme Way, Stan. HA7 117 CF51
Holmewood Gdns, SW2 203 DM87
Holmewood Rd, SE25 224 DS97
SW2 203 DL87
Holmfield Av, NW4 141 CX57
Holm Gro, Uxb. UB10 156 BN66
Holmhurst Rd, Belv. DA17 189 FB78
Holmlea Rd, Datchet SL3 174 AX81
Holmlea Wk, Datchet SL3 174 AW81
Holmleigh Av, Dart. DA1 190 FJ84
Sch Holmleigh Prim Sch, N16
off Dunsmure Rd 144 DT60
Holmleigh Rd, N16 144 DS60
Holmleigh Rd Est, N16
off Holmleigh Rd 144 DS60
Holm Oak Cl, SW15 201 CZ86
Holm Oak Ms, SW4 203 DL85
Holmsdale Cl, Iver SL0 155 BF72
Holmsdale Gro, Bexh. DA7 189 FE82
Holmshaw Cl, SE26 205 DY91
Holmshill La, Borwd. WD6 100 CS36
Holmside Ri, Wat. WD19 115 BV48
Holmside Rd, SW12 202 DG86
Holmsley Cl, N.Mal. KT3 221 CT100
Holmsley Ho, SW15
off Tangley Gro 201 CT87
Holms St, E2 10 C10
Holmstall Av, Edg. HA8 140 CQ55
Holm Wk, SE3 47 P9
Holmwood Av, Shenf. CM15 131 GA44
South Croydon CR2 242 DT113
Holmwood Cl, Add. KT15 234 BG106
East Horsley KT24 267 BS128
Harrow HA2 138 CC55
Northolt UB5 158 CB65
Sutton SM2 239 CX109
Holmwood Gdns, N3 120 DA54
Wallington SM6 241 DH107
Holmwood Gro, NW7 118 CR50
Holmwood Rd, Chess. KT9 237 CK106
Enfield EN3 105 DX36
Ilford IG3 147 ES61
Sutton SM2 239 CW110
Holmwood Vw Rd, Mid Holm.
RH5 off Horsham Rd 285 CH142
Holmwood Vil, SE7 35 P10
Holne Chase, N2 142 DC58
Morden SM4 221 CZ100
Holness Rd, E15 13 L5
Holroyd Cl, Clay. KT10 237 CF109
Holroyd Rd, SW15 181 CW84
Claygate KT10 237 CF109
Holsart Cl, Tad. KT20 255 CV122
Holstein Av, Wey. KT13 234 BN105
Holstein Way, Erith DA18 188 EY76
Holst Ho, W12 off Du Cane Rd 161 CV72
Holstock Rd, Ilf. IG1 147 EQ61
Holsworth Cl, Har. HA2 138 CC57
Holsworthy Sq, WC1 18 D5
Holsworthy Way, Chess. KT9 237 CJ106
Holt, The, Hem.H. HP2
off Turners Hill 62 BL21
Ilford IG6 125 EQ51
Morden SM4 off London Rd 222 DA98
Wallington SM6 241 DJ105
Welwyn Garden City AL7 52 DD10
Holt Cl, N10 142 DG56
SE28 168 EV73
Chigwell IG7 125 ET50
Elstree WD6 100 CM42
Holton St, E1 21 J4
Holt Rd, E16 37 H3
Romford RM3 128 FL52
Wembley HA0 139 CH62
Holtsmere Cl, Wat. WD25 98 BW35
Sch Holtsmere End Inf & Nurs Sch,
Hem.H. HP2 off Shenley Rd 63 BP15
Sch Holtsmere End Jun Sch, Hem.H.
HP2 off Shenley Rd 63 BP15
HOLTSPUR, Beac. HP9 110 AF54
Holtspur Av, Woob.Grn HP10 132 AE56
Holtspur Cl, Beac. HP9 110 AG54
Holtspur La, Woob.Grn HP10 132 AE57
Sch Holtspur Sch, Holt. HP9
off Cherry Tree Rd 110 AG54
Holtspur Top La, Beac. HP9 110 AG54
Holtspur Way, Beac. HP9 110 AG54
Holt Way, Chig. IG7 125 ET50
Holtwhite Av, Enf. EN2 104 DQ40
Holtwhites Hill, Enf. EN2 103 DP39
Holtwood Rd, Oxshott KT22 236 CC113
Holwell Caravan Site, Hat. AL9 52 DE14
Holwell Hyde, Welw.G.C. AL7 52 DC11
Holwell Hyde La, Welw.G.C.
AL7 52 DC12
Holwell La, Hat. AL9 52 DE14
Holwell Pl, Pnr. HA5 138 BY56
Sch Holwell Prim Sch, Welw.G.C.
AL7 off Holwell Rd 51 CZ10
Holwell Rd, Welw.G.C. AL7 51 CY10
Holwood Cl, Walt. KT12 218 BW103
Holwood Pk Av, Orp. BR6 245 EM105
Holwood Pl, SW4 183 DK84
Holy Acre, Roydon CM19
off Roydon Mill Pk 56 EG14
Holybourne Av, SW15 201 CU87
Sch Holy Cross Cath Prim Sch,
SE6 off Culverley Rd 205 EC88
SW6 39 J6
Harlow CM18
off Tracyes Rd 74 EU17
South Ockendon RM15
off Daiglen Dr 171 FV72
Sch Holy Cross Conv Sch, Chal.St.P.
SL9 off Gold Hill E 112 AX53
Holy Cross Hill, Brox. EN10 70 DU24
Sch Holy Cross Prep Sch, Kings.T.
KT2 off George Rd 200 CQ94
Sch Holy Cross Sch, The, N.Mal.
KT3 off Sandal Rd 220 CS99
Sch Holy Family Catholic Prim Sch,
Add. KT15 off Ongar Hill 234 BG106
Langley SL3 off High St 175 AZ78
Sch Holy Family RC Prim Sch,
E14 22 C10
SE3 off Tudway Rd 186 EJ84
Welwyn Garden City AL7
off Crookhams 52 DA06
Coll Holy Family Tech Coll, E17
off Shernhall St 145 EC55
Wiseman Ho Site, E17
off Shernhall St 145 EC56
HOLYFIELD, Wal.Abb. EN9 89 ED28
Holyfield, Wal.Abb. EN9 89 EC29
Sch Holy Ghost RC Prim Sch,
SW12 off Nightingale Sq 202 DG87
Holyhead Cl, E3 22 B3
E6 25 J6
Holyhead Ms, Slou. SL1 153 AL72

Holy Innocents Cath Prim Sch, Orp. BR6 *off Mitchell Rd* . . 227 ET104
Holyoake Av, Wok. GU21 . . . . 248 AW117
Holyoake Ct, SE16 . . . . 33 M4
Holyoake Cres, Wok. GU21 . . . 248 AW117
Holyoake Ter, Sev. TN13 . . . . 278 FG124
Holyoake Wk, N2 . . . . 142 DC55
W5 . . . . 159 CJ70
Holyoak Rd, SE11 . . . . 30 G8
HOLYPORT, Maid. SL6 . . . . 172 AC78
Holyport Rd, SW6 . . . . 38 B4
Holyrood Av, Har. HA2 . . . . 138 BY63
Holyrood Cres, St.Alb. AL1 . . . . 65 CD24
Holyrood Gdns, Edg. HA8 . . . . 140 CP55
Grays RM16 . . . . 193 GJ77
Holyrood Ms, E16 . . . . 35 P2
Holy Rood RC Prim Sch, Wat. WD17 *off Greenbank Rd* . . . 97 BR36
Holyrood Rd, New Barn. EN5 . 102 DC44
Holyrood St, SE1 . . . . 31 N3
Holy Trinity & St. Silas C of E Prim Sch, NW1 . . . . 7 J6
Holy Trinity C of E Jun Sch, Wall. SM6 *off Bute Rd* 241 DJ105
Holy Trinity C of E Jun Sch Guildford, Guil. GU1 *off Addison Rd* 281 AZ136
Holy Trinity C of E Prim Sch, E8 . . . . 10 A5
N2 *off Eagans Cl* 142 DD55
NW3 . . . . 5 P5
SE23 *off Dartmouth Rd* 204 DW89
Jun, SW1 . . . . 28 G8
SW2 *off Upper Tulse Hill* . . . 203 DM87
Inf, SW3 . . . . 28 F8
SW19 *off Effra Rd* 202 DB93
Dartford DA1 *off Chatsworth Rd* 210 FJ85
Gravesend DA12 *off Trinity Rd* 213 GJ87
Northwood HA6 *off Rickmansworth Rd* 115 BQ51
Richmond TW10 *off Carrington Rd* 180 CN84
Waltham Cross EN8 *off Crossbrook St* 89 DX32
Holy Trinity Lamorbey C of E Prim Sch, Sid. DA15 *off Burnt Oak La* 208 EU88
Holy Wk, Brox. EN10 *off St. Catharines Rd* 71 EA19
Hoddesdon EN11 *off High St* 71 EA18
HOLYWELL, Wat. WD18 . . . . 97 BS44
Holywell Cl, SE3 . . . . 47 P2
SE16 . . . . 32 F10
Orpington BR6 . . . . 246 EU105
Staines TW19 . . . . 196 BL88
Holywell Hill, St.Alb. AL1 . . . . 64 CC21
● Holywell Ind Est, Wat. WD18 . . . . 115 BR45
Holywell La, EC2 . . . . 19 P4
Holywell Prim Sch, Wat. WD18 *off Tolpits La* 97 BT44
Holywell Rd, Wat. WD18 . . . . 97 BU43
Holywell Row, EC2 . . . . 19 N5
Holywell Way, Stai. TW19 . . . . 196 BL88
Homan Ct, N12 . . . . 120 DC49
Home Barn Ct, Eff. KT24 *off The Street* 268 BX127
Home Cl, Brox. EN10 . . . . 71 DZ24
Carshalton SM5 . . . . 222 DF103
Fetcham KT22 . . . . 253 CD121
Harlow CM20 . . . . 73 ET15
Northolt UB5 . . . . 158 BZ69
Virginia Water GU25 . . . . 214 AX100
Homecroft Gdns, Loug. IG10 . . 107 EP42
Homecroft Rd, N22 . . . . 121 DP53
SE26 . . . . 204 DW92
Homedean Rd, Chipstead TN13 . . . . 278 FC122
Home Fm, Orp. BR6 . . . . 246 FA106
Home Fm Cl, Bet. RH3 . . . . 286 CS135
Esher KT10 . . . . 236 CB107
Ottershaw KT16 . . . . 233 BA108
Shepperton TW17 . . . . 217 BS98
Tadworth KT20 . . . . 255 CX117
Thames Ditton KT7 . . . . 219 CF101
Home Fm Gdns, Walt. KT12 . . 218 BW103
● Home Fm Ind Est, Stans.Abb. SG12 . . . . 56 EF10
Homefarm Rd, W7 . . . . 159 CE72
Home Fm Rd, N.Mymms AL9 . . 85 CV26
Rickmansworth WD3 . . . . 114 BN49
Home Fm Way, Stoke P. SL3 . . 154 AW67
Homefield, Bov. HP3 . . . . 79 BB28
Home Fld, Pott.End HP4 . . . . 61 BB16
Homefield, Wal.Abb. EN9 . . . . 90 EG32
Walton-on-Thames KT12 . . 236 BX105
Homefield Av, Ilf. IG2 . . . . 147 ES57
Homefield Cl, NW10 . . . . 160 CQ65
Epping CM16 . . . . 92 EU30
Hayes UB4 . . . . 158 BW70
Horley RH6 *off Tanyard Way* 291 DH147
Leatherhead KT22 . . . . 253 CJ121
St. Paul's Cray BR5 . . . . 228 EV98
Swanley BR8 . . . . 229 FF97
Woodham KT15 . . . . 233 BE112
Homefield Fm Rd, Sutt.H. DA4 . 230 FM96
Homefield Gdns, N2 . . . . 142 DD55
Mitcham CR4 . . . . 222 DC96
Tadworth KT20 . . . . 255 CW120
Homefield Ms, Beck. BR3 . . . . 225 EA95
Homefield Pk, Sutt. SM1 . . . . 240 DB107
Homefield Prep Sch, Sutt. SM1 *off Western Rd* 240 DA106
Homefield Ri, Orp. BR6 . . . . 228 EU102
Homefield Rd, SW19 . . . . 201 CX93
W4 . . . . 181 CT77
Bromley BR1 . . . . 226 EJ95
Bushey WD23 . . . . 98 CA43
Chorleywood WD3 . . . . 95 BC42
Coulsdon CR5 . . . . 257 DP119
Edgware HA8 . . . . 118 CR51
Hemel Hempstead HP2 . . . . 62 BN20
Radlett WD7 . . . . 99 CF37
Sevenoaks TN13 . . . . 278 FE122
Walton-on-Thames KT12 . . 218 BY101
Ware SG12 . . . . 55 DY05
Warlingham CR6 . . . . 258 DW119
Homefield Rd, Wem. HA0 . . . . 139 CG63
Homefield St, N1 . . . . 19 N1
Homefirs Ho, Wem. HA9 . . . . 140 CM62
Home Gdns, Dag. RM10 . . . . 149 FC62
Dartford DA1 . . . . 210 FL86
Home Hill, Swan. BR8 . . . . 209 FF94
Homeland Dr, Sutt. SM2 . . . . 240 DB109
Homelands, Lthd. KT22 . . . . 253 CJ121
Homelands Dr, SE19 . . . . 204 DS94
Home Lea, Orp. BR6 . . . . 245 ET106
Homeleigh Ct, Chsht EN8 . . . . 88 DV29
Homeleigh Rd, SE15 . . . . 205 DX85
Home Ley, Welw.G.C. AL7 . . . . 51 CY10
Homemead, SW12 . . . . 203 DH89
Home Mead, Stan. HA7 . . . . 117 CJ53
Homemead Cl, Grav. DA12 . . . 213 GH87
Homemead Ct, Grav. DA12 *off Homemead Cl* 213 GH87
Home Meadow, Bans. SM7 . . . 256 DA116
Farnham Royal SL2 . . . . 153 AQ68
Welwyn Garden City AL7 . . . 51 CZ09
Homemead Rd, Brom. BR2 . . . 227 EM99
Croydon CR0 . . . . 223 DJ100
★ Home Office, SW1 . . . . 29 P7
Home Orchard, Dart. DA1 . . . . 210 FL86
Home Pk, E.Mol. (Hampton Ct Pk) KT8 . . . . 219 CH98
Kingston upon Thames (Hampton Ct Pk) KT1 . . . . 219 CH98
Oxted RH8 . . . . 276 EG131
Home Pk Mill Link Rd, Kings L. WD4 . . . . 81 BP31
Home Pk Par, Kings.T. KT1 *off High St* 219 CK96
Home Pk Rd, SW19 . . . . 202 DA90
Home Pk Wk, Kings.T. KT1 . . . 219 CK98
Homer Cl, Bexh. DA7 . . . . 189 FC81
Homer Dr, E14 . . . . 34 A9
Homerfield, Welw.G.C. AL8 . . . 51 CW08
Homer First Sch, Wind. SL4 *off Testwood Rd* 173 AK81
Home Rd, SW11 . . . . 40 C8
Homer Rd, E9 . . . . 11 M5
Croydon CR0 . . . . 225 DX100
Homer Row, W1 . . . . 16 D7
Homersham Rd, Kings.T. KT1 . 220 CN96
Homers Rd, Wind. SL4 . . . . 173 AK81
Homer St, W1 . . . . 16 D7
Homerswood La, Welw. AL6 . . . 51 CU05
Homerswood Prim Sch, Welw.G.C. AL8 *off Kirklands* 51 CX05
HOMERTON, E9 . . . . 11 M3
Homerton 11 J4
Homerton Gro, E9 . . . . 11 J3
Homerton High St, E9 . . . . 11 H3
Homerton Rd, E9 . . . . 11 M2
Homerton Row, E9 . . . . 11 H3
Homerton Ter, E9 . . . . 11 H4
Homerton Uni Hosp, E9 . . . . 11 J2
Homesdale Cl, E11 . . . . 146 EG57
Homesdale Rd, Brom. BR1, BR2 . . . . 226 EJ98
Caterham CR3 . . . . 258 DR123
Petts Wood BR5 . . . . 227 ES101
Homesfield, NW11 . . . . 142 DA57
Homestall Rd, SE22 . . . . 204 DW85
Homestead, The, N11 . . . . 121 DH49
Dartford DA1 . . . . 210 FJ86
Homestead Cl, Park St AL2 . . . 82 CC27
Homestead Ct, Welw.G.C. AL7 . 51 CZ11
Homestead Gdns, Clay. KT10 . 237 CE106
Homestead La, Welw.G.C. AL7 . 51 CZ12
Homestead Paddock, N14 . . . 103 DH43
Homestead Pk, NW2 . . . . 141 CT62
Homestead Rd, SW6 . . . . 38 G5
Caterham CR3 . . . . 258 DR123
Dagenham RM8 . . . . 148 EZ61
Hatfield AL10 . . . . 67 CU15
Orpington BR6 . . . . 246 EV108
Rickmansworth WD3 *off Park Rd* 114 BK45
Staines TW18 . . . . 196 BH93
Homesteads, The, Hunsdon SG12 *off Hunsdon Rd* 56 EK07
Homestead Way, New Adgtn CR0 . . . . 243 EC111
Homewaters Av, Sun. TW16 . . . 217 BT95
Home Way, Mill End WD3 . . . . 113 BF46
Homeway, Rom. RM3 . . . . 128 FP51
Homewillow Cl, N21 . . . . 103 DP44
Homewood, Geo.Grn SL3 . . . . 154 AX72
Homewood Av, Cuffley EN6 . . . 87 DL27
Homewood Cl, Hmptn. TW12 . 198 BZ93
Homewood Cres, Chis. BR7 . . . 207 ES93
Homewood Indep Sch, Park St AL2 *off Hazel Rd* 82 CB28
Homewood La, Northaw EN6 . . 87 DJ27
Homewood Rd, St.Alb. AL1 . . . . 65 CH17
Homildon Ho, SE26 *off Sydenham Hill Est* 204 DU90
Honduras St, EC1 . . . . 19 J4
Honeybourne Rd, NW6 . . . . 5 L2
Honeybourne Way, Petts Wd BR5 . . . . 227 ER102
Honey Brook, Wal.Abb. EN9 . . . 90 EE33
Honeybrook Rd, SW12 . . . . 203 DJ87
Honey Cl, Dag. RM10 . . . . 169 FB65
Honeycrock La, Red. RH1 . . . . 288 DG141
Honeycroft, Loug. IG10 . . . . 107 EN42
Welwyn Garden City AL8 . . . . 51 CW10
Honeycroft Dr, St.Alb. AL4 . . . . 65 CJ22
Honeycroft Hill, Uxb. UB10 . . . 156 BL66
Honeycross Rd, Hem.H. HP1 . . . 61 BE21
Honeyden Rd, Sid. DA14 . . . . 208 EY93
Honey Hill, Uxb. UB10 . . . . 156 BM66
Honey La, EC2 . . . . 19 K9
Hertford SG14 *off Fore St* . . . 54 DR09
Waltham Abbey EN9 . . . . 106 EG35
Honeyman Cl, NW6 . . . . 4 C6
Honeymeade, Saw. CM21 . . . . 58 EW08
● Honeypot Business Cen, Stan. HA7 . . . . 118 CL53
Honeypot Cl, NW9 . . . . 140 CM56
Honeypot La, NW9 . . . . 140 CM55
Brentwood CM14 . . . . 130 FU48
Stanmore HA7 . . . . 140 CM55
Waltham Abbey EN9 . . . . 90 EJ34
Honeypots Rd, Wok. GU22 . . . 248 AX122
Honeysett Rd, N17 *off Reform Row* 122 DT54
Honeysuckle Bottom, E.Hors. KT24 . . . . 267 BS134
Honeysuckle Cl, Hert. SG13 . . . 54 DU09
Horley RH6 . . . . 291 DJ147
Iver SL0 . . . . 155 BC72
Pilgrim's Hatch CM15 . . . . 130 FV43
Romford RM3 . . . . 128 FJ51
Southall UB1 . . . . 158 BY73
Honeysuckle Fld, Chesh. HP5 . . 76 AQ30
Honeysuckle Gdns, Croy. CR0 . 225 DX101
Hatfield AL10 . . . . 67 CV19
Honeysuckle La, N.Holm. RH5 *off Treelands* 285 CJ139
Honeywell Inf & Jun Schs, SW11 *off Honeywell Rd* . . . 202 DF86
Honeywell Rd, SW11 . . . . 202 DF86
Honeywood Cl, Pot.B. EN6 . . . . 86 DE33
★ Honeywood Heritage Cen, Cars. SM5 . . . . 240 DF106
Honeywood Rd, NW10 . . . . 161 CT68
Isleworth TW7 . . . . 179 CG84
Honeywood Wk, Cars. SM5 . . . 240 DF105
Honilands Prim Sch, Enf. EN1 *off Lovell Rd* 104 DV36
Honister Cl, Stan. HA7 . . . . 117 CH53
Honister Gdns, Stan. HA7 . . . . 117 CH52
Honister Hts, Pur. CR8 . . . . 242 DR114
Honister Pl, Stan. HA7 . . . . 117 CH53
Honiton Gdns, NW7 . . . . 119 CX52
SE15 *off Gibbon Rd* 45 H9
Honiton Ho, Enf. EN3 *off Exeter Rd* 105 DX41
Honiton Rd, NW6 . . . . 4 G10
Romford RM7 . . . . 149 FD58
Welling DA16 . . . . 187 ET82
Honley Rd, SE6 . . . . 205 EB87
Honnor Gdns, Islw. TW7 . . . . 179 CD82
Honnor Rd, Stai. TW18 . . . . 196 BK94
HONOR OAK, SE23 . . . . 204 DW86
HONOR OAK PARK, SE4 . . . . 205 DY86
⇌ Honor Oak Park 205 DX86
Honor Oak Pk, SE23 . . . . 204 DW86
Honor Oak Ri, SE23 . . . . 204 DW86
Honor Oak Rd, SE23 . . . . 204 DW88
Hon St, Harl. CM17 . . . . 58 EX14
Hoo, The, Harl. CM17 . . . . 58 EW10
Hood Av, N14 . . . . 103 DH44
SW14 . . . . 200 CQ85
Orpington BR5 . . . . 228 EV99
Hood Cl, Croy. CR0 . . . . 223 DP102
Hoodcote Gdns, N21 . . . . 121 DP45
Hood Ct, EC4 . . . . 18 F9
Hood Rd, SW20 . . . . 201 CT94
Rainham RM13 . . . . 169 FE67
Hood Wk, Rom. RM7 . . . . 127 FB53
HOOK, Chess. KT9 . . . . 238 CL105
Hook, The, New Barn. EN5 . . . 102 DD44
Hooke Rd, E.Hors. KT24 . . . . 267 BT125
Hookers Rd, E17 . . . . 145 DX55
Hook Fm Rd, Brom. BR2 . . . . 226 EK99
Hookfield, Epsom KT19 . . . . 238 CQ113
Harlow CM18 . . . . 73 ES17
Hookfields, Nthflt DA11 . . . . 212 GE90
Hook Gate, Enf. EN1 . . . . 104 DV36
HOOK GREEN, Dart. DA2 . . . . 209 FG91
HOOK GREEN, Grav. DA13 . . . 212 FZ93
Hook Grn La, Dart. DA2 . . . . 209 FF90
Hook Grn Rd, Sthflt DA13 . . . . 212 FY94
HOOK HEATH, Wok. GU22 . . . 248 AV120
Hook Heath Av, Wok. GU22 . . . 248 AV119
Hook Heath Gdns, Wok. GU22 . 248 AT121
Hook Heath Rd, Wok. GU22 . . . 248 AW121
Hook Hill, S.Croy. CR2 . . . . 242 DS110
Hook Hill La, Wok. GU22 . . . . 248 AV121
Hook Hill Pk, Wok. GU22 . . . . 248 AV121
Hooking Grn, Har. HA2 . . . . 138 CB57
Hook Junct, Surb. KT6 . . . . 219 CK104
Hook La, Northaw EN6 . . . . 86 DF32
Romford RM4 . . . . 108 EZ44
Shere GU5 . . . . 282 BN141
Welling DA16 . . . . 207 ET85
Hook La Prim Sch, Well. DA16 *off Faraday Rd* 188 EU83
Hook Ri N, Surb. KT6 . . . . 220 CN104
Hook Ri S, Surb. KT6 . . . . 220 CN104
● Hook Ri S Business Cen, Surb. KT6 . . . . 220 CN104
● Hook Ri S Ind Pk, Surb. KT6 . . . . 220 CM104
Hook Rd, Chess. KT9 . . . . 237 CK106
Epsom KT19 . . . . 238 CR111
Surbiton KT6 . . . . 220 CL104
Hooks Cl, SE15 . . . . 44 F7
Hooks Hall Dr, Dag. RM10 . . . . 149 FC62
Hookstone Way, Wdf.Grn. IG8 . 124 EK52
Hook Wk, Edg. HA8 . . . . 118 CQ51
HOOKWOOD, Horl. RH6 . . . . 290 DC150
Hookwood Cor, Oxt. RH8 *off Hookwood Pk* 276 EH128
Hookwood Cotts, Headley KT18 . . . . 254 CQ123
Hookwood Pk, Oxt. RH8 . . . . 276 EH128
Hookwood Rd, Orp. BR6 . . . . 246 EW111
Hool Cl, NW9 . . . . 140 CQ57
HOOLEY, Couls. CR5 . . . . 256 DG122
Hooley La, Red. RH1 . . . . 288 DF135
Hooper Dr, Uxb. UB8 . . . . 157 BP71
Hooper Rd, E16 . . . . 23 P9
Hooper's Ct, SW3 . . . . 28 E5
Hoopers Ms, W3 . . . . 160 CQ74
Hooper's Ms, Bushey WD23 . . . 116 CB46
Hooper St, E1 . . . . 20 C10
Hoopers Yd, NW6 . . . . 4 G8
Sevenoaks TN13 . . . . 279 FJ126
Hoop La, NW11 . . . . 141 CZ59
Hope Cl, N1 . . . . 9 K4
SE12 . . . . 206 EH90
Brentford TW8 . . . . 180 CL78
Chadwell Heath RM6 . . . . 148 EW56
Sutton SM1 . . . . 240 DC106
Woodford Green IG8 *off West Gro* 124 EJ51
Hopedale Rd, SE7 . . . . 186 EH79
Hopefield Av, NW6 . . . . 4 F10
Hope Gdns, W3 *off Park Rd N* . 180 CP75
Hope Grn, Wat. WD25 . . . . 81 BU33
Hope La, SE9 . . . . 207 EP89
Hope Pk, Brom. BR1 . . . . 206 EF94
Hope Rd, Swans. DA10 . . . . 212 FZ86
Hopes Cl, Houns. TW5 *off Old Cote Dr* 178 CA79
Hope St, SW11 . . . . 182 DD83
Hope Ter, Grays RM20 . . . . 191 FX78
Hopetown St, E1 . . . . 20 B7
Hopewell Cl, Chaff.Hun. RM16 . 191 FX78
Hopewell Dr, Grav. DA12 . . . . 213 GM92
Hopewell St, SE5 . . . . 43 M5
Hopewell Yd, SE5 . . . . 43 M5
Hope Wf, SE16 *off St. Marychurch St* 32 G4
Hopfield, Horsell GU21 . . . . 248 AY116
Hopfield Av, Byfleet KT14 . . . . 234 BL112
Hopgarden La, Sev. TN13 . . . . 278 FG128
Hop Gdns, WC2 . . . . 30 A1
Hop Gdn Way, Wat. WD25 . . . . 82 BW31
Hopgood St, W12 . . . . 26 B4
Hopground Cl, St.Alb. AL1 . . . . 65 CG22
Hopkin Cl, Guil. GU2 . . . . 264 AV130
Hopkins Cl, N10 . . . . 120 DG52
Romford RM2 . . . . 150 FJ55
Hopkins Ms, E15 . . . . 13 M9
Hopkinsons Pl, NW1 . . . . 6 F8
Hopkins Rd, E10 . . . . 145 EB59
Hopkins St, W1 . . . . 17 M9
Hoppers Rd, N13 . . . . 121 DN47
N21 . . . . 121 DN47
Hoppett Rd, E4 . . . . 124 EE48
Hoppety, The, Tad. KT20 . . . . 255 CX122
Hopping La, N1 . . . . 9 H5
Hoppingwood Av, N.Mal. KT3 . 220 CS97
Hoppit Rd, Wal.Abb. EN9 . . . . 89 EB32
Hoppner Rd, Hayes UB4 . . . . 157 BQ68
Hop St, SE10 . . . . 35 M8
Hopton Ct, Guil. GU2 *off Chapelhouse Cl* 264 AS134
Hopton Gdns, N.Mal. KT3 . . . . 221 CU100
Hopton Rd, SE18 . . . . 37 P6
SW16 . . . . 203 DL92
Hopton's Gdns, SE1 . . . . 31 H2
Hopton St, SE1 . . . . 31 H2
Hoptree Cl, N12 *off Woodside Pk Rd* 120 DB49
Hopwood Cl, SW17 . . . . 202 DC90
Watford WD17 . . . . 97 BR36
Hopwood Rd, SE17 . . . . 43 M2
Hopwood Wk, E8 . . . . 10 D6
Horace Av, Rom. RM7 . . . . 149 FC60
Horace Bldg, SW8 *off Queenstown Rd* 41 J4
Horace Rd, E7 . . . . 146 EH63
Ilford IG6 . . . . 147 EQ55
Kingston upon Thames KT1 . 220 CM97
Horatio Ct, SE16 *off Rotherhithe St* 33 H3
Horatio Pl, E14 . . . . 34 F4
SW19 *off Kingston Rd* 222 DA95
Horatio St, E2 . . . . 20 B1
Horatius Way, Croy. CR0 . . . . 241 DM107
Horbury Cres, W11 . . . . 27 J1
Horbury Ms, W11 . . . . 27 H1
Horder Rd, SW6 . . . . 38 F7
Hordle Gdns, St.Alb. AL1 . . . . 65 CF21
● Horizon Business Cen, N9 *off Goodwin Rd* 123 DX46
● Horizon Business Village, Wey. KT13 . . . . 234 BN112
Horizon Ho, Enf. EN3 *off Tysoe Av* 105 DZ36
Horizon Sch, N16 . . . . 9 P1
Horizon Way, SE7 . . . . 36 B9
Horksley Gdns, Hutt. CM13 *off Bannister Dr* 131 GC44
Horle Wk, SE5 . . . . 42 G8
HORLEY, RH6 . . . . 290 DG148
⇌ Horley 291 DH149
Horley Adult Ed Cen, Horl. RH6 *off Court Lo Rd* 290 DE148
Horley Cl, Bexh. DA6 . . . . 208 FA85
Horley Inf Sch, Horl. RH6 *off Lumley Rd* 290 DG148
Horley Lo La, Red. RH1 . . . . 288 DF143
Horley Rd, SE9 . . . . 206 EL91
Redhill RH1 . . . . 288 DF136
Horley Row, Horl. RH6 . . . . 290 DF147
Hormead Rd, W9 . . . . 14 G5
Hornbeam Av, Upmin. RM14 . . 150 FN63
Hornbeam Chase, S.Ock. RM15 . . . . 171 FX69
Hornbeam Cl, NW7 . . . . 119 CT48
SE11 . . . . 30 E8
Barking IG11 . . . . 168 EU69
Borehamwood WD6 . . . . 100 CN39
Brentwood CM13 . . . . 131 GB48
Buckhurst Hill IG9 *off Hornbeam Rd* 124 EK48
Hertford SG14 . . . . 53 DP08
Ilford IG1 . . . . 147 ER64
Northolt UB5 . . . . 138 BZ64
Theydon Bois CM16 . . . . 107 ES37
Hornbeam Cres, Brent. TW8 . . 179 CH80
Hornbeam Gdns, N.Mal. KT3 . . 221 CU100
Slough SL1 *off Upton Rd* 174 AU76
Hornbeam Gro, E4 . . . . 124 EE48
Hornbeam Ho, NW3 . . . . 6 F4
Hornbeam La, E4 . . . . 106 EE43
Bexleyheath DA7 . . . . 189 FC82
Essendon AL9 . . . . 68 DE22
Hornbeam Rd, Buck.H. IG9 . . . 124 EK48
Guildford GU1 . . . . 264 AW131
Hayes UB4 . . . . 158 BW71
Reigate RH2 . . . . 288 DB137
Theydon Bois CM16 . . . . 107 ER37
Hornbeams, Brick.Wd AL2 . . . . 82 BZ30
Hornbeams, The, Harl. CM20 . . 57 EP13
Hornbeams Av, Enf. EN1 . . . . 104 DW35
Hornbeam Sq, E3 . . . . 11 N8
Hornbeams Ri, N11 . . . . 120 DG51
Hornbeam Ter, Cars. SM5 . . . . 222 DE102
Hornbeam Wk, Rich. TW10 . . . . 200 CM90
Whiteley Village KT12 *off Octagon Rd* 235 BT109
Hornbeam Way, Brom. BR2 . . . 227 EN100
Waltham Cross EN7 . . . . 88 DT29
Hornbill Cl, Uxb. UB8 . . . . 156 BK72
Hornblower Cl, SE16 . . . . 33 L8
Hornbuckle Cl, Har. HA2 . . . . 139 CD61
Hornby Cl, NW3 . . . . 6 B6
Horncastle Cl, SE12 . . . . 206 EG87
Horncastle Rd, SE12 . . . . 206 EG87
HORNCHURCH, RM11 & RM12 . 150 FJ61
⊖ Hornchurch 150 FK62
Hornchurch Cl, Kings.T. KT2 . . 199 CK91
Hornchurch Hill, Whyt. CR3 . . 258 DT117
Hornchurch Rd, Horn. RM11, RM12 . . . . 149 FG60
Horndean Cl, SW15 *off Bessborough Rd* 201 CU88
Horndon Cl, Rom. RM5 . . . . 127 FC53
Horndon Grn, Rom. RM5 . . . . 127 FC53
Horndon Rd, Rom. RM5 . . . . 127 FC53
Horner La, Mitch. CR4 . . . . 222 DD96
Horne Rd, Shep. TW17 . . . . 216 BN98
Hornets, The, Wat. WD18 . . . . 97 BV42
Horne Way, E6 . . . . 167 ER71
Horne Way, SW15 . . . . 38 A9
Hornfair Rd, SE7 . . . . 186 EJ79
Hornford Way, Rom. RM7 . . . . 149 FE59
Hornhatch, Chilw. GU4 . . . . 281 BB140
Hornhatch Cl, Chilw. GU4 . . . . 281 BB140
Hornhatch La, Guil. GU4 . . . . 281 BA140
Hornhill Rd, Ger.Cr. SL9 . . . . 113 BB50
Maple Cross WD3 . . . . 113 BD50
Horniman Dr, SE23 . . . . 204 DV88
★ Horniman Mus, SE23 . . . . 204 DV88
Horniman Prim Sch, SE23 *off Horniman Dr* 204 DV88
Horning Cl, SE9 . . . . 206 EL91
Horn La, SE10 . . . . 35 N9
W3 . . . . 160 CQ73
Woodford Green IG8 . . . . 124 EG51
Horn Link Way, SE10 . . . . 35 N8
Hornminster Glen, Horn. RM11 . . . . 150 FN61
Horn Pk Cl, SE12 . . . . 206 EH85
Horn Pk La, SE12 . . . . 206 EH85
Horn Pk Prim Sch, SE12 *off Alnwick Rd* 206 EH87
Hornsby Ho Sch, SW12 *off Hearnville Rd* 202 DG88
Hornsby La, Orsett RM16 . . . . 193 GG75
Horns Cl, Hert. SG13 . . . . 54 DQ11
Horns Cft Cl, Bark. IG11 *off Thornhill Gdns* 167 ES66
Horns End Pl, Pnr. HA5 . . . . 138 BW56
HORNSEY, N8 . . . . 143 DM55
⇌ Hornsey 143 DM56
Hornsey La, N6 . . . . 143 DH60
Hornsey La Est, N19 . . . . 143 DK59
Hornsey La Gdns, N6 . . . . 143 DJ59
Hornsey Pk Rd, N8 . . . . 143 DM55
Hornsey Ri, N19 . . . . 143 DK59
Hornsey Ri Gdns, N19 . . . . 143 DK59
Hornsey Rd, N7 . . . . 143 DM61
N19 . . . . 143 DL60
Hornsey Sch for Girls, N8 *off Inderwick Rd* 143 DM57
Hornsey St, N7 . . . . 8 D2
Hornsfield, Welw.G.C. AL7 . . . . 52 DC08
HORNS GREEN, Sev. TN14 . . . 261 ES117
Hornshay St, SE15 . . . . 45 H3
Horns Mill Rd, Hert. SG13 . . . . 54 DQ12
Horns Rd, Hert. SG13 . . . . 54 DQ10
Ilford IG2, IG6 . . . . 147 EQ57
Hornton Pl, W8 . . . . 27 K5
Hornton St, W8 . . . . 27 K4
Horsa Gdns, Hat. AL10 . . . . 66 CR16
Horsa Rd, SE12 . . . . 206 EJ87
Erith DA8 . . . . 189 FC80
Horse & Dolphin Yd, W1 . . . . 17 P10
Horsebridges Cl, Dag. RM9 . . . 168 EY67
Horsecroft, Bans. SM7 *off Lyme Regis Rd* 255 CZ117
Horsecroft Cl, Orp. BR6 . . . . 228 EV102
Horsecroft Pl, Harl. CM19 . . . . 72 EL16
Horsecroft Rd, Edg. HA8 . . . . 118 CR52
Harlow CM19 . . . . 72 EL16
Hemel Hempstead HP1 . . . . 62 BG22
Horse Fair, Kings.T. KT1 . . . . 219 CK96
Horseferry Pl, SE10 . . . . 46 E3
Horseferry Rd, E14 . . . . 21 L10
SW1 . . . . 29 N7
Horse Guards Av, SW1 . . . . 30 A3
★ Horse Guards Par, SW1 . . . . 29 P3
Horse Guards Rd, SW1 . . . . 29 P3
Horse Hill, Chesh. HP5 . . . . 78 AX32
Horsehill, Horl. RH6 . . . . 290 DA146
Horse La, Ware SG12 . . . . 55 DX05
Horse Leaze, E6 . . . . 25 M8
Horselers, Hem.H. HP3 . . . . 62 BN23
HORSELL, Wok. GU21 . . . . 248 AW116
Horsell Birch, Wok. GU21 . . . . 248 AV115
Horsell C of E Jun Sch, Horsell GU21 *off Meadway Dr* . . . 248 AW116
Horsell Common, Wok. GU21 . 232 AX114
Horsell Common Rd, Wok. GU21 . . . . 232 AW114
Horsell Ct, Cher. KT16 *off Stepgates* 216 BH101
Horsell Moor, Wok. GU21 . . . . 248 AX117
Horsell Pk, Wok. GU21 . . . . 248 AX116
Horsell Pk Cl, Wok. GU21 . . . . 248 AX116
Horsell Ri, Wok. GU21 . . . . 248 AX115
Horsell Ri Cl, Wok. GU21 . . . . 248 AX115
Horsell Rd, N5 . . . . 8 E3
Orpington BR5 . . . . 228 EV95
Horsell Vale, Wok. GU21 . . . . 248 AY115
Horsell Village Sch, The, Horsell GU21 *off Church Hill* . . . 248 AX116
Horsell Way, Wok. GU21 . . . . 248 AW116
Horselydown La, SE1 . . . . 32 A4
Horseman Side, Nave.S. CM14 . . . . 127 FH45
Horsemans Ride, St.Alb. AL2 . . 82 CA26
Horsemongers Ms, SE1 . . . . 31 K5
Horsemoor Cl, Slou. SL3 . . . . 175 BA77
Horsenden Av, Grnf. UB6 . . . . 139 CE64
Horsenden Cres, Grnf. UB6 . . . 139 CF64
Horsenden La N, Grnf. UB6 . . . 159 CF65
Horsenden La S, Perivale UB6 . 159 CG67
Horsenden Prim Sch, Grnf. UB6 *off Horsenden La N* . . 159 CF65
Horse Ride, SW1 . . . . 29 N3
Dorking RH5 . . . . 285 CD144
Leatherhead KT24 . . . . 267 BR130
Tadworth KT20 . . . . 271 CY125
Horse Rd, E7 *off Centre Rd* . . . 146 EH62
Horseshoe, The, Bans. SM7 . . . 255 CZ115
Coulsdon CR5 . . . . 241 DK113
Hemel Hempstead HP3 . . . . 63 BQ22
● Horseshoe Business Pk, Brick.Wd AL2 . . . . 82 CA30
Horseshoe Cl, E14 . . . . 34 E10
NW2 . . . . 141 CV61
Waltham Abbey EN9 . . . . 90 EG34
Horse Shoe Ct, EC1 *off Brewhouse Yd* 19 H4
Horseshoe Cres, Beac. HP9 . . . 111 AL54
Horse Shoe Cres, Nthlt. UB5 . . 158 CA68
Horseshoe Dr, Uxb. UB8 . . . . 156 BN72
Horse Shoe Grn, Sutt. SM1 *off Aultone Way* 222 DB103
Horseshoe Hill, Burn. SL1 . . . . 132 AJ63
Waltham Abbey EN9 . . . . 90 EJ33
Horseshoe La, N20 . . . . 119 CX46
Enfield EN2 *off Chase Side* 104 DQ41
Watford WD25 . . . . 81 BV32
Horseshoe La E, Guil. GU1 . . . 265 BB133
Horseshoe La W, Guil. GU1 . . . 265 BB133
Horseshoe Ms, SW2 *off Acre La* 183 DL84
Horseshoe Ridge, Wey. KT13 . . 235 BQ111
Horse Yd, N1 . . . . 9 H8
Horsfeld Gdns, SE9 . . . . 206 EL85
Horsfeld Rd, SE9 . . . . 206 EK85
Horsfield Cl, Dart. DA2 . . . . 210 FQ87
Horsford Rd, SW2 . . . . 203 DM85
Horsham Av, N12 . . . . 120 DE50
Horsham Rd, Abin.Ham. RH5 . 283 BT142
Bexleyheath DA6 . . . . 208 FA85
Dorking RH4 . . . . 285 CG137
Feltham TW14 . . . . 197 BQ86
Guildford GU4, GU5 . . . . 280 AY142
Holmwood RH5 . . . . 285 CH140
Horshams, Harl. CM19 *off Little Gro Fld* 73 EQ15

Horsley 267 BS125
Horsley Cl, Epsom KT19 238 CR113
Horsleydown Old Stairs, SE1 32 A3
Horsley Dr, Kings.T. KT2 199 CK92
New Addington CR0 243 EC108
Horsley Rd, E4 123 EC47
Bromley BR1 off Palace Rd 226 EH95
Cobham KT11 251 BV119
Horsleys, Map.Cr. WD3 113 BD50
Horsley St, SE17 43 L2
Horsmonden Cl, Orp. BR6 227 ES101
Horsmonden Rd, SE4 205 DZ85
Hortensia Rd, SW10 39 N3
Horticultural Pl, W4 180 CR78
HORTON, Epsom KT19 238 CP110
HORTON, Slou. SL3 175 BA83
Horton Av, NW2 4 F1
Horton Br Rd, West Dr. UB7 156 BM74
Horton Cl, Maid. SL6 152 AC70
West Drayton UB7 156 BM74
Horton Country Pk, Epsom KT19 238 CM110
Horton Cres, Epsom KT19 238 CP110
Horton Footpath, Epsom KT19 238 CQ111
Horton Gdns, Epsom KT19 238 CQ111
Horton Hill, Epsom KT19 238 CQ111
Horton Ho, SW8 42 C4
Horton Ind Pk, West Dr. UB7 156 BM74
HORTON KIRBY, Dart. DA4 231 FR98
Horton Kirby C of E Prim Sch, Hort.Kir. DA4 off Horton Rd 230 FQ97
Horton La, Epsom KT19 238 CP110
Horton Park Children's Fm, Epsom KT19 238 CN110
Horton Pl, West. TN16 off Hortons Way 277 ER126
Horton Rd, E8 10 E4
Colnbrook SL3 175 BA81
Dartford DA4 230 FQ97
Datchet SL3 174 AV80
Poyle SL3 175 BE83
Staines TW19 196 BG85
West Drayton UB7 156 BN74
Horton St, SE13 46 D10
Hortons Way, West. TN16 277 ER126
Horton Twr, Orp. BR5 228 EW98
Horton Way, Croy. CR0 225 DX99
Farningham DA4 230 FM101
Hortus Rd, E4 123 EC47
Southall UB2 178 BZ75
Horvath Cl, Wey. KT13 235 BR105
Horwood Cl, Rick. WD3 off Thellusson Way 114 BG45
Horwood Ct, Wat. WD24 98 BX37
Hosack Rd, SW17 202 DF89
Hoser Av, SE12 206 EG89
Hosey Common La, West. TN16 277 ES130
Hosey Common Rd, Eden. TN8 277 EQ133
Westerham TN16 277 ER130
HOSEY HILL, West. TN16 277 ES127
Hosey Hill, West. TN16 277 ER127
Hosier La, EC1 18 G7
Hoskins Cl, E16 24 D8
Hayes UB3 off Cranford Dr 177 BT78
Hoskins Rd, Oxt. RH8 276 EE129
Hoskins St, SE10 47 H1
Hoskins Wk, Oxt. RH8 276 EE129
Hospital Br Rd, Twick. TW2 198 CB87
Hospital Hill, Chesh. HP5 76 AQ32
Hospital of St. John & St. Elizabeth, NW8 16 A1
Hospital Rd, E9 11 H2
Hounslow TW3 178 CA83
Sevenoaks TN13 279 FJ121
Hospital Way, SE13 205 ED87
Hotham Cl, Sutt.H. DA4 210 FP94
Swanley BR8 229 FH95
West Molesey KT8 off Garrick Gdns 218 CA97
Hotham Prim Sch, SW15 off Charlwood Rd 181 CX84
Hotham Rd, SW15 181 CW83
SW19 202 DC94
Hotham Rd Ms, SW19 off Haydons Rd 202 DC94
Hotham St, E15 13 J8
Hothfield Pl, SE16 33 H7
Hotspur Ind Est, N17 122 DV51
Hotspur Rd, Nthlt. UB5 158 CA68
Hotspur St, SE11 30 E10
Houblon Rd, Rich. TW10 200 CL85
Houblons Hill, Cooper. CM16 92 EW31
Houghton Cl, E8 10 B5
Hampton TW12 198 BY93
Houghton Rd, N15 off West Grn Rd 144 DT56
Houghton Sq, SW9 42 A9
Houghton St, WC2 18 D9
Houlder Cres, Croy. CR0 241 DP107
Hound Ho Rd, Shere GU5 282 BN141
Houndsden Rd, N21 103 DM44
Houndsditch, EC3 19 P8
Houndsfield Prim Sch, N9 off Ripon Rd 122 DV45
Houndsfield Rd, N9 122 DV45
HOUNSLOW, TW3 - TW6 178 BZ84
Hounslow 198 CB85
Hounslow Av, Houns. TW3 198 CB85
Hounslow Business Pk, Houns. TW3 off Alice Way 178 CB84
Hounslow Central 178 CA83
Hounslow East 178 CC82
Hounslow Gdns, Houns. TW3 198 CB85
Hounslow Heath, Houns. TW4 198 BY86
Hounslow Heath Inf & Nur Sch, Houns. TW4 off Martindale Rd 178 BY83
Hounslow Heath Jun Sch, Houns. TW4 off Selwyn Cl 178 BY83
Hounslow Manor Sch, Houns. TW3 off Prince Regent Rd 178 CC83
Hounslow Rd, Feltham TW14 197 BV88
Hanworth TW13 198 BX90
Twickenham TW2 198 CC86
Hounslow Town Prim Sch, Houns. TW3 off Pears Rd 178 CC83
HOUNSLOW WEST, Houns. TW4 178 BX83
Hounslow West 178 BY82
Housden Cl, Wheat. AL4 50 CL08
Housefield Way, St.Alb. AL4 65 CJ23
Household Cavalry Mus (Combermere Barracks), Wind. SL4 173 AQ83
House La, Sand. AL4 65 CK16
Houseman Way, SE5 43 M5
Houses of Parliament, SW1 30 B5
Housewood End, Hem.H. HP1 62 BH17
HOUSHAM TYE, Harl. CM17 59 FD13
Houston Pl, Esher KT10 off Lime Tree Av 219 CE102
Houston Rd, SE23 205 DY89
Long Ditton KT6 219 CH100
Hove Av, E17 145 DZ57
Hove Cl, Grays RM17 192 GA79
Hutton CM13 131 GC47
Hoveden Rd, NW2 4 E2
Hove Gdns, Sutt. SM1 222 DB102
Hoveton Rd, SE28 168 EW72
Hoveton Way, Ilf. IG6 125 EP52
Howard Agne Cl, Bov. HP3 79 BA27
Howard Av, Bex. DA5 208 EW88
Epsom KT17 239 CU110
Slough SL2 153 AR71
Howard Bldg, SW8 41 J3
Howard Business Pk, Wal.Abb. EN9 off Howard Cl 89 ED34
Howard Cen, The, Welw.G.C. AL8 51 CX09
Howard Cl, N11 120 DG47
NW2 141 CY63
W3 160 CP72
Ashtead KT21 254 CM118
Bushey Heath WD23 117 CE45
Hampton TW12 198 CC93
Leatherhead KT22 253 CJ123
Loughton IG10 106 EL44
St. Albans AL1 65 CJ22
Sunbury-on-Thames TW16 197 BT93
Waltham Abbey EN9 89 ED34
Walton on the Hill KT20 271 CT125
Watford WD24 97 BU37
West Horsley KT24 267 BR125
Howard Ct, Reig. RH2 272 DC133
Howard Cres, Seer Grn HP9 111 AQ50
Howard Dr, Borwd. WD6 100 CR42
Howard Gdns, Guil. GU1 265 BA133
Howard Ind Est, Chesh. HP5 76 AQ29
Howard Ms, N5 9 H1
Slough SL3 off Laburnum Gro 175 BB79
Howard of Effingham Sch, Eff. KT24 off Lower Rd 268 BX127
Howard Pl, Reig. RH2 272 DA132
Howard Prim Sch, Croy. CR0 off Dering Pl 242 DQ105
Howard Ridge, Burpham GU4 265 BA130
Howard Rd, E6 167 EM68
E11 146 EE62
E17 145 EA55
N15 144 DS58
N16 9 M1
NW2 4 C1
SE20 224 DW95
SE25 224 DU99
Barking IG11 167 ER67
Bookham KT23 268 CB127
Bromley BR1 226 EG94
Chafford Hundred RM16 191 FW76
Chesham HP5 76 AP28
Coulsdon CR5 257 DJ115
Dartford DA1 210 FN86
Dorking RH4 285 CG136
Effingham Junction KT24 251 BU122
Ilford IG1 147 EP63
Isleworth TW7 179 CF83
New Malden KT3 220 CS97
North Holmwood RH5 off Holmesdale Rd 285 CJ140
Reigate RH2 288 DB135
Seer Green HP9 111 AQ50
Southall UB1 158 CB72
Surbiton KT5 220 CM100
Upminster RM14 150 FQ61
Howards Cl, Pnr. HA5 115 BV54
Woking GU22 249 BA120
Howards Crest Cl, Beck. BR3 225 EC96
Howards Dr, Hem.H. HP1 61 BF17
Howards Gate, Farn.Royal SL2 off Farnham Rd 153 AQ69
Howardsgate, Welw.G.C. AL8 51 CX08
Howards La, SW15 201 CV85
Addlestone KT15 233 BE107
Howards Rd, E13 23 N2
Woking GU22 249 AZ120
Howards Thicket, Ger.Cr. SL9 134 AW61
Howard St, T.Ditt. KT7 219 CH101
Howards Wd Dr, Ger.Cr. SL9 134 AX61
Howard Wk, N2 142 DC56
Howard Way, Barn. EN5 101 CX43
Harlow CM20 74 EU15
Howarth Rd, SE2 188 EU78
Howberry Cl, Edg. HA8 117 CK51
Howberry Rd, Edg. HA8 117 CK51
Stanmore HA7 117 CK51
Thornton Heath CR7 224 DR95
Howbury La, Erith DA8 189 FG82
Howbury Rd, SE15 44 G10
Howcroft Cres, N3 120 DA52
Howcroft La, Grnf. UB6 159 CD69
Howden Cl, SE28 168 EX73
Howden Rd, SE25 224 DT96
Howden St, SE15 44 C10
Howe Cl, Rom. RM7 126 FA53
Shenley WD7 84 CL32
Howe Dell, Hat. AL10 67 CV18
Howe Dell Prim Sch, Hat. AL10 off The Runway 66 CS16
Howe Dell Sch, Hat. AL10 off The Runway 66 CS16
Howe Dr, Beac. HP9 111 AK50
Caterham CR3 258 DR122
Howell Cl, Rom. RM6 148 EX57
Howell Hill Cl, Epsom KT17 239 CW111
Howell Hill Gro, Epsom KT17 239 CW110
Howell Wk, SE1 31 H9
Howerd Way, SE18 186 EL81
Howe Rd, Hem.H. HP3 62 BN22
Howes Cl, N3 142 DA55
Howfield Grn, Hodd. EN11 55 DZ14
Howfield Pl, N17 144 DT55
Howgate Rd, SW14 180 CR83
Howick Pl, SW1 29 M7
Howicks Grn, Welw.G.C. AL7 52 DA12
Howie St, SW11 40 C5
Howitt Cl, N16 off Allen Rd 144 DS63
NW3 6 D4
Howitt Rd, NW3 6 C4
Howitts Cl, Esher KT10 236 CA107
Howland Est, SE16 33 H6
Howland Garth, St.Alb. AL1 64 CC24
Howland Ms E, W1 17 M6
Howlands, Welw.G.C. AL7 52 DB12
Howlands Ho, Welw.G.C. AL7 52 DA12
Howland St, W1 17 L6
Howland Way, SE16 33 M5
How La, Chipstead CR5 256 DG117
Howletts La, Ruis. HA4 137 BQ57
Howletts Rd, SE24 204 DQ86
Howley Pl, W2 15 P6
Howley Rd, Croy. CR0 223 DP104
Hows Cl, Uxb. UB8 156 BJ67
Howse Rd, Wal.Abb. EN9 off Deer Pk Way 105 EB35
Howsman Rd, SW13 181 CU79
Hows Mead, N.Wld Bas. CM16 75 FD24
Howson Rd, SE4 185 DY84
Howson Ter, Rich. TW10 200 CL86
Hows Rd, Uxb. UB8 156 BJ67
Hows St, E2 10 A10
Howton Pl, Bushey Hth WD23 117 CD46
HOW WOOD, St.Alb. AL2 82 CC27
How Wood 82 CC28
How Wd, Park St AL2 82 CB28
How Wd Prim Sch, Park St AL2 off Spooners Dr 82 CC27
HOXTON, N1 19 N1
Hoxton 19 P1
Hoxton Mkt, N1 19 N3
Hoxton Sq, N1 19 N3
Hoxton St, N1 19 P3
Hoylake Cl, Slou. SL1 173 AL75
Hoylake Cres, Ickhm UB10 136 BN60
Hoylake Gdns, Mitch. CR4 223 DJ97
Romford RM3 128 FN53
Ruislip HA4 137 BV60
Watford WD19 116 BX49
Hoylake Rd, W3 160 CS72
Hoyland Cl, SE15 44 E4
Hoyle Rd, SW17 202 DE92
Hoy St, E16 23 L9
Hoy Ter, Grays RM20 191 FX78
H.Q.S. Wellington, Master Mariners' Hall, WC2 18 E10
Hubbard Dr, Chess. KT9 237 CJ107
Hubbard Rd, SE27 204 DQ91
Hubbards Chase, Horn. RM11 150 FN57
Hubbards Cl, Horn. RM11 150 FN57
Uxbridge UB8 157 BP72
Hubbard's Hall Est, Harl. CM17 58 EY14
Hubbards Rd, Chorl. WD3 95 BD43
Hubbard St, E15 13 J9
Hubbinet Ind Est, Rom. RM7 149 FC55
Hubert Day Cl, Beac. HP9 off Seeleys Rd 111 AK52
Hubert Gro, SW9 183 DL83
Hubert Rd, E6 24 E2
Brentwood CM14 130 FV48
Rainham RM13 169 FF69
Slough SL3 174 AX76
Hucknall Cl, Rom. RM3 128 FM51
Huddart St, E3 21 P6
Huddleston Cl, E2 10 G10
Huddleston Cres, Merst. RH1 273 DK128
Huddlestone Rd, E7 146 EF63
NW2 161 CV65
Huddleston Rd, N7 7 N1
Hudson Apts, N8 off Chadwell La 143 DM55
Hudson Av, Denh. UB9 135 BF58
Hudson Cl, E15 13 N8
W12 off Canada Way 161 CV73
St. Albans AL1 65 CD23
Watford WD24 97 BT36
Hudson Ct, E14 off Maritime Quay 34 B10
SW19 202 DB94
Guildford GU2 off Cobbett Rd 264 AT133
Hudson Gdns, Grn St Grn BR6 off Superior Dr 245 ET107
Hudson Ho, Epsom KT19 238 CR113
Hudson Pl, SE18 187 EQ78
Slough SL3 175 AZ78
Hudson Rd, Bexh. DA7 188 EZ82
Harlington UB3 177 BR79
Hudsons, Tad. KT20 255 CX121
Hudsons Ct, Pot.B. EN6 off Darkes La 86 DA31
Hudson's Pl, SW1 29 K8
Hudson Way, N9 122 DW48
NW2 off Gratton Ter 141 CX62
Huggin Ct, EC4 19 K10
Huggin Hill, EC4 19 K10
Huggins La, N.Mymms AL9 67 CV23
Huggins Pl, SW2 203 DM88
Hughan Rd, E15 13 H2
Hugh Dalton Av, SW6 38 G3
Hughenden Av, Har. HA3 139 CH57
Hughenden Gdns, Nthlt. UB5 158 BW69
Hughenden Rd, St.Alb. AL4 65 CH17
Slough SL1 153 AR72
Worcester Park KT4 221 CU101
Hughendon Ter, E15 off Westdown Rd 145 EC63
Hughes Cl, N12 off Coleridge Rd 120 DC50
Hughes Rd, Ashf. TW15 197 BQ94
Grays RM16 193 GG76
Hayes UB3 157 BV73
Hughes Ter, SW9 off Styles Gdns 43 H10
Hughes Wk, Croy. CR0 off St. Saviours Rd 224 DQ101
Hugh Gaitskell Cl, SW6 38 G3
Hugh Herland Ho, Kings.T. KT1 220 CL97
Hugh Ms, SW1 29 K9
Hugh Myddelton Prim Sch, EC1 18 F3
Hugh's Twr, Harl. CM20 57 ER14
Hugh St, SW1 29 K9
Hugo Cl, Wat. WD18 off Malkin Way 97 BS42
Hugo Gdns, Rain. RM13 169 FF65
Hugo Gryn Way, Shenley WD7 84 CL31
Hugon Rd, SW6 39 L10
Hugo Rd, N19 143 DJ63
Huguenot Pl, E1 20 B6
SW18 202 DC85
Huguenot Sq, SE15 44 E10
HULBERRY, Dart. DA4 229 FG103
Hullbridge Ms, N1 9 L8
Hull Cl, SE16 33 K4
Cheshunt EN7 88 DR26
Slough SL1 173 AQ75
Sutton SM2 off Yarbridge Cl 240 DB110
Hulletts La, Pilg.Hat. CM15 130 FT43
Hull Gro, Harl. CM19 73 EN20
Hull Pl, E16 off Fishguard Way 167 EQ74
Hull St, EC1 19 J3
Hulme Pl, SE1 31 K5
Hulse Av, Bark. IG11 167 ER65
Romford RM7 127 FB53
Hulse Ter, Ilf. IG1 off Buttsbury Rd 147 EQ64
Hulsewood Cl, Dart. DA2 209 FH90
Hulton Cl, Lthd. KT22 253 CJ123
Hulverston Cl, Sutt. SM2 240 DB110
Humber Av, S.Ock. RM15 171 FT72
Humber Cl, West Dr. UB7 156 BK74
Humber Dr, W10 14 C5
Upminster RM14 151 FR58
Humber Rd, NW2 141 CV61
SE3 47 L2
Dartford DA1 210 FK85
Humberstone Rd, E13 24 C3
Humberton Cl, E9 11 L3
Humber Way, Slou. SL3 175 BA77
Humbolt Cl, Guil. GU2 264 AS134
Humbolt Rd, W6 38 E3
Hume Av, Til. RM18 193 GG83
Hume Cl, Til. RM18 193 GG83
Hume Ms, Til. RM18 off Hume Cl 193 GG83
Humes Av, W7 179 CE76
Hume Ter, E16 24 C7
Hume Way, Ruis. HA4 137 BU58
Hummer Rd, Egh. TW20 195 BA91
Humphrey Cl, Fetch. KT22 252 CC122
Ilford IG5 125 EM53
Humphrey St, SE1 32 A10
Humphries Cl, Dag. RM9 148 EZ63
Hundred Acre, NW9 119 CT54
Hundred Acres La, Amer. HP7 77 AR40
Hungerdown, E4 123 EC46
Hungerford Av, Slou. SL2 154 AS71
Hungerford Br, SE1 30 B2
WC2 30 B2
Hungerford La, WC2 30 A2
Hungerford Prim Sch, N7 7 P4
Hungerford Rd, N7 7 P4
Hungerford Sq, Wey. KT13 off Rosslyn Pk 235 BR105
Hungerford St, E1 20 F8
Hungry Hill, Ripley GU23 250 BK124
Hungry Hill La, Send GU23 250 BK124
HUNSDON, Ware SG12 56 EJ06
Hunsdon, Welw.G.C. AL7 52 DD09
HUNSDONBURY, Ware SG12 56 EJ08
Hunsdon Cl, Dag. RM9 168 EY65
Hunsdon Dr, Sev. TN13 279 FH123
Hunsdon JMI Sch, Hunsdon SG12 off High St 56 EK06
Hunsdon Pound, Stans.Abb. SG12 56 EL12
Hunsdon Rd, SE14 45 J4
Stanstead Abbotts SG12 56 EE11
Hunslett St, E2 21 H1
Hunstanton Cl, Colnbr. SL3 175 BC80
Hunston Rd, Mord. SM4 222 DB102
Hunt Cl, W11 26 D2
St. Albans AL4 off Villiers Cres 65 CK17
Hunter Av, Shenf. CM15 131 GA44
Hunter Cl, SE1 31 M7
SW12 202 DG88
Borehamwood WD6 100 CQ43
Potters Bar EN6 86 DB33
Wallington SM6 241 DL108
Huntercombe Cl, Tap. SL6 152 AH72
Huntercombe La N, Slou. SL1 152 AJ71
Taplow SL6 152 AJ71
Huntercombe La S, Tap. SL6 152 AH74
Huntercombe Manor, Tap. SL6 152 AJ73
Huntercombe Spur, Slou. SL1 152 AJ73
Huntercrombe Gdns, Wat. WD19 116 BW50
Hunter Dr, Horn. RM12 150 FJ63
Hunter Ho, Felt. TW13 197 BU88
Hunter Rd, SW20 221 CW95
Guildford GU1 280 AY135
Ilford IG1 147 EP64
Thornton Heath CR7 224 DR97
Hunters, The, Beck. BR3 225 EC95
Hunters Cl, Bex. DA5 209 FE90
Bovingdon HP3 79 BA29
Chesham HP5 76 AN30
Epsom KT19 off Marshalls Cl 238 CQ113
Hunters Ct, Rich. TW9 199 CK85
Huntersfield Cl, Reig. RH2 272 DB131
Hunters Gate, Nutfld RH1 273 DM133
Watford WD25 off Hunters La 81 BU33
Hunters Gro, Har. HA3 139 CJ56
Hayes UB3 157 BU74
Orpington BR6 245 EP105
Romford RM5 127 FB50
Hunters Hall Prim Sch, Dag. RM10 off Alibon Rd 149 FB64
Hunters Hall Rd, Dag. RM10 148 FA63
Hunters Hill, Ruis. HA4 138 BW62
Hunters La, Wat. WD25 81 BT33
Hunters Meadow, SE19 off Dulwich Wd Av 204 DS91
Hunters Oak, Hem.H. HP2 63 BP15
Hunters Pk, Berk. HP4 60 AY18
Hunters Reach, Wal.Cr. EN7 88 DT29
Hunters Ride, Brick.Wd AL2 82 CA31
Hunters Rd, Chess. KT9 220 CL104
Hunters Sq, Dag. RM10 148 FA63
Hunter St, WC1 18 B4
Hunters Wk, Knock.P. TN14 246 EY114
Hunters Way, Croy. CR0 242 DS105
Enfield EN2 103 DN39
Slough SL1 173 AL75
Welwyn Garden City AL7 51 CZ12
Hunter Wk, E13 13 N10
Borehamwood WD6 off Hunter Cl 100 CQ43
Hunting Cl, Esher KT10 236 CA105
Huntingdon Cl, Brox. EN10 71 DY24
Mitcham CR4 223 DL97
Northolt UB5 158 CA65
Huntingdon Gdns, W4 180 CQ80
Worcester Park KT4 221 CW104
Huntingdon Rd, N2 142 DE55
N9 122 DW46
Redhill RH1 272 DF134
Woking GU21 248 AT117
Huntingdon St, E16 23 M9
N1 8 C7
Huntingfield, Croy. CR0 243 DZ108
Huntingfield Rd, SW15 181 CU84
Huntingfield Way, Egh. TW20 195 BD94
Hunting Gate, Hem.H. HP2 62 BL16
Hunting Gate Cl, Enf. EN2 103 DN41
Hunting Gate Dr, Chess. KT9 238 CL108
Hunting Gate Ms, Sutt. SM1 222 DB104
Twickenham TW2 off Colne Rd 199 CE88
Huntings Rd, Dag. RM10 168 FA65
Huntington Pl, Langley SL3 175 BB76
Huntland Cl, Rain. RM13 169 FH71
Huntley Av, Nthflt DA11 212 GB86
Huntley Cl, Stanw. TW19 off Cambria Gdns 196 BL87
Huntley Ho, Walt. KT12 off Octagon Rd 235 BT109
Huntley St, WC1 17 M5
Huntley Way, SW20 221 CU96
Huntly Dr, N3 120 DA51
Huntly Rd, SE25 224 DS98
HUNTON BRIDGE, Kings L. WD4 81 BP33
Hunton Br Hill, Hunt.Br. WD4 81 BQ33
Hunton Br Interchange, Wat. WD17 97 BQ35
Hunton St, E1 20 C5
Hunt Rd, Nthflt DA11 212 GE90
Southall UB2 178 CA76
Hunt's Cl, SE3 47 P8
Hunt's Ct, WC2 29 P1
Hunts La, E15 22 E1
Taplow SL6 152 AE68
Huntsman Rd, Ilf. IG6 126 EU51
Huntsmans Cl, Felt. TW13 197 BV91
Fetcham KT22 off The Green 253 CD124
Warlingham CR6 258 DW119
Huntsmans Dr, Upmin. RM14 150 FQ64
Huntsman St, SE17 31 M9
Hunts Mead, Enf. EN3 105 DX41
Hunts Mead Cl, Chis. BR7 207 EM94
Huntsmill Rd, Hem.H. HP1 61 BE21
Huntsmoor Rd, Epsom KT19 238 CR106
Huntspill St, SW17 202 DC90
Hunts Slip Rd, SE21 204 DS90
Huntswood La, Slou. SL1 152 AE66
Taplow SL6 152 AE66
Huntsworth Ms, NW1 16 E5
Hurdwick Pl, NW1 off Harrington Sq 7 L10
Hurley Cl, Walt. KT12 217 BV103
Hurley Cres, SE16 33 K4
Hurley Gdns, Guil. GU4 265 AZ130
Hurley Ho, SE11 30 F9
Hurley Rd, Grnf. UB6 158 CB72
Hurlfield, Dart. DA2 210 FJ90
Hurlford, Wok. GU21 248 AU117
Hurlingham & Chelsea Sch, SW6 39 K10
Hurlingham Business Pk, SW6 182 DA83
Hurlingham Club, SW6 181 CZ83
Hurlingham Ct, SW6 38 G10
Hurlingham Gdns, SW6 38 G10
Hurlingham Park, SW6 39 H10
Hurlingham Retail Pk, SW6 off Carnwath Rd 182 DB83
Hurlingham Rd, SW6 38 G9
Bexleyheath DA7 188 EZ80
Hurlingham Sch, SW15 off Putney Br Rd 181 CZ84
Hurlingham Sq, SW6 182 DA83
Hurlock St, N5 143 DP62
Hurlstone Rd, SE25 224 DR99
Hurn Ct Rd, Houns. TW4 off Renfrew Rd 178 BX82
Hurnford Cl, S.Croy. CR2 242 DS110
Huron Cl, Grn St Grn BR6 off Winnipeg Dr 245 ET107
Huron Rd, SW17 202 DG89
Broxbourne EN10 89 DY26
Huron Uni USA in London, WC1 18 A6
Hurren Cl, SE3 47 J10
Hurricane Rd, Wall. SM6 241 DL108
Hurricane Trd Cen, NW9 119 CU53
Hurricane Way, Abb.L. WD5 off Abbey Dr 81 BU32
North Weald Bassett CM16 92 EZ27
Slough SL3 175 BB78
Hurry Cl, E15 13 K7
Hursley Rd, Chig. IG7 125 ET50
Hurst Av, E4 123 EA49
N6 143 DJ58
Hurstbourne, Clay. KT10 237 CF107
Hurstbourne Gdns, Bark. IG11 167 ES65
Hurstbourne Ho, SW15 off Tangley Gro 201 CT86
Hurstbourne Rd, SE23 205 DY88
Hurst Cl, E4 123 EA48
NW11 142 DB58
Bromley BR2 226 EF102
Chessington KT9 238 CN106
Headley KT18 254 CQ124
Northolt UB5 158 BZ65
Welwyn Garden City AL7 52 DC10
Woking GU22 248 AW120
Hurstcourt Rd, Sutt. SM1 222 DB103
Hurst Cft, Guil. GU1 280 AY137
Hurstdene Av, Brom. BR2 226 EF102
Staines TW18 196 BH93
Hurstdene Gdns, N15 144 DS59
Hurst Dr, Wal.Cr. EN8 89 DX34
Walton on the Hill KT20 271 CU126
Hurst Dr Prim Sch, Wal.Cr. EN8 off Hurst Dr 89 DX34
Hurst Est, SE2 188 EX78
Hurstfield, Brom. BR2 226 EG99
Hurstfield Cres, Hayes UB4 157 BS70
Hurstfield Dr, Tap. SL6 152 AH72
Hurstfield Rd, W.Mol. KT8 218 CA97
HURST GREEN, Oxt. RH8 276 EG132
Hurst Green 276 EF132
Hurst Grn Cl, Oxt. RH8 276 EG132
Hurst Grn Rd, Oxt. RH8 276 EF132
Hurst Grn Sch, Oxt. RH8 off Wolfs Wd 276 EG132
Hurst Gro, Walt. KT12 217 BT102
Hurstlands, Oxt. RH8 276 EG132
Hurstlands Cl, Horn. RM11 150 FJ59
Hurst La, SE2 188 EX78
East Molesey KT8 218 CC98
Egham TW20 215 BA96
Headley KT18 254 CQ124
Hurstleigh Cl, Red. RH1 272 DF132
Hurstleigh Dr, Red. RH1 272 DF132

Hurstleigh Gdns, Ilf. IG5 125 EM53
Hurstlings, Welw.G.C. AL7 52 DB10
Hurstmead Ct, Edg. HA8 118 CP49
Sch Hurstmere Sch, Sid.
DA15 off Hurst Rd 208 EW88
Hurst Pk Av, Horn. RM12
off Crystal Av 150 FL63
Sch Hurst Pk Prim Sch, W.Mol.
KT8 off Hurst Rd 218 CA97
Hurst Pl, Nthwd. HA6 115 BP53
Sch Hurst Prim Sch, Bex. DA5
off Dorchester Av 208 EX87
Hurst Ri, Barn. EN5 102 DA41
Hurst Rd, E17 145 EB55
N21 121 DN46
Bexley DA5 208 EX88
Buckhurst Hill IG9 124 EK46
Croydon CR0 242 DR106
East Molesey KT8 218 CA97
Epsom KT19 238 CR111
Erith DA8 189 FC80
Headley KT18 254 CR123
Horley RH6 290 DE147
Sidcup DA15 208 EU89
Slough SL1 153 AK71
Walton on the Hill KT20 254 CR123
Walton-on-Thames KT12 218 BW99
West Molesey KT8 218 BY97
Hurst Springs, Bex. DA5 208 EY88
Hurst St, SE24 203 DP86
Hurst Vw Rd, S.Croy. CR2 242 DS108
Hurst Way, Pyrford GU22 233 BE114
Sevenoaks TN13 279 FJ127
South Croydon CR2 242 DS107
Hurstway Wk, W11 14 D10
Hurstwood Av, E18 146 EH56
Bexley DA5 208 EY88
Bexleyheath DA7 189 FE81
Erith DA8 189 FE81
Pilgrim's Hatch CM15 130 FV45
Hurstwood Ct, Upmin. RM14 150 FP60
Hurstwood Dr, Brom. BR1 227 EM97
Hurstwood Rd, NW11 141 CY56
Hurtwood Rd, Walt. KT12 218 BZ101
Hurworth Av, Slou. SL3 174 AW76
Huson Cl, NW3 6 C6
Hussain Cl, Har. HA1 139 CF63
Hussars Cl, Houns. TW4 178 BY83
Husseywell Cres, Brom. BR2 226 EG102
Hutchingsons Rd, New Adgtn
CR0 243 EC111
Hutchings Rd, Beac. HP9 111 AK50
Hutchings St, E14 34 A5
Hutchings Wk, NW11 142 DB56
Hutchins Cl, E15 12 F7
Hornchurch RM12 150 FL62
Hutchinson Ter, Wem. HA9 139 CK62
Hutchins Rd, SE28 168 EU73
Hutchins Way, Horl. RH6 290 DF146
Hutson Ter, Purf. RM19
off London Rd Purfleet 191 FR79
HUTTON, Brwd. CM13 131 GD44
Sch Hutton All Saints' C of E
Prim Sch, Hutt. CM13
off Claughton Way 131 GD44
Hutton Cl, Grnf. UB6
off Mary Peters Dr 139 CD64
Hertford SG14 53 DN09
Walton-on-Thames KT12 235 BV106
Woodford Green IG8 124 EH51
Hutton Dr, Hutt. CM13 131 GD45
Hutton Gdns, Har. HA3 116 CC52
Hutton Gate, Hutt. CM13 131 GB45
Hutton Gro, N12 120 DB50
Hutton La, Har. HA3 116 CC52
Hutton Ms, SW15 201 CV85
HUTTON MOUNT,
Brwd. CM13 131 GB46
Hutton Pl, Hutt. CM13 131 GB44
Hutton Rd, Shenf. CM15 131 FZ45
Hutton Row, Edg. HA8 118 CQ52
Hutton St, EC4 18 F9
Hutton Village, Hutt. CM13 131 GE45
Hutton Wk, Har. HA3 116 CC52
Huxbear St, SE4 205 DZ85
Huxley Cl, Nthlt. UB5 158 BY67
Uxbridge UB8 156 BK70
Wexham SL3 154 AV70
Huxley Dr, Rom. RM6 148 EV59
Huxley Gdns, NW10 160 CM69
Huxley Par, N18 122 DR50
Huxley Pl, N13 121 DP49
Huxley Rd, E10 145 EC61
N18 122 DR49
Welling DA16 187 ET83
Huxley Sayze, N18 122 DR50
Huxley St, W10 14 E3
Huxtable Gdns, Maid. SL6 172 AD79
Hyacinth Cl, Hmptn. TW12
off Gresham Rd 198 CA93
Ilford IG1 167 EP65
Hyacinth Ct, Pnr. HA5
off Tulip Ct 138 BW55
Hyacinth Dr, Uxb. UB10 156 BL66
Hyacinth Rd, SW15 201 CU88
Hyburn Cl, Brick.Wd AL2 82 BZ30
Hemel Hempstead HP3 63 BP21
Hycliffe Gdns, Chig. IG7 125 EQ49
HYDE, THE, NW9 141 CT56
Hyde, The, NW9 140 CS57
Ware SG12 54 DV05
Hyde Av, Pot.B. EN6 86 DB33
Hyde Cl, E13 13 P10
Ashford TW15 off Hyde Ter 197 BS93
Barnet EN5 101 CZ41
Chafford Hundred RM16 191 FX76
Romford RM1 127 FD51
Hyde Ct, N20 120 DD48
Waltham Cross EN8
off Parkside 89 DY34
Hyde Cres, NW9 140 CS57
Hyde Dr, St.P.Cray BR5 228 EV98
Hyde Est Rd, NW9 141 CT57
Hyde Fm Ms, SW12 203 DK88
Hydefield Cl, N21 122 DR46
Hydefield Ct, N9 122 DS47
Hyde Grn, Beac. HP9 111 AM52
● Hyde Ho, NW9 140 CS57
Hyde La, SW11 40 C6
Bovingdon HP3 79 BA27
Frogmore AL2 83 CE28
Hyde La, Hem.H. HP3 81 BR26
Ockham GU23 250 BN120
Park Street AL2 82 CC28
Hyde Mead, Lwr Naze. EN9 72 EE23
Hyde Meadows, Bov. HP3 79 BA28
★ Hyde Park, W2 28 C2
Hyde Pk, SW7 28 C2
W1 28 C2
Hyde Pk Av, N21 122 DQ47
⊖ Hyde Park Corner 28 G4
Hyde Pk Cor, W1 29 H4
Hyde Pk Cres, W2 16 C9
Hyde Pk Gdns, N21 122 DQ46
W2 16 B10
Hyde Pk Gdns Ms, W2 16 B10
Hyde Pk Gate, SW7 27 P5
Hyde Pk Gate Ms, SW7 27 P5
Hyde Pk Pl, W2 16 D10
Hyde Pk Sq, W2 16 C9
Hyde Pk Sq Ms, W2 16 C9
Hyde Pk St, W2 16 C9
Sch Hyde Prim Sch, The,
NW9 off Hyde Cres 141 CT57
Hyderabad Way, E15 13 J6
Hyde Rd, N1 9 M9
Bexleyheath DA7 188 EZ82
Richmond TW10
off Albert Rd 200 CM85
South Croydon CR2 242 DS113
Watford WD17 97 BU40
Hyder Rd, Grays RM16 193 GJ76
Hydeside Gdns, N9 122 DT47
Hydes Pl, N1 8 G6
Hyde St, SE8 46 A3
Hyde Ter, Ashf. TW15 197 BS93
Hydethorpe Av, N9 122 DT47
Hydethorpe Rd, SW12 203 DJ88
Hyde Vale, SE10 46 F5
Hyde Valley, Welw.G.C. AL7 51 CZ11
Hyde Wk, Mord. SM4 222 DA101
Hyde Way, N9 122 DT47
Hayes UB3 177 BT77
Welwyn Garden City AL7 51 CY09
Hydro Ho, Cher. KT16
off Bridge Wf 216 BJ101
Hyland Cl, Horn. RM11 149 FH59
Sch Hyland Ho Sch, E17
off Forest Rd 123 ED54
Hylands Cl, Epsom KT18 254 CQ115
Hylands Ms, Epsom KT18 254 CQ115
Hylands Rd, E17 123 ED54
Epsom KT18 254 CQ115
Hyland Way, Horn. RM11 149 FH59
Hylle Cl, Wind. SL4 173 AL81
Hylton St, SE18 187 ET77
Hyndewood, SE23 205 DX90
Hyndford Cres, Green. DA9
off Ingress Pk Av 211 FW85
Hyndman St, SE15 44 E3
Hynton Rd, Dag. RM8 148 EW61
Hyperion Ct, Hem.H. HP2 62 BM17
Hyperion Ho, E3 21 L1
Hyperion Pl, Epsom KT19 238 CR109
Hyperion Wk, Horl. RH6 291 DH150
Hyrons Cl, Amer. HP6 77 AS38
Hyrons La, Amer. HP6 77 AR38
Hyrstdene, S.Croy. CR2 241 DP105
Hyson Rd, SE16 32 F10
Hythe, The, Stai. TW18 195 BE92
Hythe Av, Bexh. DA7 188 EZ80
Hythe Cl, N18 122 DU49
Orpington BR5
off Sandway Rd 228 EW98
HYTHE END, Stai. TW19 195 BB90
Hythe End Rd, Wrays. TW19 195 BA89
Hythe Fld Av, Egh. TW20 195 BD93
Hythe Pk Rd, Egh. TW20 195 BC92
Hythe Path, Th.Hth. CR7 224 DR97
Hythe Rd, NW10 161 CU70
Staines TW18 195 BD92
Thornton Heath CR7 224 DR96
● Hythe Rd Ind Est, NW10 161 CU69
Sch Hythe Sch, The, Stai. TW18
off Thorpe Rd 195 BD92
Hythe St, Dart. DA1 210 FL86
Hythe St Lwr, Dart. DA1 210 FL85
Hyver Hill, NW7 100 CR44

I

Sch Ian Mikardo High Sch, E3 22 D3
Ian Sq, Enf. EN3
off Lansbury Rd 105 DX39
Ibbetson Path, Loug. IG10 107 EP41
Ibbotson Av, E16 23 M8
Ibbott St, E1 21 H4
Iberian Av, Wall. SM6 241 DK105
Ibex Ho, E15 13 K4
Ibis La, W4 180 CQ81
Ibis Way, Hayes UB4
off Cygnet Way 158 BX72
Ibscott Cl, Dag. RM10 169 FC65
Ibsley Gdns, SW15 201 CU88
Ibsley Way, Cockfos. EN4 102 DE43
Sch Ibstock Pl Sch, SW15
off Clarence La 200 CS86
Icehouse Wd, Oxt. RH8 276 EE131
Iceland Rd, E3 12 B9
Iceland Wf, SE16 33 L8
Iceni Ct, E3 11 P9
Ice Wf, N1 8 B10
Ice Wf Marina, N1
off New Wf Rd 8 B10
Ickburgh Est, E5 144 DV61
Ickburgh Rd, E5 144 DV62
Sch Ickburgh Sch, E5
off Ickburgh Rd 144 DV62
ICKENHAM, Uxb. UB10 137 BQ62
⊖ Ickenham 137 BQ63
Ickenham Cl, Ruis. HA4 137 BR61
Ickenham Rd, Ickhm UB10 137 BQ61
Ruislip HA4 137 BR60
Ickleton Rd, SE9 206 EL91
Icklingham Gate, Cob. KT11 236 BW112
Icklingham Rd, Cob. KT11 236 BW112
Icknield Cl, St.Alb. AL3 64 BZ22
Icknield Dr, Ilf. IG2 147 EP57
Ickworth Pk Rd, E17 145 DY56
Idaho Bldg, SE13
off Deals Gateway 46 C7
Ida Rd, N15 144 DR57
Ida St, E14 22 E9
Iden Cl, Brom. BR2 226 EE97
Idlecombe Rd, SW17 202 DG93
Idmiston Rd, E15 13 L3
SE27 204 DQ90
Idmiston Rd, Wor.Pk. KT4 221 CT101
Idmiston Sq, Wor.Pk. KT4 221 CT101
Idol La, EC3 31 N1
Idonia St, SE8 45 P4
Idris Ct, N9 off Galahad Rd 122 DU48
Iffley Cl, Uxb. UB8 156 BK66
Iffley Rd, W6 181 CV76
IFIELD, Grav. DA13 213 GH94
Ifield Cl, Red. RH1 288 DE137
Ifield Rd, SW10 39 M2
Sch Ifield Sch, Grav. DA12
off Cedar Av 213 GJ92
Ifield Way, Grav. DA12 213 GK93
Ifold Rd, Red. RH1 288 DG136
Ifor Evans Pl, E1 21 K5
Ightham Rd, Erith DA8 188 FA80
Igraine Ct, N9
off Galahad Rd 122 DU48
Ret IKEA Ampere Way 223 DM101
Ikona Ct, Wey. KT13 235 BQ106
Ilbert St, W10 14 D3
Ilchester Gdns, W2 15 L10
Ilchester Pl, W14 26 G6
Ilchester Rd, Dag. RM8 148 EV64
Ildersly Gro, SE21 204 DR89
Sch Ilderton Prim Sch, SE16 44 G1
Ilderton Rd, SE15 44 G2
SE16 32 F10
Ilex Cl, Eng.Grn TW20 194 AV94
Sunbury-on-Thames TW16
off Oakington Dr 218 BW96
Ilex Ct, Berk. HP4 60 AV19
Ilex Ho, N4 143 DM59
Ilex Rd, NW10 161 CT65
Ilex Way, SW16 203 DN92
ILFORD, IG1 - IG6 147 EQ62
⇌ Ilford 147 EN62
Sch Ilford Co High Sch, Ilf.
IG6 off Fremantle Rd 125 EP54
Ilford Hill, Ilf. IG1 147 EN62
Sch Ilford Jewish Prim Sch,
Barkingside IG6
off Carlton Dr 147 ER55
Ilford La, Ilf. IG1 147 EP62
Sch Ilford Ursuline High Sch,
Ilf. IG1 off Morland Rd 147 EP61
Sch Ilford Ursuline Prep Sch,
Ilf. IG1 off Coventry Rd 147 EN61
Ilfracombe Cres, Horn. RM12 150 FJ63
Ilfracombe Gdns, Rom. RM6 148 EV59
Ilfracombe Rd, Brom. BR1 206 EF90
Iliffe St, SE17 31 H10
Iliffe Yd, SE17 31 H10
Ilkeston Ct, E5
off Overbury St 145 DX63
Ilkley Cl, SE19 204 DR93
Ilkley Rd, E16 24 C7
Watford WD19 116 BX50
Illingworth, Wind. SL4 173 AL84
Illingworth Cl, Mitch. CR4 222 DD97
Illingworth Way, Enf. EN1 104 DS42
Ilmington Rd, Har. HA3 139 CK58
Ilminster Gdns, SW11 182 DE84
Imber Cl, N14 121 DJ45
Esher KT10 219 CD102
● Imber Ct Trd Est,
E.Mol. KT8 219 CD100
Imber Gro, Esher KT10 219 CD101
Imber Pk Rd, Esher KT10 219 CD102
Imber St, N1 9 L9
Imer Pl, T.Ditt. KT7 219 CF101
Sch Immanuel & St. Andrew
C of E Prim Sch, SW16
off Buckleigh Rd 203 DL93
Sch Immanuel Coll, Bushey
WD23 off Elstree Rd 117 CE45
Sch Immanuel Sch, Rom. RM1
off Havering Rd 127 FD50
Imperial Av, N16 144 DT62
● Imperial Business Est,
Grav. DA11 213 GF86
Imperial Cl, NW2 141 CV64
Harrow HA2 138 CA58
Uni Imperial Coll London,
Charing Cross Campus, W6 38 C1
Hammersmith Campus,
W12 off Du Cane Rd 161 CU72
St. Mary's Campus, W2 16 B8
South Kensington Campus,
SW7 28 A6
Imperial Coll Rd, SW7 28 A7
Imperial Ct, NW8 6 D10
Imperial Cres, SW6 39 N8
Weybridge KT13 217 BQ104
Imperial Dr, Grav. DA12 213 GM92
Harrow HA2 138 CA59
Imperial Gdns, Mitch. CR4 223 DH97
Imperial Ms, E6 24 E1
● Imperial Pk, Wat. WD24 98 BW39
Imperial Pl, Chis. BR7
off Forest Cl 227 EN95
🔒 Imperial Retail Pk,
Grav. DA11 213 GG86
Imperial Rd, N22 121 DL53
SW6 39 M6
Feltham TW14 197 BS87
Windsor SL4 173 AN83
Imperial Sq, SW6 39 M6
Imperial St, E3 22 E3
● Imperial Trd Est,
Rain. RM13 170 FJ70
★ Imperial War Mus, SE1 30 F7
Imperial Way, Chis. BR7 207 EQ90
Croydon CR0 241 DM107
Harrow HA3 140 CL58
Hemel Hempstead HP3 62 BL24
Watford WD24 98 BW39
Imperial Wf, SW6 39 N8
● Impresa Pk, Hodd. EN11 71 EC16
● Imprimo Pk, Loug. IG10 107 EQ42
Imre Cl, W12
off Ellerslie Rd 161 CV74
Inca Dr, SE9 207 EP87
Inca Ter, N15 off Milton Rd 143 DP55
Ince Rd, Hersham KT12 235 BS107
Coll Inchbald Sch of Design,
Garden Design Faculty, SW1 29 K9
Interior Design Faculty, SW1 28 G8
Inchmery Rd, SE6 205 EB89
Inchwood, Croy. CR0 243 EB105
Indells, Hat. AL10 67 CT19
Independence Ho, SW19
off Chapter Way 222 DD95
Sch Independent Jewish Day Sch,
The, NW4 off Green La 141 CX57
Independent Pl, E8 10 B2
Independents Rd, SE3 47 L10
Inderwick Rd, N8 143 DM57
Indescon Ct, E14 34 B5
Index Apts, Rom. RM1
off Mercury Gdns 149 FF56
Indiana Bldg, SE13
off Deals Gateway 46 B7
India Pl, WC2 18 C10
India Rd, Slou. SL1 174 AV75
India St, EC3 20 A9
India Way, W12 161 CV73
Indigo Ms, E14 22 F9
N16 144 DR62
Indigo Wk, N2 142 DF56
N6 142 DF56
Indus Rd, SE7 186 EJ80
Industry Ter, SW9
off Canterbury Cres 183 DN83
Inforum Ms, SE15 44 D4
Ingal Rd, E13 23 N5
Ingate Pl, SW8 41 K7
Ingatestone Rd, E12 146 EJ60
SE25 224 DV98
Woodford Green IG8 124 EG52
Ingelow Rd, SW8 41 J9
Ingels Mead, Epp. CM16 91 ET29
Ingersoll Rd, W12 161 CV74
Enfield EN3 104 DW38
Ingestre Ct, W1
off Ingestre Pl 17 M10
Ingestre Pl, W1 17 M9
Ingestre Rd, E7 146 EG63
NW5 143 DH63
Ingham Cl, S.Croy. CR2 243 DX109
Ingham Rd, NW6 5 J1
South Croydon CR2 242 DW109
Inglebert St, EC1 18 E2
Ingleboro Dr, Pur. CR8 242 DR113
Ingleborough St, SW9 42 E8
Ingleby Dr, Har. HA1 139 CD62
Ingleby Gdns, Chig. IG7 126 EV48
Ingleby Rd, N7 off Bryett Rd 143 DL62
Dagenham RM10 169 FB65
Grays RM16 193 GH76
Ilford IG1 147 EP60
Ingleby Way, Chis. BR7 207 EN92
Wallington SM6 241 DK109
Ingle Cl, Pnr. HA5 138 BY55
Ingledew Rd, SE18 187 ER78
Inglefield, Pot.B. EN6 86 DA30
Ingleglen, Farn.Com. SL2 133 AP64
Hornchurch RM11 150 FN59
Inglehurst, New Haw KT15 234 BH110
Inglehurst Gdns, Ilf. IG4 147 EM57
Inglemere Rd, SE23 205 DX90
Mitcham CR4 202 DF94
Ingle Ms, EC1 18 E2
Ingles, Welw.G.C. AL8 51 CX06
Inglesham Wk, E9 11 P4
Ingleside, Colnbr. SL3 175 BE81
Ingleside Cl, Beck. BR3 205 EA94
Ingleside Gro, SE3 47 M3
Inglethorpe St, SW6 38 C6
Ingleton Av, Well. DA16 208 EU85
Ingleton Rd, N18 122 DU51
Carshalton SM5 240 DE109
Ingleton St, SW9 42 E8
Ingleway, N12 120 DD51
Inglewood, Cher. KT16 215 BF104
Croydon CR0 243 DY109
Woking GU21 248 AV118
Inglewood Cl, E14 34 B8
Hornchurch RM12 150 FK63
Ilford IG6 125 ET51
Inglewood Copse, Brom. BR1 226 EL96
Inglewood Gdns, St.Alb. AL2
off North Orbital Rd 83 CE25
Inglewood Ms, Surb. KT6 220 CN102
Inglewood Rd, NW6 5 K3
Bexleyheath DA7 189 FD84
Inglis Barracks, NW7 119 CX50
Inglis Rd, W5 160 CM73
Croydon CR0 224 DT102
Inglis St, SE5 43 H7
Ingoldsby Rd, Grav. DA12 213 GL88
Ingram Av, NW11 142 DC59
Ingram Cl, SE11 30 D8
Stanmore HA7 117 CJ50
Ingram Ho, E3 11 L10
Ingram Rd, N2 142 DE56
Dartford DA1 210 FL88
Grays RM17 192 GD77
Thornton Heath CR7 224 DQ95
Ingrams Cl, Hersham KT12 236 BW106
Ingram Way, Grnf. UB6 159 CD67
Ingrave Ho, Dag. RM9 168 EV67
Ingrave Rd, Brwd. CM13,
CM14, CM15 130 FX47
Romford RM1 149 FD56
Ingrave St, SW11 40 B10
Ingrebourne Gdns, Upmin.
RM14 150 FQ60
Sch Ingrebourne Prim Sch,
Harold Hill RM3
off Taunton Rd 128 FJ49
Ingrebourne Rd, Rain. RM13 169 FH70
Ingrebourne Valley Grn Way,
Horn. RM12 150 FK64
Ingress Gdns, Green. DA9 211 FX85
Ingress Pk, Green. DA9
off Ingress Pk Av 191 FW84
Ingress Pk Av, Green. DA9 191 FV84
Ingress St, W4
off Devonshire Rd 180 CS78
Ingreway, Rom. RM3 128 FP52
Inholms La, Dor. RH5 285 CH140
Inigo Jones Rd, SE7 186 EL80
Inigo Pl, WC2 18 A10
Inkerman Rd, NW5 7 J4
Eton Wick SL4 173 AM77
Knaphill GU21 248 AS118
St. Albans AL1 65 CE21
Inkerman Ter, W8
off Allen St 27 K7
Chesham HP5 76 AQ33
Inkerman Way, Wok. GU21 248 AS118
Inks Grn, E4 123 EC50
Inkster Ho, SW11
off Ingrave St 40 C10
Inkwell Cl, N12 120 DC48
Inman Rd, NW10 160 CS67
SW18 202 DC87
Inmans Row, Wdf.Grn. IG8 124 EG49
Inner Circle, NW1 16 G3
Inner Pk Rd, SW19 201 CX88
Inner Ring E, Lon.Hthrw Air.
TW6 177 BP83
Inner Ring W, Lon.Hthrw Air.
TW6 176 BN83
Inner Temple La, EC4 18 E9
Innes Cl, SW20 221 CY96
Innes Ct, Hem.H. HP3 62 BK22
Innes Gdns, SW15 201 CV86
Innes St, SE15 43 P4
Innes Yd, Croy. CR0
off Whitgift St 224 DQ104
Inniskilling Rd, E13 24 D1
● Innova Business Pk,
Enf. EN3 105 DZ36
Innovation Cl, Wem. HA0 160 CL67
Innova Way, Enf. EN3 105 DZ36
Inskip Cl, E10 145 EB61
Inskip Dr, Horn. RM11 150 FL60
Inskip Rd, Dag. RM8 148 EX60
Insley Ho, E3 off Bow Rd 22 C2
Uni Institute of Cancer Research,
The, Sutton Site, Sutt. SM2
off Cotswold Rd 240 DC110
★ Institute of Contemporary
Arts (I.C.A.), SW1 29 P3
Uni Institute of Ed, WC1 17 P5
Institute Pl, E8 10 E3
Institute Rd, Cooper. CM16 92 EX29
Taplow SL6 152 AF72
Westcott RH4
off Guildford Rd 284 CC137
Instone Rd, Dart. DA1 210 FK87
Integer Gdns, E11 145 ED59
● Interchange E Ind Est, E5
off Grosvenor Way 144 DW61
International Av, Houns. TW5 178 BW78
Sch International Comm Sch,
NW1 17 H5
Sch International Sch of London,
W3 off Gunnersbury Av 180 CN77
● International Trd Est,
Sthl. UB2 177 BV76
International Way, Sun. TW16 217 BS95
Inveraray Pl, SE18
off Old Mill Rd 187 ER79
Inver Cl, E5 off Theydon Rd 144 DW61
Inverclyde Gdns, Rom. RM6 148 EX56
Inver Ct, W2 15 M9
W6 off Invermead Cl 181 CU76
Inveresk Gdns, Wor.Pk. KT4 221 CT104
Inverforth Cl, NW3
off North End Way 142 DC61
Inverforth Rd, N11 121 DH50
Inverine Rd, SE7 186 EH78
Invermead Cl, W6 181 CU77
Invermore Pl, SE18 187 EQ77
Inverness Av, Enf. EN1 104 DS39
Inverness Dr, Ilf. IG6 125 ES51
Inverness Gdns, W8 27 L3
Inverness Ms, E16 167 EQ74
W2 15 M10
Inverness Pl, W2 15 M10
Inverness Rd, N18
off Aberdeen Rd 122 DV50
Hounslow TW3 178 BZ84
Southall UB2 178 BY77
Worcester Park KT4 221 CX102
Inverness St, NW1 7 J8
Inverness Ter, W2 15 M10
Inverton Rd, SE15 185 DX84
Invicta Cl, E3 22 B7
Chislehurst BR7 207 EN92
Feltham TW14 197 BT88
Invicta Gro, Nthlt. UB5 158 BZ69
Invicta Plaza, SE1 30 G2
Sch Invicta Prim Sch, SE3 47 P3
Invicta Rd, SE3 47 P4
Dartford DA2 210 FP86
Inville Rd, SE17 43 M1
Inwen Ct, SE8 45 M1
Inwood Av, Couls. CR5 257 DN120
Hounslow TW3 178 CC83
Inwood Cl, Croy. CR0 225 DY103
Inwood Ct, Walt. KT12 218 BW103
Inwood Ho, SE22
off Pytchley Rd 184 DS83
Inwood Rd, Houns. TW3 178 CB84
Inworth St, SW11 40 D8
Inworth Wk, N1 9 J8
● IO Cen, SE18
off Armstrong Rd 187 EQ76
Barking IG11 167 ET70
Hatfield AL10 66 CS16
Waltham Abbey EN9 105 EA35
Iona Cl, SE6 205 EA87
Morden SM4 222 DB101
Iona Cres, Slou. SL1 153 AL72
Ionian Bldg, E14 21 L10
Ionian Way, Hem.H. HP2
off Jupiter Dr 62 BM18
Ionia Wk, Grav. DA12 213 GM90
Ion Sq, E2 20 C1
Ipswich Rd, SW17 202 DG93
Slough SL1 153 AN73
Ireland Cl, E6 25 J7
Ireland Pl, N22 121 DL52
Ireland Yd, EC4 19 H9
Irene Rd, SW6 39 J7
Orpington BR6 227 ET101
Stoke D'Abernon KT11 236 CA114
Ireton Av, Walt. KT12 217 BS103
Ireton Cl, N10 120 DG52
Ireton Pl, Grays RM17
off Russell Rd 192 GA77
Ireton St, E3 22 A4
Iris Av, Bex. DA5 208 EY85
Iris Cl, E6 25 H6
Croydon CR0 225 DX102
Pilgrim's Hatch CM15 130 FV43
Surbiton KT6 220 CM101
Iris Ct, Pnr. HA5 138 BW55
Iris Cres, Bexh. DA7 188 EZ79
Iris Path, Rom. RM3
off Clematis Cl 128 FJ52
Iris Rd, W.Ewell KT19 238 CP106
Iris Wk, Edg. HA8 off Ash Cl 118 CQ49
Irkdale Av, Enf. EN1 104 DT39
Iron Br Cl, NW10 140 CS64
Southall UB2 158 CC74
Ironbridge Rd N, Uxb. UB11 176 BN75
Ironbridge Rd S, West Dr. UB7 176 BN75
Iron Dr, Hert. SG13 54 DV08
Iron Mill La, Dart. DA1 189 FE84
Iron Mill Pl, SW18
off Garratt La 202 DB86
Dartford DA1 189 FF84
Iron Mill Rd, SW18 202 DB86
Ironmonger La, EC2 19 L9
Ironmonger Pas, EC1 19 K4
Ironmonger Row, EC1 19 K3
Ironmongers Pl, E14 34 B9
IRONS BOTTOM, Reig. RH2 288 DA142
Ironsbottom, Horl. RH6 290 DA146
Sidlow RH2 288 DB141
Ironside Cl, SE16 33 J4
Ironside Rd, Brent. TW8 179 CJ80

Irons Way, Rom. RM5 127 FC52
Iron Wks, E3 12 A8
Irvine Av, Har. HA3 139 CG55
Irvine Cl, E14 22 D6
N20 120 DE47
Irvine Gdns, S.Ock. RM15 171 FT72
Irvine Pl, Vir.W. GU25 214 AY99
Irvine Way, Orp. BR6 227 ET101
Irving Av, Nthlt. UB5 158 BX67
Irving Gro, SW9 42 C9
Irving Ms, N1 9 J5
Irving Rd, W14 26 D6
Irving St, WC2 29 P1
Irving Wk, Swans. DA10 212 FY87
Irving Way, NW9 141 CT57
Swanley BR8 229 FD96
Irwell Est, SE16
off Neptune St 32 G5
Irwin Av, SE18 187 ES80
Irwin Cl, Uxb. UB10 136 BN62
Irwin Gdns, NW10 161 CV67
Irwin Rd, Guil. GU2 280 AU135
Isaac Way, SE1 31 K4
Isabel Ct, Hodd. EN11 71 EB15
Isabel Gate, Chshl EN8 89 DZ26
Isabel Hill Cl, Hmptn. TW12
off Upper Sunbury Rd 218 CB95
Isabella Cl, N14 121 DJ45
Isabella Ct, Rich. TW10
off Grove Rd 200 CM86
Isabella Dr, Orp. BR6 245 EQ105
Isabella Ms, N1 9 N4
Isabella Pl, Kings.T. KT2 200 CM92
Isabella Rd, E9 11 H3
Isabella St, SE1 30 G3
Isabelle Cl, Goffs Oak EN7 88 DQ29
Isabel St, SW9 42 D6
Isambard Ms, E14 34 F7
Isambard Pl, SE16 33 H3
Isbell Gdns, Rom. RM1 127 FE52
Isbells Dr, Reig. RH2 288 DB135
Isel Way, SE22
off East Dulwich Gro 204 DS85
Isenburg Way, Hem.H. HP2 62 BK15
Isham Rd, SW16 223 DL96
Isis Cl, SW15 181 CW84
Ruislip HA4 137 BQ58
Isis Dr, Upmin. RM14 151 FS58
Isis Ho, Cher. KT16
off Bridge Wf 216 BJ101
● Isis Reach, Belv. DA17 169 FB74
Isis St, SW18 202 DC89
Sch Islamia Prim Sch, NW6 4 F8
Coll Islamic Coll for Advanced Studies, NW10
off High Rd 161 CV65
Island, The, West Dr. UB7 176 BH81
Wraysbury TW19 195 BA90
Island Cen Way, Enf. EN3 105 EA37
Island Cl, Stai. TW18 195 BE91
Island Fm Av, W.Mol. KT8 218 BZ99
Island Fm Rd, W.Mol. KT8 218 BZ99
DLR Island Gardens 34 E9
Island Ho, E3 22 E2
Island Rd, SE16 33 J9
Mitcham CR4 202 DF94
Island Row, E14 21 N9
Isla Rd, SE18 187 EQ79
Islay Gdns, Houns. TW4 198 BX85
Islay Wk, N1 9 K5
Isledon Rd, N7 143 DN62
Islehurst Cl, Chis. BR7 227 EN95
Islet Pk, Maid. SL6 152 AC68
Islet Pk Dr, Maid. SL6 152 AC68
ISLEWORTH, TW7 179 CF83
⇌ Isleworth 179 CF82
Sch Isleworth & Syon Sch for Boys, Islw. TW7 off Ridgeway Rd 179 CE80
● Isleworth Business Complex, Islw. TW7 off St. John's Rd 179 CF82
Isleworth Prom, Twick. TW1 179 CH84
Sch Isleworth Town Prim Sch, Islw. TW7 off Twickenham Rd 179 CG82
ISLINGTON, N1 8 E9
Sch Islington Arts & Media Sch, N4 off Turle Rd 143 DM60
Coll Islington City Learning Cen, N5 9 J3
Islington Grn, N1 8 G9
Islington High St, N1 18 F1
Islington Pk Ms, N1 8 G6
Islington Pk St, N1 8 F6
Islip Gdns, Edg. HA8 118 CR52
Northolt UB5 158 BY66
Islip Manor Rd, Nthlt. UB5 158 BY66
Islip St, NW5 7 L3
Ismailia Rd, E7 166 EH66
★ Ismaili Cen, SW7 28 B8
Isom Cl, E13 24 B3
Issa Rd, Houns. TW3 178 BZ84
Issigonis Ho, W3
off Cowley Rd 161 CT74
ISTEAD RISE, Grav. DA13 212 GE94
Istead Ri, Grav. DA13 213 GF94
Sch Italia Conti Acad of Thea Arts, EC1 19 J5
Coll Italia Conti Arts Cen, Guil. GU1 off Epsom Rd 265 BD133
Itchingwood Common Rd, Oxt. RH8 276 EJ133
Ivanhoe Cl, Uxb. UB8 156 BK71
Ivanhoe Dr, Har. HA3 139 CG55
Ivanhoe Rd, SE5 184 DT83
Hounslow TW4 178 BX83
Ivatt Pl, W14 39 H1
Ivatt Way, N17 143 DP55
Iveagh Av, NW10 160 CN68
Iveagh Cl, E9 11 K8
NW10 160 CN68
Northwood HA6 115 BP53
Iveagh Ct, Hem.H. HP2 62 BK19
Iveagh Rd, Guil. GU2 280 AV135
Woking GU21 248 AT118
Iveagh Ter, NW10
off Iveagh Av 160 CN68
Ivedon Rd, Well. DA16 188 EW82
Ive Fm Cl, E10 145 EA61
Ive Fm La, E10 145 EA61
Iveley Rd, SW4 41 L9
IVER, SL0 155 BF72
⇌ Iver 175 BF75
Iverdale Cl, Iver SL0 155 BC73
Ivere Dr, New Barn. EN5 102 DB44
IVER HEATH, Iver SL0 155 BD69
Sch Iver Heath Inf Sch & Nurs, Iver SL0 off Slough Rd 155 BD69
Sch Iver Heath Jun Sch, Iver SL0 off St. Margarets Cl 155 BD68
Iverhurst Cl, Bexh. DA6 208 EX85
Iver La, Iver SL0 156 BH71
Uxbridge UB8 156 BH71
Iverna Ct, W8 27 K6
Iverna Gdns, W8 27 K6
Feltham TW14 197 BR85
Iver Rd, Iver SL0 156 BG72
Pilgrim's Hatch CM15 130 FV44
Iverson Rd, NW6 5 H5
Ivers Way, New Adgtn CR0 243 EB108
Sch Iver Village Inf Sch, Iver SL0 off West Sq 155 BF72
Sch Iver Village Jun Sch, Iver SL0 off High St 155 BE72
Ives Gdns, Rom. RM1
off Sims Cl 149 FF56
Ives Rd, E16 23 J7
Hertford SG14 53 DP08
Slough SL3 175 AZ76
Ives St, SW3 28 D8
Ivestor Ter, SE23 204 DW87
Ivimey St, E2 20 D2
Ivinghoe Cl, Enf. EN1 104 DS40
St. Albans AL4
off Highview Gdns 65 CJ15
Watford WD25 98 BX35
Ivinghoe Rd, Bushey WD23 117 CD45
Dagenham RM8 148 EV64
Mill End WD3 114 BG45
Ivins Rd, Beac. HP9 110 AG54
Ivor Cl, Guil. GU1 281 AZ135
Ivor Gro, SE9 207 EP88
Ivor Pl, NW1 16 E5
Ivor St, NW1 7 L7
Ivory Cl, St.Alb. AL4 65 CJ22
Ivory Ct, Felt. TW13 197 BU88
Hemel Hempstead HP3 62 BL23
Ivorydown, Brom. BR1 206 EG91
Ivory Sq, SW11
off Gartons Way 182 DC83
Ivy Bower Cl, Green. DA9
off Riverview Rd 211 FV85
Ivybridge, Brox. EN10 71 EA19
Ivybridge Cl, Twick. TW1 199 CG86
Uxbridge UB8 156 BL69
Ivybridge Est, Islw. TW7 199 CF85
Ivybridge Ho, SE22
off Pytchley Rd 184 DS83
Ivybridge La, WC2 30 B1
Sch Ivybridge Prim Sch, Islw. TW7
off Summerwood Rd 199 CF86
IVY CHIMNEYS, Epp. CM16 91 ES32
Sch Ivy Chimneys Prim Sch, Epp. CM16
off Ivy Chimneys Rd 91 ET32
Ivy Chimneys Rd, Epp. CM16 91 ES32
Ivychurch Cl, SE20 204 DW94
Ivychurch La, SE17 32 A10
Ivy Cl, Chesh. HP5 76 AP30
Dartford DA1 210 FN87
Gravesend DA12 213 GJ90
Harrow HA2 138 BZ63
Pinner HA5 138 BW59
Sunbury-on-Thames TW16 218 BW96
Ivy Cotts, E14 22 D10
Ivy Ct, SE16 44 D1
Ivy Cres, W4 180 CQ77
Slough SL1 153 AM73
Sch Ivydale Prim Sch, SE15
off Ivydale Rd 185 DX84
Ivydale Rd, SE15 185 DX83
Carshalton SM5 222 DF103
Ivyday Gro, SW16 203 DM90
Ivydene, W.Mol. KT8 218 BZ99
Ivydene Cl, Red. RH1 289 DH139
Sutton SM1 240 DC105
Ivy Gdns, N8 143 DL58
Mitcham CR4 223 DK97
Ivy Ho La, Berk. HP4 60 AY19
Sevenoaks TN14 263 FD118
Ivyhouse Rd, Dag. RM9 168 EX65
Ivy Ho Rd, Uxb. UB10 137 BP62
Ivy La, Houns. TW4 178 BZ84
Knockholt Pound TN14 262 EY116
Woking GU22 249 BB118
Ivy Lea, Rick. WD3
off Springwell Av 114 BG46
Ivy Lo La, Rom. RM3 128 FP53
Ivy Mill Cl, Gdse. RH9 274 DV132
Ivy Mill La, Gdse. RH9 274 DU132
Ivymount Rd, SE27 203 DN90
Ivy Rd, E16 23 N8
E17 145 EA58
N14 121 DJ45
NW2 141 CW63
SE4 185 DZ84
SW17 off Tooting High St 202 DE92
Hounslow TW3 178 CB84
Surbiton KT6 220 CN102
Ivy St, N1 9 N10
Ivy Ter, Hodd. EN11 71 EC15
Ivy Wk, Dag. RM9 168 EY65
Hatfield AL10 66 CS15
Ixworth Pl, SW3 28 C10
Izane Rd, Bexh. DA6 188 EZ84

J

Jacaranda Cl, N.Mal. KT3 220 CS97
Jacaranda Gro, E8 10 B7
Sch Jack & Jill Sch, Hmptn. TW12 off Nightingale Rd 198 CA93
Jackass La, Kes. BR2 244 EH107
Tandridge RH8 275 DZ131
Jack Barnett Way, N22 121 DM54
Jack Clow Rd, E15 23 K1
Jack Cornwell St, E12 147 EN63
Jack Dash Way, E6 24 G5
Jackdaws, Welw.G.C. AL7 52 DC09
Jackets La, Hare. UB9 114 BN52
Northwood HA6 115 BP53
Jacketts Fld, Abb.L. WD5 81 BT31
Jack Goodchild Way, Kings.T. KT1 off Kingston Rd 220 CP97
Jacklin Grn, Wdf.Grn. IG8 124 EG49
Jackman Ms, NW2 140 CS62
Jackmans La, Wok. GU21 248 AU119
Jackman St, E8 10 E9
JACKS HATCH, Epp. CM16 73 EN21
Jacks La, Hare. UB9 114 BG53
Jackson Cl, E9 11 H7
Epsom KT18 238 CR114
Greenhithe DA9
off Cowley Av 211 FU85
Hornchurch RM11 150 FM56
Slough SL3 174 AY76
Jackson Ct, E11
off Brading Cres 146 EH60
Dagenham RM10
off St. Mark's Pl 168 FA65
Jackson Rd, N7 8 D1
Barking IG11 167 ER67
Barnet EN4 102 DE44
Bromley BR2 226 EL103
Jacksons Dr, Chshl EN7 88 DU28
Jacksons La, N6 142 DG59
Jacksons Pl, Croy. CR0
off Cross Rd 224 DR102
Jackson St, SE18 187 EN79
Jacksons Way, Croy. CR0 225 EA104
Jackson Way, Epsom KT19
off Lady Harewood Way 238 CN109
Southall UB2 178 CB75
Jack Stevens Cl, Harl. CM17
off Potter St 74 EW17
Sch Jack Taylor Sch, NW8 5 N8
Sch Jack Tizard Sch, W12
off South Africa Rd 161 CV74
Jack Walker Ct, N5 9 H1
Jacob Cl, Wind. SL4 173 AL81
Jacob Ct, Enf. EN3
off Baddeley Cl 105 EA37
Jacob Ho, Erith DA18
off Kale Rd 188 EX75
Jacob Ms, Stan. HA7 117 CG47
Jacobs Av, Harold Wd RM3 128 FL54
Jacobs Cl, Dag. RM10 149 FB62
Jacobs Ho, E13 24 C2
Jacobs Ladder, Hat. AL9
off The Broadway 67 CW18
Jacobs La, Hort.Kir. DA4 230 FQ97
Jacob St, SE1 32 B4
JACOBS WELL, Guil. GU4 264 AY129
Jacob's Well Ms, W1 17 H8
Jacob's Well Rd, Jacobs Well GU4 264 AX129
Jacqueline Cl, Nthlt. UB5 158 BY67
Jade Cl, E16 24 F9
NW2 141 CX59
Dagenham RM8 148 EW60
Jaffe Rd, Ilf. IG1 147 EQ60
Jaffray Pl, SE27
off Chapel Rd 203 DP91
Jaffray Rd, Brom. BR2 226 EK98
Jaggard Way, SW12 202 DF87
Jagger Cl, Dart. DA2 210 FQ87
Jago Cl, SE18 187 EQ79
Jago Wk, SE5 43 L5
Jail La, Bigg.H. TN16 260 EK116
Jake's Vw, Park St AL2 82 CC27
Sch Jamahiriya Sch, SW3 40 C2
Jamaica Rd, SE1 32 B5
SE16 32 E6
Thornton Heath CR7 223 DP100
Jamaica St, E1 21 H8
Sch James Allen's Girls' Sch, SE22
off East Dulwich Gro 204 DS85
Sch James Allen's Prep Sch, Pre-Prep Sch, SE21
off Dulwich Village 204 DR86
Mid Sch, SE22
off East Dulwich Gro 204 DS85
James Av, NW2 4 B2
Dagenham RM8 148 EZ60
James Bedford Cl, Pnr. HA5 116 BW54
James Boswell Cl, SW16
off Samuel Johnson Cl 203 DN91
James Clavell Sq, SE18 37 P6
James Cl, E13 13 P10
NW11 off Woodlands 141 CY58
Bushey WD23 98 BY43
Romford RM2 149 FG57
James Collins Cl, W9 14 G5
James Ct, N1 9 K7
Sch James Dixon Prim Sch, SE20
off William Booth Rd 224 DU95
James Dudson Ct, NW10 160 CQ66
Sch James Elliman Prim Sch, Slou. SL2 off Elliman Av 154 AT73
James Gdns, N22 121 DP52
James Hammett Ho, E2 20 B1
James Joyce Wk, SE24
off Shakespeare Rd 183 DP84
James La, E10 145 ED59
E11 145 ED58
James Lee Sq, Enf. EN3
off Harston Dr 105 EA38
James Martin Cl, Denh. UB9 136 BG58
James Meadow, Slou. SL3 175 AZ79
James Newman Ct, SE9
off Great Harry Dr 207 EN90
Sch James Oglethorpe Prim Sch, The, Upmin. RM14
off Ashvale Gdns 151 FT61
Jameson Cl, W3 off Acton La 180 CQ75
Jameson Ct, E2 20 G1
St. Albans AL1
off Avenue Rd 65 CF19
Jameson Ho, SE11
off Glasshouse Wk 30 C10
Jameson St, W8 27 K2
James Pl, N17 122 DT53
James Riley Pt, E15 12 F8
James Rd, Dart. DA1 209 FG87
Peasmarsh GU3 280 AW142
James's Cotts, Rich. TW9 180 CN80
James St, W1 17 H8
WC2 18 B10
Barking IG11 167 EQ66
Enfield EN1 104 DT43
Epping CM16 91 ET28
Hounslow TW3 179 CD83
Windsor SL4 173 AR81
James Ter, SW14
off Mullins Path 180 CR83
Jamestown Rd, NW1 7 J8
Jamestown Way, E14 35 H1
James Voller Way, E1 20 G9
James Watt Way, Erith DA8 189 FE79
James Way, Wat. WD19 116 BX49
Sch James Wolfe Prim Sch, SE10 46 E4
James Yd, E4 123 ED51
Jamieson Ho, Houns. TW4 198 BZ87
Jamnagar Cl, Stai. TW18 195 BF93
Jamuna Cl, E14 21 M7
Jane Cl, Hem.H. HP2 63 BP15
Jane Seymour Ct, SE9
off Avery Hill Rd 207 ER87
Jane St, E1 20 E8
Janet St, E14 34 B6
Janeway Pl, SE16 32 E5
Janeway St, SE16 32 D5
Janice Ms, Ilf. IG1
off Oakfield Rd 147 EP62
Janmead, Hutt. CM13 131 GB45
Janoway Hill La, Wok. GU21 248 AW119
Jansen Wk, SW11 off Hope St 182 DD84
Janson Cl, E15 13 J2
NW10 140 CR62
Janson Rd, E15 13 J2
Jansons Rd, N15 144 DS55
Japan Cres, N4 143 DM60
Sch Japanese Sch, The, W3
off Creffield Rd 160 CN73
Japan Rd, Rom. RM6 148 EX58
Japonica Cl, Wok. GU21 248 AW118
Jardine Rd, E1 21 K10
Jarman Cl, Hem.H. HP3 62 BL22
Jarman Ho, E1 20 G7
🔒 Jarman Pk, Hem.H. HP2 62 BM21
Jarman Way, Hem.H. HP2 62 BM21
Jarrah Cotts, Purf. RM19 191 FR79
Jarrett Cl, SW2 203 DP88
Jarrow Cl, Mord. SM4 222 DB99
Jarrow Rd, N17 144 DV56
SE16 32 G9
Romford RM6 148 EW58
Jarrow Way, E9 11 M1
Jarvis Cleys, Chshl EN7 88 DT26
Jarvis Cl, Bark. IG11
off Westbury Rd 167 ER67
Barnet EN5 101 CX43
Jarvis Rd, SE22
off Melbourne Gro 184 DS84
South Croydon CR2 242 DR107
Jarvis Way, Harold Wd RM3 128 FL54
Jasmin Cl, Nthwd. HA6 115 BT53
Jasmine Cl, Ilf. IG1 147 EP64
Orpington BR6 227 EP103
Redhill RH1
off Spencer Way 288 DG139
Southall UB1 158 BY73
Woking GU21 248 AT116
Jasmine Dr, Hert. SG13 54 DU09
Jasmine Gdns, Croy. CR0 225 EB104
Harrow HA2 138 CA61
Hatfield AL10 67 CU16
Jasmine Gro, SE20 224 DV95
Jasmine Rd, Rush Grn RM7 149 FE61
Jasmine Sq, E3 11 N9
Jasmine Ter, West Dr. UB7 176 BN75
Jasmine Wk, Chesh. HP5 76 AN30
Jasmine Way, E.Mol. KT8
off Hampton Ct Way 219 CE98
Jasmin Rd, Epsom KT19 238 CP106
Jasmin Way, Hem.H. HP1
off Larkspur Cl 61 BE19
Jason Cl, Brwd. CM14 130 FT49
Redhill RH1 288 DE139
Weybridge KT13 235 BQ106
Jason Ct, W1
off Marylebone La 17 H8
Jasons Dr, Guil. GU4 265 BC131
Jasons Hill, Chesh. HP5 78 AV30
Jason Wk, SE9 207 EN91
Jasper Cl, Enf. EN3 104 DW38
Jasper Pas, SE19 204 DT93
Jasper Rd, E16 24 F9
SE19 204 DT92
Jasper Wk, N1 19 L2
Javelin Way, Nthlt. UB5 158 BX69
Jaycroft, Enf. EN2
off The Ridgeway 103 DN39
Jay Gdns, Chis. BR7 207 EM91
Jay Ms, SW7 27 P5
Jays Cl, Brick.Wd AL2 82 CA31
Jays Covert, Couls. CR5 256 DG119
Jazzfern Ter, Wem. HA0
off Maybank Av 139 CG64
Jean Batten Cl, Wall. SM6 241 DM108
Jebb Av, SW2 203 DL86
Jebb St, E3 22 B1
Jedburgh Rd, E13 24 C2
Jedburgh St, SW11 182 DG84
Jeddo Rd, W12 181 CT75
Jeeva Mans, N16
off Shacklewell La 10 B1
Jefferson Cl, W13 179 CH76
Ilford IG2 147 EP57
Slough SL3 175 BA77
Jefferson Wk, SE18
off Kempt St 187 EN79
Jeffreys Pl, NW1 7 L6
Jeffreys Rd, SW4 42 A8
Enfield EN3 105 DZ41
Jeffreys St, NW1 7 K6
Jeffreys Wk, SW4 42 A8
Jeffries Ho, NW10 160 CQ67
Jeffries Pas, Guil. GU1
off High St 280 AX135
Jeffries Rd, Ware SG12 55 DY06
West Horsley KT24 267 BQ130
Jeffs Cl, Hmptn. TW12 198 CB93
Jeffs Rd, Sutt. SM1 239 CZ105
Coll Jeff Wooller Coll, WC1 18 B6
Jeger Av, E2 10 A9
Jeken Rd, SE9 186 EJ84
Jelf Rd, SW2 203 DN85
Jellicoe Av, Grav. DA12 213 GJ90
Jellicoe Av W, Grav. DA12
off Kitchener Av 213 GJ90
Jellicoe Cl, Slou. SL1 173 AP75
Jellicoe Gdns, Stan. HA7 117 CF51
Jellicoe Ho, SW8
off St. George Wf 42 A2
Jellicoe Rd, E13 23 P5
N17 122 DR52
Watford WD18 97 BU44
Jemma Knowles Cl, SW2
off Neil Wates Cres 203 DN88
Jemmett Cl, Kings.T. KT2 220 CP95
Jengar Cl, Sutt. SM1 240 DB105
Jenkins Av, Brick.Wd AL2 82 BY30
Jenkins Cl, Nthflt DA11 213 GF90
Jenkins La, E6 25 M1
Barking IG11 25 P1
Jenkinson Ho, E2 off Usk St 21 J2
Jenkins Rd, E13 24 B5
Jenner Av, W3 160 CR71
Jenner Cl, Sid. DA14 208 EU91
Jenner Pl, SW13 181 CV79
Jenner Rd, N16 144 DT61
Guildford GU1 280 AY135
Jenner Way, Epsom KT19
off Monro Pl 238 CN109
Jennery La, Burn. SL1 152 AJ69
Jennett Rd, Croy. CR0 223 DN104
Jennifer Rd, Brom. BR1 206 EF90
Jennings Cl, Long Dit. KT6 219 CJ101
New Haw KT15
off Woodham La 234 BJ109
Jennings Fld, Flack.Hth HP10 132 AC56
Jennings Rd, SE22 204 DT86
St. Albans AL1 65 CG19
Jennings Way, Barn. EN5 101 CW41
Hemel Hempstead HP3 62 BL22
Horley RH6 291 DK148
Jenningtree Rd, Erith DA8 189 FH80
Jenningtree Way, Belv. DA17 189 FC75
Jenny Hammond Cl, E11
off Newcomen Rd 146 EF62
Sch Jenny Hammond Prim Sch, E11 off Worsley Rd 146 EE63
Jenny Path, Rom. RM3 128 FK52
Jennys Way, Couls. CR5 257 DJ122
Jenson Way, SE19 204 DT94
Jenton Av, Bexh. DA7 188 EY81
Jephson Rd, E7 166 EJ66
Jephson St, SE5 43 L7
Jephtha Rd, SW18 202 DA86
Jeppos La, Mitch. CR4 222 DF98
Jepps Cl, Chshl EN7 88 DS27
Jepson Ho, SW6
off Pearscroft Rd 39 M7
Jerdan Pl, SW6 39 K4
Jeremiah Ct, Red. RH1 273 DJ131
Jeremiah St, E14 22 C9
Jeremys Grn, N18 122 DV49
Jermyn St, SW1 29 L2
Jernigham Av, Ilf. IG5 125 EP54
Jerningham Rd, SE14 45 L6
Jerome Cres, NW8 16 C4
Jerome Dr, St.Alb. AL3 64 CA22
Jerome Pl, Kings.T. KT1
off Wadbrook St 219 CK96
Jerome St, E1 20 A6
Jerome Twr, W3 180 CP75
Jerounds, Harl. CM19 73 EP17
Sch Jerounds Comm Inf Sch, Harl. CM19 off Pyenest Rd 73 EP18
Sch Jerounds Comm Jun Sch, Harl. CM19 off Pyenest Rd 73 EP18
Jerrard St, N1 19 P1
SE13 46 D10
Jersey Av, Stan. HA7 117 CH54
Jersey Cl, Cher. KT16 215 BF104
Guildford GU4
off Weybrook Dr 265 BB129
Hoddesdon EN11 71 EA16
Jersey Dr, Petts Wd BR5 227 ER100
JERSEY FARM, St.Alb. AL4 65 CJ15
Jersey Ho, N1 9 K5
Enfield EN3
off Eastfield Rd 105 DX38
Jersey La, St.Alb. AL4 65 CH18
Jersey Par, Houns. TW5 178 CB81
Jersey Rd, E11 145 ED60
E16 24 C8
SW17 203 DH93
W7 179 CG75
Hounslow TW3, TW5 178 CB81
Ilford IG1 147 EP63
Isleworth TW7 179 CE79
Rainham RM13 169 FG66
Jersey St, E2 20 F3
Jerusalem Pas, EC1 18 G5
Jervis Av, Enf. EN3 105 DY35
Jervis Ct, W1 17 K9
Jervis Rd, SW6 39 H3
Jerviston Gdns, SW16 203 DN93
Jesmond Av, Wem. HA9 160 CM65
Jesmond Cl, Mitch. CR4 223 DH97
Jesmond Rd, Croy. CR0 224 DT101
Jesmond Way, Stan. HA7 118 CL50
Jessam Av, E5 144 DV60
Jessamine Pl, Dart. DA2 210 FQ87
Jessamine Rd, W7 159 CE74
Jessamy Rd, Wey. KT13 217 BP103
Jessel Dr, Loug. IG10 107 EQ39
Jessel Ho, SW1 off Page St 29 P8
Jesse Rd, E10 145 EC60
Jesses La, Peasl. GU5 283 BQ144
Jessett Cl, Erith DA8
off West St 189 FD77
Jessica Rd, SW18 202 DC86
Jessie Blythe La, N19 143 DL59
Jessiman Ter, Shep. TW17 216 BN99
Jessop Av, Sthl. UB2 178 BZ77
Jessop Ct, N1 off Graham St 19 H1
Sch Jessop Prim Sch, SE24
off Lowden Rd 184 DQ84
Jessop Rd, SE24
off Milkwood Rd 183 DP84
Jessop Sq, E14 34 A3
Jessops Way, Croy. CR0 223 DJ100
Jessup Cl, SE18 187 EQ77
Jethou Ho, N1
off Nightingale Rd 9 K5
Jetstar Way, Nthlt. UB5 158 BY69
Jetty Wk, Grays RM17 192 GA79
Jevington Way, SE12 206 EH88
Jewel Rd, E17 145 EA55
Jewels Hill, Bigg.H. TN16 244 EG112
★ Jewel Twr (Hos of Parliament), SW1 30 A6
★ Jewish Mus, NW1 7 J9
Jewry St, EC3 20 A9
Jew's Row, SW18 182 DB84
Jews Wk, SE26 204 DV91
Jeymer Av, NW2 141 CV64
Jeymer Dr, Grnf. UB6 158 CC67
Jeypore Pas, SW18
off Jeypore Rd 202 DC86
Jeypore Rd, SW18 202 DC87
Sch JFS, Har. HA3 off The Mall 140 CN58
Jigger Mast Ho, SE18 37 K6
Jillian Cl, Hmptn. TW12 198 CA94
Jim Bradley Cl, SE18 37 M8
Jim Desormeaux Bungalows, Harl. CM20 off School La 57 ES13
Jim Griffiths Ho, SW6
off Clem Attlee Ct 39 H3
Jim O'Neill Wk, Ruis. HA4
off Sidmouth Dr 137 BU62
Jim Veal Dr, N7 8 B4
Jinnings, The, Welw.G.C. AL7 52 DA12
Joan Cres, SE9 206 EK87
Joan Gdns, Dag. RM8 148 EY61
Joan Rd, Dag. RM8 148 EY61
Joan St, SE1 30 G3
Jocelyn Rd, Rich. TW9 180 CL83
Jocelyns, Harl. CM17 58 EW11
Jocelyn St, SE15 44 C6

Jocketts Hill, Hem.H. HP1 . . . . . 61 BF20
Jocketts Rd, Hem.H. HP1 . . . . . . 61 BF21
Jockey's Flds, WC1 . . . . 18 D6
Jodane St, SE8 . . . . 33 N9
Jodies Ct, St.Alb. AL4 . . . . 65 CJ18
Jodrell Cl, Islw. TW7 . . . . 179 CG81
Jodrell Rd, E3 . . . . 11 P8
Jodrell Way, W.Thur. RM20 . . . 191 FT78
Joel St, Nthwd. HA6 . . . . 137 BU55
Pinner HA5 . . . . 137 BU55
Sch Johanna Prim Sch, SE1 . . . . 30 E5
Johanna St, SE1 . . . . 30 E5
John Adam St, WC2 . . . . 30 B2
John Aird Ct, W2 . . . . 15 P6
John Archer Way, SW18 . . . . . . 202 DD86
John Ashby Cl, SW2 . . . . 203 DL86
John Austin Cl, Kings.T. KT2
off Queen Elizabeth Rd 220 CM95
Sch John Ball Prim Sch, SE3 . . . 47 K9
John Barnes Wk, E15 . . . . 13 L4
Sch John Betts Prim Sch, W6
off Paddenswick Rd 181 CV76
John Bradshaw Rd, N14 . . . . . . 121 DK46
Sch John Bramston Prim Sch,
Ilf. IG6 *off Newcastle Av* . . . 126 EU51
John Burns Dr, Bark. IG11 . . . . 167 ES66
Sch John Burns Prim Sch, SW11 . 41 H9
Johnby Cl, Enf. EN3 . . . . 105 DY37
John Campbell Rd, N16 . . . . 9 P3
John Carpenter St, EC4 . . . . 18 G10
Sch John Chiltern Sch, Nthlt.
UB5 *off Compton Cres* 158 BY67
John Cobb Rd, Wey. KT13 . . . . 234 BN108
John Cornwell VC Ho, E12 . . . . 147 EN63
John Ct, Hodd. EN11
off Molesworth 55 EA14
Sch John Donne Prim Sch,
SE15 . . . . 44 E7
John Drinkwater Cl, E11
off Browning Rd 146 EF59
John Eliot Cl, Lwr Naze. EN9 . . . 72 EE21
John Fearon Wk, W10 . . . . 14 F2
John Felton Rd, SE16 . . . . 32 C5
Sch John Fisher Sch, The, Pur.
CR8 *off Peaks Hill* 241 DL110
John Fisher St, E1 . . . . 20 C10
Sch John F. Kennedy Post 16
(Beckton) Annexe, E16 . . . . . 24 E6
Sch John F. Kennedy RC Sch, Hem.H.
HP1 *off Hollybush La* 61 BF19
Sch John F. Kennedy Sch, E15 . . 13 H8
John Gale Ct, Ewell KT17
off West St 239 CT109
John Gooch Dr, Enf. EN2 . . . . . 103 DP39
John Harrison Ho, E1
off Philpot St 20 F8
John Harrison Way, SE10 . . . . . . 35 L7
John Horner Ms, N1 . . . . 9 J10
H John Howard Cen, E9 . . . . . . 11 K3
John Islip St, SW1 . . . . 30 A9
John Keats Ho, N22 . . . . 121 DM52
Sch John Keble C of E Prim Sch,
NW10 *off Crownhill Rd* 161 CT67
Sch John Kelly Boys' Tech Coll,
NW2 *off Crest Rd* 141 CU62
Sch John Kelly Girls' Tech Coll,
NW2 *off Crest Rd* 141 CU62
John Kennedy Ho, SE16 . . . . 33 H8
Sch John Loughborough Sch, The,
N17 *off Holcombe Rd* 122 DU54
Sch John Lyon Sch, The, Har.
HA2 *off Middle Rd* 139 CD60
John Maurice Cl, SE17 . . . . 31 L8
John McKenna Wk, SE16 . . . . . . 32 D6
John Mills Ct, Denh. UB9 . . . . . 135 BF58
John Newton Ct, Well. DA16 . . 188 EV83
John Parker Cl, Dag. RM10 . . . 169 FB66
John Parker Sq, SW11
off Thomas Baines Rd 182 DD83
Sch John Paul II RC Sch, SW19
off Princes Way 201 CX87
John Penn St, SE13 . . . . 46 D7
John Perrin Pl, Har. HA3 . . . . . 140 CL59
Sch John Perryn Prim Sch, W3
off Long Dr 160 CS72
Sch John Perry Prim Sch, Dag.
RM10 *off Charles Rd* 169 FD65
John Princes St, W1 . . . . 17 K8
John Rennie Wk, E1 . . . . 32 F2
Sch John Roan Sch, The, SE3 . . . 47 K4
John Roll Way, SE16 . . . . 32 D6
Sch John Ruskin Prim Sch, SE5 . 43 J3
Coll John Ruskin 6th Form Coll,
S.Croy. CR2
off Selsdon Pk Rd 243 DY108
John Ruskin St, SE5 . . . . 42 G4
John Russell Cl, Guil. GU2 . . . . 264 AU131
Johns Av, NW4 . . . . 141 CW56
Johns Cl, Ashf. TW15 . . . . 197 BQ91
Sch John Scurr Prim Sch, E1 . . . 20 G5
Johnsdale, Oxt. RH8 . . . . 276 EF129
John Silkin La, SE8 . . . . 33 K9
Johns La, Mord. SM4 . . . . 222 DC99
John's Ms, WC1 . . . . 18 D5
John Smith Av, SW6 . . . . 38 G4
John Smith Ms, E14 . . . . 22 G10
Johnson Cl, E8 . . . . 10 C8
Northfleet DA11 . . . . 212 GD90
Johnson Ct, Hem.H. HP3 . . . . . . 62 BL22
Johnson Ho, E2 . . . . 20 D2
Johnson Rd, NW10 . . . . 160 CR67
Bromley BR2 . . . . 226 EK99
Croydon CR0 . . . . 224 DR101
Hounslow TW5 . . . . 178 BW80
Johnsons Av, Bad.Mt TN14 . . . 247 FB110
Johnsons Cl, Cars. SM5 . . . . . . 222 DF104
Johnson's Ct, EC4
off Fleet St 18 F9
Johnsons Ct, Seal TN15
off School La 279 FM121
Johnsons Dr, Hmptn. TW12 . . . 218 CC95
Johnson's Pl, SW1 . . . . 41 L1
Johnson St, E1 . . . . 21 H9
Southall UB2 . . . . 178 BW76
Johnsons Way, NW10 . . . . 160 CP70
Greenhithe DA9 . . . . 211 FW86
Johnsons Yd, Uxb. UB8
off Redford Way 156 BJ66
John Spencer Sq, N1 . . . . 9 H5
John's Pl, E1 . . . . 20 F8
Johns Rd, Tats. TN16 . . . . 260 EK120
Sch John Stainer Prim Sch,
SE4 *off St. Asaph Rd* 185 DY83
John's Ter, Croy. CR0 . . . . 224 DR102
Romford RM3 . . . . 128 FP51
Johnston Cl, SW9 . . . . 42 D7
Johnston Ct, E10
off Oliver Rd 145 EB62
Johnstone Rd, E6 . . . . 25 K3
Johnston Grn, Guil. GU2 . . . . . 264 AU130
Johnston Rd, Wdf.Grn. IG8 . . . 124 EG50
Johnston Ter, NW2
off Kara Way 141 CX62
Johnston Wk, Guil. GU2 . . . . . 264 AU130
John St, E15 . . . . 13 L9
SE25 . . . . 224 DU98
WC1 . . . . 18 D5
Enfield EN1 . . . . 104 DT43
Grays RM17 . . . . 192 GC79
Hounslow TW3 . . . . 178 BY82
Johns Wk, Whyt. CR3 . . . . 258 DU119
John's Way, S.Ock. RM15 . . . . 171 FX72
John Tate Rd, Hert. SG13 . . . . . 54 DT10
John Trundle Ct, EC2
off The Barbican 19 J6
John Walsh Twr, E11 . . . . 146 EF61
Sch John Warner Sch, The, Hodd.
EN11 *off Stanstead Rd* 55 EB14
John Watkin Cl, Epsom KT19 . . 238 CP109
John Wesley Cl, E6 . . . . 25 K2
John William Cl, Chaff.Hun.
RM16 . . . . 191 FX78
John Williams Cl, SE14 . . . . 45 J3
Kingston upon Thames KT2
off Henry Macaulay Av 219 CK95
John Wilson St, SE18 . . . . 37 L7
John Woolley Cl, SE13 . . . . 186 EE84
Joiner's Arms Yd, SE5 . . . . 43 L7
Joiners Cl, Chal.St.P. SL9 . . . . . 113 AZ52
Ley Hill HP5 . . . . 78 AV30
Joiners La, Chal.St.P. SL9 . . . . . 112 AY53
Joiners Pl, N5 . . . . 9 L1
Joiner St, SE1 . . . . 31 M3
Joiners Way, Chal.St.P. SL9 . . . 112 AY52
Joiners Yd, N1
off Caledonia St 18 B1
Joinville Pl, Add. KT15 . . . . . . 234 BK105
Jolles Ho, E3
off Bromley High St 22 D2
Jolliffe Rd, Red. RH1 . . . . 273 DJ126
Jollys La, Har. HA2 . . . . 139 CD60
Hayes UB4 . . . . 158 BX71
Jonathan Ct, W4
off Windmill Rd 180 CS77
Jonathan St, SE11 . . . . 30 C10
Jones Ho, N16
off Stamford Hill 144 DS60
Jones Rd, E13 . . . . 24 B5
Goffs Oak EN7 . . . . 87 DP30
Jones St, W1 . . . . 29 J1
Jones Wk, Rich. TW10
off Lower Gro Rd 200 CM86
Jones Way, Hedg. SL2 . . . . 133 AR61
Jonquil Cl, Welw.G.C. AL7 . . . . . 52 DB11
Jonquil Gdns, Hmptn. TW12
off Partridge Rd 198 CA93
Jonson Cl, Hayes UB4 . . . . 157 BU71
Mitcham CR4 . . . . 223 DH98
Jordan Cl, Har. HA2
off Hamilton Cres 138 BZ62
South Croydon CR2 . . . . 242 DT111
Watford WD25 . . . . 97 BT35
Jordan Ct, SW15
off Charlwood Rd 181 CX84
Jordan Rd, Perivale UB6 . . . . . 159 CH67
JORDANS, Beac. HP9 . . . . 112 AT52
Jordans Cl, Dag. RM10 . . . . 149 FB63
Guildford GU1
off Beatty Av 265 BA133
Isleworth TW7 . . . . 179 CE81
Redhill RH1 . . . . 288 DG139
Stanwell TW19 . . . . 196 BJ87
Jordans La, Jordans HP9 . . . . . . 112 AS53
Jordans Ms, Twick. TW2 . . . . . . 199 CE89
Jordans Rd, Rick. WD3 . . . . 114 BG45
Sch Jordans Sch, Jordans
HP9 *off Puers La* 112 AT51
Jordans Way, Brick.Wd AL2 . . . . 82 BZ30
Jordans HP9 . . . . 112 AT51
Rainham RM13 . . . . 170 FK68
Sch Jo Richardson Comm Sch,
The, Dag. RM9 *off Gale St* . 168 EX67
Joseph Av, W3 . . . . 160 CR72
Sch Joseph Clarke Sch, E4
off Vincent Rd 123 ED51
Joseph Conrad Ho, SW1
off Tachbrook St 29 M9
Joseph Hardcastle Cl, SE14 . . . . 45 K4
Sch Joseph Hood Prim Sch,
SW20 *off Whatley Av* 221 CY97
Josephine Av, SW2 . . . . 203 DM85
Lower Kingswood KT20 . . . . . 271 CZ126
Josephine Cl, Lwr Kgswd KT20 . 271 CZ127
Joseph Locke Way, Esher KT10 . 218 CA103
Joseph Powell Cl, SW12 . . . . . . 203 DJ86
Joseph Ray Rd, E11 . . . . 146 EE61
Joseph's Rd, Guil. GU1 . . . . 264 AX133
Joseph St, E3 . . . . 21 P5
Joseph Trotter Cl, EC1
off Myddelton St 18 F3
Joshua Cl, N10 . . . . 121 DH52
South Croydon CR2 . . . . 241 DP108
Joshua St, E14 . . . . 22 E8
Joshua Wk, Wal.Cr. EN8
off Longcroft Dr 89 EA34
Josling Cl, Grays RM17 . . . . . . 192 FZ79
Joslings Cl, W12 . . . . 161 CV73
Joslin Rd, Purf. RM19 . . . . 190 FQ78
Joslyn Cl, Enf. EN3 . . . . 105 EA38
Joubert St, SW11 . . . . 40 E8
Journeys End, Stoke P. SL2 . . . 154 AS71
Jowett St, SE15 . . . . 44 B5
Joyce Av, N18 . . . . 122 DT50
Joyce Ct, Wal.Abb. EN9 . . . . 89 ED34
Joyce Dawson Way, SE28
off Thamesmere Dr 168 EU73
🔒 Joyce Dawson Way Shop Arc,
SE28 *off Thamesmere Dr* . . . 168 EU73
Joyce Grn La, Dart. DA1 . . . . . . 190 FL81
Joyce Grn Wk, Dart. DA1 . . . . . 190 FM84
Joyce Lattimore Ct, N9
off Colthurst Dr 122 DV48
Joyce Page Cl, SE7 . . . . 186 EK79
Joyce Wk, SW2 . . . . 203 DN86
JOYDENS WOOD, Bex. DA5 . . . 209 FC92
Sch Joydens Wd Inf Sch, Bex.
DA5 *off Park Way* 209 FE90
Sch Joydens Wd Jun Sch, Wilm.
DA2 *off Birchwood Dr* 209 FE91
Joydens Wd Rd, Bex. DA5 . . . . 209 FD91
Joydon Dr, Rom. RM6 . . . . 148 EV58
Joyes Cl, Rom. RM3 . . . . 128 FK49
Joyners Cl, Dag. RM9 . . . . 148 EZ63
Joyners Fld, Harl. CM18 . . . . 73 EQ19
Joy Rd, Grav. DA12 . . . . 213 GJ88
Jubb Powell Ho, N15 . . . . 144 DS58
Jubilee Arch, Wind. SL4
off High St 173 AR81
Jubilee Av, E4 . . . . 123 EC51
London Colney AL2 . . . . 83 CK26
Romford RM7 . . . . 149 FB57
Twickenham TW2 . . . . 198 CC88
Ware SG12 . . . . 55 DZ05
Jubilee Cl, NW9 . . . . 140 CR58
NW10 . . . . 160 CS68
Greenhithe DA9 . . . . 211 FW86
Kingston upon Thames KT1
off High St 219 CJ95
Pinner HA5 . . . . 116 BW54
Romford RM7 . . . . 149 FB57
Stanwell TW19 . . . . 196 BJ87
Jubilee Ct, Hat. AL10 . . . . 67 CV15
Staines TW18 . . . . 196 BG91
Waltham Abbey EN9 . . . . 90 EF33
Jubilee Cres, E14 . . . . 34 F7
N9 . . . . 122 DU46
Addlestone KT15 . . . . 234 BK106
Gravesend DA12 . . . . 213 GL89
Jubilee Dr, Ruis. HA4 . . . . 138 BX63
★ Jubilee Gdns, SE1 . . . . 30 C3
Jubilee Gdns, Sthl. UB1 . . . . . . 158 CA72
Sch Jubilee High Sch, Add.
KT15 *off School La* 234 BG106
Sch Jubilee La, W5 *off Haven La* . 160 CL72
🔒 Jubilee Mkt Hall, WC2 . . . . . 18 B10
Jubilee Par, Wdf.Grn. IG8
off Snakes La E 124 EJ51
Jubilee Pl, SW3 . . . . 28 D10
Sch Jubilee Prim Sch, N16
off Filey Av 144 DU60
SE28 *off Crossway* 168 EW73
SW2 *off Tulse Hill* 203 DN86
Jubilee Ri, Seal TN15 . . . . 279 FM121
Jubilee Rd, Grays RM20 . . . . . . 191 FV79
Orpington BR6 . . . . 246 FA107
Perivale UB6 . . . . 159 CH67
Sutton SM3 . . . . 239 CX108
Watford WD24 . . . . 97 BU38
Jubilee St, E1 . . . . 20 G8
Jubilee Ter, Bet. RH3 . . . . 286 CP138
Dorking RH4 . . . . 285 CH135
Jubilee Trust, SE10
off Egerton Dr 46 D5
Jubilee Wk, Kings L. WD4 . . . . . 80 BN30
Watford WD19 . . . . 115 BV49
Jubilee Way, SW19 . . . . 222 DB95
Chessington KT9 . . . . 238 CN105
Datchet SL3 . . . . 174 AW80
Feltham TW14 . . . . 197 BT88
Sidcup DA14 . . . . 208 EU89
Judd Apts, N8
off Great Amwell La 143 DM55
Judd St, WC1 . . . . 18 A3
Jude St, E16 . . . . 23 L9
Judeth Gdns, Grav. DA12 . . . . . 213 GL92
Judge Heath La, Hayes UB3 . . . 157 BQ72
Uxbridge UB8 . . . . 157 BQ72
Judges Hill, Northaw EN6 . . . . . 86 DE29
Judge St, Wat. WD24 . . . . 97 BV38
Judge Wk, Clay. KT10 . . . . 237 CE107
Judith Av, Rom. RM5 . . . . 127 FB51
Juer St, SW11 . . . . 40 D5
Jug Hill, Bigg.H. TN16
off Hillcrest Rd 260 EK116
Juglans Rd, Orp. BR6 . . . . 228 EU102
Jules Thorn Av, Enf. EN1 . . . . . 104 DT41
Julia Gdns, Bark. IG11 . . . . 168 EX68
Julia Garfield Ms, E16 . . . . 36 B2
Juliana Cl, N2 . . . . 142 DC55
Julian Av, W3 . . . . 160 CP73
Julian Cl, New Barn. EN5 . . . . . 102 DB41
Woking GU21 . . . . 248 AW118
Julian Hill, Har. HA1 . . . . 139 CE61
Weybridge KT13 . . . . 234 BN108
Julian Ho, SE21
off Kingswood Est 204 DS91
Julian Pl, E14 . . . . 34 D10
Julian Rd, Orp. BR6 . . . . 246 EU107
Julians Cl, Sev. TN13 . . . . 278 FG127
Sch Julian's Prim Sch, SW16
off Leigham Ct Rd 203 DN91
Julians Way, Sev. TN13 . . . . 278 FG127
Julia Tayler Path, SE23 . . . . 204 DV89
Julia St, NW5 . . . . 6 G1
Julien Rd, W5 . . . . 179 CJ76
Coulsdon CR5 . . . . 257 DK115
Juliette Cl, Aveley RM15 . . . . . 190 FN75
Juliette Rd, E13 . . . . 23 M1
Juliette Way, Aveley RM15 . . . . 190 FM75
Julius Caesar Way, Stan. HA7 . 117 CK49
Julius Nyerere Cl, N1 . . . . 8 C9
🔒 Junction, The, Grays RM20 . 191 FT77
Junction App, SE13 . . . . 46 E10
SW11 . . . . 182 DE83
Junction Av, W10 . . . . 14 B3
Junction Ms, W2 . . . . 16 C8
Junction Pl, W2 . . . . 16 B8
Junction Rd, E13 . . . . 166 EH68
N9 . . . . 122 DU46
N17 . . . . 144 DU55
N19 . . . . 143 DJ63
W5 . . . . 179 CJ77
Ashford TW15 . . . . 197 BQ92
Brentford TW8 . . . . 179 CJ77
Dartford DA1 . . . . 210 FK86
Dorking RH4 . . . . 285 CG136
Harrow HA1 . . . . 139 CE58
Romford RM1 . . . . 149 FF56
South Croydon CR2 . . . . 242 DR106
Warley CM14 . . . . 130 FW49
Junction Rd E, Rom. RM6
off Kenneth Rd 148 EY59
Junction Rd W, Rom. RM6 . . . . 148 EY59
🔒 Junction Shop Cen, The,
SW11 *off St. John's Hill* . . . 182 DE84
🔒 Junction, Wembley Retail Pk,
The, Wem. HA9 . . . . 140 CP63
June Cl, Couls. CR5 . . . . 241 DH114
June La, Red. RH1 . . . . 289 DH141
Junewood Cl, Wdhm KT15 . . . . 233 BF111
Juniper Av, Brick.Wd AL2 . . . . . 82 CA31
Juniper Cl, Barn. EN5 . . . . 101 CX43
Biggin Hill TN16 . . . . 260 EL117
Broxbourne EN10 . . . . 89 DZ25
Chesham HP5 . . . . 76 AN30
Chessington KT9 . . . . 238 CM107
Guildford GU1 . . . . 264 AV129
Oxted RH8 . . . . 276 EH133
Reigate RH2 . . . . 288 DC136
Juniper Cl, Rick. WD3 . . . . 114 BK48
Wembley HA9 . . . . 140 CM64
Juniper Ct, Slou. SL1
off Nixey Cl 174 AU75
Juniper Cres, NW1 . . . . 7 H7
Juniper Dr, SW18 . . . . 182 DC84
Juniper Gdns, SW16
off Leonard Rd 223 DJ95
Shenley WD7 . . . . 84 CL33
Sunbury-on-Thames TW16 . . 197 BT93
Juniper Gate, Rick. WD3 . . . . . 114 BK47
Juniper Grn, Hem.H. HP1 . . . . . . 61 BE20
Juniper Gro, Wat. WD17 . . . . . . 97 BU38
Juniper La, E6 . . . . 25 H7
High Wycombe HP10 . . . . 132 AD56
Juniper Pl, Shalf. GU4 . . . . 280 AX141
Juniper Rd, Ilf. IG1 . . . . 147 EN63
Reigate RH2 . . . . 288 DC136
Juniper St, E1 . . . . 20 G10
Juniper Ter, Shalf. GU4 . . . . 280 AX141
Juniper Wk, Brock. RH3 . . . . . . 286 CQ136
Swanley BR8 . . . . 229 FD96
Juniper Way, Hayes UB3 . . . . . 157 BR73
Romford RM3 . . . . 128 FL53
Juno Ho, E3 *off Garrison Rd* . . 12 A9
Juno Rd, Hem.H. HP2
off Saturn Way 62 BM17
Juno Way, SE14 . . . . 45 K2
Jupiter Ct, Slou. SL1 . . . . 153 AL73
Jupiter Dr, Hem.H. HP2 . . . . 62 BM18
Sch Jupiter Dr Prim Sch, Hem.H.
HP2 *off Jupiter Dr* 62 BM18
Jupiter Way, N7 . . . . 8 D4
Jupp Rd, E15 . . . . 12 G7
Jupp Rd W, E15 . . . . 12 F8
Jury St, Grav. DA11
off Princes St 213 GH86
Justice Wk, SW3 . . . . 40 C3
Justin Cl, Brent. TW8 . . . . 179 CK80
Justines Pl, E2 . . . . 21 K2
Justin Rd, E4 . . . . 123 DZ51
Jute La, Enf. EN3 . . . . 105 DY40
Jutland Cl, N19 . . . . 143 DL60
Jutland Gdns, Couls. CR5 . . . . 257 DM120
Jutland Pl, Egh. TW20 . . . . 195 BC92
Jutland Rd, E13 . . . . 23 P5
SE6 . . . . 205 EC87
Jutsums Av, Rom. RM7 . . . . 149 FB58
Jutsums La, Rom. RM7 . . . . 149 FB58
Juxon Cl, Har. HA3
off Augustine Rd 116 CB53
Juxon St, SE11 . . . . 30 D8

K

Kaduna Cl, Pnr. HA5 . . . . 137 BU57
Sch Kaizen Prim Sch, E13 . . . . . . 24 A5
Kale Rd, Erith DA18 . . . . 188 EY75
Kambala Rd, SW11 . . . . 40 B9
Kandlewood, Hutt. CM13 . . . . . 131 GB45
Kangley Br Rd, SE26 . . . . 205 DZ93
Kaplan Dr, N21 . . . . 103 DL43
Kapuvar Cl, SE15 . . . . 44 D9
Kara Way, NW2 . . . . 141 CX63
Karen Cl, Brwd. CM15 . . . . 130 FW45
Rainham RM13 . . . . 169 FE68
Karen Ct, SE4 . . . . 45 P10
Bromley BR1 . . . . 226 EF95
Karen Ter, E11
off Montague Rd 146 EF61
Karenza Ct, Wem. HA9
off Lulworth Av 139 CJ59
Kariba Cl, N9 . . . . 122 DW48
Karina Cl, Chig. IG7 . . . . 125 ES50
Karma Way, Har. HA2 . . . . 138 CA60
Karoline Gdns, Grnf. UB6
off Oldfield La N 159 CD68
Kashgar Rd, SE18 . . . . 187 ET78
Kashmir Cl, New Haw KT15 . . . 234 BK109
Kashmir Rd, SE7 . . . . 186 EK80
Kassala Rd, SW11 . . . . 40 F7
● Katella Trd Est, Bark. IG11 . 167 ES69
Kates Cl, Barn. EN5 . . . . 101 CU43
Katescroft, Welw.G.C. AL7 . . . . . 51 CY13
Katharine St, Croy. CR0 . . . . . . 224 DQ104
Katherine Cl, SE16 . . . . 33 J3
Addlestone KT15 . . . . 234 BG107
Hemel Hempstead HP3 . . . . . . 62 BL23
Penn HP10 . . . . 110 AC47
Katherine Gdns, SE9 . . . . 186 EK84
Ilford IG6 . . . . 125 EQ52
Katherine Ms, Whyt. CR3 . . . . . 258 DT117
Katherine Pl, Abb.L. WD5 . . . . . . 81 BU32
Katherine Rd, E6 . . . . 166 EK66
E7 . . . . 146 EJ64
Twickenham TW1
off London Rd 199 CG88
KATHERINES, Harl. CM19 . . . . . 73 EM18
Katherines Hatch, Harl. CM19
off Brookside 73 EN17
Sch Katherines Prim Sch, Harl.
CM19 *off Brookside* 73 EN17
Katherine Sq, W11 . . . . 26 E2
Katherines Way, Harl. CM19 . . . 73 EN18
Kathleen Av, W3 . . . . 160 CQ71
Wembley HA0 . . . . 160 CL66
Kathleen Rd, SW11 . . . . 182 DF83
Katrine Sq, Hem.H. HP2 . . . . 62 BK16
Kavanaghs Rd, Brwd. CM14 . . . 130 FU48
Kavanaghs Ter, Brwd. CM14
off Kavanaghs Rd 130 FV48
Kaye Ct, Guil. GU1 . . . . 264 AW131
Kaye Don Way, Wey. KT13 . . . . 234 BN111
Kayemoor Rd, Sutt. SM2 . . . . . 240 DE108
Kay Rd, SW9 . . . . 42 B9
Kays Ter, E18 *off Walpole Rd* . 124 EF53
Kay St, E2 . . . . 10 D10
Welling DA16 . . . . 188 EV81
Kay Wk, St.Alb. AL4 . . . . 65 CK20
Kay Way, SE10 . . . . 46 D4
Kaywood Cl, Slou. SL3 . . . . 174 AW76
Kean St, WC2 . . . . 18 C9
Kearton Cl, Ken. CR8 . . . . 258 DQ117
Keary Rd, Swans. DA10 . . . . . . 212 FY87
Keate's La, Eton SL4 . . . . 173 AR79
Keatley Grn, E4 . . . . 123 DZ51
Keats Av, E16 . . . . 36 A2
Redhill RH1 . . . . 272 DG132
Romford RM3 . . . . 127 FH52
Keats Cl, E11
off Nightingale La 146 EH57
NW3 . . . . 6 C1
SE1 . . . . 32 A9
SW19 . . . . 202 DD93
Chigwell IG7 . . . . 125 EQ51
Enfield EN3 . . . . 105 DX43
Keats Cl, Hayes UB4 . . . . 157 BU71
Keats Gdns, Til. RM18 . . . . 193 GH82
Keats Gro, NW3 . . . . 6 B1
★ Keats Ho, NW3 . . . . 6 C1
Keats Ho, SW1 . . . . 41 M2
Beckenham BR3 . . . . 205 EA93
Keats Pl, EC2 . . . . 19 L7
Keats Rd, Belv. DA17 . . . . 189 FC76
Welling DA16 . . . . 187 ES81
Keats Wk, Hutt. CM13
off Byron Rd 131 GD45
Keats Way, Croy. CR0 . . . . 224 DW100
Greenford UB6 . . . . 158 CB71
West Drayton UB7 . . . . 176 BM77
Kebbell Ter, E7 . . . . 146 EH64
Keble Cl, Nthlt. UB5 . . . . 138 CC64
Worcester Park KT4 . . . . 221 CT102
Keble Pl, SW13
off Somerville Av 181 CV79
Sch Keble Sch, N21
off Wades Hill 121 DN45
Keble St, SW17 . . . . 202 DC91
Keble Ter, Abb.L. WD5 . . . . 81 BT32
Kechill Gdns, Brom. BR2 . . . . . 226 EG101
Kedelston Ct, E5
off Redwald Rd 145 DY63
Kedeston Ct, Sutt. SM1
off Hurstcourt Rd 222 DB102
Kedleston Dr, Orp. BR5 . . . . . . 227 ET100
Kedleston Wk, E2 . . . . 20 F2
Keedonwood Rd, Brom. BR1 . . 206 EE92
Keefield, Harl. CM19 . . . . 73 EP20
Keel Cl, SE16 . . . . 33 K3
Barking IG11 . . . . 168 EW68
Keel Ct, E14 *off Newport Av* . . 23 H10
Keel Dr, Slou. SL1 . . . . 173 AQ75
Keele Cl, Wat. WD24 . . . . 98 BW40
Keeler Cl, Wind. SL4 . . . . 173 AL83
Keeley Rd, Croy. CR0 . . . . 224 DQ103
Keeley St, WC2 . . . . 18 C9
Keeling Ho, E2 . . . . 20 E1
Keeling Rd, SE9 . . . . 206 EK85
Keely Cl, Barn. EN4 . . . . 102 DE43
Keemor Cl, SE18 . . . . 187 EN80
Keensacre, Iver SL0 . . . . 155 BD68
Keens Cl, SW16 . . . . 203 DK92
Keens La, Guil. GU3 . . . . 264 AT130
Keens Pk Rd, Guil. GU3 . . . . . . 264 AT130
Keens Rd, Croy. CR0 . . . . 242 DQ105
Sch Keen Students Sch, E1 . . . . 20 D6
Keens Yd, N1 . . . . 9 H5
Keep, The, SE3 . . . . 47 N9
Kingston upon Thames KT2 . 200 CM93
Keepers Cl, Guil. GU4 . . . . 265 BD131
Keepers Fm Cl, Wind. SL4 . . . . 173 AL82
Keepers Ms, Tedd. TW11 . . . . . 199 CJ93
Keepers Wk, Vir.W. GU25 . . . . . 214 AX99
Keep La, N11
off Gardeners Cl 120 DG47
Keetons Rd, SE16 . . . . 32 E6
Keevil Dr, SW19 . . . . 201 CX87
Keighley Cl, N7 . . . . 8 B1
Keighley Rd, Rom. RM3 . . . . . . 128 FL52
Keightley Dr, SE9 . . . . 207 EQ88
Keilder Cl, Uxb. UB10 . . . . 156 BN68
Keildon Rd, SW11 . . . . 182 DF84
Keir, The, SW19 . . . . 201 CW92
Keir Hardie Est, E5
off Springfield 144 DV60
Keir Hardie Ho, W6 . . . . 38 B2
Sch Keir Hardie Prim Sch, E16 . . 23 N7
Keir Hardie Way, Bark. IG11 . . . 168 EU66
Hayes UB4 . . . . 157 BU69
Keith Av, Sutt.H. DA4 . . . . 210 FP93
Keith Connor Cl, SW8 . . . . 41 J10
Keith Gro, W12 . . . . 181 CU75
Keith Pk Cres, Bigg.H. TN16 . . . 244 EH112
Keith Pk Rd, Uxb. UB10 . . . . . . 156 BM66
Keith Rd, E17 . . . . 123 DZ53
Barking IG11 . . . . 167 ER68
Hayes UB3 . . . . 177 BS76
Keiths Rd, Hem.H. HP3 . . . . 62 BN21
Keith Way, Horn. RM11 . . . . . . 150 FL59
Kelbrook Rd, SE3 . . . . 186 EL83
Kelburn Way, Rain. RM13
off Dominion Way 169 FG69
Kelby Path, SE9 . . . . 207 EP90
Kelbys, Welw.G.C. AL7 . . . . 52 DC08
Kelceda Cl, NW2 . . . . 141 CU61
Kelday Hts, E1 . . . . 20 F9
Kelf Gro, Hayes UB3 . . . . 157 BT72
Kelfield Gdns, W10 . . . . 14 B8
Kelfield Ms, W10 . . . . 14 C7
Kelland Cl, N8 . . . . 143 DK57
Kelland Rd, E13 . . . . 23 P4
Kellaway Rd, SE3 . . . . 186 EJ82
Keller Cres, E12 . . . . 146 EK63
Kellerton Rd, SE13 . . . . 206 EE85
Kellett Rd, SW2 . . . . 183 DN84
Kelling Gdns, Croy. CR0 . . . . . . 223 DP101
Kellino St, SW17 . . . . 202 DF91
Kellner Rd, SE28 . . . . 187 ET76
Kell St, SE1 . . . . 31 H6
Kelly Av, SE15 . . . . 44 A5
Kelly Cl, NW10 . . . . 140 CR62
Shepperton TW17 . . . . 217 BS96
Kelly Ct, Borwd. WD6 . . . . 100 CQ40
Kelly Ms, W9 . . . . 15 H5
Kelly Rd, NW7 . . . . 119 CY51
Kelly St, NW1 . . . . 7 K5
Kelly Way, Rom. RM6 . . . . 148 EY57
Kelman Cl, SW4 . . . . 41 P9
Waltham Cross EN8 . . . . 89 DX31
Kelmore Gro, SE22 . . . . 184 DU84
Kelmscott Cl, E17 . . . . 123 DZ54
Watford WD18 . . . . 97 BU43
Kelmscott Cres, Wat. WD18 . . . . 97 BU43
Kelmscott Gdns, W12 . . . . 181 CU76
Kelmscott Pl, Ashtd. KT21 . . . . 253 CJ117
Kelmscott Rd, SW11 . . . . 202 DE85
Sch Kelmscott Sch, E17
off Markhouse Rd 145 DZ58
Kelpatrick Rd, Slou. SL1 . . . . . . 153 AK72
Kelross Pas, N5
off Kelross Rd 144 DQ63
Kelross Rd, N5 . . . . 143 DP63
Kelsall Cl, SE3 . . . . 186 EH82
Kelsall Ms, Rich. TW9 . . . . 180 CP81
Kelsey Cl, Horl. RH6
off Court Lo Rd 290 DF148
Kelsey Gate, Beck. BR3 . . . . 225 EB96
Kelsey La, Beck. BR3 . . . . 225 EA97
Kelsey Pk Av, Beck. BR3 . . . . . . 225 EB96
Kelsey Pk Rd, Beck. BR3 . . . . . . 225 EA96
Sch Kelsey Pk Sports Coll, Beck.
BR3 *off Manor Way* 225 EA97
Kelsey Rd, Orp. BR5 . . . . 228 EV96
Kelsey Sq, Beck. BR3 . . . . 225 EA96
Kelsey St, E2 . . . . 20 D4

Kelsey Way, Beck. BR3 . . . . 225 EA97
Kelshall, Wat. WD25 . . . . 98 BY36
Kelshall Ct, N4
off Brownswood Rd 144 DQ61
Kelsie Way, Ilf. IG6 . . . . 125 ES52
Kelso Dr, Grav. DA12 . . . . 213 GM91
Kelson Ho, E14 . . . . 34 F6
Kelso Pl, W8. . . . . 27 M6
Kelso Rd, Cars. SM5. . . . . 222 DC101
Kelston Rd, Ilf. IG6 . . . . 125 EP54
Kelvedon Av, Hersham KT12 . . 235 BS108
Kelvedon Cl, Hutt. CM13 . . . . . 131 GE44
Kingston upon Thames KT2. 200 CM93
Kelvedon Ho, SW8 . . . . 42 B6
Kelvedon Rd, SW6 . . . . 39 H5
Kelvedon Wk, Rain. RM13
off Ongar Way. 169 FE66
Kelvedon Way, Wdf.Grn. IG8 . . 125 EM51
Kelvin Av, N13. . . . . 121 DM51
Leatherhead KT22. . . . . 253 CF119
Teddington TW11. . . . . 199 CE93
Kelvinbrook, W.Mol. KT8 . . . . . 218 CB97
Kelvin Cl, Epsom KT19 . . . . . . 238 CN107
Kelvin Cres, Har. HA3 . . . . 117 CE52
Kelvin Dr, Twick. TW1 . . . . 199 CH86
Kelvin Gdns, Croy. CR0 . . . . 223 DL101
Southall UB1. . . . . 158 CA72
Kelvin Gro, SE26. . . . . 204 DV90
Chessington KT9. . . . . 219 CK104
Sch Kelvin Gro Prim Sch,
SE26 off Kirkdale 204 DV90
Kelvington Cl, Croy. CR0 . . . . . 225 DY101
Kelvington Rd, SE15. . . . . 205 DX85
● Kelvin Ind Est, Grnf. UB6. . 158 CB66
Kelvin Par, Orp. BR6 . . . . 227 ES102
Kelvin Rd, N5. . . . . 9 H1
Tilbury RM18. . . . . 193 GG82
Welling DA16. . . . . 188 EU83
Kember St, N1. . . . . 8 C7
Kemble Cl, Pot.B. EN6 . . . . 86 DD33
Weybridge KT13 . . . . 235 BR105
Kemble Cotts, Add. KT15
off Emley Rd 234 BG105
Kemble Dr, Brom. BR2 . . . . 226 EL104
Kemble Par, Pot.B. EN6
off High St. 86 DC32
Kemble Rd, N17 . . . . 122 DU53
SE23. 205 DX88
Croydon CR0. . . . . 223 DN104
Kembleside Rd, Bigg.H. TN16 . 260 EJ118
Kemble St, WC2 . . . . 18 C9
Kemerton Rd, SE5. . . . . 184 DQ83
Beckenham BR3 . . . . 225 EB96
Croydon CR0. . . . . 224 DT101
Kemeys St, E9. . . . . 11 L3
Kemishford, Wok. GU22 . . . . . . 248 AU123
Kemnal Rd, Chis. BR7. . . . . 207 ER91
Sch Kemnal Tech Coll,
Sid. DA14
off Sevenoaks Way 208 EV94
Kemp Ct, SW8. . . . . 42 A5
Kempe Cl, St.Alb. AL1 . . . . 64 CC24
Slough SL3 . . . . 175 BC77
Kempe Rd, NW6 . . . . 14 C1
Enfield EN1 . . . . 104 DV36
Kemp Gdns, Croy. CR0
off St. Saviours Rd 224 DQ100
Kemp Ho, W1 off Berwick St . . . 17 N10
Kempis Way, SE22
off East Dulwich Gro. 204 DS85
Kemplay Rd, NW3. . . . . 6 A1
Kemp Pl, Bushey WD23 . . . . 98 CA44
Kemp Rd, Dag. RM8. . . . . 148 EX60
Kemprow, Ald. WD25 . . . . 99 CD36
Kemp's Ct, W1. . . . . 17 M9
Kemps Dr, E14. . . . . 22 B10
Northwood HA6 . . . . 115 BT52
Kempsford Gdns, SW5. . . . . 39 K1
Kempsford Rd, SE11 . . . . 30 F9
Kemps Gdns, SE13
off Thornford Rd 205 EC85
Kempshott Rd, SW16. . . . . 203 DK94
Kempson Rd, SW6. . . . . 39 K6
Kempthorne Rd, SE8 . . . . 33 M8
Kempton Av, Horn. RM12 . . . . 150 FM63
Northolt UB5. . . . . 158 CA65
Sunbury-on-Thames TW16. . 217 BV95
Kempton Cl, Erith DA8. . . . . . . 189 FC79
Uxbridge UB10 . . . . 137 BQ63
Kempton Ct, E1. . . . . 20 E6
Sunbury-on-Thames TW16. . 217 BV95
⇌ Kempton Park
(Race days only) 197 BV94
★ Kempton Park Racecourse,
Sun. TW16 . . . . 198 BW94
Kempton Rd, E6 . . . . 167 EM67
Hampton TW12 . . . . 218 BZ96
Kempton Wk, Croy. CR0. . . . . . 225 DY100
Kempt St, SE18. . . . . 187 EN79
Kemsing Cl, Bex. DA5 . . . . 208 EY87
Bromley BR2. . . . . 226 EF103
Thornton Heath CR7. . . . . . . 224 DQ98
Kemsing Rd, SE10. . . . . 35 N10
Kemsley, SE13. . . . . 205 EC85
Kemsley Chase, Farn.Royal
SL2. . . . . 153 AR67
Kemsley Cl, Green. DA9. . . . . . 211 FV86
Northfleet DA11. . . . . 213 GF91
Kemsley Rd, Tats. TN16. . . . . . 260 EK119
Kenbury Cl, Uxb. UB10. . . . . . . 136 BN62
Kenbury Gdns, SE5. . . . . 43 J8
Kenbury St, SE5 . . . . 43 J8
Kenchester Cl, SW8 . . . . 42 B5
Kencot Cl, Erith DA18. . . . . 188 EZ75
Kendal, Purf. RM19. . . . . 190 FQ78
Kendal Av, N18 . . . . 122 DR49
W3 . . . . 160 CN70
Barking IG11 . . . . 167 ES66
Epping CM16. . . . . 92 EU30
Kendal Cl, N20. . . . . 120 DE47
SW9. . . . . 42 G4
Feltham TW14
off Ambleside Dr. 197 BT88
Hayes UB4. . . . . 157 BS68
Reigate RH2. . . . . 272 DD133
Slough SL2 . . . . 154 AU73
Woodford Green IG8 . . . . . . 124 EF47
Kendal Cft, Horn. RM12 . . . . . 149 FG64
Kendal Dr, Slou. SL2 . . . . 154 AU73
Kendale, Grays RM16. . . . . 193 GH76
Hemel Hempstead HP3 . . . . . . 63 BP21
Kendale Rd, Brom. BR1 . . . . . . 206 EE92
Kendal Gdns, N18. . . . . 122 DR49
Sutton SM1 . . . . 222 DC103
Kendal Ho, N1. . . . . 8 D10
Kendall Av, Beck. BR3 . . . . 225 DY96
South Croydon CR2 . . . . 242 DR109
Kendall Av S, S.Croy. CR2 . . . 242 DQ110
Kendall Cl, Welw.G.C. AL7 . . . . . 51 CY13
Kendall Ct, SW19 . . . . 202 DD93
Borehamwood WD6
off Gregson Cl. 100 CQ39
Kendall Gdns, Grav. DA11 . . . . 213 GF87
Kendall Pl, W1 . . . . 16 G7
Kendall Rd, SE18. . . . . 186 EL81
Beckenham BR3 . . . . 225 DY96
Isleworth TW7 . . . . 179 CG82
Kendalmere Cl, N10 . . . . 121 DH53
Kendal Par, N18
off Great Cambridge Rd. . . 122 DR49
Kendal Pl, SW15 . . . . 201 CZ85
Kendal Rd, NW10 . . . . 141 CU63
Waltham Abbey EN9. . . . . . . 105 EC35
Kendals Cl, Rad. WD7 . . . . 99 CE36
Kendal Steps, W2
off St. Georges Flds 16 D9
Kendal St, W2 . . . . 16 D9
Sch Kender Prim Sch, SE14 . . . . 45 H6
Kender St, SE14 . . . . 45 H5
Kendoa Rd, SW4. . . . . 183 DK84
Kendon Cl, E11 . . . . 146 EH57
Kendor Av, Epsom KT19. . . . . . 238 CQ111
Kendra Hall Rd, S.Croy. CR2 . . 241 DP108
Kendrey Gdns, Twick. TW2 . . . . 199 CE86
Kendrick Ms, SW7. . . . . 28 A8
Kendrick Pl, SW7. . . . . 28 A9
Kendrick Rd, Slou. SL3. . . . . . . 174 AV76
Kenelm Cl, Har. HA1. . . . . 139 CG62
Kenerne Dr, Barn. EN5 . . . . 101 CY43
Kenford Cl, Wat. WD25 . . . . 81 BV32
Kenia Wk, Grav. DA12. . . . . 213 GM90
Kenilford Rd, SW12. . . . . 203 DH87
Kenilworth Av, E17 . . . . 123 EA54
SW19 . . . . 202 DA92
Harrow HA2. . . . . 138 BZ63
Romford RM3 . . . . 128 FP50
Stoke D'Abernon KT11 . . . . . 236 CB114
Kenilworth Cl, Bans. SM7 . . . . 256 DB116
Borehamwood WD6 . . . . 100 CQ41
Hemel Hempstead HP2 . . . . . . 62 BL21
Slough SL1 . . . . 174 AT76
Kenilworth Ct, SW15
off Lower Richmond Rd . . . 181 CY83
Watford WD17. . . . . 97 BU39
Kenilworth Cres, Enf. EN1 . . . . 104 DS39
Kenilworth Dr, Borwd. WD6. . . 100 CQ41
Croxley Green WD3 . . . . 97 BP42
Walton-on-Thames KT12 . . . 218 BX104
Kenilworth Gdns, SE18 . . . . . . 187 EP82
Hayes UB4. . . . . 157 BT71
Hornchurch RM12 . . . . 150 FJ62
Ilford IG3 . . . . 147 ET61
Loughton IG10. . . . . 107 EM44
Southall UB1. . . . . 158 BZ69
Staines TW18. . . . . 196 BJ92
Watford WD19 . . . . 116 BW50
Sch Kenilworth Prim Sch, Borwd.
WD6 off Kenilworth Dr 100 CR41
Kenilworth Rd, E3. . . . . 11 L10
NW6. . . . . 5 H8
SE20. 225 DX95
W5 . . . . 160 CL74
Ashford TW15 . . . . 196 BK90
Edgware HA8. . . . . 118 CQ48
Epsom KT17 . . . . 239 CU107
Petts Wood BR5. . . . . 227 EQ100
KENLEY, CR8. . . . . 258 DQ116
⇌ Kenley 242 DQ114
Kenley, N17 . . . . 122 DR54
Kenley Av, NW9. . . . . 118 CS54
Kenley Cl, Barn. EN4. . . . . 102 DE42
Bexley DA5 . . . . 208 FA87
Caterham CR3. . . . . 258 DR120
Chislehurst BR7 . . . . 227 ES97
Kenley Gdns, Horn. RM12 . . . . 150 FM61
Thornton Heath CR7. . . . . 223 DP98
Kenley La, Ken. CR8 . . . . 242 DQ114
Sch Kenley Prim Sch, Whyt.
CR3 off New Barn La 258 DS116
Kenley Rd, SW19. . . . . 221 CZ96
Kingston upon Thames KT1. 220 CP96
Twickenham TW1 . . . . 199 CG86
Kenley Wk, W11. . . . . 26 E1
Sutton SM3 . . . . 239 CX105
Kenlor Rd, SW17. . . . . 202 DD92
Kenmare Dr, N17 . . . . 122 DT54
Mitcham CR4. . . . . 202 DF94
Kenmare Gdns, N13. . . . . 121 DP49
Kenmare Rd, Th.Hth. CR7. . . . . 223 DN100
Kenmere Gdns, Wem. HA0 . . . . 160 CN67
Kenmere Rd, Well. DA16 . . . . . . 188 EW82
Kenmont Gdns, NW10 . . . . 161 CV69
Sch Kenmont Prim Sch, NW10
off Valliere Rd 161 CV69
Kenmore Av, Har. HA3 . . . . 139 CG56
Kenmore Cl, Rich. TW9
off Kent Rd. 180 CN80
Kenmore Cres, Hayes UB4. . . . . 157 BT69
Kenmore Gdns, Edg. HA8. . . . . 178 CP54
Sch Kenmore Pk First & Mid Schs,
Kenton HA3
off Moorhouse Rd. 140 CL55
Kenmore Rd, Har. HA3. . . . . . . 139 CK55
Kenley CR8 . . . . 241 DP114
Kenmure Rd, E8 . . . . 10 F3
Kenmure Yd, E8. . . . . 10 F3
Kennacraig Cl, E16 . . . . 35 P3
Kennard Rd, E15 . . . . 12 G7
N11 . . . . 120 DF50
Kennard St, E16 . . . . 37 J3
SW11 . . . . 40 G7
Kenneally, Wind. SL4 . . . . 172 AJ82
Kenneally Cl, Wind. SL4
off Kenneally 172 AJ82
Kenneally Pl, Wind. SL4
off Kenneally 172 AJ82
Kenneally Row, Wind. SL4
off Kenneally 172 AJ82
Kenneally Wk, Wind. SL4
off Kenneally 172 AJ82
Kennedy Av, Enf. EN3. . . . . 104 DW44
Hoddesdon EN11 . . . . 71 DZ17
Kennedy Cl, E13 . . . . 23 P1
Cheshunt EN8. . . . . 89 DX28
Farnham Common SL2 . . . . . 153 AQ65
London Colney AL2 . . . . 83 CK26
Mitcham CR4. . . . . 222 DG96
Petts Wood BR5. . . . . 227 ER102
Pinner HA5. . . . . 116 BZ51
Kennedy Gdns, Sev. TN13 . . . . 279 FJ123
Kennedy Ho, SE11
off Vauxhall Wk 30 C10
Kennedy Path, W7 off Harp Rd . 159 CF70
Kennedy Rd, W7 . . . . 159 CE71
Barking IG11 . . . . 167 ES67
Kennedy Wk, SE17
off Flint St 31 M9
Kennel Cl, Fetch. KT22 . . . . 252 CC124
Kennel La, Fetch. KT22. . . . . . . 252 CC122
Hookwood RH6. . . . . 290 DD149
Kennelwood Cres, New Adgtn
CR0. . . . . 243 ED111
Kennelwood La, Hat. AL10. . . . . 67 CV17
Kennet Cl, SW11
off Maysoule Rd 182 DD84
Upminster RM14. . . . . 151 FS58
Kennet Grn, S.Ock. RM15. . . . . 171 FV73
Kenneth Av, Ilf. IG1 . . . . 147 EP63
Kenneth Cres, NW2 . . . . 141 CV64
Kenneth Gdns, Stan. HA7 . . . . . 117 CG51
Kenneth More Rd, Ilf. IG1
off Oakfield Rd 147 EP62
Kennet Ho, NW8. . . . . 16 B6
Kenneth Rd, Bans. SM7 . . . . . . 256 DD115
Romford RM6 . . . . 148 EX59
Kenneth Robbins Ho, N17. . . . . 122 DV52
Kennet Rd, W9 . . . . 15 H4
Dartford DA1 . . . . 189 FG83
Isleworth TW7 . . . . 179 CF83
Kennet Sq, Mitch. CR4 . . . . 222 DE95
Kennet St, E1 . . . . 32 D2
Kennett Ct, Swan. BR8. . . . . . . 229 FE97
Kennett Dr, Hayes UB4 . . . . . . 158 BY71
Kennett Rd, Slou. SL3 . . . . 175 BB76
Kennet Wf La, EC4 . . . . 19 K10
Jct Kenninghall, N18 . . . . 122 DV50
Kenninghall Rd, E5. . . . . 144 DU62
N18. 122 DW50
Kenning Rd, Hodd. EN11 . . . . . . 71 EA15
Kenning St, SE16 . . . . 33 H4
Kennings Way, SE11 . . . . 30 F10
Kenning Ter, N1. . . . . 9 N8
KENNINGTON, SE11. . . . . 42 E3
⊖ Kennington 30 G10
Kennington Grn, SE11 . . . . 42 E1
Kennington La, SE11 . . . . 30 F10
Kennington Oval, SE11. . . . . 42 D2
● Kennington Pk, SW9 . . . . 42 F4
Kennington Pk Est, SE11 . . . . . . 42 E3
Kennington Pk Gdns, SE11 . . . . 42 G2
Kennington Pk Pl, SE11 . . . . 42 F1
Kennington Pk Rd, SE11. . . . . . . 42 F2
Kennington Rd, SE1 . . . . 30 E6
SE11 . . . . 30 E7
Sch Kenningtons Prim Sch, Aveley
RM15 off Tamar Dr 170 FQ72
Kennoldes, SE21 . . . . 204 DR89
Kenny Dr, Cars. SM5 . . . . 240 DF109
Kenrick Pl, W1 . . . . 16 G6
Kenrick Sq, Bletch. RH1 . . . . . . 274 DS133
KENSAL GREEN, NW10 . . . . 14 B2
⊜ Kensal Green. 14 B2
⊖ Kensal Green. 14 B2
★ Kensal Green Cem, W10. . . . 14 A3
KENSAL RISE, NW6 . . . . 14 C1
⊜ Kensal Rise 14 B1
Sch Kensal Ri Prim Sch, NW6. . . 14 C1
Kensal Rd, W10 . . . . 14 F4
KENSAL TOWN, W10 . . . . 14 E4
Kensal Wf, W10 . . . . 14 D4
KENSINGTON, W8 . . . . 27 H3
Coll Kensington & Chelsea Coll,
Hortensia Cen, SW10 . . . . 39 N4
Marlborough Cen, SW3 . . . . . . 28 D9
Wornington Cen, W10. . . . . . . 14 F6
Kensington Av, E12. . . . . 166 EL65
Thornton Heath CR7. . . . . . . 223 DN95
Watford WD18. . . . . 97 BT42
Sch Kensington Av Prim Sch, Th.Hth.
CR7 off Kensington Av 223 DN95
Kensington Ch Ct, W8 . . . . 27 L5
Kensington Ch St, W8 . . . . 27 K2
Kensington Ch Wk, W8. . . . . 27 L4
Kensington Cl, N11 . . . . 120 DG50
St. Albans AL1 . . . . 65 CG22
Coll Kensington Coll of Business,
WC2 . . . . 18 C8
Kensington Ct, NW7
off Grenville Pl. 118 CR50
W8 . . . . 27 M5
Kensington Ct Gdns, W8
off Kensington Ct Pl 27 M6
Kensington Ct Ms, W8 . . . . 27 M5
Kensington Ct Pl, W8 . . . . 27 M6
Kensington Dr, Wdf.Grn. IG8 . . 124 EK53
★ Kensington Gdns, W2. . . . . . . 27 P3
Kensington Gdns, Ilf. IG1. . . . . 147 EM61
Kingston upon Thames KT1
off Portsmouth Rd. 219 CK97
Kensington Gdns Sq, W2. . . . . . 15 L9
Kensington Gate, W8 . . . . 27 N6
Kensington Gore, SW7. . . . . 28 A5
Kensington Grn, W8 . . . . 27 L7
Kensington Hall Gdns, W14. . . . 26 G10
Kensington High St, W8. . . . . . . 27 J6
W14 . . . . 26 G7
Kensington Mall, W8 . . . . 27 K2
⊜ Kensington (Olympia) 26 E6
⊖ Kensington (Olympia) 26 E6
★ Kensington Palace, W8. . . . . 27 M3
Kensington Palace Gdns, W8. . . 27 L2
Kensington Pk Gdns, W11 . . . . . 26 G1
Kensington Pk Ms, W11 . . . . 14 G9
Kensington Pk Rd, W11 . . . . 14 G10
Kensington Pl, W8. . . . . 27 J3
Sch Kensington Prim Sch, E12
off Kensington Av 167 EM65
Kensington Rd, SW7 . . . . 28 B5
W8 . . . . 27 M5
Northolt UB5. . . . . 158 CA69
Pilgrim's Hatch CM15 . . . . . . 130 FU44
Romford RM7 . . . . 149 FC58
Kensington Sq, W8 . . . . 27 L5
Kensington Ter, S.Croy. CR2 . . 242 DR108
Kensington Village, W14. . . . . . . 27 H9
Kensington Way, Borwd. WD6. 100 CR41
Coll Kensit Mem Coll, N3
off Hendon La 119 CY54
Kent Av, W13 . . . . 159 CH71
Dagenham RM9 . . . . 168 FA70
Slough SL1 . . . . 153 AQ71
Welling DA16. . . . . 207 ET85
Kent Cl, Borwd. WD6 . . . . 100 CR38
Mitcham CR4. . . . . 223 DL98
Orpington BR6 . . . . 245 ES107
Staines TW18. . . . . 196 BK93
Uxbridge UB8 . . . . 156 BJ65
Kent Dr, Cockfos. EN4 . . . . 102 DG42
Hornchurch RM12. . . . . 150 FK63
Teddington TW11. . . . . 199 CE92
Kentford Way, Nthlt. UB5. . . . . 158 BY67
Kent Gdns, W13 . . . . 159 CH71
Ruislip HA4 . . . . 137 BV58
Kent Gate Way, Croy. CR0 . . . . 243 EA106
KENT HATCH, Eden. TN8 . . . . . 277 EP131
Kent Hatch Rd, Crock.H. TN8 . . 277 EM131
Oxted RH8 . . . . 276 EJ129
⇌ Kent House 225 DY95
Kent Ho La, Beck. BR3 . . . . 205 DY92
Kent Ho Rd, SE26. . . . . 225 DX95
Beckenham BR3 . . . . 205 DY92
Kentish Bldgs, SE1 . . . . 31 L3
Kentish La, Hat. AL9. . . . . 86 DC25
Kentish Rd, Belv. DA17. . . . . . . 188 FA77
KENTISH TOWN, NW5 . . . . 7 L4
⇌ Kentish Town. 7 L3
⊖ Kentish Town. 7 L3
Sch Kentish Town C of E
Prim Sch, NW5. . . . . 7 L3
Kentish Town Rd, NW1. . . . . 7 K7
NW5. . . . . 7 K7
⊜ Kentish Town West 7 H5
Kentish Way, Brom. BR1 . . . . . 226 EG96
● Kent Kraft Ind Est,
Nthflt DA11 . . . . 212 FZ85
Kentlea Rd, SE28 . . . . 187 ES75
Kentmere Rd, SE18. . . . . 187 ES77
KENTON, Har. HA3 . . . . 139 CH57
⊜ Kenton 139 CH58
⊖ Kenton 139 CH58
Kenton Av, Har. HA1. . . . . 139 CF59
Southall UB1. . . . . 158 CA73
Sunbury-on-Thames TW16. . 218 BY96
Kenton Ct, W14. . . . . 26 G7
Kenton Gdns, Har. HA3 . . . . . . 139 CJ57
St. Albans AL1. . . . . 65 CF21
Kenton La, Har. HA3. . . . . 139 CJ55
Kenton Pk Av, Har. HA3 . . . . . . 139 CK56
Kenton Pk Cl, Har. HA3 . . . . . . 139 CJ56
Kenton Pk Cres, Har. HA3 . . . . 139 CK56
Kenton Pk Par, Har. HA3 . . . . . 139 CJ57
Kenton Pk Rd, Har. HA3. . . . . . 139 CJ56
Kenton Rd, E9 . . . . 11 J5
Harrow HA1, HA3. . . . . 139 CK57
Kentons La, Wind. SL4 . . . . 173 AL82
Kenton St, WC1. . . . . 18 A4
Kenton Way, Hayes UB4
off Exmouth Rd. 157 BS69
Woking GU21 . . . . 248 AT117
● Kent Pk Ind Est, SE15. . . . . . . 44 E2
Kent Pas, NW1 . . . . 16 E4
Kent Rd, N21. . . . . 122 DR46
W4 . . . . 180 CQ76
Dagenham RM10 . . . . 149 FB64
Dartford DA1 . . . . 210 FK86
East Molesey KT8. . . . . 218 CC98
Gravesend DA11 . . . . 213 GG88
Grays RM17. . . . . 192 GC79
Kingston upon Thames KT1
off The Bittoms 219 CK97
Longfield DA3 . . . . 231 FX96
Orpington BR5 . . . . 228 EV100
Richmond TW9 . . . . 180 CN80
West Wickham BR4. . . . . 225 EB102
Woking GU22 . . . . 249 BB116
Kents Av, Hem.H. HP3 . . . . 62 BK24
Kents La, N.Wld Bas. CM16. . . . . 75 FD21
Kents Pas, Hmptn. TW12 . . . . . 218 BZ95
Kent St, E2. . . . . 10 B10
E13 . . . . 24 B3
Kent Ter, NW1 . . . . 16 D3
Kent Vw, Aveley RM15 . . . . 190 FQ75
Kent Vw Gdns, Ilf. IG3 . . . . 147 ES61
Kent Way, Surb. KT6. . . . . 220 CL104
Kentwell Cl, SE4 . . . . 185 DY84
Kentwode Grn, SW13. . . . . 181 CU80
Kentwyns Ri, S.Nutfld RH1 . . . 289 DM135
Kent Yd, SW7 . . . . 28 D5
Kenver Av, N12 . . . . 120 DD51
Kenward Rd, SE9 . . . . 206 EJ85
Kenway, Rain. RM13. . . . . 170 FJ69
Romford RM5 . . . . 127 FC54
Ken Way, Wem. HA9 . . . . 140 CQ61
Kenway Cl, Rain. RM13 . . . . . . 170 FJ69
Kenway Dr, Amer. HP7. . . . . 94 AV39
Kenway Rd, SW5 . . . . 27 L9
Kenway Wk, Rain. RM13. . . . . . 170 FK69
Kenwood Av, N14 . . . . 103 DK43
SE14. . . . . 45 H6
Kenwood Cl, NW3 . . . . 142 DD60
Sipson UB7 . . . . 176 BN79
Kenwood Dr, Beck. BR3 . . . . . . 225 EC97
Hersham KT12 . . . . 235 BV107
Mill End WD3. . . . . 113 BF47
Kenwood Gdns, E18. . . . . 146 EH55
Ilford IG2 . . . . 147 EN56
★ Kenwood Ho, NW3. . . . . 142 DE60
Kenwood Pk, Wey. KT13. . . . . . 235 BR107
Kenwood Ridge, Ken. CR8. . . . . 257 DP117
Kenwood Rd, N6. . . . . 142 DF58
N9. . . . . 122 DU46
Kenworth Cl, Wal.Cr. EN8. . . . . . 89 DX33
Kenworthy Rd, E9 . . . . 11 L3
Kenwyn Dr, NW2 . . . . 140 CS62
Kenwyn Rd, SW4 . . . . 183 DK84
SW20. . . . . 221 CW95
Dartford DA1 . . . . 210 FK85
Kenya Rd, SE7. . . . . 186 EK80
Kenyngton Dr, Sun. TW16 . . . . 197 BU92
Sch Kenyngton Manor Prim Sch,
Sun. TW16 off Bryony Way. 197 BU93
Kenyngton Pl, Har. HA3 . . . . . . 139 CJ57
Kenyon Pl, Welw.G.C. AL7
off Twelve Acres 51 CY12
Kenyons, W.Hors. KT24 . . . . . . 267 BP128
Kenyon St, SW6 . . . . 38 C6
Keogh Rd, E15. . . . . 13 K4
Kepler Rd, SW4. . . . . 183 DL84
Keppel Rd, E6 . . . . 167 EM66
Dagenham RM9 . . . . 148 EY63
Dorking RH4 . . . . 269 CH134
Keppel Row, SE1 . . . . 31 J3
Keppel Spur, Old Wind. SL4 . . 194 AV87
Keppel St, WC1 . . . . 17 P6
Windsor SL4 . . . . 173 AR82
Kerbela St, E2 . . . . 20 C4
Kerbey St, E14. . . . . 22 D8
Kerdistone Cl, Pot.B. EN6. . . . . . 86 DB30
Sch Kerem Sch, N2
off Norrice Lea 142 DD57
Kerfield Cres, SE5. . . . . 43 L7
Kerfield Pl, SE5 . . . . 43 L7
Kernow Cl, Horn. RM12 . . . . . . 150 FL61
Kerri Cl, Barn. EN5. . . . . 101 CW42
Kerridge Ct, N1 . . . . 9 P4
Kerril Cft, Harl. CM20 . . . . 57 EN14
Kerrill Av, Couls. CR5 . . . . 257 DN119
Kerrison Pl, W5 . . . . 159 CK74
Kerrison Rd, E15 . . . . 12 G8
SW11 . . . . 40 C10
W5 . . . . 159 CK74
Kerrison Vil, W5
off Kerrison Pl 159 CK74
Kerry Av, Aveley RM15 . . . . 190 FM75
Stanmore HA7. . . . . 117 CK49
Kerry Av N, Stan. HA7. . . . . 117 CK49
Kerry Cl, E16 . . . . 24 A9
N13. 121 DM47
Upminster RM14. . . . . 151 FT59
Kerry Ct, Stan. HA7. . . . . 117 CK49
Kerry Dr, Upmin. RM14 . . . . . . 151 FT59
Kerry Ho, E1 off Sidney St. 20 G8
Kerry Path, SE14 . . . . 45 N3
Kerry Rd, SE14 . . . . 45 N3
Kerry Ter, Wok. GU21 . . . . 249 BB116
Kersey Dr, S.Croy. CR2. . . . . . . 242 DW112
Kersey Gdns, SE9. . . . . 206 EL91
Romford RM3 . . . . 128 FL52
Kersfield Rd, SW15. . . . . 201 CX86
Kershaw Cl, SW18 . . . . 202 DC86
Chafford Hundred RM16 . . . 191 FW77
Hornchurch RM11 . . . . 150 FK59
Kershaw Rd, Dag. RM10 . . . . . . 148 FA62
Kersley Ms, SW11 . . . . 40 E7
Kersley Rd, N16. . . . . 144 DS62
Kersley St, SW11. . . . . 40 E8
Kerstin Cl, Hayes UB3 . . . . 157 BT73
Kerswell Cl, N15 . . . . 144 DS57
Kerwick Cl, N7. . . . . 8 B6
Keslake Rd, NW6 . . . . 14 C1
Kessock Cl, N17 . . . . 144 DV57
Kesters Rd, Chesh. HP5 . . . . 76 AR32
Kesteven Cl, Ilf. IG6 . . . . 125 ET51
Kestlake Rd, Bex. DA5
off East Rochester Way. . . . 208 EW86
KESTON, BR2 . . . . 244 EJ106
Keston Av, Couls. CR5 . . . . 257 DN119
Keston BR2 . . . . 244 EJ106
New Haw KT15 . . . . 234 BG111
Keston Cl, N18 . . . . 122 DR48
Welling DA16. . . . . 188 EW80
Sch Keston C of E Prim Sch,
Kes. BR2 off Lakes Rd 244 EK106
Keston Gdns, Kes. BR2. . . . . . . 244 EJ105
Jct Keston Mark, Kes. BR2. . . . . 226 EL104
Keston Ms, Wat. WD17
off Nascot Rd 97 BV40
Keston Pk Cl, Kes. BR2 . . . . . . 227 EM104
Sch Keston Prim Sch, Couls.
CR5 off Keston Av. 257 DN119
Keston Rd, N17. . . . . 144 DR55
SE15. 184 DU83
Thornton Heath CR7. . . . . . . 223 DN100
Kestral Ct, Wall. SM6
off Carew Rd 241 DJ106
Kestrel Av, E6 . . . . 24 G7
SE24. 203 DP85
Staines TW18. . . . . 195 BF90
Kestrel Cl, NW9 . . . . 118 CS54
NW10 . . . . 140 CR64
Berkhamsted HP4 . . . . 60 AW20
Epsom KT19 . . . . 238 CN111
Guildford GU4. . . . . 265 BD132
Hornchurch RM12. . . . . 169 FH66
Ilford IG6 . . . . 126 EW49
Kingston upon Thames KT2. 199 CK91
Watford WD25. . . . . 82 BY34
Kestrel Grn, Hat. AL10 . . . . 67 CU19
Kestrel Ho, EC1 . . . . 19 J2
SW8 off St. George Wf. 42 A2
W13 . . . . 159 CF70
Enfield EN3 off Alma Rd. . . . 105 DY43
Kestrel Path, Slou. SL2. . . . . . . 153 AL70
Kestrel Pl, SE14
off Milton Ct Rd. 45 M3
Kestrel Rd, Wal.Abb. EN9. . . . . . 90 EG34
Kestrels, The, Brick.Wd AL2 . . . . 82 BZ31
Kestrel Way, Felt. TW14. . . . . . 197 BV85
Hayes UB3. . . . . 177 BR75
New Addington CR0. . . . . . . 243 ED109
Welwyn Garden City AL7. . . . . 51 CZ07
Woking GU21 . . . . 248 AV115
Keswick Av, SW15 . . . . 200 CS92
SW19 . . . . 222 DA96
Hornchurch RM11 . . . . 150 FK60
Keswick Bdy, SW15
off Upper Richmond Rd . . . 201 CZ85
Keswick Cl, St.Alb. AL1 . . . . 65 CH21
Sutton SM1 . . . . 240 DC105
Keswick Ct, Slou. SL2
off Stoke Rd. 154 AT73
Keswick Dr, Enf. EN3 . . . . 104 DW36
Keswick Gdns, Ilf. IG4 . . . . 146 EL57
Purfleet RM19 . . . . 190 FQ79
Ruislip HA4 . . . . 137 BR58
Wembley HA9. . . . . 140 CL63
Keswick Ms, W5 . . . . 160 CL74
Keswick Rd, SW15 . . . . 201 CY85
Bexleyheath DA7 . . . . 188 FA82
Egham TW20. . . . . 195 BB94
Leatherhead KT22, KT23 . . . 268 CC125
Orpington BR6 . . . . 227 ET102
Twickenham TW2 . . . . 198 CC86
West Wickham BR4. . . . . 226 EE103
Kettering Rd, Enf. EN3
off Beaconsfield Rd. 105 DX37
Romford RM3 . . . . 128 FL52
Kettering St, SW16. . . . . 203 DJ93
Kett Gdns, SW2 . . . . 203 DM85
Kettlebaston Rd, E10 . . . . 145 DZ60
Kettlewell Cl, N11 . . . . 120 DG51
Woking GU21 . . . . 232 AX114
Kettlewell Ct, Swan. BR8. . . . . . 229 FF96
Kettlewell Dr, Wok. GU21. . . . . 232 AY114
Kettlewell Hill, Wok. GU21. . . . 232 AY114
Ketton Grn, Merst. RH1
off Malmstone Av 273 DK128
Kevan Dr, Send GU23. . . . . 249 BE124
Kevan Ho, SE5. . . . . 43 J5
Kevelioc Rd, N17. . . . . 122 DQ53
Kevin Cl, Houns. TW4 . . . . 178 BX82
Kevington Cl, Orp. BR5 . . . . . . 227 ET98
Kevington Dr, Chis. BR7. . . . . . 227 ET98
Orpington BR5 . . . . 227 ET98
KEW, Rich. TW9. . . . . 180 CN79
⇌ Kew Bridge 180 CM78
Jct Kew Br, Brent. TW8. . . . . . . 180 CM78
Kew Br, Brent. TW8. . . . . 180 CM79
Richmond TW9 . . . . 180 CM79
Kew Br Arches, Rich. TW9
off Kew Br 180 CM79
Kew Br Ct, W4. . . . . 180 CN78
● Kew Br Distribution Cen,
Brent. TW8. . . . . 180 CM78
Kew Br Rd, Brent. TW8. . . . . . . 180 CM79
★ Kew Bridge Steam Mus,
Brent. TW8. . . . . 180 CM78

Kew Cl, Rom. RM1 . . . 127 FE51
Uxbridge UB8 . . . 156 BK68
Sch Kew Coll, Kew TW9 off Cumberland Rd . . . 180 CN80
Kew Cres, Sutt. SM3 . . . 221 CY104
Kewferry Dr, Nthwd. HA6 . . . 115 BP50
Kewferry Rd, Nthwd. HA6 . . . 115 BQ51
Kew Foot Rd, Rich. TW9 . . . 180 CL84
⇌ Kew Gardens . . . 180 CM81
⊖ Kew Gardens . . . 180 CM81
Kew Gdns Rd, Rich. TW9 . . . 180 CM80
Jct Kew Grn, Rich. TW9 . . . 180 CM80
Kew Grn, Rich. TW9 . . . 180 CN80
Kew Meadows Path, Rich. TW9 . . . 180 CP82
★ Kew Observatory, Rich. TW9 . . . 179 CH83
★ Kew Palace (Royal Botanic Gdns), Rich. TW9 . . . 180 CL80
Kew Retail Pk, Rich. TW9 . . . 180 CP81
Sch Kew Riverside Prim Sch, Rich. TW9 off Courtlands Av . . . 180 CP82
Kew Rd, Rich. TW9 . . . 180 CN79
Key Cl, E1 . . . 20 F5
Keyes Rd, NW2 . . . 4 D2
Dartford DA1 . . . 190 FM84
Keyfield Ter, St.Alb. AL1 . . . 65 CD21
Keyham Ho, W2 . . . 15 J7
Keymer Cl, Bigg.H. TN16 . . . 260 EK116
Keymer Rd, SW2 . . . 203 DM89
Keynes Cl, N2 . . . 142 DF55
Keynsham Av, Wdf.Grn. IG8 . . . 124 EE49
Keynsham Gdns, SE9 . . . 206 EL85
Keynsham Rd, SE9 . . . 206 EK85
Morden SM4 . . . 222 DB102
Keynsham Wk, Mord. SM4 . . . 222 DB102
Keynton Cl, Hert. SG14 . . . 53 DM08
Keys, The, Gt Warley CM13 off Eagle Way . . . 129 FW51
Keyse Rd, SE1 . . . 32 A7
Keysers Est, Brox. EN10 . . . 71 EB21
Keysers Rd, Brox. EN10 . . . 71 EA22
Keysham Av, Houns. TW5 off The Avenue . . . 177 BU81
Keys Ho, Enf. EN3 off Beaconsfield Rd . . . 105 DX37
Sch Keys Meadow Prim Sch, Enf. EN3 off Tysoe Av . . . 105 DZ36
Keystone Cres, N1 . . . 18 B1
Keywood Dr, Sun. TW16 . . . 197 BU93
Keyworth Cl, E5 . . . 145 DY63
Keyworth Pl, SE1 . . . 31 H6
Sch Keyworth Prim Sch, SE17 . . . 42 G1
Keyworth St, SE1 . . . 31 H6
Kezia Ms, SE8 . . . 33 L10
Kezia St, SE8 . . . 45 L1
Khalsa Av, Grav. DA12 . . . 213 GJ87
Khalsa Ct, N22 off Acacia Rd . . . 121 DP53
Sch Khalsa Prim Sch, Slou. SL2 off Wexham Rd . . . 154 AU72
Khama Rd, SW17 . . . 202 DE91
Khartoum Pl, Grav. DA12 . . . 213 GJ86
Khartoum Rd, E13 . . . 24 A3
SW17 . . . 202 DD91
Ilford IG1 . . . 147 EP64
Khyber Rd, SW11 . . . 40 C9
Kibes La, Ware SG12 . . . 55 DX06
Kibworth St, SW8 . . . 42 C5
Kidborough Down, Bkhm KT23 . . . 268 CA127
KIDBROOKE, SE3 . . . 186 EH83
⇌ Kidbrooke . . . 186 EH83
Kidbrooke Gdns, SE3 . . . 47 N8
Kidbrooke Gro, SE3 . . . 47 P6
Jct Kidbrooke Interchange, SE3 . . . 186 EJ83
Kidbrooke La, SE9 . . . 186 EL84
Kidbrooke Pk Cl, SE3 . . . 186 EH81
Sch Kidbrooke Pk Prim Sch, SE3 off Hargood Rd . . . 186 EJ81
Kidbrooke Pk Rd, SE3 . . . 186 EH81
Sch Kidbrooke Sch, SE3 off Corelli Rd . . . 186 EK82
Kidbrooke Way, SE3 . . . 186 EH82
Kidderminster Pl, Croy. CR0 off Kidderminster Rd . . . 223 DP102
Kidderminster Rd, Croy. CR0 . . . 223 DP102
Slough SL2 . . . 153 AN69
Kidderpore Av, NW3 . . . 142 DA63
Kidderpore Gdns, NW3 . . . 142 DA63
Kidd Pl, SE7 . . . 37 H10
Kidman Cl, Gidea Pk RM2 . . . 150 FJ55
Kidworth Cl, Horl. RH6 . . . 290 DF147
Kielder Cl, Ilf. IG6 . . . 125 ET51
Kiffen St, EC2 . . . 19 M4
Kilberry Cl, Islw. TW7 . . . 179 CD81
Kilbride Ct, Hem.H. HP2 off Aycliffe Dr . . . 62 BM16
KILBURN, NW6 . . . 5 J10
⊖ Kilburn . . . 4 F5
Kilburn Br, NW6 . . . 5 K9
Kilburn Gate, NW6 . . . 5 L10
⇌ Kilburn High Road . . . 5 K9
Kilburn High Rd, NW6 . . . 5 H6
Kilburn La, W9 . . . 14 D3
W10 . . . 14 D3
⊖ Kilburn Park . . . 5 J10
Sch Kilburn Pk Jun Sch, NW6 . . . 15 H1
Kilburn Pk Rd, NW6 . . . 15 J3
Kilburn Pl, NW6 . . . 5 K9
Kilburn Priory, NW6 . . . 5 L9
Kilburn Sq, NW6 . . . 5 J8
Kilburn Vale, NW6 . . . 5 L9
Kilby Cl, Wat. WD25 . . . 98 BX35
Kilby Ct, SE10 off Child La . . . 35 M7
Kilcorral Cl, Epsom KT17 . . . 239 CU114
Kildare Cl, Ruis. HA4 . . . 138 BW60
Kildare Gdns, W2 . . . 15 K8
Kildare Rd, E16 . . . 23 N6
Kildare Ter, W2 . . . 15 K8
Kildare Wk, E14 . . . 22 A9
Kildonan Cl, Wat. WD17 . . . 97 BT39
Kildoran Rd, SW2 . . . 203 DL85
Kildowan Rd, Ilf. IG3 . . . 148 EU60
Kilfillan Gdns, Berk. HP4 . . . 60 AU20
Kilgour Rd, SE23 . . . 205 DY86
Kilkie St, SW6 . . . 39 N9
Killarney Rd, SW18 . . . 202 DC86
Killasser Ct, Tad. KT20 . . . 255 CW123
Killburns Mill Cl, Wall. SM6 off London Rd . . . 223 DH103
Killearn Rd, SE6 . . . 205 ED88
Killester Gdns, Wor.Pk. KT4 . . . 239 CV105
Killewarren Way, Orp. BR5 . . . 228 EW100
Killick Cl, Dunt.Grn TN13 . . . 278 FE121
Killick St, N1 . . . 8 C10
Killieser Av, SW2 . . . 203 DL89
Sch Killigrew Inf & Nurs Sch, St.Alb. AL2 off West Av . . . 82 CB25
Sch Killigrew Jun Sch, St.Alb. AL2 off West Av . . . 82 CB25
Killip Cl, E16 . . . 23 M8
Killowen Av, Nthlt. UB5 . . . 138 CC64
Killowen Rd, E9 . . . 11 J5
Killy Hill, Chobham GU24 . . . 232 AS108
Killyon Rd, SW8 . . . 41 M8
Killyon Ter, SW8 . . . 41 M9
Kilmaine Rd, SW6 . . . 38 F5
Kilmarnock Gdns, Dag. RM8 off Lindsey Rd . . . 148 EW62
Kilmarnock Pk, Reig. RH2 . . . 272 DB133
Kilmarnock Rd, Wat. WD19 . . . 116 BX49
Kilmarsh Rd, W6 . . . 26 A8
Kilmartin Av, SW16 . . . 223 DM97
Kilmartin Rd, Ilf. IG3 . . . 148 EU61
Kilmartin Way, Horn. RM12 . . . 149 FH64
Kilmington Cl, Hutt. CM13 . . . 131 GB47
Kilmington Rd, SW13 . . . 181 CU79
Kilmiston Av, Shep. TW17 . . . 217 BQ100
Kilmorey Gdns, Twick. TW1 . . . 199 CH85
Kilmorey Rd, Twick. TW1 . . . 179 CH84
Sch Kilmorie Prim Sch, SE23 off Kilmorie Rd . . . 205 DY89
Kilmorie Rd, SE23 . . . 205 DY88
Kiln Av, Amer. HP6 . . . 94 AW38
Kiln Cl, Harling. UB3 off Brickfield La . . . 177 BR79
Potten End HP4 . . . 61 BB17
Kiln Ct, Beac. HP9 . . . 132 AG55
Kilncroft, Hem.H. HP3 . . . 63 BP22
Kilndown, Grav. DA12 . . . 213 GK93
Kilner St, E14 . . . 22 A7
Kilnfield, Welw.G.C. AL7 . . . 51 CZ06
Kiln Flds, Woob.Grn HP10 . . . 132 AE61
Kiln Grd, Hem.H. HP3 . . . 62 BN22
Kiln Ho Cl, Ware SG12 . . . 55 DY05
Kiln La, B.End SL8 . . . 132 AC60
Brockham RH3 . . . 286 CP135
Church Langley CM17 . . . 74 EW16
Epsom KT17 . . . 238 CS111
Hedgerley SL2 . . . 133 AQ60
Horley RH6 . . . 290 DG146
Ley Hill HP5 . . . 78 AV31
Ripley GU23 . . . 250 BH124
Wooburn Green HP10 . . . 132 AC60
Kiln Ms, SW17 . . . 202 DD92
Kiln Pl, NW5 . . . 7 H2
Kiln Rd, N.Wld Bas. CM16 . . . 92 FA27
Kilnside, Clay. KT10 . . . 237 CG108
Kiln Wk, Red. RH1 . . . 288 DG139
Kiln Way, Bad.Dene RM17 . . . 192 FZ78
Northwood HA6 . . . 115 BS51
Kilnwood, Halst. TN14 . . . 246 EZ113
Kiln Wd La, Hav.at.Bow. RM4 . . . 127 FD50
Kilpatrick Way, Hayes UB4 . . . 158 BY71
Kilravock St, W10 . . . 14 E3
Kilross Rd, Felt. TW14 . . . 197 BR88
Kilrue La, Hersham KT12 . . . 235 BT105
Kilrush Ter, Wok. GU21 . . . 249 BA116
Kilsby Wk, Dag. RM9 off Rugby Rd . . . 168 EV65
Kilsha Rd, Walt. KT12 . . . 217 BV100
Kilsmore La, Chsht EN8 . . . 89 DX28
Kilvinton Dr, Enf. EN2 . . . 104 DR38
Kilworth Av, Shenf. CM15 . . . 131 GA44
Kilworth Cl, Welw.G.C. AL7 . . . 52 DB11
Kimbell Gdns, SW6 . . . 38 E7
Kimbell Pl, SE3 off Tudway Rd . . . 186 EJ84
Kimber Cl, Wind. SL4 . . . 173 AM83
Kimber Ct, Guil. GU4 off Gilliat Dr . . . 265 BD132
Kimberley Av, E6 . . . 166 EL68
SE15 . . . 44 F9
Ilford IG2 . . . 147 ER59
Romford RM7 . . . 149 FC58
Kimberley Cl, Horl. RH6 . . . 290 DE148
Slough SL3 . . . 175 AZ77
Kimberley Dr, Sid. DA14 . . . 208 EX89
Kimberley Gdns, N4 . . . 143 DP57
Enfield EN1 . . . 104 DT41
● Kimberley Ind Est, E17 . . . 123 DZ53
Kimberley Pl, Pur. CR8 off Brighton Rd . . . 241 DN111
Kimberley Ride, Cob. KT11 . . . 236 CB113
Kimberley Rd, E4 . . . 124 EE46
E11 . . . 145 ED61
E16 . . . 23 L4
E17 . . . 123 DZ53
N17 . . . 122 DU54
N18 . . . 122 DV51
NW6 . . . 4 F8
SW9 . . . 42 B9
Beckenham BR3 . . . 225 DX96
Croydon CR0 . . . 223 DP100
St. Albans AL3 . . . 64 CC19
Kimberley Wk, Walt. KT12 off Cottimore La . . . 217 BV101
Kimberley Way, E4 . . . 124 EE46
Kimber Rd, SW18 . . . 202 DA87
Kimbers Dr, Burn. SL1 . . . 153 AK69
Kimble Cl, Wat. WD18 . . . 97 BS44
Kimble Cres, Bushey WD23 . . . 116 CC45
Kimble Rd, SW19 . . . 202 DD93
Kimbolton Cl, SE12 . . . 206 EF86
Kimbolton Grn, Borwd. WD6 . . . 100 CQ42
Kimbolton Row, SW3 . . . 28 C9
Kimmeridge Gdns, SE9 . . . 206 EL91
Kimmeridge Rd, SE9 . . . 206 EL91
Kimps Way, Hem.H. HP3 . . . 62 BN23
Kimpton Av, Brwd. CM15 . . . 130 FV45
Kimpton Cl, Hem.H. HP2 . . . 63 BP15
Kimpton Ho, SW15 off Fontley Way . . . 201 CU87
● Kimpton Link Business Cen, Sutt. SM3 off Kimpton Rd . . . 221 CZ103
Kimpton Pk Way, Sutt. SM3 . . . 221 CZ103
Kimpton Pl, Wat. WD25 . . . 82 BX34
Kimpton Rd, SE5 . . . 43 L6
Sutton SM3 . . . 221 CZ103
Kimptons Cl, Pot.B. EN6 . . . 85 CX33
Kimptons Mead, Pot.B. EN6 . . . 85 CX32
● Kimpton Trade & Business Cen, Sutt. SM3 . . . 221 CZ103
Kinburn Dr, Egh. TW20 . . . 194 AY92
Kinburn St, SE16 . . . 33 J4
Kincaid Rd, SE15 . . . 44 E5
Kincardine Gdns, W9 . . . 15 J5
Kinch Gro, Wem. HA9 . . . 140 CM59
Kincraig Dr, Sev. TN13 . . . 278 FG124
Kinder Cl, SE28 . . . 168 EX73
Kinderscout, Hem.H. HP3 . . . 62 BN22
Kindersley Way, Abb.L. WD5 . . . 81 BQ31
Kinder St, E1 . . . 20 E9
Kinderton Cl, N14 . . . 121 DJ46
Kinefold Ho, N7 . . . 8 A4
● Kinetic Business Cen, Borwd. WD6 . . . 100 CM41
Kinetic Cres, Enf. EN3 . . . 105 DZ36
Kinfauns Av, Horn. RM11 . . . 150 FJ58
Kinfauns Rd, SW2 . . . 203 DN89
Ilford IG3 . . . 148 EU60
Kingaby Gdns, Rain. RM13 . . . 169 FG66
King Acre Ct, Stai. TW18 . . . 195 BE90
King Alfred Av, SE6 . . . 205 EA90
King Alfred Rd, Rom. RM3 . . . 128 FM54
Sch King Alfred Sch, The, NW11 off North End Rd . . . 142 DB60
King & Queen Cl, SE9 off St. Keverne Rd . . . 206 EL91
King & Queen St, SE17 . . . 31 K9
King & Queen Wf, SE16 . . . 33 J2
King Arthur Cl, SE15 . . . 44 G5
King Arthur Ct, Chsht EN8 . . . 89 DX31
Sch King Athelstan Prim Sch, Kings.T. KT1 off Villiers Rd . . . 220 CM97
Coll King Charles Cen, Surb. KT5 off Hollyfield Rd . . . 220 CM101
King Charles Cres, Surb. KT5 . . . 220 CM101
King Charles Rd, Shenley WD7 . . . 84 CL32
Surbiton KT5 . . . 220 CM99
King Charles St, SW1 . . . 29 P4
King Charles Ter, E1 off Sovereign Cl . . . 32 F1
King Charles Wk, SW19 off Princes Way . . . 201 CY88
Kingcup Cl, Croy. CR0 . . . 225 DX101
King David La, E1 . . . 20 G10
Kingdom St, W2 . . . 15 N7
Kingdon Rd, NW6 . . . 5 K4
King Edward Av, Dart. DA1 . . . 210 FK86
Rainham RM13 . . . 170 FK68
King Edward Ct, Wem. HA9 off Elm Rd . . . 140 CL64
Windsor SL4 . . . 173 AR81
King Edward Dr, Chess. KT9 off Kelvin Gro . . . 220 CL104
Grays RM16 . . . 192 GE75
King Edward Ms, SW13 . . . 181 CU81
King Edward Rd, E10 . . . 145 EC60
E17 . . . 145 DY55
Barnet EN5 . . . 102 DA42
Brentwood CM14 . . . 130 FW48
Greenhithe DA9 . . . 211 FU85
Romford RM1 . . . 149 FF58
Shenley WD7 . . . 84 CM33
Waltham Cross EN8 . . . 89 DY33
Watford WD19 . . . 98 BY44
King Edward VII Av, Wind. SL4 . . . 174 AS80
H King Edward VII Hosp, Wind. SL4 . . . 173 AQ83
H King Edward VII's Hosp for Officers, W1 . . . 17 H6
King Edward's Gdns, W3 . . . 160 CN74
King Edwards Gro, Tedd. TW11 . . . 199 CH93
King Edward's Pl, W3 . . . 160 CN74
King Edwards Rd, E9 . . . 10 F8
N9 . . . 122 DV45
Barking IG11 . . . 167 ER67
King Edward's Rd, Enf. EN3 . . . 105 DX42
King Edwards Rd, Ruis. HA4 . . . 137 BR60
Ware SG12 . . . 55 DY05
King Edward St, EC1 . . . 19 J8
Hemel Hempstead HP3 . . . 62 BJ24
Slough SL1 . . . 173 AR75
King Edward III Ms, SE16 . . . 32 F5
King Edward Wk, SE1 . . . 30 F6
Sch King Fahad Acad, The, W3 off Bromyard Av . . . 160 CS73
Girls Upr Sch, W5 off Little Ealing La . . . 179 CJ77
Kingfield Cl, Wok. GU22 . . . 249 AZ120
Kingfield Dr, Wok. GU22 . . . 249 AZ120
Kingfield Gdns, Wok. GU22 . . . 249 AZ120
Kingfield Grn, Wok. GU22 . . . 249 AZ120
Kingfield Rd, W5 . . . 159 CK70
Woking GU22 . . . 248 AY120
Sch Kingfield Sch, Wok. GU22 off Kingfield Rd . . . 249 BA120
Kingfield St, E14 . . . 34 F9
Kingfisher Av, E11 off Eastern Av . . . 146 EH58
Kingfisher Cl, SE28 . . . 168 EW73
Broxbourne EN10 . . . 71 EA20
Harrow Weald HA3 . . . 117 CF52
Hersham KT12 . . . 236 BY106
Hutton CM13 . . . 131 GA45
Northwood HA6 . . . 115 BP53
Orpington BR5 . . . 228 EX98
Stanstead Abbotts SG12 off Lawrence Av . . . 55 EC12
Kingfisher Ct, SW19 off Queensmere Rd . . . 201 CY89
Enfield EN2 off Mount Vw . . . 103 DM38
Sheerwater GU21 off Blackmore Cres . . . 233 BC114
Surbiton KT6 off Ewell Rd . . . 220 CM101
Sutton SM1 off Sandpiper Rd . . . 239 CZ106
Woking GU21 off Vale Fm Rd . . . 248 AX117
Kingfisher Dr, Green. DA9 . . . 211 FU85
Guildford GU4 . . . 265 BC132
Hemel Hempstead HP3 . . . 80 BM25
Redhill RH1 . . . 272 DG131
Richmond TW10 . . . 199 CH91
Staines TW18 . . . 195 BF91
Kingfisher Gdns, S.Croy. CR2 . . . 243 DX111
Kingfisher Height, Grays RM17 . . . 192 GA78
Kingfisher Ho, SW18 off Juniper Dr . . . 182 DC83
Kingfisher Lure, Kings L. WD4 . . . 81 BP29
Loudwater WD3 . . . 96 BH42
Kingfisher Ms, SE13 . . . 185 EB84
Kingfisher Pl, N22 off Clarendon Rd . . . 121 DM54
Kingfisher Rd, Upmin. RM14 . . . 151 FT60
Kingfisher Sq, SE8 . . . 45 P3
Kingfisher St, E6 . . . 25 H6
Kingfisher Wk, NW9 . . . 118 CS54
Kingfisher Way, NW10 . . . 140 CR64
Beckenham BR3 . . . 225 DX99
King Frederik IX Twr, SE16 . . . 33 N6
King Gdns, Croy. CR0 . . . 241 DP106
King George Av, E16 . . . 24 E8
Bushey WD23 . . . 98 CB44
Ilford IG2 . . . 147 ER57
Walton-on-Thames KT12 . . . 218 BX102
King George Cl, Rom. RM7 . . . 149 FC55
Sunbury-on-Thames TW16 . . . 197 BS92
King George Cres, Wem. HA0 . . . 139 CK64
DLR King George V . . . 37 M3
King George V Dock, E16 . . . 37 J2
King George V Rd, Amer. HP6 . . . 77 AR38
H King George Hosp, Ilf. IG3 . . . 148 EV57
King George Rd, Wal.Abb. EN9 . . . 89 EC34
Ware SG12 . . . 55 DY05
King Georges Av, Wat. WD18 . . . 97 BS43
King Georges Dr, New Haw KT15 . . . 234 BG110
Southall UB1 . . . 158 BZ71
King George VI Av, Mitch. CR4 . . . 222 DF98
Westerham TN16 . . . 260 EK116
King George Sq, Rich. TW10 . . . 200 CM86
King Georges Rd, Pilg.Hat. CM15 . . . 130 FV44
● King George's Trd Est, Chess. KT9 . . . 238 CN105
King George St, SE10 . . . 46 F5
Kingham Cl, SW18 . . . 202 DC87
W11 . . . 26 E4
King Harold Ct, Wal.Abb. EN9 off Sun St . . . 89 EC33
Sch King Harold Sch, Wal.Abb. EN9 off Broomstick Hall Rd . . . 90 EE33
King Harolds Way, Bexh. DA7 . . . 188 EX80
King Harry La, St.Alb. AL3 . . . 64 CA21
King Harry St, Hem.H. HP2 . . . 62 BK21
King Henry Ms, Har. HA2 . . . 139 CE60
Orpington BR6 off Osgood Av . . . 245 ET106
King Henrys Ct, Wal.Abb. EN9 off Deer Pk Way . . . 105 EC36
Trm King Henry's Drive . . . 243 EB109
King Henry's Dr, New Adgtn CR0 . . . 243 EC109
King Henry's Ms, Enf. EN3 . . . 105 EA37
King Henry's Reach, W6 . . . 38 B2
King Henry's Rd, NW3 . . . 6 D7
Kingston upon Thames KT1 . . . 220 CP97
King Henry St, N16 . . . 9 N2
King Henry's Wk, N1 . . . 9 N4
King Henry Ter, E1 . . . 32 F1
Kinghorn St, EC1 . . . 19 J7
King James Av, Cuffley EN6 . . . 87 DL29
King James Ct, SE1 . . . 31 H5
King James St, SE1 . . . 31 H5
King John Ct, EC2 . . . 19 P4
King Johns Cl, Wrays. TW19 . . . 194 AW86
King John St, E1 . . . 21 K7
King Johns Wk, SE9 . . . 206 EK88
Kinglake Ct, Wok. GU21 off Raglan Rd . . . 248 AS118
Kinglake Est, SE17 . . . 31 P10
Kinglake St, SE17 . . . 43 N1
Kinglet Cl, E7 . . . 13 N4
● Kingley Pk, Kings L. WD4 . . . 81 BP29
Kingly Ct, W1 . . . 17 M10
Kingly St, W1 . . . 17 L9
Kingsand Rd, SE12 . . . 206 EG89
Kings Arbour, Sthl. UB2 . . . 178 BY78
Kings Arms Ct, E1 . . . 20 C7
Kings Arms Yd, EC2 . . . 19 L8
Kingsash Dr, Hayes UB4 . . . 158 BY70
Kings Av, N10 . . . 142 DG55
N21 . . . 121 DP46
King's Av, SW4 . . . 203 DK87
SW12 . . . 203 DK88
Kings Av, W5 . . . 159 CK72
Bromley BR1 . . . 206 EF93
Buckhurst Hill IG9 . . . 124 EK47
Byfleet KT14 . . . 234 BK112
Carshalton SM5 . . . 240 DE108
Greenford UB6 . . . 158 CB72
Hemel Hempstead HP3 . . . 62 BM24
Hounslow TW3 . . . 178 CB81
New Malden KT3 . . . 220 CS98
Redhill RH1 . . . 288 DE136
Romford RM6 . . . 148 EZ58
Sunbury-on-Thames TW16 . . . 197 BT92
Watford WD18 . . . 97 BT42
Woodford Green IG8 . . . 124 EH51
Sch King's Av Prim Sch, SW4 off King's Av . . . 203 DL85
Sch King's Av Sch Early Years Cen, SW4 off Park Hill . . . 203 DL85
Kings Bench St, SE1 . . . 31 H4
Kings Bench Wk, EC4 . . . 18 F9
Kingsbridge Av, W3 . . . 180 CM75
Kingsbridge Circ, Rom. RM3 . . . 128 FL51
Kingsbridge Cl, Rom. RM3 . . . 128 FL51
Kingsbridge Ct, E14 off Dockers Tanner Rd . . . 34 B7
Kingsbridge Cres, Sthl. UB1 . . . 158 BZ71
Kingsbridge Dr, NW7 . . . 119 CX52
Kingsbridge Rd, W10 . . . 14 B8
Barking IG11 . . . 167 ER68
Morden SM4 . . . 221 CX101
Romford RM3 . . . 128 FL51
Southall UB2 . . . 178 BZ77
Walton-on-Thames KT12 . . . 217 BV101
Kingsbridge Way, Hayes UB4 . . . 157 BS69
Kingsbrook, Lthd. KT22 off Ryebrook Rd . . . 253 CG118
KINGSBURY, NW9 . . . 140 CP58
⊖ Kingsbury . . . 140 CN57
Kingsbury Av, St.Alb. AL3 . . . 64 CC19
Kingsbury Circle, NW9 . . . 140 CN57
H Kingsbury Comm Hosp, NW9 . . . 140 CN56
Kingsbury Cres, Stai. TW18 . . . 195 BD91
Kingsbury Dr, Old Wind. SL4 . . . 194 AV86
Sch Kingsbury Grn Prim Sch, NW9 off Old Kenton La . . . 140 CQ57
Sch Kingsbury High Sch, Lwr Sch, NW9 off Bacon La . . . 140 CQ56
Upr Sch, NW9 off Princes Av . . . 140 CP56
Kingsbury Ms, St.Alb. AL3 . . . 64 CB19
Kingsbury Rd, N1 . . . 9 P4
NW9 . . . 140 CP57
Kingsbury Ter, N1 . . . 9 P4
● Kingsbury Trd Est, NW9 . . . 140 CQ58
★ Kingsbury Watermill, St.Alb. AL3 . . . 64 CB19
Kings Butts, SE9 off Strongbow Cres . . . 207 EM85
Kings Chace Vw, Enf. EN2 off Crofton Way . . . 103 DN40
Kings Chase, Brwd. CM14 . . . 130 FW48
East Molesey KT8 . . . 218 CC97
Kingsclere Cl, SW15 . . . 201 CU87
Kingsclere Ct, Barn. EN5 off Gloucester Rd . . . 102 DC43
Kingsclere Pl, Enf. EN2 . . . 104 DQ40
Kingscliffe Gdns, SW19 . . . 201 CZ88
Kings Cl, E10 . . . 145 EB59
NW4 . . . 141 CX56
Beaconsfield HP9 . . . 132 AG55
Chalfont St. Giles HP8 . . . 112 AX47
Chipperfield WD4 . . . 80 BH31
Dartford DA1 . . . 189 FE84
Northwood HA6 . . . 115 BT51
Staines TW18 . . . 196 BK94
Thames Ditton KT7 . . . 219 CG100
Walton-on-Thames KT12 . . . 217 BV102
King's Cl, Wat. WD18 off Lady's Cl . . . 98 BW42
Sch Kings Coll, Guil. GU2 off Southway . . . 264 AS134
Uni King's Coll - Denmark Hill Campus, SE5 off Champion Hill . . . 184 DR83
Uni King's Coll - Guy's Campus, SE1 . . . 31 L6
Uni King's Coll - Half Moon La, SE24 off Half Moon La . . . 204 DR86
Uni King's Coll - Hampstead Campus, NW3 off Kidderpore Av . . . 142 DA63
Uni King's Coll - Maughan Lib & Information Services Cen, WC2 . . . 18 E8
Uni King's Coll - Strand Campus, WC2 . . . 18 D10
Uni King's Coll - Waterloo Campus, SE1 . . . 30 E3
H King's Coll Hosp, SE5 . . . 43 L9
Kings Coll Rd, NW3 . . . 6 C6
Ruislip HA4 . . . 137 BT58
Sch King's Coll Sch, SW19 off Southside Common . . . 201 CW93
Kingscote Rd, W4 . . . 180 CR76
Croydon CR0 . . . 224 DV101
New Malden KT3 . . . 220 CR97
Sch Kingscote Sch, Ger.Cr. SL9 off Oval Way . . . 134 AY55
Kingscote St, EC4 . . . 18 G10
Kings Ct, E13 . . . 166 EH67
W6 off Hamlet Gdns . . . 181 CU77
Berkhamsted HP4 off Lower Kings Rd . . . 60 AW18
Tadworth KT20 . . . 255 CW122
Wembley HA9 . . . 140 CP61
Sch Kings Ct First Sch, Old Wind. SL4 off Ashbrook Rd . . . 194 AV87
Kingscourt Rd, SW16 . . . 203 DK90
Kings Ct S, SW3 off Chelsea Manor Gdns . . . 40 D1
Kings Cres, N4 . . . 144 DQ62
Kings Cres Est, N4 . . . 144 DQ61
Kingscroft, Welw.G.C. AL7 . . . 52 DB08
Sch Kingscroft Jun Sch, Stai. TW18 off Park Av . . . 196 BG93
Kingscroft Rd, NW2 . . . 4 F4
Banstead SM7 . . . 256 DD115
Leatherhead KT22 . . . 253 CH120
KING'S CROSS, N1 . . . 7 P8
⇌ King's Cross . . . 18 A1
King's Cross Br, N1 . . . 18 B2
Kings Cross La, S.Nutfld RH1 . . . 289 DL136
King's Cross Rd, WC1 . . . 18 D2
⊖ King's Cross St. Pancras . . . 18 A1
Kingsdale Ct, Wal.Abb. EN9 off Lamplighters Cl . . . 90 EG34
Sch Kingsdale Foundation Sch, SE21 off Alleyn Pk . . . 204 DS90
Kingsdale Gdns, W11 . . . 26 D3
Kingsdale Rd, SE18 . . . 187 ET80
SE20 . . . 205 DX94
Berkhamsted HP4 . . . 60 AU20
Kingsdene, Tad. KT20 . . . 255 CV121
Kingsdon La, Harl. CM17 . . . 74 EW16
Kingsdown Av, W3 . . . 160 CS73
W13 . . . 179 CH75
South Croydon CR2 . . . 241 DP109
Kingsdown Cl, SE16 . . . 44 F1
W10 . . . 14 D9
Gravesend DA12 off Farley Rd . . . 213 GM88
Kingsdowne Rd, Surb. KT6 . . . 220 CL101
Kingsdown Rd, E11 . . . 146 EE62
N19 . . . 143 DL61
Epsom KT17 . . . 239 CU113
Sutton SM3 . . . 239 CY106
Kingsdown Way, Brom. BR2 . . . 226 EG101
Kings Dr, Edg. HA8 . . . 118 CM49
Gravesend DA12 . . . 213 GH90
Surbiton KT5 . . . 220 CN101
Teddington TW11 . . . 199 CD92
Thames Ditton KT7 . . . 219 CH100
Wembley HA9 . . . 140 CP61
Kings Dr, The, Hersham KT12 . . . 235 BT110
Kingsend, Ruis. HA4 . . . 137 BR60
KINGS FARM, Grav. DA12 . . . 213 GJ90
Kings Fm Av, Rich. TW10 . . . 180 CN84
Sch King's Fm Prim Sch, Grav. DA12 off Cedar Av . . . 213 GJ91
Kings Fm Rd, Chorl. WD3 . . . 95 BD44
Kingsfield, Albury GU5 . . . 282 BL144
Hoddesdon EN11 . . . 71 EA15
Windsor SL4 . . . 173 AK81
Kingsfield Av, Har. HA2 . . . 138 CB56
● Kingsfield Business Cen, Red. RH1 . . . 288 DG135
Kingsfield Ct, Wat. WD19 . . . 116 BX45
Kingsfield Dr, Enf. EN3 . . . 105 DX35
Kingsfield Ho, SE9 . . . 206 EK90
Kingsfield Rd, Har. HA1 . . . 139 CD59
Watford WD19 . . . 116 BX45
Kingsfield Ter, Dart. DA1 . . . 210 FK85
Kingsfield Way, Enf. EN3 . . . 105 DX35
Redhill RH1 . . . 288 DG135
Sch Kingsford Comm Sch, E6 . . . 25 J8
Kingsford St, NW5 . . . 6 E3
Kingsford Way, E6 . . . 25 K7
Kings Gdns, NW6 . . . 5 K7
Ilford IG1 . . . 147 ER60
Upminster RM14 . . . 151 FS59
King's Garth Ms, SE23 off London Rd . . . 204 DW89
Kings Gate, Add. KT15 . . . 234 BH105
Kingsgate, St.Alb. AL3 off King Harry La . . . 64 CB22
Wembley HA9 . . . 140 CQ62
Kingsgate Av, N3 . . . 142 DA55
Kingsgate Cl, Bexh. DA7 . . . 188 EY81
Orpington BR5 off Main Rd . . . 228 EW97
Kingsgate Est, N1 . . . 9 P5
Kingsgate Pl, NW6 . . . 5 J7
Sch Kingsgate Prim Sch, NW6 . . . 5 J6
Kingsgate Rd, NW6 . . . 5 J6
Kingston upon Thames KT2 . . . 220 CL95
Kings Grn, Loug. IG10 . . . 106 EL41
Kingsground, SE9 . . . 206 EL87

Kings Gro, SE15 44 F5
Romford RM1 149 FG57
Kings Hall Ms, SE13 46 F10
Kings Hall Rd, Beck. BR3 205 DY94
Kings Head Hill, E4 123 EB45
Kings Head La, Byfleet KT14 234 BK111
Kings Head Yd, SE1 31 L3
Kings Highway, SE18 187 ES79
Kingshill, SE17 31 K9
Kings Hill, Loug. IG10 106 EL40
Kingshill Av, Har. HA3 139 CH56
Hayes UB4 157 BS69
Northolt UB5 157 BU69
Romford RM5 127 FC51
St. Albans AL4 65 CG17
Worcester Park KT4 221 CU101
Kingshill Cl, Hayes UB4 157 BU69
Kingshill Dr, Har. HA3 139 CH55
Kingshill Way, Berk. HP4 60 AU21
Kingshold Est, E9 10 G8
Kingshold Rd, E9 11 H7
Kingsholm Gdns, SE9 186 EK84
King's Ho, SW8 42 B4
King's Ho Sch, Jun Dept, Rich. TW10 *off Kings Rd* 200 CM85
Sen Dept, Rich. TW10 *off Kings Rd* 200 CM85
Kingshurst Rd, SE12 206 EG87
● **Kingside**, SE18 36 G7
King's Keep, SW15 *off Westleigh Av* 201 CX85
Kings Keep, Kings.T. KT1 *off Beaufort Rd* 220 CL98
KINGSLAND, N1 9 N5
Kingsland, NW8 6 D9
Harlow CM18 73 EQ17
Potters Bar EN6 85 CZ33
Kingsland Basin, N1 9 P8
Kingsland Grn, E8 9 P4
Kingsland High St, E8 10 A4
Kingsland Pas, E8 9 P4
Kingsland Rd, E2 19 P2
E8 9 P8
E13 24 C3
Hemel Hempstead HP1 62 BG22
Kingsland Shop Cen, E8 10 A4
Kings La, Chipper. WD4 80 BG31
Englefield Green TW20 194 AU92
Sutton SM1 240 DD107
KINGS LANGLEY, WD4 80 BM30
⇌ **Kings Langley** 81 BQ30
Kings Langley Bypass, Hem.H. HP1, HP3 62 BG23
Kings Langley WD4 80 BK28
Kings Langley Prim Sch, Kings L. WD4 *off Common La* 80 BM28
Kings Langley Sch, Kings L. WD4 *off Love La* 80 BL28
Kingslawn Cl, SW15 201 CV85
Kingslea, Lthd. KT22 253 CG120
Kingsleigh Cl, Brent. TW8 179 CK79
Kingsleigh Pl, Mitch. CR4 222 DF97
Kingsleigh Wk, Brom. BR2 *off Stamford Dr* 226 EF98
Kingsley Av, W13 159 CG72
Banstead SM7 256 DA115
Borehamwood WD6 100 CM40
Cheshunt EN8 88 DV29
Dartford DA1 210 FN85
Englefield Green TW20 194 AV93
Hounslow TW3 178 CC82
Southall UB1 158 CA73
Sutton SM1 240 DD105
Kingsley Cl, N2 142 DC57
Dagenham RM10 149 FB63
Horley RH6 290 DF146
Kingsley Ct, Edg. HA8 118 CP47
Welwyn Garden City AL7 51 CZ13
Kingsley Dr, Wor.Pk. KT4 *off Badgers Copse* 221 CT103
Kingsley Flats, SE1 31 N8
Kingsley Gdns, E4 123 EA50
Hornchurch RM11 150 FK56
Ottershaw KT16 233 BD107
Kingsley Gro, Reig. RH2 288 DA137
Kingsley High Sch, Har. HA3 *off Whittlesea Rd* 116 CC52
Kingsley Ms, E1 32 F1
W8 27 M7
Chislehurst BR7 207 EP93
Kingsley Path, Slou. SL2 153 AK70
Kingsley Pl, N6 142 DG59
Kingsley Prim Sch, Croy. CR0 *off Thomson Cres* 223 DN102
Kingsley Rd, E7 13 P6
E17 123 EC54
N13 121 DN49
NW6 5 H8
SW19 202 DB92
Croydon CR0 223 DN102
Harrow HA2 138 CC63
Horley RH6 290 DF146
Hounslow TW3 178 CC82
Hutton CM13 131 GD45
Ilford IG6 125 EQ53
Loughton IG10 107 ER41
Orpington BR6 245 ET107
Pinner HA5 138 BZ56
Kingsley St, SW11 40 F10
Kingsley Wk, Grays RM16 193 GG77
Kingsley Way, N2 142 DC58
Kingsley Wd Dr, SE9 207 EM90
Kingslyn Cres, SE19 224 DS95
Kings Lynn Cl, Rom. RM3 *off Kings Lynn Dr* 128 FK51
Kings Lynn Dr, Rom. RM3 128 FK51
Kings Lynn Path, Rom. RM3 *off Kings Lynn Dr* 128 FK51
Kings Mall, W6 26 A9
Kingsman Par, SE18 37 K7
Kingsman St, SE18 37 K7
Kingsmead, Barn. EN5 102 DA42
Biggin Hill TN16 260 EK116
Cuffley EN6 87 DL28
Richmond TW10 200 CM86
St. Albans AL4 65 CK17
Sawbridgeworth CM21 58 EY06
Kings Mead, Smallfield RH6 291 DP148
South Nutfield RH1 289 DL136
Kingsmead, Wal.Cr. EN8 89 DX28
Kingsmead Av, N9 122 DV46
NW9 140 CR59
Mitcham CR4 223 DJ97
Romford RM1 149 FE58
Sunbury-on-Thames TW16 218 BW97
Surbiton KT6 220 CN103
Worcester Park KT4 221 CV104
Kingsmead Cl, Epsom KT19 238 CR108
Roydon CM19 72 EH16
Sidcup DA15 208 EU89
Teddington TW11 199 CH93
Kingsmead Dr, Nthlt. UB5 158 BZ66
Kingsmead Est, E9 11 M2
Kingsmead Hill, Roydon CM19 72 EH16
Kingsmead Ho, E9 *off Kingsmead Way* 11 M1
Kings Meadow, Kings L. WD4 80 BN28
Kings Mead Pk, Clay. KT10 237 CE108
Kingsmead Prim Sch, E9 11 M1
Kingsmead Rd, SW2 203 DN89
Kingsmead Sch, Enf. EN1 *off Southbury Rd* 104 DU41
Kingsmead Way, E9 11 M1
Kingsmere Cl, SW15 *off Felsham Rd* 181 CX83
Kingsmere Pk, NW9 140 CP60
Kingsmere Pl, N16 144 DR60
Kingsmere Rd, SW19 201 CX89
Kings Ms, SW4 *off King's Av* 203 DL85
King's Ms, WC1 18 D5
Kings Ms, Chig. IG7 125 EQ47
● **Kingsmill Business Pk**, Kings.T. KT1 220 CM97
Kingsmill Ct, Hat. AL10 *off Drakes Way* 67 CV20
Kingsmill Gdns, Dag. RM9 148 EZ64
Kings Mill La, Red. RH1 289 DK138
Kingsmill Rd, Dag. RM9 148 EZ64
Kingsmill Ter, NW8 6 B10
KINGSMOOR, Harl. CM19 73 EQ20
Kingsmoor Inf Sch, Harl. CM18 *off Ployters Rd* 73 EQ19
Kingsmoor Jun Sch, Harl. CM18 *off Ployters Rd* 73 EQ19
Kingsmoor Rd, Harl. CM19 73 EP18
Kingsnympton Pk, Kings.T. KT2 200 CP93
Kings Oak, Rom. RM7 148 FA55
Kings Oak Hosp, The, Enf. EN2 103 DN38
King Solomon Acad, NW1 16 C6
King Solomon High Sch, Ilf. IG6 *off Forest Rd* 125 ER54
King's Orchard, SE9 206 EL86
Kings Paddock, Hmptn. TW12 218 CC95
Kings Par, Cars. SM5 *off Wrythe La* 222 DE104
Kings Pk, Colnbr. SL3 175 BD80
Kingspark Ct, E18 146 EG55
King's Pas, E11 146 EE59
Kings Pas, Kings.T. KT1 219 CK96
★ **Kings Pl**, N1 8 B10
King's Pl, SE1 31 J5
W4 180 CQ78
Buckhurst Hill IG9 124 EJ47
Loughton IG10 124 EK45
King Sq, EC1 19 J3
King's Quay, SW10 39 P6
● **King's Reach Twr**, SE1 30 F2
Kings Ride Gate, Rich. TW10 180 CN84
Kingsridge, SW19 201 CY89
Kingsridge Gdns, Dart. DA1 210 FK86
Kings Rd, E4 123 ED46
E6 166 EJ67
E11 146 EE59
King's Rd, N17 122 DT53
Kings Rd, N18 122 DU50
N22 121 DM53
NW10 161 CV66
SE25 224 DU97
King's Rd, SW3 28 D10
SW6 39 M5
SW10 39 M5
Kings Rd, SW14 180 CR83
SW19 202 DA93
W5 159 CK71
Barking IG11 *off North St* 167 EQ66
Barnet EN5 101 CW41
Berkhamsted HP4 60 AU20
Biggin Hill TN16 260 EJ116
Brentwood CM14 130 FW48
Chalfont St. Giles HP8 112 AX47
Egham TW20 195 BA91
Feltham TW13 198 BW88
Guildford GU1 264 AX134
Harrow HA2 138 BZ61
King's Rd, Hert. SG13 54 DU08
Kings Rd, Horl. RH6 290 DG148
Kingston upon Thames KT2 200 CL94
London Colney AL2 83 CJ26
Long Ditton KT6 219 CJ102
Mitcham CR4 222 DG97
New Haw KT15 234 BH110
Orpington BR6 227 ET105
Richmond TW10 200 CM85
Romford RM1 149 FG57
St. Albans AL3 64 CB19
Shalford GU4 280 AY141
Slough SL1 174 AS76
Sutton SM2 240 DA110
Teddington TW11 199 CD92
Twickenham TW1 199 CH86
King's Rd, Uxb. UB8 156 BK68
Kings Rd, Wal.Cr. EN8 89 DY34
Walton-on-Thames KT12 217 BV103
West Drayton UB7 176 BM75
King's Rd, Wind. SL4 173 AR82
Kings Rd, Wok. GU21 249 BA116
Kings Rd Bungalows, Har. HA2 *off Kings Rd* 138 BZ62
King's Scholars' Pas, SW1 29 L7
King Stable Ct, Wind. SL4 *off King Stable St* 173 AR80
King Stable St, Eton SL4 173 AR80
King Stairs Cl, SE16 32 F4
King's Ter, NW1 7 L9
Kings Ter, Islw. TW7 *off South St* 179 CG83
Kingsthorpe Rd, SE26 205 DX91
⇌ **Kingston** 200 CL95
Kingston Av, E.Hors. KT24 267 BS126
Feltham TW14 197 BS86
Leatherhead KT22 253 CH121
Sutton SM3 221 CY104
West Drayton UB7 156 BM73
Kingston Br, Kings.T. KT1 219 CK96
● **Kingston Business Cen**, Chess. KT9 220 CL104
Kingston Bypass, SW15 200 CS93
SW20 200 CS93
Esher KT10 219 CG104
New Malden KT3 221 CU96
Surbiton KT5, KT6 220 CL104
Kingston Cl, Nthlt. UB5 158 BZ66
Romford RM6 148 EY55
Teddington TW11 199 CH93
Kingston Coll, Kings.T. KT1 *off Kingston Hall Rd* 219 CK97
Sch of Art & Design, Kings.T. KT2 *off Richmond Rd* 200 CL95
Kingston Ct, Nthflt DA11 212 GB85
Kingston Cres, Ashf. TW15 196 BJ92
Beckenham BR3 225 DZ95
Kingston Gdns, Croy. CR0 223 DL104
Kingston Gram Sch, Kings.T. KT2 *off London Rd* 220 CM96
Kingston Hall Rd, Kings.T. KT1 219 CK97
Kingston Hill, Kings.T. KT2 200 CQ93
Kingston Hill Av, Rom. RM6 126 EY54
Kingston Hill Pl, Kings.T. KT2 200 CQ91
Kingston Hosp, Kings.T. KT2 220 CP95
● **Kingston Ho Est**, Long Dit. KT6 219 CH100
Kingston Ho Gdns, Lthd. KT22 *off Upper Fairfield Rd* 253 CH121
Kingston La, Lthd. KT24 266 BM127
Teddington TW11 199 CG92
Uxbridge UB8 156 BL69
West Drayton UB7 176 BM75
Kingston Lo, N.Mal. KT3 *off Kingston Rd* 220 CS98
★ **Kingston Mus & Heritage Cen**, Kings.T. KT1 220 CL96
Kingston Pk Est, Kings.T. KT2 200 CP93
Kingston Pl, Har. HA3 *off Richmond Gdns* 117 CF52
Kingston Ri, New Haw KT15 234 BG110
Kingston Rd, N9 122 DU47
SW15 201 CU88
SW19 221 CZ95
SW20 221 CW96
Ashford TW15 196 BL93
Barnet EN4 102 DD43
Epsom KT17, KT19 238 CS106
Ilford IG1 147 EP63
Kingston upon Thames KT1 220 CP97
Leatherhead KT22 253 CG117
New Malden KT3 220 CR98
Romford RM1 149 FF56
Southall UB2 178 BZ75
Staines TW18 196 BJ93
Surbiton KT5 220 CP103
Teddington TW11 199 CH92
Worcester Park KT4 220 CP103
Kingston Sq, SE19 204 DR92
Leatherhead KT22 *off Kingston Rd* 253 CG119
Kingston Uni, Clayhills Halls of Res, Surb. KT5 *off Clayhill* 220 CN99
Kingston Hill, Kings.T. KT2 *off Kingston Hill* 200 CR92
Kingston Vale, SW15 *off Kingston Vale* 200 CR91
Knights Pk, Kings.T. KT1 *off Grange Rd* 220 CL97
Penrhyn Rd, Kings.T. KT1 *off Penrhyn Rd* 220 CL98
Roehampton Vale, SW15 *off Friars Av* 201 CT90
Seething Wells Halls of Res, Surb. KT6 *off Portsmouth Rd* 219 CJ100
KINGSTON UPON THAMES, KT1 & KT2 220 CL96
KINGSTON VALE, SW15 200 CS91
Kingston Vale, SW15 200 CR91
Kingstown St, NW1 6 G8
King St, E13 23 N5
EC2 19 K9
N2 142 DD55
N17 122 DT53
SW1 29 M3
W3 160 CP74
W6 181 CU77
WC2 18 A10
Chertsey KT16 216 BG102
Chesham HP5 76 AP32
Gravesend DA12 213 GH86
Richmond TW9 199 CK85
Southall UB2 178 BY76
Twickenham TW1 199 CG88
Watford WD18 98 BW42
King St Ms, N2 *off King St* 142 DD55
Kings Wk, Grays RM17 192 GA79
King's Wk, Kings.T. KT2 219 CK95
Kings Wk, S.Croy. CR2 242 DV114
Kings Wk Shop Mall, SW3 *off King's Rd* 28 E10
Kings Warren, Oxshott KT22 236 CC111
Kingswater Pl, SW11 *off Battersea Ch Rd* 40 C5
Kingsway, N12 120 DC51
SW14 180 CP83
WC2 18 C8
Chalfont St. Peter SL9 134 AY55
Kings Way, Croy. CR0 241 DM106
Kingsway, Cuffley EN6 87 DL30
Enfield EN3 104 DV43
Farnham Common SL2 153 AP65
Kings Way, Har. HA1 139 CE56
Kingsway, Hayes UB3 157 BQ71
Iver SL0 155 BE72
New Malden KT3 221 CW98
Petts Wood BR5 227 ES99
Staines TW19 196 BK88
Watford WD25 82 BW34
Wembley HA9 140 CL63
West Wickham BR4 226 EE104
Woking GU21 248 AX118
Woodford Green IG8 124 EJ50
Kingsway, The, Epsom KT17 239 CT111
Kingsway Av, S.Croy. CR2 242 DW109
Woking GU21 248 AX118
● **Kingsway Business Pk**, Hmptn. TW12 218 BZ95
Kingsway Cres, Har. HA2 138 CC56
Kingsway Infants' Sch, Wat. WD25 *off North App* 81 BU34
Kingsway Jun Sch, Wat. WD25 *off Briar Rd* 81 BU34
Kingsway Ms, Farn.Com. SL2 153 AQ65
Kingsway Pl, EC1 18 F4
Kingsway Rd, Sutt. SM3 239 CY108
Kingsway Shop Cen, NW3 *off Hampstead High St* 142 DC63
Kingswear Rd, NW5 143 DH62
Ruislip HA4 137 BU61
Kingswell Ride, Cuffley EN6 87 DL30
● **Kingswey Business Pk**, Wok. GU21 233 BC114
Kings Wf, E8 9 P8
KINGSWOOD, Tad. KT20 255 CY123
KINGSWOOD, Wat. WD25 81 BV34
⇌ **Kingswood** 255 CZ121
Kingswood Av, NW6 4 E9
Belvedere DA17 188 EZ77
Bromley BR2 226 EE97
Hampton TW12 198 CB93
Hounslow TW3 178 BZ81
South Croydon CR2 258 DV115
Swanley BR8 229 FF98
Thornton Heath CR7 223 DN99
Kingswood Cl, N20 102 DC44
SW8 42 B5
Ashford TW15 197 BQ91
Dartford DA1 210 FJ85
Enfield EN1 104 DS43
Englefield Green TW20 194 AX91
Guildford GU1 265 BC133
New Malden KT3 221 CT100
Orpington BR6 227 ER101
Surbiton KT6 220 CL101
Weybridge KT13 235 BP108
Kingswood Ct, SE13 *off Hither Grn La* 205 ED86
Kingswood Creek, Wrays. TW19 194 AX85
Kingswood Dr, SE19 204 DS91
Carshalton SM5 222 DF102
Sutton SM2 240 DB109
Kingswood Est, SE21 204 DS91
Kingswood Gra, Lwr Kgswd KT20 272 DA128
Kingswood Ho Sch, Epsom KT19 *off West Hill* 238 CQ113
Kingswood La, S.Croy. CR2 242 DW113
Warlingham CR6 258 DW115
Kingswood Ms, N15 *off Harringay Rd* 143 DP57
Kingswood Pk, N3 119 CZ54
Kingswood Pl, SE13 186 EE84
Kingswood Prim Sch, SE27 *off Gipsy Rd* 204 DR92
Lower Kingswood KT20 *off Buckland Rd* 271 CZ128
Kingswood Ri, Eng.Grn TW20 194 AX92
Kingswood Rd, E11 146 EE59
SE20 204 DW93
SW2 203 DL86
SW19 201 CZ94
W4 180 CQ76
Bromley BR2 225 ED98
Dunton Green TN13 263 FE120
Ilford IG3 148 EU60
Tadworth KT20 255 CV121
Watford WD25 81 BV34
Wembley HA9 140 CN62
King's Wd Sch, Harold Hill RM3 *off Settle Rd* 128 FN49
Kingswood Ter, W4 *off Kingswood Rd* 180 CQ76
Kingswood Way, S.Croy. CR2 242 DW113
Wallington SM6 241 DL106
Kingsworth Cl, Beck. BR3 225 DY99
Kingsworthy Cl, Kings.T. KT1 220 CM97
King's Yd, SW15 *off Stanbridge Rd* 38 B10
Kingthorpe Rd, NW10 160 CR66
Kingthorpe Ter, NW10 160 CR65
Kingwell Rd, Barn. EN4 102 DD38
Kingweston Cl, NW2 141 CY62
King William Ct, Wal.Abb. EN9 *off Kendal Rd* 105 EC35
King William IV Gdns, SE20 *off St. John's Rd* 204 DW93
King William La, SE10 47 J1
King William St, EC4 31 M1
King William Wk, SE10 46 F2
Kingwood City Learning Cen, The, SW6 38 E6
Kingwood Rd, SW6 38 D6
Kinlet Rd, SE18 187 EQ81
Kinloch Dr, NW9 140 CS59
Kinloch St, N7 143 DM62
Kinloss Ct, N3 *off Kinloss Gdns* 141 CZ56
Kinloss Gdns, N3 141 CZ56
Kinloss Rd, Cars. SM5 222 DC101
Kinnaird Av, W4 180 CQ80
Bromley BR1 206 EF93
Kinnaird Cl, Brom. BR1 206 EF93
Slough SL1 152 AJ72
Kinnaird Ho, N6 143 DK59
Kinnaird Way, Wdf.Grn. IG8 125 EM51
Kinnear Apts, N8 *off Chadwell La* 143 DM55
Kinnear Rd, W12 181 CT75
Kinnersley Manor, Reig. RH2 288 DC142
Kinnersley Wk, Reig. RH2 288 DB139
Kinnerton Pl N, SW1 28 F5
Kinnerton Pl S, SW1 28 F5
Kinnerton St, SW1 28 G5
Kinnerton Yd, SW1 28 F5
Kinnoul Rd, W6 38 E2
Kinross Av, Wor.Pk. KT4 221 CU103
Kinross Cl, Edg. HA8 *off Tayside Dr* 118 CP47
Harrow HA3 140 CM57
Sunbury-on-Thames TW16 197 BT92
Kinross Dr, Sun. TW16 197 BT92
Kinross Ter, E17 123 DZ54
Kinsale Rd, SE15 184 DU83
Kinsella Gdns, SW19 201 CV92
Kinsey Ho, SE21 *off Kingswood Est* 204 DS91
Kintore Way, SE1 32 A8
Kintyre Cl, SW16 223 DM96
Kinveachy Gdns, SE7 36 G9
Kinver Rd, SE26 204 DW91
Kipings, Tad. KT20 255 CX122
Kipling Av, Til. RM18 193 GH81
Kipling Cl, Warley CM14 130 FV50
Kipling Dr, SW19 202 DD93
Kipling Est, SE1 31 M5
Kipling Pl, Stan. HA7 117 CF51
Kipling Rd, Bexh. DA7 188 EY81
Dartford DA1 210 FP85
Kipling St, SE1 31 M5
Kipling Ter, N9 122 DR48
Kipling Twr, W3 180 CQ76
Kipling Twrs, Rom. RM3 127 FH52
KIPPINGTON, Sev. TN13 278 FG126
Kippington Cl, Sev. TN13 278 FF124
Kippington Dr, SE9 206 EK88
Kippington Ho, Sev. TN13 *off Kippington Rd* 278 FG126
Kippington Rd, Sev. TN13 278 FG124
Kirby Cl, Epsom KT19 239 CT106
Ilford IG6 125 ES51
Loughton IG10 124 EL45
Northwood HA6 115 BT51
Romford RM3 128 FN50
Kirby Est, SE16 32 E6
Kirby Gro, SE1 31 N4
Kirby Rd, Dart. DA2 210 FQ87
Woking GU21 248 AW117
Kirby St, EC1 18 F6
Kirby Way, Uxb. UB8 156 BM70
Walton-on-Thames KT12 218 BW100
Kirchen Rd, W13 159 CH73
Kirkby Cl, N11 *off Coverdale Rd* 120 DG51
Kirkcaldy Grn, Wat. WD19 *off Trevose Way* 116 BW48
Kirk Ct, Sev. TN13 278 FG123
Kirkdale, SE26 204 DV89
Kirkdale Rd, E11 146 EE60
Kirkefields, Guil. GU2 264 AU131
Kirkfield Cl, W13 *off Broomfield Rd* 159 CH74
Kirkham Rd, E6 25 H8
Kirkham St, SE18 187 ES79
Kirkland Av, Ilf. IG5 125 EN54
Woking GU21 248 AS116
Kirkland Cl, Sid. DA15 207 ES86
Kirkland Dr, Enf. EN2 103 DP39
Kirklands, Welw.G.C. AL8 51 CX05
Kirkland Wk, E8 10 A5
Kirk La, SE18 187 EQ79
Kirkleas Rd, Surb. KT6 220 CL102
Kirklees Rd, Dag. RM8 148 EW64
Thornton Heath CR7 223 DN99
Kirkley Rd, SW19 222 DA95
Kirkly Cl, S.Croy. CR2 242 DS109
Kirkman Pl, W1 17 N7
Kirkmichael Rd, E14 22 F8
Kirk Ri, Sutt. SM1 222 DB104
Kirk Rd, E17 145 DZ58
Kirkside Rd, SE3 47 N2
Kirkstall Av, N17 144 DR56
Kirkstall Gdns, SW2 203 DK88
Kirkstall Rd, SW2 203 DK88
Kirkstead Ct, E5 *off Mandeville St* 145 DY63
Kirksted Rd, Mord. SM4 222 DB102
Kirkstone Lo, Islw. TW7 *off Summerwood Rd* 199 CF85
Kirkstone Way, Brom. BR1 206 EE94
Kirk St, WC1 18 C5
Kirkton Rd, N15 144 DS56
Kirkwall Pl, E2 21 H2
Kirkwall Spur, Slou. SL1 154 AS71
Kirkwood Rd, SE15 44 F8
Kirn Rd, W13 *off Kirchen Rd* 159 CH73
Kirrane Cl, N.Mal. KT3 221 CT99
Kirsty Cl, Dor. RH5 285 CJ138
Kirtle Rd, Chesh. HP5 76 AQ31
Kirtley Ho, N16 *off Stamford Hill* 144 DS60
Kirtley Rd, SE26 205 DY91
Kirtling St, SW8 41 L4
Kirton Cl, W4 180 CR77
Hornchurch RM12 170 FJ65
Kirton Gdns, E2 20 B3
Kirton Rd, E13 166 EJ68
Kirton Wk, Edg. HA8 118 CQ52
Kirwyn Way, SE5 43 H4
Kisharon Coll, NW4 *off Parson St* 141 CW55
Kisharon Day Sch, NW11 *off Finchley Rd* 141 CZ58
Kitcat Ter, E3 22 B2
Kitchen Ct, E10 *off Brisbane Rd* 145 EB61
Kitchener Av, Grav. DA12 213 GJ90
Kitchener Cl, St.Alb. AL1 65 CH21
Kitchener Rd, E7 166 EH65
E17 123 EB53
N2 142 DE55
N17 144 DR55
Dagenham RM10 169 FB65
Thornton Heath CR7 224 DR97
Kitcheners Mead, St.Alb. AL3 64 CC20
Kitchenride Cor, Cher. KT16 233 BA105
Kite Fld, Nthch HP4 60 AS16
Kite Pl, E2 20 D2
Kite Yd, SW11 40 E7
Kitley Gdns, SE19 224 DT95
Kitsbury Rd, Berk. HP4 60 AV19
Kitsbury Ter, Berk. HP4 60 AV19
Kitsmead La, Longcr. KT16 214 AX103
Kitson Rd, SE5 43 K4
SW13 181 CU81
Kitson Way, Harl. CM20 57 EQ14
Kitswell Way, Rad. WD7 83 CF33
Kitten La, Stans.Abb. SG12 56 EE11
Kitters Grn, Abb.L. WD5 *off High St* 81 BS31
Kittiwake Cl, S.Croy. CR2 243 DY110
Kittiwake Pl, Sutt. SM1 *off Sandpiper Rd* 239 CZ106
Kittiwake Rd, Nthlt. UB5 158 BX69
Kittiwake Way, Hayes UB4 158 BX71
Kitto Rd, SE14 45 J9
KITT'S END, Barn. EN5 101 CY37
Kitts End Rd, Barn. EN5 101 CX36
Kiver Rd, N19 143 DK61
Klea Av, SW4 203 DJ86
Kleine Wf, N1 9 P9
Knapdale Cl, SE23 204 DV89
Knapmill Rd, SE6 205 EA89
Knapmill Way, SE6 205 EB89
Knapp Cl, NW10 160 CS65
Knapp Rd, E3 22 A5
Ashford TW15 196 BM91
Knapton Ms, SW17 *off Seely Rd* 202 DG93
Knaresborough Dr, SW18 202 DB88
Knaresborough Pl, SW5 27 L8
Knatchbull Rd, NW10 160 CR67
SE5 43 J7
Knaves Beech, Loud. HP10 110 AD53
● **Knaves Beech Business Cen**, H.Wyc. HP10 *off Boundary Rd* 110 AC54
● **Knaves Beech Ind Est**, Loud. HP10 110 AC54
Knaves Beech Way, Loud. HP10 110 AC54
Knaves Hollow, Woob.Moor HP10 110 AD54
Knebworth Av, E17 123 EA53
Knebworth Cl, Barn. EN5 102 DB42

Knebworth Path, Borwd. WD6 100 CR42
Knebworth Rd, N16 144 DS63
Knee Hill, SE2 188 EW77
Knee Hill Cres, SE2 188 EW77
Knella Grn, Welw.G.C. AL7 52 DA09
Knella Rd, Welw.G.C. AL7 51 CY10
Kneller Gdns, Islw. TW7 199 CD85
Kneller Rd, SE4 185 DY84
New Malden KT3 220 CS101
Twickenham TW2 198 CC86
Knevett Ter, Houns. TW3 178 CA84
Knight Cl, Dag. RM8 148 EW61
Knight Ct, E4
off The Ridgeway 123 EC46
Knighten St, E1 32 E3
Knighthead Pt, E14 34 A6
Knightland Rd, E5 144 DV61
Knighton Cl, Rom. RM7 149 FD58
South Croydon CR2 241 DP108
Woodford Green IG8 124 EH49
Knighton Dr, Wdf.Grn. IG8 124 EG49
Knighton Grn, Buck.H. IG9
off High Rd 124 EH47
Knighton La, Buck.H. IG9 124 EH47
Knighton Pk Rd, SE26 205 DX92
Knighton Rd, E7 146 EG62
Otford TN14 263 FF116
Redhill RH1 288 DG136
Romford RM7 149 FC58
Knighton Way La, Denh. UB9 156 BH65
Knightrider Ct, EC4
off Knightrider St 19 J10
Knightrider St, EC4 19 J10
Knights Av, W5 180 CL75
⊖ Knightsbridge 28 E5
Knightsbridge, SW1 28 F5
SW7 28 D5
Knightsbridge Apts, The, SW7
off Knightsbridge 28 E5
Knightsbridge Ct, Langley
SL3 off High St 175 BA77
Knightsbridge Cres, Stai.
TW18 196 BH93
Knightsbridge Gdns, Rom.
RM7 149 FD57
Knightsbridge Grn, SW1 28 E5
Knightsbridge Way, Hem.H.
HP2 62 BL20
Knights Cl, E9 11 H3
Egham TW20 195 BD93
West Molesey KT8 218 BZ99
Windsor SL4 173 AK81
Knightscote Cl, Hare. UB9 114 BK54
Knights Ct, Kings.T. KT1 220 CL97
Romford RM6 148 EY58
Knights Fld, Eyns. DA4 230 FL104
Knightsfield, Welw.G.C. AL8 51 CY06
Knights Hill, SE27 203 DP92
Knights Hill Sq, SE27 203 DP91
Knights La, N9 122 DU48
Knights Manor Way,
Dart. DA1 210 FM86
Knights Ms, Sutt. SM2
off York Rd 240 DA108
Knights Orchard, Hem.H. HP1 61 BF18
Knights Pk, Kings.T. KT1 220 CL97
Knights Pl, Red. RH1
off Noke Dr 272 DG133
Knight's Pl, Twick. TW2
off May Rd 199 CE88
Knights Pl, Wind. SL4
off Frances Rd 173 AQ82
Knights Ridge, Orp. BR6
off Stirling Dr 246 EV106
Knights Rd, E16 35 P4
Stanmore HA7 117 CJ49
Knight St, Saw. CM21 58 EY05
Knights Wk, SE11 30 G9
Abridge RM4 108 EV41
Knight's Way, Brwd. CM13 131 GA48
Knights Way, Ilf. IG6 125 EQ51
Knightswood, Wok. GU21 248 AT118
Knightswood Cl, Edg. HA8 118 CQ47
Knightswood Rd, Rain. RM13 169 FG68
Knightwood Cl, Reig. RH2 288 DA136
Knightwood Cres, N.Mal. KT3 220 CS100
Knipp Hill, Cob. KT11 236 BZ113
Knivet Rd, SW6 39 J3
Knobfield, Abin.Ham. RH5 283 BT143
KNOCKHALL, Green. DA9 211 FW85
Knockhall Chase, Green. DA9 211 FV85
Sch Knockhall Comm Prim Sch,
Green. DA9
off Eynsford Rd 211 FW85
Knockhall Rd, Green. DA9 211 FW86
KNOCKHOLT, Sev. TN14 262 EU116
⇌ Knockholt 246 EY109
Knockholt Cl, Sutt. SM2 240 DB110
Knockholt Main Rd, Knock.P.
TN14 262 EY115
KNOCKHOLT POUND,
Sev. TN14 262 EX115
Knockholt Rd, SE9 206 EK85
Halstead TN14 246 EZ113
Knole, The, SE9 207 EN91
Istead Rise DA13 212 GE94
Knole Cl, Croy. CR0 224 DW100
Knole Gate, Sid. DA15
off Woodside Cres 207 ES90
★ Knole Ho & Pk, Sev. TN15 279 FL126
Knole La, Sev. TN13 279 FJ126
Knole Rd, Dart. DA1 209 FG87
Sevenoaks TN13 279 FK123
Knole Way, Sev. TN13 279 FJ125
Knoll, The, W13 159 CJ71
Beckenham BR3 225 EB95
Bromley BR2 226 EG103
Chertsey KT16 215 BF102
Cobham KT11 236 CA113
Hertford SG13 54 DV08
Leatherhead KT22 253 CJ121
Knoll Ct, SE19 204 DS92
Knoll Cres, Nthwd. HA6 115 BS53
Knoll Dr, N14 120 DG45
Knolles Cres, N.Mymms AL9 67 CV24
Knollmead, Surb. KT5 220 CQ102
Sch Knollmead Prim Sch,
Surb. KT5
off Knollmead 220 CQ103
Knoll Pk Rd, Cher. KT16 215 BF102
Knoll Ri, Orp. BR6 227 ET102
Knoll Rd, SW18 202 DC85
Bexley DA5 208 FA87
Dorking RH4 285 CG138
Sidcup DA14 208 EV92
Jct Knoll Rbt, Lthd. KT22 253 CJ121
Knolls, The, Epsom KT17 255 CW116
Knolls Cl, Wor.Pk. KT4 221 CV104
Knollys Cl, SW16 203 DN90
Knollys Rd, SW16 203 DN90
Knolton Way, Slou. SL2 154 AW72
Knottisford St, E2 21 H2
Knottocks Cl, Beac. HP9 110 AJ50
Knottocks Dr, Beac. HP9 110 AJ50
Knottocks End, Beac. HP9 111 AK50
Knotts Grn Ms, E10 145 EB58
Knotts Grn Rd, E10 145 EB58
Knotts Pl, Sev. TN13 278 FG124
KNOTTY GREEN, Beac. HP9 110 AJ49
Knowle, The, Hodd. EN11 71 EA18
Tadworth KT20 255 CW121
Knowle Av, Bexh. DA7 188 EY80
Knowle Cl, SW9 42 E10
Knowle Gdns, W.Byf. KT14
off Madeira Rd 233 BF113
Knowle Grn, Stai. TW18 196 BG92
Knowle Gro, Vir.W. GU25 214 AW101
Knowle Gro Cl, Vir.W. GU25 214 AW101
Knowle Hill, Vir.W. GU25 214 AV101
Knowle Pk, Cob. KT11 252 BY115
Knowle Pk Av, Stai. TW18 196 BH93
Sch Knowle Pk Inf Sch, Stai.
TW18 off Knowle Grn 196 BG92
Knowle Rd, Brom. BR2 226 EL103
Twickenham TW2 199 CE88
Knowles Cl, West Dr. UB7 156 BL74
Knowles Hill Cres, SE13 205 ED85
Knowles Ho, SW18
off Neville Gill Cl 202 DB86
Knowles Wk, SW4 41 M10
Knowl Hill, Wok. GU22 249 BB119
Knowl Pk, Els. WD6 100 CL43
Knowlton Grn, Brom. BR2 226 EF99
Knowl Way, Els. WD6 100 CL42
Knowsley Av, Sthl. UB1 158 CA74
Knowsley Rd, SW11 40 E9
Knoxfield Caravan Pk, Dart.
DA2 211 FS90
Knox Rd, E7 13 M5
Guildford GU2 264 AU129
Knox St, W1 16 E6
Knoyle St, SE14 45 L3
Knutsford Av, Wat. WD24 98 BX38
Sch Knutsford Prim Sch, Wat.
WD24 off Knutsford Av 98 BX38
Sch Kobi Nazrul Prim Sch, E1 20 D8
Kohat Rd, SW19 202 DB92
Koh-i-noor Av, Bushey WD23 98 CA44
Koonowla Cl, Bigg.H. TN16 260 EK115
Kooringa, Warl. CR6 258 DV119
Korda Cl, Shep. TW17 216 BM97
Kossuth St, SE10 35 J10
Kotan Dr, Stai. TW18 195 BC90
Kotree Way, SE1 32 D9
Kramer Ms, SW5 39 K1
Kreedman Wk, E8 10 C3
Kreisel Wk, Rich. TW9 180 CM79
Kuala Gdns, SW16 223 DM95
● Kubrick Business Est, E7
off Woodgrange Rd 146 EH63
Kuhn Way, E7 13 P2
Kydbrook Cl, Petts Wd BR5 227 EQ101
Kylemore Cl, E6 off Parr Rd 166 EK68
Kylemore Rd, NW6 5 J6
Kymberley Rd, Har. HA1 139 CE58
Kyme Rd, Horn. RM11 149 FF58
Kynance Cl, Rom. RM3 128 FJ48
Kynance Gdns, Stan. HA7 117 CJ53
Kynance Ms, SW7 27 N7
Kynance Pl, SW7 27 N7
Kynaston Av, N16
off Dynevor Rd 144 DT62
Thornton Heath CR7 224 DQ99
Kynaston Cl, Har. HA3 117 CD52
Kynaston Cres, Th.Hth. CR7 224 DQ99
Kynaston Rd, N16 144 DS62
Bromley BR1 206 EG92
Enfield EN2 104 DR39
Orpington BR5 228 EV101
Thornton Heath CR7 224 DQ99
Kynaston Wd, Har. HA3 117 CD52
Kynersley Cl, Cars. SM5
off William St 222 DF104
Kyngeshene Gdns, Guil. GU1 281 BA135
Kynoch Rd, N18 122 DW49
Kyrle Rd, SW11 202 DG85
Kytes Dr, Wat. WD25 82 BX33
Kytes Est, Wat. WD25 82 BX33
Kyverdale Rd, N16 144 DT61

L

Laburnham Cl, Upmin. RM14 151 FU59
Laburnham Gdns, Upmin.
RM14 151 FT59
Laburnum Av, N9 122 DS47
N17 122 DR52
Dartford DA1 210 FJ88
Hornchurch RM12 149 FF62
Sutton SM1 222 DE104
Swanley BR8 229 FC97
West Drayton UB7 156 BM73
Laburnum Cl, E4 123 DZ51
N11 120 DG51
SE15 44 G5
Cheshunt EN8 89 DX31
Guildford GU1 264 AW131
Sheering CM22 59 FC07
Wembley HA0 160 CN66
Laburnum Ct, E2 10 A9
Stanmore HA7 117 CJ49
Laburnum Cres, Sun. TW16
off Batavia Rd 217 BV95
Laburnum Gdns, N21 122 DQ47
Croydon CR0 225 DX101
Laburnum Gro, N21 122 DQ47
NW9 140 CQ59
Hounslow TW3 178 BZ84
New Malden KT3 220 CR96
Northfleet DA11 212 GD87
Ruislip HA4 137 BR58
St. Albans AL2 82 CB25
Slough SL3 175 BB79
South Ockendon RM15 171 FW69
Southall UB1 158 BZ70
Laburnum Ho, Dag. RM10
off Bradwell Av 148 FA61
Laburnum Pl, Eng.Grn TW20 194 AV93
Laburnum Rd, SW19 202 DC94
Chertsey KT16 216 BG102
Coopersale CM16 92 EW29
Epsom KT18 238 CS113
Hayes UB3 177 BT77
Hoddesdon EN11 71 EB15
Mitcham CR4 222 DG96
Woking GU22 248 AX120
Laburnum St, E2 10 A9
Laburnum Wk, Horn. RM12 150 FJ64
Laburnum Way, Brom. BR2 227 EN101
Goffs Oak EN7
off Millcrest Rd 87 DP28
Staines TW19 196 BM88
Lacebark Cl, Sid. DA15 207 ET87
Lacewing Cl, E13 23 P2
Lacey Av, Couls. CR5 257 DN120
Lacey Cl, N9 122 DU47
Egham TW20 195 BD94
Lacey Dr, Couls. CR5 257 DN120
Dagenham RM8 148 EV63
Edgware HA8 118 CL49
Hampton TW12 218 BZ95
Lacey Grn, Couls. CR5 257 DN120
Lacey Ms, E3 12 A10
Lackford Rd, Chipstead CR5 256 DF118
Lackington St, EC2 19 M6
Lackmore Rd, Enf. EN1 104 DW35
Lacock Cl, SW19 202 DC93
Lacock Ct, W13
off Singapore Rd 159 CG74
Lacon Rd, SE22 184 DU84
Lacrosse Way, SW16 223 DK95
Lacy Rd, SW15 181 CX84
Ladas Rd, SE27 204 DQ91
Ladbroke Ct, Red. RH1 272 DG132
Ladbroke Cres, W11 14 F9
Ladbroke Gdns, W11 14 G10
⊖ Ladbroke Grove 14 F8
Ladbroke Gro, W10 14 D4
W11 14 F9
Redhill RH1 272 DG133
Ladbroke Ms, W11 26 F3
Ladbroke Rd, W11 26 F2
Enfield EN1 104 DT44
Epsom KT18 238 CR114
Horley RH6 290 DG146
Redhill RH1 272 DG133
Ladbroke Sq, W11 26 G1
Ladbroke Ter, W11 27 H1
Ladbroke Wk, W11 27 H2
Ladbrook Cl, Pnr. HA5 138 BZ57
Ladbrooke Cl, Pot.B. EN6
off Strafford Gate 86 DA32
Ladbrooke Cres, Sid. DA14 208 EX90
Ladbrooke Dr, Pot.B. EN6 86 DA32
Sch Ladbrooke JMI Sch, Pot.B. EN6
off Watkins Ri 86 DB32
Ladbrooke Rd, Slou. SL1 173 AQ76
Ladbrook Rd, SE25 224 DR97
Ladderstile Ride, Kings.T. KT2 200 CP92
Ladderswood Way, N11 121 DJ50
Ladds Way, Swan. BR8 229 FD98
Ladies Gro, St.Alb. AL3 64 CB18
Ladlands, SE22 204 DU87
Lady Aylesford Av, Stan. HA7 117 CH50
Sch Lady Bankes Inf & Jun Schs,
Hlgdn HA4 off Dawlish Dr 137 BU61
Lady Booth Rd, Kings.T. KT1 220 CL96
Sch Lady Boswell's C of E Prim Sch,
Sev. TN13 off Plymouth Dr 279 FJ125
Lady Cooper Ct, Berk. HP4
off Benningfield Gdns 60 AY17
Lady Craig Ct, Uxb. UB8
off Harlington Rd 157 BP71
Ladycroft Gdns, Orp. BR6 245 EQ106
Ladycroft Rd, SE13 185 EB83
Ladycroft Wk, Stan. HA7 117 CK53
Ladycroft Way, Orp. BR6 245 EQ106
Ladyday Pl, Slou. SL1
off Glentworth Pl 153 AQ74
Lady Dock Path, SE16 33 L5
Ladyegate Cl, Dor. RH5 285 CK135
Ladyegate Rd, Dor. RH5 285 CJ136
Sch Lady Eleanor Holles Sch, The,
Hmptn. TW12
off Hanworth Rd 198 CB92
Jun Dept, Hmptn. TW12
off Uxbridge Rd 198 CB92
Ladyfield Cl, Loug. IG10 107 EP42
Ladyfields, Loug. IG10 107 EP42
Northfleet DA11 213 GF91
Lady Forsdyke Way, Epsom
KT19 238 CN109
Ladygate La, Ruis. HA4 137 BP58
Ladygrove, Croy. CR0 243 DY109
Lady Gro, Welw.G.C. AL7 51 CY12
Ladygrove Dr, Guil. GU4 265 BA129
Lady Harewood Way, Epsom
KT19 238 CN109
Lady Hay, Wor.Pk. KT4 221 CT103
Sch Lady Margaret Prim Sch,
Sthl. UB1
off Lady Margaret Rd 158 BZ71
Lady Margaret Rd, N19 7 M1
NW5 7 L2
Southall UB1 158 BZ71
Sch Lady Margaret Sch, SW6 39 J7
Ladymead, Guil. GU1 264 AW133
Lady Meadow, Kings L. WD4 80 BK27
🛍 Ladymead Retail Pk, Guil.
GU1 264 AW133
Lady's Cl, Wat. WD18 97 BV42
Ladyshot, Harl. CM20 58 EU14
Ladysmith Av, E6 166 EL68
Ilford IG2 147 ER59
Ladysmith Cl, NW7 119 CU52
Ladysmith Rd, E16 23 L3
N17 122 DU54
N18 122 DV50
SE9 207 EN86
Enfield EN1 104 DS41
Harrow HA3 117 CE54
St. Albans AL3 65 CD19
Lady Somerset Rd, NW5 7 K1
Ladythorpe Cl, Add. KT15
off Church Rd 234 BH105
Ladywalk, Map.Cr. WD3 113 BE50
LADYWELL, SE13 205 EA85
⇌ Ladywell 205 EB85
Ladywell Cl, SE4
off Adelaide Av 185 EA84
Ladywell Hts, SE4 205 DZ86
Ladywell Prospect, Saw. CM21 58 FA06
Ladywell Rd, SE13 205 EA85
Ladywell St, E15 13 L9
Ladywood Av, Petts Wd BR5 227 ES99
Ladywood Cl, Rick. WD3 96 BH41
Ladywood Rd, Hert. SG14 53 DM09
Lane End DA2 211 FS92
Surbiton KT6 220 CN103
Lady Yorke Pk, Iver SL0 155 BD65
Lafone Av, Felt. TW13
off Alfred Rd 198 BW88
Lafone St, SE1 32 A4
Lagado Ms, SE16 33 K3
Lagger, The, Ch.St.G. HP8 112 AV48
Lagger Cl, Ch.St.G. HP8 112 AV48
Laglands Cl, Reig. RH2 272 DC132
Lagonda Av, Ilf. IG6 125 ET51
Lagonda Way, Dart. DA1 190 FJ84
Lagoon Rd, Orp. BR5 228 EV99
Laidlaw Dr, N21 103 DM42
Laidon Sq, Hem.H. HP2 62 BK16
Laing Cl, Ilf. IG6 125 ER51
Laing Dean, Nthlt. UB5 158 BW67
Laing Ho, SE5 off Comber Gro 43 J5
Laings Av, Mitch. CR4 222 DF96
Lainlock Pl, Houns. TW3
off Spring Gro Rd 178 CB81
Lainson St, SW18 202 DA87
Lairdale Cl, SE21 204 DQ88
Laird Av, Grays RM16 192 GD75
Laird Ho, SE5 43 J5
Lairs Cl, N7 8 B4
Lait Ho, Beck. BR3 225 EA95
Laitwood Rd, SW12 203 DH88
Lakanal, SE5 off Sceaux Gdns 43 P6
Lake, The, Bushey Hth WD23 116 CC46
Lake Av, Brom. BR1 206 EG93
Rainham RM13 170 FK68
Slough SL1 153 AR73
● Lake Business Cen, N17
off Tariff Rd 122 DU52
Lake Cl, SW19 off Lake Rd 201 CZ92
Byfleet KT14 234 BK112
Dagenham RM8 148 EW62
Lakedale Rd, SE18 187 ES79
Lake Dr, Bushey Hth WD23 116 CC47
Lake End Ct, Tap. SL6
off Taplow Rd 152 AH72
Lake End Rd, Dorney SL4 172 AH76
Taplow SL6 152 AH73
Lakefield Cl, SE20
off Limes Av 204 DV94
Lakefield Rd, N22 121 DP54
Lakefields Cl, Rain. RM13 170 FK68
Lake Gdns, Dag. RM10 148 FA64
Richmond TW10 199 CH89
Wallington SM6 223 DH104
Lakehall Gdns, Th.Hth. CR7 223 DP99
Lakehall Rd, Th.Hth. CR7 223 DP99
Lake Ho Rd, E11 146 EG62
Lakehurst Rd, Epsom KT19 238 CS106
Lakeland Cl, Chig. IG7 126 EV49
Harrow HA3 117 CD51
Lake La, Horl. RH6 289 DJ144
Lakenheath, N14 103 DK44
Lake Ri, Grays RM20 191 FU77
Romford RM1 149 FF55
Lake Rd, E10 145 EB59
SW19 201 CZ92
Croydon CR0 225 DZ103
Lower Nazeing EN9 72 EE21
Romford RM6 148 EX56
Virginia Water GU25 214 AV98
Laker Pl, SW15 201 CY86
Lakers Ri, Bans. SM7 256 DE116
Lakes Cl, Chilw. GU4 281 BB140
Lakes Ct, Stans.Abb. SG12 55 EB11
◆ Lakeside 191 FV76
🛍 Lakeside, Grays RM20 191 FV77
Lakeside, W13 off Edgehill Rd 159 CJ72
Beckenham BR3 225 EB97
Enfield EN2 103 DK42
Rainham RM13 170 FL68
Redhill RH1 272 DG132
Wallington SM6
off Derek Av 223 DH104
Weybridge KT13 217 BS103
Woking GU21 248 AS119
Lakeside Av, SE28 168 EU74
Ilford IG4 146 EK56
Lakeside Cl, SE25 224 DU96
Chigwell IG7 125 ET49
Ruislip HA4 137 BR56
Sidcup DA15 208 EW85
Woking GU21 248 AS119
Lakeside Ct, N4 143 DP61
Elstree WD6
off Cavendish Cres 100 CN43
Lakeside Cres, Barn. EN4 102 DF43
Brentwood CM14 130 FX48
Weybridge KT13
off Churchill Dr 217 BQ104
Lakeside Dr, NW10 160 CM69
Bromley BR2 226 EL104
Chobham GU24 232 AS113
Esher KT10 236 CC107
Stoke Poges SL2 154 AS67
Lakeside Gra, Wey. KT13 217 BQ104
● Lakeside Ind Est, Colnbr.
SL3 176 BG79
Lakeside Pl, Lon.Col. AL2 83 CK27
🛍 Lakeside Retail Pk, Grays
RM20 191 FU77
Lakeside Rd, N13 121 DM49
W14 26 C6
Cheshunt EN8 88 DW28
Slough SL3 175 BF80
Sch Lakeside Sch, Welw.G.C. AL8
off Lemsford La 51 CV11
Lakeside Way, Wem. HA9 140 CM63
Lakes La, Beac. HP9 111 AM54
Lakes Rd, Kes. BR2 244 EJ106
Lakeswood Rd, Petts Wd BR5 227 EP100
Lake Vw, Edg. HA8 118 CM50
North Holmwood RH5 285 CJ139
Potters Bar EN6 86 DC33
Lakeview Ct, SW19
off Victoria Dr 201 CY89
Lakeview Est, E3 11 K10
Lakeview Rd, SE27 203 DN92
Lake Vw Rd, Sev. TN13 278 FG122
Lakeview Rd, Well. DA16 188 EV84
Lakis Cl, NW3 off Flask Wk 142 DC63
LALEHAM, Stai. TW18 216 BJ97
Laleham Av, NW7 118 CR48
Laleham Cl, Stai. TW18
off Worple Rd 216 BH95
Sch Laleham C of E Prim Sch,
Laleham TW18
off The Broadway 216 BJ96
Laleham Ct, Wok. GU21 248 AY116
Sch Laleham Lea Prep Sch, Pur.
CR8 off Peaks Hill 241 DL110
Laleham Pk, Stai. TW18 216 BJ98
Laleham Reach, Cher. KT16 216 BH96
Laleham Rd, SE6 205 EC86
Shepperton TW17 216 BM98
Staines TW18 195 BF92
Lalor St, SW6 38 E8
Lamb All, St.Alb. AL3
off Market Pl 65 CD20
Lambarde Av, SE9 207 EN91
Lambarde Dr, Sev. TN13 278 FG123
Lambarde Rd, Sev. TN13 278 FG122
Lambardes Cl, Pr.Bot. BR6 246 EW110
Lamb Cl, Hat. AL10 67 CV19
Northolt UB5 158 BY69
Tilbury RM18
off Coleridge Rd 193 GJ82
Watford WD25 82 BW34
Lamberhurst Cl, Orp. BR5 228 EX102
Lamberhurst Rd, SE27 203 DN91
Dagenham RM8 148 EZ60
Lambert Av, Rich. TW9 180 CP83
Slough SL3 174 AY75
Lambert Cl, Bigg.H. TN16 260 EK116
Lambert Ct, Bushey WD23 98 BX42
Lambert Jones Ms, EC2
off The Barbican 19 J6
Lambert Rd, E16 24 A8
N12 120 DC50
SW2 203 DL85
Banstead SM7 240 DA114
Lamberts Pl, Croy. CR0 224 DR102
Lamberts Rd, Surb. KT5 220 CL99
Lambert St, N1 8 E7
Lambert Wk, Wem. HA9 139 CK62
Lambert Way, N12
off Woodhouse Rd 120 DC50
LAMBETH, SE1 30 C6
Sch Lambeth Acad, SW4
off Elms Rd 203 DJ85
Lambeth Br, SE1 30 B8
SW1 30 B8
Coll Lambeth Coll, Adare Cen,
SW16 off Adare Wk 203 DM89
Brixton Cen, SW2
off Brixton Hill 203 DM85
Clapham Cen, SW4 off Clapham
Common S Side 203 DJ85
Vauxhall Cen, SW8 41 P6
Lambeth High St, SE1 30 C9
Lambeth Hill, EC4 19 J10
H Lambeth Hosp, SW9 42 B10
⊖ Lambeth North 30 E5
★ Lambeth Palace, SE1 30 C7
Lambeth Palace Rd, SE1 30 C7
Lambeth Pier, SE1 30 B7
Lambeth Rd, SE1 30 D7
SE11 30 D7
Croydon CR0 223 DN101
Lambeth Twrs, SE11 30 E7
Lambeth Wk, SE1 30 D8
SE11 30 D8
Lambfold Ho, N7 8 A4
Lambkins Ms, E17 145 EC56
Lamb La, E8 10 E7
Lamble St, NW5 6 G2
Lambley Rd, Dag. RM9 168 EV65
Lambly Hill, Vir.W. GU25 214 AY97
Lambolle Pl, NW3 6 D5
Lambolle Rd, NW3 6 C5
Lambourn Chase, Rad. WD7 99 CF36
Lambourn Cl, W7 179 CF75
South Croydon CR2 241 DP109
Lambourne Av, SW19 201 CZ91
Lambourne Cl, Chig. IG7 126 EV48
Lambourne Ct, Wdf.Grn. IG8
off Navestock Cres 124 EJ53
Lambourne Cres, Chig. IG7 126 EV47
Woking GU21 233 BD113
Lambourne Dr, Cob. KT11 252 BX115
Hutton CM13 131 GE45
LAMBOURNE END, Rom.
RM4 108 EX44
Lambourne Gdns, E4 123 EA47
Barking IG11
off Lambourne Rd 167 ET66
Enfield EN1 104 DT40
Hornchurch RM12 150 FK61
Lambourne Gro, SE16 33 J9
Lambourne Pl, SE3
off Shooters Hill Rd 186 EH81
Sch Lambourne Prim Sch, Abridge
RM4 off Hoe La 108 EV42
Lambourne Rd, E11 145 EC59
Barking IG11 167 ES66
Chigwell IG7 125 ES49
Ilford IG3 147 ES61
Lambourn Gro, Kings.T. KT1 220 CP96
Lambourn Rd, SW4 41 K10
Lambrook Ter, SW6 38 E6
Lamb's Bldgs, EC1 19 L5
Lambs Cl, N9
off Winchester Rd 122 DU47
Cuffley EN6 87 DM29
Lambs Conduit Pas, WC1 18 C6
Lamb's Conduit St, WC1 18 C5
Lambscroft Av, SE9 206 EJ90
Lambscroft Way, Chal.St.P.
SL9 112 AY54
Lambs La N, Rain. RM13 170 FJ70
Lambs La S, Rain. RM13 169 FH71
Lambs Meadow, Wdf.Grn.
IG8 124 EK54
Lambs Ms, N1 8 G9
Lamb's Pas, EC1 19 L6
Lambs Ter, N9 122 DR47
Lamb St, E1 20 A6
Lambs Wk, Enf. EN2 104 DQ40
Lambton Av, Wal.Cr. EN8 89 DX32
Lambton Ms, N19
off Lambton Rd 143 DL60
Lambton Pl, W11 15 H10
Lambton Rd, N19 143 DL60
SW20 221 CW95
Lamb Wk, SE1 31 N5
Lambyn Cft, Horl. RH6 291 DJ147
Lamerock Rd, Brom. BR1 206 EF91
Lamerton Rd, Ilf. IG6 125 EP54
Lamerton St, SE8 46 A3
Lamford Cl, N17 122 DR52
Lamington St, W6 181 CV77
Lamlash St, SE11 30 G8
Lammas Av, Mitch. CR4 222 DG96
Lammas Cl, Stai. TW18 195 BE90
Lammas Ct, Stai. TW19 195 BD89
Windsor SL4 173 AQ82
Lammas Dr, Stai. TW18 195 BD90
Lammas Grn, SE26 204 DV90
Lammas La, Esher KT10 236 CA106
Lammasmead, Brox. EN10 71 DZ23
Lammas Pk, W5 179 CJ75

Lammas Pk Gdns, W5 179 CJ75
Lammas Pk Rd, W5 159 CJ74
Lammas Rd, E9 11 K7
E10 145 DY61
Richmond TW10 199 CJ91
Slough SL1 153 AK71
Watford WD18 98 BW43
Sch Lammas Sch, The, E10
off Seymour Rd 145 DZ60
Lammas Way, Loud. HP10 110 AC54
Lammermoor Rd, SW12 203 DH87
Lammtarra Pl, Epsom KT17
off Windmill La 239 CT112
Lamont Rd, SW10 39 P3
Lamont Rd Pas, SW10
off Lamont Rd 40 A3
LAMORBEY, Sid. DA15 207 ET88
Lamorbey Cl, Sid. DA15 207 ET88
Lamorna Av, Grav. DA12 213 GJ90
Lamorna Cl, E17 123 EC54
Orpington BR6 228 EU101
Radlett WD7 83 CH34
Lamorna Gro, Stan. HA7 117 CK53
Lampard Gro, N16 144 DT60
Lampern Sq, E2 20 D2
Lampeter Cl, NW9 140 CS58
Woking GU22 248 AY118
Lampeter Sq, W6 38 E3
Lampits, Hodd. EN11 71 EB17
Lamplighter Cl, E1 20 G5
Lamplighters Cl, Dart. DA1 210 FM86
Waltham Abbey EN9 90 EG34
Lampmead Rd, SE12 206 EE85
Lamp Office Ct, WC1 18 C5
Lamport Cl, SE18 37 K8
LAMPTON, Houns. TW3 178 CB81
Lampton Av, Houns. TW3 178 CB81
Lampton Ho Cl, SW19 201 CX91
Lampton Pk Rd, Houns. TW3 178 CB82
Lampton Rd, Houns. TW3 178 CB82
Sch Lampton Sch, Houns. TW3
off Lampton Av 178 CA81
Lamsey Rd, Hem.H. HP3 62 BK22
Lamson Rd, Rain. RM13 169 FF70
Lanacre Av, NW9 119 CT53
Lanadron Cl, Islw. TW7 179 CF82
Lanark Cl, W5 159 CJ71
Lanark Ms, W9 15 N3
Lanark Pl, W9 15 P4
Lanark Rd, W9 15 N3
Lanark Sq, E14 34 D6
Lanata Wk, Hayes UB4
off Ramulis Dr 158 BX70
Lanbury Rd, SE15 185 DX84
Lancashire Ct, W1 17 K10
Lancaster Av, E18 146 EH56
SE27 203 DP89
SW19 201 CX92
Barking IG11 167 ES66
Barnet EN4 102 DD38
Guildford GU1 281 AZ136
Mitcham CR4 223 DL99
Slough SL2 153 AQ70
Lancaster Cl, N1 9 P7
N17 off Park La 122 DU52
NW9 119 CT52
Ashford TW15 196 BL91
Bromley BR2 226 EF98
Egham TW20 194 AX92
Kingston upon Thames KT2 199 CK92
Pilgrim's Hatch CM15 130 FU43
Stanwell TW19 196 BL86
Woking GU21 249 BA116
Lancaster Cotts, Rich. TW10
off Lancaster Pk 200 CL86
Lancaster Ct, SE27 203 DP89
SW6 39 J5
W2 27 P1
Banstead SM7 239 CZ114
Walton-on-Thames KT12 217 BU101
Lancaster Dr, E14 34 F3
NW3 6 C5
Bovingdon HP3 79 AZ27
Hornchurch RM12 149 FH64
Loughton IG10 106 EL44
Lancaster Gdns, SW19 201 CY92
W13 179 CH75
Bromley BR1 226 EL99
Kingston upon Thames KT2 199 CK92
⊖ Lancaster Gate 16 A10
Lancaster Gate, W2 27 P1
Lancaster Gro, NW3 6 B5
★ Lancaster Ho, SW1 29 L4
Sch Lancasterian Prim Sch, N17
off King's Rd 122 DT53
Lancaster Ms, SW18
off East Hill 202 DB85
W2 15 P10
Richmond TW10
off Richmond Hill 200 CL86
Lancaster Pk, Rich. TW10 200 CL85
Lancaster Pl, SW19 201 CX92
WC2 18 C10
Hounslow TW4 178 BW82
Ilford IG1 off Staines Rd 147 EQ63
Twickenham TW1 199 CG86
Lancaster Rd, E7 13 P6
E11 146 EE61
E17 123 DX54
N4 143 DN59
N11 121 DK51
N18 122 DT50
NW10 141 CT64
SE25 224 DT96
SW19 201 CX92
W11 14 E9
Barnet EN4 102 DD43
Chafford Hundred RM16 191 FX78
Enfield EN2 104 DR39
Harrow HA2 138 CA57
North Weald Bassett CM16 92 FA26
Northolt UB5 158 CC65
St. Albans AL1 65 CF18
Southall UB1 158 BY73
Uxbridge UB8 156 BK65
Lancaster St, SE1 31 H5
Lancaster Ter, W2 16 A10
Lancaster Wk, W2 28 A4
Hayes UB3 157 BQ72
Lancaster Way, Abb.L. WD5 81 BT31
Worcester Park KT4 221 CV101
Lancaster W, W11
off Grenfell Rd 14 D10
Lancastrian Rd, Wall. SM6 241 DL108
Lancefield St, W10 14 G2
Lancell St, N16 144 DS62
Lancelot Av, Wem. HA0 139 CK63
Lancelot Cl, Slou. SL1 173 AN75
Lancelot Cres, Wem. HA0 139 CK63
Lancelot Gdns, E.Barn. EN4 120 DG45
Lancelot Pl, SW7 28 E5
Lancelot Rd, Ilf. IG6 125 ES51
Welling DA16 188 EU84
Wembley HA0 139 CK64
Lance Rd, Har. HA1 138 CC59
Lancer Sq, W8 27 L4
Lancey Cl, SE7 36 F8
Lanchester Rd, N6 142 DF57
Lanchester Way, SE14 45 H6
Lancing Gdns, N9 122 DT46
Lancing Rd, W13
off Drayton Grn Rd 159 CH73
Croydon CR0 223 DM100
Feltham TW13 197 BT89
Ilford IG2 147 ER58
Orpington BR6 228 EU103
Romford RM3 128 FL52
Lancing St, NW1 17 N3
Lancing Way, Crox.Grn WD3 97 BP43
Lancresse Cl, Uxb. UB8 156 BK65
Lancresse Ct, N1 9 N8
Landale Gdns, Dart. DA1 210 FJ87
Landau Way, Brox. EN10 89 DZ26
Erith DA8 190 FK78
Landcroft Rd, SE22 204 DT86
Landells Rd, SE22 204 DT86
Landen Pk, Horl. RH6 290 DE146
Lander Rd, Grays RM17 192 GD78
Landford Cl, Rick. WD3 114 BL47
Landford Rd, SW15 181 CW83
Landgrove Rd, SW19 202 DA92
Landmann Ho, SE16 32 F9
Landmann Way, SE14 45 K2
● Landmark Commercial Cen,
N18 122 DS51
Landmark Hts, E5 11 L1
Landmead Rd, Chsht EN8 89 DY29
Landon Pl, SW1 28 E6
Landons Cl, E14 34 F2
Landon Wk, E14 22 D10
Landon Way, Ashf. TW15
off Courtfield Rd 197 BP93
Landor Rd, SW9 183 DL83
Landor Wk, W12 181 CU75
Landra Gdns, N21 103 DP44
Landridge Dr, Enf. EN1 104 DV38
Landridge Rd, SW6 38 F8
Landrock Rd, N8 143 DL58
Landscape Rd, Warl. CR6 258 DV119
Woodford Green IG8 124 EH52
Landsdown Cl, New Barn.
EN5 102 DC42
Landseer Av, E12 147 EN64
Northfleet DA11 212 GD90
Landseer Cl, SW19
off Thorburn Way 222 DD95
Edgware HA8 118 CN54
Hornchurch RM11 149 FH60
Landseer Rd, N19 143 DL62
Enfield EN1 104 DU43
New Malden KT3 220 CR101
Sutton SM1 240 DA107
Lands End, Els. WD6 99 CK44
Landstead Rd, SE18 187 ER80
Landway, The, Orp. BR5 228 EW97
Lane, The, NW8 5 N10
SE3 47 P10
Chertsey KT16 216 BG97
Virginia Water GU25 214 AY97
Lane Av, Green. DA9 211 FW86
Lane Cl, NW2 141 CV62
Addlestone KT15 234 BG106
LANE END, Dart. DA2 211 FR92
Lane End, Berk. HP4 60 AT19
Bexleyheath DA7 189 FB83
Epsom KT18 238 CP114
Harlow CM17 74 EY15
Hatfield AL10 67 CT21
Lanefield Wk, Welw.G.C. AL8 51 CW09
Lane Gdns, Bushey Hth WD23 117 CE45
Claygate KT10 237 CF108
Lane Ms, E12
off Colchester Av 147 EM62
Lanercost Cl, SW2 203 DN89
Lanercost Gdns, N14 121 DL45
Lanercost Rd, SW2 203 DN89
Lanes Av, Nthflt DA11 213 GG90
Lanesborough Pl, SW1 29 H4
Sch Lanesborough Sch, Guil. GU1
off Maori Rd 265 AZ134
Laneside, Chis. BR7 207 EP92
Edgware HA8 118 CQ50
Laneside Av, Dag. RM8 148 EZ59
Laneway, SW15 201 CV85
Lane Wd Cl, Amer. HP7 94 AT39
Lanfranc Rd, E3 21 L1
Lanfrey Pl, W14 38 G1
Langaller La, Fetch. KT22 252 CB122
Langbourne Av, N6 142 DG61
Langbourne Pl, E14 34 C10
Sch Langbourne Prim Sch, SE21
off Lyall Av 204 DS90
Langbourne Way, Clay. KT10 237 CG107
Langbrook Rd, SE3 186 EK83
Lang Cl, Fetch. KT22 252 CB123
Langcroft Cl, Cars. SM5 222 DF104
Langdale, NW1 17 L2
Langdale Av, Mitch. CR4 222 DF97
Langdale Cl, SE17 43 J2
SW14 180 CP84
Dagenham RM8 148 EW60
Orpington BR6
off Grasmere Rd 227 EP104
Woking GU21 248 AW116
Langdale Ct, Hem.H. HP2
off Wharfedale 62 BL17
Langdale Cres, Bexh. DA7 188 FA80
Langdale Dr, Hayes UB4 157 BS68
Langdale Gdns, Horn. RM12 149 FG64
Perivale UB6 159 CH69
Waltham Cross EN8 105 DX35
Langdale Rd, SE10 46 E5
Thornton Heath CR7 223 DN98
Langdale St, E1 20 E9
Langdale Wk, Nthflt DA11
off Landseer Av 212 GE90
Langdon Ct, EC1 off City Rd 19 H1
NW10 160 CS67
Langdon Cres, E6 167 EN68
Langdon Dr, NW9 140 CQ60
DLR Langdon Park 22 D7
Langdon Pk, Tedd. TW11 199 CJ94
Langdon Pk Rd, N6 143 DJ59
Sch Langdon Pk Sch, E14 22 D8
Langdon Pl, SW14 180 CQ83
Langdon Rd, E6 167 EN67
Bromley BR2 226 EH97
Morden SM4 222 DC99
Sch Langdon Sch, E6
off Sussex Rd 167 EP67
Langdons Ct, Sthl. UB2 178 CA76
Langdon Shaw, Sid. DA14 207 ET92
Langdon Wk, Mord. SM4 222 DC99
Langdon Way, SE1 32 D9
Langfield Cl, Lwr Naze. EN9 72 EE22
Langford Cl, E8 10 C2
N15 144 DS58
NW8 5 P10
W3 180 CP75
St. Albans AL4 65 CJ18
Langford Ct, NW8 15 N1
Langford Cres, Cockfos. EN4 102 DF42
Langford Grn, SE5 184 DS83
Hutton CM13 131 GC44
Langford Ms, N1 8 F6
Langford Pl, NW8 15 P1
Sidcup DA14 208 EU90
Sch Langford Prim Sch, SW6 39 M8
Langford Rd, SW6 39 M8
Cockfosters EN4 102 DE42
Woodford Green IG8 124 EJ51
Langfords, Buck.H. IG9 124 EK47
Langfords Way, Croy. CR0 243 DY111
Langham Cl, N15
off Langham Rd 143 DP55
St. Albans AL4 65 CK15
Langham Ct, Horn. RM11 150 FK59
Langham Dene, Ken. CR8 257 DP115
Langham Dr, Rom. RM6 148 EV58
Langham Gdns, N21 103 DN43
W13 159 CH73
Edgware HA8 118 CQ52
Richmond TW10 199 CJ91
Wembley HA0 139 CJ61
Langham Ho Cl, Rich. TW10 199 CK91
Langham Pk Pl, Brom. BR2 226 EF98
Langham Pl, N15 143 DP55
W1 17 K7
W4 180 CS79
Egham TW20 195 AZ92
Langham Rd, N15 143 DP55
SW20 221 CW95
Edgware HA8 118 CQ51
Teddington TW11 199 CH92
Langham St, W1 17 K7
Langhedge Cl, N18 122 DT51
Langhedge La, N18 122 DT50
● Langhedge La Ind Est,
N18 122 DT51
Langholm Cl, SW12 203 DK87
Langholme, Bushey WD23 116 CC46
Langhorn Dr, Twick. TW2 199 CE87
Langhorne Ho, SE7
off Springfield Gro 186 EJ79
Langhorne Rd, Dag. RM10 168 FA66
Langland Ct, Nthwd. HA6 115 BQ52
Langland Cres, Stan. HA7 140 CL55
Langland Dr, Pnr. HA5 116 BY52
Langland Gdns, NW3 5 M2
Croydon CR0 225 DZ103
Langlands Dr, Lane End DA2 211 FS92
Langlands Ri, Epsom KT19
off Burnet Gro 238 CQ113
Langler Rd, NW10 14 B1
LANGLEY, Slou. SL3 175 BA76
⇌ Langley 175 BA75
Sch Langley Acad, Langley SL3
off Langley Rd 174 AY76
Langley Av, Hem.H. HP3 62 BL23
Ruislip HA4 137 BV60
Surbiton KT6 219 CK102
Worcester Park KT4 221 CX103
Langley Broom, Slou. SL3 175 AZ78
LANGLEYBURY, Kings L. WD4 81 BP34
Langleybury La, Kings L. WD4 97 BP37
● Langley Business Cen, Langley
SL3 175 BA75
Langley Cl, Epsom KT18 254 CR119
Guildford GU1 264 AW133
Romford RM3 128 FK52
Jct Langley Cor, Fulmer SL3 155 AZ65
● Langley Ct, Beck. BR3 225 EB99
Langley Ct, WC2 18 A10
Langley Cres, E11 146 EJ59
Dagenham RM9 168 EW66
Edgware HA8 118 CQ48
Hayes UB3 177 BT80
Kings Langley WD4 80 BN30
St. Albans AL3 64 CC18
Langley Dr, E11 146 EH59
W3 160 CP74
Brentwood CM14 130 FU48
Langley Gdns, Brom. BR2
off Great Elms Rd 226 EJ98
Dagenham RM9 168 EW66
Petts Wood BR5 227 EP100
Sch Langley Gram Sch, Langley
SL3 off Reddington Dr 175 AZ77
Langley Gro, N.Mal. KT3 220 CS96
Langley Hill, Kings L. WD4 80 BM29
Langley Hill Cl, Kings L. WD4 80 BN29
Langley La, SW8 42 B2
Abbots Langley WD5 81 BT31
Headley KT18 270 CP125
Langley Lo La, Kings L. WD4 80 BN31
Sch Langley Manor Sch, Langley
SL3 off St. Mary's Rd 154 AY74
Langley Meadow, Loug. IG10 107 ER40
Langley Oaks Av, S.Croy. CR2 242 DU110
Langley Pk, NW7 118 CS51
★ Langley Park Country Pk,
Slou. SL3 155 BA70
Langley Pk Rd, Iver SL0 155 BC72
Slough SL3 175 BA75
Sutton SM1, SM2 240 DC106
Sch Langley Pk Sch for Boys,
Beck. BR3
off Hawksbrook La 225 EB100
Sch Langley Pk Sch for Girls, Beck.
BR3 off Hawksbrook La 225 EC100
Langley Quay, Langley SL3 175 BA75
Langley Rd, SW19 221 CZ95
Abbots Langley WD5 81 BS31
Beckenham BR3 225 DY98
Chipperfield WD4 80 BH30
Isleworth TW7 179 CF82
Slough SL3 174 AW75
South Croydon CR2 243 DX109
Staines TW18 195 BF93
Surbiton KT6 220 CL101
Watford WD17 97 BU39
Welling DA16 188 EW79
Langley Row, Barn. EN5 101 CZ39
Langley St, WC2 18 A9
LANGLEY VALE, Epsom KT18 254 CR120
Langley Vale Rd, Epsom KT18 254 CR118
Langley Wk, Wok. GU22 248 AY119
Langley Way, Wat. WD17 97 BS40
West Wickham BR4 225 ED102
Langmans La, Wok. GU21 248 AV118
Langmans Way, Wok. GU21 248 AS116
Langmead Dr, Bushey Hth
WD23 117 CD46
Langmead St, SE27
off Beadman St 203 DP91
Langmore Ct, Bexh. DA6
off Regency Way 188 EX83
Langport Ct, Walt. KT12 218 BW102
Langridge Ms, Hmptn. TW12
off Oak Av 198 BZ93
Langroyd Rd, SW17 202 DF89
Langshott, Horl. RH6 291 DH146
Langshott Cl, Wdhm KT15 233 BE111
Sch Langshott Inf Sch, Horl. RH6
off Smallfield Rd 291 DJ148
Langshott La, Horl. RH6 291 DJ147
Langside Av, SW15 181 CU84
Langside Cres, N14 121 DK48
Langstone Ley, Welw.G.C. AL7 52 DB09
Langstone Way, NW7 119 CX52
Langston Hughes Cl, SE24
off Shakespeare Rd 183 DP84
Langston Rd, Loug. IG10 107 EQ43
Lang St, E1 20 G4
Langthorn Ct, EC2 19 L8
Langthorne Cres, Grays RM17 192 GC77
Langthorne Rd, E11 145 ED62
Langthorne St, SW6 38 C5
Langton Av, E6 25 L2
N20 120 DC45
Epsom KT17 239 CT111
Langton Cl, WC1 18 D3
Addlestone KT15 216 BH104
Slough SL1 153 AK74
Woking GU21 248 AT117
Langton Gro, Nthwd. HA6 115 BQ50
Langton Ho, SW16
off Colson Way 203 DJ91
Langton Pl, SW18
off Merton Rd 202 DA88
Langton Ri, SE23 204 DV87
Langton Rd, NW2 141 CW62
SW9 43 H5
Harrow HA3 116 CC52
Hoddesdon EN11 71 DZ17
West Molesey KT8 218 CC98
Sch Langtons Inf & Jun Schs, Horn.
RM11 off Westland Av 150 FL60
Langton's Meadow, Farn.Com.
SL2 153 AQ65
Langton St, SW10 39 P3
Langton Way, SE3 47 M6
Croydon CR0 242 DS105
Egham TW20 195 BC93
Grays RM16 193 GJ77
Langtry Pl, SW6 39 K2
Langtry Rd, NW8 5 L9
Northolt UB5 158 BX68
Langtry Wk, NW8 5 N8
Langwood Chase, Tedd. TW11 199 CJ93
Langwood Cl, Ashtd. KT21 254 CN117
Langwood Gdns, Wat. WD17 97 BU39
Langworth Cl, Dart. DA2 210 FK90
Langworth Dr, Hayes UB4 157 BU72
Lanherne Ho, SW20 201 CX94
Lanhill Rd, W9 15 J4
Lanier Rd, SE13 205 EC86
Lanigan Dr, Houns. TW3 198 CB85
Lankaster Gdns, N2 120 DD53
Lankers Dr, Har. HA2 138 BZ58
Lankester Sq, Oxt. RH8 275 ED128
Lankton Cl, Beck. BR3 225 EC95
Lannock Rd, Hayes UB3 157 BS74
Lannoy Pt, SW6
off Pellant Rd 38 F4
Lannoy Rd, SE9 207 EQ88
Lanrick Copse, Berk. HP4 60 AY18
Lanrick Rd, E14 23 H8
Lanridge Rd, SE2 188 EX76
Lansbury Av, N18 122 DR50
Barking IG11 168 EU66
Feltham TW14 197 BV86
Romford RM6 148 EY57
Lansbury Cl, NW10 140 CQ64
Lansbury Cres, Dart. DA1 210 FN85
Lansbury Dr, Hayes UB4 157 BT71
Lansbury Est, E14 22 C8
Lansbury Gdns, E14 22 G8
Tilbury RM18 193 GG81
Sch Lansbury Lawrence Prim Sch,
E14 22 C9
Lansbury Rd, Enf. EN3 105 DX39
Lansbury Way, N18 122 DS50
Lanscombe Wk, SW8 42 A6
Lansdell Rd, Mitch. CR4 222 DG96
Lansdown, Guil. GU1 265 BA134
Lansdown Cl, Walt. KT12 218 BW102
Woking GU21 248 AT119
Lansdowne Av, Bexh. DA7 188 EX80
Orpington BR6 227 EP102
Slough SL1 154 AS74
Lansdowne Cl, SW20 201 CX94
Surbiton KT5 220 CP103
Twickenham TW1 199 CF88
Watford WD25 98 BX35
Coll Lansdowne Coll, W2 27 L1
Lansdowne Copse, Wor.Pk.
KT4 221 CU103
Lansdowne Ct, Pur. CR8 241 DP110
Slough SL1 154 AS74
Worcester Park KT4 221 CU103
Lansdowne Cres, W11 26 F1
Lansdowne Dr, E8 10 D5
Lansdowne Gdns, SW8 42 A6
Lansdowne Grn, SW8 41 P5
Lansdowne Gro, NW10 140 CS63
Lansdowne Hill, SE27 203 DP90
Lansdowne La, SE7 186 EK79
Lansdowne Ms, SE7 186 EK78
W11 26 G2
Lansdowne Pl, SE1 31 M6
SE19 204 DT94
Sch Lansdowne Prim Sch, Til.
RM18 off Alexandra Rd 193 GF82
Lansdowne Ri, W11 26 F1
Lansdowne Rd, E4 123 EA47
E11 146 EF61
E17 145 EA57
E18 146 EG55
N3 119 CZ52
N10 121 DJ54
N17 122 DT53
SW20 201 CW94
W11 14 F10
Bromley BR1 206 EG94
Chesham HP5 76 AQ29
Lansdowne Rd, Croy. CR0 224 DR103
Epsom KT19 238 CQ108
Harrow HA1 139 CE59
Hounslow TW3 178 CB83
Ilford IG3 147 ET60
Purley CR8 241 DN112
Sevenoaks TN13 279 FK122
Staines TW18 196 BH94
Stanmore HA7 117 CJ51
Tilbury RM18 193 GF82
Uxbridge UB8 157 BP72
Lansdowne Row, W1 29 K2
Sch Lansdowne Sch, SW9 42 C10
Lansdowne Sq, Nthflt DA11 213 GF86
Lansdowne Ter, WC1 18 B5
Lansdowne Wk, W11 26 F2
Lansdowne Way, SW8 41 P6
Lansdowne Wd Cl, SE27 203 DP90
Lansdown Pl, Nthflt DA11 213 GF88
Lansdown Rd, E7 166 EJ66
Chalfont St. Peter SL9 112 AX53
Sidcup DA14 208 EV90
Lansfield Av, N18 122 DU49
Lanson Bldg, SW8 41 J4
Lantern Cl, SW15 181 CU84
Orpington BR6 245 EP105
Wembley HA0 139 CK64
Lanterns Ct, E14 34 B5
Lantern Way, West Dr. UB7 176 BL75
Lanthorn Cl, Brox. EN10 71 DY19
Lant St, SE1 31 J4
Lanvanor Rd, SE15 44 G8
Lapford Cl, W9 15 H4
Lapis Cl, NW10 160 CN69
La Plata Gro, Brwd. CM14 130 FV48
Lapponum Wk, Hayes UB4
off Lochan Cl 158 BY70
Lapse Wd Wk, SE23 204 DV89
Lapstone Gdns, Har. HA3 139 CJ58
Lapwing Cl, Erith DA8 189 FH80
Hemel Hempstead HP2 62 BL16
South Croydon CR2 243 DY110
Lapwing Ct, Surb. KT6
off Chaffinch Cl 220 CN104
Lapwing Gro, Guil. GU4 265 BD132
Lapwings, The, Grav. DA12 213 GK89
Lapwing Ter, E7
off Hampton Rd 146 EK64
Lapwing Twr, SE8 45 N2
Lapwing Way, Abb.L. WD5 81 BU31
Hayes UB4 158 BX72
Lapworth Cl, Orp. BR6 228 EW103
Lara Cl, SE13 205 EC86
Chessington KT9 238 CL108
Larbert Rd, SW16 223 DJ95
Larby Pl, Epsom KT17 238 CS110
Larch Av, W3 160 CS74
Bricket Wood AL2 82 BY30
Guildford GU1 264 AW132
Larch Cl, E13 24 C4
N11 120 DG52
N19 off Bredgar Rd 143 DJ61
SE8 45 P3
SW12 203 DH89
Cheshunt EN7 off The Firs 88 DS27
Kingswood KT20 256 DC121
Penn HP10 110 AC45
Redhill RH1 288 DC136
Slough SL2 153 AP71
Warlingham CR6 259 DY119
Larch Cres, Epsom KT19 238 CP107
Hayes UB4 158 BW70
Larch Dene, Orp. BR6 227 EN103
Larch Dr, W4
off Gunnersbury Av 180 CN78
Larches, The, N13 122 DQ48
Amersham HP6 94 AV38
Bushey WD23 98 BY43
Northwood HA6
off Rickmansworth Rd 115 BQ51
St. Albans AL4 65 CK16
Uxbridge UB10 157 BP69
Woking GU21 248 AY116
Larches Av, SW14 180 CR84
Enfield EN1 104 DW35
Larch Grn, NW9
off Clayton Fld 118 CS53
Larch Gro, Sid. DA15 207 ET88
Larchlands, The, Penn HP10 110 AD46
Larchmoor Pk, Stoke P. SL2 134 AU64
Larch Ri, Berk. HP4 60 AU18
Larch Rd, E10 145 EA61
NW2 141 CW63
Dartford DA1 210 FK87
Larch Tree Way, Croy. CR0 225 EA104
Larch Wk, Swan. BR8 229 FD96
Larch Way, Brom. BR2 227 EN101
Larchwood Av, Rom. RM5 127 FB51
Larchwood Cl, Bans. SM7 255 CY116
Romford RM5 127 FC51
Larchwood Dr, Eng.Grn TW20 194 AV93
Larchwood Gdns, Pilg.Hat.
CM15 130 FU44
Larchwood Ho, Chig. IG7 126 EV49
Sch Larchwood Prim Sch, Pilg.Hat.
CM15 off Larchwood Gdns 130 FU44
Larchwood Rd, SE9 207 EP89
Hemel Hempstead HP2 62 BM18
Larcombe Cl, Croy. CR0 242 DT105
Larcom St, SE17 31 K9
Larden Rd, W3 160 CS74
Sch La Retraite RC Girls' Sch,
SW12 off Atkins Rd 203 DJ87
Largewood Av, Surb. KT6 220 CN103
Largo Wk, Erith DA8
off Selkirk Dr 189 FE81
Larissa St, SE17 31 M10
Lark Av, Stai. TW18 195 BF90
Larkbere Rd, SE26 205 DY91
Lark Cl, Warley CM14 130 FV49
Larken Cl, Bushey WD23
off Larken Dr 116 CC46
Larken Dr, Bushey WD23 116 CC46
Larkfield, Cob. KT11 235 BU113
Larkfield Av, Har. HA3 139 CH55
Larkfield Cl, Brom. BR2 226 EF103
Larkfield Cl, Smallfield RH6
off Cooper Cl 291 DN148
Larkfield Rd, Rich. TW9 180 CL84
Sevenoaks TN13 278 FC123
Sidcup DA14 207 ET90

Larkfields, Nthflt DA11 212 GE90
Larkhall Cl, Hersham KT12 236 BW107
Larkhall La, SW4 41 N9
Larkhall Prim Sch, SW4 41 P9
Larkhall Ri, SW4 41 M10
Larkham Cl, Felt. TW13 197 BS90
Larkhill Ter, SE18
off Prince Imperial Rd 187 EN80
Larkin Cl, Couls. CR5 257 DM117
Hutton CM13 131 GC45
Larkings La, Stoke P. SL2 154 AV67
Larkins Rd, Lon.Gat.Air. RH6 290 DD152
Lark Ri, E.Hors. KT24 267 BS131
Hatfield AL10 67 CU20
Lark Row, E2 10 G9
Larksfield, Eng.Grn TW20 194 AW94
Horley RH6 291 DH147
Larksfield Gro, Enf. EN1 104 DV39
Larks Gro, Bark. IG11 167 ES66
Larkshall Ct, Rom. RM7 127 FC54
Larkshall Cres, E4 123 EC49
Larkshall Rd, E4 123 EC50
Larkspur Cl, E6 24 G6
N17 off Fryatt Rd 122 DR52
NW9 140 CP57
Hemel Hempstead HP1 61 BE19
Orpington BR6 228 EW103
Ruislip HA4 137 BQ59
South Ockendon RM15 171 FW69
Larkspur Gro, Edg. HA8 118 CQ49
Larkspur Way, Epsom KT19 238 CQ106
North Holmwood RH5 285 CK139
Larks Ri, Chesh. HP5 76 AR33
Larkswood, Harl. CM17 74 EW17
Larkswood Cl, Erith DA8 189 FG81
Larkswood Ct, E4 123 ED50
Larkswood Leisure Pk, E4
off New Rd 123 EC49
Larkswood Prim Sch, E4
off New Rd 123 EB49
Larkswood Ri, Pnr. HA5 138 BW56
St. Albans AL4 65 CJ15
Larkswood Rd, E4 123 EA49
Lark Way, Cars. SM5 222 DE101
Larkway Cl, NW9 140 CR56
Larmans Rd, Enf. EN3 104 DW36
Larmenier & Sacred Heart Prim Sch, W6 26 D9
Larnach Rd, W6 38 C3
Larner Ct, W12
off Heathstan Rd 161 CU72
Larne Rd, Ruis. HA4 137 BT59
Larner Rd, Erith DA8 189 FE80
La Roche Cl, Slou. SL3 174 AW76
Larpent Av, SW15 201 CW85
Larsen Dr, Wal.Abb. EN9 89 ED34
Larwood Cl, Grnf. UB6 139 CD64
La Sainte Union Cath Sch, NW5 off Highgate Rd 142 DG62
La Salette Cath Prim Sch, Rain. RM13 off Dunedin Rd 169 FF69
Lascelles Av, Har. HA1 139 CD59
Lascelles Cl, E11 145 ED61
Pilgrim's Hatch CM15 130 FU43
Lascelles Rd, Slou. SL3 174 AV76
Lascotts Rd, N22 121 DM51
Las Palmas Est, Shep. TW17 217 BQ101
Lassa Rd, SE9 206 EL85
Lassell St, SE10 47 H1
Lasseter Pl, SE3 47 K2
Lasswade Rd, Cher. KT16 215 BF101
Latchett Rd, E18 124 EH53
Latchford Pl, Chig. IG7 126 EV49
Hemel Hempstead HP1 62 BG21
Latching Cl, Rom. RM3
off Troopers Dr 128 FK49
Latchingdon Ct, E17 145 DX56
Latchingdon Gdns, Wdf.Grn. IG8 124 EL51
Latchmere Cl, Rich. TW10 200 CL92
Latchmere Inf Sch, Kings.T. KT2 off Latchmere Rd 200 CM93
Latchmere Jun Sch, Kings.T. KT2 off Latchmere Rd 200 CM93
Latchmere La, Kings.T. KT2 200 CM93
Latchmere Pas, SW11 40 D9
Latchmere Rd, SW11 40 E8
Kingston upon Thames KT2 200 CL94
Latchmere St, SW11 40 E8
Latchmoor Av, Chal.St.P. SL9 134 AX56
Latchmoor Gro, Chal.St.P. SL9 134 AX56
Latchmoor Way, Chal.St.P. SL9 134 AX56
Lateward Rd, Brent. TW8 179 CK79
Latham Cl, E6 25 H8
Biggin Hill TN16 260 EJ116
Dartford DA2 211 FS89
Twickenham TW1 199 CG87
Latham Gra, Upmin. RM14 150 FQ61
Latham Ho, E1 21 K8
Latham Rd, Bexh. DA6 208 FA85
Twickenham TW1 199 CF87
Lathams Way, Croy. CR0 223 DM102
Lathkill Cl, Enf. EN1 122 DU45
Lathom Jun Sch, E6
off Lathom Rd 166 EL66
Lathom Rd, E6 167 EM66
LATIMER, Chesh. HP5 94 AY36
Latimer, SE17 43 N1
Latimer Av, E6 167 EM67
Latimer Cl, Amer. HP6 94 AW39
Hemel Hempstead HP2 62 BN15
Pinner HA5 116 BW53
Watford WD18 115 BS45
Woking GU22 249 BB116
Worcester Park KT4 239 CV105
Latimer Ct, Earls. RH1 288 DF136
Latimer Dr, Horn. RM12 150 FK62
Latimer Gdns, Pnr. HA5 116 BW53
Welwyn Garden City AL7 52 DB09
Latimer Ind Est, W10 14 B8
Latimer Pl, W10 14 B8
Latimer Road 14 D10
Latimer Rd, E7 146 EH63
N15 144 DS58
SW19 202 DB93
W10 14 A7
Barnet EN5 102 DB41
Chenies WD3 95 BB38
Chesham HP5 94 AU36
Latimer Rd, Croy. CR0
off Abbey Rd 223 DP104
Teddington TW11 199 CF92
Latimer Way, Knot.Grn HP9 110 AJ49
Latitude Apts, N16 144 DS60
Latitude Ct, E16
off Albert Basin Way 167 EQ73
Latium Cl, St.Alb. AL1 65 CD21
Latona Dr, Grav. DA12 213 GM92
Latona Rd, SE15 44 C3
La Tourne Gdns, Orp. BR6 227 EQ104
Lattimer Pl, W4 180 CS79
Lattimore Rd, St.Alb. AL1 65 CE21
LATTON BUSH, Harl. CM18 74 EU18
Latton Cl, Esher KT10 236 CB105
Walton-on-Thames KT12 218 BY101
Latton Common, Harl. CM17 74 EV18
Latton Common Rd, Harl. CM18 74 EU18
Latton Grn, Harl. CM18 73 ET19
Latton Grn Prim Sch, Harl. CM18 off Riddings La 73 ET19
Latton Hall Cl, Harl. CM20 58 EU14
Latton Ho, Harl. CM18 74 EV18
Latton St, Harl. CM20 58 EU14
Potter Street CM17 74 EW18
Latymer All Saints C of E Prim Sch, N9
off Hydethorpe Av 122 DT47
Latymer Cl, Wey. KT13 235 BQ105
Latymer Ct, W6 26 D9
Latymer Rd, N9 122 DT46
Latymer Sch, The, N9
off Haselbury Rd 122 DS47
Latymer Upr Sch, W6
off King St 181 CU77
Latymer Way, N9 122 DR47
Laubin Cl, Twick. TW1 179 CH84
Lauder Cl, Nthlt. UB5 158 BX68
Lauderdale Dr, Rich. TW10 199 CK90
Lauderdale Pl, EC2
off The Barbican 19 J6
Lauderdale Rd, W9 15 L3
Hunton Bridge WD4 81 BQ33
Lauderdale Twr, EC2 19 J6
Laud St, SE11 30 C10
Croydon CR0 224 DQ104
Laugan Wk, SE17 off East St 31 K10
Laughton Ct, Borwd. WD6
off Banks Rd 100 CR40
Laughton Rd, Nthlt. UB5 158 BX67
Launcelot Prim Sch, Downham BR1 off Launcelot Rd 206 EG91
Launcelot Rd, Brom. BR1 206 EG91
Launcelot St, SE1 30 E5
Launceston, Chorl. WD3 95 BB44
Launceston Cl, Rom. RM3 128 FJ53
Launceston Gdns, Perivale UB6 159 CJ67
Launceston Pl, W8 27 N6
Launceston Rd, Perivale UB6 159 CJ67
Launch St, E14 34 E6
Launders Gate, W3 180 CP75
Launders La, Rain. RM13 170 FM69
Laundress La, N16 144 DU62
Laundry La, N1 9 J7
Lower Nazeing EN9 90 EE25
Laundry Ms, SE23 205 DY87
Laundry Rd, W6 38 E3
Guildford GU1 280 AW135
Launton Dr, Bexh. DA6 188 EX84
Laura Cl, E11 146 EJ57
Enfield EN1 104 DS43
Lauradale Rd, N2 142 DF56
Laura Dr, Swan. BR8 209 FG94
Laurance Haines Prim & Nurs Sch, Wat. WD18
off Vicarage Rd 97 BU44
Laura Pl, E5 10 G1
Laureate Way, Hem.H. HP1 62 BG18
Laurel Apts, SE17
off Townsend St 31 N8
Laurel Av, Eng.Grn TW20 194 AV92
Gravesend DA12 213 GJ89
Potters Bar EN6 85 CZ32
Slough SL3 174 AY75
Twickenham TW1 199 CF88
Laurel Bk, Felden HP3 61 BF23
Laurel Bk Gdns, SW6 39 H8
Laurel Bk Rd, Enf. EN2 104 DQ39
Laurel Bk Vil, W7
off Lower Boston Rd 159 CE74
Laurel Cl, N19
off Hargrave Pk 143 DJ61
SW17 202 DE92
Colnbrook SL3 175 BE80
Dartford DA1
off Willow Rd 210 FJ88
Hemel Hempstead HP2 62 BM19
Hutton CM13 131 GB43
Ilford IG6 125 EQ51
Sidcup DA14 208 EU90
Watford WD19 116 BX45
Woking GU21 233 BD113
Laurel Ct, Amer. HP6 77 AQ36
Cuffley EN6
off Station Rd 87 DM29
Laurel Cres, Croy. CR0 225 EA104
Romford RM7 149 FE60
Woking GU21 233 BC113
Laurel Dr, N21 121 DN45
Oxted RH8 276 EF131
South Ockendon RM15 171 FX70
Laurel Flds, Pot.B. EN6 85 CZ31
Laurel Gdns, E4 123 EB45
NW7 118 CR48
W7 159 CE74
Bromley BR1 226 EL98
Hounslow TW4 178 BY84
New Haw KT15 234 BH110
Laurel Gro, SE20 204 DV94
SE26 205 DX91
Laurel La, Horn. RM12
off Station La 150 FL61
West Drayton UB7 176 BL77
Laurel Lo La, Barn. EN5 101 CW36
Laurel Manor, Sutt. SM2 240 DC108
Laurel Pk, Har. HA3 117 CF52
Laurel Rd, SW13 181 CU82
SW20 221 CV95
Chalfont St. Peter SL9 112 AX53
Hampton Hill TW12 199 CD92
St. Albans AL1 65 CF20
Laurels, The, Bans. SM7 255 CZ117
Cobham KT11 252 BY115
Dartford DA2 210 FJ90
Potten End HP4 61 BB17
Waltham Cross EN7 88 DS27
Weybridge KT13 217 BR104
Laurelsfield, St.Alb. AL3 64 CB23
Laurels Rd, Iver SL0 155 BD68
Laurel St, E8 10 B5
Laurel Vw, N12 120 DB48
Laurel Way, E18 146 EF56
N20 120 DA48
Laurence Ms, W12
off Askew Rd 181 CU75
Laurence Pountney Hill, EC4 19 L10
Laurence Pountney La, EC4 19 M10
Laurie Gro, SE14 45 M6
Laurie Rd, W7 159 CE71
Laurier Rd, NW5 143 DH62
Croydon CR0 224 DT101
Lauries Cl, Hem.H. HP1 61 BB22
Laurie Wk, Rom. RM1
off Market Pl 149 FE56
Laurimel Cl, Stan. HA7
off September Way 117 CH51
Laurino Pl, Bushey Hth WD23 116 CC47
Lauriston Prim Sch, E9 11 J8
Lauriston Rd, E9 11 J8
SW19 201 CX93
Lausanne Rd, N8 143 DN56
SE15 45 H7
Lauser Rd, Stanw. TW19 196 BJ87
Laustan Cl, Guil. GU1 265 BC134
Lavell St, N16 9 M1
Lavender Av, NW9 140 CQ60
Mitcham CR4 222 DE95
Pilgrim's Hatch CM15 130 FV43
Worcester Park KT4 221 CW104
Lavender Cl, SW3 40 B3
Bromley BR2 226 EL100
Carshalton SM5 240 DG105
Chaldon CR3 274 DQ125
Cheshunt EN7 88 DT27
Coulsdon CR5 257 DJ119
Harlow CM20 57 ES14
Hatfield AL10 66 CS15
Leatherhead KT22 253 CJ123
Redhill RH1 289 DH139
Romford RM3 128 FK52
Lavender Ct, W.Mol. KT8
off Molesham Way 218 CB97
Lavender Cres, St.Alb. AL3 64 CC18
Lavender Dr, Uxb. UB8 156 BM71
Lavender Gdns, SW11 182 DF84
Enfield EN2 103 DP39
Harrow Weald HA3 117 CE51
Lavender Gate, Oxshott KT22 236 CB113
Lavender Gro, E8 10 B7
Mitcham CR4 222 DE95
Lavender Hill, SW11 182 DE84
Enfield EN2 103 DN39
Swanley BR8 229 FD97
Lavender Pk Rd, W.Byf. KT14 234 BG112
Lavender Pl, Ilf. IG1 147 EP64
Lavender Prim Sch, Enf. EN2
off Lavender Rd 104 DS39
Lavender Ri, West Dr. UB7 176 BN75
Lavender Rd, SE16 33 L2
SW11 40 B10
Carshalton SM5 240 DG105
Croydon CR0 223 DM100
Enfield EN2 104 DR39
Epsom KT19 238 CP106
Sutton SM1 240 DD105
Uxbridge UB8 156 BM71
Woking GU22 249 BB116
Lavender St, E15 13 J4
Lavender Sweep, SW11 182 DF84
Lavender Ter, SW11 40 D10
Lavender Vale, Wall. SM6 241 DK107
Lavender Wk, SW11 182 DF84
Hemel Hempstead HP2 62 BK18
Mitcham CR4 222 DG97
Lavender Way, Croy. CR0 225 DX100
Lavengro Rd, SE27 204 DQ89
Lavenham Rd, SW18 201 CZ89
Lavernock Rd, Bexh. DA7 188 FA82
Laverock Sch, Oxt. RH8
off Bluehouse La 276 EE128
Lavers Rd, N16 144 DS62
Laverstoke Gdns, SW15 201 CU87
Laverton Ms, SW5 27 M9
Laverton Pl, SW5 27 M9
Lavidge Rd, SE9 206 EL89
Lavina Gro, N1 8 C10
Lavington Cl, E9 11 N4
Lavington Rd, W13 159 CH74
Croydon CR0 223 DM104
Lavington St, SE1 31 H3
Lavinia Av, Wat. WD25 82 BX34
Lavinia Rd, Dart. DA1 210 FM86
Lavrock La, Rick. WD3 114 BM45
Lawbrook La, Guil. GU5 283 BQ144
Lawdale Jun Sch, E2 20 D2
Lawdons Gdns, Croy. CR0 241 DP105
Lawford Av, Chorl. WD3 95 BC44
Lawford Cl, Chorl. WD3 95 BC44
Hornchurch RM12 150 FJ63
Lawford Gdns, Dart. DA1 210 FJ85
Kenley CR8 258 DQ116
Lawford Rd, N1 9 N7
NW5 7 L5
W4 180 CQ80
Law Ho, Bark. IG11 168 EU68
Lawkland, Farn.Royal SL2 153 AQ69
Lawless St, E14 22 D10
Lawley Rd, N14 121 DH45
Lawley St, E5 144 DW63
Lawn, The, Harl. CM20 58 EV12
Southall UB2 178 CA78
Lawn Av, West Dr. UB7 176 BJ75
Lawn Cl, N9 122 DT45
Bromley BR1 206 EH93
Datchet SL3 174 AW80
New Malden KT3 220 CS96
Ruislip HA4 137 BT62
Swanley BR8 229 FC96
Lawn Cres, Rich. TW9 180 CM82
Lawn Fm Gro, Rom. RM6 148 EY56
Lawn Gdns, W7 159 CE74
Lawn Ho Cl, E14 34 E4
Lawn La, SW8 42 B2
Hemel Hempstead HP3 62 BK22
Lawn Pk, Sev. TN13 279 FH127
Lawn Prim Sch, Nthflt DA11
off High St 212 GC86
Lawn Rd, NW3 6 E2
Beckenham BR3 205 DZ94
Gravesend DA11 212 GC86
Guildford GU2 280 AW137
Uxbridge UB8 156 BJ66
Lawns, The, E4 123 EA50
SE3 47 K10
SE19 224 DR95
Colnbrook SL3 175 BE81
Lawns, The, Hem.H. HP1 61 BE19
Pinner HA5 116 CB52
St. Albans AL3 64 CC19
Shenley WD7 84 CL33
Sidcup DA14 208 EV91
Sutton SM2 239 CY108
Welwyn Garden City AL8 51 CX06
Lawns Ct, Wem. HA9
off The Avenue 140 CM61
Lawns Cres, Grays RM17 192 GD79
Lawns Dr, The, Brox. EN10 71 DZ21
Lawnside, SE3 186 EF84
Lawnsmead, Won. GU5 281 BB144
Lawns Way, Rom. RM5 127 FC52
Lawn Ter, SE3 47 K10
Lawn Vale, Pnr. HA5 116 BX54
Lawrance Gdns, Chsht EN8 89 DX28
Lawrance Rd, St.Alb. AL3 64 CC16
Lawrance Sq, Nthflt DA11 213 GF90
Lawrence Av, E12 147 EN63
E17 123 DX53
N13 121 DP49
NW7 118 CS49
NW10 160 CR67
New Malden KT3 220 CR100
Stanstead Abbotts SG12 55 EC11
Lawrence Bldgs, N16 144 DT62
Lawrence Campe Cl, N20
off Friern Barnet La 120 DD48
Lawrence Cl, E3 22 A1
N15 144 DS55
W12 off Australia Rd 161 CV73
Guildford GU4
off Ladygrove Dr 265 BB129
Hertford SG14 53 DL08
Lawrence Ct, NW7 118 CS50
Lawrence Cres, Dag. RM10 149 FB62
Edgware HA8 118 CN54
Lawrence Dr, Uxb. UB10 137 BQ63
Lawrence Gdns, NW7 119 CT48
Tilbury RM18 193 GH80
Lawrence Hall, E13 24 A4
Lawrence Hall End, Welw.G.C. AL7 51 CY12
Lawrence Hill, E4 123 EA47
Lawrence Hill Gdns, Dart. DA1 210 FJ86
Lawrence Hill Rd, Dart. DA1 210 FJ86
Lawrence La, EC2 19 K9
Buckland RH3 271 CV131
Lawrence Moorings, Saw. CM21 58 EZ06
Lawrence Orchard, Chorl. WD3 95 BD43
Lawrence Pl, N1 8 B8
Lawrence Rd, E6 166 EK67
E13 166 EH67
N15 144 DS56
N18 122 DV49
SE25 224 DT98
W5 179 CJ77
Erith DA8 189 FB80
Hampton TW12 198 BZ94
Hayes UB4 157 BQ68
Hounslow TW4 178 BW84
Pinner HA5 138 BX57
Richmond TW10 199 CJ91
Romford RM2 149 FH57
West Wickham BR4 244 EG105
Lawrence St, E16 23 M7
NW7 119 CT49
SW3 40 C3
Lawrence Way, NW10 140 CQ62
Slough SL1 153 AK71
Lawrence Weaver Cl, Mord. SM4
off Green La 222 DA100
Lawrie Pk Av, SE26 204 DV92
Lawrie Pk Cres, SE26 204 DV92
Lawrie Pk Gdns, SE26 204 DV91
Lawrie Pk Rd, SE26 204 DV93
Laws Cl, SE25 224 DR98
Lawson Cl, E16 24 D7
SW19 201 CX90
Ilford IG1 147 ER64
Lawson Ct, N11 off Ringway 121 DJ51
Lawson Est, SE1 31 L7
Lawson Gdns, Dart. DA1 210 FK85
Pinner HA5 137 BV55
Lawson Rd, Dart. DA1 190 FK84
Enfield EN3 104 DW39
Southall UB1 158 BZ70
Lawson Wk, Cars. SM5 240 DF110
Law St, SE1 31 M6
Lawton Rd, E3 21 M3
E10 145 EC60
Cockfosters EN4 102 DD41
Loughton IG10 107 EP41
Laxcon Cl, NW10 140 CQ64
Laxey Rd, Orp. BR6 245 ET107
Laxley Cl, SE5 43 H4
Laxton Gdns, Merst. RH1 273 DK128
Shenley WD7 84 CL32
Laxton Pl, NW1 17 K4
Layard Rd, SE16 32 F8
Enfield EN1 104 DT39
Thornton Heath CR7 224 DR96
Layard Sq, SE16 32 F8
Layborne Av, Noak Hill RM3
off North End 128 FJ47
Laybrook, St.Alb. AL4 65 CG16
Layburn Cres, Slou. SL3 175 BB79
Laycock Prim Sch, N1 8 G5
Laycock St, N1 8 F5
Layer Gdns, W3 160 CN73
Layfield Cl, NW4 141 CV59
Layfield Cres, NW4 141 CV59
Layfield Rd, NW4 141 CV59
Layhams Rd, Kes. BR2 244 EF106
West Wickham BR4 225 ED104
Layhill, Hem.H. HP2 62 BK18
Laymarsh Cl, Belv. DA17 188 EZ76
Laymead Cl, Nthlt. UB5 158 BY65
Laystall St, EC1 18 E5
Layters Av, Chal.St.P. SL9 112 AW54
Layters Av S, Chal.St.P. SL9 112 AW54
Layters Cl, Chal.St.P. SL9 112 AW54
Layters End, Chal.St.P. SL9 112 AW54
LAYTER'S GREEN, Ger.Cr. SL9 112 AV54
Layters Grn La, Chal.St.P. SL9 134 AU55
Layter's Grn Mobile Home Pk, Chal.St.P. SL9
off Layters Grn La 112 AV54
Layters Way, Ger.Cr. SL9 134 AX56
Layton Ct, Wey. KT13 235 BP105
Layton Cres, Croy. CR0 241 DN106
Layton Pl, Kew TW9
off Station Av 180 CN81
Layton Rd, Brent. TW8 179 CK78
Hounslow TW3 178 CB84
Laytons Bldgs, SE1 31 K4
Laytons La, Sun. TW16 217 BT96
Layton St, Welw.G.C. AL7 51 CY12
Layzell Wk, SE9
off Mottingham La 206 EK88
Lazar Wk, N7 off Briset Way 143 DM61
Lazell Gdns, Bet. RH3 286 CQ140
Lazenby Ct, WC2 18 A10
Lea, The, Egh. TW20 215 BB95
Leabank Cl, Har. HA1 139 CE62
Leabank Sq, E9 12 A4
Leabank Vw, N15 144 DU58
Leabourne Rd, N16 144 DU58
LEA BRIDGE, E5 145 DX62
Lea Br Rd, E5 144 DW62
E10 145 DY60
E17 145 ED56
Lea Bushes, Wat. WD25 98 BY35
Leachcroft, Chal.St.P. SL9 112 AV53
Leach Gro, Lthd. KT22 253 CJ122
Lea Cl, Bushey WD23 98 CB43
Twickenham TW2 198 BZ87
Lea Ct, N15 off Broad La 144 DU56
Lea Cres, Ruis. HA4 137 BT63
Leacroft, Stai. TW18 196 BH91
Leacroft Av, SW12 202 DF87
Leacroft Cl, N21 121 DP47
Kenley CR8 258 DQ116
Staines TW18 196 BH91
West Drayton UB7 156 BL72
Leacroft Rd, Iver SL0 155 BD72
Leadale Av, E4 123 EA47
Leadale Rd, N15 144 DU58
N16 144 DU58
Leadbeaters Cl, N11
off Goldsmith Rd 120 DF50
Leadbetter Dr, Wat. WD25 97 BR36
Leadenhall Mkt, EC3 19 N9
Leadenhall Pl, EC3 19 N9
Leadenhall St, EC3 19 N9
Leadenham Ct, E3 22 A5
Leader Av, E12 147 EN64
Leadings, The, Wem. HA9 140 CQ62
Leaf Cl, Nthwd. HA6 115 BR52
Thames Ditton KT7 219 CE99
Leaf Gro, SE27 203 DN92
Leafield Cl, SW16 203 DP93
Woking GU21
off Winnington Way 248 AV118
Leafield La, Sid. DA14 208 EZ91
Leafield Rd, SW20 221 CZ97
Sutton SM1 222 DA103
Leaford Cres, Wat. WD24 97 BT37
Leaforis Rd, Wal.Cr. EN7 88 DU28
Leaf Way, St.Alb. AL1 65 CD23
Leafy Gro, Croy. CR0 243 DY111
Keston BR2 244 EJ106
Leafy Oak Rd, SE12 206 EJ90
Leafy Way, Croy. CR0 224 DT103
Hutton CM13 131 GD46
Lea Gdns, Wem. HA9 140 CL63
Leagrave St, E5 144 DW62
Lea Hall Gdns, E10
off Lea Hall Rd 145 EA60
Lea Hall Rd, E10 145 EA60
Leahoe Gdns, Hert. SG13 54 DQ10
Leaholme Gdns, Slou. SL1 152 AJ71
Leaholme Way, Ruis. HA4 137 BP58
Leahurst Rd, SE13 205 ED85
Lea Interchange, E9 12 B2
Leake St, SE1 30 D4
Lealand Rd, N15 144 DT58
Leamington Av, E17 145 EA57
Bromley BR1 206 EJ92
Morden SM4 221 CZ98
Orpington BR6 245 ES105
Leamington Cl, E12 146 EL64
Bromley BR1 206 EJ91
Hounslow TW3 198 CC85
Romford RM3 128 FM51
Leamington Cres, Har. HA2 138 BY62
Leamington Gdns, Ilf. IG3 147 ET61
Leamington Pk, W3 160 CR71
Leamington Pl, Hayes UB4 157 BT70
Leamington Rd, Rom. RM3 128 FN50
Southall UB2 178 BX77
Leamington Rd Vil, W11 15 H7
Leamore St, W6 181 CV77
Lea Mt, Goffs Oak EN7 88 DS28
Leamouth Rd, E6 24 G8
E14 23 H9
Leander Ct, SE8 46 A7
Leander Dr, Grav. DA12 213 GM91
Leander Gdns, Wat. WD25 98 BY37
Leander Rd, SW2 203 DM86
Northolt UB5 158 CA68
Thornton Heath CR7 223 DM98
Leapale La, Guil. GU1 280 AX135
Leapale Rd, Guil. GU1 280 AX135
Lea Pk Trd Estates, E10
off Warley Cl 145 DZ60
Learner Dr, Har. HA2 138 CA61
Lea Rd, Beck. BR3
off Fairfield Rd 225 EA96
Enfield EN2 104 DR39
Grays RM16 193 GG78
Hoddesdon EN11 71 EC15
Sevenoaks TN13 279 FJ127
Southall UB2 178 BY77
Waltham Abbey EN9 89 EA34
Watford WD24 97 BV38
Learoyd Gdns, E6 25 L10
Leas, The, Bushey WD23 98 BZ39
Hemel Hempstead HP3 62 BN24
Staines TW18
off Raleigh Ct 196 BG91
Upminster RM14 151 FR59
Leas Cl, Chess. KT9 238 CM108
Leas Dale, SE9 207 EN90
Leas Dr, Iver SL0 155 BE72
Leas Grn, Chis. BR7 207 ET93
Leaside, Bkhm KT23 252 CA123
Hemel Hempstead HP2 63 BQ21
Leaside Av, N10 142 DG55
Leaside Ct, Uxb. UB10 157 BP69
Leaside Rd, E5 144 DW60
Leaside Wk, Ware SG12
off East St 55 DX06
Leas La, Warl. CR6 259 DX118
Leasowes Rd, E10 145 EA60
Lea Sq, E3 11 P9
Leas Rd, Guil. GU1 280 AW135
Warlingham CR6 259 DX118
Leasway, Brwd. CM14 130 FX48
Upminster RM14 150 FQ62
Leathart Cl, Horn. RM12
off Dowding Way 169 FH66
Leatherbottle Grn, Erith DA18 188 EZ76
Leather Bottle La, Belv. DA17 188 EY77
Leather Cl, Mitch. CR4 222 DG96

Leatherdale St, E1 . . . . 21 J3
Leather Gdns, E15 . . . . 13 K9
LEATHERHEAD, KT22 - KT24 . . 253 CF121
⇌ Leatherhead 253 CG121
Leatherhead Bypass Rd, Lthd. KT22 . . . . 253 CJ120
Leatherhead Cl, N16 . . . . 144 DT60
LEATHERHEAD COMMON, Lthd. KT22 . . . . 253 CF119
H Leatherhead Hosp, Lthd. KT22 . . . . 253 CJ122
★ Leatherhead Mus of Local History, Lthd. KT22 . . . . 253 CH122
Leatherhead Rd, Ashtd. KT21 . 253 CK121
Bookham KT22, KT23 . . . . 268 CB126
Chessington KT9 . . . . 237 CJ111
Leatherhead KT22 . . . . 253 CK121
Oxshott KT22 . . . . 237 CD114
● Leatherhead Trade Pk, Lthd. KT22 . . . . 253 CG121
Sch Leatherhead Trinity Sch, Lthd. KT22 off Woodvill Rd 253 CH120
Leatherhead KT22 off Fortyfoot Rd 253 CJ122
Leather La, EC1 . . . . 18 F7
Gomshall GU5 . . . . 283 BQ139
Hornchurch RM11 off North St 150 FK60
Leather Mkt, The, SE1 . . . . 31 N5
Leathermarket Ct, SE1 . . . . 31 N5
Leathermarket St, SE1 . . . . 31 N5
Leather Rd, SE16 . . . . 33 J9
Leathersellers Cl, Barn. EN5 off The Avenue 101 CY42
Leathsail Rd, Har. HA2 . . . . 138 CB62
Leathwaite Rd, SW11 . . . . 182 DF84
Leathwell Rd, SE8 . . . . 46 D8
Lea Vale, Dart. DA1 . . . . 189 FD84
● Lea Valley Business Pk, E10 off Lammas Rd 145 DY61
Sch Lea Valley High Sch, Enf. EN3 off Bullsmoor La 104 DW35
Sch Lea Valley Prim Sch, N17 off Somerford Gro 122 DU52
Lea Valley Rd, E4 . . . . 105 DY43
Enfield EN3 . . . . 105 DY43
● Lea Valley Trd Est, N18 . . . . 123 DX50
Lea Valley Viaduct, E4 . . . . 123 DX50
N18 . . . . 123 DX50
Lea Valley Wk, E3 . . . . 22 E1
E5 . . . . 145 DY62
E9 . . . . 11 P2
E10 . . . . 145 DY62
E14 . . . . 22 A8
E15 . . . . 12 B8
E17 . . . . 122 DW53
N9 . . . . 123 DY46
N15 . . . . 144 DU58
N16 . . . . 144 DU58
N17 . . . . 122 DW53
N18 . . . . 122 DW53
Broxbourne EN10 . . . . 71 EB21
Enfield EN3 . . . . 105 DZ41
Hatfield AL9 . . . . 68 DA15
Hertford SG13, SG14 . . . . 53 DP11
Hoddesdon EN11 . . . . 71 ED18
Waltham Abbey EN9 . . . . 89 DZ30
Waltham Cross EN8 . . . . 89 DZ30
Ware SG12 . . . . 54 DW06
Welwyn Garden City AL7, AL8 . . . . 51 CW13
Leaveland Cl, Beck. BR3 . . . . 225 EA98
Leaver Gdns, Grnf. UB6 . . . . 159 CD68
Leavesden Ct, Abb.L. WD5 . . . . 81 BU31
LEAVESDEN GREEN, Wat. WD25 . . . . 81 BS34
Sch Leavesden Grn JMI Sch, Lvsdn WD25 off High Rd 81 BU34
Leavesden Rd, Stan. HA7 . . . . 117 CG51
Watford WD24 . . . . 97 BV38
Weybridge KT13 . . . . 235 BP106
LEAVES GREEN, Kes. BR2 . . . . 244 EK109
Leaves Grn Cres, Kes. BR2 . . . . 244 EJ111
Leaves Grn Rd, Kes. BR2 . . . . 244 EK111
Leaview, Wal.Abb. EN9 . . . . 89 EB33
Lea Vw Ho, E5 off Springfield 144 DV60
Leaway, E10 . . . . 145 DX60
Leazes Av, Chaldon CR3 . . . . 257 DN123
Leazes La, Cat. CR3 . . . . 257 DN123
Lebanon Av, Felt. TW13 . . . . 198 BX92
Lebanon Cl, Wat. WD17 . . . . 97 BR36
Lebanon Ct, Twick. TW1 . . . . 199 CH87
Lebanon Dr, Cob. KT11 . . . . 236 CA113
Lebanon Gdns, SW18 . . . . 202 DA86
Biggin Hill TN16 . . . . 260 EK117
Lebanon Pk, Twick. TW1 . . . . 199 CH87
Tra Lebanon Road 224 DS103
Lebanon Rd, SW18 . . . . 202 DA85
Croydon CR0 . . . . 224 DS102
Lebrun Sq, SE3 . . . . 186 EH83
Lechford Rd, Horl. RH6 . . . . 290 DG149
Lechmere App, Wdf.Grn. IG8 . . . . 124 EJ54
Lechmere Av, Chig. IG7 . . . . 125 EQ49
Woodford Green IG8 . . . . 124 EK54
Lechmere Rd, NW2 . . . . 161 CV65
Leckford Rd, SW18 . . . . 202 DC89
Leckhampton Pl, SW2 off Scotia Rd 203 DN87
Leckwith Av, Bexh. DA7 . . . . 188 EY79
Lecky St, SW7 . . . . 28 A10
Leclair Ho, SE3 off Gallus Sq 186 EH83
Leconfield Av, SW13 . . . . 181 CT83
Leconfield Rd, N5 . . . . 9 L1
Leconfield Wk, Horn. RM12 off Airfield Way 170 FJ65
Le Corte Cl, Kings L. WD4 . . . . 80 BM29
Lectern La, St.Alb. AL1 . . . . 65 CD24
Leda Av, Enf. EN3 . . . . 105 DX39
Leda Rd, SE18 . . . . 37 J7
Ledborough Gate, Beac. HP9 . . . . 111 AM51
Ledborough La, Beac. HP9 . . . . 111 AK52
Ledborough Wd, Beac. HP9 . . . . 111 AL51
Ledbury Est, SE15 . . . . 44 E4
Ledbury Ho, SE22 off Pytchley Rd 184 DS83
Ledbury Ms N, W11 . . . . 15 J10
Ledbury Ms W, W11 . . . . 15 J10
Ledbury Pl, Croy. CR0 . . . . 242 DR105
Ledbury Rd, W11 . . . . 15 H8
Croydon CR0 . . . . 242 DQ105
Reigate RH2 . . . . 271 CZ133
Ledbury St, SE15 . . . . 44 D4
Ledger Cl, Guil. GU1 . . . . 265 BB132
Ledger Dr, Add. KT15 . . . . 233 BF106
Ledger La, Fifield SL6 . . . . 172 AD82
Ledgers Rd, Slou. SL1 . . . . 173 AR75
Warlingham CR6 . . . . 259 EA116
Ledrington Rd, SE19 . . . . 204 DU93
Ledway Dr, Wem. HA9 . . . . 140 CM59
LEE, SE12 . . . . 186 EE84
⇌ Lee 206 EG86
Lee, The, Nthwd. HA6 . . . . 115 BT50
Lee Av, Rom. RM6 . . . . 148 EY58
Lee Br, SE13 . . . . 185 EC83
Leechcroft Av, Sid. DA15 . . . . 207 ET85
Swanley BR8 . . . . 229 FF97
Leechcroft Rd, Wall. SM6 . . . . 222 DG104
Leech La, Headley KT18 . . . . 270 CQ126
Leatherhead KT22 . . . . 270 CQ126
Lee Ch St, SE13 . . . . 186 EE84
Lee Cl, E17 . . . . 123 DX53
Barnet EN5 . . . . 102 DC42
Hertford SG13 . . . . 54 DQ11
Stanstead Abbotts SG12 . . . . 55 EC11
Lee Conservancy Rd, E9 . . . . 11 P3
Leecroft Rd, Barn. EN5 . . . . 101 CY43
Leeds Cl, Orp. BR6 . . . . 228 EX103
Leeds Pl, N4 . . . . 143 DM60
Leeds Rd, Ilf. IG1 . . . . 147 ER60
Slough SL1 . . . . 154 AS73
Leeds St, N18 . . . . 122 DU50
Lee Fm Cl, Chesh. HP5 . . . . 78 AU30
Leefern Rd, W12 . . . . 181 CU75
Leefe Way, Cuffley EN6 . . . . 87 DK28
Lee Gdns Av, Horn. RM11 . . . . 150 FN60
Leegate, SE12 . . . . 206 EF85
Leegate Cl, Wok. GU21 off Sythwood 248 AV116
Jct Lee Grn, SE12 off Lee High Rd 206 EF85
Lee Grn, Orp. BR5 . . . . 228 EU99
Lee Grn La, Epsom KT18 . . . . 254 CP124
Lee Gro, Chig. IG7 . . . . 125 EN47
Lee High Rd, SE12 . . . . 185 ED83
SE13 . . . . 185 ED83
Leeke St, WC1 . . . . 18 C2
Leeland Rd, W13 . . . . 159 CG74
Leeland Ter, W13 . . . . 159 CG74
Leeland Way, NW10 . . . . 140 CS63
Sch Lee Manor Prim Sch, SE13 off Leahurst Rd 206 EE86
Leeming Rd, Borwd. WD6 . . . . 100 CM39
Lee Pk, SE3 . . . . 186 EF84
Lee Pk Way, N9 . . . . 123 DX49
N18 . . . . 123 DX49
Leerdam Dr, E14 . . . . 34 F7
Lee Rd, NW7 . . . . 119 CX52
SE3 . . . . 47 L10
SW19 . . . . 222 DB95
Enfield EN1 . . . . 104 DU44
Perivale UB6 . . . . 159 CJ67
Lees, The, Croy. CR0 . . . . 225 DZ103
Lees Av, Nthwd. HA6 . . . . 115 BT53
Leeside, Barn. EN5 . . . . 101 CY43
Potters Bar EN6 off Wayside 86 DD32
● Leeside Business Cen, Enf. EN3 . . . . 105 DZ40
Leeside Ct, SE16 . . . . 33 J2
Leeside Cres, NW11 . . . . 141 CZ58
● Leeside Ind Est, N17 off Garman Rd 122 DW52
Leeside Rd, N17 . . . . 122 DV51
Leeson Gdns, Eton Wick SL4 off Victoria Rd 173 AL77
Leeson Rd, SE24 . . . . 183 DN84
Leesons Hill, Chis. BR7 . . . . 227 ES97
Orpington BR5 . . . . 228 EU97
Sch Leesons Prim Sch, St.P.Cray BR5 off Leesons Hill 228 EV97
Leesons Way, Orp. BR5 . . . . 227 ET96
Lees Pl, W1 . . . . 16 G10
Lees Rd, Uxb. UB8 . . . . 157 BP70
Lee St, E8 . . . . 10 A8
Horley RH6 . . . . 290 DE148
Lee Ter, SE3 . . . . 186 EE83
SE13 . . . . 186 EE83
Lee Valley Cycle Route, Harl. CM19 . . . . 72 EF15
Hoddesdon EN11 . . . . 56 EE13
Waltham Abbey EN9 . . . . 71 ED20
Ware SG12 . . . . 55 EB09
★ Lee Valley Pk, E10 . . . . 89 DZ31
Lee Valley Pathway, E9 . . . . 145 DZ62
E10 . . . . 144 DW59
E17 . . . . 144 DW59
Waltham Abbey EN9 . . . . 89 EA31
● Lee Valley Technopark, N17 . . . . 144 DU55
Lee Vw, Enf. EN2 . . . . 103 DP39
Leeward Gdns, SW19 . . . . 201 CZ93
Leeway, SE8 . . . . 33 N10
Leeway Cl, Hatch End HA5 . . . . 116 BZ52
Leewood Cl, SE12 off Upwood Rd 206 EF86
Leewood Pl, Swan. BR8 . . . . 229 FD98
Leewood Way, Eff. KT24 . . . . 268 BW127
Le Fay Ct, N9 off Galahad Rd . . 122 DU48
Lefevre Wk, E3 . . . . 12 A10
Lefroy Rd, W12 . . . . 181 CT75
Legard Rd, N5 . . . . 143 DP63
Legatt Rd, SE9 . . . . 206 EK85
Leggatt Rd, E15 . . . . 12 F10
Leggatts Cl, Wat. WD24 . . . . 97 BT36
Leggatts Pk, Pot.B. EN6 . . . . 86 DD29
Leggatts Ri, Wat. WD25 . . . . 97 BU35
Leggatts Way, Wat. WD24 . . . . 97 BT36
Leggatts Wd Av, Wat. WD24 . . . . 97 BV36
Legge St, SE13 . . . . 205 EC85
Leggfield Ter, Hem.H. HP1 . . . . 61 BF20
Leghorn Rd, NW10 . . . . 161 CT68
SE18 . . . . 187 ER78
Legion Cl, N1 . . . . 8 F5
Legion Ct, Mord. SM4 . . . . 222 DA100
Legion Rd, Grnf. UB6 . . . . 158 CC67
Legion Ter, E3 . . . . 11 P9
Legion Way, N12 . . . . 120 DE52
Legon Av, Rom. RM7 . . . . 149 FC60
Legra Av, Hodd. EN11 . . . . 71 EA17
Legrace Av, Houns. TW4 . . . . 178 BX82
Leicester Av, Mitch. CR4 . . . . 223 DL98
Leicester Cl, Wor.Pk. KT4 . . . . 239 CW105
Leicester Ct, WC2 . . . . 17 P10
Leicester Gdns, Ilf. IG3 . . . . 147 ES59
Leicester Ms, N2 . . . . 142 DE55
Leicester Pl, WC2 . . . . 17 P10
Leicester Rd, E11 . . . . 146 EH57
N2 . . . . 142 DE55
Barnet EN5 . . . . 102 DB43
Croydon CR0 . . . . 224 DS101
Tilbury RM18 . . . . 193 GF81
⊖ Leicester Square 17 P10
Leicester Sq, WC2 . . . . 29 P1
Leicester St, WC2 . . . . 17 P10
LEIGH, Reig. RH2 . . . . 287 CU141
Leigh, The, Kings.T. KT2 . . . . 200 CS93
Leigham Av, SW16 . . . . 203 DL90
Leigham Cl, SW16 . . . . 203 DM90
Leigham Ct, Wall. SM6 off Clyde Rd 241 DJ107
Leigham Ct Rd, SW16 . . . . 203 DL89
Leigham Dr, Islw. TW7 . . . . 179 CE80
Leigham Vale, SW2 . . . . 203 DN90
SW16 . . . . 203 DM90
Leigh Av, Ilf. IG4 . . . . 146 EK56
Leigh Cl, Add. KT15 . . . . 233 BF108
New Malden KT3 . . . . 220 CQ98
● Leigh Cl Ind Est, N.Mal. KT3 off Leigh Cl 220 CR98
Leigh Common, Welw.G.C. AL7 . 51 CY11
Leigh Cor, Cob. KT11 off Leigh Hill Rd 252 BW115
Leigh Ct, SE4 off Lewisham Way 46 A8
Borehamwood WD6 off Banks Rd 100 CR40
Harrow HA2 . . . . 139 CE60
Leigh Ct Cl, Cob. KT11 . . . . 236 BW114
Leigh Cres, New Adgtn CR0 . . . . 243 EB108
Leigh Dr, Rom. RM3 . . . . 128 FK49
Leigh Gdns, NW10 . . . . 14 A1
Leigh Hill Rd, Cob. KT11 . . . . 236 BW114
Leigh Hunt Dr, N14 . . . . 121 DK46
Leigh Hunt St, SE1 . . . . 31 J4
Leigh Orchard Cl, SW16 . . . . 203 DM90
Leigh Pk, Datchet SL3 . . . . 174 AV80
Leigh Pl, EC1 . . . . 18 E6
Cobham KT11 . . . . 252 BW115
Dartford DA2 . . . . 210 FN92
Feltham TW13 . . . . 198 BW88
Welling DA16 . . . . 188 EU82
Leigh Pl La, Reig. RH2 . . . . 287 DY132
Leigh Pl Rd, Reig. RH2 . . . . 287 CU140
Leigh Rd, E6 . . . . 167 EN65
E10 . . . . 145 EC59
N5 . . . . 8 G1
Betchworth RH3 . . . . 286 CQ140
Cobham KT11 . . . . 235 BV113
Gravesend DA11 . . . . 213 GH89
Hounslow TW3 . . . . 179 CD84
Slough SL1 . . . . 153 AP73
Leigh Rodd, Wat. WD19 . . . . 116 BZ48
Leigh Sq, Wind. SL4 . . . . 173 AK82
Leigh St, WC1 . . . . 18 A4
Sch Leigh Tech Acad, The, Dart. DA1 off Green St Grn Rd 210 FP88
Leigh Ter, Orp. BR5 off Saxville Rd 228 EV97
Leighton Av, E12 . . . . 147 EN64
Pinner HA5 . . . . 138 BY55
Leighton Buzzard Rd, Hem.H. HP1 . . . . 62 BJ19
Leighton Cl, Edg. HA8 . . . . 118 CN54
Leighton Cres, NW5 . . . . 7 M2
Leighton Gdns, NW10 . . . . 161 CV68
South Croydon CR2 . . . . 242 DV113
Tilbury RM18 . . . . 193 GG80
Leighton Gro, NW5 . . . . 7 M3
★ Leighton Ho Mus, W14 . . . . 27 H6
Leighton Pl, NW5 . . . . 7 L3
Leighton Rd, NW5 . . . . 7 N3
W13 . . . . 179 CG75
Enfield EN1 . . . . 104 DT43
Harrow Weald HA3 . . . . 117 CD54
Leighton St, Croy. CR0 . . . . 223 DP102
Leighton Way, Epsom KT18 . . . . 238 CR114
Leila Parnell Pl, SE7 . . . . 186 EJ79
Leinster Av, SW14 . . . . 180 CQ83
Leinster Gdns, W2 . . . . 15 N9
Leinster Ms, W2 . . . . 15 N10
Barnet EN5 . . . . 101 CY41
Leinster Pl, W2 . . . . 15 N9
Leinster Rd, N10 . . . . 143 DH56
Leinster Sq, W2 . . . . 15 K10
Leinster Ter, W2 . . . . 15 N10
Leiston Spur, Slou. SL1 . . . . 154 AS72
Leisure La, W.Byf. KT14 . . . . 234 BH112
Leisure Way, N12 . . . . 120 DD52
Leith Cl, NW9 . . . . 140 CR60
Slough SL1 . . . . 154 AU74
Leithcote Gdns, SW16 . . . . 203 DM91
Leithcote Path, SW16 . . . . 203 DM90
Leith Hill, Orp. BR5 . . . . 228 EU95
Leith Hill Grn, Orp. BR5 off Leith Hill 228 EU95
Leith Hill Rd, Abin.Com. RH5 . . 284 BY144
Leith Pk Rd, Grav. DA12 . . . . 213 GH88
Leith Rd, N22 . . . . 121 DP53
Epsom KT17 . . . . 238 CS112
Leith Twrs, Sutt. SM2 . . . . 240 DB108
Leith Vw, N.Holm. RH5 . . . . 285 CJ140
Leith Yd, NW6 . . . . 5 J8
Lela Av, Houns. TW4 . . . . 178 BW82
Lelitia Cl, E8 . . . . 10 C9
Leman St, E1 . . . . 20 B9
Lemark Cl, Stan. HA7 . . . . 117 CJ50
Le May Av, SE12 . . . . 206 EH90
Le May Cl, Horl. RH6 . . . . 290 DG147
Lemmon Rd, SE10 . . . . 47 J2
Lemna Rd, E11 . . . . 146 EE59
Lemonfield Dr, Wat. WD25 . . . . 82 BY32
Lemon Gro, Felt. TW13 . . . . 197 BU88
Lemonwell Ct, SE9 off Lemonwell Dr 207 EQ85
Lemonwell Dr, SE9 . . . . 207 EQ85
LEMSFORD, Welw.G.C. AL8 . . . . 51 CT10
Lemsford Cl, N15 . . . . 144 DU57
Lemsford Ct, N4 off Brownswood Rd 144 DQ61
Borehamwood WD6 . . . . 100 CQ42
Lemsford La, Welw.G.C. AL8 . . . . 51 CV10
Lemsford Rd, Hat. AL10 . . . . 67 CT17
Lemsford AL8 . . . . 51 CT10
St. Albans AL1 . . . . 65 CF20
Lemsford Village, Lmsfd AL8 . . . . 51 CU10
Lemuel St, SW18 . . . . 202 DB86
Lena Cres, N9 . . . . 122 DW47
Lena Gdns, W6 . . . . 26 B7
Sch Lena Gdns Prim Sch, W6 . . . . 26 B6
Lena Kennedy Cl, E4 . . . . 123 EB51
Lenanton Steps, E14 . . . . 34 B4
Lendal Ter, SW4 . . . . 183 DK83
Lenelby Rd, Surb. KT6 . . . . 220 CN102
Len Freeman Pl, SW6 . . . . 38 G3
Lenham Rd, SE12 . . . . 186 EF84
Bexleyheath DA7 . . . . 188 EZ79
Sutton SM1 . . . . 240 DB105
Thornton Heath CR7 . . . . 224 DR96
Lenmore Av, Grays RM17 . . . . 192 GC76
Lennard Av, W.Wick. BR4 . . . . 226 EE103
Lennard Cl, W.Wick. BR4 . . . . 226 EE103
Lennard Rd, SE20 . . . . 204 DW93
Beckenham BR3 . . . . 205 DX93
Bromley BR2 . . . . 227 EM102
Croydon CR0 . . . . 224 DQ102
Lennard Rd, Dunt.Grn TN13 . . . . 263 FE120
Lennard Row, Aveley RM15 . . . . 171 FR74
Lennon Rd, NW2 . . . . 4 A3
Lennox Av, Grav. DA11 . . . . 213 GF86
Lennox Cl, Chaff.Hun. RM16 . . . . 191 FW77
Romford RM1 . . . . 149 FF58
Lennox Gdns, NW10 . . . . 141 CT63
SW1 . . . . 28 E7
Croydon CR0 . . . . 241 DP105
Ilford IG1 . . . . 147 EM60
Lennox Gdns Ms, SW1 . . . . 28 E7
Lennox Rd, E17 . . . . 145 DZ58
N4 . . . . 143 DM61
Gravesend DA11 . . . . 213 GF86
Lennox Rd E, Grav. DA11 . . . . 213 GG87
Lenor Cl, Bexh. DA6 . . . . 188 EY84
Lensbury Av, SW6 . . . . 39 P8
Lensbury Cl, Chsht EN8 . . . . 89 DY28
Lensbury Way, SE2 . . . . 188 EW76
Lens Rd, E7 . . . . 166 EJ66
Len Taylor Cl, Hayes UB4 off Welwyn Way 157 BS70
Lenten Cl, Peasl. GU5 . . . . 283 BR142
Lent Grn, Burn. SL1 . . . . 152 AH70
Lent Grn La, Burn. SL1 . . . . 152 AH70
Lenthall Av, Grays RM17 . . . . 192 GA75
Lenthall Ho, SW1 . . . . 41 M1
Lenthall Rd, E8 . . . . 10 B6
Loughton IG10 . . . . 107 ER42
Lenthorp Rd, SE10 . . . . 35 L10
Lentmead Rd, Brom. BR1 . . . . 206 EF90
Lenton Path, SE18 . . . . 187 ER79
Lenton Ri, Rich. TW9 . . . . 180 CL83
Lenton St, SE18 . . . . 187 ER77
Lenton Ter, N4 off Fonthill Rd 143 DN61
LENT RISE, Slou. SL1 . . . . 152 AH72
Sch Lent Ri Comb Sch, Burn. SL1 off Coulson Way 152 AH71
Lent Ri Rd, Burn. SL1 . . . . 152 AH72
Taplow SL6 . . . . 152 AH72
Coll Leo Baeck Coll, N3 off East End Rd 120 DA54
Leof Cres, SE6 . . . . 205 EB92
Leominster Rd, Mord. SM4 . . . . 222 DC100
Leominster Wk, Mord. SM4 . . . . 222 DC100
Leonard Av, Mord. SM4 . . . . 222 DC99
Otford TN14 . . . . 263 FH116
Romford RM7 . . . . 149 FD60
Swanscombe DA10 . . . . 212 FY87
Leonard Pl, N16 off Allen Rd 144 DS63
Leonard Rd, E4 . . . . 123 EA51
E7 . . . . 13 N1
N9 . . . . 122 DT48
SW16 . . . . 223 DJ95
Southall UB2 . . . . 178 BX76
Leonard Robbins Path, SE28 off Tawney Rd 168 EV73
Leonard St, E16 . . . . 37 H3
EC2 . . . . 19 M4
Leonard Way, Brwd. CM14 . . . . 130 FS49
Leontine Cl, SE15 . . . . 44 D5
Leopards Ct, EC1 . . . . 18 E6
Leopold Av, SW19 . . . . 201 CZ92
Leopold Ms, E9 . . . . 10 G8
Sch Leopold Prim Sch, NW10 off Hawkshead Rd 161 CT66
Leopold Rd, E17 . . . . 145 EA57
N2 . . . . 142 DD55
N18 . . . . 122 DV50
NW10 . . . . 160 CS66
SW19 . . . . 201 CZ91
W5 . . . . 160 CM74
Leopold St, E3 . . . . 21 P6
Leopold Ter, SW19 . . . . 201 CZ92
Leo St, SE15 . . . . 44 F4
Leo Yd, EC1 . . . . 19 H5
Le Personne Rd, Cat. CR3 . . . . 258 DR122
Leppoc Rd, SW4 . . . . 203 DK85
Leret Way, Lthd. KT22 . . . . 253 CH121
Leroy St, SE1 . . . . 31 N8
Lerry Cl, W14 . . . . 39 H2
Lerwick Dr, Slou. SL1 . . . . 154 AS71
Lesbourne Rd, Reig. RH2 . . . . 288 DB135
Lescombe Cl, SE23 . . . . 205 DY90
Lescombe Rd, SE23 . . . . 205 DY90
Lesley Cl, Bex. DA5 . . . . 209 FB87
Istead Rise DA13 . . . . 213 GF94
Swanley BR8 . . . . 229 FD97
Leslie Gdns, Sutt. SM2 . . . . 240 DA108
Leslie Gro, Croy. CR0 . . . . 224 DS102
Leslie Gro Pl, Croy. CR0 off Leslie Gro 224 DS102
Leslie Pk Rd, Croy. CR0 . . . . 224 DS102
Leslie Rd, E11 . . . . 12 F1
E16 . . . . 24 A9
N2 . . . . 142 DD55
Chobham GU24 . . . . 232 AS110
Dorking RH4 . . . . 269 CK134
Leslie Smith Sq, SE18 off Nightingale Vale 187 EN79
★ Lesnes Abbey (ruins), Erith DA18 . . . . 188 EX77
Lesney Fm Est, Erith DA8 . . . . 189 FD80
Lesney Pk, Erith DA8 . . . . 189 FD79
Lesney Pk Rd, Erith DA8 . . . . 189 FD79
Lessar Av, SW4 . . . . 203 DJ85
Lessingham Av, SW17 . . . . 202 DF91
Ilford IG5 . . . . 147 EN55
Lessing St, SE23 . . . . 205 DY87
Lessington Av, Rom. RM7 . . . . 149 FC58
Lessness Av, Bexh. DA7 . . . . 188 EX80
LESSNESS HEATH, Belv. DA17 . . . . 189 FB78
Sch Lessness Heath Prim Sch, Belv. DA17 off Erith Rd 188 FA78
Lessness Pk, Belv. DA17 . . . . 188 EZ78
Lessness Rd, Belv. DA17 off Stapley Rd 188 FA78
Morden SM4 . . . . 222 DC100
Lester Av, E15 . . . . 23 K3
Lestock Cl, SE25 . . . . 224 DU97
Leston Cl, Rain. RM13 . . . . 169 FH69
Leswin Pl, N16 . . . . 144 DT62
Leswin Rd, N16 . . . . 144 DT62
Letchfield, Ley Hill HP5 . . . . 78 AV31
Letchford Gdns, NW10 . . . . 161 CU69
Letchford Ms, NW10 off Letchford Gdns 161 CU69
Letchford Ter, Har. HA3 . . . . 116 CB53
LETCHMORE HEATH, Wat. WD25 . . . . 99 CD38
Letchmore Rd, Rad. WD7 . . . . 99 CG36
Letchworth Av, Felt. TW14 . . . . 197 BT87
Letchworth Cl, Brom. BR2 . . . . 226 EG99
Watford WD19 . . . . 116 BX50
Letchworth Dr, Brom. BR2 . . . . 226 EG99
Letchworth St, SW17 . . . . 202 DF91
Lethbridge Cl, SE13 . . . . 46 E7
Letter Box La, Sev. TN13 . . . . 279 FJ129
Letterstone Rd, SW6 . . . . 38 G5
Lettice St, SW6 . . . . 38 G7
Lett Rd, E15 . . . . 12 G7
Lettsom St, SE5 . . . . 43 N8
Lettsom Wk, E13 . . . . 13 N10
LETTY GREEN, Hert. SG14 . . . . 53 DH13
Leucha Rd, E17 . . . . 145 DY57
Levana Cl, SW19 . . . . 201 CY88
Levehurst Ho, SE27 off Elder Rd 204 DQ92
Levehurst Way, SW4 . . . . 42 B8
Leven Cl, Wal.Cr. EN8 . . . . 89 DX33
Watford WD19 . . . . 116 BX50
Levendale Rd, SE23 . . . . 205 DY89
Leven Dr, Wal.Cr. EN8 . . . . 89 DX33
Leven Rd, E14 . . . . 22 F7
Leven Way, Hayes UB3 . . . . 157 BS72
Hemel Hempstead HP2 . . . . 62 BK16
Leveret Cl, New Adgtn CR0 . . . . 243 ED111
Watford WD25 . . . . 81 BU34
Leverett St, SW3 . . . . 28 D8
Leverholme Gdns, SE9 . . . . 207 EN90
Leverson St, SW16 . . . . 203 DJ93
Lever Sq, Grays RM16 . . . . 193 GG77
LEVERSTOCK GREEN, Hem.H. HP3 . . . . 63 BQ21
Sch Leverstock Grn C of E Prim Sch, Hem.H. HP2 off Green La 63 BR21
Leverstock Grn Rd, Hem.H. HP2, HP3 . . . . 63 BQ21
Leverstock Grn Way, Hem.H. HP3 . . . . 63 BQ20
Lever St, EC1 . . . . 19 H3
Sch Leverton Inf & Nurs Sch, Wal.Abb. EN9 off Honey La 90 EF34
Sch Leverton Jun Sch, Wal.Abb. EN9 off Honey La 90 EF34
Leverton Pl, NW5 . . . . 7 K3
Leverton St, NW5 . . . . 7 L3
Leverton Way, Wal.Abb. EN9 . . . . 89 EC33
Leveson Rd, Grays RM16 . . . . 193 GH76
Levett Gdns, Ilf. IG3 . . . . 147 ET63
Levett Rd, Bark. IG11 . . . . 167 ES65
Leatherhead KT22 . . . . 253 CH120
Levine Gdns, Bark. IG11 . . . . 168 EX68
Levison Way, N19 off Grovedale Rd 143 DK61
Levylsdene, Guil. GU1 . . . . 265 BD134
Lewes Cl, Grays RM17 . . . . 192 GA79
Northolt UB5 . . . . 158 CA65
Lewes Ct, Slou. SL1 off Chalvey Gro 173 AQ75
Lewesdon Cl, SW19 . . . . 201 CX88
Lewes Rd, N12 . . . . 120 DE50
Bromley BR1 . . . . 226 EK96
Romford RM3 . . . . 128 FJ49
Leweston Pl, N16 . . . . 144 DT59
Lewes Way, Crox.Grn WD3 . . . . 97 BQ42
Lewey Ho, E3 . . . . 21 P5
Lewgars Av, NW9 . . . . 140 CQ58
Lewing Cl, Orp. BR6 off Place Fm Av 227 ES102
Lewington Ct, Enf. EN3 off Hertford Rd 105 DX37
Lewin Rd, SW14 . . . . 180 CR83
SW16 . . . . 203 DK93
Bexleyheath DA6 . . . . 188 EY84
Lewins Rd, Chal.St.P. SL9 . . . . 134 AX55
Epsom KT18 . . . . 238 CP114
Lewins Way, Slou. SL1 . . . . 153 AM73
Lewin Ter, Felt. TW14 . . . . 197 BR87
Lewis Av, E17 . . . . 123 EA53
Lewis Cl, N14 off Orchid Rd 121 DJ45
Addlestone KT15 . . . . 234 BJ105
Harefield UB9 . . . . 114 BJ54
Shenfield CM15 . . . . 131 FZ45
Lewis Cres, NW10 . . . . 140 CQ64
Lewis Gdns, N2 . . . . 120 DD54
N16 . . . . 144 DT58
Lewis Gro, SE13 . . . . 185 EC83
LEWISHAM, SE13 . . . . 185 EB84
⇌ Lewisham 46 D10
DLR Lewisham 46 E10
⊖ Lewisham 46 E10
Sch Lewisham Br Prim Sch, SE13 off Elmira St 185 EB83
🔒 Lewisham Cen, SE13 . . . . 185 EC83
Coll Lewisham City Learning Cen, SE23 off Mayow Rd 205 DX90
Coll Lewisham Coll, Deptford Campus, SE8 . . . . 46 B6
Lewisham Way Campus, SE4 . . . . 46 A9
Lewisham Ct, Enf. EN3 off Hodson Pl 105 EA38
Lewisham High St, SE13 . . . . 46 F10
Lewisham Hill, SE13 . . . . 46 F9
Lewisham Pk, SE13 . . . . 205 EB86
Lewisham Rd, SE13 . . . . 46 D7
Lewisham St, SW1 . . . . 29 P5
Lewisham Way, SE4 . . . . 45 N6
SE14 . . . . 45 N6
Lewis La, Chal.St.P. SL9 . . . . 112 AY53
Lewis Pl, E8 . . . . 10 C3
Lewis Rd, Horn. RM11 . . . . 150 FJ58
Mitcham CR4 . . . . 222 DD96
Richmond TW10 off Red Lion St 199 CK85
Sidcup DA14 . . . . 208 EW90
Southall UB1 . . . . 178 BY75
Sutton SM1 . . . . 240 DB105
Swanscombe DA10 . . . . 212 FY86
Welling DA16 . . . . 188 EW83
Lewis St, NW1 . . . . 7 K5
Lewiston Cl, Wor.Pk. KT4 . . . . 221 CV101
Lewis Way, Dag. RM10 . . . . 169 FB65
Leworth Pl, Wind. SL4 off Bachelors Acre 173 AR81
Lexden Dr, Rom. RM6 . . . . 148 EV58
Lexden Rd, W3 . . . . 160 CP73
Mitcham CR4 . . . . 223 DK98
Lexham Ct, Grnf. UB6 off Oldfield La N 159 CD67
Lexham Gdns, W8 . . . . 27 L8
Amersham HP6 . . . . 77 AQ37
Lexham Gdns Ms, W8 . . . . 27 M7
Lexham Ho, Bark. IG11 off St. Margarets 167 ER67
Lexham Ms, W8 . . . . 27 K8
Lexham Wk, W8 . . . . 27 M7

Lexicon Apts, Rom. RM1
off *Mercury Gdns* 149 FE56
Lexington Apts, EC1 19 L4
Lexington Bldg, E3
off *Fairfield Rd* 22 B1
Lexington Cl, Borwd. WD6 100 CM41
Lexington Ct, Pur. CR8 242 DQ110
Lexington Pl, Kings.T. KT1 199 CK94
Lexington St, W1 17 M9
Lexington Way, Barn. EN5 101 CX42
Upminster RM14 151 FT58
Lexton Gdns, SW12 203 DK88
Leyborne Av, W13 179 CH75
Leyborne Pk, Rich. TW9 180 CN81
Leybourne Av, Byfleet KT14 234 BM113
Leybourne Cl, Brom. BR2 226 EG100
Byfleet KT14 234 BM113
Leybourne Rd, E11 146 EF60
NW1 7 K7
NW9 140 CN57
Uxbridge UB10 157 BQ67
Leybourne St, NW1 7 J7
Leybridge Ct, SE12 206 EG85
Leyburn Cl, E17 145 EB56
Leyburn Cres, Rom. RM3 128 FL52
Leyburn Gdns, Croy. CR0 224 DS103
Leyburn Gro, N18 122 DU51
Leyburn Rd, N18 122 DU51
Romford RM3 128 FL52
Leycroft Cl, Loug. IG10 107 EN43
Leycroft Gdns, Erith DA8 189 FH81
Leydenhatch La, Swan. BR8 229 FC95
Leyden St, E1 20 A7
Leydon Cl, SE16 33 K3
Leyfield, Wor.Pk. KT4 220 CS102
Leyhill Cl, Swan. BR8 229 FE99
Ley Hill Rd, Bov. HP3 78 AX30
Sch **Ley Hill Sch**, Ley Hill HP5
off *Jasons Hill* 78 AV30
Leyland Av, Enf. EN3 105 DY40
St. Albans AL1 65 CD22
Leyland Cl, Chsht EN8 88 DW28
Leyland Gdns, Wdf.Grn. IG8 124 EJ50
Leyland Rd, SE12 206 EG85
Leylands La, Stai. TW19 195 BF85
Leylang Rd, SE14 45 K4
Sch **Ley Pk Prim Sch**, Brox. EN10
off *Cozens La E* 71 DZ22
Leys, The, N2 142 DC56
Amersham HP6 77 AP35
Harrow HA3 140 CM58
St. Albans AL4 65 CK17
Leys Av, Dag. RM10 169 FC66
Leys Cl, Dag. RM10 169 FC66
Harefield UB9 114 BK53
Harrow HA1 139 CD57
Leysdown, Welw.G.C. AL7 52 DD09
Leysdown Av, Bexh. DA7 189 FC84
Leysdown Rd, SE9 206 EL89
Leysfield Rd, W12 181 CU75
Leys Gdns, Barn. EN4 102 DG43
Sch **Leys Prim Sch, The**, Dag. RM10
off *Leys Av* 169 FC66
Leyspring Rd, E11 146 EF60
Leys Rd, Hem.H. HP3 62 BL22
Oxshott KT22 237 CD112
Leys Rd E, Enf. EN3 105 DY39
Leys Rd W, Enf. EN3 105 DY39
Ley St, Ilf. IG1, IG2 147 EP61
Leyswood Dr, Ilf. IG2 147 ES57
Leythe Rd, W3 180 CQ75
LEYTON, E11 145 EB60
⊖ **Leyton** 145 EC62
● **Leyton Business Cen**, E10 145 EA61
Leyton Cross Rd, Dart. DA2 209 FF90
Leyton Gra, E10 145 EA61
Leyton Gra Est, E10
off *Leyton Gra* 145 EA61
Leyton Grn Rd, E10 145 EC58
● **Leyton Ind Village**, E10 145 DX59
⊖ **Leyton Midland Road** 145 EC60
★ **Leyton Orient FC**, E10 145 EB62
Leyton Pk Rd, E10 145 EC62
Leyton Rd, E15 12 G3
SW19 202 DC94
Coll **Leyton 6th Form Coll**, E10
off *Essex Rd* 145 ED58
LEYTONSTONE, E11 145 ED59
⊖ **Leytonstone** 146 EE60
⊖ **Leytonstone High Road** 146 EE61
Leytonstone Rd, E15 13 J3
Sch **Leytonstone Sch**, E11
off *Colworth Rd* 146 EE58
Ley Wk, Welw.G.C. AL7 52 DC09
Leywick St, E15 13 J10
Leywood Cl, Amer. HP7 77 AR40
Lezayre Rd, Orp. BR6 245 ET107
Liardet St, SE14 45 M3
Liberia Rd, N5 9 H4
★ **Liberty**, W1 17 L9
Liberty, The, Rom. RM1 149 FE57
Liberty Av, SW19 222 DD95
● **Liberty Cen**, Wem. HA0
off *Mount Pleasant* 160 CM67
Liberty Cl, N18 122 DT49
Hertford SG13 54 DQ11
Liberty Hall Rd, Add. KT15 234 BG106
Liberty Ho, Cher. KT16
off *Guildford St* 215 BF102
Liberty La, Add. KT15 234 BG106
Liberty Ms, SW12 203 DH86
Sch **Liberty Prim Sch**, Mitch. CR4
off *Western Rd* 222 DE96
Liberty Ri, Add. KT15 234 BG107
Liberty St, SW9 42 D7
Liberty Wk, St.Alb. AL1 65 CJ21
Libra Rd, E3 11 P9
E13 13 N10
Library Hill, Brwd. CM14
off *Coptfold Rd* 130 FX47
Library Pl, E1 20 F10
Library St, SE1 30 G5
Library Way, Twick. TW2
off *Nelson Rd* 198 CC87
Lichfield Cl, Barn. EN4 102 DF41
Lichfield Ct, Rich. TW9
off *Sheen Rd* 200 CL85
Lichfield Gdns, Rich. TW9 180 CL84
Lichfield Gro, N3 120 DA53
Lichfield Pl, St.Alb. AL1
off *Avenue Rd* 65 CF19
Lichfield Rd, E3 21 M2
E6 24 E3
N9 off *Winchester Rd* 122 DU47
NW2 141 CY63
Dagenham RM8 148 EV63
Hounslow TW4 178 BW83
Northwood HA6 137 BU55
Richmond TW9 180 CM81
Woodford Green IG8 124 EE49
Lichfield Ter, Upmin. RM14 151 FS61
Lichfield Way, Brox. EN10 71 DZ22
South Croydon CR2 243 DX110
Lichlade Cl, Orp. BR6 245 ET105
Lickey Ho, W14
off *North End Rd* 39 H2
Lidbury Rd, NW7 119 CY51
Lidcote Gdns, SW9 42 E9
Liddall Way, West Dr. UB7 156 BM74
Liddell, Wind. SL4 172 AJ83
Liddell Cl, Har. HA3 139 CK55
Liddell Gdns, NW10 4 A10
Liddell Pl, Wind. SL4
off *Liddell* 172 AJ82
Liddell Rd, NW6 5 J4
Liddell Sq, Wind. SL4
off *Liddell* 172 AJ82
Liddell Way, Wind. SL4
off *Liddell* 172 AJ83
Lidding Rd, Har. HA3 139 CK57
Liddington Hall Dr, Rydes.
GU3 264 AS131
Liddington New Rd, Rydes.
GU3 264 AS131
Liddington Rd, E15 13 L8
Liddon Rd, E13 24 A3
Bromley BR1 226 EJ97
Liden Cl, E17 145 DZ59
Lidfield Rd, N16 9 L1
Lidgate Rd, SE15 44 A5
Lidiard Rd, SW18 202 DC89
Lidlington Pl, NW1 17 L1
Lido Ho, W13
off *Northfield Av* 159 CH74
Lido Sq, N17 122 DR53
Lidstone Cl, Wok. GU21 248 AV117
Lidstone Ct, Geo.Grn SL3 154 AX72
Lidyard Rd, N19 143 DJ60
Lieutenant Ellis Way, Wal.Cr.
EN7, EN8 88 DT31
Coll **Lifelong Learning**,
The Shadwell Cen, E1 21 J10
★ **Lifetimes Mus** (Croydon
Cen Lib), Croy. CR0 224 DQ104
Liffler Rd, SE18 187 ES78
Liffords Pl, SW13 181 CT82
Lifford St, SW15 181 CX84
Lightcliffe Rd, N13 121 DN49
Lighter Cl, SE16 33 M8
Lighterman Ms, E1 21 K8
Lighterman's Ms, Grav. DA11 212 GE87
Lightermans Rd, E14 34 B5
Lightermans Way, Green. DA9 191 FW84
Lightfoot Rd, N8 143 DL57
Lightley Cl, Wem. HA0 160 CM67
Lightswood Cl, Chsht EN7 88 DR27
Ligonier St, E2 20 A4
Lilac Av, Enf. EN1 104 DW36
Woking GU22 248 AX120
Lilac Cl, E4 123 DZ51
Cheshunt EN7 88 DV31
Guildford GU1 264 AW130
Pilgrim's Hatch CM15
off *Magnolia Way* 130 FV43
Lilac Ct, Slou. SL2 153 AM69
Lilac Gdns, W5 179 CK76
Croydon CR0 225 EA104
Hayes UB3 157 BS72
Romford RM7 149 FE60
Swanley BR8 229 FD97
Lilac Ms, N8 off *Courcy Rd* 143 DN55
Lilac Pl, SE11 30 C9
West Drayton UB7 156 BM73
Lilac Rd, Hodd. EN11 71 EB15
Lilac St, W12 161 CU73
Lilah Ms, Brom. BR2
off *Beckenham La* 226 EE96
Lila Pl, Swan. BR8 229 FE98
Lilbourne Dr, Hert. SG13 54 DU08
Lilburne Gdns, SE9 206 EL85
Lilburne Rd, SE9 206 EL85
Lilburne Wk, NW10 160 CQ65
Lile Cres, W7 159 CE71
Lilestone St, NW8 16 C4
Lilford Rd, SE5 42 G8
Lilian Barker Cl, SE12 206 EG85
Sch **Lilian Baylis Tech Sch**, SE11 42 D1
Lilian Board Way, Grnf. UB6 139 CD64
Lilian Cl, N16 144 DS62
Lilian Cres, Hutt. CM13 131 GC47
Lilian Gdns, Wdf.Grn. IG8 124 EH53
Lilian Rd, SW16 223 DJ95
Lillechurch Rd, Dag. RM8 168 EV65
Lilleshall Rd, Mord. SM4 222 DD100
Lilley Cl, E1 32 D3
Brentwood CM14 130 FT49
Lilley Dr, Kgswd KT20 256 DB122
Lilley La, NW7 118 CR50
Lilley Mead, Red. RH1 273 DJ131
Lilley Way, Slou. SL1 153 AL74
Lillian Av, W3 180 CN75
Lillian Rd, SW13 181 CU79
Lilliards Cl, Hodd. EN11 55 EB13
Lillie Rd, SW6 38 D3
Biggin Hill TN16 260 EK118
Lillieshall Rd, SW4 183 DH83
Lillie Yd, SW6 39 J2
Lillingston Ho, N7
off *Harvist Est* 143 DN63
Lillington Gdns Est, SW1 29 M9
Lilliots La, Lthd. KT22
off *Kingston Rd* 253 CG119
Lilliput Av, Nthlt. UB5 158 BZ67
Lilliput Rd, Rom. RM7 149 FD59
Lillyfee Fm La, Woob.Grn
HP10 132 AG57
Lilly La, Hem.H. HP2 63 BR16
Lily Cl, W14 26 E9
Lily Dr, West Dr. UB7 176 BK77
Lily Gdns, Wem. HA0 159 CJ68
Lily Pl, EC1 18 F6
Lily Rd, E17 145 EA58
Lilyville Rd, SW6 38 G6
Limbourne Av, Dag. RM8 148 EZ59
Limburg Rd, SW11 182 DF84
Lime Av, Brwd. CM13 131 FZ48
Northfleet DA11 212 GD87
Upminster RM14 150 FN63
West Drayton UB7 156 BM73
Windsor SL4 174 AT80
Limeburner La, EC4 18 G9
Limebush Cl, New Haw KT15 234 BJ109
Lime Cl, E1 32 D2
Bromley BR1 226 EL98
Buckhurst Hill IG9 124 EK48
Carshalton SM5 222 DF103
Harrow HA3 117 CF54
Pinner HA5 137 BT55
Reigate RH2 288 DB137
Romford RM7 149 FC56
South Ockendon RM15 171 FW69
Ware SG12 55 DY05
Watford WD19 116 BX45
West Clandon GU4 266 BH128
Lime Ct, Mitch. CR4 222 DD96
Lime Cres, Sun. TW16 218 BW96
Limecroft Cl, Epsom KT19 238 CR108
Limedene Cl, Pnr. HA5 116 BX53
Lime Gro, E4 123 DZ51
N20 119 CZ46
W12 26 A4
Addlestone KT15 234 BG105
Guildford GU1 264 AV130
Hayes UB3 157 BR73
Ilford IG6 125 ET51
New Malden KT3 220 CR97
Orpington BR6 227 EP103
Ruislip HA4 137 BV59
Sidcup DA15 207 ET86
Twickenham TW1 199 CF86
Warlingham CR6 259 DY118
West Clandon GU4 266 BG128
Woking GU22 248 AY121
Limeharbour, E14 34 D5
LIMEHOUSE, E14 21 M10
⇌ **Limehouse** 21 L9
DLR **Limehouse** 21 L9
Limehouse Causeway, E14 21 P10
Limehouse Link, E14 33 P1
Limekiln Dr, SE7 186 EH79
Limekiln Pl, SE19 204 DT94
Lime Meadow Av, S.Croy.
CR2 242 DU113
Lime Pit La, Dunt.Grn TN13 263 FC117
Lime Quarry Ms, Guil. GU1 265 BD133
Limerick Cl, SW12 203 DJ87
Limerick Gdns, Upmin. RM14 151 FT59
Limerick Ms, N2 142 DE55
Lime Rd, Epp. CM16 91 ET31
Richmond TW9 180 CM84
Swanley BR8 229 FD97
Lime Row, Erith DA18
off *Northwood Pl* 188 EZ76
Limerston St, SW10 39 P2
Limes, The, SW18 202 DA86
W2 27 K1
Amersham HP6 77 AP35
Brentwood CM13 131 FZ48
Bromley BR2 226 EL103
Hornchurch RM11 150 FK55
Horsell GU21 248 AX115
Purfleet RM19
off *Tank Hill Rd* 190 FN78
St. Albans AL1 65 CE18
Welwyn Garden City AL7 52 DA11
Windsor SL4 172 AJ82
Limes Av, E11 146 EH56
N12 120 DC49
NW7 118 CS51
NW11 141 CY59
SE20 204 DV94
SW13 181 CT82
Carshalton SM5 222 DF102
Chigwell IG7 125 EQ50
Croydon CR0 223 DN104
Horley RH6 291 DH150
Limes Av, The, N11 121 DH50
Limes Cl, Ashf. TW15 196 BN92
Leatherhead KT22
off *Linden Gdns* 253 CJ120
Limes Ct, Brwd. CM15
off *Sawyers Hall La* 130 FX46
Hoddesdon EN11
off *Conduit La* 71 EA17
Limesdale Gdns, Edg. HA8 118 CQ54
Sch **Limes Fm Inf & Nurs &
Jun Schs**, Chig. IG7
off *Limes Av* 125 ER50
Limes Fld Rd, SW14
off *First Av* 180 CS83
Limesford Rd, SE15 185 DX84
Limes Gdns, SW18 202 DA86
Limes Gro, SE13 185 EC84
Limes Ms, Egh. TW20
off *Limes Rd* 195 AZ92
Limes Pl, Croy. CR0 224 DR101
Limes Rd, Beck. BR3 225 EB96
Cheshunt EN8 89 DX32
Croydon CR0 224 DR100
Egham TW20 195 AZ92
Weybridge KT13 234 BN105
Limes Row, Farnboro. BR6 245 EP106
Limestone Wk, Erith DA18 188 EX76
Lime St, E17 145 DY56
EC3 19 N10
Lime St Pas, EC3 19 N9
Limes Wk, SE15 184 DV84
W5 179 CK75
Lime Ter, W7 off *Manor Ct Rd* 159 CE73
Lime Tree Av, Bluewater DA9 211 FU88
Esher KT10 219 CD102
Thames Ditton KT7 219 CD102
Lime Tree Cl, E18 146 EJ56
Limetree Cl, SW2 203 DM88
Lime Tree Ct, Bkhm KT23 252 CA124
Lime Tree Ct, Ashtd. KT21
off *Greville Pk Rd* 254 CL118
London Colney AL2 83 CH26
Lime Tree Gro, Croy. CR0 225 DZ104
Lime Tree Pl, Mitch. CR4 223 DH95
St. Albans AL1 65 CF21
Lime Tree Rd, Houns. TW5 178 CB81
Limetree Wk, SW17
off *Hawthorn Cres* 202 DG92
Lime Tree Wk, Amer. HP7 94 AT39
Bushey Heath WD23 117 CE46
Enfield EN2 104 DQ38
Rickmansworth WD3 96 BH43
Sevenoaks TN13 279 FH125
Virginia Water GU25 214 AY98
West Wickham BR4 244 EF105
Lime Wk, E15 13 K8
Denham UB9 136 BJ64
Hemel Hempstead HP3 62 BM22
Shere GU5 282 BM139
Sch **Lime Wk Prim Sch**,
Hem.H. HP3
off *Lime Wk* 62 BM22
Limeway Ter, Dor. RH4 269 CG134
Limewood Cl, E17 145 DZ56
W13 159 CH72
Beckenham BR3 225 EC99
Limewood Ct, Ilf. IG4 147 EM57
Limewood Rd, Erith DA8 189 FC80
Lime Wks Rd, Merst. RH1 273 DJ126
LIMPSFIELD, Oxt. RH8 276 EG128
Limpsfield Av, SW19 201 CX89
Thornton Heath CR7 223 DM99
LIMPSFIELD CHART, Oxt.
RH8 276 EL130
Sch **Limpsfield C of E Inf Sch**, Oxt.
RH8 off *Westerham Rd* 276 EJ129
Sch **Limpsfield Gra Sch**, Oxt. RH8
off *Bluehouse La* 276 EG127
Limpsfield Rd, S.Croy. CR2 242 DU112
Warlingham CR6 258 DW116
Linacre Cl, SE15 44 F10
Linacre Ct, W6 26 D10
Linacre Rd, NW2 161 CV65
Linale Ho, N1 off *Murray Gro* 19 L1
Linberry Wk, SE8 33 M9
Lince La, Westc. RH4 285 CD136
Linces Way, Welw.G.C. AL7 52 DB11
Linchfield Rd, Datchet SL3 174 AW81
Linchmere Rd, SE12 206 EF87
Lincoln Av, N14 121 DJ48
SW19 201 CX90
Romford RM7 149 FD60
Twickenham TW2 198 CB89
Lincoln Cl, SE25
off *Woodside Grn* 224 DV100
Erith DA8 189 FF82
Greenford UB6 158 CC67
Harrow HA2 138 BZ57
Horley RH6 290 DF149
Hornchurch RM11 150 FN57
Welwyn Garden City AL7 52 DD08
Lincoln Ct, N16 144 DR59
Berkhamsted HP4 60 AV19
Borehamwood WD6 100 CR43
Denham UB9 135 BF58
Lincoln Cres, Enf. EN1 104 DS43
Lincoln Dr, Crox.Grn WD3 97 BP42
Watford WD19 116 BW48
Woking GU22 249 BE115
Lincoln Gdns, Ilf. IG1 146 EL59
Lincoln Grn Rd, Orp. BR5 227 ET99
Lincoln Hatch La, Burn. SL1 152 AJ70
Lincoln Ms, N15 144 DQ56
NW6 4 G8
SE21 204 DR88
Lincoln Pk, Amer. HP7 77 AS39
Lincoln Rd, E7 166 EK65
E13 24 A5
E18 off *Grove Rd* 124 EG53
N2 142 DE55
SE25 224 DV97
Chalfont St. Peter SL9 112 AY53
Dorking RH4 269 CJ134
Enfield EN1, EN3 104 DU43
Erith DA8 189 FF82
Feltham TW13 198 BZ90
Guildford GU2 264 AT132
Harrow HA2 138 BZ57
Mitcham CR4 223 DL99
New Malden KT3 220 CQ97
Northwood HA6 137 BT55
Sidcup DA14 208 EV92
Wembley HA0 159 CK65
Worcester Park KT4 221 CV102
Lincolns, The, NW7 119 CT48
Lincolns Cl, St.Alb. AL4 65 CJ15
Lincolns Fld, Epp. CM16 91 ET29
Lincolnshott, Sthflt DA13 212 GB92
★ **Lincoln's Inn**, WC2 18 D8
Lincoln's Inn Flds, WC2 18 C8
Lincoln St, E11 146 EE61
SW3 28 E9
Lincoln Wk, Epsom KT19 238 CR110
Lincoln Way, Crox.Grn WD3 97 BP42
Enfield EN1 104 DV43
Slough SL1 153 AK73
Sunbury-on-Thames TW16 217 BS95
Lincombe Rd, Brom. BR1 206 EF90
Lindal Cres, Enf. EN2 103 DL42
Lindale Cl, Vir.W. GU25 214 AT98
Lindales, The, N17
off *Brantwood Rd* 122 DT51
Lindal Rd, SE4 205 DZ85
Lindbergh, Welw.G.C. AL7 52 DC09
Lindbergh Rd, Wall. SM6 241 DL108
Linden Av, NW10 14 C1
Coulsdon CR5 257 DH116
Dartford DA1 210 FJ88
Enfield EN1 104 DU39
Hounslow TW3 198 CB85
Ruislip HA4 137 BU60
Thornton Heath CR7 223 DP98
Watford WD18 97 BS42
Wembley HA9 140 CM64
Sch **Linden Br Sch**, Wor.Pk. KT4
off *Grafton Rd* 220 CS104
Linden Chase, Sev. TN13 279 FH122
Linden Cl, N14 103 DJ44
Iver SL0 155 BD68
New Haw KT15 234 BG111
Orpington BR6 246 EU106
Purfleet RM19 190 FQ79
Ruislip HA4 137 BU60
Stanmore HA7 117 CH50
Tadworth KT20 255 CX120
Thames Ditton KT7 219 CF101
Waltham Cross EN7 88 DV30
Linden Ct, W12 26 A2
Englefield Green TW20 194 AV93
Leatherhead KT22 253 CH121
Linden Cres, Grnf. UB6 159 CF65
Kingston upon Thames KT1 220 CM96
St. Albans AL1 65 CJ20
Woodford Green IG8 124 EH51
Linden Dr, Chaldon CR3 258 DQ124
Chalfont St. Peter SL9 112 AY53
Farnham Royal SL2 153 AQ66
Lindenfield, Chis. BR7 227 EP96
Linden Gdns, W2 27 K1
W4 180 CR78
Enfield EN1 104 DU39
Leatherhead KT22 253 CJ121
Linden Glade, Hem.H. HP1 62 BG21
Linden Gro, SE15 184 DV83
SE26 204 DW93
New Malden KT3 220 CS97
Teddington TW11
off *Waldegrave Rd* 199 CF92
Walton-on-Thames KT12 217 BT103
Warlingham CR6 259 DY118
Linden Ho, Slou. SL3 175 BB78
Linden Lawns, Wem. HA9 140 CM63
Linden Lea, N2 142 DC57
Dorking RH4 285 CJ138
Watford WD25 81 BU33
Linden Leas, W.Wick. BR4 225 ED103
Sch **Linden Lo Sch**, SW19
off *Princes Way* 201 CY88
Linden Mans, N6
off *Hornsey La* 143 DH60
Linden Ms, N1 9 M3
W2 27 K1
Linden Pas, W4
off *Linden Gdns* 180 CR78
Linden Pit Path, Lthd. KT22 253 CH121
Linden Pl, Epsom KT17
off *East St* 238 CS112
Leatherhead KT24
off *Station App* 267 BS126
Mitcham CR4 222 DE98
Linden Ri, Warley CM14 130 FX50
Linden Rd, E17
off *High St* 145 DZ57
N10 143 DH56
N11 120 DF47
N15 144 DQ56
Guildford GU1 264 AX134
Hampton TW12 198 CA94
Leatherhead KT22 253 CH121
Weybridge KT13 235 BQ109
Lindens, The, N12 120 DD50
W4 180 CQ81
Hemel Hempstead HP3 61 BF23
Loughton IG10 107 EM43
New Addington CR0 243 EC107
Lindens Cl, Eff. KT24 268 BY128
Linden Sq, Hare. UB9 114 BG51
Sevenoaks TN13
off *London Rd* 278 FE122
Linden St, Rom. RM7 149 FD56
Linden Wk, N19
off *Hargrave Pk* 143 DJ61
Linden Way, N14 103 DJ44
Purley CR8 241 DJ110
Ripley GU23 249 BF124
Shepperton TW17 217 BQ99
Woking GU22 249 AZ121
Lindeth Cl, Stan. HA7 117 CH51
Lindfield Gdns, NW3 5 M2
Guildford GU1 265 AZ133
Lindfield Rd, W5 159 CJ70
Croydon CR0 224 DT100
Romford RM3 128 FL50
Lindfield St, E14 22 A8
Lindhill Cl, Enf. EN3 105 DX39
Lindisfarne Cl, Grav. DA12 213 GL89
Lindisfarne Rd, SW20 201 CU94
Dagenham RM8 148 EW62
Lindisfarne Way, E9 11 M1
Lindley Est, SE15 44 C4
Lindley Pl, Kew TW9 180 CN81
Lindley Rd, E10 145 EB61
Godstone RH9 274 DW130
Walton-on-Thames KT12 218 BX104
Lindley St, E1 20 G6
Lindlings, Hem.H. HP1 61 BE21
Lindo Cl, Chesh. HP5 76 AP30
Sch **Lindon Bennett Sch**,
Han. TW13
off *Main St* 198 BX92
Lindore Rd, SW11 182 DF84
Lindores Rd, Cars. SM5 222 DC101
Lindo St, SE15 45 H9
Lind Rd, Sutt. SM1 240 DC106
Lindrop St, SW6 39 N8
Lindsay Cl, Chess. KT9 238 CL108
Epsom KT19 238 CQ113
Stanwell TW19 196 BK85
Lindsay Ct, SW11 40 B7
Lindsay Dr, Har. HA3 140 CL58
Shepperton TW17 217 BR100
Lindsay Pl, Wal.Cr. EN7 88 DV30
Lindsay Rd, Hmptn H. TW12 198 CB91
New Haw KT15 234 BG110
Worcester Park KT4 221 CV103
Lindsay Sq, SW1 29 P10
Lindsell St, SE10 46 E6
Lindsey Cl, Brwd. CM14 130 FU49
Bromley BR1 226 EK97
Mitcham CR4 223 DL98
Lindsey Gdns, Felt. TW14 197 BR87
Lindsey Ms, N1 9 K6
Lindsey Rd, Dag. RM8 148 EW63
Denham UB9 136 BG62
Lindsey St, EC1 19 H6
Epping CM16 91 ER28
Lindsey Way, Horn. RM11 150 FJ57
Lind St, SE8 46 B8
Lindum Pl, St.Alb. AL3 64 BZ22
Lindum Rd, Tedd. TW11 199 CJ94
Lindvale, Wok. GU21 248 AY115
Lindway, SE27 203 DP92
Lindwood Cl, E6 25 H7
Linfield Cl, NW4 141 CW55
Hersham KT12 235 BV106
Linfield Ct, Hert. SG14 53 DM08
Linfields, Amer. HP7 94 AW40
LINFORD, S.le H. SS17 193 GM75
Linford Cl, Harl. CM19 73 EP17
Linford End, Harl. CM19 73 EQ17
Linford Rd, E17 145 EC55
Grays RM16 193 GH78
West Tilbury RM18 193 GJ77
Linford St, SW8 41 L6
Lingards Rd, SE13 185 EC84
Lingey Cl, Sid. DA15 207 ET89
Lingfield Av, Dart. DA2 210 FP87
Kingston upon Thames KT1 220 CL98
Upminster RM14 150 FM62
Lingfield Cl, Enf. EN1 104 DS44
Northwood HA6 115 BS52
Lingfield Cres, SE9 187 ER84
Lingfield Gdns, N9 122 DV45
Coulsdon CR5 257 DP119
Lingfield Rd, SW19 201 CX92
Gravesend DA12 213 GH89
Worcester Park KT4 221 CW104
Lingfield Way, Wat. WD17 97 BT38
Lingham St, SW9 42 B8
Lingholm Way, Barn. EN5 101 CX43
Lingmere Cl, Chig. IG7 125 EQ47
Lingmoor Dr, Wat. WD25 82 BW33
Ling Rd, E16 23 P6
Erith DA8 189 FC79
Lingrove Gdns, Buck.H. IG9 124 EH48
Lings Coppice, SE21 204 DR89
Lingwell Rd, SW17 202 DE90
Lingwood Gdns, Islw. TW7 179 CE80
Lingwood Rd, E5 144 DU59
Linhope St, NW1 16 E4
Linington Av, Chesh. HP5 78 AU30

Link,The, SE9 207 EN90
W3 160 CP72
Eastcote HA5 138 BW59
Enfield EN3 105 DY39
Northolt UB5 off Eastcote La 138 BZ64
Slough SL2 154 AV72
Wembley HA0 off Nathans Rd 139 CJ60
Link Av, Wok. GU22 249 BD115
Link Cen,The, Dag. RM10 off Heathway 168 FA65
Link Cl, Hat. AL10 67 CV18
Link Dr, Hat. AL10 67 CV18
Linkfield, Brom. BR2 226 EG100
Welwyn Garden City AL7 51 CY13
West Molesey KT8 218 CA97
Linkfield Cor, Red. RH1 off Hatchlands Rd 272 DE133
Linkfield Gdns, Red. RH1 off Hatchlands Rd 272 DE134
Linkfield La, Red. RH1 272 DE133
Linkfield Rd, Islw. TW7 179 CF82
Linkfield St, Red. RH1 272 DE134
Link La, Wall. SM6 241 DK107
Linklea Cl, NW9 118 CS52
Link Prim Sch,The, Croy. CR0 off Croydon Rd 241 DL105
Link Rd, N11 120 DG49
Addlestone KT15 off Weybridge Rd 234 BL105
Chenies WD3 95 BA37
Dagenham RM9 169 FB68
Datchet SL3 174 AW80
Feltham TW14 197 BT87
Hemel Hempstead HP1, HP2 62 BJ17
Wallington SM6 222 DG102
Watford WD24 98 BX40
Links,The, E17 145 DY56
Cheshunt EN8 89 DX26
Walton-on-Thames KT12 217 BU103
Welwyn Garden City AL8 off Applecroft Rd 51 CV09
Links Av, Hert. SG13 54 DV08
Morden SM4 222 DA98
Romford RM2 127 FH54
Links Brow, Fetch. KT22 253 CE124
Links Cl, Ashtd. KT21 253 CJ117
Linkscroft Av, Ashf. TW15 197 BP93
Links Dr, N20 120 DA46
Elstree WD6 100 CM41
Radlett WD7 83 CF33
Link Sec Sch,The, Bedd. CR0 off Croydon Rd 241 DM105
Links Gdns, SW16 203 DN94
Links Grn Way, Cob. KT11 236 CA114
Linkside, N12 119 CZ51
Chigwell IG7 125 EQ50
New Malden KT3 220 CS96
Linkside Cl, Enf. EN2 103 DM41
Linkside Gdns, Enf. EN2 103 DM41
Links Pl, Ashtd. KT21 253 CK117
Links Prim Sch, SW17 off Frinton Rd 202 DG93
Links Rd, NW2 141 CT61
SW17 202 DF93
W3 160 CN72
Ashford TW15 196 BL92
Ashtead KT21 253 CJ118
Bramley GU5 280 AY144
Epsom KT17 239 CU113
Flackwell Heath HP10 132 AC56
West Wickham BR4 225 EC102
Woodford Green IG8 124 EG50
Links Side, Enf. EN2 103 DN41
Link St, E9 11 H4
Links Vw, N3 119 CZ52
Dartford DA1 210 FJ88
St. Albans AL3 64 CB18
Links Vw Av, Brock. RH3 270 CN134
Links Vw Cl, Stan. HA7 117 CG51
Links Vw Rd, Croy. CR0 225 EA104
Hampton Hill TW12 198 CC92
Linksway, NW4 119 CX54
Links Way, Beck. BR3 225 EA100
Bookham KT23 268 BY128
Croxley Green WD3 97 BQ41
Linksway, Nthwd. HA6 115 BQ53
Linkswood Rd, Burn. SL1 152 AJ68
Links Yd, E1 20 C6
Link Wk, Hat. AL10 67 CV17
Linkway, N4 144 DQ59
SW20 221 CW97
Link Way, Brom. BR2 226 EL101
Linkway, Dag. RM8 148 EW63
Link Way, Denh. UB9 136 BG58
Linkway, Guil. GU2 264 AT133
Harlow CM20 off North Gate 57 EQ14
Link Way, Horn. RM11 150 FL60
Pinner HA5 116 BX53
Linkway, Rich. TW10 199 CH89
Link Way, Stai. TW18 196 BH93
Linkway, Wok. GU22 249 BC117
Linkway,The, Barn. EN5 102 DB44
Sutton SM2 240 DC109
Linkway Rd, Brwd. CM14 130 FT48
Linkwood Wk, NW1 7 P6
Linley Cres, Rom. RM7 149 FB55
Linley Rd, N17 122 DS54
★ Linley Sambourne Ho, W8 27 K5
Linnell Cl, NW11 142 DB58
Linnell Dr, NW11 142 DB58
Linnell Rd, N18 off Fairfield Rd 122 DU50
SE5 43 P8
Redhill RH1 288 DG135
Linnet Cl, N9 123 DX46
SE28 168 EW73
Bushey WD23 116 CC45
South Croydon CR2 243 DX110
Linnet Gro, Guil. GU4 off Partridge Way 265 BD132
Linnet Ms, SW12 202 DG87
Linnet Rd, Abb.L. WD5 81 BU31
Linnett Cl, E4 123 EC49
Linnet Ter, Ilf. IG5 off Tiptree Cres 147 EN55
Linnet Wk, Hat. AL10 off Lark Ri 67 CU20
Linnet Way, Purf. RM19 190 FP78
Linom Rd, SW4 183 DL84
Linscott Rd, E5 10 G1
Linsdell Rd, Bark. IG11 167 EQ67
Linsey Cl, Hem.H. HP3 62 BN24
Linsey St, SE16 32 C8
Linslade Cl, Houns. TW4 off Heathlands Way 198 BY85
Pinner HA5 137 BV55
Linslade Rd, Orp. BR6 246 EU107
Linstead St, NW6 5 J6
Linstead Way, SW18 201 CY87
Linsted Ct, SE9 207 ES86
Linster Gro, Borwd. WD6 100 CQ43
Lintaine Cl, W6 38 F3
Linthorpe Av, Wem. HA0 159 CJ65
Linthorpe Rd, N16 144 DS59
Cockfosters EN4 102 DE41
Linton Av, Borwd. WD6 100 CM39
Linton Cl, Mitch. CR4 222 DF101
Welling DA16 188 EV81
Linton Gdns, E6 24 G8
Linton Glade, Croy. CR0 243 DY109
Linton Gro, SE27 203 DP92
Linton Mead Prim Sch, SE28 off Central Way 168 EV73
Linton Rd, Bark. IG11 167 EQ66
Lintons Cl, Hodd. EN11 off Essex Rd 71 EB16
Lintons La, Epsom KT17 238 CS112
Linton St, N1 9 K9
Lintott Ct, Stanw. TW19 196 BK86
Linver Rd, SW6 39 H8
Linwood, Saw. CM21 58 EY05
Linwood Cl, SE5 44 A9
Linwood Cres, Enf. EN1 104 DU39
Linzee Rd, N8 143 DL56
Lion Av, Twick. TW1 off Lion Rd 199 CF88
Lion Cl, SE4 205 EA86
Shepperton TW17 216 BL97
Lion Ct, Borwd. WD6 100 CQ39
Lionel Gdns, SE9 206 EK85
Lionel Ms, W10 14 E6
Lionel Oxley Ho, Grays RM17 off New Rd 192 GB79
Lionel Prim Sch, Brent. TW8 off Lionel Rd N 180 CL77
Lionel Rd, SE9 206 EK85
Lionel Rd N, Brent. TW8 180 CL77
Lionel Rd S, Brent. TW8 180 CM78
● Liongate Enterprise Pk, Mitch. CR4 222 DD98
Lion Gate Gdns, Rich. TW9 180 CM83
Lion Gate Ms, SW18 202 DA87
Lion Grn Rd, Couls. CR5 257 DK115
Lion La, Red. RH1 272 DF133
Lion Mills, E2 20 D1
Lion Pk Av, Chess. KT9 238 CN105
Lion Plaza, EC2 off Lothbury 19 L8
Lion Rd, E6 25 K7
N9 122 DU47
Bexleyheath DA6 188 EZ84
Croydon CR0 224 DQ99
Twickenham TW1 199 CF88
Lions Cl, SE9 206 EJ90
Lion Way, Brent. TW8 179 CK80
Lion Wf Rd, Islw. TW7 179 CH83
Lion Yd, SW4 off Tremadoc Rd 183 DK84
Liphook Cl, Horn. RM12 off Petworth Way 149 FF63
Liphook Cres, SE23 204 DW87
Liphook Rd, Wat. WD19 116 BX49
Lippitts Hill, High Beach IG10 106 EE39
Lipsham Cl, Bans. SM7 240 DD113
Lipton Cl, SE28 off Aisher Rd 168 EW73
Lipton Rd, E1 21 J9
Lisbon Av, Twick. TW2 198 CC89
Lisbon Cl, E17 123 DZ54
Lisburne Rd, NW3 6 E1
Lisford St, SE15 44 B6
Lisgar Ter, W14 26 G8
Liskeard Cl, Chis. BR7 207 EQ93
Liskeard Gdns, SE3 47 P7
Liskeard Lo, Cat. CR3 274 DU126
Lisle Cl, SW17 203 DH91
Lisle Pl, Grays RM17 192 GA76
Lisle St, WC2 17 P10
Lismore, Hem.H. HP3 63 BQ22
Lismore Circ, NW5 off Wellesley Rd 6 G2
Lismore Cl, Islw. TW7 179 CG82
Lismore Pk, Slou. SL2 154 AT72
Lismore Rd, N17 144 DR55
South Croydon CR2 242 DS107
Lismore Wk, N1 9 K4
Lissant Cl, Long Dit. KT6 219 CK101
Lissenden Gdns, NW5 142 DG63
Lissoms Rd, Chipstead CR5 256 DG118
Lisson Grn Est, NW8 16 C3
LISSON GROVE, NW8 16 B4
Lisson Gro, NW1 16 C4
NW8 16 B3
Lisson St, NW1 16 C6
Lister Av, Rom. RM3 128 FK54
Lister Cl, W3 160 CR71
Mitcham CR4 222 DE95
Lister Comm Sch, E13 off St. Marys Rd 166 EH68
Lister Ct, NW9 118 CS54
Lister Gdns, N18 122 DQ50
Lister Hosp,The, SW1 41 J1
Lister Rd, E11 146 EE60
Tilbury RM18 193 GG82
Lister Wk, SE28 off Haldane Rd 168 EX73
Liston Rd, N17 122 DU53
SW4 183 DJ83
Liston Way, Wdf.Grn. IG8 off Navestock Cres 124 EJ52
Listowel Cl, SW9 42 F4
Listowel Rd, Dag. RM10 148 FA62
Listria Pk, N16 144 DS61
Litcham Spur, Slou. SL1 153 AR72
Litchfield Av, E15 13 J5
Morden SM4 221 CZ101
Litchfield Gdns, NW10 161 CU65
Cobham KT11 235 BU114
Litchfield Rd, Sutt. SM1 240 DC105
Litchfield St, WC2 17 P10
Litchfield Way, NW11 142 DB57
Guildford GU2 280 AT136
Lithos Rd, NW3 5 M4
Little Acre, Beck. BR3 225 EA97
Bookham KT23 252 BZ124
St. Albans AL3 65 CD17
Little Acres, Ware SG12 55 DX07
Little Albany St, NW1 17 K4
Little Argyll St, W1 17 L9
Little Aston Rd, Rom. RM3 128 FM52
Little Belhus Cl, S.Ock. RM15 171 FU70
Little Benty, West Dr. UB7 176 BK78
LITTLE BERKHAMSTED, Hert. SG13 69 DH18
Little Berkhamsted La, Lt.Berk. SG13 69 DH20
Little Birch Cl, New Haw KT15 234 BK109
Little Birches, Sid. DA15 207 ES89
Little Boltons,The, SW5 27 M10
SW10 27 M10
LITTLE BOOKHAM, Lthd. KT23 268 BY125
Little Bookham Common, Bkhm KT23 252 BY122
Little Bookham St, Bkhm KT23 252 BZ124
Little Bornes, SE21 204 DS91
Little Borough, Brock. RH3 286 CN135
Little Brays, Harl. CM18 74 EU16
Little Br Rd, Berk. HP4 60 AX19
Little Britain, EC1 19 J8
Littlebrook Av, Slou. SL2 153 AL70
Littlebrook Cl, Croy. CR0 225 DX100
Littlebrook Gdns, Chsht EN8 88 DW30
Littlebrook Interchange, Dart. DA1 190 FP84
Littlebrook Manor Way, Dart. DA1 210 FN85
Little Brook Rd, Roydon CM19 72 EJ15
Little Brownings, SE23 204 DV89
Little Buntings, Wind. SL4 173 AM83
Little Burrow, Welw.G.C. AL7 51 CX11
Littlebury Rd, SW4 41 N10
Little Bury St, N9 122 DR46
Little Bushey La, Bushey WD23 99 CD44
Little Bushey La Footpath, Bushey WD23 off Little Bushey La 117 CD45
Little Catherells, Hem.H. HP1 61 BE18
Little Cattins, Harl. CM19 73 EM19
Little Cedars, N12 off Woodside Av 120 DC49
LITTLE CHALFONT, Amer. HP7 94 AW40
LITTLE CHALFONT, Ch.St.G. HP8 94 AW40
Little Chalfont Prim Sch, Lt.Chal. HP6 off Oakington Av 94 AY39
Little Chapels Way, Slou. SL1 153 AN74
Little Chester St, SW1 29 H6
Little Cloisters, SW1 off College Ms 30 A6
Little Coll La, EC4 off College St 19 L10
Little Coll St, SW1 30 A6
Little Collins, Outwood RH1 289 DP144
Littlecombe, SE7 186 EH79
Littlecombe Cl, SW15 201 CX86
Little Common, Stan. HA7 117 CG48
Little Common La, Bletch. RH1 273 DP132
Littlecote Cl, SW19 201 CX87
Littlecote Pl, Pnr. HA5 116 BY53
Little Cottage Pl, SE10 46 D4
Little Ct, W.Wick. BR4 226 EE103
Littlecourt Rd, Sev. TN13 278 FG124
Little Cranmore La, W.Hors. KT24 267 BP128
Littlecroft, SE9 187 EN83
Istead Rise DA13 212 GE94
Littlecroft Rd, Egh. TW20 195 AZ92
Littledale, SE2 188 EU79
Dartford DA2 210 FQ90
Little Dean's Yd, SW1 30 A6
Little Dell, Welw.G.C. AL8 51 CX07
Little Dimocks, SW12 203 DH89
Little Dormers, Ger.Cr. SL9 135 AZ56
Little Dorrit Ct, SE1 31 K4
Littledown Rd, Slou. SL1 154 AT74
Little Dragons, Loug. IG10 106 EK42
LITTLE EALING, W5 179 CJ77
Little Ealing La, W5 179 CJ77
Little Ealing Prim Sch, W5 off Weymouth Av 179 CJ76
Little E Fld, Couls. CR5 257 DK121
Little Edward St, NW1 17 K2
Little Elms, Harling. UB3 177 BR80
Little Essex St, WC2 18 E10
Little Ferry Rd, Twick. TW1 off Ferry Rd 199 CH88
Littlefield Cl, N19 off Tufnell Pk Rd 143 DJ63
Kingston upon Thames KT1 off Fairfield W 220 CL96
Littlefield Rd, Edg. HA8 118 CQ52
Littleford La, Guil. GU4, GU5 281 BE142
Little Friday Rd, E4 124 EE47
Little Gaynett, Welw.G.C. AL7 52 DB11
Little Gaynes Gdns, Upmin. RM14 150 FP63
Little Gaynes La, Upmin. RM14 150 FM63
Little Gearies, Ilf. IG6 147 EP56
Little George St, SW1 30 A5
Little Gerpins La, Upmin. RM14 170 FM67
Little Gra, Grnf. UB6 off Perivale La 159 CG69
Little Graylings, Abb.L. WD5 81 BS33
Little Grn, Rich. TW9 179 CK84
Little Greencroft, Chesh. HP5 76 AN27
Little Grn Jun Sch, Crox.Grn WD3 off Lincoln Dr 97 BP41
Little Grn La, Cher. KT16 215 BE104
Croxley Green WD3 97 BP41
Little Grn St, NW5 7 J1
Little Gregories La, They.B. CM16 107 ER35
Little Gro, Bushey WD23 98 CB42
Littlegrove, E.Barn. EN4 102 DE44
Little Gro Av, Chsht EN7 88 DS27
Little Gro Fld, Harl. CM19 73 EQ15
Little Halliards, Walt. KT12 off Felix Rd 217 BU100
Little Hardings, Welw.G.C. AL7 52 DC08
Little Hayes, Kings L. WD4 80 BN29
Little Heath, Rom. RM6 148 EV56
Little Heath, SE7 186 EL79
Chadwell Heath RM6 148 EV56
Little Heath La, Berk. HP4 61 BB21
Chobham GU24 232 AS109
Littleheath La, Cob. KT11 236 CA114
Little Heath Prim Sch, Pot.B. EN6 off School Rd 86 DC30
Little Heath Rd, Bexh. DA7 188 EZ81
Chobham GU24 232 AS109
Littleheath Rd, S.Croy. CR2 242 DV108
Little Heath Sch, Rom. RM6 off Hainault Rd 148 EV56
Little Henleys, Hunsdon SG12 56 EK06
Little Hide, Guil. GU1 265 BB132
Little Hill, Herons. WD3 95 BC44
Little Hivings, Chesh. HP5 76 AN27
★ Little Holland Ho, Cars. SM5 240 DE108
Little How Cft, Abb.L. WD5 81 BQ31
LITTLE ILFORD, E12 146 EL64
Little Ilford La, E12 147 EM63
Little Ilford Sch, E12 off Browning Rd 147 EM64
Littlejohn Rd, W7 159 CF72
Orpington BR5 228 EU100
Little Julians Hill, Sev. TN13 278 FG128
Little Kiln, Gdmg. GU7 280 AS143
Little Lake, Welw.G.C. AL7 52 DB12
Little Ley, Welw.G.C. AL7 51 CY12
Little London, Chig. IG7 107 ET42
Little London, Albury GU5 282 BL141
Little London Cl, Uxb. UB8 157 BP71
Little London Ct, SE1 off Mill St 32 B5
Little Marlborough St, W1 off Foubert's Pl 17 L9
Little Martins, Bushey WD23 98 CB43
Littlemead, Esher KT10 237 CD105
Little Mead, Hat. AL10 67 CV15
Woking GU21 248 AT116
Littlemede, SE9 207 EM90
Little Mimms, Hem.H. HP2 62 BK19
Littlemoor Rd, Ilf. IG1 147 ER62
Littlemore Rd, SE2 188 EU75
Little Moreton Cl, W.Byf. KT14 234 BH112
Little Moss La, Pnr. HA5 116 BY54
Little Mundells, Welw.G.C. AL7 51 CZ07
Little Newport St, WC2 17 P10
Little New St, EC4 18 F8
Little Oaks Cl, Shep. TW17 216 BM98
Little Orchard, Hem.H. HP2 62 BN18
Woking GU21 233 BA114
Woodham KT15 233 BF111
Little Orchard Cl, Abb.L. WD5 81 BR32
Pinner HA5 off Barrow Pt La 116 BY54
Little Orchard Way, Shalf. GU4 280 AY141
Little Oxhey La, Wat. WD19 116 BX50
Little Pk, Bov. HP3 79 BA28
Little Pk Dr, Felt. TW13 198 BX89
Little Pk Gdns, Enf. EN2 104 DQ41
LITTLE PARNDON, Harl. CM20 57 EP14
Little Parndon Prim Sch, Harl. CM20 off Park Mead 57 EP14
Little Pipers Cl, Goffs Oak EN7 87 DP29
Little Pluckets Way, Buck.H. IG9 124 EJ46
Little Portland St, W1 17 L8
Littleport Spur, Slou. SL1 154 AS72
Little Potters, Bushey WD23 117 CD45
Little Pynchons, Harl. CM18 73 ET18
Little Queens Rd, Tedd. TW11 199 CF93
Little Queen St, Dart. DA1 210 FM87
Little Reddings Prim Sch, Bushey WD23 off Harcourt Rd 98 CB43
Little Redlands, Brom. BR1 226 EL96
Little Reeves Av, Amer. HP7 94 AT39
Little Ridge, Welw.G.C. AL7 52 DA09
Little Riding, Wok. GU22 249 BB116
Little Rivers, Welw.G.C. AL7 52 DA08
Little Rd, Croy. CR0 off Lower Addiscombe Rd 224 DS102
Hayes UB3 177 BT75
Hemel Hempstead HP2 62 BM19
Little Roke Av, Ken. CR8 241 DP114
Little Roke Rd, Ken. CR8 242 DQ114
Littlers Cl, SW19 off Runnymede 222 DD95
Little Russell St, WC1 18 A7
Little Russets, Hutt. CM13 off Hutton Village 131 GE45
Little St. James's St, SW1 29 L3
Little St. Leonards, SW14 180 CQ83
Little Sanctuary, SW1 29 P5
Little Shardeloes, Amer. HP7 77 AN39
Little Smith St, SW1 29 P6
Little Somerset St, E1 20 A9
Little Spring, Chesh. HP5 76 AP28
Little Spring Prim Sch, Chesh. HP5 off Greenway 76 AP28
Little Stanmore First & Mid Sch, Edg. HA8 off St. Davids Dr. 118 CM53
Little Stock Rd, Chsht EN7 88 DR26
Littlestone Cl, Beck. BR3 205 EA93
Little Strand, NW9 119 CT54
Little Stream Cl, Nthwd. HA6 115 BS50
Little St, Guil. GU2 264 AV130
Waltham Abbey EN9 off Greenwich Way 105 EC36
Little Sutton La, Slou. SL3 175 BC78
Little Thistle, Welw.G.C. AL7 52 DC12
Little Thrift, Petts Wd BR5 227 EQ98
LITTLE THURROCK, Grays RM17 192 GD76
Little Thurrock Prim Sch, Grays RM17 off Rectory Rd 192 GD76
Little Titchfield St, W1 17 L7
LITTLETON, Guil. GU3 280 AU140
LITTLETON, Shep. TW17 217 BP97
Littleton Av, E4 124 EF46
Littleton C of E Inf Sch, Littleton TW17 off Rectory Cl 216 BN97
Littleton Cres, Har. HA1 139 CF61
Littleton Ho, SW1 off Lupus St 41 L1
Littleton La, Littleton GU3 280 AU139
Reigate RH2 287 CX136
Shepperton TW17 216 BK101
Littleton Rd, Ashf. TW15 197 BQ94
Harrow HA1 139 CF61
Littleton St, SW18 202 DC89
Little Trinity La, EC4 19 K10
Little Tumners Ct, Gdmg. GU7 280 AS144
Little Turnstile, WC1 18 C8
★ Little Venice (Waterbuses), W2 15 N6
Little Wade, Welw.G.C. AL7 51 CZ12
Little Wk, Harl. CM20 73 EQ15
Little Warren Cl, Guil. GU4 281 BB136
Littlewick Common, Knap. GU21 248 AS115
Littlewick Rd, Wok. GU21 232 AW114
Little Widbury, Ware SG12 55 DZ06
Little Widbury La, Ware SG12 55 DZ06
Little Windmill Hill, Chipper. WD4 79 BE32
Littlewood, SE13 205 EC85
Little Wd, Sev. TN13 279 FJ122
Littlewood Cl, W13 179 CH76
Little Wd Cl, Orp. BR5 228 EU95
LITTLE WOODCOTE, Cars. SM5 240 DG111
Little Woodcote Est, Cars. SM5 240 DG111
Wallington SM6 240 DG111
Little Woodcote La, Cars. SM5 241 DH112
Purley CR8 241 DH112
Wallington SM6 241 DH112
Little Woodlands, Wind. SL4 173 AM83
Littleworth Av, Esher KT10 237 CD106
Littleworth Common Rd, Esher KT10 219 CD104
Littleworth La, Esher KT10 237 CD105
Littleworth Pl, Esher KT10 237 CD105
Littleworth Rd, Burn. SL1 133 AK61
Esher KT10 237 CE105
Little Youngs, Welw.G.C. AL8 51 CW09
Litton Ct, Loud. HP10 110 AC53
Livermere Rd, E8 10 A8
Liverpool Gro, SE17 43 K1
Liverpool Rd, E10 145 EC58
E16 23 K6
N1 8 F7
N7 8 E4
W5 179 CK75
Kingston upon Thames KT2 200 CN94
St. Albans AL1 65 CE20
Slough SL1 153 AP72
Thornton Heath CR7 224 DQ97
Watford WD18 97 BV43
⇌ Liverpool Street 19 N7
⊖ Liverpool Street 19 N7
Liverpool St, EC2 19 N7
Liveryman Wk, Green. DA9 off Capability Way 191 FW84
Livesey Cl, SE28 187 EQ76
Kingston upon Thames KT1 220 CM97
Livesey Pl, SE15 44 D2
Livingstone Ct, E10 off Matlock Rd 145 EC58
Barnet EN5 off Christchurch La 101 CY40
Livingstone Gdns, Grav. DA12 213 GK92
Livingstone Hosp, Dart. DA1 210 FM87
Livingstone Pl, E14 46 E1
Livingstone Prim Sch, New Barn. EN4 off Baring Rd 102 DD41
Livingstone Rd, E15 12 F9
E17 145 EB58
N13 121 DL51
SW11 off Winstanley Rd 182 DD83
Caterham CR3 258 DR122
Gravesend DA12 213 GK92
Hounslow TW3 178 CC84
Southall UB1 158 BX73
Thornton Heath CR7 224 DQ96
Livingstone Ter, Rain. RM13 169 FE67
Livingstone Wk, SW11 182 DD83
Hemel Hempstead HP2 62 BM16
Livity Sch, SW2 off Mandrell Rd 203 DL85
Livonia St, W1 17 M9
Lizard St, EC1 19 K3
Lizban St, SE3 186 EH80
Llanbury Cl, Chal.St.P. SL9 112 AY52
Llanelly Rd, NW2 141 CZ61
Llanover Rd, SE18 187 EN79
Wembley HA9 139 CK62
Llanthony Rd, Mord. SM4 222 DD100
Llanvanor Rd, NW2 141 CZ61
Llewellyn St, SE16 32 D5
Lloyd Av, SW16 223 DL95
Coulsdon CR5 240 DG114
Lloyd Baker St, WC1 18 D3
Lloyd Ct, Pnr. HA5 138 BX57
Lloyd Ms, Enf. EN3 105 EA38
Lloyd Park 242 DT105
Lloyd Pk, E17 123 EA54
Lloyd Pk Av, Croy. CR0 242 DT105
Lloyd Rd, E6 167 EM67
E17 145 DX56
Dagenham RM9 168 EZ65
Worcester Park KT4 221 CW104
Lloyd's Av, EC3 19 P9
★ Lloyd's of London, EC3 19 N9
Lloyds Pl, SE3 47 K9
Lloyd Sq, WC1 18 E2
Lloyd's Row, EC1 18 F3
Lloyd St, WC1 18 E2
Lloyds Way, Beck. BR3 225 DY99
Lloyd Vil, SE4 46 A8
Lloyd Williamson Sch, W10 14 E6
Loampit Hill, SE13 46 B9
Loampit Vale, SE13 46 E10
Loampit Vale, SE13 46 D10
Loanda Cl, E8 10 A8
Loates La, Wat. WD17 98 BW41
Loats Rd, SW2 203 DL86
Lobelia Cl, E6 24 G6
Local Board Rd, Wat. WD17 98 BX43
Locarno Rd, W3 160 CQ74
Greenford UB6 158 CC70
Lochaber Rd, SE13 186 EE84
Lochaline St, W6 38 B2
Lochan Cl, Hayes UB4 158 BY70
Lochinvar Cl, Slou. SL1 173 AP75
Lochinvar St, SW12 203 DH87
Lochinver Ho Sch, Pot.B. EN6 off Heath Rd 86 DB30
Lochmere Cl, Erith DA8 189 FB79
Lochnagar St, E14 22 F7
Lochnell Rd, Berk. HP4 60 AT17
Lock Av, Maid. SL6 152 AC69
Lock Bldg,The, E15 12 E10
Lock Chase, SE3 186 EE83
Lock Cl, Sthl. UB2 off Navigator Dr 178 CC75
Woodham KT15 233 BE113
Locke Cl, Rain. RM13 169 FF65
Locke Gdns, Slou. SL3 174 AW75
Locke Ho, N16 off Stamford Hill 144 DS60
Locke King Cl, Wey. KT13 234 BN108
Locke King Rd, Wey. KT13 234 BN108
Lockers Pk La, Hem.H. HP1 62 BH20
Lockers Pk Sch, Hem.H. HP1 off Lockers Pk La 62 BH20

Lockesfield Pl, E14 34 D10
Lockesley Dr, Orp. BR5 227 ET100
Lockesley Sq, Surb. KT6
off Lovelace Gdns 219 CK100
Lockestone, Wey. KT13 234 BM107
Lockestone Cl, Wey. KT13 234 BM107
Locket Rd, Har. HA3 139 CE55
Locket Rd Ms, Har. HA3
off Locket Rd 139 CE55
Lockets Cl, Wind. SL4 173 AL81
Locke Way, Wok. GU21
off The Broadway 249 AZ117
Lockfield Av, Enf. EN3 105 DY40
Lockfield Dr, Wok. GU21 248 AT118
Lockgate Cl, E9 11 N2
Lockhart Cl, N7 8 C4
Enfield EN3 104 DV43
Lockhart Rd, Cob. KT11 236 BW113
Lockhart St, E3 21 P5
● Lock Ho Ind Est, Hert.
SG13 54 DS08
Lockhursthatch La, Far.Grn
GU5 282 BM144
Lockhurst St, E5 145 DX63
Lockie Pl, SE25 224 DU97
Lockier Wk, Wem. HA9 139 CK62
Lockington Rd, SW8 41 K6
Lock Island, Shep. TW17 216 BN103
Lock La, Wok. GU22 250 BH116
Lockley Cres, Hat. AL10 67 CV16
Lock Mead, Maid. SL6 152 AC69
Lockmead Rd, N15 144 DU58
SE13 46 F10
Lock Ms, NW1 7 N4
Lockner Holt, Chilw. GU4 281 BF141
Lock Path, Dorney SL4 173 AL79
Lock Rd, Guil. GU1 264 AX131
Richmond TW10 199 CJ91
Locks La, Mitch. CR4 222 DF95
Locksley Dr, Wok. GU21
off Robin Hood Rd 248 AT118
Locksley Est, E14 21 N8
Locksley St, E14 21 N7
Locksmeade Rd, Rich. TW10 199 CJ91
Locksons Cl, E14 22 C7
Lockswood Cl, Barn. EN4 102 DF42
Lockton St, W10 14 C10
Lockwell Rd, Dag. RM10 148 EZ62
Lockwood Cl, SE26 205 DX91
Lockwood Ho, SE11
off Kennington Oval 42 E3
● Lockwood Ind Pk, N17 144 DV55
Lockwood Path, Wok. GU21 233 BD113
Lockwood Pl, E4 123 EA51
Lockwood Sq, SE16 32 E6
Lockwood Wk, Rom. RM1
off Western Rd 149 FE57
Lockwood Way, E17 123 DX54
Chessington KT9 238 CN106
Lockyer Est, SE1 31 M4
Lockyer Ms, Enf. EN3 105 EB38
Lockyer Rd, Purf. RM19 190 FQ79
Lockyer St, SE1 31 M5
Locomotive Dr, Felt. TW14 197 BU88
Locton Grn, E3 11 P8
Loddiges Rd, E9 10 G6
Loddon Spur, Slou. SL1 154 AS73
Loder Cl, Wok. GU21 233 BD113
Loder St, SE15 44 G6
Lodge Av, SW14 180 CS83
Croydon CR0 223 DN104
Dagenham RM8, RM9 168 EU67
Dartford DA1 210 FJ86
Elstree WD6 100 CM43
Harrow HA3 140 CL56
Romford RM2 149 FG56
Lodge Av Junct, Bark.
IG11 168 EU67
Lodgebottom Rd, Lthd. KT22 270 CM127
Lodge Cl, N18 122 DQ50
Chigwell IG7 126 EU48
Edgware HA8 118 CM51
Englefield Green TW20 194 AX92
Epsom KT17
off Howell Hill Gro 239 CW110
Fetcham KT22 253 CD122
Hertford SG14 54 DQ07
Hutton CM13 131 GE45
Isleworth TW7 179 CH81
North Holmwood RH5 285 CJ140
Orpington BR6 228 EV102
Slough SL1 173 AQ75
Stoke D'Abernon KT11 252 BZ115
Uxbridge UB8 156 BJ70
Wallington SM6 222 DG102
Lodge Ct, Horn. RM12 150 FL61
Wembley HA0 140 CL64
Lodge Cres, Orp. BR6 228 EV102
Waltham Cross EN8 89 DX34
Lodge Dr, N13 121 DN49
Hatfield AL9 67 CX15
Loudwater WD3 96 BJ42
Lodge End, Crox.Grn WD3 97 BR42
Radlett WD7 83 CH34
Lodgefield, Welw.G.C. AL7 51 CY06
Lodge Gdns, Beck. BR3 225 DZ99
Lodge Hall, Harl. CM18 73 ES19
Lodge Hill, SE2 188 EV80
Ilford IG4 146 EL56
Purley CR8 257 DN115
Welling DA16 188 EV80
Lodgehill Pk Cl, Har. HA2 138 CB61
Lodge La, N12 120 DC50
Bexley DA5 208 EX86
Chalfont St. Giles HP8 95 AZ41
Grays RM16, RM17 192 GA75
New Addington CR0 243 EA107
Redhill RH1 288 DE143
Romford RM5 126 FA52
South Holmwood RH5 286 CL144
Waltham Abbey EN9 105 ED35
Westerham TN16 277 EQ127
Lodge Pl, Sutt. SM1 240 DB106
Lodge Rd, NW4 141 CW56
NW8 16 B3
Bromley BR1 206 EH94
Croydon CR0 223 DP100
Epping CM16
off Crown Hill 91 EN34
Fetcham KT22 252 CC122
Wallington SM6 241 DH106
Lodge Sch, Commonweal Lo,
Pur. CR8
off Woodcote La 241 DK112
Downside Lo, Pur. CR8
off Woodcote La 241 DK111
Lodge Vil, Wdf.Grn. IG8 124 EF52
Lodge Wk, Warl. CR6 259 EA116
Lodge Way, Ashf. TW15 196 BL89
Shepperton TW17 217 BQ96
Windsor SL4 173 AL83
Lodore Gdns, NW9 140 CS57
Lodore Grn, Uxb. UB10 136 BL62
Lodore St, E14 22 E9
Loewen Rd, Grays RM16 193 GG76
Lofthouse Pl, Chess. KT9 237 CJ107
Loftie St, SE16 32 D5
Lofting Rd, N1 8 E7
Loftus Rd, W12 161 CV74
Barking IG11 167 EQ65
Logan Cl, Enf. EN3 105 DX39
Hounslow TW4 178 BZ83
Logan Ct, Rom. RM1
off Logan Ms 149 FE57
Logan Ms, W8 27 J8
Romford RM1 149 FE57
Logan Pl, W8 27 J8
Logan Rd, N9 122 DV47
Wembley HA9 140 CL61
Loggetts, The, SE21 204 DS90
Logmore La, Dor. RH4 284 CB138
Logs Hill, Brom. BR1 206 EL94
Chislehurst BR7 206 EL94
Logs Hill Cl, Chis. BR7 226 EL95
Lohmann Ho, SE11
off Kennington Oval 42 E2
Lois Dr, Shep. TW17 217 BP99
Lolesworth Cl, E1 20 A7
Lollards Cl, Amer. HP6 77 AQ37
Lollard St, SE11 30 D8
Lollesworth La, W.Hors. KT24 267 BQ126
Loman Path, S.Ock. RM15 171 FT72
Loman St, SE1 31 H4
Lomas Cl, Croy. CR0 243 EC108
Lomas Dr, E8 10 B6
Lomas St, E1 20 D6
Lombard Av, Enf. EN3 104 DW39
Ilford IG3 147 ES60
● Lombard Business Pk,
SW19 222 DB96
Lombard Ct, EC3 19 M10
W3 off Crown St 160 CP74
Lombard La, EC4 18 F9
Lombard Rd, N11 121 DH50
SW11 40 A9
SW19 222 DB96
Lombard Rbt, Croy. CR0 223 DM101
Lombards, The, Horn. RM11 150 FM59
Lombard St, EC3 19 M9
Horton Kirby DA4 230 FQ99
Lombard Wall, SE7 36 A7
Lombardy Cl, Hem.H. HP2 63 BR21
Ilford IG6 off Hazel La 125 EP52
Woking GU21
off Nethercote Av 248 AT117
Lombardy Dr, Berk. HP4 60 AX20
Lombardy Pl, W2 27 L1
● Lombardy Retail Pk, Hayes
UB3 157 BV73
Lombardy Way, Borwd. WD6 100 CL39
Lomond Cl, N15 144 DS56
Wembley HA0 160 CM66
Lomond Gdns, S.Croy. CR2 243 DY108
Lomond Gro, SE5 43 L4
Lomond Rd, Hem.H. HP2 62 BK16
Loncin Mead Av, New Haw
KT15 234 BJ109
Loncroft Rd, SE5 43 P2
Londesborough Rd, N16 144 DS63
Londinium Twr, E1
off Mansell St 20 B10
★ London 2012 Olympic Park Site,
E15 12 B4
London Acad, Edg. HA8
off Spur Rd 118 CM49
London Acad of Computing &
Electronics, SW17
off Upper Tooting Rd 202 DF90
London Acad of Management
Sciences, Ilf. IG1
off Cranbrook Rd 147 EN61
London Acad of Music &
Dramatic Art, W14 26 D10
★ London Aquarium, SE1 30 C4
★ London Biggin Hill Airport,
West. TN16 244 EK113
★ London Brass Rubbing Cen
(St. Martin-in-the-Fields Ch),
WC2 30 A1
⇌ London Bridge 31 N3
⊖ London Bridge 31 N3
London Br, EC4 31 M2
SE1 31 M2
London Bridge City Pier 31 N2
London Br Hosp, SE1 31 M2
London Br St, SE1 31 L3
London Business Sch,
NW1 16 E4
★ London Canal Mus, The, N1
off New Wf Rd 8 B10
London Cen Mkts, EC1 18 G6
★ London Cen Mosque, NW8 16 D2
London Chest Hosp, E2 11 H10
★ London City Airport, E16 36 G2
London City Airport 36 G2
London City Coll, SE1 30 E3
London Clinic, The, W1 17 H5
★ London Coliseum, WC2 30 A1
London Coll of Beauty Therapy,
W1 17 L9
London Coll of Communication,
SE1 31 H7
London Coll of Fashion,
Barrett St, W1 17 H9
Curtain Rd, EC2 19 P4
John Princes St, W1 17 K8
Lime Gro, W12 26 A4
Mare St, E8 10 F6
LONDON COLNEY, St.Alb. AL2 84 CL26
London Colney Bypass, Lon.Col.
AL2 83 CK25
London Colney JMI Sch,
Lon.Col. AL2
off Alexander Rd 83 CK26
★ London Dungeon, SE1 31 M3
London Electronics Coll,
SW5 27 L10
London End, Beac. HP9 111 AM54
★ London Eye, SE1 30 C4
⇌ London Fields 10 E7
London Flds, E8 10 E6
London Flds E Side, E8 10 E7
London Flds Prim Sch, E8 10 E8
London Flds W Side, E8 10 D6
★ London Fire Brigade Mus,
SE1 31 J4
London Fruit Ex, E1
off Brushfield St 20 A7
★ London Gatwick Airport,
Gat. RH6 290 DD153
London Gatwick Airport 291 DH152
★ London Heathrow Airport,
Houns. TW6 177 BP81
London Heathrow Airport
Central 177 BP83
London Heathrow Airport
Terminal 4 197 BQ85
London Indep Hosp, E1 21 J6
● London Ind Est, E6 25 M6
London La, E8 10 F6
Bromley BR1 206 EF94
East Horsley KT24 267 BU131
Shere GU5 282 BN138
London Master Bakers Almshouses,
E10 off Lea Br Rd 145 EB58
★ London Met Archives, EC1 18 F4
London Met Uni - London City
Campus, Calcutta Ho, E1 20 B8
Central Ho, E1 20 C8
Commercial Rd, E1 20 D8
Goulston St, E1 20 A8
Jewry St, EC3 20 A9
Moorgate, EC2 19 M7
Students Union, E1 20 B8
Tower Hill, EC3 20 A10
Whitechapel High St, E1 20 B8
London Met Uni - London N
Campus, Carleton Gra
Hall of Res, N7 7 P1
Dept of Architecture, N7 8 F4
Eden Gro, N7 8 D2
Harglenis, N7 8 E2
James Leicester Hall of Res,
N7 8 B4
Ladbroke Ho, N5 9 H2
Learning Cen, N7 8 D1
Science Cen, N7 8 E1
Stapleton Ho, N7 8 D2
The Arc Hall of Res, N7
off Holloway Rd 143 DL63
Tower Bldg, N7 8 E2
Tufnell Pk Hall of Res, N7
off Huddleston Rd 143 DJ62
London Ms, W2 16 B9
London Nautical Sch, SE1 30 F2
London Oratory Sch, The,
SW6 39 L4
★ London Palladium, W1 17 L9
★ London Peace Pagoda,
SW11 40 F4
★ London Regatta Cen, E16 36 F1
London Rd, E13 13 N10
SE1 30 G6
SE23 204 DV88
SW16 223 DM95
SW17 222 DF96
Abridge RM4 107 ET42
Amersham HP7 77 AQ40
Ashford TW15 196 BH90
Aveley RM15 170 FM74
Barking IG11 167 EP66
Beaconsfield HP9 111 AM54
Beddington Corner CR4 222 DG101
Berkhamsted HP4 60 AY20
Borehamwood WD6 84 CN34
Brentford TW8 179 CJ80
Brentwood CM14 130 FS49
Bromley BR1 206 EF94
Bushey WD23 98 BY44
Caterham CR3 258 DR123
Chadwell Heath RM6, RM7 148 FA58
Chalfont St. Giles HP8 112 AW47
Crayford DA1 209 FD85
Croydon CR0 223 DP101
Datchet SL3 174 AV80
Dorking RH4, RH5 269 CJ133
Dunton Green TN13 263 FD118
Enfield EN2 104 DR41
Englefield Green TW20 214 AV95
Ewell KT17 239 CT109
Farningham DA4 230 FL100
Feltham TW14 196 BH90
Gatwick RH6 290 DF150
Grays RM17, RM20 191 FW79
Greenhithe DA9 211 FS86
Guildford GU1, GU4 265 BB129
Halstead TN14 247 FB112
Harrow HA1 139 CE61
Hemel Hempstead HP1, HP3 62 BK24
Hertford SG13 54 DT10
High Wycombe HP10 110 AD54
Hounslow TW3 178 CC83
Isleworth TW7 179 CF82
Kingston upon Thames KT2 220 CM96
Mitcham CR4 222 DF96
Morden SM4 222 DA99
Northfleet DA11 212 GD86
Old Harlow CM17 74 EV16
Potter Street CM17 74 EW18
Redhill RH1 272 DG132
Reigate RH2 272 DA134
Rickmansworth WD3 114 BM47
St. Albans AL1 65 CH24
Sawbridgeworth CM21 74 EW15
Send GU23 265 BC128
Sevenoaks TN13 278 FF123
Shenley WD7 84 CM33
Slough SL3 175 AZ78
Staines TW18 195 BF91
Stanford Rivers CM5 109 FH36
Stanmore HA7 117 CJ50
Stapleford Tawney RM4 109 FC40
Stone DA2 210 FP87
Sutton SM3 221 CX104
Swanley BR8 229 FC95
Swanscombe DA10 211 FV85
Thornton Heath CR7 223 DN99
Thornwood CM17 74 EV23
Tilbury RM18 193 GG82
Twickenham TW1 199 CG85
Virginia Water GU25 214 AU97
Wallington SM6 241 DH105
Ware SG12 55 DY07
Wembley HA9 160 CL65
Westerham TN16 261 EQ123
● London Rd Business Pk,
St.Alb. AL1 65 CF22
London Rd E, Amer. HP7 94 AT42
⇌ London Road (Guildford) 264 AY134
London Rd N, Merst. RH1 273 DH125
London Rd Purfleet, Purf.
RM19 190 FN78
London Rd Rbt, Twick.
TW1 199 CG86
London Rd S, Merst. RH1 272 DG130
London Rd W, Amer. HP7 77 AQ40
London Rd W Thurrock, Grays
RM20 191 FS79
London Sch of Economics &
Political Science, WC2 18 D9
London Sch of Flying, Borwd.
WD6 off Hogg La 99 CF42
London Sch of Hygiene &
Tropical Medicine, WC1 17 P6
London Sch of Jewish Studies,
NW4 off Albert Rd 141 CX56
London Sch of Theology,
Nthwd. HA6 off Green La 115 BR51
Londons Cl, Upmin. RM14 150 FQ64
London Silver Vaults, WC2 18 E7
London S Bk Uni, SE1 31 H6
Caxton Ho, SE1 30 G6
● London Sq, Guil. GU1 264 AY134
London Stile, W4
off Wellesley Rd 180 CN78
★ London Stone, EC4 19 L10
London St, EC3 19 P10
W2 16 A9
Chertsey KT16 216 BG101
London Studio Cen, N1 8 B10
★ London Television Cen, SE1 30 E2
London Ter, E2 20 C1
★ London Transport Mus,
WC2 18 B10
London Trocadero, The, W1 29 N1
London Wall, EC2 19 K7
London Wall Bldgs, EC2 19 M7
★ London Zoo, NW1 6 G10
Londrina Ct, Berk. HP4 60 AX19
Londrina Ter, Berk. HP4 60 AX19
Lone Oak, Smallfield RH6 291 DP150
Lonesome La, Reig. RH2 288 DB138
Lonesome Prim Sch,
Mitch. CR4
off Grove Rd 223 DH96
Lonesome Way, SW16 223 DH95
Long Acre, WC2 18 A10
Longacre, Harl. CM17 58 EV11
Long Acre, Orp. BR6 228 EX103
Longacre Pl, Cars. SM5
off Beddington Gdns 240 DG107
Longacre Rd, E17 123 ED53
Longacres, St.Alb. AL4 65 CK20
Longaford Way, Hutt. CM13 131 GC46
Long Arrotts, Hem.H. HP1 62 BH18
Long Banks, Harl. CM18 73 ER19
Long Barn Cl, Wat. WD25 81 BU32
Longbeach Rd, SW11 182 DF83
Longberrys, NW2 141 CZ62
Longboat Row, Sthl. UB1 158 BZ72
Long Bottom La, Beac. HP9 111 AR52
Longbourn, Wind. SL4 173 AN83
Longbourne Grn, Gdmg. GU7 280 AS143
Longbourne Way, Cher. KT16 215 BF100
Longboyds, Cob. KT11 235 BV114
Longbridge Ho, E16 37 N1
Longbridge Rd, Bark. IG11 167 EQ66
Dagenham RM8 148 EU63
Horley RH6 290 DF150
Longbridge Rbt, Horl. RH6 290 DE149
Longbridge Vw, Chipstead
CR5 256 DF120
Longbridge Wk, Horl. RH6 290 DF150
Longbridge Way, SE13 205 EC85
Cowley UB8 156 BH68
London Gatwick Airport
RH6 290 DF150
Longbury Cl, Orp. BR5 228 EV97
Longbury Dr, Orp. BR5 228 EV97
Longchamp Cl, Horl. RH6 291 DJ148
Long Chaulden, Hem.H. HP1 61 BE20
Longcliffe Path, Wat. WD19 115 BU48
Long Cl, Farn.Com. SL2 153 AP66
Long Cl Sch, Slou. SL3
off Upton Ct Rd 174 AU76
Long Copse Cl, Bkhm KT23 252 CB123
Long Ct, Purf. RM19 190 FN77
Longcourt Ms, E11 146 EJ56
Longcroft, SE9 207 EM90
Watford WD19 115 BV45
Longcroft Av, Bans. SM7 240 DC114
Longcroft Dr, Wal.Cr. EN8 89 DZ34
Longcrofte Rd, Edg. HA8 117 CK52
Longcroft Gdns, Welw.G.C.
AL8 51 CX10
Longcroft Grn, Welw.G.C. AL8
off Stanborough Rd 51 CX10
Longcroft La, Hem.H. HP3 79 BC28
Welwyn Garden City AL8 51 CX10
Longcroft Ri, Loug. IG10 107 EN43
Longcroft Rd, Map.Cr. WD3 113 BD50
Longcrofts, Wal.Abb. EN9
off Roundhills 90 EE34
LONGCROSS, Cher. KT16 214 AU104
⇌ Longcross 214 AT102
Longcross Rd, Longcr. KT16 214 AY104
Long Deacon Rd, E4 124 EE46
Longdean Pk, Hem.H. HP3 62 BN24
Longdean Sch, Hem.H. HP3
off Rumballs Rd 63 BP23
LONG DITTON, Surb. KT6 219 CJ102
Long Ditton Inf & Nurs Sch,
Long Dit. KT6
off Ditton Hill Rd 219 CJ102
Long Ditton St. Mary's C of E
Jun Sch, Long Dit. KT7
off Sugden Rd 219 CH102
Longdon Wd, Kes. BR2 244 EL105
Longdown La N, Epsom KT17 239 CU114
Longdown La S, Epsom KT17 239 CU114
Longdown Rd, SE6 205 EA91
Epsom KT17 239 CU114
Guildford GU4 281 BB137
Long Dr, W3 160 CS72
Burnham SL1 152 AJ69
Greenford UB6 158 CB67
Ruislip HA4 138 BX63
Long Dyke, Guil. GU1 265 BB132
Long Elmes, Har. HA3 116 CB53
Long Elms, Abb.L. WD5 81 BR33
Long Elms Cl, Abb.L. WD5
off Long Elms 81 BR33
Long Fallow, St.Alb. AL2 82 CA27
Longfellow Dr, Hutt. CM13 131 GC45
Longfellow Rd, E17 145 DZ58
Worcester Park KT4 221 CU103
Longfellow Way, SE1 32 B9
Long Fld, NW9 118 CS52
Longfield, Brom. BR1 226 EF95
Harlow CM18 74 EU17
Hedgerley SL2 133 AR61
Hemel Hempstead HP3 63 BP22
Loughton IG10 106 EJ43
Longfield Av, E17 145 DY56
NW7 119 CU52
W5 159 CJ73
Enfield EN3 104 DW37
Hornchurch RM11 149 FF59
Wallington SM6 222 DG102
Wembley HA9 140 CL60
Longfield Cres, SE26 204 DW90
Tadworth KT20 255 CW120
Longfield Dr, SW14 200 CP85
Amersham HP6 77 AP38
Mitcham CR4 202 DE94
Longfield Est, SE1 32 B9
Longfield First & Mid Schs,
Har. HA2 off Dukes Av 138 CA58
Longfield La, Chsht EN7 88 DU27
Longfield Rd, W5 159 CJ73
Chesham HP5 76 AM29
Dorking RH4 285 CF137
Longfield St, SW18 202 DA87
Longfield Wk, W5 159 CJ72
LONGFORD, Sev. TN13 263 FD120
LONGFORD, West Dr. UB7 176 BH81
Longford Av, Felt. TW14 197 BS86
Southall UB1 158 CA73
Staines TW19 196 BL88
Longford Cl, Hmptn H. TW12 198 CA91
Hanworth TW13 198 BY90
Hayes UB4 158 BX73
Longford Comm Sch, Felt.
TW14 off Tachbrook Rd 197 BT87
Longford Ct, E5 off Pedro St 145 DX63
NW4 141 CX56
Epsom KT19 238 CQ105
Longford Gdns, Hayes UB4 158 BX73
Sutton SM1 222 DC104
Longford Ho, E1
off Jubilee St 20 G8
Longford Rd, Twick. TW2 198 CA88
Longford Rbt, Stai. TW19 176 BG81
Longford St, NW1 17 K4
Longford Wk, SW2
off Papworth Way 203 DN87
Longford Way, Stai. TW19 196 BL88
Long Furlong Dr, Slou. SL2 153 AN70
Long Gore, Gdmg. GU7 280 AS142
Long Grn, Chig. IG7 125 ES49
Nazeing Gate EN9 90 EH25
Long Gro, Harold Wd RM3 128 FL54
Seer Green HP9 111 AQ51
Long Gro Cl, Brox. EN10 71 DY19
Long Gro Rd, Epsom KT19 238 CQ111
Longhayes Av, Rom. RM6 148 EX56
Longhayes Ct, Rom. RM6
off Longhayes Av 148 EX56
Longheath Dr, Bkhm KT23 252 BY124
Longheath Gdns, Croy. CR0 224 DW99
Longhedge Ho, SE26 204 DT91
Long Hedges, Houns. TW3 178 CA81
Longhedge St, SW11 41 H8
Long Hill, Wold. CR3 259 DX121
Longhill Rd, SE6 205 ED89
Longhook Gdns, Nthlt. UB5 157 BU68
Longhope Cl, SE15 44 A3
Long Ho, Harl. CM18
off Bush Fair 73 ET17
Longhouse Rd, Grays RM16 193 GH76
Longhurst Rd, SE13 205 ED85
Croydon CR0 224 DV100
East Horsley KT24 267 BS129
Long John, Hem.H. HP3 62 BM22
Longland Br, Sheering CM22 59 FC07
Longland Ct, SE1 32 C10
Longland Dr, N20 120 DB48
LONGLANDS, Chis. BR7 207 EQ90
Longlands, Hem.H. HP2 62 BN20
Longlands Av, Couls. CR5 240 DG114
Longlands Cl, Chsht EN8 89 DX32
Longlands Ct, W11 15 H10
Mitcham CR4
off Summerhill Way 222 DG95
Longlands Pk Cres, Sid. DA15 207 ES90
Longlands Prim Sch, Sid.
DA15 off Woodside Rd 207 ES90
Longlands Prim Sch & Nurs,
Turnf. EN10
off Nunsbury Dr 89 DZ25
Longlands Rd, Sid. DA15 207 ES90
Welwyn Garden City AL7 51 CY11
Long La, EC1 19 H6
N2 120 DC54
N3 120 DB52
SE1 31 L5
Bexleyheath DA7 188 EX80
Bovingdon HP3 79 AZ31
Croydon CR0 224 DW99
Grays RM16 192 GA75
Heronsgate WD3 95 BC44
Mill End WD3 113 BF47
Stanwell TW19 196 BM87
Uxbridge UB10 156 BN69
Longleat Ho, SW1
off Rampayne St 29 N10
Longleat Ms, Orp. BR5
off High St 228 EW98
Longleat Rd, Enf. EN1 104 DS43
Longleat Way, Felt. TW14 197 BR87
Longlees, Map.Cr. WD3 113 BC50
Longleigh La, SE2 188 EW79
Bexleyheath DA7 188 EW79
Longlents Ho, NW10 160 CR67
Long Ley, Harl. CM20 73 ET15
Welwyn Garden City AL7 52 DC09
Longley Av, Wem. HA0 160 CM67
Longley Ct, SW8 42 A6
Longley Rd, SW17 202 DE93
Croydon CR0 223 DP101
Harrow HA1 138 CC57
Long Leys, E4 123 EB51
Longley St, SE1 32 C9
Longley Way, NW2 141 CW62
Long Lo Dr, Walt. KT12 218 BW104
Longman Ct, Hem.H. HP3 80 BL25
Longmans Cl, Wat. WD18 97 BQ44
Long Mark Rd, E16 24 E7
Longmarsh La, SE28 167 ES74
Longmarsh Vw, Sutt.H. DA4 230 FP95
Long Mead, NW9 119 CT53
Longmead, Chis. BR7 227 EN96
Guildford GU1 265 BC134
Hatfield AL10 67 CV15
Windsor SL4 173 AL81
Longmead Adult Ed Cen, Red.
RH1 off Holland Cl 272 DF134

● Longmead Business Cen, Epsom KT19 238 CR111
● Longmead Business Pk, Epsom KT19 238 CR111
Longmead Cl, Cat. CR3 258 DS122
Shenfield CM15 130 FY46
Longmead Dr, Sid. DA14 208 EX89
Longmeade, Grav. DA12 213 GM88
Longmead Ho, SE27 off Elder Rd 204 DQ92
● Longmead Ind Est, Epsom KT19 238 CS111
Longmead La, Slou. SL1 153 AK66
Long Meadow, NW5 7 N3
Longmeadow, Bkhm KT23 268 BZ125
Long Meadow, Chesh. HP5 77 AQ28
Hutton CM13 131 GC47
Noak Hill RM3 128 FJ48
Riverhead TN13 278 FD121
Long Meadow Cl, W.Wick. BR4 225 EC101
Longmeadow Rd, Sid. DA15 207 ES88
Sch Longmead Prim Sch, West Dr. UB7 off Laurel La 176 BL77
Longmead Rd, SW17 202 DF92
Epsom KT19 238 CR111
Hayes UB3 157 BT73
Thames Ditton KT7 219 CE101
Longmere Gdns, Tad. KT20 255 CW119
Long Mimms, Hem.H. HP2 62 BL19
Long Moor, Chsht EN8 89 DY29
Longmoore St, SW1 29 L9
Longmoor Pt, SW15 off Norley Vale 201 CU88
Longmore Av, Barn. EN4, EN5 102 DC44
Longmore Cl, Map.Cr. WD3 113 BF49
Longmore Gdns, Welw.G.C. AL7 51 CZ09
Longmore Rd, Hersham KT12 236 BY105
Longnor Rd, E1 21 K3
Long Orchard Dr, Penn HP10 110 AC47
Long Pk, Amer. HP6 77 AQ36
Long Pk Cl, Amer. HP6 77 AQ36
Long Pk Way, Amer. HP6 77 AQ35
Long Pond Rd, SE3 47 K7
Longport Cl, Ilf. IG6 126 EU51
Long Reach, Ock. GU23 250 BN123
West Horsley KT24 267 BP125
Long Reach Ct, Bark. IG11 167 ER68
Longreach Rd, Bark. IG11 167 ET70
Erith DA8 189 FH80
Long Readings La, Slou. SL2 153 AP70
Long Ride, The, Hat. AL9 67 CZ18
Longridge, Rad. WD7 83 CH34
Longridge Gro, Wok. GU22 233 BF114
Longridge Ho, SE1 31 K7
Longridge La, Sthl. UB1 158 CB73
Longridge Rd, SW5 27 J9
Long Ridings Av, Hutt. CM13 131 GB43
Sch Long Ridings Prim Sch, Hutt. CM13 off Long Ridings Av 131 GB43
Long Rd, SW4 183 DH84
Longs Cl, Wok. GU22 250 BG116
Long's Ct, WC2 17 N10
Longs Ct, Rich. TW9 off Crown Ter 180 CM84
Longsdon Way, Cat. CR3 258 DU124
Longshaw, Lthd. KT22 253 CG119
Sch Longshaw Prim Sch, E4 off Longshaw Rd 123 ED48
Longshaw Rd, E4 123 ED48
Longshore, SE8 33 N9
Longside Cl, Egh. TW20 215 BC95
Long Spring, Port.Wd AL3 65 CF16
Longspring, Wat. WD24 97 BV38
Longspring Wd, Sev. TN14 278 FF130
Longstaff Cres, SW18 202 DA86
Longstaff Rd, SW18 202 DA86
Longstone Av, NW10 161 CT66
Longstone Ct, SE1 31 K5
Longstone Rd, SW17 203 DH92
Iver SL0 155 BC68
Long St, E2 20 A2
Waltham Abbey EN9 90 EL32
Longthornton Rd, SW16 223 DJ96
Longthorpe Ct, W6 off Invermead Cl 181 CU76
Longton Av, SE26 204 DU91
Longton Gro, SE26 204 DV91
Longton Ho, SE11 off Lambeth Wk 30 D8
Longtown Cl, Rom. RM3 128 FJ50
Longtown Rd, Rom. RM3 128 FJ50
Longview, Beac. HP9 132 AF55
Long Vw, Berk. HP4 60 AU17
Longview Way, Rom. RM5 127 FD53
Longville Rd, SE11 30 G8
Long Wk, SE1 31 P6
SE18 187 EP79
SW13 180 CS82
Chalfont St. Giles HP8 94 AX41
Epsom KT18 255 CX119
New Malden KT3 220 CQ97
Waltham Abbey EN9 89 EA30
West Byfleet KT14 234 BJ114
West Horsley KT24 266 BN128
Long Wk, The, Wind. SL4 173 AR83
Longwalk Rd, Uxb. UB11 157 BP74
Longwood, Harl. CM18 73 ER20
Longwood Av, Slou. SL3 175 BB78
● Longwood Business Pk, Sun. TW16 217 BT99
Longwood Cl, Upmin. RM14 150 FQ64
Longwood Dr, SW15 201 CU86
Long Wd Dr, Jordans HP9 112 AT51
Longwood Gdns, Ilf. IG5, IG6 147 EM56
Longwood La, Amer. HP7 77 AR39
Longwood Rd, Hert. SG14 53 DM08
Kenley CR8 258 DR116
Sch Longwood Sch, Bushey WD23 off Bushey Hall Dr 98 BZ42
Longworth Cl, SE28 168 EX72
Longworth Dr, Maid. SL6 152 AC70
Long Yd, WC1 18 C5
Loning, The, NW9 140 CS56
Enfield EN3 104 DW38
Lonsdale, Hem.H. HP2 62 BL17
Lonsdale Av, E6 24 E3
Hutton CM13 131 GD44
Romford RM7 149 FC58
Wembley HA9 140 CL64
Lonsdale Cl, E6 24 G4
SE9 206 EK90
Edgware HA8 118 CM50
Pinner HA5 116 BY52
Uxbridge UB8 157 BQ71
Lonsdale Cres, Dart. DA2 210 FQ88
Ilford IG2 147 EP58
Lonsdale Dr, Enf. EN2 103 DL43
Lonsdale Gdns, Th.Hth. CR7 223 DM98
Lonsdale Ms, W11 15 H9
Richmond TW9 off Elizabeth Cotts 180 CN81
Lonsdale Pl, N1 8 F7
Dorking RH4 off Lonsdale Rd 285 CH135
Lonsdale Rd, E11 146 EF59
NW6 4 G10
SE25 224 DV98
SW13 181 CU79
W4 181 CT77
W11 15 H9
Bexleyheath DA7 188 EZ82
Dorking RH4 285 CH135
Southall UB2 178 BX76
Weybridge KT13 234 BN108
Lonsdale Sq, N1 8 F7
Lonsdale Way, Maid. SL6 172 AC78
Loobert Rd, N15 144 DS55
Looe Gdns, Ilf. IG6 147 EP55
Loom La, Rad. WD7 99 CG37
Loom Pl, Rad. WD7 99 CG36
Loop Rd, Chis. BR7 207 EQ93
Epsom KT18 off Woodcote Side 254 CQ116
Waltham Abbey EN9 89 EB32
Woking GU22 249 AZ121
Lopen Rd, N18 122 DS49
Loraine Cl, Enf. EN3 104 DW43
Loraine Gdns, Ashtd. KT21 254 CL117
Loraine Rd, N7 143 DM63
W4 180 CP79
Lorane Ct, Wat. WD17 97 BU40
Lord Amory Way, E14 34 E4
Lord Av, Ilf. IG5 147 EM56
Lord Chancellor Wk, Kings.T. KT2 220 CQ95
Lord Chatham's Ride, Sev. TN14 262 EX117
Lord Darby Ms, Cudham TN14 261 ER115
Lordell Pl, SW19 201 CW93
Lorden Wk, E2 20 C3
Lord Gdns, Ilf. IG5 146 EL56
Lord Hills Br, W2 15 M7
Lord Hills Rd, W2 15 M6
Lord Holland La, SW9 42 F8
Lord Knyvett Cl, Stanw. TW19 196 BK86
Lord Knyvetts Ct, Stanw. TW19 off De Havilland Way 196 BL86
Lord Mayors Dr, Farn.Com. SL2 133 AN64
Lord Napier Pl, W6 off Oil Mill La 181 CU78
Lord N St, SW1 30 A7
Lord Roberts Ms, SW6 39 L5
Lord Roberts Ter, SE18 187 EN78
★ Lord's (Marylebone CC & Mus, Middlesex CCC), NW8 16 B2
Lordsbury Fld, Wall. SM6 241 DJ110
Lord's Cl, SE21 204 DQ89
Lords Cl, Felt. TW13 198 BY89
Shenley WD7 84 CL32
Lordsgrove Cl, Tad. KT20 off Whitegate Way 255 CV120
Lordship Cl, Hutt. CM13 131 GD46
Lordship Gro, N16 144 DR61
Lordship La, N17 122 DQ53
N22 121 DN54
SE22 204 DT86
Lordship La Est, SE22 204 DU88
Sch Lordship La Prim Sch, N22 off Lordship La 122 DQ53
Lordship Pk, N16 144 DQ61
Lordship Pk Ms, N16 144 DQ61
Lordship Pl, SW3 40 C3
Lordship Rd, N16 144 DR61
Cheshunt EN7 88 DV30
Northolt UB5 158 BY66
Lordship Ter, N16 144 DR61
Lordsmead Rd, N17 122 DS53
Lord St, E16 37 H3
Gravesend DA12 213 GH87
Hoddesdon EN11 70 DV17
Watford WD17 98 BW41
Lord's Vw, NW8 16 B3
Lords Wd, Welw.G.C. AL7 52 DC09
Lordswood Cl, Bexh. DA6 208 EY85
Lane End DA2 211 FS91
Lord Warwick St, SE18 37 J7
Lorenzo St, WC1 18 C2
Sch Loreto Coll, St.Alb. AL1 off Hatfield Rd 65 CE20
Loretto Gdns, Har. HA3 140 CL56
Lorian Cl, N12 120 DB49
Lorian Dr, Reig. RH2 272 DC133
Loriners Cl, Cob. KT11 235 BU114
Loring Rd, N20 120 DE47
SE14 45 M6
Berkhamsted HP4 60 AW20
Isleworth TW7 179 CF82
Windsor SL4 173 AM81
Loris Rd, W6 26 B7
Lorn Ct, SW9 42 E8
Lorne, The, Bkhm KT23 268 CA126
Lorne Av, Croy. CR0 225 DX101
Lorne Cl, NW8 16 D3
Slough SL1 173 AP76
Lorne Gdns, E11 146 EJ56
W11 26 D4
Croydon CR0 225 DX101
Lorne Rd, E7 146 EH63
E17 145 EA57
N4 143 DM60
Harrow HA3 117 CF54
Richmond TW10 off Albert Rd 200 CM85
Warley CM14 130 FW49
Lorn Rd, SW9 42 D8
Lorraine Pk, Har. HA3 117 CE52
Lorrimore Rd, SE17 43 H2
Lorrimore Sq, SE17 43 H2
Lorton Cl, Grav. DA12 213 GL89
Loseberry Rd, Clay. KT10 237 CD106
Sch Loseley Flds Prim Sch, Farnc. GU7 off Green La 280 AS143
★ Loseley Ho & Pk, Guil. GU3 280 AS140
Loseley Pk, Littleton GU3 280 AS140
Loseley Rd, Gdmg. GU7 280 AS143
Losfield Rd, Wind. SL4 173 AL81
Lossie Dr, Iver SL0 155 BB73
Lothair Rd, W5 179 CK75
Lothair Rd N, N4 143 DP58
Lothair Rd S, N4 143 DN59
Lothair St, SW11 off Grant Rd 182 DE83
Lothbury, EC2 19 L8
Lothian Av, Hayes UB4 157 BV71
Lothian Cl, Wem. HA0 139 CG63
Lothian Rd, SW9 43 H6
Lothian Wd, Tad. KT20 255 CV122
Lothrop St, W10 14 E2
Lots Rd, SW10 39 N5
Lotus Cl, SE21 204 DQ90
Lotus Rd, Bigg.H. TN16 261 EM118
Loubet St, SW17 202 DF93
Loudhams Rd, Amer. HP7 94 AW39
Loudhams Wd La, Ch.St.G. HP8 94 AX40
Loudoun Av, Ilf. IG6 147 EP57
Loudoun Rd, NW8 5 P10
LOUDWATER, H.Wyc. HP10 110 AD53
LOUDWATER, Rick. WD3 96 BK41
Loudwater Cl, Sun. TW16 217 BU98
Loudwater Dr, Loud. WD3 96 BJ42
Loudwater Hts, Loud. WD3 96 BH41
Loudwater La, Rick. WD3 96 BK42
Loudwater Ridge, Loud. WD3 96 BJ42
Loudwater Rd, Sun. TW16 217 BU98
Loughborough Est, SW9 42 F9
⇌ Loughborough Junction 43 H10
Loughborough Pk, SW9 183 DP84
Sch Loughborough Prim Sch, SW9 42 G9
Loughborough Rd, SW9 42 E8
Loughborough St, SE11 30 D10
Lough Rd, N7 8 D4
LOUGHTON, IG10 107 EM43
⊖ Loughton 106 EL43
Loughton Business Cen, Loug. IG10 off Langston Rd 107 EQ42
Loughton Ct, Wal.Abb. EN9 90 EH33
Loughton La, They.B. CM16 107 ER38
● Loughton Seedbed Cen, Loug. IG10 off Langston Rd 107 ER42
Loughton Way, Buck.H. IG9 124 EK46
Louisa Cl, E9 11 K8
Louisa Gdns, E1 21 J5
Louisa Ho, SW15 180 CS84
Coll Louisa Oakes Cen, E4 off Hall La 123 DZ49
Louisa St, E1 21 J5
Louise Aumonier Wk, N19 off Hillrise Rd 143 DL59
Louise Bennett Cl, SE24 off Shakespeare Rd 183 DP84
Louise Ct, E11 146 EH57
Louise Gdns, Rain. RM13 169 FE69
Louise Rd, E15 13 K4
Louise Wk, Bov. HP3 79 BA28
Louis Gdns, Chis. BR7 207 EM91
Louis Ms, N10 121 DH53
Louisville Cl, Stans.Abb. SG12 55 EC11
Louisville Rd, SW17 202 DG90
Louvaine Rd, SW11 182 DD84
Louvain Rd, Green. DA9 211 FS87
Louvain Way, Wat. WD25 81 BV32
Lovage App, E6 25 H7
Lovat Cl, NW2 141 CT62
Lovat La, EC3 31 N1
Lovatt Cl, Edg. HA8 118 CP51
Lovatt Dr, Ruis. HA4 137 BT57
Lovatts, Crox.Grn WD3 96 BN42
Lovat Wk, Houns. TW5 off Cranford La 178 BY80
Loveday Rd, W13 159 CH74
Love Grn La, Iver SL0 155 BD71
Lovegrove Dr, Slou. SL2 153 AM70
Lovegrove St, SE1 44 D1
Lovegrove Wk, E14 34 E3
Love Hill La, Slou. SL3 155 BA73
Lovejoy La, Wind. SL4 173 AK83
Lovekyn Cl, Kings.T. KT2 off Queen Elizabeth Rd 220 CM96
Lovelace Av, Brom. BR2 227 EN100
Lovelace Cl, Eff.Junct. KT24 251 BU123
Lovelace Dr, Wok. GU22 249 BF115
Lovelace Gdns, Bark. IG11 148 EU63
Hersham KT12 236 BW106
Surbiton KT6 219 CK101
Lovelace Grn, SE9 187 EM83
Lovelace Ho, W13 159 CH73
Sch Lovelace Prim Sch, Chess. KT9 off Mansfield Rd 237 CJ106
Lovelace Rd, SE21 204 DQ89
Barnet EN4 120 DE45
Surbiton KT6 219 CJ101
Lovelands La, Lwr Kgswd KT20 272 DB127
Love La, EC2 19 K8
N17 122 DT52
SE18 37 M9
SE25 224 DV97
Abbots Langley WD5 81 BT30
Aveley RM15 190 FQ75
Bexley DA5 208 EZ86
Godstone RH9 274 DW132
Gravesend DA12 213 GJ87
Iver SL0 155 BD72
Kings Langley WD4 80 BL29
Mitcham CR4 222 DE97
Morden SM4 222 DA101
Pinner HA5 138 BY55
Surbiton KT6 219 CK103
Sutton SM3 239 CY107
Walton on the Hill KT20 271 CT126
Woodford Green IG8 125 EM51
Lovel Av, Well. DA16 188 EU82
Lovel Cl, Hem.H. HP1 62 BG20
Lovel End, Chal.St.P. SL9 112 AW52
Lovelinch Cl, SE15 45 H3
Lovell Ho, E8 10 C8
Lovell Pl, SE16 33 M6
Lovell Rd, Enf. EN1 104 DV35
Richmond TW10 199 CJ90
Southall UB1 158 CB72
Lovell Wk, Rain. RM13 169 FG65
Lovel Mead, Chal.St.P. SL9 112 AW52
Lovelock Cl, Ken. CR8 258 DQ117
Lovel Rd, Chal.St.P. SL9 112 AW52
Loveridge Ms, NW6 5 H5
Loveridge Rd, NW6 5 H5
Lovering Rd, Chsht EN7 88 DQ26
Lovers La, Green. DA9 191 FX84
Lovers Wk, N3 120 DA52
NW7 119 CZ51
SE10 47 J3
Lover's Wk, W1 28 G2
Lovet Rd, Harl. CM19 73 EN16
Lovett Dr, Cars. SM5 222 DC101
Lovett Rd, Hare. UB9 136 BJ55
London Colney AL2 83 CG26
Staines TW18 195 BB91
Lovett's Pl, SW18 off Old York Rd 182 DB84
Lovett Way, NW10 140 CQ64
Love Wk, SE5 43 L8
Lovibonds Av, Orp. BR6 245 EP105
West Drayton UB7 156 BM72
Lowbell La, Lon.Col. AL2 84 CL27
Lowbrook Rd, Ilf. IG1 147 EP64
Lowburys, Dor. RH4 285 CH139
Low Cl, Green. DA9 211 FU85
Low Cross Wd La, SE21 204 DT90
Lowdell Cl, West Dr. UB7 156 BL72
Lowden Rd, N9 122 DV46
SE24 183 DP84
Southall UB1 158 BY73
Lowe, The, Chig. IG7 126 EU50
Lowe Av, E16 23 P7
Lowe Cl, Chig. IG7 126 EU50
Lowell St, E14 21 M9
Lowen Rd, Rain. RM13 169 FD68
Lower Addiscombe Rd, Croy. CR0 224 DS102
Lower Addison Gdns, W14 26 D5
Lower Adeyfield Rd, Hem.H. HP2 62 BK19
Lower Alderton Hall La, Loug. IG10 107 EN43
LOWER ASHTEAD, Ashtd. KT21 253 CJ119
Lower Barn, Hem.H. HP3 62 BM23
Lower Barn Rd, Pur. CR8 242 DR112
Lower Bedfords Rd, Rom. RM1 127 FE51
Lower Belgrave St, SW1 29 J7
Lower Bobbingworth Grn, Ong. CM5 75 FG24
LOWER BOIS, Chesh. HP5 76 AR34
Lower Boston Rd, W7 159 CE74
Lower Br Rd, Red. RH1 272 DF134
Lower Britwell Rd, Slou. SL2 153 AK70
Lower Broad St, Dag. RM10 168 FA67
Lower Bury La, Epp. CM16 91 ES31
Lower Camden, Chis. BR7 207 EM94
Lower Ch Hill, Green. DA9 211 FS85
Lower Ch St, Croy. CR0 off Waddon New Rd 223 DP103
Lower Cippenham La, Slou. SL1 153 AN74
Lower Clabdens, Ware SG12 55 DZ06
LOWER CLAPTON, E5 11 H1
Lower Clapton Rd, E5 10 G3
Lower Clarendon Wk, W11 off Lancaster Rd 14 E9
Lower Common S, SW15 181 CV83
Lower Coombe St, Croy. CR0 242 DQ105
Lower Ct Rd, Epsom KT19 238 CQ111
Lower Cft, Swan. BR8 229 FF98
Lower Dagnall St, St.Alb. AL3 64 CC20
Lower Derby Rd, Wat. WD17 off Water La 98 BW42
Lower Downs Rd, SW20 221 CX95
Lower Drayton Pl, Croy. CR0 off Drayton Rd 223 DP103
Lower Dr, Beac. HP9 111 AK50
Lower Dunnymans, Bans. SM7 off Upper Sawley Wd 239 CZ114
Lower Edgeborough Rd, Guil. GU1 281 AZ135
LOWER EDMONTON, N9 122 DU46
Lower Emms, Hem.H. HP2 off Hunters Oak 63 BQ15
Lower Fm Rd, Eff. KT24 251 BV124
LOWER FELTHAM, Felt. TW13 197 BS90
Lowerfield, Welw.G.C. AL7 52 DA10
Lower George St, Rich. TW9 199 CK85
Lower Gravel Rd, Brom. BR2 226 EL102
LOWER GREEN, Esher KT10 218 CA103
Lower Grn, Tewin AL6 52 DE05
Lower Grn Gdns, Wor.Pk. KT4 221 CU102
Lower Grn Rd, Esher KT10 218 CB103
Lower Grn W, Mitch. CR4 222 DE97
Lower Grosvenor Pl, SW1 29 J6
Lower Gro Rd, Rich. TW10 200 CM86
🔒 Lower Guild Hall, Bluewater DA9 off Bluewater Shop Cen 211 FT87
Lower Hall La, E4 123 DY50
Lower Hampton Rd, Sun. TW16 218 BW97
Lower Ham Rd, Kings.T. KT2 199 CK93
Lower Hatfield Rd, Hert. SG13 69 DK15
Lower Higham Rd, Grav. DA12 213 GM88
Lower High St, Wat. WD17 98 BX43
Lower Hill Rd, Epsom KT19 238 CP112
LOWER HOLLOWAY, N7 8 C2
Lower James St, W1 17 M10
Lower John St, W1 17 M10
Lower Kenwood Av, Enf. EN2 103 DK43
Lower Kings Rd, Berk. HP4 60 AW19
Kingston upon Thames KT2 220 CL95
LOWER KINGSWOOD, Tad. KT20 272 DA127
Lower Lea Crossing, E14 23 J10
E16 23 J10
Lower Lees Rd, Slou. SL2 153 AN69
Lower Maidstone Rd, N11 off Telford Rd 121 DJ51
Lower Mall, W6 181 CV78
Lower Mardyke Av, Rain. RM13 169 FC68
Lower Marsh, SE1 30 E5
Lower Marsh La, Kings.T. KT1 220 CM98
Lower Mast Ho, SE18 37 K6
Lower Mead, Iver SL0 155 BD69
Lowermead, Red. RH1 272 DF132
Lower Meadow, Chsht EN8 89 DX27
Harlow CM18 73 ES19
Lower Merton Ri, NW3 6 D6
Lower Morden La, Mord. SM4 221 CW100
Lower Mortlake Rd, Rich. TW9 180 CL84
LOWER NAZEING, Wal.Abb. EN9 72 EE23
Lower Noke Cl, Brwd. CM14 128 FL47
Lower Northfield, Bans. SM7 239 CZ114
Lower Paddock Rd, Wat. WD19 98 BY44
Lower Pk Rd, N11 121 DJ50
Belvedere DA17 188 FA76
Chipstead CR5 256 DE118
Loughton IG10 106 EK43
Lower Paxton Rd, St.Alb. AL1 65 CE21
Lower Peryers, E.Hors. KT24 267 BS128
Lower Pillory Down, Cars. SM5 240 DG113
● Lower Pl Business Cen, NW10 off Steele Rd 160 CQ68
Lower Plantation, Loud. WD3 96 BJ41
Lower Queens Rd, Buck.H. IG9 124 EK47
Lower Range Rd, Grav. DA12 213 GL87
Lower Richmond Rd, SW14 180 CP83
SW15 181 CW83
Richmond TW9 180 CN83
Lower Riding, Beac. HP9 110 AH53
Lower Rd, SE1 30 E4
SE8 32 G6
SE16 33 J8
Belvedere DA17 188 FA76
Chorleywood WD3 95 BC42
Denham UB9 135 BC59
Erith DA8 189 FD77
Gerrards Cross SL9 112 AY53
Great Amwell SG12 55 DZ08
Harrow HA2 139 CD61
Hemel Hempstead HP3 80 BN25
Kenley CR8 241 DP113
Leatherhead KT22, KT23, KT24 253 CD123
Loughton IG10 107 EN40
Mountnessing CM13, CM15 131 GD41
Northfleet DA11 192 FY84
Orpington BR5 228 EV101
Redhill RH1 288 DD136
Sutton SM1 240 DC105
Swanley BR8 209 FF94
Lower Robert St, WC2 off John Adam St 30 B1
🔒 Lower Rose Gall, Bluewater DA9 off Bluewater Shop Cen 211 FU87
Lower Sales, Hem.H. HP1 61 BF21
Lower Sandfields, Send GU23 249 BD124
Lower Sand Hills, Long Dit. KT6 219 CJ101
Lower Sawley Wd, Bans. SM7 off Upper Sawley Wd 239 CZ114
Lower Shott, Bkhm KT23 268 CA126
Cheshunt EN7 88 DT26
Lower Sloane St, SW1 28 G9
Lower Sq, Islw. TW7 179 CH83
Lower Sta Rd, Cray. DA1 209 FE86
Lower Strand, NW9 119 CT54
Lower St, Shere GU5 282 BN139
Lower Sunbury Rd, Hmptn. TW12 218 BZ96
Lower Swaines, Epp. CM16 91 ES30
LOWER SYDENHAM, SE26 205 DX91
⇌ Lower Sydenham 205 DZ92
● Lower Sydenham Ind Est, SE26 off Kangley Br Rd 205 DZ92
Lower Tail, Wat. WD19 116 BY48
Lower Talbot Wk, W11 off Talbot Wk 161 CY72
Lower Teddington Rd, Kings.T. KT1 219 CK95
Lower Ter, NW3 142 DC62
Lower Thames St, EC3 31 M1
🔒 Lower Thames Wk, Bluewater DA9 off Bluewater Shop Cen 211 FT88
Lower Tub, Bushey WD23 117 CD45
Lower Wd Rd, Clay. KT10 237 CG107
Lower Woodside, Hat. AL9 67 CZ22
Lower Yott, Hem.H. HP2 62 BM21
Lowestoft Cl, E5 off Theydon Rd 144 DW61
Lowestoft Dr, Slou. SL1 152 AJ72
Lowestoft Ms, E16 37 P4
Lowestoft Rd, Wat. WD24 97 BV39
Loweswater Cl, Wat. WD25 82 BW33
Wembley HA9 139 CK61
★ Lowewood Mus, Hodd. EN11 71 EA18
Lowfield, Saw. CM21 58 EX06
● Lowfield Heath Ind Est, Craw. RH11 290 DE154
Lowfield La, Hodd. EN11 71 EA17
Lowfield Rd, NW6 5 J6
W3 160 CQ72
Lowfield St, Dart. DA1 210 FL89
Low Hall Cl, E4 123 EA45
Low Hall La, E17 145 DY58
Low Hill Rd, Roydon CM19 72 EF17
Lowick Rd, Har. HA1 139 CE56
Lowlands, Hat. AL9 67 CW15
Lowlands Dr, Stanw. TW19 196 BK85
Lowlands Gdns, Rom. RM7 149 FB58
Lowlands Rd, Aveley RM15 170 FP74
Harrow HA1 139 CE59
Pinner HA5 138 BW59
Lowman Rd, N7 8 D1
Lowndes Av, Chesh. HP5 76 AP30
Lowndes Cl, SW1 29 H7
Lowndes Ct, W1 17 L9
Bromley BR1 off Queens Rd 226 EG96
Lowndes Pl, SW1 28 G7
Lowndes Sq, SW1 28 F5
Lowndes St, SW1 28 F6
Lowood Ct, SE19 204 DT92
Lowood St, E1 20 F10
Low Rd, Hat. AL9 68 DF15
Lowry Cl, Erith DA8 189 FD77
Lowry Cres, Mitch. CR4 222 DE96
Lowry Ho, E14 off Cassilis Rd 34 B5
Lowry Rd, Dag. RM8 148 EV63
Lowshoe La, Rom. RM5 127 FB53
Lowson Gro, Wat. WD19 116 BY45
LOW STREET, Til. RM18 193 GM79
Low St La, E.Til. RM18 193 GM78
Lowswood Cl, Nthwd. HA6 115 BQ53
Lowther Cl, Els. WD6 100 CM43
Lowther Dr, Enf. EN2 103 DL42
Lowther Gdns, SW7 28 A6
Lowther Hill, SE23 205 DY87
Sch Lowther Prim Sch, SW13 off Stillingfleet Rd 181 CU79
Lowther Rd, E17 123 DY54
N7 8 E3
SW13 181 CT81
Kingston upon Thames KT2 220 CM95
Stanmore HA7 140 CM55
Lowthorpe, Wok. GU21 off Shilburn Way 248 AU118
Lowth Rd, SE5 43 J7
LOXFORD, Ilf. IG1 147 EQ64
Loxford Av, E6 166 EK68
Loxford La, Ilf. IG1, IG3 147 EQ64
Loxford Rd, Bark. IG11 167 EP65
Caterham CR3 274 DT125

Sch Loxford Sch of Science & Tech, Ilf. IG1 off Loxford La 147 ER64
Loxford Ter, Bark. IG11
off Fanshawe Av 167 EQ65
Loxford Way, Cat. CR3 274 DT125
Loxham Rd, E4 123 EA52
Loxham St, WC1 18 B3
Loxley Cl, SE26 205 DX92
Byfleet KT14 234 BL114
Loxley Ct, Ware SG12 55 DY06
Loxley Rd, SW18 202 DD88
Berkhamsted HP4 60 AS17
Hampton TW12 198 BZ91
Loxton Rd, SE23 205 DX88
Loxwood Cl, Felt. TW14 197 BR88
Hemel Hempstead HP3 61 BF23
Orpington BR5 228 EX103
Loxwood Rd, N17 144 DS55
Sch Loyola Prep Sch, Buck.H. IG9
off Palmerston Rd 124 EJ46
Coll L.S.O. St. Luke's, EC1 19 K4
Sch Lubavitch Girls Prim Sch, N16
off Stamford Hill 144 DT59
Sch Lubavitch Ho Boys' Sch, E5
off Clapton Common 144 DT59
Lubbock Rd, Chis. BR7 207 EM94
Lubbock St, SE14 45 H5
Lucan Dr, Stai. TW18 196 BK94
Lucan Pl, SW3 28 C9
Lucan Rd, Barn. EN5 101 CY41
Lucas Av, E13 166 EH67
Harrow HA2 138 CA61
Lucas Cl, NW10 off Pound La 161 CU66
Lucas Ct, SW11 41 H7
Harrow HA2 138 CA60
Waltham Abbey EN9 90 EF33
Lucas Cres, Green. DA9
off Ingress Pk Av 211 FW85
Lucas Gdns, N2 120 DC54
Lucas Rd, SE20 204 DW93
Grays RM17 192 GA76
Lucas Sq, NW11
off Hampstead Way 142 DA58
Lucas St, SE8 46 A8
Sch Lucas Vale Prim Sch, SE8 46 A7
Lucern Cl, Chsht EN7 88 DS27
Lucerne Cl, N13 121 DL49
Woking GU22 248 AY119
Lucerne Ct, Erith DA18
off Middle Way 188 EY76
Lucerne Gro, E17 145 ED56
Lucerne Ms, W8 27 K2
Lucerne Rd, N5 143 DP63
Orpington BR6 227 ET102
Thornton Heath CR7 223 DP99
Lucerne Way, Rom. RM3 128 FK51
Lucey Rd, SE16 32 C7
Lucey Way, SE16 32 D7
Lucida Ct, Wat. WD18
off Whippendell Rd 97 BS43
Lucie Av, Ashf. TW15 197 BP93
Lucien Rd, SW17 202 DG91
SW19 202 DB89
Lucknow St, SE18 187 ES80
Lucks Hill, Hem.H. HP1 61 BE20
Lucorn Cl, SE12 206 EF86
Lucton Ms, Loug. IG10 107 EP42
Luctons Av, Buck.H. IG9 124 EJ46
Lucy Cres, W3 160 CQ71
Lucy Gdns, Dag. RM8 148 EY62
Luddesdon Rd, Erith DA8 188 FA80
Luddington Av, Vir.W. GU25 215 AZ96
Ludford Cl, Croy. CR0
off Warrington Rd 241 DP105
Ludgate Bdy, EC4 18 G9
Ludgate Circ, EC4 18 G9
Ludgate Hill, EC4 18 G9
Ludgate Sq, EC4 19 H9
Ludham Cl, SE28
off Rollesby Way 168 EW72
Ilford IG6 125 EQ53
Ludlow Cl, Brom. BR2
off Aylesbury Rd 226 EG97
Harrow HA2 138 BZ63
Ludlow Ct, Dag. RM10
off St. Mark's Pl 168 FA65
Ludlow Mead, Wat. WD19 115 BV48
Ludlow Pl, Grays RM17 192 GB76
Ludlow Rd, W5 159 CJ70
Feltham TW13 197 BU91
Guildford GU2 280 AV135
Ludlow St, EC1 19 J4
Ludlow Way, N2 142 DC56
Croxley Green WD3 97 BQ42
Ludovick Wk, SW15 180 CS84
Ludwick Cl, Welw.G.C. AL7 51 CZ11
Ludwick Grn, Welw.G.C. AL7 51 CZ10
Ludwick Ms, SE14 45 M4
Ludwick Way, Welw.G.C. AL7 51 CZ09
Luff Cl, Wind. SL4 173 AL83
Luffield Rd, SE2 188 EV76
Luffman Rd, SE12 206 EH90
Lugard Rd, SE15 44 F8
Lugg App, E12 147 EN62
Luke Ho, E1 20 E9
Luke St, EC2 19 N4
Lukin Cres, E4 123 ED48
Lukin St, E1 21 H9
Lukintone Cl, Loug. IG10 106 EL44
Lullarook Cl, Bigg.H. TN16 260 EJ116
Lullingstone Av, Swan. BR8 229 FF97
Lullingstone Cl, Orp. BR5 208 EV94
Lullingstone Cres, Orp. BR5 208 EU94
Lullingstone La, SE13 205 ED86
Eynsford DA4 230 FJ104
★ Lullingstone Park Visitor Cen, Dart. DA4 247 FG107
Lullingstone Rd, Belv. DA17 188 EZ79
★ Lullingstone Roman Vil, Dart. DA4 229 FH104
Lullington Garth, N12 119 CZ50
Borehamwood WD6 100 CP43
Bromley BR1 206 EE94
Lullington Rd, SE20 204 DU94
Dagenham RM9 168 EY66
Lulot Gdns, N19 143 DH61
Lulworth, NW1 7 M7
SE17 31 L10
Lulworth Av, Goffs Oak EN7 87 DP29
Hounslow TW5 178 CB80
Wembley HA9 139 CJ59
Lulworth Cl, Har. HA2 138 BZ62
Lulworth Cres, Mitch. CR4 222 DE96
Lulworth Dr, Pnr. HA5 138 BX59
Romford RM5 127 FB50
Lulworth Gdns, Har. HA2 138 BY61
Lulworth Ho, SW8 42 C4
Lulworth Rd, SE9 206 EL89
SE15 44 F8
Welling DA16 187 ET82
Lulworth Waye, Hayes UB4 158 BW72
Lumbards, Welw.G.C. AL7 52 DA06
Lumen Rd, Wem. HA9 139 CK61
Lumiere Ct, SW17 202 DG89
Lumley Cl, Belv. DA17 188 FA79
Lumley Ct, WC2 30 B1
Horley RH6 290 DG147
Lumley Flats, SW1
off Holbein Pl 28 G10
Lumley Gdns, Sutt. SM3 239 CY106
Lumley Rd, Horl. RH6 290 DG147
Sutton SM3 239 CY107
Lumley St, W1 17 H9
Luna Ho, SE16 32 D4
Luna Pl, St.Alb. AL1 65 CG20
Lunar Cl, Bigg.H. TN16 260 EK116
Luna Rd, Th.Hth. CR7 224 DQ97
Lundin Wk, Wat. WD19 116 BX49
Lund Pt, E15 12 E8
Lundy Dr, Hayes UB3 177 BS77
Lundy Wk, N1 9 K5
Lunedale Rd, Dart. DA2 210 FQ88
Lunedale Wk, Dart. DA2
off Lunedale Rd 210 FQ88
Lunghurst Rd, Wold. CR3 259 DZ120
Lunham Rd, SE19 204 DS93
Lupin Cl, SW2
off Palace Rd 203 DP89
Croydon CR0
off Primrose La 225 DX102
Rush Green RM7 149 FD61
West Drayton UB7
off Magnolia St 176 BK78
Lupin Cres, Ilf. IG1
off Bluebell Way 167 EP65
Lupino Ct, SE11 30 D9
Lupin Pt, SE1 32 B5
Luppit Cl, Hutt. CM13 131 GA46
Lupton Cl, SE12 206 EH91
Lupton St, NW5 7 L1
Lupus St, SW1 41 M1
Luralda Gdns, E14 34 F10
Lurgan Av, W6 38 D2
Lurline Gdns, SW11 41 H6
Luscombe Ct, Brom. BR2 226 EE96
Luscombe Way, SW8 42 A4
Lushes Ct, Loug. IG10
off Lushes Rd 107 EP43
Lushes Rd, Loug. IG10 107 EP43
Lushington Dr, Cob. KT11 235 BV114
Lushington Rd, NW10 161 CV68
SE6 205 EB92
Lushington Ter, E8 10 D3
Lusted Hall La, Tats. TN16 260 EJ120
Lusted Rd, Sev. TN13 263 FE120
Lusteds Cl, Dor. RH4
off Glory Mead 285 CJ139
Luther Cl, Edg. HA8 118 CQ47
Luther King Cl, E17 145 DY58
Luther Ms, Tedd. TW11
off Luther Rd 199 CF92
Luther Rd, Tedd. TW11 199 CF92
Luton Pl, SE10 46 F5
Luton Rd, E13 23 N5
E17 145 DZ55
Sidcup DA14 208 EW90
Luton St, NW8 16 B5
Lutton Ter, NW3 142 DC63
Luttrell Av, SW15 201 CV85
Lutwyche Rd, SE6 205 DZ89
Lutyens Cl, Eff. KT24 268 BX127
Lutyens Ho, SW1
off Churchill Gdns 41 L1
Luxborough La, Chig. IG7 124 EL48
Luxborough St, W1 16 G6
Luxborough Twr, W1
off Luxborough St 16 G6
Luxembourg Ms, E15 13 J3
Luxemburg Gdns, W6 26 C8
Luxfield Rd, SE9 206 EL88
Luxford Pl, Saw. CM21 58 EZ06
Luxford St, SE16 33 J9
Luxmore St, SE4 45 P7
Luxor St, SE5 43 H9
Luxted Rd, Downe BR6 245 EN112
Lyall Av, SE21 204 DS90
Lyall Ms, SW1 28 G7
Lyall Ms W, SW1 28 G7
Lyall St, SW1 28 G7
Lyal Rd, E3 21 M1
Lycaste Cl, St.Alb. AL1 65 CF21
Lycée, The, SE11 42 F1
Sch Lycée Français Charles de Gaulle, SW7 28 A8
Lycett Pl, W12
off Becklow Rd 181 CU75
Lych Gate, Wat. WD25 82 BX33
Lych Gate Rd, Orp. BR6 228 EU102
Lych Gate Wk, Hayes UB3 157 BT73
Lych Way, Wok. GU21 248 AX116
Lyconby Gdns, Croy. CR0 225 DY101
Lycrome La, Chesh. HP5 76 AR28
Lycrome Rd, Chesh. HP5 76 AS28
Lydd Cl, Sid. DA14 207 ES90
Lydden Ct, SE9 207 ES86
Lydden Gro, SW18 202 DB87
Lydden Rd, SW18 202 DB87
Lydd Rd, Bexh. DA7 188 EZ80
Lydeard Rd, E6 167 EM66
Lydele Cl, Wok. GU21 249 AZ115
Lydford Av, Slou. SL2 153 AR71
Lydford Cl, N16 9 P2
Lydford Rd, N15 144 DR57
NW2 4 B5
W9 15 H4
Lydger Cl, Wok. GU22 249 BB120
Lydhurst Av, SW2 203 DM89
Lydia Ms, N.Mymms AL9 67 CW24
Lydia Rd, Erith DA8 189 FF79
Lydney Cl, SW19
off Princes Way 201 CY89
Lydon Rd, SW4 183 DJ83
Lydsey Cl, Slou. SL2 153 AN69
Lydstep Rd, Chis. BR7 207 EN91
Lye, The, Tad. KT20 255 CW122
LYE GREEN, Chesh. HP5 78 AT27
Lye Grn Rd, Chesh. HP5 76 AR30
Lye La, Brick.Wd AL2 82 CA30
Lyell Pl E, Wind. SL4
off Lyell Rd 172 AJ83
Lyell Pl W, Wind. SL4
off Lyell Rd 172 AJ83
Lyell Rd, Wind. SL4 172 AJ83
Lyell Wk E, Wind. SL4
off Lyell Rd 172 AJ83
Lyell Wk W, Wind. SL4
off Lyell Rd 172 AJ83
Lyfield, Oxshott KT22 236 CB114
Lyford Rd, SW18 202 DD87
Lyford St, SE18 37 H9
Lygean Av, Ware SG12 55 DY06
Lygon Ho, SW6 38 E6
Lygon Pl, SW1 29 J7
Lyham Cl, SW2 203 DL86
Lyham Rd, SW2 203 DL85
Lyle Cl, Mitch. CR4 222 DG101
Lyle Pk, Sev. TN13 279 FH123
Lymbourne Cl, Sutt. SM2 240 DA110
Lymden Gdns, Reig. RH2 288 DB135
Lyme Fm Rd, SE12 186 EG84
Lyme Gro, E9 10 G6
Lymer Av, SE19 204 DT92
Lyme Regis Rd, Bans. SM7 255 CZ117
Lyme Rd, Well. DA16 188 EV81
Lymescote Gdns, Sutt. SM1 222 DA103
Lyme St, NW1 7 L7
Lyme Ter, NW1 7 L7
Lyminge Cl, Sid. DA14 207 ET91
Lyminge Gdns, SW18 202 DE88
Lymington Av, N22 121 DN54
Lymington Cl, E6 25 J6
SW16 223 DK96
Lymington Ct, Sutt. SM1
off All Saints Rd 222 DC104
Lymington Dr, Ruis. HA4 137 BR61
Lymington Gdns, Epsom KT19 239 CT106
Lymington Rd, NW6 5 L4
Dagenham RM8 148 EX60
Lyminster Cl, Hayes UB4
off West Quay Dr 158 BY71
Lympstone Gdns, SE15 44 D4
Lynbridge Gdns, N13 121 DP49
Lynbrook Cl, Rain. RM13 169 FD68
Lynbrook Gro, SE15 43 P4
Lynceley Gra, Epp. CM16 92 EU29
Lynch, The, Hodd. EN11 71 EB17
Uxbridge UB8 156 BJ66
Lynch Cl, SE3 47 L9
Uxbridge UB8 off Cross Rd 156 BJ66
Lynchen Cl, Houns. TW5
off The Avenue 177 BU81
Lynch Hill La, Slou. SL2 153 AL70
Sch Lynch Hill Prim Sch, Slou. SL2
off Garrard Rd 153 AM69
Lynchmere Pl, Guil. GU2
off Peak Rd 264 AU131
Lynch Wk, SE8 45 P2
Lyncott Cres, SW4 183 DH84
Lyncroft Av, Pnr. HA5 138 BY57
Lyncroft Gdns, NW6 5 K2
W13 179 CJ75
Epsom KT17 239 CT109
Hounslow TW3 178 CC84
Lyndale, NW2 141 CZ63
Lyndale Av, NW2 141 CZ62
Lyndale Cl, SE3 47 L3
Lyndale Ct, W.Byf. KT14
off Parvis Rd 234 BG113
● Lyndale Est, Grays RM20 191 FV79
Lyndale Rd, Red. RH1 272 DF131
Lynden Hyrst, Croy. CR0
off Addiscombe Rd 224 DT103
Lynden Way, Swan. BR8 229 FC97
Lyndhurst Av, N12 120 DF51
NW7 118 CS51
SW16 223 DK96
Pinner HA5 115 BV53
Southall UB1 158 CB74
Sunbury-on-Thames TW16 217 BU97
Surbiton KT5 220 CP102
Twickenham TW2 198 BZ88
Lyndhurst Cl, NW10 140 CR62
Bexleyheath DA7 189 FB83
Croydon CR0 224 DT104
Orpington BR6 245 EP105
Woking GU21 248 AX115
Lyndhurst Ct, E18
off Churchfields 124 EG53
Sutton SM2 off Overton Rd 240 DA108
Lyndhurst Dr, E10 145 EC59
Hornchurch RM11 150 FJ60
New Malden KT3 220 CS100
Sevenoaks TN13 278 FE124
Lyndhurst Gdns, N3 119 CY53
NW3 6 B2
Barking IG11 167 ES65
Enfield EN1 104 DS42
Ilford IG2 147 ER58
Pinner HA5 115 BV53
Lyndhurst Gro, SE15 43 P8
Lyndhurst Ho, SW15
off Ellisfield Dr 201 CU87
Sch Lyndhurst Ho Prep Sch, NW3 6 B2
Sch Lyndhurst Prim Sch, SE5 43 M8
Lyndhurst Ri, Chig. IG7 125 EN49
Lyndhurst Rd, E4 123 EC52
N18 122 DU49
N22 121 DM51
NW3 6 B2
Bexleyheath DA7 189 FB83
Chesham HP5 76 AP28
Coulsdon CR5 256 DG116
Greenford UB6 158 CB70
Reigate RH2 288 DA137
Thornton Heath CR7 223 DN98
Lyndhurst Sq, SE15 44 B7
Lyndhurst Ter, NW3 6 A2
Lyndhurst Wk, Borwd. WD6 100 CM39
Lyndhurst Way, SE15 44 B6
Chertsey KT16 215 BE104
Hutton CM13 131 GC46
Sutton SM2 240 DA108
Lyndon Av, Pnr. HA5 116 BY51
Sidcup DA15 207 ET85
Wallington SM6 222 DG104
Lyndon Rd, Belv. DA17 188 FA77
Lyndon Yd, SW17 202 DB91
Lyndwood Dr, Old Wind. SL4 194 AU86
LYNE, Cher. KT16 215 BA102
Sch Lyne & Long Cross C of E Inf Sch, Lyne KT16
off Lyne La 215 BB103
Lyne Cl, Vir.W. GU25 215 AZ100
Lyne Cres, E17 123 DZ53
Lyne Crossing Rd, Lyne KT16 215 BA100
Lyne Gdns, Bigg.H. TN16 260 EL118
Lynegrove Av, Ashf. TW15 197 BQ92
Lyneham Dr, NW9 118 CS53
Lyneham Wk, E5
off Boscombe Cl 11 L2
Pinner HA5 137 BT55
Lyne La, Egh. TW20 215 BA99
Lyne KT16 215 BA100
Virginia Water GU25 215 BA100
Lyne Rd, Vir.W. GU25 214 AX100
Lynette Av, SW4 203 DH86
Lynett Rd, Dag. RM8 148 EX61
Lyne Way, Hem.H. HP1 61 BF18
Lynford Cl, Barn. EN5
off Rowley La 101 CT43
Edgware HA8 118 CQ52
Lynford Gdns, Edg. HA8 118 CP48
Ilford IG3 147 ET61
Lyngarth Cl, Bkhm KT23 268 CC125
Lyngfield Pk, Maid. SL6 172 AD79
Lynhurst Cres, Uxb. UB10 157 BQ66
Lynhurst Rd, Uxb. UB10 157 BQ66
Lynmere Rd, Well. DA16 188 EV82
Lyn Ms, E3 21 N3
N16 9 P1
Lynmouth Av, Enf. EN1 104 DT44
Morden SM4 221 CX101
Lynmouth Dr, Ruis. HA4 137 BV61
Lynmouth Gdns, Houns. TW5 178 BX81
Perivale UB6 159 CH67
Lynmouth Ri, Orp. BR5 228 EV98
Lynmouth Rd, E17 145 DY58
N2 142 DF55
N16 144 DT60
Perivale UB6 159 CH67
Welwyn Garden City AL7 51 CZ09
Lynn Cl, Ashf. TW15 197 BR92
Harrow HA3 117 CD54
Lynne Cl, Grn St Grn BR6 245 ET107
South Croydon CR2 242 DW111
Lynne Wk, Esher KT10 236 CC106
Lynne Way, Nthlt. UB5 158 BX68
Lynn Ms, E11 off Lynn Rd 146 EE61
Lynn Rd, E11 146 EE61
SW12 203 DH87
Ilford IG2 147 ER59
Lynn St, Enf. EN2 104 DR39
Lynn Wk, Reig. RH2 288 DB137
Lynross Cl, Rom. RM3 128 FM54
Lynscott Way, S.Croy. CR2 241 DP109
Lynsted Cl, Bexh. DA6 209 FB85
Bromley BR1 226 EJ96
Lynsted Ct, Beck. BR3
off Churchfields Rd 225 DY96
Lynsted Gdns, SE9 186 EK83
Lynton Av, N12 120 DD49
NW9 141 CT56
W13 159 CG72
Orpington BR5 228 EV98
Romford RM7 126 FA53
St. Albans AL1 65 CJ21
Lynton Cl, NW10 140 CS64
Chessington KT9 238 CL105
Isleworth TW7 179 CF84
Lynton Cres, Ilf. IG2 147 EP58
Lynton Crest, Pot.B. EN6
off Strafford Gate 86 DA32
Lynton Est, SE1 32 C9
Lynton Gdns, N11 121 DK51
Enfield EN1 122 DS45
Lynton Mead, N20 120 DA48
Lynton Par, Chsht EN8
off Turners Hill 89 DX30
Lynton Rd, E4 123 EB50
N8 143 DK57
NW6 5 H9
SE1 32 B9
W3 160 CN73
Chesham HP5 76 AP28
Croydon CR0 223 DN100
Gravesend DA11 213 GG88
Harrow HA2 138 BY61
New Malden KT3 220 CR99
Lynton Rd S, Grav. DA11 213 GG88
Lynton Ter, W3 160 CP72
Lynton Wk, Hayes UB4 157 BS69
Lynwood, Guil. GU2 280 AV135
Lynwood Av, Couls. CR5 257 DH115
Egham TW20 194 AY93
Epsom KT17 239 CT114
Slough SL3 174 AX76
Lynwood Cl, E18 124 EJ53
Harrow HA2 138 BY62
Romford RM5 127 FB51
Woking GU21 233 BD113
Lynwood Dr, Nthwd. HA6 115 BS53
Romford RM5 127 FB51
Worcester Park KT4 221 CU103
Lynwood Gdns, Croy. CR0 241 DM105
Southall UB1 158 BZ72
Lynwood Gro, N21 121 DN46
Orpington BR6 227 ES101
Lynwood Hts, Rick. WD3 96 BH43
Lynwood Rd, SW17 202 DF90
W5 160 CL70
Epsom KT17 239 CT114
Redhill RH1 272 DG132
Thames Ditton KT7 219 CF103
Lynx Hill, E.Hors. KT24 267 BT128
Lynx Way, E16 24 E10
● Lyon Business Pk, Bark. IG11 167 ES68
Lyon Meade, Stan. HA7 117 CJ53
Lyon Pk Av, Wem. HA0 160 CL65
Sch Lyon Pk Inf & Jun Schs, Wem. HA0 off Vincent Rd 160 CM66
Lyon Rd, SW19 222 DC95
Harrow HA1 139 CF58
Romford RM1 149 FF59
Walton-on-Thames KT12 218 BY103
Lyons Ct, Dor. RH4 285 CH136
Lyonsdene, Lwr Kgswd KT20 271 CZ127
Lyonsdown Av, New Barn. EN5 102 DC44
Lyonsdown Rd, New Barn. EN5 102 DC44
Sch Lyonsdown Sch, New Barn. EN5 off Richmond Rd 102 DC43
Lyons Dr, Guil. GU2 264 AU129
Lyons Pl, NW8 16 A4
Lyon St, N1 8 C7
Lyons Wk, W14 26 E8
Lyon Way, Grnf. UB6 159 CE67
St. Albans AL4 66 CN20
Lyoth Rd, Orp. BR5 227 EQ103
Lyrical Way, Hem.H. HP1 62 BH18
Lyric Dr, Grnf. UB6 158 CB70
★ Lyric Hammersmith, W6 26 A9
Lyric Ms, SE26 204 DW91
Lyric Rd, SW13 181 CT81
Lyric Sq, W6 off King St 26 A9
Lysander Cl, Bov. HP3 79 AZ27
Lysander Gdns, Surb. KT6
off Ewell Rd 220 CM100
Lysander Gro, N19 143 DK60
Lysander Ho, E2 20 E1
Lysander Ms, N19 143 DJ60
Lysander Rd, Croy. CR0 241 DM107
Ruislip HA4 137 BR61
Lysander Way, Abb.L. WD5 81 BU32
Orpington BR6 227 EQ104
Welwyn Garden City AL7 52 DD08
Lys Hill Gdns, Hert. SG14 53 DP07
Lysias Rd, SW12 202 DG86
Lysia St, SW6 38 C5
Lysley Pl, Brook.Pk AL9 86 DC27
Lysnader Ct, N.Wld Bas. CM16
off High St 93 FB26
Lysons Wk, SW15 201 CU85
Lyster Ms, Cob. KT11 235 BV113
Lytchet Rd, Brom. BR1 206 EH94
Lytchet Way, Enf. EN3 104 DW39
Lytchgate Cl, S.Croy. CR2 242 DS108
Lytcott Dr, W.Mol. KT8
off Freeman Dr 218 BZ98
Lytcott Gro, SE22 204 DT85
Lyte St, E2 10 G10
Lytham Av, Wat. WD19 116 BX50
Lytham Cl, SE28 168 EY72
Lytham Gro, W5 160 CM69
Lytham St, SE17 43 L1
Lyttelton Cl, NW3 6 C7
Lyttelton Rd, E10 145 EB62
N2 142 DC57
Lyttleton Rd, N8 143 DN55
Lytton Av, N13 121 DN47
Enfield EN3 105 DY38
Lytton Cl, N2 142 DD58
Loughton IG10 107 ER41
Northolt UB5 158 BZ66
Lytton Gdns, Wall. SM6 241 DK105
Welwyn Garden City AL8 51 CX09
Lytton Gro, SW15 201 CX85
Lytton Pk, Cob. KT11 236 BZ112
Lytton Rd, E11 146 EE59
Barnet EN5 102 DC42
Grays RM16 193 GG77
Pinner HA5 116 BY52
Romford RM2 149 FH57
Woking GU22 249 BB116
Lytton Strachey Path, SE28
off Titmuss Av 168 EV73
Lyttons Way, Hodd. EN11 55 EA14
Lyveden Rd, SE3 186 EH80
SW17 202 DE93
Lywood Cl, Tad. KT20 255 CW122

M

Mabbotts, Tad. KT20 255 CX121
Mabbutt Cl, Brick.Wd AL2 82 BY30
Mabel Rd, Swan. BR8 209 FG93
Mabel St, Wok. GU21 248 AX117
Maberley Cres, SE19 204 DU94
Maberley Rd, SE19 224 DT95
Beckenham BR3 225 DX97
Mabeys Wk, High Wych CM21 58 EV06
Mabledon Pl, WC1 17 P3
Mablethorpe Rd, SW6 38 E5
Mabley St, E9 11 L4
McAdam Cl, Hodd. EN11 71 EA15
McAdam Dr, Enf. EN2 103 DP40
McArdle Way, Colnbr. SL3 175 BD80
Macaret Cl, N20 120 DB45
MacArthur Cl, E7 13 P5
Erith DA8 189 FE78
Wembley HA9 160 CP65
MacArthur Ter, SE7 186 EK79
Macaulay Av, Esher KT10 219 CE103
Sch Macaulay C of E Prim Sch, SW4 off Victoria Ri 183 DH83
Macaulay Ct, SW4 183 DH83
Macaulay Rd, E6 166 EK68
SW4 183 DH83
Caterham CR3 258 DS122
Macaulay Sq, SW4 183 DJ84
Macaulay Way, SE28
off Booth Cl 168 EV73
McAuley Cl, SE1 30 E6
SE9 207 EP85
Macauley Ms, SE13 46 F7
McAuliffe Dr, Slou. SL2 133 AM63
Macbean St, SE18 37 M7
Macbeth St, W6 181 CV78
McCabe Ct, E16 23 L7
McCall Cl, SW4 42 A8
McCall Cres, SE7 186 EL78
McCall Ho, N7
off Tufnell Pk Rd 143 DL62
McCarthy Rd, Felt. TW13 198 BX92
Macclesfield Br, NW1 6 D10
Macclesfield Rd, EC1 19 J2
SE25 224 DV99
Macclesfield St, W1 17 P10
McClintock Pl, Enf. EN3 105 EB37
McCoid Way, SE1 31 J5
McCrone Ms, NW3 6 B4
McCudden Rd, Dart. DA1
off Cornwall Rd 190 FM83
McCullum Rd, E3 11 N9
McDermott Cl, SW11 40 C10
McDermott Rd, SE15 44 C10
Macdonald Av, Dag. RM10 149 FB62
Hornchurch RM11 150 FL56
● McDonald Business Pk, Hem.H. HP2 63 BP17
Macdonald Cl, Amer. HP6 77 AR35
McDonald Ct, Hat. AL10 67 CU20
Macdonald Rd, E7 13 N1
E17 123 EC54
N11 120 DF50
N19 143 DJ61
Macdonald Way, Horn. RM11 150 FL56
Macdonnell Gdns, Wat. WD25 97 BT35
McDonough Cl, Chess. KT9 238 CL105
McDougall Rd, Berk. HP4 60 AX19
McDowall Cl, E16 23 M7
McDowall Rd, SE5 43 J7
Macdowall Rd, Guil. GU2 264 AV129
Macduff Rd, SW11 41 H6
Mace Cl, E1 32 E2
Mace Ct, Grays RM17 192 GE79
Mace La, Cudham TN14 245 ER113
McEntee Av, E17 123 DY53
Macers Ct, Brox. EN10 71 DZ24
Macers La, Brox. EN10 71 DZ24
Mace St, E2 21 J1

McEwen Way, E15 13 H8
Macey Ho, SW11 off Surrey La 40 D7
Macfarland Gro, SE15 43 P4
MacFarlane La, Islw. TW7 179 CF79
Macfarlane Rd, W12 26 A2
Macfarren Pl, NW1 17 H5
McGrath Rd, E15 13 L3
McGredy, Chsht EN7 88 DV29
Macgregor Rd, E16 24 D6
McGregor Rd, W11 14 G8
Machell Rd, SE15 44 G10
Macintosh Cl, Chsht EN7 88 DR26
McIntosh Cl, Rom. RM1 149 FE55
Wallington SM6 241 DL108
McIntosh Rd, Rom. RM1 149 FE55
Mackay Rd, SW4 41 K10
McKay Rd, SW20 201 CV94
● McKay Trd Est, Colnbr. SL3 175 BE82
McKellar Cl, Bushey Hth WD23 116 CC47
Mackennal St, NW8 16 D1
Mackenzie Cl, W12 off Australia Rd 161 CV73
Mackenzie Rd, N7 8 C4
Beckenham BR3 224 DW96
McKenzie Rd, Brox. EN10 71 DZ20
Mackenzie St, Slou. SL1 154 AT74
Mackenzie Wk, E14 34 B3
McKenzie Way, Epsom KT19 238 CN110
Mackenzie Way, Grav. DA12 213 GK93
McKerrell Rd, SE15 44 D7
Mackeson Rd, NW3 6 E1
Mackie Rd, SW2 203 DN87
Mackies Hill, Peasl. GU5 283 BR144
Mackintosh La, E9 11 K3
Macklin St, WC2 18 B8
Mackrells, Red. RH1 288 DC137
Mackrow Wk, E14 22 E10
Macks Rd, SE16 32 D8
Mackworth St, NW1 17 L2
Maclaren Ms, SW15 181 CW84
Maclean Rd, SE23 205 DY86
Maclennan Av, Rain. RM13 170 FK69
Macleod Cl, Grays RM17 192 GD77
Macleod Rd, N21 103 DL43
McLeod Rd, SE2 188 EW77
McLeod's Ms, SW7 27 M7
Macleod St, SE17 43 K1
Maclise Rd, W14 26 E7
Macmahon Cl, Chobham GU24 232 AS110
McMillan Cl, Grav. DA12 213 GJ91
Mcmillan Gdns, Dart. DA1 190 FN84
McMillan St, SE8 46 A3
McMillan Student Village, SE8 46 B3
Macmillan Way, SW17 203 DH91
McNair Rd, Sthl. UB2 178 CB75
McNeil Rd, SE5 43 N9
McNicol Dr, NW10 160 CQ68
Macoma Rd, SE18 187 ER79
Macoma Ter, SE18 187 ER79
Maconochies Rd, E14 34 C10
Macon Way, Upmin. RM14 151 FT59
Macquarie Way, E14 34 D9
McRae La, Mitch. CR4 222 DF101
Macroom Rd, W9 15 H2
Mac's Pl, EC4 18 F8
★ Madame Tussauds, NW1 16 G5
Madan Cl, West. TN16 277 ES125
Sch Madani Girls Sch, E1 20 D8
Madan Rd, West. TN16 277 ER125
Madans Wk, Epsom KT18 238 CR114
Mada Rd, Orp. BR6 227 EP104
Maddams St, E3 22 C5
Madden Cl, Swans. DA10 211 FX86
Maddison Cl, N2 off Long La 120 DC54
Teddington TW11 199 CF93
Maddocks Cl, Sid. DA14 208 EY92
Maddock Way, SE17 43 H3
Maddox La, Bkhm KT23 252 BY123
Maddox Pk, Bkhm KT23 252 BY123
Maddox Rd, Harl. CM20 57 ES14
Hemel Hempstead HP2 63 BP20
Maddox St, W1 17 K10
Madeira Av, Brom. BR1 206 EE94
Madeira Cl, W.Byf. KT14 off Brantwood Gdns 234 BG113
Madeira Cres, W.Byf. KT14 off Brantwood Gdns 234 BG113
Madeira Gro, Wdf.Grn. IG8 124 EJ51
Madeira Rd, E11 145 ED60
N13 121 DP49
SW16 203 DL92
Mitcham CR4 222 DF98
West Byfleet KT14 233 BF113
Madeira Wk, Brwd. CM15 130 FY48
Reigate RH2 272 DD133
Windsor SL4 173 AR81
Madeleine Cl, Rom. RM6 148 EW58
Madeley Cl, Amer. HP6 77 AR36
Madeley Rd, W5 160 CL72
Madeline Gro, Ilf. IG1 147 ER64
Madeline Rd, SE20 224 DU95
Madells, Epp. CM16 91 ET31
Madford Retail Pk, Hert. SG13 54 DS09
Madge Gill Way, E6 off Ron Leighton Way 166 EL67
Madgeways Cl, Gt Amwell SG12 55 DZ09
Madgeways La, Gt Amwell SG12 55 DZ10
Madinah Rd, E8 10 C3
Madingley, Kings.T. KT1 off St. Peters Rd 220 CN96
Madison Bldg, SE10 off Blackheath Rd 46 C6
Madison Cl, Dag. RM10 off St. Mark's Pl 169 FB65
Madison Cres, Bexh. DA7 188 EW80
Madison Gdns, Bexh. DA7 188 EW80
Bromley BR2 226 EF97
Madison Hts, Houns. TW3 178 CC83
Madison Way, Sev. TN13 278 FF123
Madras Pl, N7 8 E4
Madras Rd, Ilf. IG1 147 EP63
Madresfield Ct, Shenley WD7 off Russet Dr 84 CL32
Madrid Rd, SW13 181 CU81
Guildford GU2 280 AV135
Madrigal La, SE5 43 H5
Madron St, SE17 31 P10
Maesmaur Rd, Tats. TN16 260 EK121
Mafeking Av, E6 166 EK68
Brentford TW8 180 CL79
Ilford IG2 147 ER59
Mafeking Rd, E16 23 L4
N17 122 DU54
Enfield EN1 104 DT41
Wraysbury TW19 195 BB89
Magazine Pl, Lthd. KT22 253 CH122
Magazine Rd, Cat. CR3 257 DP122
Magdala Av, N19 143 DH61
Magdala Rd, Islw. TW7 179 CG83
South Croydon CR2 off Napier Rd 242 DR108
Magdalen Cl, Byfleet KT14 234 BL114
Magdalen Cres, Byfleet KT14 234 BL114
Magdalene Cl, SE15 44 E9
Magdalene Gdns, E6 25 L4
N20 120 DF46
Magdalene Rd, Shep. TW17 216 BM98
Magdalen Gdns, Hutt. CM13 131 GE44
Magdalen Gro, Orp. BR6 246 EV105
MAGDALEN LAVER, Ong. CM5 75 FE17
Magdalen Ms, NW3 5 N4
Magdalen Pas, E1 20 B10
Magdalen Rd, SW18 202 DC88
Magdalen St, SE1 31 N3
Magee St, SE11 42 E2
Magellan Pl, E14 off Maritime Quay 34 B9
Maggie Blakes Causeway, SE1 off Shad Thames 32 A3
Magna Carta La, Wrays. TW19 194 AX88
★ Magna Carta Monument, Egh. TW20 194 AX89
Sch Magna Carta Sch, The, Stai. TW18 off Thorpe Rd 195 BD93
Magna Rd, Eng.Grn TW20 194 AV93
Magnaville Rd, Bushey Hth WD23 117 CE45
● Magnet Est, Grays RM20 191 FW78
Magnet Rd, Wem. HA9 139 CK61
West Thurrock RM20 191 FW79
Magnin Cl, E8 10 D8
Magnolia Av, Abb.L. WD5 81 BU32
Magnolia Cl, E10 145 EA61
Hertford SG13 54 DU09
Kingston upon Thames KT2 200 CP93
Park Street AL2 83 CD27
Magnolia Ct, Felt. TW13 off Highfield Rd 197 BU88
Harrow HA3 140 CM59
Horley RH6 290 DG148
Wallington SM6 off Parkgate Rd 241 DH106
Magnolia Dr, Bigg.H. TN16 260 EK116
Magnolia Gdns, Edg. HA8 118 CQ49
Slough SL3 174 AW76
Magnolia Pl, SW4 203 DK85
W5 159 CK71
Magnolia Rd, W4 180 CP79
Magnolia St, West Dr. UB7 176 BK77
Magnolia Way, Epsom KT19 238 CQ106
North Holmwood RH5 285 CK139
Pilgrim's Hatch CM15 130 FV43
Wooburn Green HP10 off Glory Mill La 132 AE56
Magnum Cl, Rain. RM13 170 FJ70
Magnum Ho, Kings.T. KT2 off London Rd 220 CN95
Magnus Ct, N9 off Bedevere Rd 122 DU48
Magpie All, EC4 18 F9
Magpie Cl, E7 13 M2
NW9 off Eagle Dr 118 CS54
Coulsdon CR5 off Ashbourne Cl 257 DJ118
Enfield EN1 104 DU39
Magpie Hall Cl, Brom. BR2 226 EL100
Magpie Hall La, Brom. BR2 227 EM99
Magpie Hall Rd, Bushey Hth WD23 117 CE47
Magpie La, Colesh. HP7 111 AM45
Little Warley CM13 129 FW54
Magpie Pl, SE14 off Milton Ct Rd 45 M3
Magpies, The, Epp.Grn CM16 73 EN24
Magpie Wk, Hat. AL10 off Lark Ri 67 CU20
Magpie Way, Slou. SL2 off Pemberton Rd 153 AL70
Magri Wk, E1 20 G7
Maguire Dr, Rich. TW10 199 CJ91
Maguire St, SE1 32 B4
● Mahatma Gandhi Ind Est, SE24 off Milkwood Rd 183 DP84
Mahlon Av, Ruis. HA4 137 BV64
Mahogany Cl, SE16 33 M3
Mahon Cl, Enf. EN1 104 DT39
Maida Av, E4 123 EB45
W2 15 P6
MAIDA HILL, W9 15 J4
Maida Rd, Belv. DA17 188 FA76
MAIDA VALE, W9 15 M4
⊖ Maida Vale 15 M2
Maida Vale, W9 15 N3
Maida Vale Rd, Dart. DA1 209 FG85
Maida Way, E4 123 EB45
Maiden Erlegh Av, Bex. DA5 208 EY88
Maidenhead Rd, Wind. SL4 173 AK80
Maidenhead St, Hert. SG14 54 DR09
Maiden La, NW1 7 P6
SE1 31 K2
WC2 30 B1
Dartford DA1 189 FG83
Maiden Pl, NW5 143 DJ62
Maiden Rd, E15 13 K6
Maiden's Br, Enf. EN2 104 DU37
Maidensfield, Welw.G.C. AL8 51 CX06
Maidenshaw Rd, Epsom KT19 238 CR112
Maidenstone Hill, SE10 46 E6
Maids of Honour Row, Rich. TW9 off The Green 199 CK85
Maidstone Av, Rom. RM5 127 FC54
Maidstone Bldgs Ms, SE1 31 K3
Maidstone Ho, E14 22 C8
Maidstone Rd, N11 121 DJ51
Grays RM17 192 GA79
Seal TN15 279 FN121
Sevenoaks TN13 278 FE122
Sidcup DA14 208 EX93
Swanley BR8 229 FB95
Main Av, Enf. EN1 104 DT43
Northwood HA6 115 BQ48
Main Dr, Ger.Cr. SL9 134 AW57
Iver SL0 175 BE76
Wembley HA9 139 CK62
Main Par, Chorl. WD3 off Whitelands Av 95 BC42
Main Par Flats, Chorl. WD3 off Whitelands Av 95 BC42
Main Ride, Egh. TW20 194 AS93
Mainridge Rd, Chis. BR7 207 EN91
Main Rd, Crock. BR8 229 FD100
Crockham Hill TN8 277 EQ134
Farningham DA4 230 FL100
Hextable BR8 209 FF94
Knockholt TN14 262 EV117
Longfield DA3 231 FX96
Orpington BR5 228 EW95
Romford RM1, RM2, RM7 149 FF56
Sidcup DA14 207 ES90
Sundridge TN14 262 EX124
Sutton at Hone DA4 210 FP93
Westerham TN16 244 EJ113
Windsor SL4 172 AJ80
Main St, Felt. TW13 198 BX92
Maisie Webster Cl, Stanw. TW19 off Lauser Rd 196 BK87
Maismore St, SE15 44 D3
Maisonettes, The, Sutt. SM1 239 CZ106
Maitland Cl, Houns. TW4 178 BZ83
Walton-on-Thames KT12 218 BY103
West Byfleet KT14 234 BG113
Maitland Cl Est, SE10 46 D5
Maitland Pk Est, NW3 6 F4
Maitland Pk Rd, NW3 6 F5
Maitland Pk Vil, NW3 6 F4
Maitland Pl, E5 10 G1
Maitland Rd, E15 13 L5
SE26 205 DX93
Maize Cft, Horl. RH6 291 DJ147
Maizey Ct, Pilg.Hat. CM15 off Danes Way 130 FU43
Majendie Rd, SE18 187 ER78
Majestic Way, Mitch. CR4 222 DF96
Major Cl, SW9 43 H10
Sch Majorie McClure Sch, Chis. BR7 off Hawkwood La 227 EQ96
Major Rd, E15 12 F2
SE16 32 D6
Majors Fm Rd, Slou. SL3 174 AX80
Makepeace Av, N6 142 DG61
Makepeace Rd, E11 146 EG56
Northolt UB5 158 BY68
Makins St, SW3 28 D9
Malabar St, E14 34 A5
Malacca Fm, W.Clan. GU4 266 BH127
Malam Ct, SE11 30 E9
Malam Gdns, E14 22 C10
Malan Cl, Bigg.H. TN16 260 EL117
Malan Sq, Rain. RM13 169 FH65
Malbrook Rd, SW15 181 CV84
Malcolm Ct, Stan. HA7 117 CJ50
Malcolm Cres, NW4 141 CU58
Malcolm Dr, Surb. KT6 220 CL102
Malcolm Gdns, Hkwd RH6 290 DD150
Malcolm Pl, E2 20 G4
Sch Malcolm Prim Sch, SE20 off Malcolm Rd 204 DW94
Malcolm Rd, E1 20 G4
SE20 204 DW94
SE25 224 DU100
SW19 201 CY93
Coulsdon CR5 257 DK115
Uxbridge UB10 136 BM63
Malcolms Way, N14 103 DJ43
Malcolm Way, E11 146 EG57
Malden Av, SE25 224 DV98
Greenford UB6 139 CE64
Malden Ct, Amer. HP6 94 AT38
Malden Ct, N.Mal. KT3 221 CV97
Malden Cres, NW1 7 H5
Malden Flds, Bushey WD23 98 BX42
Malden Grn Av, Wor.Pk. KT4 221 CT102
Malden Grn Ms, Wor.Pk. KT4 off Malden Rd 221 CU102
Malden Hill, N.Mal. KT3 221 CT97
Malden Hill Gdns, N.Mal. KT3 221 CT97
Jct Malden Junct, N.Mal. KT3 221 CT99
≠ Malden Manor 220 CS101
Sch Malden Manor Prim & Nurs Sch, N.Mal. KT3 off Lawrence Av 220 CS101
Malden Pk, N.Mal. KT3 221 CT100
Sch Malden Parochial C of E Prim Sch, Wor.Pk. KT4 off The Manor Drive 220 CS102
Malden Pl, NW5 6 G3
Malden Rd, NW5 6 F3
Borehamwood WD6 100 CN41
New Malden KT3 220 CS99
Sutton SM3 239 CX105
Watford WD17 97 BU40
Worcester Park KT4 221 CT101
MALDEN RUSHETT, Chess. KT9 237 CH111
Malden Way, N.Mal. KT3 221 CT99
Maldon Cl, E15 13 J3
N1 9 J8
SE5 43 N10
Maldon Ct, Wall. SM6 241 DJ106
Maldon Rd, N9 122 DT48
W3 160 CQ73
Romford RM7 149 FC59
Wallington SM6 241 DH106
Maldon Wk, Wdf.Grn. IG8 124 EJ51
Malet Cl, Egh. TW20 195 BD93
Malet Pl, WC1 17 N5
Malet St, WC1 17 N5
Maley Av, SE27 203 DP89
Malford Ct, E18 124 EG54
Malford Gro, E18 146 EF56
Malfort Rd, SE5 43 P10
Malham Cl, N11 off Catterick Cl 120 DG51
Malham Rd, SE23 205 DX88
Malham Ter, N18 off Dysons Rd 122 DV51
Malin Ct, Hem.H. HP3 62 BJ23
Malins Cl, Barn. EN5 101 CV43
Malkin Dr, Beac. HP9 110 AJ52
Church Langley CM17 74 EY16
Malkin Way, Wat. WD18 97 BS42
Mall, The, Brom. BR1 226 EG97
Croydon CR0 224 DQ103
Romford RM1 149 FF56
Mall, The, N14 121 DL48
SW1 29 M4
SW14 200 CQ85
W5 160 CL73
Harrow HA3 140 CM58
Hornchurch RM11 149 FH60
Park Street AL2 82 CC27
Surbiton KT6 219 CK99
Swanley BR8 off London Rd 229 FE97
Mallams Ms, SW9 42 F10
Mallard Cl, E9 11 P4
NW6 5 K9
W7 179 CE75
Mallard Cl, Burn. SL1 152 AH68
Dartford DA1 210 FM85
Horley RH6 290 DG146
New Barnet EN5 off The Hook 102 DD44
Redhill RH1 272 DG131
Twickenham TW2 off Stephenson Rd 198 CA87
Upminster RM14 151 FT59
Mallard Dr, Slou. SL1 153 AM73
Mallard Path, SE28 off Goosander Way 187 ER76
Mallard Pl, Twick. TW1 199 CG90
Mallard Pt, E3 22 C3
Mallard Rd, Abb.L. WD5 81 BU31
South Croydon CR2 243 DX110
Mallards, E11 146 EG59
Mallards, The, Hem.H. HP3 80 BM25
Staines TW18 216 BH96
Mallards Reach, Wey. KT13 217 BR103
Mallards Ri, Harl. CM17 74 EX15
Mallards Rd, Bark. IG11 168 EU69
Woodford Green IG8 124 EH52
Mallard Wk, Beck. BR3 225 DX99
Sidcup DA14 208 EW92
Mallard Way, NW9 140 CQ59
Hutton CM13 131 GB45
Northwood HA6 115 BQ52
Wallington SM6 241 DJ109
Watford WD25 98 BY37
Mall Chambers, W8 off Kensington Mall 27 K2
Mallet Dr, Nthlt. UB5 138 BZ64
Mallet Rd, SE13 205 ED86
Mall Ex, The, Ilf. IG1 147 EP61
★ Mall Galleries, SW1 29 P2
Malling, SE13 205 EC85
Malling Cl, Croy. CR0 224 DW100
Malling Gdns, Mord. SM4 222 DC100
Malling Way, Brom. BR2 226 EF101
Mallinson Cl, Horn. RM12 150 FJ64
Mallinson Rd, SW11 202 DE85
Croydon CR0 223 DK104
Mallion Ct, Wal.Abb. EN9 90 EF33
Mallord St, SW3 40 B2
Mallory Cl, E14 22 D6
SE4 185 DY84
Mallory Gdns, E.Barn. EN4 120 DG45
Mallory St, NW8 16 D4
Mallow Cl, Croy. CR0 off Marigold Way 225 DX102
Northfleet DA11 212 GE91
Tadworth KT20 255 CV119
● Mallow Ct, Welw.G.C. AL7 52 DA08
Mallow Ct, Grays RM17 192 GD79
Mallow Cres, Guil. GU4 265 BB131
Mallow Cft, Hat. AL10 off Oxlease Dr 67 CV19
Mallow Mead, NW7 119 CY52
Mallows, The, Uxb. UB10 137 BP62
Mallows Grn, Harl. CM19 73 EN19
Mallow St, EC1 19 L4
Mallow Wk, Goffs Oak EN7 88 DR28
Mall Rd, W6 181 CV78
Sch Mall Sch, The, Twick. TW2 off Hampton Rd 199 CD90
Mall Shop, Dag. RM10 off Heathway 168 FA65
Mall Walthamstow, The, E17 145 DZ56
Mallys Pl, S.Darenth DA4 230 FQ95
Malmains Cl, Beck. BR3 225 ED99
Malmains Way, Beck. BR3 225 EC98
Malm Cl, Rick. WD3 114 BK47
Malmesbury, E2 20 G1
Malmesbury Cl, Pnr. HA5 137 BT56
Sch Malmesbury Prim Sch, E3 21 P2
Morden SM4 off Malmesbury Rd 222 DC100
Malmesbury Rd, E3 21 N2
E16 23 K6
E18 124 EF53
Morden SM4 222 DC101
Malmesbury Ter, E16 23 L6
Malmes Cft, Hem.H. HP3 63 BQ22
Malmsdale, Welw.G.C. AL8 51 CX05
Malmsmead Ho, E9 off Kingsmead Way 11 M2
Sch Malorees Inf & Jun Schs, NW6 4 D7
Malory Cl, Beck. BR3 225 DY96
Malory Ct, N9 off Galahad Rd 122 DU48
Malpas Dr, Pnr. HA5 138 BX57
Malpas Rd, E8 10 E4
SE4 45 N9
Dagenham RM9 168 EX65
Grays RM16 193 GJ76
Slough SL2 154 AV73
Malta Rd, E10 145 EA60
Tilbury RM18 193 GF82
Malta St, EC1 19 H4
Maltby Cl, Orp. BR6 228 EU102
Maltby Dr, Enf. EN1 104 DV38
Maltby Rd, Chess. KT9 238 CN107
Maltby St, SE1 32 A5
Malt Hill, Egh. TW20 194 AY92
Malt Ho Cl, Old Wind. SL4 194 AV87
Malthouse Dr, W4 180 CS79
Feltham TW13 198 BX92
Malthouse Pas, SW13 off The Terrace 180 CS82
Malthouse Pl, Rad. WD7 83 CG34
Malt Ho Pl, Rom. RM1 off Exchange St 149 FE57
Malthouse Sq, Beac. HP9 133 AM55
Malthus Path, SE28 off Byron Cl 168 EW74
Malting Ho, E14 21 N10
Malting Mead, Hat. AL10 off Endymion Rd 67 CW17
● Maltings, The, Saw. CM21 58 FA05
Stanstead Abbotts SG12 55 ED11
Maltings, The, St.Alb. AL1 65 CD20
Maltings, The, Byfleet KT14 234 BM113
Hunton Bridge WD4 81 BQ33
Orpington BR6 227 ET102
Oxted RH8 276 EF131
Romford RM1 149 FF59
Staines TW18 off Church St 195 BE91
Worcester Park KT4 off Sherbrooke Way 221 CV101
Maltings Cl, E3 22 E3
SW13 off Cleveland Gdns 180 CS82
Maltings Dr, Epp. CM16 off Palmers Hill 92 EU29
Maltings La, Epp. CM16 92 EU29
Maltings Ms, Amer. HP7 77 AP40
Sidcup DA15 off Station Rd 208 EU90
Maltings Pl, SE1 31 P5
SW6 39 M7
Malting Way, Islw. TW7 179 CF83
Malt La, Rad. WD7 99 CG35
Sch Maltman's Grn Sch, Chal.St.P. SL9 off Maltmans La 134 AW55
Maltmans La, Chal.St.P. SL9 134 AW55
Malton Av, Slou. SL1 153 AP72
Malton Ms, SE18 off Malton St 187 ES79
W10 off Malton Rd 14 E8
Malton Rd, W10 14 E8
Malton St, SE18 187 ES79
Maltravers St, WC2 18 D10
Malt St, SE1 44 C2
Malus Cl, Add. KT15 233 BF108
Hemel Hempstead HP2 62 BN19
Malus Dr, Add. KT15 233 BF107
Malva Cl, SW18 off St. Ann's Hill 202 DB85
Malvern Av, E4 123 ED52
Bexleyheath DA7 188 EY80
Harrow HA2 138 BY62
Malvern Cl, SE20 off Derwent Rd 224 DU96
W10 14 G7
Bushey WD23 98 CC44
Hatfield AL10 67 CT17
Mitcham CR4 223 DJ97
Ottershaw KT16 233 BC107
St. Albans AL4 65 CH16
Surbiton KT6 220 CL102
Uxbridge UB10 137 BP61
Malvern Ct, SE14 45 H4
SW7 28 B9
Slough SL3 off Hill Ri 175 BA79
Sutton SM2 off Overton Rd 240 DA108
Malvern Dr, Felt. TW13 198 BX92
Ilford IG3 147 ET63
Woodford Green IG8 124 EJ50
Malvern Gdns, NW2 141 CY61
NW6 15 H1
Harrow HA3 140 CL55
Loughton IG10 107 EM44
Malvern Ms, NW6 15 J3
Malvern Pl, NW6 15 H2
Malvern Rd, E6 166 EL67
E8 10 C7
E11 146 EE61
N8 143 DM55
N17 144 DU55
NW6 15 J2
Enfield EN3 105 DY37
Grays RM17 192 GD77
Hampton TW12 198 CA94
Hayes UB3 177 BS80
Hornchurch RM11 149 FG58
Orpington BR6 246 EV105
Surbiton KT6 220 CL103
Thornton Heath CR7 223 DN98
Malvern Ter, N1 8 E8
N9 off Latymer Rd 122 DT46
Malvern Way, W13 off Templewood 159 CH71
Croxley Green WD3 97 BP43
Hemel Hempstead HP2 62 BM18
Sch Malvern Way Inf & Nurs Sch, Crox.Grn WD3 off Malvern Way 97 BQ43
Malvina Av, Grav. DA12 213 GH89
Malwood Rd, SW12 203 DH86
Malyons, The, Shep. TW17 off Gordon Rd 217 BR100
Malyons Rd, SE13 205 EB85
Swanley BR8 209 FF94
Malyons Ter, SE13 205 EB85
Managers St, E14 34 F3
Manan Cl, Hem.H. HP3 63 BQ22
Manatee Pl, Wall. SM6 off Croydon Rd 223 DK104
Manaton Cl, SE15 44 E10
Manaton Cres, Sthl. UB1 158 CA72
Manbey Gro, E15 13 J4
Manbey Pk Rd, E15 13 J4
Manbey Rd, E15 13 J4
Manbey St, E15 13 J5
Manbre Rd, W6 38 B2
Manbrough Av, E6 25 K3
Sch Manby Lo Inf Sch, Wey. KT13 off Princes Rd 235 BQ105
Manchester Ct, E16 24 B9
Manchester Dr, W10 14 E5
Manchester Gro, E14 34 E10
Manchester Ms, W1 16 G7
Manchester Rd, E14 34 E10
N15 144 DR58
Thornton Heath CR7 224 DQ97
Manchester Sq, W1 16 G8
Manchester St, W1 16 G7
Manchester Way, Dag. RM10 149 FB63
Manchuria Rd, SW11 202 DG86
Manciple St, SE1 31 L5
Mandalay Rd, SW4 203 DJ85
Mandarin St, E14 22 A10
Mandarin Way, Hayes UB4 158 BX72
Mandela Av, Harl. CM20 57 ES13
Mandela Cl, NW10 160 CQ66
Mandela Rd, E16 23 P9
Mandela St, NW1 7 M8
SW9 42 E5
Mandela Way, SE1 31 P8
Mandel Ho, SW18 off Eastfields Av 182 DA84
Mandelyns, Nthch HP4 60 AS16
Coll Mander Portman Woodward 6th Form Tutorial Coll, SW7 28 A9
Mandeville Cl, SE3 47 M5
SW20 221 CY95
Broxbourne EN10 71 DZ20
Guildford GU2 264 AU131
Harlow CM17 74 EW17
Hertford SG13 54 DQ12
Watford WD17 97 BT38
Mandeville Ct, E4 123 DY49
Egham TW20 195 BA91
Mandeville Dr, St.Alb. AL1 65 CD23
Surbiton KT6 219 CK102
Mandeville Ho, SE1 32 B10

Mandeville Ms, SW4
off Clapham Pk Rd 183 DL84
Mandeville Pl, W1 . . . . 17 H8
Mandeville Prim Sch, E5
off Oswald St. 145 DX62
St. Albans AL1
off Mandeville Dr 65 CD23
Mandeville Ri, Welw.G.C. AL8 . . 51 CX07
Mandeville Rd, N14 . . . . 121 DH47
Enfield EN3 . . . . 105 DX36
Hertford SG13 . . . . 54 DQ12
Isleworth TW7 . . . . 179 CG82
Northolt UB5 . . . . 158 CA66
Potters Bar EN6 . . . . 86 DC32
Shepperton TW17 . . . . 216 BN99
Mandeville Sch, Grnf. UB6
off Horsenden La N 159 CE65
Mandeville St, E5 . . . . 145 DY62
Mandeville Wk, Hutt. CM13 . . . 131 GE44
Mandrake Rd, SW17 . . . . 202 DF90
Mandrake Way, E15 . . . . 13 J6
Mandrell Rd, SW2 . . . . 203 DL85
Manette St, W1 . . . . 17 P9
Manfield Cl, Slou. SL2 . . . . 153 AN69
Manford Cl, Chig. IG7 . . . . 126 EU49
Manford Ct, Chig. IG7
off Manford Way 126 EU50
Manford Cross, Chig. IG7 . . . . . 126 EU50
● Manford Ind Est, Erith
DA8 . . . . 189 FG79
Manford Prim Sch, Chig. IG7
off Manford Way 125 ET50
Manford Way, Chig. IG7 . . . . . . 125 ES49
Manfred Rd, SW15 . . . . 201 CZ85
Manger Rd, N7 . . . . 8 B4
Mangles Rd, Guil. GU1 . . . . 264 AX132
Mangold Way, Erith DA18 . . . . 188 EY76
Mangrove Dr, Hert. SG13 . . . . . . 54 DS11
Mangrove La, Hert. SG13 . . . . . . 70 DT16
Mangrove Rd, Hert. SG13 . . . . . . 54 DS10
Manhattan Av, Wat. WD18 . . . . . 97 BT42
Manhattan Bldg, E3 . . . . 12 B10
Manhattan Wf, E16 . . . . 35 N4
Manilla St, E14 . . . . 34 A4
Manister Rd, SE2 . . . . 188 EU76
Manitoba Ct, SE16 . . . . 33 H5
Manitoba Gdns, Grn St Grn BR6
off Superior Dr 245 ET107
Manley Ct, N16 . . . . 144 DT62
Manley Rd, Hem.H. HP2
off Knightsbridge Way 62 BL19
Manley St, NW1 . . . . 6 G8
Manly Dixon Dr, Enf. EN3 . . . . 105 DY37
Mannamead, Epsom KT18 . . . . 254 CS119
Mannamead Cl, Epsom KT18
off Mannamead 254 CS119
Mann Cl, Croy. CR0
off Scarbrook Rd 224 DQ104
Manneby Prior, N1
off Cumming St 18 D1
Mannicotts, Welw.G.C. AL8 . . . . 51 CV09
Manningford Cl, EC1 . . . . 18 G2
Manning Gdns, Har. HA3 . . . . . 139 CK59
Manning Pl, Rich. TW10
off Grove Rd 200 CM86
Manning Rd, E17
off Southcote Rd 145 DY57
Dagenham RM10 . . . . 168 FA65
Orpington BR5 . . . . 228 EX99
Manning St, Aveley RM15 . . . . 170 FQ74
Manningtree Cl, SW19 . . . . 201 CY88
Manningtree Rd, Ruis. HA4 . . . . 137 BV63
Manningtree St, E1 . . . . 20 C8
Mannin Rd, Rom. RM6 . . . . 148 EV59
Mannock Dr, Loug. IG10 . . . . . . 107 EQ40
Mannock Ms, E18 . . . . 124 EH53
Mannock Rd, N22 . . . . 143 DP55
Dartford DA1
off Barnwell Rd 190 FM83
Manns Cl, Islw. TW7 . . . . 199 CF85
Manns Rd, Edg. HA8 . . . . 118 CN51
Manoel Rd, Twick. TW2 . . . . 198 CC89
Manor Av, SE4 . . . . 45 P9
Caterham CR3 . . . . 258 DS124
Hemel Hempstead HP3 . . . . . 62 BK23
Hornchurch RM11 . . . . 150 FJ57
Hounslow TW4 . . . . 178 BX83
Northolt UB5 . . . . 158 BZ66
Manorbrook, SE3 . . . . 186 EG84
Manor Chase, Wey. KT13 . . . . . 235 BP106
Manor Circ, Rich. TW9 . . . . 180 CN83
Manor Cl, E17 off Manor Rd . . 123 DY54
NW7 off Manor Dr. 118 CR50
NW9 . . . . 140 CP57
SE28 . . . . 168 EW72
Aveley RM15 . . . . 170 FQ74
Barnet EN5 . . . . 101 CY42
Berkhamsted HP4 . . . . 60 AW19
Crayford DA1 . . . . 189 FD84
Dagenham RM10 . . . . 169 FD65
East Horsley KT24 . . . . 267 BS128
Hatfield AL10 . . . . 67 CT15
Hertford SG14 . . . . 54 DR07
Horley RH6 . . . . 290 DF148
Romford RM1
off Manor Rd 149 FG57
Ruislip HA4 . . . . 137 BT60
Warlingham CR6 . . . . 259 DY117
Wilmington DA2 . . . . 209 FG90
Woking GU22 . . . . 249 BF116
Worcester Park KT4 . . . . 220 CS102
Manor Cl S, Aveley RM15
off Manor Cl 170 FQ74
Manor Comm Prim Sch,
Swans. DA10
off Keary Rd 212 FZ87
Manor Cotts, Nthwd. HA6 . . . . . 115 BT53
Manor Cotts App, N2 . . . . 120 DC54
Manor Ct, E10
off Grange Pk Rd 145 EB60
N2 . . . . 142 DF57
SW6 . . . . 39 M7
Enfield EN1 . . . . 104 DV36
Harefield UB9 . . . . 114 BJ54
Radlett WD7 . . . . 99 CF38
Slough SL1
off Richards Way 153 AM74
Twickenham TW2 . . . . 198 CC89
Wembley HA9 . . . . 140 CL64
Weybridge KT13 . . . . 235 BP105
Manor Ct Rd, W7 . . . . 159 CE73
Manor Cres, Byfleet KT14 . . . . 234 BM113
Epsom KT19 . . . . 238 CN112
Guildford GU2 . . . . 264 AV132
Hornchurch RM11 . . . . 150 FJ57
Seer Green HP9 . . . . 111 AR51
Surbiton KT5 . . . . 220 CN100
Manorcroft Prim Sch,
Egh. TW20
off Wesley Dr 195 BA93
Manorcrofts Rd, Egh. TW20 . . . 195 BA93
Manordene Cl, T.Ditt. KT7 . . . . 219 CG102
Manordene Rd, SE28 . . . . 168 EW72
Manor Dr, N14 . . . . 121 DH45
N20 . . . . 120 DE48
NW7 . . . . 118 CR50
Amersham HP6 . . . . 77 AP36
Epsom KT19 . . . . 238 CS107
Esher KT10 . . . . 219 CF103
Feltham TW13
off Lebanon Av 198 BX92
Horley RH6 . . . . 290 DF148
New Haw KT15 . . . . 234 BG110
St. Albans AL2 . . . . 82 CA27
Sunbury-on-Thames TW16 . . 217 BU96
Surbiton KT5 . . . . 220 CM100
Wembley HA9 . . . . 140 CM63
Manor Dr, The, Wor.Pk. KT4 . . . 220 CS102
Manor Dr N, N.Mal. KT3 . . . . . 220 CR101
Worcester Park KT4 . . . . 220 CS102
Manor Est, SE16 . . . . 32 E9
Manor Fm, Fnghm DA4 . . . . . . 230 FM101
Manor Fm Av, Shep. TW17 . . . . 217 BP100
Manor Fm Cl, Wind. SL4 . . . . . . 173 AM83
Worcester Park KT4 . . . . 220 CS102
Manor Fm Ct, Egh. TW20
off Manor Fm La 195 BA92
Manor Fm Dr, E4 . . . . 124 EE48
Manor Fm La, Egh. TW20 . . . . . 195 BA92
Manor Fm Rd, Enf. EN1 . . . . . . 104 DV35
Thornton Heath CR7 . . . . 223 DN96
Wembley HA0 . . . . 159 CK68
Manor Fm Way, Seer Grn HP9
off Orchard Rd 111 AR51
Manorfield Cl, N19
off Junction Rd 143 DJ63
Manorfield Prim & Nurs Sch,
Horl. RH6 off Sangers Dr . . 290 DF148
Manorfield Prim Sch, E14 . . 22 D6
Manor Flds, SW15 . . . . 201 CX86
Manorfields Cl, Chis. BR7 . . . . 227 ET97
Manor Gdns, N7 . . . . 143 DL62
SW20 . . . . 221 CZ96
W3 . . . . 180 CN77
W4 off Devonshire Rd 180 CS78
Effingham KT24 . . . . 268 BX128
Godalming GU7
off Farncombe St 280 AS144
Guildford GU2 . . . . 264 AV132
Hampton TW12 . . . . 198 CB94
Richmond TW9 . . . . 180 CM84
Ruislip HA4 . . . . 138 BW64
South Croydon CR2 . . . . 242 DT107
Sunbury-on-Thames TW16 . . 217 BU96
Wooburn Green HP10 . . . . . . 132 AE58
Manor Gate, Nthlt. UB5 . . . . . . 158 BY66
Manorgate Rd, Kings.T. KT2 . . 220 CN95
Manor Grn Rd, Epsom KT19 . . 238 CP113
Manor Gro, SE15 . . . . 44 G3
Beckenham BR3 . . . . 225 EB96
Fifield SL6 . . . . 172 AD80
Richmond TW9 . . . . 180 CN84
Manor Hall Av, NW4 . . . . 119 CW54
Manor Hall Dr, NW4 . . . . 119 CX54
Manorhall Gdns, E10 . . . . 145 EA60
Manor Hatch Cl, Harl. CM18 . . . 74 EV16
⊖ Manor House 143 DP59
Manor Ho Ct, Epsom KT18 . . . . 238 CQ113
Shepperton TW17 . . . . 217 BP101
Manor Ho Dr, NW6 . . . . 4 D7
Hersham KT12 . . . . 235 BT107
Northwood HA6 . . . . 115 BP52
Manor Ho Est, Stan. HA7 . . . . . 117 CH51
Manor Ho Gdns, Abb.L. WD5 . . . 81 BR31
Manor Ho La, Bkhm KT23 . . . . 268 BY126
Datchet SL3 . . . . 174 AV81
Manor Ho Sch, Bkhm KT23
off Manor Ho La 268 BY127
Manor Ho Way, Islw. TW7 . . . . . 179 CH83
Manor Inf & Nurs Sch, Til.
RM18 off Dickens Av 193 GH80
Manor Inf Sch, Bark. IG11
off Sandringham Rd 167 ET65
Manor Jun Sch, Bark. IG11
off Sandringham Rd 167 ET65
Manor La, SE12 . . . . 206 EE86
SE13 . . . . 186 EE84
Fawkham Green DA3 . . . . 231 FW101
Feltham TW13 . . . . 197 BU89
Gerrards Cross SL9 . . . . 134 AX59
Harlington UB3 . . . . 177 BR79
Lower Kingswood KT20 . . . . . 272 DA129
Sevenoaks TN15 . . . . 231 FW103
Sunbury-on-Thames TW16 . . 217 BU96
Sutton SM1 . . . . 240 DC106
Manor La Ter, SE13 . . . . 186 EE84
Manor Leaze, Egh. TW20 . . . . . 195 BB92
Manor Lo, Guil. GU2 . . . . 264 AV132
Manor Lo Sch, Shenley WD7
off Rectory La 84 CQ30
Manor Mead Sch, Shep. TW17
off Laleham Rd 217 BP99
Manor Ms, NW6 . . . . 5 K10
SE4 . . . . 45 P8
Manor Mt, SE23 . . . . 204 DW88
Manor Oak Prim Sch, Orp. BR5
off Sweeps La 228 EX99
Manor Par, NW10
off Station Rd 161 CT68
Hatfield AL10 . . . . 67 CT15
MANOR PARK, E12 . . . . 146 EL63
MANOR PARK, Slou. SL2 . . . . . 153 AQ70
⇌ Manor Park 146 EK63
Manor Pk, SE13 . . . . 185 ED84
Chislehurst BR7 . . . . 227 ER96
Richmond TW9 . . . . 180 CM84
Staines TW18 . . . . 195 BD90
Manor Pk Cl, W.Wick. BR4 . . . . 225 EB102
Manor Pk Cres, Edg. HA8 . . . . . 118 CN51
Manor Pk Dr, Har. HA2 . . . . 138 CB55
Manor Pk Gdns, Edg. HA8 . . . . 118 CN50
Manor Pk Par, SE13
off Lee High Rd 185 ED84
Manor Pk Prim Sch, Sutt. SM1
off Greyhound Rd 240 DC106
Manor Pk Rd, E12 . . . . 146 EK63
N2 . . . . 142 DC55
NW10 . . . . 161 CT67
Chislehurst BR7 . . . . 227 EQ95
Sutton SM1 . . . . 240 DC106
Manor Pk Rd, W.Wick. BR4 . . . 225 EB102
Manor Pl, SE17 . . . . 43 H1
Bookham KT23 . . . . 268 CA126
Chislehurst BR7 . . . . 227 ER95
Feltham TW14 . . . . 197 BU88
Mitcham CR4 . . . . 223 DJ97
Staines TW18 . . . . 196 BH92
Sutton SM1 . . . . 240 DB105
Walton-on-Thames KT12 . . . 217 BT101
Manor Prim Sch, E15 . . . . . . 13 J10
Manor Prim Sch, The, Rom.
RM1 off Shaftesbury Rd . . . 149 FF57
Manor Rd, E10 . . . . 145 EA59
E15 . . . . 23 J1
E16 . . . . 23 J4
E17 . . . . 123 DY54
N16 . . . . 144 DR61
N17 . . . . 122 DU53
N22 . . . . 121 DL51
SE25 . . . . 224 DU98
SW20 . . . . 221 CZ96
W13 . . . . 159 CG73
Ashford TW15 . . . . 196 BM92
Barking IG11 . . . . 167 ET65
Barnet EN5 . . . . 101 CY43
Beckenham BR3 . . . . 225 EB96
Bexley DA5 . . . . 209 FB88
Chadwell Heath RM6 . . . . 148 EX58
Chesham HP5
off Lansdowne Rd 76 AQ29
Chigwell IG7 . . . . 125 EP50
Dagenham RM10 . . . . 169 FC65
Dartford DA1 . . . . 189 FE84
East Molesey KT8 . . . . 219 CD98
Enfield EN2 . . . . 104 DR40
Erith DA8 . . . . 189 FF79
Gravesend DA12 . . . . 213 GH86
Grays RM17 . . . . 192 GC79
Guildford GU2 . . . . 264 AV132
Harlow CM17 . . . . 58 EW10
Harrow HA1 . . . . 139 CG58
Hatfield AL10 . . . . 67 CT15
Hayes UB3 . . . . 157 BU72
High Beach IG10 . . . . 106 EH38
Hoddesdon EN11 . . . . 71 EA16
Lambourne End RM4 . . . . 126 EW47
London Colney AL2 . . . . 83 CJ26
Loughton IG10 . . . . 106 EH44
Mitcham CR4 . . . . 223 DJ98
Potters Bar EN6 . . . . 85 CZ31
Reigate RH2 . . . . 271 CZ132
Richmond TW9 . . . . 180 CM83
Ripley GU23 . . . . 249 BF123
Romford RM1 . . . . 149 FG57
Ruislip HA4 . . . . 137 BR60
St. Albans AL1 . . . . 65 CE19
Seer Green HP9 . . . . 111 AR50
Sidcup DA15 . . . . 207 ET90
South Merstham RH1 . . . . 273 DJ129
Sundridge TN14 . . . . 262 EX124
Sutton SM2 . . . . 239 CZ108
Swanscombe DA10 . . . . 211 FX86
Tatsfield TN16 . . . . 260 EL120
Teddington TW11 . . . . 199 CH92
Tilbury RM18 . . . . 193 GG82
Twickenham TW2 . . . . 198 CC89
Wallington SM6 . . . . 241 DH105
Waltham Abbey EN9 . . . . 89 ED33
Walton-on-Thames KT12 . . . 217 BT101
Watford WD17 . . . . 97 BV39
West Thurrock RM20 . . . . 191 FW79
West Wickham BR4 . . . . 225 EB103
Windsor SL4 . . . . 173 AL82
Woking GU21 . . . . 248 AW116
Woodford Green IG8 . . . . 125 EM51
Manor Rd N, Esher KT10 . . . . . 219 CF104
Thames Ditton KT7 . . . . 219 CG103
Wallington SM6 . . . . 241 DH105
Manor Rd S, Esher KT10 . . . . . 237 CE105
Manor Sch, NW10 . . . . 4 B9
Manorside, Barn. EN5 . . . . 101 CY42
Manorside Cl, SE2 . . . . 188 EW77
Manorside Prim Sch, N3
off Squires La 120 DC53
Manor Sq, Dag. RM8 . . . . 148 EX61
Manor St, Berk. HP4 . . . . 60 AX19
Manor Vale, Brent. TW8 . . . . . . 179 CJ78
Manor Vw, N3 . . . . 120 DB54
Manorville Rd, Hem.H. HP3 . . . . 62 BJ24
Manor Wk, Wey. KT13 . . . . 235 BP106
Manor Way, E4 . . . . 123 ED49
NW9 . . . . 140 CS55
SE3 . . . . 186 EF84
SE23 . . . . 204 DW87
SE28 . . . . 168 EW74
Banstead SM7 . . . . 256 DF116
Beckenham BR3 . . . . 225 EA96
Bexley DA5 . . . . 208 FA88
Bexleyheath DA7 . . . . 189 FD83
Borehamwood WD6 . . . . 100 CQ42
Brentwood CM14 . . . . 130 FU48
Bromley BR2 . . . . 226 EL100
Chesham HP5 . . . . 76 AR30
Cheshunt EN8
off Russells Ride 89 DY31
Coleshill HP7 . . . . 77 AM44
Croxley Green WD3 . . . . 96 BN42
Egham TW20 . . . . 195 AZ93
Manorway, Enf. EN1 . . . . 122 DS45
Manor Way, Grays RM17 . . . . . 192 GB80
Guildford GU2 . . . . 280 AS137
Harrow HA2 . . . . 138 CB56
Mitcham CR4 . . . . 223 DJ97
Oxshott KT22 . . . . 252 CC115
Petts Wood BR5 . . . . 227 EQ98
Potters Bar EN6 . . . . 86 DA30
Purley CR8 . . . . 241 DL112
Rainham RM13 . . . . 169 FE70
Ruislip HA4 . . . . 137 BS59
South Croydon CR2 . . . . 242 DS107
Southall UB2 . . . . 178 BX77
Swanscombe DA10 . . . . 191 FX84
Woking GU22 . . . . 249 BB121
Manorway, Wdf.Grn. IG8 . . . . . 124 EJ50
Manor Way, Wor.Pk. KT4 . . . . . 220 CS102
Manor Way, The, Wall. SM6 . . . 241 DH105
Manor Waye, Uxb. UB8 . . . . . . 156 BK67
● Manor Way Ind Est, Grays
RM17 . . . . 192 GC80
Manor Wd Rd, Pur. CR8 . . . . . . 241 DL113
Manpreet Ct, E12 . . . . 147 EM64
Manresa Rd, SW3 . . . . 40 C1
Mansard Beeches, SW17 . . . . . 202 DG92
Mansard Cl, Horn. RM12 . . . . . 149 FG61
Pinner HA5 . . . . 138 BX55
Mansards, The, St.Alb. AL1
off Avenue Rd 65 CE19
Manscroft Rd, Hem.H. HP1 . . . . 62 BH17
Manse Cl, Harling. UB3 . . . . . . 177 BR79
Mansel Cl, Guil. GU2 . . . . 264 AV129
Slough SL2 . . . . 154 AV71
Mansel Gro, E17 . . . . 123 EA53
Mansell Cl, Wind. SL4 . . . . 173 AL82
Mansell Rd, W3 . . . . 180 CR75
Greenford UB6 . . . . 158 CB71
Mansell St, E1 . . . . 32 B1
Mansell Way, Cat. CR3 . . . . 258 DQ122
Mansel Rd, SW19 . . . . 201 CY93
Mansergh Cl, SE18 . . . . 186 EL80
Manse Rd, N16 . . . . 144 DT62
Manser Rd, Rain. RM13 . . . . . . 169 FE69
Manse Way, Swan. BR8 . . . . . . 229 FG98
Mansfield, High Wych CM21 . . . 58 EU06
Mansfield Av, N15 . . . . 144 DR56
Barnet EN4 . . . . 102 DF44
Ruislip HA4 . . . . 137 BV60
Mansfield Cl, N9 . . . . 104 DU44
Orpington BR5 . . . . 228 EX101
Weybridge KT13 . . . . 235 BP106
Mansfield Dr, Hayes UB4 . . . . . 157 BS70
Merstham RH1 . . . . 273 DK128
Mansfield Gdns, Hert. SG14 . . . 54 DQ07
Hornchurch RM12 . . . . 150 FK61
Mansfield Hill, E4 . . . . 123 EB46
Mansfield Ms, W1 . . . . 17 J7
Mansfield Pl, NW3
off New End 142 DC63
South Croydon CR2 . . . . 242 DR107
Mansfield Rd, E11 . . . . 146 EH58
E17 . . . . 145 DZ56
NW3 . . . . 6 F2
W3 . . . . 160 CP70
Chessington KT9 . . . . 237 CJ106
Ilford IG1 . . . . 147 EN61
South Croydon CR2 . . . . 242 DR107
Swanley BR8 . . . . 209 FE93
Mansfield St, W1 . . . . 17 J7
Mansford St, E2 . . . . 20 D1
Manship Rd, Mitch. CR4 . . . . . . 202 DG94
Mansion, The, Albury GU5 . . . . 282 BL139
Berkhamsted HP4 . . . . 60 AY17
Mansion Apts, Ald. WD25 . . . . . 98 CB36
Mansion Cl, SW9 . . . . 42 F6
Mansion Gdns, NW3 . . . . 142 DB62
★ Mansion Ho, EC4 . . . . 19 L9
⊖ Mansion House 19 K10
Mansion Ho Pl, EC4 . . . . 19 L9
Mansion Ho St, EC4 . . . . 19 L9
Mansion La, Iver SL0 . . . . 155 BC74
Mansion La Caravan Site, Iver
SL0 . . . . 155 BC74
Mansions, The, SW5
off Earls Ct Rd 27 L10
Manson Ms, SW7 . . . . 27 P9
Manson Pl, SW7 . . . . 28 A9
Manstead Gdns, Rain. RM13 . . 169 FH72
Mansted Gdns, Rom. RM6 . . . . 148 EW59
Manston Av, Sthl. UB2 . . . . 178 CA77
Manston Cl, SE20
off Garden Rd 224 DW95
Cheshunt EN8 . . . . 88 DW30
Manstone Rd, NW2 . . . . 4 E2
Manston Gro, Kings.T. KT2 . . . 199 CK92
Manston Rd, Guil. GU4 . . . . . . 265 BA130
Harlow CM20 . . . . 73 ES15
Manston Way, Horn. RM12 . . . . 169 FH65
St. Albans AL4 . . . . 65 CK21
Manthorp Rd, SE18 . . . . 187 EQ78
Mantilla Rd, SW17 . . . . 202 DG91
Mantle Rd, SE4 . . . . 185 DY83
Mantlet Cl, SW16 . . . . 203 DJ94
Mantle Way, E15 . . . . 13 J6
Manton Av, W7 . . . . 179 CF75
Manton Cl, Hayes UB3 . . . . 157 BS73
Manton Rd, SE2 . . . . 188 EU77
Enfield EN3 . . . . 105 EA37
Mantua St, SW11 . . . . 40 B10
Mantus Cl, E1 . . . . 21 H4
Mantus Rd, E1 . . . . 20 G4
Manuka Cl, W7 . . . . 159 CG74
Manus Way, N20
off Blakeney Cl 120 DC46
Manville Gdns, SW17 . . . . 203 DH90
Manville Rd, SW17 . . . . 202 DG89
Manwood Rd, SE4 . . . . 205 DZ85
Manwood St, E16 . . . . 37 K3
Manygate La, Shep. TW17 . . . . 217 BQ101
Manygates, SW12 . . . . 203 DH89
Maori Rd, Guil. GU1 . . . . 265 AZ134
Mapesbury Ms, NW4
off Station Rd 141 CU58
Mapesbury Rd, NW2 . . . . 4 E4
Mapeshill Pl, NW2 . . . . 4 B5
Mape St, E2 . . . . 20 E4
Maple Av, E4 . . . . 123 DZ50
W3 . . . . 160 CS74
Harrow HA2 . . . . 138 CB61
St. Albans AL3 . . . . 64 CC16
Upminster RM14 . . . . 150 FP62
West Drayton UB7 . . . . 156 BL73
Maple Cl, N3 . . . . 120 DA51
N16 . . . . 144 DU58
SW4 . . . . 203 DK86
Brentwood CM13
off Cherry Av 131 FZ48
Buckhurst Hill IG9 . . . . 124 EK48
Bushey WD23 . . . . 98 BY40
Hampton TW12 . . . . 198 BZ93
Hatfield AL10 off Elm Dr 67 CU19
Hayes UB4 . . . . 158 BX69
Hornchurch RM12 . . . . 149 FH62
Ilford IG6 . . . . 125 ES50
Mitcham CR4 . . . . 223 DH95
Petts Wood BR5 . . . . 227 ER99
Ruislip HA4 . . . . 137 BV58
Swanley BR8 . . . . 229 FE96
Theydon Bois CM16
off Loughton La 107 ER36
Whyteleafe CR3 . . . . 258 DT117
Maple Ct, Eng.Grn TW20
off Ashwood Rd 194 AV93
Erith DA8 . . . . 189 FF80
New Malden KT3 . . . . 220 CR97
Stanstead Abbotts SG12 . . . . . 55 ED11
Maplecourt Wk, Wind. SL4
off Common Rd 173 AN78
Maple Cres, Sid. DA15 . . . . 208 EU86
Slough SL2 . . . . 154 AV73
Maplecroft Cl, E6 . . . . 24 G8
Maplecroft La, Lwr Naze. EN9 . . 72 EE21
MAPLE CROSS, Rick. WD3 . . . . 113 BD49
Maple Cross JMI Sch, Rick.
WD3 off Denham Way 113 BE50
Maple Cross Rbt, Rick.
WD3 . . . . 113 BE48
Mapledale Av, Croy. CR0 . . . . . 224 DU103
Mapledene, Chis. BR7 . . . . 207 EQ92
Mapledene Est, E8 . . . . 10 C6
Mapledene Rd, E8 . . . . 10 B6
Mapledown Spec Sch, NW2
off Claremont Rd 141 CW59
Maple Dr, Bkhm KT23 . . . . 268 CB125
South Ockendon RM15 . . . . . 171 FX70
Maplefield, Park St AL2 . . . . 82 CB29
Maplefield La, Ch.St.G. HP8 . . . . 94 AV41
Maple Gdns, Edg. HA8 . . . . 118 CS52
Staines TW19 . . . . 196 BL89
Maple Gate, Loug. IG10 . . . . . . 107 EN40
Maple Grn, Hem.H. HP1 . . . . 61 BE18
Maple Gro, NW9 . . . . 140 CQ59
W5 . . . . 179 CK76
Bookham KT23 . . . . 268 CA127
Brentford TW8 . . . . 179 CH80
Guildford GU1 . . . . 264 AX132
Southall UB1 . . . . 158 BZ71
Watford WD17 . . . . 97 BU39
Welwyn Garden City AL7 . . . . . 51 CZ06
Woking GU22 . . . . 248 AY121
Maple Ho, NW3
off Maitland Pk Vil 6 F4
Maplehurst, Lthd. KT22 . . . . . . 253 CD123
Maplehurst Cl, Dart. DA2
off Sandringham Dr 209 FE89
Kingston upon Thames KT1 . 220 CL98
● Maple Ind Est, Felt. TW13
off Maple Way 197 BV90
Maple Inf Sch, Surb. KT6
off Maple Rd 219 CK99
Maple Leaf Cl, Abb.L. WD5 . . . . 81 BU32
Biggin Hill TN16
off Main Rd 260 EK116
Mapleleaf Cl, S.Croy. CR2 . . . . 243 DX111
Maple Leaf Cl, Stans.Abb.
SG12 . . . . 55 ED12
Maple Leaf Dr, Sid. DA15 . . . . . 207 ET88
Mapleleafe Gdns, Ilf. IG6 . . . . . 147 EP55
Maple Leaf Sq, SE16 . . . . 33 K5
Maple Lo Cl, Map.Cr. WD3 . . . . 113 BE49
Maple Ms, NW6 . . . . 5 L10
SW16 . . . . 203 DM92
● Maple Pk, Hodd. EN11 . . . . . . 71 EC17
Maple Pl, N17 off Park La 122 DU52
W1 . . . . 17 M5
Banstead SM7 . . . . 239 CX114
West Drayton UB7 . . . . 156 BL73
● Maple River Ind Est, Harl.
CM20 . . . . 58 EV09
Maple Rd, E11 . . . . 146 EE58
SE20 . . . . 224 DV95
Ashtead KT21 . . . . 253 CK119
Dartford DA1 . . . . 210 FJ88
Gravesend DA12 . . . . 213 GJ91
Grays RM17 . . . . 192 GC79
Hayes UB4 . . . . 158 BW69
Redhill RH1 . . . . 288 DF138
Ripley GU23 . . . . 250 BG124
Surbiton KT6 . . . . 220 CL99
Whyteleafe CR3 . . . . 258 DT117
Maples, The, Bans. SM7 . . . . . . 240 DB114
Claygate KT10 . . . . 237 CG108
Goffs Oak EN7 . . . . 88 DS28
Harlow CM19 . . . . 73 EP19
Ottershaw KT16 . . . . 233 BB107
St. Albans AL1
off Granville Rd 65 CF20
Maple Sch, St.Alb. AL1
off Hall Pl Gdns 65 CE19
Maplescombe La, Fnghm
DA4 . . . . 230 FN104
Maples Pl, E1 . . . . 20 F6
Maple Springs, Wal.Abb. EN9 . . 90 EG33
Maplestead Rd, SW2 . . . . 203 DM87
Dagenham RM9 . . . . 168 EV67
Maple St, E2 . . . . 20 D1
W1 . . . . 17 L6
Romford RM7 . . . . 149 FC56
Maplethorpe Rd, Th.Hth. CR7 . 223 DN98
Mapleton Cl, Brom. BR2 . . . . . . 226 EG100
Mapleton Cres, SW18 . . . . 202 DB86
Enfield EN3 . . . . 104 DW38
Mapleton Rd, E4 . . . . 123 EC48
SW18 . . . . 202 DB86
Edenbridge TN8 . . . . 277 ET133
Enfield EN1 . . . . 104 DV40
Westerham TN16 . . . . 277 ES130
Maple Wk, W10 . . . . 14 D4
Sutton SM2 . . . . 240 DB110
Maple Way, Couls. CR5 . . . . . . 257 DH121
Feltham TW13 . . . . 197 BU90
Waltham Abbey EN9 off Breach
Barn Mobile Home Pk 90 EH29
Maplewood Gdns, Beac. HP9 . . 110 AH54
Maplin Cl, N21 . . . . 103 DM44
Maplin Ho, SE2
off Wolvercote Rd 188 EX75
Maplin Pk, Slou. SL3 . . . . 175 BC75
Maplin Rd, E16 . . . . 24 A8
Maplin St, E3 . . . . 21 N3
Mapperley Dr, Wdf.Grn. IG8
off Forest Dr 124 EE52
Marabou Cl, E12 . . . . 146 EL64
Maran Way, Erith DA18 . . . . 188 EX75
Marathon Ho, NW1 . . . . 16 E6
Marathon Way, SE28 . . . . 187 ET75
Marban Rd, W9 . . . . 14 G2
Marbeck Cl, Wind. SL4 . . . . 173 AK81
★ Marble Arch, W1 . . . . 16 F10
⊖ Marble Arch 16 F10
Marble Arch Apts, W1
off Harrowby St 16 D8
Marble Cl, W3 . . . . 160 CP74
Marble Dr, NW2 . . . . 141 CX60
Marble Hill Cl, Twick. TW1 . . . . 199 CH87
Marble Hill Gdns, Twick. TW1 . . 199 CH87
★ Marble Hill Ho, Twick. TW1 . 199 CJ87
Marble Ho, SE18
off Felspar Cl 187 ET78
Marble Quay, E1 . . . . 32 C2
Marbles Way, Tad. KT20 . . . . . . 255 CX119
Marbrook Ct, SE12 . . . . 206 EJ90
Marcella Rd, SW9 . . . . 42 F9
Marcellina Way, Orp. BR6 . . . . . 227 ES104
Marcet Rd, Dart. DA1 . . . . 210 FJ85
Marchant Rd, E11 . . . . 145 ED61
Marchant St, SE14 . . . . 45 L3
Marchbank Rd, W14 . . . . 39 H2
Marchmant Cl, Horn. RM12 . . . 150 FJ62
Marchmont Gdns, Rich. TW10
off Marchmont Rd 200 CM85
Marchmont Grn, Hem.H. HP2
off Paston Rd 62 BK18
Marchmont Rd, Rich. TW10 . . . 200 CM85
Wallington SM6 . . . . 241 DJ108
Marchmont St, WC1 . . . . 18 A4
March Rd, Twick. TW1 . . . . 199 CG87
Weybridge KT13 . . . . 234 BN106
Marchside Cl, Houns. TW5 . . . . 178 BX81

Marchwood Cl, SE5 43 P5
Marchwood Cres, W5 159 CJ72
Marcia Ct, Slou. SL1 153 AM74
Marcia Rd, SE1 31 P9
Marcilly Rd, SW18 202 DD85
Marco Dr, Pnr. HA5 116 BZ52
Marconi Gdns, Pilg.Hat. CM15 130 FW43
Marconi Pl, N11 121 DH49
Marconi Rd, E10 145 EA60
Northfleet DA11 212 GD90
Marconi Way, St.Alb. AL4 65 CK20
Southall UB1 158 CB72
Marcon Pl, E8 10 E3
Marco Rd, W6 181 CW76
Marcourt Lawns, W5 160 CL70
Marcus Ct, E15 13 K8
Marcuse Rd, Cat. CR3 258 DR123
Marcus Garvey Ms, SE22
off St. Aidan's Rd 204 DV85
Marcus Garvey Way, SE24 183 DN84
Marcus Rd, Dart. DA1 209 FG87
Marcus St, E15 13 K8
SW18 202 DB86
Marcus Ter, SW18 202 DB86
Mardale Dr, NW9 140 CR57
Mardell Rd, Croy. CR0 225 DX99
Marden Av, Brom. BR2 226 EG100
Marden Cl, Chig. IG7 126 EV47
Marden Cres, Bex. DA5 209 FC85
Croydon CR0 223 DM100
Marden Ho, E8 10 E2
Sch **Marden Lo Prim Sch**, Cat. CR3
off Croydon Rd 258 DV121
Marden Pk, Wold. CR3 275 DZ125
Marden Rd, N17 144 DS55
Croydon CR0 223 DM100
Romford RM1 149 FE58
Marden Sq, SE16 32 E7
Marder Rd, W13 179 CG75
Mardyke Cl, Rain. RM13 169 FC68
Mardyke Ho, SE17
off Crosslet St 31 M8
Rainham RM13
off Lower Mardyke Av 169 FD68
Mardyke Rd, Harl. CM20 58 EU13
Marechal Niel Av, Sid. DA15 207 ER90
Mareschal Rd, Guil. GU2 280 AW136
Marescroft Rd, Slou. SL2 153 AL70
Maresfield, Croy. CR0 224 DS104
Maresfield Gdns, NW3 5 P3
Mare St, E8 10 F9
Marfleet Cl, Cars. SM5 222 DE103
Marford Rd, Welw.G.C. AL8 50 CS10
Wheathampstead AL4 50 CN07
Margaret Av, E4 105 EB44
St. Albans AL3 65 CD18
Shenfield CM15 131 FZ45
Margaret Bondfield Av, Bark.
IG11 168 EU66
Margaret Bldgs, N16
off Margaret Rd 144 DT60
Margaret Cl, Abb.L. WD5 81 BT32
Epping CM16
off Margaret Rd 92 EU29
Potters Bar EN6 86 DC33
Romford RM2
off Margaret Rd 149 FH57
Staines TW18
off Charles Rd 196 BK93
Waltham Abbey EN9 89 ED33
Margaret Ct, W1 17 L8
Margaret Dr, Horn. RM11 150 FM60
Margaret Gardner Dr, SE9 207 EM89
Margaret Ingram Cl, SW6 38 G3
Margaret Lockwood Cl, Kings.T.
KT1 220 CM98
Margaret McMillan Ho, E16 24 C9
Margaret Rd, N16 144 DT60
Barnet EN4 102 DD43
Bexley DA5 208 EX86
Epping CM16 92 EU29
Guildford GU1 280 AW135
Romford RM2 149 FH57
Sch **Margaret Roper Cath Prim Sch**,
Pur. CR8 *off Russell Hill Rd* 241 DN110
Margaret Sq, Uxb. UB8 156 BJ67
Margaret St, W1 17 K8
Margaretta Ter, SW3 40 C2
Margaretting Rd, E12 146 EJ61
Margaret Way, Couls. CR5 257 DP118
Ilford IG4 146 EL58
Sch **Margaret Wix Prim Sch**, St.Alb.
AL3 *off High Oaks* 64 CC16
Margate Rd, SW2 203 DL85
Margeholes, Wat. WD19 116 BY47
MARGERY, Tad. KT20 272 DA129
Margery Fry Ct, N7 143 DL62
Margery Gro, Lwr Kgswd
KT20 271 CY129
Margery La, Lwr Kgswd KT20 271 CZ129
Tewin AL6 52 DD05
Margery Pk Rd, E7 13 N6
Margery Rd, Dag. RM8 148 EX62
Margery St, WC1 18 E3
Margery Wd, Welw.G.C. AL7 52 DA06
Margery Wd La, Lwr Kgswd
KT20 271 CZ129
Margherita Pl, Wal.Abb. EN9 90 EF34
Margherita Rd, Wal.Abb. EN9 90 EG34
Margin Dr, SW19 201 CX92
Margravine Gdns, W6 26 D10
Margravine Rd, W6 38 D1
Marham Dr, NW9
off Kenley Av 118 CS53
Marham Gdns, SW18 202 DE88
Morden SM4 222 DC100
Mar Ho, SE7
off Springfield Gro 186 EJ79
Maria Cl, SE1 32 D8
Sch **Maria Fidelis Conv Sch**,
Lwr Sch, NW1 17 M3
Upr Sch, NW1 17 N2
Mariam Gdns, Horn. RM12 150 FM61
Marian Cl, Hayes UB4 158 BX70
Marian Ct, Sutt. SM1 240 DB106
Marian Lawson Ct, Chig. IG7
off Manford Way 126 EU50
Marian Pl, E2 10 E10
Marian Rd, SW16 223 DJ95
Marian Sq, E2 10 D10
Marian St, E2 10 E10
Sch **Marian Vian Prim Sch**, Beck.
BR3 *off Shirley Cres* 225 DY99
Marian Way, NW10 161 CT66
Maria Ter, E1 21 J6
Maria Theresa Cl, N.Mal. KT3 220 CR99
Maricas Av, Har. HA3 117 CD53
Marie Curie, SE5
off Sceaux Gdns 43 P6
Marie Lloyd Gdns, N19 143 DL59
Marie Lloyd Ho, N1 19 L1
Marie Lloyd Wk, E8 10 B5
Marie Manor Way, Dart. DA2 191 FS84
Mariette Way, Wall. SM6 241 DL109
Marigold All, SE1 30 G1
Marigold Cl, Sthl. UB1
off Lancaster Rd 158 BY73
Marigold Ct, Guil. GU1 264 AY131
Marigold Pl, Harl. CM17 58 EV11
Marigold Rd, N17 122 DW52
Marigold St, SE16 32 E5
Marigold Way, E4
off Silver Birch Av 123 DZ51
Croydon CR0 225 DX102
H **Marillac Hosp**, Warley
CM13 129 FX51
Marina App, Hayes UB4 158 BY71
Marina Av, N.Mal. KT3 221 CV99
Marina Cl, Brom. BR2 226 EG97
Chertsey KT16 216 BH102
Marina Dr, Dart. DA1 210 FN88
Northfleet DA11 213 GF87
Welling DA16 187 ES82
Marina Gdns, Chsht EN8 88 DW30
Romford RM7 149 FC58
Marina Pl, Hmptn W. KT1 219 CK95
Marina Way, Iver SL0 155 BF73
Slough SL1 153 AK73
Teddington TW11
off Fairways 199 CK94
Marine Dr, SE18 37 K9
Barking IG11 168 EV70
Marinefield Rd, SW6 39 M8
● **Mariner Business Cen**,
Croy. CR0 241 DM106
Mariner Gdns, Rich. TW10 199 CJ90
Mariner Rd, E12
off Dersingham Av 147 EN63
Mariners Cl, Barn. EN4 102 DD43
Mariners Ct, Green. DA9
off High St 191 FV84
Mariners Ms, E14 34 G8
Mariners Wk, Erith DA8
off Cornwallis Cl 189 FF79
Mariner's Way, Grav. DA11 212 GE87
Mariner Way, Hem.H. HP2 62 BN21
Marine St, SE16 32 C6
Marine Twr, SE8 45 N2
Marion Av, Shep. TW17 217 BP99
Marion Cl, Bushey WD23 98 BZ39
Ilford IG6 125 ER52
Marion Cres, Orp. BR5 228 EU99
Marion Gro, Wdf.Grn. IG8 124 EE50
Marion Ms, SE21 204 DR90
Sch **Marion Richardson Prim Sch**,
E1 21 J9
Marion Rd, NW7 119 CU50
Thornton Heath CR7 224 DQ99
Marion Wk, Hem.H. HP2
off Washington Av 62 BM15
Marischal Rd, SE13 185 ED83
Marisco Cl, Grays RM16 193 GH77
Marish La, Denh. UB9 135 BC56
Sch **Marish Prim Sch**,
Langley SL3
off Swabey Rd 175 BA76
Marish Wf, Mdgrn SL3 174 AY75
Sch **Marist Catholic Prim Sch, The**,
W.Byf. KT14
off Old Woking Rd 233 BF113
Maritime Cl, Green. DA9 211 FV85
Maritime Gate, Grav. DA11 212 GE87
Maritime Ho, SE18 37 N8
Maritime Quay, E14 34 B10
Maritime St, E3 21 P5
Marius Pas, SW17
off Marius Rd 202 DG89
Marius Rd, SW17 202 DG89
Marjoram Cl, Guil. GU2 264 AU130
Marjorams Av, Loug. IG10 107 EM40
Marjorie Gro, SW11 182 DF84
Marjorie Ms, E1 21 J9
Sch **Marjory Kinnon Sch**, Felt.
TW14 *off Hatton Rd* 197 BS85
Markab Rd, Nthwd. HA6 115 BT50
Mark Av, E4 105 EB44
Mark Cl, Bexh. DA7 188 EY81
Southall UB1
off Longford Av 158 CB74
Mark Dr, Chal.St.P. SL9 112 AX49
Marke Cl, Kes. BR2 244 EL105
Markedge La, Chipstead CR5 256 DE124
Merstham RH1 272 DF126
Markenfield Rd, Guil. GU1 264 AX134
Markeston Grn, Wat. WD19 116 BX49
Market, The, Cars. SM5
off Wrythe La 222 DC102
Sutton SM1 *off Rose Hill* 222 DC102
Market App, W12 26 A4
Market Ct, W1 17 L8
Market Dr, W4 180 CS80
Market Est, N7 8 A4
Marketfield Rd, Red. RH1 272 DF134
Marketfield Way, Red. RH1 272 DF134
Market Hill, SE18 37 M7
Market Ho, Harl. CM20
off Birdcage Wk 57 ER14
Market La, W12 26 A5
Edgware HA8 118 CQ53
Iver SL0 175 BC75
Slough SL3 175 BC76
Market Link, Rom. RM1 149 FE56
Market Meadow, Orp. BR5 228 EW98
Market Ms, W1 29 J3
Market Oak La, Hem.H. HP3 62 BN24
Market Pl, N2 142 DE55
SE16 32 D8
W1 17 L8
W3 160 CQ74
Abridge RM4 108 EV41
Beaconsfield HP9
off London End 111 AM54
Bexleyheath DA6 188 FA84
Brentford TW8 179 CJ80
Chalfont St. Peter SL9 112 AX53
Dartford DA1
off Market St 210 FL87
Enfield EN2 *off The Town* 104 DR41
Hatfield AL10
off Kennelwood La 67 CV17
Hertford SG14 *off Fore St* 54 DR09
Kingston upon Thames KT1 219 CK96
Romford RM1 149 FE57
St. Albans AL3 65 CD20
Tilbury RM18 193 GF82
Market Pl, The, NW11 142 DB56
Market Rd, N7 8 A5
Richmond TW9 180 CN83
Market Row, SW9
off Atlantic Rd 183 DN84
Market Service Rd, The, Sutt. SM1
off Rosehill Av 222 DC102
🔒 **Market Sq**, N9 *off Edmonton*
Grn Shop Cen 122 DV47
Uxbridge UB8
off The Pavilions 156 BJ66
Market Sq, E14 22 D9
Amersham HP7 *off High St* 77 AP40
Bromley BR1 226 EG96
Chesham HP5 *off High St* 76 AP31
Harlow CM20 *off East Gate* 57 ER14
Staines TW18
off Clarence St 195 BE91
Waltham Abbey EN9
off Church St 89 EC33
Westerham TN16 277 EQ127
Woking GU21
off Cawsey Way 248 AY117
Market St, E1 20 A6
E6 167 EM68
SE18 37 M8
Dartford DA1 210 FL87
Guildford GU1 280 AX135
Harlow CM17 58 EW11
Hertford SG14 54 DR09
Watford WD18 97 BV42
Windsor SL4 173 AR81
Market Way, E14 22 D9
Wembley HA0 *off Turton Rd* 140 CL64
Westerham TN16
off Costell's Meadow 277 ER126
Market Yd Ms, SE1 31 N6
Markfield, Croy. CR0 243 DZ110
Markfield Gdns, E4 123 EB45
Markfield Rd, N15 144 DU56
Caterham CR3 274 DV126
Sch **Mark Hall Comm Sch &**
Sports Coll, Harl. CM17
off First Av 58 EW12
Mark Hall Moors, Harl. CM20 58 EV12
MARK HALL NORTH, Harl.
CM20 58 EU12
MARK HALL SOUTH, Harl.
CM20 58 EV14
Markham Cl, Borwd. WD6 100 CM41
Markham Pl, SW3 28 E10
Markham Rd, Chsht EN7 88 DQ26
Markham Sq, SW3 28 E10
Markham St, SW3 28 D10
Markhole Cl, Hmptn. TW12 198 BZ94
Markhouse Av, E17 145 DY58
Markhouse Rd, E17 145 DZ57
Markland Ho, W10 14 C10
Mark La, EC3 31 P1
Gravesend DA12 213 GL86
Markmanor Av, E17 145 DY59
Mark Oak La, Lthd. KT22 252 CA122
Mark Rd, N22 121 DP54
Hemel Hempstead HP2 62 BN18
Marksbury Av, Rich. TW9 180 CN83
MARK'S GATE, Rom. RM6 126 EY54
Sch **Marks Gate Inf Sch**,
Chad.Hth RM6
off Lawn Fm Gro 148 EY55
Sch **Marks Gate Jun Sch**,
Chad.Hth RM6
off Rose La 148 EY55
Mark Sq, EC2 19 N4
Marks Rd, Rom. RM7 149 FC57
Warlingham CR6 259 DY118
Marks Sq, Nthflt DA11 213 GF91
Mark St, E15 13 J7
EC2 19 N4
Reigate RH2 272 DB133
Markville Gdns, Cat. CR3 274 DU125
Mark Wade Cl, E12 146 EK60
Markway, Sun. TW16 218 BW96
Mark Way, Swan. BR8 229 FG99
Markwell Cl, SE26 204 DV91
Markwell Wd, Harl. CM19 73 EP21
Markyate Rd, Dag. RM8 148 EV64
Marlands Rd, Ilf. IG5 146 EL55
Marlborough, SW3 28 D8
Marlborough Av, E8 10 C9
N14 121 DJ48
Edgware HA8 118 CP48
Ruislip HA4 137 BQ58
Marlborough Cl, N20
off Marlborough Gdns 120 DF48
SE17 31 H9
SW19 202 DE93
Grays RM16 192 GC75
Hersham KT12 218 BX104
Orpington BR6
off Aylesham Rd 227 ET100
Upminster RM14 151 FS60
Marlborough Ct, W1 17 L9
W8 27 J8
Dorking RH4
off Marlborough Hill 285 CH136
Wallington SM6
off Cranley Gdns 241 DJ108
Marlborough Cres, W4 180 CR76
Harlington UB3 177 BR80
Sevenoaks TN13 278 FE124
Marlborough Dr, Ilf. IG5 146 EL55
Weybridge KT13 217 BQ104
Sch **Marlborough First & Mid Sch**,
Har. HA1
off Marlborough Hill 139 CE56
Marlborough Gdns, N20 120 DF48
Upminster RM14 151 FR60
Marlborough Gate, St.Alb. AL1 65 CE20
Marlborough Gate Ho, W2 16 A10
Marlborough Gro, SE1 44 C1
Marlborough Hill, NW8 5 P9
Dorking RH4 285 CH136
Harrow HA1 139 CF56
★ **Marlborough Ho**, SW1 29 M3
Marlborough La, SE7 186 EJ79
Marlborough Ms, SW2
off Acre La 183 DM84
Banstead SM7 256 DA115
Marlborough Pk Av, Sid.
DA15 208 EU87
Marlborough Pl, NW8 15 N1
Sch **Marlborough Prim Sch**,
SW3 28 D9
Isleworth TW7
off London Rd 179 CG81
Marlborough Ri, Hem.H. HP2 62 BL17
Marlborough Rd, E4 123 EA51
E7 166 EJ66
E15 13 K1
E18 146 EG55
N9 122 DT46
N19 143 DK61
Marlborough Rd, N22 121 DL52
SE18 37 P6
SW1 29 M3
SW19 202 DE93
W4 180 CQ78
W5 179 CK75
Ashford TW15 196 BK92
Bexleyheath DA7 188 EX83
Bromley BR2 226 EJ98
Dagenham RM8 148 EV63
Dartford DA1 210 FJ86
Dorking RH4 285 CH136
Feltham TW13 198 BX89
Hampton TW12 198 CA93
Isleworth TW7 179 CH81
Pilgrim's Hatch CM15 130 FU44
Richmond TW10 200 CL86
Romford RM7 148 FA56
St. Albans AL1 65 CE20
Slough SL3 174 AX77
South Croydon CR2 242 DQ108
Southall UB2 178 BW76
Sutton SM1 222 DA104
Uxbridge UB10 157 BP70
Watford WD18 97 BV42
Woking GU21 249 BA116
Sch **Marlborough Sch**, St.Alb. AL1
off Watling St 64 CC23
Sidcup DA15
off Marlborough Pk Av 208 EU87
Marlborough St, SW3 28 C9
Marlborough Yd, N19 143 DK61
Marld, The, Ashtd. KT21 254 CM118
Marle Gdns, Wal.Abb. EN9 89 EC32
Marler Rd, SE23 205 DY88
Marlescroft Way, Loug. IG10 107 EP43
Marley Av, Bexh. DA7 188 EX79
Marley Cl, N15 143 DP56
Addlestone KT15 233 BF107
Greenford UB6 158 CA69
Marley Ct, Brox. EN10 71 DZ23
Marley Ho, E16
off University Way 37 N1
Marley Ri, Dor. RH4 285 CG139
Marley Rd, Welw.G.C. AL7 52 DA11
Marley St, SE16 33 J9
Marley Wk, NW2 4 A3
Marl Fld Cl, Wor.Pk. KT4 221 CU102
Marlin Cl, Berk. HP4 60 AT18
Sunbury-on-Thames TW16 197 BS93
Marlin Copse, Berk. HP4 60 AU20
Marlin End, Berk. HP4 60 AT20
Marlingdene Cl, Hmptn. TW12 198 CA93
Marlings Cl, Chis. BR7 227 ES98
Whyteleafe CR3 258 DS117
Marlings Pk Av, Chis. BR7 227 ES98
Marling Way, Grav. DA12 213 GL92
Marlins, The, Nthwd. HA6 115 BT51
Marlins Cl, Chorl. WD3 95 BE40
Sutton SM1
off Turnpike La 240 DC106
Marlins Meadow, Wat. WD18 97 BR44
Marlin Sq, Abb.L. WD5 81 BT31
Marlins Turn, Hem.H. HP1 62 BH17
Marloes Cl, Wem. HA0 139 CK63
Marloes Rd, W8 27 L7
Marlow Av, Purf. RM19 190 FN77
Marlow Cl, SE20 224 DV97
Marlow Ct, NW6 4 D6
NW9 141 CT55
Marlow Cres, Twick. TW1 199 CF86
Marlow Dr, Sutt. SM3 221 CX103
Marlowe Cl, Chis. BR7 207 ER93
Ilford IG6 125 EQ53
Marlowe Ct, SE19
off Lymer Av 204 DT92
Marlowe Gdns, SE9 207 EN86
Romford RM3 128 FJ53
Marlowe Path, SE8 46 C2
Marlowe Rd, E17 145 EC56
Marlowes, Hem.H. HP1 62 BK21
Marlowes, The, NW8 6 A9
Dartford DA1 189 FD84
🔒 **Marlowes Cen, The**, Hem.H.
HP1 62 BK21
Marlowe Sq, Mitch. CR4 223 DJ98
Marlowe Way, Croy. CR0 223 DL103
Marlow Gdns, Hayes UB3 177 BR76
Marlow Rd, E6 25 J3
SE20 224 DV97
Southall UB2 178 BZ76
Marlow Way, SE16 33 J4
Marlpit Av, Couls. CR5 257 DL117
Marlpit La, Couls. CR5 257 DK116
Marl Rd, SW18 182 DB84
Marlton St, SE10 35 M10
Marlwood Cl, Sid. DA15 207 ES89
Marlyns Cl, Guil. GU4 265 BA130
Marlyns Dr, Guil. GU4 265 BA130
Marlyon Rd, Ilf. IG6 126 EV50
Marmadon Rd, SE18 187 ET77
Marmara Apts, E16
off Western Gateway 35 P1
Marmion App, E4 123 EA49
Marmion Av, E4 123 DZ49
Marmion Cl, E4 123 DZ49
Marmion Ms, SW11
off Taybridge Rd 182 DG83
Marmion Rd, SW11 182 DG84
Marmont Rd, SE15 44 D6
Marmora Rd, SE22 204 DW86
Marmot Rd, Houns. TW4 178 BX83
Marne Av, N11 121 DH49
Welling DA16 188 EU83
Marnell Way, Houns. TW4 178 BX83
Sch **Marner Prim Sch**, E3 22 D4
Marne St, W10 14 E2
Marney Rd, SW11 182 DG84
Marneys Cl, Epsom KT18 254 CN115
Marnfield Cres, SW2 203 DM88
Marnham Av, NW2 141 CY63
Marnham Cres, Grnf. UB6 158 CB69
Marnham Pl, Add. KT15 234 BJ105
Marnham Ri, Hem.H. HP1 62 BG18
Marnock Rd, SE4 205 DY85
Maroon St, E14 21 L7
Maroons Way, SE6 205 EA92
Marquess Est, N1 9 K4
Marquess Rd, N1 9 L5
Marquis Cl, Wem. HA0 160 CM66
Marquis Rd, N4 143 DM60
N22 121 DM51
NW1 7 P5
Marrabon Cl, Sid. DA15 208 EU88
Marram Ct, Grays RM17
off Medlar Rd 192 GE79
Marrick Cl, SW15 181 CU84
Marrilyne Av, Enf. EN3 105 DZ38
Marriott Cl, Felt. TW14 197 BR86
Marriot Ter, Chorl. WD3 95 BF42
Marriott Lo Cl, Add. KT15 234 BJ105
Marriott Rd, E15 13 J8
N4 143 DM60
N10 120 DF53
Barnet EN5 101 CX41
Dartford DA1 210 FN87
Marriotts, Harl. CM17 58 EW10
Marriotts Cl, NW9 141 CT58
Marriotts Way, Hem.H. HP3 62 BK22
Mar Rd, S.Ock. RM15 171 FW70
Marrods Bottom, Beac. HP9 110 AJ47
Marrowells, Wey. KT13 217 BS104
Marryat Cl, Houns. TW4 178 BZ84
Marryat Pl, SW19 201 CY91
Marryat Rd, SW19 201 CX92
Enfield EN1 104 DV35
Marryat Sq, SW6 38 E6
Marsala Rd, SE13 185 EB84
Marsden Cl, Welw.G.C. AL8 51 CV11
Marsden Grn, Welw.G.C. AL8 51 CV10
Marsden Rd, N9 122 DW47
SE15 184 DT83
Welwyn Garden City AL8 51 CV10
Marsden St, NW5 6 G5
Marsden Way, Orp. BR6 245 ET105
Marshall, W2
off Hermitage St 16 A7
Marshall Av, St.Alb. AL3 65 CE17
Marshall Cl, SW18
off Allfarthing La 202 DC86
Harrow HA1 *off Bowen Rd* 139 CD59
Hounslow TW4 198 BZ85
South Croydon CR2 242 DU113
Marshall Dr, Hayes UB4 157 BT71
Marshall Est, NW7 119 CU49
Marshall Path, SE28
off Attlee Rd 168 EV73
Marshall Pl, New Haw KT15 234 BJ109
Marshall Rd, E10 145 EB62
N17 122 DR53
Marshalls Cl, N11 121 DH49
Epsom KT19 238 CQ113
Marshalls Dr, Rom. RM1 149 FE55
Marshall's Gro, SE18 37 H8
Sch **Marshalls Pk Sch**, Rom. RM1
off Pettits La 127 FE54
Marshalls Pl, SE16 32 B7
Marshalls Rd, Rom. RM7 149 FD56
Marshall's Rd, Sutt. SM1 240 DB105
Marshall St, NW10 160 CR66
W1 17 M9
Marshals Dr, St.Alb. AL1 65 CG17
Marshalsea Rd, SE1 31 K4
MARSHALSWICK, St.Alb. AL1 65 CG17
Marshalswick La, St.Alb. AL1 65 CH17
Marsham Cl, Chis. BR7 207 EP92
Marsham La, Ger.Cr. SL9 134 AY58
Marsham Lo, Ger.Cr. SL9 134 AY58
Marsham St, SW1 29 P7
Marsham Way, Ger.Cr. SL9 134 AY57
Marsh Av, Epsom KT19 238 CS110
Mitcham CR4 222 DF96
Marshbrook Cl, SE3 186 EK83
Marsh Cl, NW7 119 CT48
Waltham Cross EN8 89 DZ33
Marsh Ct, SW19 222 DC95
Marshcroft Dr, Chsht EN8 89 DY30
Marsh Dr, NW9 141 CT58
Marshe Cl, Pot.B. EN6 86 DD32
Marsh Fm Rd, Twick. TW2 199 CF88
Marshfield, Datchet SL3 174 AW81
Sch **Marshfields C of E Inf Sch**,
Ott. KT16 *off Fletcher Cl* 233 BE107
Marshfield St, E14 34 E6
Jct **Marshfoot Interchange**, Grays
RM16, RM17 192 GE79
Marshfoot Rd, Grays
RM16, RM17 192 GE78
Marshgate, Harl. CM20
off School La 57 ES12
● **Marshgate Cen**, Harl. CM19 72 EK15
Marshgate Dr, Hert. SG13 54 DS08
Marshgate La, E15 12 E10
Marshgate Path, SE28
off Tom Cribb Rd 187 EQ76
Sch **Marshgate Prim Sch**, Rich.
TW10 *off Queens Rd* 180 CM84
● **Marshgate Trd Est**, Tap.
SL6 152 AG72
Sch **Marsh Grn Prim Sch**, Dag.
RM10 *off South Cl* 168 FA67
Marsh Grn Rd, Dag. RM10 168 FA67
Marsh Hill, E9 11 L3
Marsh La, E10 145 EA61
N17 122 DV52
NW7 118 CS49
Addlestone KT15 234 BH105
Dorney SL4 172 AF75
Harlow CM17 58 EY10
Maidenhead SL6 172 AF75
Stanmore HA7 117 CJ50
Stanstead Abbotts SG12 55 ED12
Ware SG12 55 DY07
Marshmoor Cres, N.Mymms
AL9 67 CW22
Marshmoor La, N.Mymms
AL9 67 CW22
Marsh Rd, Pnr. HA5 138 BY56
Wembley HA0 159 CK68
Marshside Cl, N9 122 DW46
Marsh St, E14 34 C9
Dartford DA1 190 FN82
Marsh Ter, Orp. BR5
off Buttermere Rd 228 EX98
Marsh Vw, Grav. DA12 213 GM88
Marsh Wall, E14 34 A3
Marsh Way, Rain. RM13 169 FD70
Marsland Cl, SE17 43 H1
Marston, SE17 *off Deacon Way* 31 K8
Epsom KT19 238 CQ111
Marston Av, Chess. KT9 238 CL107
Dagenham RM10 148 FA61
Marston Cl, NW6 5 P6
Chesham HP5 76 AN27
Dagenham RM10 148 FA62
Hemel Hempstead HP3 62 BN21
Marston Ct, Green. DA9 191 FU84
Walton-on-Thames KT12
off St. Johns Dr 218 BW102
Marston Dr, Warl. CR6 259 DY118

Marston Ho, Grays RM17 192 GA79
Marston Rd, Hodd. EN11 71 EB16
Ilford IG5 124 EL53
Teddington TW11 199 CH92
Woking GU21 248 AV117
Marston Way, SE19 203 DP94
Marsworth Av, Pnr. HA5 116 BX53
Marsworth Cl, Hayes UB4 158 BY71
Watford WD18 97 BS44
Marsworth Ho, E2 10 C9
Martaban Rd, N16 144 DS61
Martara Ms, SE17 43 J1
Martello St, E8 10 E6
Martello Ter, E8 10 E6
Martell Rd, SE21 204 DR90
Martel Pl, E8 10 B4
Marten Gate, St.Alb. AL4 65 CG16
Marten Rd, E17 123 EA54
Martens Av, Bexh. DA7 189 FC84
Martens Cl, Bexh. DA7 189 FC84
Martha Ct, E2 10 F10
Martham Cl, SE28 168 EX73
Ilford IG6 125 EP53
Martha Rd, E15 13 K4
Martha's Bldgs, EC1 19 L4
Martha St, E1 20 F9
Marthorne Cres, Har. HA3 117 CD54
Martian Av, Hem.H. HP2 62 BM17
Martina Ter, Chig. IG7
off Manford Way 125 ES50
Martin Bowes Rd, SE9 187 EM83
● Martinbridge Trd Est, Enf.
EN1 104 DU43
Martin Cl, N9 123 DX46
Hatfield AL10 67 CU20
South Croydon CR2 243 DX111
Uxbridge UB10 156 BL68
Warlingham CR6 258 DV116
Windsor SL4 172 AJ81
Martin Cres, Croy. CR0 223 DN102
Martindale, SW14 200 CQ85
Iver SL0 155 BD70
Martindale Av, E16 23 P10
Orpington BR6 246 EU106
Martindale Cl, Guil. GU4
off Gilliat Dr 265 BD132
Sch Martindale Prim & Nurs Sch,
Hem.H. HP1 off Boxted Rd 61 BF19
Martindale Rd, SW12 203 DH87
Hemel Hempstead HP1 61 BF19
Hounslow TW4 178 BY83
Woking GU21 248 AT118
Martin Dene, Bexh. DA6 208 EZ85
Martin Dr, Nthlt. UB5 138 BZ64
Rainham RM13 169 FH70
Stone DA2 210 FQ86
Martineau Cl, Esher KT10 237 CD105
Martineau Dr, Dor. RH4 285 CH138
Twickenham TW1 179 CH84
Martineau Ms, N5 8 G1
Martineau Rd, N5 8 F1
Martineau St, E1 20 G9
Martinfield, Welw.G.C. AL7 51 CZ08
● Martinfield Business Pk,
Welw.G.C. AL7
off Martinfield 51 CZ08
Martingale Cl, Sun. TW16 217 BU98
Martingales Cl, Rich. TW10 199 CK90
Martin Gdns, Dag. RM8 148 EW63
Martin Gro, Mord. SM4 222 DA97
Martin Ho, SE1 31 K7
Martini Dr, Enf. EN3 105 EA37
Martin La, EC4 19 M10
Sch Martin Prim Sch, N2
off Plane Tree Wk 120 DE54
Martin Ri, Bexh. DA6 208 EZ85
Martin Rd, Aveley RM15 171 FR73
Dagenham RM8 148 EW63
Dartford DA2 210 FJ90
Guildford GU2 264 AU132
Slough SL1 174 AS76
Martins, The, Wem. HA9 140 CM62
Martins Cl, Guil. GU1 265 BC133
Orpington BR5 228 EX97
Radlett WD7 99 CE36
West Wickham BR4 225 ED102
Martins Ct, St.Alb. AL1
off Swallow La 65 CJ23
Martins Dr, Chsht EN8 89 DY28
Hertford SG13 54 DV09
Martinsfield Cl, Chig. IG7 125 ES49
Martins Mt, New Barn. EN5 102 DA42
Martins Pl, SE28
off Martin St 167 ES74
Martin's Plain, Stoke P. SL2 154 AT69
Martins Rd, Brom. BR2 226 EE96
Martins Shaw, Chipstead
TN13 278 FC122
Martinstown Cl, Horn. RM11 150 FN58
Martin St, SE28 167 ES74
Martins Wk, N8
off Alexandra Rd 143 DN55
N10 120 DG53
SE28 167 ES74
Borehamwood WD6
off Siskin Cl 100 CN42
Martinsyde, Wok. GU22 249 BC117
Martin Way, SW20 221 CY97
Morden SM4 221 CY97
Woking GU21 248 AU118
● Martlands Ind Est, Wok.
GU22 248 AU123
Martlesham, Welw.G.C. AL7 52 DE09
Martlesham Cl, Horn. RM12 150 FJ64
Martlesham Wk, NW9
off Kenley Av 118 CS54
Martlet Gro, Nthlt. UB5 158 BX69
Martlett Ct, WC2 18 B9
Martley Dr, Ilf. IG2 147 EP57
Martock Cl, Har. HA3 139 CG56
Martock Gdns, N11 120 DF50
Marton Cl, SE6 205 EA90
Marton Rd, N16 144 DS61
Martyr Cl, St.Alb. AL1
off Creighton Av 65 CD24
Martyr Rd, Guil. GU1 280 AX135
MARTYR'S GREEN, Wok.
GU23 251 BR120
Martyrs La, Wok. GU21 233 BB112
Martys Yd, NW3 6 A1
Marunden Grn, Slou. SL2 153 AM69
Marvell Av, Hayes UB4 157 BU71
Marvels Cl, SE12 206 EH89
Marvels La, SE12 206 EH89
Sch Marvels La Prim Sch, SE12
off Riddons Rd 206 EJ91
Marville Rd, SW6 38 G5
Marvin St, E8 10 F4
Marwell, West. TN16 277 EP126
Marwell Cl, Rom. RM1 149 FG57
West Wickham BR4
off Deer Pk Way 226 EF103
Marwood Cl, Kings L. WD4 80 BN29
Welling DA16 188 EV83
Marwood Dr, NW7 119 CX52
Mary Adelaide Cl, SW15 200 CS91
Mary Ann Gdns, SE8 46 A3
Maryatt Av, Har. HA2 138 CB61
Marybank, SE18 37 J8
Mary Cl, Stan. HA7 140 CM56
Mary Datchelor Cl, SE5 43 M6
Maryfield Cl, Bex. DA5 209 FE90
Marygold Wk, Amer. HP6 94 AV39
Mary Grn, NW8 5 M9
Maryhill Cl, Ken. CR8 258 DQ117
⇌ Maryland 13 J4
Maryland, Hat. AL10 67 CT19
Maryland Conv, St.Alb. AL3
off Townsend Dr 65 CD18
● Maryland Ind Est, E15
off Maryland Rd 13 H3
Maryland Pk, E15 13 K3
Maryland Pt, E15
off The Grove 13 J4
Sch Maryland Prim Sch, E15 13 K2
Maryland Rd, E15 13 H3
N22 121 DM51
Thornton Heath CR7 223 DP95
Maryland Sq, E15 13 K3
Marylands Rd, W9 15 K5
Maryland St, E15 13 H3
Maryland Wk, N1 9 J8
Maryland Way, Sun. TW16 217 BU96
Mary Lawrenson Pl, SE3 47 N5
MARYLEBONE, NW1 16 E8
⇌ Marylebone 16 E5
⊖ Marylebone 16 E5
Marylebone Flyover, NW1 16 B7
W2 16 B7
Marylebone Gdns, Rich. TW9
off Manor Rd 180 CM84
Marylebone High St, W1 17 H6
Marylebone La, W1 17 J9
Marylebone Ms, W1 17 J7
Marylebone Pas, W1 17 M8
Marylebone Rd, NW1 16 D6
Marylebone St, W1 17 H7
Marylee Way, SE11 30 D10
Mary Macarthur Ho, E2 21 J2
W6 38 E2
Mary Morgan Ct, Slou. SL2
off Douglas Rd 153 AR71
Sch Marymount Int Sch, Kings.T.
KT2 off George Rd 200 CQ94
Maryon Gro, SE7 37 H9
Maryon Ms, NW3 6 C1
Maryon Rd, SE7 36 G8
SE18 36 G8
Mary Peters Dr, Grnf. UB6 139 CD64
Mary Pl, W11 26 E1
Mary Rd, Guil. GU1 280 AW135
Mary Rose Cl, Chaff.Hun.
RM16 191 FW77
Hampton TW12
off Ashley Rd 218 CA95
Mary Rose Mall, E6 25 K7
Maryrose Way, N20 120 DD46
Mary Seacole Cl, E8 10 A8
Mary Seacole Ho, W6
off Invermead Cl 181 CU76
Maryside, Slou. SL3 174 AY75
Mary's Ter, Twick. TW1 199 CG87
Mary St, E16 23 L6
N1 9 K9
Mary Ter, NW1 7 K9
Coll Mary Ward Adult Ed Cen, The,
WC1 18 B6
Mary Way, Wat. WD19 116 BW49
Masbro Rd, W14 26 D7
Mascalls Ct, SE7 186 EJ79
Mascalls Gdns, Brwd. CM14 130 FT49
Mascalls La, Brwd. CM14 130 FT49
H Mascalls Pk, Gt Warley
CM14 129 FV51
Mascalls Rd, SE7 186 EJ79
Mascoll Path, Slou. SL2 153 AM69
Mascotte Rd, SW15 181 CX84
Mascotts Cl, NW2 141 CV62
Masefield Av, Borwd. WD6 100 CP43
Southall UB1 158 CA73
Stanmore HA7 117 CF50
Masefield Cl, Chesh. HP5 76 AP28
Erith DA8 189 FF81
Romford RM3 128 FJ53
Masefield Ct, Brwd. CM14 130 FW49
Masefield Cres, N14 103 DJ44
Romford RM3 128 FJ53
Masefield Dr, Upmin. RM14 150 FQ59
Masefield Gdns, E6 25 L4
Masefield La, Hayes UB4 157 BV70
Masefield Rd, Dart. DA1 210 FP85
Grays RM16 192 GE75
Hampton TW12
off Wordsworth Rd 198 BZ91
Northfleet DA11 212 GD90
Masefield Vw, Orp. BR6 227 EQ104
Masefield Way, Stai. TW19 196 BM88
Masham Ho, Erith DA18
off Kale Rd 188 EX75
Mashie Rd, W3 160 CS72
Mashiters Hill, Rom. RM1 127 FD53
Mashiters Wk, Rom. RM1 149 FE55
Maskall Cl, SW2 203 DN88
Maskani Wk, SW16
off Bates Cres 203 DJ94
Maskell Rd, SW17 202 DC90
Maskelyne Cl, SW11 40 D6
Maslen Rd, St.Alb. AL4 65 CJ23
Mason Cl, E16 23 N10
SE16 32 D10
SW20 221 CX95
Bexleyheath DA7 189 FB83
Borehamwood WD6 100 CQ40
Hampton TW12 218 BZ95
Waltham Abbey EN9 90 EF34
Mason Ct, Wem. HA9
off The Avenue 140 CN61
Mason Dr, Harold Wd RM3
off Whitmore Av 128 FL54
Masonic Hall Rd, Cher. KT16 215 BF100
Mason Rd, Sutt. SM1
off Manor Pl 240 DB106
Woodford Green IG8 124 EE49
Masons Arms Ms, W1 17 K9
Masons Av, EC2 19 L8
Croydon CR0 224 DQ104
Harrow HA3 139 CF56
Masons Br Rd, Red. RH1 289 DH139
Masons Ct, Slou. SL1 153 AL73
Masons Grn La, W3 160 CN71
Masons Hill, SE18 37 P9
Bromley BR1, BR2 226 EG97
Masons Paddock, Dor. RH4 269 CG134
Masons Pl, EC1 19 H2
Mitcham CR4 222 DF95
Masons Rd, Enf. EN1 104 DW36
Hemel Hempstead HP2 63 BP19
Slough SL1 153 AL73
Mason St, SE17 31 M9
Masons Yd, EC1 19 H2
Mason's Yd, SW1 29 M2
SW19
off High St Wimbledon 201 CX92
Mason Way, Wal.Abb. EN9 90 EF34
Massetts Rd, Horl. RH6 290 DF149
Massey Cl, N11 off Grove Rd 121 DH50
Massey Ct, E6 166 EJ67
Massie Rd, E8 10 C5
Massingberd Way, SW17 203 DH91
Massinger St, SE17 31 N9
Massingham St, E1 21 J4
Masson Av, Ruis. HA4 158 BW65
Mast, The, E16 37 P1
Master Cl, Oxt. RH8
off Church La 276 EE129
Master Gunner Pl, SE18 186 EL80
Masterman Ho, SE5 43 K4
Masterman Rd, E6 24 G3
Masters Cl, SW16 203 DJ93
Masters Dr, SE16 44 E1
Masters St, E1 21 K6
Masthead Cl, Dart. DA2 190 FQ84
Riv Masthouse Terrace 34 B10
Mast Ho Ter, E14 34 B9
🔒 Mast Leisure Pk, SE16 33 K7
Mastmaker Rd, E14 34 B5
Mast Quay, SE18
off Woolwich Ch St 37 K6
Maswell Pk Cres, Houns. TW3 198 CC85
Maswell Pk Rd, Houns. TW3 198 CB85
Matcham Rd, E11 146 EE62
Matching Rd, Hat.Hth CM22 59 FH06
Old Harlow CM17 59 FB11
Ongar CM5 75 FH18
MATCHING TYE, Harl. CM17 59 FF12
Matchless Dr, SE18 187 EN80
Matfield Cl, Brom. BR2 226 EG99
Matfield Rd, Belv. DA17 188 FA79
Matham Gro, SE22 184 DT84
Matham Rd, E.Mol. KT8 219 CD99
Matheson Rd, W14 26 G9
Mathews Av, E6 25 M1
Mathews Pk Av, E15 13 M5
Mathias Cl, Epsom KT18 238 CQ113
Sch Mathilda Marks-Kennedy
Prim Sch, NW7
off Hale La 118 CR50
Mathisen Way, Colnbr. SL3 175 BE81
Mathon Ct, Guil. GU1 265 AZ134
Matilda Cl, SE19
off Elizabeth Way 204 DR94
Matilda Gdns, E3 22 A1
Matilda St, N1 8 D9
Matisse Rd, Houns. TW3 178 CB83
Matlock Cl, SE24 184 DQ84
Barnet EN5 101 CX43
Matlock Ct, SE5
off Denmark Hill Est 184 DR84
Matlock Cres, Sutt. SM3 239 CY105
Watford WD19 116 BW48
Matlock Gdns, Horn. RM12 150 FL62
Sutton SM3 239 CY105
Matlock Pl, Sutt. SM3 239 CY105
Matlock Rd, E10 145 EC58
Caterham CR3 258 DS121
Matlock St, E14 21 L8
Matlock Way, N.Mal. KT3 220 CR95
Matrimony Pl, SW8 41 L9
Matson Ct, Wdf.Grn. IG8
off The Bridle Path 124 EE52
Matson Ho, SE16 32 F6
Matthew Arnold Cl, Cob.
KT11 235 BU114
Staines TW18
off Elizabeth Av 196 BJ93
Sch Matthew Arnold Sch, The, Stai.
TW18 off Kingston Rd 196 BJ93
Matthew Cl, W10 14 C5
Matthew Ct, Mitch. CR4 223 DK99
Matthew Parker St, SW1 29 P5
Matthews Cl, Rom. RM3
off Oak Rd 128 FM53
Matthews Gdns, New Adgtn
CR0 243 ED111
Matthews La, Stai. TW18
off Kingston Rd 196 BG91
Matthews Rd, Grnf. UB6 139 CD64
Matthews St, SW11 40 E8
Reigate RH2 288 DA138
Matthews Yd, WC2 18 A9
Matthias Rd, N16 9 M2
Mattingley Way, SE15 44 A4
Mattison Rd, N4 143 DN58
Mattock La, W5 159 CH74
W13 159 CH74
Maud Cashmore Way, SE18 37 K7
Maud Chadburn Pl, SW4
off Balham Hill 203 DH86
Maude Cres, Wat. WD24 97 BV37
Maude Rd, E17 145 DY57
SE5 43 N7
Beaconsfield HP9 111 AN54
Swanley BR8 209 FG93
Maudesville Cotts, W7 159 CE74
Maude Ter, E17 145 DY56
Maud Gdns, E13 13 M10
Barking IG11 167 ET68
Maudlin's Grn, E1 32 C2
Maud Rd, E10 145 EC62
E13 13 M10
Maudslay Rd, SE9 187 EM83
H Maudsley Hosp, SE5 43 M8
Maudsley Ho, Brent. TW8
off Green Dragon La 180 CL78
Maud St, E16 23 L7
Maud Wilkes Cl, NW5 7 L3
Mauleverer Rd, SW2 203 DL85
Maundeby Wk, NW10
off Neasden La 160 CS65
Maunder Cl, Chaff.Hun. RM16 191 FX77
Maunder Rd, W7 159 CF74
Maunds Fm, Harl. CM18 73 ER20
Maunds Hatch, Harl. CM18 73 ER19
Maunsel St, SW1 29 N8
Maurer Ct, SE10 35 M6
Maurice Av, N22 121 DP54
Caterham CR3 258 DR122
Maurice Brown Cl, NW7 119 CX50
Maurice St, W12 161 CV72
Maurice Wk, NW11 142 DC56
Maurier Cl, Nthlt. UB5 158 BW67
Mauritius Rd, SE10 35 K9
Maury Rd, N16 144 DU61
Mauveine Gdns, Houns. TW3 178 CA84
Mavelstone Cl, Brom. BR1 226 EL95
Mavelstone Rd, Brom. BR1 226 EL95
Maverton Rd, E3 12 A9
Mavis Av, Epsom KT19 238 CS106
Mavis Cl, Epsom KT19 238 CS106
Mavis Gro, Horn. RM12 150 FL61
Mavis Wk, E6 24 G7
Mawbey Est, SE1 44 C1
Mawbey Ho, SE1
off Old Kent Rd 44 B1
Mawbey Pl, SE1 44 B1
Mawbey Rd, SE1 44 B1
Ottershaw KT16 233 BD107
Mawbey St, SW8 42 A5
Mawney Cl, Rom. RM7 127 FB54
Sch Mawney Prim Sch, The,
Rom. RM7
off Mawney Rd 149 FD57
Mawney Rd, Rom. RM7 149 FC56
Mawson Cl, SW20 221 CY96
Mawson La, W4
off Great W Rd 181 CT79
Maxey Gdns, Dag. RM9 148 EY63
Maxey Rd, SE18 187 EQ77
Dagenham RM9 148 EY63
Maxfield Cl, N20 120 DC45
Maxilla Gdns, W10 14 D8
Maxilla Wk, W10 14 D9
Maximfeldt Rd, Erith DA8 189 FE78
Maxim Rd, N21 103 DN44
Dartford DA1 209 FE85
Erith DA8 189 FE78
Maxim Twr, Rom. RM1
off Mercury Gdns 149 FE56
Maxted Cl, Hem.H. HP2 63 BQ18
Maxted Pk, Har. HA1 139 CE59
Maxted Rd, SE15 44 B10
Hemel Hempstead HP2 63 BP17
Maxwell Cl, Croy. CR0 223 DL102
Hayes UB3 157 BU73
Mill End WD3 114 BG47
Maxwell Dr, W.Byf. KT14 234 BJ111
Maxwell Gdns, Orp. BR6 227 ET104
Maxwell Ri, Wat. WD19 116 BY45
Maxwell Rd, SW6 39 L5
Ashford TW15 197 BQ93
Beaconsfield HP9 111 AK52
Borehamwood WD6 100 CP41
Northwood HA6 115 BR52
St. Albans AL1 65 CH21
Welling DA16 187 ET83
West Drayton UB7 176 BM77
● Maxwells W, Chsht EN8 88 DW31
Maxwelton Av, NW7 118 CR50
Maxwelton Cl, NW7 118 CR50
Maya Angelou Ct, E4
off Bailey Cl 123 EC49
Maya Cl, SE15 44 E8
Mayall Cl, Enf. EN3 105 EA38
Mayall Rd, SE24 203 DP85
Maya Pl, N11 121 DK52
Maya Rd, N2 142 DC56
May Av, Nthflt DA11 213 GF88
Orpington BR5 228 EV99
● May Av Ind Est, Nthflt DA11
off May Av 213 GF88
Maybank Av, E18 124 EH54
Hornchurch RM12 149 FH64
Wembley HA0 139 CF64
Maybank Gdns, Pnr. HA5 137 BU57
Maybank Lo, Horn. RM12
off Maybank Av 150 FJ64
Maybank Rd, E18 124 EH53
May Bate Av, Kings.T. KT2 219 CK95
● Maybells Commercial Est,
Bark. IG11 168 EX68
Mayberry Pl, Surb. KT5 220 CM101
Maybourne Cl, SE26 204 DV92
Maybourne Ri, Wok. GU22 248 AX124
Maybrick Rd, Horn. RM11 150 FJ58
Maybrook Meadow Est,
Bark. IG11 168 EU66
MAYBURY, Wok. GU22 249 BB117
Maybury Av, Chsht EN8 88 DV28
Dartford DA2 210 FQ88
Maybury Cl, Enf. EN1 104 DV38
Loughton IG10 107 EP42
Petts Wood BR5 227 EP99
Slough SL1 153 AK72
Tadworth KT20
off Ballards Grn 255 CY119
Maybury Gdns, NW10 161 CV65
Maybury Hill, Wok. GU22 249 BB116
Sch Maybury Inf Sch,
Wok. GU21
off Walton Rd 249 BA116
Maybury Ms, N6 143 DJ59
Maybury Rd, E13 24 C5
Barking IG11 167 ET68
Woking GU21 249 AZ117
Maybury St, SW17 202 DE92
Maybush Rd, Horn. RM11 150 FL59
Maychurch Cl, Stan. HA7 117 CK52
May Cl, Chess. KT9 238 CM107
St. Albans AL3 65 CD18
Maycock Gro, Nthwd. HA6 115 BT51
May Cotts, Wat. WD18 98 BW43
May Ct, SW19 222 DB95
Grays RM17 off Medlar Rd 192 GE79
Maycroft, Pnr. HA5 115 BV54
Maycroft Av, Grays RM17 192 GD78
Maycroft Gdns, Grays RM17 192 GD78
Maycroft Rd, Chsht EN7 88 DS26
Maycross Av, Mord. SM4 221 CZ97
Mayday Gdns, SE3 186 EL82
Mayday Rd, Th.Hth. CR7 223 DP100
H Mayday Uni Hosp, Th.Hth.
CR7 223 DP100
Maydew Ho, SE16 32 G8
Maydwell Lo, Borwd. WD6 100 CM40
Mayell Cl, Lthd. KT22 253 CJ123
Mayerne Rd, SE9 206 EK85
Mayer Rd, Wal.Abb. EN9
off Deer Pk Way 105 EB36
Mayesbrook Rd, Bark. IG11 167 ET67
Dagenham RM8 148 EU62
Ilford IG3 148 EU62
Mayes Cl, Swan. BR8 229 FG98
Warlingham CR6 259 DX118
Mayesford Rd, Rom. RM6 148 EW59
Sch Mayespark Prim Sch, Ilf. IG3
off Goodmayes La 148 EU62
Mayes Rd, N22 121 DN54
Mayeswood Rd, SE12 206 EJ90
MAYFAIR, W1 29 J1
Mayfair Av, Bexh. DA7 188 EX81
Ilford IG1 147 EM61
Romford RM6 148 EX58
Twickenham TW2 198 CC87
Worcester Park KT4 221 CU102
Mayfair Cl, Beck. BR3 225 EB95
St. Albans AL4 65 CJ15
Surbiton KT6 220 CL102
Mayfair Gdns, N17 122 DR51
Woodford Green IG8 124 EG52
Mayfair Ms, NW1 6 F7
Mayfair Pl, W1 29 K2
Mayfair Rd, Dart. DA1 210 FK85
Mayfair Ter, N14 121 DK45
Mayfare, Crox.Grn WD3 97 BR43
Mayfield, Bexh. DA7 188 EZ83
Leatherhead KT22 253 CJ121
Waltham Abbey EN9 89 ED34
Welwyn Garden City AL8 51 CW05
Mayfield Av, N12 120 DC49
N14 121 DJ47
W4 180 CS77
W13 179 CH76
Gerrards Cross SL9 134 AX56
Harrow HA3 139 CH57
New Haw KT15 234 BH110
Orpington BR6 227 ET102
Woodford Green IG8 124 EG52
Mayfield Cl, E8 10 A5
SW4 203 DK85
Ashford TW15 197 BP93
Harlow CM17 58 EZ11
Hersham KT12 235 BU105
New Haw KT15 234 BJ110
Redhill RH1 288 DG140
Thames Ditton KT7 219 CH102
Uxbridge UB10 157 BP69
Mayfield Cres, N9 104 DV44
Thornton Heath CR7 223 DM98
Mayfield Dr, Pnr. HA5 138 BZ56
Windsor SL4 173 AN83
Mayfield Gdns, NW4 141 CX58
W7 159 CD72
Brentwood CM14 130 FV46
Hersham KT12 235 BU105
New Haw KT15 234 BH110
Staines TW18 195 BF93
Mayfield Grn, Bkhm KT23 268 CA126
Sch Mayfield Inf & Nurs Sch, Wal.Cr.
EN8 off Cheshunt Wash 89 DY27
Mayfield Mans, SW15
off West Hill 201 CX87
Mayfield Pk, West Dr. UB7 176 BJ76
Sch Mayfield Prim Sch, W7
off High La 159 CD72
Mayfield Rd, E4 123 EC47
E8 10 A7
E13 23 M5
E17 123 DY54
N8 143 DM58
SW19 221 CZ95
W3 160 CP73
W12 180 CS75
Belvedere DA17 189 FC77
Bromley BR1 226 EL99
Dagenham RM8 148 EW60
Enfield EN3 105 DX40
Gravesend DA11 213 GF87
Hersham KT12 235 BU105
South Croydon CR2 242 DR109
Sutton SM2 240 DD107
Thornton Heath CR7 223 DM98
Weybridge KT13 234 BM106
Wooburn Green HP10 132 AE57
Mayfields, Grays RM16 192 GC75
Swanscombe DA10 211 FX86
Wembley HA9 140 CN61
Sch Mayfield Sch & Coll, Dag. RM8
off Pedley Rd 148 EW60
Mayfields Cl, Wem. HA9 140 CN61
Mayflower Av, Hem.H. HP2 62 BK20
Mayflower Cl, SE16 33 K8
Hertingfordbury SG14 53 DL11
Lower Nazeing EN9 72 EE22
Ruislip HA4 137 BQ58
South Ockendon RM15 171 FW70
Mayflower Ct, SE16
off St. Marychurch St 32 G5
Harlow CM19 73 EP19
Sch Mayflower Prim Sch, E14 22 C9
Mayflower Rd, SW9 42 A10
Chafford Hundred RM16 191 FW78
Park Street AL2 82 CB27
Mayflower St, SE16 32 G5
Mayflower Way, Beac. HP9 132 AG55
Farnham Common SL2 133 AQ64
Mayfly Cl, Eastcote HA5 138 BW59
Orpington BR5 228 EX98
Mayfly Gdns, Nthlt. UB5
off Seasprite Cl 158 BX69
MAYFORD, Wok. GU22 248 AW122
Mayford Cl, SW12 202 DF87
Beckenham BR3 225 DX97
Woking GU22 248 AX122
Mayford Grn, Wok. GU22
off Smarts Heath Rd 248 AX122
Mayford Rd, SW12 202 DF87
May Gdns, Els. WD6 99 CK44
Wembley HA0 159 CJ68
Maygoods Cl, Uxb. UB8 156 BK71
Maygoods Grn, Uxb. UB8 156 BK71
Maygoods La, Uxb. UB8 156 BK71
Maygood St, N1 8 D10
Maygoods Vw, Cowley UB8 156 BJ71
Maygreen Cres, Horn. RM11 149 FG59
Maygrove Rd, NW6 4 G5
Mayhall La, Amer. HP6 77 AP35
Mayhew Cl, E4 123 EA48
Mayhill Rd, SE7 186 EH79
Barnet EN5 101 CY44
Mayhurst Av, Wok. GU22 249 BC116
Mayhurst Cl, Wok. GU22 249 BC116
Mayhurst Cres, Wok. GU22 249 BC116
Maylands Av, Hem.H. HP2 63 BP17
Hornchurch RM12 149 FH63
Maylands Dr, Sid. DA14 208 EX90
Uxbridge UB8 156 BK65
Maylands Rd, Wat. WD19 116 BW49

Maylands Way, Rom. RM3 . . . . 128 FQ51
Maylins Dr, Saw. CM21 . . . . . . 58 EX05
Maynard Cl, N15
off Brunswick Rd. 144 DS57
SW6 . . . . 39 M5
Erith DA8 . . . . 189 FF80
Maynard Ct, Enf. EN3
off Harston Dr 105 EA38
Waltham Abbey EN9 . . . . 90 EF34
Maynard Dr, St.Alb. AL1 . . . . . . 65 CD23
Maynard Path, E17 . . . . 145 EC57
Maynard Pl, Cuffley EN6 . . . . . . 87 DL29
Maynard Rd, E17. . . . . 145 EC57
Hemel Hempstead HP2 . . . . . 62 BK21
Maynards, Horn. RM11. . . . . . . 150 FL59
Maynards Quay, E1 . . . . 32 G1
Mayne Av, St.Alb. AL3 . . . . 64 BZ22
Maynooth Gdns, Cars. SM5 . . 222 DF101
Mayo Cl, Chsht EN8 . . . . 88 DW28
Mayo Gdns, Hem.H. HP1 . . . . . 62 BH21
Mayola Rd, E5. . . . . 144 DW63
Mayo Rd, NW10 . . . . 160 CS65
Croydon CR0. . . . . 224 DR99
Walton-on-Thames KT12 . . . 217 BT101
Mayor's La, Dart. DA2. . . . . . . 210 FJ92
Mayow Rd, SE23. . . . . 205 DX90
SE26 . . . . 205 DX91
Mayplace Av, Dart. DA1 . . . . . . 189 FG84
Mayplace Cl, Bexh. DA7 . . . . . 189 FB83
Mayplace La, SE18 . . . . 187 EP80
Sch Mayplace Prim Sch, Barne. DA7
off Woodside Rd 189 FD84
Mayplace Rd E, Bexh. DA7 . . . 189 FB83
Dartford DA1 . . . . 189 FC83
Mayplace Rd W, Bexh. DA7 . . . 188 FA84
MAYPOLE, Orp. BR6. . . . . 246 EZ106
Maypole Cres, Erith DA8 . . . . . 190 FK79
Ilford IG6 . . . . 125 ER52
Maypole Dr, Chig. IG7 . . . . 126 EU48
Sch Maypole Prim Sch, Dart. DA2
off Franklin Rd. 209 FE90
Maypole Rd, Grav. DA12 . . . . . 213 GM88
Orpington BR6 . . . . 246 EZ106
Taplow SL6 . . . . 152 AG71
Maypole St, Harl. CM17
off Alba Rd. 58 EW14
May Rd, E4 . . . . 123 EA51
E13 . . . . 13 P10
Hawley DA2. . . . . 210 FM91
Twickenham TW2 . . . . 199 CE88
Mayroyd Av, Surb. KT6. . . . . . . 220 CN103
May's Bldgs Ms, SE10 . . . . 46 F6
Mays Cl, Wey. KT13 . . . . 234 BM110
Mays Ct, WC2 . . . . 30 A1
Maysfield Rd, Send GU23 . . . . 249 BD123
MAY'S GREEN, Cob. KT11 . . . . 251 BT121
Mays Gro, Send GU23 . . . . 249 BD124
Mays Hill Rd, Brom. BR2 . . . . . 226 EE96
Mays La, E4 . . . . 123 ED47
Barnet EN5. . . . . 101 CY43
Maysoule Rd, SW11 . . . . 182 DD84
Mays Rd, Tedd. TW11. . . . . 199 CD92
Mayston Ms, SE10
off Westcombe Hill 47 P1
May St, W14 . . . . 39 H1
Mayswood Gdns, Dag. RM10 . . 169 FC65
Maythorne Cl, Wat. WD18 . . . . . 97 BS42
Mayton St, N7. . . . . 143 DM62
Maytree Cl, Edg. HA8 . . . . 118 CQ48
Guildford GU1. . . . . 264 AV131
Rainham RM13 . . . . 169 FE68
Maytree Cres, Wat. WD24. . . . . . 97 BT35
Maytree Gdns, W5 . . . . 179 CK76
May Tree La, Stan. HA7. . . . . . . 117 CF52
Maytrees, Rad. WD7 . . . . 99 CG37
Maytree Wk, SW2. . . . . 203 DN89
Mayville Est, N16 . . . . 9 N2
Sch Mayville Prim Sch, E11
off Lincoln St. 146 EE62
Mayville Rd, E11 . . . . 146 EE61
Ilford IG1 . . . . 147 EP64
May Wk, E13 . . . . 166 EH68
Maywater Cl, S.Croy. CR2 . . . . 242 DR111
Maywin Dr, Horn. RM11. . . . . . 150 FM60
Maywood Cl, Beck. BR3 . . . . . . 205 EB94
⇌ Maze Hill 47 J2
Maze Hill, SE3. . . . . 47 J3
SE10. 47 J2
Mazenod Av, NW6 . . . . 5 K7
Maze Rd, Rich. TW9 . . . . 180 CN80
Mead, The, N2 . . . . 120 DC54
W13 . . . . 159 CH71
Ashtead KT21 . . . . 254 CL119
Beaconsfield HP9. . . . . 111 AL53
Beckenham BR3 . . . . 225 EC95
Cheshunt EN8. . . . . 88 DW29
Uxbridge UB10 . . . . 136 BN61
Wallington SM6 . . . . 241 DK107
Watford WD19 . . . . 116 BY48
West Wickham BR4. . . . . 225 ED102
Mead Av, Red. RH1 . . . . 288 DG142
Slough SL3 . . . . 175 BB75
● Mead Business Cen, Hert.
SG13 . . . . 54 DS08
● Mead Business Pk, Chesh. HP5
off Berkhampstead Rd 76 AQ30
Mead Cl, NW1 . . . . 7 H6
Addlestone KT15. . . . . 216 BK104
Denham UB9. . . . . 136 BG61
Egham TW20. . . . . 195 BB93
Grays RM16. . . . . 192 GB75
Harrow HA3. . . . . 117 CD53
Loughton IG10. . . . . 107 EP40
Redhill RH1 . . . . 272 DG131
Romford RM2 . . . . 127 FG54
Slough SL3 . . . . 175 BB75
Swanley BR8. . . . . 229 FG99
Mead Ct, NW9. . . . . 140 CQ57
Egham TW20
off Holbrook Meadow. 195 BC93
Knaphill GU21. . . . . 248 AS116
Waltham Abbey EN9 . . . . 89 EB34
Mead Cres, E4. . . . . 123 EC49
Bookham KT23 . . . . 268 CA125
Dartford DA1 off Beech Rd. . 210 FK88
Sutton SM1 . . . . 240 DE105
Meadcroft Rd, SE11 . . . . 42 G3
Meade Cl, W4 . . . . 180 CN79
Meade Ct, Walt.Hill KT20 . . . . 255 CU124
Mead End, Ashtd. KT21 . . . . . . 254 CM116
Meades, The, Wey. KT13. . . . . . 235 BQ107
Meades La, Chesh. HP5 . . . . 76 AP32
Meadfield, Edg. HA8. . . . . 118 CP47
Mead Fld, Har. HA2
off Kings Rd. 138 BZ62
Meadfield Av, Slou. SL3. . . . . . 175 BA76
Meadfield Grn, Edg. HA8 . . . . . 118 CP47
Meadfield Rd, Slou. SL3. . . . . . 175 BA76
Meadfoot Rd, SW16 . . . . 203 DJ94
Meadgate Av, Wdf.Grn. IG8 . . . 124 EL50
Meadgate Rd, Lwr Naze. EN9 . . 71 ED20
Roydon CM19 . . . . 71 ED20
Mead Gro, Rom. RM6. . . . . 148 EX55
Mead Ho La, Hayes UB4 . . . . . 157 BR70
Meadhurst Pk, Sun. TW16 . . . . 197 BS93
Meadhurst Rd, Cher. KT16. . . . 216 BH102
Sch Mead Inf Sch, The, Ewell KT19
off Newbury Gdns 239 CT105
Meadlands Dr, Rich. TW10 . . . . 199 CK89
Sch Meadlands Prim Sch, Rich.
TW10 off Broughton Av 199 CJ91
Mead La, Cher. KT16 . . . . 216 BH102
Hertford SG13 . . . . 54 DR08
● Mead La Ind Est, Hert.
SG13 . . . . 54 DT08
Meadow, The, Chis. BR7. . . . . . 207 EQ93
Hailey SG13. . . . . 55 DY13
Meadow Av, Croy. CR0. . . . . . . 225 DX100
Meadow Bk, N21. . . . . 103 DM44
Meadowbank, NW3 . . . . 6 E7
SE3. 186 EF83
Meadow Bk, E.Hors. KT24. . . . 267 BT128
Guildford GU1
off Stoughton Rd 264 AW132
Meadowbank, Kings L. WD4 . . . 80 BN30
Surbiton KT5. . . . . 220 CM100
Watford WD19 . . . . 116 BW45
Meadowbank Cl, SW6 . . . . 38 B5
Meadow Bk Cl, Amer. HP7. . . . . 77 AS38
Meadowbank Cl, Bov. HP3. . . . . 79 BB28
Meadowbank Gdns, Houns.
TW5 . . . . 177 BU82
Meadowbank Rd, NW9 . . . . . . 140 CR59
Meadowbanks, Barn. EN5 . . . . 101 CT43
Meadowbrook, Oxt. RH8 . . . . . 275 EC130
Meadowbrook Cl, Colnbr. SL3. 175 BF82
Meadowbrook Rd, Dor. RH4 . . 285 CG135
Meadow Bungalows, Chilw.
GU4 . . . . 281 BB140
Meadow Cl, E4 . . . . 123 EB46
E9 . . . . 11 P3
SE6. 205 EA92
SW20 . . . . 221 CW98
Barking IG11 . . . . 167 ET67
Barnet EN5. . . . . 101 CZ44
Bexleyheath DA6 . . . . 208 EZ85
Bricket Wood AL2 . . . . 82 CA29
Chesham HP5
off Little Hivings 76 AN27
Chislehurst BR7 . . . . 207 EP92
Enfield EN3 . . . . 105 DY38
Esher KT10. . . . . 219 CF104
Godalming GU7 . . . . 280 AS144
Hersham KT12 . . . . 236 BZ105
Hertford SG13 . . . . 54 DT08
Hounslow TW4 . . . . 198 CA86
London Colney AL2 . . . . 83 CK27
North Mymms AL9. . . . . 67 CX24
Northolt UB5. . . . . 158 CA68
Old Windsor SL4. . . . . 194 AV86
Purley CR8. . . . . 241 DK113
Richmond TW10 . . . . 200 CL88
Ruislip HA4 . . . . 137 BT58
St. Albans AL4. . . . . 65 CJ17
Sevenoaks TN13 . . . . 278 FG123
Sutton SM1
off Aultone Way. 222 DC103
Meadowcot La, Colesh. HP7 . . . 77 AM44
Meadow Cotts, Beac. HP9 . . . . 111 AL54
Meadow Ct, Epsom KT18 . . . . . 238 CQ113
Harlow CM18
off Lodge Hall 73 ES19
Redhill RH1 . . . . 273 DJ130
Staines TW18. . . . . 195 BE90
Meadowcourt Rd, SE3 . . . . 186 EF84
Meadowcroft, Brom. BR1. . . . . 227 EM97
Bushey WD23 . . . . 98 CB44
Chalfont St. Peter SL9. . . . . . 112 AX54
Meadow Cft, Hat. AL10. . . . . . . 67 CT18
Meadowcroft, St.Alb. AL1 . . . . . 65 CG23
Meadowcroft Cl, Horl. RH6 . . . 291 DJ151
Sch Meadowcroft Comm Inf Sch,
Cher. KT16 off Little Grn La. 215 BF104
Meadowcroft Rd, N13 . . . . 121 DN47
Meadowcross, Wal.Abb. EN9. . . . 90 EE34
Meadow Dell, Hat. AL10. . . . . . . 67 CT18
Meadow Dr, N10. . . . . 143 DH55
NW4 . . . . 119 CW54
Amersham HP6. . . . . 77 AS37
Ripley GU23 . . . . 249 BF123
Meadowford Cl, SE28. . . . . 168 EU73
Meadow Gdns, Edg. HA8. . . . . . 118 CP51
Staines TW18. . . . . 195 BD92
Meadow Garth, NW10 . . . . 160 CQ66
Meadow Gate, Ashtd. KT21 . . . 254 CL117
Meadowgate Cl, NW7. . . . . 119 CT50
Sch Meadowgate Sch, SE4
off Revelon Rd. 185 DY83
Meadow Grn, Welw.G.C. AL8. . . 51 CW09
Sch Meadow High Sch, Hlgdn UB8
off Royal La 156 BM71
Meadow Hill, Couls. CR5 . . . . . 241 DJ113
New Malden KT3 . . . . 220 CS100
Purley CR8. . . . . 241 DJ113
Meadowlands, Cob. KT11 . . . . 235 BU113
Hornchurch RM11 . . . . 150 FL59
Oxted RH8 . . . . 276 EG134
West Clandon GU4. . . . . 266 BH130
Meadowlands Pk, Add. KT15. . 216 BL104
Meadow La, SE12. . . . . 206 EH90
Beaconsfield HP9. . . . . 111 AM53
Eton SL4 . . . . 173 AQ80
Fetcham KT22 . . . . 252 CC121
Meadowlea Cl, Harm. UB7. . . . 176 BK79
Meadow Ms, SW8 . . . . 42 C3
Meadow Pl, SW8 . . . . 42 B4
W4 off Edensor Rd 180 CS80
Sch Meadow Prim Sch, Epsom
KT17 off Sparrow Fm Rd . . 239 CV105
Meadow Ri, Couls. CR5 . . . . . . 241 DK113
Meadow Rd, SW8. . . . . 42 C4
SW19 . . . . 202 DC94
Ashford TW15 . . . . 197 BR92
Ashtead KT21 . . . . 254 CL117
Barking IG11 . . . . 167 ET66
Berkhamsted HP4. . . . . 60 AU17
Borehamwood WD6 . . . . 100 CP40
Bromley BR2 . . . . 226 EE95
Bushey WD23 . . . . 98 CB43
Claygate KT10. . . . . 237 CE107
Dagenham RM9 . . . . 168 EZ65
Epping CM16. . . . . 91 ET29
Feltham TW13 . . . . 198 BY89
Gravesend DA11 . . . . 213 GG89
Guildford GU4. . . . . 265 BA130
Hemel Hempstead HP3 . . . . . . 62 BN24
Loughton IG10. . . . . 106 EL43
Pinner HA5 . . . . 138 BX57
Meadow Rd, Rom. RM7. . . . . . . 149 FC60
Slough SL3 . . . . 174 AY76
Southall UB1 . . . . 158 BZ73
Sutton SM1 . . . . 240 DE106
Virginia Water GU25. . . . . 214 AS99
Watford WD25. . . . . 81 BU34
Meadow Row, SE1. . . . . 31 J7
Meadows, The, Amer. HP7. . . . . 77 AS39
Guildford GU2. . . . . 280 AW137
Halstead TN14 . . . . 246 EZ113
Hemel Hempstead HP1 . . . . . . 61 BE19
Orpington BR6 . . . . 246 EW107
Sawbridgeworth CM21 . . . . . . 58 FA05
Warlingham CR6. . . . . 259 DX117
Welwyn Garden City AL7. . . . . 52 DC09
Meadows Cl, E10 . . . . 145 EA61
Meadows End, Sun. TW16. . . . . 217 BU95
Meadowside, SE9. . . . . 186 EJ84
Bookham KT23 . . . . 252 CA123
Dartford DA1 . . . . 210 FK88
Horley RH6 off Stockfield. . . 291 DH147
Jordans HP9 . . . . 112 AT52
Walton-on-Thames KT12 . . . 218 BW103
Meadow Side, Wat. WD25 . . . . . 81 BV31
Meadowside Rd, Sutt. SM2. . . 239 CY109
Upminster RM14. . . . . 150 FQ64
Meadows Leigh Cl, Wey.
KT13. . . . . 217 BQ104
Sch Meadows Sch, The, Woob.Grn
HP10 off School Rd. 132 AE57
Meadow Stile, Croy. CR0
off High St 224 DQ104
Meadowsweet Cl, E16 . . . . 24 E7
SW20 . . . . 221 CW98
Meadow Vw, Ch.St.G. HP8. . . . 112 AU48
Chertsey KT16. . . . . 216 BJ102
Harrow HA1. . . . . 139 CE60
Orpington BR5 . . . . 228 EW97
Sidcup DA15 . . . . 208 EV87
Staines TW19. . . . . 195 BF85
Meadowview Rd, SE6 . . . . 205 DZ92
Bexley DA5 . . . . 208 EY86
Epsom KT19 . . . . 238 CS109
Meadow Vw Rd, Hayes UB4 . . 157 BQ70
Thornton Heath CR7. . . . . . . 223 DP99
Meadow Wk, E18 . . . . 146 EG56
Dagenham RM9 . . . . 168 EZ65
Dartford DA2 . . . . 210 FJ91
Epsom KT17, KT19 . . . . 238 CS107
Penn HP10 . . . . 110 AC46
Wallington SM6 . . . . 223 DH104
Walton on the Hill KT20. . . . . 255 CV124
Meadow Way, NW9 . . . . 140 CR57
Addlestone KT15. . . . . 234 BH105
Bedmond WD5 . . . . 81 BT27
Bookham KT23 . . . . 252 CB123
Chessington KT9. . . . . 238 CL106
Chigwell IG7 . . . . 125 EQ48
Dartford DA2 . . . . 210 FQ87
Dorney Reach SL6. . . . . 172 AF75
Fifield SL6 . . . . 172 AD81
Hemel Hempstead HP3 . . . . . . 61 BF23
Kings Langley WD4. . . . . 80 BN30
Old Windsor SL4. . . . . 194 AV86
Orpington BR6 . . . . 227 EN104
Potters Bar EN6. . . . . 86 DA34
Reigate RH2. . . . . 288 DB138
Rickmansworth WD3. . . . . 114 BJ45
Ruislip HA4 . . . . 137 BV58
Sawbridgeworth CM21 . . . . 58 FA06
Tadworth KT20 . . . . 255 CY118
Upminster RM14. . . . . 150 FQ62
Wembley HA9 . . . . 139 CK63
West Horsley KT24 . . . . 267 BR125
Meadow Way, The, Har. HA3 . . 117 CE53
Meadow Waye, Houns. TW5. . . 178 BY79
Sch Meadow Wd Sch, Bushey
WD23 off Coldharbour La . . . 98 CC43
● Mead Pk, Harl. CM20 . . . . 57 ET11
Mead Path, SW17. . . . . 202 DC92
Mead Pl, E9 . . . . 11 H5
Croydon CR0. . . . . 223 DP102
Rickmansworth WD3. . . . . 114 BH46
Mead Plat, NW10 . . . . 160 CQ65
Sch Mead Prim Sch, Harold Hill
RM3 off Amersham Rd. 128 FM51
Mead Rd, Cat. CR3 . . . . 258 DT123
Chislehurst BR7 . . . . 207 EQ93
Dartford DA1 . . . . 210 FK88
Edgware HA8. . . . . 118 CN51
Gravesend DA11 . . . . 213 GH89
Hersham KT12 . . . . 236 BY105
Richmond TW10 . . . . 199 CJ90
Shenley WD7. . . . . 84 CN33
Uxbridge UB8 . . . . 156 BK65
Sch Mead Rd Inf Sch, Chis. BR7
off Mead Rd. 207 EQ93
Mead Row, SE1. . . . . 30 E6
Meads, The, Brick.Wd AL2 . . . . . 82 BZ29
Edgware HA8. . . . . 118 CR51
Northchurch HP4. . . . . 60 AS17
Sutton SM3 . . . . 221 CY104
Upminster RM14. . . . . 151 FS61
Uxbridge UB8 . . . . 156 BL70
Jct Meads Cor, Purf. RM19. . . . . 190 FP77
Meadside Cl, Beck. BR3 . . . . . . 225 DY95
Meads La, Ilf. IG3 . . . . 147 ES59
Meads Rd, N22 . . . . 121 DP54
Enfield EN3 . . . . 105 DY39
Guildford GU1. . . . . 265 BA134
Meadsway, Gt Warley CM13 . . 129 FV51
Mead Ter, Wem. HA9
off Meadow Way. 139 CK63
MEAD VALE, Red. RH1 . . . . . . 288 DD136
Meadvale Rd, W5 . . . . 159 CH70
Croydon CR0. . . . . 224 DT101
Meadview Rd, Ware SG12 . . . . . 55 DX07
Mead Wk, Slou. SL3 . . . . 175 BB75
Meadway, N14 . . . . 121 DK47
NW11 . . . . 142 DB58
SW20 . . . . 221 CW98
Ashford TW15 . . . . 196 BN91
Barnet EN5. . . . . 102 DA42
Beckenham BR3 . . . . 225 EC95
Berkhamsted HP4. . . . . 60 AY18
Mead Way, Brom. BR2 . . . . . . 226 EF100
Bushey WD23 . . . . 98 BY40
Meadway, Coln.Hth AL4. . . . . . . 66 CR23
Mead Way, Couls. CR5 . . . . . . 257 DL118
Croydon CR0. . . . . 225 DY103
Meadway, Eff. KT24 . . . . 268 BY128
Enfield EN3 . . . . 104 DW36
Epsom KT19 . . . . 238 CQ112
Esher KT10 . . . . 236 CB109
Grays RM17. . . . . 192 GD77
Mead Way, Guil. GU4 . . . . 265 BC129
Meadway, Halst. TN14 . . . . . . 246 EZ113
Hoddesdon EN11 . . . . 71 EA19
Ilford IG3 . . . . 147 ES63
Meadway, Oxshott KT22 . . . . . 237 CD114
Romford RM2 . . . . 127 FG54
Ruislip HA4 . . . . 137 BR58
Mead Way, Slou. SL1 . . . . 153 AK71
Meadway, Stai. TW18. . . . . 196 BG94
Surbiton KT5. . . . . 220 CQ102
Twickenham TW2 . . . . 199 CD88
Warlingham CR6. . . . . 258 DW115
Welwyn Garden City AL7. . . . . 51 CZ11
Woodford Green IG8 . . . . 124 EJ50
Meadway, The, SE3. . . . . 47 H9
Buckhurst Hill IG9. . . . . 124 EK46
Cuffley EN6 . . . . 87 DM28
Horley RH6 . . . . 291 DJ148
Loughton IG10. . . . . 107 EM44
Orpington BR6 . . . . 246 EV106
Sevenoaks TN13 . . . . 278 FF122
Meadway Cl, NW11 . . . . 142 DB58
Barnet EN5. . . . . 102 DA42
Pinner HA5
off Highbanks Rd. 116 CB51
Staines TW18. . . . . 195 BF94
Meadway Ct, NW11 . . . . 142 DB58
Meadway Dr, Add. KT15 . . . . . 234 BJ108
Woking GU21 . . . . 248 AW116
Meadway Gdns, Ruis. HA4 . . . 137 BR58
Meadway Gate, NW11 . . . . 142 DA58
Meadway Pk, Ger.Cr. SL9. . . . . 134 AX60
Meaford Way, SE20. . . . . 204 DV94
Meakin Est, SE1 . . . . 31 N6
Meanley Rd, E12. . . . . 146 EL63
Meard St, W1. . . . . 17 N9
Meare Cl, Tad. KT20 . . . . 255 CW123
Meare Est, Woob.Grn HP10 . . 132 AD55
Meath Cl, Orp. BR5. . . . . 228 EV99
Meath Cres, E2 . . . . 21 J3
Meath Gdns, Horl. RH6 . . . . . . 290 DE146
MEATH GREEN, Horl. RH6 . . . . 290 DE146
Meath Grn Av, Horl. RH6 . . . . 290 DF146
Sch Meath Grn Inf Sch, Horl. RH6
off Kiln La 290 DF146
Sch Meath Grn Jun Sch, Horl. RH6
off Greenfields Rd. 290 DF146
Meath Grn La, Horl. RH6 . . . . 288 DE143
Meath Rd, E15. . . . . 13 L1
Ilford IG1 . . . . 147 EQ62
Sch Meath Sch, Ott. KT16
off Brox Rd 233 BD108
Meath St, SW11 . . . . 41 J6
Meautys, St.Alb. AL3 . . . . 64 BZ22
Sch Mechinah Liyeshiva Zichron
Moshe Sch, N16
off Amhurst Pk 144 DR59
Mecklenburgh Pl, WC1 . . . . 18 C4
Mecklenburgh Sq, WC1 . . . . 18 C4
Mecklenburgh St, WC1. . . . . 18 C4
Medburn St, NW1. . . . . 7 N10
Medbury Rd, Grav. DA12 . . . . 213 GM88
Medcalf Rd, Enf. EN3 . . . . 105 DZ37
Medcroft Gdns, SW14 . . . . 180 CQ84
Medebourne Cl, SE3. . . . . 47 P10
Mede Cl, Wrays. TW19 . . . . . . 194 AX88
Mede Fld, Fetch. KT22 . . . . 253 CD124
Medesenge Way, N13. . . . . 121 DP51
Medfield St, SW15 . . . . 201 CV87
Medhurst Cl, E3 . . . . 21 M1
Chobham GU24 . . . . 232 AT109
Medhurst Cres, Grav. DA12 . . . 213 GM90
Medhurst Gdns, Grav. DA12 . . 213 GM90
Median Rd, E5. . . . . 10 G2
★ Medici Galleries, W1. . . . . 29 K1
Medick Ct, Grays RM17 . . . . . . 192 GE79
Medina Av, Esher KT10. . . . . . . 219 CE104
Medina Gro, N7. . . . . 143 DN62
Medina Ho, Erith DA8
off Waterhead Cl 189 FE80
Medina Rd, N7 . . . . 143 DN62
Grays RM17. . . . . 192 GD77
Medina Sq, Epsom KT19 . . . . . 238 CN109
Medlake Rd, Egh. TW20 . . . . . 195 BC93
Medland Cl, Wall. SM6. . . . . . . 222 DG102
Medland Ho, E14. . . . . 21 L10
Medlar Cl, Guil. GU1 . . . . 264 AW132
Northolt UB5
off Parkfield Av 158 BY68
Medlar Ct, Slou. SL2 . . . . 154 AW74
Medlar Rd, Grays RM17. . . . . . 192 GD79
Medlar St, SE5 . . . . 43 K6
Medley Rd, NW6. . . . . 5 K5
Medman Cl, Uxb. UB8 . . . . 156 BJ68
Medora Rd, SW2. . . . . 203 DM87
Romford RM7 . . . . 149 FD56
Medow Mead, Rad. WD7 . . . . . . 83 CF33
Medusa Rd, SE6 . . . . 205 EB86
Medway Bldgs, E3 . . . . 21 M1
Medway Cl, Croy. CR0 . . . . . . 224 DW100
Ilford IG1 . . . . 147 EQ64
Watford WD25. . . . . 82 BW34
Medway Dr, Perivale UB6 . . . . 159 CF68
Medway Gdns, Wem. HA0. . . . 139 CG63
Medway Ms, E3 . . . . 21 M1
Medway Par, Perivale UB6 . . . 159 CF68
Medway Rd, E3. . . . . 21 M1
Dartford DA1. . . . . 189 FG83
Hemel Hempstead HP2 . . . . . . 62 BM15
Medway St, SW1 . . . . 29 P7
Medwick Ms, Hem.H. HP2
off Hunters Oak. 63 BP15
Medwin St, SW4. . . . . 183 DM84
Meecham Ct, SW11 . . . . 40 B8
Meerbrook Rd, SE3. . . . . 186 EJ83
Meeson Rd, E15 . . . . 13 L8
Meesons La, Grays RM17 . . . . 192 FZ77
Meeson St, E5 . . . . 11 L1
Meeting Fld Path, E9 . . . . 11 H4
Meeting Ho All, E1 . . . . 32 F2
Meeting Ho La, SE15 . . . . 44 E6
Megg La, Chipper. WD4 . . . . . . 80 BH29
Mehetabel Rd, E9 . . . . 10 G4
Meister Cl, Ilf. IG1 . . . . 147 ER60
Melancholy Wk, Rich. TW10 . . 199 CJ89
Melanda Cl, Chis. BR7 . . . . 207 EM92
Melanie Cl, Bexh. DA7 . . . . . . 188 EY81
Melba Gdns, Til. RM18 . . . . . . 193 GG80
Melba Way, SE13 . . . . 46 D7
Melbourne Av, N13. . . . . 121 DM51
W13 . . . . 159 CG74
Pinner HA5 . . . . 138 CB55
Slough SL1 . . . . 153 AQ72
Melbourne Cl, Orp. BR6. . . . . . 227 ES101
St. Albans AL3. . . . . 65 CF16
Uxbridge UB10 . . . . 136 BN63
Wallington SM6
off Melbourne Rd 241 DJ106
Melbourne Ct, E5
off Daubeney Rd. 145 DY63
SE20. . . . . 204 DU94
Waltham Cross EN8
off Alexandra Way. 89 DZ34
Melbourne Ct, Welw.G.C. AL8 . . 51 CV10
Melbourne Gdns, Rom. RM6 . . 148 EY57
Melbourne Gro, SE22. . . . . 184 DS84
Melbourne Ho, Hayes UB4. . . . 158 BW70
Melbourne Ms, SE6 . . . . 205 EC87
SW9 . . . . 42 E7
Melbourne Pl, WC2. . . . . 18 D10
Melbourne Rd, E6. . . . . 167 EM67
E10 . . . . 145 EB59
E17 . . . . 145 DY56
SW19 . . . . 222 DA95
Bushey WD23 . . . . 98 CB44
Ilford IG1 . . . . 147 EP60
Teddington TW11. . . . . 199 CJ93
Tilbury RM18. . . . . 192 GE81
Wallington SM6 . . . . 241 DH106
Melbourne Sq, SW9 . . . . 42 E7
Melbourne Ter, SW6
off Moore Pk Rd 39 L5
Melbourne Way, Enf. EN1. . . . . 104 DT44
Melbray Ms, SW6. . . . . 38 G9
Melbreak Ho, SE22
off Pytchley Rd 184 DS83
Melbury Av, Sthl. UB2 . . . . 178 CB76
Melbury Cl, Cher. KT16 . . . . . . 216 BG101
Chislehurst BR7 . . . . 206 EL93
Claygate KT10. . . . . 237 CH107
West Byfleet KT14. . . . . 234 BG114
Melbury Ct, W8. . . . . 27 H6
Melbury Dr, SE5 . . . . 43 N5
Melbury Gdns, SW20. . . . . 221 CV95
Melbury Rd, W14. . . . . 26 G6
Harrow HA3. . . . . 140 CM57
Melchester Ho, N19
off Wedmore St. 143 DK62
Melcombe Gdns, Har. HA3 . . . 140 CM58
Melcombe Ho, SW8
off Dorset Rd. 42 C5
Melcombe Pl, NW1. . . . . 16 E6
Sch Melcombe Prim Sch, W6 . . . 38 C2
Melcombe St, NW1 . . . . 16 F5
Meldex Cl, NW7 . . . . 119 CW51
Meldon Cl, SW6 . . . . 39 M7
Meldone Cl, Surb. KT5. . . . . . . 220 CP100
Meldrum Cl, Orp. BR5
off Killewarren Way. 228 EW100
Oxted RH8 . . . . 276 EF132
Meldrum Rd, Ilf. IG3. . . . . 148 EU61
Melfield Gdns, SE6. . . . . 205 EB91
Melford Av, Bark. IG11 . . . . . . 167 ES65
Melford Cl, Chess. KT9. . . . . . 238 CM106
Melford Rd, E6 . . . . 25 J4
E11 . . . . 146 EE61
E17 . . . . 145 DY56
SE22. . . . . 204 DU87
Ilford IG1 . . . . 147 ER61
Melfort Av, Th.Hth. CR7 . . . . . 223 DP97
Melfort Rd, Th.Hth. CR7 . . . . . 223 DP97
Melgund Rd, N5 . . . . 8 F3
Melia Cl, Wat. WD25. . . . . 98 BW35
Melina Cl, Hayes UB3. . . . . 157 BR71
Melina Pl, NW8. . . . . 16 A3
Melina Rd, W12. . . . . 181 CV75
Melings, The, Hem.H. HP2 . . . . . 63 BP15
Melior Pl, SE1 . . . . 31 N4
Melior St, SE1. . . . . 31 M4
Meliot Rd, SE6 . . . . 205 ED89
Melksham Cl, Rom. RM3 . . . . . 128 FL52
Melksham Dr, Rom. RM3
off Melksham Gdns 128 FM52
Melksham Gdns, Rom. RM3 . . 128 FL52
Melksham Grn, Rom. RM3
off Melksham Gdns 128 FM52
Meller Cl, Croy. CR0 . . . . 223 DL104
Mellersh Hill Rd, Won. GU5. . . 281 BB144
Mellifont Cl, Cars. SM5 . . . . . . 222 DD101
Melling Dr, Enf. EN1 . . . . 104 DU39
Melling St, SE18. . . . . 187 ES79
Mellish Cl, Bark. IG11 . . . . 167 ET67
Mellish Gdns, Wdf.Grn. IG8. . . 124 EG50
● Mellish Ind Est, SE18. . . . . . . 36 F6
Mellish St, E14 . . . . 34 A6
Mellish Way, Horn. RM11 . . . . 150 FJ57
Mellison Rd, SW17. . . . . 202 DE92
Melliss Av, Rich. TW9 . . . . 180 CP81
Mellitus St, W12 . . . . 161 CT72
Mellor Cl, Walt. KT12 . . . . 218 BZ101
Mellor Wk, Wind. SL4 . . . . 173 AR81
Mellow Cl, Bans. SM7 . . . . 240 DB114
Mellow La E, Hayes UB4 . . . . . 157 BQ69
Sch Mellow La Sch, Hayes End
UB4 off Hewens Rd 157 BQ70
Mellow La W, Uxb. UB10 . . . . . 157 BQ69
Mellows Rd, Ilf. IG5 . . . . 147 EM55
Wallington SM6 . . . . 241 DK106
Mells Cres, SE9. . . . . 207 EM91
Mell St, SE10. . . . . 47 J1
Melody La, N5. . . . . 9 H2
Melody Rd, SW18. . . . . 202 DC85
Biggin Hill TN16 . . . . 260 EJ118
Melon Pl, W8. . . . . 27 L4
Melon Rd, E11 . . . . 146 EE62
SE15. 44 C6
Melrose Av, N22 . . . . 121 DP53
NW2. . . . . 4 B2
SW16 . . . . 223 DM97
SW19 . . . . 202 DA89
Borehamwood WD6 . . . . 100 CP43
Dartford DA1 . . . . 209 FE87
Greenford UB6 . . . . 158 CB68
Mitcham CR4. . . . . 203 DH94
Potters Bar EN6. . . . . 86 DB32
Twickenham TW2 . . . . 198 CB87
Melrose Cl, SE12. . . . . 206 EG88
Greenford UB6 . . . . 158 CB68
Hayes UB4. . . . . 157 BU71
Melrose Ct, W13
off Williams Rd 159 CG74
Melrose Cres, Orp. BR6 . . . . . . 245 ER105
Melrose Dr, Sthl. UB1. . . . . 158 CA74
Melrose Gdns, W6. . . . . 26 B6
Edgware HA8. . . . . 118 CP54
Hersham KT12 . . . . 236 BW106
New Malden KT3 . . . . 220 CR97
Melrose Pl, Wat. WD17. . . . . 97 BT38
Melrose Rd, SW13 . . . . 181 CT82
SW18 . . . . 201 CZ86
SW19 . . . . 222 DA96
W3 off Stanley Rd. 180 CQ76
Biggin Hill TN16 . . . . 260 EJ116
Coulsdon CR5 . . . . 257 DH115

Melrose Rd, Pnr. HA5 . . . 138 BZ56
Weybridge KT13 . . . 234 BN106
Sch Melrose Sch, Mitch. CR4 off Church Rd . . . 222 DE97
Melrose Ter, W6 . . . 26 B5
Melsa Rd, Mord. SM4 . . . 222 DC100
Melsted Rd, Hem.H. HP1 . . . 62 BH20
Melstock Av, Upmin. RM14 . . . 150 FQ63
Melthorne Dr, Ruis. HA4 . . . 138 BW62
Melthorpe Gdns, SE3 . . . 186 EL81
Melton Cl, Ruis. HA4 . . . 138 BW60
Melton Ct, SW7 . . . 28 B9
Sutton SM2 . . . 240 DC108
Melton Flds, Epsom KT19 . . . 238 CR109
Melton Gdns, Rom. RM1 . . . 149 FF59
Melton Pl, Epsom KT19 . . . 238 CR109
Melton Rd, S.Merst. RH1 . . . 273 DJ130
Melton St, NW1 . . . 17 M3
Melville Av, SW20 . . . 201 CU94
Greenford UB6 . . . 139 CF64
South Croydon CR2 . . . 242 DT106
Melville Cl, Uxb. UB10 . . . 137 BR62
Melville Ct, W12 off Goldhawk Rd . . . 181 CV76
Melville Gdns, N13 . . . 121 DP50
Melville Pl, N1 . . . 9 J7
Melville Rd, E17 . . . 145 DZ55
NW10 . . . 160 CR66
SW13 . . . 181 CU81
Rainham RM13 . . . 169 FG70
Romford RM5 . . . 127 FB52
Sidcup DA14 . . . 208 EW89
Melville Vil Rd, W3 off High St . . . 160 CR74
Melvin Rd, SE20 . . . 224 DW95
Melvinshaw, Lthd. KT22 . . . 253 CJ121
Melvyn Cl, Goffs Oak EN7 . . . 87 DP28
Melwas Ct, N9 off Galahad Rd . . . 122 DU48
Melyn Cl, N7 . . . 7 M1
Memel Ct, EC1 . . . 19 J5
Memel St, EC1 . . . 19 J5
Memess Path, SE18 . . . 187 EN79
Memorial Av, E15 . . . 23 J2
Memorial Cl, Houns. TW5 . . . 178 BZ79
Oxted RH8 . . . 275 ED127
Memorial Hts, Ilf. IG2 . . . 147 ER58
H Memorial Hosp, SE18 . . . 187 EN82
Menai Pl, E3 . . . 12 A10
Mendip Cl, SE26 . . . 204 DW91
Harlington UB3 . . . 177 BR80
St. Albans AL4 . . . 65 CJ15
Slough SL3 . . . 175 BA78
Worcester Park KT4 . . . 221 CW102
Mendip Dr, NW2 . . . 141 CX61
Mendip Ho, N9 off Edmonton Grn Shop Cen . . . 122 DU47
Mendip Hos, E2 . . . 21 H2
Mendip Rd, SW11 . . . 182 DC83
Bexleyheath DA7 . . . 189 FE81
Bushey WD23 . . . 98 CC44
Hornchurch RM11 . . . 149 FG59
Ilford IG2 . . . 147 ES57
Mendip Way, Hem.H. HP2 . . . 62 BL17
Mendlesham, Welw.G.C. AL7 . . . 52 DE09
Mendora Rd, SW6 . . . 38 F4
Mendoza Cl, Horn. RM11 . . . 150 FL57
Menelik Rd, NW2 . . . 4 F2
★ Menier Chocolate Factory, SE1 off Southwark St . . . 31 K3
Menlo Gdns, SE19 . . . 204 DR94
Menon Dr, N9 . . . 122 DV48
Sch Menorah Foundation Sch, Edg. HA8 off Abbots Rd . . . 118 CQ52
Sch Menorah Gram Sch, Edg. HA8 off Abbots Rd . . . 118 CQ52
Sch Menorah Prim Sch, NW11 off Woodstock Av . . . 141 CY59
Menotti St, E2 . . . 20 D4
Menthone Pl, Horn. RM11 . . . 150 FK59
Mentmore Cl, Har. HA3 . . . 139 CJ58
Mentmore Rd, St.Alb. AL1 . . . 65 CD22
Mentmore Ter, E8 . . . 10 F7
Meon Cl, Tad. KT20 . . . 255 CV122
Meon Ct, Islw. TW7 . . . 179 CE82
Meon Rd, W3 . . . 180 CQ75
Meopham Rd, Mitch. CR4 . . . 223 DJ95
Mepham Cres, Har. HA3 . . . 116 CC52
Mepham Gdns, Har. HA3 . . . 116 CC52
Mepham St, SE1 . . . 30 D3
Mera Dr, Bexh. DA7 . . . 188 FA84
Merantun Way, SW19 . . . 222 DC95
Merbury Cl, SE13 . . . 205 EC85
SE28 . . . 167 ER74
Merbury Rd, SE28 . . . 187 ES75
Mercator Pl, E14 . . . 34 B10
Mercator Rd, SE13 . . . 185 ED84
Mercer Cl, T.Ditt. KT7 . . . 219 CF101
Merceron Hos, E2 off Globe Rd . . . 20 G2
Merceron St, E1 . . . 20 E5
Mercer Pl, Pnr. HA5 . . . 116 BW54
Mercers, Harl. CM19 . . . 73 EN18
Hemel Hempstead HP2 . . . 62 BL18
Mercers Cl, SE10 . . . 35 L9
Mercers Ms, N19 . . . 143 DK62
Mercers Pl, W6 . . . 26 B8
Mercers Rd, N19 . . . 143 DK62
Mercers Row, St.Alb. AL1 . . . 64 CC22
Mercer St, WC2 . . . 18 A9
Mercer Wk, Uxb. UB8 off The Pavilions . . . 156 BJ66
Merchant Dr, Hert. SG13 . . . 54 DT08
Merchants Cl, SE25 off Clifford Rd . . . 224 DU98
Merchants Ho, SE10 off Collington St . . . 47 H1
Merchants Row, SE10 off Hoskins St . . . 47 H1
Merchant St, E3 . . . 21 P3
Sch Merchant Taylors' Sch, Nthwd. HA6 off Sandy Lo La . . . 115 BS46
Merchiston Rd, SE6 . . . 205 ED89
Merchland Rd, SE9 . . . 207 EQ88
Mercia Gro, SE13 . . . 185 EC84
Mercian Way, Slou. SL1 . . . 153 AK74
Mercia Wk, Wok. GU21 off Commercial Way . . . 249 AZ117
Mercier Rd, SW15 . . . 201 CY85
● Mercury Cen, Felt. TW14 . . . 197 BU85
Mercury Gdns, Rom. RM1 . . . 149 FE56
Mercury Ho, E3 off Garrison Rd . . . 12 A9
● Mercury Pk, Woob.Grn HP10 . . . 132 AE56
Mercury Wk, Hem.H. HP2 . . . 62 BM17
Mercury Way, SE14 . . . 45 J2
Mercy Ter, SE13 . . . 185 EB84
Merebank La, Croy. CR0 . . . 241 DM106
Mere Cl, SW15 . . . 201 CX87
Orpington BR6 . . . 227 EP103
Meredith Av, NW2 . . . 4 B2
Meredith Cl, Pnr. HA5 . . . 116 BX52
Meredith Ms, SE4 . . . 185 DZ84
Meredith Rd, Grays RM16 . . . 193 GG77
Meredith St, E13 . . . 23 P3
EC1 . . . 18 G3
Meredyth Rd, SW13 . . . 181 CU82
Mere End, Croy. CR0 . . . 225 DX101
Merefield, Saw. CM21 . . . 58 EY06
Merefield Gdns, Tad. KT20 . . . 255 CX119
Mere Rd, Shep. TW17 . . . 217 BP100
Slough SL1 . . . 174 AT76
Tadworth KT20 . . . 255 CV124
Weybridge KT13 . . . 217 BR104
Mereside, Orp. BR6 . . . 227 EN103
Mereside Pl, Vir.W. GU25 . . . 214 AX100
Meretone Cl, SE4 . . . 185 DY84
Mereton Mans, SE8 . . . 46 B6
Merevale Cres, Mord. SM4 . . . 222 DC100
Mereway Rd, Twick. TW2 . . . 199 CD88
Merewood Cl, Brom. BR1 . . . 227 EN96
Merewood Gdns, Croy. CR0 . . . 225 DX101
Merewood Rd, Bexh. DA7 . . . 189 FC82
Mereworth Cl, Brom. BR2 . . . 226 EF99
Mereworth Dr, SE18 . . . 187 EP80
Merganser Gdns, SE28 off Avocet Ms . . . 187 ER76
MERIDEN, Wat. WD25 . . . 98 BY35
Meriden Cl, Brom. BR1 . . . 206 EK94
Ilford IG6 . . . 125 EQ53
Meriden Way, Wat. WD25 . . . 98 BY36
● Meridian Business Pk, Enf. EN3 . . . 105 DY44
Waltham Abbey EN9 . . . 105 EB35
Meridian Cl, NW7 . . . 118 CR49
Meridian Ct, SE16 off East La . . . 32 C4
Meridian Gate, E14 . . . 34 E4
Meridian Gro, Horl. RH6 . . . 291 DJ147
Meridian Pl, E14 . . . 34 D4
Sch Meridian Prim Sch, SE10 . . . 47 H1
Meridian Rd, SE7 . . . 186 EK80
Meridian Sq, E15 . . . 12 G6
● Meridian Trd Est, SE7 . . . 36 B8
Meridian Wk, N17 off Commercial Rd . . . 122 DS51
Meridian Way, N9 . . . 122 DW50
N18 . . . 122 DW51
Enfield EN3 . . . 105 DX44
Stanstead Abbotts SG12 . . . 55 EB10
Waltham Abbey EN9 . . . 105 EB35
Meriel Wk, Green. DA9 off The Avenue . . . 191 FV84
Merifield Rd, SE9 . . . 186 EJ84
Merino Cl, E11 . . . 146 EJ56
Merino Pl, Sid. DA15 off Blackfen Rd . . . 208 EU86
Merivale Rd, SW15 . . . 181 CY84
Harrow HA1 . . . 138 CC59
Merland Cl, Tad. KT20 . . . 255 CW120
Merland Grn, Tad. KT20 . . . 255 CW120
Merland Ri, Epsom KT18 . . . 255 CW119
Tadworth KT20 . . . 255 CW119
Sch Merland Ri Comm Prim Sch, Epsom KT18 off Merland Ri . . . 255 CW119
Merle Av, Hare. UB9 . . . 114 BH54
Merlewood, Sev. TN13 . . . 279 FH123
Merlewood Cl, Cat. CR3 . . . 258 DR120
Merlewood Dr, Chis. BR7 . . . 227 EM95
Merley Ct, NW9 . . . 140 CQ60
Merlin Cl, Chaff.Hun. RM16 . . . 192 FY76
Croydon CR0 . . . 242 DS105
Ilford IG6 . . . 126 EW50
Mitcham CR4 . . . 222 DE97
Northolt UB5 . . . 158 BW69
Romford RM5 . . . 127 FD51
Slough SL3 . . . 175 BB79
Wallington SM6 . . . 241 DM107
Waltham Abbey EN9 . . . 90 EG34
Merlin Ct, Brom. BR2 off Durham Av . . . 226 EF98
Woking GU21 off Blackmore Cres . . . 233 BC114
Merlin Cres, Edg. HA8 . . . 118 CM53
Merlin Gdns, Brom. BR1 . . . 206 EG90
Romford RM5 . . . 127 FD51
Merling Cl, Chess. KT9 off Coppard Gdns . . . 237 CK106
Merling Cft, Nthch HP4 . . . 60 AS17
Merlin Gro, Beck. BR3 . . . 225 DZ98
Ilford IG6 . . . 125 EP52
Merlin Ho, Enf. EN3 off Allington Ct . . . 105 DX43
Sch Merlin Prim Sch, Downham BR1 off Ballamore Rd . . . 206 EG90
Merlin Rd, E12 . . . 146 EJ61
Romford RM5 . . . 127 FD51
Welling DA16 . . . 188 EU84
Merlin Rd N, Well. DA16 . . . 188 EU84
Merlins Av, Har. HA2 . . . 138 BZ62
Sch Merlin Sch, SW15 off Carlton Dr . . . 201 CX85
Merlin St, WC1 . . . 18 E3
Merlin Way, Lvsdn WD25 . . . 81 BT34
North Weald Bassett CM16 . . . 92 FA27
Merlot Ms, St.Alb. AL3 . . . 65 CD16
Mermagen Dr, Rain. RM13 . . . 169 FH66
Mermaid Cl, Grav. DA11 . . . 212 GD87
Mermaid Ct, SE1 . . . 31 L4
SE16 . . . 33 N3
Mermaid Twr, SE8 . . . 45 N3
Mermerus Gdns, Grav. DA12 . . . 213 GM91
Merredene St, SW2 . . . 203 DM86
Merriam Av, E9 . . . 11 P4
Merriam Cl, E4 . . . 123 EC50
Merrick Rd, Sthl. UB2 . . . 178 BZ75
Merrick Sq, SE1 . . . 31 K6
Merridale, SE12 . . . 206 EG85
Merridene, N21 . . . 103 DP44
Merrielands Cres, Dag. RM9 . . . 168 EZ67
Merrifield Ct, Welw.G.C. AL7 . . . 51 CX12
Merrilands Rd, Wor.Pk. KT4 . . . 221 CW102
Merrilees Rd, Sid. DA15 . . . 207 ES88
Merrilyn Cl, Clay. KT10 . . . 237 CG107
Merriman Rd, SE3 . . . 186 EJ81
Merrington Rd, SW6 . . . 39 K2
Merrin Hill, S.Croy. CR2 . . . 242 DS111
Merrion Av, Stan. HA7 . . . 117 CK50
Merritt Gdns, Chess. KT9 . . . 237 CJ107
Merritt Rd, SE4 . . . 205 DZ85
Merritt Wk, N.Mymms AL9 . . . 67 CV23
Merrivale, N14 . . . 103 DK44
Merrivale Av, Ilf. IG4 . . . 146 EK56
Merrivale Gdns, Wok. GU21 . . . 248 AW117
MERROW, Guil. GU1 . . . 265 BB133
● Merrow Business Cen, Guil. GU4 . . . 265 BD131
Merrow Chase, Guil. GU1 . . . 265 BC134
Sch Merrow C of E Inf Sch, Guil. GU4 off Kingfisher Dr . . . 265 BD132
Merrow Common Rd, Guil. GU4 . . . 265 BC131
Merrow Copse, Guil. GU1 . . . 265 BB133
Merrow Ct, Guil. GU1 . . . 265 BD134
Merrow Cft, Guil. GU1 . . . 265 BC133
Merrow Downs, Guil. GU1 . . . 281 BD135
Merrow Dr, Hem.H. HP1 . . . 61 BE19
● Merrow Ind Est, Guil. GU4 . . . 265 BD131
Merrow La, Guil. GU4 . . . 265 BC129
Merrow Pl, Guil. GU4 . . . 265 BD132
Merrow Rd, Sutt. SM2 . . . 239 CX109
Merrows Cl, Nthwd. HA6 off Rickmansworth Rd . . . 115 BQ51
Merrow St, SE17 . . . 43 L2
Guildford GU4 . . . 265 BD132
Merrow Wk, SE17 . . . 31 M10
Merrow Way, Guil. GU1 . . . 265 BD133
New Addington CR0 . . . 243 EC107
Merrow Wds, Guil. GU1 . . . 265 BB132
Merrydown Way, Chis. BR7 . . . 226 EL95
Merryfield, SE3 . . . 47 M9
Merryfield Gdns, Stan. HA7 . . . 117 CJ50
Merryfield Ho, SE9 off Grove Pk Rd . . . 206 EJ90
Merryfields, St.Alb. AL4 off Firwood Av . . . 66 CL20
Uxbridge UB8 . . . 156 BK68
Merryfields Way, SE6 . . . 205 EB87
MERRY HILL, Bushey WD23 . . . 116 CA46
Merryhill Cl, E4 . . . 123 EB45
Sch Merry Hill Inf Sch & Nurs, Bushey WD23 off School La . . . 116 CB45
Merry Hill Mt, Bushey WD23 . . . 116 CB46
Merry Hill Rd, Bushey WD23 . . . 116 CB46
Merryhills Cl, Bigg.H. TN16 . . . 260 EK116
Merryhills Ct, N14 . . . 103 DJ43
Merryhills Dr, Enf. EN2 . . . 103 DK42
Sch Merryhills Prim Sch, Enf. EN2 off Bincote Rd . . . 103 DM41
Merrylands, Cher. KT16 . . . 215 BE104
Merrylands Rd, Bkhm KT23 . . . 252 BZ123
Merrymeade Chase, Brwd. CM15 . . . 130 FX46
Merrymeet, Bans. SM7 . . . 240 DF114
Merryweather Cl, Dart. DA1 . . . 210 FM86
Merryweather Ct, N.Mal. KT3 off Rodney Cl . . . 220 CS99
Merrywood Gro, Lwr Kgswd KT20 . . . 271 CX130
Merrywood Pk, Box H. KT20 . . . 270 CP130
Reigate RH2 . . . 272 DB132
Mersea Ho, Bark. IG11 . . . 167 EP65
Mersey Av, Upmin. RM14 . . . 151 FR58
Mersey Pl, Hem.H. HP2 off Colne Way . . . 62 BM15
Mersey Rd, E17 . . . 145 DZ55
Mersey Wk, Nthlt. UB5 off Brabazon Rd . . . 158 CA68
Mersham Dr, NW9 . . . 140 CN57
Mersham Pl, SE20 . . . 224 DV95
Mersham Rd, Th.Hth. CR7 . . . 224 DR97
MERSTHAM, Red. RH1 . . . 273 DJ128
⇌ Merstham . . . 273 DJ128
Sch Merstham Prim Sch, Merst. RH1 off London Rd S . . . 273 DJ129
Merstham Rd, Red. RH1 . . . 273 DN129
Merten Rd, Rom. RM6 . . . 148 EY59
Merthyr Ter, SW13 . . . 181 CV79
MERTON, SW19 . . . 222 DA95
Merton Abbey Mills, SW19 off Watermill Way . . . 222 DC95
Sch Merton Abbey Prim Sch, SW19 off High Path . . . 222 DB95
Coll Merton Adult Ed, SW20 off Whatley Av . . . 221 CY97
Merton Av, W4 . . . 181 CT77
Northolt UB5 . . . 138 CC64
Uxbridge UB10 . . . 157 BP66
Coll Merton Coll, Mord. SM4 off London Rd . . . 222 DA99
Merton Ct, Ilf. IG1 off Castleview Gdns . . . 146 EL58
Sch Merton Ct Sch, Sid. DA14 off Knoll Rd . . . 208 EW91
Merton Gdns, Petts Wd BR5 . . . 227 EP99
Tadworth KT20 . . . 255 CX119
Merton Hall Gdns, SW20 . . . 221 CY95
Merton Hall Rd, SW19 . . . 221 CY95
Merton High St, SW19 . . . 202 DB94
● Merton Ind Pk, SW19 . . . 222 DC95
Merton La, N6 . . . 142 DF61
Merton Mans, SW20 . . . 221 CX96
MERTON PARK, SW19 . . . 222 DA96
Tram Merton Park . . . 222 DA95
Merton Pk Par, SW19 off Kingston Rd . . . 221 CZ95
Sch Merton Pk Prim Sch, SW19 off Church La . . . 222 DA96
Merton Pl, Grays RM16 . . . 193 GG77
Merton Ri, NW3 . . . 6 D7
Merton Rd, E17 . . . 145 EC57
SE25 . . . 224 DU99
SW18 . . . 202 DA85
SW19 . . . 202 DB94
Barking IG11 . . . 167 ET66
Enfield EN2 . . . 104 DR38
Harrow HA2 . . . 138 CC60
Ilford IG3 . . . 147 ET59
Slough SL1 . . . 174 AU76
Watford WD18 . . . 97 BV42
Merton Wk, Lthd. KT22 . . . 253 CG118
Merton Way, Lthd. KT22 . . . 253 CG119
Uxbridge UB10 . . . 157 BP66
West Molesey KT8 . . . 218 CB98
Merttins Rd, SE15 . . . 205 DX85
Meru Cl, NW5 . . . 7 H2
Mervan Rd, SW2 . . . 183 DN84
Mervyn Av, SE9 . . . 207 EQ90
Mervyn Rd, W13 . . . 179 CG76
Shepperton TW17 . . . 217 BQ101
Merwin Way, Wind. SL4 . . . 173 AK83
Meryfield Cl, Borwd. WD6 . . . 100 CM40
Sch Meryfield Comm Prim Sch, Borwd. WD6 off Theobald St . . . 100 CM39
Mesne Way, Shore. TN14 . . . 247 FF112
Messaline Av, W3 . . . 160 CQ72
Messant Cl, Harold Wd RM3 . . . 128 FK54
Messent Rd, SE9 . . . 206 EJ85
Messeter Pl, SE9 . . . 207 EN86
Messina Av, NW6 . . . 5 J7
Metcalfe Ct, SE10 . . . 35 M6
Metcalf Rd, Ashf. TW15 . . . 197 BP92
Metcalf Wk, Felt. TW13 off Cresswell Rd . . . 198 BY91
Meteor St, SW11 . . . 182 DG84
Meteor Way, Wall. SM6 . . . 241 DL108
Metford Cres, Enf. EN3 . . . 105 EA38
Methley St, SE11 . . . 42 F1
★ Methodist Cen Hall, SW1 . . . 29 P5
Methuen Cl, Edg. HA8 . . . 118 CN52
Methuen Pk, N10 . . . 121 DH54
Methuen Rd, Belv. DA17 . . . 189 FB77
Bexleyheath DA6 . . . 188 EZ84
Edgware HA8 . . . 118 CN52
Methven Ct, N9 off The Broadway . . . 122 DU48
Methwold Rd, W10 . . . 14 C6
Metro Apts, The, Wok. GU21 off Goldsworth Rd . . . 248 AY117
● Metro Business Cen, SE26 . . . 205 DZ92
Metro Cen Hts, SE1 . . . 31 J7
● Metro Cen, St.Alb. AL4 . . . 65 CF16
● Metro Ind Cen, Islw. TW7 . . . 179 CE82
Metropolis Cen, Borwd. WD6 . . . 100 CN41
● Metropolitan Cen, The, Grnf. UB6 . . . 158 CB67
Metropolitan Cl, E14 . . . 22 B7
Metropolitan Ho, Pot.B. EN6 . . . 86 DA32
Metropolitan Ms, Wat. WD18 . . . 97 BS42
Coll Metropolitan Pol Cadet Training Cen, Loug. IG10 off Lippitts Hill . . . 106 EF40
Coll Metropolitan Pol Mounted Branch Training Sch, E.Mol. KT8 off Ember La . . . 219 CD100
Metropolitan Sta App, Wat. WD18 . . . 97 BT41
Meux Cl, Chsht EN7 . . . 88 DU31
Mews, The, N1 . . . 9 K8
N8 off Turnpike La . . . 143 DN55
Grays RM17 . . . 192 GC77
Guildford GU1 off Walnut Tree Cl . . . 280 AW135
Harlow CM18 off Lodge Hall . . . 73 ES19
Ilford IG4 . . . 146 EK57
Romford RM1 off Market Link . . . 149 FE56
Sevenoaks TN13 . . . 278 FG123
Twickenham TW1 off Bridge Rd . . . 199 CH86
Mews Deck, E1 . . . 32 F1
Mews End, Bigg.H. TN16 . . . 260 EK118
Mews Pl, Wdf.Grn. IG8 . . . 124 EG49
Mews St, E1 . . . 32 C2
Mexfield Rd, SW15 . . . 201 CZ85
Meyer Grn, Enf. EN1 . . . 104 DU38
Meyer Rd, Erith DA8 . . . 189 FC79
Meymott St, SE1 . . . 30 G3
Meynell Cres, E9 . . . 11 J6
Meynell Gdns, E9 . . . 11 J6
Meynell Rd, E9 . . . 11 J6
Romford RM3 . . . 127 FH52
Meyrick Cl, Knap. GU21 . . . 248 AS116
Meyrick Rd, NW10 . . . 161 CU65
SW11 . . . 40 B10
Mezen Cl, Nthwd. HA6 . . . 115 BR50
★ MI5 (Security Service) Thames Ho, SW1 . . . 30 A8
Miah Ter, E1 . . . 32 D3
Miall Wk, SE26 . . . 205 DY91
Micawber Av, Uxb. UB8 . . . 156 BN70
Micawber St, N1 . . . 19 K2
Michael Cliffe Ho, EC1 . . . 18 F3
Michael Cres, Horl. RH6 . . . 290 DG150
Michael Faraday Ho, SE17 . . . 43 M1
Sch Michael Faraday Prim Sch, SE17 . . . 43 M2
Michael Gdns, Grav. DA12 . . . 213 GL92
Hornchurch RM11 . . . 150 FK56
Michael Gaynor Cl, W7 . . . 159 CF74
Michael La, Guil. GU2 . . . 264 AV129
Michaelmas Cl, SW20 . . . 221 CW97
Coll Michael Reid Ministries - Peniel Coll, Pilg.Hat. CM14 off Coxtie Grn Rd . . . 130 FS43
Michael Rd, E11 . . . 146 EE60
SE25 . . . 224 DS97
SW6 . . . 39 M6
Michaels Cl, SE13 . . . 186 EE84
Michaels La, Ash TN15 . . . 231 FV103
Fawkham Green DA3 . . . 231 FV103
Sch Michael Sobell Sinai Sch, Har. HA3 off Shakespeare Dr . . . 140 CN58
Michael Stewart Ho, SW6 off Clem Attlee Ct . . . 39 H3
Sch Michael Tippett Sch, SE24 off Heron Rd . . . 184 DQ84
Micheldever Rd, SE12 . . . 206 EE86
Michelham Gdns, Tad. KT20 off Waterfield . . . 255 CW120
Twickenham TW1 . . . 199 CF90
Michels Row, Rich. TW9 off Kew Foot Rd . . . 180 CL84
Michel Wk, SE18 . . . 187 EP78
Michigan Av, E12 . . . 146 EL63
Michigan Bldg, E14 . . . 34 F1
Michigan Cl, Brox. EN10 . . . 89 DY26
Michleham Down, N12 . . . 119 CZ49
Micholls Av, Ger.Cr. SL9 . . . 112 AY49
Micklefield Rd, Hem.H. HP2 . . . 63 BQ20
Sch Micklefield Sch, Reig. RH2 off Somers Rd . . . 272 DA133
Micklefield Way, Borwd. WD6 . . . 100 CL38
MICKLEHAM, Dor. RH5 . . . 269 CJ128
Mickleham Bypass, Mick. RH5 . . . 269 CH127
Mickleham Cl, Orp. BR5 . . . 227 ET96
Mickleham Downs, Mick. RH5 . . . 269 CK127
Mickleham Dr, Lthd. KT22 . . . 269 CJ126
Mickleham Gdns, Sutt. SM3 . . . 239 CY107
Mickleham Rd, Orp. BR5 . . . 227 ET95
Mickleham Way, New Adgtn CR0 . . . 243 ED108
Micklem Dr, Hem.H. HP1 . . . 61 BF19
Sch Micklem Prim Sch, Hem.H. HP1 off Boxted Rd . . . 62 BG19
Micklethwaite Rd, SW6 . . . 39 K3
● Midas Ind Est, Cowley UB8 . . . 156 BH68
Midcot Way, Berk. HP4 . . . 60 AT17
Midcroft, Ruis. HA4 . . . 137 BS60
Slough SL2 . . . 153 AP70
Mid Cross La, Chal.St.P. SL9 . . . 112 AY50
Middle Boy, Abridge RM4 . . . 108 EW41
Middle Cl, Amer. HP6 . . . 94 AT37
Coulsdon CR5 . . . 257 DN120
Epsom KT17 off Middle La . . . 238 CS112
Middle Cres, Denh. UB9 . . . 135 BD59
Middle Dartrey Wk, SW10 off Blantyre St . . . 40 A4
Middle Dene, NW7 . . . 118 CR48
Middledown, Ald. WD25 . . . 98 CB36
Middle Dr, Beac. HP9 . . . 111 AK50
Middle Fm Cl, Eff. KT24 . . . 268 BX127
Middle Fm Pl, Eff. KT24 . . . 268 BW127
Middle Fld, NW8 . . . 6 A8
Middlefield, Hat. AL10 . . . 67 CU17
Horley RH6 . . . 291 DJ147
Welwyn Garden City AL7 . . . 51 CY13
Middlefield Av, Hodd. EN11 . . . 71 EA15
Middlefield Cl, Hodd. EN11 . . . 71 EA15
St. Albans AL4 . . . 65 CJ17
Middlefielde, W13 . . . 159 CH71
Middlefield Gdns, Ilf. IG2 . . . 147 EP58
Middlefield Rd, Hodd. EN11 . . . 71 EA15
Middlefields, Croy. CR0 . . . 243 DY109
Middle Furlong, Bushey WD23 . . . 98 CB42
Middle Gorse, Croy. CR0 . . . 243 DY112
MIDDLE GREEN, Slou. SL3 . . . 154 AY73
Middle Grn, Brock. RH3 . . . 286 CP136
Slough SL3 . . . 154 AY74
Staines TW18 . . . 196 BK94
Middle Grn Cl, Surb. KT5 off Alpha Rd . . . 220 CM100
Middle Grn Rd, Slou. SL3 . . . 174 AX75
Middleham Gdns, N18 . . . 122 DU51
Middleham Rd, N18 . . . 122 DU51
Middle Hill, Egh. TW20 . . . 194 AW91
Hemel Hempstead HP1 . . . 61 BE20
Middleknights Hill, Hem.H. HP1 . . . 62 BG17
Middle La, N8 . . . 143 DL57
Bovingdon HP3 . . . 79 BA29
Epsom KT17 . . . 238 CS112
Seal TN15 off Church Rd . . . 279 FM121
Teddington TW11 . . . 199 CF93
Middle La Ms, N8 off Middle La . . . 143 DL57
Middlemead Cl, Bkhm KT23 . . . 268 CA125
Middle Meadow, Ch.St.G. HP8 . . . 112 AW48
Middlemead Rd, Bkhm KT23 . . . 268 BZ125
Middle Ope, Wat. WD24 . . . 97 BV37
Middle Pk Av, SE9 . . . 206 EK86
Sch Middle Pk Prim Sch, SE9 off Middle Pk Av . . . 206 EK87
Middle Path, Har. HA2 off Middle Rd . . . 139 CD60
Middle Rd, E13 . . . 23 N1
SW16 . . . 223 DK96
Berkhamsted HP4 . . . 60 AV19
Denham UB9 . . . 135 BC59
East Barnet EN4 . . . 102 DE44
Harrow HA2 . . . 139 CD61
Ingrave CM13 . . . 131 GC50
Leatherhead KT22 . . . 253 CH121
Waltham Abbey EN9 . . . 89 EB32
Middle Row, W10 . . . 14 E5
Sch Middle Row Prim Sch, W10 . . . 14 E4
Middlesborough Rd, N18 . . . 122 DU51
● Middlesex Business Cen, Sthl. UB2 . . . 178 BZ75
Middlesex Cl, Sthl. UB1 . . . 158 CB70
Middlesex Ct, W4 . . . 181 CT78
Addlestone KT15 off Garfield Rd . . . 234 BJ105
Middlesex Ho, Wem. HA0 . . . 159 CK67
Middlesex Pas, EC1 . . . 19 H7
Middlesex Rd, Mitch. CR4 . . . 223 DL99
Middlesex St, E1 . . . 19 P7
Uni Middlesex Uni, Cat Hill Campus, Barn. EN4 off Cat Hill . . . 102 DG43
Hendon Campus, NW4 off The Burroughs . . . 141 CV56
New Southgate Campus, N11 off Oakleigh Rd S . . . 120 DG48
Trent Pk Campus, N14 off Bramley Rd . . . 103 DJ40
Middlesex Wf, E5 . . . 144 DW61
Middle St, EC1 . . . 19 J6
Betchworth RH3 . . . 286 CP136
Croydon CR0 off Surrey St . . . 224 DQ103
Lower Nazeing EN9 . . . 72 EG23
Shere GU5 . . . 282 BN139
Middle Temple, EC4 . . . 18 E10
Middle Temple La, EC4 . . . 18 E9
Middleton Av, E4 . . . 123 DZ49
Greenford UB6 . . . 159 CD68
Sidcup DA14 . . . 208 EW93
Middleton Cl, E4 . . . 123 DZ48
Middleton Dr, SE16 . . . 33 K5
Pinner HA5 . . . 137 BU55
Middleton Gdns, Ilf. IG2 . . . 147 EP58
Middleton Gro, N7 . . . 8 A2
Middleton Hall La, Brwd. CM15 . . . 130 FY47
Middleton Ms, N7 . . . 8 A2
Middleton Pl, W1 . . . 17 L7
Middleton Rd, E8 . . . 10 B7
NW11 . . . 142 DA59
Carshalton SM5 . . . 222 DE101
Downside KT11 . . . 251 BV119
Epsom KT19 . . . 238 CR110
Hayes UB3 . . . 157 BR71
Mill End WD3 . . . 114 BG46
Morden SM4 . . . 222 DC100
Shenfield CM15 . . . 130 FY46
Middleton St, E2 . . . 20 E2
Middleton Way, SE13 . . . 185 ED84
Middle Wk, Burn. SL1 . . . 152 AH69
Woking GU21 off Commercial Way . . . 248 AY117
Middleway, NW11 . . . 142 DB57
Middle Way, SW16 . . . 223 DK96
Erith DA18 . . . 188 EY76
Hayes UB4 . . . 158 BW70
Watford WD24 . . . 97 BV37
Middle Way, The, Har. HA3 . . . 117 CF54
Middle Yd, SE1 . . . 31 M2
Middlings, The, Sev. TN13 . . . 278 FF125
Middlings Ri, Sev. TN13 . . . 278 FF126
Middlings Wd, Sev. TN13 . . . 278 FF125
Coll Mid Essex Adult Comm Coll, Bishops Hill, Hutt. CM13 off Rayleigh Rd . . . 131 GB44
Warley Cen, Warley CM13 off Essex Way . . . 129 FW51
Midfield Av, Bexh. DA7 . . . 189 FC83
Swanley BR8 . . . 209 FH93
Midfield Par, Bexh. DA7 . . . 189 FC83

Midfield Prim Sch, St.P.Cray BR5 off Grovelands Rd 208 EU94
Midfield Way, Orp. BR5 228 EV95
Midford Pl, W1 17 M5
Midgarth Cl, Oxshott KT22 236 CC114
Mid Herts Music Cen, Hat. AL10 off Birchwood Av 67 CV16
Midholm, NW11 142 DB56
Wembley HA9 140 CN60
Midholm Cl, NW11 142 DB56
Midholm Rd, Croy. CR0 225 DY103
MID HOLMWOOD, Dor. RH5 285 CJ142
Mid Holmwood La, Mid Holm. RH5 285 CJ142
Midhope Cl, Wok. GU22 248 AY119
Midhope Gdns, Wok. GU22 off Midhope Rd 248 AY119
Midhope Rd, Wok. GU22 248 AY119
Midhope St, WC1 18 B3
Midhurst Av, N10 142 DG55
Croydon CR0 223 DN101
Midhurst Cl, Horn. RM12 149 FG63
Midhurst Gdns, Uxb. UB10 157 BQ66
Midhurst Hill, Bexh. DA6 208 FA86
Midhurst Rd, W13 179 CG75
Midhurst Way, E5 144 DU63
Midland Cres, NW3 5 N4
Midland Pl, E14 34 E10
Midland Rd, E10 145 EC59
NW1 17 P1
Hemel Hempstead HP2 62 BK20
Midland Ter, NW2 141 CX62
NW10 160 CS70
● Midleton Ind Est, Guil. GU2 264 AV133
Midleton Rd, Guil. GU2 264 AV133
New Malden KT3 220 CQ97
Midlothian Rd, E3 21 N5
Midmoor Rd, SW12 203 DJ88
SW19 221 CX95
Midship Cl, SE16 33 K3
Midship Pt, E14 34 A5
Midstrath Rd, NW10 140 CS63
Mid St, S.Nutfld RH1 273 DM134
Midsummer Av, Houns. TW4 178 BZ84
Midsummer Wk, Wok. GU21 248 AX116
Midway, St.Alb. AL3 64 CB23
Sutton SM3 221 CZ101
Walton-on-Thames KT12 217 BV103
Midway Av, Cher. KT16 216 BG97
Egham TW20 215 BB97
Midway Cl, Stai. TW18 196 BH90
Midwinter Cl, Well. DA16 188 EU83
Midwood Cl, NW2 141 CV62
Miena Way, Ashtd. KT21 253 CK117
Miers Cl, E6 167 EN67
Mighell Av, Ilf. IG4 146 EK57
Mike Spring Ct, Grav. DA12 213 GK91
Milan Rd, Sthl. UB1 178 BZ75
Milborne Gro, SW10 39 P1
Milborne St, E9 11 H5
Milborough Cres, SE12 206 EE86
Milbourne La, Esher KT10 236 CC107
Milbourne Lo Jun Sch, Esher KT10 off Milbourne La 236 CC107
Milbourne Lo Sch, Esher KT10 off Arbrook La 237 CD107
Milbrook, Esher KT10 236 CC107
Milburn Dr, West Dr. UB7 156 BL73
Milburn Wk, Epsom KT18 254 CS115
Milcombe Cl, Wok. GU21 off Inglewood 248 AV118
Milcote St, SE1 30 G5
Mildenhall Rd, E5 144 DW63
Slough SL1 154 AS72
Mildmay Av, N1 9 M4
Mildmay Gro N, N1 9 M3
Mildmay Gro S, N1 9 M3
Mildmay Pk, N1 9 M2
Mildmay Pl, N16 9 P3
Shoreham TN14 247 FF111
Mildmay Rd, N1 9 M2
Ilford IG1 off Albert Rd 147 EP62
Romford RM7 149 FC57
Mildmay St, N1 9 M4
Mildred Av, Borwd. WD6 100 CN42
Hayes UB3 177 BR77
Northolt UB5 138 CB64
Watford WD18 97 BT42
Mildred Cl, Dart. DA1 210 FN86
Mildred Rd, Erith DA8 189 FE78
Mile Cl, Wal.Abb. EN9 89 EC33
MILE END, E1 21 L3
⊖ Mile End 21 N4
Mile End, The, E17 123 DX53
MILE END GREEN, Dart. DA2 231 FW96
Mile End Hosp, E1 21 K4
Mile End Pl, E1 21 J4
Mile End Rd, E1 20 F6
E3 20 F6
Mile Ho Cl, St.Alb. AL1 65 CG23
Mile Ho La, St.Alb. AL1 65 CG23
Mile Path, Wok. GU22 248 AV120
Mile Rd, Wall. SM6 222 DG102
Miles Cl, SE28 167 ER74
Harlow CM19 73 EP16
Miles Coverdale Prim Sch, W12 26 A4
Miles Dr, SE28 167 ER74
Miles La, Cob. KT11 236 BY113
Milespit Hill, NW7 119 CV50
Miles Pl, NW1 16 B6
Surbiton KT5 off Villiers Av 220 CM98
Miles Rd, N8 143 DL55
Epsom KT19 238 CR112
Mitcham CR4 222 DE97
Miles St, SW8 42 A3
Milestone Cl, N9 off Chichester Rd 122 DU47
Ripley GU23 250 BG122
Sutton SM2 240 DD107
Milestone Dr, Pur. CR8 241 DM114
Milestone Grn, SW14 180 CQ84
Milestone Rd, SE19 204 DT93
Dartford DA2 210 FP86
Harlow CM17 58 EW13
Miles Way, N20 120 DE47
Milfoil St, W12 161 CU73
Milford Cl, SE2 188 EY79
St. Albans AL4 65 CK16
Milford Gdns, Croy. CR0 off Tannery Cl 225 DX99
Edgware HA8 118 CN52
Wembley HA0 139 CK64
Milford Gro, Sutt. SM1 240 DC105
Milford La, WC2 18 D10
Milford Ms, SW16 203 DM90
Milford Rd, W13 159 CH74
Southall UB1 158 CA73
Milford Twrs, SE6 off Thomas La 205 EB87
Milkhouse Gate, Guil. GU1 off High St 280 AX136
Milking La, Downe BR6 244 EL112
Keston BR2 244 EK111
Milk St, E16 37 N3
EC2 19 K9
Bromley BR1 206 EH93
Milkwell Gdns, Wdf.Grn. IG8 124 EH52
Milkwell Yd, SE5 43 K7
Milkwood Rd, SE24 203 DP85
Milk Yd, E1 32 G1
Mill, The, Hertingfordbury SG14 53 DM10
Millacres, Ware SG12 55 DX06
Millais Av, E12 147 EN64
Millais Cres, Epsom KT19 238 CS106
Millais Gdns, Edg. HA8 118 CN54
Millais Pl, Til. RM18 193 GG80
Millais Rd, E11 145 EC63
Enfield EN1 104 DT43
New Malden KT3 220 CS101
Millais Way, Epsom KT19 238 CQ105
Millan Cl, New Haw KT15 234 BH110
Milland Ct, Borwd. WD6 100 CR39
Millard Cl, N16 9 P2
Millard Rd, SE8 33 N10
Millard Ter, Dag. RM10 off Church Elm La 168 FA65
Mill Av, Uxb. UB8 156 BJ68
Millbank, SW1 30 A7
Hemel Hempstead HP3 62 BK24
Millbank Ct, SW1 30 A8
Millbank Millennium Pier 30 B9
Millbank Prim Sch, SW1 29 P9
● Millbank Twr, SW1 30 A9
Millbank Way, SE12 206 EG85
Mill Bottom, S.Holm. RH5 285 CK144
Millbourne Rd, Felt. TW13 198 BY91
Mill Br, Barn. EN5 101 CZ44
Millbridge, Hert. SG14 54 DQ09
Millbridge Ms, Hert. SG14 off Millbridge 54 DQ09
Mill Br Pl, Uxb. UB8 156 BH68
Millbro, Swan. BR8 209 FG94
Millbrook, Guil. GU1 280 AX136
Weybridge KT13 235 BS105
Millbrook Av, Well. DA16 187 ER84
Millbrook Ct, Ware SG12 55 DX05
Millbrook Gdns, Chad.Hth RM6 148 EZ58
Gidea Park RM2 127 FE54
Millbrook Pl, NW1 off Hampstead Rd 7 L10
Millbrook Prim Sch, Chsht EN8 off Gews Cor 89 DX29
Millbrook Rd, N9 122 DV46
SW9 183 DP83
Bushey WD23 98 BZ39
Mill Brook Rd, St.M.Cray BR5 228 EW98
Millbrook Way, Colnbr. SL3 175 BE82
Mill Cl, Bkhm KT23 252 CA124
Carshalton SM5 222 DG103
Chesham HP5 76 AS34
Hemel Hempstead HP3 80 BN25
Horley RH6 290 DE147
Lemsford AL8 51 CU10
Piccotts End HP1 62 BH16
Ware SG12 55 DX06
West Drayton UB7 176 BK76
Mill Cor, Barn. EN5 101 CZ39
Mill Ct, E10 145 EC62
Harlow CM20 57 ER12
Millcrest Rd, Goffs Oak EN7 87 DP28
Millcroft Ho, SE6 205 EC91
Millen Ct, Hort.Kir. DA4 230 FP98
MILL END, Rick. WD3 113 BF46
Millender Wk, SE16 33 H9
Millennium Br, EC4 19 J10
SE1 19 J10
● Millennium Business Cen, NW2 141 CV61
Millennium Cl, E16 23 P8
Uxbridge UB8 156 BH68
Millennium Dr, E14 34 G8
Millennium Harbour, E14 33 P4
Millennium Pl, E2 20 F1
Millennium Prim Sch, SE10 35 L7
Millennium Sq, SE1 32 A4
Millennium Way, SE10 35 J4
Millennium Wf, Rick. WD3 off Wharf La 114 BL45
Miller Av, Enf. EN3 105 EA38
Miller Cl, Brom. BR1 206 EG92
Collier Row RM5 126 FA52
Mitcham CR4 222 DF101
Pinner HA5 116 BW54
Miller Pl, Ger.Cr. SL9 134 AX57
Miller Rd, SW19 202 DD93
Croydon CR0 223 DM102
Guildford GU4 265 BC131
Miller's Av, E8 10 A2
Millers Cl, NW7 119 CU49
Chigwell IG7 126 EV47
Chorleywood WD3 95 BE41
Dartford DA1 210 FK87
Staines TW18 196 BH92
Millers Copse, Epsom KT18 254 CR119
Redhill RH1 289 DP144
Millers Ct, W4 off Chiswick Mall 181 CT78
Hertford SG14 off Parliament Sq 54 DR10
Millersdale, Harl. CM19 73 EP19
Millers Grn Cl, Enf. EN2 103 DP41
Miller's La, Chig. IG7 126 EV46
Millers La, Stans.Abb. SG12 55 EC11
Windsor SL4 194 AT86
Millers Meadow Cl, SE3 off Meadowcourt Rd 206 EF85
Millers Ri, St.Alb. AL1 65 CE21
Miller's Ter, E8 10 A2
Miller St, NW1 7 L10
Millers Way, W6 26 B5
Miller Wk, SE1 30 F3
Millet Rd, Grnf. UB6 158 CB69
Mill Fm Av, Sun. TW16 197 BS94
Mill Fm Cl, Pnr. HA5 116 BW54
Mill Fm Cres, Houns. TW4 198 BY88
Millfield, N4 off Six Acres Est 143 DN61
Berkhamsted HP4 60 AX18
Mill Fld, Harl. CM17 58 EW11
Millfield, Sun. TW16 217 BR95
Welwyn Garden City AL7 52 DC08
Millfield Av, E17 123 DY53
Millfield Dr, Nthflt DA11 212 GE89
Millfield La, N6 142 DF61
Lower Kingswood KT20 271 CZ125
Millfield Pl, N6 142 DG61
Millfield Rd, Edg. HA8 118 CQ54
Hounslow TW4 198 BY88
Millfields, Chesh. HP5 76 AQ33
Millfields Cl, Orp. BR5 228 EV97
Millfields Comm Sch, E5 off Hilsea St 144 DW63
Millfields Cotts, Orp. BR5 off Millfields Cl 228 EV98
Millfields Est, E5 145 DX62
Millfields Rd, E5 144 DW63
Millfield Wk, Hem.H. HP3 62 BN22
Millford, Wok. GU21 248 AV117
Mill Gdns, SE26 204 DV91
MILL GREEN, Hat. AL9 67 CY15
Mill Grn, Mitch. CR4 222 DG101
● Mill Grn Business Pk, Mitch. CR4 off Mill Grn Rd 222 DG101
Mill Grn La, Hat. AL9 67 CY15
★ Mill Green Mus, Hat. AL9 67 CX15
Mill Grn Rd, Mitch. CR4 222 DF101
Welwyn Garden City AL7 51 CY10
Millgrove St, SW11 40 G8
Millharbour, E14 34 C6
Millhaven Cl, Rom. RM6 148 EV58
Millhedge Cl, Cob. KT11 252 BY116
MILL HILL, NW7 119 CU50
Mill Hill, SW13 181 CU83
Shenfield CM15 130 FY45
≠ Mill Hill Broadway 118 CS51
Mill Hill Circ, NW7 119 CT50
Mill Hill Co High Sch, NW7 off Worcester Cres 118 CS47
Oakhill Campus, Barn. EN4 off Church Hill Rd 120 DF46
⊖ Mill Hill East 119 CX52
Mill Hill Gro, W3 160 CP74
● Mill Hill Ind Est, NW7 119 CT51
Mill Hill La, Brock. RH3 270 CP134
Mill Hill Rd, SW13 181 CU82
W3 180 CP75
Mill Hill Sch, NW7 off The Ridgeway 119 CV49
Millhoo Ct, Wal.Abb. EN9 90 EF34
Mill Ho Cl, Eyns. DA4 off Mill La 230 FL102
Millhouse La, Bedmond WD5 81 BT27
Mill Ho La, Cher. KT16 215 BB98
Egham TW20 215 BB98
Millhouse Pl, SE27 203 DP91
Millhurst Ms, Harl. CM17 58 EY11
Millicent Rd, E10 145 DZ60
Milligan St, E14 33 P1
Milliners Ct, Loug. IG10 off The Croft 107 EN40
Milliner's Ct, St.Alb. AL1 65 CE20
Milliners Ho, SW18 off Eastfields Av 182 DA84
Milling Rd, Edg. HA8 118 CR52
Millington Rd, Hayes UB3 177 BS76
Mill La, E4 105 EB41
NW6 5 H3
SE18 37 M10
Albury GU5 281 BF139
Amersham HP7 77 AN39
Beaconsfield HP9 111 AL54
Broxbourne EN10 71 DZ21
Byfleet KT14 234 BM113
Carshalton SM5 240 DF105
Chadwell Heath RM6 148 EY58
Chafford Hundred RM16 191 FX77
Chalfont St. Giles HP8 112 AU47
Cheshunt EN8 89 DY28
Chilworth GU4 281 BF139
Croxley Green WD3 97 BQ44
Croydon CR0 223 DM104
Dorking RH4 285 CH135
Downe BR6 245 EN110
Egham TW20 215 BB98
Epsom KT17 239 CT109
Eynsford DA4 230 FL102
Fetcham KT22 253 CG122
Gerrards Cross SL9 135 AZ58
Grays RM20 191 FX78
Guildford GU1 off Quarry St 280 AX136
Harlow CM17 58 EY11
Hookwood RH6 290 DD148
Horton SL3 175 BB83
Kings Langley WD4 80 BN29
Limpsfield Chart RH8 277 EM131
Navestock RM4 109 FH40
Oxted RH8 276 EF132
Ripley GU23 250 BK119
Sevenoaks TN14 279 FJ121
Shoreham TN14 247 FF110
South Merstham RH1 273 DJ131
Taplow SL6 152 AC71
Toot Hill CM5 93 FE29
Westerham TN16 277 EQ127
Windsor SL4 173 AN80
Woodford Green IG8 124 EF50
Mill La Cl, Brox. EN10 71 DZ21
● Mill La Trd Est, Croy. CR0 223 DM104
Millman Ms, WC1 18 C5
Millman Pl, WC1 off Millman St 18 C5
Millman St, WC1 18 C5
Millmark Gro, SE14 45 M9
Millmarsh La, Enf. EN3 105 DY40
Millmead, Byfleet KT14 234 BM112
Guildford GU1, GU2 280 AW136
Mill Mead, Stai. TW18 195 BF91
Mill Mead Rd, N17 144 DV56
Mill Mead Sch, Hert. SG14 off Port Vale 54 DQ09
Millmead Ter, Guil. GU2 280 AW136
Millmead Way, Hert. SG14 53 DP08
Mill Pk Av, Horn. RM12 150 FL61
Mill Pl, E14 21 M9
Chislehurst BR7 off Old Hill 227 EP95
Dartford DA1 189 FG84
Datchet SL3 174 AX82
Kingston upon Thames KT1 220 CM97
Mill Pl Caravan Pk, Datchet SL3 174 AW82
Mill Plat, Islw. TW7 179 CG82
Mill Plat Av, Islw. TW7 179 CG82
Mill Pond Cl, SW8 41 P5
Sevenoaks TN14 279 FK121
Millpond Ct, Add. KT15 234 BL106
Millpond Est, SE16 32 E5
Mill Pond Pl, Cars. SM5 222 DG104
Mill Pond Rd, Dart. DA1 210 FL86
Mill Race, Stans.Abb. SG12 55 ED11
Mill Ridge, Edg. HA8 118 CM50
Mill Rd, E16 36 B2
SW19 202 DC94
Aveley RM15 170 FQ73
Cobham KT11 252 BW115
Dunton Green TN13 278 FE121
Epsom KT17 239 CT112
Erith DA8 189 FC80
Esher KT10 218 CA103
Hawley DA2 210 FM91
Hertford SG14 54 DR08
Ilford IG1 147 EN62
Northfleet DA11 212 GE87
Purfleet RM19 190 FP79
South Holmwood RH5 285 CJ144
Tadworth KT20 255 CX123
Twickenham TW2 198 CC89
West Drayton UB7 176 BJ76
Mill Row, N1 9 P9
Mills Cl, Uxb. UB10 156 BN68
Mills Ct, EC2 19 P3
Mills Gro, E14 22 E7
NW4 141 CX55
Mill Shaw, Oxt. RH8 276 EF132
Millshot Dr, Amer. HP7 77 AR40
Millshott Cl, SW6 38 B6
Millside, B.End SL8 132 AC60
Carshalton SM5 222 DF103
Millside Ct, Iver SL0 176 BH75
● Millside Ind Est, Dart. DA1 190 FK84
Millside Pl, Islw. TW7 179 CH82
Millsmead Way, Loug. IG10 107 EM40
Millson Cl, N20 120 DD47
Mills Rd, Hersham KT12 236 BW106
Mills Row, W4 180 CR77
Mills Spur, Old Wind. SL4 194 AV87
Millstead Cl, Tad. KT20 255 CV122
Millstone Cl, E15 13 H4
South Darenth DA4 230 FQ96
Millstone Ms, S.Darenth DA4 230 FQ95
Millstream Cl, N13 121 DN50
Hertford SG14 53 DP09
Millstream La, Slou. SL1 153 AL74
Millstream Rd, SE1 32 A5
Millstream Way, Woob.Moor HP10 132 AD55
Mill St, SE1 32 B5
W1 17 K10
Berkhamsted HP4 60 AW19
Colnbrook SL3 175 BD80
Harlow CM17 74 EY17
Hemel Hempstead HP3 off Fourdinier Way 62 BK23
Kingston upon Thames KT1 220 CL97
Redhill RH1 288 DE135
Slough SL2 154 AT74
Westerham TN16 277 ER127
Mills Way, Hutt. CM13 131 GC46
Mills Yd, SW6 39 L10
Millthorne Cl, Crox.Grn WD3 96 BM43
Mill Vale, Brom. BR2 226 EF96
Mill Vw, Park St AL2 off Park St 83 CD27
Mill Vw Cl, Ewell KT17 239 CT108
Millview Cl, Reig. RH2 272 DD132
Mill Vw Gdns, Croy. CR0 225 DX104
MILLWALL, E14 34 C8
Millwall Dock Rd, E14 34 A6
★ Millwall FC, SE16 45 H1
Millwards, Hat. AL10 67 CV21
Millway, NW7 118 CS50
Mill Way, Bushey WD23 98 BY40
Feltham TW14 197 BV85
Leatherhead KT22 254 CM124
Mill End WD3 113 BF46
Millway, Reig. RH2 272 DD134
Millway Gdns, Nthlt. UB5 158 BZ65
Millwell Cres, Chig. IG7 125 ER50
Millwood Rd, Houns. TW3 198 CC85
Orpington BR5 228 EW97
Millwood St, W10 14 E7
Millwrights Wk, Hem.H. HP3 off Stephenson Wf 80 BM25
Mill Yd, E1 20 C10
● Mill Yd Indusrial Est, Edg. HA8 118 CP53
Milman Cl, Pnr. HA5 138 BX55
Milman Rd, NW6 4 D10
Milman's St, SW10 40 A3
● Milmead Ind Cen, N17 122 DV54
Milne Ct, E18 off Churchfields 124 EG53
Milne Feild, Pnr. HA5 116 CA52
Milne Gdns, SE9 206 EL85
Milne Pk E, New Adgtn CR0 243 ED111
Milne Pk W, New Adgtn CR0 243 ED111
Milner App, Cat. CR3 258 DU121
Milner Cl, Cat. CR3 258 DT121
Watford WD25 81 BV34
Milner Ct, Bushey WD23 98 CB44
Milner Dr, Cob. KT11 236 BZ112
Twickenham TW2 199 CD87
Milner Pl, N1 8 F8
Carshalton SM5 off High St 240 DG105
Milner Rd, E15 23 J3
SW19 222 DB95
Burnham SL1 152 AG71
Caterham CR3 258 DU122
Dagenham RM8 148 EW61
Kingston upon Thames KT1 219 CK97
Morden SM4 222 DD99
Thornton Heath CR7 224 DR97
Milner Sq, N1 8 G7
Milner St, SW3 28 E8
Milner Wk, SE9 207 ER89
Milne Way, Hare. UB9 114 BH53
Milnthorpe Rd, W4 180 CR79
Milo Gdns, SE22 off Milo Rd 204 DT86
Milo Rd, SE22 204 DT86
Milroy Av, Nthflt DA11 212 GE89
Milroy Wk, SE1 30 G2
Milson Rd, W14 26 D6
Milstead Ho, E5 10 F2
MILTON, Grav. DA12 213 GK86
Milton Av, E6 166 EK66
N6 143 DJ59
NW9 140 CQ55
NW10 160 CQ67
Badgers Mount TN14 247 FB110
Barnet EN5 101 CZ43
Chalfont St. Peter SL9 134 AX56
Croydon CR0 224 DR101
Gravesend DA12 213 GJ88
Hornchurch RM12 149 FF61
Sutton SM1 222 DD104
Westcott RH4 285 CD137
Milton Cl, N2 142 DC58
SE1 32 A9
Hayes UB4 157 BU72
Horton SL3 175 BA83
Sutton SM1 222 DD104
Milton Ct, EC2 19 L6
Chadwell Heath RM6 off Cross Rd 148 EW59
Hemel Hempstead HP2 off Milton Dene 63 BP15
Uxbridge UB10 137 BP62
Waltham Abbey EN9 89 EC34
Milton Ct La, Dor. RH4 285 CF136
Milton Ct Rd, SE14 45 M3
Milton Cres, Ilf. IG2 147 EQ59
Milton Dene, Hem.H. HP2 63 BP15
Milton Dr, Borwd. WD6 100 CP43
Shepperton TW17 216 BL98
Milton Flds, Ch.St.G. HP8 112 AV48
Milton Gdn Est, N16 9 N1
Milton Gdns, Epsom KT18 238 CS114
Staines TW19 off Chesterton Dr 196 BM88
Tilbury RM18 193 GH81
Milton Gro, N11 121 DJ50
N16 9 M1
Milton Hall Rd, Grav. DA12 213 GK88
Milton Hill, Ch.St.G. HP8 112 AV48
Milton Lawns, Amer. HP6 77 AR36
● Milton Pk, Egh. TW20 195 BA94
Milton Pk, N6 143 DJ59
Milton Pl, N7 8 E2
Gravesend DA12 213 GJ86
Milton Rd, E17 145 EA56
N6 143 DJ59
N15 143 DP56
NW7 119 CU50
NW9 off West Hendon Bdy 141 CU59
SE24 203 DP85
SW14 180 CR83
SW19 202 DC93
W3 160 CR74
W7 159 CF73
Addlestone KT15 234 BG107
Belvedere DA17 188 FA77
Caterham CR3 258 DR121
Chesham HP5 76 AP29
Croydon CR0 224 DR102
Dunton Green TN13 278 FE121
Egham TW20 195 AZ92
Gravesend DA12 213 GJ86
Grays RM17 192 GB78
Hampton TW12 198 CA94
Harrow HA1 139 CE56
Mitcham CR4 202 DG94
Romford RM1 149 FG58
Slough SL2 153 AR70
Sutton SM1 222 DA104
Swanscombe DA10 212 FY86
Uxbridge UB10 136 BN63
Wallington SM6 241 DJ107
Walton-on-Thames KT12 218 BX104
Ware SG12 55 DX05
Warley CM14 130 FV49
Welling DA16 187 ET81
★ Milton's Cottage, Ch.St.G. HP8 112 AV48
Milton St, EC2 19 L6
Swanscombe DA10 211 FX86
Waltham Abbey EN9 89 EC34
Watford WD24 97 BV38
Westcott RH4 285 CD137
Milton Way, Fetch. KT22 253 CC125
West Drayton UB7 176 BM77
Milverton Dr, Uxb. UB10 137 BQ63
Milverton Gdns, Ilf. IG3 147 ET61
Milverton Ho, SE23 205 DY90
Milverton Rd, NW6 4 B7
Milverton St, SE11 42 F1
Milverton Way, SE9 207 EN91
Milwards, Harl. CM19 73 EP19
Milwards Prim Sch & Nurs, Harl. CM19 off Paringdon Rd 73 EP19
Milward St, E1 20 F7
Milward Wk, SE18 off Spearman St 187 EN79
Mimas Rd, Hem.H. HP2 off Saturn Way 62 BM17
MIMBRIDGE, Wok. GU24 232 AV113
Mimms Hall Rd, Pot.B. EN6 85 CX31
Mimms La, Ridge EN6 84 CQ33
Shenley WD7 84 CN33
Mimosa Cl, Orp. BR6 228 EW103
Pilgrim's Hatch CM15 130 FV43
Romford RM3 128 FJ52
Mimosa Rd, Hayes UB4 158 BW71
Mimosa St, SW6 38 G7
Mimram Rd, Hert. SG14 53 DP10
Mina Av, Slou. SL3 174 AX75
Minard Rd, SE6 206 EE87
Mina Rd, SE17 43 P1
SW19 222 DA95
Minchenden Cres, N14 121 DJ48
Minchen Rd, Harl. CM20 57 ET13
Minchin Cl, Lthd. KT22 253 CG122
Mincing La, EC3 19 N10
Chobham GU24 232 AT108
Minden Rd, SE20 224 DV95
Sutton SM3 221 CZ103
Minehead Rd, SW16 203 DM92
Harrow HA2 138 CA62
Mineral Cl, Barn. EN5 101 CW44
Mineral La, Chesh. HP5 76 AQ32
Mineral St, SE18 187 ES77
Minera Ms, SW1 29 H8
Minerva Cl, SW9 42 F5
Sidcup DA14 207 ES90
Staines TW19 196 BG85
Minerva Dr, Wat. WD24 97 BS36
Minerva Rd, E4 123 EB52
NW10 160 CQ70
Kingston upon Thames KT1 220 CM96
Minerva St, E2 20 E1
Minerva Way, Beac. HP9 111 AP54
Minet Av, NW10 160 CS68
Minet Dr, Hayes UB3 157 BU74
Minet Gdns, NW10 160 CS68
Hayes UB3 157 BU74
Minet Inf Sch, Hayes UB3 off Avondale Dr 157 BV74

Minet Jun Sch, Hayes UB3 off Avondale Dr 157 BV74
Minet Rd, SW9 42 G8
Minford Gdns, W14 26 C5
Mingard Wk, N7 off Hornsey Rd 143 DM62
Ming St, E14 22 B10
Minims, The, Hat. AL10 67 CU17
Minister Ct, Frog. AL2 83 CE28
Ministers Gdns, St.Alb. AL2 off Frogmore 83 CE28
★ Ministry of Defence, SW1 30 A4
★ Ministry of Justice, SW1 29 M6
Ministry Way, SE9 207 EM89
Miniver Pl, EC4 off Garlick Hill 19 K10
Mink Ct, Houns. TW4 178 BW83
Minniecroft Rd, Burn. SL1 152 AH69
Minniedale, Surb. KT5 220 CM99
Minnow St, SE17 31 P9
Minnow Wk, SE17 off Minnow St 31 P9
Minoan Dr, Hem.H. HP3 62 BL24
Minorca Rd, Wey. KT13 234 BN105
Minories, EC3 20 A10
Minshull Pl, Beck. BR3 205 EA94
Minshull St, SW8 41 N7
Minson Rd, E9 11 K8
Minstead Gdns, SW15 201 CT87
Minstead Way, N.Mal. KT3 220 CS100
Minster Av, Sutt. SM1 off Leafield Rd 222 DA103
Minster Cl, Hat. AL10 67 CU20
● Minster Ct, EC3 19 N10
Minster Ct, Horn. RM11 150 FN61
Minster Dr, Croy. CR0 242 DS105
Minster Gdns, W.Mol. KT8 218 BZ98
Minsterley Av, Shep. TW17 217 BS98
Minster Pavement, EC3 off Mincing La 19 N10
Minster Rd, NW2 4 F3
Bromley BR1 206 EH94
Minster Wk, N8 off Lightfoot Rd 143 DL56
Minster Way, Horn. RM11 150 FM60
Slough SL3 175 AZ75
Minstrel Cl, Hem.H. HP1 62 BH19
Minstrel Gdns, Surb. KT5 220 CM98
● Mint Business Pk, E16 23 P7
Mint Cl, Hlgdn UB10 157 BP69
Mintern Cl, N13 121 DP48
Minterne Av, Sthl. UB2 178 CA77
Minterne Rd, Har. HA3 140 CM57
Minterne Waye, Hayes UB4 158 BW72
Mintern St, N1 9 M10
Mint Gdns, Dor. RH4 off Church St 285 CG136
Mint La, Lwr Kgswd KT20 272 DA129
Minton Ho, SE11 off Walnut Tree Wk 30 E8
Minton La, Harl. CM17 74 EW15
Minton Ms, NW6 5 M4
Minton Ri, Tap. SL6 152 AH72
Mint Rd, Bans. SM7 256 DC116
Wallington SM6 241 DH105
Mint St, SE1 31 J4
Mint Wk, Croy. CR0 off High St 224 DQ104
Knaphill GU21 248 AS117
Warlingham CR6 259 DX118
Mintwater Cl, Ewell KT17 239 CU110
Mirabel Rd, SW6 39 H4
Mirador Cres, Slou. SL2 154 AV73
Miramar Way, Horn. RM12 150 FK64
Miranda Cl, E1 20 G7
Miranda Ct, W3 off Queens Dr 160 CM72
Miranda Rd, N19 143 DJ60
Mirfield St, SE7 36 E8
Miriam Rd, SE18 187 ES78
● Mirravale Trd Est, Dag. RM8 148 EZ59
Mirren Cl, Har. HA2 138 BZ63
Mirrie La, Denh. UB9 135 BC57
Mirror Path, SE9 off Lambscroft Av 206 EJ90
Misbourne Av, Chal.St.P. SL9 112 AY50
Misbourne Cl, Chal.St.P. SL9 112 AY50
Misbourne Ct, Slou. SL3 off High St 175 BA77
Misbourne Meadows, Denh. UB9 135 BC60
Misbourne Rd, Uxb. UB10 156 BN67
Misbourne Vale, Chal.St.P. SL9 112 AX50
Miskin Rd, Dart. DA1 210 FJ87
Miskin Way, Grav. DA12 213 GK93
Missden Dr, Hem.H. HP3 63 BQ22
Missenden Cl, Felt. TW14 197 BT88
Missenden Gdns, Burn. SL1 152 AH72
Morden SM4 222 DC100
Missenden Rd, Amer. HP7 77 AL39
Chesham HP5 76 AL32
Mission Gro, E17 145 DY57
Mission Gro Prim Sch, E17 off Buxton Rd 145 DZ56
Mission Pl, SE15 44 D6
Mission Sq, Brent. TW8 180 CL79
Mistletoe Cl, Croy. CR0 off Marigold Way 225 DX102
Mistley Gdns, Hkwd RH6 290 DD149
Mistley Rd, Harl. CM20 58 EU13
Mistral, SE5 off Sceaux Gdns 43 P6
Misty's Fld, Walt. KT12 218 BW102
Mitali Pas, E1 20 C9
MITCHAM, CR4 222 DG97
Mitcham 222 DE98
⇌ Mitcham Eastfields 222 DG96
Mitcham Gdn Village, Mitch. CR4 222 DG99
● Mitcham Ind Est, Mitch. CR4 222 DG95
⇌ Mitcham Junction 222 DG99
Mitcham Junction 222 DG99
Mitcham La, SW16 203 DJ93
Mitcham Pk, Mitch. CR4 222 DF98
Mitcham Rd, E6 25 H2
SW17 202 DF92
Croydon CR0 223 DL100
Ilford IG3 147 ET59
Mitchell Av, Nthflt DA11 212 GD89
Mitchell Brook Prim Sch, NW10 off Bridge Rd 160 CR65
Mitchellbrook Way, NW10 160 CR65
Mitchell Cl, SE2 188 EW77
Abbots Langley WD5 81 BU32
Belvedere DA17 189 FC76
Bovingdon HP3 79 AZ27
Dartford DA1 210 FL89
Rainham RM13 170 FJ68
St. Albans AL1 65 CD24
Slough SL1 173 AN75
Welwyn Garden City AL7 52 DC09
Mitchell Rd, N13 121 DP50
Orpington BR6 245 ET105
Mitchells Cl, Shalf. GU4 off Station Rd 280 AY140
Mitchell's Pl, SE21 off Dulwich Village 204 DS87
Mitchells Row, Shalf. GU4 280 AY141
Mitchell St, EC1 19 J4
Mitchell Wk, E6 24 G7
Amersham HP6 77 AS38
Swanscombe DA10 212 FY87
Mitchell Way, NW10 160 CQ65
Bromley BR1 226 EG95
Mitchison Rd, N1 9 L5
Mitchley Av, Pur. CR8 242 DQ113
South Croydon CR2 242 DQ113
Mitchley Gro, S.Croy. CR2 242 DU113
Mitchley Hill, S.Croy. CR2 242 DT113
Mitchley Rd, N17 144 DU55
Mitchley Vw, S.Croy. CR2 242 DU113
Mitford Cl, Chess. KT9 off Merritt Gdns 237 CJ107
Mitford Rd, N19 143 DL61
Mitre, The, E14 21 N10
Mitre Av, E17 off Greenleaf Rd 145 DZ55
● Mitre Br Ind Est, W10 161 CV70
Mitre Cl, Brom. BR2 off Beckenham La 226 EF96
Shepperton TW17 217 BR100
Sutton SM2 240 DC108
Mitre Ct, EC2 19 K8
Hertford SG14 54 DR09
Mitre Rd, E15 13 J10
SE1 30 F4
Mitre Sq, EC3 19 P9
Mitre St, EC3 19 P9
Mitre Way, W10 161 CV70
Mitre Wf, NW10 161 CV70
Mixbury Gro, Wey. KT13 235 BR107
Mixnams La, Cher. KT16 216 BG97
Mizen Cl, Cob. KT11 236 BX114
Mizen Way, Cob. KT11 252 BW115
Mizzen Mast Ho, SE18 37 L6
Moat, The, N.Mal. KT3 220 CS95
Toot Hill CM5 93 FF29
Moatbridge Sch, SE9 off Eltham Palace Rd 206 EK86
Moat Cl, Bushey WD23 98 CB43
Chipstead TN13 278 FB123
Orpington BR6 245 ET107
Moat Ct, Ashtd. KT21 254 CL117
Moat Cres, N3 142 DB55
Moat Cft, Well. DA16 188 EW83
Moat Dr, E13 24 D1
Harrow HA1 138 CC56
Ruislip HA4 137 BS59
Slough SL2 154 AW71
Moated Fm Dr, Add. KT15 234 BJ108
Moat Fm Rd, Nthlt. UB5 158 BZ65
Moatfield Rd, Bushey WD23 98 CB43
Moat La, Erith DA8 189 FG81
Moat Pl, SW9 42 D10
W3 160 CP72
Denham UB9 136 BH63
Moatside, Enf. EN3 105 DX42
Feltham TW13 198 BW91
Moats La, S.Nutfld RH1 289 DN140
Moatview Ct, Bushey WD23 98 CB43
Moatwood Grn, Welw.G.C. AL7 51 CY10
Moberly Rd, SW4 203 DK87
Moberly Way, Ken. CR8 258 DR120
Moby Dick, Rom. RM6 148 EZ56
Mocatta Ms, Red. RH1 273 DJ131
Mockford Ms, Red. RH1 273 DJ131
Modbury Gdns, NW5 6 F5
Modder Pl, SW15 181 CX84
Model Cotts, SW14 180 CQ83
Model Fm Cl, SE9 206 EL90
Modena Ms, Wat. WD18 97 BS42
Modling Ho, E2 21 J1
Moelwyn Hughes Ct, N7 7 P3
Moelyn Ms, Har. HA1 139 CG57
Moffat Ho, SE5 off Comber Gro 43 J5
Moffat Rd, N13 121 DL51
SW17 202 DE91
Thornton Heath CR7 224 DQ96
Moffats Cl, Brook.Pk AL9 86 DA26
Moffats La, Brook.Pk AL9 85 CZ27
MOGADOR, Tad. KT20 271 CY129
Mogador Cotts, Tad. KT20 off Mogador Rd 271 CX128
Mogador Rd, Lwr Kgswd KT20 271 CX128
Mogden La, Islw. TW7 199 CE85
Mohmmad Khan Rd, E11 off Harvey Rd 146 EF60
Moira Cl, N17 122 DS54
Moira Ct, SW17 off Balham High Rd 202 DG89
Moira Rd, SE9 187 EM84
Moir Cl, S.Croy. CR2 242 DU109
Molash Rd, Orp. BR5 228 EX98
Molasses Row, SW11 39 P10
Mole Abbey Gdns, W.Mol. KT8 218 CA97
● Mole Business Pk, Lthd. KT22 253 CG121
Mole Ct, Epsom KT19 238 CQ105
Molember Ct, E.Mol. KT8 219 CE99
Molember Rd, E.Mol. KT8 219 CE99
Mole Rd, Fetch. KT22 253 CD121
Hersham KT12 236 BX106
Molescroft, SE9 207 EQ90
Molesey Adult Learning Cen, W.Mol. KT8 off Ray Rd 218 CB99
Molesey Av, W.Mol. KT8 218 BZ98
Molesey Cl, Hersham KT12 236 BY105
Molesey Dr, Sutt. SM3 221 CY103
Molesey Hosp, W.Mol. KT8 218 CA99
Molesey Pk Av, W.Mol. KT8 218 CB99
Molesey Pk Cl, E.Mol. KT8 218 CC99
Molesey Pk Rd, E.Mol. KT8 219 CD99
West Molesey KT8 218 CB99
Molesey Rd, Walt. KT12 236 BX106
West Molesey KT8 218 BY99
Molesford Rd, SW6 39 J7
Molesham Cl, W.Mol. KT8 218 CB97
Molesham Way, W.Mol. KT8 218 CB97
Moles Hill, Oxshott KT22 237 CD111
Molesworth, Hodd. EN11 55 EA13
Molesworth Rd, Cob. KT11 235 BU113
Molesworth St, SE13 185 EC83
Mole Valley Pl, Ashtd. KT21 253 CK119
Molewood Rd, Hert. SG14 53 DP08
Mollands La, S.Ock. RM15 171 FW70
Mollison Av, Enf. EN3 105 DY43
Mollison Dr, Wall. SM6 241 DL107
Mollison Ri, Grav. DA12 213 GL92
Mollison Sq, Wall. SM6 off Mollison Dr 241 DL108
Mollison Way, Edg. HA8 118 CN54
Molloy Ct, Wok. GU21 off Courtenay Rd 249 BA116
Molly Huggins Cl, SW12 203 DJ87
Molteno Rd, Wat. WD17 97 BU39
Molyneaux Av, Bov. HP3 79 AZ27
Molyneux Dr, SW17 203 DH91
Molyneux Rd, Gdmg. GU7 280 AT144
Weybridge KT13 234 BN106
Molyneux St, W1 16 D7
Molyns Ms, Slou. SL1 off Nicholas Gdns 153 AL74
Momples Rd, Harl. CM20 58 EV13
Monahan Av, Pur. CR8 241 DM112
Monarch Cl, Felt. TW14 197 BS87
Rainham RM13 off Wymark Cl 169 FG68
Tilbury RM18 193 GH82
West Wickham BR4 244 EF105
Monarch Dr, E16 24 E7
Monarch Ms, E17 145 EB57
SW16 203 DN92
Monarch Par, Mitch. CR4 off London Rd 222 DF96
Monarch Pl, Buck.H. IG9 124 EJ47
Monarch Rd, Belv. DA17 188 FA76
Monarchs Ct, NW7 off Grenville Pl 118 CR50
Monarchs Way, Ruis. HA4 137 BR60
Waltham Cross EN8 89 DY34
Monarch Way, Ilf. IG2 147 ER58
Mona Rd, SE15 45 H8
Monastery Gdns, Enf. EN2 104 DR40
Mona St, E16 23 M7
Monaveen Gdns, W.Mol. KT8 218 CA97
Monck St, SW1 29 P7
Monclar Rd, SE5 184 DR84
Moncorvo Cl, SW7 28 C5
Moncrieff Cl, E6 24 G8
Moncrieff Pl, SE15 44 C8
Moncrieff St, SE15 44 D8
Mondial Way, Harling. UB3 177 BQ80
Monega Prim Sch, E12 off Monega Rd 166 EK65
Monega Rd, E7 166 EJ65
E12 166 EK65
Money Av, Cat. CR3 258 DR122
MONEYHILL, Rick. WD3 114 BH46
Moneyhill Par, Rick. WD3 off Uxbridge Rd 114 BH46
Money Hill Rd, Rick. WD3 114 BJ46
Money Hole La, Tewin AL6 52 DE08
Money La, West Dr. UB7 176 BK76
Money Rd, Cat. CR3 258 DR122
Mongers La, Epsom KT17 239 CT110
Monica Cl, Wat. WD24 98 BW40
Monier Rd, E3 12 A7
Monivea Rd, Beck. BR3 205 DZ94
Monkchester Cl, Loug. IG10 107 EN39
Monk Dr, E16 23 N9
MONKEN HADLEY, Barn. EN5 101 CZ39
Monken Hadley C of E Prim Sch, Barn. EN4 off Camlet Way 102 DA39
Monkey Island La, Bray SL6 172 AE78
Monkfrith Av, N14 103 DH44
Monkfrith Cl, N14 121 DH45
Monkfrith Prim Sch, N14 off Knoll Dr 120 DG45
Monkfrith Way, N14 120 DG45
Monkhams, Wal.Abb. EN9 89 EC29
Monkhams Av, Wdf.Grn. IG8 124 EG50
Monkhams Dr, Wdf.Grn. IG8 124 EH49
Monkhams La, Buck.H. IG9 124 EH48
Woodford Green IG8 124 EG50
Monkleigh Rd, Mord. SM4 221 CY97
Monk Pas, E16 23 N10
Monks Av, Barn. EN5 102 DC44
West Molesey KT8 218 BZ99
Monksbury, Harl. CM18 74 EU18
Monks Chase, Ingrave CM13 131 GC50
Monks Cl, SE2 188 EX77
Broxbourne EN10 71 EA20
Enfield EN2 104 DQ40
Harrow HA2 138 CB61
Ruislip HA4 138 BX63
St. Albans AL1 65 CE22
Monks Cres, Add. KT15 234 BH106
Walton-on-Thames KT12 217 BV102
Monksdene Gdns, Sutt. SM1 222 DB104
Monks Dr, W3 160 CN71
Monksfield Way, Slou. SL2 153 AN69
Monksgate, St.Alb. AL1 off Monks Cl 65 CE22
Monks Grn, Fetch. KT22 252 CC121
Monksgrove, Loug. IG10 107 EN43
Monks Horton Way, St.Alb. AL1 65 CH18
Monksmead, Borwd. WD6 100 CQ42
Monksmead Sch, Borwd. WD6 off Hillside Av 100 CQ41
MONKS ORCHARD, Croy. CR0 225 DZ101
Monks Orchard, Dart. DA1 210 FJ89
Monks Orchard Prim Sch, Croy. CR0 off The Glade 225 DX99
Monks Orchard Rd, Beck. BR3 225 EA102
Monks Pk, Wem. HA9 160 CQ65
Monks Pk Gdns, Wem. HA9 160 CP65
Monks Pl, Cat. CR3 off Tillingdown Hill 258 DV122
Monk's Ridge, N20 119 CV46
Monks Ri, Welw.G.C. AL8 51 CX05
Monks Rd, Bans. SM7 256 DA116
Enfield EN2 104 DQ40
Virginia Water GU25 214 AX98
Windsor SL4 173 AK82
Monk St, SE18 37 M8
Monks Wk, Cher. KT16 215 BE98
Monk's Wk, Reig. RH2 272 DB134
Monks Wk, Sthflt DA13 212 GA93
Monks Way, NW11 off Hurstwood Rd 141 CZ56
Beckenham BR3 225 EA100
Harmondsworth UB7 176 BL79
Orpington BR5 227 EQ102
Staines TW18 196 BK94
Monks Well, Green. DA9 191 FV84
Monkswell Ct, N10 120 DG53
Monkswell La, Chipstead CR5 256 DB124
Monkswick Rd, Harl. CM20 57 ET13
Monkswood, Welw.G.C. AL8 51 CW05
Monkswood Av, Wal.Abb. EN9 89 ED33
Monkswood Gdns, Borwd. WD6 100 CR43
Ilford IG5 147 EN55
Monkton Ho, E5 off Pembury Rd 10 E2
Monkton Rd, Well. DA16 187 ET82
Monkton St, SE11 30 F8
Monkville Av, NW11 141 CZ56
Monkwell Sq, EC2 19 K7
Monkwood Cl, Rom. RM1 149 FG57
Monmouth Av, E18 146 EH56
Kingston upon Thames KT1 199 CJ94
Monmouth Cl, W4 180 CR76
Mitcham CR4 off Recreation Way 223 DL98
Welling DA16 188 EU84
Monmouth Gro, Brent. TW8 off Sterling Pl 180 CL77
Monmouth Ho, NW5 7 K4
Monmouth Pl, W2 15 K9
Monmouth Rd, E6 25 J3
N9 122 DV47
W2 15 K9
Dagenham RM9 148 EZ64
Hayes UB3 177 BS77
Watford WD17 97 BV41
Monmouth St, WC2 18 A9
Monnery Rd, N19 143 DJ62
Monnow Grn, Aveley RM15 off Monnow Rd 170 FQ73
Monnow Rd, SE1 32 C10
Aveley RM15 170 FQ73
Mono La, Felt. TW13 197 BV89
Monoux Gro, E17 123 EA53
Monro Dr, Guil. GU2 264 AU131
Monroe Cres, Enf. EN1 104 DV39
Monroe Dr, SW14 200 CP85
Monro Gdns, Har. HA3 117 CE52
● Monro Ind Est, Wal.Cr. EN8 89 DY34
Monro Pl, Epsom KT19 238 CN109
Monro Way, E5 144 DU63
Monsal Ct, E5 off Redwald Rd 145 DY63
Monsell Ct, N4 off Monsell Rd 143 DP62
Monsell Gdns, Stai. TW18 195 BE92
Monsell Rd, N4 143 DP62
Monson Prim Sch, SE14 45 J4
Monson Rd, NW10 161 CU68
SE14 45 J5
Broxbourne EN10 71 DZ20
Redhill RH1 272 DF130
Mons Wk, Egh. TW20 195 BC92
Mons Way, Brom. BR2 226 EL100
Montacute Rd, SE6 205 DZ87
Bushey Heath WD23 117 CE45
Morden SM4 222 DD100
New Addington CR0 243 EC109
Montagu Cres, N18 122 DV49
Montague Av, SE4 185 DZ84
W7 159 CF74
South Croydon CR2 242 DS112
Montague Cl, SE1 31 L2
Barnet EN5 101 CZ42
Farnham Royal SL2 153 AP68
Walton-on-Thames KT12 217 BU101
Montague Dr, Cat. CR3 258 DQ122
Montague Gdns, W3 160 CN73
Montague Hall Pl, Bushey WD23 98 CA44
Montague Pl, WC1 17 P6
Montague Rd, E8 10 C3
E11 146 EF61
N8 143 DM57
N15 144 DU56
SW19 202 DB94
W7 159 CF74
W13 159 CH72
Berkhamsted HP4 60 AV19
Croydon CR0 223 DP102
Hounslow TW3 178 CB83
Richmond TW10 200 CL86
Slough SL1 154 AT73
Southall UB2 178 BY77
Uxbridge UB8 156 BK66
Montague Sq, SE15 45 H5
Montague St, EC1 19 J7
WC1 18 A6
Montague Waye, Sthl. UB2 178 BY76
Montagu Gdns, N18 122 DV49
Wallington SM6 241 DJ105
Montagu Mans, W1 16 F6
Montagu Ms N, W1 16 F7
Montagu Ms S, W1 16 F8
Montagu Ms W, W1 16 F8
Montagu Pl, W1 16 E7
Montagu Rd, N9 122 DW49
N18 122 DV50
NW4 141 CU58
Datchet SL3 174 AV81
● Montagu Rd Ind Est, N18 122 DW49
Montagu Row, W1 16 F7
Montagu Sq, W1 16 F7
Montagu St, W1 16 F8
Montaigne Cl, SW1 29 P9
Montalt Rd, Wdf.Grn. IG8 124 EF50
Montana Bldg, SE13 off Deals Gateway 46 C6
Montana Cl, S.Croy. CR2 242 DR110
Montana Gdns, SE26 205 DZ92
Sutton SM1 off Lind Rd 240 DC106
Montana Rd, SW17 202 DG91
SW20 221 CW95
Montayne Rd, Chsht EN8 89 DX32
Montbelle Prim Sch, SE9 off Milverton Way 207 EN91
Montbelle Rd, SE9 207 EP90
Montbretia Cl, Orp. BR5 228 EW98
Montcalm Cl, Brom. BR2 226 EG100
Hayes UB4 157 BV69
Montcalm Rd, SE7 186 EK80
Montclare St, E2 20 A3
Monteagle Av, Bark. IG11 167 EQ65
Monteagle Prim Sch, Dag. RM9 off Burnham Rd 168 EV67
Monteagle Way, E5 144 DU62
SE15 44 F10
Montefiore St, SW8 41 K9
Montego Cl, SE24 off Railton Rd 183 DN84
Montem La, Slou. SL1 153 AR74
Montem Prim Sch, N7 off Hornsey Rd 143 DM62
Slough SL1 off Chalvey Gro 173 AP75
Montem Rd, SE23 205 DZ87
New Malden KT3 220 CS98
Montem St, N4 off Thorpedale Rd 143 DM60
Montenotte Rd, N8 143 DJ57
Monterey Cl, NW7 off The Broadway 118 CS50
Bexley DA5 209 FC89
Montesole Ct, Pnr. HA5 116 BW54
Montevetro, SW11 40 A6
Montford Pl, SE11 42 E1
Montford Rd, Sun. TW16 217 BU98
Montfort Gdns, Ilf. IG6 125 EQ51
Montfort Pl, SW19 201 CX88
Montfort Ri, Red. RH1 288 DF142
Montgolfier Wk, Nthlt. UB5 off Wayfarer Rd 158 BY69
Montgomerie Cl, Berk. HP4 off Mortain Dr 60 AU17
Montgomerie Dr, Guil. GU2 264 AU129
Montgomerie Ms, SE23 204 DW87
Montgomery Av, Esher KT10 219 CE104
Hemel Hempstead HP2 62 BN19
Montgomery Cl, Grays RM16 192 GC75
Mitcham CR4 223 DL98
Sidcup DA15 207 ET86
Montgomery Ct, W2 off Harrow Rd 16 A7
W4 off St. Thomas' Rd 180 CQ79
Dagenham RM10 off St. Mark's Pl 168 FA65
Montgomery Cres, Rom. RM3 128 FJ50
Montgomery Dr, Chsht EN8 89 DY28
Montgomery Gdns, Sutt. SM2 240 DD108
Montgomery Pl, Slou. SL2 154 AW72
Montgomery Rd, W4 180 CQ77
Edgware HA8 118 CM51
South Darenth DA4 231 FR95
Woking GU22 248 AY118
Montgomery St, E14 34 D3
Montgomery Way, Ken. CR8 258 DR120
Montholme Rd, SW11 202 DF86
Monthope Rd, E1 20 C7
Montolieu Gdns, SW15 201 CV85
Montpelier Av, W5 159 CJ71
Bexley DA5 208 EX87
Montpelier Cl, Uxb. UB10 156 BN67
Montpelier Ct, Wind. SL4 off St. Leonards Rd 173 AQ82
Montpelier Gdns, E6 24 F2
Romford RM6 148 EW59
Montpelier Gro, NW5 7 M2
Montpelier Ms, SW7 28 D6
Montpelier Pl, E1 20 G9
SW7 28 D6
Montpelier Prim Sch, W5 off Montpelier Rd 159 CK71
Montpelier Ri, NW11 141 CY59
Wembley HA9 139 CK60
Montpelier Rd, N3 120 DC53
SE15 44 F6
W5 159 CK71
Purley CR8 241 DP110
Sutton SM1 240 DC105
Montpelier Row, SE3 47 L9
Twickenham TW1 199 CH87
Montpelier Sq, SW7 28 D5
Montpelier St, SW7 28 D5
Montpelier Ter, SW7 28 D5
Montpelier Vale, SE3 47 L9
Montpelier Wk, SW7 28 D6
Montpelier Way, NW11 141 CY59
Montrave Rd, SE20 204 DW93
Montreal Pl, WC2 18 C10
Montreal Rd, Ilf. IG1 147 EQ59
Sevenoaks TN13 278 FE123
Tilbury RM18 193 GG83
Montrell Rd, SW2 203 DL88
Montrose Av, NW6 4 F10
Datchet SL3 174 AW80
Edgware HA8 118 CQ54
Romford RM2 128 FJ54
Sidcup DA15 208 EU87
Slough SL1 153 AP72
Twickenham TW2 198 CB87
Welling DA16 187 ER83
Montrose Cl, Ashf. TW15 197 BQ93
Welling DA16 187 ET83
Woodford Green IG8 124 EG49
Montrose Ct, SW7 28 B5
Montrose Cres, N12 120 DC51
Wembley HA0 160 CL65
Montrose Gdns, Mitch. CR4 222 DF97
Oxshott KT22 237 CD112
Sutton SM1 222 DB103
Montrose Pl, SW1 29 H5
Montrose Rd, Felt. TW14 197 BR86
Harrow HA3 117 CE54
Montrose Wk, Wey. KT13 217 BP104
Montrose Way, SE23 205 DX88
Datchet SL3 174 AX81
Montrouge Cres, Epsom KT17 255 CW116
Montserrat Av, Wdf.Grn. IG8 123 ED52
Montserrat Cl, SE19 204 DR92
Montserrat Rd, SW15 181 CY84
⊖ Monument 19 M10
★ Monument, The, EC3 19 M10
● Monument Business Cen, Wok. GU21 off Monument Way E 249 BB115
Monument Gdns, SE13 205 EC85
Monument Grn, Wey. KT13 217 BP104
Monument Hill, Wey. KT13 235 BP105
Monument La, Chal.St.P. SL9 112 AY51
Monument Rd, Wey. KT13 235 BP105
Woking GU21 233 BA114
Monument St, EC3 31 M1
Monument Way, N17 144 DT55
Monument Way E, Wok. GU21 249 BB115
Monument Way W, Wok. GU21 249 BA115
Monza St, E1 32 G1
Moodkee St, SE16 32 G6
Moody Rd, SE15 44 A5
Moody St, E1 21 K3
Moon La, Barn. EN5 101 CZ41
Moon St, N1 8 G8
Moorcroft Gdns, Brom. BR2 off Southborough Rd 226 EL99
Moorcroft La, Uxb. UB8 156 BN71

Moorcroft Rd, SW16 203 DL90
[Sch] Moorcroft Sch, Hlgdn UB8
off Bramble Cl 156 BM72
Moorcroft Way, Pnr. HA5 138 BY57
Moordown, SE18 187 EP81
Moore Av, Grays RM20 192 FY78
Tilbury RM18 193 GH82
Moore Cl, SW14 180 CQ83
Addlestone KT15 234 BH106
Dartford DA2 211 FR89
Mitcham CR4 223 DH96
Slough SL1 173 AP75
Moore Cres, Dag. RM9 168 EV67
Moorefield Rd, N17 122 DT54
Moore Gro Cres, Egh.TW20 194 AY94
Moorehead Way, SE3 186 EH83
Moore Ho, E14 34 B5
Mooreland Rd, Brom. BR1 206 EF94
Moor End, Maid. SL6 172 AC78
Moorend, Welw.G.C. AL7 52 DA12
Moor End Rd, Hem.H. HP1 62 BJ21
Moore Pk Rd, SW6 39 L5
Moore Rd, SE19 204 DQ93
Berkhamsted HP4 60 AT17
Swanscombe DA10 212 FY86
Moores La, Eton Wick SL4 173 AM77
Moores Pl, Brwd. CM14 130 FX47
Moores Rd, Dor. RH4 285 CH135
Moore St, SW3 28 E8
Moore Wk, E7 13 P2
Moore Way, Sutt. SM2 240 DA109
Moorey Cl, E15 13 L9
Moorfield, Harl. CM18 73 EQ20
South Holmwood RH5 285 CK144
Moorfield Av, W5 159 CK70
● Moorfield Pt, Guil. GU1 264 AY130
Moorfield Rd, Chess. KT9 238 CL106
Denham UB9 136 BG59
Enfield EN3 104 DW39
Guildford GU1 264 AX130
Orpington BR6 228 EU101
Uxbridge UB8 156 BK72
Moorfields, EC2 19 L7
Moorfields Cl, Stai. TW18 215 BE95
[H] Moorfields Eye Hosp, EC1 19 L3
Moorfields Highwalk, EC2 19 L7
Moor Furlong, Slou. SL1 153 AL74
⇌ Moorgate 19 L7
⊖ Moorgate 19 L7
Moorgate, EC2 19 L8
Moorgate Pl, EC2 19 L8
Moorhall Rd, Hare. UB9 136 BH58
Moor Hall Rd, Harl. CM17 58 EZ11
Moorhayes Dr, Stai.TW18 216 BJ97
Moorhen Cl, Erith DA8 189 FH80
Moorholme, Wok. GU22
off Oakbank 248 AY119
MOORHOUSE, West.TN16 277 EM127
MOORHOUSE BANK, West.
TN16 277 EM128
Moorhouse Rd, W2 15 J8
Harrow HA3 139 CK55
Oxted RH8 277 EM131
Westerham TN16 277 EM128
[Sch] Moor Ho Sch, Oxt. RH8
off Mill La 276 EF132
Moorhurst Av, Goffs Oak EN7 87 DN29
Moorings, SE28 168 EV73
Moorings, The, E16
off Prince Regent La 24 C7
Bookham KT23 268 CA125
Windsor SL4
off Straight Rd 194 AW87
Moorings Ho, Brent. TW8
off Tallow Rd 179 CJ80
Moorland Cl, Rom. RM5 127 FB52
Twickenham TW2 198 CA87
Moorland Rd, SW9 183 DP84
Harmondsworth UB7 176 BJ79
Hemel Hempstead HP1 62 BG22
Moorlands, Frog. AL2 83 CD28
Welwyn Garden City AL7 52 DA12
Moorlands, The, Wok. GU22 249 AZ121
Moorlands Av, NW7 119 CV51
Moorlands Est, SW9 183 DN84
Moorlands Reach, Saw. CM21 58 EZ06
Moor La, EC2 19 L7
Chessington KT9 238 CL105
Harmondsworth UB7 176 BJ79
Rickmansworth WD3 114 BM47
Sarratt WD3 95 BE36
Staines TW18, TW19 195 BE90
Upminster RM14 151 FS60
Woking GU22 248 AY122
Moor La Crossing, Wat. WD18 115 BQ46
Moormead Dr, Epsom KT19 238 CS106
Moor Mead Rd, Twick. TW1 199 CG86
Moormede Cres, Stai. TW18 195 BF91
Moor Mill La, Coln.St AL2 99 CE29
MOOR PARK, Nthwd. HA6 115 BQ49
★ Moor Park, Rick. WD3 114 BN48
⊖ Moor Park 115 BR48
Moor Pk Est, Nthwd. HA6 115 BQ49
Moor Pk Gdns, Kings.T. KT2 200 CS94
● Moor Pk Ind Cen, Wat.
WD18 115 BQ45
Moor Pk Rd, Nthwd. HA6 115 BR50
Moor Pl, EC2 19 L7
Moor Rd, Chesh. HP5 76 AQ32
Sevenoaks TN14 263 FH120
Moors, The, Welw.G.C. AL7 52 DA08
Moorside, Hem.H. HP3 62 BH23
Welwyn Garden City AL7 52 DA12
Wooburn Green HP10 132 AE55
Moorside Rd, Brom. BR1 206 EE90
Moors La, Orch.L. HP5 78 AV28
Moorsom Way, Couls. CR5 257 DK117
Moorstown Ct, Slou. SL1 174 AS75
Moor St, W1 17 P9
Moors Wk, Welw.G.C. AL7 52 DC09
Moor Twr, Harl. CM18 73 ET16
Moortown Rd, Wat. WD19 116 BW49
Moor Vw, Wat. WD18 115 BU45
Moot Ct, NW9 140 CN57
Moran Cl, Brick.Wd AL2 82 BZ31
Morant Gdns, Rom. RM5 127 FB50
Morant Pl, N22
off Commerce Rd 121 DM53
Morant Rd, Grays RM16 193 GH76
[Jct] Morants Ct Cross, Dunt.Grn
TN14 263 FB118
Morants Ct Rd, Dunt.Grn
TN13 263 FC118
Morant St, E14 22 B10
[Sch] Mora Prim Sch, NW2
off Mora Rd 141 CW63
Mora Rd, NW2 141 CW63
Mora St, EC1 19 K3
Morat St, SW9 42 D6
Moravian Pl, SW10 40 B3
Moravian St, E2 20 G1
Moray Av, Hayes UB3 157 BT74
Moray Cl, Edg. HA8
off Pentland Av 118 CP47
Romford RM1 127 FE52
Moray Dr, Slou. SL2 154 AU72
Moray Ms, N7 143 DM61
Moray Rd, N4 143 DM61
Moray Way, Rom. RM1 127 FD52
Morcote Cl, Shalf. GU4 280 AY141
Mordaunt Gdns, Dag. RM9 168 EY66
Mordaunt Ho, NW10 160 CR67
Mordaunt St, SW9 42 C10
MORDEN, SM4 222 DA97
⊖ Morden 222 DB97
Morden Cl, Tad. KT20 255 CX120
Morden Ct, Mord. SM4 222 DB98
Morden Gdns, Grnf. UB6 139 CF64
Mitcham CR4 222 DD98
★ Morden Hall Pk NT, Mord.
SM4 222 DB97
Morden Hall Rd, Mord. SM4 222 DB97
Morden Hill, SE13 46 E8
Morden La, SE13 46 F7
[Sch] Morden Mt Prim Sch, SE13 46 D8
MORDEN PARK, Mord. SM4 221 CY99
[Sch] Morden Prim Sch,
Mord. SM4
off London Rd 222 DA99
[Tra] Morden Road 222 DB96
Morden Rd, SE3 47 N8
SW19 202 DB94
Mitcham CR4 222 DC98
Romford RM6 148 EY59
Morden Rd Ms, SE3 47 N9
⇌ Morden South 222 DA99
Morden St, SE13 46 D7
Morden Way, Sutt. SM3 222 DA101
Morden Wf Rd, SE10 35 J7
Mordon Rd, Ilf. IG3 147 ET59
Mordred Ct, N9
off Galahad Rd 122 DU47
Mordred Rd, SE6 206 EE89
Moreau Wk, Geo.Grn SL3
off Alan Way 154 AY72
Morecambe Cl, E1 21 J6
Hornchurch RM12 149 FH64
Morecambe Gdns, Stan. HA7 117 CK49
Morecambe St, SE17 31 K9
Morecambe Ter, N18 122 DR49
More Circle, Gdmg. GU7 280 AS144
More Cl, E16 23 M8
W14 26 D9
Purley CR8 241 DN111
Morecoombe Cl, Kings.T. KT2 200 CP94
Moree Way, N18 122 DU49
[Sch] More Ho Sch, SW1 28 F7
Moreland Av, Colnbr. SL3 175 BC80
Grays RM16 192 GC75
Moreland Cl, Colnbr. SL3
off Moreland Av 175 BC80
Moreland Dr, Ger.Cr. SL9 135 AZ59
[Sch] Moreland Prim Sch, EC1 19 H2
Moreland St, EC1 19 H2
Moreland Way, E4 123 EB48
More La, Esher KT10 218 CB103
Morel Ct, Sev. TN13 279 FH122
Morella Cl, Vir.W. GU25 214 AW98
Morella Rd, SW12 202 DF87
Morell Cl, Barn. EN5 102 DC41
Morello Av, Uxb. UB8 157 BP71
Morello Cl, Swan. BR8 229 FD98
Morello Dr, Slou. SL3 155 AZ74
More London Pl, SE1 31 N3
More London Riverside, SE1 31 P3
Moremead, Wal.Abb. EN9 89 ED33
Moremead Rd, SE6 205 DZ91
Morena St, SE6 205 EB87
More Rd, Gdmg. GU7 280 AS144
Moresby Av, Surb. KT5 220 CP101
Moresby Rd, E5 144 DV60
Moresby Wk, SW8 41 L9
Moretaine Rd, Ashf. TW15
off Hengrove Cres 196 BK90
MORETON, Ong. CM5 75 FH20
Moreton Av, Islw. TW7 179 CE81
Moreton Cl, E5 144 DW61
N15 144 DR58
NW7 119 CW51
SW1 29 M10
Cheshunt EN7 88 DV27
Swanley BR8 229 FE96
Moreton Gdns, Wdf.Grn. IG8 124 EL50
Moreton Ho, SE16 32 F6
● Moreton Ind Est, Swan.
BR8 229 FG98
Moreton Pl, SW1 29 M10
Moreton Rd, N15 144 DR58
Moreton CM5 75 FG24
South Croydon CR2 242 DR106
Worcester Park KT4 221 CU103
Moreton St, SW1 29 M10
Moreton Ter, SW1 29 M10
Moreton Ter Ms N, SW1 29 M10
Moreton Ter Ms S, SW1 29 M10
Moreton Twr, W3 160 CP74
Moreton Way, Slou. SL1 153 AK74
Morewood Cl, Sev. TN13 278 FF123
● Morewood Cl Ind Pk, Sev.
TN13 off Morewood Cl 278 FF123
Morford Cl, Ruis. HA4 137 BV59
Morford Way, Ruis. HA4 137 BV59
Morgan Av, E17 145 ED56
Morgan Cl, Dag. RM10 168 FA66
Northwood HA6 115 BT51
Morgan Ct, N9
off Galahad Rd 122 DU48
SW11
off Battersea High St 40 B7
Morgan Cres, They.B. CM16 107 ER36
Morgan Dr, Green. DA9 211 FS87
Morgan Gdns, Ald. WD25 98 CB38
Morgan Ho, SW1
off Vauxhall Br Rd 29 M9
Morgan Rd, N7 8 E3
W10 14 G6
Bromley BR1 206 EG94
Morgans Cl, Hert. SG13 54 DR11
[Sch] Morgans JMI Sch, Hert. SG13
off Morgans Rd 54 DR11
Morgans La, SE1 31 N3
Hayes UB3 157 BR71
Morgans Rd, Hert. SG13 54 DR11
Morgan St, E3 21 M3
E16 23 M6
Morgans Wk, Hert. SG13 54 DR12
Morgan Way, Rain. RM13 170 FJ69
Woodford Green IG8 124 EL51
[Sch] Moriah Jewish Day Sch, Pnr.
HA5 off Cannon La 138 BY60
Moriarty Cl, Brom. BR1 227 EP98
Moriatry Cl, N7 143 DL63
Morice Rd, Hodd. EN11 71 DZ15
Morie St, SW18 182 DB84
Morieux Rd, E10 145 DZ60
Moring Rd, SW17 202 DG91
Morkyns Wk, SE21 204 DS90
Morland Av, Croy. CR0 224 DS102
Dartford DA1 209 FH85
Morland Cl, NW11 142 DB60
Hampton TW12 198 BZ92
Mitcham CR4 222 DE97
Morland Est, E8 10 D6
Morland Gdns, NW10 160 CR66
Southall UB1 158 CB74
Morland Ms, N1 8 F7
Morland Pl, N15 144 DS56
Morland Rd, E17 145 DX57
SE20 205 DX93
Croydon CR0 224 DS102
Dagenham RM10 168 FA66
Harrow HA3 140 CL57
Ilford IG1 147 EP61
Sutton SM1 240 DC106
Morland Way, Chsht EN8 89 DY28
Morley Av, E4 123 ED52
N18 122 DU49
N22 121 DN54
Morley Cl, Orp. BR6 227 EP103
Slough SL3 175 AZ75
[Coll] Morley Coll, SE1 30 F6
Morley Cres, Edg. HA8 118 CQ47
Ruislip HA4 138 BW61
Morley Cres E, Stan. HA7 117 CJ54
Morley Cres W, Stan. HA7 117 CJ54
Morley Gro, Harl. CM20 57 EQ13
Morley Hill, Enf. EN2 104 DR38
Morley Rd, E10 145 EC60
E15 13 L10
SE13 185 EC84
Barking IG11 167 ER67
Chislehurst BR7 227 EQ95
Romford RM6 148 EY57
South Croydon CR2 242 DT110
Sutton SM3 221 CZ102
Twickenham TW1 199 CK86
Morley Sq, Grays RM16 193 GG77
Morley St, SE1 30 F6
Morna Rd, SE5 43 K8
Morning La, E9 10 G4
Morning Ri, Loud. WD3 96 BK41
[Sch] Morningside Prim Sch, E9 11 H4
Morningside Rd, Wor.Pk. KT4 221 CV103
Mornington Av, W14 26 G9
Bromley BR1 226 EJ97
Ilford IG1 147 EN59
Mornington Cl, Bigg.H. TN16 260 EK117
Woodford Green IG8 124 EG49
Mornington Ct, Bex. DA5 209 FC88
⊖ Mornington Crescent 7 L10
Mornington Cres, NW1 7 L10
Hounslow TW5 177 BV81
Mornington Gro, E3 22 A3
Mornington Ms, SE5 43 J6
Mornington Pl, NW1 7 K10
Mornington Rd, E4 123 ED45
E11 146 EF60
SE8 45 P5
Ashford TW15 197 BQ92
Greenford UB6 158 CB71
Loughton IG10 107 EQ41
Radlett WD7 83 CG34
Woodford Green IG8 124 EF49
Morningtons, Harl. CM19 73 EQ19
Mornington St, NW1 7 K10
Mornington Ter, NW1 7 K9
Mornington Wk, Rich. TW10 199 CJ91
Morocco St, SE1 31 N5
Morpeth Av, Borwd. WD6 100 CM38
Morpeth Cl, Hem.H. HP2
off York Way 62 BL21
Morpeth Gro, E9 11 J8
Morpeth Rd, E9 11 H9
[Sch] Morpeth Sch, E2 21 H3
Annexe, E2 20 G3
Morpeth St, E2 21 J2
Morpeth Ter, SW1 29 L7
Morpeth Wk, N17 off West Rd 122 DV52
Morrab Gdns, Ilf. IG3 147 ET62
Morrell Cl, Welw.G.C. AL7 51 CZ08
Morrells Yd, SE11 30 F10
Morrice Cl, Slou. SL3 175 AZ77
Morris Av, E12 147 EM64
Morris Cl, Chal.St.P. SL9 113 AZ53
Croydon CR0 225 DY100
Orpington BR6 227 ES104
Morris Ct, E4 123 EB48
Enfield EN3 off Rigby Pl 105 EA37
Waltham Abbey EN9 90 EF34
Morris Gdns, SW18 202 DA87
Dartford DA1 210 FN85
Morris Ho, W3
off Swainson Rd 181 CT75
Harlow CM18 73 EQ18
Morrish Rd, SW2 203 DL87
Morrison Av, E4 123 EA51
N17 144 DS55
Morrison Rd, SW9 42 F9
Barking IG11 168 EY68
Hayes UB4 157 BV69
Morrison St, SW11 40 G10
Morris Pl, N4 143 DN61
Morris Rd, E14 22 C6
E15 146 EE63
Dagenham RM8 148 EZ61
Isleworth TW7 179 CF83
Romford RM3 127 FH52
South Nutfield RH1 289 DL136
Morris St, E1 20 F9
Morriston Cl, Wat. WD19 116 BW50
Morris Way, Lon.Col. AL2 85 CK26
Morse Cl, E13 23 N3
Harefield UB9 114 BJ54
Morshead Rd, W9 15 K3
Morson Rd, Enf. EN3 105 DY44
Morston Cl, Tad. KT20
off Waterfield 255 CV120
Morston Gdns, SE9 207 EM91
Mortain Dr, Berk. HP4 60 AT17
Morten Cl, SW4 203 DK86
Morten Gdns, Denh. UB9 136 BG59
Mortens Wd, Amer. HP7 77 AR40
Morteyne Rd, N17 122 DR53
Mortham St, E15 13 J9
Mortimer Cl, NW2 141 CZ62
SW16 203 DK89
Bushey WD23 98 CB44
Mortimer Cres, NW6 5 L9
Worcester Park KT4 220 CR104
Mortimer Dr, Enf. EN1 104 DR43
Mortimer Est, NW6 5 L9
Mortimer Gate, Chsht EN8 89 DZ27
Mortimer Ho, W11
off St. Anns Rd 26 D2
Mortimer Mkt, WC1 17 M5
Mortimer Pl, NW6 5 L9
Mortimer Rd, E6 25 J3
N1 9 P7
NW10 14 A2
W13 159 CJ72
Erith DA8 189 FD79
Mitcham CR4 222 DF95
Orpington BR6 228 EU103
Slough SL3 174 AX76
Mortimer Sq, W11 26 D1
Mortimer St, W1 17 L8
Mortimer Ter, NW5
off Gordon Ho Rd 143 DH63
MORTLAKE, SW14 180 CQ83
⇌ Mortlake 180 CQ83
Mortlake Cl, Croy. CR0 223 DL104
Mortlake Dr, Mitch. CR4 222 DE95
Mortlake High St, SW14 180 CR83
Mortlake Rd, E16 24 B8
Ilford IG1 147 EQ63
Richmond TW9 180 CN80
Mortlake Sta Pas, SW14
off Sheen La 180 CQ83
Mortlake Ter, Rich. TW9
off Kew Rd 180 CN80
Mortlock Cl, SE15 44 E7
Morton, Tad. KT20 255 CX121
Morton Cl, E1 20 G9
Uxbridge UB8 156 BM70
Wallington SM6 241 DM108
Woking GU21 248 AW115
Morton Ct, Nthlt. UB5 138 CC64
Morton Cres, N14 121 DK49
Morton Dr, Slou. SL2 133 AL64
Morton Gdns, Wall. SM6 241 DJ106
Morton Ms, SW5 27 L9
Morton Pl, SE1 30 E7
Morton Rd, E15 13 L7
N1 9 K7
Morden SM4 222 DD99
Woking GU21 248 AW115
Morton Way, N14 121 DJ48
Morvale Cl, Belv. DA17 188 EZ77
Morval Rd, SW2 203 DN85
Morven Cl, Pot.B. EN6 86 DC31
Morven Rd, SW17 202 DF90
Morville Ho, SW18
off Fitzhugh Gro 202 DD86
Morville St, E3 12 A10
Morwell St, WC1 17 P7
Mosbach Gdns, Hutt. CM13 131 GB47
Moscow Pl, W2 15 L10
Moscow Rd, W2 15 L10
Moseley Row, SE10 35 M8
Moselle Av, N22 121 DN54
Moselle Cl, N8 off Miles Rd 143 DL55
Moselle Ho, N17
off William St 122 DT52
Moselle Pl, N17 off High Rd 122 DT52
Moselle Rd, Bigg.H. TN16 260 EL118
[Sch] Moselle Sch, Main Site, N17
off Adams Rd 122 DS54
[Sch] Moselle Spec Sch, Upr Sch,
N17 off Downhills Pk Rd 144 DQ55
Moselle St, N17 122 DT52
Mosford Cl, Horl. RH6 290 DF146
Mospey Cres, Epsom KT17 255 CT115
Mosquito Way, Hat. AL10 66 CS17
Moss Bk, Grays RM17 192 FZ78
Mossborough Cl, N12 120 DB51
[Sch] Mossbourne Comm Acad,
E5 10 D2
Mossbury Rd, SW11 182 DE83
Moss Cl, E1 20 D6
N9 122 DU46
Pinner HA5 116 BZ54
Rickmansworth WD3 114 BK47
Moss Ct, Seer Grn HP9
off Orchard Rd 111 AR51
Mossdown Cl, Belv. DA17 188 FA77
Mossendew Cl, Hare. UB9 114 BK53
Mossfield, Cob. KT11 235 BU113
Mossford Ct, Ilf. IG6 147 EP55
Mossford Grn, Ilf. IG6 147 EP55
[Sch] Mossford Grn Prim Sch,
Barkingside IG6
off Fairlop Rd 125 EQ54
Mossford La, Ilf. IG6 125 EP54
Mossford St, E3 21 N4
Moss Gdns, Felt. TW13 197 BU89
South Croydon CR2
off Warren Av 243 DX108
Moss Grn, Welw.G.C. AL7 51 CY11
Moss Hall Ct, N12 120 DB51
Moss Hall Cres, N12 120 DB51
Moss Hall Gro, N12 120 DB51
[Sch] Moss Hall Inf Sch, N12
off Moss Hall Gro 120 DB51
[Sch] Moss Hall Jun Sch, N3
off Nether St 120 DB51
Mossington Gdns, SE16 32 G9
Moss La, Pnr. HA5 138 BZ55
Romford RM1 off Albert Rd 149 FF58
Mosslea Rd, SE20 204 DW94
Bromley BR2 226 EK99
Orpington BR6 227 EQ104
Whyteleafe CR3 258 DT116
Mossop St, SW3 28 D8
Moss Rd, Dag. RM10 168 FA66
South Ockendon RM15 171 FW71
Watford WD25 81 BV34
Moss Side, Brick.Wd AL2 82 BZ30
Mossville Gdns, Mord. SM4 221 CZ97
Moss Way, Beac. HP9 110 AJ51
Lane End DA2 211 FR91
Moston Cl, Hayes UB3
off Fuller Way 177 BT78
Mostyn Av, Wem. HA9 140 CM64
Mostyn Gdns, NW10 14 C2
Mostyn Gro, E3 21 P1
Mostyn Rd, SW9 42 E7
SW19 221 CZ95
Bushey WD23 98 CC43
Edgware HA8 118 CR52
Mostyn Ter, Red. RH1 288 DG135
Mosul Way, Brom. BR2 226 EL100
Mosyer Dr, Orp. BR5 228 EX103
Motcomb St, SW1 28 F6
Moth Cl, Wall. SM6 241 DL108
Mothers' Sq, E5 10 F1
Motherwell Way, Grays RM20 191 FU78
Motley Av, EC2 19 N4
Motley St, SW8 41 L8
MOTSPUR PARK, N.Mal. KT3 221 CV100
⇌ Motspur Park 221 CV99
Motspur Pk, N.Mal. KT3 221 CT100
MOTTINGHAM, SE9 206 EJ89
⇌ Mottingham 206 EL88
Mottingham Gdns, SE9 206 EK88
Mottingham La, SE9 206 EJ88
SE12 206 EJ88
[Sch] Mottingham Prim Sch, SE9
off Ravensworth Rd 207 EM90
Mottingham Rd, N9 105 DX44
SE9 206 EL89
Mottisfont Rd, SE2 188 EU76
Motts Hill La, Tad. KT20 255 CU123
Motts La, Dag. RM8
off Becontree Av 148 EZ61
Mott St, E4 105 ED38
High Beach IG10 106 EF39
Mouchotte Cl, Bigg.H. TN16 244 EH112
Moulins Rd, E9 11 H7
Moulsford Ho, N7 7 P3
Moultain Hill, Swan. BR8 229 FG98
Moulton Av, Houns. TW3 178 BY82
Moultrie Way, Upmin. RM14 151 FS59
Mound, The, SE9 207 EN90
Moundfield Rd, N16 144 DU58
Moundsfield Way, Slou. SL1 173 AL75
Mount, The, E5 144 DV61
N20 120 DC47
NW3 off Heath St 142 DC63
W3 160 CP74
Brentwood CM14 130 FW48
Cheshunt EN7 88 DR26
Coulsdon CR5 256 DG115
Esher KT10 236 CA107
Ewell KT17 239 CT110
Fetcham KT22 253 CE123
Guildford GU1, GU2 280 AV137
Lower Kingswood KT20 271 CZ126
New Malden KT3 221 CT97
Potters Bar EN6 86 DB30
Rickmansworth WD3 96 BJ44
Romford RM3 128 FJ48
St. John's GU21 248 AU119
Virginia Water GU25 214 AX100
Warlingham CR6 258 DU119
Wembley HA9 140 CP61
Weybridge KT13 217 BS103
Woking GU21 248 AX118
Worcester Park KT4 239 CV105
Mountacre Cl, SE26 204 DT91
Mount Adon Pk, SE22 204 DU87
Mountague Pl, E14 22 E10
Mountain Ho, SE11 30 C10
[H] Mount Alvernia Hosp,
Guil. GU1 280 AY136
Mount Angelus Rd, SW15 201 CT87
Mount Ararat Rd, Rich. TW10 200 CL85
Mount Ash Rd, SE26 204 DV90
Mount Av, E4 123 EA48
W5 159 CK71
Brentwood CM13 131 GA44
Chaldon CR3 258 DQ124
Romford RM3 128 FQ51
Southall UB1 158 CA72
Mountbatten Cl, SE18 187 ES79
SE19 204 DS92
St. Albans AL1 65 CH23
Slough SL1 174 AU76
Mountbatten Ct, SE16
off Rotherhithe St 33 H3
Buckhurst Hill IG9 124 EK47
Mountbatten Gdns, Beck. BR3
off Balmoral Av 225 DY98
Mountbatten Ms, SW18
off Inman Rd 202 DC88
Mountbatten Sq, Wind. SL4
off Ward Royal 173 AQ81
Mountbel Rd, Stan. HA7 117 CG53
[Sch] Mount Carmel RC Prim Sch,
W5 off Little Ealing La 179 CJ77
[Sch] Mount Carmel RC Tech Coll
for Girls, N19
off Holland Wk 143 DK60
Mount Cl, W5 159 CJ71
Bromley BR1 226 EL95
Carshalton SM5 240 DG109
Cockfosters EN4 102 DG42
Farnham Common SL2 133 AQ63
Fetcham KT22 253 CE123
Hemel Hempstead HP1 61 BF20
Kenley CR8 258 DQ116
Sevenoaks TN13 278 FF123
Woking GU22 248 AV121
Mount Cl, The, Vir.W. GU25 214 AX100
Mountcombe Cl, Surb. KT6 220 CL101
Mount Cor, Felt. TW13 198 BX89
Mount Ct, SW15
off Weimar St 181 CY83
Guildford GU2
off The Mount 280 AW136
West Wickham BR4 226 EE103
Mount Cres, Warley CM14 130 FX49
Mount Culver Av, Sid. DA14 208 EX93
Mount Dr, Bexh. DA6 208 EY85
Harrow HA2 138 BZ57
Park Street AL2 83 CD25
Wembley HA9 140 CQ61
Mount Dr, The, Reig. RH2 272 DC132
Mountearl Gdns, SW16 203 DM90
Mount Echo Av, E4 123 EB47
Mount Echo Dr, E4 123 EB46
MOUNT END, Epp. CM16 92 EZ32
Mount Ephraim La, SW16 203 DK90
Mount Ephraim Rd, SW16 203 DK90
Mount Felix, Walt. KT12 217 BT102
Mountfield Cl, SE6 205 ED87
Mountfield Rd, E6 25 L1
N3 142 DA55
W5 159 CK72
Hemel Hempstead HP2 62 BL20
Mountfield Ter, SE6
off Mountfield Cl 205 ED87
Mountfield Way, Orp. BR5 228 EW98
Mountford Mans, SW11 41 H7
Mountfort Cres, N1 8 E6
Mountfort Ter, N1 8 E7
Mount Gdns, SE26 204 DV90
Mount Grace Rd, Pot.B. EN6 86 DA31

Sch **Mount Grace Sch**, Pot.B. EN6 off Church Rd 86 DB30
Mount Gro, Edg. HA8 118 CQ48
Mountgrove Rd, N5 143 DP62
Mount Harry Rd, Sev. TN13 278 FG123
MOUNT HERMON, Wok. GU22 248 AX118
Mount Hermon Cl, Wok. GU22 248 AX118
Mount Hermon Rd, Wok. GU22 248 AX119
Mount Hill La, Ger.Cr. SL9 134 AV60
Mount Holme, T.Ditt. KT7 219 CH101
Mounthurst Rd, Brom. BR2 226 EF101
Mountington Pk Cl, Har. HA3 139 CK58
Mountjoy Cl, SE2 188 EV75
Mountjoy Ho, EC2 off The Barbican 19 K7
Mount La, Denh. UB9 135 BD61
Mount Lee, Egh. TW20 194 AY92
Mount Ms, Hmptn. TW12 218 CB95
Mount Mills, EC1 19 H3
Mountnessing Bypass, Brwd. CM15 131 GD41
Jct **Mountnessing Rbt**, Brwd. CM15 131 GC41
Mount Nod Rd, SW16 203 DM90
Mount Nugent, Chesh. HP5 76 AN27
Mount Pk, Cars. SM5 240 DG109
Mount Pk Av, Har. HA1 139 CD61
South Croydon CR2 241 DP109
Mount Pk Cres, W5 159 CK72
Mount Pk Rd, W5 159 CK71
Harrow HA1 139 CD62
Pinner HA5 137 BU57
Mount Pl, W3 off High St 160 CP74
Guildford GU2 off The Mount 280 AW136
Mount Pleasant, SE27 204 DQ91
WC1 18 D5
Barnet EN4 102 DE42
Biggin Hill TN16 260 EK117
Effingham KT24 268 BY128
Epsom KT17 239 CT110
Guildford GU2 280 AW136
Harefield UB9 114 BG53
Hertford Heath SG13 54 DW11
Ruislip HA4 138 BW61
St. Albans AL3 64 CB19
Wembley HA0 160 CL67
West Horsley KT24 267 BP129
Weybridge KT13 216 BN104
Mount Pleasant Av, Hutt. CM13 131 GE44
Mount Pleasant Cl, Hat. AL9 67 CW15
Mount Pleasant Cres, N4 143 DM59
Mount Pleasant Est, Ilf. IG1 off Ilford La 147 EQ64
Mount Pleasant Hill, E5 144 DV61
Mount Pleasant La, E5 144 DV61
Bricket Wood AL2 82 BY30
Hatfield AL9 51 CW14
Sch **Mount Pleasant La JMI Sch**, Brick.Wd AL2 off Mount Pleasant La 82 BY30
Mount Pleasant Pl, SE18 187 ER77
Mount Pleasant Rd, E17 123 DY54
N17 122 DS54
NW10 4 B7
SE13 205 EB86
W5 159 CJ70
Caterham CR3 258 DU123
Chigwell IG7 125 ER49
Dartford DA1 210 FM86
New Malden KT3 220 CQ97
Romford RM5 127 FD51
Mount Pleasant Vil, N4 143 DM59
Mount Pleasant Wk, Bex. DA5 209 FC85
Sch **Mount Prim Sch, The**, N.Mal. KT3 off Dickerage La 220 CP97
Mount Ri, Red. RH1 288 DD136
Mount Rd, NW2 141 CV62
NW4 141 CU58
SE19 204 DR93
SW19 202 DA89
Barnet EN4 102 DE43
Bexleyheath DA6 208 EX85
Chessington KT9 238 CM106
Chobham GU24 232 AV112
Dagenham RM8 148 EZ60
Dartford DA1 209 FF86
Epping CM16 92 EW32
Feltham TW13 198 BY90
Hayes UB3 177 BT75
Hertford SG14 53 DN10
Ilford IG1 147 EP64
Mitcham CR4 222 DE96
New Malden KT3 220 CR97
Woking GU22 248 AV121
Mount Row, W1 29 J1
Sch **Mount Sch, The**, NW7 off Milespit Hill 119 CV50
Mountsfield Cl, Stai. TW19 196 BG86
Mountsfield Ct, SE13 205 ED86
Mountside, Felt. TW13 198 BY90
Guildford GU2 280 AV136
Stanmore HA7 117 CF53
Mountsorrel, Hert. SG13 54 DT08
Mounts Pond Rd, SE3 46 G8
Mount Sq, The, NW3 off Heath St 142 DC62
Mounts Rd, Green. DA9 211 FV85
Mount Stewart Av, Har. HA3 139 CK58
Sch **Mount Stewart Inf Sch**, Kenton HA3 off Carlisle Gdns 139 CK59
Sch **Mount Stewart Jun Sch**, Kenton HA3 off Mount Stewart Av 139 CK59
Mount St, W1 29 H1
Dorking RH4 285 CG136
Mount St Ms, W1 29 J1
Mount Ter, E1 20 E7
Mount Vernon, NW3 142 DC63
H **Mount Vernon Hosp**, Nthwd. HA6 115 BP51
Mount Vw, NW7 118 CR48
W5 159 CK70
Enfield EN2 103 DM38
London Colney AL2 84 CL27
Mountview, Nthwd. HA6 115 BT51
Mount Vw, Rick. WD3 114 BH46
Coll **Mountview Acad of Thea Arts**, Crouch End, N8 off Crouch Hill 143 DL58
Wood Grn, N22 off Kingfisher Pl 121 DM54
Mountview Cl, NW11 142 DB60
Redhill RH1 288 DE136
Mountview Ct, N8 off Green Las 143 DP56
Mountview Dr, Red. RH1 288 DD136
Mount Vw Rd, E4 123 EC45
N4 143 DL59
NW9 140 CR56
Mountview Rd, Chsht EN7 88 DS26
Claygate KT10 237 CH108
Orpington BR6 228 EU101
Mount Vil, SE27 203 DP90
Mount Way, Cars. SM5 240 DG109
Mountway, Pot.B. EN6 86 DA30
Welwyn Garden City AL7 51 CZ12
Mountway Cl, Welw.G.C. AL7 51 CZ12
Mountwood, W.Mol. KT8 218 CA97
Mountwood Cl, S.Croy. CR2 242 DV110
Jct **Movers La**, Bark. IG11 167 ES68
Movers La, Bark. IG11 167 ER67
★ **Movieum of London, The**, SE1 30 C4
● **Mowat Ind Est**, Wat. WD24 98 BW38
Mowatt Cl, N19 143 DK60
Mowbray Av, Byfleet KT14 234 BL113
Mowbray Cres, Egh. TW20 195 BA92
Mowbray Gdns, Dor. RH4 269 CH134
Mowbray Rd, NW6 4 E6
SE19 224 DT95
Edgware HA8 118 CN49
Harlow CM20 57 ET13
New Barnet EN5 102 DC42
Richmond TW10 199 CJ90
Mowbrays Cl, Rom. RM5 127 FC53
Mowbrays Rd, Rom. RM5 127 FC54
Mowbrey Gdns, Loug. IG10 107 EQ40
Sch **Mowlem Prim Sch**, E2 10 G10
Mowlem St, E2 10 F10
● **Mowlem Trd Est**, N17 122 DW52
Mowll St, SW9 42 E5
Moxom Av, Chsht EN8 89 DY30
Moxon Cl, E13 23 M1
Moxon St, W1 16 G7
Barnet EN5 101 CZ41
Moye Cl, E2 10 D10
Moyers Rd, E10 145 EC59
Moylan Rd, W6 38 F3
Moyne Ct, Wok. GU21 off Iveagh Rd 248 AT118
Moyne Pl, NW10 160 CN68
Moynihan Dr, N21 103 DL43
Moys Cl, Croy. CR0 223 DL100
Moyser Rd, SW16 203 DH92
Mozart St, W10 14 G3
Mozart Ter, SW1 29 H9
Muchelney Rd, Mord. SM4 222 DC100
Muckhatch La, Egh. TW20 215 BB97
MUCKINGFORD, S.le H. SS17 193 GM76
Muckingford Rd, Linford SS17 193 GM77
West Tilbury RM18 193 GL77
DLR **Mudchute** 34 D9
Muddy La, Slou. SL2 154 AS71
● **Mudlands Ind Est**, Rain. RM13 169 FE69
Mud La, W5 159 CK71
Mudlarks Boul, SE10 off John Harrison Way 35 M6
Muggeridge Cl, S.Croy. CR2 242 DR106
Muggeridge Rd, Dag. RM10 149 FB63
MUGSWELL, Couls. CR5 272 DB125
Muirdown Av, SW14 180 CQ84
Muir Dr, SW18 202 DE86
Muirfield, W3 160 CS72
Muirfield Cl, SE16 44 F1
Watford WD19 116 BW49
Muirfield Cres, E14 34 C6
Muirfield Grn, Wat. WD19 116 BW49
Muirfield Rd, Wat. WD19 116 BX49
Woking GU21 248 AU118
Muirkirk Rd, SE6 205 EC88
Muir Rd, E5 144 DU62
Muir St, E16 37 J3
Mulberry Av, Stai. TW19 196 BL88
Windsor SL4 174 AT82
● **Mulberry Business Cen**, SE16 33 K5
Mulberry Cl, E4 123 EA47
N8 143 DL57
NW3 6 A1
NW4 141 CW55
SE7 186 EK79
SE22 204 DU85
SW3 off Beaufort St 40 B3
SW16 203 DJ91
Amersham HP7 94 AT39
Barnet EN4 102 DD42
Broxbourne EN10 71 DZ24
Northolt UB5 off Parkfield Av 158 BY68
Park Street AL2 82 CB28
Romford RM2 149 FH56
Watford WD17 97 BS36
Weybridge KT13 217 BP104
Woking GU21 232 AY114
● **Mulberry Ct**, Dart. DA1 off Bourne Ind Pk 209 FE85
Mulberry Ct, EC1 off Tompion St 19 H3
N2 off Great N Rd 142 DE55
Barking IG11 off Westrow Dr 167 ET65
Beaconsfield HP9 133 AM55
Guildford GU4 off Gilliat Dr 265 BD132
Surbiton KT6 219 CK101
Mulberry Cres, Brent. TW8 179 CH80
West Drayton UB7 176 BN75
Mulberry Dr, Purf. RM19 190 FM77
Slough SL3 174 AY78
Mulberry Gdns, Harl. CM17 58 EX11
Shenley WD7 84 CL33
Mulberry Gate, Bans. SM7 255 CZ116
Mulberry Grn, Harl. CM17 58 EX11
Mulberry Hill, Shenf. CM15 131 FZ45
Sch **Mulberry Ho Sch, The**, NW2 4 F3
Mulberry La, Croy. CR0 224 DT102
Mulberry Mead, Hat. AL10 51 CT14
Mulberry Ms, SE14 45 N6
Wallington SM6 241 DJ107
Mulberry Par, West Dr. UB7 176 BN76
Mulberry Pl, SE9 186 EK84
W6 off Chiswick Mall 181 CU78
Sch **Mulberry Prim Sch**, N17 off Parkhurst Rd 122 DU54
Mulberry Rd, E8 10 A6
Northfleet DA11 212 GE90
Sch **Mulberry Sch for Girls**, E1 20 E9
Coll **Mulberry Sch for Girls - St. George's**, E1 20 E10
Mulberry St, E1 20 C8
Mulberry Tree Ms, W4 off Clovelly Rd 180 CQ75
Mulberry Trees, Shep. TW17 217 BQ101
Mulberry Wk, SW3 40 B2
Mulberry Way, E18 124 EH54
Belvedere DA17 189 FC75
Ilford IG6 147 EQ56
Mulgrave Rd, NW10 141 CT63
SE18 37 K9
SW6 38 G2
W5 159 CK69
Croydon CR0 224 DR104
Harrow HA1 139 CG61
Sutton SM2 240 DA107
Sch **Mulgrave Sch & Early Years Cen**, SE18 37 N7
Mulgrave Way, Knap. GU21 248 AS118
Mulholland Cl, Mitch. CR4 223 DH96
Mulkern Rd, N19 143 DK60
Mullards Cl, Mitch. CR4 222 DF102
Mullein Ct, Grays RM17 192 GD79
Mullens Rd, Egh. TW20 195 BB92
Muller Ho, SE18 37 M10
Muller Rd, SW4 203 DK86
Mullet Gdns, E2 20 D2
Mullins Path, SW14 180 CR83
Mullion Cl, Har. HA3 116 CB53
Mullion Wk, Wat. WD19 off Ormskirk Rd 116 BX49
Mull Wk, N1 9 K5
Mulready St, NW8 16 C5
Mulready Wk, Hem.H. HP3 62 BL24
Multi-way, W3 off Valetta Rd 180 CS75
Multon Rd, SW18 202 DD87
Mulvaney Way, SE1 31 M5
Mumford Mills, SE10 46 C6
Mumford Rd, SE24 203 DP85
Mumfords La, Chal.St.P. SL9 134 AU55
Muncaster Cl, Ashf. TW15 196 BN91
Muncaster Rd, SW11 202 DF85
Ashford TW15 197 BP92
Muncies Ms, SE6 205 EC89
Mundania Rd, SE22 204 DV86
Munday Rd, E16 23 N9
Mundells, Chsht EN7 88 DU27
Welwyn Garden City AL7 51 CZ07
Mundells Ct, Welw.G.C. AL7 51 CZ07
MUNDEN, Wat. WD25 82 CB34
Munden Dr, Wat. WD25 98 BY37
Munden Gro, Wat. WD24 98 BW38
Munden Ho, E3 off Bromley High St 22 D2
Munden St, W14 26 E8
Munden Vw, Wat. WD25 98 BX36
Mundesley Cl, Wat. WD19 116 BW49
Mundesley Spur, Slou. SL1 154 AS72
Mundford Rd, E5 144 DW61
Mundon Gdns, Ilf. IG1 147 ER60
Mund St, W14 39 H1
Mundy Ct, Eton SL4 off Eton Ct 173 AR80
Mundy St, N1 19 N2
Munford Dr, Swans. DA10 212 FY87
Mungo Pk Cl, Bushey Hth WD23 116 CC47
Mungo Pk Rd, Grav. DA12 213 GK92
Rainham RM13 169 FG65
Mungo Pk Way, Orp. BR5 228 EW101
Munkenbeck, W2 off Hermitage St 16 A7
Munnery Way, Orp. BR6 227 EN104
Munnings Gdns, Islw. TW7 199 CD85
Munro Dr, N11 121 DJ51
Munro Ms, W10 14 F6
Munro Rd, Bushey WD23 98 CB43
Munro Ter, SW10 40 A3
Munslow Gdns, Sutt. SM1 240 DD105
Munstead Vw, Art. GU3 280 AV138
Munster Av, Houns. TW4 178 BZ84
Munster Ct, Tedd. TW11 199 CJ93
Munster Gdns, N13 121 DP49
Munster Ms, SW6 38 E4
Munster Rd, SW6 38 E4
Teddington TW11 199 CH93
Munster Sq, NW1 17 K3
Munton Rd, SE17 31 K8
Murchison Av, Bex. DA5 208 EX88
Murchison Rd, E10 145 EC61
Hoddesdon EN11 55 EB14
Murdoch Cl, Stai. TW18 196 BG92
Murdock Cl, E16 23 M8
Murdock St, SE15 44 E3
Murfett Cl, SW19 201 CY89
Murfitt Way, Upmin. RM14 150 FN63
Muriel Av, Wat. WD18 98 BW43
Muriel St, N1 8 D10
Murillo Rd, SE13 185 ED84
Murphy St, SE1 30 E5
Murray Av, Brom. BR1 226 EH96
Hounslow TW3 198 CB85
● **Murray Business Cen**, Orp. BR5 228 EV97
Murray Cl, SE28 167 ES74
Murray Ct, W7 179 CE76
Murray Cres, Pnr. HA5 116 BX53
Murray Grn, Wok. GU21 off Bunyard Dr 233 BC114
Murray Gro, N1 19 K1
Murray Ms, NW1 7 N6
Murray Rd, SW19 201 CX93
W5 179 CJ77
Berkhamsted HP4 60 AV18
Northwood HA6 115 BS53
Orpington BR5 228 EV97
Ottershaw KT16 233 BC107
Richmond TW10 199 CH89
Murrays La, Byfleet KT14 234 BK114
Murray Sq, E16 23 P9
Murray St, NW1 7 M6
Murrays Yd, SE18 37 N8
Murray Ter, NW3 off Flask Wk 142 DD63
W5 off Murray Rd 179 CK77
Murrells Wk, Bkhm KT23 252 CA123
Murreys, The, Ashtd. KT21 253 CK118
Mursell Est, SW8 42 C6
Murthering La, Rom. RM4 109 FG43
Murton Ct, St.Alb. AL1 65 CE19
Murtwell Dr, Chig. IG7 125 EQ51
Musard Rd, W6 38 F2
W14 38 F2
Musbury St, E1 20 G8
Muscal, W6 38 E2
Muscatel Pl, SE5 43 P5
Sch **Muschamp Prim Sch**, Cars. SM5 off Muschamp Rd 222 DE103
Muschamp Rd, SE15 184 DT83
Carshalton SM5 222 DE103
Muscovy Ho, Erith DA18 off Kale Rd 188 EY75
Muscovy St, EC3 31 P1
★ **Museum in Docklands**, E14 34 B1
Museum La, SW7 28 B7
★ **Museum of Childhood at Bethnal Grn**, E2 20 F2
★ **Museum of Croydon**, Croy. CR0 224 DQ104
★ **Museum of Gdn History**, SE1 30 C7
★ **Museum of Harlow**, Harl. CM20 58 EV12
★ **Museum of Instruments** (Royal Coll of Music), SW7 28 A6
★ **Museum of London**, EC2 19 J7
★ **Museum of Richmond**, Rich. TW9 199 CK85
★ **Museum of St. Albans**, St.Alb. AL1 65 CE19
Museum Pas, E2 20 G2
Museum St, WC1 18 A7
Museum Way, W3 180 CN75
Musgrave Cl, Barn. EN4 102 DC39
Cheshunt EN7 off Allwood Rd 88 DT27
Musgrave Cres, SW6 39 K5
Musgrave Rd, Islw. TW7 179 CF81
Musgrove Rd, SE14 45 K7
Musjid Rd, SW11 40 B9
Muskalls Cl, Chsht EN7 88 DU27
Musket Cl, E.Barn. EN4 off East Barnet Rd 102 DD43
Muskham Rd, Harl. CM20 58 EU12
Musk Hill, Hem.H. HP1 61 BE21
Musleigh Manor, Ware SG12 55 DZ06
Musley Hill, Ware SG12 55 DY05
Musley La, Ware SG12 55 DY05
Musquash Way, Houns. TW4 178 BW82
Mussenden La, Fawk.Grn DA3 231 FS101
Horton Kirby DA4 230 FQ99
Mustard Mill Rd, Stai. TW18 195 BF91
Muston Rd, E5 144 DV61
Mustow Pl, SW6 39 H8
Muswell Av, N10 121 DH54
MUSWELL HILL, N10 143 DH55
Muswell Hill, N10 143 DH55
Muswell Hill Bdy, N10 143 DH55
Muswell Hill Pl, N10 143 DH56
Sch **Muswell Hill Prim Sch**, N10 off Muswell Hill 143 DH55
Muswell Hill Rd, N6 142 DG58
N10 142 DG56
Muswell Ms, N10 143 DH55
Muswell Rd, N10 143 DH55
Mutchetts Cl, Wat. WD25 82 BY33
Mutrix Rd, NW6 5 K8
Mutton La, Pot.B. EN6 85 CY31
Mutton Pl, NW1 7 H5
Muybridge Rd, N.Mal. KT3 220 CQ96
Sch **Myatt Gdn Prim Sch**, SE4 45 P8
Myatt Rd, SW9 42 G6
Myatts Flds S, SW9 off St. Lawrence Way 42 F8
Myatts N, SW9 off Fairbairn Grn 42 F6
Mycenae Rd, SE3 47 N4
Myddelton Av, Enf. EN1 104 DS38
Myddelton Cl, Enf. EN1 104 DT39
Myddelton Gdns, N21 121 DP45
Myddelton Pk, N20 120 DD48
Myddelton Pas, EC1 18 F2
Myddelton Rd, N8 143 DL56
Myddelton Sq, EC1 18 F2
Myddelton St, EC1 18 F3
Myddleton Av, N4 144 DQ61
Myddleton Cl, Stan. HA7 117 CG47
Myddleton Ct, Horn. RM11 149 FF59
Myddleton Ms, N22 121 DL52
Myddleton Path, Chsht EN7 88 DV31
Myddleton Rd, N22 121 DL52
Uxbridge UB8 156 BJ67
Ware SG12 55 DX07
Myers Cl, Shenley WD7 84 CL32
Myers Dr, Slou. SL2 133 AP64
Myers La, SE14 45 J2
Mygrove Cl, Rain. RM13 170 FK68
Mygrove Gdns, Rain. RM13 170 FK68
Mygrove Rd, Rain. RM13 170 FK68
Myles Ct, Goffs Oak EN7 88 DQ29
Mylis Cl, SE26 204 DV91
Mylius Cl, SE14 45 H6
Mylne Cl, W6 181 CU78
Cheshunt EN8 88 DW27
Mylner Ct, Hodd. EN11 off Ditchfield Rd 71 EA15
Mylne St, EC1 18 E1
Mylor Cl, Wok. GU21 232 AY114
Mymms Dr, Brook.Pk AL9 86 DA26
Mynchen Cl, Beac. HP9 111 AK49
Mynchen End, Beac. HP9 111 AK49
Mynchen Rd, Beac. HP9 111 AK50
Mynns Cl, Epsom KT18 238 CP114
Mynterne Ct, SW19 off Swanton Gdns 201 CX88
MYNTHURST, Reig. RH2 287 CV144
Myra St, SE2 188 EU78
Myrdle St, E1 20 D7
Myrke, The, Datchet SL3 174 AT77
Myrna Cl, SW19 202 DE94
Myron Pl, SE13 185 EC83
Myrtle Av, Felt. TW14 177 BS84
Ruislip HA4 137 BU59
Myrtleberry Cl, E8 10 A5
Myrtle Cl, Colnbr. SL3 175 BE81
East Barnet EN4 120 DF46
Erith DA8 189 FE81
Uxbridge UB8 off Violet Av 156 BM71
West Drayton UB7 176 BM76
Myrtle Cres, Slou. SL2 154 AT73
Myrtledene Rd, SE2 188 EU78
Myrtle Gdns, W7 159 CE74
Myrtle Grn, Hem.H. HP1 off Newlands Rd 61 BE19
Myrtle Gro, Aveley RM15 190 FQ75
Enfield EN2 104 DR38
New Malden KT3 220 CQ96
Myrtle Pl, Dart. DA2 211 FR87
Myrtle Rd, E6 166 EL67
E17 145 DY58
N13 122 DQ48
W3 160 CQ74
Croydon CR0 225 EA104
Myrtle Rd, Dart. DA1 210 FK88
Dorking RH4 285 CG135
Hampton Hill TW12 198 CC93
Hounslow TW3 178 CC82
Ilford IG1 147 EP61
Romford RM3 128 FJ51
Sutton SM1 240 DC106
Warley CM14 130 FW49
Myrtleside Cl, Nthwd. HA6 115 BR52
Myrtle Wk, N1 19 N1
Mysore Rd, SW11 182 DF83
Myton Rd, SE21 204 DR90

N

● **N17 Studios**, N17 122 DT52
🔒 **N1 Shop Cen**, N1 8 F10
Nadine Ct, Wall. SM6 off Woodcote Rd 241 DJ109
Nadine St, SE7 186 EJ78
Nafferton Ri, Loug. IG10 106 EK43
Nagle Cl, E17 123 ED54
Jct **Nags Head**, N7 143 DM63
🔒 **Nags Head Cen**, N7 143 DM63
Nags Head Cl, Hert. SG13 54 DV08
Nag's Head Ct, EC1 19 J5
Nags Head La, Brwd. CM14 129 FR51
Upminster RM14 128 FQ53
Welling DA16 188 EV83
Nags Head Rd, Enf. EN3 104 DW42
Nailsworth Cres, Merst. RH1 273 DK129
Nailzee Cl, Ger.Cr. SL9 134 AY59
Nairn Ct, Til. RM18 off Dock Rd 193 GF82
Nairne Gro, SE24 204 DR85
Nairn Grn, Wat. WD19 115 BU48
Nairn Rd, Ruis. HA4 158 BW65
Nairn St, E14 22 F7
Nalders Rd, Chesh. HP5 76 AR29
NALDERSWOOD, Reig. RH2 287 CW144
Nallhead Rd, Felt. TW13 198 BW92
Namba Roy Cl, SW16 203 DM91
Namton Dr, Th.Hth. CR7 223 DM98
Nan Clark's La, NW7 119 CT47
Nancy Downs, Wat. WD19 116 BW45
Nankin St, E14 22 B9
Nansen Rd, SW11 182 DG84
Gravesend DA12 213 GK92
Nansen Village, N12 120 DB49
Nant Ct, NW2 off Granville Rd 141 CZ61
Nantes Cl, SW18 182 DC84
Nantes Pas, E1 20 A6
Nant Rd, NW2 141 CZ61
Nant St, E2 20 F2
Naoroji St, WC1 18 E3
Nap, The, Kings L. WD4 80 BN29
Napier Av, E14 34 B10
SW6 38 G10
Napier Cl, SE8 45 P4
W14 26 G6
Hornchurch RM11 149 FH60
London Colney AL2 83 CK25
West Drayton UB7 176 BM76
Napier Ct, SE12 206 EH90
SW6 off Ranelagh Gdns 38 G10
Cheshunt EN8 off Flamstead End Rd 88 DV28
Surbiton KT6 219 CK100
Napier Dr, Bushey WD23 98 BY42
Napier Gdns, Guil. GU1 265 BB133
Napier Gro, N1 19 K1
Napier Ho, Rain. RM13 169 FF69
Napier Pl, W14 26 G7
Napier Rd, E6 167 EN67
E11 146 EE63
E15 23 K1
N17 144 DS55
NW10 161 CV69
SE25 224 DV98
W14 26 G7
Ashford TW15 197 BR94
Belvedere DA17 188 EZ77
Bromley BR2 226 EH98
Enfield EN3 105 DX43
Isleworth TW7 179 CG84
London Heathrow Airport TW6 176 BK81
Northfleet DA11 213 GF88
South Croydon CR2 242 DR108
Wembley HA0 139 CK64
Napier Ter, N1 8 G7
Napier Wk, Ashf. TW15 197 BR94
Napoleon Rd, E5 144 DV62
Twickenham TW1 199 CH87
Napsbury Av, Lon.Col. AL2 83 CJ26
Napsbury La, St.Alb. AL1 65 CG23
Napton Cl, Hayes UB4 158 BY70
Narbonne Av, SW4 203 DJ85
Narboro Ct, Rom. RM1 149 FG58
Narborough Cl, Uxb. UB10 137 BQ61
Narborough St, SW6 39 L9
Narcissus Rd, NW6 5 J3
Narcot La, Ch.St.G. HP8 112 AU48
Chalfont St. Peter SL9 112 AV52
Narcot Rd, Ch.St.G. HP8 112 AU48
Narcot Way, Ch.St.G. HP8 112 AU49
Nare Rd, Aveley RM15 170 FQ73
Naresby Fold, Stan. HA7 117 CJ51
Narford Rd, E5 144 DU62
Narrow Boat Cl, SE28 off Ridge Cl 187 ER75
Narrow La, Warl. CR6 258 DV119
Narrow St, E14 21 L10
Narrow Way, Brom. BR2 226 EL100
Nascot Pl, Wat. WD17 97 BV39
Nascot Rd, Wat. WD17 97 BV40
Nascot St, W12 14 A8
Watford WD17 97 BV40
Sch **Nascot Wd Inf & Nurs Sch**, Wat. WD17 off Nascot Wd Rd 97 BU38
Sch **Nascot Wd Jun Sch**, Wat. WD17 off Nascot Wd Rd 97 BU38
Nascot Wd Rd, Wat. WD17 97 BT37
Naseberry Ct, E4 off Merriam Cl 123 EC50
Naseby Cl, NW6 5 P6
Isleworth TW7 179 CE81
Naseby Ct, Walt. KT12 off Clements Rd 218 BW103
Naseby Rd, SE19 204 DR93
Dagenham RM10 148 FA62
Ilford IG5 125 EM53
Nash Cl, Els. WD6 100 CM42
North Mymms AL9 67 CX23
Sutton SM1 222 DD104

Coll Nash Coll, Brom. BR2
off Croydon Rd 226 EF104
Nash Cft, Nthflt DA11 212 GE91
Nashdom La, Burn. SL1 152 AG66
Nash Dr, Red. RH1 272 DF132
Nash Gdns, Red. RH1 272 DF132
Nash Grn, Brom. BR1 206 EG93
Hemel Hempstead HP3 80 BM25
Nash Ho, SW1 41 K1
Nash La, Kes. BR2 244 EG106
Nashleigh Hill, Chesh. HP5 76 AQ29
Sch Nash Mills C of E Prim Sch, Hem.H. HP3
off Belswains La 80 BM25
Nash Mills La, Hem.H. HP3 80 BM26
Nash Rd, N9 122 DW47
SE4 185 DX84
Romford RM6 148 EX56
Slough SL3 175 AZ77
Nash St, NW1 17 K3
Nash's Yd, Uxb. UB8
off George St 156 BK66
Nash Way, Kenton HA3 139 CH58
Nasmyth St, W6 181 CV76
Nassau Path, SE28
off Disraeli Cl 168 EW74
Nassau Rd, SW13 181 CT81
Nassau St, W1 17 L7
Nassington Rd, NW3 142 DE63
Natalie Cl, Felt. TW14 197 BR87
Natalie Ms, Twick. TW2
off Sixth Cross Rd 199 CD90
Natal Rd, N11 121 DL51
SW16 203 DK93
Ilford IG1 147 EP63
Thornton Heath CR7 224 DR97
Nathan Cl, Upmin. RM14 151 FS60
Nathaniel Cl, E1 20 B7
Nathans Rd, Wem. HA0 139 CJ61
Nathan Way, SE28 187 ES77
★ National Archives, The, Rich.
TW9 180 CP80
★ National Army Mus, SW3 40 F2
H National Blood Service,
Brentwood Transfusion Cen,
Brwd. CM15 131 FZ46
N London Blood Transfusion Cen,
NW9 118 CR54
S Thames Blood Transfusion Cen,
SW17 202 DD92
Coll National Film & Television Sch
Beaconsfield Studios, Beac.
HP9 off Station Rd 111 AL54
★ National Gall, WC2 29 P1
H National Hosp for Neurology &
Neurosurgery, The, WC1 18 B5
★ National Maritime Mus,
SE10 46 G3
★ National Portrait Gall, WC2 29 P1
Coll National Sch of Govt, SW1 29 L9
National Ter, SE16
off Bermondsey Wall E 32 E5
★ National Thea, SE1 30 D2
Nation Way, E4 123 EC46
★ Natural History Mus, SW7 28 A7
Natwoke Cl, Beac. HP9 111 AK50
Naunton Way, Horn. RM12 150 FK62
Naval Row, E14 22 F10
Naval Wk, Brom. BR1
off High St 226 EG96
Navarino Gro, E8 10 D4
Navarino Rd, E8 10 D4
Navarre Gdns, Rom. RM5 127 FB51
Navarre Rd, E6 166 EL68
Navarre St, E2 20 A4
Navenby Wk, E3 22 B4
Navestock Cl, E4
off Mapleton Rd 123 EC48
Navestock Cres, Wdf.Grn. IG8 124 EJ53
Navigation Ct, E16
off Armada Way 167 EQ73
Navigation Dr, Enf. EN3 105 EA38
Navigator Dr, Sthl. UB2 178 CC75
● Navigator Pk, Sthl. UB2 178 BW77
Navy St, SW4 41 N10
Naxos Bldg, E14 34 A5
Nayim Pl, E8 10 E3
Nayland Ct, Rom. RM1
off Market Pl 149 FE56
Naylor Gro, Enf. EN3
off South St 105 DX43
Naylor Rd, N20 120 DC47
SE15 44 E4
Naylor Ter, Colnbr. SL3
off Vicarage Way 175 BC80
Nazareth Gdns, SE15 44 E8
NAZEING, Wal.Abb. EN9 72 EJ22
Nazeingbury Cl, Lwr Naze.
EN9 71 ED22
Nazeingbury Par, Wal.Abb. EN9
off Nazeing Rd 71 ED22
Nazeing Common, Naze. EN9 72 EH24
NAZEING GATE, Wal.Abb. EN9 90 EJ25
Nazeing New Rd, Brox. EN10 71 EA21
Sch Nazeing Prim Sch, Naze. EN9
off Hyde Mead 72 EE23
Nazeing Rd, Lwr Naze. EN9 71 EC22
Nazeing Wk, Rain. RM13
off Ongar Way 169 FF67
Nazrul St, E2 20 A2
● NCR Business Cen, NW10
off Great Cen Way 140 CS64
Neagle Cl, Borwd. WD6
off Balcon Way 100 CQ39
Neal Av, Sthl. UB1 158 BZ70
Neal Cl, Ger.Cr. SL9 135 BB60
Northwood HA6 115 BU53
Neal Ct, Hert. SG14 54 DQ09
Waltham Abbey EN9 90 EF33
Nealden St, SW9 42 C10
Neale Cl, N2 142 DC55
Neal St, WC2 18 A9
Watford WD18 98 BW43
Neal's Yd, WC2 18 A9
Near Acre, NW9 119 CT53
NEASDEN, NW2 140 CS62
⊖ Neasden 140 CS64
Neasden Cl, NW10 140 CS64
Jct Neasden Junct, NW10
off North Circular Rd 140 CS63
Neasden La, NW10 140 CS63
Neasden La N, NW10 140 CR62
Neasham Rd, Dag. RM8 148 EV64
Neatby Ct, Chsht EN8
off Coopers Wk 89 DX28
Neate St, SE5 44 A2
Neath Gdns, Mord. SM4 222 DC100
Neathouse Pl, SW1 29 L8
Neats Acre, Ruis. HA4 137 BR59
Neatscourt Rd, E6 24 F7
Neave Cres, Rom. RM3 128 FJ53
Neb La, Oxt. RH8 275 EC131
Nebraska Bldg, SE13
off Deals Gateway 46 C7
Nebraska St, SE1 31 L5
★ NEC Harlequins RFC, Twick.
TW2 199 CE87
Neckinger, SE16 32 B6
Neckinger Est, SE16 32 B6
Neckinger St, SE1 32 B5
Nectarine Way, SE13 46 D8
Necton Rd, Wheat. AL4 50 CL07
Needham Cl, Wind. SL4 173 AL81
Needham Ct, Enf. EN3
off Manton Rd 105 EA37
Needham Rd, W11 15 J9
Needham Ter, NW2
off Kara Way 141 CX62
Needleman St, SE16 33 J5
Needles Bk, Gdse. RH9 274 DV131
Neela Cl, Uxb. UB10 137 BP63
Neeld Cres, NW4 141 CV57
Wembley HA9 140 CN64
Neeld Par, Wem. HA9
off Harrow Rd 140 CN64
Neil Cl, Ashf. TW15 197 BQ92
Neild Way, Rick. WD3 113 BF45
Neil Wates Cres, SW2 203 DN88
Nelgarde Rd, SE6 205 EA87
Nella Rd, W6 38 C3
Nelldale Rd, SE16 32 G8
Nellgrove Rd, Uxb. UB10 157 BP70
Nell Gwynn Cl, Shenley WD7 84 CL32
Nell Gwynne Av, Shep. TW17 217 BR100
Nell Gwynne Cl, Epsom KT19 238 CN111
Nello James Gdns, SE27 204 DR91
Nelmes Cl, Horn. RM11 150 FM57
Nelmes Cres, Horn. RM11 150 FL57
Sch Nelmes Prim Sch, Horn. RM11
off Wingletye La 150 FM56
Nelmes Rd, Horn. RM11 150 FL59
Nelmes Way, Horn. RM11 150 FL56
Nelson Av, St.Alb. AL1 65 CH23
Nelson Cl, NW6 15 J3
Biggin Hill TN16 260 EL117
Croydon CR0 223 DP102
Feltham TW14 197 BT88
Romford RM7 127 FB53
Slough SL3 174 AX77
Uxbridge UB10 157 BP69
Walton-on-Thames KT12 217 BV102
Warley CM14 130 FX50
Nelson Ct, SE16
off Brunel Rd 33 H3
Gravesend DA12 213 GJ88
Nelson Gdns, E2 20 D2
Guildford GU1 265 BA133
Hounslow TW3 198 CA86
Nelson Gro Rd, SW19 222 DB95
H Nelson Hosp, SW20 221 CZ96
Nelson La, Uxb. UB10 157 BP69
Nelson Mandela Cl, N10 120 DG54
Nelson Mandela Rd, SE3 186 EJ83
Nelson Pas, EC1 19 K3
Nelson Pl, N1 19 H1
Sidcup DA14
off Sidcup High St 208 EU91
Sch Nelson Prim Sch, E6
off Napier Rd 167 EN68
Whitton TW2 off Nelson Rd 198 CB87
Nelson Rd, E4 123 EB51
E11 146 EG56
N8 143 DM57
N9 122 DV47
N15 144 DS56
SE10 46 F3
SW19 202 DB94
Ashford TW15 196 BL92
Belvedere DA17 188 EZ78
Bromley BR2 226 EJ98
Caterham CR3 258 DR123
Dartford DA1 210 FJ86
Enfield EN3 105 DX44
Harrow HA1 139 CD60
Hounslow TW3, TW4 198 CA86
London Heathrow Airport
TW6 176 BM81
New Malden KT3 220 CR99
Northfleet DA11 213 GF89
Rainham RM13 169 FF68
Sidcup DA14
off Sidcup High St 208 EU91
South Ockendon RM15 171 FW68
Stanmore HA7 117 CJ51
Twickenham TW2 198 CC86
Uxbridge UB10 157 BP69
Windsor SL4 173 AM83
★ Nelson's Column, WC2 30 A2
Nelson Sq, SE1 30 G4
Nelson's Row, SW4 183 DK84
Nelson St, E1 20 E8
E6 167 EM68
E16 23 L10
Hertford SG14 53 DP08
Nelsons Yd, NW1 7 L10
Nelson Ter, N1 19 H1
● Nelson Trd Est, SW19 222 DB95
Nelson Wk, SE16 33 M3
Epsom KT19 238 CN109
Nelwyn Av, Horn. RM11 150 FM57
Nemoure Rd, W3 160 CQ73
Nene Gdns, Felt. TW13 198 BZ89
Nene Rd, Lon.Hthrw Air. TW6 177 BP81
Nepaul Rd, SW11 40 C9
Nepean St, SW15 201 CU86
Neptune Cl, Rain. RM13 169 FF68
Neptune Ct, Borwd. WD6
off Clarendon Rd 100 CN41
Neptune Dr, Hem.H. HP2 62 BL18
Neptune Ho, E3
off Garrison Rd 12 A9
Neptune Rd, Har. HA1 139 CD58
London Heathrow Airport
TW6 177 BR81
Neptune St, SE16 32 G6
Neptune Wk, Erith DA8 189 FD77
Neptune Way, Slou. SL1
off Hunters Way 173 AL75
Nero Ct, Brent. TW8
off Justin Cl 179 CK80
Nesbit Rd, SE9 186 EK84
Nesbitt Cl, SE3 47 J9
Nesbitts All, Barn. EN5
off Bath Pl 101 CZ41
Nesbitt Sq, SE19
off Coxwell Rd 204 DS94
Coll Nescot, Ewell KT17
off Reigate Rd 239 CU111
Nesham St, E1 32 C2
Ness Rd, Erith DA8 190 FK79
Ness St, SE16 32 C6
Nesta Rd, Wdf.Grn. IG8 124 EE51
Nestles Av, Hayes UB3 177 BT76
Neston Rd, Wat. WD24 98 BW37
Nestor Av, N21 103 DP44
Nethan Dr, Aveley RM15 170 FQ73
Netheravon Rd, W4 181 CT77
W7 159 CF74
Netheravon Rd S, W4 181 CT78
Netherbury Rd, W5 179 CK76
Netherby Gdns, Enf. EN2 103 DL42
Netherby Pk, Wey. KT13 235 BS106
Netherby Rd, SE23 204 DW87
Nether Cl, N3 120 DA52
Nethercote Av, Wok. GU21 248 AT117
Nethercourt Av, N3 120 DA51
Netherfield Ct, Stans.Abb.
SG12 55 ED12
Netherfield Gdns, Bark. IG11 167 ER65
Netherfield La, Stans.Abb.
SG12 56 EE12
Netherfield Rd, N12 120 DB50
SW17 202 DG90
Netherford Rd, SW4 41 M9
Netherhall Gdns, NW3 5 P4
Netherhall Rd, Roydon CM19 72 EF17
Netherhall Way, NW3 5 P3
Netherlands, The, Couls. CR5 257 DJ119
Netherlands Rd, New Barn.
EN5 102 DD44
Netherleigh Cl, N6 143 DH60
Netherleigh Pk, Red. RH1 289 DK136
Nether Mt, Guil. GU2 280 AV136
Nethern Ct Rd, Wold. CR3 259 EA123
Netherne Dr, Couls. CR5 257 DH121
Netherne La, Couls. CR5 257 DK121
Merstham RH1 257 DJ123
Netherpark Dr, Rom. RM2 127 FF54
Nether St, N3 120 DA53
N12 120 DB50
Netherton Gro, SW10 39 P3
Netherton Rd, N15 144 DR58
Twickenham TW1 199 CG85
Netherway, St.Alb. AL3 64 CA23
Netherwood, N2 120 DD54
Netherwood Pl, W14 26 C6
Netherwood Rd, W14 26 C6
Beaconsfield HP9 111 AK50
Netherwood St, NW6 5 H6
Netley Cl, Goms. GU5 283 BQ138
New Addington CR0 243 EC108
Sutton SM3 239 CX106
Netley Dr, Walt. KT12 218 BZ101
Netley Gdns, Mord. SM4 222 DC101
Sch Netley Prim Sch, NW1 17 L3
Netley Rd, E17 145 DZ57
Brentford TW8 180 CL79
Ilford IG2 147 ER57
London Heathrow Airport
TW6 177 BR81
Morden SM4 222 DC101
Netley St, NW1 17 L3
NETTESWELL, Harl. CM20 57 ET14
Netteswellbury Fm, Harl.
CM18 73 ET16
Netteswell Orchard, Harl.
CM20 57 ER14
Netteswell Rd, Harl. CM20 57 ES12
Netteswell Twr, Harl. CM20 57 ER14
Nettlecombe Cl, Sutt. SM2 240 DB109
Nettlecroft, Hem.H. HP1 62 BH21
Welwyn Garden City AL7 52 DB08
Nettleden Av, Wem. HA9 160 CN65
Nettleden Rd, Hem.H. HP1 61 BB15
Potten End HP4 61 BA16
Nettlefold Pl, SE27 203 DP90
Nettlestead Cl, Beck. BR3 225 DZ95
Nettles Ter, Guil. GU1 264 AX134
Nettleton Rd, SE14 45 K6
London Heathrow Airport
TW6 177 BP81
Uxbridge UB10 136 BM63
Nettlewood Rd, SW16 203 DK94
Neuchatel Rd, SE6 205 DZ89
Nevada Bldg, SE10
off Blackheath Rd 46 C6
Nevada Cl, N.Mal. KT3 220 CQ98
Nevada St, SE10 46 F4
Nevell Rd, Grays RM16 193 GH76
Nevern Pl, SW5 27 K9
Nevern Rd, SW5 27 J9
Nevern Sq, SW5 27 K9
Nevil Cl, Nthwd. HA6 115 BQ50
Neville Av, N.Mal. KT3 220 CR95
Neville Cl, E11 146 EF62
NW1 17 P1
NW6 15 H1
SE15 44 C5
W3 off Acton La 180 CQ75
Banstead SM7 240 DB114
Esher KT10 236 BZ107
Hounslow TW3 178 CB82
Potters Bar EN6 85 CZ31
Sidcup DA15 207 ET91
Stoke Poges SL2 154 AT65
Neville Ct, Slou. SL1
off Dropmore Rd 152 AJ69
Neville Dr, N2 142 DC58
Neville Gdns, Dag. RM8 148 EX62
Neville Gill Cl, SW18 202 DA86
Neville Pl, N22 121 DM53
Neville Rd, E7 13 P7
NW6 15 H1
W5 159 CK70
Croydon CR0 224 DR101
Dagenham RM8 148 EX61
Ilford IG6 125 EQ53
Kingston upon Thames KT1 220 CN96
Richmond TW10 199 CJ90
Nevilles Ct, NW2 141 CU62
Neville St, SW7 28 A10
Neville Ter, SW7 28 A10
Neville Wk, Cars. SM5 222 DE101
Nevill Gro, Wat. WD24 97 BV39
Nevill Rd, N16 144 DS63
Nevill Way, Loug. IG10
off Valley Hill 106 EL44
Nevin Dr, E4 123 EB46
Nevinson Cl, SW18 202 DD86
Nevis Cl, Rom. RM1 127 FE51
Nevis Rd, SW17 202 DG89
New Acres Rd, SE28 187 ES75
NEW ADDINGTON, Croy. CR0 243 ED109
Tra New Addington 243 EC110
Newall Ct, W12
off Heathstan Rd 161 CU72
Newall Ho, SE1 31 K6
Newall Rd, Lon.Hthrw Air.
TW6 177 BQ81
New Arc, Uxb. UB8
off High St 156 BK67
Newark Cl, Guil. GU4
off Dairyman's Wk 265 BB129
Ripley GU23 250 BG121
Newark Cotts, Ripley GU23 250 BG121
Newark Ct, Walt. KT12 218 BW102
Newark Cres, NW10 160 CR69
Newark Grn, Borwd. WD6 100 CR41
Newark Knok, E6 25 L8
Newark La, Ripley
GU22, GU23 249 BF118
Newark Rd, S.Croy. CR2 242 DR107
Newark St, E1 20 E7
Newark Way, NW4 141 CU56
New Ash Cl, N2 142 DD55
New Atlas Wf, E14 33 P7
New Barn Cl, Wall. SM6 241 DM107
New Barnes Av, St.Alb. AL1 65 CG23
NEW BARNET, Barn. EN5 102 DB42
⇌ New Barnet 102 DD43
New Barn La, Cudham TN14 261 EQ116
Newbarn La, Seer Grn HP9 112 AS49
New Barn La, West. TN16 261 EQ118
Whyteleafe CR3 258 DS117
New Barn Rd, Sthflt DA13 212 GC90
Swanley BR8 229 FE95
New Barns Av, Mitch. CR4 223 DK98
New Barn St, E13 23 P4
New Barns Way, Chig. IG7 125 EP48
New Battlebridge La, Red.
RH1 273 DH130
Sch New Beacon Sch, The,
Sev. TN13
off Brittains La 278 FG127
NEW BECKENHAM, Beck.
BR3 205 DZ93
⇌ New Beckenham 205 DZ94
Newberries Av, Rad. WD7 99 CJ35
Sch Newberries Prim Sch, Rad.
WD7 off Newberries Av 99 CJ36
Newberry Cres, Wind. SL4 173 AK82
New Berry La, Hersham KT12 236 BX106
Newbery Rd, Erith DA8 189 FF81
Newbery Way, Slou. SL1 173 AR75
Newbiggin Path, Wat. WD19 116 BW49
Newbolt Av, Sutt. SM3 239 CW106
Newbolt Rd, Stan. HA7 117 CF51
New Bond St, W1 17 J9
Newborough Grn, N.Mal. KT3 220 CR98
New Brent St, NW4 141 CW57
Newbridge Pt, SE23
off Windrush La 205 DX90
Sch Newbridge Sch,
Barley La Campus, Ilf. IG3
off Barley La 148 EV57
Loxford La Campus, Ilf. IG3
off Loxford La 147 ES63
New Br St, EC4 18 G9
New Broad St, EC2 19 N7
New Bdy, W5 159 CJ73
Hampton Hill TW12
off Hampton Rd 199 CD92
New Bdy Bldgs, W5
off New Bdy 159 CK73
Newburgh Rd, W3 160 CQ74
Grays RM17 192 GD78
Newburgh St, W1 17 L9
New Burlington Ms, W1 17 L10
New Burlington Pl, W1 17 L10
New Burlington St, W1 17 L10
Newburn St, SE11 42 D1
Newbury Av, Enf. EN3 105 DZ38
Newbury Cl, Dart. DA2
off Lingfield Av 210 FP87
Northolt UB5 158 BZ65
Romford RM3 128 FK51
Newbury Gdns, Epsom KT19 239 CT105
Romford RM3 128 FK51
Upminster RM14 150 FM62
Newbury Ho, N22 121 DL53
Newbury Ms, NW5 7 H5
NEWBURY PARK, Ilf. IG2 147 ER57
⊖ Newbury Park 147 ER58
Sch Newbury Pk Prim Sch,
Barkingside IG2
off Perrymans Fm Rd 147 ER58
Newbury Rd, E4 123 EC51
Bromley BR2 226 EG97
Ilford IG2 147 ES58
London Heathrow Airport
TW6 176 BM81
Romford RM3 128 FK50
Newbury St, EC1 19 J7
Newbury Wk, Rom. RM3 128 FK50
Newbury Way, Nthlt. UB5 158 BY65
New Butt La, SE8 46 B5
New Butt La N, SE8 46 B5
Newby Cl, Enf. EN1 104 DS40
Newby Pl, E14 22 E10
Newby St, SW8 41 K10
New Caledonian Wf, SE16 33 N6
Newcastle Av, Ilf. IG6 126 EU51
Newcastle Cl, EC4 18 G8
Newcastle Pl, W2 16 B7
Newcastle Row, EC1 18 F4
New Causeway, Reig. RH2 288 DB137
New Cavendish St, W1 17 K6
New Change, EC4 19 J9
New Chapel Rd, Felt. TW13
off High St 197 BV88
New Chapel Sq, Felt. TW13 197 BV88
New Charles St, EC1 19 H2
NEW CHARLTON, SE7 36 C8
New Ch Ct, SE19
off Waldegrave Rd 204 DU94
New Ch Rd, SE5 43 K4
Newchurch Rd, Slou. SL2 153 AM71
Sch New City Prim Sch, E13 24 D3
New City Rd, E13 24 C2
New Clock Twr Pl, N7 8 A4
New Cl, SW19 222 DC97
Feltham TW13 198 BY92
New Coll Ct, NW3
off Finchley Rd 5 P5
New Coll Ms, N1 8 F6
New Coll Par, NW3
off Finchley Rd 6 A5
Newcombe Gdns, SW16 203 DL91
Hounslow TW4 178 BZ84
Newcombe Pk, NW7 118 CS50
Wembley HA0 160 CM67
Newcombe Ri, West Dr. UB7 156 BL72
Newcombe St, W8 27 K2
Newcomen Rd, E11 146 EF62
SW11 182 DD83
Newcomen St, SE1 31 L4
Newcome Path, Shenley WD7
off Newcome Rd 84 CN34
Newcome Rd, Shenley WD7 84 CN34
New Compton St, WC2 17 P9
New Concordia Wf, SE1 32 B4
New Coppice, Wok. GU21 248 AT119
New Cotts, Wenn. RM13 170 FJ72
New Ct, EC4 18 E10
Addlestone KT15 216 BJ104
Newcourt, Uxb. UB8 156 BJ71
Newcourt St, NW8 16 C1
🔒 New Covent Gdn Flower Mkt,
SW8 41 P3
🔒 New Covent Gdn Mkt,
SW8 41 N5
New Crane Pl, E1 32 G2
Newcroft Cl, Uxb. UB8 156 BM71
NEW CROSS, SE14 45 L6
⇌ New Cross 45 P5
⊖ New Cross 45 P5
Jct New Cross, SE14 45 N5
NEW CROSS GATE, SE14 45 J6
⇌ New Cross Gate 45 L5
⊖ New Cross Gate 45 L5
New Cross Rd, SE14 45 H5
Guildford GU2 264 AU132
New Cut, Slou. SL1 152 AG70
Newdales Cl, N9 122 DU47
Newdene Av, Nthlt. UB5 158 BX68
Newdigate Grn, Hare. UB9 114 BK53
Newdigate Rd, Hare. UB9 114 BJ53
Leigh RH2 286 CS141
Newdigate Rd E, Hare. UB9 114 BK53
New Ealing Bdy, W5
off Haven Grn 159 CK73
Newell Ri, Hem.H. HP3 62 BL23
Newell Rd, Hem.H. HP3 62 BL23
Newell St, E14 21 N9
NEW ELTHAM, SE9 207 EN89
⇌ New Eltham 207 EP88
New End, NW3 142 DC63
Sch New End Prim Sch, NW3
off Streatley Pl 142 DC63
New End Sq, NW3 142 DD63
● New England Ind Est, Bark.
IG11 167 EQ68
New England St, St.Alb. AL3 64 CC20
Newenham Rd, Bkhm KT23 268 CA126
Newent Cl, SE15 43 N4
Carshalton SM5 222 DF102
H New Epsom & Ewell Cottage
Hosp, Epsom KT19 238 CL111
New Fm Av, Brom. BR2 226 EG98
New Fm Cl, Stai. TW18 216 BJ95
New Fm Dr, Abridge RM4 108 EV41
New Fm La, Nthwd. HA6 115 BS53
New Ferry App, SE18 37 L6
New Fetter La, EC4 18 F8
Newfield Cl, Hmptn. TW12 218 CA95
Newfield La, Hem.H. HP2 62 BL20
Sch Newfield Prim Sch, NW10
off Longstone Av 161 CT66
Newfield Ri, NW2 141 CV62
Newfields, Welw.G.C. AL8 51 CV10
Newfield Way, St.Alb. AL4 65 CJ22
● New Ford Business Cen,
Wal.Cr. EN8 89 DZ34
Newford Cl, Hem.H. HP2 63 BP19
New Ford Rd, Wal.Cr. EN8 89 DZ34
New Forest La, Chig. IG7 125 EN51
● New Frontiers Science Pk,
Harl. CM19 73 EM16
Newgale Gdns, Edg. HA8 118 CM53
New Gdn Dr, West Dr. UB7
off Drayton Gdns 176 BL75
Newgate, Croy. CR0 224 DQ102
Newgate Cl, Felt. TW13 198 BY89
St. Albans AL4 65 CK17
NEWGATE STREET, Hert. SG13 69 DK24
Newgate St, E4 124 EF48
EC1 19 H8
Hertford SG13 69 DK22
Newgatestreet Rd, Goffs Oak
EN7 87 DP27
Newgate St Village,
Hert. SG13 87 DL25
New Globe Wk, SE1 31 J2
New Goulston St, E1 20 A8
New Grn Pl, SE19 204 DS93
NEW GREENS, St.Alb. AL3 65 CD16
New Grns Av, St.Alb. AL3 65 CD15
New Hall Cl, Bov. HP3 79 BA27
Newhall Ct, Wal.Abb. EN9 90 EF33
New Hall Dr, Rom. RM3 128 FL53
Newhall Gdns, Walt. KT12 218 BW103
Coll Newham Acad of Music, E6
off Wakefield St 166 EL67
H Newham Cen for Mental
Health, E13 24 E5
Coll Newham Coll of Further Ed,
SE1 31 P4
East Ham Campus, E6
off High St S 167 EM68
Little Ilford Cen, E12
off Browning Rd 147 EM64
Stratford Campus, E15 13 K7
Coll Newham 6th Form Coll,
Main Site, E13 24 B4
Stratford Site, E15 13 H7
Newhams Row, SE1 31 P5
H Newham Uni Hosp, E13 24 D4
Gateway Surgical Cen, E13 24 E5
Newham Way, E6 25 P2
E16 23 N7
Newhaven Cl, Hayes UB3 177 BT77
Newhaven Cres, Ashf. TW15 197 BR92
Newhaven Gdns, SE9 186 EK84
Newhaven La, E16 23 M5
Newhaven Rd, SE25 224 DR99
Newhaven Spur, Slou. SL2 153 AP70
NEW HAW, Add. KT15 234 BK108
Sch New Haw Comm Jun Sch,
New Haw KT15
off The Avenue 234 BG110
New Haw Rd, Add. KT15 234 BJ106
New Heston Rd, Houns. TW5 178 BZ80
● New Horizons Ct, Brent.
TW8 179 CG79
Newhouse Av, Rom. RM6 148 EX55
Newhouse Cl, N.Mal. KT3 220 CS101
Newhouse Cres, Wat. WD25 81 BV32

New Ho La, Grav. DA11 . . . . . . **213** GF90
North Weald Bassett CM16 . . **75** FC24
Redhill RH1 . . . . **289** DK142
New Ho Pk, St.Alb. AL1 . . . . **65** CG23
Newhouse Rd, Bov. HP3 . . . . . . **79** BA26
Newhouse Wk, Mord. SM4 . . . **222** DC101
Newick Cl, Bex. DA5 . . . . **209** FB86
Newick Rd, E5 . . . . **144** DV62
Newing Grn, Brom. BR1 . . . . . . **206** EK94
NEWINGTON, SE1 . . . . **31** J8
Newington Barrow Way, N7 . . **143** DM62
Newington Butts, SE1 . . . . **31** H9
SE11 . . . . **31** H9
Newington Causeway, SE1 . . . . **31** H7
Newington Grn, N1 . . . . **9** M2
N16 . . . . **9** M2
Newington Grn Prim Sch,
N16 . . . . **9** M2
Newington Grn Rd, N1 . . . . **9** L3
New Inn Bdy, EC2 . . . . **19** P4
New Inn La, Guil. GU4 . . . . **265** BB130
New Inn Pas, WC2 . . . . **18** D9
New Inn Sq, EC2 . . . . **19** P4
New Inn St, EC2 . . . . **19** P4
New Inn Yd, EC2 . . . . **19** P4
New James Ct, SE15
off Nunhead La **184** DV83
New Jersey Ter, SE15
off Nunhead La **184** DV83
New Jubilee Ct, Wdf.Grn. IG8
off Grange Av **124** EG52
New Kent Rd, SE1 . . . . **31** J7
St. Albans AL1 . . . . **65** CD20
New King's Prim Sch, SW6 . **39** H8
New Kings Rd, SW6 . . . . **38** F9
New King St, SE8 . . . . **46** A2
Newland Cl, Pnr. HA5 . . . . **116** BY51
St. Albans AL1 . . . . **65** CG23
Newland Ct, EC1
off St. Luke's Est **19** L4
Wembley HA9 . . . . **140** CN61
Newland Dr, Enf. EN1 . . . . **104** DV39
Newland Gdns, W13 . . . . **179** CG75
Hertford SG13 . . . . **54** DS09
Newland Ho Sch, Twick. TW1
off Waldegrave Pk **199** CF91
Newland Rd, N8 . . . . **143** DL55
Newlands, Hat. AL9 . . . . **67** CW16
Newlands, The, Wall. SM6 . . . . **241** DJ108
Newlands Av, Rad. WD7 . . . . . . **83** CF34
Thames Ditton KT7 . . . . **219** CE102
Woking GU22 . . . . **249** AZ121
Newlands Cl, Edg. HA8 . . . . . . **118** CL48
Hersham KT12 . . . . **236** BY105
Horley RH6 . . . . **290** DF146
Hutton CM13 . . . . **131** GD45
Southall UB2 . . . . **178** BY78
Wembley HA0 . . . . **159** CJ65
Newlands Cor, Guil. GU4 . . . . **282** BG136
Newlands Ct, SE9 . . . . **207** EN86
Caterham CR3 . . . . **258** DQ121
Newlands Cres, Guil. GU1 . . . . **281** AZ136
Newlands Dr, Colnbr. SL3 . . . . **175** BE83
Newlands Pk, SE26 . . . . **205** DX92
Bedmond WD5 . . . . **81** BT26
Newlands Pl, Barn. EN5 . . . . . . **101** CX43
Newlands Quay, E1 . . . . **32** G1
Newlands Rd, SW16 . . . . **223** DL96
Hemel Hempstead HP1 . . . . . **61** BE19
Woodford Green IG8 . . . . . . **124** EF47
Newlands Ter, SW8
off Queenstown Rd **41** J8
Newland St, E16 . . . . **37** H3
Newlands Wk, Wat. WD25 . . . . . **82** BX33
Newlands Way, Chess. KT9 . . . **237** CJ106
Potters Bar EN6 . . . . **86** DB30
Newlands Wds, Croy. CR0 . . . . **243** DZ109
New La, Sutt.Grn GU4 . . . . **248** AY122
Newling Cl, E6 . . . . **25** K8
New Lo Dr, Oxt. RH8 . . . . **276** EF128
New Lo Sch, Dor. RH4
off Chichester Rd **269** CH134
New London St, EC3 . . . . **19** P10
● **New Lydenburg Commercial Est**,
SE7 *off New Lydenburg St* . . **36** D7
New Lydenburg St, SE7 . . . . **36** D7
Newlyn Cl, Brick.Wd AL2 . . . . . . **82** BY30
Orpington BR6 . . . . **245** ET105
Uxbridge UB8 . . . . **156** BN71
Newlyn Gdns, Har. HA2 . . . . . . **138** BZ59
Newlyn Rd, N17 . . . . **122** DT53
Barnet EN5 . . . . **101** CZ42
Welling DA16 . . . . **187** ET82
NEW MALDEN, KT3 . . . . **220** CR97
⇌ **New Malden** **220** CS97
Newman Cl, Horn. RM11 . . . . . **150** FL57
Newman Pas, W1 . . . . **17** M7
Newman Rd, E13 . . . . **24** A3
E17 . . . . **145** DX56
Bromley BR1 . . . . **226** EG95
Croydon CR0 . . . . **223** DM102
Hayes UB3 . . . . **157** BV73
Newmans Cl, Loug. IG10 . . . . . **107** EP41
Newman's Ct, EC3 . . . . **19** M9
Newmans Dr, Hutt. CM13 . . . . **131** GC45
NEWMAN'S END, Harl. CM17 . . **59** FE10
Newmans La, Loug. IG10 . . . . . **107** EN41
Surbiton KT6 . . . . **219** CK100
Newmans Rd, Nthflt DA11 . . . . **213** GF89
Newman's Row, WC2 . . . . **18** D7
Newman St, W1 . . . . **17** M7
Newmans Way, Barn. EN4 . . . . **102** DC39
Newman Yd, W1 . . . . **17** M8
Newmarket Av, Nthlt. UB5 . . . **138** CA64
Newmarket Ct, St.Alb. AL3 . . . . **64** CC19
Newmarket Grn, SE9
off Middle Pk Av **206** EK87
Newmarket Way, Horn. RM12 . **150** FL63
Newmarsh Rd, SE28 . . . . **167** ET74
New Mill Rd, Orp. BR5 . . . . **228** EW95
Newminster Rd, Mord. SM4 . . **222** DC100
New Monument Prim Sch,
Wok. GU22 *off Alpha Rd* . . **249** BC115
New Mt St, E15 . . . . **13** H8
Newnes Path, SW15
off Putney Pk La **181** CV84
Newnham Av, Ruis. HA4 . . . . . **138** BW60
Newnham Cl, Loug. IG10 . . . . . **106** EK44
Northolt UB5 . . . . **138** CC64
Slough SL2 . . . . **154** AU74
Thornton Heath CR7 . . . . **224** DQ96
Newnham Gdns, Nthlt. UB5 . . **138** CC64
Newnham Inf & Jun Schs, Ruis.
HA4 *off Newnham Av* **138** BW60
Newnham Ms, N22
off Newnham Rd **121** DM53
Newnham Pl, Grays RM16 . . . . **193** GG77
Newnham Rd, N22 . . . . **121** DM53
Newnhams Cl, Brom. BR1 . . . . **227** EM97
Newnham Ter, SE1 . . . . **30** E6
Newnham Way, Har. HA3 . . . . . **140** CL57
New N Comm Sch, N1 . . . . **9** J8
New N Pl, EC2 . . . . **19** N5
New N Rd, N1 . . . . **19** M1
Ilford IG6 . . . . **125** ER52
Reigate RH2 . . . . **287** CZ137
New N St, WC1 . . . . **18** C6
Newnton Cl, N4 . . . . **144** DR59
New Oak Rd, N2 . . . . **120** DC54
New Orleans Wk, N19 . . . . **143** DK59
New Oxford St, WC1 . . . . **17** P8
New Par, Ashf. TW15
off Church Rd **196** BM91
Chorleywood WD3
off Whitelands Av **95** BC42
Croxley Green WD3
off The Green **96** BM44
New Par Flats, Chorl. WD3
off Whitelands Av **95** BC42
New Pk Av, N13 . . . . **122** DQ48
New Pk Cl, Nthlt. UB5 . . . . **158** BY65
New Pk Ct, SW2 . . . . **203** DL87
New Pk Dr, Hem.H. HP2 . . . . . . **63** BP19
● **New Pk Ind Est**, N18 . . . . . **122** DW50
New Pk Par, SW2
off New Pk Rd **203** DL87
New Pk Rd, SW2 . . . . **203** DK88
Ashford TW15 . . . . **197** BQ92
Harefield UB9 . . . . **114** BJ53
Newgate Street SG13 . . . . **69** DK24
New Peachey La, Uxb. UB8 . . . **156** BK72
Newpiece, Loug. IG10 . . . . **107** EP41
New Pl Gdns, Upmin. RM14 . . **151** FR61
New Pl Sq, SE16 . . . . **32** E6
New Plaistow Rd, E15 . . . . **13** K8
New Plymouth Ho, Rain.
RM13 . . . . **169** FF69
Newport Av, E13 . . . . **24** B5
E14 . . . . **35** H1
Newport Cl, Enf. EN3 . . . . **105** DY37
Newport Ct, WC2 . . . . **17** P10
Newport Mead, Wat. WD19
off Kilmarnock Rd **116** BX49
Newport Pl, WC2 . . . . **17** P10
Newport Rd, E10 . . . . **145** EC61
E17 . . . . **145** DY56
SW13 . . . . **181** CU81
W3 . . . . **180** CQ75
Hayes UB4 . . . . **157** BR71
London Heathrow Airport
TW6 . . . . **176** BN81
Slough SL2 . . . . **153** AL70
Newports, Saw. CM21 . . . . **58** EW06
Swanley BR8 . . . . **229** FD101
Newport Sch, E10
off Newport Rd **145** EC61
Newport St, SE11 . . . . **30** C9
New Priory Ct, NW6 . . . . **5** K7
New Providence Wf, E14 . . . . . . **34** G2
New Provident Pl, Berk. HP4
off Holliday St **60** AX19
Newquay Cres, Har. HA2 . . . . . **138** BY61
Newquay Gdns, Wat. WD19
off Fulford Gro **115** BV47
Newquay Rd, SE6 . . . . **205** EB89
New Quebec St, W1 . . . . **16** F9
New Ride, SW7 . . . . **28** E4
New River Arms, Brox.
EN10 . . . . **89** DY25
New River Av, N8 . . . . **143** DM55
Stanstead Abbotts SG12 . . . . **55** EB11
New River Cl, Hodd. EN11 . . . . . **71** EB16
New River Ct, N5 . . . . **9** L1
Cheshunt EN7 . . . . **88** DV31
New River Cres, N13 . . . . **121** DP49
New River Head, EC1 . . . . **18** F2
● **New River Trd Est**, Chsht
EN8 . . . . **89** DX26
New River Wk, N1 . . . . **9** J5
New River Way, N4 . . . . **144** DR59
New Rd, E1 . . . . **20** E7
E4 . . . . **123** EB49
N8 . . . . **143** DL57
N9 . . . . **122** DV47
N17 . . . . **122** DT53
N22 . . . . **122** DQ53
NW7 . . . . **119** CY52
NW7 (Barnet Gate) **119** CT45
SE2 . . . . **188** EX77
Albury GU5 . . . . **282** BK139
Amersham HP6 . . . . **77** AS37
Berkhamsted HP4 . . . . **60** AX18
Brentford TW8 . . . . **179** CK79
Brentwood CM14 . . . . **130** FX47
Broxbourne EN10 . . . . **71** DZ19
Chalfont St. Giles HP8 . . . . . . **94** AY41
Chilworth GU4 . . . . **281** BB141
Chipperfield WD4 . . . . **79** BF30
Church End WD3 . . . . **95** BF39
Claygate KT10 . . . . **237** CF110
Coleshill HP7 . . . . **77** AM42
Croxley Green WD3 . . . . **96** BN43
Dagenham RM9, RM10 . . . . . **168** FA67
Datchet SL3 . . . . **174** AX81
Dorking RH5 . . . . **285** CK137
East Bedfont TW14 . . . . **197** BR86
East Clandon GU4 . . . . **266** BL131
Elstree WD6 . . . . **99** CK44
Epping CM16 . . . . **92** FA32
Esher KT10 . . . . **218** CC104
Feltham TW14 . . . . **197** BV88
Gomshall GU5 . . . . **283** BQ139
Gravesend DA11 . . . . **213** GH86
Grays RM17 . . . . **192** GA79
Grays (Bridge Rd) RM17 . . . . **192** GB79
Hanworth TW13 . . . . **198** BY92
Harlington UB3 . . . . **177** BQ80
Harlow CM17 . . . . **58** EX11
Harrow HA1 . . . . **139** CF63
Hertford SG14 . . . . **54** DQ07
Hextable BR8 . . . . **209** FF94
Hounslow TW3 . . . . **178** CB84
Ilford IG3 . . . . **147** ES61
Kingston upon Thames KT2 . **200** CN94
Lambourne End RM4 . . . . **108** EX44
Langley SL3 . . . . **175** BA76
Leatherhead KT22 . . . . **237** CF110
Letchmore Heath WD25 . . . . . **99** CE39
Limpsfield RH8 . . . . **276** EH130
Mitcham CR4 . . . . **222** DF102
New Rd, Nthch HP4 . . . . **60** AS17
Orpington BR6 . . . . **228** EU101
Penn HP10 . . . . **110** AC47
Radlett WD7 . . . . **99** CE36
Rainham RM13 . . . . **169** FG69
Richmond TW10 . . . . **199** CJ91
Shenley WD7 . . . . **84** CN34
Shepperton TW17 . . . . **217** BP97
Smallfield RH6 . . . . **291** DP148
South Darenth DA4 . . . . **230** FQ96
South Mimms EN6 . . . . **85** CU33
Staines TW18 . . . . **195** BC92
Stanborough AL8 . . . . **51** CU12
Sundridge TN14 . . . . **262** EX124
Swanley BR8 . . . . **229** FF97
Tadworth KT20 . . . . **255** CW123
Uxbridge UB8 . . . . **157** BQ70
Ware SG12 . . . . **55** DX06
Watford WD17 . . . . **98** BW42
Welling DA16 . . . . **188** EV82
West Molesey KT8 . . . . **218** CA97
Weybridge KT13 . . . . **235** BQ106
Wonersh GU5 . . . . **281** BB143
New Rd Hill, Downe BR6 . . . . . **244** EL109
Keston BR2 . . . . **244** EL109
New Row, WC2 . . . . **18** A10
New Rush Hall Sch, Ilf. IG6
off Fencepiece Rd **125** EQ52
Newry Rd, Twick. TW1 . . . . **179** CG84
Newsam Av, N15 . . . . **144** DR57
New Sch at W Heath, The, Sev.
TN13 *off Ashgrove Rd* **279** FH129
★ **New Scotland Yd**, SW1 . . . . . **29** N6
Newsham Rd, Wok. GU21 . . . . . **248** AT117
Newsholme Dr, N21 . . . . **103** DM43
NEW SOUTHGATE, N11 . . . . **121** DK49
⇌ **New Southgate** **121** DH50
● **New Southgate Ind Est**,
N11 . . . . **121** DJ50
🔒 **New Spitalfields Mkt**, E10 . **145** EA62
New Spring Gdns Wk, SE11 . . . . **42** B1
● **New Sq**, Felt. TW14 . . . . **197** BQ88
New Sq, WC2 . . . . **18** D8
Slough SL1 . . . . **174** AS75
Newstead, Hat. AL10 . . . . **67** CT21
Newstead Av, Orp. BR6 . . . . . . **227** ER104
Newstead Ri, Cat. CR3 . . . . **274** DV126
Newstead Rd, SE12 . . . . **206** EE87
Newstead Wk, Cars. SM5 . . . . . **222** DC101
Newstead Way, SW19 . . . . **201** CX91
Harlow CM20 . . . . **57** EQ13
Newstead Wd Sch for Girls,
Orp. BR6 *off Avebury Rd* . . **227** ER104
New St, EC2 . . . . **19** P7
Berkhamsted HP4 . . . . **60** AX19
Staines TW18 . . . . **196** BG91
Watford WD18 . . . . **98** BW42
Westerham TN16 . . . . **277** EQ127
New St Hill, Brom. BR1 . . . . **206** EH92
New St Sq, EC4 . . . . **18** F8
New Swan Yd, Grav. DA12
off Bank St **213** GH86
New Tank Hill Rd, Purf. RM19 . **190** FN76
Newteswell Dr, Wal.Abb. EN9 . . **89** ED32
Newton Abbot Rd, Nthflt
DA11 . . . . **213** GF89
Newton Av, N10 . . . . **120** DG53
W3 . . . . **180** CQ75
Newton Cl, E17 . . . . **145** DY58
Harrow HA2 . . . . **138** CA61
Hoddesdon EN11 . . . . **55** EB13
Slough SL3 . . . . **175** AZ75
Newton Ct, Old Wind. SL4 . . . . **194** AU86
Newton Cres, Borwd. WD6 . . . . **100** CQ42
Newton Dr, Saw. CM21 . . . . **58** EX06
Newton Fm First & Mid Sch,
S.Har. HA2
off Ravenswood Cres **138** BZ61
Newton Gro, W4 . . . . **180** CS77
Newton Ho, Enf. EN3
off Exeter Rd **105** DX41
Newton La, Old Wind. SL4 . . . . **194** AV86
Newton Lo, SE10 . . . . **35** M7
Newton Pl, E14 . . . . **34** A8
Newton Prep Sch, SW8 . . . . **41** K6
Newton Rd, E15 . . . . **13** H2
N15 . . . . **144** DT57
NW2 . . . . **141** CW62
SW19 . . . . **201** CY94
W2 . . . . **15** K9
Chigwell IG7 . . . . **126** EV50
Harrow HA3 . . . . **117** CE54
Isleworth TW7 . . . . **179** CF82
Purley CR8 . . . . **241** DJ112
Tilbury RM18 . . . . **193** GG82
Welling DA16 . . . . **188** EU83
Wembley HA0 . . . . **160** CM66
Newtons Cl, Rain. RM13 . . . . . . **169** FF66
Newtons Cor, Rain. RM13 . **169** FE66
● **Newtons Ct**, Dart. DA2 . . . . **191** FR84
Newtonside Orchard, Wind.
SL4 . . . . **194** AU86
Newtons Prim Sch, Rain.
RM13 *off Lowen Rd* **169** FD68
Newton St, WC2 . . . . **18** B8
Newtons Yd, SW18
off Wandsworth High St . . . **202** DA85
Newton Wk, Edg. HA8
off Roscoff Cl **118** CQ53
Newton Way, N18 . . . . **122** DQ50
Newton Wd, Ashtd. KT21 . . . . . **238** CL114
Newton Wd Rd, Ashtd. KT21 . . **254** CM116
NEWTOWN, Chesh. HP5 . . . . **76** AP30
NEW TOWN, Dart. DA1 . . . . **210** FN86
Newtown Inf Sch & Nurs,
Chesh. HP5
off Berkhampstead Rd **76** AQ29
Newtown Rd, Denh. UB9 . . . . . **156** BH65
Newtown St, SW11 . . . . **41** J6
New Trinity Rd, N2 . . . . **142** DD55
New Turnstile, WC1 . . . . **18** C7
New Union Cl, E14 . . . . **34** F6
New Union St, EC2 . . . . **19** L7
New Victoria Hosp, The,
Kings.T. KT2 . . . . **220** CS95
New Wanstead, E11 . . . . **146** EF58
New Way La, Thres.B. CM17 . . . **75** FB16
New Way Rd, NW9 . . . . **140** CS56
New Wf Rd, N1 . . . . **8** B10
New Wickham La, Egh. TW20 . **195** BA94
New Windsor St, Uxb. UB8 . . . . **156** BJ67
New Wd, Welw.G.C. AL7 . . . . **52** DC08
New Woodlands Sch, Brom.
BR1 *off Shroffold Rd* **206** EE91
NEWYEARS GREEN, Uxb.
UB9 . . . . **136** BN59
New Years Grn La, Hare. UB9 . **136** BL58
New Years La, Knock. TN14 . . . **261** ET116
New Zealand Av, Walt. KT12 . . **217** BT102
New Zealand Way, W12 . . . . . . **161** CV73
Rainham RM13 . . . . **169** FF69
Nexus Ct, E11
off Kirkdale Rd **146** EE59
Niagara Av, W5 . . . . **179** CJ77
Niagara Cl, N1
off Cropley St **9** K10
Cheshunt EN8 . . . . **89** DX29
Nibthwaite Rd, Har. HA1 . . . . . **139** CE57
● **Nice Business Pk**, SE15 . . . . **44** F3
Nicholas Breakspear RC Sch,
St.Alb. AL4
off Colney Heath La **66** CL21
Nicholas Cl, Grnf. UB6 . . . . **158** CB68
St. Albans AL3 . . . . **65** CD17
South Ockendon RM15 . . . . . **171** FW69
Watford WD24 . . . . **97** BV37
Nicholas Ct, E13 . . . . **24** B3
N7 . . . . **8** C3
Nicholas Gdns, W5 . . . . **179** CK75
Slough SL1 . . . . **153** AL74
Woking GU22 . . . . **249** BE116
Nicholas La, EC4 . . . . **19** M10
Hertford SG14
off Old Cross **54** DQ09
Nicholas Ms, W4
off Short Rd **180** CS79
Nicholas Pas, EC4 . . . . **19** M10
Nicholas Rd, E1 . . . . **21** H4
W11 . . . . **26** C1
Croydon CR0 . . . . **241** DL105
Dagenham RM8 . . . . **148** EZ61
Elstree WD6 . . . . **100** CM44
Nicholas Way, Hem.H. HP2 . . . . **62** BM18
Northwood HA6 . . . . **115** BQ53
Nicholay Rd, N19 . . . . **143** DK61
Nichol Cl, N14 . . . . **121** DK46
Nicholes Rd, Houns. TW3 . . . . . **178** CA84
Nichol La, Brom. BR1 . . . . **206** EG94
Nicholl Rd, Epp. CM16 . . . . **91** ET31
Nicholls, Wind. SL4 . . . . **172** AJ83
Nicholls Av, Uxb. UB8 . . . . **156** BN70
Nicholls Cl, Cat. CR3 . . . . **258** DQ122
Nicholls Fld, Harl. CM18 . . . . **74** EV16
Nichollsfield Wk, N7 . . . . **8** C3
Nicholls Pt, E15 . . . . **13** P8
Nicholls Twr, Harl. CM18 . . . . . . **74** EU16
Nicholl St, E2 . . . . **10** C9
Nichols Cl, N4
off Osborne Rd **143** DN60
Chessington KT9
off Merritt Gdns **237** CJ107
Nichols Ct, E2 . . . . **20** A1
Nichols Grn, W5 . . . . **160** CL71
● **Nicholson Ct**, Hodd. EN11 . . **71** EB17
Nicholson Rd, Croy. CR0 . . . . . **224** DT102
Nicholson St, SE1 . . . . **30** G3
Nicholson Wk, Egh. TW20 . . . . **195** BA92
Nicholson Way, Sev. TN13 . . . . **279** FK122
Nickelby Cl, SE28 . . . . **168** EW72
Nickleby Cl, Uxb. UB8 . . . . **157** BP72
Nickols Wk, SW18
off Jew's Row **182** DB84
Nicola Cl, Har. HA3 . . . . **117** CD54
South Croydon CR2 . . . . **242** DQ107
Nicola Ms, Ilf. IG6 . . . . **125** EP52
Nicolas Wk, Grays RM16
off Godman Rd **193** GH75
Nicol Cl, Chal.St.P. SL9 . . . . **112** AX53
Twickenham TW1
off Cassilis Rd **199** CH86
Nicol End, Chal.St.P. SL9 . . . . . **112** AW53
Nicoll Pl, NW4 . . . . **141** CV58
Nicoll Rd, NW10 . . . . **160** CS67
Nicoll Way, Borwd. WD6 . . . . . . **100** CR43
Nicol Rd, Chal.St.P. SL9 . . . . **112** AW53
Nicolson Dr, Bushey Hth
WD23 . . . . **116** CC46
Nicolson Rd, Orp. BR5 . . . . **228** EX101
Nicosia Rd, SW18 . . . . **202** DE87
Nidderdale, Hem.H. HP2
off Wharfedale **62** BM17
Niederwald Rd, SE26 . . . . **205** DY91
Nield Rd, Hayes UB3 . . . . **177** BT75
Nigel Cl, Nthlt. UB5
off Church Rd **158** BY67
Nigel Fisher Way, Chess. KT9 . **237** CJ108
Nigel Ms, Ilf. IG1 . . . . **147** EP63
Nigel Playfair Av, W6
off King St **181** CV77
Nigel Rd, E7 . . . . **146** EJ64
SE15 . . . . **44** C10
Nigeria Rd, SE7 . . . . **186** EJ80
Nightingale Av, E4 . . . . **124** EE50
Harrow HA1 . . . . **139** CH59
Upminster RM14 . . . . **151** FT60
West Horsley KT24 . . . . **251** BR124
Nightingale Cl, E4 . . . . **124** EE49
W4 . . . . **180** CQ79
Abbots Langley WD5 . . . . **81** BU31
Biggin Hill TN16 . . . . **260** EJ115
Carshalton SM5 . . . . **222** DG103
Cobham KT11 . . . . **236** BX111
Epsom KT19 . . . . **238** CN112
Northfleet DA11 . . . . **212** GE91
Pinner HA5 . . . . **138** BW57
Radlett WD7 . . . . **99** CF36
Nightingale Ct, E11
off Nightingale La **146** EH57
Hertford SG14 . . . . **54** DQ09
Slough SL1
off St. Laurence Way **174** AU76
Sutton SM1 *off Lind Rd* **240** DC106
Woking GU21
off Inkerman Way **248** AT118
Nightingale Cres, Harold Wd
RM3 . . . . **128** FL54
West Horsley KT24 . . . . **251** BQ124
Nightingale Dr, Epsom KT19 . . **238** CP107
Nightingale Est, E5 . . . . **144** DU62
Nightingale Gro, SE13 . . . . **205** ED85
Dartford DA1 . . . . **190** FN84
Nightingale Hts, SE18
off Nightingale Vale **187** EP79
Nightingale Ho, E1
off Thomas More St **32** C2
W12 *off Du Cane Rd* **14** A9
Nightingale La, E11 . . . . **146** EG57
N6 . . . . **142** DE60
N8 . . . . **143** DL56
SW4 . . . . **202** DF87
SW12 . . . . **202** DF87
Bromley BR1 . . . . **226** EJ96
Ide Hill TN14 . . . . **278** FB130
Richmond TW10 . . . . **200** CL87
St. Albans AL1 . . . . **65** CJ24
Nightingale Ms, E3 . . . . **11** L10
E11 . . . . **146** EG57
SE11 . . . . **30** F8
Nightingale Ms, Kings.T. KT1
off South La **219** CK97
Nightingale Pk, Farn.Com.
SL2 . . . . **153** AM66
Nightingale Pl, SE18 . . . . **187** EN79
SW10 . . . . **39** P2
Rickmansworth WD3
off Nightingale Rd **114** BK45
Nightingale Prim Sch, E5
off Rendlesham Rd **144** DU63
E18 *off Ashbourne Av* **146** EJ56
N22 *off Bounds Grn Rd* **121** DM53
SE18 *off Bloomfield Rd* **187** EP78
Nightingale Rd, E5 . . . . **144** DV62
N1 . . . . **9** K5
N9 . . . . **104** DW44
N22 . . . . **121** DL53
NW10 . . . . **161** CT68
W7 . . . . **159** CF74
Bushey WD23 . . . . **98** CA43
Carshalton SM5 . . . . **222** DF104
Chesham HP5 . . . . **76** AP29
Cheshunt EN7 . . . . **88** DQ25
East Horsley KT24 . . . . **267** BT125
Esher KT10 . . . . **236** BZ106
Guildford GU1 . . . . **264** AX134
Hampton TW12 . . . . **198** CA92
Petts Wood BR5 . . . . **227** EQ100
Rickmansworth WD3 . . . . **114** BJ46
South Croydon CR2 . . . . **243** DX111
Walton-on-Thames KT12 . . . . **217** BV101
West Molesey KT8 . . . . **218** CB99
Nightingales, Harl. CM17 . . . . . . **74** EW17
Waltham Abbey EN9
off Roundhills **90** EE34
Nightingales, The, Stai. TW19 . **196** BM87
Nightingale Sch, SW17
off Beechcroft Rd **202** DE89
Nightingales Cor, Amer. HP7
off Chalfont Sta Rd **94** AW40
Nightingale Shott, Egh. TW20 . **195** AZ93
Nightingales La, Ch.St.G. HP8 . **112** AX46
Nightingale Sq, SW12 . . . . **202** DG87
Nightingale Vale, SE18 . . . . **187** EN79
Nightingale Wk, SW4 . . . . **203** DH86
Windsor SL4 . . . . **173** AQ83
Nightingale Way, E6 . . . . **25** H6
Bletchingley RH1 . . . . **274** DS134
Denham UB9 . . . . **135** BF59
Swanley BR8 . . . . **229** FE97
Nile Cl, N16 . . . . **144** DT62
Nile Dr, N9 . . . . **122** DW47
Nile Path, SE18
off Jackson St **187** EN79
Nile Rd, E13 . . . . **24** C1
Nile St, N1 . . . . **19** K2
Nile Ter, SE15 . . . . **44** A1
Nimbus Rd, Epsom KT19 . . . . . **238** CR110
Nimegen Way, SE22 . . . . **204** DS85
Nimmo Dr, Bushey Hth WD23 . **117** CD45
Nimrod Cl, Nthlt. UB5 . . . . **158** BX69
St. Albans AL4 . . . . **65** CJ18
Nimrod Dr, Hat. AL10 . . . . **66** CR17
Nimrod Pas, N1 . . . . **9** P5
Nimrod Rd, SW16 . . . . **203** DH93
Nina Mackay Cl, E15 . . . . **13** J8
Nine Acre La, Hat. AL10 . . . . **67** CT19
Nine Acres, Slou. SL1 . . . . **153** AM74
Nine Acres Cl, E12 . . . . **146** EL64
Hayes UB3 . . . . **177** BQ76
Nineacres Way, Couls. CR5 . . . **257** DL116
Nine Ashes, Hunsdon SG12
off Acorn St **56** EK08
NINE ELMS, SW8 . . . . **41** M4
Nine Elms Av, Uxb. UB8 . . . . **156** BK71
Nine Elms Cl, Felt. TW14 . . . . . **197** BT88
Uxbridge UB8 . . . . **156** BK72
Nine Elms Gro, Grav. DA11 . . . . **213** GG87
Nine Elms La, SW8 . . . . **41** M3
Ninefields, Wal.Abb. EN9 . . . . . . **90** EF33
Ninehams Cl, Cat. CR3 . . . . **258** DR120
Ninehams Gdns, Cat. CR3 . . . . **258** DR120
Ninehams Rd, Cat. CR3 . . . . **258** DR121
Tatsfield TN16 . . . . **260** EJ121
Nine Stiles Cl, Denh. UB9 . . . . . **156** BH65
Nineteenth Rd, Mitch. CR4 . . . . **223** DL98
Ninhams Wd, Orp. BR6 . . . . **245** EN105
Ninian Rd, Hem.H. HP2 . . . . **62** BL15
Ninnings Rd, Chal.St.P. SL9 . . . . **113** AZ52
Ninnings Way, Chal.St.P. SL9 . . **113** AZ52
Ninth Av, Hayes UB3 . . . . **157** BU73
Nisbet Ho, E9 . . . . **11** K3
Nisbett Wk, Sid. DA14
off Sidcup High St **208** EU91
Nita Rd, Warley CM14 . . . . **130** FW50
Nithdale Rd, SE18 . . . . **187** EP80
Nithsdale Gro, Uxb. UB10 . . . . **137** BQ62
Niton Cl, Barn. EN5 . . . . **101** CX44
Niton Rd, Rich. TW9 . . . . **180** CN83
Niton St, SW6 . . . . **38** C4
Niven Cl, Borwd. WD6 . . . . **100** CQ39
Nixey Cl, Slou. SL1 . . . . **174** AU75
N.L.A. Twr, Croy. CR0 . . . . **224** DR103
No. 1 St, SE18 . . . . **37** P7
Noahs Ct Gdns, Hert. SG13 . . . . . **54** DS10
NOAK HILL, Rom. RM4 . . . . **128** FK47
Noak Hill Rd, Rom. RM3 . . . . . . **128** FJ49
Nobel Dr, Harling. UB3 . . . . **177** BR80
Nobel Rd, N18 . . . . **122** DW50
Noble Cl, Mitch. CR4 . . . . **222** DD96
Slough SL2 . . . . **154** AT74
Noble St, EC2 . . . . **19** J8
Walton-on-Thames KT12 . . . . **217** BV104
Nobles Way, Egh. TW20 . . . . . . **194** AY93
Noel Coward Ho, SW1
off Vauxhall Br Rd **29** M9
NOEL PARK, N22 . . . . **121** DN54
Noel Pk Prim Sch, N22
off Gladstone Av **121** DN54
Noel Pk Rd, N22 . . . . **121** DN54
Noel Rd, E6 . . . . **24** G5
N1 . . . . **8** G10
W3 . . . . **160** CP72
Noel Sq, Dag. RM8 . . . . **148** EW63
Noel St, W1 . . . . **17** M9
Noel Ter, SE23
off Dartmouth Rd **204** DW89
Noke Dr, Red. RH1 . . . . **272** DG133
Noke Fm Barns, Couls. CR5 . . . **256** DF122
Noke La, St.Alb. AL2 . . . . **82** BY26
Nokes, The, Hem.H. HP1 . . . . **62** BG18
Noke Side, St.Alb. AL2 . . . . **82** CA27
Noko, W10 . . . . **14** D2
Nolan Way, E5 . . . . **144** DU63
Nolton Pl, Edg. HA8 . . . . **118** CM53
Nonsuch Cl, Ilf. IG6 . . . . **125** EP51
Nonsuch Ct Av, Epsom KT17 . . **239** CV110
Nonsuch High Sch for Girls,
Cheam SM3 *off Ewell Rd* . . **239** CX108

Nonsuch Ho, SW19
off Chapter Way 222 DD95
● Nonsuch Ind Est, Epsom KT17 238 CS111
★ Nonsuch Mansion, Sutt. SM3 239 CW107
Sch Nonsuch Prim Sch, Stoneleigh KT17
off Chadacre Rd 239 CV106
Nonsuch Wk, Sutt. SM2 239 CW110
Nook, The, Stans.Abb. SG12 55 EB11
Noons Cor Rd, Dor. RH5 284 BZ143
Nora Gdns, NW4 141 CX56
NORBITON, Kings.T. KT2 220 CP96
⇌ Norbiton 220 CN95
Norbiton Av, Kings.T. KT1 220 CN96
Norbiton Common Rd, Kings.T. KT1 220 CP97
Norbiton Rd, E14 21 N8
Norbreck Gdns, NW10
off Lytham Gro 160 CM69
Norbreck Par, NW10
off Lytham Gro 160 CM69
Norbroke St, W12 161 CT73
Norburn St, W10 14 E7
NORBURY, SW16 223 DN95
⇌ Norbury 223 DM95
Norbury Av, SW16 223 DM95
Hounslow TW3 199 CD85
Thornton Heath CR7 223 DN96
Watford WD24 98 BW39
Norbury Cl, SW16 223 DN95
Norbury Ct Rd, SW16 223 DL97
Norbury Cres, SW16 223 DM95
Norbury Cross, SW16 223 DL97
Norbury Gdns, Rom. RM6 148 EX57
Norbury Gro, NW7 118 CS48
Norbury Hill, SW16 203 DN94
Sch Norbury Manor Business & Enterprise Coll for Girls, Th.Hth. CR7
off Kensington Av 223 DN95
Sch Norbury Manor Prim Sch, SW16 off Abingdon Rd 223 DL95
Norbury Pk, Mick. RH5 269 CF127
Norbury Ri, SW16 223 DL97
Norbury Rd, E4 123 EA50
Feltham TW13 197 BT90
Reigate RH2 271 CZ134
Thornton Heath CR7 224 DQ96
Sch Norbury Sch, Har. HA1
off Welldon Cres 139 CE57
Norbury Way, Bkhm KT23 268 CC125
Norcombe Gdns, Har. HA3 139 CJ58
Norcombe Ho, N19
off Wedmore St 143 DK62
Norcott Cl, Hayes UB4 158 BW70
Norcott Rd, N16 144 DU61
Norcroft Gdns, SE22 204 DU87
Norcutt Rd, Twick. TW2 199 CE88
Nordenfeldt Rd, Erith DA8 189 FD78
Nordmann Pl, S.Ock. RM15 171 FX70
Norelands Dr, Burn. SL1 152 AJ68
Norfield Rd, Dart. DA2 209 FC91
Norfolk Av, N13 121 DP51
N15 144 DT58
Slough SL1 153 AQ71
South Croydon CR2 242 DU110
Watford WD24 98 BW38
Norfolk Cl, N2 142 DE55
N13 121 DP51
Barnet EN4 102 DG42
Dartford DA1 210 FN86
Horley RH6 290 DF149
Twickenham TW1
off Cassilis Rd 199 CH86
Norfolk Ct, Dor. RH5 285 CK140
Norfolk Cres, W2 16 D8
Sidcup DA15 207 ES87
Norfolk Fm Cl, Wok. GU22 249 BD116
Norfolk Fm Rd, Wok. GU22 249 BD115
Norfolk Gdns, Bexh. DA7 188 EZ81
Borehamwood WD6 100 CR42
Norfolk Ho, SE3 47 K2
SW1 off Regency St 29 P8
Norfolk Ho Rd, SW16 203 DK90
Norfolk La, Mid Holm. RH5 285 CH142
Norfolk Ms, W10 14 F7
Norfolk Pl, W2 16 B8
Chafford Hundred RM16 191 FW78
Welling DA16 188 EU82
Norfolk Rd, E6 167 EM67
E17 123 DX54
NW8 6 B9
NW10 160 CS66
SW19 202 DE94
Barking IG11 167 ES66
Barnet EN5 102 DA41
Claygate KT10 237 CE106
Dagenham RM10 149 FB64
Dorking RH4 285 CG136
Enfield EN3 104 DV44
Feltham TW13 198 BW88
Gravesend DA12 213 GK86
Harrow HA1 138 CB57
Ilford IG3 147 ES60
Rickmansworth WD3 114 BL46
Romford RM7 149 FC58
South Holmwood RH5 285 CJ144
Thornton Heath CR7 224 DQ97
Upminster RM14 150 FN62
Uxbridge UB8 156 BK65
Norfolk Row, SE1 30 C8
Norfolk Sq, W2 16 B9
Norfolk Sq Ms, W2 16 B9
Norfolk St, E7 13 N2
Norfolk Ter, W6 38 E1
Norgrove Pk, Ger.Cr. SL9 134 AY56
Norgrove St, SW12 202 DG87
Norheads La, Bigg.H. TN16 260 EJ116
Warlingham CR6 260 EG119
Norhyrst Av, SE25 224 DT97
NORK, Bans. SM7 255 CY115
Nork Gdns, Bans. SM7 239 CY114
Nork Ri, Bans. SM7 255 CX116
Nork Way, Bans. SM7 255 CY115
Norland Ho, W11 26 D3
Norland Pl, W11 26 F3
Sch Norland Pl Sch, W11 26 E3
Norland Rd, W11 26 D3
Norlands Cres, Chis. BR7 227 EP95
Norlands Gate, Chis. BR7 227 EP95
Norlands La, Egh. TW20 215 BE97
Norland Sq, W11 26 F3
Norley Vale, SW15 201 CU88
Norlington Rd, E10 145 EC60
E11 145 EC60
Sch Norlington Sch, E10
off Norlington Rd 145 ED60
Norman Av, N22 121 DP53
Epsom KT17 239 CT112
Feltham TW13 198 BY89
Richmond TW9
off Sandycombe Rd 180 CN81
South Croydon CR2 242 DQ110
Southall UB1 158 BY73
Twickenham TW1 199 CH87
Normanby Cl, SW15 201 CZ85
Normanby Rd, NW10 141 CT63
Norman Cl, Epsom KT18 255 CV119
Orpington BR6 227 EQ104
Romford RM5 127 FB54
St. Albans AL1 65 CE23
Waltham Abbey EN9 89 ED33
Norman Colyer Ct, Epsom KT19
off Hollymoor La 238 CR110
Norman Ct, Ilf. IG2 147 ER59
Potters Bar EN6 86 DC30
Woodford Green IG8
off Monkhams Av 124 EH50
Norman Cres, Brwd. CM13 131 GA48
Hounslow TW5 178 BX81
Pinner HA5 116 BW53
Sch Normand Cft Comm Sch for Early Years & Prim Ed, W14 39 H2
Normand Gdns, W14
off Greyhound Rd 38 F2
Normand Ms, W14 38 F2
Normand Rd, W14 38 G2
Normandy Av, Barn. EN5 101 CZ43
Normandy Cl, SE26 205 DY90
Normandy Ct, Hem.H. HP2 62 BK19
Normandy Dr, Berk. HP4 60 AV17
Hayes UB3 157 BQ72
Normandy Ho, Enf. EN2
off Cedar Rd 104 DQ38
Sch Normandy Prim Sch, Barne. DA7 off Fairford Av 189 FD81
Normandy Rd, SW9 42 E7
St. Albans AL3 65 CD18
Normandy Ter, E16 24 A9
Normandy Wk, Egh. TW20
off Mullens Rd 195 BC92
Normandy Way, Erith DA8 189 FE81
Hoddesdon EN11 71 EC16
Norman Gro, E3 21 M1
Normanhurst, Ashf. TW15 196 BN92
Hutton CM13 131 GC44
Normanhurst Av, Bexh. DA7 188 EX81
Normanhurst Dr, Twick. TW1
off St. Margarets Rd 199 CH85
Normanhurst Rd, SW2 203 DM89
Orpington BR5 228 EV96
Walton-on-Thames KT12 218 BX103
Sch Normanhurst Sch, E4
off Station Rd 123 ED45
Norman Rd, E6 25 K4
E11 145 ED61
N15 144 DT57
SE10 46 D4
SW19 202 DC94
Ashford TW15 197 BR93
Belvedere DA17 189 FB76
Dartford DA1 210 FL88
Hornchurch RM11 149 FG59
Ilford IG1 147 EP64
Sutton SM1 240 DA106
Thornton Heath CR7 223 DP99
Normans, The, Slou. SL2 154 AV72
Normans Cl, NW10 160 CR65
Gravesend DA11 213 GG87
Uxbridge UB8 156 BL71
Normansfield Av, Tedd. TW11 199 CJ94
Normansfield Cl, Bushey WD23 116 CB45
Normanshire Av, E4 123 EC49
Normanshire Dr, E4 123 EA49
Normans Mead, NW10 160 CR65
Norman St, EC1 19 J3
Normanton Av, SW19 202 DA89
Normanton Pk, E4 124 EE48
Normanton Rd, S.Croy. CR2 242 DS107
Normanton St, SE23 205 DX89
Norman Way, N14 121 DL47
W3 160 CP71
Normington Cl, SW16 203 DN92
Norrels Dr, E.Hors. KT24 267 BT126
Norrels Ride, E.Hors. KT24 267 BT125
Norrice Lea, N2 142 DD57
Norris Cl, Epsom KT19 238 CP111
London Colney AL2 83 CH26
Norris Gro, Brox. EN10 71 DY20
Norris La, Hodd. EN11 71 EA16
Norris Ri, Hodd. EN11 71 DZ16
Norris Rd, Hodd. EN11 71 EA17
Staines TW18 195 BF91
Norris St, SW1 29 N1
Norris Way, Dart. DA1 189 FF83
Norroy Rd, SW15 181 CX84
Norrys Cl, Cockfos. EN4 102 DF43
Norrys Rd, Cockfos. EN4 102 DF42
Norseman Cl, Ilf. IG3 148 EV60
Norseman Way, Grnf. UB6
off Olympic Way 158 CB67
Norstead Pl, SW15 201 CU89
Norsted La, Pr.Bot. BR6 246 EU110
North Access Rd, E17 145 DX58
North Acre, NW9 118 CS53
Banstead SM7 255 CZ116
NORTH ACTON, W3 160 CR70
⊖ North Acton 160 CR70
North Acton Rd, NW10 160 CR69
Northallerton Way, Rom. RM3 128 FK50
Northall Rd, Bexh. DA7 189 FC82
Northampton Av, Slou. SL1 153 AQ72
Northampton Gro, N1 9 L3
Northampton Pk, N1 9 K4
Northampton Rd, EC1 18 F4
Croydon CR0 224 DU103
Enfield EN3 105 DY42
Northampton Row, EC1 18 F3
Northampton Sq, EC1 18 G3
Northampton St, N1 9 J6
Coll North & W Essex Adult Comm Coll, Epping Cen, Epp. CM16
off St. John's Rd 91 ET30
Northbrooks Ho, Harl. CM19
off Northbrooks 73 EQ16
Rivermill Cen, Harl. CM20
off Hodings Rd 57 EQ13
Northanger Rd, SW16 203 DL93
North App, Nthwd. HA6 115 BQ47
Watford WD25 97 BT35
North Arc, Croy. CR0
off North End 224 DQ103
North Audley St, W1 16 G9
North Av, N18 122 DU49
W13 159 CH72
Brentwood CM14 129 FR45
Carshalton SM5 240 DG108
North Av, Har. HA2 138 CB58
Hayes UB3 157 BU73
Richmond TW9
off Sandycombe Rd 180 CN81
Shenley WD7 84 CL32
Southall UB1 158 BZ73
Whiteley Village KT12 235 BS109
NORTHAW, Pot.B. EN6 86 DF30
Northaw Cl, Hem.H. HP2 63 BP15
Sch Northaw C of E Prim Sch, Northaw EN6
off Vineyards Rd 86 DG30
Northaw Pl, Northaw EN6 86 DD30
Northaw Rd E, Cuffley EN6 87 DK31
Northaw Rd W, Northaw EN6 86 DG30
North Bk, NW8 16 B3
Northbank Rd, E17 123 EC54
North Barn, Brox. EN10 71 EA21
NORTH BECKTON, E6 25 H5
Sch North Beckton Prim Sch, E6 25 K6
North Birkbeck Rd, E11 145 ED62
Northborough Rd, SW16 223 DK97
Slough SL2 153 AN70
Northbourne, Brom. BR2 226 EG101
Godalming GU7 280 AT143
Northbourne Ho, E5
off Pembury Rd 10 E2
Northbourne Rd, SW4 183 DK84
North Branch Av, W10 14 B3
Sch North Br Ho Jun Sch, NW3 5 P3
Sch North Br Ho Sen Sch, NW1 7 J9
Northbridge Rd, Berk. HP4 60 AT17
Sch Northbrook C of E Sch, SE13
off Leahurst Rd 205 ED85
Northbrook Dr, Nthwd. HA6 115 BS53
Northbrook Rd, N22 121 DL52
SE13 205 ED85
Barnet EN5 101 CY44
Croydon CR0 224 DR99
Ilford IG1 147 EN61
Northbrooks, Harl. CM19 73 EQ16
Northburgh St, EC1 19 H4
North Burnham Cl, Burn. SL1
off Wyndham Cres 152 AH68
Sch Northbury Inf & Jun Schs, Bark. IG11 off North St 167 EQ65
North Carriage Dr, W2 16 C10
NORTH CHEAM, Sutt. SM3 239 CW105
NORTHCHURCH, Berk. HP4 60 AT17
Northchurch, SE17 31 M10
Northchurch Rd, N1 9 L6
Wembley HA9 160 CM65
Northchurch Ter, N1 9 N7
North Circular Rd, E4 (A406) 123 DZ52
E6 (A406) 167 EP68
E11 (A406) 124 EJ54
E12 (A406) 147 EP64
E17 (A406) 123 DZ52
E18 (A406) 124 EJ54
N3 (A406) 142 DB55
N11 (A406) 120 DD53
N12 (A406) 120 DD53
N13 (A406) 121 DN50
N18 (A406) 122 DS50
NW2 (A406) 140 CS62
NW10 (A406) 160 CP66
NW11 (A406) 141 CY56
W3 (A406) 180 CM75
W4 (A406) 180 CM75
W5 (A406) 180 CM75
Barking (A406) IG11 167 EP68
Ilford (A406) IG1, IG4 146 EL60
Northcliffe Cl, Wor.Pk. KT4 220 CS104
Northcliffe Dr, N20 119 CZ46
North Cl, Barn. EN5 101 CW43
Beaconsfield HP9 132 AH55
Bexleyheath DA6 188 EX84
Chigwell IG7 126 EU50
Dagenham RM10 168 FA67
Feltham TW14 off North Rd 197 BR86
Morden SM4 221 CY98
North Holmwood RH5 285 CJ140
St. Albans AL2 82 CB25
Windsor SL4 173 AM81
North Colonnade, The, E14 34 B2
North Common, Wey. KT13 235 BP105
North Common Rd, W5 160 CL73
Uxbridge UB8 136 BK64
Northcote, Add. KT15 234 BK105
Oxshott KT22 236 CC114
Pinner HA5 116 BW54
Northcote Av, W5 160 CL73
Isleworth TW7 199 CG85
Southall UB1 158 BY73
Surbiton KT5 220 CN101
Northcote Cl, W.Hors. KT24 267 BQ125
Northcote Cres, W.Hors. KT24 267 BQ125
Sch Northcote Lo Sch, SW11
off Bolingbroke Gro 202 DF86
Northcote Ms, SW11
off Northcote Rd 182 DE84
Northcote Rd, E17 145 DY56
NW10 160 CS66
SW11 182 DE84
Croydon CR0 224 DR100
Gravesend DA11 213 GF88
New Malden KT3 220 CQ97
Sidcup DA14 207 ES91
Twickenham TW1 199 CG85
West Horsley KT24 267 BQ125
North Cotts, Lon.Col. AL2 83 CG25
Northcott Av, N22 121 DL53
Northcotts, Abb.L. WD5
off Long Elms 81 BR33
Hatfield AL9 67 CW17
North Countess Rd, E17 123 DZ54
Northcourt, Mill End WD3
off Springwell Av 114 BG46
NORTH CRAY, Sid. DA14 208 FA90
North Cray Rd, Bex. DA5 208 EZ90
Sidcup DA14 208 EY93
North Cres, E16 23 H5
N3 119 CZ54
WC1 17 N6
Northcroft, Slou. SL2 153 AP70
Wooburn Green HP10 132 AE56
Northcroft Cl, Eng.Grn TW20 194 AV92
Northcroft Gdns, Eng.Grn TW20 194 AV92
Northcroft Rd, W13 179 CH75
Englefield Green TW20 194 AV92
Epsom KT19 238 CR108
Northcroft Ter, W13
off Northcroft Rd 179 CH75
Northcroft Vil, Eng.Grn TW20 194 AV92
North Cross Rd, SE22 204 DT85
Ilford IG6 147 EQ56
North Dene, NW7 118 CR48
Northdene, Chig. IG7 125 ER50
North Dene, Houns. TW3 178 CB81
Northdene Gdns, N15 144 DT58
North Down, S.Croy. CR2 242 DS111
Northdown Cl, Ruis. HA4 137 BT62
Northdown Gdns, Ilf. IG2 147 ES57
Northdown La, Guil. GU1 280 AY137
Northdown Rd, Chal.St.P. SL9 112 AY51
Hatfield AL10 67 CU21
Hornchurch RM11 149 FH59
Longfield DA3 231 FX96
Sutton SM2 240 DA110
Welling DA16 188 EV82
Woldingham CR3 259 EA123
● North Downs Business Pk, Dunt.Grn TN13 263 FC117
North Downs Cres, New Adgtn CR0 243 EB110
H North Downs Private Hosp, The, Cat. CR3 274 DT125
North Downs Rd, New Adgtn CR0 243 EB110
Northdown St, N1 8 B10
North Downs Way, Bet. RH3 271 CU130
Caterham CR3 273 DN126
Dorking RH5 269 CE133
Godstone RH9 275 DY128
Guildford GU3, GU4 280 AT138
Oxted RH8 276 EE126
Redhill RH1 272 DG128
Reigate RH2 272 DD130
Sevenoaks TN13, TN14 263 FD118
Tadworth KT20 271 CX130
Westerham TN16 261 ER121
North Dr, SW16 203 DJ91
Beaconsfield HP9 132 AG55
Beckenham BR3 225 EB98
Hatfield AL9
off Great N Rd 67 CW16
Hounslow TW3 178 CC82
Oaklands AL4 66 CL18
Orpington BR6 245 ES105
Romford RM2 150 FJ55
Ruislip HA4 137 BS59
Slough SL2 154 AS69
Virginia Water GU25 214 AS100
⇌ North Dulwich 204 DR85
⊖ North Ealing 160 CM72
Sch North Ealing Prim Sch, W5
off Pitshanger La 159 CH70
North End, NW3 142 DC61
Buckhurst Hill IG9 124 EJ45
Croydon CR0 224 DQ103
Northend, Hem.H. HP3 63 BP22
North End, Noak Hill RM3 128 FJ47
Northend, Warley CM14 130 FW50
North End Av, NW3 142 DC61
Northend Cl, Flack.Hth HP10 132 AC56
North End Cres, W14 26 G9
North End Ho, W14 26 F9
North End La, Downe BR6 245 EN110
North End Par, W14 26 F9
Sch Northend Prim Sch, Erith DA8
off Peareswood Rd 189 FF81
North End Rd, NW11 142 DA60
SW6 39 H2
W14 26 G10
Northend Rd, Dart. DA1 189 FF80
Erith DA8 189 FF80
North End Rd, Wem. HA9 140 CN62
● Northend Trd Est, Erith DA8 189 FE81
North End Way, NW3 142 DC61
Northern Av, N9 122 DT47
Northernhay Wk, Mord. SM4 221 CY98
Northern Perimeter Rd, Lon.Hthrw Air. TW6 177 BQ81
Northern Perimeter Rd W, Lon.Hthrw Air. TW6 176 BK81
Northern Relief Rd, Bark. IG11 167 EP66
Northern Rd, E13 166 EH67
Slough SL2 153 AR70
Northern Service Rd, Barn. EN5 101 CY41
Northern Wds, Flack.Hth HP10 132 AC56
Northey Av, Sutt. SM2 239 CZ110
North Eyot Gdns, W6 181 CU78
Northey St, E14 21 M10
Northfield, Hat. AL10
off Longmead 67 CV15
Loughton IG10 106 EK42
Shalford GU4 280 AY142
Northfield Av, W5 179 CH75
W13 179 CH75
Orpington BR5 228 EW100
Pinner HA5 138 BX56
Northfield Cl, Brom. BR1 226 EL95
Hayes UB3 177 BS76
Northfield Ct, Stai. TW18 216 BH95
Northfield Cres, Sutt. SM3 239 CY105
Northfield Fm Ms, Cob. KT11 235 BU113
Northfield Gdns, Dag. RM9
off Northfield Rd 148 EZ63
Watford WD24 98 BW37
Northfield Pk, Hayes UB3 177 BT76
Northfield Path, Dag. RM9 148 EZ62
Northfield Pl, Wey. KT13 235 BP108
Northfield Rd, E6 167 EM66
N16 144 DS59
W13 179 CH75
Barnet EN4 102 DE41
Borehamwood WD6 100 CP39
Cobham KT11 235 BU113
Dagenham RM9 148 EZ63
Enfield EN3 104 DV43
Eton Wick SL4 173 AM77
Hounslow TW5 178 BX79
Staines TW18 216 BH95
Waltham Cross EN8 89 DY32
⊖ Northfields 179 CH76
Northfields, SW18 182 DA84
Ashtead KT21 254 CL119
Grays RM17 192 GC77
● Northfields Ind Est, Wem. HA0 160 CN67
Northfields Rd, W3 160 CP71
NORTH FINCHLEY, N12 120 DD50
NORTHFLEET, Grav. DA10 212 GD86
⇌ Northfleet 212 GA86
NORTHFLEET GREEN, Grav. DA13 212 GC92
Northfleet Grn Rd, Grav. DA13 212 GC93
● Northfleet Ind Est, Nthflt DA11 192 GA84
Sch Northfleet Sch for Girls, Grav. DA11 off Hall Rd 212 GD89
Sch Northfleet Tech Coll, Nthflt DA11 off Colyer Rd 212 GD88
North Flockton St, SE16 32 C4
North Gdn, E14
off Westferry Circ 33 P2
North Gdns, SW19 202 DD94
North Gate, NW8 16 C1
Northgate, Gat. RH6 290 DF151
North Gate, Harl. CM20 57 EQ14
Northgate, Nthwd. HA6 115 BQ52
Northgate Ct, SW9
off Canterbury Cres 183 DN83
Northgate Dr, NW9 140 CS58
● Northgate Ind Pk, Rom. RM5 126 EZ54
Northgate Path, Borwd. WD6 100 CM38
North Glade, The, Bex. DA5 208 EZ87
North Gower St, NW1 17 M3
North Grn, NW9
off Clayton Fld 118 CS52
Slough SL1 154 AS73
⊖ North Greenwich 35 J4
North Greenwich 35 J4
North Gro, N6 142 DG59
N15 144 DR57
Chertsey KT16 215 BF100
Harlow CM18 74 EU16
Sch North Harringay Prim Sch, N8
off Falkland Rd 143 DN56
NORTH HARROW, Har. HA2 138 CA58
⊖ North Harrow 138 CA57
North Hatton Rd, Lon.Hthrw Air. TW6 177 BR81
North Hill, N6 142 DF57
Rickmansworth WD3 95 BE40
North Hill Av, N6 142 DF58
North Hill Dr, Rom. RM3 128 FK48
North Hill Grn, Rom. RM3 128 FK49
NORTH HILLINGDON, Uxb. UB10 157 BQ66
Coll North Hillingdon Adult Ed Cen, Uxb. UB10 off Long La 137 BP64
NORTH HOLMWOOD, Dor. RH5 285 CH141
North Ho, Harl. CM18
off Bush Fair 73 ET17
NORTH HYDE, Sthl. UB2 177 BY77
North Hyde Gdns, Hayes UB3 177 BU77
North Hyde La, Houns. TW5 178 BY78
Southall UB2 178 BY78
North Hyde Rd, Hayes UB3 177 BT76
Northiam, N12 120 DA48
Northiam St, E9 10 F9
Northington St, WC1 18 C5
NORTH KENSINGTON, W10 14 D7
North Kent Av, Nthflt DA11 212 GC86
Coll North Kingston Cen, Kings.T. KT2 off Richmond Rd 200 CL93
Northlands, Pot.B. EN6 86 DD31
Northlands Av, Orp. BR6 245 ES105
Northlands St, SE5 43 J9
North La, Tedd. TW11 199 CF93
North Lo Cl, SW15 201 CX85
● North London Business Pk, N11 120 DF47
Sch North London Collegiate Sch, Edg. HA8 off Canons Dr 118 CL50
Sch North London Int Sch, The, IB Diploma Cen, N11
off Friern Barnet La 120 DF50
Upr Sch, N11
off Friern Barnet Rd 120 DF50
Lwr Sch, N12
off Woodside Av 120 DC48
Lwr Sch, N12
off Woodside Pk Rd 120 DB49
NORTH LOOE, Epsom KT17 239 CW113
North Mall, N9 off Edmonton Grn Shop Cen 122 DV47
North Mead, Red. RH1 272 DF131
Sch Northmead Jun Sch, Guil. GU2 off Grange Rd 264 AV131
Northmead Rd, Slou. SL2 153 AM70
North Ms, WC1 18 D5
H North Middlesex Uni Hosp, N18 122 DS50
North Moors, Guil. GU1 264 AY130
NORTH MYMMS, Hat. AL9 85 CU25
North Mymms Pk, N.Mymms AL9 85 CT25
NORTH OCKENDON, Upmin. RM14 151 FV64
Northolm, Edg. HA8 118 CR49
Northolme Cl, Grays RM16
off Premier Av 192 GC76
Northolme Gdns, Edg. HA8 118 CN53
Northolme Ri, Orp. BR6 227 ES103
Northolme Rd, N5 144 DQ63
NORTHOLT, UB5 158 BZ66
⊖ Northolt 158 CA66
Northolt, N17 122 DR54
Northolt Av, Ruis. HA4 137 BV64
Northolt Gdns, Grnf. UB6 139 CF64
Sch Northolt High Sch, Nthlt. UB5
off Eastcote La 158 BZ65
⇌ Northolt Park 138 CB63
Northolt Rd, Har. HA2 138 CB63
London Heathrow Airport TW6 176 BK81
Northolt Way, Horn. RM12 170 FJ65
● North Orbital Commercial Pk, St.Alb. AL1 65 CG24
North Orbital Rd, Denh. UB9 135 BF60
Hatfield AL10 51 CV14
Rickmansworth WD3 135 BF55
St. Albans AL1, AL2, AL4 83 CK25
Watford WD25 81 BU34
Northover, Brom. BR1 206 EF90
North Par, Chess. KT9 238 CL106
Edgware HA8
off Mollison Way 118 CN54
North Pk, SE9 207 EM86
Chalfont St. Peter SL9 134 AY56
Iver SL0 175 BC76
North Pk La, Gdse. RH9 274 DU129
North Pas, SW18 182 DA84
North Perimeter Rd, Uxb. UB8
off Kingston La 156 BL69
North Pl, Guil. GU1 280 AX135
Mitcham CR4 202 DF94
Teddington TW11 199 CF93
Waltham Abbey EN9
off Highbridge St 89 EB33

North Pt, N8 ... 143 DM57
Northpoint, Brom. BR1
off Sherman Rd ... 226 EG95
Northpoint Cl, Sutt. SM1 ... 222 DC104
Northpoint Ho, N1
off Essex Rd ... 9 L5
Northpoint Sq, NW1 ... 7 N4
North Pole La, Kes. BR2 ... 244 EF107
North Pole Rd, W10 ... 14 A7
Northport St, N1 ... 9 M9
Sch North Prim Sch, Sthl. UB1
off Meadow Rd ... 158 BZ73
North Ride, W2 ... 28 C1
Northridge Rd, Grav. DA12 ... 213 GJ90
Northridge Way, Hem.H. HP1 ... 61 BF21
North Riding, Brick.Wd AL2 ... 82 CA30
North Ri, W2
off St. Georges Flds ... 16 D9
North Rd, N6 ... 142 DG59
N7 ... 7 P4
N9 ... 122 DV46
SE18 ... 187 ES77
SW19 ... 202 DC93
W5 ... 179 CK76
Belvedere DA17 ... 189 FB76
Berkhamsted HP4 ... 60 AV19
Brentford TW8 ... 180 CL79
Brentwood CM14 ... 130 FW46
Bromley BR1 ... 226 EH95
Chadwell Heath RM6 ... 148 EY57
Chesham Bois HP6 ... 77 AQ36
Chorleywood WD3 ... 95 BD43
Dartford DA1 ... 209 FF86
Edgware HA8 ... 118 CP53
Feltham TW14 ... 197 BR86
Guildford GU2 ... 264 AV131
Havering-atte-Bower RM4 ... 127 FE48
Hayes UB3 ... 157 BR71
Hersham KT12 ... 236 BW106
Hertford SG14 ... 54 DQ09
Hoddesdon EN11 ... 71 EA16
Ilford IG3 ... 147 ES61
Purfleet RM19 ... 190 FQ77
Reigate RH2 ... 287 CZ137
Richmond TW9 ... 180 CN83
South Ockendon RM15 ... 171 FW68
Southall UB1 ... 158 CA73
Surbiton KT6 ... 219 CK100
Waltham Cross EN8 ... 89 DY33
West Drayton UB7 ... 176 BM76
West Wickham BR4 ... 225 EB102
Woking GU21 ... 249 BA116
North Rd Av, Brwd. CM14 ... 130 FW46
Hertford SG14 ... 53 DN08
North Rd Gdns, Hert. SG14 ... 53 DP09
Northrop Rd, Lon.Hthrw Air.
TW6 ... 177 BS81
North Row, W1 ... 16 F10
North Several, SE3 ... 47 H8
NORTH SHEEN, Rich. TW9 ... 180 CN82
⇌ North Sheen ... 180 CN84
Sch Northside Prim Sch, N12
off Albert St ... 120 DC50
Northside Rd, Brom. BR1
off Mitchell Way ... 226 EG95
North Side Wandsworth Common,
SW18 ... 202 DC85
Northspur Rd, Sutt. SM1 ... 222 DA104
North Sq, N9 *off Edmonton
Grn Shop Cen* ... 122 DV47
North Sq, NW11 ... 142 DA57
North Sta App, S.Nutfld RH1 ... 289 DM136
Northstead Rd, SW2 ... 203 DN89
North St, E13 ... 24 A1
NW4 ... 141 CW57
SW4 ... 41 L10
Barking IG11 ... 167 EP65
Bexleyheath DA7 ... 188 FA84
Bromley BR1 ... 226 EG95
Carshalton SM5 ... 222 DF104
Dartford DA1 ... 210 FK87
Dorking RH4 ... 285 CG136
Egham TW20 ... 195 AZ92
Godalming GU7
off Station Rd ... 280 AT144
Gravesend DA12
off South St ... 213 GH87
Guildford GU1 ... 280 AX135
Hornchurch RM11 ... 150 FK59
Isleworth TW7 ... 179 CG83
Leatherhead KT22 ... 253 CG121
Lower Nazeing EN9 ... 72 EE22
Redhill RH1 ... 272 DF133
Romford RM1, RM5 ... 149 FD55
Westcott RH4 ... 284 CC137
North St Pas, E13 ... 166 EH68
North Tenter St, E1 ... 20 B9
North Ter, SW3 ... 28 C7
Windsor SL4
off Windsor Castle ... 174 AS80
Northumberland All, EC3 ... 19 P9
Northumberland Av, E12 ... 146 EJ60
WC2 ... 30 A2
Enfield EN1 ... 104 DV39
Hornchurch RM11 ... 150 FJ57
Isleworth TW7 ... 179 CF81
Welling DA16 ... 187 ER84
Northumberland Cl, Erith DA8 ... 189 FC80
Stanwell TW19 ... 196 BL86
Northumberland Cres, Felt.
TW14 ... 197 BS86
Northumberland Gdns, N9 ... 122 DT48
Bromley BR1 ... 227 EN98
Isleworth TW7 ... 179 CG80
Mitcham CR4 ... 223 DK99
Northumberland Gro, N17 ... 122 DV52
NORTHUMBERLAND HEATH,
Erith DA8 ... 189 FC80
Sch Northumberland Heath Prim Sch,
Erith DA8 *off Byron Dr* ... 189 FB80
⇌ Northumberland Park ... 122 DV53
Northumberland Pk, N17 ... 122 DT52
Erith DA8 ... 189 FC80
Sch Northumberland Pk Comm Sch,
N17 *off Trulock Rd* ... 122 DU52
● Northumberland Pk Ind Est,
N17 *off Willoughby La* ... 122 DV52
Northumberland Pl, W2 ... 15 J8
Richmond TW10 ... 199 CK85
Northumberland Rd, E6 ... 25 H8
E17 ... 145 EA59
Northumberland Rd, Har. HA2 ... 138 BZ57
Istead Rise DA13 ... 213 GF94
New Barnet EN5 ... 102 DC44
Northumberland Row, Twick. TW2
off Colne Rd ... 199 CE88
Northumberland St, WC2 ... 30 A2
Northumberland Way, Erith
DA8 ... 189 FC81
Northumbria St, E14 ... 22 B8
North Verbena Gdns, W6
off St. Peter's Sq ... 181 CU78
Northview, N7 ... 143 DL62
North Vw, SW19 ... 201 CV92
W5 ... 159 CJ70
Northview, Hem.H. HP1
off Winkwell ... 61 BD22
North Vw, Ilf. IG6 ... 126 EU52
Pinner HA5 ... 138 BW59
Northview, Swan. BR8 ... 229 FE96
North Vw Av, Til. RM18 ... 193 GG81
Northview Cres, NW10 ... 141 CT63
North Vw Cres, Epsom KT18 ... 255 CV117
North Vw Dr, Wdf.Grn. IG8 ... 124 EK54
Sch Northview Prim Sch, NW10
off Northview Cres ... 141 CT64
North Vw Rd, N8 ... 143 DK55
Sevenoaks TN14 *off Seal Rd* ... 279 FJ121
North Vil, NW1 ... 7 N5
North Wk, W2 ... 27 N1
New Addington CR0 ... 243 EB106
NORTH WATFORD, Wat. WD24 ... 97 BV37
North Way, N9 ... 122 DW47
N11 ... 121 DJ51
NW9 ... 140 CP55
Northway, NW11 ... 142 DB57
Guildford GU2 ... 264 AU132
Morden SM4 ... 221 CY97
North Way, Pnr. HA5 ... 138 BW55
Northway, Rick. WD3 ... 114 BK45
North Way, Uxb. UB10 ... 156 BL66
Northway, Wall. SM6 ... 241 DJ105
Welwyn Garden City AL7
off Nursery Hill ... 51 CZ06
Northway Circ, NW7 ... 118 CR49
Northway Cres, NW7 ... 118 CR49
Northway Ho, N20 ... 120 DC46
Northway Rd, SE5 ... 184 DQ83
Croydon CR0 ... 224 DT100
Sch Northway Sch, NW7
off The Fairway ... 118 CR48
Northways Par, NW3
off Finchley Rd ... 6 A6
North Weald Airfield, N.Wld Bas.
CM16 ... 92 EZ26
NORTH WEALD BASSETT, Epp.
CM16 ... 93 FB27
North Weald Cl, Horn. RM12 ... 169 FH66
Northweald La, Kings.T. KT2 ... 199 CK92
NORTH WEMBLEY, Wem.
HA0 ... 139 CH61
⇌ North Wembley ... 139 CK62
⊖ North Wembley ... 139 CK62
North Western Av, Wat.
WD24, WD25 ... 97 BU35
● North Western Commercial Cen,
NW1 *off Broadfield La* ... 8 A7
Coll North W Kent Coll,
Dartford Campus, Dart.
DA1 *off Oakfield La* ... 210 FJ89
Gravesend Campus, Grav.
DA12 *off Dering Way* ... 213 GM88
H North West London Health
Protection Unit, NW9 ... 140 CR55
Sch North W London Jewish
Prim Sch, NW6 ... 4 E6
Northwest Pl, N1 ... 8 F10
North Wf Rd, W2 ... 16 A7
Northwick Av, Har. HA3 ... 139 CG58
Northwick Circle, Har. HA3 ... 139 CJ58
Northwick Cl, NW8 ... 16 A4
Harrow HA1 ... 139 CH60
⊖ Northwick Park ... 139 CG59
H Northwick Pk Hosp, Har.
HA1 ... 139 CG59
Northwick Pk Rd, Har. HA1 ... 139 CF58
Northwick Rd, Wat. WD19 ... 116 BW49
Wembley HA0 ... 159 CK67
Northwick Ter, NW8 ... 16 A4
Northwick Wk, Har. HA1 ... 139 CF59
Northwold Dr, Pnr. HA5
off Cuckoo Hill ... 138 BW55
Northwold Est, E5 ... 144 DU61
Sch Northwold Prim Sch, E5
off Northwold Rd ... 144 DU61
Northwold Rd, E5 ... 144 DT61
N16 ... 144 DT61
NORTHWOOD, HA6 ... 115 BR51
⊖ Northwood ... 115 BS52
Northwood, Grays RM16 ... 193 GH75
Welwyn Garden City AL7 ... 52 DD09
Northwood Av, Horn. RM12 ... 149 FG63
Purley CR8 ... 241 DN113
Northwood Cl, Chsht EN7 ... 88 DT27
Coll Northwood Coll, Nthwd. HA6
off Maxwell Rd ... 115 BR52
North Wd Ct, SE25
off Regina Rd ... 224 DU97
Northwood Dr, Green. DA9 ... 211 FU86
Northwood Gdns, N12 ... 120 DD50
Greenford UB6 ... 139 CF64
Ilford IG5 ... 147 EN56
Northwood Hall, N6 ... 143 DJ59
NORTHWOOD HILLS, Nthwd.
HA6 ... 115 BT54
⊖ Northwood Hills ... 115 BU54
Northwood Ho, SE27 ... 204 DR91
Northwood Pl, Erith DA18 ... 188 EZ76
Sch Northwood Prep Sch, Rick.
WD3 *off Sandy Lo Rd* ... 115 BQ47
Sch Northwood Prim Sch, Erith
DA18 *off Northwood Pl* ... 188 EZ76
Northwood Rd, N6 ... 143 DH59
SE23 ... 205 DZ88
Carshalton SM5 ... 240 DG107
Harefield UB9 ... 114 BJ53
London Heathrow Airport
TW6 ... 176 BK81
Thornton Heath CR7 ... 223 DP96
Sch Northwood Sch, Nthwd. HA6
off Potter St ... 115 BU53
Northwood Twr, E17 ... 145 EC56
Northwood Way, SE19
off Roman Ri ... 204 DR93
Harefield UB9 ... 114 BK53
Northwood HA6 ... 115 BU52
NORTH WOOLWICH, E16 ... 37 H4
★ North Woolwich Old Sta Mus,
E16 ... 37 M4
North Woolwich Rd, E16 ... 35 M2
Jct North Woolwich Rbt, E16 ... 36 E3
North Worple Way, SW14 ... 180 CR83
Nortoft Rd, Chal.St.P. SL9 ... 113 AZ51
Norton Av, Surb. KT5 ... 220 CP101
Norton Cl, E4 ... 123 EA50
Borehamwood WD6 ... 100 CN39
Enfield EN1 *off Brick La* ... 104 DV40
Norton Folgate, E1 ... 19 P6
Norton Gdns, SW16 ... 223 DL96
Norton La, Cob. KT11 ... 251 BT119
Norton Rd, E10 ... 145 DZ60
Dagenham RM10 ... 169 FD65
Uxbridge UB8 ... 156 BK69
Wembley HA0 ... 159 CK65
Norval Rd, Wem. HA0 ... 139 CH61
Norvic Ho, Erith DA8
off Waterhead Cl ... 189 FF80
Norway Dr, Slou. SL2 ... 154 AV71
Norway Gate, SE16 ... 33 M6
Norway Pl, E14 ... 21 N9
Norway St, SE10 ... 46 D3
Norway Wk, Rain. RM13
off The Glen ... 170 FJ70
Sch Norwegian Sch in London, The,
SW20 *off Arterberry Rd* ... 201 CW94
Norwich Cres, Chad.Hth RM6 ... 148 EV57
Norwich Ho, E14 ... 22 D8
Norwich Ms, Ilf. IG3 ... 148 EU60
Norwich Pl, Bexh. DA6 ... 188 FA84
Norwich Rd, E7 ... 13 N3
Dagenham RM9 ... 168 FA68
Greenford UB6 ... 158 CB67
Northwood HA6 ... 137 BT55
Thornton Heath CR7 ... 224 DQ97
Norwich St, EC4 ... 18 E8
Norwich Wk, Edg. HA8 ... 118 CQ52
Norwich Way, Crox.Grn WD3 ... 97 BP41
NORWOOD, SE19 ... 204 DR93
Norwood Av, Rom. RM7 ... 149 FE59
Wembley HA0 ... 160 CM67
Norwood Cl, NW2 ... 141 CY62
Effingham KT24 ... 268 BY128
Hertford SG14 ... 53 DM08
Southall UB2 ... 178 CA77
Twickenham TW2
off Fourth Cross Rd ... 199 CD89
Norwood Ct, Amer. HP7 ... 77 AP40
Norwood Cres, Lon.Hthrw Air.
TW6 ... 177 BQ81
Norwood Dr, Har. HA2 ... 138 BZ58
Norwood Fm La, Cob. KT11 ... 235 BU111
Norwood Gdns, Hayes UB4 ... 158 BW70
Southall UB2 ... 178 BZ77
NORWOOD GREEN, Sthl.
UB2 ... 178 CA77
Sch Norwood Grn Inf & Nurs Sch,
Sthl. UB2 *off Thorncliffe Rd* ... 178 BZ78
Sch Norwood Grn Jun Sch, Sthl.
UB2 *off Thorncliffe Rd* ... 178 BY78
Norwood Grn Rd, Sthl. UB2 ... 178 CA77
Norwood High St, SE27 ... 203 DP90
⇌ Norwood Junction ... 224 DT98
Norwood La, Iver SL0 ... 155 BD70
NORWOOD NEW TOWN,
SE19 ... 204 DQ93
Norwood Pk Rd, SE27 ... 204 DQ92
Norwood Rd, SE24 ... 203 DP88
SE27 ... 203 DP89
Cheshunt EN8 ... 89 DY30
Effingham KT24 ... 268 BY128
Southall UB2 ... 178 BZ77
Sch Norwood Sch, The, SE19
off Crown Dale ... 204 DQ92
Norwood Ter, Sthl. UB2
off Tentelow La ... 178 CB77
Notley End, Eng.Grn TW20 ... 194 AW93
Notley St, SE5 ... 43 L4
Notre Dame Est, SW4 ... 183 DJ84
Sch Notre Dame Prep Sch, Cob.
KT11 *off Burwood Pk* ... 235 BT112
Sch Notre Dame RC Prim Sch,
SE18 *off Eglinton Rd* ... 187 EP79
Sch Notre Dame Sch, SE1 ... 30 G6
Sch Notre Dame Sen Sch, Cob.
KT11 *off Burwood Pk* ... 235 BT111
Notson Rd, SE25 ... 224 DV98
Notting Barn Rd, W10 ... 14 C5
Nottingdale Sq, W11 ... 26 E1
Nottingham Av, E16 ... 24 C7
Nottingham Cl, Wat. WD25 ... 81 BU33
Woking GU21 ... 248 AT118
Nottingham Ct, WC2 ... 18 A9
St. John's GU21
off Nottingham Cl ... 248 AT118
Nottingham Pl, W1 ... 16 G5
Nottingham Rd, E10 ... 145 EC58
SW17 ... 202 DF88
Heronsgate WD3 ... 113 BC45
Isleworth TW7 ... 179 CF82
South Croydon CR2 ... 242 DQ105
Nottingham St, W1 ... 16 G6
Nottingham Ter, NW1 ... 16 G5
NOTTING HILL, W11 ... 14 F10
Sch Notting Hill & Ealing High Sch,
Sen Sch & 6th Form, W13
off Cleveland Rd ... 159 CH71
⊖ Notting Hill Gate ... 27 J1
Notting Hill Gate, W11 ... 27 J2
Nova, E14 ... 34 A8
Nova Ms, Sutt. SM3 ... 221 CY102
Novar Cl, Orp. BR6 ... 227 ET101
Nova Rd, Croy. CR0 ... 223 DP102
Novar Rd, SE9 ... 207 EQ88
Novello St, SW6 ... 39 J7
Novello Way, Borwd. WD6 ... 100 CR39
Nowell Rd, SW13 ... 181 CU79
Nower, The, Sev. TN14 ... 261 ET119
Nower Cl E, Dor. RH4 ... 285 CF137
Nower Cl W, Dor. RH4 ... 285 CF137
Nower Hill, Pnr. HA5 ... 138 BZ56
Sch Nower Hill High Sch,
Pnr. HA5
off George V Av ... 138 CA56
Nower Rd, Dor. RH4 ... 285 CG136
Noyna Rd, SW17 ... 202 DF90
Nubia Way, Brom. BR1 ... 206 EE90
Nuding Cl, SE13 ... 185 EA83
H Nuffield Hosp Brentwood,
Brwd. CM15 ... 130 FY46
H Nuffield Hosp N London
(Enfield), Enf. EN2 ... 103 DN40
Nuffield Rd, Swan. BR8 ... 209 FG93
H Nuffield Speech & Language
Unit, W5 ... 159 CJ71
● Nugent Ind Pk, Orp. BR5 ... 228 EW99
Nugent Rd, N19 ... 143 DL60
SE25 ... 224 DT97
Nugents Ct, Pnr. HA5
off St. Thomas' Dr ... 116 BY53
Nugent Shop Pk, Orp.
BR5 ... 228 EW98
Nugents Pk, Pnr. HA5 ... 116 BY53
Nugent Ter, NW8 ... 15 P1
Numa Ct, Brent. TW8
off Justin Cl ... 179 CK80
Nunappleton Way, Oxt. RH8 ... 276 EG132
Nun Ct, EC2 ... 19 L8
Nuneaton Rd, Dag. RM9 ... 168 EX66
Nuneham Est, SW16
off Prentis Rd ... 203 DK91
Nunfield, Chipper. WD4 ... 80 BH31
NUNHEAD, SE15 ... 184 DW83
⇌ Nunhead ... 44 G9
Nunhead Cres, SE15 ... 184 DV83
Nunhead Est, SE15 ... 184 DV84
Nunhead Grn, SE15 ... 44 F10
Nunhead Gro, SE15 ... 184 DV83
Nunhead La, SE15 ... 184 DV83
Nunhead Pas, SE15
off Peckham Rye ... 184 DU83
Nunnery Cl, St.Alb. AL1 ... 65 CD22
Nunnery Stables, St.Alb. AL1 ... 65 CD22
Nunnington Cl, SE9 ... 206 EL90
Nunns Rd, Enf. EN2 ... 104 DQ40
Nunns Way, Grays RM17 ... 192 GD77
Nunsbury Dr, Brox. EN10 ... 89 DY25
Nuns La, St.Alb. AL1 ... 65 CE24
Nuns Wk, Vir.W. GU25 ... 214 AX99
NUPER'S HATCH, Rom. RM4 ... 127 FE45
Nupton Dr, Barn. EN5 ... 101 CW44
Nurse Cl, Edg. HA8
off Gervase Rd ... 118 CQ53
Nurseries Rd, Wheat. AL4 ... 50 CL08
Nursery, The, Erith DA8 ... 189 FF80
Nursery Av, N3 ... 120 DC54
Bexleyheath DA7 ... 188 EZ83
Croydon CR0 ... 225 DX103
Nursery Cl, SE4 ... 45 N9
SW15 ... 181 CX84
Amersham HP7 ... 77 AS39
Croydon CR0 ... 225 DX103
Dartford DA2 ... 210 FQ87
Enfield EN3 ... 105 DX39
Epsom KT17 ... 238 CS110
Feltham TW14 ... 197 BV87
Orpington BR6 ... 227 ET101
Penn HP10 ... 110 AC47
Romford RM6 ... 148 EX58
Sevenoaks TN13 ... 279 FJ122
South Ockendon RM15 ... 171 FW70
Swanley BR8 ... 229 FC96
Walton on the Hill KT20 ... 271 CV125
Watford WD19 ... 115 BV46
Woking GU21 ... 248 AW116
Woodford Green IG8 ... 124 EH50
Woodham KT15 ... 233 BF110
Nursery Ct, N17
off Nursery St ... 122 DT52
Nursery Flds, Saw. CM21 ... 58 EX05
Nursery Gdns, Chilw. GU4 ... 281 BB140
Chislehurst BR7 ... 207 EP93
Enfield EN3 ... 105 DX39
Goffs Oak EN7 ... 88 DR28
Hampton TW12 ... 198 BZ91
Hounslow TW4 ... 198 BZ85
Staines TW18 ... 196 BH94
Sunbury-on-Thames TW16 ... 217 BT96
Ware SG12 ... 55 DY06
Welwyn Garden City AL7 ... 51 CY06
Nursery Hill, Welw.G.C. AL7 ... 51 CY06
Nursery La, E2 ... 10 A9
E7 ... 13 P4
W10 ... 14 A7
Hookwood RH6 ... 290 DD149
Penn HP10 ... 110 AC47
Slough SL3 ... 154 AW74
Uxbridge UB8 ... 156 BK70
Nurserymans Rd, N11 ... 120 DG47
Nursery Pl, Old Wind. SL4
off Gregory Dr ... 194 AV86
Sevenoaks TN13 ... 278 FD122
Nursery Rd, E9 ... 10 G4
N2 ... 120 DD53
N14 ... 121 DJ45
SW9 ... 183 DM84
Broxbourne EN10 ... 89 DY25
Godalming GU7 ... 280 AT144
Hoddesdon EN11 ... 55 EB14
Loughton IG10 ... 106 EJ43
Lower Nazeing EN9 ... 71 ED22
Pinner HA5 ... 138 BW55
Sunbury-on-Thames TW16 ... 217 BS96
Sutton SM1 ... 240 DC105
Taplow SL6 ... 152 AH72
Thornton Heath CR7 ... 224 DR98
Walton on the Hill KT20 ... 271 CU125
Nursery Rd Merton, SW19 ... 222 DB96
Nursery Rd Mitcham, Mitch.
CR4 ... 222 DE97
Nursery Rd Wimbledon, SW19
off Worple Rd ... 201 CY94
Nursery Row, SE17 ... 31 L9
Barnet EN5
off St. Albans Rd ... 101 CY41
Nursery St, N17 ... 122 DT52
Nursery Ter, Pott.End HP4
off The Front ... 61 BB16
Nursery Wk, NW4 ... 141 CV55
Romford RM7 ... 149 FD59
Nursery Way, Wrays. TW19 ... 194 AX86
Nursery Waye, Uxb. UB8 ... 156 BK67
Nurstead Rd, Erith DA8 ... 188 FA80
Nutberry Av, Grays RM16 ... 192 GA75
Nutberry Cl, Grays RM16
off Long La ... 192 GA75
Nutbourne St, W10 ... 14 E2
Nutbrook St, SE15 ... 184 DU83
Nutbrowne Rd, Dag. RM9 ... 168 EZ67
Nutcombe La, Dor. RH4 ... 285 CF136
Nutcroft Gro, Fetch. KT22 ... 253 CE121
Nutcroft Rd, SE15 ... 44 E4
NUTFIELD, Red. RH1 ... 273 DM133
⇌ Nutfield ... 289 DL136
Nutfield, Welw.G.C. AL7 ... 52 DA06
Sch Nutfield Ch C of E Prim Sch,
S.Nutfld RH1 *off Mid St* ... 289 DM135
Nutfield Cl, N18 ... 122 DU51
Carshalton SM5 ... 222 DE104
Nutfield Gdns, Ilf. IG3 ... 147 ET61
Northolt UB5 ... 158 BW68
Nutfield Marsh Rd, Nutfld
RH1 ... 273 DJ130
Nutfield Pk, S.Nutfld RH1 ... 289 DN137
Nutfield Rd, E15 ... 145 EC63
NW2 ... 141 CU61
SE22 ... 204 DT85
Coulsdon CR5 ... 256 DG116
Redhill RH1 ... 272 DG134
Nutfield Rd, S.Merst. RH1 ... 273 DJ129
Thornton Heath CR7 ... 223 DP98
Nutfield Way, Orp. BR6 ... 227 EN103
Nutford Pl, W1 ... 16 D8
Nut Gro, Welw.G.C. AL8 ... 51 CX06
Nuthatch Cl, Stai. TW19 ... 196 BM88
Nuthatch Gdns, SE28 ... 187 ER75
Reigate RH2 ... 288 DC138
Nuthurst Av, SW2 ... 203 DM89
Nutkins Way, Chesh. HP5 ... 76 AQ29
Nutkin Wk, Uxb. UB8 ... 156 BL66
Nutley Cl, Swan. BR8 ... 229 FF95
Nutley Ct, Reig. RH2
off Nutley La ... 271 CZ134
Nutley La, Reig. RH2 ... 271 CZ133
Nutley Ter, NW3 ... 5 P4
Nutmead Cl, Bex. DA5 ... 209 FC88
Nutmeg Cl, E16 ... 23 K4
Nutmeg La, E14 ... 22 G9
Nuttall St, N1 ... 9 P10
Nutter La, E11 ... 146 EJ58
Nuttfield Cl, Crox.Grn WD3 ... 97 BP44
Nutt Gro, Edg. HA8 ... 117 CK47
Nut Tree Cl, Orp. BR6 ... 228 EX104
Nutt St, SE15 ... 44 B4
Nutty La, Shep. TW17 ... 217 BQ98
Nutwell St, SW17 ... 202 DE92
Nutwood Av, Brock. RH3 ... 286 CQ135
Nutwood Cl, Brock. RH3 ... 286 CQ135
Nutwood Gdns, Chsht EN7
off Great Stockwood Rd ... 88 DS26
Nuxley Rd, Belv. DA17 ... 188 EZ79
Nyall Ct, Gidea Pk RM2 ... 150 FJ56
Nyanza St, SE18 ... 187 ER79
Nye Bevan Est, E5 ... 145 DX62
Nyefield Pk, Walt.Hill KT20 ... 271 CU126
Nye Way, Bov. HP3 ... 79 BA28
Nylands Av, Rich. TW9 ... 180 CN81
Nymans Gdns, SW20
off Hidcote Gdns ... 221 CV97
Nynehead St, SE14 ... 45 L4
Nyon Gro, SE6 ... 205 DZ89
Nyssa Cl, Wdf.Grn. IG8
off Gwynne Pk Av ... 125 EM51
Nyth Cl, Upmin. RM14 ... 151 FR58
Nyton Cl, N19
off Courtauld Rd ... 143 DL60

O

★ O2, The, SE10 ... 35 J3
O2 Shop Cen, NW3 ... 5 N4
Oakapple Cl, S.Croy. CR2 ... 242 DV114
Oak Apple Ct, SE12 ... 206 EG89
Oak Av, N8 ... 143 DL56
N10 ... 121 DH52
N17 ... 122 DR52
Bricket Wood AL2 ... 82 CA30
Croydon CR0 ... 225 EA103
Egham TW20 ... 195 BC94
Enfield EN2 ... 103 DM38
Hampton TW12 ... 198 BY92
Hounslow TW5 ... 178 BX80
Sevenoaks TN13 ... 279 FH128
Upminster RM14 ... 150 FP62
Uxbridge UB10 ... 137 BP61
West Drayton UB7 ... 176 BN76
Oakbank, Fetch. KT22 ... 252 CC123
Hutton CM13 ... 131 GE43
Oak Bk, New Adgtn CR0 ... 243 EC107
Oakbank, Wok. GU22 ... 248 AY119
Oakbank Av, Walt. KT12 ... 218 BZ101
Oakbank Gro, SE24 ... 184 DQ84
Oakbark Ho, Brent. TW8
off High St ... 179 CJ80
Oakbrook Cl, Brom. BR1 ... 206 EH91
Oakbury Rd, SW6 ... 39 M9
Oak Cl, N14 ... 121 DH45
Box Hill KT20 ... 270 CP130
Dartford DA1 ... 189 FE84
Godalming GU7 ... 280 AS143
Hemel Hempstead HP3 ... 62 BM24
Sutton SM1 ... 222 DC103
Waltham Abbey EN9 ... 89 ED34
Oakcombe Cl, N.Mal. KT3 ... 220 CS95
Oak Cottage Cl, SE6 ... 206 EE88
Oak Cres, E16 ... 23 K7
Oakcroft Cl, Pnr. HA5 ... 115 BV54
West Byfleet KT14 ... 233 BF114
Oakcroft Rd, SE13 ... 46 G9
Chessington KT9 ... 238 CM105
West Byfleet KT14 ... 233 BF114
Oakcroft Vil, Chess. KT9 ... 238 CM105
Oakdale, N14 ... 121 DH46
Welwyn Garden City AL8 ... 51 CW05
Oakdale Av, Har. HA3 ... 140 CL57
Northwood HA6 ... 115 BU54
Oakdale Cl, Wat. WD19 ... 116 BW49
Oakdale Gdns, E4 ... 123 EC50
Sch Oakdale Infants' Sch, E18
off Woodville Rd ... 124 EH54
Sch Oakdale Jun Sch, E18
off Oakdale Rd ... 124 EH54
Oakdale La, Crock.H. TN8 ... 277 EP133
Oakdale Rd, E7 ... 166 EH66
E11 ... 145 ED61
E18 ... 124 EH54
N4 ... 144 DQ58
SE15 ... 45 H10
SW16 ... 203 DL92
Epsom KT19 ... 238 CR109
Watford WD19 ... 116 BW48
Weybridge KT13 ... 216 BN104
Oakdale Way, Mitch. CR4 ... 222 DG101
Oakdene, SE15 ... 44 E6
Oak Dene, W13
off The Dene ... 159 CH71
Oakdene, Beac. HP9 ... 111 AL52
Cheshunt EN8 ... 89 DY30
Chobham GU24 ... 232 AT110
Romford RM3 ... 128 FM54
Tadworth KT20 ... 255 CY120
Oakdene Av, Chis. BR7 ... 207 EN92
Erith DA8 ... 189 FC79
Thames Ditton KT7 ... 219 CG102
Oakdene Cl, Bkhm KT23 ... 268 CC127
Brockham RH3 ... 286 CQ136
Hornchurch RM11 ... 149 FH58
Pinner HA5 ... 116 BZ52
Oakdene Ct, Walt. KT12 ... 217 BV104
Oakdene Dr, Surb. KT5 ... 220 CQ101
Oakdene Ms, Sutt. SM3 ... 221 CZ102
Oakdene Par, Cob. KT11
off Anyards Rd ... 235 BV114
Oakdene Pk, N3 ... 119 CZ52
Oakdene Pl, Peasm. GU3 ... 280 AW142

Oakdene Rd, Bkhm KT23 252 BZ124
Brockham RH3 286 CQ136
Cobham KT11 235 BV114
Hemel Hempstead HP3 62 BM24
Hillingdon UB10 157 BP68
Orpington BR5 227 ET99
Peasmarsh GU3 280 AW142
Redhill RH1 272 DE134
Sevenoaks TN13 278 FG122
Watford WD24 97 BV36
Oakdene Way, St.Alb. AL1 65 CJ20
Oakden St, SE11 30 F8
Oak Dr, Berk. HP4 60 AX20
Box Hill KT20 270 CP130
Sawbridgeworth CM21 58 EW07
Oake Ct, SW15
off Portinscale Rd 201 CY85
Oaken Coppice, Ashtd. KT21 254 CN119
Oak End, Harl. CM18 73 ET17
Oak End Dr, Iver SL0 155 BC68
Oaken Dr, Clay. KT10 237 CF107
Oak End Way, Ger.Cr. SL9 135 AZ57
Woodham KT15 233 BE112
Oakengate Wd, Tad. KT20 270 CQ131
Oaken Gro, Welw.G.C. AL7 51 CY11
Oakenholt Ho, SE2
off Hartslock Dr 188 EX75
Oaken La, Clay. KT10 237 CE106
Oakenshaw Cl, Surb. KT6 220 CL101
Oakes Cl, E6 25 K9
Oakeshott Av, N6 142 DG61
Oakey La, SE1 30 E6
Oak Fm, Borwd. WD6 100 CQ43
Sch Oak Fm Inf & Jun Schs, Hlgdn UB10 off Windsor Av 157 BP67
Oakfield, E4 123 EB50
Oak Fld, Chesh. HP5 76 AP30
Oakfield, Mill End WD3 113 BF45
Woking GU21 248 AS116
Oakfield Av, Har. HA3 139 CH55
Slough SL1 153 AP74
Oakfield Cl, Amer. HP6 77 AQ37
New Malden KT3
off Blakes La 221 CT99
Potters Bar EN6 85 CZ31
Ruislip HA4 137 BT58
Weybridge KT13 235 BQ105
Sch Oakfield Co Inf & Nurs Sch, Dart. DA1 off Oakfield La 210 FL89
Oakfield Ct, N8 143 DL59
NW2 off Hendon Way 141 CX59
Borehamwood WD6 100 CP41
Oakfield Dr, Reig. RH2 272 DA132
Sch Oakfield First Sch, Wind. SL4
off Imperial Rd 173 AP82
Oakfield Gdns, N18 122 DS49
SE19 204 DS92
Beckenham BR3 225 EA99
Carshalton SM5 222 DE102
Greenford UB6 159 CD70
Oakfield Glade, Wey. KT13 235 BQ105
Sch Oakfield Jun Sch, Dart. DA1
off Oakfield La 210 FK89
Fetcham KT22 off Bell La 253 CD123
Oakfield La, Bex. DA5 209 FF89
Dartford DA1, DA2 209 FG89
Keston BR2 244 EJ105
Oakfield Lo, Ilf. IG1
off Albert Rd 147 EP62
Oakfield Pk Rd, Dart. DA1 210 FK89
Oakfield Pl, Dart. DA1 210 FK89
Sch Oakfield Prep Sch, SE21
off Thurlow Pk Rd 204 DR88
Oakfield Rd, E6 166 EL67
E17 123 DY54
N3 120 DB53
N4 143 DN58
N14 121 DL48
SE20 204 DV94
SW19 201 CX90
Ashford TW15 197 BP92
Ashtead KT21 253 CK117
Cobham KT11 235 BV113
Croydon CR0 224 DQ102
Ilford IG1 147 EP61
● Oakfield Rd Ind Est, SE20
off Oakfield Rd 204 DV94
Oakfields, Guil. GU3 264 AS132
Sevenoaks TN13 279 FH126
Walton-on-Thames KT12 217 BU102
West Byfleet KT14 234 BH114
Sch Oakfield Sch, Pyrford GU22
off Coldharbour Rd 249 BF115
Oakfields Rd, NW11 141 CY58
Oakfield St, SW10 39 N2
Oakford Rd, NW5 7 L1
Oak Gdns, Croy. CR0 225 EA103
Edgware HA8 118 CQ54
Oak Glade, Cooper. CM16
off Coopersale Common 92 EX29
Epsom KT19
off Christ Ch Rd 238 CN112
Northwood HA6 115 BP53
Oak Glen, Horn. RM11 150 FL55
Oak Gra Rd, W.Clan. GU4 266 BH128
Oak Grn, Abb.L. WD5 81 BS32
Oak Grn Way, Abb.L. WD5 81 BS32
Oak Gro, NW2 141 CY63
Hatfield AL10 67 CT18
Hertford SG13 54 DS11
Ruislip HA4 137 BV59
Sunbury-on-Thames TW16 197 BV94
West Wickham BR4 225 EC103
Oak Gro Rd, SE20 224 DW95
Oakhall Ct, E11 146 EH58
Oak Hall Ct, Sun. TW16 197 BT92
Oakhall Dr, Sun. TW16 197 BT92
Oak Hall Rd, E11 146 EH58
Oakham Cl, SE6
off Rutland Wk 205 DZ89
Barnet EN4 102 DF41
Oakham Dr, Brom. BR2 226 EF98
Oakhampton Rd, NW7 119 CX52
Oak Hill, Burpham GU4 265 BC129
Oakhill, Clay. KT10 237 CG107
Oak Hill, Epsom KT18 254 CR116
Surbiton KT6 220 CL101
Woodford Green IG8 123 ED52
Oakhill Av, NW3 5 L1
Pinner HA5 116 BY54
Oakhill Cl, Ashtd. KT21 253 CJ118
Maple Cross WD3 113 BE49
Oak Hill Cl, Wdf.Grn. IG8 123 ED52
Coll Oak Hill Coll, N14
off Chase Side 102 DG44
Oakhill Ct, SW19 201 CX94
Oak Hill Cres, Surb. KT6 220 CL101
Woodford Green IG8 123 ED52
Oakhill Dr, Surb. KT6 220 CL101
Oakhill Gdns, Wey. KT13 217 BS103
Oak Hill Gdns, Wdf.Grn. IG8 124 EE53
Oak Hill Gro, Surb. KT6 220 CL100
Oak Hill Pk, NW3 142 DB63
Oak Hill Pk Ms, NW3 142 DC63
Oakhill Path, Surb. KT6 220 CL100
Oakhill Pl, SW15
off Oakhill Rd 202 DA85
Sch Oakhill Prim Sch, Wdf.Grn. IG8 off Alders Av 124 EE51
Oakhill Rd, SW15 201 CZ85
SW16 223 DL95
Addlestone KT15 233 BF107
Ashtead KT21 253 CJ118
Beckenham BR3 225 EC96
Maple Cross WD3 113 BD49
Orpington BR6 227 ET102
Purfleet RM19 190 FP78
Reigate RH2 288 DB135
Sevenoaks TN13 278 FG124
Oak Hill Rd, Stap.Abb. RM4 127 FD45
Surbiton KT6 220 CL100
Oakhill Rd, Sutt. SM1 222 DB104
Oak Hill Way, NW3 142 DC63
Oak Ho, NW3
off Maitland Pk Vil 6 F4
Oakhouse Rd, Bexh. DA6 208 FA85
Oakhurst, Chobham GU24 232 AS109
Oakhurst Av, Bexh. DA7 188 EY80
East Barnet EN4 120 DE45
Oakhurst Cl, E17 146 EE56
Chislehurst BR7 227 EM95
Ilford IG6 125 EQ53
Teddington TW11 199 CE92
Oakhurst Gdns, E4 124 EF46
E17 146 EE56
Bexleyheath DA7 188 EY80
Oakhurst Gro, SE22 184 DU84
Oakhurst Pl, Wat. WD18
off Cherrydale 97 BT42
Oakhurst Ri, Cars. SM5 240 DE110
Oakhurst Rd, Enf. EN3 105 DX36
Epsom KT19 238 CQ107
Sch Oakhyrst Gra Sch, Cat. CR3
off Stanstead Rd 274 DR126
Oakington, Welw.G.C. AL7 52 DD08
Oakington Av, Amer. HP6 94 AY39
Harrow HA2 138 CA59
Hayes UB3 177 BR77
Wembley HA9 140 CM62
Oakington Cl, Sun. TW16 218 BW96
Oakington Dr, Sun. TW16 218 BW96
Oakington Manor Dr, Wem. HA9 140 CN64
Sch Oakington Manor Prim Sch, Wem. HA9
off Oakington Manor Dr 140 CP64
Oakington Rd, W9 15 K4
Oakington Way, N8 143 DL58
Oakland Gdns, Hutt. CM13 131 GC43
Oakland Pl, Buck.H. IG9 124 EG47
Oakland Rd, E15 13 H1
Oaklands, N21 121 DM47
Berkhamsted HP4 60 AU19
Fetcham KT22 253 CD124
Horley RH6 291 DJ148
Kenley CR8 242 DQ114
Twickenham TW2 198 CC87
Oaklands Av, N9 104 DV44
Brookmans Park AL9 85 CY27
Esher KT10 219 CD102
Isleworth TW7 179 CF79
Romford RM1 149 FE55
Sidcup DA15 207 ET87
Thornton Heath CR7 223 DN98
Watford WD19 115 BV46
West Wickham BR4 225 EB104
Oaklands Cl, Bexh. DA6 208 EZ85
Chessington KT9 237 CJ105
Petts Wood BR5 227 ES100
Shalford GU4 280 AY142
Coll Oaklands Coll, Borehamwood Campus, Borwd. WD6
off Elstree Way 100 CQ40
Cen for Construction Crafts, St.Alb. AL4
off Acrewood Way 66 CN20
St. Albans City Campus, St.Alb. AL1 off St. Peters Rd 65 CE20
St. Albans Smallford Campus, St.Alb. AL4 off Hatfield Rd 66 CL19
Welwyn Gdn City Campus, Welw.G.C. AL8
off The Campus 51 CX08
Oaklands Ct, W12
off Uxbridge Rd 161 CV74
Addlestone KT15 216 BH104
Watford WD17 97 BU39
Wembley HA0 139 CK64
Oaklands Dr, Harl. CM17 74 EW16
Redhill RH1 289 DH136
South Ockendon RM15 171 FW71
Oaklands Est, SW4 203 DJ86
Oaklands Gdns, Ken. CR8 242 DQ114
Oaklands Gate, Nthwd. HA6
off Green La 115 BS51
Oaklands Gro, W12 161 CU74
Broxbourne EN10 71 DY24
Sch Oaklands Inf Sch, Bigg.H. TN16 off Norheads La 260 EJ116
Sch Oaklands Jun Sch, Bigg.H. TN16 off Oaklands La 260 EJ116
Oaklands La, Barn. EN5 101 CV42
Biggin Hill TN16 244 EH113
Smallford AL4 66 CL18
Oaklands Ms, NW2 4 C1
Oaklands Pk, Hutt. CM13 131 GB46
Oaklands Pk Av, Ilf. IG1
off High Rd 147 ER61
Oaklands Pl, SW4
off St. Alphonsus Rd 183 DJ84
Sch Oaklands Prim Sch, W7
off Oaklands Rd 179 CF75
Oaklands Rd, N20 119 CZ45
NW2 4 C2
SW14 180 CR83
W7 179 CF75
Bexleyheath DA6 188 EZ84
Bromley BR1 206 EE94
Cheshunt EN7 88 DS26
Dartford DA2 210 FP88
Northfleet DA11 213 GF91
Sch Oaklands Sch, E2 20 E2
Isleworth TW7
off Woodlands Rd 179 CD83
Loughton IG10
off Albion Hill 106 EK43
Oaklands Way, Tad. KT20 255 CW122
Wallington SM6 241 DK108
Oaklands Wd, Hat. AL10 67 CU18
Oakland Way, Epsom KT19 238 CR107
Oak La, E14 21 N10
N2 120 DD54
N11 121 DK51
Cuffley EN6 87 DM28
Englefield Green TW20 194 AW90
Isleworth TW7 179 CE84
Sevenoaks TN13 278 FG127
Twickenham TW1 199 CG87
Windsor SL4 173 AN81
Woking GU22
off Beaufort Rd 249 BC116
Woodford Green IG8 124 EF49
Oaklawn Rd, Lthd. KT22 253 CE118
Oak Leaf Cl, Epsom KT19 238 CQ112
Oakleafe Gdns, Ilf. IG6 147 EP55
Oaklea Pas, Kings.T. KT1 219 CK97
Oakleigh Av, N20 120 DD47
Edgware HA8 118 CP54
Surbiton KT6 220 CN102
Oakleigh Cl, N20 120 DF48
Swanley BR8 229 FE97
Oakleigh Ct, N1 19 L1
Barnet EN4 102 DE44
Edgware HA8 118 CQ54
Oakleigh Cres, N20 120 DE47
Oakleigh Dr, Crox.Grn WD3 97 BQ44
Oakleigh Gdns, N20 120 DC46
Edgware HA8 118 CM50
Orpington BR6 245 ES105
Oakleigh Ms, N20
off Oakleigh Rd N 120 DC47
OAKLEIGH PARK, N20 120 DD46
⇌ Oakleigh Park 120 DD45
Oakleigh Pk Av, Chis. BR7 227 EN95
Oakleigh Pk N, N20 120 DD46
Oakleigh Pk S, N20 120 DE47
Oakleigh Ri, Epp. CM16
off Bower Hill 92 EU32
Oakleigh Rd, Pnr. HA5 116 BZ51
Uxbridge UB10 157 BQ66
Oakleigh Rd N, N20 120 DD47
Oakleigh Rd S, N11 120 DG48
Sch Oakleigh Spec Sch, N20
off Oakleigh Rd N 120 DF48
Oakleigh Way, Mitch. CR4 223 DH95
Surbiton KT6 220 CN102
Oakley Av, W5 160 CN73
Barking IG11 167 ET66
Croydon CR0 241 DL105
Oakley Cl, E4 123 EC48
E6 25 H8
W7 159 CE73
Addlestone KT15 234 BK105
Grays RM20 191 FW79
Isleworth TW7 179 CD81
Oakley Ct, Loug. IG10
off Hillyfields 107 EN40
Mitcham CR4 222 DG101
Oakley Cres, EC1 19 H1
Slough SL1 154 AS73
Oakley Dell, Guil. GU4 265 BC132
Oakley Dr, SE9 207 ER88
SE13 205 ED86
Bromley BR2 226 EL104
Romford RM3 128 FN50
Oakley Gdns, N8 143 DM57
SW3 40 D2
Banstead SM7 256 DB115
Betchworth RH3 286 CQ140
OAKLEY GREEN, Wind. SL4 172 AH82
Oakley Grn Rd, Oakley Grn SL4 172 AG82
Oakley Pk, Bex. DA5 208 EW87
Oakley Pl, SE1 44 A1
Oakley Rd, N1 9 L6
SE25 224 DV99
Bromley BR2 226 EL104
Harrow HA1 139 CE58
Warlingham CR6 258 DU118
Oakley Sq, NW1 17 M1
Oakley St, SW3 40 C2
Oakley Wk, W6 38 D2
Oakley Yd, E2 20 B4
Oak Lo Av, Chig. IG7 125 ER50
Oak Lo Cl, Hersham KT12 236 BW106
Stanmore HA7
off Dennis La 117 CJ50
Oak Lo Dr, Red. RH1 288 DG142
West Wickham BR4 225 EB101
Oak Lo La, West. TN16 277 ER125
Sch Oak Lo Prim Sch, W.Wick. BR4
off Chamberlain Cres 225 EB101
Sch Oak Lo Sch, SW12
off Nightingale La 202 DG87
Sch Oak Lo Spec Sch, N2
off Heath Vw 142 DC56
Oaklodge Way, NW7 119 CT50
Oak Manor Dr, Wem. HA9
off Oakington Manor Dr 140 CM64
Oakmead Av, Brom. BR2 226 EG100
Oakmeade, Pnr. HA5 116 CA51
Oakmead Gdns, Edg. HA8 118 CR49
Oakmead Grn, Epsom KT18 254 CP115
Oakmead Pl, Mitch. CR4 222 DE95
Oakmead Rd, SW12 202 DG88
Croydon CR0 223 DK100
Oakmere Av, Pot.B. EN6 86 DC33
Oakmere Cl, Pot.B. EN6 86 DD31
Oakmere La, Pot.B. EN6 86 DC32
Oakmere Ms, Pot.B. EN6 86 DC32
Sch Oakmere Prim Sch, Pot.B. EN6
off Chace Av 86 DD32
Oakmere Rd, SE2 188 EU79
Oakmont Pl, Orp. BR6 227 ER102
Oakmoor Way, Chig. IG7 125 ES50
Oak Pk, Hunsdon SG12 56 EH06
West Byfleet KT14 233 BE113
Oak Pk Gdns, SW19 201 CX87
Oak Pk Ms, N16 144 DT62
Oak Path, Bushey WD23
off Mortimer Cl 98 CB44
Oak Piece, N.Wld Bas. CM16 93 FC25
Oak Pl, SW18 off East Hill 202 DB85
Oakridge, Brick.Wd AL2 82 BZ29
Oak Ridge, Dor. RH4 285 CH139
Oakridge Av, Rad. WD7 83 CF34
Oakridge Dr, N2 142 DD55
Oakridge La, Ald. WD25 99 CD35
Bromley BR1 205 ED92
Radlett WD7 83 CF33
Oakridge Rd, Brom. BR1 205 ED91
Oak Ri, Buck.H. IG9 124 EK48
Oak Rd, W5 off The Broadway 159 CK73
Caterham CR3 258 DS122
Cobham KT11 252 BX115
Epping CM16 91 ET30
Gravesend DA12 213 GJ90
Oak Rd, Grays RM17 192 GC79
Greenhithe DA9 211 FS86
Leatherhead KT22 253 CG118
New Malden KT3 220 CR96
Northumberland Heath DA8 189 FC80
Orpington BR6 246 EU108
Reigate RH2 272 DB133
Romford RM3 128 FM53
Slade Green DA8 189 FG81
Westerham TN16 277 ER125
Oak Row, SW16 223 DJ96
Oakroyd Av, Pot.B. EN6 85 CZ33
Oakroyd Cl, Pot.B. EN6 85 CZ34
Oaks, The, N12 120 DB49
SE18 187 EQ78
Berkhamsted HP4 60 AU19
Dartford DA2 210 FP86
Dorking RH4 off Oak Ridge 285 CH139
Epsom KT18 239 CT114
Fetcham KT22 252 CC123
Hayes UB4 157 BQ68
Morden SM4 221 CY98
Ruislip HA4 137 BS59
Staines TW18
off Moormede Cres 195 BF91
Swanley BR8 229 FE96
Tadworth KT20 255 CW123
Watford WD19 116 BW46
West Byfleet KT14 234 BG113
Woodford Green IG8 124 EE51
Oaks Av, SE19 204 DS92
Feltham TW13 198 BY89
Romford RM5 127 FC54
Worcester Park KT4 221 CV104
Oaks Cl, Lthd. KT22 253 CG121
Radlett WD7 99 CF35
Oaksford Av, SE26 204 DV90
Oaks Gro, E4 124 EE47
Oakshade Rd, Brom. BR1 205 ED91
Oxshott KT22 236 CC114
Oakshaw, Oxt. RH8 275 ED127
Oakshaw Rd, SW18 202 DB87
Oakside, Denh. UB9 156 BH65
Oakside Ct, Horl. RH6
off Oakside La 291 DJ147
Ilford IG6 125 ER53
Oakside La, Horl. RH6 291 DJ147
Oaks La, Croy. CR0 224 DW104
Ilford IG2 147 ES57
Mid Holmwood RH5 285 CH143
Sch Oaks Pk High Sch, Ilf. IG2
off Oaks La 147 ES57
Oak Sq, Sev. TN13
off High St 279 FJ126
Oaks Retail Pk, The, Harl. CM20 57 ET12
Oaks Rd, Croy. CR0 242 DV106
Kenley CR8 241 DP114
Reigate RH2 272 DC133
Stanwell TW19 196 BK86
Woking GU21 248 AY117
Oaks Shop Cen, W3
off High St 160 CQ74
Oaks Sq, The, Epsom KT19
off Waterloo Rd 238 CR113
Oaks Track, Cars. SM5 240 DF111
Wallington SM6 241 DH110
Oak St, Hem.H. HP3 62 BM24
Romford RM7 149 FC57
Oak Stubbs La, Dorney R. SL6 172 AF75
Oaks Way, Cars. SM5 240 DF108
Epsom KT18
off Epsom La N 255 CV119
Kenley CR8 242 DQ114
Long Ditton KT6 219 CK103
Ripley GU23 250 BG124
Sch Oakthorpe Prim Sch, N13
off Tile Kiln La 122 DQ50
Oakthorpe Rd, N13 121 DN50
Oaktree Av, N13 121 DP48
Oak Tree Av, Bluewater DA9 211 FT87
Oak Tree Cl, W5 159 CJ72
Abbots Langley WD5 81 BR32
Oaktree Cl, Brwd. CM13
off Hawthorn Av 131 FZ48
Oak Tree Cl, Burpham GU4 265 BB129
Oaktree Cl, Goffs Oak EN7 87 DP28
Oak Tree Cl, Hat. AL10 67 CU17
Hertford Heath SG13 54 DW12
Jacobs Well GU4 264 AW128
Loughton IG10 107 EQ39
Stanmore HA7 117 CJ52
Virginia Water GU25 214 AX101
Oak Tree Ct, Els. WD6 99 CK44
Oak Tree Dell, NW9 140 CQ57
Oak Tree Dr, N20 120 DB46
Englefield Green TW20 194 AW92
Guildford GU1 264 AW130
Slough SL3 175 BB78
Oak Tree Gdns, Brom. BR1 206 EH92
Oaktree Gdns, Ch.Lang. CM17
off Burley Hill 74 EX16
Oak Tree Gdns, Guil. GU1 265 BB131
Oaktree Garth, Welw.G.C. AL7 51 CY10
Oaktree Gro, Ilf. IG1 147 ER64
Oak Tree Rd, NW8 16 B3
Sch Oaktree Sch, N14
off Chase Side 102 DG44
Sch Oaktree Sch, The, St.John's GU21 off Gorsewood Rd 248 AS119
Oaktree Wk, Cat. CR3 258 DS122
Oak Vw, Wat. WD18 97 BS41
Oakview Cl, Chsht EN7 88 DV28
Watford WD19 98 BW44
Oakview Gdns, N2 142 DD56
Oak Vw Gdns, Slou. SL3 175 AZ77
Oakview Gro, Croy. CR0 225 DY102
Sch Oak Vw Prim & Nurs Sch, Hat. AL10 off Woods Av 67 CV19
Oakview Rd, SE6 205 EB92
Sch Oak Vw Sch, Loug. IG10
off Whitehills Rd 107 EN42
Oak Village, NW5 7 H2
Oak Wk, Saw. CM21 58 EX07
Wallington SM6
off Helios Rd 222 DG102
Oak Warren, Sev. TN13 278 FG129
Oak Way, N14 121 DH45
Oakway, SW20 221 CW98
Oak Way, W3 160 CS74
Oakway, Amer. HP6 77 AP35
Oak Way, Ashtd. KT21 254 CN116
Oakway, Brom. BR2 225 ED96
Oak Way, Croy. CR0 225 DX100
Feltham TW14 197 BS88
Reigate RH2 288 DD135
Oakway, Wok. GU21 248 AS119
Oakway Cl, Bex. DA5 208 EY86
Oakway Pl, Rad. WD7
off Watling St 83 CG34
Oakways, SE9 207 EP86
Oakwell Dr, Northaw EN6 87 DH32
OAKWOOD, N14 103 DK44
⊖ Oakwood 103 DJ43
Oakwood, Berk. HP4 60 AT20
Guildford GU2 264 AU129
Wallington SM6 241 DH109
Waltham Abbey EN9
off Fairways 90 EE34
Oakwood Av, N14 121 DK45
Beckenham BR3 225 EC96
Borehamwood WD6 100 CP42
Bromley BR2 226 EH97
Epsom KT19 238 CN109
Hutton CM13 131 GE44
Mitcham CR4 222 DD96
Purley CR8 242 DP112
Southall UB1 158 CA73
Oakwood Chase, Horn. RM11 150 FM58
Oakwood Cl, N14 103 DJ44
SE13 205 ED87
Chislehurst BR7 207 EM93
Dartford DA1 210 FP88
East Horsley KT24 267 BS127
Redhill RH1 272 DG134
South Nutfield RH1
off Mid St 289 DM136
Woodford Green IG8
off Green Wk 124 EL51
Oakwood Ct, W14 26 G6
Slough SL1
off Oatlands Dr 154 AS72
Oakwood Cres, N21 103 DL44
Greenford UB6 159 CG65
Oakwood Dr, SE19 204 DR93
Bexleyheath DA7 189 FD84
East Horsley KT24 267 BS127
Edgware HA8 118 CQ51
St. Albans AL4 65 CJ19
Sevenoaks TN13 279 FH123
● Oakwood Est, Harl. CM20 58 EV11
Oakwood Gdns, Ilf. IG3 147 ET61
Orpington BR6 227 EQ103
Sutton SM1 222 DA103
Oakwood Hill, Loug. IG10 107 EM44
● Oakwood Hill Ind Est, Loug. IG10 107 EP43
Oakwood La, W14 26 G6
Oakwood Ms, Harl. CM17
off Station Rd 58 EW11
Oakwood Pk Rd, N14 121 DK45
Oakwood Pl, Croy. CR0 223 DN100
Sch Oakwood Prim Sch, St.Alb. AL4 off Oakwood Dr 65 CJ19
Oakwood Ri, Cat. CR3 274 DS125
Oakwood Rd, NW11 142 DB57
SW20 221 CU95
Bricket Wood AL2 82 BY29
Croydon CR0 223 DN100
Horley RH6 290 DG147
Merstham RH1 273 DN129
Orpington BR6 227 EQ103
Pinner HA5 115 BV54
Virginia Water GU25 214 AW99
Woking GU21 248 AS119
Sch Oakwood Sch, Bexh. DA7
off Woodside Rd 189 FD84
Horley RH6
off Balcombe Rd 291 DJ148
Purley CR8
off Godstone Rd 241 DP113
Oakwood Vw, N14 103 DK44
Oakworth Rd, W10 14 B6
Oarsman Pl, E.Mol. KT8 219 CE98
Sch Oasis Acad Enfield, Enf. EN3
off Kinetic Cres 105 DZ37
Oast Ho Cl, Wrays. TW19 194 AY87
Oasthouse Way, Orp. BR5 228 EV98
Oast Rd, Oxt. RH8 276 EF131
Oates Cl, Brom. BR2 225 ED97
Oates Rd, Rom. RM5 127 FB50
Oatfield Ho, N15 144 DS58
Oatfield Rd, Orp. BR6 227 ET102
Tadworth KT20 255 CV120
Oatland Ri, E17 123 DY54
Oatlands, Horl. RH6 291 DH147
Oatlands Av, Wey. KT13 235 BR106
Oatlands Chase, Wey. KT13 217 BS104
Oatlands Cl, Wey. KT13 235 BQ105
Oatlands Dr, Slou. SL1 153 AR72
Weybridge KT13 217 BR104
Oatlands Grn, Wey. KT13 217 BR104
Sch Oatlands Inf Sch, Wey. KT13
off St. Marys Rd 235 BR105
Oatlands Mere, Wey. KT13 217 BR104
OATLANDS PARK, Wey. KT13 235 BR105
Oatlands Rd, Enf. EN3 104 DW39
Tadworth KT20 255 CY119
Oat La, EC2 19 J8
Oatridge Gdns, Hem.H. HP2 63 BP19
Oban Cl, E13 24 C5
Oban Ct, Slou. SL1
off Montem La 173 AR75
Oban Ho, E14 23 H8
Barking IG11
off Wheelers Cross 167 ER68
Oban Rd, E13 24 D3
SE25 224 DR98
Oban St, E14 23 H8
Obelisk Ride, Egh. TW20 194 AS93
Oberon Cl, Borwd. WD6 100 CQ39
Oberon Way, Shep. TW17 216 BL97
Oberstein Rd, SW11 182 DD84
Oborne Cl, SE24 203 DP85
O'Brien Ho, E2 21 K2
Observatory Gdns, W8 27 J4
Observatory Ms, E14 34 G9
Observatory Rd, SW14 180 CQ84
Observatory Shop Cen, Slou. SL1 174 AU75
Observatory Wk, Red. RH1
off Lower Br Rd 272 DF134
Observer Dr, Wat. WD18 97 BS42
Occupation La, SE18 187 EP81
W5 179 CK77
Roydon CM19 72 EH15

Occupation Rd, SE17 31 J10
W13 179 CH75
Watford WD18 97 BV43
Ocean Est, E1 21 K5
Oceanis, E16 off Seagull La 23 N10
Ocean St, E1 21 K6
Ocean Wf, E14 34 A5
Ockenden Cl, Wok. GU22
off Ockenden Rd 249 AZ118
Ockenden Gdns, Wok. GU22
off Ockenden Rd 249 AZ118
Ockenden Rd, Wok. GU22 249 AZ118
⇌ Ockendon 171 FX69
Ockendon Ms, N1 9 L5
Ockendon Rd, N1 9 L5
Upminster RM14 150 FQ64
Sch Ockendon Sch, The, S.Ock. RM15
off Erriff Dr 171 FU71
OCKHAM, Wok. GU23 250 BN121
Ockham Dr, Orp. BR5 208 EU94
West Horsley KT24 251 BR124
Ockham La, Cob. KT11 251 BT118
Ockham GU23 251 BP120
Jct Ockham Pk, Wok. GU23 250 BL119
Ockham Rd N, Lthd. KT24 251 BQ124
Ockham GU23 250 BN121
Ockham Rd S, E.Hors. KT24 251 BS126
Ockley Ct, Guil. GU4
off Cotts Wd Dr 265 BB129
Sutton SM1 off Oakhill Rd 240 DC105
Ockley Rd, SW16 203 DL90
Croydon CR0 223 DM101
Ockleys Mead, Gdse. RH9 274 DW129
Octagon, The, Ware SG12 55 DX05
Octagon Arc, EC2 19 N7
Octagon Rd, Whiteley Vill. KT12 235 BS109
Octavia Cl, Mitch. CR4 222 DE99
Octavia Ms, W9 14 G4
Octavia Rd, Islw. TW7 179 CF82
Octavia St, SW11 40 C7
Octavia Way, SE28
off Booth Cl 168 EV73
Staines TW18 196 BG93
Octavius St, SE8 46 A4
Odard Rd, W.Mol. KT8
off Down St 218 CA98
Oddesey Rd, Borwd. WD6 100 CP39
Odds Fm Est, Woob.Grn HP10 132 AH59
Odell Cl, Bark. IG11 167 ET66
Odell Wk, SE13
off Bankside Av 185 EB83
Odencroft Rd, Slou. SL2 153 AN69
Odeon, The, Bark. IG11
off Longbridge Rd 167 ER66
Sch Odessa Inf Sch, E7 13 N2
Odessa Rd, E7 13 M1
NW10 161 CU68
Odessa St, SE16 33 N5
Odger St, SW11 40 F8
Odhams Wk, WC2 18 B9
● Odyssey Business Pk, Ruis. HA4 137 BV64
Offa Rd, St.Alb. AL3 64 CC20
Offa's Mead, E9 11 M1
Offenbach Ho, E2 21 J1
Offenham Rd, SE9 207 EM91
Offers Ct, Kings.T. KT1
off Winery La 220 CM97
Offerton Rd, SW4 183 DJ83
Offham Slope, N12 119 CZ50
Offley Pl, Islw. TW7 179 CD82
Offley Rd, SW9 42 E4
Offord Cl, N17 122 DU51
Offord Rd, N1 8 C6
Offord St, N1 8 C6
Ogard Rd, Hodd. EN11 71 EC15
Ogilby St, SE18 37 J9
Oglander Rd, SE15 184 DT84
Ogle St, W1 17 L6
Oglethorpe Rd, Dag. RM10 148 EZ62
Ohio Bldg, SE13
off Deals Gateway 46 C7
Ohio Rd, E13 23 M5
Oil Mill La, W6 181 CU78
Okeburn Rd, SW17 202 DG92
Okehampton Cl, N12 120 DD50
Okehampton Cres, Well. DA16 188 EV81
Okehampton Rd, NW10 4 B9
Romford RM3 128 FJ51
Okehampton Sq, Rom. RM3 128 FJ51
Okemore Gdns, Orp. BR5 228 EW98
Olaf St, W11 26 D1
Old Acre, Wok. GU22 234 BG114
Oldacre Ms, SW12
off Balham Gro 203 DH87
★ Old Admiralty Bldg (MoD), SW1 29 P3
Old Amersham Rd, Ger.Cr. SL9 135 BB60
Old Av, W.Byf. KT14 233 BE113
Weybridge KT13 235 BR107
Old Av Cl, W.Byf. KT14 233 BE113
Old Bailey, EC4 19 H9
Old Bakery Ms, Albury GU5 282 BH139
Old Barge Ho All, SE1
off Upper Grd 30 F2
Old Barn Cl, Sutt. SM2 239 CY108
Old Barn La, Crox.Grn WD3 96 BM43
Kenley CR8 258 DT116
Old Barn Ms, Crox.Grn WD3
off Old Barn La 96 BM43
Old Barn Rd, Epsom KT18 254 CQ117
Old Barn Way, Bexh. DA7 189 FD83
Old Barrack Yd, SW1 28 G4
Old Barrowfield, E15 13 K9
Old Bath Rd, Colnbr. SL3 175 BE81
Old Beaconsfield Rd, Farn.Com. SL2 153 AQ65
Old Bell Ct, Hem.H. HP2
off George St 62 BK19
Old Bellgate Pl, E14 34 A7
Oldberry Rd, Edg. HA8 118 CR51
Old Bethnal Grn Rd, E2 20 D2
OLD BEXLEY, Bex. DA5 209 FB87
Sch Old Bexley C of E Prim Sch, Bex. DA5 off Hurst Rd 208 EZ88
Old Bexley La, Bex. DA5 209 FD89
Dartford DA1 209 FF88
★ Old Billingsgate Mkt, EC3 31 N1
Old Billingsgate Wk, EC3
off Lower Thames St 31 N1
Old Bond St, W1 29 L1
Oldborough Rd, Wem. HA0 139 CJ61
Old Brewers Yd, WC2 18 A9
Old Brewery Ms, NW3 6 A1
Old Br Cl, Nthlt. UB5 158 CA68
Old Br St, Hmptn W. KT1 219 CK96
Old Broad St, EC2 19 M9
Old Bromley Rd, Brom. BR1 205 ED92
Old Brompton Rd, SW5 39 K1
SW7 39 K1
Old Bldgs, WC2 18 E8
Old Burlington St, W1 17 L10
Oldbury Cl, Cher. KT16
off Oldbury Rd 215 BE101
Orpington BR5 228 EX98
Oldbury Gro, Beac. HP9 111 AK50
Old Bury Hill, Westc. RH4 285 CE138
Oldbury Pl, W1 17 H6
Oldbury Rd, Cher. KT16 215 BE101
Enfield EN1 104 DU40
Old Canal Ms, SE15 44 B1
Old Carriageway, The, Sev. TN13 278 FC123
Old Castle St, E1 20 A7
Old Cavendish St, W1 17 J8
Old Change Ct, EC4
off Carter La 19 J9
Old Chapel Rd, Swan. BR8 229 FC101
Old Charlton Rd, Shep. TW17 217 BQ99
● Old Char Wf, Dor. RH4 285 CF135
Old Chelsea Ms, SW3 40 B3
Old Chertsey Rd, Chobham GU24 232 AV110
Old Chestnut Av, Esher KT10 236 CA107
Old Chorleywood Rd, Rick. WD3
off Chorleywood Rd 96 BK44
Old Ch Cl, Orp. BR6 228 EV102
Oldchurch Gdns, Rom. RM7 149 FD59
Old Ch La, NW9 140 CQ61
Mountnessing CM13 131 GE42
Perivale UB6
off Perivale La 159 CG69
Stanmore HA7 117 CJ52
Old Ch Path, Esher KT10
off High St 236 CB105
Oldchurch Ri, Rom. RM7 149 FE58
Old Ch Rd, E1 21 J9
E4 123 EA49
Oldchurch Rd, Rom. RM7 149 FD59
Old Ch St, SW3 40 B1
Old Claygate La, Clay. KT10 237 CG107
Old Clem Sq, SE18
off Kempt St 187 EN79
Old Coach Rd, Cher. KT16 215 BD99
Old Coach Rd, The, Cole Grn SG14 52 DF12
Old Coal Yd, SE28
off Pettman Cres 187 ER77
Old Common Rd, Chorl. WD3
off Common Rd 95 BD42
Cobham KT11 235 BU112
Old Compton St, W1 17 N10
Old Cote Dr, Houns. TW5 178 CA79
OLD COULSDON, Couls. CR5 257 DN119
Old Ct, Ashtd. KT21 254 CL119
Old Ct Grn, Pott.End HP4
off Hempstead La 61 BC17
Old Ct Pl, W8 27 L4
Old Ct Rd, Guil. GU2 280 AU135
Old Crabtree La, Hem.H. HP2 62 BL21
Old Cross, Hert. SG14 54 DQ09
Old Cross Wf, Hert. SG14
off Old Cross 54 DQ09
★ Old Curiosity Shop, WC2 18 C8
Old Dairy, The, Wok. GU21
off Goldsworth Rd 248 AX117
Old Dairy Ms, SW4
off Tintern St 183 DL84
SW12 202 DG88
Old Dairy Sq, N21
off Wades Hill 121 DN45
Old Dartford Rd, Fnghm DA4 230 FM100
Old Dean, Bov. HP3 79 BA27
Old Deer Pk Gdns, Rich. TW9 180 CL83
Old Devonshire Rd, SW12 203 DH87
Old Dock App Rd, Grays RM17 192 GE77
Old Dock Cl, Rich. TW9 180 CN79
Old Dover Rd, SE3 47 P4
Old Dr, The, Welw.G.C. AL8 51 CV10
Olden La, Pur. CR8 241 DN112
Old Esher Cl, Hersham KT12 236 BX106
Old Esher Rd, Hersham KT12 236 BX106
Old Farleigh Rd, S.Croy. CR2 242 DW110
Warlingham CR6 243 DY113
Old Fm Av, N14 121 DJ45
Sidcup DA15 207 ER88
Old Fm Cl, Houns. TW4 178 BZ84
Knotty Green HP9 110 AJ50
Old Fm Gdns, Swan. BR8 229 FF97
Old Farmhouse Dr, Oxshott KT22 253 CD115
Old Fm Pas, Hmptn. TW12 218 CC95
Old Fm Rd, N2 120 DD53
Guildford GU1 264 AX131
Hampton TW12 198 BZ93
West Drayton UB7 176 BK75
Old Fm Rd E, Sid. DA15 208 EU89
Old Fm Rd W, Sid. DA15 207 ET89
Old Fm Yd, The, Sheering CM22 59 FC07
Old Ferry Dr, Wrays. TW19 194 AW86
Sch Oldfield Cen, Hmptn. TW12
off Oldfield Rd 218 BZ95
Oldfield Circ, Nthlt. UB5 158 CC65
Old Fld Cl, Amer. HP6 94 AY39
Oldfield Cl, Brom. BR1 227 EM98
Cheshunt EN8 89 DY28
Greenford UB6 139 CE64
Horley RH6
off Oldfield Rd 290 DF150
Stanmore HA7 117 CG50
Oldfield Dr, Chsht EN8 89 DY28
Oldfield Fm Gdns, Grnf. UB6 159 CD67
Oldfield Gdns, Ashtd. KT21 253 CK119
Oldfield Gro, SE16 33 J9
Oldfield La N, Grnf. UB6 159 CE65
Oldfield La S, Grnf. UB6 158 CC70
Oldfield Ms, N6 143 DJ59
Sch Oldfield Prim Sch, Grnf. UB6
off Oldfield La N 159 CD68
Oldfield Rd, N16 144 DS62
NW10 161 CT66
SW19 201 CY93
W3 off Valetta Rd 181 CT75
Bexleyheath DA7 188 EY82
Bromley BR1 227 EM98
Oldfield Rd, Hmptn. TW12 218 BZ95
Hemel Hempstead HP1 61 BE21
Horley RH6 290 DF150
London Colney AL2 83 CK25
Oldfields Rd, Sutt. SM1 221 CZ104
● Oldfields Trd Est, Sutt. SM1 222 DA104
Oldfield Wd, Wok. GU22
off Maybury Hill 249 BB117
Old Fishery La, Hem.H. HP1 61 BF22
Old Fish St Hill, EC4 19 J10
Old Fives Ct, Burn. SL1 152 AH69
Old Fleet La, EC4 18 G8
Old Fold Cl, Barn. EN5
off Old Fold La 101 CZ39
Old Fold La, Barn. EN5 101 CZ39
Old Fold Vw, Barn. EN5 101 CW41
OLD FORD, E3 11 N7
Sch Old Ford Prim Sch, E3 11 N10
Old Ford Rd, E2 20 F2
E3 11 K10
Old Forge Cl, Stan. HA7 117 CG49
Watford WD25 81 BU33
Welwyn AL6 51 CZ05
Old Forge Cres, Shep. TW17 217 BP100
Old Forge Ms, W12
off Goodwin Rd 181 CV75
Old Forge Rd, N19 143 DK61
Enfield EN1 104 DT38
Loudwater HP10 110 AC53
Old Forge Way, Sid. DA14 208 EV91
Old Fox Cl, Cat. CR3 257 DP121
Old Fox Footpath, S.Croy. CR2
off Essenden Rd 242 DS108
Old French Horn La, Hat. AL10 67 CV17
Old Gannon Cl, Nthwd. HA6 115 BQ50
Old Gdn, The, Sev. TN13 278 FD123
Old Gdn Ct, St.Alb. AL3 64 CC20
Old Gloucester St, WC1 18 B6
Old Gro Cl, Chsht EN7 88 DR26
Old Hall Cl, Pnr. HA5 116 BY53
Old Hall Dr, Pnr. HA5 116 BY53
Old Hall Ri, Harl. CM17 74 EY15
Old Hall St, Hert. SG14 54 DR09
Oldham Ter, W3 160 CQ74
OLD HARLOW, Harl. CM17 58 EX11
Old Harpenden Rd, St.Alb. AL3 65 CE17
Old Harrow La, West. TN16 261 EQ119
Old Hatch Manor, Ruis. HA4 137 BT59
OLD HATFIELD, Hat. AL9 67 CX17
Old Heath Rd, Wey. KT13 234 BN107
Old Herns La, Welw.G.C. AL7
off Herns La 52 DC07
Old Hertford Rd, Hat. AL9 67 CW16
Old Highway, Hodd. EN11 55 EB14
Old Hill, Chis. BR7 227 EN95
Orpington BR6 245 ER107
Woking GU22 248 AX120
Oldhill St, N16 144 DU60
Old Homesdale Rd, Brom. BR2 226 EJ98
Old Hosp Cl, SW12 202 DF88
Old Ho Cl, SW19 201 CY92
Epsom KT17 239 CT110
Old Ho Ct, Hem.H. HP2 62 BM20
Oldhouse Cft, Harl. CM20 57 ES13
Old Ho Gdns, Twick. TW1 199 CJ85
Old Ho La, Kings L. WD4 96 BL35
Lower Nazeing EN9 72 EF23
Roydon CM19 72 EK18
Old Ho Rd, Hem.H. HP2 62 BM20
Old Howlett's La, Ruis. HA4 137 BQ58
Old Jamaica Rd, SE16 32 C6
Old James St, SE15 184 DV83
Old Jewry, EC2 19 L9
Old Kenton La, NW9 140 CP57
Old Kent Rd, SE1 31 M7
SE15 44 D2
Old Kiln La, Brock. RH3 286 CQ135
Old Kiln Rd, Penn HP10 110 AC45
Old Kingston Rd, Wor.Pk. KT4 220 CQ104
Old La, Cob. KT11 251 BP117
Oxted RH8 276 EF129
Tatsfield TN16 260 EK121
Old La Gdns, Cob. KT11 251 BT122
Old Leys, Hat. AL10 67 CU22
Old Lib La, Hert. SG14
off Old Cross 54 DQ09
Old Lo Dr, Beac. HP9 111 AL54
Old Lo La, Ken. CR8 257 DN115
Purley CR8 241 DM113
Old Lo Pl, Twick. TW1
off St. Margarets Rd 199 CH86
Old Lo Way, Stan. HA7 117 CG50
Old London Rd, Bad.Mt TN14 246 FA110
East Horsley KT24 267 BU126
Epsom KT18 255 CU118
Hertford SG13 54 DS09
Kingston upon Thames KT2 220 CL96
Knockholt Pound TN14 262 EY115
Mickleham RH5 269 CJ127
St. Albans AL1 65 CD21
Old Long Gro, Beac. HP9 111 AQ51
Old Maidstone Rd, Sid. DA14 208 EZ94
OLD MALDEN, Wor.Pk. KT4 220 CR102
Old Malden La, Wor.Pk. KT4 220 CR103
Old Malt Way, Wok. GU21 248 AX117
Old Manor Dr, Grav. DA12 213 GJ88
Isleworth TW7 198 CC86
Old Manor Gdns, Chilw. GU4 281 BD140
Old Manor Ho Ms, Shep. TW17
off Squires Br Rd 216 BN97
Old Manor La, Chilw. GU4 281 BC140
Old Manor Rd, Sthl. UB2 178 BX77
Old Manor Way, Bexh. DA7 189 FD82
Chislehurst BR7 207 EM92
Old Manor Yd, SW5 27 K10
Old Mkt Sq, E2 20 A2
Old Marsh La, Tap. SL6 172 AF75
Old Marylebone Rd, NW1 16 D7
Old Mead, Chal.St.P. SL9 112 AY51
Old Meadow Cl, Berk. HP4 60 AU21
Old Merrow St, Guil. GU4 265 BC131
Old Ms, Har. HA1
off Hindes Rd 139 CE57
Old Mill Cl, Eyns. DA4 230 FL102
Old Mill Ct, E18 146 EJ55
Old Mill Gdns, Berk. HP4 60 AX19
Old Mill La, Bray SL6 172 AD75
Merstham RH1 273 DH128
Uxbridge UB8 156 BH72
Old Mill Pl, Rom. RM7 149 FD58
Wraysbury TW19 195 BB86
Old Mill Rd, SE18 187 ER79
Denham UB9 136 BG62
Hunton Bridge WD4 81 BQ33
Old Mitre Ct, EC4 18 F9
Old Montague St, E1 20 C7
Old Moor La, Woob.Moor HP10 132 AE55
Old Nazeing Rd, Brox. EN10 71 EA21
Old Nichol St, E2 20 A4
Old N St, WC1 18 C6
Old Nurs Ct, Hedg. SL2 133 AQ61
Old Nurs Pl, Ashf. TW15
off Park Rd 197 BP92
Old Oak, St.Alb. AL1 65 CE23
Old Oak Av, Chipstead CR5 256 DE119
Old Oak Cl, Chess. KT9 238 CM105
Cobham KT11 235 BV113
OLD OAK COMMON, NW10 161 CT71
Old Oak Common La, NW10 160 CS71
W3 160 CS71
Old Oak La, NW10 160 CS69
Sch Old Oak Prim Sch, W12
off Mellitus St 161 CT72
Old Oak Rd, W3 161 CT73
Old Oaks, Wal.Abb. EN9 90 EE32
★ Old Operating Thea Mus & Herb Garret, SE1 31 M3
Old Orchard, Byfleet KT14 234 BM112
Harlow CM18 73 ER17
Park Street AL2 82 CC26
Sunbury-on-Thames TW16 218 BW96
Old Orchard, The, NW3
off Nassington Rd 142 DF63
Iver SL0 155 BF72
Old Orchard Cl, Barn. EN4 102 DD38
Uxbridge UB8 156 BN72
Old Orchard Ms, Berk. HP4 60 AW20
Old Otford Rd, Sev. TN14 263 FH117
Old Palace La, Rich. TW9 199 CJ85
Sch Old Palace of John Whitgift Jun Sch, S.Croy. CR2
off Melville Av 242 DT107
Sch Old Palace of John Whitgift Sen Sch, Croy. CR0
off Old Palace Rd 223 DP104
Sch Old Palace Prim Sch, E3 22 D2
Old Palace Rd, Croy. CR0 223 DP104
Guildford GU2 280 AU135
Weybridge KT13 217 BP104
Old Palace Ter, Rich. TW9
off King St 199 CK85
Old Palace Yd, SW1 30 A6
Richmond TW9 199 CJ85
Old Papermill Cl, Woob.Grn HP10
off Glory Mill La 132 AE56
Old Paradise St, SE11 30 C8
Old Pk Av, SW12 202 DG86
Enfield EN2 104 DQ42
Old Parkbury La, Coln.St AL2 83 CF30
Old Pk Gro, Enf. EN2 104 DQ42
Old Pk La, W1 29 H3
Old Pk Ms, Houns. TW5 178 BZ80
Old Pk Ride, Wal.Cr. EN7 88 DT33
Old Pk Ridings, N21 103 DP44
Old Pk Rd, N13 121 DM49
SE2 188 EU78
Enfield EN2 103 DP41
Old Pk Rd S, Enf. EN2 103 DP42
Old Pk Vw, Enf. EN2 103 DN41
Old Parsonage Yd, Hort.Kir. DA4 230 FQ97
Old Parvis Rd, W.Byf. KT14 234 BK112
Old Pearson St, SE10 46 D4
Old Perry St, Chis. BR7 207 ES94
Northfleet DA11 212 GE89
Old Polhill, Sev. TN14 263 FD115
Old Portsmouth Rd, Gdmg. GU7 280 AV142
Guildford GU3 280 AV142
Old PO La, SE3 186 EH83
Old Pottery Cl, Reig. RH2 288 DB136
Old Pound Cl, Islw. TW7 179 CG81
Old Priory, Hare. UB9 137 BP59
Old Pye St, SW1 29 N6
Old Quebec St, W1 16 F9
Old Queen St, SW1 29 P5
Old Rectory Cl, Walt.Hill KT20 255 CU124
Old Rectory Dr, Hat. AL10 67 CV18
Old Rectory Gdns, Edg. HA8 118 CN51
Old Rectory La, Denh. UB9 135 BE59
East Horsley KT24 267 BS126
Old Redding, Har. HA3 116 CC49
Old Redstone Dr, Red. RH1 288 DG135
Old Reigate Rd, Bet. RH3 270 CP134
Dorking RH4 270 CL134
Oldridge Rd, SW12 202 DG87
Old Rd, SE13 186 EE84
Addlestone KT15 233 BF108
Buckland RH3 270 CS134
Dartford DA1 189 FD84
Enfield EN3 104 DW39
Harlow CM17 58 EX11
Old Rd E, Grav. DA12 213 GH88
Old Rd W, Grav. DA11 213 GF88
Old Rope Wk, Sun. TW16
off The Avenue 217 BV97
Old Royal Free Pl, N1
off Old Royal Free Sq 8 F9
Old Royal Free Sq, N1 8 F9
Old Ruislip Rd, Nthlt. UB5 158 BX68
Old St. Mary's, W.Hors. KT24
off Ripley La 267 BP129
Olds App, Wat. WD18 115 BP46
Old Savill's Cotts, Chig. IG7
off The Chase 125 EQ49
Old Sch Cl, SE10 35 K7
SW19 222 DA96
Beckenham BR3 225 DX96
Guildford GU1
off Markenfield Rd 264 AX134
Old Sch Ct, Wrays. TW19 194 AY87
Old Sch Cres, E7 13 N5
Old Sch Ho, Godden Grn TN15 279 FN124
Old Sch La, Brock. RH3 286 CN138
Old Sch Ms, Stai. TW18 195 BD92
Weybridge KT13 235 BR105
Old Sch Pl, Croy. CR0 241 DN105
Woking GU22 248 AY121
Old Sch Rd, Uxb. UB8 156 BM70
Old Schs La, Epsom KT17 239 CT109
Old Sch Sq, E14 22 A9
Thames Ditton KT7 219 CF100
Olds Cl, Wat. WD18 115 BP46
Old Seacoal La, EC4 18 G8
Old Shire La, Chorl. WD3 95 BB44
Gerrards Cross SL9 113 BA46
Waltham Abbey EN9 106 EG35
Old Slade La, Iver SL0 175 BE76
Old Solesbridge La, Chorl. WD3 96 BG41
Old Sopwell Gdns, St.Alb. AL1 65 CE22
Old S Cl, Hatch End HA5 116 BX53
Old S Lambeth Rd, SW8 42 B4
Old Spitalfields Mkt, E1 20 A6
Old Sq, WC2 18 D8
Old Sta App, Lthd. KT22 253 CG121
Old Sta Pas, Rich. TW9
off Little Grn 179 CK84
Old Sta Rd, Hayes UB3 177 BT76
Loughton IG10 106 EL43
Old Sta Way, SW4
off Voltaire Rd 183 DK83
Wooburn Green HP10 132 AE58
Old Sta Yd, Brom. BR2
off Bourne Way 226 EF102
Oldstead Rd, Brom. BR1 205 ED91
Old Stede Cl, Ashtd. KT21 254 CM117
Old Stockley Rd, West Dr. UB7 177 BP75
⇌ Old Street 19 L3
⊖ Old Street 19 L3
Old St, E13 24 B1
EC1 19 J4
Old St, The, Fetch. KT22 253 CD123
Old Studio Cl, Croy. CR0 224 DR101
Old Swan Yd, Cars. SM5 240 DF105
Old Thea Ct, SE1
off Porter St 31 K2
Old Thieves La, Hertingfordbury SG14 off Thieves La 53 DM10
Old Tilburstow Rd, Gdse. RH9 274 DW134
Old Town, SW4 183 DJ83
Croydon CR0 223 DP104
Old Town Cl, Beac. HP9 111 AL54
★ Old Town Hall Arts Cen, Hem.H. HP1 62 BK19
Old Tram Yd, SE18
off Lakedale Rd 187 ES77
Old Twelve Cl, W7 159 CE70
Old Tye Av, Bigg.H. TN16 260 EL116
Old Uxbridge Rd, W.Hyde WD3 113 BE53
Sch Old Vicarage Sch, Rich. TW10
off Richmond Hill 200 CL86
Old Vicarage Way, Woob.Grn HP10 132 AE59
Old Wk, The, Otford TN14 263 FH117
Old Watery La, Woob.Grn HP10 132 AE55
Old Watford Rd, Brick.Wd AL2 82 BY30
Old Watling St, Grav. DA11 213 GG92
Oldway La, Slou. SL1 173 AK75
Old Westhall Cl, Warl. CR6 258 DW119
Old Wf Way, Wey. KT13
off Weybridge Rd 234 BM105
OLD WINDSOR, Wind. SL4 194 AU86
Old Windsor Lock, Old Wind. SL4 194 AW85
OLD WOKING, Wok. GU22 249 BA121
Old Woking Rd, W.Byf. KT14 233 BF113
Woking GU22 249 BE116
Old Woolwich Rd, SE10 47 H2
Old Yd, The, West. TN16 262 EW124
Old York Rd, SW18 202 DB85
Oleander Cl, Orp. BR6 245 ER106
O'Leary Sq, E1 20 G6
Sch Olga Prim Sch, E3 21 M1
Olga St, E3 21 M1
Olinda Rd, N16 144 DT58
Oliphant St, W10 14 D2
Olive Cl, St.Alb. AL1 65 CH21
Olive Gro, N15 144 DQ56
Oliver Av, SE25 224 DT97
● Oliver Business Pk, NW10
off Oliver Rd 160 CQ68
Oliver Cl, W4 180 CP79
Addlestone KT15 234 BG105
Grays RM20 191 FT80
Hemel Hempstead HP3 62 BL24
Hoddesdon EN11 71 EB15
Park Street AL2 83 CD27
Oliver Cres, Fnghm DA4 230 FM101
Oliver Gdns, E6 25 H8
Oliver-Goldsmith Est, SE15 44 D6
Sch Oliver Goldsmith Prim Sch, NW9 off Coniston Gdns 140 CR57
SE5 44 A6
Oliver Gro, SE25 224 DT98
Oliver Ms, SE15 44 C8
Olive Rd, E13 24 D3
NW2 141 CW63
SW19 off Norman Rd 202 DC94
W5 179 CK76
Dartford DA1 210 FK88
Oliver Ri, Hem.H. HP3 62 BL24
Oliver Rd, E10 145 EB61
E17 145 EC57
NW10 160 CQ68
Grays RM20 191 FU80
Hemel Hempstead HP3 62 BL24
New Malden KT3 220 CQ96
Rainham RM13 169 FF67
Shenfield CM15 131 GA43
Sutton SM1 240 DD105
Swanley BR8 229 FD97
Olivers Cl, Pott.End HP4 61 BC16
Olivers Yd, EC1 19 M4
Olive St, Rom. RM7 149 FD57
Olivette St, SW15 181 CX83
Olivia Dr, Slou. SL3 175 AZ78
Olivia Gdns, Hare. UB9 114 BJ53
Olivier Cres, Dor. RH4
off Stubs Cl 285 CJ138
Ollards Gro, Loug. IG10 106 EK42
Olleberrie La, Sarratt WD3 79 BD32
Ollerton Grn, E3 11 P8
Ollerton Rd, N11 121 DK50
Olley Cl, Wall. SM6 241 DL108
Ollgar Cl, W12 161 CT74
Olliffe St, E14 34 F7
Olmar St, SE1 44 C2
Olney Rd, SE17 43 J2
Olron Cres, Bexh. DA6 208 EX85
Olven Rd, SE18 187 EQ80
Olveston Wk, Cars. SM5 222 DD100
Olwen Ms, Pnr. HA5 116 BX54
Olyffe Av, Well. DA16 188 EU82
Olyffe Dr, Beck. BR3 225 EC95
★ Olympia, W14 26 F7
Olympia Ms, W2 27 M1
Olympia Way, W14 26 F7
H Olympic Med Inst, Har. HA1 139 CH59
Olympic Sq, Wem. HA9 140 CN62
Olympic Way, Grnf. UB6 158 CB67
Wembley HA9 140 CN63
Olympus Gro, N22 121 DN53
Olympus Sq, E5
off Nolan Way 144 DU62
Oman Av, NW2 141 CW63
O'Meara St, SE1 31 K3

Omega Bldg, SW18
off Smugglers Way . . . 182 DB84
Omega Cl, E14 . . . 34 C6
Omega Ct, Rom. RM7 . . . 149 FC58
Ware SG12 off Crib St . . . 55 DX06
Omega Maltings, Ware SG12
off Star St . . . 55 DY06
Omega Pl, N1 . . . 18 B1
Omega Rd, Wok. GU21 . . . 249 BA115
Omega St, SE14 . . . 45 P6
Omega Way, Egh. TW20 . . . 215 BC95
● Omega Wks, E3 . . . 12 B6
Ommaney Rd, SE14 . . . 45 L7
Omnibus Way, E17 . . . 123 EA54
Ondine Rd, SE15 . . . 184 DT84
Onega Gate, SE16 . . . 33 L6
O'Neill Path, SE18
off Kempt St . . . 187 EN79
One Pin La, Farn.Com. SL2 . . . 133 AQ63
One Tree Cl, SE23 . . . 204 DW86
One Tree Hill Rd, Guil. GU4 . . . 281 BB135
One Tree La, Beac. HP9 . . . 111 AL52
Ongar Cl, Add. KT15 . . . 233 BF107
Romford RM6 . . . 148 EW57
Ongar Hill, Add. KT15 . . . 234 BG107
Ongar Par, Add. KT15
off Ongar Hill . . . 234 BG107
Ongar Pl, Add. KT15 . . . 234 BG107
Sch Ongar Pl Inf Sch, Add. KT15
off Milton Rd . . . 234 BG107
Ongar Rd, SW6 . . . 39 J2
Addlestone KT15 . . . 234 BG106
Brentwood CM15 . . . 130 FV45
Romford RM4 . . . 108 EW40
Ongar Way, Rain. RM13 . . . 169 FE67
Onra Rd, E17 . . . 145 EA59
Onslow Av, Rich. TW10 . . . 200 CL85
Sutton SM2 . . . 239 CZ110
Onslow Cl, E4 . . . 123 EC47
W10 . . . 14 G2
Hatfield AL10 . . . 67 CV18
Thames Ditton KT7 . . . 219 CE102
Woking GU22 . . . 249 BA117
Onslow Cres, SW7 . . . 28 B9
Chislehurst BR7 . . . 227 EP95
Woking GU22 . . . 249 BA117
Onslow Dr, Sid. DA14 . . . 208 EX89
Onslow Gdns, E18 . . . 146 EH55
N10 . . . 143 DH57
N21 . . . 103 DN43
SW7 . . . 28 A9
South Croydon CR2 . . . 242 DU112
Thames Ditton KT7 . . . 219 CE102
Wallington SM6 . . . 241 DJ107
Sch Onslow Inf Sch, Ons.Vill.
GU2 off Powell Cl . . . 280 AT136
Onslow Ms, Cher. KT16 . . . 216 BG100
Onslow Ms E, SW7 . . . 28 A9
Onslow Ms W, SW7 . . . 28 A9
Onslow Par, N14
off Osidge La . . . 121 DH46
Onslow Rd, Croy. CR0 . . . 223 DM101
Guildford GU1 . . . 264 AX134
Hersham KT12 . . . 235 BT105
New Malden KT3 . . . 221 CU98
Richmond TW10 . . . 200 CL85
Sch Onslow St. Audrey's Sch, Hat.
AL10 off Old Rectory Dr . . . 67 CV18
Onslow Sq, SW7 . . . 28 B8
Onslow St, EC1 . . . 18 F5
Guildford GU1 . . . 280 AW135
ONSLOW VILLAGE, Guil. GU2 . . . 280 AS136
Onslow Way, T.Ditt. KT7 . . . 219 CE102
Woking GU22 . . . 249 BF115
Ontario Cl, Brox. EN10 . . . 89 DY25
Smallfield RH6 . . . 291 DN149
Ontario St, SE1 . . . 31 H7
Ontario Twr, E14 . . . 34 F1
Ontario Way, E14 . . . 34 A1
On The Hill, Wat. WD19 . . . 116 BY47
Onyx Ms, E15 off Vicarage La . . . 13 K5
Opal Cl, E16 . . . 24 F9
Opal Ct, Wexham SL3 . . . 154 AW70
Opal Ms, NW6 . . . 5 H8
Ilford IG1 . . . 147 EP61
Opal St, SE11 . . . 30 G9
Opecks Cl, Wexham SL2 . . . 154 AV70
Opendale Rd, Burn. SL1 . . . 152 AH71
Openshaw Rd, SE2 . . . 188 EV77
Uni Open Uni in London, The,
NW1 . . . 7 K6
Openview, SW18 . . . 202 DC88
Ophelia Gdns, NW2
off Hamlet Sq . . . 141 CY62
Ophir Ter, SE15 . . . 44 C7
Opossum Way, Houns. TW4 . . . 178 BW82
Oppenheim Rd, SE13 . . . 46 E8
Oppidans Ms, NW3 . . . 6 E7
Oppidans Rd, NW3 . . . 6 E7
● Optima Business Pk, Hodd.
EN11 . . . 71 EC16
● Optima Pk, Cray. DA1 . . . 189 FG83
Opulens Pl, Nthwd. HA6 . . . 115 BP52
Oram Pl, Hem.H. HP3 . . . 62 BK23
Orange Ct, E1
off Hermitage Wall . . . 32 D3
Orange Ct La, Downe BR6 . . . 245 EN109
Orange Gro, E11 . . . 145 ED62
Chigwell IG7 . . . 125 EQ51
Orange Hill Rd, Edg. HA8 . . . 118 CQ52
Orange Pl, SE16 . . . 33 H7
Orangery, The, Rich. TW10 . . . 199 CJ89
Orangery La, SE9 . . . 207 EM85
Orange Sq, SW1 . . . 29 H9
Orange St, WC2 . . . 29 N1
Orange Tree Hill, Hav.at.Bow.
RM4 . . . 127 FD50
Orange Yd, W1 . . . 17 P9
Oransay Rd, N1 . . . 9 K5
Oransay Wk, N1
off Oransay Rd . . . 9 K5
Oratory La, SW3 . . . 28 B10
Sch Oratory RC Prim Sch, SW3 . . . 28 C10
Orbain Rd, SW6 . . . 38 F5
Orbel St, SW11 . . . 40 C7
● Orbital 25 Business Pk, Wat.
WD18 . . . 115 BR45
Orbital Cres, Wat. WD25 . . . 97 BT35
Orbital One, Dart. DA1 . . . 210 FP89
Orb St, SE17 . . . 31 L9
Orchard, The, N14 . . . 103 DH43
N20 . . . 120 DB46
N21 . . . 104 DR44
NW11 . . . 142 DA57
SE3 . . . 47 H8
W4 . . . 180 CR77
W5 off Montpelier Rd . . . 159 CK71
Banstead SM7 . . . 256 DA115
Dunton Green TN13 . . . 263 FE120
Orchard, The, Epsom KT17 . . . 239 CT108
Ewell KT17
off Tayles Hill Dr . . . 239 CT110
Hertford SG14 . . . 54 DQ06
Hounslow TW3 . . . 178 CC82
Kings Langley WD4 . . . 80 BN29
North Holmwood RH5 . . . 285 CJ140
Swanley BR8 . . . 229 FD96
Virginia Water GU25 . . . 214 AY99
Welwyn Garden City AL8 . . . 51 CX07
Weybridge KT13 . . . 235 BP105
Woking GU22 . . . 249 AY122
Orchard Av, N3 . . . 142 DA55
N14 . . . 103 DJ44
N20 . . . 120 DD47
Ashford TW15 . . . 197 BQ93
Belvedere DA17 . . . 188 EY79
Berkhamsted HP4 . . . 60 AU19
Brentwood CM13 . . . 131 FZ48
Croydon CR0 . . . 225 DY101
Dartford DA1 . . . 209 FH87
Feltham TW14 . . . 197 BR85
Gravesend DA11 . . . 213 GH92
Hounslow TW5 . . . 178 BY80
Mitcham CR4 . . . 222 DG102
New Malden KT3 . . . 220 CS96
Rainham RM13 . . . 170 FJ70
Slough SL1 . . . 153 AK71
Southall UB1 . . . 158 BY74
Thames Ditton KT7 . . . 219 CG102
Watford WD25 . . . 81 BV32
Windsor SL4 . . . 173 AN81
Woodham KT15 . . . 233 BF111
Orchard Bungalow Caravan Site,
Slou. SL2 . . . 153 AM66
● Orchard Business Cen, Red.
RH1 . . . 289 DH143
Orchard Cl, E4
off Chingford Mt Rd . . . 123 EA49
E11 . . . 146 EH56
N1 . . . 9 K7
NW2 . . . 141 CU62
SE23 . . . 204 DW86
SW20 off Grand Dr . . . 221 CW98
W10 . . . 14 F6
Ashford TW15 . . . 197 BQ93
Banstead SM7 . . . 240 DB114
Beaconsfield HP9
off Seeleys Rd . . . 111 AK52
Bexleyheath DA7 . . . 188 EY81
Bushey Heath WD23 . . . 117 CD46
Chorleywood WD3 . . . 95 BD42
Cuffley EN6 . . . 87 DL28
Denham UB9 . . . 156 BH65
East Horsley KT24 . . . 251 BT124
Edgware HA8 . . . 118 CL51
Egham TW20 . . . 195 BB92
Elstree WD6 . . . 100 CM42
Fetcham KT22 . . . 253 CD122
Guildford GU1 . . . 265 BB134
Hemel Hempstead HP2 . . . 62 BM18
Horley RH6 . . . 290 DF147
Leatherhead KT22 . . . 253 CF119
Little Berkhamsted SG13 . . . 69 DJ19
Long Ditton KT6 . . . 219 CH101
Northolt UB5 . . . 138 CC64
Radlett WD7 . . . 99 CE37
Ruislip HA4 . . . 137 BQ59
St. Albans AL1 . . . 65 CF21
Sheering CM22 . . . 59 FC07
South Ockendon RM15 . . . 171 FW70
Stanstead Abbotts SG12 . . . 55 EC11
Walton-on-Thames KT12 . . . 217 BV101
Ware SG12 . . . 55 DX05
Watford WD17 . . . 97 BT40
Wembley HA0 . . . 160 CL67
West Ewell KT19 . . . 238 CP107
Woking GU22 . . . 249 BB116
Orchard Ct, Bov. HP3 . . . 79 BA27
Twickenham TW2 . . . 199 CD89
Wallington SM6
off Parkgate Rd . . . 241 DH106
Worcester Park KT4 . . . 221 CU102
Orchard Cres, Edg. HA8 . . . 118 CQ50
Enfield EN1 . . . 104 DT39
Orchard Cft, Harl. CM20 . . . 58 EU13
Orchard Dr, SE3 . . . 47 H8
Ashtead KT21 . . . 253 CK120
Chorleywood WD3 . . . 95 BC41
Edgware HA8 . . . 118 CM50
Grays RM17 . . . 192 GA75
Park Street AL2 . . . 82 CB27
Theydon Bois CM16 . . . 107 ES36
Uxbridge UB8 . . . 156 BK70
Watford WD17 . . . 97 BT39
Woking GU21 . . . 249 AZ115
Wooburn Green HP10 . . . 132 AD59
Orchard End, Cat. CR3 . . . 258 DS122
Fetcham KT22 . . . 252 CC124
Weybridge KT13 . . . 217 BS103
Orchard End Av, Amer. HP7 . . . 94 AT39
Orchard Est, Wdf.Grn. IG8 . . . 124 EJ52
Orchard Fm Pk, Red. RH1 . . . 289 DM143
Orchard Fld Rd, Gdmg. GU7 . . . 280 AT144
Orchard Gdns, Chess. KT9 . . . 238 CL105
Effingham KT24 . . . 268 BY128
Epsom KT18 . . . 238 CQ114
Sutton SM1 . . . 240 DA106
Waltham Abbey EN9 . . . 89 EC34
Orchard Gate, NW9 . . . 140 CS56
Esher KT10 . . . 219 CD102
Farnham Common SL2 . . . 133 AQ64
Greenford UB6 . . . 159 CH65
Orchard Grn, Orp. BR6 . . . 227 ES103
Orchard Gro, SE20 . . . 204 DU94
Chalfont St. Peter SL9 . . . 112 AW53
Croydon CR0 . . . 225 DY101
Edgware HA8 . . . 118 CN53
Harrow HA3 . . . 140 CM57
Orpington BR6 . . . 227 ET103
Orchard Hill, SE13 . . . 46 D8
Carshalton SM5 . . . 240 DF106
Dartford DA1 . . . 209 FE85
Coll Orchard Hill Coll, Wall. SM6
off Woodcote Rd . . . 241 DH107
Orchard Ho, Erith DA8
off Northend Rd . . . 189 FF81
Sch Orchard Inf & Nurs & Jun
Schs, The, Houns. TW4
off Orchard Rd . . . 198 CA85
Orchard La, SW20 . . . 221 CV95
Amersham HP6 . . . 77 AR38
East Molesey KT8 . . . 219 CD100
Pilgrim's Hatch CM15 . . . 130 FT43
Woodford Green IG8 . . . 124 EJ49
Orchard Lea, Saw. CM21 . . . 58 EW06
Orchard Lea Cl, Wok. GU22 . . . 249 BE115
ORCHARD LEIGH, Chesh. HP5 . . . 78 AV28
Orchard Leigh, Chesh. HP5 . . . 78 AU28
Orchardleigh, Lthd. KT22 . . . 253 CH122
Orchardleigh Av, Enf. EN3 . . . 104 DW40
Orchard Mains, Wok. GU22 . . . 248 AW119
Orchard Mead, Hat. AL10
off Days Mead . . . 67 CT18
Orchard Mead Ho, NW11 . . . 141 CZ61
Orchardmede, N21 . . . 104 DR44
Orchard Ms, N1 . . . 9 M7
N6 off Orchard Rd . . . 143 DH59
SW17 off Franche Ct Rd . . . 202 DC90
Seer Green HP9
off Orchard Rd . . . 111 AR51
Orchard Path, Slou. SL3 . . . 155 BA72
Orchard Pl, E5 . . . 10 F3
E14 . . . 23 J10
N17 . . . 122 DT52
Cheshunt EN8
off Turners Hill . . . 89 DX30
Keston BR2 . . . 244 EJ109
Sundridge TN14 . . . 262 EY124
Sch Orchard Prim Sch, E9 . . . 11 H7
SW2 off Christchurch Rd . . . 203 DM88
Sidcup DA14 off Oxford Rd . . . 208 EV92
Sch Orchard Prim Sch, The, Wat.
WD24 off Gammons La . . . 97 BT36
Orchard Ri, Croy. CR0 . . . 225 DY102
Kingston upon Thames KT2 . . . 220 CQ95
Pinner HA5 . . . 137 BT55
Richmond TW10 . . . 180 CP84
Orchard Ri E, Sid. DA15 . . . 207 ET85
Orchard Ri W, Sid. DA15 . . . 207 ES85
Orchard Rd, N6 . . . 143 DH59
SE3 . . . 47 J8
SE18 . . . 187 ER77
Barnet EN5 . . . 101 CZ42
Beaconsfield HP9 . . . 111 AM54
Belvedere DA17 . . . 188 FA77
Brentford TW8 . . . 179 CJ79
Bromley BR1 . . . 226 EJ95
Burpham GU4 . . . 265 BB130
Chalfont St. Giles HP8 . . . 112 AW47
Chessington KT9 . . . 238 CL105
Dagenham RM10 . . . 168 FA67
Dorking RH4 . . . 285 CH137
Enfield EN3 . . . 104 DW43
Farnborough BR6 . . . 245 EP106
Feltham TW13 . . . 197 BU88
Hampton TW12 . . . 198 BZ94
Hayes UB3 . . . 157 BT73
Hounslow TW4 . . . 198 BZ85
Kingston upon Thames KT1 . . . 220 CL96
Mitcham CR4 . . . 222 DG102
Northfleet DA11 . . . 212 GC89
Old Windsor SL4 . . . 194 AV86
Onslow Village GU2 . . . 264 AT136
Otford TN14 . . . 263 FF116
Pratt's Bottom BR6 . . . 246 EW110
Reigate RH2 . . . 272 DB134
Richmond TW9 . . . 180 CN83
Riverhead TN13 . . . 278 FE122
Romford RM7 . . . 127 FB53
Seer Green HP9 . . . 111 AQ50
Shalford GU4 . . . 280 AY140
Shere GU5 . . . 282 BN139
Sidcup DA14 . . . 207 ES91
Smallfield RH6 . . . 291 DP148
South Croydon CR2 . . . 242 DV114
South Ockendon RM15 . . . 171 FW70
Sunbury-on-Thames TW16
off Hanworth Rd . . . 197 BV94
Sutton SM1 . . . 240 DA106
Swanscombe DA10 . . . 212 FY85
Twickenham TW1 . . . 199 CG85
Welling DA16 . . . 188 EV83
Orchards, The, Epp. CM16 . . . 92 EU32
Sawbridgeworth CM21 . . . 58 EY05
Sch Orchard Sch, The, E.Mol. KT8
off Bridge Rd . . . 219 CD98
Orchards Cl, W.Byf. KT14 . . . 234 BG114
Sch Orchards Inf Sch, Reig. RH2
off Alexander Rd . . . 288 DA137
Orchardson Ho, NW8
off Orchardson St . . . 16 B4
Orchardson St, NW8 . . . 16 A5
Orchard Sq, W14 . . . 38 G1
Broxbourne EN10 . . . 71 DZ24
Orchards Residential Pk, The,
Slou. SL3 . . . 155 AZ74
Orchards Shop Cen, Dart.
DA1 . . . 210 FL86
Orchard St, E17 . . . 145 DY56
W1 . . . 16 G9
Dartford DA1 . . . 210 FL86
Hemel Hempstead HP3 . . . 62 BK24
St. Albans AL3 . . . 64 CC21
Orchard Ter, Enf. EN1 . . . 104 DU44
Orchard Vw, Cher. KT16 . . . 216 BG100
Uxbridge UB8 . . . 156 BK70
Orchard Vil, Sid. DA14 . . . 208 EV93
Orchardville, Burn. SL1 . . . 152 AH70
Orchard Wk, Kings.T. KT2
off Clifton Rd . . . 220 CN95
Orchard Way, Add. KT15 . . . 234 BH106
Ashford TW15 . . . 196 BM89
Beckenham BR3 . . . 225 DY99
Bovingdon HP3 . . . 79 BA28
Chigwell IG7 . . . 126 EU48
Croydon CR0 . . . 225 DY102
Dartford DA2 . . . 210 FK90
Dorking RH4 . . . 285 CH137
Enfield EN1 . . . 104 DS41
Esher KT10 . . . 236 CC107
Goffs Oak EN7 . . . 87 DP27
Lower Kingswood KT20 . . . 271 CZ126
Mill End WD3 . . . 114 BG45
Oxted RH8 . . . 276 EG133
Potters Bar EN6 . . . 86 DB28
Reigate RH2 . . . 288 DB138
Send GU23 . . . 265 BC125
Slough SL3 . . . 154 AY74
Sutton SM1 . . . 240 DD105
Orchard Waye, Uxb. UB8 . . . 156 BK68
Sch Orchard Way Prim Sch, Croy.
CR0 off Orchard Way . . . 225 DY101
Orchehill Av, Ger.Cr. SL9 . . . 134 AX56
Orchehill Ct, Ger.Cr. SL9 . . . 134 AY57
Orchehill Ri, Ger.Cr. SL9 . . . 134 AY57
Orchestra Cl, Edg. HA8
off Symphony Cl . . . 118 CP52
Orchid Cl, E6 . . . 24 G6
SE13 . . . 205 ED85
Abridge RM4 . . . 108 EV41
Chessington KT9 . . . 237 CJ108
Goffs Oak EN7 . . . 88 DQ30
Hatfield AL10 . . . 51 CT14
Southall UB1 . . . 158 BY72
Orchid Ct, Egh. TW20 . . . 195 BB91
Romford RM7 . . . 149 FE61
Orchid Gdns, Houns. TW3 . . . 178 BZ84
Orchid Rd, N14 . . . 121 DJ45
Orchid St, W12 . . . 161 CU73
Orchis Gro, Bad.Dene RM17 . . . 192 FZ78
Orchis Way, Rom. RM3 . . . 128 FM51
Orde Hall St, WC1 . . . 18 C5
Ordell Rd, E3 . . . 21 P1
Ordnance Cl, Felt. TW13 . . . 197 BU89
Ordnance Cres, SE10 . . . 35 H4
Ordnance Hill, NW8 . . . 6 B9
Ordnance Ms, NW8 . . . 6 B10
Ordnance Rd, E16 . . . 23 L6
SE18 . . . 187 EN79
Enfield EN3 . . . 105 DX37
Gravesend DA12 . . . 213 GJ86
Oregano Cl, West Dr. UB7
off Camomile Way . . . 156 BL72
Oregano Dr, E14 . . . 23 H9
Oregano Way, Guil. GU2 . . . 264 AU129
Oregon Av, E12 . . . 147 EM63
Oregon Bldg, SE13
off Deals Gateway . . . 46 C6
Oregon Cl, N.Mal. KT3
off Georgia Rd . . . 220 CQ98
Oregon Sq, Orp. BR6 . . . 227 ER102
Orestan La, Eff. KT24 . . . 267 BV127
Orestes Ms, NW6 . . . 5 J2
Oreston Rd, Rain. RM13 . . . 170 FK69
Orewell Gdns, Reig. RH2 . . . 288 DB136
Orford Ct, SE27 . . . 203 DP89
Orford Gdns, Twick. TW1 . . . 199 CF89
Orford Rd, E17 . . . 145 EA57
E18 . . . 146 EH55
SE6 . . . 205 EB90
Jct Organ Crossroads, Epsom
KT17 . . . 239 CU108
Organ Hall Rd, Borwd. WD6 . . . 100 CL39
Organ La, E4 . . . 123 EC47
Oriel Cl, Mitch. CR4 . . . 223 DK98
Oriel Ct, NW3 . . . 5 P1
Oriel Dr, SW13 . . . 181 CV79
Oriel Gdns, Ilf. IG5 . . . 147 EM55
Oriel Pl, NW3 . . . 5 P1
Sch Oriel Prim Sch, Han. TW13
off Hounslow Rd . . . 198 BY90
Oriel Rd, E9 . . . 11 K4
Oriel Way, Nthlt. UB5 . . . 158 CB66
Oriental City, NW9 . . . 140 CR55
Oriental Cl, Wok. GU22
off Oriental Rd . . . 249 BA117
Oriental Rd, E16 . . . 36 F2
Woking GU22 . . . 249 BA117
Oriental St, E14 . . . 22 B10
Orient Cl, St.Alb. AL1 . . . 65 CE22
● Orient Ind Pk, E10 . . . 145 EA61
Orient St, SE11 . . . 30 G8
Orient Way, E5 . . . 145 DX62
E10 . . . 145 DY61
Oriole Cl, Abb.L. WD5 . . . 81 BU31
Oriole Way, SE28 . . . 168 EV73
● Orion Business Cen, SE14 . . . 45 J1
● Orion Cen, The, Croy. CR0 . . . 223 DL103
Orion Ho, E1 . . . 20 F5
Orion Pt, E14 . . . 34 A8
Sch Orion Prim Sch, The, NW9
off Lanacre Av . . . 119 CT54
Orion Rd, N11 . . . 121 DH51
Orion Way, Nthwd. HA6 . . . 115 BT49
Orissa Rd, SE18 . . . 187 ES78
Orkney Ct, Tap. SL6 . . . 152 AE66
Orkney St, SW11 . . . 40 G8
Orlando Gdns, Epsom KT19 . . . 238 CR110
Orlando Rd, SW4 . . . 183 DJ83
Orleans Cl, Esher KT10 . . . 219 CD103
★ Orleans Ho Gall, Twick.
TW1 . . . 199 CH88
Sch Orleans Inf Sch, Twick. TW1
off Hartington Rd . . . 199 CH87
Sch Orleans Pk Sch, Twick. TW1
off Richmond Rd . . . 199 CH87
Orleans Rd, SE19 . . . 204 DR93
Twickenham TW1 . . . 199 CH87
Orlestone Gdns, Orp. BR6 . . . 246 EY106
Orleston Ms, N7 . . . 8 F4
Orleston Rd, N7 . . . 8 F4
Orley Fm Rd, Har. HA1 . . . 139 CE62
Sch Orley Fm Sch, Har.Hill HA1
off South Hill Av . . . 139 CD62
Orlop St, SE10 . . . 47 J1
Ormanton Rd, SE26 . . . 204 DU91
Orme Ct, W2 . . . 27 L1
Orme Ct Ms, W2 . . . 27 M1
Orme La, W2 . . . 27 L1
Ormeley Rd, SW12 . . . 203 DH88
Orme Rd, Kings.T. KT1 . . . 220 CP96
Sutton SM1 off Grove Rd . . . 240 DB107
Ormerod Gdns, Mitch. CR4 . . . 222 DG96
Ormesby Cl, SE28
off Wroxham Rd . . . 168 EX73
Ormesby Dr, Pot.B. EN6 . . . 85 CX32
Ormesby Way, Har. HA3 . . . 140 CM58
Orme Sq, W2 . . . 27 L1
Ormiston Gro, W12 . . . 161 CV74
Ormiston Rd, SE10 . . . 47 N1
Ormond Av, Hmptn. TW12 . . . 218 CB95
Richmond TW10
off Ormond Rd . . . 199 CK85
Ormond Cl, WC1 . . . 18 B6
Harold Wood RM3
off Chadwick Dr . . . 128 FK54
Ormond Cres, Hmptn. TW12 . . . 218 CB95
Ormond Dr, Hmptn. TW12 . . . 198 CB94
Ormonde Av, Epsom KT19 . . . 238 CR109
Orpington BR6 . . . 227 EQ103
Ormonde Gate, SW3 . . . 40 F1
Ormonde Pl, SW1 . . . 28 G9
Ormonde Ri, Buck.H. IG9 . . . 124 EJ46
Ormonde Rd, SW14 . . . 180 CP83
Northwood HA6 . . . 115 BR49
Woking GU21 . . . 248 AW116
Ormonde Ter, NW8 . . . 6 E9
Ormond Ms, WC1 . . . 18 B5
Ormond Rd, N19 . . . 143 DL60
Richmond TW10 . . . 199 CK85
Ormond Yd, SW1 . . . 29 M2
Ormsby, Sutt. SM2
off Grange Rd . . . 240 DB108
Ormsby Gdns, Grnf. UB6 . . . 158 CC68
Ormsby Pl, N16 . . . 144 DT62
Ormsby Pt, SE18 . . . 37 P9
Ormsby St, E2 . . . 10 A10
Ormside St, SE15 . . . 44 G3
Ormside Way, Red. RH1 . . . 273 DH130
Ormskirk Rd, Wat. WD19 . . . 116 BX49
Ornan Rd, NW3 . . . 6 C3
Oronsay, Hem.H. HP3
off Northend . . . 63 BP22
Orpen Wk, N16 . . . 144 DS62
Orphanage Rd, Wat.
WD17, WD24 . . . 98 BW40
Coll Orpheus Cen, Gdse. RH9
off North Pk La . . . 274 DU130
Orpheus St, SE5 . . . 43 L7
ORPINGTON, BR5 & BR6 . . . 227 ES102
⇌ Orpington . . . 227 ET103
Orpington . . . 227 ET103
Orpington Bypass, Orp. BR6 . . . 228 EV103
Sevenoaks TN14 . . . 246 FA109
Coll Orpington Coll, Orp. BR6
off The Walnuts . . . 228 EU102
Orpington Gdns, N18 . . . 122 DS48
H Orpington Hosp, Orp. BR6 . . . 245 ET105
Orpington Rd, N21 . . . 121 DP46
Chislehurst BR7 . . . 227 ES97
Orpin Rd, S.Merst. RH1 . . . 273 DH130
Orpwood Cl, Hmptn. TW12 . . . 198 BZ92
ORSETT HEATH, Grays RM16 . . . 193 GG75
Orsett Heath Cres, Grays
RM16 . . . 193 GG76
Orsett Rd, Grays RM17 . . . 192 GA78
Orsett St, SE11 . . . 30 D10
Orsett Ter, W2 . . . 15 M8
Woodford Green IG8 . . . 124 EJ52
Orsman Rd, N1 . . . 9 N9
Orton Cl, St.Alb. AL4 . . . 65 CG16
Orton Gro, Enf. EN1 . . . 104 DU39
Orton Pl, SW19 . . . 202 DB94
Orton St, E1 . . . 32 C3
Orville Rd, SW11 . . . 40 B8
Orwell Cl, Hayes UB3 . . . 157 BS73
Rainham RM13 . . . 169 FD71
Windsor SL4 . . . 173 AR83
Orwell Ct, N5 . . . 9 K1
Orwell Rd, E13 . . . 166 EJ68
Osbaldeston Rd, N16 . . . 144 DU61
Osberton Rd, SE12 . . . 206 EG85
Osbert St, SW1 . . . 29 N9
Osborn Cl, E8 . . . 10 C8
Osborne Av, Stai. TW19 . . . 196 BL88
Osborne Cl, Barn. EN4 . . . 102 DF41
Beckenham BR3 . . . 225 DY98
Feltham TW13 . . . 198 BX92
Hornchurch RM11 . . . 149 FH58
Osborne Ct, Pot.B. EN6 . . . 86 DB29
Windsor SL4
off Osborne Rd . . . 173 AQ82
Osborne Gdns, Pot.B. EN6 . . . 86 DB30
Thornton Heath CR7 . . . 224 DQ96
Osborne Gro, E17 . . . 145 DZ56
N4 . . . 143 DN60
Osborne Hts, Warley CM14 . . . 130 FV49
Osborne Ms, E17
off Osborne Gro . . . 145 DZ56
Windsor SL4 . . . 173 AQ82
Osborne Pl, Sutt. SM1 . . . 240 DD106
Osborne Rd, E7 . . . 146 EH64
E9 . . . 11 P4
E10 . . . 145 EB62
N4 . . . 143 DM60
N13 . . . 121 DN48
NW2 . . . 161 CV65
W3 . . . 180 CP76
Belvedere DA17 . . . 188 EZ78
Broxbourne EN10 . . . 71 EA19
Buckhurst Hill IG9 . . . 124 EH46
Cheshunt EN8 . . . 89 DY27
Dagenham RM9 . . . 148 EZ64
Egham TW20 . . . 195 AZ93
Enfield EN3 . . . 105 DY40
Hornchurch RM11 . . . 149 FH58
Hounslow TW3 . . . 178 BZ83
Kingston upon Thames KT2 . . . 200 CL94
Pilgrim's Hatch CM15 . . . 130 FU44
Potters Bar EN6 . . . 86 DB30
Redhill RH1 . . . 272 DG131
Southall UB1 . . . 158 CC72
Thornton Heath CR7 . . . 224 DQ96
Uxbridge UB8
off Oxford Rd . . . 156 BJ66
Walton-on-Thames KT12 . . . 217 BU102
Watford WD24 . . . 98 BW38
Windsor SL4 . . . 173 AQ82
Osborne Sq, Dag. RM9 . . . 148 EZ63
Osborne St, Slou. SL1 . . . 174 AT75
Osborne Ter, SW17
off Church La . . . 202 DG92
Osborne Way, Chess. KT9
off Bridge Rd . . . 238 CM106
Osborn Gdns, NW7 . . . 119 CX52
Osborn La, SE23 . . . 205 DY87
Osborn St, E1 . . . 20 B7
Osborn Ter, SE3 off Lee Rd . . . 186 EF84
Osborn Way, Welw.G.C. AL8 . . . 51 CX10
Osborn Way Tunnel, Welw.G.C.
AL8 off Osborn Way . . . 51 CX09
Osbourne Av, Kings L. WD4 . . . 80 BM28
Osbourne Ct, W5 . . . 160 CL71
Osbourne Rd, Dart. DA2 . . . 210 FP86
Oscar Faber Pl, N1 . . . 9 P7
Oscar St, SE8 . . . 46 A8
Oseney Cres, NW5 . . . 7 M4
Osgood Av, Orp. BR6 . . . 245 ET106
Osgood Gdns, Orp. BR6 . . . 245 ET106
OSIDGE, N14 . . . 121 DH46
Osidge La, N14 . . . 120 DG46
Sch Osidge Prim Sch, N14
off Chase Side . . . 121 DJ46
Osier Cres, N10 . . . 120 DF53
Osier La, SE10 . . . 35 M7
Osier Ms, W4 . . . 181 CT79
Osier Pl, Egh. TW20 . . . 195 BC93
Osiers, The, Crox.Grn WD3 . . . 97 BQ44
Osiers Rd, SW18 . . . 182 DA84
Osier St, E1 . . . 21 H5
Osier Way, E10 . . . 145 EB62
Banstead SM7 . . . 239 CY114
Mitcham CR4 . . . 222 DE99
Oslac Rd, SE6 . . . 205 EB92
Oslo Ct, NW8 . . . 16 C1
Oslo Sq, SE16 . . . 33 M6
Osman Cl, N15 off Pulford Rd . . . 144 DR58
Sch Osmani Prim Sch, E1 . . . 20 D6
Osman Rd, N9 . . . 122 DU48
W6 . . . 26 B6
Osmington Ho, SW8 . . . 42 C5
Osmond Cl, Har. HA2 . . . 138 CC61
Osmond Gdns, Wall. SM6 . . . 241 DJ106
Osmund St, W12
off Braybrook St . . . 161 CT71
Osnaburgh St, NW1 . . . 17 K5
NW1 (north section) . . . 17 K3

Osnaburgh Ter, NW1 17 K4
Osney Ho, SE2
off Hartslock Dr 188 EX75
Osney Wk, Cars. SM5 222 DD100
Osney Way, Grav. DA12 213 GM89
Osprey Cl, E6 24 G7
E11 146 EG56
E17 123 DY52
Bromley BR2 226 EL102
Fetcham KT22 252 CC122
Sutton SM1
off Sandpiper Rd 239 CZ106
Watford WD25 82 BY34
West Drayton UB7 176 BK75
Osprey Ct, Wal.Abb. EN9 90 EG34
Osprey Gdns, S.Croy. CR2 243 DX110
Osprey Hts, SW11
off Bramlands Cl 182 DE83
Osprey Ms, Enf. EN3 104 DV43
Osprey Rd, Wal.Abb. EN9 90 EG34
Ospringe Cl, SE20 204 DW94
Ospringe Ct, SE9 207 ER86
Ospringe Rd, NW5 7 L1
Osram Ct, W6 26 B7
Osram Rd, Wem. HA9 139 CK62
Osric Path, N1 19 N1
Ossian Ms, N4 143 DM59
Ossian Rd, N4 143 DM59
Jct Ossie Garvin Rbt, Hayes UB4 158 BW73
Ossington Bldgs, W1 16 G6
Ossington Cl, W2 27 K1
Ossington St, W2 27 K1
Ossory Rd, SE1 44 C1
Ossulston St, NW1 17 N1
Ossulton Pl, N2 142 DC55
Ossulton Way, N2 142 DC56
Ostade Rd, SW2 203 DM87
Ostell Cres, Enf. EN3 105 EA38
Osten Ms, SW7 27 M7
Osterberg Rd, Dart. DA1 190 FM84
OSTERLEY, Islw. TW7 178 CC80
⊖ Osterley 179 CD80
Osterley Av, Islw. TW7 179 CD80
Osterley Cl, Orp. BR5 228 EU95
Osterley Ct, Islw. TW7 179 CD81
Osterley Cres, Islw. TW7 179 CE81
Osterley Gdns, Sthl. UB2 178 CC75
Thornton Heath CR7 224 DQ96
Osterley Ho, E14 22 C8
Osterley La, Islw. TW7 179 CE78
Southall UB2 178 CA78
Osterley Pk, Islw. TW7 179 CD78
★ Osterley Park Ho, Islw. TW7 178 CC78
Osterley Pk Rd, Sthl. UB2 178 BZ76
Osterley Pk Vw Rd, W7 179 CE75
Osterley Rd, N16 144 DS63
Isleworth TW7 179 CE80
Osterley Views, Sthl. UB2 158 CC74
Oster St, St.Alb. AL3 64 CC19
Oster Ter, E17
off Southcote Rd 145 DX57
Ostlers Dr, Ashf. TW15 197 BQ92
Ostliffe Rd, N13 122 DQ50
Oswald Bldg, SW8 41 J3
Oswald Cl, Fetch. KT22 252 CC122
Oswald Rd, Fetch. KT22 252 CC122
St. Albans AL1 65 CE21
Southall UB1 158 BY74
Oswald's Mead, E9
off Lindisfarne Way 145 DY63
Oswald St, E5 145 DX62
Oswald Ter, NW2
off Temple Rd 141 CW62
Osward, Croy. CR0 243 DZ109
Osward Pl, N9 122 DV47
Osward Rd, SW17 202 DF89
Oswell Ho, E1 32 F2
Oswin St, SE11 31 H8
Oswyth Rd, SE5 43 P8
OTFORD, Sev. TN14 263 FH116
Otford Cl, SE20 224 DW95
Bexley DA5
off Southwold Rd 209 FB86
Bromley BR1 227 EN97
Otford Cres, SE4 205 DZ86
Otford La, Halst. TN14 246 EZ112
Sch Otford Prim Sch, Otford TN14
off High St 263 FH116
Otford Rd, Sev. TN14 263 FH118
Othello Cl, SE11 30 G10
Otho Ct, Brent. TW8 179 CK80
Otis St, E3 22 E2
Otley App, Ilf. IG2 147 EP58
Otley Dr, Ilf. IG2 147 EP57
Otley Rd, E16 24 C8
Otley Ter, E5 145 DX61
Otley Way, Wat. WD19 116 BW48
Otlinge Rd, Orp. BR5 228 EX98
Ottawa Ct, Brox. EN10 89 DY25
Ottawa Gdns, Dag. RM10 169 FD66
Ottawa Rd, Til. RM18 193 GG82
Ottaway St, E5 144 DU62
Ottenden Cl, Orp. BR6
off Southfleet Rd 245 ES105
Otterbourne Rd, E4 123 ED48
Croydon CR0 224 DQ103
Otterburn Gdns, Islw. TW7 179 CG80
Otterburn Ho, SE5 43 J4
Otterburn St, SW17 202 DF93
Otter Cl, E15 12 E9
Ottershaw KT16 233 BB107
Otterden St, SE6 205 EA91
Otterfield Rd, West Dr. UB7 156 BL73
Otter Gdns, Hat. AL10 67 CV19
Ottermead La, Ott. KT16 233 BC107
Otter Meadow, Lthd. KT22 253 CF119
Otter Rd, Grnf. UB6 158 CC70
Otters Cl, Orp. BR5 228 EX98
OTTERSHAW, Cher. KT16 233 BC106
Ottershaw Pk, Ott. KT16 233 BA109
Otterspool La, Wat. WD25 98 BY38
Otterspool Service Rd, Wat. WD25 98 BZ39
Otterspool Way, Wat. WD25 98 BY37
Otto Cl, SE26 204 DV90
Ottoman Ter, Wat. WD17
off Ebury Rd 98 BW41
Otto St, SE17 42 G3
Ottways Av, Ashtd. KT21 253 CK119
Ottways La, Ashtd. KT21 253 CK120
Otway Gdns, Bushey WD23 117 CE45
Otways Cl, Pot.B. EN6 86 DB32
Oulton Cl, E5
off Mundford Rd 144 DW61
SE28 off Rollesby Way 168 EW72
Oulton Cres, Bark. IG11 167 ET65
Potters Bar EN6 85 CX32
Oulton Rd, N15 144 DR57
Oulton Way, Wat. WD19 116 BY49
Oundle Av, Bushey WD23 98 CC44
Sch Our Lady & St. John's RC Prim Sch, Brent. TW8
off Boston Pk Rd 179 CJ78
Sch Our Lady & St. Joseph RC Prim Sch, N1 9 N5
Sch Our Lady & St. Philip Neri Prim Sch, Annexe, SE23
off Mayow Rd 205 DX90
SE26 off Sydenham Rd 205 DY91
Sch Our Lady Immaculate Cath Prim Sch, Surb. KT6
off Ewell Rd 220 CP102
Sch Our Lady of Dolours RC Prim Sch, W2 15 L6
Sch Our Lady of Grace Inf Sch, NW2 off Dollis Hill Av 141 CW61
Sch Our Lady of Grace Jun Sch, NW2 off Dollis Hill La 141 CV62
Sch Our Lady of Grace RC Prim Sch, SE7 off Charlton Rd 186 EH79
Sch Our Lady of Lourdes Cath Prim Sch, E11
off Chestnut Dr 146 EG58
SE13 off Belmont Hill 185 ED83
Sch Our Lady of Lourdes Prim Sch, NW10 off Wesley Rd 160 CQ67
Sch Our Lady of Lourdes RC Prim Sch, N11
off The Limes Avenue 121 DJ50
N12 off Bow La 120 DC53
Sch Our Lady of Muswell Cath Prim Sch, N10 off Pages La 142 DG55
Sch Our Lady of Peace Catholic Inf & Nurs Sch, Slou. SL1
off Derwent Dr 152 AJ71
Sch Our Lady of Peace Catholic Jun Sch, Slou. SL1
off Derwent Dr 152 AJ71
Sch Our Lady of the Rosary RC Prim Sch, Sid. DA15
off Holbeach Gdns 207 ES86
Staines TW18 off Park Av 196 BG93
Sch Our Lady of the Visitation RC Prim Sch, Grnf. UB6
off Greenford Rd 158 CC70
Sch Our Lady of Victories RC Prim Sch, SW7 27 P9
SW15 off Clarendon Dr 181 CX84
Sch Our Lady Queen of Heaven RC Prim Sch, SW19
off Victoria Dr 201 CX87
Sch Our Lady's Catholic Prim Sch, Chesh.B. HP6
off Amersham Rd 77 AP35
Dartford DA1
off King Edward Av 210 FK86
Sch Our Lady's Conv High Sch, N16 off Amhurst Pk 144 DS59
Sch Our Lady's Prim Sch, E14 21 P9
Sch Our Lady's RC Prim Sch, NW1 7 L8
Welwyn Garden City AL7
off Woodhall La 51 CY11
Ousden Cl, Chsht EN8 89 DY30
Ousden Dr, Chsht EN8 89 DY30
Ouseley Rd, SW12 202 DF88
Old Windsor SL4 194 AW87
Wraysbury TW19 194 AW87
Outdowns, Eff. KT24 267 BV129
Outer Circle, NW1 16 G5
Outfield Rd, Chal.St.P. SL9 112 AX52
Outgate Rd, NW10 161 CT66
Outlook Dr, Ch.St.G. HP8 112 AX48
Outlook Ho, Enf. EN3
off Tysoe Av 105 DZ36
Outram Pl, N1 8 B8
Weybridge KT13 235 BQ106
Outram Rd, E6 166 EL67
N22 121 DK53
Croydon CR0 224 DT102
Outwich St, EC3 19 P8
OUTWOOD, Red. RH1 289 DP143
Outwood La, Chipstead CR5 256 DF118
Kingswood KT20 256 DB122
⊖ Oval 42 E3
★ Oval, The (Surrey CCC), SE11 42 D2
Oval, The, E2 10 E10
Banstead SM7 240 DA114
Broxbourne EN10 89 DY25
Godalming GU7 280 AT144
Guildford GU2 280 AU135
Sidcup DA15 208 EU87
Oval Gdns, Grays RM17 192 GC76
Oval Pl, SW8 42 C4
Sch Oval Prim Sch, Croy. CR0
off Cherry Orchard Rd 224 DS102
Oval Rd, NW1 7 J7
Croydon CR0 224 DS102
Oval Rd N, Dag. RM10 169 FB67
Oval Rd S, Dag. RM10 169 FB68
Ovaltine Ct, Kings L. WD4 81 BP29
Ovaltine Dr, Kings L. WD4 81 BP29
Oval Way, SE11 42 D1
Gerrards Cross SL9 134 AY56
Ovanna Ms, N1 9 P5
Ovenden Rd, Sund. TN14 262 EX120
Overbrae, Beck. BR3 205 EA93
Overbrook, W.Hors. KT24 267 BP129
Overbrook Wk, Edg. HA8 118 CN52
Overbury Av, Beck. BR3 225 EB97
Overbury Cres, New Adgtn CR0 243 EC110
Overbury Rd, N15 144 DR58
Overbury St, E5 145 DX63
Overchess Ridge, Chorl. WD3 95 BF41
Overcliffe, Grav. DA11 213 GG86
Overcliff Rd, SE13 185 EA83
Grays RM17 192 GD77
Overcourt Cl, Sid. DA15 208 EV86
Overdale, Ashtd. KT21 254 CL115
Bletchingley RH1 274 DQ133
Dorking RH5 285 CJ135
Overdale Av, N.Mal. KT3 220 CQ96
Overdale Rd, W5 179 CJ76
Chesham HP5 76 AP28
Overdown Rd, SE6 205 EA91
Overhill, Warl. CR6 258 DW119
Overhill Rd, SE22 204 DU87
Purley CR8 241 DN109
Overhill Way, Beck. BR3 225 ED99
Overlea Rd, E5 144 DU59
Overlord Cl, Brox. EN10 71 DY20
Overlord Ct, Lthd. KT22 253 CD121
Overmead, Sid. DA15 207 ER87
Swanley BR8 229 FE99
Oversley Ho, W2 15 J6
Overstand Cl, Beck. BR3 225 EA99
Overstone Gdns, Croy. CR0 225 DZ101
Overstone Rd, W6 26 A7
Overstrand Ho, Horn. RM12 149 FH61
Overstream, Loud. WD3 96 BH42
Over The Misbourne, Denh. UB9 135 BC58
Gerrards Cross SL9 135 BA58
Overthorpe Cl, Knap. GU21 248 AS117
Overton Cl, NW10 160 CQ65
Isleworth TW7 179 CF81
Overton Ct, E11 146 EG59
Overton Dr, E11 146 EH59
Romford RM6 148 EW59
Sch Overton Gra Sch, Sutt. SM2
off Stanley Rd 240 DB109
Overton Ho, SW15
off Tangley Gro 201 CT87
Overton Rd, E10 145 DY60
N14 103 DL43
SE2 188 EW76
SW9 42 F9
Sutton SM2 240 DA107
Overton Rd E, SE2 188 EX76
Overtons Yd, Croy. CR0 224 DQ104
Overy St, Dart. DA1 210 FL86
Ovesdon Av, Har. HA2 138 BZ60
Oveton Way, Bkhm KT23 268 CA126
Ovett Cl, SE19 204 DS93
Ovex Cl, E14 34 F5
Ovington Ct, Wok. GU21
off Roundthorn Way 248 AT116
Ovington Gdns, SW3 28 D7
Ovington Ms, SW3 28 D7
Ovington Sq, SW3 28 D7
Ovington St, SW3 28 D7
Owen Cl, SE28 168 EW74
Croydon CR0 224 DR100
Hayes UB4 157 BV69
Northolt UB5 158 BY65
Romford RM5 127 FB51
Slough SL3 off Parsons Rd 175 AZ78
Owen Gdns, Wdf.Grn. IG8 124 EL51
Owenite St, SE2 188 EV77
Owen Pl, Lthd. KT22
off Church Rd 253 CH122
Owen Rd, N13 122 DQ50
Hayes UB4 157 BV69
Owens Ms, E11 off Short Rd 146 EE61
Owen's Row, EC1 18 G2
Owen St, EC1 18 G1
Owens Way, SE23 205 DY87
Croxley Green WD3 96 BN43
Owen Wk, SE20
off Sycamore Gro 224 DU95
Owen Waters Ho, Ilf. IG5 125 EM53
Owen Way, NW10 160 CQ65
Owgan Cl, SE5 43 M5
Owl, The, High Beach IG10 106 EF40
Owl Cl, S.Croy. CR2 243 DX110
Owlets Hall Cl, Horn. RM11
off Prospect Rd 150 FM55
Owlsears Cl, Beac. HP9 111 AK51
Ownstead Gdns, S.Croy. CR2 242 DT111
Ownsted Hill, New Adgtn CR0 243 EC110
Oxberry Av, SW6 38 F8
Oxdowne Cl, Stoke D'Ab. KT11 236 CB114
Oxenden Dr, Hodd. EN11 71 EA18
Oxenden Wd Rd, Orp. BR6 246 EV107
Oxendon St, SW1 29 N1
Oxenford St, SE15 184 DT83
Oxenholme, NW1 17 M1
Oxenpark Av, Wem. HA9 140 CL59
Oxestalls Rd, SE8 33 M10
Oxfield Cl, Berk. HP4 60 AU20
Oxford Av, N14 121 DJ46
SW20 221 CY96
Burnham SL1 152 AG68
Grays RM16 193 GG77
Hayes UB3 177 BT80
Hornchurch RM11 150 FN56
Hounslow TW5 178 CA78
St. Albans AL1 65 CJ21
Slough SL1 153 AM71
⊖ Oxford Circus 17 L9
Oxford Circ Av, W1 17 L9
Oxford Cl, N9 122 DV47
Ashford TW15 197 BQ94
Cheshunt EN8 89 DX29
Gravesend DA12 213 GM89
Mitcham CR4 223 DJ97
Northwood HA6 115 BQ49
Romford RM2 149 FG57
Oxford Ct, EC4 19 L10
W3 160 CN72
Feltham TW13
off Oxford Way 198 BX91
Warley CM14 130 FX49
Oxford Cres, N.Mal. KT3 220 CR100
Oxford Dr, SE1 31 N3
Ruislip HA4 138 BW61
Oxford Gdns, N20 120 DD46
N21 122 DQ45
W4 180 CN78
W10 14 F7
Denham UB9 135 BF62
Sch Oxford Gdns Prim Sch, W10 14 C8
Oxford Gate, W6 26 D8
Oxford Ms, Bex. DA5 208 FA88
Oxford Pl, NW10 off Press Rd 140 CR62
Hatfield AL10 66 CS16
Oxford Rd, E15 13 H5
N4 143 DN60
N9 122 DV47
NW6 15 K1
SE19 204 DR93
SW15 181 CY84
W5 159 CK73
Beaconsfield HP9 133 AP55
Carshalton SM5 240 DE107
Enfield EN3 104 DV43
Gerrards Cross SL9 135 BA60
Guildford GU1 280 AX136
Harrow HA1 138 CC58
High Wycombe HP10 110 AE54
Holtspur HP9 110 AE54
Ilford IG1 147 EQ63
Redhill RH1 272 DE133
Oxford Rd, Rom. RM3 128 FM51
Sidcup DA14 208 EV92
Teddington TW11 199 CD92
Uxbridge UB8, UB9 156 BJ65
Wallington SM6 241 DJ106
Wealdstone HA3 139 CF55
Windsor SL4 173 AQ81
Woodford Green IG8 124 EJ50
Oxford Rd E, Wind. SL4 173 AQ81
Oxford Rd N, W4 180 CP78
Oxford Rd S, W4 180 CN78
Oxford Sq, W2 16 D9
Oxford St, W1 17 M8
Watford WD18 97 BV43
Oxford Ter, Guil. GU1
off Pewley Hill 280 AX136
Oxford Wk, Sthl. UB1 158 BZ74
Oxford Way, Felt. TW13 198 BX91
● Oxgate Cen Ind Est, The, NW2 141 CV60
Oxgate Gdns, NW2 141 CV62
Oxgate La, NW2 141 CV61
Oxhawth Cres, Brom. BR2 227 EN99
OXHEY, Wat. WD19 98 BW44
Oxhey Av, Wat. WD19 116 BX45
Oxhey Dr, Nthwd. HA6 115 BV50
Watford WD19 116 BW48
Oxhey Dr S, Nthwd. HA6 115 BV50
Oxhey La, Har. HA3 116 CA50
Pinner HA5 116 CA50
Watford WD19 116 BZ47
Oxhey Ridge Cl, Nthwd. HA6 115 BU50
Oxhey Rd, Wat. WD19 98 BW44
Sch Oxhey Wd Prim Sch, S.Oxhey WD19 off Oxhey Dr 116 BW48
Ox La, Epsom KT17 239 CU109
Oxleas, E6 25 N8
Oxleas Cl, Well. DA16 187 ER82
OXLEASE, Hat. AL10 67 CV19
Oxlease Dr, Hat. AL10 67 CV19
Oxleay Ct, Har. HA2 138 CA60
Oxleay Rd, Har. HA2 138 CA60
Oxleigh Cl, N.Mal. KT3 220 CS99
Oxley Cl, SE1 32 B10
Romford RM2 128 FJ54
Oxleys, The, Harl. CM17 58 EX11
Oxleys Rd, NW2 141 CV62
Waltham Abbey EN9 90 EG32
Oxlip Cl, Croy. CR0
off Marigold Way 225 DX102
Oxlow La, Dag. RM9, RM10 148 FA63
Oxonian St, SE22 184 DT84
Oxo Twr Wf, SE1 30 F1
OXSHOTT, Lthd. KT22 237 CD113
⇌ Oxshott 236 CC113
Oxshott Ri, Cob. KT11 236 BX113
Oxshott Rd, Lthd. KT22 253 CE115
Oxshott Way, Cob. KT11 252 BY115
OXTED, RH8 275 ED129
⇌ Oxted 276 EE129
Oxted Cl, Mitch. CR4 222 DD97
Oxted Rd, Gdse. RH9 274 DW130
Sch Oxted Sch, Oxt. RH8
off Bluehouse La 276 EF128
Oxtoby Way, SW16 223 DK96
Oxygen, E16 23 N10
Oyster Catchers Cl, E16 24 A8
Oyster Catcher Ter, Ilf. IG5
off Tiptree Cres 147 EN55
Oysterfields, St.Alb. AL3 64 CB19
Oystergate Wk, EC4
off Swan La 31 L1
Oyster La, Byfleet KT14 234 BK110
Oyster Row, E1 21 H9
Oyster Wf, SW11 40 A8
Ozolins Way, E16 23 N8

P

Pablo Neruda Cl, SE24
off Shakespeare Rd 183 DP84
Paceheath Cl, Rom. RM5 127 FD51
Pace Pl, E1 20 F9
PACHESHAM PARK, Lthd. KT22 253 CF116
Pachesham Pk, Lthd. KT22 253 CG117
Pacific Cl, Felt. TW14 197 BT88
Swanscombe DA10 212 FY85
Pacific Ms, SW9
off Saltoun Rd 183 DN84
Pacific Rd, E16 23 N8
● Pacific Wf, Bark. IG11 167 EP66
Pacific Wf, SE16
off Rotherhithe St 33 J3
Packet Boat La, Uxb. UB8 156 BH72
Packham Cl, Orp. BR6 228 EV104
Packham Ct, Wor.Pk. KT4
off Lavender Av 221 CW104
Packham Rd, Nthflt DA11 213 GF90
Packhorse Cl, St.Alb. AL4 65 CJ17
Packhorse La, Borwd. WD6 100 CS37
Ridge EN6 84 CR31
Packhorse Rd, Ger.Cr. SL9 134 AY58
Sevenoaks TN13 278 FC123
Packington Rd, W3 180 CQ76
Packington Sq, N1 9 J9
Packington St, N1 9 H8
Packmores Rd, SE9 207 ER85
Padbrook, Oxt. RH8 276 EG129
Padbrook Cl, Oxt. RH8 276 EH128
Padbury, SE17 43 N1
Padbury Cl, Felt. TW14 197 BR88
Padbury Ct, E2 20 B3
Padcroft Rd, West Dr. UB7 156 BK74
Paddenswick Rd, W6 181 CU76
Paddick Cl, Hodd. EN11 71 DZ16
PADDINGTON, W2 15 N7
⇌ Paddington 16 A8
⊖ Paddington 16 A8
Sch Paddington Acad, W9 15 K5
Paddington Cl, Hayes UB4 158 BX70
Paddington Grn, W2 16 B6
Sch Paddington Grn Prim Sch, W2 16 A5
Paddington St, W1 16 G6
Paddock, The, Brox. EN10 71 EA20
Chalfont St. Peter SL9 112 AY50
Dartford DA2 211 FS89
Datchet SL3 174 AV81
Guildford GU1 265 BD133
Hatfield AL10 67 CU16
Ickenham UB10 137 BP63
Westcott RH4 284 CB137
Westerham TN16 277 EQ126
Paddock Cl, SE3 47 P9
SE26 205 DX91
Paddock Cl, Farnboro. BR6
off State Fm Av 245 EP105
Hunsdon SG12 56 EK06
Northolt UB5 158 CA68
Oxted RH8 276 EF131
South Darenth DA4 230 FQ95
Watford WD19 98 BY44
Worcester Park KT4 220 CS102
Paddock Gdns, SE19
off Westow St 204 DS93
Paddock Mead, Harl. CM18 73 EQ20
Paddock Rd, NW2 141 CU62
Bexleyheath DA6 188 EY84
Ruislip HA4 138 BX62
Paddocks, The, NW7 119 CY51
Bookham KT23
off Leatherhead Rd 268 CB126
Chorleywood WD3 95 BF42
Cockfosters EN4 102 DF41
Hertford Heath SG13 54 DV12
New Haw KT15 234 BH110
Sevenoaks TN13 279 FK124
Stapleford Abbotts RM4 109 FF44
Virginia Water GU25 214 AY100
Welwyn Garden City AL7 52 DB08
Wembley HA9 140 CP61
Weybridge KT13 217 BS104
Sch Paddock Sch, SW15
off Priory La 181 CT84
Paddocks Cl, Ashtd. KT21 254 CL118
Cobham KT11 236 BW114
Harrow HA2 138 CB63
Orpington BR5 228 EX103
Paddocks End, Seer Grn HP9
off Orchard Rd 111 AR51
Paddocks Mead, Wok. GU21 248 AS116
Paddocks Retail Pk, Wey. KT13 234 BL111
Paddocks Rd, Guil. GU4 265 BA130
Paddocks Way, Ashtd. KT21 254 CL118
Chertsey KT16 216 BH102
Paddock Wk, Warl. CR6 258 DV119
Paddock Way, SW15 201 CW87
Ashley Green HP5 78 AT25
Chislehurst BR7 207 ER94
Hemel Hempstead HP1 61 BE20
Oxted RH8 276 EF131
Woking GU21 233 BB114
Padfield Ct, Wem. HA9
off Forty Av 140 CM62
Padfield Rd, SE5 43 J10
Padgets, The, Wal.Abb. EN9 89 ED34
Padley Cl, Chess. KT9 238 CM106
Padnall Ct, Rom. RM6
off Padnall Rd 148 EX55
Padnall Rd, Rom. RM6 148 EX56
Padstow Cl, Orp. BR6 245 ET105
Slough SL3 174 AY76
Padstow Rd, Enf. EN2 103 DP40
Padstow Wk, Felt. TW14 197 BT88
Padua Rd, SE20 224 DW95
Pagden St, SW8 41 K6
Pageant Av, NW9 118 CR53
Pageant Cl, Til. RM18 193 GJ81
Pageant Cres, SE16 33 M2
Pageantmaster Ct, EC4 18 G9
Pageant Rd, St.Alb. AL1 65 CD21
Pageant Wk, Croy. CR0 224 DS104
Page Av, Wem. HA9 140 CQ62
Page Cl, Bean DA2 211 FW90
Dagenham RM9 148 EY64
Hampton TW12 198 BY93
Harrow HA3 140 CM58
Page Cres, Croy. CR0 241 DN106
Erith DA8 189 FF80
Page Grn Rd, N15 144 DU57
Page Grn Ter, N15 144 DT57
Page Heath La, Brom. BR1 226 EK97
Page Heath Vil, Brom. BR1 226 EK97
Page Hill, Ware SG12 54 DV05
Pagehurst Rd, Croy. CR0 224 DV101
Page Meadow, NW7 119 CU52
Page Rd, Felt. TW14 197 BR86
Hertford SG13 54 DU9
Pages Cft, Berk. HP4 60 AU17
Pages Hill, N10 120 DG54
Pages La, N10 120 DG54
Romford RM3 128 FP54
Uxbridge UB8 156 BJ65
Page St, NW7 119 CU53
SW1 29 P8
Pages Wk, SE1 31 N8
Pages Yd, W4 off Church St 180 CS79
Paget Av, Sutt. SM1 222 DD104
Paget Cl, Hmptn. TW12 199 CD91
Paget Gdns, Chis. BR7 227 EP95
Paget La, Islw. TW7 179 CD83
Paget Pl, Kings.T. KT2 200 CQ93
Thames Ditton KT7
off Brooklands Rd 219 CG102
Paget Ri, SE18 187 EN80
Paget Rd, N16 144 DR60
Ilford IG1 147 EP63
Slough SL3 175 AZ77
Uxbridge UB10 157 BQ70
Paget St, EC1 18 G2
Paget Ter, SE18 187 EN79
Pagette Way, Bad.Dene RM17 192 GA77
Pagitts Gro, Barn. EN4 102 DB39
Paglesfield, Hutt. CM13 131 GC44
Pagnell St, SE14 45 N4
Pagoda Av, Rich. TW9 180 CM83
Pagoda Gdns, SE3 46 G9
Pagoda Gro, SE27 204 DQ89
Pagoda Vista, Rich. TW9 180 CM82
Paignton Cl, Rom. RM3 128 FK53
Paignton Rd, N15 144 DS58
Ruislip HA4 137 BU62
Paines Brook Rd, Rom. RM3
off Paines Brook Way 128 FM51
Paines Brook Way, Rom. RM3 128 FM51
Paines Cl, Pnr. HA5 138 BY55
Painesfield Dr, Cher. KT16 216 BG103
Paines La, Pnr. HA5 116 BY53
Pains Cl, Mitch. CR4 223 DH96
Jct Painshill, Cob. KT11 235 BT113
Pains Hill, Oxt. RH8 276 EJ132
★ Painshill Park, Cob. KT11 235 BS114
Painsthorpe Rd, N16
off Oldfield Rd 144 DS62
Painters Ash La, Nthflt DA11 212 GD90
Sch Painters Ash Prim Sch, Nthflt DA11 off Masefield Rd 212 GD90
Painters La, Enf. EN3 105 DY35
Painters Ms, SE16
off Macks Rd 32 D8
Painters Rd, Ilf. IG2 147 ET55
Paisley Rd, N22 121 DP53
Carshalton SM5 222 DD102

Paisley Ter, Cars. SM5 222 DD101
Sch Pakeman Prim Sch, N7
off Hornsey Rd 143 DM62
Pakeman St, N7 143 DM62
Pakenham Cl, SW12
off Balham Pk Rd 202 DG88
Pakenham St, WC1 18 D3
Pakes Way, They.B. CM16 107 ES37
Palace Av, W8 27 M3
Palace Cl, E9 11 P5
Kings Langley WD4 80 BM30
Slough SL1 153 AM74
Palace Ct, NW3 5 M2
W2 15 L10
Harrow HA3 140 CL58
Palace Ct Gdns, N10 143 DJ55
Palace Dr, Wey. KT13 217 BP104
🔒 Palace Ex, Enf. EN2 104 DR42
🔒 Palace Gdns, Enf. EN2 104 DR42
Palace Gdns, Buck.H. IG9 124 EK46
Palace Gdns Ms, W8 27 K2
Palace Gdns Ter, W8 27 K2
Palace Gate, W8 27 N5
Palace Gates Rd, N22 121 DK53
Palace Grn, W8 27 M4
Croydon CR0 243 DZ108
Palace Gro, SE19 204 DT94
Bromley BR1 226 EH95
Palace Ms, E17 145 DZ56
SW1 29 H9
SW6 39 H5
● Palace of Industry,
Wem. HA9
off Fulton Rd 140 CN63
Palace Par, E17 145 DZ56
Palace Pl, SW1 29 L6
Palace Rd, N8 143 DK57
N11 121 DL52
SE19 204 DT94
SW2 203 DM88
Bromley BR1 226 EH95
East Molesey KT8 219 CD97
Kingston upon Thames KT1 219 CK98
Ruislip HA4 138 BY63
Westerham TN16 261 EN121
Palace Rd Est, SW2 203 DM88
Palace Sq, SE19 204 DT94
Palace St, SW1 29 L6
Palace Vw, SE12 206 EG89
Bromley BR1 226 EG97
Croydon CR0 243 DZ105
Palace Vw Rd, E4 123 EB50
Palace Way, Wey. KT13
off Palace Dr 217 BP104
Woking GU22 249 BB120
Palamos Rd, E10 145 EA60
Palatine Av, N16 9 P1
Palatine Rd, N16 9 P1
Palemead Cl, SW6 38 C6
Palermo Rd, NW10 161 CU68
Palestine Gro, SW19 222 DD95
Palewell Cl, Orp. BR5 228 EV96
Palewell Common Dr, SW14 200 CR85
Palewell Pk, SW14 200 CR85
Paley Gdns, Loug. IG10 107 EP41
Palfrey Cl, St.Alb. AL3 65 CD18
Palfrey Pl, SW8 42 D4
Palgrave Av, Sthl. UB1 158 CA73
Palgrave Gdns, NW1 16 D4
Palgrave Ho, NW3 6 E2
Palgrave Rd, W12 181 CT76
Palissy St, E2 20 A3
Palladian Circ, Green. DA9 191 FW84
Palladino Ho, SW17
off Laurel Cl 202 DE92
Palladio Ct, SW18
off Mapleton Rd 202 DB86
Pallant Way, Orp. BR6 227 EN104
Pallas Rd, Hem.H. HP2 62 BM18
Pallet Way, SE18 186 EL81
Palliser Dr, Rain. RM13 169 FG71
Palliser Rd, W14 26 E10
Chalfont St. Giles HP8 112 AU48
Pallister Ter, SW15
off Roehampton Vale 201 CT90
Pall Mall, SW1 29 M3
Pall Mall E, SW1 29 P2
Palmar Cres, Bexh. DA7 188 FA83
Palmar Rd, Bexh. DA7 188 FA82
Palmarsh Rd, Orp. BR5
off Wotton Grn 228 EX98
Palm Av, Sid. DA14 208 EX93
Palm Cl, E10 145 EB62
Palmeira Rd, Bexh. DA7 188 EX83
Palmer Av, Bushey WD23 98 CB43
Gravesend DA12 213 GK91
Sutton SM3 239 CW105
Palmer Cl, Hert. SG14 54 DQ07
Horley RH6 290 DF145
Hounslow TW5 178 CA81
Northolt UB5 158 BY65
Redhill RH1 288 DG135
West Wickham BR4 225 ED104
Palmer Cres, Kings.T. KT1 220 CL97
Ottershaw KT16 233 BD107
Palmer Dr, Brom. BR1 227 EP98
Palmer Gdns, Barn. EN5 101 CX43
Palmer Ho, SE14
off Lubbock St 45 J5
Palmer Pl, N7 8 E3
Palmer Rd, E13 24 B5
Dagenham RM8 148 EX60
Hertford SG14 54 DR07
Palmers Av, Grays RM17 192 GC78
Coll Palmer's Coll,
Grays RM17
off Chadwell Rd 192 GE77
Palmers Dr, Grays RM17 192 GC77
Palmersfield Rd, Bans. SM7 240 DA114
PALMERS GREEN, N13 121 DN48
⇌ Palmers Green 121 DM49
Sch Palmers Grn High Sch,
N21 off Hoppers Rd 121 DN47
Palmers Gro, Lwr Naze. EN9 72 EF22
West Molesey KT8 218 CA98
Palmers Hill, Epp. CM16 92 EU29
Palmers La, Enf. EN1, EN3 104 DV39
Palmer's Lo, Guil. GU2
off Old Palace Rd 280 AV135
Palmers Moor La, Iver SL0 156 BG70
Palmers Orchard, Shore. TN14 247 FF111
Palmers Pas, SW14
off Palmers Rd 180 CQ83
Palmers Rd, E2 21 K1
N11 121 DJ50
SW14 180 CQ83
SW16 223 DM96
Borehamwood WD6 100 CP39
Palmerston Av, Slou. SL3 174 AV76
Palmerston Cl, Red. RH1
off Reed Dr 288 DG137
Welwyn Garden City AL8 51 CW09
Woking GU21 233 AZ114
Palmerston Cres, N13 121 DM50
SE18 187 EQ79
Palmerstone Ct, Vir.W. GU25
off Sandhills La 214 AY99
Palmerston Gdns, Grays
RM20 191 FX78
Palmerston Gro, SW19 202 DA94
Palmerston Ho, SW11
off Strasburg Rd 41 H7
W8 27 J3
Palmerston Rd, E7 146 EH64
E17 145 DZ56
N22 121 DM52
NW6 5 J6
SW14 180 CQ84
SW19 202 DA94
W3 180 CQ76
Buckhurst Hill IG9 124 EH47
Carshalton SM5 240 DF105
Croydon CR0 224 DR99
Grays RM20 191 FX78
Harrow HA3 139 CF55
Hounslow TW3 178 CC81
Orpington BR6 245 EQ105
Rainham RM13 170 FJ68
Sutton SM1 off Vernon Rd 240 DC106
Twickenham TW2 199 CE86
Palmerston Way, SW8 41 K5
Palmer St, SW1 29 N5
Palmers Way, Chsht EN8 89 DY29
Palm Gro, W5 180 CL76
Guildford GU1 264 AW129
Palm Rd, Rom. RM7 149 FC57
Pamela Av, Hem.H. HP3 62 BM23
Pamela Gdns, Pnr. HA5 137 BV57
Pamela Wk, E8 10 C8
Pampisford Rd, Pur. CR8 241 DN111
South Croydon CR2 241 DP108
Pams Way, Epsom KT19 238 CR106
Pancake La, Hem.H. HP2 63 BR21
Pancras La, EC4 19 K9
Pancras Rd, NW1 7 N10
Pancras Way, E3 12 A10
Pancroft, Abridge RM4 108 EV41
Pandian Way, NW1 7 N4
Pandora Rd, NW6 5 J4
Panfield Ms, Ilf. IG2 147 EN58
Panfield Rd, SE2 188 EU76
Pangbourne Av, W10 14 B6
Pangbourne Dr, Stan. HA7 117 CK50
Pangbourne Ho, N7 7 P3
Panhard Pl, Sthl. UB1 158 CB73
Pank Av, Barn. EN5 102 DC43
Pankhurst Av, E16 36 B2
Pankhurst Cl, SE14 45 J5
Isleworth TW7 179 CF83
Pankhurst Rd, Walt. KT12 218 BW101
Panmuir Rd, SW20 221 CV95
Panmure Cl, N5 9 H1
Panmure Rd, SE26 204 DV90
Pannells Cl, Cher. KT16 215 BF102
Pannells Ct, Guil. GU1 280 AX135
Hounslow TW5 178 BZ79
Panoramic, The, NW3 6 D2
PANSHANGER, Welw.G.C. AL7 52 DB09
Panshanger Dr, Welw.G.C. AL7 52 DB09
Panshanger La, Cole Grn SG14 52 DF10
Sch Panshanger Prim Sch, Welw.G.C.
AL7 off Daniells 52 DA08
Pansy Gdns, W12 161 CU73
Panters, Swan. BR8 209 FF94
Panther Dr, NW10 140 CR64
Pantile Rd, Wey. KT13 235 BR105
Pantile Row, Slou. SL3 175 BA77
Pantiles, The, NW11 141 CZ56
Bexleyheath DA7 188 EZ80
Bromley BR1 226 EL97
Bushey Heath WD23 117 CD45
Pantiles Cl, N13 121 DP50
Woking GU21 248 AV118
🔒 Pantile Wk, Uxb. UB8
off The Pavilions 156 BJ66
Panton Cl, Croy. CR0 223 DP102
Panton St, SW1 29 N1
Panxworth Rd, Hem.H. HP3 62 BL22
Panyer All, EC4 19 J9
Papercourt La, Ripley GU23 249 BF122
Paper Ms, Dor. RH4 285 CH135
Papermill Cl, Cars. SM5 240 DG105
Paper Mill La, Dart. DA1
off Lawson Rd 190 FK84
Sch Papillon Ho Sch, Tad. KT20
off Pebble Cl 270 CS129
Papillons Wk, SE3 47 N9
Papworth Gdns, N7 8 D3
Papworth Way, SW2 203 DN87
Parade, The, SW11 40 F4
Aveley RM15 190 FQ75
Brentwood CM14
off Kings Rd 130 FW48
Burgh Heath KT20 255 CY119
Carpenders Park WD19 116 BY48
Carshalton SM5
off Beynon Rd 240 DF106
Claygate KT10 237 CE107
Dartford DA1
off Crayford Way 209 FF85
Epsom KT17, KT18 238 CR113
Epsom Common KT18
off Spa Dr 238 CN114
Hampton TW12
off Hampton Rd 199 CD92
Romford RM3 128 FP51
South Oxhey WD19
off Prestwick Rd 116 BX48
Sunbury-on-Thames TW16 197 BT94
Virginia Water GU25 214 AX100
Watford WD17 97 BV41
Windsor SL4 173 AK81
Parade Ms, SE27
off Norwood Rd 203 DP89
Paradise, Hem.H. HP2 62 BK21
Paradise Cl, Chsht EN7 88 DV28
Paradise Pas, N7 8 E3
Paradise Path, SE28
off Birchdene Dr 168 EU74
Paradise Pl, SE18 37 H9
Paradise Rd, SW4 42 A8
Richmond TW9 199 CK85
Waltham Abbey EN9 89 EC34
Paradise Row, E2 20 F2
Paradise St, SE16 32 E5
Paradise Wk, SW3 40 E2
Paragon, The, SE3 47 M8
Paragon Cl, E16 23 N8
Paragon Gro, Surb. KT5 220 CM100
Paragon Ms, SE1 31 M8
Paragon Pl, SE3 47 M8
Surbiton KT5
off Berrylands Rd 220 CM100
Paragon Rd, E9 10 F5
Parbury Ri, Chess. KT9 238 CL107
Parbury Rd, SE23 205 DY86
Parchment Cl, Amer. HP6 77 AS37
Parchmore Rd, Th.Hth. CR7 223 DP96
Parchmore Way, Th.Hth. CR7 223 DP96
Par Cl, Hert. SG13
off Birdie Way 54 DV08
Sch Pardes Ho Gram Sch, N3
off Hendon La 119 CZ54
Sch Pardes Ho Prim Sch, N3
off Hendon La 119 CZ54
Pardoe Rd, E10 145 EB59
Pardoner St, SE1 31 M6
Pardon St, EC1 19 H4
Pares Cl, Wok. GU21 248 AX116
Parfett St, E1 20 D7
Parfitt Cl, NW3
off North End 142 DC61
Parfour Dr, Ken. CR8 258 DQ116
Parfrey St, W6 38 B2
Parham Dr, Ilf. IG2 147 EP58
Parham Way, N10 121 DJ54
Sch Paringdon Jun Sch, Harl.
CM18 off Paringdon Rd 73 ER19
Paringdon Rd, Harl.
CM18, CM19 73 EP19
Paris Gdn, SE1 30 G2
Sch Parish Ch C of E Junior, Inf &
Nurs Schs, Croy. CR0
off Warrington Rd 223 DP104
Parish Cl, Horn. RM11 149 FH61
Watford WD25 off Crown Ri 82 BX34
Sch Parish C of E Prim Sch, Brom.
BR1 off London La 206 EG94
Parish Gate Dr, Sid. DA15 207 ES86
Parish La, SE20 205 DX93
Farnham Common SL2 133 AP61
Parish Ms, SE20 205 DX94
Parish Wf, SE18 37 H8
Park, The, N6 142 DG58
NW11 142 DB60
SE19 204 DS94
SE23 off Park Hill 204 DW88
W5 159 CK74
Bookham KT23 252 CA123
Carshalton SM5 240 DF106
St. Albans AL1 65 CG18
Sidcup DA14 208 EU92
Park App, Well. DA16 188 EV84
Park Av, E6 167 EN67
E15 13 J5
N3 120 DB53
N13 121 DN48
N18 122 DU49
N22 121 DL54
NW2 161 CV65
NW10 160 CM69
NW11 142 DB60
SW14 180 CR84
Barking IG11 167 EQ65
Bromley BR1 206 EF93
Bushey WD23 98 BZ40
Carshalton SM5 240 DG107
Caterham CR3 258 DS124
Chorleywood WD3 96 BG43
Egham TW20 195 BC93
Enfield EN1 104 DS44
Farnborough BR6 227 EM104
Gravesend DA12 213 GJ88
Grays RM20 191 FU79
Harlow CM17 74 EW18
Hounslow TW3 198 CB86
Hutton CM13 131 GC46
Ilford IG1 147 EN61
Mitcham CR4 203 DH94
Northfleet DA11 212 GE88
Orpington BR6 228 EU103
Potters Bar EN6 86 DC34
Radlett WD7 83 CH33
Redhill RH1 288 DF142
Ruislip HA4 137 BR58
St. Albans AL1 65 CG19
Southall UB1 158 CA74
Staines TW18 195 BF93
Upminster RM14 151 FS59
Watford WD18 97 BU42
West Wickham BR4 225 EC103
Woodford Green IG8 124 EH50
Wraysbury TW19 194 AX85
Park Av E, Epsom KT17 239 CU107
Park Av Ms, Mitch. CR4
off Park Av 203 DH94
Park Av N, N8 143 DK55
NW10 141 CV64
Park Av Rd, N17 122 DV52
Park Av S, N8 143 DK56
Park Av W, Epsom KT17 239 CU107
PARK BARN, Guil. GU2 264 AS133
Park Barn Dr, Guil. GU2 264 AS132
Park Barn E, Guil. GU2 264 AT133
Park Boul, Rom. RM2 127 FF53
Park Cen Bldg, E3
off Fairfield Rd 12 B10
Park Chase, Guil. GU1 264 AY134
Wembley HA9 140 CM63
Park Cliff Rd, Green. DA9 191 FW84
Park Cl, E9 11 H8
NW2 141 CV62
NW10 160 CM69
SW1 28 E5
W4 180 CR78
W14 27 H6
Brookmans Park AL9 85 CZ26
Bushey WD23 98 BX41
Carshalton SM5 240 DF107
Esher KT10 236 BZ107
Fetcham KT22 253 CD124
Hampton TW12 218 CC95
Harrow HA3 117 CE53
Hatfield AL9 67 CW17
Hounslow TW3 198 CC85
Kingston upon Thames KT2 220 CN95
New Haw KT15 234 BH110
North Weald Bassett CM16 92 FA27
Oxted RH8 276 EF128
Rickmansworth WD3 115 BP49
Strood Green RH3 286 CP139
Walton-on-Thames KT12 217 BT103
Windsor SL4 173 AR82
Park Copse, Dor. RH5 285 CK136
Park Cor, Coln.Hth AL4 66 CP23
Windsor SL4 173 AL83
Park Cor Dr, E.Hors. KT24 267 BS128
Park Cor Rd, Sthflt DA13 212 FZ91
Park Ct, SE21 204 DQ90
SE26 204 DV93
SW11 41 J6
Bookham KT23 268 CA125
Hampton Wick KT1 219 CJ95
Harlow CM20 57 ER14
New Malden KT3 220 CR98
Wembley HA9 140 CL64
West Byfleet KT14 234 BG113
Woking GU22 off Park Dr 249 AZ118
Park Cres, N3 120 DB52
W1 17 J5
Elstree WD6 100 CM41
Enfield EN2 104 DR42
Erith DA8 189 FC79
Harrow HA3 117 CE53
Hornchurch RM11 149 FG59
Twickenham TW2 199 CD88
Park Cres Ms E, W1 17 K5
Park Cres Ms W, W1 17 J6
Park Cres Rd, Erith DA8 189 FD79
Park Cft, Edg. HA8 118 CQ53
Parkcroft Rd, SE12 206 EF87
Park Dale, N11 121 DK51
Parkdale Cres, Wor.Pk. KT4 220 CR104
Parkdale Rd, SE18 187 ES78
Park Dr, N21 104 DQ44
NW11 142 DB60
SE7 186 EL79
SW14 180 CR84
W3 180 CN76
Ashtead KT21 254 CN118
Dagenham RM10 149 FC62
Harrow Weald HA3 117 CE51
Hatfield Heath CM22 59 FH05
North Harrow HA2 138 CA59
Potters Bar EN6 86 DA31
Romford RM1 149 FD56
Upminster RM14 150 FQ63
Weybridge KT13 235 BP106
Woking GU22 249 AZ118
Park Dr Cl, SE7 186 EL78
Park E Bldg, E3
off Fairfield Rd 12 B10
Park End, NW3 6 D1
Bromley BR1 226 EF95
Park End Rd, Rom. RM1 149 FE56
Parker Av, Hert. SG14 54 DR07
Tilbury RM18 193 GJ81
Parker Cl, E16 36 G3
Carshalton SM5 240 DF107
Parker Ms, WC2 18 B8
Parke Rd, SW13 181 CU81
Sunbury-on-Thames TW16 217 BU98
Parker Rd, Croy. CR0 242 DQ105
Grays RM17 192 FZ78
Parkers Cl, Ashtd. KT21 254 CL119
Parkers Hill, Ashtd. KT21 254 CL119
Parkers La, Ashtd. KT21 254 CL119
Parkers Row, SE1 32 B5
Parker St, E16 36 G3
WC2 18 B8
Watford WD24 97 BV39
Parkes Rd, Chig. IG7 125 ES50
Park Fm Cl, N2 142 DC55
Pinner HA5 137 BV57
Park Fm Rd, Brom. BR1 226 EK95
Kingston upon Thames KT2 200 CL94
Upminster RM14 150 FM64
Parkfield, Chorl. WD3 95 BF42
Sevenoaks TN15 279 FM123
Parkfield Av, SW14 180 CS84
Amersham HP6 77 AR37
Feltham TW13 197 BU90
Harrow HA2 116 CC54
Hillingdon UB10 157 BP69
Northolt UB5 158 BX68
Parkfield Cl, Edg. HA8 118 CP51
Northolt UB5 158 BY68
Parkfield Cres, Felt. TW13 197 BU90
Harrow HA2 116 CC54
Ruislip HA4 138 BY62
Parkfield Dr, Nthlt. UB5 158 BX68
Parkfield Gdns, Har. HA2 138 CB55
Sch Parkfield Prim Sch, NW4
off Park Rd 141 CV59
Parkfield Rd, NW10 161 CU66
SE14 45 N6
Feltham TW13 197 BU90
Harrow HA2 138 CC62
Ickenham UB10 137 BP61
Northolt UB5 158 BY68
Parkfields, SW15 181 CW84
Croydon CR0 225 DZ102
Oxshott KT22 237 CD111
Roydon CM19 72 EH16
Welwyn Garden City AL8 51 CX09
Parkfields Av, NW9 140 CR60
SW20 221 CV95
Parkfields Cl, Cars. SM5 240 DG105
Parkfields Rd, Kings.T. KT2 200 CM92
Parkfield St, N1 8 F10
Parkfield Vw, Pot.B. EN6 86 DB32
Parkfield Way, Brom. BR2 227 EM100
Park Gdns, NW9 140 CP55
Erith DA8 off Valley Rd 189 FD77
Kingston upon Thames KT2 200 CM92
Park Gate, N2 142 DD55
N21 121 DM45
Parkgate, SE3 186 EF83
Park Gate, W5 159 CK71
Parkgate, Burn. SL1 152 AJ70
Parkgate Av, Barn. EN4 102 DC39
Parkgate Cl, Kings.T. KT2
off Warboys App 200 CP93
Park Gate Ct, Wok. GU22
off Constitution Hill 248 AY118
Parkgate Cres, Barn. EN4 102 DC40
Parkgate Gdns, SW14 200 CR85
Sch Parkgate Inf & Nurs Sch, Wat.
WD24 off Northfield Gdns 98 BW37
Sch Parkgate Jun Sch, Wat. WD24
off Southwold Rd 98 BW37
Parkgate Ms, N6 143 DJ59
Parkgate Rd, SW11 40 C5
Orpington BR6 247 FB105
Reigate RH2 288 DB135
Wallington SM6 240 DG106
Watford WD24 98 BW37
Park Gates, Har. HA2 138 CA63
Park Gra Gdns, Sev. TN13
off Solefields Rd 279 FJ127
Park Grn, Bkhm KT23 252 CA124
Park Gro, E15 13 N8
N11 121 DK52
Bexleyheath DA7 189 FC84
Bromley BR1 226 EH95
Chalfont St. Giles HP8 94 AX41
Park Gro, Edg. HA8 118 CM50
Knotty Green HP9 110 AJ48
Park Gro Rd, E11 146 EE61
Park Hall Rd, N2 142 DE56
SE21 204 DQ90
Reigate RH2 272 DA132
● Park Hall Trd Est, SE21 204 DQ90
Parkham Ct, Brom. BR2 226 EE96
Parkham St, SW11 40 B7
Park Hts, Wok. GU22
off Constitution Hill 248 AY118
Sch Park High Sch, Stan. HA7
off Thistlecroft Gdns 117 CK54
Park Hill, SE23 204 DV89
SW4 203 DK85
W5 159 CK71
Bromley BR1 226 EL98
Carshalton SM5 240 DE107
Harlow CM17 58 EV12
Loughton IG10 106 EK43
Richmond TW10 200 CM86
Park Hill Cl, Cars. SM5 240 DE106
Parkhill Cl, Horn. RM12 150 FJ62
Park Hill Ct, SW17
off Beeches Rd 202 DF90
Sch Parkhill Inf & Jun Schs, Ilf. IG5
off Lord Av 147 EN55
Sch Park Hill Inf Sch, Croy. CR0
off Stanhope Rd 224 DS104
Sch Park Hill Jun Sch, Croy. CR0
off Stanhope Rd 224 DS104
Park Hill Ri, Croy. CR0 224 DS103
Parkhill Rd, E4 123 EC46
NW3 6 F4
Bexley DA5 208 EZ87
Park Hill Rd, Brom. BR2 226 EE96
Croydon CR0 224 DS103
Epsom KT17 239 CT111
Parkhill Rd, Hem.H. HP1 62 BH20
Sidcup DA15 207 ER90
Park Hill Rd, Wall. SM6 241 DH108
Sch Park Hill Sch, Kings.T. KT2
off Queens Rd 200 CN94
Parkhill Wk, NW3 6 F3
Parkholme Rd, E8 10 B4
Park Homes, Lon.Col. AL2
off Peters Av 83 CJ26
Park Horsley, E.Hors. KT24 267 BU129
◆ Parkhouse 67 CT17
Park Ho, N21 121 DM45
Parkhouse Ct, Hat. AL10 66 CS17
Park Ho Dr, Reig. RH2 287 CZ136
Park Ho Gdns, Twick. TW1 199 CJ86
Parkhouse St, SE5 43 M4
Parkhurst, Epsom KT19 238 CQ110
Parkhurst Gdns, Bex. DA5 208 FA87
Parkhurst Gro, Horl. RH6 290 DE147
Parkhurst Ho, W12 14 A9
Parkhurst Rd, E12 147 EN63
E17 145 DY56
N7 8 A1
N11 120 DG49
N17 122 DU54
N22 121 DM52
Bexley DA5 208 FA87
Guildford GU2 264 AU133
Hertford SG14 53 DP08
Horley RH6 290 DE147
Sutton SM1 240 DD105
● Park Ind Est, Frog. AL2 83 CE27
Parkinson Ho, SW1
off Tachbrook St 29 N10
Parkland Av, Rom. RM1 149 FE55
Slough SL3 174 AX77
Upminster RM14 150 FP64
Parkland Cl, Chig. IG7 125 EQ48
Hoddesdon EN11 55 EB14
Sevenoaks TN13 279 FJ129
Parkland Dr, St.Alb. AL3 64 CA21
Parkland Gdns, SW19 201 CX88
Parkland Gro, Ashf. TW15 196 BN91
Parkland Mead, Brom. BR1
off Gardenia Rd 227 EP97
Parkland Rd, N22 121 DM54
Ashford TW15 196 BN91
Woodford Green IG8 124 EG52
Parklands, N6 143 DH59
Addlestone KT15 234 BJ106
Bookham KT23 252 CA123
Chigwell IG7 125 EQ48
Coopersale CM16 92 EX29
Guildford GU2 264 AU130
Hemel Hempstead HP1 61 BF18
North Holmwood RH5 285 CH140
Oxted RH8 276 EE131
Shere GU5 282 BN141
Surbiton KT5 220 CM99
Waltham Abbey EN9 89 ED32
Parklands Cl, SW14 200 CQ85
Barnet EN4 102 DD38
Ilford IG2 147 EQ59
Parklands Ct, Houns. TW5 178 BX82
Parklands Dr, N3 141 CY55
Parklands Gro, Islw. TW7 179 CF81
Sch Parklands Inf Sch, Rom. RM1
off Havering Rd 127 FD54
Sch Parklands Jun Sch, Rom. RM1
off Havering Rd 149 FD55
Parklands Pl, Guil. GU1 265 BB134
Parklands Rd, SW16 203 DH92
Parklands Way, Wor.Pk. KT4 220 CS104
Parkland Wk, N4 143 DM59
N6 143 DK59
N10 143 DH56
Park La, E15 12 G8
N9 122 DT48
N17 122 DU52
W1 29 H3
Ashtead KT21 254 CM118
Aveley RM15 171 FR74
Banstead SM7 256 DD118
Beaconsfield HP9 111 AM54
Broxbourne EN10 71 DY19
Burnham SL1 133 AL64
Carshalton SM5 240 DG105
Chadwell Heath RM6 148 EX58
Cheshunt EN7 88 DU26
Colney Heath AL4 66 CP23
Coulsdon CR5 257 DK121
Cranford TW5 177 BU80
Croydon CR0 224 DR104

Park La, Elm Pk RM12 169 FH65
Greenhithe DA9 211 FU86
Guildford GU4 265 BC131
Harefield UB9 114 BG53
Harlow CM20 57 ER13
Harrow HA2 138 CB62
Hayes UB4 157 BS71
Hemel Hempstead HP1, HP2 62 BK21
Hornchurch RM11 149 FG58
Horton SL3 175 BA83
Reigate RH2 287 CY135
Richmond TW9 179 CK84
Seal TN15 279 FN121
Sevenoaks TN13 279 FJ124
Slough SL3 174 AV76
Stanmore HA7 117 CG48
Sutton SM3 239 CY107
Swanley BR8 230 FJ96
Teddington TW11 199 CF93
Wallington SM6 240 DG105
Waltham Cross EN8 89 DX33
Wembley HA9 140 CL64
Wormley EN10 70 DV22
Park La Cl, N17 122 DU52
Park La E, Reig. RH2 288 DA136
Park La Paradise, Chsht EN7 70 DU24
Sch **Park La Prim Sch**, Wem. HA9
off Park La 140 CL63
PARK LANGLEY, Beck. BR3 225 EC99
Park Lawn, Farn.Royal SL2 153 AQ69
Parklawn Av, Epsom KT18 238 CP113
Horley RH6 290 DF146
Park Lawn Rd, Wey. KT13 235 BQ105
Park Lawns, Wem. HA9 140 CM63
Parklea Cl, NW9 118 CS53
Parkleigh Rd, SW19 222 DB96
Park Ley Rd, Wold. CR3 259 DX120
Parkleys, Rich. TW10 199 CK91
Park Lo Av, West Dr. UB7 176 BM75
Park Mans, SW1
off Knightsbridge 28 E5
SW8 42 B2
Parkmead, SW15 201 CV86
Park Mead, Harl. CM20 57 EP14
Harrow HA2 138 CB62
Parkmead, Loug. IG10 107 EN43
Park Mead, Sid. DA15 208 EV85
Parkmead Gdns, NW7 119 CT51
Park Meadow, Hat. AL9 67 CW17
Park Ms, SE10 47 M1
SE24 *off Croxted Rd* 204 DQ86
Chislehurst BR7 207 EP93
East Molesey KT8 218 CC98
Hatfield AL9 67 CW16
Oxted RH8 276 EF128
Rainham RM13 169 FG65
Parkmore Cl, Wdf.Grn. IG8 124 EG49
Park Nook Gdns, Enf. EN2 104 DR37
Parkpale La, Bet. RH3 286 CN139
Park Par, NW10 161 CT68
Park Piazza, SE13
off Highfield Cl 205 ED86
Park Pl, E14 34 A2
N1 9 M8
SW1 29 L3
W3 180 CN77
W5 159 CK74
Amersham HP6 94 AT38
Gravesend DA12 213 GJ86
Hampton Hill TW12 198 CC93
Park Street AL2 83 CD27
Seer Green HP9 111 AR50
Sevenoaks TN13 278 FD123
Wembley HA9 140 CM63
Woking GU22
off Hill Vw Rd 249 AZ118
Park Pl Vil, W2 15 P6
Sch **Park Prim Sch**, E15 13 M6
Park Ridings, N8 143 DN55
Park Ri, SE23 205 DY88
Harrow HA3 117 CE53
Leatherhead KT22 253 CH121
Northchurch HP4 60 AS17
Park Ri Cl, Lthd. KT22 253 CH121
Park Ri Rd, SE23 205 DY88
Park Rd, E6 166 EJ67
E10 145 EA60
E12 146 EH60
E15 13 N8
E17 145 DZ57
N2 142 DD55
N8 143 DJ56
N11 121 DK52
N14 121 DK45
N15 143 DP56
N18 122 DT49
NW1 16 C2
NW4 141 CU59
NW8 16 C2
NW9 140 CR59
NW10 160 CS67
SE25 224 DS98
SW19 202 DD93
W4 180 CQ80
W7 159 CF73
Albury GU5 282 BL140
Amersham HP6 94 AT37
Ashford TW15 197 BP92
Ashtead KT21 254 CL118
Banstead SM7 256 DB115
Beckenham BR3 205 DZ94
Brentwood CM14 130 FV46
Bromley BR1 226 EH95
Bushey WD23 98 CA44
Caterham CR3 258 DS123
Chesham HP5 76 AP31
Chislehurst BR7 207 EP93
Dartford DA1 210 FN87
East Molesey KT8 218 CC98
Egham TW20 195 BA91
Enfield EN3 105 DY36
Esher KT10 236 CB105
Feltham TW13 198 BX91
Gravesend DA11 213 GH88
Grays RM17 192 GB78
Guildford GU1 264 AX134
Hackbridge SM6 223 DH103
Hampton Hill TW12 198 CB91
Hampton Wick KT1 219 CJ95
Hayes UB4 157 BS71
Hemel Hempstead HP1 62 BJ22
Park Rd, Hert. SG13 54 DS09
High Barnet EN5 101 CZ42
Hoddesdon EN11 71 EA17
Hounslow TW3 178 CC84
Ilford IG1 147 ER62
Isleworth TW7 179 CH81
Kenley CR8 257 DP115
Kingston upon Thames KT2 200 CM92
New Barnet EN4 102 DE42
New Malden KT3 220 CR98
Northaw EN6 86 DG30
Orpington BR5 228 EW99
Oxted RH8 276 EF128
Radlett WD7 99 CG35
Redhill RH1 272 DF132
Richmond TW10 200 CM86
Rickmansworth WD3 114 BK45
Shepperton TW17 216 BN102
Slough SL2 153 AQ68
Stanwell TW19 196 BH86
Sunbury-on-Thames TW16 197 BV94
Surbiton KT5 220 CM99
Sutton SM3 239 CY107
Swanley BR8 229 FF97
Swanscombe DA10 212 FY86
Teddington TW11 199 CF93
Twickenham TW1 199 CJ86
Uxbridge UB8 156 BL66
Wallington SM6 241 DH106
Waltham Cross EN8 89 DX33
Ware SG12 54 DV05
Warlingham CR6 244 EE114
Watford WD17 97 BU39
Wembley HA0 160 CL65
Woking GU22 249 BA117
Park Rd E, W3 180 CP75
Uxbridge UB10 156 BK68
Park Rd N, W3 180 CP75
W4 180 CR78
Park Row, SE10 46 G2
PARK ROYAL, NW10 160 CN69
⊖ **Park Royal** 160 CN70
H **Park Royal Cen for Mental Health**, NW10 160 CQ68
● **Park Royal Metro Cen**, NW10 160 CP70
Park Royal Rd, NW10 160 CQ69
W3 160 CQ69
Sch **Park Sch, The**, Wok. GU22
off Onslow Cres 249 BA117
Sch **Park Sch for Girls**, Ilf. IG1
off Park Av 147 EP60
Parkshot, Rich. TW9 180 CL84
Parkside, N3 120 DB53
NW2 141 CU62
NW7 119 CU51
SE3 47 L4
SW19 201 CX91
Buckhurst Hill IG9 124 EH47
Chalfont St. Peter SL9
off Lower Rd 135 AZ56
Park Side, Epp. CM16 92 EV29
Parkside, Grays RM16 192 GE76
Halstead TN14 246 EZ113
Hampton Hill TW12 199 CD92
Matching Tye CM17 59 FE12
New Haw KT15 234 BH110
Potters Bar EN6
off High St 86 DC32
Sidcup DA14 208 EV89
Sutton SM3 239 CY107
Waltham Cross EN8 89 DY34
Watford WD19 98 BW44
Parkside Av, SW19 201 CX92
Bexleyheath DA7 189 FD82
Bromley BR1 226 EL98
Romford RM1 149 FD55
Tilbury RM18 193 GH82
● **Parkside Business Est**, SE8 45 M2
Parkside Cl, SE20 204 DW94
East Horsley KT24 267 BT125
Sch **Parkside Comm Prim Sch**, Borwd. WD6
off Aycliffe Rd 100 CM38
Parkside Ct, Wey. KT13 234 BN105
Parkside Cres, N7 143 DN62
Surbiton KT5 220 CQ100
Parkside Cross, Bexh. DA7 189 FE82
Parkside Dr, Edg. HA8 118 CN48
Watford WD17 97 BS40
Parkside Est, E9 11 H8
Parkside Gdns, SW19 201 CX91
Coulsdon CR5 257 DH117
East Barnet EN4 120 DF46
H **Parkside Hosp**, SW19 201 CX90
Parkside Ho, Dag. RM10 149 FC62
Parkside Ms, Warl. CR6 259 EA116
H **Parkside Oncology Clinic**, SW19 201 CX90
Parkside Pl, E.Hors. KT24 267 BS125
Staines TW18 196 BG93
Parkside Rd, SW11 40 G7
Belvedere DA17 189 FC77
Hounslow TW3 198 CB85
Northwood HA6 115 BT50
Sch **Parkside Sch**, Stoke D'Ab. KT11 *off Stoke Rd* 252 CA118
Parkside Ter, N18
off Great Cambridge Rd 122 DR49
Orpington BR6
off Willow Wk 227 EP104
Parkside Wk, SE10 35 J7
Slough SL1 174 AU76
Parkside Way, Har. HA2 138 CB56
Park S, SW11 40 G7
Park Sq, Esher KT10
off Park Rd 236 CB105
Lambourne End RM4 108 EY44
Park Sq E, NW1 17 J4
Park Sq Ms, NW1 17 J5
Park Sq W, NW1 17 J4
Parkstead Rd, SW15 201 CU85
Park Steps, W2
off St. Georges Flds 16 D10
Parkstone Av, N18 122 DT50
Hornchurch RM11 150 FK58
Parkstone Rd, E17 145 EC55
SE15 44 D9
PARK STREET, St.Alb. AL2 83 CD26
⇌ **Park Street** 83 CD26
Park St, SE1 31 J2
W1 16 G10
Berkhamsted HP4 60 AV18
Colnbrook SL3 175 BD80
Croydon CR0 224 DQ103
Guildford GU1 280 AW136
Hatfield AL9 67 CW17
St. Albans AL2 83 CD26
Slough SL1 174 AT76
Park St, Tedd. TW11 199 CE93
Windsor SL4 173 AR81
Sch **Park St C of E Prim Sch & Nurs**, Park St AL2 *off Branch Rd* 83 CD27
Park St La, Park St AL2 82 CB30
Park Ter, Green. DA9 211 FV85
Sundridge TN14
off Main Rd 262 EX124
Worcester Park KT4 221 CU102
Parkthorne Cl, Har. HA2 138 CB58
Parkthorne Dr, Har. HA2 138 CA58
Parkthorne Rd, SW12 203 DK87
Park Twrs, W1 *off Brick St* 29 J3
Park Vw, N21 121 DM45
W3 160 CQ71
Aveley RM15 171 FR74
Bookham KT23 268 CA125
Caterham CR3 274 DU125
Hatfield AL9 67 CW16
Hoddesdon EN11 71 EA18
Horley RH6
off Brighton Rd 290 DG148
New Malden KT3 221 CT97
Pinner HA5 116 BZ53
Potters Bar EN6 86 DC33
Parkview, St.Alb. AL1 65 CG21
Park Vw, Wem. HA9 140 CP64
Sch **Park Vw Acad**, N15
off Langham Rd 144 DQ56
Parkview Chase, Slou. SL1 153 AL72
Parkview Cl, Cars. SM5 240 DF108
Park Vw Cl, St.Alb. AL1 65 CG21
Parkview Ct, SW18
off Broomhill Rd 202 DA86
Park Vw Ct, Ilf. IG2 147 ES58
Woking GU22 248 AY119
Park Vw Cres, N11 121 DH49
Parkview Dr, Mitch. CR4 222 DD96
Park Vw Est, E2 11 H10
N5 144 DQ63
Park Vw Gdns, NW4 141 CW57
Grays RM17 192 GB78
Ilford IG4 147 EM56
Park Vw Ho, SE24
off Hurst St 203 DP86
Parkview Ho, Horn. RM12 149 FH61
Park Vw Ms, SW9 42 D8
Parkview Ms, Rain. RM13 169 FH71
Park Vw Rd, N3 120 DB53
N17 144 DU55
NW10 141 CT63
Parkview Rd, SE9 207 EP88
Park Vw Rd, W5 160 CL71
Berkhamsted HP4 60 AV19
Parkview Rd, Croy. CR0 224 DU102
Park Vw Rd, Lthd. KT22 253 CF120
Pinner HA5 115 BV52
Redhill RH1 288 DG141
Southall UB1 158 CA74
Uxbridge UB8 156 BN72
Welling DA16 188 EW83
Woldingham CR3 259 DY122
Park Vw Rd Est, N17 122 DV54
Parkview Vale, Guil. GU4 265 BC131
Park Village E, NW1 7 J9
Park Village W, NW1 7 J10
Park Vil, Rom. RM6 148 EX58
Parkville Rd, SW6 38 G5
Park Vista, SE10 47 H3
Park Wk, N6 *off North Rd* 142 DG59
SE10 46 G5
SW10 39 P2
Ashtead KT21
off Rectory La 254 CM119
Sch **Park Wk Prim Sch**, SW10 40 A3
Parkway, N14 121 DL47
Park Way, N20 120 DF49
Parkway, NW1 7 J9
Park Way, NW11 141 CY57
Parkway, SW20 221 CX98
Park Way, Bex. DA5 209 FE90
Bookham KT23 252 CA123
Parkway, Dor. RH4 285 CG135
Park Way, Edg. HA8 118 CP53
Enfield EN2 103 DN40
Parkway, Erith DA18 188 EY76
Park Way, Felt. TW14 197 BV87
Parkway, Guil. GU1 264 AY133
Harlow CM19 72 EL15
Park Way, Horl. RH6 290 DG148
Parkway, Ilf. IG3 147 ET62
New Addington CR0 243 EC109
Porters Wood AL3 65 CF16
Rainham RM13
off Upminster Rd S 169 FG70
Park Way, Rick. WD3 114 BJ46
Parkway, Rom. RM2 149 FF55
Park Way, Ruis. HA4 137 BU60
Parkway, Saw. CM21 58 EY06
Park Way, Shenf. CM15 131 FZ46
Parkway, Uxb. UB10 156 BN66
Welwyn Garden City AL8 51 CW11
Park Way, W.Mol. KT8 218 CB97
Parkway, Wey. KT13 235 BR105
Woodford Green IG8 124 EJ50
Parkway, The, Cran. TW4, TW5 177 BV82
Hayes UB3, UB4 158 BW72
Iver SL0 155 BC68
Northolt UB5 158 BX69
Southall UB2 177 BU78
Parkway Cl, Welw.G.C. AL8 51 CW09
Parkway Ct, St.Alb. AL1 65 CH23
Parkway Cres, E15 12 F2
Parkway Gdns, Welw.G.C. AL8 51 CW10
Sch **Parkway Prim Sch**, Erith DA18 *off Alsike Rd* 188 EY76
● **Parkway Trd Est**, Houns. TW5 178 BW79
Park W, W2 16 D9
Park W Bldg, E3
off Fairfield Rd 12 B10
Park W Pl, W2 16 D8
Parkwood, N20 120 DF48
Beckenham BR3 225 EA95
Parkwood Av, Esher KT10 218 CC102
Parkwood Cl, Bans. SM7 255 CX115
Broxbourne EN10 71 DZ19
Parkwood Dr, Hem.H. HP1 61 BF20
Parkwood Gro, Sun. TW16 217 BU97
Sch **Parkwood Hall Sch**, Swan. BR8 *off Beechenlea La* 229 FH97
Parkwood Ms, N6 143 DH58
Sch **Parkwood Prim Sch**, N4
off Queens Dr 143 DP61
Parkwood Rd, SW19 201 CZ92
Banstead SM7 255 CX115
Bexley DA5 208 EZ87
Isleworth TW7 179 CF81
Nutfield RH1 273 DL133
Parkwood Rd, Tats. TN16 260 EL121
Parkwood Vw, Bans. SM7 255 CW116
Park Wks Rd, Red. RH1 273 DM133
Sch **Parlaunt Pk Prim Sch**, Langley SL3 *off Kennett Rd* 175 BB76
Parlaunt Rd, Slou. SL3 175 BA77
Parley Dr, Wok. GU21 248 AW117
Parliament Ct, E1 19 P7
Parliament Hill, NW3 6 D1
Sch **Parliament Hill Sch**, NW5
off Highgate Rd 142 DG63
Parliament La, Burn. SL1 152 AF66
Parliament Ms, SW14
off Thames Bk 180 CQ82
Parliament Sq, SW1 30 A5
Hertford SG14 54 DR09
Parliament St, SW1 30 A5
Parliament Vw Apts, SE1 30 C8
Parma Cres, SW11 182 DF84
● **Parmiter Ind Cen**, E2 10 F10
Sch **Parmiter's Sch**, Wat. WD25
off High Elms La 82 BW31
Parmiter St, E2 10 F10
Parmoor Ct, EC1 19 J4
Parnall Rd, Harl. CM18 73 ER18
Parndon Mill La, Harl. CM20 57 EP12
Parndon Wd Rd, Harl. CM19 73 EQ20
Parnell Cl, W12 181 CV76
Abbots Langley WD5 81 BT30
Chafford Hundred RM16 191 FW78
Edgware HA8 118 CP49
Parnell Gdns, Wey. KT13 234 BN111
Parnell Rd, E3 11 P9
Parnel Rd, Ware SG12 55 DZ05
Parnham Cl, Brom. BR1
off Stoneleigh Rd 227 EP97
Parnham St, E14 21 M8
Parolles Rd, N19 143 DJ60
Paroma Rd, Belv. DA17 188 FA76
Parr Av, Epsom KT17 239 CV109
Parr Cl, N9 122 DV49
N18 122 DV49
Chafford Hundred RM16 191 FW77
Leatherhead KT22 253 CF120
Parr Ct, N1 9 L10
Feltham TW13 198 BW91
Parr Cres, Hem.H. HP2 63 BP15
Parris Cft, Dor. RH4
off Goodwyns Rd 285 CJ139
Parritt Rd, Red. RH1 273 DH132
Parrock, The, Grav. DA12 213 GJ88
Parrock Av, Grav. DA12 213 GJ88
PARROCK FARM, Grav. DA12 213 GK91
Parrock Rd, Grav. DA12 213 GJ88
Parrock St, Grav. DA12 213 GH87
Parrotts Cl, Crox.Grn WD3 96 BN42
Parrotts Fld, Hodd. EN11 71 EB16
Parr Pl, W4
off Chiswick High Rd 181 CT77
Parr Rd, E6 166 EK67
Stanmore HA7 117 CK53
Parrs Cl, S.Croy. CR2 242 DR109
Parrs Pl, Hmptn. TW12 198 CA94
Parr St, N1 9 L10
Parry Av, E6 25 J9
Parry Cl, Epsom KT17 239 CU108
Parry Dr, Wey. KT13 234 BN110
Parry Grn N, Slou. SL3 175 AZ77
Parry Grn S, Slou. SL3 175 AZ77
Parry Pl, SE18 37 P8
Parry Rd, SE25 224 DS97
W10 14 F2
Parry St, SW8 42 A2
Parsifal Rd, NW6 5 K2
Parsley Gdns, Croy. CR0
off Primrose La 225 DX102
Parsloe Rd, Epp.Grn CM16 73 EN21
Harlow CM19 73 EP20
Parsloes Av, Dag. RM9 148 EX63
Sch **Parsloes Prim Sch**, Dag. RM9
off Spurling Rd 168 EZ65
Parsonage Bk, Eyns. DA4
off Pollyhaugh 230 FL103
Parsonage Cl, Abb.L. WD5 81 BS30
Hayes UB3 157 BT72
Warlingham CR6 259 DY116
Westcott RH4 284 CC138
Sch **Parsonage Fm Prim Sch**, Rain. RM13 *off Farm Rd* 170 FJ69
Parsonage Gdns, Enf. EN2 104 DQ40
Parsonage La, Chesh. HP5
off Blucher St 76 AP31
Enfield EN1, EN2 104 DR40
North Mymms AL9 67 CV23
Sidcup DA14 208 EZ91
Slough SL2 153 AQ68
Sutton at Hone DA4 210 FP93
Westcott RH4 284 CC137
Windsor SL4 173 AN81
Parsonage Leys, Harl. CM20 57 ET14
Parsonage Manorway, Belv. DA17 188 FA79
Parsonage Rd, Ch.St.G. HP8 112 AV48
Englefield Green TW20 194 AX92
Grays RM20 191 FW79
North Mymms AL9 67 CV23
Rainham RM13 170 FJ69
Rickmansworth WD3 114 BK45
Parsonage Sq, Dor. RH4 285 CG135
Parsonage St, E14 34 F9
Parsons Cl, Horl. RH6 290 DE147
Sutton SM1 222 DB104
Parsons Cres, Edg. HA8 118 CN48
Parsonsfield Cl, Bans. SM7 255 CX115
Parsonsfield Rd, Bans. SM7 255 CX116
PARSONS GREEN, SW6 39 J6
⊖ **Parsons Green** 39 H7
Parsons Grn, SW6 39 J7
Guildford GU1
off Bellfields Rd 264 AX132
Parsons Grn Ct, Guil. GU1
off Bellfields Rd 264 AX132
Parsons Grn La, SW6 39 J6
Parsons Gro, Edg. HA8 118 CN48
Parsons Ho, SW2
off New Pk Rd 203 DL87
Parson's Ho, W2 16 A5
Parsons La, Dart. DA2 209 FH90
Parson's Mead, Croy. CR0 223 DP102
Parsons Mead, E.Mol. KT8 218 CC97
Parsons Pightle, Couls. CR5 257 DN120
Parsons Rd, E13 24 C1
Slough SL3 175 AZ79
Parson St, NW4 141 CW56
Parsons Wd, Farn.Com. SL2 153 AQ65
Parthenia Rd, SW6 39 K7
Parthia Cl, Tad. KT20 255 CV119
Partingdale La, NW7 119 CX50
Partington Cl, N19 143 DK60
Partridge Cl, E16 24 E7
Barnet EN5 101 CW44
Bushey WD23 116 CB46
Chesham HP5 76 AS28
Stanmore HA7 118 CL49
Partridge Ct, Harl. CM18 73 ER17
Partridge Dr, Orp. BR6 227 EQ104
Partridge Grn, SE9 207 EN90
Partridge Knoll, Pur. CR8 241 DP112
Partridge Mead, Bans. SM7 255 CW116
Partridge Rd, Hmptn. TW12 198 BZ93
Harlow CM18 73 ER17
St. Albans AL3 65 CD16
Sidcup DA14 207 ES90
Partridges, Hem.H. HP3
off Reddings 62 BN22
Partridge Sq, E6 25 H6
Partridge Way, N22 121 DL53
Guildford GU4 265 BD132
Parvills, Wal.Abb. EN9 89 ED32
Parvin St, SW8 41 N6
Parvis Rd, W.Byf. KT14 234 BG113
Pasadena Cl, Hayes UB3 177 BV75
● **Pasadena Trd Est**, Hayes UB3 177 BU75
Pascal Ms, SE19
off Anerley Hill 204 DU94
Pascal St, SW8 41 P4
Pascoe Rd, SE13 205 ED85
Pasfield, Wal.Abb. EN9 89 ED33
Pasgen Ct, N9
off Galahad Rd 122 DU47
Pasley Cl, SE17 43 J1
Pasquier Rd, E17 145 DY55
Passey Pl, SE9 207 EM86
Passfield Dr, E14 22 D6
Passfield Path, SE28
off Booth Cl 168 EV73
Passing All, EC1 19 H5
Passmore Gdns, N11 121 DK51
PASSMORES, Harl. CM18 73 ER17
Sch **Passmores Sch & Tech Coll**, Harl. CM18
off Tendring Rd 73 ER17
Passmore St, SW1 28 G9
★ **Passport Office**, SW1 29 K8
Pastens Rd, Oxt. RH8 276 EJ131
Pasteur Cl, NW9 118 CS54
Pasteur Dr, Harold Wd RM3 128 FK54
Pasteur Gdns, N18 121 DP50
Paston Cl, E5
off Caldecott Way 145 DX62
Wallington SM6 223 DJ104
Paston Cres, SE12 206 EH87
Paston Rd, Hem.H. HP2 62 BK18
Pastoral Way, Warley CM14 130 FV50
Pastor St, SE11 31 H8
Pasture Cl, Bushey WD23 116 CC45
Wembley HA0 139 CH62
Pasture Rd, SE6 206 EF88
Dagenham RM9 148 EZ63
Wembley HA0 139 CH61
Pastures, The, N20 119 CZ46
Hatfield AL10 67 CV19
Hemel Hempstead HP1 61 BE19
St. Albans AL2 64 CA24
Watford WD19 116 BW45
Welwyn Garden City AL7 52 DA11
Pastures Mead, Uxb. UB10 156 BN65
Pastures Path, E11
off Lister Rd 146 EE60
Patch, The, Sev. TN13 278 FE122
Patcham Ct, Sutt. SM2 240 DC109
Patcham Ter, SW8 41 K6
Patch Cl, Uxb. UB10 156 BM67
PATCHETTS GREEN, Wat. WD25 98 CC39
Patching Way, Hayes UB4 158 BY71
Paternoster Cl, Wal.Abb. EN9 90 EF33
Paternoster Hill, Wal.Abb. EN9 90 EF32
Paternoster La, EC4
off Warwick La 19 H9
Paternoster Row, EC4 19 J9
Noak Hill RM4 128 FJ47
Paternoster Sq, EC4 19 H9
Paterson Ct, EC1
off St. Luke's Est 19 L3
Paterson Rd, Ashf. TW15 196 BK92
Pater St, W8 27 J7
Pates Manor Dr, Felt. TW14 197 BR87
Path, The, SW19 222 DB95
Pathfield Rd, SW16 203 DK93
Pathfields, Shere GU5 282 BN140
Pathway, The, Rad. WD7 99 CF36
Send GU23 265 BF125
Watford WD19
off Anthony Cl 116 BX46
Patience Rd, SW11 40 C9
Patio Cl, SW4 203 DK86
Patmore Est, SW8 41 L6
Patmore La, Hersham KT12 235 BT107
Patmore Link Rd, Hem.H. HP2 63 BQ20
Patmore Rd, Wal.Abb. EN9 90 EE34
Patmore St, SW8 41 M6
Patmore Way, Rom. RM5 127 FB50
Patmos Rd, SW9 42 G5
Paton Cl, E3 22 B2
Paton St, EC1 19 J3
Patricia Cl, Slou. SL1 153 AL73
Patricia Ct, Chis. BR7
off Manor Pk Rd 227 ER95
Welling DA16 188 EV80
Patricia Dr, Horn. RM11 150 FL60
Patricia Gdns, Sutt. SM2 240 DA111
Patrick Connolly Gdns, E3 22 D3
Patrick Gro, Wal.Abb. EN9
off Beaulieu Dr 89 EB33
Patrick Rd, E13 24 D3
Patrington Cl, Uxb. UB8 156 BJ69
Patriot Sq, E2 20 F1
Patrol Pl, SE6 205 EB86
Patshull Pl, NW5 7 L5
Patshull Rd, NW5 7 K4
Patten All, Rich. TW10
off The Hermitage 199 CK85
Pattenden Rd, SE6 205 DZ88
Patten Rd, SW18 202 DE87
Patterdale Cl, Brom. BR1 206 EF93
Patterdale Rd, SE15 44 G4
Dartford DA2 211 FR88
Patterson Ct, SE19 204 DT94
Dartford DA1 210 FN85
Wooburn Green HP10
off Glory Mill La 132 AE56
Patterson Rd, SE19 204 DT93
Chesham HP5 76 AP28
Pattina Wk, SE16 33 M3
Pattison Rd, NW2 142 DA62
Pattison Wk, SE18 187 EQ78

Paul Cl, E15 .... 13 J7
Cheshunt EN7
off Gladding Rd 88 DQ25
Paulet Rd, SE5 .... 43 H8
Paulet Way, NW10 .... 160 CS66
Paul Gdns, Croy. CR0 .... 224 DT103
Paulhan Rd, Har. HA3 .... 139 CK56
Paulin Dr, N21 .... 121 DN45
Pauline Cres, Twick. TW2 .... 198 CC88
Pauline Ho, E1 .... 20 D6
Paulinus Cl, Orp. BR5 .... 228 EW96
Paul Julius Cl, E14 .... 34 G1
Paul Robeson Cl, E6 .... 25 M2
Pauls Grn, Wal.Cr. EN8 .... 89 DY33
Pauls Hill, Penn HP10 .... 110 AF48
Pauls La, Hodd. EN11
off Taverners Way 71 EA17
Paul's Nurs Rd, High Beach
IG10 .... 106 EH39
Paul's Pl, Ashtd. KT21 .... 254 CP119
Paul St, E15 .... 13 J8
EC2 .... 19 M5
Paul's Wk, EC4 .... 19 H10
Paultons Sq, SW3 .... 40 B2
Paultons St, SW3 .... 40 B3
Pauntley St, N19 .... 143 DJ60
Paved Ct, Rich. TW9 .... 199 CK85
Paveley Ct, NW7 .... 119 CX52
Paveley Dr, SW11 .... 40 C5
Paveley Ho, N1
off Priory Grn Est 18 C1
Paveley St, NW8 .... 16 D4
Pavement, The, SW4 .... 183 DJ84
W5 *off Popes La* 180 CL76
Isleworth TW7
off South St 179 CG83
Pavement Ms, Rom. RM6
off Clarissa Rd 148 EX59
Pavement Sq, Croy. CR0 .... 224 DU102
Pavet Cl, Dag. RM10 .... 169 FB65
Pavilion End, Knot.Grn HP9 .... 110 AJ50
Pavilion Gdns, Stai. TW18 .... 196 BH94
Pavilion Ho, SE16
off Canada St 33 J5
Pavilion La, Beck. BR3 .... 205 DZ93
Pavilion Ms, N3
off Windermere Av 120 DA54
Pavilion Par, W12 .... 14 A8
Pavilion Rd, SW1 .... 28 F7
Ilford IG1 .... 147 EM59
Pavilions, Wind. SL4 .... 173 AP81
Pavilions, The, Uxb. UB8 .... 156 BJ66
Pavilions, The, Byfleet KT14 .... 234 BK111
North Weald Bassett CM16 .... 93 FC25
Pavilion Sq, SW17 .... 202 DE90
Pavilions Shop Cen, Wal.Cr.
EN8 .... 89 DX34
Pavilion St, SW1 .... 28 F7
Pavilion Ter, W12 .... 14 A8
East Molesey KT8 .... 219 CF98
Ilford IG2
off Southdown Cres 147 ES57
Pavilion Way, Amer. HP6 .... 94 AW39
Edgware HA8 .... 118 CP52
Ruislip HA4 .... 138 BW61
Pavillion Ms, N4 .... 143 DM61
Pawleyne Cl, SE20 .... 204 DW94
Pawsey Cl, E13 .... 13 P8
Pawson's Rd, Croy. CR0 .... 224 DQ100
Paxford Rd, Wem. HA0 .... 139 CH61
Paxton Av, Slou. SL1 .... 173 AQ76
Paxton Cl, Rich. TW9 .... 180 CM82
Walton-on-Thames KT12 .... 218 BW101
Paxton Ct, Borwd. WD6
off Manor Way 100 CQ42
Paxton Gdns, Wok. GU21 .... 233 BE112
Paxton Pl, SE27 .... 204 DS91
Sch **Paxton Prim Sch**, SE19
off Woodland Rd 204 DS93
Paxton Rd, N17 .... 122 DT52
SE23 .... 205 DY90
W4 .... 180 CS79
Berkhamsted HP4 .... 60 AX19
Bromley BR1 .... 206 EG94
St. Albans AL1 .... 65 CE21
Paxton Ter, SW1 .... 41 K2
Paycock Rd, Harl. CM19 .... 73 EN17
Payne Cl, Bark. IG11 .... 167 ES66
Paynell Ct, SE3 .... 47 K10
Payne Rd, E3 .... 22 C1
Paynesfield Av, SW14 .... 180 CR83
Paynesfield Rd, Bushey Hth
WD23 .... 117 CF45
Tatsfield TN16 .... 260 EK119
Paynes La, Lwr Naze. EN9 .... 71 EC24
Payne St, SE8 .... 45 P3
Paynes Wk, W6 .... 38 E3
Paynetts Ct, Wey. KT13 .... 235 BR106
Payzes Gdns, Wdf.Grn. IG8
off Chingford La 124 EF50
Peabody Av, SW1 .... 29 J10
Peabody Cl, SE10 .... 46 D6
SW1 .... 41 K2
Croydon CR0 .... 224 DW102
Peabody Cotts, SE24
off Rosendale Rd 204 DQ87
Peabody Ct, Enf. EN3
off Martini Dr 105 EA37
Peabody Dws, WC1 .... 18 A4
Peabody Est, EC1 (Clerkenwell)
off Farringdon La 18 F5
EC1 (St. Luke's) 19 K5
N1 (Islington) 9 J7
N17 .... 122 DS53
SE1 .... 30 F3
SE17 .... 31 L9
SE24 .... 203 DP87
SW1 .... 29 L8
SW3 .... 40 D2
SW6 .... 39 J2
W6 .... 38 B1
W10 .... 14 B6
Peabody Hill, SE21 .... 203 DP88
Peabody Hill Est, SE21 .... 203 DP87
Peabody Sq, SE1 .... 30 G5
Peabody Twr, EC1
off Golden La 19 K5
Peabody Trust, SE1 .... 31 J3
Peabody Trust Camberwell Grn Est,
SE5 .... 43 L6
Peabody Trust Old Pye St Est,
SW1 *off Old Pye St* 29 N7
Peabody Yd, N1 .... 9 J8
Peace Cl, N14 .... 103 DH43
SE25 .... 224 DS98
Cheshunt EN7 *off Goffs La* 88 DU29
Greenford UB6 .... 159 CD67
Peace Dr, Wat. WD17 .... 97 BU41
Peace Gro, Wem. HA9 .... 140 CP62
Peace Prospect, Wat. WD17 .... 97 BU41
Peace Rd, Iver SL0 .... 155 BA67
Slough SL3 .... 155 BA68
Peace St, SE18
off Nightingale Vale 187 EP79
Peach Cft, Nthflt DA11 .... 212 GE90
Peaches Cl, Sutt. SM2 .... 239 CY108
Peachey Cl, Uxb. UB8 .... 156 BK72
Peachey La, Uxb. UB8 .... 156 BK71
Peach Gro, E11 .... 145 ED62
Peach Rd, W10 .... 14 D2
Feltham TW13 .... 197 BU88
Peach Tree Av, West Dr. UB7
off Pear Tree Av 156 BM72
Peachum Rd, SE3 .... 47 M2
Peachwalk Ms, E3 .... 11 K10
Peachy Cl, Edg. HA8
off Manor Pk Cres 118 CN51
Peacock Av, Felt. TW14 .... 197 BR88
Peacock Cl, E4 .... 123 DZ52
Dagenham RM8 .... 148 EW60
Hornchurch RM11 .... 150 FL56
Peacock Gdns, S.Croy. CR2 .... 243 DY110
● **Peacock Ind Est**, N17 .... 122 DT52
Peacocks, Harl. CM19 .... 73 EM17
Peacocks Cen, The, Wok.
GU21 .... 248 AY117
Peacocks Cl, Berk. HP4 .... 60 AT16
Peacock St, SE17 .... 31 H9
Gravesend DA12 .... 213 GJ87
Peacock Wk, E16 .... 24 B8
Abbots Langley WD5 .... 81 BU31
Dorking RH4 *off Rose Hill* 285 CG137
Peacock Yd, SE17 .... 31 H9
Peak, The, SE26 .... 204 DW90
Peakes La, Chsht EN7 .... 88 DT27
Peakes Pl, St.Alb. AL1
off Granville Rd 65 CF20
Peakes Way, Chsht EN7 .... 88 DT27
Peaketon Av, Ilf. IG4 .... 146 EK56
Peak Hill, SE26 .... 204 DW91
Peak Hill Av, SE26 .... 204 DW91
Peak Hill Gdns, SE26 .... 204 DW91
Peak Rd, Guil. GU2 .... 264 AU131
Peaks Hill, Pur. CR8 .... 241 DK110
Peaks Hill Ri, Pur. CR8 .... 241 DL110
Pea La, Upmin. RM14 .... 171 FU66
Peal Gdns, W13
off Ruislip Rd E 159 CG70
Peall Rd, Croy. CR0 .... 223 DM100
Pearce Cl, Mitch. CR4 .... 222 DG96
Pearcefield Av, SE23 .... 204 DW88
Pearce Rd, Chesh. HP5 .... 76 AP29
Pearces Wk, St.Alb. AL1
off Albert St 65 CD21
Pear Cl, NW9 .... 140 CR56
SE14 .... 45 M5
Pearcroft Rd, E11 .... 145 ED61
Pearcy Cl, Harold Hill RM3 .... 128 FL52
Peardon St, SW8 .... 41 K9
Peareswood Gdns, Stan. HA7 .... 117 CK53
Peareswood Rd, Erith DA8 .... 189 FF81
Pearfield Rd, SE23 .... 205 DY90
Pearl Cl, E6 .... 25 L8
NW2 .... 141 CX59
Pearl Ct, Wok. GU21
off Langmans Way 248 AS116
Pearl Gdns, Slou. SL1 .... 153 AP74
Pearl Rd, E17 .... 145 EA55
Pearl St, E1 .... 32 F2
Pearmain Cl, Shep. TW17 .... 217 BP99
Pearman St, SE1 .... 30 F6
Pear Pl, SE1 .... 30 E4
Pear Rd, E11 .... 145 ED62
Pearscroft Ct, SW6 .... 39 M7
Pearscroft Rd, SW6 .... 39 L8
Pearse St, SE15 .... 43 P3
Pearson Av, Hert. SG13 .... 54 DQ11
Pearson Cl, SE5 .... 43 K6
Barnet EN5 .... 102 DB42
Hertford SG13
off Pearson Av 54 DQ11
Purley CR8 .... 241 DP111
Pearson Ms, SW4 .... 183 DK83
Pearsons Av, SE14 .... 46 A6
Pearson St, E2 .... 9 P10
Pearson Way, Dart. DA1 .... 210 FM89
Mitcham CR4 .... 222 DG95
Pears Rd, Houns. TW3 .... 178 CC83
PEARTREE, Welw.G.C. AL7 .... 51 CZ09
Peartree Av, SW17 .... 202 DC90
Pear Tree Av, West Dr. UB7 .... 156 BM72
Pear Tree Cl, E2 .... 10 A9
Addlestone KT15
off Pear Tree Rd 234 BG106
Amersham HP7
off Orchard End Av 94 AT39
Bromley BR2 .... 226 EK99
Chessington KT9 .... 238 CN106
Peartree Cl, Erith DA8 .... 189 FD81
Hemel Hempstead HP1 .... 62 BG19
Pear Tree Cl, Mitch. CR4 .... 222 DE96
Seer Green HP9 .... 111 AQ51
Slough SL1 .... 153 AM74
Peartree Cl, S.Croy. CR2 .... 242 DV114
South Ockendon RM15 .... 171 FW68
Pear Tree Cl, Swan. BR8 .... 229 FD96
Peartree Cl, Welw.G.C. AL7 .... 51 CY09
Peartree Ct, E18
off Churchfields 124 EH53
Pear Tree Ct, EC1 .... 18 F5
Peartree Ct, Welw.G.C. AL7 .... 51 CY10
Peartree Fm, Welw.G.C. AL7 .... 51 CY09
Peartree Gdns, Dag. RM8 .... 148 EV63
Romford RM7 .... 127 FB54
Pear Tree Hill, Salf. RH1 .... 288 DG143
Peartree La, E1 .... 33 H1
Welwyn Garden City AL7 .... 51 CY10
Pear Tree Mead, Harl. CM18 .... 74 EU18
Sch **Pear Tree Mead Prim & Nurs Sch**, Harl. CM18
off Pear Tree Mead 74 EU18
Sch **Peartree Prim Sch**, Welw.G.C.
AL7 *off Peartree La* 51 CY10
Pear Tree Rd, Add. KT15 .... 234 BG106
Ashford TW15 .... 197 BQ92
Peartree Rd, Enf. EN1 .... 104 DS41
Hemel Hempstead HP1 .... 62 BG19
Pear Tree St, EC1 .... 19 H4
Pear Tree Wk, Chsht EN7 .... 88 DR26
Peartree Way, SE10 .... 35 N8
Peary Pl, E2 .... 21 H2
Peascod Pl, Wind. SL4
off Peascod St 173 AR81
Peascod St, Wind. SL4 .... 173 AR81
Peascroft Rd, Hem.H. HP3 .... 62 BN23
Pease Cl, Horn. RM12
off Dowding Way 169 FH66
PEASMARSH, Guil. GU3 .... 280 AW142
Peatfield Cl, Sid. DA15
off Woodside Rd 207 ES90
Peatmore Av, Wok. GU22 .... 250 BG116
Peatmore Cl, Wok. GU22 .... 250 BG116
Pebble Cl, Tad. KT20 .... 270 CS128
PEBBLE COOMBE, Tad. KT20 .... 270 CS128
Pebble Hill, Lthd. KT24 .... 267 BQ133
Pebble Hill Rd, Bet. RH3 .... 270 CS131
Tadworth KT20 .... 270 CS131
Pebble La, Epsom KT18 .... 254 CN121
Leatherhead KT22 .... 270 CL125
Pebble Way, W3 .... 160 CP74
Pebworth Rd, Har. HA1 .... 139 CG61
Peckarmans Wd, SE26 .... 204 DU90
Peckett Sq, N5 .... 9 H1
Peckford Pl, SW9 .... 42 F9
PECKHAM, SE15 .... 44 A8
Peckham Gro, SE15 .... 43 P4
Peckham High St, SE15 .... 44 C7
Peckham Hill St, SE15 .... 44 C4
Peckham Pk Rd, SE15 .... 44 C4
Sch **Peckham Pk Sch**, SE15 .... 44 D5
Peckham Rd, SE5 .... 43 N7
SE15 .... 43 N7
⇌ **Peckham Rye** 44 C8
Peckham Rye, SE15 .... 44 D10
SE22 .... 184 DU84
Pecks Hill, Lwr Naze. EN9 .... 72 EE21
Pecks Yd, E1 .... 20 A6
Peckwater St, NW5 .... 7 L3
● **Pedham Pl Ind Est**, Swan.
BR8 .... 229 FG99
Pedlars End, Moreton CM5 .... 75 FH21
Pedlars Wk, N7 .... 8 B4
Pedley Rd, Dag. RM8 .... 148 EW60
Pedley St, E1 .... 20 B5
PEDNORMEAD END, Chesh.
HP5 .... 76 AN32
Pednormead End, Chesh. HP5 .... 76 AP32
Pednor Rd, Chesh. HP5 .... 76 AM30
Pedro St, E5 .... 145 DX62
Pedworth Gdns, SE16 .... 32 G9
Peek Cres, SW19 .... 201 CX92
Peeks Brook La, Horl. RH6 .... 291 DM150
Coll **Peel Cen (Met Pol Training & Driving Sch)**, NW9
off Aerodrome Rd 141 CT55
Peel Cl, E4 .... 123 EB47
N9 *off Plevna Rd* 122 DU48
Windsor SL4 .... 173 AP83
Peel Ct, Slou. SL1 .... 153 AP71
Peel Cres, Hert. SG14 .... 53 DP07
Peel Dr, NW9 .... 141 CT55
Ilford IG5 .... 146 EL55
Peel Gro, E2 .... 20 G1
Peel Pas, W8 .... 27 J3
Peel Pl, Ilf. IG5 .... 124 EL54
Peel Prec, NW6 .... 15 J1
Peel Rd, E18 .... 124 EF53
Orpington BR6 .... 245 EQ106
Wealdstone HA3 .... 139 CF55
Wembley HA9 .... 139 CK62
Peel St, W8 .... 27 J3
Peel Way, Rom. RM3 .... 128 FM54
Uxbridge UB8 .... 156 BL71
Peerage Way, Horn. RM11 .... 150 FL59
● **Peerglow Cen**, Ware SG12 .... 55 DY07
● **Peerglow Est**, Enf. EN3 .... 104 DW43
Peerless Dr, Hare. UB9 .... 136 BJ57
Peerless St, EC1 .... 19 L3
Pegamoid Rd, N18 .... 122 DW48
Pegasus Cl, N16 .... 9 L1
Pegasus Ct, W3 *off Horn La* 160 CQ72
Abbots Langley WD5
off Furtherfield 81 BT32
Gravesend DA12 .... 213 GJ90
Harrow HA3 .... 139 CK57
Pegasus Pl, SE11 .... 42 E2
SW6 *off Ackmar Rd* 39 J7
St. Albans AL3 .... 65 CD18
Pegasus Rd, Croy. CR0 .... 241 DN107
Pegasus Way, N11 .... 121 DH51
Pegelm Gdns, Horn. RM11 .... 150 FM59
Peggotty Way, Uxb. UB8 .... 157 BP72
Pegg Rd, Houns. TW5 .... 178 BX80
Pegley Gdns, SE12 .... 206 EG89
Pegmire La, Ald. WD25 .... 98 CC39
Pegrams Rd, Harl. CM18 .... 73 EQ18
Pegrum Dr, Lon.Col. AL2 .... 83 CH26
Pegs La, Hert. SG13 .... 54 DR11
Pegwell St, SE18 .... 187 ES80
Peket Cl, Stai. TW18 .... 215 BE95
Pekin Cl, E14 .... 22 B9
Pekin St, E14 .... 22 B9
Peldon Ct, Rich. TW9 .... 180 CM84
Peldon Pas, Rich. TW10
off Worple Way 180 CM84
Peldon Rd, Harl. CM19 .... 73 EN17
Peldon Wk, N1 .... 9 H8
Pelham Av, Bark. IG11 .... 167 ET67
Pelham Cl, SE5 .... 43 P10
Pelham Ct, Hem.H. HP2 .... 63 BQ20
Welwyn Garden City AL7 .... 52 DC10
Pelham Cres, SW7 .... 28 C9
Pelham Ho, W14 .... 26 G9
Pelham La, Ald. WD25 .... 98 CB36
Pelham Pl, SW7 .... 28 C9
W13 *off Ruislip Rd E* 159 CF70
Sch **Pelham Prim Sch**, SW19
off Southey Rd 202 DA94
Bexleyheath DA7
off Pelham Rd 188 FA83
Pelham Rd, E18 .... 146 EH55
N15 .... 144 DT56
N22 .... 121 DN54
SW19 .... 202 DA94
Beckenham BR3 .... 224 DW96
Bexleyheath DA7 .... 188 FA83
Gravesend DA11 .... 213 GF87
Ilford IG1 .... 147 ER61
Pelham Rd S, Grav. DA11 .... 213 GF88
Pelhams, The, Wat. WD25 .... 98 BX35
Pelhams Cl, Esher KT10 .... 236 CA105
Pelham St, SW7 .... 28 B8
Pelhams Wk, Esher KT10 .... 218 CA104
Pelham Ter, Grav. DA11
off Campbell Rd 213 GF87
Pelham Way, Bkhm KT23 .... 268 CB126
Pelican Est, SE15 .... 44 A7
Pelican Ho, SE5
off Peckham Rd 44 A7
Pelican Pas, E1 .... 20 G4
Pelier St, SE17 .... 43 K2
Pelinore Rd, SE6 .... 206 EE89
Pellant Rd, SW6 .... 38 F3
Pellatt Gro, N22 .... 121 DN53
Pellatt Rd, SE22 .... 204 DT85
Wembley HA9 .... 140 CL61
Pellerin Rd, N16 .... 9 P2
Pelling Hill, Old Wind. SL4 .... 194 AV87
Pellings Cl, Brom. BR2 .... 226 EE97
Pelling St, E14 .... 22 A8
Pellipar Cl, N13 .... 121 DN48
Pellipar Gdns, SE18 .... 37 J10
Pelly Ct, Epp. CM16 .... 91 ET31
Pelly Rd, E13 .... 13 P10
Pelman Way, Epsom KT19 .... 238 CP110
Pelter St, E2 .... 20 A2
Pelton Av, Sutt. SM2 .... 240 DB110
Pelton Rd, SE10 .... 35 J10
Pembar Av, E17 .... 145 DY55
Pemberley Chase, W.Ewell
KT19 .... 238 CP106
Pemberley Cl, W.Ewell KT19 .... 238 CP106
Pember Rd, NW10 .... 14 C3
Pemberton Av, Rom. RM2 .... 149 FH55
Pemberton Cl, St.Alb. AL1 .... 65 CD23
Pemberton Gdns, N19 .... 143 DJ62
Romford RM6 .... 148 EY57
Swanley BR8 .... 229 FE97
Pemberton Ho, SE26
off High Level Dr 204 DU91
Pemberton Pl, E8 .... 10 F7
Esher KT10
off Carrick Gate 218 CC104
Pemberton Rd, N4 .... 143 DN57
East Molesey KT8 .... 218 CC98
Slough SL2 .... 153 AL70
Pemberton Row, EC4 .... 18 F8
Pemberton Ter, N19 .... 143 DJ62
Pembrey Way, Horn. RM12 .... 170 FJ65
Pembridge Av, Twick. TW2 .... 198 BZ88
Pembridge Chase, Bov. HP3 .... 79 AZ28
Pembridge Cl, Bov. HP3 .... 79 AZ28
Pembridge Cres, W11 .... 15 J10
Pembridge Gdns, W2 .... 27 J1
Coll **Pembridge Hall**, W2 .... 27 K1
Sch **Pembridge Hall Sch**, W2 .... 27 K1
Pembridge La, Brickendon
SG13 .... 70 DQ19
Broxbourne EN10 .... 70 DR21
Pembridge Ms, W11 .... 15 J10
Pembridge Pl, SW15 .... 202 DA85
W2 .... 15 K10
Pembridge Rd, W11 .... 27 J1
Bovingdon HP3 .... 79 BA28
Pembridge Sq, W2 .... 27 J1
Pembridge Vil, W2 .... 15 J10
W11 .... 15 J10
Pembroke Av, N1 .... 8 B8
Enfield EN1 .... 104 DV38
Harrow HA3 .... 139 CG55
Hersham KT12 .... 236 BX105
Pinner HA5 .... 138 BX60
Surbiton KT5 .... 220 CP99
Pembroke Cl, SW1 .... 29 H5
Banstead SM7 .... 256 DB117
Broxbourne EN10 .... 71 DY23
Erith DA8 *off Pembroke Rd* 189 FD77
Hornchurch RM11 .... 150 FM56
Pembroke Cotts, W8
off Pembroke Sq 27 J7
Pembroke Dr, Aveley RM15 .... 190 FP75
Goffs Oak EN7 .... 87 DP29
Pembroke Gdns, W8 .... 27 H8
Dagenham RM10 .... 149 FB62
Woking GU22 .... 249 BA118
Pembroke Gdns Cl, W8 .... 27 H7
Pembroke Ms, E3 .... 21 M2
N10 .... 120 DG53
W8 .... 27 J7
Sevenoaks TN13 .... 279 FH125
Pembroke Pl, W8 .... 27 J7
Edgware HA8 .... 118 CN52
Isleworth TW7
off Thornbury Rd 179 CE82
Sutton at Hone DA4 .... 230 FP95
Pembroke Rd, E6 .... 25 J6
E17 .... 145 EB57
N8 .... 143 DL56
N10 .... 120 DG53
N13 .... 122 DQ48
N15 .... 144 DT57
SE25 .... 224 DS98
W8 .... 27 J8
Bromley BR1 .... 226 EJ96
Erith DA8 .... 189 FC78
Greenford UB6 .... 158 CB70
Ilford IG3 .... 147 ET60
Mitcham CR4 .... 222 DG96
Northwood HA6 .... 115 BQ48
Ruislip HA4 .... 137 BS60
Sevenoaks TN13 .... 279 FH125
Wembley HA9 .... 139 CK62
Woking GU22 .... 249 BA118
Pembroke Sq, W8 .... 27 J7
Pembroke St, N1 .... 8 B7
Pembroke Studios, W8 .... 27 H7
Pembroke Vil, W8 .... 27 J8
Richmond TW9 .... 179 CK84
Pembroke Wk, W8 .... 27 J8
Pembroke Way, Hayes UB3 .... 177 BQ76
Pembry Cl, SW9 .... 42 E7
Pembury Av, Wor.Pk. KT4 .... 221 CU101
Pembury Cl, E5 .... 10 F2
Bromley BR2 .... 226 EF101
Coulsdon CR5 .... 240 DG114
Pembury Ct, Harling. UB3 .... 177 BR79
Pembury Cres, Sid. DA14 .... 208 EY89
Pembury Pl, E5 .... 10 E3
Pembury Rd, E5 .... 10 E3
N17 .... 122 DT54
SE25 .... 224 DU98
Bexleyheath DA7 .... 188 EY80
Pemdevon Rd, Croy. CR0 .... 223 DN101
Pemell Cl, E1 .... 21 H4
Pemerich Cl, Hayes UB3 .... 177 BT78
Pempath Pl, Wem. HA9 .... 139 CK61
Pemsel Ct, Hem.H. HP3
off Crabtree La 62 BL22
Penally Pl, N1 .... 9 M8
Penang St, E1 .... 32 F2
Penard Rd, Sthl. UB2 .... 178 CA76
Penarth St, SE15 .... 44 G2
Penates, Esher KT10 .... 237 CD105
Penberth Rd, SE6 .... 205 EC89
Penbury Rd, Sthl. UB2 .... 178 BZ77
Pencombe Ms, W11 .... 15 H10
Pencraig Way, SE15 .... 44 E3
Pencroft Dr, Dart. DA1
off Shepherds La 210 FJ87
Pendall Cl, Barn. EN4 .... 102 DE42
Penda Rd, Erith DA8 .... 189 FB80
Pendarves Rd, SW20 .... 221 CW95
Penda's Mead, E9 .... 11 M1
Pendell Av, Hayes UB3 .... 177 BT80
Pendell Ct, Bletch. RH1 .... 273 DP131
Pendell Rd, Bletch. RH1 .... 273 DP131
Pendennis Cl, W.Byf. KT14 .... 234 BG114
Pendennis Rd, N17 .... 144 DR55
SW16 .... 203 DL91
Orpington BR6 .... 228 EW103
Sevenoaks TN13 .... 279 FH123
Pendenza, Cob. KT11 .... 252 BY116
Penderel Rd, Houns. TW3 .... 198 CA85
Penderry Ri, SE6 .... 205 ED89
Penderyn Way, N7 .... 143 DK63
Pendle Rd, SW16 .... 203 DH93
Pendlestone Rd, E17 .... 145 EB57
Pendleton Cl, Red. RH1 .... 288 DF136
Pendleton Rd, Red. RH1 .... 288 DE136
Reigate RH2 .... 288 DC137
Pendlewood Cl, W5 .... 159 CJ71
Pendolino Way, NW10 .... 160 CN66
Pendragon Rd, Brom. BR1 .... 206 EF90
Sch **Pendragon Sch**, Downham
BR1 *off Pendragon Rd* 206 EG90
Pendragon Wk, NW9 .... 140 CS58
Pendrell Rd, SE4 .... 45 L9
Pendrell St, SE18 .... 187 ER80
Pendula Dr, Hayes UB4 .... 158 BX70
Pendulum Ms, E8 .... 10 A3
Penerley Rd, SE6 .... 205 EB88
Rainham RM13 .... 169 FH71
Penfields Ho, N7 .... 8 A5
Penfold Cl, Croy. CR0 .... 223 DN104
Penfold La, Bex. DA5 .... 208 EX89
Penfold Pl, NW1 .... 16 B6
Penfold Rd, N9 .... 123 DX46
Penfold St, NW1 .... 16 B5
NW8 .... 16 B5
Penford Gdns, SE9 .... 186 EK83
Penford St, SE5 .... 42 G8
Pengarth Rd, Bex. DA5 .... 208 EX85
PENGE, SE20 .... 204 DW94
⇌ **Penge East** 204 DW93
Penge Ho, SW11 .... 40 B10
Penge La, SE20 .... 204 DW94
Pengelly Cl, Chsht EN7 .... 88 DV30
Penge Rd, E13 .... 166 EJ66
SE20 .... 224 DU97
SE25 .... 224 DU97
⇌ **Penge West** 204 DV93
Penhale Cl, Orp. BR6 .... 246 EU105
Penhall Rd, SE7 .... 36 E8
Penhill Rd, Bex. DA5 .... 208 EW87
Penhurst, Wok. GU21 .... 233 AZ114
Penhurst Pl, SE1 .... 30 D7
Penhurst Rd, Ilf. IG6 .... 125 EP52
Penifather La, Grnf. UB6 .... 159 CD69
Penington Rd, Beac. HP9 .... 132 AH55
Peninsula Apts, W2
off Praed St 16 C7
Peninsula Hts, SE1 .... 30 B10
Peninsular Cl, Felt. TW14 .... 197 BR86
Peninsular Pk Rd, SE7 .... 35 P9
Peninsula Sq, SE10 .... 35 J4
Penistone Rd, SW16 .... 203 DL94
Penistone Wk, Rom. RM3
off Okehampton Rd 128 FJ51
Penketh Dr, Har. HA1 .... 139 CD62
Penlow Rd, Harl. CM18 .... 73 EQ18
Penman Cl, St.Alb. AL2 .... 82 CA27
Penman's Grn, Kings L. WD4 .... 79 BF32
Penmans Hill, Chipper. WD4 .... 79 BF33
Penmon Rd, SE2 .... 188 EU76
PENN, H.Wyc. HP10 .... 110 AE48
Pennack Rd, SE15 .... 44 B3
Pennant Ms, W8 .... 27 L8
Pennant Ter, E17 .... 123 DZ54
Pennard Mans, W12 .... 26 A5
Pennard Rd, W12 .... 26 A4
Pennards, The, Sun. TW16 .... 218 BW96
Penn Av, Chesh. HP5 .... 76 AN30
Penn Bottom, Penn HP10 .... 110 AG47
Penn Cl, Chorl. WD3 .... 95 BD44
Greenford UB6 .... 158 CB68
Harrow HA3 .... 139 CJ56
Uxbridge UB8 .... 156 BK70
Penn Dr, Denh. UB9 .... 135 BF58
Penne Cl, Rad. WD7 .... 83 CF34
Penner Cl, SW19 .... 201 CY89
Penners Gdns, Surb. KT6 .... 220 CL101
Pennethorne Cl, E9 .... 10 G9
Pennethorne Ho, SW11 .... 40 B10
Pennethorne Rd, SE15 .... 44 E5
Penney Cl, Dart. DA1 .... 210 FK87
Penn Gdns, Chis. BR7 .... 227 EP96
Romford RM5 .... 126 FA52
Penn Gaskell La, Chal.St.P.
SL9 .... 113 AZ50
Penn Grn, Beac. HP9 .... 111 AK51
Penn Ho, Burn. SL1 .... 152 AJ69
Pennine Dr, NW2 .... 141 CY61
Pennine Ho, N9 *off Edmonton Grn Shop Cen* 122 DU48
Pennine La, NW2 .... 141 CY61
Pennine Rd, Slou. SL2 .... 153 AN71
Pennine Way, Bexh. DA7 .... 189 FE81
Harlington UB3 .... 177 BR80
Hemel Hempstead HP2 .... 62 BM17
Northfleet DA11 .... 212 GE90
Pennings Av, Guil. GU2 .... 264 AT132
Pennington Cl, SE27
off Hamilton Rd 204 DR91
Romford RM5 .... 126 FA50
Pennington Dr, N21 .... 103 DL43
Weybridge KT13 .... 217 BS104
Pennington Rd, Chal.St.P. SL9 .... 112 AX52
Penningtons, The, Amer. HP6 .... 77 AS37
Pennington St, E1 .... 32 D1
Pennington Way, SE12 .... 206 EH89
Pennis La, Fawk.Grn DA3 .... 231 FX100
Penniston Cl, N17 .... 122 DQ54
Penn La, Bex. DA5 .... 208 EX85
Penn Meadow, Stoke P. SL2 .... 154 AT67
Penn Pl, Rick. WD3
off Northway 114 BK45
Penn Rd, N7 .... 8 B2
Beaconsfield HP9 .... 110 AJ48
Chalfont St. Peter SL9 .... 112 AX53
Datchet SL3 .... 174 AX81
Mill End WD3 .... 113 BF46
Park Street AL2 .... 82 CC27
Slough SL2 .... 153 AR70
Watford WD24 .... 97 BV39
Sch **Penn Sch**, Penn HP10
off Church Rd 110 AD48
Penn St, N1 .... 9 M9

Penn Way, Chorl. WD3 95 BD44
Penny Cl, Rain. RM13 169 FH69
Pennycroft, Croy. CR0 243 DY109
Pennyfather La, Enf. EN2 104 DQ40
Pennyfield, Cob. KT11 235 BU113
Pennyfields, E14 22 A10
  Warley CM14 130 FW49
Penny La, Shep. TW17 217 BS101
Pennylets Grn, Stoke P. SL2 154 AT66
Pennymead, Harl. CM20 74 EU15
Pennymead Dr, E.Hors. KT24 267 BT127
Pennymead Ri, E.Hors. KT24 267 BT127
Pennymead Twr, Harl. CM20 74 EU15
Penny Ms, SW12 203 DH87
Pennymoor Wk, W9 15 H4
Penny Rd, NW10 160 CP69
Pennyroyal Av, E6 25 L9
Pennys La, High Wych CM21 57 ER05
Penpoll Rd, E8 10 E4
Penpool La, Well. DA16 188 EV83
Penrhyn Av, E17 123 DZ53
Penrhyn Cl, Cat. CR3 258 DR120
Penrhyn Cres, E17 123 EA53
  SW14 180 CQ84
Penrhyn Gdns, Kings.T. KT1
  off Surbiton Rd 219 CK98
Penrhyn Gro, E17 123 EA53
Penrhyn Rd, Kings.T. KT1 220 CL97
Penrith Cl, SW15 201 CY85
  Beckenham BR3 225 EB95
  Reigate RH2 272 DE133
  Uxbridge UB8 156 BK66
Penrith Cres, Rain. RM13 149 FG64
Penrith Pl, SE27 203 DP89
Penrith Rd, N15 144 DR57
  Ilford IG6 125 ET51
  New Malden KT3 220 CR98
  Romford RM3 128 FN51
  Thornton Heath CR7 224 DQ96
Penrith St, SW16 203 DJ93
Penrose Av, Wat. WD19 116 BX47
Penrose Ct, Eng.Grn TW20 194 AW93
  Hemel Hempstead HP2 62 BL16
Penrose Dr, Epsom KT19 238 CN111
Penrose Gro, SE17 43 J1
Penrose Ho, SE17 43 J1
Penrose Rd, Fetch. KT22 252 CC122
Penrose St, SE17 43 J1
Penryn St, NW1 7 N10
Penry St, SE1 31 P9
Pensbury Pl, SW8 41 M8
Pensbury St, SW8 41 M8
Penscroft Gdns, Borwd. WD6 100 CR42
Pensford Av, Rich. TW9 180 CN82
Penshurst, Harl. CM17 58 EV12
Penshurst Av, Sid. DA15 208 EU86
Penshurst Cl, Chal.St.P. SL9 112 AX54
Penshurst Gdns, Edg. HA8 118 CP50
Penshurst Grn, Brom. BR2 226 EF99
Penshurst Rd, E9 11 J7
  N17 122 DT52
  Bexleyheath DA7 188 EZ81
  Potters Bar EN6 86 DD31
  Thornton Heath CR7 223 DP99
Penshurst Wk, Brom. BR2
  off Penshurst Grn 226 EF99
Penshurst Way, Orp. BR5
  off Star La 228 EW98
  Sutton SM2 240 DA108
Pensilver Cl, Barn. EN4 102 DE42
Pensons La, Ong. CM5 93 FG28
Penstemon Cl, N3 120 DA52
Penstock Footpath, N22 143 DL55
Pentavia Retail Pk, NW7 119 CT52
Pentelow Gdns, Felt. TW14 197 BU86
Pentire Cl, Horsell GU21 232 AY114
  Upminster RM14 151 FS58
Pentire Rd, E17 123 ED53
Pentland, Hem.H. HP2
  off Mendip Way 62 BM17
Pentland Av, Edg. HA8 118 CP47
  Shepperton TW17 216 BN99
Pentland Cl, N9 122 DW47
  NW11 141 CY61
Pentland Gdns, SW18 202 DC86
Pentland Pl, Nthlt. UB5 158 BY67
Pentland Rd, NW6 15 J2
  Bushey WD23 98 CC44
  Slough SL2 153 AN71
Pentlands Cl, Mitch. CR4 223 DH97
Pentland St, SW18 202 DC86
Pentland Way, Uxb. UB10 137 BQ62
Pentley Cl, Welw.G.C. AL8 51 CX06
Pentley Pk, Welw.G.C. AL8 51 CX06
Pentlow St, SW15 38 B10
Pentlow Way, Buck.H. IG9 124 EL45
Pentney Rd, E4 123 ED46
  SW12 203 DJ88
  SW19 off Midmoor Rd 221 CY95
Penton Av, Stai. TW18 195 BF94
Penton Dr, Chsht EN8 89 DX29
Penton Gro, N1 18 E1
Penton Hall Dr, Stai. TW18 216 BG95
Penton Hook Rd, Stai. TW18 196 BG94
Penton Ho, SE2
  off Hartslock Dr 188 EX75
Penton Pk, Cher. KT16 216 BG97
Penton Pl, SE17 31 H10
Penton Ri, WC1 18 D2
Penton Rd, Stai. TW18 195 BF94
Penton St, N1 8 E10
PENTONVILLE, N1 18 E1
Pentonville Rd, N1 18 C1
Pentreath Av, Guil. GU2 280 AT135
Pentrich Av, Enf. EN1 104 DU38
Pentridge St, SE15 44 A4
Pentstemon Dr, Swans. DA10 212 FY85
Pentyre Av, N18 122 DR50
Penwerris Av, Islw. TW7 178 CC80
Penwith Rd, SW18 202 DB89
Penwith Wk, Wok. GU22 248 AX119
Penwood End, Wok. GU22 248 AV121
Penwood Ho, SW15
  off Tunworth Cres 201 CT86
Sch Penwortham Prim Sch, SW16
  off Penwortham Rd 203 DH93
Penwortham Rd, SW16 203 DH93
  South Croydon CR2 242 DQ110
Penylan Pl, Edg. HA8 118 CN52
Penywern Rd, SW5 27 K10
Penzance Cl, Hare. UB9 114 BK53
Penzance Gdns, Rom. RM3 128 FN51
Penzance Pl, W11 26 E2
Penzance Rd, Rom. RM3 128 FN51
Penzance Spur, Slou. SL2 153 AP70
Penzance St, W11 26 E2
Peony Cl, Pilg.Hat. CM15 130 FV44
Peony Ct, Wdf.Grn. IG8
  off The Bridle Path 124 EE52
Peony Gdns, W12 161 CU73
● Peoplebuilding, Hem.H.
  HP2 63 BP19
Pepler Ms, SE5 44 A2
Pepler Way, Burn. SL1 152 AH69
Peplins Cl, Brook.Pk AL9 85 CY26
Peplins Way, Brook.Pk AL9 85 CY25
Peploe Rd, NW6 4 D10
Peplow Cl, West Dr. UB7
  off Tavistock Rd 156 BK74
Pepper All, High Beach IG10 106 EG39
Pepper Cl, E6 25 K6
  Caterham CR3 274 DS125
Peppercorn Cl, Th.Hth. CR7 224 DR96
Pepper Hill, Gt Amwell SG12 55 DZ10
  Northfleet DA11 212 GC90
Pepperhill La, Nthflt DA11 212 GC90
Peppermead Sq, SE13 205 EA85
Peppermint Cl, Croy. CR0 223 DL101
Peppermint Pl, E11
  off Birch Gro 146 EE62
Pepper St, E14 34 C6
  SE1 31 J4
Peppie Cl, N16 144 DS61
Pepys Cl, Ashtd. KT21 254 CN117
  Dartford DA1 190 FN84
  Northfleet DA11 212 GD90
  Slough SL3 175 BB79
  Tilbury RM18 193 GJ81
  Uxbridge UB10 137 BP63
Pepys Cres, E16 35 P2
  Barnet EN5 101 CW43
Pepys Ri, Orp. BR6 227 ET102
Pepys Rd, SE14 45 K7
  SW20 221 CW95
Pepys St, EC3 19 P10
Perceval Av, NW3 6 C2
Percheron Cl, Islw. TW7 179 CG83
Percheron Rd, Borwd. WD6 100 CR44
Perch St, E8 10 B1
Percival Cl, Oxshott KT22 236 CB111
Percival Ct, N17 off High Rd 122 DT52
  Northolt UB5 138 CA64
★ Percival David Foundation of
  Chinese Art, WC1
  off Gordon Sq 17 P5
Percival Gdns, Rom. RM6 148 EW58
Percival Rd, SW14 180 CQ84
  Enfield EN1 104 DT42
  Feltham TW13 197 BT89
  Hornchurch RM11 150 FJ58
  Orpington BR6 227 EP103
Percival St, EC1 18 G4
Percival Way, Epsom KT19 238 CQ105
Percy Av, Ashf. TW15 196 BN92
Percy Bryant Rd, Sun. TW16 197 BS94
Percy Bush Rd, West Dr. UB7 176 BM76
Percy Circ, WC1 18 D2
Percy Gdns, Enf. EN3 105 DX43
  Hayes UB4 157 BS69
  Isleworth TW7 179 CG82
  Worcester Park KT4 220 CR102
Percy Ho, SW16
  off Pringle Gdns 203 DJ91
Percy Ms, W1 17 N7
Percy Pas, W1 17 M7
Percy Pl, Datchet SL3 174 AV81
Percy Rd, E11 146 EE59
  E16 23 K6
  N12 120 DC50
  N21 122 DQ45
  SE20 225 DX95
  SE25 224 DU99
  W12 181 CU75
  Bexleyheath DA7 188 EY82
  Guildford GU1 264 AV132
  Hampton TW12 198 CA94
  Ilford IG3 148 EU59
  Isleworth TW7 179 CG84
  Mitcham CR4 222 DG101
  Romford RM7 149 FB55
  Twickenham TW2 198 CB88
  Watford WD18 97 BV42
Percy St, W1 17 N7
  Grays RM17 192 GC79
Percy Ter, Brom. BR1 227 EP97
Percy Way, Twick. TW2 198 CC88
Percy Yd, WC1 18 D2
Peregrine Cl, NW10 140 CR64
  Watford WD25 82 BY34
Peregrine Ct, SW16 203 DM91
  Welling DA16 187 ET81
Peregrine Gdns, Croy. CR0 225 DY103
Peregrine Ho, EC1 19 H2
Peregrine Rd, N17 122 DQ52
  Ilford IG6 126 EV50
  Sunbury-on-Thames TW16 217 BT96
  Waltham Abbey EN9 90 EG34
Peregrine Wk, Horn. RM12
  off Heron Flight Av 169 FH65
Peregrine Way, SW19 201 CW94
Perham Rd, W14 38 F1
Perham Way, Lon.Col. AL2 83 CK26
Peridot St, E6 25 H6
Perifield, SE21 204 DQ88
Perimeade Rd, Perivale UB6 159 CJ68
Perimeter Rd E, Lon.Gat.Air.
  RH6 290 DG154
Perimeter Rd N, Lon.Gat.Air.
  RH6 290 DF151
Perimeter Rd S, Lon.Gat.Air.
  RH6 290 DC154
Periton Rd, SE9 186 EK84
PERIVALE, Grnf. UB6 159 CJ67
⊖ Perivale 159 CG68
Sch Perivale, Grnf. UB6 159 CF69
Perivale Gdns, W13 159 CH70
  Watford WD25 81 BV34
Perivale Gra, Perivale UB6 159 CG69
● Perivale Ind Pk, Perivale
  UB6 159 CG68
Perivale La, Perivale UB6 159 CG69
● Perivale New Business Cen,
  Perivale UB6 159 CH68
Sch Perivale Prim Sch, Perivale
  UB6 off Federal Rd 159 CJ68
Periwood Cres, Perivale UB6 159 CG67
Perkin Cl, Houns. TW3 178 CB84
  Wembley HA0 139 CH64
Perkins Cl, Green. DA9 211 FT85
Perkins Ct, Ashf. TW15 196 BM92
Perkin's Rents, SW1 29 N6
Perkins Rd, Ilf. IG2 147 ER57
Perkins Sq, SE1 31 K2
Perks Cl, SE3 47 J9
Perleybrooke La, Wok. GU21
  off Bampton Way 248 AU117
Permain Cl, Shenley WD7 83 CK33
Perpins Rd, SE9 207 ES86
Perram Cl, Brox. EN10 89 DY26
Perran Rd, SW2
  off Christchurch Rd 203 DP89
Perran Wk, Brent. TW8 180 CL78
Perren St, NW5 7 J4
Perrers Rd, W6 181 CV77
Perrett Gdns, Hert. SG14 53 DL08
Perrin Cl, Ashf. TW15
  off Fordbridge Rd 196 BM92
Perrin Ct, Wok. GU21
  off Blackmore Cres 249 BB115
Perrin Rd, Wem. HA0 139 CG63
Perrins Ct, NW3 5 P1
Perrins La, NW3 5 P1
Perrin's Wk, NW3 5 P1
Perrior Rd, Gdmg. GU7 280 AS144
Perriors Cl, Chsht EN7 88 DU27
Perrott St, SE18 187 EQ77
Perry Av, W3 160 CR72
Perry Cl, Rain. RM13
  off Lowen Rd 169 FD68
  Uxbridge UB8 157 BP72
Perry Ct, E14
  off Maritime Quay 34 B10
  N15 144 DS58
Perrycroft, Wind. SL4 173 AL83
Perryfields Way, Burn. SL1 152 AH70
Perryfield Way, NW9 141 CT58
  Richmond TW10 199 CH89
Perry Gdns, N9 off Deansway 122 DS48
Perry Garth, Nthlt. UB5 158 BW67
Perry Gro, Dart. DA1 190 FN84
Perry Hall Cl, Orp. BR6 228 EU101
Sch Perry Hall Prim Sch,
  Orp. BR6
  off Perry Hall Rd 227 ET100
Perry Hall Rd, Orp. BR6 227 ET100
Perry Hill, SE6 205 DZ90
  Lower Nazeing EN9 72 EF23
  Worplesdon GU3 264 AS128
Perry Ho, SW2 off Tierney Rd 203 DL87
  Rainham RM13
  off Lowen Rd 169 FD68
Perry How, Wor.Pk. KT4 221 CT102
Perrylands La, Smallfield RH6 291 DM149
Perryman Ho, Bark. IG11 167 EQ67
Perrymans Fm Rd, Ilf. IG2 147 ER58
Perryman Way, Slou. SL2 153 AM69
Perry Mead, Bushey WD23 116 CB45
  Enfield EN2 103 DP40
Perrymead St, SW6 39 K7
Sch Perrymount Prim Sch, SE23
  off Sunderland Rd 205 DX89
Perryn Rd, SE16 32 E6
  W3 160 CR73
Perry Ri, SE23 205 DY90
Perry Rd, Dag. RM9 168 EZ70
  Harlow CM18 73 EQ18
Perrysfield Rd, Chsht EN8 89 DY27
Perrys La, Knock.P. TN14 246 EV113
Perrys Pl, W1 17 N8
Perry Spring, Harl. CM17 74 EW17
PERRY STREET, Grav. DA11 212 GE88
Perry St, Chis. BR7 207 ER93
  Dartford DA1 189 FE84
  Northfleet DA11 212 GE88
Perry St Gdns, Chis. BR7
  off Old Perry St 207 ES93
Perry Vale, SE23 204 DW89
Perry Way, Aveley RM15 170 FQ73
● Perrywood Business Pk,
  Red. RH1 289 DH142
Perrywood Ho, E5
  off Pembury Rd 10 E2
Persant Rd, SE6 206 EE89
Perseverance Cotts, Ripley
  GU23 250 BJ121
Perseverance Pl, SW9 42 F5
  Richmond TW9
  off Shaftesbury Rd 180 CL83
Persfield Cl, Epsom KT17 239 CT110
Pershore Cl, Ilf. IG2 147 EP57
Pershore Gro, Cars. SM5 222 DD100
Perspective Ho, Enf. EN3
  off Tysoe Av 105 DY36
Pert Cl, N10 121 DH52
Perth Av, NW9 140 CR59
  Hayes UB4 158 BW70
  Slough SL1 153 AP72
Perth Cl, SW20
  off Huntley Way 221 CU96
  Northolt UB5 138 CA64
Perth Rd, E10 145 DY60
  E13 24 A1
  N4 143 DN60
  N22 121 DP53
  Barking IG11 167 ER68
  Beckenham BR3 225 EC96
  Ilford IG2 147 EN58
Perth Ter, Ilf. IG2 147 EQ59
● Perth Trd Est, Slou. SL1 153 AP71
Perwell Av, Har. HA2 138 BZ60
Perwell Ct, Har. HA2 138 BZ60
Pescot Hill, Hem.H. HP1 62 BH18
Sch Petchey Acad, E8 10 B2
Peter Av, NW10 161 CV66
  Oxted RH8 275 ED129
Peterboat Cl, SE10 35 K8
Sch Peterborough & St. Margaret's
  Sch, Stan. HA7
  off Common Rd 117 CE48
Peterborough Av, Upmin.
  RM14 151 FS60
Peterborough Gdns, Ilf. IG1 146 EL59
Peterborough Ms, SW6 39 J8
Sch Peterborough Prim Sch,
  SW6 39 K9
Peterborough Rd, E10 145 EC57
  SW6 39 J8
  Carshalton SM5 222 DE100
  Guildford GU2 264 AT132
  Harrow HA1 139 CE60
Peterborough Vil, SW6 39 L6
Peterchurch Ho, SE15 44 E4
Peter Dwight Dr, Amer. HP6
  off Woodside Rd 77 AS38
Petergate, SW11 182 DC84
Peterhead Ms, Slou. SL3 175 BA78
Peter Heathfield Ho, E15
  off Wise Rd 12 G8
Peterhill Cl, Chal.St.P. SL9 112 AY50
Sch Peter Hills with St. Mary's &
  St. Paul's C of E Prim Sch,
  SE16 33 K2
Peterhouse Gdns, SW6 39 M7
● Peter James Business Cen,
  Hayes UB3 177 BU75
Peterlee Ct, Hem.H. HP2 62 BM16
● Peterley Business Cen, E2 20 E1
Peter Moore Ct, N9
  off Menon Dr 122 DV48
★ Peter Pan Statue, W2 28 A2
Peters Av, Lon.Col. AL2 83 CJ26
Peters Cl, Dag. RM8 148 EX60
  Stanmore HA7 117 CK51
  Welling DA16 187 ES82
Petersfield Av, Rom. RM3 128 FL51
  Slough SL2 154 AU74
  Staines TW18 196 BJ92
Petersfield Cl, N18 122 DQ50
  Romford RM3 128 FN51
Petersfield Cres, Couls. CR5 257 DL115
Petersfield Ri, SW15 201 CV88
Petersfield Rd, W3 180 CQ75
  Staines TW18 196 BJ92
PETERSHAM, Rich. TW10 200 CL88
Petersham Av, Byfleet KT14 234 BL112
Petersham Cl, Byfleet KT14 234 BL112
  Richmond TW10 199 CK89
  Sutton SM1 240 DA106
Petersham Dr, Orp. BR5 227 ET96
Petersham Gdns, Orp. BR5 227 ET96
Petersham La, SW7 27 N6
Petersham Ms, SW7 27 N7
Petersham Pl, SW7 27 N6
Petersham Rd, Rich. TW10 200 CL86
Peters Hill, EC4 19 J10
Peter's La, EC1 19 H6
Peterslea, Kings L. WD4 81 BP29
Petersmead Cl, Tad. KT20 255 CW123
Peters Path, SE26 204 DV91
Peterstone Rd, SE2 188 EV76
Peterstow Cl, SW19 201 CY89
Peter St, W1 17 M10
  Gravesend DA12 213 GH87
Peterswood, Harl. CM18 73 ER19
Peters Wd Hill, Ware SG12 55 DX07
Sch Peterswood Inf Sch & Nurs,
  Harl. CM18
  off Paringdon Rd 73 ER19
Peterwood Way, Croy. CR0 223 DM103
Petham Ct, Swan. BR8 229 FF100
Petherton Rd, N5 9 K3
Petiver Cl, E9 11 H6
Petley Rd, W6 38 B3
Peto Pl, NW1 17 K4
Peto St N, E16 23 L9
Petridge Rd, Red. RH1 288 DF139
Petridgewood Common, Red.
  RH1 288 DF140
Petrie Cl, NW2 4 F4
★ Petrie Mus of Egyptian
  Archaeology, WC1
  off Malet Pl 17 N5
Petros Gdns, NW3 5 N3
Pettacre Cl, SE28 187 EQ76
Pett Cl, Horn. RM11 149 FH61
Petten Cl, Orp. BR5 228 EX102
Petten Gro, Orp. BR5 228 EW102
Petters Rd, Ashtd. KT21 254 CM116
Petticoat La, E1 19 P7
Petticoat Sq, E1 20 A8
Petticoat Twr, E1 20 A8
Pettits Boul, Rom. RM1 127 FE53
Pettits Cl, Rom. RM1 127 FE54
Pettits La, Rom. RM1 127 FE54
Pettits La N, Rom. RM1 127 FD53
Pettits Pl, Dag. RM10 148 FA64
Pettits Rd, Dag. RM10 148 FA64
Pettiward Cl, SW15 181 CW84
Pettley Gdns, Rom. RM7 149 FD57
Pettman Cres, SE28 187 ER76
Pettsgrove Av, Wem. HA0 139 CJ64
Petts Hill, Nthlt. UB5 138 CB64
Sch Petts Hill Prim Sch, Nthlt.
  UB5 off Newmarket Av 138 CB64
Petts La, Shep. TW17 216 BN98
Pett St, SE18 36 G8
PETTS WOOD, Orp. BR5 227 ER99
⇌ Petts Wood 227 EQ99
Petts Wd Rd, Petts Wd BR5 227 EQ99
Petty Cross, Slou. SL1 153 AL72
Petty France, SW1 29 M6
Pettys Cl, Chsht EN8 89 DX28
Petty Wales, EC3 31 P1
Petworth Cl, Couls. CR5 257 DJ119
  Northolt UB5 158 BZ66
Petworth Ct, Wind. SL4 173 AP81
Petworth Gdns, SW20
  off Hidcote Gdns 221 CV97
  Uxbridge UB10 157 BQ67
Petworth Ho, SE22
  off Pytchley Rd 184 DS83
Petworth Rd, N12 120 DE50
  Bexleyheath DA6 208 FA85
Petworth St, SW11 40 D6
Petworth Way, Horn. RM12 149 FF63
Petyt Pl, SW3 40 C3
Petyward, SW3 28 D9
Pevensey Av, N11 121 DK50
  Enfield EN1 104 DR40
Pevensey Cl, Islw. TW7 178 CC80
Pevensey Rd, E7 146 EF63
  SW17 202 DD91
  Feltham TW13 198 BY88
  Slough SL2 153 AN71
Peverel, E6 25 L8
Peverel Ho, Dag. RM10 148 FA61
Peveret Cl, N11
  off Woodland Rd 121 DH50
Peveril Dr, Tedd. TW11 199 CD92
Pewley Bk, Guil. GU1 280 AY136
Sch Pewley Down Inf Sch, Guil.
  GU1 off Semaphore Rd 280 AY136
Pewley Hill, Guil. GU1 280 AX136
Pewley Pt, Guil. GU1 280 AY136
Pewley Way, Guil. GU1 280 AY136
Pewsey Cl, E4 123 EA50
Peyton Pl, SE10 46 E4
Peyton's Cotts, Red. RH1 273 DM132
Pharaoh Cl, Mitch. CR4 222 DF101
Pharaoh's Island, Shep. TW17 216 BM103
Pheasant Cl, E16 23 P8
  Berkhamsted HP4 60 AW20
  Purley CR8
  off Partridge Knoll 241 DP113
Pheasant Hill, Ch.St.G. HP8 112 AW47
Pheasant Ri, Chesh. HP5 76 AR33
Pheasants Way, Rick. WD3 114 BH45
Pheasant Wk, Chal.St.P. SL9 112 AX49
Phelips Rd, Harl. CM19 73 EN20
Phelp St, SE17 43 L2
Phelps Way, Hayes UB3 177 BT77
Phene St, SW3 40 D2
Philanthropic Rd, Red. RH1 288 DG135
Philan Way, Rom. RM5 127 FD51
Philbeach Gdns, SW5 27 H10
Phil Brown Pl, SW8 41 K10
Philbye Ms, Slou. SL1 173 AM75
Philchurch Pl, E1 20 D9
Philimore Cl, SE18 187 ES78
Philip Av, Rom. RM7 149 FD60
  Swanley BR8 229 FD98
Philip Cl, Pilg.Hat. CM15 130 FV44
  Romford RM7 off Philip Av 149 FD60
Philip Dr, Flack.Hth HP10 132 AC56
Philip Gdns, Croy. CR0 225 DZ103
Philip La, N15 144 DR56
Philipot Path, SE9 207 EM86
Philippa Gdns, SE9 206 EK85
Philippa Way, Grays RM16 193 GH77
Philip Rd, Rain. RM13 169 FE69
  Staines TW18 196 BK93
Philips Cl, Cars. SM5 222 DG102
Philip Sidney Ct, Chaff.Hun.
  RM16 191 FX78
Sch Philip Southcote Sch, Add.
  KT15 off Addlestone Moor 216 BJ103
Philip St, E13 23 N4
Philip Sydney Rd, Grays
  RM16 191 FX78
Philip Wk, SE15 44 D10
Phillida Rd, Rom. RM3 128 FN54
Phillimore Gdns, NW10 4 A8
  W8 27 J5
Phillimore Gdns Cl, W8 27 J6
Phillimore Pl, W8 27 J5
  Radlett WD7 99 CE36
Phillimore Wk, W8 27 J6
Phillipers, Wat. WD25 98 BY35
Phillipp St, N1 9 N9
Phillips Cl, Dart. DA1 209 FH86
Phillips Hatch, Won. GU5 281 BC143
Philpot La, EC3 19 N10
  Chobham GU24 232 AV113
Philpot Path, Ilf. IG1
  off Richmond Rd 147 EQ62
Philpots Cl, West Dr. UB7 156 BK73
Philpot Sq, SW6
  off Peterborough Rd 182 DB83
Philpot St, E1 20 F8
Phineas Pett Rd, SE9 186 EL83
[rail] Phipps Bridge 222 DC97
Phipps Br Rd, SW19 222 DC96
  Mitcham CR4 222 DC96
Phipps Hatch La, Enf. EN2 104 DQ38
Phipp's Ms, SW1 29 K7
Phipps Rd, Slou. SL1 153 AK71
Phipp St, EC2 19 N4
Phoebe Rd, Hem.H. HP2 62 BM17
Phoebeth Rd, SE4 205 EA85
● Phoenix Business Cen, Chesh.
  HP5 off Higham Rd 76 AP30
Phoenix Cl, E8 10 A8
  E17 123 DZ54
  W12 161 CV73
  Epsom KT19 238 CN112
  Northwood HA6 115 BT49
  West Wickham BR4 226 EE103
Phoenix Ct, Felt. TW13 197 BS91
  Guildford GU1 off High St 280 AX136
  New Malden KT3 221 CT97
  Northfleet DA11 212 GA85
Phoenix Dr, Kes. BR2 226 EK104
Sch Phoenix High Sch, W12
  off The Curve 161 CU73
● Phoenix Pk, Brent. TW8 179 CK78
Phoenix Pl, WC1 18 D4
  Dartford DA1 210 FK87
Phoenix Rd, NW1 17 N2
  SE20 204 DW93
Sch Phoenix Sch, E3 21 P2
Sch Phoenix Sch, The, NW3 5 P5
Phoenix St, WC2 17 P9
● Phoenix Trd Est, Perivale
  UB6 159 CJ67
Phoenix Way, SW18 off North Side
  Wandsworth Common 202 DC85
  Hounslow TW5 178 BW79
Phoenix Wf, SE10 35 L4
Phoenix Wf Rd, SE1 32 B5
Phoenix Yd, WC1 18 D3
★ Photographers' Gall, WC2 17 P10
Phygtle, The, Chal.St.P. SL9 112 AY51
Phyllis Av, N.Mal. KT3 221 CV99
★ Physical Energy Statue, W2 27 P3
Physic Pl, SW3 40 E2
Picardy Ho, Enf. EN2
  off Cedar Rd 104 DQ38
Picardy Manorway, Belv.
  DA17 189 FB76
Picardy Rd, Belv. DA17 188 FA78
Picardy St, Belv. DA17 188 FA76
Piccadilly, W1 29 K3
Piccadilly Arc, SW1 29 L2
⊖ Piccadilly Circus 29 M1
Piccadilly Circ, W1 29 N1
Piccadilly Ct, N7 8 C4
Piccadilly Pl, W1 29 M1
Piccards, The, Guil. GU2
  off Chestnut Av 280 AW138
PICCOTTS END, Hem.H. HP2 62 BJ16
Piccotts End La, Hem.H. HP2 62 BJ17
Piccotts End Rd, Hem.H. HP1 62 BJ18
Pickard Cl, N14 121 DK46
Pickard St, EC1 19 H2
Pickering Av, E6 25 M1
Pickering Cl, E9 11 J6
Pickering Gdns, N11 120 DG51
  Croydon CR0 224 DT100
Pickering Ms, W2 15 M8
Pickering Pl, SW1 29 M3
  Guildford GU2 264 AU132
Pickering Rd, Bark. IG11 167 EQ65
Pickering St, N1 9 H8
Pickets Cl, Bushey Hth WD23 117 CD46
Pickets St, SW12 203 DH87
Pickett Cft, Stan. HA7 117 CK53
Picketts, Welw.G.C. AL8 51 CX06
Picketts La, Red. RH1 289 DJ144
Picketts Lock La, N9 122 DW47
Pickford Cl, Bexh. DA7 188 EY82
Pickford Dr, Slou. SL3 155 AZ74
Pickford La, Bexh. DA7 188 EY82
Pickford Rd, Bexh. DA7 188 EY83
  St. Albans AL1 65 CH20
Pickfords Gdns, Slou. SL1 153 AR73
Pickfords Wf, N1 19 J1
Pick Hill, Wal.Abb. EN9 90 EF32

Pickhurst Grn, Brom. BR2 226 EF101
Pickhurst Inf Sch, W.Wick. BR4 off Pickhurst La 226 EF100
Pickhurst Jun Sch, W.Wick. BR4 off Pickhurst La 226 EF100
Pickhurst La, Brom. BR2 226 EF102
West Wickham BR4 226 EE100
Pickhurst Mead, Brom. BR2 226 EF101
Pickhurst Pk, Brom. BR2 226 EE99
Pickhurst Ri, W.Wick. BR4 225 EC101
Pickins Piece, Horton SL3 175 BA82
Pickmoss La, Otford TN14 263 FH116
Pickwick Cl, Houns. TW4 off Dorney Way 198 BY85
Pickwick Ct, SE9 206 EL88
Pickwick Gdns, Nthflt DA11 212 GD90
Pickwick Ms, N18 122 DS50
Pickwick Pl, Har. HA1 139 CE59
Pickwick Rd, SE21 204 DR87
Pickwick St, SE1 31 J5
Pickwick Ter, Slou. SL2 off Maple Cres 154 AV73
Pickwick Way, Chis. BR7 207 EQ93
Pickworth Cl, SW8 42 B5
Picquets Way, Bans. SM7 255 CY116
Picton Pl, W1 17 H9
Surbiton KT6 220 CN102
Picton St, SE5 43 L5
Picture Ho, SW16 off Streatham High Rd 203 DL89
Pied Bull Yd, N1 off Theberton St 8 G8
Piedmont Rd, SE18 187 ER78
Pield Heath Av, Uxb. UB8 156 BN70
Pield Heath Ho Sch, Uxb. UB8 off Pield Heath Rd 156 BL70
Pield Heath Rd, Uxb. UB8 156 BM71
Piercing Hill, They.B. CM16 107 ER35
Pier Head, E1 32 E3
Pierian Spring, Hem.H. HP1 62 BH18
Pieris Ho, Felt. TW13 off High St 197 BU89
Piermont Grn, SE22 204 DV85
Piermont Pl, Brom. BR1 226 EL96
Piermont Rd, SE22 204 DV85
Pier Par, E16 37 L3
Pierrepoint Arc, N1 8 G10
Pierrepoint Rd, W3 160 CP73
Pierrepoint Row, N1 8 G10
Pier Rd, E16 37 L5
Erith DA8 189 FE79
Feltham TW14 197 BV85
Greenhithe DA9 191 FV84
Northfleet DA11 213 GF86
Pierson Rd, Wind. SL4 173 AK82
Pier St, E14 34 F8
Pier Ter, SW18 off Jew's Row 182 DB84
Pier Wk, Grays RM17 192 GA80
Pier Way, SE28 187 ER76
Pigeonhouse La, Chipstead CR5 272 DC125
Pigeon La, Hmptn. TW12 198 CA91
Piggotts End, Amer. HP7 77 AP40
Piggotts Orchard, Amer. HP7 77 AP40
Piggs Cor, Grays RM17 192 GC76
Piggy La, Chorl. WD3 95 BB44
Pigott St, E14 22 A9
Pike Cl, Brom. BR1 206 EH92
Uxbridge UB10 156 BM67
Pike La, Upmin. RM14 151 FT64
Pike Rd, NW7 off Ellesmere Av 118 CR49
Pikes End, Pnr. HA5 137 BV56
Pikes Hill, Epsom KT17 238 CS113
Pikestone Cl, Hayes UB4 off Berrydale Rd 158 BY70
Pike Way, N.Wld Bas. CM16 92 FA27
Pilgrimage St, SE1 31 L5
Pilgrim Cl, Mord. SM4 222 DB101
Park Street AL2 82 CC27
Pilgrim Hill, SE27 204 DQ91
Orpington BR5 228 EY96
Pilgrims Cl, N13 121 DM49
Northolt UB5 138 CC64
Pilgrim's Hatch CM15 130 FT43
Shere GU5 282 BN139
Watford WD25 off Kytes Dr 82 BX33
Westhumble RH5 269 CG131
Pilgrims Ct, SE3 47 P6
Dartford DA1 210 FN85
PILGRIM'S HATCH, Brwd. CM15 130 FU42
Pilgrim's La, NW3 6 B1
Pilgrims La, Chaldon CR3 273 DM125
North Stifford RM16 171 FW74
Titsey RH8 276 EH125
Westerham TN16 260 EL123
Pilgrims Ms, E14 23 H10
Pilgrims Pl, NW3 6 A1
Reigate RH2 272 DA132
Pilgrims Ri, Barn. EN4 102 DE43
Pilgrim St, EC4 18 G9
Pilgrims Vw, Green. DA9 211 FW86
Pilgrims Way, E6 off High St N 166 EL67
N19 143 DK60
Pilgrims' Way, Albury GU5 282 BL138
Betchworth RH3 271 CY131
Caterham CR3 273 DP126
Pilgrims Way, Chev. TN14 262 EV121
Dartford DA1 210 FN88
Pilgrims' Way, Dor. RH4 269 CE134
Pilgrims Way, Guil. GU4 280 AX138
Pilgrims' Way, Red. RH1 273 DJ127
Pilgrims Way, Reig. RH2 272 DA131
Shere GU5 282 BN139
South Croydon CR2 242 DT106
Pilgrim's Way, Wem. HA9 140 CP60
Pilgrims Way, West. TN16 261 EM123
Westhumble RH5 269 CH131
Pilgrims' Way Prim Sch, SE15 44 G3
Pilgrims Way W, Otford TN14 263 FD116
Pilkington Rd, SE15 44 E9
Orpington BR6 227 EQ103
Pilkingtons, Harl. CM17 74 EX15
Pillions La, Hayes UB4 157 BR70
Pilot Busway, SE10 35 K5
Pilot Cl, SE8 45 N2
Pilots Pl, Grav. DA12 213 GJ86
Pilsdon Cl, SW19 201 CX88
Piltdown Rd, Wat. WD19 116 BX49
● Pilton Ind Est, Croy. CR0 223 DP103
Pilton Pl, SE17 31 K10
Pimento Ct, W5 off Olive Rd 179 CK76
PIMLICO, SW1 29 L10
⊖ Pimlico 29 N10
Pimlico Acad, SW1 41 M1
Pimlico Rd, SW1 28 G10
Pimlico Wk, N1 19 N2
Pimms Cl, Guil. GU4 265 BA130
Pimpernel Way, Rom. RM3 128 FK51
Pinceybrook Rd, Harl. CM18 73 EQ19
Pinchbeck Rd, Orp. BR6 245 ET107
Pinchfield, Map.Cr. WD3 113 BE50
Pinchin St, E1 20 D10
Pincott La, W.Hors. KT24 267 BP129
Pincott Pl, SE4 45 K10
Pincott Rd, SW19 202 DC94
Bexleyheath DA6 208 FA85
Pindar Rd, Hodd. EN11 71 EC16
Pindar St, EC2 19 N6
PINDEN, Dart. DA2 231 FW96
Pindock Ms, W9 15 M5
Pineapple Ct, SW1 29 L6
Pineapple Rd, Amer. HP7 94 AT39
Pine Av, E15 13 H2
Gravesend DA12 213 GK88
West Wickham BR4 225 EB102
Pine Cl, E10 145 EA61
N14 121 DJ45
N19 143 DJ61
SE20 224 DW95
Berkhamsted HP4 60 AV19
Cheshunt EN8 89 DX28
Kenley CR8 258 DR117
New Haw KT15 234 BH111
Stanmore HA7 117 CH49
Swanley BR8 229 FF98
Woking GU21 248 AW117
Pine Coombe, Croy. CR0 243 DX105
Pine Ct, Upmin. RM14 150 FN63
Pine Cres, Cars. SM5 240 DD111
Hutton CM13 131 GD43
Pinecrest Gdns, Orp. BR6 245 EP105
Pinecroft, Gidea Pk RM2 150 FJ56
Hemel Hempstead HP3 62 BM24
Hutton CM13 131 GB45
Pinecroft Cres, Barn. EN5 off Hillside Gdns 101 CY42
Pine Dean, Bkhm KT23 268 CB125
Pinedene, SE15 44 E6
Pinefield Cl, E14 22 A10
Pine Gdns, Horl. RH6 290 DG149
Ruislip HA4 137 BV60
Surbiton KT5 220 CN100
Pine Glade, Orp. BR6 245 EM105
Pine Gro, N4 143 DL61
N20 119 CZ46
SW19 201 CZ92
Bricket Wood AL2 82 BZ30
Brookmans Park AL9 86 DB25
Bushey WD23 98 BZ40
Weybridge KT13 235 BP106
Pine Gro Ms, Wey. KT13 235 BQ106
Pine Hill, Epsom KT18 254 CR115
Pinehurst, Sev. TN14 279 FL121
Pinehurst Cl, Abb.L. WD5 81 BS32
Kingswood KT20 256 DA122
Pinehurst Gdns, W.Byf. KT14 234 BJ112
Pinehurst Wk, Orp. BR6 227 ES102
Pinelands Cl, SE3 47 M5
Pinel Cl, Vir.W. GU25 214 AY98
Pinemartin Cl, NW2 141 CW62
Pine Ms, NW10 4 C10
Pineneedle La, Sev. TN13 279 FH123
Pine Pl, Bans. SM7 239 CX114
Hayes UB4 157 BT70
Pine Ridge, Cars. SM5 240 DG109
Pineridge Cl, Wey. KT13 235 BS105
Pine Rd, N11 120 DG47
NW2 141 CW63
Woking GU22 248 AW120
Pines, The, N14 103 DJ43
Borehamwood WD6 off Anthony Rd 100 CM40
Coulsdon CR5 257 DH118
Dorking RH4 off South Ter 285 CH137
Hemel Hempstead HP3 61 BF24
Purley CR8 241 DP113
Slough SL3 155 AZ74
Sunbury-on-Thames TW16 217 BU97
Woking GU21 233 AZ114
Woodford Green IG8 124 EG48
Pines Av, Enf. EN1 104 DV36
Pines Cl, Amer. HP6 77 AP36
Northwood HA6 115 BS51
Pines Rd, Brom. BR1 226 EL96
● Pines Trd Est, The, Guil. GU3 264 AS132
Pine St, EC1 18 E4
Pinetree Cl, Chal.St.P. SL9 112 AW52
Pine Tree Cl, Hem.H. HP2 62 BK19
Hounslow TW5 177 BV81
Pinetree Gdns, Hem.H. HP3 62 BL22
Pine Tree Hill, Wok. GU22 249 BD116
Pine Trees Dr, Uxb. UB10 136 BL63
Pine Tree Way, SE13 off Elmira St 185 EB83
Pine Vw Cl, Chilw. GU4 281 BF140
Pine Vw Manor, Epp. CM16 92 EU30
Pine Wk, Bans. SM7 256 DF117
Pinewalk, Bkhm KT23 268 CB125
Pine Wk, Brom. BR1 226 EJ95
Carshalton SM5 240 DD110
Caterham CR3 258 DS122
Cobham KT11 236 BX114
East Horsley KT24 267 BT128
Surbiton KT5 220 CN100
Pine Way, Eng.Grn TW20 off Ashwood Rd 194 AV93
Pine Wd, Sun. TW16 217 BU95
Pinewood, Welw.G.C. AL7 51 CY11
Pinewood Av, New Haw KT15 234 BJ109
Pinner HA5 116 CB51
Rainham RM13 169 FH70
Sevenoaks TN14 279 FK121
Sidcup DA15 207 ES88
Uxbridge UB8 156 BM72
Pinewood Cl, Borwd. WD6 100 CR39
Croydon CR0 225 DY104
Gerrards Cross SL9 off Oxford Rd 134 AY59
Harlow CM17 74 EW16
Iver SL0 155 BC66
Northwood HA6 115 BV50
Orpington BR6 227 ER103
Pinner HA5 116 CB51
St. Albans AL4 65 CJ20
Watford WD17 97 BU39
Woking GU21 233 BA114
Pinewood Dr, Orp. BR6 245 ES106
Potters Bar EN6 85 CZ31
Staines TW18 196 BG92
Pinewood Gdns, Hem.H. HP1 62 BH20
Pinewood Grn, Iver SL0 155 BC66
Pinewood Gro, W5 159 CJ72
New Haw KT15 234 BH110
Pinewood Ms, Stanw. TW19 196 BK86
Pinewood Pk, New Haw KT15 234 BH111
Pinewood Pl, Dart. DA2 209 FE89
Epsom KT19 238 CR105
Pinewood Prim Sch, Coll.Row RM5 off Thistledene Av 127 FB50
Pinewood Ride, Iver SL0 155 BA68
Slough SL3 155 BA68
Pinewood Rd, SE2 188 EX79
Bromley BR2 226 EG98
Feltham TW13 197 BV90
Havering-atte-Bower RM4 127 FC49
Iver SL0 155 BB67
Virginia Water GU25 214 AU98
Pinewood Sch, Ware SG12 off Hoe La 55 DX08
Pinewood Way, Hutt. CM13 131 GD43
Pinfold Rd, SW16 203 DL91
Bushey WD23 98 BZ40
Pinglestone Cl, Harm. UB7 176 BL80
Pinkcoat Cl, Felt. TW13 off Tanglewood Way 197 BV90
Pinkerton Pl, SW16 203 DK91
Pinkham Way, N11 120 DG52
Pink La, Burn. SL1 152 AH68
Pinkneys Ct, Tap. SL6 152 AG72
Pinks Hill, Swan. BR8 229 FE99
Pinkwell Av, Hayes UB3 177 BR77
Pinkwell La, Hayes UB3 177 BQ77
Pinkwell Prim Sch, Hayes UB3 off Pinkwell La 177 BQ77
Pinley Gdns, Dag. RM9 off Stamford Rd 168 EV67
Pinnacle Hill, Bexh. DA7 189 FB84
Pinnacle Hill N, Bexh. DA7 189 FB83
PINNACLES, Harl. CM19 73 EN15
Pinnacles, Wal.Abb. EN9 90 EE34
Pinnate Pl, Welw.G.C. AL7 51 CY13
Pinn Cl, Uxb. UB8 156 BK72
Pinnell Rd, SE9 186 EK84
PINNER, HA5 138 BY56
⊖ Pinner 138 BY56
Pinner Ct, Pnr. HA5 138 CA56
PINNER GREEN, Pnr. HA5 116 BX54
Pinner Grn, Pnr. HA5 116 BW54
Pinner Gro, Pnr. HA5 138 BY56
Pinner Hill, Pnr. HA5 116 BW53
Pinner Hill Rd, Pnr. HA5 116 BW54
Pinner Pk, Pnr. HA5 116 CA53
Pinner Pk Av, Har. HA2 138 CB55
Pinner Pk First Sch, Pnr. HA5 off Melbourne Av 138 CB55
Pinner Pk Gdns, Har. HA2 116 CC54
Pinner Pk Mid Sch, Pnr. HA5 off Melbourne Av 138 CB55
Pinner Rd, Har. HA1, HA2 138 CB57
Northwood HA6 115 BT53
Pinner HA5 138 BZ56
Watford WD19 98 BX44
Pinner Vw, Har. HA1, HA2 138 CC58
PINNERWOOD PARK, Pnr. HA5 116 BW52
Pinner Wd Sch, Pnr. HA5 off Latimer Gdns 116 BW53
Pinnocks Av, Grav. DA11 213 GH88
Pinn Way, Ruis. HA4 137 BS59
Pinstone Way, Ger.Cr. SL9 135 BB61
Pintail Cl, E6 24 G7
Pintail Rd, Wdf.Grn. IG8 124 EH52
Pintail Way, Hayes UB4 158 BX71
Pinter Ho, SW9 42 B9
Pinto Cl, Borwd. WD6 off Percheron Rd 100 CR44
Pinto Way, SE3 186 EH84
Pioneer Cl, E14 22 C7
Pioneer Pl, Croy. CR0 243 EA109
● Pioneers Ind Pk, Croy. CR0 223 DL102
Pioneer St, SE15 44 C6
Pioneer Way, W12 off Du Cane Rd 161 CV72
Swanley BR8 229 FE97
Watford WD18 97 BT44
Piper Cl, N7 8 C3
Piper Rd, Kings.T. KT1 220 CN97
Pipers Cl, Burn. SL1 152 AJ69
Cobham KT11 252 BX115
PIPERS END, Hert. SG14 53 DJ13
Pipers End, Hert. SG14 53 DJ13
Virginia Water GU25 214 AX97
Piper's Gdns, Croy. CR0 225 DY101
Pipers Grn, NW9 140 CQ57
Pipers Grn La, Edg. HA8 118 CL48
Piper Way, Ilf. IG1 147 ER60
Pipewell Rd, Cars. SM5 222 DE100
Pippbrook, Dor. RH4 285 CH135
Pippbrook Gdns, Dor. RH4 off London Rd 285 CH135
Pippens, Welw.G.C. AL8 51 CY06
Pippin Cl, NW2 141 CV62
Croydon CR0 225 DZ102
Shenley WD7 84 CL33
Pippins, The, Slou. SL3 off Pickford Dr 155 AZ74
Watford WD25 82 BW34
Pippins Cl, West Dr. UB7 176 BK76
Pippins Ct, Ashf. TW15 197 BP93
Pippins Sch, Colnbr. SL3 off Raymond Cl 175 BF81
Pippit Ct, Enf. EN3 off Teal Cl 104 DW37
Piquet Rd, SE20 224 DW96
Pirbright Cres, New Adgtn CR0 243 EC107
Pirbright Rd, SW18 201 CZ88
Pirie Cl, SE5 43 M10
Pirie St, E16 36 B3
Pirrip Cl, Grav. DA12 213 GM89
Pirton Cl, St.Alb. AL4 65 CJ15
Pishiobury Dr, Saw. CM21 58 EW07
Pishiobury Ms, Saw. CM21 58 EX08
Pitcairn Cl, Rom. RM7 148 FA56
Pitcairn Rd, Mitch. CR4 202 DF94
Pitcairn's Path, Har. HA2 off Eastcote Rd 138 CC62
Pitchfont La, Oxt. RH8 260 EF124
Pitchford St, E15 13 H7
PITCH PLACE, Guil. GU3 264 AT129
Pitch Pond Cl, Knot.Grn HP9 110 AH50
Pit Fm Rd, Guil. GU1 265 BA134
Pitfield Cres, SE28 168 EU74
Pitfield Est, N1 19 M2
Pitfield St, N1 19 N3
Pitfield Way, NW10 160 CQ65
Enfield EN3 104 DW39
Pitfold Cl, SE12 206 EG86
Pitfold Rd, SE12 206 EG86
Pitlake, Croy. CR0 223 DP103
Pitman Ho, SE8 off Tanners Hill 46 A6
Pitman St, SE5 43 J4
Pitmaston Ho, SE13 46 E8
Pitmaston Rd, SE13 46 E8
Pitsea Pl, E1 21 K9
Pitsea St, E1 21 K9
Pitsfield, Welw.G.C. AL8 51 CX06
Pitshanger La, W5 159 CH70
★ Pitshanger Manor Ho & Gall, W5 159 CJ74
Pitshanger Pk, W13 159 CH69
Pitson Cl, Add. KT15 234 BK105
Pitstone Cl, St.Alb. AL4 off Highview Gdns 65 CJ15
Pitt Cres, SW19 202 DB91
Pitt Dr, St.Alb. AL4 65 CJ23
Pitteway Wk, Hert. SG14 off Port Vale 54 DQ09
Pitt Ho, SW11 off Maysoule Rd 182 DD84
Pittman Cl, Ingrave CM13 131 GC50
Pittman Gdns, Ilf. IG1 147 EQ64
Pittmans Fld, Harl. CM20 57 ET14
Pitt Pl, Epsom KT17 238 CS114
Pitt Rd, Croy. CR0 224 DQ99
Epsom KT17 238 CS114
Orpington BR6 245 EQ105
Thornton Heath CR7 224 DQ99
Pitt's Head Ms, W1 29 H3
Pittsmead Av, Brom. BR2 226 EG101
Pitts Rd, Slou. SL1 153 AQ74
Pitt St, W8 27 K4
Pittville Gdns, SE25 224 DU97
Pittwood, Shenf. CM15 131 GA46
Pitwood Grn, Tad. KT20 255 CW120
● Pitwood Pk Ind Est, Tad. KT20 off Waterfield 255 CV120
Pix Fm La, Hem.H. HP1 61 BB21
Pixfield Ct, Brom. BR2 off Beckenham La 226 EF96
PIXHAM, Dor. RH4 269 CJ133
● Pixham End, Dor. RH4 269 CJ133
Pixham La, Dor. RH4 269 CJ133
Pixholme Gro, Dor. RH4 269 CJ134
Pixies Hill Cres, Hem.H. HP1 61 BF22
Pixies Hill JMI Sch, Hem.H. HP1 off Hazeldell Rd 61 BF21
Pixies Hill Rd, Hem.H. HP1 61 BF21
Pixley St, E14 21 P8
Pixton Way, Croy. CR0 243 DY109
Place Fm Av, Orp. BR6 227 ER102
Place Fm Rd, Bletch. RH1 274 DR130
Placehouse La, Couls. CR5 257 DM119
Plackett Way, Slou. SL1 153 AK74
Plain, The, Epp. CM16 92 EV29
Plaines Cl, Slou. SL1 153 AM74
PLAISTOW, E13 23 L2
PLAISTOW, Brom. BR1 206 EF93
⊖ Plaistow 13 M10
Plaistow Gro, E15 13 L9
Bromley BR1 206 EH94
Plaistow Hosp, E13 24 C1
Plaistow La, Brom. BR1 206 EG94
Plaistow Pk Rd, E13 166 EH68
Plaistow Prim Sch, E13 off Junction Rd 166 EH68
Plaistow Rd, E13 13 L9
E15 13 L9
Plaitford Cl, Rick. WD3 114 BL47
Plane Av, Nthflt DA11 212 GD87
Planes, The, Cher. KT16 216 BJ101
Plane St, SE26 204 DV90
Plane Tree Cres, Felt. TW13 197 BV90
Plane Tree Wk, N2 142 DD55
SE19 off Lunham Rd 204 DS93
Plantaganet Pl, Wal.Abb. EN9 89 EB33
Plantagenet Cl, Wor.Pk. KT4 238 CR105
Plantagenet Gdns, Rom. RM6 148 EX59
Plantagenet Pl, Rom. RM6 148 EX59
Plantagenet Rd, Barn. EN5 102 DC42
Plantain Gdns, E11 off Hollydown Way 145 ED62
Plantain Pl, SE1 31 L4
Plantation, The, SE3 47 P9
Plantation Cl, SW4 off King's Av 203 DL85
Greenhithe DA9 211 FT86
Plantation Dr, Orp. BR5 228 EX102
Plantation La, EC3 off Rood La 19 N10
Warlingham CR6 259 DY119
Plantation Rd, Amer. HP6 77 AS37
Erith DA8 189 FG81
Swanley BR8 209 FG94
Plantation Wk, Hem.H. HP1 62 BG17
Plantation Way, Amer. HP6 77 AS37
Plantation Wf, SW11 39 P10
Plashet Gdns, Brwd. CM13 131 GA49
Plashet Gro, E6 166 EJ67
Plashet Rd, E13 13 P8
Plashets, The, Sheering CM22 59 FC07
Plashet Sch, E6 off Plashet Gro 166 EL66
Plassy Rd, SE6 205 EB87
Platford Grn, Horn. RM11 150 FL56
Platina St, EC2 19 M4
Platinum Ho, Har. HA1 139 CF58
Platinum Ms, N15 off Crowland Rd 144 DT57
Plato Rd, SW2 183 DL84
Platt, The, SW15 38 D10
Amersham HP7 77 AP40
Platt Meadow, Guil. GU4 off Eustace Rd 265 BD131
Platts Av, Wat. WD17 97 BV41
Platt's Eyot, Hmptn. TW12 218 CA96
Platt's La, NW3 142 DA63
Platts Rd, Enf. EN3 104 DW39
Platt St, NW1 7 N10
Plawsfield Rd, Beck. BR3 225 DX95
Plaxtol Cl, Brom. BR1 226 EJ95
Plaxtol Rd, Erith DA8 188 FA80
Plaxton Ct, E11 off Woodhouse Rd 146 EF62
Playfair St, W6 38 B1
Playfield Av, Rom. RM5 127 FC53
Playfield Cres, SE22 204 DT85
Playfield Rd, Edg. HA8 118 CQ54
Playford Rd, N4 143 DM61
Playgreen Way, SE6 205 EA91
Playground Cl, Beck. BR3 off Churchfields Rd 225 DX96
Playhouse Ct, SE1 off Southwark Br Rd 31 J4
Playhouse Sq, Harl. CM20 off College Gate 73 EQ15
Playhouse Yd, EC4 18 G9
● Plaza Business Cen, Enf. EN3 off Stockingswater La 105 DZ40
Plaza Par, NW6 off Kilburn High Rd 5 L10
Plaza Shop Cen, The, W1 17 M8
Plaza W, Houns. TW3 178 CB81
Pleasance, The, SW15 181 CV84
Pleasance Rd, SW15 201 CV85
Orpington BR5 228 EV96
Pleasant Gro, Croy. CR0 225 DZ104
Pleasant Pl, N1 9 H7
Hersham KT12 236 BW107
West Hyde WD3 113 BE52
Pleasant Ri, Hat. AL9 67 CW15
Pleasant Row, NW1 7 K9
Pleasant Vw, Erith DA8 189 FE78
Pleasant Vw Pl, Orp. BR6 off High St 245 EP106
Pleasant Way, Wem. HA0 159 CJ68
Pleasure Pit Rd, Ashtd. KT21 254 CP118
Plender St, NW1 7 L9
Pleshey Rd, N7 7 N1
Plesman Way, Wall. SM6 241 DL109
Plevna Cres, N15 144 DS58
Plevna Rd, N9 122 DU48
Hampton TW12 218 CB95
Plevna St, E14 34 E6
Pleydell Av, SE19 204 DT94
W6 181 CT77
Pleydell Ct, EC4 18 F9
Pleydell Est, EC1 off Radnor St 19 K3
Pleydell St, EC4 18 F9
Plimley Pl, W12 26 C4
Plimsoll Cl, E14 22 C9
Plimsoll Rd, N4 143 DN62
Plomer Av, Hodd. EN11 55 DZ14
Plough Ct, EC3 19 M10
Plough Fm Cl, Ruis. HA4 137 BR58
Plough Hill, Cuffley EN6 87 DL28
● Plough Ind Est, Lthd. KT22 253 CG120
Plough La, SE22 204 DT86
SW17 202 DB92
SW19 202 DB92
Downside KT11 251 BU116
Harefield UB9 114 BJ51
Potten End HP4 61 BB16
Purley CR8 241 DL109
Sarratt WD3 79 BF33
Stoke Poges SL2 154 AV67
Teddington TW11 199 CG92
Wallington SM6 241 DL105
Plough La Cl, Wall. SM6 241 DL106
Ploughlees La, Slou. SL1 154 AS73
Ploughmans Cl, NW1 7 N8
Ploughmans End, Islw. TW7 199 CD85
Welwyn Garden City AL7 52 DC10
Ploughmans Wk, N2 off Long La 120 DC54
Plough Ms, SW11 off Plough Ter 182 DD84
Plough Pl, EC4 18 F8
Plough Ri, Upmin. RM14 151 FS59
Plough Rd, SW11 40 A10
Epsom KT19 238 CR109
Smallfield RH6 291 DP148
Plough Rbt, Hem.H. HP1 62 BK22
Plough St, E1 20 C8
Plough Ter, SW11 182 DD84
Plough Way, SE16 33 K8
Plough Yd, EC2 19 P5
Plover Cl, Berk. HP4 60 AW20
Staines TW18 195 BF90
Plover Ct, Enf. EN3 off Teal Cl 104 DW36
Plover Gdns, Upmin. RM14 151 FT60
Plover Way, SE16 33 L6
Hayes UB4 158 BX72
Plowden Bldgs, EC4 off Middle Temple La 18 E10
Plowman Cl, N18 122 DR50
Plowman Way, Dag. RM8 148 EW60
Ployters Rd, Harl. CM18 73 EQ18
Plumbers Row, E1 20 C7
Plumbridge St, SE10 46 E6
Plum Cl, Felt. TW13 197 BU88
Plumcroft Prim Sch, SE18 off Plum La 187 EQ79
Plum Garth, Brent. TW8 179 CK77
Plum La, SE18 187 EP80
Plummer La, Mitch. CR4 222 DF96
Plummer Rd, SW4 203 DK87
Plummers Cft, Dunt.Grn TN13 278 FE121
Plumpton Av, Horn. RM12 150 FL63
Plumpton Cl, Nthlt. UB5 158 CA65
Plumpton Rd, Hodd. EN11 71 EC15
Plumpton Way, Cars. SM5 222 DE104
PLUMSTEAD, SE18 187 ES78
⇌ Plumstead 187 ER77
Plumstead Common Rd, SE18 187 EP79
Plumstead High St, SE18 187 ES77
Plumstead Manor Sch, SE18 off Old Mill Rd 187 ER79
Plumstead Rd, SE18 37 P8
Plumtree Cl, Dag. RM10 169 FB65
Wallington SM6 241 DK108
Plumtree Ct, EC4 18 F8
Plumtree Mead, Loug. IG10 107 EN41
Pluto Cl, Slou. SL1 173 AL75
Pluto Ri, Hem.H. HP2 62 BL18
Plymouth Dr, Sev. TN13 279 FJ124
Plymouth Pk, Sev. TN13 279 FJ124
Plymouth Rd, E16 23 N7
Bromley BR1 226 EH95
Chafford Hundred RM16 191 FW77
Slough SL1 153 AL71
Plymouth Wf, E14 34 G8
Plympton Av, NW6 4 G7
Plympton Cl, Belv. DA17 off Halifield Dr 188 EY76
Plympton Pl, NW8 16 C5
Plympton Rd, NW6 4 G7
Plympton St, NW8 16 C5
Plymstock Rd, Well. DA16 188 EW80
Pocket Hill, Sev. TN13 278 FG128
Pocketsdell La, Bov. HP3 78 AX28
Pocklington Cl, NW9 118 CS54
Pocock Av, West Dr. UB7 176 BM76
Pococks La, Eton SL4 174 AS78

Pocock St, SE1 30 G4
Podium, The, E2 21 H2
Podmore Rd, SW18 182 DC84
Poets Chase, Hem.H. HP1
off Laureate Way 62 BH18
Poets Gate, Chsht EN7 88 DR28
Poets Rd, N5 9 L2
Poets Way, Har. HA1
off Blawith Rd 139 CE56
Point, The, E17 *off Tower Ms* 145 EA56
Ruislip HA4 137 BU63
Pointalls Cl, N3 120 DC54
Point Cl, SE10 46 F6
Pointer Cl, SE28 168 EX72
Pointers, The, Ashtd. KT21 254 CL120
Pointer Sch, The, SE3 47 N5
Pointers Cl, E14 34 C10
Pointers Hill, Westc. RH4 284 CC138
Pointers Rd, Cob. KT11 251 BQ116
Point Hill, SE10 46 F5
Point of Thomas Path, E1 33 H1
Point Pl, Wem. HA9 160 CP66
Point Pleasant, SW18 182 DA84
Point W, SW7 27 M8
Point Wf La, Brent. TW8
off Town Meadow 180 CL80
Poland Ho, E15 12 G8
Poland St, W1 17 M9
● **Polar Pk**, West Dr. UB7 176 BM80
Polayn Garth, Welw.G.C. AL8 51 CW08
Polebrook Rd, SE3 186 EJ83
Pole Cat All, Brom. BR2 226 EF103
Polecroft La, SE6 205 DZ89
Polehamptons, The, Hmptn.
TW12 218 CC95
Polehanger La, Hem.H. HP1 61 BE18
Pole Hill Rd, E4 123 EC45
Hayes UB4 157 BQ69
Uxbridge UB10 157 BQ69
Pole La, Ong. CM5 75 FE17
Polesden Gdns, SW20 221 CV96
★ **Polesden Lacey, Ho & Gdn**,
Dor. RH5 268 CA130
Polesden La, Ripley GU23 249 BF122
Polesden Rd, Bkhm KT23 268 CB129
Polesden Vw, Bkhm KT23 268 CB127
Poles Hill, Chesh. HP5 76 AN29
Sarratt WD3 79 BE33
Polesteeple Hill, Bigg.H. TN16 260 EK117
Polesworth Ho, W2 15 K6
Polesworth Rd, Dag. RM9 168 EX66
Polhill, Halst. TN13, TN14 263 FC115
Polhill Pk, Halst. TN14 263 FD117
Police Sta La, Bushey WD23
off Sparrows Herne 116 CB45
Police Sta Rd, Hersham KT12 236 BW107
★ **Polish Inst & Sikorski Mus**,
SW7 *off Princes Gate* 28 B5
Polish War Mem, Ruis.
HA4 157 BV66
Pollard Av, Denh. UB9 135 BF58
Pollard Cl, E16 23 N10
N7 8 D2
Chigwell IG7 126 EU50
Old Windsor SL4 194 AV85
Pollard Hatch, Harl. CM19 73 EP18
Pollard Rd, N20 120 DE47
Morden SM4 222 DD99
Woking GU22 249 BB116
Pollard Row, E2 20 D2
Pollards, Map.Cr. WD3 113 BD50
Pollards Cl, Goffs Oak EN7 88 DQ29
Loughton IG10 106 EJ43
Pollards Cres, SW16 223 DL97
Pollards Hill E, SW16 223 DM97
Pollards Hill N, SW16 223 DL97
Pollards Hill S, SW16 223 DL97
Pollards Hill W, SW16 223 DL97
Pollards Oak Cres, Oxt. RH8 276 EG132
Pollards Oak Rd, Oxt. RH8 276 EG132
Pollard St, E2 20 D2
Pollards Wd Hill, Oxt. RH8 276 EH130
Pollards Wd Rd, SW16 223 DL96
Oxted RH8 276 EH131
Pollard Wk, Sid. DA14 208 EW93
Pollen St, W1 17 K9
Pollicott Cl, St.Alb. AL4 65 CJ15
Pollitt Dr, NW8 16 A4
★ **Pollock's Toy Mus**, W1 17 M6
Pollyhaugh, Eyns. DA4 230 FL104
Polperro Cl, Orp. BR6
off Cotswold Ri 227 ET100
Polperro Ms, SE11 30 F8
Polsted Rd, SE6 205 DZ87
Polsten Ms, Enf. EN3 105 EA37
Polthorne Est, SE18 187 EQ77
Polthorne Gro, SE18 187 EQ77
Poltimore Rd, Guil. GU2 280 AU136
Polworth Rd, SW16 203 DL92
Polygon, The, SW4
off Old Town 183 DJ84
Polygon Rd, NW1 17 N1
Polytechnic St, SE18 37 M8
Pomell Way, E1 20 B8
Pomeroy Cl, Amer. HP7 77 AR40
Twickenham TW1 179 CH84
Pomeroy Cres, Wat. WD24 97 BV36
Pomeroy St, SE14 45 H5
Pomfret Rd, SE5 43 H10
Pomoja La, N19 143 DK61
Pompadour Cl, Warley CM14
off Queen St 130 FW50
Pond Cl, N12 120 DE51
SE3 47 M9
Ashtead KT21 254 CL117
Harefield UB9 114 BJ54
Hersham KT12 235 BU107
Pond Cottage La, W.Wick.
BR4 225 EA102
Pond Cotts, SE21 204 DS88
Pond Cft, Hat. AL10 67 CT18
Pondcroft, Welw.G.C. AL7 51 CY10
PONDERS END, Enf. EN3 104 DW43
⇌ **Ponders End** 105 DX43
● **Ponders End Ind Est**, Enf.
EN3 105 DZ42
Ponder St, N7 8 C6
Pond Fm Cl, Walt.Hill KT20 255 CU124
Pond Fm Est, E5
off Millfields Rd 144 DW62
Pond Fld, Welw.G.C. AL7 52 DA06
Pondfield Cres, St.Alb. AL4 65 CH16
Pond Fld End, Loug. IG10 124 EJ45
Pondfield Ho, SE27
off Elder Rd 204 DQ92
Pondfield La, Brwd. CM13 131 GA49
Pondfield Rd, Brom. BR2 226 EE102
Dagenham RM10 149 FB64
Godalming GU7 280 AT144
Kenley CR8 257 DP116
Orpington BR6 227 EP104
Pond Grn, Ruis. HA4 137 BS61
Pond Hill Gdns, Sutt. SM3 239 CY107
Pond La, Chal.St.P. SL9 112 AV53
Peaslake GU5 283 BQ144
Pond Lees Cl, Dag. RM10
off Leys Av 169 FD66
Pond Mead, SE21 204 DR86
Pond Meadow, Guil. GU2 264 AS134
Pond Meadow Sch,
Guil. GU1
off Larch Av 264 AW131
Pond Pk Rd, Chesh. HP5 76 AP29
Pond Path, Chis. BR7
off Heathfield La 207 EQ93
Pond Piece, Oxshott KT22 236 CB114
Pond Pl, SW3 28 C9
Pond Rd, E15 13 J10
SE3 47 M8
Egham TW20 195 BC93
Hemel Hempstead HP3 80 BN25
Woking GU22 248 AU120
Ponds, The, Wey. KT13
off Ellesmere Rd 235 BS107
Pondside Cl, Harling. UB3
off Providence La 177 BR80
Ponds La, Guil. GU5 282 BL142
Pond Sq, N6 *off South Gro* 142 DG60
Pond St, NW3 6 C2
Pond Wk, Upmin. RM14 151 FS61
Pond Way, Tedd. TW11
off Holmesdale Rd 199 CJ93
Pondwicks, Amer. HP7 77 AP39
Pondwicks Cl, St.Alb. AL1 64 CC21
Pondwood Ri, Orp. BR6 227 ES101
Ponler St, E1 20 E9
Ponsard Rd, NW10 161 CV69
**Ponsbourne St. Mary's C of E
Prim Sch**, Hert. SG13
off Newgate St Village 69 DL24
Ponsford St, E9 11 H4
Ponsonby Pl, SW1 29 P10
Ponsonby Rd, SW15 201 CV87
Ponsonby Ter, SW1 29 P10
Pontefract Rd, Brom. BR1 206 EF92
Pontoise Cl, Sev. TN13 278 FF122
Ponton Rd, SW8 41 P3
Pontoon Dock 36 C3
Pont St, SW1 28 E7
Pont St Ms, SW1 28 E7
Pontypool Pl, SE1 30 G4
Pontypool Wk, Rom. RM3 128 FJ51
Pony Chase, Cob. KT11 236 BZ113
Pool Cl, Beck. BR3 205 EA92
West Molesey KT8 218 BZ99
Pool Ct, SE6 205 EA89
Poole Cl, Ruis. HA4 137 BS61
Poole Ct Rd, Houns. TW4 178 BY82
Poole Ho, SE11
off Lambeth Wk 30 D7
Grays RM16 193 GJ75
Pool End Cl, Shep. TW17 216 BN99
Poole Rd, E9 11 J5
Epsom KT19 238 CR107
Hornchurch RM11 150 FM59
Woking GU21 248 AY117
Pooles Bldgs, EC1 18 E5
Pooles La, SW10 39 N5
Dagenham RM9 168 EY68
Pooles Pk, N4 143 DN61
Pooles Pk Prim Sch, N4
off Lennox Rd 143 DM61
Poole St, N1 9 L9
Poole Way, Hayes UB4 157 BR69
Pooley Av, Egh. TW20 195 BB92
Pooley Dr, SW14
off Sheen La 180 CQ83
POOLEY GREEN, Egh. TW20 195 BC92
Pooley Grn Cl, Egh. TW20 195 BC92
Pooley Grn Rd, Egh. TW20 195 BB92
Pooleys La, N.Mymms AL9 67 CV23
Pool Gro, Croy. CR0 243 DY112
Pool La, Slou. SL1 154 AS73
Poolmans Rd, Wind. SL4 173 AK83
Poolmans St, SE16 33 J4
Pool Rd, Har. HA1 139 CD59
West Molesey KT8 218 BZ100
Poolsford Rd, NW9 140 CS56
Poonah St, E1 21 H9
Pootings Rd, Crock.H. TN8 277 ER134
Pope Cl, SW19 202 DD93
Feltham TW14 197 BT88
Pope Ho, SE16 32 E9
Pope John RC Prim Sch, W12
off Commonwealth Av 161 CV73
Pope Paul Cath Prim Sch,
Pot.B. EN6 *off Baker St* 85 CZ33
Pope Rd, Brom. BR2 226 EK99
Popes Av, Twick. TW2 199 CE89
Popes Cl, Amer. HP6 94 AT37
Colnbrook SL3 175 BB80
Popes Dr, N3 120 DA53
Popes Gro, Croy. CR0 225 DZ104
Twickenham TW1, TW2 199 CF89
Pope's Head All, EC3
off Cornhill 19 M9
Popes La, W5 179 CK76
Oxted RH8 276 EE134
Watford WD24 97 BV37
Popes Rd, SW9 183 DN83
Abbots Langley WD5 81 BS31
Pope St, SE1 31 P5
Popham Cl, Han. TW13 198 BZ90
Popham Gdns, Rich. TW9
off Lower Richmond Rd 180 CN83
Popham Rd, N1 9 J9
Popham St, N1 9 H8
● **Popin Business Cen**,
Wem. HA9 140 CP64
POPLAR, E14 34 C2
Poplar 34 C1
Poplar Av, Amer. HP7 94 AT39
Gravesend DA12 213 GJ91
Leatherhead KT22 253 CH122
Mitcham CR4 222 DF95
Orpington BR6 227 EP103
Southall UB2 178 CB76
West Drayton UB7 156 BM73
Poplar Bath St, E14 22 D10
● **Poplar Business Pk**, E14 34 E1
Poplar Cl, E9 11 N2
Chesham HP5 76 AQ28
Colnbrook SL3 175 BE81
Pinner HA5 116 BX53
South Ockendon RM15 171 FX70
Poplar Ct, SW19 202 DA92
Poplar Cres, Epsom KT19 238 CQ107
Poplar Dr, Bans. SM7 239 CX114
Hutton CM13 131 GC44
Poplar Fm Cl, Epsom KT19 238 CQ107
Poplar Gdns, N.Mal. KT3 220 CR96
Poplar Gro, N11 120 DG51
W6 26 B5
New Malden KT3 220 CR97
Wembley HA9 160 CQ62
Woking GU22 248 AY119
Poplar High St, E14 22 C10
Poplar Ho, Langley SL3 175 AZ78
Poplar Mt, Belv. DA17 189 FB77
Poplar Pl, SE28 168 EW73
W2 15 L10
Hayes UB3 157 BU73
Poplar Prim Sch, SW19
off Poplar Rd S 222 DA97
Poplar Rd, SE24 184 DQ84
SW19 222 DA96
Ashford TW15 197 BQ92
Denham UB9 136 BJ64
Leatherhead KT22 253 CH122
Shalford GU4 280 AY141
Sutton SM3 221 CZ102
Wooburn Green HP10
off Glory Mill La 132 AE56
Poplar Rd S, SW19 222 DA97
Poplar Row, They.B. CM16 107 ES37
Poplars, Welw.G.C. AL7 52 DB08
Poplars, The, N14 103 DH43
Abridge RM4 *off Hoe La* 108 EV41
Borehamwood WD6
off Grove Rd 100 CN39
Cheshunt EN7 88 DS26
Gravesend DA12 213 GL87
Hemel Hempstead HP1 62 BH21
Magdalen Laver CM5 75 FB19
St. Albans AL1 65 CH24
Poplars Av, NW10 4 A5
Hatfield AL10 66 CR18
Poplars Cl, Hat. AL10 66 CQ18
Ruislip HA4 137 BS60
Watford WD25 81 BV32
Poplar Shaw, Wal.Abb. EN9 90 EF33
Poplars Rd, E17 145 EB58
Poplar St, Rom. RM7 149 FC56
Poplar Vw, Wem. HA9
off Magnet Rd 139 CK61
Poplar Wk, SE24 184 DQ84
Caterham CR3 258 DS123
Croydon CR0 224 DQ103
Poplar Way, Felt. TW13 197 BU90
Ilford IG6 147 EQ56
Poppins Ct, EC4 18 G9
Poppleton Rd, E11 146 EE58
Poppy Cl, Barn. EN5 102 DC44
Belvedere DA17 189 FB76
Hemel Hempstead HP1 61 BE19
Northolt UB5 158 BZ65
Pilgrim's Hatch CM15 130 FV43
Wallington SM6 222 DG102
★ **Poppy Factory Mus, The**,
Rich. TW10 199 CK86
Poppyfields, Welw.G.C. AL7 52 DC09
Poppy La, Croy. CR0 224 DW101
Poppy Wk, Hat. AL10 67 CT15
Waltham Cross EN7 88 DR28
Porchester Cl, SE5 184 DQ84
Hornchurch RM11 150 FL58
Porchester Gdns, W2 15 L10
Porchester Gdns Ms, W2 15 M9
Porchester Gate, W2
off Bayswater Rd 27 N1
Porchester Mead, Beck. BR3 205 EA93
Porchester Ms, W2 15 M8
Porchester Pl, W2 16 D9
Porchester Rd, W2 15 L8
Kingston upon Thames KT1 220 CP96
Porchester Sq, W2 15 M8
Porchester Sq Ms, W2 15 M8
Porchester Ter, W2 15 N9
Porchester Ter N, W2 15 M8
Porchfield Cl, Grav. DA12 213 GJ89
Sutton SM2 240 DB110
Porch Way, N20 120 DF48
Porcupine Cl, SE9 206 EL89
Porden Rd, SW2 183 DM84
Porlock Av, Har. HA2 138 CC60
Porlock Rd, Enf. EN1 122 DT45
Porlock St, SE1 31 L4
Porridge Pot All, Guil. GU2
off Bury Flds 280 AW136
Porrington Cl, Chis. BR7 227 EM95
Portal Cl, SE27 203 DN90
Ruislip HA4 137 BU63
Uxbridge UB10 156 BL66
Portal Way, W3 160 CR71
Port Av, Green. DA9 211 FV86
Portbury Cl, SE15 44 D7
Port Cres, E13 24 A5
★ **Portcullis Ho**, SW1
off Bridge St 30 B5
Portcullis Lo Rd, Enf. EN2 104 DR41
Portelet Ct, N1 9 M8
Portelet Rd, E1 21 J3
Porten Rd, W14 26 E7
Porter Cl, Grays RM20 191 FW79
Porter Rd, E6 25 K8
Porters Av, Dag. RM8, RM9 168 EV65
Porters Cl, Brwd. CM14 130 FU46
Portersfield Rd, Enf. EN1 104 DS42
Porters Pk Dr, Shenley WD7 83 CK33
Porter Sq, N19 143 DL60
Porter St, SE1 31 K2
W1 16 F6
Porters Wk, E1 32 F1
Porters Way, N12 120 DE52
West Drayton UB7 176 BM76
Porters Wd, St.Alb. AL3 65 CE16
Porteus Rd, W2 15 P7
Portgate Cl, W9 15 H4
Porthallow Cl, Orp. BR6 245 ET105
Porthcawe Rd, SE26 205 DY91
Port Hill, Hert. SG14 54 DQ09
Orpington BR6 246 EV112
Porthkerry Av, Well. DA16 188 EU84
Portia Way, E3 21 N5
Portico City Learning Cen,
E5 10 G1
Portinscale Rd, SW15 201 CY85
Portland Av, N16 144 DT59
Gravesend DA12 213 GH89
Portland Av, N.Mal. KT3 221 CT101
Sidcup DA15 208 EU86
● **Portland Business Cen**, Datchet
SL3 *off Manor Ho La* 174 AV81
Portland Cl, Rom. RM6 148 EY57
Slough SL2 153 AK70
Worcester Park KT4 221 CV101
Portland Ct, SE1
off Falmouth Rd 31 L6
Portland Cres, SE9 206 EL89
Feltham TW13 197 BR91
Greenford UB6 158 CB70
Stanmore HA7 117 CK54
Portland Dr, Chsht EN7 88 DU31
Enfield EN2 104 DS38
Merstham RH1 273 DK129
Portland Gdns, N4 143 DP58
Romford RM6 148 EX57
Portland Gro, SW8 42 C6
Portland Hts, Nthwd. HA6 115 BT49
**Portland Hosp for Women &
Children, The**, W1 17 K5
Portland Ho, Merst. RH1 273 DJ129
Portland Ms, W1 17 M9
Portland Pk, Ger.Cr. SL9 134 AX58
Portland Pl, W1 17 J5
Epsom KT17 238 CS112
Greenhithe DA9 191 FW84
Hertford Heath SG13 54 DW11
Portland Pl Sch, W1 17 K6
Portland Ri, N4 143 DP60
Portland Ri Est, N4 143 DP60
Portland Rd, N15 144 DT56
SE9 206 EL89
SE25 224 DU98
W11 26 F2
Ashford TW15 196 BL90
Bromley BR1 206 EJ91
Dorking RH4 285 CG135
Gravesend DA12 213 GH88
Hayes UB4 157 BS69
Kingston upon Thames KT1 220 CL97
Mitcham CR4 222 DE96
Southall UB2 178 BZ76
Portland Sq, E1 32 E2
Portland St, SE17 31 L10
St. Albans AL3 64 CC20
Portland Ter, Rich. TW9 179 CK84
Portland Wk, SE17 43 M2
Portley La, Cat. CR3 258 DS121
Portley Wd Rd, Whyt. CR3 258 DT120
Portman Av, SW14 180 CR83
Portman Cl, W1 16 F8
Bexley DA5 209 FE88
Bexleyheath DA7
off Queen Anne's Gate 188 EX83
St. Albans AL4 65 CJ15
Portman Dr, Wdf.Grn. IG8 124 EK54
Portman Gdns, NW9 118 CR54
Uxbridge UB10 156 BN66
Portman Gate, NW1 16 D5
Portman Hall, Har. HA3 117 CD50
Portman Ho, St.Alb. AL3 65 CD17
Portman Ms S, W1 16 G9
Portman Pl, E2 21 H3
Portman Rd, Kings.T. KT1 220 CM96
Portman Sq, W1 16 F8
Portman St, W1 16 G9
Portmeadow Wk, SE2 188 EX75
Portmeers Cl, E17
off Lennox Rd 145 EA58
Portmore Gdns, Rom. RM5 126 FA50
Portmore Pk Rd, Wey. KT13 234 BN105
Portmore Quays, Wey. KT13
off Weybridge Rd 234 BM105
Portmore Way, Wey. KT13 216 BN104
Portnall Dr, Vir.W. GU25 214 AT99
Portnall Ri, Vir.W. GU25 214 AT99
Portnall Rd, W9 14 G4
Virginia Water GU25 214 AT99
Portnalls Cl, Couls. CR5 257 DH116
Portnalls Ri, Couls. CR5 257 DH116
Portnalls Rd, Couls. CR5 257 DH118
Portnoi Cl, Rom. RM1 127 FD54
Portobello Cl, Chesh. HP5 76 AN29
Portobello Ct, W11 15 H9
Portobello Ms, W11 27 J1
Portobello Rd, W10 14 G8
W11 15 H10
Port of Tilbury, Til. RM18 192 GE84
Porton Ct, Surb. KT6 219 CJ100
Portpool La, EC1 18 E6
Portree Cl, N22 121 DM52
Portree St, E14 23 H8
Portsdown, Edg. HA8
off Rectory La 118 CN50
Portsdown Av, NW11 141 CZ58
Portsdown Ms, NW11 141 CZ58
Portsea Ms, W2 16 D9
Portsea Pl, W2 16 D9
Portsea Rd, Til. RM18 193 GJ81
Portslade Rd, SW8 41 L8
Portsmouth Av, T.Ditt. KT7 219 CG101
Portsmouth Ct, Slou. SL1 154 AS73
Portsmouth Ms, E16 36 B2
Portsmouth Rd, SW15 201 CV87
Cobham KT11 235 BU114
Esher KT10 236 CC105
Guildford GU2, GU3 280 AW138
Kingston upon Thames KT1 219 CJ99
Surbiton KT6 219 CJ99
Thames Ditton KT7 219 CE103
Woking GU23 250 BM119
Portsmouth St, WC2 18 C9
Portsoken St, E1 20 A10
Portugal Gdns, Twick. TW2
off Fulwell Pk Av 198 CC89
Portugal Rd, Wok. GU21 249 AZ116
Portugal St, WC2 18 C9
Port Vale, Hert. SG14 53 DP08
Portway, E15 13 M8
Epsom KT17 239 CU110
Rainham RM13 169 FG67
Portway Cres, Epsom KT17 239 CU109
Portway Gdns, SE18
off Shooters Hill Rd 186 EK81
Portway Prim Sch, E15 13 N9
Postern Grn, Enf. EN2 103 DN40
Postfield, Welw.G.C. AL7 52 DA06
Post Ho La, Bkhm KT23 268 CA125
Post La, Twick. TW2 199 CD88
Post Meadow, Iver SL0 155 BD69
Postmill Cl, Croy. CR0 225 DX104
Post Office App, E7 146 EH64
Post Office Ct, EC3 19 M9
Post Office La, Beac. HP9 111 AK52
George Green SL3 154 AX72
Post Office Rd, Harl. CM20 57 EQ14
Post Office Row, Oxt. RH8 276 EL131
Post Office Wk, Harl. CM20 57 ER14
Post Office Way, SW8 41 N4
Post Rd, Sthl. UB2 178 CB76
Postway Ms, Ilf. IG1
off Clements Rd 147 EP62
Postwood Grn, Hert.Hth SG13 54 DW12
Post Wd Rd, Ware SG12 55 DY08
Potier St, SE1 31 M7
Potiphar Pl, Warley CM14 130 FV49
Potkiln La, Jordans HP9 133 AQ55
POTTEN END, Berk. HP4 61 BC16
Potten End First Sch, Pott.End
HP4 *off Church Rd* 61 BB17
Potten End Hill, Hem.H. HP1 61 BD16
Potten End HP4 61 BD16
Potter Cl, Mitch. CR4 223 DH96
Potterells, N.Mymms AL9 85 CX25
Potteries, The, Barn. EN5 102 DA43
Ottershaw KT16 233 BE107
Potterne Cl, SW19 201 CX87
POTTERS BAR, EN6 86 DA32
⇌ **Potters Bar** 86 DA32
Potters Bar Comm Hosp,
Pot.B. EN6 86 DC34
★ **Potters Bar Mus**
(The Wyllyotts Cen), Pot.B.
EN6 85 CZ32
Potters Cl, SE15 43 P4
Croydon CR0 225 DY102
Loughton IG10 106 EL40
Potters Ct, Pot.B. EN6 86 DA32
Potters Cross, Iver SL0 155 BE69
POTTERS CROUCH, St.Alb.
AL2 82 BX25
Potters Fld, Harl. CM17 74 EX17
St. Albans AL3 65 CE16
Potters Flds, SE1 31 P3
Potters Gro, N.Mal. KT3 220 CQ98
Potters Hts Cl, Pnr. HA5 115 BV52
Potters La, SW16 203 DK93
Barnet EN5 102 DA42
Borehamwood WD6 100 CQ39
Send GU23 249 BB123
Potters Ms, Els. WD6 99 CK44
Potters Rd, SW6 39 N9
Barnet EN5 102 DB42
POTTER STREET, Harl. CM17 74 EW16
Potter St, Harl. CM17 74 EW16
Northwood HA6 115 BU53
Pinner HA5 115 BV53
Potter St Hill, Pnr. HA5 115 BV51
Potter St Prim Sch, Harl. CM17
off Carters Mead 74 EW17
Potters Way, Reig. RH2 288 DC138
Pottery La, W11 26 E1
Pottery Rd, Bex. DA5 209 FC89
Brentford TW8 180 CL79
Pottery St, SE16 32 E5
Pott St, E2 20 F3
Pouchen End La, Hem.H. HP1 61 BD21
Poulcott, Wrays. TW19 194 AY86
Poulett Gdns, Twick. TW1 199 CG88
Poulett Rd, E6 167 EM68
Poulters Wd, Kes. BR2 244 EK106
Poultney Cl, Shenley WD7 84 CM32
Poulton Av, Sutt. SM1 222 DD104
Poulton Cl, E8 10 E4
Poulton Ct, W3
off Victoria Rd 160 CR71
Poultry, EC2 19 L9
Pound, The, Burn. SL1
off Hogfair La 152 AJ70
Pound Cl, Epsom KT19 238 CR111
Long Ditton KT6 219 CJ102
Lower Nazeing EN9 72 EE23
Orpington BR6 227 ER103
Pound Ct, Ashtd. KT21 254 CM118
Pound Ct Dr, Orp. BR6 227 ER103
Pound Cres, Fetch. KT22 253 CD121
Pound Fm Cl, Esher KT10 219 CD102
Pound Fld, Guil. GU1 264 AX133
Poundfield, Wat. WD25 97 BT35
Poundfield Ct, Wok. GU22
off High St 249 BC121
Poundfield Gdns, Wok. GU22 249 BC120
Poundfield Rd, Loug. IG10 107 EN43
Pound La, NW10 161 CU65
Epsom KT19 238 CR112
Knockholt Pound TN14 262 EX115
Sevenoaks TN13 279 FH124
Shenley WD7 84 CM33
Pound Pk Rd, SE7 36 E9
Pound Pl, SE9 207 EN86
Shalford GU4 281 AZ140
Pound Pl Cl, Shalf. GU4 281 AZ140
Pound Rd, Bans. SM7 255 CZ117
Chertsey KT16 216 BH101
Pound St, Cars. SM5 240 DF106
Poundwell, Welw.G.C. AL7 52 DA10
Pounsley Rd, Dunt.Grn TN13 278 FE121
Pountney Rd, SW11 40 G10
POVEREST, Orp. BR5 227 ET99
Poverest Prim Sch, St.M.Cray
BR5 *off Tillingbourne Grn* 228 EU99
Poverest Rd, Orp. BR5 227 ET99
Povey Cross Rd, Horl. RH6 290 DD150
Powder Mill La, Dart. DA1 210 FL89
Twickenham TW2 198 BZ88
Powdermill La, Wal.Abb. EN9 89 EB33
Powdermill Ms, Wal.Abb. EN9
off Powdermill La 89 EB33
Powdermill Way, Wal.Abb. EN9 89 EB32
Powell Av, Dart. DA2 211 FS89
Powell Cl, Chess. KT9
off Coppard Gdns 237 CK106
Edgware HA8 118 CM51
Guildford GU2 280 AT136
Horley RH6 290 DE147
Wallington SM6 241 DK108
Powell Corderoy Prim Sch, Dor.
RH4 *off Longfield Rd* 285 CF137
Powell Gdns, Dag. RM10 148 FA63
Redhill RH1 273 DH132
Powell Rd, E5 144 DV62
Buckhurst Hill IG9 124 EJ45
Powells Cl, Dor. RH4
off Goodwyns Rd 285 CJ139
Powell's Wk, W4 180 CS79
Power Cl, Guil. GU1 264 AW133
● **Powergate Business Pk**,
NW10 160 CR69
● **Power Ind Est**, Erith DA8 189 FG81
Power Rd, W4 180 CN77
Powers Ct, Twick. TW1 199 CK87
Powerscroft Rd, E5 10 G1
Sidcup DA14 208 EW93
Powis Ct, Pot.B. EN6 86 DC34
Powis Gdns, NW11 141 CZ59
W11 15 H8

Powis Ms, W11 . . . . **15** H8
Powis Pl, WC1 . . . . **18** B5
Powis Rd, E3 . . . . **22** D3
Powis Sq, W11 . . . . **15** H8
Powis St, SE18 . . . . **37** L7
Powis Ter, W11 . . . . **15** H8
Powle Ter, Ilf. IG1
off Oaktree Gro **147** ER64
Powlett Pl, NW1 . . . . **7** H6
Pownall Gdns, Houns.TW3 . . . **178** CB84
Pownall Rd, E8 . . . . **10** B9
HounslowTW3 . . . . **178** CB84
Pownsett Ter, Ilf. IG1
off Buttsbury Rd **147** EQ64
Powster Rd, Brom. BR1 . . . . . . **206** EH92
Powys Cl, Bexh. DA7 . . . . **188** EX79
Powys Ct, Borwd. WD6 . . . . . . **100** CR41
Powys La, N13 . . . . **121** DL50
N14 . . . . **121** DL49
POYLE, Slou. SL3 . . . . **175** BE81
Poyle La, Burn. SL1 . . . . **152** AH67
Poyle New Cotts, Colnbr. SL3 . **175** BF82
Poyle Pk, Colnbr. SL3 . . . . **175** BE83
Poyle Rd, Colnbr. SL3 . . . . **175** BE83
Guildford GU1 . . . . **280** AY136
● **Poyle Tech Cen**, Slou. SL3 . **175** BE82
Poyle Ter, Guil. GU1
off Sydenham Rd **280** AX136
Poynder Rd, Til. RM18 . . . . **193** GH81
Poynders Ct, SW4
off Poynders Rd **203** DJ86
Poynders Gdns, SW4 . . . . **203** DJ87
Poynders Hill, Hem.H. HP2 . . . . . . **63** BQ21
Poynders Rd, SW4 . . . . **203** DJ86
Poynes Rd, Horl. RH6 . . . . **290** DE146
Poynings, The, Iver SL0 . . . . . . **175** BF77
Poynings Cl, Orp. BR6 . . . . . . **228** EV103
Poynings Rd, N19 . . . . **143** DJ62
Poynings Way, N12 . . . . **120** DA50
Romford RM3
off Arlington Gdns **128** FL53
Poyntell Cres, Chis. BR7 . . . . . . **227** ER95
Poynter Ho, W11 . . . . **26** D2
Poynter Rd, Enf. EN1 . . . . **104** DU43
Poynton Rd, N17 . . . . **122** DU54
Poyntz Rd, SW11 . . . . **40** E9
Poyser St, E2 . . . . **20** F1
Prae, The, Wok. GU22 . . . . **249** BF118
Prae Cl, St.Alb. AL3 . . . . **64** CB19
Praed Ms, W2 . . . . **16** B8
Praed St, W2 . . . . **16** C7
Praetorian Ct, St.Alb. AL1 . . . . . **64** CC23
Sch **Prae Wd Prim Sch**, St.Alb.
AL3 *off King Harry La* **64** CA22
Pragel St, E13 . . . . **24** B1
Pragnell Rd, SE12 . . . . **206** EH89
Prague Pl, SW2 . . . . **203** DL85
Prah Rd, N4 . . . . **143** DN61
Prairie Cl, Add. KT15 . . . . **216** BH104
Prairie Rd, Add. KT15 . . . . **216** BH104
Prairie St, SW8 . . . . **41** H9
Pratt Ms, NW1 . . . . **7** L9
PRATT'S BOTTOM, Orp. BR6 . . **246** EV110
Sch **Pratts Bottom Prim Sch**, Pr.Bot.
BR6 *off Hookwood Rd* **246** EW111
Pratts La, Hersham KT12
off Molesey Rd **236** BX105
Pratts Pas, Kings.T. KT1
off Clarence St **220** CL96
Pratt St, NW1 . . . . **7** L9
Pratt Wk, SE11 . . . . **30** D8
Prayle Gro, NW2 . . . . **141** CX60
Prebend Gdns, W4 . . . . **181** CT76
W6 . . . . **181** CT76
Prebend St, N1 . . . . **9** J9
Precinct, The, Egh. TW20
off High St **195** BA92
West Molesey KT8
off Victoria Av **218** CB97
Precinct Rd, Hayes UB3 . . . . . . **157** BV73
Precincts, The, Burn. SL1 . . . . . **152** AH70
Morden SM4 *off Green La* . . **222** DA100
Premier Av, Grays RM16 . . . . . **192** GC75
Premier Cor, W9 . . . . **14** G1
Premiere Pl, E14 . . . . **34** A1
● **Premier Pk**, NW10 . . . . **160** CP67
Premier Pk Rd, NW10 . . . . **160** CP68
Premier Pl, Wat. WD18 . . . . **97** BT43
Sch **Prendergast - Hilly Flds Coll**,
SE4 *off Adelaide Av* **185** EA84
Sch **Prendergast - Ladywell Flds
Coll**, SE4 *off Manwood Rd* . **205** EA86
Prendergast Rd, SE3 . . . . **47** K10
Prentice Pl, Harl. CM17 . . . . **74** EW17
Prentis Rd, SW16 . . . . **203** DK91
Prentiss Ct, SE7 . . . . **36** E9
Presburg Rd, N.Mal. KT3 . . . . . . **220** CS99
Prescelly Pl, Edg. HA8 . . . . **118** CM53
Prescot St, E1 . . . . **20** B10
Prescott Av, Petts Wd BR5 . . . . **227** EP100
Prescott Cl, SW16 . . . . **203** DL94
Prescott Grn, Loug. IG10 . . . . . **107** EQ41
Prescott Ho, SE17 . . . . **43** H3
Prescott Pl, SW4 . . . . **183** DK83
Prescott Rd, Chshr EN8 . . . . **89** DY27
Colnbrook SL3 . . . . **175** BE82
Presdales Ct, Ware SG12
off Presdales Dr **55** DY07
Presdales Dr, Ware SG12 . . . . . . **55** DX07
Sch **Presdales Sch**, Ware SG12
off Hoe La **55** DX08
Presentation Ms, SW2 . . . . **203** DM89
Preshaw Cres, Mitch. CR4
off Lower Grn W **222** DE97
President Dr, E1 . . . . **32** E2
President St, EC1 . . . . **19** J2
Prespa Cl, N9 *off Hudson Way* . **122** DW47
Press Ct, SE1 . . . . **32** C10
Press Rd, NW10 . . . . **140** CR62
Uxbridge UB8 . . . . **156** BK65
Prestage Way, E14 . . . . **22** F10
Prestbury Ct, Wok. GU21
off Muirfield Rd **248** AU118
Prestbury Cres, Bans. SM7 . . . **256** DF116
Prestbury Rd, E7 . . . . **166** EJ66
Prestbury Sq, SE9 . . . . **207** EM91
Prested Rd, SW11
off St. John's Hill **182** DE84
Prestige Way, NW4
off Heriot Rd **141** CW57
PRESTON, Wem. HA9 . . . . **139** CK59
Preston Av, E4 . . . . **123** ED51
Preston Cl, SE1 . . . . **31** N8
TwickenhamTW2 . . . . **199** CE90
Preston Ct, Walt. KT12 . . . . **218** BW102
Jct **Preston Cross**, Lthd. KT23 . **268** BZ126
Preston Dr, E11 . . . . **146** EJ57
Bexleyheath DA7 . . . . **188** EX81
Epsom KT19 . . . . **238** CS107
Preston Gdns, NW10
off Church Rd **160** CS65
Enfield EN3 . . . . **105** DY37
Ilford IG1 . . . . **146** EL58
Preston Gro, Ashtd. KT21 . . . . . **253** CJ117
Preston Hill, Chesh. HP5 . . . . . . **76** AR29
Harrow HA3 . . . . **140** CM58
Preston La, Tad. KT20 . . . . **255** CV121
Sch **Preston Manor High Sch**, Wem.
HA9 *off Carlton Av E* **140** CM61
Sch **Preston Pk Prim Sch**, Wem.
HA9 *off College Rd* **139** CK60
Preston Pl, NW2 . . . . **161** CU65
RichmondTW10 . . . . **200** CL85
⊖ **Preston Road** **140** CL60
Preston Rd, E11 . . . . **146** EE58
SE19 . . . . **203** DP93
SW20 . . . . **201** CT94
Harrow HA3 . . . . **140** CL59
Northfleet DA11 . . . . **212** GE88
Romford RM3 . . . . **128** FK49
SheppertonTW17 . . . . **216** BN99
Slough SL2 . . . . **154** AW73
Wembley HA9 . . . . **140** CL61
Prestons Rd, E14 . . . . **34** F4
Bromley BR2 . . . . **226** EG104
Preston Waye, Har. HA3 . . . . . . **140** CL60
Prestwick Cl, Sthl. UB2
off Ringway **178** BY78
Prestwick Rd, Wat. WD19 . . . . . **116** BX50
Prestwood, Slou. SL2 . . . . **154** AV72
Prestwood Av, Har. HA3 . . . . . . **139** CH56
Prestwood Cl, SE18 . . . . **188** EU80
Harrow HA3 . . . . **139** CH56
Prestwood Dr, Rom. RM5 . . . . . **127** FC50
Prestwood Gdns, Croy. CR0 . . **224** DQ101
Prestwood St, N1 . . . . **19** K1
Pretoria Av, E17 . . . . **145** DY56
Pretoria Cl, N17 . . . . **122** DT52
Pretoria Cres, E4 . . . . **123** EC46
Pretoria Ho, Erith DA8
off Waterhead Cl **189** FE80
Pretoria Rd, E4 . . . . **123** EC46
E11 . . . . **145** ED60
E16 . . . . **23** L4
N17 . . . . **122** DT52
SW16 . . . . **203** DH93
Chertsey KT16 . . . . **215** BF102
Ilford IG1 . . . . **147** EP64
Romford RM7 . . . . **149** FC56
Watford WD18 . . . . **97** BU42
Pretoria Rd N, N18 . . . . **122** DT51
Pretty La, Couls. CR5 . . . . **257** DJ121
Prevost Rd, N11 . . . . **120** DG47
Prey Heath, Wok. GU22 . . . . . . **248** AV123
Prey Heath Cl, Wok. GU22 . . . . **248** AW124
Prey Heath Rd, Wok. GU22 . . . **248** AV124
Price Cl, NW7 . . . . **119** CY51
SW17 . . . . **202** DF90
Price Rd, Croy. CR0 . . . . **241** DP106
Price's Ct, SW11 . . . . **40** A10
Prices La, Reig. RH2 . . . . **288** DA137
Prices Ms, N1 . . . . **8** D8
Price's St, SE1 . . . . **31** H3
Price Way, Hmptn. TW12
off Victors Dr **198** BY93
Prichard Ct, N7 . . . . **8** C3
Pricklers Hill, Barn. EN5 . . . . . . **102** DB44
Prickley Wd, Brom. BR2 . . . . . . **226** EF102
Priddy Pl, Red. RH1 . . . . **273** DJ131
Priddy's Yd, Croy. CR0
off Church St **224** DQ103
Prideaux Pl, W3 . . . . **160** CR73
WC1 . . . . **18** D2
Prideaux Rd, SW9 . . . . **42** B10
Pridham Rd, Th.Hth. CR7 . . . . . **224** DR98
Priest Ct, EC2 . . . . **19** J8
Priestfield Rd, SE23 . . . . **205** DY90
Priest Hill, Egh. TW20 . . . . **194** AW90
Old Windsor SL4 . . . . **194** AW90
Priestland Gdns, Berk. HP4 . . . . **60** AY17
Priestlands Cl, Horl. RH6 . . . . **290** DF147
Priestlands Pk Rd, Sid. DA15 . . **207** ET90
Priestley Cl, N16 . . . . **144** DT59
Priestley Gdns, Rom. RM6 . . . . **148** EV58
Priestley Rd, Mitch. CR4 . . . . . **222** DG96
Priestley Way, E17 . . . . **145** DX55
NW2 . . . . **141** CU60
Priestly Gdns, Wok. GU22 . . . . **249** BA120
Priestman Pt, E3 . . . . **22** C3
Sch **Priestmead First & Mid Schs**,
Kenton HA3
off Hartford Av **139** CH55
Priest Pk Av, Har. HA2 . . . . **138** CA61
Priests Av, Rom. RM1 . . . . **127** FD54
Priests Br, SW14 . . . . **180** CS84
SW15 . . . . **180** CS84
Priests Fld, Ingrave CM13 . . . . **131** GC50
Priests La, Brwd. CM15 . . . . . . **130** FY47
Priests Paddock, Knot.Grn
HP9 . . . . **110** AJ50
Prima Rd, SW9 . . . . **42** E4
Prime Zone Ms, N8 . . . . **143** DL58
Primley La, Sheering CM22 . . . . **59** FC06
Primrose Av, Enf. EN2 . . . . **104** DR39
Horley RH6 . . . . **291** DH150
Romford RM6 . . . . **148** EV59
Primrose Cl, E3 . . . . **22** A1
N3 . . . . **120** DB54
SE6 . . . . **205** EC92
Harrow HA2 . . . . **138** BZ62
Hatfield AL10 . . . . **67** CV19
Hemel Hempstead HP1 . . . . . . **61** BE21
Wallington SM6 . . . . **223** DH102
Primrose Dr, Hert. SG13 . . . . . . **54** DV09
West Drayton UB7 . . . . **176** BK77
Primrose Fld, Harl. CM18 . . . . . . **73** ET18
Primrose Gdns, NW3 . . . . **6** D4
Bushey WD23 . . . . **116** CB45
Radlett WD7
off Aldenham Rd **99** CG35
Ruislip HA4 . . . . **138** BW64
Primrose Glen, Horn. RM11 . . . **150** FL56
PRIMROSE HILL, NW8 . . . . **6** E8
Primrose Hill, EC4 . . . . **18** F9
Brentwood CM14 . . . . **130** FW48
Kings Langley WD4 . . . . **81** BP28
Primrose Hill Ct, NW3 . . . . **6** E7
Sch **Primrose Hill Prim Sch**,
NW1 . . . . **7** H8
Primrose Hill Rd, NW3 . . . . **6** E6
Primrose Hill Studios, NW1 . . . . . **6** G8
Primrose La, Ald. WD25 . . . . **99** CD38
Croydon CR0 . . . . **225** DX102
Primrose Ms, NW1 . . . . **6** F7
SE3 . . . . **186** EH80
W5 *off St. Mary's Rd* **179** CK75
Primrose Path, Chsht EN7 . . . . . . **88** DU31
Primrose Pl, Islw. TW7 . . . . **179** CF82
Primrose Rd, E10 . . . . **145** EB60
E18 . . . . **124** EH54
Hersham KT12 . . . . **236** BW106
Primrose Sq, E9 . . . . **11** H7
Primrose St, EC2 . . . . **19** N6
Primrose Wk, SE14 . . . . **45** M4
Ewell KT17 . . . . **239** CT108
Primrose Way, Wem. HA0 . . . . . **159** CK68
Primula St, W12 . . . . **161** CU72
Prince Albert Rd, NW1 . . . . **16** D1
NW8 . . . . **16** D1
Prince Albert Sq, Red. RH1 . . . **288** DF139
Prince Alberts Wk, Wind. SL4 . . **174** AU81
Prince Arthur Ms, NW3 . . . . **5** P1
Prince Arthur Rd, NW3 . . . . **5** P2
Prince Charles Av, S.Darenth
DA4 . . . . **231** FR96
Prince Charles Dr, NW4 . . . . . . **141** CW59
Prince Charles Rd, SE3 . . . . **47** L6
Prince Charles Way, Wall.
SM6 . . . . **223** DH104
Prince Consort Cotts, Wind.
SL4 . . . . **173** AR82
Prince Consort Dr, Chis. BR7 . . **227** ER95
Prince Consort Rd, SW7 . . . . **27** P6
Princedale Rd, W11 . . . . **26** F2
Prince Edward Rd, E9 . . . . **11** P5
Prince Edward St, Berk. HP4 . . . **60** AW19
Prince George Av, N14 . . . . **103** DJ42
Prince George Duke of Kent Ct,
Chis. BR7 *off Holbrook La* . **207** ER94
Prince George Rd, N16 . . . . **9** P1
Prince George's Av, SW20 . . . . **221** CW96
Prince George's Rd, SW19 . . . . **222** DD95
Prince Henry Rd, SE7 . . . . **186** EK80
★ **Prince Henry's Room**, EC4 . . **18** E9
Prince Imperial Rd, SE18 . . . . . **187** EM81
Chislehurst BR7 . . . . **207** EP94
Prince John Rd, SE9 . . . . **206** EL85
Princelet St, E1 . . . . **20** B6
Prince of Orange La, SE10 . . . . . **46** E4
Prince of Wales Cl, NW4
off Church Ter **141** CV56
Prince of Wales Dr, SW8 . . . . **41** K5
SW11 . . . . **40** E7
Prince of Wales Footpath, Enf.
EN3 . . . . **105** DY38
Prince of Wales Gate, SW7 . . . . . **28** C4
Prince of Wales Pas, NW1 . . . . . . **17** L3
Sch **Prince of Wales Prim Sch**, Enf.
EN3 *off Salisbury Rd* **105** DZ37
Prince of Wales Rd, NW5 . . . . **7** H5
SE3 . . . . **47** M7
Outwood RH1 . . . . **289** DN143
Sutton SM1 . . . . **222** DD103
Prince of Wales Ter, W4 . . . . . . **180** CS78
W8 . . . . **27** M5
Prince Pk, Hem.H. HP1 . . . . **62** BG21
DLR **Prince Regent** **24** C10
⊖ **Prince Regent** **24** D10
Prince Regent La, E13 . . . . **24** C7
E16 . . . . **24** C7
Prince Regent Ms, NW1 . . . . **17** L3
Prince Regent Rd, Houns.
TW3 . . . . **178** CC83
Prince Rd, SE25 . . . . **224** DS99
Prince Rupert Rd, SE9 . . . . **187** EM84
Prince's Arc, SW1 . . . . **29** M2
Princes Av, N3 . . . . **120** DA53
N10 . . . . **142** DG55
N13 . . . . **121** DN50
N22 . . . . **121** DK53
NW9 . . . . **140** CP56
W3 . . . . **180** CN76
Carshalton SM5 . . . . **240** DF108
Dartford DA2 . . . . **210** FP88
Enfield EN3 . . . . **105** DY36
Greenford UB6 . . . . **158** CB72
Petts Wood BR5 . . . . **227** ES99
South Croydon CR2 . . . . **258** DV115
Surbiton KT6 . . . . **220** CN102
Watford WD18 . . . . **97** BT43
Woodford Green IG8 . . . . **124** EH49
Princes Cl, N4 . . . . **143** DP60
NW9 . . . . **140** CN56
SW4 *off Old Town* **183** DJ83
Berkhamsted HP4 . . . . **60** AU17
Edgware HA8 . . . . **118** CN50
Eton Wick SL4 . . . . **173** AM78
North Weald Bassett CM16 . . . **93** FC25
Sidcup DA14 . . . . **208** EX90
South Croydon CR2 . . . . **258** DV115
TeddingtonTW11 . . . . **199** CD91
Princes Ct, SE16 . . . . **33** N7
SW3 *off Brompton Rd* **28** E6
Hemel Hempstead HP3 . . . . . . **62** BH23
Wembley HA9 . . . . **140** CL64
● **Princes Ct Business Cen**,
E1 . . . . **32** F1
Princes Dr, Har. HA1 . . . . **139** CE55
Prince's Dr, Oxshott KT22 . . . . **237** CE112
Princesfield Rd, Wal.Abb. EN9 . . **90** EH33
Coll **Prince's Foundation, The**,
EC2 . . . . **19** N4
Princes Gdns, SW7 . . . . **28** B6
W3 . . . . **160** CN71
W5 . . . . **159** CJ70
🔒 **Princes Gate**, Harl. CM20 . . . **57** ES12
Princes Gate, SW7 . . . . **28** C5
Princes Gate Ct, SW7 . . . . **28** B5
Princes Gate Ms, SW7 . . . . **28** B6
Princes La, N10 . . . . **143** DH55
Ruislip HA4 . . . . **137** BS60
Princes Ms, W2 . . . . **15** L10
HounslowTW3 . . . . **178** CA84
Princes Par, Pot.B. EN6
off High St **86** DC32
Princes Pk, Rain. RM13 . . . . **169** FG66
Princes Pk Av, NW11 . . . . **141** CY58
Hayes UB3 . . . . **157** BR73
Princes Pk Circle, Hayes UB3 . . **157** BR73
Princes Pk Cl, Hayes UB3 . . . . . **157** BR73
Princes Pk La, Hayes UB3 . . . . . **157** BR73
Princes Pk Par, Hayes UB3 . . . . **157** BR73
Princes Pl, SW1 . . . . **29** M2
W11 . . . . **26** E2
Princes Plain, Brom. BR2 . . . . . **226** EL101
Sch **Princes Plain Prim Sch**, Brom.
BR2 *off Church La* **226** EL101
Princes Ri, SE13 . . . . **46** F8
Princes Riverside Rd, SE16 . . . . **33** J2
Princes Rd, N18 . . . . **122** DW49
SE20 . . . . **205** DX93
SW14 . . . . **180** CR83
SW19 . . . . **202** DA93
W13 *off Broomfield Rd* **159** CH74
AshfordTW15 . . . . **196** BM92
Bourne End SL8 . . . . **132** AC60
Buckhurst Hill IG9 . . . . **124** EJ47
Princes Rd, Dart. DA1, DA2 . . . **209** FG86
Egham TW20 . . . . **195** AZ93
FelthamTW13 . . . . **197** BT89
Gravesend DA12 . . . . **213** GJ90
Ilford IG6 . . . . **147** ER56
KewTW9 . . . . **180** CM81
Kingston uponThames KT2 . **200** CN94
Redhill RH1 . . . . **288** DF136
RichmondTW10 . . . . **200** CM85
Romford RM1 . . . . **149** FG57
Swanley BR8 . . . . **209** FG93
TeddingtonTW11 . . . . **199** CD91
Weybridge KT13 . . . . **235** BP106
Jct **Princes Rd Interchange**,
Dart. DA1 . . . . **210** FP88
H **Princess Alexandra Hosp**,
Harl. CM20 . . . . **57** EP14
Princess Alice Way, SE28 . . . . **187** ER75
Princess Av, Wem. HA9 . . . . **140** CL61
Windsor SL4 . . . . **173** AP83
Princess Cl, SE28 . . . . **168** EX72
Princess Cres, N4 . . . . **143** DP61
Princess Diana Dr, St.Alb. AL4 . . **65** CK21
Princesses Wk, KewTW9
off Royal Botanic Gdns . . . **180** CL80
Sch **Princess Frederica C of E
Prim Sch**, NW10 . . . . **14** A1
Princess Gdns, Wok. GU22 . . . . **249** BB116
H **Princess Grace Hosp, The**,
W1 . . . . **16** G5
Princess Gro, Seer Grn HP9 . . . **111** AR49
Princess Louise Cl, W2 . . . . **16** B6
H **Princess Margaret Hosp**,
Wind. SL4 . . . . **173** AR82
Princess Mary Cl, Guil. GU2 . . **264** AU130
Princess Mary's Rd, Add.
KT15 . . . . **234** BJ105
Sch **Princess May Prim Sch**,
N16 . . . . **10** A2
Princess May Rd, N16 . . . . **9** P1
Princess Ms, NW3 . . . . **6** B4
Kingston uponThames KT1 . **220** CM97
Princess Par, Orp. BR6
off Crofton Rd **227** EN104
Princess Pk Manor, N11 . . . . . . **120** DG50
Princess Prec, Horl. RH6
off High St **291** DH148
Princes Sq, W2 . . . . **15** L10
Princess Rd, NW1 . . . . **6** G8
NW6 . . . . **15** J1
Croydon CR0 . . . . **224** DQ100
Woking GU22 . . . . **249** BB116
H **Princess Royal Uni Hosp, The**,
Orp. BR6 . . . . **227** EN104
Princess St, SE1 . . . . **31** H7
Princes St, EC2 . . . . **19** L8
N17 *off Queen St* **122** DS51
W1 . . . . **17** K9
Bexleyheath DA7 . . . . **188** EZ84
Gravesend DA11 . . . . **213** GH86
RichmondTW9
off Sheen Rd **200** CL85
Slough SL1 . . . . **174** AV75
Sutton SM1 . . . . **240** DD105
Ware SG12 . . . . **55** DX05
Princess Way, Red. RH1 . . . . . . **272** DG133
Princes Ter, E13 . . . . **166** EH67
Prince St, SE8 . . . . **45** P2
Watford WD17 . . . . **98** BW41
Princes Vw, Dart. DA1 . . . . **210** FN88
Princes Way, SW19 . . . . **201** CX87
Buckhurst Hill IG9 . . . . **124** EJ47
Croydon CR0 . . . . **241** DM106
Hutton CM13 . . . . **131** GA46
Ruislip HA4 . . . . **138** BY63
West Wickham BR4 . . . . **244** EF105
Princes Yd, W11 . . . . **26** F3
Princethorpe Ho, W2 . . . . **15** K6
Princethorpe Rd, SE26 . . . . **205** DX91
Princeton Ct, SW15
off Felsham Rd **181** CX83
Princeton St, WC1 . . . . **18** C6
Principal Cl, N14 . . . . **121** DJ46
Principal Sq, E9
off Chelmer Rd **11** K2
Pringle Gdns, SW16 . . . . **203** DJ91
Purley CR8 . . . . **241** DM110
Sch **Prins Willem Alexander Sch**,
Wok. GU22
off Old Woking Rd **249** BC117
Printers Av, Wat. WD18 . . . . **97** BS43
Printers Inn Ct, EC4 . . . . **18** E8
Printers Ms, E3 . . . . **11** M9
Printer St, EC4 . . . . **18** F8
Printers Way, Harl. CM20 . . . . . . **58** EU10
Printing Ho La, Hayes UB3 . . . . **177** BS75
Printing Ho Sq, Guil. GU1
off Martyr Rd **280** AX135
Printing Ho Yd, E2 . . . . **19** P2
Print Village, SE15 . . . . **44** B9
Priolo Rd, SE7 . . . . **186** EJ78
Prior Av, Sutt. SM2 . . . . **240** DE108
Prior Bolton St, N1 . . . . **9** H5
Prior Chase, Bad.Dene RM17 . . **192** FZ77
Prioress Cres, Green. DA9 . . . . **191** FW84
Prioress Ho, E3
off Bromley High St **22** D2
Prioress Rd, SE27 . . . . **203** DP90
Prioress St, SE1 . . . . **31** M7
Prior Gro, Chesh. HP5 . . . . **76** AQ30
Prior Rd, Ilf. IG1 . . . . **147** EN62
Priors, The, Ashtd. KT21 . . . . . **253** CK119
Priors Cl, Hert.Hth SG13 . . . . . . **54** DV12
Slough SL1 . . . . **174** AU76
Priors Ct, Wok. GU21 . . . . **248** AU118
Priors Cft, E17 . . . . **123** DY54
Woking GU22 . . . . **249** BA120
Priors Fm La, Nthlt. UB5 . . . . . **158** BZ65
Priors Fld, Nthlt. UB5
off Arnold Rd **158** BY65
Priorsford Av, Orp. BR5 . . . . . . **228** EU98
Priors Gdns, Ruis. HA4 . . . . **138** BW64
Priors Mead, Bkhm KT23 . . . . . **268** CC125
Enfield EN1 . . . . **104** DS39
Priors Pk, Horn. RM12 . . . . **150** FJ62
Priors Rd, Wind. SL4 . . . . **173** AK83
Prior St, SE10 . . . . **46** E5
Priors Wd Rd, Hert.Hth SG13 . . . **54** DW12
Sch **Prior Weston Prim Sch**, EC1 . **19** K5
Priory, The, SE3 . . . . **186** EF84
Croydon CR0 *off Epsom Rd* . **241** DN105
Godstone RH9 . . . . **274** DV131
Priory Av, E4 . . . . **123** DZ48
E17 . . . . **145** EA57
N8 . . . . **143** DK56
W4 . . . . **180** CS77
Harefield UB9 . . . . **136** BJ56
Harlow CM17 . . . . **58** EW10
Petts Wood BR5 . . . . **227** ER100
Priory Av, Sutt. SM3 . . . . **239** CX105
Wembley HA0 . . . . **139** CF63
Priory Cl, E4 . . . . **123** DZ48
E18 . . . . **124** EG53
N3 *off Church Cres* **119** CZ53
N14 . . . . **103** DH43
N20 . . . . **119** CZ45
SW19 *off High Path* **222** DB95
Beckenham BR3 . . . . **225** DY97
Broxbourne EN10
off High Rd Turnford **71** DY24
Chislehurst BR7 . . . . **227** EM95
Dartford DA1 . . . . **210** FJ85
Denham UB9 . . . . **136** BG62
Dorking RH4 . . . . **285** CG138
HamptonTW12 . . . . **218** BZ95
Harefield UB9 . . . . **136** BH56
Hayes UB3 . . . . **157** BV73
Hoddesdon EN11 . . . . **71** EA18
Horley RH6 . . . . **290** DF147
Pilgrim's Hatch CM15 . . . . **130** FU43
Ruislip HA4 . . . . **137** BT60
Stanmore HA7 . . . . **117** CF48
Sudbury HA0 . . . . **139** CF63
Sunbury-on-ThamesTW16
off Staines Rd E **197** BU94
Walton-on-Thames KT12 . . . **217** BU104
Woking GU21 . . . . **233** BD113
Sch **Priory C of E Prim Sch, The**,
SW19 *off Queens Rd* **202** DB92
Priory Ct, E17 . . . . **145** DZ55
EC4 *off Carter La* **19** H9
SW8 . . . . **41** P7
Berkhamsted HP4 . . . . **60** AW19
Bushey WD23
off Sparrows Herne **116** CC46
Epsom KT17
off Old Schs La **239** CT109
Guildford GU2
off Portsmouth Rd **280** AW137
Harlow CM18 . . . . **74** EV17
Priory Ct Est, E17
off Priory Ct **123** DZ54
Priory Cres, SE19 . . . . **204** DQ94
Sutton SM3 . . . . **239** CX105
Wembley HA0 . . . . **139** CG62
Priory Dr, SE2 . . . . **188** EX78
Reigate RH2 . . . . **288** DA136
Stanmore HA7 . . . . **117** CF48
Priory Fld Dr, Edg. HA8 . . . . **118** CP49
Priory Flds, Eyns. DA4 . . . . **230** FM103
Watford WD17 . . . . **97** BT39
Priory Gdns, N6 . . . . **143** DH58
SE25 . . . . **224** DT98
SW13 . . . . **181** CT83
W4 . . . . **180** CS77
W5 *off Hanger La* **160** CM69
AshfordTW15 . . . . **197** BR92
Berkhamsted HP4 . . . . **60** AW19
Dartford DA1 . . . . **210** FK85
HamptonTW12 . . . . **198** BZ94
Harefield UB9 . . . . **136** BJ56
Wembley HA0 . . . . **139** CG63
Priory Gate, Chsht EN8 . . . . **89** DZ27
Priory Grn, Stai. TW18 . . . . **196** BH92
Priory Grn Est, N1 . . . . **8** C10
Priory Gro, SW8 . . . . **42** A8
Barnet EN5 . . . . **102** DA43
Romford RM3 . . . . **128** FL48
Priory Hts, N1 . . . . **8** C10
Slough SL1
off Buckingham Av **153** AL72
Priory Hill, Dart. DA1 . . . . **210** FK86
Wembley HA0 . . . . **139** CG63
H **Priory Hosp, The**, SW15 . . . **181** CT84
H **Priory Hosp Hayes Gro, The**,
Hayes BR2 . . . . **226** EG103
H **Priory Hosp N London**,
N14 . . . . **121** DL46
Priory Ho, SE7
off Springfield Gro **186** EJ79
Priory La, SW15 . . . . **200** CS86
Eynsford DA4 . . . . **230** FM102
RichmondTW9 . . . . **180** CN80
West Molesey KT8 . . . . **218** CA98
Priory Ms, SW8 . . . . **42** A7
Hornchurch RM11 . . . . **149** FH60
StainesTW18 . . . . **196** BH92
Priory Pk, SE3 . . . . **186** EF83
Priory Pk Rd, NW6 . . . . **5** H8
Wembley HA0 . . . . **139** CG63
Priory Path, Rom. RM3 . . . . **128** FL48
Priory Pl, Dart. DA1 . . . . **210** FK86
Walton-on-Thames KT12 . . . **217** BU104
Priory Rd, E6 . . . . **166** EK67
N8 . . . . **143** DK56
NW6 . . . . **5** L8
SW19 . . . . **202** DD94
W4 . . . . **180** CR76
Barking IG11 . . . . **167** ER66
Chalfont St. Peter SL9 . . . . . **134** AX55
Chessington KT9 . . . . **220** CL104
Croydon CR0 . . . . **223** DN101
HamptonTW12 . . . . **198** BZ94
HounslowTW3 . . . . **198** CC85
Loughton IG10 . . . . **106** EL42
Reigate RH2 . . . . **288** DA136
RichmondTW9 . . . . **180** CN79
Romford RM3 . . . . **128** FL48
Slough SL1 . . . . **152** AJ71
Sutton SM3 . . . . **239** CX105
Priory Rd N, Dart. DA1 . . . . **190** FK84
Priory Rd S, Dart. DA1 . . . . **210** FK85
Sch **Priory Sch**, SE25
off Tennison Rd **224** DT98
Slough SL1 *off Orchard Av* . **153** AK71
Sch **Priory Sch, The**, Bans. SM7
off Bolters La **256** DA115
Dorking RH4 *off West Bk* . . . **285** CF137
Orpington BR5
off Tintagel Rd **228** EW102
🔒 **Priory Shop Cen**, Dart.
DA1 . . . . **210** FL86
Priory St, E3 . . . . **22** D2
Hertford SG14 . . . . **54** DR09
Ware SG12 . . . . **54** DW06
Priory Ter, NW6 . . . . **5** L8
Sunbury-on-ThamesTW16
off Staines Rd E **197** BU94
Priory Vw, Bushey Hth WD23 . . **117** CE45
Priory Wk, SW10 . . . . **39** P1

A
B
C
D
E
F
G
H
I
J
K
L
M
N
O
P
Q
R
S
T
U
V
W
X
Y
Z

Priory Wk, St.Alb. AL1 65 CE23
Priory Way, Chal.St.P. SL9 134 AX55
Datchet SL3 174 AV80
Harmondsworth UB7 176 BL79
Harrow HA2 138 CB56
Southall UB2 178 BX76
Priory Wf, Hert. SG14
off Priory St 54 DR09
Priscilla Cl, N15 144 DQ57
Pritchard's Rd, E2 10 D9
Pritchett Cl, Enf. EN3 105 EA37
Priter Rd, SE16 32 D7
Private Rd, Enf. EN1 104 DS43
Probert Rd, SW2 203 DN85
Probyn Ho, SW1 *off Page St* 29 P8
Probyn Rd, SW2 203 DP89
Procter Ho, SE1 32 C10
Procter St, WC1 18 C7
Proctor Cl, Mitch. CR4 222 DG95
Proctor Gdns, Bkhm KT23 268 CB125
Proctors Cl, Felt. TW14 197 BU88
Profumo Rd, Hersham KT12 236 BX106
● **Progress Business Cen**, Slou.
SL1 153 AK72
● **Progress Business Pk**, Croy.
CR0 223 DM103
● **Progression Cen, The**, Hem.H.
HP2 62 BN17
Progress Way, N22 121 DN53
Croydon CR0 223 DM103
Enfield EN1 104 DU43
Promenade, Edg. HA8 118 CN50
Promenade, The, W4 180 CS81
Promenade App Rd, W4 180 CS80
Promenade de Verdun, Pur.
CR8 241 DK111
Promenade Mans, Edg. HA8
off Hale La 118 CN50
● **Prospect Business Pk**, Loug.
IG10 107 ER42
Prospect Cl, SE26 204 DV91
Belvedere DA17 188 FA77
Hounslow TW3 178 BZ81
Ruislip HA4 138 BX59
Prospect Cotts, SW18 182 DA84
Prospect Cres, Twick. TW2 198 CC86
Prospect Gro, Grav. DA12 213 GK87
Prospect Hill, E17 145 EB56
Prospect Ho, SW19
off Chapter Way 222 DD95
Prospect La, Eng.Grn TW20 194 AT92
Prospect Pl, Dart. DA1 210 FK86
Prospect Pl, E1 32 G2
N2 142 DD56
N7 8 B1
N17 122 DS52
NW2 *off Ridge Rd* 141 CZ62
NW3 5 N1
SW20 201 CV94
W4 *off Chiswick High Rd* 180 CR78
Bromley BR2 226 EH97
Epsom KT17 *off Clayton Rd* 238 CS113
Gravesend DA12 213 GK87
Grays RM17 192 GB79
Romford RM5 127 FC54
Staines TW18 195 BF92
Prospect Quay, SW18 182 DA84
Prospect Ring, N2 142 DD55
Prospect Rd, NW2 141 CZ62
Barnet EN5 102 DA43
Cheshunt EN8 88 DW29
Hornchurch RM11 150 FM55
Long Ditton KT6 219 CJ100
St. Albans AL1 65 CD22
Sevenoaks TN13 279 FJ123
Woodford Green IG8 124 EJ50
Prospect St, SE16 32 F6
Prospect Vale, SE18 36 G8
Prospect Way, Hutt. CM13 131 GE42
Prospero Rd, N19 143 DJ60
Prossers, Tad. KT20 255 CX121
Protea Cl, E16 23 L4
Prothero Gdns, NW4 141 CV57
Prothero Rd, SW6 38 F4
Prout Gro, NW10 140 CS63
Prout Rd, E5 144 DV62
Provence St, N1 9 J10
Providence Av, Har. HA2
off Goodwill Dr 138 CA60
Providence Cl, E9 11 K8
Providence Ct, W1 17 H10
Providence La, Harling. UB3 177 BR80
Providence Pl, N1 8 G8
Epsom KT17 238 CS112
Romford RM5 126 EZ54
Woking GU22 234 BG114
Providence Rd, West Dr. UB7 156 BL74
Providence Row, N1
off Pentonville Rd 18 C1
Providence Row Cl, E2
off Ainsley St 20 F3
Providence Sq, SE1
off Jacob St 32 C4
Providence St, Green. DA9 211 FU85
Providence Yd, E2 20 C2
● **Provident Ind Est**, Hayes
UB3 177 BU75
Provost Est, N1 19 L2
Provost Rd, NW3 6 F6
Provost St, N1 19 L3
Prowse Av, Bushey Hth WD23 116 CC47
Prowse Pl, NW1 7 L6
Prudence La, Orp. BR6 245 EN105
Pruden Cl, N14 121 DJ47
Prudent Pas, EC2 19 K8
Prune Hill, Eng.Grn TW20 194 AX94
Prusom St, E1 32 F3
Pryor Cl, Abb.L. WD5 81 BT32
Pryors, The, NW3 142 DD62
★ **P.S. Tattershall Castle**, SW1 30 B3
Puck La, Wal.Abb. EN9 89 ED29
Pucknells Cl, Swan. BR8 229 FC95
Puddenhole Cotts, Bet. RH3 270 CN133
Pudding La, EC3 31 M1
Chigwell IG7 125 ET46
Hemel Hempstead HP1 62 BG18
St. Albans AL3
off Market Pl 65 CD20
Seal TN15 *off Church St* 279 FN121
Pudding Mill Lane 12 C9
Pudding Mill La, E15 12 D9
Puddingstone Dr, St.Alb. AL4 65 CJ22
Puddle Dock, EC4 19 H10
Puddledock La, Dart. DA2 209 FE92
Westerham TN16 277 ET133
PUDDS CROSS, Hem.H. HP3 78 AX29
Puers Fld, Jordans HP9 112 AS51
Puers La, Jordans HP9 112 AS51
Puffin Cl, Bark. IG11 168 EV69
Beckenham BR3 225 DX99
Puffin Ter, Ilf. IG5
off Tiptree Cres 147 EN55
Pulborough Rd, SW18 201 CZ87
Pulborough Way, Houns. TW4 178 BW84
Pulford Rd, N15 144 DR58
Pulham Av, N2 142 DC56
Broxbourne EN10 71 DX21
Pulham Ho, SW8
off Dorset Rd 42 C5
Puller Rd, Barn. EN5 101 CY40
Hemel Hempstead HP1 62 BG21
Pulleyns Av, E6 25 H2
Pulleys Cl, Hem.H. HP1 61 BF19
Pulleys La, Hem.H. HP1 61 BF19
Pullfields, Chesh. HP5 76 AN30
Pullman Cl, St.Alb. AL1
off Ramsbury Rd 65 CE22
Pullman Ct, SW2 203 DL88
Pullman Gdns, SW15 201 CW86
Pullman Ms, SE12 206 EH90
Pullman Pl, SE9 206 EL85
Pullmans Pl, Stai. TW18 196 BG92
Pulpit Cl, Chesh. HP5 76 AN29
Pulross Rd, SW9 183 DM83
Pulse, The, Colnbr. SL3 175 BE81
Pulse Apts, NW6 5 M3
Pulteney Cl, E3 11 N9
Isleworth TW7
off Gumley Gdns 179 CG83
Pulteney Gdns, E18
off Pulteney Rd 146 EH55
Pulteney Rd, E18 146 EH55
Pulteney Ter, N1 8 D9
Pulton Pl, SW6 39 J5
Puma Ct, E1 20 A6
Pump All, Brent. TW8 179 CK80
Pump Cl, Nthlt. UB5
off Union Rd 158 CA68
Pump Ct, EC4 18 E9
Pumphandle Path, N2
off Tarling Rd 120 DC54
Pump Hill, Loug. IG10 107 EM40
Pump Ho Cl, SE16 33 H5
Bromley BR2 226 EF96
★ **Pumphouse Ed Mus, Rotherhithe**, SE16 33 M2
Pump Ho Ms, E1 20 C10
Pumping Sta Rd, W4 180 CS80
Pumpkin Hill, Burn. SL1 153 AL65
Pump La, SE14 45 H4
Chesham HP5 76 AS32
Epping Green CM16 73 EP24
Hayes UB3 177 BV75
Orpington BR6 247 FB106
Pump Pail N, Croy. CR0
off Old Town 224 DQ104
Pump Pail S, Croy. CR0
off Southbridge Rd 224 DQ104
Punchard Cres, Enf. EN3 105 EB38
Punch Bowl La, Chesh. HP5
off Red Lion St 76 AQ32
Punchbowl La, Dor. RH5 285 CK135
Punch Bowl La, Hem.H. HP2 63 BR17
St. Albans AL3 63 BT16
Pundersons Gdns, E2 20 F2
Punjab La, Sthl. UB1
off Herbert Rd 158 BZ74
Purbeck Av, N.Mal. KT3 221 CT100
Purbeck Cl, Merst. RH1 273 DK128
Purbeck Ct, Guil. GU2 264 AS134
Purbeck Dr, NW2 141 CY61
Woking GU21 233 AZ114
Purbeck Ho, SW8
off Bolney St 42 C5
Purbeck Rd, Horn. RM11 149 FG60
Purberry Gro, Epsom KT17 239 CT110
Purbrock Av, Wat. WD25 98 BW36
Purbrook Est, SE1 31 P5
Purbrook St, SE1 31 P6
Purcell Cl, Borwd. WD6 99 CK39
Kenley CR8 242 DR114
Purcell Cres, SW6 38 E4
Purcell Ho, Enf. EN1 104 DT38
Purcell Rd, Grnf. UB6 158 CB71
Purcells Av, Edg. HA8 118 CN50
Purcell Sch, The, Bushey
WD23 *off Aldenham Rd* 98 CA41
Purcells Cl, Ashtd. KT21
off Albert Rd 254 CM118
Purcell St, N1 9 N10
Purchese St, NW1 7 P10
Purdom Rd, Welw.G.C. AL7 51 CY12
Purdy St, E3 22 C4
Purelake Ms, SE13 185 ED83
PURFLEET, RM19 190 FP77
Purfleet 190 FN78
Purfleet Bypass, Purf. RM19 190 FP77
● **Purfleet Ind Pk**, Aveley
RM15 190 FM75
Purfleet Prim Sch, Purf.
RM19 *off Tank Hill Rd* 190 FN77
Purfleet Rd, Aveley RM15 190 FN75
● **Purfleet Thames Terminal**,
Purf. RM19 190 FQ80
Purford Grn, Harl. CM18 74 EU16
Purford Grn Inf Sch, Harl.
CM18 *off Purford Grn* 74 EU17
Purford Grn Jun Sch, Harl.
CM18 *off Purford Grn* 74 EU17
Purkis Cl, Uxb. UB8
off Dawley Rd 157 BQ72
Purkiss Rd, Hert. SG13 54 DQ12
Purland Cl, Dag. RM8 148 EZ60
Purland Rd, SE28 187 ET75
Purleigh Av, Wdf.Grn. IG8 124 EL51
PURLEY, CR8 241 DM111
Purley 241 DP112
Purley Av, NW2 141 CY62
Purley Bury Av, Pur. CR8 242 DQ110
Purley Bury Cl, Pur. CR8 242 DQ111
Purley Cl, Ilf. IG5 125 EN54
Purley Cross, Pur. CR8 241 DN111
Purley Downs Rd, Pur. CR8 242 DQ110
South Croydon CR2 242 DR111
Purley Hill, Pur. CR8 241 DP112
Purley Knoll, Pur. CR8 241 DM111
Purley Oaks 242 DQ109
Purley Oaks Prim Sch, S.Croy.
CR2 *off Bynes Rd* 242 DR108
Purley Oaks Rd, S.Croy. CR2 242 DR109
Purley Par, Pur. CR8
off High St 241 DN111
Purley Pk Rd, Pur. CR8 241 DP110
Purley Pl, N1 8 G6
Purley Ri, Pur. CR8 241 DM112
Purley Rd, N9 122 DR48
Purley CR8 241 DN111
South Croydon CR2 242 DR108
Purley Vale, Pur. CR8 241 DP113
Purley War Mem Hosp, Pur.
CR8 241 DN111
Purley Way, Croy. CR0 223 DM101
Purley CR8 241 DN108
Purley Way Cres, Croy. CR0
off Purley Way 223 DM101
Purlieu Way, They.B. CM16 107 ES35
Purlings Rd, Bushey WD23 98 CB43
Purneys Rd, SE9 186 EK84
Purrett Rd, SE18 187 ET78
Pursers Ct, Slou. SL2 154 AS72
Purser's Cross Rd, SW6 39 H6
Pursers La, Peasl. GU5 283 BR142
Pursers Lea, Peasl. GU5 283 BR144
Pursewardens Cl, W13 159 CJ74
Pursley Gdns, Borwd. WD6 100 CN38
Pursley Rd, NW7 119 CV52
Purton Ct, Farn.Royal SL2 153 AQ66
Purton La, Farn.Royal SL2 153 AQ66
Purves Rd, NW10 14 A1
Puteaux Ho, E2 21 J1
PUTNEY, SW15 181 CY84
Putney 181 CY84
Putney Bridge 38 G10
Putney Br, SW6 181 CY83
SW15 181 CY83
Putney Br App, SW6 38 F10
Putney Br Rd, SW15 181 CY84
SW18 181 CY84
Putney Common, SW15 38 A10
Putney Ex Shop Cen,
SW15 181 CX84
Putney Gdns, Chad.Hth RM6
off Heathfield Pk Dr 148 EV57
PUTNEY HEATH, SW15 201 CW86
Putney Heath, SW15 201 CW86
Putney Heath La, SW15 201 CX86
Putney High Sch, SW15
off Putney Hill 201 CX85
Putney High St, SW15 181 CX84
Putney Hill, SW15 201 CX86
Putney Pk Av, SW15 181 CU84
Putney Pk La, SW15 181 CV84
Putney Pk Sch, SW15
off Woodborough Rd 181 CV84
Putney Pier 38 E10
Putney Rd, Enf. EN3 105 DX36
Putney Sch of Art & Design,
SW15 *off Oxford Rd* 181 CY84
PUTNEY VALE, SW15 201 CT90
Putney Wf Twr, SW15 181 CY83
Puttenham Cl, Wat. WD19 116 BW48
Putters Cft, Hem.H. HP2 62 BM15
Puttocks Cl, N.Mymms AL9 67 CW23
Puttocks Dr, N.Mymms AL9 67 CW23
Pycroft Way, N9 122 DU49
Pyebush La, Beac. HP9 133 AN56
Pye Cl, Cat. CR3
off St. Lawrence Way 258 DR123
Pyecombe Cor, N12 119 CZ49
PYE CORNER, Harl. CM20 57 ER10
Pyenest Rd, Harl. CM19 73 ER17
Pyghtle, The, Denh. UB9 136 BG60
Pylbrook Rd, Sutt. SM1 222 DA104
Pyle Hill, Wok. GU22 248 AX124
● **Pylon Trd Est**, E16 23 J5
Pylon Way, Croy. CR0 223 DL102
Pym Cl, E.Barn. EN4 102 DD43
Pymers Mead, SE21 204 DQ88
Pymmes Brook Dr, Barn. EN4 102 DE42
Pymmes Cl, N13 121 DM50
N17 122 DV53
Pymmes Gdns N, N9 122 DT48
Pymmes Gdns S, N9 122 DT48
Pymmes Grn Rd, N11 121 DH49
Pymmes Rd, N13 121 DL51
Pym Orchard, Brasted TN16 262 EW124
Pym Pl, Grays RM17 192 GA77
Pynchester Cl, Uxb. UB10 136 BN61
Pyne Rd, Surb. KT6 220 CN102
Pynest Grn La, Wal.Abb. EN9 106 EG38
Pynfolds, SE16 32 F5
Pynham Cl, SE2 188 EU76
Pynnacles Cl, Stan. HA7 117 CH50
Pypers Hatch, Harl. CM20 73 ET15
Pyrcroft Gra Prim Sch, Cher.
KT16 *off Pyrcroft Rd* 215 BF100
Pyrcroft La, Wey. KT13 235 BP106
Pyrcroft Rd, Cher. KT16 215 BF101
PYRFORD, Wok. GU22 249 BE115
Pyrford C of E Prim Sch, Pyrford
GU22 *off Coldharbour Rd* 250 BG116
Pyrford Common Rd, Wok.
GU22 249 BD116
Pyrford Ct, Wok. GU22 249 BE117
PYRFORD GREEN, Wok. GU22 250 BH117
Pyrford Heath, Wok. GU22 249 BF116
Pyrford Lock, Wisley GU23 250 BJ116
Pyrford Rd, W.Byf. KT14 234 BG113
Woking GU22 234 BG114
PYRFORD VILLAGE, Wok.
GU22 250 BG118
Pyrford Wds, Wok. GU22 249 BE115
Pyrford Wds Cl, Wok. GU22 249 BF115
Pyrford Wds Rd, Wok. GU22 249 BE115
Pyrgo Priory Prim Sch,
Harold Hill RM3
off Dagnam Pk Dr 128 FN50
Pyrian Cl, Wok. GU22 249 BD117
Pyrland Rd, N5 9 L2
Richmond TW10 200 CM86
Pyrles Grn, Loug. IG10 107 EP39
Pyrles La, Loug. IG10 107 EP40
Pyrmont Gro, SE27 203 DP90
Pyrmont Rd, W4 180 CN79
Pytchley Cres, SE19 204 DQ93
Pytchley Rd, SE22 184 DS83
Pytt Fld, Harl. CM17 74 EV16

Q

Quadrangle, The, SE24 204 DQ85
SW10 39 P6
W2 16 C8
Guildford GU2
off The Oval 280 AU135
Horley RH6 291 DH148
Quadrangle, The, Welw.G.C.
AL8 51 CW08
Quadrangle Cl, SE1 31 N8
Quadrangle Ho, E15 13 K5
Quadrangle Ms, Stan. HA7 117 CJ52
Quadrant, The, Epsom
KT17 238 CR113
Quadrant, The, SW20 221 CY95
Bexleyheath DA7 188 EX80
Purfleet RM19 190 FQ77
Richmond TW9 180 CL84
Rickmansworth WD3 114 BL45
St. Albans AL4 65 CH17
Sutton SM2 240 DC107
Quadrant Arc, Rom. RM1 149 FE57
Quadrant Arc, W1 29 M1
Quadrant Cl, NW4
off The Burroughs 141 CV57
● **Quadrant Ct**, Green. DA9 191 FT84
Quadrant Gro, NW5 6 F3
Quadrant Ho, Sutt. SM2 240 DC107
● **Quadrant Pk**, Welw.G.C.
AL7 51 CZ07
Quadrant Rd, Rich. TW9 179 CK84
Thornton Heath CR7 223 DP98
Quadrant Way, Wey. KT13 234 BM105
Quadrivium Pt, Slou. SL1 153 AQ74
Quad Rd, Wem. HA9 139 CK62
● **Quadrum Ind Pk**, Peasm.
GU3 280 AV141
Quaggy Wk, SE3 186 EG84
Quail Gdns, S.Croy. CR2 243 DY110
Quainton Hall Sch, Har. HA1
off Hindes Rd 139 CE57
Quainton St, NW10 140 CR62
Quaker Cl, Sev. TN13 279 FK123
Quaker Ct, E1 20 A5
EC1 19 L4
Quaker La, Sthl. UB2 178 CA76
Waltham Abbey EN9 89 EC34
Quakers Course, NW9 119 CT53
Quakers Hall La, Sev. TN13 279 FJ122
Quakers La, Islw. TW7 179 CG81
Potters Bar EN6 86 DB30
Quaker's Pl, E7 146 EK64
Quaker St, E1 20 A5
Quakers Wk, N21 104 DR44
Quality Ct, WC2 18 E8
Quality St, Merst. RH1 273 DH128
Quantock Cl, Harling. UB3 177 BR80
St. Albans AL4 65 CJ16
Slough SL3 175 BA78
Quantock Dr, Wor.Pk. KT4 221 CW103
Quantock Gdns, NW2 141 CX61
Quantock Ms, SE15 44 C9
Quantock Rd, Bexh. DA7
off Cumbrian Av 189 FE82
Quantocks, Hem.H. HP2 62 BM17
Quarles Cl, Rom. RM5 126 FA52
Quarles Pk Rd, Chad.Hth RM6 148 EV58
Quarrendon Fm La, Colesh.
HP7 77 AQ42
Quarrendon Rd, Amer. HP7 77 AR40
Quarrendon St, SW6 39 K7
Quarr Rd, Cars. SM5 222 DD100
Quarry, The, Bet. RH3 270 CR132
Quarry Cl, Lthd. KT22 253 CK121
Oxted RH8 276 EE130
Quarry Cotts, Sev. TN13 278 FG123
Quarry Gdns, Lthd. KT22 253 CK121
Quarry Hill, Grays RM17 192 GA78
Sevenoaks TN15 279 FK123
Quarry Hill Inf Sch, Grays
RM17 *off Dell Rd* 192 GB78
Quarry Hill Jun Sch, Grays
RM17 *off Bradleigh Av* 192 GB78
Quarry Hill Pk, Reig. RH2 272 DC131
Quarry Ms, Purf. RM19 190 FN77
Quarry Pk Rd, Sutt. SM1 239 CZ107
Quarry Ri, Sutt. SM1 239 CZ107
Quarry Rd, SW18 202 DC86
Godstone RH9 274 DW128
Oxted RH8 276 EE130
● **Quarryside Business Pk**, Red.
RH1 273 DH130
Quarry Spring, Harl. CM20 74 EU15
Quarry St, Guil. GU1 280 AX136
Quarterdeck, The, E14 34 A5
Quartermaine Av, Wok. GU22 249 AZ122
Quartermass Cl, Hem.H. HP1
off Quartermass Rd 62 BG19
Quartermass Rd, Hem.H. HP1 62 BG19
Quarter Mile La, E10 12 C1
Quaves Rd, Slou. SL3 174 AV76
Quay La, Green. DA9 191 FV84
Quayside Wk, Kings.T. KT1
off Bishop's Hall 219 CK96
Quay W, Tedd. TW11 199 CH92
Quebec Av, West. TN16 277 ER126
Quebec Cl, Smallfield RH6
off Alberta Dr 291 DN148
★ **Quebec Ho** (Wolfe's Ho),
West. TN16 277 ER126
Quebec Ms, W1 16 F9
Quebec Rd, Hayes UB4 158 BW73
Ilford IG1, IG2 147 EP59
Tilbury RM18 193 GG82
Quebec Sq, West. TN16 277 ER126
Quebec Way, SE16 33 K5
Queen Adelaide Rd, SE20 204 DW93
Queen Alexandra's Ct, SW19 201 CZ92
Queen Alexandra's Way, Epsom
KT19 238 CN111
Queen Anne Av, N15
off Suffield Rd 144 DT57
Bromley BR2 226 EF97
Queen Anne Dr, Clay. KT10 237 CE108
Queen Anne Ms, W1 17 K7
Queen Anne Rd, E9 11 J5
**Queen Anne Royal Free C of E
First Sch, The**, Wind. SL4
off Chaucer Cl 173 AR83
Queen Anne's Cl, Twick. TW2 199 CD90
Queen Anne's Gdns, W4 180 CS76
Queen Annes Gdns, W5 180 CL75
Enfield EN1 104 DS44
Leatherhead KT22
off Linden Rd 253 CH121
Queen Anne's Gdns, Mitch.
CR4 222 DF97
Queen Anne's Gate, SW1 29 N5
Bexleyheath DA7 188 EX83
Queen Anne's Gro, W4 180 CS76
Queen Annes Gro, W5 180 CL75
Enfield EN1 122 DR45
Queen Anne's Ms, Lthd. KT22
off Fairfield Rd 253 CH121
Queen Annes Pl, Enf. EN1 104 DS44
Queen Annes Rd, Wind. SL4 173 AQ84
Queen Annes Sq, SE1 32 C8
Queen Annes Ter, Lthd. KT22
off Fairfield Rd 253 CH121
Queen Anne St, W1 17 J8
Queen Anne's Wk, WC1
off Queen Sq 18 B5
Queen Anne Ter, E1
off Sovereign Cl 32 F1
Queen Bee Ct, Hat. AL10 66 CR16
Queenborough Gdns, Chis.
BR7 207 ER93
Ilford IG2 147 EN56
Queen Caroline Est, W6 38 A1
Queen Caroline St, W6 26 B9
**Queen Charlotte's & Chelsea
Hosp**, W12 161 CU72
Queen Charlotte St, Wind. SL4
off High St 173 AR81
Queendale Ct, Wok. GU21
off Roundthorn Way 248 AT116
**Queen Eleanor's C of E
Jun Sch**, Guil. GU2
off Queen Eleanor's Rd 280 AU135
Queen Eleanor's Rd, Guil.
GU2 280 AT135
Queen Elizabeth Ct, Brox. EN10
off Groom Rd 89 DZ26
Queen Elizabeth Gdns, Mord.
SM4 222 DA98
★ **Queen Elizabeth Hall &
Purcell Room**, SE1 30 C2
Queen Elizabeth Hosp,
SE18 186 EL80
Queen Elizabeth Rd, E17 145 DY55
Kingston upon Thames KT2 220 CM95
Queen Elizabeths Cl, N16 144 DR61
Queen Elizabeth's Coll, SE10 46 E4
Queen Elizabeth's Ct, Wal.Abb.
EN9 *off Greenwich Way* 105 EC36
Queen Elizabeths Dr, N14 121 DL46
Queen Elizabeth's Dr, New Adgtn
CR0 243 ED110
Queen Elizabeth II Br, Dart.
DA1 191 FR82
Purfleet RM19 191 FR82
★ **Queen Elizabeth II Conf Cen**,
SW1 29 P5
Queen Elizabeth II Hosp,
Welw.G.C. AL7 52 DA13
Queen Elizabeth II Jubilee Sch,
W9 15 H4
**Queen Elizabeth's Foundation,
Training Coll**, Lthd. KT22
off Woodlands Rd 253 CD117
Queen Elizabeth's Gdns,
New Adgtn CR0 243 ED110
Queen Elizabeth's Girls' Sch,
Barn. EN5 *off High St* 101 CZ42
★ **Queen Elizabeth's Hunting Lo**,
E4 124 EF45
Queen Elizabeth's Sch,
Barn. EN5
off Queens Rd 101 CX41
Queen Elizabeth St, SE1 31 P4
Queen Elizabeths Wk, N16 144 DR61
Queen Elizabeth's Wk, Wall.
SM6 241 DK105
Queen Elizabeth Wk, SW13 181 CV81
Windsor SL4 174 AS82
Queen Elizabeth Way, Wok.
GU22 249 AZ119
Queenhill Rd, S.Croy. CR2 242 DV110
Queenhithe, EC4 19 K10
Queenhythe Cres, Guil. GU4 264 AX128
Queenhythe Rd, Jacobs Well
GU4 264 AX128
Queen Margaret's Gro, N1 9 N3
Queen Mary, Mile End Campus,
E1 21 L4
**Queen Mary - Barts & The
London Sch of Med &
Dentistry**, EC1 19 H5
Royal London Hosp, E1 20 E7
Queen Mary Av, Mord. SM4 221 CX99
Queen Mary Cl, Rom. RM1 149 FF58
Surbiton KT6 220 CN104
Woking GU22 249 BC116
Queen Mary Ct, Stai. TW19
off Victory Cl 196 BL88
Queen Mary Rd, SE19 203 DP93
Shepperton TW17 217 BQ96
Queen Mary's Av, Cars. SM5 240 DF108
Queen Marys Av, Wat. WD18 97 BS42
Queen Marys Bldgs, SW1
off Stillington St 29 M8
Queen Mary's Ct,
Wal.Abb. EN9
off Greenwich Way 105 EC35
Queen Marys Dr, New Haw
KT15 233 BF110
★ **Queen Mary's Gdns**, NW1 16 G3
Queen Mary's Hosp, NW3 142 DC62
Sidcup DA14 208 EU93
**Queen Mary's Hosp for
Children**, Cars. SM5 222 DC102
**Queen Mary's Hosp
(Roehampton)**, SW15 201 CU86
Queen Mother's Dr, Denh.
UB9 135 BF58
Queen of Denmark Ct, SE16 33 N6
Queens Acre, Sutt. SM3 239 CX108
Windsor SL4 173 AR84
Queens All, Epp. CM16 91 ET31
Queens Av, N3 120 DC52
N10 142 DG55
N20 120 DD47
Queen's Av, N21 121 DP46
Queens Av, Byfleet KT14 234 BK112
Feltham TW13 198 BW91
Greenford UB6 158 CB72
Stanmore HA7 139 CJ55
Watford WD18 97 BT42
Woodford Green IG8 124 EH50
Queensberry Ms W, SW7 28 A8
Queensberry Pl, E12 146 EK64
SW7 28 A8
Richmond TW9
off Friars La 199 CK85
Queensberry Way, SW7 28 A8
Queensborough Ms, W2 15 N10
Queensborough Pas, W2 15 N10
Queensborough Studios, W2 15 N10
Queensborough Ter, W2 15 M10
Queensbridge Pk, Islw. TW7 199 CE85
Queensbridge Prim Sch, E8 10 B7
Queensbridge Rd, E2 10 B8
E8 10 B5
QUEENSBURY, Har. HA3 139 CK55
Queensbury 140 CM55

Queensbury Circle Par, Har. HA3
off Streatfield Rd **140** CL55
Stanmore HA7
off Streatfield Rd **140** CL55
Queensbury Rd, NW9 . . . . **140** CR59
Wembley HA0 . . . . **160** CM68
Queensbury Sta Par, Edg.
HA8 . . . . **140** CM55
Queensbury St, N1 . . . . **9** K7
Queen's Circ, SW8 . . . . **41** J5
SW11 . . . . **41** J5
Queens Cl, Edg. HA8 . . . . **118** CN50
Old Windsor SL4 . . . . **194** AU85
Wallington SM6
off Queens Rd **241** DH106
Walton on the Hill KT20 . . . . **255** CU124
★ **Queens Club (Tennis Cen)**,
W14 . . . . **38** E1
Queens Club Gdns, W14 . . . . . . **38** F2
Sch **Queen's C of E Prim Sch, The**,
Kew TW9
off Cumberland Rd **180** CN80
Sch **Queen's Coll**, W1 . . . . **17** J7
Queen's Cotts, Wind. SL4 . . . . . **173** AR84
Queens Ct, SE23 . . . . **204** DW88
Broxbourne EN10 . . . . **71** DZ24
Hertford SG13
off Queens Rd **54** DR10
Richmond TW10 . . . . **200** CM86
St. Albans AL1 . . . . **65** CH20
Slough SL1 . . . . **154** AT73
Waltham Cross EN8
off Queens Way **89** DZ34
Queenscourt, Wem. HA9 . . . . . **140** CL63
Queens Ct, Wey. KT13 . . . . **235** BR106
Woking GU22
off Hill Vw Rd **249** AZ118
Queens Ct Ride, Cob. KT11 . . . **235** BU113
Queen's Cres, NW5 . . . . **6** G5
Queens Cres, Rich. TW10 . . . . . **200** CM85
St. Albans AL4 . . . . **65** CH17
Queenscroft Rd, SE9 . . . . **206** EK85
Queensdale Cres, W11 . . . . **26** D2
Queensdale Pl, W11 . . . . **26** E2
Queensdale Rd, W11 . . . . **26** D3
Queensdale Wk, W11 . . . . **26** E3
Queensdown Rd, E5 . . . . **144** DV63
Queens Dr, E10 . . . . **145** EA59
N4 . . . . **143** DP61
W3 . . . . **160** CM72
W5 . . . . **160** CM72
Abbots Langley WD5 . . . . **81** BT32
Guildford GU2 . . . . **264** AU131
Oxshott KT22 . . . . **236** CC111
Queen's Dr, Slou. SL3 . . . . **155** AZ66
Queens Dr, Surb. KT5 . . . . **220** CN101
Thames Ditton KT7 . . . . **219** CG101
Waltham Cross EN8 . . . . **89** EA34
Queens Dr, The, Mill End WD3 . **113** BF45
Queens Elm Par, SW3
off Old Ch St **28** B10
Queen's Elm Sq, SW3 . . . . **40** B1
Queensferry Wk, N17
off Jarrow Rd **144** DV56
★ **Queen's Gall, The**, SW1 . . . . . **29** K5
Queens Gdns, NW4 . . . . **141** CW57
W2 . . . . **15** N10
W5 . . . . **159** CJ71
Dartford DA2 . . . . **210** FP88
Queen's Gdns, Houns. TW5 . . . **178** BY81
Queens Gdns, Rain. RM13 . . . . **169** FD68
Upminster RM14 . . . . **151** FT58
Queen's Gate, SW7 . . . . **27** P5
Queensgate, Cob. KT11 . . . . . . **236** BX112
Queen's Gate, Gat. RH6 . . . . . . **290** DG152
Queensgate, Wal.Cr. EN8 . . . . . . **89** DZ34
🛍 **Queensgate Cen**, Harl.
CM20 . . . . **57** ES11
Queen's Gate Gdns, SW7 . . . . . . **27** P7
Queens Gate Gdns, SW15 . . . . **181** CV84
Queensgate Gdns, Chis. BR7 . . **227** ER95
Queensgate Ho, E3
off Hereford Rd **21** P1
Queen's Gate Ms, SW7 . . . . **27** P5
Queensgate Ms, Beck. BR3
off Queens Rd **225** DY95
Queensgate Pl, NW6 . . . . **5** J7
Queen's Gate Pl, SW7 . . . . **27** P7
Queen's Gate Pl Ms, SW7 . . . . . **27** P7
Sch **Queen's Gate Sch**, SW7 . . . . . **28** A8
Queen's Gate Ter, SW7 . . . . **27** N6
Queen's Gro, NW8 . . . . **6** A9
Queen's Gro Ms, NW8 . . . . **6** A9
Queens Gro Rd, E4 . . . . **123** ED46
Queen's Head Pas, EC4 . . . . **19** J8
Queen's Head St, N1 . . . . **9** H9
Queens Head Wk, Brox. EN10
off High Rd Wormley **71** DY23
Queens Head Yd, SE1 . . . . **31** L3
H **Queen's Hosp**, Rom. RM7 . . **149** FE59
Queens Ho, Tedd. TW11 . . . . . . **199** CF93
★ **Queen's Ho, The**, SE10 . . . . **46** G3
★ **Queen's Ice & Bowl**, W2 . . . . . . **27** M1
Queenside Ms, Horn. RM12 . . . **150** FL61
Queensland Av, N18 . . . . **122** DQ51
SW19 . . . . **222** DB95
Queensland Cl, E17 . . . . **123** DZ54
Queensland Ho, E16
off Rymill St **37** L3
Queensland Rd, N7 . . . . **8** E1
Queens La, N10 . . . . **143** DH55
Ashford TW15
off Clarendon Rd **196** BM91
Sch **Queen's Manor Prim Sch**,
SW6 . . . . **38** C5
● **Queens Mkt**, E13
off Green St **166** EJ67
Queensmead, NW8 . . . . **6** B8
Datchet SL3 . . . . **174** AV80
Queens Mead, Edg. HA8 . . . . . **118** CM51
Queensmead, Oxshott KT22 . . **236** CC111
Queensmead Av, Epsom
KT17 . . . . **239** CV110
Queensmead Rd, Brom. BR2 . . **226** EF96
Sch **Queensmead Sch**,
S.Ruis. HA4
off Queens Wk **138** BX63
Queensmere Cl, SW19 . . . . **201** CX89
Queensmere Rd, SW19 . . . . **201** CX89
Slough SL1
off Wellington St **174** AU75
🛍 **Queensmere Shop Cen**,
Slou. SL1 . . . . **174** AT75
Queens Ms, W2 . . . . **15** M10
Queensmill Rd, SW6 . . . . **38** C5
Sch **Queensmill Sch**, SW6 . . . . . . **39** K9
Queens Par, N11
off St. Johns Av **120** DF50
W5 . . . . **160** CM72
Queens Par Cl, N11
off Colney Hatch La **120** DF50
⊖ **Queen's Park** **14** F1
⊖ **Queen's Park** **14** F1
Sch **Queens Pk Comm Sch**,
NW6 . . . . **4** C8
Queens Pk Ct, W10 . . . . **14** D3
Queens Pk Gdns, Felt. TW13
off Vernon Rd **197** BU90
Sch **Queen's Pk Prim Sch**, W10 . . **14** F4
★ **Queens Park Rangers FC**,
W12 . . . . **161** CV74
Queens Pk Rd, Cat. CR3 . . . . . **258** DS123
Romford RM3 . . . . **128** FM53
Queens Pas, Chis. BR7
off High St **207** EP93
Queens Pl, Mord. SM4 . . . . **222** DA98
Watford WD17 . . . . **98** BW41
Queen's Prom, Kings.T. KT1
off High St **219** CK97
Queen Sq, WC1 . . . . **18** B5
Queen Sq Pl, WC1 . . . . **18** B5
Queens Reach, E.Mol. KT8 . . . . **219** CE98
Queens Ride, SW13 . . . . **181** CU83
SW15 . . . . **181** CU83
Queen's Ride, Rich. TW10 . . . . **200** CP88
Queens Ri, Rich. TW10 . . . . . . **200** CM86
Queens Rd, E11 . . . . **145** ED59
E13 . . . . **166** EH67
Queen's Rd, E17 . . . . **145** DZ58
Queens Rd, N3 . . . . **120** DC53
N9 . . . . **122** DV48
Queen's Rd, N11 . . . . **121** DL52
Queens Rd, NW4 . . . . **141** CW57
SE14 . . . . **44** E6
SE15 . . . . **44** E6
SW14 . . . . **180** CR83
SW19 . . . . **201** CZ93
W5 . . . . **160** CL72
Barking IG11 . . . . **167** EQ66
Barnet EN5 . . . . **101** CX41
Beckenham BR3 . . . . **225** DY96
Berkhamsted HP4 . . . . **60** AU18
Brentwood CM14 . . . . **130** FW48
Bromley BR1 . . . . **226** EG96
Buckhurst Hill IG9 . . . . **124** EH47
Chesham HP5 . . . . **76** AQ30
Chislehurst BR7 . . . . **207** EP93
Queen's Rd, Croy. CR0 . . . . . . **223** DP100
Queens Rd, Datchet SL3 . . . . . **174** AU81
Egham TW20 . . . . **195** AZ93
Enfield EN1 . . . . **104** DS42
Queen's Rd, Erith DA8 . . . . . . **189** FE79
Queens Rd, Eton Wick SL4 . . . . **173** AL78
Feltham TW13 . . . . **197** BV88
Gravesend DA12 . . . . **213** GJ90
Guildford GU1 . . . . **264** AX134
Hampton Hill TW12 . . . . **198** CB91
Hayes UB3 . . . . **157** BS72
Hersham KT12 . . . . **235** BV106
Hertford SG13, SG14 . . . . **54** DR11
Horley RH6 . . . . **290** DG148
Queen's Rd, Houns. TW3 . . . . . **178** CB83
Queens Rd, Kings.T. KT2 . . . . . **200** CN94
Loughton IG10 . . . . **106** EL41
Morden SM4 . . . . **222** DA98
New Malden KT3 . . . . **221** CT98
North Weald Bassett CM16 . . **93** FB26
Richmond TW10 . . . . **200** CM85
Queen's Rd, Slou. SL1 . . . . **154** AT73
Queens Rd, Sthl. UB2 . . . . **178** BX75
Sutton SM2 . . . . **240** DA110
Queen's Rd, Tedd. TW11 . . . . . . **199** CE93
Thames Ditton KT7 . . . . **219** CF99
Queens Rd, Twick. TW1 . . . . . . **199** CF88
Queens Rd, Uxb. UB8 . . . . **156** BJ69
Queens Rd, Wall. SM6 . . . . **241** DH106
Waltham Cross EN8 . . . . **89** DY34
Ware SG12 . . . . **55** DZ05
Watford WD17 . . . . **98** BW42
Queen's Rd, Well. DA16 . . . . . **188** EV82
Queens Rd, West Dr. UB7 . . . . . **176** BM75
Weybridge KT13 . . . . **235** BQ105
Windsor SL4 . . . . **173** AQ82
⇌ **Queens Road Peckham** **44** F6
Queens Rd W, E13 . . . . **13** P10
Queen's Row, SE17 . . . . **43** L2
Sch **Queens' Sch**, Bushey WD23
off Aldenham Rd **98** BZ41
Queen's Sq, The, Hem.H. HP2 . . **62** BM20
Queens Ter, E13 . . . . **166** EH67
Queen's Ter, NW8 . . . . **6** A10
Queens Ter, Islw. TW7 . . . . **179** CG84
Queens Ter Cotts, W7
off Boston Rd **179** CE75
Queensthorpe Rd, SE26 . . . . . . **205** DX91
★ **Queen's Twr**, SW7 . . . . **28** A6
Queenstown Gdns, Rain.
RM13 . . . . **169** FF69
Queenstown Ms, SW8 . . . . **41** J7
Queenstown Rd, SW8 . . . . **41** J3
⇌ **Queenstown Road**
(Battersea) **41** K6
Queen St, EC4 . . . . **19** K10
N17 . . . . **122** DS51
W1 . . . . **29** J2
Bexleyheath DA7 . . . . **188** EZ83
Chertsey KT16 . . . . **216** BG102
Chipperfield WD4 . . . . **80** BG31
Croydon CR0 . . . . **242** DQ105
Erith DA8 . . . . **189** FE79
Gomshall GU5 . . . . **283** BQ139
Gravesend DA12 . . . . **213** GH86
Romford RM7 . . . . **149** FD58
St. Albans AL3 . . . . **64** CC20
Warley CM14 . . . . **130** FW50
Queen St Pl, EC4 . . . . **31** K1
Queensville Rd, SW12 . . . . **203** DK87
Queens Wk, E4 . . . . **123** ED46
NW9 . . . . **140** CQ61
Queen's Wk, SW1 . . . . **29** L3
Queens Wk, W5 . . . . **159** CJ70
Ashford TW15 . . . . **196** BK91
Queen's Wk, Har. HA1 . . . . **139** CE56
Queens Wk, Ruis. HA4 . . . . **138** BX62
Queen's Wk, The, SE1 . . . . **30** C3
⊖ **Queensway** **27** M1
Queens Way, NW4 . . . . **141** CW57
Queensway, W2 . . . . **15** M9
Queens Way, Croy. CR0 . . . . . . **241** DM107
Queensway, Enf. EN3 . . . . **104** DV42
Queens Way, Felt. TW13 . . . . . . **198** BW91
Queensway, Hat. AL10 . . . . **67** CU18
Hemel Hempstead
HP1, HP2 . . . . **62** BM18
Petts Wood BR5 . . . . **227** EQ99
Redhill RH1 . . . . **272** DF133
Queens Way, Shenley WD7 . . . . **84** CL32
Queensway, Sun. TW16 . . . . **217** BV96
Queens Way, Wal.Cr. EN8 . . . . . . **89** DZ34
Queensway, W.Wick. BR4 . . . . **226** EE104
Queensway, The, Chal.St.P.
SL9 . . . . **134** AX55
● **Queensway Business Cen**,
Enf. EN3 *off Queensway* . . . **104** DW42
Queensway N, Hersham KT12
off Robinsway **236** BW105
Queensway S, Hersham KT12
off Trenchard Cl **236** BW106
Queenswell Av, N20 . . . . **120** DE49
Sch **Queenswell Inf & Nurs Sch**,
N20 *off Sweets Way* **120** DD47
Sch **Queenswell Jun Sch**, N20
off Sweets Way **120** DD47
Queenswood Av, E17 . . . . **123** EC53
Hampton TW12 . . . . **198** CB93
Hounslow TW3 . . . . **178** BZ82
Hutton CM13 . . . . **131** GD43
Thornton Heath CR7 . . . . **223** DN99
Wallington SM6 . . . . **241** DK105
Queenswood Cres, Wat. WD25 . **81** BU33
Queenswood Gdns, E11 . . . . . . **146** EG60
Queenswood Pk, N3 . . . . **119** CY54
Queen's Wd Rd, N10 . . . . **143** DH58
Queenswood Rd, SE23 . . . . **205** DX90
Sidcup DA15 . . . . **207** ET85
Sch **Queenswood Sch**, Brook.Pk
AL9 *off Shepherds Way* **86** DD28
Queens Yd, WC1 . . . . **17** M5
Jct **Queen Victoria**, Sutt. SM3 . **239** CW105
Queen Victoria Av, Wem. HA0 . **159** CK66
★ **Queen Victoria Mem**, SW1 . . **29** L4
Queen Victoria St, EC4 . . . . **19** H10
Queen Victoria's Wk, Wind.
SL4 . . . . **174** AS81
Queen Victoria Ter, E1
off Sovereign Cl **32** F1
Quemerford Rd, N7 . . . . **8** C2
Quendell Wk, Hem.H. HP2 . . . . **62** BL20
Quendon Dr, Wal.Abb. EN9 . . . . **89** ED33
Quennell Cl, Ashtd. KT21
off Parkers La **254** CM119
Quennell Way, Hutt. CM13 . . . . **131** GC45
Quentin Pl, SE13 . . . . **186** EE83
Quentin Rd, SE13 . . . . **186** EE83
Quentins Dr, Berry's Grn
TN16 . . . . **261** EP116
Quentins Wk, Berry's Grn TN16
off St. Anns Way **261** EP116
Quentin Way, Vir.W. GU25 . . . **214** AV98
Quernmore Cl, Brom. BR1 . . . . **206** EG93
Quernmore Rd, N4 . . . . **143** DN58
Bromley BR1 . . . . **206** EG93
Querrin St, SW6 . . . . **39** N9
● **Questor**, Dart. DA1 . . . . **210** FL89
Quex Ms, NW6 . . . . **5** K8
Quex Rd, NW6 . . . . **5** K8
Quickbeams, Welw.G.C. AL7 . . . **52** DA06
Quickberry Pl, Amer. HP7 . . . . . **77** AR39
Quickley La, Chorl. WD3 . . . . . . **95** BB44
Quickley Ri, Chorl. WD3 . . . . . . **95** BC44
Quickmoor La, Kings L. WD4 . . . **80** BH33
Quick Rd, W4 . . . . **180** CS78
Quicks Rd, SW19 . . . . **202** DB94
Quick St, N1 . . . . **19** H1
Quick St Ms, N1 . . . . **18** G1
Quickswood, NW3 . . . . **6** D6
Quickwood Cl, Rick. WD3 . . . . . **96** BG44
Quiet Cl, Add. KT15 . . . . **234** BG105
Quiet Nook, Brom. BR2
off Croydon Rd **226** EK104
Quill Hall La, Amer. HP6 . . . . . . **94** AT37
Quill La, SW15 . . . . **181** CX84
Quillot, The, Hersham KT12 . . **235** BT106
Quill St, N4 . . . . **143** DN62
W5 . . . . **160** CL69
Quilp St, SE1 . . . . **31** J4
Quilter Gdns, Orp. BR5
off Tintagel Rd **228** EW102
Quilter Rd, Orp. BR5 . . . . **228** EW102
Quilter St, E2 . . . . **20** C2
SE18 . . . . **187** ET78
Quilting Ct, SE16
off Poolmans St **33** J4
Quinbrookes, Slou. SL2 . . . . . **154** AW72
Quince Ho, Felt. TW13
off High St **197** BV88
Quince Rd, SE13 . . . . **46** D8
Quinces Cft, Hem.H. HP1 . . . . . **62** BG18
Quince Tree Cl, S.Ock. RM15 . . **171** FW70
Quincy Rd, Egh. TW20 . . . . **195** BA92
Quinnell Cl, SE18
off Rippolson Rd **187** ET78
Quinta Dr, Barn. EN5 . . . . **101** CV43
Quintin Av, SW20 . . . . **221** CZ95
Quintin Cl, Pnr. HA5
off High Rd **137** BV57
Sch **Quintin Kynaston Sch**,
NW8 . . . . **6** A9
Quinton Cl, Beck. BR3 . . . . **225** EC97
Hounslow TW5 . . . . **177** BV80
Wallington SM6 . . . . **241** DH105
Quinton Rd, T.Ditt. KT7 . . . . . **219** CG102
Quinton St, SW18 . . . . **202** DC89
Quintrell Cl, Wok. GU21 . . . . . **248** AV117
Quixley St, E14 . . . . **22** G10
Quorn Rd, SE22 . . . . **184** DS84

R

Raans Rd, Amer. HP6 . . . . **94** AT38
Rabbit La, Hersham KT12 . . . . **235** BU108
Rabbit Row, W8 . . . . **27** K2
Rabbits Rd, E12 . . . . **146** EL63
South Darenth DA4 . . . . **231** FR96
Sch **Rabbsfarm Prim Sch**, Yiew.
UB7 *off Gordon Rd* **156** BL73
Rabbs Mill Ho, Uxb. UB8 . . . . **156** BJ68
Rabies Heath Rd, Bletch. RH1 . **274** DS133
Godstone RH9 . . . . **274** DU134
Rabournmead Dr, Nthlt. UB5 . . **138** BY64
Raby Rd, N.Mal. KT3 . . . . **220** CR98
Raby St, E14 . . . . **21** L8
Raccoon Way, Houns. TW4 . . . **178** BW82
Racecourse Way, Gat. RH6 . . . **290** DF151
Rachel Cl, Ilf. IG6 . . . . **147** ER55
Rachels Way, Chesh. HP5
off Cresswell Rd **76** AR34
Rackham Cl, Well. DA16 . . . . . **188** EV82
Rackham Ms, SW16 . . . . **203** DJ93
Racks Ct, Guil. GU1 . . . . **280** AX136
Racton Rd, SW6 . . . . **39** J3
Radbourne Av, W5 . . . . **179** CJ77
Radbourne Cl, E5 . . . . **145** DX63
Radbourne Cres, E17 . . . . **123** ED54
Radbourne Rd, SW12 . . . . **203** DK88
Radburn Cl, Harl. CM18 . . . . **74** EU19
Radcliffe Av, NW10 . . . . **161** CU68
Enfield EN2 . . . . **104** DQ39
Radcliffe Gdns, Cars. SM5 . . . . **240** DE108
Radcliffe Ms, Hmptn H. TW12
off Taylor Cl **198** CC92
Radcliffe Path, SW8 . . . . **41** K9
Radcliffe Rd, N21 . . . . **121** DP46
SE1 . . . . **31** P6
Croydon CR0 . . . . **224** DT103
Harrow HA3 . . . . **117** CG54
Radcliffe Sq, SW15 . . . . **201** CX86
Radcliffe Way, Nthlt. UB5 . . . . **158** BX69
Radcot Av, Slou. SL3 . . . . **175** BB76
Radcot Pt, SE23 . . . . **205** DX90
Radcot St, SE11 . . . . **42** F1
Raddington Rd, W10 . . . . **14** F7
Radfield Dr, Dart. DA2
off Teynham Rd **210** FQ87
Radfield Way, Sid. DA15 . . . . . **207** ER87
Radford Rd, SE13 . . . . **205** EC86
Radford Way, Bark. IG11 . . . . . **167** ET69
Radipole Rd, SW6 . . . . **38** G6
● **Radius Pk**, Felt. TW14 . . . . . **177** BT84
Radland Rd, E16 . . . . **23** M9
Rad La, Abin.Ham. RH5 . . . . . . **283** BS141
Peaslake GU5 . . . . **283** BS140
Radlet Av, SE26 . . . . **204** DV90
RADLETT, WD7 . . . . **99** CH35
⇌ **Radlett** **99** CG35
Radlett Cl, E7 . . . . **13** M4
Radlett La, Shenley WD7 . . . . . . **99** CK35
Sch **Radlett Lo Sch**, Rad. WD7
off Harper La **83** CH31
Radlett Pk Rd, Rad. WD7 . . . . . . **83** CG34
Radlett Pl, NW8 . . . . **6** C8
Sch **Radlett Prep Sch**, Rad. WD7
off Watling St **99** CJ38
Radlett Rd, Ald. WD25 . . . . **98** CB39
St. Albans AL2 . . . . **83** CE28
Watford WD17, WD24 . . . . **98** BW41
Radley Av, Ilf. IG3 . . . . **147** ET63
Radley Cl, Felt. TW14 . . . . **197** BT88
Radley Ct, SE16 . . . . **33** K4
Radley Gdns, Har. HA3 . . . . **140** CL56
Radley Ho, SE2
off Wolvercote Rd **188** EX75
Radley Ms, W8 . . . . **27** K7
Radley Rd, N17 . . . . **122** DS54
Radley's La, E18 . . . . **124** EG54
Radleys Mead, Dag. RM10 . . . . **169** FB65
Radley Sq, E5
off Dudlington Rd **144** DW61
Radlix Rd, E10 . . . . **145** EA60
Radnor Av, Har. HA1 . . . . **139** CE57
Welling DA16 . . . . **208** EV85
Radnor Cl, Chis. BR7 . . . . **207** ES93
Mitcham CR4 . . . . **223** DL98
Radnor Cres, SE18 . . . . **188** EU79
Ilford IG4 . . . . **147** EM57
Radnor Gdns, Enf. EN1 . . . . . . **104** DS39
Twickenham TW1 . . . . **199** CF89
Radnor Gro, Uxb. UB10 . . . . . . **156** BN68
Radnor Ho, SW16 . . . . **223** DM96
Radnor La, Holm.St.M. RH5 . . . **283** BU144
Radnor Ms, W2 . . . . **16** B9
Radnor Pl, W2 . . . . **16** C9
Radnor Rd, NW6 . . . . **4** E9
SE15 . . . . **44** C4
Harrow HA1 . . . . **139** CD57
Twickenham TW1 . . . . **199** CF89
Weybridge KT13 . . . . **216** BN104
Radnor St, EC1 . . . . **19** K3
Radnor Ter, W14 . . . . **26** G8
Radnor Wk, E14 . . . . **34** B8
SW3 . . . . **40** D1
Croydon CR0 . . . . **225** DZ100
Radnor Way, NW10 . . . . **160** CP70
Slough SL3 . . . . **174** AY77
Radolphs, Tad. KT20 . . . . **255** CX122
Radstock Av, Har. HA3 . . . . **139** CG55
Radstock Cl, N11 . . . . **120** DG50
Radstock St, SW11 . . . . **40** C5
Radstock Way, Merst. RH1 . . . . **273** DK128
Radstone Ct, Wok. GU22 . . . . . **249** AZ118
Radzan Cl, Dart. DA2 . . . . **209** FE89
Raebarn Gdns, Barn. EN5 . . . . . **101** CV43
Raeburn Av, Dart. DA1 . . . . **209** FH85
Surbiton KT5 . . . . **220** CP100
Raeburn Cl, NW11 . . . . **142** DC58
Kingston upon Thames KT1 . **199** CK94
Raeburn Ct, Wok. GU21
off Martin Way **248** AU118
Raeburn Rd, Edg. HA8 . . . . **118** CN54
Hayes UB4 . . . . **157** BR68
Sidcup DA15 . . . . **207** ES86
Raeburn St, SW2 . . . . **183** DL84
Raeside Cl, Seer Grn HP9 . . . . . **111** AQ51
Raffles Ct, Edg. HA8 . . . . **118** CM49
Rafford Way, Brom. BR1 . . . . . . **226** EH96
★ **R.A.F. Northolt**, Ruis. HA4 . **137** BT64
Raft Rd, SW18 *off North Pas* . . **182** DA84
Ragged Hall La, St.Alb. AL2 . . . . **64** BZ24
★ **Ragged Sch Mus**, E3 . . . . **21** M6
Raggleswood, Chis. BR7 . . . . . . **227** EN95
Rag Hill Cl, Tats. TN16 . . . . **260** EL121
Rag Hill Rd, Tats. TN16 . . . . . . **260** EK121
Raglan Av, Wal.Cr. EN8 . . . . **89** DX34
Raglan Cl, Houns. TW4 . . . . **198** BZ85
Reigate RH2 . . . . **272** DC132
Raglan Ct, SE12 . . . . **206** EG85
South Croydon CR2 . . . . **241** DP106
Wembley HA9 . . . . **140** CM63
Raglan Gdns, Wat. WD19 . . . . . **115** BV46
Sch **Raglan Inf Sch**, Enf. EN1
off Wellington Rd **122** DS45
Sch **Raglan Jun Sch**, Enf. EN1
off Raglan Rd **122** DS45
Raglan Prec, Cat. CR3 . . . . **258** DS122
Sch **Raglan Prim Sch**, Brom. BR2
off Raglan Rd **226** EJ98
Raglan Rd, E17 . . . . **145** EC57
SE18 . . . . **37** P10
Belvedere DA17 . . . . **188** EZ77
Bromley BR2 . . . . **226** EJ98
Enfield EN1 . . . . **122** DS45
Knaphill GU21 . . . . **248** AS118
Reigate RH2 . . . . **272** DB131
Raglan St, NW5 . . . . **7** K4
Raglan Ter, Har. HA2 . . . . **138** CB63
Raglan Way, Nthlt. UB5 . . . . . . **158** CC65
Ragley Cl, W3 *off Church Rd* . . **180** CQ75
Rags La, Chsht EN7 . . . . **88** DS27
Ragstone Rd, Slou. SL1 . . . . **173** AR76
Ragwort Ct, SE26 . . . . **204** DV92
Rahere Ho, EC1 . . . . **19** J2
Rahn Rd, Epp. CM16 . . . . **92** EU31
Raider Cl, Rom. RM7 . . . . **126** FA53
Raikes Hollow, Abin.Ham.
RH5 . . . . **283** BV142
Raikes La, Abin.Ham. RH5 . . . . **283** BV141
Railey Ms, NW5 . . . . **7** L2
Railpit La, Warl. CR6 . . . . **260** EE115
Railshead Rd, Islw. TW7 . . . . . . **179** CH84
Railstore, The, Gidea Pk RM2 . . **150** FJ55
Railton Rd, SE24 . . . . **183** DN84
Guildford GU2 . . . . **264** AV130
Railway App, N4
off Wightman Rd **143** DN58
SE1 . . . . **31** M2
Harrow HA1, HA3 . . . . **139** CF56
Hertford SG14 . . . . **54** DQ09
Twickenham TW1 . . . . **199** CG87
Wallington SM6 . . . . **241** DH107
Railway Arches, W12 . . . . **26** A5
Railway Av, SE16 . . . . **33** H4
Railway Children Wk, SE12 . . . **206** EG89
Bromley BR1 . . . . **206** EG89
Railway Cotts, Rad. WD7 . . . . . . **99** CH35
Watford WD24 . . . . **97** BV39
Railway Ms, E3 . . . . **22** A3
W10 . . . . **14** F8
Railway Pas, Tedd. TW11
off Victoria Rd **199** CG93
Railway Pl, SW19
off Hartfield Rd **201** CZ93
Belvedere DA17 . . . . **188** FA76
Gravesend DA12
off Stone St **213** GH86
Hertford SG13 . . . . **54** DS09
Railway Ri, SE22
off Grove Vale **184** DS84
Railway Rd, Tedd. TW11 . . . . . . **199** CF91
Waltham Cross EN8 . . . . **89** DY33
Railway Side, SW13 . . . . **180** CS83
Railway Sq, Brwd. CM14
off Fairfield Rd **130** FW48
Railway St, N1 . . . . **18** B1
Hertford SG13, SG14 . . . . **54** DR09
Northfleet DA11 . . . . **212** GA85
Romford RM6 . . . . **148** EW60
Railway Ter, E17 . . . . **123** EC53
SE13 *off Ladywell Rd* **205** EB85
Kings Langley WD4 . . . . **80** BN27
Slough SL2 . . . . **154** AT74
Staines TW18 . . . . **195** BD92
Westerham TN16 . . . . **277** ER125
Rainborough Cl, NW10 . . . . **160** CQ65
Rainbow Av, E14 . . . . **34** C10
Rainbow Ct, Wat. WD19
off Oxhey Rd **98** BW44
Woking GU21
off Langmans Way **248** AS116
● **Rainbow Ind Est**, West Dr.
UB7 . . . . **156** BK73
● **Rainbow Ind Pk**, SW20 . . . . **221** CV96
Rainbow Quay, SE16 . . . . **33** M7
Rainbow Rd, Chaff.Hun.
RM16 . . . . **191** FW77
Matching Tye CM17 . . . . **59** FE12
Rainbow St, SE5 . . . . **43** N5
Rainer Cl, Chsht EN8 . . . . **89** DX29
Raines Ct, N16
off Northwold Rd **144** DT61
Sch **Raine's Foundation Sch**,
Lwr Sch, E2 . . . . **20** F2
Upr Sch, E2 . . . . **21** H1
Raine St, E1 . . . . **32** F2
RAINHAM, RM13 . . . . **169** FG69
⇌ **Rainham** **169** FF70
Rainham Cl, SE9 . . . . **207** ER86
SW11 . . . . **202** DE86
★ **Rainham Hall**, Rain. RM13 . **169** FG70
Rainham Rd, NW10 . . . . **14** B3
Rainham RM13 . . . . **169** FE66
Rainham Rd N, Dag. RM10 . . . . **149** FB61
Rainham Rd S, Dag. RM10 . . . . **149** FB63
Sch **Rainham Village Prim Sch**,
Rain. RM13
off Upminster Rd S **169** FG70
Rainhill Way, E3 . . . . **22** B2
Rainsborough Av, SE8 . . . . **33** L9
Rainsborough Ct, Hert. SG13
off Lilbourne Dr **54** DU08
Rainsford Cl, Stan. HA7 . . . . . . **117** CJ49
Rainsford Rd, NW10 . . . . **160** CP69
Rainsford St, W2 . . . . **16** C8
Rainsford Way, Horn. RM12 . . . **149** FG60
Rainton Rd, SE7 . . . . **35** P10
Rainville Rd, W6 . . . . **38** B3
Raisins Hill, Pnr. HA5 . . . . **138** BW55
Raith Av, N14 . . . . **121** DK48
Raleana Rd, E14 . . . . **34** F2
Raleigh Av, Hayes UB4 . . . . **157** BV71
Wallington SM6 . . . . **241** DK105
Raleigh Cl, NW4 . . . . **141** CW57
Erith DA8 . . . . **189** FF79
Pinner HA5 . . . . **138** BX59
Ruislip HA4 . . . . **137** BT61
Slough SL1 . . . . **153** AN74
Raleigh Ct, SE19
off Lymer Av **204** DT92
Beckenham BR3 . . . . **225** EB95
Staines TW18 . . . . **196** BG91
Wallington SM6 . . . . **241** DH107
Raleigh Dr, N20 . . . . **120** DE48
Claygate KT10 . . . . **237** CD106
Smallfield RH6 . . . . **291** DN148
Surbiton KT5 . . . . **220** CQ102
Raleigh Gdns, SW2
off Brixton Hill **203** DM86
Mitcham CR4 . . . . **222** DF96
Raleigh Ms, N1
off Queen's Head St **9** H9
Orpington BR6
off Osgood Av **245** ET106
Raleigh Rd, N8 . . . . **143** DN56
SE20 . . . . **205** DX94
Enfield EN2 . . . . **104** DR42
Feltham TW13 . . . . **197** BT90
Richmond TW9 . . . . **180** CM83
Southall UB2 . . . . **178** BY78
Sch **Raleigh Sch, The**, W.Hors.
KT24 *off Northcote Cres* . . . **267** BQ125
Raleigh St, N1 . . . . **9** H9
Raleigh Way, N14 . . . . **121** DK46
Feltham TW13 . . . . **198** BW92
Ralliwood Rd, Ashtd. KT21 . . . **254** CN119
Ralph Ct, W2 . . . . **15** M8

Ralph Perring Ct, Beck. BR3 225 EA98
Ralston Ct, Wind. SL4
off Russell St 173 AR81
Ralston St, SW3 40 E1
Ralston Way, Wat. WD19 116 BX47
Rama Cl, SW16 203 DK94
Rama Ct, Har. HA1 139 CE61
Ramac Way, SE7 36 A9
Rama La, SE19 204 DT94
Rambert Sch of Ballet & Contemporary Dance, Twick. TW1 off St. Margarets Rd 199 CH85
Rambler Cl, SW16 203 DJ91
Taplow SL6 152 AH72
Rambler La, Slou. SL3 174 AW76
Ramblers La, Harl. CM17
off Crossway 58 EX14
Ramblers Way, Welw.G.C. AL7 52 DB10
Rambling Way, Pott.End HP4 61 BC17
Rame Cl, SW17 202 DG92
Ram Gorse, Harl. CM20 57 EP13
Ramilles Cl, SW2 203 DL86
Ramillies Pl, W1 17 L9
Ramillies Rd, NW7 118 CS47
W4 180 CR77
Sidcup DA15 208 EV86
Ramillies St, W1 17 L9
Ramin Ct, Guil. GU1 264 AW131
Ramney Dr, Enf. EN3 105 DY37
Ramornie Cl, Hersham KT12 236 BZ106
Ramparts, The, St.Alb. AL3 64 CB21
Rampart St, E1 20 E9
Ram Pas, Kings.T. KT1
off High St 219 CK96
Rampayne St, SW1 29 N10
Ram Pl, E9 11 H4
Rampton Cl, E4 123 EA48
Ramsay Cl, Brox. EN10 71 DY21
Ramsay Gdns, Rom. RM3 128 FJ53
Ramsay Ms, SW3 40 C2
Ramsay Pl, Har. HA1 139 CE60
Ramsay Rd, E7 146 EE63
W3 180 CQ76
Ramsbury Rd, St.Alb. AL1 65 CE21
Ramscote La, Bell. HP5 76 AN25
Ramscroft Cl, N9 122 DS45
Ramsdale Rd, SW17 202 DG92
RAMSDEN, Orp. BR5 228 EW102
Ramsden Cl, Orp. BR5 228 EW102
Ramsden Dr, Rom. RM5 126 FA52
Ramsden Rd, N11 120 DF50
SW12 202 DG86
Erith DA8 189 FD80
Orpington BR5, BR6 228 EV101
Ramsey Cl, NW9 141 CT58
Brookmans Park AL9 86 DD27
Greenford UB6 139 CD64
Horley RH6 290 DF148
St. Albans AL1 65 CG22
Ramsey Ct, Slou. SL2
off Lower Britwell Rd 153 AK70
Ramsey Ho, SW11
off Maysoule Rd 182 DD84
Wembley HA9 160 CL65
Ramsey Lo Ct, St.Alb. AL1 65 CE19
Ramsey Pl, Cat. CR3 258 DQ122
Ramsey Rd, Th.Hth. CR7 223 DM100
Ramsey St, E2 20 D4
Ramsey Wk, N1 9 L5
Ramsey Way, N14 121 DJ45
Ramsfort Ho, SE16
off Manor Est 32 E9
Ramsgate Cl, E16 36 A3
Ramsgate St, E8 10 B4
Ramsgill App, Ilf. IG2 147 ET56
Ramsgill Dr, Ilf. IG2 147 ET57
Rams Gro, Rom. RM6 148 EY56
Ramson Ri, Hem.H. HP1 61 BE21
Ram St, SW18 202 DB85
Ramulis Dr, Hayes UB4 158 BX70
Ramus Wd Av, Orp. BR6 245 ES106
Rancliffe Gdns, SE9 186 EL84
Rancliffe Rd, E6 25 H1
Randal Cremer Prim Sch, E2 10 A10
Randal Cres, Reig. RH2 288 DA136
Randall Av, NW2 141 CT62
Randall Cl, SW11 40 C6
Erith DA8 189 FC79
Slough SL3 175 AZ78
Randall Ct, NW7 119 CU52
Randall Dr, Horn. RM12 150 FJ63
Randall Pl, SE10 46 E4
Randall Rd, SE11 30 C10
Randall Row, SE11 30 C9
Randalls Cres, Lthd. KT22 253 CG120
Randalls Dr, Hutt. CM13 131 GE44
Randalls Pk Av, Lthd. KT22 253 CG120
Randalls Pk Dr, Lthd. KT22
off Randalls Rd 253 CG121
Randalls Ride, Hem.H. HP2 62 BK18
Randalls Rd, Lthd. KT22 253 CE119
Randall's Wk, Brick.Wd AL2 82 BZ30
Randalls Way, Lthd. KT22 253 CG121
Randell's Rd, N1 8 B8
Randisbourne Gdns, SE6 205 EB90
Randle Rd, Rich. TW10 199 CJ91
Randlesdown Rd, SE6 205 EA91
Randles La, Knock.P. TN14 262 EX115
Randolph App, E16 24 D9
Randolph Av, W9 15 P4
Randolph Cl, Bexh. DA7 189 FC83
Kingston upon Thames KT2 200 CQ92
Knaphill GU21
off Creston Av 248 AS117
Stoke D'Abernon KT11 252 CA115
Randolph Cres, W9 15 N5
Randolph Gdns, NW6 15 L1
Randolph Gro, Rom. RM6
off Donald Dr 148 EW57
● Randolph Ho, Croy. CR0 224 DQ102
Randolph Ms, W9 15 P5
Randolph Rd, E17 145 EB57
W9 15 N5
Bromley BR2 227 EM102
Epsom KT17 239 CT114
Slough SL3 174 AY76
Southall UB1 178 BZ75
Randolph's La, West. TN16 277 EP126
Randolph St, NW1 7 L7
Randon Cl, Har. HA2 116 CB54
Ranelagh Av, SW6 38 G10
SW13 181 CU82
Ranelagh Br, W2
off Gloucester Ter 15 M7
Ranelagh Cl, Edg. HA8 118 CN49
Ranelagh Dr, Edg. HA8 118 CN49
Twickenham TW1 199 CH85
★ Ranelagh Gdns, SW3 40 G1
Ranelagh Gdns, E11 146 EJ57
SW6 38 G10
W4 180 CQ80
W6 181 CT76
Ilford IG1 147 EN60
Northfleet DA11 213 GF87
Ranelagh Gdns Mans, SW6
off Ranelagh Gdns 38 F10
Ranelagh Gro, SW1 29 H10
Ranelagh Ms, W5 179 CK75
Ranelagh Pl, N.Mal. KT3 220 CS99
Ranelagh Prim Sch, E15 13 K10
Ranelagh Rd, E6 167 EN67
E11 146 EE63
E15 13 K9
N17 144 DS55
N22 121 DM53
NW10 161 CT68
SW1 41 M1
W5 179 CK75
Hemel Hempstead HP2 63 BP20
Redhill RH1 272 DE134
Southall UB1 158 BX74
Wembley HA0 139 CK64
Ranfurly Rd, Sutt. SM1 222 DA103
Rangefield Prim Sch, Downham BR1 off Glenbow Rd 206 EE92
Rangefield Rd, Brom. BR1 206 EE92
Rangemoor Rd, N15 144 DT57
Range Rd, Grav. DA12 213 GL87
Rangers Rd, E4 124 EE45
Loughton IG10 124 EE45
Rangers Sq, SE10 46 G6
Ranger Wk, Add. KT15
off Monks Cres 234 BH106
Range Way, Shep. TW17 216 BN101
Rangeworth Pl, Sid. DA15
off Priestlands Pk Rd 207 ET90
Rangoon St, EC3 20 A9
Rankin Cl, NW9 140 CS55
Rankine Ho, SE1 off Bath Ter 31 J7
Ranleigh Gdns, Bexh. DA7 188 EZ80
Ranmere St, SW12
off Ormeley Rd 203 DH88
Ranmoor Cl, Har. HA1 139 CD56
Ranmoor Gdns, Har. HA1 139 CD56
Ranmore Av, Croy. CR0 224 DT104
Ranmore Cl, Red. RH1 272 DG131
★ Ranmore Common, Dor. RH5 268 CB133
Ranmore Common Rd, Westh. RH5 269 CD133
Ranmore Path, Orp. BR5 228 EU98
Ranmore Rd, Dor. RH4 268 CC134
Sutton SM2 239 CX109
Rannoch Cl, Edg. HA8 118 CP47
Rannoch Rd, W6 38 B2
Rannoch Wk, Hem.H. HP2 62 BK16
Rannock Av, NW9 140 CS59
Ranskill Rd, Borwd. WD6 100 CN39
Ransom Cl, Wat. WD19 116 BW45
● Ransome's Dock Business Cen, SW11 40 D5
Ransom Rd, SE7 36 D10
Ransom Wk, SE7 36 D9
Ranston Cl, Denh. UB9
off Nightingale Way 135 BF58
Ranston St, NW1 16 C6
Rant Meadow, Hem.H. HP3 62 BN22
Ranulf Cl, Harl. CM17 58 EW09
Ranulf Rd, NW2 141 CZ63
Ranwell Cl, E3 11 N9
Ranwell St, E3 11 N9
Ranworth Av, Hodd. EN11 55 EB13
Ranworth Cl, Erith DA8 189 FE82
Hemel Hempstead HP3
off Panxworth Rd 62 BK22
Ranworth Gdns, Pot.B. EN6 85 CX31
Ranworth Rd, N9 122 DW47
Ranyard Cl, Chess. KT9 220 CM104
Raphael Av, Rom. RM1 149 FF55
Tilbury RM18 193 GG80
Raphael Cl, Shenley WD7 84 CL32
Raphael Dr, T.Ditt. KT7 219 CF101
Watford WD24 98 BX40
Raphael Indep Sch, Horn. RM11 off Park La 149 FG59
Raphael Rd, Grav. DA12 213 GK87
Raphael St, SW7 28 E5
Rapier Cl, Purf. RM19 190 FN77
Rasehill Cl, Rick. WD3 96 BJ43
Rashleigh St, SW8 41 K9
Rashleigh Way, Hort.Kir. DA4 230 FQ98
Rasper Rd, N20 120 DC47
Rastell Av, SW2 203 DK89
Ratcliffe Cl, SE12 206 EG87
Uxbridge UB8 156 BK69
Ratcliffe Cross St, E1 21 K9
Ratcliffe La, E14 21 L9
Ratcliffe Orchard, E1 21 K10
Ratcliff Rd, E7 146 EJ64
Rathbone Ed Cen, The, E16 23 M6
Rathbone Mkt, E16 23 L7
Rathbone Pl, W1 17 N8
Rathbone St, E16 23 L7
W1 17 M7
Rathcoole Av, N8 143 DM56
Rathcoole Gdns, N8 143 DM57
Rathfern Prim Sch, SE6
off Rathfern Rd 205 DZ88
Rathfern Rd, SE6 205 DZ88
Rathgar Av, W13 159 CH74
Rathgar Cl, N3 119 CZ54
Redhill RH1 288 DG139
Rathgar Rd, SW9 43 H10
Rathlin, Hem.H. HP3 63 BP22
Rathmell Dr, SW4 203 DK86
Rathmore Rd, SE7 36 A10
Gravesend DA11 213 GH87
Rathwell Path, Borwd. WD6 100 CL39
Rats La, High Beach IG10 106 EH38
Rattray Rd, SW2 183 DN84
Ratty's La, Hodd. EN11 71 ED17
Raul Rd, SE15 44 D8
Raveley St, NW5 7 L1
Ravel Gdns, Aveley RM15 170 FQ72
Ravel Rd, Aveley RM15 170 FQ72
Raven Cl, NW9 118 CS54
Rickmansworth WD3 114 BJ45
Raven Ct, E5 off Stellman Cl 144 DU62
Hatfield AL10 67 CU19
Ravencroft, Grays RM16
off Alexandra Cl 193 GH75
Ravendale Rd, Sun. TW16 217 BT96
Ravenet St, SW11 41 J7
Ravenfield, Eng.Grn TW20 194 AW93
Ravenfield Rd, SW17 202 DF90
Welwyn Garden City AL7 51 CZ09
Ravenhill Rd, E13 166 EJ68
Ravenna Rd, SW15 201 CX85
Ravenoak Way, Chig. IG7 125 ES50
Ravenor Pk Rd, Grnf. UB6 158 CB69
Ravenor Prim Sch, Grnf. UB6
off Greenway Gdns 158 CA69
Raven Rd, E18 124 EJ54
Raven Row, E1 20 F6
⇌ Ravensbourne 205 ED94
Ravensbourne Av, Beck. BR3 205 ED94
Bromley BR2 205 ED94
Staines TW19 196 BL88
● Ravensbourne Business Cen, Kes. BR2 244 EK105
Ravensbourne Coll of Design & Communication, Chis. BR7
off Walden Rd 207 EM92
Ravensbourne Cres, Rom. RM3 150 FM55
Ravensbourne Gdns, W13 159 CH71
Ilford IG5 125 EN53
Ravensbourne Pk, SE6 205 EA87
Ravensbourne Pk Cres, SE6 205 DZ87
Ravensbourne Pl, SE13 46 D8
Ravensbourne Rd, SE6 205 DZ87
Bromley BR1 226 EG97
Dartford DA1 189 FG83
Twickenham TW1 199 CJ86
Ravensbourne Sch, Rom. RM3
off Neave Cres 128 FK53
Ravensbourne Sch, The, Brom. BR2 off Hayes La 226 EH98
Ravensbourne Ter, Stanw. TW19
off Ravensbourne Av 196 BM88
Ravensbury Av, Mord. SM4 222 DC99
Ravensbury Ct, Mitch. CR4
off Ravensbury Gro 222 DD98
Ravensbury Gro, Mitch. CR4 222 DD98
Ravensbury La, Mitch. CR4 222 DD98
Ravensbury Path, Mitch. CR4 222 DD98
Ravensbury Rd, SW18 202 DA89
Orpington BR5 227 ET98
Ravensbury Ter, SW18 202 DB89
Ravenscar Rd, Brom. BR1 206 EE91
Surbiton KT6 220 CM103
Ravens Cl, Brom. BR2 226 EF96
Enfield EN1 104 DS40
Redhill RH1 272 DF132
Surbiton KT6 219 CK100
Ravens Ct, Berk. HP4
off Benningfield Gdns 60 AY17
Ravenscourt, Sun. TW16 217 BT95
Ravenscourt Av, W6 181 CU77
Ravenscourt Cl, Horn. RM12
off Ravenscourt Dr 150 FL62
Ruislip HA4 137 BQ59
Ravenscourt Dr, Horn. RM12 150 FL62
Ravenscourt Gdns, W6 181 CU77
Ravenscourt Gro, Horn. RM12 150 FL61
⊖ Ravenscourt Park 181 CU77
Ravenscourt Pk, W6 181 CU76
Ravenscourt Pl, W6 181 CV77
Ravenscourt Rd, W6 181 CV77
Orpington BR5 228 EU97
Ravenscourt Sq, W6 181 CU76
Ravenscraig Rd, N11 121 DH49
Ravenscroft, Brox. EN10 71 DZ20
Watford WD25 82 BY34
Ravenscroft Av, NW11 141 CZ59
Wembley HA9 140 CM60
Ravenscroft Cl, E16 23 N6
Ravenscroft Cres, SE9 207 EM90
Ravenscroft Pk, Barn. EN5 101 CX42
Ravenscroft Pt, E9 11 J5
Ravenscroft Prim Sch, E16 23 P5
Ravenscroft Rd, E16 23 P6
W4 180 CQ77
Beckenham BR3 224 DW96
Weybridge KT13 235 BQ111
Ravenscroft Sch, The, N20
off Barnet La 119 CZ45
Ravenscroft St, E2 20 B1
Ravensdale Av, N12 120 DC49
Ravensdale Gdns, SE19 204 DR94
Hounslow TW4 178 BY83
Ravensdale Ms, Stai. TW18
off Worple Rd 196 BH93
Ravensdale Rd, N16 144 DT59
Hounslow TW4 178 BY83
Ravensdell, Hem.H. HP1 61 BF19
Ravensdon St, SE11 42 F1
Ravensfield, Slou. SL3 174 AX75
Ravensfield Cl, Dag. RM9 148 EX63
Ravensfield Gdns, Epsom KT19 238 CS106
Ravens Gate Ms, Brom. BR2
off Meadow Rd 226 EE96
Ravenshaw St, NW6 5 H3
Ravenshead Cl, S.Croy. CR2 242 DW111
Ravenshill, Chis. BR7 227 EP95
Ravenshurst Av, NW4 141 CW56
Ravenside Cl, N18 123 DX51
Ravenside Retail Pk, N18 123 DX50
Ravens La, Berk. HP4 60 AX19
Ravenslea Rd, SW12 202 DF87
Ravensleigh Gdns, Brom. BR1
off Pike Cl 206 EH92
Ravensmead, Chal.St.P. SL9 113 AZ50
Ravensmead Rd, Brom. BR2 205 ED94
Ravensmede Way, W4 181 CT77
Ravensmere, Epp. CM16 92 EU31
Ravens Ms, SE12
off Ravens Way 206 EG85
Ravenstone, SE17 43 P1
Ravenstone Prim Sch, SW12
off Ravenstone St 203 DH88
Ravenstone Rd, N8 143 DN55
NW9 off West Hendon Bdy 141 CT58
Ravenstone St, SW12 202 DG88
Ravens Way, SE12 206 EG85
Ravens Wf, Berk. HP4 60 AX19
Ravenswold, Ken. CR8 258 DQ115
Ravenswood, Bex. DA5 208 EY88
Ravenswood Av, Surb. KT6 220 CM103
West Wickham BR4 225 EC102
Ravenswood Cl, Cob. KT11 252 BX115
Romford RM5 127 FB50
Ravenswood Ct, Kings.T. KT2 200 CP93
Woking GU22 249 AZ118
Ravenswood Cres, Har. HA2 138 BZ61
West Wickham BR4 225 EC102
Ravenswood Gdns, Islw. TW7 179 CE81
● Ravenswood Ind Est, E17
off Shernhall St 145 EC56
Ravenswood Pk, Nthwd. HA6 115 BU51
Ravenswood Rd, E17 145 EB56
SW12 203 DH87
Croydon CR0 223 DP104
Ravens Wd Sch, Brom. BR2
off Oakley Rd 226 EK104
Ravensworth Rd, NW10 161 CV69
SE9 207 EM91
Slough SL2 153 AN69
Ravey St, EC2 19 N4
Ravine Gro, SE18 187 ES79
Rav Pinter Cl, N16 144 DS59
Rawdon Dr, Hodd. EN11 71 EA18
Rawlings Cl, Beck. BR3 225 EC99
Orpington BR6 245 ET106
Rawlings Cres, Wem. HA9 140 CP62
Rawlings La, Seer Grn HP9 111 AQ48
Rawlings St, SW3 28 E8
Rawlins Cl, N3 141 CY55
South Croydon CR2 243 DY108
Rawlinson Ho, SE13
off Mercator Rd 185 ED84
Rawlyn Cl, Chaff.Hun. RM16 191 FV78
Rawnsley Av, Mitch. CR4 222 DD99
Rawreth Wk, N1 9 K8
Rawson Ct, SW11
off Strasburg Rd 41 J7
Rawson St, SW11 41 H7
Rawsthorne Cl, E16 37 J3
Rawstone Wk, E13 13 P10
Rawstorne Pl, EC1 18 G2
Rawstorne St, EC1 18 G2
Raybarn Rd, Hem.H. HP1 62 BG18
Rayburn Rd, Horn. RM11 150 FN59
Ray Cl, Chess. KT9 237 CJ107
Raydean Rd, New Barn. EN5 102 DB43
Raydon Rd, Chsht EN8 89 DX32
Raydons Gdns, Dag. RM9 148 EY63
Raydons Rd, Dag. RM9 148 EY64
Raydon St, N19 143 DH61
Rayfield, Epp. CM16 92 EU30
Welwyn Garden City AL8 51 CX06
Rayfield Cl, Brom. BR2 226 EL100
Rayford Av, SE12 206 EF87
Rayford Cl, Dart. DA1 210 FJ85
Ray Gdns, Bark. IG11 168 EU68
Stanmore HA7 117 CH50
Ray Lamb Way, Erith DA8 189 FH79
Raylands Mead, Ger.Cr. SL9 134 AW57
Rayleas Cl, SE18 187 EP81
Rayleigh Av, Tedd. TW11 199 CE93
Rayleigh Cl, N13
off Rayleigh Rd 122 DR48
Hutton CM13 131 GC44
Rayleigh Ct, Kings.T. KT1 220 CM96
Rayleigh Ri, S.Croy. CR2 242 DS107
Rayleigh Rd, E16 36 B2
N13 122 DQ48
SW19 221 CZ95
Hutton CM13 131 GB44
Woodford Green IG8 124 EJ51
Rayley La, N.Wld Bas. CM16 74 FA24
Ray Lo Prim Sch, Wdf.Grn. IG8
off Snakes La E 124 EK51
Ray Lo Rd, Wdf.Grn. IG8 124 EJ51
Ray Massey Way, E6
off Ron Leighton Way 166 EL67
Raymead, NW4 141 CW56
Raymead Av, Th.Hth. CR7 223 DN99
Raymead Cl, Fetch. KT22 253 CE122
Ray Mead Ct, Maid. SL6
off Boulters La 152 AC70
Raymead Pas, Th.Hth. CR7
off Raymead Av 223 DN99
Ray Mead Rd, Maid. SL6 152 AC72
Raymead Way, Fetch. KT22 253 CE122
Raymer Cl, St.Alb. AL1 65 CE19
Raymere Gdns, SE18 187 ER80
Raymer Wk, Horl. RH6 291 DJ147
Raymond Av, E18 146 EF55
W13 179 CG76
Raymond Bldgs, WC1 18 D6
Raymond Cl, SE26 204 DW92
Abbots Langley WD5 81 BR32
Colnbrook SL3 175 BE81
Raymond Ct, N10
off Pembroke Rd 120 DG52
Potters Bar EN6
off St. Francis Cl 86 DC34
Raymond Cres, Guil. GU2 280 AT135
Raymond Gdns, Chig. IG7 126 EV48
Raymond Rd, E13 166 EJ66
SW19 201 CY93
Beckenham BR3 225 DY98
Ilford IG2 147 ER59
Slough SL3 175 BA76
Raymonds Cl, Welw.G.C. AL7 51 CY11
Raymonds Plain, Welw.G.C. AL7 51 CY11
Raymond Way, Clay. KT10 237 CG107
Raymouth Rd, SE16 32 F8
Rayne Ct, E18 146 EF56
Raynehurst Comm Prim Sch, Grav. DA12
off Cerne Rd 213 GM90
Rayners Av Mobile Home Pk, Loud. HP10 110 AC52
Rayners Cl, Colnbr. SL3 175 BC80
Loudwater HP10 110 AC52
Wembley HA0 139 CK64
Rayners Ct, Grav. DA11 212 GB86
Harrow HA2 138 CA60
Rayners Cres, Nthlt. UB5 157 BV69
Rayners Gdns, Nthlt. UB5 157 BV68
RAYNERS LANE, Har. HA2 138 BZ60
⊖ Rayners Lane 138 BZ59
Rayners La, Har. HA2 138 CB61
Pinner HA5 138 BZ58
Rayners Rd, SW15 201 CY85
Rayner Twrs, E10 145 EA59
Raynes Av, E11 146 EJ59
RAYNES PARK, SW20 221 CV97
⇌ Raynes Park 221 CW96
Raynes Pk High Sch, SW20
off Bushey Rd 221 CV97
Raynham, W2 16 C9
Raynham Av, N18 122 DU51
Raynham Prim Sch, N18
off Raynham Av 122 DU50
Raynham Rd, N18 122 DU50
W6 181 CV77
Raynham St, Hert. SG13 54 DS08
Raynham Ter, N18 122 DU50
Raynor Cl, Sthl. UB1 158 BZ74
Raynor Pl, N1 9 K7
Raynsford Rd, Ware SG12 55 DY06
Raynton Cl, Har. HA2 138 BY60
Hayes UB4 157 BT70
Raynton Dr, Hayes UB4 157 BT70
Raynton Rd, Enf. EN3 105 DX37
Ray Rd, Rom. RM5 127 FB50
West Molesey KT8 218 CB99
Rays Av, N18 122 DW49
Windsor SL4 173 AM80
Rays Hill, Hort.Kir. DA4 230 FQ98
Rays La, Penn HP10 110 AC47
Rays Rd, N18 122 DW49
West Wickham BR4 225 EC101
Ray St, EC1 18 F5
Ray St Br, EC1 18 F5
Ray Wk, N7 off Andover Rd 143 DM61
Raywood Cl, Harling. UB3 177 BQ80
Reach, The, SE28 187 ES75
Reachview Cl, NW1 7 M7
Read Cl, T.Ditt. KT7 219 CG101
Read Ct, Wal.Abb. EN9 90 EG33
Reade Ct, Farn.Com. SL2
off Victoria Rd 153 AQ65
Readens, The, Bans. SM7 256 DF116
Reading Arch Rd, Red. RH1 272 DF134
Reading La, E8 10 E5
Reading Rd, Nthlt. UB5 138 CB64
Sutton SM1 240 DC106
Readings, The, Chorl. WD3 95 BF41
Harlow CM18 73 ET18
Reading Way, NW7 119 CX50
Read Rd, Ashtd. KT21 253 CK117
Reads Cl, Ilf. IG1
off Chapel Rd 147 EP62
Reads Rest La, Tad. KT20 255 CZ119
Read Way, Grav. DA12 213 GK92
Reapers Cl, NW1 7 N8
Reapers Way, Islw. TW7
off Hall Rd 199 CD85
Reardon Ct, N21
off Cosgrove Cl 122 DQ47
Reardon Path, E1 32 F3
Reardon St, E1 32 E2
Reaston St, SE14 45 H4
Reay Prim Sch, SW9 42 D5
Reckitt Rd, W4 180 CS78
Record St, SE15 44 G2
Recovery St, SW17 202 DE92
Recreation Av, Harold Wd RM3 128 FM54
Romford RM7 149 FC57
Recreation Rd, SE26 205 DX91
Bromley BR2 226 EF96
Guildford GU1 264 AW134
Sidcup DA15
off Woodside Rd 207 ES90
Southall UB2 178 BY77
Recreation Way, Mitch. CR4 223 DK97
Rector St, N1 9 J9
Rectory Chase, Lt.Warley CM13 151 FX56
Rectory Cl, E4 123 EA48
N3 119 CZ53
SW20 221 CW97
Ashtead KT21 254 CM119
Byfleet KT14 234 BL113
Dartford DA1 189 FE84
Essendon AL9 68 DF17
Farnham Royal SL2 153 AQ69
Guildford GU4 265 BD132
Hunsdon SG12 56 EK07
Long Ditton KT6 219 CJ102
Shepperton TW17 216 BN97
Sidcup DA14 208 EV91
Stanmore HA7 117 CH51
Windsor SL4 173 AN81
Rectory Ct, E11 146 EJ58
Rectory Fm Rd, Enf. EN2 103 DM38
Rectory Fld, Harl. CM19 73 EP17
Rectory Fld Cres, SE7 186 EJ80
Rectory Gdns, N8 143 DL56
SW4 41 L10
Chalfont St. Giles HP8 112 AV48
Hatfield AL10 67 CV18
Northolt UB5 158 BZ67
Upminster RM14 151 FR61
Rectory Grn, Beck. BR3 225 DZ95
Rectory Gro, SW4 41 L10
Croydon CR0 223 DP103
Hampton TW12 198 BZ91
Rectory Hill, Amer. HP6, HP7 77 AP39
Rectory La, SW17 202 DG93
Ashtead KT21 254 CM118
Banstead SM7 240 DF114
Berkhamsted HP4 60 AW19
Bookham KT23 268 BZ126
Brasted TN16 262 EW123
Buckland RH3 271 CT131
Byfleet KT14 234 BL113
Edgware HA8 118 CN51
Harlow CM19 73 EP17
Kings Langley WD4 80 BN28
Long Ditton KT6 219 CH102
Loughton IG10 107 EN40
Rickmansworth WD3 114 BK46
Sevenoaks TN13 279 FJ126
Shenley WD7 84 CN33
Shere GU5 282 BM139
Sidcup DA14 208 EV91
Stanmore HA7 117 CH50
Wallington SM6 241 DJ105
Westerham TN16 260 EL123
Rectory Meadow, Sthflt DA13 212 GA93
Rectory Orchard, SW19 201 CY91
Rectory Pk, S.Croy. CR2 242 DS113
Rectory Pk Av, Nthlt. UB5 158 BZ69
Rectory Pl, SE18 37 L7
⇌ Rectory Road 144 DT62
Rectory Rd, E12 147 EM64
E17 145 EB55
N16 144 DT62
SW13 181 CU82
W3 160 CP74
Beckenham BR3 225 EA95
Chipstead CR5 272 DD125
Dagenham RM10 168 FA66
Grays RM17 192 GD76
Hayes UB3 157 BU72
Hounslow TW4 177 BV81
Keston BR2 244 EK108
Rickmansworth WD3 114 BK46
Southall UB2 178 BZ76
Sutton SM1 222 DA104
Swanscombe DA10 212 FY87
Taplow SL6 152 AD70
Welwyn Garden City AL8 51 CV06
West Tilbury RM18 193 GK79
Rectory Sq, E1 21 K6
Rectory Way, Amer. HP7 77 AP39
Uxbridge UB10 137 BP62

Rectory Wd, Harl. CM20 57 EQ14
Reculver Ms, N18
off Lyndhurst Rd 122 DU49
Reculver Rd, SE16 33 J10
Red Anchor Cl, SW3 40 C3
Redan Pl, W2 15 L9
Redan St, W14 26 D6
Redan Ter, SE5 43 H8
Redbarn Cl, Pur. CR8
off Whytecliffe Rd N 241 DP111
Red Barracks Rd, SE18 37 J7
Redberry Gro, SE26 204 DW90
Redbourne Av, N3 120 DA53
Redbourne Dr, SE28 168 EX72
Redbourn Rd, Hem.H. HP2 62 BN16
St. Albans AL3 64 CA18
REDBRIDGE, Ilf. IG1 147 EM58
⊖ **Redbridge** 146 EK58
Coll **Redbridge Coll**, Rom. RM6
off Little Heath 148 EV57
Coll **Redbridge Drama Cen**, E18
off Churchfields 124 EG53
● **Redbridge Enterprise Cen**,
Ilf. IG1 147 EQ61
Redbridge Gdns, SE5 43 P5
Redbridge Ho, E16
off University Way 37 N1
Coll **Redbridge Inst of Adult Ed**,
Ilf. IG2 *off Gaysham Av* 147 EP57
Redbridge La E, Ilf. IG4 146 EK58
Redbridge La W, E11 146 EH58
Coll **Redbridge Music Sch**, Ilf. IG6
off Fencepiece Rd 125 EQ52
Sch **Redbridge Prim Sch**, Ilf. IG4
off College Gdns 146 EL57
Jct **Redbridge Rbt**, Ilf. IG4 146 EJ58
Redburn St, SW3 40 E2
Redbury Cl, Rain. RM13
off Deri Av 169 FH70
Redcar Cl, Nthlt. UB5 138 CB64
Redcar Rd, Rom. RM3 128 FM50
Redcar St, SE5 43 J5
Redcastle Cl, E1 20 G10
Red Cedars Rd, Orp. BR6 227 ES101
Redchurch St, E2 20 A4
Redcliffe Cl, SW5
off Old Brompton Rd 39 L1
Redcliffe Ct, E5
off Napoleon Rd 144 DV62
Redcliffe Gdns, SW5 39 M1
SW10 39 M1
W4 180 CP80
Ilford IG1 147 EN60
Redcliffe Ms, SW10 39 M1
Redcliffe Pl, SW10 39 N3
Redcliffe Rd, SW10 39 N1
Sch **Redcliffe Sch**, SW10 39 N2
Redcliffe Sq, SW10 39 M1
Redcliffe St, SW10 39 M2
Redclose Av, Mord. SM4 222 DA99
Redclyffe Rd, E6 166 EJ67
Redcote Pl, Dor. RH4 269 CK134
Red Cottage Ms, Slou. SL3 174 AW76
Red Ct, Slou. SL1 154 AS74
Redcourt, Wok. GU22 249 BD115
Jct **Red Cow**, Slou. SL1 174 AT76
Redcroft Rd, Sthl. UB1 158 CC73
Redcross Way, SE1 31 K4
Redden Ct Rd, Rom. RM3 150 FL55
Sch **Redden Ct Sch**, Harold Wd
RM3 *off Cotswold Rd* 150 FM55
Redding Cl, Dart. DA2 211 FS89
Redding Dr, Amer. HP6 77 AN37
Reddings, Hem.H. HP3 62 BM22
Welwyn Garden City AL8 51 CW08
Reddings, The, NW7 119 CT48
Borehamwood WD6 100 CM41
Reddings Av, Bushey WD23 98 CB43
Reddings Cl, NW7 119 CT49
Sch **Reddings Prim & Nurs Sch,
The**, Hem.H. HP3
off Bennetts End Rd 62 BN22
Reddington Cl, S.Croy. CR2 242 DR109
Reddington Dr, Slou. SL3 174 AY76
Reddington Ho, N1 8 D10
Reddins Rd, SE15 44 C3
Redditch Ct, Hem.H. HP2 62 BM16
Reddons Rd, Beck. BR3 205 DY94
Reddown Rd, Couls. CR5 257 DK118
Reddy Rd, Erith DA8 189 FF79
Rede Ct, Wey. KT13 217 BP104
Redehall Rd, Smallfield RH6 291 DP148
Redenham Ho, SW15
off Tangley Gro 201 CT87
Rede Pl, W2 15 K9
Redesdale Gdns, Islw. TW7 179 CG80
Redesdale St, SW3 40 D2
Redfern Av, Houns. TW4 198 CA87
Redfern Cl, Uxb. UB8 156 BJ67
Redfern Gdns, Rom. RM2 128 FK54
Redfern Rd, NW10 160 CS66
SE6 205 EC87
Redfield La, SW5 27 K8
Redfield Ms, SW5 27 K8
Redford Av, Couls. CR5 241 DH114
Thornton Heath CR7 223 DM98
Wallington SM6 241 DL107
Redford Cl, Felt. TW13 197 BT89
H **Redford Lo Psychiatric Hosp**,
N9 122 DU47
Redford Rd, Wind. SL4 173 AK81
Redford Wk, N1 9 H8
Redford Way, Uxb. UB8 156 BJ66
Redgate Dr, Brom. BR2 226 EH103
Sch **Red Gates Sch**, Croy. CR0
off Purley Way 241 DN106
Redgate Ter, SW15 201 CY86
Redgrave Cl, Croy. CR0 224 DT100
Redgrave Rd, SW15 181 CX83
Redhall Cl, Hat. AL10 67 CT21
Redhall Ct, Cat. CR3 258 DR123
Redhall Dr, Hat. AL10 67 CT22
Redhall End, St.Alb. AL4
off Roestock La 66 CS22
Redhall La, Chan.Cr. WD3 96 BL39
Redheath Cl, Wat. WD25 97 BT35
REDHILL, RH1 272 DG134
⇌ **Redhill** 272 DG133
⇌ **Redhill** 272 DG133
Red Hill, Chis. BR7 207 EN92
Denham UB9 135 BD61
Coll **Redhill Coll (Royal Nat Inst for
the Blind)**, Red. RH1
off Philanthropic Rd 289 DH136
Redhill Common, Red. RH1 288 DE135
Redhill Dr, Edg. HA8 118 CQ54
Sch **Red Hill Prim Sch**, Chis. BR7
off Red Hill 207 EP92
Redhill Rd, Cob. KT11 235 BP113
Red Hills, Hodd. EN11 70 DV19
Redhill St, NW1 17 K2
★ **Red Ho, The** (William Morris Ho),
Bexh. DA6 188 EY84
Red Ho Cl, Knot.Grn HP9 110 AH51
Ware SG12 55 DY07
Red Ho La, Bexh. DA6 188 EX84
Walton-on-Thames KT12 217 BU103
Red Ho Rd, Croy. CR0 223 DK100
Redhouse Rd, Tats. TN16 260 EJ120
Red Ho Sq, N1 9 K5
Redington Gdns, NW3 142 DB63
Redington Rd, NW3 142 DB63
Redland Gdns, W.Mol. KT8
off Dunstable Rd 218 BZ98
Redlands, Couls. CR5 257 DL116
Sch **Redlands C of E Prim Sch, The**,
Dor. RH4 *off Goodwyns Rd* 285 CH139
Redlands Ct, Brom. BR1 206 EF94
Redlands La, Mid Holm. RH5 285 CG142
Sch **Redlands Prim Sch**, E1 21 H6
Redlands Rd, Enf. EN3 105 DY39
Sevenoaks TN13 278 FF124
Redlands Way, SW2 203 DM87
Red La, Clay. KT10 237 CG107
Dorking RH5 286 CL142
Oxted RH8 276 EH133
Redleaf Cl, Belv. DA17 188 FA79
Fetcham KT22 253 CE124
Red Leaf Cl, Slou. SL3
off Pickford Dr 155 AZ74
Redleaves Av, Ashf. TW15 197 BP93
Redlees Cl, Islw. TW7 179 CG84
Red Leys, Uxb. UB8 156 BL66
● **Red Lion Business Pk**, Surb.
KT6 220 CM103
Red Lion Cl, SE17 43 K2
Aldenham WD25
off Church La 98 CC37
Orpington BR5 228 EW100
Red Lion Ct, EC4 18 F8
Hatfield AL9 67 CW16
Red Lion Cres, Harl. CM17 74 EW17
Red Lion Dr, Hem.H. HP3 80 BM25
Red Lion Hill, N2 120 DD54
Red Lion La, SE18 187 EN80
Chobham GU24 232 AS109
Harlow CM17 74 EW17
Hemel Hempstead HP3 80 BM26
Sarratt WD3 96 BG35
Red Lion Pl, SE18
off Shooters Hill Rd 187 EN81
Red Lion Rd, Chobham GU24 232 AS109
Surbiton KT6 220 CM103
Red Lion Row, SE17 43 K2
Red Lion Sq, SW18
off Wandsworth High St 202 DA85
WC1 18 C7
Red Lion St, WC1 18 C6
Chesham HP5 76 AP32
Richmond TW9 199 CK85
Red Lion Way, Woob.Grn
HP10 132 AE57
Red Lion Yd, W1 29 H2
Red Lo Cres, Bex. DA5 209 FD90
Red Lo Gdns, Berk. HP4 60 AU20
Red Lo Rd, Beck. BR3 225 ED100
Bexley DA5 209 FD90
West Wickham BR4 225 EC102
Redman Cl, Nthlt. UB5 158 BW68
Redmans La, Shore. TN14 247 FE107
Redman's Rd, E1 20 G6
Redmead La, E1 32 C3
Redmead Rd, Hayes UB3 177 BS77
Redmore Rd, W6 181 CV77
Red Oak Cl, Orp. BR6 227 EP104
Red Oaks Mead, They.B.
CM16 107 ER37
Red Path, E9 11 M4
Red Pl, W1 16 G10
Redpoll Way, Erith DA18 188 EX76
Red Post Hill, SE21 204 DR85
SE24 184 DR84
Redricks La, Saw. CM21 57 ES09
Redriffe Rd, E13 13 M9
Redriff Est, SE16 33 M6
Sch **Redriff Prim Sch**, SE16 33 M4
Redriff Rd, SE16 33 K7
Romford RM7 127 FB54
Red Rd, Borwd. WD6 100 CM41
Warley CM14 130 FV49
Redroofs Cl, Beck. BR3 225 EB95
Coll **Red Rover**, SW15 181 CT83
Redruth Cl, N22 121 DM52
Redruth Gdns, Clay. KT10 237 CF108
Romford RM3 128 FM50
Redruth Rd, E9 11 H8
Romford RM3 128 FM50
Redruth Wk, Rom. RM3 128 FN50
Red Sq, N16 144 DR62
Redstart Cl, E6 24 G6
SE14 45 L4
New Addington CR0 243 ED110
Redstart Mans, Ilf. IG1
off Mill Rd 147 EN62
Redstone Hill, Red. RH1 272 DG134
Redstone Hollow, Red. RH1 288 DG135
Redstone Manor, Red. RH1 272 DG134
Redstone Pk, Red. RH1 272 DG134
Redstone Rd, Red. RH1 288 DG135
Redston Rd, N8 143 DK56
REDSTREET, Grav. DA13 212 GB93
Red St, Sthflt DA13 212 GA93
Redtiles Gdns, Ken. CR8 257 DP115
Redvers Rd, N22 121 DN54
Warlingham CR6 258 DW118
Redvers St, N1 19 P2
Redwald Rd, E5 11 K1
Redway Dr, Twick. TW2 198 CC87
Red Willow, Harl. CM19 73 EM18
Redwing Cl, S.Croy. CR2 243 DX111
Redwing Gdns, W.Byf. KT14 234 BH112
Redwing Gro, Abb.L. WD5 81 BU31
Redwing Ms, SE5 43 J9
Redwing Path, SE28 187 ER75
Redwing Ri, Guil. GU4 265 BD132
Redwing Rd, Wall. SM6 241 DL108
Redwood, Burn. SL1 152 AG68
Egham TW20 215 BE96
Redwood Chase, S.Ock.
RM15 171 FW70
Redwood Cl, E3 12 A10
N14 *off The Vale* 121 DK45
SE16 33 M3
Kenley CR8 242 DQ114
St. Albans AL1 65 CJ20
Sidcup DA15 208 EU87
Uxbridge UB10 157 BP68
Watford WD19 116 BW49
Redwood Ct, NW6 4 E7
Redwood Dr, Hem.H. HP3 62 BL22
Redwood Est, Houns. TW5 177 BV79
Redwood Gdns, E4 105 EB44
Chigwell IG7 126 EU50
Slough SL1
off Godolphin Rd 153 AR73
Redwood Gro, W5 179 CH76
Chilworth GU4 281 BC140
Redwood Ms, SW4 41 K10
Ashford TW15
off Napier Wk 197 BR94
Redwood Mt, Reig. RH2 272 DA131
Redwood Pl, Beac. HP9 111 AK54
Redwood Ri, Borwd. WD6 100 CN37
Redwoods, SW15 201 CU88
Addlestone KT15 234 BG107
Hertford SG14 54 DQ08
Redwoods, The, Wind. SL4 173 AR83
Redwoods Cl, Buck.H. IG9 124 EH47
Redwood Wk, Surb. KT6 219 CK102
Redwood Way, Barn. EN5 101 CX43
Reece Ms, SW7 28 A8
Reed Av, Orp. BR6 227 ES104
Reed Cl, E16 23 N7
SE12 206 EG85
Iver SL0 155 BE72
London Colney AL2 83 CK27
Reed Ct, Green. DA9 191 FW84
Reed Dr, Red. RH1 288 DG137
Reede Gdns, Dag. RM10 149 FB64
Reede Rd, Dag. RM10 168 FA65
Reede Way, Dag. RM10 149 FB64
⇌ **Reedham** 241 DM113
Reedham Cl, N17 144 DV56
Bricket Wood AL2 82 CA29
Reedham Dr, Pur. CR8 241 DM113
Reedham Pk Av, Pur. CR8 257 DN116
Reedham Rd, Burn. SL1 152 AJ69
Reedham St, SE15 44 C9
Reedholm Vil, N16 144 DR63
Reed Pl, SW4 183 DK84
Shepperton TW17 216 BM102
West Byfleet KT14 233 BE113
Reed Pond Wk, Rom. RM2 127 FF54
Reed Rd, N17 122 DT54
Reeds, The, Welw.G.C. AL7 51 CX10
Reeds Cres, Wat. WD24 98 BW40
Reedsfield Cl, Ashf. TW15
off Reedsfield Rd 197 BP91
Reedsfield Rd, Ashf. TW15 197 BP91
Reeds Pl, NW1 7 L6
Sch **Reed's Sch**, Cob. KT11
off Sandy La 236 CA112
Reeds Wk, Wat. WD24 98 BW40
Reedworth St, SE11 30 F9
Ree La Cotts, Loug. IG10
off Englands La 107 EN39
Reenglass Rd, Stan. HA7 117 CK49
Rees Dr, Stan. HA7 118 CL49
Rees Gdns, Croy. CR0 224 DT100
Reesland Cl, E12 167 EN65
Rees St, N1 9 K9
Reets Fm Cl, NW9 140 CS58
Reeve Rd, Reig. RH2 288 DC138
Reeves Av, NW9 140 CR59
Tra **Reeves Corner** 223 DP103
Reeves Cor, Croy. CR0
off Roman Way 223 DP103
Reeves Cres, Swan. BR8 229 FD97
Reeves La, Roydon CM19 72 EJ19
Reeves Ms, W1 28 G1
Reeves Rd, E3 22 C4
SE18 187 EP79
Reflection, The, E16 37 N4
Reform Row, N17 122 DT54
Reform St, SW11 40 E8
Regal Cl, E1 20 D6
W5 159 CK71
Regal Ct, N18 *off College Cl* 122 DT50
Regal Cres, Wall. SM6 223 DH104
Regal Dr, N11 121 DH50
Regalfield Cl, Guil. GU2 264 AU130
Regal Ho, SW6
off Lensbury Av 39 P8
Ilford IG2 *off Royal Cres* 147 ER58
Regal La, NW1 7 H9
Regal Pl, E3 21 P3
SW6 39 M5
Regal Row, SE15 44 G6
Regal Way, Har. HA3 140 CL58
Watford WD24 98 BW38
Regan Cl, Guil. GU2 264 AV129
Regan Way, N1 19 N1
Regarder Rd, Chig. IG7 126 EU50
Regarth Av, Rom. RM1 149 FE58
Regatta Ho, Tedd. TW11
off Twickenham Rd 199 CG91
Regency Cl, W5 160 CL72
Chigwell IG7 125 EQ50
Hampton TW12 198 BZ92
Regency Ct, E18 124 EG54
Brentwood CM14 130 FW47
Broxbourne EN10
off Berners Way 71 DZ23
Harlow CM18 74 EU18
Hemel Hempstead HP2
off Alexandra Rd 62 BK20
Sutton SM1
off Brunswick Rd 240 DB105
Regency Cres, NW4 119 CX54
Regency Dr, Ruis. HA4 137 BS60
West Byfleet KT14 233 BF113
Regency Gdns, Horn. RM11 150 FJ59
Walton-on-Thames KT12 218 BW102
Regency Ho, SW6
off The Boulevard 39 P7
Regency Lo, Buck.H. IG9 124 EK47
Regency Ms, NW10 161 CU65
SW9 43 H5
Beckenham BR3 225 EC95
Isleworth TW7
off Queensbridge Pk 199 CE85
Regency Pl, SW1 29 P8
Regency St, NW10 160 CS70
SW1 29 N8
Regency Ter, SW7
off Fulham Rd 28 A10
Regency Wk, Croy. CR0 225 DY100
Richmond TW10
off Grosvenor Rd 200 CL85
Regency Way, Bexh. DA6 188 EX83
Woking GU22 249 BD115
Regeneration Rd, SE16 33 J9
Regent Av, Uxb. UB10 157 BP66
Regent Cl, N12 *off Nether St* 120 DC50
Grays RM16 192 GC75
Harrow HA3 140 CL58
Hounslow TW4 177 BV81
Regent Cl, Kings L. WD4 80 BN29
New Haw KT15 234 BK109
Redhill RH1 273 DJ129
St. Albans AL4 65 CJ16
Coll **Regent Coll**, Har. HA2
off Imperial Dr 138 CA59
Regent Ct, Slou. SL1 154 AS72
Welwyn Garden City AL7 51 CY10
Windsor SL4 173 AR81
Regent Cres, Red. RH1 272 DF132
Regent Gdns, Ilf. IG3 148 EU58
Regent Gate, Wal.Cr. EN8 89 DX34
● **Regent Pk**, Lthd. KT22 253 CG118
Regent Pk, Barn. EN4 102 DB39
Regent Pl, SW19
off Haydons Rd 202 DB92
W1 17 M10
Croydon CR0 *off Grant Rd* 224 DT102
Regent Rd, SE24 203 DP86
Epping CM16 91 ET30
Surbiton KT5 220 CM99
Regents Av, N13 121 DM50
Regents Br Gdns, SW8 42 B4
Regents Cl, Hayes UB4 157 BS71
Radlett WD7 83 CG34
South Croydon CR2 242 DS107
Whyteleafe CR3 258 DS118
Coll **Regent's Coll**, NW1 16 G4
Regents Dr, Kes. BR2 244 EK106
Woodford Green IG8 125 EN51
Regents Ms, NW8 5 P10
Horley RH6
off Victoria Rd 290 DG148
REGENT'S PARK, NW1 17 H1
⊖ **Regent's Park** 17 J5
★ **Regent's Park, The**, NW1 16 F1
Regent's Pk Est, NW1 17 K3
Regents Pk Rd, N3 141 CZ55
NW1 6 F8
Regents Pk Ter, NW1 7 J8
Regent's Pl, SE3 47 N8
Regents Pl, Loug. IG10 124 EK45
Regent Sq, E3 22 C3
WC1 18 B3
Belvedere DA17 189 FB77
Regents Row, E8 10 C9
Regent St, NW10 14 D3
SW1 29 N1
W1 17 K8
W4 180 CN78
Watford WD24 97 BV38
Regents Wf, N1 8 C10
Regina Cl, Barn. EN5 101 CX41
Sch **Regina Coeli Catholic Prim Sch**,
S.Croy. CR2
off Pampisford Rd 241 DP108
Reginald Ms, Harl. CM17
off Green St 58 EX14
Reginald Rd, E7 13 N6
SE8 46 A5
Northwood HA6 115 BT53
Romford RM3 128 FN53
Reginald Sq, SE8 46 A5
Regina Pt, SE16 33 H6
Regina Rd, N4 143 DM60
SE25 224 DU97
W13 159 CG74
Southall UB2 178 BY77
Regina Ter, W13 159 CG74
Regis Pl, SW2 183 DM84
Regis Rd, NW5 7 J3
Regius Ct, Penn HP10 110 AD47
Regnart Bldgs, NW1 17 M4
Reid Av, Cat. CR3 258 DR121
Reid Cl, Couls. CR5 257 DH116
Hayes UB3 157 BS72
Pinner HA5 137 BU56
Reidhaven Rd, SE18 187 ES77
REIGATE, RH2 272 DA134
⇌ **Reigate** 272 DA133
Reigate Av, Sutt. SM1 222 DA102
● **Reigate Business Ms**, Reig.
RH2 *off Albert Rd N* 271 CZ133
Coll **Reigate Coll**, Reig. RH2
off Castlefield Rd 272 DB134
Sch **Reigate Gram Sch**, Reig. RH2
off Reigate Rd 272 DC134
Reigate Heath, Reig. RH2 287 CX135
Reigate Hill, Reig. RH2 272 DB130
Reigate Hill Cl, Reig. RH2 272 DA131
Jct **Reigate Hill Interchange**, Tad.
KT20 272 DB129
Sch **Reigate Parish Ch Sch**, Reig.
RH2 *off Blackborough Rd* 272 DC134
Sch **Reigate Priory Sch**,
Reig. RH2
off Bell St 272 DA134
Reigate Rd, Bet. RH3 270 CS132
Bromley BR1 206 EF90
Dorking RH4 285 CJ135
Epsom KT17, KT18 239 CT110
Hookwood RH6 290 DC146
Ilford IG3 147 ET61
Leatherhead KT22 253 CJ123
Redhill RH1 272 DB134
Reigate RH2 272 DB134
Sidlow RH2 288 DB141
Tadworth KT20 255 CX117
Sch **Reigate St. Mary's Prep &
Choir Sch**, Reig. RH2
off Chart La 272 DB134
Sch **Reigate Sch**, Reig. RH2
off Pendleton Rd 288 DC137
Reigate Way, Wall. SM6 241 DL106
Reighton Rd, E5 144 DU62
Reindeer Cl, E13 13 P9
Reindorp Cl, Guil. GU2
off Old Ct Rd 280 AU135
Reinickendorf Av, SE9 207 EQ85
Reizel Cl, N16 144 DT60
Relay Rd, W12 26 B1
Relf Rd, SE15 44 D10
Reliance Sq, EC2 19 P4
Relko Ct, Epsom KT19 238 CR110
Relko Gdns, Sutt. SM1 240 DD106
Relton Ms, SW7 28 D6
Rembrandt Cl, E14 34 G7
SW1 28 G9
Rembrandt Ct, Epsom KT19 239 CT107
Rembrandt Dr, Nthflt DA11 212 GD90
Rembrandt Rd, SE13 186 EE84
Edgware HA8 118 CN54
Rembrandt Way, Walt. KT12 217 BV104
Remington Rd, E6 24 G8
N15 144 DR58
Remington St, N1 19 H1
Remnant St, WC2 18 C8
Remus Cl, St.Alb. AL1 65 CD24
Remus Rd, E3 12 A7
Renaissance Ct, Houns. TW3
off Prince Regent Rd 178 CC83
Renaissance Wk, SE10 35 M6
Rendel Ho, Bans. SM7 256 DC118
Rendle Cl, Croy. CR0 224 DT99
Rendlesham Av, Rad. WD7 99 CF37
Rendlesham Cl, Ware SG12 54 DV05
Rendlesham Rd, E5 144 DU63
Enfield EN2 103 DP39
Rendlesham Way, Chorl. WD3 95 BC44
Renforth St, SE16 33 H5
Renfree Way, Shep. TW17 216 BM101
Renfrew Cl, E6 25 L9
Renfrew Ho, E17
off Sherwood Cl 123 DZ54
Renfrew Rd, SE11 30 G8
Hounslow TW4 178 BX82
Kingston upon Thames KT2 200 CP94
Renmans, The, Ashtd. KT21 254 CM116
Renmuir St, SW17 202 DF93
Rennell St, SE13 185 EC83
Rennels Way, Islw. TW7 179 CE82
Renness Rd, E17 145 DY55
Rennets Cl, SE9 207 ES85
Rennets Wd Rd, SE9 207 ER85
Rennie Cl, Ashf. TW15 196 BK90
Rennie Ct, SE1 *off Upper Grd* 30 G2
Enfield EN3
off Brunswick Rd 105 EA38
Rennie Est, SE16 32 F9
Rennie Ho, SE1 *off Bath Ter* 31 J7
Rennie St, SE1 30 G2
Rennie Ter, Red. RH1 288 DG135
Rennison Cl, Chsht EN7 88 DT27
Renovation, The, E16 37 N4
Renown Cl, Croy. CR0 223 DP102
Romford RM7 126 FA53
Rensburg Rd, E17 145 DX57
Renshaw Cl, Belv. DA17
off Grove Rd 188 EZ79
Renters Av, NW4 141 CW58
Renton Dr, Orp. BR5 228 EX101
● **Renwick Ind Est**, Bark.
IG11 168 EV67
Renwick Rd, Bark. IG11 168 EV70
Repens Way, Hayes UB4 158 BX70
Rephidim St, SE1 31 N7
Replingham Rd, SW18 201 CZ88
Reporton Rd, SW6 38 F5
Repository Rd, SE18 187 EM79
Repton Av, Hayes UB3 177 BR77
Romford RM2 149 FG55
Wembley HA0 139 CJ63
Repton Cl, Cars. SM5 240 DE106
Repton Ct, Beck. BR3 225 EB95
Ilford IG5 *off Repton Gro* 125 EM53
Repton Dr, Rom. RM2 149 FG56
Repton Gdns, Rom. RM2 149 FG55
Repton Grn, St.Alb. AL3 65 CD16
Repton Gro, Ilf. IG5 125 EM53
Repton Pl, Amer. HP7 94 AU39
Repton Rd, Har. HA3 140 CM56
Orpington BR6 228 EU104
Repton St, E14 21 M8
Repton Way, Crox.Grn WD3 96 BN43
Repulse Cl, Rom. RM5 126 FA53
Reservoir Cl, Green. DA9 211 FW86
Thornton Heath CR7 224 DR98
Reservoir Rd, N14 103 DJ43
SE4 45 L9
Ruislip HA4 137 BQ57
Resham Cl, Sthl. UB2 178 BW76
Resolution Wk, SE18 37 J6
Resolution Way, SE8 46 A4
Reson Way, Hem.H. HP1 62 BH21
Restavon Pk, Berry's Grn
TN16 261 EP116
Restell Cl, SE3 47 K2
Restmor Way, Wall. SM6 222 DG103
Reston Cl, Borwd. WD6 100 CN38
Reston Path, Borwd. WD6 100 CN38
Reston Pl, SW7 27 N5
Restons Cres, SE9 207 ER86
Restoration Sq, SW11 40 B7
Restormel Cl, Houns. TW3 198 CA85
Retcar Cl, N19
off Dartmouth Pk Hill 143 DH61
Retcar Pl, N19 143 DH61
Retford Cl, Borwd. WD6
off The Campions 100 CN38
Romford RM3 128 FN51
Retford Path, Rom. RM3 128 FN51
Retford Rd, Rom. RM3 128 FM51
Retford St, N1 19 P1
Retingham Way, E4 123 EB47
Retreat, The, NW9 140 CR57
SW14
off South Worple Way 180 CS83
Addlestone KT15 234 BK106
Amersham HP6 94 AY39
Brentwood CM14 130 FV46
Englefield Green TW20 194 AX92
Fifield SL6 172 AD80
Grays RM17 192 GB79
Harrow HA2 138 CA59
Hutton CM13 131 GB44
Kings Langley WD4 81 BQ31
Orpington BR6 246 EV107
Surbiton KT5 220 CM100
Thornton Heath CR7 224 DR98
Worcester Park KT4 221 CV104
Retreat Cl, Har. HA3 139 CJ57
Retreat Pl, E9 11 H5
Retreat Rd, Rich. TW9 199 CK85
Retreat Way, Chig. IG7 126 EV48
Reubens Rd, Hutt. CM13 131 GB44
Reunion Row, E1
off Tobacco Dock 32 F1
Reuters Plaza, E14 34 B3
Reveley Sq, SE16 33 M5
Revell Cl, Fetch. KT22 252 CB122
Revell Dr, Fetch. KT22 252 CB122
Revell Ri, SE18 187 ET79
Revell Rd, Kings.T. KT1 220 CP95
Sutton SM1 239 CZ107
Revelon Rd, SE4 185 DY84
Revel Rd, Woob.Grn HP10 132 AD55
Revels Cl, Hert. SG14 54 DR07
Revels Rd, Hert. SG14 54 DR07
Revelstoke Rd, SW18 201 CZ89
Reventlow Rd, SE9 207 EQ88

A B C D E F G H I J K L M N O P Q R S T U V W X Y Z

Reverdy Rd, SE1 32 C9
Reverend Cl, Har. HA2 138 CB62
Revere Way, Epsom KT19 238 CS109
Revesby Rd, Cars. SM5 222 DD100
Review Rd, NW2 141 CT61
Dagenham RM10 169 FB67
Rewell St, SW6 39 N5
Rewley Rd, Cars. SM5 222 DD100
Rex Av, Ashf. TW15 196 BN93
Rex Cl, Rom. RM5 127 FB52
Rex Pl, W1 29 H1
Reydon Av, E11 146 EJ58
Reynard Cl, SE4 45 M10
Bromley BR1 227 EM97
Reynard Ct, Pur. CR8 241 DN111
Reynard Dr, SE19 204 DT94
Reynard Pl, SE14
off Milton Ct Rd 45 M3
Reynardson Rd, N17 122 DQ52
Reynards Way, Brick.Wd AL2 82 BZ29
Reynard Way, Hert. SG13 54 DU09
Reynolah Gdns, SE7 36 B10
Reynolds Av, E12 147 EN64
Chessington KT9 238 CL108
Redhill RH1 273 DH132
Romford RM6 148 EW59
Reynolds Cl, NW11 142 DB59
SW19 222 DD95
Carshalton SM5 222 DF102
Hemel Hempstead HP1 62 BG19
Reynolds Ct, E11
off Cobbold Rd 146 EF62
Romford RM6 148 EX55
Reynolds Cres, Sand. AL4 65 CH15
Reynolds Dr, Edg. HA8 140 CM55
Reynolds Pl, SE3 186 EH80
Richmond TW10
off Cambrian Rd 200 CM86
Reynolds Rd, SE15 204 DW85
W4 180 CQ76
Beaconsfield HP9 110 AJ52
Hayes UB4 158 BW70
New Malden KT3 220 CR101
Reynolds Wk, Chesh. HP5
off Great Hivings 76 AN27
Reynolds Way, Croy. CR0 242 DS105
Rhapsody Cres, Warley CM14 130 FV50
Rheidol Ms, N1 9 J10
Rheidol Ter, N1 9 H10
Rheingold Way, Wall. SM6 241 DL109
Rheola Cl, N17 122 DT53
Rhoda St, E2 20 B4
Rhodes Av, N22 121 DJ53
Rhodes Av Prim Sch, N22
off Rhodes Av 121 DJ53
Rhodes Cl, Egh. TW20 195 BB92
Rhodesia Rd, E11 145 ED61
SW9 42 B9
Rhodes Moorhouse Ct, Mord.
SM4 222 DA100
Rhodes St, N7 8 D3
Rhodes Way, Wat. WD24 98 BX40
Rhodeswell Rd, E14 21 M6
Rhododendron Ride, Egh.
TW20 194 AT94
Slough SL3 155 AZ69
Rhodrons Av, Chess. KT9 238 CL106
Rhondda Gro, E3 21 M3
Rhyl Prim Sch, NW5 7 H4
Rhyl Rd, Perivale UB6 159 CF68
Rhyl St, NW5 7 H4
Rhymes, The, Hem.H. HP1 62 BH18
Rhys Av, N11 121 DK52
Rialto Rd, Mitch. CR4 222 DG96
Ribble Cl, Wdf.Grn. IG8
off Prospect Rd 124 EJ51
Ribbledale, Lon.Col. AL2 84 CM27
Ribblesdale, Dor. RH4
off Roman Rd 285 CH138
Hemel Hempstead HP2 62 BL17
Ribblesdale Av, N11 120 DG51
Northolt UB5 158 CB65
Ribblesdale Rd, N8 143 DM56
SW16 203 DH93
Dartford DA2 210 FQ88
Ribbon Dance Ms, SE5 43 M7
Ribchester Av, Perivale UB6 159 CF69
Ribston Cl, Brom. BR2 227 EM102
Shenley WD7 83 CK33
Rib Vale, Hert. SG14 54 DR06
Ricardo Path, SE28
off Byron Cl 168 EW74
Ricardo Rd, Old Wind. SL4 194 AV86
Ricardo St, E14 22 C9
Ricards Lo High Sch, SW19
off Lake Rd 201 CZ92
Ricards Rd, SW19 201 CZ92
Ricebridge La, Reig. RH2 287 CV137
Rice Cl, Hem.H. HP2 62 BM19
Rices Cor, Shalf. GU4 281 BA141
Richard Alibon Prim Sch, Dag.
RM10 *off Alibon Rd* 148 FA64
Richard Atkins Prim Sch, SW2
off New Pk Rd 203 DL87
Richard Challoner Sch, N.Mal.
KT3 *off Manor Dr N* 220 CR101
Richard Cl, SE18 37 H9
Richard Cloudesley Sch,
EC1 19 J5
Richard Cobden Prim Sch,
NW1 7 M10
Richard Fell Ho, E12
off Walton Rd 147 EN63
Richard Foster Cl, E17 145 DZ59
Richard Hale Sch, Hert. SG13
off Hale Rd 54 DR10
Richard Ho Dr, E16 24 F9
Richard Meyjes Rd, Guil. GU2 280 AS135
Richard Robert Res, The, E15
off Salway Pl 13 H5
Richards Av, Rom. RM7 149 FC57
Richards Cl, Bushey WD23 117 CD45
Harlington UB3 177 BR79
Harrow HA1 139 CG57
Uxbridge UB10 156 BN67
Richards Fld, Epsom KT19 238 CR109
Richardson Cl, E8 10 A8
Greenhithe DA9
off Steele Av 211 FU85
London Colney AL2 84 CL27
Richardson Cres, Chsht EN7 87 DP25
Richardson Pl, Coln.Hth AL4 66 CP22
Richardson Rd, E15 13 J10
Richardson's Ms, W1 17 L5
Richards Pl, E17 145 EA55
SW3 28 D8
Richards Rd, Stoke D'Ab. KT11 236 CB114
Richards St, Hat. AL10 66 CR16
Richard Stagg Cl, St.Alb. AL1 65 CJ22
Richard St, E1 20 E9
Richards Way, Slou. SL1 153 AN74
Richbell Cl, Ashtd. KT21 253 CK118
Richbell Pl, WC1 18 C6
Richborne Ter, SW8 42 D4
Richborough Cl, Orp. BR5 228 EX98
Richborough Ho, E5
off Pembury Rd 10 E2
Richborough Rd, NW2 4 D1
Richbourne Ct, W1
off Harrowby St 16 D8
Richens Cl, Houns. TW3 179 CD82
Riches Rd, Ilf. IG1 147 EQ61
Richfield Rd, Bushey WD23 116 CC45
Richford Gate, W6 26 A6
Richford Rd, E15 13 L8
Richford St, W6 26 A5
● **Rich Ind Est**, SE1 31 P7
RICHINGS PARK, Iver SL0 175 BE76
Richings Pl, Iver SL0 175 BE76
Richings Way, Iver SL0 175 BF76
Richland Av, Couls. CR5 240 DG114
Richlands Av, Epsom KT17 239 CU105
Rich La, SW5 39 L1
Richmer Rd, Erith DA8 189 FG80
★ **Rich Mix Cen, The**, E1
off Bethnal Grn Rd 20 B4
RICHMOND, TW9 & TW10 200 CL86
⇌ **Richmond** 180 CL84
⊖ **Richmond** 180 CL84
⊖ **Richmond** 199 CK85
Richmond Adult Comm Coll,
Clifden, Twick. TW1
off Clifden Rd 199 CF88
Parkshot, Rich. TW9
off Parkshot 179 CK84
Richmond Av, E4 123 ED50
N1 8 C8
NW10 4 A5
SW20 221 CY95
Feltham TW14 197 BS86
Uxbridge UB10 157 BP65
Richmond Br, Rich. TW9 199 CK86
Twickenham TW1 199 CK86
Richmond Bldgs, W1 17 N9
Richmond Circ, Rich. TW9 180 CL84
Richmond Cl, E17 145 DZ58
Amersham HP6 94 AT38
Biggin Hill TN16 260 EH119
Borehamwood WD6 100 CR43
Cheshunt EN8 88 DW29
Epsom KT18 238 CS114
Fetcham KT22 252 CC124
Richmond Ct, Brox. EN10 71 DZ20
Hatfield AL10
off Cooks Way 67 CV20
Mitcham CR4
off Phipps Br Rd 222 DD97
Potters Bar EN6 86 DC31
Richmond Cres, E4 123 ED50
N1 8 D8
N9 122 DU46
Slough SL1 154 AU74
Staines TW18 195 BF92
Richmond Dr, Grav. DA12 213 GL89
Shepperton TW17 217 BQ100
Watford WD17 97 BS39
Woodford Green IG8 125 EN52
Richmond Gdns, NW4 141 CU57
Harrow HA3 117 CF51
Richmond Grn, Croy. CR0 223 DL104
Richmond Gro, N1 8 G7
Surbiton KT5 *off Ewell Rd* 220 CM100
Richmond Hill, Rich. TW10 200 CL86
Richmond Hill Ct, Rich. TW10 200 CL86
Richmond Ho, Hmptn. TW12
off Buckingham Rd 198 BZ92
Richmond Ho, NW1
off Park Village E 17 K1
Richmond Ms, W1 17 N9
Teddington TW11
off Church Rd 199 CF92
★ **Richmond Park**, Rich.
TW10 200 CN88
Richmond Pk, Kings.T. KT2 200 CN88
Loughton IG10
off Fallow Flds 124 EK45
Richmond TW10 200 CN88
Richmond Pk Rd, SW14 200 CQ85
Kingston upon Thames KT2 200 CL94
Richmond Pl, SE18 187 EQ77
Richmond Rd, E4 123 ED46
E7 146 EH64
E8 10 A6
E11 145 ED61
N2 120 DC54
N11 121 DL51
N15 144 DS58
SW20 221 CV95
W5 180 CL75
Coulsdon CR5 257 DH115
Croydon CR0 223 DL104
Grays RM17 192 GC79
Ilford IG1 147 EQ62
Isleworth TW7 179 CG83
Kingston upon Thames KT2 199 CK92
New Barnet EN5 102 DB43
Potters Bar EN6 86 DC31
Romford RM1 149 FF58
Staines TW18 195 BF92
Thornton Heath CR7 223 DP97
Twickenham TW1 199 CJ86
Richmond Royal Hosp, Rich.
TW9 180 CL83
Richmond St, E13 23 P1
Richmond Ter, SW1 30 A4
Richmond Uni - The American Int Uni In London,
Kensington Campus, W8 27 M6
Richmond Hill Campus, Rich.
TW10 *off Queens Rd* 200 CL87
Richmond upon Thames Coll,
Twick. TW2 *off Egerton Rd* 199 CE87
Richmond Wk, St.Alb. AL4 65 CK16
Richmond Way, E11 146 EG61
W12 26 D5
W14 26 D6
Croxley Green WD3 97 BQ42
Fetcham KT22 252 CB123
Richmount Gdns, SE3 186 EG83
Rich St, E14 21 P10
Rickard Cl, NW4 141 CV56
SW2 203 DM88
West Drayton UB7 176 BK76
Rickards Cl, Surb. KT6 220 CL102
Ricketts Hill Rd, Tats. TN16 260 EK118
Rickett St, SW6 39 K2
Rickfield Cl, Hat. AL10 67 CU20
Rickman Ct, Add. KT15
off Rickman Cres 216 BH104
Rickman Cres, Add. KT15 216 BH104
Rickman Hill, Couls. CR5 257 DH118
Rickman Hill Rd, Chipstead
CR5 257 DH118
Rickmans La, Stoke P. SL2 134 AS64
Rickman St, E1 21 H4
RICKMANSWORTH, WD3 114 BL45
⇌ **Rickmansworth** 114 BK45
⊖ **Rickmansworth** 114 BK45
Rickmansworth La, Chal.St.P.
SL9 113 AZ50
Rickmansworth Pk, Rick. WD3 114 BK45
Rickmansworth Pk JMI Sch,
Rick. WD3 *off Park Rd* 114 BL45
Rickmansworth PNEU Sch,
Rick. WD3 *off The Drive* 96 BJ44
Rickmansworth Rd, Amer. HP6 77 AQ37
Chorleywood WD3 95 BE41
Harefield UB9 114 BJ53
Northwood HA6 115 BR52
Pinner HA5 115 BV54
Watford WD17, WD18 97 BS42
Rickmansworth Sch, Crox.Grn
WD3 *off Scots Hill* 96 BM44
Rick Roberts Way, E15 12 F9
Ricksons La, W.Hors. KT24 267 BP127
Rickthorne Rd, N19 143 DL61
Rickwood, Horl. RH6 291 DH147
Rickyard Path, SE9 186 EL84
Ridding La, Grnf. UB6 139 CF64
Riddings, The, Cat. CR3 274 DT125
Riddings La, Harl. CM18 73 ET19
⇌ **Riddlesdown** 242 DR113
Riddlesdown Av, Pur. CR8 242 DQ112
Riddlesdown High Sch, Pur.
CR8 *off Dunmail Dr* 242 DS114
Riddlesdown Rd, Pur. CR8 242 DQ111
Riddons Rd, SE12 206 EJ90
Ride, The, Brent. TW8 179 CH78
Enfield EN3 104 DW41
Ride La, Far.Grn GU5 282 BK144
Rideout St, SE18 37 J9
Rider Cl, Sid. DA15 207 ES86
Riders Way, Gdse. RH9 274 DW131
Ridgdale St, E3 22 B1
RIDGE, Pot.B. EN6 84 CS34
Ridge, The, Barn. EN5 101 CZ43
Bexley DA5 208 EZ87
Coulsdon CR5 241 DL114
Epsom KT18 254 CP117
Fetcham KT22 253 CD124
Orpington BR6 227 ER103
Purley CR8 241 DJ110
Surbiton KT5 220 CN99
Twickenham TW2 199 CD87
Woking GU22 249 BB117
Woldingham CR3 275 EB126
Ridge Av, N21 122 DQ45
Dartford DA1 209 FF86
Ridgebank, Slou. SL1 153 AM73
Ridgebrook Rd, SE3 186 EJ84
Ridge Cl, NW4 119 CX54
NW9 140 CR56
SE28 187 ER75
Strood Green RH3 286 CP138
Woking GU22 248 AV121
Ridge Crest, Enf. EN2 103 DM39
Ridgecroft Cl, Bex. DA5 209 FC88
Ridgefield, Wat. WD17 97 BS37
Ridgegate Cl, Reig. RH2 272 DD132
RIDGE GREEN, Red. RH1 289 DL137
Ridge Grn, S.Nutfld RH1 289 DL137
Ridge Grn Cl, S.Nutfld RH1 289 DL137
RIDGE HILL, Rad. WD7 84 CQ30
Ridge Hill, NW11 141 CY60
Ridgehurst Av, Wat. WD25 81 BT34
Ridgelands, Fetch. KT22 253 CD124
Ridge La, Wat. WD17 97 BS38
Ridge Langley, S.Croy. CR2 242 DU109
Ridge Lea, Hem.H. HP1 61 BF20
Ridgemead Cl, N14 121 DL47
Ridgemead Rd, Eng.Grn
TW20 194 AU90
Ridgemont Gdns, Edg. HA8 118 CQ49
Ridgemount, Guil. GU2 280 AV135
Weybridge KT13
off Oatlands Dr 217 BS103
Ridgemount Av, Couls. CR5 257 DH117
Croydon CR0 225 DX102
Ridgemount Cl, SE20 204 DV94
Ridgemount End, Chal.St.P.
SL9 112 AY50
Ridgemount Gdns, Enf. EN2 103 DP40
Ridgemount Way, Red. RH1 288 DD136
Ridge Pk, Pur. CR8 241 DK110
Ridge Rd, N8 143 DM58
N21 122 DQ46
NW2 141 CZ62
Mitcham CR4 203 DH94
Sutton SM3 221 CY102
Ridges, The, Art. GU3 280 AW139
Ridge St, Wat. WD24 97 BV38
Ridgeview Cl, Barn. EN5 101 CX44
Ridgeview Lo, Lon.Col. AL2 84 CM28
Ridgeview Rd, N20 120 DB48
Ridge Way, SE19
off Vicars Oak Rd 204 DS93
Ridgeway, SE28
off Pettman Cres 187 ER77
Berkhamsted HP4 60 AT19
Bromley BR2 226 EG103
Ridge Way, Cray. DA1 209 FF86
Ridgeway, Epsom KT19 238 CQ112
Ridge Way, Felt. TW13 198 BY90
Ridgeway, Grays RM17 192 GE77
Horsell GU21 248 AX115
Hutton CM13 131 GB46
Iver SL0 155 BF73
Lane End DA2 211 FS92
Rickmansworth WD3 114 BH45
Virginia Water GU25 214 AY99
Welwyn Garden City AL7 52 DA09
Woodford Green IG8 124 EJ49
Ridgeway, The, E4 123 EB47
N3 120 DB52
N11 120 DF49
N14 121 DL47
NW7 119 CU49
NW9 140 CS56
NW11 141 CZ60
Ridgeway, The, W3 180 CN75
Amersham HP7 77 AR40
Chalfont St. Peter SL9 134 AY55
Croydon CR0 223 DM104
Cuffley EN6 86 DE28
Enfield EN2 103 DN39
Fetcham KT22 253 CD123
Gidea Park RM2 149 FG56
Guildford GU1 281 BA135
Harold Wood RM3 128 FL53
Hertford SG14 53 DM08
Horley RH6 290 DG150
Kenton HA3 139 CJ58
North Harrow HA2 138 CA58
Oxshott KT22 236 CC114
Potters Bar EN6 86 DD34
Radlett WD7 99 CF37
Ruislip HA4 137 BU59
St. Albans AL4 65 CH17
Ridge Way, The, S.Croy. CR2 242 DS110
Ridgeway, The, Stan. HA7 117 CJ51
Walton-on-Thames KT12 217 BT102
Watford WD17 97 BS37
Ridgeway Av, Barn. EN4 102 DF44
Gravesend DA12 213 GH90
Ridgeway Cl, Chesh. HP5 76 AP28
Dorking RH4 285 CG138
Fetcham KT22 253 CE124
Hemel Hempstead HP3
off London Rd 80 BM25
Oxshott KT22 236 CC114
Woking GU21 248 AX116
Ridgeway Ct, Red. RH1 288 DE135
Ridgeway Cres, Orp. BR6 227 ES104
Ridgeway Cres Gdns, Orp.
BR6 227 ES103
Ridgeway Dr, Brom. BR1 206 EH91
Dorking RH4 285 CG139
Ridgeway E, Sid. DA15 207 ET85
Ridgeway Gdns, N6 143 DJ59
Ilford IG4 146 EL57
Woking GU21 248 AX115
Ridgeway Prim Sch, S.Croy.
CR2 *off Southcote Rd* 242 DS110
Ridgeway Rd, SW9 183 DP83
Chesham HP5 76 AN28
Dorking RH4 285 CG139
Isleworth TW7 179 CE80
Redhill RH1 272 DE134
Ridgeway Rd N, Islw. TW7 179 CE79
Ridgeways, Harl. CM17 74 EY15
Ridgeway Wk, Nthlt. UB5
off Arnold Rd 158 BY65
Ridgeway W, Sid. DA15 207 ES85
Ridgewell Cl, N1 9 K8
SE26 205 DZ91
Dagenham RM10 169 FB67
Ridgewell Gro, Horn. RM12
off North Weald Cl 169 FH66
Ridgmont Rd, St.Alb. AL1 65 CE21
Ridgmount Gdns, WC1 17 N5
Ridgmount Pl, WC1 17 N6
Ridgmount Rd, SW18 202 DB85
Ridgmount St, WC1 17 N6
Ridgway, SW19 201 CX93
Pyrford GU22 249 BF115
Ridgway, The, Sutt. SM2 240 DD108
Ridgway Gdns, SW19 201 CX93
Ridgway Pl, SW19 201 CY93
Ridgway Rd, Pyrford GU22 249 BF115
Ridgwell Rd, E16 24 D6
Riding, The, NW11
off Golders Grn Rd 141 CZ59
Woking GU21 233 BB114
Riding Ct Rd, Datchet SL3 174 AW80
Riding Hill, S.Croy. CR2 242 DU113
Riding Ho St, W1 17 L7
Riding La, Beac. HP9 110 AF53
Ridings, The, E11
off Malcolm Way 146 EG57
W5 160 CM70
Addlestone KT15 233 BF107
Amersham HP6 77 AR35
Ashtead KT21 253 CK117
Biggin Hill TN16 260 EL117
Chigwell IG7 126 EV49
Cobham KT11 236 CA112
East Horsley KT24 267 BS125
Epsom KT18 254 CS115
Ewell KT17 239 CT109
Hertford SG14 53 DN10
Iver SL0 175 BF77
Kingswood KT20 255 CZ120
Latimer HP5 94 AX36
Reigate RH2 272 DD131
Ripley GU23 250 BG123
Sunbury-on-Thames TW16 217 BU95
Surbiton KT5 220 CN99
Windsor SL4 *off River Rd* 173 AK80
Ridings Av, N21 103 DP42
Ridings Cl, N6 143 DJ59
Ridings La, Wok. GU23 250 BN123
Ridlands Gro, Oxt. RH8 276 EL130
Ridlands La, Oxt. RH8 276 EK130
Ridlands Ri, Oxt. RH8 276 EL130
Ridler Rd, Enf. EN1 104 DS38
Ridley Av, W13 179 CH76
Ridley Cl, Bark. IG11 167 ET66
Romford RM3 127 FH53
Ridley Rd, E7 146 EJ63
E8 10 A3
NW10 161 CU68
SW19 202 DB94
Bromley BR2 226 EF97
Warlingham CR6 258 DW118
Welling DA16 188 EV81
Ridsdale Rd, SE20 224 DV95
Woking GU21 248 AV117
Riefield Rd, SE9 187 EQ84
Riesco Dr, Croy. CR0 242 DW107
Riffel Rd, NW2 4 A2
Riffhams, Brwd. CM13 131 GB48
Rifle Butts All, Epsom KT18 255 CT115
Rifle Ct, SE11 42 F2
Rifle Pl, W11
off St. Anns Rd 26 D2
Rifle St, E14 22 D7
Riga Ms, E1
off Commercial Rd 20 C8
Rigault Rd, SW6 38 F9
Rigby Cl, Croy. CR0 223 DN104
Rigby Gdns, Grays RM16 193 GH77
Rigby La, Hayes UB3 177 BR75
Rigby Ms, Ilf. IG1 147 EN61
Rigby Pl, Enf. EN3 105 EA37
Rigden St, E14 22 C9
Rigeley Rd, NW10 161 CU69
Rigg App, E10 145 DX60
Rigge Pl, SW4 183 DK84
Riggindale Rd, SW16 203 DK92
Riley Cl, Epsom KT19 238 CP111
Riley Rd, SE1 31 P6
Enfield EN3 104 DW38
Riley St, SW10 40 A4
Rill Ct, Bark. IG11
off Spring Pl 167 EQ68
Rinaldo Rd, SW12 203 DH87
Ring, The, W2 16 C10
Ring Cl, Brom. BR1 206 EH94
Ringcroft St, N7 8 E3
Ringers Rd, Brom. BR1 226 EG97
Ringford Rd, SW18 201 CZ85
Ringlet Cl, E16 24 A7
Ringlewell Cl, Enf. EN1
off Central Av 104 DV40
Ringley Av, Horl. RH6 290 DG148
Ringley Pk Av, Reig. RH2 288 DD135
Ringley Pk Rd, Reig. RH2 272 DC134
Ringmer Av, SW6 38 F7
Ringmer Gdns, N19 143 DL61
Ringmer Ho, SE22
off Pytchley Rd 184 DS83
Ringmer Pl, N21 104 DR43
Ringmer Way, Brom. BR1 227 EM99
Ringmore Dr, Guil. GU4 265 BC131
Ringmore Ri, SE23 204 DV87
Ringmore Rd, Walt. KT12 218 BW104
Ringmore Vw, SE23
off Ringmore Ri 204 DV87
Ring Rd, W12 26 A1
Ring Rd N, Gat. RH6 291 DH152
Ring Rd S, Gat. RH6 291 DH152
Ringshall Rd, Orp. BR5 228 EU97
Ringslade Rd, N22 121 DM54
Ringstead Rd, SE6 205 EB87
Sutton SM1 240 DD105
Ringway, N11 121 DJ51
Southall UB2 178 BY78
Ringway Rd, Park St AL2 82 CB27
Ringwold Cl, Beck. BR3 205 DY94
Ringwood Av, N2 120 DF54
Croydon CR0 223 DL101
Hornchurch RM12 150 FK61
Orpington BR6 246 EW110
Redhill RH1 272 DF131
Ringwood Cl, Pnr. HA5 138 BW55
Ringwood Gdns, E14 34 B8
SW15 201 CU89
Ringwood Rd, E17 145 DZ58
Ringwood Way, N21 121 DP46
Hampton Hill TW12 198 CA91
RIPLEY, Wok. GU23 250 BJ122
Ripley Av, Egh. TW20 194 AY93
Ripley Bypass, Wok. GU23 250 BK122
Ripley Cl, Brom. BR1 227 EM99
New Addington CR0 243 EC107
Slough SL3 174 AY77
Ripley C of E Inf Sch,
Ripley GU23
off Georgelands 250 BH121
Ripley Ct Sch, Ripley
GU23 *off Rose La* 250 BJ122
Ripley Gdns, SW14 180 CR83
Sutton SM1 240 DC105
Ripley La, W.Hors. KT24 266 BN125
Woking GU23 250 BL123
Ripley Ms, E11 146 EE58
Ripley Rd, E16 24 C8
Belvedere DA17 188 FA77
East Clandon GU4 266 BJ127
Enfield EN2 104 DQ39
Hampton TW12 198 CA94
Ilford IG3 147 ET61
Send GU23 266 BJ127
★ **Ripley's Believe It or Not!**
W1 29 N1
RIPLEY SPRINGS, Egh. TW20 194 AY93
Ripley Vw, Loug. IG10 107 EP38
Ripley Vil, W5 159 CJ72
Ripley Way, Chsht EN7 88 DV30
Epsom KT19 238 CN111
Hemel Hempstead HP1 61 BE19
Riplington Ct, SW15 201 CU87
Ripon Cl, Guil. GU2 264 AT131
Northolt UB5 138 CA64
Ripon Gdns, Chess. KT9 237 CK106
Ilford IG1 146 EL58
Ripon Rd, N9 122 DV45
N17 144 DR55
SE18 187 EP79
Ripon Way, Borwd. WD6 100 CQ43
St. Albans AL4 65 CK16
Rippersley Rd, Well. DA16 188 EU81
Ripple Inf & Jun Schs, Bark. IG11
off Suffolk Rd 167 ES67
Ripple Rd, Bark. IG11 167 EQ66
Dagenham RM9 168 EV67
● **Rippleside Commercial Est**,
Bark. IG11 168 EW68
Ripplevale Gro, N1 8 D7
Rippolson Rd, SE18 187 ET78
Ripston Rd, Ashf. TW15 197 BR92
Risborough, SE17
off Deacon Way 31 J8
Risborough Dr, Wor.Pk. KT4 221 CU101
Risborough St, SE1 31 H4
Risdens, Harl. CM18 73 EQ19
Risdon St, SE16 33 H5
Rise, The, E11 146 EG57
N13 121 DN49
NW7 119 CT51
NW10 140 CR63
Amersham HP7 77 AQ39
Bexley DA5 208 EW87
Buckhurst Hill IG9 124 EK45
Dartford DA1 189 FF84
East Horsley KT24 267 BS126
Edgware HA8 118 CP50
Elstree WD6 100 CM43
Epsom KT17 239 CT110
Gravesend DA12 213 GL91
Greenford UB6 139 CG64
Greenhithe DA9 211 FU86
Park Street AL2 83 CD25
Sevenoaks TN13 279 FJ129
South Croydon CR2 242 DW109
Tadworth KT20 255 CW121
Uxbridge UB10 156 BM68
Waltham Abbey EN9
off Breach Barn
Mobile Home Pk 90 EH30
Risebridge Chase, Rom. RM1 127 FF52
Risebridge Rd, Rom. RM2 127 FF54
Rise Cotts, Ware SG12
off Widford Rd 56 EK05
Risedale Cl, Hem.H. HP3
off Risedale Hill 62 BL23
Risedale Hill, Hem.H. HP3 62 BL23

Risedale Rd, Bexh. DA7 189 FB83
Hemel Hempstead HP3 62 BL23
Riseholme Ho, SE22
off Albrighton Rd 184 DS83
Riseldine Rd, SE23 205 DY86
Rise Pk Boul, Rom. RM1 127 FF53
Sch Rise Pk Inf Sch, Rom. RM1
off Annan Way 127 FD53
Sch Rise Pk Jun Sch,
Rom. RM1
off Annan Way 127 FD53
Rise Pk Par, Rom. RM1 127 FE54
Riseway, Brwd. CM15 130 FY48
Rising Hill Cl, Nthwd. HA6
off Ducks Hill Rd 115 BQ51
Risinghill St, N1 8 D10
Risingholme Cl, Bushey
WD23 116 CB45
Harrow HA3 117 CE53
Risingholme Rd, Har. HA3 117 CE54
Risings, The, E17 145 ED56
Rising Sun Ct, EC1 19 H7
Risley Av, N17 122 DQ53
Sch Risley Av Prim Sch, N17
off The Roundway 122 DS53
Rita Rd, SW8 42 B3
Ritches Rd, N15 144 DQ57
Ritchie Rd, Croy. CR0 224 DV100
Ritchie St, N1 8 F10
Ritchings Av, E17 145 DY56
Ritcroft Cl, Hem.H. HP3 63 BP21
Ritcroft Dr, Hem.H. HP3 63 BP21
Ritcroft St, Hem.H. HP3 63 BP21
Ritherdon Rd, SW17 202 DG89
Ritson Rd, E8 10 B4
Ritter St, SE18 187 EN79
Ritz Ct, Pot.B. EN6 86 DA31
Ritz Par, W5
off Connell Cres 160 CM70
Rivaz Pl, E9 11 H4
Rivenhall End, Welw.G.C. AL7 52 DC09
Rivenhall Gdns, E18 146 EF56
River App, Edg. HA8 118 CQ53
River Ash Est, Shep. TW17 217 BS101
River Av, N13 121 DP48
Hoddesdon EN11 71 EB16
Thames Ditton KT7 219 CG101
River Bk, N21 122 DQ45
East Molesey KT8 219 CE97
Riverbank, Picc.End HP1
off Piccotts End Rd 62 BJ16
Staines TW18 195 BF93
River Bk, T.Ditt. KT7 219 CF99
West Molesey KT8 218 BZ97
Riverbank, The, Wind. SL4 173 AP80
Riverbank Rd, Brom. BR1 206 EG90
Riverbank Way, Brent. TW8 179 CJ79
River Barge Cl, E14 34 F5
● River Brent Business Pk,
W7 179 CE76
River Cl, E11 146 EJ58
Guildford GU1 264 AW132
Rainham RM13 169 FH71
Ruislip HA4 137 BT58
Southall UB2 178 CC75
Surbiton KT6
off Catherine Rd 219 CK99
Waltham Cross EN8 89 EA34
● River Ct, Wok. GU21 249 BC115
River Ct, SE1 30 G1
Shepperton TW17 217 BQ101
Taplow SL6 152 AC72
Rivercourt Rd, W6 181 CV77
River Crane Wk, Felt. TW13 198 BX88
Hounslow TW4 198 BX88
River Crane Way, Felt. TW13
off Watermill Way 198 BZ89
Riverdale, SE13
off Lewisham High St 185 EC83
Riverdale Cl, Bark. IG11 168 EV70
Riverdale Dr, SW18
off Knaresborough Dr 202 DB88
Woking GU22 249 AZ121
Riverdale Gdns, Twick. TW1 199 CJ86
Riverdale Rd, SE18 187 ET78
Bexley DA5 208 EZ87
Erith DA8 189 FB78
Feltham TW13 198 BY91
Twickenham TW1 199 CJ86
Riverdene, Edg. HA8 118 CQ48
Riverdene Rd, Ilf. IG1 147 EN62
River Dr, Upmin. RM14 150 FQ58
Riverfield Rd, Stai. TW18 195 BF93
River Front, Enf. EN1 104 DR41
River Gdns, Bray SL6 172 AD75
Carshalton SM5 222 DG103
Feltham TW14 197 BV85
River Gro Pk, Beck. BR3 225 DZ95
RIVERHEAD, Sev. TN13 278 FD122
Riverhead Cl, E17 123 DX54
Riverhead Dr, Sutt. SM2 240 DA110
Sch Riverhead Infants' Sch, Sev.
TN13 off Worships Hill 278 FE123
Riverhill, Cob. KT11 251 BV115
Sevenoaks TN15 279 FL130
Worcester Park KT4 220 CR103
Riverhill Ms, Wor.Pk. KT4 220 CR104
Riverholme Dr, Epsom KT19 238 CR109
River Island Cl, Fetch. KT22 253 CD121
River La, Lthd. KT22 253 CD120
Richmond TW10 199 CK88
Sch Riverley Prim Sch, E10
off Park Rd 145 EA60
Rivermead, Byfleet KT14 234 BM113
East Molesey KT8 218 CC97
Kingston upon Thames KT1 219 CK99
Rivermead Cl, Add. KT15 234 BJ108
Teddington TW11 199 CH92
Rivermead Ct, SW6 38 G10
Rivermead Ho, E9
off Kingsmead Way 11 M2
Rivermead Rd, N18 123 DX51
River Meads, Stans.Abb. SG12 55 EC10
Rivermeads Av, Twick. TW2 198 CA90
Rivermill, SW1 41 P1
Harlow CM20 57 EQ13
River Mt, Walt. KT12 217 BT101
Rivermount Gdns, Guil. GU2 280 AW137
Rivernook Cl, Walt. KT12 218 BW99
River Pk, Berk. HP4 60 AU18
Hemel Hempstead HP1 62 BG22
River Pk Av, Stai. TW18 195 BD91
River Pk Gdns, Brom. BR2 205 ED94
River Pk Rd, N22 121 DM54
River Pk Vw, Orp. BR6 228 EV101
River Pl, N1 9 J7
River Reach, Tedd. TW11 199 CJ92
River Rd, Bark. IG11 167 ES68
Brentwood CM14 130 FS49
River Rd, Buck.H. IG9 124 EL46
Staines TW18 215 BF95
Taplow SL6 152 AC73
Windsor SL4 172 AJ80
● River Rd Business Pk,
Bark. IG11 167 ET69
Riversdale, Nthflt DA11 212 GE89
Sch Riversdale Prim Sch,
SW18 off Merton Rd 202 DA88
Riversdale Rd, N5 143 DP62
Romford RM5 127 FB52
Thames Ditton KT7 219 CG99
Riversdell Cl, Cher. KT16 215 BF101
Riversend Rd, Hem.H. HP3 62 BJ23
Riversfield Rd, Enf. EN1 104 DS41
H Rivers Hosp, The,
Saw. CM21 58 EW06
Rivers Ho, Brent. TW8
off Chiswick High Rd 180 CN78
Riverside, Hem.H. HP1 62 BJ22
Riverside, NW4 141 CV59
SE7 36 A7
Chertsey KT16 216 BG97
Dorking RH4 269 CK134
Eynsford DA4 230 FK103
Guildford GU1 264 AX132
Hertford SG14
off The Folly 54 DR09
Horley RH6 290 DG150
London Colney AL2 84 CL27
Richmond TW9, TW10
off Water La 199 CK85
Runnymede TW20 195 BA90
Shepperton TW17 217 BS101
Staines TW18 215 BF95
Stanstead Abbotts SG12 55 EC11
Twickenham TW1 199 CH88
Wraysbury TW19 194 AW87
Riverside, The, E.Mol. KT8 219 CD97
Riverside Av, Brox. EN10 71 EA22
East Molesey KT8 219 CD99
● Riverside Business Cen,
SW18 202 DB88
Guildford GU1 264 AW134
Tilbury RM18 193 GH84
Riverside Cl, E5 144 DW60
W7 159 CE70
Kings Langley WD4 81 BP29
Kingston upon Thames KT1 219 CK98
Orpington BR5 228 EW96
Romford RM1 149 FD56
St. Albans AL1
off Riverside Rd 65 CE22
Staines TW18 215 BF95
Wallington SM6 223 DH104
Riverside Cotts, Woob.Moor
HP10 132 AE55
Riverside Ct, E4
off Chelwood Cl 105 EB44
SW8 41 P2
Harlow CM17 58 EW09
St. Albans AL1 65 CE22
Riverside Dr, NW11 141 CY58
W4 180 CS80
Bramley GU5 281 BA144
Esher KT10 236 CA105
Mitcham CR4 222 DE99
Richmond TW10 199 CH89
Rickmansworth WD3 114 BK46
Staines TW18 195 BE92
● Riverside Est, Lon.Col. AL2 84 CL27
Riverside Gdns, N3 141 CY55
W6 181 CV78
Berkhamsted HP4 60 AU18
Enfield EN2 104 DQ40
Old Woking GU22 249 BB121
Wembley HA0 160 CL68
Riverside Hts, Til. RM18
off Dock Rd 193 GG82
● Riverside Ind Est, Bark.
IG11 168 EU69
Dartford DA1 210 FL85
Enfield EN3 105 DY44
Riverside Mans, E1 32 G1
Riverside Pk, West Dr. UB7 176 BJ76
Weybridge KT13 234 BL106
Riverside Path, Chsht EN8
off Dewhurst Rd 88 DW29
Riverside Pl, Stanw. TW19 196 BK86
Sch Riverside Prim Sch, SE16 32 D5
Riverside Retail Pk,
Sev. TN14 263 FH119
Riverside Rd, E15 22 F1
N15 144 DU58
SW17 202 DB91
Hersham KT12 236 BX105
St. Albans AL1 65 CE21
Sidcup DA14 208 EY90
Staines TW18 215 BF94
Stanwell TW19 196 BK85
Watford WD19 97 BV44
Sch Riverside Sch, St.P.Cray
BR5 off Main Rd 228 EW96
Riverside Twr, SW6 39 P8
Riverside Wk, E14
off Ferry St 46 E1
Bexley DA5 208 EW87
Isleworth TW7 179 CE83
Kingston upon Thames KT1
off High St 219 CK97
Loughton IG10 107 EP44
West Wickham BR4
off The Alders 225 EB102
Windsor SL4 off Farm Yd 173 AR80
Riverside Way, Cowley UB8 156 BH67
Dartford DA1 210 FL85
St. Albans AL2 83 CD32
● Riverside W, Woob.Grn
HP10 132 AE55
Riverside Yd, SW17 202 DC91
Riversmead, Hodd. EN11 71 EA18
Riversmeet, Hert. SG14 53 DP10
Riverstone Cl, Har. HA2 139 CD60
Riverstone Ct, Kings.T. KT2
off Queen Elizabeth Rd 220 CM95
Sch Riverston Sch, SE12
off Eltham Rd 206 EG85
River St, EC1 18 E2
Ware SG12 55 DY06
Windsor SL4 173 AR80
River Ter, W6 38 A1
Riverton Cl, W9 15 H3
River Vw, Enf. EN2
off Chase Side 104 DQ41
Grays RM16 193 GG77
Welwyn Garden City AL7 51 CZ05
Sch Riverview C of E Prim Sch &
Nurs, W.Ewell KT19
off Riverview Rd 238 CR105
Riverview Gdns, SW13 181 CV79
Cobham KT11 235 BU113
Twickenham TW1 199 CF89
Riverview Gro, W4 180 CP79
River Vw Hts, SE16 32 C4
Sch Riverview Inf Sch, Grav.
DA12 off Cimba Wd 213 GL91
Sch Riverview Jun Sch, Grav.
DA12 off Cimba Wd 213 GL91
RIVERVIEW PARK, Grav.
DA12 213 GK92
Riverview Pk, SE6 205 EA89
Riverview Rd, W4 180 CP80
Epsom KT19 238 CQ105
Greenhithe DA9 211 FU85
River Wk, E4
off Winchester Rd 123 EC52
Denham UB9 136 BJ64
Walton-on-Thames KT12 217 BU100
● Riverwalk Business Pk,
Enf. EN3 105 DZ41
Riverwalk Rd, Enf. EN3 105 DZ42
Riverway, N13 121 DN50
River Way, SE10 35 L6
Epsom KT19 238 CR106
Harlow CM20 58 EU10
Loughton IG10 107 EN44
Riverway, Stai. TW18 216 BH95
River Way, Twick. TW2 198 CB89
● Riverway Est, Peasm.
GU3 280 AW142
River Wey Navigation,
Guil. GU1 264 AX132
Woking GU23 249 BB122
Riverwood La, Chis. BR7 227 ER95
Rivet Ho, SE1 32 B10
Rivett-Drake Cl, Guil. GU2 264 AV130
Rivey Cl, W.Byf. KT14 233 BF114
Rivington Av, Wdf.Grn. IG8 124 EK54
Rivington Ct, NW10 161 CU67
Dagenham RM10
off St. Mark's Pl 169 FB65
Rivington Cres, NW7 119 CT52
Rivington Pl, EC2 19 P3
Rivington St, EC2 19 N3
Rivington Wk, E8 10 D8
Rivulet Rd, N17 122 DQ52
Rixon Cl, Geo.Grn. SL3 154 AY72
Rixon Ho, SE18 187 EP79
Rixon St, N7 143 DN62
Rixsen Rd, E12 146 EL64
Sch R.J. Mitchell Prim Sch, The,
Horn. RM12
off Tangmere Cres 169 FH65
Roach Rd, E3 12 A6
Road Ho Est, Old Wok. GU22
off High St 249 BA120
Roads Pl, N19 143 DL61
Roakes Av, Add. KT15 216 BH103
Roan St, SE10 46 E3
Roasthill La, Dorney SL4 173 AK79
Robarts Cl, Pnr. HA5 137 BV57
Robb Rd, Stan. HA7 117 CG51
Robbs Cl, Hem.H. HP1 62 BG17
Robe End, Hem.H. HP1 61 BF18
Robert Adam St, W1 16 G8
Roberta St, E2 20 C2
Robert Av, St.Alb. AL1 64 CB24
Sch Robert Blair Prim Sch, N7 8 B5
Sch Robert Browning Prim Sch,
SE17 31 L10
Robert Burns Ms, SE24
off Mayall Rd 203 DP85
Sch Robert Clack Sch, Lwr Site,
Dag. RM8 off Green La 148 EZ61
Upr Site, Dag. RM8
off Gosfield Rd 148 FA60
Robert Cl, W9 15 P5
Chigwell IG7 125 ET50
Hersham KT12 235 BV106
Potters Bar EN6 85 CY33
Robert Daniels Ct, They.B.
CM16 107 ES37
Robert Dashwood Way, SE17 31 J9
Robert Keen Cl, SE15 44 D7
Robert Lowe Cl, SE14 45 K4
Roberton Dr, Brom. BR1 226 EJ95
Robert Owen Ho, SW6 38 D6
Robert Rd, Hedg. SL2 133 AR61
Robertsbridge Rd, Cars. SM5 222 DC102
Roberts Cl, SE9 207 ER88
SE16 33 K5
Barking IG11
off Tanner St 167 EQ65
Cheshunt EN8
off Norwood Rd 89 DY30
Orpington BR5
off Sholden Gdns 228 EW99
Romford RM3 127 FH53
Stanwell TW19 196 BJ86
Sutton SM3 239 CX108
Thornton Heath CR7
off Kitchener Rd 224 DR97
West Drayton UB7 156 BL74
Roberts La, Chal.St.P. SL9 113 BA50
Roberts Ms, SW1 28 G7
Orpington BR6 228 EU102
Robertson Cl, Brox. EN10 89 DY26
Robertson Ct, Wok. GU21 248 AS118
Robertson Rd, E15 12 F8
Berkhamsted HP4 60 AX19
Robertson St, SW8 41 J10
Robert's Pl, EC1 18 F4
Roberts Pl, Dag. RM10 168 FA65
Robert Sq, SE13 185 EC84
Roberts Rd, E17 123 EB53
NW7 119 CY51
Belvedere DA17 188 FA78
Watford WD18
off Tucker St 98 BW43
Robert St, E16 37 N3
NW1 17 K3
SE18 187 ER77
WC2 30 B1
Croydon CR0 off High St 224 DQ104
Robert Sutton Ho, E1
off Tarling St 20 G9
Roberts Way, Eng.Grn TW20 194 AW94
Hatfield AL10 67 CT19
Sch Robertswood Comb Sch,
Chal.St.P. SL9
off Denham La 113 AZ52
Roberts Wd Dr, Chal.St.P. SL9 113 AZ50
Robeson St, E3 21 P6
Robeson Way, Borwd. WD6 100 CQ39
Robina Cl, Bexh. DA6 188 EX84
Northwood HA6 115 BT53
Robin Cl, NW7 118 CS48
Addlestone KT15 234 BK106
Robin Cl, Hmptn. TW12 198 BY92
Romford RM5 127 FD52
Stanstead Abbotts SG12 55 EC12
Robin Ct, SE16 32 C8
Wallington SM6
off Carew Rd 241 DJ107
Robin Cres, E6 24 F6
Robin Gdns, Red. RH1 272 DG131
Robin Gro, N6 142 DG61
Brentford TW8 179 CJ79
Harrow HA3 140 CM58
Robin Hill, Berk. HP4 60 AW20
Robin Hill Dr, Chis. BR7 206 EL93
Robin Hood, SW15 200 CS90
Robinhood Cl, Mitch. CR4 223 DJ97
Robin Hood Cl, Slou. SL1 153 AL74
Woking GU21 248 AT118
Robin Hood Cres, Knap.
GU21 248 AS117
Robin Hood Dr, Bushey WD23 98 BZ39
Harrow HA3 117 CF52
Robin Hood Gdns, E14 22 F10
Robin Hood Grn, Orp. BR5 228 EU99
Sch Robin Hood Infants' Sch, Sutt.
SM1 off Robin Hood La 240 DA106
Sch Robin Hood Jun Sch, Sutt.
SM1 off Thorncroft Rd 240 DB106
Robin Hood La, E14 22 F10
SW15 200 CS91
Bexleyheath DA6 208 EY85
Hatfield AL10 67 CU17
Robinhood La, Mitch. CR4 223 DJ97
Robin Hood La, Sutt. SM1 240 DA106
Sutton Green GU4 249 AZ124
Robin Hood Meadow, Hem.H.
HP2 62 BM15
Sch Robin Hood Prim Sch, SW15
off Bowness Cres 200 CS92
Robin Hood Rd, SW19 201 CV92
Brentwood CM15 130 FV45
Woking GU21 248 AT118
Robin Hood Way, SW15 200 CS91
SW20 200 CS91
Greenford UB6 159 CF65
● Robin Hood Wks, Knap. GU21
off Robin Hood Rd 248 AS117
Robin Ho, NW8
off Newcourt St 16 C1
Robinia Av, Nthflt DA11 212 GD87
Robinia Cl, SE20
off Sycamore Gro 224 DU95
Ilford IG6 125 ES51
Robinia Cres, E10 145 EB61
Robin La, NW4 141 CX55
Robin Mead, Welw.G.C. AL7 52 DA06
Robins, The, Harl. CM17 58 EW09
Robins Cl, Lon.Col. AL2 84 CL27
Uxbridge UB8
off Newcourt 156 BJ71
Robins Ct, SE12 206 EJ90
Robinscroft Ms, SE10 46 D7
Robinsfield, Hem.H. HP1 62 BG20
Sch Robinsfield Inf Sch, NW8 6 C10
Robins Gro, W.Wick. BR4 226 EG104
Robins La, They.B. CM16 107 EQ36
Robins Nest Hill, Lt.Berk. SG13 69 DJ19
Robinson Av, Goffs Oak EN7 87 DP28
Robinson Cl, E11 146 EE62
Enfield EN2 104 DQ41
Hornchurch RM12 169 FH66
Woking GU22 249 BC120
Robinson Cres, Bushey Hth
WD23 116 CC46
Robinson Ho, W10 14 D9
Robinson Rd, E2 20 G1
SW17 202 DE93
Dagenham RM10 148 FA63
Robinsons Cl, W13 159 CG71
Robinson St, SW3 40 E2
Robinson Way, Nthflt DA11 212 GA85
Robins Orchard, Chal.St.P.
SL9 112 AY51
Robins Rd, Hem.H. HP3 62 BN22
Robins Way, Hat. AL10 67 CT21
Robinsway, Hersham KT12 236 BW105
Waltham Abbey EN9
off Roundhills 90 EE34
Robinswood Cl, Beac. HP9 110 AJ50
Robinswood Ms, N5 8 G3
Robin Way, Cuffley EN6 87 DL28
Guildford GU2 264 AV130
Orpington BR5 228 EV97
Staines TW18 195 BF90
Robin Willis Way, Old Wind.
SL4 194 AU86
Robinwood Gro, Uxb. UB8 156 BM70
Robinwood Pl, SW15 200 CR91
Roborough Wk, Horn. RM12 170 FJ65
Robsart St, SW9 42 D8
Robson Av, NW10 161 CU67
Robson Cl, E6 24 G8
Chalfont St. Peter SL9 112 AY50
Enfield EN2 103 DP40
Robson Rd, SE27 203 DP90
Robsons Cl, Chsht EN8 88 DW29
Robyns Cft, Nthflt DA11 212 GE90
Robyns Way, Sev. TN13 278 FF122
Rocastle Rd, SE4 205 DY85
Roch Av, Edg. HA8 118 CM54
Rochdale Rd, E17 145 EA59
SE2 188 EV78
Rochdale Way, SE8 46 A4
Rochelle Cl, SW11 182 DD84
Rochelle St, E2 20 A3
Rochemont Wk, E8 10 B9
Roche Rd, SW16 223 DM95
Sch Roche Sch, The, SW18
off Frogmore 202 DA85
Rochester Av, E13 166 EJ67
Bromley BR1 226 EH96
Feltham TW13 197 BT89
Rochester Cl, SW16 203 DL94
Enfield EN1 104 DS39
Sidcup DA15 208 EV86
Rochester Dr, Bex. DA5 208 EZ86
Pinner HA5 138 BX57
Watford WD25 82 BW34
Rochester Gdns, Cat. CR3 258 DS122
Croydon CR0 224 DS104
Ilford IG1 147 EM59
Rochester Ms, NW1 7 L6
Rochester Pl, NW1 7 M6
Rochester Rd, NW1 7 L5
Carshalton SM5 240 DF105
Dartford DA1 210 FN87
Gravesend DA12 213 GL87
Hornchurch RM12 169 FH66
Northwood HA6 137 BT55
Staines TW18 195 BD92
Rochester Row, SW1 29 M8
Rochester Sq, NW1 7 M6
Rochester St, SW1 29 N7
Rochester Ter, NW1 7 L5
Rochester Wk, SE1 31 L2
Reigate RH2 off Castle Dr 288 DB139
Rochester Way, SE3 186 EH81
SE9 187 EM83
Croxley Green WD3 97 BP42
Dartford DA1 209 FD87
Rochester Way Relief Rd, SE3 186 EH81
SE9 186 EL84
Roche Wk, Cars. SM5 222 DD100
Rochford Av, Loug. IG10 107 EQ41
Romford RM6 148 EW57
Shenfield CM15 131 GA43
Waltham Abbey EN9 89 ED33
Rochford Cl, E6
off Boleyn Rd 166 EK68
Broxbourne EN10 89 DY26
Hornchurch RM12 169 FH65
Rochford Grn, Loug. IG10 107 EQ41
Rochfords Gdns, Slou. SL2 154 AW74
Rochford St, NW5 6 F2
Rochford Wk, E8 10 D6
Rochford Way, Croy. CR0 223 DL100
Taplow SL6 152 AG73
Rockall Ct, Slou. SL3 175 BB76
Rock Av, SW14
off South Worple Way 180 CR83
Rockbourne Rd, SE23 205 DX88
Rockchase Gdns, Horn. RM11 150 FL58
Sch Rockcliffe Manor Prim Sch,
SE18 off Bassant Rd 187 ET79
Rock Cl, Mitch. CR4 222 DD96
Rockdale Gdns, Sev. TN13 279 FH125
Rockdale Rd, Sev. TN13 279 FH125
Rockells Pl, SE22 204 DV86
Rockfield Cl, Oxt. RH8 276 EF131
Rockfield Rd, Oxt. RH8 276 EF129
Rockford Av, Perivale UB6 159 CG68
Rock Gdns, Dag. RM10 149 FB64
Rock Gro Way, SE16 32 D8
Rockhall Rd, NW2 4 C1
Rockhall Way, NW2
off Midland Ter 141 CX62
Rockhampton Cl, SE27 203 DN91
Rockhampton Rd, SE27 203 DN91
South Croydon CR2 242 DS107
Rock Hill, SE26 204 DT91
Orpington BR6 246 FA107
Rockingham Av, Horn. RM11 149 FH58
Rockingham Cl, SW15 181 CT84
Uxbridge UB8 156 BJ67
Rockingham Est, SE1 31 J7
Rockingham Gate, Bushey
WD23 98 CC44
Rockingham Par, Uxb. UB8 156 BJ66
Rockingham Pl, Beac. HP9 111 AM54
Rockingham Rd, Uxb. UB8 156 BH67
Rockingham St, SE1 31 J7
Rockland Rd, SW15 181 CY84
Rocklands Dr, Stan. HA7 117 CH54
Rockleigh, Hert. SG14 53 DP09
Rockleigh Ct, Shenf. CM15 131 GA45
Rockley Rd, W14 26 C5
Rockliffe Av, Kings L. WD4 80 BN30
Sch Rockmount Prim Sch, SE19
off Chevening Rd 204 DR93
Rockmount Rd, SE18 187 ET78
SE19 204 DR93
Rockshaw Rd, Merst. RH1 273 DM127
Rocks La, SW13 181 CU81
Rock St, N4 143 DN61
Rockware Av, Grnf. UB6 159 CD67
Rockways, Barn. EN5 101 CT44
Rockwell Gdns, SE19 204 DS92
Rockwell Rd, Dag. RM10 149 FB64
Rockwood Pl, W12 26 B4
Rocky La, Merst. RH1 272 DG129
Reigate RH2 272 DF128
Rocliffe St, N1 19 H1
Rocombe Cres, SE23 204 DW87
Rocque La, SE3 47 M10
Rodborough Rd, NW11 142 DA60
Roden Cl, Harl. CM17 58 EZ11
Roden Ct, N6 143 DK59
Roden Gdns, Croy. CR0 224 DS100
Rodenhurst Rd, SW4 203 DJ86
Roden St, N7 143 DM62
Ilford IG1 147 EN62
Rodeo Cl, Erith DA8 189 FH81
Roderick Rd, NW3 6 F1
Rodgers Cl, Els. WD6 99 CK44
Roding Av, Wdf.Grn. IG8 124 EL51
Roding Gdns, Loug. IG10 106 EL44
Roding La, Buck.H. IG9 124 EL46
Chigwell IG7 125 EN46
Roding La N, Wdf.Grn. IG8 124 EK54
Roding La S, Ilf. IG4 146 EK56
Woodford Green IG8 146 EK56
Roding Ms, E1 32 D2
Sch Roding Prim Sch, Dag. RM8
off Hewett Rd 148 EX63
Woodford Green IG8
off Roding La N 124 EL52
Roding Rd, E5 11 K1
E6 25 N6
Loughton IG10 106 EL43
Rodings, The, Upmin. RM14 151 FR58
Woodford Green IG8 124 EJ51
Rodings Row, Barn. EN5
off Leecroft Rd 101 CY43
⊖ Roding Valley 124 EK49
Sch Roding Valley High Sch, Loug.
IG10 off Alderton Hill 106 EL43
Roding Vw, Buck.H. IG9 124 EK46
Roding Way, Rain. RM13 170 FK68
Rodmarton St, W1 16 F7
Rodmell Cl, Hayes UB4 158 BY70
Rodmell Slope, N12 119 CZ50
Rodmere St, SE10 47 K1
Rodmill La, SW2 203 DL87
Rodney Av, St.Alb. AL1 65 CG22
Rodney Cl, Croy. CR0 223 DP102
New Malden KT3 220 CS99
Pinner HA5 138 BY59
Walton-on-Thames KT12 218 BW102
Rodney Ct, W9 15 P4
Rodney Cres, Hodd. EN11 71 EA15
Rodney Gdns, Pnr. HA5 137 BV57

Rodney Gdns, W.Wick. BR4 . . . 244 EG105
Rodney Grn, Walt. KT12 . . . . . 218 BW103
Rodney Pl, E17 . . . . 123 DY54
SE17 . . . . 31 K8
SW19 . . . . 222 DC95
Rodney Rd, E11 . . . . 146 EH56
SE17 . . . . 31 K8
Mitcham CR4 . . . . 222 DE96
New Malden KT3 . . . . 220 CS99
Twickenham TW2 . . . . 198 CA86
Walton-on-Thames KT12 . . . 218 BW103
Rodney St, N1 . . . . 8 D10
Rodney Way, Colnbr. SL3 . . . . . 175 BE81
Guildford GU1 . . . . 265 BA133
Romford RM7 . . . . 126 FA53
Rodona Rd, Wey. KT13 . . . . . . 235 BR111
Rodway Rd, SW15 . . . . 201 CU87
Bromley BR1 . . . . 226 EH95
Rodwell Cl, Ruis. HA4 . . . . 138 BW60
Rodwell Ct, Add. KT15
off Garfield Rd 234 BJ105
Rodwell Pl, Edg. HA8
off Whitchurch La 118 CN51
Rodwell Rd, SE22 . . . . 204 DT86
Roebourne Way, E16 . . . . 37 L4
Roebuck Cl, Ashtd. KT21 . . . . 254 CL120
Feltham TW13 . . . . 197 BV91
Hertford SG13 . . . . 54 DU09
Reigate RH2 . . . . 272 DB134
Roebuck Grn, Slou. SL1 . . . . . 153 AL74
Roebuck La, N17 off High Rd . . 122 DT51
Buckhurst Hill IG9 . . . . 124 EJ45
Roebuck Rd, Chess. KT9 . . . . 238 CN106
Ilford IG6 . . . . 126 EV50
Roedean Av, Enf. EN3 . . . . 104 DW39
Roedean Cl, Enf. EN3 . . . . 104 DW39
Orpington BR6 . . . . 246 EV105
Roedean Cres, SW15 . . . . 200 CS86
Roedean Dr, Rom. RM1 . . . . . . 149 FE56
Roe End, NW9 . . . . 140 CQ56
Roefields Cl, Felden HP3 . . . . . 62 BG24
ROE GREEN, Hat. AL10 . . . . 67 CU18
Roe Grn, NW9 . . . . 140 CQ57
Roe Grn Cl, Hat. AL10 . . . . 66 CS19
Sch Roe Grn Inf & Jun Schs, NW9
off Princes Av 140 CP56
Roe Grn La, Hat. AL10 . . . . 67 CT18
ROEHAMPTON, SW15 . . . . 201 CU85
Roehampton Cl, SW15 . . . . . . 181 CU84
Gravesend DA12 . . . . 213 GL87
Sch Roehampton C of E Prim Sch,
SW15 off Roehampton La . 201 CV87
Roehampton Dr, Chis. BR7 . . . 207 EQ93
Roehampton Gate, SW15 . . . . 200 CS86
Roehampton High St, SW15 . . 201 CV87
Jct Roehampton La, SW15 . . . . 201 CV88
Roehampton La, SW15 . . . . . 181 CU84
Uni Roehampton Uni -
Digby Stuart Coll, SW15
off Roehampton La 201 CU85
Coll Roehampton Uni -
Downshire Ho, SW15
off Roehampton La 201 CU86
Uni Roehampton Uni - Froebel Coll,
SW15 off Roehampton La . 201 CT86
Halls of Res, SW15
off Minstead Gdns 201 CT87
Uni Roehampton Uni -
Southlands Coll, SW15
off Roehampton La 201 CU85
Uni Roehampton Uni -
Whitelands Coll, SW15
off Holybourne Av 201 CU87
Roehampton Vale, SW15 . . . . . 200 CS90
Roe Hill Cl, Hat. AL10 . . . . 67 CT19
Roehyde Way, Hat. AL10 . . . . . . 66 CS20
Roe La, NW9 . . . . 140 CP56
ROESTOCK, St.Alb. AL4 . . . . 66 CR23
Roestock Gdns, Coln.Hth AL4 . . 66 CS22
Roestock La, Coln.Hth AL4 . . . 66 CR23
Roe Way, Wall. SM6 . . . . 241 DL107
Rofant Rd, Nthwd. HA6 . . . . . . 115 BS51
Roffes La, Chaldon CR3 . . . . . 258 DR124
Roffey Cl, Horl. RH6 . . . . 290 DF148
Purley CR8 . . . . 257 DP116
Roffey St, E14 . . . . 34 E5
Roffords, Wok. GU21 . . . . 248 AV117
Rogate Ho, E5 off Muir Rd 144 DV62
Sch Roger Ascham Prim Sch, E17
off Wigton Rd 123 DZ53
Roger Dowley Ct, E2 . . . . 10 G10
Rogers Cl, Cat. CR3
off Tillingdown Hill 258 DV122
Cheshunt EN7 . . . . 88 DR26
Coulsdon CR5 . . . . 257 DP118
Rogers Ct, Swan. BR8 . . . . 229 FG98
Rogers Est, E2 off Globe Rd 21 H3
Rogers Gdns, Dag. RM10 . . . . . 148 FA64
Rogers Ho, SW1 off Page St 29 P8
Rogers La, Stoke P. SL2 . . . . . . 154 AT67
Warlingham CR6 . . . . 259 DZ118
Rogers Mead, Gdse. RH9
off Ivy Mill La 274 DV132
Rogers Rd, E16 . . . . 23 M9
SW17 . . . . 202 DD91
Dagenham RM10 . . . . 148 FA64
Grays RM17 . . . . 192 GC77
Rogers Ruff, Nthwd. HA6 . . . . . 115 BQ53
Roger St, WC1 . . . . 18 D5
Rogers Wk, N12
off Holden Rd 120 DB48
Rojack Rd, SE23 . . . . 205 DX88
Rokeby Ct, Wok. GU21 . . . . . . 248 AT117
Rokeby Gdns, Wdf.Grn. IG8 . . . 124 EG53
Rokeby Pl, SW20 . . . . 201 CV94
Rokeby Rd, SE4 . . . . 45 N8
Sch Rokeby Sch, E15 . . . . 13 H7
Kingston upon Thames KT2
off George Rd 200 CQ94
Rokeby St, E15 . . . . 13 H8
Roke Cl, Ken. CR8 . . . . 242 DQ114
Rokefield, Dor. RH4 . . . . 284 CB136
Roke Lo Rd, Ken. CR8 . . . . 241 DP113
Sch Roke Prim Sch, Ken. CR8
off Little Roke Rd 242 DQ114
Roke Rd, Ken. CR8 . . . . 258 DQ115
Roker Pk Av, Uxb. UB10 . . . . . 136 BL63
Rokesby Cl, Well. DA16 . . . . . . 187 ER82
Rokesby Pl, Wem. HA0 . . . . . . 139 CK64
Rokesby Rd, Slou. SL2 . . . . 153 AM69
Rokesly Av, N8 . . . . 143 DL57
Sch Rokesly Inf Sch, N8
off Hermiston Av 143 DL57
Sch Rokesly Jun Sch, N8
off Rokesly Av 143 DL57
Rokewood Ms, Ware SG12 . . . . 55 DX05
Roland Gdns, SW7 . . . . 27 P10
Feltham TW13 . . . . 198 BY90
Roland Ms, E1 . . . . 21 J6
Roland Rd, E17 . . . . 145 ED56
Roland St, St.Alb. AL1 . . . . 65 CG20
Roland Way, SE17 . . . . 43 M1
SW7 . . . . 27 P10
Worcester Park KT4 . . . . 221 CT103
Roles Gro, Rom. RM6 . . . . 148 EX56
Rolfe Cl, Barn. EN4 . . . . 102 DE42
Beaconsfield HP9 . . . . 111 AL54
Rolinsden Way, Kes. BR2 . . . . . 244 EK105
Rollason Way, Brwd. CM14 . . . 130 FV48
Rollesby Rd, Chess. KT9 . . . . . 238 CN107
Rollesby Way, SE28 . . . . 168 EW73
Rolleston Av, Petts Wd BR5 . . . 227 EP100
Rolleston Cl, Petts Wd BR5 . . . 227 EP101
Rolleston Rd, S.Croy. CR2 . . . . 242 DR108
Roll Gdns, Ilf. IG2 . . . . 147 EN57
Rollins St, SE15 . . . . 45 H2
Rollit Cres, Houns. TW3 . . . . . . 198 CA85
Rollit St, N7 . . . . 8 E2
Rollo Rd, Swan. BR8 . . . . 209 FF94
Rolls Bldgs, EC4 . . . . 18 E8
Rolls Cotts, Magd.Lav. CM5
off Hastingwood Rd 75 FB19
Rollscourt Av, SE24 . . . . 204 DQ85
Rolls Pk Av, E4 . . . . 123 EA51
Rolls Pk Rd, E4 . . . . 123 EB50
Jct Rolls Pk Rbt, Chig. IG7 . . . . 125 ER45
Rolls Pas, EC4 . . . . 18 E8
Rolls Rd, SE1 . . . . 32 B10
Rolls Royce Cl, Wall. SM6 . . . . 241 DL108
Rollswood, Welw.G.C. AL7 . . . . . 51 CY12
Rolt St, SE8 . . . . 45 L2
Rolvenden Gdns, Brom. BR1 . . 206 EK94
Rolvenden Pl, N17 . . . . 122 DU52
Romanby Ct, Red. RH1
off Mill St 288 DF135
Roman Cl, W3
off Avenue Gdns 180 CP75
Feltham TW14 . . . . 198 BW85
Harefield UB9 . . . . 114 BH53
Rainham RM13 . . . . 169 FD68
Romanfield Rd, SW2 . . . . 203 DM87
Roman Gdns, Kings L. WD4 . . . . 81 BP30
Roman Ho, Rain. RM13
off Roman Cl 169 FD68
Romanhurst Av, Brom. BR2 . . . 226 EE98
Romanhurst Gdns, Brom.
BR2 . . . . 226 EE98
● Roman Ind Est, Croy. CR0 . 224 DS101
Roman Ms, Hodd. EN11
off North Rd 71 EA16
Roman Ri, SE19 . . . . 204 DR93
Sawbridgeworth CM21 . . . . . . 58 EX05
Roman Rd, E2 . . . . 20 G3
E3 . . . . 21 L1
E6 . . . . 24 F5
N10 . . . . 121 DH52
NW2 . . . . 141 CW62
W4 . . . . 180 CS77
Brentwood CM15 . . . . 131 GC41
Dorking RH4 . . . . 285 CG138
Ilford IG1 . . . . 167 EP65
Northfleet DA11 . . . . 212 GC90
Sch Roman Rd Prim Sch, E6 . . . . 24 F4
Jct Roman Rbt, Harl. CM20 . . . . 58 EU11
Romans End, St.Alb. AL3 . . . . . . 64 CC22
Roman Sq, SE28 . . . . 168 EU74
Roman St, Hodd. EN11 . . . . 71 EA16
Romans Way, Wok. GU22 . . . . . 250 BG115
Roman Vale, Harl. CM17 . . . . . . 58 EW10
Roman Vil Rd, Dart. DA2, DA4 . 210 FQ92
Roman Way, N7 . . . . 8 D5
SE15 . . . . 44 G5
Carshalton SM5 . . . . 240 DF109
Croydon CR0 . . . . 223 DP103
Dartford DA1 . . . . 209 FE85
Enfield EN1 . . . . 104 DT43
Waltham Abbey EN9 . . . . 105 EB35
● Roman Way Ind Est, N1 . . . . . 8 C6
Romany Ct, Hem.H. HP2
off Wood End Cl 63 BQ19
Romany Gdns, E17
off McEntee Av 123 DY53
Sutton SM3 . . . . 222 DA101
Romany Ri, Orp. BR5 . . . . 227 EQ102
Roma Read Cl, SW15 . . . . 201 CV87
Roma Rd, E17 . . . . 145 DY55
Romberg Rd, SW17 . . . . 202 DG90
Romborough Gdns, SE13 . . . . . 205 EC85
Romborough Way, SE13 . . . . . . 205 EC85
Rom Cres, Rom. RM7 . . . . 149 FF59
Romeland, Els. WD6 . . . . 99 CK44
St. Albans AL3 . . . . 64 CC20
Waltham Abbey EN9 . . . . 89 EC33
Romeland Hill, St.Alb. AL3 . . . . . 64 CC20
Romero Cl, SW9 . . . . 42 D10
Romero Sq, SE3 . . . . 186 EJ84
Romeyn Rd, SW16 . . . . 203 DM90
ROMFORD, RM1 - RM7 . . . . . . 149 FF57
⇌ Romford 149 FE58
Romford Rd, E7 . . . . 13 M4
E12 . . . . 146 EL63
E15 . . . . 13 J6
Aveley RM15 . . . . 170 FQ73
Chigwell IG7 . . . . 126 EU48
Romford RM5 . . . . 126 EY52
● Romford Seedbed Cen, Rom.
RM7 . . . . 149 FE59
Romford St, E1 . . . . 20 D7
Romilly Dr, Wat. WD19 . . . . . . 116 BY49
Romilly Rd, N4 . . . . 143 DP61
Romilly St, W1 . . . . 17 N10
Rommany Rd, SE27 . . . . 204 DR91
Romney Chase, Horn. RM11 . . 150 FM58
Romney Cl, N17 . . . . 122 DV53
NW11 . . . . 142 DC60
SE14 . . . . 45 H5
Ashford TW15 . . . . 197 BQ92
Chessington KT9 . . . . 238 CL105
Harrow HA2 . . . . 138 CA59
Romney Dr, Brom. BR1 . . . . . . 206 EK94
Harrow HA2 . . . . 138 CA59
Romney Gdns, Bexh. DA7 . . . . 188 EZ81
Romney Lock, Wind. SL4 . . . . . 174 AS79
Romney Lock Rd, Wind. SL4 . . 173 AR80
Romney Ms, W1 . . . . 16 G6
Romney Par, Hayes UB4
off Romney Rd 157 BR68
Romney Rd, SE10 . . . . 46 F3
Hayes UB4 . . . . 157 BR68
New Malden KT3 . . . . 220 CR100
Romney Rd, Nthflt DA11 . . . . . 212 GE90
Romney Row, NW2
off Brent Ter 141 CX61
Romney St, SW1 . . . . 29 P7
Romola Rd, SE24 . . . . 203 DP88
Romsey Cl, Orp. BR6 . . . . 245 EP105
Slough SL3 . . . . 175 AZ76
Romsey Dr, Farn.Com. SL2 . . . . 133 AR62
Romsey Gdns, Dag. RM9 . . . . . 168 EX67
Romsey Rd, W13 . . . . 159 CG73
Dagenham RM9 . . . . 168 EX67
Romside Pl, Rom. RM7
off Brooklands La 149 FD56
Romulus Ct, Brent. TW8
off Justin Cl 179 CK80
Rom Valley Way, Rom. RM7 . . . 149 FE59
Ronald Av, E15 . . . . 23 K3
Ronald Cl, Beck. BR3 . . . . 225 DZ98
Ronald Ct, St.Alb. AL2 . . . . 82 BY29
Ronald Rd, Beac. HP9 . . . . 111 AM53
Romford RM3 . . . . 128 FN53
Sch Ronald Ross Prim Sch,
SW19
off Castlecombe Dr 201 CY87
Ronaldsay Spur, Slou. SL1 . . . . 154 AS71
Ronalds Rd, N5 . . . . 8 F3
Bromley BR1 . . . . 226 EG95
Ronaldstone Rd, Sid. DA15 . . . 207 ES86
Ronald St, E1 . . . . 21 H9
Rona Way, Denh. UB9 . . . . 135 BF61
Rona Rd, NW3 . . . . 6 G1
Ronart St, Wealds. HA3 . . . . . . 139 CF55
Rona Wk, N1 . . . . 9 L5
Rondu Rd, NW2 . . . . 4 E2
Ronelean Rd, Surb. KT6 . . . . . 220 CM104
Roneo Cor, Horn. RM12 . . . . . 149 FF60
Roneo Link, Horn. RM12 . . . . . 149 FF60
Ronfearn Av, Orp. BR5 . . . . 228 EX99
Ron Grn Ct, Erith DA8 . . . . 189 FD79
Ron Leighton Way, E6 . . . . 166 EL67
Ronneby Cl, Wey. KT13 . . . . . . 217 BS104
Ronnie La, E12 . . . . 147 EN63
Ronsons Way, St.Alb. AL4 . . . . . 65 CF17
Ronson Way, Lthd. KT22 . . . . . 253 CF121
Ron Todd Cl, Dag. RM10 . . . . . 168 FA67
Ronver Rd, SE12 . . . . 206 EF87
Rood La, EC3 . . . . 19 N10
Roof of the World Pk Homes Est,
Box H. KT20 . . . . 270 CP132
Rookby Ct, N21 . . . . 121 DP47
Rook Cl, Horn. RM12 . . . . 169 FG66
Wembley HA9 . . . . 140 CP62
Rookdean, Chipstead TN13 . . . 278 FC122
Rookeries Cl, Felt. TW13 . . . . . 197 BV90
Rookery, The, Grays RM20 . . . . 191 FU79
Westcott RH4 . . . . 284 CA138
Rookery Cl, NW9 . . . . 141 CT57
Fetcham KT22 . . . . 253 CE124
Rookery Ct, Grays RM20 . . . . . 191 FU79
Rookery Cres, Dag. RM10 . . . . 169 FB66
Rookery Dr, Chis. BR7 . . . . 227 EN95
Westcott RH4 . . . . 284 CA138
Rookery Gdns, Orp. BR5 . . . . . 228 EW99
Rookery Hill, Ashtd. KT21 . . . . 254 CN118
Outwood RH1 . . . . 291 DN145
Rookery La, Brom. BR2 . . . . . . 226 EK100
Grays RM17 . . . . 192 GD78
Smallfield RH6 . . . . 291 DN146
Rookery Mead, Couls. CR5 . . . 257 DJ122
Rookery Rd, SW4 . . . . 183 DJ84
Downe BR6 . . . . 245 EM110
Staines TW18 . . . . 196 BH92
Rookery Vw, Grays RM17 . . . . 192 GD78
Rookery Way, NW9 . . . . 141 CT57
Lower Kingswood KT20 . . . . 271 CZ127
Rookes All, Hert. SG13
off Mangrove Rd 54 DS10
Rookesley Rd, Orp. BR5 . . . . . . 228 EX101
Rooke Way, SE10 . . . . 35 L10
Rookfield Av, N10 . . . . 143 DJ56
Rookfield Cl, N10 . . . . 143 DJ56
Rook La, Chaldon CR3 . . . . . . 257 DM124
Rookley Cl, Sutt. SM2 . . . . 240 DB110
Rook Rd, Woob.Grn HP10 . . . . 132 AD59
Rooks Cl, Welw.G.C. AL8 . . . . . . 51 CX10
Sch Rooks Heath Coll,
S.Har. HA2
off Eastcote La 138 CA62
Rooks Hill, Loud. WD3 . . . . 96 BJ42
Welwyn Garden City AL8 . . . . 51 CW10
Rooksmead Rd, Sun. TW16 . . . 217 BT96
Rooks Nest, Gdse. RH9 . . . . . . 275 DY130
Rookstone Rd, SW17 . . . . 202 DF92
Rook Wk, E6 . . . . 24 G8
Rookwood Av, Loug. IG10 . . . . 107 EQ41
New Malden KT3 . . . . 221 CU98
Wallington SM6 . . . . 241 DK105
Rookwood Cl, Grays RM17 . . . . 192 GB77
Merstham RH1 . . . . 273 DH129
Rookwood Ct, Guil. GU2 . . . . . 280 AW137
Rookwood Gdns, E4 . . . . 124 EF47
Loughton IG10 . . . . 107 EQ41
Rookwood Ho, Bark. IG11
off St. Marys 167 ER68
Rookwood Rd, N16 . . . . 144 DT59
★ Roosevelt Mem, W1 . . . . 17 H10
Roosevelt Way, Dag. RM10 . . . . 169 FD65
Rootes Dr, W10 . . . . 14 C5
Roothill La, Bet. RH3 . . . . 286 CN140
Ropemaker Rd, SE16 . . . . 33 L5
Ropemakers Flds, E14 . . . . 33 N1
Ropemaker St, EC2 . . . . 19 L6
Roper La, SE1 . . . . 31 P4
Ropers Av, E4 . . . . 123 EC50
Ropers Orchard, SW3 . . . . 40 B3
Roper St, SE9 . . . . 207 EM86
Ropers Wk, SW2
off Brockwell Pk Gdns 203 DN87
Roper Way, Mitch. CR4 . . . . 222 DG96
● Ropery Business Pk, SE7 . . . 36 C8
Ropery St, E3 . . . . 21 N5
Rope St, SE16 . . . . 33 M7
Rope Wk, Sun. TW16 . . . . 218 BW97
Ropewalk Gdns, E1 . . . . 20 D9
Ropewalk Ms, E8 . . . . 10 C7
Rope Yd Rails, SE18 . . . . 37 N7
Ropley St, E2 . . . . 20 C1
Rosa Alba Ms, N5
off Kelross Rd 144 DQ63
Rosa Av, Ashf. TW15 . . . . 196 BN91
Rosalind Franklin Cl, Guil.
(Surr.Res.Pk) GU2 . . . . 280 AS135
Rosaline Rd, SW6 . . . . 38 F5
Rosamond St, SE26 . . . . 204 DV90
Rosamund Cl, S.Croy. CR2 . . . . 242 DR105
Rosamun St, Sthl. UB2 . . . . 178 BY77
Rosary, The, Egh. TW20 . . . . . . 215 BD96
Rosary Cl, Houns. TW3 . . . . . . 178 BY82
Rosary Ct, Pot.B. EN6 . . . . 86 DB30
Rosary Gdns, SW7 . . . . 27 N9
Ashford TW15 . . . . 197 BP91
Bushey WD23 . . . . 117 CE45
Sch Rosary RC Prim Sch, NW3 . . . 6 C2
Heston TW5 off The Green . . 178 CA79
Rosaville Rd, SW6 . . . . 38 G5
Roscoe St, EC1 . . . . 19 K5
Roscoff Cl, Edg. HA8 . . . . 118 CQ53
Roseacre, Oxt. RH8 . . . . 276 EG134
Roseacre Cl, W13 . . . . 159 CH71
Hornchurch RM11 . . . . 150 FM60
Shepperton TW17 . . . . 216 BN99
Sutton SM1 . . . . 222 DC103
Roseacre Gdns, Chilw. GU4 . . . 281 BF140
Welwyn Garden City AL7 . . . . 52 DC09
Roseacre Rd, Well. DA16 . . . . . 188 EV83
Rose All, EC2 off New St 19 P7
SE1 . . . . 31 K2
Rose & Crown Ct, EC2 . . . . 19 J8
Rose & Crown Yd, SW1 . . . . 29 M2
Roseary Cl, West Dr. UB7 . . . . 176 BK77
Rose Av, E18 . . . . 124 EH54
Gravesend DA12 . . . . 213 GL88
Mitcham CR4 . . . . 222 DF95
Morden SM4 . . . . 222 DC99
Rosebank, SE20 . . . . 204 DV94
Rose Bk, Brwd. CM14 . . . . 130 FX48
Rosebank, Epsom KT18 . . . . . . 238 CQ114
Waltham Abbey EN9 . . . . 90 EE33
Rosebank Av, Horn. RM12 . . . . 150 FJ64
Wembley HA0 . . . . 139 CF63
Rosebank Cl, N12 . . . . 120 DE50
Teddington TW11 . . . . 199 CG93
Rose Bk Cotts, Wok. GU22 . . . . 248 AY122
Rosebank Gdns, E3 . . . . 21 M1
Northfleet DA11 . . . . 212 GE88
Rosebank Gro, E17 . . . . 145 DZ55
Rosebank Rd, E17 . . . . 145 EB58
W7 . . . . 179 CE75
Rosebank Vil, E17 . . . . 145 EA56
Rosebank Wk, NW1 . . . . 7 P6
SE18 . . . . 37 H8
Rosebank Way, W3 . . . . 160 CR72
Rose Bates Dr, NW9 . . . . 140 CN56
Roseberry Cl, Upmin. RM14 . . . 151 FT58
Roseberry Ct, Wat. WD17
off Grandfield Av 97 BU39
Roseberry Gdns, N4 . . . . 143 DP58
Dartford DA1 . . . . 210 FJ87
Orpington BR6 . . . . 227 ES104
Upminster RM14 . . . . 151 FT59
Roseberry Pl, E8 . . . . 10 A5
Roseberry St, SE16 . . . . 32 E9
Rosebery Av, E12 . . . . 166 EL65
EC1 . . . . 18 E5
N17 . . . . 122 DU54
Epsom KT17 . . . . 238 CS114
Harrow HA2 . . . . 138 BY63
New Malden KT3 . . . . 221 CT96
Sidcup DA15 . . . . 207 ES87
Thornton Heath CR7 . . . . 224 DQ96
Rosebery Cl, Mord. SM4 . . . . . 221 CX100
Rosebery Ct, EC1
off Rosebery Av 18 E4
Northfleet DA11 . . . . 213 GF88
Rosebery Cres, Wok. GU22 . . . . 249 AZ121
Rosebery Gdns, N8 . . . . 143 DL57
W13 . . . . 159 CG72
Sutton SM1 . . . . 240 DB105
● Rosebery Ind Pk, N17 . . . . . 122 DV54
Rosebery Ms, N10 . . . . 121 DJ54
SW2 off Rosebery Rd 203 DL86
Rosebery Rd, N10 . . . . 121 DJ54
SW2 . . . . 203 DL86
Bushey WD23 . . . . 116 CB45
Epsom KT18 . . . . 254 CR119
Grays RM17 . . . . 192 FY79
Hounslow TW3 . . . . 198 CC85
Kingston upon Thames KT1 . 220 CP96
Sutton SM1 . . . . 239 CZ107
Sch Rosebery Sch, Epsom KT18
off White Horse Dr 238 CQ114
Rosebery Sq, EC1 . . . . 18 E5
Kingston upon Thames KT1 . 220 CN96
Rosebine Av, Twick. TW2 . . . . . 199 CD87
Rosebriar Cl, Wok. GU22 . . . . . 250 BG116
Rosebriars, Cat. CR3 . . . . 258 DS120
Esher KT10 . . . . 236 CC106
Rosebriar Wk, Wat. WD24 . . . . . 97 BT36
Coll Rose Bruford Coll,
Sid. DA15
off Burnt Oak La 208 EV88
Rosebury Rd, SW6 . . . . 39 M9
Rosebury Sq, Wdf.Grn. IG8 . . . 125 EN52
Rosebury Vale, Ruis. HA4 . . . . . 137 BT60
Rose Bushes, Epsom KT17 . . . . 255 CV116
Rose Ct, E1 . . . . 20 A7
Amersham HP6
off Chestnut La 77 AS37
Pinner HA5 off Nursery Rd . . 138 BW55
Waltham Cross EN7 . . . . 88 DU27
Rosecourt Rd, Croy. CR0 . . . . . 223 DM100
Rosecroft Av, NW3 . . . . 142 DA62
Rosecroft Cl, Bigg.H. TN16
off Lotus Rd 261 EM118
Orpington BR5 . . . . 228 EW100
Rosecroft Dr, Wat. WD17 . . . . . 97 BS36
Rosecroft Gdns, NW2 . . . . 141 CU62
Twickenham TW2 . . . . 199 CD88
Rosecroft Rd, Sthl. UB1 . . . . . . 158 CA70
Rosecroft Wk, Pnr. HA5 . . . . . . 138 BX57
Wembley HA0 . . . . 139 CK64
Rosedale, Ashtd. KT21 . . . . 253 CJ118
Caterham CR3 . . . . 258 DS123
Rose Dale, Orp. BR6 . . . . 227 EP103
Rosedale, Welw.G.C. AL7 . . . . . . 51 CZ05
Rosedale Av, Chsht EN7 . . . . . . 88 DT29
Hayes UB3 . . . . 157 BR71
Rosedale Cl, SE2 . . . . 188 EV76
W7 off Boston Rd 179 CF75
Bricket Wood AL2 . . . . 82 BY30
Dartford DA2 . . . . 210 FP87
Stanmore HA7 . . . . 117 CH51
Sch Rosedale Coll, Hayes UB3
off Wood End Grn Rd 157 BS72
Rosedale Ct, N5 . . . . 8 G1
Rosedale Dr, Dag. RM9 . . . . . . 168 EV67
Rosedale Gdns, Dag. RM9 . . . . 168 EV66
Rosedale Pl, Croy. CR0 . . . . . . 225 DX101
Rosedale Rd, E7 . . . . 146 EJ64
Dagenham RM9 . . . . 168 EV66
Epsom KT17 . . . . 239 CU106
Grays RM17 . . . . 192 GD78
Richmond TW9 . . . . 180 CL84
Romford RM1 . . . . 127 FC54
Rosedale Ter, W6
off Dalling Rd 181 CV76
Rosedale Way, Chsht EN7 . . . . . 88 DU29
Rosedene, NW6 . . . . 4 D8
Rosedene Av, SW16 . . . . 203 DM90
Croydon CR0 . . . . 223 DM101
Greenford UB6 . . . . 158 CA69
Morden SM4 . . . . 222 DA99
Rosedene Ct, Dart. DA1
off Shepherds La 210 FJ87
Ruislip HA4 . . . . 137 BS60
Rosedene Gdns, Ilf. IG2 . . . . . 147 EN56
Rosedene Ter, E10 . . . . 145 EB61
Rosedew Rd, W6 . . . . 38 C3
Rose Dr, Chesh. HP5 . . . . 76 AS32
Rose End, Wor.Pk. KT4 . . . . 221 CX102
Rosefield, Sev. TN13 . . . . 278 FG124
Rosefield Cl, Cars. SM5 . . . . . . 240 DE106
Rosefield Gdns, E14 . . . . 22 A10
Ottershaw KT16 . . . . 233 BD107
Rosefield Rd, Stai. TW18 . . . . . 196 BG91
Roseford Ct, W12 . . . . 26 C5
Rose Gdn Cl, Edg. HA8 . . . . 118 CL51
Rose Gdns, W5 . . . . 179 CK76
Feltham TW13 . . . . 197 BU89
Southall UB1 . . . . 158 CA70
Stanwell TW19 . . . . 196 BK87
Watford WD18 . . . . 97 BU43
Rosegate Ho, E3 . . . . 21 P1
Rose Glen, NW9 . . . . 140 CR56
Romford RM7 . . . . 149 FE60
Rosehart Ms, W11 . . . . 15 J9
Rose Hatch Av, Rom. RM6 . . . . 148 EX55
Roseheath, Hem.H. HP1 . . . . 61 BE19
Roseheath Rd, Houns. TW4 . . . 198 BZ85
ROSE HILL, Dor. RH4 . . . . 285 CG136
ROSEHILL, Sutt. SM1 . . . . 222 DB102
Jct Rose Hill, Sutt. SM1 . . . . . . 222 DB101
Rose Hill, Burn. SL1 . . . . 152 AG66
Rosehill, Clay. KT10 . . . . 237 CG107
Rose Hill, Dor. RH4 . . . . 285 CH136
Rosehill, Hmptn. TW12 . . . . . . 218 CA95
Rose Hill, Sutt. SM1 . . . . 222 DB103
Rose Hill App, Dor. RH4
off Rose Hill 285 CG136
Rosehill Av, Sutt. SM1 . . . . 222 DC102
Woking GU21 . . . . 248 AW116
Rosehill Cl, Hodd. EN11 . . . . 71 DZ17
Rosehill Ct, Hem.H. HP1
off Green End Rd 62 BG22
Slough SL1 . . . . 174 AU76
Rosehill Fm Meadow, Bans.
SM7 . . . . 256 DB115
Rosehill Gdns, Abb.L. WD5 . . . . 81 BQ32
Greenford UB6 . . . . 139 CF64
Sutton SM1 . . . . 222 DB103
Rose Hill Pk W, Sutt. SM1 . . . . 222 DC102
Rosehill Rd, SW18 . . . . 202 DC86
Biggin Hill TN16 . . . . 260 EJ117
Rose Joan Ms, NW6 . . . . 5 J1
Roseland Cl, N17
off Cavell Rd 122 DR52
Roselands Av, Hodd. EN11 . . . . . 71 DZ15
Sch Roselands Prim Sch, Hodd.
EN11 off High Wd Rd 55 DZ14
Rose La, Ripley GU23 . . . . 250 BJ121
Romford RM6 . . . . 148 EX55
Rose Lawn, Bushey Hth
WD23 . . . . 116 CC46
Roseleigh Av, N5 . . . . 9 H1
Roseleigh Cl, Twick. TW1 . . . . . 199 CK86
Roseley Cotts, Eastwick CM20 . . 57 EP11
Rosemary Av, N3 . . . . 120 DB54
N9 . . . . 122 DV46
Enfield EN2 . . . . 104 DR39
Hounslow TW4 . . . . 178 BX82
Romford RM1 . . . . 149 FF55
West Molesey KT8 . . . . 218 CA97
Rosemary Cl, Croy. CR0 . . . . . . 223 DL100
Harlow CM17 . . . . 58 EW11
Oxted RH8 . . . . 276 EG133
South Ockendon RM15 . . . . . 171 FW69
Uxbridge UB8 . . . . 156 BN71
Rosemary Ct, Horl. RH6 . . . . . . 290 DE147
Rosemary Cres, Guil. GU2 . . . . 264 AT130
Rosemary Dr, E14 . . . . 22 G9
Ilford IG4 . . . . 146 EK57
London Colney AL2 . . . . 83 CG26
Rosemary Gdns, SW14
off Rosemary La 180 CQ83
Chessington KT9 . . . . 238 CL105
Dagenham RM8 . . . . 148 EZ60
Rosemary La, SW14 . . . . 180 CQ83
Egham TW20 . . . . 215 BB97
Horley RH6 . . . . 291 DH149
Rosemary Rd, SE15 . . . . 44 B4
SW17 . . . . 202 DC90
Welling DA16 . . . . 187 ET81
Rosemary St, N1 . . . . 9 L8
Rosemead, NW9 . . . . 141 CT59
Chertsey KT16 . . . . 216 BH101
Potters Bar EN6 . . . . 86 DC30
Rosemead Av, Felt. TW13 . . . . . 197 BT89
Mitcham CR4 . . . . 223 DJ96
Wembley HA9 . . . . 140 CL64
Rosemead Cl, Red. RH1 . . . . . . 288 DD136
Rosemead Gdns, Hutt. CM13 . . 131 GD42
Sch Rosemead Prep Sch, SE21
off Thurlow Pk Rd 204 DQ89
Rose Ms, N18 . . . . 122 DV49
Rosemont Av, N12 . . . . 120 DC51
Rosemont Rd, NW3 . . . . 5 N4
W3 . . . . 160 CP73
New Malden KT3 . . . . 220 CQ97
Richmond TW10 . . . . 200 CL86
Wembley HA0 . . . . 160 CL67
Rosemoor Cl, Welw.G.C. AL7 . . . 51 CZ10
Rosemoor St, SW3 . . . . 28 E9
Rosemount, Harl. CM19 . . . . 73 EP18
Wallington SM6 . . . . 241 DJ107
Rosemount Av, W.Byf. KT14 . . 234 BG113
Rosemount Cl, Wdf.Grn. IG8
off Chapelmount Rd 125 EM51
Rosemount Dr, Brom. BR1 . . . . 227 EM98
Rosemount Pt, SE23
off Dacres Rd 205 DX90
Rosemount Rd, W13 . . . . 159 CG72
Rosenau Cres, SW11 . . . . 40 D7
Rosenau Rd, SW11 . . . . 40 D6
Sch Rosendale Prim Sch, SE21
off Rosendale Rd 204 DQ87
Rosendale Rd, SE21 . . . . 204 DQ87
SE24 . . . . 204 DQ87
Roseneath Av, N21 . . . . 121 DP46
Roseneath Cl, Orp. BR6 . . . . . . 246 EW108
Roseneath Pl, SW16
off Curtis Fld Rd 203 DM91
Roseneath Rd, SW11 . . . . 202 DG86
Roseneath Wk, Enf. EN1 . . . . . . 104 DR42
Rosens Wk, Edg. HA8 . . . . 118 CP48
Rosenthal Rd, SE6 . . . . 205 EB86
Rosenthorpe Rd, SE15 . . . . 205 DX85
Rose Pk, Add. KT15 . . . . 233 BE109

Rose Pk Cl, Hayes UB4 158 BW70
Rosepark Ct, Ilf. IG5 125 EM54
Roserton St, E14 34 E5
Rosery, The, Croy. CR0 225 DX100
Roses, The, Wdf.Grn. IG8 124 EF52
Roses La, Wind. SL4 173 AK82
Rose Sq, SW3 28 B10
Rose St, EC4 19 H8
WC2 18 A10
Northfleet DA11 212 GB86
Rosethorn Cl, SW12 203 DJ87
Rose Tree Ms, Wdf.Grn. IG8
off Chigwell Rd 124 EL51
Rosetree Pl, Hmptn. TW12 198 CA94
Rosetrees, Guil. GU1 281 BA135
Rosetta Cl, SW8 42 B5
Rosetta Prim Sch, E16 24 B7
Rosetti Ter, Dag. RM8
off Marlborough Rd 148 EV63
Rose Vale, Hodd. EN11 71 EA17
Rose Valley, Brwd. CM14 130 FW48
Roseveare Rd, SE12 206 EJ91
Rose Vil, Dart. DA1 210 FP87
Roseville Av, Houns. TW3 198 CA85
Roseville Rd, Hayes UB3 177 BU78
Rosevine Rd, SW20 221 CW95
Rose Wk, Pur. CR8 241 DK111
St. Albans AL4 65 CJ18
Slough SL2 153 AP71
Surbiton KT5 220 CP99
West Wickham BR4 225 ED103
Rose Wk, The, Rad. WD7 99 CH37
Rosewarne Cl, Wok. GU21
off Muirfield Rd 248 AU118
Rose Way, SE12 206 EG85
Roseway, SE21 204 DR86
Rose Way, Edg. HA8 118 CQ49
Rosewell Cl, SE20 204 DV94
Rosewood, Dart. DA2 209 FE91
Esher KT10 219 CG103
Sutton SM2 240 DC110
Woking GU22 249 BA119
Rosewood Av, Grnf. UB6 139 CG64
Hornchurch RM12 149 FG64
Rosewood Cl, Sid. DA14 208 EW90
Rosewood Ct, Brom. BR1 226 EJ95
Hemel Hempstead HP1 61 BE19
Romford RM6 148 EW57
Rosewood Dr, Enf. EN2 103 DN35
Shepperton TW17 216 BM99
Rosewood Gdns, SE13
off Morden Hill 46 E8
Rosewood Gro, Sutt. SM1 222 DC103
Rosewood Sq, W12
off Primula St 161 CU72
Rosewood Ter, SE20
off Laurel Gro 204 DW94
Rosewood Way, Farn.Com.
SL2 133 AQ64
Rosher Cl, E15 12 G7
ROSHERVILLE, Grav. DA11 212 GF85
Rosherville C of E Prim Sch,
Nthflt DA11 off London Rd 212 GE86
Rosherville Way, Grav. DA11 212 GE87
Rosh Pinah Jewish Prim Sch,
Edg. HA8 off Glengall Rd 118 CP48
Rosie's Way, S.Ock. RM15 171 FX72
Rosina St, E9 11 J3
Roskell Rd, SW15 181 CX83
Rosken Gro, Farn.Royal SL2 153 AP68
Roslin Rd, W3 180 CP76
● Roslin Sq, W3 180 CP76
Roslin Way, Brom. BR1 206 EG92
Roslyn Cl, Brox. EN10 71 DY21
Mitcham CR4 222 DD96
Roslyn Ct, Wok. GU21
off St. John's Rd 248 AU118
Roslyn Gdns, Rom. RM2 127 FF54
Roslyn Rd, N15 144 DR57
Rosmead Rd, W11 14 F10
Rosoman Pl, EC1 18 F4
Rosoman St, EC1 18 F3
Ross, E16 off Seagull La 23 N10
Rossall Cl, Horn. RM11 149 FG58
Rossall Cres, NW10 160 CM69
Ross Av, Dag. RM8 148 EZ61
Ross Cl, Har. HA3 116 CC52
Hatfield AL10
off Homestead Rd 67 CU15
Hayes UB3 177 BR77
Northolt UB5 139 CD63
Ross Ct, E5 off Napoleon Rd 144 DV63
SW15 201 CX87
Ross Cres, Wat. WD25 97 BU35
Rossdale, Sutt. SM1 240 DE106
Rossdale Dr, N9 104 DW44
NW9 140 CQ60
Rossdale Rd, SW15 181 CW84
Rosse Gdns, SE13
off Desvignes Dr 205 ED86
Rosse Ms, SE3 186 EH81
Rossendale Cl, Enf. EN2 103 DP37
Rossendale St, E5 144 DV61
Rossendale Way, NW1 7 M7
Rossetti Gdns, Couls. CR5 257 DM118
Rossetti Ms, NW8 6 B9
Rossetti Rd, SE16 32 E10
Rossgate, Hem.H. HP1
off Galley Hill 62 BG18
Rossgate Prim Sch, Hem.H.
HP1 off Galley Hill 62 BG18
Ross Haven Pl, Nthwd. HA6 115 BT53
Rossignol Gdns, Cars. SM5 222 DG103
Rossindel Rd, Houns. TW3 198 CA85
Rossington Av, Borwd. WD6 100 CL38
Rossington Cl, Enf. EN1 104 DV38
Rossington St, E5 144 DU61
Rossiter Cl, Slou. SL3 174 AY77
Rossiter Flds, Barn. EN5 101 CY44
Rossiter Rd, SW12 203 DH88
Rossland Cl, Bexh. DA6 209 FB85
Rosslare Cl, West. TN16 277 ER125
Rosslyn Av, E4 124 EF47
SW13 180 CS83
Dagenham RM8 148 EZ59
East Barnet EN4 102 DE44
Feltham TW14 197 BU86
Romford RM3 128 FM54
Rosslyn Cl, Hayes UB3 157 BR71
Sunbury-on-Thames TW16
off Cadbury Rd 197 BS93
West Wickham BR4 226 EF104
Rosslyn Cres, Har. HA1 139 CF57
Wembley HA9 140 CL63
Rosslyn Gdns, Wem. HA9
off Rosslyn Cres 140 CL62
Rosslyn Hill, NW3 6 B1
Rosslyn Ms, NW3 6 B1
Rosslyn Pk, Wey. KT13 235 BR105
Rosslyn Pk Ms, NW3 6 B2
Rosslyn Rd, E17 145 EC56
Barking IG11 167 ER66
Twickenham TW1 199 CJ86
Watford WD18 97 BV41
Rossmore Cl, Enf. EN3 105 DX42
Rossmore Ct, NW1 16 E4
Rossmore Rd, NW1 16 D5
Ross Par, Wall. SM6 241 DH107
Ross Rd, SE25 224 DR97
Cobham KT11 236 BW113
Dartford DA1 209 FG86
Twickenham TW2 198 CB88
Wallington SM6 241 DJ106
Ross Way, SE9 186 EL83
Northwood HA6 115 BT49
Rossway Dr, Bushey WD23 98 CC43
Rosswood Gdns, Wall. SM6 241 DJ107
Rostella Rd, SW17 202 DD91
Rostrevor Av, N15 144 DT58
Rostrevor Gdns, Hayes UB3 157 BS74
Iver SL0 155 BD68
Southall UB2 178 BY78
Rostrevor Ms, SW6 38 G7
Rostrevor Rd, SW6 38 G6
SW19 202 DA92
Roswell Cl, Chsht EN8 89 DY30
Rotary St, SE1 30 G6
Rothbury Av, Rain. RM13 169 FH71
Rothbury Gdns, Islw. TW7 179 CG80
Rothbury Rd, E9 11 P6
Rothbury Wk, N17 122 DU52
Roth Dr, Hutt. CM13 131 GB47
Rother Cl, Wat. WD25 82 BW34
Rotherfield Prim Sch, N1 9 K8
Rotherfield Rd, Cars. SM5 240 DG105
Enfield EN3 105 DX37
Rotherfield St, N1 9 K7
Rotherham Wk, SE1 30 G3
Rotherhill Av, SW16 203 DK93
ROTHERHITHE, SE16 33 J6
⊖ Rotherhithe 33 H4
Rotherhithe New Rd, SE16 44 D1
Rotherhithe Old Rd, SE16 33 J7
Rotherhithe Prim Sch,
SE16 33 J8
Rotherhithe St, SE16 33 H4
Rotherhithe Tunnel, E1 33 J2
Rotherhithe Tunnel App, E14 21 L10
SE16 32 G5
Rothervale, Horl. RH6 290 DF145
Rotherwick Hill, W5 160 CM70
Rotherwick Rd, NW11 142 DA59
Rotherwood Cl, SW20 221 CY95
Rotherwood Rd, SW15 38 C10
Rothery St, N1 8 G8
Rothery Ter, SW9 42 G5
Rothesay Av, SW20 221 CY96
Greenford UB6 159 CD65
Richmond TW10 180 CP84
Rothesay Rd, SE25 224 DR98
Rothes Rd, Dor. RH4 285 CH135
Rothsay Rd, E7 166 EJ66
Rothsay St, SE1 31 N6
Rothsay Wk, E14 34 B8
Rothschild Rd, W4 180 CQ77
Rothschild St, SE27 203 DP91
Roth Wk, N7 off Durham Rd 143 DN61
Rothwell Gdns, Dag. RM9 168 EW67
Rothwell Ho, Houns. TW5
off Biscoe Cl 178 CA79
Rothwell Rd, Dag. RM9 168 EW67
Rothwell St, NW1 6 F8
Rotten Row, SW1 28 G4
SW7 28 C4
Rotterdam Dr, E14 34 F7
Rouel Rd, SE16 32 C7
Rouge La, Grav. DA12 213 GH88
Rougemont Av, Mord. SM4 222 DA100
Roughdown Av, Hem.H. HP3 62 BG23
Roughdown Rd, Hem.H. HP3 62 BH23
Roughdown Vil Rd, Hem.H.
HP3 62 BG23
Roughets La, Bletch. RH1 274 DS129
Godstone RH9 274 DS129
Roughlands, Wok. GU22 249 BE115
Rough Rew, Dor. RH4 285 CH139
Roughs, The, Nthwd. HA6 115 BT48
Roughtallys, N.Wld Bas. CM16 92 EZ27
Roughwood Cl, Wat. WD17 97 BS38
Roughwood La, Ch.St.G. HP8 112 AY45
Roundacre, SW19 201 CX89
Roundaway Rd, Ilf. IG5 125 EM54
ROUND BUSH, Wat. WD25 98 CC38
Roundbush La, Ald. WD25 98 CC38
Roundcroft, Chsht EN7 88 DT26
Roundel Cl, SE4 185 DZ84
Round Gro, Croy. CR0 225 DX101
Roundhay Cl, SE23 205 DX89
Roundheads End, Forty Grn
HP9 110 AH51
Roundhedge Way, Enf. EN2 103 DM38
Round Hill, SE26 204 DW89
Roundhill, Wok. GU22 249 BB119
Roundhill Dr, Enf. EN2 103 DM42
Woking GU22 249 BB118
Roundhills, Wal.Abb. EN9 90 EE34
Roundhill Way, Cob. KT11 236 CB111
Guildford GU2 264 AT134
Round Ho Ct, Chsht EN8
off Hobbs Cl 89 DX29
Roundings, The, Hert.Hth SG13 54 DV14
Roundlyn Gdns, St.M.Cray BR5
off Lynmouth Ri 228 EV98
Roundmead Av, Loug. IG10 107 EN41
Roundmead Cl, Loug. IG10 107 EN41
Roundmoor Dr, Chsht EN8 89 DX29
Round Oak Rd, Wey. KT13 234 BM105
Roundtable Rd, Brom. BR1 206 EF90
Roundthorn Way, Wok. GU21 248 AT116
Roundtree Rd, Wem. HA0 139 CH64
Roundway, Bigg.H. TN16
off Norheads La 260 EK116
Egham TW20 195 BC92
Roundway, The, N17 122 DQ53
Claygate KT10 237 CF106
Watford WD18 97 BT44
Roundways, Ruis. HA4 137 BT62
Roundwood, Chis. BR7 227 EP96
Kings Langley WD4 80 BL26
Roundwood Av, Hutt. CM13 131 GA46
Uxbridge UB11 157 BQ74
Roundwood Cl, Ruis. HA4 137 BR59
Roundwood Dr, Welw.G.C.
AL8 51 CW07
Roundwood Gro, Hutt. CM13 131 GB45
Roundwood Lake, Hutt. CM13 131 GB46
Roundwood Pk, NW10 161 CU66
Roundwood Rd, NW10 161 CT65
Roundwood Rd, Amer. HP6 77 AS38
Roundwood Vw, Bans. SM7 255 CX115
Roundwood Way, Bans. SM7 255 CX115
Rounton Rd, E3 22 B4
Waltham Abbey EN9 90 EE33
Roupell Rd, SW2 203 DM88
Roupell St, SE1 30 F3
Rousden St, NW1 7 L7
Rousebarn La, Rick. WD3 97 BQ41
Rouse Gdns, SE21 204 DS91
Rous Rd, Buck.H. IG9 124 EL46
Routemaster Cl, E13 24 A2
Routh Ct, Felt. TW14 197 BR88
Routh Rd, SW18 202 DE87
Routh St, E6 25 K7
Rover Av, Ilf. IG6 125 ET51
Rover Ho, N1 off Phillipp St 9 P9
Rowallan Rd, SW6 38 E5
Rowan Av, E4 123 DZ51
Egham TW20 195 BC92
Rowan Cl, SW16 223 DJ95
W5 180 CL75
Ashford TW15 196 BK91
Beaconsfield HP9 110 AH54
Bricket Wood AL2 82 CA31
Guildford GU1 264 AV131
Ilford IG1 147 ER64
New Malden KT3 220 CS96
Reigate RH2 288 DC136
St. Albans AL4 66 CL20
Shenley WD7
off Juniper Gdns 84 CL33
Stanmore HA7 117 CF51
Wembley HA0 139 CG62
Rowan Ct, Borwd. WD6
off Theobald St 100 CL39
Rowan Cres, SW16 223 DJ95
Dartford DA1 210 FJ88
Rowan Dr, NW9 141 CU56
Broxbourne EN10 89 DZ25
Rowan Gdns, Croy. CR0 224 DT104
Iver SL0 155 BC68
Rowan Grn, Wey. KT13 235 BR105
Rowan Grn E, Brwd. CM13 131 FZ48
Rowan Grn W, Brwd. CM13 131 FZ49
Rowan Gro, Aveley RM15 170 FQ73
Coulsdon CR5 257 DH121
Rowan Ho, NW3
off Maitland Pk Rd 6 F4
Rowanhurst Dr, Farn.Com.
SL2 133 AQ64
Rowan Pl, Amer. HP6 94 AT38
Hayes UB3 157 BT73
Rowan Prep Sch, Rowan Brae,
Esher KT10 off Gordon Rd 237 CE108
Rowan Hill, Esher KT10
off Fitzalan Rd 237 CF108
Rowan Rd, SW16 223 DJ96
W6 26 C9
Bexleyheath DA7 188 EY83
Brentford TW8 179 CH80
Swanley BR8 229 FD97
West Drayton UB7 176 BK77
Rowans, Welw.G.C. AL7 52 DA06
Rowans, The, N13 122 DQ48
Aveley RM15
off Purfleet Rd 170 FQ74
Chalfont St. Peter SL9 134 AX55
Hemel Hempstead HP1 62 BG20
Sunbury-on-Thames TW16 197 BT92
Woking GU22 248 AY118
Rowans Cl, Long. DA3 231 FX96
Rowans Prim Sch, Welw.G.C.
AL7 off Rowans 52 DA06
Rowans Sch, The, SW20
off Drax Av 201 CU94
Rowans Way, Loug. IG10 107 EM42
Rowan Ter, SE20
off Sycamore Gro 224 DU95
W6 26 C9
Rowantree Cl, N21 122 DR46
Rowantree Rd, N21 122 DR46
Enfield EN2 103 DP40
Rowan Wk, N2 142 DC58
N19 off Bredgar Rd 143 DJ61
W10 14 E4
Barnet EN5 102 DB43
Bromley BR2 227 EM104
Chesham HP5 76 AN30
Hatfield AL10 67 CU21
Hornchurch RM11 150 FK56
Rowan Way, Rom. RM6 148 EW55
Slough SL2 153 AP71
South Ockendon RM15 171 FX70
Rowanwood Av, Sid. DA15 208 EU88
Rowanwood Ms, Enf. EN2 103 DP40
Rowbarns Way, E.Hors. KT24 267 BT130
Rowben Cl, N20 120 DB46
Rowberry Cl, SW6 38 B5
Rowbourne Pl, Cuffley EN6 87 DK28
Rowbury, Gdmg. GU7 280 AU143
Rowcroft, Hem.H. HP1 61 BE21
Rowcross St, SE1 32 A10
Rowdell Rd, Nthlt. UB5 158 CA67
Rowden Pk Gdns, E4
off Rowden Rd 123 EA51
Rowden Rd, E4 123 EA51
Beckenham BR3 225 DY95
Epsom KT19 238 CP105
Rowditch La, SW11 40 G8
Rowdon Av, NW10 161 CV66
Rowdown Cres, New Adgtn
CR0 243 ED109
Rowdown Inf Sch, New Adgtn
CR0 off Calley Down Cres 243 ED110
Rowdowns Rd, Dag. RM9 168 EZ67
Rowe Gdns, Bark. IG11 167 ET68
Rowe La, E9 10 G2
Rowena Cres, SW11 40 D9
Rowe Wk, Har. HA2 138 CA62
Rowfant Rd, SW17 202 DG88
Rowhedge, Brwd. CM13 131 GA48
Rowhill Rd, E5 10 F1
Dartford DA2 209 FF93
Swanley BR8 209 FF93
Rowhill Sch, Wilm. DA2
off Stock La 210 FJ91
Rowhurst Av, Add. KT15 234 BH107
Leatherhead KT22 253 CF117
Rowington Cl, W2 15 L6
Rowland Av, Har. HA3 139 CJ55
Rowland Cl, Wind. SL4 173 AK83
Rowland Ct, E16 23 L4
Rowland Cres, Chig. IG7 125 ES49
Rowland Gro, SE26
off Dallas Rd 204 DV90
Rowland Hill Av, N17 122 DQ52
Rowland Hill St, NW3 6 C2
Rowlands Av, Pnr. HA5 116 CA51
Rowlands Cl, N6 142 DG58
NW7 119 CU52
Cheshunt EN8 89 DX30
Rowlands Flds, Chsht EN8 89 DX29
Rowlands Rd, Dag. RM8 148 EZ61
Rowland Wk, Hav.at.Bow.
RM4 127 FE48
Rowland Way, SW19
off Hayward Cl 222 DB95
Ashford TW15
off Littleton Rd 197 BQ94
Rowlatt Cl, Dart. DA2 210 FJ91
Rowlatt Ct, St.Alb. AL1
off Hillside Rd 65 CE19
Rowlatt Dr, St.Alb. AL3 64 CA22
Rowlatt Rd, Dart. DA2
off Whitehead Cl 210 FJ90
Rowley Av, Sid. DA15 208 EV87
Rowley Cl, Pyrford GU22 250 BG116
Watford WD19
off Lower Paddock Rd 98 BY44
Wembley HA0 160 CM66
Rowley Ct, Cat. CR3 258 DQ122
Rowley Gdns, N4 144 DQ59
Cheshunt EN8 89 DX28
ROWLEY GREEN, Barn. EN5 101 CT42
Rowley Grn Rd, Barn. EN5 101 CT43
● Rowley Ind Pk, W3 180 CP76
Rowley La, Barn. EN5 101 CT43
Borehamwood WD6 100 CR39
Wexham SL3 154 AW67
Rowley Mead, Thnwd CM16 92 EW25
Rowley Rd, N15 144 DQ57
Rowleys Rd, Hert. SG13 54 DT08
Rowley Wk, Hem.H. HP2 63 BQ15
Rowley Way, NW8 5 M8
Rowlheys Pl, West Dr. UB7 176 BL76
Rowlls Rd, Kings.T. KT1 220 CM97
Rowmarsh Cl, Nthflt DA11 212 GD91
Rowney Gdns, Dag. RM9 168 EW65
Sawbridgeworth CM21 58 EW07
Rowney Rd, Dag. RM9 168 EV65
Rowney Wd, Saw. CM21 58 EW06
Rowntree Clifford Cl, E13 24 A4
Rowntree Cl, NW6 5 K5
Rowntree Path, SE28
off Booth Cl 168 EV73
Rowntree Rd, Twick. TW2 199 CE88
Rows, The, Harl. CM20
off East Gate 57 ER14
Rowse Cl, E15 12 F8
Rowsley Av, NW4 141 CW55
Rowstock Gdns, N7 7 P3
Rowton Rd, SE18 187 EQ80
ROWTOWN, Add. KT15 233 BF108
Rowtown, Add. KT15 233 BF108
Rowzill Rd, Swan. BR8 209 FF93
Roxborough Av, Har. HA1 139 CD59
Isleworth TW7 179 CF80
Roxborough Pk, Har. HA1 139 CE59
Roxborough Rd, Har. HA1 139 CD57
Roxbourne Cl, Nthlt. UB5 158 BX65
Roxbourne First & Mid Schs,
S.Har. HA2 off Torbay Rd 138 BY61
Roxburgh Av, Upmin. RM14 150 FQ62
Roxburgh Rd, SE27 203 DP92
Roxburn Way, Ruis. HA4 137 BT62
Roxby Pl, SW6 39 K2
ROXETH, Har. HA2 139 CD61
Roxeth Ct, Ashf. TW15 196 BN92
Roxeth First & Mid Sch, Har.
HA2 off Brickfields 139 CD61
Roxeth Grn Av, Har. HA2 138 CB62
Roxeth Gro, Har. HA2 138 CB63
Roxeth Hill, Har. HA2 139 CD61
Roxeth Manor First & Mid Schs,
S.Har. HA2 off Eastcote La 138 CA62
Roxford Cl, Shep. TW17 217 BS99
Roxley Rd, SE13 205 EB86
Roxton Gdns, Croy. CR0 243 EA106
Roxwell Cl, Slou. SL1 153 AL74
Roxwell Gdns, Hutt. CM13 131 GC43
Roxwell Rd, W12 181 CU75
Barking IG11 168 EU68
● Roxwell Trd Pk, E10 145 DX59
Roxwell Way, Wdf.Grn. IG8 124 EJ52
Roxy Av, Rom. RM6 148 EW59
★ Royal Acad of Arts, W1 29 L1
Royal Acad of Dance, SW11 40 B7
★ Royal Acad of Dramatic Art
(R.A.D.A.), WC1 17 P6
Royal Acad of Music, NW1 17 H5
★ Royal Air Force Mus, NW9 119 CU54
Royal Albert 24 G10
Royal Albert Dock, E16 37 J1
★ Royal Albert Hall, SW7 28 A5
Royal Albert Rbt, E16 24 G10
Royal Albert Way, E16 24 F10
Royal Alexandra & Albert Sch,
Reig. RH2
off Rocky La 272 DE129
Royal Arc, W1 29 L1
Royal Artillery Barracks, SE18 37 L10
Royal Av, SW3 28 E10
Waltham Cross EN8 89 DY33
Worcester Park KT4 220 CS103
Royal Ballet Sch, The, Upr Sch,
WC2 18 B9
Royal Ballet Sch, The, Lwr Sch,
Rich. TW10
off Richmond Pk 200 CR88
★ Royal Berkshire Yeomanry
Mus (Windsor TA Cen),
Wind. SL4 173 AR83
★ Royal Botanic Gdns, Kew,
Rich. TW9 180 CL80
Royal Brompton Hosp,
SW3 28 C10
Annexe, SW3 28 B10
Royal Circ, SE27 203 DN90
Royal Cl, N16 144 DS60
SE8 45 N2
SW19 201 CX90
Ilford IG3 148 EU59
Orpington BR6 245 EP105
Uxbridge UB8 156 BM72
Worcester Park KT4 220 CS103
Royal Coll of Anaesthetists,
The, WC1 18 C7
Royal Coll of Art, SW7 27 P5
Royal Coll of Art, Sculpture Sch,
SW11 40 C5
Royal Coll of Defence Studies,
SW1 29 H6
Royal Coll of Music, SW7 28 A6
Royal Coll of Nursing, W1 17 J8
Royal Coll of Obstetricians &
Gynaecologists, NW1 16 E4
Royal Coll of Physicians,
NW1 17 K4
★ Royal Coll of Surgeons of
England, WC2 18 D8
Royal Coll St, NW1 7 L6
Royal Ct, EC3
off Royal Ex Bldgs 19 M9
SE16 33 N6
Hemel Hempstead HP3 62 BL23
★ Royal Courts of Justice,
WC2 18 D9
Royal Cres, W11 26 D3
Ilford IG2 147 ER58
Ruislip HA4 138 BY63
Royal Cres Ms, W11 26 D3
Royal Docks Comm Sch, The,
E16 24 D9
Royal Docks Rd, E6 25 P10
★ Royal Dress Collection
(Kensington Palace), W8 27 M3
Royal Dr, N11 120 DG50
Epsom KT18 255 CV118
Royal Duchess Ms, SW12
off Dinsmore Rd 203 DH87
Royal Earlswood Pk, Red.
RH1 288 DG138
Royale Leisure Pk, W3 160 CN70
Royal Ex, EC3 19 M9
Royal Ex Av, EC3 19 M9
Royal Ex Bldgs, EC3 19 M9
★ Royal Festival Hall, SE1 30 D3
Royal Free & Uni Coll Med Sch,
Royal Free Campus, NW3 6 D2
Royal Free Hosp, The, NW3 6 D2
Royal Gdns, W7 179 CG76
★ Royal Geographical Society,
SW7 28 A5
Royal Gram Sch, Guil. GU1
off High St 280 AY135
Royal Herbert Pavilions, SE18 187 EM81
Royal Hill, SE10 46 E4
Royal Holloway Coll, Egh.
TW20 off Egham Hill 194 AX93
Inst for Environmental Research,
Vir.W. GU25 off Callow Hill 214 AW96
Kingswood Hall of Res, Egh.
TW20 off Coopers Hill La 194 AX91
Royal Horticultural Society Cotts,
Wisley GU23 off Wisley La 250 BL116
★ Royal Horticultural Society Gdn
Wisley, Wok. GU22 250 BL119
★ Royal Horticultural Society
(Lawrence Hall), SW1 29 N7
★ Royal Horticultural Society
(Lindley Hall), SW1 29 N8
★ Royal Hosp Chelsea & Mus,
SW3 40 G1
Royal Hosp for Neuro-Disability,
SW15 201 CY86
Royal Hosp Rd, SW3 40 E2
Royal Jubilee Ct, Rom. RM2 149 FG55
Royal Kent C of E Prim Sch,
The, Oxshott KT22
off Oakshade Rd 236 CC114
Royal La, Uxb. UB8 156 BM69
West Drayton UB7 156 BM72
Royal Liberty Sch, The,
Gidea Pk RM2
off Upper Brentwood Rd 150 FJ55
Royal London Homoeopathic
Hosp, WC1 18 B6
Royal London Hosp, The,
St. Clements, E3 21 P3
Whitechapel, E1 20 E7
Whitechapel - Dentistry Cen,
E1 20 E7
Royal Marsden Hosp, The,
SW3 28 B10
Sutton SM2 240 DC110
Royal Masonic Sch for Girls,
The, Rick. WD3
off Chorleywood Rd 96 BK44
★ Royal Mews, The, SW1 29 K6
Royal Military Sch of Music,
Twick. TW2 off Kneller Rd 199 CD86
Royal Mint Ct, EC3 32 B1
Royal Mint Pl, E1 20 B10
Royal Mint St, E1 20 B10
Royal Mt Ct, Twick. TW2 199 CE90
Royal Nat Inst for the Blind
Sunshine Ho Sch, Nthwd.
HA6 off Dene Rd 115 BR51
Royal Nat Orthopaedic Hosp,
W1 17 K5
Stanmore HA7 117 CJ47
★ Royal National Rose Society -
Gdns of the Rose, The,
St.Alb. AL2 82 BY26
Royal National Throat, Nose &
Ear Hosp, WC1 18 C2
Royal Naval Pl, SE14 45 N4
⊖ Royal Oak 15 M7
Royal Oak Ct, N1 19 N2
Royal Oak Ms, Tedd. TW11
off High St 199 CG92
Royal Oak Pl, SE22 204 DV86
Royal Oak Rd, E8 10 E4
Bexleyheath DA6 208 EZ85
Woking GU21 248 AW118
Royal Oak Ter, Grav. DA12
off Constitution Hill 213 GJ88
Royal Oak Yd, SE1 31 N5
★ Royal Observatory Greenwich
(Flamsteed Ho), SE10 47 H4
Royal Opera Arc, SW1 29 N2
★ Royal Opera Ho, WC2 18 B10
Royal Orchard Cl, SW18 201 CY87
Royal Par, SE3 47 L9
SW6 off Dawes Rd 38 E4
W5 off Western Av 160 CL69
Chislehurst BR7 207 EQ94
Richmond TW9
off Station App 180 CN81
Royal Par Ms, SE3 47 L9
Chislehurst BR7 207 EQ94
Royal Pk Prim Sch, Sid. DA14
off Riverside Rd 208 EY90
Royal Pier Ms, Grav. DA12
off Royal Pier Rd 213 GH86
Royal Pier Rd, Grav. DA12 213 GH86
Royal Pl, SE10 46 F5

Royal Quarter, Kings.T. KT2 . . . **220** CL95
Royal Rd, E16 . . . **24** E9
SE17 . . . **42** G2
Darenth DA2 . . . **210** FN92
St. Albans AL1 . . . **65** CH20
Sidcup DA14 . . . **208** EX90
Teddington TW11 . . . **199** CD92
Royal Route, Wem. HA9 . . . **140** CM63
Royal Russell Prep Sch, Croy.
CR0 *off Coombe La* . . . **242** DV106
Royal Russell Sen Sch, Croy.
CR0 *off Coombe La* . . . **242** DV107
● **Royals Business Pk, The**,
E16 . . . **36** G1
Royal Sch Hampstead, The,
NW3 . . . **6** A1
Royal Sch of Needlework,
E.Mol. KT8
off Hampton Ct Palace . . . **219** CF98
Royal St, SE1 . . . **30** D6
Royal Surrey Co Hosp, Guil.
GU2 . . . **264** AS134
Royal Swan Quarter, Lthd. KT22
off Leret Way . . . **253** CH121
Royalty Ms, W1 . . . **17** N9
Royal Vet Coll - Boltons Pk Fm,
Pot.B. EN6
off Hawkshead Rd . . . **86** DA29
Royal Vet Coll - Camden Campus,
Beaumont Animal's Hosp,
NW1 . . . **7** M9
Royal Coll St, NW1 . . . **7** N9
Royal Vet Coll - Hawkshead Campus, N.Mymms AL9
off Hawkshead La . . . **85** CX28
Royal Victoria . . . **23** N10
Royal Victoria Dock, E16 . . . **36** A1
● **Royal Victoria Patriotic Bldg**,
SW18 . . . **202** DD86
Royal Victoria Pl, E16 . . . **36** B2
Royal Victoria Sq, E16 . . . **36** A1
Royal Victor Pl, E3 . . . **21** K1
Royal Wk, Wall. SM6
off Prince Charles Way . . . **223** DH104
Royce Cl, Brox. EN10 . . . **71** DZ21
Royce Gro, Lvsdn WD25 . . . **81** BT34
Roycraft Av, Bark. IG11 . . . **167** ET68
Roycraft Cl, Bark. IG11 . . . **167** ET68
Roycroft Cl, E18 . . . **124** EH53
SW2 . . . **203** DN88
Roydene Rd, SE18 . . . **187** ES79
ROYDON, Harl. CM19 . . . **72** EH15
Roydon . . . **56** EG13
● **Roydonbury Ind Est**, Harl.
CM19 . . . **72** EL15
Roydon Cl, SW11 . . . **40** F8
Loughton IG10 . . . **124** EL45
Roydon Ct, Hersham KT12 . . . **235** BU105
ROYDON HAMLET, Harl. CM19 . **72** EJ19
Roydon Lo Chalet Est, Roydon
CM19 . . . **56** EJ14
Roydon Mill Pk, Roydon CM19 . **56** EG14
Roydon Prim Sch, Roydon
CM19 *off Epping Rd* . . . **72** EH15
Roydon Rd, Harl. CM19 . . . **56** EL14
Stanstead Abbotts SG12 . . . **56** EE11
Roydon St, SW11 . . . **41** J6
Roy Gdns, Ilf. IG2 . . . **147** ES56
Roy Gro, Hmptn. TW12 . . . **198** CB93
Royle Bldg, N1 . . . **9** J10
Royle Cl, Chal.St.P. SL9 . . . **113** AZ52
Romford RM2 . . . **149** FH57
Royle Cres, W13 . . . **159** CG70
Roy Rd, Nthwd. HA6 . . . **115** BT52
Roy Sq, E14 . . . **21** M10
Royston Av, E4 . . . **123** EA50
Byfleet KT14 . . . **234** BL112
Sutton SM1 . . . **222** DD104
Wallington SM6 . . . **241** DK105
Royston Cl, Hert. SG14 . . . **53** DP09
Hounslow TW5 . . . **177** BV81
Walton-on-Thames KT12 . . . **217** BU102
Royston Ct, SE24 . . . **204** DQ86
Richmond TW9 . . . **180** CM81
Surbiton KT6 . . . **220** CN104
Royston Gdns, Ilf. IG1 . . . **146** EK58
Royston Gro, Pnr. HA5 . . . **116** BZ51
Royston Par, Ilf. IG1 . . . **146** EK58
Royston Pk Rd, Pnr. HA5 . . . **116** BZ51
Royston Prim Sch, SE20
off High St . . . **225** DX95
Royston Rd, SE20 . . . **225** DX95
Byfleet KT14 . . . **234** BL112
Dartford DA1 . . . **209** FF86
Richmond TW10 . . . **200** CL85
Romford RM3 . . . **128** FN52
St. Albans AL1 . . . **65** CH21
Roystons, The, Surb. KT5 . . . **220** CP99
Royston St, E2 . . . **21** H1
Royston Way, Slou. SL1 . . . **152** AJ71
Rozel Ct, N1 . . . **9** N8
Rozel Rd, SW4 . . . **41** L9
Rubastic Rd, Sthl. UB2 . . . **178** BW76
Rubeck Cl, Red. RH1 . . . **273** DH132
Rubens Pl, SW4
off Dolman St . . . **183** DM84
Rubens Rd, Nthlt. UB5 . . . **158** BW68
Rubens St, SE6 . . . **205** DZ89
Rubin Pl, Enf. EN3 . . . **105** EA37
Ruby Cl, Slou. SL1 . . . **173** AN75
Ruby Ms, E17 *off Ruby Rd* . . . **145** EA55
Ruby Rd, E17 . . . **145** EA55
Ruby St, NW10 . . . **160** CQ66
SE15 . . . **44** E2
Ruby Triangle, SE15 . . . **44** E2
Ruby Way, NW9 . . . **119** CT53
Ruckholt Cl, E10 . . . **145** EB62
Ruckholt Rd, E10 . . . **12** B1
Rucklers La, Kings L. WD4 . . . **80** BK27
Ruckles Way, Amer. HP7 . . . **77** AQ40
Rucklidge Av, NW10 . . . **161** CT68
Rudall Cres, NW3
off Willoughby Rd . . . **142** DD63
Ruddington Cl, E5 . . . **145** DY63
Ruddlesway, Wind. SL4 . . . **173** AK81
Ruddock Cl, Edg. HA8 . . . **118** CQ52
Ruddstreet Cl, SE18 . . . **37** P9
Ruden Way, Epsom KT17 . . . **255** CV116
Rudge Ri, Add. KT15 . . . **233** BF106
Rudgwick Keep, Horl. RH6
off Langshott La . . . **291** DJ147
Rudgwick Ter, NW8 . . . **6** D9
Rudland Rd, Bexh. DA7 . . . **189** FB83
Rudloe Rd, SW12 . . . **203** DJ87
Rudolf Pl, SW8 . . . **42** B3
Rudolf Steiner Sch - Kings Langley, Kings L.
WD4 *off Langley Hill* . . . **80** BM29
Rudolph Rd, E13 . . . **23** M1
NW6 . . . **15** K1
Bushey WD23 . . . **98** CA44
Rudstone Ho, E3
off Bromley High St . . . **22** C2
Rudsworth Cl, Colnbr. SL3 . . . **175** BD80
Rudyard Gro, NW7 . . . **118** CQ51
Rue de St. Lawrence, Wal.Abb.
EN9 *off Quaker La* . . . **89** EC34
Ruffets Wd, Grav. DA12 . . . **213** GJ93
Ruffetts, The, S.Croy. CR2 . . . **242** DV108
Ruffetts Cl, S.Croy. CR2 . . . **242** DV108
Ruffetts Way, Tad. KT20 . . . **255** CY118
Ruffle Cl, West Dr. UB7 . . . **176** BL75
Rufford Cl, Har. HA3 . . . **139** CG58
Watford WD17 . . . **97** BT37
Rufford St, N1 . . . **8** B8
Rufford Twr, W3 . . . **160** CP74
● **Rufus Business Cen**,
SW18 . . . **202** DB89
Rufus Cl, Ruis. HA4 . . . **138** BY62
Rufus St, N1 . . . **19** N3
Rugby Av, N9 . . . **122** DT46
Greenford UB6 . . . **159** CD65
Wembley HA0 . . . **139** CH64
Rugby Cl, Har. HA1 . . . **139** CE57
★ **Rugby Football Union Twickenham**, Twick. TW1 . . . **199** CE86
Rugby Gdns, Dag. RM9 . . . **168** EW65
Rugby La, Sutt. SM2
off Nonsuch Wk . . . **239** CX109
Rugby Rd, NW9 . . . **140** CP56
W4 . . . **180** CS75
Dagenham RM9 . . . **168** EV66
Twickenham TW1 . . . **199** CE86
Rugby St, WC1 . . . **18** C5
Rugby Way, Crox.Grn WD3 . . . **97** BP43
Rugged La, Wal.Abb. EN9 . . . **90** EK33
Ruggles-Brise Rd, Ashf. TW15 . **196** BK92
Rugg St, E14 . . . **22** A10
RUISLIP, HA4 . . . **137** BS59
Ruislip . . . **137** BS60
Ruislip Adult Learning Cen,
Ruis. HA4
off Sidmouth Dr . . . **137** BU62
Ruislip Cl, Grnf. UB6 . . . **158** CB70
RUISLIP COMMON, Ruis.
HA4 . . . **137** BR57
Ruislip Ct, Ruis. HA4
off Courtfield Gdns . . . **137** BT61
RUISLIP GARDENS, Ruis.
HA4 . . . **137** BS63
Ruislip Gardens . . . **137** BU63
Ruislip Gdns Prim Sch, Ruis.
HA4 *off Stafford Rd* . . . **137** BT63
Ruislip High Sch, Ruis. HA4
off Sidmouth Dr . . . **137** BU62
RUISLIP MANOR, Ruis. HA4 . . **137** BU61
Ruislip Manor . . . **137** BU60
● **Ruislip Retail Pk**, Ruis.
HA4 . . . **138** BY63
Ruislip Rd, Grnf. UB6 . . . **158** CA69
Northolt UB5 . . . **158** BX69
Ruislip Rd E, W7 . . . **159** CD70
W13 . . . **159** CD70
Greenford UB6 . . . **159** CD70
Ruislip St, SW17 . . . **202** DF91
Rumania Wk, Grav. DA12 . . . **213** GM90
Rumballs Cl, Hem.H. HP3 . . . **62** BN23
Rumballs Rd, Hem.H. HP3 . . . **62** BN23
Rumbold Rd, SW6 . . . **39** M5
Hoddesdon EN11 . . . **71** EC15
Rum Cl, E1 . . . **32** G1
Rumford Ho, SE1 *off Bath Ter* . . **31** J6
Rumford Shop Hall, Rom.
RM1 *off Market Pl* . . . **149** FE56
Rumsey Cl, Hmptn. TW12 . . . **198** BZ93
Rumsey Ms, N4 . . . **143** DP62
Rumsey Rd, SW9 . . . **42** D10
Rumsley, Wal.Cr. EN7 . . . **88** DU27
Runbury Circle, NW9 . . . **140** CR61
Runcie Cl, St.Alb. AL4 . . . **65** CG16
Runciman Cl, Orp. BR6 . . . **246** EW110
Runcorn Cl, N17 . . . **144** DV56
Runcorn Cres, Hem.H. HP2 . . . **62** BM16
Runcorn Pl, W11 . . . **14** E10
Rundell Cres, NW4 . . . **141** CV57
Rundells, Harl. CM18 . . . **74** EU19
Rundell Twr, SW8 . . . **42** C6
Runes Cl, Mitch. CR4 . . . **222** DD98
Runham Rd, Hem.H. HP3 . . . **62** BL22
Runnel Ct, Bark. IG11
off Spring Pl . . . **167** EQ68
Runnelfield, Har. HA1 . . . **139** CE62
Runnemede Rd, Egh. TW20 . . . **195** AZ91
Running Horse Yd, Brent. TW8
off Pottery Rd . . . **180** CL79
Running Waters, Brwd. CM13 . **131** GA49
Runnymede, SW19 . . . **222** DD95
Runnymede Cen, The, Add.
KT15 *off Chertsey Rd* . . . **216** BH103
Runnymede Cl, Twick. TW2 . . . **198** CB86
Runnymede Ct, SW15 . . . **201** CU88
Croydon CR0 . . . **224** DT103
Egham TW20 . . . **195** BA91
Runnymede Cres, SW16 . . . **223** DK95
Runnymede Gdns, Grnf. UB6 . **159** CD68
Twickenham TW2 . . . **198** CB86
Runnymede Hosp, Cher.
KT16 . . . **215** BD104
Runnymede Ho, E9
off Kingsmead Way . . . **11** M1
Runnymede Rd, Twick. TW2 . . . **198** CB86
Runrig Hill, Amer. HP6 . . . **77** AS35
Runsley, Welw.G.C. AL7 . . . **51** CZ06
Runtley Wd La, Sutt.Grn GU4 . **265** AZ125
Runway, The, Hat. AL10 . . . **66** CR16
Ruislip HA4 . . . **137** BV64
Runway Cl, NW9
off Great Strand . . . **119** CT54
Rupack St, SE16 . . . **32** G5
Rupert Av, Wem. HA9 . . . **140** CL64
Rupert Ct, W1 . . . **17** N10
West Molesey KT8
off St. Peter's Rd . . . **218** CA98
Rupert Gdns, SW9 . . . **42** G9
Rupert Rd, N19
off Holloway Rd . . . **143** DK61
NW6 . . . **15** H1
W4 . . . **180** CS76
Guildford GU2 . . . **280** AV135
Rupert St, W1 . . . **17** N10
Rural Cl, Horn. RM11 . . . **149** FH60
Rural Vale, Nthflt DA11 . . . **212** GE87
Rural Way, SW16 . . . **203** DH94
Redhill RH1 . . . **272** DG134
Rusbridge Cl, E8 . . . **10** C2
Ruscoe Dr, Wok. GU22
off Pembroke Rd . . . **249** BA117
Ruscoe Rd, E16 . . . **23** L8
Ruscombe Dr, Park St AL2 . . . **82** CB26
Ruscombe Gdns, Datchet SL3 . **174** AU80
Ruscombe Way, Felt. TW14 . . . **197** BT87
Rush, The, SW19
off Kingston Rd . . . **221** CZ95
Rusham Ct, Egh. TW20
off Rusham Pk Av . . . **195** BA93
Rusham Pk Av, Egh. TW20 . . . **195** AZ93
Rusham Rd, SW12 . . . **202** DF86
Egham TW20 . . . **195** AZ93
Rushbrook Cres, E17 . . . **123** DZ53
Rushbrook Rd, SE9 . . . **207** EQ89
Rushburn, Woob.Grn HP10 . . . **132** AF57
Rush Cl, Stans.Abb. SG12 . . . **55** EC11
Rush Common Ms, SW2 . . . **203** DM87
Rush Cft, Gdmg. GU7 . . . **280** AU143
Rushcroft Rd, E4 . . . **123** EA52
SW2 . . . **183** DN84
Rush Cft Sch, E4
off Rushcroft Rd . . . **123** EB52
Rushden Cl, SE19 . . . **204** DR94
Rushdene, SE2 . . . **188** EX76
Rushdene Av, Barn. EN4 . . . **120** DE45
Rushdene Cl, Nthlt. UB5 . . . **158** BW68
Rushdene Cres, Nthlt. UB5 . . . **158** BW68
Rushdene Rd, Brwd. CM15 . . . **130** FW45
Pinner HA5 . . . **138** BX58
Rushdene Wk, Bigg.H. TN16 . . . **260** EK117
Rushden Gdns, NW7 . . . **119** CW51
Ilford IG5 . . . **147** EN55
Rushdon Cl, Grays RM17 . . . **192** GA76
Romford RM1 . . . **149** FG57
Rush Dr, Wal.Abb. EN9 . . . **105** EC36
Rushen Dr, Hert.Hth SG13 . . . **54** DW12
Rushen Wk, Cars. SM5
off Paisley Rd . . . **222** DD102
Rushes Mead, Harl. CM18 . . . **73** ES17
Uxbridge UB8
off Frays Waye . . . **156** BJ67
Rushet Rd, Orp. BR5 . . . **228** EU96
Rushett Cl, T.Ditt. KT7 . . . **219** CH102
Rushett Dr, Dor. RH4 . . . **285** CH139
Rushett La, Epsom KT18 . . . **237** CJ111
Rushett Rd, T.Ditt. KT7 . . . **219** CH101
Rushetts Rd, Reig. RH2 . . . **288** DC138
Rushey Cl, N.Mal. KT3 . . . **220** CR98
Rushey Grn, SE6 . . . **205** EB87
Rushey Grn Prim Sch, SE6
off Culverley Rd . . . **205** EB88
Rushey Hill, Enf. EN2 . . . **103** DM42
Rushey Mead, SE4 . . . **205** EA85
Rushfield, Pot.B. EN6 . . . **85** CX33
Sawbridgeworth CM21 . . . **58** EY05
Rushford Rd, SE4 . . . **205** DZ86
RUSH GREEN, Rom. RM7 . . . **149** FC59
Rush Grn Gdns, Rom. RM7 . . . **149** FC60
Rush Grn Inf Sch, Rom. RM7
off Dagenham Rd . . . **149** FD60
Rush Grn Jun Sch, Rom. RM7
off Dagenham Rd . . . **149** FE60
Rush Grn Rd, Rom. RM7 . . . **149** FC60
Rushgrove Av, NW9 . . . **141** CT57
Rushgrove St, SE18 . . . **37** K9
Rush Hill Ms, SW11
off Rush Hill Rd . . . **182** DG83
Rush Hill Rd, SW11 . . . **182** DG83
Rushleigh Av, Chsht EN8 . . . **89** DX31
Rushley Cl, Kes. BR2 . . . **244** EK105
Rushmead, E2 . . . **20** E3
Richmond TW10 . . . **199** CH90
Rushmead Cl, Croy. CR0 . . . **242** DT105
Rushmere Av, Upmin. RM14 . . . **150** FQ62
Rushmere Ct, Wor.Pk. KT4
off The Avenue . . . **221** CU103
Rushmere Ho, SW15
off Fontley Way . . . **201** CU88
Rushmere La, Orch.L. HP5 . . . **78** AU28
Rushmere Pl, SW19 . . . **201** CX92
Englefield Green TW20 . . . **194** AY92
Rushmon Gdns, Walt. KT12
off Collingwood Pl . . . **217** BV104
Rushmoor Cl, Guil. GU2 . . . **264** AT131
Pinner HA5 . . . **137** BV56
Rickmansworth WD3 . . . **114** BK47
Rushmore Cl, Brom. BR1 . . . **226** EL97
Rushmore Cres, E5
off Rushmore Rd . . . **145** DX63
Rushmore Hill, Knock.P. TN14 . **246** EX112
Orpington BR6 . . . **246** EW110
Rushmore Prim Sch, E5
off Elderfield Rd . . . **145** DX63
Rushmore Rd, E5 . . . **144** DW63
Rusholme Av, Dag. RM10 . . . **148** FA62
Rusholme Gro, SE19 . . . **204** DS92
Rusholme Rd, SW15 . . . **201** CX86
Rushout Av, Har. HA3 . . . **139** CH58
Rushton Av, Wat. WD25 . . . **97** BU35
Rushton Gro, Harl. CM17 . . . **74** EX15
Rushton St, N1 . . . **9** M10
Rushworth Rd, Reig. RH2 . . . **272** DA133
Rushworth St, SE1 . . . **31** H4
Rushy Meadow La, Cars.
SM5 . . . **222** DE103
Rushy Meadow Prim Sch,
Cars. SM5
off Rushy Meadow La . . . **222** DE104
Ruskin Av, E12 . . . **166** EL65
Feltham TW14 . . . **197** BT86
Richmond TW9 . . . **180** CN80
Upminster RM14 . . . **150** FQ59
Waltham Abbey EN9 . . . **90** EE34
Welling DA16 . . . **188** EU83
Ruskin Cl, NW11 . . . **142** DB58
Cheshunt EN7 . . . **88** DS26
Ruskin Dr, Orp. BR6 . . . **227** ES104
Welling DA16 . . . **188** EU83
Worcester Park KT4 . . . **221** CV103
Ruskin Gdns, W5 . . . **159** CK70
Harrow HA3 . . . **140** CM56
Romford RM3 . . . **127** FH52
Ruskin Gro, Dart. DA1 . . . **210** FN85
Welling DA16 . . . **188** EU82
Ruskin Pk Ho, SE5 . . . **43** M10
Ruskin Rd, N17 . . . **122** DT53
Belvedere DA17 . . . **188** FA77
Carshalton SM5 . . . **240** DF106
Croydon CR0 . . . **223** DP103
Grays RM16 . . . **193** GG77
Isleworth TW7 . . . **179** CF83
Southall UB1 . . . **158** BY73
Staines TW18 . . . **195** BF94
Ruskin Wk, N9 . . . **122** DU47
SE24 . . . **204** DQ85
Bromley BR2 . . . **227** EM100
Ruskin Way, SW19 . . . **222** DD95
Rusland Av, Orp. BR6 . . . **227** ER104
Rusland Hts, Har. HA1
off Rusland Pk Rd . . . **139** CE56
Rusland Pk Rd, Har. HA1 . . . **139** CE56
Rusper Cl, NW2 . . . **141** CW62
Stanmore HA7 . . . **117** CJ49
Rusper Rd, N22 . . . **122** DQ54
Dagenham RM9 . . . **168** EW65
Russell Av, N22 . . . **121** DP54
St. Albans AL3 . . . **65** CD20
Russell Cl, NW10 . . . **160** CQ66
SE7 . . . **186** EJ80
W4 . . . **181** CT79
Amersham HP6 . . . **94** AX39
Beckenham BR3 . . . **225** EB97
Bexleyheath DA7 . . . **188** FA84
Brentwood CM15 . . . **130** FV45
Dartford DA1 . . . **189** FG83
Northwood HA6 . . . **115** BQ50
Ruislip HA4 . . . **138** BW61
Walton on the Hill KT20 . . . **271** CU125
Woking GU21 . . . **248** AW115
Russell Ct, SW1 . . . **29** M3
Bricket Wood AL2 . . . **82** CA30
Chesham HP5 . . . **76** AR29
Guildford GU1 . . . **264** AW131
Leatherhead KT22 . . . **253** CH122
Surbiton KT6 . . . **220** CL101
Russell Cres, Wat. WD25 . . . **97** BT35
Russellcroft Rd, Welw.G.C. AL8 . **51** CW08
Russell Dr, Stanw. TW19 . . . **196** BK86
Russell Gdns, N20 . . . **120** DE47
NW11 . . . **141** CY58
W14 . . . **26** E6
Richmond TW10 . . . **199** CJ89
Sipson UB7 . . . **176** BN78
Russell Gdns Ms, W14 . . . **26** E5
Russell Grn Cl, Pur. CR8 . . . **241** DN110
Russell Gro, NW7 . . . **118** CS50
SW9 . . . **42** F5
Russell Hill, Pur. CR8 . . . **241** DM110
Russell Hill Pl, Pur. CR8 . . . **241** DN111
Russell Hill Rd, Pur. CR8 . . . **241** DN110
Russell Kerr Cl, W4 . . . **180** CQ80
Russell La, N20 . . . **120** DE47
Watford WD17 . . . **97** BR36
Russell Lo, SE1
off Spurgeon St . . . **31** L6
Russell Mead, Har.Wld HA3 . . . **117** CF53
Russell Par, NW11
off Golders Grn Rd . . . **141** CY58
Russell Pl, NW3 . . . **6** D2
SE16 . . . **33** L7
Hemel Hempstead HP3 . . . **62** BH23
Sutton at Hone DA4 . . . **230** FN95
Russell Prim Sch, The, Rich.
TW10 *off Petersham Rd* . . . **199** CK88
Russell Rd, E4 . . . **123** DZ49
E10 . . . **145** EB58
E16 . . . **23** P8
E17 . . . **145** DZ55
N8 . . . **143** DK58
N13 . . . **121** DM51
N15 . . . **144** DS57
N20 . . . **120** DE47
NW9 . . . **141** CT58
SW19 . . . **202** DA94
W14 . . . **26** E6
Buckhurst Hill IG9 . . . **124** EH46
Enfield EN1 . . . **104** DT38
Gravesend DA12 . . . **213** GK86
Grays RM17 . . . **192** GA77
Mitcham CR4 . . . **222** DE97
Northolt UB5 . . . **138** CC64
Northwood HA6 . . . **115** BQ49
Shepperton TW17 . . . **217** BQ101
Tilbury RM18 . . . **192** GE81
Tilbury (cul-de-sac) RM18 . . . **193** GF82
Twickenham TW2 . . . **199** CF86
Walton-on-Thames KT12 . . . **217** BU100
Woking GU21 . . . **248** AW115
Russells, Tad. KT20 . . . **255** CX122
Russell Sch, The, Chorl. WD3
off Brushwood Dr . . . **95** BB42
Russells Cres, Horl. RH6 . . . **290** DG149
Russell's Footpath, SW16 . . . **203** DL92
Russell Square . . . **18** A5
Russell Sq, WC1 . . . **18** A5
Longfield DA3
off Cavendish Sq . . . **231** FX97
Russells Ride, Chsht EN8 . . . **89** DX31
Russell St, WC2 . . . **18** B10
Hertford SG14 . . . **54** DQ09
Windsor SL4 . . . **173** AR81
Russell's Way, S.Ock. RM15 . . . **171** FX72
Russell's Wf Flats, W10 . . . **14** G4
Russell Wk, Rich. TW10
off Park Hill . . . **200** CM86
Russell Way, Sutt. SM1 . . . **240** DA106
Watford WD19 . . . **115** BV45
Russell Wilson Ct, Rom. RM3
off Church Rd . . . **128** FN53
Russet Cl, Chsht EN7 . . . **88** DS26
Hersham KT12 . . . **218** BX104
Horley RH6
off Carlton Tye . . . **291** DJ148
Staines TW19 . . . **195** BF86
Uxbridge UB10
off Uxbridge Rd . . . **157** BQ70
Russet Cres, N7 . . . **8** C2
Russet Dr, Croy. CR0 . . . **225** DY102
St. Albans AL4 . . . **65** CJ21
Shenley WD7 . . . **84** CL32
Russet Ho Sch, Enf. EN1
off Autumn Cl . . . **104** DV39
Russets, The, Chal.St.P. SL9
off Austenwood Cl . . . **112** AX54
Russets Cl, E4
off Larkshall Rd . . . **123** ED49
Russett Cl, Orp. BR6 . . . **246** EV106
Russett Ct, Cat. CR3 . . . **274** DU125
Russett Hill, Chal.St.P. SL9 . . . **134** AY55
Russetts, Horn. RM11 . . . **150** FL56
Russetts Cl, Wok. GU21 . . . **249** AZ115
Russett Way, Swan. BR8 . . . **229** FD96
Russettwood, Welw.G.C. AL7 . . **52** DD10
Russet Way, N.Holm. RH5 . . . **285** CK140
Russia Dock Rd, SE16 . . . **33** M3
Russia La, E2 . . . **10** G10
Russia Row, EC2 . . . **19** K9
Russia Wk, SE16 . . . **33** K5
Russington Rd, Shep. TW17 . . . **217** BR100
Rusthall Av, W4 . . . **180** CR77
Rusthall Cl, Croy. CR0 . . . **224** DW100
Rustic Av, SW16 . . . **203** DH94
Rustic Cl, Upmin. RM14 . . . **151** FS60
Rustic Pl, Wem. HA0 . . . **139** CK63
Rustic Wk, E16 . . . **24** A8
Rustington Wk, Mord. SM4 . . . **221** CZ101
Ruston Av, Surb. KT5 . . . **220** CP101
Ruston Gdns, N14 *off Byre Rd* . **102** DG44
Ruston Ms, W11 . . . **14** E9
Ruston Rd, SE18 . . . **36** G7
Ruston St, E3 . . . **11** P8
Rust Sq, SE5 . . . **43** L4
Rutford Rd, SW16 . . . **203** DL92
Ruth Cl, Stan. HA7 . . . **140** CM56
Ruthen Cl, Epsom KT18 . . . **238** CP114
Rutherford Cl, Borwd. WD6 . . . **100** CQ40
Sutton SM2 . . . **240** DD107
Uxbridge UB8 . . . **156** BM70
Windsor SL4 . . . **173** AM81
Rutherford Sch, S.Croy. CR2
off Melville Av . . . **242** DT106
Rutherford St, SW1 . . . **29** N8
Rutherford Twr, Sthl. UB1 . . . **158** CB72
Rutherford Way, Bushey Hth
WD23 . . . **117** CD46
Wembley HA9 . . . **140** CN63
Rutherglen Rd, SE2 . . . **188** EU79
Rutherwick Cl, Horl. RH6 . . . **290** DF148
Rutherwick Ri, Couls. CR5 . . . **257** DL117
Rutherwyke Cl, Epsom KT17 . . **239** CU107
Rutherwyk Rd, Cher. KT16 . . . **215** BE101
Ruthin Cl, NW9 . . . **140** CS58
Ruthin Rd, SE3 . . . **47** N2
Ruthven Av, Wal.Cr. EN8 . . . **89** DX33
Ruthven St, E9 . . . **11** J8
Rutland App, Horn. RM11 . . . **150** FN57
Rutland Av, Sid. DA15 . . . **208** EU87
Slough SL1 . . . **153** AR71
Rutland Cl, SW14 . . . **180** CP83
SW19 *off Rutland Rd* . . . **202** DE94
Ashtead KT21 . . . **254** CL117
Bexley DA5 . . . **208** EX88
Chessington KT9 . . . **238** CM107
Dartford DA1 . . . **210** FK87
Epsom KT19 . . . **238** CR110
Redhill RH1 . . . **272** DF133
Rutland Ct, SW7
off Rutland Gdns . . . **28** D5
Enfield EN3 . . . **104** DW43
Rutland Dr, Horn. RM11 . . . **150** FN57
Morden SM4 . . . **221** CZ100
Richmond TW10 . . . **199** CK88
Rutland Gdns, N4 . . . **143** DP58
SW7 . . . **28** D5
W13 . . . **159** CG71
Croydon CR0 . . . **242** DS105
Dagenham RM8 . . . **148** EW64
Hemel Hempstead HP2 . . . **62** BM19
Rutland Gdns Ms, SW7 . . . **28** D5
Rutland Gate, SW7 . . . **28** D5
Belvedere DA17 . . . **189** FB78
Bromley BR2 . . . **226** EF98
Rutland Gate Ms, SW7 . . . **28** C5
Rutland Gro, W6 . . . **181** CV78
Rutland Ms, NW8 . . . **5** M9
Rutland Ms E, SW7 . . . **28** C6
Rutland Ms S, SW7 . . . **28** C6
Rutland Ms W, SW7
off Ennismore St . . . **28** C6
Rutland Pk, NW2 . . . **4** B5
SE6 . . . **205** DZ89
Rutland Pk Gdns, NW2
off Rutland Pk . . . **4** B5
Rutland Pk Mans, NW2
off Rutland Pk . . . **4** B5
Rutland Pl, EC1 . . . **19** J5
Bushey Heath WD23
off The Rutts . . . **117** CD46
Rutland Rd, E7 . . . **166** EK66
E9 . . . **11** H8
E11 . . . **146** EH57
E17 . . . **145** EA58
SW19 . . . **202** DE94
Harrow HA1 . . . **138** CC58
Hayes UB3 . . . **177** BR77
Ilford IG1 . . . **147** EP63
Southall UB1 . . . **158** CA71
Twickenham TW2 . . . **199** CD89
Rutland St, SW7 . . . **28** D6
Rutland Wk, SE6 . . . **205** DZ89
Rutland Way, Orp. BR5 . . . **228** EW100
Rutley Cl, SE17 . . . **42** G2
Harold Wood RM3
off Pasteur Dr . . . **128** FK54
Rutlish Rd, SW19 . . . **222** DA95
Rutlish Sch, SW20
off Watery La . . . **221** CZ96
Rutson Rd, Byfleet KT14 . . . **234** BM114
Rutter Gdns, Mitch. CR4 . . . **222** DC98
Rutters Cl, West Dr. UB7 . . . **176** BN75
Rutts, The, Bushey Hth WD23 . **117** CD46
Rutts Ter, SE14 . . . **45** J7
Ruvigny Gdns, SW15 . . . **38** D10
Ruxbury Rd, Cher. KT16 . . . **215** BC100
Ruxley Cl, Epsom KT19 . . . **238** CP106
Sidcup DA14 . . . **208** EX93
Ruxley Cor, Sid. DA14 . . . **208** EY93
● **Ruxley Cor Ind Est**, Sid.
DA14 . . . **208** EX93
Ruxley Cres, Clay. KT10 . . . **237** CH107
Ruxley Gdns, Shep. TW17 . . . **217** BQ99
Ruxley La, Epsom KT19 . . . **238** CR106
Ruxley Ms, Epsom KT19 . . . **238** CP106
Ruxley Ridge, Clay. KT10 . . . **237** CG108
Ruxton Cl, Couls. CR5 . . . **257** DJ115
Swanley BR8 . . . **229** FE97
Ryall Cl, Brick.Wd AL2 . . . **82** BY29
Ryalls Ct, N20 . . . **120** DF48
Ryan Cl, SE3 . . . **186** EJ84
Ruislip HA4 . . . **137** BV60
Ryan Dr, Brent. TW8 . . . **179** CG79
Ryan Way, Wat. WD24 . . . **98** BW39
Ryarsh Cres, Orp. BR6 . . . **245** ES105
Rybrook Dr, Walt. KT12 . . . **218** BW103
Rycott Path, SE22
off Lordship La . . . **204** DU87
Rycroft, Wind. SL4 . . . **173** AM83
Rycroft La, Sev. TN14 . . . **278** FE130
Rycroft Way, N17 . . . **144** DT55
Ryculff Sq, SE3 . . . **47** M8
Rydal Cl, NW4 . . . **119** CY53
Purley CR8 . . . **242** DR113
Rydal Ct, Wat. WD25
off Grasmere Cl . . . **81** BV32
Rydal Cres, Perivale UB6 . . . **159** CH69
Rydal Dr, Bexh. DA7 . . . **188** FA81
West Wickham BR4 . . . **226** EE103
Rydal Gdns, NW9 . . . **140** CS57
SW15 . . . **200** CS92
Hounslow TW3 . . . **198** CB86
Wembley HA9 . . . **139** CJ60

Rydal Rd, SW16 . . . 203 DK91
Rydal Way, Egh. TW20 . . . 195 BB94
Enfield EN3 . . . 104 DW44
Ruislip HA4 . . . 138 BW63
RYDE, THE, Hat. AL9 . . . 67 CW15
Ryde, The, Hat. AL9 . . . 67 CW16
Staines TW18 . . . 216 BH95
Ryde Cl, Ripley GU23 . . . 250 BJ121
Ryde Heron, Knap. GU21 . . . 248 AS117
RYDENS, Walt. KT12 . . . 218 BW103
Rydens Av, Walt. KT12 . . . 217 BV103
Rydens Cl, Walt. KT12 . . . 218 BW103
Rydens Gro, Hersham KT12 . . . 236 BX105
Rydens Pk, Walt. KT12 . . . 218 BX103
Rydens Rd, Walt. KT12 . . . 218 BX103
Sch Rydens Sch, Hersham KT12
off Hersham Rd . . . 236 BW105
Rydens Way, Wok. GU22 . . . 249 BA120
Ryde Pl, Twick. TW1 . . . 199 CJ86
Ryder Cl, Bov. HP3 . . . 79 BA28
Bromley BR1 . . . 206 EH92
Bushey WD23 . . . 98 CB44
Hertford SG13 . . . 54 DV08
Ryder Ct, SW1 . . . 29 M2
Ryder Dr, SE16 . . . 44 E1
Ryder Gdns, Rain. RM13 . . . 169 FF65
Ryder Ms, E9 . . . 11 H3
Ryders Av, Coln.Hth AL4 . . . 66 CS20
Ryder Seed Ms, St.Alb. AL1
off Pageant Rd . . . 65 CD21
Ryders Ter, NW8 . . . 5 N10
Ryder St, SW1 . . . 29 M2
Ryder Yd, SW1 . . . 29 M2
Rydes Av, Guil. GU2 . . . 264 AT131
Sch Ryde Sch, The, Hat. AL9
off Pleasant Ri . . . 67 CW15
Rydes Cl, Wok. GU22 . . . 249 BC120
RYDESHILL, Guil. GU3 . . . 264 AS131
Rydes Hill Cres, Guil. GU2 . . . 264 AT130
Sch Rydes Hill Prep Sch, Guil.
GU2 off Aldershot Rd . . . 264 AT132
Rydes Hill Rd, Guil. GU2 . . . 264 AT132
Ryde Vale Rd, SW12 . . . 203 DH89
Rydings, Wind. SL4 . . . 173 AM83
● Rydon Business Cen, Lthd.
KT22 . . . 253 CH119
Rydon Ms, SW19 . . . 201 CW94
Rydons Cl, SE9 . . . 186 EL83
Rydon's La, Couls. CR5 . . . 258 DQ120
Rydon St, N1 . . . 9 K8
Rydons Way, Red. RH1 . . . 288 DG135
Rydon's Wd Cl, Couls. CR5 . . . 258 DQ120
Rydston Cl, N7 . . . 8 B6
Rye, The, N14 . . . 121 DJ45
Ryebridge Cl, Lthd. KT22 . . . 253 CG118
Ryebrook Rd, Lthd. KT22 . . . 253 CG118
Rye Cl, Bex. DA5 . . . 209 FB86
Guildford GU2 . . . 264 AS132
Hornchurch RM12 . . . 150 FJ64
Ryecotes Mead, SE21 . . . 204 DS88
Rye Ct, Slou. SL1
off Alpha St S . . . 174 AU76
Rye Cres, Orp. BR5 . . . 228 EW102
Ryecroft, Grav. DA12 . . . 213 GL92
Harlow CM19 . . . 73 EP15
Hatfield AL10 . . . 67 CT20
Ryecroft Av, Ilf. IG5 . . . 125 EP54
Twickenham TW2 . . . 198 CB87
Ryecroft Cl, Hem.H. HP2
off Poynders Hill . . . 63 BQ21
Ryecroft Ct, St.Alb. AL4 . . . 66 CM20
Ryecroft Cres, Barn. EN5 . . . 101 CV43
Ryecroft Rd, SE13 . . . 205 EC85
SW16 . . . 203 DN93
Chesham HP5 . . . 76 AN32
Otford TN14 . . . 263 FG116
Petts Wood BR5 . . . 227 ER100
Ryecroft St, SW6 . . . 39 L7
Ryedale, SE22 . . . 204 DV86
● Ryedale Ct, Sev. TN13
off London Rd . . . 278 FE121
Ryefeld Cl, Hodd. EN11 . . . 55 EB13
Rye Fld, Ashtd. KT21 . . . 253 CK117
Orpington BR5 . . . 228 EX102
Ryefield Av, Uxb. UB10 . . . 157 BP66
Ryefield Ct, Nthwd. HA6
off Ryefield Cres . . . 115 BU54
Ryefield Cres, Nthwd. HA6 . . . 115 BU54
Ryefield Par, Nthwd. HA6
off Ryefield Cres . . . 115 BU54
Ryefield Path, SW15 . . . 201 CU88
Sch Ryefield Prim Sch, Hlgdn
UB10 off Ryefield Av . . . 157 BQ67
Ryefield Rd, SE19 . . . 204 DQ93
Ryegates, SE15 . . . 44 F8
RYE HILL, Harl. CM18 . . . 73 ES22
Rye Hill Pk, SE15 . . . 184 DW84
Rye Hill Rd, Harl. CM18 . . . 73 ES22
Thornwood CM16 . . . 74 EU23
⇌ Rye House . . . 71 EC15
Ryeland Cl, West Dr. UB7 . . . 156 BL72
Ryelands, Horl. RH6 . . . 291 DJ147
Welwyn Garden City AL7 . . . 51 CZ12
Ryelands Cl, Cat. CR3 . . . 258 DS121
Ryelands Ct, Lthd. KT22 . . . 253 CG118
Ryelands Cres, SE12 . . . 206 EJ86
Ryelands Pl, Wey. KT13 . . . 217 BS104
Sch Ryelands Prim Sch, SE25
off Albert Rd . . . 224 DV99
Rye La, SE15 . . . 44 C7
Sevenoaks TN14 . . . 263 FG117
Sch Rye Oak Prim Sch, SE15
off Whorlton Rd . . . 184 DV83
RYE PARK, Hodd. EN11 . . . 71 EB16
● Rye Pk Ind Est, Hodd. EN11
off Salisbury Rd . . . 71 EC15
Rye Pas, SE15 . . . 44 D10
Ryepeck Meadow Moorings,
Shep. TW17 . . . 216 BL101
Rye Rd, SE15 . . . 185 DX84
Hoddesdon EN11 . . . 71 EB15
Stanstead Abbotts SG12 . . . 56 EE13
Rye Wk, SW15 . . . 201 CX85
Rye Way, Edg. HA8
off Canons Dr . . . 118 CM51
Ryfold Rd, SW19 . . . 202 DA90
Ryhope Rd, N11 . . . 121 DH49
Rykens La, Bet. RH3 . . . 286 CQ139
Rykhill, Grays RM16 . . . 193 GH76
Ryland Cl, Felt. TW13 . . . 197 BT91
Rylandes Rd, NW2 . . . 141 CU62
South Croydon CR2 . . . 242 DV109
● Ryland Ho, Croy. CR0 . . . 224 DQ104
Ryland Rd, NW5 . . . 7 J4
Rylett Cres, W12 . . . 181 CT76
Rylett Rd, W12 . . . 181 CT75
Rylston Rd, N13 . . . 122 DR48
SW6 . . . 38 G3
Rymer Rd, Croy. CR0 . . . 224 DS101
Rymer St, SE24 . . . 203 DP86
Rymill Cl, Bov. HP3 . . . 79 BA28
Rymill St, E16 . . . 37 L3
Rysbrack St, SW3 . . . 28 E6
Rysted La, West. TN16 . . . 277 EQ126
Rythe Cl, Chess. KT9
off Nigel Fisher Way . . . 237 CJ108
Claygate KT10 . . . 237 CE106
Rythe Ct, T.Ditt. KT7 . . . 219 CG101
Rythe Rd, Clay. KT10 . . . 237 CD106
Sch Ryvers Comb Sch, Langley
SL3 off Trelawney Av . . . 174 AX76
Ryvers Rd, Slou. SL3 . . . 175 AZ76

S

★ Saatchi Gall, The, SW3 . . . 28 F9
Sabah Ct, Ashf. TW15 . . . 196 BN91
Sabbarton St, E16 . . . 23 L9
Sabella Ct, E3 . . . 21 P1
Sabina Rd, Grays RM16 . . . 193 GJ77
Sabine Rd, SW11 . . . 40 E10
Sable Cl, Houns. TW4 . . . 178 BW83
Sable St, N1 . . . 9 H6
Sachfield Dr, Chaff.Hun.
RM16 . . . 192 FY76
Sach Rd, E5 . . . 144 DV61
Sackville Av, Brom. BR2 . . . 226 EG102
Sackville Cl, Har. HA2 . . . 139 CD62
Sevenoaks TN13 . . . 279 FH122
Sackville Ct, Rom. RM3
off Sackville Cres . . . 128 FL53
Sackville Cres, Rom. RM3 . . . 128 FL53
Sackville Est, SW16 . . . 203 DL90
Sackville Gdns, Ilf. IG1 . . . 147 EM60
Sackville Rd, Dart. DA2 . . . 210 FK89
Sutton SM2 . . . 240 DA108
Sackville St, W1 . . . 29 M1
Sacombe Rd, Hem.H. HP1 . . . 61 BF18
Sch Sacred Heart Cath Prim Sch,
N.Mal. KT3
off Burlington Rd . . . 221 CU98
Sch Sacred Heart Cath Prim Sch &
Nurs, Bushey WD23
off Merry Hill Rd . . . 98 BZ44
Sch Sacred Heart High Sch, W6 . . . 26 B9
Sch Sacred Heart Language Coll, The,
Wealds. HA3 off High St . . . 117 CE54
Sch Sacred Heart of Mary Girls' Sch,
Upmin. RM14
off St. Mary's La . . . 150 FP61
Sch Sacred Heart RC Prim Sch,
N7 . . . 8 D3
N20 off Oakleigh Pk S . . . 120 DE47
SW11 . . . 40 D9
SW15 off Roehampton La . . . 201 CU85
Ruislip HA4
off Herlwyn Av . . . 137 BS61
Teddington TW11
off St. Mark's Rd . . . 199 CH94
Ware SG12 off Broadmeads . . . 55 DX06
Sch Sacred Heart RC Sch, SE5 . . . 43 J6
Saddington St, Grav. DA12 . . . 213 GH87
Saddlebrook Pk, Sun. TW16 . . . 197 BS94
Saddlers Cl, Arkley EN5 . . . 101 CV43
Borehamwood WD6
off Farriers Way . . . 100 CR44
Pinner HA5 . . . 116 CA51
Saddlers Ms, SW8
off Portland Gro . . . 42 B6
Hampton Wick KT1 . . . 219 CJ95
Wembley HA0
off The Boltons . . . 139 CF63
Saddler's Pk, Eyns. DA4 . . . 230 FK104
Saddlers Path, Borwd. WD6 . . . 100 CR43
Saddlers Way, Epsom KT18 . . . 254 CR119
Saddlescombe Way, N12 . . . 120 DA50
Saddleworth Rd, Rom. RM3 . . . 128 FJ51
Saddleworth Sq, Rom. RM3 . . . 128 FJ51
Saddle Yd, W1 . . . 29 J2
Sadleir Rd, St.Alb. AL1 . . . 65 CE22
Sadler Cl, Chsht EN7
off Markham Rd . . . 88 DQ25
Mitcham CR4 . . . 222 DF96
Sadler Ho, E3
off Bromley High St . . . 22 D2
Sadlers Cl, Guil. GU4 . . . 265 BD133
Sadlers Gate Ms, SW15 . . . 38 A10
Sadlers Mead, Harl. CM18 . . . 74 EU16
Sadlers Ride, W.Mol. KT8 . . . 218 CC96
Sadlers Way, Hert. SG14 . . . 53 DN09
★ Sadler's Wells Thea, EC1 . . . 18 G2
Coll SAE Inst, N7 . . . 8 B3
Saffron Av, E14 . . . 22 G10
Saffron Cl, NW11 . . . 141 CZ57
Croydon CR0 . . . 223 DL100
Datchet SL3 . . . 174 AV81
Hoddesdon EN11 . . . 71 DZ16
Saffron Ct, Felt. TW14
off Staines Rd . . . 197 BQ87
Sch Saffron Grn First Sch, Borwd.
WD6 off Nicoll Way . . . 100 CR42
Saffron Hill, EC1 . . . 18 F5
Saffron La, Hem.H. HP1 . . . 62 BH19
Saffron Platt, Guil. GU2 . . . 264 AU130
Saffron Rd, Chaff.Hun. RM16 . . . 191 FW77
Romford RM5 . . . 127 FC54
Saffron St, EC1 . . . 18 F6
Saffron Way, Surb. KT6 . . . 219 CK102
Sage Cl, E6 . . . 25 J7
Sage Ms, SE22
off Lordship La . . . 204 DT85
Sage St, E1 . . . 20 G10
Sage Way, WC1 . . . 18 C3
Saigasso Cl, E16 . . . 24 E9
Sailacre Ho, SE10
off Calvert Rd . . . 186 EF78
Sail Ct, E14 off Newport Av . . . 23 H10
Sailmakers Ct, SW6 . . . 39 N10
Sail St, SE11 . . . 30 D8
Sainfoin Rd, SW17 . . . 202 DG89
Sainsbury Cen, The, Cher.
KT16 off Guildford St . . . 216 BG101
Sainsbury Rd, SE19 . . . 204 DS92
Sch St. Adrian's RC Prim Sch &
Nurs, St.Alb. AL1
off Watling View . . . 64 CC23
Sch St. Agatha's Cath Prim Sch,
Kings.T. KT2
off St. Agatha's Dr . . . 200 CM93
St. Agatha's Dr, Kings.T. KT2 . . . 200 CM93
St. Agathas Gro, Cars. SM5 . . . 222 DF102
St. Agnells Ct, Hem.H. HP2 . . . 62 BN16
St. Agnells La, Hem.H. HP2 . . . 62 BM15
St. Agnes Cl, E9 . . . 10 G9
St. Agnes Pl, SE11 . . . 42 G3
Sch St. Agnes RC Prim Sch, E3 . . . 22 C2
Sch St. Agnes' RC Prim Sch, NW2
off Thorverton Rd . . . 141 CY62
St. Agnes Well, EC1
off Old St . . . 19 M4
Sch St. Aidan's Cath Prim Sch,
Couls. CR5 off Portnalls Rd . . . 257 DJ116
Ilford IG1 off Benton Rd . . . 147 ER60
St. Aidans Ct, W13
off St. Aidans Rd . . . 179 CJ75
Barking IG11
off Choats Rd . . . 168 EV69
Sch St. Aidan's Prim Sch, N4
off Albany Rd . . . 143 DN59
St. Aidan's Rd, SE22 . . . 204 DV86
St. Aidans Rd, W13 . . . 179 CH75
St. Aidan's Way, Grav. DA12 . . . 213 GL90
Sch St. Alban & Stephen RC Inf &
Nurs Sch, St.Alb. AL1
off Vanda Cres . . . 65 CF21
Sch St. Alban & Stephen RC
Jun Sch, St.Alb. AL1
off Cecil Rd . . . 65 CG20
ST. ALBANS, AL1 - AL4 . . . 65 CE20
⇌ St. Albans Abbey . . . 65 CD22
St. Albans Av, E6 . . . 25 K2
St. Alban's Av, W4 . . . 180 CR77
St. Albans Av, Felt. TW13 . . . 198 BX92
Upminster RM14 . . . 151 FS60
Weybridge KT13 . . . 216 BN104
★ St. Albans Cath, St.Alb.
AL3 . . . 65 CD20
Sch St. Alban's Catholic Prim Sch,
E.Mol. KT8
off Beauchamp Rd . . . 218 CC99
Sch St. Albans Catholic Prim Sch,
Harl. CM20 off First Av . . . 57 ET13
Sch St. Alban's Cath Prim Sch, Horn.
RM12 off Heron Flight Av . . . 169 FH66
⇌ St. Albans City . . . 65 CE20
H St. Albans City Hosp, St.Alb.
AL3 . . . 64 CC18
St. Albans Cl, NW11 . . . 142 DA60
Gravesend DA12 . . . 213 GK90
Windsor SL4
off St. Alban's St . . . 173 AR81
Sch St. Alban's C of E Prim Sch,
EC1 . . . 18 E6
St. Albans Ct, EC2 . . . 19 K8
St. Albans Cres, N22 . . . 121 DN53
St. Alban's Cres, Wdf.Grn. IG8 . . . 124 EG52
● St. Albans Enterprise Cen,
St.Alb. AL3 off Long Spring . . . 65 CF16
St. Albans Gdns, Grav. DA12 . . . 213 GK90
St. Alban's Gdns, Tedd. TW11 . . . 199 CG92
Sch St. Albans Girls' Sch, St.Alb.
AL3 off Sandridgebury La . . . 65 CE16
St. Albans Gro, W8 . . . 27 M6
St. Alban's Gro, Cars. SM5 . . . 222 DE101
Sch St. Albans High Sch for Girls,
St.Alb. AL1
off Townsend Av . . . 65 CE19
St. Albans Hill, Hem.H. HP3 . . . 62 BL23
St. Albans La, NW11 . . . 142 DA60
Bedmond WD5 . . . 81 BT26
Sch St. Albans Music Sch, St.Alb.
AL3 off Townsend Dr . . . 65 CD17
★ St. Albans Organ Mus, St.Alb.
AL1 off Camp Rd . . . 65 CH21
St. Alban's Pl, N1 . . . 8 G9
St. Albans Retail Pk, St.Alb.
AL1 . . . 65 CD22
St. Albans Rd, NW5 . . . 142 DG62
NW10 . . . 160 CS67
Barnet EN5 . . . 101 CX39
Coopersale CM16 . . . 92 EX29
Dancers Hill EN6 . . . 101 CV35
Dartford DA1 . . . 210 FM87
Hemel Hempstead HP2, HP3 . . . 62 BN21
Ilford IG3 . . . 147 ET60
St. Alban's Rd, Kings.T. KT2 . . . 200 CL93
St. Albans Rd, Lon.Col. AL2 . . . 84 CS28
Reigate RH2 . . . 272 DA133
Sandridge AL4 . . . 65 CF17
Shenley WD7 . . . 84 CN28
South Mimms EN6 . . . 85 CV34
St. Alban's Rd, Sutt. SM1 . . . 239 CZ105
St. Albans Rd, Wat. WD17, WD24,
WD25 . . . 97 BV40
St. Alban's Rd, Wdf.Grn. IG8 . . . 124 EG52
St. Albans Rd E, Hat. AL10 . . . 67 CV17
Sch St. Albans Rd Inf Sch, Dart.
DA1 off St. Albans Rd . . . 210 FM86
St. Albans Rd W, Hat. AL10 . . . 66 CR18
Roe Green AL10 . . . 67 CT17
Sch St. Albans Sch, St.Alb. AL3
off Abbey Gateway . . . 64 CC20
St. Albans St, SW1 . . . 29 N1
St. Alban's St, Wind. SL4 . . . 173 AR81
St. Albans Ter, W6 . . . 38 E2
St. Alban's Vil, NW5
off Highgate Rd . . . 142 DG62
Sch St. Albert the Gt RC Prim Sch,
Hem.H. HP3 off Acorn Rd . . . 62 BN21
St. Alfege Pas, SE10 . . . 46 E3
St. Alfege Rd, SE7 . . . 186 EK79
Sch St. Alfege with St. Peter's
C of E Prim Sch, SE10 . . . 46 E3
Sch St. Aloysius' Coll, N6
off Hornsey La . . . 143 DJ60
Sch St. Aloysius RC Inf Sch,
NW1 . . . 17 N2
Sch St. Aloysius RC Jun Sch,
NW1 . . . 17 M1
St. Alphage Gdns, EC2 . . . 19 K7
St. Alphage Highwalk, EC2 . . . 19 L7
St. Alphage Wk, Edg. HA8 . . . 118 CQ54
St. Alphege Rd, N9 . . . 122 DW45
St. Alphonsus Rd, SW4 . . . 183 DJ84
St. Amunds Cl, SE6 . . . 205 EA91
Sch St. Andrew & St. Francis
C of E Prim Sch, NW2
off Belton Rd . . . 161 CU65
St. Andrew Ms, Hert. SG14 . . . 54 DQ09
Sch St. Andrew's & St. Mark's
C of E Jun Sch, Surb. KT6
off Maple Rd . . . 219 CK99
St. Andrews Av, Horn. RM12 . . . 149 FG64
Wembley HA0 . . . 139 CG63
Windsor SL4 . . . 173 AM82
St. Andrew's Cl, N12
off Woodside Av . . . 120 DC49
St. Andrews Cl, NW2 . . . 141 CV62
SE16 . . . 44 F1
SE28 . . . 168 EX72
SW19 . . . 202 DB93
St. Andrew's Cl, Islw. TW7 . . . 179 CD81
St. Andrews Cl, N.Wld Bas.
CM16 . . . 75 FC24
St. Andrew's Cl, Old Wind.
SL4 . . . 194 AU86
St. Andrews Cl, Reig. RH2
off St. Marys Rd . . . 288 DB135
Ruislip HA4 . . . 138 BX61
St. Andrew's Cl, Shep. TW17 . . . 217 BR98
St. Andrews Cl, Stan. HA7 . . . 117 CJ54
Thames Ditton KT7 . . . 219 CH102
Woking GU21 . . . 248 AW117
St. Andrew's Cl, Wrays. TW19 . . . 194 AY87
Sch St. Andrews C of E High Sch,
Croy. CR0
off Warrington Rd . . . 241 DP105
Sch St. Andrew's C of E Prim Sch,
N1 . . . 8 D8
N14 off Chase Rd . . . 121 DK46
N20 off Totteridge Village . . . 119 CZ47
SW9 . . . 42 B9
Enfield EN1
off Churchbury La . . . 104 DS40
North Weald Bassett CM16
off School Grn La . . . 93 FC25
Stanstead Abbotts SG12
off Mill Race . . . 55 ED11
Uxbridge UB8
off Nursery Waye . . . 156 BK67
St. Andrew's Ct, SW18 . . . 202 DC89
St. Andrews Ct, Colnbr. SL3
off High St . . . 175 BD80
Watford WD17 . . . 97 BV39
St. Andrews Cres, Wind. SL4 . . . 173 AM82
St. Andrews Dr, Orp. BR5 . . . 228 EV100
St. Albans AL1 . . . 65 CH23
Stanmore HA7 . . . 117 CJ53
St. Andrews Gdns, Cob. KT11 . . . 236 BW113
St. Andrew's Gro, N16 . . . 144 DR60
St. Andrew's Hill, EC4 . . . 19 H10
St. Andrews Meadow, Harl.
CM18 . . . 73 ET16
St. Andrew's Ms, N16 . . . 144 DS60
St. Andrews Ms, SE3 . . . 47 N4
SW12 off Emmanuel Rd . . . 203 DK88
Sch St. Andrew's Montessori Sch,
Wat. WD25 off High Elms La . . . 82 BW31
St. Andrews Pl, NW1 . . . 17 K4
Shenfield CM15 . . . 131 FZ47
Sch St. Andrew's Prim Sch,
Cob. KT11
off Lockhart Rd . . . 236 BW113
Sch St. Andrew's RC Prim Sch,
SW16 off Polworth Rd . . . 203 DL92
St. Andrews Rd, E11 . . . 146 EE58
E13 . . . 24 A3
E17 . . . 123 DX54
N9 . . . 122 DW45
NW9 . . . 140 CR60
NW10 . . . 161 CV65
NW11 . . . 141 CZ58
W3 . . . 160 CS73
W7 off Churchfield Rd . . . 179 CE75
W14 . . . 38 F2
Carshalton SM5 . . . 222 DE104
Coulsdon CR5 . . . 256 DG116
Croydon CR0
off Lower Coombe St . . . 242 DQ105
Enfield EN1 . . . 104 DR41
St. Andrew's Rd, Grav. DA12 . . . 213 GJ87
St. Andrews Rd, Hem.H. HP3
off West Valley Rd . . . 62 BJ24
Ilford IG1 . . . 147 EM59
Romford RM7 . . . 149 FD58
Sidcup DA14 . . . 208 EX90
St. Andrew's Rd, Surb. KT6 . . . 219 CK100
St. Andrews Rd, Til. RM18 . . . 192 GE81
Uxbridge UB10 . . . 156 BM66
Watford WD19 . . . 116 BX48
Sch St. Andrew's Sch, Lthd. KT22
off Grange Rd . . . 253 CK120
Woking GU21
off Wilson Way . . . 248 AX116
St. Andrews Sq, W11 . . . 14 E9
St. Andrew's Sq, Surb. KT6 . . . 219 CK100
St. Andrews Twr, Sthl. UB1 . . . 158 CC73
St. Andrew St, EC4 . . . 18 F7
Hertford SG14 . . . 54 DQ09
St. Andrews Wk, Cob. KT11 . . . 251 BV115
St. Andrews Way, E3 . . . 22 C5
Oxted RH8 . . . 276 EL130
Slough SL1 . . . 153 AK73
Sch St. Angela's Ursuline Sch, E7
off St. Georges Rd . . . 166 EH65
St. Anna Rd, Barn. EN5
off Sampson Av . . . 101 CX43
St. Annes Av, Stanw. TW19 . . . 196 BK87
St. Annes Boul, Red. RH1 . . . 273 DH132
Sch St. Anne's Cath High Sch for
Girls, Upr Sch, N13
off Oakthorpe Rd . . . 121 DN49
Lwr Sch, Enf. EN2
off London Rd . . . 104 DR42
Sch St. Anne's Catholic Prim Sch,
Bans. SM7 off Court Rd . . . 256 DA116
Chertsey KT16
off Free Prae Rd . . . 216 BG102
St. Annes Cl, N6 . . . 142 DG62
St. Annes Cl, Chsht EN7 . . . 88 DU28
St. Anne's Cl, Wat. WD19 . . . 116 BW49
Sch St. Anne's C of E Prim Sch,
SW18 off St. Ann's Hill . . . 202 DB85
St. Anne's Ct, W1 . . . 17 N9
St. Anne's Dr, Red. RH1 . . . 272 DG133
St. Annes Dr N, Red. RH1 . . . 272 DG132
St. Annes Gdns, NW10 . . . 160 CM69
St. Anne's Mt, Red. RH1 . . . 272 DG133
St. Annes Pk, Brox. EN10 . . . 71 EA20
St. Annes Pas, E14 . . . 21 N9
Sch St. Anne's Prim Sch, E1 . . . 20 C5
Sch St. Anne's RC Prim Sch,
SE11 . . . 42 C2
St. Annes Ri, Red. RH1 . . . 272 DG133
St. Annes Rd, E11 . . . 145 ED61
St. Anne's Rd, Hare. UB9 . . . 136 BJ55
London Colney AL2 . . . 83 CK27
Wembley HA0 . . . 139 CK64
St. Anne's Row, E14 . . . 21 P9
St. Anne St, E14 . . . 21 P9
St. Anne's Way, Red. RH1
off St. Anne's Dr . . . 272 DG133
St. Ann's, Bark. IG11 . . . 167 EQ67
St. Anns Cl, Cher. KT16 . . . 215 BF100
Sch St. Ann's C of E Prim Sch,
N15 off Avenue Rd . . . 144 DR57
St. Ann's Cres, SW18 . . . 202 DC86
St. Ann's Gdns, NW5 . . . 6 G4
Sch St. Ann's Heath Jun Sch, Vir.W.
GU25 off Sandhills La . . . 214 AY99
St. Anns Hill, SW18 . . . 202 DB85
St. Anns Hill Rd, Cher. KT16 . . . 215 BC100
H St. Ann's Hosp, N15 . . . 144 DQ57
St. Ann's La, SW1 . . . 29 P6
St. Ann's Pk Rd, SW18 . . . 202 DC86
St. Ann's Pas, SW13 . . . 180 CS83
St. Anns Rd, N9 . . . 122 DT47
St. Ann's Rd, N15 . . . 143 DP57
SW13 . . . 181 CT82
St. Anns Rd, W11 . . . 26 D1
St. Ann's Rd, Bark. IG11
off Axe St . . . 167 EQ67
St. Anns Rd, Cher. KT16 . . . 215 BF100
St. Ann's Rd, Har. HA1 . . . 139 CE58
Sch St. Ann's Sch, W7
off Springfield Rd . . . 159 CE74
Morden SM4
off Bordesley Rd . . . 222 DB99
St. Ann's Shop Cen, Har.
HA1 . . . 139 CE58
St. Ann's St, SW1 . . . 29 P6
St. Ann's Ter, NW8 . . . 6 B10
St. Anns Vil, W11 . . . 26 D3
St. Anns Way, Berry's Grn
TN16 . . . 261 EP116
South Croydon CR2 . . . 241 DP107
Sch St. Anselm's Cath Prim Sch,
Dart. DA1 off Littlebrook
Manor Way . . . 210 FN85
St. Anselm's Pl, W1 . . . 17 J9
Sch St. Anselm's RC Prim Sch,
SW17 off Tooting Bec Rd . . . 202 DG90
Harrow HA1
off Roxborough Pk . . . 139 CE59
Sch St. Anselms RC Prim Sch,
Sthl. UB2 off Church Av . . . 178 BZ76
St. Anselms Rd, Hayes UB3 . . . 177 BT75
St. Anthonys Av, Hem.H. HP3 . . . 63 BP22
Woodford Green IG8 . . . 124 EJ51
Sch St. Anthony's Cath Prim Sch,
SE20 off Genoa Rd . . . 224 DV95
SE22 off Etherow St . . . 204 DU86
Farnham Royal SL2
off Farnham Rd . . . 153 AQ70
Woodford Green IG8
off Mornington Rd . . . 124 EG49
St. Anthonys Cl, E1 . . . 32 C2
SW17 off College Gdns . . . 202 DE89
St. Anthonys Ct, Beac. HP9
off Walkwood Ri . . . 132 AJ55
H St. Anthony's Hosp, Sutt.
SM3 . . . 221 CX102
Sch St. Anthony's Prep Sch,
NW3 . . . 6 A2
Sch St. Anthony's RC Prim Sch,
Wat. WD18 off Croxley Vw . . . 97 BS43
St. Anthony's Way, Felt. TW14 . . . 177 BT84
Sch St. Antony's RC Prim Sch, E7
off Upton Av . . . 166 EH66
St. Antony's Rd, E7 . . . 166 EH66
St. Arvans Cl, Croy. CR0 . . . 224 DS104
St. Asaph Rd, SE4 . . . 45 J10
St. Aubins Ct, N1
off De Beauvoir Est . . . 9 M8
St. Aubyn's Av, SW19 . . . 201 CZ92
St. Aubyns Av, Houns. TW3 . . . 198 CA85
St. Aubyns Cl, Orp. BR6 . . . 227 ET104
St. Aubyns Gdns, Orp. BR6 . . . 227 ET103
St. Aubyn's Rd, SE19 . . . 204 DT93
Sch St. Aubyn's Sch, Wdf.Grn.
IG8 off Bunces La . . . 124 EF52
St. Audrey Av, Bexh. DA7 . . . 188 FA82
St. Audreys Cl, Hat. AL10 . . . 67 CV21
St. Audreys Grn, Welw.G.C.
AL7 . . . 51 CZ10
Sch St. Augustine of Canterbury
C of E Prim Sch, Belv. DA17
off St. Augustine's Rd . . . 188 EZ76
St. Augustine Rd, Grays
RM16 . . . 193 GH77
St. Augustines Av, W5 . . . 160 CL68
St. Augustines Av, Brom. BR2 . . . 226 EL99
St. Augustine's Av, S.Croy.
CR2 . . . 242 DQ107
St. Augustines Av, Wem. HA9 . . . 140 CL62
Sch St. Augustine's Cath Prim Sch,
Ilf. IG2 off Cranbrook Rd . . . 147 EP57
St. Augustines Cl, Brox. EN10 . . . 71 DZ20
Sch St. Augustine's C of E High Sch,
NW6 . . . 15 K1
Sch St. Augustine's C of E Prim Sch,
NW6 . . . 5 L10
St. Augustines Ct, SE1 . . . 32 E10
St. Augustines Dr, Brox. EN10 . . . 71 DZ19
St. Augustine's Path, N5 . . . 9 K1
Sch St. Augustine's Priory Sch, W5
off Hillcrest Rd . . . 160 CM71
Sch St. Augustine's RC Prim Sch,
SE6 off Dunfield Rd . . . 205 EC92
W6 . . . 38 F3
Hoddesdon EN11
off Riversmead . . . 71 EA17
St. Augustines Rd, NW1 . . . 7 N6
St. Augustine's Rd, Belv.
DA17 . . . 188 EZ77
St. Austell Cl, Edg. HA8 . . . 118 CM54
St. Austell Rd, SE13 . . . 46 F8
St. Awdry's Rd, Bark. IG11 . . . 167 ER66
St. Awdry's Wk, Bark. IG11
off Station Par . . . 167 EQ66
Sch St. Barnabas & St. Philip's
C of E Prim Sch, W8 . . . 27 J7
St. Barnabas Cl, SE22
off East Dulwich Gro . . . 204 DS85
Beckenham BR3 . . . 225 EC96
Sch St. Barnabas C of E Prim Sch,
SW1 . . . 29 H10
St. Barnabas Ct, Har. HA3 . . . 116 CC53
St. Barnabas Gdns, W.Mol.
KT8 . . . 218 CA99
St. Barnabas Rd, E17 . . . 145 EA58
Mitcham CR4 . . . 202 DG94
Sutton SM1 . . . 240 DD106
Woodford Green IG8 . . . 124 EH53
St. Barnabas St, SW1 . . . 29 H10
St. Barnabas Ter, E9 . . . 11 J3
St. Barnabas Vil, SW8 . . . 42 B6
Sch St. Bartholomew's Catholic
Prim Sch, Swan. BR8
off Sycamore Dr . . . 229 FE97
St. Bartholomews Cl, SE26 . . . 204 DW91
Sch St. Bartholomew's C of E
Prim Sch, SE26
off The Peak . . . 204 DW91

St. Bartholomews Ct, Guil. GU1 281 AZ135
St. Bartholomew's Hosp, EC1 19 H7
St. Bartholomew's Rd, E6 166 EL67
★ St. Bartholomew-the-Great Ch, EC1 19 H7
St. Bart's Cl, St.Alb. AL4 65 CK21
St. Bede's Cath Prim Sch, Chad.Hth RM6 off Canon Av 148 EW57
St. Bede's C of E Jun Sch, Send GU23 off Bush La 249 BD124
St. Bede's RC Inf Sch, SW12 off Thornton Rd 203 DK88
St. Bede's Sch, Red. RH1 off Carlton Rd 272 DE131
St. Benedict's Av, Grav. DA12 213 GK89
St. Benedict's Cl, SW17 off Church La 202 DG92
St. Benedict's Sch, Nurs & Jun Sch, W5 off Montpelier Av 159 CJ71
Sen Sch & 6th Form, W5 off Eaton Ri 159 CK71
St. Benet's Cl, SW17 off College Gdns 202 DE89
St. Benet's Gro, Cars. SM5 222 DC101
St. Benet's Pl, EC3 19 M10
St. Benjamins Dr, Pr.Bot. BR6 246 EW109
St. Bernadette Cath Prim Sch, Uxb. UB10 off Long La 157 BP67
St. Bernadette RC Nurs & Prim Sch, Lon.Col. AL2 off Walsingham Way 83 CK27
St. Bernadette's Catholic Prim Sch, Kenton HA3 off Clifton Rd 140 CM56
St. Bernadette's RC Jun Sch, SW12 off Atkins Rd 203 DJ87
St. Bernards, Croy. CR0 224 DS104
St. Bernard's Cl, SE27 204 DR91
St. Bernard's Conv Sch, Slou. SL3 off Langley Rd 174 AW75
St. Bernard's Hosp, Sthl. UB1 179 CD75
St. Bernard's Prep Sch, Slou. SL1 off Hawtrey Cl 174 AV75
St. Bernard's Rd, E6 166 EK67
St. Bernards Rd, St.Alb. AL3 65 CD19
Slough SL3 174 AW76
St. Blaise Av, Brom. BR1 226 EH96
St. Bonaventure's Cath Comp Sch, E7 13 P7
St. Boniface RC Prim Sch, SW17 off Undine St 202 DF92
St. Botolph Rd, Nthflt DA11 212 GC90
St. Botolph Row, EC3 20 A9
St. Botolph's Av, Sev. TN13 278 FG124
St. Botolph's C of E Prim Sch, Nthflt DA11 off Dover Rd 212 GD87
St. Botolph's Rd, Sev. TN13 278 FG124
St. Botolph St, EC3 20 A9
St. Brelades Cl, Dor. RH4 285 CG138
St. Brelades Ct, N1 off Balmes Rd 9 M8
St. Brelades Pl, St.Alb. AL4 off Harvesters 65 CK16
St. Brides Av, EC4 18 G9
Edgware HA8 118 CM53
★ St. Bride's Ch, EC4 18 G9
St. Brides Cl, Erith DA18 off St. Katherines Rd 188 EX75
St. Bride's Pas, EC4 off Salisbury Ct 18 G9
St. Bride St, EC4 18 G8
St. Catharines Rd, Brox. EN10 71 EA19
St. Catherine of Siena Cath Prim Sch, Wat. WD25 off Horseshoe La 82 BX33
St. Catherines, Wok. GU22 248 AW119
St. Catherine's Bletchingley Village Sch, Bletch. RH1 off Coneybury 274 DS133
St. Catherine's Cath Sch for Girls, Bexh. DA6 off Watling St 189 FB84
St. Catherines Cl, SW17 202 DE89
Chessington KT9 237 CK107
St. Catherine's C of E Prim Sch, Hodd. EN11 off Haslewood Av 71 EA17
Ware SG12 off Park Rd 54 DV05
St. Catherines Ct, Felt. TW13 197 BU88
St. Catherines Cross, Bletch. RH1 274 DS134
St. Catherines Dr, SE14 45 K9
Guildford GU2 280 AV138
St. Catherines Fm Ct, Ruis. HA4 137 BQ58
St. Catherines Hill, Guil. GU2 off Portsmouth Rd 280 AW138
St. Catherine's Ms, SW3 28 E8
St. Catherines Pk, Guil. GU1 281 AZ136
St. Catherine's RC Prim Sch, Barn. EN5 off Vale Dr 102 DA42
West Drayton UB7 off Money La 176 BK75
St. Catherines Rd, E4 123 EA47
Ruislip HA4 137 BR57
St. Catherine's Sch, Sen Sch, Bramley GU5 off Station Rd 281 AZ144
Twickenham TW1 off Cross Deep 199 CG89
St. Cecelia's Pl, SE3 47 N1
St. Cecilia Rd, Grays RM16 193 GH77
St. Cecilia's Cl, Sutt. SM3 221 CY102
St. Cecilia's RC Prim Sch, Sutt. SM3 off London Rd 221 CX103
St. Cecilia's, Wandsworth Sch, SW18 off Sutherland Gro 201 CZ87
St. Chad's Cath Prim Sch, SE25 off Alverston Gdns 224 DS99
St. Chads Cl, Long Dit. KT6 219 CJ101
St. Chad's Dr, Grav. DA12 213 GL90
St. Chad's Gdns, Rom. RM6 148 EY59
St. Chad's Pl, WC1 18 B2
St. Chad's Rd, Rom. RM6 148 EY58
Tilbury RM18 193 GG80
St. Chad's St, WC1 18 B2
St. Charles Borromeo Catholic Prim Sch, Wey. KT13 off Portmore Way 216 BN104
St. Charles Catholic 6th Form Coll, W10 14 D7
St. Charles Ct, Wey. KT13 234 BN106
St. Charles Hosp, W10 14 D6
St. Charles Pl, W10 14 E7
Weybridge KT13 234 BN106
St. Charles RC Prim Sch, W10 14 D6
St. Charles Rd, Brwd. CM14 130 FV46
St. Charles Sq, W10 14 E6
St. Christina's Sch, NW8 6 D10
St. Christopher Rd, Uxb. UB8 156 BK71
St. Christopher's Cl, Islw. TW7 179 CE81
St. Christopher's Dr, Hayes UB3 157 BV73
St. Christophers Gdns, Th.Hth. CR7 223 DN97
St. Christophers Ms, Wall. SM6 241 DJ106
St. Christopher's Pl, W1 17 H8
St. Christopher's Sch, NW3 6 B3
Epsom KT18 off Downs Rd 238 CS114
Wembley HA9 off Wembley Pk Dr 140 CM62
St. Christopher's The Hall Sch, Beck. BR3 off Bromley Rd 225 EC96
St. Clair Cl, Ilf. IG5 125 EM54
Oxted RH8 275 EC130
Reigate RH2 272 DC134
St. Clair Dr, Wor.Pk. KT4 221 CV104
St. Clair Rd, E13 24 B1
St. Clair's Rd, Croy. CR0 224 DS103
● St. Clare Business Pk, Hmptn. TW12 198 CC93
St. Clare St, EC3 20 A9
St. Clement Cl, Uxb. UB8 156 BK72
★ St. Clement Danes Ch, WC2 18 D9
St. Clement Danes C of E Prim Sch, WC2 18 C9
St. Clement Danes Sch, Chorl. WD3 off Chenies Rd 95 BD40
St. Clements & St. James C of E Prim Sch, W11 26 E2
St. Clements Av, Grays RM20 191 FV79
St. Clement's Catholic Prim Sch, Ewell KT17 off Fennells Mead 239 CT109
St. Clement's Cl, Nthflt DA11 off Coldharbour Rd 213 GF90
St. Clement's C of E Jun Sch, Wal.Cr. EN8 off Cheshunt Wash 89 DY27
St. Clements Ct, EC4 off Clements La 19 M10
N7 8 E5
Purfleet RM19 190 FN77
St. Clements Hts, SE26 204 DU90
St. Clement's La, WC2 18 D9
St. Clements Rd, Grays RM20 191 FW80
Greenhithe DA9 191 FW84
St. Clements St, N7 8 E5
St. Clements Way, Grays RM20 191 FT79
Greenhithe DA9 211 FU85
St. Clements Yd, SE22 off Archdale Rd 204 DT85
St. Cloud Rd, SE27 204 DQ91
St. Columba's Cath Boys' Sch, Bexh. DA6 off Halcot Av 209 FB85
St. Columba's Cl, Grav. DA12 213 GL90
St. Columba's Coll, St.Alb. AL3 off King Harry La 64 CC22
St. Crispins Cl, NW3 6 D1
Southall UB1 158 BZ72
St. Crispins Way, Ott. KT16 233 BC109
St. Cross Ct, Hodd. EN11 71 EA19
St. Cross RC Prim Sch, Hodd. EN11 off Upper Marsh La 71 EA19
St. Cross St, EC1 18 F6
St. Cuthbert La, Uxb. UB8 156 BK72
St. Cuthbert Mayne Catholic Jun Sch, Hem.H. HP1 off Clover Way 62 BH19
St. Cuthbert's Catholic Prim Sch, Eng.Grn TW20 off Bagshot Rd 194 AW94
St. Cuthberts Cl, Eng.Grn TW20 194 AX92
St. Cuthberts Gdns, Pnr. HA5 off Westfield Pk 116 BZ52
St. Cuthberts Rd, N13 121 DN51
NW2 4 G4
Hoddesdon EN11 55 EC14
St. Cuthbert with St. Matthias C of E Prim Sch, SW5 27 L10
St. Cyprian's Greek Orthodox Prim Sch, Th.Hth. CR7 off Springfield Rd 224 DQ95
St. Cyprian's St, SW17 202 DF91
St. David Cl, Uxb. UB8 156 BK71
St. Davids, Couls. CR5 257 DM117
St. Davids Cl, SE16 44 F1
Hemel Hempstead HP3 63 BR21
Iver SL0 155 BD67
St. David's Cl, Reig. RH2 272 DC133
St. Davids Cl, Wem. HA9 140 CQ62
St. David's Cl, W.Wick. BR4 225 EB101
St. David's Coll, W.Wick. BR4 off Beckenham Rd 225 EB101
St. David's Ct, E17 145 EC55
St. David's Cres, Grav. DA12 213 GK91
St. David's Dr, Brox. EN10 71 DZ19
St. Davids Dr, Edg. HA8 118 CM53
St. David's Dr, Eng.Grn TW20 194 AW94
St. Davids Ms, E3 off Morgan St 21 M3
St. Davids Pl, NW4 141 CV59
St. Davids Rd, Swan. BR8 209 FF93
St. David's Sch, Ashf. TW15 off Church Rd 196 BM90
Purley CR8 off Woodcote Valley Rd 241 DM111
St. Davids Sq, E14 34 D10
St. Denis Rd, SE27 204 DR91
St. Denys Cl, Pur. CR8 241 DP110
St. Dionis Rd, SW6 39 H8
St. Dominic's RC Prim Sch, E9 11 L4
NW5 6 F3
St. Dominic's 6th Form Coll, Har.Hill HA1 off Mount Pk Av 139 CE61
St. Donatts Rd, SE14 45 N7
St. Dunstans, Sutt. SM1 off Cheam Rd 239 CZ107
St. Dunstan's All, EC3 19 N10
St. Dunstans Av, W3 160 CR73
St. Dunstan's Catholic Prim Sch, Wok. GU22 off Onslow Cres 249 BA117
St. Dunstans Cl, Hayes UB3 177 BT77
St. Dunstan's C of E Prim Sch, Cheam SM3 off Anne Boleyn's Wk 239 CY108
St. Dunstan's Coll, SE6 off Stanstead Rd 205 EA88
St. Dunstan's Ct, EC4 off Fleet St 18 F9
St. Dunstan's Dr, Grav. DA12 213 GL91
St. Dunstans Gdns, W3 160 CR73
St. Dunstan's Hill, EC3 31 N1
Sutton SM1 239 CY106
St. Dunstan's La, EC3 31 N1
Beckenham BR3 225 EC100
St. Dunstan's Rd, E7 166 EJ65
St. Dunstans Rd, SE25 224 DT98
W6 38 C1
W7 179 CE75
St. Dunstan's Rd, Felt. TW13 197 BT90
St. Dunstans Rd, Houns. TW4 178 BW82
Hunsdon SG12 56 EK07
St. Ebba's Hosp, Epsom KT19 238 CQ109
St. Edith Cl, Epsom KT18 off St. Elizabeth Dr 238 CQ114
St. Edmunds, Berk. HP4 60 AW20
St. Edmunds Av, Ruis. HA4 137 BR58
St. Edmunds Cl, NW8 6 E9
SW17 off College Gdns 202 DE89
Erith DA18 off St. Katherines Rd 188 EX75
St. Edmunds Dr, Stan. HA7 117 CG53
St. Edmund's La, Twick. TW2 198 CB87
St. Edmund's RC Prim Sch, E14 34 B8
N9 off Hertford Rd 122 DV46
Whitton TW2 off Nelson Rd 198 CB87
St. Edmunds Rd, N9 122 DU45
Dartford DA1 190 FM84
Ilford IG1 147 EM58
St. Edmunds Sq, SW13 38 A3
St. Edmunds Ter, NW8 6 D10
St. Edmunds Wk, St.Alb. AL4 65 CJ21
St. Edmunds Way, Harl. CM17 58 EW11
St. Edward's Catholic First Sch, Wind. SL4 off Parsonage La 173 AN81
St. Edwards Cl, NW11 142 DA58
New Addington CR0 243 ED111
St. Edward's C of E Comp Sch, Rom. RM7 off London Rd 148 FA58
St. Edward's C of E Prim Sch, Rom. RM1 off Havering Dr 149 FE56
St. Edward's RC Prim Sch, E13 off Green St 166 EJ67
NW1 16 D5
St. Edward's Royal Free Ecumenical Mid Sch, Wind. SL4 off Parsonage La 173 AN81
St. Edwards Way, Rom. RM1 149 FD57
St. Egberts Way, E4 123 EC46
St. Elizabeth Dr, Epsom KT18 238 CQ114
St. Elizabeth's Catholic Prim Sch, Rich. TW10 off Queens Rd 200 CM86
St. Elizabeth's Prim Sch, E2 11 H10
St. Elmo Cl, Slou. SL2 off St. Elmo Cres 153 AR70
St. Elmo Cres, Slou. SL2 153 AR70
St. Elmo Rd, W12 161 CT74
St. Elmos Rd, SE16 33 L4
St. Elphege's RC Infants' & Jun Schs, Wall. SM6 off Mollison Dr 241 DL107
St. Erkenwald Ms, Bark. IG11 off St. Erkenwald Rd 167 ER67
St. Erkenwald Rd, Bark. IG11 167 ER67
St. Ermin's Hill, SW1 29 N6
St. Ervans Rd, W10 14 F6
St. Ethelbert's Catholic Prim Sch, Slou. SL2 off Wexham Rd 154 AV72
St. Etheldredas Dr, Hat. AL10 67 CW18
St. Eugene de Mazenod RC Prim Sch, NW6 5 K7
St. Faiths Cl, Enf. EN2 104 DQ39
St. Faith's C of E Prim Sch, SW18 off Alma Rd 202 DC85
St. Faith's Rd, SE21 203 DP88
St. Fidelis Cath Prim Sch, Erith DA8 off Bexley Rd 189 FC79
St. Fidelis Rd, Erith DA8 189 FD77
St. Fillans Rd, SE6 205 EC88
St. Francesca Cabrini RC Prim Sch, SE23 off Honor Oak Pk 204 DW86
St. Francis Av, Grav. DA12 213 GL91
St. Francis Cath Prim Sch, SE15 44 D4
Caterham CR3 off Whyteleafe Rd 258 DT121
St. Francis Cl, Petts Wd BR5 227 ES100
Potters Bar EN6 86 DC33
Watford WD19 115 BV46
St. Francis de Sales RC Inf & Jun Schs, N17 off Church Rd 122 DT52
St. Francis of Assisi RC Prim Sch, W11 26 D1
St. Francis Pl, SW12 off Malwood Rd 203 DH86
St. Francis' RC Prim Sch, E15 13 J3
St. Francis Rd, SE22 184 DS84
Denham UB9 135 BF58
Erith DA8 off West St 189 FD77
St. Francis Way, Grays RM16 193 GJ77
Ilford IG1 147 ES63
St. Francis Xavier 6th Form Coll, SW12 off Malwood Rd 203 DH86
St. Frideswides Ms, E14 22 E9
St. Gabriel's Cl, E11 146 EH61
E14 22 C7
St. Gabriel's C of E Prim Sch, SW1 41 L1
St. Gabriels Rd, NW2 4 C3
St. George's, SW17 off Cranmer Ter 202 DD92
St. George's, Har. HA1 139 CE58
St. Georges Av, E7 166 EH66
N7 143 DK63
NW9 140 CQ56
St. George's Av, W5 179 CK75
St. Georges Av, Grays RM17 192 GC77
Hornchurch RM11 150 FM59
Southall UB1 158 BZ73
St. George's Av, Wey. KT13 235 BP107
St. George's Bickley C of E Prim Sch, Brom. BR1 off Tylney Rd 226 EK96
St. George's Cath RC Prim Sch, SE1 30 G6
St. George's Cath School, Maida Vale, W9 15 M1
St. George's Cen, Grav. DA11 213 GH86
St. Georges Circ, SE1 30 G6
St. Georges Cl, NW11 141 CZ58
SE28 off Redbourne Dr 168 EX72
St. George's Cl, SW8 41 M6
St. Georges Cl, Horl. RH6 291 DH148
Wembley HA0 139 CG62
St. George's Cl, Wey. KT13 235 BQ106
Windsor SL4 173 AL81
St. George's C of E Inf Sch, Amer. HP7 off White Lion Rd 94 AT39
St. George's C of E Prim Sch, SE5 43 N4
SW8 41 M5
St. George's C of E Sch, Grav. DA11 off Meadow Rd 213 GG89
St. George's Coll, Add. KT15 off Weybridge Rd 216 BK104
Jun Sch, Wey. KT13 off Thames St 217 BP104
St. Georges Ct, E6 25 J4
EC4 18 G8
SW7 27 N6
St. Georges Cres, Grav. DA12 213 GK91
St. George's Cres, Slou. SL1 153 AK73
St. George's Dr, SW1 29 K9
St. Georges Dr, Uxb. UB10 136 BM62
Watford WD19 116 BY48
St. Georges Flds, W2 16 D9
St. Georges Gdns, Epsom KT17 239 CT114
St. George's Gdns, Surb. KT6 220 CP103
St. Georges Gro, SW17 202 DD90
St. George's Hanover Sq Prim Sch, W1 29 H1
ST. GEORGE'S HILL, Wey. KT13 235 BQ110
St. George's Hosp, SW17 202 DD92
Hornchurch RM12 150 FK63
● St. George's Ind Est, N22 121 DP52
● St. Georges Ind Est, Kings.T. KT2 199 CK92
St. Georges La, EC3 off Pudding La 19 M10
St. George's Lo, Wey. KT13 235 BR106
St. Georges Ms, NW1 6 F7
SE1 30 F6
SE8 33 N8
St. Georges Pl, Twick. TW1 off Church St 199 CG88
St. George's RC Prim Sch, Enf. EN2 off Gordon Rd 104 DR40
Harrow HA1 off Sudbury Hill 139 CF62
St. Georges Rd, E7 166 EH65
E10 145 EC62
N9 122 DU48
N13 121 DM48
NW11 141 CZ58
SE1 30 F6
St. George's Rd, SW19 201 CZ93
St. Georges Rd, W4 180 CS75
W7 159 CF74
Addlestone KT15 234 BJ105
St. George's Rd, Beck. BR3 225 EB95
St. Georges Rd, Brom. BR1 227 EM96
Dagenham RM9 148 EY64
Enfield EN1 104 DT38
St. George's Rd, Felt. TW13 198 BX91
St. Georges Rd, Hem.H. HP3 62 BJ24
Ilford IG1 147 EM59
St. George's Rd, Kings.T. KT2 200 CN94
Mitcham CR4 223 DH97
Petts Wood BR5 227 ER100
St. Georges Rd, Red. RH1 289 DK142
Richmond TW9 180 CM83
St. George's Rd, Sev. TN13 279 FH122
Sidcup DA14 208 EX93
St. Georges Rd, Swan. BR8 229 FF98
Twickenham TW1 199 CH85
Wallington SM6 241 DH106
Watford WD24 97 BV38
St. George's Rd, Wey. KT13 235 BR107
St. Georges Rd W, Brom. BR1 226 EL95
St. George's Sch, Wind. SL4 off Windsor Castle 173 AR80
St. Georges Sq, E7 166 EH66
E14 21 L10
SE8 33 N8
St. George's Sq, SW1 29 N10
New Malden KT3 off High St 220 CS97
St. George's Sq Ms, SW1 41 N1
St. Georges Ter, NW1 6 F7
St. George St, W1 17 K9
St. Georges Wk, Croy. CR0 224 DQ104
St. Georges Way, SE15 43 N3
St. George the Martyr C of E Prim Sch, WC1 18 C5
St. George Wf, SW8 42 A1
St. Gerards Cl, SW4 203 DJ85
St. German's Pl, SE3 47 N7
St. Germans Rd, SE23 205 DY88
St. Gilda's RC Jun Sch, N8 off Oakington Way 143 DL59
St. Giles Av, Dag. RM10 169 FB66
South Mimms EN6 85 CV32
Uxbridge UB10 137 BQ63
St. Giles Cl, Dag. RM10 off St. Giles Av 169 FB66
Hounslow TW5 178 BY80
Orpington BR6 245 ER106
St. Giles C of E Inf Sch, Ashtd. KT21 off Dene Rd 254 CM118
St. Giles' C of E Prim Sch, S.Mimms EN6 off Blanche La 85 CU32
St. Giles Coll, London Cen, WC1 18 B6
London Highgate, N6 off Shepherds Hill 143 DJ58
St. Giles Ct, WC2 off St. Giles High St 18 A8
St. Giles High St, WC2 17 P8
St. Giles Pas, WC2 17 P9
St. Giles Rd, SE5 43 N5
St. Giles' Sch, S.Croy. CR2 off Pampisford Rd 241 DP107
St. Gilles Ho, E2 21 J1
St. Gothard Rd, SE27 204 DR91
St. Gregory Cl, Ruis. HA4 138 BW63
St. Gregory's Catholic Science Coll, Kenton HA3 off Donnington Rd 139 CK57
St. Gregorys Cres, Grav. DA12 213 GL89
St. Gregory's RC Prim Sch, W5 off Woodfield Rd 159 CK71
St. Helena Rd, SE16 33 J9
St. Helena St, WC1 18 E3
St. Helen's Cath Inf Sch, E17 off Shernhall St 145 EC57
Brentwood CM14 off Queens Rd 130 FX47
St. Helen's Catholic Jun Sch, Brwd. CM15 off Sawyers Hall La 130 FX45
St. Helens Cl, Uxb. UB8 156 BK72
St. Helen's Coll, Uxb. UB10 off Parkway 157 BP66
St. Helens Ct, Epp. CM16 off Hemnall St 92 EU30
Rainham RM13 169 FG70
St. Helens Cres, SW16 off St. Helens Rd 223 DM95
St. Helens Gdns, W10 14 C7
St. Helens Pl, E10 145 DY59
EC3 19 N8
St. Helen's RC Prim Sch, E13 23 N4
SW9 42 E10
St. Helens Rd, SW16 223 DM95
St. Helen's Rd, W13 off Dane Rd 159 CJ74
St. Helens Rd, Erith DA18 188 EX75
Ilford IG1 147 EM58
St. Helen's Sch, Nthwd. HA6 off Eastbury Rd 115 BS51
ST. HELIER, Cars. SM5 222 DD101
⇌ St. Helier 222 DA100
St. Helier Av, Mord. SM4 222 DC101
St. Helier Hosp, Cars. SM5 222 DC102
St. Helier Rd, Sand. AL4 65 CH15
St. Heliers Av, Houns. TW3 198 CA85
St. Heliers Rd, E10 145 EC58
St. Hildas Av, Ashf. TW15 196 BL92
St. Hildas Cl, NW6 4 D7
SW17 202 DE89
Horley RH6 291 DH148
St. Hilda's Rd, SW13 181 CV79
St. Hilda's Sch, Bushey WD23 off High St 116 CB45
St. Hilda's Way, Grav. DA12 213 GK91
St. Huberts Cl, Ger.Cr. SL9 134 AY60
St. Huberts La, Ger.Cr. SL9 135 AZ61
St. Hughe's Cl, SW17 202 DE89
St. Hughs Rd, SE20 off Ridsdale Rd 224 DV95
St. Ignatious RC Prim Sch, N15 off St. Ann's Rd 144 DT58
St. Ignatius Coll, Enf. EN1 off Turkey St 104 DV37
St. Ignatius RC Prim Sch, Sun. TW16 off Green St 217 BU95
St. Ives Cl, Rom. RM3 128 FM52
St. Ivians Dr, Rom. RM2 149 FG55
St. James' & St. Michael's C of E Prim Sch, W2 15 P10
St. James Av, N20 120 DE48
W13 159 CG74
Epsom KT17 239 CT111
Sutton SM1 240 DA106
St. James' Cath High Sch, NW9 off Great Strand 119 CT53
St. James' Cath Prim Sch, Orp. BR5 off Maybury Cl 227 EP99
St. James Cen, Harl. CM20 58 EU11
St. James Cl, N20 120 DE48
NW8 off St. James's Ter 6 E9
SE18 off Congleton Gro 187 EQ78
Barnet EN4 102 DD42
Epsom KT18 238 CS114
New Malden KT3 221 CT99
Ruislip HA4 138 BW61
Woking GU21 248 AU118
St. James' C of E Jun Sch, E7 13 N2
St. James C of E Prim Sch, N10 off Woodside Av 142 DG56
St. James' C of E Prim Sch, SE16 32 C6
Enfield EN3 off Frederick Cres 104 DW40
Harlow CM18 off Paringdon Rd 73 ER19
St. James C of E Prim Sch, Wey. KT13 off Grotto Rd 217 BQ104
St. James Ct, Green. DA9 211 FT86
St. James Gdns, Lt.Hth RM6 148 EV56
Wembley HA0 159 CK66
St. James Gate, NW1 7 P7
St. James Gro, SW11 40 F8
St. James Hatcham C of E Prim Sch, SE14 45 M6
St. James Indep Sch for Sen Boys, Twick. TW1 off Cross Deep 199 CG89
St. James Indep Schs for Jun Boys & Girls & Sen Girls, W14 26 F8
St. James La, Green. DA9 211 FS88
St. James Ms, E14 34 F7
E17 145 DY57
Weybridge KT13 235 BP105
St. James Oaks, Grav. DA11 213 GG87
St. James Pl, Dart. DA1 off Spital St 210 FK86
Slough SL1 off Greenfern Av 152 AJ72
St. James Rd, E15 13 L2
N9 off Queens Rd 122 DV47
Brentwood CM14 130 FW48
Carshalton SM5 222 DE104
Goffs Oak EN7 88 DQ28
Kingston upon Thames KT1 220 CL96
Mitcham CR4 202 DG94
Purley CR8 241 DP113
Sevenoaks TN13 279 FH122
Surbiton KT6 219 CK100
Sutton SM1 240 DA106
Watford WD18 97 BV43
ST. JAMES'S, SW1 29 N3
St. James's, SE14 45 M6

St. James's & Lucie Clayton Coll, SW5 . . . 27 N9
St. James's Av, E2 . . . 21 H1
Beckenham BR3 . . . 225 DY97
Gravesend DA11 . . . 213 GG87
Hampton Hill TW12 . . . 198 CC92
St. James's Cath Prim Sch, Twick. TW2
off Stanley Rd . . . 199 CD90
St. James's Cl, SW17 . . . 202 DF89
St. James's Cotts, Rich. TW9
off Paradise Rd . . . 200 CL85
St. James's Ct, SW1 . . . 29 M6
St. James's Cres, SW9 . . . 42 F10
St. James's Dr, SW12 . . . 202 DF88
SW17 . . . 202 DF88
St. James's Gdns, W11 . . . 26 E2
St. James's La, N10 . . . 143 DH56
St. James's Mkt, SW1 . . . 29 N1
★ St. James's Palace, SW1 . . . 29 M4
★ St. James's Park, SW1 . . . 29 N4
⊖ St. James's Park . . . 29 N6
St. James's Pk, Croy. CR0 . . . 224 DQ101
St. James's Pas, EC3 . . . 19 P9
St. James's Pl, SW1 . . . 29 L3
St. James's Rd, SE1 . . . 32 D10
SE16 . . . 32 D6
Croydon CR0 . . . 223 DP101
Gravesend DA11 . . . 213 GG86
Hampton Hill TW12 . . . 198 CB92
St. James's Sq, SW1 . . . 29 M2
St. James's St, E17 . . . 145 DY57
SW1 . . . 29 L2
Gravesend DA11 . . . 213 GG86
St. James's Ter, NW8 . . . 6 E10
St. James's Ter Ms, NW8 . . . 6 E9
⇌ St. James Street . . . 145 DY57
St. James St, W6 . . . 38 A1
St. James's Wk, EC1 . . . 18 G4
St. James Ter, SW12 . . . 202 DG88
St. James the Gt Cath Prim & Nurs Sch, Th.Hth. CR7
off Windsor Rd . . . 223 DP96
St. James the Gt Cath Prim Sch, SE15 . . . 44 B6
St. James Wk, Iver SL0 . . . 175 BE75
St. James Way, Sid. DA14 . . . 208 EY92
St. Jeromes Gro, Hayes UB3 . . 157 BQ72
St. Joachim's RC Prim Sch, E16 . . . 24 C9
St. Joan of Arc Cath Sch, Rick. WD3 off High St . . . 114 BL45
St. Joan of Arc RC Prim Sch, N5 off Northolme Rd . . . 144 DQ63
St. Joans Rd, N9 . . . 122 DT46
St. John & St. James C of E Prim Sch, E9 . . . 10 G3
N18 off Grove St . . . 122 DT50
St. John Baptist Prim Sch, Downham BR1
off Beachborough Rd . . . 205 EC91
St. John Evangelist RC Prim Sch, N1 . . . 8 G10
St. John Fisher Cath Prim Sch, Erith DA18 off Kale Rd . . . 188 EY76
Loughton IG10
off Burney Dr . . . 107 EQ40
St. John Fisher RC First & Mid Sch, Pnr. HA5
off Melrose Rd . . . 138 CA56
St. John Fisher RC Prim Sch, SW20 off Grand Dr . . . 221 CX99
Perivale UB6
off Thirlmere Av . . . 159 CJ69
St. Albans AL4
off Hazelmere Rd . . . 65 CJ17
St. John Fisher Rd, Erith DA18 . . . 188 EX76
St. John of Jerusalem C of E Prim Sch, E9 . . . 11 H7
ST. JOHN'S, SE8 . . . 46 A8
ST. JOHN'S, Wok. GU21 . . . 248 AV118
⇌ St. John's . . . 46 B8
St. Johns, N.Holm. RH5 . . . 285 CH140
St. John's, Red. RH1 . . . 288 DE136
St. John's & St. Clement's C of E Prim Sch, SE15
off Adys Rd . . . 184 DU83
St. John's (Angell Town) C of E Prim Sch, SW9 . . . 42 F9
St. Johns Av, N11 . . . 120 DF50
St. John's Av, NW10 . . . 161 CT67
SW15 . . . 201 CX85
Epsom KT17 . . . 239 CT112
Harlow CM17 . . . 58 EW11
St. Johns Av, Lthd. KT22 . . . 253 CH121
Warley CM14 . . . 130 FX49
St. John's Beaumont Sch, Old Wind. SL4
off Priest Hill . . . 194 AV89
St. John's Catholic Comp Sch, Grav. DA12
off Rochester Rd . . . 213 GK88
St. John's Catholic Prim Sch, Grav. DA12
off Rochester Rd . . . 213 GK87
Mill End WD3 off Berry La . . 114 BH46
St. John's Ch Rd, E9 . . . 10 G3
Wotton RH5
off Coast Hill . . . 284 BZ139
St. Johns Cl, N14 . . . 103 DJ44
St. John's Cl, SW6 . . . 39 J4
St. Johns Cl, Berry's Grn TN16
off St. Johns Ri . . . 261 EP116
St. John's Cl, Guil. GU2
off St. John's Rd . . . 280 AU135
St. Johns Cl, Hem.H. HP1
off Anchor La . . . 62 BH22
Leatherhead KT22 . . . 253 CJ120
St. John's Cl, Pot.B. EN6 . . . 86 DC33
St. Johns Cl, Rain. RM13 . . . 169 FG66
St. John's Cl, Uxb. UB8 . . . 156 BH67
Wembley HA9 . . . 140 CL64
St. John's C of E Prim Sch, N11 off Crescent Rd . . . 120 DF49
N20 off Swan La . . . 120 DC47
SE20 off Maple Rd . . . 204 DW94
Buckhurst Hill IG9
off High Rd . . . 124 EH46
Caterham CR3
off Markfield Rd . . . 274 DV125
Croydon CR0
off Spring Pk Rd . . . 225 DX104
Enfield EN2
off Theobalds Pk Rd . . . 103 DP36
Kingston upon Thames KT1
off Portland Rd . . . 220 CL97
Lemsford AL8
off Lemsford Village . . . 51 CT10
St. John's C of E Prim Sch, Sevenoaks TN13
off Bayham Rd . . . 279 FK123
Welwyn AL6
off Hertford Rd . . . 51 CZ05
St. John's C of E Sch, Epp. CM16 off Tower Rd . . . 91 ES30
St. John's C of E School, Stanmore, Stan. HA7
off Green La . . . 117 CG49
St. John's C of E Walham Grn Prim Sch, SW6 . . . 38 F6
St. John's Cotts, SE20
off Maple Rd . . . 204 DW94
St. Johns Cotts, Rich. TW9
off Kew Foot Rd . . . 180 CL83
St. Johns Ct, Buck.H. IG9 . . . 124 EH46
St. John's Ct, Egh. TW20 . . . 195 BA92
St. Johns Ct, Hert. SG14
off St. John's St . . . 54 DR09
St. John's Ct, Islw. TW7 . . . 179 CF82
St. Johns Ct, Nthwd. HA6
off Murray Rd . . . 115 BS52
St. Albans AL1 . . . 65 CH19
Westcott RH4
off St. John's Rd . . . 284 CC137
St. John's Ct, Wok. GU21
off St. Johns Hill Rd . . . 248 AU119
St. John's Cres, SW9 . . . 42 E10
St. Johns Dr, SW18 . . . 202 DB88
Walton-on-Thames KT12 . . 218 BW102
Windsor SL4 . . . 173 AM82
St. John's Est, N1 . . . 19 M1
SE1 . . . 32 A5
St. John's Gdns, W11 . . . 26 G1
★ St. John's Gate & Mus of the Order of St. John, EC1 . . . 18 G5
St. Johns Gro, N19 . . . 143 DJ61
SW13 off Terrace Gdns . . . 181 CT82
Richmond TW9
off Kew Foot Rd . . . 180 CL84
St. John's Highbury Vale C of E Prim Sch, N5
off Conewood St . . . 143 DP62
St. John's Hill, SW11 . . . 182 DD84
Coulsdon CR5 . . . 257 DN117
Purley CR8 . . . 257 DN116
Sevenoaks TN13 . . . 279 FJ123
St. John's Hill Gro, SW11 . . . 182 DD84
St. Johns Hill Rd, Wok. GU21 . 248 AU119
★ St. John's Jerusalem, Dart. DA4 . . . 210 FP94
St. John's La, EC1 . . . 18 G5
Great Amwell SG12 . . . 55 EA09
St. Johns Lo, Wok. GU21 . . . 248 AU119
St. John's Lye, Wok. GU21 . . . 248 AT119
St. John's Ms, W11 . . . 15 J9
Woking GU21 . . . 248 AU119
St. Johns Par, Sid. DA14 . . . 208 EU91
St. John's Pk, SE3 . . . 47 M5
St. Johns Pk Home Est, Enf. EN2 . . . 103 DP37
St. John's Pas, SW19
off Ridgway Pl . . . 201 CY93
St. John's Path, EC1 . . . 18 G5
St. Johns Pathway, SE23
off Devonshire Rd . . . 204 DW88
St. John's Pl, EC1 . . . 18 G5
St. John's Prep Sch, Pot.B. EN6 off The Ridgeway . . . 86 DE34
St. John's Prim Sch, E2 . . . 20 G1
W13 off Felix Rd . . . 159 CG73
Knaphill GU21
off Victoria Rd . . . 248 AS118
Redhill RH1
off Pendleton Rd . . . 288 DE136
St. John's RC Prim Sch, SE16 . . . 33 L5
St. John's R. C. Sch, Wdf.Grn. IG8 off Turpins La . . . 125 EN50
St. Johns Ri, Berry's Grn TN16 . . . 261 EP116
Woking GU21 . . . 248 AV119
St. John's Rd, E4 . . . 123 EB48
E6 off Ron Leighton Way . . . 166 EL67
St. Johns Rd, E16 . . . 23 N8
St. John's Rd, E17 . . . 123 EB54
N15 . . . 144 DS58
St. Johns Rd, NW11 . . . 141 CZ58
St. John's Rd, SE20 . . . 204 DW94
SW11 . . . 182 DE84
SW19 . . . 201 CY94
Barking IG11 . . . 167 ES67
Carshalton SM5 . . . 222 DE104
St. Johns Rd, Croy. CR0
off Waddon Rd . . . 223 DP104
St. John's Rd, Dart. DA2 . . . 210 FQ87
St. Johns Rd, E.Mol. KT8 . . . 219 CD98
St. John's Rd, Epp. CM16 . . . 91 ET30
St. Johns Rd, Erith DA8 . . . 189 FD78
St. John's Rd, Felt. TW13 . . . 198 BY91
St. Johns Rd, Grav. DA12 . . . 213 GK87
Grays RM16 . . . 193 GH78
St. John's Rd, Guil. GU2 . . . 280 AT135
Hampton Wick KT1 . . . 219 CJ96
Harrow HA1 . . . 139 CF58
St. Johns Rd, Hem.H. HP1 . . . 62 BG22
Ilford IG2 . . . 147 ER59
St. John's Rd, Islw. TW7 . . . 179 CE82
St. Johns Rd, Lthd. KT22 . . . 253 CJ121
Loughton IG10 . . . 107 EM40
New Malden KT3 . . . 220 CQ97
St. John's Rd, Petts Wd BR5 . . 227 ER100
Redhill RH1 . . . 288 DF136
Richmond TW9 . . . 180 CL84
St. Johns Rd, Rom. RM5 . . . 127 FC50
St. John's Rd, Sev. TN13 . . . 279 FH121
St. Johns Rd, Sid. DA14 . . . 208 EV91
Slough SL2 . . . 154 AU74
Southall UB2 . . . 178 BY76
Sutton SM1 . . . 222 DA103
Uxbridge UB8 . . . 156 BH67
Watford WD17 . . . 97 BV40
St. John's Rd, Well. DA16 . . . 188 EV83
Wembley HA9 . . . 139 CK63
Westcott RH4 . . . 284 CC137
St. Johns Rd, Wind. SL4 . . . 173 AN82
St. John's Rd, Wok. GU21 . . . 248 AV118
St. John's Sch, Lthd. KT22
off Epsom Rd . . . 253 CH121
Northwood HA6
off Wieland Rd . . . 115 BV51
St. John's Seminary, Won. GU5 off Cranleigh Rd . . . 281 BC144
St. John's Sen Sch, Enf. EN2
off The Ridgeway . . . 102 DG35
St. John's Sq, EC1 . . . 18 G5
St. John's St, Gdmg. GU7 . . . 280 AT144
Hertford SG14 . . . 54 DR09
St. Johns Ter, E7 . . . 166 EH65
SE18 . . . 187 EQ79
SW15 off Kingston Vale . . . 200 CS90
W10 . . . 14 D4
St. John's Ter, Enf. EN2 . . . 104 DR37
Redhill RH1
off St. John's Ter Rd . . . 288 DF136
St. John's Ter Rd, Red. RH1 . . . 288 DF136
St. John St, EC1 . . . 19 H5
St. John's Upr Holloway C of E Prim Sch, N19
off Pemberton Gdns . . . 143 DK61
St. Johns Vale, SE8 . . . 46 B8
St. Johns Vil, N19 . . . 143 DK61
St. John's Vil, W8 . . . 27 M7
St. Johns Wk, Harl. CM17 . . . 58 EW11
St. John's Walworth C of E Prim Sch, SE17 . . . 31 K9
St. John's Waterside, Wok. GU21
off Copse Rd . . . 248 AT118
St. Johns Way, N19 . . . 143 DK60
St. John's Way, Cher. KT16 . . 216 BG102
St. Johns Well Ct, Berk. HP4 . . 60 AV18
St. Johns Well La, Berk. HP4 . . 60 AV18
ST. JOHN'S WOOD, NW8 . . . 16 A2
⊖ St. John's Wood . . . 6 A10
St. John's Wd Ct, NW8 . . . 16 B3
St. John's Wd High St, NW8 . . . 16 B1
St. John's Wd Pk, NW8 . . . 6 B9
St. John's Wd Rd, NW8 . . . 16 A4
St. John's Wd Ter, NW8 . . . 6 C10
St. John the Baptist C of E Jun Sch, Hmptn W. KT1
off Lower Teddington Rd . . 199 CK94
St. John the Baptist C of E Prim Sch, N1 . . . 19 N1
Great Amwell SG12
off Hillside La . . . 55 EA10
St. John the Baptist Sch, Wok. GU22 off Elmbridge La . . . 249 BA119
St. John the Divine C of E Prim Sch, SE5 . . . 42 G4
St. John Vianney RC Prim Sch, N15 off Stanley Rd . . . 143 DP56
St. Joseph's Catholic Comb Sch, Chal.St.P. SL9
off Priory Rd . . . 134 AW55
St. Joseph's Catholic High Sch, Slou. SL2
off Shaggy Calf La . . . 154 AU73
St. Joseph's Cath Infants' & Jun Schs, SE5 . . . 43 J4
St. Joseph's Cath Inf Sch, E10
off Marsh La . . . 145 EA61
St. Joseph's Cath Jun Sch, E10
off Vicarage Rd . . . 145 EB60
St. Joseph's Cath Prim Sch, Bark. IG11 off Broadway . . . 167 EQ67
Bromley BR1
off Plaistow La . . . 206 EH94
Crayford DA1 off Old Rd . . . 189 FE84
Dagenham RM9
off Connor Rd . . . 148 EZ63
Dorking RH4
off Norfolk Rd . . . 285 CG136
Epsom KT18 off Rosebank . . 238 CQ114
Guildford GU2
off Aldershot Rd . . . 264 AT132
Harrow HA3 off Dobbin Cl . . 117 CG54
Hertford SG14
off North Rd . . . 53 DN08
Kingston upon Thames KT1
off Fairfield S . . . 220 CM96
Northfleet DA11
off Springhead Rd . . . 212 GD87
South Oxhey WD19
off Ainsdale Rd . . . 116 BW48
Upminster RM14
off St. Mary's La . . . 150 FP61
St. Joseph's Catholic Prim Sch Redhill, Red. RH1
off Linkfield La . . . 272 DE133
St. Josephs Cl, W10 . . . 14 F7
St. Joseph's Cl, Orp. BR6 . . . 245 ET105
St. Joseph's Coll, SE19
off Beulah Hill . . . 203 DP93
St. Joseph's Conv Prep Sch, Grav. DA12 off Old Rd E . . . 213 GJ89
St. Joseph's Conv Sch, E11
off Cambridge Pk . . . 146 EG58
St. Joseph's Ct, SE7 . . . 186 EH79
St. Josephs Dr, Sthl. UB1 . . . 158 BY74
St. Josephs Grn, Welw.G.C. AL7 . . . 51 CX12
St. Joseph's Gro, NW4 . . . 141 CV56
St. Joseph's In The Pk Sch, Hertingfordbury SG14
off St. Mary's La . . . 53 DN11
St. Joseph's Ms, Beac. HP9 . . . 111 AM53
St. Joseph's Prim Sch, SE8 . . 46 A4
SW3 . . . 28 E9
St. Joseph's RC Inf & Jun Schs, NW4 off Watford Way . . . 141 CV56
St. Joseph's RC Inf Sch, SE19
off Crown Dale . . . 204 DQ93
Wembley HA9
off Waverley Av . . . 140 CM64
St. Joseph's RC Jun Sch, SE19
off Woodend . . . 204 DQ93
Wembley HA9
off Chatsworth Av . . . 140 CM64
St. Joseph's RC Prim Sch, N19
off Highgate Hill . . . 143 DH60
NW10 off Goodson Rd . . . 160 CS66
SE1 . . . 31 K4
SE10 . . . 35 K10
Bermondsey, SE16 . . . 32 C5
Rotherhithe, SE16 . . . 33 H7
SW15 off Oakhill Rd . . . 202 DA85
W7 off York Av . . . 159 CE74
W9 . . . 15 N3
WC2 . . . 18 B8
Waltham Cross EN8
off Royal Av . . . 89 DY32
St. Josephs Rd, N9 . . . 122 DV45
St. Joseph's Rd, Wal.Cr. EN8 . . 89 DY33
St. Josephs St, SW8 . . . 41 K6
St. Joseph's Vale, SE3 . . . 47 H9
St. Joseph the Worker Catholic Prim Sch, Hutt. CM13
off Highview Cres . . . 131 GC44
St. Jude's & St. Paul's C of E Prim Sch, N1 . . . 9 N4
St. Judes Cl, Eng.Grn TW20 . . 194 AW92
St. Jude's C of E Prim Sch, SE1 . . . 30 G6
SE24 off Regent Rd . . . 203 DP85
St. Jude's C of E Sch, Eng.Grn TW20 off Bagshot Rd . . . 194 AW93
St. Jude's Rd, E2 . . . 20 F1
Englefield Green TW20 . . . 194 AW90
St. Jude St, N16 . . . 9 P3
ST. JULIANS, St.Alb. AL1 . . . 65 CD23
St. Julians, Sev. TN15 . . . 279 FN128
St. Julian's Cl, SW16 . . . 203 DN91
St. Julian's Fm Rd, SE27 . . . 203 DN91
St. Julian's Rd, NW6 . . . 5 H7
St. Julians Rd, St.Alb. AL1 . . . 65 CD22
St. Justin Cl, Orp. BR5 . . . 228 EX97
★ St. Katharine Docks, E1 . . . 32 B1
St. Katharine's Pier . . . 32 A2
St. Katharines Prec, NW1 . . . 7 J10
St. Katharine's Way, E1 . . . 32 B2
St. Katharine's Knockholt C of E Prim Sch, Knock. TN14 off Main Rd . . . 262 EV117
St. Katherines Rd, Cat. CR3 . . 274 DU125
Erith DA18 . . . 188 EX75
St. Katherine's Row, EC3
off Fenchurch St . . . 19 P9
St. Katherine's Wk, W11 . . . 26 D2
St. Katherines Way, Berk. HP4 . . 60 AT16
St. Keverne Rd, SE9 . . . 206 EL91
St. Kilda Rd, W13 . . . 159 CG74
Orpington BR6 . . . 227 ET102
St. Kilda's Rd, N16 . . . 144 DR60
Brentwood CM15 . . . 130 FV45
Harrow HA1 . . . 139 CE58
St. Kitts Ter, SE19 . . . 204 DS92
St. Laurence Cl, NW6 . . . 4 D9
Orpington BR5 . . . 228 EX97
Uxbridge UB8 . . . 156 BJ71
St. Laurence Dr, Brox. EN10 . . 71 DZ23
St. Laurence Way, Slou. SL1 . . 174 AU76
St. Lawrence Cl, Abb.L. WD5 . . 81 BS30
Bovingdon HP3 . . . 79 BA27
Edgware HA8 . . . 118 CM52
St. Lawrence C of E Jun Sch, E.Mol. KT8
off Church Rd . . . 218 CC98
St. Lawrence Ct, Abb.L. WD5
off St. Lawrence Cl . . . 81 BS30
St. Lawrence Dr, Pnr. HA5 . . . 137 BV58
★ St. Lawrence Jewry Ch, EC2 . . . 19 K8
St. Lawrence Prim Sch, Eff. KT24 off Lower Rd . . . 268 BX127
Feltham TW13
off Victoria Rd . . . 197 BV88
St. Lawrence Rd, Upmin. RM14 . . . 150 FQ61
St. Lawrence St, E14 . . . 34 F2
St. Lawrence's Way, Reig. RH2
off Church St . . . 272 DA134
St. Lawrence Ter, W10 . . . 14 E6
St. Lawrence Way, SW9 . . . 42 F7
Bricket Wood AL2 . . . 82 BZ30
Caterham CR3 . . . 258 DQ123
St. Leonards Av, E4 . . . 123 ED51
Harrow HA3 . . . 139 CJ56
Windsor SL4 . . . 173 AQ82
St. Leonards Cl, Bushey WD23 . 98 BY42
Grays RM17 . . . 192 FZ79
Hertford SG14 . . . 54 DS07
St. Leonard's Cl, Well. DA16 . . . 188 EU83
St. Leonard's C of E Prim Sch, SW16
off Mitcham La . . . 203 DK92
St. Leonards Ct, N1 . . . 19 M2
St. Leonard's Gdns, Houns. TW5 . . . 178 BY80
St. Leonards Gdns, Ilf. IG1 . . . 147 EQ64
St. Leonards Hill, Wind. SL4 . . . 173 AK84
St. Leonards Ri, Orp. BR6 . . . 245 ES105
St. Leonards Rd, E14 . . . 22 D7
NW10 . . . 160 CR70
St. Leonard's Rd, SW14 . . . 180 CP83
St. Leonards Rd, W13 . . . 159 CJ73
Amersham HP6 . . . 77 AS35
Claygate KT10 . . . 237 CF107
Croydon CR0 . . . 223 DP104
Epsom KT18 . . . 255 CW119
Hertford SG14 . . . 54 DR07
Nazeing EN9 . . . 90 EE25
St. Leonard's Rd, Surb. KT6 . . . 219 CK99
St. Leonards Rd, T.Ditt. KT7 . . 219 CG100
Windsor SL4 . . . 173 AQ82
St. Leonards Sq, NW5 . . . 7 H5
St. Leonard's Sq, Surb. KT6 . . . 219 CK99
St. Leonards St, E3 . . . 22 D2
St. Leonard's Ter, SW3 . . . 40 E1
St. Leonards Wk, SW16 . . . 203 DM94
Iver SL0 . . . 175 BF76
St. Leonards Way, Horn. RM11 . . . 149 FH61
St. Loo Av, SW3 . . . 40 D2
St. Louis Cl, Pot.B. EN6 . . . 86 DC33
St. Louis Rd, SE27 . . . 204 DQ91
St. Loy's Rd, N17 . . . 122 DS54
St. Lucia Dr, E15 . . . 13 L8
St. Luke Cl, Uxb. UB8 . . . 156 BK72
ST. LUKE'S, EC1 . . . 19 K4
St. Luke's Av, SW4 . . . 183 DK84
St. Lukes Av, Enf. EN2 . . . 104 DR38
St. Luke's Av, Ilf. IG1 . . . 147 EP64
St. Luke's Catholic Prim Sch, Harl. CM19
off Pyenest Rd . . . 73 EQ17
St. Luke's Cl, EC1 . . . 19 K4
SE25 . . . 224 DV100
St. Lukes Cl, Lane End DA2 . . . 211 FS92
Swanley BR8 . . . 229 FD96
St. Luke's C of E Prim Sch, EC1 . . . 19 K3
SE27 off Linton Gro . . . 204 DQ92
W9 . . . 14 G2
Kingston upon Thames KT2
off Acre Rd . . . 220 CM95
St. Luke's C of E (VA) Prim Sch, E16 . . . 23 M8
St. Lukes Ct, Hat. AL10 . . . 67 CV17
St. Luke's Est, EC1 . . . 19 L3
St. Luke's Hosp for the Clergy, W1 . . . 17 L5
St. Lukes Ms, W11 . . . 15 H8
St. Luke's Prim Sch, E14 . . . 34 G9
St. Lukes Rd, W11 . . . 15 H7
Old Windsor SL4 . . . 194 AU86
Whyteleafe CR3
off Whyteleafe Hill . . . 258 DT118
St. Lukes Sq, E16 . . . 23 M9
Guildford GU1 . . . 281 AZ135
St. Luke's St, SW3 . . . 28 C10
St. Luke's Woodside Hosp, N10 . . . 142 DG56
St. Luke's Yd, W9 . . . 14 G1
St. Magnus Ct, Hem.H. HP3 . . . 63 BP22
St. Malo Av, N9 . . . 122 DW48
St. Margaret Clitherow RC Prim Sch, NW10
off Quainton St . . . 140 CR63
SE28 off Cole Cl . . . 168 EV74
St. Margaret Dr, Epsom KT18 . 238 CR114
ST. MARGARETS, Twick. TW1 . . 199 CG85
ST. MARGARETS, Ware SG12 . . 55 EB10
St. Margarets, Bark. IG11 . . . 167 ER67
Guildford GU1 . . . 265 AZ133
St. Margarets Av, N15 . . . 143 DP56
N20 . . . 120 DC47
Ashford TW15 . . . 197 BP92
Berry's Green TN16
off St. Anns Way . . . 261 EP116
Harrow HA2 . . . 138 CC62
Sidcup DA15 . . . 207 ER90
St. Margaret's Av, Sutt. SM3 . . 221 CY104
St. Margarets Av, Uxb. UB8 . . . 156 BN70
St. Margarets Cl, EC2
off Lothbury . . . 19 L8
Berkhamsted HP4 . . . 60 AX20
Dartford DA2 . . . 211 FR89
Iver SL0 . . . 155 BD68
Orpington BR6 . . . 246 EV105
Penn HP10 . . . 110 AC47
St. Margaret's C of E Prim Sch, SE18
off St. Margaret's Gro . . . 187 EQ78
Barking IG11 off North St . . . 167 EQ66
St. Margaret's Ct, SE1 . . . 31 K3
St. Margaret's Cres, SW15 . . . 201 CV85
Gravesend DA12 . . . 213 GL90
St. Margaret's Dr, Twick. TW1 . . 199 CH85
St. Margarets Gate, Iver SL0
off St. Margarets Cl . . . 155 BD68
St. Margaret's Gro, E11 . . . 146 EF62
SE18 . . . 187 EQ79
St. Margarets Gro, Twick. TW1 . 199 CG86
St. Margaret's Hosp, Epp. CM16 . . . 92 EV29
St. Margarets La, W8 . . . 27 L7
St. Margaret's Lee C of E Prim Sch, SE13
off Lee Ch St . . . 186 EE84
St. Margarets Pas, SE13
off Church Ter . . . 186 EE83
St. Margarets Path, SE18 . . . 187 EQ78
St. Margarets Rd, E12 . . . 146 EJ61
St. Margaret's Rd, N17 . . . 144 DS55
NW10 . . . 14 A1
St. Margarets Rd, SE4 . . . 185 DZ84
W7 . . . 179 CE75
Coulsdon CR5 . . . 257 DH121
Edgware HA8 . . . 118 CP50
Isleworth TW7 . . . 179 CH84
St. Margaret's Rd, Nthflt DA11 . 212 GE89
Ruislip HA4 . . . 137 BR58
St. Margarets Rd, S.Darenth DA2, DA4 . . . 211 FS93
St. Margaret's Rd, Stans.Abb. SG12 . . . 55 EA13
St. Margarets Rd, Twick. TW1 . . 179 CH84
St. Margarets Rbt, Twick. TW1 . . . 199 CH85
St. Margaret's Sch, NW3
off Kidderpore Gdns . . . 142 DB63
Tadworth KT20
off Tadworth Ct . . . 255 CX121
St. Margaret's Sch Bushey, Bushey WD23
off Merry Hill Rd . . . 116 CA45
Prep Sch, Bushey WD23
off Merry Hill Rd . . . 116 CA46
⇌ St. Margarets (SG12) . . . 55 EC11
St. Margarets Sq, SE4
off Adelaide Av . . . 185 DZ84
St. Margaret's St, SW1 . . . 30 A5
St. Margaret's Ter, SE18 . . . 187 EQ78
⇌ St. Margarets (TW1) . . . 199 CH86
St. Margarets Way, Hem.H. HP2 . . . 63 BR20
St. Marks Av, Nthflt DA11 . . . 213 GF87
St. Mark's Catholic Sch, Houns. TW3 off Bath Rd . . . 178 BZ83
St. Marks Cl, SE10 . . . 46 E5
SW6 . . . 39 J7
W11 . . . 14 E9
St. Mark's Cl, Barn. EN5 . . . 102 DB41
St. Marks Cl, Coln.Hth AL4 . . . 66 CP22
Harrow HA1
off Nightingale Av . . . 139 CH59
St. Mark's C of E Acad, Mitch. CR4 off Acacia Rd . . . 223 DH96
St. Mark's C of E Prim Sch, N19 off Sussex Way . . . 143 DL61
SE11 . . . 42 D2
SE25 off Albert Rd . . . 224 DU98
Bromley BR2
off Aylesbury Rd . . . 226 EG97
St. Marks Cres, NW1 . . . 7 H8
St. Mark's Gate, E9 . . . 11 P7
St. Mark's Gro, SW10 . . . 39 M3
St. Mark's Hill, Surb. KT6 . . . 220 CL100
St. Mark's Hosp, Har. HA1 . 139 CH59
St. Mark's Pl, SW19
off Wimbledon Hill Rd . . . 201 CZ93
St. Marks Pl, W11 . . . 14 F9
St. Mark's Pl, Dag. RM10 . . . 169 FB65
St. Marks Pl, Wind. SL4 . . . 173 AQ82
St. Mark's Prim Sch, W7
off Lower Boston Rd . . . 179 CE75
Mitcham CR4
off St. Marks Rd . . . 222 DF96
St. Marks Ri, E8 . . . 10 B3
St. Marks Rd, SE25
off Coventry Rd . . . 224 DU98
St. Mark's Rd, W5 . . . 160 CL74
St. Marks Rd, W7 . . . 179 CE75
W10 . . . 14 D8
W11 . . . 14 E9
Bromley BR2 . . . 226 EH97
Enfield EN1 . . . 104 DT44
St. Mark's Rd, Epsom KT18 . . . 255 CW118
St. Marks Rd, Mitch. CR4 . . . 222 DF96
St. Mark's Rd, Tedd. TW11 . . . 199 CH94
St. Marks Rd, Wind. SL4 . . . 173 AQ82
St. Marks Sq, NW1 . . . 6 G8
St. Mark St, E1 . . . 20 B9
St. Mark's W Essex Catholic Sch, Harl. CM18 off Tripton Rd . . 73 ES16
St. Martha's Av, Wok. GU22 . . . 249 AZ121

St. Martha's Conv Jun Sch, Barn. EN5 off Wood St . . . 101 CY42
St. Martha's Conv Sen Sch, Had.Wd EN4 off Camlet Way . . . 102 DA39
St. Marthas Ct, Chilw. GU4 off Nursery Gdns . . . 281 BB140
St. Martin Cl, Uxb. UB8 . . . 156 BK72
★ St. Martin-in-the-Fields Ch, WC2 . . . 30 A1
St. Martin-in-the-Fields High Sch for Girls, SW2 off Tulse Hill . . . 203 DP88
St. Martin of Porres RC Prim Sch, N11 off Blake Rd . . . 121 DJ51
St. Martins, Nthwd. HA6 . . . 115 BR50
St. Martins App, Ruis. HA4 . . . 137 BS59
St. Martins Av, E6 . . . 24 E1
Epsom KT18 . . . 238 CS114
St. Martins Cl, NW1 . . . 7 L8
East Horsley KT24 . . . 267 BS129
Enfield EN1 . . . 104 DV39
Epsom KT17 . . . 239 CT113
Erith DA18 off St. Helens Rd . . . 188 EX75
St. Martin's Cl, Wat. WD19 . . . 116 BW49
West Drayton UB7 off St. Martin's Rd . . . 176 BK76
St. Martin's C of E Inf & Jun Schs, Epsom KT18 off Worple Rd . . . 254 CR115
St. Martin's C of E Prim Sch, Pixham La, Dor. RH4 off Pixham La . . . 269 CJ134
Ranmore Rd, Dor. RH4 off Ranmore Rd . . . 285 CG135
St. Martin's Coll, E3 . . . 21 N5
St. Martin's Ct, WC2 off St. Martin's La . . . 18 A10
Ashford TW15 . . . 196 BJ92
St. Martins Dr, Walt. KT12 . . . 218 BW104
St. Martins Est, SW2 . . . 203 DN88
St. Martin's La, WC2 . . . 18 A10
St. Martins La, Beck. BR3 . . . 225 EB99
St. Martin's-le-Grand, EC1 . . . 19 J8
St. Martins Meadow, Brasted TN16 . . . 262 EW123
St. Martin's Ms, WC2 . . . 30 A1
St. Martins Ms, Dor. RH4 off Church St . . . 285 CG136
Pyrford GU22 . . . 250 BG116
St. Martin's Pl, WC2 . . . 30 A1
St. Martins Rd, N9 . . . 122 DV47
St. Martin's Rd, SW9 . . . 42 C8
St. Martins Rd, Dart. DA1 . . . 210 FM86
Hoddesdon EN11 . . . 71 EC17
St. Martin's Rd, West Dr. UB7 . . . 176 BJ76
St. Martin's Sch, Hutt. CM13 off Hanging Hill La . . . 131 GC46
Northwood HA6 off Moor Pk Rd . . . 115 BR50
St. Martin's St, WC2 . . . 29 P1
St. Martins Ter, N10 off Pages La . . . 120 DG54
St. Martins Wk, Dor. RH4 off High St . . . 285 CH136
St. Martins Way, SW17 . . . 202 DC90
St. Mary Abbots C of E Prim Sch, W8 . . . 27 L5
St. Mary Abbots Pl, W8 . . . 27 H7
St. Mary Abbots Ter, W14 . . . 27 H7
St. Mary & All Saints C of E Prim Sch, Beac. HP9 off Maxwell Rd . . . 111 AL52
St. Mary & St. Joseph's Cath Sch, Sid. DA14 off Chislehurst Rd . . . 208 EU92
St. Mary & St. Michael Prim Sch, E1 . . . 20 G9
St. Mary & St. Pancras C of E Prim Sch, NW1 . . . 17 N1
St. Mary at Hill, EC3 . . . 31 N1
★ St. Mary at Hill Ch, EC3 . . . 31 N1
St. Mary Av, Wall. SM6 . . . 222 DG104
St. Mary Axe, EC3 . . . 19 N9
St. Marychurch St, SE16 . . . 32 G5
ST. MARY CRAY, Orp. BR5 . . . 228 EW99
≠ St. Mary Cray . . . 228 EU98
St. Mary Cray Prim Sch, St.M.Cray BR5 off High St . . . 228 EW100
St. Mary Graces Ct, E1 . . . 20 B10
St. Marylebone Cl, NW10 off Craven Pk . . . 160 CS67
St. Marylebone C of E Sch, W1 . . . 17 H6
★ St. Mary-le-Bow Ch, EC2 . . . 19 K9
St. Mary Magdalene Acad, N7 . . . 8 E4
St. Mary Magdalene C of E Prim Sch, SE15 . . . 44 E9
SE18 . . . 37 L8
St. Mary Magdalene's Cath Prim Sch, SW14 off Worple St . . . 180 CR83
St. Mary Magdalene's C of E Prim Sch, W2 . . . 15 L6
St. Mary Magdalen's Cath Prim Sch, SE4 off Howson Rd . . . 185 DY84
St. Mary Magdalen's RC Jun Sch, NW2 off Linacre Rd . . . 161 CV65
St. Mary Newington Cl, SE17 off Surrey Sq . . . 31 P10
St. Mary of the Angels RC Prim Sch, W2 . . . 15 J8
St. Mary Rd, E17 . . . 145 EA56
St. Marys, Bark. IG11 . . . 167 ER67
St. Mary's & St. John's C.E. Prim Sch, NW4 off Prothero Gdns . . . 141 CV57
St. Mary's & St. Peter's C of E Prim Sch, Tedd. TW11 off Somerset Rd . . . 199 CF92
St. Marys App, E12 . . . 147 EM64
St. Marys Av, E11 . . . 146 EH58
St. Mary's Av, N3 . . . 119 CY54
Bromley BR2 . . . 226 EE97
Northwood HA6 . . . 115 BS50
St. Marys Av, Shenf. CM15 . . . 131 GA43
St. Mary's Av, Stanw. TW19 . . . 196 BK87
Teddington TW11 . . . 199 CF93
St. Mary's Av Cen, Sthl. UB2 . . . 178 CB77
St. Mary's Av N, Sthl. UB2 . . . 178 CB77
St. Mary's Av S, Sthl. UB2 . . . 178 CB77
St. Mary's Bryanston Sq C of E Prim Sch, W1 . . . 16 E6
St. Mary's Cath Inf Sch, Croy. CR0 off Bedford Pk . . . 224 DR102
St. Mary's Cath Jun Sch, E17 off Shernhall St . . . 145 EC55
Croydon CR0 off Sydenham Rd . . . 224 DR102
St. Mary's Cath Prim Sch, E4 off Station Rd . . . 123 ED46
SW19 off Russell Rd . . . 202 DA94
Beckenham BR3 off Westgate Rd . . . 205 EC94
Hornchurch RM12 off Hornchurch Rd . . . 149 FG60
Uxbridge UB8 off Rockingham Cl . . . 156 BJ67
St. Mary's Ch Rd, Hat. AL9 . . . 85 CU25
St. Mary's Cl, N17 off Kemble Rd . . . 122 DU53
St. Marys Cl, Chess. KT9 . . . 238 CM108
Epsom KT17 . . . 239 CU108
St. Mary's Cl, Fetch. KT22 . . . 253 CD123
Gravesend DA12 . . . 213 GJ89
St. Marys Cl, Grays RM17 off Dock Rd . . . 192 GD79
St. Mary's Cl, Hare. UB9 . . . 136 BH55
St. Marys Cl, Orp. BR5 . . . 228 EV96
St. Mary's Cl, Oxt. RH8 . . . 276 EE129
Stanwell TW19 . . . 196 BK87
Sunbury-on-Thames TW16 off Green Way . . . 217 BU98
St. Marys Cl, Wat. WD18 off Church St . . . 98 BW42
St. Mary's C of E Comb Sch, Amer. HP7 off School La . . . 77 AP39
St. Mary's C of E First Sch, Nthch HP4 off New Rd . . . 60 AS17
St. Mary's C of E High Sch, NW4 off Downage . . . 141 CW55
St. Mary's C of E Inf Sch, N8 off Church La . . . 143 DM56
St. Mary's C of E Jun Sch, N8 off Rectory Gdns . . . 143 DL56
Oxted RH8 off Silkham Rd . . . 276 EE128
St. Mary's C of E Prim Sch, E17 off The Drive . . . 145 EB56
N1 . . . 9 H8
N3 off Dollis Pk . . . 119 CZ52
NW10 off Garnet Rd . . . 160 CS65
SE13 off Lewisham High St . . . 205 EC85
SW15 off Felsham Rd . . . 181 CX83
Barnet EN4 off Littlegrove . . . 102 DE44
Byfleet KT14 off Hart Rd . . . 234 BL113
Chessington KT9 off Church La . . . 238 CM107
North Mymms AL9 off Dellsome La . . . 67 CV23
Rickmansworth WD3 off Stockers Fm Rd . . . 114 BK48
Shenfield CM15 off Hall La . . . 131 FZ44
Slough SL1 off Yew Tree Rd . . . 174 AU76
Swanley BR8 off St. Marys Rd . . . 229 FE98
Inf Site, Twick. TW1 off Amyand Pk Rd . . . 199 CG87
Jun Site, Twick. TW1 off Richmond Rd . . . 199 CH88
St. Mary's C of E Prim School, Stoke Newington, N16 off Lordship Rd . . . 144 DS61
St. Mary's Coll, Twick. TW1 off Waldegrave Rd . . . 199 CF90
St. Mary's Copse, Wor.Pk. KT4 . . . 220 CS103
St. Marys Ct, E6 . . . 25 J3
St. Mary's Ct, SE7 . . . 186 EK80
W5 off St. Mary's Rd . . . 179 CK75
Beaconsfield HP9 off Malthouse Sq . . . 133 AM55
St. Marys Cres, NW4 . . . 141 CV55
Hayes UB3 . . . 157 BT73
St. Marys Cres, Islw. TW7 . . . 179 CD80
St. Mary's Cres, Stanw. TW19 . . . 196 BK87
St. Marys Dr, Felt. TW14 . . . 197 BQ87
St. Mary's Dr, Sev. TN13 . . . 278 FE123
St. Marys Est, SE16 off St. Marychurch St . . . 32 G5
St. Mary's Gdns, SE11 . . . 30 F8
St. Mary's Gate, W8 . . . 27 L7
St. Marys Grn, N2 off Thomas More Way . . . 142 DC55
Biggin Hill TN16 . . . 260 EJ118
St. Mary's Gro, N1 . . . 9 H5
SW13 . . . 181 CV83
W4 . . . 180 CP79
St. Marys Gro, Bigg.H. TN16 . . . 260 EJ118
St. Mary's Gro, Rich. TW9 . . . 180 CM84
St. Mary's Hare Pk Sch, Gidea Pk RM2 off South Dr . . . 150 FJ55
St. Mary's High Sch, Chsht EN8 off Churchgate . . . 88 DV30
Croydon CR0 off Woburn Rd . . . 224 DQ102
St. Mary's Hosp, W2 . . . 16 B8
St. Mary's Kilburn C of E Prim Sch, NW6 . . . 5 K8
St. Mary's La, Hert. SG14 . . . 53 DM11
Upminster RM14 . . . 150 FN61
St. Marys Mans, W2 . . . 16 A6
St. Mary's Ms, NW6 . . . 5 L7
Richmond TW10 off Wiggins La . . . 199 CJ89
St. Mary's Mt, Cat. CR3 . . . 258 DT124
St. Marys Path, N1 . . . 9 H8
St. Mary's Pl, SE9 off Eltham High St . . . 207 EN86
W5 . . . 179 CK75
W8 . . . 27 L7
St. Mary's RC Inf Sch, N15 off Hermitage Rd . . . 144 DR58
St. Mary's RC Infants' Sch, Cars. SM5 off West St . . . 240 DF105
St. Mary's RC Jun Sch, N15 off Hermitage Rd . . . 144 DR57
Carshalton SM5 off Shorts Rd . . . 240 DF106
St. Mary's RC Prim Sch, NW6 . . . 5 J10
SE9 off Glenure Rd . . . 207 EN85
SW4 off Crescent La . . . 183 DJ84
SW8 . . . 41 K6
W4 off Duke Rd . . . 180 CS78
St. Mary's RC Prim Sch, W10 . . . 14 E5
W14 . . . 26 D7
Enfield EN3 off Durants Rd . . . 105 DX42
Isleworth TW7 off South St . . . 179 CG83
Tilbury RM18 off Calcutta Rd . . . 193 GF82
St. Marys Rd, E10 . . . 145 EC62
E13 . . . 166 EH68
N8 off High St . . . 143 DL56
N9 . . . 122 DW46
St. Mary's Rd, NW10 . . . 160 CS67
St. Marys Rd, NW11 . . . 141 CY59
St. Mary's Rd, SE15 . . . 44 G7
SE25 . . . 224 DS97
SW19 (Wimbledon) . . . 201 CY92
W5 . . . 179 CK75
Barnet EN4 . . . 120 DF45
Bexley DA5 . . . 209 FC88
Cheshunt EN8 . . . 88 DW29
Denham UB9 . . . 135 BF58
St. Marys Rd, E.Mol. KT8 . . . 219 CD99
St. Mary's Rd, Grays RM16 . . . 193 GH77
Greenhithe DA9 . . . 211 FS85
Harefield UB9 . . . 136 BH56
Hayes UB3 . . . 157 BT73
Hemel Hempstead HP2 . . . 62 BK19
St. Marys Rd, Ilf. IG1 . . . 147 EQ61
Leatherhead KT22 . . . 253 CH122
Long Ditton KT6 . . . 219 CJ101
Reigate RH2 . . . 288 DB135
St. Mary's Rd, Slou. SL3 . . . 154 AY74
South Croydon CR2 . . . 242 DR110
St. Marys Rd, Surb. KT6 . . . 219 CK100
Swanley BR8 . . . 229 FD98
St. Mary's Rd, Wat. WD18 . . . 97 BV42
St. Marys Rd, Wey. KT13 . . . 235 BR105
St. Mary's Rd, Wok. GU21 . . . 248 AW117
Worcester Park KT4 . . . 220 CS103
St. Mary's Sch, NW3 . . . 6 A3
Gerrards Cross SL9 off Packhorse Rd . . . 134 AY56
St. Marys Sq, W2 . . . 16 A6
St. Mary's Sq, W5 off St. Mary's Rd . . . 179 CK75
St. Marys Ter, W2 . . . 16 A6
St. Mary's Twr, EC1 off Fortune St . . . 19 K5
St. Mary St, SE18 . . . 37 K8
St. Marys Vw, Har. HA3 . . . 139 CJ57
St. Mary's Vw, Wat. WD18 . . . 98 BW42
St. Mary's Wk, SE11 . . . 30 F8
Bletchingley RH1 . . . 274 DR133
Hayes UB3 . . . 157 BT73
St. Marys Wk, St.Alb. AL4 . . . 65 CH16
St. Mary's Way, Chal.St.P. SL9 . . . 112 AX54
Chesham HP5 . . . 76 AP31
Chigwell IG7 . . . 125 EN50
Guildford GU2 . . . 264 AS132
St. Matthew Acad, SE3 . . . 47 J10
St. Matthew Cl, Uxb. UB8 . . . 156 BK72
St. Matthew's Av, Surb. KT6 . . . 220 CL102
St. Matthews Cl, Rain. RM13 . . . 169 FG66
Watford WD19 . . . 98 BX44
St. Matthew's C of E Inf Sch, Cob. KT11 off Downside Rd . . . 251 BV118
St. Matthew's C of E Prim Sch, SW1 . . . 29 P6
Enfield EN3 off South St . . . 104 DW43
St. Matthews C of E Prim Sch, Red. RH1 off Linkfield La . . . 272 DF132
St. Matthew's C of E Prim Sch, Surb. KT6 off Langley Rd . . . 220 CL101
St. Matthew's Dr, Brom. BR1 . . . 227 EM97
St. Matthews Prim Sch, SW20 off Cottenham Pk Rd . . . 221 CU95
St. Matthew's Prim Sch, Yiew. UB7 off High St . . . 156 BL74
St. Matthew's Rd, SW2 . . . 183 DM84
St. Matthews Rd, W5 off The Common . . . 160 CL74
St. Matthew's Rd, Red. RH1 . . . 272 DF133
St. Matthew's Row, E2 . . . 20 C3
St. Matthew St, SW1 . . . 29 N7
St. Matthias Cl, NW9 . . . 141 CT57
St. Matthias C of E Prim Sch, E2 . . . 20 B4
N16 . . . 9 N2
St. Maur Rd, SW6 . . . 39 H6
St. Mellion Cl, SE28 . . . 168 EX72
St. Merryn Cl, SE18 . . . 187 ER80
St. Meryl Sch, Carp.Pk WD19 off The Mead . . . 116 BY48
St. Michael & All Angels C of E Acad, SE5 . . . 43 J5
St. Michael & St. Martin RC Prim Sch, Houns. TW4 off Belgrave Rd . . . 178 BZ83
St. Michael at Bowes C of E Jun Sch, N13 off Tottenhall Rd . . . 121 DN51
St. Michael Cath Prim Sch, Ashf. TW15 off Feltham Hill Rd . . . 196 BN92
St. Michael's, Oxt. RH8 . . . 276 EG129
St. Michael's All, EC3 . . . 19 M9
St. Michaels Av, N9 . . . 122 DW45
Hemel Hempstead HP3 . . . 63 BP21
St. Michael's Av, Wem. HA9 . . . 160 CN65
St. Michael's Camden Town C of E Prim Sch, NW1 . . . 7 L8
St. Michael's Catholic Gram Sch, N12 off Nether St . . . 120 DC50
St. Michael's Catholic High Sch, Wat. WD25 off High Elms La . . . 82 BX32
St. Michaels Cl, E16 . . . 24 E7
St. Michael's Cl, N3 . . . 119 CZ54
St. Michaels Cl, N12 . . . 120 DE50
Aveley RM15 . . . 170 FQ73
Bromley BR1 . . . 226 EL97
Erith DA18 off St. Helens Rd . . . 188 EX75
Harlow CM20 . . . 57 ES14
Walton-on-Thames KT12 . . . 218 BW103
Worcester Park KT4 . . . 221 CT103
St. Michael's C of E First Sch, Mick. RH5 off School La . . . 269 CJ127
St. Michael's C of E Prim Sch, N6 off North Rd . . . 142 DG59
N22 off Bounds Grn Rd . . . 121 DM53
SE26 off Champion Rd . . . 205 DY91
SW18 off Granville Rd . . . 201 CZ87
Enfield EN2 off Brigadier Hill . . . 104 DQ39
St. Albans AL3 off St. Michaels St . . . 64 CB20
St. Michael's C of E Prim Sch, Well. DA16 off Wrotham Rd . . . 188 EW81
St. Michael's Ct, Slou. SL2 . . . 153 AK70
St. Michaels Cres, Pnr. HA5 . . . 138 BY58
St. Michaels Dr, Wat. WD25 . . . 81 BV33
St. Michaels Gdns, W10 . . . 14 E7
St. Michael's Grn, Beac. HP9 . . . 111 AL52
St. Michael's Ms, SW1 . . . 28 G9
St. Michael's RC Prim Sch, E6 off Howard Rd . . . 167 EM68
St. Michael's RC Sch, SE16 . . . 32 C5
St. Michaels Rd, NW2 . . . 141 CW63
St. Michael's Rd, SW9 . . . 42 C8
Ashford TW15 . . . 196 BN92
St. Michaels Rd, Brox. EN10 . . . 71 DZ20
Caterham CR3 . . . 258 DR122
Croydon CR0 . . . 224 DQ102
Grays RM16 . . . 193 GH78
Wallington SM6 . . . 241 DJ107
Welling DA16 . . . 188 EV83
St. Michael's Rd, Wok. GU21 . . . 233 BD114
St. Michaels St, W2 . . . 16 B8
St. Albans AL3 . . . 64 CB20
St. Michaels Ter, N22 . . . 121 DL54
St. Michaels Vw, Hat. AL10 off Homestead Rd . . . 67 CV16
St. Michaels Way, Pot.B. EN6 . . . 86 DB30
St. Mildred's Ct, EC2 off Poultry . . . 19 L9
St. Mildreds Rd, SE12 . . . 206 EE87
Guildford GU1 . . . 265 AZ133
St. Monica's RC Prim Sch, N1 . . . 19 N2
N14 off Cannon Rd . . . 121 DL48
St. Monica's Rd, Kgswd KT20 . . . 255 CZ121
St. Nazaire Cl, Egh. TW20 off Mullens Rd . . . 195 BC92
St. Neots Cl, Borwd. WD6 . . . 100 CN38
St. Neots Rd, Rom. RM3 . . . 128 FM52
St. Nicholas Av, Bkhm KT23 . . . 268 CB125
Hornchurch RM12 . . . 149 FG62
St. Nicholas Cen, Sutt. SM1 off St. Nicholas Way . . . 240 DB106
St. Nicholas Cl, Amer. HP7 . . . 94 AV39
Elstree WD6 . . . 99 CK44
Uxbridge UB8 . . . 156 BK72
St. Nicholas C of E Prim Sch, Els. WD6 off St. Nicholas Cl . . . 99 CK44
Shepperton TW17 off Manor Fm Av . . . 217 BP100
St. Nicholas Cres, Pyrford GU22 . . . 250 BG116
St. Nicholas Dr, Sev. TN13 . . . 279 FH126
Shepperton TW17 . . . 216 BN101
St. Nicholas Glebe, SW17 . . . 202 DG93
St. Nicholas Grn, Harl. CM17 . . . 58 EW14
St. Nicholas Gro, Ingrave CM13 . . . 131 GC50
St. Nicholas Hill, Lthd. KT22 . . . 253 CH122
St. Nicholas Ho, Enf. EN2 . . . 103 DH35
St. Nicholas Mt, Hem.H. HP1 . . . 61 BF20
St. Nicholas Pl, Loug. IG10 . . . 107 EN42
St. Nicholas Prep Sch, SW7 . . . 28 B5
St. Nicholas Rd, SE18 . . . 187 ET78
Sutton SM1 . . . 240 DB106
Thames Ditton KT7 . . . 219 CF100
St. Nicholas Sch, Harl. CM17 off Hobbs Cross Rd . . . 58 EY12
Merstham RH1 off Taynton Dr . . . 273 DK129
Purley CR8 off Old Lo La . . . 241 DN113
St. Nicholas St, SE8 . . . 45 P7
St. Nicholas Way, Sutt. SM1 . . . 240 DB105
St. Nicholas' C of E Comb Sch, Tap. SL6 off Rectory Rd . . . 152 AE70
St. Nicolas C of E Inf Sch, Guil. GU2 off Portsmouth Rd . . . 280 AW136
St. Nicolas La, Chis. BR7 . . . 226 EL95
St. Ninian's Ct, N20 . . . 120 DF48
St. Norbert Grn, SE4 . . . 185 DY84
St. Norbert Rd, SE4 . . . 185 DY84
St. Normans Way, Epsom KT17 . . . 239 CU110
St. Olaf's Rd, SW6 . . . 38 F5
St. Olaves Cl, Stai. TW18 . . . 195 BF94
St. Olaves Ct, EC2 . . . 19 L9
St. Olave's Est, SE1 . . . 31 P4
St. Olaves Gdns, SE11 . . . 30 E8
St. Olave's Gram Sch, Orp. BR6 off Goddington La . . . 228 EV104
St. Olave's Prep Sch, SE9 off Southwood Rd . . . 207 EP89
St. Olaves Rd, E6 . . . 167 EN67
St. Olave's Wk, SW16 . . . 223 DJ96
St. Olav's Sq, SE16 . . . 32 G6
St. Omer Ridge, Guil. GU1 . . . 281 BA135
St. Omer Rd, Guil. GU1 . . . 281 BA135
St. Osmund's Cath Prim Sch, SW13 off Church Rd . . . 181 CT81
St. Oswald's Pl, SE11 . . . 42 C1
St. Oswald's Rd, SW16 . . . 223 DP95
St. Oswulf St, SW1 . . . 29 P9
ST. PANCRAS, WC1 . . . 18 A3
● St. Pancras Commercial Cen, NW1 off Pratt St . . . 7 M8
St. Pancras Hosp, NW1 . . . 7 N9
≠ St. Pancras . . . 18 A1
⊖ Saint Pancras International . . . 18 A1
St. Pancras Way, NW1 . . . 7 M8
St. Patrick's Cath Prim Sch, E17 off Longfield Av . . . 145 DY56
NW5 . . . 7 K4
Collier Row RM5 off Lowshoe La . . . 127 FB53
St. Patrick's Ct, Wdf.Grn. IG8 . . . 124 EE52
St. Patrick's Gdns, Grav. DA12 . . . 213 GK90
St. Patricks Pl, Grays RM16 . . . 193 GJ77
St. Patrick's RC Prim Sch, SE18 off Griffin Rd . . . 187 ER77
St. Paul & All Hallows C.E. Inf & Jun Schs, N17 off Park La . . . 122 DU52
St. Paul Cl, Uxb. UB8 . . . 156 BK71
St. Paulinus C of E Prim Sch, Cray. DA1 off Iron Mill La . . . 189 FE84
⊖ St. Paul's . . . 19 J8
St. Paul's Acad, SE2 off Wickham La . . . 188 EU79
St. Paul's All, EC4 off St. Paul's Chyd . . . 19 H9
St. Paul's Av, NW2 . . . 161 CV65
SE16 . . . 33 K2
St. Pauls Av, Har. HA3 . . . 140 CM57
Slough SL2 . . . 154 AT73
★ St. Paul's Cath, EC4 . . . 19 J9
St. Paul's Cath Sch, EC4 . . . 19 J9
St. Paul's Catholic Coll, Sun. TW16 off Green St . . . 217 BU95
St. Paul's Cath Prim Sch, T.Ditt. KT7 off Hampton Ct Way . . . 219 CE101
St. Paul's Chyd, EC4 . . . 19 H9
St. Paul's Cl, SE7 . . . 186 EK78
W5 . . . 180 CM75
St. Pauls Cl, Add. KT15 . . . 234 BG106
St. Paul's Cl, Ashf. TW15 . . . 197 BQ92
St. Pauls Cl, Aveley RM15 . . . 170 FQ73
Borehamwood WD6 . . . 100 CQ43
St. Paul's Cl, Cars. SM5 . . . 222 DE102
St. Pauls Cl, Chess. KT9 . . . 237 CK105
Harlington UB3 . . . 177 BR78
St. Paul's Cl, Houns. TW3 . . . 178 BY82
St. Pauls Cl, Swans. DA10 . . . 212 FY87
St. Paul's C of E Comb Sch, Woob.Grn HP10 off Stratford Dr . . . 132 AD59
St. Paul's C of E Jun Sch, Kings.T. KT2 off Princes Rd . . . 200 CN94
St. Paul's C of E Prim Sch, E1 . . . 20 D10
N11 off The Avenue . . . 121 DH50
N21 off Ringwood Way . . . 121 DP45
NW3 . . . 6 E7
NW7 off The Ridgeway . . . 119 CV49
SE17 . . . 43 J1
W6 . . . 26 A10
Addlestone KT15 off School La . . . 234 BG105
Brentford TW8 off St. Paul's Rd . . . 179 CK79
St. Pauls C of E Prim Sch, Chess. KT9 off Orchard Rd . . . 238 CL105
St. Paul's C of E Prim Sch, Chipper. WD4 off The Common . . . 80 BG31
Dorking RH4 off St. Pauls Rd W . . . 285 CH137
Hunton Bridge WD4 off Langleybury La . . . 81 BQ34
Swanley BR8 off School La . . . 229 FH95
St. Paul's Ct, W14 . . . 26 D9
St. Pauls Ct, Chipper. WD4 off The Common . . . 80 BG31
St. Pauls Ctyd, SE8 off Mary Ann Gdns . . . 46 A3
ST. PAUL'S CRAY, Orp. BR5 . . . 228 EU96
St. Paul's Cray C of E Prim Sch, St.P.Cray BR5 off Buttermere Rd . . . 228 EX97
St. Pauls Cray Rd, Chis. BR7 . . . 227 ER95
St. Paul's Cres, NW1 . . . 7 P6
St. Pauls Dr, E15 . . . 12 G3
St. Paul's Girls' Sch, W6 . . . 26 C8
St. Paul's Ms, NW1 . . . 7 P6
St. Pauls Ms, Dor. RH4 . . . 285 CH137
St. Paul's Pl, N1 . . . 9 L4
St. Pauls Pl, Aveley RM15 . . . 170 FQ73
St. Albans AL1 . . . 65 CG20
St. Paul's Prep Sch, SW13 off Lonsdale Rd . . . 181 CU78
St. Paul's RC Prim Sch, N22 off Bradley Rd . . . 121 DM54
Cheshunt EN7 off Park La . . . 88 DV27
St. Pauls Ri, N13 . . . 121 DP51
St. Paul's Rd, N1 . . . 8 G5
N17 . . . 122 DU52
Barking IG11 . . . 167 EQ67
Brentford TW8 . . . 179 CK79
Erith DA8 . . . 189 FC80
St. Pauls Rd, Hem.H. HP2 . . . 62 BK19
St. Paul's Rd, Rich. TW9 . . . 180 CM83
Staines TW18 . . . 195 BD92
Thornton Heath CR7 . . . 224 DQ97
St. Pauls Rd, Wok. GU22 . . . 249 BA117
St. Pauls Rd E, Dor. RH4 . . . 285 CH137
St. Pauls Rd W, Dor. RH4 . . . 285 CG137
St. Paul's Sch, SW13 off Lonsdale Rd . . . 181 CU78
St. Paul's Shrubbery, N1 . . . 9 L4
St. Pauls Sq, Brom. BR2 . . . 226 EG96
St. Paul's Ter, SE17 . . . 43 H2
St. Paul St, N1 . . . 9 J9
St. Pauls Wk, Kings.T. KT2 off Alexandra Rd . . . 200 CN94
St. Pauls Way, E3 . . . 21 N7
E14 . . . 21 N7
St. Paul's Way, N3 . . . 120 DB52
St. Pauls Way, Wal.Abb. EN9 off Rochford Av . . . 89 ED33
Watford WD24 . . . 98 BW40
St. Paul's Way Comm Sch, E3 . . . 22 A6
St. Paul's with St. Luke's Prim Sch, E3 . . . 21 P6
St. Paul's with St. Michael's C of E Prim Sch, E8 . . . 10 D8
St. Pauls Wd Hill, Orp. BR5 . . . 227 ES96
St. Peter & Paul's Cath Prim Sch, Ilf. IG1 off Gordon Rd . . . 147 ER62
St. Peter & St. Paul Cath Prim Sch, St.P.Cray BR5 off St. Pauls Wd Hill . . . 227 ES96
St. Peter & St. Paul C of E Inf Sch, Chaldon CR3 off Rook La . . . 273 DN125
St. Peter & St. Paul RC Prim Sch, Mitch. CR4 off Cricket Grn . . . 222 DF98
St. Peter & St. Paul's RC Prim Sch, EC1 . . . 19 H4
St. Peter Chanel Cath Prim Sch, Sid. DA14 off Baugh Rd . . . 208 EW92
St. Peter in Chains RC Inf Sch, N8 off Elm Gro . . . 143 DL58
St. Peter's All, EC3 . . . 19 M9
St. Peter's Av, E2 . . . 20 D1
E17 . . . 146 EE56
St. Peters Av, N18 . . . 122 DU49
Berry's Green TN16 . . . 261 EP116
St. Petersburgh Ms, W2 . . . 15 L10
St. Petersburgh Pl, W2 . . . 15 L10
St. Peter's Catholic Comp Sch, Guil. GU1 off Horseshoe La E . . . 265 BC133
St. Peter's Cath Prim Sch, Dag. RM9 off Goresbrook Rd . . . 168 EZ67
Leatherhead KT22 off Grange Rd . . . 253 CJ120
Romford RM1 off Dorset Av . . . 149 FE55
St. Peter's Cl, E2 . . . 20 D1
St. Peters Cl, SW17 . . . 202 DE89
St. Peter's Cl, Barn. EN5 . . . 101 CV43
Burnham SL1 . . . 152 AH70
St. Peters Cl, Bushey Hth WD23 . . . 117 CD46
Chalfont St. Peter SL9 off Lewis La . . . 112 AY53
Chislehurst BR7 . . . 207 ER94

St. Peters Cl, Hat. AL10 . . . 67 CU17
Ilford IG2 . . . 147 ES56
Mill End WD3 . . . 114 BH46
Old Windsor SL4
off Church Rd . . . 194 AU85
St. Peter's Cl, Ruis. HA4 . . . 138 BX61
St. Peters Cl, St.Alb. AL1 . . . 65 CD19
Staines TW18 . . . 195 BF93
Swanscombe DA10 . . . 212 FZ87
Woking GU22 . . . 249 BC120
St. Peter's C of E Comb Sch, Burn. SL1
off Minniecroft Rd . . . 152 AH69
St. Peter's C of E Inf Sch, Tand. RH8
off Tandridge La . . . 275 EA133
St. Peter's C of E Mid Sch, Old Wind. SL4
off Crimp Hill Rd . . . 194 AT86
St. Peter's C of E Prim Sch, SE17 . . . 43 L1
W6 off St. Peter's Rd . . . 181 CU77
W9 . . . 15 J5
Mill End WD3
off Church La . . . 114 BH46
South Weald CM14
off Wigley Bush La . . . 130 FS47
St. Peters Ct, Chal.St.P. SL9
off High St . . . 112 AY53
St. Peter's Ct, NW4 . . . 141 CW57
St. Peters Ct, SE3
off Eltham Rd . . . 206 EF85
SE4 . . . 45 P9
West Molesey KT8 . . . 218 CA98
St. Peter's Eaton Sq C of E Prim Sch, SW1 . . . 29 K7
St. Peter's Gdns, SE27 . . . 203 DN90
St. Peter's Gro, W6 . . . 181 CU77
St. Peter's Hosp, Cher. KT16 . . . 215 BD104
St. Peters La, St.P.Cray BR5 . . . 228 EU96
St. Peters Ms, N4 . . . 143 DP57
St. Peter's Pl, W9 . . . 15 L5
St. Peter's Prim Sch, E1 . . . 32 G2
South Croydon CR2
off Normanton Rd . . . 242 DS107
St. Peter's RC Prim Sch, SE18 . . . 37 N10
St. Peters Rd, N9 . . . 122 DW46
St. Peter's Rd, W6 . . . 181 CU78
Croydon CR0 . . . 242 DR105
Grays RM16 . . . 193 GH77
St. Peters Rd, Kings.T. KT1 . . . 220 CN96
St. Albans AL1 . . . 65 CE20
Southall UB1 . . . 158 CA71
Twickenham TW1 . . . 199 CH85
Uxbridge UB8 . . . 156 BK71
Warley CM14
off Crescent Rd . . . 130 FV49
St. Peter's Rd, W.Mol. KT8 . . . 218 CA98
St. Peters Rd, Wok. GU22 . . . 249 BB121
St. Peter's Sch, St.Alb. AL1
off Cottonmill La . . . 65 CE21
St. Peter's Sq, E2 . . . 20 D1
W6 . . . 181 CU78
St. Peters St, N1 . . . 9 H9
St. Albans AL1 . . . 65 CD20
St. Peter's St, S.Croy. CR2 . . . 242 DR106
St. Peter's St Ms, N1 . . . 9 H10
St. Peters Ter, SW6 . . . 38 F5
St. Peter's Vil, W6 . . . 181 CT77
St. Peter's Way, N1 . . . 9 P7
St. Peters Way, W5 . . . 159 CK71
St. Peter's Way, Add. KT15 . . . 216 BG104
Chertsey KT16 . . . 233 BD105
St. Peters Way, Chorl. WD3 . . . 95 BB43
Harlington UB3 . . . 177 BR78
St. Philip Howard RC Prim Sch, Hat. AL10 off Woods Av . . . 67 CV18
St. Philip's Av, Wor.Pk. KT4 . . . 221 CV103
St. Philips Gate, Wor.Pk. KT4 . . . 221 CV103
St. Philip Sq, SW8 . . . 41 J8
St. Philip's Rd, E8 . . . 10 C5
St. Philips Rd, Surb. KT6 . . . 219 CK100
St. Philip's Sch, SW7 . . . 27 P9
Chessington KT9
off Harrow Cl . . . 237 CK107
St. Philip St, SW8 . . . 41 J10
St. Philip's Way, N1 . . . 9 K8
St. Philomena's Cath Prim Sch, Orp. BR5 off Chelsfield Rd . . . 228 EW101
St. Philomena's Sch, Cars. SM5 off Pound St . . . 240 DF106
St. Pinnock Av, Stai. TW18 . . . 216 BG95
St. Quentin Ho, SW18
off Fitzhugh Gro . . . 202 DD86
St. Quentin Rd, Well. DA16 . . . 187 ET83
St. Quintin Av, W10 . . . 14 B7
St. Quintin Gdns, W10 . . . 14 A7
St. Quintin Rd, E13 . . . 24 A1
St. Raphaels Ct, St.Alb. AL1
off Avenue Rd . . . 65 CE19
St. Raphael's RC Prim Sch, Nthlt. UB5 off Hartfield Av . . . 157 BV68
St. Raphael's Way, NW10 . . . 140 CQ64
St. Regis Cl, N10 . . . 121 DH54
St. Richard's with St. Andrew's C of E Prim Sch, Rich. TW10
off Ashburnham Rd . . . 199 CH90
St. Robert Southwell Cath Prim Sch, NW9
off Slough La . . . 140 CQ58
St. Ronan's Cl, Barn. EN4 . . . 102 DD38
St. Ronans Cres, Wdf.Grn. IG8 . 124 EG52
St. Ronans Vw, Dart. DA1 . . . 210 FM87
St. Rose's Catholic Inf Sch, Hem.H. HP1
off Green End Rd . . . 62 BG22
St. Rule St, SW8 . . . 41 L8
St. Saviour's & St. Olave's Sch, SE1 . . . 31 M7
St. Saviour's C of E Inf Sch, W5 off The Grove . . . 159 CK74
St. Saviour's C of E Prim Sch, E17 off Verulam Av . . . 145 DZ59
SE24 off Herne Hill Rd . . . 184 DQ83
W9 . . . 15 M5
St. Saviour's Est, SE1 . . . 32 A6
St. Saviours Pl, Guil. GU1
off Leas Rd . . . 264 AW134
St. Saviour's Prim Sch, E14 . 22 C7
St. Saviour's RC Prim Sch, SE13 off Bonfield Rd . . . 185 EC84
St. Saviour's Rd, SW2 . . . 203 DM85
St. Saviours Rd, Croy. CR0 . . . 224 DQ100
St. Saviours Vw, St.Alb. AL1
off Summerhill Ct . . . 65 CF19
St. Scholastica's RC Prim Sch, E5 off Kenninghall Rd . . . 144 DU62
Saints Cl, SE27
off Wolfington Rd . . . 203 DP91
Saints Dr, E7 . . . 146 EK64
St. Silas Pl, NW5 . . . 6 G5
St. Silas St Est, NW5 . . . 6 G4
St. Simon's Av, SW15 . . . 201 CW85
ST. STEPHENS, St.Alb. AL3 . . . 64 CC22
St. Stephens Av, E17 . . . 145 EC57
W12 . . . 181 CV75
W13 . . . 159 CH72
St. Stephen's Av, Ashtd. KT21 . 254 CL116
St. Stephens Av, St.Alb. AL3 . . . 64 CB22
St. Stephen's Cath Prim Sch, Well. DA16
off Deepdene Rd . . . 188 EU82
St. Stephens Cl, E17 . . . 145 EB57
NW8 . . . 6 D9
St. Albans AL3 . . . 64 CB23
Southall UB1 . . . 158 CA71
St. Stephen's C of E Jun Sch, Twick. TW1
off Winchester Rd . . . 199 CH86
St. Stephen's C of E Prim Sch, SE8 . . . 46 B8
SW8 . . . 42 C4
W2 . . . 15 K7
W12 . . . 26 A4
St. Stephens Cres, W2 . . . 15 K8
Brentwood CM13 . . . 131 GA49
Thornton Heath CR7 . . . 223 DN97
St. Stephens Gdn Est, W2 . . . 15 J8
St. Stephens Gdns, SW15
off Manfred Rd . . . 201 CZ85
W2 . . . 15 K7
Twickenham TW1 . . . 199 CJ86
St. Stephens Gro, SE13 . . . 46 F10
St. Stephens Hill, St.Alb. AL1 . . 64 CC22
St. Stephens Ms, W2 . . . 15 K7
St. Stephen's Par, E7
off Green St . . . 166 EJ66
St. Stephen's Pas, Twick. TW1
off Richmond Rd . . . 199 CJ86
St. Stephen's Prim Sch, E6
off Whitfield Rd . . . 166 EJ66
St. Stephen's Rd, E3 . . . 11 N10
St. Stephens Rd, E6 . . . 166 EJ66
St. Stephen's Rd, E17 . . . 145 EB57
St. Stephens Rd, W13 . . . 159 CH72
St. Stephen's Rd, Barn. EN5 . . . 101 CX43
St. Stephens Rd, Enf. EN3 . . . 105 DX37
Hounslow TW3 . . . 198 CA86
St. Stephen's Rd, West Dr. UB7 . . . 156 BK74
St. Stephens Row, EC4 . . . 19 L9
St. Stephens Ter, SW8 . . . 42 C5
St. Stephen's Wk, SW7 . . . 27 N8
Saints Wk, Grays RM16 . . . 193 GJ77
St. Swithin's La, EC4 . . . 19 L10
St. Swithun's Rd, SE13 . . . 205 ED85
St. Swithun Wells RC Prim Sch, Hlgdn HA4 off Hunters Hill . 138 BX62
St. Teresa Cath Prim Sch, The, Dag. RM8 off Bowes Rd . . . 148 EW63
St. Teresa's Cath Prim Sch, Borwd. WD6 off Brook Rd . . . 100 CP40
St. Teresa's Prep Sch, Dor. RH5
off Effingham Hill . . . 268 BX132
St. Teresa's RC First & Mid Sch, Har.Wld HA3
off Long Elmes . . . 116 CC53
St. Teresa's RC Prim Sch, Mord. SM4 off Montacute Rd . . . 222 DD100
St. Teresa's Sch, Dor. RH5
off Effingham Hill . . . 268 BX132
St. Teresa Wk, Grays RM16 . . . 193 GH76
St. Theresa Cl, Epsom KT18 . . . 238 CQ114
St. Theresa's Prim Sch, N3
off East End Rd . . . 142 DB55
St. Theresa's Rd, Felt. TW14 . . . 177 BT84
St. Thomas à Becket RC Prim Sch, SE2 off Mottisfont Rd . 188 EU76
St. Thomas Becket Cath Prim Sch, SE25 off Becket Cl . . . 224 DU100
St. Thomas' Catholic Prim Sch, Sev. TN13 off South Pk . . . 279 FH125
St. Thomas Cl, Chilw. GU4 . . . 281 BC140
St. Thomas' Cl, Surb. KT6 . . . 220 CM102
St. Thomas Cl, Wok. GU21
off St. Mary's Rd . . . 248 AW117
St. Thomas C of E Prim Sch, W10 . . . 14 F5
St. Thomas Ct, Bex. DA5 . . . 208 FA87
St. Thomas Dr, E.Clan. GU4
off The Street . . . 266 BL131
Orpington BR5 . . . 227 EQ102
St. Thomas' Dr, Pnr. HA5 . . . 116 BY53
St. Thomas Gdns, Ilf. IG1 . . . 167 EQ65
St. Thomas' Hosp, SE1 . . . 30 C6
St. Thomas' Med Sch & the Nightingale Sch, SE1 . . . 30 C7
St. Thomas More Cath Prim Sch, Bexh. DA7
off Sheldon Rd . . . 188 EZ82
St. Thomas More RC Prim Sch, SE9 off Appleton Rd . . . 186 EL83
Berkhamsted HP4
off Greenway . . . 60 AU19
St. Thomas More RC Sch, N22 off Glendale Av . . . 121 DN52
SE9 off Footscray Rd . . . 207 EN86
St. Thomas More Sch, SW3 . 28 E9
St. Thomas of Canterbury Cath Prim Sch, SW6 . . . 38 G4
Grays RM17 off Ward Av . . . 192 GB77
Guildford GU1
off Horseshoe La W . . . 265 BB134
Mitcham CR4
off Commonside E . . . 222 DG97
St. Thomas of Canterbury C of E Inf & Jun Schs, Brwd. CM15 off Sawyers Hall La . 130 FX45
St. Thomas Rd, E16 . . . 23 N8
N14 . . . 121 DK45
St. Thomas' Rd, W4 . . . 180 CQ79
St. Thomas Rd, Belv. DA17 . . . 189 FC75
Brentwood CM14 . . . 130 FX47
Northfleet DA11
off St. Margaret's Rd . . . 212 GE89
St. Thomas's Av, Grav. DA11 . . 213 GH88
St. Thomas's Cl, Wal.Abb. EN9 . 90 EH33
St. Thomas's Gdns, NW5 . . . 6 G4
St. Thomas's Ms, Guil. GU1
off St. Catherines Pk . . . 281 AZ136
St. Thomas's Pl, E9 . . . 10 G6
St. Thomas's Rd, N4 . . . 143 DN61
NW10 . . . 160 CS67
St. Thomas's Sq, E9 . . . 10 F6
St. Thomas St, SE1 . . . 31 L3
St. Thomas's Way, SW6 . . . 38 G4
St. Thomas the Apostle Coll, SE15 . . . 44 G8
St. Thomas Wk, Colnbr. SL3 . . . 175 BD80
St. Timothy's Ms, Brom. BR1
off Wharton Rd . . . 226 EH95
St. Ursula Gro, Pnr. HA5 . . . 138 BX57
St. Ursula Rd, Sthl. UB1 . . . 158 CA72
St. Ursula's Cath Inf Sch, Harold Hill RM3
off Straight Rd . . . 128 FJ51
St. Ursula's Conv Sch, SE10 . . . 46 G5
St. Ursula's Jun Sch, Harold Hill RM3 off Straight Rd . . . 127 FH51
St. Vincent Cl, SE27 . . . 203 DP92
St. Vincent de Paul RC Prim Sch, SW1 . . . 29 L7
St. Vincent Dr, St.Alb. AL1 . . . 65 CG23
St. Vincent Rd, Twick. TW2 . . . 198 CC86
Walton-on-Thames KT12 . . . 217 BV104
St. Vincents Av, Dart. DA1 . . . 210 FN85
St. Vincent's Cath Prim Sch, SE9 off Harting Rd . . . 206 EL91
Dagenham RM8
off Burnside Rd . . . 148 EW61
ST. VINCENT'S HAMLET, Brwd. CM14 . . . 128 FP46
St. Vincents La, NW7 . . . 119 CW50
St. Vincent's RC Prim Sch, NW7 off The Ridgeway . . . 119 CW50
W1 . . . 17 H7
W3 off Pierrepoint Rd . . . 160 CP73
St. Vincents Rd, Dart. DA1 . . . 210 FN86
St. Vincent St, W1 . . . 17 H7
St. Vincents Way, Pot.B. EN6 . . . 86 DC33
St. Wilfrids Cl, Barn. EN4 . . . 102 DE43
St. Wilfrids Rd, Barn. EN4 . . . 102 DD43
St. William of York RC Prim Sch, SE23 off Brockley Pk . . . 205 DY88
St. Winefride's Av, E12 . . . 147 EM64
St. Winefride's RC Prim Sch, E12 off Church Rd . . . 147 EM64
St. Winifreds, Ken. CR8 . . . 258 DQ115
St. Winifred's Catholic Jun Sch, SE12 off Newstead Rd . . . 206 EF86
St. Winifred's Catholic Nurs & Inf Sch, SE12
off Effingham Rd . . . 206 EE85
St. Winifreds Cl, Chig. IG7 . . . 125 EQ50
St. Winifred's Rd, Bigg.H. TN16 . . . 261 EM118
Teddington TW11 . . . 199 CH93
St. Yon Ct, St.Alb. AL4 . . . 65 CK20
Sakins Cft, Harl. CM18 . . . 73 ET18
Sakura Dr, N22 . . . 121 DK53
Saladin Dr, Purf. RM19 . . . 190 FN77
Salamanca Pl, SE1 . . . 30 C9
Salamanca St, SE1 . . . 30 B9
Salamander Cl, Kings.T. KT2 . . 199 CJ92
Salamander Quay, Hare. UB9 . 114 BG52
Salamons Way, Rain. RM13 . . . 169 FE72
Salbrook Rd, Salf. RH1 . . . 288 DG142
Salcombe Dr, Mord. SM4 . . . 221 CX102
Romford RM6 . . . 148 EZ58
Salcombe Gdns, NW7 . . . 119 CW51
Salcombe Pk, Loug. IG10 . . . 106 EK43
Salcombe Prep Sch, Inf Dept, N14 off Green Rd . . . 103 DH43
Jun Dept, N14
off Chase Side . . . 121 DH45
Salcombe Rd, E17 . . . 145 DZ59
N16 . . . 9 P2
Ashford TW15 . . . 196 BL91
Salcombe Vil, Rich. TW10
off The Vineyard . . . 200 CL85
Salcombe Way, Hayes UB4 . . . 157 BS69
Ruislip HA4 . . . 137 BU61
Salcot Cres, New Adgtn CR0 . . 243 EC110
Salcote Rd, Grav. DA12 . . . 213 GL92
Salcott Rd, SW11 . . . 202 DE85
Croydon CR0 . . . 223 DL104
Salehurst Cl, Har. HA3 . . . 140 CL57
Salehurst Rd, SE4 . . . 205 DZ86
Salem Pl, Croy. CR0 . . . 224 DQ104
Northfleet DA11 . . . 212 GD87
Salem Rd, W2 . . . 15 M10
Sale Pl, W2 . . . 16 C7
Salesian Coll, SW11 . . . 40 C7
Salesian Gdns, Cher. KT16 . . . 216 BG102
Salesian Sch, Cher. KT16
off Highfield Rd . . . 216 BG102
Sale St, E2 . . . 20 C4
Salford Rd, SW2 . . . 203 DK88
SALFORDS, Red. RH1 . . . 288 DF142
Salfords . . . 288 DG142
Salfords Prim Sch, Salf. RH1
off Copsleigh Av . . . 288 DG140
Salfords Way, Red. RH1 . . . 288 DG142
Salhouse Cl, SE28
off Rollesby Way . . . 168 EW72
Salisbury Av, N3 . . . 141 CZ55
Barking IG11 . . . 167 ER66
St. Albans AL1 . . . 65 CH19
Slough SL2 . . . 153 AQ70
Sutton SM1 . . . 239 CZ107
Swanley BR8 . . . 229 FG98
Salisbury Cl, SE17 . . . 31 L8
Amersham HP7 . . . 77 AS39
Potters Bar EN6 . . . 86 DC32
Upminster RM14
off Canterbury Av . . . 151 FT61
Worcester Park KT4 . . . 221 CT104
Salisbury Ct, EC4 . . . 18 G9
Edgware HA8 . . . 118 CM49
Salisbury Cres, Chsht EN8 . . . 89 DX32
Salisbury Gdns, SW19 . . . 201 CY94
Buckhurst Hill IG9 . . . 124 EK47
Welwyn Garden City AL7 . . . 51 CZ10
Salisbury Hall Dr, Hat. AL10 . . . 66 CR16
Salisbury Hall Gdns, E4 . . . 123 EA51
Salisbury Ho, E14 . . . 22 C8
Salisbury Ms, SW6 . . . 38 G5
Bromley BR2 . . . 226 EL99
Salisbury Pl, SW9 . . . 43 H5
W1 . . . 16 E6
West Byfleet KT14 . . . 234 BJ111
Salisbury Prim Sch, E12
off Romford Rd . . . 146 EL64
Salisbury Rd, E4 . . . 123 EA48
E7 . . . 13 N5
E10 . . . 145 EC61
E12 . . . 146 EK64
E17 . . . 145 EC57
N4 . . . 143 DP57
N22 . . . 121 DP53
SE25 . . . 224 DU100
SW19 . . . 201 CY94
W13 . . . 179 CG75
Banstead SM7 . . . 240 DB114
Salisbury Rd, Barn. EN5 . . . 101 CY41
Bexley DA5 . . . 208 FA88
Bromley BR2 . . . 226 EL99
Carshalton SM5 . . . 240 DF107
Dagenham RM10 . . . 169 FB65
Dartford DA2 . . . 210 FQ88
Enfield EN3 . . . 105 DZ37
Feltham TW13 . . . 198 BW88
Godstone RH9 . . . 274 DW131
Gravesend DA11 . . . 213 GF88
Grays RM17 . . . 192 GC79
Harrow HA1 . . . 139 CD57
Hoddesdon EN11 . . . 71 EC15
Hounslow TW4 . . . 178 BW83
Ilford IG3 . . . 147 ES61
London Heathrow Airport TW6 . . . 197 BQ85
New Malden KT3 . . . 220 CR97
Pinner HA5 . . . 137 BU56
Richmond TW9 . . . 180 CL84
Romford RM2 . . . 149 FH57
Southall UB2 . . . 178 BY77
Uxbridge UB8 . . . 156 BH68
Watford WD24 . . . 97 BV38
Welwyn Garden City AL7 . . . 51 CZ10
Woking GU22 . . . 248 AY119
Worcester Park KT4 . . . 221 CT104
Salisbury Sch, Lwr Sch, N9
off Turin Rd . . . 122 DW45
Upr Sch, N9
off Nightingale Rd . . . 122 DW45
Salisbury Sq, EC4 . . . 18 F9
Hatfield AL9 off Park St . . . 67 CW17
Hertford SG14
off Railway St . . . 54 DR09
Salisbury St, NW8 . . . 16 B5
W3 . . . 180 CQ75
Salisbury Ter, SE15 . . . 45 H10
Salisbury Wk, N19 . . . 143 DJ61
Salix Cl, Fetch. KT22 . . . 252 CB123
Sunbury-on-Thames TW16
off Oak Gro . . . 197 BV94
Salix Rd, Grays RM17 . . . 192 GD79
Salliesfield, Twick. TW2 . . . 199 CD86
Sally Murray Cl, E12 . . . 147 EN63
Salmen Rd, E13 . . . 23 M1
Salmon Cl, Welw.G.C. AL7 . . . 52 DA06
Salmond Cl, Stan. HA7 . . . 117 CG51
Salmonds Gro, Ingrave CM13 . 131 GC50
Salmon La, E14 . . . 21 L8
Salmon Meadow Footpath, Hem.H. HP3 . . . 62 BK24
Salmon Rd, Belv. DA17 . . . 188 FA78
Dartford DA1 . . . 190 FM83
Salmons La, Whyt. CR3 . . . 258 DU119
Salmons La W, Cat. CR3 . . . 258 DS120
Salmons Rd, N9 . . . 122 DU46
Chessington KT9 . . . 237 CK107
Effingham KT24 . . . 267 BV129
Salmon St, E14 . . . 21 N9
NW9 . . . 140 CP60
Salomons Rd, E13 . . . 24 C6
Salop Rd, E17 . . . 145 DX58
Saltash Cl, Sutt. SM1 . . . 239 CZ105
Saltash Rd, Ilf. IG6 . . . 125 ER52
Welling DA16 . . . 188 EW81
Salt Box Hill, Bigg.H. TN16 . . . 244 EH113
Salt Box Rd, Guil. GU3, GU4 . . 264 AT129
Saltcoats Rd, W4 . . . 180 CS75
Saltcote Cl, Dart. DA1 . . . 209 FE86
Saltcroft Cl, Wem. HA9 . . . 140 CP60
Salter Cl, Har. HA2 . . . 138 BZ62
Salterford Rd, SW17 . . . 202 DG93
Saltern Ct, Bark. IG11
off Puffin Cl . . . 168 EV69
Salter Rd, SE16 . . . 33 J3
Salters Cl, Berk. HP4 . . . 60 AT17
Rickmansworth WD3 . . . 114 BL46
Salters Gdns, Wat. WD17 . . . 97 BU39
Salters Hall Ct, EC4 . . . 19 L10
Salters Hill, SE19 . . . 204 DR92
Salters Rd, E17 . . . 145 ED56
W10 . . . 14 C5
Salter St, E14 . . . 22 A10
NW10 . . . 161 CU69
Salter St Alleyway, NW10
off Hythe Rd . . . 161 CU70
Salterton Rd, N7 . . . 143 DL62
Saltford Cl, Erith DA8 . . . 189 FE78
Salt Hill Av, Slou. SL1 . . . 153 AQ74
Salthill Cl, Uxb. UB8 . . . 136 BL64
Salt Hill Dr, Slou. SL1 . . . 153 AQ74
Salt Hill Way, Slou. SL1 . . . 153 AQ74
Saltings, The, Green. DA9 . . . 191 FW84
Saltley Cl, E6 . . . 25 H8
Salton Cl, N3
off East End Rd . . . 120 DA54
Saltoun Rd, SW2 . . . 183 DN84
Saltram Cl, N15 . . . 144 DT56
Saltram Cres, W9 . . . 15 H2
Saltwell St, E14 . . . 22 B10
Saltwood Cl, Orp. BR6 . . . 246 EW105
Saltwood Gro, SE17 . . . 43 L1
Salusbury Prim Sch, NW6 . . . 4 G9
Salusbury Rd, NW6 . . . 14 G1
Salutation Rd, SE10 . . . 35 K8
Salvatorian Coll, Wealds. HA3 off High St . . . 117 CE54
Salvia Gdns, Perivale UB6 . . . 159 CG68
Salvin Rd, SW15 . . . 181 CX83
Salway Cl, Wdf.Grn. IG8 . . . 124 EF52
Salway Pl, E15 . . . 13 H5
Salway Rd, E15 . . . 13 H5
Salwey Cres, Brox. EN10 . . . 71 DZ20
Samantha Cl, E17 . . . 145 DZ59
Samantha Ms, Hav.at.Bow. RM4 . . . 127 FE48
Sam Bartram Cl, SE7 . . . 36 D10
Sambrook Ho, SE11 . . . 30 E9
Sambruck Ms, SE6 . . . 205 EB88
Samels Ct, W6
off South Black Lion La . . . 181 CU78
Samford Ho, N1 . . . 8 E9
Samford St, NW8 . . . 16 B5
Samian Gate, St.Alb. AL3 . . . 64 BZ22
Samira Cl, E17
off Colchester Rd . . . 145 DZ58
Samos Rd, SE20 . . . 224 DV96
Samphire Ct, Grays RM17
off Salix Rd . . . 192 GE79
Sample Oak La, Chilw. GU4 . . 281 BE140
Sampson Av, Barn. EN5 . . . 101 CX43
Sampson Cl, Belv. DA17
off Carrill Way . . . 188 EX76
Sampsons Ct, Shep. TW17
off Linden Way . . . 217 BQ99
Sampsons Grn, Slou. SL2 . . . 153 AM69
Sampson St, E1 . . . 32 D3
Samson St, E13 . . . 24 C1
Samuel Cl, E8 . . . 10 B8
SE14 . . . 45 J3
SE18 . . . 37 H8
Stanmore HA7 . . . 117 CG47
Samuel Gray Gdns, Kings.T. KT2 . . . 219 CK95
Samuel Johnson Cl, SW16 . . . 203 DM91
Samuel Lewis Trust Dws, N1 . . . 8 F5
SW3 . . . 28 C9
SW6 . . . 39 K4
W14 . . . 26 F8
Samuel Lewis Trust Est, SE5
off Warner Rd . . . 43 K7
Samuel Rhodes Sch, N1 . . . 8 E8
Samuels Cl, W6 . . . 181 CU78
Samuel Sq, St.Alb. AL1
off Pageant Rd . . . 65 CD21
Samuel St, SE15 . . . 44 A4
SE18 . . . 37 J8
Sancroft Cl, NW2 . . . 141 CV62
Sancroft Rd, Har. HA3 . . . 117 CF54
Sancroft St, SE11 . . . 30 D10
Sanctuary, The, SW1 . . . 29 P5
Bexley DA5 . . . 208 EX86
Morden SM4 . . . 222 DA100
Sanctuary Cl, Dart. DA1 . . . 210 FJ86
Harefield UB9 . . . 114 BJ52
Sanctuary Ms, E8 . . . 10 B5
Sanctuary Rd, Lon.Hthrw Air. TW6 . . . 196 BN86
Sanctuary St, SE1 . . . 31 K5
Sandall Cl, W5 . . . 160 CL70
Sandall Ho, E3 . . . 11 M10
Sandall Rd, NW5 . . . 7 M5
W5 . . . 160 CL70
Sandalls Spring, Hem.H. HP1 . . 61 BF18
Sandal Rd, N18 . . . 122 DU50
New Malden KT3 . . . 220 CR99
Sandal St, E15 . . . 13 J8
Sandalwood, Guil. GU2 . . . 280 AV135
Sandalwood Av, Cher. KT16 . . 215 BD104
Sandalwood Cl, E1 . . . 21 L5
Sandalwood Dr, Ruis. HA4 . . . 137 BQ59
Sandalwood Rd, Felt. TW13 . . . 197 BV90
Sanday Cl, Hem.H. HP3 . . . 63 BP22
Sandbach Pl, SE18 . . . 187 EQ78
Sandbanks, Felt. TW14 . . . 197 BS88
Sandbanks Hill, Bean DA2 . . . 211 FV93
Sandbourne Av, SW19 . . . 222 DB97
Sandbourne Rd, SE4 . . . 45 L8
Sandbrook Cl, NW7 . . . 118 CR51
Sandbrook Rd, N16 . . . 144 DS62
Sandby Grn, SE9 . . . 186 EL83
Sandcliff Rd, Erith DA8 . . . 189 FD77
Sandcroft Cl, N13 . . . 121 DP51
Sandcross La, Reig. RH2 . . . 287 CZ137
Sandcross Sch, Reig. RH2
off Sandcross La . . . 287 CZ137
Sandells Av, Ashf. TW15 . . . 197 BQ91
Sandell St, SE1 . . . 30 E4
Sandels Way, Beac. HP9 . . . 111 AK51
Sandelswood End, Beac. HP9 . 111 AK50
Sandelswood Gdns, Beac. HP9 . . . 111 AK51
Sandeman Gdns, Ware SG12 . . 55 DY05
Sanderling Way, Green. DA9 . . 211 FU85
Sanders Cl, Hmptn H. TW12 . . . 198 CC92
Hemel Hempstead HP3 . . . 62 BM24
London Colney AL2 . . . 83 CK27
Sanders Draper Sch, The, Horn. RM12
off Suttons La . . . 150 FK63
Sandersfield Gdns, Bans. SM7 . . . 256 DA115
Sandersfield Rd, Bans. SM7 . . 256 DB115
Sanders La, NW7 . . . 119 CX52
Sanderson Cl, NW5 . . . 7 J1
Sanderson Rd, Uxb. UB8 . . . 156 BJ65
Sandersons Av, Bad.Mt TN14 . . 246 FA110
Sanderson Sq, Brom. BR1 . . . 227 EN97
Sanders Rd, Hem.H. HP3 . . . 62 BM23
SANDERSTEAD, S.Croy. CR2 . . 242 DT111
Sanderstead . . . 242 DR109
Sanderstead Av, NW2 . . . 141 CY61
Sanderstead Cl, SW12 . . . 203 DJ87
Sanderstead Ct Av, S.Croy. CR2 . . . 242 DU113
Sanderstead Hill, S.Croy. CR2 . 242 DS111
Sanderstead Rd, E10 . . . 145 DY60
Orpington BR5 . . . 228 EV100
South Croydon CR2 . . . 242 DR108
Sanders Way, N19
off Sussex Way . . . 143 DK60
Sandes Pl, Lthd. KT22 . . . 253 CG118
Sandfield Gdns, Th.Hth. CR7 . . 223 DP97
Sandfield Pas, Th.Hth. CR7 . . . 224 DQ97
Sandfield Prim Sch, Guil. GU1 off York Rd . . . 280 AX135
Sandfield Rd, St.Alb. AL1 . . . 65 CG20
Thornton Heath CR7 . . . 223 DP97
Sandfields, Send GU23 . . . 249 BD124
Sandfield Ter, Guil. GU1 . . . 280 AX135
Sandford Av, N22 . . . 122 DQ52
Loughton IG10 . . . 107 EQ41
Sandford Cl, E6 . . . 25 J4
Sandford Ct, N16 . . . 144 DS60
Sandford Rd, E6 . . . 25 H2
Bexleyheath DA7 . . . 188 EY84
Bromley BR2 . . . 226 EG98
Sandford St, SW6 . . . 39 M5
Sandgate Cl, Rom. RM7 . . . 149 FD59
Sandgate Ho, E5 . . . 10 F1
W5 . . . 159 CJ71
Sandgate La, SW18 . . . 202 DE88
Sandgate Rd, Well. DA16 . . . 188 EW80
Sandgates, Cher. KT16 . . . 215 BE103
Sandgate St, SE15 . . . 44 E2
Sandham Pt, SE18 . . . 37 P9
Sandhills, Wall. SM6 . . . 241 DK105
Sandhills, The, SW10
off Limerston St . . . 39 P2
Sandhills Ct, Vir.W. GU25 . . . 214 AY99
Sandhills La, Vir.W. GU25 . . . 214 AY99
Sandhills Meadow, Shep. TW17 . . . 217 BQ101
Sandhills Rd, Reig. RH2 . . . 288 DA136
Sandhurst Av, Har. HA2 . . . 138 CB58
Surbiton KT5 . . . 220 CP101
Sandhurst Cl, NW9 . . . 140 CN55
South Croydon CR2 . . . 242 DS109
Sandhurst Dr, Ilf. IG3 . . . 147 ET63

Sandhurst Inf & Jun Schs, SE6 off Minard Rd 206 EE88
Sandhurst Rd, N9 . . . . 104 DW44
NW9 . . . . 140 CN55
SE6 . . . . 205 ED88
Bexley DA5 . . . . 208 EX85
Orpington BR6 . . . . 228 EU104
Sidcup DA15 . . . . 207 ET90
Tilbury RM18 . . . . 193 GJ82
Sandhurst Way, S.Croy. CR2 . . 242 DS108
Sandifer Dr, NW2 . . . . 141 CX62
Sandifield, Hat. AL10 . . . . 67 CU21
Sandiford Rd, Sutt. SM3 . . . . . 221 CZ103
Sandiland Cres, Brom. BR2 . . . 226 EF103
Sandilands 224 DT103
Sandilands, Croy. CR0 . . . . . . 224 DU103
Sevenoaks TN13 . . . . 278 FD122
Sandilands Rd, SW6 . . . . 39 L7
Sandison St, SE15 . . . . 44 B10
Sandlands Gro, Walt.Hill KT20 . 255 CU123
Sandlands Rd, Walt.Hill KT20 . 255 CU123
Sandland St, WC1 . . . . 18 D7
Sandlers End, Slou. SL2 . . . . . . 153 AP70
Sandlewood Cl, Barn. EN5 . . . . 101 CT43
Sandling Ri, SE9 . . . . 207 EN90
Sandlings, The, N22 . . . . 121 DN54
Sandlings Cl, SE15 . . . . 44 E9
Sandmartin Way, Wall. SM6 . . . 222 DG101
Sandmere Cl, Hem.H. HP2 off St. Albans Rd 62 BN21
Sandmere Rd, SW4 . . . . 183 DL84
Sandon Cl, Esher KT10 . . . . . . 219 CD101
Sandon Rd, Chsht EN8 . . . . 88 DW30
Sandow Cres, Hayes UB3 . . . . 177 BT76
Sandown Av, Dag. RM10 . . . . . 169 FC65
Esher KT10 . . . . 236 CC106
Hornchurch RM12 . . . . 150 FK61
Sandown Cl, Houns. TW5 . . . . . 177 BU81
Sandown Ct, Sutt. SM2 off Grange Rd 240 DB108
Sandown Dr, Cars. SM5 . . . . . . 240 DG109
Sandown Gate, Esher KT10 . . . 218 CC104
● Sandown Ind Pk, Esher KT10 . . . . 218 CA103
★ Sandown Park Racecourse, Esher KT10 . . . . 218 CB104
Sandown Rd, SE25 . . . . 224 DV99
Coulsdon CR5 . . . . 256 DG116
Esher KT10 . . . . 236 CC105
Gravesend DA12 . . . . 213 GJ93
Slough SL2 . . . . 153 AM71
Watford WD24 . . . . 98 BW38
● Sandown Rd Ind Est, Wat. WD24 . . . . 98 BW37
Sandown Way, Nthlt. UB5 . . . . 158 BY65
Sandpiper Cl, E17 . . . . 123 DX53
SE16 . . . . 33 N4
Greenhithe DA9 . . . . 211 FU85
Sandpiper Dr, Erith DA8 . . . . . . 189 FH80
Sandpiper Rd, S.Croy. CR2 . . . 243 DX111
Sutton SM1 . . . . 239 CZ106
Sandpipers, The, Grav. DA12 . . 213 GK89
Sandpiper Way, Orp. BR5 . . . . . 228 EX98
Sandpit Hall Rd, Chobham GU24 . . . . 232 AU112
Sandpit La, Brwd. CM14, CM15 . . . . 130 FT46
St. Albans AL1, AL4 . . . . 65 CJ18
Sandpit Pl, SE7 . . . . 37 H10
Sandpit Rd, Brom. BR1 . . . . 206 EE92
Dartford DA1 . . . . 190 FJ84
Redhill RH1 . . . . 288 DE135
Welwyn Garden City AL7 . . . . . 51 CY11
Sandpits La, Penn HP10 . . . . . . 110 AC48
Sandpits Rd, Croy. CR0 . . . . . . 243 DX105
Richmond TW10 . . . . 199 CK89
Sandra Cl, N22 off New Rd 122 DQ53
Hounslow TW3 . . . . 198 CB85
Sandridgebury La, St.Alb. AL3 . . 65 CE16
Sandridge Cl, Barn. EN4 . . . . . . 102 DE37
Harrow HA1 . . . . 139 CE56
● Sandridge Gate Business Cen, St.Alb. AL4 . . . . 65 CF16
● Sandridge Pk, Port.Wd AL3 . . 65 CF15
Sandridge Rd, St.Alb. AL1 . . . . . 65 CE18
Sandridge St, N19 . . . . 143 DJ61
Sandringham Av, SW20 . . . . . . 221 CY95
Harlow CM19 . . . . 72 EL15
Sandringham Cl, SW19 . . . . . . 201 CX88
Enfield EN1 . . . . 104 DS40
Ilford IG6 . . . . 147 EQ55
Woking GU22 . . . . 250 BG116
Sandringham Ct, W9 . . . . 15 P3
Kingston upon Thames KT2 off Skerne Wk 219 CK95
Slough SL1 . . . . 153 AK72
Sandringham Cres, Har. HA2 . . 138 CA61
St. Albans AL4 . . . . 65 CJ15
Sandringham Dr, Ashf. TW15 . . 196 BK91
Dartford DA2 . . . . 209 FE89
Welling DA16 . . . . 187 ES82
Sandringham Flats, WC2 off Charing Cross Rd 17 P10
Sandringham Gdns, N8 . . . . 143 DL58
N12 . . . . 120 DC51
Hounslow TW5 . . . . 177 BU81
Ilford IG6 . . . . 147 EQ55
West Molesey KT8 . . . . 218 CA98
Sandringham Lo, Hodd. EN11 off Taverners Way 71 EA17
Sandringham Ms, W5 off High St 159 CK73
Hampton TW12 . . . . 218 BZ95
Sandringham Pk, Cob. KT11 . . 236 BZ112
Sandringham Prim Sch, E7 off Sandringham Rd 146 EJ64
Sandringham Rd, E7 . . . . 146 EJ64
E8 . . . . 10 A3
E10 . . . . 145 ED58
N22 . . . . 144 DQ55
NW2 . . . . 161 CV65
NW11 . . . . 141 CY59
Barking IG11 . . . . 167 ET65
Bromley BR1 . . . . 206 EG92
London Heathrow Airport TW6 . . . . 196 BL85
Northolt UB5 . . . . 158 CA66
Pilgrim's Hatch CM15 . . . . 130 FV43
Potters Bar EN6 . . . . 86 DB30
Thornton Heath CR7 . . . . 224 DQ99
Watford WD24 . . . . 98 BW37
Sandringham Rd, Wor.Pk. KT4 . 221 CU104
Sandringham Sch, St.Alb. AL4 off The Ridgeway 65 CH16
Sandringham Way, Wal.Cr. EN8 . 89 DX34
Sandrock Pl, Croy. CR0 . . . . . . 243 DX105
Sandrock Rd, SE13 . . . . 46 B10
Westcott RH4 . . . . 284 CB138
Sandroyd Way, Cob. KT11 . . . . 236 CA113
SANDS END, SW6 . . . . 39 N7
Sand's End La, SW6 . . . . 39 M6
Sands Fm Dr, Burn. SL1 . . . . . . 152 AJ70
Sandstone La, E16 . . . . 24 B10
Sandstone Pl, N19 . . . . 143 DH61
Sandstone Rd, SE12 . . . . 206 EH89
Sands Way, Wdf.Grn. IG8 . . . . . 124 EL51
Sandtoft Rd, SE7 . . . . 186 EH79
Sandway Path, St.M.Cray BR5 off Okemore Gdns 228 EW98
Sandway Rd, Orp. BR5 . . . . 228 EW98
Sandwell Cres, NW6 . . . . 5 K4
Sandwich St, WC1 . . . . 18 A3
Sandwick Cl, NW7 . . . . 119 CU52
Sandy Bk Rd, Grav. DA12 . . . . . 213 GH88
Sandy Bury, Orp. BR6 . . . . 227 ER104
Sandy Cl, Hert. SG14 . . . . 53 DP09
Woking GU22 off Sandy La . 249 BC117
Sandycombe Rd, Felt. TW14 . . 197 BU88
Richmond TW9 . . . . 180 CN83
Sandycoombe Rd, Twick. TW1 . 199 CJ86
Sandycroft, SE2 . . . . 188 EU79
Sandy Cft, Epsom KT17 . . . . . . 239 CW110
Sandycroft Rd, Amer. HP6 . . . . . 94 AV39
Sandy Dr, Cob. KT11 . . . . 236 CA111
Feltham TW14 . . . . 197 BS88
Sandy Gro, Borwd. WD6 . . . . . . 100 CM40
Sandy Hill Av, SE18 . . . . 187 EP78
Sandy Hill Rd, SE18 . . . . 37 N9
Sandyhill Rd, Ilf. IG1 . . . . 147 EP63
Sandy Hill Rd, Wall. SM6 . . . . . 241 DJ109
Sandy La, Alb.Hth GU5 . . . . 282 BJ141
Aveley RM15 . . . . 170 FM73
Bean DA2 . . . . 211 FW89
Betchworth RH3 . . . . 286 CS135
Bletchingley RH1 . . . . 273 DP132
Bushey WD23 . . . . 98 CC41
Chadwell St. Mary RM16 . . . . 193 GH79
Chobham GU24 . . . . 232 AS109
Cobham KT11 . . . . 236 CA112
Guildford GU3 . . . . 280 AU139
Harrow HA3 . . . . 140 CM58
Kingston upon Thames KT1 . 199 CG94
Kingswood KT20 . . . . 256 DA123
Leatherhead KT22 . . . . 236 CA112
Limpsfield RH8 . . . . 276 EH127
Mitcham CR4 . . . . 222 DG95
Northwood HA6 . . . . 115 BU50
Orpington BR6 . . . . 228 EU101
Oxted RH8 . . . . 275 EC129
Pyrford GU22 . . . . 249 BF117
Reigate RH2 . . . . 287 CW135
Richmond TW10 . . . . 199 CJ89
St. Paul's Cray BR5 . . . . 228 EX95
Send GU23 . . . . 249 BC123
Sevenoaks TN13 . . . . 279 FJ123
Shere GU5 . . . . 282 BN139
Sidcup DA14 . . . . 208 EX94
South Nutfield RH1 . . . . 289 DK135
Sutton SM2 . . . . 239 CY108
Teddington TW11 . . . . 199 CG94
Virginia Water GU25 . . . . 214 AY98
Walton-on-Thames KT12 . . . . 217 BV100
Watford WD25 . . . . 98 CC41
West Thurrock RM20 off London Rd W Thurrock . 191 FV79
Westerham TN16 . . . . 277 ER125
Woking GU22 . . . . 249 BC116
Sandy La Caravan Site, Wat. WD25 off Sandy La 98 CC41
Sandy La Est, Rich. TW10 . . . . 199 CK89
Sandy La N, Wall. SM6 . . . . 241 DK107
Sandy La S, Wall. SM6 . . . . 241 DK107
Sandy Lo, Nthwd. HA6 . . . . 115 BS47
Sandy Lo La, Nthwd. HA6 . . . . 115 BR47
Sandy Lo Rd, Rick. WD3 . . . . . . 115 BP47
Sandy Lo Way, Nthwd. HA6 . . . 115 BS50
Sandy Mead, Epsom KT19 . . . . 238 CN109
Maidenhead SL6 . . . . 172 AC78
Sandymount Av, Stan. HA7 . . . . 117 CJ50
Sandy Ridge, Chis. BR7 . . . . . . 207 EN93
Sandy Ri, Chal.St.P. SL9 . . . . . 112 AY53
Sandy Rd, NW3 . . . . 142 DB62
Addlestone KT15 . . . . 234 BG107
Sandy's Row, E1 . . . . 19 P7
Sandy Way, Cob. KT11 . . . . 236 CA112
Croydon CR0 . . . . 225 DZ104
Walton-on-Thames KT12 . . . . 217 BT102
Woking GU22 . . . . 249 BC117
Sanfoin End, Hem.H. HP2 . . . . . 62 BN18
Sanford La, N16 off Lawrence Bldgs 144 DT61
Sanford St, SE14 . . . . 45 L3
Sanford Ter, N16 . . . . 144 DT62
Sanford Wk, N16 off Sanford Ter 144 DT61
SE14 . . . . 45 L3
Sangam Cl, Sthl. UB2 . . . . 178 BY76
Sanger Av, Chess. KT9 . . . . 238 CL106
Sanger Dr, Send GU23 . . . . 249 BC123
Sangers Dr, Horl. RH6 . . . . 290 DF148
Sangers Wk, Horl. RH6 off Sangers Dr 290 DF148
Sangley Rd, SE6 . . . . 205 EB87
SE25 . . . . 224 DS98
Sangora Rd, SW11 . . . . 182 DD84
San Ho, E9 . . . . 11 K5
San Juan Dr, Chaff.Hun. RM16 . . . . 191 FW77
San Luis Dr, Chaff.Hun. RM16 . 191 FW77
San Marcos Dr, Chaff.Hun. RM16 . . . . 191 FW77
Sansom Rd, E11 . . . . 146 EE61
Sansom St, SE5 . . . . 43 M5
Sans Wk, EC1 . . . . 18 F4
Santers La, Pot.B. EN6 . . . . 85 CY33
Santiago Way, Chaff.Hun. RM16 . . . . 191 FX78
Santley St, SW4 . . . . 183 DM84
Santos Rd, SW18 . . . . 202 DA85
Santway, The, Stan. HA7 . . . . . . 117 CE50
Sanway Cl, Byfleet KT14 . . . . . 234 BL114
Sanway Rd, Byfleet KT14 . . . . . 234 BL114
● Sapcote Trd Cen, NW10 . . . 141 CT64
Saperton Wk, SE11 . . . . 30 D8
Sapho Pk, Grav. DA12 . . . . 213 GM91
Saphora Cl, Orp. BR6 . . . . 245 ER106
Sappers Cl, Saw. CM21 . . . . 58 EZ05
Sapperton Ct, EC1 . . . . 19 J4
Sapphire Cl, E6 . . . . 25 K8
Dagenham RM8 . . . . 148 EW60
Sapphire Rd, NW10 . . . . 160 CQ66
SE8 . . . . 33 M9
Sappho Ct, Wok. GU21 off Langmans Way 248 AS116
Saracen Cl, Croy. CR0 . . . . 224 DR100
● Saracen Ind Area, Hem.H. HP2 . . . . 63 BP18
Saracens Head, Hem.H. HP2 off Adeyfield Rd 62 BN19
Saracen's Head Yd, EC3 . . . . . . 19 P9
★ Saracens RFC, Wat. WD18 . . 97 BV43
Saracen St, E14 . . . . 22 B9
Sara Ct, Beck. BR3 . . . . 225 EB95
Sara Cres, Green. DA9 . . . . 191 FU84
Sarah Bonnell Sch, E15 . . . . . 13 K5
Sarah Ho, SW15 . . . . 181 CT84
Sara Ho, Erith DA8 off Larner Rd 189 FE80
Sara Pk, Grav. DA12 . . . . 213 GL91
Saratoga Rd, E5 . . . . 144 DW63
Sarbir Ind Pk, Harl. CM20 . . 58 EW10
Sardinia St, WC2 . . . . 18 C9
Sarel Way, Horl. RH6 . . . . 291 DH146
Sargeant Cl, Uxb. UB8 . . . . 156 BK69
Sarita Cl, Har. HA3 . . . . 117 CD54
Sarjant Path, SW19 off Queensmere Rd 201 CX89
Sark Cl, Houns. TW5 . . . . 178 CA80
Sark Ho, N1 off Clifton Rd 9 K5
Enfield EN3 off Eastfield Rd 105 DX38
Sark Twr, SE28 . . . . 187 EQ75
Sark Wk, E16 . . . . 24 B8
Sarnesfield Ho, SE15 . . . . 44 E3
Sarnesfield Rd, Enf. EN2 off Church St 104 DR41
SARRATT, Rick. WD3 . . . . 96 BG35
Sarratt Bottom, Sarratt WD3 . . . 95 BE36
Sarratt C of E Sch, Sarratt WD3 off The Green 96 BG36
Sarratt La, Rick. WD3 . . . . 96 BH40
Sarratt Rd, Rick. WD3 . . . . 96 BM41
Sarre Av, Horn. RM12 . . . . 170 FJ65
Sarre Rd, NW2 . . . . 4 G2
Orpington BR5 . . . . 228 EW99
Sarsby Dr, Stai. TW19 . . . . 195 BA89
Sarsen Av, Houns. TW3 . . . . . . 178 BZ82
Sarsfeld Rd, SW12 . . . . 202 DF88
Sarsfield Rd, Perivale UB6 . . . . 159 CH68
Sartor Rd, SE15 . . . . 185 DX84
● Sarum Complex, Uxb. UB8 . . . . 156 BH68
Sarum Grn, Wey. KT13 . . . . 217 BS104
Sarum Hall Sch, NW3 . . . . 6 C6
Sarum Pl, Hem.H. HP2 . . . . 62 BL16
Sarum Ter, E3 . . . . 21 N5
Satanita Cl, E16 . . . . 24 E8
Satchell Mead, NW9 . . . . 119 CT53
Satchwell Rd, E2 . . . . 20 C3
Satinwood Ct, Hem.H. HP3 . . . . 62 BL22
Satis Ct, Epsom KT17 off Windmill Av 239 CT111
Sattar Ms, N16 off Clissold Rd 144 DR62
Saturn Ho, E3 off Garrison Rd 12 A9
Saturn Way, Hem.H. HP2 . . . . . . 62 BM18
Sauls Grn, E11 off Napier Rd . . 146 EE62
Saunder Cl, Chsht EN8 off Welsummer Way 89 DX27
Saunders Cl, E14 . . . . 21 P10
Ilford IG1 . . . . 147 ER60
Northfleet DA11 . . . . 212 GE89
Saunders Copse, Wok. GU22 . . 248 AV122
Saunders La, Wok. GU22 . . . . . 248 AS122
Saunders Ness Rd, E14 . . . . 34 F10
Saunders Rd, SE18 . . . . 187 ET78
Uxbridge UB10 . . . . 156 BM66
Saunders St, SE11 . . . . 30 E9
Saunders Way, SE28 off Oriole Way 168 EV73
Dartford DA1 . . . . 210 FM89
Saunderton Rd, Wem. HA0 . . . . 139 CH64
Saunton Av, Hayes UB3 . . . . . . 177 BT80
Saunton Rd, Horn. RM12 . . . . . 149 FG61
Savage Gdns, E6 . . . . 25 K9
EC3 . . . . 19 P10
Savannah Cl, SE15 . . . . 44 A5
Savay Cl, Denh. UB9 . . . . 136 BG59
Savay La, Denh. UB9 . . . . 136 BG58
Savera Cl, Sthl. UB2 . . . . 178 BW76
Savernake Rd, N9 . . . . 104 DU44
NW3 . . . . 6 F1
Savery Dr, Long Dit. KT6 . . . . . 219 CJ101
Savile Cl, N.Mal. KT3 . . . . 220 CS99
Thames Ditton KT7 . . . . 219 CF102
Savile Gdns, Croy. CR0 . . . . 224 DT103
Savile Row, W1 . . . . 17 L10
Savill Cl, Chsht EN7 off Markham Rd 88 DQ25
Saville Cl, Epsom KT19 . . . . . . 238 CP111
Saville Cres, Ashf. TW15 . . . . . 197 BR93
Saville Ho, E16 off Robert St 37 N3
Saville Rd, E16 . . . . 37 H3
W4 . . . . 180 CR76
Romford RM6 . . . . 148 EZ58
Twickenham TW1 . . . . 199 CF88
Saville Row, Brom. BR2 . . . . . . 226 EF102
Enfield EN3 . . . . 105 DX40
Savill Gdns, SW20 off Bodnant Gdns 221 CU97
Savill Ms, Eng.Grn TW20 . . . . . 194 AX93
Savill Row, Wdf.Grn. IG8 . . . . . 124 EF51
Savona Cl, SW19 . . . . 201 CY94
Savona Est, SW8 . . . . 41 L5
Savona St, SW8 . . . . 41 L5
Savoy Av, Hayes UB3 . . . . 177 BS78
Savoy Bldgs, WC2 . . . . 30 C1
Savoy Circ, W3 . . . . 161 CT73
Savoy Cl, E15 . . . . 13 J8
Edgware HA8 . . . . 118 CN50
Harefield UB9 . . . . 114 BK54
Savoy Ct, WC2 . . . . 30 B1
Savoy Hill, WC2 . . . . 30 C1
Savoy Ms, SW9 . . . . 42 A9
St. Albans AL1 . . . . 65 CB23
Savoy Pier 30 C1
Savoy Pl, WC2 . . . . 30 B1
Savoy Rd, Dart. DA1 . . . . 210 FK85
Savoy Row, WC2 . . . . 18 C10
Savoy Steps, WC2 off Savoy Row 30 C1
Savoy St, WC2 . . . . 18 C10
Savoy Way, WC2 . . . . 30 C1
Savoy Wd, Harl. CM19 . . . . 73 EN20
Sawbill Cl, Hayes UB4 . . . . 158 BX71
SAWBRIDGEWORTH, CM21 . . . . 58 EW05
Sawells, Brox. EN10 . . . . 71 DZ21
Sawkins Cl, SW19 . . . . 201 CY89
Sawley Rd, W12 . . . . 161 CU74
Sawmill Yd, E3 . . . . 11 M9
Sawpit La, E.Clan. GU4 . . . . . . 266 BL131
Sawtry Cl, Cars. SM5 . . . . 222 DD101
Sawtry Way, Borwd. WD6 . . . . 100 CN38
Sawyer Cl, N9 . . . . 122 DU47
Sawyers Chase, Abridge RM4 . 108 EV41
Sawyers Cl, Dag. RM10 . . . . . . 169 FC65
Windsor SL4 . . . . 173 AL80
Sawyers Ct, Wal.Cr. EN8 off Sturlas Way 89 DY33
Sawyers Gro, Brwd. CM15 . . . . 130 FX46
Sawyers Hall Coll of Science & Tech, The, Brwd. CM15 off Sawyers Hall La 130 FW45
Sawyers Hall La, Brwd. CM15 . 130 FW45
Sawyer's Hill, Rich. TW10 . . . . 200 CP87
Sawyers La, Els. WD6 . . . . 99 CH40
Potters Bar EN6 . . . . 85 CX34
Sawyers Lawn, W13 . . . . 159 CF72
Sawyer St, SE1 . . . . 31 J4
Sawyers Way, Hem.H. HP2 . . . . 62 BM20
Saxby Rd, SW2 . . . . 203 DL87
Saxham Rd, Bark. IG11 . . . . 167 ES68
Saxley, Horl. RH6 off Ewelands 291 DJ147
Saxlingham Rd, E4 . . . . 123 ED48
Saxon Av, Felt. TW13 . . . . 198 BZ89
Saxonbury Av, Sun. TW16 . . . . 217 BV97
Saxonbury Cl, Mitch. CR4 . . . . 222 DD97
Saxonbury Gdns, Long Dit. KT6 . . . . 219 CJ102
Saxon Cl, E17 . . . . 145 EA59
Amersham HP6 . . . . 77 AR38
Brentwood CM13 . . . . 131 GA48
Northfleet DA11 . . . . 212 GC90
Otford TN14 . . . . 263 FF117
Romford RM3 . . . . 128 FM54
Slough SL3 . . . . 175 AZ75
Surbiton KT6 . . . . 219 CK100
Uxbridge UB8 . . . . 156 BM71
Saxon Ct, Borwd. WD6 . . . . 100 CL40
Whyteleafe CR3 off Godstone Rd 258 DU119
Saxon Dr, W3 . . . . 160 CP72
Saxonfield Cl, SW2 . . . . 203 DM87
Saxon Gdns, Sthl. UB1 . . . . 158 BY73
Taplow SL6 . . . . 152 AD70
Saxon Pl, Hort.Kir. DA4 . . . . . . 230 FQ99
Saxon Prim Sch, Shep. TW17 off Briar Rd 216 BN99
Saxon Rd, E3 . . . . 21 N1
E6 . . . . 25 J5
N22 . . . . 121 DP53
SE25 . . . . 224 DR99
Ashford TW15 . . . . 197 BR93
Bromley BR1 . . . . 206 EF94
Hawley DA2 . . . . 210 FL91
Ilford IG1 . . . . 167 EP65
Kingston upon Thames KT2 . 220 CL95
Southall UB1 . . . . 158 BY74
Walton-on-Thames KT12 . . . . 218 BX104
Wembley HA9 . . . . 140 CQ62
Saxons, Tad. KT20 . . . . 255 CX121
Saxon Shore Way, Grav. DA12 . 213 GM86
Saxon Ter, SE6 off Neuchatel Rd 205 DZ89
Saxon Wk, Sid. DA14 . . . . 208 EW93
Saxon Way, N14 . . . . 103 DK44
Harmondsworth UB7 . . . . 176 BJ79
Old Windsor SL4 . . . . 194 AV86
Reigate RH2 . . . . 271 CZ133
Waltham Abbey EN9 . . . . 89 EC33
Saxony Par, Hayes UB3 . . . . . . 157 BQ71
Saxton Cl, SE13 . . . . 185 ED83
Saxton Ms, Wat. WD17 . . . . 97 BU40
Saxville Rd, Orp. BR5 . . . . 228 EV97
Sayer Cl, Green. DA9 . . . . 211 FU85
Sayers Cl, Fetch. KT22 . . . . 252 CC124
Sayers Gdns, Berk. HP4 . . . . 60 AU16
Sayers Wk, Rich. TW10 off Stafford Pl 200 CM87
Sayesbury La, N18 . . . . 122 DU50
Sayesbury Rd, Saw. CM21 . . . . . 58 EX05
Sayes Ct, SE8 . . . . 45 P2
Addlestone KT15 . . . . 234 BJ106
Sayes Ct Fm Dr, Add. KT15 . . . 234 BH106
Sayes Ct Jun Sch, Add. KT15 off Sayes Ct Fm Dr 234 BH106
Sayes Ct Rd, Orp. BR5 . . . . 228 EU98
Sayes Ct St, SE8 . . . . 45 P2
Sayes Gdns, Saw. CM21 . . . . 58 EZ05
Sayward Cl, Chesh. HP5 . . . . 76 AR29
Scadbury Gdns, Orp. BR5 . . . . . 228 EU96
Scadbury Pk, Chis. BR7 . . . . 207 ET93
Scads Hill Cl, Orp. BR6 . . . . . . 227 ET100
Scafell Rd, Slou. SL2 . . . . 153 AM71
Scala St, W1 . . . . 17 M6
Scales Rd, N17 . . . . 144 DT55
Scammell Way, Wat. WD18 . . . . 97 BT44
Scampston Ms, W10 . . . . 14 D8
Scampton Rd, Lon.Hthrw Air. TW6 off Southampton Rd E 196 BM86
Scandrett St, E1 . . . . 32 E3
Scarab Cl, E16 . . . . 35 L1
Scarba Wk, N1 . . . . 9 L5
Scarborough Cl, Bigg.H. TN16 . 260 EJ118
Sutton SM2 . . . . 239 CZ111
Scarborough Rd, E11 . . . . 145 ED60
N4 . . . . 143 DN59
N9 . . . . 122 DW45
London Heathrow Airport TW6 off Southern Perimeter Rd . 197 BQ86
Scarborough St, E1 . . . . 20 B9
Scarborough Way, Slou. SL1 . . 173 AP75
Scarbrook Rd, Croy. CR0 . . . . . 224 DQ104
Scargill Inf & Jun Schs, Rain. RM13 off Mungo Pk Rd 169 FG65
Scarle Rd, Wem. HA0 . . . . 159 CK65
Scarlet Cl, St.P.Cray BR5 . . . . . 228 EV98
Scarlet Rd, SE6 . . . . 206 EE90
Scarlett Cl, Wok. GU21 . . . . 248 AT118
Scarlette Manor Way, SW2 off Papworth Way 203 DN87
Scarsbrook Rd, SE3 . . . . 186 EK83
Scarsdale Pl, W8 . . . . 27 L6
Scarsdale Rd, Har. HA2 . . . . . . 138 CC62
Scarsdale Vil, W8 . . . . 27 K7
Scarth Rd, SW13 . . . . 181 CT83
Scatterdells La, Chipper. WD4 . . 79 BF30
Scawen Cl, Cars. SM5 . . . . 240 DG105
Scawen Rd, SE8 . . . . 45 L1
Scawfell St, E2 . . . . 20 B1
Scaynes Link, N12 . . . . 120 DA50
Sceaux Gdns, SE5 . . . . 43 P6
Sceptre Rd, E2 . . . . 21 H3
Schiller Int Uni, SE1 . . . . 30 E3
Schofield Wk, SE3 off Dornberg Cl 186 EH80
Scholars Cl, Barn. EN5 . . . . 101 CY42
Scholars Ms, Welw.G.C. AL8 . . . 51 CX07
Scholars Pl, N16 . . . . 144 DS62
Scholars Rd, E4 . . . . 123 EC46
SW12 . . . . 203 DJ88
Scholars Wk, Chal.St.P. SL9 . . . 112 AY51
Guildford GU2 . . . . 280 AV135
Hatfield AL10 . . . . 67 CU21
Langley SL3 . . . . 175 BA75
Scholars Way, Amer. HP6 . . . . . 94 AT38
Romford RM2 . . . . 149 FG57
Scholefield Rd, N19 . . . . 143 DK60
Schomberg Ho, SW1 off Page St 29 P8
Schonfeld Sq, N16 . . . . 144 DR61
Schoolbank Rd, SE10 . . . . 35 L8
Schoolbell Ms, E3 . . . . 21 M1
School Cl, Chesh. HP5 . . . . 76 AP28
Essendon AL9 off School La 68 DF17
Guildford GU1 . . . . 264 AX132
School Cres, Cray. DA1 . . . . . . 189 FF84
Schoolfield Rd, Grays RM20 . . 191 FU79
School Gdns, Pott.End HP4 . . . . 61 BB17
School Grn La, N.Wld Bas. CM16 . . . . 93 FC25
School Hill, Merst. RH1 . . . . . . 273 DJ128
Schoolhouse Gdns, Loug. IG10 . . . . 107 EP42
Schoolhouse La, E1 . . . . 21 J10
School Ho La, Tedd. TW11 . . . . 199 CH94
Schoolhouse Yd, SE18 off Bloomfield Rd 187 EP78
School La, Add. KT15 . . . . 234 BG105
Amersham Old Town HP7 . . . 77 AM39
Bean DA2 . . . . 211 FW90
Bricket Wood AL2 . . . . 82 CA31
Bushey WD23 . . . . 116 CB45
Caterham CR3 . . . . 274 DT126
Chalfont St. Giles HP8 . . . . . . 112 AV47
Chalfont St. Peter SL9 . . . . . . 112 AX54
Chigwell IG7 . . . . 125 ET49
East Clandon GU4 . . . . 266 BL131
Egham TW20 . . . . 195 BA92
Essendon AL9 . . . . 68 DE17
Fetcham KT22 . . . . 253 CD122
Harlow CM20 . . . . 57 ES12
Hatfield AL10 . . . . 67 CV17
Horton Kirby DA4 . . . . 230 FQ98
Kingston upon Thames KT1 off School Rd 219 CJ95
Longfield DA3 . . . . 231 FT100
Magdalen Laver CM5 . . . . 75 FD17
Mickleham RH5 . . . . 269 CJ127
Ockham GU23 . . . . 251 BP122
Pinner HA5 . . . . 138 BY56
Seal TN15 . . . . 279 FM121
Seer Green HP9 . . . . 111 AR51
Shepperton TW17 . . . . 217 BP100
Slough SL2 . . . . 154 AT73
Stoke Poges SL2 . . . . 154 AV67
Surbiton KT6 . . . . 220 CN102
Swanley BR8 . . . . 229 FH95
Tewin AL6 . . . . 52 DE06
Walton on the Hill KT20 off Chequers La 271 CU125
Welling DA16 . . . . 188 EV83
West Horsley KT24 . . . . 267 BP129
Westcott RH4 . . . . 285 CD137
School Mead, Abb.L. WD5 . . . . . 81 BS32
School Meadow, Guil. GU2 . . . 264 AS132
School of Economic Science, W1 . . . . 17 H8
School of Horticulture, Rich. TW9 off Kew Grn 180 CM80
School of Oriental & African Studies, Russell Sq Campus, WC1 . . . . 17 P5
Vernon Sq Campus, WC1 . . . 18 D2
School of Pharmacy, WC1 . . . 18 B4
School of the Islamic Republic of Iran, The, NW6 . . . . 15 J1
School Pas, Kings.T. KT1 . . . . . 220 CM96
Southall UB1 . . . . 158 BZ74
School Rd, E12 off Sixth Av . . . 147 EM63
NW10 . . . . 160 CR70
Ashford TW15 . . . . 197 BP93
Chislehurst BR7 . . . . 227 EQ95
Dagenham RM10 . . . . 168 FA67
East Molesey KT8 . . . . 219 CD98
Hampton Hill TW12 . . . . 198 CC93
Harmondsworth UB7 . . . . 176 BK79
Hounslow TW3 . . . . 178 CC83
Kingston upon Thames KT1 . 219 CJ95
Ongar CM5 . . . . 93 FG32
Penn HP10 . . . . 110 AC47
Potters Bar EN6 . . . . 86 DC30
Wooburn Green HP10 . . . . 132 AE57
School Rd Av, Hmptn H. TW12 . 198 CC93
School Row, Hem.H. HP1 . . . . . . 61 BF21
School Sq, SE10 off Greenroof Way 35 M7
School Wk, Horl. RH6 off Thornton Cl 290 DE148
Slough SL2 off Grasmere Av 154 AV73
Sunbury-on-Thames TW16 . . 217 BT98
School Way, N12 off High Rd . . 120 DC49
Schoolway, N12 (Woodhouse Rd) 120 DD51
School Way, Dag. RM8 . . . . 148 EW62
Schooner Cl, E14 . . . . 34 G7
SE16 . . . . 33 J4
Barking IG11 . . . . 168 EV69
Schooner Ct, Dart. DA2 . . . . . . 190 FQ84
Schrier, Bark. IG11 off Ripple Rd 167 EQ66
Schroder Ct, Eng.Grn TW20 . . . 194 AV92
Schubert Rd, SW15 . . . . 201 CZ85
Elstree WD6 . . . . 99 CK44
★ Science Mus, SW7 . . . . 28 B7
Scilla Ct, Grays RM17 . . . . 192 GD79
Scillonian Rd, Guil. GU2 . . . . . 280 AU135
Scilly Isles, Esher KT10 . . . . . 219 CE103
● Scimitar Pk, Harl. CM19 . . . . . 56 EL14
Sclater St, E1 . . . . 20 A4
Scoble Pl, N16 . . . . 10 B1
Scoles Cres, SW2 . . . . 203 DN88
Scope Way, Kings.T. KT1 . . . . . 220 CL98
Scoresby St, SE1 . . . . 30 G3
Scorton Av, Perivale UB6 . . . . . 159 CG68
Scotch Common, W13 . . . . 159 CG71
Scoter Cl, Wdf.Grn. IG8 off Mallards Rd 124 EH52
Scot Gro, Pnr. HA5 . . . . 116 BX52
Scotia Rd, SW2 . . . . 203 DN87

Scotland Br Rd, New Haw KT15 234 BG111
Scotland Grn, N17 122 DT54
Scotland Grn Rd, Enf. EN3 105 DX43
Scotland Grn Rd N, Enf. EN3 105 DX42
Scotland Pl, SW1 30 A2
Scotland Rd, Buck.H. IG9 124 EJ46
Scotlands Dr, Farn.Com. SL2 153 AP65
Scotney Cl, Orp. BR6 245 EN105
Scotney Wk, Horn. RM12 off Bonington Rd 150 FK64
Scotscraig, Rad. WD7 99 CF35
Scotsdale Cl, Petts Wd BR5 227 ES98
Sutton SM3 239 CY108
Scotsdale Rd, SE12 206 EH85
Scotshall La, Warl. CR6 243 EC114
Scots Hill, Crox.Grn WD3 96 BM44
Scots Hill Cl, Crox.Grn WD3 96 BM44
Scotsmill La, Crox.Grn WD3 96 BM44
Scotswood Cl, Beac. HP9 111 AK50
Scotswood St, EC1 18 F4
Scotswood Wk, N17 122 DU52
Scott Av, SW15 201 CY86
Stanstead Abbotts SG12 55 EB11
Scott Cl, SW16 223 DM95
Epsom KT19 238 CQ106
Farnham Common SL2 133 AQ64
Guildford GU2 264 AU132
West Drayton UB7 176 BM77
Scott Ct, SW8 off Silverthorne Rd 41 K9
W3 off Petersfield Rd 180 CR75
Scott Cres, Erith DA8 off Cloudesley Rd 189 FF81
Harrow HA2 138 CB60
Scott Ellis Gdns, NW8 16 A3
Scottes La, Dag. RM8 off Valence Av 148 EX60
Scott Fm Cl, T.Ditt. KT7 219 CH102
Scott Gdns, Houns. TW5 178 BX80
Scott Ho, E13 13 P10
N18 122 DU50
Scott Lidgett Cres, SE16 32 C5
Scott Rd, Edg. HA8 118 CP54
Gravesend DA12 213 GK92
Grays RM16 193 GG77
Scott Russell Pl, E14 34 C10
Scotts Av, Brom. BR2 225 ED96
Sunbury-on-Thames TW16 197 BS94
Scotts Cl, Horn. RM12 off Rye Cl 150 FJ64
Staines TW19 196 BK88
Ware SG12 55 DX07
Scotts Dr, Hmptn. TW12 198 CB94
Scotts Fm Rd, Epsom KT19 238 CQ107
Scotts La, Brom. BR2 225 ED97
Walton-on-Thames KT12 236 BX105
Sch Scotts Pk Prim Sch, Brom. BR1 off Orchard Rd 226 EJ95
Scotts Pas, SE18 off Spray St 37 P8
Sch Scotts Prim Sch, Horn. RM12 off Bonington Rd 150 FJ64
Scotts Rd, E10 145 EC60
W12 181 CV75
Bromley BR1 206 EG94
Southall UB2 178 BW76
Ware SG12 55 DX07
Scott St, E1 20 E5
Scotts Vw, Welw.G.C. AL8 51 CW10
Scotts Way, Sev. TN13 278 FE122
Sunbury-on-Thames TW16 197 BS93
Scottswood Cl, Bushey WD23 off Scottswood Rd 98 BY40
Scottswood Rd, Bushey WD23 98 BY40
Scott Trimmer Way, Houns. TW3 178 BY82
Scottwell Dr, NW9 141 CT57
Sch Scott Wilkie Prim Sch, E16 24 E8
Scoulding Rd, E16 23 M8
Scouler St, E14 34 G1
Scout App, NW10 140 CS63
Scout La, SW4 off Old Town 183 DJ83
Scout Way, NW7 118 CR49
Scovell Cres, SE1 31 J5
Scovell Rd, SE1 31 J5
Scratchers La, Fawk.Grn DA3 231 FR103
Scrattons Ter, Bark. IG11 168 EX67
Scriveners Cl, Hem.H. HP2 62 BL20
Scriven St, E8 10 B8
Scrooby St, SE6 205 EB86
Scrubbitts Pk Rd, Rad. WD7 99 CG35
Scrubbitts Sq, Rad. WD7 99 CG35
Scrubs La, NW10 161 CU69
W10 161 CU69
Scrutton Cl, SW12 203 DK87
Scrutton St, EC2 19 N5
Scudamore La, NW9 140 CQ55
Scudders Hill, Fawk.Grn DA3 231 FV100
Scutari Rd, SE22 204 DW85
Scylla Cres, Lon.Hthrw Air. TW6 197 BP87
Scylla Pl, St.John's GU21 off Church Rd 248 AU119
Scylla Rd, SE15 44 D10
London Heathrow Airport TW6 197 BP86
Seaborough Rd, Grays RM16 193 GJ76
Seabright St, E2 20 E3
Seabrook Ct, Pot.B. EN6 off Station Cl 86 DA32
Seabrook Dr, W.Wick. BR4 226 EE103
Seabrooke Ri, Grays RM17 192 GB79
Seabrook Gdns, Rom. RM7 148 FA59
Seabrook Rd, Dag. RM8 148 EX62
Kings Langley WD4 81 BR27
Seaburn Cl, Rain. RM13 169 FE68
Seacole Cl, W3 160 CR71
Seacon Twr, E14 33 P5
Seacourt Rd, SE2 188 EX75
Slough SL3 175 BB77
Seacroft Gdns, Wat. WD19 116 BX48
Seafield Rd, N11 121 DK49
Seaford Cl, Ruis. HA4 137 BR61
Seaford Rd, E17 145 EB55
N15 144 DR57
W13 159 CH74
Enfield EN1 104 DS42
London Heathrow Airport TW6 196 BK85
Seaford St, WC1 18 B3
Seaforth Av, N.Mal. KT3 221 CV99
Seaforth Cl, Rom. RM1 127 FE52
Seaforth Cres, N5 9 J2
Seaforth Dr, Wal.Cr. EN8 89 DX34
Seaforth Gdns, N21 121 DM45
Epsom KT19 239 CT105
Woodford Green IG8 124 EJ50
Seaforth Pl, SW1 off Buckingham Gate 29 M6
Seagrave Cl, E1 21 J7
Seagrave Rd, SW6 39 K2
Beaconsfield HP9 111 AJ51
Seagry Rd, E11 146 EG58
Seagull Cl, Bark. IG11 168 EU69
Seagull La, E16 23 P10
SEAL, Sev. TN15 279 FN121
Sealand Rd, Lon.Hthrw Air. TW6 196 BN86
Sealand Wk, Nthlt. UB5 off Wayfarer Rd 158 BY69
Seal Dr, Seal TN15 279 FM121
Seale Hill, Reig. RH2 288 DA136
Seal Hollow Rd, Sev. TN13, TN15 279 FJ124
Seally Rd, Grays RM17 192 GA78
Seal Rd, Sev. TN14, TN15 279 FJ121
Seal St, E8 10 B1
Seaman Cl, Park St AL2 83 CD25
Searches La, Bedmond WD5 81 BV28
Searchwood Rd, Warl. CR6 258 DV118
Searle Pl, N4 143 DM60
Searles Cl, SW11 40 D5
Searles Dr, E6 25 N7
Searles Rd, SE1 31 M8
Sears St, SE5 43 L4
Seasons Cl, W7 off Boston Rd 159 CE74
Seasprite Cl, Nthlt. UB5 158 BX69
Seaton Av, Ilf. IG3 147 ES64
Seaton Cl, E13 23 P5
SE11 30 F10
SW15 201 CV88
Twickenham TW2 199 CD86
Seaton Dr, Ashf. TW15 196 BL89
Seaton Gdns, Ruis. HA4 137 BU62
Sch Seaton Ho Sch, Sutt. SM2 off Banstead Rd S 240 DD110
Seaton Pt, E5 144 DU63
Seaton Rd, Dart. DA1 209 FG87
Hayes UB3 177 BR77
Hemel Hempstead HP3 62 BK23
London Colney AL2 83 CK26
Mitcham CR4 222 DE96
Twickenham TW2 198 CC86
Welling DA16 188 EW80
Wembley HA0 160 CL68
Seaton Sq, NW7 off Tavistock Av 119 CX52
Seaton St, N18 122 DU50
Seawall Ct, Bark. IG11 off Dock Rd 167 EQ68
Sebastian Av, Shenf. CM15 131 GA44
Sebastian Ct, Bark. IG11 off Meadow Rd 167 ET66
Sebastian St, EC1 19 H3
Sebastopol Rd, N9 122 DU49
Sebbon St, N1 9 H7
Sebergham Gro, NW7 119 CU52
Sebert Rd, E7 146 EH64
Sebright Pas, E2 20 D1
Sch Sebright Prim Sch, E2 20 C10
Sebright Rd, Barn. EN5 101 CX40
Hemel Hempstead HP1 62 BG21
Secker Cres, Har. HA3 116 CC53
Secker St, SE1 30 E3
Second Av, E12 146 EL63
E13 23 N2
E17 145 EA57
N18 122 DW49
NW4 141 CX56
SW14 180 CS83
W3 161 CT74
W10 14 F4
Dagenham RM10 169 FB67
Enfield EN1 104 DT43
Grays RM20 191 FU79
Harlow CM18 73 ES15
Hayes UB3 157 BT74
Romford RM6 148 EW57
Waltham Abbey EN9 off Breach Barn Mobile Home Pk 90 EH30
Walton-on-Thames KT12 217 BV100
Watford WD25 98 BX35
Wembley HA9 139 CK61
Second Cl, W.Mol. KT8 218 CC98
Second Cres, Slou. SL1 153 AQ71
Second Cross Rd, Twick. TW2 199 CE89
Second Way, Wem. HA9 140 CP63
Sedan Way, SE17 31 N10
Sedcombe Cl, Sid. DA14 208 EV91
Sedcote Rd, Enf. EN3 104 DW43
Sedding St, SW1 28 G8
Seddon Highwalk, EC2 off The Barbican 19 J6
Seddon Ho, EC2 off The Barbican 19 J6
Seddon Rd, Mord. SM4 222 DD99
Seddon St, WC1 18 D3
Sedgebrook Rd, SE3 186 EK82
Sedgecombe Av, Har. HA3 139 CJ57
Sedge Ct, Grays RM17 192 GE80
Sedgefield Cl, Rom. RM3 128 FM49
Sedgefield Cres, Rom. RM3 128 FM49
Sedgeford Rd, W12 161 CT74
Sedge Grn, Lwr Naze. EN9 72 EE20
Roydon CM19 72 EE20
Sedgehill Rd, SE6 205 EA91
Sch Sedgehill Sch, SE6 off Sedgehill Rd 205 EB92
Sedgemere Av, N2 142 DC55
Sedgemere Rd, SE2 188 EW76
Sedgemoor Dr, Dag. RM10 148 FA63
Sedge Rd, N17 122 DW52
Sedgeway, SE6 206 EF88
Sedgewick Av, Uxb. UB10 157 BP66
Sedgewood Cl, Brom. BR2 226 EF101
Sedgmoor Pl, SE5 43 P5
Sedgwick Rd, E10 145 EC61
Sedgwick St, E9 11 J3
Sedleigh Rd, SW18 201 CZ86
Sedlescombe Rd, SW6 39 H3
Sedley, Sthflt DA13 212 GA93
Sedley Cl, Enf. EN1 104 DV38
Sedley Gro, Hare. UB9 136 BJ56
Sedley Pl, W1 17 J9
Sedley Ri, Loug. IG10 107 EM40
Sch Sedley's C of E Prim Sch, Sthflt DA13 off Church St 212 GA92
Sedum Cl, NW9 140 CP57
Seeley Dr, SE21 204 DS91
Seeleys, Harl. CM17 58 EW12
Seeleys Cl, Beac. HP9 110 AJ51
Seeleys La, Beac. HP9 off Seeleys Wk 111 AK52
Seeleys Rd, Beac. HP9 110 AJ50
Seeleys Wk, Beac. HP9 110 AJ52
Seelig Av, NW9 141 CU59
Seely Rd, SW17 202 DG93
SEER GREEN, Beac. HP9 111 AR52
⇌ Seer Green 111 AR52
Sch Seer Grn C of E Comb Sch, Seer Grn HP9 off School La 111 AQ51
Seer Grn La, Jordans HP9 112 AS52
Seer Mead, Seer Grn HP9 111 AR52
Seething La, EC3 31 P1
Seething Wells La, Surb. KT6 219 CJ100
Sefton Av, NW7 118 CR50
Harrow HA3 117 CD53
Sefton Cl, Petts Wd BR5 227 ET98
St. Albans AL1 off Blenheim Rd 65 CF19
Stoke Poges SL2 154 AT66
Sefton Ct, Welw.G.C. AL8 51 CV11
Sefton Paddock, Stoke P. SL2 154 AU66
● Sefton Pk, Stoke P. SL2 154 AU66
Sefton Rd, Croy. CR0 224 DU102
Epsom KT19 238 CR110
Petts Wood BR5 227 ET98
Sefton St, SW15 38 B9
Sefton Way, Uxb. UB8 156 BJ72
Segal Cl, SE23 205 DY87
Segrave Cl, Wey. KT13 234 BN108
Sekforde St, EC1 18 G5
Sekhon Ter, Felt. TW13 198 CA90
Selah Dr, Swan. BR8 229 FC95
Selan Gdns, Hayes UB4 157 BV71
Selbie Av, NW10 141 CT64
Selborne Av, E12 off Walton Rd 147 EN63
Bexley DA5 208 EY88
Selborne Gdns, NW4 141 CU56
Perivale UB6 159 CG67
Sch Selborne Prim Sch, Perivale UB6 off Conway Cres 159 CF68
Selborne Rd, E17 145 DZ57
N14 121 DL48
N22 121 DM53
SE5 43 L8
Croydon CR0 224 DS104
Ilford IG1 147 EN61
New Malden KT3 220 CS96
Sidcup DA14 208 EV91
Selborne Wk, E17 off The Mall Walthamstow 145 DZ56
Selbourne Av, E17 145 DZ56
New Haw KT15 234 BH110
Surbiton KT6 220 CM103
Selbourne Cl, New Haw KT15 234 BH109
Selbourne Rd, Guil. GU4 265 BA131
Selbourne Sq, Gdse. RH9 274 DW130
Selby Av, St.Alb. AL3 65 CD20
Selby Chase, Ruis. HA4 137 BV61
Selby Cl, E6 24 G7
Chessington KT9 238 CL108
Chislehurst BR7 207 EN93
Selby Gdns, Sthl. UB1 158 CA70
Selby Grn, Cars. SM5 222 DE101
Selby Rd, E11 146 EE62
E13 24 B6
N17 122 DS51
SE20 224 DU96
W5 159 CH70
Ashford TW15 197 BQ93
Carshalton SM5 222 DE101
Selby Sq, W10 14 F2
Selby St, E1 20 D5
Selby Wk, Wok. GU21 off Wyndham Rd 248 AV118
Selcroft Rd, Pur. CR8 241 DP112
Selden Hill, Hem.H. HP2 62 BK21
Selden Rd, SE15 45 H9
Selden Wk, N7 off Durham Rd 143 DM61
Seldon Ho, SW8 41 L5
Sele Mill, Hert. SG14 53 DP09
Sele Rd, Hert. SG14 53 DP09
Sch Sele Sch, The, Hert. SG14 off Welwyn Rd 53 DM09
★ Selfridges, W1 16 G9
SELHURST, SE25 224 DS100
⇌ Selhurst 224 DS99
Selhurst Cl, SW19 201 CX88
Woking GU21 249 AZ115
Selhurst New Rd, SE25 224 DS100
Selhurst Pl, SE25 224 DS100
Selhurst Rd, N9 122 DR48
SE25 224 DS99
Selinas La, Dag. RM8 148 EY59
Selkirk Dr, Erith DA8 189 FE81
Selkirk Rd, SW17 202 DE91
Twickenham TW2 198 CC89
Sell Cl, Chsht EN7 off Gladding Rd 88 DQ26
Sellers Cl, Borwd. WD6 100 CQ39
Sellers Hall Cl, N3 120 DA52
Sch Sellincourt Prim Sch, SW17 off Sellincourt Rd 202 DE93
Sellincourt Rd, SW17 202 DE92
Sellindge Cl, Beck. BR3 205 DZ94
Sellons Av, NW10 161 CT67
Sells Cl, Guil. GU1 281 AZ136
Sells Rd, Ware SG12 55 DZ05
Sellwood Dr, Barn. EN5 101 CX43
Sellwood St, SW2 off Brockwell Pk Row 203 DN87
SELSDON, S.Croy. CR2 242 DW110
Selsdon Av, S.Croy. CR2 242 DR107
Selsdon Cl, Rom. RM5 127 FC53
Surbiton KT6 220 CL99
Selsdon Cres, S.Croy. CR2 242 DW109
Sch Selsdon High Sch, S.Croy. CR2 off Farnborough Av 243 DX108
Selsdon Pk Rd, S.Croy. CR2 243 DX109
Sch Selsdon Prim Sch, S.Croy. CR2 off Addington Rd 242 DW109
Selsdon Rd, E11 146 EG59
E13 166 EJ67
NW2 141 CT61
SE27 203 DP90
New Haw KT15 234 BG111
South Croydon CR2 242 DR106
● Selsdon Rd Ind Est, S.Croy. CR2 off Selsdon Rd 242 DR108
Selsdon Way, E14 34 D7
Selsea Pl, N16 9 P2
Selsey Cres, Well. DA16 188 EX81
Selsey St, E14 22 A7
Selvage La, NW7 118 CR50
Selway Cl, Pnr. HA5 137 BV56
Selway Ho, SW8 off South Lambeth Rd 42 B6
Selwood Cl, Stanw. TW19 196 BJ86
Selwood Gdns, Stanw. TW19 196 BJ86
Selwood Pl, SW7 28 A10
Selwood Rd, Brwd. CM14 130 FT48
Chessington KT9 237 CK105
Croydon CR0 224 DV103
Selwood Rd, Sutt. SM3 221 CZ102
Woking GU22 249 BB120
Selwood Ter, SW7 28 A10
Selworthy Cl, E11 146 EG57
Selworthy Ho, SW11 40 B6
Selworthy Rd, SE6 205 DZ90
Selwyn Av, E4 123 EC51
Hatfield AL10 66 CR19
Ilford IG3 147 ES58
Richmond TW9 180 CL83
Selwyn Cl, Houns. TW4 178 BY84
Windsor SL4 173 AL82
Selwyn Ct, SE3 47 L10
Edgware HA8 118 CP52
Selwyn Cres, Hat. AL10 66 CS18
Welling DA16 188 EV84
Selwyn Dr, Hat. AL10 66 CR18
Selwyn Pl, Orp. BR5 228 EV97
Sch Selwyn Prim Sch, E4 off Selwyn Av 123 EC51
E13 13 P8
Selwyn Rd, E3 21 N1
E13 166 EH67
NW10 160 CR66
New Malden KT3 220 CR99
Tilbury RM18 off Dock Rd 193 GF82
Semaphore Rd, Guil. GU1 280 AY136
Semley Pl, SW1 29 H9
Semley Rd, SW16 223 DL96
Semper Cl, Knap. GU21 248 AS117
Semper Rd, Grays RM16 193 GJ75
Sempill Rd, Hem.H. HP3 62 BL23
Senate St, SE15 45 H9
Senator Wk, SE28 off Garrick Dr 187 ER76
SEND, Wok. GU23 249 BC124
Sendall Ct, SW11 182 DD83
Send Barns La, Send GU23 249 BD124
Send Cl, Send GU23 249 BC123
Sch Send C of E First Sch, Send GU23 off Send Barns La 249 BE124
SENDGROVE, Wok. GU23 265 BC126
Send Hill, Send GU23 265 BC125
SEND MARSH, Wok. GU23 249 BF124
Send Marsh Grn, Send M. GU23 off Send Marsh Rd 249 BF123
Send Marsh Rd, Wok. GU23 249 BF123
Send Par Cl, Send GU23 off Send Rd 249 BC123
Send Rd, Send GU23 249 BB122
Seneca Rd, Th.Hth. CR7 224 DQ98
Senga Rd, Wall. SM6 222 DG102
Senhouse Rd, Sutt. SM3 221 CX104
Senior St, W2 15 L6
Senlac Rd, SE12 206 EH88
Sennen Rd, Enf. EN1 122 DT45
Sennen Wk, SE9 206 EL90
Senrab St, E1 21 J8
Sentamu Cl, SE24 203 DP88
Sentinel Cl, Nthlt. UB5 158 BY70
Sentinel Pt, SW8 off St. George Wf 42 A2
Sentinel Sq, NW4 141 CW56
Sentis Ct, Nthwd. HA6 off Carew Rd 115 BT51
September Way, Stan. HA7 117 CH51
Sequoia Cl, Bushey Hth WD23 off Giant Tree Hill 117 CD46
Sequoia Gdns, Orp. BR6 227 ET101
Sequoia Pk, Pnr. HA5 116 CB51
Serbin Cl, E10 145 EC59
Serenaders Rd, SW9 42 F9
Sergeants Grn La, Wal.Abb. EN9 90 EJ33
Sergeants Pl, Cat. CR3 258 DQ122
Sergehill La, Bedmond WD5 81 BT27
Serjeants Inn, EC4 18 F9
Serle St, WC2 18 D8
Sermed Ct, Slou. SL2 154 AW74
Sermon Dr, Swan. BR8 229 FC97
Sermon La, EC4 19 J9
★ Serpentine, The, W2 28 C3
Serpentine Ct, Sev. TN13 279 FK122
★ Serpentine Gall, W2 28 B3
Serpentine Grn, Merst. RH1 off Malmstone Av 273 DK129
Serpentine Rd, W2 28 E3
Sevenoaks TN13 279 FJ123
Service Rd, The, Pot.B. EN6 86 DA32
Serviden Dr, Brom. BR1 226 EK95
Sch Servite RC Prim Sch, SW10 39 N2
Setchell Rd, SE1 32 A8
Setchell Way, SE1 32 A8
Seth St, SE16 33 H5
Seton Gdns, Dag. RM9 168 EW66
Settle Pt, E13 23 N1
Settle Rd, E13 13 N10
Romford RM3 128 FN49
Settlers Ct, E14 off Newport Av 23 H10
Settles St, E1 20 D7
Settrington Rd, SW6 39 L9
Seven Acres, Cars. SM5 222 DE103
Northwood HA6 115 BU51
Swanley BR8 229 FD100
Seven Arches App, Wey. KT13 234 BM108
Seven Arches Rd, Brwd. CM14 130 FX48
Seven Hills Cl, Walt. KT12 235 BS109
Seven Hills Rd, Cob. KT11 235 BS111
Iver SL0 155 BC65
Walton-on-Thames KT12 235 BS109
Seven Hills Rd S, Cob. KT11 235 BS113
SEVEN KINGS, Ilf. IG3 147 ES59
⇌ Seven Kings 147 ES60
Sch Seven Kings High Sch, Ilf. IG2 off Ley St 147 ER59
Seven Kings Rd, Ilf. IG3 147 ET61
Seven Kings Way, Kings.T. KT2 220 CL95
Sch Seven Mills Prim Sch, E14 34 B5
SEVENOAKS, TN13 - TN15 279 FJ125
⇌ Sevenoaks 278 FG124
Sevenoaks 279 FJ125
Coll Sevenoaks Adult Ed Cen, Sev. TN13 off Bradbourne Rd 279 FH122
● Sevenoaks Business Cen, Sev. TN14 279 FH121
Sevenoaks Bypass, Sev. TN14 278 FC123
Sevenoaks Cl, Bexh. DA7 189 FC84
Romford RM3 128 FJ49
Sutton SM2 240 DA110
SEVENOAKS COMMON, Sev. TN13 279 FH129
Sevenoaks Ct, Nthwd. HA6 115 BQ52
H Sevenoaks Hosp, Sev. TN13 279 FJ121
Sevenoaks Ho, SE25 224 DU97
★ Sevenoaks Mus, Sev. TN13 279 FJ125
Sch Sevenoaks Prep Sch, Godden Grn TN15 off Fawke Common Rd 279 FN126
Sch Sevenoaks Prim Sch, Sev. TN13 off Bradbourne Pk Rd 279 FH122
Sevenoaks Rd, SE4 205 DY86
Orpington BR6 245 ET106
Otford TN14 263 FH116
Pratt's Bottom BR6 245 ET108
Sch Sevenoaks Sch, Sev. TN13 off High St 279 FJ126
Sevenoaks Way, Orp. BR5 208 EW94
Sidcup DA14 208 EW94
Sevens Cl, Berk. HP4 60 AX19
Sevenseas Rd, Lon.Hthrw Air. TW6 197 BQ86
⇌ Seven Sisters 144 DS57
⊖ Seven Sisters 144 DS57
Sch Seven Sisters Prim Sch, N15 off South Gro 144 DR57
Seven Sisters Rd, N4 143 DM62
N7 143 DM62
N15 144 DQ59
Seven Stars Cor, W12 off Goldhawk Rd 181 CU76
Seven Stars Yd, E1 20 B6
Seventh Av, E12 147 EM63
Hayes UB3 157 BU74
Severalls Av, Chesh. HP5 76 AQ30
Severnake Cl, E14 34 B8
Severn Av, W10 14 F2
Romford RM2 149 FH55
Severn Cres, Slou. SL3 175 BB78
Severn Dr, Enf. EN1 104 DU38
Esher KT10 219 CG103
Upminster RM14 151 FR58
Walton-on-Thames KT12 218 BX103
Severnmead, Hem.H. HP2 62 BL17
Severn Rd, Aveley RM15 170 FQ72
Severns Fld, Epp. CM16 92 EU29
Severnvale, Lon.Col. AL2 off Thamesdale 84 CM27
Severn Way, NW10 141 CT64
Watford WD25 82 BW34
Severus Rd, SW11 182 DE84
Seville Ms, N1 9 N7
Seville St, SW1 28 F5
Sevington Rd, NW4 141 CV58
Sevington St, W9 15 L5
Seward Rd, W7 179 CG75
Beckenham BR3 225 DX96
SEWARDSTONE, E4 105 EC39
SEWARDSTONEBURY, E4 106 EE42
Sewardstone Gdns, E4 105 EB43
Sewardstone Grn, E4 106 EE42
Sewardstone Rd, E2 11 H10
E4 123 EB45
Waltham Abbey EN9 105 EC38
Jct Sewardstone Rbt, Wal.Abb. EN9 105 ED35
Sewardstone St, Wal.Abb. EN9 89 EC34
Seward St, EC1 19 H4
Sewdley St, E5 145 DX62
Sewell Cl, Chaff.Hun. RM16 191 FW78
St. Albans AL4 66 CL20
Sewell Harris Cl, Harl. CM20 57 ET14
Sewell Rd, SE2 188 EU76
Sewells, Welw.G.C. AL8 51 CY05
Sewell St, E13 23 P2
Sextant Av, E14 34 G8
Sexton Cl, Chsht EN7 off Shambrook Rd 88 DQ25
Rainham RM13 off Blake Cl 169 FF67
Sexton Ct, E14 off Newport Av 23 H10
Sexton Rd, Til. RM18 193 GF81
Seymer Rd, Rom. RM1 149 FD55
Seymour Av, N17 122 DU54
Caterham CR3 258 DQ123
Epsom KT17 239 CV109
Morden SM4 221 CX101
Seymour Cl, E.Mol. KT8 218 CC99
Loughton IG10 106 EL44
Pinner HA5 116 BZ53
Seymour Ct, E4 124 EF47
Seymour Cres, Hem.H. HP2 62 BL20
Seymour Dr, Brom. BR2 227 EM102
Seymour Gdns, SE4 45 L10
Feltham TW13 198 BW91
Ilford IG1 147 EM60
Ruislip HA4 138 BX60
Surbiton KT5 220 CM99
Twickenham TW1 199 CH87
Seymour Ms, W1 16 G8
Ewell KT17 239 CU110
Sawbridgeworth CM21 58 EY08
Seymour Pl, SE25 224 DV98
W1 16 E7
Hornchurch RM11 150 FK59
Seymour Rd, E4 123 EB46
E6 166 EK68
E10 145 DZ60
N3 120 DB52
N8 143 DN57
N9 122 DV47
SW18 201 CZ87
SW19 201 CX89
W4 180 CQ77
Carshalton SM5 240 DG106
Chalfont St. Giles HP8 112 AW49
East Molesey KT8 218 CC99
Hampton Hill TW12 198 CC92
Kingston upon Thames KT1 219 CK95
Mitcham CR4 222 DG101
Northchurch HP4 60 AS17
Northfleet DA11 213 GF88
St. Albans AL3 65 CE17
Slough SL1 173 AR75
Tilbury RM18 193 GF81
Seymours, Harl. CM19 73 EM18
Seymours, The, Loug. IG10 107 EN39
Seymour St, SE18 187 EQ76
W1 16 E9
W2 16 E9
Seymour Ter, SE20 224 DV95
Seymour Vil, SE20 224 DV95
Seymour Wk, SW10 39 N2
Swanscombe DA10 212 FY87
Seymour Way, Sun. TW16 197 BS93

Seyssel St, E14 34 F8
Shaa Rd, W3 160 CR73
Shacklands Rd, Sev.TN14 247 FB111
Shackleford Rd, Wok. GU22 249 BA121
Shacklegate La, Tedd.TW11 199 CE91
Shackleton Cl, SE23
off Featherstone Av 204 DV89
Shackleton Ct, E14
off Maritime Quay 34 B10
W12 181 CV75
Shackleton Rd, Slou. SL1 154 AT73
Southall UB1 158 BZ73
Shackleton Wk, Guil. GU2
off Humbolt Cl 264 AT134
Shackleton Way, Abb.L. WD5
off Lysander Way 81 BU32
Welwyn Garden City AL7 52 DD09
SHACKLEWELL, N16 10 A1
Shacklewell Grn, E8 10 B1
Shacklewell La, E8 10 A2
N16 10 A2
Shacklewell Prim Sch, E8 10 A1
Shacklewell Rd, N16 10 B1
Shacklewell Row, E8 10 B1
Shacklewell St, E2 20 B4
Shadbolt Av, E4 123 DY50
Shadbolt Cl, Wor.Pk. KT4 221 CT103
Shad Thames, SE1 32 A3
SHADWELL, E1 32 G1
Shadwell 20 F10
Shadwell 20 F10
Shadwell Ct, Nthlt. UB5
off Shadwell Dr 158 BZ68
Shadwell Dr, Nthlt. UB5 158 BZ69
Shadwell Gdns Est, E1 20 G10
Shadwell Pierhead, E1 33 H1
Shadwell Pl, E1 20 G10
Shady Bush Cl, Bushey WD23 116 CC45
Shady La, Wat. WD17 97 BV40
Shaef Way, Tedd. TW11 199 CG94
Shafter Rd, Dag. RM10 169 FC65
Shaftesbury, Loug. IG10 106 EK41
Shaftesbury Av, W1 17 N10
WC2 17 N10
Enfield EN3 105 DX40
Feltham TW14 197 BU86
Kenton HA3 139 CK58
New Barnet EN5 102 DC42
South Harrow HA2 138 CB60
Southall UB2 178 CA77
Shaftesbury Circle, S.Har. HA2
off Shaftesbury Av 138 CC60
Shaftesbury Ct, N1 19 L1
SE1 off Alderney Ms 31 L6
Shaftesbury Cres, Stai. TW18 196 BK94
Shaftesbury Gdns, NW10 160 CS70
Shaftesbury High Sch, Har.Wld
HA3 off Headstone La 116 CB53
Shaftesbury La, Dart. DA1 190 FP84
Shaftesbury Ms, SW4 203 DJ85
W8 27 K7
Shaftesbury Pk Prim Sch,
SW11 40 G9
Shaftesbury Pl, W14 27 H9
Shaftesbury Pt, E13 23 P1
Shaftesbury Prim Sch, E7
off Shaftesbury Rd 166 EJ66
Shaftesbury Quay, Hert. SG14
off Railway St 54 DR09
Shaftesbury Rd, E4 123 ED46
E7 166 EJ66
E10 145 EA60
E17 145 EB58
N18 122 DS51
N19 143 DL60
Beckenham BR3 225 DZ96
Carshalton SM5 222 DD101
Epping CM16 91 ET29
Richmond TW9 180 CL83
Romford RM1 149 FF58
Watford WD17 98 BW41
Woking GU22 249 BA117
Shaftesburys, The, Bark. IG11 167 EQ67
Shaftesbury St, N1 19 K1
Shaftesbury Way, Kings L.
WD4 81 BQ28
Twickenham TW2 199 CD90
Shaftesbury Waye, Hayes
UB4 157 BV71
Shafto Ms, SW1 28 E7
Shafton Rd, E9 11 K8
Shaggy Calf La, Slou. SL2 154 AU73
Shakespeare Av, N11 121 DJ50
NW10 160 CR67
Feltham TW14 197 BU86
Hayes UB4 157 BV70
Tilbury RM18 193 GH82
Shakespeare Cres, E12 167 EM65
Shakespeare Dr, Har. HA3 140 CM58
Shakespeare Gdns, N2 142 DF56
● Shakespeare Ind Est, Wat.
WD24 97 BU38
Shakespeare Rd, E17 123 DX54
N3 off Popes Dr 120 DA53
NW7 119 CT49
NW10 160 CR67
SE24 203 DP85
W3 160 CQ74
W7 159 CF73
Addlestone KT15 234 BK105
Bexleyheath DA7 188 EY81
Dartford DA1 190 FN84
Romford RM1 149 FF58
★ Shakespeare's Globe Thea,
SE1 31 J1
Shakespeare Sq, Ilf. IG6 125 EQ51
Shakespeare St, Wat. WD24 97 BV38
Shakespeare Twr, EC2 19 K6
Shakespeare Way, Felt. TW13 198 BW91
Shakspeare Ms, N16
off Shakspeare Wk 144 DS63
Shakspeare Wk, N16 9 N1
Shalbourne Sq, E9 11 N4
Shalcomb St, SW10 39 P3
Shalcross Dr, Chsht EN8 89 DZ30
Shalden Ho, SW15
off Tunworth Cres 201 CT86
Shaldon Dr, Mord. SM4 221 CY99
Ruislip HA4 138 BW62
Shaldon Rd, Edg. HA8 118 CM53
Shaldon Way, Walt. KT12 218 BW104
Shale Grn, Merst. RH1
off Bletchingley Rd 273 DK129
Shalfleet Dr, W10 14 C10
SHALFORD, Guil. GU4 280 AX141
⇌ Shalford 280 AY140
Shalford Cl, Orp. BR6 245 EQ105
Shalford Inf Sch, Guil. GU4
off Station Row 280 AY140
Shalford Rd, Guil. GU1, GU4 280 AX137
Shalimar Gdns, W3 160 CQ73
Shalimar Rd, W3 160 CQ73
Shallcross Cres, Hat. AL10 67 CU21
Shallons Rd, SE9 207 EP91
Shalstone Rd, SW14 180 CP83
Shalston Vil, Surb. KT6 220 CM100
Shambles, The, Sev. TN13
off London Rd 279 FJ125
Shambrook Rd, Chsht EN7 87 DP25
Shamrock Cl, Fetch. KT22 253 CD121
Shamrock Ho, SE26
off Talisman Sq 204 DU91
Shamrock Rd, Croy. CR0 223 DM100
Gravesend DA12 213 GL87
Shamrock St, SW4 41 N10
Shamrock Way, N14 121 DH46
Shandon Rd, SW4 203 DJ86
Shand St, SE1 31 N4
Shandy St, E1 21 K5
Shanklin Cl, Chsht EN7 88 DT29
Shanklin Gdns, Wat. WD19 116 BW49
Shanklin Ho, E17
off Sherwood Cl 123 DZ54
Shanklin Rd, N8 143 DK57
N15 144 DU56
Shannon Cl, NW2 141 CX62
Southall UB2 178 BX78
● Shannon Commercial Cen,
N.Mal. KT3
off Beverley Way 221 CU98
Shannon Cor, N.Mal. KT3 221 CU98
Shannon Cor Retail Pk,
N.Mal. KT3 221 CU98
Shannon Gro, SW9 183 DM84
Shannon Pl, NW8 6 D10
Shannon Way, Aveley RM15 170 FQ73
Beckenham BR3 205 EB93
Shantock Hall La, Bov. HP3 78 AY29
Shantock La, Bov. HP3 78 AX30
Shap Cres, Cars. SM5 222 DF102
Shapland Way, N13 121 DM50
Shapla Prim Sch, E1 20 C10
Shapwick Cl, N11 120 DF50
Shardcroft Av, SE24 203 DP85
Shardeloes Rd, SE4 45 N9
SE14 45 N8
Sharland Cl, Th.Hth. CR7
off Dunheved Rd N 223 DN100
Sharland Rd, Grav. DA12 213 GJ89
Sharman Ct, Sid. DA14 208 EU91
Sharman Row, Slou. SL3 175 AZ78
Sharnbrooke Cl, Well. DA16 188 EW83
Sharnbrook Ho, W14 39 J2
Sharney Av, Slou. SL3 175 BB76
Sharon Cl, Bkhm KT23 252 CA124
Epsom KT19 238 CQ113
Long Ditton KT6 219 CJ102
Sharon Gdns, E9 10 G8
Sharon Rd, W4 180 CR78
Enfield EN3 105 DY40
Sharpcroft, Hem.H. HP2 62 BK18
Sharpe Cl, W7
off Templeman Rd 159 CF71
Sharpecroft, Harl. CM19 73 EQ15
Sharpes La, Hem.H. HP1 61 BB21
Sharpleshall St, NW1 6 F7
Sharpness Cl, Hayes UB4 158 BY71
Sharps La, Ruis. HA4 137 BR60
Sharp Way, Dart. DA1 190 FM83
Sharratt St, SE15 45 H2
Sharsted St, SE17 42 G1
Sharvel La, Nthlt. UB5 157 BU67
Shavers Pl, SW1 29 N1
Shaw Av, Bark. IG11 168 EY68
Shawbridge, Harl. CM19 73 EQ18
Shawbrooke Rd, SE9 206 EJ85
Shawbury Cl, NW9 118 CS54
Shawbury Rd, SE22 204 DT85
Shaw Cl, SE28 168 EV74
Bushey Heath WD23 117 CE47
Cheshunt EN8 88 DW28
Epsom KT17 239 CT111
Hornchurch RM11 149 FH60
Ottershaw KT16 233 BC107
South Croydon CR2 242 DT112
Shaw Ct, SW11 182 DD83
Morden SM4 222 DC101
Windsor SL4 194 AU85
Shaw Cres, E14 21 M7
Hutton CM13 131 GD43
South Croydon CR2 242 DT112
Tilbury RM18 193 GH81
Shaw Dr, Walt. KT12 218 BW101
Shawfield Ct, West Dr. UB7 176 BL76
Shawfield Pk, Brom. BR1 226 EK96
Shawfield St, SW3 40 D1
Shawford Ct, SW15 201 CU87
Shawford Rd, Epsom KT19 238 CR107
Shaw Gdns, Bark. IG11 168 EY68
Slough SL3 175 AZ78
Shaw Ho, E16
off Claremont St 37 M3
N17 off Queen St 122 DS51
Banstead SM7 256 DC118
Shawley Comm Prim Sch,
Epsom KT18
off Shawley Way 255 CW118
Shawley Cres, Epsom KT18 255 CW118
Shawley Way, Epsom KT18 255 CV118
Shaw Path, Brom. BR1
off Shroffold Rd 206 EF90
Shaw Prim Sch, S.Ock. RM15
off Avon Grn 171 FV72
Shaw Rd, SE22 184 DS84
Bromley BR1 206 EF90
Enfield EN3 105 DX39
Tatsfield TN16 260 EJ120
Shaws, The, Welw.G.C. AL7 52 DC10
Shaws Cotts, SE23 205 DY90
Shaw Sq, E17 123 DY53
Shaw Way, Wall. SM6 241 DL108
Shaxton Cres, New Adgtn
CR0 243 EC109
Sheares Hoppit, Hunsdon
SG12 56 EK05
Shearing Dr, Cars. SM5
off Stavordale Rd 222 DC101
Shearling Way, N7 8 B4
Shearman Rd, SE3 186 EF84
Shears, The, Sun. TW16 197 BS94
Shears Cl, Dart. DA1 210 FJ89
Shears Ct, Sun. TW16
off Staines Rd W 197 BS94
Shears Grn Inf Sch, Nthflt
DA11 off Packham Rd 213 GF90
Shears Grn Jun Sch, Nthflt
DA11 off White Av 213 GF90
Shearsmith Ho, E1 20 D10
Shearwater Cl, Bark. IG11 168 EU69
Shearwater Rd, Sutt. SM1 239 CZ106
Shearwater Way, Hayes UB4 158 BX72
Shearwood Cres, Dart. DA1 189 FF83
Sheath La, Oxshott KT22 236 CB113
Sheaveshill Av, NW9 140 CS56
Sheba Pl, E1 20 B5
Sheehy Way, Slou. SL2 154 AV73
Sheen Common, SW14 200 CP85
Sheen Common Dr, Rich.
TW10 180 CN84
Sheen Ct, Rich. TW10 180 CN84
Sheen Ct Rd, Rich. TW10 180 CN84
Sheendale Rd, Rich. TW9 180 CM84
Sheenewood, SE26 204 DV92
Sheen Gate Gdns, SW14 180 CQ84
Sheen Gate Mans Pas, SW14
off East Sheen Av 180 CR84
Sheen Gro, N1 8 E8
Sheen La, SW14 180 CQ83
Sheen Mt Prim Sch, SW14
off West Temple Sheen 200 CP85
Sheen Pk, Rich. TW9 180 CM84
Sheen Rd, Orp. BR5 227 ET98
Richmond TW9, TW10 200 CL85
Sheen Sch, SW14
off Park Av 180 CS84
Sheen Way, Wall. SM6 241 DM106
Sheen Wd, SW14 200 CQ85
Sheepbarn La, Warl. CR6 244 EF112
Sheepcot Dr, Wat. WD25 82 BW34
Sheepcote, Welw.G.C. AL7 52 DA12
Sheepcote Cl, Beac. HP9 110 AJ51
Hounslow TW5 177 BU80
Sheepcote Gdns, Denh. UB9 136 BG58
Sheepcote La, SW11 40 E9
Burnham SL1 132 AF62
Orpington BR5 228 EZ99
Swanley BR8 228 EZ98
Wheathampstead AL4 50 CL07
Wooburn Green HP10 132 AG61
Sheepcote Rd, Eton Wick SL4 173 AN78
Harrow HA1 139 CF58
Hemel Hempstead HP2 62 BM20
Windsor SL4 173 AL82
Sheepcotes Rd, Rom. RM6 148 EX56
Sheepcot La, Wat. WD25 81 BV34
Sheepfold La, Amer. HP7 77 AR39
Sheepfold Rd, Guil. GU2 264 AT131
Sheephouse Grn, Wotton RH5 284 BZ140
Sheephouse La, Dor. RH5 284 BZ139
Sheephouse Rd, Hem.H. HP3 62 BM22
Sheephouse Way, N.Mal. KT3 220 CS101
Sheeplands Av, Guil. GU1 265 BC132
Sheep La, E8 10 E9
Sheep Wk, Epsom KT18 254 CR122
Reigate RH2 271 CY131
Shepperton TW17 216 BM101
Sheep Wk, The, Wok. GU22 249 BE118
Sheepwalk La, E.Hors. KT24 267 BT134
Sheep Wk Ms, SW19 201 CX93
SHEERING, B.Stort. CM22 59 FC07
Sheering C of E Prim Sch,
Sheering CM22
off The Street 59 FD06
Sheering Dr, Harl. CM17 58 EX12
Sheering Hall Dr, Harl. CM17 58 FA08
Sheering Lwr Rd, Harl. CM17 58 EZ09
Sawbridgeworth CM21 58 FA06
Sheering Mill La, Saw. CM21 58 EZ05
Sheering Rd, Harl. CM17 58 EY11
Hatfield Heath CM22 59 FF05
Sheerness Ms, E16 37 P4
SHEERWATER, Wok. GU21 233 BC113
Sheerwater Av, Wdhm KT15 233 BE112
Sheerwater Rd, E16 24 E6
West Byfleet KT14 233 BE112
Woking GU21 233 BE112
Woodham KT15 233 BE112
Sheethanger La, Felden HP3 62 BG24
Sheet St, Wind. SL4 173 AR82
Sheffield Dr, Rom. RM3 128 FN50
Sheffield Gdns, Rom. RM3 128 FN50
Sheffield Rd, Lon.Hthrw Air. TW6
off Shrewsbury Rd 197 BQ86
Slough SL1 153 AQ72
Sheffield Sq, E3 21 P2
Sheffield St, WC2 18 C9
Sheffield Ter, W8 27 J3
Shefton Ri, Nthwd. HA6 115 BU52
Sheila Cl, Rom. RM5 127 FB52
Sheila Rd, Rom. RM5 127 FB52
Sheilings, The, Horn. RM11 150 FM57
Shelbourne Cl, Pnr. HA5 138 BZ55
Shelbourne Pl, Beck. BR3 205 DZ94
Shelbourne Rd, N17 122 DV54
Shelburne Dr, Houns. TW4
off Hanworth Rd 198 CA86
Shelburne Rd, N7 143 DM63
Shelbury Cl, Sid. DA14 208 EU90
Shelbury Rd, SE22 204 DV85
Sheldon Av, N6 142 DE59
Ilford IG5 125 EP54
Sheldon Cl, SE12 206 EH85
SE20 224 DV95
Cheshunt EN7 88 DS26
Harlow CM17 74 EY15
Reigate RH2 288 DB135
Sheldon Ct, SW8
off Thorncroft St 42 A5
Guildford GU1 off Lower
Edgeborough Rd 281 AZ135
Sheldon Pl, E2 20 D1
Sheldon Rd, N18 122 DS49
NW2 4 D1
Bexleyheath DA7 188 EZ81
Dagenham RM9 168 EY66
Sheldon Sq, W2 15 P7
Sheldon St, Croy. CR0 224 DQ104
Sheldrake Cl, E16 37 J3
Sheldrake Pl, W8 27 J4
Sheldrick Cl, SW19 222 DD96
Shelduck Cl, E15 13 M2
Sheldwich Ter, Brom. BR2 226 EL100
Shelford Pl, N16 144 DR62
Shelford Ri, SE19 204 DT94
Shelford Rd, Barn. EN5 101 CW44
Shelgate Rd, SW11 202 DE85
Shellbank La, Dart. DA2 211 FU93
★ Shell Cen, SE1 30 D3
Shell Cl, Brom. BR2 226 EL100
Shellduck Cl, NW9
off Swan Dr 118 CS54
Shelley Av, E12 166 EL65
Greenford UB6 159 CD69
Hornchurch RM12 149 FF61
Shelley Cl, SE15 44 F8
Banstead SM7 255 CX115
Borehamwood WD6 100 CN42
Coulsdon CR5 257 DM117
Edgware HA8 118 CN49
Greenford UB6 159 CD69
Hayes UB4 157 BU71
Northwood HA6 115 BT50
Orpington BR6 227 ES104
Slough SL3 175 AZ78
Wooburn Moor HP10
off Falcons Cft 132 AE55
Shelley Ct, N4 143 DM60
Waltham Abbey EN9
off Bramley Shaw 90 EF33
Shelley Cres, Houns. TW5 178 BX82
Southall UB1 158 BZ72
Shelley Dr, Well. DA16 187 ES81
Shelley Gdns, Wem. HA0 139 CJ61
Shelley Gro, Loug. IG10 107 EM42
Shelley Ho, SW1 41 M2
Shelley La, Hare. UB9 114 BG53
Shelley Pl, Til. RM18 193 GH81
Shelley Rd, NW10 160 CR67
Chesham HP5 76 AP29
Hutton CM13 131 GD45
Shelleys La, Knock. TN14 261 ET116
Shelley Way, SW19 202 DD93
Shellfield Cl, Stai. TW19 196 BG85
Shellgrove Est, N16 9 P2
Shellness Rd, E5 10 F2
Shell Rd, SE13 185 EB83
Shellwood Dr, N.Holm. RH5 285 CJ140
Shellwood Rd, SW11 40 E9
Leigh RH2 286 CQ141
Shelmerdine Cl, E3 22 A6
Shelson Av, Felt. TW13 197 BT90
Shelton Av, Warl. CR6 258 DW117
Shelton Cl, Guil. GU2 264 AU129
Warlingham CR6 258 DW117
Shelton Rd, SW19 222 DA95
Shelton St, WC2 18 A9
Shelvers Grn, Tad. KT20 255 CW121
Shelvers Hill, Tad. KT20
off Ashurst Rd 255 CV121
Shelvers Spur, Tad. KT20 255 CW121
Shelvers Way, Tad. KT20 255 CW121
Shenden Cl, Sev. TN13 279 FJ128
Shenden Way, Sev. TN13 279 FJ128
Shendish Edge, Hem.H. HP3
off London Rd 80 BM25
SHENFIELD, Brwd. CM15 131 GA45
⇌ Shenfield 131 GA45
Shenfield Cl, Couls. CR5
off Woodfield Cl 257 DJ119
Shenfield Common, Brwd.
CM15 130 FY48
Shenfield Cres, Brwd. CM15 130 FY47
Shenfield Gdns, Hutt. CM13 131 GB44
Shenfield Grn, Shenf. CM15 131 GA45
Shenfield High Sch,
Shenf. CM15
off Alexander La 131 GA43
Shenfield Ho, SE18
off Shooters Hill Rd 186 EK80
Shenfield Pl, Shenf. CM15 130 FY45
Shenfield Rd, Brwd. CM15 130 FX46
Woodford Green IG8 124 EH52
Shenfield St, N1 19 P1
SHENLEY, Rad. WD7 84 CN33
Shenley Av, Ruis. HA4 137 BT61
Shenleybury, Shenley WD7 84 CL30
Shenleybury Cotts, Shenley
WD7 84 CL31
Shenley Cl, S.Croy. CR2 242 DT110
Shenley Hill, Rad. WD7 99 CG35
Shenley La, Lon.Col. AL2 83 CJ27
Shenley Prim Sch, Shenley
WD7 off London Rd 84 CM34
Shenley Rd, SE5 43 P7
Borehamwood WD6 100 CN42
Dartford DA1 210 FN86
Hounslow TW5 178 BY81
Radlett WD7 83 CH34
Shenstone Cl, Dart. DA1 189 FD84
Shenstone Dr, Burn. SL1 153 AK70
Shenstone Gdns, Rom. RM3 128 FJ53
Shenstone Hill, Berk. HP4 60 AX18
Shenstone Sch, Cray. DA1
off Old Rd 189 FD84
Shepcot Ho, N14 103 DJ44
Shepherd Cl, Abb.L. WD5 81 BT30
Hanworth TW13 198 BY91
Shepherdess Pl, N1 19 K2
Shepherdess Wk, N1 9 K10
Shepherd Ho, E16 37 N1
Shepherd Mkt, W1 29 J2
Shepherd Prim Sch, Mill End
WD3 off Shepherds La 114 BG46
SHEPHERD'S BUSH, W12 26 B2
Shepherd's Bush 26 C4
Shepherd's Bush 26 C4
Shepherds Bush Grn, W12 26 B4
Shepherd's Bush Market 26 A3
Shepherds Bush Mkt, W12 26 A5
Shepherds Bush Pl, W12 26 C4
Shepherds Bush Rd, W6 26 B9
Shepherds Cl, N6 143 DH58
W1 off Lees Pl 16 G10
Beaconsfield HP9 111 AM54
Cowley UB8 off High St 156 BJ70
Leatherhead KT22 254 CL124
Orpington BR6
off Stapleton Rd 227 ET104
Romford RM6 148 EX57
Shepperton TW17 217 BP100
Stanmore HA7 117 CG50
Shepherds Ct, W12 26 C4
Hertford SG14 54 DQ06
Shepherds Grn, Chis. BR7 207 ER94
Hemel Hempstead HP1 61 BE21
Shepherds Hill, N6 143 DH58
Guildford GU2 264 AU132
Merstham RH1 273 DJ126
Romford RM3 128 FN54
Shepherds Ho, N7
off York Way 8 A5
Shepherds La, E9 11 J3
SE28 167 ES74
Beaconsfield HP9 111 AM54
Shepherd's La, Brwd. CM14 130 FS45
Shepherds La, Dart. DA1 209 FG88
Guildford GU2 264 AT131
Rickmansworth WD3 113 BF45
Shepherds Path, Nthlt. UB5
off Cowings Mead 158 BY65
Shepherd's Pl, W1 16 G10
Shepherds Rd, Wat. WD18 97 BT41
Shepherd St, W1 29 J3
Northfleet DA11 212 GD87
Shepherds Wk, NW2 141 CU61
NW3 6 A2
Bushey Heath WD23 117 CD47
Shepherds' Wk, Epsom KT18 254 CP121
Shepherds Way, Brook.Pk AL9 86 DC27
Chesham HP5 76 AR33
Rickmansworth WD3 114 BH45
Shalford GU4 280 AY138
South Croydon CR2 243 DX108
Shepiston La, Hayes UB3 177 BR77
West Drayton UB7 177 BQ77
Shepley Cl, Cars. SM5 222 DG104
Shepley Ms, Enf. EN3 105 EA37
Sheppard Cl, Enf. EN1 104 DV38
Kingston upon Thames KT1
off Beaufort Rd 220 CL98
Sheppard Dr, SE16 32 E10
Sheppards, Harl. CM19
off Heighams 73 EM18
Sheppards Cl, St.Alb. AL3 65 CE17
Sheppard St, E16 23 M4
SHEPPERTON, TW17 216 BN101
⇌ Shepperton 217 BQ99
● Shepperton Business Pk,
Shep. TW17 217 BQ99
Shepperton Cl, Borwd. WD6 100 CR39
Shepperton Ct, Shep. TW17 217 BP100
Shepperton Ct Dr, Shep.
TW17 217 BP99
Shepperton Rd, N1 9 K8
Petts Wood BR5 227 EQ100
Staines TW18 216 BJ97
Shepperton Studios, Shep.
TW17 216 BM97
Sheppey Cl, Erith DA8 189 FH80
Sheppey Gdns, Dag. RM9
off Sheppey Rd 168 EW66
Sheppey Rd, Dag. RM9 168 EV66
Sheppeys La, Bedmond WD5 81 BS28
Sheppey Wk, N1 9 K6
Sheppy Pl, Grav. DA12 213 GH87
Shepton Hos, E2
off Welwyn St 21 H2
Sherard Ct, N7
off Manor Gdns 143 DL62
Sherard Rd, SE9 206 EL85
Sherards Orchard, Harl. CM19 73 EP17
● Sheraton Business Cen,
Perivale UB6 159 CH68
Sheraton Cl, Els. WD6 100 CM43
Sheraton Dr, Epsom KT19 238 CQ113
Sheraton Ms, Wat. WD18 97 BS42
Sheraton St, W1 17 N9
Sherborne Av, Enf. EN3 104 DW40
Southall UB2 178 CA77
Sherborne Cl, Colnbr. SL3 175 BE81
Epsom KT18 255 CW117
Hayes UB4 158 BW72
Sherborne Ct, Guil. GU2
off The Mount 280 AW136
Sherborne Cres, Cars. SM5 222 DE101
Sherborne Gdns, NW9 140 CN55
W13 159 CH72
Romford RM5 126 FA50
Sherborne Ho, SW8
off Bolney St 42 C5
Sherborne La, EC4 19 L10
Sherborne Pl, Nthwd. HA6 115 BR51
Sherborne Rd, Chess. KT9 238 CL106
Feltham TW14 197 BR87
Orpington BR5 227 ET98
Sutton SM3 222 DA103
Sherborne St, N1 9 L8
Sherborne Wk, Lthd. KT22
off Windfield 253 CJ121
Sherborne Way, Crox.Grn
WD3 97 BP42
Sherboro Rd, N15 144 DT58
Sherbourne, Albury GU5 282 BK139
Sherbourne Cl, Hem.H. HP2 62 BL21
Sherbourne Cotts, Albury
GU5 282 BL138
Watford WD18
off Lammas Rd 98 BW43
Sherbourne Dr, Wind. SL4 173 AM84
Sherbourne Gdns, Shep.
TW17 217 BS101
Sherbourne Pl, Stan. HA7 117 CG51
Sherbourne Wk, Farn.Com.
SL2 133 AQ63
Sherbrooke Cl, Bexh. DA6 188 FA84
Sherbrooke Rd, SW6 38 F5
Sherbrooke Way, Wor.Pk. KT4 221 CV101
Sherbrook Gdns, N21 121 DP45
SHERE, Guil. GU5 282 BN139
Shere Av, Sutt. SM2 239 CW110
Shere Cl, Chess. KT9 237 CK106
North Holmwood RH5 285 CJ140
Shere C of E Inf Sch,
Shere GU5
off Gomshall La 282 BN139
Sheredan Rd, E4 123 ED50
Sheredes Dr, Hodd. EN11 71 DZ19
Sheredes Prim Sch, Hodd.
EN11 off Benford Rd 71 DZ19
Sheredes Sch, Hodd. EN11
off Cock La 71 DZ18
Shere La, Shere GU5 282 BN139
★ Shere Mus, Guil. GU5 282 BN139
Shere Rd, Guil. GU4, GU5 282 BL138
Ilford IG2 147 EN57
West Horsley KT24 267 BP130
Sherfield Av, Rick. WD3 114 BK47
Sherfield Cl, N.Mal. KT3 220 CP98
Sherfield Gdns, SW15 201 CT86
Sherfield Rd, Grays RM17 192 GB79
Sheridan Cl, Hem.H. HP1 62 BH21
Romford RM3 127 FH52
Swanley BR8 off Willow Av 229 FF97
Uxbridge UB10
off Alpha Rd 157 BQ70
Sheridan Ct, Houns. TW4
off Vickers Way 198 BY85
Northolt UB5 138 CB64
Sheridan Cres, Chis. BR7 227 EP96
Sheridan Dr, Reig. RH2 272 DB132
Sheridan Gdns, Har. HA3 139 CK58
Sheridan Hts, E1
off Spencer Way 20 F9
Sheridan Ho, Lthd. KT22
off Highbury Dr 253 CG121
Sheridan Ms, E11
off Woodbine Pl 146 EH58

Sheridan Pl, SW13 181 CT82
Bromley BR1 226 EK96
Hampton TW12 218 CB95
Sheridan Rd, E7 146 EF62
E12 146 EL64
SW19 221 CZ95
Belvedere DA17 188 FA77
Bexleyheath DA7 188 EY83
Richmond TW10 199 CJ90
Watford WD19 116 BX45
Sheridans Rd, Bkhm KT23 268 CC126
Sheridan Ter, Nthlt. UB5 138 CB64
Sheridan Wk, NW11 142 DA58
Broxbourne EN10 71 DY20
Carshalton SM5
off Carshalton Pk Rd 240 DF106
Sheridan Way, Beck. BR3
off Turners Meadow Way 225 DZ95
Sheriff Way, Wat. WD25 81 BU33
Sch Sheringdale Prim Sch, SW18
off Standen Rd 201 CZ88
Sheringham Av, E12 147 EM63
N14 103 DK43
Feltham TW13 197 BU90
Romford RM7 149 FC58
Twickenham TW2 198 BZ88
Sheringham Ct, Hayes UB3 177 BT75
Sheringham Dr, Bark. IG11 147 ET64
Sch Sheringham Jun Sch, E12
off Sheringham Av 147 EM63
Sheringham Rd, N7 8 D4
SE20 224 DV97
Sheringham Twr, Sthl. UB1 158 CB73
Sherington Av, Pnr. HA5 116 CA52
Sch Sherington Prim Sch, SE7
off Sherington Rd 186 EH79
Sherington Rd, SE7 186 EH79
Sherland Rd, Twick. TW1 199 CF88
Sherlies Av, Orp. BR6 227 ES103
★ Sherlock Holmes Mus,
NW1 16 F5
Sherlock Ms, W1 16 G6
Shermanbury Cl, Erith DA8 189 FF80
Sherman Gdns, Chad.Hth
RM6 148 EW58
Sherman Rd, Brom. BR1 226 EG95
Slough SL1 154 AS71
Shernbroke Rd, Wal.Abb. EN9 90 EF34
Shernhall St, E17 145 EC57
Sherpa Rd, Hem.H. HP2 62 BN19
Sherrard Rd, E7 166 EJ65
E12 166 EK65
Sherrards, Welw.G.C. AL8 51 CV06
Sherrards Mansion, Welw.G.C.
AL8 off Sherrards 51 CV06
Sherrards Ms, Welw.G.C. AL8
off Sherrards 51 CV06
SHERRARDSPARK, Welw.G.C.
AL8 51 CV07
Sherrardspark Rd, Welw.G.C.
AL8 51 CW07
Sherrards Way, Barn. EN5 102 DA43
Sherrick Grn Rd, NW10 141 CV64
Sherriff Cl, Esher KT10 218 CB103
Sherriff Rd, NW6 5 K5
Sherringham Av, N17 122 DU54
Sherrin Rd, E10 145 EA63
Sherrock Gdns, NW4 141 CU56
Sherry Ms, Bark. IG11 167 ER66
Sherwin Rd, SE14 45 J7
Sherwood Av, E18 146 EH55
SW16 203 DK94
Greenford UB6 159 CE65
Hayes UB4 157 BV70
Potters Bar EN6 85 CY32
Ruislip HA4 137 BS58
St. Albans AL4 65 CH17
Sherwood Cl, E17 123 DZ54
SW13 off Lower Common S 181 CV83
W13 159 CH74
Bexley DA5 208 EW86
Fetcham KT22 252 CC122
Slough SL3 174 AY76
Sherwood Ct, Colnbr. SL3
off High St 175 BD80
Watford WD25 off High Rd 81 BU34
Sherwood Cres, Reig. RH2 288 DB138
Sherwood Gdns, E14 34 B8
SE16 44 D1
Barking IG11 167 ER66
Sherwood Ho, Harl. CM18
off Bush Fair 73 ET17
Sherwood Pk Av, Sid. DA15 208 EU87
Sch Sherwood Pk Prim Sch, Sid.
DA15 off Sherwood Pk Av 208 EV86
Sherwood Pk Rd, Mitch. CR4 223 DJ98
Sutton SM1 240 DA106
Sch Sherwood Pk Sch, Wall. SM6
off Streeters La 223 DK104
Sherwood Pl, Hem.H. HP2
off Turnpike Grn 62 BN18
Sherwood Rd, NW4 141 CW55
SW19 201 CZ94
Coulsdon CR5 257 DJ116
Croydon CR0 224 DV101
Hampton Hill TW12 198 CC92
Harrow HA2 138 CC61
Ilford IG6 147 ER56
Knaphill GU21 248 AS117
Welling DA16 187 ES82
Sch Sherwood Sch, The, Mitch.
CR4 off Abbotts Rd 223 DJ98
Sherwoods Rd, Wat. WD19 116 BY45
Sherwood St, N20 120 DD48
W1 17 M10
Sherwood Ter, N20
off Green Rd 120 DD48
Sherwood Way, W.Wick. BR4 225 EB103
Shetland Cl, Borwd. WD6 100 CR44
Guildford GU4
off Weybrook Dr 265 BB129
Shetland Rd, E3 21 N1
Shevon Way, Brwd. CM14 130 FT49
Shewens Rd, Wey. KT13 235 BR105
Shey Copse, Wok. GU22 249 BC117
Shield Dr, Brent. TW8 179 CG79
Shieldhall St, SE2 188 EW77
Shield Rd, Ashf. TW15 197 BQ91
Shifford Path, SE23 205 DX90
Shilburn Way, Wok. GU21 248 AU118
Shillibeer Pl, W1 16 D6
Shillibeer Wk, Chig. IG7 125 ET48
Shillingford Cl, NW7 119 CX52
Shillingford St, N1 9 H7
Shillitoe Av, Pot.B. EN6 85 CX32
Shimmings, The, Guil. GU1 265 BA133
Shinecroft, Otford TN14 263 FG116
Shinfield St, W12 14 A9
Shingle Ct, Wal.Abb. EN9 90 EG33
Shinglewell Rd, Erith DA8 188 FA80
Shinners Cl, SE25 224 DU99
Ship All, W4 off Thames Rd 180 CN79
Ship & Half Moon Pas, SE18 37 N6
Ship & Mermaid Row, SE1 31 M4
Shipfield Cl, Tats. TN16 260 EJ121
Ship Hill, H.Wyc. HP10 133 AL60
Tatsfield TN16 260 EJ121
Shipka Rd, SW12 203 DH88
Ship La, SW14 180 CQ82
Aveley RM15 191 FR75
Mountnessing CM13 131 GF41
Purfleet RM19 191 FS76
Sutton at Hone DA4 230 FK95
Swanley BR8 230 FK95
Ship La Caravan Site,
Aveley RM15 191 FR76
SHIPLEY BRIDGE, Horl. RH6 291 DM153
Shipman Rd, E16 24 B9
SE23 205 DX89
Ship St, SE8 46 A6
Ship Tavern Pas, EC3 19 N10
Shipton Cl, Dag. RM8 148 EX62
Shipton St, E2 20 B2
Shipwright Rd, SE16 33 L5
Shipwright Yd, SE1 31 N3
Ship Yd, E14 34 C10
Weybridge KT13
off High St 235 BP105
Shirburn Cl, SE23
off Tyson Rd 204 DW87
Shirbutt St, E14 22 C10
Shirebrook Rd, SE3 186 EK82
Shire Cl, Brox. EN10
off Groom Rd 89 DZ26
Shire Ct, Epsom KT17 239 CT108
Erith DA18
off St. John Fisher Rd 188 EX76
Shirehall Cl, NW4 141 CX58
Shirehall Gdns, NW4 141 CX58
Shirehall La, NW4 141 CX58
Shirehall Pk, NW4 141 CX58
Shirehall Rd, Dart. DA2 210 FK92
Shire Horse Way, Islw. TW7 179 CF83
Shire La, Chal.St.P. SL9 113 BD54
Chorleywood WD3 95 BB43
Denham UB9 135 BE55
Keston BR2 245 EM108
Orpington BR6 245 ER107
Shiremeade, Els. WD6 100 CM43
Shire Ms, Whitton TW2 198 CC86
● Shire Pk, Welw.G.C. AL7 51 CY07
Shire Pl, SW18 202 DB87
Redhill RH1 288 DF136
Shires, The, Ham TW10 200 CL91
Watford WD25 81 BV31
Shires Cl, Ashtd. KT21 253 CK118
Shires Ho, Byfleet KT14 234 BL113
Shirland Ms, W9 15 H3
Shirland Rd, W9 15 J3
SHIRLEY, Croy. CR0 225 DX104
Shirley Av, Bex. DA5 208 EX87
Cheam SM2 239 CZ109
Coulsdon CR5 257 DP119
Croydon CR0 224 DW102
Redhill RH1 288 DF139
Sutton SM1 240 DE105
Windsor SL4 173 AM81
Shirley Ch Rd, Croy. CR0 225 DX104
Shirley Cl, E17
off Addison Rd 145 EB57
Broxbourne EN10 71 DZ24
Cheshunt EN8 88 DW29
Dartford DA1 190 FJ84
Hounslow TW3 198 CC85
Shirley Ct, Croy. CR0 225 DX104
Shirley Cres, Beck. BR3 225 DY98
Shirley Dr, Houns. TW3 198 CC85
Shirley Gdns, W7 159 CF74
Barking IG11 167 ES65
Hornchurch RM12 150 FJ61
Shirley Gro, N9 122 DW45
SW11 182 DG83
Shirley Hts, Wall. SM6 241 DJ109
Sch Shirley High Sch,
Croy. CR0
off Shirley Ch Rd 225 DX104
Shirley Hills Rd, Croy. CR0 243 DX106
Shirley Ho Dr, SE7 186 EJ80
H Shirley Oaks Hosp, Croy.
CR0 224 DW101
Shirley Oaks Rd, Croy. CR0 225 DX102
Shirley Pk Rd, Croy. CR0 224 DV102
Shirley Rd, E15 13 K6
W4 180 CR75
Abbots Langley WD5 81 BT32
Croydon CR0 224 DV101
Enfield EN2 104 DQ41
St. Albans AL1 65 CF21
Sidcup DA15 207 ES90
Wallington SM6 241 DJ109
Shirley St, E16 23 L8
Shirley Way, Croy. CR0 225 DY104
Shirlock Rd, NW3 6 F1
Shirwell Cl, NW7 119 CX52
Coll SHL Management Training
Cen, Long Dit. KT6
off Woodstock La N 219 CJ103
Shobden Rd, N17 122 DR53
Shobroke Cl, NW2 141 CW62
Shoebury Rd, E6 167 EM66
Shoe La, EC4 18 F8
Harlow CM17 74 EZ16
Sholden Gdns, Orp. BR5 228 EW99
Sholto Rd, Lon.Hthrw Air.
TW6 196 BM85
Shona Ho, E13 24 C6
Shonks Mill Rd, Nave. RM4 109 FG37
Shooters Av, Har. HA3 139 CJ56
Shooters Dr, Lwr Naze. EN9 72 EE22
SHOOTER'S HILL, SE18 187 EQ81
Shooters Hill, SE18 187 EN81
Welling DA16 187 EN81
Coll Shooters Hill Post 16
Campus, SE18
off Red Lion La 187 EN81
Shooters Hill Rd, SE3 47 M6
SE10 46 F7
SE18 186 EH80
Shooters Rd, Enf. EN2 103 DP39
Shootersway, Berk. HP4 60 AU20
Shootersway La, Berk. HP4 60 AT20
Shootersway Pk, Berk. HP4 60 AT20
Shoot Up Hill, NW2 4 E3
Shophouse La, Albury GU5 282 BK144
Shoplands, Welw.G.C. AL8 51 CX05
Shord Hill, Ken. CR8 258 DR116
Shore, The, Nthflt DA11 212 GD85
Rosherville DA11 213 GF86
Shore Cl, Felt. TW14 197 BU87
Hampton TW12
off Stewart Cl 198 BY92
Shorediche Cl, Uxb. UB10 136 BM62
SHOREDITCH, E1 20 A5
⊖ Shoreditch High Street 19 P5
Shoreditch High St, E1 19 P5
Shoreditch Ho, N1 19 M3
Shore Gro, Felt. TW13 198 CA89
SHOREHAM, Sev. TN14 247 FG111
⇌ Shoreham 247 FG111
Shoreham Cl, SW18
off Ram St 202 DB85
Bexley DA5 208 EX88
Croydon CR0 224 DW100
Shoreham La, Halst. TN14 246 EZ112
Orpington BR6 246 FA107
Sevenoaks TN13 278 FF122
Shoreham Pl, Shore. TN14 247 FG112
Shoreham Ri, Slou. SL2
off Lower Britwell Rd 153 AK70
Shoreham Rd, Orp. BR5 228 EV95
Sevenoaks TN14 247 FH111
Shoreham Rd E, Lon.Hthrw Air.
TW6 196 BL85
Shoreham Rd W, Lon.Hthrw Air.
TW6 196 BL85
Sch Shoreham Village Sch, Shore.
TN14 off Church St 247 FF111
Shoreham Way, Brom. BR2 226 EG100
Shore Pl, E9 10 G7
Shore Pt, Buck.H. IG9 124 EH47
Shore Rd, E9 10 G7
Shores Rd, Wok. GU21 232 AY114
Shore Way, SW9 42 F8
Shorncliffe Rd, SE1 32 A10
Shorndean St, SE6 205 EC88
Shorne Cl, Orp. BR5 228 EX98
Sidcup DA15 208 EV86
Shornefield Cl, Brom. BR1 227 EN97
Shornells Way, SE2
off Willrose Cres 188 EW78
Shorrolds Rd, SW6 39 H4
Shortacres, Red. RH1 273 DM133
Shortcroft Rd, Epsom KT17 239 CT108
Shortcrofts Rd, Dag. RM9 168 EZ65
Shorter Av, Shenf. CM15 131 FZ44
Shorter St, E1 20 A10
Shortfern, Slou. SL2 154 AW72
Shortgate, N12 119 CZ49
Short Hedges, Houns.
TW3, TW5 178 CB81
Short Hill, Har. HA1
off High St 139 CE60
SHORTLANDS, Brom. BR1 226 EE97
⇌ Shortlands 226 EE96
Shortlands, W6 26 C9
Harlington UB3 177 BR79
Shortlands Cl, N18 122 DR48
Belvedere DA17 188 EZ76
Shortlands Gdns, Brom. BR2 226 EE96
Shortlands Grn, Welw.G.C. AL7 51 CZ10
Shortlands Gro, Brom. BR2 225 ED97
Shortlands Rd, E10 145 EB59
Bromley BR2 225 ED97
Kingston upon Thames KT2 200 CM94
Short La, Brick.Wd AL2 82 BZ30
Oxted RH8 276 EH132
Staines TW19 196 BM88
Shortmead Dr, Chsht EN8 89 DY31
Short Path, SE18 off Long Wk 187 EP79
Short Rd, E11 146 EE61
W4 180 CS79
London Heathrow Airport
TW6 196 BL86
Shorts Cft, NW9 140 CP56
Shorts Gdns, WC2 18 A9
Shorts Rd, Cars. SM5 240 DE105
Short St, NW4
off New Brent St 141 CW56
SE1 30 F4
Short Wall, E15 22 F2
Shortway, N12 120 DE51
Short Way, SE9 186 EL83
Shortway, Amer. HP6 77 AR37
Chesham HP5 76 AP29
Short Way, Twick. TW2 198 CC87
Shortwood Av, Stai. TW18 196 BH90
Shortwood Common, Stai.
TW18 196 BH91
Sch Shortwood Inf Sch,
Stai. TW18
off Stanwell New Rd 196 BH90
Shotfield, Wall. SM6 241 DH107
Shothanger Way, Bov. HP3 79 BC26
Shott Cl, Sutt. SM1
off Turnpike La 240 DC106
Shottendane Rd, SW6 39 J6
Shottery Cl, SE9 206 EL90
Shottfield Av, SW14 180 CS84
Shoulder of Mutton All, E14 21 M10
Shouldham St, W1 16 D7
Showers Way, Hayes UB3 157 BU74
Shrapnel Cl, SE18 186 EL80
Shrapnel Rd, SE9 187 EM83
SHREDING GREEN, Iver SL0 155 BB72
Shrewsbury Av, SW14 180 CQ84
Harrow HA3 140 CL56
Shrewsbury Cl, Surb. KT6 220 CL103
Shrewsbury Ct, EC1
off Whitecross St 19 K5
Shrewsbury Cres, NW10 160 CR67
Sch Shrewsbury Ho Sch, Surb.
KT6 off Ditton Rd 220 CL103
Shrewsbury La, SE18 187 EP81
Shrewsbury Ms, W2 15 J7
Shrewsbury Rd, E7 146 EK64
N11 121 DJ51
NW10 off Shakespeare Rd 160 CR67
W2 15 J8
Beckenham BR3 225 DY97
Carshalton SM5 222 DE100
London Heathrow Airport
TW6 197 BQ86
Redhill RH1 272 DE134
Shrewsbury St, W10 14 B5
Shrewsbury Wk, Islw. TW7
off South St 179 CG83
Shrewton Rd, SW17 202 DF94
Shrimpton Cl, Beac. HP9 111 AK49
Shrimpton Rd, Beac. HP9 111 AK49
Shroffold Rd, Brom. BR1 206 EE91
Shropshire Cl, Mitch. CR4 223 DL98
Shropshire Ho, N18 122 DV50
Shropshire Pl, WC1 17 M5
Shropshire Rd, N22 121 DM52
Shroton St, NW1 16 C6
Shrubberies, The, E18 124 EG54
Chigwell IG7 125 EQ50
Shrubbery, The, E11 146 EH57
Hemel Hempstead HP1 61 BE19
Upminster RM14 150 FQ62
Shrubbery Cl, N1 9 K9
Shrubbery Gdns, N21 121 DP45
Shrubbery Rd, N9 122 DU48
SW16 203 DL91
Gravesend DA12 213 GH88
South Darenth DA4 231 FR95
Southall UB1 158 BZ74
Shrubhill Rd, Hem.H. HP1 61 BF21
Shrubland Gro, Wor.Pk. KT4 221 CW104
Shrubland Rd, E8 10 B8
E10 145 EA59
E17 145 EA57
Banstead SM7 255 CZ116
Shrublands, Brook.Pk AL9 86 DB26
Shrublands, The, Pot.B. EN6 85 CY33
Shrublands Av, Berk. HP4 60 AU19
Croydon CR0 243 EA105
Shrublands Cl, N20 120 DD46
SE26 204 DW90
Chigwell IG7 125 EQ51
Shrublands Rd, Berk. HP4 60 AU18
Shrubsall Cl, SE9 206 EL88
Shrubs Rd, Rick. WD3 114 BM51
Shuna Wk, N1
off St. Paul's Rd 9 L4
Shurland Av, Barn. EN4 102 DD44
Shurland Gdns, SE15 44 B4
Shurlock Av, Swan. BR8 229 FD96
Shurlock Dr, Orp. BR6 245 EQ105
Shuters Sq, W14 38 G1
Shuttle Cl, Sid. DA15 207 ET87
Shuttlemead, Bex. DA5 208 EZ87
Shuttle Rd, Dart. DA1 189 FG83
Shuttle St, E1 20 C5
Shuttleworth Rd, SW11 40 B8
Siamese Ms, N3
off Station Rd 120 DA53
Siani Ms, N8 143 DP56
Sibella Rd, SW4 41 N9
Sibford Ct, Mitch. CR4
off Lower Grn W 222 DF97
Sibley Cl, Bexh. DA6 208 EY85
Bromley BR1 226 EL99
Sibley Gro, E12 166 EL66
Sibneys Grn, Harl. CM18 73 ES19
Sibthorpe Rd, SE12 206 EH86
North Mymms AL9 67 CX24
Sibthorp Rd, Mitch. CR4
off Holborn Way 222 DF96
Sibton Rd, Cars. SM5 222 DE101
Sicilian Av, WC1 18 B7
Sicklefield Cl, Chsht EN7 88 DT26
Sidbury St, SW6 38 E6
SIDCUP, DA14 & DA15 207 ET91
⇌ Sidcup 208 EU89
Coll Sidcup Arts & Adult Ed Cen,
Sid. DA14 off Alma Rd 208 EV90
Sidcup Bypass, Chis. BR7 207 ES91
Orpington BR5 208 EX94
Sidcup DA14 207 ES91
Sidcup High St, Sid. DA14 208 EU91
Sidcup Hill, Sid. DA14 208 EV91
Sidcup Hill Gdns, Sid. DA14
off Sidcup Hill 208 EW92
Sidcup Pl, Sid. DA14 208 EU92
Sidcup Rd, SE9 206 EK87
SE12 206 EH85
● Sidcup Tech Cen, Sid.
DA14 208 EX92
Siddeley Dr, Houns. TW4 178 BY83
Siddons La, NW1 16 F5
Siddons Rd, N17 122 DU53
SE23 205 DY89
Croydon CR0 223 DN104
Side Rd, E17 145 DZ57
Denham UB9 135 BD59
Sideways La, Hkwd RH6 290 DD149
Sidewood Rd, SE9 207 ER88
Sidford Cl, Hem.H. HP1 61 BF20
Sidford Ho, SE1
off Briant Est 30 D7
Sidford Pl, SE1 30 D7
Sidi Ct, N15 143 DP55
Sidings, The, E11 145 EC60
Dunton Green TN13 263 FE120
Hatfield AL10 66 CS19
Loughton IG10 106 EL44
Staines TW18 196 BH91
Sidings Ct, Hert. SG14 54 DQ09
Sidings Ms, N7 143 DN62
Sidings Way, Lon.Col. AL2 83 CH26
SIDLOW, Reig. RH2 288 DB141
Sidmouth Av, Islw. TW7 179 CE82
Sidmouth Cl, Wat. WD19 115 BV47
Sidmouth Dr, Ruis. HA4 137 BU62
Sidmouth Par, NW2
off Sidmouth Rd 4 A7
Sidmouth Rd, E10 145 EC62
NW2 4 B6
Orpington BR5 228 EV99
Welling DA16 188 EW80
Sidmouth St, WC1 18 B3
Sidney Av, N13 121 DM50
Sidney Cl, Uxb. UB8 156 BJ66
Sidney Ct, Wal.Cr. EN8
off Queens Way 89 DZ34
Sidney Elson Way, E6 25 L1
Sidney Gdns, Brent. TW8 179 CJ79
Sidney Gro, EC1 18 G1
Sidney Rd, E7 146 EG62
N22 121 DM52
SE25 224 DU99
SW9 42 C9
Beckenham BR3 225 DY96
Harrow HA2 138 CC55
Staines TW18 196 BG91
Theydon Bois CM16 107 ER36
Twickenham TW1 199 CG86
Walton-on-Thames KT12 217 BU101
Windsor SL4 172 AJ83
Sidney Sq, E1 20 G7
Sidney St, E1 20 G8
Sidney Webb Ho, SE1 31 M6
Sidworth St, E8 10 F7
Siebert Rd, SE3 47 P3
Siemens Rd, SE18 36 F7
Sienna Cl, Chess. KT9 237 CK107
Sigdon Pas, E8 10 D3
Sigdon Rd, E8 10 D3
Sigers, The, Pnr. HA5 137 BV58
Signmakers Yd, NW1 7 K9
Sigrist Sq, Kings.T. KT2 220 CL95
Silbury Av, Mitch. CR4 222 DE95
Silbury Ho, SE26
off Sydenham Hill Est 204 DU90
Silbury St, N1 19 L2
Sch Silchester Manor Sch,
Tap. SL6
off Bath Rd 152 AD72
Silchester Rd, W10 14 D9
Silecroft Rd, Bexh. DA7 188 FA81
Jct Silent Pool Junct, Guil.
GU5 282 BK138
Silesia Bldgs, E8 10 F6
Silex St, SE1 31 H5
Silk Br Retail Pk, NW9 141 CT58
Silk Cl, SE12 206 EG85
Silkfield Rd, NW9 140 CS57
Silkham Rd, Oxt. RH8 275 ED127
Silkin Ms, SE15 44 D5
Silk Mill Ct, Wat. WD19
off Silk Mill Rd 115 BV45
Silk Mill Rd, Wat. WD19 115 BV45
Silk Mills Cl, Sev. TN14 279 FJ121
Silk Mills Pas, SE13 46 D8
Silk Mills Path, SE13 46 D9
Silk Mills Sq, E9 11 P4
Silkmore La, W.Hors. KT24 266 BN125
Silkstream Rd, Edg. HA8 118 CQ53
Silk St, EC2 19 K6
Silo Cl, Gdmg. GU7 280 AT143
Silo Dr, Gdmg. GU7 280 AT143
Silo Rd, Gdmg. GU7 280 AT143
Silsden Cres, Ch.St.G. HP8
off London Rd 112 AX48
Silsoe Ho, NW1
off Park Village E 17 K1
Silsoe Rd, N22 121 DM54
Silverbeck Way, Stanw.M.
TW19 196 BG85
Silver Birch Av, E4 123 DZ51
North Weald Bassett CM16 92 EY27
Silver Birch Cl, N11 120 DG51
SE6 205 DZ90
SE28 168 EU74
Dartford DA2 209 FE91
Uxbridge UB10 136 BL63
Woodham KT15 233 BE112
Silver Birch Ct, Chsht EN8 89 DX31
Silver Birches, Hutt. CM13 131 GA46
Silver Birch Gdns, E6 25 J5
Silver Birch Ms, Ilf. IG6
off Fencepiece Rd 125 EQ51
Silverbirch Wk, NW3 6 F5
Silvercliffe Gdns, Barn. EN4 102 DE42
Silver Cl, SE14 45 L4
Harrow HA3 117 CD52
Kingswood KT20 255 CY124
● Silver Ct, Welw.G.C. AL7 52 DA08
Silver Cres, W4 180 CP77
Silverdale, NW1 17 L2
SE26 204 DW91
Enfield EN2 103 DL42
Silverdale Av, Ilf. IG3 147 ES57
Oxshott KT22 236 CC114
Walton-on-Thames KT12 217 BT104
Silverdale Cl, W7 159 CE74
Brockham RH3 286 CP138
Northolt UB5 138 BZ64
Sutton SM1 239 CZ105
Silverdale Ct, Stai. TW18
off Leacroft 196 BH92
Silverdale Dr, SE9 206 EL89
Hornchurch RM12 149 FH64
Sunbury-on-Thames TW16 217 BV96
Silverdale Gdns, Hayes UB3 177 BU75
Silverdale Rd, E4 123 ED51
Bexleyheath DA7 189 FB82
Bushey WD23 98 BY43
Hayes UB3 177 BU75
Petts Wood BR5 227 EQ98
St. Paul's Cray BR5 228 EU97
Silver Dell, Wat. WD24 97 BT35
Silverfield, Brox. EN10 71 DZ22
Silvergate, Epsom KT19 238 CQ106
● Silverglade Business Pk,
Chess. KT9 237 CJ112
Silverhall St, Islw. TW7 179 CG83
Silver Hill, Ch.St.G. HP8 112 AV47
Well End WD6 100 CQ36
Silverholme Cl, Har. HA3 139 CK59
Silver Jubilee Way, Houns.
TW4 177 BV82
Silverlands Cl, Ott. KT16 215 BD104
Silverland St, E16 37 K3
Silver La, Pur. CR8 241 DK112
West Wickham BR4 225 ED103
Silverlea Gdns, Horl. RH6 291 DJ149
Silverleigh Rd, Th.Hth. CR7 223 DM98
Silverlocke Rd, Grays RM17 192 GD79
Silvermead, E18
off Churchfields 124 EG53
Silvermere Av, Rom. RM5 127 FB51
Silvermere Dr, N18 123 DX51
Silvermere Rd, SE6 205 EB86
Silver Pl, W1 17 M10
Watford WD18
off Metropolitan Ms 97 BS42
Silver Rd, SE13 185 EB83
W12 26 C1
Gravesend DA12 213 GL89
Silversmiths Way, Wok. GU21 248 AW118
Silver Spring Cl, Erith DA8 189 FB79
Silverstead La, West. TN16 261 ER121
Silverstone Cl, Red. RH1
off Goodwood Rd 272 DF132
Silverston Way, Stan. HA7 117 CJ51
⇌ Silver Street 122 DT50
Silver St, N18 122 DS49
Abridge RM4 108 EV41
Enfield EN1 104 DR41
Goffs Oak EN7 88 DR30
Waltham Abbey EN9 89 EC33
Silverthorn Dr, Hem.H. HP3 63 BP24
Silverthorne Rd, SW8 41 J8
Silverthorn Gdns, E4 123 EA47
Silverton Rd, W6 38 C3
SILVERTOWN, E16 36 C4
Silvertown Way, E16 23 K8
Silver Tree Cl, Walt. KT12 217 BU104
Silvertree La, Grnf. UB6 159 CD69
Silver Trees, Brick.Wd AL2 82 BZ30
Silver Wk, SE16 33 N3
Silver Way, Hlgdn UB10 157 BP68
Romford RM7 149 FB55
● Silverwing Ind Est, Croy.
CR0 241 DM106

Silverwood Cl, Beck. BR3 . . . . . **205** EA94
Croydon CR0 . . . . . **243** DZ109
Northwood HA6 . . . . . **115** BQ53
Silverwood Cotts, Shere GU5 . **282** BL138
Silvester Rd, SE22 . . . . . **204** DT85
Silvesters, Harl. CM19 . . . . . **73** EM17
Silvester St, SE1 . . . . . **31** K5
Silvocea Way, E14 . . . . . **23** H9
Silwood Est, SE16
off Concorde Way **33** J9
Silwood St, SE16 . . . . . **33** H9
Sime Cl, Guil. GU3 . . . . . **264** AT130
Simla Ho, SE1 . . . . . **31** M5
Simmil Rd, Clay. KT10 . . . . . **237** CE106
Simmonds Ri, Hem.H. HP3 . . . . **62** BK22
Simmons Cl, N20 . . . . . **120** DE46
Chessington KT9 . . . . . **237** CJ107
Slough SL3 *off Common Rd* . **175** BA77
Simmons Ct, Guil. GU1 . . . . . **264** AW130
Simmons Dr, Dag. RM8 . . . . . **148** EY62
Simmons Gate, Esher KT10 . . . **236** CC106
Simmons La, E4 . . . . . **123** ED47
Simmons Pl, Stai. TW18
off Chertsey La **195** BE92
Simmons Rd, SE18 . . . . . **37** N10
Simmons Way, N20 . . . . . **120** DE47
Simms Cl, Cars. SM5 . . . . . **222** DE103
Simms Gdns, N2 . . . . . **120** DC54
Simms Rd, SE1 . . . . . **32** C9
Simnel Rd, SE12 . . . . . **206** EH87
Simon Balle Sch, Hert. SG13
off Mangrove Rd **54** DS10
Simon Cl, W11 . . . . . **15** H10
Simon Ct, N11 *off Ringway* . . **121** DJ51
Simon Dean, Bov. HP3 . . . . . **79** BA27
Simonds Rd, E10 . . . . . **145** EA61
Simone Cl, Brom. BR1 . . . . . **226** EK95
Simone Dr, Ken. CR8 . . . . . **258** DQ116
Simon Marks Jewish Prim Sch,
N16 *off Cazenove Rd* **144** DT61
Simons Cl, Ott. KT16 . . . . . **233** BC107
Simons Wk, E15 . . . . . **13** H3
Englefield Green TW20 . . . . **194** AW94
Simplemarsh Ct, Add. KT15
off Simplemarsh Rd **234** BH105
Simplemarsh Rd, Add. KT15 . . **234** BG105
Simplicity La, Harl. CM17 . . . . **58** EX14
Simpson Cl, N21
off Macleod Rd **103** DL43
Simpson Dr, W3 . . . . . **160** CR72
Simpson Rd, Houns. TW4 . . . . **198** BZ86
Rainham RM13 . . . . . **169** FF65
Richmond TW10 . . . . . **199** CJ91
Simpsons Rd, E14 . . . . . **34** D1
Bromley BR2 . . . . . **226** EG97
Simpson St, SW11 . . . . . **40** C8
Simpsons Way, Slou. SL1 . . . . **154** AS74
Simpson Way, Long Dit. KT6 . . **219** CJ100
Simrose Ct, SW18
off Wandsworth High St . . . **202** DA85
Sims Cl, Rom. RM1 . . . . . **149** FF56
Sims Wk, SE3 . . . . . **186** EF84
Sinclair Ct, Beck. BR3 . . . . . **205** EA94
Sinclair Dr, Sutt. SM2 . . . . . **240** DB109
Sinclair Gdns, W14 . . . . . **26** D5
Sinclair Gro, NW11 . . . . . **141** CX58
Sinclair Pl, SE4 . . . . . **205** EA86
Sinclair Rd, E4 . . . . . **123** DZ50
W14 . . . . . **26** D5
Windsor SL4 . . . . . **173** AQ83
Sinclair Way, Lane End DA2 . . **211** FR91
Sinclare Cl, Enf. EN1 . . . . . **104** DT39
Sincots Rd, Red. RH1
off Lower Br Rd **272** DF134
Sinderby Cl, Borwd. WD6 . . . . **100** CL39
Singapore Rd, W13 . . . . . **159** CG74
Singer St, EC2 . . . . . **19** M3
Singlegate Prim Sch, SW19
off South Gdns **202** DD94
Singles Cross La, Knock.P.
TN14 . . . . . **246** EW114
SINGLE STREET, West. TN16 . . **261** EN115
Single St, Berry's Grn TN16 . . **261** EP115
Singleton Cl, SW17 . . . . . **202** DF94
Croydon CR0
off St. Saviours Rd **224** DQ101
Hornchurch RM12
off Carfax Rd **149** FF63
Singleton Rd, Dag. RM9 . . . . . **148** EZ64
Singleton Scarp, N12 . . . . . **120** DA50
SINGLEWELL, Grav. DA12 . . . . **213** GK93
Singlewell Prim Sch, Grav.
DA12 *off Mackenzie Way* . . **213** GK93
Singlewell Rd, Grav. DA11 . . . . **213** GH89
Singret Pl, Cowley UB8 . . . . . **156** BJ70
Sinnott Rd, E17 . . . . . **123** DX53
Sion-Manning RC Girls' Sch,
W10 . . . . . **14** E7
Sion Rd, Twick. TW1 . . . . . **199** CH88
SIPSON, West Dr. UB7 . . . . . **176** BN79
Sipson Cl, Sipson UB7 . . . . . **176** BN79
Sipson La, Harling. UB3 . . . . . **176** BN79
Sipson UB7 . . . . . **176** BN79
Sipson Rd, West Dr. UB7 . . . . **176** BN78
Sipson Way, Sipson UB7 . . . . **176** BN80
Sir Alexander Cl, W3 . . . . . **161** CT74
Sir Alexander Rd, W3 . . . . . **161** CT74
Sir Cyril Black Way, SW19 . . **202** DA94
Sirdar Rd, N22 . . . . . **143** DP55
W11 . . . . . **26** D1
Mitcham CR4
off Grenfell Rd **202** DG93
Sirdar Strand, Grav. DA12 . . . **213** GM92
Sir Francis Drake Prim Sch,
SE8 . . . . . **45** L1
Sir Francis Way, Brwd. CM14 . . **130** FV47
Sir Frederic Osborn Sch,
Welw.G.C. AL7
off Herns La **52** DB08
Sir George Monoux Coll, E17
off Chingford Rd **123** EB54
Sir Giles Gilbert Scott Bldg, The,
SW15 . . . . . **201** CY86
Sir Henry Peek's Dr, Slou.
SL2 . . . . . **153** AN65
Sirinham Pt, SW8 . . . . . **42** C3
Sirius Rd, Nthwd. HA6 . . . . . **115** BU50
Sir James Barrie Prim Sch,
SW8 . . . . . **41** M7
Sir James Black Ho, SE5
off Coldharbour La **43** L8
Sir John Cass's Foundation &
Redcoat Sch, E1 . . . . . **21** K7
Sir John Cass's Foundation
C of E Prim Sch, EC3 . . . . . **20** A9
Sir John Heron Prim Sch, E12
off School Rd **147** EM63
Sir John Kirk Cl, SE5 . . . . . **43** J4
Sir John Lillie Prim Sch,
SW6 . . . . . **38** F3
Sir John Lyon Ho, EC4
off Gardners La **19** J10
Sir John Newsom Way, Welw.G.C.
AL7 . . . . . **51** CY12
★ **Sir John Soane's Mus**, WC2
off Lincoln's Inn Flds **18** C8
Sir Martin Bowles Ho, SE18
off Calderwood St **37** M8
Sir Robert Ms, Slou. SL3
off Cheviot Rd **175** BA78
Sir Thomas Abney Sch, N16
off Fairholt Rd **144** DR60
Sir Thomas More Est, SW3 . . . **40** B3
Sir William Burrough Prim Sch,
E14 . . . . . **21** M8
Sir William Perkin's Sch, Cher.
KT16 *off Guildford Rd* **215** BF102
Sise La, EC4 . . . . . **19** L9
Siskin Cl, Borwd. WD6 . . . . . **100** CN42
Bushey WD23 . . . . . **98** BY42
Sisley Rd, Bark. IG11 . . . . . **167** ES67
Sispara Gdns, SW18 . . . . . **201** CZ86
Sissinghurst Cl, Brom. BR1 . . . **206** EE92
Sissinghurst Rd, Croy. CR0 . . . **224** DU101
Sissulu Ct, E6 . . . . . **166** EJ67
Sister Mabel's Way, SE15 . . . . **44** C4
Sisters Av, SW11 . . . . . **182** DF84
Sistova Rd, SW12 . . . . . **203** DH88
Sisulu Pl, SW9 . . . . . **183** DN83
Sittingbourne Av, Enf. EN1 . . . **104** DR44
Sitwell Gro, Stan. HA7 . . . . . **117** CF50
Siverst Cl, Nthlt. UB5 . . . . . **158** CB65
Sivill Ho, E2 . . . . . **20** B2
Siviter Way, Dag. RM10 . . . . . **169** FB66
Siward Rd, N17 . . . . . **122** DR53
SW17 . . . . . **202** DC90
Bromley BR2 . . . . . **226** EH97
Six Acres, Hem.H. HP3 . . . . . **62** BN23
Six Acres Est, N4 . . . . . **143** DN61
Six Bells La, Sev. TN13 . . . . . **279** FJ126
● **Six Bridges Trd Est**, SE1 . . . . **44** D1
Sixpenny Ct, Bark. IG11 . . . . . **167** EQ65
Sixth Av, E12 . . . . . **147** EM63
W10 . . . . . **14** E3
Hayes UB3 . . . . . **157** BT74
Watford WD25 . . . . . **98** BX35
Sixth Cross Rd, Twick. TW2 . . **198** CC90
Skardu Rd, NW2 . . . . . **4** E2
Skarnings Ct, Wal.Abb. EN9 . . . **90** EG33
Skeena Hill, SW18 . . . . . **201** CY87
Skeet Hill La, Orp. BR5, BR6 . . **228** EY103
Skeffington Rd, E6 . . . . . **166** EL67
Skeffington St, SE18 . . . . . **187** EQ76
Skelbrook St, SW18 . . . . . **202** DB89
Skelgill Rd, SW15 . . . . . **181** CZ84
Skelley Rd, E15 . . . . . **13** L7
Skelton Cl, E8 . . . . . **10** B5
Beaconsfield HP9 . . . . . **132** AG55
Skelton Rd, E7 . . . . . **13** P5
Skeltons La, E10 . . . . . **145** EB59
Skelwith Rd, W6 . . . . . **38** B3
Skenfrith Ho, SE15 . . . . . **44** E3
Skerne Rd, Kings.T. KT2 . . . . . **219** CK95
Skerne Wk, Kings.T. KT2 . . . . . **219** CK95
Sketchley Gdns, SE16 . . . . . **33** J10
Sketty Rd, Enf. EN1 . . . . . **104** DS41
Skibbs La, Orp. BR5, BR6 . . . . **228** EZ103
Skid Hill La, Warl. CR6 . . . . . **244** EF113
Skidmore Way, Rick. WD3 . . . . **114** BL46
Skiers St, E15 . . . . . **13** J9
Skiffington Cl, SW2 . . . . . **203** DN88
Skillet Hill, Wal.Abb. EN9 . . . **106** EH35
Skimpans Cl, N.Mymms AL9 . . . **67** CX24
Skinner Ct, E2 . . . . . **10** F10
Skinner Pl, SW1 . . . . . **28** G9
Skinners' Company's Sch for
Girls, The, Lwr Sch, E5
off Mount Pleasant La **144** DV60
Upr Sch, N16
off Stamford Hill **144** DT59
★ **Skinners' Hall**, EC4
off Dowgate Hill **19** L10
Skinners La, EC4 . . . . . **19** K10
Ashtead KT21 . . . . . **253** CK118
Hounslow TW5 . . . . . **178** CB81
Skinner St, EC1 . . . . . **18** F3
Skinney La, Hort.Kir. DA4 . . . . **230** FQ97
Skip La, Hare. UB9 . . . . . **136** BL60
Skippers Cl, Green. DA9 . . . . . **211** FV85
Skipsea Ho, SW18 . . . . . **202** DD86
Skipsey Av, E6 . . . . . **25** K3
Skipton Cl, N11 . . . . . **120** DG51
Skipton Dr, Hayes UB3 . . . . . **177** BQ76
Skipton Way, Horl. RH6 . . . . . **291** DH145
Skipworth Rd, E9 . . . . . **11** H8
Skomer Wk, N1 *off Ashby Gro* . . **9** K6
● **Sky Business Pk**, Egh. TW20
off Eversley Way **215** BC96
Skydmore Path, Slou. SL2
off Umberville Way **153** AM69
Skylark Av, Green. DA9 . . . . . **211** FU86
Skylark Rd, Denh. UB9 . . . . . **135** BC60
Skylines Village, E14 . . . . . **34** E5
Sky Peals Rd, Wdf.Grn. IG8 . . **123** ED53
Skyport Dr, Harm. UB7 . . . . . **176** BK80
Skyswood Prim Sch, St.Alb.
AL4 *off Chandlers Rd* **65** CJ16
Skys Wd Rd, St.Alb. AL4 . . . . . **65** CH16
Skyvan Cl, Lon.Hthrw Air.
TW6 . . . . . **197** BQ85
Slacksbury Hatch, Harl. CM19
off Helions Rd **73** EP15
Slade, The, SE18 . . . . . **187** ES79
Sladebrook Rd, SE3 . . . . . **186** EK83
Slade Ct, Ott. KT16 . . . . . **233** BD107
Radlett WD7 . . . . . **99** CG35
Sladedale Rd, SE18 . . . . . **187** ES78
Slade End, They.B. CM16 . . . . . **107** ES36
Slade Gdns, Erith DA8 . . . . . **189** FF81
⇌ **Slade Green** **189** FG81
Slade Grn Inf Sch, Erith DA8
off Slade Grn Rd **189** FG80
Slade Grn Jun Sch, Erith DA8
off Slade Grn Rd **189** FG80
Slade Grn Rd, Erith DA8 . . . . . **189** FG80
Slade Ho, Houns. TW4 . . . . . **198** BZ86
Slade Oak La, Denh. UB9 . . . . . **135** BD59
Gerrards Cross SL9 . . . . . **135** BB55
Slade Rd, Ott. KT16 . . . . . **233** BD107
Slades Cl, Enf. EN2 . . . . . **103** DN41
Slades Dr, Chis. BR7 . . . . . **207** EQ90
Slades Gdns, Enf. EN2 . . . . . **103** DN40
Slades Hill, Enf. EN2 . . . . . **103** DN41
Slades Ri, Enf. EN2 . . . . . **103** DN41
Slade Twr, E10 . . . . . **145** EA61
Slade Wk, SE17 . . . . . **43** H3
Slade Way, Mitch. CR4 . . . . . **222** DG95
Slagrove Pl, SE13 . . . . . **205** EA85
Slaidburn St, SW10 . . . . . **39** P3
Slaithwaite Rd, SE13 . . . . . **185** EC84
Slaney Pl, N7 . . . . . **8** E2
Slaney Rd, Rom. RM1 . . . . . **149** FE57
Slapleys, Wok. GU22 . . . . . **248** AX120
Slater Cl, SE18 . . . . . **37** M9
Slattery Rd, Felt. TW13 . . . . . **198** BW88
Sleaford Grn, Wat. WD19 . . . . **116** BX48
Sleaford Ho, E3 . . . . . **22** B5
Sleaford St, SW8 . . . . . **41** L4
Sleapcross Gdns, Smallford
AL4 . . . . . **66** CP21
SLEAPSHYDE, St.Alb. AL4 . . . . . **66** CP21
Sleapshyde La, Smallford AL4 . . **66** CP21
Sleddale, Hem.H. HP2 . . . . . **62** BL17
Sledmere Ct, Felt. TW14
off Kilross Rd **197** BS88
Sleepers Fm Rd, Grays RM16 . **193** GH75
Sleets End, Hem.H. HP1 . . . . . **62** BH18
Slewins Cl, Horn. RM11 . . . . . **150** FJ57
Slewins La, Horn. RM11 . . . . . **150** FJ57
Slievemore Cl, SW4
off Voltaire Rd **183** DK83
Slimmons Dr, St.Alb. AL4 . . . . . **65** CG16
Slines Oak Rd, Warl. CR6 . . . . **259** EA119
Woldingham CR3 . . . . . **259** EA123
Slingsby Pl, WC2 . . . . . **18** A10
Slip, The, West. TN16 . . . . . **277** EQ126
Slipe La, Brox. EN10 . . . . . **71** DZ24
Slippers Hill, Hem.H. HP2 . . . . **62** BK19
Slippers Pl, SE16 . . . . . **32** F6
Slippers Pl Est, SE16 . . . . . **32** F7
Slipshatch Rd, Reig. RH2 . . . . **287** CX138
Slipshoe St, Reig. RH2
off West St **272** DA134
Sloane Av, SW3 . . . . . **28** D9
Sloane Ct E, SW3 . . . . . **28** G10
Sloane Ct W, SW3 . . . . . **28** G10
Sloane Gdns, SW1 . . . . . **28** G9
Orpington BR6 . . . . . **227** EQ104
Sloane Hosp, The, Beck.
BR3 . . . . . **225** ED95
Sloane Ms, N8 . . . . . **143** DL57
⊖ **Sloane Square** **28** G9
Sloane Sq, SW1 . . . . . **28** G9
Sloane St, SW1 . . . . . **28** F6
Sloane Ter, SW1 . . . . . **28** F8
Sloane Wk, Croy. CR0 . . . . . **225** DZ100
Sloansway, Welw.G.C. AL7 . . . . **51** CZ06
Slocock Hill, Wok. GU21 . . . . . **248** AW117
Slocum Cl, SE28 . . . . . **168** EW73
SLOUGH, SL1 - SL3 . . . . . **154** AS74
⇌ **Slough** **154** AT74
Slough & Eton C of E Sch,
Slou. SL1 *off Ragstone Rd* . **173** AR76
Slough Gram Sch, Slou. SL3
off Lascelles Rd **174** AV76
● **Slough Interchange**, Slou.
SL2 . . . . . **154** AU74
Slough Islamic Sch, Slou.
SL2 *off Wexham Rd* **154** AV73
Slough La, NW9 . . . . . **140** CQ58
Buckland RH3 . . . . . **271** CU133
Epping CM16 . . . . . **75** FD24
Headley KT18 . . . . . **270** CQ125
★ **Slough Mus**, Slou. SL1 . . . . . **174** AU75
Slough Retail Pk, Slou.
SL1 . . . . . **153** AP74
Slough Rd, Datchet SL3 . . . . . **174** AU78
Eton SL4 . . . . . **173** AR78
Iver SL0 . . . . . **155** BE68
● **Slough Trd Est**, Slou. SL1 . . **153** AN72
Slowmans Cl, Park St AL2 . . . . **82** CC28
Slyfield Ct, Guil. GU1
off Slyfield Grn **264** AY131
Slyfield Grn, Guil. GU1 . . . . . **264** AX130
● **Slyfield Ind Est**, Guil. GU1 . **264** AY130
Sly St, E1 . . . . . **20** E9
Smaldon Cl, West Dr. UB7
off Walnut Av **176** BN76
Small Acre, Hem.H. HP1 . . . . . **61** BF20
Smallberry Av, Islw. TW7 . . . . . **179** CF82
Smallberry Grn Prim Sch,
Islw. TW7 *off Turnpike Way* . **179** CG81
Smallbrook Ms, W2 . . . . . **16** A9
Smallcroft, Welw.G.C. AL7 . . . . **52** DB08
Smalley Cl, N16 . . . . . **144** DT62
Smalley Rd Est, N16
off Smalley Cl **144** DT61
SMALLFIELD, Horl. RH6 . . . . . **291** DP149
Smallfield Rd, Horl. RH6 . . . . . **291** DH148
SMALLFORD, St.Alb. AL4 . . . . . **66** CP19
Smallford La, Smallford AL4 . . . **66** CP21
Small Grains, Fawk.Grn DA3 . . **231** FV104
Smallholdings Rd, Epsom
KT17 . . . . . **239** CW114
Smallmead, Horl. RH6 . . . . . **291** DH148
Small's Hill Rd, Leigh RH2 . . . . **287** CU141
Smallwood Cl, Wheat. AL4 . . . . **50** CL08
Smallwood Prim Sch, SW17
off Smallwood Rd **202** DD91
Smallwood Rd, SW17 . . . . . **202** DD91
Smardale Rd, SW18
off Alma Rd **202** DC85
Smarden Cl, Belv. DA17
off Essenden Rd **188** FA78
Smarden Gro, SE9 . . . . . **207** EM91
Smart Cl, Rom. RM3 . . . . . **127** FH53
Smarts Grn, Chsht EN7 . . . . . **88** DT27
Smarts Heath La, Wok. GU22 . **248** AU123
Smarts Heath Rd, Wok. GU22 . **248** AT123
Smarts La, Loug. IG10 . . . . . **106** EK42
Smarts Pl, N18 *off Fore St* . . . **122** DU50
Smart's Pl, WC2 . . . . . **18** B8
Smarts Rd, Grav. DA12 . . . . . **213** GH89
Smart St, E2 . . . . . **21** J2
Smead Way, SE13 . . . . . **185** EB83
Smeaton Cl, Chess. KT9 . . . . . **237** CK107
Waltham Abbey EN9 . . . . . **90** EE32
Smeaton Ct, SE1 . . . . . **31** J7
Smeaton Dr, Wok. GU22 . . . . . **249** BB120
Smeaton Rd, SW18 . . . . . **202** DA87
Enfield EN3 . . . . . **105** EA37
Woodford Green IG8 . . . . . **125** EM50
Smeaton St, E1 . . . . . **32** E2
Smedley St, SW4 . . . . . **41** P8
SW8 . . . . . **41** P8
Smeed Rd, E3 . . . . . **12** A7
Smiles Pl, SE13 . . . . . **46** E8
Woking GU22 . . . . . **249** BB116
⇌ **Smitham** **257** DL115
Smitham Bottom La, Pur.
CR8 . . . . . **241** DJ111
Smitham Downs Rd, Pur. CR8 . **241** DK113
Smitham Prim Sch, Couls.
CR5 *off Portnalls Rd* **257** DJ116
Smithbarn Cl, Horl. RH6 . . . . . **291** DH147
Smith Cl, SE16 . . . . . **33** J3
Smithers, The, Brock. RH3 . . . . **286** CP136
Smithfield, Hem.H. HP2 . . . . . **62** BK18
Smithfield St, EC1 . . . . . **18** G7
Smithies Rd, SE2 . . . . . **188** EV77
Smith Rd, Reig. RH2 . . . . . **287** CZ137
Smith's Ct, W1 . . . . . **17** M10
Smiths Ct, Thnwd CM16 . . . . . **92** EW25
Smiths Cres, Smallford AL4 . . . **66** CP21
Smiths Fm Est, Nthlt. UB5 . . . . **158** CA68
Smiths La, Chsht EN7 . . . . . **88** DR26
Crockham Hill TN8 . . . . . **277** EQ133
Windsor SL4 . . . . . **173** AL82
Smithson Rd, N17 . . . . . **122** DR53
Smiths Pt, E13 . . . . . **13** N9
Smith Sq, SW1 . . . . . **30** A7
Smith St, SW3 . . . . . **28** E10
Surbiton KT5 . . . . . **220** CM100
Watford WD18 . . . . . **98** BW42
Smiths Yd, SW18
off Summerley St **202** DC89
Smith's Yd, Croy. CR0
off St. Georges Wk **224** DQ104
Smith Ter, SW3 . . . . . **40** E1
Smithwood Cl, SW19 . . . . . **201** CY88
Smithy Cl, Lwr Kgswd KT20 . . **271** CZ126
Smithy La, Lwr Kgswd KT20 . . **271** CZ127
Smithy St, E1 . . . . . **20** G6
Smithy St Prim Sch, E1 . . . . **21** H6
Smock Wk, Croy. CR0 . . . . . **224** DQ100
Smokehouse Yd, EC1 . . . . . **19** H6
Smoke La, Reig. RH2 . . . . . **288** DB136
SMOKY HOLE, Guil. GU5 . . . . . **283** BR144
Smugglers Wk, Green. DA9 . . . **211** FV85
Smugglers Way, SW18 . . . . . **182** DB84
● **Smug Oak Grn Business Cen**,
Brick.Wd AL2 . . . . . **82** CA29
Smug Oak La, St.Alb. AL2 . . . . **82** CB30
Smyrks Rd, SE17 . . . . . **43** P1
Smyrna Rd, NW6 . . . . . **5** J7
Smythe Cl, N9 . . . . . **122** DU48
Smythe Rd, Sutt.H. DA4 . . . . . **230** FN95
Smythe St, E14 . . . . . **22** D10
Snag La, Cudham TN14 . . . . . **245** ES109
Snakeley Cl, Loud. HP10 . . . . . **110** AC54
Snakes La, Barn. EN4 . . . . . **103** DH41
Snakes La E, Wdf.Grn. IG8 . . . **124** EJ51
Snakes La W, Wdf.Grn. IG8 . . **124** EG51
Snakey La, Felt. TW13 . . . . . **197** BU91
Snape Spur, Slou. SL1 . . . . . **154** AS72
SNARESBROOK, E11 . . . . . **146** EE57
⊖ **Snaresbrook** **146** EG57
Snaresbrook Coll, E18
off Woodford Rd **146** EG55
Snaresbrook Dr, Stan. HA7 . . . **117** CK49
Snaresbrook Prim Sch, E18
off Meadow Wk **146** EG56
Snaresbrook Rd, E11 . . . . . **146** EE56
Snarsgate St, W10 . . . . . **14** A7
Snatts Hill, Oxt. RH8 . . . . . **276** EF129
Sneath Av, NW11 . . . . . **141** CZ59
Snelling Av, Nthflt DA11 . . . . . **212** GE89
Snellings Rd, Hersham KT12 . . **236** BW106
Snells La, Amer. HP7 . . . . . **94** AV39
Snells Pk, N18 . . . . . **122** DT51
Snells Wd Ct, Amer. HP7 . . . . . **94** AW40
Sneyd Rd, NW2 . . . . . **4** A2
Sniggs La, Penn HP10
off Beacon Hill **110** AD50
Snipe Cl, Erith DA8 . . . . . **189** FH80
Snodland Cl, Downe BR6
off Mill La **245** EN110
Snowberry Cl, E15 . . . . . **13** H1
Snowbury Rd, SW6 . . . . . **39** M9
Snowden Av, Hlgdn UB10 . . . . **157** BP68
Snowden Cl, Wind. SL4 . . . . . **173** AK84
Snowden Hill, Nthflt DA11 . . . . **212** GA85
Snowden St, EC2 . . . . . **19** N5
Snowdon Cres, Hayes UB3 . . . **177** BQ76
Snowdon Dr, NW9 . . . . . **140** CS58
Snowdon Rd, Lon.Hthrw Air. TW6
off Southern Perimeter Rd . **197** BQ85
Snowdown Cl, SE20 . . . . . **225** DX95
Snowdrop Cl, Hmptn. TW12
off Gresham Rd **198** CA93
Snowdrop Path, Rom. RM3 . . . . **128** FK52
Snowerhill Rd, Bet. RH3 . . . . . **286** CS136
Snow Hill, EC1 . . . . . **18** G7
Snowhill Cotts, Chesh. HP5 . . . **60** AT24
Snow Hill Ct, EC1 . . . . . **19** H8
Snowman Ho, NW6 . . . . . **5** L8
Snowsfields, SE1 . . . . . **31** M4
Snowsfields Prim Sch, SE1 . **31** N4
Snowshill Rd, E12 . . . . . **146** EL64
Snowy Fielder Waye, Islw.
TW7 . . . . . **179** CH82
Soames Pl, Barn. EN4 . . . . . **102** DB40
Soames St, SE15 . . . . . **184** DT83
Soames Wk, N.Mal. KT3 . . . . . **220** CS95
Soane Cl, W5 . . . . . **179** CK75
Soap Ho La, Brent. TW8
off Ferry La **180** CL79
Socket La, Brom. BR2 . . . . . **226** EH100
SOCKETT'S HEATH, Grays
RM16 . . . . . **192** GD76
Soham Rd, Enf. EN3 . . . . . **105** DZ37
SOHO, W1 . . . . . **17** N10
Soho Cres, Woob.Grn HP10 . . . **132** AD59
● **Soho Mills Ind Est**, Woob.Grn
HP10 . . . . . **132** AD59
Soho Parish Sch, W1 . . . . . **17** N10
Soho Sq, W1 . . . . . **17** N8
Soho St, W1 . . . . . **17** N8
Sojourner Truth Cl, E8 . . . . . **10** F5
Solander Gdns, E1 . . . . . **20** G10
Solar Way, Enf. EN3 . . . . . **105** DZ36
Soldene Ct, N7 . . . . . **8** C4
Solebay St, E1 . . . . . **21** L5
Solecote, Bkhm KT23 . . . . . **268** CA125
Sole Fm Av, Bkhm KT23 . . . . . **268** BZ125
Sole Fm Cl, Bkhm KT23 . . . . . **252** BZ124
Sole Fm Rd, Bkhm KT23 . . . . . **268** BZ125
Solefield Sch, Sev. TN13
off Solefields Rd **279** FJ126
Solefields Rd, Sev. TN13 . . . . . **279** FH128
Solent Ri, E13 . . . . . **23** N3
Solent Rd, NW6 . . . . . **5** J3
Soleoak Dr, Sev. TN13 . . . . . **279** FH127
Solesbridge Cl, Chorl. WD3 . . . . **95** BF41
Solesbridge La, Rick. WD3 . . . . **96** BG40
Soley Ms, WC1 . . . . . **18** E2
Solna Av, SW15 . . . . . **201** CW85
Solna Rd, N21 . . . . . **122** DR46
Solomon Av, N9 . . . . . **122** DU49
Solomons Hill, Rick. WD3
off Northway **114** BK45
Solomon's Pas, SE15 . . . . . **184** DV84
Solom's Ct Rd, Bans. SM7 . . . . **256** DD117
Solon New Rd, SW4 . . . . . **183** DL84
Solon Rd, SW2 . . . . . **183** DL84
Solway, Hem.H. HP2 . . . . . **62** BM18
Solway Cl, E8 . . . . . **10** B5
Hounslow TW4 . . . . . **178** BY83
Solway Rd, N22 . . . . . **121** DP53
SE22 . . . . . **184** DU84
Somaford Gro, Barn. EN4 . . . . **102** DD44
Somali Rd, NW2 . . . . . **4** G1
Somborne Ho, SW15
off Fontley Way **201** CU87
Somerby Cl, Brox. EN10 . . . . . **71** EA21
Somerby Rd, Bark. IG11 . . . . . **167** ER66
Somercoates Cl, Barn. EN4 . . . **102** DE41
Somerden Rd, Orp. BR5 . . . . . **228** EX101
Somerfield Cl, Tad. KT20 . . . . . **255** CY119
Somerfield Rd, N4 . . . . . **143** DP61
Somerfield St, SE16 . . . . . **33** J10
Somerford Cl, Eastcote HA5 . . **137** BU56
Somerford Gro, N16 . . . . . **10** A1
N17 . . . . . **122** DU52
Somerford Gro Est, N16 . . . . . **10** A1
Somerford Pl, Beac. HP9 . . . . . **111** AK52
Somerford St, E1 . . . . . **20** E5
Somerford Way, SE16 . . . . . **33** L5
Somerhill Av, Sid. DA15 . . . . . **208** EV87
Somerhill Rd, Well. DA16 . . . . . **188** EV82
Someries Rd, Hem.H. HP1 . . . . **61** BF18
Somerleyton Pas, SW9 . . . . . **183** DP84
Somerleyton Rd, SW9 . . . . . **183** DN84
Somersby Gdns, Ilf. IG4 . . . . . **147** EM57
Somers Cl, NW1 . . . . . **7** N10
Reigate RH2 . . . . . **272** DA133
Somers Cres, W2 . . . . . **16** C9
Somerset Av, SW20 . . . . . **221** CV96
Chessington KT9 . . . . . **237** CK105
Welling DA16 . . . . . **207** ET85
Somerset Cl, N17 . . . . . **122** DR54
Epsom KT19 . . . . . **238** CS109
Hersham KT12
off Queens Rd **235** BV106
New Malden KT3 . . . . . **220** CS100
Woodford Green IG8 . . . . . **124** EG53
Somerset Est, SW11 . . . . . **40** B6
Somerset Gdns, N6 . . . . . **142** DG59
N17 . . . . . **122** DS52
SE13 . . . . . **46** C9
SW16 . . . . . **223** DM97
Hornchurch RM11 . . . . . **150** FN60
Teddington TW11 . . . . . **199** CE92
Somerset Hall, N17 . . . . . **122** DS52
★ **Somerset Ho**, WC2 . . . . . **18** C10
Somerset Ho, SW19 . . . . . **201** CX90
Somerset Rd, E17 . . . . . **145** EA57
N17 . . . . . **144** DT55
N18 . . . . . **122** DT50
NW4 . . . . . **141** CW56
SW19 . . . . . **201** CY91
W4 . . . . . **180** CR76
W13 . . . . . **159** CH74
Brentford TW8 . . . . . **179** CJ79
Dartford DA1 . . . . . **209** FH86
Enfield EN3 . . . . . **105** EA38
Harrow HA1 . . . . . **138** CC58
Kingston upon Thames KT1 . **220** CM96
New Barnet EN5 . . . . . **102** DB43
Orpington BR6 . . . . . **228** EU101
Redhill RH1 . . . . . **288** DD136
Southall UB1 . . . . . **158** BZ71
Teddington TW11 . . . . . **199** CE92
Somerset Sq, W14 . . . . . **26** F5
Somerset Way, Iver SL0 . . . . . **175** BF75
Somerset Waye, Houns. TW5 . . **178** BY79
Somersham, Welw.G.C. AL7 . . . **52** DD09
Somersham Rd, Bexh. DA7 . . . **188** EY82
Somers Heath Prim Sch,
S.Ock. RM15
off Foyle Dr **171** FU73
Somers Ms, W2 . . . . . **16** C9
Somers Pl, SW2 . . . . . **203** DM87
Reigate RH2 . . . . . **272** DA133
Somers Rd, E17 . . . . . **145** DZ56
SW2 . . . . . **203** DM86
North Mymms AL9 . . . . . **67** CW24
Reigate RH2 . . . . . **271** CZ133
Somers Sq, N.Mymms AL9 . . . . **67** CW23
SOMERS TOWN, NW1 . . . . . **17** P2
Somers Way, Bushey WD23 . . . **116** CC45
Somerswey, Shalf. GU4 . . . . . **280** AY142
Somerton Av, Rich. TW9 . . . . . **180** CP83
Somerton Cl, Pur. CR8 . . . . . **257** DN115
Somerton Rd, NW2 . . . . . **141** CY62
SE15 . . . . . **184** DV84
Somertons Cl, Guil. GU2 . . . . . **264** AU131
Somertrees Av, SE12 . . . . . **206** EH89
Somervell Rd, Har. HA2 . . . . . **138** BZ64
Somerville Av, SW13 . . . . . **181** CV79
Somerville Cl, SW9 . . . . . **42** D8
Somerville Rd, SE20 . . . . . **205** DX94
Cobham KT11 . . . . . **236** CA114
Dartford DA1 . . . . . **210** FM86
Eton SL4 . . . . . **173** AQ78
Romford RM6 . . . . . **148** EW58
Sommer's Ct, Ware SG12
off Crane Mead **55** DY07
Sommerville Ct, Borwd. WD6
off Alconbury Cl **100** CM39
Sonderburg Rd, N7 . . . . . **143** DM61
Sondes Fm, Dor. RH4 . . . . . **285** CF136
Sondes Pl Dr, Dor. RH4 . . . . . **285** CF136
Sondes St, SE17 . . . . . **43** L2
Songhurst Cl, Croy. CR0 . . . . . **223** DM100
Sonia Cl, Wat. WD19 . . . . . **116** BW45
Sonia Ct, Har. HA1 . . . . . **139** CF58
Sonia Gdns, N12
off Woodside Av **120** DC49
NW10 . . . . . **141** CT63
Hounslow TW5 . . . . . **178** CA80
Sonic Ct, Guil. GU1 . . . . . **264** AW133
Sonnets, The, Hem.H. HP1 . . . . **62** BH19
Sonnet Wk, Bigg.H. TN16
off Kings Rd **260** EH118
Sonning Gdns, Hmptn. TW12 . **198** BY93
Sonning Rd, SE25 . . . . . **224** DU100
Soothouse Spring, St.Alb. AL3 . **65** CF16
Soper Cl, E4 . . . . . **123** DZ50
SE23 . . . . . **205** DX88
Soper Dr, Cat. CR3 . . . . . **258** DR123
Soper Ms, Enf. EN3
off Harston Dr **105** EA38
Soper Sq, Harl. CM17
off Square St **58** EW14
Sopers Rd, Cuffley EN6 . . . . . **87** DM29
Sophia Cl, N7 . . . . . **8** C4

Sophia Rd, E10 145 EB60
E16 24 A8
Sophia Sq, SE16 33 L1
Sophie Gdns, Slou. SL3 174 AX75
Sopwell La, St.Alb. AL1 65 CD21
Sopwith Av, Chess. KT9 238 CL106
Sopwith Cl, Bigg.H. TN16 260 EK116
Kingston upon Thames KT2 200 CM92
Sopwith Dr, W.Byf. KT14 234 BL111
Weybridge KT13 234 BL111
Sopwith Rd, Houns. TW5 178 BW80
Sopwith Way, SW8 41 J4
Kingston upon Thames KT2 220 CL95
Sorbie Cl, Wey. KT13 235 BR107
Sorrel Bk, Croy. CR0 243 DY110
Sorrel Cl, SE28 168 EU74
Sorrel Ct, Grays RM17
off Salix Rd 192 GD79
Sorrel Gdns, E6 24 G6
Sorrel La, E14 23 H9
Sorrell Cl, SE14 45 L4
SW9 42 F8
Sorrel Wk, Rom. RM1 149 FF55
Sorrel Way, Nthflt DA11 212 GE91
Sorrento Rd, Sutt. SM1 222 DB104
Sospel Ct, Farn.Royal SL2 153 AQ68
Sotheby Rd, N5 143 DP62
Sotheran Cl, E8 10 D8
Sotheron Rd, SW6 39 M5
Watford WD17 98 BW40
Soudan Rd, SW11 40 E7
Souldern Rd, W14 26 D7
Souldern St, Wat. WD18 97 BU43
Sounds Lo, Swan. BR8 229 FC100
South Access Rd, E17 145 DY59
Southacre Way, Pnr. HA5 116 BW53
SOUTH ACTON, W3 180 CN76
⊖ South Acton 180 CQ76
South Acton Est, W3 180 CP75
South Africa Rd, W12 161 CV74
South Albert Rd, Reig. RH2 271 CZ133
SOUTHALL, UB1 & UB2 158 BX74
⇌ Southall 178 BZ75
Coll Southall & W London Coll, Sthl.
UB1 off Beaconsfield Rd 158 BY74
Southall Cl, Ware SG12 55 DX05
Southall La, Houns. TW5 177 BV79
Southall UB2 177 BV79
Southall Pl, SE1 31 L5
Southall Way, Brwd. CM14 130 FT49
Southampton Bldgs, WC2 18 E8
Southampton Gdns, Mitch.
CR4 223 DL99
Southampton Ms, E16 36 A2
Southampton Pl, WC1 18 B7
Southampton Rd, NW5 6 F3
Southampton Rd E, Lon.Hthrw Air.
TW6 196 BN86
Southampton Rd W, Lon.Hthrw Air.
TW6 196 BL86
Southampton Row, WC1 18 B6
Southampton St, WC2 18 B10
Southampton Way, SE5 43 M4
Southam St, W10 14 F5
South App, Nthwd. HA6 115 BR48
South Audley St, W1 29 H1
South Av, E4 123 EB45
Carshalton SM5 240 DG108
Egham TW20 195 BC93
Richmond TW9
off Sandycombe Rd 180 CN82
Southall UB1 158 BZ73
Whiteley Village KT12 235 BS110
South Av Gdns, Sthl. UB1 158 BZ73
South Bk, Chis. BR7 207 EQ90
Southbank, Hext. BR8 209 FF94
South Bk, Surb. KT6 220 CL100
Southbank, T.Ditt. KT7 219 CH101
South Bk, West. TN16 277 ER126
● Southbank Business Cen,
SW8 41 P3
Sch Southbank Int Sch -
Hampstead Campus, NW3 5 P4
Sch Southbank Int Sch -
Kensington Campus, W11 27 J1
Sch Southbank Int Sch -
Westminster Campus,
Conway St, W1 17 L5
Portland Pl, W1 17 J6
South Bk Rd, Berk. HP4 60 AT17
South Bk Ter, Surb. KT6 220 CL100
SOUTH BEDDINGTON, Wall.
SM6 241 DK107
⇌ South Bermondsey 32 G10
South Birkbeck Rd, E11 145 ED62
South Black Lion La, W6 181 CU78
South Bolton Gdns, SW5 27 M10
Sch South Bookham Sch, Bkhm
KT23 off Oakdene Cl 268 CC127
South Border, The, Pur. CR8 241 DK111
SOUTHBOROUGH, Brom.
BR2 227 EM100
Southborough Cl, Surb. KT6 219 CK102
Southborough La, Brom. BR2 226 EL99
Sch Southborough Prim Sch, Brom.
BR2 off Southborough La 227 EN99
Southborough Rd, E9 11 J8
Bromley BR1 226 EL97
Surbiton KT6 220 CL102
Sch Southborough Sch, Surb.
KT6 off Hook Rd 220 CL104
Southbourne, Brom. BR2 226 EG101
Southbourne Av, NW9 118 CQ54
Southbourne Cl, Pnr. HA5 138 BY59
Southbourne Cres, NW4 141 CY56
Southbourne Gdns, SE12 206 EH85
Ilford IG1 147 EQ64
Ruislip HA4 137 BV60
Southbridge Pl, Croy. CR0 242 DQ105
Southbridge Rd, Croy. CR0 242 DQ105
Southbridge Way, Sthl. UB2 178 BY75
Southbrook, Saw. CM21 58 EY06
Southbrook Dr, Chsht EN8 89 DX28
Southbrook Ms, SE12 206 EF86
Southbrook Rd, SE12 206 EF86
SW16 223 DL95
⇌ Southbury 104 DV42
Southbury Av, Enf. EN1 104 DU43
Southbury Cl, Horn. RM12 150 FK64
Sch Southbury Prim Sch, Enf.
EN3 off Swansea Rd 104 DW42
Southbury Rd, Enf. EN1, EN3 104 DR41
Coll South Camden City Learning
Cen, NW1 7 N10
Sch South Camden Comm Sch,
NW1 7 N10
South Carriage Dr, SW1 28 E4
SW7 28 B5
SOUTH CHINGFORD, E4 123 DZ50
Southchurch Rd, E6 25 J1
South Circular Rd, SE6 (A205) 205 ED87
SE9 (A205) 187 EM83
SE12 (A205) 206 EH86
SE18 (A205) 187 EN79
SE21 (A205) 204 DS88
SE22 (A205) 204 DV88
SE23 (A205) 205 DZ88
SW2 (A205) 203 DN88
SW4 (A205) 202 DG85
SW11 (A3) 202 DE85
SW12 (A205) 203 DN88
SW14 (A205) 180 CS84
SW15 (A205) 181 CW84
SW18 (A3) 202 DE85
W4 (A205) 180 CN78
Brentford (A205) TW8 180 CN78
Richmond (A205) TW9 180 CP82
South City Ct, SE15 43 P4
Southcliffe Dr, Chal.St.P. SL9 112 AY50
South Cl, N6 143 DH58
Barnet EN5 101 CZ41
Bexleyheath DA6 188 EX84
Dagenham RM10 168 FA67
Morden SM4 222 DA100
Pinner HA5 138 BZ59
St. Albans AL2 82 CB25
Slough SL1
off St. George's Cres 153 AK73
Twickenham TW2 198 CA90
West Drayton UB7 176 BM76
Woking GU21 248 AW116
South Cl Grn, Merst. RH1 273 DH129
South Colonnade, The, E14 34 B2
Southcombe St, W14 26 E8
South Common Rd, Uxb.
UB8 156 BL65
Southcote, Wok. GU21 248 AX115
Southcote Av, Felt. TW13 197 BT89
Surbiton KT5 220 CP101
Southcote Ri, Ruis. HA4 137 BR59
Southcote Rd, E17 145 DX57
N19 143 DJ63
SE25 224 DV100
South Croydon CR2 242 DS110
South Merstham RH1 273 DJ129
South Cottage Dr, Chorl.
WD3 95 BF43
South Cottage Gdns, Chorl.
WD3 95 BF43
Southcott Ms, NW8 16 C1
South Countess Rd, E17 145 DZ55
South Cres, E16 22 G5
WC1 17 N7
South Cft, Eng.Grn TW20 194 AV92
Southcroft, Slou. SL2 153 AP70
Southcroft Av, Well. DA16 187 ES83
West Wickham BR4 225 EC103
Southcroft Rd, SW16 202 DG93
SW17 202 DG93
Orpington BR6 227 ES104
South Cross Rd, Ilf. IG6 147 EQ57
South Croxted Rd, SE21 204 DR90
SOUTH CROYDON, CR2 242 DQ107
⇌ South Croydon 242 DR106
Southdale, Chig. IG7 125 ER51
SOUTH DARENTH, Dart. DA4 231 FR95
Southdean Gdns, SW19 201 CZ89
South Dene, NW7 118 CR48
Southdene, Halst. TN14 246 EY113
Southdown Av, W7 179 CG76
Southdown Ct, Hat. AL10 67 CV21
Southdown Cres, Har. HA2 138 CB60
Ilford IG2 147 ES57
Southdown Dr, SW20 201 CX94
Southdown Rd, SW20 221 CX95
Carshalton SM5 240 DG109
Hatfield AL10 67 CU21
Hersham KT12 236 BY105
Hornchurch RM11 149 FH59
Woldingham CR3 259 DZ122
Southdowns, S.Darenth DA4 231 FR96
South Dr, Bans. SM7 240 DE113
Beaconsfield HP9 132 AH55
Coulsdon CR5 257 DK115
Cuffley EN6 87 DL30
Dorking RH5 285 CJ136
Orpington BR6 245 ES106
Romford RM2 150 FJ55
Ruislip HA4 137 BS60
St. Albans AL4 65 CK20
Sutton SM2 239 CY110
Virginia Water GU25 214 AU102
Warley CM14 130 FX49
⊖ South Ealing 179 CJ76
South Ealing Rd, W5 179 CK75
South Eastern Av, N9 122 DT48
Coll South E London Coll, SE4 45 M10
South Eaton Pl, SW1 29 H8
South Eden Pk Rd, Beck. BR3 225 EB100
South Edwardes Sq, W8 27 H7
SOUTHEND, SE6 205 EB91
South End, W8 27 M6
Bookham KT23 268 CB126
Croydon CR0 242 DQ105
Southend Arterial Rd, Brwd.
CM13 151 FV57
Hornchurch RM11 128 FK54
Romford RM2, RM3 128 FK54
Upminster RM14 151 FR57
South End Cl, NW3 6 D1
Southend Cl, SE9 207 EP86
Southend Cres, SE9 207 EN86
South End Grn, NW3 6 D1
Southend La, SE6 205 DZ91
SE26 205 DZ91
Waltham Abbey EN9 90 EH34
Southend Rd, E4 123 DY50
E6 167 EM66
E17 123 EB53
E18 124 EG53
South End Rd, NW3 6 C1
Southend Rd, Beck. BR3 205 EA94
Grays RM17 192 GC77
South End Rd, Horn. RM12 169 FH65
Rainham RM13 169 FG67
Southend Rd, Wdf.Grn. IG8 124 EJ54
South End Row, W8 27 M6
Southerland Cl, Wey. KT13 235 BQ105
Southern Av, SE25 224 DT97
Feltham TW14 197 BU88
Redhill RH1 288 DG141
Southern Dr, Loug. IG10 107 EM44
Southerngate Way, SE14 45 L4
Southern Gro, E3 21 N4
Southernhay, Loug. IG10 106 EK43
Southern Lo, Harl. CM19 73 EQ18
Southern Perimeter Rd,
Lon.Hthrw Air. TW6 197 BR85
Southern Pl, Har. HA1 139 CF63
Swanley BR8 229 FD98
Southern Rd, E13 24 B1
N2 142 DF56
Sch Southern Rd Prim Sch, E13
off Southern Rd 166 EH68
Southern Row, W10 14 E5
Southerns La, Chipstead CR5 272 DC125
Southern St, N1 8 C10
Southern Way, SE10 35 M8
Harlow CM17, CM18 73 EN18
Romford RM7 148 FA58
Southernwood Cl, Hem.H. HP2 62 BN19
Southerton Rd, W6 26 A7
Southerton Way, Shenley WD7 84 CL33
South Esk Rd, E7 166 EJ65
Southey Ms, E16 35 P2
Southey Rd, N15 144 DS57
SW9 42 E6
SW19 202 DA94
Southey St, SE20 205 DX94
Southey Wk, Til. RM18 193 GH81
Southfield, Barn. EN5 101 CX44
Welwyn Garden City AL7 51 CX11
Southfield Av, Wat. WD24 98 BW38
Southfield Cl, Dorney SL4 172 AJ76
Uxbridge UB8 156 BN69
Southfield Cotts, W7
off Oaklands Rd 179 CF75
Southfield Gdns, Burn. SL1 152 AH71
Twickenham TW1 199 CF91
Southfield Pk, Har. HA2 138 CB56
Sch Southfield Pk Prim Sch, Epsom
KT19 off Long Gro Rd 238 CQ111
Southfield Pl, Wey. KT13 235 BP108
Sch Southfield Prim Sch, W4
off Southfield Rd 180 CS75
Southfield Rd, N17
off The Avenue 122 DS54
W4 180 CS76
Chislehurst BR7 227 ET97
Enfield EN3 104 DV44
Hoddesdon EN11 71 EA15
Waltham Cross EN8 89 DY32
SOUTHFIELDS, SW18 202 DA88
⊖ Southfields 201 CZ88
Southfields, NW4 141 CU55
East Molesey KT8 219 CE100
Swanley BR8 229 FE94
Southfields Av, Ashf. TW15 197 BP93
Sch Southfield Sch, Hat. AL10
off Travellers La 67 CV21
Sch Southfields Comm Coll, SW18
off Merton Rd 202 DA88
Southfields Ct, SW19 201 CY88
Sutton SM1
off Sutton Common Rd 222 DA103
Southfields Grn, Grav. DA11 213 GH92
Southfields Ms, SW18
off Southfields Rd 202 DA86
Southfields Pas, SW18 202 DA86
Southfields Rd, SW18 202 DA86
Woldingham CR3 259 EB123
Southfield Way, St.Alb. AL4 65 CK18
SOUTHFLEET, Grav. DA13 212 GB93
Southfleet Rd, Bean DA2 211 FW91
Northfleet DA11 213 GF89
Orpington BR6 227 ES104
Swanscombe DA10 212 FZ87
South Gdns, SW19 202 DD94
Wembley HA9
off The Avenue 140 CM61
SOUTHGATE, N14 121 DJ47
⊖ Southgate 121 DJ46
South Gate, Harl. CM20 73 ER15
Southgate, Purf. RM19 190 FQ77
Southgate Av, Felt. TW13 197 BR91
Southgate Circ, N14
off The Bourne 121 DK46
Coll Southgate Coll, N14
off High St 121 DK46
Minchenden Complex, N14
off High St 121 DK47
Southgate Gro, N1 9 M7
Southgate Rd, N1 9 M8
Potters Bar EN6 86 DC33
Sch Southgate Sch, Cockfos.
EN4 off Sussex Way 103 DH43
South Gipsy Rd, Well. DA16 188 EX83
South Glade, The, Bex. DA5 208 EZ88
South Grn, NW9
off Clayton Fld 118 CS53
Slough SL1 154 AS73
⇌ South Greenford 159 CE69
South Gro, E17 145 DZ57
N6 142 DG60
N15 144 DR57
Chertsey KT16 215 BF100
South Gro Ho, N6 142 DG60
Sch South Gro Prim Sch, E17
off Ringwood Rd 145 DZ58
SOUTH HACKNEY, E9 10 F7
South Hall Cl, Fnghm DA4 230 FM101
South Hall Dr, Rain. RM13 169 FH71
SOUTH HAMPSTEAD, NW6 5 M6
⇌ South Hampstead 5 P7
Sch South Hampstead High Sch,
NW3 5 P5
Jun Dept, NW3 5 P4
SOUTH HAREFIELD, Uxb.
UB9 136 BJ56
Sch South Harringay Inf Sch, N4
off Pemberton Rd 143 DP57
Sch South Harringay Jun Sch, N4
off Mattison Rd 143 DP57
SOUTH HARROW, Har. HA2 138 CB62
⊖ South Harrow 138 CC62
SOUTH HATFIELD, Hat. AL10 67 CU20
South Hill, Chis. BR7 207 EM93
Guildford GU1 280 AX136
South Hill Av, Har. HA1, HA2 138 CC62
South Hill Gro, Har. HA1 139 CE63
South Hill Pk, NW3 6 C1
South Hill Pk Gdns, NW3 142 DE63
Sch South Hill Prim Sch, Hem.H.
HP1 off Heath La 62 BJ21
South Hill Rd, Brom. BR2 226 EE97
Gravesend DA12 213 GH88
Hemel Hempstead HP1 62 BJ20
Southholme Cl, SE19 224 DS95
SOUTH HOLMWOOD, Dor.
RH5 285 CJ144
SOUTH HORNCHURCH, Rain.
RM13 169 FE67
South Huxley, N18 122 DR50
Southill La, Pnr. HA5 137 BU56
Southill Rd, Chis. BR7 206 EL94
Southill St, E14 22 D8
South Island Pl, SW9 42 D5
SOUTH KENSINGTON, SW7 27 N9
⊖ South Kensington 28 B8
South Kensington Sta Arc, SW7
off Pelham St 28 B8
South Kent Av, Nthflt DA11 212 GC86
⇌ South Kenton 139 CJ60
⊖ South Kenton 139 CJ60
SOUTH LAMBETH, SW8 42 B6
South Lambeth Est, SW8
off Dorset Rd 42 C5
South Lambeth Pl, SW8 42 B2
South Lambeth Rd, SW8 42 B3
Southland Rd, SE18 187 ET80
Southlands Av, Horl. RH6 290 DF147
Orpington BR6 245 ER105
Southlands Cl, Couls. CR5 257 DM117
Southlands Dr, SW19 201 CX89
Southlands Gro, Brom. BR1 226 EL97
Southlands La, Tand. RH8 275 EB134
Southlands Rd, Brom.
BR1, BR2 226 EJ99
Denham UB9 135 BF63
Iver SL0 135 BF64
Southland Way, Houns. TW3 199 CD85
South La, Kings.T. KT1 219 CK97
New Malden KT3 220 CR98
South La W, N.Mal. KT3 220 CR98
SOUTHLEA, Slou. SL3 174 AV82
Southlea Rd, Datchet SL3 174 AV81
Windsor SL4 174 AU84
South Ley, Welw.G.C. AL7 51 CY12
South Ley Ct, Welw.G.C. AL7
off South Ley 51 CY12
South Lo, NW8 16 A2
SW7 off Knightsbridge 28 D5
South Lo Av, Mitch. CR4 223 DL98
South Lo Cres, Enf. EN2 103 DK42
South Lo Dr, N14 103 DL43
South Lo Rd, Walt. KT12 235 BU109
★ South London Art Gall,
SE5 43 P6
Southly Cl, Sutt. SM1 222 DA104
South Mall, N9 off Edmonton
Grn Shop Cen 122 DU48
South Mead, NW9 119 CT53
Epsom KT19 238 CS108
Redhill RH1 272 DF131
Southmead Cres, Chsht EN8 89 DY30
Southmead Gdns, Tedd. TW11 199 CG93
South Meadow La, Eton SL4 173 AQ80
South Meadows, Wem. HA9 140 CL64
Sch Southmead Prim Sch, SW19
off Princes Way 201 CY88
Southmead Rd, SW19 201 CY88
SOUTH MERSTHAM, Red.
RH1 273 DJ130
⇌ South Merton 221 CZ97
SOUTH MIMMS, Pot.B. EN6 85 CT32
South Molton La, W1 17 J9
South Molton Rd, E16 23 P8
South Molton St, W1 17 J9
Southmont Rd, Esher KT10 219 CE103
Southmoor Way, E9 11 P4
South Mundells, Welw.G.C.
AL7 51 CZ08
SOUTH NORWOOD, SE25 224 DT97
Coll South Norwood CETS Cen,
SE25 off Sandown Rd 224 DV99
South Norwood Hill, SE25 224 DS96
Sch South Norwood Prim Sch,
SE25 off Crowther Rd 224 DU98
SOUTH NUTFIELD, Red. RH1 289 DL136
South Oak Rd, SW16 203 DM91
SOUTH OCKENDON, RM15 171 FW70
Southold Ri, SE9 207 EM90
Southolm St, SW11 41 J7
South Ordnance Rd, Enf. EN3 105 EA37
Southover, N12 120 DA49
Bromley BR1 206 EG92
SOUTH OXHEY, Wat. WD19 116 BW48
South Par, SW3 28 B10
W4 180 CR77
Edgware HA8
off Mollison Way 118 CN54
SOUTH PARK, Reig. RH2 287 CZ138
South Pk, SW6 39 K9
Gerrards Cross SL9 135 AZ57
Sevenoaks TN13 279 FH125
South Pk Av, Chorl. WD3 95 BF43
South Pk Cres, SE6 206 EF88
Gerrards Cross SL9 134 AY56
Ilford IG1 147 ER62
South Pk Dr, Bark. IG11 147 ES63
Gerrards Cross SL9 134 AY56
Ilford IG3 147 ES63
South Pk Gdns, Berk. HP4 60 AV18
South Pk Gro, N.Mal. KT3 220 CQ98
South Pk Hill Rd, S.Croy. CR2 242 DR106
South Pk Ms, SW6 39 L10
Sch South Pk Prim Sch,
Seven Kings IG3
off Water La 147 ES62
South Pk Rd, SW19 202 DA93
Ilford IG1 147 ER62
South Pk Ter, Ilf. IG1 147 ER62
South Pk Vw, Ger.Cr. SL9 135 AZ56
South Pk Way, Ruis. HA4 158 BW65
South Path, Wind. SL4 173 AQ81
South Penge Pk Est, SE20 224 DV96
South Perimeter Rd, Uxb. UB8
off Kingston La 156 BL69
South Pier Rd, Gat. RH6 291 DH152
South Pl, EC2 19 M6
Enfield EN3 104 DW43
Harlow CM20 58 EU12
Surbiton KT5 220 CM101
Waltham Abbey EN9
off Sun St 89 EC33
South Pl Ms, EC2 19 M7
South Pt, Sutt. SM1 240 DC107
Southport Rd, SE18 187 ER77
DLR South Quay 34 D5
● South Quay Plaza, E14 34 C4
South Quay Sq, E14 34 C4
South Ridge, Wey. KT13 235 BP110
Southridge Pl, SW20 201 CX94
South Riding, Brick.Wd AL2 82 CA30
South Ri, Cars. SM5 240 DE109
Sch South Ri Prim Sch, SE18
off Brewery Rd 187 ER78
South Ri Way, SE18 187 ER78
South Rd, N9 122 DU46
SE23 205 DX89
SW19 202 DC93
W5 179 CK77
Amersham HP6 77 AQ36
Chadwell Heath RM6 148 EY58
Chorleywood WD3 95 BC43
Edgware HA8 118 CP53
South Rd, Eng.Grn TW20 194 AW93
Erith DA8 189 FF79
Feltham TW13 198 BX92
Guildford GU2 264 AV132
Hampton TW12 198 BY93
Harlow CM20 58 EU12
Little Heath RM6 148 EW57
Reigate RH2 288 DB135
St. George's Hill KT13 235 BP109
South Ockendon RM15 171 FW72
Southall UB1 178 BZ75
Twickenham TW2 199 CD90
West Drayton UB7 176 BM76
Weybridge KT13 235 BQ106
Woking GU21 232 AX114
South Row, SE3 47 M8
SOUTH RUISLIP, Ruis. HA4 138 BW63
⇌ South Ruislip 138 BW63
⊖ South Ruislip 138 BW63
Southsea Av, Wat. WD18 97 BU42
Southsea Rd, Kings.T. KT1 220 CL98
South Sea St, SE16 33 N6
South Side, W6 181 CT76
Southside, Chal.St.P. SL9 134 AX55
South Side, Cher. KT16 216 BG97
Southside Common, SW19 201 CW93
Southside Shop Cen,
SW18 202 DB86
Southspring, Sid. DA15 207 ER87
South Sq, NW11 142 DB58
WC1 18 E7
South Sta App, S.Nutfld RH1 289 DL136
SOUTH STIFFORD, Grays
RM20 191 FW78
SOUTH STREET, West. TN16 261 EM119
South St, W1 29 H2
Brentwood CM14 130 FW47
Bromley BR1 226 EG96
Dorking RH4 285 CG137
Enfield EN3 105 DX43
Epsom KT18 238 CR113
Gravesend DA12 213 GH87
Hertford SG14 54 DR09
Isleworth TW7 179 CG83
Rainham RM13 169 FC68
Romford RM1 149 FF58
Staines TW18 195 BF92
Stanstead Abbotts SG12 55 EC11
South Tenter St, E1 20 B10
South Ter, SW7 28 C8
Dorking RH4 285 CH137
Surbiton KT6 220 CL100
Coll South Thames Coll,
Putney Cen, SW15
off Putney Hill 201 CX85
Roehampton Cen, SW15
off Roehampton La 201 CU86
Tooting Cen, SW17
off Tooting High St 202 DE92
Wandsworth Cen, SW18
off Wandsworth High St 202 DB85
SOUTH TOTTENHAM, N15 144 DS57
⇌ South Tottenham 144 DT57
South Vale, SE19 204 DS93
Harrow HA1 139 CE63
Southvale Rd, SE3 47 K9
South Vw, Brom. BR1 226 EH96
Epsom KT19 238 CN110
Southview Av, NW10 141 CT64
South Vw Av, Til. RM18 193 GG81
Southview Cl, SW17 202 DG92
South Vw Cl, Bex. DA5 208 EZ86
Southview Cl, Chsht EN7 88 DS26
Swanley BR8 229 FF98
South Vw Ct, Wok. GU22
off Constitution Hill 248 AY118
Southview Cres, Ilf. IG2 147 EP58
South Vw Dr, E18 146 EH55
Upminster RM14 150 FN62
Southview Gdns, Wall. SM6 241 DJ108
South Vw Rd, N8 143 DK55
Ashtead KT21 253 CK119
Southview Rd, Brom. BR1 205 ED91
South Vw Rd, Dart. DA2 210 FK90
Gerrards Cross SL9 134 AX56
Grays RM20 191 FW79
Loughton IG10 107 EM44
Pinner HA5 115 BV51
Southview Rd, Warl. CR6 258 DU119
Woldingham CR3 259 EB124
Southviews, S.Croy. CR2 243 DX109
South Vil, NW1 7 P5
Southville, SW8 41 P6
Southville Cl, Epsom KT19 238 CR109
Feltham TW14 197 BS88
Southville Cres, Felt. TW14 197 BS88
Sch Southville Inf & Nurs &
Jun Schs, Felt. TW14
off Bedfont La 197 BT88
Southville Rd, Felt. TW14 197 BS88
Thames Ditton KT7 219 CG101
South Wk, Hayes UB3
off Middleton Rd 157 BR71
Reigate RH2 off Chartway 272 DB134
West Wickham BR4 226 EE104
SOUTHWARK, SE1 31 H3
⊖ Southwark 30 G3
Coll Southwark Adult Ed,
Nunhead Cen, SE15
off Whorlton Rd 184 DV83
Thomas Calton Cen, SE15 44 C9
Southwark Br, EC4 31 K2
SE1 31 K2
Southwark Br Rd, SE1 31 H6
★ Southwark Cath, SE1 31 L2
Coll Southwark Coll,
Bermondsey Cen, SE16 32 E6
Camberwell Cen, SE5 43 N5
Grange Cen, SE1 31 P7
Waterloo Cen, SE1 30 G4
Southwark Pk, SE16 32 F7
Southwark Pk Est, SE16 32 F8
Sch Southwark Pk Prim Sch,
SE16 32 F7
Southwark Pk Rd, SE16 32 B8
Southwark Pl, Brom. BR1 227 EM97
Southwark St, SE1 31 H2
Southwater Cl, E14 21 N8
Beckenham BR3 205 EB94
South Way, N9 122 DW47
N11 off Ringway 121 DJ51

Southway, N20 120 DA47
NW11 142 DB58
SW20 221 CW98
South Way, Abb.L. WD5 81 BT33
Beaconsfield HP9 132 AG55
Southway, Cars. SM5 240 DD110
South Way, Croy. CR0 225 DY104
Southway, Guil. GU2 264 AT134
South Way, Har. HA2 138 CA56
Southway, Hat. AL10 67 CU22
South Way, Hayes BR2 226 EG101
Purfleet RM19 191 FS76
Southway, Wall. SM6 241 DJ105
South Way, Wem. HA9 140 CN64
Southway Cl, W12 181 CV75
Southway Ct, Guil. GU2 264 AS134
SOUTH WEALD, Brwd. CM14 130 FS47
South Weald Dr, Wal.Abb. EN9 89 ED33
South Weald Rd, Brwd. CM14 130 FU48
Southwell Av, Nthlt. UB5 158 CA65
Southwell Cl, Chaff.Hun. RM16 191 FW78
Southwell Gdns, SW7 27 N8
Southwell Gro Rd, E11 146 EE61
Southwell Rd, SE5 43 J10
Croydon CR0 223 DN100
Kenton HA3 139 CK58
South Western Rd, Twick. TW1 199 CG86
Southwest Rd, E11 145 ED60
South Wf Rd, W2 16 A8
Southwick Ms, W2 16 B8
Southwick Pl, W2 16 C9
Southwick St, W2 16 C8
SOUTH WIMBLEDON, SW19 202 DB94
⊖ South Wimbledon 202 DB94
Southwold Dr, Bark. IG11 148 EU64
Sch Southwold Prim Sch, E5
off Detmold Rd 144 DW61
Southwold Rd, E5 144 DV61
Bexley DA5 209 FB86
Watford WD24 98 BW38
Southwold Spur, Slou. SL3 175 BC75
Southwood Av, N6 143 DH59
Coulsdon CR5 257 DJ115
Kingston upon Thames KT2 220 CQ95
Ottershaw KT16 233 BC108
Southwood Cl, Brom. BR1 227 EM98
Worcester Park KT4 221 CX102
Southwood Dr, Surb. KT5 220 CQ101
SOUTH WOODFORD, E18 124 EF54
⊖ South Woodford 124 EG54
Southwood Gdns, Esher KT10 219 CG104
Ilford IG2 147 EP56
Southwood La, N6 142 DG59
Southwood Lawn Rd, N6 142 DG59
Southwood Pk, N6 142 DG59
Sch Southwood Prim Sch, Dag. RM9 off Keppel Rd 148 EY63
Southwood Rd, SE9 207 EP89
SE28 168 EV74
Southwood Smith St, N1 8 G9
South Worple Av, SW14 180 CS83
South Worple Way, SW14 180 CR83
Soval Ct, Nthwd. HA6 off Maxwell Rd 115 BR52
● Sovereign Business Cen, Enf. EN3 105 DZ40
Sovereign Cl, E1 32 F1
W5 159 CJ71
Purley CR8 241 DM110
Ruislip HA4 137 BS60
Sovereign Ct, Harl. CM19 off Rosemount 73 EP18
West Molesey KT8 218 BZ98
Sovereign Cres, SE16 33 L1
Sovereign Gro, Wem. HA0 139 CK62
Sovereign Hts, Slou. SL3 175 BA79
Sovereign Ms, E2 10 A10
Barnet EN4 102 DF41
Sovereign Pk, NW10 160 CP70
St. Albans AL4 65 CK21
Sovereign Pl, Har. HA1 139 CF57
Sovereign Rd, Bark. IG11 168 EW69
Sowerby Cl, SE9 206 EL85
Sowrey Av, Rain. RM13 169 FF65
Soyer Ct, Wok. GU21 off Raglan Rd 248 AS118
Space Waye, Felt. TW14 197 BV85
Spackmans Way, Slou. SL1 173 AQ76
Spa Cl, SE25 224 DS95
Spa Dr, Epsom KT18 238 CN114
Spafield St, EC1 18 E4
Spa Grn Est, EC1 18 F2
Spa Hill, SE19 224 DR95
Spalding Cl, Edg. HA8 118 CS52
Spalding Rd, NW4 141 CW58
SW17 203 DH92
Spalt Cl, Hutt. CM13 131 GB47
Spanby Rd, E3 22 B5
Spaniards Cl, NW11 142 DD60
Spaniards End, NW3 142 DC60
Spaniards Rd, NW3 142 DC61
Spanish Pl, W1 17 H8
Spanish Rd, SW18 202 DC85
Spareleaze Hill, Loug. IG10 107 EM43
Sparepenny La, Dart. DA4 230 FL102
Sparkbridge Rd, Har. HA1 139 CE56
Sparkes Cl, Brom. BR2 226 EH98
Sparke Ter, E16 23 L8
Sparkford Gdns, N11 120 DG50
Sparkford Ho, SW11 40 B6
Sparks Cl, W3 160 CR72
Dagenham RM8 148 EX61
Hampton TW12 off Victors Dr 198 BY93
Spa Rd, SE16 32 A7
Sparrow Cl, Hmptn. TW12 198 BY93
Sparrow Dr, Orp. BR5 227 EQ102
Sparrow Fm Dr, Felt. TW14 198 BX87
Sch Sparrow Fm Inf & Nurs Sch, Felt. TW14 off Denham Rd 198 BW87
Sch Sparrow Fm Jun Sch, Felt. TW14 off Sparrow Fm Dr 198 BW87
Sparrow Fm Rd, Epsom KT17 239 CU105
Sparrow Grn, Dag. RM10 149 FB62
Sparrows Herne, Bushey WD23 116 CB45
Sparrows La, SE9 207 EQ87
Sparrows Mead, Red. RH1 272 DG131
Sparrows Way, Bushey WD23 116 CC45
Sparrowswick Ride, St.Alb. AL3 64 CC15
Sparrow Wk, Wat. WD25 off Gullet Wd Rd 97 BU35
Sparsholt Rd, N19 143 DL60
Barking IG11 167 ES67
Spartan Cl, Wall. SM6 241 DL108
Sparta St, SE10 46 D7
Sch Spa Sch, SE1 32 C9
★ Speaker's Cor, W2 16 F10
Speaker's Ct, Croy. CR0 off St. James's Rd 224 DR102
Spearman St, SE18 187 EN79
Spear Ms, SW5 27 K9
Spearpoint Gdns, Ilf. IG2 147 ET56
Spears Rd, N19 143 DL60
Speart La, Houns. TW5 178 BY80
Spectacle Wks, E13 24 C2
Spectrum Ho, Enf. EN3 off Tysoe Av 105 DY36
Spectrum Pl, SE17 43 L2
Spedan Cl, NW3 142 DB62
Speechly Ms, E8 10 B2
Speedbird Way, Harm. UB7 176 BH80
Speedgate Hill, Fawk.Grn DA3 231 FU103
Speed Highwalk, EC2 off Silk St 19 K6
Speed Ho, EC2 19 L6
Speedwell Cl, Guil. GU4 265 BB131
Hemel Hempstead HP1 off Campion Rd 61 BE21
Speedwell Ct, Grays RM17 192 GE80
Speedwell St, SE8 46 A5
Speedy Pl, WC1 18 A3
Speer Rd, T.Ditt. KT7 219 CF99
Speirs Cl, N.Mal. KT3 221 CT100
Spekehill, SE9 207 EM90
Speke Rd, Th.Hth. CR7 224 DR96
Speldhurst Cl, Brom. BR2 226 EF99
Speldhurst Rd, E9 11 J7
W4 180 CR76
Spellbrook Wk, N1 9 K8
Spelman St, E1 20 C6
Spelthorne Gro, Sun. TW16 197 BT94
Sch Spelthorne Inf & Nurs Sch, Ashf. TW15 off Chertsey Rd 197 BS93
Sch Spelthorne Jun Sch, Ashf. TW15 off Feltham Hill Rd 197 BR93
Spelthorne La, Ashf. TW15 217 BQ95
Spence Av, Byfleet KT14 234 BL114
Spence Cl, SE16 33 N5
Spencer Av, N13 121 DM51
Cheshunt EN7 88 DS26
Hayes UB4 157 BU71
Spencer Cl, N3 119 CZ54
NW10 160 CM69
Epping CM16 92 EV29
Epsom KT18 254 CS119
Orpington BR6 227 ES103
Uxbridge UB8 156 BJ69
Woking GU21 233 BC113
Woodford Green IG8 124 EJ50
H Spencer Cl Hosp, Epp. CM16 92 EV29
Spencer Ctyd, N3 off Regents Pk Rd 119 CZ54
Spencer Dr, N2 142 DC58
Spencer Gdns, SE9 207 EM85
SW14 200 CQ85
Englefield Green TW20 194 AX92
Spencer Gate, St.Alb. AL1 65 CE18
Spencer Hill, SW19 201 CY93
Spencer Hill Rd, SW19 201 CY94
★ Spencer Ho, SW1 29 L3
Spencer Ms, SW8 42 C7
W6 38 E2
Spencer Pk, SW18 202 DD85
Spencer Pas, E2 10 E10
Spencer Pl, N1 8 G6
Croydon CR0 224 DR101
Spencer Ri, NW5 143 DH63
Spencer Rd, E6 166 EK67
E17 123 EC54
N8 143 DM57
N11 121 DH49
N17 122 DU53
SW18 182 DD84
SW20 221 CV95
W3 160 CQ74
W4 180 CQ80
Beddington Corner CR4 222 DG101
Bromley BR1 206 EE94
Caterham CR3 258 DR121
Cobham KT11 251 BV115
East Molesey KT8 218 CC99
Harrow HA3 117 CE54
Ilford IG3 147 ET60
Isleworth TW7 179 CD81
Mitcham CR4 222 DG97
Rainham RM13 169 FD69
Slough SL3 175 AZ76
South Croydon CR2 242 DS106
Twickenham TW2 199 CE90
Wembley HA0 139 CJ61
Spencers Cft, Harl. CM18 74 EV17
Spencer St, EC1 18 G3
Gravesend DA11 213 GG87
Hertford SG13 54 DS08
St. Albans AL3 65 CD20
Southall UB2 178 BX75
Spencer Wk, NW3 5 P1
SW15 181 CX84
Rickmansworth WD3 96 BJ43
Tilbury RM18 193 GG82
Spencer Way, E1 20 F9
Hemel Hempstead HP1 62 BG17
Redhill RH1 288 DG139
Spencer Yd, SE3 47 L9
Spenser Av, Wey. KT13 234 BN108
Spenser Cres, Upmin. RM14 150 FQ59
Spenser Gro, N16 9 N1
Spenser Ms, SE21 204 DR88
Spenser Rd, SE24 203 DN85
Spenser St, SW1 29 M6
Spensley Wk, N16 144 DR62
Speranza St, SE18 187 ET78
Sperling Rd, N17 122 DS54
Spert St, E14 21 L10
Speyhawk Pl, Pot.B. EN6 86 DB30
Speyside, N14 103 DJ44
Spey St, E14 22 E7
Spey Way, Rom. RM1 127 FE52
Spezia Rd, NW10 161 CU68
Sphere, The, E16 23 L9
● Sphere Ind Est, St.Alb. AL1 65 CG20
Spice Quay Hts, SE1 32 B3
Spicer Cl, SW9 43 H8
Walton-on-Thames KT12 218 BW100
Spicersfield, Chsht EN7 88 DU27
Spicers Fld, Oxshott KT22 237 CD113
Spicers La, Harl. CM17 off Wayre St 58 EW11
Spicer St, St.Alb. AL3 64 CC20
Spice's Yd, Croy. CR0 242 DQ105
Spielman Rd, Dart. DA1 190 FM84
Spiers Way, Horl. RH6 291 DH150
Spigurnell Rd, N17 122 DR53
Spikes Br Moorings, Hayes UB4 158 BY73
Spikes Br Rd, Sthl. UB1 158 BY72
Spilsby Rd, Rom. RM3 128 FK52
Spindle Cl, SE18 37 H7
Spindles, Til. RM18 193 GG80
Spindlewood Gdns, Croy. CR0 242 DS105
Spindlewoods, Tad. KT20 255 CV122
Spindrift Av, E14 34 C8
Spinel Cl, SE18 187 ET78
Spingate Cl, Horn. RM12 150 FK64
Spinnaker Cl, Bark. IG11 168 EV69
Spinnells Rd, Har. HA2 138 BZ60
Spinners Wk, Wind. SL4 173 AQ81
Spinney, Slou. SL1 153 AP74
Spinney, The, N21 121 DN45
SW16 203 DK90
Aldenham WD25 99 CD38
Barnet EN5 102 DB40
Beaconsfield HP9 133 AK55
Berkhamsted HP4 60 AT20
Bookham KT23 252 CB124
Broxbourne EN10 71 DZ19
Chesham HP5 76 AR29
Epsom KT18 255 CV119
Gerrards Cross SL9 134 AX60
Guildford GU2 off Southway 264 AU133
Headley KT18 270 CQ126
Hertford SG13 54 DT09
Horley RH6 290 DG146
Hutton CM13 131 GC44
Loughton IG10 107 EP42
Oxshott KT22 236 CC112
Potters Bar EN6 86 DD31
Purley CR8 241 DP111
Send GU23 266 BJ127
Sidcup DA14 208 EY92
Stanmore HA7 118 CL49
Sunbury-on-Thames TW16 217 BU95
Sutton SM3 239 CW105
Swanley BR8 229 FE96
Watford WD17 97 BU39
Welwyn Garden City AL7 51 CY10
Wembley HA0 139 CG62
Spinney Cl, Beck. BR3 225 EB98
Cobham KT11 236 CA111
New Malden KT3 220 CS99
Rainham RM13 169 FE68
West Drayton UB7 156 BL73
Worcester Park KT4 221 CT104
Spinneycroft, Oxshott KT22 253 CD115
Spinney Dr, Felt. TW14 197 BQ87
Spinney Gdns, SE19 204 DT92
Dagenham RM9 148 EY64
Spinney Hill, Add. KT15 233 BE106
Sch Spinney Inf Sch, Harl. CM20 off Cooks Spinney 58 EU14
Sch Spinney Jun Sch, Harl. CM20 off Cooks Spinney 58 EU14
Spinney Oak, Brom. BR1 226 EL96
Ottershaw KT16 233 BD107
Spinneys, The, Brom. BR1 227 EM96
Spinneys Dr, St.Alb. AL3 64 CB22
Spinney St, Hert. SG13 54 DU09
Spinney Way, Cudham TN14 245 ER111
Spinning Wk, The, Shere GU5 282 BN139
Spinning Wheel Mead, Harl. CM18 74 EU18
H Spire Bushey Hosp, Bushey WD23 117 CF46
Spire Cl, Grav. DA12 213 GH88
H Spire Gatwick Pk Hosp, Horl. RH6 290 DE149
● Spire Grn Cen, Harl. CM19 72 EL16
H Spire Hartswood Hosp, Warley CM13 129 FV51
Spire Ho, W2 15 P10
Spire Pl, Warl. CR6 259 DY118
H Spire Roding Hosp, Ilf. IG4 146 EK55
Spires, The, Dart. DA1 210 FK89
🛍 Spires Shop Cen, The, Barn. EN5 101 CY41
Spirit Quay, E1 32 D2
SPITALBROOK, Hodd. EN11 71 EA19
★ Spitalfields City Fm, E1 20 C5
Spital Heath, Dor. RH4 285 CJ135
Spital La, Brwd. CM14 130 FT48
Spital Sq, E1 19 P6
Spital St, E1 20 C6
Dartford DA1 210 FK86
Spital Yd, E1 19 P6
● Spitfire Business Pk, Croy. CR0 241 DN107
Spitfire Cl, Slou. SL3 175 BA77
● Spitfire Est, Houns. TW5 178 BW78
Spitfire Rd, Wall. SM6 241 DL108
Spitfire Way, Houns. TW5 178 BW78
Spode Ho, SE11 off Lambeth Wk 30 E7
Spode Wk, NW6 5 M3
Spondon Rd, N15 144 DU56
Spook Hill, N.Holm. RH5 285 CH141
Spoonbill Way, Hayes UB4 off Cygnet Way 158 BX71
Spooners Dr, Park St AL2 82 CC27
Spooners Ms, W3 off Churchfield Rd 160 CR74
Spooner Wk, Wall. SM6 241 DK106
Sporle Ct, SW11 182 DD83
Sportsbank St, SE6 205 EC87
Sportsman Ms, E2 10 C9
Spotted Dog Path, E7 13 P5
Spottons Gro, N17 off Gospatrick Rd 122 DQ53
Spout Hill, Croy. CR0 243 EA106
Spout La, Crock.H. TN8 277 EQ134
Staines TW19 196 BG85
Spout La N, Stai. TW19 176 BH84
Spratt Hall Rd, E11 146 EG58
Spratts All, Ott. KT16 233 BE107
Spratts La, Ott. KT16 233 BE107
Spray La, Twick. TW2 199 CE86
Spray St, SE18 37 P8
🛍 Spread Eagle Wk Shop Cen, Epsom KT19 off High St 238 CR113
Spreighton Rd, W.Mol. KT8 218 CB98
Spriggs Oak, Epp. CM16 off Palmers Hill 92 EU29
Sprimont Pl, SW3 28 E10
Springall St, SE15 44 F5
Springate Fld, Slou. SL3 174 AY75
Spring Av, Egh. TW20 194 AY93
Springbank, N21 103 DM44
Springbank Av, Horn. RM12 150 FJ64
Springbank Rd, SE13 205 ED86
Springbank Wk, NW1 7 P6
Springbottom La, Bletch. RH1 273 DN127
Springbourne Ct, Beck. BR3 225 EC95
Spring Br Ms, W5 off Spring Br Rd 159 CK73
Spring Br Rd, W5 159 CK73
Spring Cl, Barn. EN5 101 CX43
Borehamwood WD6 100 CN39
Dagenham RM8 148 EX60
Godalming GU7 280 AS143
Harefield UB9 114 BK53
Latimer HP5 94 AX36
Springclose La, Sutt. SM3 239 CY107
Springcopse Rd, Reig. RH2 288 DC135
Spring Cotts, Surb. KT6 219 CK99
Spring Ct, Guil. GU2 off Dayspring 264 AV130
Sidcup DA15 off Station Rd 208 EU90
Spring Ct Rd, Enf. EN2 103 DN38
Springcroft Av, N2 142 DF56
Spring Cfts, Bushey WD23 98 CA43
Springdale Ms, N16 9 L1
Springdale Rd, N16 9 L1
Spring Dr, Maid. SL6 152 AE65
Pinner HA5 137 BU58
Spring Fm Cl, Rain. RM13 170 FK69
Springfield, E5 144 DV60
Bushey Heath WD23 117 CD46
Epping CM16 91 ET32
Oxted RH8 275 ED130
Springfield Av, N10 143 DJ55
SW20 221 CZ97
Hampton TW12 198 CB93
Hutton CM13 131 GE45
Swanley BR8 229 FF98
Springfield Cl, N12 120 DB50
Chesham HP5 76 AQ33
Croxley Green WD3 97 BP43
Knaphill GU21 248 AS118
Potters Bar EN6 86 DD31
Stanmore HA7 117 CG48
Windsor SL4 173 AP82
Sch Springfield Comm Prim Sch, N16 off Castlewood Rd 144 DU58
Springfield Ct, Wall. SM6 off Springfield Rd 241 DH106
Springfield Dr, Ilf. IG2 147 EQ58
Leatherhead KT22 253 CE119
Springfield Gdns, E5 144 DV60
NW9 140 CR57
Bromley BR1 227 EM98
Ruislip HA4 137 BV60
Upminster RM14 150 FP62
West Wickham BR4 225 EB103
Woodford Green IG8 124 EJ52
Springfield Gro, SE7 186 EJ79
Sunbury-on-Thames TW16 217 BT95
Springfield Gro Est, SE7 186 EJ79
Springfield La, NW6 5 L9
Weybridge KT13 235 BP105
Springfield Meadows, Wey. KT13 235 BP105
Springfield Mt, NW9 140 CS57
Springfield Pl, Ger.Cr. SL9 134 AY57
New Malden KT3 220 CQ98
Sch Springfield Prim Sch, Sun. TW16 off Nursery Rd 217 BT96
Springfield Ri, SE26 204 DV90
Springfield Rd, E4 124 EE46
E6 167 EM66
E15 23 K2
E17 145 DZ58
N11 121 DH50
N15 144 DU56
NW8 5 N9
SE26 204 DV92
SW19 201 CZ92
W7 159 CE74
Ashford TW15 196 BM92
Berkhamsted HP4 60 AT16
Bexleyheath DA7 189 FB83
Bromley BR1 227 EM98
Chesham HP5 76 AQ33
Cheshunt EN8 89 DY32
Epsom KT17 239 CW110
Grays RM16 192 GD75
Guildford GU1 280 AY135
Harrow HA1 139 CE58
Hayes UB4 158 BW74
Hemel Hempstead HP2 62 BM19
Kingston upon Thames KT1 220 CL97
St. Albans AL1 65 CG21
Slough SL3 175 BB80
Smallford AL4 66 CP20
Teddington TW11 199 CG92
Thornton Heath CR7 224 DQ95
Twickenham TW2 198 CA88
Wallington SM6 241 DH106
Watford WD25 off Haines Way 81 BV33
Welling DA16 188 EV83
Westcott RH4 284 CB137
Windsor SL4 173 AP82
● Springfield Rd Business Cen, Hayes UB4 158 BW74
Springfields, Amer. HP6 77 AQ37
Broxbourne EN10 71 DZ19
Waltham Abbey EN9 90 EE34
Welwyn Garden City AL8 51 CV11
Springfields Cl, Cher. KT16 216 BH102
H Springfield Uni Hosp, SW17 202 DE89
Springfield Wk, NW6 5 L9
Orpington BR6 off Place Fm Av 227 ER102
Spring Gdns, N5 9 J3
SW1 29 P2
Biggin Hill TN16 260 EJ118
Dorking RH4 285 CG136
Hornchurch RM12 149 FH63
Orpington BR6 246 EV107
Romford RM7 149 FC57
Wallington SM6 241 DJ106
Watford WD25 98 BW35
West Molesey KT8 218 CC99
Wooburn Green HP10 132 AE55
Woodford Green IG8 124 EJ52
● Spring Gdns Business Pk, Rom. RM7 149 FC57
Spring Glen, Hat. AL10 67 CT19
SPRING GROVE, Islw. TW7 179 CF81
Spring Gro, SE19 off Alma Pl 204 DT94
W4 180 CN78
Fetcham KT22 252 CB123
Godalming GU7 280 AS143
Gravesend DA12 213 GH88
Hampton TW12 off Plevna Rd 218 CB95
Loughton IG10 106 EK44
Mitcham CR4 222 DG95
Spring Gro Cres, Houns. TW3 178 CC81
Sch Spring Gro Prim Sch, Islw. TW7 off Star Rd 179 CD82
Spring Gro Rd, Houns. TW3 178 CB81
Isleworth TW7 178 CB81
Richmond TW10 200 CM85
Springhall La, Saw. CM21 58 EY06
Sch Springhallow Sch, W13 off Compton Cl 159 CG72
Springhall Rd, Saw. CM21 58 EY05
Springhaven Cl, Guil. GU1 265 BA134
● Springhead Enterprise Pk, Nthflt DA11 212 GC88
Springhead Rd, Erith DA8 189 FF79
Northfleet DA11 212 GC87
Spring Hill, E5 144 DU59
SE26 204 DW91
Springhill Cl, SE5 184 DR83
Spring Hills, Harl. CM20 57 EN14
Springholm Cl, Bigg.H. TN16 260 EJ118
Springhurst Cl, Croy. CR0 243 DZ105
Spring Lake, Stan. HA7 117 CH49
Spring La, E5 144 DV60
N10 142 DG55
SE25 224 DV100
Farnham Royal SL2 153 AP66
Hemel Hempstead HP1 61 BF18
Oxted RH8 275 ED131
Slough SL1 153 AM74
Springle La, Hailey SG13 55 DZ12
Sch Springmead JMI Sch, Welw.G.C. AL7 off Hilly Flds 52 DC08
Spring Ms, W1 16 F6
Epsom KT17 off Old Schs La 239 CT109
Richmond TW9 off Rosedale Rd 180 CL84
Spring Pk Av, Croy. CR0 225 DX103
Spring Pk Dr, N4 144 DQ60
Springpark Dr, Beck. BR3 225 EC97
Sch Spring Pk Prim Sch, Croy. CR0 off Bridle Rd 225 EA104
Spring Pk Rd, Croy. CR0 225 DX103
Spring Pas, SW15 38 C10
Spring Path, NW3 6 A3
Spring Pl, N3 off Windermere Av 120 DA54
NW5 7 J3
Barking IG11 167 EQ68
Springpond Rd, Dag. RM9 148 EY64
Springrice Rd, SE13 205 EC86
Spring Ri, Egh. TW20 194 AY93
Spring Rd, Felt. TW13 197 BT90
Springs, The, Brox. EN10 89 DY25
Hertford SG13 54 DT08
Springshaw Cl, Sev. TN13 278 FD123
Spring Shaw Rd, Orp. BR5 228 EU95
Springside Ct, Guil. GU1 264 AW133
Spring St, W2 16 A9
Epsom KT17 239 CT109
Spring Ter, Rich. TW9 200 CL85
Spring Tide Cl, SE15 44 D6
Spring Vale, Bexh. DA7 189 FB84
Greenhithe DA9 211 FW86
Springvale Av, Brent. TW8 179 CK78
Springvale Cl, Bkhm KT23 268 CB126
Spring Vale Cl, Swan. BR8 229 FF95
Springvale Est, W14 26 D7
Spring Vale N, Dart. DA1 210 FK87
🛍 Springvale Retail Pk, Orp. BR5 228 EW97
Spring Vale S, Dart. DA1 210 FK87
Springvale Ter, W14 26 D7
Springvale Way, Orp. BR5 228 EW97
● Spring Valley Enterprise Cen, Port.Wd AL3 65 CE16
Spring Vw Rd, Ware SG12 54 DW07
Spring Vil Rd, Edg. HA8 118 CN52
Spring Wk, E1 20 D6
Broxbourne EN10 70 DW22
Horley RH6 off Court Lo Rd 290 DF148
Springwater Cl, SE18 187 EN81
Springway, Har. HA1 139 CD59
Spring Way, Hem.H. HP2 63 BP18
Springwell Av, NW10 161 CT67
Mill End WD3 114 BG47
Springwell Cl, SW16 off Etherstone Rd 203 DN91
Springwell Ct, Houns. TW4 178 BX82
Stanstead Abbotts SG12 55 EC11
Springwell Hill, Hare. UB9 114 BH51
Sch Springwell Inf & Nurs Sch, Heston TW5 off Speart La 178 BY80
Sch Springwell Jun Sch, Heston TW5 off Vicarage Fm Rd 178 BY80
Springwell La, Hare. UB9 114 BG49
Rickmansworth WD3 114 BG49
Springwell Rd, SW16 203 DN91
Hounslow TW4, TW5 178 BX81
Springwood, Chsht EN7 88 DU26
Springwood Cl, E3 22 A1
Harefield UB9 114 BK53
Springwood Cres, Edg. HA8 118 CP47
Springwood Pl, Wey. KT13 235 BP108
Spring Wds, Vir.W. GU25 214 AV98
Springwood Wk, St.Alb. AL4 65 CK17
Springwood Way, Rom. RM1 149 FG57
Sprowston Ms, E7 13 N4
Sprowston Rd, E7 13 P3
Spruce Cl, Red. RH1 272 DF133
Spruce Ct, W5 180 CL76
Sprucedale Cl, Swan. BR8 229 FE96
Sprucedale Gdns, Croy. CR0 243 DX105
Wallington SM6 241 DK109
Spruce Hill, Harl. CM18 73 ES20
Spruce Hills Rd, E17 123 EC54
Spruce Pk, Brom. BR2 off Cumberland Rd 226 EF98
Spruce Rd, Bigg.H. TN16 260 EK116
Spruce Way, Park St AL2 82 CB27
Sprules Rd, SE4 45 L9
Spur, The, Chsht EN8 off Welsummer Way 89 DX28
Slough SL1 153 AK71
Walton-on-Thames KT12 218 BW103

Spur Cl, Abb.L. WD5 . . . . . 81 BR33
Abridge RM4 . . . . . 108 EV41
Spurfield, W.Mol. KT8 . . . . . 218 CB97
Spurgate, Hutt. CM13 . . . . . 131 GA47
Spurgeon Av, SE19 . . . . . 224 DR95
Spurgeon Cl, Grays RM17 . . . . 192 GC79
Spurgeon Rd, SE19 . . . . . 224 DR95
Sch Spurgeon's Coll, SE25
off South Norwood Hill . . . 224 DS96
Spurgeon St, SE1 . . . . . 31 L7
Spurling Rd, SE22 . . . . . 184 DT84
Dagenham RM9 . . . . . 168 EZ65
Spurrell Av, Bex. DA5 . . . . . 209 FD91
Spur Rd, N15 off Philip La 144 DR56
SE1 . . . . . 30 E4
SW1 . . . . . 29 L5
Barking IG11 . . . . . 167 EQ68
Edgware HA8 . . . . . 118 CL49
Feltham TW14 . . . . . 197 BV85
Isleworth TW7 . . . . . 179 CH80
Orpington BR6 . . . . . 228 EU103
Spur Rd Est, Edg. HA8
off Green La 118 CM49
Spurstowe Rd, E8 . . . . . 10 E3
Spurstowe Ter, E8 . . . . . 10 E3
Squadrons App, Horn. RM12 . . 170 FJ65
Square, The, E10 . . . . . 145 EC62
W6 . . . . . 38 B1
Broxbourne EN10 . . . . . 71 DY23
Carshalton SM5 . . . . . 240 DG106
Caterham CR3
off Godstone Rd 258 DU124
Guildford GU2 . . . . . 280 AT136
Hemel Hempstead HP1
off Marlowes 62 BK20
Ilford IG1 . . . . . 147 EN59
Potten End HP4 . . . . . 61 BB16
Richmond TW9 . . . . . 199 CK85
Sawbridgeworth CM21 . . . . . 58 EY05
Sevenoaks TN13
off Amherst Hill 278 FE122
Shere GU5 . . . . . 282 BN139
Swanley BR8 . . . . . 229 FD97
Tatsfield TN16 . . . . . 260 EJ120
Uxbridge UB11 . . . . . 157 BR74
Watford WD24 . . . . . 97 BV37
West Drayton UB7 . . . . . 176 BH81
Weybridge KT13 . . . . . 235 BQ105
Wisley GU23 . . . . . 250 BL116
Woodford Green IG8 . . . . . 124 EG50
Square Rigger Row, SW11
off York Pl 182 DC83
Square St, Harl. CM17 . . . . . 58 EW14
Squarey St, SW17 . . . . . 202 DC90
Squerryes, The, Cat. CR3 . . . . 258 DS121
★ Squerryes Ct & Gdns, West.
TN16 . . . . . 277 EQ128
Squerryes Mede, West. TN16 . . 277 EQ127
Squire Gdns, NW8 . . . . . 16 A3
Squires, The, Rom. RM7 . . . . . 149 FC58
Squires Br Rd, Shep. TW17 . . . . 216 BM98
Squires Ct, SW19 . . . . . 202 DA91
Chertsey KT16
off Springfields Cl 216 BH102
Squires Fld, Swan. BR8 . . . . . 229 FF95
Squires La, N3 . . . . . 120 DB54
Squires Mt, NW3
off East Heath Rd 142 DD62
Squires Rd, Shep. TW17 . . . . . 216 BM98
Squire's Wk, Ashf. TW15 . . . . . 197 BR94
Squires Way, Dart. DA2 . . . . . 209 FD91
Squires Wd Dr, Chis. BR7 . . . . 206 EL94
Squirrel Chase, Hem.H. HP1 . . . 61 BE19
Squirrel Cl, Houns. TW4 . . . . . 178 BW82
Squirrel Keep, W.Byf. KT14 . . . 234 BH112
Squirrel Ms, W13 . . . . . 159 CG73
Squirrels, The, SE13 . . . . . 185 ED83
Bushey WD23 . . . . . 99 CD44
Hertford SG13 . . . . . 54 DU09
Pinner HA5 . . . . . 138 BZ55
Welwyn Garden City AL7 . . . . 52 DC10
Squirrels Chase, Orsett RM16
off Hornsby La 193 GG75
Squirrels Cl, N12
off Woodside Av 120 DC49
Orpington BR6 . . . . . 227 ES102
Uxbridge UB10 . . . . . 156 BN66
Squirrels Grn, Bkhm KT23 . . . . 252 CA123
Worcester Park KT4 . . . . . 221 CT102
Squirrels Heath Av, Rom.
RM2 . . . . . 149 FH55
Sch Squirrels Heath Inf & Jun
Schs, Rom. RM2
off Salisbury Rd 149 FH57
Squirrels Heath La, Horn.
RM11 . . . . . 150 FJ56
Romford RM2 . . . . . 150 FJ56
Squirrels Heath Rd, Rom.
RM3 . . . . . 150 FL55
Squirrels La, Buck.H. IG9 . . . . 124 EK48
● Squirrels Trd Est, Hayes
UB3 . . . . . 177 BU76
Squirrels Way, Epsom KT18 . . . 254 CR115
Squirrel Wd, W.Byf. KT14 . . . . 234 BH112
Squirries St, E2 . . . . . 20 D2
Stable Cl, Epsom KT18 . . . . . 254 CS119
Kingston upon Thames KT2 . 200 CM93
Northolt UB5 . . . . . 158 CA68
Stable La, Seer Grn HP9 . . . . . 111 AQ51
Stable Ms, NW5 . . . . . 7 J4
Twickenham TW1 . . . . . 199 CF88
Stables, The, Ald. WD25 . . . . . 98 CB36
Buckhurst Hill IG9 . . . . . 124 EJ45
Cobham KT11 . . . . . 236 BZ114
Guildford GU1
off Old Fm Rd 264 AX131
Stables End, Orp. BR6 . . . . . 227 EQ104
Stables Ms, SE27 . . . . . 204 DQ92
Stables Way, SE11 . . . . . 30 E10
Stable Wk, N1
off Wharfdale Rd 163 DL68
N2 off Old Fm Rd 120 DD53
Stable Way, W10 . . . . . 14 B9
Stable Yd, SW1 . . . . . 29 L4
SW9 . . . . . 42 D9
SW15 . . . . . 38 B10
Stable Yd Rd, SW1 . . . . . 29 L3
Staburn Ct, Edg. HA8 . . . . . 118 CQ54
Stacey Av, N18 . . . . . 122 DW49
Stacey Cl, E10 . . . . . 145 ED57
Gravesend DA12 . . . . . 213 GL92
Stacey St, N7 . . . . . 143 DN62
WC2 . . . . . 17 P9
Stackfield, Harl. CM20 . . . . . 58 EU12
Stackhouse St, SW3 . . . . . 28 E6
Stacklands, Welw.G.C. AL8 . . . . 51 CV11
Stack Rd, Hort.Kir. DA4 . . . . . 231 FR97
Stacy Path, SE5 . . . . . 43 N5
Staddon Cl, Beck. BR3 . . . . . 225 DY98
● Stadium Business Cen, Wem.
HA9 . . . . . 140 CP62
Stadium Retail Pk, Wem.
HA9 . . . . . 140 CN62
Stadium Rd, NW2 . . . . . 141 CV59
SE18 . . . . . 186 EL80
Stadium Rd E, NW2 . . . . . 141 CW59
Stadium St, SW10 . . . . . 39 P5
Stadium Way, Dart. DA1 . . . . . 209 FE85
Harlow CM19 . . . . . 57 EM14
Wembley HA9 . . . . . 140 CM63
Staffa Rd, E10 . . . . . 145 DY60
Stafford Av, Horn. RM11 . . . . . 150 FK55
Slough SL2 . . . . . 153 AQ70
Stafford Cl, E17 . . . . . 145 DZ58
N14 . . . . . 103 DJ43
NW6 . . . . . 15 J3
Caterham CR3 . . . . . 258 DT123
Chafford Hundred RM16 . . . 191 FW77
Cheshunt EN8 . . . . . 88 DV29
Greenhithe DA9 . . . . . 211 FT85
Sutton SM3 . . . . . 239 CY107
Taplow SL6 . . . . . 152 AH72
Stafford Ct, SW8
off Allen Edwards Dr 42 A5
W8 . . . . . 27 J6
Stafford Cripps Ho, E2 . . . . . 21 H3
SW6 off Clem Attlee Ct 39 H3
● Stafford Cross Business Pk,
Croy. CR0 . . . . . 241 DM106
Stafford Dr, Brox. EN10 . . . . . 71 EA20
Stafford Gdns, Croy. CR0 . . . . 241 DM106
Stafford Pl, SW1 . . . . . 29 L6
Richmond TW10 . . . . . 200 CM87
Stafford Ri, Cat. CR3 . . . . . 258 DU122
Stafford Rd, E3 . . . . . 21 N1
E7 . . . . . 166 EJ66
NW6 . . . . . 15 J2
Caterham CR3 . . . . . 258 DT122
Croydon CR0 . . . . . 241 DN105
Harrow HA3 . . . . . 116 CC52
New Malden KT3 . . . . . 220 CQ97
Ruislip HA4 . . . . . 137 BT63
Sidcup DA14 . . . . . 207 ES91
Wallington SM6 . . . . . 241 DJ107
Staffords, Harl. CM17 . . . . . 58 EY11
Staffordshire St, SE15 . . . . . 44 D6
Staffords Pl, Horl. RH6 . . . . . 291 DH150
Stafford Sq, Wey. KT13
off Rosslyn Pk 235 BR105
Stafford St, W1 . . . . . 29 L2
Stafford Ter, W8 . . . . . 27 J6
Stafford Way, Sev. TN13 . . . . . 279 FJ127
Staff St, EC1 . . . . . 19 M3
Stagbury Av, Chipstead CR5 . . 256 DE118
Stagbury Cl, Chipstead CR5 . . 256 DE119
Stag Cl, Edg. HA8 . . . . . 118 CP54
Staggart Grn, Chig. IG7 . . . . . 125 ET51
Stagg Hill, Barn. EN4 . . . . . 102 DD35
Potters Bar EN6 . . . . . 102 DD35
Stag Grn Av, Hat. AL9 . . . . . 67 CW16
STAG HILL, Guil. GU2 . . . . . 280 AU135
Stag Hill, Guil. GU2 . . . . . 280 AU135
Jct Stag La, SW15 . . . . . 201 CT89
Stag La, NW9 . . . . . 140 CQ55
SW15 . . . . . 201 CT89
Berkhamsted HP4 . . . . . 60 AU18
Buckhurst Hill IG9 . . . . . 124 EH47
Chorleywood WD3 . . . . . 95 BC44
Edgware HA8 . . . . . 118 CP54
Sch Stag La First & Mid Schs,
Edg. HA8 off Collier Dr 118 CN54
Stag Leys, Ashtd. KT21 . . . . . 254 CL120
Stag Leys Cl, Bans. SM7 . . . . . 256 DD115
Stag Ride, SW19 . . . . . 201 CT90
Stagshaw Ho, SE22
off Pytchley Rd 184 DS83
Stags Way, Islw. TW7 . . . . . 179 CF79
Stainash Cres, Stai. TW18 . . . . 196 BH92
Stainash Par, Stai. TW18
off Kingston Rd 196 BH92
Stainbank Rd, Mitch. CR4 . . . . 223 DH97
Stainby Cl, West Dr. UB7 . . . . . 176 BL76
Stainby Rd, N15 . . . . . 144 DT56
Stainer Rd, Borwd. WD6 . . . . . 99 CK39
Stainer St, SE1 . . . . . 31 M3
STAINES, TW18 & TW19 . . . . . 196 BG91
≠ Staines 196 BG92
⊖ Staines 195 BF92
Staines Av, Sutt. SM3 . . . . . 221 CX103
Staines Br, Stai. TW18 . . . . . 195 BE92
Staines Bypass, Ashf. TW15 . . . 196 BH91
Staines TW18, TW19 . . . . . 196 BH91
Staines Grn, Hert. SG14 . . . . . 53 DK11
Staines La, Cher. KT16 . . . . . 215 BF99
Staines La Cl, Cher. KT16 . . . . 215 BF100
Sch Staines Prep Sch,
Stai. TW18
off Gresham Rd 196 BG92
Staines Rd, Cher. KT16 . . . . . 215 BF97
Feltham TW14 . . . . . 197 BR87
Hounslow TW3, TW4 . . . . . 178 CB83
Ilford IG1 . . . . . 147 EQ63
Staines TW18 . . . . . 216 BH95
Twickenham TW2 . . . . . 198 CA90
Wraysbury TW19 . . . . . 194 AY87
Staines Rd E, Sun. TW16 . . . . . 197 BU94
Staines Rd W, Ashf. TW15 . . . . 197 BP93
Sunbury-on-Thames TW16 . . 197 BP93
Staines Wk, Sid. DA14
off Evry Rd 208 EW93
Stainford Cl, Ashf. TW15 . . . . . 197 BR92
Stainforth Rd, E17 . . . . . 145 EA56
Ilford IG2 . . . . . 147 ER59
Staining La, EC2 . . . . . 19 K8
Stainmore Cl, Chis. BR7 . . . . . 227 ER95
Stainsbury St, E2 . . . . . 21 H1
Stainsby Rd, E14 . . . . . 22 A8
Stains Cl, Chsht EN8 . . . . . 89 DY28
Stainton Rd, SE6 . . . . . 205 ED86
Enfield EN3 . . . . . 104 DW39
Stainton Wk, Wok. GU21
off Inglewood 248 AW118
Stairfoot La, Chipstead TN13 . . 278 FC122
Staithes Way, Tad. KT20 . . . . . 255 CV120
Stakescorner Rd, Littleton
GU3 . . . . . 280 AU142
Stalbridge St, NW1 . . . . . 16 D6
Stalham St, SE16 . . . . . 32 F7
Stalham Way, Ilf. IG6 . . . . . 125 EP53
Stalisfield Pl, Downe BR6
off Mill La 245 EN110
Stambourne Way, SE19 . . . . . 204 DS94
West Wickham BR4 . . . . . 225 EC104
⊖ Stamford Brook 181 CT77
Stamford Brook Av, W6 . . . . . 181 CT76
Stamford Brook Gdns, W6
off Stamford Brook Rd 181 CT76
Stamford Brook Rd, W6 . . . . . 181 CT76
Stamford Cl, N15 . . . . . 144 DU56
Harrow HA3 . . . . . 117 CE52
Potters Bar EN6 . . . . . 86 DD32
Southall UB1 . . . . . 158 CA73
Stamford Cotts, SW10 . . . . . 39 M4
Stamford Ct, W6 . . . . . 181 CU77
Edgware HA8 . . . . . 118 CM49
Stamford Dr, Brom. BR2 . . . . . 226 EF98
Stamford Gdns, Dag. RM9 . . . . 168 EW66
Stamford Grn, Epsom KT18 . . . 238 CP113
Sch Stamford Grn Prim Sch, Epsom
KT19 off Christ Ch Mt 238 CP112
Stamford Grn Rd, Epsom
KT18 . . . . . 238 CP113
Stamford Gro E, N16 . . . . . 144 DU60
Stamford Gro W, N16 . . . . . 144 DU60
STAMFORD HILL, N16 . . . . . 144 DS60
≠ Stamford Hill 144 DS59
Stamford Hill, N16 . . . . . 144 DT61
Stamford Hill Est, N16 . . . . . 144 DT60
Sch Stamford Hill Prim Sch, N15
off Berkeley Rd 144 DR58
Stamford Rd, E6 . . . . . 166 EL67
N1 . . . . . 9 P6
N15 . . . . . 144 DU57
Dagenham RM9 . . . . . 168 EV67
Walton-on-Thames KT12
off Kenilworth Dr 218 BX104
Watford WD17 . . . . . 97 BV40
Stamford St, SE1 . . . . . 30 E3
Stamp Pl, E2 . . . . . 20 A2
Stanard Cl, N16 . . . . . 144 DS59
STANBOROUGH, Welw.G.C.
AL8 . . . . . 51 CT12
Stanborough Av, Borwd. WD6 . 100 CN37
Stanborough Cl, Borwd. WD6 . 100 CN38
Hampton TW12 . . . . . 198 BZ93
Welwyn Garden City AL8 . . . 51 CW10
Stanborough Grn, Welw.G.C.
AL8 . . . . . 51 CW11
Stanborough Ms, Welw.G.C.
AL8 . . . . . 51 CX11
Stanborough Pk, Wat. WD25 . . . 97 BV35
Stanborough Pas, E8 . . . . . 10 A4
Sch Stanborough Prim Sch, Wat.
WD25 off Appletree Wk . . . 98 BW35
Stanborough Rd, Houns. TW3 . 179 CD83
Welwyn Garden City AL8 . . . 51 CV12
Sch Stanborough Sch, Wat. WD25
off Stanborough Pk 97 BV35
Welwyn Garden City AL8
off Lemsford La 51 CV11
Stanbridge Pl, N21 . . . . . 121 DP47
Stanbridge Rd, SW15 . . . . . 181 CW83
Stanbrook Rd, SE2 . . . . . 188 EV75
Gravesend DA11 . . . . . 213 GF88
Sch Stanburn First & Mid Schs,
Stan. HA7 off Abercorn Rd . 117 CJ52
Stanbury Av, Wat. WD17 . . . . . 97 BS37
Stanbury Rd, SE15 . . . . . 44 F7
Stancroft, NW9 . . . . . 140 CS56
Standale Gro, Ruis. HA4 . . . . . 137 BQ57
● Standard Ind Est, E16 . . . . . 37 J4
Standard Pl, EC2 . . . . . 19 P3
Standard Rd, NW10 . . . . . 160 CQ70
Belvedere DA17 . . . . . 188 FA78
Bexleyheath DA6 . . . . . 188 EY84
Downe BR6 . . . . . 245 EN110
Enfield EN3 . . . . . 105 DY38
Hounslow TW4 . . . . . 178 BY83
Standen Av, Horn. RM12 . . . . . 150 FK62
Standen Rd, SW18 . . . . . 201 CZ87
Standfield, Abb.L. WD5 . . . . . 81 BS31
Standfield Gdns, Dag. RM10
off Standfield Rd 168 FA65
Standfield Rd, Dag. RM10 . . . . 148 FA64
Standingford, Harl. CM19 . . . . 73 EP20
Standish Ho, SE3
off Elford Cl 186 EJ84
Standish Rd, W6 . . . . . 181 CU77
Standlake Pt, SE23 . . . . . 205 DX90
Standring Ri, Hem.H. HP3 . . . . 62 BH23
Stane Cl, SW19
off Hayward Cl 202 DB94
Stane Gro, SW9 . . . . . 42 A9
Stane St, Lthd. KT22 . . . . . 270 CL126
Mickleham RH5 . . . . . 269 CK127
Stane Way, SE18 . . . . . 186 EK80
Epsom KT17 . . . . . 239 CU110
Stanfield Ho, NW8
off Frampton St 16 B4
Stanfield Rd, E3 . . . . . 21 M1
Stanfields Ct, Harl. CM20
off Broadfield 57 ES14
Stanford Cl, Hmptn. TW12 . . . . 198 BZ93
Romford RM7 . . . . . 149 FB58
Ruislip HA4 . . . . . 137 BQ58
Woodford Green IG8 . . . . . 124 EL50
Stanford Ct, SW6 . . . . . 39 M7
Waltham Abbey EN9 . . . . . 90 EG33
Stanford Gdns, Aveley RM15 . . 171 FR74
Stanford Ms, E8 . . . . . 10 C3
Stanford Pl, SE17 . . . . . 31 N9
Sch Stanford Prim Sch, SW16
off Chilmark Rd 223 DK95
Stanford Rd, N11 . . . . . 120 DF50
SW16 . . . . . 223 DK96
W8 . . . . . 27 M6
Grays RM16 . . . . . 192 GD76
Stanford St, SW1 . . . . . 29 N9
Stanford Way, SW16 . . . . . 223 DK96
Stangate, SE1 . . . . . 30 C6
Stangate Cres, Borwd. WD6 . . 100 CS43
Stangate Gdns, Stan. HA7 . . . . 117 CH49
Stanger Rd, SE25 . . . . . 224 DU98
Stanham Pl, Dart. DA1
off Crayford Way 189 FG84
Stanham Rd, Dart. DA1 . . . . . 210 FJ85
Stanhope Av, N3 . . . . . 141 CZ55
Bromley BR2 . . . . . 226 EF102
Harrow HA3 . . . . . 117 CD53
Stanhope Cl, SE16 . . . . . 33 K4
Stanhope Gdns, N4 . . . . . 143 DP58
N6 . . . . . 143 DH58
NW7 . . . . . 119 CT50
SW7 . . . . . 27 P8
Dagenham RM8 . . . . . 148 EZ62
Ilford IG1 . . . . . 147 EM60
Stanhope Gate, W1 . . . . . 29 H2
Stanhope Gro, Beck. BR3 . . . . . 225 DZ99
Stanhope Heath, Stanw.
TW19 . . . . . 196 BJ86
Stanhope Ms E, SW7 . . . . . 27 P8
Stanhope Ms S, SW7 . . . . . 27 P9
Stanhope Ms W, SW7 . . . . . 27 P8
Stanhope Par, NW1
off Stanhope St 17 L2
Stanhope Pk Rd, Grnf. UB6 . . . 158 CC70
Stanhope Pl, W2 . . . . . 16 E9
Sch Stanhope Prim Sch, Grnf.
UB6 off Mansell Rd 158 CC70
Stanhope Rd, E17 . . . . . 145 EB57
N6 . . . . . 143 DJ58
N12 . . . . . 120 DC50
Barnet EN5 . . . . . 101 CW44
Bexleyheath DA7 . . . . . 188 EY82
Carshalton SM5 . . . . . 240 DG108
Croydon CR0 . . . . . 224 DS104
Dagenham RM8 . . . . . 148 EZ61
Greenford UB6 . . . . . 158 CC71
Rainham RM13 . . . . . 169 FG68
St. Albans AL1 . . . . . 65 CF21
Sidcup DA15 . . . . . 208 EU91
Slough SL1 . . . . . 153 AK72
Swanscombe DA10 . . . . . 212 FZ85
Waltham Cross EN8 . . . . . 89 DY33
Stanhope Row, W1 . . . . . 29 J3
Stanhopes, Oxt. RH8 . . . . . 276 EH128
Stanhope St, NW1 . . . . . 17 L3
Stanhope Ter, W2 . . . . . 16 B10
Stanhope Way, Sev. TN13 . . . . 278 FD122
Stanwell TW19 . . . . . 196 BJ86
Stanier Cl, W14 . . . . . 39 H1
Stanier Ri, Berk. HP4 . . . . . 60 AT16
Staniland Dr, Wey. KT13 . . . . . 234 BM111
Stanlake Ms, W12 . . . . . 26 A3
Stanlake Rd, W12 . . . . . 161 CV74
Stanlake Vil, W12 . . . . . 26 A3
Stanley Av, Bark. IG11 . . . . . 167 ET68
Beckenham BR3 . . . . . 225 EC96
Chesham HP5 . . . . . 76 AP31
Dagenham RM8 . . . . . 148 EZ60
Greenford UB6 . . . . . 158 CC67
New Malden KT3 . . . . . 221 CU99
Romford RM2 . . . . . 149 FG56
St. Albans AL2 . . . . . 82 CA25
Wembley HA0 . . . . . 160 CL66
Stanley Cl, SE9 . . . . . 207 EQ88
SW8 . . . . . 42 C3
Coulsdon CR5 . . . . . 257 DM117
Greenhithe DA9 . . . . . 211 FS85
Hornchurch RM12
off Stanley Rd 150 FJ61
Romford RM2 . . . . . 149 FG56
Uxbridge UB8 . . . . . 156 BK67
Wembley HA0 . . . . . 160 CL66
Stanley Cotts, Slou. SL2 . . . . . 154 AT74
Stanley Ct, Cars. SM5
off Stanley Pk Rd 240 DG108
Stanley Cres, W11 . . . . . 14 G10
Gravesend DA12 . . . . . 213 GK92
Stanleycroft Cl, Islw. TW7 . . . . 179 CE81
Stanley Dr, Hat. AL10 . . . . . 67 CV20
Stanley Gdns, NW2 . . . . . 4 B3
W3 . . . . . 160 CS74
W11 . . . . . 14 G10
Borehamwood WD6 . . . . . 100 CL39
Hersham KT12 . . . . . 236 BW107
Mitcham CR4
off Ashbourne Rd 202 DG93
South Croydon CR2 . . . . . 242 DU112
Wallington SM6 . . . . . 241 DJ107
Stanley Gdns Ms, W11 . . . . . 15 H10
Stanley Gdns Rd, Tedd. TW11 . . 199 CE92
Stanley Grn E, Slou. SL3 . . . . . 175 AZ77
Stanley Grn W, Slou. SL3 . . . . . 175 AZ77
Stanley Gro, SW8 . . . . . 41 H9
Croydon CR0 . . . . . 223 DN100
Stanley Hill, Amer. HP7 . . . . . 77 AR40
Stanley Hill Av, Amer. HP7 . . . . 77 AR39
Sch Stanley Inf & Nurs Sch, Tedd.
TW11 off Strathmore Rd . . . 199 CE91
Sch Stanley Jun Sch, Tedd. TW11
off Stanley Rd 199 CE91
Stanley Pk Dr, Wem. HA0 . . . . . 160 CM66
Sch Stanley Pk High Sch, Cars.
SM5 off Stanley Pk Rd . . . 240 DG107
Sch Stanley Pk Infants' Sch, Cars.
SM5 off Stanley Pk Rd . . . 240 DF108
Sch Stanley Pk Jun Sch, Cars.
SM5 off Stanley Pk Rd . . . 240 DF108
Stanley Pk Rd, Cars. SM5 . . . . 240 DF108
Wallington SM6 . . . . . 241 DH107
Stanley Rd, E4 . . . . . 123 ED46
E10 . . . . . 145 EB58
E12 . . . . . 146 EL64
E15 . . . . . 12 G9
E18 . . . . . 124 EF53
N2 . . . . . 142 DD55
N9 . . . . . 122 DT46
N10 . . . . . 121 DH52
N11 . . . . . 121 DK51
N15 . . . . . 143 DP56
NW9 off West Hendon Bdy . 141 CU59
SW14 . . . . . 180 CP84
SW19 . . . . . 202 DA94
W3 . . . . . 180 CQ76
Ashford TW15 . . . . . 196 BL92
Bromley BR2 . . . . . 226 EH98
Carshalton SM5 . . . . . 240 DG108
Croydon CR0 . . . . . 223 DN101
Enfield EN1 . . . . . 104 DS41
Grays RM17 . . . . . 192 GB78
Harrow HA2 . . . . . 138 CC61
Hertford SG13 . . . . . 54 DS09
Hornchurch RM12 . . . . . 150 FJ61
Hounslow TW3 . . . . . 178 CC84
Ilford IG1 . . . . . 147 ER61
Mitcham CR4 . . . . . 202 DG94
Morden SM4 . . . . . 222 DA98
Northfleet DA11 . . . . . 212 GE88
Northwood HA6 . . . . . 115 BU53
Orpington BR6 . . . . . 228 EU102
Sidcup DA14 . . . . . 208 EU90
Southall UB1 . . . . . 158 BY73
Sutton SM2 . . . . . 240 DB107
Swanscombe DA10 . . . . . 212 FZ86
Teddington TW11 . . . . . 199 CE91
Twickenham TW2 . . . . . 199 CD90
Watford WD17 . . . . . 98 BW41
Wembley HA9 . . . . . 160 CM65
Woking GU21 . . . . . 249 AZ116
Stanley Rd N, Rain. RM13 . . . . 169 FE67
Stanley Rd S, Rain. RM13 . . . . 169 FF68
Stanley Sq, Cars. SM5 . . . . . 240 DF109
Stanley St, SE8 . . . . . 45 P5
Caterham CR3 . . . . . 258 DQ121
Stanley Ter, N19 . . . . . 143 DL61
Stanley Way, Orp. BR5 . . . . . 228 EV99
Stanliff Ho, E14 . . . . . 34 B6
Stanmer St, SW11 . . . . . 40 D7
STANMORE, HA7 . . . . . 117 CG50
⊖ Stanmore 117 CK50
Stanmore Chase, St.Alb. AL4 . . 65 CK21
Sch Stanmore Coll, Stan. HA7
off Elm Pk 117 CJ51
Stanmore Gdns, Rich. TW9 . . . . 180 CM83
Sutton SM1 . . . . . 222 DC104
Stanmore Hall, Stan. HA7 . . . . 117 CH48
Stanmore Hill, Stan. HA7 . . . . 117 CG48
Stanmore Rd, E11 . . . . . 146 EF60
N15 . . . . . 143 DP56
Belvedere DA17 . . . . . 189 FC77
Richmond TW9 . . . . . 180 CM83
Watford WD24 . . . . . 97 BV39
Stanmore St, N1 . . . . . 8 C8
Stanmore Ter, Beck. BR3 . . . . . 225 EA96
Stanmore Way, Loug. IG10 . . . . 107 EN39
Stanmount Rd, St.Alb. AL2 . . . . 82 CA25
Stannard Ms, E8 . . . . . 10 C4
Stannard Rd, E8 . . . . . 10 C4
Stannary St, SE11 . . . . . 42 F2
Stannet Way, Wall. SM6 . . . . . 241 DJ105
Stannington Path, Borwd.
WD6 . . . . . 100 CN39
Stansbury Sq, W10 . . . . . 14 F2
Stansfeld Rd, E6 . . . . . 24 F7
E16 . . . . . 24 F7
Stansfield Ho, SE1 . . . . . 32 B9
Stansfield Rd, SW9 . . . . . 183 DM83
Hounslow TW4 . . . . . 177 BV82
Stansgate Rd, Dag. RM10 . . . . 148 FA61
STANSTEAD ABBOTTS, Ware
SG12 . . . . . 55 ED11
Stanstead Bury, Stans.Abb.
SG12 . . . . . 56 EF12
Stanstead Cl, Brom. BR2 . . . . . 226 EF99
Caterham CR3 . . . . . 258 DS124
Stanstead Dr, Hodd. EN11 . . . . 71 EB15
Stanstead Gro, SE6
off Stanstead Rd 205 DZ88
Stanstead Manor, Sutt. SM1 . . 240 DA107
Stanstead Rd, E11 . . . . . 146 EH57
SE6 . . . . . 205 DX88
SE23 . . . . . 205 DX88
Caterham CR3 . . . . . 274 DR125
Hertford SG13 . . . . . 54 DT08
Hoddesdon EN11 . . . . . 71 EB15
Hunsdon SG12 . . . . . 56 EG09
London Heathrow Airport
TW6 . . . . . 196 BM86
Stanstead Abbotts SG12 . . . . 56 EH12
Ware SG12 . . . . . 54 DW09
Stansted Cl, Horn. RM12 . . . . . 169 FH65
Stansted Cres, Bex. DA5 . . . . . 208 EX88
Stanswood Gdns, SE5 . . . . . 43 P5
● Stanta Business Cen, St.Alb.
AL3 off Soothouse Spring . . 65 CF16
Stanthorpe Cl, SW16 . . . . . 203 DL92
Stanthorpe Rd, SW16 . . . . . 203 DL92
Stanton Av, Tedd. TW11 . . . . . 199 CE93
Stanton Cl, Epsom KT19 . . . . . 238 CP106
Orpington BR5 . . . . . 228 EW101
St. Albans AL4 . . . . . 65 CK16
Worcester Park KT4 . . . . . 221 CX102
Stanton Ct, Dag. RM10
off St. Mark's Pl 168 FA65
Stanton Ho, SE16 . . . . . 33 N4
Stanton Rd, SE26
off Stanton Way 205 DZ91
SW13 . . . . . 181 CT82
SW20 . . . . . 221 CX96
Croydon CR0 . . . . . 224 DQ101
Stantons, Harl. CM20 . . . . . 73 EN15
Stanton Sq, SE26
off Stanton Way 205 DZ91
Stantons Wf, Bramley GU5 . . . 281 BA144
Stanton Way, SE26 . . . . . 205 DZ91
Slough SL3 . . . . . 174 AY77
Stants Vw, Hert. SG13
off Rowleys Rd 54 DT08
Stanway Cl, Chig. IG7 . . . . . 125 ES50
Stanway Ct, N1 . . . . . 19 P1
Stanway Gdns, W3 . . . . . 160 CN74
Edgware HA8 . . . . . 118 CQ50
Stanway Rd, Wal.Abb. EN9 . . . . 90 EG33
Stanway St, N1 . . . . . 9 P10
STANWELL, Stai. TW19 . . . . . 196 BL87
Stanwell Cl, Stanw. TW19 . . . . 196 BK86
Sch Stanwell Flds C of E
Prim Sch, Stanw. TW19
off Clare Rd 196 BL87
Stanwell Gdns, Stanw. TW19 . . 196 BK86
STANWELL MOOR, Stai.
TW19 . . . . . 196 BG85
Stanwell Moor Rd, Stai. TW19 . 196 BH85
Stanwell New Rd, Stai. TW18 . 196 BH90
Stanwell Rd, Ashf. TW15 . . . . . 196 BL89
Feltham TW14 . . . . . 197 BQ87
Horton SL3 . . . . . 175 BA83
Stanwick Rd, W14 . . . . . 26 G9
Stanworth St, SE1 . . . . . 32 A5
Stanwyck Dr, Chig. IG7 . . . . . 125 EQ50
Stanwyck Gdns, Rom. RM3 . . . 127 FH50
Stapenhill Rd, Wem. HA0 . . . . . 139 CH62
Staple Cl, Bex. DA5 . . . . . 209 FD90
Staplefield Cl, SW2 . . . . . 203 DL88
Pinner HA5 . . . . . 116 BY52
Stapleford, Welw.G.C. AL7 . . . . 52 DD09
STAPLEFORD ABBOTTS,
Rom. RM4 . . . . . 109 FC43
Sch Stapleford Abbotts Prim Sch,
Stap.Abb. RM4
off Stapleford Rd 109 FB43
★ Stapleford Aerodrome,
Rom. RM4 . . . . . 108 EZ40
Stapleford Av, Ilf. IG2 . . . . . 147 ES57
Stapleford Cl, E4 . . . . . 123 EC48
SW19 . . . . . 201 CY87
Kingston upon Thames KT1 . 220 CN97
Stapleford Ct, Sev. TN13 . . . . . 278 FF123
Stapleford Gdns, Rom. RM5 . . 126 FA51
Stapleford Rd, Rom. RM4 . . . . 109 FB42
Wembley HA0 . . . . . 159 CK66
STAPLEFORD TAWNEY, Rom.
RM4 . . . . . 109 FC37
Stapleford Way, Bark. IG11 . . . . 168 EV69
Staple Hill Rd, Chob.Com.
GU24 . . . . . 232 AS105
Staplehurst Cl, Reig. RH2 . . . . 288 DC138
Staplehurst Rd, SE13 . . . . . 206 EE85
Carshalton SM5 . . . . . 240 DE108
Reigate RH2 . . . . . 288 DC138
Staple Inn, WC1 . . . . . 18 E7
Staple Inn Bldgs, WC1 . . . . . 18 E7
Staple La, Shere GU5 . . . . . 266 BK132
Staples, The, Swan. BR8 . . . . . 229 FH95
Staples Cl, SE16 . . . . . 33 L2
Jct Staples Cor, NW2 . . . . . 141 CV60

● **Staples Cor Retail Pk**, NW2
off Geron Way 141 CV61
Staples Rd, Loug. IG10 106 EL41
Sch **Staples Rd Inf Sch**, Loug.
IG10 *off Staples Rd* 106 EL41
Sch **Staples Rd Jun Sch**, Loug.
IG10 *off Staples Rd* 106 EL41
Staple St, SE1 31 M5
Stapleton Cl, Pot.B. EN6 86 DD31
Stapleton Cres, Rain. RM13 169 FG65
Stapleton Gdns, Croy. CR0 241 DN106
Stapleton Hall Rd, N4 143 DM59
Stapleton Rd, SW17 202 DG90
Bexleyheath DA7 188 EZ80
Borehamwood WD6 100 CN38
Orpington BR6 227 ET104
Staple Tye Shop Cen,
Harl. CM18 73 EQ18
Staple Tye Shop Ms, Harl.
CM18 *off Perry Rd* 73 EQ18
Stapley Rd, Belv. DA17 188 FA78
St. Albans AL3 65 CD19
Stapylton Rd, Barn. EN5 101 CY41
Star All, EC3 19 P10
Star & Garter Hill, Rich. TW10 200 CL88
Starboard Av, Green. DA9 211 FV86
Starboard Way, E14 34 B6
Starbuck Cl, SE9 207 EN87
Starch Ho La, Ilf. IG6 125 ER54
Star Cl, Enf. EN3 104 DW44
Starcross St, NW1 17 M3
Starfield Rd, W12 181 CU75
Star Hill, Dart. DA1 209 FE85
Woking GU22 248 AW119
Star Hill Rd, Dunt.Grn TN14 262 EZ116
Star Holme Ct, Ware SG12 55 DY06
Sch **Starhurst Sch**, Dor. RH5
off Chart La S 285 CJ138
Starkey Cl, Chsht EN7
off Shambrook Rd 88 DQ25
Sch **Starks Fld Prim Sch**, N9
off Church St 122 DS47
Star La, E16 23 J5
Coulsdon CR5 256 DG122
Epping CM16 92 EU30
Orpington BR5 228 EW98
Starlight Way, Lon.Hthrw Air.
TW6 197 BQ85
St. Albans AL4 65 CJ22
Starling Cl, Buck.H. IG9 124 EG46
Croydon CR0 225 DY100
Pinner HA5 138 BW55
Starling La, Cuffley EN6 87 DM28
Starlings, The, Oxshott KT22 236 CC113
Starling Wk, Hmptn. TW12
off Oak Av 198 BY92
Starmans Cl, Dag. RM9 168 EY67
Star Path, Nthlt. UB5
off Brabazon Rd 158 CA68
Star Pl, E1 32 B1
Sch **Star Prim Sch**, E16 23 K5
Star Rd, W14 38 G2
Isleworth TW7 179 CD82
Uxbridge UB10 157 BQ70
Starrock La, Chipstead CR5 256 DF120
Starrock Rd, Couls. CR5 257 DH119
Star St, E16 23 M6
W2 16 B8
Ware SG12 55 DY06
Starts Cl, Orp. BR6 227 EN104
Starts Hill Av, Farnboro. BR6 245 EP106
Starts Hill Rd, Orp. BR6 227 EN104
Starveall Cl, West Dr. UB7 176 BM76
Star Wf, NW1 7 M8
Starwood Cl, W.Byf. KT14 234 BJ111
Star Yd, WC2 18 E8
State Fm Av, Orp. BR6 245 EP105
Staten Bldg, E3
off Fairfield Rd 12 B10
Staten Gdns, Twick. TW1 199 CF88
Statham Ct, N7 143 DL62
Statham Gro, N16
off Green Las 144 DR63
N18 122 DS50
Station App, E4 (Chingford)
off Station Rd 124 EE45
E4 (Highams Pk)
off The Avenue 123 ED51
E7 *off Woodgrange Rd* 146 EH63
E11 (Snaresbrook)
off High St 146 EG57
N11 *off Friern Barnet Rd* 121 DH50
N12 (Woodside Pk) 120 DB49
N16 (Stoke Newington)
off Stamford Hill 144 DT61
NW10 *off Station Rd* 161 CT69
SE1 30 D3
SE3 *off Kidbrooke Pk Rd* 186 EH83
SE9 (Mottingham) 207 EM88
SE26 (Lwr Sydenham)
off Worsley Br Rd 205 DZ92
SE26 (Sydenham)
off Sydenham Rd 204 DW91
SW6 38 F10
SW16 203 DK92
SW20 221 CW96
W7 159 CE74
Amersham HP6 77 AQ38
Ashford TW15 196 BM91
Barnehurst DA7 189 FC82
Beckenham BR3
off Rectory Rd 225 EA95
Belmont SM2
off Brighton Rd 240 DB110
Berkhamsted HP4
off Brownlow Rd 60 AW18
Bexley DA5
off Bexley High St 208 FA87
Bexleyheath DA7
off Avenue Rd 188 EY82
Buckhurst Hill IG9
off Cherry Tree Ri 124 EK49
Carpenders Park WD19
off Prestwick Rd 116 BX48
Cheam SM2 239 CY108
Chelsfield BR6 246 EV106
Cheshunt EN8 89 DZ30
Chipstead CR5 256 DF118
Chislehurst BR7 227 EN95
Chorleywood WD3 95 BD42
Coulsdon CR5 257 DK116
Station App, Cray. DA1 209 FF86
Dartford DA1 210 FL86
Debden IG10 107 EQ42
Denham UB9 *off Middle Rd* 135 BD59
Dorking RH4 269 CJ134
Dunton Green TN13 263 FE120
East Horsley KT24 267 BS126
Elmstead Woods BR7 206 EL93
Epping CM16 92 EU31
Epsom KT19 238 CR113
Ewell East KT17 239 CV110
Ewell West KT19
off Chessington Rd 239 CT109
Gerrards Cross SL9 134 AY57
Gomshall GU5 283 BR139
Grays RM17 192 GA79
Greenford UB6 159 CD66
Guildford GU1 280 AY135
Hampton TW12
off Milton Rd 218 CA95
Harlow (Harl. Mill) CM20 58 EW10
Harlow (Harl. Town) CM20 57 EQ12
Harrow HA1 139 CE59
Hatch End HA5
off Uxbridge Rd 116 CA52
Hayes BR2 226 EG102
Hemel Hempstead HP3 62 BG23
High Barnet EN5
off Barnet Hill 102 DA42
Hinchley Wood KT10 219 CF104
Horley RH6 291 DH148
Kenley CR8 *off Hayes La* 242 DQ114
Kingston upon Thames KT1 220 CN95
Leatherhead KT22 253 CG121
Little Chalfont HP7
off Chalfont Sta Rd 94 AX39
Loughton IG10 106 EL43
New Barnet EN5 102 DC42
Northwood HA6 115 BS52
Orpington BR6 227 ET103
Oxshott KT22 236 CC113
Oxted RH8 276 EE128
Pinner HA5 138 BY55
Purley CR8 241 DN111
Radlett WD7
off Shenley Hill 99 CG35
Richmond TW9 180 CN81
Ruislip HA4 137 BS60
St. Mary Cray BR5 228 EV98
Shalford GU4
off Horsham Rd 280 AY140
Shepperton TW17 217 BQ100
South Croydon CR2
off Sanderstead Rd 242 DR109
South Ruislip HA4 137 BV64
Staines TW18 196 BG92
Stoneleigh KT19 239 CU106
Sunbury-on-Thames TW16 217 BU95
Swanley BR8 229 FE98
Tadworth KT20 255 CW122
Theydon Bois CM16
off Coppice Row 107 ES36
Upminster RM14 150 FQ61
Virginia Water GU25 214 AX98
Waltham Cross EN8 89 DY34
Watford WD18
off Cassiobury Pk Av 97 BT41
Wembley HA0 159 CH65
West Byfleet KT14 234 BG112
West Drayton UB7 156 BL74
West Wickham BR4 225 EC102
Weybridge KT13 234 BN107
Whyteleafe CR3 258 DU117
Woking GU22 249 AZ117
Woodford Green IG8
off The Broadway 124 EH51
Worcester Park KT4 221 CU102
Station App E, Earls. RH1
off Earlsbrook Rd 288 DF136
Station App N, Sid. DA15 208 EU89
Station App Path, SE9
off Glenlea Rd 207 EM85
Station App Rd, W4 180 CQ80
Coulsdon CR5 257 DK115
Gatwick RH6
off London Rd 291 DH151
Station App W, Earls. RH1
off Earlswood Rd 288 DF136
Station Av, SW9 43 H10
Caterham CR3 258 DU124
Epsom KT19 238 CS109
Kew TW9 180 CN81
New Malden KT3 220 CS97
Walton-on-Thames KT12 235 BU105
Station Cl, N3 120 DA53
N12 (Woodside Pk) 120 DB49
Brookmans Park AL9 85 CY26
Hampton TW12 218 CB95
Potters Bar EN6 85 CZ31
Station Ct, SW6 39 N7
Station Cres, N15 144 DR56
SE3 47 N1
Ashford TW15 196 BK90
Wembley HA0 159 CH65
Stationers Hall Ct, EC4
off Ludgate Hill 19 H9
Stationers Pl, Hem.H. HP3 80 BL25
● **Station Est**, E18
off George La 124 EH54
Station Est, Beck. BR3
off Elmers End Rd 225 DX98
Station Est Rd, Felt. TW14 197 BV88
Station Footpath, Kings L.
WD4 81 BP31
Station Forecourt, Rick. WD3
off Rectory Rd 114 BK45
Station Gar Ms, SW16
off Estreham Rd 203 DK93
Station Gdns, W4 180 CQ80
Station Gro, Wem. HA0 160 CL65
Station Hill, Brom. BR2 226 EG103
Station Ho Ms, N9
off Fore St 122 DU49
Station La, Horn. RM12 150 FK62
Station Ms Ter, SE3
off Halstow Rd 47 N1
Station Par, E11 146 EG57
N14 *off High St* 121 DK46
NW2 4 B4
SW12 *off Balham High Rd* 202 DG88
W3 160 CN72
W5 *off Uxbridge Rd* 160 CM74
Ashford TW15
off Woodthorpe Rd 196 BM91
Barking IG11 167 EQ66
Barnet EN4
off Cockfosters Rd 102 DG42
Beaconsfield HP9 111 AK52
Denham UB9 136 BG59
Station Par, E.Hors. KT24
off Ockham Rd S 267 BS126
Edgware HA8 118 CL52
Feltham TW14 197 BV87
Hornchurch RM12
off Rosewood Av 149 FH63
Richmond TW9 180 CN81
Sevenoaks TN13
off London Rd 278 FG124
Virginia Water GU25 214 AX98
Station Pas, E18
off Cowslip Rd 124 EH54
SE15 44 G6
Station Path, E8 10 F4
Staines TW18 195 BF91
Station Pl, N4
off Seven Sisters Rd 143 DN61
Godalming GU7
off Summers Rd 280 AT144
Station Ri, SE27
off Norwood Rd 203 DP89
Station Rd, E4 (Chingford) 123 ED46
E7 146 EG63
E12 146 EK63
E17 145 DY58
N3 120 DA53
N11 121 DH50
N17 144 DU55
N19 143 DJ62
N21 121 DP46
N22 121 DM54
NW4 141 CU58
NW7 118 CS50
NW10 161 CT68
SE13 46 E10
SE20 204 DW93
SE25 (Norwood Junct.) 224 DT98
SW13 181 CU83
SW19 222 DC95
W5 160 CM72
W7 (Hanwell) 159 CE74
Addlestone KT15 234 BJ105
Amersham HP6, HP7 77 AQ38
Ashford TW15 196 BM91
Barkingside IG6 147 ER55
Beaconsfield HP9 111 AK52
Belmont SM2 240 DA110
Belvedere DA17 188 FA76
Berkhamsted HP4 60 AW18
Betchworth RH3 270 CS131
Bexleyheath DA7 188 EY83
Borehamwood WD6 100 CN42
Bramley GU5 281 AZ144
Brasted TN16 262 EV123
Brentford TW8 179 CJ79
Bricket Wood AL2 82 CA31
Bromley BR1 226 EG95
Broxbourne EN10 71 DZ20
Carshalton SM5 240 DF105
Chadwell Heath RM6 148 EX59
Chertsey KT16 215 BF102
Chesham HP5 76 AP31
Chessington KT9 238 CL106
Chigwell IG7 125 EP48
Chobham GU24 232 AT111
Cippenham SL1 153 AL72
Claygate KT10 237 CD106
Crayford DA1 209 FF86
Croydon CR0 224 DQ102
Cuffley EN6 87 DM29
Dorking RH4 285 CG135
Dunton Green TN13 263 FE120
Edgware HA8 118 CN51
Egham TW20 195 BA92
Epping CM16 91 ET31
Esher KT10 219 CD103
Eynsford DA4 230 FK104
Farncombe GU7 280 AT144
Gerrards Cross SL9 134 AY57
Gidea Park RM2 149 FH56
Gomshall GU5 283 BQ139
Greenhithe DA9 191 FU84
Halstead TN14 246 EZ111
Hampton TW12 218 CA95
Hampton Wick KT1 219 CJ95
Harlow CM17 58 EW11
Harold Wood RM3 128 FM53
Harrow HA1 139 CF59
Hayes UB3 177 BS77
Hemel Hempstead HP1 62 BH22
Horley RH6 291 DH148
Hounslow TW3 178 CB84
Ilford IG1 147 EP62
Kenley CR8 242 DQ114
Kings Langley WD4 81 BP29
Kingston upon Thames KT2 220 CN95
Langley SL3 175 BA76
Leatherhead KT22 253 CG121
Letty Green SG14 52 DG12
Loudwater HP10 110 AC53
Loughton IG10 106 EL42
Merstham RH1 273 DJ128
Motspur Park KT3 221 CV99
New Barnet EN5 102 DB43
North Harrow HA2 138 CB57
North Mymms AL9 85 CX25
North Weald Bassett CM16 93 FB27
Northfleet DA11 212 GB86
Orpington BR6 227 ET103
Otford TN14 263 FH116
Radlett WD7 99 CG35
Redhill RH1 272 DG133
Rickmansworth WD3 114 BK45
St. Paul's Cray BR5 228 EW98
Shalford GU4 280 AY140
Shepperton TW17 217 BQ99
Shoreham TN14 247 FG111
Shortlands BR2 226 EE96
Sidcup DA15 208 EU91
Smallford AL4 66 CP19
South Darenth DA4 230 FP96
Southfleet DA13 212 GA91
Stanstead Abbotts SG12 55 EA11
Stoke D'Abernon KT11 252 BY117
Sunbury-on-Thames TW16 197 BU94
Swanley BR8 229 FE98
Taplow SL6 152 AF72
Teddington TW11 199 CF92
Thames Ditton KT7 219 CF101
Twickenham TW1 199 CF88
Upminster RM14 150 FQ61
Uxbridge UB8 156 BJ70
Waltham Abbey EN9 89 EA34
Waltham Cross EN8 89 EA34
Ware SG12 55 DX06
Watford WD17 97 BV40
West Byfleet KT14 234 BG112
West Drayton UB7 156 BK74
West Wickham BR4 225 EC102
Station Rd, Whyt. CR3 258 DT118
Woldingham CR3 259 DZ123
Wraysbury TW19 195 AZ86
Station Rd E, Oxt. RH8 276 EE128
Station Rd N, Belv. DA17 189 FB76
Egham TW20 195 BA92
Merstham RH1 273 DJ128
Station Rd S, Merst. RH1 273 DJ128
Station Rd W, Oxt. RH8 276 EE129
Station Row, Shalf. GU4 280 AY140
Station Sq, Petts Wd BR5 227 EQ99
Romford RM2 149 FH56
Station St, E15 12 G6
E16 37 N3
Station Ter, NW10 14 C1
SE5 43 K6
Dorking RH4
off Chalkpit La 285 CG135
Park Street AL2
off Park St 83 CD26
Station Vw, Grnf. UB6 159 CD67
Guildford GU1 280 AW135
Station Way, Cheam SM3 239 CY107
Claygate KT10 237 CE107
Epsom KT19 238 CR113
Roding Valley IG9 124 EJ49
St. Albans AL1 65 CF20
Station Yd, Denh. UB9 136 BG59
Smallford AL4 66 CP20
Twickenham TW1 199 CG87
Staunton Rd, Kings.T. KT2 200 CL93
Slough SL2 153 AR71
Staunton St, SE8 45 P2
★ **Stave Hill Ecological Pk**,
SE16 33 L4
Staveley Cl, E9 11 H2
N7 8 B1
SE15 44 F6
Staveley Gdns, W4 180 CR81
Staveley Rd, W4 180 CR80
Ashford TW15 197 BR93
Staveley Way, Knap. GU21 248 AS117
Staverton Rd, NW2 4 A6
Hornchurch RM11 150 FK58
Stave Yd Rd, SE16 33 L3
Stavordale Rd, N5 143 DP63
Carshalton SM5 222 DC101
Stayne End, Vir.W. GU25 214 AU98
Stayner's Rd, E1 21 J4
Stayton Rd, Sutt. SM1 222 DA104
Steadfast Rd, Kings.T. KT1 219 CK95
Stead St, SE17 31 L9
Steam Fm La, Felt. TW14 177 BT84
Stean St, E8 10 A8
Stebbing Ho, W11 26 D2
Stebbing Way, Bark. IG11 168 EU68
Stebondale St, E14 34 F10
Sch **Stebon Prim Sch**, E14 22 A7
Stedham Pl, WC1 18 A8
Stedman Cl, Bex. DA5 209 FE90
Uxbridge UB10 136 BN62
Steed Cl, Horn. RM11 149 FH61
Steedman St, SE17 31 J9
Steeds Rd, N10 120 DF53
Steeds Way, Loug. IG10 106 EL41
Steele Av, Green. DA9 211 FT85
Steele Rd, E11 146 EE63
N17 144 DS55
NW10 160 CQ68
W4 180 CQ76
Isleworth TW7 179 CG84
Steeles Ms N, NW3 6 E5
Steeles Ms S, NW3 6 F5
Steeles Rd, NW3 6 E5
Steele Wk, Erith DA8 189 FB79
Steel's La, E1 21 H9
Steels La, Oxshott KT22 236 CB114
Steelyard Pas, EC4 31 L1
Steen Way, SE22
off East Dulwich Gro 204 DS85
Steep Cl, Orp. BR6 245 ET107
Steep Hill, SW16 203 DK90
Croydon CR0 242 DS105
Steeplands, Bushey WD23 116 CB45
Steeple Cl, SW6 38 F9
SW19 201 CY92
Steeple Ct, E1
off Coventry Rd 20 F4
Egham TW20
off The Chantries 195 BA92
Steeple Gdns, Add. KT15
off Weatherall Cl 234 BH106
Steeple Hts Dr, Bigg.H. TN16 260 EK117
Steeplestone Cl, N18 122 DQ50
Steeple Wk, N1 9 K8
Steerforth St, SW18 202 DB89
Steering Cl, N9 122 DW46
Steers Mead, Mitch. CR4 222 DF95
Steers Way, SE16 33 M5
Stella Cl, Uxb. UB8 157 BP71
Stellar Ho, N17 122 DT51
Stella Rd, SW17 202 DF93
Stelling Rd, Erith DA8 189 FD80
Stellman Cl, E5 144 DU62
Stembridge Rd, SE20 224 DV96
Sten Cl, Enf. EN3 105 EA37
Stents La, Cob. KT11 252 BZ120
Stepbridge Path, Wok. GU21
off Goldsworth Rd 248 AX117
Stepgates, Cher. KT16 216 BH101
Stepgates Cl, Cher. KT16 216 BH101
Sch **Stepgates Comm Sch**, Cher.
KT16 *off Stepgates* 216 BH101
Stephan Cl, E8 10 D8
Stephen Av, Rain. RM13 169 FG65
Stephen Cl, Egh. TW20 195 BC93
Orpington BR6 227 ET104
Stephendale Rd, SW6 39 M8
Sch **Stephen Hawking Sch**, E14 21 M9
Stephen Ms, W1 17 N7
Stephen Pl, SW4 41 L10
Stephen Rd, Bexh. DA7 189 FC83
Stephens Cl, Rom. RM3 128 FJ50
Stephenson Av, Til. RM18 193 GG81
Stephenson Cl, E3 22 C3
Hoddesdon EN11 71 ED17
Welling DA16 188 EU82
Stephenson Ct, Ware SG12 55 DY07
Stephenson Dr, Wind. SL4 173 AP80
Stephenson Ho, SE1
off Bath Ter 31 J6
Stephenson Rd, E17 145 DY57
W7 159 CF72
Twickenham TW2 198 CA87
Stephenson St, E16 23 J5
NW10 160 CS69
Stephenson Way, NW1 17 M4
Watford WD24 98 BX41
Stephenson Wf, Hem.H. HP3 80 BL25
Stephen's Rd, E15 13 K9
Stephen St, W1 17 N7
Stephyns Chambers, Hem.H.
HP1 *off Waterhouse St* 62 BJ21
STEPNEY, E1 21 J7
Stepney Causeway, E1 21 K9
Stepney Cl, Mitch. CR4 222 DG95
⊖ **Stepney Green** 21 J5
Stepney Grn, E1 21 H6
Sch **Stepney Greencoat C of E
Prim Sch**, E14 21 N8
Sch **Stepney Grn Sch**, E1 21 K7
Stepney High St, E1 21 K7
Stepney Way, E1 20 E7
Sterling Av, Edg. HA8 118 CM49
Waltham Cross EN8 89 DX34
Sterling Cl, NW10 161 CU66
Sterling Gdns, SE14 45 L3
● **Sterling Ind Est**, Dag.
RM10 149 FB63
Sterling Pl, W5 180 CL77
Weybridge KT13 235 BS105
Sterling Rd, Enf. EN2 104 DR39
Sterling St, SW7 28 D6
Sterling Way, N18 122 DR50
★ **Sternberg Cen**, N3 120 DB54
Stern Cl, Bark. IG11 168 EW68
Sterndale Rd, W14 26 C7
Dartford DA1 210 FM87
Sterne St, W12 26 C4
Sternhall La, SE15 44 D10
Sternhold Av, SW2 203 DK89
Sterry Cres, Dag. RM10
off Alibon Rd 148 FA64
Sterry Dr, Epsom KT19 238 CS105
Thames Ditton KT7 219 CE100
Sterry Gdns, Dag. RM10 168 FA65
Sterry Rd, Bark. IG11 167 ET67
Dagenham RM10 148 FA63
Sterry St, SE1 31 L5
Steucers La, SE23 205 DY87
Steve Biko La, SE6 205 EA91
Steve Biko Rd, N7 143 DN62
Steve Biko Way, Houns. TW3 178 CA83
Stevedale Rd, Well. DA16 188 EW82
Stevedore St, E1 32 E2
Stevenage Cres, Borwd. WD6 100 CL39
Stevenage Ri, Hem.H. HP2 62 BM16
Stevenage Rd, E6 167 EN65
SW6 38 C5
Stevens Av, E9 11 H4
Stevens Cl, Beck. BR3 205 EA93
Bexley DA5 209 FD91
Epsom KT17
off Upper High St 238 CS113
Hampton TW12 198 BY93
Steven's Cl, Lane End DA2 211 FS92
Stevens Cl, Pnr. HA5 138 BW57
Potters Bar EN6 85 CX33
Stevens Grn, Bushey Hth
WD23 116 CC46
Stevens La, Clay. KT10 237 CG108
Stevenson Cl, Barn. EN5 102 DD44
Erith DA8 189 FH80
Stevenson Cres, SE16 32 D10
Stevenson Rd, Hedg. SL2 133 AR61
Stevens Pl, Pur. CR8 241 DP113
Stevens Rd, Dag. RM8 148 EV62
Stevens St, SE1 31 P6
Steven's Wk, Croy. CR0 243 DY111
Stevens Way, Amer. HP7 77 AP40
Chigwell IG7 125 ES49
Steventon Rd, W12 161 CT73
Steward Cl, Chsht EN8 89 DY30
STEWARDS, Harl. CM18 73 ER19
Stewards Cl, Epp. CM16 92 EU33
Stewards Grn La, Epp. CM16 92 EV32
Stewards Grn Rd, Epp. CM16 92 EU33
Stewards Holte Wk, N11
off Coppies Gro 121 DH49
Sch **Stewards Sch**, Harl. CM18
off Parnall Rd 73 ER19
Steward St, E1 19 P7
Stewards Wk, Rom. RM1
off Western Rd 149 FE57
Stewart, Tad. KT20 255 CX121
Stewart Av, Shep. TW17 216 BN98
Slough SL1 154 AT71
Upminster RM14 150 FP62
Stewart Cl, NW9 140 CQ58
Abbots Langley WD5 81 BT32
Chislehurst BR7 207 EP92
Fifield SL6 172 AD81
Hampton TW12 198 BY92
Woking GU21 248 AT117
Stewart Ct, Denh. UB9 135 BF58
Sch **Stewart Fleming Prim Sch**,
SE20 *off Witham Rd* 224 DW97
Sch **Stewart Headlam Prim Sch**,
E1 20 E4
Stewart Pl, Ware SG12 55 DX06
Stewart Rainbird Ho, E12 147 EN64
Stewart Rd, E15 12 F1
Stewartsby Cl, N18 122 DQ50
Stewart's Dr, Farn.Com. SL2 133 AP64
Stewart's Gro, SW3 28 B10
Stewart's Rd, SW8 41 L5
Stewart St, E14 34 F5
Stew La, EC4 19 J10
Steyne Rd, W3 160 CQ74
Steyning Cl, Ken. CR8 257 DP116
Steyning Gro, SE9 207 EM91
Steynings Way, N12 120 DA50
Steyning Way, Houns. TW4 178 BW84
Steynton Av, Bex. DA5 208 EX89
Stickland Rd, Belv. DA17 188 FA77
Stickleton Cl, Grnf. UB6 158 CB69
Stifford Hill, N.Stfd RM16 171 FX74
South Ockendon RM15 171 FW73
Sch **Stifford Prim Sch**, Grays
RM17 *off Parker Rd* 192 FY78
Stifford Rd, S.Ock. RM15 171 FR74
Stile Cft, Harl. CM18 74 EU17
Stilecroft Gdns, Wem. HA0 139 CH62
Stile Hall Gdns, W4 180 CN78
Stile Hall Par, W4
off Chiswick High Rd 180 CN78
Stile Meadow, Beac. HP9 111 AL52
Stile Path, Sun. TW16 217 BU98
Stile Rd, Slou. SL3 174 AX76
Stiles Cl, Brom. BR2 227 EM100
Erith DA8
off Riverdale Rd 189 FB78
Stillingfleet Rd, SW13 181 CU79
Stillington St, SW1 29 M8
Sch **Stillness Inf & Jun Schs**,
SE23 *off Brockley Ri* 205 DY86
Stillness Rd, SE23 205 DY86
Stilton Path, Borwd. WD6 100 CN38

Stilwell Dr, Uxb. UB8 156 BM70
Jct Stilwell Rbt, Uxb. UB8 157 BP72
Stipularis Dr, Hayes UB4 158 BX70
Stirling Av, Pnr. HA5 138 BY59
Wallington SM6 241 DL108
Stirling Cl, SW16 223 DJ95
Banstead SM7 255 CZ117
Rainham RM13 169 FH69
Sidcup DA14 207 ES91
Uxbridge UB8
off Ferndale Cres 156 BJ69
Windsor SL4 173 AK82
Jct Stirling Cor, Barn. EN5 100 CR44
Borehamwood WD6 100 CR44
Stirling Dr, Cat. CR3 258 DQ121
Orpington BR6 246 EV106
Stirling Gro, Houns. TW3 178 CC82
● Stirling Ind Cen, Borwd.
WD6 100 CR43
Stirling Retail Pk, Borwd.
WD6 100 CR44
Stirling Rd, E13 24 A1
E17 145 DY55
N17 122 DU53
N22 121 DP53
SW9 42 A9
W3 180 CP76
Harrow HA3 139 CF55
Hayes UB3 157 BV73
London Heathrow Airport
TW6 196 BM86
Slough SL1 153 AP72
Twickenham TW2 198 CA87
Stirling Rd Path, E17 145 DY55
Stirling Wk, N.Mal. KT3 220 CQ99
Surbiton KT5 220 CP100
Stirling Way, Abb.L. WD5 81 BU32
Borehamwood WD6 100 CR44
Croydon CR0 223 DL101
Welwyn Garden City AL7 52 DE09
Stites Hill Rd, Couls. CR5 257 DP120
Stiven Cres, Har. HA2 138 BZ62
Sch St John's Inf & Nurs Sch,
Rad. WD7 off Gills Hill La 99 CF36
Sch St. Mary's Farnham Royal
C of E Prim Sch, Farn.Royal
SL2 off Church Rd 153 AQ69
Stoat Cl, Hert. SG13 54 DU09
Stoats Nest Rd, Couls. CR5 241 DL114
Stoats Nest Village, Couls.
CR5 257 DL115
Stockbreach Cl, Hat. AL10 67 CU17
Stockbreach Rd, Hat. AL10 67 CU17
Stockbury Rd, Croy. CR0 224 DW100
Stockdale Rd, Dag. RM8 148 EZ61
Stockdales Rd, Eton Wick SL4 173 AM77
Stockdove Way, Perivale UB6 159 CF69
Stocker Gdns, Dag. RM9 168 EW66
Stockers Fm Rd, Rick. WD3 114 BK48
Stockers La, Wok. GU22 249 AZ120
★ Stock Exchange, EC4 19 H8
Stockfield, Horl. RH6 291 DH147
Stockfield Av, Hodd. EN11 71 EA15
Stockfield Rd, SW16 203 DM90
Claygate KT10 237 CE106
Stockford Av, NW7 119 CX52
Stockham's Cl, S.Croy. CR2 242 DR111
Stock Hill, Bigg.H. TN16 260 EK116
Stockholm Ho, E1 20 E10
Stockholm Rd, SE16 45 H1
Stockholm Way, E1 32 C2
Stockhurst Cl, SW15 38 B9
Stocking La, Bayford SG13 69 DN18
Stockings La, Lt.Berk. SG13 69 DK18
Stockingswater La, Enf. EN3 105 DY41
Stockland Rd, Rom. RM7 149 FD58
Stock La, Dart. DA2 210 FJ91
Stockleigh Hall, NW8
off Prince Albert Rd 6 E10
Sch Stockley Acad, Yiew. UB7
off Apple Tree Av 156 BM72
Stockley Cl, West Dr. UB7 177 BP75
Stockley Fm Rd, West Dr. UB7
off Stockley Rd 177 BP76
● Stockley Pk, Uxb. UB11 157 BP74
Jct Stockley Pk Rbt, Uxb.
UB11 156 BN74
Stockley Rd, Uxb. UB8 157 BP73
West Drayton UB7 177 BP77
Stock Orchard Cres, N7 8 C2
Stock Orchard St, N7 8 C3
Stockport Rd, SW16 223 DK95
Heronsgate WD3 113 BC45
Stocksbridge Cl, Chsht EN7 88 DS26
Stocks Cl, Horl. RH6 291 DH149
Stocksfield Rd, E17 145 EC55
Stocks Meadow, Hem.H. HP2 62 BN19
Stocks Pl, E14 21 P10
Hillingdon UB10 156 BN67
Stock St, E13 23 N1
Stockton Cl, New Barn. EN5 102 DC42
Stockton Gdns, N17
off Stockton Rd 122 DQ52
NW7 118 CR48
Stockton Ho, E2
off Ellsworth St 20 E2
Stockton Rd, N17 122 DQ52
N18 122 DU51
Reigate RH2 288 DA137
STOCKWELL, SW9 42 E9
⊖ Stockwell 42 B8
Stockwell Av, SW9 183 DM83
Stockwell Cl, Brom. BR1 226 EH96
Cheshunt EN7 88 DU28
Edgware HA8 118 CQ54
Stockwell Gdns, SW9 42 C7
Stockwell Gdns Est, SW9 42 B8
Stockwell Grn, SW9 42 C9
Stockwell La, SW9 42 D9
Cheshunt EN7 88 DU28
Stockwell Ms, SW9 42 C9
Stockwell Pk Cres, SW9 42 D8
Stockwell Pk Est, SW9 42 D9
Stockwell Pk Rd, SW9 42 C7
Sch Stockwell Pk Sch, SW9 42 C7
Stockwell Pk Wk, SW9 42 D10
Sch Stockwell Prim Sch, SW9 42 D10
Stockwell Rd, SW9 42 C8
Stockwells, Tap. SL6 152 AD70
Stockwell St, SE10 46 F3
Stockwell Ter, SW9 42 C7
Stocton Cl, Guil. GU1 264 AW133
Stocton Rd, Guil. GU1 264 AW133
Stodart Rd, SE20 224 DW95
Stofield Gdns, SE9
off Aldersgrove Av 206 EK90
Stoford Cl, SW19 201 CY87
Stoke Av, Ilf. IG6 126 EU51
Stoke Cl, Stoke D'Ab. KT11 252 BZ116
Stoke Common Rd, Fulmer
SL3 134 AU63
Stoke Ct Dr, Stoke P. SL2 154 AS67
STOKE D'ABERNON, Cob.
KT11 252 BZ116
Stoke Flds, Guil. GU1
off Stoke Rd 264 AX134
Stoke Gdns, Slou. SL1 154 AS74
STOKE GREEN, Slou. SL2 154 AU70
Stoke Grn, Stoke P. SL2 154 AU70
Stoke Gro, Guil. GU1
off Stoke Rd 264 AX134
Stoke Hosp, Guil. GU1
off Stoke Rd 264 AX134
Stoke Ms, Guil. GU1
off Stoke Rd 280 AX135
Stoke Mill Cl, Guil. GU1
off Mangles Rd 264 AX132
Stokenchurch St, SW6 39 L7
STOKE NEWINGTON, N16 144 DS61
⇌ Stoke Newington 144 DT61
Stoke Newington Ch St, N16 144 DR62
Stoke Newington Common,
N16 144 DT62
Stoke Newington High St,
N16 144 DT62
Stoke Newington Rd, N16 10 A2
Sch Stoke Newington Sch, N16
off Clissold Rd 144 DR62
Stoke Pk Av, Farn.Royal SL2 153 AQ69
Stoke Pl, NW10 161 CT69
STOKE POGES, Slou. SL2 154 AT66
Stoke Poges La, Slou.
SL1, SL2 154 AS72
Sch Stoke Poges Sch, The, Stoke P.
SL2 off Rogers La 154 AT66
Stoke Rd, Cob. KT11 252 BW115
Guildford GU1 264 AX133
Kingston upon Thames KT2 200 CQ94
Rainham RM13 170 FK68
Slough SL2 154 AT71
Walton-on-Thames KT12 218 BW104
Stokers Cl, Gat. RH6 290 DE151
Stokesay, Slou. SL2 154 AT73
Stokesby Rd, Chess. KT9 238 CM107
Stokesheath Rd, Oxshott
KT22 236 CC111
Stokesley Ri, Woob.Grn HP10 132 AE55
Stokesley St, W12 161 CT72
Stokes Ridings, Tad. KT20 255 CX123
Stokes Rd, E6 24 G5
Croydon CR0 225 DX100
Stoke Wd, Stoke P. SL2 134 AT63
Stoll Cl, NW2 141 CW62
Stompond La, Walt. KT12 217 BU103
Stomp Rd, Burn. SL1 152 AJ71
Stonard Rd, N13 121 DN48
Dagenham RM8 148 EV64
Stonards Hill, Epp. CM16 92 EW31
Loughton IG10 107 EM44
Stondon Pk, SE23 205 DY87
Stondon Wk, E6 166 EK68
STONE, Green. DA9 211 FT85
Stonebank, Welw.G.C. AL8
off Stonehills 51 CX08
Stonebanks, Walt. KT12 217 BU101
STONEBRIDGE, NW10 160 CP67
STONEBRIDGE, Dor. RH5 286 CL139
Stonebridge Common, E8 10 A7
Stonebridge Fld, Eton SL4 173 AP78
Stonebridge Flds, Shalf. GU4 280 AX141
⇌ Stonebridge Park 160 CN66
⊖ Stonebridge Park 160 CN66
Stonebridge Pk, NW10 160 CR66
Sch Stonebridge Prim Sch, The,
NW10 off Shakespeare Av 160 CQ67
Stonebridge Rd, N15 144 DS57
Northfleet DA11 212 GA85
Stonebridge Shop Cen, NW10
off Shakespeare Rd 160 CR67
Stonebridge Way, Wem. HA9 160 CP65
Stonebridge Wf, Shalf. GU4 280 AX141
Stone Bldgs, WC2 18 D7
Stonechat Sq, E6 25 H6
Stone Cl, SW4 41 M9
Dagenham RM8 148 EZ61
West Drayton UB7 156 BM74
Stonecot Cl, Sutt. SM3 221 CY102
Stonecot Hill, Sutt. SM3 221 CY102
Stonecourt Cl, Horl. RH6 291 DJ148
Stone Cres, Felt. TW14 197 BT87
Stonecroft Av, Iver SL0 155 BE72
Stonecroft Cl, Barn. EN5 101 CV42
Stonecroft Rd, Erith DA8 189 FC80
Stonecroft Way, Croy. CR0 223 DL101
Stonecrop Cl, NW9 140 CR55
Stonecrop Rd, Guil. GU4 265 BC132
Stone Cross, Harl. CM20
off Post Office Rd 57 ER14
Stonecross, St.Alb. AL1 65 CE19
Stonecross Cl, St.Alb. AL1 65 CE19
⇌ Stone Crossing 211 FS85
Stonecross Rd, Hat. AL10 67 CV16
Stonecutter St, EC4 18 G8
Stonefield, N4 143 DM61
Stonefield Cl, Bexh. DA7 188 FA83
Ruislip HA4 138 BY64
Stonefield St, N1 8 F8
Stonefield Way, SE7
off Greenbay Rd 186 EK80
Ruislip HA4 138 BY63
Stonegate Cl, Orp. BR5
off Main Rd 228 EW97
Stonegrove, Edg. HA8 118 CL49
Stonegrove Est, Edg. HA8
off Lacey Dr 118 CM49
Stonegrove Gdns, Edg. HA8 118 CM50
Stonehall Av, Ilf. IG1 146 EL58
● Stonehall Business Pk,
Match.Grn CM17 59 FH10
Stone Hall Gdns, W8 27 L7
Stone Hall Pl, W8 27 L7
Stone Hall Rd, N21 121 DM45
Stoneham Rd, N11 121 DJ51
STONEHILL, Cher. KT16 232 AY107
● Stonehill Business Pk, N18
off Silvermere Dr 123 DX51
Stonehill Cl, SW14 200 CR85
Bookham KT23 268 CA125
Stonehill Cres, Ott. KT16 232 AY107
Stonehill Grn, Dart. DA2 209 FC94
Stonehill Rd, SW14 200 CQ85
W4 180 CN78
Chobham GU24 232 AW108
Ottershaw KT16 233 BA105
Stonehills, Welw.G.C. AL8 51 CX09
Stonehills Ct, SE21 204 DS90
Stonehill Wds Pk, Sid. DA14 209 FB93
Stonehorse Rd, Enf. EN3 104 DW43
Jct Stonehouse Cor, Purf.
RM19 191 FR79
Stone Ho Ct, EC3 19 N8
Stone Ho Gdns, Cat. CR3 274 DS125
Stonehouse La, Halst. TN14 246 EX109
Purfleet RM19 191 FS78
Stonehouse Rd, Halst. TN14 246 EW110
Stoneings La, Knock. TN14 261 ET118
Stone Lake Retail Pk, SE7 36 B9
Jct Stone Lake Rbt, SE7 36 C9
Stonelea Rd, Hem.H. HP3 62 BM23
STONELEIGH, Epsom KT17 239 CU106
⇌ Stoneleigh 239 CU106
Stoneleigh Av, Enf. EN1 104 DV39
Worcester Park KT4 239 CU105
Stoneleigh Bdy, Epsom KT17 239 CU106
Stoneleigh Cl, Wal.Cr. EN8 89 DX33
Stoneleigh Cres, Epsom KT19 239 CT106
Stoneleigh Dr, Hodd. EN11 55 EB14
Stoneleigh Ms, E3 21 M1
Stoneleigh Pk, Wey. KT13 235 BQ106
Stoneleigh Pk Av, Croy. CR0 225 DX100
Stoneleigh Pk Rd, Epsom
KT19 239 CT107
Stoneleigh Pl, W11 26 D1
Stoneleigh Rd, N17 144 DT55
Bromley BR1 227 EP97
Carshalton SM5 222 DE101
Ilford IG5 146 EL55
Oxted RH8 276 EL130
Stoneleigh St, W11 14 D10
Stoneleigh Ter, N19 143 DH61
Stoneley Cres, Green. DA9 191 FW84
Stonells Rd, SW11
off Chatham Rd 202 DF85
Stonemasons Cl, N15 144 DR56
Stoneness Rd, Grays RM20 191 FV79
Stonenest St, N4 143 DM60
Stone Pk Av, Beck. BR3 225 EA98
Stone Pl, Wor.Pk. KT4 221 CU103
Stone Pl Rd, Green. DA9 211 FS85
Stone Rd, Brom. BR2 226 EF99
Sch Stone St. Mary's C of E
Prim Sch, Stone DA9
off Hayes Rd 211 FS87
Stones All, Wat. WD18 97 BV42
Stones Cross Rd, Swan. BR8 229 FC99
Stones End St, SE1 31 J5
Stones La, Westc. RH4 284 CC137
Stones Rd, Epsom KT17 238 CS112
Stone St, Grav. DA11 213 GH86
Stoneswood Rd, Oxt. RH8 276 EH130
Stonewall, E6 25 M7
Stonewood, Bean DA2 211 FW90
Stonewood Rd, Erith DA8 189 FE78
Stoney All, SE18 187 EN82
Stoneyard La, E14 34 C1
Stoney Br Dr, Wal.Abb. EN9 90 EG34
Stoney Brook, Guil. GU2 264 AS133
Stoney Cl, Nthch HP4 60 AT17
Stoney Cft, Couls. CR5 257 DJ122
Stoneycroft, Hem.H. HP1 62 BG20
Welwyn Garden City AL7 52 DA08
Stoneycroft Cl, SE12 206 EF87
Stoneycroft Rd, Wdf.Grn. IG8 124 EL51
Stoneydeep, Tedd. TW11
off Twickenham Rd 199 CG91
Stoneydown, E17 145 DY56
Stoneydown Av, E17 145 DY56
Sch Stoneydown Pk Prim Sch,
E17 off Pretoria Av 145 DY56
Stoneyfield, Ger.Cr. SL9 134 AW60
Stoneyfield Rd, Couls. CR5 257 DM117
Stoneyfields Gdns, Edg. HA8 118 CQ49
Stoneyfields La, Edg. HA8 118 CQ50
Stoney Gro, Chesh. HP5 76 AR30
Stoneylands Ct, Egh. TW20 195 AZ92
Stoneylands Rd, Egh. TW20 195 AZ92
Stoney La, E1 19 P8
SE19 off Church Rd 204 DT93
Bovingdon HP3 79 BB27
Chipperfield WD4 79 BE30
East Burnham SL2 153 AN67
Hemel Hempstead HP1 61 BB23
Stoney Meade, Slou. SL1
off Weekes Dr 153 AP74
Stoney St, SE1 31 L2
Stonhouse St, SW4 183 DK83
Stonny Cft, Ashtd. KT21 254 CM117
Stonor Rd, W14 26 G9
Stonycroft Cl, Enf. EN3
off Brimsdown Av 105 DY40
Sch Stony Dean Sch, Amer. HP7
off Orchard End Av 94 AT39
Stony La, Amer. HP6 94 AY38
Stony Path, Loug. IG10 107 EM40
Stonyrock La, Dor. RH5 268 BY131
Stonyshotts, Wal.Abb. EN9 90 EE34
Stony Wd, Harl. CM18 73 ES16
Stoop Ct, W.Byf. KT14 234 BH112
Stopes St, SE15 44 B5
Stopford Rd, E13 13 P8
SE17 43 H1
Store Rd, E16 37 L4
Storers Quay, E14 34 G9
Store St, E15 13 H3
WC1 17 N7
Storey Ct, NW8
off St. John's Wd Rd 16 A3
Storey Rd, E17 145 DZ56
N6 142 DF58
Storey's Gate, SW1 29 P5
Storey St, E16 37 M3
Hemel Hempstead HP3 62 BK24
Stories Ms, SE5 43 N9
Stories Rd, SE5 43 N10
Stork Rd, E7 13 M5
Storksmead Rd, Edg. HA8 118 CS52
Storks Rd, SE16 32 D7
Sch Stormont Ho Sch, E5 10 E1
Stormont Rd, N6 142 DF59
SW11 182 DG83
Sch Stormont Sch, Pot.B. EN6
off The Causeway 86 DD31
Stormont Way, Chess. KT9 237 CJ106
Stormount Dr, Hayes UB3 177 BQ75
Stornaway Rd, Slou. SL3 175 BC77
Stornaway Strand, Grav.
DA12 213 GM91
Stornoway, Hem.H. HP3 63 BP22
Storr Gdns, Hutt. CM13 131 GD43
Storrington Rd, Croy. CR0 224 DT102
Stortford Rd, Hodd. EN11 71 EB16
Stort Mill, Harl. CM20 58 EV09
Stort Twr, Harl. CM20 57 ET13
Story St, N1 8 C7
Stothard Pl, E1
off Spital Yd 19 P6
Stothard St, E1 20 G4
Stott Cl, SW18 202 DD86
STOUGHTON, Guil. GU2 264 AV131
Stoughton Av, Sutt. SM3 239 CX106
Stoughton Cl, SE11 30 D9
SW15 off Bessborough Rd 201 CU88
Sch Stoughton Inf Sch, Guil.
GU2 off Stoughton Rd 264 AV131
Stoughton Rd, Guil.
GU1, GU2 264 AU131
Stour Av, Sthl. UB2 178 CA76
Stourcliffe St, W1 16 E9
Stour Cl, Kes. BR2 244 EJ105
Slough SL1 173 AP76
Stourhead Cl, SW19 201 CX87
Stourhead Gdns, SW20 221 CU97
Stourhead Ho, SW1
off Tachbrook St 29 N10
Stour Rd, E3 12 A7
Dagenham RM10 148 FA61
Dartford DA1 189 FG83
Grays RM16 193 GG78
Stourton Av, Felt. TW13 198 BZ91
Stour Way, Upmin. RM14 151 FS58
Stovell Rd, Wind. SL4 173 AP80
Stow, The, Harl. CM20 57 ET13
Stowage, SE8 46 B3
Stow Cres, E17 123 DY52
Stowe Ct, Dart. DA2 210 FQ87
Stowe Cres, Ruis. HA4 137 BP58
Stowe Gdns, N9 122 DT46
Stowell Av, New Adgtn CR0 243 ED110
Stowe Pl, N15 144 DS55
Stowe Rd, W12 181 CV75
Orpington BR6 246 EV105
Slough SL1 153 AL73
Sch Stowford Coll, Sutt. SM2
off Brighton Rd 240 DC108
Stowting Rd, Orp. BR6 245 ES105
Stox Mead, Har. HA3 117 CD53
Stracey Rd, E7 13 P1
NW10 160 CR67
Strachan Pl, SW19 201 CW93
Stradbroke Dr, Chig. IG7 125 EN51
Stradbroke Gro, Buck.H. IG9 124 EK46
Ilford IG5 146 EL55
Stradbroke Pk, Chig. IG7 125 EP51
Stradbroke Rd, N5 9 K1
Stradbrook Cl, Har. HA2
off Stiven Cres 138 BZ62
Stradella Rd, SE24 204 DQ86
Strafford Av, Ilf. IG5 125 EN54
Strafford Cl, Pot.B. EN6
off Strafford Gate 86 DA32
Strafford Gate, Pot.B. EN6 86 DA32
Strafford Rd, W3 180 CQ75
Barnet EN5 101 CY41
Hounslow TW3 178 BZ83
Twickenham TW1 199 CG87
Strafford St, E14 34 A4
Strahan Rd, E3 21 M2
Straight, The, Sthl. UB1 178 BX75
Straight Bit, Flack.Hth HP10 132 AC56
Straight Rd, Old Wind. SL4 194 AU85
Romford RM3 128 FJ52
Straightsmouth, SE10 46 E4
Strait Rd, E6 25 K10
Straker's Rd, SE15 184 DV84
STRAND, WC2 18 A10
Strand, WC2 30 A1
Strand Cl, Epsom KT18 254 CR119
Strand Ct, SE18
off Strandfield Cl 187 ES78
Strand Dr, Rich. TW9 180 CP80
Strandfield Cl, SE18 187 ES78
Strand Ho, SE28
off Merbury Cl 167 ER74
Strand La, WC2 18 D10
Strand on the Grn, W4 180 CN79
Sch Strand-on-the-Grn Inf &
Nurs & Jun Schs, W4
off Thames Rd 180 CN79
Strand Pl, N18 122 DR49
Strand Sch App, W4
off Thames Rd 180 CN79
Strangeways, Wat. WD17 97 BS36
Strangways Ter, W14 26 G6
Stranraer Gdns, Slou. SL1 154 AS74
Stranraer Rd, Lon.Hthrw Air.
TW6 196 BL86
Stranraer Way, N1 8 B7
Strasburg Rd, SW11 41 H7
Stratfield Dr, Brox. EN10 71 DY19
Stratfield Pk Cl, N21 121 DP45
Stratfield Rd, Borwd. WD6 100 CN41
Slough SL1 174 AU75
STRATFORD, E15 12 F4
⊖ Stratford 12 G6
Stratford Av, W8 27 K7
Uxbridge UB10 156 BM68
Stratford Cen, The, E15 13 H6
Stratford Cl, Bark. IG11 168 EU66
Dagenham RM10 169 FC66
Slough SL2 153 AK70
Stratford Ct, N.Mal. KT3 220 CR98
Stratford Dr, Woob.Grn HP10 132 AD59
Stratford Gro, SW15 181 CX84
Stratford Ho Av, Brom. BR1 226 EL97
● Stratford Hub, E15 12 C10
⇌ Stratford International 12 D5
● Stratford Office Village, The,
E15 13 J6
Stratford Pl, W1 17 J9
Stratford Regional 12 F6
⊖ Stratford Regional 12 F6
DLR Stratford Regional 12 F6
Stratford Rd, E13 13 M9
NW4 141 CX56
W8 27 K8
Hayes UB4 157 BV70
London Heathrow Airport
TW6 197 BP86
Southall UB2 178 BY77
Thornton Heath CR7 223 DN98
Watford WD17 97 BU40
Sch Stratford Sch, E7 13 P6
Stratford Vil, NW1 7 M6
Stratford Way, Brick.Wd AL2 82 BZ29
Hemel Hempstead HP3 62 BH23
Watford WD17 97 BT40
Strathan Cl, SW18 201 CY86
Strathaven Rd, SE12 206 EH86
Strathblaine Rd, SW11 182 DD84
Strathbrook Rd, SW16 203 DM94
Strathcona Av, Bkhm KT23 268 BY128
Strathcona Cl, Flack.Hth HP10 132 AC56
Strathcona Rd, Wem. HA9 139 CK61
Strathcona Way, Flack.Hth
HP10 132 AC56
Strathdale, SW16 203 DM92
Strathdon Dr, SW17 202 DD90
Strathearn Av, Hayes UB3 177 BT80
Twickenham TW2 198 CB88
Strathearn Pl, W2 16 B10
Strathearn Rd, SW19 202 DA92
Sutton SM1 240 DA106
Stratheden Par, SE3
off Stratheden Rd 47 P5
Stratheden Rd, SE3 47 N6
Strathfield Gdns, Bark. IG11 167 ER65
Strathleven Rd, SW2 203 DL85
Strathmore Cl, Cat. CR3 258 DS121
Strathmore Gdns, N3 120 DB53
W8 27 K2
Edgware HA8 118 CP54
Hornchurch RM12 149 FF60
Strathmore Rd, SW19 202 DA90
Croydon CR0 224 DQ101
Teddington TW11 199 CE91
Sch Strathmore Sch, Rich. TW10
off Meadlands Dr 199 CK89
Strathnairn St, SE1 32 D9
Strathray Gdns, NW3 6 C5
Strath Ter, SW11 182 DE84
Strathville Rd, SW18 202 DB89
Strathyre Av, SW16 223 DN97
Stratton Av, Enf. EN2 104 DR37
Wallington SM6 241 DK109
Stratton Chase Dr, Ch.St.G.
HP8 112 AU47
Stratton Cl, SW19 222 DA96
Bexleyheath DA7 188 EY83
Edgware HA8 118 CM52
Hounslow TW3 178 BZ81
Walton-on-Thames KT12
off St. Johns Dr 218 BW102
Stratton Ct, Surb. KT6
off Adelaide Rd 220 CL99
Strattondale St, E14 34 E6
Stratton Dr, Bark. IG11 147 ET64
Stratton Gdns, Sthl. UB1 158 BZ72
Stratton Rd, SW19 222 DA96
Beaconsfield HP9 110 AH53
Bexleyheath DA7 188 EY83
Romford RM3 128 FN50
Sunbury-on-Thames TW16 217 BT96
Stratton St, W1 29 K2
Stratton Ter, West. TN16
off High St 277 EQ127
Stratton Wk, Rom. RM3 128 FN50
Strauss Rd, W4 180 CR75
Strawberry Cres, Lon.Col. AL2 83 CH26
Strawberry Fld, Hat. AL10 67 CU21
Strawberry Flds, Farnboro.
BR6 245 EP106
Swanley BR8 229 FE95
Ware SG12 54 DV05
STRAWBERRY HILL, Twick.
TW1 199 CE90
⇌ Strawberry Hill 199 CE90
Strawberry Hill, Twick. TW1 199 CF90
Strawberry Hill Cl, Twick. TW1 199 CF90
Strawberry Hill Rd, Twick.
TW1 199 CF90
Strawberry La, Cars. SM5 222 DF104
Strawberry Vale, N2 120 DD53
Twickenham TW1 199 CG90
Straw Cl, Cat. CR3 258 DQ123
Strawfields, Welw.G.C. AL7 52 DB08
Strawmead, Hat. AL10 67 CV16
Strawson Ct, Horl. RH6 290 DF147
Strayfield Rd, Enf. EN2 103 DP37
Streakes Fld Rd, NW2 141 CU61
Stream Cl, Byfleet KT14 234 BK112
Streamdale, SE2 188 EU79
Stream La, Edg. HA8 118 CP50
Streamline Ms, SE22 204 DU88
Streamside, Slou. SL1
off Richards Way 153 AM74
Streamside Cl, N9 122 DT46
Bromley BR2 226 EG98
Streamway, Belv. DA17 188 FA79
Streatfeild Av, E6 167 EM67
Streatfield Rd, Har. HA3 139 CK55
STREATHAM, SW16 203 DL91
⇌ Streatham 203 DL92
Sch Streatham & Clapham High
Sch, Jun Dept, SW2
off Wavertree Rd 203 DM88
SW16 off Abbotswood Rd 203 DK90
Streatham Cl, SW16 203 DL89
⇌ Streatham Common 203 DK94
Streatham Common N, SW16 203 DL92
Streatham Common S, SW16 203 DL93
Streatham Ct, SW16 203 DL90
Streatham High Rd, SW16 203 DL92
STREATHAM HILL, SW2 203 DM87
⇌ Streatham Hill 203 DL89
Streatham Hill, SW2 203 DL89
STREATHAM PARK, SW16 203 DJ91
Streatham Pl, SW2 203 DL87
Streatham Rd, SW16 222 DG95
Mitcham CR4 222 DG95
Streatham St, WC1 17 P8
STREATHAM VALE, SW16 203 DK94
Streatham Vale, SW16 203 DJ94
Sch Streatham Wells Prim Sch,
SW2 off Palace Rd 203 DN89
Streathbourne Rd, SW17 202 DG89
Streatley Pl, NW3
off New End 142 DC63
Streatley Rd, NW6 4 G7
Street, The, Albury GU5 282 BH139
Ashtead KT21 254 CL119
Betchworth RH3 286 CS135
Chipperfield WD4 80 BG31
East Clandon GU4 266 BK131
Effingham KT24 268 BX127
Fetcham KT22 253 CD122
Horton Kirby DA4 230 FP98
Shalford GU4 280 AY139
Sheering CM22 59 FC07
West Clandon GU4 266 BH131
West Horsley KT24 267 BP129
Wonersh GU5 281 BA144
Streeters La, Wall. SM6 223 DK104
Streetfield Ms, SE3 47 P10
Streimer Rd, E15 12 F10
Strelley Way, W3 160 CS73
Stretton Mans, SE8 46 B1
Stretton Pl, Amer. HP6 94 AT38

Stretton Rd, Croy. CR0 . . . . **224** DS101
Richmond TW10 . . . . **199** CJ89
Stretton Way, Borwd. WD6 . . . **100** CL38
Strickland Av, Dart. DA1 . . . . . . **190** FL83
Strickland Row, SW18 . . . . **202** DD87
Strickland St, SE8. . . . . **46** B7
Strickland Way, Orp. BR6 . . . . . **245** ET105
Stride Rd, E13 . . . . **23** M1
Strides Ct, Ott. KT16
off Brox Rd **233** BC107
Strimon Cl, N9 . . . . **122** DW47
Stringers Av, Jacobs Well
GU4 . . . . **264** AX128
Stringer's Common, Guil.
GU1, GU4 . . . . **264** AV129
Stringhams Copse, Ripley
GU23 . . . . **249** BF124
Stripling Way, Wat. WD18. . . . . . **97** BU44
Strode Cl, N10. . . . . **120** DG52
Strode Rd, E7 . . . . **146** EG63
N17. **122** DS54
NW10. . . . . **161** CU65
SW6 . . . . **38** D4
Strodes Coll, Egh. TW20
off High St. **195** AZ92
Strodes Coll La, Egh. TW20 . . . **195** AZ92
Strodes Cres, Stai. TW18 . . . . . **196** BJ92
Strode St, Egh. TW20 . . . . **195** BA91
Stroma Cl, Hem.H. HP3 . . . . **63** BQ22
Stroma Ct, Slou. SL1
off Lincoln Way. **153** AK73
Strone Rd, E7 . . . . **166** EJ65
E12 . . . . **166** EK65
Strone Way, Hayes UB4 . . . . . . **158** BY70
Strongbow Cres, SE9. . . . . **207** EM85
Strongbow Rd, SE9 . . . . **207** EM85
Strongbridge Cl, Har. HA2 . . . . . **138** CA60
Stronsa Rd, W12 . . . . **181** CT75
Stronsay Cl, Hem.H. HP3
off Northend **63** BQ22
Strood Av, Rom. RM7. . . . . **149** FD60
STROOD GREEN, Bet. RH3 . . . **286** CP138
Stroud Cl, Wind. SL4 . . . . **173** AK83
Stroud Cres, SW15 . . . . **201** CU90
STROUDE, Vir.W. GU25 . . . . . . **215** AZ96
Stroude Rd, Egh. TW20 . . . . . . **195** BA93
Virginia Water GU25. . . . . . . **214** AY98
Stroudes Cl, Wor.Pk. KT4 . . . . . **220** CS101
Stroud Fld, Nthlt. UB5 . . . . **158** BY65
Stroud Gate, Har. HA2 . . . . **138** CB63
STROUD GREEN, N4 . . . . **143** DM58
Stroud Grn Gdns, Croy. CR0 . . . **224** DW101
Stroud Grn Prim Sch, N4
off Woodstock Rd **143** DN60
Stroud Grn Rd, N4 . . . . **143** DM60
Stroud Grn Way, Croy. CR0 . . . **224** DV101
Stroudley Wk, E3 . . . . **22** C2
Stroud Rd, SE25 . . . . **224** DU100
SW19 . . . . **202** DA90
Strouds Cl, Chad.Hth RM6. . . . . **148** EV57
Stroudwater Pk, Wey. KT13 . . . **235** BP107
Stroud Way, Ashf. TW15
off Courtfield Rd. **197** BP93
Strouts Pl, E2 . . . . **20** A2
Struan Gdns, Wok. GU21 . . . . . **248** AY115
Strutton Grd, SW1 . . . . **29** N6
Struttons Av, Nthflt DA11 . . . . . **213** GF89
Strype St, E1 . . . . **20** A7
Stuart Av, NW9. . . . . **141** CU59
W5 . . . . **160** CM74
Bromley BR2. . . . . **226** EG102
Harrow HA2. . . . . **138** BZ62
Walton-on-Thames KT12 . . . **217** BV102
Stuart Cl, Pilg.Hat. CM15 . . . . . . **130** FV43
Swanley BR8. . . . . **209** FF94
Uxbridge UB10 . . . . **156** BN65
Windsor SL4 . . . . **173** AM82
Stuart Ct, Els. WD6
off High St. **99** CK44
Stuart Cres, N22 . . . . **121** DM53
Croydon CR0. . . . . **225** DZ104
Hayes UB3. . . . . **157** BQ72
Reigate RH2. . . . . **288** DA137
Stuart Evans Cl, Well. DA16. . . **188** EW83
Stuart Gro, Tedd. TW11 . . . . . . **199** CE92
Stuart Mantle Way,
Erith DA8 . . . . **189** FD80
Stuart Pl, Mitch. CR4 . . . . **222** DF95
Stuart Rd, NW6. . . . . **15** J3
SE15 . . . . **184** DW84
SW19 . . . . **202** DA90
W3 . . . . **160** CQ74
Barking IG11 . . . . **167** ET66
East Barnet EN4 . . . . **120** DE45
Gravesend DA11 . . . . **213** GG86
Grays RM17. . . . . **192** GB78
Harrow HA3. . . . . **117** CF54
Reigate RH2. . . . . **288** DA137
Richmond TW10 . . . . **199** CH89
Thornton Heath CR7. . . . . . . **224** DQ98
Warlingham CR6. . . . . **258** DV120
Welling DA16. . . . . **188** EV81
Stuarts Cl, Hem.H. HP3
off Marriotts Way **62** BK22
Stuart Twr, W9. . . . . **15** P3
Stuart Way, Chsht EN7. . . . . **88** DV31
Staines TW18. . . . . **196** BH93
Virginia Water GU25. . . . . . . **214** AU97
Windsor SL4 . . . . **173** AL82
Stubbers La, Upmin. RM14 . . . **171** FR65
Stubbins Hall La, Wal.Abb.
EN9. . . . . **89** EB28
Stubbs Cl, NW9. . . . . **140** CQ57
Stubbs Dr, SE16 . . . . **32** E10
Stubbs End Cl, Amer. HP6 . . . . . **77** AS36
Stubbs Hill, Knock.P. TN14 . . . . **246** EW113
Stubbs La, Lwr Kgswd KT20 . . **271** CZ128
Stubbs Ms, Dag. RM8 . . . . **148** EV63
Stubbs Pt, E13. . . . . **24** A5
Stubbs Way, SW19
off Ruskin Way **222** DD95
Stubbs Wd, Amer. HP6. . . . . **77** AS36
Stubs Cl, Dor. RH4 . . . . **285** CJ138
Stubs Hill, Dor. RH4 . . . . **285** CJ139
Stucley Pl, NW1 . . . . **7** K7
Stucley Rd, Houns. TW5. . . . . . **178** CC80
Studdridge St, SW6 . . . . **39** K9
Studd St, N1. . . . . **8** G8
Stud Grn, Wat. WD25 . . . . **81** BV32
Studholme Ct, NW3 . . . . **5** K1
Studholme St, SE15. . . . . **44** E5
Studio Ms, NW4
off Glebe Cres. **141** CW56
Studio Pl, SW1 . . . . **28** F5
Studios, The, Bushey WD23. . . . **98** CA44
Studios Rd, Shep. TW17. . . . . . **216** BM97
Studio Way, Borwd. WD6. . . . . . **100** CQ40
Studland, SE17 . . . . **31** L10
Studland Cl, Sid. DA15. . . . . . . **207** ET90
Studland Ho, E14 . . . . **21** L8
Studland Rd, SE26 . . . . **205** DX92
W7 . . . . **159** CD72
Byfleet KT14 . . . . **234** BM113
Kingston upon Thames KT2. **200** CL93
Studland St, W6 . . . . **181** CV77
Studley Av, E4. . . . . **123** ED52
Studley Cl, E5 . . . . **11** L3
Studley Ct, E14
off Jamestown Way **35** H1
Sidcup DA14 . . . . **208** EV92
Studley Dr, Ilf. IG4 . . . . **146** EK58
Studley Est, SW4 . . . . **42** A7
Studley Gra Rd, W7 . . . . **179** CE75
Studley Rd, E7. . . . . **166** EH65
SW4 . . . . **42** A7
Dagenham RM9 . . . . **168** EX66
Study Prep Sch, The,
Spencer Ho, SW19
off Peek Cres **201** CX92
Wilberforce Ho, SW19
off Camp Rd **201** CW92
Study Sch, The,
N.Mal. KT3
off Thetford Rd **220** CS99
Stukeley Rd, E7. . . . . **166** EH66
Stukeley St, WC1 . . . . **18** B8
WC2 . . . . **18** B8
Stump Rd, Epp. CM16 . . . . **92** EW27
Stumps Hill La, Beck. BR3 . . . . **205** EA93
Stumps La, Whyt. CR3 . . . . **258** DS117
Stumpwell La, Penn HP10 . . . . **110** AD48
Sturdy Rd, SE15 . . . . **44** E9
Sturge Av, E17. . . . . **123** EB54
Sturgeon Rd, SE17 . . . . **43** J1
Sturges Fld, Chis. BR7 . . . . **207** ER93
Sturgess Av, NW4. . . . . **141** CV59
Sturge St, SE1. . . . . **31** J4
Sturla Cl, Hert. SG14. . . . . **53** DP08
Sturlas Way, Wal.Cr. EN8 . . . . . . **89** DX33
Sturmer Cl, St.Alb. AL4 . . . . **65** CJ21
Sturmer Way, N7. . . . . **8** C2
Sturminster Cl, Hayes UB4 . . . **158** BW72
Sturrock Cl, N15 . . . . **144** DR56
Sturry St, E14 . . . . **22** C9
Sturt Ct, Guil. GU4 . . . . **265** BB132
Sturts La, Walt.Hill KT20 . . . . . **271** CT127
Sturt St, N1 . . . . **19** K1
Stutfield St, E1 . . . . **20** D9
Stychens Cl, Bletch. RH1 . . . . . **274** DQ133
Stychens La, Bletch. RH1 . . . . . **274** DQ132
Stylecroft Rd, Ch.St.G. HP8 . . . **112** AX47
Styles End, Bkhm KT23 . . . . . . **268** CB127
Styles Gdns, SW9. . . . . **43** H10
Styles Way, Beck. BR3 . . . . **225** EC98
Stylus Ho, E1
off Devonport St. **21** H9
Styventon Pl, Cher. KT16. . . . . . **215** BF101
Subrosa Dr, Merst. RH1 . . . . . . **273** DH130
● **Subrosa Pk**, Merst. RH1 . . . **273** DH130
Succombs Hill, Warl. CR6. . . . . . **258** DV120
Whyteleafe CR3. . . . . **258** DV120
Succombs Pl, Warl. CR6. . . . . . **258** DV120
Sudbourne Prim Sch, SW2
off Hayter Rd **203** DM85
Sudbourne Rd, SW2. . . . . **203** DL85
Sudbrooke Rd, SW12. . . . . **202** DF86
Sudbrook Gdns, Rich. TW10. . . . **199** CK90
Sudbrook La, Rich. TW10. . . . . . **200** CL88
SUDBURY, Wem. HA0 . . . . **139** CG64
Sudbury, E6. . . . . **25** M8
⇌ **Sudbury & Harrow Road** . . **139** CH64
Sudbury Av, Wem. HA0 . . . . **139** CK62
Sudbury Ct, SW8
off Allen Edwards Dr **42** A6
Sudbury Ct Dr, Har. HA1 . . . . . . **139** CF62
Sudbury Ct Rd, Har. HA1 . . . . . . **139** CF62
Sudbury Cres, Brom. BR1 . . . . . **206** EG93
Wembley HA0. . . . . **139** CH64
Sudbury Cft, Wem. HA0. . . . . . . **139** CF63
Sudbury Gdns, Croy. CR0 . . . . . **242** DS105
Sudbury Hts Av, Grnf. UB6 . . . . **139** CF64
⊖ **Sudbury Hill** **139** CE63
Sudbury Hill, Har. HA1 . . . . **139** CE61
Sudbury Hill Cl, Wem. HA0 . . . . **139** CF63
⇌ **Sudbury Hill Harrow**. **139** CE63
Sudbury Ho, SW18
off Wandsworth High St. . . **202** DB85
Sudbury Prim Sch, Wem.
HA0 *off Watford Rd*. **139** CH63
Sudbury Rd, Bark. IG11 . . . . **147** ET64
⊖ **Sudbury Town** **159** CH65
Sudeley St, N1 . . . . **19** H1
Sudicamps Ct, Wal.Abb. EN9. . . . **90** EG33
Sudlow Rd, SW18. . . . . **182** DA84
Sudrey St, SE1 . . . . **31** J5
Suez Av, Grnf. UB6. . . . . **159** CF68
Suez Rd, Enf. EN3. . . . . **105** DY42
Suffield Cl, S.Croy. CR2 . . . . . . **243** DX112
Suffield Rd, E4. . . . . **123** EB48
N15. . . . . **144** DT57
SE20. **224** DW96
Suffolk Cl, Borwd. WD6 . . . . . . **100** CR43
Horley RH6 . . . . **290** DG149
London Colney AL2 . . . . **83** CJ25
Slough SL1 . . . . **153** AL72
Suffolk Ct, E10. . . . . **145** EA59
Ilford IG3 . . . . **147** ES58
Suffolk Dr, Guil. GU4 . . . . **265** BB129
Suffolk La, EC4 . . . . **19** L10
Suffolk Pk Rd, E17 . . . . **145** DY56
Suffolk Pl, SW1 . . . . **29** P2
Suffolk Rd, E13 . . . . **23** M3
N15. . . . . **144** DR58
NW10. . . . . **160** CS66
SE25. **224** DT98
SW13 . . . . **181** CT80
Barking IG11 . . . . **167** ER66
Dagenham RM10 . . . . **149** FC64
Dartford DA1 . . . . **210** FL86
Enfield EN3 . . . . **104** DV43
Gravesend DA12. . . . . **213** GK86
Harrow HA2. . . . . **138** BZ58
Ilford IG3 . . . . **147** ES58
Potters Bar EN6. . . . . **85** CY32
Sidcup DA14 . . . . **208** EW93
Worcester Park KT4 . . . . **221** CT103
Suffolks Prim Sch, Enf. EN1
off Brick La. **104** DV40
Suffolk St, E7 . . . . **13** N2
SW1 . . . . **29** P2
Suffolk Way, Horn. RM11 . . . . . **150** FN56
Sevenoaks TN13 . . . . **279** FJ125
Sugar Bakers Ct, EC3
off Creechurch La **19** P9
Sugar Ho La, E15 . . . . **12** E10
Sugar La, Berk. HP4 . . . . **61** AZ22
Hemel Hempstead HP1 . . . . . **61** BB22
Sugar Loaf Wk, E2 . . . . **20** G2
Sugar Quay Wk, EC3. . . . . **31** P1
Sugden Rd, SW11. . . . . **182** DG83
Thames Ditton KT7. . . . . **219** CH102
Sugden Way, Bark. IG11 . . . . . . **167** ET68
Sulgrave Gdns, W6. . . . . **26** B5
Sulgrave Rd, W6. . . . . **26** B5
Sulina Rd, SW2. . . . . **203** DL87
Sulivan Ct, SW6 . . . . **39** J9
● **Sulivan Enterprise Cen**, SW6
off Sulivan Rd. **182** DA83
Sulivan Prim Sch, SW6 . . . . **39** J9
Sulivan Rd, SW6. . . . . **182** DA83
Sulkin Ho, E2
off Knottisford St **21** J2
Sullivan Av, E16. . . . . **24** E6
Sullivan Cl, SW11 . . . . **40** C10
Dartford DA1 . . . . **209** FH86
Hayes UB4. . . . . **158** BW71
Sullivan Cres, Hare. UB9 . . . . . **114** BK54
Sullivan Ho, SW1
off Churchill Gdns. **41** K1
Sullivan Rd, SE11 . . . . **30** F8
Tilbury RM18. . . . . **193** GG81
Sullivans Reach, Walt. KT12 . . **217** BT101
Sullivan Way, Els. WD6. . . . . **99** CJ44
Sultan Rd, E11. . . . . **146** EH56
Sultan St, SE5. . . . . **43** J4
Beckenham BR3 . . . . **225** DX96
Sultan Ter, N22
off Vincent Rd **121** DN54
Sumatra Rd, NW6. . . . . **5** K4
Sumburgh Rd, SW12 . . . . **202** DG86
Sumburgh Way, Slou. SL1 . . . . **154** AS71
Summer Av, E.Mol. KT8 . . . . . . **219** CE99
Summer Cl, Byfleet KT14. . . . . . **234** BM114
Summer Ct, Hem.H. HP2
off Townsend. **62** BK18
Summercourt Rd, E1 . . . . **21** H8
Summer Crossing, T.Ditt. KT7 . **219** CE98
Summerdale, Welw.G.C. AL8. . . **51** CX05
Summerene Cl, SW16 . . . . **203** DJ94
Summerfield, Ashtd. KT21. . . . . **253** CK119
Hatfield AL10. . . . . **67** CU21
Summerfield Av, NW6 . . . . **4** F10
Summerfield Cl, Add. KT15
off Spinney Hill. **233** BF106
London Colney AL2 . . . . **83** CJ26
Summerfield La, Long Dit.
KT6. . . . . **219** CK103
Summerfield Pl, Ott. KT16
off Crawshaw Rd **233** BD107
Summerfield Rd, W5 . . . . **159** CH70
Loughton IG10. . . . . **106** EK44
Watford WD25. . . . . **97** BU35
Summerfields Av, N12 . . . . **120** DE51
Summerfield St, SE12 . . . . **206** EF87
Summer Gdns, E.Mol. KT8 . . . . **219** CE99
Summer Gro, Els. WD6 . . . . **99** CK44
West Wickham BR4. . . . . **226** EE103
Summerhayes Cl, Wok. GU21 . **232** AY114
Summerhays, Cob. KT11 . . . . . . **236** BX113
Summer Hill, Chis. BR7 . . . . . . **227** EN96
Elstree WD6. . . . . **100** CN43
Summerhill Cl, Orp. BR6 . . . . . **227** ES104
Summerhill Ct, St.Alb. AL1 . . . . . **65** CF19
Summerhill Gro, Enf. EN1 . . . . **104** DS44
Summerhill Rd, N15. . . . . **144** DR56
Dartford DA1 . . . . **210** FK87
Summer Hill Vil, Chis. BR7. . . . . **227** EN95
Summerhill Way, Mitch. CR4 . . **222** DG95
Summerhouse Av, Houns.
TW5 . . . . **178** BY81
Summerhouse Dr, Bex. DA5 . . **209** FD91
Dartford DA2 . . . . **209** FD91
Summerhouse La, Ald. WD25 . . **98** CC40
Harefield UB9 . . . . **114** BG52
Harmondsworth UB7 . . . . . . **176** BK79
Summerhouse Rd, N16 . . . . **144** DS61
Summerhouse Way, Abb.L.
WD5 . . . . **81** BT30
Summerland Gdns, N10. . . . . . **143** DH55
Summerlands Av, W3. . . . . **160** CQ73
Summerlands Rd, St.Alb. AL4. . **65** CJ16
Summerlay Cl, Kgswd KT20 . . . **255** CY120
Summerlea, Slou. SL1 . . . . **153** AP74
Summerleas Cl, Hem.H. HP2. . . **62** BL20
Summerlee Av, N2 . . . . **142** DF56
Summerlee Gdns, N2. . . . . **142** DF56
Summerley St, SW18. . . . . **202** DB89
Summerly Av, Reig. RH2
off Burnham Dr. **272** DA133
Summer Pl, Chal.St.P. SL9 . . . . **112** AY52
Summer Rd, E.Mol. KT8. . . . . . **219** CE99
Thames Ditton KT7. . . . . **219** CF99
Summersbury Dr, Shalf. GU4 . **280** AY142
Summersbury Hall, Shalf. GU4
off Summersbury Dr **280** AY142
Summersby Rd, N6 . . . . **143** DH58
Summers Cl, Sutt. SM2
off Overton Rd. **240** DA108
Wembley HA9. . . . . **140** CP60
Weybridge KT13 . . . . **234** BN111
Summerside Prim Sch, N12
off Crossway **120** DD51
Summerskill Cl, SE15. . . . . **44** E10
Summerskille Cl, N9
off Plevna Rd. **122** DV47
Summers La, N12 . . . . **120** DD52
Summers Rd, Burn. SL1. . . . . . . **152** AJ69
Godalming GU7 . . . . **280** AT144
Summers Row, N12 . . . . **120** DE51
Summers St, EC1 . . . . **18** E5
SUMMERSTOWN, SW17 . . . . . **202** DB90
Summerstown, SW17 . . . . **202** DC90
Summerswood Cl, Ken. CR8
off Longwood Rd **258** DR116
Summerswood La, Borwd.
WD6 . . . . **84** CS34
Summerswood Prim Sch,
Borwd. WD6
off Furzehill Rd **100** CP42
Summerton Way, SE28. . . . . . . **168** EX72
Summer Trees, Sun. TW16
off The Avenue. **217** BV95
Summerville Gdns, Sutt. SM1. **239** CZ107
Summerwood Rd, Islw. TW7 . . . **199** CF85
Summit, The, Loug. IG10 . . . . . **107** EM39
Summit Av, NW9 . . . . **140** CR57
Summit Cl, N14. . . . . **121** DJ47
NW9. . . . . **140** CR56
Edgware HA8. . . . . **118** CN52
Summit Ct, NW2 . . . . **4** F4
Summit Dr, Wdf.Grn. IG8. . . . . . **124** EK54
Summit Est, N16. . . . . **144** DU59
Summit Pl, Wey. KT13 . . . . **234** BN108
Summit Rd, E17 . . . . **145** EB56
Northolt UB5. . . . . **158** CA66
Potters Bar EN6. . . . . **85** CY30
Summit Way, N14. . . . . **121** DH47
SE19. **204** DS94
Sumner Av, SE15 . . . . **44** B6
Sumner Cl, Fetch. KT22 . . . . . . **253** CD124
Orpington BR6 . . . . **245** EQ105
Sumner Ct, SW8
off Darsley Dr **42** A6
Sumner Gdns, Croy. CR0 . . . . . **223** DN102
Sumner Pl, SW7 . . . . **28** B9
Addlestone KT15. . . . . **234** BG106
Sumner Pl Ms, SW7. . . . . **28** B9
Sumner Rd, SE15 . . . . **44** B3
Croydon CR0. . . . . **223** DN102
Harrow HA1. . . . . **138** CC59
Sumner Rd S, Croy. CR0 . . . . . **223** DN102
SUMNERS, Harl. CM19. . . . . **73** EN19
Sumners Fm Cl, Harl. CM19 . . . **73** EN20
Sumner St, SE1 . . . . **31** H2
Sumpter Cl, NW3 . . . . **5** P5
Sumpter Yd, St.Alb. AL1. . . . . . . **65** CD20
Sun All, Rich. TW9
off Kew Rd. **180** CL84
Sunbeam Cres, W10 . . . . **14** B5
Sunbeam Rd, NW10. . . . . **160** CQ70
SUNBURY, Sun. TW16 . . . . **217** BV97
⇌ **Sunbury**. **217** BT95
Sunbury Adult Learning Cen,
Sun. TW16
off The Avenue. **217** BV95
Sunbury Av, NW7 . . . . **118** CR50
SW14 . . . . **180** CR84
Sunbury Cl, Walt. KT12. . . . . . . **217** BU100
Sunbury Ct, Sun. TW16 . . . . . . **218** BX96
Sunbury Ct Island, Sun. TW16. **218** BX97
Sunbury Ct Ms, Sun. TW16
off Lower Hampton Rd. . . . **218** BX97
Sunbury Ct Rd, Sun. TW16 . . . **218** BW96
Sunbury Cres, Felt. TW13
off Ryland Cl **197** BT91
Sunbury Cross, Sun.
TW16 . . . . **197** BT94
Sunbury Cross Cen, Sun.
TW16 . . . . **197** BT94
Sunbury Gdns, NW7. . . . . **118** CR50
Sunbury La, SW11 . . . . **40** B6
Walton-on-Thames KT12 . . . **217** BU100
Sunbury Lock Ait, Walt. KT12 . **217** BV98
Sunbury Manor Sch, Sun.
TW16 *off Nursery Rd* **217** BT95
Sunbury Rd, Eton SL4 . . . . **173** AR79
Feltham TW13 . . . . **197** BT90
Sutton SM3 . . . . **221** CX104
Sunbury St, SE18 . . . . **37** K7
Sunbury Training Cen (Met Pol),
Sun. TW16 *off Green St* . . . **217** BU98
Sunbury Way, Han. TW13. . . . . **198** BW92
● **Sunbury Workshops**, E2
off Swanfield St **20** A3
Sun Ct, EC3 . . . . **19** M9
Erith DA8 . . . . **189** FF82
Suncroft Pl, SE26 . . . . **204** DW90
Sundale Av, S.Croy. CR2 . . . . . **242** DW110
Sunderland Av, St.Alb. AL1 . . . . **65** CG18
Sunderland Ct, SE22 . . . . **204** DU87
Sunderland Gro, Lvsdn WD25 . . **81** BT34
Sunderland Mt, SE23 . . . . **205** DX89
Sunderland Rd, SE23 . . . . **205** DX88
W5 . . . . **179** CK76
Sunderland Ter, W2. . . . . **15** L8
Sunderland Way, E12 . . . . **146** EK61
Sundew Av, W12. . . . . **161** CU73
Sundew Cl, W12 . . . . **161** CU73
Sundew Ct, Grays RM17
off Salix Rd **192** GD79
Sundew Rd, Hem.H. HP1. . . . . . . **61** BE21
Sundial Av, SE25. . . . . **224** DT97
Sundon Cres, Vir.W. GU25 . . . . **214** AV99
Sundorne Rd, SE7. . . . . **186** EH78
Sundown Av, S.Croy. CR2 . . . . . **242** DT111
Sundown Rd, Ashf. TW15. . . . . . **197** BQ92
Sundra Wk, E1. . . . . **21** J5
SUNDRIDGE, Brom. BR1 . . . . . **206** EJ93
SUNDRIDGE, Sev. TN14 . . . . . . **262** EZ124
Sundridge Av, Brom. BR1 . . . . **226** EK95
Chislehurst BR7 . . . . **206** EK94
Welling DA16. . . . . **187** ER82
Sundridge Cl, Dart. DA1 . . . . . . **210** FN86
Sundridge Hill, Sev. TN14. . . . . . **262** EW118
Sundridge Ho, Brom. BR1
off Burnt Ash La **206** EH92
Sundridge La, Sev. TN14 . . . . . **262** EV117
⇌ **Sundridge Park** **206** EH94
Sundridge Pl, Croy. CR0
off Inglis Rd. **224** DU102
Sundridge Rd, Croy. CR0 . . . . . **224** DT101
Dunton Green TN14 . . . . **262** FA120
Woking GU22 . . . . **249** BA119
Sunfields Pl, SE3. . . . . **186** EH80
Sunflower Way, Rom. RM3 . . . . **128** FK53
Sun Hill, Fawk.Grn DA3 . . . . . . **231** FU104
Woking GU22 . . . . **248** AU121
Sun-In-The-Sands, SE3 . . . **186** EH80
Sunken Rd, Croy. CR0 . . . . **242** DW106
Sunkist Way, Wall. SM6 . . . . . . **241** DL109
Sunland Av, Bexh. DA6 . . . . . . **188** EY84
Sun La, SE3. . . . . **186** EH80
Gravesend DA12. . . . . **213** GJ89
Sunleigh Rd, Wem. HA0. . . . . . **160** CL67
Sunley Gdns, Perivale UB6 . . . **159** CG67
Sunlight Cl, SW19. . . . . **202** DC93
Sunlight Sq, E2. . . . . **20** F3
Sunmead Cl, Fetch. KT22. . . . . **253** CF122
Sunmead Rd, Hem.H. HP2. . . . . **62** BK18
Sunbury-on-Thames TW16. . **217** BU97
Sunna Gdns, Sun. TW16. . . . . . **217** BV96
Sunningdale, N14
off Wilmer Way **121** DK50
Sunningdale Av, W3. . . . . **160** CS73
Barking IG11 . . . . **167** ER67
Feltham TW13 . . . . **198** BY89
Rainham RM13 . . . . **169** FH70
Ruislip HA4 . . . . **138** BW60
Sunningdale Cl, E6. . . . . **25** J2
SE16. . . . . **44** E1
SE28. **168** EY72
Stanmore HA7. . . . . **117** CG52
Surbiton KT6
off Culsac Rd. **220** CL103
Sunningdale Gdns, NW9. . . . . **140** CQ57
W8 . . . . **27** K7
Sunningdale Ms, Welw.G.C.
AL7. . . . . **51** CY05
Sunningdale Rd, Brom. BR1 . . **226** EL98
Rainham RM13 . . . . **169** FG66
Sutton SM1 . . . . **239** CZ105
Sunningfields Cres, NW4 . . . . . **119** CV54
Sunningfields Rd, NW4 . . . . . . **119** CV54
Sunning Hill, Nthflt DA11 . . . . . **212** GE89
Sunninghill Ct, W3
off Bollo Br Rd. **180** CQ75
Sunninghill Rd, SE13 . . . . **46** C9
Sunnings La, Upmin. RM14. . . . **170** FQ65
Sunningvale Av, Bigg.H. TN16 . **260** EJ115
Sunningvale Cl, Bigg.H. TN16 . **260** EK116
Sunny Bk, SE25. . . . . **224** DU97
Sunnybank, Epsom KT18. . . . . . **254** CQ116
Sunny Bk, Warl. CR6. . . . . **259** DY117
Sunny Bk Prim Sch, Pot.B.
EN6 *off Field Vw Rd* **86** DA34
Sunnybank Rd, Pot.B. EN6. . . . . **86** DA33
Sunnybank Vil, Red. RH1 . . . . . **274** DT132
Sunny Cres, NW10 . . . . **160** CQ66
Sunny Cft, Harl. CM18 . . . . **73** ET18
Sunnycroft Gdns, Upmin.
RM14 . . . . **151** FT59
Sunnycroft Rd, SE25. . . . . **224** DU97
Hounslow TW3 . . . . **178** CB82
Southall UB1. . . . . **158** CA71
Sunnydale, Orp. BR6 . . . . **227** EN103
Sunnydale Gdns, NW7. . . . . . . **118** CR51
Sunnydale Rd, SE12. . . . . **206** EH85
Sunnydell, St.Alb. AL2 . . . . **82** CB26
Sunnydene Av, E4. . . . . **123** ED50
Ruislip HA4 . . . . **137** BU60
Sunnydene Cl, Rom. RM3 . . . . **128** FM52
Sunnydene Gdns, Wem. HA0. . **159** CJ65
Sunnydene Rd, Pur. CR8 . . . . . **241** DP113
Sunnydene St, SE26. . . . . **205** DY91
Sunnydown Sch, Cat. CR3
off Whyteleafe Rd **258** DT121
Sunnyfield, NW7. . . . . **119** CT49
Hatfield AL9. . . . . **67** CX15
Sunnyfield Rd, Chis. BR7. . . . . **228** EU97
Sunnyfields Prim Sch, NW4
off Hatchcroft. **141** CV55
Sunny Gdns Par, NW4
off Great N Way. **119** CW54
Sunny Gdns Rd, NW4. . . . . **119** CV54
Sunny Hill, NW4 . . . . **141** CV55
Sunnyhill Cl, E5. . . . . **145** DY63
Sunnyhill Prim Sch, SW16
off Sunnyhill Rd **203** DM91
Sunnyhill Rd, SW16 . . . . **203** DL91
Hemel Hempstead HP1 . . . . . **62** BH20
West Hyde WD3. . . . . **113** BD51
Sunnyhurst Cl, Sutt. SM1 . . . . . **222** DA104
Sunnymead Av, Mitch. CR4 . . . **223** DJ97
Sunnymead Rd, NW9. . . . . **140** CR59
SW15 . . . . **201** CV85
⇌ **Sunnymeads** **174** AY83
SUNNYMEADS, Stai. TW19 . . . **174** AY84
Sunnymede, Chig. IG7 . . . . **126** EV48
Sunnymede Av, Cars. SM5 . . . **240** DD111
Chesham HP5 . . . . **76** AS28
Epsom KT19 . . . . **238** CS109
Sunnymede Dr, Ilf. IG6. . . . . . . **147** EP56
Sunny Ms, Rom. RM5. . . . . **127** FC52
Sunny Nook Gdns, S.Croy.
CR2. **242** DR107
Sunny Pl, NW4
off Sunny Gdns Rd. **141** CW56
Sunny Ri, Chaldon CR3 . . . . . . **258** DR124
Sunny Rd, The, Enf. EN3. . . . . . **105** DX39
Sunnyside, NW2 . . . . **141** CZ62
SW19 . . . . **201** CY93
Lower Nazeing EN9 . . . . **72** EF22
Walton-on-Thames KT12 . . . **218** BW99
Sunnyside Cotts, Chesh. HP5 . . **78** AU26
Sunnyside Dr, E4 . . . . **123** EC45
Sunnyside Gdns, Upmin.
RM14 . . . . **150** FQ61
Sunnyside Pas, SW19. . . . . **201** CY93
Sunnyside Pl, SW19
off Sunnyside **201** CY93
Sunnyside Rd, E10 . . . . **145** EA60
N19. . . . . **143** DK59
W5 . . . . **159** CK74
Chesham HP5 . . . . **76** AP30
Epping CM16. . . . . **91** ET32
Ilford IG1 . . . . **147** EQ62
Teddington TW11. . . . . **199** CD91
Sunnyside Rd E, N9 . . . . **122** DU48
Sunnyside Rd N, N9 . . . . **122** DT48
Sunnyside Rd S, N9 . . . . **122** DT48
Sunnyside Ter, NW9
off Edgware Rd. **140** CR55
Sunny Vw, NW9 . . . . **140** CR56
Sunny Way, N12 . . . . **120** DE52
Sun Pas, SE16. . . . . **32** C6
Windsor SL4
off Bachelors Acre. **173** AR81
Sunray Av, SE24 . . . . **184** DR84
Bromley BR2. . . . . **226** EL100
Hutton CM13. . . . . **131** GE44
Surbiton KT5. . . . . **220** CP103
West Drayton UB7 . . . . **176** BK75
Sunrise Av, Horn. RM12. . . . . . **150** FJ62
Sunrise Cl, Felt. TW13
off Exeter Rd **198** BZ90
Sunrise Cres, Hem.H. HP3 . . . . . **62** BL23
Sun Rd, W14 . . . . **38** G1
Swanscombe DA10. . . . . **212** FZ86
Sunset Av, E4 . . . . **123** EB46
Woodford Green IG8 . . . . . . **124** EF49
Sunset Cl, Erith DA8. . . . . **189** FH80
Sunset Ct, Wdf.Grn. IG8
off Navestock Cres **124** EJ52
Sunset Dr, Hav.at.Bow. RM4 . . **127** FH50
Sunset Gdns, SE25. . . . . **224** DT96
Sunset Ms, Rom. RM5. . . . . . . **127** FC51
Sunset Rd, SE5 . . . . **184** DQ84
SE28. **188** EU75
Sunset Vw, Barn. EN5 . . . . **101** CY40
Sunshine Way, Mitch. CR4 . . . . **222** DF96
Sun Sq, Hem.H. HP1
off High St. **62** BK19
Sunstone Gro, Merst. RH1. . . . . **273** DL129
Sun St, EC2 . . . . **19** N7
Sawbridgeworth CM21 . . . . . **58** EZ06
Waltham Abbey EN9 . . . . **89** EC33
Sun Wk, E1 . . . . **32** C1
Sunwell Cl, SE15. . . . . **44** E7
Superior Dr, Grn St Grn BR6 . . **245** ET107
SURBITON, KT5 & KT6. . . . . . . **220** CM101
⇌ **Surbiton**. **219** CK100
Surbiton Ct, Surb. KT6 . . . . **219** CJ100
Surbiton Cres, Kings.T. KT1 . . **220** CL98
Surbiton Hall Cl, Kings.T. KT1 . **220** CL98
Surbiton High Sch, Kings.T.
KT1 *off Surbiton Cres*. **220** CL98
Surbiton Hill Pk, Surb. KT5 . . . **220** CN99

Surbiton Hill Rd, Surb. KT6 220 CL98
Surbiton Hosp, Surb. KT6 220 CL100
Surbiton Jun Girls' Sch, Kings.T. KT1
off Surbiton Rd 220 CL98
Surbiton Par, Surb. KT6
off St. Mark's Hill 220 CL100
Surbiton Prep Sch, Surb. KT6 *off Avenue Elmers* 220 CL99
Surbiton Rd, Kings.T. KT1 220 CL98
Surlingham Cl, SE28 168 EX73
Surly Hall Wk, Wind. SL4 173 AM81
Surma Cl, E1 20 E5
Surman Cres, Hutt. CM13 131 GC45
Surmans Cl, Dag. RM9 168 EW67
Surrendale Pl, W9 15 K5
Surrey Av, Slou. SL2 153 AQ71
Surrey Canal Rd, SE14 45 H2
SE15 45 H2
Surrey Cl, N3 141 CY55
Surrey Cres, W4 180 CN78
★ **Surrey Docks Fm**, SE16 33 N5
Surrey Dr, Horn. RM11 150 FN56
Surrey Gdns, N4 144 DQ58
Effingham Junction KT24 251 BT123
Surrey Gro, SE17 43 N1
Sutton SM1 222 DD104
Surrey Hills Av, Box H. KT20 270 CQ130
● **Surrey Hills Business Pk**, Wotton RH5 284 BZ139
Surrey Hills Pk, Box H. KT20 270 CP130
Surrey Inst of Art & Design, The, Epsom KT18
off Ashley Rd 238 CS114
Surrey La, SW11 40 C7
Surrey La Est, SW11 40 C6
Surrey Ms, SE27
off Hamilton Rd 204 DS91
Surrey Mt, SE23 204 DV88
Surrey Quays 33 J8
Surrey Quays Rd, SE16 33 H6
Surrey Quays Shop Cen, SE16 33 J7
Surrey Rd, SE15 205 DX85
Barking IG11 167 ES67
Dagenham RM10 149 FB64
Harrow HA1 138 CC57
West Wickham BR4 225 EB102
Surrey Row, SE1 30 G4
Surrey Sq, SE17 31 N10
Surrey Sq Inf & Jun Schs, SE17 31 N10
Surrey St, E13 24 B3
WC2 18 D10
Croydon CR0 224 DQ104
Surrey Ter, SE17 31 P9
Surrey Twrs, Add. KT15
off Garfield Rd 234 BJ106
Surrey Water Rd, SE16 33 K3
Surridge Cl, Rain. RM13 170 FJ69
Surridge Gdns, SE19
off Hancock Rd 204 DR93
Surr St, N7 8 B3
Sury Basin, Kings.T. KT2 220 CL95
Susan Cl, Rom. RM7 149 FC55
Susan Constant Ct, E14
off Newport Av 23 H10
Susan Lawrence Ho, E12
off Walton Rd 147 EN63
Susannah St, E14 22 D9
Susan Rd, SE3 186 EH82
Susan Wd, Chis. BR7 227 EN95
Sussex Av, Islw. TW7 179 CE83
Romford RM3 128 FM52
Sussex Border Path, Horl. RH6 290 DF150
Sussex Cl, N19 143 DL61
Chalfont St. Giles HP8 112 AV47
Hoddesdon EN11
off Roman St 71 EA16
Ilford IG4 147 EM58
New Malden KT3 220 CS98
Reigate RH2 288 DD135
Slough SL1 174 AV75
Twickenham TW1
off Westmorland Cl 199 CH86
Sussex Ct, Add. KT15
off Garfield Rd 234 BJ106
Sussex Cres, Nthlt. UB5 158 CA65
Sussex Gdns, N4 144 DQ57
N6 142 DF57
W2 16 A10
Chessington KT9 237 CK107
Sussex Ho Sch, SW1 28 E8
Sussex Keep, Slou. SL1
off Sussex Cl 174 AV75
Sussex Ms, SE6
off Ravensbourne Pk 205 EA87
Sussex Ms E, W2 16 B9
Sussex Ms W, W2 16 B10
Sussex Pl, NW1 16 E3
W2 16 B9
W6 26 A10
Erith DA8 189 FB80
New Malden KT3 220 CS98
Slough SL1 174 AV75
Sussex Ring, N12 120 DA50
Sussex Rd, E6 167 EN67
Carshalton SM5 240 DF107
Dartford DA1 210 FN87
Erith DA8 189 FB80
Harrow HA1 138 CC57
Mitcham CR4
off Lincoln Rd 223 DL99
New Malden KT3 220 CS98
Orpington BR5 228 EW100
Sidcup DA14 208 EV92
South Croydon CR2 242 DR107
Southall UB2 178 BX76
Uxbridge UB10 137 BQ63
Warley CM14 130 FV49
Watford WD24 97 BU38
West Wickham BR4 225 EB102
Sussex Sq, W2 16 B10
Sussex St, E13 24 B3
SW1 41 K1
Sussex Way, N7 143 DL61
N19 143 DL60
Cockfosters EN4 102 DG43
Sutcliffe Cl, NW11 142 DB57
Bushey WD23 98 CC42
Sutcliffe Ho, Hayes UB3 157 BU72
Sutcliffe Rd, SE18 187 ES79
Welling DA16 188 EW82
Sutherland Av, W9 15 N3
W13 159 CH72
Biggin Hill TN16 260 EK117
Cuffley EN6 87 DK28
Hayes UB3 177 BU77
Sutherland Av, Jacobs Well GU4 264 AX128
Petts Wood BR5 227 ET100
Sunbury-on-Thames TW16 217 BT96
Welling DA16 187 ES84
Sutherland Cl, Barn. EN5 101 CY42
Greenhithe DA9 211 FT85
Sutherland Ct, NW9 140 CP57
Welwyn Garden City AL7 51 CZ08
Sutherland Dr, SW19 222 DD95
Burpham GU4 265 AZ131
Sutherland Gdns, SW14 180 CS83
Sunbury-on-Thames TW16
off Sutherland Av 217 BT96
Worcester Park KT4 221 CV102
Sutherland Gro, SW18 201 CY86
Teddington TW11 199 CE92
Sutherland Pl, W2 15 J8
Sutherland Rd, E17 123 DX54
N9 122 DU46
N17 122 DU52
W4 180 CS79
W13 159 CG72
Belvedere DA17 188 FA76
Croydon CR0 223 DN101
Enfield EN3 105 DX43
Southall UB1 158 BZ72
Sutherland Rd Path, E17 145 DX55
Sutherland Row, SW1 29 K10
Sutherland Sq, SE17 43 J1
Sutherland St, SW1 29 J10
Sutherland Wk, SE17 43 K1
Sutherland Way, Cuffley EN6 87 DK28
Sutlej Rd, SE7 186 EJ80
Sutterton St, N7 8 C5
SUTTON, SM1 - SM3 240 DB107
Sutton 240 DC107
SUTTON ABINGER, Dor. RH5 283 BU143
SUTTON AT HONE, Dart. DA4 230 FN95
Sutton at Hone C of E Prim Sch, Sutt.H. DA4 *off Church Rd* 210 FN94
Sutton Av, Slou. SL3 174 AW75
Woking GU21 248 AS119
Sutton Cl, Beck. BR3 225 EB95
Broxbourne EN10 71 DY19
Loughton IG10 124 EL45
Pinner HA5 137 BU57
Sutton Coll of Learning for Adults, Sutton Cen, Sutt. SM1 *off St. Nicholas Way* 240 DB106
Sutton W Cen, Sutt. SM1
off Robin Hood La 240 DA106
Sutton Common 222 DB103
Sutton Common Rd, Sutt. SM1, SM3 221 CZ101
Sutton Ct, W4 180 CQ79
Sutton SM2 240 DC107
Ware SG12 *off Crane Mead* 55 DY07
Sutton Ct Rd, E13 24 C3
W4 180 CQ80
Sutton SM1 240 DC107
Uxbridge UB10 157 BP67
Sutton Cres, Barn. EN5 101 CX43
Sutton Dene, Houns. TW3 178 CB81
Sutton Est, SW3 28 D10
W10 14 A6
Sutton Est, The, N1 8 G6
Sutton Gdns, Bark. IG11
off Sutton Rd 167 ES68
Croydon CR0 224 DT99
Merstham RH1 273 DK129
Sutton Gram Sch for Boys, Sutt. SM1 *off Manor La* 240 DC106
SUTTON GREEN, Guil. GU4 265 AZ125
Sutton Grn, Bark. IG11
off Sutton Rd 167 ES67
Sutton Grn Rd, Sutt.Grn GU4 264 AY126
Sutton Gro, Sutt. SM1 240 DD105
Sutton Hall Rd, Houns. TW5 178 CA80
Sutton Hts, Sutt. SM2 240 DD108
Sutton High Sch, Sutt. SM1
off Cheam Rd 240 DB107
Sutton Hill, Guil. GU4 265 BC129
Sutton Hosp, Sutt. SM2 240 DB110
★ **Sutton Ho**, E9 10 G3
Sutton Ho, Hem.H. HP2 62 BL16
Sutton La, EC1 19 H5
Abinger Common RH5 283 BV143
Banstead SM7 256 DB115
Hounslow TW3 178 BZ83
Slough SL3 175 BC78
Sutton SM2 240 DB111
Sutton La N, W4 180 CQ78
Sutton La S, W4 180 CQ79
Sutton Par, NW4
off Church Rd 141 CW56
Sutton Pk, Sutt.Grn GU4 265 AZ127
Sutton Pk Rd, Sutt. SM1 240 DB107
Sutton Path, Borwd. WD6
off Stratfield Rd 100 CN40
★ **Sutton Pl**, Guil. GU4 265 BA127
Sutton Pl, E9 10 G3
Abinger Hammer RH5 283 BT143
Dartford DA4 210 FN92
Slough SL3 175 BB79
Sutton Rd, E13 23 M4
E17 123 DX53
N10 120 DG54
Barking IG11 167 ES68
Hounslow TW5 178 CA81
St. Albans AL1 65 CH21
Watford WD17 98 BW41
Sutton Row, W1 17 P8
Suttons Av, Horn. RM12 150 FJ62
Suttons Gdns, Horn. RM12 150 FK62
Suttons La, Horn. RM12 150 FK64
Suttons Prim Sch, Horn. RM12 *off Suttons La* 150 FK63
Sutton Sq, E9 10 G3
Hounslow TW5 178 BZ81
Sutton St, E1 20 G10
Sutton's Way, EC1 19 K5
Sutton Wk, SE1 30 D3
Sutton Way, W10 14 A5
Hounslow TW5 178 BZ81
Swabey Rd, Slou. SL3 175 BA77
Swaby Rd, SW18 202 DC88
Swaffham Way, N22 121 DP52
Swaffield Prim Sch, SW18
off St. Ann's Hill 202 DC86
Swaffield Rd, SW18 202 DB87
Sevenoaks TN13 279 FJ122
Swain Cl, SW16 203 DH93
Swain Rd, Th.Hth. CR7 224 DQ99
Swains Cl, West Dr. UB7 176 BL75
Swains La, N6 142 DG62
Swainson Rd, W3 181 CT75
Swains Rd, SW17 202 DF94
Swain St, NW8 16 C4
Swaisland Dr, Cray. DA1 209 FF85
Swaisland Rd, Dart. DA1 209 FH85
Swakeleys Dr, Uxb. UB10 136 BM63
Swakeleys Rd, Ickhm UB10 136 BM62
Swakeleys Rbt, Uxb. UB9 136 BL63
Swakeleys Sch, Hlgdn UB10
off Clifton Gdns 157 BP68
Swale Cl, Aveley RM15 170 FQ72
Swaledale Cl, N11
off Ribblesdale Av 120 DG51
Swaledale Rd, Dart. DA2 210 FQ88
Swale Rd, Dart. DA1 189 FG83
Swaley's Way, S.Ock. RM15 171 FX72
Swallands Rd, SE6 205 EA90
Swallow Cl, SE14 45 H7
Bushey WD23 116 CC46
Chafford Hundred RM16 191 FW77
Erith DA8 189 FE81
Greenhithe DA9 211 FT85
Rickmansworth WD3 114 BJ45
Staines TW18 195 BF91
Swallow Ct, Hert. SG14 54 DQ09
Swallowdale, Iver SL0 155 BD69
South Croydon CR2 243 DX109
Swallowdale La, Hem.H. HP2 63 BP17
Swallow Dell Prim Sch, Welw.G.C. AL7
off Blackthorn Rd 52 DA10
Swallow Dr, NW10
off Kingfisher Way 160 CR65
Northolt UB5 158 CA68
Swallow End, Welw.G.C. AL7 51 CZ09
Swallowfield, NW1
off Munster Sq 17 K3
Englefield Green TW20
off Heronfield 194 AV93
Swallowfield Rd, SE7 186 EH78
Swallow Flds, Iver SL0 155 BD70
Swallowfields, Nthflt DA11 212 GE90
Welwyn Garden City AL7 51 CZ09
Swallowfield Way, Hayes UB3 177 BR75
Swallow Gdns, SW16 203 DK92
Hatfield AL10 67 CU20
Swallow Ho, NW8
off Allitsen Rd 6 C10
Swallow La, Mid Holm. RH5 285 CH142
St. Albans AL1 65 CH23
Swallow Pas, W1
off Swallow Pl 17 K9
Swallow Pl, W1 17 K9
Swallows, Harl. CM17 58 EW11
Swallows, The, Welw.G.C. AL7 51 CZ05
Swallows Oak, Abb.L. WD5 81 BT31
Swallow St, E6 25 H7
W1 29 M1
Iver SL0 155 BD69
Swallowtail Cl, Orp. BR5 228 EX98
Swallowtail Wk, Berk. HP4
off Springfield Rd 60 AT16
Swallow Wk, Horn. RM12
off Heron Flight Av 169 FH65
Swaminarayan Sch, The, NW10 *off Brentfield Rd* 160 CR65
Swanage Ho, SW8 42 C5
Swanage Rd, E4 123 EC52
SW18 202 DC86
Swanage Waye, Hayes UB4 158 BW72
Swan All, Wat. WD18
off Lower High St 98 BW43
Swan & Pike Rd, Enf. EN3 105 EA38
Swan App, E6 24 G7
Swan Av, Upmin. RM14 151 FT60
Swanbourne, SE17 31 J9
Swanbourne Dr, Horn. RM12 150 FJ64
Swanbridge Rd, Bexh. DA7 188 FA81
● **Swan Business Pk**, Dart. DA1 190 FJ84
● **Swan Cen, The**, SW17
off Rosemary Rd 202 DC90
Swan Cl, E17 123 DY53
Chesham HP5 76 AP27
Croydon CR0 224 DS101
Feltham TW13 198 BY91
Orpington BR5 228 EU97
Rickmansworth WD3
off Parsonage Rd 114 BK45
Swan Ct, SW3 40 D1
Guildford GU1 264 AX132
Hemel Hempstead HP1
off Waterhouse St 62 BJ21
Swandon Way, SW18 202 DB85
Swan Dr, NW9 118 CS54
Swanfield Rd, Wal.Cr. EN8 89 DY33
Swanfield St, E2 20 A3
Swanhill, Welw.G.C. AL7 52 DA06
Swan Junct, The, W.Wick. BR4 225 EC103
Swanland Rd, N.Mymms AL9 85 CV28
South Mimms EN6 85 CV33
Swan La, EC4 31 L1
N20 120 DC48
Dartford DA1 209 FF87
Guildford GU1 280 AX135
Loughton IG10 124 EJ45
Swanlea Sch, E1 20 E6
SWANLEY, BR8 229 FE98
Swanley 229 FD98
Swanley Adult Ed Cen, Swan. BR8 *off St. Marys Rd* 229 FE97
Swanley Bar La, Pot.B. EN6 86 DB28
Swanley Bypass, Sid. DA14 229 FC97
Swanley BR8 229 FC97
Swanley Cen, Swan. BR8 229 FE97
Swanley Cres, Pot.B. EN6 86 DB29
Swanley La, Swan. BR8 229 FF97
Swanley Rd, Well. DA16 188 EW81
Swanley Sch, Swan. BR8
off St. Marys Rd 229 FE97
SWANLEY VILLAGE, Swan. BR8 230 FJ95
Swanley Village Rd, Swan. BR8 229 FH95
Swan Mead, SE1 31 N7
Hemel Hempstead HP3 80 BM25
Swan Ms, SW6
off Purser's Cross Rd 39 J6
Romford RM7 149 FB56
Swan Mill Gdns, Dor. RH4 269 CJ134
Swanns Meadow, Bkhm KT23 268 CA126
Swan Pas, E1
off Cartwright St 32 B1
Swan Path, E10 *off Jesse Rd* 145 EC60
Kingston upon Thames KT1
off Villiers Rd 220 CL97
Swan Pl, SW13 181 CT82
Swan Rd, SE16 33 H4
SE18 36 F7
Feltham TW13 198 BY92
Swan Rd, Iver SL0 155 BF72
Southall UB1 158 CB72
West Drayton UB7 176 BK75
Swans Cl, St.Alb. AL4 66 CL21
SWANSCOMBE, DA10 212 FZ86
Swanscombe 212 FZ85
Swanscombe Ho, W11
off St. Anns Rd 26 D2
Swanscombe Rd, W4 180 CS78
W11 26 D3
Swanscombe St, Swans. DA10 212 FY87
Swansea Cl, Coll.Row RM5 127 FD52
Swansea Ct, E16 37 P3
Swansea Rd, Enf. EN3 104 DW42
London Heathrow Airport TW6
off Shrewsbury Rd 197 BR86
Swanshope, Loug. IG10 107 EP40
Swansland Gdns, E17
off McEntee Av 123 DY53
Swanston Path, Wat. WD19 116 BW48
Swan St, SE1 31 K6
Isleworth TW7 179 CH83
Swan Ter, Wind. SL4
off Mill La 173 AN80
Swanton Gdns, SW19 201 CX88
Swanton Rd, Erith DA8 189 FB80
Swan Valley Comm Sch, Swans. DA10 *off Southfleet Rd* 212 FZ87
Swan Wk, Rom. RM1
off Market Pl 149 FE57
Swan Wk, SW3 40 E2
Shepperton TW17 217 BS101
Swan Way, Enf. EN3 105 DX40
Swanwick Cl, SW15 201 CT87
Swanworth La, Mick. RH5 269 CH128
Swan Yd, N1 8 G5
Swaton Rd, E3 22 B5
Swaylands Rd, Belv. DA17 188 FA79
Swaynesland Rd, Eden. TN8 277 EM134
Swaynes La, Guil. GU1 265 BE134
Swaythling Cl, N18 122 DV49
Swaythling Ho, SW15
off Tunworth Cres 201 CT86
Swedenborg Gdns, E1 20 D10
Sweden Gate, SE16 33 L7
Swedish Sch, The, SW13
off Lonsdale Rd 181 CT79
Sweeney Cres, SE1 32 B5
Sweeps Ditch Cl, Stai. TW18 216 BG95
Sweeps La, Egh. TW20 195 AZ92
Orpington BR5 228 EX99
Sweet Briar, Welw.G.C. AL7 52 DA11
Sweetbriar Cl, Hem.H. HP1 62 BG17
Sweet Briar Grn, N9 122 DT48
Sweet Briar Gro, N9 122 DT48
Sweet Briar La, Epsom KT18 238 CR114
Sweet Briar Wk, N18 122 DT49
Sweetcroft La, Uxb. UB10 156 BN66
Sweet La, Peasl. GU5 283 BR143
Sweetmans Av, Pnr. HA5 138 BX55
Sweets Way, N20 120 DD47
Swetenham Wk, SE18
off Raglan Rd 187 EQ78
Swete St, E13 23 P1
Sweyne Rd, Swans. DA10 212 FY86
Sweyn Pl, SE3 47 P9
Sweyns, Harl. CM17 74 EW17
Swievelands Rd, Bigg.H. TN16 260 EH119
Swift Cl, E17 123 DY52
SE28 168 EV73
Harrow HA2 138 CB61
Hayes UB3 *off Church Rd* 157 BT72
Stanstead Abbotts SG12 55 EC12
Upminster RM14 151 FS60
Swiftfields, Welw.G.C. AL7 51 CZ08
Swift Rd, Felt. TW13 198 BY90
Southall UB2 178 BZ76
Swiftsden Way, Brom. BR1 206 EE93
Swift St, SW6 38 F6
Swiftsure Rd, Chaff.Hun. RM16 191 FW77
SWILLET, THE, Rick. WD3 95 BB44
Swinbrook Rd, W10 14 F6
Swinburne Ct, SE5
off Basingdon Way 184 DR84
Swinburne Cres, Croy. CR0 224 DW100
Swinburne Gdns, Til. RM18 193 GH82
Swinburne Rd, SW15 181 CU84
Swinderby Rd, Wem. HA0 160 CL65
Swindon Cl, Ilf. IG3
off Salisbury Rd 147 ES61
Romford RM3 128 FM50
Swindon Gdns, Rom. RM3 128 FM50
Swindon La, Rom. RM3 128 FM50
Swindon Rd, Lon.Hthrw Air. TW6 197 BQ85
Swindon St, W12 161 CV74
Swinfield Cl, Felt. TW13 198 BY91
Swinford Gdns, SW9 42 G10
Swingate La, SE18 187 ES79
Swing Gate First & Nurs Sch, Berk. HP4
off Swing Gate La 60 AX20
Swing Gate La, Berk. HP4 60 AX22
Swinnerton St, E9 11 L3
Swinton Cl, Wem. HA9 140 CP60
Swinton Pl, WC1 18 C2
Swinton St, WC1 18 C2
Swires Shaw, Kes. BR2 244 EK105
Swiss Av, Wat. WD18 97 BS42
Swiss Cl, Wat. WD18 97 BS41
Swiss Cottage 6 A6
Swiss Cottage Sch, NW8 6 B7
Swiss Ct, W1 29 P1
Swiss Ter, NW6 6 A6
Switch Ho, E14 23 H10
Swithland Gdns, SE9 207 EN91
Sword Cl, Brox. EN10 71 DX20
Swyncombe Av, W5 179 CH77
Swynford Gdns, NW4 141 CU56
Sybil Elgar Sch, W5
off Florence Rd 160 CL73
Southall UB2
off Havelock Rd 178 BZ76
Sybil Ms, N4 143 DP58
Sybil Phoenix Cl, SE8 33 K10
Sybourn Infants' Sch, E17
off Sybourn St 145 DZ59
Sybourn Jun Sch, E17
off Sybourn St 145 DZ59
Sybourn St, E17 145 DZ59
Sycamore App, Crox.Grn WD3 97 BQ43
Sycamore Av, E3 11 N8
W5 179 CK76
Hatfield AL10 67 CU19
Hayes UB3 157 BS73
Sycamore Av, Sid. DA15 207 ET86
Upminster RM14 150 FN62
Sycamore Cl, E16 23 J5
N9 *off Pycroft Way* 122 DU49
SE9 206 EL89
W3 *off Bromyard Av* 160 CS74
Amersham HP6 77 AR37
Barnet EN4 102 DD44
Bushey WD23 98 BY40
Carshalton SM5 240 DF105
Chalfont St. Giles HP8 112 AU48
Cheshunt EN7 88 DT27
Edgware HA8 *off Ash Cl* 118 CQ49
Feltham TW13 197 BU90
Fetcham KT22 253 CE123
Gravesend DA12 213 GK87
Loughton IG10 107 EP40
Northolt UB5 158 BY67
South Croydon CR2 242 DS106
Tilbury RM18 193 GG81
Watford WD25 97 BV35
West Drayton UB7 156 BM73
Sycamore Ct, Surb. KT6
off Penners Gdns 220 CL101
Sycamore Dene, Chesh. HP5 76 AR28
Sycamore Dr, Brwd. CM14
off Copperfield Gdns 130 FW46
Park Street AL2 83 CD27
Swanley BR8 229 FE97
Sycamore Fld, Harl. CM19 73 EN19
Sycamore Gdns, W6 181 CV75
Mitcham CR4 222 DD96
Sycamore Gro, NW9 140 CQ59
SE6 205 EC86
SE20 204 DU94
New Malden KT3 220 CR97
Romford RM2 127 FG54
Sycamore Hill, N11 120 DG51
Sycamore Ho, NW3
off Maitland Pk Vil 6 F4
Warlingham CR6
off East Parkside 259 EB115
Sycamore Ms, SW4 183 DJ83
Sycamore Pl, Brom. BR1 227 EN97
Sycamore Ri, Bans. SM7 239 CX114
Berkhamsted HP4 60 AX20
Chalfont St. Giles HP8 112 AU48
Sycamore Rd, SW19 201 CW93
Amersham HP6 77 AR37
Chalfont St. Giles HP8 112 AU48
Croxley Green WD3 97 BQ43
Dartford DA1 210 FK88
Guildford GU1 264 AX134
Sycamores, The, Aveley RM15
off Dacre Av 171 FR74
Bookham KT23 252 CC124
Hemel Hempstead HP3 61 BF23
Radlett WD7 83 CH34
Sycamore St, EC1 19 J5
Sycamore Wk, W10 14 E4
Englefield Green TW20 194 AV93
George Green SL3 154 AY72
Ilford IG6 *off Civic Way* 147 EQ56
Reigate RH2 288 DC137
Sycamore Way, S.Ock. RM15 171 FX70
Teddington TW11 199 CJ93
Thornton Heath CR7 223 DN99
SYDENHAM, SE26 204 DW92
Sydenham 204 DW91
Sydenham Av, N21
off Fleming Dr 103 DM43
SE26 204 DV92
Sydenham Cl, Rom. RM1 149 FF56
Sydenham Cotts, SE12 206 EJ89
Sydenham Gdns, Slou. SL1 173 AQ76
Sydenham High Sch, SE26
off Westwood Hill 204 DV92
Jun Dept, SE26
off Westwood Hill 204 DV91
Sydenham Hill 204 DT90
Sydenham Hill, SE23 204 DV88
SE26 204 DU90
Sydenham Hill Est, SE26 204 DU90
Sydenham Pk, SE26 204 DW90
Sydenham Pk Rd, SE26 204 DW90
Sydenham Pl, SE27
off Lansdowne Hill 203 DP90
Sydenham Ri, SE23 204 DV89
Sydenham Rd, SE26 204 DW91
Croydon CR0 224 DR101
Guildford GU1 280 AX136
Sydenham Sch, SE26
off Dartmouth Rd 204 DV90
Sydmons Ct, SE23 204 DW87
Sydner Ms, N16 144 DT63
Sydner Rd, N16 144 DT63
Sydney Av, Pur. CR8 241 DM112
Sydney Chapman Way, Barn. EN5 101 CZ40
Sydney Cl, SW3 28 B9
Sydney Cres, Ashf. TW15 197 BP93
Sydney Gro, NW4 141 CW57
Slough SL1 153 AQ72
Sydney Ms, SW3 28 B9
Sydney Pl, SW7 28 B9
Guildford GU1 281 AZ135
Sydney Rd, E11
off Mansfield Rd 146 EH58
N8 143 DN56
N10 120 DG53
SE2 188 EW76
SW20 221 CX96
W13 159 CG74
Bexleyheath DA6 188 EX84
Enfield EN2 104 DR42
Feltham TW14 197 BU88
Guildford GU1 281 AZ135
Ilford IG6 125 EQ54
Richmond TW9 180 CL84
Sidcup DA14 207 ES91
Sutton SM1 240 DA105
Teddington TW11 199 CF92
Tilbury RM18 193 GG82
Watford WD18 97 BS43
Woodford Green IG8 124 EG49
Sydney Russell Comp Sch, Dag. RM9 *off Parsloes Av* 148 EX64
Sydney St, SW3 28 C10
Syke Cluan, Iver SL0 175 BE75
Syke Ings, Iver SL0 175 BE76
Sykes Dr, Stai. TW18 196 BH92

Sykes Rd, Slou. SL1 153 AP72
Sylvana Cl, Uxb. UB10 156 BM67
Sylvan Av, N3 120 DA54
N22 121 DM52
NW7 119 CT51
Hornchurch RM11 150 FL58
Romford RM6 148 EZ58
Sylvan Cl, Chaff.Hun. RM16 192 FY77
Hemel Hempstead HP3 62 BN21
Oxted RH8 276 EH129
South Croydon CR2 242 DV110
Woking GU22 249 BB117
Sylvan Ct, N12 120 DB49
Sylvandale, Welw.G.C. AL7 52 DC10
Sylvan Est, SE19 224 DT95
Sylvan Gdns, Surb. KT6 219 CK101
Sylvan Gro, NW2 4 D1
SE15 44 F4
Sylvan Hill, SE19 224 DS95
Sylvan Ms, Green. DA9
off Watermans Way 191 FV84
Sylvan Rd, E7 13 P4
E11 146 EG57
E17 145 EA57
SE19 224 DT95
Ilford IG1 147 EQ61
Sylvan Wk, Brom. BR1 227 EM97
Sylvan Way, Chig. IG7 126 EV48
Dagenham RM8 148 EV62
Redhill RH1 288 DG135
Welwyn Garden City AL7 52 DC10
West Wickham BR4 244 EE105
Sylverdale Rd, Croy. CR0 223 DP104
Purley CR8 241 DP113
Sylvester Av, Chis. BR7 207 EM93
Sylvester Gdns, Ilf. IG6 126 EV50
Sylvester Path, E8 10 F4
Sylvester Rd, E8 10 F4
E17 145 DZ59
N2 120 DC54
Wembley HA0 139 CJ64
Sylvestres, Rvrhd TN13 278 FD121
Sylvestrus Cl, Kings.T. KT1 220 CN95
Sylvia Av, Hutt. CM13 131 GC47
Pinner HA5 116 BZ51
Sylvia Ct, Wem. HA9
off Harrow Rd 160 CP66
Sylvia Gdns, Wem. HA9 160 CP66
Sch Sylvia Young Thea Sch, NW1 16 D5
Symes Ms, NW1 7 L10
Symington Ho, SE1 31 L7
Symington Ms, E9 11 K2
Symister Ms, N1 19 N3
Symonds Ct, Chsht EN8 89 DX28
Symonds Hyde, Hat. AL10 50 CP13
Symons Cl, SE15 44 G9
Symons St, SW3 28 F9
Symphony Cl, Edg. HA8 118 CP52
Symphony Ms, W10 14 F2
Syon Gate Way, Brent. TW8 179 CG80
★ Syon Ho & Pk, Brent. TW8 179 CJ81
⇌ Syon Lane 179 CG80
Syon La, Islw. TW7 179 CH80
Syon Pk Gdns, Islw. TW7 179 CF80
Sch Syon Pk Sch, Islw. TW7
off Twickenham Rd 179 CH81
Syon Vista, Rich. TW9 179 CK81
Syracuse Av, Rain. RM13 170 FL69
Uni Syracuse Uni - London Program, WC1 18 B6
Syringa Ct, Grays RM17 192 GD80
Sythwood, Wok. GU21 248 AV117
Sch Sythwood Prim Sch, Horsell GU21 *off Sythwood* 248 AV116

T

Tabard Cen, SE1
off Prioress St 31 M7
Tabard Gdns Est, SE1 31 M5
Tabard St, SE1 31 L5
Tabarin Way, Epsom KT17 255 CW116
Tabernacle Av, E13 23 N5
Tabernacle St, EC2 19 M5
Tableer Av, SW4 203 DJ85
Tabley Rd, N7 143 DL63
Tabor Gdns, Sutt. SM3 239 CZ107
Tabor Gro, SW19 201 CY94
Tabor Rd, W6 181 CV76
Tabors Ct, Shenf. CM15
off Shenfield Rd 131 FZ45
Tabrums Way, Upmin. RM14 151 FS59
Tachbrook Est, SW1 41 P1
Tachbrook Ms, SW1 29 L8
Tachbrook Rd, Felt. TW14 197 BT87
Southall UB2 178 BX77
Uxbridge UB8 156 BJ68
Tachbrook St, SW1 29 M9
Tack Ms, SE4 46 A10
Tadema Ho, NW8 16 B5
Tadema Rd, SW10 39 P4
Tadlows Cl, Upmin. RM14 150 FP64
Tadmor Cl, Sun. TW16 217 BT98
Tadmor St, W12 26 C3
Tadorne Rd, Tad. KT20 255 CW121
TADWORTH, KT20 255 CV121
⇌ Tadworth 255 CW122
Tadworth Av, N.Mal. KT3 221 CT99
Tadworth Cl, Tad. KT20 255 CX122
Tadworth Par, Horn. RM12
off Maylands Av 149 FH63
Sch Tadworth Prim Sch, Tad. KT20
off Tadworth St 255 CX122
Tadworth Rd, NW2 141 CU61
Tadworth St, Tad. KT20 255 CW123
Taeping St, E14 34 C8
Taffy's How, Mitch. CR4 222 DE97
Taft Way, E3 22 D2
Tagalie Pl, Shenley WD7 84 CL32
Tagg's Island, Hmptn. TW12 219 CD96
Tailworth St, E1 20 C7
Tait Ct, SW8 *off Darsley Dr* 41 P6
Tait Rd, Croy. CR0 224 DS101
● Tait Rd Ind Est, Croy. CR0 224 DS101
Tait St, E1 20 E9
Takeley Cl, Rom. RM5 127 FD54
Waltham Abbey EN9 89 ED33
Takhar Ms, SW11 40 D9
Talacre Rd, NW5 7 H4
Jct Talbot, The, N.Wld Bas. CM16 75 FD24
Talbot Av, N2 142 DD55
Slough SL3 175 AZ76
Watford WD19 116 BY45
Talbot Cl, N15 144 DT56
Reigate RH2 288 DB135
Talbot Ct, EC3 19 M10
Hemel Hempstead HP3
off Forest Av 62 BK22
Talbot Cres, NW4 141 CU57
Talbot Gdns, Ilf. IG3 148 EU61
Talbot Ho, E14 22 C8
N7 *off Harvist Est* 143 DN62
Talbot Pl, SE3 47 J8
Datchet SL3 174 AW81
Talbot Rd, E6 167 EN68
E7 146 EG63
N6 142 DG58
N15 144 DT56
N22 121 DJ54
SE22 184 DS84
W2 15 K8
W11 15 H8
W13 159 CG73
Ashford TW15 196 BK92
Carshalton SM5 240 DG106
Dagenham RM9 168 EZ65
Harrow HA3 117 CF54
Hatfield AL10 67 CU15
Isleworth TW7 179 CG84
Rickmansworth WD3 114 BL46
Southall UB2 178 BY77
Thornton Heath CR7 224 DR98
Twickenham TW2 199 CE88
Wembley HA0 139 CK64
Talbot Sq, W2 16 B9
Talbot St, Hert. SG13 54 DS09
Talbot Wk, NW10
off Garnet Rd 160 CS65
W11 14 E9
Talbot Yd, SE1 31 L3
Talbrook, Brwd. CM14 130 FT48
Taleworth Cl, Ashtd. KT21 253 CK120
Taleworth Pk, Ashtd. KT21 253 CK120
Taleworth Rd, Ashtd. KT21 253 CK119
Talfourd Pl, SE15 44 A7
Talfourd Rd, SE15 44 A7
Talfourd Way, Red. RH1 288 DF137
Talgarth Rd, W6 26 B10
W14 26 D10
Talgarth Wk, NW9 140 CS57
Talisman Cl, Ilf. IG3 148 EV60
Talisman Sq, SE26 204 DU91
Talisman Way, Epsom KT17 255 CW116
Wembley HA9 140 CM62
Tallack Cl, Har. HA3 117 CE52
Tallack Rd, E10 145 DZ60
Tall Elms Cl, Brom. BR2 226 EF99
Tallents Cl, Sutt.H. DA4 210 FP94
Tallis Cl, E16 24 A9
Tallis Ct, Gidea Pk RM2 150 FJ55
Tallis Gro, SE7 186 EH79
Tallis St, EC4 18 F10
Tallis Vw, NW10 160 CR65
Tallis Way, Borwd. WD6 99 CK39
Warley CM14 130 FV50
Tall Oaks, Amer. HP6 77 AR37
Tallon Rd, Hutt. CM13 131 GE43
Tallow Cl, Dag. RM9 168 EX65
Tallow Rd, Brent. TW8 179 CJ79
Tall Trees, SW16 223 DM97
Colnbrook SL3 175 BE81
Tall Trees Cl, Horn. RM11 150 FK58
Jct Tally Ho Cor, N12 120 DC50
Tally Rd, Oxt. RH8 276 EL131
Talma Gdns, Twick. TW2 199 CE86
Talmage Cl, SE23
off Tyson Rd 204 DW87
Talman Gro, Stan. HA7 117 CK51
Talma Rd, SW2 183 DN84
Sch Talmud Torah Machzikei Hadass Sch, E5
off Clapton Common 144 DU59
Talus Cl, Purf. RM19
off Brimfield Rd 191 FR77
Talwin St, E3 22 D3
Tamar Cl, E3 11 P9
Upminster RM14 151 FS58
Tamar Dr, Aveley RM15 170 FQ72
Tamar Grn, Hem.H. HP2 62 BM15
Tamarind Cl, Guil. GU2 264 AU129
Tamarind Yd, E1 32 D2
Tamarisk Cl, St.Alb. AL3
off New Grns Av 65 CD16
South Ockendon RM15 171 FW70
Tamarisk Rd, S.Ock. RM15 171 FW69
Tamarisk Sq, W12 161 CT73
Tamarisk Way, Slou. SL1 173 AN75
Tamarix Cres, Lon.Col. AL2 83 CG26
Tamar Sq, Wdf.Grn. IG8 124 EH51
Tamar St, SE7 36 G8
Tamar Way, N17
off Park Vw Rd 144 DU55
Slough SL3 175 BB78
Tamblin Way, Hat. AL10 66 CS17
Tamerton Sq, Wok. GU22 249 AY119
Tamesis Gdns, Wor.Pk. KT4 220 CS102
Tamesis Strand, Grav. DA12 213 GL92
Tamian Way, Houns. TW4 178 BW84
Tamworth Av, Wdf.Grn. IG8 124 EE51
Tamworth La, Mitch. CR4 223 DH96
Tamworth Pk, Mitch. CR4 223 DH98
Tamworth Pl, Croy. CR0 224 DQ103
Tamworth Rd, Croy. CR0 223 DP103
Hertford SG13 54 DS08
Tamworth St, SW6 39 J2
Tancred Rd, N4 143 DP58
🔒 Tandem Cen, SW19 222 DD95
Tandem Way, SW19 222 DD95
TANDRIDGE, Oxt. RH8 275 EA133
Tandridge Ct, Cat. CR3 258 DU122
Tandridge Dr, Orp. BR6 227 ER102
Tandridge Gdns, S.Croy. CR2 242 DT113
Tandridge Hill La, Gdse. RH9 275 DZ128
Tandridge La, Tand. RH8 275 EA131
Tandridge Pl, Orp. BR6 227 ER102
Tandridge Rd, Warl. CR6 259 DX119
Tanfield Av, NW2 141 CT63
Tanfield Cl, Chsht EN7 88 DU27
Tanfield Rd, Croy. CR0 242 DQ105
Tangent Link, Harold Hill RM3 128 FK53
Tangent Rd, Rom. RM3
off Ashton Rd 128 FK53
Tangier La, Eton SL4 173 AR79
Tangier Rd, Guil. GU1 281 BA135
Richmond TW10 180 CP83
Tangier Way, Tad. KT20 255 CY117
Tangier Wd, Tad. KT20 255 CY118
Tangleberry Cl, Brom. BR1 226 EL98
Tangle Tree Cl, N3 120 DB54
Tanglewood Cl, Croy. CR0 224 DW104
Longcross KT16 214 AV104
Stanmore HA7 117 CE47
Uxbridge UB10 156 BN69
Woking GU22 249 BD116
Tanglewood Way, Felt. TW13 197 BV90
Tangley Gro, SW15 201 CT87
Tangley La, Guil. GU3 264 AT130
Tangley Pk Rd, Hmptn. TW12 198 BZ93
Tanglyn Av, Shep. TW17 217 BP99
Tangmere Cres, Horn. RM12 169 FH65
Tangmere Gdns, Nthlt. UB5 158 BW68
Tangmere Gro, Kings.T. KT2 199 CK92
Tangmere Way, NW9 118 CS54
Tanhouse Rd, Oxt. RH8 275 ED132
Tanhurst Wk, SE2
off Alsike Rd 188 EX76
Tankerton Rd, Surb. KT6 220 CM103
Tankerton St, WC1 18 B3
Tankerton Ter, Croy. CR0
off Mitcham Rd 223 DM101
Tankerville Rd, SW16 203 DK93
Tank Hill Rd, Purf. RM19 190 FN78
Tank La, Purf. RM19 190 FN77
Tankridge Rd, NW2 141 CV61
Tanner Pt, E13 13 N9
Tanners Cl, St.Alb. AL3 64 CC19
Walton-on-Thames KT12 217 BV100
Tanners Ct, Brock. RH3 286 CQ138
Tanners Cres, Hert. SG13 54 DQ11
Tanners Dean, Lthd. KT22 253 CJ122
Tanners End La, N18 122 DS49
Tannersfield, Shalf. GU4 280 AY142
Tanners Hill, SE8 45 P7
Abbots Langley WD5 81 BT31
Tanners La, Ilf. IG6 147 EQ55
Tanners Meadow, Brock. RH3 286 CP138
Tanners Ms, SE8 45 P7
Tanner St, SE1 31 P5
Barking IG11 167 EQ65
Tanners Way, Hunsdon SG12 56 EJ06
Tanners Wd Cl, Abb.L. WD5
off Tanners Wd La 81 BS32
Sch Tanners Wd JMI Sch, Abb.L. WD5
off Hazelwood La 81 BS32
Tanners Wd La, Abb.L. WD5 81 BS32
Tanners Yd, E2 20 E1
Tannery, The, Red. RH1 272 DE134
Tannery Cl, Beck. BR3 225 DX99
Dagenham RM10 149 FB62
Tannery La, Bramley GU5 280 AY144
Send GU23 249 BF122
Tannington Ter, N5 143 DN62
Tannsfeld Rd, SE26 205 DX92
Tannsfield Dr, Hem.H. HP2 62 BM18
Tannsmore Cl, Hem.H. HP2 62 BM18
Tansley Cl, N7 7 P2
Tanswell Est, SE1 30 E5
Tanswell St, SE1 30 E5
Tansy Cl, E6 25 M9
Guildford GU4 265 BC132
Romford RM3 128 FL51
Tansycroft, Welw.G.C. AL7 52 DB08
Tantallon Rd, SW12 202 DG88
Tant Av, E16 23 L8
Tantony Gro, Rom. RM6 148 EX55
Tanworth Cl, Nthwd. HA6 115 BQ51
Tanworth Gdns, Pnr. HA5 115 BV54
Tanyard Ho, Brent. TW8
off London Rd 179 CJ80
Tanyard La, Bex. DA5 208 FA88
Tanyard Way, Horl. RH6 291 DH146
Tanys Dell, Harl. CM20 58 EU12
Sch Tany's Dell Comm Prim Sch, Harl. CM20 *off Mowbray Rd* 58 EU12
Tanza Rd, NW3 142 DF63
Tapestry Cl, Sutt. SM2 240 DB108
TAPLOW, Maid. SL6 152 AE70
⇌ Taplow 152 AF72
Taplow, NW3 6 B7
SE17 31 M10
Taplow Common Rd, Burn. SL1 152 AG67
Taplow Rd, N13 122 DQ49
Taplow SL6 152 AG71
Taplow St, N1 19 K1
Tapners Rd, Bet. RH3 287 CT139
Leigh RH2 287 CT139
Tappesfield Rd, SE15 44 G10
Tapp St, E1 20 E4
Tapster St, Barn. EN5 101 CZ42
Tara Ms, N8 143 DK58
Taransay, Hem.H. HP3 63 BP22
Taransay Wk, N1 9 L4
Tarbay La, Oakley Grn SL4 172 AH82
Tarbert Ms, N15 144 DS57
Tarbert Rd, SE22 204 DS85
Tarbert Wk, E1 20 G10
Target Cl, Felt. TW14 197 BS86
Jct Target Rbt, Nthlt. UB5
off Western Av 158 BZ67
Tarham Cl, Horl. RH6 290 DE146
Tariff Cres, SE8 33 N8
Tariff Rd, N17 122 DU51
Tarleton Gdns, SE23 204 DV88
Tarling Cl, Sid. DA14 208 EV90
Tarling Rd, E16 23 M9
N2 120 DC54
Tarling St, E1 20 G9
Tarling St Est, E1 20 G9
Tarmac Way, West Dr. UB7 176 BH80
Tarnbank, Enf. EN2 103 DL43
Tarn St, SE1 31 J7
Tarnwood Pk, SE9 207 EM88
Tarnworth Rd, Rom. RM3 128 FN50
Tarpan Way, Brox. EN10 89 DZ26
Tarquin Ho, SE26 204 DU91
Tarragon Cl, SE14 45 L4
Tarragon Dr, Guil. GU2 264 AU129
Tarragon Gro, SE26 205 DX93
Tarrant Pl, W1 16 E7
Tarrington Cl, SW16 203 DK90
Tartar Rd, Cob. KT11 236 BW113
Tarver Rd, SE17 43 H1
Tarves Way, SE10 46 D4
Tash Pl, N11 *off Woodland Rd* 121 DH50
Sch TASIS, The American Sch in England, Thorpe TW20
off Coldharbour La 215 BC97
Tasker Cl, Harling. UB3 177 BQ80
Tasker Ho, Bark. IG11
off Dovehouse Mead 167 ER68
Tasker Rd, NW3 6 E3
Grays RM16 193 GH76
Tasman Ct, E14
off Westferry Rd 34 C9
Sunbury-on-Thames TW16 197 BS94
Tasmania Ho, Til. RM18
off Hobart Rd 193 GG81
Tasmania Ter, N18 122 DQ51
Tasman Rd, SW9 183 DL83
Tasman Wk, E16 24 E9
Tasso Rd, W6 38 E2
Tatam Rd, NW10 160 CQ66
Tatchbury Ho, SW15
off Tunworth Cres 201 CT86
Tate & Lyle Jetty, E16 36 G5
★ Tate Britain, SW1 30 A9
Tate Cl, Lthd. KT22 253 CJ123
Tate Gdns, Bushey WD23 117 CE45
★ Tate Modern, SE1 31 H2
Tate Rd, E16 37 J3
Chalfont St. Peter SL9 113 AZ50
Sutton SM1 240 DA106
Tatham Pl, NW8 6 B10
TATLING END, Ger.Cr. SL9 135 BB61
Tatnell Rd, SE23 205 DY86
TATSFIELD, West. TN16 260 EL120
Tatsfield App Rd, Tats. TN16 260 EH123
Tatsfield Av, Lwr Naze. EN9 71 ED23
Tatsfield La, Tats. TN16 261 EM121
Sch Tatsfield Prim Sch, Tats. TN16
off Church La 260 EK121
TATTENHAM CORNER, Epsom KT18 255 CV118
⇌ Tattenham Corner 255 CV118
Tattenham Cor Rd, Epsom KT18 255 CT117
Tattenham Cres, Epsom KT18 255 CU118
Tattenham Gro, Epsom KT18 255 CV118
Tattenham Way, Tad. KT20 255 CX118
Tattersall Cl, SE9 206 EL85
Tattle Hill, Hert. SG14 53 DL05
Tatton Cres, N16 144 DT59
Tatton St, Harl. CM17 58 EW14
Tatum St, SE17 31 M9
Tauber Cl, Els. WD6 100 CM42
Tauheed Cl, N4 144 DQ61
Taunton Av, SW20 221 CV96
Caterham CR3 258 DT123
Hounslow TW3 178 CC82
Taunton Cl, Bexh. DA7 189 FD82
Ilford IG6 125 ET51
Sutton SM3 222 DA102
Taunton Dr, N2 120 DC54
Enfield EN2 103 DN41
Taunton La, Couls. CR5 257 DN119
Taunton Ms, NW1 16 E5
Taunton Pl, NW1 16 E4
Taunton Rd, SE12 206 EE85
Greenford UB6 158 CB67
Northfleet DA11 212 GA85
Romford RM3 128 FJ49
Taunton Vale, Grav. DA12 213 GK90
Taunton Way, Stan. HA7 140 CL55
Tavern Cl, Cars. SM5 222 DE101
Taverners, Hem.H. HP2 62 BL18
Taverners Cl, W11 26 E3
Taverner Sq, N5 9 J1
Taverners Way, E4 124 EE46
Hoddesdon EN11 71 EA17
Tavern La, SW9 42 F8
Tavistock Av, E17 145 DY55
NW7 119 CX52
Perivale UB6 159 CG68
St. Albans AL1 64 CC23
Tavistock Cl, N16 9 P3
Potters Bar EN6 86 DD31
Romford RM3 128 FK53
St. Albans AL1 65 CD24
Staines TW18 196 BK94
Tavistock Ct, WC2
off Tavistock St 18 B10
Tavistock Cres, W11 15 H7
Mitcham CR4 223 DL98
Tavistock Gdns, Ilf. IG3 147 ES63
Tavistock Gate, Croy. CR0 224 DR102
Tavistock Gro, Croy. CR0 224 DR101
Tavistock Ms, E18
off Tavistock Pl 146 EG56
Tavistock Pl, E18 146 EG56
N14 103 DH44
WC1 17 P4
Tavistock Rd, E7 146 EF63
E15 13 L5
E18 146 EG55
N4 144 DR58
NW10 161 CT68
W11 14 G8
Bromley BR2 226 EF98
Carshalton SM5 222 DD102
Croydon CR0 224 DR102
Edgware HA8 118 CN53
Uxbridge UB10 137 BQ64
Watford WD24 98 BX39
Welling DA16 188 EW81
West Drayton UB7 156 BK74
Tavistock Sq, WC1 17 P4
Tavistock St, WC2 18 B10
Tavistock Ter, N19 143 DK62
Tavistock Twr, SE16 33 L7
Tavistock Wk, Cars. SM5
off Tavistock Rd 222 DD102
Taviton St, WC1 17 N4
Tavy Cl, SE11 30 F10
Tawney Common, They.Mt CM16 92 FA32
Tawney La, Ong. CM5 93 FC32
Stapleford Tawney RM4 109 FD35
Tawney Rd, SE28 168 EV73
Tawneys Rd, Harl. CM18 73 ES16
Tawny Av, Upmin. RM14 150 FP64
Tawny Cl, W13 159 CH74
Feltham TW13
off Chervil Cl 197 BU90
Tawny Way, SE16 33 K8
Tayben Av, Twick. TW2 199 CE86
Taybridge Rd, SW11 182 DG83
Tayburn Cl, E14 22 E8
Tayfield Cl, Uxb. UB10 137 BQ62
Tayler Cotts, Ridge EN6
off Crossoaks La 85 CT34
Tayles Hill, Epsom KT17
off Tayles Hill Dr 239 CT110
Tayles Hill Dr, Epsom KT17 239 CT110
Taylifers, Harl. CM19 73 EN20
Taylor Av, Rich. TW9 180 CP82
Taylor Cl, N17 122 DU52
SE8 45 N2
Epsom KT19 238 CN111
Hampton Hill TW12 198 CC92
Harefield UB9 *off High St* 114 BJ53
Taylor Cl, Houns. TW3 178 CC81
Orpington BR6 245 ET105
Romford RM5 126 FA52
St. Albans AL4 65 CG16
Taylor Rd, Ashtd. KT21 253 CK117
Mitcham CR4 202 DE94
Wallington SM6 241 DH106
Taylor Row, Dart. DA2 210 FJ90
Noak Hill RM3
off Cummings Hall La 128 FJ47
Taylors Av, Hodd. EN11 71 EA18
Taylors Bldgs, SE18 37 P8
Taylors Cl, Sid. DA14 207 ET91
Taylors Ct, Felt. TW13 197 BU89
Taylors Grn, W3 160 CS72
Taylors La, SE26 204 DV91
Barnet EN5 101 CZ39
Taylors Rd, Chesh. HP5 76 AR29
Taymount Ri, SE23 204 DW89
Taynton Dr, Merst. RH1 273 DK129
Tayport Cl, N1 8 B7
Tayside Dr, Edg. HA8 118 CP48
Tay Way, Rom. RM1 127 FF53
Taywood Rd, Nthlt. UB5 158 BZ69
Teak Cl, SE16 33 M3
Teal Av, Orp. BR5 228 EX98
Tealby Ct, N7 8 C4
Teal Cl, E16 24 E7
Enfield EN3 104 DW37
South Croydon CR2 243 DX111
Teal Ct, Wall. SM6
off Carew Rd 241 DJ107
Teal Dr, Nthwd. HA6 115 BQ52
Teale St, E2 10 D10
Tealing Dr, Epsom KT19 238 CR105
Teal Pl, Sutt. SM1
off Sandpiper Rd 239 CZ106
Teal St, SE10 35 M6
Teal Way, Hem.H. HP3 80 BM25
● Teardrop Cen, Swan. BR8 229 FH99
Teasel Cl, Croy. CR0 225 DX102
Teasel Cres, SE28 167 ES74
Teasel Way, E15 23 K2
Teazle Meade, Thnwd CM16 92 EV25
Teazle Wd Hill, Lthd. KT22 253 CE117
Teazlewood Pk, Lthd. KT22 253 CG117
Tebworth Rd, N17 122 DT52
● Technology Pk, The, NW9 140 CR55
Teck Cl, Islw. TW7 179 CG82
Tedder Cl, Chess. KT9 237 CJ107
Ruislip HA4
off West End Rd 137 BV64
Uxbridge UB10 156 BM66
Tedder Rd, Hem.H. HP2 62 BN19
South Croydon CR2 242 DW108
TEDDINGTON, TW11 199 CG93
⇌ Teddington 199 CG93
Teddington Cl, Epsom KT19 238 CR110
Teddington Lock, Tedd. TW11 199 CG91
H Teddington Mem Hosp, Tedd. TW11 199 CE93
Teddington Pk, Tedd. TW11 199 CF92
Teddington Pk Rd, Tedd. TW11 199 CF91
Sch Teddington Sch, Tedd. TW11
off Broom Rd 199 CJ93
Tedworth Gdns, SW3 40 E1
Tedworth Sq, SW3 40 E1
Tee, The, W3 160 CS72
Tees Av, Perivale UB6 159 CE68
Tees Cl, Upmin. RM14 151 FR59
Teesdale, Hem.H. HP2 62 BL17
Teesdale Av, Islw. TW7 179 CG81
Teesdale Cl, E2 20 D1
Teesdale Gdns, SE25 224 DS96
Isleworth TW7 179 CG81
Teesdale Rd, E11 146 EF58
Dartford DA2 210 FQ88
Slough SL2 153 AM71
Teesdale St, E2 20 E1
Teesdale Yd, E2 10 D10
Tees Dr, Rom. RM3 128 FK48
Tee Side, Hert. SG13 54 DV08
Teeswater Ct, Erith DA18
off Middle Way 188 EX76
Teevan Cl, Croy. CR0 224 DU101
Teevan Rd, Croy. CR0 224 DU101
Teggs La, Wok. GU22 249 BF116
Teign Ms, SE9 206 EL89
Teignmouth Cl, SW4 183 DK84
Edgware HA8 118 CM54
Teignmouth Gdns, Perivale UB6 159 CF68
Teignmouth Par, Perivale UB6
off Teignmouth Gdns 159 CH68
Teignmouth Rd, NW2 4 C3
Welling DA16 188 EW82
Sch Teikyo Sch UK Teikyo Women's Coll London, Stoke P. SL2
off Framewood Rd 154 AX66
Telcote Way, Ruis. HA4
off Woodlands Av 138 BW59
★ Telecom Twr, W1 17 L6
Telegraph Hill, NW3 142 DB62
Telegraph La, Clay. KT10 237 CF107
Telegraph Ms, Ilf. IG3 148 EU60
Telegraph Path, Chis. BR7 207 EP92
Telegraph Pl, E14 34 C8
Telegraph Rd, SW15 201 CV87
Telegraph St, EC2 19 L8
Telegraph Track, Cars. SM5 240 DG110
Telemann Sq, SE3 186 EH83
Telephone Pl, SW6 39 H2
Telfer Cl, W3 *off Church Rd* 180 CQ75
Sch Telferscot Prim Sch, SW12
off Telferscot Rd 203 DK88
Telferscot Rd, SW12 203 DK88
Telford Av, SW2 203 DL88
Telford Cl, E17 145 DY59
SE19 *off St. Aubyn's Rd* 204 DT93
Watford WD25 98 BX35
Telford Ct, Guil. GU1 265 AZ134
St. Albans AL1 65 CE21
Telford Dr, Slou. SL1 173 AN75
Walton-on-Thames KT12 218 BW101
Telford Ho, SE1 31 J7
Telford Rd, N11 121 DJ51
NW9 *off West Hendon Bdy* 141 CU58
SE9 207 ER89
W10 14 E6
London Colney AL2 83 CJ27
Southall UB1 158 CB73
Twickenham TW2 198 CA87
Telfords Yd, E1 32 D1
Telford Ter, SW1 41 L2
Telford Way, W3 160 CS71
Hayes UB4 158 BY71
Telham Rd, E6 25 L1
Tell Gro, SE22 184 DT84
Tellisford, Esher KT10 236 CB105

Tellson Av, SE18 . . . . **186** EL81
Telscombe Cl, Orp. BR6 . . . . . . **227** ES103
Telston La, Otford TN14 . . . . . . **263** FF117
Temair Ho, SE10
off Tarves Way **46** D4
Temeraire Pl, Brent. TW8 . . . . . **180** CM78
Temeraire St, SE16 . . . . **33** H5
Temperance St, St.Alb. AL3 . . . . **64** CC20
Temperley Rd, SW12 . . . . **202** DG87
Tempest Av, Pot.B. EN6 . . . . **86** DC32
Tempest Mead, N.Wld Bas.
CM16 . . . . **93** FB27
Tempest Rd, Egh. TW20 . . . . . . **195** BC93
Tempest Way, Rain. RM13 . . . . **169** FG65
Templar Ct, NW8
off St. John's Wd Rd **16** A3
Templar Dr, SE28 . . . . **168** EX72
Gravesend DA11 . . . . **213** GG92
Templar Ho, NW2 . . . . **4** G4
Harrow HA2
off Northolt Rd **139** CD61
Rainham RM13
off Chantry Way **169** FD68
Templar Pl, Hmptn. TW12 . . . . . **198** CA94
Templars Av, NW11 . . . . **141** CZ58
Templars Cres, N3 . . . . **120** DA54
Templars Dr, Har. HA3 . . . . **117** CD51
Templars Ho, E16
off University Way **37** P1
Templar St, SE5 . . . . **43** H7
⊖ **Temple** **18** D10
★ **Temple, The**, EC4 . . . . **18** E10
Temple Av, EC4 . . . . **18** F10
N20 . . . . **120** DD45
Croydon CR0 . . . . **225** DZ103
Dagenham RM8 . . . . **148** FA60
Temple Bk, Harl. CM20 . . . . **58** EV09
★ **Temple Bar**, EC4 . . . . **19** H9
★ **Temple Bar Mem**, EC4 . . . . . . **18** E9
Temple Bar Rd, Wok. GU21 . . . . **248** AT119
Temple Cl, E11 . . . . **146** EE59
N3 . . . . **119** CZ54
SE28 . . . . **187** EQ76
Cheshunt EN7 . . . . **88** DU31
Epsom KT19 . . . . **238** CR112
Watford WD17 . . . . **97** BT40
Templecombe Ms, Wok. GU22
off Dorchester Ct **249** BA116
Templecombe Rd, E9 . . . . **10** G8
Templecombe Way, Mord.
SM4 . . . . **221** CY99
Temple Ct, E1 *off Rectory Sq* . . . **21** J6
SW8 *off Thorncroft St* **42** A5
Hertford SG14 . . . . **54** DR06
Potters Bar EN6 . . . . **85** CY31
Templecroft, Ashf. TW15 . . . . . . **197** BR93
Templedene Av, Stai. TW18 . . . . **196** BH94
Temple Dws, E2 *off Temple Yd* . . **20** E1
Templefield Cl, Add. KT15 . . . . . **234** BH107
● **Temple Flds**, Harl. CM20 . . . . **58** EU11
Temple Flds, Hert. SG14 . . . . **54** DR06
Temple Fortune Hill, NW11 . . . . **142** DA57
Temple Fortune La, NW11 . . . . **142** DA58
Temple Fortune Mans, NW11
off Finchley Rd **141** CZ57
Temple Fortune Par, NW11
off Finchley Rd **141** CZ57
Temple Gdns, N21
off Barrowell Grn **121** DP47
NW11 . . . . **141** CZ58
Dagenham RM8 . . . . **148** EX62
Rickmansworth WD3 . . . . **115** BP49
Staines TW18 . . . . **215** BF95
Temple Gro, NW11 . . . . **142** DA58
Enfield EN2 . . . . **103** DP41
Temple Hill, Dart. DA1 . . . . **210** FM86
Sch **Temple Hill Comm Prim & Nurs Sch**, Dart. DA1
off St. Edmunds Rd **210** FN85
Temple Hill Sq, Dart. DA1 . . . . . **210** FM85
Templehof Av, NW2 . . . . **141** CW59
Temple La, EC4 . . . . **18** F9
Templeman Cl, Pur. CR8
off Croftleigh Av **257** DP116
Templeman Rd, W7 . . . . **159** CF71
Temple Mead, Hem.H. HP2 . . . . **62** BK18
Roydon CM19 . . . . **72** EH15
Templemead Cl, W3 . . . . **160** CS72
Temple Mead Cl, Stan. HA7 . . . **117** CH51
Templemead Ho, E9
off Kingsmead Way **11** M1
Templemere, Wey. KT13 . . . . . . **217** BR104
Temple Mill La, E15 . . . . **145** EB63
★ **Temple of Mithras**, EC4
off Queen Victoria St **19** L9
Templepan La, Chan.Cr. WD3 . . **96** BL37
Temple Pk, Uxb. UB8 . . . . **156** BN69
Temple Pl, WC2 . . . . **18** D10
Temple Av, Grays RM16 . . . . . **193** GG77
Temple Rd, E6 . . . . **166** EL67
N8 . . . . **143** DM56
NW2 . . . . **141** CW63
W4 . . . . **180** CQ76
W5 . . . . **179** CK76
Biggin Hill TN16 . . . . **260** EK117
Croydon CR0 . . . . **242** DR105
Epsom KT19 . . . . **238** CR112
Hounslow TW3 . . . . **178** CB84
Richmond TW9 . . . . **180** CM83
Windsor SL4 . . . . **173** AQ82
Temple Sheen, SW14 . . . . **200** CQ85
Temple Sheen Rd, SW14 . . . . . **180** CP84
Temple St, E2 . . . . **20** E1
Templeton Av, E4 . . . . **123** EA49
Templeton Cl, N16 . . . . **9** P2
SE19 . . . . **224** DR95
Templeton Ct, NW7
off Kingsbridge Dr **119** CX52
Templeton Pl, SW5 . . . . **27** K9
Templeton Rd, N15 . . . . **144** DR58
Temple Vw, St.Alb. AL3 . . . . . . **64** CC18
Temple Way, Farn.Com. SL2 . . **133** AQ64
Sutton SM1 . . . . **222** DD104
Temple W Ms, SE11 . . . . **30** G7
Templewood, W13 . . . . **159** CH71
Welwyn Garden City AL8 . . . . **51** CX06
Templewood Av, NW3 . . . . **142** DB62
Temple Wd Dr, Red. RH1 . . . . **272** DF131
Templewood Gdns, NW3 . . . . . **142** DB62
Templewood Gate, Farn.Com.
SL2 . . . . **133** AQ64
Templewood La, Slou. SL2 . . . **134** AS63
Templewood Pk, Slou. SL2 . . . **134** AT63
Templewood Pt, NW2 . . . . **141** CZ61
Sch **Templewood Prim Sch**, Welw.G.C. AL8
off Pentley Pk **51** CX07
Temple Yd, E2 . . . . **20** E1
Tempsford, Welw.G.C. AL7 . . . . **52** DD09
Tempsford Av, Borwd. WD6 . . . **100** CR42
Tempsford Cl, Enf. EN2
off Gladbeck Way **104** DQ41
Tempus Ct, E18 . . . . **124** EG53
Temsford Cl, Har. HA2 . . . . **116** CC54
Ten Acre, Wok. GU21
off Chirton Wk **248** AU118
Ten Acre La, Egh. TW20 . . . . . . **215** BC96
Ten Acres, Fetch. KT22 . . . . . . **253** CD124
Ten Acres Cl, Fetch. KT22 . . . . **253** CD124
Tenbury Cl, E7
off Romford Rd **146** EK64
Tenbury Ct, SW2 . . . . **203** DK88
Tenby Av, Har. HA3 . . . . **117** CH54
Tenby Cl, N15 . . . . **144** DT56
Romford RM6 . . . . **148** EY58
Tenby Gdns, Nthlt. UB5 . . . . . . **158** CA65
Tenby Rd, E17 . . . . **145** DY57
Edgware HA8 . . . . **118** CM53
Enfield EN3 . . . . **104** DW41
Romford RM6 . . . . **148** EY58
Welling DA16 . . . . **188** EX81
Tenchleys La, Oxt. RH8 . . . . . . **276** EK131
Tench St, E1 . . . . **32** E3
Tenda Rd, SE16 . . . . **32** E9
Tendring Ms, Harl. CM18 . . . . . . **73** ES16
Tendring Rd, Harl. CM18 . . . . . . **73** EQ17
Tendring Way, Rom. RM6 . . . . . **148** EW57
Tenham Av, SW2 . . . . **203** DK88
Tenison Ct, W1 . . . . **17** L10
Tenison Way, SE1 . . . . **30** E3
Tennand Cl, Chsht EN7 . . . . **88** DT26
Tenniel Cl, W2 . . . . **15** N9
Guildford GU2 . . . . **264** AV132
Tennis Ct La, E.Mol. KT8
off Hampton Ct Way **219** CE97
Tennison Av, Borwd. WD6 . . . . **100** CP43
Tennison Cl, Couls. CR5 . . . . . . **257** DP120
Tennison Rd, SE25 . . . . **224** DT98
Tennis St, SE1 . . . . **31** L4
Tenniswood Rd, Enf. EN1 . . . . . **104** DT39
Tennyson Av, E11 . . . . **146** EG59
E12 . . . . **166** EL66
NW9 . . . . **140** CQ55
Grays RM17 . . . . **192** GB76
New Malden KT3 . . . . **221** CV99
Twickenham TW1 . . . . **199** CF88
Waltham Abbey EN9 . . . . **90** EE34
Tennyson Cl, Enf. EN3 . . . . **105** DX43
Feltham TW14 . . . . **197** BT86
Welling DA16 . . . . **187** ES81
Tennyson Rd, E10 . . . . **145** EB61
E15 . . . . **13** J6
E17 . . . . **145** DZ58
NW6 . . . . **4** G8
NW7 . . . . **119** CU50
SE20 . . . . **205** DX94
SW19 . . . . **202** DC93
W7 . . . . **159** CF73
Addlestone KT15 . . . . **234** BL105
Ashford TW15 . . . . **196** BL92
Dartford DA1 . . . . **210** FN85
Hounslow TW3 . . . . **178** CC82
Hutton CM13 . . . . **131** GC45
Romford RM3 . . . . **128** FJ52
St. Albans AL2 . . . . **82** CA26
Tennyson St, SW8 . . . . **41** J9
Tennyson Wk, Nthflt DA11 . . . . **212** GD90
Tilbury RM18 . . . . **193** GH82
Tennyson Way, Horn. RM12 . . . **149** FF61
Slough SL2 . . . . **153** AL70
Tensing Av, Nthflt DA11 . . . . . **212** GE90
Tensing Rd, Sthl. UB2 . . . . **178** CA76
Tentelow La, Sthl. UB2 . . . . . . **178** CA78
Tenterden Cl, NW4 . . . . **141** CX55
SE9 . . . . **207** EM91
Tenterden Dr, NW4 . . . . **141** CX55
Tenterden Gdns, NW4 . . . . **141** CX55
Croydon CR0 . . . . **224** DU101
Tenterden Gro, NW4 . . . . **141** CW56
Tenterden Rd, N17 . . . . **122** DT52
Croydon CR0 . . . . **224** DU101
Dagenham RM8 . . . . **148** EZ61
Tenterden St, W1 . . . . **17** K9
Tenter Grd, E1 . . . . **20** A7
Tenter Pas, E1 . . . . **20** B9
Tent Peg La, Orp. BR5 . . . . **227** EQ99
Tent St, E1 . . . . **20** E4
Tenzing Rd, Hem.H. HP2 . . . . . . **62** BN20
Tequila Wf, E14
off Commercial Rd **21** M9
Terborch Way, SE22
off East Dulwich Gro **204** DS85
Tercel Path, Chig. IG7 . . . . **126** EV49
Teredo St, SE16 . . . . **33** K7
Terence Cl, Grav. DA12 . . . . **213** GM88
Terence Ct, Belv. DA17
off Nuxley Rd **188** EZ79
Teresa Gdns, Wal.Cr. EN8 . . . . . **88** DW34
Teresa Ms, E17 . . . . **145** EA56
Teresa Wk, N10
off Connaught Gdns **143** DH57
Terling Cl, E11 . . . . **146** EF62
Terling Rd, Dag. RM8 . . . . **148** FA61
Terlings, The, Brwd. CM14 . . . . **130** FU48
Terling Wk, N1 . . . . **9** J8
Jct **Terminal Four Rbt**, Lon.Hthrw Air. TW6 . . . . **197** BQ86
Terminus Pl, SW1 . . . . **29** K7
Terminus St, Harl. CM20 . . . . . . **57** ER14
Tern Gdns, Upmin. RM14 . . . . . **151** FS60
Tern Way, Brwd. CM14 . . . . **130** FS49
Terrace, The, E4
off Chingdale Rd **124** EE48
N3 *off Hendon La* **119** CZ54
NW6 . . . . **5** J8
SW13 . . . . **180** CS82
Addlestone KT15 . . . . **234** BL106
Bray SL6 . . . . **172** AC76
Dorking RH5 . . . . **285** CJ137
Gravesend DA12 . . . . **213** GH86
Sevenoaks TN13 . . . . **278** FD122
Woodford Green IG8
off Broadmead Rd **124** EG51
Terrace Apts, N5
off Drayton Pk **8** F2
Terrace Gdns, SW13 . . . . **181** CT82
Watford WD17 . . . . **97** BV40
Terrace La, Rich. TW10 . . . . **200** CL86
Terrace Rd, E9 . . . . **11** H6
E13 . . . . **13** P9
Walton-on-Thames KT12 . . . **217** BU101
Terraces, The, Dart. DA2 . . . . . . **210** FQ87
Terrace St, Grav. DA12 . . . . **213** GH86
Terrace Wk, Dag. RM9 . . . . **148** EY64
Terrapin Rd, SW17 . . . . **203** DH90
Terretts Pl, N1 . . . . **8** G7
Terrick Rd, N22 . . . . **121** DL53
Terrick St, W12 . . . . **161** CV72
Terrilands, Pnr. HA5 . . . . **138** BZ55
Terront Rd, N15 . . . . **144** DQ57
Tersha St, Rich. TW9 . . . . **180** CM84
Tessa Sanderson Pl, SW8 . . . . . . **41** K10
Tessa Sanderson Way, Grnf.
UB6 *off Lilian Board Way* . . **139** CD64
Testard Rd, Guil. GU2 . . . . . . **280** AW136
Testers Cl, Oxt. RH8 . . . . **276** EH132
Testerton Wk, W11 . . . . **14** D10
Testwood Rd, Wind. SL4 . . . . . . **173** AK81
Tetbury Pl, N1 . . . . **8** G9
Tetcott Rd, SW10 . . . . **39** N4
Tetherdown, N10 . . . . **142** DG55
Coll **Tetherdown Adult Ed Cen**,
N10 *off Tetherdown* **142** DG55
Sch **Tetherdown Prim Sch**, N10
off Grand Av **142** DG56
Tethys Rd, Hem.H. HP2 . . . . **62** BM17
Tetty Way, Brom. BR2 . . . . **226** EG96
Teversham La, SW8 . . . . **42** B6
Teviot Av, Aveley RM15 . . . . . . **170** FQ72
Teviot Cl, Guil. GU2 . . . . **264** AU131
Welling DA16 . . . . **188** EV81
Teviot St, E14 . . . . **22** E6
TEWIN, Welw. AL6 . . . . **52** DE05
Tewin Cl, St.Alb. AL4 . . . . **65** CJ16
Tewin Ct, Welw.G.C. AL7 . . . . . . **51** CZ08
Sch **Tewin Cowper C of E Prim Sch**,
Tewin AL6
off Cannons Meadow **52** DE05
Tewin Mill Ho, Tewin AL6 . . . . . . **52** DE07
Tewin Rd, Hem.H. HP2 . . . . **63** BQ20
Welwyn Garden City AL7 . . . . . **51** CZ09
Tewin Water, Welw. AL6 . . . . **52** DB05
Tewkesbury Av, SE23 . . . . **204** DV88
Pinner HA5 . . . . **138** BY57
Tewkesbury Cl, N15
off Pulford Rd **144** DR58
Barnet EN4
off Approach Rd **102** DD42
Byfleet KT14 . . . . **234** BK111
Loughton IG10 . . . . **106** EL44
Tewkesbury Gdns, NW9 . . . . . . **140** CP55
Tewkesbury Rd, N15 . . . . **144** DR58
W13 . . . . **159** CG73
Carshalton SM5 . . . . **222** DD102
Tewkesbury Ter, N11 . . . . **121** DJ51
Tewson Rd, SE18 . . . . **187** ES78
Teynham Av, Enf. EN1 . . . . **104** DR44
Teynham Grn, Brom. BR2 . . . . . **226** EG99
Teynham Rd, Dart. DA2 . . . . **210** FQ87
Teynton Ter, N17 . . . . **122** DQ53
Thackeray Av, N17 . . . . **122** DU54
Tilbury RM18 . . . . **193** GH81
Thackeray Cl, SW19 . . . . **201** CX94
Isleworth TW7 . . . . **179** CG82
Uxbridge UB8 . . . . **157** BP72
Thackeray Dr, Rom. RM6 . . . . . **148** EU59
Thackeray Rd, E6 . . . . **166** EK68
SW8 . . . . **41** J9
Thackeray St, W8 . . . . **27** M5
Thakeham Cl, SE26 . . . . **204** DV92
Thalia Cl, SE10 . . . . **47** H2
Thalmassing Cl, Hutt. CM13 . . **131** GB47
Thame Rd, SE16 . . . . **33** K4
Thames Av, SW10 . . . . **39** P6
Chertsey KT16 . . . . **216** BG97
Dagenham RM9 . . . . **169** FB70
Hemel Hempstead HP2 . . . . . . **62** BM15
Perivale UB6 . . . . **159** CF68
Windsor SL4 . . . . **173** AR80
Thames Bk, SW14 . . . . **180** CQ82
Thamesbank Pl, SE28 . . . . **168** EW72
★ **Thames Barrier Information & Learning Cen**, SE18 . . . . **36** E6
Sch **Thames Christian Coll**,
SW11 . . . . **40** B10
Thames Circle, E14 . . . . **34** B8
Thames Cl, Cher. KT16 . . . . **216** BH101
Hampton TW12 . . . . **218** CB96
Rainham RM13 . . . . **169** FH72
Thames Ct, W.Mol. KT8 . . . . **218** CB96
Thames Cres, W4
off Corney Rd **180** CS80
Thamesdale, Lon.Col. AL2 . . . . . **84** CM27
THAMES DITTON, KT7 . . . . **219** CF100
⇌ **Thames Ditton** **219** CF101
Sch **Thames Ditton Inf Sch**, T.Ditt.
KT7 *off Speer Rd* **219** CF100
Thames Ditton Island, T.Ditt.
KT7 . . . . **219** CG99
Sch **Thames Ditton Jun Sch**, T.Ditt.
KT7 *off Mercer Cl* **219** CF101
Thames Dr, Grays RM16 . . . . . . **193** GG78
Ruislip HA4 . . . . **137** BQ58
Thames Edge Ct, Stai. TW18
off Clarence St **195** BE91
● **Thames Europort**, Dart.
DA2 . . . . **191** FS84
Thamesfield Ct, Shep. TW17 . . **217** BQ101
Thames Gate, Dart. DA1 . . . . . . **210** FN85
Thamesgate Cl, Rich. TW10 . . . . **199** CH91
🔒 **Thamesgate Shop Cen**,
Grav. DA11 *off New Rd* **213** GH86
Thames Gateway, Dag. RM9 . . . **168** EZ68
Rainham RM13 . . . . **169** FG72
South Ockendon RM15 . . . . . **190** FP75
Coll **Thames Gateway Coll**,
CEME Campus, Rain.
RM13 *off Marsh Way* **169** FD70
● **Thames Gateway Pk**, Dag.
RM9 . . . . **168** EZ69
Thameshill Av, Rom. RM5 . . . . . **127** FC54
Thameside, Cher. KT16 . . . . . . **216** BJ101
Staines TW18 . . . . **216** BH97
Teddington TW11 . . . . **199** CK94
● **Thameside Cen**, Brent.
TW8 . . . . **180** CM79
● **Thameside Ind Est**, E16 . . . . . **36** F4
Sch **Thameside Inf Sch**, Grays
RM17 *off Manor Rd* **192** GC79
Sch **Thameside Jun Sch**, Grays
RM17 *off Manor Rd* **192** GC79
Thameside Wk, SE28 . . . . **167** ET72
Thames Link, SE16 . . . . **33** J3
THAMESMEAD, SE28 . . . . **167** ET73
Thames Mead, Walt. KT12 . . . . **217** BU101
Windsor SL4 . . . . **173** AL81
Coll **Thamesmead Cen**, Erith DA18
off Yarnton Way **188** EY75
THAMESMEAD NORTH, SE28 . **168** EX72
Thames Meadow, Shep.
TW17 . . . . **217** BR102
West Molesey KT8 . . . . **218** CA96
Sch **Thamesmead Sch**, Shep.
TW17 *off Manygate La* **217** BQ100
Thamesmead Spine Rd, Belv.
DA17 . . . . **189** FB75
THAMESMEAD WEST, SE18 . . **187** EP76
Thamesmere Dr, SE28 . . . . **168** EU73
Thames Pl, SW15 . . . . **181** CX83
Thames Pt, SW6 . . . . **39** P7
Thamespoint, Tedd. TW11 . . . . . **199** CK94
Thames Quay, SW10 . . . . **39** P7
Thames Rd, E16 . . . . **36** E3
W4 . . . . **180** CN79
Barking IG11 . . . . **167** ET69
Dartford DA1 . . . . **189** FG82
Grays RM17 . . . . **192** GB80
Slough SL3 . . . . **175** BA77
Thames Side, Kings.T. KT1 . . . **219** CK95
Windsor SL4 . . . . **173** AR80
Thames St, SE10 . . . . **46** D2
Greenhithe DA9 . . . . **191** FT84
Hampton TW12 . . . . **218** CB95
Kingston upon Thames KT1 . **219** CK96
Staines TW18 . . . . **195** BE91
Sunbury-on-Thames TW16 . . **217** BV98
Walton-on-Thames KT12 . . . **217** BT101
Weybridge KT13 . . . . **217** BP103
Windsor SL4 . . . . **173** AR81
Thames Tunnel Mills, SE16
off Rotherhithe St **32** G4
Thamesvale Cl, Houns. TW3 . . . **178** CA83
H **Thames Valley Nuffield Hosp**,
Wexham SL2 . . . . **154** AW67
H **Thames Valley Nuffield Hosp, The**, Wexham Pk Hall,
Wexham SL3 . . . . **154** AV68
Uni **Thames Valley Uni - Ealing Campus**, W5
off St. Mary's Rd **159** CK74
Grove Ho, W5
off The Grove **159** CK74
London Coll of Music, W5
off Ranelagh Rd **179** CK75
Paragon Site, Brent. TW8
off Boston Manor Rd **179** CJ78
Walpole Ho, W5
off Bond St **159** CK73
Westel Ho, W5
off Uxbridge Rd **159** CJ73
Uni **Thames Valley Uni - Faculty of Health & Human Sciences**,
Slou. SL2 *off Wexham St* . . **154** AV70
Uni **Thames Valley Uni - Slough Campus**, Slou. SL1
off Wellington St **154** AS74
Thames Vw, Grays RM16 . . . . . . **193** GG78
Ilford IG1 *off Axon Pl* **147** EQ61
Sch **Thames Vw Inf Sch**, Bark.
IG11 *off Bastable Av* **168** EU68
Sch **Thames Vw Jun Sch**, Bark.
IG11 *off Bastable Av* **167** ET68
Sch **Thamesview Sch**, Grav. DA12
off Thong La **213** GM90
Thames Village, W4 . . . . **180** CQ81
Thames Way, Grav. DA11 . . . . . **212** GB86
Thames Wf, E16 . . . . **35** L2
Thamley, Purf. RM19 . . . . **190** FN77
Thanescroft Gdns, Croy. CR0 . . **224** DS104
Thanet Dr, Kes. BR2
off Phoenix Dr **226** EK104
Thanet Pl, Croy. CR0 . . . . **242** DQ105
Thanet Rd, Bex. DA5 . . . . **208** FA87
Erith DA8 . . . . **189** FE80
Thanet St, WC1 . . . . **18** A3
Thane Vil, N7 . . . . **143** DM62
Thane Wks, N7 . . . . **143** DM62
Thanington Ct, SE9 . . . . **207** ES86
Thanstead Copse, Loud. HP10 . **110** AC53
Thanstead Ct, Loud. HP10 . . . . **110** AC53
Thant Cl, E10 . . . . **145** EB62
Tharp Rd, Wall. SM6 . . . . **241** DK106
Thatcham Gdns, N20 . . . . **120** DC45
Thatcher Cl, West Dr. UB7
off Classon Cl **176** BL75
Thatcher Ct, Dart. DA1
off Heath St **210** FK87
Thatchers Cl, Horl. RH6
off Wheatfield Way **291** DH146
Loughton IG10 . . . . **107** EQ40
Thatchers Cft, Hem.H. HP2 . . . . **62** BL16
Thatchers Way, Islw. TW7 . . . . **199** CD85
Thatches Gro, Rom. RM6 . . . . . **148** EY56
Thavies Inn, EC1 . . . . **18** F8
Thaxted Ct, N1 . . . . **19** L1
Thaxted Grn, Hutt. CM13 . . . . . **131** GC43
Thaxted Ho, Dag. RM10 . . . . . . **169** FB66
Thaxted Pl, SW20 . . . . **201** CX94
Thaxted Rd, SE9 . . . . **207** EQ89
Buckhurst Hill IG9 . . . . **124** EL45
Thaxted Wk, Rain. RM13
off Ongar Way **169** FF67
Thaxted Way, Wal.Abb. EN9 . . . . **89** ED33
Thaxton Rd, W14 . . . . **39** H2
Thayers Fm Rd, Beck. BR3 . . . . **225** DY95
Thayer St, W1 . . . . **17** H7
Thaynesfield, Pot.B. EN6 . . . . . . **86** DD31
★ **Theatre Royal**, WC2 . . . . **18** B9
Theatre Sq, E15 . . . . **13** H5
Theatre St, SW11 . . . . **40** F10
Theberton St, N1 . . . . **8** F8
Theed St, SE1 . . . . **30** E3
Thele Av, Stans.Abb. SG12 . . . . **55** ED11
Theleway Cl, Hodd. EN11 . . . . . . **55** EB14
Thellusson Way, Rick. WD3 . . . . **113** BF45
Thelma Cl, Grav. DA12 . . . . **213** GM92
Thelma Gdns, SE3 . . . . **186** EK81
Feltham TW13 . . . . **198** BY90
Thelma Gro, Tedd. TW11 . . . . . **199** CG93
Theobald Cres, Har. HA3 . . . . . **116** CB53
Theobald Rd, E17 . . . . **145** DZ59
Croydon CR0 . . . . **223** DP103
Theobalds Av, N12 . . . . **120** DC49
Grays RM17 . . . . **192** GC78
Theobalds Cl, Cuffley EN6 . . . . . **87** DM30
Theobalds Ct, N4
off Queens Dr **144** DQ62
⇌ **Theobalds Grove** **89** DX32
Theobalds La, Chsht EN7, EN8 . **88** DV32
Theobalds Pk Rd, Enf. EN2 . . . **103** DP35
Theobald's Rd, WC1 . . . . **18** C6
Theobalds Rd, Cuffley EN6 . . . . **87** DL30
Theobald St, SE1 . . . . **31** L7
Borehamwood WD6 . . . . **100** CM40
Radlett WD7 . . . . **99** CH36
Theodora Way, Pnr. HA5 . . . . . **137** BT55
Theodore Rd, SE13 . . . . **205** EC86
Thepps Cl, S.Nutfld RH1 . . . . . **289** DM137
Tra **Therapia Lane** **223** DL101
Therapia La, Croy. CR0 . . . . . . **223** DL100
Therapia Rd, SE22 . . . . **204** DW86
Theresa Rd, W6 . . . . **181** CU77
Theresas Wk, S.Croy. CR2
off St. Mary's Rd **242** DR110
Therfield Ct, N4
off Brownswood Rd **144** DQ61
Therfield Rd, St.Alb. AL3 . . . . . . **65** CD16
Sch **Therfield Sch**, Lthd. KT22
off Dilston Rd **253** CG119
Thermopylae Gate, E14 . . . . **34** D9
Theseus Wk, N1 . . . . **19** H1
Thesiger Rd, SE20 . . . . **205** DX94
Thessaly Ho, SW8 . . . . **41** L5
Thessaly Rd, SW8 . . . . **41** L5
Thetford Cl, N13 . . . . **121** DP52
Thetford Gdns, Dag. RM9 . . . . . **168** EX66
Thetford Rd, Ashf. TW15 . . . . . . **196** BL91
Dagenham RM9 . . . . **168** EX67
New Malden KT3 . . . . **220** CR100
Thetis Ter, Rich. TW9
off Kew Grn **180** CN79
THEYDON BOIS, Epp. CM16 . . . **107** ET36
⊖ **Theydon Bois** **107** ET36
Sch **Theydon Bois Prim Sch**, They.B.
CM16 *off Orchard Dr* **107** ES36
Theydon Bower, Epp. CM16 . . . . **92** EU31
Theydon Ct, Wal.Abb. EN9 . . . . . **90** EG33
Theydon Gdns, Rain. RM13 . . . **169** FE66
THEYDON GARNON, Epp.
CM16 . . . . **108** EW35
Theydon Gate, They.B. CM16
off Coppice Row **107** ES36
Theydon Gro, Epp. CM16 . . . . . . **92** EU30
Woodford Green IG8 . . . . **124** EJ51
THEYDON MOUNT, Epp.
CM16 . . . . **92** FA34
Theydon Pk Rd, They.B. CM16 . **107** ES39
Theydon Pl, Epp. CM16 . . . . **91** ET31
Theydon Rd, E5 . . . . **144** DW61
Epping CM16 . . . . **91** ER34
Theydon St, E17 . . . . **145** DZ59
Thicket, The, West Dr. UB7 . . . . **156** BL72
Thicket Cres, Sutt. SM1 . . . . . . **240** DC105
Thicket Gro, SE20
off Anerley Rd **204** DU94
Dagenham RM9 . . . . **168** EW65
Thicket Rd, SE20 . . . . **204** DU94
Sutton SM1 . . . . **240** DC105
Thicketts, Sev. TN13 . . . . **279** FJ123
Thickthorne La, Stai. TW18 . . . **196** BJ94
Thieves La, Hert. SG14 . . . . **53** DM10
Ware SG12 . . . . **54** DW08
Third Av, E12 . . . . **146** EL63
E13 . . . . **23** P2
E17 . . . . **145** EA57
W3 . . . . **161** CT74
W10 . . . . **14** F4
Dagenham RM10 . . . . **169** FB67
Enfield EN1 . . . . **104** DT43
Grays RM20 . . . . **191** FU79
Harlow CM18, CM19 . . . . **73** EM16
Hayes UB3 . . . . **157** BT74
Romford RM6 . . . . **148** EW57
Waltham Abbey EN9 *off Breach Barn Mobile Home Pk* **90** EH30
Watford WD25 . . . . **98** BX35
Wembley HA9 . . . . **139** CK61
Third Cl, W.Mol. KT8 . . . . **218** CB98
Third Cres, Slou. SL1 . . . . **153** AQ71
Third Cross Rd, Twick. TW2 . . . **199** CD89
Third Way, Wem. HA9 . . . . **140** CP63
Thirkleby Cl, Slou. SL1 . . . . **153** AQ74
Thirleby Rd, SW1 . . . . **29** M7
Edgware HA8 . . . . **118** CR53
Thirlmere Av, Perivale UB6 . . . **159** CJ69
Slough SL1 . . . . **152** AJ71
Thirlmere Cl, Egh. TW20 . . . . . . **195** BB94
Thirlmere Dr, St.Alb. AL1 . . . . . . **65** CH22
Thirlmere Gdns, Nthwd. HA6 . . **115** BQ51
Wembley HA9 . . . . **139** CJ60
Thirlmere Ho, Islw. TW7
off Summerwood Rd **199** CF85
Thirlmere Ri, Brom. BR1 . . . . . . **206** EF93
Thirlmere Rd, N10 . . . . **121** DH53
SW16 . . . . **203** DK91
Bexleyheath DA7 . . . . **189** FC82
Thirlstane, St.Alb. AL1 . . . . **65** CE19
Thirsk Cl, Nthlt. UB5 . . . . **158** CA65
Thirsk Rd, SE25 . . . . **224** DR98
SW11 . . . . **182** DG83
Borehamwood WD6 . . . . **100** CN37
Mitcham CR4 . . . . **202** DG94
Thirston Path, Borwd. WD6 . . . **100** CN40
Thirza Rd, Dart. DA1 . . . . **210** FM86
Thistlebrook, SE2 . . . . **188** EW76
● **Thistlebrook Ind Est**, SE2 . **188** EW75
Thistle Cl, Hem.H. HP1 . . . . **61** BE21
Thistlecroft, Hem.H. HP1 . . . . . . **62** BH21
Thistlecroft Gdns, Stan. HA7 . . **117** CK53
Thistlecroft Rd, Hersham
KT12 . . . . **236** BW105
Thistledene, T.Ditt. KT7 . . . . . . **219** CE100
West Byfleet KT14 . . . . **233** BF113
Thistledene Av, Har. HA2 . . . . . **138** BY62
Romford RM5 . . . . **127** FB50
Thistledown, Grav. DA12 . . . . . **213** GK93
Thistle Dr, Hat. AL10 . . . . **67** CT15
Thistlefield Cl, Bex. DA5 . . . . . . **208** EX88
Thistle Gro, SW10 . . . . **27** P10
Welwyn Garden City AL7 . . . . . **52** DC12
Thistlemead, Chis. BR7 . . . . . . **227** EP96
Thistle Mead, Loug. IG10 . . . . . **107** EN41
Thistle Rd, Grav. DA12 . . . . **213** GL87
Thistles, The, Hem.H. HP1 . . . . . **62** BH19
Leatherhead KT22 . . . . **253** CJ122
Thistlewaite Rd, E5 . . . . **144** DV62
Thistlewood Cl, N7 . . . . **143** DM61
Thistlewood Cres, New Adgtn
CR0 . . . . **243** ED112
Thistleworth Cl, Islw. TW7 . . . . **179** CD80
Thistley Cl, N12
off Summerfields Av **120** DE51
Coulsdon CR5 . . . . **257** DK122
Thistley Ct, SE8
off Glaisher St **46** C2
Thomas a'Beckett Cl, Wem.
HA0 . . . . **139** CF63
Sch **Thomas Arnold Prim Sch**, Dag.
RM9 *off Rowdowns Rd* **168** EZ66
Thomas Av, Cat. CR3 . . . . **258** DQ121
Thomas Baines Rd, SW11 . . . . . **182** DD83
Sch **Thomas Buxton Inf & Jun Schs**,
E1 . . . . **20** D5
Thomas Cl, Brwd. CM15 . . . . . . **130** FY48
Sch **Thomas Coram Mid Sch, The**,
Berk. HP4 *off Swing Gate La* . **60** AX21
Thomas Cribb Ms, E6 . . . . **25** K8

Thomas Darby Ct, W11 14 E9
Thomas Dean Rd, SE26
off Kangley Br Rd 205 DZ91
Thomas Dinwiddy Rd, SE12 206 EH89
Thomas Doyle St, SE1 30 G6
Thomas Dr, Grav. DA12 213 GK89
Thomas Fairchild Comm Sch, N1 9 K10
Thomas Gamuel Prim Sch, E17 off Colchester Rd 145 EA58
Thomas Harding Jun Sch, Chesh. HP5 off Fullers Hill 76 AP32
Thomas Hardy Ho, N22 121 DM52
Thomas Hollywood Ho, E2 20 G1
Thomas Jones Prim Sch, W11 14 E9
Thomas Knyvett Coll, Ashf. TW15 off Stanwell Rd 196 BL90
Thomas La, SE6 205 EA87
Thomas More Bldg, The, Ruis. HA4 137 BS60
Thomas More Cath Sch, Pur. CR8
off Russell Hill Rd 241 DN110
Thomas More Ho, EC2
off The Barbican 19 J7
Thomas More St, E1 32 C1
Thomas More Way, N2 142 DC55
Thomas N Ter, E16
off Barking Rd 23 L7
Thomas Pl, W8 27 L7
Thomas Rd, E14 21 P8
Crayford DA1 189 FG82
Wooburn Green HP10 132 AD59
● Thomas Rd Ind Est, E14 22 A7
Thomas Rochford Way, Chsht EN8 89 DZ27
Thomas Sims Ct, Horn. RM12 149 FH64
Thomas's School, Battersea, SW11 40 B7
Thomas's School, Clapham, SW11 off Broomwood Rd 202 DF86
Thomas's School, Fulham, SW6 39 L10
Thomas's School, Kensington, Lwr Sch, W8 27 N6
Prep Sch, W8 27 M6
Thomas St, SE18 37 M8
Thomas Tallis Sch, SE3
off Kidbrooke Pk Rd 186 EH83
Thomas Wall Cl, Sutt. SM1
off Clarence Rd 240 DB106
Thomas Willingale Sch, Loug. IG10
off The Broadway 107 EQ41
Thompkins La, Farn.Royal SL2 153 AM66
Thompson Av, Rich. TW9 180 CN83
Thompson Cl, Ilf. IG1
off High Rd 147 EQ61
Slough SL3 175 BA77
Sutton SM3
off Barrington Rd 222 DA102
Thompson Rd, SE22 204 DT86
Dagenham RM9 148 EZ62
Hounslow TW3 178 CB84
Thompsons Av, SE5 43 J4
Thompsons Cl, Chsht EN7 88 DT29
Thompson's La, High Beach IG10 106 EF39
Thompson Way, Rick. WD3 114 BG45
Thomson Cres, Croy. CR0 223 DN102
Thomson Rd, Har. HA3 139 CE55
Thong La, Grav. DA12 213 GM90
Thorburn Sq, SE1 32 C9
Thorburn Way, SW19 222 DC95
Thoresby St, N1 19 K2
Thorkhill Gdns, T.Ditt. KT7 219 CG102
Thorkhill Rd, T.Ditt. KT7 219 CH101
Thorley Cl, W.Byf. KT14 234 BG114
Thorley Gdns, Wok. GU22 234 BG114
Thornaby Gdns, N18 122 DU51
Thornaby Pl, Woob.Grn HP10 132 AE55
Thornash Cl, Wok. GU21 248 AW115
Thornash Rd, Wok. GU21 248 AW115
Thornash Way, Wok. GU21 248 AW115
Thorn Av, Bushey Hth WD23 116 CC46
Thorn Bk, Guil. GU2 280 AU136
Thornbank Cl, Stai. TW19 196 BG85
Thornberry Way, Guil. GU1 265 AZ130
Thornbridge Rd, Iver SL0 155 BC67
Thornbrook, Thnwd CM16 92 EX25
Thornbury Av, Islw. TW7 179 CD80
Thornbury Cl, N16 9 P2
NW7 off Kingsbridge Dr 119 CX52
Hoddesdon EN11 55 EB13
Thornbury Gdns, Borwd. WD6 100 CQ42
Thornbury Rd, SW2 203 DL86
Isleworth TW7 179 CD81
Thornbury Sq, N6 143 DJ60
Thornby Rd, E5 144 DW62
Thorncliffe Rd, SW2 203 DL86
Southall UB2 178 BZ78
Thorn Cl, Brom. BR2 227 EN100
Northolt UB5 158 BZ69
Thorncombe Rd, SE22 204 DS85
Thorncroft, Eng.Grn TW20 194 AW94
Hemel Hempstead HP3 63 BP22
Hornchurch RM11 149 FH58
Thorncroft Cl, Couls. CR5
off Waddington Av 257 DN119
Thorncroft Dr, Lthd. KT22 253 CH123
Thorncroft Rd, Sutt. SM1 240 DB105
Thorncroft St, SW8 42 A5
Thorndales, Warley CM14 130 FX49
Thorndean St, SW18 202 DC89
Thorndene Av, N11 120 DG46
Thorndike, Slou. SL2 153 AN71
Thorndike Av, Nthlt. UB5 158 BX67
Thorndike Cl, SW10 39 N4
Thorndike Ho, SW1
off Vauxhall Br Rd 29 N10
Thorndike Rd, N1 9 K5
Thorndike St, SW1 29 N9
Thorndon Cl, Orp. BR5 227 ET96
Thorndon Ct, Gt Warley CM13 129 FW51
Thorndon Gdns, Epsom KT19 238 CS105
Thorndon Gate, Ingrave CM13 131 GC50
Thorndon Rd, Orp. BR5 227 ET96
Thorn Dr, Geo.Grn SL3 154 AY72
Thorndyke Ct, Pnr. HA5
off Westfield Pk 116 BZ52
Thorne Cl, E11 146 EE63
E16 23 N8
Ashford TW15 197 BQ94
Claygate KT10 237 CG108
Erith DA8 189 FC79
Hemel Hempstead HP1 62 BH22
Thorneloe Gdns, Croy. CR0 241 DN106
Thorne Pas, SW13 180 CS82
Thorne Rd, SW8 42 A5
Thornes Cl, Beck. BR3 225 EC97
Thorne St, E16 23 M8
SW13 180 CS83
Thornet Wd Rd, Brom. BR1 227 EN97
THORNEY, Iver SL0 176 BH76
Thorney Cres, SW11 40 B5
Thorneycroft Cl, Walt. KT12 218 BW100
Thorneycroft Dr, Enf. EN3 105 EA38
Thorney Hedge Rd, W4 180 CP77
Thorney La N, Iver SL0 155 BF74
Thorney La S, Iver SL0 175 BF75
Thorney Mill Rd, Iver SL0 176 BG76
West Drayton UB7 176 BG76
Thorney St, SW1 30 A8
Thornfield Av, NW7 119 CY53
Thornfield Rd, W12 181 CV75
Banstead SM7 256 DA117
Thornford Rd, SE13 205 EC85
Thorngate Rd, W9 15 K4
Thorngrove Rd, E13 166 EH67
Thornham Gro, E15 12 G3
Thornham St, SE10 46 D3
Thornhaugh Ms, WC1 17 P5
Thornhaugh St, WC1 17 P6
Thornhill, N.Wld Bas. CM16 93 FC26
Thornhill Av, SE18 187 ES80
Surbiton KT6 220 CL103
Thornhill Br Wf, N1 8 C9
Thornhill Cl, Amer. HP7 77 AP40
Thornhill Cres, N1 8 C7
Thornhill Gdns, E10 145 EB61
Barking IG11 167 ES66
Thornhill Gro, N1 8 D7
Thornhill Prim Sch, N1 8 E7
Thornhill Rd, E10 145 EB61
N1 8 E6
Croydon CR0 224 DQ101
Northwood HA6 115 BQ49
Surbiton KT6 220 CL103
Uxbridge UB10 136 BM63
Thornhill Sq, N1 8 D7
Thornhill Way, Shep. TW17 216 BN99
Thorn Ho, Beck. BR3 225 DY95
Thorn La, Rain. RM13 170 FK68
Thornlaw Rd, SE27 203 DN91
Thornleas Pl, E.Hors. KT24
off Station App 267 BS126
Thornley Cl, N17 122 DU52
Thornley Dr, Har. HA2 138 CB61
Thornley Pl, SE10 47 J1
Thornridge, Brwd. CM14 130 FV45
Thornsbeach Rd, SE6 205 EC88
Thornsett Pl, SE20 224 DV96
Thornsett Rd, SE20 224 DV96
SW18 202 DB89
Thornside, Edg. HA8
off High St 118 CN51
Thorns Meadow, Brasted TN16 262 EW123
Thorn Ter, SE15
off Nunhead Gro 184 DW83
Thornton Av, SW2 203 DK88
W4 180 CS77
Croydon CR0 223 DM100
West Drayton UB7 176 BM76
Thornton Cl, Guil. GU2 264 AU130
Horley RH6 290 DE148
West Drayton UB7 176 BM76
Thornton Ct, SW20 221 CX99
Thornton Cres, Couls. CR5 257 DN119
Thornton Dene, Beck. BR3 225 EA96
Thornton Gdns, SW12 203 DK88
Thornton Gro, Pnr. HA5 116 CA51
THORNTON HEATH, CR7 223 DP98
⇌ Thornton Heath 224 DQ98
⊖ Thornton Heath 223 DN99
Thornton Heath Pond, Th.Hth. CR7 223 DN99
Thornton Hill, SW19 201 CY94
Thornton Ho, SE17 31 M9
Thornton Pl, W1 16 F6
Horley RH6 290 DE148
Thornton Rd, E11 145 ED61
N18 122 DW48
SW12 203 DK87
SW14 180 CR83
SW19 201 CX93
Barnet EN5 101 CY41
Belvedere DA17 189 FB77
Bromley BR1 206 EG92
Carshalton SM5 222 DD102
Croydon CR0 223 DM101
Ilford IG1 147 EP63
Potters Bar EN6 86 DC30
Thornton Heath CR7 223 DM101
Thornton Rd E, SW19
off Thornton Rd 201 CX93
● Thornton Rd Ind Est, Croy. CR0 223 DL100
Thornton Row, Th.Hth. CR7
off London Rd 223 DN99
Thorntons Fm Av, Rom. RM7 149 FD60
Thornton Side, Red. RH1 273 DH131
Thornton St, SW9 42 E8
Hertford SG14 54 DR09
St. Albans AL3 64 CC19
Thornton Wk, Horl. RH6
off Thornton Pl 290 DE148
Thornton Way, NW11 142 DB57
Thorntree Prim Sch, SE7 36 F10
Thorntree Rd, SE7 186 EK78
Thornville Gro, Mitch. CR4 222 DC96
Thornville St, SE8 46 A7
THORNWOOD, Epp. CM16 92 EW25
Thornwood Cl, E18 124 EH54
Thornwood Gdns, W8 27 J4
Thornwood Rd, SE13 206 EE85
Epping CM16 92 EW29
Thorogood Gdns, E15 13 K3
Thorogood Way, Rain. RM13 169 FE67
Thorold Cl, S.Croy. CR2 243 DX110
Thorold Rd, N22 121 DL52
Ilford IG1 147 EP61
Thoroughfare, The, Walt.Hill KT20 271 CU125
Thorparch Rd, SW8 41 P6
THORPE, Egh. TW20 215 BC97
Thorpebank Rd, W12 161 CU74
Thorpe Bypass, Egh. TW20 215 BB96
Thorpe Cl, W10 14 F8
New Addington CR0 243 EC111
Orpington BR6 227 ES103
Thorpe C of E Inf Sch, Thorpe TW20 off The Bence 215 BB97
Thorpe Coombe Hosp, E17 145 EC55
Thorpe Cres, E17 123 DZ54
Watford WD19 116 BW45
Thorpedale Gdns, Ilf. IG2, IG6 147 EN56
Thorpedale Rd, N4 143 DL60
Thorpefield Cl, St.Alb. AL4 65 CK17
THORPE GREEN, Egh. TW20 215 BA98
Thorpe Hall Prim Sch, E17
off Hale End Rd 123 EC53
Thorpe Hall Rd, E17 123 EC53
Thorpe Ho Sch, Ger.Cr. SL9
off Oval Way 134 AY56
● Thorpe Ind Est, Egh. TW20 215 BC96
THORPE LEA, Egh. TW20 195 BB93
Thorpe Lea Prim Sch, Egh. TW20 off Huntingfield Way 195 BD93
Thorpe Lea Rd, Egh. TW20 195 BB93
Thorpe Lo, Horn. RM11 150 FK59
★ Thorpe Park, Cher. KT16 215 BE98
Thorpe Rd, E6 167 EM67
E7 146 EF63
E17 123 EC54
N15 144 DS58
Barking IG11 167 ER66
Chertsey KT16 215 BD99
Kingston upon Thames KT2 200 CL94
St. Albans AL1 65 CD21
Staines TW18 195 BD93
Thorpes Cl, Guil. GU2 264 AU131
Thorpeside Cl, Stai. TW18 215 BE96
Thorpe Wk, Grnf. UB6 159 CE68
Thorpewood Av, SE26 204 DV89
Thorpland Av, Uxb. UB10 137 BQ62
Thorsden Cl, Wok. GU22 248 AY118
Thorsden Ct, Wok. GU22
off Guildford Rd 248 AY118
Thorsden Way, SE19
off Oaks Av 204 DS92
Thorverton Rd, NW2 141 CY62
Thoydon Rd, E3 21 L1
Thrale Rd, SW16 203 DJ92
Thrale St, SE1 31 K3
Thrasher Cl, E8 10 A8
Thrawl St, E1 20 B7
Threadneedle St, EC2 19 M9
Three Arches Pk, Red. RH1 288 DF138
Three Arch Rd, Red. RH1 288 DF138
Three Barrels Wk, EC4 31 K1
Three Bridges Path, Kings.T. KT1
off Portland Rd 220 CL97
Three Bridges Prim Sch, Sthl. UB2 off Melbury Av 178 CB76
Three Cherry Trees La, Hem.H. HP2 63 BP16
Three Cl La, Berk. HP4 60 AW20
Three Colts Cor, E2 20 C4
Three Colts La, E2 20 E4
Three Colt St, E14 21 P9
Three Cors, Bexh. DA7 189 FB82
Hemel Hempstead HP3 62 BN22
Three Cranes Wk, EC4
off Bell Wf La 31 K1
Three Cups Yd, WC1 18 D7
Three Forests Way, Broad.Com. EN9 72 EL21
Chigwell IG7 126 EW48
Epping CM16 73 EM23
Harlow CM19 72 EH18
Loughton IG10
off The Clay Rd 106 EK38
Mark Hall North CM20 58 EU10
Romford RM4 126 EW48
Waltham Abbey EN9 106 EK36
Ware SG12 56 EL12
Three Gates, Guil. GU1 265 BC132
Three Gates Rd, Fawk.Grn DA3 231 FU102
Three Horseshoes Rd, Harl. CM19 73 EP17
Three Households, Ch.St.G. HP8 112 AT49
Three Kings Rd, Mitch. CR4 222 DG97
Three Kings Yd, W1 17 J10
Three Meadows Ms, Har. HA3 117 CF53
Three Mill La, E3 22 E2
Three Oak La, SE1 32 A4
Three Oaks Cl, Uxb. UB10 136 BM62
Three Pears Rd, Guil. GU1 265 BE134
Three Quays Wk, EC3 31 P1
Three Valleys Way, Bushey WD23 98 BX43
THRESHERS BUSH, Harl. CM17 75 FB16
Threshers Bush, Harl. CM17 58 FA14
Threshers Pl, W11 14 E10
Thriffwood, SE26 204 DW90
Thrift, The, Bean DA2 211 FW90
Thrift Fm La, Borwd. WD6 100 CP40
Thriftfield, Hem.H. HP2 62 BK18
Thrift Grn, Brwd. CM13
off Knight's Way 131 GA48
Thrift La, Cudham TN14 261 ER117
Ware SG12 55 DZ08
Thrifts Mead, They.B. CM16 107 ES37
Thrift Vale, Guil. GU4 265 BD131
Thrigby Rd, Chess. KT9 238 CM107
Throckmorton Rd, E16 24 B9
Throgmorton Av, EC2 19 M8
Throgmorton St, EC2 19 M8
Thrower Pl, Dor. RH5 285 CJ138
Throwley Cl, SE2 188 EW76
Throwley Rd, Sutt. SM1 240 DB106
Throwley Way, Sutt. SM1 240 DB105
Thrums, The, Wat. WD24 97 BV37
Thrupp Cl, Mitch. CR4 223 DH96
Thrupps Av, Hersham KT12 236 BX106
Thrupps La, Hersham KT12 236 BX106
Thrush Av, Hat. AL10 67 CU20
Thrush Grn, Har. HA2 138 CA56
Rickmansworth WD3 114 BJ45
Thrush La, Cuffley EN6 87 DL28
Thrush St, SE17 31 J10
Thumbswood, Welw.G.C. AL7 52 DA12
Thumpers, Hem.H. HP2 62 BL18
Thundercourt, Ware SG12 55 DX05
Thunderer Rd, Dag. RM9 168 EY70
Thundridge Cl, Welw.G.C. AL7
off Amwell Common 52 DB10
Thurbarn Rd, SE6 205 EB92
Thurgood Rd, Hodd. EN11 71 EA15
Thurland Ho, SE16
off Manor Est 32 E9
Thurland Rd, SE16 32 C6
Thurlby Cl, Har. HA1
off Gayton Rd 139 CG58
Woodford Green IG8 125 EM50
Thurlby Rd, SE27 203 DN91
Wembley HA0 159 CK65
Thurleigh Av, SW12 202 DG86
Thurleigh Rd, SW12 202 DG86
Thurleston Av, Mord. SM4 221 CY99
Thurlestone Av, N12 120 DF51
Ilford IG3 147 ET63
Thurlestone Cl, Shep. TW17 217 BQ100
Thurlestone Rd, SE27 203 DN90
Thurloe Cl, SW7 28 C8
Thurloe Gdns, Rom. RM1 149 FF58
Thurloe Pl, SW7 28 B8
Thurloe Pl Ms, SW7 28 B8
Thurloe Sq, SW7 28 C8
Thurloe St, SW7 28 B8
Thurloe Wk, Grays RM17 192 GA76
Thurlow Cl, E4
off Higham Sta Av 123 EB51
Thurlow Gdns, Ilf. IG6 125 ER51
Wembley HA0 139 CK64
Thurlow Hill, SE21 204 DQ88
Thurlow Pk Rd, SE21 203 DP88
Thurlow Rd, NW3 6 A2
W7 179 CG75
Thurlow St, SE17 31 M10
Thurlow Ter, NW5 6 G3
Thurlstone Rd, Ruis. HA4 137 BU62
Thurlton Ct, Wok. GU21
off Chobham Rd 248 AY116
Thurnby Ct, Twick. TW2 199 CE90
Thurnham Way, Tad. KT20 255 CW120
Thurrock Adult Comm Coll - Grays Adult Ed Cen, Grays RM17
off Richmond Rd 192 GB78
Thurrock & Basildon Coll, Woodview Campus, Grays RM16 off Woodview 193 GF77
Thurrock Pk Way, Til. RM18 192 GD80
Thursby Rd, Wok. GU21 248 AU118
Thursland Rd, Sid. DA14 208 EY92
Thursley Cres, New Adgtn CR0 243 ED108
Thursley Gdns, SW19 201 CX89
Thursley Rd, SE9 207 EM90
Thurso Cl, Rom. RM3 128 FP51
Thurso Ho, NW6 15 L1
Thurso St, SW17 202 DD91
Thurstan Rd, SW20 201 CV94
Thurstans, Harl. CM19 73 EP20
Thurston Rd, SE13 46 D9
Slough SL1 154 AS72
Southall UB1 158 BZ72
● Thurston Rd Ind Est, SE13 46 C10
Thurtle Rd, E2 10 B9
Thwaite Cl, Erith DA8 189 FC79
Thyer Cl, Orp. BR6
off Isabella Dr 245 EQ105
Thyme Cl, SE3 186 EJ83
Thyme Ct, Guil. GU4
off Mallow Cres 265 BB131
Thyra Gro, N12 120 DB51
Tibbatts Rd, E3 22 C4
Tibbenham Pl, SE6 205 EA89
Tibbenham Wk, E13 23 M1
Tibberton Sq, N1 9 J7
Tibbets Cl, SW19 201 CX88
Tibbet's Cor, SW15 201 CX87
Tibbet's Cor Underpass, SW15
off West Hill 201 CX87
Tibbet's Ride, SW15 201 CX87
Tibbles Cl, Wat. WD25 98 BY35
Tibbs Hill Rd, Abb.L. WD5 81 BT30
Tiber Cl, E3 12 A9
Tiber Gdns, N1 8 B9
Ticehurst Cl, Orp. BR5 208 EU94
Ticehurst Rd, SE23 205 DY89
Tichborne, Map.Cr. WD3 113 BD50
Tichmarsh, Epsom KT19 238 CQ110
Tickenhall Dr, Harl. CM17 74 EX15
Tickford Cl, SE2
off Ampleforth Rd 188 EW75
Tidal Basin Rd, E16 35 M1
Tideham Ho, SE28
off Merbury Cl 167 ER74
Tidemill Prim Sch, SE8 46 B5
Tidenham Gdns, Croy. CR0 224 DS104
Tideslea Path, SE28 167 ER74
Tideslea Twr, SE28 187 ER75
Tideswell Rd, SW15 201 CW85
Croydon CR0 225 EA104
Tideway Cl, Rich. TW10 199 CH91
● Tideway Ind Est, SW8 41 M3
Tideway Wk, SW8 41 L3
Tidey St, E3 22 B6
Tidford Rd, Well. DA16 187 ET82
Tidlock Ho, SE28 187 ER75
Tidworth Ho, SE22
off Albrighton Rd 184 DS83
Tidworth Rd, E3 22 A4
Tidy's La, Epp. CM16 92 EV29
Tiepigs La, Brom. BR2 226 EE103
West Wickham BR4 226 EE103
Tierney Rd, SW2 203 DL88
Tiffin Girl's Sch, The, Kings.T. KT2 off Richmond Rd 200 CL93
Tiffin Sch for Boys, Kings.T. KT2 off Queen Elizabeth Rd 220 CM96
Tiger Moth Way, Hat. AL10 66 CR17
Tiger Way, E5 144 DV63
Tigris Cl, N9 122 DW47
Tilbrook Rd, SE3 186 EJ83
Tilburstow Hill Rd, Gdse. RH9 274 DW132
TILBURY, RM18 193 GG81
Tilbury Cl, SE15 44 B4
Orpington BR5 228 EV96
Pinner HA5 116 BZ52
Tilbury Energy & Environment Cen, Til. RM18 off Fort Rd 193 GK83
★ Tilbury Fort, Til. RM18 193 GJ84
Tilbury Manor Jun Sch, Til. RM18 off Dickens Av 193 GH80
Tilbury Mead, Harl. CM18 74 EU17
Tilbury Rd, E6 25 J1
E10 145 EC59
⇌ Tilbury Town 192 GE82
Tilbury Wk, Slou. SL3 175 BB76
Tildesley Rd, SW15 201 CW86
Tilecroft, Welw.G.C. AL8 51 CX06
Tile Fm Rd, Orp. BR6 227 ER104
Tilegate Rd, Harl. CM18 73 ET17
Ongar CM5 75 FC19
Tilehouse Cl, Borwd. WD6 100 CM41
Tilehouse Comb Sch, Denh. UB9
off Nightingale Way 135 BF58
Tilehouse La, Denh. UB9 135 BE58
Gerrards Cross SL9 113 BE53
West Hyde WD3 113 BE53
Tilehouse Rd, Guil. GU4 280 AY138
Tilehouse Way, Denh. UB9 135 BF59
Tilehurst La, Dor. RH5 286 CL137
Tilehurst Pt, SE2
off Yarnton Way 188 EW75
Tilehurst Rd, SW18 202 DD88
Sutton SM3 239 CY106
Tilekiln Cl, Chsht EN7 88 DS29
Tile Kiln Cl, Hem.H. HP3 63 BP21
Tile Kiln Cres, Hem.H. HP3 63 BP21
Tile Kiln La, N6 143 DJ60
N13 122 DQ50
Bexley DA5 209 FC89
Harefield UB9 137 BP59
Hemel Hempstead HP3 62 BN21
Tilers Cl, S.Merst. RH1 273 DJ131
Tiler's Wk, Reig. RH2 288 DC138
Tiler's Way, Reig. RH2 288 DC138
Tile Yd, E14 21 P9
Tileyard Rd, N7 8 A6
Tilford Av, New Adgtn CR0 243 EC109
Tilford Gdns, SW19 201 CX89
Tilgate Common, Bletch. RH1 274 DQ133
Tilia Cl, Sutt. SM1 239 CZ106
Tilia Rd, E5 10 F1
Tilia Wk, SW9 183 DP84
Till Av, Fnghm DA4 230 FM102
Tiller Rd, E14 34 A6
Tillett Cl, NW10 160 CQ65
Tillett Sq, SE16 33 M5
Tillett Way, E2 20 C2
Tilley La, Headley KT18 254 CQ123
Tilley Rd, Felt. TW13 197 BU88
Tillingbourne Gdns, N3 141 CZ55
Tillingbourne Grn, Orp. BR5 228 EU98
Tillingbourne Jun Sch, Chilw. GU4 off New Rd 281 BB141
Tillingbourne Rd, Shalf. GU4 280 AY140
Tillingbourne Way, N3
off Tillingbourne Gdns 141 CZ56
Tillingdown Hill, Cat. CR3 258 DU122
Tillingdown La, Cat. CR3 258 DV124
Tillingham Ct, Wal.Abb. EN9 90 EG33
Tillingham Way, N12 120 DA49
Tilling Rd, NW2 141 CW60
Tillings Cl, SE5 43 K7
Tilling Way, Wem. HA9 139 CK61
Tillman St, E1 20 F9
Tilloch St, N1 8 C7
Tillotson Ct, SW8
off Wandsworth Rd 42 A5
Tillotson Rd, N9 122 DT47
Harrow HA3 116 CB52
Ilford IG1 147 EN59
Tillwicks Rd, Harl. CM18 74 EU17
Tilly's La, Stai. TW18 195 BF91
Tilmans Mead, Fnghm DA4 230 FM101
Tilney Cl, Lthd. KT22
off Randalls Cres 253 CG120
Tilney Ct, EC1 19 K4
Tilney Dr, Buck.H. IG9 124 EG47
Tilney Gdns, N1 9 M5
Tilney Rd, Dag. RM9 168 EZ65
Southall UB2 178 BW77
Tilney St, W1 29 H2
Tilson Cl, SE5 43 N4
Tilson Gdns, SW2 203 DL87
Tilson Ho, SW2 203 DL87
Tilson Rd, N17 122 DU53
Tilston Cl, E11
off Matcham Rd 146 EF62
Tilstone Av, Eton Wick SL4 173 AL78
Tilstone Cl, Eton Wick SL4 173 AL78
Tilsworth Rd, Beac. HP9 132 AJ55
Tilsworth Wk, St.Alb. AL4
off Larkswood Ri 65 CJ15
Tilt Cl, Cob. KT11 252 BY116
Tilthams Cor Rd, Gdmg. GU7 280 AV143
Tilthams Grn, Gdmg. GU7 280 AV143
Tilt Meadow, Cob. KT11 252 BY116
Tilton St, SW6 38 F3
Tilt Rd, Cob. KT11 252 BW115
Tiltwood, The, W3 160 CQ73
Tilt Yd App, SE9 207 EM86
Timber Cl, Bkhm KT23 268 CC126
Chislehurst BR7 227 EN96
Woking GU22 233 BF114
Timber Ct, Grays RM17
off Columbia Wf Rd 192 GA79
Timbercroft, Epsom KT19 238 CS105
Welwyn Garden City AL7 51 CZ06
Timbercroft La, SE18 187 ES79
Timbercroft Prim Sch, SE18
off Timbercroft La 187 ES80
Timberdene, NW4 119 CX54
Timberdene Av, Ilf. IG6 125 EP53
Timberham Fm Rd, Gat. RH6 290 DD151
Timberham Way, Horl. RH6 290 DE152
Timberhill, Ashtd. KT21 254 CL119
Timber Hill Cl, Ott. KT16 233 BC108
Timber Hill Rd, Cat. CR3 258 DU124
Timberidge, Loud. WD3 96 BJ42
Timberland Cl, SE15 44 C5
Timberland Rd, E1
off Hainton Cl 20 F9
Timber La, Cat. CR3
off Timber Hill Rd 258 DU124
Timberling Gdns, S.Croy. CR2
off St. Mary's Rd 242 DR110
Timber Mill Way, SW4 41 N10
Timber Orchard, Waterf. SG14 53 DN05
Timber Pond Rd, SE16 33 K3
Timberslip Dr, Wall. SM6 241 DK109
Timber St, EC1 19 J4
Timbertop Rd, Bigg.H. TN16 260 EJ118
Timber Wf, E2 10 A9
Timberwharf Rd, N16 144 DU58
Timberwood, Slou. SL2 133 AR62
Timbrell Pl, SE16 33 N3
Time Sq, E8 10 A3
Times Sq, Sutt. SM1 240 DB106
Times Sq, E1 20 C9
Times Sq Shop Cen, Sutt. SM1 off High St 240 DB106
Timms Cl, Brom. BR1 227 EM98
Timothy Cl, SW4 off Elms Rd 203 DJ85
Bexleyheath DA6 208 EY85
Timothy Ho, Erith DA18
off Kale Rd 188 EY75
Timperley Gdns, Red. RH1 272 DE132
Timplings Row, Hem.H. HP1 62 BH18
Timsbury Wk, SW15 201 CU88
Timsway, Stai. TW18 195 BF92
Tindale Cl, S.Croy. CR2 242 DR111
Tindall Cl, Rom. RM3 128 FM54
Tindall Ms, Horn. RM12 150 FJ62

Tindal St, SW9 42 G6
Tinderbox All, SW14 180 CR83
Tine Rd, Chig. IG7 125 ES50
Tingeys Top La, Enf. EN2 103 DN36
Tinkers La, Roydon CM19 72 EJ20
Windsor SL4 173 AK82
Tinniswood Cl, N5
off Drayton Pk 8 E2
Tinsey Cl, Egh. TW20 195 BB92
Tinsley Cl, SE25 224 DV97
Tinsley Rd, E1 21 H6
Tintagel Cl, Epsom KT17 239 CT114
Hemel Hempstead HP2 62 BK15
Tintagel Cres, SE22 184 DT84
Tintagel Dr, Stan. HA7 117 CK49
Tintagel Gdns, SE22
off Oxonian St 184 DT84
Tintagel Rd, Orp. BR5 228 EW103
Tintagel Way, Wok. GU22 249 BA116
Tintells La, W.Hors. KT24 267 BP128
Tintern Av, NW9 140 CP55
Tintern Cl, SW15 201 CY85
SW19 202 DC94
Slough SL1 173 AQ76
Tintern Ct, W13
off Green Man La 159 CG73
Tintern Gdns, N14 121 DL45
Tintern Path, NW9
off Ruthin Cl 140 CS58
Tintern Rd, N22 122 DQ53
Carshalton SM5 222 DD102
Tintern St, SW4 183 DL84
Tintern Way, Har. HA2 138 CB60
Tinto Rd, E16 23 P5
Tinwell Ms, Borwd. WD6
off Cranes Way 100 CQ43
Tinworth St, SE11 30 B10
Tippendell La, St.Alb. AL2 82 CB26
Tippetts Cl, Enf. EN2 104 DQ39
Tipthorpe Rd, SW11 40 G10
Tipton Cotts, Add. KT15
off Oliver Cl 234 BH105
Tipton Dr, Croy. CR0 242 DS105
Tiptree Cl, E4
off Mapleton Rd 123 EC48
Hornchurch RM11 150 FN60
Tiptree Cres, Ilf. IG5 147 EN55
Tiptree Dr, Enf. EN2 104 DR42
Tiptree Est, Ilf. IG5 147 EN55
Tiptree Rd, Ruis. HA4 137 BV63
Tiree Cl, Hem.H. HP3 63 BP22
Tirlemont Rd, S.Croy. CR2 242 DQ108
Tirrell Rd, Croy. CR0 224 DQ100
Tisbury Ct, W1 off Rupert St 17 N10
Tisbury Rd, SW16 223 DL96
Tisdall Pl, SE17 31 M9
Tissington Ct, SE16
off Rotherhithe New Rd 33 J9
Titan Rd, Grays RM17 192 GA78
Hemel Hempstead HP2 62 BM17
Titchborne Row, W2 16 D9
Titchfield Rd, NW8 6 D9
Carshalton SM5 222 DD102
Enfield EN3 105 DY37
Titchfield Wk, Cars. SM5
off Titchfield Rd 222 DD101
Titchwell Rd, SW18 202 DD87
Tite Hill, Egh. TW20 194 AX92
Tite St, SW3 40 E1
Tithe Barn Cl, Kings.T. KT2 220 CM95
St. Albans AL1 64 CC23
Tithe Barn Ct, Abb.L. WD5
off Dairy Way 81 BT29
Tithe Barn Dr, Maid. SL6 172 AE78
Tithebarns La, Send GU23 266 BG126
Tithe Barn Way, Nthlt. UB5 157 BV68
Tithe Cl, NW7 119 CU53
Hayes UB4 157 BT71
Maidenhead SL6 172 AC78
Virginia Water GU25 214 AX100
Walton-on-Thames KT12 217 BV100
Tithe Ct, Slou. SL3 175 BA77
Tithe Fm Av, Har. HA2 138 CA62
Tithe Fm Cl, Har. HA2 138 CA62
Tithelands, Harl. CM19 73 EM18
Tithe La, Wrays. TW19 195 BA86
Tithe Meadows, Vir.W. GU25 214 AW100
Tithepit Shaw La, Warl. CR6 258 DV115
Tithe Wk, NW7 119 CU53
Titian Av, Bushey Hth WD23 117 CE45
Titley Cl, E4 123 EA50
Titmus Cl, Uxb. UB8 157 BQ72
Titmuss Av, SE28 168 EV73
Titmuss St, W12
off Goldhawk Rd 181 CW75
TITSEY, Oxt. RH8 276 EH125
Titsey Hill, Titsey RH8 260 EF123
Titsey Rd, Oxt. RH8 276 EH125
Tiverton Av, Ilf. IG5 147 EN55
Tiverton Cl, Croy. CR0
off Exeter Rd 224 DT101
Tiverton Dr, SE9 207 EQ88
Tiverton Gro, Rom. RM3 128 FN50
Tiverton Ho, Enf. EN3 105 DX41
Tiverton Prim Sch, N15
off Pulford Rd 144 DR58
Tiverton Rd, N15 144 DR58
N18 122 DS50
NW10 4 C9
Edgware HA8 118 CM54
Hounslow TW3 178 CC82
Potters Bar EN6 86 DD31
Ruislip HA4 137 BU62
Thornton Heath CR7
off Willett Rd 223 DN99
Wembley HA0 160 CL68
Tiverton St, SE1 31 J7
Tiverton Way, NW7 119 CX52
Chessington KT9 237 CJ106
Tivoli Ct, SE16 33 N4
Tivoli Gdns, SE18 36 G8
Tivoli Rd, N8 143 DK57
SE27 204 DQ92
Hounslow TW4 178 BY84
Toad La, Houns. TW4 178 BZ84
Tobacco Dock, E1 32 E1
Tobacco Quay, E1 32 E1
Tobago St, E14 34 A4
Tobermory Cl, Slou. SL3 174 AY77
Tobin Cl, NW3 6 D6
Epsom KT19 238 CP111
Toby La, E1 21 L5
Toby Way, Surb. KT5 220 CP103
Tockley Rd, Burn. SL1 152 AH68
Todd Brook, Harl. CM19 73 EP16
Todd Cl, Rain. RM13 170 FK70
Todds Cl, Horl. RH6 290 DE146
Todds Wk, N7
off Andover Rd 143 DM61
Todhunter Ter, Barn. EN5
off Prospect Rd 102 DA42
Toft Av, Grays RM17 192 GD77
Tokenhouse Yd, EC2 19 L8
Token Yd, SW15 181 CY84
TOKYNGTON, Wem. HA9 160 CP65
Tokyngton Av, Wem. HA9 160 CN65
Toland Sq, SW15 201 CU85
Tolcarne Dr, Pnr. HA5 137 BV55
Toldene Ct, Couls. CR5 257 DM120
Toley Av, Wem. HA9 140 CL59
Tolhurst Dr, W10 14 F2
Toll Bar Ct, Sutt. SM2 240 DB109
Tollbridge Cl, W10 14 F4
Tolldene Cl, Knap. GU21
off Robin Hood Rd 248 AS117
Tollers La, Couls. CR5 257 DM119
Tollesbury Gdns, Ilf. IG6 147 ER55
Tollet St, E1 21 J4
Tollgate, Guil. GU1 265 BD133
Tollgate Av, Red. RH1 288 DF139
Tollgate Cl, Chorl. WD3 95 BF41
Tollgate Dr, SE21 204 DS89
Hayes UB4 158 BX73
Tollgate Gdns, NW6 5 L10
Tollgate Ho, NW6 5 K10
Tollgate Prim Sch, E13 24 D4
Tollgate Rd, E6 24 E7
E16 24 C6
Colney Heath AL4 66 CS24
Dartford DA2 211 FR87
Dorking RH4 285 CH139
North Mymms AL9 85 CU25
Waltham Cross EN8 105 DX35
Tollhouse La, Wall. SM6 241 DJ109
Tollhouse Way, N19 143 DJ61
Tollington Pk, N4 143 DM61
Tollington Pl, N4 143 DM61
Tollington Rd, N7 143 DM63
Tollington Way, N7 143 DL62
Tollpit End, Hem.H. HP1 62 BG17
Tolmers Av, Cuffley EN6 87 DL28
Tolmers Gdns, Cuffley EN6 87 DL29
Tolmers Ms, Newgate St SG13 87 DL25
Tolmers Pk, Newgate St SG13 87 DL25
Tolmers Rd, Cuffley EN6 87 DL27
Tolmers Sq, NW1 17 M4
Tolpaide Ho, SE11 30 E9
Tolpits Cl, Wat. WD18 97 BT43
Tolpits La, Wat. WD18 97 BT44
Tolpuddle Av, E13
off Rochester Av 166 EJ67
Tolpuddle St, N1 8 E10
Tolsford Rd, E5 10 F2
Tolson Rd, Islw. TW7 179 CG83
Tolvaddon, Wok. GU21
off Cardingham 248 AU117
Tolverne Rd, SW20 221 CW95
TOLWORTH, Surb. KT6 220 CN103
⇌ Tolworth 220 CP103
Tolworth Bdy, Surb. KT6 220 CP102
Tolworth Cl, Surb. KT6 220 CP102
Tolworth Gdns, Rom. RM6 148 EX57
Tolworth Girls' Sch & Cen for Cont Ed, Surb. KT6
off Fullers Way N 220 CM104
Tolworth Hosp, Surb. KT6 220 CN103
Tolworth Infants' Sch, Surb. KT6 off School La 220 CM102
Tolworth Junct, Surb. KT5 220 CP103
Tolworth Jun Sch, Surb. KT6 off Douglas Rd 220 CM102
Tolworth Pk Rd, Surb. KT6 220 CM103
Tolworth Ri N, Surb. KT5
off Elmbridge Av 220 CQ101
Tolworth Ri S, Surb. KT5
off Warren Dr S 220 CQ102
Tolworth Rd, Surb. KT6 220 CL103
Tolworth Twr, Surb. KT6 220 CP103
Tomahawk Gdns, Nthlt. UB5
off Javelin Way 158 BX69
Tom Coombs Cl, SE9 186 EL84
Tom Cribb Rd, SE28 187 EQ76
Tom Gros Cl, E15 13 H3
Tom Hood Cl, E15 13 H3
Tom Hood Sch, E11
off Terling Cl 146 EF62
Tom Jenkinson Rd, E16 35 P2
Tomkins Cl, Borwd. WD6
off Tallis Way 100 CL39
Tomkyns La, Upmin. RM14 151 FR56
Tomlin Cl, Epsom KT19 238 CR111
Tomlin Rd, Slou. SL2 153 AL70
Tomlins Gro, E3 22 B2
Tomlinson Cl, E2 20 B3
W4 180 CP78
Tomlins Orchard, Bark. IG11 167 EQ67
Tomlins Ter, E14 21 M8
Tomlins Wk, N7
off Briset Way 143 DM61
Tomlyns Cl, Hutt. CM13 131 GE44
Tom Mann Cl, Bark. IG11 167 ES67
Tom Nolan Cl, E15 23 K1
● Tomo Ind Est, Uxb. UB8 156 BJ72
Tompion Ho, EC1
off Percival St 19 H4
Tompion St, EC1 18 G3
Toms Cft, Hem.H. HP2 62 BL21
Tomsfield, Hat. AL10 66 CS19
Toms Hill, Kings L. WD4 96 BL36
Rickmansworth WD3 96 BL36
Toms La, Bedmond WD5 81 BR28
Kings Langley WD4 81 BP29
Tom Smith Cl, SE10 47 J2
Tomswood Ct, Ilf. IG6 125 EQ53
Tomswood Hill, Ilf. IG6 125 EP52
Tomswood Rd, Chig. IG7 125 EN51
Tom Thumbs Arch, E3
off Malmesbury Rd 22 A1
Tom Williams Ho, SW6
off Clem Attlee Ct 38 G3
Tonbridge Cl, Bans. SM7 240 DF114
Tonbridge Cres, Har. HA3 140 CL56
Tonbridge Ho, SE25 224 DU97
Tonbridge Rd, Harold Hill RM3 128 FK52
Sevenoaks TN13 279 FJ127
West Molesey KT8 218 BY98
Tonbridge St, WC1 18 A2
Tonbridge Wk, WC1
off Bidborough St 18 A2
Tonfield Rd, Sutt. SM3 221 CZ102
Tonge Cl, Beck. BR3 225 EA99
Tonsley Hill, SW18 202 DB85
Tonsley Pl, SW18 202 DB85
Tonsley Rd, SW18 202 DB85
Tonsley St, SW18 202 DB85
Tonstall Rd, Epsom KT19 238 CR110
Mitcham CR4 222 DG96
Tony Cannell Ms, E3 21 N3
Tooke Cl, Pnr. HA5 116 BY53
Tookey Cl, Har. HA3 140 CM59
Took's Ct, EC4 18 E8
Tooley St, SE1 31 M2
Northfleet DA11 212 GD87
Toorack Rd, Har. HA3 117 CD54
TOOT HILL, Ong. CM5 93 FF30
Toot Hill Rd, Ong. CM5 93 FF29
⇌ Tooting 202 DG93
⊖ Tooting Bec 202 DF90
Tooting Bec, SW17 202 DF90
Tooting Bec Gdns, SW16 203 DK91
Tooting Bec Rd, SW16 202 DG90
SW17 202 DG90
⊖ Tooting Broadway 202 DE92
Tooting Bdy, SW17 202 DE91
TOOTING GRAVENEY, SW17 202 DE93
Tooting Gro, SW17 202 DE92
Tooting High St, SW17 202 DE93
Tooting Mkt, SW17
off Tooting High St 202 DF91
Tootswood Rd, Brom. BR2 226 EE99
Tooveys Mill Cl, Kings L. WD4 80 BN28
Topaz Cl, Slou. SL1
off Pearl Gdns 153 AP74
Topaz Ct, E11
off High Rd Leytonstone 146 EE60
Topaz Ho, E15 off Romford Rd 13 L5
Topaz Wk, NW2 off Marble Dr 141 CX59
Topcliffe Dr, Orp. BR6 245 ER105
Top Dartford Rd, Dart. DA2 209 FF94
Swanley BR8 209 FF94
Top Fm Cl, Beac. HP9 110 AG54
Topham Sq, N17 122 DQ53
Topham St, EC1 18 E4
Top Ho Ri, E4
off Parkhill Rd 123 EC45
Topiary, The, Ashtd. KT21 254 CL120
Topiary Sq, Rich. TW9 180 CM83
Topland Rd, Chal.St.P. SL9 112 AX52
Toplands Av, Aveley RM15 170 FP74
Topley St, SE9 186 EK84
Topmast Pt, E14 34 A5
Top Pk, Beck. BR3 226 EE99
Gerrards Cross SL9 134 AW58
Topping La, Uxb. UB8 156 BK69
Topp Wk, NW2 141 CW61
Topsfield Cl, N8 143 DK57
Topsfield Par, N8
off Tottenham La 143 DL57
Topsfield Rd, N8 143 DL57
Topsham Rd, SW17 202 DF90
Torbay Rd, NW6 4 G7
Harrow HA2 138 BY61
Torbay St, NW1 7 K7
Torbitt Way, Ilf. IG2 147 ET57
Torbridge Cl, Edg. HA8 118 CL52
Torbrook Cl, Bex. DA5 208 EY86
Torcross Dr, SE23 204 DW89
Torcross Rd, Ruis. HA4 137 BV62
Tor Gdns, W8 27 J4
Tor Gro, SE28 167 ES74
Torin Ct, Eng.Grn TW20 194 AW92
Torland Dr, Oxshott KT22 237 CD114
Tor La, Wey. KT13 235 BQ111
Tormead Cl, Sutt. SM1 240 DA107
Tormead Rd, Guil. GU1 265 AZ134
Tormead Sch, Jun Sch, Guil. GU1 off Cranley Rd 265 AZ134
Sen Sch, Guil. GU1
off Cranley Rd 265 AZ134
Tormount Rd, SE18 187 ES79
Tornay Ho, N1
off Priory Grn Est 8 C10
Toronto Av, E12 147 EM63
Toronto Dr, Smallfield RH6 291 DN148
Toronto Rd, Ilf. IG1 147 EP60
Tilbury RM18 193 GG82
Torquay Gdns, Ilf. IG4 146 EK56
Torquay Spur, Slou. SL2 153 AP70
Torquay St, W2 15 L7
Torrance Cl, SE7 186 EK79
Hornchurch RM11 149 FH60
Torrens Cl, Guil. GU2 264 AU131
Torrens Rd, E15 13 L4
SW2 203 DM85
Torrens Sq, E15 13 K4
Torrens St, EC1 18 F1
Torrens Wk, Grav. DA12 213 GL92
Torres Sq, E14
off Maritime Quay 34 B10
Torre Wk, Cars. SM5 222 DE102
Torrey Dr, SW9 42 F8
Torriano Av, NW5 7 N3
Torriano Cotts, NW5 7 M3
Torriano Inf Sch, NW5 7 N4
Torriano Jun Sch, NW5 7 N3
Torriano Ms, NW5 7 M2
Torridge Gdns, SE15 184 DW84
Torridge Rd, Slou. SL3 175 BB79
Thornton Heath CR7 223 DP99
Torridge Wk, Hem.H. HP2
off The Dee 62 BM15
Torridon Cl, Wok. GU21 248 AV117
Torridon Ho, NW6 15 L1
Torridon Inf Sch, SE6
off Torridon Rd 205 ED89
Torridon Jun Sch, SE6
off Hazelbank Rd 205 ED89
Torridon Rd, SE6 205 ED88
SE13 205 ED87
Torrington Av, N12 120 DD50
Torrington Cl, N12 120 DD49
Claygate KT10 237 CE107
Torrington Dr, Har. HA2 138 CB63
Loughton IG10 107 EQ42
Potters Bar EN6 86 DD32
Torrington Gdns, N11 121 DJ51
Loughton IG10 107 EQ42
Perivale UB6 159 CJ67
Torrington Gro, N12 120 DE50
Torrington Pk, N12 120 DC50
Torrington Pl, E1 32 D2
WC1 17 M6
Torrington Rd, E18 146 EG55
Berkhamsted HP4 60 AV19
Claygate KT10 237 CE107
Dagenham RM8 148 EZ60
Perivale UB6 159 CJ67
Ruislip HA4 137 BT62
Torrington Sq, WC1 17 P5
Croydon CR0
off Tavistock Gro 224 DR101
Torrington Way, Mord. SM4 222 DA100
Tor Rd, Well. DA16 188 EW81
Torr Rd, SE20 205 DX94
Tortoiseshell Way, Berk. HP4 60 AT17
Torver Rd, Har. HA1 139 CE56
Torver Way, Orp. BR6 227 ER104
Torwood Cl, Berk. HP4 60 AT19
Torwood La, Whyt. CR3 258 DT120
Torwood Rd, SW15 201 CU85
Torworth Rd, Borwd. WD6 100 CM39
Tothill Ho, SW1 off Page St 29 P8
Tothill St, SW1 29 N5
Totnes Rd, Well. DA16 188 EV80
Totnes Wk, N2 142 DD56
Tottan Ter, E1 21 K8
Tottenhall Inf Sch, N13
off Tottenhall Rd 121 DN51
Tottenhall Rd, N13 121 DN51
TOTTENHAM, N17 122 DS53
⊖ Tottenham Court Road 17 N8
Tottenham Ct Rd, W1 17 M5
Tottenham Grn E, N15 144 DT56
TOTTENHAM HALE, N17 144 DV55
⇌ Tottenham Hale 144 DV55
⊖ Tottenham Hale 144 DV55
Tottenham Hale, N17 144 DT56
Tottenham Hale Retail Pk, N15 144 DU56
★ Tottenham Hotspur FC, N17 122 DT52
Tottenham La, N8 143 DL57
Tottenham Ms, W1 17 M6
Tottenham Rd, N1 9 N5
Tottenham St, W1 17 M7
Totterdown St, SW17 202 DF91
TOTTERIDGE, N20 119 CY46
⊖ Totteridge & Whetstone 120 DB47
Totteridge Common, N20 119 CU47
Totteridge Grn, N20 120 DA47
Totteridge Ho, SW11 40 B9
Totteridge La, N20 120 DA47
Totteridge Rd, Enf. EN3 105 DX37
Totteridge Village, N20 119 CY46
Totternhoe Cl, Har. HA3 139 CJ57
Totton Rd, Th.Hth. CR7 223 DN97
Toucan Cl, NW10 160 CN69
Toulmin Dr, St.Alb. AL3 64 CC16
Toulmin St, SE1 31 J5
Toulon St, SE5 43 J4
Tournay Rd, SW6 39 H4
Tours Pas, SW11 182 DD84
Toussaint Wk, SE16 32 D6
Tovey Av, Hodd. EN11 71 EA15
Tovey Cl, Lon.Col. AL2 83 CK26
Lower Nazeing EN9 72 EE23
Tovil Cl, SE20 224 DU96
Tovy Ho, SE1 44 C1
Towcester Rd, E3 22 D5
Tower, The, Couls. CR5 257 DK122
● Tower 42, EC2 19 N8
Tower Br, E1 32 A3
SE1 32 A3
Tower Br App, E1 32 A2
★ Tower Br Exhib, SE1 32 A3
Tower Br Ms, Har. HA1
off Greenford Rd 139 CF63
Tower Br Piazza, SE1 32 A3
Tower Br Prim Sch, SE1 32 A4
Tower Br Rd, SE1 31 N7
Tower Br Wf, E1 32 C3
Tower Bldgs, E1
off Brewhouse La 32 F3
● Tower Cen, Hodd. EN11 71 EA17
Tower Cl, NW3 6 B2
SE20 204 DV94
Berkhamsted HP4 60 AU20
Flackwell Heath HP10 132 AC56
Gravesend DA12 213 GL92
Hertford Heath SG13 54 DW13
Horley RH6 290 DF148
Ilford IG6 125 EP51
North Weald Bassett CM16 75 FD24
Orpington BR6 227 ET103
Woking GU21 248 AX117
Tower Ct, WC2 18 A9
Brentwood CM14 130 FV47
Egham TW20
off The Chantries 195 BA92
Tower Cft, Eyns. DA4 230 FL103
Tower Gdns, Clay. KT10 237 CG108
Tower Gdns Rd, N17 122 DQ53
Towergate Cl, Uxb. UB8 136 BL64
Tower Gateway 20 B10
Tower Gro, Wey. KT13 217 BS103
Tower Hamlets Coll, Arbour Sq Cen, E1 21 J8
Bethnal Grn Cen, E2 20 C3
East India Dock Rd, E14 22 D9
Poplar Cen, E14 34 C1
Tower Hamlets Rd, E7 13 M1
E17 145 EA55
Tower Hts, Hodd. EN11
off Amwell St 71 EA17
TOWER HILL, Dor. RH4 285 CH138
⊖ Tower Hill 19 P10
Tower Hill, EC3 32 A1
Brentwood CM14 130 FW47
Chipperfield WD4 79 BE29
Dorking RH4 285 CH138
Gomshall GU5 283 BQ140
Tower Hill La, Goms. GU5 283 BQ140
Sandridge AL4 50 CM10
Tower Hill Ri, Goms. GU5 283 BQ140
Tower Hill Rd, Dor. RH4 285 CH138
Tower Hill Ter, EC3
off Byward St 31 P1
Tower Ho, Slou. SL1 174 AS75
Tower Ho Sch, SW14
off Sheen La 180 CQ84
Tower La, Wem. HA9
off Main Dr 139 CK62
Tower Ms, E17 145 EA56
★ Tower Millennium Pier, EC3 31 P2
Tower Mill Rd, SE15 43 N3
★ Tower of London, EC3 32 A1
Tower Pk Rd, Cray. DA1 209 FF85
Tower Pl, Warl. CR6 259 EA115
● Tower Pl E, EC3 31 P1
● Tower Pl W, EC3 31 P1
Tower Pt, Enf. EN2 104 DR42
Tower Retail Pk, Cray. DA1 209 FF85
Tower Ri, Rich. TW9
off Jocelyn Rd 180 CL83
Tower Rd, NW10 161 CU66
Belvedere DA17 189 FC77
Bexleyheath DA7 189 FB84
Coleshill HP7 77 AN43
Dartford DA1 210 FJ86
Epping CM16 91 ES30
Orpington BR6 227 ET103
Tadworth KT20 255 CW123
Twickenham TW1 199 CF90
Ware SG12 55 DY05
Tower Royal, EC4 19 K10
Towers, The, Ken. CR8 258 DQ115
Towers Av, Hlgdn UB10 157 BQ69
● Towers Business Pk, Wem. HA9 off Carey Way 140 CQ63
Towers Inf Sch, Horn. RM11
off Osborne Rd 150 FJ59
Towers Jun Sch, Horn. RM11
off Windsor Rd 150 FJ59
Towers Pl, Rich. TW9 200 CL85
Towers Rd, Grays RM17 192 GC78
Hemel Hempstead HP2 62 BL19
Pinner HA5 116 BY53
Southall UB1 158 CA70
Tower St, WC2 17 P9
Hertford SG14 54 DQ07
Towers Wk, Wey. KT13 235 BP107
Towers Wd, S.Darenth DA4 231 FR95
Tower Ter, N22 off Mayes Rd 121 DM54
SE4 off Foxberry Rd 185 DY84
Tower Vw, Bushey Hth WD23 117 CE45
Croydon CR0 225 DX101
Towfield Rd, Felt. TW13 198 BZ89
Towing Path, Guil. GU1 280 AW138
Towing Path Wk, N1 8 A10
Town, The, Enf. EN2 104 DR41
Town Br Ct, Chesh. HP5
off Watermeadow 76 AP32
Town Cen, Hat. AL10 67 CU17
Towncourt Cres, Petts Wd BR5 227 EQ99
Towncourt La, Petts Wd BR5 227 ER100
Town Ct Path, N4 144 DQ60
Town End, Cat. CR3 258 DS122
Town End Cl, Cat. CR3 258 DS122
Towney Mead, Nthlt. UB5 158 BZ68
Towney Mead Ct, Nthlt. UB5
off Towney Mead 158 BZ68
Town Fm Prim Sch, Stanw. TW19 off St. Mary's Cres 196 BK87
Town Fm Way, Stanw. TW19
off Town La 196 BK87
Townfield, Chesh. HP5 76 AP32
Rickmansworth WD3 114 BJ45
Townfield Cor, Grav. DA12 213 GJ88
Townfield Ct, Dor. RH4
off Horsham Rd 285 CG137
Town Fld La, Ch.St.G. HP8 112 AW48
Townfield Rd, Dor. RH4 285 CG137
Hayes UB3 157 BT74
Townfields, Hat. AL10 67 CU17
Townfield Sq, Hayes UB3 157 BT74
Town Fld Way, Islw. TW7 179 CG82
Towngate, Cob. KT11 252 BY115
Town Hall App, N16 9 M1
Town Hall App Rd, N15 144 DT56
Town Hall Av, W4 180 CR78
Town Hall Rd, SW11 182 DF83
Townholm Cres, W7 179 CF76
Town La, Stanw. TW19 196 BK86
Wooburn Green HP10 132 AD59
Townley Ct, E15 13 L5
Townley Gram Sch for Girls, Bexh. DA6 off Townley Rd 208 EZ85
Townley Rd, SE22 204 DS85
Bexleyheath DA6 208 EZ85
Townley St, SE17 31 L10
Town Mead, Bletch. RH1 274 DR133
● Townmead Business Cen, SW6 39 N10
Town Meadow, Brent. TW8 179 CK79
Townmead Rd, SW6 39 N9
Richmond TW9 180 CP82
Waltham Abbey EN9 89 EC34
Town Mill Ms, Hert. SG14
off Millbridge 54 DQ09
Town Path, Egh. TW20 195 BA92
Town Pier, Grav. DA11
off West St 213 GH86
Town Quay, Bark. IG11 167 EP67
Town Rd, N9 122 DV47
TOWNSEND, St.Alb. AL3 65 CD17
Townsend, Hem.H. HP2 62 BK18
Townsend Av, N14 121 DK49
St. Albans AL1 65 CE19
Townsend C of E Sch, St.Alb. AL3 off Sparrowswick Ride 64 CC15
Townsend Dr, St.Alb. AL3 65 CD18
● Townsend Ind Est, NW10 160 CQ68
Townsend La, NW9 140 CR59
Woking GU22
off St. Peters Rd 249 BB121
Townsend Ms, SW18
off Waynflete St 202 DC89
Townsend Prim Sch, SE17 31 N8
Townsend Rd, N15 144 DT57
Ashford TW15 196 BL92
Chesham HP5 76 AP30
Southall UB1 158 BY74
Townsend St, SE17 31 M9
Townsend Way, Nthwd. HA6 115 BT52
Townsend Yd, N6 143 DH60
Townshend Cl, Sid. DA14 208 EW93
Townshend Est, NW8 6 C10
Townshend Rd, NW8 6 C9
Chislehurst BR7 207 EP92
Richmond TW9 180 CM84
Townshend St, Hert. SG13 54 DS09
Townshend Ter, Rich. TW9 180 CM84
Townshott Cl, Bkhm KT23 268 CA125
Townslow La, Wisley GU23 250 BK116
Townson Av, Nthlt. UB5 157 BU69
Townson Way, Nthlt. UB5
off Townson Av 157 BU68
Town Sq, Bark. IG11
off Clockhouse Av 167 EQ67
Erith DA8 off Pier Rd 189 FE79
Woking GU21
off Church St E 249 AZ117
Town Sq Cres, Bluewater DA9 211 FT87
Town Tree Rd, Ashf. TW15 196 BN92
Towpath, Shep. TW17 216 BM103
Towpath Rd, N18 123 DX51
Towpath Wk, E9 11 N2
Towpath Way, Croy. CR0 224 DT100
Towton Rd, SE27 204 DQ89
Toynbec Cl, Chis. BR7
off Beechwood Ri 207 EP91
Toynbee Rd, SW20 221 CY95
Toynbee St, E1 20 A7
Toyne Way, N6 142 DF58

Tozer Wk, Wind. SL4 . . . 173 AK83
Tracery, The, Bans. SM7 . . . 256 DB115
Tracey Av, NW2 . . . 4 A2
Tracious Cl, Wok. GU21
off Sythwood . . . 248 AV116
Tracious La, Wok. GU21 . . . 248 AV116
Tracy Av, Slou. SL3 . . . 175 AZ78
Tracy Ct, Stan. HA7 . . . 117 CJ52
Tracyes Rd, Harl. CM18 . . . 74 EV17
● Trade City, Wey. KT13 . . . 234 BL110
Trade Cl, N13 . . . 121 DN49
Trader Rd, E6 . . . 25 N9
Tradescant Rd, SW8 . . . 42 B5
Trading Est Rd, NW10 . . . 160 CQ70
Trafalgar Av, N17 . . . 122 DS51
SE15 . . . 44 B1
Broxbourne EN10 . . . 71 DZ21
Worcester Park KT4 . . . 221 CX102
● Trafalgar Business Cen, Bark.
IG11 . . . 167 ET70
Trafalgar Cl, SE16 . . . 33 L8
Trafalgar Ct, E1 . . . 33 H1
Cobham KT11 . . . 235 BU113
Trafalgar Dr, Walt. KT12 . . . 217 BV104
Trafalgar Gdns, E1 . . . 21 K6
W8 . . . 27 L6
Trafalgar Gro, SE10 . . . 47 H2
Sch Trafalgar Inf Sch, Twick. TW2
off Elmsleigh Rd . . . 199 CD89
Sch Trafalgar Jun Sch, Twick. TW2
off Elmsleigh Rd . . . 199 CD89
Trafalgar Ms, E9 . . . 11 N4
Trafalgar Pl, E11 . . . 146 EG56
N18 . . . 122 DU50
Trafalgar Rd, SE10 . . . 47 H2
SW19 . . . 202 DB94
Dartford DA1 . . . 210 FL89
Gravesend DA11 . . . 213 GG87
Rainham RM13 . . . 169 FF68
Twickenham TW2 . . . 199 CD89
Trafalgar Sq, SW1 . . . 29 P2
WC2 . . . 29 P2
Trafalgar St, SE17 . . . 31 L10
Trafalgar Ter, Har. HA1
off Nelson Rd . . . 139 CE60
● Trafalgar Trd Est, Enf. EN3 . 105 DY42
Trafalgar Way, E14 . . . 34 E2
Croydon CR0 . . . 223 DM103
Trafford Cl, Ilf. IG6 . . . 125 ET51
Shenley WD7 . . . 84 CL32
Trafford Rd, Th.Hth. CR7 . . . 223 DM99
Trahorn Cl, E1 . . . 20 E5
Tralee Ct, SE16 . . . 32 E10
Tram Cl, SE24 off Hinton Rd . . 183 DP83
● Tramsheds Ind Est, Croy.
CR0 . . . 223 DK101
Tramway Av, E15 . . . 13 J6
N9 . . . 122 DV45
Tramway Cl, SE20 . . . 224 DW95
Tramway Ho, Erith DA8
off Stonewood Rd . . . 189 FE78
Tramway Path, Mitch. CR4 . . . 222 DF99
Tranby Pl, E9 . . . 11 K3
Tranley Ms, NW3 . . . 6 D2
Tranmere Rd, N9 . . . 122 DT45
SW18 . . . 202 DC89
Twickenham TW2 . . . 198 CB87
Tranquil Dale, Buckland RH3 . . 271 CT132
Tranquil Pas, SE3 . . . 47 L9
Tranquil Ri, Erith DA8
off West St . . . 189 FE78
Tranquil Vale, SE3 . . . 47 K9
Transept St, NW1 . . . 16 C7
Transmere Cl, Petts Wd BR5 . . 227 EQ100
Transmere Rd, Petts Wd BR5 . . 227 EQ100
Transom Cl, SE16 . . . 33 M8
Transom Sq, E14 . . . 34 C9
Transport Av, Brent. TW8 . . . 179 CG78
Tranton Rd, SE16 . . . 32 D6
Trappes Ho, SE16
off Manor Est . . . 32 E9
Trapps La, Chesh. HP5 . . . 76 AR32
Traps Hill, Loug. IG10 . . . 107 EM41
Traps La, N.Mal. KT3 . . . 220 CS95
Trapstyle Rd, Ware SG12 . . . 54 DU05
Trasher Mead, Dor. RH4 . . . 285 CJ139
Travellers Cl, N.Mymms AL9 . . 67 CW23
Travellers La, Hat. AL10 . . . 67 CV22
North Mymms AL9 . . . 67 CW22
Travellers Way, Houns. TW4 . . 178 BW82
Travers Cl, E17 . . . 123 DX53
Travers Rd, N7 . . . 143 DN62
Travic Rd, Slou. SL2 . . . 153 AM69
Travis Ct, Farn.Royal SL2 . . . 153 AP69
Treachers Cl, Chesh. HP5 . . . 76 AP31
Jct Treacle Mine Rbt, Grays
RM16 . . . 192 FZ75
Treacy Cl, Bushey Hth WD23 . . 116 CC47
Treadgold St, W11 . . . 14 D10
Treadway St, E2 . . . 20 E1
Treadwell Rd, Epsom KT18 . . . 254 CS115
Treasury Cl, Wall. SM6 . . . 241 DK106
Treaty Cen, Houns. TW3 . . . 178 CB83
Treaty St, N1 . . . 8 C9
Trebble Rd, Swans. DA10 . . . 212 FY86
Trebeck St, W1 . . . 29 J2
Trebellan Dr, Hem.H. HP2 . . . 62 BM19
Treboyir Rd, SW5 . . . 27 K10
Treby St, E3 . . . 21 N5
Trecastle Way, N7 . . . 7 P1
Tredegar Ms, E3 . . . 21 N2
Tredegar Rd, E3 . . . 21 N1
N11 . . . 121 DK52
Dartford DA2 . . . 209 FG89
Tredegar Sq, E3 . . . 21 N2
Tredegar Ter, E3 . . . 21 N2
Trederwen Rd, E8 . . . 10 D8
Tredown Rd, SE26 . . . 204 DW92
Tredwell Cl, SW2
off Hillside Rd . . . 203 DM89
Bromley BR2 . . . 226 EL98
Tredwell Rd, SE27 . . . 203 DP91
Treebourne Rd, Bigg.H. TN16 . . 260 EJ117
Treeby Ct, Enf. EN3
off George Lovell Dr . . . 105 EA37
Treebys Av, Jacobs Well GU4 . . 264 AX128
Tree Cl, Rich. TW10 . . . 199 CK88
Sch Treehouse Sch, N10
off Woodside Av . . . 142 DG56
Treelands, N.Holm. RH5 . . . 285 CJ139
Treemount Ct, Epsom KT17 . . . 238 CS113
Treen Av, SW13 . . . 181 CT83
Tree Rd, E16 . . . 24 C8
Treeside Cl, West Dr. UB7 . . . 176 BK77
Tree Tops, Brwd. CM15 . . . 130 FW46
Treetops, Grav. DA12 . . . 213 GH92
Whyteleafe CR3 . . . 258 DU118
Treetops Cl, SE2 . . . 188 EY78
Northwood HA6 . . . 115 BR50
Sch Treetops Sch, Grays RM17
off Dell Rd . . . 192 GB77
Treetops Vw, Loug. IG10 . . . 124 EK45
Treeview Cl, SE19 . . . 224 DS95
Treewall Gdns, Brom. BR1 . . . 206 EH91
Tree Way, Reig. RH2 . . . 272 DB131
Trefgarne Rd, Dag. RM10 . . . 148 FA61
Trefil Wk, N7 . . . 143 DL63
Trefoil Ho, Erith DA18
off Kale Rd . . . 188 EY75
Trefoil Rd, SW18 . . . 202 DC85
Trefusis Wk, Wat. WD17 . . . 97 BS39
Tregaron Av, N8 . . . 143 DL58
Tregaron Gdns, N.Mal. KT3
off Avenue Rd . . . 220 CS98
Tregarthen Pl, Lthd. KT22 . . . 253 CJ121
Tregarth Pl, Wok. GU21 . . . 248 AT117
Tregarvon Rd, SW11 . . . 182 DG84
Tregelles Rd, Hodd. EN11 . . . 55 EA14
Tregenna Av, Har. HA2 . . . 138 BZ63
Tregenna Cl, N14 . . . 103 DJ43
Tregenna Ct, Har. HA2 . . . 138 CA63
Tregony Rd, Orp. BR6 . . . 245 ET105
Trego Rd, E9 . . . 11 P6
Tregothnan Rd, SW9 . . . 42 A10
Tregunter Rd, SW10 . . . 39 N2
Trehaven Par, Reig. RH2
off Hornbeam Rd . . . 288 DB137
Trehearn Rd, Ilf. IG6 . . . 125 ER52
Treherne Ct, SW9 . . . 42 F6
SW17 . . . 202 DG91
Trehern Rd, SW14 . . . 180 CR83
Trehurst St, E5 . . . 11 L2
Trelawn Cl, Ott. KT16 . . . 233 BC108
Trelawney Av, Slou. SL3 . . . 174 AX76
Trelawney Cl, E17
off Orford Rd . . . 145 EB56
Trelawney Est, E9 . . . 10 G5
Trelawney Gro, Wey. KT13 . . . 234 BN107
Trelawney Rd, Ilf. IG6 . . . 125 ER52
Trelawn Rd, E10 . . . 145 EC62
SW2 . . . 203 DN85
Trellick Twr, W10 . . . 14 G5
Trellis Sq, E3 . . . 21 P2
Treloar Gdns, SE19
off Hancock Rd . . . 204 DR93
Tremadoc Rd, SW4 . . . 183 DK84
Tremaine Cl, SE4 . . . 46 A9
Tremaine Gro, Hem.H. HP2 . . . 62 BL16
Tremaine Rd, SE20 . . . 224 DV96
Trematon Pl, Tedd. TW11 . . . 199 CJ94
Tremlett Gro, N19 . . . 143 DJ62
Tremlett Ms, N19 . . . 143 DJ62
Trenance, Wok. GU21
off Cardingham . . . 248 AU117
Trenance Gdns, Ilf. IG3 . . . 148 EU62
Trenchard Av, Ruis. HA4 . . . 137 BV63
Trenchard Cl, NW9
off Fulbeck Dr . . . 118 CS53
Hersham KT12 . . . 236 BW106
Stanmore HA7 . . . 117 CG51
Trenchard Ct, Mord. SM4
off Green La . . . 222 DA100
Trenchard St, SE10 . . . 47 H1
Trenches La, Slou. SL3 . . . 155 BA73
Trenchold St, SW8 . . . 42 A3
Trenear Cl, Orp. BR6 . . . 246 EU105
Trenham Dr, Warl. CR6 . . . 258 DW116
Trenholme Cl, SE20 . . . 204 DV94
Trenholme Ct, Cat. CR3 . . . 258 DU122
Trenholme Rd, SE20 . . . 204 DV94
Trenholme Ter, SE20 . . . 204 DV94
Trenmar Gdns, NW10 . . . 161 CV69
Trent Av, W5 . . . 179 CJ76
Upminster RM14 . . . 151 FR58
Trentbridge Cl, Ilf. IG6 . . . 125 ET51
Trent Cl, Shenley WD7
off Edgbaston Dr . . . 84 CL32
Sch Trent C of E Prim Sch, Cockfos.
EN4 off Church Way . . . 102 DF42
Trent Gdns, N14 . . . 103 DH44
Trentham Ct, W3
off Victoria Rd . . . 160 CR71
Trentham Cres, Wok. GU22 . . . 249 BA121
Trentham Dr, Orp. BR5 . . . 228 EU98
Trentham Rd, Red. RH1 . . . 288 DF136
Trentham St, SW18 . . . 202 DA88
★ Trent Park Country Pk, Barn.
EN4 . . . 102 DG40
Trent Rd, SW2 . . . 203 DM85
Buckhurst Hill IG9 . . . 124 EH46
Slough SL3 . . . 175 BB79
Trent Way, Hayes UB4 . . . 157 BS69
Worcester Park KT4 . . . 221 CW104
Trentwood Side, Enf. EN2 . . . 103 DM41
Treport St, SW18 . . . 202 DB87
Tresco Cl, Brom. BR1 . . . 206 EE93
Trescoe Gdns, Har. HA2 . . . 138 BY59
Romford RM5 . . . 127 FC50
Tresco Gdns, Ilf. IG3 . . . 148 EU61
Tresco Rd, SE15 . . . 184 DV84
Berkhamsted HP4 . . . 60 AT19
Tresham Cres, NW8 . . . 16 C4
Tresham Rd, Bark. IG11 . . . 167 ET66
Tresham Wk, E9 . . . 11 H2
Tresilian Av, N21 . . . 103 DM43
Tresilian Sq, Hem.H. HP2 . . . 62 BM15
Tresillian Way, Wok. GU21 . . . 248 AU116
Tressell Cl, N1 . . . 9 H7
Tressillian Cres, SE4 . . . 46 A10
Tressillian Rd, SE4 . . . 185 DZ84
Tresta Wk, Wok. GU21 . . . 248 AU115
Trestis Cl, Hayes UB4
off Jollys La . . . 158 BY71
Treston Ct, Stai. TW18 . . . 195 BF92
Treswell Rd, Dag. RM9 . . . 168 EY67
Tretawn Gdns, NW7 . . . 118 CS49
Tretawn Pk, NW7 . . . 118 CS49
Trevalga Way, Hem.H. HP2 . . . 62 BL16
Trevanion Rd, W14 . . . 26 F10
Treve Av, Har. HA1 . . . 138 CC59
Trevellance Way, Wat. WD25 . . . 82 BW33
Trevelyan Av, E12 . . . 147 EM63
Trevelyan Cl, Dart. DA1 . . . 190 FM84
Trevelyan Ct, Wind. SL4 . . . 173 AP82
Trevelyan Cres, Har. HA3 . . . 139 CK59
Trevelyan Gdns, NW10 . . . 4 A9
Trevelyan Ho, E2
off Morpeth St . . . 21 J3
Sch Trevelyan Mid Sch, Wind.
SL4 off Wood Cl . . . 173 AQ84
Trevelyan Rd, E15 . . . 13 K1
SW17 . . . 202 DE92
Trevelyan Way, Berk. HP4 . . . 60 AV17
Trevera Ct, Wal.Cr. EN8
off Eleanor Rd . . . 89 DY33
Trevereux Hill, Oxt. RH8 . . . 277 EM131
Treveris St, SE1 . . . 30 G3
Treverton St, W10 . . . 14 D5
Treves Cl, N21 . . . 103 DM43
Treville St, SW15 . . . 201 CV87
Treviso Rd, SE23
off Farren Rd . . . 205 DY89
Trevithick Cl, Felt. TW14 . . . 197 BT88
Trevithick Dr, Dart. DA1 . . . 190 FM84
Trevithick Ho, SE16 . . . 32 F9
Trevithick St, SE8 . . . 46 A2
Trevone Gdns, Pnr. HA5 . . . 138 BY58
Trevor Cl, Brom. BR2 . . . 226 EF101
East Barnet EN4 . . . 102 DD43
Harrow HA3 off Kenton La . . 117 CF52
Isleworth TW7 . . . 199 CF85
Northolt UB5 . . . 158 BW68
Trevor Cres, Ruis. HA4 . . . 137 BT63
Trevor Gdns, Edg. HA8 . . . 118 CR53
Northolt UB5 . . . 158 BW68
Ruislip HA4
off Clyfford Rd . . . 137 BU63
Trevor Pl, SW7 . . . 28 D5
Trevor Rd, SW19 . . . 201 CY94
Edgware HA8 . . . 118 CR53
Hayes UB3 . . . 177 BS75
Woodford Green IG8 . . . 124 EG52
Trevor Sq, SW7 . . . 28 E5
Trevor St, SW7 . . . 28 D5
Trevor Wk, SW7 off Trevor Sq . 28 E5
Trevose Av, W.Byf. KT14 . . . 233 BF114
Trevose Rd, E17 . . . 123 ED53
Trevose Way, Wat. WD19 . . . 116 BW48
Trewarden Av, Iver SL0 . . . 155 BD68
Trewenna Dr, Chess. KT9 . . . 237 CK106
Potters Bar EN6 . . . 86 DD32
Trewince Rd, SW20 . . . 221 CW95
Trewint St, SW18 . . . 202 DC89
Trewsbury Ho, SE2
off Hartslock Dr . . . 188 EX75
Trewsbury Rd, SE26 . . . 205 DX92
Triandra Way, Hayes UB4 . . . 158 BX71
Triangle, The, EC1 . . . 19 H4
N13 off Green Las . . . 121 DM49
Barking IG11
off Tanner St . . . 167 EQ65
Kingston upon Thames KT1
off Kenley Rd . . . 220 CQ96
Woking GU21 . . . 248 AW118
● Triangle Business Cen, NW10
off Enterprise Way . . . 161 CU69
Triangle Ct, E16 . . . 24 E6
Triangle Est, SE11 . . . 42 E1
Triangle Pas, Barn. EN4
off Station App . . . 102 DC42
Triangle Pl, SW4 . . . 183 DK84
Triangle Rd, E8 . . . 10 E8
● Triangle Wks, N9
off Centre Way . . . 122 DW47
Tricorn Ho, SE28
off Miles Dr . . . 167 ER74
● Trident Cen, Wat. WD24 . . . 98 BW39
Trident Gdns, Nthlt. UB5
off Jetstar Way . . . 158 BX69
Trident Ho, SE28
off Merbury Rd . . . 167 ER74
● Trident Ind Est, Colnbr.
SL3 . . . 175 BE83
Hoddesdon EN11 . . . 71 EC17
Trident Rd, Wat. WD25 . . . 81 BT34
Trident St, SE16 . . . 33 K8
Trident Way, Sthl. UB2 . . . 177 BV76
Trigg's Cl, Wok. GU22 . . . 248 AX119
Trigg's La, Wok. GU21, GU22 . . 248 AW118
Trig La, EC4 . . . 19 J10
Trigo Ct, Epsom KT19
off Blakeney Cl . . . 238 CR111
Trigon Rd, SW8 . . . 42 D4
Trilby Rd, SE23 . . . 205 DX89
Trimmer Wk, Brent. TW8 . . . 180 CL79
Trim St, SE14 . . . 45 N3
Trinder Gdns, N19 . . . 143 DL60
Trinder Ms, Tedd. TW11 . . . 199 CG92
Trinder Rd, N19 . . . 143 DL60
Barnet EN5 . . . 101 CW43
Trindles Rd, S.Nutfld RH1 . . . 289 DM136
Tring Av, W5 . . . 160 CM74
Southall UB1 . . . 158 BZ72
Wembley HA9 . . . 160 CN65
Tring Cl, Ilf. IG2 . . . 147 EQ57
Romford RM3 . . . 128 FM49
Tring Gdns, Rom. RM3 . . . 128 FL49
Tring Grn, Rom. RM3 . . . 128 FM49
Tringham Cl, Ott. KT16 . . . 233 BC107
Tring Wk, Rom. RM3 . . . 128 FL49
Trinidad Gdns, Dag. RM10 . . . 169 FD66
Trinidad St, E14 . . . 21 P10
Trinity Av, N2 . . . 142 DD55
Enfield EN1 . . . 104 DT44
Trinity Buoy Wf, E14 . . . 35 L1
● Trinity Business Pk, E4
off Trinity Way . . . 123 DZ51
Sch Trinity Cath High Sch, Lwr Sch,
Wdf.Grn. IG8
off Sydney Rd . . . 124 EG49
Upr Sch, Wdf.Grn. IG8
off Mornington Rd . . . 124 EG49
Trinity Ch Pas, SW13 . . . 181 CV79
Trinity Ch Rd, SW13 . . . 181 CV79
Trinity Ch Sq, SE1 . . . 31 K6
Trinity Chyd, Guil. GU1
off High St . . . 280 AX135
Trinity Cl, E8 . . . 10 B4
E11 . . . 146 EE61
NW3 . . . 6 A1
SE13 . . . 185 ED84
SW4 off The Pavement . . . 183 DJ84
Bromley BR2 . . . 226 EL102
Hounslow TW4 . . . 178 BY84
Northwood HA6 . . . 115 BS51
South Croydon CR2 . . . 242 DS109
Stanwell TW19 . . . 196 BJ86
Coll Trinity Coll of Music, SE10 . . 46 F2
Trinity Cotts, Rich. TW9
off Trinity Rd . . . 180 CM83
Trinity Ct, N1 . . . 9 N8
NW2 . . . 4 A1
SE7 . . . 36 E9
Trinity Cres, SW17 . . . 202 DF89
Trinity Dr, Uxb. UB8 . . . 157 BQ72
Trinity Gdns, E16 . . . 23 M6
SW9 . . . 183 DM84
Dartford DA1
off Summerhill Rd . . . 210 FK86
Trinity Gate, Guil. GU1
off Epsom Rd . . . 280 AY135
Trinity Gro, SE10 . . . 46 E6
Hertford SG14 . . . 54 DQ07
Trinity Hall Cl, Wat. WD24 . . . 98 BW41
★ Trinity Ho, EC3 . . . 19 P10
Trinity Ho, SE1 off Bath Ter . . 31 K6
Trinity La, Wal.Cr. EN8 . . . 89 DY32
Trinity Ms, SE20 . . . 224 DV95
W10 . . . 14 D8
Hemel Hempstead HP2 . . . 63 BR21
Trinity Path, SE26 . . . 204 DW90
Trinity Pl, EC3 . . . 32 A1
Bexleyheath DA6 . . . 188 EZ84
Windsor SL4 . . . 173 AQ82
Trinity Ri, SW2 . . . 203 DN88
Trinity Rd, N2 . . . 142 DD55
N22 . . . 121 DL53
SW17 . . . 202 DF89
SW18 . . . 202 DD85
SW19 . . . 202 DA93
Gravesend DA12 . . . 213 GJ87
Hertford Heath SG13 . . . 54 DW12
Ilford IG6 . . . 147 EQ55
Richmond TW9 . . . 180 CM83
Southall UB1 . . . 158 BY74
Ware SG12 . . . 55 DY05
Sch Trinity St. Mary's C of E
Prim Sch, SW12
off Balham Pk Rd . . . 202 DG88
Sch Trinity St. Stephen C of E
First Sch, Wind. SL4
off Vansittart Rd . . . 173 AP81
Sch Trinity Sch, Belv. DA17
off Erith Rd . . . 189 FC77
Dagenham RM10
off Heathway . . . 148 FA63
Sch Trinity Sch of John Whitgift,
Croy. CR0 off Shirley Rd . . 224 DW103
Trinity Sq, EC3 . . . 31 P1
Trinity St, E16 . . . 23 N7
SE1 . . . 31 K5
Enfield EN2 . . . 104 DQ40
Trinity Wk, NW3 . . . 5 P5
Hemel Hempstead HP2 . . . 63 BR21
Hertford Heath SG13 . . . 54 DW12
Trinity Way, E4 . . . 123 DZ51
W3 . . . 160 CS73
Trio Pl, SE1 . . . 31 K5
Tripps Hill, Ch.St.G. HP8 . . . 112 AU48
Tripps Hill Cl, Ch.St.G. HP8 . . . 112 AU48
Tripton Rd, Harl. CM18 . . . 73 ES16
Tristan Ct, Wem. HA0
off King George Cres . . . 139 CK64
Tristan Sq, SE3 . . . 186 EE83
Tristram Cl, E17 . . . 145 ED55
Tristram Dr, N9 . . . 122 DU48
Tristram Rd, Brom. BR1 . . . 206 EF91
● Triton Sq, NW1 . . . 17 L4
Triton Way, Hem.H. HP2 . . . 62 BM18
Tritton Av, Croy. CR0 . . . 241 DL105
Tritton Rd, SE21 . . . 204 DR90
Trittons, Tad. KT20 . . . 255 CW121
Triumph Cl, Chaff.Hun. RM16 . . 191 FW77
Harlington UB3 . . . 177 BQ80
Triumph Ho, Bark. IG11 . . . 168 EU69
Triumph Rd, E6 . . . 25 K8
● Triumph Trd Est, N17 . . . 122 DU51
Trivett Cl, Green. DA9 . . . 211 FU85
Trocette Mansion, SE1
off Bermondsey St . . . 31 P6
Trodd's La, Guil. GU1 . . . 281 BF135
Trojan Way, Croy. CR0 . . . 223 DM104
Trolling Down Hill, Dart. DA2 . . 210 FP89
Troon Cl, SE16 . . . 32 F10
SE28 off Fairway Dr . . . 168 EX72
Troon St, E1 . . . 21 L8
Troopers Dr, Rom. RM3 . . . 128 FK49
Trosley Av, Grav. DA11 . . . 213 GH89
Trosley Rd, Belv. DA17 . . . 188 FA79
Trossachs Rd, SE22 . . . 204 DS85
Trothy Rd, SE1 . . . 32 D8
Trotsworth Av, Vir.W. GU25 . . . 214 AX98
Trotsworth Ct, Vir.W. GU25 . . . 214 AX98
Trotters Bottom, Barn. EN5 . . . 101 CU37
Trotters Gap, Stans.Abb. SG12 . 55 ED11
Trotters La, Mimbr. GU24 . . . 232 AV112
Trotters Rd, Harl. CM18 . . . 74 EU17
Trotter Way, Epsom KT19 . . . 238 CN112
Trott Rd, N10 . . . 120 DF52
Trotts La, West. TN16 . . . 277 EQ127
Trott St, SW11 . . . 40 C7
Trotwood, Chig. IG7 . . . 125 ER51
Trotwood Cl, Shenf. CM15
off Middleton Rd . . . 130 FY46
Troughton Rd, SE7 . . . 36 A10
Troutbeck Cl, Slou. SL2 . . . 154 AU73
Troutbeck Rd, SE14 . . . 45 L6
Trout La, West Dr. UB7 . . . 156 BJ73
Trout Ri, Loud. WD3 . . . 96 BH41
Trout Rd, West Dr. UB7 . . . 156 BK74
Troutstream Way, Loud. WD3 . . 96 BH42
Trouvere Pk, Hem.H. HP1 . . . 62 BH18
Trouville Rd, SW4 . . . 203 DJ86
Trowbridge Est, E9 . . . 11 N4
Trowbridge Rd, E9 . . . 11 P5
Romford RM3 . . . 128 FK51
Trowers Way, Red. RH1 . . . 273 DH131
Trowley Ri, Abb.L. WD5 . . . 81 BS31
Trowlock Av, Tedd. TW11 . . . 199 CJ93
Trowlock Island, Tedd. TW11 . . 199 CK92
Trowlock Way, Tedd. TW11 . . . 199 CK93
Troy Cl, Tad. KT20 . . . 255 CV120
Troy Ct, SE18 . . . 37 P9
W8 . . . 27 J6
Troy Rd, SE19 . . . 204 DR93
Troy Town, SE15 . . . 44 D10
Trubshaw Rd, Sthl. UB2
off Havelock Rd . . . 178 CB76
Trueman Cl, Edg. HA8 . . . 118 CQ52
Trueman Rd, Ken. CR8 . . . 258 DR120
Truesdale Dr, Hare. UB9 . . . 136 BJ56
Truesdale Rd, E6 . . . 25 K9
Trulock Ct, N17 . . . 122 DU52
Trulock Rd, N17 . . . 122 DU52
Truman's Rd, N16 . . . 9 P2
Trumpers Way, W7 . . . 179 CE76
Trumper Way, Slou. SL1 . . . 153 AM74
Uxbridge UB8 . . . 156 BJ67
Trumpets Hill Rd, Reig. RH2 . . 287 CU135
Trumpington Dr, St.Alb. AL1 . . 65 CD23
Trumpington Rd, E7 . . . 146 EF63
Trumps Grn Av, Vir.W. GU25 . . 214 AX100
Trumps Grn Cl, Vir.W. GU25
off Trumpsgreen Rd . . . 214 AY99
Sch Trumps Grn Inf Sch, Vir.W.
GU25 off Crown Rd . . . 214 AX100
Trumpsgreen Rd, Vir.W. GU25 . 214 AX100
Trumps Mill La, Vir.W. GU25 . . 215 AZ100
Trump St, EC2 . . . 19 K9
Trundlers Way, Bushey Hth
WD23 . . . 117 CE46
Trundle St, SE1 . . . 31 J4
Trundleys Rd, SE8 . . . 33 K10
Trundleys Ter, SE8 . . . 33 K9
Trunks All, Swan. BR8 . . . 229 FB96
Trunley Heath Rd, Bramley
GU5 . . . 280 AW144
Truro Gdns, Ilf. IG1 . . . 146 EL59
Truro Rd, E17 . . . 145 DZ56
N22 . . . 121 DL52
Gravesend DA12 . . . 213 GK90
Truro St, NW5 . . . 6 G5
Truro Wk, Rom. RM3 . . . 128 FJ51
Truro Way, Hayes UB4 . . . 157 BS69
Truslove Rd, SE27 . . . 203 DN92
Trussley Rd, W6 . . . 26 A7
Trustees Cl, Denh. UB9 . . . 135 BF58
Trustees Way, Denh. UB9 . . . 135 BF57
Trustons Gdns, Horn. RM11 . . . 149 FG59
Trust Rd, Wal.Cr. EN8 . . . 89 DY34
Trust Wk, SE21
off Peabody Hill . . . 203 DP88
Tryfan Cl, Ilf. IG4 . . . 146 EK57
Tryon Cres, E9 . . . 10 G8
Tryon St, SW3 . . . 28 E10
Trys Hill, Lyne KT16 . . . 215 AZ103
Trystings Cl, Clay. KT10 . . . 237 CG107
Tuam Rd, SE18 . . . 187 ER79
Tubbenden Cl, Orp. BR6 . . . 227 ES103
Tubbenden Dr, Orp. BR6 . . . 245 ER105
Sch Tubbenden Inf Sch, Orp.
BR6 off Sandy Bury . . . 227 ER104
Sch Tubbenden Jun Sch, Orp.
BR6 off Sandy Bury . . . 227 ER104
Tubbenden La, Orp. BR6 . . . 227 ES104
Tubbenden La S, Orp. BR6 . . . 245 ER106
Tubbs Cft, Welw.G.C. AL7 . . . 52 DB10
Tubbs Rd, NW10 . . . 161 CT68
Tubs Hill Par, Sev. TN13 . . . 278 FG124
Tubwell Rd, Stoke P. SL2 . . . 154 AV67
Tucker Rd, Ott. KT16 . . . 233 BD107
Tucker St, Wat. WD18 . . . 98 BW43
Tuckey Gro, Ripley GU23 . . . 249 BF124
Tuck Rd, Rain. RM13 . . . 169 FG65
Tudor Av, Chsht EN7 . . . 88 DU31
Hampton TW12 . . . 198 CA93
Romford RM2 . . . 149 FG55
Watford WD24 . . . 98 BX38
Worcester Park KT4 . . . 221 CV104
Tudor Circle, Gdmg. GU7 . . . 280 AS144
Tudor Cl, N6 . . . 143 DJ59
NW3 . . . 6 C3
NW7 . . . 119 CU51
NW9 . . . 140 CQ61
SW2 . . . 203 DM86
Ashford TW15 . . . 196 BL91
Banstead SM7 . . . 255 CY115
Bookham KT23 . . . 252 CA124
Cheshunt EN7 . . . 88 DV31
Chessington KT9 . . . 238 CL106
Chigwell IG7 . . . 125 EN49
Chislehurst BR7 . . . 227 EM95
Cobham KT11 . . . 236 BZ113
Coulsdon CR5 . . . 257 DN118
Dartford DA1 . . . 209 FH86
Epsom KT17 . . . 239 CT110
Hatfield AL10 . . . 66 CS21
Hunsdon SG12 . . . 56 EK07
Northfleet DA11 . . . 212 GE88
Pinner HA5 . . . 137 BU57
Shenfield CM15 . . . 131 FZ44
Smallfield RH6 . . . 291 DP148
South Croydon CR2 . . . 258 DV115
Sutton SM3 . . . 239 CX106
Wallington SM6 . . . 241 DJ108
Woking GU22 . . . 249 BA117
Woodford Green IG8 . . . 124 EH50
Tudor Ct, E17 . . . 145 DY59
Borehamwood WD6 . . . 100 CL40
Crockenhill BR8 . . . 229 FC101
Egham TW20
off The Chantries . . . 195 BA92
Feltham TW13 . . . 198 BW91
Tudor Ct N, Wem. HA9 . . . 140 CN64
Sch Tudor Ct Prim Sch, Chaff.Hun.
RM16 off Bark Burr Rd . . . 192 FZ75
Tudor Ct S, Wem. HA9 . . . 140 CN64
Tudor Cres, Enf. EN2 . . . 103 DP39
Ilford IG6 . . . 125 EP51
Tudor Dr, Kings.T. KT2 . . . 200 CL92
Morden SM4 . . . 221 CX100
Romford RM2 . . . 149 FG56
Walton-on-Thames KT12 . . . 218 BX102
Watford WD24 . . . 98 BX38
Wooburn Green HP10 . . . 132 AD55
● Tudor Est, NW10 . . . 160 CP68
Tudor Gdns, NW9 . . . 140 CQ61
SW13 off Treen Av . . . 180 CS83
W3 . . . 160 CN72
Harrow HA3 off Tudor Rd . . . 117 CD54
Romford RM2 . . . 149 FG56
Slough SL1 . . . 152 AJ72
Twickenham TW1 . . . 199 CF88
Upminster RM14 . . . 150 FQ61
West Wickham BR4 . . . 225 EC104
Tudor Gro, E9 . . . 10 G7
N20 off Church Cres . . . 120 DE48
Tudor Ho, Surb. KT6
off Lenelby Rd . . . 220 CN102
Tudor La, Old Wind. SL4 . . . 194 AW87
Tudor Manor Gdns, Wat. WD25 . 82 BX32
Tudor Ms, Rom. RM1
off Eastern Rd . . . 149 FF57
Tudor Par, Rick. WD3
off Berry La . . . 114 BG45
Tudor Pk, Amer. HP6 . . . 77 AR37
Tudor Pl, Mitch. CR4 . . . 202 DE94
Sch Tudor Prim Sch, N3
off Queens Rd . . . 120 DC53
Hemel Hempstead HP3
off Redwood Dr . . . 62 BL22
Southall UB1 off Tudor Rd . . 158 BY73
Tudor Ri, Brox. EN10 . . . 71 DY21
Tudor Rd, E4 . . . 123 EB51
E6 . . . 166 EJ67
E9 . . . 10 F8
N9 . . . 122 DV45
SE19 . . . 204 DT94
SE25 . . . 224 DV99
Ashford TW15 . . . 197 BR93
Barking IG11 . . . 167 ET67
Barnet EN5 . . . 102 DA41
Beckenham BR3 . . . 225 EB97
Godalming GU7 . . . 280 AS144
Hampton TW12 . . . 198 CA94
Harrow HA3 . . . 117 CD54
Hayes UB3 . . . 157 BR72

Tudor Rd, Haz. HP15 110 AC45
Hounslow TW3 179 CD84
Kingston upon Thames KT2 208 CN94
Pinner HA5 116 BW54
St. Albans AL3 65 CE16
Southall UB1 158 BY73
Wheathampstead AL4 50 CL07
Tudors, The, Reig. RH2 272 DC131
Tudor Sq, Hayes UB3 157 BR71
Tudor St, EC4 18 F10
Tudor Wk, Bex. DA5 208 EY86
Leatherhead KT22 253 CF120
Watford WD24 98 BX37
Weybridge KT13
off West Palace Gdns 217 BP104
Tudor Way, N14 121 DK46
W3 180 CN75
Hertford SG14 53 DN09
Petts Wood BR5 227 ER100
Rickmansworth WD3 114 BG46
Uxbridge UB10 156 BN65
Waltham Abbey EN9 89 ED33
Windsor SL4 173 AL81
Tudor Well Cl, Stan. HA7 117 CH50
Tudway Rd, SE3 186 EH83
Tufnell Ct, Chsht EN8
off Coopers Wk 89 DX28
Tufnail Rd, Dart. DA1 210 FM86
TUFNELL PARK, N7 143 DK63
⊖ Tufnell Park 143 DJ63
Sch Tufnell Pk Prim Sch, N7 7 P1
Tufnell Pk Rd, N7 143 DJ63
N19 143 DJ63
Tufter Rd, Chig. IG7 125 ET50
Tufton Gdns, W.Mol. KT8 218 CB96
Tufton Rd, E4 123 EA49
Tufton St, SW1 29 P6
Tugboat St, SE28 187 ES75
Tugela Rd, Croy. CR0 224 DR100
Tugela St, SE6 205 DZ89
Tugmutton Cl, Orp. BR6 245 EP105
Tugswood Cl, Couls. CR5 257 DK121
Tuilerie St, E2 10 C10
Coll Tuition Cen, The, NW4
off Lodge Rd 141 CW56
Sch Tuke Sch, SE15 44 E7
Tulip Cl, E6 25 J7
Croydon CR0 225 DX102
Hampton TW12
off Partridge Rd 198 BZ93
Pilgrim's Hatch CM15
off Poppy Cl 130 FV43
Romford RM3 128 FJ51
Southall UB2 off Chevy Rd 178 CC75
Tulip Ct, Pnr. HA5 138 BW55
Tulip Gdns, Ilf. IG1 167 EP65
Tulip Tree Ct, Sutt. SM2
off The Crescent 240 DA111
Tulip Way, West Dr. UB7 176 BK77
Tull St, Mitch. CR4 222 DF101
Tulse Cl, Beck. BR3 225 EC97
TULSE HILL, SE21 204 DQ88
⇌ Tulse Hill 203 DP89
Jct Tulse Hill, SW2 203 DP88
Tulse Hill, SW2 203 DN86
Tulse Hill Est, SW2 203 DN86
Tulsemere Rd, SE27 204 DQ89
Tulyar Cl, Tad. KT20 255 CV120
Tumber St, Headley KT18 270 CQ125
Tumbler Rd, Harl. CM18 74 EU17
Tumblewood Rd, Bans. SM7 255 CY116
Tumbling Bay, Walt. KT12 217 BU100
Tummons Gdns, SE25 224 DS96
Tump Ho, SE28 167 ES74
Tuncombe Rd, N18 122 DS49
Tunfield Rd, Hodd. EN11 55 EB14
Tunis Rd, W12 161 CV74
Tunley Grn, E14
off Burdett Rd 21 P7
Tunley Rd, NW10 160 CS67
SW17 202 DG88
Tunmarsh La, E13 24 B2
Tunmers End, Chal.St.P. SL9 112 AW53
Tunnan Leys, E6 25 M8
Tunnel Av, SE10 35 H4
● Tunnel Av Trd Est, SE10 35 H5
Tunnel Gdns, N11 121 DJ52
Tunnel Rd, SE16 32 G4
Reigate RH2 off Church St 272 DA134
Tunnel Wd Cl, Wat. WD17 97 BT37
Tunnel Wd Rd, Wat. WD17 97 BT37
Tunnmeade, Harl. CM20 58 EU14
Tunsgate, Guil. GU1 280 AX136
🛍 Tunsgate Sq, Guil. GU1
off High St 280 AX136
Tuns La, Slou. SL1 173 AQ76
Tunstall Av, Ilf. IG6 126 EU51
Tunstall Cl, Orp. BR5 245 ES105
Tunstall Rd, SW9 183 DM84
Croydon CR0 224 DS102
Tunstall Wk, Brent. TW8 180 CL79
Tunstock Way, Belv. DA17 188 EY76
Tunworth Cl, NW9 140 CQ58
Tunworth Cres, SW15 201 CT86
Tun Yd, SW8 41 K10
Tupelo Rd, E10 145 EB61
Tuppy St, SE28 187 EQ76
Tupwood Ct, Cat. CR3 274 DU125
Tupwood La, Cat. CR3 274 DU125
Tupwood Scrubbs Rd, Cat.
CR3 274 DU128
Turenne Cl, SW18 182 DC84
Turfhouse La, Chobham
GU24 232 AS109
Turin Rd, N9 122 DW45
Turin St, E2 20 C3
Turkey Oak Cl, SE19 224 DS95
⇌ Turkey Street 104 DW37
Turkey St, Enf. EN1, EN3 104 DV37
Turks Cl, Uxb. UB8 156 BN69
Turks Head Ct, Eton SL4
off High St 173 AR80
Turk's Head Yd, EC1 18 G6
Turks Row, SW3 28 F10
Turle Rd, N4 143 DM60
SW16 223 DL96
Turleway Cl, N4 143 DM60
Turley Cl, E15 13 K9
Turmore Dale, Welw.G.C. AL8 51 CW10
Turnagain La, EC4 18 G8
Dartford DA2 209 FG90
Turnage Rd, Dag. RM8 148 EY60
Turnberry Cl, NW4 119 CX54
SE16 44 F1
Turnberry Ct, Wat. WD19 116 BW48
Turnberry Dr, Brick.Wd AL2 82 BY30
Turnberry Quay, E14 34 D6
Turnberry Way, Orp. BR6 227 ER102
Turnbull Cl, Green. DA9 211 FS87
Turnbury Cl, SE28 168 EX72
Turnchapel Ms, SW4
off Cedars Rd 183 DH83
Turner Av, N15 144 DS56
Mitcham CR4 222 DF95
Twickenham TW2 198 CC90
Turner Cl, NW11 142 DB58
SW9 43 H6
Guildford GU4 265 AZ131
Hayes UB4 157 BQ68
Wembley HA0 139 CK64
Turner Ct, N15
off St. Ann's Rd 144 DR57
Dartford DA1 210 FJ85
Turner Dr, NW11 142 DB58
Turner Ho, E14
off Cassilis Rd 34 B5
Turner Ms, Sutt. SM2 240 DB108
Turner Pl, SW11 202 DE85
Turner Rd, E17 145 EC55
Bean DA2 211 FV90
Bushey WD23 98 CC42
Edgware HA8 140 CM55
Hornchurch RM12 149 FF61
New Malden KT3 220 CR101
Slough SL3 174 AW75
Turners Cl, N20
off Oakleigh Rd N 120 DF48
Staines TW18 196 BH92
Turners Ct, Abridge RM4 108 EV41
Turners Gdns, Sev. TN13 279 FJ128
Turners Hill, Chsht EN8 89 DX30
Hemel Hempstead HP2 62 BL21
Turners La, Hersham KT12 235 BV107
Turners Meadow Way, Beck.
BR3 225 DZ95
Turners Rd, E3 21 N7
Turner St, E1 20 E7
E16 23 L9
Turners Wk, Chesh. HP5 76 AQ30
Turners Way, Croy. CR0 223 DN103
Turners Wd, NW11 142 DC60
Turners Wd Dr, Ch.St.G. HP8 112 AX48
Turneville Rd, W14 38 G2
Sch Turney Prim & Sec Spec Sch,
SE21 off Turney Rd 204 DQ87
Turney Rd, SE21 204 DR87
Turneys Orchard, Chorl. WD3 95 BD43
TURNFORD, Brox. EN10 89 DZ26
Jct Turnford, Brox. EN10 89 DY25
Sch Turnford Sch, Chsht EN8
off Mill La 89 DY28
Turnford Vil, Turnf. EN10 89 DZ26
Turnham Cl, Guil. GU2 280 AW138
⊖ Turnham Green 180 CS77
Turnham Grn Ter, W4 180 CS77
Turnham Grn Ter Ms, W4 180 CS77
Sch Turnham Prim Sch, SE4
off Turnham Rd 185 DY84
Turnham Rd, SE4 205 DY85
Turnmill St, EC1 18 F5
Turnoak Av, Wok. GU22 248 AY120
Turnoak La, Wok. GU22 248 AY120
Turnoak Pk, Wind. SL4 173 AL84
Turnors, Harl. CM20 73 EQ15
Turnpike Cl, SE8 45 P4
Turnpike Dr, Orp. BR6 246 EW109
Turnpike Grn, Hem.H. HP2 62 BL16
Turnpike Ho, EC1 19 H3
⊖ Turnpike Lane 143 DN55
⊖ Turnpike Lane 143 DP55
Turnpike La, N8 143 DM56
Sutton SM1 240 DC106
Uxbridge UB10 156 BL69
West Tilbury RM18 193 GK78
Turnpike Link, Croy. CR0 224 DS103
Turnpike Ms, N8 143 DN56
Turnpike Way, Islw. TW7 179 CG81
Turnpin La, SE10 46 F3
Turnstone Cl, E13 23 N3
NW9 off Kestrel Cl 118 CS54
Ickenham UB10 137 BP64
South Croydon CR2 243 DY110
Turnstones, The, Grav. DA12 213 GK89
Watford WD25 98 BY36
Turp Av, Grays RM16 192 GC75
Turpentine La, SW1 29 K10
Turpin Av, Rom. RM5 126 FA52
Turpin Cl, Enf. EN3 105 EA37
Turpington Cl, Brom. BR2 226 EL100
Turpington La, Brom. BR2 226 EL101
Turpin Ho, SW11 41 J6
Turpin La, Erith DA8 189 FG80
Turpin Rd, Felt. TW14
off Staines Rd 197 BT86
Turpins Cl, Hert. SG14 53 DM09
Turpins La, Wdf.Grn. IG8 125 EM50
Turpin Way, N19 143 DK61
Wallington SM6 241 DH108
Turquand St, SE17 31 K9
Turret Gro, SW4 41 L10
Turton Rd, Wem. HA0 140 CL64
Turton Way, Slou. SL1 173 AR76
Turville Ct, Bkhm KT23
off Proctor Gdns 268 CB125
Turville St, E2 20 A4
Tuscan Ho, E2 21 H2
Tuscan Rd, SE18 187 ER78
Tuscany Ho, E17
off Sherwood Cl 123 DZ54
Tuskar St, SE10 47 J1
Tussauds Cl, Crox.Grn WD3 96 BN43
Tustin Est, SE15 44 G3
Tuttlebee La, Buck.H. IG9 124 EG47
Tuxford Cl, Borwd. WD6 100 CL38
Twankhams All, Epp. CM16
off Hemnall St 92 EU30
Tweed Cl, Berk. HP4 60 AV18
Tweeddale Gro, Uxb. UB10 137 BQ62
Sch Tweeddale Prim Sch, Cars.
SM5 off Tweeddale Rd 222 DD101
Tweeddale Rd, Cars. SM5 222 DD102
Tweed Glen, Rom. RM1 127 FD52
Tweed Grn, Rom. RM1 127 FD52
Tweed Ho, E14 22 E5
Tweed La, Strood Grn RH3 286 CP139
Tweedmouth Rd, E13 24 A1
Tweed Rd, Slou. SL3 175 BA79
Tweed Way, Rom. RM1 127 FD52
Tweedy Cl, Enf. EN1 104 DT43
Tweedy Rd, Brom. BR1 226 EF95
Tweenways, Chesh. HP5 76 AR30
Tweezer's All, WC2 18 E10
Twelve Acre Cl, Bkhm KT23 252 BZ124
Twelve Acre Ho, E12
off Grantham Rd 147 EN62
Twelve Acres, Welw.G.C. AL7 51 CY11
● Twelvetrees Business Pk,
E3 22 G5
Twelvetrees Cres, E3 22 E4
Twentyman Cl, Wdf.Grn. IG8 124 EG50
TWICKENHAM, TW1 & TW2 199 CG89
⇌ Twickenham 199 CF87
Twickenham Br, Rich. TW9 199 CJ85
Twickenham TW1 199 CJ85
Twickenham Cl, Croy. CR0 223 DM104
Twickenham Gdns, Grnf. UB6 139 CG64
Harrow HA3 117 CE52
Sch Twickenham Prep Sch, Hmptn.
TW12 off High St 218 CC95
Twickenham Rd, E11 145 ED61
Feltham TW13 198 BZ90
Isleworth TW7 179 CG83
Richmond TW9 179 CJ84
Teddington TW11 199 CG92
● Twickenham Trd Est, Twick.
TW1 199 CF86
Twig Folly Cl, E2 21 K1
Twigg Cl, Erith DA8 189 FE80
Twilley St, SW18 202 DB87
Twinches La, Slou. SL1 153 AP74
Twine Cl, Bark. IG11
off Thames Rd 168 EV69
Twine Ct, E1 20 G10
Twineham Grn, N12 120 DA49
Twine Ter, E3 off Ropery St 21 N5
Twining Av, Twick. TW2 198 CC90
Twinn Rd, NW7 119 CY51
Twinoaks, Cob. KT11 236 CA113
Twin Tumps Way, SE28 168 EU73
Twisden Rd, NW5 143 DH63
Twisleton Ct, Dart. DA1
off Priory Hill 210 FK86
Twitchells La, Jordans HP9 112 AT51
TWITTON, Sev. TN14 263 FF116
Twitton La, Otford TN14 263 FD115
Twitton Meadows, Otford
TN14 263 FE116
Two Acres, Welw.G.C. AL7 51 CZ11
Two Beeches, Hem.H. HP2 62 BM15
Two Dells La, Chesh. HP5 60 AT24
Two Mile Dr, Slou. SL1 153 AK74
🛍 Two Rivers Retail Pk, Stai.
TW18 195 BE91
Sch Two Waters Prim Sch, Hem.H.
HP3 off High Ridge Cl 80 BK25
Two Waters Rd, Hem.H. HP3 62 BJ22
Two Waters Way, Hem.H. HP3 62 BJ24
Twybridge Way, NW10 160 CQ66
Twycross Ms, SE10 35 K9
Twyford Abbey Rd, NW10 160 CM69
Twyford Av, N2 142 DF55
W3 160 CN73
Sch Twyford C of E High Sch, W3
off Twyford Cres 160 CP74
Twyford Cres, W3 160 CN74
Twyford Ho, N15 144 DS58
Twyford Pl, WC2 18 C8
Twyford Rd, Cars. SM5 222 DD102
Harrow HA2 138 CB60
Ilford IG1 147 EQ64
St. Albans AL4 65 CJ16
Twyford St, N1 8 C8
Twyner Cl, Horl. RH6 291 DK147
Twynersh Av, Cher. KT16 215 BF100
Twysdens Ter, N.Mymms AL9
off Dellsome La 67 CW24
Tyas Rd, E16 23 L5
Tybenham Rd, SW19 222 DA97
Tyberry Rd, Enf. EN3 104 DV41
Tyburn La, Har. HA1 139 CE59
Tyburns, The, Hutt. CM13 131 GC47
Tyburn Way, W1 16 F10
Tycehurst Hill, Loug. IG10 107 EM42
Tychbourne Dr, Guil. GU4 265 BC131
Tydcombe Rd, Warl. CR6 258 DW119
TYE GREEN, Harl. CM18 73 ES17
Tye Grn Village, Harl. CM18 73 ES18
Tye La, Headley KT18 270 CR127
Orpington BR6 245 EQ106
Tadworth KT20 270 CS128
Tyers Est, SE1 31 N4
Tyers Gate, SE1 31 N4
Tyers St, SE11 30 C10
Tyers Ter, SE11 42 C1
Tyeshurst Cl, SE2 188 EY78
Tyfield Cl, Chsht EN8 88 DW30
Tykeswater La, Els. WD6 99 CJ39
Tylecroft Rd, SW16 223 DL96
Tyle Grn, Horn. RM11 150 FL56
Tylehost, Guil. GU2 264 AU130
Tylehurst Dr, Red. RH1 288 DF135
Tylehurst Gdns, Ilf. IG1 147 EQ64
Tyle Pl, Old Wind. SL4 194 AU85
Tyler Cl, E2 10 A10
Erith DA8 189 FB80
Tyler Gdns, Add. KT15 234 BJ105
Tyler Gro, Dart. DA1
off Spielman Rd 190 FM84
Tyler Rd, Sthl. UB2
off McNair Rd 178 CB76
TYLERS CAUSEWAY, Hert.
SG13 69 DK22
Tylers Causeway, Newgate St
SG13 69 DH23
Tylers Cl, Gdse. RH9 274 DV130
Kings Langley WD4 80 BL28
Loughton IG10 124 EL45
Tyler's Ct, W1 17 N9
Tylers Cres, Horn. RM12 150 FJ64
Tylersfield, Abb.L. WD5 81 BT31
Tylers Gate, Har. HA3 140 CL58
Sch Tylers Grn First Sch, Penn
HP10 off School Rd 110 AD47
Tylers Grn Rd, Swan. BR8 229 FC100
Tylers Hill Rd, Chesh. HP5 78 AT30
Tylers Path, Cars. SM5
off Rochester Rd 240 DF105
Tylers Rd, Roydon CM19 72 EJ19
Tyler St, SE10 47 K1
Tylers Way, Wat. WD25 99 CD42
Tyler Wk, Slou. SL3
off Gilbert Way 175 AZ78
Tyler Way, Brwd. CM14 130 FV46
Tylney Av, SE19 204 DT92
Tylney Cl, Chig. IG7 125 ET49
Tylney Cft, Harl. CM19 73 EP17
Tylney Rd, E7 146 EJ63
Bromley BR1 226 EK96
Tylsworth Cl, Amer. HP6 77 AR38
Tymperley Ct, SW19
off Windlesham Gro 201 CY88
Tynan Cl, Felt. TW14
off Sandycombe Rd 197 BU88
Tyndale Ct, E14 34 C10
Tyndale La, N1 8 G6
Tyndale Ms, Slou. SL1 173 AP75
Tyndale Ter, N1 8 G6
Tyndall Rd, E10 145 EC61
Welling DA16 187 ET83
Tyne Cl, Upmin. RM14 151 FR58
Tynedale, Lon.Col. AL2
off Thamesdale 84 CM27
Tynedale Cl, Dart. DA2 211 FR88
Tynedale Rd, Strood Grn RH3 286 CP138
Tyne Gdns, Aveley RM15 170 FQ73
Tyneham Cl, SW11 41 H10
Tyneham Rd, SW11 41 H9
Tynemouth Cl, E6 25 N9
Tynemouth Dr, Enf. EN1 104 DU38
Tynemouth Rd, N15 144 DT56
SE18 187 ET78
Mitcham CR4 202 DG94
Tynemouth St, SW6 39 N8
Tyne St, E1
off Old Castle St 20 B8
Tynley Gro, Jacobs Well GU4 264 AX128
Tynsdale Rd, NW10 160 CS66
Tynwald Ho, SE26
off Sydenham Hill Est 204 DU90
Type St, E2 21 J1
Typhoon Way, Wall. SM6 241 DL108
Typleden Cl, Hem.H. HP2 62 BK18
Tyrawley Rd, SW6 39 L6
Tyre La, NW9 140 CS56
Tyrell Cl, Har. HA1 139 CE63
Tyrell Ct, Cars. SM5 240 DF105
Tyrell Gdns, Wind. SL4 173 AM83
Tyrell Ri, Warley CM14 130 FW50
Tyrells Cl, Upmin. RM14 150 FN61
Tyrells Pl, Guil. GU1 281 AZ135
Tyrols Rd, SE23
off Wastdale Rd 205 DX88
Tyrone Rd, E6 25 K1
Tyron Way, Sid. DA14 207 ES91
Tyrrell Av, Well. DA16 208 EU85
Tyrrell Rd, SE22 184 DU84
Tyrrells Hall Cl, Grays RM17 192 GD79
Tyrrell Sq, Mitch. CR4 222 DE95
TYRRELL'S WOOD, Lthd. KT22 254 CM123
Tyrrel Way, NW9 141 CT59
Tyrwhitt Ct, Guil. GU2
off Henderson Av 264 AV130
Tyrwhitt Rd, SE4 185 EA83
Tysea Cl, Harl. CM18 73 ET18
Tysea Hill, Stap.Abb. RM4 127 FF45
Tysea Rd, Harl. CM18 73 ET18
Tysoe Av, Enf. EN3 105 DZ36
Tysoe St, EC1 18 E3
Tyson Rd, SE23 204 DW87
Sch Tyssen Comm Prim Sch,
N16 off Oldhill St 144 DU60
Tyssen Pas, E8 10 A4
Tyssen Pl, S.Ock. RM15 171 FW69
Tyssen Rd, N16 144 DT62
Tyssen St, E8 10 B4
N1 9 P10
Tythebarn Cl, Guil. GU4
off Dairyman's Wk 265 BB129
Tytherton Rd, N19 143 DK62
TYTTENHANGER, St.Alb. AL4 65 CK23
Tyttenhanger Grn, Tytten. AL4 65 CK23

U

Uamvar St, E14 22 D6
Uckfield Gro, Mitch. CR4 222 DG95
Uckfield Rd, Enf. EN3 105 DX37
Udall Gdns, Rom. RM5 126 FA51
Udall St, SW1 29 M9
Udney Pk Rd, Tedd. TW11 199 CG92
Uffington Rd, NW10 161 CU67
SE27 203 DN91
Ufford Cl, Har. HA3 116 CB52
Ufford Rd, Har. HA3 116 CB52
Ufford St, SE1 30 F4
Ufton Gro, N1 9 M6
Ufton Rd, N1 9 M7
Uhura Sq, N16 144 DS62
Ujima Ct, SW16 203 DL91
Ullathorne Rd, SW16 203 DJ91
Ulleswater Rd, N14 121 DL49
Ullin St, E14 22 E7
● Ullswater Business Pk,
Couls. CR5 257 DL116
Ullswater Cl, SW15 200 CR91
Bromley BR1 206 EE93
Hayes UB4 157 BS68
Slough SL1
off Buttermere Av 152 AJ71
Ullswater Ct, Har. HA2 138 CA59
Ullswater Cres, SW15 200 CR91
Coulsdon CR5 257 DL116
Ullswater Rd, SE27 203 DP89
SW13 181 CU80
Hemel Hempstead HP3 63 BQ22
Ullswater Way, Horn. RM12 149 FG64
Ulstan Cl, Wold. CR3 259 EA123
Ulster Gdns, N13 122 DQ49
Ulster Pl, NW1 17 J5
Ulster Ter, NW1 17 J5
Ulundi Rd, SE3 47 K3
Ulva Rd, SW15 201 CX85
Ulverscroft Rd, SE22 204 DT85
Ulverston, Purf. RM19 190 FQ78
Ulverston Cl, St.Alb. AL1 65 CF20
Ulverstone Rd, SE27 203 DP89
Ulverston Rd, E17 123 ED54
Ulwin Av, Byfleet KT14 234 BL113
Ulysses Rd, NW6 5 H2
Umberstones, Vir.W. GU25 214 AX100
Umberston St, E1 20 E8
Umberville Way, Slou. SL2 153 AM70
Umbria St, SW15 201 CU86
Umfreville Rd, N4 143 DP58
Underacres Cl, Hem.H. HP2 62 BN19
Undercliff Rd, SE13 46 B10
UNDERHILL, Barn. EN5 102 DA43
Underhill, Barn. EN5 102 DA43
Sch Underhill Inf Sch, Barn. EN5
off Mays La 101 CY43
Sch Underhill Jun Sch, Barn. EN5
off Mays La 101 CY43
Underhill Pk Rd, Reig. RH2 272 DA131
Underhill Pas, NW1 7 K8
Underhill Rd, SE22 204 DV86
Underhill St, NW1 7 K9
Underne Av, N14 121 DH47
UNDERRIVER, Sev. TN15 279 FN130
Underriver Ho Rd, Undrvr
TN15 279 FP130
Undershaft, EC3 19 N9
Undershaw Rd, Brom. BR1 206 EE90
Underwood, New Adgtn CR0 243 EC106
Underwood, The, SE9 207 EM89
Underwood Rd, E1 20 C5
E4 123 EB50
Caterham CR3 274 DS126
Woodford Green IG8 124 EK52
Underwood Row, N1 19 K2
Underwood St, N1 19 K2
Undine Rd, E14 34 D8
Undine St, SW17 202 DF92
Uneeda Dr, Grnf. UB6 159 CD67
Unicorn Pas, SE1
off Tooley St 31 P3
Sch Unicorn Prim Sch,
Beck. BR3
off Creswell Dr 225 EB99
Sch Unicorn Sch, Rich. TW9
off Kew Rd 180 CM81
Unicorn Wk, Green. DA9 211 FT85
● Union Business Pk, Uxb.
UB8 156 BH66
Union Cl, E11 145 ED63
Union Cotts, E15 13 K6
Union Ct, EC2 19 N8
Richmond TW9 off Eton St 200 CL85
Union Dr, E1 21 M4
Union Grn, Hem.H. HP2
off Church St 62 BK19
Union Gro, SW8 41 N9
Union Jack Club, SE1 30 E4
Union Pk, SE10 47 L1
Union Rd, N11 121 DK51
SW4 41 N8
SW8 41 N8
Bromley BR2 226 EK99
Croydon CR0 224 DQ101
Northolt UB5 158 CA68
Wembley HA0 160 CL65
Union Sq, N1 9 J9
Union St, E15 12 G9
SE1 31 H3
Barnet EN5 101 CY42
Kingston upon Thames KT1 219 CK96
Union Wk, E2 19 P2
Union Wf, N1 19 J1
West Drayton UB7
off Bentinck Rd 156 BL74
Unity Cl, NW10 161 CU65
SE19 off Crown Dale 204 DQ92
New Addington CR0 243 EB109
Unity Ct, SE1 off Mawbey Pl 32 B10
Unity Rd, Enf. EN3 104 DW37
Unity Ter, Har. HA2
off Scott Cres 138 CB60
● Unity Trd Est, Wdf.Grn.
IG8 146 EK55
Unity Way, SE18 36 E6
Unity Wf, SE1 32 B4
University Cl, NW7 119 CT52
Bushey WD23 98 CA42
H University Coll Hosp, NW1 17 M4
Elizabeth Garrett Anderson
Wing, NW1 17 M4
Hosp for Tropical Diseases,
WC1 17 M5
Obstetric Hosp, WC1 17 M5
Private Wing, WC1 17 M5
Uni University Coll London,
WC1 17 N4
Arthur Stanley Ho, W1 17 M6
Dorville & Doran Ho, W1 17 L7
Eastman Dental Inst, WC1 18 C3
Inst of Ophthalmology, EC1 19 L3
Ludwig Inst for Cancer
Research, W1 17 M6
Prankerd Ho, NW1 17 M4
Ramsay Hall, W1 17 L5
Slade Research Cen, WC1 17 P5
The Inst of Neurology, WC1 18 B5
The Warburg Inst, WC1 17 P5
Windeyer Bldg, W1 17 M6
Wolfson Ho, NW1 17 M3
Wolfson Inst for Biomedical
Research, WC1 17 M5
Sch University Coll Sch,
Jun Branch, NW3
off Holly Hill 142 DC63
Sen Sch, NW3 5 N2
University Gdns, Bex. DA5 208 EZ87
H University Hosp Lewisham,
SE13 205 EB85
Uni University of E London -
London Docklands Campus,
E16 25 M10
Uni University of E London -
Stratford Campus,
Arthur Edwards Bldg, E15 13 K4
Cen for Clinical Ed, E15 13 K5
Duncan Ho, E15 12 G8
Sch of Ed, E15 13 K4
Student Services Cen, E15 13 K4
Uni Ho, E15 13 K5
Uni University of Gloucestershire,
Urban Learning Foundation,
E14 22 A10
Uni University of Greenwich -
Avery Hill Campus, Mansion
Site, SE9 off Bexley Rd 207 EQ86
Southwood Site, SE9
off Avery Hill Rd 207 EQ87
Uni University of Greenwich -
Maritime Greenwich Campus,
Cooper Bldg, SE10 46 G2
Old Royal Naval Coll, SE10 46 G2
Uni University of Hertfordshire,
Bayfordbury Fld Sta &
Observatory, Hert. SG13
off Lower Hatfield Rd 53 DN14
College La Campus, Hat.
AL10 off College La 67 CT20
de Havilland Campus, Hat.
AL10 off Mosquito Way 66 CR18
St. Albans Campus, St.Alb.
AL1 off Hatfield Rd 65 CE19
Uni University of London,
Canterbury Hall, WC1 18 A3
Commonwealth Hall, WC1 18 A3
Hughes Parry Hall, WC1 18 A3
International Hall, WC1 18 B5
Senate Ho, WC1 17 P6
Stewart Ho, WC1 17 P6
Union, WC1 17 N5

University of Surrey,
Frances Harrison Ho,
Guil. GU2 *off Gill Av* 280 AS135
Guildford Pk, Guil. GU2
off Alresford Rd 264 AV134
HPRU, Guil. GU2
off Gill Av 280 AS135
Post Grad Med Sch, Guil.
GU2 *off Gill Av* 280 AS135
Wealden Ho, Guil. GU2
off Gill Av 280 AS135
University of the Arts, W1 . . 17 J9
University of Westminster - Cavendish Campus, W1 . . . . 17 L6
University of Westminster - Harrow Campus,
Har. HA1
off Watford Rd 139 CG59
University of Westminster - Marylebone Campus, NW1 . 16 G6
University of Westminster - Regent Campus, W1 . . . . . . 17 K8
Great Portland St, W1 . . . . 17 K6
Little Titchfield St, W1 . . . . . . 17 L7
Riding Ho St, W1 . . . . 17 L7
University Pl, Erith DA8
off Belmont Rd 189 FC80
University Rd, SW19 . . . . 202 DD93
University St, WC1 . . . . 17 M5
University Way, E16 . . . . 37 M1
Dartford DA1 . . . . 190 FP84
Unstead La, Bramley GU5 . . . . 280 AW144
Unstead Wd, Peasm. GU3 . . . . 280 AW142
Unwin Av, Felt. TW14 . . . . 197 BR85
Unwin Cl, SE15 . . . . 44 C3
Unwin Rd, SW7 . . . . 28 B6
Isleworth TW7 . . . . 179 CE83
Upbrook Ms, W2 . . . . 15 P9
Upcerne Rd, SW10 . . . . 39 P5
Upchurch Cl, SE20 . . . . 204 DV94
Up Cor, Ch.St.G. HP8 . . . . 112 AW47
Up Cor Cl, Ch.St.G. HP8 . . . . . . 112 AV47
Upcroft, Wind. SL4 . . . . 173 AP83
Upcroft Av, Edg. HA8 . . . . 118 CQ50
Updale Cl, Pot.B. EN6 . . . . 85 CY33
Updale Rd, Sid. DA14 . . . . 207 ET91
Upfield, Croy. CR0 . . . . 224 DV103
Horley RH6 . . . . 290 DG149
Upfield Cl, Horl. RH6 . . . . 290 DG150
Upfield Rd, W7 . . . . 159 CF71
Upfolds Grn, Guil. GU4 . . . . . . 265 BC130
Upgrove Manor Way, SW2
off Trinity Ri 203 DN87
Uphall Prim Sch, Ilf. IG1
off Uphall Rd 147 EP64
Uphall Rd, Ilf. IG1 . . . . 147 EP64
Upham Pk Rd, W4 . . . . 180 CS77
Uphavering Ho, Horn. RM12 . . 149 FH61
Uphill Dr, NW7 . . . . 118 CS50
NW9 . . . . 140 CQ57
Uphill Gro, NW7 . . . . 118 CS49
Uphill Rd, NW7 . . . . 118 CS49
Upland Av, Chesh. HP5 . . . . 76 AP28
Upland Ct Rd, Rom. RM3 . . . . . 128 FM54
Upland Dr, Brook.Pk AL9 . . . . . . 86 DB25
Upland Ms, SE22 . . . . 204 DU85
Upland Prim Sch, Bexh.
DA7 *off Church Rd* 188 EZ83
Upland Rd, E13 . . . . 23 M4
SE22 . . . . 204 DU85
Bexleyheath DA7 . . . . 188 EZ83
Caterham CR3 . . . . 259 EB120
Epping CM16 . . . . 91 ET25
South Croydon CR2 . . . . 242 DR106
Sutton SM2 . . . . 240 DD108
Uplands, Ashtd. KT21 . . . . 253 CK120
Beckenham BR3 . . . . 225 EA96
Croxley Green WD3 . . . . 96 BM44
Ware SG12 . . . . 55 DZ05
Welwyn Garden City AL8 . . . . 51 CW05
Uplands, The, Brick.Wd AL2 . . . 82 BY30
Gerrards Cross SL9 . . . . 134 AY60
Loughton IG10 . . . . 107 EM41
Ruislip HA4 . . . . 137 BU60
Uplands Av, E17
off Blackhorse La 123 DX54
● **Uplands Business Pk**, E17 . 123 DX54
Uplands Cl, SW14
off Monroe Dr 200 CP85
Gerrards Cross SL9 . . . . 134 AY60
Sevenoaks TN13 . . . . 278 FF123
Uplands Dr, Oxshott KT22 . . . 237 CD113
Uplands End, Wdf.Grn. IG8 . . . 124 EL52
Uplands Pk Rd, Enf. EN2 . . . . . 103 DN41
Uplands Rd, N8 . . . . 143 DM57
East Barnet EN4 . . . . 120 DG46
Kenley CR8 . . . . 258 DQ116
Orpington BR6 . . . . 228 EV102
Romford RM6 . . . . 148 EX55
Warley CM14 . . . . 130 FY50
Woodford Green IG8 . . . . . . 124 EL52
Uplands Way, N21 . . . . 103 DN43
Sevenoaks TN13 . . . . 278 FF123
Upland Way, Epsom KT18 . . . . 255 CW118
UPMINSTER, RM14 . . . . 150 FQ62
⇌ **Upminster** 150 FQ61
⊖ **Upminster** 150 FQ61
⊖ **Upminster Bridge** 150 FN61
Upminster Inf Sch, Upmin.
RM14 *off St. Mary's La* 150 FQ62
Upminster Jun Sch, Upmin.
RM14 *off St. Mary's La* 150 FQ62
Upminster Rd, Horn.
RM11, RM12 . . . . 150 FM61
Upminster RM14 . . . . 150 FM61
Upminster Rd N, Rain. RM13 . . 170 FJ69
Upminster Rd S, Rain. RM13 . . 169 FG70
★ **Upminster Tithe Barn Mus of Nostalgia**, Upmin. RM14 . . 150 FQ59
● **Upminster Trd Pk**, Upmin.
RM14 . . . . 151 FX59
⊖ **Upney** 167 ET66
Upney Cl, Horn. RM12
off Tylers Cres 150 FK64
Upney La, Bark. IG11 . . . . 167 ES65
Upnor Way, SE17 . . . . 31 P10
Uppark Dr, Ilf. IG2 . . . . 147 EQ58
Upper Abbey Rd, Belv. DA17 . . 188 EZ77
Upper Addison Gdns, W14 . . . . . 26 E4
Upper Ashlyns Rd, Berk. HP4 . . 60 AV20
Upper Bk St, E14 . . . . 34 C3
Upper Bardsey Wk, N1
off Bardsey Wk 9 K4
Upper Barn, Hem.H. HP3 . . . . . . 62 BM23
Upper Belgrave St, SW1 . . . . . . 29 H6
Upper Belmont Rd, Chesh.
HP5 . . . . 76 AP28
Upper Berenger Wk, SW10
off Blantyre St 40 A4
Upper Berkeley St, W1 . . . . 16 E9
Upper Beulah Hill, SE19 . . . . . . 224 DS95
Upper Blantyre Wk, SW10
off Blantyre St 40 A4
Upper Bourne End La, Hem.H.
HP1 . . . . 79 BA25
Upper Bray Rd, Bray SL6 . . . . . 172 AC77
Upper Brentwood Rd, Rom.
RM2 . . . . 150 FJ56
Upper Br Rd, Red. RH1 . . . . 272 DE134
Upper Brighton Rd, Surb. KT6 . 219 CK100
Upper Brockley Rd, SE4 . . . . 45 P8
Upper Brook St, W1 . . . . 28 G1
Upper Butts, Brent. TW8 . . . . . 179 CJ79
Upper Caldy Wk, N1
off Clifton Rd 164 DQ65
Upper Camelford Wk, W11
off St. Marks Rd 161 CY72
Upper Cavendish Av, N3 . . . . . 142 DA55
Upper Cheyne Row, SW3 . . . . . . 40 C3
Upper Ch Hill, Green. DA9 . . . . 211 FS85
Upper Clabdens, Ware SG12 . . . 55 DZ05
UPPER CLAPTON, E5 . . . . 144 DV60
Upper Clapton Rd, E5 . . . . 144 DV60
Upper Clarendon Wk, W11
off Clarendon Wk 161 CY72
Upper Cornsland, Brwd.
CM14 . . . . 130 FX48
Upper Ct Rd, Epsom KT19 . . . . 238 CQ111
Woldingham CR3 . . . . 259 EA123
Upper Culver Rd, St.Alb. AL1 . . 65 CE18
Upper Dagnall St, St.Alb. AL3 . . 65 CD20
Upper Dartrey Wk, SW10
off Blantyre St 40 A4
Upper Dengie Wk, N1
off Popham Rd 164 DQ67
Upper Dr, Beac. HP9 . . . . 111 AK50
Biggin Hill TN16 . . . . 260 EJ118
Upper Dunnymans, Bans. SM7
off Basing Rd 239 CZ114
Upper Edgeborough Rd, Guil.
GU1 . . . . 281 AZ135
UPPER EDMONTON, N18 . . . . . 122 DU51
UPPER ELMERS END, Beck.
BR3 . . . . 225 DZ100
Upper Elmers End Rd, Beck.
BR3 . . . . 225 DY98
Upper Fairfield Rd, Lthd.
KT22 . . . . 253 CH121
Upper Fm Rd, W.Mol. KT8 . . . . 218 BZ98
Upperfield Rd, Welw.G.C. AL7 . . 51 CZ11
Upper Forecourt, Gat. RH6 . . . 291 DH152
Upper Fosters, NW4
off New Brent St 141 CW57
UPPER GATTON, Reig. RH2 . . . 272 DC127
Upper George St, Chesh. HP5
off Frances St 76 AQ30
Upper Gladstone Rd, Chesh.
HP5 . . . . 76 AQ30
Upper Grn E, Mitch. CR4 . . . . . 222 DF97
Upper Grn Rd, Tewin AL6 . . . . . . 52 DE05
Upper Grn W, Mitch. CR4
off London Rd 222 DF97
Upper Grosvenor St, W1 . . . . 28 G1
Upper Grotto Rd, Twick. TW1 . . 199 CF89
Upper Grd, SE1 . . . . 30 E2
Upper Gro, SE25 . . . . 224 DS98
Upper Gro Rd, Belv. DA17 . . . . 188 EZ79
Upper Guild Hall,
Bluewater DA9
off Bluewater Shop Cen . . . 211 FT87
Upper Guildown Rd, Guil.
GU2 . . . . 280 AV137
Upper Gulland Wk, N1
off Nightingale Rd 9 K5
UPPER HALLIFORD, Shep.
TW17 . . . . 217 BS97
⇌ **Upper Halliford** 217 BS96
Upper Halliford Bypass, Shep.
TW17 . . . . 217 BS99
Upper Halliford Grn, Shep.
TW17 . . . . 217 BS98
Upper Halliford Rd, Shep.
TW17 . . . . 217 BS96
Upper Hall Pk, Berk. HP4 . . . . . . 60 AX20
Upper Hampstead Wk, NW3
off New End 142 DC63
Upper Ham Rd, Kings.T. KT2 . . 199 CK91
Richmond TW10 . . . . 199 CK91
Upper Handa Wk, N1
off Handa Wk 9 K4
Upper Harestone, Cat. CR3 . . . 274 DU127
Upper Hawkwell Wk, N1
off Popham Rd 164 DQ67
Upper Heath Rd, St.Alb. AL1 . . . 65 CF18
Upper High St, Epsom KT17 . . 238 CS113
Upper Highway, Abb.L. WD5 . . . 81 BR33
Kings Langley WD4 . . . . 81 BQ32
Upper Hill Ri, Rick. WD3 . . . . . . 96 BH44
Upper Hitch, Wat. WD19 . . . . . 116 BY46
UPPER HOLLOWAY, N19 . . . . . 143 DJ62
⊖ **Upper Holloway** 143 DK61
Upper Holly Hill Rd, Belv.
DA17 . . . . 189 FB78
Upper Hook, Harl. CM18 . . . . . . 73 ET17
Upper James St, W1 . . . . 17 M10
Upper John St, W1 . . . . 17 M10
Upper Lattimore Rd, St.Alb.
AL1 . . . . 65 CE20
Upper Lees Rd, Slou. SL2 . . . . 153 AP69
Upper Lismore Wk, N1
off Mull Wk 9 K5
Upper Lo Way, Couls. CR5
off Netherne Dr 257 DK122
Upper Mall, W6 . . . . 181 CU78
Upper Manor Rd, Gdmg. GU7 . 280 AS144
Upper Marlborough Rd, St.Alb.
AL1 . . . . 65 CE20
Upper Marsh, SE1 . . . . 30 D6
Upper Marsh La, Hodd. EN11 . . 71 EA18
Upper Meadow, Chesh. HP5
off Stanley Av 76 AP30
Gerrards Cross SL9 . . . . 134 AW60
Upper Mealines, Harl. CM18 . . . 74 EU18
Upper Montagu St, W1 . . . . 16 E6
Upper Mulgrave Rd, Sutt.
SM2 . . . . 239 CY108
Upper N St, E14 . . . . 22 B10
UPPER NORWOOD, SE19 . . . . . 204 DR94
Upper Paddock Rd, Wat. WD19 . 98 BY44
Upper Palace Rd, E.Mol. KT8 . . 218 CC97
Upper Pk, Harl. CM20 . . . . 57 EP14
Loughton IG10 . . . . 106 EK42
Upper Pk Rd, N11 . . . . 121 DH50
NW3 . . . . 6 E4
Belvedere DA17 . . . . 189 FB77
Bromley BR1 . . . . 226 EH95
Kingston upon Thames KT2 . 200 CN93
Upper Phillimore Gdns, W8 . . . 27 J5
Upper Pillory Down, Cars.
SM5 . . . . 240 DG113
Upper Pines, Bans. SM7 . . . . . 256 DF117
Upper Rainham Rd, Horn.
RM12 . . . . 149 FF63
Upper Ramsey Wk, N1
off Ramsey Wk 9 L5
Upper Rawreth Wk, N1
off Popham Rd 164 DQ67
Upper Richmond Rd, SW15 . . . 181 CY84
Upper Richmond Rd W, SW14 . 180 CP84
Richmond TW10 . . . . 180 CN84
Upper Riding, Beac. HP9 . . . . . 110 AG54
Upper Rd, E13 . . . . 23 N2
Denham UB9 . . . . 135 BD59
Wallington SM6 . . . . 241 DK106
Upper Rose Gall,
Bluewater DA9
off Bluewater Shop Cen . . . 211 FU87
Upper Rose Hill, Dor. RH4 . . . . 285 CH137
Upper Ryle, Brwd. CM14 . . . . . 130 FV45
Upper St. Martin's La, WC2 . . . . 18 A10
Upper Sales, Hem.H. HP1 . . . . . 61 BF21
Upper Sawley Wd, Bans. SM7 . 239 CZ114
Upper Selsdon Rd, S.Croy.
CR2 . . . . 242 DT108
Upper Sheridan Rd, Belv. DA17
off Coleman Rd 188 FA77
Upper Shirley Rd, Croy. CR0 . . 224 DW103
Upper Shot, Welw.G.C. AL7 . . . . 52 DA08
Upper Shott, Chsht EN7 . . . . 88 DT26
Upper Sq, Islw. TW7 . . . . 179 CG83
Upper Sta Rd, Rad. WD7 . . . . . . 99 CG35
Upper Stoneyfield, Harl. CM19 . 73 EP15
Upper St, N1 . . . . 8 F10
Shere GU5 . . . . 282 BM138
Upper Sunbury Rd, Hmptn.
TW12 . . . . 218 BY95
Upper Sutton La, Houns. TW5 . 178 CA80
Upper Swaines, Epp. CM16 . . . . 91 ET30
UPPER SYDENHAM, SE26 . . . . 204 DU91
Upper Tachbrook St, SW1 . . . . . 29 L8
Upper Tail, Wat. WD19 . . . . 116 BY48
Upper Talbot Wk, W11
off Talbot Wk 161 CY72
Upper Teddington Rd, Kings.T.
KT1 . . . . 219 CJ95
Upper Ter, NW3 . . . . 142 DC62
Upper Thames St, EC4 . . . . 19 H10
Upper Thames Wk,
Bluewater DA9
off Bluewater Shop Cen . . . 211 FT88
Upper Tollington Pk, N4 . . . . . 143 DN60
Upperton Rd, Guil. GU2 . . . . . . 280 AW136
Sidcup DA14 . . . . 207 ET92
Upperton Rd E, E13 . . . . 24 D2
Upperton Rd W, E13 . . . . 24 C3
UPPER TOOTING, SW17 . . . . . . 202 DE90
Upper Tooting Pk, SW17 . . . . . 202 DF89
Upper Tooting Rd, SW17 . . . . . 202 DF91
Upper Town Rd, Grnf. UB6 . . . . 158 CB70
Upper Tulse Hill, SW2 . . . . 203 DM87
Upper Vernon Rd, Sutt. SM1 . . 240 DD106
Upper Wk, Vir.W. GU25 . . . . . . 214 AY98
UPPER WALTHAMSTOW, E17 . 145 EB56
Upper Walthamstow Rd, E17 . . 145 ED56
⇌ **Upper Warlingham** 258 DU118
Upper W St, Reig. RH2 . . . . 271 CZ134
Upper Whistler Wk, SW10
off Blantyre St 39 P4
Upper Wickham La, Well.
DA16 . . . . 188 EV80
Upper Wimpole St, W1 . . . . 17 J6
Upper Woburn Pl, WC1 . . . . 17 P3
Upper Woodcote Village, Pur.
CR8 . . . . 241 DK112
Uppingham Av, Stan. HA7 . . . . 117 CH53
Upsdell Av, N13 . . . . 121 DN51
UPSHIRE, Wal.Abb. EN9 . . . . . . 90 EJ32
Upshirebury Grn, Wal.Abb. EN9
off Horseshoe Hill 90 EK33
Upshire Prim Foundation Sch,
Wal.Abb. EN9
off Upshire Rd 90 EH33
Upshire Rd, Wal.Abb. EN9 . . . . . 90 EF32
Upshot La, Wok. GU22 . . . . 249 BF117
Upstall St, SE5 . . . . 43 H7
UPTON, E7 . . . . 166 EH66
UPTON, Slou. SL1 . . . . 174 AU76
Upton, Wok. GU21 . . . . 248 AV117
Upton Av, E7 . . . . 13 P6
St. Albans AL3 . . . . 65 CD19
Upton Cl, NW2 . . . . 141 CY62
Bexley DA5 . . . . 208 EZ86
Park Street AL2 . . . . 83 CD25
Slough SL1 . . . . 174 AT76
Upton Ct, SE20 *off Blean Gro* . 204 DW94
Upton Ct Rd, Slou. SL3 . . . . . . 174 AU76
Upton Cross Prim Sch, E13
off Churston Av 166 EH67
Upton Dene, Sutt. SM2 . . . . 240 DB108
Upton Gdns, Har. HA3 . . . . 139 CH57
Upton Hosp, Slou. SL1 . . . . 174 AT76
Upton Ho Sch, Wind. SL4
off St. Leonards Rd 173 AQ82
Upton La, E7 . . . . 13 P8
Upton Lo Cl, Bushey WD23 . . . 116 CC45
UPTON PARK, E6 . . . . 166 EJ67
UPTON PARK, Slou. SL1 . . . . . . 174 AT76
⊖ **Upton Park** 166 EH67
Upton Pk, Slou. SL1 . . . . 174 AT76
Upton Pk Rd, E7 . . . . 166 EH66
Upton Prim Sch, Bexh. DA6
off Upton Rd 208 EZ85
Upton Rd, N18 . . . . 122 DU50
SE18 . . . . 187 EQ79
Bexley DA5 . . . . 208 EZ86
Bexleyheath DA6 . . . . 188 EY84
Hounslow TW3 . . . . 178 CA83
Slough SL1 . . . . 174 AU76
Thornton Heath CR7 . . . . 224 DR96
Watford WD18 . . . . 97 BV42
Upton Rd S, Bex. DA5 . . . . 208 EZ86
Upway, N12 . . . . 120 DE52
Chalfont St. Peter SL9 . . . . . . 113 AZ53
Upwood Rd, SE12 . . . . 206 EF86
SW16 . . . . 223 DL95
Uranus Rd, Hem.H. HP2 . . . . 62 BM18
Urban Av, Horn. RM12 . . . . 150 FJ62
Urban Ms, N4 . . . . 143 DP59
Urdang Acad, The, EC1 . . . . 18 F3
Urlwin St, SE5 . . . . 43 J3
Urlwin Wk, SW9 . . . . 42 F7
Urmston Dr, SW19 . . . . 201 CY88
Ursula Ms, N4 . . . . 143 DP60
Ursula St, SW11 . . . . 40 C7
Ursuline Conv Prep Sch,
SW20 *off The Downs* 201 CX94
Ursuline High Sch, SW20
off Crescent Rd 221 CX95
Urswick Gdns, Dag. RM9 . . . . . 168 EY66
Urswick Rd, E9 . . . . 10 G2
Dagenham RM9 . . . . 168 EX66
Usborne Ms, SW8 . . . . 42 C4
Usher Rd, E3 . . . . 11 P10
Usherwood Cl, Box H. KT20 . . 270 CP131
Usk Rd, SW11 . . . . 182 DC84
Aveley RM15 . . . . 170 FQ72
Usk St, E2 . . . . 21 J2
Utah Bldg, SE13
off Deals Gateway 46 C6
Utopia Village, NW1 . . . . 6 G8
Uvedale Cl, New Adgtn CR0
off Uvedale Cres 243 ED111
Uvedale Cres, New Adgtn
CR0 . . . . 243 ED111
Uvedale Rd, Dag. RM10 . . . . . . 148 FA62
Enfield EN2 . . . . 104 DR43
Oxted RH8 . . . . 276 EF129
Uverdale Rd, SW10 . . . . 39 P5
UXBRIDGE, UB8 - UB11 . . . . . . 156 BK66
⊖ **Uxbridge** 156 BK66
● **Uxbridge Business Pk**, Uxb.
UB8 . . . . 136 BJ64
Uxbridge Coll, Hayes Comm
Campus, Hayes UB3
off Coldharbour La 157 BU73
Uxbridge Campus, Uxb. UB8
off Park Rd 156 BL65
Uxbridge High Sch, Uxb.
UB8 *off The Greenway* 156 BK68
UXBRIDGE MOOR, Iver SL0 . . . 156 BG67
UXBRIDGE MOOR, Uxb. UB8 . 156 BG67
Uxbridge Rd, W3 . . . . 160 CL73
W5 . . . . 159 CJ73
W5 (Ealing Com.) 160 CL73
W7 . . . . 159 CE74
W12 . . . . 26 B4
W13 . . . . 159 CH74
Feltham TW13 . . . . 198 BW89
Hampton TW12 . . . . 198 CA91
Harrow HA3 . . . . 116 CC52
Hayes UB4 . . . . 158 BW73
Iver SL0 . . . . 154 AY71
Kingston upon Thames KT1 . 219 CK98
Pinner HA5 . . . . 116 CB52
Rickmansworth WD3 . . . . 113 BF47
Slough SL1, SL2, SL3 . . . . 174 AU75
Southall UB1 . . . . 158 CA74
Stanmore HA7 . . . . 117 CF51
Uxbridge UB10 . . . . 156 BN69
Uxbridge St, W8 . . . . 27 J2
Uxendon Cres, Wem. HA9 . . . . 140 CL60
Uxendon Hill, Wem. HA9 . . . . . 140 CM60
Uxendon Manor Prim Sch,
Kenton HA3 *off Vista Way* . 140 CL57

V

Vache La, Ch.St.G. HP8 . . . . . . 112 AW47
Vache Ms, Ch.St.G. HP8 . . . . . . 112 AX46
Vaillant Rd, Wey. KT13 . . . . . . 235 BQ105
Valance Av, E4 . . . . 124 EF46
Valan Leas, Brom. BR2 . . . . 226 EE97
Vale, The, N10 . . . . 120 DG53
N14 . . . . 121 DK45
NW11 . . . . 141 CX62
SW3 . . . . 40 A2
W3 . . . . 160 CR74
Brentwood CM14 . . . . 130 FW46
Chalfont St. Peter SL9 . . . . . . 112 AX53
Coulsdon CR5 . . . . 241 DK114
Croydon CR0 . . . . 225 DX103
Feltham TW14 . . . . 197 BV86
Hounslow TW5 . . . . 178 BY79
Ruislip HA4 . . . . 138 BW63
Sunbury-on-Thames TW16 . . 197 BU93
Woodford Green IG8 . . . . 124 EG52
Vale Av, Borwd. WD6 . . . . 100 CP43
Vale Border, Croy. CR0 . . . . 243 DX111
Vale Cl, N2 . . . . 142 DF55
W9 . . . . 15 N3
Chalfont St. Peter SL9 . . . . . . 112 AX53
Epsom KT18 . . . . 254 CS119
Orpington BR6 . . . . 245 EN105
Pilgrim's Hatch CM15 . . . . . . 130 FT43
Weybridge KT13 . . . . 217 BR104
Woking GU21 . . . . 248 AY116
Vale Cotts, SW15 . . . . 200 CS90
Vale Ct, W3 *off The Vale* 161 CT74
W9 . . . . 15 N3
Weybridge KT13 . . . . 217 BR104
Vale Cres, SW15 . . . . 200 CS90
Vale Cft, Clay. KT10 . . . . 237 CE109
Pinner HA5 . . . . 138 BY57
Vale Dr, Barn. EN5 . . . . 101 CZ42
Vale End, SE22
off Grove Vale 184 DS84
Vale Fm Rd, Wok. GU21 . . . . . 248 AX117
Vale Gro, N4 . . . . 144 DQ59
W3 *off The Vale* 160 CS74
Slough SL1 . . . . 174 AS76
● **Vale Ind Est**, Wat. WD18 . . . 115 BP46
Vale La, W3 . . . . 160 CN71
Valence Av, Dag. RM8 . . . . 148 EX62
Valence Circ, Dag. RM8 . . . . . . 148 EX62
Valence Dr, Chsht EN7 . . . . 88 DU28
★ **Valence Ho Mus**, Dag.
RM8 . . . . 148 EX62
Valence Inf & Jun Schs, Dag.
RM8 *off Bonham Rd* 148 EX61
Valence Rd, Erith DA8 . . . . 189 FD80
Valence Sch, West. TN16
off Westerham Rd 277 ET126
Valence Wd Rd, Dag. RM8 . . . . 148 EX62
Valencia Rd, Stan. HA7 . . . . . . 117 CJ49
Valency Cl, Nthwd. HA6 . . . . . . 115 BT49
Valentia Pl, SW9
off Brixton Sta Rd 183 DN84
Valentine Av, Bex. DA5 . . . . . . 208 EY89
Valentine Ct, SE23 . . . . 205 DX89
Valentine Ho, E3
off Garrison Rd 11 P9
Valentine Pl, SE1 . . . . 30 G4
Valentine Rd, E9 . . . . 11 J5
Harrow HA2 . . . . 138 CC62
Valentine Row, SE1 . . . . 30 G5
Valentines High Sch, Ilf. IG2
off Cranbrook Rd 147 EN58
Valentines Rd, Ilf. IG1 . . . . 147 EP60
Valentines Way, Rom. RM7 . . . 149 FE61
Valentine Way, Ch.St.G. HP8 . . 112 AX48
Valentyne Cl, New Adgtn CR0 . 244 EE111
Vale of Health, NW3 . . . . 142 DD62
Vale Par, SW15
off Kingston Vale 200 CS90
Vale Prim Sch, The, Epsom
KT18 *off Beaconsfield Rd* . . 254 CS119
Valerian Wk, N11
off Nurserymans Rd 120 DG47
Valerian Way, E15 . . . . 23 K3
Valerie Cl, St.Alb. AL1 . . . . 65 CH20
Valerie Ct, Bushey WD23 . . . . . 116 CC45
Sutton SM2 *off Stanley Rd* . 240 DB108
Vale Ri, NW11 . . . . 141 CZ60
Chesham HP5 . . . . 76 AQ28
Vale Rd, E7 . . . . 166 EH65
N4 . . . . 144 DQ59
Bromley BR1 . . . . 227 EN96
Bushey WD23 . . . . 98 BY43
Chesham HP5 . . . . 76 AQ27
Claygate KT10 . . . . 237 CE109
Dartford DA1 . . . . 209 FH88
Epsom KT19 . . . . 239 CT105
Mitcham CR4 . . . . 223 DK97
Northfleet DA11 . . . . 212 GD87
Sutton SM1 . . . . 240 DB105
Weybridge KT13 . . . . 217 BR104
Windsor SL4 . . . . 173 AM80
Worcester Park KT4 . . . . 239 CT105
Vale Rd N, Surb. KT6 . . . . 220 CL103
Vale Rd S, Surb. KT6 . . . . 220 CL103
Vale Row, N5
off Gillespie Rd 143 DP62
Vale Royal, N7 . . . . 8 A7
Valery Pl, Hmptn. TW12 . . . . . . 198 CA94
Vale Sch, The, SW7 . . . . 27 N7
Valeside, Hert. SG14 . . . . 53 DN10
Vale St, SE27 . . . . 204 DR90
Valeswood Rd, Brom. BR1 . . . . 206 EF92
Vale Ter, N4 . . . . 144 DQ58
Valetta Gro, E13 . . . . 13 N10
Valetta Rd, W3 . . . . 180 CS75
Valette St, E9 . . . . 10 F4
Valiant Cl, Nthlt. UB5
off Ruislip Rd 158 BX69
Romford RM7 . . . . 126 FA54
Valiant Ho, SE7 . . . . 36 D10
Valiant Path, NW9 . . . . 118 CS53
Valiant Way, E6 . . . . 25 J7
Vallance Rd, E1 . . . . 20 D3
E2 . . . . 20 D3
N22 . . . . 121 DJ54
Vallentin Rd, E17 . . . . 145 EC56
Valley, The, Guil. GU2
off Portsmouth Rd 280 AW138
Valley Av, N12 . . . . 120 DD49
Valley Cl, Dart. DA1 . . . . 209 FF86
Hertford SG13 . . . . 54 DR10
Loughton IG10 . . . . 107 EM44
Pinner HA5 . . . . 115 BV54
Waltham Abbey EN9 . . . . 89 EC32
Ware SG12 . . . . 54 DV05
Valley Ct, Cat. CR3
off Beechwood Gdns 258 DU122
Kenley CR8 *off Hayes La* . . . 242 DQ114
Valley Dr, NW9 . . . . 140 CN58
Gravesend DA12 . . . . 213 GK91
Sevenoaks TN13 . . . . 279 FH125
Valleyfield Rd, SW16 . . . . 203 DM92
Valley Flds Cres, Enf. EN2 . . . . 103 DN40
Valley Gdns, SW19 . . . . 202 DD94
Greenhithe DA9 . . . . 211 FV86
Wembley HA0 . . . . 160 CM66
★ **Valley Gdns, The**, Egh.
TW20 . . . . 214 AS96
Valley Grn, The, Welw.G.C. AL8 . 51 CW08
Valley Gro, SE7 . . . . 36 D10
Valley Hill, Loug. IG10 . . . . 124 EL45
● **Valleylink Est**, Enf. EN3
off Meridian Way 105 DY44
Valley Ms, Twick. TW1
off Cross Deep 199 CG89
● **Valley Pt Ind Est**, Croy.
CR0 . . . . 223 DL101
Valley Prim Sch, Brom. BR2
off Beckenham La 226 EF96
Valley Ri, Wat. WD25 . . . . 81 BV33
Valley Rd, SW16 . . . . 203 DM91
Belvedere DA17 . . . . 189 FB77
Bromley BR2 . . . . 226 EE96
Dartford DA1 . . . . 209 FF86
Erith DA8 . . . . 189 FD77
Fawkham Green DA3 . . . . 231 FV102
Kenley CR8 . . . . 258 DR115
Northchurch HP4 . . . . 60 AT17
Orpington BR5 . . . . 228 EV95
Rickmansworth WD3 . . . . 96 BG43
St. Albans AL3 . . . . 65 CE15
Uxbridge UB10 . . . . 156 BL68
Welwyn Garden City AL8 . . . . . 51 CV10
Valley Side, E4 . . . . 123 EA47
Valleyside, Hem.H. HP1 . . . . 61 BF20
Valley Side Par, E4
off Valley Side 123 EA47
Valley Vw, Barn. EN5 . . . . 101 CY44
Biggin Hill TN16 . . . . 260 EJ118
Chesham HP5 . . . . 76 AN29
Goffs Oak EN7 . . . . 88 DQ28
Greenhithe DA9 . . . . 211 FV86
Valley Vw Gdns, Ken. CR8 . . . . 258 DS115
Valley Wk, Crox.Grn WD3 . . . . . 97 BQ43
Croydon CR0 . . . . 224 DW103
Valley Way, Ger.Cr. SL9 . . . . . . 134 AW58
Valliere Rd, NW10 . . . . 161 CV69
Valliers Wd Rd, Sid. DA15 . . . . 207 ER88
Vallis Way, W13 . . . . 159 CG71
Chessington KT9 . . . . 237 CK105
Valmar Rd, SE5 . . . . 43 K7
● **Valmar Trd Est**, SE5 . . . . 43 K7
Val McKenzie Av, N7
off Parkside Cres 143 DN62
Valnay St, SW17 . . . . 202 DF92
Valognes Av, E17 . . . . 123 DY53
Valonia Gdns, SW18 . . . . 201 CZ86
Vambery Rd, SE18 . . . . 187 EQ79
Vanbrough Cres, Nthlt. UB5 . . 158 BW67
Vanbrugh Cl, E16 . . . . 24 E7
Vanbrugh Dr, Walt. KT12 . . . . . 218 BW101
Vanbrugh Flds, SE3 . . . . 47 L3
Vanbrugh Hill, SE3 . . . . 47 L2
SE10 . . . . 47 K1
Vanbrugh Pk, SE3 . . . . 47 L5
Vanbrugh Pk Rd, SE3 . . . . 47 M4
Vanbrugh Pk Rd W, SE3 . . . . 47 L4
Vanbrugh Rd, W4 . . . . 180 CR76

Vanbrugh Ter, SE3 47 M6
Vanburgh Cl, Orp. BR6 227 ES102
Vancouver Cl, Epsom KT19 238 CQ111
Orpington BR6 246 EU105
Vancouver Ct, Smallfield RH6 291 DN148
Vancouver Rd, SE23 205 DY89
Broxbourne EN10 89 DY25
Edgware HA8 118 CP53
Hayes UB4 157 BV70
Richmond TW10 199 CJ91
Vanda Cres, St.Alb. AL1 65 CF21
Vanderbilt Rd, SW18 202 DB88
Vanderville Gdns, N2 120 DC54
Vandome Cl, E16 24 A9
Vandon Pas, SW1 29 M6
Vandon St, SW1 29 M6
Van Dyck Av, N.Mal. KT3 220 CR101
Vandyke Cl, SW15 201 CX87
Redhill RH1 272 DF131
Vandyke Cross, SE9 206 EL85
Vandy St, EC2 19 N5
Vane Cl, NW3 6 A1
Harrow HA3 140 CM58
Vanessa Cl, Belv. DA17 188 FA78
Vanessa Wk, Grav. DA12 213 GM92
Vanessa Way, Bex. DA5 209 FD90
Vane St, SW1 29 M8
Van Gogh Cl, Islw. TW7
off Twickenham Rd 179 CG83
Vanguard Cl, E16 23 P7
Croydon CR0 223 DP102
Romford RM7 127 FB54
Vanguard Ho, E8 10 F6
Vanguard St, SE8 46 A6
Vanguard Way, Cat. CR3 259 EB121
Wallington SM6 241 DL108
Warlingham CR6 259 EB121
Vanneck Sq, SW15 201 CU85
Vanner Pt, E9 11 J5
Vanners Par, Byfleet KT14
off Brewery La 234 BL113
Vanoc Gdns, Brom. BR1 206 EG91
Vanquisher Wk, Grav. DA12 213 GM90
● **Vansittart Est**, Wind. SL4 173 AQ81
Vansittart Rd, E7 13 M1
Windsor SL4 173 AP80
Vansittart St, SE14 45 M4
Vanston Pl, SW6 39 J4
Vantage Ms, E14 34 F3
Northwood HA6 115 BR51
Vantage Pl, W8 27 K7
Feltham TW14 197 BU86
Vantage Pt, S.Croy. CR2
off Sanderstead Rd 242 DR109
Vantage Rd, Slou. SL1 153 AP74
Vantorts Cl, Saw. CM21 58 EY05
Vantorts Rd, Saw. CM21 58 EY06
Vant Rd, SW17 202 DF92
Varcoe Rd, SE16 44 F1
Vardens Rd, SW11 182 DD84
Varden St, E1 20 E8
Vardon Cl, W3 160 CR72
Varley Par, NW9 140 CS56
Varley Rd, E16 24 B8
Varley Way, Mitch. CR4 222 DD96
Varna Rd, SW6 38 F4
Hampton TW12 218 CB95
Varndell St, NW1 17 L2
Varney Cl, Chsht EN7 88 DU27
Hemel Hempstead HP1 61 BF20
Varney Rd, Hem.H. HP1 61 BF20
Varnishers Yd, N1 18 B1
Varsity Dr, Twick. TW1 199 CE85
Varsity Row, SW14 180 CQ82
Vartry Rd, N15 144 DR58
Vassall Rd, SW9 42 E5
Vauban Est, SE16 32 B7
Vauban St, SE16 32 B7
Vaughan Av, NW4 141 CU57
W6 181 CT77
Hornchurch RM12 150 FK63
Vaughan Cl, Hmptn. TW12
off Oak Av 198 BY93
Vaughan Ct, Guil. GU2
off Railton Rd 264 AV130
Sch **Vaughan First & Mid Sch**,
Har. HA1
off Vaughan Rd 138 CC58
Vaughan Gdns, Eton Wick SL4
off Moores La 173 AM77
Ilford IG1 147 EM59
Vaughan Rd, E15 13 L5
SE5 43 J9
Harrow HA1 138 CC59
Thames Ditton KT7 219 CH101
Welling DA16 187 ET82
Vaughan St, SE16 33 N5
Vaughan Way, E1 32 C1
Dorking RH4 285 CG136
Slough SL2 153 AL70
Vaughan Williams Cl, SE8 46 A5
Vaughan Williams Way, Warley
CM14 129 FU51
Vaux Cres, Hersham KT12 235 BV107
VAUXHALL, SE11 42 B1
⇌ **Vauxhall** 42 B2
⊖ **Vauxhall** 42 B2
Vauxhall Br, SE1 42 A1
SW1 42 A1
Vauxhall Br Rd, SW1 29 M8
Vauxhall Cl, Nthflt DA11 213 GF87
Vauxhall Gdns, S.Croy. CR2 242 DQ107
Vauxhall Gdns Est, SE11 42 C1
Vauxhall Gro, SW8 42 C2
Vauxhall Pl, Dart. DA1 210 FL87
Sch **Vauxhall Prim Sch**, SE11 30 D10
Vauxhall Rd, Hem.H. HP2 62 BN20
Vauxhall St, SE11 30 D10
Vauxhall Wk, SE11 30 C10
Vawdrey Cl, E1 20 G5
Veals Mead, Mitch. CR4 222 DE95
Vectis Gdns, SW17
off Vectis Rd 203 DH93
Vectis Rd, SW17 203 DH93
Veda Rd, SE13 185 EA84
Vega Cres, Nthwd. HA6 115 BT50
Vegal Cres, Eng.Grn TW20 194 AW92
Vega Rd, Bushey WD23 116 CC45
Veitch Cl, Felt. TW14 197 BT88
Veldene Way, Har. HA2 138 BZ62
Velde Way, SE22
off East Dulwich Gro 204 DS85
Velizy Av, Harl. CM20 73 ER15
Velletri Ho, E2 21 J1
Vellum Dr, Cars. SM5 222 DG104
Venables Cl, Dag. RM10 149 FB63
Venables St, NW8 16 B5
Vencourt Pl, W6 181 CU78
Venetian Rd, SE5 43 K9
Venetia Rd, N4 143 DP58
W5 179 CK75
Venette Cl, Rain. RM13 169 FH71
Venice Av, Wat. WD18 97 BS42
Venice Wk, W2 15 P6
Venner Cl, Red. RH1 272 DG133
Venner Rd, SE26 204 DW93
Venners Cl, Bexh. DA7 189 FE82
Venn St, SW4 183 DJ84
Ventnor Av, Stan. HA7 117 CH53
Ventnor Dr, N20 120 DB48
Ventnor Gdns, Bark. IG11 167 ES65
Ventnor Rd, SE14 45 K5
Sutton SM2 240 DB108
Venton Cl, Wok. GU21 248 AV117
● **Ventura Pk**, Coln.St AL2 83 CF29
Venture Cl, Bex. DA5 208 EY87
Venue St, E14 22 E6
Venus Cl, Slou. SL2 153 AM70
Venus Hill, Bov. HP3 79 BA31
Venus Ho, E3 *off Garrison Rd* 12 A9
E14 *off Crews St* 34 A8
Venus Ms, Mitch. CR4 222 DE97
Venus Rd, SE18 37 J7
Veny Cres, Horn. RM12 150 FK64
Vera Av, N21 103 DN43
Vera Ct, Wat. WD19 116 BX45
Vera Lynn Cl, E7 13 P1
Vera Rd, SW6 38 F7
Verbena Cl, E16 23 L4
South Ockendon RM15 171 FW72
West Drayton UB7
off Magnolia St 176 BK78
Verbena Gdns, W6 181 CU78
Verdant La, SE6 206 EE88
Verdayne Av, Croy. CR0 225 DX102
Verdayne Gdns, Warl. CR6 258 DW116
Verderers Rd, Chig. IG7 126 EU50
Verdi Cres, W10 14 F1
Verdun Rd, SE18 188 EU79
SW13 181 CU79
Verdure Cl, Wat. WD25 82 BY32
Vereker Dr, Sun. TW16 217 BU97
Vereker Rd, W14 38 F1
Vere Rd, Loug. IG10 107 EQ42
Vere St, W1 17 J9
Veridion Way, Erith DA18 188 EZ75
Verity Cl, W11 14 E9
Veritys, Hat. AL10 67 CU18
Vermeer Gdns, SE15
off Elland Rd 184 DW84
Vermont Cl, Enf. EN2 103 DP42
Vermont Rd, SE19 204 DR93
SW18 202 DB86
Slough SL2 153 AM70
Sutton SM1 222 DB104
Verney Cl, Berk. HP4 60 AT18
Verney Gdns, Dag. RM9 148 EY63
Verney Rd, SE16 44 D2
Dagenham RM9 148 EY64
Slough SL3 175 BA77
Verney St, NW10 140 CR62
Verney Way, SE16 44 E1
Vernham Rd, SE18 187 EQ79
Vernon Av, E12 147 EM63
SW20 221 CX96
Enfield EN3 105 DY36
Woodford Green IG8 124 EH52
Vernon Cl, Epsom KT19 238 CQ107
Orpington BR5 228 EV97
Ottershaw KT16 233 BD107
St. Albans AL1 65 CE21
Staines TW19 196 BL88
Vernon Ct, Stan. HA7
off Vernon Dr 117 CH53
Vernon Cres, Barn. EN4 102 DG44
Brentwood CM13 131 GA48
Vernon Dr, Cat. CR3 258 DQ122
Harefield UB9 114 BJ53
Stanmore HA7 117 CG53
Sch **Vernon Ho Sch**, NW10
off Drury Way 140 CR64
Vernon Ms, E17 *off Vernon Rd* 145 DZ56
W14 26 F9
Vernon Pl, WC1 18 B7
Vernon Ri, WC1 18 D2
Greenford UB6 139 CD64
Vernon Rd, E3 11 P10
E11 146 EE60
E15 13 K6
E17 145 DZ57
N8 143 DN55
SW14 180 CR83
Bushey WD23 98 BY43
Feltham TW13 197 BT89
Ilford IG3 147 ET60
Romford RM5 127 FC50
Sutton SM1 240 DC106
Swanscombe DA10 212 FZ86
Vernon Sq, WC1 18 D2
Vernon St, W14 26 E9
Vernon Wk, Tad. KT20 255 CX120
Vernon Way, Guil. GU2 264 AT133
Vernon Yd, W11 14 G10
Vern Pl, Tats. TN16
off Paynesfield Rd 260 EJ121
Veroan Rd, Bexh. DA7 188 EY82
Verona Cl, Uxb. UB8 156 BJ72
Verona Ct, W4
off Chiswick La 180 CS78
Verona Dr, Surb. KT6 220 CL103
Verona Gdns, Grav. DA12 213 GL91
Verona Ho, Erith DA8
off Waterhead Cl 189 FF80
Verona Rd, E7 13 P6
Veronica Cl, Rom. RM3 128 FJ52
Veronica Gdns, SW16 223 DJ95
Veronica Rd, SW17 203 DH90
Veronique Gdns, Ilf. IG6 147 EP57
Verralls, Wok. GU22 249 BB117
Verran Rd, SW12 203 DH87
Ver Rd, St.Alb. AL3 64 CC20
Versailles Rd, SE20 204 DU94
Verulam Av, E17 145 DZ58
Purley CR8 241 DJ112
Verulam Bldgs, WC1 18 D6
Verulam Cl, Welw.G.C. AL7 51 CZ09
Verulam Ct, NW9 141 CU59
Verulam Ho, W6
off Hammersmith Gro 26 A5
● **Verulam Ind Est**, St.Alb.
AL1 65 CF22
★ **Verulamium Mus & Pk**, St.Alb.
AL3 64 CB20
Verulam Pas, Wat. WD17 97 BV40
Verulam Rd, Grnf. UB6 158 CA70
St. Albans AL3 64 CB19
Sch **Verulam Sch**, St.Alb. AL1
off Brampton Rd 65 CG19
Verulam St, WC1 18 E6
Verwood Dr, Barn. EN4 102 DF41
Verwood Rd, Har. HA2 116 CC54
Veryan, Wok. GU21 248 AU117
Veryan Cl, Orp. BR5 228 EW98
Vesage Ct, EC1 18 F7
Vesey Path, E14 22 D9
Vespan Rd, W12 181 CU75
Vesta Av, St.Alb. AL1 64 CC23
Vesta Ct, SE1 *off Morocco St* 31 N5
Vesta Ho, E3 *off Garrison Rd* 12 A9
Vesta Rd, SE4 45 L9
Hemel Hempstead HP2
off Saturn Way 62 BM18
Vestris Rd, SE23 205 DX89
Vestry Ms, SE5 43 N7
Vestry Rd, E17 145 EB56
SE5 43 N7
Vestry St, N1 19 L2
Vevers Rd, Reig. RH2 288 DB137
Vevey St, SE6 205 DZ89
Vexil Cl, Purf. RM19 191 FR77
Veysey Cl, Hem.H. HP1
off Halwick Cl 62 BH22
Veysey Gdns, Dag. RM10 148 FA62
Viaduct Pl, E2 20 E3
Viaduct Rd, Ware SG12 55 DY06
Viaduct St, E2 20 E3
Viaduct Way, Welw.G.C. AL7 51 CZ06
Vian Av, Enf. EN3 105 DY35
Vian St, SE13 46 D10
Vibart Gdns, SW2 203 DM87
Vibart Wk, N1 8 B8
Vibia Cl, Stanw. TW19 196 BK87
Vicarage Av, SE3 47 P5
Egham TW20 195 BB93
Vicarage Causeway, Hert.Hth
SG13 54 DV11
Vicarage Cl, Bkhm KT23 268 CA125
Brentwood CM14 130 FS49
Erith DA8 189 FC79
Hemel Hempstead HP1 62 BJ22
Kingswood KT20 255 CY124
Northaw EN6 86 DF30
Northolt UB5 158 BZ66
Potters Bar EN6 85 CY32
Ruislip HA4 137 BR59
St. Albans AL1 64 CC23
Seer Green HP9 111 AQ52
Worcester Park KT4 220 CS102
Vicarage Ct, W8
off Vicarage Gate 27 L4
Egham TW20 195 BB93
Feltham TW14 197 BQ87
Vicarage Cres, SW11 40 A7
Egham TW20 195 BB92
Vicarage Dr, SW14 200 CR85
Barking IG11 167 EQ66
Beckenham BR3 225 EA95
Bray SL6 172 AC75
Northfleet DA11 212 GC86
Vicarage Fm Rd, Houns.
TW3, TW5 178 BY82
Vicarage Flds, Walt. KT12 218 BW100
🔒 **Vicarage Fld Shop Cen**, Bark.
IG11 167 EQ66
Vicarage Gdns, SW14
off Vicarage Rd 200 CQ85
W8 27 K3
Mitcham CR4 222 DE97
Potten End HP4 61 BB16
Vicarage Gate, W8 27 L4
Guildford GU2 280 AU136
Vicarage Gate Ms, Tad. KT20 255 CY124
Vicarage Gro, SE5 43 M6
Vicarage Hill, West. TN16 277 ER126
Vicarage La, E6 25 K2
E15 13 K8
Bovingdon HP3 79 BB26
Chigwell IG7 125 EQ47
Dunton Green TN13
off London Rd 263 FD119
Epsom KT17 239 CU109
Horley RH6 290 DF147
Ilford IG1 147 ER60
Kings Langley WD4 80 BM29
Laleham TW18 216 BH97
Leatherhead KT22 253 CH122
North Weald Bassett CM16 74 FA24
Send GU23 265 BC126
Wraysbury TW19 194 AY88
Vicarage Par, N15
off West Grn Rd 144 DQ56
Vicarage Pk, SE18 187 EQ78
Vicarage Path, N8 143 DL59
Vicarage Pl, Slou. SL1 174 AU76
Sch **Vicarage Prim Sch**, E6 25 K2
Vicarage Rd, E10 145 EB60
E15 13 L6
N17 122 DU52
NW4 141 CU58
SE18 187 EQ78
SW14 200 CQ85
Bexley DA5 209 FB88
Coopersale CM16 92 EW29
Croydon CR0 223 DN104
Dagenham RM10 169 FB65
Egham TW20 195 BB93
Hampton Wick KT1 219 CJ95
Hornchurch RM12 149 FG60
Kingston upon Thames KT1 219 CK96
Potten End HP4 61 BA16
Staines TW18 195 BE91
Sunbury-on-Thames TW16 197 BT92
Sutton SM1 240 DB105
Teddington TW11 199 CG92
Twickenham TW2 199 CE89
Ware SG12 55 DY06
Watford WD18 97 BU44
Whitton TW2 198 CC86
Woking GU22 249 AZ121
Woodford Green IG8 124 EL52
Vicarage Sq, Grays RM17 192 GA79
Vicarage Wk, SW11 40 A7
Reigate RH2 *off Chartway* 272 DB134
Vicarage Way, NW10 140 CR62
Colnbrook SL3 175 BC80
Gerrards Cross SL9 135 AZ58
Harrow HA2 138 CA59
Vicarage Wd, Harl. CM20 58 EU14
Vicars Br Cl, Wem. HA0 160 CL68
Vicars Cl, E9 10 G9
E15 13 N8
Enfield EN1 104 DS40
Sch **Vicar's Grn Prim Sch**, Wem.
HA0 *off Lily Gdns* 159 CJ68
Vicars Hill, SE13 185 EB84
Vicars Moor La, N21 121 DN45
Vicars Oak Rd, SE19 204 DS93
Vicars Rd, NW5 6 G2
Vicars Wk, Dag. RM8 148 EV62
Viceroy Cl, N2 142 DE55
Viceroy Ct, NW8 6 D10
Viceroy Par, N2 *off High Rd* 142 DE56
Viceroy Rd, SW8 42 A6
Vickers Cl, Wall. SM6 241 DM108
Vickers Dr N, Wey. KT13 234 BL110
Vickers Dr S, Wey. KT13 234 BL111
Vickers Rd, Erith DA8 189 FD78
Vickers Way, Houns. TW4 198 BY85
Vickery's Wf, E14 22 A8
Victor App, Horn. RM12
off Abbs Cross Gdns 150 FK60
Victor Cl, Horn. RM12 150 FK60
Victor Ct, Horn. RM12 150 FK60
Rainham RM13
off Askwith Rd 169 FD68
Victor Gdns, Horn. RM12 150 FK60
Victor Gro, Wem. HA0 160 CL66
⇌ **Victoria** 29 K8
⊖ **Victoria** 29 K8
★ **Victoria & Albert Mus**, SW7 28 B7
Victoria Arc, SW1
off Terminus Pl 29 K7
Victoria Av, E6 166 EK67
EC2 19 P7
N3 119 CZ53
Barnet EN4 102 DD42
Gravesend DA12
off Sheppy Pl 213 GH87
Grays RM16 192 GC75
Hounslow TW3 198 BZ85
Romford RM5 127 FB51
South Croydon CR2 242 DQ110
Surbiton KT6 219 CK101
Uxbridge UB10 157 BP66
Wallington SM6 222 DG104
Wembley HA9 160 CP65
West Molesey KT8 218 CA97
🚌 **Victoria Bus Sta** 29 K7
H **Victoria Cen**, Rom. RM1 149 FF56
Victoria Cl, SE22
off Underhill Rd 204 DU85
Barnet EN4 102 DD42
Cheshunt EN8 89 DX30
Grays RM16 192 GC75
Hayes UB3
off Commonwealth Av 157 BR72
Horley RH6 290 DG148
Rickmansworth WD3
off Nightingale Rd 114 BK45
West Molesey KT8
off Victoria Av 218 CA97
Weybridge KT13 217 BR104
🚌 **Victoria Coach Sta** 29 J9
Sch **Victoria C of E First Sch**, Berk.
HP4 *off Prince Edward St* 60 AW19
Victoria Cotts, Rich. TW9 180 CM81
Victoria Ct, Red. RH1 288 DG137
Wembley HA9 160 CN65
Victoria Cres, N15 144 DS57
SE19 204 DS93
SW19 201 CZ94
Iver SL0 156 BG73
Victoria Dock Rd, E16 24 B10
Victoria Dr, SW19 201 CX87
Slough SL1, SL2 153 AL65
South Darenth DA4 231 FR96
Victoria Embk, EC4 30 C1
SW1 30 B4
WC2 30 C1
★ **Victoria Embankment Gdns**,
WC2 30 B1
Victoria Gdns, W11 27 J2
Biggin Hill TN16 260 EJ115
Hounslow TW5 178 BY81
Victoria Gate, Harl. CM17 74 EW15
Victoria Gro, N12 120 DC50
W8 27 N6
Victoria Gro Ms, W2 27 K1
Victoria Hill Rd, Swan. BR8 229 FF95
Victoria Ho, SW8
off South Lambeth Rd 42 B4
● **Victoria Ind Est**, NW10 160 CS69
W3 160 CR71
● **Victoria Ind Pk**, Dart. DA1 210 FL85
Sch **Victoria Jun Sch**, Felt. TW13
off Victoria Rd 197 BV88
Victoria La, Barn. EN5 101 CZ42
Harlington UB3 177 BQ78
Victoria Mans, SW8
off South Lambeth Rd 42 B4
Victoria Ms, E8 10 C4
NW6 5 J8
SW4 *off Victoria Ri* 183 DH84
SW18 202 DC88
Bayfordbury SG13 53 DN14
Englefield Green TW20 194 AW93
Victoria Mills Studios, E15 12 G8
Victorian Gro, N16 144 DS62
Victorian Hts, SW8
off Thackeray Rd 41 K9
Victorian Rd, N16 144 DS62
★ **Victoria Park**, E9 11 L8
● **Victoria Pk Ind Cen**, E9 11 P6
Victoria Pk Rd, E9 10 F9
Victoria Pk Sq, E2 20 G2
Victoria Pas, NW8 16 A4
Watford WD18 97 BV42
● **Victoria Pl**, SW1 29 K8
Victoria Pl, Epsom KT17 238 CS112
Richmond TW9 199 CK85
Victoria Pt, E13 13 N10
🔒 **Victoria Retail Pk**, Ruis.
HA4 138 BX64
Victoria Ri, SW4 183 DH83
Victoria Rd, E4 124 EE46
E11 146 EE63
E13 23 N1
E17 123 EC54
E18 124 EH54
N4 143 DM59
N9 122 DT49
N15 144 DU56
N18 122 DT49
N22 121 DJ53
NW4 141 CW56
NW6 5 H9
NW7 119 CT50
NW10 160 CR71
SW14 180 CR83
W3 160 CR71
W5 159 CH71
W8 27 N7
Addlestone KT15 234 BK105
Barking IG11 167 EP65
Barnet EN4 102 DD42
Berkhamsted HP4 60 AW20
Victoria Rd, Bexh. DA6 188 FA84
Bromley BR2 226 EK99
Buckhurst Hill IG9 124 EK47
Bushey WD23 116 CB46
Chesham HP5 76 AQ31
Chislehurst BR7 207 EN92
Coulsdon CR5 257 DK115
Dagenham RM10 149 FB64
Dartford DA1 210 FK85
Erith DA8 189 FE79
Eton Wick SL4 173 AM78
Farnham Common SL2 153 AQ65
Feltham TW13 197 BV88
Guildford GU1 264 AY134
Horley RH6 290 DG148
Kingston upon Thames KT1 220 CM96
Mitcham CR4 202 DE94
Northfleet DA11 213 GF88
Redhill RH1 288 DG135
Romford RM1 149 FE58
Ruislip HA4 138 BW64
Sevenoaks TN13 279 FH125
Sidcup DA15 207 ET90
Slough SL2 154 AV74
Southall UB2 178 BZ76
Staines TW18 195 BE90
Surbiton KT6 219 CK100
Sutton SM1 240 DD106
Teddington TW11 199 CG93
Twickenham TW1 199 CH87
Uxbridge UB8 156 BJ66
Waltham Abbey EN9 89 EC34
Warley CM14 130 FW49
Watford WD24 97 BV38
Weybridge KT13 217 BR104
Woking GU22 248 AY117
Victoria Scott Ct, Dart. DA1 189 FE83
● **Victoria Sq**, St.Alb. AL1 65 CF21
Victoria Sq, SW1 29 K6
Victoria Steps, Brent. TW8
off Kew Br Rd 180 CM79
Victoria St, E15 13 J6
SW1 29 L7
Belvedere DA17 188 EZ78
Englefield Green TW20 194 AW93
St. Albans AL1 65 CD20
Slough SL1 174 AT75
Windsor SL4 173 AQ81
Victoria's Way, S.Ock. RM15 171 FW72
Victoria Ter, N4 143 DN60
NW10 *off Old Oak La* 160 CS70
Dorking RH4 *off South St* 285 CG136
Harrow HA1 139 CE60
Victoria Vil, Rich. TW9 180 CM83
Victoria Way, SE7 36 A10
Ruislip HA4 138 BX64
Weybridge KT13 217 BR104
Woking GU21 248 AY117
Victoria Wf, E14 33 M1
Victoria Yd, E1 20 D9
Victor Rd, NW10 161 CV69
SE20 205 DX94
Harrow HA2 138 CC55
Teddington TW11 199 CE91
Windsor SL4 173 AQ83
Victors Cres, Hutt. CM13 131 GB47
Victors Dr, Hmptn. TW12 198 BY93
Sch **Victor Seymour Infants' Sch**,
Cars. SM5
off Denmark Rd 240 DF105
Victor Smith Ct, Brick.Wd AL2 82 CA31
Victors Way, Barn. EN5 101 CZ41
Victor Vil, N9 122 DR48
Victor Wk, NW9 118 CS54
Hornchurch RM12
off Abbs Cross Gdns 150 FK60
Victory Av, Mord. SM4 222 DC99
● **Victory Business Cen**, Islw.
TW7 179 CF83
Victory Cl, Chaff.Hun. RM16 191 FW77
Staines TW19 196 BL88
Victory Pk Rd, Add. KT15 234 BJ105
Victory Pl, E14 21 M10
SE17 31 L8
SE19 *off Westow St* 204 DS93
Sch **Victory Prim Sch**, SE17 31 K8
Victory Rd, E11 146 EH56
SW19 202 DC94
Berkhamsted HP4
off Gossoms End 60 AU18
Chertsey KT16 216 BG102
Rainham RM13 169 FG68
Victory Rd Ms, SW19
off Victory Rd 202 DC94
Victory Wk, SE8 46 A6
Victory Way, SE16 33 M5
Dartford DA2 190 FQ84
Hounslow TW5 178 BW78
Romford RM7 127 FB54
Vidler Cl, Chess. KT9
off Merritt Gdns 237 CJ107
Vienna Cl, Ilf. IG5 146 EK55
View, The, SE2 188 EY78
View Cl, N6 142 DF59
Biggin Hill TN16 260 EJ116
Chigwell IG7 125 ER50
Harrow HA1 139 CD56
View Cres, N8 143 DK57
Viewfield Cl, Har. HA3 140 CL59
Viewfield Rd, SW18 201 CZ86
Bexley DA5 208 EW88
Viewland Rd, SE18 187 ET78
Viewlands Av, West. TN16 261 ES120
View Rd, N6 142 DF59
Potters Bar EN6 86 DC32
Viga Rd, N21 103 DN44
Vigerons Way, Grays RM16 193 GH77
Viggory La, Wok. GU21 248 AW115
Vigilant Cl, SE26 204 DU91
Vigilant Way, Grav. DA12 213 GL92
Vignoles Rd, Rom. RM7 148 FA59
Vigors Cft, Hat. AL10 67 CT19
Vigo St, W1 29 L1
Viking Cl, E3 21 M1
Viking Ct, SW6 39 K2
Viking Gdns, E6 24 G5
Viking Pl, E10 145 DZ60
Sch **Viking Prim Sch**, Nthlt. UB5
off Radcliffe Way 158 BX69
Viking Rd, Nthflt DA11 212 GC90
Southall UB1 158 BY73

Viking Way, Erith DA8 189 FC76
Pilgrim's Hatch CM15 130 FV45
Rainham RM13 169 FG70
Villa Ct, Dart. DA1
off Greenbanks 210 FL89
Villacourt Rd, SE18 188 EU80
Village, The, Bluewater
DA9 211 FT87
Slough SL1 174 AT75
Village, The, SE7 186 EJ79
Village Arc, E4
off Station Rd 123 ED46
Village Cl, E4 123 EC50
NW3 6 B3
Hoddesdon EN11 71 ED15
Weybridge KT13 217 BR104
Village Ct, E17 off Eden Rd 145 EB57
Village Gdns, Epsom KT17 239 CT110
Village Grn Av, Bigg.H. TN16 260 EL117
Village Grn Rd, Dart. DA1 189 FG84
Village Grn Way, Bigg.H. TN16
off Main Rd 260 EL117
Village Hts, Wdf.Grn. IG8 124 EF50
Village Infants' Sch, Dag.
RM10 off Ford Rd 168 FA66
Village La, Hedg. SL2 133 AR60
Village Ms, NW9 140 CR61
Village Pk Cl, Enf. EN1 104 DS44
Village Rd, N3 119 CY53
Coleshill HP7 77 AM44
Denham UB9 135 BF61
Dorney SL4 172 AH76
Egham TW20 215 BC97
Enfield EN1 104 DS44
Village Row, Sutt. SM2 240 DA108
Village Sq, The, Couls. CR5
off Netherne Dr 257 DK122
Village Way, NW10 140 CR63
SE21 204 DR86
Amersham HP7 94 AX40
Ashford TW15 196 BM91
Beckenham BR3 225 EA96
Ilford IG6 147 EQ55
Pinner HA5 138 BY59
South Croydon CR2 242 DU113
Village Way E, Har. HA2 138 BZ59
Villa Rd, SW9 42 E10
Villas Rd, SE18 187 EQ77
Villa St, SE17 43 M1
Villiers, The, Wey. KT13 235 BR107
Villiers Av, Surb. KT5 220 CM99
Twickenham TW2 198 BZ88
Villiers Cl, E10 145 EA61
Surbiton KT5 220 CM98
Villiers Ct, N20
off Buckingham Av 120 DC45
Villiers Cres, St.Alb. AL4 65 CK17
Villiers Gro, Sutt. SM2 239 CX109
Villiers High Sch,
Sthl. UB1
off Boyd Av 158 BZ74
Villiers Path, Surb. KT5 220 CL99
Villiers Rd, NW2 161 CU65
Beckenham BR3 225 DX96
Isleworth TW7 179 CE82
Kingston upon Thames KT1 220 CM97
Slough SL2 153 AR71
Southall UB1 158 BZ74
Watford WD19 98 BY44
Villiers St, WC2 30 A1
Hertford SG13 54 DS09
Villier St, Uxb. UB8 156 BK68
Vimy Cl, Houns. TW4 198 BZ85
Vincam Cl, Twick. TW2 198 CA87
Vince Ct, N1 off Charles Sq 19 M3
Vincent Av, Cars. SM5 240 DD111
Croydon CR0 243 DY111
Surbiton KT5 220 CP102
Vincent Cl, SE16 33 L5
Barnet EN5 102 DA41
Bromley BR2 226 EH98
Chertsey KT16 215 BE101
Cheshunt EN8 89 DY28
Esher KT10 218 CB104
Fetcham KT22 252 CB123
Ilford IG6 125 EQ51
Sidcup DA15 207 ES88
Sipson UB7 176 BN79
Vincent Dr, Dor. RH4 285 CG137
Shepperton TW17 217 BS97
Uxbridge UB10
off Birch Cres 156 BM67
Vincent Gdns, NW2 141 CT62
Vincent Grn, Couls. CR5 256 DF120
Vincent La, Dor. RH4 285 CG136
Vincent Ms, E3 off Menai Pl 12 A10
Vincent Rd, E4 123 ED51
N15 144 DQ56
N22 121 DN54
SE18 37 N8
W3 180 CQ76
Chertsey KT16 215 BE101
Coulsdon CR5 257 DJ116
Croydon CR0 224 DS101
Dagenham RM9 168 EY66
Dorking RH4 285 CG136
Hounslow TW4 178 BX82
Isleworth TW7 179 CD81
Kingston upon Thames KT1 220 CN97
Rainham RM13 170 FJ70
Stoke D'Abernon KT11 252 BY116
Wembley HA0 160 CM66
Vincent Row, Hmptn H. TW12 198 CC93
Vincents Cl, Chipstead CR5 256 DF120
Vincents Dr, Dor. RH4
off Nower Rd 285 CG137
Vincents Path, Nthlt. UB5
off Arnold Rd 158 BY65
Vincent Sq, N22 121 DN54
SW1 29 M8
Biggin Hill TN16 244 EJ113
Vincent St, E16 23 M7
SW1 29 N8
Vincents Wk, Dor. RH4
off Arundel Rd 285 CG136
Vincent Ter, N1 8 G10
Vincent Wks, Dor. RH4 285 CG136
Vincenzo Cl, N.Mymms AL9 67 CW23
Vince St, EC1 19 M3
Vine, The, Sev. TN13 279 FH124
Vine Av, Sev. TN13 279 FH124
Vine Cl, E5
off Rendlesham Rd 144 DU63
Staines TW19 196 BG85
Surbiton KT5 220 CM100
Sutton SM1 222 DC104
Welwyn Garden City AL8 51 CY07
West Drayton UB7 176 BN77
Vine Ct, E1 20 D7
Harrow HA3 140 CL58
Vine Ct Rd, Sev. TN13 279 FJ124
Vinegar All, E17 145 EB56
Vine Gdns, Ilf. IG1 147 EQ64
Vinegar St, E1 32 E2
Vinegar Yd, SE1 31 N4
Vine Gate, Farn.Com. SL2 153 AQ65
Vine Gro, Harl. CM20 57 ER10
Uxbridge UB10 156 BN66
Vine Hill, EC1 18 E5
Vine La, SE1 31 P3
Uxbridge UB10 156 BM67
Vine Pl, W5
off St. Mark's Rd 160 CL74
Hounslow TW3 178 CB84
Viner Cl, Walt. KT12 218 BW100
Vineries, The, N14 103 DJ44
SE6 205 EA88
Enfield EN1 104 DS41
Vineries Bk, NW7 119 CV50
Vineries Cl, Dag. RM9
off Heathway 168 FA65
Sipson UB7 176 BN79
Vine Rd, E15 13 L6
SW13 181 CT83
East Molesey KT8 218 CC98
Orpington BR6 245 ET107
Stoke Poges SL2 154 AT65
Vines Av, N3 120 DB53
Vine Sq, W14 39 H1
Vine St, EC3 20 A10
W1 29 M1
Romford RM7 149 FC57
Uxbridge UB8 156 BK67
Vine St Br, EC1 18 F5
Vine Way, Brwd. CM14 130 FW46
Vine Yd, SE1 31 K4
Vineyard, The, Hert. SG14 54 DR07
Richmond TW10 200 CL85
Ware SG12 55 EA05
Welwyn Garden City AL8 51 CX07
Vineyard Av, NW7 119 CY52
Vineyard Cl, SE6 205 EA88
Kingston upon Thames KT1 220 CM97
Vineyard Gro, N3 120 DB53
Vineyard Hill, Northaw EN6 86 DG29
Vineyard Hill Rd, SW19 202 DA91
Vineyard Pas, Rich. TW9
off Paradise Rd 200 CL85
Vineyard Path, SW14 180 CR83
Vineyard Prim Sch, The,
Rich. TW10
off Friars Stile Rd 200 CL86
Vineyard Rd, Felt. TW13 197 BU90
Vineyard Row, Hmptn W. KT1 219 CJ95
Vineyards Rd, Northaw EN6 86 DF30
Vineyard Wk, EC1 18 E4
Viney Bk, Croy. CR0 243 DZ109
Viney Rd, SE13 185 EB83
Vining St, SW9 183 DN84
Vinlake Av, Uxb. UB10 136 BM62
Vinopolis, SE1 31 K2
Vinson Cl, Orp. BR6 228 EU102
Vintners Ct, EC4 19 K10
Vintners Pl, EC4
off Vintners Ct 19 K10
Vintry Ms, E17
off Cleveland Pk Cres 145 EA56
Viola Av, SE2 188 EV77
Feltham TW14 198 BW86
Staines TW19 196 BK88
Viola Cl, S.Ock. RM15 171 FW69
Viola Sq, W12 161 CT73
Violet Av, Enf. EN2 104 DR38
Uxbridge UB8 156 BM71
Violet Cl, E16 23 K5
SE8 45 N2
Sutton SM3 221 CY102
Wallington SM6 222 DG102
Violet Gdns, Croy. CR0 241 DP106
Violet Hill, NW8 15 N1
Violet La, Croy. CR0 241 DP106
Violet Rd, E3 22 C5
E17 145 EA58
E18 124 EH54
Violet St, E2 20 F4
Violet Way, Loud. WD3 96 BJ42
Virgil Dr, Brox. EN10 71 DZ23
Virgil Pl, W1 16 E7
Virgil St, SE1 30 D6
Virginia Av, Vir.W. GU25 214 AW99
Virginia Beeches, Vir.W. GU25 214 AW97
Virginia Cl, Ashtd. KT21
off Skinners La 253 CK118
New Malden KT3
off Willow Rd 220 CQ98
Romford RM5 127 FC52
Staines TW18
off Blacksmiths La 216 BJ97
Weybridge KT13 235 BQ107
Virginia Dr, Vir.W. GU25 214 AW99
Virginia Gdns, Ilf. IG6 125 EQ54
Virginia Pl, Cob. KT11 235 BU114
Virginia Prim Sch, E2 20 A3
Virginia Rd, E2 20 A3
Thornton Heath CR7 223 DP95
Virginia St, E1 32 D1
Virginia Wk, SW2 203 DM86
Gravesend DA12 213 GK93
VIRGINIA WATER, GU25 214 AX99
Virginia Water 214 AY99
Virgo Fidelis Conv Sen Sch,
SE19 off Central Hill 204 DR93
Virgo Fidelis Prep Sch, SE19
off Central Hill 204 DR93
Viridian Apts, SW8 41 L5
Visage Apts, NW3 6 B7
Viscount Cl, N11 121 DH50
Viscount Dr, E6 25 J6
Viscount Gdns, W.Byf. KT14 234 BL112
Viscount Gro, Nthlt. UB5 158 BX69
Viscount Rd, Stanw. TW19 196 BK88
Viscount St, EC1 19 J5
Viscount Way, Lon.Hthrw Air.
TW6 177 BS84
Vista, The, E4 123 ED45
SE9 206 EK86
Sidcup DA14 207 ET92
Vista Av, Enf. EN3 105 DX40
Vista Bldg, The, SE18 37 M8
Vista Dr, Ilf. IG4 146 EK57
Vista Ho, SW19
off Chapter Way 222 DD95
Vista Way, Har. HA3 140 CL58
Vitae, W6 off Goldhawk Rd 181 CU76
Vita et Pax Sch, N14
off Priory Cl 103 DH43
Vittoria Prim Sch, N1 8 E10
Viveash Cl, Hayes UB3 177 BT76
Vivian Av, NW4 141 CV57
Wembley HA9 140 CN64
Vivian Cl, Wat. WD19 115 BU46
Vivian Comma Cl, N4 143 DP62
Vivian Ct, W9 5 L10
Vivian Gdns, Wat. WD19 115 BU46
Wembley HA9 140 CN64
Vivian Rd, E3 11 L10
Vivian Sq, SE15 44 E10
Vivian Way, N2 142 DD57
Vivien Cl, Chess. KT9 238 CL108
Vivien Ct, N9 off Galahad Rd 122 DU47
Vivienne Cl, Twick. TW1 199 CJ86
Vixen Ct, Hat. AL10 67 CV16
Vixen Dr, Hert. SG13 54 DU09
Voce Rd, SE18 187 ER80
Voewood Cl, N.Mal. KT3 221 CT100
Vogan Cl, Reig. RH2 288 DB137
Vogans Mill, SE1 32 B4
Volta Cl, N9 off Hudson Way 122 DW48
Voltaire Bldgs, SW18 202 DB88
Voltaire Rd, SW4 183 DK83
Voltaire Way, Hayes UB3 157 BS73
Volt Av, NW10 160 CR69
Volta Way, Croy. CR0 223 DM102
Voluntary Pl, E11 146 EG58
Vorley Rd, N19 143 DJ61
Voss Ct, SW16 203 DL93
Voss St, E2 20 D3
Voyager Business Est, SE16
off Spa Rd 32 C6
Voyagers Cl, SE28 168 EW72
Voysey Cl, N3 141 CY55
Vulcan Cl, E6 25 M9
Vulcan Gate, Enf. EN2 103 DN40
Vulcan Rd, SE4 45 N8
Vulcan Sq, E14 34 B9
Vulcan Ter, SE4 45 N8
Vulcan Way, N7 8 D4
New Addington CR0 244 EE110
Wallington SM6 241 DL109
Vyne, The, Bexh. DA7 189 FB83
Vyner Rd, W3 160 CR73
Vyners Sch, Ickhm UB10
off Warren Rd 136 BM63
Vyner St, E2 10 F10
Vyners Way, Uxb. UB10 136 BN64
Vyse Cl, Barn. EN5 101 CW42

W

Wacketts, Chsht EN7 88 DU27
Wadbrook St, Kings.T. KT1 219 CK96
Wadding St, SE17 31 L9
Waddington Av, Couls. CR5 257 DN120
Waddington Cl, Couls. CR5 257 DP119
Enfield EN1 104 DS42
Waddington Rd, E15 13 H3
St. Albans AL3 65 CD20
Waddington St, E15 13 H4
Waddington Way, SE19 204 DQ94
WADDON, Croy. CR0 223 DN103
Waddon 241 DN105
Waddon Cl, Croy. CR0 223 DN104
Waddon Ct Rd, Croy. CR0 241 DN105
Waddon Inf & Nurs Sch, Croy.
CR0 off Purley Way 241 DN106
Waddon Marsh 223 DN103
Waddon Marsh Way, Croy.
CR0 223 DM102
Waddon New Rd, Croy. CR0 223 DP104
Waddon Pk Av, Croy. CR0 241 DN105
Waddon Rd, Croy. CR0 223 DN104
Waddon Way, Croy. CR0 241 DP107
Wade, The, Welw.G.C. AL7 51 CZ12
Wade Av, Orp. BR5 228 EX101
Wade Dr, Slou. SL1 153 AN74
Wades, The, Hat. AL10 67 CU21
Wades Gro, N21 121 DN45
Wades Hill, N21 103 DN44
Wades La, Tedd. TW11
off High St 199 CG92
Wadesmill Rd, Chap.End SG12 54 DQ06
Hertford SG14 54 DQ06
Wadeson St, E2 10 F10
Wades Pl, E14 22 C10
Wadeville Av, Rom. RM6 148 EZ59
Wadeville Cl, Belv. DA17 188 FA79
Wadham Av, E17 123 EB52
Wadham Cl, Shep. TW17 217 BQ101
Wadham Gdns, NW3 6 C8
Greenford UB6 159 CD65
Wadham Rd, E17 123 EB53
SW15 181 CY84
Abbots Langley WD5 81 BT31
Wadhurst Cl, SE20 224 DV96
Wadhurst Rd, SW8 41 L6
W4 180 CR76
Wadley Cl, Hem.H. HP2
off White Hart Dr 62 BM21
Wadley Rd, E11 146 EE59
Wadsworth Business Cen,
Grnf. UB6 159 CJ68
Wadsworth Cl, Enf. EN3 105 DX43
Perivale UB6 159 CJ68
Wadsworth Rd, Perivale UB6 159 CH68
Wager St, E3 21 N5
Waggon Cl, Guil. GU2 264 AS133
Waggoners Rbt, Houns.
TW5 177 BV81
Waggon Ms, N14
off Chase Side 121 DJ46
Waggon Rd, Barn. EN4 102 DC37
Waghorn Rd, E13 166 EJ67
Harrow HA3 139 CK55
Waghorn St, SE15 44 C10
Wagner St, SE15 44 G4
Wagon Rd, Barn. EN4 102 DB36
Wagon Way, Loud. WD3 96 BJ41
Wagstaff Gdns, Dag. RM9 168 EW66
Wagtail Cl, NW9 118 CS54
Enfield EN1 104 DV39
Wagtail Gdns, S.Croy. CR2 243 DY110
Wagtail Wk, Beck. BR3 225 EC99
Wagtail Way, Orp. BR5 228 EX98
Waid Cl, Dart. DA1 210 FM86
Waight Cl, Hat. AL10 66 CS16
Waights Ct, Kings.T. KT2 220 CL95
Wain Cl, Pot.B. EN6 86 DB29
Wainfleet Av, Rom. RM5 127 FC54
Wainford Cl, SW19
off Windlesham Gro 201 CX88
Wainwright Av, Hutt. CM13 131 GD44
Wainwright Gro, Islw. TW7 179 CD84
Waite Davies Rd, SE12 206 EF87
Waite St, SE15 44 A2
Waithman St, EC4 18 G9
Wake Arms, Epp. CM16 107 EM36
Wake Cl, Guil. GU2 264 AV129
Wakefield Cl, Byfleet KT14 234 BL112
Wakefield Cres, Stoke P. SL2 154 AT66
Wakefield Gdns, SE19 204 DS94
Ilford IG1 146 EL58
Wakefield Ms, WC1 18 B3
Wakefield Rd, N11 121 DK50
N15 144 DT57
Greenhithe DA9 211 FW85
Richmond TW10 199 CK85
Wakefield St, E6 166 EK67
N18 122 DU50
WC1 18 B4
Wakefields Wk, Chsht EN8 89 DY31
Wakeford Cl, SW4 203 DJ85
Wakehams Hill, Pnr. HA5 138 BZ55
Wakeham St, N1 9 L5
Wakehurst Path, Wok. GU21 233 BC114
Wakehurst Rd, SW11 202 DE85
Wakeling La, Wem. HA0 139 CH62
Wakeling Rd, W7 159 CF71
Wakeling St, E14 21 L9
Wakelin Rd, E15 13 J10
Wakely Cl, Bigg.H. TN16 260 EJ118
Wakeman Rd, NW10 14 C2
Wakemans Hill Av, NW9 140 CR57
Wakerfield Cl, Horn. RM11 150 FM57
Wakering Rd, Bark. IG11 167 EQ66
Wakerley Cl, E6 25 J9
Wake Rd, High Beach IG10 106 EJ38
Wakley St, EC1 18 G2
Walberswick St, SW8 42 B5
Walbrook, EC4 19 L10
Walbrook Ho, N9 122 DW47
Walbrook Wf, EC4
off Bell Wf La 31 K1
Walburgh St, E1 20 E9
Walburton Rd, Pur. CR8 241 DJ113
Walcorde Av, SE17 31 K9
Walcot Ho, SE22
off Albrighton Rd 184 DS83
Walcot Rd, Enf. EN3 105 DZ40
Walcot Sq, SE11 30 F8
Walcott St, SW1 29 M8
Waldair Ct, E16 37 N4
Waldair Wf, E16 37 N4
Waldeck Gro, SE27 203 DP90
Waldeck Rd, N15 143 DP56
SW14
off Lower Richmond Rd 180 CQ83
W4 180 CN79
W13 159 CH72
Dartford DA1 210 FM86
Waldeck Ter, SW14
off Lower Richmond Rd 180 CQ83
Waldegrave Av, Tedd. TW11
off Waldegrave Rd 199 CF92
Waldegrave Ct, Upmin. RM14 150 FP60
Waldegrave Gdns, Twick. TW1 199 CF89
Upminster RM14 150 FP60
Waldegrave Pk, Twick. TW1 199 CF91
Waldegrave Rd, N8 143 DN55
SE19 204 DT94
W5 160 CM72
Bromley BR1 226 EL98
Dagenham RM8 148 EW61
Teddington TW11 199 CF91
Twickenham TW1 199 CF91
Waldegrave Sch for Girls, Twick.
TW2 off Fifth Cross Rd 199 CD90
Waldegrove, Croy. CR0 224 DT104
Waldemar Av, SW6 38 F7
W13 159 CJ74
Waldemar Rd, SW19 202 DA92
Walden Av, N13 122 DQ49
Chislehurst BR7 207 EM91
Rainham RM13 169 FD68
Waldenbury Pl, Beac. HP9 132 AG55
Walden Cl, Belv. DA17 188 EZ78
Walden Ct, SW8
off Wandsworth Rd 41 P6
Walden Gdns, Th.Hth. CR7 223 DM97
Waldenhurst Rd, Orp. BR5 228 EX101
Walden Par, Chis. BR7
off Walden Rd 207 EM93
Walden Pl, Welw.G.C. AL8 51 CX07
Walden Rd, N17 122 DR53
Chislehurst BR7 207 EM93
Hornchurch RM11 150 FK58
Welwyn Garden City AL8 51 CX07
Waldens Cl, Orp. BR5 228 EX101
Waldenshaw Rd, SE23 204 DW88
Waldens Pk Rd, Wok. GU21 248 AW116
Waldens Rd, Orp. BR5 228 EY101
Woking GU21 248 AX117
Walden St, E1 20 E8
Walden Way, NW7 119 CX51
Hornchurch RM11 150 FK58
Ilford IG6 125 ES52
Waldo Cl, SW4 203 DJ85
Waldo Pl, Mitch. CR4 202 DE94
Waldorf Cl, S.Croy. CR2 241 DP109
Waldorf Sch of S W London,
The, SW16
off Abbotswood Rd 203 DJ89
Waldo Rd, NW10 161 CU69
Bromley BR1 226 EK97
Waldram Cres, SE23 204 DW88
Waldram Pk Rd, SE23 205 DX88
Waldram Pl, SE23
off Waldram Cres 204 DW88
Waldrist Way, Erith DA18 188 EZ75
Waldron Gdns, Brom. BR2 225 ED97
Waldronhyrst, S.Croy. CR2 241 DP105
Waldron Ms, SW3 40 B2
Waldron Rd, SW18 202 DC90
Harrow HA1, HA2 139 CE60
Waldrons, The, Croy. CR0 241 DP105
Oxted RH8 276 EF131
Waldrons Path, S.Croy. CR2 242 DQ105
Waldrons Yd, Har. HA2
off Northolt Rd 139 CD61
Waldstock Rd, SE28 168 EU73
Waleran Cl, Stan. HA7 117 CF51
Walerand Rd, SE13 46 F9
Waleran Flats, SE1 31 N8
Wales Av, Cars. SM5 240 DF106
Wales Cl, SE15 44 E4
Wales Fm Rd, W3 160 CR71
Waleton Acres, Wall. SM6 241 DJ107
Waley St, E1 21 K6
Walfield Av, N20 120 DB45
Walford Rd, N16 144 DS63
North Holmwood RH5 285 CH140
Uxbridge UB8 156 BJ68
Walfords Cl, Harl. CM17 58 EW12
Walfrey Gdns, Dag. RM9 168 EY66
WALHAM GREEN, SW6 39 L5
Walham Grn Ct, SW6 39 L5
Walham Gro, SW6 39 J4
Walham Ri, SW19 201 CY93
Walham Yd, SW6 39 J4
Walk, The, Eton Wick SL4 173 AN78
Hertford SG14
off Chelmsford Rd 53 DN10
Hornchurch RM11 150 FM61
Potters Bar EN6 86 DA32
Sunbury-on-Thames TW16 197 BT94
Tandridge RH8 275 EA133
Walkden Rd, Chis. BR7 207 EN92
Walker Cl, N11 121 DJ49
SE18 187 EQ77
W7 159 CE74
Dartford DA1 189 FF83
Feltham TW14 197 BT87
Hampton TW12
off Fearnley Cres 198 BZ93
Walker Cres, Slou. SL3 175 AZ78
Walker Gro, Hat. AL10 66 CR17
Walker Ms, SW2 off Effra Rd 203 DN85
Walker Prim Sch, N14
off Waterfall Rd 121 DK47
Walkers Ct, E8 10 C4
W1 17 N10
Walkerscroft Mead, SE21 204 DQ88
Walkers Pl, SW15
off Felsham Rd 181 CY84
Walkfield Dr, Epsom KT18 255 CV117
Walkley Rd, Dart. DA1 209 FH85
Walks, The, N2 142 DD55
Walkwood End, Beac. HP9 110 AJ54
Walkwood Ri, Beac. HP9 132 AJ55
Walkynscroft, SE15 44 F8
Wallace Cl, SE28
off Haldane Rd 168 EX73
Shepperton TW17 217 BR98
Uxbridge UB10 156 BL68
Wallace Collection, W1 16 G8
Wallace Ct, Enf. EN3
off Eden Cl 105 EA37
Wallace Cres, Cars. SM5 240 DF106
Wallace Flds, Epsom KT17 239 CT112
Wallace Flds Inf Sch, Ewell
KT17 off Wallace Flds 239 CU113
Wallace Flds Jun Sch, Ewell
KT17 off Dorling Dr 239 CU112
Wallace Gdns, Swans. DA10 212 FY86
Wallace Rd, N1 9 K4
Grays RM17 192 GA76
Wallace Sq, Couls. CR5
off Cayton Rd 257 DK122
Wallace Wk, Add. KT15 234 BJ105
Wallace Way, N19
off Giesbach Rd 143 DK61
Romford RM1 127 FD53
Wallasey Cres, Uxb. UB10 136 BN61
Wallbutton Rd, SE4 45 L9
Wallcote Av, NW2 141 CX60
Walled Gdn, The, Bet. RH3 286 CR135
Tadworth KT20 255 CX122
Walled Gdn Cl, Beck. BR3 225 EB98
Wall End Rd, E6 167 EM66
Wallenger Av, Rom. RM2 149 FH55
Waller Dr, Nthwd. HA6 115 BU54
Waller La, Cat. CR3 258 DT123
Waller Rd, SE14 45 J7
Beaconsfield HP9 111 AM53
Wallers Cl, Dag. RM9 168 EY67
Woodford Green IG8 125 EM51
Waller's Hoppet, Loug. IG10 106 EL40
Wallers Way, Hodd. EN11 55 EB14
Waller Way, SE10 46 D4
Wallfield All, Hert. SG13 54 DQ10
Wallflower St, W12 161 CT73
Wallgrave Rd, SW5 27 L8
Wall Hall Dr, Ald. WD25 98 CB36
Wallhouse Rd, Erith DA8 189 FH80
Wallingford Av, W10 14 C7
Wallingford Rd, Uxb. UB8 156 BH68
Wallingford Wk, St.Alb. AL1 65 CD23
WALLINGTON, SM6 241 DJ106
Wallington 241 DH107
Wallington Cl, Ruis. HA4 137 BQ58
Wallington Cor, Wall. SM6
off Manor Rd N 241 DH105
Wallington Co Gram Sch,
Wall. SM6 off Croydon Rd 241 DH105
Wallington Grn, Wall. SM6
off Croydon Rd 241 DH105
Wallington High Sch for Girls,
Wall. SM6 off Woodcote Rd 241 DH109
Wallington Rd, Chesh. HP5 76 AP30
Ilford IG3 147 ET59
Wallington Sq, Wall. SM6
off Woodcote Rd 241 DH107
Wallis All, SE1 31 K4
Wallis Cl, SW11 182 DD83
Dartford DA2 209 FF90
Hornchurch RM11 149 FH60
Wallis Ct, Slou. SL1 174 AU75
Wallis Ms, N8 off Courcy Rd 143 DN55
Fetcham KT22 253 CG122
Wallis Pk, Nthflt DA11 212 GB85
Wallis Rd, E9 11 P5
Southall UB1 158 CB72
Wallis's Cotts, SW2 203 DL87
Wallman Pl, N22
off Bounds Grn Rd 121 DM53
Wallorton Gdns, SW14 180 CR84
Wallside, EC2 19 K7
Wall St, N1 9 M5
Wallwood Rd, E11 145 ED60
Wallwood St, E14 21 P7
Walmar Cl, Barn. EN4 102 DD39
Walmer Cl, E4 123 EB47
Farnborough BR6
off Tubbenden La S 245 ER105
Romford RM7 127 FB54
Walmer Gdns, W13 179 CG75
Walmer Ho, N9 122 DT45
Walmer Pl, W1 16 E6
Walmer Rd, W10 14 B9
W11 14 E10
Walmer St, W1 16 E6
Walmer Ter, SE18 187 EQ77
Walmgate Rd, Perivale UB6 159 CH67
Walmington Fold, N12 120 DA51
Walm La, NW2 4 B5

Walmsley Ho, SW16
off Colson Way 203 DJ91
Walney Wk, N1 9 K4
Walnut Av, West Dr. UB7 176 BN76
Walnut Cl, SE8 45 P3
Carshalton SM5 240 DF106
Epsom KT18 255 CT115
Eynsford DA4 230 FK104
Hayes UB3 157 BS73
Ilford IG6 147 EQ56
Park Street AL2 82 CB27
Walnut Ct, W5 180 CL75
Welwyn Garden City AL7 51 CY12
Walnut Dr, Kgswd KT20 255 CY123
Walnut Gdns, E15 13 H2
Walnut Grn, Bushey WD23 98 BZ40
Walnut Gro, Bans. SM7 239 CX114
Enfield EN1 104 DR43
Harlow CM20 57 EP14
Hemel Hempstead HP2 62 BK20
Hornchurch RM12 150 FK60
Welwyn Garden City AL7 51 CY12
Wooburn Green HP10 132 AE57
Walnut Ms, Sutt. SM2 240 DC108
Wooburn Green HP10 132 AE57
Walnut Rd, E10 145 EA61
Walnuts, The, Orp. BR6
off High St 228 EU102
Walnut Shop Cen,
Orp. BR6 228 EU102
Walnuts Rd, Orp. BR6 228 EU102
Walnut Tree Av, Dart. DA1 210 FL89
Mitcham CR4
off De'Arn Gdns 222 DE97
Walnut Tree Cl, SW13 181 CT81
Banstead SM7 239 CY112
Cheshunt EN8 89 DX31
Chislehurst BR7 227 EQ95
Guildford GU1 264 AW134
Hoddesdon EN11 71 EA17
Westerham TN16 277 ER126
Walnut Tree Cotts, SW19
off Church Rd 201 CY92
Walnut Tree Gdns, Gdmg.
GU7 280 AS144
Walnut Tree La, Byfleet KT14 234 BK112
Walnut Tree Pk, Guil. GU1 264 AW134
Walnut Tree Pl, Send GU23 249 BD123
Walnut Tree Rd, SE10 47 K1
Brentford TW8 180 CL79
Dagenham RM8 148 EX61
Erith DA8 189 FE78
Hounslow TW5 178 BZ79
Shepperton TW17 217 BQ96
Walnut Tree Wk, SE11 30 E8
Ware SG12 55 DX09
Walnut Tree Wk Prim Sch,
SE11 30 E8
Walnut Way, Buck.H. IG9 124 EK48
Ruislip HA4 158 BW65
Swanley BR8 229 FD96
Walpole Av, Chipstead CR5 256 DF118
Richmond TW9 180 CM82
Walpole Cl, W13 179 CJ75
Grays RM17
off Palmers Dr 192 GC77
Pinner HA5 116 CA51
Walpole Cres, Tedd. TW11 199 CF92
Walpole Gdns, W4 180 CQ78
Twickenham TW2 199 CE89
Walpole Ms, NW8 6 A9
SW19 off Walpole Rd 202 DD93
Walpole Pk, W5 159 CJ74
Weybridge KT13 234 BN108
Walpole Pl, SE18 37 N9
Teddington TW11 199 CF92
Walpole Rd, E6 166 EJ66
E17 145 DY56
E18 124 EF53
N17 (Downhills Way) 144 DQ55
N17 (Lordship La) 122 DQ54
SW19 202 DD93
Bromley BR2 226 EK99
Croydon CR0 224 DR103
Old Windsor SL4 194 AV87
Slough SL1 153 AK72
Surbiton KT6 220 CL101
Teddington TW11 199 CF92
Twickenham TW2 199 CE89
Walpole St, SW3 28 E10
Walrond Av, Wem. HA9 140 CL64
Walsham Cl, N16
off Clarke Path 144 DU60
SE28 168 EX73
Walsham Rd, SE14 45 J8
Feltham TW14 197 BV87
Walsh Cres, New Adgtn CR0 244 EE112
Walshford Way, Borwd. WD6 100 CN38
Walsingham Cl, Hat. AL10 67 CT17
Walsingham Gdns, Epsom
KT19 238 CS105
Walsingham Pk, Chis. BR7 227 ER96
Walsingham Pl, SW4 off
Clapham Common W Side 182 DF84
SW11 202 DG86
Walsingham Rd, E5 144 DU62
W13 159 CG74
Enfield EN2 104 DR42
Mitcham CR4 222 DF99
New Addington CR0 243 EC110
Orpington BR5 228 EV95
Walsingham Wk, Belv. DA17 188 FA79
Walsingham Way, Lon.Col.
AL2 83 CJ27
Walter Hurford Par, E12
off Walton Rd 147 EN63
Walter Rodney Cl, E6
off Stevenage Rd 167 EM65
Walters Cl, SE17 31 K9
Cheshunt EN7 87 DP25
Hayes UB3 177 BT75
Walters Ho, SE17 42 G3
Walters Mead, Ashtd. KT21 254 CL117
Walters Rd, SE25 224 DS98
Enfield EN3 104 DW43
Walter St, E2 21 J3
Kingston upon Thames KT2
off Sopwith Way 220 CL95
Walters Way, SE23 205 DX86
Walters Yd, Brom. BR1 226 EG96
Walter Ter, E1 21 K8
Walterton Rd, W9 15 H5
Walter Wk, Edg. HA8 118 CQ51
WALTHAM ABBEY, EN9 106 EF35
★ Waltham Abbey (ruins),
Wal.Abb. EN9 89 EC33
Waltham Av, NW9 140 CN58
Guildford GU2 264 AV131
Hayes UB3 177 BQ76
Waltham Cl, Dart. DA1 209 FG86
Hutton CM13
off Bannister Dr 131 GC44
Orpington BR5 228 EX102
WALTHAM CROSS, EN7 & EN8 89 DZ33
Waltham Cross 89 DY34
Waltham Cross 89 DY34
Waltham Dr, Edg. HA8 118 CN54
Waltham Forest Coll, E17
off Forest Rd 145 EB55
Waltham Gdns, Enf. EN3 104 DW36
Waltham Gate, Wal.Cr. EN8 89 DZ26
Waltham Holy Cross Inf Sch,
Wal.Abb. EN9
off Quendon Dr 89 ED33
Waltham Holy Cross Jun Sch,
Wal.Abb. EN9
off Quendon Dr 89 ED33
Waltham Pk Way, E17 123 EA53
Waltham Rd, Cars. SM5 222 DD101
Caterham CR3 258 DV122
Nazeing Gate EN9 90 EF26
Southall UB2 178 BY76
Woodford Green IG8 124 EL51
WALTHAMSTOW, E17 123 EB54
Walthamstow Acad, E17
off Billet Rd 123 DZ53
Walthamstow Adult Ed Cen,
E17 off Greenleaf Rd 145 DZ55
Walthamstow Av, E4 123 DZ52
Walthamstow Business Cen,
E17 123 EC54
Walthamstow Central 145 EA56
Walthamstow Central 145 EA56
Walthamstow Central 145 EA56
Walthamstow Hall Sch,
Jun Sch, Sev. TN13
off Bradbourne Pk Rd 279 FH122
Sen Sch, Sev. TN13
off Holly Bush La 279 FJ123
Walthamstow Queens
Road 145 DZ57
Walthamstow Sch for Girls,
E17 off Church Hill 145 EB56
Waltham Way, E4 123 DZ49
Waltheof Av, N17 122 DR53
Waltheof Gdns, N17 122 DR53
Walton Av, Har. HA2 138 BZ64
New Malden KT3 221 CT98
Sutton SM3 221 CZ104
Wembley HA9 140 CP62
Walton Br, Shep. TW17 217 BS101
Walton-on-Thames KT12 217 BS101
Walton Br Rd, Shep. TW17 217 BS101
Walton Cl, E5 off Orient Way 145 DX62
NW2 141 CV61
SW8 42 B4
Harrow HA1 139 CD56
Walton Comm Hosp, Walt.
KT12 217 BV103
Walton Ct, Wok. GU21 249 BA116
Walton Cres, Har. HA2 138 BZ63
Walton Dr, NW10 160 CR65
Harrow HA1 139 CD56
Walton Gdns, W3 160 CP71
Feltham TW13 197 BT91
Hutton CM13 131 GC43
Waltham Abbey EN9 89 EB33
Wembley HA9 140 CL61
Walton Grn, New Adgtn CR0 243 EC108
Walton La, Farn.Royal SL2 153 AL69
Shepperton TW17 217 BR101
Walton-on-Thames KT12 217 BQ102
Weybridge KT13 217 BP103
Walton Leigh Sch, Walt.
KT12 off Queens Rd 235 BT105
Walton Oak Sch,
Walt. KT12
off Ambleside Av 218 BW102
WALTON-ON-THAMES, KT12 217 BT103
Walton-on-Thames 235 BU105
WALTON ON THE HILL, Tad.
KT20 271 CT125
Walton-on-the-Hill Prim Sch,
Walt.Hill KT20
off Walton St 255 CV124
Walton Pk, Walt. KT12 218 BX103
Walton Pk La, Walt. KT12 218 BX103
Walton Pl, SW3 28 E6
Walton Rd, E12 147 EN63
E13 166 EJ68
N15 144 DT56
Bushey WD23 98 BX42
East Molesey KT8 218 CA98
Epsom Downs KT18 255 CT118
Harrow HA1 139 CD56
Headley KT18 254 CQ121
Hoddesdon EN11 71 EB15
Romford RM5 126 EZ52
Sidcup DA14 208 EW89
Walton-on-Thames KT12 218 BW99
Ware SG12 55 DX07
West Molesey KT8 218 BY99
Woking GU21 249 AZ116
Walton St, SW3 28 D8
Enfield EN2 104 DR39
St. Albans AL1 65 CF19
Walton on the Hill KT20 255 CU124
Walton Ter, Wok. GU21 249 BB115
Walton Way, W3 160 CP71
Mitcham CR4 223 DJ98
Walt Whitman Cl, SE24
off Shakespeare Rd 183 DP84
Walverns Cl, Wat. WD19 98 BW44
WALWORTH, SE17 31 J10
Walworth Acad, SE1 43 P1
★ Walworth Garden Fm -
Horticultural Training Cen,
SE17 43 H1
Walworth Pl, SE17 43 K1
Walworth Rd, SE1 31 J8
SE17 31 J8
Walwyn Av, Brom. BR1 226 EK97
Wambrook Cl, Hutt. CM13 131 GC46
Wanborough Dr, SW15 201 CV88
Wanderer Dr, Bark. IG11 168 EV69
Wander Wf, Kings L. WD4 81 BP30
Wandle Bk, SW19 202 DD93
Croydon CR0 223 DL104
Wandle Ct, Epsom KT19 238 CQ105
Wandle Ct Gdns, Croy. CR0 223 DL104
Wandle Park 223 DN103
Wandle Rd, SW17 202 DE89
Beddington CR0 223 DL104
Croydon CR0 224 DQ104
Morden SM4 222 DC98
Wallington SM6 223 DH103
Wandle Side, Croy. CR0 223 DM104
Wallington SM6 223 DH104
Wandle Tech Pk, Mitch.
CR4 222 DF101
Wandle Trd Est, Mitch. CR4
off Budge La 222 DF101
Wandle Valley Sch, Cars.
SM5 off Welbeck Rd 222 DE101
Wandle Way, SW18 202 DB88
Mitcham CR4 222 DF99
Wandon Rd, SW6 39 M5
WANDSWORTH, SW18 201 CZ85
Wandsworth Br, SW6 182 DB83
SW18 182 DB83
Wandsworth Br Rd, SW6 39 L6
Wandsworth Common 202 DF88
Wandsworth Common, SW12 202 DE86
Wandsworth Common W Side,
SW18 202 DC85
Wandsworth High St, SW18 202 DA85
Wandsworth Plain, SW18 202 DB85
Wandsworth Riverside
Quarter Pier 182 DA84
Wandsworth Road 41 M9
Wandsworth Rd, SW8 42 A2
Wandsworth Town 182 DB84
Wandsworth Town, SW18 202 DA85
Wangey Rd, Rom. RM6 148 EX59
Wanless Rd, SE24 184 DQ83
Wanley Rd, SE5 184 DR84
Wanlip Rd, E13 24 A4
Wanmer Ct, Reig. RH2
off Birkheads Rd 272 DA133
Wannions Cl, Chesh. HP5 78 AU30
Wannock Gdns, Ilf. IG6 125 EP52
Wansbeck Rd, E3 11 P6
E9 11 P6
Wansbury Way, Swan. BR8 229 FG99
Wansdown Pl, SW6 39 L4
Wansey St, SE17 31 K9
Wansford Cl, Brwd. CM14 130 FT48
Wansford Grn, Wok. GU21 248 AT117
Wansford Pk, Borwd. WD6 100 CS42
Wansford Rd, Wdf.Grn. IG8 124 EJ53
WANSTEAD, E11 146 EH59
Wanstead 146 EH58
Wanstead Ch Prim Sch, E11
off Church Path 146 EG57
Wanstead Cl, Brom. BR1 226 EJ96
Wanstead High Sch, E11
off Redbridge La W 146 EJ58
Wanstead La, Ilf. IG1 146 EK58
Wanstead Park 146 EH63
Wanstead Pk, E11 146 EK59
Wanstead Pk Av, E12 146 EK61
Wanstead Pk Rd, Ilf. IG1 147 EM60
Wanstead Pl, E11 146 EG58
Wanstead Rd, Brom. BR1 226 EJ96
Wansunt Rd, Bex. DA5 209 FC88
Wantage Rd, SE12 206 EF85
Wantz La, Rain. RM13 169 FH70
Wantz Rd, Dag. RM10 149 FB63
Waplings, The, Tad. KT20 255 CV124
WAPPING, E1 32 D2
Wapping 32 G3
Wapping Dock St, E1 32 F3
Wapping High St, E1 32 C3
Wapping La, E1 32 F1
Wapping Wall, E1 32 G2
Wapseys La, Hedg. SL2 134 AS58
Wapshott Rd, Stai. TW18 195 BE93
Warbank Cl, New Adgtn CR0 244 EE111
Warbank Cres, New Adgtn
CR0 244 EE110
Warbank La, Kings.T. KT2 201 CT94
Warbeck Rd, W12 161 CV74
Warberry Rd, N22 121 DM54
Warblers Grn, Cob. KT11 236 BZ114
Warboys App, Kings.T. KT2 200 CP93
Warboys Cres, E4 123 EC50
Warboys Rd, Kings.T. KT2 200 CP93
Warburton Cl, N1 9 N4
Harrow HA3 117 CD51
Warburton Ho, E8
off Warburton Rd 10 E8
Warburton Rd, E8 10 E8
Twickenham TW2 198 CB88
Warburton St, E8 10 E8
Warburton Ter, E17 123 EB54
War Coppice Rd, Cat. CR3 274 DR127
Wardalls Gro, SE14 45 H4
Ward Av, Grays RM17 192 GA77
Ward Cl, Chsht EN7 88 DU27
Erith DA8 189 FD79
Iver SL0 155 BF72
South Croydon CR2 242 DS106
Ware SG12 54 DW05
Wardell Cl, NW7 118 CS52
Wardell Fld, NW9 118 CS53
Warden Av, Har. HA2 138 BZ60
Romford RM5 127 FC50
Warden Rd, NW5 7 H4
Wardens Fld Cl, Grn St Grn
BR6 245 ES107
Wardens Gro, SE1 31 J3
Ward Gdns, Harold Wd RM3
off Whitmore Av 128 FL54
Slough SL1 153 AL73
Ward Hatch, Harl. CM20 58 EU12
Ward La, Warl. CR6 258 DW116
Wardle St, E9 11 J3
Wardley St, SW18 202 DB87
Wardo Av, SW6 38 E7
Wardour Ms, W1 17 M9
Wardour St, W1 17 N10
Ward Pl, Amer. HP7 77 AP40
Ward Pt, SE11 30 E9
Ward Rd, E15 12 G8
N19 143 DJ62
Wardrobe Pl, EC4
off St. Andrew's Hill 19 H9
Wardrobe Ter, EC4 19 H9
Ward Royal, Wind. SL4 173 AQ81
Wards Dr, Sarratt WD3 95 BF36
Wards La, Els. WD6 99 CG40
Ward's Pl, Egh. TW20 195 BC93
Wards Rd, Ilf. IG2 147 ER59
Ward St, Guil. GU1
off Martyr Rd 280 AX135
Wards Wf App, E16 36 E4
WARE, SG12 55 DX06
Ware 55 DY07
Wareham Cl, Houns. TW3 178 CB84
Wareham Ho, SW8 42 C4
Warehams La, Hert. SG14 54 DQ10
Warehouse W, E16 24 A10
Waremead Rd, Ilf. IG2 147 EP57
★ Ware Mus, Ware SG12 55 DX06
Warenford Way, Borwd. WD6 100 CN39
Warenne Hts, Red. RH1 288 DD136
Warenne Rd, Fetch. KT22 252 CC122
WARE PARK, Ware SG12 54 DT06
Ware Pk Rd, Hert. SG14 54 DR07
Ware Pt Dr, SE28 187 ER75
Ware Rd, Chad.Spr. SG12 54 DU08
Hailey SG13 55 EA12
Hertford SG13, SG14 54 DS09
Hoddesdon EN11 55 EA14
Widford SG12 55 EC05
Warescot Cl, Brwd. CM15 130 FV45
Warescot Rd, Brwd. CM15 130 FV45
Wareside Cl, Welw.G.C. AL7 52 DB10
Warfield Rd, NW10 14 C3
Feltham TW14 197 BS87
Hampton TW12 218 CB95
Warfield Yd, NW10 14 C3
Wargrave Av, N15 144 DT58
Wargrave Rd, Har. HA2 138 CC62
Warham Rd, N4 143 DN57
Harrow HA3 117 CF54
Otford TN14 263 FH116
South Croydon CR2 242 DP106
Warham St, SE5 43 H4
Waring Cl, Orp. BR6 245 ET107
Waring Dr, Orp. BR6 245 ET107
Waring Rd, Sid. DA14 208 EW93
Waring St, SE27 204 DQ91
Warkworth Gdns, Islw. TW7 179 CG80
Warkworth Rd, N17 122 DR52
Warland Rd, SE18 187 ER80
WARLEY, Brwd. CM14 130 FW50
Warley Av, Dag. RM8 148 EZ59
Hayes UB4 157 BU71
Warley Cl, E10 145 DZ60
Warley Gap, Lt.Warley CM13 129 FV52
Warley Hill, Brwd.
CM13, CM14 129 FV51
Warley Mt, Warley CM14 130 FW49
Warley Prim Sch, Warley
CM14 off Chindits La 130 FW50
Warley Rd, N9 122 DW47
Great Warley CM13 129 FT54
Hayes UB4 157 BU72
Ilford IG5 125 EN53
Upminster RM14 128 FQ54
Woodford Green IG8 124 EH52
Warley St, E2 21 J2
Great Warley CM13 151 FW58
Upminster RM14 151 FW58
Warley St Flyover, Brwd.
CM13 151 FX57
Warley Wds Cres, Brwd. CM14
off Crescent Rd 130 FV49
WARLINGHAM, CR6 259 DX118
Warlingham Pk Sch, Warl. CR6
off Chelsham Common 259 EA116
Warlingham Rd, Th.Hth. CR7 223 DP98
Warlingham Sch, Warl. CR6
off Tithepit Shaw La 258 DV116
Warlock Rd, W9 15 J4
Warlow Cl, Enf. EN3 105 EA37
Warlters Cl, N7
off Warlters Rd 143 DL63
Warlters Rd, N7 143 DL63
Warltersville Rd, N19 143 DL59
Warltersville Way, Horl. RH6 291 DJ150
Warmark Rd, Hem.H. HP1 61 BE18
Warmington Cl, E5
off Denton Way 145 DX62
Warmington Rd, SE24 204 DQ86
Warmington St, E13 23 P4
Warminster Gdns, SE25 224 DU96
Warminster Rd, SE25 224 DT96
Warminster Sq, SE25 224 DU96
Warminster Way, Mitch. CR4 223 DH95
Warmwell Av, NW9 118 CS53
Warndon St, SE16 33 H9
Warneford Pl, Wat. WD19 98 BY44
Warneford Rd, Har. HA3 139 CK55
Warneford St, E9 10 F8
Warne Pl, Sid. DA15
off Shorne Cl 208 EV86
Warner Av, Sutt. SM3 221 CY103
Warner Cl, E15 13 K3
NW9 141 CT59
Barnet EN4 102 DE37
Hampton TW12
off Tangley Pk Rd 198 BZ92
Harlington UB3 177 BR80
Slough SL1 153 AL74
Warner Ho, SE13 46 D8
Warner Par, Hayes UB3 177 BR80
Warner Pl, E2 20 D1
Warner Rd, E17 145 DY56
N8 143 DK56
SE5 43 J7
Bromley BR1 206 EF94
Ware SG12 54 DW07
Warners Av, Hodd. EN11 71 DZ19
Warners Cl, Wdf.Grn. IG8 124 EG50
WARNERS END, Hem.H. HP1 61 BE19
Warners End Rd, Hem.H. HP1 62 BG20
Warners La, Albury GU5 282 BL141
Kingston upon Thames KT2 199 CK91
Warners Path, Wdf.Grn. IG8 124 EG50
Warner St, EC1 18 E5
Warner Ter, E14 22 B7
Warner Yd, EC1 18 E5
Warnford Ho, SW15
off Tunworth Cres 200 CS86
Warnford Ind Est, Hayes
UB3 177 BS75
Warnford Rd, Orp. BR6 245 ET106
Warnham Ct Rd, Cars. SM5 240 DF108
Warnham Rd, N12 120 DE50
Warple Ms, W3
off Warple Way 180 CS75
Warple Way, W3 160 CS74
Warren, The, E12 146 EL63
Ashtead KT21 254 CL119
Carshalton SM5 240 DD109
Chalfont St. Peter SL9 113 AZ52
Chesham HP5 76 AL28
East Horsley KT24 267 BT130
Gravesend DA12 213 GK91
Hayes UB4 157 BU72
Hounslow TW5 178 BZ80
Kings Langley WD4 80 BM29
Kingswood KT20 255 CY123
Oxshott KT22 236 CC112
Park Street AL2
off How Wd 82 CC28
Radlett WD7 83 CG33
Worcester Park KT4 238 CR105
Warren Av, E10 145 EC62
Bromley BR1 206 EE94
Orpington BR6 245 ET106
Richmond TW10 180 CP84
South Croydon CR2 243 DX108
Sutton SM2 239 CZ110
Warren Cl, N9 123 DX45
SE21 204 DQ87
Bexleyheath DA6 208 FA85
Esher KT10 236 CB105
Hatfield AL10 67 CV15
Hayes UB4 158 BW71
Slough SL3 174 AY76
Wembley HA9 139 CK61
Warren Comp Sch, The,
Chad.Hth RM6
off Whalebone La N 148 EZ57
Warren Ct, N17
off High Cross Rd 144 DU55
SE7 186 EJ78
Ashtead KT21
off Ashfield Cl 254 CL119
Chigwell IG7 125 ER49
Sevenoaks TN13 279 FJ125
Weybridge KT13 234 BN106
Warren Cres, N9 122 DT45
Warren Cutting, Kings.T. KT2 200 CR94
Warren Dale, Welw.G.C. AL8 51 CX06
Warren Dell Prim Sch, S.Oxhey
WD19 off Gosforth La 116 BW48
Warrender Prim Sch, Ruis.
HA4 off Old Hatch Manor 137 BT59
Warrender Rd, N19 143 DJ62
Chesham HP5 76 AS29
Warrender Way, Ruis. HA4 137 BU59
Warren Dr, Grnf. UB6 158 CB70
Hornchurch RM12 149 FG62
Kingswood KT20 255 CZ122
Orpington BR6 246 EV106
Ruislip HA4 138 BX59
Warren Dr, The, E11 146 EJ59
Warren Dr N, Surb. KT5 220 CP102
Warren Dr S, Surb. KT5 220 CQ102
Warreners La, Wey. KT13 235 BR109
Warren Fm Home Pk, Wok.
GU22 250 BH119
Warren Fld, Epp. CM16 92 EU32
Iver SL0 155 BC68
Warrenfield Cl, Chsht EN7 88 DU31
Warren Flds, Stan. HA7
off Valencia Rd 117 CJ49
Warren Footpath, Twick. TW1 199 CK87
Warren Gdns, E15 12 G3
Orpington BR6 246 EU106
Warrengate La, S.Mimms EN6 85 CW31
Warrengate Rd, N.Mymms AL9 85 CW28
Warren Grn, Hat. AL10 67 CV15
Warren Gro, Borwd. WD6 100 CR42
Warren Hastings Ct, Grav. DA11
off Pier Rd 213 GF86
Warren Hts, Chaff.Hun. RM16 192 FY77
Loughton IG10 106 EJ43
Warren Hill, Epsom KT18 254 CR116
Loughton IG10 106 EJ44
Warren Ho, E3 22 C2
W14 27 H8
Warrenhyrst, Guil. GU1
off Warren Rd 281 BA135
Warren Jun Sch, Chad.Hth
RM6 off Gordon Rd 148 EZ57
Warren La, SE18 37 N7
Albury GU5 282 BJ139
Grays RM16 191 FX77
Oxshott KT22 236 CC111
Oxted RH8 276 EF134
Stanmore HA7 117 CF48
Woking GU22 250 BH118
Warren La Gate, SE18 37 N7
Warren Lo, Kgswd KT20 255 CY124
Warren Mead, Bans. SM7 255 CW115
Warren Mead Inf Sch, Bans.
SM7 off Partridge Mead 255 CX115
Warren Mead Jun Sch, Nork
SM7 off Roundwood Way 255 CX115
Warren Ms, W1 17 L5
Warrenne Rd, Brock. RH3 286 CP136
Warrenne Way, Reig. RH2 272 DA134
Warren Pk, Box H. KT20 270 CQ131
Kingston upon Thames KT2 200 CQ93
Warlingham CR6 259 DX118
Warren Pk Rd, Hert. SG14 54 DQ08
Sutton SM1 240 DD107
Warren Pond Rd, E4 124 EF46
Warren Prim Sch, Chaff.Hun.
RM16 off Gilbert Rd 191 FW76
Warren Ri, N.Mal. KT3 220 CR95
Warren Rd, E4 123 EC47
E10 145 EC62
E11 146 EJ60
NW2 141 CT61
SW19 202 DE93
Ashford TW15 197 BS94
Banstead SM7 239 CW114
Bexleyheath DA6 208 FA85
Bromley BR2 226 EG103
Bushey Heath WD23 116 CC46
Croydon CR0 224 DS102
Dartford DA1 210 FK90
Godalming GU7 280 AS144
Guildford GU1 281 AZ135
Ilford IG6 147 ER57
Kingston upon Thames KT2 200 CQ93
New Haw KT15 234 BG110
Orpington BR6 245 ET106
Purley CR8 241 DP111
Reigate RH2 272 DB133
St. Albans AL1 64 CC24
Sidcup DA14 208 EW90
Southfleet DA13 212 GB92
Twickenham TW2 198 CC86
Uxbridge UB10 136 BL63
Warren Rd Prim Sch, Orp.
BR6 off Warren Rd 245 ET106
Warrens Shawe La, Edg. HA8 118 CP46
Warren Street 17 M4
Warren St, W1 17 K5
Warren Ter, Grays RM16
off Arterial Rd W Thurrock 191 FX75
Hertford SG14 54 DR07
Romford RM6 148 EX56
Warren Wk, SE7 186 EJ79
Warren Way, Edg. HA8 118 CP54
Weybridge KT13 235 BQ106
Warren Wd Cl, Brom. BR2 226 EF103
Warren Wd Ms, Hat. AL9 68 DD22
Warriner Av, Horn. RM12 150 FK61
Warriner Dr, N9 122 DU48

Warriner Gdns, SW11 ... 40 F7
Warrington Av, Slou. SL1 ... 153 AQ72
Warrington Cres, W9 ... 15 N5
Warrington Gdns, W9 ... 15 N5
Hornchurch RM11 ... 150 FJ58
Warrington Rd, Croy. CR0 ... 223 DP104
Dagenham RM8 ... 148 EX61
Harrow HA1 ... 139 CE57
Richmond TW10 ... 199 CK85
Warrington Spur, Old Wind. SL4 ... 194 AV87
Warrington Sq, Dag. RM8 ... 148 EX61
Warrior Av, Grav. DA12 ... 213 GJ91
Warrior Cl, SE28 ... 167 ER74
Warrior Sq, E12 ... 147 EN63
Warsaw Cl, Ruis. HA4
off Glebe Av ... 157 BV65
Warsdale Dr, NW9
off Mardale Dr ... 140 CR57
Warspite Rd, SE18 ... 36 G6
Warton Rd, E15 ... 12 E8
Warwall, E6 ... 25 N8
⊖ Warwick Avenue ... 15 N5
Warwick Av, W2 ... 15 N5
W9 ... 15 N5
Cuffley EN6 ... 87 DK27
Edgware HA8 ... 118 CP48
Egham TW20 ... 215 BC95
Harrow HA2 ... 138 BZ63
Slough SL2 ... 153 AQ70
Staines TW18 ... 196 BJ93
Warwick Bldg, SW8 ... 41 J4
Warwick Chambers, W8
off Pater St ... 27 J6
Warwick Cl, Barn. EN4 ... 102 DD43
Bexley DA5 ... 208 EZ87
Bushey Heath WD23
off Magnaville Rd ... 117 CE45
Cuffley EN6 ... 87 DK27
Hampton TW12 ... 198 CC94
Hertford SG13 ... 54 DQ11
Hornchurch RM11 ... 150 FM56
Orpington BR6 ... 228 EU104
South Holmwood RH5 ... 285 CH144
Warwick Ct, SE15 ... 44 D9
WC1 ... 18 D7
Chorleywood WD3 ... 95 BF41
Surbiton KT6 ... 220 CL103
Warwick Cres, W2 ... 15 N6
Hayes UB4 ... 157 BT70
Warwick Deeping, Ott. KT16 ... 233 BC106
Warwick Dene, W5 ... 160 CL74
Warwick Dr, SW15 ... 181 CV83
Cheshunt EN8 ... 89 DX28
Warwick Est, W2 ... 15 L7
Warwick Gdns, N4 ... 144 DQ57
W14 ... 27 H7
Ashtead KT21 ... 253 CJ117
Barnet EN5 off Great N Rd ... 101 CZ38
Ilford IG1 ... 147 EP60
Romford RM2 ... 150 FJ55
Thames Ditton KT7 ... 219 CF99
Thornton Heath CR7
off London Rd ... 223 DN97
Warwick Gro, E5 ... 144 DV60
Surbiton KT5 ... 220 CM101
Warwick Ho St, SW1 ... 29 P2
Warwick La, EC4 ... 19 H9
Rainham RM13 ... 170 FM68
Upminster RM14 ... 170 FP68
Woking GU21 ... 248 AU119
Warwick Ms, Crox.Grn WD3 ... 96 BN44
Warwick Pas, EC4 ... 19 H8
Warwick Pl, W5
off Warwick Rd ... 179 CK75
W9 ... 15 N6
Northfleet DA11 ... 212 GB85
Uxbridge UB8 ... 156 BJ66
Warwick Pl N, SW1 ... 29 L9
Warwick Quad Shop Mall,
Red. RH1 off London Rd ... 272 DG133
Warwick Rd, E4 ... 123 EA50
E11 ... 146 EH57
E12 ... 146 EL64
E15 ... 13 M5
E17 ... 123 DZ53
N11 ... 121 DK51
N18 ... 122 DS49
SE20 ... 224 DV97
SW5 ... 26 G8
W5 ... 179 CK75
W14 ... 26 G8
Ashford TW15 ... 196 BL92
Barnet EN5 ... 102 DB42
Beaconsfield HP9 ... 111 AK52
Borehamwood WD6 ... 100 CR41
Coulsdon CR5 ... 241 DJ114
Enfield EN3 ... 105 DZ37
Hounslow TW4 ... 177 BV83
Kingston upon Thames KT1 ... 219 CJ95
New Malden KT3 ... 220 CQ97
Rainham RM13 ... 170 FJ70
Redhill RH1 ... 272 DF133
St. Albans AL1 ... 65 CF18
Sidcup DA14 ... 208 EV92
Southall UB2 ... 178 BZ76
Sutton SM1 ... 240 DC105
Thames Ditton KT7 ... 219 CF99
Thornton Heath CR7 ... 223 DN97
Twickenham TW2 ... 199 CE88
Welling DA16 ... 188 EW83
West Drayton UB7 ... 176 BL75
Warwick Row, SW1 ... 29 K6
Warwicks Bench, Guil. GU1 ... 280 AX136
Warwicks Bench La, Guil.
GU1 ... 280 AY137
Warwicks Bench Rd, Guil.
GU1 ... 280 AY137
Sch Warwick Sch, The, Red. RH1
off Noke Dr ... 272 DG133
Warwickshire Path, SE8 ... 45 P4
Warwick Sq, EC4 ... 19 H8
SW1 ... 29 L10
Warwick Sq Ms, SW1 ... 29 L9
Warwick St, W1 ... 17 M10
Warwick Ter, SE18 ... 187 ER79
Warwick Way, SW1 ... 29 L9
Croxley Green WD3 ... 97 BQ42
Dartford DA1 ... 210 FL89
WARWICK WOLD, Red. RH1 ... 273 DN129
Warwick Wold Rd, Red. RH1 ... 273 DN128
Warwick Yd, EC1 ... 19 K5
Wash, The, Hert. SG14 ... 54 DR09
Wash Hill, Woob.Grn HP10 ... 132 AE60
Wash Hill Lea, Woob.Grn
HP10 ... 132 AD59
Washington Av, E12 ... 146 EL63
Hemel Hempstead HP2 ... 62 BM15
Washington Bldg, SE13
off Deals Gateway ... 46 C6
Washington Cl, E3 ... 22 D2
Reigate RH2 ... 272 DA131
Washington Dr, Slou. SL1 ... 153 AK73
Windsor SL4 ... 173 AL83
Washington Rd, E6
off St. Stephens Rd ... 166 EJ66
E18 ... 124 EF54
SW13 ... 181 CU80
Kingston upon Thames KT1 ... 220 CN96
Worcester Park KT4 ... 221 CV103
Washington Row, Amer. HP7
off London Rd W ... 77 AQ40
Wash La, S.Mimms EN6 ... 85 CV33
Washneys Rd, Orp. BR6 ... 246 EV113
Washpond La, Warl. CR6 ... 259 EC118
Wash Rd, Hutt. CM13 ... 131 GD44
Wasp Grn La, Outwood RH1 ... 289 DP143
Wastdale Rd, SE23 ... 205 DX88
Watchfield Ct, W4 ... 180 CQ78
Watchgate, Lane End DA2 ... 211 FR91
Watchlytes, Welw.G.C. AL7 ... 52 DC09
Sch Watchlytes Sch, Welw.G.C.
AL7 off Watchlytes ... 52 DC09
Watchmead, Welw.G.C. AL7 ... 52 DA09
Watcombe Cotts, Rich. TW9 ... 180 CN79
Watcombe Pl, SE25
off Albert Rd ... 224 DV98
Watcombe Rd, SE25 ... 224 DV99
Waterbank Rd, SE6 ... 205 EC91
Waterbeach, Welw.G.C. AL7 ... 52 DD08
Waterbeach Cl, Slou. SL1 ... 153 AR72
Waterbeach Rd, Dag. RM9 ... 168 EW65
Slough SL1 ... 153 AR72
Waterbourne Way, Ken. CR8 ... 242 DR114
Water Brook La, NW4 ... 141 CW57
Water Circ, Bluewater DA9 ... 211 FT88
Watercress Pl, N1 ... 9 P7
Watercress Rd, Chsht EN7 ... 88 DR26
Watercress Way, Wok. GU21 ... 248 AV117
Watercroft Rd, Halst. TN14 ... 246 EZ110
Jct Waterdale, Wat. WD25 ... 82 BX30
Waterdale, Hert. SG13 ... 54 DQ11
Waterdale Rd, SE2 ... 188 EU79
Waterdales, Nthflt DA11 ... 212 GD88
Waterdell Pl, Rick. WD3
off Uxbridge Rd ... 114 BG47
Waterden Cl, Guil. GU1 ... 281 AZ135
Waterden Rd, E15 off Eastway ... 12 B2
Guildford GU1 ... 280 AY135
WATER END, Hat. AL9 ... 85 CV26
Water End Cl, Borwd. WD6 ... 100 CM40
Waterend La, Ayot St.P. AL6 ... 50 CQ07
Wheathampstead AL4 ... 50 CQ07
Water End Rd, Pott.End HP4 ... 61 BB17
Waterer Gdns, Tad. KT20 ... 255 CX118
Waterer Ri, Wall. SM6 ... 241 DK107
Waterfall Cl, N14 ... 121 DJ48
Hoddesdon EN11 ... 71 DZ16
Virginia Water GU25 ... 214 AU97
Waterfall Cotts, SW19 ... 202 DD93
Waterfall Rd, N11 ... 121 DH49
N14 ... 121 DJ48
SW19 ... 202 DD93
Waterfall Ter, SW17 ... 202 DE93
Waterfield, Herons. WD3 ... 113 BC45
Tadworth KT20 ... 255 CV119
Welwyn Garden City AL7 ... 52 DB08
Waterfield Cl, SE28 ... 168 EV74
Belvedere DA17 ... 188 FA76
Waterfield Dr, Warl. CR6 ... 258 DW119
Waterfield Gdns, SE25 ... 224 DR98
Waterfield Grn, Tad. KT20 ... 255 CW120
Waterfields, Lthd. KT22 ... 253 CH119
Waterfields Shop Pk, Wat.
WD17 ... 98 BX42
Waterfields Way, Wat. WD17 ... 98 BX42
WATERFORD, Hert. SG14 ... 53 DM05
Waterford Cl, Cob. KT11 ... 236 BY111
Waterford Common, Waterf.
SG14 ... 53 DP05
Waterford Grn, Welw.G.C. AL7 ... 52 DB09
Waterford Rd, SW6 ... 39 M6
Waterford Way, NW10 ... 141 CV64
Waterfront, The, Hert. SG14 ... 54 DR09
● Waterfront Studios Business
Cen, E16 ... 35 N2
Water Gdns, Harl. CM20 ... 73 ER15
Water Gdns, Stan. HA7 ... 117 CH51
Water Gdns, The, W2 ... 16 D8
Watergardens, The, Kings.T.
KT2 ... 200 CQ93
Water Gdns Sq, SE16
off Canada St ... 33 J5
Watergate, EC4 ... 18 G10
Watergate, The, Wat. WD19 ... 116 BX47
Sch Watergate Sch, SE6
off Lushington Rd ... 205 EB92
Watergate St, SE8 ... 46 A3
Watergate Wk, WC2 ... 30 B2
● Waterglade Ind Pk, Grays
RM20 ... 191 FT78
Waterglades, Knot.Grn HP9 ... 110 AJ49
Waterhall Av, E4 ... 124 EE49
Waterhall Cl, E17 ... 123 DX53
Waterhead Cl, Erith DA8 ... 189 FE80
Waterhouse Cl, E16 ... 24 E6
NW3 ... 6 B2
W6 ... 26 D10
Waterhouse La, Bletch. RH1 ... 274 DT132
Kenley CR8 ... 258 DQ119
Kingswood KT20 ... 255 CY121
Waterhouse Moor, Harl. CM18 ... 73 ES16
Waterhouse Sq, EC1 ... 18 E7
Waterhouse St, Hem.H. HP1 ... 62 BJ20
Wateridge Cl, E14 ... 34 A7
Wateringbury Cl, Orp. BR5 ... 228 EV97
Water La, E15 ... 13 K4
EC3 ... 31 N1
N9 ... 122 DV46
NW1 ... 7 K7
SE14 ... 45 H4
Abinger Hammer RH5 ... 283 BV143
Albury GU5 ... 282 BH137
Berkhamsted HP4 ... 60 AW19
Bookham KT23 ... 268 BY125
Bovingdon HP3 ... 79 BA29
Chesham HP5 ... 76 AP32
Cobham KT11 ... 252 BY115
Hertford SG14 ... 54 DQ10
Ilford IG3 ... 147 ES62
Water La, Kings L. WD4 ... 81 BP29
Kingston upon Thames KT1 ... 219 CK95
Purfleet RM19 ... 190 FN77
Redhill RH1 ... 273 DP130
Richmond TW9 ... 199 CK85
Roydon CM19 ... 72 EL19
Shoreham TN14 ... 247 FF112
Sidcup DA14 ... 208 EZ89
Titsey RH8 ... 276 EG126
Twickenham TW1
off The Embankment ... 199 CG88
Watford WD17 ... 98 BW42
Westerham TN16 ... 277 ER127
Sch Water La Prim Sch, Harl.
CM19 off Broadley Rd ... 73 EN19
Water Lily Cl, Sthl. UB2
off Navigator Dr ... 178 CC75
⇌ Waterloo ... 30 E4
⊖ Waterloo ... 30 E4
Waterloo Br, SE1 ... 30 C1
WC2 ... 30 C1
Waterloo Cl, E9 ... 11 H2
Feltham TW14 ... 197 BT88
⇌ Waterloo East ... 30 E3
Waterloo Est, E2 ... 10 G10
Waterloo Gdns, E2 ... 10 G10
N1 ... 8 G7
Romford RM7 ... 149 FD58
Riv Waterloo Millennium Pier ... 30 B4
Waterloo Pas, NW6 ... 5 H7
Waterloo Pl, SW1 ... 29 N2
Kew TW9 off Kew Grn ... 180 CN79
Richmond TW9
off The Quadrant ... 180 CL84
Waterloo Rd, E6 ... 166 EJ66
E7 ... 13 M2
E10 ... 145 EA59
NW2 ... 141 CU60
SE1 ... 30 E4
Brentwood CM14 ... 130 FW46
Epsom KT19 ... 238 CR112
Ilford IG6 ... 125 EQ54
Romford RM7 ... 149 FE57
Sutton SM1 ... 240 DD106
Uxbridge UB8 ... 156 BJ67
Waterloo St, Grav. DA12 ... 213 GJ87
Waterloo Ter, N1 ... 8 G7
Waterlow Ct, NW11
off Heath Cl ... 142 DB59
Waterlow Rd, N19 ... 143 DJ60
Reigate RH2 ... 288 DC135
Waterman Cl, Wat. WD19 ... 97 BV44
Waterman Ct, Slou. SL1 ... 153 AL74
● Watermans, The, Stai.
TW18 ... 195 BE91
★ Watermans Art Cen, Brent.
TW8 ... 180 CL79
Waterman's Cl, Kings.T. KT2
off Woodside Rd ... 200 CL94
Waterman St, SW15 ... 181 CX83
Waterman's Wk, EC4
off Allhallows La ... 31 L1
Watermans Wk, SE16 ... 33 L6
Watermans Way, Green. DA9 ... 191 FV84
North Weald Bassett CM16 ... 92 FA27
Waterman Way, E1 ... 32 E2
Watermark Way, Hert. SG13 ... 54 DT09
Water Mead, Chipstead CR5 ... 256 DF117
Watermead, Felt. TW14 ... 197 BS88
Tadworth KT20 ... 255 CV121
Woking GU21 ... 248 AT116
Watermead Ho, E9
off Kingsmead Way ... 11 M2
Watermead La, Cars. SM5
off Middleton Rd ... 222 DF101
Watermeadow, Chesh. HP5 ... 76 AP32
Watermeadow Cl, Erith DA8 ... 189 FH80
Watermeadow La, SW6 ... 39 N9
Water Meadows, Frog. AL2
off Frogmore ... 83 CE28
Watermead Rd, SE6 ... 205 EC91
Watermead Way, N17 ... 144 DV55
Watermen's Sq, SE20 ... 204 DW94
Water Ms, SE15 ... 184 DW84
● Watermill Business Cen, Enf.
EN3 ... 105 DZ40
Watermill Cl, Rich. TW10 ... 199 CJ90
Watermill La, N18 ... 122 DS50
Hertford SG14 ... 54 DR06
Watermill La N, Hert. SG14 ... 54 DQ06
Watermill Way, SW19 ... 222 DC95
Feltham TW13 ... 198 BZ89
Water Mill Way, S.Darenth
DA4 ... 230 FP96
Watermint Cl, Orp. BR5
off Wagtail Way ... 228 EX98
Watermint Quay, N16 ... 144 DU59
Waterperry La, Chobham
GU24 ... 232 AT110
Water Rd, Wem. HA0 ... 160 CM67
Water Row, Ware SG12 ... 55 DX06
Waters Dr, Rick. WD3 ... 114 BL46
Staines TW18 ... 195 BF90
Watersedge, Epsom KT19 ... 238 CQ105
Waters Edge Ct, Erith DA8
off Erith High St ... 189 FF78
Watersfield Way, Edg. HA8 ... 117 CK52
Waters Gdns, Dag. RM10 ... 148 FA64
WATERSIDE, Chesh. HP5 ... 76 AR32
Waterside, Beck. BR3
off Rectory Rd ... 225 EA95
Berkhamsted HP4
off Holliday St ... 60 AX19
Chesham HP5 ... 76 AQ32
Dartford DA1 ... 209 FE85
Gravesend DA11 ... 212 GE86
Horley RH6 ... 290 DG146
Water Side, Kings L. WD4 ... 80 BN29
Waterside, Lon.Col. AL2 ... 84 CL27
Radlett WD7 ... 83 CH34
Uxbridge UB8 ... 156 BJ71
Welwyn Garden City AL7 ... 52 DA07
Wooburn Green HP10 ... 132 AE56
Waterside Av, Beck. BR3
off Brockwell Av ... 225 EB99
Waterside Cl, E3 ... 11 N8
SE16 ... 32 D5
SE28 ... 167 ET74
Barking IG11 ... 148 EU63
Harold Wood RM3 ... 128 FN52
Northolt UB5 ... 158 BZ69
Surbiton KT6
off Culsac Rd ... 220 CL103
Sch Waterside Comb Sch, Chesh.
HP5 off Blackhorse Av ... 76 AR33
Waterside Ct, SE13
off Weardale Rd ... 185 ED84
Kings Langley WD4
off Water Side ... 81 BP29
Waterside Dr, Langley SL3 ... 175 AZ75
Walton-on-Thames KT12 ... 217 BU99
Waterside Ms, Guil. GU1 ... 264 AW132
Harefield UB9 ... 114 BG51
Waterside Path, SW18
off Smugglers Way ... 182 DB84
Waterside Pl, NW1 ... 7 H8
Sawbridgeworth CM21 ... 58 FA05
Waterside Pt, SW11 ... 40 D4
Waterside Rd, Guil. GU1 ... 264 AX131
Southall UB2 ... 178 CA76
Sch Waterside Sch, SE18
off Robert St ... 187 ER78
Waterside Twr, SW6 ... 39 P8
● Waterside Trd Cen, W7 ... 179 CE76
Waterside Way, SW17 ... 202 DC91
Woking GU21
off Winnington Way ... 248 AV118
Waterslade, Red. RH1 ... 272 DE134
Watersmeet, Harl. CM19 ... 73 EP19
Watersmeet Cl, Guil. GU4
off Cotts Wd Dr ... 265 BA129
Watersmeet Way, SE28 ... 168 EW72
Waterson Rd, Grays RM16 ... 193 GH77
Waterson St, E2 ... 19 P2
Waters Pl, SW15 ... 38 B9
Watersplash Cl, Kings.T. KT1 ... 220 CL97
Watersplash Ct, Lon.Col. AL2
off Thamesdale ... 84 CM27
Watersplash La, Hayes UB3 ... 177 BU77
Hounslow TW5 ... 177 BV78
Watersplash Rd, Shep. TW17 ... 216 BN98
Waters Rd, SE6 ... 206 EE90
Kingston upon Thames KT1 ... 220 CP96
Waters Sq, Kings.T. KT1 ... 220 CP97
Water St, WC2 ... 18 D10
Waterton, Swan. BR8 ... 229 FD98
Waterton Av, Grav. DA12 ... 213 GL87
Water Twr Cl, Uxb. UB8 ... 136 BL64
Water Twr Hill, Croy. CR0 ... 242 DR105
Water Twr Pl, N1 ... 8 F9
Water Twr Rd, Gt Warley
CM14 ... 130 FW50
Water Vw, Horl. RH6
off Carlton Tye ... 291 DJ148
Waterview Cl, Bexh. DA6 ... 208 EX85
Waterview Ho, E14 ... 21 M7
Waterway Av, SE13 ... 185 EB83
Waterway Rd, Lthd. KT22 ... 253 CG122
● Waterways Business Cen,
Enf. EN3 ... 105 EA38
Jct Waterworks Cor, E18 ... 124 EE54
Waterworks Cotts, Brox. EN10 ... 71 DY22
Waterworks La, E5 ... 145 DX61
Waterworks Rd, SW2 ... 203 DL86
Waterworks Yd, Croy. CR0
off Surrey St ... 224 DQ104
Watery La, SW20 ... 221 CZ96
Flamstead AL3 ... 83 CK28
Hatfield AL10 ... 66 CS19
Lyne KT16 ... 215 BD101
Northolt UB5 ... 158 BW68
Sidcup DA14 ... 208 EV93
Wooburn Green HP10 ... 110 AE54
Wates Way, Brwd. CM15 ... 130 FX46
Mitcham CR4 ... 222 DF100
● Wates Way Ind Est, Mitch.
CR4 ... 222 DF100
Wateville Rd, N17 ... 122 DQ53
WATFORD, WD17 - WD19;
WD24 & WD25 ... 97 BT41
⊖ Watford ... 97 BT41
Watford Arches Retail Pk,
Wat. WD17 ... 98 BX43
● Watford Business Pk, Wat.
WD18 ... 97 BS44
Watford Bypass, Borwd. WD6 ... 117 CG45
Watford Cl, SW11 ... 40 D6
Guildford GU1 ... 265 AZ134
Watford Fld Rd, Wat. WD18 ... 98 BW43
★ Watford FC, Wat. WD18 ... 97 BV43
H Watford Gen Hosp, Wat.
WD18 ... 97 BV43
Sch Watford Gram Sch for Boys,
Wat. WD18
off Rickmansworth Rd ... 97 BT42
Sch Watford Gram Sch for Girls,
Wat. WD18 off Lady's Cl ... 98 BW43
WATFORD HEATH, Wat. WD19 ... 116 BY46
Watford Heath, Wat. WD19 ... 116 BX45
⇔ Watford High Street ... 98 BW42
⇌ Watford Junction ... 98 BW40
● Watford Metro Cen, Wat.
WD18 ... 115 BQ45
★ Watford Mus, Wat. WD17 ... 98 BW42
⇌ Watford North ... 98 BW37
Watford Rd, E16 ... 23 P7
Croxley Green WD3 ... 97 BQ43
Elstree WD6 ... 99 CJ44
Harrow HA1 ... 139 CG61
Kings Langley WD4 ... 81 BP32
Northwood HA6 ... 115 BT52
Radlett WD7 ... 99 CE36
St. Albans AL1, AL2 ... 82 CA27
Wembley HA0 ... 139 CG61
Coll Watford Sch of Music, Wat.
WD17 off Nascot Wd Rd ... 97 BU38
Watford Way, NW4 ... 141 CU56
NW7 ... 119 CT51
Wathen Rd, Dor. RH4 ... 285 CH135
Watkin Ms, Enf. EN3 ... 105 EA37
Watkin Rd, Wem. HA9 ... 140 CP62
Watkins Cl, Nthwd. HA6
off Chestnut Av ... 115 BT53
Watkinson Rd, N7 ... 8 C4
Watkins Ri, Pot.B. EN6
off The Walk ... 86 DB32
Watling Av, Edg. HA8 ... 118 CR52
Watling Cl, Hem.H. HP2 ... 62 BL17
Watling Ct, EC4 ... 19 K9
Borehamwood WD6 ... 99 CK44
Watling Fm Cl, Stan. HA7 ... 117 CJ46
Watling Gdns, NW2 ... 4 F5
Watling Knoll, Rad. WD7 ... 83 CF33
Watlings Cl, Croy. CR0 ... 225 DY100
Watling St, EC4 ... 19 J9
SE15 ... 43 P3
Bexleyheath DA6 ... 189 FB84
Dartford DA1, DA2 ... 210 FP87
Elstree WD6 ... 99 CJ40
Gravesend DA11, DA12,
DA13 ... 213 GL94
Radlett WD7 ... 83 CF32
St. Albans AL1, AL2 ... 82 CC25
Watling St Caravan Site (Travellers),
Park St AL2 ... 82 CC25
Watlington Gro, SE26 ... 205 DY92
Watlington Rd, Harl. CM17 ... 58 EX11
Watling Vw, St.Alb. AL1 ... 64 CC24
Sch Watling Vw Sch, St.Alb. AL1
off Watling Vw ... 65 CD24
Watney Cl, Pur. CR8 ... 241 DM113
Watney Cotts, SW14
off Lower Richmond Rd ... 180 CQ83
Watney Mkt, E1 ... 20 F9
Watney Rd, SW14 ... 180 CQ83
Watneys Rd, Mitch. CR4 ... 223 DK99
Watney St, E1 ... 20 F9
Watson Av, E6 ... 167 EN66
St. Albans AL3 ... 65 CF17
Sutton SM3 ... 221 CY103
Watson Cl, N16 ... 9 M2
SW19 ... 202 DE93
Grays RM20 ... 191 FU81
Watson Gdns, Harold Wd
RM3 ... 128 FK54
Watson Rd, Westc. RH4 ... 284 CC137
Watsons Ms, W1 ... 16 D7
Watsons Rd, N22 ... 121 DM53
Watson's St, SE8 ... 46 A5
Watson St, E13 ... 166 EH68
Watsons Wk, St.Alb. AL1 ... 65 CE21
Sch Wattenden Prim Sch, The,
Pur. CR8 off Old Lo La ... 257 DP116
Wattendon Rd, Ken. CR8 ... 257 DP116
Wattisfield Rd, E5 ... 144 DW62
Wattleton Rd, Beac. HP9 ... 111 AK54
Watton Rd, Ware SG12 ... 54 DW05
Watts Cl, N15 off Seaford Rd ... 144 DS57
Tadworth KT20 ... 255 CX122
Watts Cres, Purf. RM19 ... 190 FQ77
Watts Down Cl, E13 ... 13 N9
Watts Fm Par, Chobham GU24
off Barnmead ... 232 AT110
Watts Gro, E3 ... 22 C6
Watts La, Chis. BR7 ... 227 EP95
Tadworth KT20 ... 255 CX122
Teddington TW11 ... 199 CG92
Watts Lea, Horsell GU21 ... 248 AU115
Watts Mead, Tad. KT20 ... 255 CX122
Watts Rd, T.Ditt. KT7 ... 219 CG101
Watts St, E1 ... 32 F2
SE15 ... 44 B6
Watts Way, SW7 ... 28 B6
Wat Tyler Rd, SE3 ... 46 F8
SE10 ... 46 F8
Wauthier Cl, N13 ... 121 DP50
Wavell Cl, Chsht EN8 ... 89 DY27
Wavell Dr, Sid. DA15 ... 207 ES86
Wavell Gdns, Slou. SL2 ... 153 AM69
Wavell Rd, Beac. HP9 ... 111 AP54
Wavel Ms, N8 ... 143 DK56
NW6 ... 5 L7
Wavel Pl, SE26
off Sydenham Hill ... 204 DT91
Wavendene Av, Egh. TW20 ... 195 BB94
Wavendon Av, W4 ... 180 CR78
Waveney, Hem.H. HP2 ... 62 BM15
Waveney Av, SE15 ... 184 DV84
Waveney Cl, E1 ... 32 D2
Waverley Av, E4 ... 123 DZ49
E17 ... 145 ED55
Kenley CR8 ... 258 DS116
Surbiton KT5 ... 220 CP100
Sutton SM1 ... 222 DB103
Twickenham TW2 ... 198 BZ88
Wembley HA9 ... 140 CM64
Waverley Cl, E18 ... 124 EJ53
Bromley BR2 ... 226 EK99
Hayes UB3 ... 177 BR77
West Molesey KT8 ... 218 CA99
Waverley Ct, Wok. GU22 ... 248 AY118
Waverley Cres, SE18 ... 187 ER78
Romford RM3 ... 128 FJ51
Waverley Dr, Cher. KT16 ... 215 BD104
Virginia Water GU25 ... 214 AU97
Waverley Gdns, E6 ... 25 H7
NW10 ... 160 CM69
Barking IG11 ... 167 ES68
Grays RM16 ... 192 GA75
Ilford IG6 ... 125 EQ54
Northwood HA6 ... 115 BU53
Waverley Gro, N3 ... 141 CX55
● Waverley Ind Est, Har.
HA1 ... 139 CD55
Waverley Pl, N4 ... 143 DP60
NW8 ... 6 A10
Leatherhead KT22
off Church Rd ... 253 CH122
Waverley Rd, E17 ... 145 EC55
E18 ... 124 EJ53
N8 ... 143 DK58
N17 ... 122 DV52
SE18 ... 187 EQ78
SE25 ... 224 DV98
Enfield EN2 ... 103 DP42
Epsom KT17 ... 239 CV106
Harrow HA2 ... 138 BZ60
Oxshott KT22 ... 236 CB114
Rainham RM13 ... 169 FH69
St. Albans AL3 ... 65 CD18
Slough SL1 ... 153 AQ71
Southall UB1 ... 158 CA73
Stoke D'Abernon KT11 ... 236 CB114
Weybridge KT13 ... 234 BN106
Sch Waverley Sch, Enf. EN3
off The Ride ... 104 DW42
Waverley Vil, N17 ... 122 DT54
Waverley Wk, W2 ... 15 K6
Waverley Way, Cars. SM5 ... 240 DE107
Waverton Ho, E3 ... 11 P8
Waverton Rd, SW18 ... 202 DC87
Waverton St, W1 ... 29 H2
Wavertree Ct, SW2
off Streatham Hill ... 203 DL88
Wavertree Rd, E18 ... 124 EG54
SW2 ... 203 DL88
Waxham, NW3 ... 6 F2
Waxlow Cres, Sthl. UB1 ... 158 CA72
Waxlow Rd, NW10 ... 160 CQ68
Waxlow Way, Nthlt. UB5 ... 158 BZ70
Waxwell Cl, Pnr. HA5 ... 116 BX54
Waxwell La, Pnr. HA5 ... 116 BX54
Way, The, Reig. RH2 ... 272 DD133
Wayborne Gro, Ruis. HA4 ... 137 BQ58
Waycross Rd, Upmin. RM14 ... 151 FS58
Waye Av, Houns. TW5 ... 177 BU81
Wayfarer Rd, Nthlt. UB5 ... 158 BX70
Wayfarers Pk, Berk. HP4 ... 60 AT19
Wayfaring Grn, Bad.Dene RM17
off Curling La ... 192 FZ78
Wayfield Link, SE9 ... 207 ER86
Wayford St, SW11 ... 40 D9
Wayland Av, E8 ... 10 D3
Wayland Ho, SW9 ... 42 E8
Waylands, Hayes UB3 ... 157 BR71
Swanley BR8 ... 229 FF98
Wraysbury TW19 ... 194 AY86

Waylands Cl, Knock.P. TN14 . . . **262** EY115
Waylands Mead, Beck. BR3 . . . **225** EB95
Wayleave, The, SE28 . . . **168** EV73
Waylett Ho, SE11 . . . **42** E1
Waylett Pl, SE27 . . . **203** DP90
Wembley HA0 . . . **139** CK63
Wayman Ct, E8 . . . **10** E5
Wayne Cl, Orp. BR6 . . . **227** ET104
Wayneflete Pl, Esher KT10
off More La . . . **218** CB104
Wayneflete Twr Av, Esher
KT10 . . . **218** CA104
Waynflete Av, Croy. CR0 . . . **223** DP104
Waynflete Sq, W10 . . . **14** C10
Waynflete St, SW18 . . . **202** DC89
Wayre, The, Harl. CM17 . . . **58** EW11
Wayre St, Harl. CM17 . . . **58** EW11
Wayside, NW11 . . . **141** CY60
SW14 . . . **200** CQ85
Chipperfield WD4 . . . **80** BH30
New Addington CR0 . . . **243** EB107
Potters Bar EN6 . . . **86** DD33
Shenley WD7 . . . **83** CK33
Wayside, The, Hem.H. HP3 . . . **63** BQ21
Wayside Av, Bushey WD23 . . . **99** CD44
Hornchurch RM12 . . . **150** FK61
Wayside Cl, N14 . . . **103** DJ44
Romford RM1 . . . **149** FF55
● **Wayside Commercial Est**,
Bark. IG11 . . . **168** EU67
Wayside Ct, Twick. TW1 . . . **199** CJ86
Wembley HA9 . . . **140** CN62
Woking GU21
off Langmans Way . . . **248** AS116
Wayside Gdns, SE9
off Wayside Gro . . . **207** EM91
Dagenham RM10 . . . **148** FA64
Gerrards Cross SL9 . . . **134** AX59
Wayside Gro, SE9 . . . **207** EM91
Wayside Ms, Ilf. IG2
off Gaysham Av . . . **147** EN57
Wayville Rd, Dart. DA1 . . . **210** FP87
Way Volante, Grav. DA12 . . . **213** GL91
Weald, The, Chis. BR7 . . . **207** EM93
Weald Br Rd, N.Wld Bas. CM16 . **75** FD24
Weald Cl, SE16 . . . **32** E10
Brentwood CM14 . . . **130** FU48
Bromley BR2 . . . **226** EL103
Istead Rise DA13 . . . **212** GE94
Shalford GU4
off Station Rd . . . **280** AY140
★ **Weald Country Pk**, Brwd.
CM14 . . . **130** FS45
Sch **Weald First & Mid Schs**,
Har. HA3
off Robin Hood Dr . . . **117** CF52
● **Weald Hall Fm Commercial**
Cen, Hast. CM17 . . . **92** EZ25
Weald Hall La, Thnwd CM16 . . . **92** EW25
Weald La, Har. HA3 . . . **117** CD54
Wealdon Ct, Guil. GU2
off Chapelhouse Cl . . . **264** AS134
Weald Pk Way, S.Wld CM14 . . . **130** FS48
Weald Ri, Har. HA3 . . . **117** CF52
Weald Rd, Brwd. CM14 . . . **129** FR46
Sevenoaks TN13 . . . **279** FH129
Uxbridge UB10 . . . **156** BN68
Weald Sq, E5 . . . **144** DU61
WEALDSTONE, Har. HA3 . . . **139** CF55
Wealdstone Rd, Sutt. SM3 . . . **221** CZ103
Weald Way, Cat. CR3 . . . **274** DS128
Wealdway, Grav. DA13 . . . **213** GH93
Weald Way, Hayes UB4 . . . **157** BS69
Reigate RH2 . . . **288** DC138
Romford RM7 . . . **149** FB58
Wealdwood Gdns, Pnr. HA5
off Highbanks Rd . . . **116** CB51
Weale Rd, E4 . . . **123** ED48
Weall Cl, Pur. CR8 . . . **241** DM113
Weall Grn, Wat. WD25 . . . **81** BV32
Weardale Av, Dart. DA2 . . . **210** FQ89
Weardale Gdns, Enf. EN2 . . . **104** DR39
Weardale Rd, SE13 . . . **185** ED84
Wear Pl, E2 . . . **20** E3
Wearside Rd, SE13 . . . **185** EB84
Weasdale Ct, Wok. GU21
off Roundthorn Way . . . **248** AT116
Weatherall Cl, Add. KT15 . . . **234** BH106
Weatherbury Ho, N19
off Wedmore St . . . **143** DK62
Weatherhill Cl, Horl. RH6 . . . **291** DM148
Weatherhill Common,
Smallfield RH6 . . . **291** DM147
Weatherhill Rd, Smallfield
RH6 . . . **291** DM148
Weatherley Cl, E3 . . . **21** P6
Weaver Cl, E6 . . . **25** N10
Croydon CR0 . . . **242** DT105
Weavers Almshouses, E11
off New Wanstead . . . **146** EG58
Weavers Cl, Grav. DA11 . . . **213** GG88
Isleworth TW7 . . . **179** CE84
Weavers La, SE1 . . . **31** P3
Sevenoaks TN14 . . . **279** FJ121
Weavers Orchard, Sthflt DA13 . **212** GA93
Weavers Ter, SW6 . . . **39** K3
Weaver St, E1 . . . **20** C5
Weavers Way, NW1 . . . **7** N8
Weaver Wk, SE27 . . . **203** DP91
Webb Cl, W10 . . . **14** A5
Chesham HP5 . . . **76** AP30
Slough SL3 . . . **174** AX77
Webber Cl, Els. WD6
off Rodgers Cl . . . **99** CK44
Erith DA8 . . . **189** FH80
Webber Row, SE1 . . . **30** F5
Webber St, SE1 . . . **30** F4
Webb Est, E5 . . . **144** DU59
Webb Gdns, E13 . . . **23** P4
Webb Ho, SW8 . . . **41** P5
Webb Pl, NW10 . . . **161** CT69
Webb Rd, SE3 . . . **47** M2
Webb's All, Sev. TN13, TN15 . . . **279** FJ125
Webbscroft Rd, Dag. RM10 . . . **149** FB63
Webbs Rd, SW11 . . . **202** DF85
Hayes UB4 . . . **157** BV69
Webb St, SE1 . . . **31** N7
Webheath Est, NW6 . . . **5** H6
Webley Ct, Enf. EN3
off Sten Cl . . . **105** EA37
Webster Cl, Horn. RM12 . . . **150** FK62
Oxshott KT22 . . . **236** CB114
Waltham Abbey EN9 . . . **90** EG33
Webster Gdns, W5 . . . **159** CK74
Webster Rd, E11 . . . **145** EC62
SE16 . . . **32** D7
Websters Cl, Wok. GU22 . . . **248** AU120
Wedderburn Rd, NW3 . . . **6** A3
Barking IG11 . . . **167** ER67

Wedgewood Cl, Epp. CM16 . . . **92** EU30
Northwood HA6 . . . **115** BQ52
Wedgewood Dr, Harl. CM17 . . . **74** EX16
Wedgwood Ho, SE11 . . . **30** E7
Wedgwood Ms, W1 . . . **17** P9
Wedgwood Pl, Cob. KT11 . . . **235** BU114
Wedgwoods, Tats. TN16
off Redhouse Rd . . . **260** EJ121
Wedgwood Wk, NW6
off Dresden Cl . . . **5** M3
Wedgwood Way, SE19 . . . **204** DQ94
Wedhey, Harl. CM19 . . . **73** EQ15
Wedlake Cl, Horn. RM11 . . . **150** FL60
Wedlake St, W10 . . . **14** F4
Wedmore Av, Ilf. IG5 . . . **125** EN53
Wedmore Gdns, N19 . . . **143** DK61
Wedmore Ms, N19 . . . **143** DK62
Wedmore Rd, Grnf. UB6 . . . **159** CD69
Wedmore St, N19 . . . **143** DK62
Wednesbury Gdns, Rom.
RM3 . . . **128** FM52
Wednesbury Grn, Rom. RM3
off Wednesbury Gdns . . . **128** FM52
Wednesbury Rd, Rom. RM3 . . . **128** FM52
Weech Rd, NW6 . . . **5** J1
Weedington Rd, NW5 . . . **6** G2
Weedon Cl, Chal.St.P. SL9 . . . **112** AV53
Weedon La, Amer. HP6 . . . **77** AN36
Weekes Dr, Slou. SL1 . . . **153** AP74
Weekley Sq, SW11
off Thomas Baines Rd . . . **182** DD83
Weigall Rd, SE12 . . . **186** EG84
Weighhouse St, W1 . . . **17** H9
Weighton Rd, SE20 . . . **224** DV96
Harrow HA3 . . . **117** CD53
Weihurst Gdns, Sutt. SM1 . . . **240** DD106
Weimar St, SW15 . . . **181** CY83
Weind, The, They.B. CM16 . . . **107** ES36
Weirdale Av, N20 . . . **120** DF47
Weir Est, SW12 . . . **203** DJ87
Weir Hall Av, N18 . . . **122** DR51
Weir Hall Gdns, N18 . . . **122** DR50
Weir Hall Rd, N17 . . . **122** DR50
N18 . . . **122** DR50
Weir Pl, Stai. TW18 . . . **215** BE95
Weir Rd, SW12 . . . **203** DJ87
SW19 . . . **202** DB90
Bexley DA5 . . . **209** FB87
Chertsey KT16 . . . **216** BH101
Walton-on-Thames KT12 . . . **217** BU100
Weirside Gdns, West Dr. UB7 . **156** BK74
Weir's Pas, NW1 . . . **17** P2
Weiss Rd, SW15 . . . **181** CX83
Welbeck Av, Brom. BR1 . . . **206** EG91
Hayes UB4 . . . **157** BV70
Sidcup DA15 . . . **208** EU88
Welbeck Cl, N12
off Torrington Pk . . . **120** DD50
Borehamwood WD6 . . . **100** CN41
Epsom KT17 . . . **239** CU108
New Malden KT3 . . . **221** CT99
Welbeck Rd, E6 . . . **24** E2
Barnet EN4 . . . **102** DD44
Carshalton SM5 . . . **222** DE102
Harrow HA2 . . . **138** CB60
Sutton SM1 . . . **222** DD103
Welbeck St, W1 . . . **17** J8
Welbeck Wk, Cars. SM5
off Welbeck Rd . . . **222** DE102
Welbeck Way, W1 . . . **17** J8
Sch **Welbourne Prim Sch**, N17
off High Cross Rd . . . **144** DU55
Welby St, SE5 . . . **43** H7
Welch Ho, Enf. EN3
off Beaconsfield Rd . . . **105** DX37
Welch Pl, Pnr. HA5 . . . **116** BW53
Welclose St, St.Alb. AL3 . . . **64** CC20
Welcomes Rd, Ken. CR8 . . . **258** DQ115
Welcote Dr, Nthwd. HA6 . . . **115** BR51
Welden, Slou. SL2 . . . **154** AW72
Welders La, Chal.St.P. SL9 . . . **112** AT52
Jordans HP9 . . . **112** AT52
Weldon Cl, Ruis. HA4 . . . **157** BV65
Weldon Dr, W.Mol. KT8 . . . **218** BZ98
Weldon Way, Merst. RH1 . . . **273** DK129
Weld Pl, N11 . . . **121** DH50
Welfare Rd, E15 . . . **13** K6
Welford Cl, E5
off Denton Way . . . **145** DX62
Welford Pl, SW19 . . . **201** CY91
Welham Cl, N.Mymms AL9 . . . **67** CW24
Welham Ct, N.Mymms AL9
off Dixons Hill Rd . . . **67** CW24
WELHAM GREEN, Hat. AL9 . . . **67** CV23
⇌ **Welham Green** . . . **67** CX23
Welham Manor, N.Mymms
AL9 . . . **67** CW24
Welham Rd, SW16 . . . **202** DG92
SW17 . . . **202** DG92
Welhouse Rd, Cars. SM5 . . . **222** DE102
Welkin Grn, Hem.H. HP2
off Wood End Cl . . . **63** BQ19
Wellacre Rd, Har. HA3 . . . **139** CH58
Wellan Cl, Sid. DA15 . . . **208** EV85
Welland Cl, Slou. SL3 . . . **175** BA79
Welland Gdns, Perivale UB6 . . **159** CF68
Welland Ms, E1 . . . **32** D2
Wellands, Hat. AL10 . . . **67** CU16
Wellands Cl, Brom. BR1 . . . **227** EM96
Welland St, SE10 . . . **46** E2
Well App, Barn. EN5 . . . **101** CW43
Wellbank, Tap. SL6
off Rectory Rd . . . **152** AE70
Wellbrook Rd, Orp. BR6 . . . **245** EN105
Wellbury Ter, Hem.H. HP2 . . . **63** BQ20
Wellby Cl, N9 . . . **122** DU46
Well Cl, SW16 . . . **203** DM91
Ruislip HA4
off Parkfield Cres . . . **138** BY62
Woking GU21 . . . **248** AW117
Wellclose Sq, E1 . . . **20** D10
Wellclose St, E1 . . . **32** D1
Wellcome Av, Dart. DA1 . . . **190** FM84
Coll **Wellcome Trust**, NW1 . . . **17** N4
Well Cottage Cl, E11 . . . **146** EJ59
Well Ct, EC4 . . . **19** K9
SW16 . . . **203** DM91
Wellcroft, Hem.H. HP1
off Gadebridge Rd . . . **62** BH19
Wellcroft Cl, Welw.G.C. AL7 . . . **52** DA11
Wellcroft Rd, Slou. SL1 . . . **153** AP74
Welwyn Garden City AL7 . . . **52** DA11
Welldon Cres, Har. HA1 . . . **139** CE58
Sch **Welldon Pk First Sch**, S.Har.
HA2 *off Kingsley Rd* . . . **138** CC63
Sch **Welldon Pk Mid Sch**, S.Har.
HA2 *off Wyvenhoe Rd* . . . **138** CC63
WELL END, Borwd. WD6 . . . **100** CR38
Well End Rd, Borwd. WD6 . . . **100** CQ37

Wellen Ri, Hem.H. HP3 . . . **62** BL23
Weller Cl, Amer. HP6 . . . **77** AS37
Weller Ms, Brom. BR2 . . . **226** EH98
Weller Pl, Downe BR6 . . . **245** EN111
Weller Rd, Amer. HP6 . . . **77** AS37
Wellers Cl, West. TN16 . . . **277** EQ127
Wellers Ct, Shere GU5 . . . **282** BN139
Wellers Gro, Chsht EN7 . . . **88** DU28
Weller St, SE1 . . . **31** J4
Wellesford Cl, Bans. SM7 . . . **255** CZ117
Wellesley, Harl. CM19 . . . **73** EN20
Wellesley Av, W6 . . . **181** CV76
Iver SL0 . . . **175** BF76
Northwood HA6 . . . **115** BT50
Wellesley Cl, SE7
off Wellington Gdns . . . **186** EJ78
Wellesley Ct, W9 . . . **15** N2
Sutton SM3
off Stonecot Hill . . . **221** CY102
Wellesley Ct Rd, Croy. CR0 . . . **224** DR103
Wellesley Cres, Pot.B. EN6 . . . **85** CY33
Twickenham TW2 . . . **199** CE89
Wellesley Gro, Croy. CR0 . . . **224** DR103
Wellesley Pk Ms, Enf. EN2 . . . **103** DP40
Wellesley Pas, Croy. CR0
off Wellesley Rd . . . **224** DQ103
Wellesley Path, Slou. SL1
off Wellesley Rd . . . **174** AU75
Wellesley Pl, NW1 . . . **17** N3
Tra **Wellesley Road** . . . **224** DQ103
Wellesley Rd, E11 . . . **146** EG57
E17 . . . **145** EA58
N22 . . . **121** DN54
NW5 . . . **6** G3
W4 . . . **180** CN78
Brentwood CM14 . . . **130** FW46
Croydon CR0 . . . **224** DQ102
Harrow HA1 . . . **139** CE57
Ilford IG1 . . . **147** EP61
Slough SL1 . . . **174** AU75
Sutton SM2 . . . **240** DC107
Twickenham TW2 . . . **199** CD90
Wellesley St, E1 . . . **21** J7
Wellesley Ter, N1 . . . **19** K2
Welley Av, Wrays. TW19 . . . **174** AY84
Welley Rd, Horton SL3 . . . **174** AY84
Wraysbury TW19 . . . **194** AX85
Well Fm Rd, Cat. CR3 . . . **258** DU119
Wellfield Av, N10 . . . **143** DH55
Wellfield Cl, Hat. AL10 . . . **67** CU17
Wellfield Gdns, Cars. SM5 . . . **240** DE109
Wellfield Rd, SW16 . . . **203** DL91
Hatfield AL10 . . . **67** CU16
Wellfields, Loug. IG10 . . . **107** EN41
Wellfield Wk, SW16 . . . **203** DM92
Wellfit St, SE24
off Hinton Rd . . . **183** DP83
Wellgarth, Grnf. UB6 . . . **159** CH65
Welwyn Garden City AL7 . . . **51** CY10
Wellgarth Rd, NW11 . . . **142** DB60
Well Gro, N20 . . . **120** DC45
Well Hall Par, SE9
off Well Hall Rd . . . **187** EM84
Well Hall Rd, SE9 . . . **187** EM83
Jct **Well Hall Rbt**, SE9 . . . **186** EL83
WELL HILL, Orp. BR6 . . . **247** FB107
Well Hill, Orp. BR6 . . . **247** FB107
Well Hill La, Orp. BR6 . . . **247** FB108
Well Hill Rd, Sev. TN14 . . . **247** FC107
Wellhouse La, Barn. EN5 . . . **101** CW42
Betchworth RH3 . . . **286** CQ138
Wellhouse Rd, Beck. BR3 . . . **225** DZ98
Wellhurst Cl, Orp. BR6 . . . **245** ET108
WELLING, DA16 . . . **188** EU83
⇌ **Welling** . . . **188** EU82
Welling High St, Well. DA16 . . . **188** EV83
Sch **Welling Sch**, Well. DA16
off Elsa Rd . . . **188** EV81
Wellings Ho, Hayes UB3 . . . **157** BV74
★ **Wellington Arch**, W1 . . . **29** H4
Wellington Av, E4 . . . **123** EA47
N9 . . . **122** DV48
N15 . . . **144** DT58
Hounslow TW3 . . . **198** CA85
Pinner HA5 . . . **116** BZ53
Sidcup DA15 . . . **208** EU86
Virginia Water GU25 . . . **214** AV99
Worcester Park KT4 . . . **221** CW104
Wellington Bldgs, SW1 . . . **41** H1
Wellington Cl, SE14 . . . **45** J7
W11 . . . **15** J9
Dagenham RM10 . . . **169** FC66
Walton-on-Thames KT12 . . . **217** BT102
Watford WD19 . . . **116** BZ48
Wellington Cotts, E.Hors.
KT24 . . . **267** BS129
Wellington Ct, NW8 . . . **16** A1
Ashford TW15
off Wellington Rd . . . **196** BL92
Staines TW19 *off Clare Rd* . . **196** BL87
Wellington Cres, N.Mal. KT3 . . **220** CQ97
Wellington Dr, Dag. RM10 . . . **169** FC66
Purley CR8 . . . **241** DM110
Welwyn Garden City AL7 . . . **52** DC09
Wellington Gdns, SE7 . . . **186** EJ79
Twickenham TW2 . . . **199** CD91
Wellington Gro, SE10 . . . **46** G5
Wellington Hill, High Beach
IG10 . . . **106** EG37
H **Wellington Hosp**, NW8 . . . **16** B1
Wellington Ho, Gidea Pk RM2
off Kidman Cl . . . **150** FJ55
Wellingtonia Av, Hav.at.Bow.
RM4 . . . **127** FE48
Wellington Ms, SE7 . . . **186** EJ79
SE22 . . . **184** DU84
SW16 *off Woodbourne Av* . . **203** DK90
Wellington Par, Sid. DA15 . . . **208** EU85
● **Wellington Pk Est**, NW2 . . . **141** CU61
Wellington Pas, E11 . . . **146** EG57
Wellington Pl, N2 . . . **142** DE57
NW8 . . . **16** B2
Broxbourne EN10 . . . **70** DW23
Cobham KT11 . . . **236** BZ112
Warley CM14 . . . **130** FW50
Sch **Wellington Prim Sch**, E3 . . **22** A3
E4 *off Wellington Av* . . . **123** EB47
Hounslow TW3
off Sutton La . . . **178** BZ82
Wellington Rd, E6 . . . **167** EM68
E7 . . . **13** M1
E10 . . . **145** DY60
E11 . . . **146** EG57
E17 . . . **145** DY55
NW8 . . . **6** A10
NW10 . . . **14** D3
SW19 . . . **202** DA89
W5 . . . **179** CJ76
Ashford TW15 . . . **196** BL92

Wellington Rd, Belv. DA17 . . . **188** EZ78
Bexley DA5 . . . **208** EX86
Bromley BR2 . . . **226** EJ98
Caterham CR3 . . . **258** DQ122
Croydon CR0 . . . **223** DP101
Dartford DA1 . . . **210** FJ86
Enfield EN1 . . . **104** DS42
Feltham TW14 . . . **197** BS85
Hampton TW12 . . . **199** CD91
Harrow HA3 . . . **139** CE55
London Colney AL2 . . . **83** CK26
North Weald Bassett CM16 . . **92** FA27
Orpington BR5 . . . **228** EV100
Pinner HA5 . . . **116** BZ53
St. Albans AL1 . . . **65** CH21
Tilbury RM18 . . . **193** GG83
Twickenham TW2 . . . **199** CD91
Uxbridge UB8 . . . **156** BJ67
Watford WD17 . . . **97** BV40
Wellington Rd N, Houns. TW4 . **178** BZ83
Wellington Rd S, Houns. TW4 . **178** BZ84
Wellington Row, E2 . . . **20** B2
Wellington Sq, N1 . . . **8** C8
SW3 . . . **28** E10
Wellington St, SE18 . . . **37** L9
WC2 . . . **18** B10
Gravesend DA12 . . . **213** GJ87
Hertford SG14 . . . **53** DP08
Slough SL1 . . . **174** AT75
Wellington Ter, E1 . . . **32** E2
W2 *off Notting Hill Gate* . . . **27** L1
Harrow HA1 *off West St* . . . **139** CD60
Knaphill GU21
off Victoria Rd . . . **248** AS118
Wellington Way, E3 . . . **22** A3
Horley RH6 . . . **290** DF146
Weybridge KT13 . . . **234** BN110
Welling Way, SE9 . . . **187** ER83
Welling DA16 . . . **187** ER83
Well La, SW14 . . . **200** CQ85
Harlow CM19 . . . **57** EN14
Pilgrim's Hatch CM15 . . . **130** FT41
Woking GU21 . . . **248** AW117
Wellmeade Dr, Sev. TN13 . . . **279** FH127
Wellmeadow Rd, SE6 . . . **206** EE87
SE13 . . . **206** EE86
W7 . . . **179** CG77
Wellow Wk, Cars. SM5 . . . **222** DD102
Well Pas, NW3 . . . **142** DD62
Well Path, Wok. GU21
off Well La . . . **248** AW117
Well Rd, NW3 . . . **142** DD62
Barnet EN5 . . . **101** CW43
Northaw EN6 . . . **86** DE28
Well Row, Bayford SG13 . . . **69** DM17
Wells, The, N14 . . . **121** DK45
Wells Cl, Chsht EN7
off Bloomfield Rd . . . **88** DQ25
Leatherhead KT23 . . . **252** CB124
Northolt UB5
off Yeading La . . . **158** BW69
St. Albans AL3
off Artisan Cres . . . **64** CC19
South Croydon CR2 . . . **242** DS106
Windsor SL4 . . . **173** AN81
Wells Ct, Rom. RM1
off Regarth Av . . . **149** FE58
Wells Dr, NW9 . . . **140** CR60
Wellsfield, Bushey WD23 . . . **98** BY43
Wells Gdns, Dag. RM10 . . . **149** FB64
Ilford IG1 . . . **146** EL59
Rainham RM13 . . . **169** FF65
Wells Ho Rd, NW10 . . . **160** CS71
Wellside Cl, Barn. EN5 . . . **101** CW42
Wellside Gdns, SW14
off Well La . . . **200** CQ85
Wells Ms, W1 . . . **17** M7
Wellsmoor Gdns, Brom. BR1 . . **227** EN97
Wells Pk Rd, SE26 . . . **204** DU90
Sch **Wells Pk Sch & Training Cen**,
Chig. IG7
off Lambourne Rd . . . **125** ET49
Wells Path, Hayes UB4 . . . **157** BS69
Wells Pl, SW18 . . . **202** DC87
Merstham RH1 . . . **273** DH130
Westerham TN16 . . . **277** EQ127
Sch **Wells Prim Sch**, Wdf.Grn.
IG8 *off Barclay Oval* . . . **124** EG49
Wellspring Cres, Wem. HA9 . . . **140** CP62
Wellspring Ms, SE26
off Wells Pk Rd . . . **204** DV91
Wells Ri, NW8 . . . **6** E9
Wells Rd, W12 . . . **26** A5
Bromley BR1 . . . **227** EM96
Epsom KT18 . . . **238** CN114
Guildford GU4 . . . **265** BC131
Wells Sq, WC1 . . . **18** C3
Wells St, W1 . . . **17** L7
Wellstead Av, N9 . . . **122** DW45
Wellstead Rd, E6 . . . **25** L1
Wells Ter, N4 . . . **143** DN61
Wellstones, Wat. WD17 . . . **97** BV41
Wellstones Yd, Wat. WD17
off Wellstones . . . **97** BV41
Well St, E9 . . . **10** F7
E15 . . . **13** J4
Wells Way, SE5 . . . **43** M2
SW7 . . . **28** A6
Wellswood Cl, Hem.H. HP2 . . . **63** BP19
Wells Yd S, N7 . . . **8** E2
Well Wk, NW3 . . . **142** DD63
Well Way, Epsom KT18 . . . **254** CN115
Wellwood Cl, Couls. CR5
off The Vale . . . **241** DL114
Wellwood Rd, Ilf. IG3 . . . **148** EU60
Welmar Ms, SW4 . . . **183** DK84
Welsford St, SE1 . . . **32** C10
Welsh Cl, E13 . . . **23** N3
Welshpool Ho, E8 . . . **10** D8
Welshpool St, E8 . . . **10** D8
Sch **Welsh Sch, The**, NW10
off Shakespeare Av . . . **160** CQ67
Welshside Wk, NW9
off Fryent Gro . . . **140** CS58
Welstead Way, W4 . . . **181** CT77
Welsummer Way, Chsht EN8 . . . **89** DX27
● **Weltech Business Cen**,
Welw.G.C. AL7 . . . **52** DA09
Weltje Rd, W6 . . . **181** CU78
Welton Rd, SE18 . . . **187** ES80
Welwyn Av, Felt. TW14 . . . **197** BT86
Welwyn Ct, Hem.H. HP2 . . . **62** BM16
WELWYN GARDEN CITY,
AL7 & AL8 . . . **51** CX09
⇌ **Welwyn Garden City** . . . **51** CY09
◆ **Welwyn Garden City** . . . **51** CX08
Welwyn Rd, Hert. SG14 . . . **52** DG08
Welwyn St, E2 . . . **21** H2
Welwyn Way, Hayes UB4 . . . **157** BS70

WEMBLEY, HA0 & HA9 . . . **140** CL64
★ **Wembley Arena**, Wem.
HA9 . . . **140** CN63
⊖ **Wembley Central** . . . **140** CL64
⊖ **Wembley Central** . . . **140** CL64
● **Wembley Commercial Cen**,
Wem. HA9 . . . **139** CK61
Sch **Wembley High Tech Coll**,
Wem. HA0 *off East La* . . . **139** CJ62
Wembley Hill Rd, Wem. HA9 . . **140** CM64
WEMBLEY PARK, Wem. HA9 . . **140** CM61
⊖ **Wembley Park** . . . **140** CN62
● **Wembley Pk Business Cen**,
Wem. HA9 . . . **140** CP62
Wembley Pk Dr, Wem. HA9 . . . **140** CM62
Wembley Pt, Wem. HA9 . . . **160** CP66
Sch **Wembley Prim Sch**, Wem.
HA9 *off East La* . . . **140** CL62
Wembley Rd, Hmptn. TW12 . . . **198** CA94
★ **Wembley Stadium**, Wem.
HA9 . . . **140** CN63
⇌ **Wembley Stadium** . . . **140** CM64
Wembley Way, Wem. HA9 . . . **160** CP65
Wemborough Rd, Stan. HA7 . . **117** CJ52
Wembury Ms, N6
off Wembury Rd . . . **143** DH59
Wembury Rd, N6 . . . **143** DH59
Wemyss Rd, SE3 . . . **47** L9
Wend, The, Couls. CR5 . . . **241** DK114
Croydon CR0 . . . **243** DZ111
Wendela Cl, Wok. GU22 . . . **249** AZ118
Wendela Ct, Har. HA1 . . . **139** CE62
Sch **Wendell Pk Prim Sch**, W12
off Cobbold Rd . . . **181** CT75
Wendell Rd, W12 . . . **181** CT75
Wendle Ct, SW8 . . . **42** A3
Wendle Sq, SW11 . . . **40** D6
Wendley Dr, New Haw KT15 . . **233** BF110
Wendling, NW5 . . . **6** F2
Wendling Rd, Sutt. SM1 . . . **222** DD102
Wendon St, E3 . . . **11** P8
Wendover, SE17 . . . **31** N10
Wendover Cl, Hayes UB4 . . . **158** BX70
St. Albans AL4
off Highview Gdns . . . **65** CJ15
Wendover Ct, W3 . . . **160** CP70
Wendover Dr, N.Mal. KT3 . . . **221** CT100
Wendover Gdns, Brwd. CM13 . **131** GB47
Wendover Pl, Stai. TW18 . . . **195** BD92
Wendover Rd, NW10 . . . **161** CT68
SE9 . . . **186** EK83
Bromley BR2 . . . **226** EH97
Burnham SL1 . . . **152** AH71
Staines TW18 . . . **195** BC92
Wendover Way, Bushey WD23 . . **98** CC44
Hornchurch RM12 . . . **150** FJ64
Orpington BR6
off Glendower Cres . . . **228** EU100
Welling DA16 . . . **208** EU85
Wendron Cl, Wok. GU21 . . . **248** AU118
Wendy Cl, Enf. EN1 . . . **104** DT44
Wendy Cres, Guil. GU2 . . . **264** AU132
Wendy Way, Wem. HA0 . . . **160** CL67
Wengeo La, Ware SG12 . . . **54** DV05
Wenham Gdns, Hutt. CM13
off Bannister Dr . . . **131** GC44
Wenham Ho, SW8
off Ascalon St . . . **41** L5
Wenham Pl, Hat. AL10 . . . **67** CU17
Wenlack Cl, Denh. UB9 . . . **136** BG62
Wenlock Ct, N1 . . . **19** M1
Wenlock Edge, Dor. RH4 . . . **285** CJ138
Wenlock Gdns, NW4 . . . **141** CU56
Wenlock Rd, N1 . . . **9** J10
Edgware HA8 . . . **118** CP52
Wenlock St, N1 . . . **19** K1
WENNINGTON, Rain. RM13 . . . **170** FK73
Wennington Rd, E3 . . . **21** K1
Rainham RM13 . . . **169** FG70
Wensley Av, Wdf.Grn. IG8 . . . **124** EF52
Wensley Cl, N11 . . . **120** DG51
SE9 . . . **207** EM86
Romford RM5 . . . **126** FA50
Wensleydale, Hem.H. HP2 . . . **62** BM17
Wensleydale Av, Ilf. IG5 . . . **124** EL54
Wensleydale Gdns, Hmptn.
TW12 . . . **198** CB94
Wensleydale Pas, Hmptn.
TW12 . . . **218** CA95
Wensleydale Rd, Hmptn.
TW12 . . . **198** CA93
Wensley Rd, N18 . . . **122** DV51
Wensum Way, Rick. WD3 . . . **114** BK46
Wentbridge Path, Borwd.
WD6 . . . **100** CN38
Wentland Cl, SE6 . . . **205** ED89
Wentland Rd, SE6 . . . **205** ED89
WENTWORTH, Vir.W. GU25 . . . **214** AS100
Wentworth Av, N3 . . . **120** DA52
Elstree WD6 . . . **100** CM43
Slough SL2 . . . **153** AN68
🔒 **Wentworth Av Shop Par**,
Slou. SL2
off Wentworth Av . . . **153** AN69
Wentworth Cl, N3 . . . **120** DB52
SE28 . . . **168** EX72
Ashford TW15
off Reedsfield Rd . . . **197** BP91
Gravesend DA11 . . . **213** GG92
Hayes BR2 *off Hillside La* . . . **226** EG103
Long Ditton KT6 . . . **219** CK103
Morden SM4 . . . **222** DA101
Orpington BR6 . . . **245** ES106
Potters Bar EN6
off Strafford Gate . . . **86** DA31
Ripley GU23 . . . **250** BH121
Watford WD17 . . . **97** BT38
Wentworth Cotts, Brox. EN10 . . **71** DY22
Wentworth Ct, Surb. KT6
off Culsac Rd . . . **220** CL103
Wentworth Cres, SE15 . . . **44** D5
Hayes UB3 . . . **177** BR76
Wentworth Dene, Wey. KT13 . . **235** BP106
Wentworth Dr, Dart. DA1 . . . **209** FG86
Pinner HA5 . . . **137** BU57
Virginia Water GU25 . . . **214** AT98
Watford WD19 . . . **116** BX50
Wentworth Gdns, N13 . . . **121** DP49
★ **Wentworth Golf Course**,
Vir.W. GU25 . . . **214** AT100
Wentworth Hill, Wem. HA9 . . . **140** CM60

● Wentworth Ind Ct, Slou. SL2 off Goodwin Rd 153 AN69
Wentworth Ms, E3 21 M4
W3 160 CS72
Wentworth Pk, N3 120 DA52
Wentworth Pl, Grays RM16 192 GD76
Stanmore HA7 off Greenacres Dr 117 CH51
Sch Wentworth Prim Sch, Dart. DA1 off Wentworth Dr 209 FG87
Wentworth Rd, E12 146 EK63
NW11 141 CZ58
Barnet EN5 101 CX41
Croydon CR0 223 DN101
Hertford SG13 54 DQ12
Southall UB2 178 BW77
Wentworth St, E1 20 A8
Wentworth Way, Pnr. HA5 138 BX56
Rainham RM13 169 FH69
South Croydon CR2 242 DU114
Wenvoe Av, Bexh. DA7 189 FB82
Wepham Cl, Hayes UB4 158 BX71
Wernbrook St, SE18 187 EQ79
Werndee Rd, SE25 224 DU98
Werneth Hall Rd, Ilf. IG5 147 EM55
Werrington St, NW1 17 M1
Werter Rd, SW15 181 CY84
Wescott Way, Uxb. UB8 156 BJ68
Wesleyan Pl, NW5 7 J1
Wesley Av, E16 35 P2
NW10 160 CR69
Hertford SG13 off Hale Rd 54 DR10
Hounslow TW3 178 BY82
Wesley Cl, N7 143 DM61
SE17 31 H9
Goffs Oak EN7 88 DQ28
Harrow HA2 138 CC61
Horley RH6 290 DG146
Orpington BR5 228 EW97
Reigate RH2 287 CZ135
Wesley Dr, Egh. TW20 195 BA93
Wesley Hill, Chesh. HP5 76 AP30
Wesley Rd, E10 145 EC59
NW10 160 CQ67
Hayes UB3 157 BU73
★ Wesley's Ho, EC1 19 L5
Wesley Sq, W11 14 E9
Wesley St, W1 17 H7
Wessels, Tad. KT20 255 CX121
Wessex Av, SW19 222 DA96
Wessex Cl, Ilf. IG3 147 ES58
Kingston upon Thames KT1 220 CP95
Thames Ditton KT7 219 CF103
Wessex Ct, Wem. HA9 140 CM61
Wessex Dr, Erith DA8 189 FE81
Pinner HA5 116 BY52
Wessex Gdns, NW11 141 CY60
Sch Wessex Gdns Prim Sch, NW11 off Wessex Gdns 141 CY60
Wessex Ho, SE1 32 B10
Wessex La, Grnf. UB6 159 CD68
Wessex St, E2 21 H3
Wessex Wk, Dart. DA2 off Sandringham Dr 209 FE89
Wessex Way, NW11 141 CY59
Wessonmead, SE5 off Camberwell Rd 43 K5
🔒 West 12 Shop Cen, W12 26 C4
Westacott, Hayes UB4 157 BS71
Westacott Cl, N19 143 DK60
West Acres, Amer. HP7 77 AR40
Westacres, Esher KT10 236 BZ108
WEST ACTON, W3 160 CN72
⊖ West Acton 160 CN72
Sch West Acton Prim Sch, W3 off Noel Rd 160 CP72
Westall Cl, Hert. SG13 54 DQ10
Westall Ms, Hert. SG13 off West St 54 DQ10
Westall Rd, Loug. IG10 107 EP41
Westanley Av, Amer. HP7 77 AR39
West App, Petts Wd BR5 227 EQ99
West Arbour St, E1 21 H8
Sch West Ashtead Prim Sch, Ashtd. KT21 off Taleworth Rd 254 CL120
West Av, E17 145 EB56
N3 120 DA51
NW4 141 CX57
Hayes UB3 157 BT73
Penn HP10 110 AC46
Pinner HA5 138 BZ58
Redhill RH1 288 DG140
St. Albans AL2 82 CB25
Southall UB1 158 BZ73
Wallington SM6 241 DL106
Whiteley Village KT12 235 BS109
West Av Rd, E17 145 EA56
West Bk, N16 144 DS59
Barking IG11 off Highbridge Rd 167 EP67
Dorking RH4 285 CF137
Enfield EN2 104 DQ40
Westbank Rd, Hmptn H. TW12 198 CC93
WEST BARNES, N.Mal. KT3 221 CU99
West Barnes La, SW20 221 CV96
New Malden KT3 221 CV97
Westbeech Rd, N22 143 DN55
Westbere Dr, Stan. HA7 117 CK49
Westbere Rd, NW2 4 G2
Westbourne Av, W3 160 CR72
Sutton SM3 221 CY103
Westbourne Br, W2 15 N7
Westbourne Cl, Hayes UB4 157 BV70
Westbourne Cres, W2 16 A10
Westbourne Cres Ms, W2 16 A10
Westbourne Dr, SE23 205 DX89
Brentwood CM14 130 FT49
Westbourne Gdns, W2 15 L8
WESTBOURNE GREEN, W2 15 J7
Westbourne Gro, W2 15 K9
W11 15 H10
Westbourne Gro Ms, W11 15 J9
Westbourne Gro Ter, W2 15 L8
Westbourne Ho, Houns. TW5 178 CA79
Westbourne Ms, St.Alb. AL1 off London Rd 65 CD20
⊖ Westbourne Park 15 H6
Westbourne Pk Ms, W2 15 L8
Westbourne Pk Pas, W2 15 K7
Westbourne Pk Rd, W2 15 K7
W11 14 F9
Westbourne Pk Vil, W2 15 K7
Westbourne Pl, N9 122 DV48
Sch Westbourne Prim Sch, Sutt. SM1 off Anton Cres 222 DA104
Westbourne Rd, N7 8 E5
SE26 205 DX93
Bexleyheath DA7 188 EY80
Croydon CR0 224 DT100
Feltham TW13 197 BT90
Staines TW18 196 BH94
Uxbridge UB8 157 BP70
Westbourne St, W2 16 A10
Westbourne Ter, SE23 off Westbourne Dr 205 DX89
W2 15 P8
Westbourne Ter Ms, W2 15 N8
Westbourne Ter Rd, W2 15 N7
West Br Cl, W12 off Percy Rd 161 CU74
Sch Westbridge Prim Sch, SW11 40 C6
Westbridge Rd, SW11 40 B7
WEST BROMPTON, SW10 39 L2
⇌ West Brompton 39 K1
⊖ West Brompton 39 K1
Westbrook, Maid. SL6 172 AE78
Westbrook Av, Hmptn. TW12 198 BZ94
Westbrook Cl, Barn. EN4 102 DD41
Westbrook Cres, Cockfos. EN4 102 DD41
Westbrook Dr, Orp. BR5 228 EW102
Westbrooke Cres, Well. DA16 188 EW83
Westbrooke Rd, Sid. DA15 207 ER89
Welling DA16 188 EV83
Sch Westbrooke Sch, Well. DA16 off South Gipsy Rd 188 EX83
Sch Westbrook Hay Prep Sch, Hem.H. HP1 off London Rd 61 BD24
Westbrook Rd, SE3 186 EH81
Hounslow TW5 178 BZ80
Staines TW18 off South St 195 BF92
Thornton Heath CR7 224 DR95
Westbrook Sq, Barn. EN4 off Westbrook Cres 102 DD41
West Burrowfield, Welw.G.C. AL7 51 CX11
Westbury, Chsht EN8 off Turners Hill 89 DX30
Westbury Av, N22 143 DP55
Claygate KT10 237 CF107
Southall UB1 158 CA70
Wembley HA0 160 CL66
Westbury Cl, Ruis. HA4 137 BU59
Shepperton TW17 off Burchetts Way 217 BP100
Whyteleafe CR3 off Station App 258 DU118
Westbury Dr, Brwd. CM14 130 FV47
Westbury Gro, N12 120 DA51
Sch Westbury Ho Sch, N.Mal. KT3 off Westbury Rd 220 CR99
Westbury La, Buck.H. IG9 124 EJ47
Westbury Lo Cl, Pnr. HA5 138 BX55
Westbury Par, SW12 off Balham Hill 203 DH86
Westbury Pl, Brent. TW8 179 CK79
Westbury Ri, Harl. CM17 74 EX16
Westbury Rd, E7 146 EH64
E17 145 EA56
N11 121 DL51
N12 120 DA51
SE20 225 DX95
W5 160 CL72
Barking IG11 167 ER67
Beckenham BR3 225 DY97
Brentwood CM14 130 FW47
Bromley BR1 226 EK95
Buckhurst Hill IG9 124 EJ47
Croydon CR0 224 DR100
Feltham TW13 198 BX88
Ilford IG1 147 EM61
New Malden KT3 220 CR98
Northwood HA6 115 BS49
Watford WD18 97 BV43
Wembley HA0 160 CL66
Westbury St, SW8 41 L9
Westbury Ter, E7 166 EH65
Upminster RM14 151 FS61
Westerham TN16 277 EQ127
Westbush Cl, Hodd. EN11 55 DZ14
WEST BYFLEET, KT14 234 BH113
⇌ West Byfleet 234 BG112
Sch West Byfleet Comm Inf Sch, W.Byf. KT14 off Camphill Rd 234 BH112
Sch West Byfleet Jun Sch, W.Byf. KT14 off Camphill Rd 234 BH112
Westcar La, Hersham KT12 235 BV107
West Carriage Dr, W2 28 B3
West Cen St, WC1 18 A8
West Cen Av, W10 off Harrow Rd 161 CV69
West Chantry, Har. HA3 off Chantry Rd 116 CB53
Westchester Dr, NW4 141 CX55
WEST CLANDON, Guil. GU4 266 BH129
Westcliffe Apts, W2 16 B7
West Cl, N9 122 DT48
Ashford TW15 196 BL91
Barnet EN5 101 CV43
Cockfosters EN4 102 DG42
Greenford UB6 158 CC68
Hampton TW12 off Oak Av 198 BY93
Hoddesdon EN11 71 EA16
Rainham RM13 169 FH70
Wembley HA9 140 CM60
Westcombe Av, Croy. CR0 223 DL100
Westcombe Ct, SE3 47 L4
Westcombe Dr, Barn. EN5 102 DA43
Westcombe Hill, SE3 47 P2
SE10 47 N1
Westcombe Lo Dr, Hayes UB4 157 BR71
⇌ Westcombe Park 47 P1
Westcombe Pk Rd, SE3 47 K3
West Common, Ger.Cr. SL9 134 AX57
West Common Cl, Ger.Cr. SL9 134 AY57
West Common Rd, Brom. BR2 226 EG103
Keston BR2 244 EH105
Uxbridge UB8 136 BK64
Westcoombe Av, SW20 221 CT95
Westcote Ri, Ruis. HA4 137 BQ59
Westcote Rd, SW16 203 DJ92
Epsom KT19 238 CP111
WESTCOTT, Dor. RH4 284 CC138
Westcott, Welw.G.C. AL7 52 DD08
West Cotts, NW6 5 K3
Westcott Av, Nthflt DA11 213 GG90
Westcott Cl, N15 144 DT58
Bromley BR1 226 EL99
New Addington CR0 off Castle Hill Av 243 EB109
Sch Westcott C of E First Sch, Westc. RH4 off School La 285 CD137
Westcott Common, Westc. RH4 284 CB138
Westcott Cres, W7 159 CE72
Westcott Ho, E14 22 B10
Westcott Keep, Horl. RH6 off Langshott La 291 DJ147
Westcott Rd, SE17 42 G2
Dorking RH4 285 CE137
Westcott St, Westc. RH4 284 CB137
Westcott Way, Sutt. SM2 239 CW110
WESTCOURT, Grav. DA12 213 GL89
West Ct, SE18 off Prince Imperial Rd 187 EM81
Westcourt, Sun. TW16 217 BV96
West Ct, Wem. HA0 139 CJ61
Coll Westcourt Cen, The, Grav. DA12 off Jubilee Cres 213 GL89
Sch Westcourt Prim Sch, Grav. DA12 off Silver Rd 213 GL89
West Cres, Wind. SL4 173 AM81
West Cres Rd, Grav. DA12 213 GH86
Westcroft, Slou. SL2 153 AP70
Westcroft Cl, NW2 4 F2
Enfield EN3 104 DW38
Westcroft Ct, Brox. EN10 71 EA19
Westcroft Gdns, Mord. SM4 221 CZ97
Westcroft Rd, Cars. SM5 240 DG105
Wallington SM6 240 DG105
Westcroft Sq, W6 181 CU77
Westcroft Way, NW2 141 CY63
West Cromwell Rd, SW5 27 J9
W14 26 G10
● West Cross Cen, Brent. TW8 179 CG79
West Cross Route, W10 14 C10
W11 14 C10
West Cross Way, Brent. TW8 179 CH79
⇌ West Croydon 224 DQ102
Tra West Croydon 224 DQ102
⊖ West Croydon 224 DQ102
Westdale Pas, SE18 187 EP79
Westdale Rd, SE18 187 EP79
Westdean Av, SE12 206 EH88
Westdean Cl, SW18 202 DB85
Westdene, Hersham KT12 235 BV105
West Dene, Sutt. SM3 off Park La 239 CY107
West Dene Dr, Rom. RM3 128 FK50
Sch West Dene Sch, Pur. CR8 off Brighton Rd 241 DM114
Westdene Way, Wey. KT13 217 BS104
West Down, Bkhm KT23 268 CB127
Westdown Rd, E15 145 EC63
SE6 205 EA87
WEST DRAYTON, UB7 176 BK76
⇌ West Drayton 156 BL74
West Drayton Pk Av, West Dr. UB7 176 BL76
Sch West Drayton Prim Sch, West Dr. UB7 off Kingston La 176 BL75
West Drayton Rd, Hayes End UB8 157 BP71
Uxbridge UB8 156 BM72
West Dr, SW16 203 DJ91
Carshalton SM5 240 DD110
Cheam SM2 239 CX109
Harrow HA3 117 CD51
Tadworth KT20 255 CX118
Virginia Water GU25 214 AT101
Watford WD25 97 BV36
West Dr Gdns, Har. HA3 117 CD51
WEST DULWICH, SE21 204 DR90
⇌ West Dulwich 204 DR88
⇌ West Ealing 159 CH73
West Eaton Pl, SW1 28 G8
West Eaton Pl Ms, SW1 28 G8
Wested La, Swan. BR8 229 FG101
West Ella Rd, NW10 160 CS66
WEST END, Esher KT10 236 BZ107
WEST END, Hat. AL9 68 DC18
West End Av, E10 145 EC57
Pinner HA5 138 BX56
West End Cl, NW10 160 CQ66
West End Ct, Pnr. HA5 138 BX56
Stoke Poges SL2 154 AT67
West End Gdns, Esher KT10 236 BZ106
Northolt UB5 158 BW68
West End La, NW6 5 K9
Barnet EN5 101 CX42
Esher KT10 236 BZ107
Essendon AL9 68 DC18
Harlington UB3 177 BQ80
Pinner HA5 138 BX55
Stoke Poges SL2 154 AS67
West End Rd, Brox. EN10 70 DS23
Northolt UB5 158 BW66
Ruislip HA4 137 BV64
Southall UB1 158 BY74
Westerdale, Hem.H. HP2 62 BL17
Westerdale Rd, SE10 47 N1
Westerfield Rd, N15 144 DT57
Westerfolds Cl, Wok. GU22 249 BC116
Westergate Rd, SE2 188 EY79
WESTERHAM, TN16 277 EQ126
Westerham Av, N9 122 DR48
Westerham Cl, Add. KT15 234 BJ107
Sutton SM2 240 DA110
Westerham Dr, Sid. DA15 208 EV86
Westerham Hill, West. TN16 261 EN121
Westerham Rd, E10 145 EB58
Keston BR2 244 EK107
Oxted RH8 276 EF129
Sevenoaks TN13 278 FC123
Westerham TN16 277 EM128
● Westerham Trade Cen, West. TN16 off The Flyer's Way 277 ER126
Westerley Cres, SE26 205 DZ92
Westerley Ware, Rich. TW9 off Kew Grn 180 CN79
Westermain, New Haw KT15 234 BJ110
Western Av, NW11 141 CX58
W3 160 CR71
W5 160 CM69
Brentwood CM14 130 FW46
Chertsey KT16 216 BG97
Dagenham RM10 169 FC65
Denham UB9 136 BJ63
Egham TW20 215 BB97
Epping CM16 91 ET32
Greenford UB6 159 CF69
Western Av, Ickhm UB10 157 BP65
Northolt UB5 158 BZ67
Romford RM2 128 FJ54
Ruislip HA4 157 BP65
● Western Av Business Pk, W3 off Mansfield Rd 160 CP70
Western Av Underpass, W5 off Western Av 160 CM69
Western Beach Apts, E16 35 N2
Western Cl, Cher. KT16 off Western Av 216 BG97
Western Ct, N3 off Huntly Dr 120 DA51
Western Cross Cl, Green. DA9 off Johnsons Way 211 FW86
Western Dr, Shep. TW17 217 BR100
Wooburn Green HP10 132 AE58
H Western Eye Hosp, NW1 16 E6
Western Gdns, W5 160 CN73
Brentwood CM14 130 FW47
Western Gateway, E16 35 N1
Sch Western Ho Sch, Slou. SL1 off Richards Way 153 AL74
🔒 Western Int Mkt, Sthl. UB2 177 BV77
Western La, SW12 202 DG87
Western Ms, W9 15 H5
Western Par, New Barn. EN5 off Great N Rd 102 DA43
Reigate RH2 off Prices La 288 DB137
Western Pathway, Horn. RM12 170 FJ65
Western Perimeter Rd, Lon.Hthrw Air. TW6 176 BH83
Western Pl, SE16 33 H4
Western Rd, E13 166 EJ67
E17 145 EC57
N2 142 DF56
N22 121 DM54
NW10 160 CQ70
SW9 183 DN83
SW19 222 DD95
W5 159 CK73
Brentwood CM14 130 FW47
Epping CM16 91 ET32
Lower Nazeing EN9 72 EE22
Mitcham CR4 222 DD95
Romford RM1 149 FE57
Southall UB2 178 BX76
Sutton SM1 240 DA106
Western Ter, W6 off Chiswick Mall 181 CU78
● Western Trd Est, NW10 160 CQ70
Western Vw, Hayes UB3 177 BT75
Westernville Gdns, Ilf. IG2 147 EQ59
Western Way, SE28 187 ER76
Barnet EN5 102 DA44
WEST EWELL, Epsom KT19 238 CS108
Sch West Ewell Inf Sch, W.Ewell KT19 off Ruxley La 238 CR106
West Fm Av, Ashtd. KT21 253 CJ118
West Fm Cl, Ashtd. KT21 253 CJ119
West Fm Dr, Ashtd. KT21 253 CK119
DLR Westferry 22 A10
Westferry Circ, E14 34 A2
Westferry Rd, E14 33 P2
WESTFIELD, Wok. GU22 249 AZ122
Westfield, Abin.Ham. RH5 283 BS143
Ashtead KT21 254 CM118
Harlow CM18 73 ES16
Hatfield AL9 68 DA23
Loughton IG10 106 EJ43
Reigate RH2 272 DB131
Sevenoaks TN13 279 FJ122
Welwyn Garden City AL7 52 DA08
Westfield Av, S.Croy. CR2 242 DR113
Watford WD24 98 BW37
Woking GU22 248 AY121
Westfield Cl, NW9 140 CQ55
SW10 39 N5
Enfield EN3 105 DY41
Gravesend DA12 213 GJ93
Sutton SM1 239 CZ105
Waltham Cross EN8 89 DZ31
Westfield Common, Wok. GU22 248 AY122
Sch Westfield Comm Prim Sch, Hodd. EN11 off Westfield Rd 71 DZ16
Sch Westfield Comm Tech Coll, Wat. WD18 off Tolpits La 97 BT44
Westfield Ct, St.Alb. AL4 65 CK17
Westfield Dr, Bkhm KT23 252 CA122
Harrow HA3 139 CK57
Sch Westfield First Sch, Berk. HP4 off Durrants La 60 AT18
Westfield Gdns, Dor. RH4 off Westcott Rd 285 CG136
Harrow HA3 139 CK56
Romford RM6 148 EW58
Westfield Gro, Wok. GU22 248 AY120
Westfield La, Geo.Grn SL3 154 AX73
Harrow HA3 139 CK57
🔒 Westfield London, W12 26 C3
Westfield Par, New Haw KT15 234 BK110
Westfield Pk, Pnr. HA5 116 BZ52
Westfield Pk Dr, Wdf.Grn. IG8 124 EL51
Sch Westfield Prim Sch, Wok. GU22 off Bonsey La 248 AY121
Westfield Rd, NW7 118 CR48
W13 159 CG74
Beaconsfield HP9 110 AJ54
Beckenham BR3 225 DZ96
Berkhamsted HP4 60 AS17
Bexleyheath DA7 189 FC82
Croydon CR0 223 DP103
Dagenham RM9 148 EY63
Guildford GU1 264 AY130
Hertford SG14 53 DP07
Hoddesdon EN11 71 DZ16
Mitcham CR4 222 DF96
Slough SL2 153 AP70
Surbiton KT6 219 CK99
Sutton SM1 239 CZ105
Walton-on-Thames KT12 218 BY101
Woking GU22 248 AX122
Westfields, SW13 181 CT83
St. Albans AL3 64 CA22
Westfields Av, SW13 180 CS83
Westfields Rd, W3 160 CP71
Westfield St, SE18 36 E7
Westfield Wk, Wal.Cr. EN8 89 DZ31
Westfield Way, E1 21 L3
Ruislip HA4 137 BS62
Woking GU22 248 AY122
⊖ West Finchley 120 DB51
West Gdn Pl, W2 16 D9
West Gdns, E1 32 F1
SW17 202 DE93
Epsom KT17 238 CS110
Westgate, E16 23 P10
West Gate, W5 160 CL69
Harlow CM20 73 EQ15
Westgate Cl, Epsom KT18 off Chalk La 254 CR115
Westgate Ct, SW9 off Canterbury Cres 183 DN83
Waltham Cross EN8 off Holmesdale 105 DX35
Westgate Cres, Slou. SL1 153 AM73
● Westgate Est, Felt. TW14 196 BN88
Sch Westgate Prim Sch, Dart. DA1 off Summerhill Rd 210 FK87
🔒 Westgate Retail Pk, Slou. SL1 153 AN73
Westgate Rd, SE25 224 DV98
Beckenham BR3 225 EB96
Dartford DA1 210 FK86
Sch Westgate Sch, Slou. SL1 off Cippenham La 153 AN74
Westgate St, E8 10 E8
Westgate Ter, SW10 39 M1
Westglade Ct, Har. HA3 139 CK57
West Gorse, Croy. CR0 243 DY112
WEST GREEN, N15 144 DQ55
West Grn Pl, Grnf. UB6 off Uneeda Dr 159 CD67
Sch West Grn Prim Sch, N15 off Woodlands Pk Rd 144 DQ56
West Grn Rd, N15 143 DP56
West Gro, SE10 46 F6
Hersham KT12 235 BV105
Woodford Green IG8 124 EJ51
Westgrove La, SE10 46 F6
Sch West Gro Prim Sch, N14 off Chase Rd 121 DK45
West Halkin St, SW1 28 G6
West Hallowes, SE9 206 EK88
Westhall Pk, Warl. CR6 258 DW119
West Hall Rd, Rich. TW9 180 CP81
Westhall Rd, Warl. CR6 258 DV119
WEST HAM, E15 13 M7
⇌ West Ham 23 K2
⊖ West Ham 23 K2
Sch West Ham Ch Prim Sch, E15 13 L8
West Ham La, E15 13 J7
West Ham Pk, E7 13 N6
WEST HAMPSTEAD, NW6 5 L3
⊖ West Hampstead 5 K5
⊖ West Hampstead 5 L5
West Hampstead Ms, NW6 5 L5
⇌ West Hampstead (Thameslink) 5 K4
★ West Ham United FC, E13 166 EJ68
West Harding St, EC4 18 F8
West Harold, Swan. BR8 229 FD97
WEST HARROW, Har. HA1 138 CC59
⊖ West Harrow 138 CC58
Sch West Hatch High Sch, Chig. IG7 off High Rd 125 EM50
West Hatch Manor, Ruis. HA4 137 BT60
Westhay Gdns, SW14 200 CP85
WEST HEATH, SE2 188 EX79
West Heath, Oxt. RH8 276 EG130
West Heath Av, NW11 142 DA60
West Heath Cl, NW3 142 DA62
Dartford DA1 off West Heath Rd 209 FF86
West Heath Dr, NW11 142 DA60
West Heath Gdns, NW3 142 DA61
West Heath La, Sev. TN13 279 FH128
West Heath Rd, NW3 142 DA61
SE2 188 EW79
Dartford DA1 209 FF86
WEST HENDON, NW9 140 CS59
West Hendon Bdy, NW9 141 CT58
● West Herts Business Cen, Borwd. WD6 off Brook Rd 100 CP41
Coll West Herts Coll, Cassio Campus, Wat. WD17 off Langley Rd 97 BU38
Dacorum Campus, Hem.H. HP1 off Marlowes 62 BJ19
Watford Campus, Wat. WD17 off Hempstead Rd 97 BU41
West Hill, SW15 201 CX87
SW18 202 DA85
Dartford DA1 210 FK86
Downe BR6 245 EM112
Epsom KT19 238 CQ113
Harrow HA2 139 CE61
Oxted RH8 275 ED130
South Croydon CR2 242 DS110
Wembley HA9 140 CM60
West Hill Av, Epsom KT19 238 CQ112
West Hill Bk, Oxt. RH8 275 ED130
Westhill Cl, Grav. DA12 off Leith Pk Rd 213 GH88
West Hill Ct, N6 142 DG62
West Hill Dr, Dart. DA1 210 FJ86
West Hill Pk, N6 142 DF61
Sch West Hill Prim Sch, SW18 off Merton Rd 202 DA85
Dartford DA1 off Dartford Rd 210 FJ86
Westhill Ri, Dart. DA1 210 FK86
West Hill Rd, SW18 202 DA86
Westhill Rd, Hodd. EN11 71 DZ16
West Hill Rd, Wok. GU22 248 AX119
Sch West Hill Sch, Lthd. KT22 off Kingston Rd 253 CG118
West Hill Way, N20 120 DB46
Westholm, NW11 142 DB56
West Holme, Erith DA8 189 FC81
Westholme, Orp. BR6 227 ES101
Westholme Gdns, Ruis. HA4 137 BU60
Westhorne Av, SE9 206 EJ86
SE12 206 EG87
Westhorpe Gdns, NW4 141 CW55
Westhorpe Rd, SW15 181 CW83
WEST HORSLEY, Lthd. KT24 267 BP127
West Ho Cl, SW19 201 CY88
WESTHUMBLE, Dor. RH5 269 CG131
Westhumble St, Westh. RH5 269 CH131
Westhurst Dr, Chis. BR7 207 EP92
WEST HYDE, Rick. WD3 113 BE52
West Hyde La, Chal.St.P. SL9 113 AZ52
West India Av, E14 34 A2
West India Dock Rd, E14 21 P9
DLR West India Quay 34 C1
⊖ West Kensington 26 G10
West Kensington Ct, W14 26 G10
West Kent Av, Nthflt DA11 212 GC86
● West Kent Cold Storage, Dunt.Grn TN14 263 FF120
WEST KILBURN, W9 14 G2
Westlake Cl, N13 121 DN48
Hayes UB4 off Lochan Cl 158 BY70
Westlake Rd, Wem. HA9 139 CK61

Westland Av, Horn. RM11 . . . . **150** FL60
Westland Cl, Lvsdn WD25 . . . . . **81** BT34
Stanwell TW19. . . . . **196** BL86
Westland Dr, Brom. BR2 . . . . **226** EF103
Brookmans Park AL9 . . . . **85** CY27
Westland Ho, E16
off Rymill St. **37** L3
Westland Pl, N1 . . . . **19** L2
Westland Rd, Wat. WD17 . . . . . **97** BV40
Westlands Av, Slou. SL1 . . . . . **152** AJ72
Westlands Cl, Hayes UB3. . . . **177** BU77
Slough SL1
off Westlands Av **152** AJ72
Westlands Ct, Epsom KT18 . . . **254** CQ115
Westlands Ter, SW12
off Gaskarth Rd. **203** DJ86
Westlands Way, Oxt. RH8. . . . **275** ED127
West La, SE16. . . . . **32** E5
Abinger Hammer RH5 . . . . . **284** BX139
Westlea Av, Wat. WD25. . . . . . . **98** BY37
Westlea Cl, Brox. EN10. . . . . . . **71** DZ24
Westlea Rd, W7. . . . . **179** CG76
Broxbourne EN10. . . . . **71** DZ23
Westleas, Horl. RH6 . . . . **290** DE146
Sch **West Lea Sch**, N9
off Haselbury Rd. **122** DS48
Westlees Cl, N.Holm. RH5 . . . . **285** CJ139
Westleigh Av, SW15 . . . . **201** CV85
Coulsdon CR5 . . . . **256** DG116
Westleigh Dr, Brom. BR1 . . . . **226** EL95
Westleigh Gdns, Edg. HA8. . . . **118** CN53
● **Westlinks**, Wem. HA0
off Alperton La **159** CK68
Westlinton Cl, NW7. . . . . **119** CY51
West Lo Av, W3. . . . . **160** CN74
Sch **West Lo First Sch**, Pnr. HA5
off West End La. **138** BX56
Sch **West Lo Mid Sch**, Pnr. HA5
off West End La. **138** BX56
Sch **West Lo Sch**, Sid. DA15
off Station Rd **208** EU90
Sch **West London Acad**, Nthlt.
UB5 *off Compton Cres*. **158** BY67
Coll **West London Coll**, W1 . . . . . **17** H9
Westlyn Cl, Rain. RM13 . . . . . . **170** FJ69
Westly Wd, Welw.G.C. AL7. . . . . **52** DA08
Westmacott Dr, Felt. TW14. . . . **197** BT88
West Mall, W8. . . . . **27** K2
West Malling Way, Horn.
RM12 . . . . **150** FJ64
Westmark Pt, SW15
off Norley Vale. **201** CV88
Westmead, SW15 . . . . **201** CV86
West Mead, Epsom KT19. . . . . **238** CS107
Ruislip HA4 . . . . **138** BW63
Welwyn Garden City AL7. . . . . **52** DB12
Westmead, Wind. SL4 . . . . **173** AP83
Woking GU21 . . . . **248** AV117
Westmead Cor, Cars. SM5
off Colston Av **240** DE105
Westmead Dr, Red. RH1. . . . . . **288** DG142
Westmeade Cl, Chsht EN7. . . . . **88** DV29
Westmead Rd, Sutt. SM1. . . . . **240** DD105
West Meads, Guil. GU2 . . . . . . **280** AT135
Horley RH6 . . . . **291** DJ148
Westmede, Chig. IG7 . . . . **125** EQ51
Westmere Dr, NW7. . . . . **118** CR48
West Mersea Cl, E16. . . . . **36** A3
West Ms, N17 . . . . **122** DV51
SW1 . . . . **29** K9
H **West Middlesex Uni Hosp**,
Islw. TW7 . . . . **179** CG82
West Mill, Grav. DA11. . . . . **213** GF86
WESTMINSTER, SW1. . . . . **29** L6
⊖ **Westminster** **30** B5
★ **Westminster Abbey**, SW1 . . . **30** A6
Sch **Westminster Abbey Choir Sch**,
SW1 . . . . **29** P6
★ **Westminster Abbey Mus**,
SW1 . . . . **30** A6
Sch **Westminster Acad**, W2. . . . . **15** K6
Coll **Westminster Adult Ed Service**,
Amberley Rd Cen, W9 . . . . . . **15** L5
Ebury Br Cen, SW1. . . . . **29** J10
Frith St Cen, W1 . . . . **17** P9
Westminster Av, Th.Hth. CR7. . **223** DP96
Westminster Br, SE1 . . . . **30** B5
SW1 . . . . **30** B5
Westminster Br Rd, SE1. . . . . . . **30** D5
● **Westminster Business Sq**,
SE11 *off Durham St* **42** C1
★ **Westminster Cath**, SW1 . . . . **29** L7
Sch **Westminster Cath Choir Sch**,
SW1 . . . . **29** M7
Sch **Westminster Cath RC Prim Sch**,
SW1 . . . . **29** P10
★ **Westminster City Hall**,
SW1 . . . . **29** M6
Sch **Westminster City Sch**,
SW1 . . . . **29** M6
Westminster Cl, Felt. TW14 . . . **197** BU88
Ilford IG6 . . . . **125** ER54
Teddington TW11. . . . . **199** CG92
Westminster Ct, St.Alb. AL1 . . . **64** CC22
Waltham Cross EN8
off Eleanor Way. **89** DZ33
Westminster Dr, N13 . . . . **121** DL50
Westminster Gdns, E4. . . . . . . **124** EE46
SW1 . . . . **30** A8
Barking IG11 . . . . **167** ES68
Ilford IG6 . . . . **125** EQ54
Coll **Westminster Kingsway Coll**,
Castle La Cen, SW1 . . . . **29** M6
Kentish Town Cen, NW5. . . . . . **7** J4
Kings Cross Cen, WC1 . . . . . . **18** C3
Peter St Cen, W1 . . . . **17** N10
Regent's Pk Cen, NW1 . . . . . . **17** L4
Vincent Sq Cen, SW1. . . . . **29** N8
Riv **Westminster Millennium
Pier**. **30** B4
Westminster Palace Gdns, SW1
off Artillery Row **29** N7
Westminster Rd, N9. . . . . **122** DV46
W7 . . . . **159** CE74
Sutton SM1 . . . . **222** DD103
Sch **Westminster Sch**, SW1 . . . . **30** A6
Sch **Westminster Under Sch**,
SW1 . . . . **29** N9
Westmoat Cl, Beck. BR3. . . . . **205** EC94
WEST MOLESEY, KT8 . . . . **218** BZ99
Westmont Rd, Esher KT10. . . . **219** CE103
Westmoor Gdns, Enf. EN3. . . . **105** DX40
Westmoor Rd, Enf. EN3 . . . . . . **105** DX40
Westmoor St, SE7 . . . . **36** D7
Westmore Grn, Tats. TN16 . . . **260** EJ121
Westmoreland Av, Horn.
RM11 . . . . **150** FJ57
Welling DA16. . . . . **187** ES83
Westmoreland Dr, Sutt. SM2. . **240** DB109
● **Westmoreland Pl**, Brom.
BR1. **226** EG97
Westmoreland Pl, SW1 . . . . **41** K1
W5 . . . . **159** CK71
Westmoreland Rd, NW9. . . . . . **140** CN56
SE17. **43** K2
SW13 . . . . **181** CT81
Bromley BR1, BR2 . . . . **226** EE99
Westmoreland St, W1. . . . . **17** H7
Westmoreland Ter, SE20 . . . . . **204** DV94
SW1 . . . . **41** K1
Westmoreland Wk, SE17 . . . . . **43** M2
Westmore Rd, Tats. TN16 . . . . **260** EJ121
Westmorland Cl, E12 . . . . **146** EK61
Epsom KT19 . . . . **238** CS110
Twickenham TW1 . . . . **199** CH86
Westmorland Rd, E17. . . . . . . **145** EA58
Harrow HA1. . . . . **138** CB57
Westmorland Sq, Mitch. CR4
off Westmorland Way **223** DL99
Westmorland Way, Mitch.
CR4. **223** DK98
West Mt, Guil. GU2
off The Mount **280** AW136
Westmount Apts, Wat. WD18
off Linden Av. **97** BT42
Westmount Av, Amer. HP7 . . . . **77** AQ39
Westmount Rd, SE9. . . . . **187** EM82
WEST NORWOOD, SE27 . . . . . **204** DQ90
⇌ **West Norwood** **203** DP90
West Oak, Beck. BR3 . . . . **225** ED95
Westoe Rd, N9 . . . . **122** DV47
Weston Av, Add. KT15 . . . . . . **234** BG105
Grays RM20. . . . . **191** FT77
Thames Ditton KT7. . . . . **219** CE101
West Molesey KT8 . . . . **218** BY97
Weston Cl, Couls. CR5 . . . . . . **257** DM120
Godalming GU7 . . . . **280** AS144
Hutton CM13. . . . . **131** GC45
Potters Bar EN6. . . . . **85** CZ32
Weston Ct, N4 *off Queens Dr* . **144** DQ62
N20 *off Farnham Cl* **120** DC45
Weston Dr, Cat. CR3. . . . . **258** DQ122
Stanmore HA7. . . . . **117** CH53
🔒 **West One Shop Cen**, W1 . . . **17** H9
Weston Flds, Albury GU5. . . . . **282** BJ139
Weston Gdns, Islw. TW7. . . . . . **179** CD81
Woking GU22 . . . . **249** BE116
WESTON GREEN, T.Ditt. KT7 . . **219** CF102
Weston Grn, Dag. RM9. . . . . . . **148** EZ63
Thames Ditton KT7. . . . . **219** CE102
Weston Grn Rd, Esher KT10. . . . **219** CD102
Thames Ditton KT7. . . . . **219** CE102
Weston Gro, Brom. BR1 . . . . . . **226** EF95
Weston Lea, W.Hors. KT24. . . . **267** BR125
Weston Pk, N8 . . . . **143** DL58
Kingston upon Thames KT1
off Clarence St **220** CL96
Thames Ditton KT7. . . . . **219** CE102
Weston Pk Cl, T.Ditt. KT7 . . . . **219** CE102
Sch **Weston Pk Prim Sch**, N8
off Denton Rd **143** DM57
Weston Ri, WC1. . . . . **18** D1
Weston Rd, W4 . . . . **180** CQ76
Bromley BR1. . . . . **206** EF94
Dagenham RM9 . . . . **148** EY63
Enfield EN2 . . . . **104** DR39
Epsom KT17 . . . . **238** CS111
Guildford GU2. . . . . **264** AV133
Slough SL1 . . . . **153** AM71
Thames Ditton KT7. . . . . **219** CE102
Weston St, SE1. . . . . **31** M5
Weston Wk, E8 . . . . **10** F7
Weston Way, Wok. GU22 . . . . . **249** BE116
Weston Yd, Albury GU5 . . . . . . **282** BJ139
Westover Cl, Sutt. SM2 . . . . . . **240** DB109
Westover Hill, NW3 . . . . **142** DA61
Westover Rd, SW18 . . . . **202** DC86
Westow Hill, SE19. . . . . **204** DS93
Westow St, SE19 . . . . **204** DS93
West Palace Gdns, Wey. KT13 . **217** BP104
West Pk, SE9. . . . . **206** EL89
West Pk Av, Rich. TW9 . . . . . . **180** CN81
West Pk Cl, Houns. TW5. . . . . . **178** BZ79
Romford RM6 . . . . **148** EX57
West Pk Hill, Brwd. CM14 . . . . **130** FU48
H **West Pk Hosp**, Epsom
KT19. . . . . **238** CM112
West Pk Rd, Epsom KT19. . . . . **238** CM112
Richmond TW9 . . . . **180** CN81
Southall UB2 . . . . **158** CC74
West Parkside, SE10. . . . . **35** M7
Warlingham CR6. . . . . **259** EA115
West Pier, E1 . . . . **32** E3
● **West Pl**, Harl. CM20 . . . . **58** EU12
West Pl, SW19. . . . . **201** CW92
West Pt, SE1 . . . . **32** C10
Slough SL1 . . . . **153** AK74
Westpoint Apts, N8
off Turnpike La. **143** DM56
West Pt Cl, Houns. TW4 . . . . . **178** BZ83
● **Westpoint Trd Est**, W3 . . . . **160** CP71
Westpole Av, Cockfos. EN4 . . . **102** DG42
Westport Rd, E13 . . . . **24** A5
Westport St, E1. . . . . **21** K8
West Poultry Av, EC1 . . . . **18** G7
West Quarters, W12 . . . . **161** CU72
West Quay Dr, Hayes UB4 . . . . **158** BY71
West Ramp, Lon.Hthrw Air.
TW6 . . . . **176** BN81
Westray, Hem.H. HP3. . . . . **63** BQ22
Westridge Cl, Chesh. HP5 . . . . . **76** AM30
Hemel Hempstead HP1 . . . . . . **61** BF20
West Ridge Gdns, Grnf. UB6 . . **158** CC68
West Riding, Brick.Wd AL2 . . . . **82** BZ30
West Rd, E15. . . . . **13** M9
N17. **122** DV51
SW3 . . . . **40** F1
SW4 . . . . **203** DK85
W5 . . . . **160** CL71
Barnet EN4 . . . . **120** DG46
Berkhamsted HP4. . . . . **60** AU18
Chadwell Heath RM6 . . . . **148** EX58
Chessington KT9. . . . . **237** CJ112
Feltham TW14 . . . . **197** BR86
Guildford GU1. . . . . **280** AY135
Harlow CM20 . . . . **58** EU11
Kingston upon Thames KT2. **220** CQ95
Reigate RH2. . . . . **288** DB135
Rush Green RM7. . . . . **149** FD59
South Ockendon RM15. . . . . . **171** FV69
West Drayton UB7 . . . . **176** BM76
Weybridge KT13 . . . . **235** BP109
Westrow, SW15. . . . . **201** CW85
West Row, W10. . . . . **14** E4
Westrow Dr, Bark. IG11 . . . . . . **167** ET65
Westrow Gdns, Ilf. IG3. . . . . . . **147** ET61
⇌ **West Ruislip** **137** BQ61
⊖ **West Ruislip** **137** BQ61
West Shaw, Long. DA3 . . . . . . **231** FX96
West Sheen Vale, Rich. TW9. . . **180** CM84
Westside, NW4 . . . . **119** CV54
West Side, Turnf. EN10
off High Rd Turnford. **89** DY25
Westside Apts, Ilf. IG1
off Roden St **147** EN62
● **West Side Business Cen**,
Harl. CM19. . . . . **72** EL16
West Side Common, SW19 . . . **201** CW92
DLR **West Silvertown** **35** P3
West Smithfield, EC1 . . . . **18** G7
West Spur Rd, Uxb. UB8 . . . . . **156** BK69
West Sq, SE11. . . . . **30** G7
Harlow CM20 . . . . **57** EQ14
Iver SL0 *off High St* **155** BF72
West St, E2 . . . . **20** F1
E11 . . . . **146** EE62
E17 . . . . **145** EB57
WC2 . . . . **17** P9
Bexleyheath DA7 . . . . **188** EZ84
Brentford TW8. . . . . **179** CJ79
Bromley BR1. . . . . **226** EG95
Carshalton SM5 . . . . **222** DF104
Croydon CR0. . . . . **242** DQ105
Dorking RH4 . . . . **285** CG136
Epsom KT18 . . . . **238** CR113
Erith DA8 . . . . **189** FD77
Ewell KT17. . . . . **238** CS110
Gravesend DA11 . . . . **213** GG86
Grays RM17. . . . . **192** GA79
Harrow HA1. . . . . **139** CD60
Hertford SG13. . . . . **54** DQ10
Reigate RH2. . . . . **271** CY133
Sutton SM1 . . . . **240** DB106
Ware SG12. . . . . **55** DX06
Watford WD17. . . . . **97** BV40
Woking GU21
off Church St E **249** AZ117
West St La, Cars. SM5 . . . . **240** DF105
⇌ **West Sutton** **240** DA105
West Temple Sheen, SW14 . . . **180** CP84
West Tenter St, E1. . . . . **20** B9
Coll **West Thames Coll**, Islw. TW7
off London Rd. **179** CE81
Feltham Skills Cen, Felt. TW13
off Boundaries Rd. **198** BX88
● **West Thamesmead Business
Pk**, SE28. . . . . **187** ET76
Sch **West Thornton Prim Sch**, Croy.
CR0 *off Rosecourt Rd* **223** DM100
WEST THURROCK, Grays
RM20 . . . . **191** FU78
Sch **West Thurrock Prim Sch**, W.Thur.
RM20 *off The Rookery* **191** FU79
West Thurrock Way, Grays
RM20 . . . . **191** FT77
WEST TILBURY, Til. RM18 . . . **193** GL79
West Twrs, Pnr. HA5 . . . . **138** BX58
Sch **West Twyford Prim Sch**, NW10
off Twyford Abbey Rd. **160** CN68
Westvale Ms, W3. . . . . **160** CS74
West Valley Rd, Hem.H. HP3 . . . **80** BJ25
West Vw, NW4 . . . . **141** CW56
Ashtead KT21 . . . . **253** CJ119
Chesham HP5 . . . . **76** AR29
Feltham TW14 . . . . **197** BQ87
Hatfield AL10. . . . . **67** CU16
Loughton IG10. . . . . **107** EM41
West Vw Av, Whyt. CR3
off Station Rd **258** DT118
Westview Cl, NW10 . . . . **141** CT64
W7 . . . . **159** CE72
W10 . . . . **14** B8
Rainham RM13 . . . . **170** FJ69
Redhill RH1 . . . . **288** DE136
West Vw Ct, Els. WD6
off High St. **99** CK44
Westview Cres, N9. . . . . **122** DS45
Westview Dr, Wdf.Grn. IG8 . . . **124** EK54
West Vw Gdns, Els. WD6
off High St **99** CK44
Westview Ri, Hem.H. HP2 . . . . . **62** BK19
West Vw Rd, Crock. BR8 . . . . . **229** FD100
Dartford DA1 . . . . **210** FM86
St. Albans AL3. . . . . **65** CD19
Swanley BR8. . . . . **229** FG98
Westview Rd, Warl. CR6. . . . . . **258** DV119
Westville Rd, W12. . . . . **181** CU75
Thames Ditton KT7. . . . . **219** CG102
West Wk, W5 . . . . **160** CL71
East Barnet EN4 . . . . **120** DG45
Harlow CM20 . . . . **57** EQ14
Hayes UB3. . . . . **157** BU74
West Walkway, The, Sutt. SM1
off Cheam Rd **240** DB106
Westward Ho, Guil. GU1 . . . . . **265** AZ132
Sch **Westward Prep Sch**, Walt.
KT12 *off Hersham Rd*. **217** BV103
Westward Rd, E4 . . . . **123** DZ50
Westward Way, Har. HA3. . . . . **140** CL58
West Warwick Pl, SW1 . . . . **29** L9
WEST WATFORD, Wat. WD18. . . **97** BU42
🔒 **Westway**, Rom. RM1
off South St. **149** FE57
West Way, N18 . . . . **122** DR49
NW10. . . . . **140** CR62
Westway, SW20 . . . . **221** CV97
W2 . . . . **15** J6
W9 . . . . **15** J6
W10 . . . . **14** F8
W12 . . . . **161** CU73
West Way, Beac. HP9 . . . . **110** AF54
Brentwood CM14 . . . . **130** FU48
Carshalton SM5 . . . . **240** DD110
Westway, Cat. CR3. . . . . **258** DR122
West Way, Croy. CR0 . . . . **225** DY103
Edgware HA8. . . . . **118** CP51
Westway, Gat. RH6. . . . . **291** DH152
Guildford GU2. . . . . **264** AT132
West Way, Houns. TW5. . . . . . **178** BZ81
Petts Wood BR5. . . . . **227** ER99
Pinner HA5 . . . . **138** BX56
Rickmansworth WD3. . . . . **114** BH46
Ruislip HA4 . . . . **137** BT60
Shepperton TW17 . . . . **217** BR100
West Wickham BR4. . . . . **225** ED100
Westway Cl, SW20. . . . . **221** CV97
West Way Gdns, Croy. CR0 . . . **225** DX103
Westway Gdns, Red. RH1 . . . . **272** DG131
Westways, Epsom KT19. . . . . . **239** CT105
Westerham TN16. . . . . **277** EQ126
🔒 **Westway Shop Pk**, Grnf.
UB6 . . . . **159** CE67
Westwell Cl, Orp. BR5 . . . . **228** EX102
Westwell Rd, SW16 . . . . **203** DL93
Westwell Rd App, SW16
off Westwell Rd. **203** DL93
Westwick Cl, Hem.H. HP2 . . . . . **63** BR21
Westwick Gdns, W14 . . . . **26** C5
Hounslow TW4 . . . . **177** BV82
WEST WICKHAM, BR4 . . . . **225** EC103
⇌ **West Wickham** **225** EC101
Westwick Pl, Wat. WD25. . . . . . . **82** BW34
Westwick Row, Hem.H. HP2 . . . **63** BR20
Sch **West Wimbledon Prim Sch**,
SW20 *off Bodnant Gdns* . . **221** CV97
Westwood Av, SE19 . . . . **224** DQ95
Brentwood CM14 . . . . **130** FU49
Harrow HA2. . . . . **138** CB63
Woodham KT15 . . . . **233** BF112
Westwood Cl, Amer. HP6. . . . . . **94** AX39
Bromley BR1 . . . . **226** EK97
Esher KT10. . . . . **218** CC104
Potters Bar EN6. . . . . **86** DA30
Ruislip HA4 . . . . **137** BP58
Sch **Westwood Coll**, Well. DA16
off The Green. **187** ES84
Westwood Ct, Guil. GU2
off Hillcrest Rd **264** AT133
Westwood Dr, Amer. HP6 . . . . . **94** AX39
Westwood Gdns, SW13. . . . . . **181** CT83
Westwood Hill, SE26 . . . . **204** DU92
Westwood La, Sid. DA15 . . . . . **208** EU85
Welling DA16. . . . . **187** ET83
Sch **Westwood Language Coll
for Girls**, SE19
off Spurgeon Rd **204** DR94
Westwood Pk, SE23. . . . . **204** DV87
● **Westwood Pk Trd Est**, W3 . **160** CN71
Westwood Pl, SE26 . . . . **204** DU91
Westwood Rd, E16. . . . . **36** A3
SW13 . . . . **181** CT83
Coulsdon CR5 . . . . **257** DK118
Ilford IG3 . . . . **147** ET60
Southfleet DA13 . . . . **212** FY93
West Woodside, Bex. DA5 . . . . **208** EY87
Westwood Way, Sev. TN13. . . . **278** FF122
West Yoke, Ash TN15. . . . . **231** FX103
Wetheral Dr, Stan. HA7 . . . . . . **117** CH53
Wetherall Ms, St.Alb. AL1
off Watsons Wk **65** CE21
Wetherby Cl, Nthlt. UB5. . . . . . **158** CB65
Wetherby Gdns, SW5. . . . . **27** N9
Wetherby Ms, SW5. . . . . **27** L10
Wetherby Pl, SW7. . . . . **27** N9
Sch **Wetherby Pre-Prep Sch**,
W2 . . . . **27** K1
Wetherby Rd, Borwd. WD6 . . . **100** CL39
Enfield EN2 . . . . **104** DQ39
Wetherby Way, Chess. KT9 . . . **238** CL108
Wetherden St, E17 . . . . **145** DZ59
Wethered Dr, Burn. SL1. . . . . . **152** AH71
Wetherell Rd, E9 . . . . **11** K8
Wetherill Rd, N10 . . . . **120** DG53
Wetherly Cl, Harl. CM17. . . . . . . **58** EZ11
★ **Wetland Cen, The**, SW13 . . **181** CV80
Wettern Cl, S.Croy. CR2
off Purley Oaks Rd **242** DS110
Wetton Pl, Egh. TW20. . . . . **195** AZ92
Wexfenne Gdns, Wok. GU22 . . **250** BH116
Wexford Rd, SW12 . . . . **202** DF87
Sch **Wexham Ct Prim Sch**, Wexham
SL3 *off Church La* **154** AW71
Wexham Lo, Wexham SL2. . . . . **154** AV71
H **Wexham Pk Hosp**, Slou.
SL2. **154** AW70
Wexham Pk La, Wexham SL3 . **154** AW70
Wexham Pl, Wexham SL2 . . . . **154** AX65
Wexham Rd, Slou. SL1, SL2 . . **154** AV71
Sch **Wexham Sch**, Slou. SL2
off Norway Dr **154** AW71
● **Wexham Springs**, Wexham
SL2. **154** AW66
WEXHAM STREET, Slou. SL3 . **154** AW67
Wexham St, Slou. SL2, SL3. . . **154** AW67
Wexham Wds, Wexham SL3 . . **154** AW71
Wey Av, Cher. KT16. . . . . **216** BG97
Weybank, Wisley GU23 . . . . . . **250** BL116
Wey Barton, Byfleet KT14 . . . . **234** BM113
Weybourne Pl, S.Croy. CR2 . . . **242** DR110
Weybourne St, SW18. . . . . **202** DC89
WEYBRIDGE, KT13 . . . . **234** BN105
⇌ **Weybridge** **234** BN107
● **Weybridge Business Pk**,
Add. KT15 . . . . **234** BL105
Weybridge Ct, SE16 . . . . **44** D1
H **Weybridge Hosp**, Wey.
KT13. . . . . **234** BN105
Weybridge Pk, Wey. KT13. . . . **234** BN106
Weybridge Pt, SW11. . . . . **40** F8
Weybridge Rd, Add. KT15 . . . . **216** BK104
Thornton Heath CR7. . . . . **223** DN98
Weybridge KT13 . . . . **216** BL104
Weybrook Dr, Guil. GU4 . . . . . **265** BB129
Wey Cl, W.Byf. KT14
off Broadoaks Cres **234** BH113
Wey Ct, Epsom KT19 . . . . **238** CQ105
New Haw KT15. . . . . **234** BK109
Weydown Cl, SW19 . . . . **201** CY88
Guildford GU2. . . . . **264** AU129
Weydown La, Guil. GU2
off Cumberland Av **264** AU129
Sch **Weyfield Prim Sch**, Guil. GU1
off School Cl **264** AX131
Weyhill Rd, E1. . . . . **20** D8
Sch **Wey Ho Sch**, Bramley GU5
off Horsham Rd. **280** AY143
Weylands Cl, Walt. KT12. . . . . . **218** BZ102
Weylands Pk, Wey. KT13 . . . . . **235** BR107
Wey La, Chesh. HP5 . . . . **76** AP32
Weylea Av, Guil. GU4. . . . . **265** BA131
Weylond Rd, Dag. RM8 . . . . . . **148** EZ62
Wey Manor Rd, New Haw
KT15. . . . . **234** BK109
Weyman Rd, SE3 . . . . **186** EJ81
Weymead Cl, Cher. KT16 . . . . . **216** BJ102
Wey Meadows, Wey. KT13. . . . **234** BL106
Weymede, Byfleet KT14. . . . . . **234** BM112
Weymouth Av, NW7 . . . . **118** CS50
W5 . . . . **179** CJ76
Weymouth Cl, E6 . . . . **25** N9
Weymouth Ct, Sutt. SM2. . . . . . **240** DA108
Weymouth Dr, Chaff.Hun.
RM16 . . . . **191** FX78
Weymouth Ho, SW8. . . . . **42** C5
Weymouth Ms, W1. . . . . **17** J6
Weymouth Rd, Hayes UB4 . . . . **157** BS69
Weymouth St, W1. . . . . **17** H7
Hemel Hempstead HP3 . . . . . . **62** BK24
Weymouth Ter, E2. . . . . **10** B10
Weymouth Wk, Stan. HA7 . . . . **117** CG51
🔒 **Wey Retail Pk**, Byfleet
KT14. . . . . **234** BL112
Wey Rd, Wey. KT13. . . . . **216** BM104
Weyside Cl, Byfleet KT14 . . . . **234** BM112
Weyside Gdns, Guil. GU1 . . . . **264** AV132
Weyside Rd, Guil. GU1. . . . . . . **264** AV132
Weystone Rd, Wey. KT13
off Weybridge Rd **234** BM105
Weyver Ct, St.Alb. AL1
off Avenue Rd **65** CE19
● **Weyvern Pk**, Peasm. GU3
off Old Portsmouth Rd. . . . **280** AV142
Weyview Cl, Guil. GU1. . . . . . . **264** AW132
Wey Vw Ct, Guil. GU1
off Walnut Tree Cl **280** AW135
Whadcote St, N4. . . . . **143** DN61
Whaddon Ho, SE22
off Albrighton Rd **184** DS83
Whalebone Av, Rom. RM6. . . . **148** EZ58
Whalebone Ct, EC2. . . . . **19** L8
Whalebone Gro, Rom. RM6. . . **148** EZ58
Whalebone La, E15. . . . . **13** J7
Whalebone La N, Rom. RM6 . . **148** EY57
Whalebone La S, Dag. RM8. . . **148** EZ59
Romford RM6 . . . . **148** EZ59
Whales Yd, E15 . . . . **13** J7
Whaley Rd, Pot.B. EN6. . . . . **86** DC33
Wharfdale Cl, N11 . . . . **120** DG51
Wharfdale Ct, E5
off Pedro St **145** DX63
Wharfdale Rd, N1 . . . . **8** B10
Wharfedale, Hem.H. HP2 . . . . . . **62** BL17
Wharfedale Gdns, Th.Hth.
CR7. **223** DM98
Wharfedale Rd, Dart. DA2 . . . . **210** FQ88
Wharfedale St, SW10. . . . . **39** L1
Wharf Ho, Erith DA8
off West St. **189** FE78
Wharf La, E14 . . . . **21** N9
Rickmansworth WD3. . . . . **114** BL46
Ripley GU23 . . . . **250** BJ118
Send GU23 . . . . **249** BC123
Twickenham TW1 . . . . **199** CG88
Wharf Pl, E2. . . . . **10** D9
Wharf Rd, N1. . . . . **9** J10
N1 (King's Cross) **8** A10
Brentwood CM14 . . . . **130** FW48
Broxbourne EN10. . . . . **71** DZ23
Enfield EN3 . . . . **105** DY44
Gravesend DA12. . . . . **213** GL86
Grays RM17. . . . . **192** FZ79
Guildford GU1. . . . . **264** AW134
Hemel Hempstead HP1 . . . . . . **62** BH22
Wraysbury TW19. . . . . **194** AW87
Wharf Rd S, Grays RM17. . . . . **192** FZ79
Wharfside Cl, Erith DA8 . . . . . **189** FF78
Wharfside Rd, E16 . . . . **23** J7
Wharf St, E16 . . . . **23** J7
Wharley Hook, Harl. CM18. . . . . **73** ET18
Wharncliffe Dr, Sthl. UB1 . . . . . **159** CD74
Wharncliffe Gdns, SE25 . . . . . **224** DS96
Wharncliffe Rd, SE25 . . . . **224** DS96
Wharton Cl, NW10 . . . . **160** CS65
Wharton Cotts, WC1
off Wharton St. **18** D3
Wharton Rd, Brom. BR1. . . . . . **226** EH95
Wharton St, WC1 . . . . **18** D3
Whateley Cl, Guil. GU2 . . . . . . **264** AV129
Whateley Rd, SE20. . . . . **205** DX94
SE22. **204** DT85
Whatley Av, SW20 . . . . **221** CY97
Whatman Rd, SE23 . . . . **205** DX87
Whatmore Cl, Stai. TW19. . . . . **196** BG86
Wheatash Rd, Add. KT15 . . . . . **216** BH103
Wheatbarn, Welw.G.C. AL7 . . . . **52** DB08
Wheatbutts, The, Eton Wick
SL4. . . . . **173** AM77
Wheat Cl, Sand. AL4. . . . . **65** CG16
Wheatcroft, Chsht EN7. . . . . . . **88** DV28
Wheatcroft Ct, Sutt. SM1
off Cleeve Way **222** DB102
Sch **Wheatcroft Sch**, Hert. SG13
off Stanstead Rd. **54** DU08
Wheatfield, Hat. AL10
off Stonecross Rd. **67** CV17
Hemel Hempstead HP2 . . . . . . **62** BK18
Wheatfields, E6. . . . . **25** N8
Enfield EN3 . . . . **105** DY40
Harlow CM17. . . . . **58** EW09
Sch **Wheatfields Inf & Nurs Sch**,
St.Alb. AL4 *off Downes Rd* . **65** CH16
Sch **Wheatfields Jun Sch**, St.Alb.
AL4 *off Downes Rd*. **65** CH16
Wheatfield Way, Horl. RH6. . . . **291** DH147
Kingston upon Thames KT1. **220** CL96
WHEATHAMPSTEAD, St.Alb.
AL4. . . . . **50** CL06
Wheathill Rd, SE20. . . . . **224** DV97
Wheat Knoll, Ken. CR8. . . . . . . **258** DQ116
Wheatland Ho, SE22
off Albrighton Rd **184** DS83
Wheatlands, Houns. TW5. . . . . **178** CA79
Wheatlands Rd, SW17
off Stapleton Rd **202** DG90
Slough SL3 . . . . **174** AV76
Wheatley Cl, NW4. . . . . **119** CU54
Greenhithe DA9
off Steele Av **211** FU85
Hornchurch RM11 . . . . **150** FK58
Sawbridgeworth CM21 . . . . . . **58** EW06
Welwyn Garden City AL7. . . . . **52** DA11
Wheatley Cres, Hayes UB3 . . . **157** BU73
Wheatley Dr, Wat. WD25 . . . . . **82** BW34
Wheatley Gdns, N9. . . . . **122** DS47
Wheatley Ho, SW15
off Tangley Gro **201** CU87
Wheatley Rd, Islw. TW7 . . . . . . **179** CF83
Welwyn Garden City AL7. . . . . **51** CZ10
Wheatleys, St.Alb. AL4. . . . . . . **65** CJ18
Wheatleys Eyot, Sun. TW16. . . **217** BU99
Wheatley St, W1. . . . . **17** H7
Wheatley Ter Rd, Erith DA8 . . . **189** FF79
Wheatley Way, Chal.St.P. SL9. . **112** AY51
Wheat Sheaf Cl, E14. . . . . **34** C8
Wheatsheaf Cl, Nthlt. UB5. . . . **138** BY64
Ottershaw KT16 . . . . **233** BD107
Woking GU21 . . . . **248** AY116
Wheatsheaf Hill, Halst. TN14 . . **246** EZ109
Wheatsheaf La, SW6 . . . . **38** B4
SW8 . . . . **42** B4
Staines TW18. . . . . **195** BF94
Wheatsheaf Rd, Hunsdon
SG12 . . . . **56** EK06
Romford RM1 . . . . **149** FF58
Wheatsheaf Ter, SW6. . . . . **39** H5
Wheatstone Cl, Mitch. CR4 . . . **222** DE95
Slough SL3 . . . . **174** AU76

Wheatstone Rd, W10 14 F6
Erith DA8 189 FD78
Wheeler Av, Oxt. RH8 275 ED129
Penn HP10 110 AC47
Wheeler Cl, Wdf.Grn. IG8
off Chigwell Rd 125 EM50
Wheeler Gdns, N1 8 B8
Wheeler Pl, Brom. BR2 226 EH98
Wheelers, Epp. CM16 91 ET29
Wheelers Cl, Lwr Naze. EN9 72 EE22
Wheelers Cross, Bark. IG11 167 ER68
Wheelers Dr, Ruis. HA4
off Wallington Cl 137 BQ58
Wheelers Fm Gdns, N.Wld Bas.
CM16 93 FB26
Wheelers La, Brock. RH3 286 CP136
Epsom KT18 238 CP113
Hemel Hempstead HP3 62 BL22
Smallfield RH6 291 DN149
Wheelers Orchard, Chal.St.P.
SL9 112 AY51
Wheel Fm Dr, Dag. RM10 149 FC62
Wheelock Cl, Erith DA8 189 FB80
Wheelwright Cl, Bushey WD23
off Ashfield Av 98 CB44
Wheelwright St, N7 8 C6
Whelan Way, Wall. SM6 223 DK104
Wheler St, E1 20 A5
Whellock Rd, W4 180 CS76
WHELPLEY HILL, Chesh. HP5 78 AX26
Whelpley Hill Pk, Whel.Hill HP5 78 AX26
Whenman Av, Bex. DA5 209 FC89
Whernside Cl, SE28 168 EW73
Wherwell Rd, Guil. GU2 280 AW136
WHETSTONE, N20 120 DB47
Whetstone Cl, N20
off Oakleigh Rd N 120 DD47
Whetstone Pk, WC2 18 C8
Whetstone Rd, SE3 186 EJ82
Whewell Rd, N19 143 DL61
Whichcote Gdns, Chesh. HP5 76 AR33
Whichcote St, SE1 30 E3
Whichert Cl, Knot.Grn HP9 110 AJ49
Whidborne Cl, SE8 46 B9
Whidborne St, WC1 18 B3
Whielden Cl, Amer. HP7 77 AP40
Whielden Gate, Winch.Hill HP7 77 AL43
Whielden Grn, Amer. HP7 77 AP40
Whielden Hts, Amer. HP7 77 AN41
Whielden La, Amer. HP7 77 AL43
Whielden St, Amer. HP7 77 AN41
Whieldon Gra, Ch.Lang. CM17 74 EY16
Whiffins Orchard, Cooper.
CM16 92 EX29
Whimbrel Cl, SE28 168 EW73
South Croydon CR2 242 DR111
Whimbrel Way, Hayes UB4 158 BX72
Whinchat Rd, SE28 187 ER76
Whinfell Cl, SW16 203 DK92
Whinfell Way, Grav. DA12 213 GM91
Whinneys Rd, Loud. HP10 110 AC52
Whinyates Rd, SE9 186 EL83
Whipley Cl, Guil. GU4
off Weybrook Dr 265 BB129
Whippendell Cl, Orp. BR5 228 EV95
Whippendell Hill, Kings L. WD4 80 BJ30
Whippendell Rd, Wat. WD18 97 BU43
Whippendell Way, Orp. BR5 228 EV95
Jct Whipps Cross, E17 145 ED57
Whipps Cross Rd, E11 145 ED57
H Whipps Cross University
Hospital, E11 145 ED58
Whiskin St, EC1 18 G3
Whisperwood, Loud. WD3 96 BH41
Whisperwood Cl, Har. HA3 117 CE52
Whistler Gdns, Edg. HA8 118 CM54
Whistler Ms, SE15 44 B5
Dagenham RM8
off Fitzstephen Rd 148 EV64
Whistlers Av, SW11 40 B5
Whistlers Ct, Wold. CR3 275 ED125
Whistler St, N5 8 G2
Whistler Twr, SW10 39 P4
Whistler Wk, SW10
off Blantyre St 39 P4
Whiston Rd, E2 10 A10
Whitacre Ms, SE11 42 F1
Whitakers Way, Loug. IG10 107 EM39
Whitbread Cl, N17 122 DU53
Whitbread Rd, SE4 185 DY84
Whitburn Rd, SE13 185 EB84
Whitby Av, NW10 160 CP69
Whitby Cl, Bigg.H. TN16 260 EH119
Greenhithe DA9 211 FU85
Whitby Ct, N7 8 B1
Whitby Gdns, NW9 140 CN55
Sutton SM1 222 DD103
Whitby Rd, SE18 37 J8
Harrow HA2 138 CC62
Ruislip HA4 137 BV62
Slough SL1 153 AQ73
Sutton SM1 222 DD103
Whitby St, E1 20 A4
Whitcher Cl, SE14 45 L3
Whitcher Pl, NW1 7 L5
Whitchurch Av, Edg. HA8 118 CM52
Whitchurch Cl, Edg. HA8 118 CM51
Sch Whitchurch First & Mid Schs,
Stan. HA7
off Wemborough Rd 117 CK52
Whitchurch Gdns, Edg. HA8 118 CM51
Whitchurch La, Edg. HA8 117 CK52
Whitchurch Rd, W11 14 D10
Romford RM3 128 FK49
Whitcomb Ct, WC2
off Whitcomb St 29 P1
Whitcomb St, WC2 29 P1
Whitcome Ms, Rich. TW9 180 CP81
Whiteadder Way, E14 34 D8
Whitear Wk, E15 13 H4
White Av, Nthflt DA11 213 GF90
Whitebarn La, Dag. RM10 168 FA67
Whitebeam Av, Brom. BR2 227 EN100
Whitebeam Cl, SW9 42 D5
Shenley WD7
off Mulberry Gdns 84 CM33
Waltham Cross EN7 88 DS26
Whitebeam Dr, Reig. RH2 288 DB137
South Ockendon RM15 171 FW69
Whitebeam Ho, NW3
off Maitland Pk Rd 6 F4
Whitebeams, Hat. AL10 67 CU21
White Beams, Park St AL2 82 CC28
White Beam Way, Tad. KT20 255 CU121
White Bear Pl, NW3
off New End Sq 142 DD63
Whiteberry Rd, Dor. RH5 284 CB143
White Br Av, Mitch. CR4 222 DD98
Whitebridge Cl, Felt. TW14 197 BT86
Sch White Br Comm Inf Sch, The,
Loug. IG10
off Greensted Rd 125 EM45
Sch White Br Jun Sch, The, Loug.
IG10 off Greensted Rd 125 EM45
Whitebroom Rd, Hem.H. HP1 61 BE18
WHITE BUSHES, Red. RH1 289 DH139
White Butts Rd, Ruis. HA4 138 BX62
WHITECHAPEL, E1 20 C9
⊖ Whitechapel 20 E6
★ Whitechapel Art Gall, E1 20 B8
Whitechapel High St, E1 20 B8
Whitechapel Rd, E1 20 C8
White Ch La, E1 20 C8
White Ch Pas, E1 20 C8
⊖ White City 26 B1
⊖ White City 26 B2
White City Cl, W12 26 A1
White City Est, W12 161 CV73
White City Rd, W12 14 A10
White Cl, Slou. SL1 153 AR74
White Conduit St, N1 8 F10
Whitecote Rd, Sthl. UB1 158 CB72
White Craig Cl, Pnr. HA5 116 CA50
Whitecroft, Horl. RH6
off Woodhayes 291 DH147
St. Albans AL1 65 CH23
Swanley BR8 229 FE96
Whitecroft Cl, Beck. BR3 225 ED98
Whitecroft Way, Beck. BR3 225 EC99
Whitecross Pl, EC2 19 M6
Whitecross St, EC1 19 K4
★ White Cube, N1
off Hoxton Sq 19 N3
★ White Cube, SW1 29 M2
White Down Rd, Dor. RH5 284 BW135
Whitefield Av, NW2 141 CW59
Purley CR8 257 DN116
Whitefield Cl, SW15 201 CY86
Orpington BR5 228 EW97
Sch Whitefield Sch, NW2
off Claremont Rd 141 CX59
Sch Whitefield Schs & Cen, E17
off Macdonald Rd 123 ED54
Whitefields Rd, Chsht EN8 88 DW28
Whitefoot La, Brom. BR1 205 EC91
Whitefoot Ter, Brom. BR1 206 EE90
Whiteford Rd, Slou. SL2 154 AS71
White Friars, Sev. TN13 278 FG127
Whitefriars Av, Har. HA3 117 CE54
Whitefriars Dr, Har. HA3 117 CD54
Sch Whitefriars First & Mid Sch,
Wealds. HA3
off Whitefriars Av 117 CE54
Whitefriars St, EC4 18 F9
White Gdns, Dag. RM10 168 FA65
Whitegate Gdns, Har. HA3 117 CF52
White Gates, Horn. RM12 150 FJ61
Whitegates, Whyt. CR3
off Court Bushes Rd 258 DU119
Woking GU22 off Loop Rd 249 AZ120
Whitegates Cl, Crox.Grn WD3 96 BN42
Whitegate Way, Tad. KT20 255 CV120
Whitehall, SW1 30 A2
White Hall, Abridge RM4
off Market Pl 108 EV41
Whitehall Cl, Borwd. WD6 100 CN42
Chigwell IG7 126 EU48
Lower Nazeing EN9 72 EE22
Uxbridge UB8 156 BJ67
Whitehall Ct, SW1 30 A3
Whitehall Cres, Chess. KT9 237 CK106
Whitehall Fm La, Vir.W. GU25 214 AY96
Whitehall Gdns, E4 124 EE46
SW1 30 A3
W3 160 CN74
W4 180 CP79
Sch Whitehall Inf Sch, Uxb.
UB8 off Cowley Rd 156 BJ67
Sch Whitehall Jun Sch, Uxb.
UB8 off Cowley Rd 156 BJ68
Whitehall La, Buck.H. IG9 124 EG47
Egham TW20 195 AZ94
Erith DA8 189 FF82
Grays RM17 192 GC78
South Park RH2 287 CZ138
Wraysbury TW19 195 BA86
Whitehall Pk, N19 143 DJ60
Whitehall Pk Rd, W4 180 CP79
Whitehall Pl, E7 13 P2
SW1 30 A3
Wallington SM6
off Bernard Rd 241 DH105
Sch Whitehall Prim Sch, E4
off Normanton Pk 124 EE47
Whitehall Rd, E4 124 EE47
W7 179 CG75
Bromley BR2 226 EK99
Grays RM17 192 GC77
Harrow HA1 139 CE59
Thornton Heath CR7 223 DN99
Uxbridge UB8 156 BK67
Woodford Green IG8 124 EE47
Jct Whitehall Rbt, Harl. CM19 73 EM16
Whitehall St, N17 122 DT52
Whitehands Cl, Hodd. EN11 71 DZ17
White Hart Av, SE18 187 ET76
SE28 187 ET76
White Hart Cl, Ch.St.G. HP8 112 AU48
Sevenoaks TN13 279 FJ128
White Hart Ct, EC2 19 N7
Ripley GU23 250 BJ121
White Hart Dr, Hem.H. HP2 62 BM21
⇌ White Hart Lane 122 DT52
White Hart La, N17 122 DR52
N22 121 DN53
NW10 off Church Rd 161 CT65
SW13 180 CS83
Romford RM7 126 FA53
White Hart Meadow, Beac.
HP9 111 AL54
White Hart Meadows, Ripley
GU23 250 BJ121
White Hart Rd, SE18 187 ES77
Hemel Hempstead HP2 62 BN21
Orpington BR6 228 EU101
Slough SL1 173 AR76
Jct White Hart Rbt, Nthlt.
UB5 158 BX68
White Hart Row, Cher. KT16
off Heriot Rd 216 BG101
White Hart Slip, Brom. BR1
off Market Sq 226 EG96
White Hart St, EC4 19 H8
SE11 30 F10
White Hart Wd, Sev. TN13 279 FJ129
White Hart Yd, SE1 31 L3
Gravesend DA11
off High St 213 GH86
Whitehaven, Slou. SL1 154 AT73
Whitehaven Cl, Brom. BR2 226 EG98
Goffs Oak EN7 88 DS28
Whitehaven St, NW8 16 C5
Whitehead Cl, N18 122 DR50
SW18 202 DC87
Dartford DA2 210 FJ90
Whitehead's Gro, SW3 28 D10
Whiteheart Av, Uxb. UB8 157 BQ71
Whiteheath Av, Ruis. HA4 137 BQ59
Sch Whiteheath Inf Sch, Ruis.
HA4 off Ladygate La 137 BP58
Sch Whiteheath Jun Sch, Ruis.
HA4 off Whiteheath Av 137 BP58
White Hedge Dr, St.Alb. AL3 64 CC19
White Heron Ms, Tedd. TW11 199 CF93
White Hill, Beac. HP9 132 AG55
Whitehill, Berk. HP4 60 AX18
White Hill, Chesh. HP5 76 AQ31
Chipstead CR5 256 DC124
Hemel Hempstead HP1 61 BF21
Northwood HA6 114 BN51
Rickmansworth WD3 114 BN51
South Croydon CR2
off St. Mary's Rd 242 DR109
Whitehill, Welw. AL6 51 CU05
Whitehill Cl, Berk. HP4
off Whitehill 60 AX18
White Hill Cl, Chesh. HP5 76 AQ30
Whitehill Ct, Berk. HP4
off Whitehill 60 AX18
Sch Whitehill Infants' & Nurs Sch,
Grav. DA12 off Sun La 213 GJ90
Sch Whitehill Jun Sch, Grav.
DA12 off Sun La 213 GJ90
White Hill La, Bletch. RH1 274 DR127
Whitehill La, Grav. DA12 213 GK90
Ockham GU23 251 BQ123
Whitehill Par, Grav. DA12 213 GJ90
Whitehill Pl, Vir.W. GU25 214 AY99
White Hill Rd, Berk. HP4 60 AV21
Chesham HP5 78 AX26
Whitehill Rd, Dart. DA1 209 FG85
Gravesend DA12 213 GJ89
Longfield DA3 231 FX96
Southfleet DA13 231 FX96
Whitehills Rd, Loug. IG10 107 EN41
White Horse All, EC1 18 G6
White Horse Dr, Epsom KT18 238 CQ114
White Horse Hill, Chis. BR7 207 EN91
White Horse La, E1 21 J5
Whitehorse La, SE25 224 DR98
White Horse La, Lon.Col. AL2 84 CL25
Ripley GU23 250 BJ121
Sch Whitehorse Manor Inf &
Jun Schs, Th.Hth. CR7
off Whitehorse Rd 224 DR98
White Horse Ms, SE1 30 F6
White Horse Rd, E1 21 L9
E6 25 K2
Whitehorse Rd, Croy. CR0 224 DR100
Thornton Heath CR7 224 DR100
White Horse Rd, Wind. SL4 173 AK83
White Horse St, W1 29 J3
White Horse Yd, EC2 19 L8
Whitehouse Apts, SE1
off Belvedere Rd 30 D3
Whitehouse Av, Borwd. WD6 100 CP41
White Ho Cl, Chal.St.P. SL9 112 AY52
Whitehouse Cl, Woob.Grn
HP10 110 AE54
White Ho Dr, Guil. GU1 265 BB134
Stanmore HA7 117 CJ49
Whitehouse La, Bedmond
WD5 81 BV26
White Ho La, Enf. EN2
off Brigadier Hill 104 DQ39
Jacobs Well GU4 264 AX129
Sevenoaks TN14 278 FF130
Whitehouse La, Woob.Grn
HP10 110 AE54
White Ho Rd, Sev. TN14 278 FF130
Whitehouse Way, N14 121 DH47
Iver SL0 155 BD69
Slough SL3 174 AW76
Whitehurst Dr, N18 123 DX51
White Kennett St, E1 19 P8
White Knights Rd, Wey. KT13 235 BQ108
White Knobs Way, Cat. CR3 274 DU125
Whitelands Av, Chorl. WD3 95 BC42
Whitelands Cres, SW18 201 CY87
Whitelands Ho, SW3 28 E10
Whitelands Way, Rom. RM3 128 FK54
White La, Guil. GU4, GU5 281 BC136
Oxted RH8 260 EH123
Warlingham CR6 260 EH123
Whiteleaf Rd, Hem.H. HP3 62 BJ23
Whiteledges, W13 159 CJ72
Whitelegg Rd, E13 23 M1
Whiteley, Wind. SL4 173 AL80
Whiteley Rd, SE19 204 DR92
🔒 Whiteleys Shop Cen, W2 15 L9
Whiteleys Way, Han. TW13 198 CA90
WHITELEY VILLAGE, Walt.
KT12 235 BS110
White Lion Cl, Amer. HP7 94 AU39
White Lion Ct, EC3 19 N9
White Lion Gate, Cob. KT11 235 BU114
White Lion Hill, EC4 19 H10
White Lion Hos, Hat. AL10
off Robin Hood La 67 CU17
White Lion Rd, Amer. HP7 94 AT38
White Lion Sq, Hat. AL10
off Robin Hood La 67 CV17
White Lion St, N1 18 E1
Hemel Hempstead HP3 62 BK24
🔒 White Lion Wk, Guil. GU1
off High St 280 AX136
White Lo, SE19 203 DP94
White Lo Cl, N2 142 DD58
Isleworth TW7 179 CG82
Sevenoaks TN13 279 FH123
Sutton SM2 240 DC108
White Lo Gdns, Red. RH1 288 DG142
White Lyon Ct, EC2 19 J6
White Lyons Rd, Brwd. CM14 130 FW47
Whitemore Rd, Guil. GU1 264 AX130
White Oak Dr, Beck. BR3 225 EC96
White Oak Gdns, Sid. DA15 207 ET87
Sch White Oak Prim Sch, Swan.
BR8 off Hilda May Av 229 FE96
White Oaks, Bans. SM7 240 DB113
Whiteoaks La, Grnf. UB6 159 CD68
● White Oak Sq, Swan. BR8 229 FE97
White Orchards, N20 119 CZ45
Stanmore HA7 117 CG50
Whitepit La, H.Wyc. HP10 132 AE57
Jct White Post Cor, Rain.
RM13 170 FL68
White Post Fld, Saw. CM21 58 EX05
White Post Hill, Fnghm DA4 230 FN101
Whitepost Hill, Red. RH1 272 DE134
White Post La, E9 11 P6
SE13 185 EA83
White Post St, SE15 45 H4
White Rd, E15 13 K6
Betchworth RH3 270 CN133
Box Hill KT20 270 CN133
White Rose La, Wok. GU22 249 AZ117
Whites Av, Ilf. IG2 147 ES58
Whites Cl, Green. DA9 211 FW86
Whites Grds, SE1 31 P5
Whites Grds Est, SE1
off Whites Grds 31 P4
White Shack La, Chan.Cr. WD3 96 BM37
Whites La, Datchet SL3 174 AV79
Whites Meadow, Brom. BR1
off Blackbrook La 227 EN98
White's Row, E1 20 A7
White's Sq, SW4
off Nelson's Row 183 DK84
Whitestile Rd, Brent. TW8 179 CJ78
Whitestone La, NW3 142 DC62
Whitestone Wk, NW3
off North End Way 142 DC62
Hemel Hempstead HP1
off Fennycroft Rd 62 BG17
White St, Sthl. UB1 178 BX75
White Stubbs Fm, Brox. EN10 70 DU21
White Stubbs La, Bayford
SG13 69 DK21
Broxbourne EN10 69 DP21
White Swan Ms, W4
off Bennett St 180 CS79
Whitethorn, Welw.G.C. AL7 52 DB10
Whitethorn Av, Couls. CR5 256 DG115
West Drayton UB7 156 BL73
Whitethorn Gdns, Croy. CR0 224 DV103
Enfield EN2 104 DR43
Hornchurch RM11 150 FJ58
Whitethorn Pl, West Dr. UB7 156 BM74
Whitethorn St, E3 22 B5
White Twr Way, E1 21 L6
Whitewaits, Harl. CM20 57 ES14
White Way, Bkhm KT23 268 CB126
Whiteways Ct, Stai. TW18
off Pavilion Gdns 196 BH94
Whitewebbs La, Enf. EN2 104 DS35
Whitewebbs Pk, Enf. EN2 104 DQ35
Whitewebbs Rd, Enf. EN2 103 DP35
Whitewebbs Way, Orp. BR5 227 ET95
Whitewood Cotts, Tats. TN16 260 EJ120
Whitewood Rd, Berk. HP4 60 AU19
Whitfield Cl, Guil. GU2 264 AU131
Whitfield Cres, Dart. DA2 210 FQ87
Whitfield Pl, W1 17 L5
Whitfield Rd, E6 166 EJ66
SE3 47 H7
Bexleyheath DA7 188 EZ80
Whitfield St, W1 17 N7
Whitfield Way, Mill End WD3 113 BF46
Whitford Gdns, Mitch. CR4 222 DF97
Whitgift Av, S.Croy. CR2 241 DP106
🔒 Whitgift Cen, Croy. CR0 224 DQ103
Whitgift Ho, SW11
off Randall Cl 40 C6
Sch Whitgift Sch, S.Croy. CR2
off Haling Pk Rd 242 DQ106
Whitgift St, SE11 30 C8
Croydon CR0 224 DQ104
Whit Hern Ct, Chsht EN8 88 DW30
Whiting Av, Bark. IG11 167 EP66
Whitings, Ilf. IG2 147 ER57
Sch Whitings Hill Prim Sch, Barn.
EN5 off Whitings Rd 101 CW43
Whitings Rd, Barn. EN5 101 CW43
Whitings Way, E6 25 L6
Whitland Rd, Cars. SM5 222 DD102
Whitlars Dr, Kings L. WD4 80 BM28
Whitley Cl, Abb.L. WD5 81 BU32
Stanwell TW19 196 BL86
Whitley Ho, SW1 41 M1
Whitley Rd, N17 122 DS54
Hoddesdon EN11 71 EB15
Whitlock Dr, SW19 201 CY87
Whitman Rd, E3 21 M4
Whitmead Cl, S.Croy. CR2 242 DS107
Whitmoor Common, Worp.
GU3 264 AV127
Whitmoor La, Guil. GU4 264 AX126
Whitmore Av, Harold Wd
RM3 128 FL54
Whitmore Cl, N11 121 DH50
Whitmore Est, N1 9 P9
Whitmore Gdns, NW10 4 A10
Sch Whitmore High Sch, Har.
HA2 off Porlock Av 138 CC60
Sch Whitmore Prim Sch, N1 9 M9
Whitmore Rd, N1 9 N9
Beckenham BR3 225 DZ97
Harrow HA1 138 CC59
Whitmores Cl, Epsom KT18 254 CQ115
Whitmore's Wd, Hem.H. HP2 63 BP19
Whitmore Way, Horl. RH6 290 DE147
Whitnell Way, SW15 201 CX85
Whitney Av, Ilf. IG4 146 EK56
Whitney Ho, SE22
off Albrighton Rd 184 DS83
Whitney Rd, E10 145 EB59
Whitney Wk, Sid. DA14 208 EY93
Whitstable Cl, Beck. BR3 225 DZ95
Ruislip HA4 137 BS61
Whitstable Ho, W10 14 D9
Whitstable Pl, Croy. CR0 242 DQ105
Whitstone La, Beck. BR3 225 EB99
Whittaker Av, Rich. TW9
off Hill St 199 CK85
Whittaker Rd, E6 166 EJ66
Slough SL2 153 AK70
Sutton SM3 221 CZ104
Whittaker St, SW1 28 G9
Whittaker Way, SE1 32 D9
Whitta Rd, E12 146 EK63
Whittell Gdns, SE26 204 DW90
Whittenham Cl, Slou. SL2 154 AU74
Whittets Ait, Wey. KT13
off Jessamy Rd 216 BN103
Sch Whittingham Comm
Prim Sch, E17
off Higham Hill Rd 123 DY53
Whittingstall Rd, SW6 39 H7
Hoddesdon EN11 71 EB15
Whittington Av, EC3 19 N9
Hayes UB4 157 BT71
Whittington Ct, N2 142 DF57
H Whittington Hosp, N19 143 DJ61
Whittington Ms, N12 120 DC49
Whittington Rd, N22 121 DL52
Hutton CM13 131 GC44
Whittington Way, Pnr. HA5 138 BY57
Whittlebury Cl, Cars. SM5 240 DF108
Whittle Cl, E17 145 DY58
Leavesden WD25 81 BT34
Southall UB1 158 CB72
Whittle Parkway, Slou. SL1 153 AK72
Whittle Rd, Houns. TW5 178 BW80
Southall UB2 off Post Rd 178 CB75
Whittlesea Cl, Har. HA3 116 CC52
Whittlesea Path, Har. HA3 116 CC53
Whittlesea Rd, Har. HA3 116 CC53
Whittlesey St, SE1 30 E3
WHITTON, Twick. TW2 198 CB87
⇌ Whitton 198 CC87
Whitton Av E, Grnf. UB6 139 CE64
Whitton Av W, Grnf. UB6 138 CC64
Northolt UB5 138 CC64
Whitton Cl, Grnf. UB6 159 CH65
Whitton Dene, Houns. TW3 198 CB85
Isleworth TW7 199 CD85
Whitton Dr, Grnf. UB6 159 CG65
Whitton Manor Rd, Islw. TW7 198 CC85
Whitton Rd, Houns. TW3 178 CB84
Twickenham TW1, TW2 199 CF86
Jct Whitton Rd Rbt, Twick.
TW1 199 CF86
Sch Whitton Sch, Whitton TW2
off Percy Rd 198 CB89
Whitton Wk, E3 22 A2
Whitton Waye, Houns. TW3 198 CA86
Whitwell Rd, E13 23 N3
Watford WD25 98 BX35
Whitworth Cres, Enf. EN3 105 EA37
Whitworth Ho, SE1 31 K7
Whitworth Rd, SE18 187 EN80
SE25 224 DS97
Whitworth St, SE10 35 K10
Whopshott Av, Wok. GU21 248 AW116
Whopshott Cl, Wok. GU21 248 AW116
Whopshott Dr, Wok. GU21 248 AW116
Whorlton Rd, SE15 184 DV83
Whybridge Cl, Rain. RM13 169 FE67
Sch Whybridge Inf Sch, Rain.
RM13 off Ford La 169 FG67
Sch Whybridge Jun Sch, Rain.
RM13 off Blacksmiths La 169 FF67
Whybrow Gdns, Berk. HP4 60 AY17
Whychcote Pt, NW2
off Claremont Rd 141 CW59
Whymark Av, N22 143 DN55
Whytebeam Vw, Whyt. CR3 258 DT118
Whytecliffe Rd N, Pur. CR8 241 DP111
Whytecliffe Rd S, Pur. CR8 241 DN111
Whytecroft, Houns. TW5 178 BX80
WHYTELEAFE, Cat. CR3 258 DS118
⇌ Whyteleafe 258 DT117
● Whyteleafe Business Village,
Whyt. CR3
off Whyteleafe Hill 258 DT117
Whyteleafe Hill, Whyt. CR3 258 DT118
Whyteleafe Rd, Cat. CR3 258 DS120
Sch Whyteleafe Sch, Whyt. CR3
off Whyteleafe Hill 258 DT118
⇌ Whyteleafe South 258 DU119
Whyteville Rd, E7 166 EH65
Wichling Cl, Orp. BR5 228 EX102
Wick, The, Hert. SG14 53 DP06
Wickenden Rd, Sev. TN13 279 FJ122
Wicken's Meadow, Dunt.Grn
TN14 263 FF119
Wickersley Rd, SW11 41 H9
Wickers Oake, SE19 204 DT91
Wicker St, E1 20 E9
Wicket, The, Croy. CR0 243 EA106
Wicket Rd, Perivale UB6 159 CG69
Wickets, The, Ashf. TW15 196 BL91
Wickets End, Shenley WD7 84 CL33
Wickets Way, Ilf. IG6 125 ET51
Wickford Cl, Rom. RM3
off Wickford Dr 128 FM50
Wickford Dr, Rom. RM3 128 FM50
Wickford St, E1 20 G4
Wickford Way, E17 145 DX56
Wickham Av, Croy. CR0 225 DY103
Sutton SM3 239 CW106
Wickham Chase, W.Wick. BR4 225 ED101
Wickham Cl, E1 21 H7
Enfield EN3 104 DV41
Harefield UB9 114 BK53
Horley RH6 290 DF147
New Malden KT3 221 CT99
Sch Wickham Common Prim Sch,
W.Wick. BR4
off Gates Grn Rd 244 EG105
Wickham Ct, St.Alb. AL1 65 CH18
Wickham Ct Rd, W.Wick. BR4 225 EC103
Sch Wickham Ct Sch, W.Wick.
BR4 off Layhams Rd 244 EE105
Wickham Cres, W.Wick. BR4 225 EC103
Wickham Fld, Otford TN14 263 FF116
Wickham Gdns, SE4 185 DZ83
Wickham La, SE2 188 EU78
Egham TW20 195 BA94
Welling DA16 188 EU78
Wickham Ms, SE4 45 P9
Wickham Rd, E4 123 EC52
SE4 45 P9
Beckenham BR3 225 EB96
Croydon CR0 225 DX103
Grays RM16 193 GJ75
Harrow HA3 117 CD54
Wickham St, SE11 30 C10
Welling DA16 187 ES82
Wickhams Wf, Ware SG12
off Crane Mead 55 DY06
Wickham Way, Beck. BR3 225 EC98
Wicklands Rd, Hunsdon SG12 56 EK07
Wick La, E3 12 A10
Englefield Green TW20 194 AT92
Wickliffe Av, N3 119 CY54
Wickliffe Gdns, Wem. HA9 140 CP61
Wicklow St, WC1 18 C2
Wick Rd, E9 11 J5
Englefield Green TW20 194 AV94
Teddington TW11 199 CH94
Wicks Cl, SE9 206 EK91
Wicksteed Cl, Bex. DA5 209 FD90
Wicksteed Ho, SE1 31 K7
Brentford TW8
off Green Dragon La 180 CM78

Wick Way, St.Alb. AL1 . . . . **65** CH17
Wickway Ct, SE15. . . . . **44** A3
Wickwood St, SE5 . . . . **43** H9
Widbury Gdns, Ware SG12 . . . . **55** DZ06
Widbury Hill, Ware SG12 . . . . . **55** DZ06
Wid Cl, Hutt. CM13 . . . . **131** GD43
Widdecombe Av, Har. HA2. . . . . **138** BY61
Widdenham Rd, N7 . . . . **8** C1
Widdin St, E15 . . . . **13** H7
Widecombe Cl, Rom. RM3. . . . . **128** FK53
Widecombe Gdns, Ilf. IG4 . . . . . **146** EL56
Widecombe Rd, SE9. . . . . **206** EL90
Widecombe Way, N2 . . . . **142** DD57
Widecroft Rd, Iver SL0 . . . . **155** BE72
Widegate St, E1 . . . . **19** P7
Widenham Cl, Pnr. HA5 . . . . . . **138** BW57
Wide Way, Mitch. CR4 . . . . **223** DK97
Widewing Cl, Tedd. TW11 . . . . . **199** CH94
Widford Rd, Hunsdon SG12. . . . **56** EK05
Welwyn Garden City AL7. . . . **52** DB09
Widgeon Cl, E16 . . . . **24** A8
Widgeon Rd, Erith DA8 . . . . . . **189** FH80
Widgeon Way, Wat. WD25 . . . . . **98** BY36
Widley Rd, W9. . . . . **15** K3
Widmoor, Woob.Grn HP10. . . . **132** AE60
WIDMORE, Brom. BR1 . . . . **226** EH97
Widmore Dr, Hem.H. HP2 . . . . . **62** BN18
WIDMORE GREEN, Brom.
BR1. . . . . **226** EJ95
Widmore Lo Rd, Brom. BR1. . . **226** EK96
Widmore Rd, Brom. BR1 . . . . . **226** EG96
Uxbridge UB8 . . . . **157** BP70
Widworthy Hayes, Hutt.
CM13 . . . . **131** GB46
Wieland Rd, Nthwd. HA6 . . . . . **115** BU52
Wigan Ho, E5. . . . . **144** DV60
Wigeon Path, SE28. . . . . **187** ER76
Wigeon Way, Hayes UB4 . . . . . **158** BX72
Wiggenhall Rd, Wat. WD18 . . . . **97** BV43
Wiggie La, Red. RH1. . . . . **272** DG132
Wiggins La, Rich. TW10 . . . . . . **199** CJ89
Wiggins Mead, NW9. . . . . **119** CT52
Wigginton Av, Wem. HA9. . . . . **160** CP65
Wightman Rd, N4. . . . . **143** DN57
N8. **143** DN56
Wighton Ms, Islw. TW7. . . . . . . **179** CE82
Wigley Bush La, S.Wld CM14 . **130** FS47
Wigley Rd, Felt. TW13. . . . . **198** BX88
Wigmore Ct, W13
off Singapore Rd. **159** CG74
Wigmore Pl, W1 . . . . **17** J8
Wigmore Rd, Cars. SM5. . . . . . **222** DD103
Wigmores N, Welw.G.C. AL8 . . . **51** CX08
Wigmores S, Welw.G.C. AL8 . . . **51** CX09
Wigmore St, W1 . . . . **16** G9
Wigmore Wk, Cars. SM5 . . . . . **222** DD103
Wigram Rd, E11. . . . . **146** EJ58
Wigram Sq, E17 . . . . **123** EC54
Wigston Cl, N18 . . . . **122** DS50
Wigston Rd, E13 . . . . **24** A4
Wigton Gdns, Stan. HA7 . . . . . . **118** CL53
Wigton Pl, SE11. . . . . **42** F1
Wigton Rd, E17 . . . . **123** DZ53
Romford RM3 . . . . **128** FL49
Wigton Way, Rom. RM3 . . . . . . **128** FL49
Wilberforce Ct, Edg. HA8 . . . . . **118** CM49
Keston BR2 . . . . **244** EK107
Wilberforce Ms, SW4
off Stonhouse St. **183** DK84
Sch **Wilberforce Prim Sch**, W10 . **14** F2
Wilberforce Rd, N4. . . . . **143** DP61
NW9. . . . . **141** CU58
Wilberforce Wk, E15 . . . . **13** K3
Wilberforce Way, SW19 . . . . . . **201** CX93
Gravesend DA12. . . . . **213** GK92
Wilbraham Pl, SW1. . . . . **28** F8
Wilbury Av, Sutt. SM2 . . . . **239** CZ110
Sch **Wilbury Prim Sch**, N18
off Wilbury Way. **122** DR50
Wilbury Rd, Wok. GU21 . . . . . . **248** AX117
Wilbury Way, N18. . . . . **122** DR50
Wilby Ms, W11. . . . . **27** H2
Wilcon Way, Wat. WD25 . . . . **82** BX34
Wilcot Av, Wat. WD19 . . . . **116** BY45
Wilcot Cl, Wat. WD19
off Wilcot Av **116** BY45
Wilcox Cl, SW8 . . . . **42** B4
Borehamwood WD6 . . . . **100** CQ39
Wilcox Gdns, Shep. TW17 . . . . . **216** BM97
Wilcox Pl, SW1 . . . . **29** M7
Wilcox Rd, SW8 . . . . **42** A4
Sutton SM1 . . . . **240** DB105
Teddington TW11. . . . . **199** CD91
Wildacres, Nthwd. HA6. . . . . **115** BT49
West Byfleet KT14. . . . . **234** BJ111
Wildbank Ct, Wok. GU22
off White Rose La **249** AZ118
Wild Ct, WC2 . . . . **18** C8
Wildcroft Dr, N.Holm. RH5. . . . **285** CK139
Wildcroft Gdns, Edg. HA8 . . . . **117** CK51
Wildcroft Rd, SW15. . . . . **201** CW87
Wilde Cl, E8. . . . . **10** C8
Tilbury RM18
off Coleridge Rd **193** GJ82
Wilde Pl, N13
off Medesenge Way **121** DP51
SW18 . . . . **202** DD87
Wilder Cl, Ruis. HA4. . . . . **137** BV60
Wilderness, The, Berk. HP4 . . . . **60** AW19
East Molesey KT8 . . . . **218** CC99
Hampton Hill TW12
off Park Rd. **198** CB91
WILDERNESSE, Sev. TN15. . . . . **279** FL122
Wildernesse Av, Sev. TN15. . . . **279** FL122
Wildernesse Mt, Sev. TN13 . . . **279** FK122
Sch **Wildernesse Sch, The**,
Sev. TN13
off Seal Hollow Rd **279** FL121
Wilderness Ms, SW4 . . . . **183** DH84
Wilderness Rd, Chis. BR7. . . . . **207** EP94
Guildford GU2. . . . . **280** AT135
Oxted RH8 . . . . **276** EE130
Wilde Rd, Erith DA8 . . . . **189** FB80
Wilders Cl, Wok. GU21 . . . . . . **248** AW118
Wilderton Rd, N16 . . . . **144** DS59
Wildfell Rd, SE6 . . . . **205** EB87
Wild Goose Dr, SE14 . . . . **45** H7
Wild Grn N, Slou. SL3
off Verney Rd. **175** BA77
Wild Grn S, Slou. SL3. . . . . **175** BA77
Wild Hatch, NW11 . . . . **142** DA58
WILDHILL, Hat. AL9 . . . . **68** DD21
Wild Hill, Hat. AL9. . . . . **68** DC21
Wildhill Rd, Hat. AL9. . . . . **67** CY23
Wild Oaks Cl, Nthwd. HA6. . . . . . **115** BT51
Wild's Rents, SE1 . . . . **31** N6
Wild St, WC2 . . . . **18** B9
Wildwood, Nthwd. HA6 . . . . **115** BR51
Wildwood Av, Brick.Wd AL2 . . . **82** BZ30
Wildwood Cl, SE12. . . . . **206** EF87
East Horsley KT24. . . . . **267** BT125
Woking GU22 . . . . **249** BF115
Wildwood Ct, Ken. CR8 . . . . . . **258** DR115
Wildwood Gro, NW3
off North End Way **142** DC60
Wildwood Ri, NW11 . . . . **142** DC60
Wildwood Rd, NW11 . . . . **142** DC59
Wildwood Ter, NW3 . . . . **142** DC60
Wilford Cl, Enf. EN2 . . . . **104** DR41
Northwood HA6 . . . . **115** BR52
Wilford Rd, Slou. SL3 . . . . **174** AY77
Wilfred Av, Rain. RM13. . . . . . . **169** FG71
Wilfred Owen Cl, SW19 . . . . . . **202** DC93
Wilfred St, SW1 . . . . **29** L6
Gravesend DA12. . . . . **213** GH86
Woking GU21 . . . . **248** AX117
Wilfred Turney Est, W6
off Hammersmith Gro **181** CW75
Wilfrid Gdns, W3. . . . . **160** CQ71
Wilhelmina Av, Couls. CR5 . . . **257** DJ119
Wilkes Rd, Brent. TW8 . . . . **180** CL79
Hutton CM13 . . . . **131** GD43
Wilkes St, E1 . . . . **20** B6
Wilkins Cl, Hayes UB3 . . . . **177** BT78
Mitcham CR4. . . . . **222** DE95
WILKIN'S GREEN, Hat. AL10 . . . **66** CQ19
Wilkins Grn La, Hat. AL10 . . . . **66** CQ19
Smallford AL4. . . . . **66** CP20
Wilkins Gro, Welw.G.C. AL8. . . . **51** CX10
Wilkins Ho, SW1
off Churchill Gdns. **41** L2
Wilkinson Cl, Chsht EN7 . . . . . . **88** DQ26
Dartford DA1 . . . . **190** FM84
Uxbridge UB10 . . . . **157** BP67
Wilkinson Gdns, SE25 . . . . . . **224** DS95
Wilkinson Rd, E16. . . . . **24** D8
Wilkinson St, SW8 . . . . **42** C5
Wilkinson Way, W4 . . . . **180** CR75
Hemel Hempstead HP3 . . . . . **62** BM24
Wilkin St, NW5 . . . . **7** J4
Wilkin St Ms, NW5. . . . . **7** J4
Wilkins Way, Brasted TN16. . . . **262** EV124
Wilks Av, Dart. DA1 . . . . **210** FM89
Wilks Gdns, Croy. CR0 . . . . **225** DY102
Wilks Pl, N1. . . . . **19** P1
Willan Rd, N17 . . . . **122** DR54
Willan Wall, E16. . . . . **23** L10
Willard St, SW8. . . . . **41** J10
Willats Cl, Cher. KT16. . . . . **215** BF100
Willcocks Cl, Chess. KT9 . . . . . **220** CL104
Willcott Rd, W3. . . . . **160** CP74
Will Crooks Gdns, SE9. . . . . . . **186** EJ84
Willen Fld Rd, NW10. . . . . **160** CQ68
Willenhall Av, New Barn. EN5 . **102** DC44
Willenhall Dr, Hayes UB3. . . . . **157** BS73
Willenhall Rd, SE18 . . . . **187** EP78
Willersley Av, Orp. BR6 . . . . . . **227** ER104
Sidcup DA15 . . . . **207** ET88
Willersley Cl, Sid. DA15 . . . . . . **207** ET88
WILLESDEN, NW10. . . . . **161** CT65
WILLESDEN GREEN, NW10. . . . **161** CV66
⊖ **Willesden Green** **4** B4
⊖ **Willesden Junction**. **161** CT69
⊖ **Willesden Junction**. **161** CT69
Willesden La, NW2 . . . . **4** B5
NW6. . . . . **4** F7
Willes Rd, NW5. . . . . **7** K4
Willett Cl, Nthlt. UB5
off Broomcroft Av. **158** BW69
Petts Wood BR5. . . . . **227** ES100
Willett Ho, E13
off Queens Rd W. **166** EG68
Willett Pl, Th.Hth. CR7
off Willett Rd **223** DN99
Willett Rd, Th.Hth. CR7. . . . . . . **223** DN99
Willetts La, Denh. UB9. . . . . . . **135** BF63
Willetts Ms, Hodd. EN11 . . . . . . **71** EA16
Willett Way, Petts Wd BR5 . . . . **227** ER99
Willey Broom La, Chaldon
CR3. **273** DN125
Willey Fm La, Chaldon CR3 . . . **274** DQ126
Willey La, Chaldon CR3 . . . . . . **274** DR125
William Ash Cl, Dag. RM9 . . . . **168** EV65
William Barefoot Dr, SE9. . . . . **207** EN91
Sch **William Bellamy Inf Sch**, Dag.
RM10 *off Frizlands La* **148** FA61
Sch **William Bellamy Jun Sch**, Dag.
RM10 *off Frizlands La* **148** FA61
William Bonney Est, SW4 . . . . **183** DK84
Coll **William Booth Coll**, SE5. . . . **43** M9
William Booth Rd, SE20. . . . . . **224** DU95
Sch **William Byrd Prim Sch**,
Harling. UB3
off Victoria La **177** BR79
William Carey Way, Har. HA1. . **139** CE59
Sch **William C. Harvey Sch**, N17
off Adams Rd **122** DR54
William Cl, N2. . . . . **120** DD54
SE13. . . . . **46** F9
SW6. . . . . **38** F4
Romford RM5 . . . . **127** FC53
Southall UB2
off Windmill Av **178** CC75
William Cory Prom, Erith DA8. **189** FE78
William Ct, Hem.H. HP3
off King Edward St. **62** BK24
William Covell Cl, Enf. EN2 . . . **103** DM38
Sch **William Davies Prim Sch**,
E7 *off Stafford Rd* **166** EK65
Sch **William Davis Prim Sch**, E2 . **20** C4
William Dr, Stan. HA7. . . . . **117** CG51
William Dunbar Ho, NW6. . . . . . **14** G1
William Dyce Ms, SW16
off Babington Rd. **203** DK91
William Ellis Cl, Old Wind.
SL4. . . . . **194** AU85
Sch **William Ellis Sch**, NW5
off Highgate Rd **142** DG62
William Ellis Way, SE16 . . . . . . **32** D7
William Evans Rd, Epsom
KT19. **238** CN111
William Evelyn Ct, Wotton
RH5. . . . . **284** BZ139
Sch **William Ford C of E Jun Sch**,
Dag. RM10 *off Ford Rd*. **168** FA66
William Foster La, Well. DA16 . **188** EU82
William IV St, WC2 . . . . **30** A1
William Gdns, SW15. . . . . **201** CV85
Smallfield RH6 . . . . **291** DN148
William Guy Gdns, E3 . . . . **22** D3
William Harvey Ho, SW19
off Whitlock Dr. **201** CY88
William Henry Wk, SW8. . . . . . . **41** N3
Sch **William Hogarth Sch, The**,
W4 *off Duke Rd*. **180** CS78
William Hunter Way, Brwd.
CM14 . . . . **130** FW47
William Margrie Cl, SE15. . . . . . **44** D8
Sch **William Martin C of E Inf &
Nurs Sch**, Harl. CM18
off Tawneys Rd **73** ES17
Sch **William Martin C of E Jun Sch**,
Harl. CM18 *off Tawneys Rd* . **73** ET17
William Ms, SW1 . . . . **28** F5
William Morley Cl, E6. . . . . **166** EK67
William Morris Cl, E17 . . . . **145** DZ55
★ **William Morris Gall**, E17
off Lloyd Pk. **145** EA55
Sch **William Morris Prim Sch**, Mitch.
CR4 *off Recreation Way* . . . **223** DK97
Sch **William Morris Sch**, E17
off Folly La. **123** DY53
Coll **William Morris 6th Form**,
W6 . . . . **38** C1
William Morris Way, SW6. . . . . . **39** N10
William Moulder Ct, Chesh.
HP5. . . . . **76** AP28
William Nash Ct, Orp. BR5
off Brantwood Way. **228** EW97
Sch **William Patten Prim Sch**, N16
off Stoke Newington Ch St . **144** DT61
Sch **William Penn Sch, The**, Slou.
SL2 *off Penn Rd* **153** AR70
William Perkin Ct, Grnf. UB6
off Greenford Rd. **159** CE65
William Petty Way, Orp. BR5 . . **228** EW102
William Pl, E3 . . . . **11** N10
William Rd, NW1. . . . . **17** L3
SW19 . . . . **201** CY94
Caterham CR3. . . . . **258** DR122
Guildford GU1. . . . . **264** AW134
Sutton SM1 . . . . **240** DC106
William Rushbrooke Ho, SE16
off Eveline Lowe Est. **32** C8
William Russell Ct, Wok.
GU21 . . . . **248** AS118
Williams Av, E17 . . . . **123** DZ53
William Saville Ho, NW6 . . . . . . **15** H1
Williams Bldgs, E2 . . . . **20** G4
Williams Cl, N8
off Coolhurst Rd **143** DK58
Addlestone KT15
off Monks Cres **234** BH106
Williams Dr, Houns. TW3 . . . . . **178** CA84
Williams Gro, N22. . . . . **121** DN53
Long Ditton KT6 . . . . **219** CJ101
William's La, SW14. . . . . **180** CQ83
Williams La, Mord. SM4. . . . . . . **222** DC99
Williamson Cl, SE10 . . . . **35** L10
Williamson Rd, N4 . . . . **143** DP58
Williamson St, N7. . . . . **8** B1
Williamson Way, Rick. WD3 . . . **114** BG46
William Sq, SE16 . . . . **33** M1
Williams Rd, W13 . . . . **159** CG73
Southall UB2 . . . . **178** BY77
Williams Ter, Croy. CR0 . . . . . . **241** DN107
William St, E10 . . . . **145** EB58
N17. **122** DT52
SW1 . . . . **28** F5
Barking IG11 . . . . **167** EQ66
Berkhamsted HP4. . . . . **60** AX19
Bushey WD23 . . . . **98** BX41
Carshalton SM5 . . . . **222** DE104
Gravesend DA12. . . . . **213** GH87
Grays RM17. . . . . **192** GB79
Slough SL1 . . . . **154** AT74
Windsor SL4 . . . . **173** AR81
Williams Wk, Guil. GU2
off Grange Rd **264** AV130
Williams Way, Dart. DA2 . . . . . **209** FD89
Radlett WD7. . . . . **99** CJ35
William Swayne Pl, Guil. GU1
off Station App **280** AY135
Sch **William Torbitt Prim Sch**, Ilf.
IG2 *off Eastern Av*. **147** ET57
Sch **William Tyndale Prim Sch**,
N1. . . . . **9** H6
Willifield Way, NW11. . . . . **141** CZ56
Willingale Cl, Hutt. CM13
off Fairview Av **131** GE44
Loughton IG10
off Willingale Rd **107** EQ40
Woodford Green IG8 . . . . **124** EJ51
Willingale Rd, Loug. IG10. . . . . **107** EQ41
Willingdon Rd, N22 . . . . **121** DP54
Willinghall Cl, Wal.Abb. EN9 . . . **89** ED32
Willingham Cl, NW5. . . . . **7** M3
Willingham Ter, NW5 . . . . **7** M3
Willingham Way, Kings.T. KT1 . **220** CN97
Willington Ct, E5
off Mandeville St **145** DY62
Willington Rd, SW9 . . . . **183** DL83
Sch **Willington Sch**, SW19
off Worcester Rd **201** CZ92
Willis Av, Sutt. SM2 . . . . **240** DE107
Willis Cl, Epsom KT18 . . . . **238** CP113
Willis Ho, E12
off Grantham Rd. **147** EN62
Willis Rd, E15 . . . . **13** L10
Croydon CR0. . . . . **224** DQ101
Erith DA8 . . . . **189** FC77
Willis St, E14. . . . . **22** D9
Willmore End, SW19. . . . . **222** DB95
Willoners, Slou. SL2. . . . . **153** AN70
Willoughby Av, Croy. CR0 . . . . **241** DM105
Willoughby Cl, Brox. EN10. . . . . **71** DY21
Willoughby Ct, Lon.Col. AL2 . . . **83** CK26
Willoughby Dr, Rain. RM13 . . . **169** FE66
Willoughby Gro, N17 . . . . **122** DV52
Willoughby Ho, EC2
off The Barbican **19** L7
Willoughby La, N17 . . . . **122** DV52
Willoughby Ms, SW4
off Wixs La **183** DH84
Willoughby Pk Rd, N17 . . . . . . **122** DV52
Willoughby Pas, E14. . . . . **34** A2
Willoughby Rd, N8 . . . . **143** DN55
NW3. . . . . **6** A1
Kingston upon Thames KT2. **220** CM95
Slough SL3 . . . . **175** BA76
Twickenham TW1 . . . . **199** CK86
Willoughbys, The, SW14
off Upper Richmond Rd W. **180** CS83
Willoughby St, WC1 . . . . **18** A7
Willoughby Way, SE7 . . . . **36** A8
Willow Av, SW13. . . . . **181** CT82
Denham UB9. . . . . **136** BJ64
Sidcup DA15 . . . . **208** EU86
Swanley BR8. . . . . **229** FF97
West Drayton UB7 . . . . **156** BM73
Willow Bk, SW6. . . . . **38** F10
Richmond TW10 . . . . **199** CH90
Woking GU22 . . . . **248** AY122
Willowbank Gdns, Tad. KT20. . **255** CV122
Willowbank Pl, Pur. CR8
off Kingsdown Av. **241** DP109
Willowbay Cl, Barn. EN5 . . . . . **101** CX44
Willow Brean, Horl. RH6 . . . . . **290** DE147
Willow Br Rd, N1 . . . . **9** J5
Willowbrook, Eton SL4. . . . . . . **173** AR77
Willowbrook Est, SE15
off Shurland Gdns **44** B4
Sch **Willow Brook Prim Sch**, E10
off Church Rd **145** EA60
Sch **Willowbrook Prim Sch**,
Hutt. CM13
off Brookfield Cl **131** GD44
Willowbrook Rd, SE15 . . . . **44** B3
Southall UB2. . . . . **178** CA76
Staines TW19. . . . . **196** BL89
● **Willow Cen**, Mitch. CR4 . . . . **222** DF99
Willow Chase, Chesh. HP5. . . . . **76** AP30
Willow Cl, SE6
off Verdant La **206** EF88
Bexley DA5 . . . . **208** EZ86
Brentford TW8. . . . . **179** CJ79
Bromley BR2 . . . . **227** EM99
Buckhurst Hill IG9. . . . . **124** EK48
Chalfont St. Peter SL9. . . . . . **112** AY54
Chertsey KT16. . . . . **215** BE103
Cheshunt EN7 . . . . **88** DS26
Colnbrook SL3. . . . . **175** BC80
Erith DA8 *off Willow Rd* **189** FG81
Flackwell Heath HP10 . . . . . . **132** AC57
Hornchurch RM12. . . . . **149** FH62
Hutton CM13. . . . . **131** GB44
Orpington BR5 . . . . **228** EV101
Thornton Heath CR7. . . . . . . **223** DP100
Woodham KT15 . . . . **233** BF111
Willow Cor, Bayford SG13. . . . . **69** DM18
Willow Cotts, Mitch. CR4. . . . . **223** DJ97
Richmond TW9 *off Kew Grn*. **180** CN79
Willow Ct, EC2 . . . . **19** N4
Edgware HA8. . . . . **118** CL49
Horley RH6 . . . . **291** DH145
Sawbridgeworth CM21 . . . . . **58** EX06
Willowcourt Av, Har. HA3 . . . . **139** CH57
Willow Cres, St.Alb. AL1 . . . . . . **65** CJ20
Willow Cres E, Denh. UB9 . . . . **136** BJ64
Willow Cres W, Denh. UB9 . . . . **136** BJ64
Willowdene, N6 *off View Rd* . . **142** DF59
Willow Dene, Bushey Hth
WD23 . . . . **117** CE45
Willowdene, Chsht EN8 . . . . **89** DY27
Pilgrim's Hatch CM15 . . . . . . **130** FT43
Willow Dene, Pnr. HA5. . . . . . . **116** BX54
Willowdene Cl, Twick. TW2. . . . **198** CC87
Willowdene Ct, Warley CM14 . **130** FW49
Sch **Willow Dene Sch**, SE18
off Swingate La. **187** ES81
Willow Dr, Barn. EN5 . . . . **101** CY42
Ripley GU23 . . . . **250** BG124
Willow Edge, Kings L. WD4 . . . . **80** BN29
Willow End, N20. . . . . **120** DA47
Northwood HA6 . . . . **115** BU51
Surbiton KT6. . . . . **220** CL102
Willow Fm La, SW15
off Queens Ride **181** CV83
Willowfield, Harl. CM18. . . . . . . **73** ER17
Sch **Willowfield Sch**, E17
off Clifton Av. **145** DX55
Willowfields Cl, SE18 . . . . **187** ES78
Willow Gdns, Houns. TW3 . . . . . **178** CA81
Ruislip HA4 . . . . **137** BT61
Willow Glade, Reig. RH2
off Hornbeam Rd **288** DB137
Willow Grn, NW9
off Clayton Fld. **118** CS53
Borehamwood WD6 . . . . **100** CR43
North Holmwood RH5 . . . . . . **285** CH140
Willow Gro, E13 . . . . **13** N10
Chislehurst BR7 . . . . **207** EN93
Ruislip HA4 . . . . **137** BT61
Willowhayne Dr, Walt. KT12 . . . **217** BV101
Willowhayne Gdns, Wor.Pk.
KT4. . . . . **221** CW104
Willowherb Wk, Rom. RM3
off Clematis Cl. **128** FJ52
Willow Ho, NW3
off Maitland Pk Vil. **6** F4
Warlingham CR6
off East Parkside **259** EB115
Willow La, SE18 . . . . **37** K8
Amersham HP7. . . . . **94** AT41
Guildford GU1
off Boxgrove Rd **265** BA133
Mitcham CR4. . . . . **222** DF99
Watford WD18. . . . . **97** BU43
● **Willow La Ind Est**, Mitch.
CR4. . . . . **222** DF99
Willowmead, Chig. IG7 . . . . **126** EU48
Willow Mead, Dor. RH4 . . . . . . **285** CG135
Willowmead, Hert. SG14 . . . . . . **53** DN10
Willow Mead, Saw. CM21 . . . . . **58** EY06
Willowmead, Stai. TW18 . . . . . . **216** BH95
Willowmead Cl, W5 . . . . **159** CK71
Woking GU21 . . . . **248** AU116
Willowmere, Esher KT10 . . . . . **236** CC105
Willow Mt, Croy. CR0
off Langton Way **224** DS104
Willow Pk, Otford TN14 . . . . . . **263** FF117
Stoke Poges SL2. . . . . **154** AU66
Willow Path, Wal.Abb. EN9 . . . . **90** EE34
Willow Pl, SW1 . . . . **29** M8
Eton SL4 . . . . **173** AQ78
Hastingwood CM17 . . . . **74** EZ19
Willow Rd, NW3. . . . . **142** DD63
W5 . . . . **180** CL75
Colnbrook SL3. . . . . **175** BE82
Dartford DA1 . . . . **210** FJ88
Enfield EN1 . . . . **104** DS41
Erith DA8 . . . . **189** FG81
Godalming GU7 . . . . **280** AT143
New Malden KT3 . . . . **220** CQ98
Redhill RH1 . . . . **288** DC137
Romford RM6 . . . . **148** EY58
Wallington SM6 . . . . **241** DH108
Willows, The, Amer. HP6 . . . . . . **77** AP35
Buckhurst Hill IG9. . . . . **124** EK48
Byfleet KT14 . . . . **234** BL113
Claygate KT10. . . . . **237** CE107
Grays RM17. . . . . **192** GE79
Guildford GU4
off Collier Way. **265** BD132
Mill End WD3
off Uxbridge Rd. **114** BG47
St. Albans AL1. . . . . **65** CH24
Watford WD19
off Brookside Rd **115** BV45
Weybridge KT13 . . . . **216** BN104
Windsor SL4 . . . . **173** AK80
Willows Av, Mord. SM4 . . . . **222** DB99
Willows Cl, Pnr. HA5. . . . . **116** BW54
Willowside, Lon.Col. AL2 . . . . . . **84** CL27
Willows Path, Epsom KT18 . . . . **238** CP114
Windsor SL4 . . . . **172** AJ81
Willows Riverside Pk, Wind.
SL4. . . . . **172** AJ80
Sch **Willows Sch, The**, Hayes
UB4 *off Stipularis Dr* **158** BX70
Willow St, E4. . . . . **123** ED45
EC2. . . . . **19** N4
Romford RM7 . . . . **149** FC56
Willow Tree Cl, E3 . . . . **11** M9
SW18 *off Cargill Rd* **202** DB88
Abridge RM4 . . . . **108** EV41
Hayes UB4. . . . . **158** BW70
Northolt UB5. . . . . **158** BY65
Uxbridge UB10 . . . . **137** BQ62
Willow Tree La, Hayes UB4 . . . **158** BW70
Willowtree Marina, Hayes
UB4 . . . . **158** BY72
Sch **Willow Tree Prim Sch**, Nthlt.
UB5 *off Arnold Rd*. **158** BY65
Jct **Willow Tree Rbt**, Hayes
UB4 . . . . **158** BX71
Willow Tree Wk, Brom. BR1 . . . **226** EH95
Willowtree Way, Th.Hth. CR7
off Kensington Av. **223** DN95
Willow Vale, W12. . . . . **161** CU74
Chislehurst BR7 . . . . **207** EP93
Fetcham KT22 . . . . **252** CB123
Willow Vw, SW19 . . . . **222** DD95
Ware SG12. . . . . **55** DY07
Willow Wk, E17. . . . . **145** DZ57
N2. . . . . **120** DD54
N15. . . . . **143** DP56
N21. . . . . **103** DM44
SE1. . . . . **31** P8
Box Hill KT20 *off Oak Dr* . . . **270** CQ130
Chertsey KT16. . . . . **216** BG101
Dartford DA1 . . . . **210** FJ85
Englefield Green TW20. . . . . . **194** AW92
Orpington BR6 . . . . **227** EP104
Redhill RH1 *off Ash Dr*. **289** DH136
Shere GU5. . . . . **282** BN139
Sutton SM3 . . . . **221** CZ104
Upminster RM14. . . . . **151** FS60
Willow Way, N3. . . . . **120** DB52
SE26. . . . . **204** DV90
W11 . . . . **26** D1
Box Hill KT20 *off Oak Dr* . . . **270** CP130
Epsom KT19 . . . . **238** CR107
Godstone RH9. . . . . **274** DV132
Guildford GU1. . . . . **264** AV130
Hatfield AL10. . . . . **67** CT21
Hemel Hempstead HP1 . . . . . . **62** BH18
Potters Bar EN6. . . . . **86** DB33
Radlett WD7. . . . . **99** CE36
Romford RM3 . . . . **128** FP51
St. Albans AL2. . . . . **82** CA27
Sunbury-on-Thames TW16. . **217** BU98
Twickenham TW2 . . . . **198** CB89
Wembley HA0. . . . . **139** CG62
West Byfleet KT14. . . . . **234** BJ111
Woking GU22 . . . . **248** AX121
Willow Wd Cl, Burn. SL1 . . . . . . **152** AH68
Willow Wd Cres, SE25 . . . . **224** DS100
Willrose Cres, SE2. . . . . **188** EW78
Wills Cres, Houns. TW3 . . . . **198** CB86
Wills Gro, NW7 . . . . **119** CU50
Willson Rd, Eng.Grn TW20. . . . . **194** AV92
Wilman Gro, E8. . . . . **10** D6
Wilmar Cl, Hayes UB4 . . . . **157** BR70
Uxbridge UB8 . . . . **156** BK66
Wilmar Gdns, W.Wick. BR4 . . . **225** EB102
Wilmcote Ho, W2 . . . . **15** K6
Wilmer Cl, Kings.T. KT2 . . . . . . **200** CM92
Wilmer Cres, Kings.T. KT2 . . . . **200** CM92
Wilmer Gdns, N1 . . . . **9** N9
Wilmerhatch La, Epsom KT18 . **254** CP118
Wilmer Ho, E3. . . . . **11** M10
Wilmer Lea Cl, E15 . . . . **12** G7
Wilmer Pl, N16 . . . . **144** DT61
Wilmer Way, N14. . . . . **121** DK50
WILMINGTON, Dart. DA2. . . . . . **210** FK91
Wilmington Av, W4. . . . . **180** CR80
Orpington BR6 . . . . **228** EW103
Wilmington Ct Rd, Dart. DA2. . **209** FG90
Coll **Wilmington Enterprise Coll**,
Wilm. DA2 *off Common La*. **209** FH90
Wilmington Gdns, Bark. IG11 . . **167** ER65
Sch **Wilmington Gram Sch for Boys**,
Wilm. DA2 *off Common La*. **209** FH90
Sch **Wilmington Prim Sch**, Wilm.
DA2 *off Common La*. **209** FH90
Wilmington Sq, WC1 . . . . **18** E3
Wilmington St, WC1 . . . . **18** E3
Wilmot Cl, N2 . . . . **120** DC54
SE15. . . . . **44** C5
Wilmot Grn, Gt Warley CM13 . **129** FW51
Wilmot Pl, NW1 . . . . **7** L6
W7 *off Boston Rd* **159** CE74
Wilmot Rd, E10. . . . . **145** EB61
N17. . . . . **144** DR55
Burnham SL1 . . . . **152** AH69
Carshalton SM5 . . . . **240** DF106
Dartford DA1 . . . . **209** FG85
Purley CR8. . . . . **241** DN112
Wilmots Cl, Reig. RH2 . . . . **272** DC133
Wilmot St, E2 . . . . **20** E4
Wilmot Way, Bans. SM7. . . . . . . **240** DA114
Wilmount St, SE18. . . . . **37** N9
Wilna Rd, SW18 . . . . **202** DC87
Wilsham St, W11. . . . . **26** D2
Wilshaw Cl, NW4 . . . . **141** CU55
Wilshaw St, SE14 . . . . **46** A6
Wilshere Av, St.Alb. AL1. . . . . . . **64** CC23
Wilsman Rd, S.Ock. RM15 . . . . **171** FW68
Wilsmere Dr, Har.Wld HA3. . . . . **117** CE52
Northolt UB5. . . . . **158** BY65
Wilson Av, Mitch. CR4 . . . . **202** DE94
Wilson Cl, S.Croy. CR2
off Bartlett St. **242** DR106
Wembley HA9. . . . . **140** CM59
Wilson Dr, Ott. KT16. . . . . **233** BB106
Wembley HA9. . . . . **140** CM59
Wilson Gdns, Har. HA1. . . . . . . **138** CC59
Wilson Gro, SE16 . . . . **32** E5
Wilson Ho, SE7
off Springfield Gro **186** EJ79
Wilson La, Dart. DA4 . . . . **231** FT96
Wilson Rd, E6 . . . . **24** E2
SE5. . . . . **43** N7
Chessington KT9. . . . . **238** CM107
Ilford IG1 . . . . **147** EM59
Wilsons, Tad. KT20 . . . . **255** CX121

Wilsons Pl, E14 . . . 21 N9
Wilsons Rd, W6 . . . 26 D10
Sch Wilson's Sch, Wall. SM6
off Mollison Dr . . . 241 DL107
Wilson St, E17 . . . 145 EC57
EC2 . . . 19 M6
N21 . . . 121 DN45
Wilson Way, Wok. GU21 . . . 248 AX116
Wilstone Cl, Hayes UB4 . . . 158 BY70
Wilstone Dr, St.Alb. AL4 . . . 65 CJ15
Wilthorne Gdns, Dag. RM10
off Acre Rd . . . 169 FB66
Wilton Av, W4 . . . 180 CS78
Wilton Cl, Harm. UB7 . . . 176 BK79
Wilton Cres, SW1 . . . 28 G5
SW19 . . . 221 CZ95
Beaconsfield HP9 . . . 111 AL52
Hertford SG13 . . . 54 DQ12
Windsor SL4 . . . 173 AK84
Wilton Dr, Rom. RM5 . . . 127 FC52
Wilton Est, E8 . . . 10 D5
Wilton Gdns, Walt. KT12 . . . 218 BX102
West Molesey KT8 . . . 218 CA97
Wilton Gro, SW19 . . . 201 CZ94
New Malden KT3 . . . 221 CT100
Wilton Ho, SE22
off Albrighton Rd . . . 184 DS83
Wilton La, Jordans HP9 . . . 111 AR52
Wilton Ms, SW1 . . . 29 H6
Wilton Par, Felt. TW13
off High St . . . 197 BV88
Wilton Pk, Beac. HP9 . . . 111 AP53
Wilton Pk Ct, SE18
off Prince Imperial Rd . . . 187 EN81
Wilton Pl, SW1 . . . 28 G5
New Haw KT15 . . . 234 BK109
Wilton Rd, N10 . . . 120 DG54
SE2 . . . 188 EW76
SW1 . . . 29 K7
SW19 . . . 202 DE94
Beaconsfield HP9 . . . 111 AL51
Cockfosters EN4 . . . 102 DF42
Hounslow TW4 . . . 178 BX83
Ilford IG1 . . . 147 EP63
Redhill RH1 . . . 288 DF135
Wilton Row, SW1 . . . 28 G5
Wilton Sq, N1 . . . 9 L8
Wilton St, SW1 . . . 29 J6
Wilton Ter, SW1 . . . 28 G6
Wilton Vil, N1 . . . 9 L9
Wilton Way, E8 . . . 10 C5
Hertford SG13 . . . 54 DQ11
Wiltshire Av, Horn. RM11 . . . 150 FM56
Slough SL2 . . . 153 AQ70
Wiltshire Cl, NW7 . . . 119 CT50
SW3 . . . 28 E8
Dartford DA2 . . . 211 FR87
Wiltshire Gdns, N4 . . . 144 DQ58
Twickenham TW2 . . . 198 CC88
Wiltshire La, Pnr. HA5 . . . 137 BT55
Wiltshire Rd, SW9 . . . 183 DN83
Orpington BR6 . . . 228 EU101
Thornton Heath CR7 . . . 223 DN97
Wiltshire Row, N1 . . . 9 L9
Wilverley Cres, N.Mal. KT3 . . . 220 CS100
Wimbart Rd, SW2 . . . 203 DM87
WIMBLEDON, SW19 . . . 201 CY93
⇌ Wimbledon . . . 201 CZ93
⊖ Wimbledon . . . 201 CZ93
Tram Wimbledon . . . 201 CZ93
★ Wimbledon (All England Tenn & Croquet Club), SW19 . . . 201 CY91
Wimbledon Br, SW19 . . . 201 CZ93
⇌ Wimbledon Chase . . . 221 CY96
Sch Wimbledon Chase Prim Sch, SW19 off Merton Hall Rd . . . 221 CY95
Sch Wimbledon Coll, SW19
off Edge Hill . . . 201 CX94
★ Wimbledon Common, SW19 . . . 201 CT91
Sch Wimbledon Common Prep Sch, SW19 off Ridgway . . . 201 CX94
Sch Wimbledon High Sch, SW19
off Mansel Rd . . . 201 CZ93
Wimbledon Hill Rd, SW19 . . . 201 CY93
WIMBLEDON PARK, SW19 . . . 201 CZ90
⊖ Wimbledon Park . . . 202 DA90
Wimbledon Pk, SW19 . . . 201 CZ89
Wimbledon Pk Est, SW19 . . . 201 CY88
Sch Wimbledon Pk Prim Sch, SW19 off Havana Rd . . . 202 DB89
Wimbledon Pk Rd, SW18 . . . 201 CZ87
SW19 . . . 201 CZ88
Wimbledon Pk Side, SW19 . . . 201 CX89
Wimbledon Rd, SW17 . . . 202 DC91
Coll Wimbledon Sch of Art, SW19
off Merton Hall Rd . . . 221 CY95
Terry Bruen Bldg, SW19
off Palmerston Rd . . . 202 DA94
● Wimbledon Stadium Business Cen, SW17 . . . 202 DB90
★ Wimbledon Windmill Mus, SW19 . . . 201 CV89
Wimbolt St, E2 . . . 20 C2
Wimborne Av, Chis. BR7 . . . 227 ET98
Hayes UB4 . . . 157 BV72
Orpington BR5 . . . 227 ET98
Redhill RH1 . . . 288 DF139
Southall UB2 . . . 178 CA77
Wimborne Cl, SE12 . . . 206 EF85
Buckhurst Hill IG9 . . . 124 EH47
Epsom KT17 . . . 238 CS113
Sawbridgeworth CM21 . . . 58 EX05
Worcester Park KT4 . . . 221 CW102
Wimborne Dr, NW9 . . . 140 CN55
Pinner HA5 . . . 138 BX59
Wimborne Gdns, W13 . . . 159 CH72
Wimborne Gro, Wat. WD17 . . . 97 BS37
Wimborne Ho, SW8 . . . 42 D5
Wimborne Rd, N9 . . . 122 DU47
N17 . . . 122 DS54
Wimborne Way, Beck. BR3 . . . 225 DX97
Wimbourne Ct, N1 . . . 9 L10
Wimbourne St, N1 . . . 9 L10
Wimpole Cl, Brom. BR2 . . . 226 EJ98
Kingston upon Thames KT1 . . . 220 CM96
Wimpole Ms, W1 . . . 17 J6
Wimpole Rd, West Dr. UB7 . . . 156 BK74
Wimpole St, W1 . . . 17 J8
Wimshurst Cl, Croy. CR0 . . . 223 DL102
Winans Wk, SW9 . . . 42 E9
Wincanton Cres, Nthlt. UB5 . . . 138 CA64
Wincanton Gdns, Ilf. IG6 . . . 147 EP55
Wincanton Rd, SW18 . . . 201 CZ87
Romford RM3 . . . 128 FK48
Winchcombe Rd, Cars. SM5 . . . 222 DD101
Winchcomb Gdns, SE9 . . . 186 EK83
Winchdells, Hem.H. HP3 . . . 62 BN23
Winchelsea Av, Bexh. DA7 . . . 188 EZ80
Winchelsea Cl, SW15 . . . 201 CX85
Winchelsea Rd, E7 . . . 146 EG62
N17 . . . 144 DS55
NW10 . . . 160 CR67
Winchelsey Ri, S.Croy. CR2 . . . 242 DT107
Winchendon Rd, SW6 . . . 38 G5
Teddington TW11 . . . 199 CD91
Winchester Av, NW6 . . . 4 F8
NW9 . . . 140 CN55
Hounslow TW5 . . . 178 BZ79
Upminster RM14 . . . 151 FT60
Winchester Cl, E6 . . . 25 J9
SE17 . . . 31 H9
Amersham HP7 . . . 77 AS39
Bromley BR2 . . . 226 EF97
Colnbrook SL3 . . . 175 BE81
Enfield EN1 . . . 104 DS43
Esher KT10 . . . 236 CA105
Kingston upon Thames KT2 . . . 200 CP94
Waltham Abbey EN9
off Highbridge St . . . 89 EB33
Winchester Ct, E17
off Billet Rd . . . 123 DY53
Winchester Cres, Grav. DA12 . . . 213 GK90
Winchester Dr, Pnr. HA5 . . . 138 BX57
Winchester Gro, Sev. TN13 . . . 279 FH123
Winchester Ho, SE18
off Shooters Hill Rd . . . 186 EK80
Winchester Ms, NW3 . . . 6 B6
Worcester Park KT4 . . . 221 CX103
Winchester Pk, Brom. BR2 . . . 226 EF97
Winchester Pl, E8 . . . 10 A3
N6 . . . 143 DH60
Winchester Rd, E4 . . . 123 EC52
N6 . . . 143 DH60
N9 . . . 122 DU46
NW3 . . . 6 B6
Bexleyheath DA7 . . . 188 EX82
Bromley BR2 . . . 226 EF97
Feltham TW13 . . . 198 BZ90
Harrow HA3 . . . 140 CL56
Hayes UB3 . . . 177 BS80
Ilford IG1 . . . 147 ER62
Northwood HA6 . . . 137 BT55
Orpington BR6 . . . 246 EW105
Twickenham TW1 . . . 199 CH86
Walton-on-Thames KT12 . . . 217 BU102
Winchester Sq, SE1 . . . 31 L2
Winchester St, SW1 . . . 29 K10
W3 . . . 160 CQ74
Winchester Wk, SE1 . . . 31 L2
Winchester Way, Crox.Grn
WD3 . . . 97 BP43
Winchet Wk, Croy. CR0 . . . 224 DW100
Winchfield Cl, Har. HA3 . . . 139 CJ58
Winchfield Ho, SW15
off Highcliffe Dr . . . 201 CT86
Winchfield Rd, SE26 . . . 205 DY92
Winchfield Way, Rick. WD3 . . . 114 BJ45
Winchilsea Cres, W.Mol. KT8 . . . 218 CC96
WINCHMORE HILL, N21 . . . 121 DM45
WINCHMORE HILL, Amer.
HP7 . . . 110 AJ45
⇌ Winchmore Hill . . . 121 DN46
Winchmore Hill Rd, N14 . . . 121 DK46
N21 . . . 121 DK46
Sch Winchmore Sch, N21
off Laburnum Gro . . . 122 DQ47
Winchstone Cl, Shep. TW17 . . . 216 BM98
Winckley Cl, Har. HA3 . . . 140 CM57
Wincott St, SE11 . . . 30 F8
Wincrofts Dr, SE9 . . . 187 ER84
Windall Cl, SE19 . . . 224 DU95
Windborough Rd, Cars. SM5 . . . 240 DG108
Windermere Av, N3 . . . 142 DA55
NW6 . . . 4 F9
SW19 . . . 222 DB97
Harrow HA3 . . . 139 CJ59
Hornchurch RM12 . . . 149 FG64
Purfleet RM19 . . . 190 FQ78
Ruislip HA4 . . . 138 BW59
St. Albans AL1 . . . 65 CH22
Wembley HA9 . . . 139 CJ59
Windermere Cl, Chorl. WD3 . . . 95 BC43
Dartford DA1 . . . 209 FH88
Egham TW20 . . . 195 BB94
Feltham TW14 . . . 197 BT88
Hemel Hempstead HP3 . . . 63 BQ21
Orpington BR6 . . . 227 EP104
Staines TW19 . . . 196 BK89
Windermere Ct, SW13 . . . 181 CT79
Kenley CR8 . . . 257 DP115
Wembley HA9
off Windermere Av . . . 139 CJ59
Windermere Gdns, Ilf. IG4 . . . 146 EL57
Windermere Gro, Wem. HA9
off Windermere Av . . . 139 CJ60
Windermere Ho, Islw. TW7
off Summerwood Rd . . . 199 CF85
Windermere Pt, SE15 . . . 44 G4
Sch Windermere Prim Sch, St.Alb.
AL1 off Windermere Av . . . 65 CH22
Windermere Rd, N10 . . . 121 DH53
N19 off Holloway Rd . . . 143 DJ61
SW15 . . . 200 CS91
SW16 . . . 223 DJ95
W5 . . . 179 CJ76
Bexleyheath DA7 . . . 189 FC82
Coulsdon CR5 . . . 257 DL115
Croydon CR0 . . . 224 DT102
Southall UB1 . . . 158 BZ71
West Wickham BR4 . . . 226 EE103
Windermere Way, Reig. RH2 . . . 272 DD133
Slough SL1 . . . 152 AJ71
West Drayton UB7 . . . 156 BL74
Winders Rd, SW11 . . . 40 C8
Windfield, Lthd. KT22 . . . 253 CH121
Windfield Cl, SE26 . . . 205 DX91
Windgates, Guil. GU4
off Tychbourne Dr . . . 265 BC131
Windham Av, New Adgtn CR0 . . . 243 ED110
Windham Rd, Rich. TW9 . . . 180 CM83
Wind Hill, Magd.Lav. CM5 . . . 75 FF20
Windhill, Welw.G.C. AL7 . . . 52 DA08
Windhover Way, Grav. DA12 . . . 213 GL91
Windings, The, S.Croy. CR2 . . . 242 DT111
Winding Shot, Hem.H. HP1 . . . 62 BG19
Winding Way, Dag. RM8 . . . 148 EW62
Harrow HA1 . . . 139 CE63
Windlass Pl, SE8 . . . 33 M9
Windlesham Gro, SW19 . . . 201 CX88
Windley Cl, SE23 . . . 204 DW89
Windmill All, W4
off Windmill Rd . . . 180 CS77
Windmill Av, Epsom KT17 . . . 239 CT111
St. Albans AL4 . . . 65 CJ16
Southall UB2 . . . 178 CC75
Windmill Br Ho, Croy. CR0 . . . 224 DR102
● Windmill Business Village, Sun.
TW16 off Brooklands Cl . . . 217 BS95
Windmill Cl, SE1 . . . 32 D8
SE13 . . . 46 F8
Caterham CR3 . . . 258 DQ121
Epsom KT17 . . . 239 CT112
Horley RH6 . . . 291 DH148
Long Ditton KT6 . . . 219 CH102
Sunbury-on-Thames TW16 . . . 197 BS94
Upminster RM14 . . . 150 FN61
Waltham Abbey EN9 . . . 90 EE34
Windsor SL4 . . . 173 AP82
Windmill Ct, NW2 . . . 4 F4
Windmill Dr, NW2 . . . 141 CY62
SW4 . . . 203 DH85
Croxley Green WD3 . . . 96 BM44
Keston BR2 . . . 244 EJ105
Leatherhead KT22 . . . 253 CJ123
Reigate RH2 . . . 272 DD132
Windmill End, Epsom KT17 . . . 239 CT112
Windmill Fld, Ware SG12 . . . 55 DX07
Windmill Flds, Harl. CM17 . . . 58 EZ11
Windmill Gdns, Enf. EN2 . . . 103 DN41
Windmill Grn, Shep. TW17 . . . 217 BS101
Windmill Gro, Croy. CR0 . . . 224 DQ101
WINDMILL HILL, Grav. DA11 . . . 213 GG88
Windmill Hill, NW3 . . . 142 DC62
Chipperfield WD4 . . . 79 BF32
Coleshill HP7 . . . 111 AM45
Enfield EN2 . . . 103 DP41
Ruislip HA4 . . . 137 BT59
Windmill Ho, E14 . . . 34 A8
Windmill La, E15 . . . 13 H4
Barnet EN5 . . . 101 CT44
Bushey Heath WD23 . . . 117 CE46
Cheshunt EN8 . . . 89 DX30
Epsom KT17 . . . 239 CT112
Greenford UB6 . . . 158 CC71
Isleworth TW7 . . . 179 CE77
Long Ditton KT6 . . . 219 CH100
Southall UB2 . . . 178 CC76
Windmill Ms, W4 . . . 180 CS77
Windmill Pas, W4 . . . 180 CS77
Windmill Ri, Kings.T. KT2 . . . 200 CP94
Windmill Rd, N18 . . . 122 DR49
SW18 . . . 202 DD86
SW19 . . . 201 CV88
W4 . . . 180 CS77
W5 . . . 179 CJ77
Brentford TW8 . . . 179 CK78
Chalfont St. Peter SL9 . . . 112 AX52
Croydon CR0 . . . 224 DQ101
Fulmer SL3 . . . 134 AX64
Hampton Hill TW12 . . . 198 CB92
Hemel Hempstead HP2 . . . 62 BL21
Mitcham CR4 . . . 223 DJ99
Sevenoaks TN13 . . . 279 FH130
Slough SL1 . . . 153 AR74
Sunbury-on-Thames TW16 . . . 217 BS95
Windmill Rd W, Sun. TW16 . . . 217 BS96
Windmill Row, SE11 . . . 42 E1
Windmill Shott, Egh. TW20
off Rusham Rd . . . 195 AZ93
Windmill St, W1 . . . 17 N7
Bushey Heath WD23 . . . 117 CE46
Gravesend DA12 . . . 213 GH86
● Windmill Trd Est, Mitch.
CR4 . . . 223 DJ98
Windmill Wk, SE1 . . . 30 F3
Windmill Way, Reig. RH2 . . . 272 DD132
Ruislip HA4 . . . 137 BT60
Windmill Wd, Amer. HP6 . . . 77 AN37
Windmore Av, Pot.B. EN6 . . . 85 CW31
Windmore Cl, Wem. HA0 . . . 139 CG64
Windover Av, NW9 . . . 140 CR56
Windridge Cl, St.Alb. AL3 . . . 64 CA22
Windrose Cl, SE16 . . . 33 J4
Windrush, N.Mal. KT3 . . . 220 CP98
Windrush Av, Slou. SL3 . . . 175 BB76
Windrush Cl, N17 . . . 122 DS53
SW11 off Maysoule Rd . . . 182 DD84
W4 . . . 180 CQ81
Uxbridge UB10 . . . 136 BM63
Windrushes, Cat. CR3 . . . 274 DU125
Windrush La, SE23 . . . 205 DX90
Sch Windrush Prim Sch, SE28
off Bentham Rd . . . 168 EV74
Windrush Rd, NW10 . . . 160 CR67
Windrush Sq, SW2
off Rushcroft Rd . . . 183 DN84
Winds End Cl, Hem.H. HP2 . . . 62 BN18
Windsock Cl, SE16 . . . 33 N8
WINDSOR, SL4 . . . 174 AS82
⇌ Windsor & Eton Central . . . 173 AR81
Windsor & Eton Relief Rd, Wind.
SL4 . . . 173 AP80
⇌ Windsor & Eton Riverside . . . 173 AR80
Windsor Av, E17 . . . 123 DY54
SW19 . . . 222 DC95
Edgware HA8 . . . 118 CP49
Grays RM16 . . . 192 GB75
New Malden KT3 . . . 220 CQ99
Sutton SM3 . . . 221 CY104
Uxbridge UB10 . . . 157 BP67
West Molesey KT8 . . . 218 CA97
Sch Windsor Boys' Sch, The, Wind.
SL4 off Maidenhead Rd . . . 173 AP81
★ Windsor Castle, Wind. SL4 . . . 174 AS80
● Windsor Cen, The, SE27 . . . 204 DQ91
Windsor Cl, N3 . . . 119 CY54
SE27 . . . 204 DQ91
Borehamwood WD6 . . . 100 CN39
Bovingdon HP3 . . . 79 BA28
Brentford TW8 . . . 179 CH79
Cheshunt EN7 . . . 88 DU30
Chislehurst BR7 . . . 207 EP92
Guildford GU2 . . . 280 AT136
Harrow HA2 . . . 138 CA62
Hemel Hempstead HP2 . . . 62 BL22
Northwood HA6 . . . 115 BU54
Windsor Ct, N14 . . . 121 DJ45
Sunbury-on-Thames TW16 . . . 197 BU94
Windsor Ct Rd, Chobham
GU24 . . . 232 AS109
Windsor Cres, Har. HA2 . . . 138 CA63
Loudwater HP10 . . . 110 AC53
Wembley HA9 . . . 140 CP62
Windsor Dr, Ashf. TW15 . . . 196 BK91
Barnet EN4 . . . 102 DF44
Dartford DA1 . . . 209 FG86
Hertford SG14 . . . 53 DM09
Orpington BR6 . . . 246 EU107
Windsor End, Beac. HP9 . . . 133 AM55
Windsor Gdns, W9 . . . 15 J6
Croydon CR0
off Richmond Rd . . . 223 DL104
Hayes UB3 . . . 177 BR76
Sch Windsor Girls' Sch, Wind.
SL4 off Imperial Rd . . . 173 AN83
★ Windsor Great Pk, Ascot SL5,
Egh. TW20 & Wind. SL4 . . . 194 AS93
Windsor Gt Pk, Ascot SL5 . . . 194 AS93
Egham TW20 . . . 194 AS93
Windsor Gro, SE27 . . . 204 DQ91
Windsor Hill, Woob.Grn HP10 . . . 132 AF58
Windsor Ho, N1 . . . 9 J10
Windsor La, Burn. SL1 . . . 152 AJ70
Wooburn Green HP10 . . . 132 AE58
Windsor Ms, SE6 . . . 205 EC88
SE23 . . . 205 DY88
Windsor Pk Rd, Hayes UB3 . . . 177 BT80
Windsor Pl, SW1 . . . 29 M7
Chertsey KT16
off Windsor St . . . 216 BG100
Harlow CM20 . . . 58 EU11
★ Windsor Racecourse (Royal),
Wind. SL4 . . . 173 AM79
Windsor Rd, E4
off Chivers Rd . . . 123 EB49
E7 . . . 146 EH64
E10 . . . 145 EB61
E11 . . . 146 EG60
N3 . . . 119 CY54
N7 . . . 143 DL62
N13 . . . 121 DN48
N17 . . . 122 DU54
NW2 . . . 161 CV65
W5 . . . 160 CL73
Barnet EN5 . . . 101 CX44
Beaconsfield HP9 . . . 133 AN57
Bexleyheath DA6 . . . 188 EY84
Chesham HP5 . . . 76 AP28
Chobham GU24 . . . 232 AS109
Dagenham RM8 . . . 148 EY62
Datchet SL3 . . . 174 AT80
Enfield EN3 . . . 105 DX36
Englefield Green TW20 . . . 195 AZ90
Eton SL4 . . . 173 AR79
Gerrards Cross SL9 . . . 134 AW60
Gravesend DA12 . . . 213 GH90
Harrow HA3 . . . 117 CD53
Hornchurch RM11 . . . 150 FJ59
Hounslow TW4 . . . 177 BV82
Ilford IG1 . . . 147 EP63
Kingston upon Thames KT2 . . . 200 CL94
Old Windsor SL4 . . . 194 AX88
Pilgrim's Hatch CM15 . . . 130 FV44
Richmond TW9 . . . 180 CM82
Slough SL1 . . . 174 AS76
Southall UB2 . . . 178 BZ76
Stoke Poges SL2 . . . 134 AU63
Sunbury-on-Thames TW16 . . . 197 BU93
Teddington TW11 . . . 199 CD92
Thornton Heath CR7 . . . 223 DP96
Water Oakley SL4 . . . 172 AF79
Watford WD24 . . . 98 BW38
Worcester Park KT4 . . . 221 CU103
Wraysbury TW19 . . . 194 AY86
Windsors, The, Buck.H. IG9 . . . 124 EL47
Windsor St, N1 . . . 9 H8
Chertsey KT16 . . . 216 BG100
Uxbridge UB8 . . . 156 BJ66
Windsor Ter, N1 . . . 19 K2
Windsor Wk, SE5 . . . 43 M9
Walton-on-Thames KT12
off King George Av . . . 218 BX102
Weybridge KT13 . . . 235 BP106
Windsor Way, W14 . . . 26 D8
Rickmansworth WD3 . . . 114 BG46
Woking GU22 . . . 249 BC116
Windsor Wf, E9 . . . 11 P3
Windsor Wd, Wal.Abb. EN9
off Monkswood Av . . . 90 EE33
Windspoint Dr, SE15 . . . 44 E3
Winds Ridge, Send GU23 . . . 265 BC125
Windus Rd, N16 . . . 144 DT60
Windus Wk, N16 . . . 144 DT60
Windward Cl, Enf. EN3
off Bullsmoor La . . . 105 DX35
Windycroft Cl, Pur. CR8 . . . 241 DK113
Windy Hill, Hutt. CM13 . . . 131 GC46
Windy Ridge, Brom. BR1 . . . 226 EL95
Windy Ridge Cl, SW19 . . . 201 CX92
Wine Cl, E1 . . . 32 G1
Wine Office Ct, EC4 . . . 18 F8
Winern Glebe, Byfleet KT14 . . . 234 BK113
Winery La, Kings.T. KT1 . . . 220 CM97
Winey Cl, Chess. KT9
off Nigel Fisher Way . . . 237 CJ108
Winfield Mobile Home Pk, Wat.
WD25 . . . 98 CB39
Winford Dr, Brox. EN10 . . . 71 DZ22
Winford Ho, E3 . . . 11 P7
Winford Par, Sthl. UB1
off Telford Rd . . . 158 CB72
Winforton St, SE10 . . . 46 E6
Winfrith Rd, SW18 . . . 202 DC87
Wingate Cres, Croy. CR0 . . . 223 DK100
Wingate Rd, W6 . . . 181 CV76
Ilford IG1 . . . 147 EP64
Sidcup DA14 . . . 208 EW92
Wingate Way, St.Alb. AL1 . . . 65 CG21
Wing Cl, N.Wld Bas. CM16
off Epping Rd . . . 92 FA27
Wingfield, Bad.Dene RM17 . . . 192 FZ78
Wingfield Bk, Nthflt DA11 . . . 212 GC89
Wingfield Cl, Brwd. CM13
off Pondfield La . . . 131 GA48
New Haw KT15 . . . 234 BH110
Wingfield Ct, E14 . . . 34 G1
off Newport Av
Banstead SM7 . . . 256 DA115
Wingfield Gdns, Upmin.
RM14 . . . 151 FT58
Wingfield Ho, NW6
off Tollgate Gdns . . . 5 L10
Wingfield Ms, SE15 . . . 44 C10
Sch Wingfield Prim Sch, SE3
off Moorehead Way . . . 186 EH83
Wingfield Rd, E15 . . . 13 J1
E17 . . . 145 EB57
Gravesend DA12 . . . 213 GH87
Kingston upon Thames KT2 . . . 200 CN93
Wingfield St, SE15 . . . 44 C10
Wingfield Way, Ruis. HA4 . . . 157 BV65
Wingford Rd, SW2 . . . 203 DL86
Wingletye La, Horn. RM11 . . . 150 FM60
Wingmore Rd, SE24 . . . 184 DQ83
Wingrave Cres, Brwd. CM14 . . . 130 FS49
Wingrave Rd, W6 . . . 38 B3
Wingrove Dr, Purf. RM19 . . . 190 FP78
Wingrove Rd, SE6 . . . 206 EE89
Wings Cl, Sutt. SM1 . . . 240 DA105
Wing Way, Brwd. CM14
off Geary Dr . . . 130 FW46
Winifred Av, Horn. RM12 . . . 150 FK63
Winifred Cl, Barn. EN5 . . . 101 CT44
Winifred Gro, SW11 . . . 182 DF84
Winifred Pl, N12 off High Rd . . . 120 DC50
Winifred Rd, SW19 . . . 222 DA95
Coulsdon CR5 . . . 256 DG116
Dagenham RM8 . . . 148 EY61
Dartford DA1 . . . 209 FH85
Erith DA8 . . . 189 FE78
Hampton Hill TW12 . . . 198 CA91
Hemel Hempstead HP3 . . . 62 BK24
Winifred St, E16 . . . 37 K3
Winifred Ter, E13 . . . 23 N1
Enfield EN1 . . . 122 DT45
Winkers Cl, Chal.St.P. SL9 . . . 113 AZ53
Winkers La, Chal.St.P. SL9 . . . 113 AZ53
Winkfield Rd, E13 . . . 24 A1
N22 . . . 121 DN53
Winkley St, E2 . . . 20 E1
Winkwell, Hem.H. HP2 . . . 61 BD22
Winkworth Pl, Bans. SM7
off Bolters La . . . 239 CZ114
Winkworth Rd, Bans. SM7 . . . 239 CZ114
Winlaton Rd, Brom. BR1 . . . 205 ED91
Winmill Rd, Dag. RM8 . . . 148 EZ62
Winnards, Wok. GU21
off Abercorn Way . . . 248 AV118
Winn Common Rd, SE18 . . . 187 ES79
Winnett St, W1 . . . 17 N10
Winningales Ct, Ilf. IG5
off Vienna Cl . . . 146 EL55
Winnings Wk, Nthlt. UB5
off Arnold Rd . . . 158 BY65
Winnington Cl, N2 . . . 142 DD58
Winnington Rd, N2 . . . 142 DD59
Enfield EN3 . . . 104 DW38
Winnington Way, Wok. GU21 . . . 248 AV118
Winnipeg Dr, Grn St Grn BR6 . . . 245 ET107
Winnipeg Way, Brox. EN10 . . . 89 DY25
Winnock Rd, West Dr. UB7 . . . 156 BK74
Winn Rd, SE12 . . . 206 EG88
Winns Av, E17 . . . 145 DY55
Winns Ms, N15 . . . 144 DS56
Sch Winns Prim Sch, E17
off Fleeming Rd . . . 123 DZ54
Winns Ter, E17 . . . 123 EA54
Winsbeach, E17 . . . 145 ED55
Winscombe Cres, W5 . . . 159 CK70
Winscombe St, N19 . . . 143 DH61
Winscombe Way, Stan. HA7 . . . 117 CG50
Winsford Rd, SE6 . . . 205 DZ90
Winsford Ter, N18 . . . 122 DR50
Winsham Gro, SW11 . . . 202 DG85
Winslade Rd, SW2 . . . 203 DL85
Winslade Way, SE6
off Rushey Grn . . . 205 EB87
Winsland Ms, W2 . . . 16 A8
Winsland St, W2 . . . 16 A8
Winsley St, W1 . . . 17 L8
Winslow, SE17 . . . 43 N1
Winslow Cl, NW10
off Neasden La N . . . 140 CS62
Pinner HA5 . . . 137 BV58
Winslow Gro, E4 . . . 124 EE47
Winslow Rd, W6 . . . 38 B2
Winslow Way, Felt. TW13 . . . 198 BX90
Walton-on-Thames KT12 . . . 218 BW104
Sch Winsor Prim Sch, E6 . . . 25 L9
Winsor Ter, E6 . . . 25 L7
Winstanley Cl, Cob. KT11 . . . 235 BV114
Winstanley Est, SW11 . . . 40 B10
Winstanley Rd, SW11 . . . 182 DD83
Winstanley Wk, Cob. KT11
off Winstanley Cl . . . 235 BV114
Winstead Gdns, Dag. RM10 . . . 149 FC64
Winston Av, NW9 . . . 140 CS59
Sch Winston Churchill Sch, The,
St.John's GU21
off Hermitage Rd . . . 248 AT118
Winston Churchill Way, Chsht
EN8 . . . 88 DW33
Winston Cl, Green. DA9 . . . 211 FT86
Harrow HA3 . . . 117 CF51
Romford RM7 . . . 149 FB56
Winston Ct, Har. HA3 . . . 116 CB52
Winston Dr, Bigg.H. TN16
off Polesteeple Hill . . . 260 EK117
Stoke D'Abernon KT11 . . . 252 BY116
Winstone Cl, Amer. HP6 . . . 76 AP34
Winston Gdns, Berk. HP4 . . . 60 AT19
Winston Rd, N16 . . . 9 M2
Winston Wk, W4
off Beaconsfield Rd . . . 180 CR76
Winston Way, Ilf. IG1 . . . 147 EP62
Old Woking GU22 . . . 249 BB120
Potters Bar EN6 . . . 86 DA34
Sch Winston Way Prim Sch, Ilf.
IG1 off Winston Way . . . 147 EQ61
Winstre Rd, Borwd. WD6 . . . 100 CN39
Winter Av, E6 . . . 166 EL67
Winterbourne Av, Orp. BR6 . . . 227 ER104
Winterbourne Gro, Wey. KT13 . . . 235 BQ107
Sch Winterbourne Inf & Nurs
Sch, Th.Hth. CR7
off Winterbourne Rd . . . 223 DN98
Sch Winterbourne Jun Boys'
Sch, Th.Hth. CR7
off Winterbourne Rd . . . 223 DN98
Sch Winterbourne Jun Girls'
Sch, Th.Hth. CR7
off Winterbourne Rd . . . 223 DN98
Winterbourne Ms, Oxt. RH8
off Brook Hill . . . 275 EC130
Winterbourne Rd, SE6 . . . 205 DZ88
Dagenham RM8 . . . 148 EW61
Thornton Heath CR7 . . . 223 DN98
Winter Box Wk, Rich. TW10 . . . 180 CM84
Winterbrook Rd, SE24 . . . 204 DQ86
Winterburn Cl, N11 . . . 120 DG51
Winterdown Gdns, Esher
KT10 . . . 236 BZ107
Winterdown Rd, Esher KT10 . . . 236 BZ107
Winterfold Cl, SW19 . . . 201 CY89
🔒 Wintergarden, Bluewater
DA9 off Bluewater Parkway . . . 211 FU87
Winter Gdn Cres, Bluewater
DA9 . . . 211 FU87
Winter Gdn Ho, WC2
off Macklin St . . . 18 B8
Wintergreen Cl, E6 . . . 24 G7
Winterhill Way, Guil. GU4 . . . 265 BB130
Winters Cft, Grav. DA12 . . . 213 GK93
Winterscroft Rd, Hodd. EN11 . . . 71 DZ16
Wintersells Rd, Byfleet KT14 . . . 234 BK110
Winters Rd, T.Ditt. KT7 . . . 219 CH101

A
B
C
D
E
F
G
H
I
J
K
L
M
N
O
P
Q
R
S
T
U
V
W
X
Y
Z

Winterstoke Gdns, NW7 ...... **119** CU50
Winterstoke Rd, SE6 ...... **205** DZ88
Winters Way, Wal.Abb. EN9 .... **90** EG33
Winterton Ho, E1 ...... **20** F9
Winterton Pl, SW10 ...... **39** P2
Winterwell Rd, SW2 ...... **203** DL85
Winthorpe Gdns, Borwd.
WD6 ...... **100** CM39
Winthorpe Rd, SW15 ...... **181** CY84
Winthrop St, E1 ...... **20** E6
Winthrop Wk, Wem. HA9
off Everard Way **140** CL62
Winton App, Crox.Grn WD3 .... **97** BQ43
Winton Av, N11 ...... **121** DJ52
Winton Cl, N9 ...... **123** DX45
Winton Cres, Crox.Grn WD3 ... **97** BP43
Winton Dr, Chsht EN8 ...... **89** DY29
Croxley Green WD3 ...... **97** BP44
Winton Gdns, Edg. HA8 ...... **118** CM52
Winton Prim Sch, N1 ...... **18** C1
Winton Rd, Orp. BR6 ...... **245** EP105
Ware SG12 ...... **55** DZ06
Winton Way, SW16 ...... **203** DN92
Wintoun Path, Slou. SL2 ...... **153** AL70
Winvale, Slou. SL1 ...... **174** AS76
Winwood, Slou. SL2 ...... **154** AW72
Wireless Rd, Bigg.H. TN16 .... **260** EK115
Wirrall Ho, SE26
off Sydenham Hill Est. **204** DU90
Wirral Wd Cl, Chis. BR7 ...... **207** EN93
Wisbeach Rd, Croy. CR0 ...... **224** DR99
Wisborough Rd, S.Croy. CR2 .. **242** DT109
Wisdom Dr, Hert. SG13 ...... **54** DS09
Wisdons Cl, Dag. RM10 ...... **149** FB60
Wise La, NW7 ...... **119** CV51
West Drayton UB7 ...... **176** BK77
Wiseman Ct, SE19 ...... **204** DS92
Wiseman Rd, E10 ...... **145** EA61
Wisemans Gdns, Saw. CM21 ... **58** EW06
Wise Rd, E15 ...... **12** F9
Wise's La, Hat. AL9 ...... **85** CW27
Wiseton Rd, SW17 ...... **202** DE88
Wishart Rd, SE3 ...... **186** EK81
Wishaw Wk, N13
off Elvendon Rd **121** DL51
Wishbone Way, Wok. GU21 .... **248** AT116
Wishford Ct, Ashtd. KT21
off The Marld **254** CM118
Wishmore Cross Sch, Chobham
GU24 *off Alpha Rd* **232** AT110
WISLEY, Wok. GU23 ...... **250** BL116
Wisley Common, Wok. GU23 .. **250** BN117
Wisley Ct, S.Croy. CR2
off Sanderstead Rd **242** DR110
Wisley Interchange, Cob.
KT11 ...... **251** BQ116
Wisley La, Wisley GU23 ...... **250** BL116
Wisley Rd, SW11 ...... **202** DG85
Orpington BR5 ...... **208** EU94
Wissants, Harl. CM19 ...... **73** EP19
Wistaria Cl, Orp. BR6 ...... **227** EP103
Pilgrim's Hatch CM15 ...... **130** FW43
Wistaria Dr, Lon.Col. AL2 ...... **83** CH26
Wisteria Apts, E9
off Chatham Pl **10** G4
Wisteria Cl, NW7 ...... **119** CT51
Ilford IG1 ...... **147** EP64
Wisteria Gdns, Swan. BR8 .... **229** FD96
Wisteria Rd, SE13 ...... **185** ED84
Wistlea Cres, Coln.Hth AL4 .... **66** CP22
Witanhurst La, N6 ...... **142** DG60
Witan St, E2 ...... **20** F3
Witches La, Sev. TN13 ...... **278** FD122
Witchford, Welw.G.C. AL7 ...... **52** DD09
Witcombe Pt, SE15 ...... **44** E7
Witham Cl, Loug. IG10 ...... **106** EL44
Witham Rd, SE20 ...... **224** DW97
W13 ...... **159** CG74
Dagenham RM10 ...... **148** FA64
Isleworth TW7 ...... **179** CD81
Romford RM2 ...... **149** FH57
Withens Cl, Orp. BR5 ...... **228** EW98
Witherby Cl, Croy. CR0 ...... **242** DS106
Wither Dale, Horl. RH6 ...... **290** DE147
Witheridge La, Knot.Grn HP9 .. **110** AF48
Penn HP10 ...... **110** AF48
Witherings, The, Horn. RM11 .. **150** FL57
Witherington Rd, N5 ...... **8** F3
Withers Cl, Chess. KT9
off Coppard Gdns **237** CJ107
Withers Mead, NW9 ...... **119** CT53
Witherston Way, SE9 ...... **207** EN89
Withey Brook, Hkwd RH6 .... **290** DD150
Withey Cl, Wind. SL4 ...... **173** AL81
Witheygate Av, Stai. TW18 .... **196** BH93
Withey Meadows, Hkwd RH6 . **290** DD150
Withies, The, Knap. GU21 .... **248** AS117
Leatherhead KT22 ...... **253** CH120
Withybed Cor, Walt.Hill KT20 . **255** CV123
Withycombe Rd, SW19 ...... **201** CX87
Withycroft, Geo.Grn SL3 ...... **154** AY72
Withy La, Ruis. HA4 ...... **137** BQ57
Withy Mead, E4 ...... **123** ED48
Withy Pl, Park St AL2 ...... **82** CC28
Witley Cres, New Adgtn CR0 .. **243** EC107
Witley Gdns, Sthl. UB2 ...... **178** BZ77
Witley Pt, SW15
off Wanborough Dr **201** CV88
Witley Rd, N19 ...... **143** DJ61
Witney Cl, Pnr. HA5 ...... **116** BZ51
Uxbridge UB10 ...... **136** BM63
Witney Path, SE23 ...... **205** DX90
Wittenham Way, E4 ...... **123** ED48
Wittering Cl, Kings.T. KT2 .... **199** CK92
Wittering Wk, Horn. RM12 .... **170** FJ65
Wittersham Rd, Brom. BR1 .... **206** EF92
Wivenhoe Cl, SE15 ...... **44** E10
Wivenhoe Ct, Houns. TW3 .... **178** BZ84
Wivenhoe Rd, Bark. IG11 ...... **168** EU68
Wiverton Rd, SE26 ...... **204** DW93
Wix Hill, W.Hors. KT24 ...... **267** BP130
Wix Hill Cl, W.Hors. KT24 .... **267** BP131
Wix Prim Sch, SW4
off Wixs La **183** DH83
Wix Rd, Dag. RM9 ...... **168** EX67
Wixs La, SW4 ...... **183** DH84
Woburn Av, Horn. RM12 ...... **149** FG63
Purley CR8 *off High St* **241** DN111
Theydon Bois CM16 ...... **107** ES37
Woburn Cl, SE28
off Summerton Way **168** EX72
SW19 ...... **202** DC93
Bushey WD23 ...... **98** CC43
Woburn Ct, SE16
off Masters Dr **44** F1
Woburn Hill, Add. KT15 ...... **216** BJ103
Woburn Pl, WC1 ...... **17** P4
Woburn Rd, Cars. SM5 ...... **222** DE102
Croydon CR0 ...... **224** DQ102
Woburn Sq, WC1 ...... **17** P5
Woburn Wk, WC1 ...... **17** P3
Wodeham Gdns, E1 ...... **20** D6
Wodehouse Av, SE5 ...... **44** A6
Wodehouse Rd, Dart. DA1 ...... **190** FN84
Wodeland Av, Guil. GU2 ...... **280** AV136
Woffington Cl, Kings.T. KT1 .... **219** CJ95
Wokindon Rd, Grays RM16 .... **193** GH76
WOKING, GU22 - GU24 ...... **249** AZ117
⇌ **Woking** **249** AZ117
Woking Adult Learning Cen,
Wok. GU22 *off Bonsey La* . **248** AX121
● **Woking Business Pk**, Wok.
GU21 ...... **249** BB115
Woking Cl, SW15 ...... **181** CT84
Woking Coll, Wok. GU22
off Rydens Way **249** BA120
Woking Comm Hosp, Wok.
GU22 ...... **249** AZ118
Woking High Sch, Horsell
GU21 *off Morton Rd* **248** AX115
Woking Nuffield Hosp, The,
Wok. GU21 ...... **232** AY114
Woking Rd, Guil. GU1, GU4 .. **264** AX130
Wold, The, Wold. CR3 ...... **259** EA122
Woldham Pl, Brom. BR2 ...... **226** EJ98
Woldham Rd, Brom. BR2 ...... **226** EJ98
WOLDINGHAM, Cat. CR3 ...... **259** EB122
⇌ **Woldingham** **259** DX122
WOLDINGHAM GARDEN VILLAGE,
Cat. CR3 ...... **259** DY121
Woldingham Rd, Wold. CR3 ... **258** DV120
Woldingham Sch, Wold.
CR3 *off Marden Pk* **275** DY125
Wolds Dr, Orp. BR6 ...... **245** EN105
Wolfe Cl, Brom. BR2 ...... **226** EG100
Hayes UB4 ...... **157** BV69
Wolfe Cres, SE7 ...... **186** EK78
SE16 ...... **33** J5
Wolferton Rd, E12 ...... **147** EM63
Wolffe Gdns, E15 ...... **13** L5
Wolf Flds Prim Sch, Sthl.
UB2 *off Norwood Rd* **178** BZ77
Wolfram Cl, SE13 ...... **206** EE85
Wolfington Rd, SE27 ...... **203** DP91
Wolf La, Wind. SL4 ...... **173** AK83
Wolfs Hill, Oxt. RH8 ...... **276** EG131
Wolfson Hillel Prim Sch,
N14 *off Chase Rd* **103** DK44
**Wolfson Neurorehabilitation
Cen**, SW20 ...... **201** CV94
Wolf's Row, Oxt. RH8 ...... **276** EH130
Wolfs Wd, Oxt. RH8 ...... **276** EG132
Wolftencroft Cl, SW11 ...... **40** B10
Wollaston Cl, SE1 ...... **31** J8
Wolmer Cl, Edg. HA8 ...... **118** CP49
Wolmer Gdns, Edg. HA8 ...... **118** CN48
Wolseley Av, SW19 ...... **202** DA89
Wolseley Gdns, W4 ...... **180** CP79
Wolseley Rd, E7 ...... **166** EH66
N8 ...... **143** DK58
N22 ...... **121** DM53
W4 ...... **180** CQ77
Harrow HA3 ...... **139** CE55
Mitcham CR4 ...... **222** DG101
Romford RM7 ...... **149** FD59
Wolseley St, SE1 ...... **32** B5
Wolsey Av, E6 ...... **25** L3
E17 ...... **145** DZ55
Cheshunt EN7 ...... **88** DT29
Thames Ditton KT7 ...... **219** CF99
● **Wolsey Business Pk**, Wat.
WD18 ...... **115** BR45
Wolsey Cl, SW20 ...... **201** CV94
Hounslow TW3 ...... **178** CC84
Kingston upon Thames KT2 . **220** CP95
Southall UB2 ...... **178** CC76
Worcester Park KT4 ...... **239** CU105
Wolsey Cres, Mord. SM4 ...... **221** CY101
New Addington CR0 ...... **243** EC109
Wolsey Dr, Kings.T. KT2 ...... **200** CL92
Walton-on-Thames KT12 .... **218** BX102
Wolsey Gdns, Ilf. IG6 ...... **125** EQ51
Wolsey Gro, Edg. HA8 ...... **118** CR52
Esher KT10 ...... **236** CB105
Wolsey Inf Sch, Croy. CR0
off King Henry's Dr **243** EC108
Wolsey Jun Sch, New Adgtn
CR0 *off King Henry's Dr* ... **243** EC108
Wolsey Ms, NW5 ...... **7** L4
Orpington BR6 ...... **245** ET106
🔒 **Wolsey Pl Shop Cen**, Wok.
GU21 *off Commercial Way* . **249** AZ117
Wolsey Rd, N1 ...... **9** M3
Ashford TW15 ...... **196** BL91
East Molesey KT8 ...... **219** CD98
Enfield EN1 ...... **104** DV40
Esher KT10 ...... **236** CB105
Hampton Hill TW12 ...... **198** CB93
Hemel Hempstead HP2 ...... **62** BK21
Northwood HA6 ...... **115** BQ47
Sunbury-on-Thames TW16 .. **197** BT94
Wolsey St, E1 ...... **20** G7
Wolsey Wk, Wok. GU21 ...... **248** AY117
Wolsey Way, Chess. KT9 ...... **238** CN106
Wolsley Cl, Dart. DA1 ...... **209** FE85
Wolstan Cl, Denh. UB9 ...... **136** BG62
Wolstonbury, N12 ...... **120** DA50
Wolvens La, Dor. RH4, RH5 .. **284** CA140
Wolvercote Rd, SE2 ...... **188** EX75
Wolverley St, E2 ...... **20** E3
Wolverton, SE17 ...... **31** M10
Wolverton Av, Kings.T. KT2 .... **220** CN95
Wolverton Cl, Horl. RH6 ...... **290** DF150
Wolverton Gdns, W5 ...... **160** CM73
W6 ...... **26** C8
Horley RH6 ...... **290** DF149
Wolverton Rd, Stan. HA7 ...... **117** CH51
Wolverton Way, N14 ...... **103** DJ43
Wolves La, N13 ...... **121** DN52
N22 ...... **121** DN52
Wombwell Gdns, Nthflt DA11 . **212** GE89
WOMBWELL PARK, Grav.
DA11 ...... **212** GD89
Womersley Rd, N8 ...... **143** DM58
WONERSH, Guil. GU5 ...... **281** BB144
Wonersh Common, Won.
GU5 ...... **281** BB141
Wonersh Common Rd, Won.
GU5 ...... **281** BB142
Wonersh Way, Sutt. SM2 ...... **239** CX109
Wonford Cl, Kings.T. KT2 ...... **220** CS95
Walton on the Hill KT20 .... **271** CU126
Wonham La, Bet. RH3 ...... **286** CS135
Wonham Way, Guil. GU5 ...... **283** BR139
Wonnacott Pl, Enf. EN3 ...... **105** DX36
Wontford Rd, Pur. CR8 ...... **257** DN115
Wontner Cl, N1 ...... **9** J7
Wontner Rd, SW17 ...... **202** DF89
WOOBURN, H.Wyc. HP10 .... **132** AD58
Wooburn Cl, Uxb. UB8
off Aldenham Dr **157** BP70
Wooburn Common, Woob.Grn
HP10 ...... **132** AH59
Wooburn Common Rd, Slou.
SL1 ...... **132** AH61
Wooburn Green HP10 ...... **132** AH61
Wooburn Gra, Woob.Grn
HP10 ...... **132** AD60
WOOBURN GREEN, H.Wyc.
HP10 ...... **132** AF56
Wooburn Grn La, Beac. HP9 .. **132** AG56
● **Wooburn Ind Pk**, Woob.Grn
HP10 ...... **132** AD59
Wooburn Manor Pk, Woob.Grn
HP10 ...... **132** AE58
Wooburn Mead, Woob.Grn
HP10 ...... **132** AE57
Wooburn Ms, Woob.Grn HP10 . **132** AE58
Wooburn Town, Woob.Grn
HP10 ...... **132** AD59
Woodall Cl, E14 ...... **22** D10
Chessington KT9 ...... **237** CK108
Woodall Rd, Enf. EN3 ...... **105** DX44
Wood Av, Purf. RM19 ...... **190** FQ77
Woodbank, Rick. WD3 ...... **96** BJ44
Woodbank Av, Ger.Cr. SL9 .... **134** AX58
Woodbank Dr, Ch.St.G. HP8 .. **112** AX48
Woodbank Rd, Brom. BR1 ...... **206** EF90
Woodbastwick Rd, SE26 ...... **205** DX92
Woodberry Av, N21 ...... **121** DN47
Harrow HA2 ...... **138** CB56
Woodberry Cl, NW7 ...... **119** CX52
Sunbury-on-Thames TW16 .. **197** BU93
Woodberry Cres, N10 ...... **143** DH55
Woodberry Down, N4 ...... **144** DQ59
Epping CM16 ...... **92** EU29
**Woodberry Down Comm Prim
Sch**, N4 *off Woodberry Gro* . **144** DQ59
Woodberry Down Est, N4 .... **144** DQ59
Woodberry Gdns, N12 ...... **120** DC51
Woodberry Gro, N4 ...... **144** DQ59
N12 ...... **120** DC51
Bexley DA5 ...... **209** FD90
Woodberry Way, E4 ...... **123** EC46
N12 ...... **120** DC51
Woodbine Cl, Harl. CM19 ...... **73** EQ17
Twickenham TW2 ...... **199** CD89
Waltham Abbey EN9 ...... **106** EJ35
Woodbine Gro, SE20 ...... **204** DV94
Enfield EN2 ...... **104** DR38
Woodbine La, Wor.Pk. KT4 .... **221** CV104
Woodbine Pl, E11 ...... **146** EG58
Woodbine Rd, Sid. DA15 ...... **207** ES88
Woodbines Av, Kings.T. KT1 .. **219** CK97
Woodbine Ter, E9 ...... **11** H4
Woodborough Rd, SW15 ...... **181** CV84
Woodbourne Av, SW16 ...... **203** DK90
Woodbourne Cl, SW16
off Woodbourne Av **203** DL90
Woodbourne Dr, Clay. KT10 ... **237** CF107
Woodbourne Gdns, Wall.
SM6 ...... **241** DH108
Woodbridge Av, Lthd. KT22 .. **253** CG118
● **Woodbridge Business Pk**,
Guil. GU1 ...... **264** AW133
Woodbridge Cl, N7 ...... **143** DM61
NW2 ...... **141** CU62
Romford RM3 ...... **128** FK49
Woodbridge Ct, Wdf.Grn. IG8 . **124** EL52
Woodbridge Gro, Lthd. KT22 .. **253** CG118
**Woodbridge High Sch &
Language Coll**, Wdf.Grn.
IG8 *off St. Barnabas Rd* ... **124** EH52
WOODBRIDGE HILL, Guil.
GU2 ...... **264** AU132
Woodbridge Hill, Guil. GU2 ... **264** AV133
Woodbridge Hill Gdns, Guil.
GU2 ...... **264** AU133
Woodbridge La, Rom. RM3 ... **128** FK48
Woodbridge Meadows, Guil.
GU1 ...... **264** AW133
Woodbridge Rd, Bark. IG11 ... **147** ET64
Guildford GU1 ...... **264** AW133
Woodbridge St, EC1 ...... **18** G4
Woodbrook Gdns, Wal.Abb.
EN9 ...... **90** EE33
Woodbrook Rd, SE2 ...... **188** EU79
Woodburn Cl, NW4 ...... **141** CX57
Woodbury Cl, E11 ...... **146** EH56
Biggin Hill TN16 ...... **261** EM118
Bourne End SL8 ...... **132** AC59
Croydon CR0 ...... **224** DT103
Woodbury Dr, Sutt. SM2 ...... **240** DC110
Woodbury Gdns, SE12 ...... **206** EH90
Woodbury Hill, Loug. IG10 ...... **106** EL41
Woodbury Hollow, Loug. IG10 . **106** EL40
Woodbury Pk Rd, W13 ...... **159** CH70
Woodbury Rd, E17 ...... **145** EB56
Biggin Hill TN16 ...... **261** EM118
Woodbury St, SW17 ...... **202** DE92
Woodchester Pk, Knot.Grn
HP9 ...... **110** AJ50
Woodchester Sq, W2 ...... **15** L6
Woodchurch Cl, Sid. DA14 .... **207** ER90
Woodchurch Dr, Brom. BR1 ... **206** EK94
Woodchurch Rd, NW6 ...... **5** K7
Wood Cl, E2 ...... **20** C4
NW9 ...... **140** CR59
Bexley DA5 ...... **209** FE90
Harrow HA1 ...... **139** CD59
Hatfield AL10 ...... **67** CV18
Redhill RH1 ...... **288** DG143
Windsor SL4 ...... **173** AQ84
Woodclyffe Dr, Chis. BR7 ...... **227** EN96
Woodcock Ct, Har. HA3 ...... **140** CL59
Woodcock Dell Av, Har. HA3 .. **139** CK59
Woodcock Hill, Berk. HP4 ...... **60** AS18
Harrow HA3 ...... **139** CK59
Rickmansworth WD3 ...... **114** BL50
Sandridge AL4 ...... **66** CN15
● **Woodcock Hill Ind Est**, Rick.
WD3 ...... **114** BL49
Woodcocks, E16 ...... **24** D7
Woodcombe Cres, SE23 ...... **204** DW88
Wood Common, Hat. AL10 ...... **67** CV15
WOODCOTE, Epsom KT18 .... **254** CQ116
WOODCOTE, Pur. CR8 ...... **241** DK111
Woodcote, Guil. GU2 ...... **280** AV138
Horley RH6 ...... **291** DH147
Woodcote Av, NW7 ...... **119** CW51
Hornchurch RM12 ...... **149** FG63
Thornton Heath CR7 ...... **223** DP98
Wallington SM6 ...... **241** DH108
Woodcote Cl, Chsht EN8 ...... **88** DW30
Enfield EN3 ...... **104** DW44
Epsom KT18 ...... **238** CR114
Kingston upon Thames KT2 . **200** CM92
Woodcote Dr, Orp. BR6 ...... **227** ER102
Purley CR8 ...... **241** DK110
Woodcote End, Epsom KT18 .. **254** CR115
Woodcote Grn, Wall. SM6 .... **241** DJ109
Woodcote Grn Rd, Epsom
KT18 ...... **254** CQ116
Woodcote Gro, Couls. CR5 .... **241** DH112
Woodcote Gro Rd, Couls. CR5 . **257** DK115
Woodcote High Sch,
Couls. CR5
off Meadow Ri **241** DK113
Woodcote Hurst, Epsom
KT18 ...... **254** CQ116
Woodcote La, Pur. CR8 ...... **241** DK111
Woodcote Lawns, Chesh. HP5
off Little Hivings **76** AN27
Woodcote Ms, Loug. IG10 ...... **124** EK45
Wallington SM6 ...... **241** DH107
WOODCOTE PARK, Couls.
CR5 ...... **241** DH113
Woodcote Pk, Epsom KT18 ... **254** CQ117
Woodcote Pk Av, Pur. CR8 .... **241** DJ112
Woodcote Pk Rd, Epsom
KT18 ...... **254** CQ116
Woodcote Pl, SE27 ...... **203** DP92
Woodcote Prim Sch, Couls.
CR5 *off Dunsfold Ri* **241** DK114
Woodcote Rd, E11 ...... **146** EG59
Epsom KT18 ...... **238** CR114
Purley CR8 ...... **241** DJ109
Wallington SM6 ...... **241** DH107
Woodcote Side, Epsom KT18 . **254** CP115
Woodcote Valley Rd, Pur. CR8 . **241** DK113
Woodcott Ho, SW15
off Ellisfield Dr **201** CU87
Wood Ct, W12
off Heathstan Rd **161** CU72
Wood Cres, Hem.H. HP3 ...... **62** BK21
Woodcrest Rd, Pur. CR8 ...... **241** DL113
Woodcrest Wk, Reig. RH2 .... **272** DE132
Woodcroft, N21 ...... **121** DM46
SE9 ...... **207** EM90
Greenford UB6 ...... **159** CG65
Harlow CM18 ...... **73** EQ17
Woodcroft Av, NW7 ...... **118** CS52
Stanmore HA7 ...... **117** CF53
Stanstead Abbotts SG12 .... **55** ED11
Woodcroft Cres, Uxb. UB10 .. **157** BP67
Woodcroft Ms, SE8 ...... **33** L9
Woodcroft Prim Sch,
Edg. HA8
off Goldbeaters Gro **118** CS52
Woodcroft Rd, Chesh. HP5 .... **76** AR28
Thornton Heath CR7 ...... **223** DP99
Woodcroft Sch,
Loug. IG10
off Whitakers Way **107** EM39
Woodcutters Av, Grays RM16 . **192** GC75
Woodcutters Cl, Horn. RM11 .. **150** FK56
Wood Dr, Chis. BR7 ...... **206** EL93
Sevenoaks TN13 ...... **278** FF126
Woodedge Cl, E4 ...... **124** EF46
Wooden Br, Guil. GU2 ...... **264** AU133
Woodend, SE19 ...... **204** DQ93
Esher KT10 ...... **218** CC103
Wood End, Hayes UB3 ...... **157** BS72
Woodend, Lthd. KT22 ...... **269** CJ125
Wood End, Park St AL2 ...... **82** CC28
Woodend, Sutt. SM1 ...... **222** DC103
Wood End, Swan. BR8 ...... **229** FC98
Woodend, The, Wall. SM6 .... **241** DH109
Wood End Av, Har. HA2 ...... **138** CB63
Wood End Cl, Farn.Com. SL2 . **133** AR62
Hemel Hempstead HP2 ...... **63** BQ19
Northolt UB5 ...... **139** CD64
Woodend Cl, Wok. GU21 ...... **248** AU119
Woodend Gdns, Enf. EN2 ...... **103** DL42
Wood End Gdns, Nthlt. UB5 ... **138** CC64
Wood End Grn Rd, Hayes
UB3 ...... **157** BR71
Wood End Inf Sch, Nthlt.
UB5 *off Whitton Av W* **139** CD64
Wood End Jun Sch, Grnf.
UB6 *off Vernon Ri* **139** CD64
Wood End La, Nthlt. UB5 ...... **158** CB65
Woodend Pk, Cob. KT11 ...... **252** BX115
Wood End Pk Comm Sch,
Hayes UB3
off Judge Heath La **157** BQ73
Woodend Rd, E17 ...... **123** EC54
Wood End Rd, Har. HA1 ...... **139** CD63
Wood End Way, Nthlt. UB5 ... **138** CC64
Wooder Gdns, E7 ...... **13** N1
Wooderson Cl, SE25 ...... **224** DS98
Woodfall Av, Barn. EN5 ...... **101** CZ43
Woodfall Dr, Dart. DA1 ...... **189** FE84
Woodfall Rd, N4 ...... **143** DN60
Woodfall St, SW3 ...... **40** E1
Wood Fm Rd, Hem.H. HP2 ...... **62** BL20
Woodfarrs, SE5 ...... **184** DR84
Wood Fld, NW3 ...... **6** E3
Woodfield, Ashtd. KT21 ...... **253** CK117
Woodfield Av, NW9 ...... **140** CS56
SW16 ...... **203** DK90
W5 ...... **159** CJ70
Carshalton SM5 ...... **240** DG107
Gravesend DA11 ...... **213** GH88
Northwood HA6 ...... **115** BS49
Wembley HA0 ...... **139** CJ62
Woodfield Cl, SE19 ...... **204** DQ94
Ashtead KT21 ...... **253** CK117
Coulsdon CR5 ...... **257** DJ119
Enfield EN1 ...... **104** DS42
Redhill RH1 ...... **272** DE133
Woodfield Cres, W5 ...... **159** CJ70
Woodfield Dr, E.Barn. EN4 .... **120** DG46
Hemel Hempstead HP3 ...... **63** BR22
Romford RM2 ...... **149** FG56
Woodfield Gdns, W9 ...... **15** H6
Hemel Hempstead HP3 ...... **63** BQ22
New Malden KT3 ...... **221** CT99
Woodfield Gro, SW16 ...... **203** DK90
Woodfield Hill, Couls. CR5 .... **257** DH119
Woodfield La, SW16 ...... **203** DK90
Ashtead KT21 ...... **254** CL116
Hatfield AL9 ...... **68** DD23
Hertford SG13 ...... **68** DD23
Woodfield Pk, Amer. HP6 ...... **77** AN37
Woodfield Pl, W9 ...... **15** H5
Woodfield Ri, Bushey WD23 ... **117** CD45
Woodfield Rd, W5 ...... **159** CJ70
W9 ...... **15** H6
Ashtead KT21 ...... **253** CK117
Hounslow TW4 ...... **177** BV82
Radlett WD7 ...... **99** CG36
Thames Ditton KT7 ...... **219** CF103
Welwyn Garden City AL7 ...... **51** CZ09
Woodfields, Sev. TN13 ...... **278** FD122
Woodfields, The, S.Croy. CR2 . **242** DT111
Woodfield Sch, NW9
off Glenwood Av **140** CS60
Hemel Hempstead HP3
off Malmes Cft **63** BQ22
Merstham RH1
off Sunstone Gro **273** DL129
Woodfield Ter, Hare. UB9 ...... **114** BH54
Thornwood CM16 ...... **92** EW25
Woodfield Way, N11 ...... **121** DK52
Hornchurch RM12 ...... **150** FK60
Redhill RH1 ...... **272** DE132
St. Albans AL4 ...... **65** CJ17
Woodfines, The, Horn. RM11 .. **150** FK58
WOODFORD, Wdf.Grn. IG8 ... **124** EH51
⊖ **Woodford** **124** EH51
Woodford Av, Ilf. IG2, IG4 ...... **147** EM57
Woodford Green IG8 ...... **146** EK55
WOODFORD BRIDGE, Wdf.Grn.
IG8 ...... **125** EM52
Woodford Br Rd, Ilf. IG4 ...... **146** EK55
**Woodford Co High Sch for
Girls**, Wdf.Grn. IG8
off High Rd Woodford Grn . **124** EF51
Woodford Ct, W12 ...... **26** C4
Waltham Abbey EN9 ...... **90** EG33
Woodford Cres, Pnr. HA5 ...... **115** BV54
WOODFORD GREEN, IG8 ...... **124** EF49
Woodford Grn Prep Sch,
Wdf.Grn. IG8
off Glengall Rd **124** EG51
Woodford Grn Prim Sch,
Wdf.Grn. IG8
off Sunset Av **124** EG50
Woodford New Rd, E17 ...... **146** EE56
E18 ...... **124** EE53
Woodford Green IG8 ...... **124** EE53
Woodford Pl, Wem. HA9 ...... **140** CL60
Woodford Rd, E7 ...... **146** EH63
E18 ...... **146** EG56
Watford WD17 ...... **97** BV40
● **Woodford Trd Est**, Wdf.Grn.
IG8 ...... **124** EJ54
Woodford Way, Slou. SL2 ...... **153** AN69
WOODFORD WELLS, Wdf.Grn.
IG8 ...... **124** EH49
Woodgate, Wat. WD25 ...... **81** BV33
Woodgate Av, Chess. KT9 ...... **237** CK106
Northaw EN6 ...... **87** DH33
Woodgate Cl, Cob. KT11 ...... **235** BV113
Woodgate Ct, Horn. RM11
off Stafford Av **150** FK55
Woodgate Cres, Nthwd. HA6 .. **115** BU51
Woodgate Dr, SW16 ...... **203** DK94
Woodgate Ms, Wat. WD17
off Langwood Gdns **97** BU39
Woodgavil, Bans. SM7 ...... **255** CZ116
Woodger Cl, Guil. GU4 ...... **265** BC132
Woodger Rd, W12 ...... **26** B5
Woodgers Gro, Swan. BR8 .... **229** FF96
Woodget Cl, E6 ...... **24** G8
Woodgrange Av, N12 ...... **120** DD51
W5 ...... **160** CN74
Enfield EN1 ...... **104** DU44
Harrow HA3 ...... **139** CJ57
Woodgrange Cl, Har. HA3 .... **139** CK57
Woodgrange Gdns, Enf. EN1 .. **104** DU44
Woodgrange Inf Sch, E7
off Sebert Rd **146** EH63
⊖ **Woodgrange Park** **146** EK64
Woodgrange Rd, E7 ...... **13** P2
Woodgrange Ter, Enf. EN1 .... **104** DU44
WOOD GREEN, N22 ...... **121** DL53
⊖ **Wood Green** **121** DM54
Woodgreen Rd, Wal.Abb. EN9 . **106** EJ35
🔒 **Wood Grn Shop City**, N22 . **121** DN54
Wood Grn Way, Chsht EN8 .... **89** DY31
WOODHALL, Welw.G.C. AL7 ... **51** CY11
Woodhall, NW1 ...... **17** L3
Woodhall Av, SE21 ...... **204** DT90
Pinner HA5 ...... **116** BY54
Woodhall Cl, Hert. SG14 ...... **54** DQ07
Uxbridge UB8 ...... **136** BK64
Woodhall Ct, Welw.G.C. AL7 ... **51** CY10
Woodhall Cres, Horn. RM11 ... **150** FM59
Woodhall Dr, SE21 ...... **204** DT90
Pinner HA5 ...... **116** BX53
Woodhall Gate, Pnr. HA5 ...... **116** BX52
Woodhall Ho, SW18
off Fitzhugh Gro **202** DD86
Woodhall La, Hem.H. HP2 ...... **62** BL19
Shenley WD7 ...... **100** CL35
Watford WD19 ...... **116** BX49
Welwyn Garden City AL7 ...... **51** CY10
Woodhall Par, Welw.G.C. AL7 .. **51** CZ11
Woodhall Prim Sch, S.Oxhey
WD19 *off Woodhall La* **116** BY49
Woodhall Rd, Pnr. HA5 ...... **116** BX52
WOODHAM, Add. KT15 ...... **233** BF111
Woodham Ct, E18 ...... **146** EF56
Woodham Gate, Wok. GU21 .... **233** BC113
Woodham La, Add. KT15 ...... **234** BG110
Woking GU21 ...... **233** BB114
Woodham Lock, W.Byf. KT14 .. **233** BF112
Woodham Pk Rd, Wdhm
KT15 ...... **233** BF109
Woodham Pk Way, Wdhm
KT15 ...... **233** BF111
Woodham Ri, Wok. GU21 ...... **233** AZ114
Woodham Rd, SE6 ...... **205** EC90
Woking GU21 ...... **248** AY115
Woodham Way, Stans.Abb.
SG12 ...... **55** EC11
Woodham Waye, Wok. GU21 .. **233** BB113
WOODHATCH, Reig. RH2 ...... **288** DC137
Woodhatch Cl, E6 ...... **24** G7
Woodhatch Rd, Red. RH1 ...... **288** DB137
Reigate RH2 ...... **288** DB137
Woodhatch Spinney, Couls.
CR5 ...... **257** DL116
Woodhaven Gdns, Ilf. IG6
off Brandville Gdns **147** EQ56
Woodhaw, Egh. TW20 ...... **195** BB91
Woodhayes, Horl. RH6 ...... **291** DH147
Woodhayes Rd, SW19 ...... **201** CW94
Woodhead Dr, Orp. BR6
off Sherlies Av **227** ES103
Woodheyes Rd, NW10 ...... **140** CR64
Woodhill, SE18 ...... **37** H8
Harlow CM18 ...... **73** ES18
Send GU23 ...... **265** BD125
Woodhill Av, Ger.Cr. SL9 ...... **135** BA58

Woodhill Ct, Send GU23 . . . . . 265 BD125
Woodhill Cres, Har. HA3. . . . . . 139 CK58
Woodhill Prim Sch, SE18 . . . 37 H9
Wood Ho, SW17 off Laurel Cl . 202 DE92
Woodhouse Av, Perivale UB6 . 159 CF68
Woodhouse Cl, SE22 . . . . 184 DU84
Hayes UB3. . . . . 177 BS76
Perivale UB6 . . . . 159 CF68
Woodhouse Coll, N12
off Woodhouse Rd 120 DD51
Woodhouse Eaves, Nthwd.
HA6. . . . . 115 BU50
Woodhouse Gro, E12 . . . . 166 EL65
Wood Ho La, Brox. EN10 . . . . . . 70 DT21
Woodhouse La, Holm.St.M.
RH5. 283 BU143
Woodhouse Rd, E11 . . . . 146 EF62
N12. 120 DD51
Woodhurst Av, Petts Wd BR5. . 227 EQ100
Watford WD25. . . . . 98 BX35
Woodhurst Dr, Denh. UB9. . . . 135 BF57
Woodhurst La, Oxt. RH8 . . . . . 276 EE130
Woodhurst Pk, Oxt. RH8 . . . . . 276 EE130
Woodhurst Rd, SE2 . . . . 188 EU78
W3 . . . . 160 CQ73
Woodhyrst Gdns, Ken. CR8 . . . 257 DP115
Wooding Gro, Harl. CM19 . . . . . 73 EP15
Woodington Cl, SE9. . . . . 207 EN86
Woodknoll Dr, Chis. BR7 . . . . . 227 EM95
Woodland App, Grnf. UB6 . . . . 159 CG65
Woodland Av, Hem.H. HP1 . . . . 62 BH21
Hutton CM13. . . . . 131 GC43
Slough SL1 . . . . 153 AR73
Windsor SL4 . . . . 173 AM84
Woodland Cl, NW9. . . . . 140 CQ58
SE19. . . . . 204 DS93
Epsom KT19 . . . . 238 CS107
Hemel Hempstead HP1 . . . . . 62 BH21
Hutton CM13. . . . . 131 GC43
Ickenham UB10. . . . . 137 BP61
Weybridge KT13. . . . . 235 BR105
Woodford Green IG8 . . . . 124 EH48
Woodland Ct, Oxt. RH8 . . . . . . 275 ED128
Woodland Cres, SE10. . . . . 47 J2
SE16. 33 J5
Woodland Dr, E.Hors. KT24. . . 267 BT127
St. Albans AL4. . . . . 65 CJ18
Watford WD17. . . . . 97 BT39
Woodland Gdns, N10. . . . . 143 DH57
Isleworth TW7 . . . . 179 CE82
South Croydon CR2 . . . . 242 DW111
Woodland Glade, Farn.Com.
SL2. 133 AR62
Woodland Gra, Iver SL0. . . . . . 175 BE76
Woodland Gro, SE10 . . . . 47 J1
Epping CM16. . . . . 92 EU31
Weybridge KT13. . . . . 235 BR105
Woodland Hts, SE3. . . . . 47 K2
Woodland Hill, SE19. . . . . 204 DS93
Woodland La, Chorl. WD3 . . . . . 95 BD41
Woodland Ms, SW16 . . . . 203 DL90
Woodland Mt, Hert. SG13 . . . . . 54 DT09
Woodland Pl, Chorl. WD3. . . . . . 95 BF42
Hemel Hempstead HP1 . . . . . 62 BH21
Woodland Ri, N10. . . . . 143 DH56
Greenford UB6 . . . . 159 CG65
Oxted RH8. . . . . 276 EE130
Sevenoaks TN15 . . . . 279 FL123
Welwyn Garden City AL8. . . . . 51 CW07
Woodland Rd, E4 . . . . 123 EC46
N11 . . . . 121 DH50
SE19. . . . . 204 DS92
Hertford Heath SG13 . . . . 54 DV12
Loughton IG10. . . . . 106 EL41
Maple Cross WD3 . . . . 113 BD50
Thornton Heath CR7. . . . . . . 223 DN98
WOODLANDS, Islw. TW7 . . . . . . 179 CE82
Woodlands, NW11 . . . . 141 CY58
SW20 . . . . 221 CW98
Brookmans Park AL9 . . . . 86 DB26
Epping CM16. . . . . 92 EU31
Gerrards Cross SL9 . . . . 135 AZ57
Harrow HA2. . . . . 138 CA56
Horley RH6 . . . . 291 DJ147
Park Street AL2 . . . . 82 CC27
Radlett WD7. . . . . 83 CG34
Send Marsh GU23
off Clandon Rd 265 BF125
Woking GU22
off Constitution Hill 248 AY118
Woodlands, The, N14 . . . . 121 DH46
SE13. . . . . 205 ED87
SE19. . . . . 204 DQ94
Amersham HP6. . . . . 77 AQ35
Beckenham BR3 . . . . 225 EC95
Esher KT10. . . . . 218 CC103
Guildford GU1. . . . . 265 BC133
Isleworth TW7 . . . . 179 CF82
Orpington BR6 . . . . 246 EV107
Smallfield RH6 . . . . 291 DP148
Wallington SM6 . . . . 241 DH109
Woodlands Av, E11 . . . . 146 EH60
N3. . . . . 120 DC52
W3 . . . . 160 CP74
Berkhamsted HP4. . . . . 60 AW20
Hornchurch RM11 . . . . 150 FK57
New Malden KT3 . . . . 220 CQ95
Redhill RH1 . . . . 288 DF135
Romford RM6 . . . . 148 EY58
Ruislip HA4 . . . . 138 BW60
Sidcup DA15 . . . . 207 ES88
West Byfleet KT14. . . . . 233 BF113
Worcester Park KT4 . . . . 221 CT103
Woodlands Cl, NW11 . . . . 141 CY57
Borehamwood WD6 . . . . 100 CP42
Bromley BR1 . . . . 227 EM96
Claygate KT10. . . . . 237 CF108
East Horsley KT24. . . . . 267 BT127
Gerrards Cross SL9 . . . . 135 BA58
Grays RM16. . . . . 192 GE76
Guildford GU1. . . . . 264 AY130
Hoddesdon EN11 . . . . 71 EA18
Ottershaw KT16 . . . . 233 BB110
Swanley BR8. . . . . 229 FF97
Woodlands Copse, Ashtd.
KT21. . . . . 253 CK116
Woodlands Ct, Wok. GU22
off Constitution Hill 248 AY119
Woodlands Dr, Beac. HP9. . . . 110 AJ51
Hoddesdon EN11 . . . . 71 EA19
Kings Langley WD4. . . . . 81 BQ28
Woodlands Dr, Stan. HA7. . . . . 117 CF51
Sunbury-on-Thames TW16. . 218 BW96
Woodlands First & Mid Sch,
Edg. HA8 off Bransgrove Rd. 118 CM53
Woodlands Gdns, Epsom
KT18. . . . . 255 CW117
Woodlands Glade, Beac. HP9. . 110 AJ51
Woodlands Gro, Couls. CR5 . . 256 DG117
Isleworth TW7 . . . . 179 CE82
Woodlands Hill, Beac. HP9. . . . 133 AL58
Woodlands Inf Sch, Ilf. IG1
off Loxford La 147 ER64
Woodlands Jun Sch, Ilf. IG1
off Loxford La 147 ER64
Woodlands La, Stoke D'Ab.
KT11 . . . . 252 CA117
Woodlands Par, Ashf. TW15. . . 197 BQ93
Woodlands Pk, Add. KT15 . . . . 233 BF106
Bexley DA5 . . . . 209 FC91
Box Hill KT20. . . . . 270 CP131
Guildford GU1. . . . . 265 BB132
Woking GU21
off Blackmore Cres 233 BC114
Woodlands Pk Rd, N15. . . . . . . 143 DP57
SE10. 47 J2
Woodlands Pl, Cat. CR3 . . . . . . 274 DU126
Woodlands Prim Sch, Borwd.
WD6 off Alban Cres 100 CN39
Woodlands Ri, Swan. BR8 . . . . 229 FF96
Woodlands Rd, E11. . . . . 146 EE61
E17 . . . . 145 EC55
N9. . . . . 122 DW46
SW13 . . . . 181 CT83
Bexleyheath DA7 . . . . 188 EY83
Bookham KT23 . . . . 268 BY128
Bromley BR1 . . . . 226 EL96
Bushey WD23 . . . . 98 BY43
Enfield EN2 . . . . 104 DR39
Epsom KT18 . . . . 254 CN115
Guildford GU1. . . . . 264 AX130
Harold Wood RM3. . . . . 128 FN53
Harrow HA1. . . . . 139 CF57
Hemel Hempstead HP3 . . . . . 80 BN27
Hertford SG13. . . . . 54 DT09
Ilford IG1 . . . . 147 EQ62
Isleworth TW7 . . . . 179 CE82
Leatherhead KT22. . . . . 253 CD117
Orpington BR6 . . . . 246 EU107
Redhill RH1 . . . . 288 DF135
Romford RM1 . . . . 149 FF55
Southall UB1. . . . . 158 BX74
Surbiton KT6. . . . . 219 CK101
Virginia Water GU25. . . . . . . 214 AW98
West Byfleet KT14. . . . . 233 BF114
Woodlands Rd E, Vir.W. GU25. 214 AW98
Woodlands Rd W, Vir.W. GU25. 214 AW97
Woodlands Sch, Gt Warley
CM13 off Warley St. 151 FX56
Leatherhead KT22
off Fortyfoot Rd. 253 CJ122
Woodlands St, SE13. . . . . 205 ED87
Woodland St, E8. . . . . 10 B4
Woodlands Vw, Bad.Mt TN14 . 246 FA110
Dorking RH5 . . . . 285 CH142
Woodlands Way, SW15. . . . . . . 201 CZ85
Ashtead KT21 . . . . 254 CN116
Box Hill KT20. . . . . 270 CQ130
Woodland Ter, SE7 . . . . 36 G9
Woodland Vw, Chesh. HP5 . . . . . 76 AR32
Godalming GU7 . . . . 280 AS142
Woodland Wk, NW3 . . . . 6 D2
SE10. 47 K1
Bromley BR1 . . . . 206 EE91
Epsom KT19 . . . . 238 CN107
Woodland Way, N21 . . . . 121 DN47
NW7. 118 CS51
SE2. 188 EX77
Bedmond WD5 . . . . 81 BT27
Caterham CR3. . . . . 274 DS128
Croydon CR0. . . . . 225 DY102
Goffs Oak EN7. . . . . 87 DP28
Greenhithe DA9 . . . . 191 FU84
Kingswood KT20. . . . . 255 CY122
Mitcham CR4. . . . . 202 DG94
Morden SM4 . . . . 221 CZ98
Petts Wood BR5. . . . . 227 EQ98
Purley CR8. . . . . 241 DN113
Surbiton KT5. . . . . 220 CP103
Theydon Bois CM16 . . . . 107 ER35
West Wickham BR4. . . . . 243 EB105
Weybridge KT13. . . . . 235 BR106
Woodford Green IG8 . . . . 124 EH48
Wood Lane 26 B1
Wood La, N6. . . . . 143 DH58
NW9. 140 CS59
W12 . . . . 14 B10
Caterham CR3. . . . . 258 DR124
Dagenham RM8, RM9,
RM10 . . . . 148 EW63
Hedgerley SL2. . . . . 134 AS61
Hemel Hempstead HP2 . . . . . 62 BK21
Hornchurch RM12. . . . . 149 FG64
Isleworth TW7 . . . . 179 CF80
Iver SL0 . . . . 155 BC71
Lane End DA2 . . . . 211 FR91
Ruislip HA4 . . . . 137 BR60
Slough SL1 . . . . 173 AM76
Stanmore HA7. . . . . 117 CG48
Tadworth KT20 . . . . 255 CZ116
Ware SG12. . . . . 55 EA05
Weybridge KT13. . . . . 235 BQ109
Woodford Green IG8 . . . . 124 EF50
Wood La Cl, Iver SL0 . . . . 155 BB69
Wood La End, Hem.H. HP2 . . . . 62 BN19
Woodlane High Sch, W12
off Du Cane Rd 161 CV72
Woodlawn Cl, SW15. . . . . 201 CZ85
Woodlawn Cres, Twick. TW2. . . 198 CB89
Woodlawn Dr, Felt. TW13. . . . . 198 BX89
Woodlawn Gro, Wok. GU21 . . . 249 AZ115
Woodlawn Rd, SW6 . . . . 38 C4
Woodlea Dr, Brom. BR2. . . . . . . 226 EE99
Woodlea Gro, Nthwd. HA6. . . . 115 BQ51
Woodlea Prim Sch, Wold.
CR3 off Long Hill. 259 EA122
Woodlea Rd, N16 . . . . 144 DS62
Woodlee Cl, Vir.W. GU25 . . . . . 214 AW96
Woodleigh, E18
off Churchfields. 124 EG53
Woodleigh Av, N12. . . . . 120 DE51
Woodleigh Gdns, SW16. . . . . . . 203 DL90
Woodley Cl, SW17
off Arnold Rd. 202 DF94
Woodley Hill, Chesh. HP5 . . . . . 76 AR34
Woodley La, Cars. SM5 . . . . . . 222 DD104
Woodley Rd, Orp. BR6 . . . . 228 EW103
Ware SG12. . . . . 55 DZ05
Wood Lo Gdns, Brom. BR1 . . . 206 EL94
Wood Lo La, W.Wick. BR4 . . . . 225 EC104
Woodmancote Gdns, W.Byf.
KT14. . . . . 234 BG113
Woodman La, E4. . . . . 106 EE43
Woodman Ms, Rich. TW9 . . . . . 180 CP81
Woodman Path, Ilf. IG6 . . . . . . 125 ES51
Woodman Rd, Couls. CR5 . . . . 257 DJ115
Hemel Hempstead HP3 . . . . . 62 BL22
Warley CM14. . . . . 130 FW50
Woodmans Gro, NW10. . . . . . . 141 CT64
Woodmans Ms, W12. . . . . 161 CV71
WOODMANSTERNE, Bans.
SM7 . . . . 256 DD115
Woodmansterne 257 DH116
Woodmansterne La, Bans.
SM7 . . . . 256 DB115
Carshalton SM5 . . . . 240 DF112
Wallington SM6 . . . . 241 DH111
Woodmansterne Prim Sch,
SW16 off Stockport Rd. 223 DK95
Banstead SM7
off Carshalton Rd 240 DF114
Woodmansterne Rd, SW16 . . . 223 DK95
Carshalton SM5 . . . . 240 DE109
Coulsdon CR5 . . . . 257 DJ115
Woodmansterne St, Bans.
SM7 . . . . 256 DE115
Woodman St, E16. . . . . 37 M3
Wood Meads, Epp. CM16. . . . . . 92 EU29
Woodmere, SE9 . . . . 207 EM88
Woodmere Av, Croy. CR0. . . . . 225 DX101
Watford WD24. . . . . 98 BX38
Woodmere Cl, SW11
off Lavender Hill 182 DG83
Croydon CR0. . . . . 225 DX101
Woodmere Gdns, Croy. CR0 . . 225 DX101
Woodmere Way, Beck. BR3 . . . 225 ED99
Woodmill Ms, Hodd. EN11
off Whittingstall Rd. 71 EB15
Woodmill Rd, E5. . . . . 144 DW61
Woodmount, Swan. BR8 . . . . . 229 FC101
Woodnook Rd, SW16. . . . . 203 DH92
Woodpecker Cl, N9. . . . . 104 DV44
Bushey WD23 . . . . 116 CC46
Cobham KT11 . . . . 236 BY112
Harrow HA3. . . . . 117 CF53
Hatfield AL10. . . . . 67 CT21
Woodpecker Ms, SE13
off Mercator Rd. 185 ED84
Woodpecker Mt, Croy. CR0 . . . 243 DY109
Woodpecker Rd, SE14 . . . . 45 L3
SE28. . . . . 168 EW73
Woodpecker Way, Wok. GU22 . 248 AX123
Woodplace Cl, Couls. CR5 . . . . 257 DJ119
Woodplace La, Couls. CR5. . . . 257 DJ118
Wood Pond Cl, Seer Grn HP9. . 111 AQ51
Woodquest Av, SE24 . . . . 204 DQ85
Woodredon Cl, Roydon CM19
off Epping Rd 72 EH16
Woodredon Fm La, Wal.Abb.
EN9. 106 EK35
Wood Retreat, SE18 . . . . 187 ER80
Woodridden Hill, Wal.Abb.
EN9. 106 EK35
Wood Ride, Barn. EN4 . . . . 102 DD39
Petts Wood BR5. . . . . 227 ER98
Woodridge Cl, Enf. EN2 . . . . . . 103 DN39
Woodridge Prim Sch, N12
off Southover 120 DA48
Woodridge Way, Nthwd. HA6. . 115 BS51
Wood Riding, Wok. GU22
off Pyrford Wds. 249 BF115
Woodridings Av, Pnr. HA5 . . . . 116 BZ53
Woodridings Cl, Pnr. HA5. . . . . 116 BY52
Woodriffe Rd, E11 . . . . 145 ED59
Wood Ri, Guil. GU3 . . . . 264 AS132
Pinner HA5 . . . . 137 BU57
Wood Rd, NW10. . . . . 160 CQ66
Biggin Hill TN16 . . . . 260 EJ118
Godalming GU7 . . . . 280 AT144
Shepperton TW17 . . . . 216 BN98
Woodrow, SE18 . . . . 37 J9
Woodrow Av, Hayes UB4. . . . . 157 BT71
Woodrow Cl, Perivale UB6. . . . 159 CH66
Woodrow Ct, N17 . . . . 122 DV52
Woodroyd Av, Horl. RH6 . . . . . 290 DF149
Woodroyd Gdns, Horl. RH6 . . . 290 DF150
Woodruff Av, Guil. GU1 . . . . . . 265 BA131
Woodrush Cl, SE14. . . . . 45 L4
Woodrush Way, Rom. RM6 . . . . 148 EX56
Woods, The, Nthwd. HA6 . . . . . 115 BU50
Radlett WD7. . . . . 83 CH34
Uxbridge UB10 . . . . 137 BP63
Woods Av, Hat. AL10 . . . . 67 CV18
Wood's Bldgs, E1 . . . . 20 E6
Woods Dr, Slou. SL2 . . . . 133 AM64
Woodseer St, E1 . . . . 20 B6
Woodsford, SE17 . . . . 43 L1
Woodsford Sq, W14 . . . . 26 F5
Woodshire Rd, Dag. RM10. . . . . 149 FB62
Woodshore Cl, Vir.W. GU25 . . . 214 AV100
Woodshots Meadow, Wat.
WD18. 97 BR43
WOODSIDE, SE25. . . . . 224 DU100
WOODSIDE, Hat. AL9. . . . . 67 CZ21
WOODSIDE, Wat. WD25 . . . . 81 BT33
Woodside. 224 DV100
Woodside, NW11. . . . . 142 DA57
SW19. . . . . 201 CZ93
Buckhurst Hill IG9. . . . . 124 EJ47
Cheshunt EN7. . . . . 88 DU31
Elstree WD6 . . . . 100 CM42
Fetcham KT22 . . . . 252 CB122
Flackwell Heath HP10 . . . . . . 132 AC57
Hertford Heath SG13 . . . . 54 DW12
Lower Kingswood KT20. . . . . 271 CZ128
Orpington BR6 . . . . 246 EU106
Thornwood CM16. . . . . 92 EX27
Walton-on-Thames KT12
off Ashley Rd. 217 BU102
Watford WD24. . . . . 97 BU36
West Horsley KT24. . . . . 267 BQ126
Woodside Av, N6. . . . . 142 DF57
N10. 142 DF57
N12. 120 DC49
SE25. . . . . 224 DV100
Amersham HP6. . . . . 77 AR36
Beaconsfield HP9 . . . . 110 AJ52
Chislehurst BR7 . . . . 207 EQ92
Esher KT10. . . . . 219 CE101
Flackwell Heath HP10 . . . . . . 132 AC57
Hersham KT12 . . . . 235 BV105
Wembley HA0 . . . . 160 CL67
Woodside Cl, Amer. HP6 . . . . . . 77 AR37
Beaconsfield HP9 . . . . 110 AJ52
Bexleyheath DA7 . . . . 189 FD84
Caterham CR3. . . . . 258 DS124
Chalfont St. Peter SL9. . . . . . 112 AY54
Hutton CM13. . . . . 131 GD43
Rainham RM13 . . . . 170 FJ70
Woodside Cl, Ruis. HA4 . . . . . . 137 BR58
Stanmore HA7. . . . . 117 CH50
Surbiton KT5. . . . . 220 CQ101
Wembley HA0 . . . . 160 CL67
Woodside Commercial Est,
Thnwd CM16. . . . . 92 EX26
Woodside Ct, N12. . . . . 120 DB49
Woodside Ct Rd, Croy. CR0 . . . 224 DU101
Woodside Cres, Sid. DA15. . . . . 207 ES90
Smallfield RH6 . . . . 291 DN148
Woodside Dr, Dart. DA2. . . . . . 209 FE91
Woodside End, Wem. HA0. . . . 160 CL67
Woodside Gdns, E4 . . . . 123 EB50
N17. 122 DS54
Woodside Gra Rd, N12. . . . . . . 120 DB49
Woodside Grn, SE25. . . . . 224 DV100
Hatfield AL9. . . . . 68 DA21
Woodside Gro, N12 . . . . 120 DC48
Woodside High Sch, N22
off White Hart La 121 DP52
Woodside Hill, Chal.St.P. SL9. . 112 AY54
Woodside Junior, Inf & Nurs
Schs, Croy. CR0
off Morland Rd 224 DU101
Woodside Jun Sch, Amer.
HP6 off Mitchell Wk 77 AS38
Woodside La, N12. . . . . 120 DB48
Bexley DA5 . . . . 208 EX86
Hatfield AL9. . . . . 67 CZ21
Woodside Ms, SE22 . . . . 204 DT86
Woodside Park 120 DB49
Woodside Pk, SE25. . . . . 224 DU99
Woodside Pk Av, E17 . . . . 145 ED56
Woodside Pk Rd, N12. . . . . 120 DB49
Woodside Pl, Hat. AL9 . . . . 67 CZ21
Wembley HA0 . . . . 160 CL67
Woodside Prim Sch, Chsht
EN7 off Jones Rd 87 DP29
Grays RM16
off Grangewood Av 193 GF76
Woodside Rd, E13. . . . . 24 C4
N22. 121 DM52
SE25. . . . . 224 DV100
Abbots Langley WD5 . . . . 81 BV31
Amersham HP6. . . . . 77 AR37
Beaconsfield HP9 . . . . 110 AJ52
Bexleyheath DA7 . . . . 189 FD84
Bricket Wood AL2 . . . . 82 BZ30
Bromley BR1 . . . . 226 EL99
Cobham KT11 . . . . 236 CA113
Guildford GU2. . . . . 264 AT133
Kingston upon Thames KT2. 200 CL94
New Malden KT3 . . . . 220 CR96
Northwood HA6 . . . . 115 BT52
Purley CR8. . . . . 241 DK113
Sevenoaks TN13 . . . . 278 FG123
Sidcup DA15 . . . . 207 ES90
Sundridge TN14 . . . . 262 EX124
Sutton SM1 . . . . 222 DC104
Watford WD25. . . . . 81 BV31
Woodford Green IG8 . . . . 124 EG49
Woodside Sch, Belv. DA17
off Halt Robin Rd 189 FB77
Woodside Sch, The, E17
off Wood St 145 EC55
Woodside Way, Croy. CR0 . . . . 224 DV100
Mitcham CR4. . . . . 223 DH95
Penn HP10 . . . . 110 AC46
Redhill RH1 . . . . 288 DG135
Salfords RH1 . . . . 288 DG140
Virginia Water GU25. . . . . . . 214 AV97
Woods Ms, W1 . . . . 16 F10
Woodsome Lo, Wey. KT13. . . . 235 BQ107
Woodsome Rd, NW5 . . . . 142 DG62
Woods Pl, SE1. . . . . 31 P7
Woodspring Rd, SW19 . . . . 201 CY89
Woods Rd, SE15 . . . . 44 E7
Woodstead Gro, Edg. HA8 . . . . 118 CL51
Woodstock, W.Clan. GU4. . . . . 266 BH128
Woodstock, The, Sutt.
SM3 . . . . 221 CY101
Woodstock Av, NW11 . . . . 141 CY59
W13 . . . . 179 CG76
Isleworth TW7 . . . . 199 CG85
Romford RM3 . . . . 128 FP50
Slough SL3 . . . . 174 AX77
Southall UB1. . . . . 158 BZ69
Sutton SM3. . . . . 221 CZ101
Woodstock Cl, Bex. DA5 . . . . . . 208 EZ88
Hertford Heath SG13
off Hogsdell La 54 DV11
Stanmore HA7. . . . . 118 CL54
Woking GU21 . . . . 248 AY116
Woodstock Ct, SE12. . . . . 206 EG86
Woodstock Cres, N9. . . . . 104 DV44
Woodstock Dr, Uxb. UB10 . . . . 136 BL63
Woodstock Gdns, Beck. BR3 . . 225 EB95
Hayes UB4. . . . . 157 BT71
Ilford IG3 . . . . 148 EU61
Woodstock Gro, W12 . . . . 26 D4
Woodstock La N, Long Dit.
KT6. 219 CJ103
Woodstock La S, Chess. KT9. . 237 CJ105
Claygate KT10. . . . . 237 CH106
Woodstock Ms, W1. . . . . 17 H7
Woodstock Ri, Sutt. SM3. . . . . 221 CZ101
Woodstock Rd, E7. . . . . 166 EJ66
E17 . . . . 123 ED54
N4. . . . . 143 DN60
NW11 . . . . 141 CZ59
W4 . . . . 180 CS76
Broxbourne EN10 . . . . 71 DY19
Bushey Heath WD23 . . . . 117 CF45
Carshalton SM5 . . . . 240 DG106
Coulsdon CR5
off Chipstead Valley Rd . . . 257 DH116
Croydon CR0. . . . . 224 DR104
Wembley HA0 . . . . 160 CM66
Woodstock Rd N, St.Alb. AL1 . . 65 CH18
Woodstock Rd S, St.Alb. AL1 . . 65 CH20
Woodstock St, W1 . . . . 17 J9
Woodstock Ter, E14. . . . . 22 D10
Woodstock Way, Mitch. CR4 . . 223 DH96
Woodstone Av, Epsom KT17 . . 239 CU106
Wood Street 145 EC56
Wood St, E17 . . . . 123 EC54
Wood St, E17 . . . . 145 EC55
EC2. . . . . 19 K9
W4 . . . . 180 CS78
Barnet EN5. . . . . 101 CW42
Grays RM17. . . . . 192 GC79
Kingston upon Thames KT1. 219 CK95
Merstham RH1 . . . . 273 DJ129
Mitcham CR4. . . . . 222 DG101
Swanley BR8. . . . . 230 FJ96
Woodsway, Oxshott KT22 . . . . 237 CE114
Woodsyre, SE26 . . . . 204 DT91
Woodthorpe Rd, SW15. . . . . . . 181 CV84
Ashford TW15 . . . . 196 BL91
Woodtree Cl, NW4
off Ashley La 119 CW54
Wood Vale, N10. . . . . 143 DJ57
SE23. . . . . 204 DV88
Hatfield AL10. . . . . 67 CV18
Woodvale Av, SE25. . . . . 224 DT97
Wood Vale Est, SE23. . . . . 204 DW86
Woodvale Est, SE27 . . . . 204 DQ92
Woodvale Pk, St.Alb. AL1 . . . . . 65 CH20
Woodvale Wk, SE27 . . . . 204 DQ92
Woodvale Way, NW11. . . . . 141 CX62
Woodview, Chess. KT9 . . . . 237 CJ111
Wood Vw, Cuffley EN6. . . . . 87 DL27
Woodview, Grays
RM16, RM17 . . . . 192 GE76
Wood Vw, Hem.H. HP1. . . . . 62 BH18
Woodview Av, E4 . . . . 123 EC49
Woodview Cl, N4 . . . . 143 DP59
SW15 . . . . 200 CR91
Ashtead KT21 . . . . 254 CN116
Orpington BR6 . . . . 227 EQ103
South Croydon CR2 . . . . 242 DV114
Woodview Rd, Swan. BR8 . . . . 229 FC96
Woodville, SE3 . . . . 186 EH81
Woodville Cl, SE12 . . . . 206 EG85
Teddington TW11. . . . . 199 CG91
Woodville Ct, Wat. WD17 . . . . . . 97 BU40
Woodville Gdns, NW11. . . . . . . 141 CX59
W5 . . . . 160 CL72
Ilford IG6 . . . . 147 EP55
Ruislip HA4 . . . . 137 BQ59
Woodville Gro, Well. DA16. . . . 188 EU83
Woodville Pl, Grav. DA12. . . . . 213 GH87
Hertford SG14 . . . . 53 DP07
Woodville Rd, E11. . . . . 146 EF60
E17 . . . . 145 DY56
E18 . . . . 124 EH54
N16. . . . . 9 N3
NW6. . . . . 5 H10
NW11 . . . . 141 CX59
W5 . . . . 159 CK72
Barnet EN5. . . . . 102 DB41
Morden SM4 . . . . 222 DA98
Richmond TW10 . . . . 199 CH90
Thornton Heath CR7. . . . . . . 224 DQ98
Woodville St, SE18. . . . . 37 H9
Woodvill Rd, Lthd. KT22. . . . . . 253 CH120
Wood Wk, Chorl. WD3 . . . . 95 BE40
Woodward Av, NW4 . . . . 141 CU57
Woodward Cl, Clay. KT10. . . . . 237 CF107
Grays RM17. . . . . 192 GB77
Woodwarde Rd, SE22. . . . . 204 DS86
Woodward Gdns, Dag. RM9
off Woodward Rd 168 EW66
Stanmore HA7. . . . . 117 CF52
Woodward Hts, Grays RM17. . 192 GB77
Woodward Rd, Dag. RM9 . . . . . 168 EV66
Woodwards, Harl. CM19 . . . . . . 73 EQ17
Woodward Ter, Green. DA9 . . . 211 FS86
Woodway, Beac. HP9 . . . . 110 AF54
Brentwood CM13, CM15 . . . . 131 GA46
Guildford GU1. . . . . 265 BB133
Wood Way, Orp. BR6 . . . . 227 EN103
Woodway Cres, Har. HA1. . . . . 139 CG58
Woodwaye, Wat. WD19. . . . . . . 116 BW45
Woodwell St, SW18
off Huguenot Pl. 202 DC85
Wood Wf, SE10 . . . . 46 D2
Wood Wf Apts, SE10
off Horseferry Pl 46 E2
Woodwicks, Map.Cr. WD3 . . . . 113 BD50
Woodyard, The, Epp. CM16 . . . . 92 EW28
Woodyard Cl, NW5. . . . . 7 H3
Woodyard La, SE21 . . . . 204 DS87
Woodyates Rd, SE12 . . . . 206 EG86
Woodyers Cl, Won. GU5. . . . . . 281 BB144
Woolacombe Rd, SE3. . . . . 186 EJ81
Woolacombe Way, Hayes UB3. 177 BS77
Woolborough La, Outwood
RH1. 289 DM143
Woolbrook Rd, Dart. DA1. . . . . 209 FE86
Wooldridge Cl, Felt. TW14 . . . . 197 BQ88
Wooler St, SE17 . . . . 43 L1
Woolf Cl, SE28 . . . . 168 EV74
Woolf Ms, WC1 . . . . 17 P4
Woolf Wk, Til. RM18
off Brennan Rd 193 GJ82
Woolhampton Way, Chig. IG7 . 126 EV48
Woolhams, Cat. CR3. . . . . 274 DT126
Woollam Cres, St.Alb. AL3. . . . . . 64 CC16
Woollard St, Wal.Abb. EN9 . . . . . 89 EC34
Woollaston Rd, N4 . . . . 143 DP58
WOOLLENSBROOK, Hodd.
EN11. 71 DX15
Woollett Cl, Cray. DA1 . . . . 189 FG84
Woolmans Cl, Brox. EN10 . . . . . 71 DZ22
Woolmead Av, NW9. . . . . 141 CU59
Woolmer Cl, Borwd. WD6 . . . . . 100 CN38
Woolmerdine Ct, Bushey
WD23 . . . . 98 BX41
Woolmer Dr, Hem.H. HP2 . . . . . 63 BQ20
Woolmer Gdns, N18. . . . . 122 DU51
Woolmer Rd, N18 . . . . 122 DU50
Woolmers La, Letty Grn SG14. . 53 DH13
Woolmers Pk, Hert. SG13,
SG14 . . . . 53 DH14
Woolmers Pk Ms, Letty Grn
SG14 . . . . 53 DH14
Woolmore Prim Sch, E14. . . 22 F10
Woolmore St, E14. . . . . 22 E10
Woolneigh St, SW6 . . . . 39 L10
Woolpack Ho, Enf. EN3 . . . . . . 105 DX37
Woolridge Way, E9 . . . . 11 H6
Wool Rd, SW20. . . . . 201 CV93
Woolstaplers Way, SE16. . . . . . . 32 C8
Woolston Cl, E17
off Riverhead Cl 123 DX54
Woolstone Rd, SE23. . . . . 205 DY89
WOOLWICH, SE18. . . . . 37 M6
Woolwich Arsenal. 37 P8
Woolwich Arsenal. 37 P8
Woolwich Arsenal Pier. 37 P6
Woolwich Ch St, SE18 . . . . 36 G7
Woolwich Common, SE18. 187 EM80
Woolwich Common, SE18 . . . . 187 EN79
Woolwich Ct, Enf. EN3
off Hodson Pl. 105 EA38
Woolwich Dockyard 37 J8
Woolwich Dockyard Ind Est,
SE18. 37 H7
Woolwich Ferry Pier, E16. . . . . . 37 K5
Woolwich Foot Tunnel, E16 . . . 37 L5
SE18. 37 L5
Woolwich Garrison, SE18. . . . . 186 EL79
Woolwich High St, SE18 . . . . . . 37 L7
Woolwich Manor Way, E6 . . . . . 25 K5
E16. . . . . 37 N3
Woolwich Mkt, SE18 . . . . 37 N8
Woolwich New Rd, SE18. . . . . . 187 EN78

Woolwich Poly Sch, SE28
off Hutchins Rd 168 EU74
Woolwich Rd, SE2 188 EX79
SE7 36 D9
SE10 35 L10
Belvedere DA17 188 EX79
Bexleyheath DA6, DA7 188 FA84
● Woolwich Trade Pk, SE28 187 ER76
Wooster Gdns, E14 22 G8
Wooster Ms, Har. HA2
off Fairfield Dr 138 CC55
Wooster Pl, SE1 31 M8
Wooster Rd, Beac. HP9 110 AJ51
Wootton Cl, Epsom KT18 255 CT115
Hornchurch RM11 150 FK57
Wootton Dr, Hem.H. HP2 62 BM15
Wooburn Green HP10 132 AE55
Wootton Gro, N3 120 DA53
Wootton St, SE1 30 F4
Worbeck Rd, SE20 224 DV96
Worcester Av, N17 122 DU52
Upminster RM14 151 FT61
Worcester Cl, NW2
off Newfield Ri 141 CV62
Croydon CR0 225 DZ103
Greenhithe DA9 191 FV84
Istead Rise DA13 213 GF94
Mitcham CR4 222 DG96
Worcester Ct, Walt. KT12 218 BW103
Worcester Cres, NW7 118 CS48
Woodford Green IG8 124 EH50
Worcester Dr, W4 180 CS75
Ashford TW15 197 BP93
Worcester Gdns, SW11
off Grandison Rd 202 DF85
Greenford UB6 158 CC65
Ilford IG1 146 EL59
Slough SL1 173 AR75
Worcester Park KT4 220 CS104
Worcester Ho, SE11
off Kennington Rd 30 E7
Worcester Ms, NW6 5 M4
WORCESTER PARK, KT4 221 CT103
≠ Worcester Park 221 CU102
Worcester Pk Rd, Wor.Pk. KT4 220 CQ104
Worcester Rd, E12 147 EM63
E17 123 DX54
SW19 201 CZ92
Cowley UB8 156 BJ71
Guildford GU2 264 AT132
Hatfield AL10 67 CT17
Reigate RH2 271 CZ133
Sutton SM2 240 DB107
Worcesters Av, Enf. EN1 104 DU38
Sch Worcesters Prim Sch, Enf.
EN1 off Goat La 104 DT38
Wordsworth Av, E12 166 EL66
E18 146 EF55
Greenford UB6 159 CD68
Kenley CR8 off Valley Rd 258 DR115
Wordsworth Cl, Rom. RM3 128 FJ53
Tilbury RM18 193 GJ82
Wordsworth Dr, Sutt. SM3 239 CW105
Wordsworth Gdns, Borwd.
WD6 100 CN43
Wordsworth Mead, Red. RH1 272 DG132
Wordsworth Pl, NW5 6 F3
Wordsworth Rd, N16 9 P2
SE1 32 A9
SE20 205 DX94
Addlestone KT15 234 BK105
Hampton TW12 198 BZ91
Slough SL2 153 AK70
Wallington SM6 241 DJ107
Welling DA16 187 ES81
Wordsworth Wk, NW11 141 CZ56
Wordsworth Way, Dart. DA1 190 FN84
West Drayton UB7 176 BL77
Worfield St, SW11 40 D5
Worgan St, SE11 30 C10
SE16 33 K7
Workers Rd, Harl. CM17 75 FB16
Ongar CM5 75 FD17
Coll Working Men's Coll, The,
NW1 7 M10
Worland Rd, E15 13 K6
World Cargo Cen, Gat. RH6 290 DD152
WORLD'S END, Enf. EN2 103 DN41
World's End, Cob. KT11 235 BU114
Worlds End La, N21 103 DM43
Enfield EN2 103 DM43
Orpington BR6 245 ET107
World's End Pas, SW10 40 A4
World's End Pl, SW10
off King's Rd 39 P4
Worley Pl, Seer Grn HP9 111 AR50
Worley Rd, St.Alb. AL3 64 CC19
Worleys Dr, Orp. BR6 245 ER105
Worlidge St, W6 26 A10
Worlingham Rd, SE22 184 DT84
Sch Wormholt Pk Prim Sch, W12
off Bryony Rd 161 CU73
Wormholt Rd, W12 161 CU73
WORMLEY, Brox. EN10 71 DY24
Wormleybury, Brox. EN10 70 DW23
Wormley Ct, Wal.Abb. EN9 90 EG33
Wormley Lo Cl, Brox. EN10 71 DZ23
Sch Wormley Prim Sch, Brox.
EN10 off St. Laurence Dr 71 DY23
WORMLEY WEST END, Brox.
EN10 70 DS22
Wormwood St, EC2 19 N8
Wormyngford Ct, Wal.Abb. EN9
off Ninefields 90 EG33
Wornington Rd, W10 14 E5
Woronzow Rd, NW8 6 B9
Worple, The, Wrays. TW19 195 AZ86
Worple Av, SW19 201 CX94
Isleworth TW7 199 CG85
Staines TW18 196 BH93
Worple Cl, Har. HA2 138 BZ60
Sch Worple Prim Sch, Islw. TW7
off Queens Ter 179 CG84
Worple Rd, SW19 201 CY94
SW20 221 CW96
Epsom KT18 238 CS114
Isleworth TW7 179 CG84
Leatherhead KT22 253 CH123
Staines TW18 196 BH94
Worple Rd Ms, SW19 201 CZ93
≠ Worplesdon 248 AV124
Worplesdon Rd, Guil. GU2,
GU3 264 AT129
Worple St, SW14 180 CR83
Worple Way, Har. HA2 138 BZ60
Richmond TW10 200 CL85
Worrin Cl, Shenf. CM15 131 FZ46
Worrin Rd, Shenf. CM15 131 FZ47
Worsfold Cl, Send GU23 249 BB123
Worships Hill, Sev. TN13 278 FE123
Worship St, EC2 19 M5
Worslade Rd, SW17 202 DD91
Sch Worsley Br Jun Sch, Beck.
BR3 off Brackley Rd 205 EA94
Worsley Br Rd, SE26 205 DZ91
Beckenham BR3 205 DZ92
Worsley Gra, Chis. BR7 207 EQ93
Worsley Gro, E5 144 DU63
Worsley Rd, E11 146 EE63
Worsopp Dr, SW4 203 DJ85
Worsted Grn, Merst. RH1 273 DJ129
Worth Cl, Orp. BR6 245 ES105
Worthfield Cl, Epsom KT19 238 CR108
Worth Gro, SE17 43 L1
Worthies, The, Amer. HP7 77 AP40
Worthing Cl, E15 13 J9
Grays RM17 192 FY79
Worthing Rd, Houns. TW5 178 BZ79
Worthington Cl, Mitch. CR4 223 DH97
Worthington Rd, Surb. KT6 220 CM102
Worthy Down Ct, SE18
off Prince Imperial Rd 187 EN81
Wortley Rd, E6 166 EK66
Croydon CR0 223 DN101
Worton Gdns, Islw. TW7 179 CD82
● Worton Hall Ind Est, Islw.
TW7 179 CE84
Worton Rd, Islw. TW7 179 CE83
Worton Way, Houns. TW3 179 CD82
Isleworth TW7 178 CC81
WOTTON, Dor. RH5 284 BZ139
Wotton Dr, Dor. RH5 284 BZ139
Wotton Grn, Orp. BR5 228 EX98
Wotton Rd, NW2 141 CW63
SE8 45 P3
Wotton Way, Sutt. SM2 239 CW110
Wouldham Rd, E16 23 L8
Grays RM20 192 FY79
Wrabness Way, Stai. TW18 216 BH95
Wragby Rd, E11 146 EE62
Wrampling Pl, N9 122 DU46
Wrangley Ct, Wal.Abb. EN9 90 EG33
Wrangthorn Wk, Croy. CR0
off Fernleigh Cl 241 DN105
Wray Av, Ilf. IG5 147 EN55
Wray Cl, Horn. RM11 150 FJ59
Wray Common, Reig. RH2 272 DD132
Sch Wray Common Prim Sch, Reig.
RH2 off Kendal Cl 272 DD133
Wray Common Rd, Reig. RH2 272 DC133
Wray Cres, N4 143 DL61
Wrayfield Av, Reig. RH2 272 DC133
Wrayfield Rd, Sutt. SM3 221 CX104
Wraylands Dr, Reig. RH2 272 DD132
Wray La, Reig. RH2 272 DC130
Wraymead Pl, Reig. RH2
off Wray Pk Rd 272 DB133
Wray Mill Pk, Reig. RH2 272 DD132
Wray Pk Rd, Reig. RH2 272 DB133
Wray Rd, Sutt. SM2 239 CZ109
WRAYSBURY, Stai. TW19 195 AZ86
≠ Wraysbury 195 BA86
Wraysbury Cl, Houns. TW4 198 BY85
Wraysbury Gdns, Stai. TW18 195 BE91
Sch Wraysbury Prim Sch, Wrays.
TW19 off Welley Rd 194 AY86
Wraysbury Rd, Stai. TW18,
TW19 195 BC90
Wrays Way, Hayes UB4
off Balmoral Dr 157 BS70
Wrekin Rd, SE18 187 EQ80
Sch Wren Acad, N12
off Hilton Av 120 DD50
Wren Av, NW2 4 B2
Southall UB2 178 BZ77
Wren Cl, E16 23 M8
N9 off Chaffinch Cl 123 DX46
Orpington BR5 228 EX97
South Croydon CR2 243 DX109
Wren Ct, Slou. SL3 175 BA76
Warlingham CR6 258 DW117
Wren Cres, Add. KT15 234 BK106
Bushey WD23 116 CC46
Wren Dr, Wal.Abb. EN9 90 EG34
West Drayton UB7 176 BK76
Wren Gdns, Dag. RM9 148 EX64
Hornchurch RM12 149 FF60
Wren Landing, E14 34 B2
Wren Ms, SE13
off Lee High Rd 186 EE84
Wren Path, SE28 187 ER76
Wren Pl, Brwd. CM14 130 FX48
Wren Rd, SE5 43 L7
Dagenham RM9 148 EX64
Sidcup DA14 208 EW91
Wrens, The, Harl. CM19 73 EP15
Wrens Av, Ashf. TW15 197 BQ92
Wrens Cft, Nthflt DA11 212 GE91
Wrensfield, Hem.H. HP1 62 BG21
Wrens Hill, Oxshott KT22 252 CC115
Wren St, WC1 18 D4
Wren Ter, Ilf. IG5
off Tiptree Cres 147 EN55
Wrentham Av, NW10 4 C10
Wrenthorpe Rd, Brom. BR1 206 EE91
Wren Wk, Til. RM18 193 GH80
Wren Wd, Welw.G.C. AL7 52 DA08
Wrenwood Way, Pnr. HA5 137 BV56
Wrestlers Cl, Hat. AL10 67 CW15
Wrestlers Ct, EC3
off Camomile St 19 N8
Wrexham Rd, E3 22 B1
Romford RM3 128 FK48
Wricklemarsh Rd, SE3 186 EH81
Wrigglesworth St, SE14 45 J4
Wright, Wind. SL4 172 AJ83
Wright Cl, Swans. DA10 211 FX86
Wright Gdns, Shep. TW17
off Laleham Rd 216 BN99
Wright Rd, N1 9 P4
Hounslow TW5 178 BW80
Wrights All, SW19 201 CW93
Wrightsbridge Rd, S.Wld
CM14 128 FN46
Wrights Cl, SE13 185 ED84
Dagenham RM10 149 FB62
Wrights Ct, Harl. CM17
off Potter St 74 EW17
Wrights Grn, SW4
off Nelson's Row 183 DK84
Wrights La, W8 27 L6
Wrights Pl, NW10
off Mitchell Way 160 CQ65
Wright Sq, Wind. SL4
off Wright 173 AK83
Wrights Rd, E3 11 N10
SE25 224 DS97
Wrights Row, Wall. SM6 241 DH105
Wrights Wk, SW14 180 CR83
Wright Way, Wind. SL4
off Wright 172 AJ83
Wrigley Cl, E4 123 ED50
Wriotsley Way, Add. KT15
off Coombelands La 234 BG107
Writtle Wk, Rain. RM13 169 FF67
● Wrotham Business Pk,
Barn. EN5 101 CZ37
★ Wrotham Pk, Barn. EN5 101 CZ36
Wrotham Rd, NW1 7 M7
W13 off Mattock La 159 CJ74
Barnet EN5 101 CY40
Gravesend DA11, DA13 213 GG88
Welling DA16 188 EW81
Sch Wrotham Rd Prim Sch,
Grav. DA11
off Wrotham Rd 213 GH87
Wroths Path, Loug. IG10 107 EM39
Wrottesley Rd, NW10 161 CU68
SE18 187 EQ79
Wroughton Rd, SW11 202 DF86
Wroughton Ter, NW4 141 CW56
Wroxall Rd, Dag. RM9 168 EW65
Sch Wroxham, The,
Pot.B. EN6
off Wroxham Gdns 85 CX31
Wroxham Av, Hem.H. HP3 62 BK22
Wroxham Gdns, N11 121 DJ52
Enfield EN2 103 DN35
Potters Bar EN6 85 CX31
Wroxham Rd, SE28 168 EX73
Wroxham Way, Ilf. IG6 125 EP53
Wroxton Rd, SE15 44 F9
WRYTHE, THE, Cars. SM5 222 DF103
Wrythe Grn, Cars. SM5
off Wrythe Grn Rd 222 DF104
Wrythe Grn Rd, Cars. SM5 222 DF104
Wrythe La, Cars. SM5 222 DC102
Wulfstan St, W12 161 CT72
Wulstan Pk, Pot.B. EN6
off Tempest Av 86 DD32
Wyatt Cl, SE16 33 N5
Bushey Heath WD23 117 CE45
Feltham TW13 198 BW88
Hayes UB4 157 BU71
Wyatt Dr, SW13 181 CW80
Wyatt Pk Rd, SW2 203 DL89
Wyatt Pt, SE28 off Erebus Dr 187 EQ75
Wyatt Rd, E7 13 P5
N5 144 DQ62
Dartford DA1 189 FF83
Staines TW18 196 BG92
Windsor SL4 173 AK83
Wyatts Cl, Chorl. WD3 96 BG41
Wyatts Covert, Denh. UB9 135 BF56
Wyatts La, E17 145 EC55
Wyatts Rd, Chorl. WD3 95 BF42
Wybert St, NW1 17 K4
Sch Wyborne Prim Sch, SE9
off Footscray Rd 207 EP88
Wyborne Way, NW10 160 CQ66
Wyburn Av, Barn. EN5 101 CZ41
Wyche Gro, S.Croy. CR2 242 DQ108
Wych Elm, Harl. CM20 57 EQ14
Wych Elm Cl, Horn. RM11 150 FN59
Wych Elm Pas, Kings.T. KT2 200 CM94
Wych Elm Ri, Guil. GU1 280 AY137
Wych Elm Rd, Horn. RM11 150 FN58
Wych Elms, Park St AL2 82 CB28
Wycherley Cl, SE3 47 L4
Wycherley Cres, New Barn.
EN5 102 DB44
Wychford Dr, Saw. CM21 58 EW06
Wych Hill, Wok. GU22 248 AW119
Wych Hill La, Wok. GU22 248 AY119
Wych Hill Pk, Wok. GU22 248 AX119
Wych Hill Ri, Wok. GU22 248 AW119
Wych Hill Way, Wok. GU22 248 AX120
Wychwood Av, Edg. HA8 117 CK51
Thornton Heath CR7 224 DQ97
Wychwood Cl, Edg. HA8 117 CK51
Sunbury-on-Thames TW16 197 BU93
Wychwood End, N6 143 DJ59
Wychwood Gdns, Ilf. IG5 147 EM56
Wychwood Way, SE19
off Roman Ri 204 DR93
Northwood HA6 115 BT52
Wyclif Ct, EC1 off Wyclif St 18 G3
Wycliffe Cl, Chsht EN8 89 DX28
Welling DA16 187 ET81
Wycliffe Ct, Abb.L. WD5 81 BS32
Wycliffe Rd, SW11 41 H9
SW19 202 DB93
Wycliffe Row, Nthflt DA11 213 GF88
Wyclif St, EC1 18 G3
Wycombe End, Beac. HP9 133 AK55
Wycombe Gdns, NW11 142 DA61
Wycombe La, Woob.Grn
HP10 132 AE56
Wycombe Pl, SW18 202 DC86
St. Albans AL4 65 CH17
Wycombe Rd, N17 122 DU53
Ilford IG2 147 EM57
Wembley HA0 160 CN67
Wycombe Sq, W8 27 J3
Wycombe Way, St.Alb. AL4 65 CJ17
Wyddial Grn, Welw.G.C. AL7
off Widford Rd 52 DB09
Wydehurst Rd, Croy. CR0 224 DU101
Wydell Cl, Mord. SM4 221 CW100
Wydeville Manor Rd, SE12 206 EH91
Wye, The, Hem.H. HP2 62 BN15
Wyecliffe Gdns, S.Merst. RH1 273 DJ130
Wye Cl, Ashf. TW15 197 BP91
Orpington BR6 227 ET101
Ruislip HA4 137 BQ58
Wyedale, Lon.Col. AL2 84 CM27
Wyemead Cres, E4 124 EE47
Wye Rd, Grav. DA12 213 GK89
Wooburn Green HP10 132 AD55
Wye St, SW11 40 B9
Wyeth's Ms, Epsom KT17 239 CT113
Wyeths Rd, Epsom KT17 239 CT113
Wyevale Cl, Pnr. HA5 137 BU55
Wyfields, Ilf. IG5
off Ravensbourne Gdns 125 EP53
Wyfold Ho, SE2
off Wolvercote Rd 188 EX75
Wyfold Rd, SW6 38 E6
Wyhill Wk, Dag. RM10 169 FC65
Wyke Cl, Islw. TW7 179 CF79
Wyke Gdns, W7 179 CG76
Wykeham Av, Dag. RM9 168 EW65
Hornchurch RM11 150 FK58
Wykeham Cl, Grav. DA12 213 GL93
Sipson UB7 176 BN78
Wykeham Grn, Dag. RM9 168 EW65
Wykeham Hill, Wem. HA9 140 CM60
Sch Wykeham Prim Sch, NW10
off Aboyne Rd 140 CS62
Hornchurch RM12
off Rainsford Way 149 FG60
Wykeham Ri, N20 119 CY46
Wykeham Rd, NW4 141 CW57
Guildford GU1 265 BD133
Harrow HA3 139 CH56
Wykeridge Cl, Chesh. HP5 76 AP27
Wyke Rd, E3 12 A7
SW20 221 CW96
Wylands Rd, Slou. SL3 175 BA77
Wylchin Cl, Pnr. HA5 137 BT56
Wyldes Cl, NW11 142 DC60
Wyldfield Gdns, N9 122 DT47
Wyld Way, Wem. HA9 160 CP65
Wyldwood Cl, Harl. CM17 58 EW09
Wyleu St, SE23 205 DY87
Wylie Rd, Sthl. UB2 178 CA76
Wyllen Cl, E1 20 G5
Wyllyotts Cl, Pot.B. EN6 85 CZ32
Wyllyotts La, Pot.B. EN6 85 CZ32
Wyllyotts Pl, Pot.B. EN6 85 CZ32
Wylo Dr, Barn. EN5 101 CU44
Wymark Cl, Rain. RM13 169 FF68
Wymering Rd, W9 15 K3
Wymers Cl, Burn. SL1 152 AH68
Wymers Wd Rd, Burn. SL1 152 AG67
Wymond St, SW15 38 B10
Wynan Rd, E14 34 C10
Wynash Gdns, Cars. SM5 240 DE106
Wynaud Ct, N22
off Palmerston Rd 121 DM51
Wyncham Av, Sid. DA15 207 ES88
Wynches Fm Dr, St.Alb. AL4 65 CK19
Wynchgate, N14 121 DK46
N21 121 DL46
Harrow HA3 117 CE52
Wynchlands Cres, St.Alb. AL4 65 CK20
Wyncote Way, S.Croy. CR2 243 DX109
Wyncroft Cl, Brom. BR1 227 EM97
Wyndale Av, NW9 140 CN58
Wyndcliff Rd, SE7 186 EH79
Wyndcroft Cl, Enf. EN2 103 DP41
Wyndham Av, Cob. KT11 235 BU113
Wyndham Cl, Orp. BR6 227 EQ102
Sutton SM2 240 DA108
Wyndham Cres, N19 143 DJ62
Burnham SL1 152 AH69
Hounslow TW4 198 CA86
Wyndham Est, SE5 43 J4
Wyndham Ms, W1 16 E7
Wyndham Pl, W1 16 E7
Wyndham Rd, E6 166 EK66
SE5 43 H5
W13 179 CH76
Barnet EN4 120 DF46
Kingston upon Thames KT2 200 CM94
Woking GU21 248 AV118
Wyndhams End, Welw.G.C.
AL7 51 CZ13
Wyndham St, W1 16 E6
Wyndham Yd, W1 16 E7
Wyndhurst Cl, S.Croy. CR2 241 DP108
Wyneham Rd, SE24 204 DR85
Wynell Rd, SE23 205 DX90
Wynford Gro, Orp. BR5 228 EV97
Wynford Pl, Belv. DA17 188 FA79
Wynford Rd, N1 8 C10
Wynford Way, SE9 207 EM90
Wyngrave Pl, Knot.Grn HP9 110 AJ50
Wynlie Gdns, Pnr. HA5 115 BV54
Wynn Br Cl, Wdf.Grn. IG8
off Chigwell Rd 124 EJ53
Wynndale Rd, E18 124 EH53
Wynne Rd, SW9 42 E9
Wynns Av, Sid. DA15 208 EU85
Wynnstay Gdns, W8 27 K6
Wynnstow Pk, Oxt. RH8 276 EF131
Wynnswick Rd, Seer Grn HP9 111 AQ50
Wynter St, SW11 182 DC84
Wynton Gdns, SE25 224 DT99
Wynton Gro, Walt. KT12 217 BU104
Wynton Pl, W3 160 CP72
Wynyard Cl, Sarratt WD3 96 BG36
Wynyard Ter, SE11 30 D10
Wynyatt St, EC1 18 G3
Wyre Gro, Edg. HA8 118 CP48
Hayes UB3 177 BU77
Wyresdale Cres, Perivale UB6 159 CF69
Wysemead, Horl. RH6 291 DJ147
Wyteleaf Cl, Ruis. HA4 137 BQ58
Wythburn Pl, W1 16 E9
Wythenshawe Rd, Dag. RM10 148 FA62
Wythens Wk, SE9 207 EP86
Wythes Cl, Brom. BR1 227 EM96
Wythes Rd, E16 36 G3
Wythfield Rd, SE9 207 EM86
Wyton, Welw.G.C. AL7 52 DD09
Wyvenhoe Rd, Har. HA2 138 CC62
Wyvern Cl, Dart. DA1 210 FJ87
Orpington BR6 228 EV104
● Wyvern Est, N.Mal. KT3 221 CU98
Wyvern Gro, Hayes UB3 177 BP80
Wyvern Pl, Add. KT15
off Green La 234 BH105
Wyvern Rd, Pur. CR8 241 DP110
Wyvern Way, Uxb. UB8 156 BJ67
Wyvil Est, SW8 42 A4
Sch Wyvil Prim Sch, SW8 42 B4
Wyvil Rd, SW8 42 A3
Wyvis St, E14 22 D6

Y

Yabsley St, E14 34 F2
Yaffle Rd, Wey. KT13 235 BQ110
Yalding Gro, Orp. BR5 228 EX98
Yalding Rd, SE16 32 C7
Yale Cl, Houns. TW4 198 BZ85
Yale Way, Horn. RM12 149 FG63
Yarborough Rd, SW19 222 DD95
Yarbridge Cl, Sutt. SM2 240 DB110
Yardley Cl, E4 105 EB43
Reigate RH2 272 DB132
Yardley Ct, Sutt. SM3
off Hemingford Rd 239 CW105
Yardley La, E4 105 EB43
Sch Yardley Prim Sch, E4
off Hawkwood Cres 105 EC43
Yardley St, WC1 18 E3
Yard Mead, Egh. TW20 195 BA90
Yarm Cl, Lthd. KT22 253 CJ123
Yarm Ct Rd, Lthd. KT22 253 CJ123
Yarmouth Cres, N17 144 DV57
Yarmouth Pl, W1 29 J3
Yarmouth Rd, Slou. SL1 153 AQ73
Watford WD24 98 BW38
Yarm Way, Lthd. KT22 253 CJ123
Yarnfield Sq, SE15 44 D7
Yarnton Way, SE2 188 EX75
Erith DA18 188 EZ76
Yarrow Cres, E6 24 G6
Yarrowfield, Wok. GU22 248 AX123
Yarrowside, Amer. HP7 94 AV41
Yateley St, SE18 36 F7
Yates Ct, NW2 4 D5
Yates Ho, E2 off Roberta St 20 D2
Yattendon Rd, Horl. RH6 291 DH148
Sch Yattendon Sch, Horl. RH6
off Oakwood Rd 290 DG147
Sch Yavneh Coll, Borwd. WD6
off Hillside Av 100 CQ42
YEADING, Hayes UB4 157 BV69
Yeading Av, Har. HA2 138 BY61
Yeading Fork, Hayes UB4 158 BW71
Yeading Gdns, Hayes UB4 157 BV71
Sch Yeading Inf Sch,
Hayes UB4
off Carlyon Rd 158 BW71
Sch Yeading Jun Sch,
Hayes UB4
off Carlyon Rd 158 BW71
Yeading La, Hayes UB4 157 BV72
Northolt UB5 158 BW69
Yeames Cl, W13 159 CG72
Yearling Cl, Gt Amwell SG12 55 DZ08
Yeate St, N1 9 L7
Yeatman Rd, N6 142 DF58
Yeats Cl, NW10 160 CS65
Redhill RH1 288 DC137
Yeats Ct, N15
off Tynemouth Rd 144 DT56
Ye Cor, Wat. WD19 98 BY44
Yeend Cl, W.Mol. KT8 218 CA98
Sch Yehudi Menuhin Sch,
Stoke D'Ab. KT11
off Cobham Rd 252 CA119
Sch Yeshiva Gedolah Lubavitch
Sch, N2 off Kingsley Way 142 DC57
Yeldham Rd, W6 38 C1
Yellow Hammer Ct, NW9
off Eagle Dr 118 CS54
Yellowpine Way, Chig. IG7 126 EV49
Yellow Stock Ms, N.Ock.
RM14 151 FU64
Yelverton Cl, Rom. RM3 128 FK53
Yelverton Rd, SW11 40 B9
Ye Meads, Tap. SL6 152 AE73
Yenston Cl, Mord. SM4 222 DA100
Yeoman Cl, E6 25 N10
SE27 203 DP90
Yeoman Dr, Stai. TW19 196 BL88
Yeoman Rd, Nthlt. UB5 158 BY66
Yeomanry Cl, Epsom KT17
off Dirdene Gdns 239 CT112
Yeomans Acre, Ruis. HA4 137 BU58
Yeomans Ct, Hert. SG13 54 DS09
Yeomans Cft, Bkhm KT23
off Vicarage Cl 268 CA125
Yeomans Keep, Chorl. WD3
off Rickmansworth Rd 95 BF41
Yeomans Meadow, Sev. TN13 278 FG126
Yeoman's Ms, Islw. TW7
off Queensbridge Pk 199 CE85
Yeoman's Row, SW3 28 D7
Yeoman St, SE8 33 L8
Yeomans Way, Enf. EN3 104 DW40
Yeomans Yd, E1 20 B10
Yeoman Way, Red. RH1 289 DH139
Yeomen Way, Ilf. IG6 125 EQ51
Yeo St, E3 22 C6
Yeoveney Cl, Stai. TW19 195 BD89
Yeovil Cl, Orp. BR6 227 ES103
Yeovil Rd, Slou. SL1 153 AL72
Yeovilton Pl, Kings.T. KT2 199 CJ92
Sch Yerbury Prim Sch, N19
off Foxham Rd 143 DK62
Yerbury Rd, N19 143 DK62
Sch Yesodey Hatorah Sch,
N16 off Amhurst Pk 144 DT59
Sch Yesodey Hatorah Sec Sch
for Girls, N16
off Egerton Rd 144 DT59
Yester Dr, Chis. BR7 206 EL94
Yester Pk, Chis. BR7 207 EM94
Yester Rd, Chis. BR7 207 EM94
Yevele Way, Horn. RM11 150 FL59
Yew Av, West Dr. UB7 156 BL73
Yewbank Cl, Ken. CR8 258 DR115
Yew Cl, Buck.H. IG9 124 EK47
Cheshunt EN7 88 DS27
Yewdale Cl, Brom. BR1 206 EE93
Yewdells Cl, Buckland RH3 271 CU133
Yewfield Rd, NW10 161 CT66
Yew Gro, NW2 4 D1
Welwyn Garden City AL7 52 DC10
Yewlands, Hodd. EN11 71 EA18
Sawbridgeworth CM21 58 EY06
Yewlands Cl, Bans. SM7 256 DC115
Yewlands Dr, Hodd. EN11 71 EA18
Yew Pl, Wey. KT13 217 BT104
Yews, The, Ashf. TW15
off Reedsfield Rd 197 BP91
Gravesend DA12 213 GK88
Yews Av, Enf. EN1 104 DV36
Yew Tree Bottom Rd, Epsom
KT17, KT18 255 CV116
Yew Tree Cl, N21 121 DN45
Yewtree Cl, N22 121 DJ53
Yew Tree Cl, SE13
off Bankside Av 185 EC83
Beaconsfield HP9 111 AM54
Chipstead CR5 256 DF119
Yewtree Cl, Har. HA2 138 CB56
Yew Tree Cl, Horl. RH6 290 DF147
Hutton CM13 131 GB44
Ley Hill HP5 78 AU30
Sevenoaks TN13 278 FD123
Welling DA16 188 EU81
Worcester Park KT4 220 CS102
Yew Tree Ct, Els. WD6
off Barnet La 99 CK44
Hemel Hempstead HP1 62 BG22
Yew Tree Dr, Bov. HP3 79 BB28
Caterham CR3 274 DT125
Guildford GU1 264 AW130

Yewtree End, Park St AL2 **82** CB27
Yew Tree Gdns, Chad.Hth RM6 **148** EY57
Epsom KT18 **254** CP115
Romford RM7 **149** FD57
Yew Tree La, Reig. RH2 **272** DB131
Yew Tree Lo, SW16 **203** DJ91
Yew Tree Ms, West. TN16 **277** ER127
Yew Tree Rd, W12 **161** CT73
Beckenham BR3 **225** DZ97
Dorking RH4 **269** CG134
Slough SL1 **174** AU76
Uxbridge UB10 **156** BM67
Yew Trees, Egh. TW20 **215** BC97
Shepperton TW17
off Laleham Rd **216** BM98
Yew Tree Wk, Eff. KT24 **268** BX127
Hounslow TW4 **198** BZ85
Maidenhead SL6 **132** AD63
Purley CR8 **242** DQ110
Yew Tree Way, Croy. CR0 **243** DY110
Yew Wk, Har. HA1 **139** CE60
Hoddesdon EN11 **71** EA18
YIEWSLEY, West Dr. UB7 **156** BL74
Yoakley Rd, N16 **144** DS61
Yoga Way, Wor.Pk. KT4 **221** CU103
Yoke Cl, N7 **8** B4
Yolande Gdns, SE9 **206** EL85
Yonge Pk, N4 **143** DN62
York Av, SW14 **200** CQ85
W7 **159** CE74
Hayes UB3 **157** BQ71
Sidcup DA15 **207** ES89
Slough SL1 **153** AQ72
Stanmore HA7 **117** CH53
Windsor SL4 **173** AP82
York Br, NW1 **16** G4
York Bldgs, WC2 **30** B1
York Cl, E6 **25** J9
W7 *off York Av* **159** CE74
Amersham HP7 **94** AT39
Byfleet KT14 **234** BL112
Kings Langley WD4 **80** BN29
Morden SM4 **222** DB98
Shenfield CM15 **131** FZ45
York Cres, Borwd. WD6 **100** CR40
Loughton IG10 **106** EL41
Yorke Gdns, Reig. RH2 **272** DA133
Yorke Gate, Cat. CR3 **258** DR122
Sch **Yorke Mead Prim Sch**, Crox.Grn
WD3 *off Dulwich Way* **96** BN43
Yorke Rd, Crox.Grn WD3 **96** BN44
Reigate RH2 **271** CZ133
Yorkes, Harl. CM18 **73** ET17
York Gdns, Walt. KT12 **218** BX103
York Gate, N14 **121** DL45
NW1 **16** G5
York Gro, SE15 **44** G7
York Hill, SE27 **203** DP90
Loughton IG10 **106** EL41
York Hill Est, SE27 **203** DP90
● **York Ho**, Wem. HA9 **140** CN63
York Ho Pl, W8 **27** L4
Sch **York Ho Sch**, Rick. WD3
off Sarratt Rd **96** BM40
Yorkland Av, Well. DA16 **187** ET83
York Ms, NW5 **7** K3
Ilford IG1 **147** EN62
York Par, Brent. TW8 **179** CK78
York Pl, SW11 **182** DD83
WC2 **30** B1
Dagenham RM10 **169** FC65
Ilford IG1 *off York Rd* **147** EN61
York Ri, NW5 **143** DH62
Orpington BR6 **227** ES102
York Rd, E4 **123** EA50
E7 **13** N5
E10 **145** EC62
E17 **145** DX57
N11 **121** DK51
N18 **122** DV51
N21 **122** DR45
SE1 **30** D4
York Rd, SW11 **182** DC84
SW18 **182** DC84
SW19 **202** DC93
W3 **160** CQ72
W5 **179** CJ76
Brentford TW8 **179** CK78
Biggin Hill TN16 **260** EH119
Byfleet KT14 **234** BK112
Croydon CR0 **223** DN101
Dartford DA1 **210** FM87
Gravesend DA12 **213** GJ90
Guildford GU1 **280** AX135
Hounslow TW3 **178** CB83
Ilford IG1 **147** EN62
Kingston upon Thames KT2 **200** CM94
New Barnet EN5 **102** DD43
North Weald Bassett CM16 **92** FA27
Northfleet DA11 **212** GD87
Northwood HA6 **115** BU54
Rainham RM13 **169** FD66
Richmond TW10
off Albert Rd **200** CM85
St. Albans AL1 **65** CF19
Shenfield CM15 **131** FZ45
South Croydon CR2 **243** DX110
Sutton SM2 **240** DA107
Teddington TW11 **199** CE91
Uxbridge UB8 **156** BK66
Waltham Cross EN8 **89** DY34
Watford WD18 **98** BW43
Weybridge KT13 **235** BQ105
Windsor SL4 **173** AP82
Woking GU22 **248** AY118
Sch **York Rd Jun Sch & Language Unit**, Dart. DA1 *off York Rd* **210** FM87
Yorkshire Cl, N16 **144** DS62
Yorkshire Gdns, N18 **122** DV50
Jct **Yorkshire Grey**, SE9 **206** EK85
Yorkshire Grey Pl, NW3 **5** P1
Yorkshire Grey Yd, WC1 **18** C7
Yorkshire Rd, E14 **21** L9
Mitcham CR4 **223** DL99
York Sq, E14 **21** L9
York St, W1 **16** F6
Mitcham CR4 **222** DG101
York St, Twick. TW1 **199** CG88
York Ter, Enf. EN2 **104** DQ38
Erith DA8 **189** FC81
York Ter E, NW1 **17** H5
York Ter W, NW1 **16** G5
Yorkton St, E2 **20** C1
York Way, N1 **7** P4
N7 **8** B9
N20 **120** DF48
Borehamwood WD6 **100** CR40
Chessington KT9 **238** CL108
Feltham TW13 **198** BZ90
Hemel Hempstead HP2 **62** BL21
Watford WD25 **98** BX36
York Way Ct, N1 **8** B9
York Way Est, N7
off York Way **8** A5
Youngfield Rd, Hem.H. HP1 **61** BF19
Youngmans Cl, Enf. EN2 **104** DQ39
Young Rd, E16 **24** C7
Young's Bldgs, EC1 **19** K4
Youngs Ct, SW11 **41** H7
Youngs Ri, Welw.G.C. AL8 **51** CV09
Youngs Rd, Ilf. IG2 **147** ER57
Young St, W8 **27** L5
Fetcham KT22 **269** CE125
Youngstroat La, Wok. GU21,
GU24 **232** AY110
Yoxley App, Ilf. IG2 **147** EQ58
Yoxley Dr, Ilf. IG2 **147** EQ58
Yukon Rd, SW12 **203** DH87
Broxbourne EN10 **89** DY25
Yule Cl, Brick.Wd AL2 **82** BZ30
Yunus Khan Cl, E17 **145** EA57

Z

Zambezie Dr, N9 **122** DW48
Zampa Rd, SE16 **44** G1
Zander Ct, E2 **20** D1
Zangwill Rd, SE3 **186** EK81
Zealand Av, Harm. UB7 **176** BK80
Zealand Rd, E3 **11** L10
Zelah Rd, Orp. BR5 **228** EV101
Zennor Rd, SW12 **203** DJ88
● **Zennor Rd Ind Est**, SW12
off Zennor Rd **203** DJ88
Zenoria St, SE22 **184** DT84
Zermatt Rd, Th.Hth. CR7 **224** DQ98
Zetex Apts, Rom. RM1
off Mercury Gdns **149** FF56
Zetland St, E14 **22** D7
Zig Zag, The, Mick. RH5 **269** CK130
Zig Zag Rd, Box H. KT20 **269** CK132
Kenley CR8 **258** DQ116
Zion Ho, E1 **20** G8
Zion Pl, Grav. DA12 **213** GH87
Thornton Heath CR7 **224** DR98
Zion Rd, Th.Hth. CR7 **224** DR98
Zion St, Seal TN15
off Church Rd **279** FM121
Zoar St, SE1 **31** J2
● **Zodiac Business Pk**, Cowley
UB8 **156** BK72
Zodiac Ct, Croy. CR0
off London Rd **223** DP102
Zoffany St, N19 **143** DK61
★ **ZSL London Zoo**, NW1 **6** G10

AYLESBURY VALE
TRING
HERTFORDSHIRE
HARPENDEN
WHEATHAMPSTEAD
WELWYN
WELWYN GARDEN CITY
DACORUM
ST. ALBANS
WELWYN
WENDOVER
BERKHAMSTED
HATFIELD
ESSENDON
HATFIELD
ST. ALBANS
HEMEL HEMPSTEAD
PRINCES RISBOROUGH
LONDON COLNEY
GREAT MISSENDEN
CHESHAM
ABBOTS LANGLEY
POTTERS BAR
BUCKINGHAMSHIRE
WATFORD
HERTSMERE
CHILTERN
AMERSHAM
LITTLE CHALFONT
THREE RIVERS
WATFORD
BOREHAMWOOD
NEW BARNET
BARNET
WYCOMBE
TYLERS GREEN
CHALFONT ST. GILES
BUSHEY
EAST BARNET
HIGH WYCOMBE
RICKMANSWORTH
SOUTHGATE
BARNET
LOUDWATER
STANMORE
EDGWARE
BEACONSFIELD
HAREFIELD
NORTHWOOD
HARROW
FINCHLEY
PINNER
HENDON
GERRARDS CROSS
WOOBURN
GREAT
HARROW
MARLOW
SOUTH BUCKS
DENHAM
RUISLIP
WEMBLEY
BRENT
HAMPSTEAD
HILLINGDON
CAMDEN
STOKE POGES
UXBRIDGE
NORTHOLT
WILLESDEN
HENLEY-ON-THAMES
BURNHAM
PADDINGTON
WESTMINSTER
MAIDENHEAD
SLOUGH
IVER
EALING
EALING
KENSINGTON & CHELSEA
HAMMERSMITH & FULHAM
SLOUGH
HAYES
SOUTHALL
ACTON
LANGLEY
WEST DRAYTON
ETON
HAMMERSMITH
WINDSOR & MAIDENHEAD
London Heathrow
WINDSOR
DATCHET
KEW
BATTERSEA
TWYFORD
HOUNSLOW
HOUNSLOW
OLD WINDSOR
RICHMOND
WANDSWORTH
WRAYSBURY
RICHMOND UPON THAMES
WANDSWORTH
FELTHAM
TWICKENHAM
WINKFIELD
ASHFORD
STREATHAM
EGHAM
STAINES
WIMBLEDON
SPELTHORNE
TEDDINGTON
KINGSTON UPON THAMES
MERTON
BRACKNELL
MERTON
WOKINGHAM
ASCOT
VIRGINIA WATER
BRACKNELL FOREST
SURBITON
MORDEN
KINGSTON UPON THAMES
CHERTSEY
WALTON-ON-THAMES
LONDON
RUNNYMEDE
ESHER
SUTTON
OTTERSHAW
WEYBRIDGE
SUTTON
BAGSHOT
EWELL
ELMBRIDGE
SURREY HEATH
CHOBHAM
EPSOM & EWELL
SANDHURST
EPSOM
OXSHOTT
CAMBERLEY
BYFLEET
STOKE D'ABERNON
BANSTEAD
HART
FRIMLEY
WOKING
ASHTEAD
WOKING
RIPLEY
FETCHAM
LEATHERHEAD
TADWORTH
FARNBOROUGH
MYTCHETT
FLEET
REIGATE & BANSTEAD
GREAT BOOKHAM
HAMPSHIRE
RUSHMOOR
EAST HORSLEY
NORMANDY
EAST CLANDON
ALDERSHOT
MOLE VALLEY
GUILDFORD
REIGATE
TONGHAM
GUILDFORD
BROCKHAM
DORKING
WESTCOTT
GOMSHALL
FARNHAM
COMPTON
SHALFORD
LEIGH
SALFORDS
SHACKLEFORD
SURREY
HOLMBURY ST MARY
ELSTEAD
GODALMING
BEARE GREEN
EAST HANTS
MILFORD
WAVERLEY
CHARLWOOD
London Gatwick
WITLEY
CRAWLEY
M1
M25
A1(M)
M40
M4
A404(M)
A329(M)
M3